W9-BFD-424

ENCYCLOPEDIA
OF
LATIN
AMERICA

ENCYCLOPEDIA
OF
LATIN
AMERICA

Edited by
HELEN DELPAR

McGRAW-HILL BOOK COMPANY

NEW YORK   ST. LOUIS   SAN FRANCISCO   DÜSSELDORF   JOHANNESBURG
KUALA LUMPUR   LONDON   MEXICO   MONTREAL   NEW DELHI
PANAMA   PARIS   SÃO PAULO   SINGAPORE   SYDNEY
TORONTO   TOKYO

Staff for McGraw-Hill

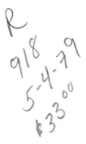

General Editor	Leonard Josephson
Editing Supervisor	Tobia L. Worth
Art Director	Edward J. Fox
Director of Production	Stephen J. Boldish
Designer	Richard A. Roth
Copy Editor	Beatrice E. Eckes
Photo Editor	Susan E. Queeney
Art Associate	Ann D. Bonardi

Map illustrations by
James Humphrey

4567890   KPKP   73210987

Library of Congress Cataloging in Publication Data

Main entry under title:

Encyclopedia of Latin America.

   1.   Latin America — Dictionaries and encyclopedias.
I. Delpar, Helen, ed.
F1406.E52   918′.03′03   74-1036

ISBN 0-07-016263-8

Introduction

The *Encyclopedia of Latin America* is designed to be a comprehensive yet concise reference book offering authoritative information on the history, economy, politics, arts, and other aspects of Latin America. In this respect it ranges far beyond the coverage to be found in other reference works on the subject, which are limited, for example, to history or literature only. It was felt that a broad overview of the entire scope of Latin American civilization was badly needed in a reference work and that heretofore this area of the world had not received proper scholarly documentation in the form of a standard and dependable encyclopedia.

Latin America, for the purposes of this book, is defined as embracing the eighteen Spanish-speaking republics plus Brazil, Haiti, and Puerto Rico, and for each of these countries there is a general article covering various aspects of its history, geography, industry, and culture. These country articles are survey articles, and references within them direct the reader to other articles in the book, where various aspects of each country are examined in greater detail—in biographical articles covering, for example, leading political and literary figures, in separate entries on such subjects as major industries, and in concise articles on a variety of subjects, for example, political parties and labor unions. Some topics, such as economic integration and trade, are dealt with in articles that describe the region as a whole.

Throughout the book emphasis has been placed on the national period of Latin American history; yet the principal colonial figures and institutions have been treated carefully, and every event of importance has been covered. If the nineteenth and twentieth centuries have been dealt with in the greatest detail, the reason is that this period has seen the most wide-ranging, variegated, and meaningful developments as they relate to the modern world. But also, it must be admitted frankly, the need to compress a vast amount of material into a predetermined number of pages meant that many topics of certain significance had to be treated in a somewhat abbreviated fashion. Efforts were made to include in the *Encyclopedia* every vital subject or person related to each country's history and position in the world, although in some cases of lesser figures of a borderline nature certain individuals had to be omitted so that others could be included.

A standard letter-by-letter alphabetical arrangement has been used in this *Encyclopedia,* and it is therefore essentially a self-indexed work. Numerous reference entries have been included, and within articles there are many cross-references to other entries. The names of individuals as they appear in the alphabetization scheme have presented problems that are understandable, given the fact that most of the names are of Spanish or Portuguese derivation. The usual practice has been to list individuals in accordance with the name by which they are most commonly known, with suitable reference entries. The dating of published works has been based on extensive research, and dates appearing in the text after such works indicate the year of first publication, unless otherwise noted. An English title placed after a foreign-language work indicates the title under which the work has been translated. The cross-references are designated with small capitals both within the running text and at the conclusion of an article. In order to provide as much information as possible to supplement each article in the book, there is liberal employment of these cross-references so that the reader will not overlook other articles where material related to the subject under consideration will be found.

To supplement certain key and longer articles in the *Encyclopedia,* brief bibliographies have been provided, and the works therein are listed alphabetically by author. Readers seeking additional information about a specific country or topic may consult the Select Bibliography of Bibliographies that appears at the end of the book. There is also included, following the basic text, a Statistical Appendix providing recent data on demography, per capita product, and the like.

The production of this *Encyclopedia* has been a collaborative enterprise, and the editor is most grateful to the contributors, whose efforts have made its appearance possible. David Bushnell, Margaret E. Crahan, and Morton D. Winsberg provided much helpful assistance in addition to their contributed articles. Special thanks are due to Charles C. Griffin, whose comments and suggestions were invaluable, and to Lewis Hanke, who in many respects can be considered the godfather of the project. Finally, the editor wishes to acknowledge the assistance of the staff of McGraw-Hill's Professional and Reference Book Division, especially Leonard Josephson, Tobia L. Worth, Beatrice E. Eckes, and Susan E. Queeney.

HELEN DELPAR

Contributors

Christopher G. Abel
Research Fellow, St. Antony's College
Oxford University

William R. Adams
Florida State University

Luis E. Agrait
University of Puerto Rico, Río Piedras

Robert J. Alexander
Professor of Economics
Rutgers University, New Brunswick

Marvin Alisky
Professor of Political Science
Arizona State University

Robin L. Anderson
University of California, Davis

Rodney D. Anderson
Assistant Professor of History
Florida State University

Werner Baer
Professor of Economics
Vanderbilt University

Samuel L. Baily
Associate Professor of History
Rutgers University, New Brunswick

John E. Baur
Professor of History
California State University, Northridge

Gerard H. Béhague
Associate Professor of Music
University of Illinois, Urbana-Champaign

Charles R. Berry
Associate Professor of History
Wright State University

Calvin P. Blair
Professor of International Business
University of Texas, Austin

Harold Blakemore
Secretary, Institute of Latin American Studies
University of London

Burr C. Brundage
Professor of History
Eckerd College

James E. Buchanan
Assistant Professor of History
Newark State College

David Bushnell
Professor of History
University of Florida

Orazio A. Ciccarelli
Assistant Professor of History
University of Southern Mississippi

James D. Cochrane
Associate Professor of Political Science
Tulane University

Simon Collier
Senior Lecturer in Latin American History
University of Essex

Robert Conrad
Associate Professor of History
University of Illinois, Chicago Circle

Donald B. Cooper
Professor of History
Ohio State University

Carlos E. Cortés
Associate Professor of History
University of California, Riverside

Taylor K. Cousins
Assistant Professor of Economics
College of William and Mary in Virginia

Edith B. Couturier
Professorial Lecturer in History
American University

Margaret E. Crahan
Assistant Professor of History
Herbert H. Lehman College, City University
of New York

David A. Crain
Assistant Professor of History
Indiana University–Purdue University

Joseph T. Criscenti
Associate Professor of History
Boston College

Donald E. Curry
New York, New York

J. Laurence Day
Associate Professor of Journalism
University of Kansas

Helen Delpar
Assistant Professor of History
University of Alabama

Elizabeth Wilkes Dore
Columbia University

James L. Dudley
University of Hawaii

William S. Dudley
Assistant Professor of History
Southern Methodist University

Joseph A. Ellis
Assistant Professor of History
City College, City University of New York

Lee C. Fennell
Assistant Professor of Political Science
University of the Pacific

Kenneth V. Finney
Assistant Professor of History
North Carolina Wesleyan College

Troy S. Floyd
Professor of History
University of New Mexico

Daniel W. Gade
Associate Professor of Geography
University of Vermont

Frederick V. Gifun
University of Florida

Alfonso González
Associate Professor of Geography
University of Calgary

Moisés González Navarro
El Colegio de México

Richard B. Gray
Professor of Government
Florida State University

George W. Grayson
Associate Professor of Government
College of William and Mary in Virginia

Terence Grieder
Associate Professor of Art History
University of Texas, Austin

William J. Griffith
Director, Center of Latin American Studies
University of Kansas

Hugh M. Hamill, Jr.
Professor of History
University of Connecticut

Timothy C. Hanley
Columbia University

John H. Hann
Assistant Professor of History
Florida State University

J. León Helguera
Professor of History
Vanderbilt University

Stanley Hochman
New York, New York

H. A. Holley
Senior Research Fellow, Institute of
    Latin American Studies
University of London

N. Gary Holten
Assistant Professor of Government
Florida Technological University

Don R. Hoy
Associate Professor of Geography
University of Georgia

Donald L. Huddle
Professor of Economics
Rice University

Allan K. Johnson
University of California, Riverside

John J. Kennedy
Director, Program of Latin American Studies
University of Notre Dame

Kenneth F. Kiple
Assistant Professor of History
Bowling Green State University

Alan Kovac
University of Florida

Michael J. Kryzanek
Teaching Associate, Department of
    Political Science
University of Massachusetts

Asunción Lavrin
Silver Spring, Maryland

John V. Lombardi
Associate Professor of History
Indiana University, Bloomington

Eileen Lord
Professor of Art History
University of Bridgeport

John D. Martz
Professor of Political Science
University of North Carolina, Chapel Hill

Kenneth R. Maxwell
Visiting Member
Institute for Advanced Study, Princeton

Arnold J. Meagher
University of California, Davis

Norman Meiklejohn, A.A.
Assistant Professor of History
Assumption College

Francesca Miller
University of California, Davis

Robert C. Mings
Associate Professor of Geography
Arizona State University

James H. Neal
Associate Professor of History
Middle Tennessee State University

Ronald C. Newton
Associate Professor of History
Simon Fraser University

Lawrence J. Nielson
University of California, Davis

Leslie S. Offutt
University of California, Riverside

Juan A. Orrego-Salas
Director, Latin American Music Center
Indiana University, Bloomington

Ann M. Pescatello
Associate Professor of History
Florida International University

Rachel Phillips
Assistant Professor of Hispanic Studies
Vassar College

John E. Pichel
University of California, Los Angeles

Larry L. Pippin
Chairman, Department of History and
    Political Science
Elbert Covell College, University of the Pacific

Rollie E. Poppino
Professor of History
University of California, Davis

Daniel R. Reedy
Professor of Spanish
University of Kentucky

J. Cordell Robinson
Assistant Professor of History
California State College, San Bernardino

Gonzalo Rubio Orbe
Director, Instituto Indigenista Interamericano

Gerardo Sáenz
Associate Professor of Spanish
University of Kentucky

Frank Safford
Associate Professor of History
Northwestern University

George Sanderlin
Professor of English
California State University, San Diego

Charles S. Sargent
Assistant Professor of History
Arizona State University

Raymond S. Sayers
Professor of Romance Languages
Queens College, City University of New York

Eugene G. Sharkey
Instructor of History
Westminster College

Brooke Larson Shute
Columbia University

Noreen F. Stack
Assistant Professor of History
Williams College

Charles L. Stansifer
Associate Professor of History
University of Kansas

Henry B. Steele
Professor of Economics
University of Houston

Charles J. Stokes
Professor of Economics
University of Bridgeport

Ádám Szászdi
Professor of History
University of Puerto Rico, Río Piedras

Gerald Theisen
Assistant Professor of History
University of Albuquerque

Jack Ray Thomas
Associate Professor of History
Bowling Green State University

Martin Torodash
Professor of History
Fairleigh Dickinson University

Paul A. Viafora
University of New Mexico, Albuquerque

Ralph H. Vigil
Director, Institute for Ethnic Studies
University of Nebraska, Lincoln

Barbara A. Waggoner
Lawrence, Kansas

George R. Waggoner
Dean, College of Arts and Sciences
University of Kansas

Lois J. Weinman
Lecturer in History
California State University, Long Beach

Howard J. Wiarda
Associate Professor of Political Science
University of Massachusetts

John Hoyt Williams
Assistant Professor of History
Indiana State University

Morton D. Winsberg
Associate Professor of Geography
Florida State University

L. Sharon Wyatt
Assistant Professor of History
Montclair State College

Gene S. Yeager
University of Kansas

Advisory Editors

Charles Griffin
Professor Emeritus of History
Vassar College

Lewis Hanke
Clarence and Helen Haring Professor
University of Massachusetts, Amherst

ENCYCLOPEDIA
OF
LATIN
AMERICA

A

Abad y Queipo, Manuel
Azuela, Mariano

ABAD Y QUEIPO, MANUEL (1751–1825). Bishop-elect of Michoacán, Mexico. Born in Oviedo, Spain, Abad y Queipo served in Honduras (1779–1784) as ecclesiastical attorney and went to Mexico with Bishop Antonio de San Miguel of Michoacán. A perceptive observer and critic of Mexican colonial society, he defended the immunity of the clergy and advocated reforms such as the abolition of the personal tribute levied on Indians and *castas* (mixed bloods) and the free distribution of uncultivated land among these social classes. After the enactment in 1804 of the Consolidation Law, which ordered the sale of clerical property and the return of clerical loans by laymen, he composed a defense of the rights of the landowners of Valladolid, who depended on church loans. During a trip to Spain in 1807 he endeavored to have the law abrogated. In 1809 he proposed the formation of a standing army to prevent revolution.

Although Abad y Queipo's ideas were reformist, he was an avowed loyalist. At the outbreak of the War of Independence he condemned both the war and its leaders, Miguel HIDALGO Y COSTILLA and José María MORELOS Y PAVÓN, and approved of an edict providing for execution of rebel clerics. In 1810 he was elected Bishop of Michoacán by the Spanish junta but did not receive papal confirmation. Recalled to Spain by King FERDINAND VII in 1814, he submitted a secret report on the war that was very critical of Viceroy Félix María Calleja. He could not return to his bishopric and remained in Madrid, where he defended himself from political charges of the Inquisition (*see* INQUISITION, HOLY OFFICE OF THE). Abad y Queipo became a deputy to the Cortes in 1820 and Bishop of Tortosa in 1822. He died in a convent near Toledo, where he had been sent by Ferdinand as a punishment for his participation in the liberal government.

ASUNCIÓN LAVRIN

ABOLITION OF SLAVERY (BRAZIL). A mainstay of the Brazilian economy and society for more than 300 years, slavery was eliminated during the nineteenth century by foreign pressure, demographic decline, the loss of its main sources of renewal, regional imbalances, and an abolitionist movement that overwhelmed the institution in the 1880s. During the first half of the century the slave population was maintained, despite a negative ratio of births to deaths, by a constant influx of slaves from Africa, but after the suppression of the traffic in mid-century as a result of the QUEIROZ LAW, the slave population decreased rapidly in most parts of the country. This decline was particularly severe in the NORTHEAST, west, and extreme south as a result of an interprovincial slave trade that uprooted tens of thousands of slaves for service on the coffee plantations of the south central provinces of Rio de Janeiro, Minas Gerais, and São Paulo, slowly decreasing the commitment to slavery in the former regions but fortifying it in the coffee provinces. Thus, in 1871, when events abroad (notably the abolition of slavery in the United States) induced the imperial government to support legislation to free the newborn children of slave women, the government's bill gained support in most slave-exporting regions but encountered strong resistance in the coffee provinces. *See* FREE BIRTH LAW.

This regional disparity was also characteristic of the abolitionist decade. Prior to the collapse of slavery in São Paulo in 1887 much of the national abolitionist leadership came from such northeastern provinces as Bahia and Pernambuco, and the most effective provincial abolitionist movements were those of Ceará, Amazonas, and Rio Grande do Sul, where slavery was all but eliminated by 1884. The coffee provinces, on the other hand, were centers of opposition, strongly resisting the Dantas bill of 1884, which was designed to liberate slaves over the age of sixty, but reluctantly accepting the less progressive Saraiva-Cotegipe law of 1885, which required as much as three more years of unpaid labor from sexagenarian slaves to compensate their masters for their freedom. The last three years of slavery were characterized by a rapid decline of the slave population, as captives abandoned plantations by the tens of thousands, masters freed them to keep them at work, and an aroused population led by abolitionist leaders such as José do PATROCINIO, Joaquim NABUCO, André REBOUÇAS, and Antônio Bento finally repudiated the slave system. Thus, when slavery was ended by the GOLDEN LAW of May 13, 1888, the institution had all but collapsed, and its abolition seemed little more than a formality to a population eager to see it finished.

ROBERT CONRAD

ABOLITION OF SLAVERY (CUBA). After the slaves in the South of the United States were emancipated in 1863, it became increasingly difficult for Cubans to justify their "peculiar institution." General abolition seemed imminent on the island. However, as the island's Atlantic slave trade ceased during the 1860s, the value of Cuba's slaves increased. Planters did not want abolition without compensation, which Spain was too poor to provide.

During the TEN YEARS' WAR the insurgents accepted the principles of abolition but did little to bring it about, for fear of alienating the island's wealthy planter class. Spain, however, took a fairly firm position on the question in order to obtain European (particularly British) support against the possibility of American intervention. The result was the Moret law of 1870, a compromise that avoided compensation by creating a patronage system to tie the slaves to the estates for ten to fifteen years while they in effect earned their freedom. Moreover, the law provided that henceforth children born of slave parents would be free, while it emancipated all slaves over the age of sixty-five (sixty as later amended) and all those belonging to the state. It also promised freedom to slaves who aided in the war.

This law, despite many qualifications, delay in implementation, and uneven application, was a big step toward total abolition. The last steps came with the law of 1880, which abolished slavery but extended the patronage system, and the decree of October 7, 1886, which ended the patronage system and with it involuntary servitude in Cuba.

KENNETH F. KIPLE

ABREU, JOÃO CAPISTRANO DE (1853–1927). Brazilian historian. Born in Maranguape, Ceará, and educated in Fortaleza and Recife, he moved to Rio de Janeiro early in 1875 to pursue his career as a scholar. After working initially as a salesman for the Livraria Garnier, he taught at Aquino College from 1876 to 1879, when he secured a post in the National Library that furnished him the opportunity for extensive research and bibliographical work. Soon after arriving in Rio de Janeiro, he also began his long career as a writer of critical articles for the city's newspapers. In 1883 he won appointment to the chair of Brazilian history at the College of Pedro II, a position he held until 1899, when he resigned in protest over an administrative move to downgrade the importance of Brazilian history in the curriculum. In 1887 he became a member of the Brazilian Historical and Geographical Institute.

Generally recognized today as the foremost Brazilian historian of the colonial period, Abreu brought a new level of sophistication to Brazilian historical writing through his insight and his application of the lessons learned from an assiduous study of the German school of historians. In his most important work, *Capítulos de História Colonial* (1907), he balanced his predecessors' heavily factual accounts, focused on the deeds of the powerful, with an interpretative approach that gave considerable attention to social, cultural, and economic developments. He was the first Brazilian historian to call attention to the importance of the hinterland as a factor in the maintenance of Brazil's unity and in the formation of a distinctively Brazilian population. Many of his seminal essays were collected in a volume entitled *Caminhos Antigos e Povoamento do Brasil* (1930) and in three volumes entitled *Ensaios e Estudos* (1931–1938). He also made substantial contributions through his editing and annotating of many traditional texts such as Francisco Adolfo de Varnhagen's *História Geral do Brasil* and Frei Vicente do Salvador's *História do Brasil, 1500–1627.*

JOHN H. HANN

ACCIÓN DEMOCRÁTICA (DEMOCRATIC ACTION; AD). Venezuelan political party. Founded in 1931 in Barranquilla, Colombia, by a group of Venezuelan exiles opposed to the regime of Juan Vicente GÓMEZ, the party was originally called the Partido Democrático Nacional. After a short courtship with the Communists, it became increasingly nationalistic. From 1937 to 1941 the party was outlawed, and it functioned underground until the elections of 1941, when under the name Acción Democrática it ran Rómulo GALLEGOS for the Presidency. Frustrated in this attempt to gain power legally, AD, led by Rómulo BETANCOURT, collaborated in the military coup against Isaías MEDINA ANGARITA in 1945. In 1947 AD elected Gallegos President, but he was overthrown in 1948. After the fall of Marcos PÉREZ JIMÉNEZ in 1958, AD reached its peak of popularity in the elections of that year, which put Betancourt in the Presidency.

Based principally in the rural areas, AD's electoral strength declined after 1958, in part because of the harsh measures taken to suppress the Cuban-inspired urban and rural insurrectionary activity of the early 1960s. Moreover, the party's substantial AGRARIAN REFORM program and a practical nationalistic industrial policy alienated other sectors of the voting public. AD managed to elect Raúl LEONI in 1964, but its plurality was so small that it had to govern by coalition arrangements. In the elections of 1968 AD was defeated by the Social Christian party, the COMITÉ DE ORGANIZACIÓN POLÍTICA ELECTORAL INDEPENDIENTE (COPEI).

Since 1958 the party has suffered from a number of serious divisions. In 1960 some young leaders left it to form the Movimiento de Izquierda Revolucionaria (MIR), and in 1961–1962 Raúl Ramos Jiménez took out a group that called itself AD-Op or AD-Ars to oppose the dominance of old guard leaders within the party. In the 1968 elections Luis Beltrán Prieto Figueroa formed the Movimiento Electoral del Pueblo in another split from the AD old guard.

JOHN V. LOMBARDI

ACCIÓN POPULAR (POPULAR ACTION; AP). First popular movement to appear in Peru since the emergence of the ALIANZA POPULAR REVOLUCIONARIA AMERICANA (APRA) in the 1930s. Acción Popular was organized in 1956 by the architect Fernando BELAÚNDE TERRY and his youthful followers just after Belaúnde's impressive showing in that year's presidential election. Like APRA, it based its power on the middle and working classes, and although its aims differed little from APRA's, the party offered a more reformist, dynamic, and youthful image.

In the election of 1963 AP, supported by the armed forces and the Christian Democratic party, won the Presidency with 39 percent of the popular vote. The following year it scored impressively in municipal elections. It appeared as if AP was on the road to becoming an established political force, but in the ensuing five years a deep division developed within the party. The leftist branch, headed by the party's secretary-general, Edgardo Seoane, accused Belaúnde and his followers of having abandoned the reformist party program. In fact, Belaúnde assumed a more moderate position after 1963 and appeared ineffective in dealing with a hostile Congress. The division, which was further deepened by the 1967–1968 economic crisis, was one factor leading to the military take-over in 1968, and it marked the likely end of AP as a viable political force.

ORAZIO A. CICCARELLI

ACEVEDO DÍAZ, EDUARDO (1851–1921). Uruguayan novelist, politician, journalist, and diplomat. Acevedo Díaz was born in Unión, Uruguay, and died in Buenos Aires. A member of the Blanco party (*see* BLANCO PARTY: URUGUAY), he spent most of the years from 1875 to 1895 in exile in Argentina and wrote his novels during this period of absence from his homeland. In 1895 he returned to Montevideo as editor of *El Nacional,* in which he attacked the government of the Colorado Juan Idiarte Borda, who was assassinated in 1897 (*see* COLORADO PARTY: URUGUAY). Through his political activity he helped revive the Blanco party, which rose in revolt in 1897. After the revolution Acevedo Díaz clashed with Aparicio SARAVIA, the party's military leader, because of the former's disapproval of the policy of reaching *acuerdos* (accords) with the ruling Colorados to determine Blanco representation in Congress. In 1903 Acevedo Díaz, now a member of the Senate, played a decisive role in the election of the Colorado José BATLLE to the Presidency. Read out of the party for this action, he later served for many years as a diplomat in the United States, Argentina, Italy, and Brazil.

It is as a novelist that Acevedo Díaz is best known abroad, being considered the first writer to succeed in producing a novel in Uruguay. His first novel, *Brenda,* originally published in *La Nación* of Buenos Aires as a serial in 1886, is a trite romantic work, but the titles that followed established him as a master of the gaucho novel. These include *Ismael* (1888), *Nativa* (1890), *Grito de Gloria* (1894), *Soledad* (1894), his masterpiece, and *Lanza y sable* (1914).

GERARDO SÁENZ

ACOSTA, JOSÉ DE (1540–1600). Jesuit naturalist, teacher, and missionary. Born in Medina del Campo in northwestern Spain, Acosta entered a Jesuit novitiate in 1552. From 1559 to 1567 he attended the University of Alcalá de Henares and in the latter year began his long career as a teacher. In 1572 he set sail for Peru, having conceived a desire to go to the Indies many years before. After teaching for a year at the Jesuit College of San Pablo in Lima, he was sent on a mission to Upper Peru (modern Bolivia). He was named rector of San Pablo in September 1575, but only four months later he was appointed Provincial of Peru, a post he retained until 1581. In 1586 he left Peru, spending a year in New Spain while en route to Spain. At the time of his death he was rector of a Jesuit college in Salamanca.

Acosta's first major work, *De procuranda Indorum salute,* was the first book to be written by a Jesuit in America. Written in 1576 and published in 1588, it is a text on the proper methods to be followed in proselytizing the Indians. His best-known work, noted for its erudition, discrimination, and usefulness to scholars, is *Historia natural y moral de las Indias,* 1590 (*The Natural and Moral History of the Indies*). Divided into seven parts, it discusses the physical geography, climate, metals, plants and animals, and native inhabitants of the Indies. Acosta's main purpose in writing the book, however, was to explore the causes of the natural phenomena observed in America and to indicate cases in which the existence of these phenomena contradicted the teachings of the ancients.

HELEN DELPAR

AD. *See* ACCIÓN DEMOCRÁTICA.

ADELANTADO. Spanish official. The title, which dates from medieval times, is derived from the verb *adelantar,* meaning "to advance," and an *adelantado* was an official who was "advanced" into the place of the King to act in his name. The office fell into disuse after the reconquest of Spain from the Moors but was revived after the discovery of America. It was analogous to the military governorship of an occupied province or a province in the process of being conquered, the district itself being known as an *adelantamiento.* Formal legislation dealing with the office is found in the RECOPILACIÓN DE LEYES DE LAS INDIAS. It was a position of great power, the term of office being for one or two lifetimes or in perpetuity. The *adelantado* possessed a combination of executive and judicial powers; the judicial function included both original and appellate jurisdiction. In addition, he possessed legislative power to make laws for the government of the *adelantamiento* and regulations for the working of the mines.

The first *adelantado* in America was Bartholomew Columbus, but only because Christopher COLUMBUS, his brother, arrogated to himself the prerogative of the

King to grant the title. Vasco Núñez de BALBOA was made *adelantado* of the South Sea on September 23, 1514, by the first such patent granted by the monarchs, although Juan PONCE DE LEÓN actually received the title earlier and was the first to exercise the powers of the office. By the end of the sixteenth century the position had been replaced by that of VICEROY.

MARTIN TORODASH

ADVANCED INSTITUTE OF BRAZILIAN STUDIES. *See* INSTITUTO SUPERIOR DE ESTUDOS BRASILEIROS.

AGRARIAN REFORM. Until recently rural society in nearly every Latin American country was characterized by extreme concentration of landownership. A relatively small number of large estates occupied thousands of acres, often monopolizing the land best suited to agriculture. While some of these holdings might be devoted to the intensive production of commercial crops such as sugar, cotton, and bananas, others were inadequately exploited, with large tracts of land lying idle or given over to extensive cattle raising. Holdings of the latter type, to which the term LATIFUNDIUM (Spanish and Portuguese *latifundio*) is frequently applied, might not yield great economic profit to the owner, but they did confer social status and political power on both the local and the national levels. Meanwhile, the vast majority of the rural population lived in conditions of extreme poverty, ignorance, and dependence. Those who owned land were likely to hold only tiny plots (*minifundios*), frequently with an insecure title. Some squatted on public or private lands, but most worked for the large estates as seasonal laborers, tenants, sharecroppers, or resident peons. *See also* AGRICULTURE (LATIN AMERICA).

Although these conditions still exist in many areas of Latin America, the twentieth century has seen drastic changes in the agrarian structure of several countries. Agrarian reform was initiated in Mexico during the second decade of the century and has continued there ever since. It began in Bolivia in 1952 and in Venezuela and Cuba in 1959. During the 1960s major agrarian reform programs were started in Chile and Peru and less significant ones in several other countries, including Colombia and the Central American republics. In 1961 nineteen of the American republics indicated their support of agrarian reform by their adherence to the Charter of the ALLIANCE FOR PROGRESS.

The term agrarian reform in Latin America usually implies the forcible transfer of landed property from its owners to the landless as a means of improving the standard of living of the rural lower classes. Agrarian reform of this kind may be accomplished in various ways, such as confiscation, expropriation (with owners usually receiving compensation in the form of long-term bonds), or the imposition of progressively mounting taxes on land. Agrarian reform laws often distinguish between the underutilized hacienda and the efficient, capital-intensive commercial holding and proceed more vigorously against the former type. The term agrarian reform is sometimes applied to less drastic methods of altering rural conditions, such as the resettlement of landless peasants on unused public lands.

Mexico. Mexico's agrarian reform was a direct result of the MEXICAN REVOLUTION. When the revolution began in 1910, approximately three-quarters of the population was rural, yet nearly all rural families were landless. During the revolution the cause of agrarian reform was upheld most forcefully and consistently by Emiliano ZAPATA, notably in his Plan of Ayala of 1911 (*see* AYALA, PLAN OF). Later Venustiano CARRANZA, finding himself pinned down in the state of Veracruz during his conflict with Zapata and Francisco VILLA, accepted the advice of his principal general, Álvaro OBREGÓN, to make an appeal to the workers and peasants. As a result, he issued what came to be regarded as Mexico's first significant agrarian reform law on January 6, 1915.

However, Carranza was unenthusiastic about agrarian reform, and although the 1915 law was incorporated into the constitution of 1917 (*see* CONSTITUTION OF 1917: MEXICO), it was not until Obregón became President in 1920 that the process of land distribution began to accelerate. An important feature of Mexico's agrarian reform program was the restitution or grant of lands to villages, many of which had been despoiled of their holdings during the nineteenth century. The communal landholdings thus formed, known as *ejidos* (*see* EJIDO), were to be inalienable. The members could decide whether to cultivate the land collectively or in individual family plots; in most cases the latter alternative was adopted.

Land distribution continued during the 1920s. Special banks were organized in this period to provide credit for the beneficiaries of agrarian reform, and a large-scale program of irrigation was undertaken to provide additional arable land. However, Obregón and his successors questioned the long-range value of the *ejido* system, conceiving of it only as a temporary expedient; they hoped that the Mexican farmer might be converted into a yeoman farmer who would own his land outright. Dissatisfaction with the results of agrarian reform led to a slowdown in the early 1930s, but the program was intensified after 1934, mainly because of the determination of President Lázaro CÁRDENAS (1934–1940) to destroy the large estate forever. During his administration he distributed nearly 18 million hectares (more than 44 million acres) of land, or more than all his predecessors put together. Moreover, Cárdenas was firmly committed to the *ejido* and in particular encouraged the formation of collective *ejidos*, as in the cotton-growing Laguna District of northern Mexico; he also expropriated profitable commercial holdings that had been left untouched by previous administrations.

Mexican Presidents since Cárdenas have continued the land distribution program, some more intensively than others. The government of President Alfonso LÓPEZ MATEOS (1958–1964) distributed almost as much land as Cárdenas, but most others did not come close to matching Cárdenas's record.

By the 1960s the government had begun to be concerned about the low productivity and incomes of those who had received land under agrarian reform. The López Mateos administration extended social security to *ejido* residents; the government of President Gustavo DÍAZ ORDAZ (1964–1970) began to invest considerably larger funds in technical and financial aid to the *ejidatarios*, and this policy was intensified by his successor, President Luis ECHEVERRÍA.

The agrarian reform problem was complicated by the rapid increase in Mexico's population. This resulted in the reduction in size of *ejido* family plots and in a continuing need for land by a sizable number of peasants. As a result, agrarian reform remained a pressing problem for Mexico.

Bolivia. Agrarian reform in Bolivia also resulted from revolution. In April 1952 the MOVIMIENTO NACIONALISTA REVOLUCIONARIO (MNR) seized power as the result of an insurrection. The first move toward agrarian reform taken by the new government of President Víctor PAZ ESTENSSORO was to establish a Ministry of Peasant Affairs. The Ministry undertook the organization of the Indian peasants into unions, militia groups, and local units of the MNR. President Paz Estenssoro also named a commission to write an agrarian reform law.

On August 2, 1953, the President officially proclaimed the Agrarian Reform Law, which provided for granting immediately to all peasants the plots of land that landlords had allowed them to use for their homes and to grow food for themselves. The law also provided for the division of the rest of the large landholdings among resident peasants and other eligible recipients as soon as the government could survey these holdings. It left to the peasants the decision whether to cultivate the land cooperatively or in individual holdings; those who received land could not sell it for twenty years except to the government. During the next decade most of the land of the ALTIPLANO of Bolivia, where most Indian peasants lived, was distributed among them. At the same time, a number of Indians were given grants in the low and humid eastern part of the country (*see* ORIENTE: BOLIVIA).

An immediate result of agrarian reform was to decrease the amount of food sold to the cities. The deficit was made up for about a decade by the provision of surplus grain by the United States. It is not clear whether total food production decreased, since the Indians consumed more than they had formerly. Indian army recruits reportedly weighed 20 pounds more in the late 1960s than they had before the 1952 revolution.

Thus far only a relatively small beginning has been made in converting the peasants from subsistence to commercial farmers. However, possession of land has made the peasants a major, if often passive, power factor in national politics. Any government seeking peasants' support has had to demonstrate a willingness to allow them to remain in possession of the land.

Venezuela. In contrast to Mexico and Bolivia, in Venezuela agrarian reform was carried out by a democratically elected regime and without major turbulence. ACCIÓN DEMOCRÁTICA, the party principally responsible for the agrarian reform, was first in power between 1945 and 1948. At that time, it began a process of land redistribution that was cut short when its government was overthrown by a military coup d'état.

With the return of Acción Democrática to power in February 1959, it again undertook agrarian reform. An agrarian reform law providing for purchase and distribution by the National Agrarian Institute of the country's large landed estates was adopted in 1960. Under its provisions the peasants were not to pay for the land they received, but they were not allowed to sell it, except to the Institute, for twenty years.

During the ten years Acción Democrática remained in power (1959–1969), approximately 150,000 landless families received land. They represented about three-fourths of those without land of their own at the time redistribution began. Agrarian reform continued after Acción Democrática had been defeated in the December 1968 election by the COMITÉ DE ORGANIZACIÓN POLÍTICA ELECTORAL INDEPENDIENTE (COPEI).

Venezuelan land redistribution has been accompanied by extensive aid to the beneficiaries. Credit has been extended by the Agricultural and Grazing Bank, and technical assistance by the National Agrarian Institute and the Ministry of Agriculture, while rural housing has been built by the Ministry of Health. The Venezuelan agrarian reform is one of the few on record in which land redistribution has been accompanied by a substantial increase in agricultural output. This has been due in large part to substantial investment by the government in agricultural development.

Cuba. Cuba's agrarian reform has been a product of the revolution of Fidel CASTRO. Although the constitution of 1940 (*see* CONSTITUTION OF 1940: CUBA) instructed the government to undertake land redistribution, the only administration that did so was that of President Carlos PRÍO SOCORRÁS (1948–1952), which set up pilot agrarian reform projects but did not launch an overall program.

The first agrarian reform law of the Castro government was enacted in May 1959. It provided for the redistribution of large landholdings to individual peasants; each peasant was to receive 66 acres free and might purchase 99 additional acres. Although peasants were authorized to form cooperatives, they were not required to do so. However, the National Institute of Agrarian Reform (INRA), in charge of the program, was staffed largely by people who believed in collectivized agriculture. Much agricultural land, including the large sugar estates, was reorganized into cooperatives under INRA supervision, while other holdings, primarily cattle ranches, became state farms under direct INRA administration. In addition, thousands of peasants were granted individual holdings.

Subsequent decrees reflected the Communist direction taken by the Castro government. In 1961–1962 the cooperatives were converted into fully state-owned people's farms (*granjas del pueblo*) that have been compared to the Russian sovkhozy. A second agrarian reform law (1963) limited private holdings to 166 acres. The remaining private landowners were organized into the National Association of Small Farmers (ANAP), which issued detailed orders to its members concerning what to produce and the prices at which to sell their crops to the government. *See also* CUBAN REVOLUTION.

Agrarian reform in Cuba since 1959 has been the most extensive and thorough to take place in Latin America. However, it has resulted in land being given not to landless peasants or rural workers but to the state.

Chile. Although an agrarian reform law was enacted in 1962, it was not until Eduardo FREI of the PARTIDO DEMÓCRATA CRISTIANO became President in 1964 that agrarian reform was seriously undertaken. It entered a new phase under Frei's Marxist successor, Salvador ALLENDE.

In 1967 Frei approved a new agrarian reform law that provided for the expropriation of estates of more than 80 hectares (approximately 200 acres) and the eventual transfer of this land to the peasants. The law also called for the establishment on expropriated estates of *asentamientos* (production cooperatives) that would last three to five years. During this period the agrarian reform agency, the Corporation for Agrarian Reform (CORA), would train the peasants to operate the land. Peasants who met CORA standards would receive title to the land and then determine whether they would cultivate their holdings communally or as individual family farms.

With the inauguration of Allende in 1970, the pace of agrarian reform quickened. Whereas 1,408 holdings occupying approximately 3.5 million hectares (9 million acres) were expropriated under Frei, the first two years of the Allende administration saw the expropriation of 3,500 holdings totaling about 5.3 million hectares (14 million acres). Moreover, the Allende government planned to convert expropriated holdings into centers of agrarian reform, or large collective farms. At the end of 1972, however, the future course of agrarian reform in Chile was clouded by several problems: uncertainty regarding the fate of properties of fewer than 80 hectares; the resistance of some peasants to the planned collectivization of agriculture; and declining food production, which, coupled with increased consumption, made it likely that food imports for 1973 would cost more than $450 million.

Peru. As in Chile, agrarian reform took place in two phases in Peru. In 1964, under democratically elected President Fernando BELAÚNDE TERRY, an agrarian reform law was passed that provided for granting peasants the small plots landlords had allowed them to use for their own purposes and the redistribution of the rest of the large estates in due time. Under this law the process of breaking up the large estates moved very slowly.

With the seizure of power by the military regime of Gen. Juan VELASCO ALVARADO in October 1968, the rhythm of agrarian reform accelerated. Within four years of General Velasco's seizure of power, the government had expropriated virtually all the traditional large estates of the highlands of Peru as well as commercial holdings in the coastal region. However, the reform was carried out with virtually no participation by the peasants. It brought into existence a series of rural institutions controlled largely by the military men who dominated the Velasco government. These institutions made little effort to mobilize rank-and-file peasants to control the new units established under the agrarian reform.

Bibliography. Pompeu Accioly Borges (ed.), *Bibliografía sôbre Reforma Agrária,* Rio de Janeiro, 1962; Thomas F. Carroll, *Land Tenure and Land Reform in Latin America: A Selected Bibliography,* Washington, 1962; Peter Dorner (ed.), *Land Reform in Latin America: Issues and Cases,* Madison, Wis., 1971; Dwight B. Heath et al., *Land Reform and Social Revolution in Bolivia,* New York, 1969; Eyler N. Simpson, *The Ejido: Mexico's Way Out,* Chapel Hill, N.C., 1937; T. Lynn Smith (ed.), *Agrarian Reform in Latin America,* New York, 1965; Nathan L. Whetten, *Rural Mexico,* Chicago, 1948; R. Wilkie, *San Miguel: A Mexican Collective Ejido,* Stanford, Calif., 1971.

ROBERT J. ALEXANDER

AGRICULTURE (ARGENTINA). Argentina is one of the great agricultural surplus producers of the world. In linseed oil it supplies 80 percent of the world market, in fresh and canned beef more than 40 percent, in oats 21 percent, in grain sorghums 18 percent, in wool 9 percent, and in wheat 7 percent. In addition, the nation is self-sufficient in almost all agricultural commodities, importing only those for which it lacks a suitable physical environment, particularly coffee and rubber. This large agricultural output is produced by only 19 percent of the labor force, for although more than 90 percent of the country's exports are agricultural commodities, Argentina is an urban, industrial nation.

Agricultural development did not begin in earnest until long after initial colonization. Throughout the colonial period most of Argentina was outside the effective control of the government and remained a domain of wild herds of cattle and horses as well as of nomadic Indians. The major export was hides, later supplemented by salt beef. Crop agriculture was confined to the immediate environs of the few small towns. After independence the agricultural economy began to expand in response to a growing demand for agricultural commodities in Europe, particularly in Great Britain. The PAMPA was rapidly cleared of Indians and incorporated into the private domain in the form of large estates. By the middle of the nineteenth century wool and wheat had been added to the important agricultural exports. In 1876 a refrigerator ship made the first successful transatlantic shipment of beef, and Argentina added what has become its most famous export, fresh beef.

The most important agricultural region of Argentina is the pampa, where most of the nation's exports are produced. Farms are large, often absentee-owned, and commonly low in efficiency as compared with United States farms. This situation can be attributed in part to government policies, but the blame also rests with the conservative attitude of many of the landowners.

Beef cattle are dominant virtually everywhere on the pampa, although they are most important in the southeast and between the Uruguay and Paraná Rivers. In addition, there have developed two important dairy regions, a fluid-milk zone surrounding Buenos Aires and a processed-milk zone in the center of Córdoba and Santa Fe. Meat other than beef plays a minor role in the diet of the Argentines. However, hogs are raised in the northern portion of the province of Buenos Aires, in a humid zone that favors corn production. Nearly half the nation's sheep also are found on the pampa, primarily in poorly drained portions of the northeast and southeast. They are raised for wool, but small amounts of lamb and mutton are exported.

During the twentieth century crops have competed successfully with animal products for primacy among Argentine exports. Wheat, the most important grain, is raised on the drier margins of the pampa, particularly north of Bahía Blanca. There oats, rye, and barley also are important. Corn is raised in the more humid center of the pampa. Sunflowers and peanuts are raised for their oil, primarily in the province of Córdoba, while flax, from which linseed oil is derived, is raised in Entre Ríos. The domestic demand for citrus is met largely in an area immediately north of Buenos Aires. Approximately a quarter of the nation's vegetables are raised on market farms near Buenos Aires, especially in the delta of the Paraná River.

Outside the pampa there has been a spectacular rise in agricultural production since 1930. Except for the large sheep stations of PATAGONIA, the greater part of agricultural production outside the pampa is intended for domestic markets, over which the government has not assumed strict control. Much of the agriculture is carried on in irrigated areas. There are major zones of oasis agriculture around Mendoza and San Juan, which are famed for their vineyards but also are important producers of fruits, vegetables, and alfalfa. The valleys of the Negro and Colorado Rivers in Patagonia also support large irrigation projects, growing much the same crops as those to the north but emphasizing deciduous fruits. Older, less efficient irrigated oases are found around the cities of Córdoba, Tucumán, and Salta. The last two produce most of the nation's sugar. Normally enough cotton is produced within the CHACO, particularly under irrigation along the Bermejo River, to supply the domestic demand.

Although only a small area in the northeast is hot and humid, this region has begun to be the focus of attention. Yerba maté, a native tea consumed in large quantities by Argentines, has been grown there since colonial times. Recently plantations of Asian tea have been laid out, particularly in Japanese and German colonies. Tobacco production has been greatly expanded, and through efforts in both northeast and northwest Argentina has recently achieved self-sufficiency. Tung nut groves have also been planted, and exports of tung oil, used as a base for paint, have greatly increased.

See also CATTLE INDUSTRY (ARGENTINA).

Bibliography. Francisco de Aparicio and Horacio A. Difrieri (eds.), *La Argentina: Suma de geografía*, 9 vols., Buenos Aires, 1958–1963; James R. Scobie, *Revolution on the Pampas: A Social History of Argentine Wheat, 1860–1910,* Austin, Tex., 1964; Carl C. Taylor, *Rural Life in Argentina*, Baton Rouge, La., 1948; United States Department of Agriculture, *Argentine Agriculture,* Economic Research Service Report 216, Washington, 1968.

MORTON D. WINSBERG

AGRICULTURE (BRAZIL). Brazil is primarily an agricultural country. In 1970 agriculture accounted for more than one-fourth of the gross national product, produced 75 percent of the nation's foreign exchange earnings, and employed half of the labor force. Excluding wheat, Brazil is self-sufficient in crop, livestock, and forest products. It is the world's leading producer of coffee, the second largest producer of cacao, and the third largest producer of sugar and corn. It is one of the largest hog-producing areas in the world, and its cattle herd ranks third, behind that of the United States and the Soviet Union. In the Americas, Brazil is the largest producer of rice and is outranked in cotton only by the United States.

Yet only one-tenth of Brazil's arable land is under cultivation, a fact underlining its enormous agricultural potential. The state of São Paulo alone produces 50 percent of the total agricultural output. The abundance of fertile land and the vast range of the nation's climate and geography encouraged centuries of speculative exploitation of successions of single crops that hindered orderly and diversified development. Hence extreme fluctuation and regional imbalance have been the dominant characteristics of the agricultural sector.

Before the coming of the Portuguese, scattered Indian tribes practiced subsistence slash-and-burn agriculture, cultivating a variety of crops: manioc, maize, sweet potatoes, squash, beans, cacao, tobacco, and cotton. The first Europeans, failing to find gold and silver, concentrated on the development of agriculture.

After depleting the lucrative groves of dyewood along the coasts, they moved inland along the rivers, adopting the wasteful Indian methods of fire agriculture, modified somewhat by iron tools. They cultivated the indigenous products and introduced the crops and livestock of Europe. Yet so persistent was the Indian heritage that such elements of European agriculture as the plow, draft animals, and crop rotation remained unused over wide areas for centuries.

The first successful agricultural colonies were concentrated in the NORTHEAST and were based on the large-scale production of imported sugarcane. The spread of sugar plantations in the coastal areas from Pernambuco to Rio de Janeiro in the second half of the sixteenth century led to Indian enslavement and subsequently to a vigorous trade in African slaves. Cattle raising developed alongside the plantation but remained subsidiary to the export-oriented sugar industry. *See* NEGRO IN BRAZIL; SUGAR INDUSTRY (COLONIAL BRAZIL).

Crops of high commercial value such as tobacco, cacao, and cotton had their era of prosperity during the colonial period, but even the gold and diamond boom of the eighteenth century did not yield as much revenue as sugar. Sugar not only brought wealth but gave to Brazil the large plantation and a patriarchal society with a slaveholding economy—patterns that fashioned the nation's economic, cultural, and political development.

The gold rush shifted the country's economic center from the Northeast to central and southern Brazil. Cattle empires that had penetrated deep into the backlands facilitated a massive internal migration southward. With increased competition from sugarcane plantations in the Caribbean, the sugar industry declined, and a new economic cycle was inaugurated.

The world demand for coffee had grown steadily from the early 1800s on. Upon the discovery that coffee flourished in the rich forest soils of Rio de Janeiro, São Paulo, and Minas Gerais, coffee cultivation spread rapidly. By the 1830s coffee was Brazil's largest export crop, and by 1900 Brazil supplied more than 70 percent of the world market. Coffee fortunes provided capital for the introduction of railroads and light industry. The ensuing prosperity encouraged large-scale European immigration (*see* IMMIGRATION: BRAZIL). Though occasionally plagued by overproduction and falling prices, coffee has maintained its position as Brazil's largest export commodity for more than 140 years.

In the last quarter of the nineteenth century the Amazon Basin became the chief world supplier of rubber (*see* AMAZON RIVER; RUBBER BOOM: BRAZIL). The boom was short-lived, for Southeast Asia captured the world market prior to World War I. An attempt by the Ford Motor Company to revive the industry between 1925 and 1946 failed, and today most of the rubber produced is used in Brazil.

In the 1930s the government of Getúlio VARGAS sought to reduce excessive dependence on monoculture and promoted industrialization at the expense of agriculture. Consequently in the 1940s and 1950s agriculture lagged behind the rest of the economy. However, in 1959 the federal government undertook a massive project to develop the arid Northeast, and in 1964 the military government extended tax incentives and special subsidies to farmers in order to facilitate the purchase of machinery and fertilizers. These policies, together with a national program of highway and dam construction and increased emphasis on the role of education and technology, stimulated a more rapid growth in the agricultural sector, particularly in products other than coffee.

See also COFFEE INDUSTRY (BRAZIL).

Bibliography. Luis Amaral, *História Geral da Agricultura Brasileira,* 2 vols., São Paulo, 1958; Rubens A. Dias and Ruy M. Paiva, "Recente Evolução da Agricultura em São Paulo," *Agricultura em São Paulo,* vol. VII, no. 1, January 1960, pp. 3–39; Celso Furtado, *The Economic Growth of Brazil: A Survey from Colonial to Modern Times,* Berkeley, Calif., 1963; E. A. Graner and C. Godoy, Jr., *Culturas da Fazenda Brasileira,* São Paulo, 1964; William S. Nicholls and Ruy M. Paiva, "Structure and Productivity of Brazilian Agriculture," *Journal of Farm Economics,* vol. XLVII, no. 2, May 1963, pp. 346–361; Ruy M. Paiva, "The Development of Brazilian Agriculture, 1945–1960," *Journal of Farm Economics,* vol. XLIII, no. 5, December 1961, pp. 1092–1102; G. Edward Schuh, *The Agricultural Development of Brazil,* New York, 1970; Lawrence W. Witt, "Changes in the Agriculture of South Central Brazil," *Journal of Farm Economics,* vol. XXV, no. 3, August 1943, pp. 622–643.

ARNOLD J. MEAGHER

AGRICULTURE (LATIN AMERICA). Agriculture is the most important sector of the Latin American economy, employing more than half of the economically active population. Unfortunately, in most countries agriculture is inefficient, and it produces only a little more than a quarter of the region's gross national product. With approximately 8 percent of the world's population and 9 percent of the world's land area, the region has a disproportionately large production of coffee, bananas, cacao, sugar, and cotton among its crops, as well as horses, cattle, and sheep. Not only does the agricultural economy supply both food and raw materials for the region, but most Latin American countries depend heavily upon the export of agricultural commodities.

The region suffers from both cultural and physical obstacles to the development of agriculture. Many parts of Latin America are dominated by traditional societies with prescientific attitudes toward agriculture. In these areas the status of the individual is usually determined from birth, and wealth is commonly based upon the ownership of land. Large estates, inefficiently operated and absentee-owned (*latifundia*), prevail. What little profits are derived from the land frequently are not returned to it but are spent on conspicuous consumption or for more land, to gain greater prestige. In some places workers for these estates are attached to them in tenure arrangements similar to those of the serfs of medieval Europe. Although this type of employment is declining, millions of Latin American farmers live a marginal existence, in crushing poverty and isolation, growing a handful of staple crops such as corn, beans, potatoes, plantains, manioc, and rice. Some must seek land arrangements with wealthy landowners, others have some form of title to their land, while many more squat without title on government or private property. Whatever the form of tenancy among the small-scale farmers, systems of agriculture that provide a barely sufficient amount of food for survival have evolved over generations. Fearful of experiments that might jeopardize his food supply, the Latin American farmer is extremely cautious about technological change. This conservatism can be understood when one recognizes the physical problems that beset agriculture throughout the region. Much of Latin America is too hot and wet for highly productive agriculture; other areas are either too dry, too high, or too steep; and many more have infertile soil. Land of the quality of the Corn Belt of the United States, the Danubian Plain, or the Yangtze River Valley is scarce.

Two distinct forms of agriculture, subsistence and commercial, prevail. Subsistence agriculture may be subdivided into migratory and sedentary types. In the hot and wet rain forests, particularly in the Amazon Basin, migratory agriculture has evolved. In an effort to lessen the effects of erosion, plants such as corn, beans, plantains, and manioc are planted together on a small plot cut from the forest. After heat and rain have robbed the soil of its fertility, normally within four years, the plot is abandoned for a new one. Today only a few million farmers continue to cultivate land in this manner. The vast majority of Latin American farmers are sedentary, cultivating the same plot for many years. Using simple tools such as a spade, a machete, a hoe, a digging stick, and perhaps a wooden plow drawn by oxen, they usually grow barely enough to survive. Most do sell some of their production in nearby markets in order to buy what they need but cannot produce themselves. The small-scale Latin American subsistence farmer is becoming increasingly conscious of the enormous disparity between his standard of living and that of the urban resident. This realization has caused a rapid rural-urban migration and a growing demand for land reform among those who remain (*see* AGRARIAN REFORM).

The importance of commercial agriculture is increasing throughout Latin America. Most commercial agriculture is large-scale, and the small-scale commercial farm found in the United States and Western Europe continues to be a rarity. Export crops began to be grown in the colonial period, particularly in the Caribbean area and Brazil, where both sugar and cacao became important. In the nineteenth century Latin America began the large-scale export of coffee, wheat, wool, and beef, and in the twentieth century bananas and cotton became significant. Today, owing to the rapidly expanding urban population, the demand to provide food for the cities has enhanced the need for greater commercialization of agriculture. The area under cultivation has been expanded by opening up isolated regions through road construction, drainage, and irrigation. Efforts to increase productivity have been made through the introduction of new seeds, new breeds of livestock, agricultural credit, and rural education programs. In several nations, particularly Mexico, Bolivia, Cuba, and Chile, evolutionary processes of agricultural development are being abandoned for revolutionary changes.

The rapid growth of agricultural production in Latin America is imperative. At present the region has the fastest rate of population growth of any cultural region in the world, and it is likely to continue to be the leader. Since 1960, although its total food production has greatly expanded, because of the rapid growth in population, it has been able only to maintain the same per capita food production. Given the already low average per capita consumption of food in Latin America, this circumstance has serious implications for the region's political stability. Latin America must begin a serious effort to overcome the cultural and physical problems that have prevented a rapid increase in agricultural productivity.

See also AGRICULTURE (ARGENTINA); AGRICULTURE (BRAZIL); BANANA INDUSTRY (CENTRAL AMERICA AND THE CARIBBEAN); BANANA INDUSTRY (ECUADOR); COFFEE INDUSTRY (BRAZIL); COFFEE INDUSTRY (CENTRAL AMERICA); COFFEE INDUSTRY (COLOMBIA); SUGAR INDUSTRY (COLONIAL BRAZIL); SUGAR INDUSTRY (CUBA).

Bibliography. Preston James, *Latin America,* 4th ed., New York, 1969; T. Lynn Smith, *The Process of Rural Development in Latin America,* Gainesville, Fla., 1967; United States Department of Agriculture, *The Latin American Farmer,* Economic Research Service Report 257, Washington, 1969; R. C. West and J. P. Augelli, *Middle America: Its Lands and Peoples,* New York, 1966.

MORTON D. WINSBERG

AGUASCALIENTES CONVENTION. Convention of 1914 during which the definitive rupture between the supporters of Venustiano CARRANZA and those of Francisco VILLA and Emiliano ZAPATA took place. Villa and Zapata had both been independent of Carranza's authority during the recently concluded struggle against Victoriano HUERTA, Villa because he was the most powerful military chief and Zapata because he had his own revolutionary program, embryonic but profound; Zapata, in fact, had not even subscribed to Carranza's Plan of Guadalupe.

Relations between Carranza and Villa had cooled after Carranza prevented Villa from moving toward Mexico City earlier in the year. In an attempt to heal the breach between the two men, discussions were held in Torreón (July 4–8, 1914), during which it was agreed to convoke a convention to determine the date of presidential elections and a program of reform. Later, on August 29, representatives of Carranza failed to persuade Zapata to lay down his arms. At a meeting in Mexico City on October 1, the partisans of Carranza refused to accept his resignation as First Chief of the revolutionary forces. The *carrancistas* now moved to Aguascalientes in order to confer in a neutral place with the supporters of Villa and Zapata. During these discussions, which lasted from October 10 until November 13, 1914, the *zapatistas* succeeded in having the convention accept the Plan of Ayala (*see* AYALA, PLAN OF). In addition, the convention asserted its sovereignty over the nation and removed Carranza from his position as First Chief and Villa from his command of the Division of the North. However, Carranza refused to step down because Villa did not surrender his command. When the convention declared Carranza in rebellion on November 10, the rupture between him and Villa became inevitable.

The convention, which adopted several important labor and agrarian measures, had three presidents. The first of these, Eulalio Gutiérrez (November 3, 1914–January 1915), though initially dependent upon Villa, ended by deposing both him and Zapata and fleeing to the north after his position became untenable. Gutiérrez was succeeded by Roque González Garza (January 18, 1915–June 10, 1915), Villa's representative in Aguascalientes, who raided the area around

Mexico City and Cuernavaca. Pressed by the *zapatistas,* he stepped down in favor of Francisco Lagos Cházaro, who was president from June 10, 1915, until January 1916.

MOISÉS GONZÁLEZ NAVARRO

AGUIRRE CERDA, PEDRO (1879–1941). President of Chile (1938–1941). Born into a large and poor family in a rural area of Aconcagua Province, Aguirre Cerda was educated locally and at the Instituto Pedagógico of the University of Chile, graduating as a teacher of Spanish. In 1904 he also qualified as a lawyer. He joined the Radical party (*see* RADICAL PARTY: CHILE) and was elected as a deputy for San Felipe (1915–1918) and Santiago (1918–1921) and as a senator for Concepción (1921–1924). While a Radical deputy, in 1918, he became Minister of Education and Justice and was largely responsible for a law making primary education compulsory. He also served three times as Minister of the Interior during the first administration of Arturo ALESSANDRI (1920–1925).

Aguirre Cerda remained outside the government in the late 1920s and early 1930s, studying in France and managing an estate he had acquired. At the same time, he added to his public reputation with two studies of Chilean national issues, *El problema agrario* (1929) and *El problema industrial* (1933). Although his party supported Alessandri's second administration (1932–1938) until 1937, he himself held no office, and although he had opposed the formation of the Popular Front, he was chosen as its candidate for the presidential election of October 1938 (*see* POPULAR FRONT: CHILE). After a countrywide campaign in which he impressed the electorate by his honest approach and sympathetic manner, Aguirre Cerda triumphed with 222,720 votes against 218,609 for his right-wing opponent, Gustavo ROSS. One of the most popular Presidents ever to hold office in Chile, Aguirre Cerda was supported by a fragile coalition that held together for only two years. Despite political problems he initiated a program of social and economic reform, establishing the CORPORACIÓN DE FOMENTO DE LA PRODUCCIÓN (Chilean Development Corporation), expanding education considerably, improving the labor laws, and passing welfare legislation. Aguirre Cerda died in office on November 25, 1941, halfway through his presidential term.

HAROLD BLAKEMORE

AGUSTINI, DELMIRA (1886–1914). Uruguayan poet. A native of Montevideo, she was murdered by her husband of a few months, Enrique Job Reyes. Three volumes of poetry appeared before her death: *El libro blanco* (1907), *Cantos de la mañana* (1910), and *Los cálices vacíos* (1913). They share a conception of love as an absolute, expressed in erotically spiritual themes by means of symbols such as the statue, the candle, the serpent, the owl, and wine. Delmira Agustini's *Obras completas,* which also include *El rosario de Eros* and *Los astros del abismo,* appeared in 1924, with a second edition in 1955.

RACHEL PHILLIPS

AIR TRANSPORT. Air transport in Latin America developed early, and by the end of the 1920s it was playing a significant role in the economic development of many countries. Growth was relatively rapid in both passenger and freight cargo movement until quite

TABLE 1. SCHEDULED PASSENGER AIR TRAFFIC IN MAJOR
LATIN AMERICAN COUNTRIES, 1953–1971
(In millions of passenger-kilometers)

	Brazil	Mexico	Argentina	Colombia	Venezuela	Chile	Peru
1953	1,482.6	630.1	316.6	415.4	268.5	95.3	78.5
1962	2,763.7	1,143.6	826.5	1,001.3	431.7	364.4	182.8
1964	2,593.5	1,506.3	1,043.8	1,319.4	543.6	511.1	369.9
1966	3,048.0	2,005.6	1,140.8	1,377.0	740.2	529.3	541.9
1968	3,692.7	2,242.5	1,748.8	1,561.9	925.3	601.5	574.2
1970	4,385.0	2,939.0	2,395.0	2,063.0	1,218.0	839.0	789.0
1971	4,882.0	3,428.0	2,700.0	2,213.0	1,292.0	1,148.0	821.0
1971 as percentage of 1953	329	544	852	533	480	1,205	1,039

SOURCES: International Civil Aviation Organization, *Monthly Bulletins;* United Nations, *Statistical Abstract, 1970.*

recently. In the late 1960s, however, Latin America's share of scheduled world air traffic declined.

The importance of air transport in Latin America is traceable to at least three basic geographical factors: (1) the vast distances between major urban centers; (2) the large stretches of mountains, deserts, jungles, and open water everywhere south of the United States border; and (3) the probably resultant inadequate surface transport. While some experts such as Robert T. Brown argue that air transport growth has deterred the development of other transport modes, especially HIGHWAYS (*see* Bibliography), perhaps a more measured judgment might be that overall transport planning in Latin America has had to take into account the relative advantages of various modes and to seek to avoid unnecessary competition, given the lack of funds.

Yet, in view of the challenging transport task facing such countries as Brazil, Colombia, Mexico, and Peru, it is not useful to approach the analysis of the role of air transport with an emphasis on competition among modes. To be sure, air transport is in many cases cheaper, more frequent, safer, and more convenient for both passenger and freight cargo movements than other forms of transport. However, as a detailed study of Colombia demonstrates, the problem is not so much which of several possible transport modes is most effective—by whatever criteria—but how to move the specific passenger and freight potential in and out of a particular city.

If a study is made of the city's industries, the inputs required in those industries, the places from which they must be brought, the markets for the city's products, and all the factors that can be derived from an intensive origin and destination analysis, it becomes clear that the basic issue is how to move goods and not which transport mode to select. The solution for each city depends upon the availability of the various transport modes, the relative costs of utilization for each type of freight, and the importance of speed, safety, and security in the movement. The result is often a very complex interrelationship. The major role played by air transport is due more to the kind of goods produced or imported and to the nature of the movement of people between places than to costs and convenience alone. For this reason, the slowdown in the growth of air cargo movements in recent years is probably traceable more to intensive local industrial development, especially in Colombia, Brazil, and Mexico, than to a loss of traffic to competing modes.

Paradoxically, however, despite the early establishment of air transport, the industry remains less developed in Latin America than might be expected. Moreover, the very reasons that made air transport essential at earlier stages in Latin American economic growth have contributed to the relative backwardness of the industry in the 1970s. Distances are so great that few passengers can afford to travel. Thus market potential is limited. Aircraft manufacturers have concentrated on building large and fast aircraft, but many Latin American airports are small and are located in jungles, deserts, or mountainous areas where specialized aircraft are necessary. Moreover, available aircraft have been very expensive to operate. What is needed is a maneuverable, large-capacity airplane that can get into difficult places and yet be operated at a relatively low cost.

Almost as important is the fact that there are probably far too many airlines in operation in Latin America. Each nation has permitted the creation of large and small companies to an excessive degree. If the international competition, especially from the airlines of Europe, North America, and Asia, and the relatively small size of the typical Latin American company are also taken into account, there is ample reason for agreeing with a pronouncement of the LATIN AMERICAN FREE TRADE ASSOCIATION that the "first priority task for the 1970s is the study of possible cooperation among the air transport companies in such areas as revenue sharing, joint agencies, joint ownership and the creation of multinational enterprises."

Passenger traffic. In the period from 1960 to 1970, scheduled passenger air traffic in the major countries in Latin America generally increased by a factor of 2 to 2.5. If Mexico, Central America, and the Caribbean are excluded, the growth for South America was more

TABLE 2. AIR FREIGHT TRAFFIC IN MAJOR
LATIN AMERICAN COUNTRIES, 1953–1971
(In millions of ton-kilometers)

	Brazil	Mexico	Argentina	Colombia	Venezuela	Chile	Peru
1953	55	157	12	97	7	20	5
1962	286	201	32	173	115	47	22
1964	259	204	34	202	155	89	34
1966	304	253	49	222	141	108	50
1968	475	301	155	216	76	185	56
1970	538	288	277	260	166	117	99
1971	590	335	329	276	181	158	102
1971 as percentage of 1953	1,073	213	2,742	285	2,585	790	2,040

SOURCE: International Civil Aviation Organization, *Monthly Bulletins.*

modest, being somewhat less than a doubling in the decade. Significantly, countries that had begun early in air transport did not show as fast a growth in passenger traffic in the 1960s and early 1970s as those that had begun later. As shown in Table 1, Argentina, with an excellent rail and surface transport system, recorded through 1971 an increase of more than 850 percent over 1953 levels, whereas the growth for the same period in Brazil was a little less than 330 percent. The growth of passenger traffic in Chile and Peru was even more dramatic.

These trends suggest that to the extent that competition among modes is important, it is of relatively recent origin insofar as passenger movement is concerned. To some extent, too, the rise in per capita incomes, accompanied by a much slower rise in passenger fares, has brought air traffic within the reach of a much larger group of Latin Americans. That tourist traffic is not a major factor in explaining this growth is revealed by the experience of Mexico and Venezuela, which registered far slower growth than nations without major tourist attractions.

Freight cargo traffic. Freight cargo traffic grew much more rapidly than passenger traffic in most of Latin America, but, as shown in Table 2, the pattern of freight traffic expansion was very uneven. Colombia, which early developed an important air cargo movement, did not record very rapid growth in the 1960s. Brazilian traffic grew only slightly faster, but Argentina, Chile, and Peru (as in the case of passenger traffic) showed very substantial gains during the 1960s and early 1970s.

Overall, freight traffic barely doubled in Latin America in the 1960s. In fact, there was hardly any growth until the latter half of the decade, and it was the emergence of air freight as a major factor in the movement of goods in Argentina and Chile that provided much of the push at that time.

Load factors. One measure of the profitability and effectiveness of air traffic is the load factor. This is the percentage of the available cargo or seat space on scheduled flights that is used for revenue-earning traffic. Thus, a passenger load factor of 60 percent means that 60 percent of the seats available on a particular flight

are occupied by revenue passengers. Table 3 shows the load factors for the 1960s. By and large, load factors on international flights were lower than those on domestic flights during most of the decade. This would seem to indicate that domestic service was more profitable, provided, of course, that domestic fares were high enough to ensure adequate revenue. Moreover, the lower load factors on international flights apparently were the result of more intensive competition.

The table also shows that as freight volume increased throughout the 1960s, load factors worsened for both domestic and international flights. For passenger traffic, in contrast, load factors worsened in the highly competitive international service area. It should be noted, of course, that the switch to large jet aircraft such as the Boeing 707 meant that much more space was available. It is also true that costs per seat-mile were lower in the larger aircraft, so that lower load factors could be sustained without necessarily worsening the net revenue picture. However, it is likely that net revenue in international traffic suffered.

TABLE 3. LOAD FACTORS

	Passenger revenue traffic		Freight cargo traffic	
	International service	Domestic service	International service	Domestic service
1960	54.0	57.9	53.3	64.6
1962	52.2	59.0	53.3	62.3
1964	53.6	57.2	55.7	63.6
1966	55.9	59.7	58.6	62.0
1968	50.2	59.1	52.7	59.0
1969	47.9	58.3	51.9	57.5

SOURCE: International Civil Aviation Organization, *Traffic Report,* February 1970.

TABLE 4. COMMERCIAL AIR FLEET, 1968

	Latin America		World	
	Number of planes	Percent	Number of planes	Percent
Jet	98	11.2	2,934	43.2
Jet-prop	123	14.1	1,381	20.3
Propeller	653	74.7	2,472	36.5
Total	874		6,787	

SOURCE: International Civil Aviation Organization, *Monthly Bulletin,* October 1970.

TABLE 5. COMMERCIAL AIR FLEET OF MAJOR LATIN AMERICAN AIRLINES, 1970

Airline	Jet	Propeller and jet-prop
Aerolineas Argentinas	19	9
Aeronaves de México *	16	5
APSA, Peru †	4	1
Avianca, Colombia	14	24
BWIA, Trinidad	5	5
Cruzeiro do Sul, Brazil	10	15
Cubana	...	26
Ecuatoriana	...	10
Ladeco, Chile	...	7
Mexicana	10	4
Varig, Brazil	15	19
VASP, Brazil	7	...
VIASA, Venezuela	7	...
Other	10	711
Total	117	836

* Renamed Aero México in 1972.
† Service discontinued in 1971.
SOURCES: International Civil Aviation Organization, *Monthly Bulletin,* October 1970; *Interavia,* 1971.

TABLE 6. PRINCIPAL LATIN AMERICAN AIRPORTS

	Passengers	Freight-tons
Mexico City		
1960	1,292,000	...
1970	3,277,000	42,306
Buenos Aires		
1960	1,019,000	9,183
1970	2,297,000	33,946
Rio de Janeiro		
1960	264,000	4,971
1970	1,066,000	21,500

SOURCE: International Civil Aviation Organization, *Monthly Bulletin,* January 1972.

Commercial air fleet. The commercial air fleet in use in Latin America by the late 1960s was quite different from the fleet in general use in the world. The International Civil Aviation Organization reported, for example, that only 11.2 percent of the Latin American commercial fleet was jet-powered in 1968, whereas the world figure was 43.2 percent (*see* Table 4). Similarly, three-quarters of the Latin American fleet was propeller-driven in 1968, in comparison with 36.5 percent of the world fleet.

An analysis of the major Latin American airlines in 1970 revealed that there had been major acquisitions of jet aircraft in recent years and that for these companies the jet-propeller ratio had improved (*see* Table 5). However, the smaller airlines still depended heavily on what in Europe and the United States would be regarded as obsolete planes.

There were at least three reasons for continued reliance on propeller aircraft. One was the lower price and the ease with which used planes could be purchased from the United States market. Another was the large number of small companies scattered across Latin America and operating very close to the margin of profit. This large number was encouraged by the fact that most Latin American nations had made access to the airways relatively easy, as well as by the fact that many nations had permitted a surprisingly large degree of competition as a result of the lack of international agreement on the matter. The third reason was that the topography of Latin America, the large number of small airports requiring frequent service, and the quality of these airports and the approaches to them often made planes such as DC3s the better aircraft for the job.

Airports. Only a handful of Latin American airports have scheduled traffic at a level comparable with North American and European operations. The leading Latin American airport is that in Mexico City, where traffic almost tripled during the 1960s. As shown in Table 6, even more rapid growth was recorded at Rio de Janeiro in these years.

Latin American airports serving major cities are often overdeveloped with respect to actual traffic, and traffic trends suggest that these airports will not be overcrowded during the 1970s. Smaller airports, especially in remote places that are difficult to reach, may be less well developed, particularly in terms of standard international safety requirements, than they should be. There is at least reason to argue that a disproportionate amount of resources has been allocated to "international" airports with display value and too little to facilities designed for normal and vital air traffic.

Air transport companies. In 1972 there were forty-eight registered airline companies in Latin America, as shown in Table 7. Twenty-four countries ranging from Brazil to Barbados had at least one airline, but only twelve of the airlines were large enough to be counted among the principal airlines of the world. (The major Latin American airlines are shown in Table 8.) Admittedly, this fact does not indicate the importance of these airlines to the nations and the places served, but given the evident economies of scale in airline operation, it is to be supposed that air service is relatively costly in Latin America. Yet, as an International Civil Aviation Organization study published in 1972

TABLE 7. AIRLINE COMPANIES IN LATIN AMERICA, 1972

Country	Number of airlines	Country	Number of airlines
Argentina	5	Jamaica	2
Colombia	5	Bolivia	1
Brazil	4	Curaçao	1
Honduras	4	Ecuador	1
Venezuela	3	El Salvador	1
Mexico	2	Cuba	1
Chile	2	Guayana	1
Panama	2	Costa Rica	1
Nicaragua	2	Barbados	1
Dominican		Guatemala	1
Republic	2	Belize	1
Trinidad	2	Uruguay	1
Peru	2		

SOURCE: *Official Airline Guide,* international ed., April 1972.

TABLE 8. PRINCIPAL AIRLINES IN LATIN AMERICA, 1970

	Passenger-kilometers (in thousands)	Freight-ton-kilometers (in millions)
Varig, Brazil	2,857.2	147.3
Aerolineas Argentinas	1,842.2	39.7
Avianca, Colombia	1,599.9	55.6
Aeronaves de México *	1,439.0	19.9
Mexicana	1,282.2	15.5
Lan-Chile	756.8	27.1
Cruzeiro do Sul, Brazil	726.0	8.0
VIASA, Venezuela	683.3	40.3
APSA, Peru †	675.9	13.4
VASP, Brazil	655.1	7.1
BWIA, Trinidad	507.1	9.7
Ecuatoriana	201.2	1.4
Ladeco, Chile	72.0	1.9

* Renamed Aero México in 1972.
† Service discontinued in 1971.
SOURCE: *Interavia,* 1971.

TABLE 9. COSTS PER SCHEDULED COMMERCIAL FLIGHT

Region	Cost	Region	Cost
Africa	$33,000	North Atlantic	$36,000
Caribbean	12,000	Pacific	27,000
Europe	22,000	South America	15,000
Middle East	24,000	Southeast Asia	14,000
Canada	33,000	World	15,000
United States	9,000		

SOURCE: International Civil Aviation Organization, *Monthly Bulletin,* May 1972.

shows, costs per flight in Latin America are about $15,000, the world average (*see* Table 9). In comparison with the United States, where per-flight costs are $9,000, there is a competitive disadvantage.

The lower costs in Latin America as compared with Africa, the Middle East, and the Pacific are in part the result of the age and quality of the air fleet in use. With passenger and freight cargo loads remaining relatively high and with as much as 75 percent of the fleet in piston planes (in contrast with a world propeller ratio of 36.5 percent), the cost performance of Latin American airlines was achieved at the expense of speed. To be sure, the kind of airport served also played a role.

More important, even with this lower cost ratio it remains difficult to cover costs of operation, and profits are rare. Brazil has begun to reduce the number of airlines, increasing the size of the remaining companies in order to ensure economic viability in both domestic and international service. In 1971 Peru lost its major international carrier, APSA, the ninth largest in Latin America, because of continued losses.

Bibliography. Robert T. Brown, *Transport and the Economic Integration of Latin America,* Washington, 1966; E. T. Haefele (ed.), *Transport and National Goals,* Washington, 1969; Charles J. Stokes, *Transportation and Economic Development in Latin America,* New York, 1968; United Nations Economic Commission for Latin America, *El transporte en América Latina,* Santiago, Chile, 1965; id., "Public Enterprises; Their Present Significance and Their Potential in Development," *Economic Bulletin for Latin America,* vol. XVI, no. 1, first half, 1971, pp. 1–70.

CHARLES J. STOKES

ALAMÁN, LUCAS (1792–1853). Mexican statesman and historian. Born in the city of Guanajuato, Alamán was trained in mineralogy and mining technology in Mexico City and Europe. His political career began in 1821 with his election as a delegate from Guanajuato to the Spanish Cortes. In that body he was a prominent advocate for American interests. After leaving the Cortes, he organized a British-backed mining company, which he later managed in Mexico. Upon his return to Mexico in 1823, he served in several administrations as Minister of Foreign Relations in the years 1823–1825, 1830–1832, and 1853 and held other important offices, such as the post of Director of Industry (1842–1846). He was the leader of the Conservative party and in this capacity was primarily responsible for recalling Antonio López de SANTA ANNA to the Presidency in 1853 and for the program which that dictator followed in his last administration.

Besides his political activities, Alamán was involved in textile manufacturing, iron smelting, legal practice (as attorney for the descendants of Hernán CORTÉS), and journalism. He strongly espoused the Conservative philosophy and the monarchical cause in his writings, most notably the three-volume *Disertaciones sobre la historia de la República Mejicana* (1844–1849) and the five-volume *Historia de Méjico desde lôs primeros movimientos que prepararon su independencia en el año 1808 hasta la época presente* (1849–1852). He organized the Banco de Avío, the Archivo General de la Nación, and the Museo de Antigüedades.

CHARLES R. BERRY

ALBERDI, JUAN BAUTISTA (1810–1884). Argentine political thinker. A prominent member of the Generation of 1837, Alberdi was born in Tucumán. His father was an important merchant, and his mother was a member of the old aristocratic family of Aráoz. After he completed his elementary education in Tucumán, he attended the Colegio de Ciencias Morales and the University of Buenos Aires and in 1834 received a law degree from the University of Córdoba. Back in Buenos Aires, he helped organize the Salón Literario and the ASOCIACIÓN DE MAYO. In 1838 he was forced to emigrate to Montevideo because of his opposition to the dictator Juan Manuel de ROSAS. There he remained, first as a journalist and then as a lawyer, until unfavorable political developments led him to leave for Italy, France, and Brazil in 1843. He established his residence in Valdivia, Chile, in 1844. Alberdi returned to Europe in 1854 as the Minister of the ARGENTINE CONFEDERATION to Great Britain and France. His mission was to nullify the efforts of the province of Buenos Aires to obtain international recognition as a sovereign state. Alberdi was not completely successful, although he did persuade Spain to acknowledge the independence of Argentina (June 9, 1859). He lost his diplomatic post in 1862 but remained in Europe, returning to Buenos Aires after his election in 1878 as the congressional representative from Tucumán. In 1881 he was back in Europe, where he died.

Alberdi was neither a philosopher nor a theorist but a statesman who knew his country and his people. Always practical, he favored policies based on conditions existing in Argentina, and although few of his partisans ever held high public office, he saw many of his ideas put into effect. His best-known work is *Bases y puntos de partida para la organización política de la república argentina* (1852), which influenced the drafting of the 1853 constitution (*see* CONSTITUTION OF 1853: ARGENTINA). Like Bernardino RIVADAVIA and Domingo Faustino SARMIENTO, he wanted to see Argentina progress materially, and for him this meant that the government should encourage commercial and pastoral development, educate the people to pursue wealth, and avoid alliances and wars. Above all, what Argentina needed were well-chosen European immigrants (*see* IMMIGRATION: ARGENTINA) and foreign capital to invest in railroads, industries, and trade. Order would come with immigrants and the elimination of poverty. Order, wealth, liberty, and civilization—these were the essential elements in Alberdi's concept of the fatherland.

JOSEPH T. CRISCENTI

ALCABALA. Ad valorem tax on the sale or exchange of most goods in colonial Spanish America. Levied in Castile at a rate of 10 percent, the *alcabala* was first introduced in New Spain in 1575 and in Peru in 1591 as an impost of 2 percent. The rate was increased to 4 percent in 1627, in the crown's effort to raise revenue to support military forces protecting the colonies. In 1639 the *alcabala* was raised to 6 percent. The tax was levied at all stages of the distribution process. A few items such as bread, books, coin, and weaponry were exempt.

Collection of the *alcabala* in the sixteenth century was often undertaken directly by royal treasury officials. Detailed laws specified how the colonists were to declare the volume and value of their commercial transactions. On that basis, the tax was computed by these officials. In large cities it was more common, however, for the municipal government to pay the *alcabala* in a lump sum, which supposedly approximated 2 percent of the value of annual trade within the city. This tax payment usually amounted to less than the full legal rate. The revenue was collected by the city government from the local guilds and wealthy citizenry, who paid a proportion of the tax based on their estimated annual sales. In this way, the tax burden fell on guild members rather than on small traders. When the tax rate rose in the seventeenth century, municipalities could no longer afford to pay the *alcabala* in one lump sum. Therefore, *cabildos* and *consulados* (merchants' guilds) often subcontracted the collection of the tax to private individuals through a public auction. Under tax farmers, collection became stricter, and a larger portion of the local population paid the tax, but ecclesiastics and Indians who sold native produce were usually exempt from the *alcabala*.

BROOKE LARSON SHUTE

ALEGRÍA, CIRO (1909–1967). Peruvian novelist. Born in the province of Huamachuco, he was a pupil of César VALLEJO in the elementary school of Trujillo, where he entered the university and became politically active, helping to found the local ALIANZA POPULAR REVOLUCIONARIA AMERICANA (APRA) party. He contributed to the newspapers *El norte, La industria,* and *La tribuna* and was exiled to Chile for political activities. He then devoted himself to literature.

His first successful novel, *La serpiente de oro,* 1935 (*The Golden Serpent*), evolved from a short story, *La balsa,* which he had first expanded into the tale *Marañon.* This work shows the elements characteristic of Alegría as a novelist: a concern for the Indian and his life that views the suffering of the Peruvian Indian as the symbol of a continental as well as a universal problem. While recovering from tuberculosis in the sanatorium of San José de Maipo (1936–1938), he wrote *Los perros hambrientos* (1938), on the theme of the persecution of the Indians in the high Andes. One chapter of this book was later developed into the novel *El mundo es ancho y ajeno,* 1941 (*Broad and Alien Is the World*), probably Alegría's most representative work. He lived in the United States from 1941 to 1949, when he began teaching at the University of Puerto Rico.

RACHEL PHILLIPS

ALEIJADINHO, O. *See* LISBÔA, ANTÔNIO FRANCISCO.

ALEM, LEANDRO (1842–1896). Founder of the Unión Cívica Radical (*see* RADICAL PARTY: ARGENTINA). Alem was born on the outskirts of the city of Buenos Aires, the son of a small storekeeper who occasionally was a police agent. In 1853 he saw his father unjustly accused and shot as a member of the pro-Rosas organization, the Sociedad Popular Restauradora (*see* ROSAS, Juan Manuel de). Alem put himself through law school and fought for the ARGENTINE CONFEDERATION at Cepeda (1859) and Pavón (1861), and as a member of the Partido Autonomista (Partido Alsinista), he defended the integrity and autonomy of his native province. Soon after returning from the PARAGUAYAN WAR, he established himself as a minor party *caudillo* and was elected to the provincial legislature in 1872 and to Congress in 1874. Four years later, unhappy with the behavior of party head Adolfo Alsina, he left the Partido Autonomista to establish the Republican party with an old childhood friend, Aristóbulo del Valle. In 1880 he was so greatly disappointed with his inability to prevent the federalization of the city of Buenos Aires that he left the legislature to resume his law practice among the poor. Poor health, a constant feature of his life, may also have contributed to his decision.

During the next decade Argentina experienced an economic and social transformation with the influx of immigrants (*see* IMMIGRATION: ARGENTINA), an increase in cereal production, the spread of the railroads, and the modernization of the livestock industry. As the decade came to a close, discontented elements in the nascent middle class (small tenant farmers and shopkeepers), military officers, conservatives, laborers, and young men, unhappy with corruption in government, minority rule, and a faltering economy, formed the Unión Cívica de la Juventud to fight for free suffrage and honest elections. Alem was their president. On July 26, 1890, he led a military revolt against President Miguel JUÁREZ CELMAN; it failed, but Juárez Celman was forced to resign.

The elections of 1890 saw a schism develop within the Unión Cívica. Alem assumed the leadership of one fraction, representing essentially the university students and immigrant interests, and with it organized the Unión Cívica Radical. In July 1893, his nephew, Hipólito YRIGOYEN, started a revolution in the province of Buenos Aires, but it was poorly coordinated with dissident elements in the interior provinces, and it failed. A disillusioned and embittered Alem continued to serve as congressman for his native city until he took his own life on July 1, 1896. Since then his reputation has grown, for he is regarded by many Argentines as an individualist, a man of principle, who represented the masses—the laborers, youth, and the middle class—and stood for honest elections, majority rule, and fiscal integrity in the government.

JOSEPH T. CRISCENTI

ALEMÁN [VALDÉS], MIGUEL (1900–   ). President of Mexico (1946–1952). Alemán was born in Sayula, Veracruz. His father, a general of the same name, died in the rebellion of 1929, the year in which the younger Alemán received his law degree. As Governor of his native state (1936–1940), he organized the peasants into a single League of Agrarian Communities, declared his desire to end land distribution, devoted half of the state budget to education, and created a department of labor. He was manager of Manuel ÁVILA CAMACHO's presidential campaign and served as Minister of the Interior (Gobernación) in the latter's Cabinet until he resigned to launch his own presidential bid.

As President he encouraged industry and developed an active irrigation policy, which was not free of corruption. He granted the right to seek writs of *amparo,* or stay writs, to landowners who could present certificates that their land was exempt from expropriation; in addition, he fixed the size of small holdings, which would be exempt from expropriation, at 200 hectares (494 acres) of seasonal land, 150 hectares (370 acres) for cotton-growing land, and 300 hectares (741 acres) for land devoted to various industrial crops. He also built large apartment buildings for federal employees, increased Mexico City's supply of potable water, and constructed the Sonora–Baja California railroad and the Southeastern Railroad. His last years in office were clouded by his devaluation of the Mexican peso in 1948, by marked corruption in his administration, and by rumors that he might seek reelection.

MOISÉS GONZÁLEZ NAVARRO

ALENCAR, JOSÉ MARTINIANO DE (1829–1877). Brazilian novelist, dramatist, essayist, critic, poet, and politician. Born in Ceará to an illustrious family of the NORTHEAST, he was brought up in Rio de Janeiro and studied law in São Paulo and Recife. He became famous in 1856 with a series of articles on *A Confederação dos Tamóios,* by Domingos José GONÇALVES DE MAGALHÃES, in which he criticized the poem for not being sufficiently Brazilian. This was only the first of several controversies in which he participated. His first work of fiction, *Viuvinha* (1856), inaugurated his series on Rio life, the most famous of which is *Senhora* (1875). In 1857 he published his first historical novel, *O Guarani,* a fantasy about colonial Brazil, the hero of which is a Rousseauan Noble Savage. *Iracema* (1865), an Indianist novel which has been called a prose poem, is an allegory about the founding of the country. Alencar also produced two excellent plays on the slavery question, *O Demonio Familiar* (1858) and *Mãe* (1860). Meanwhile, he was active in journalism and politics, holding the office of national deputy for several years and of Minister of Justice. Although even his best works are dwarfed by those of his greater contemporaries, who learned from him and surpassed him, Alencar's importance as the founder of the historical, the Indianist, and the regional novels in Brazil and his influence on the development of the urban novel are unquestioned. He fought for the use of a Brazilian Portuguese in literature and for Brazilian life as subject matter.

RAYMOND S. SAYERS

ALESSANDRI [PALMA], ARTURO (1868–1950). President of Chile (1920–1925, 1932–1938). Born of Italian ancestry on a landed estate in Linares, Alessandri graduated from the University of Chile as a lawyer in 1893. He was already a prominent young member of the Liberal party (*see* LIBERAL PARTY: CHILE) and had actively opposed President José Manuel BALMACEDA in 1891. He entered Congress in 1897 as deputy for Curicó, holding his seat in six successive elections to 1915. His first taste of higher office came in 1898, when he was appointed Minister of Public Works, a post he held briefly again in 1899, and he served as Minister of Finance for five months in 1913. His career was thus formed in the period of ministerial instability between 1891 and 1924, when Chile's social and economic problems grew rapidly and the political system seemed incapable of solving them. The impact of World War I underlined this point, and it was then, in 1915, that Alessandri emerged as a national figure, as an antigovernment candidate for a senatorial seat for Tarapacá. His natural gift for oratory and charismatic appeal to workers earned him the title "Lion of Tarapacá," and in defeating his opponent in a violent campaign he be-

Arturo Alessandri. [*Organization of American States*]

came recognized not only as a dynamic politician but also as the embodiment of a grass-roots desire for basic reform.

Alessandri was appointed Minister of the Interior in 1918, and although his program was too radical for Congress, by 1920 he had become the obvious presidential candidate for the Democratic and Radical parties against the Conservative and Liberal nominee, Luis Barros Borgoño (*see* CONSERVATIVE PARTY: CHILE; DEMOCRATIC PARTY: CHILE; RADICAL PARTY: CHILE). Alessandri ran a nationwide campaign based on impassioned and violent attacks on the existing system, but his narrow victory was disputed by the opposition, and under the constitution the issue was submitted to a special tribunal. He was finally declared elected by 177 votes to 176 in the Electoral College, after threats of violence by Alessandri and his supporters if he were denied victory. He assumed office in December 1920, but four years of frustration followed as the opposition controlled Congress and blocked reform. In March 1924, Alessandri blatantly used the Army and the state apparatus to win congressional elections, but the new Congress proved more inept than its predecessor and the state slid slowly into bankruptcy.

In June 1924, possibly to bring matters to a head, Alessandri sent Congress a bill providing for parliamentary salaries—an unconstitutional act, since the constitution forbade payment of such salaries. A long-suffering and unpaid Army intervened in September to force the withdrawal of the bill and the passage by Con-

gress in one day of all the progressive legislation held up since 1920. A last-minute attempt by Alessandri to keep himself in power failed, and faced with a demand for his withdrawal from both the Army high command and its junior officers, led by Carlos IBÁÑEZ, he sought asylum in the 'United States Embassy and then left Chile, ostensibly on a six-month leave. Meanwhile, the Army was divided between the governing conservative high command and reform-minded junior officers. Early in 1925 the latter overthrew the government formed by the generals and recalled Alessandri to the Presidency. He returned in March to massive popular demonstrations, but he was no longer a free agent, for the Army held power. He first concentrated on a cherished objective, the drafting of a new constitution, which was published in July 1925 and ratified by plebiscite in August (*see* CONSTITUTION OF 1925: CHILE). He also called in an American economic commission led by Edwin W. Kemmerer and, partly on its advice, created a Central Bank of issue and stabilized the currency. In October, however, a long-maturing conflict between Alessandri and his Minister of War, Carlos Ibáñez, reached a climax with Alessandri's resignation. He retired to Paris and remained there until the fall of Ibáñez in 1931, keeping actively in touch with Chilean politics as the focus of opposition to the dictator.

After fifteen months of near anarchy in Chile in 1931–1932, new presidential elections (October 1932) restored constitutional rule to the country and Alessandri to the Presidency as the national figure to bring order out of political and economic chaos. But the man who had horrified the oligarchy with his radical views in 1920 now saw his task as that of providing strong government under the new constitution while the Chilean economy recovered from the Great Depression. Ruling now with the support of the Conservative and Liberal parties, the strongest parties in Congress, and assisted by the brilliance of Gustavo ROSS as Minister of Finance, Alessandri restored health to the Chilean economy, but at the cost of political repression of opponents and forceful suppression of discontent. These policies united the left-wing parties and the Radicals in the Popular Front to oppose an Alessandri they no longer recognized and to fight Ross as the right-wing nominee for the presidential election of 1938 (*see* POPULAR FRONT: CHILE). The front's narrow victory was finally due to the massacre by the police of about sixty young members of the Chilean Nazi party after a pathetic attempt at a coup in September. Although final responsibility for the order to kill has not been established, many held Alessandri to be implicated. The massacre was followed by orders from the imprisoned Ibáñez and the Nazi leader, Jorge González von Marées, to their followers to vote for the front candidate, Pedro AGUIRRE CERDA. Alessandri thus handed the Presidency in 1938 to a man who had been his Minister of the Interior at the time of the military coup in 1924. After a period in which he remained aloof from politics, Alessandri returned to the Senate as member for Talca, Maule, and Linares in 1944 and for Santiago in 1949. Alessandri's remarkably long career in Chilean public life, personal impact on affairs, and polemical character made him the most controversial figure in modern Chilean history.

Bibliography. Arturo Alessandri Palma, *Revolución*

de 1891: Mi actuación, Santiago, 1950; id., *Recuerdos de gobierno,* 3 vols., Santiago, 1967; Ricardo Donoso, *Alessandri, agitador y demoledor,* 2 vols., Mexico City and Buenos Aires, 1952, 1954; Luis Durand, *Don Arturo,* Santiago, 1952; P. T. Ellsworth, *Chile: An Economy in Transition,* New York, 1945; Augusto Iglesias, *Alessandri: Una etapa de la democracia en América,* Santiago, 1960; Frederick M. Nunn, *Chilean Politics, 1920–1931,* Albuquerque, N.Mex., 1970; John Reese Stevenson, *The Chilean Popular Front,* Philadelphia, 1942.

HAROLD BLAKEMORE

ALESSANDRI [RODRÍGUEZ], JORGE (1896–   ). President of Chile (1958–1964). The son of President Arturo ALESSANDRI, he was born in Santiago and educated at the National Institute and the School of Engineering, graduating as a civil engineer in 1919. Primarily a businessman, he entered Congress as a deputy for Santiago (1926–1930), but he then remained largely outside politics for nearly twenty years and concentrated on his business interests. He did, however, serve as Minister of Finance under Gabriel GONZÁLEZ VIDELA (1947–1950). In 1956 he reentered Congress as a senator for Santiago, but two years later he was nominated for the Presidency by a loose coalition, the Alianza de Partidos y Fuerzas Populares, that drew its strength from the Conservative and Liberal parties (*see* CONSERVATIVE PARTY: CHILE; LIBERAL PARTY: CHILE). Opposed by Salvador ALLENDE of the FRENTE DE ACCIÓN POPULAR (FRAP), Eduardo FREI of the PARTIDO DEMÓCRATA CRISTIANO, and Luis Bossay for the Radicals (*see* RADICAL PARTY: CHILE), Alessandri narrowly defeated Allende by 389,909 votes to 356,493.

Alessandri formed his Cabinet from independents, Conservatives, Liberals, and Radicals and pursued orthodox financial policies to combat inflation. He initiated a housing program and carried an AGRARIAN REFORM law far in advance of previous legislation. Public works were expanded, and industry was diversified, though the fundamental problems of the Chilean economy remained unsolved. In foreign affairs, Alessandri took Chile into the LATIN AMERICAN FREE TRADE ASSOCIATION in 1960 and broke off diplomatic relations with Cuba in 1964, in pursuance of a resolution of the ORGANIZATION OF AMERICAN STATES. In 1962 he paid an official visit to the United States and a number of Latin American countries.

An honest administrator, austere and upright, Alessandri left office in 1964 as a popular President, and when, in 1970, it seemed that Unidad Popular (Popular Unity) might well win the presidential election, he was persuaded to come out of retirement at the age of seventy-four to run as an independent. His standing with the electorate was indicated by the fact that he failed to defeat Allende by a mere 39,000 votes in a poll of 3,539,000.

HAROLD BLAKEMORE

ALFARO, [JOSÉ] ELOY (1842–1912). Ecuadorian revolutionary leader and president (1895–1901, 1906–1911). Alfaro was born on June 25, 1842, in Montecristi, Manabí Province. His Spanish father, Manuel Alfaro, had arrived in Ecuador as a buyer of straw hats and settled down to live with a native girl, Natividad Delgado, the mother of Eloy and seven other children.

Eloy Alfaro's career as a revolutionary started at the age of twenty-two, when he kidnapped the governor of Manabí. For the next twenty-five years he sought stubbornly to overthrow the government of Ecuador, at times as an independent guerrilla leader, at times by financing other revolutionaries, and on one occasion by heading the Manabí revolutionaries within the general coalition that ousted Ignacio VEINTEMILLA in 1883. On this occasion he was given the title general but otherwise did not share the fruits of victory. All his other schemes and revolutionary attempts ended in failure, Alfaro having spent on them the financial means he had acquired in Panama through business activities and his marriage to the wealthy Ana Paredes Arosemena. Nonetheless, his unremitting dedication to the cause of subversion gained him international prestige as a military leader among Liberals (*see* LIBERAL PARTY: ECUADOR).

In 1895 the coalition of Moderates and Conservatives that had governed Ecuador since 1883 split (*see* CONSERVATIVE PARTY: ECUADOR). The Conservatives in the highlands took up arms against the government and forced the President to resign. This induced the Liberals of the coastal city of Guayaquil to revolt. Since they lacked the support of high-ranking officers, the Liberal revolutionaries called Alfaro back from exile. He marched with his army on Quito, defeated the government troops at Gatazo, and then turned against the Conservatives. Within a short time Alfaro was in control of the country, imposing his rule by means of an army whose key positions were given to his close relatives and friends.

Alfaro was president until 1901. He then handed over the office to his handpicked successor, Gen. Leonidas PLAZA, having failed in a last-minute scheme to impede Plaza's inauguration. He was more suc-

Eloy Alfaro. [*Organization of American States*]

cessful against the latter's successor, Lizardo García, whom he ousted after four months in office (1905).

Alfaro retained his grip on the Presidency until 1911. He picked Emilio Estrada as his successor but then changed his mind, even though Estrada had already been legally elected. The conflict ended with Alfaro's forced removal from office. He was sent into exile, but President Estrada died four months later, and Alfaro returned to Guayaquil to launch a revolt against the provisional government headed by Carlos Freile Zaldumbide. By then even the majority of Liberals had grown tired of the old *caudillo's* obsession with subversion. He and his most devoted associates were arrested and taken to Quito. They were lynched there by a mob instigated by Liberal politicians. The naked bodies of the victims were dragged through the streets, hacked to pieces, and finally incinerated (January 28, 1912).

Although after his death the figure of Alfaro assumed heroic proportions, a cool analysis of his political career reveals a negative record. For fifty years of the seventy he lived, he was a permanent menace to Ecuador's stability. After his consistent failures as a revolutionary, he reached power as an instrument of Liberal politicians. While he immediately established his own power based on the military, he could not avoid conflict with the politicians. Unable to maintain an orderly government, he would not allow others to do so. The legal reforms of the period must be ascribed to the Liberal party as a whole. In the end the conflict between the *caudillo* and the politicians came to a barbarous conclusion.

Bibliography. Francisco Guarderas, *El viejo de Montecristi,* Quito, 1953; Wilfrido Loor, *Eloy Alfaro,* 3 vols., Quito, 1947; Alfredo Pareja Diez-Canseco, *La hoguera bárbara,* Mexico City, 1944; Jorge Pérez Concha, *Eloy Alfaro: Su vida y su obra,* Quito, 1942; Luis Robalino Dávila, *Eloy Alfaro y su primera época,* 2 vols., Quito, 1969.

ÁDÁM SZÁSZDI

ALFARO, RICARDO J[OAQUÍN] (1882–1971). Panamanian jurist and President (1931–1932). Alfaro became President of Panama after the 1931 revolution. His emergency measures mitigated the effects of the economic depression. A notable achievement of his short tenure was the exemplary presidential election of 1932.

Alfaro's public life spanned many years, during which he tirelessly pleaded the case of Panama in its relations with the United States, at times as Foreign Minister and at others as Ambassador in Washington. He negotiated treaties with the United States in 1926 and 1936 (*see* HULL-ALFARO TREATY) and was an adviser to the team that negotiated the 1955 pact. It was Alfaro's statement on Panamanian sovereignty over the Canal Zone before the United Nations Political Committee in 1946 that led to an eventual decision by the United States government to allow the Panamanian flag to be flown beside that of the United States at various locations in the zone. Alfaro also served on the International Court of Justice and taught at the University of Panama. He was the author of works on a variety of subjects, ranging from the judicial code of Panama to a dictionary of anglicisms.

LARRY L. PIPPIN

ALFARO SIQUEIROS, DAVID. *See* SIQUEIROS, DAVID ALFARO.

ALIANÇA RENOVADORA NACIONAL (NATIONAL RENOVATING ALLIANCE; ARENA). The proadministration party in Brazil, ARENA commands an overwhelming majority in both houses of Congress as well as in most state legislatures, and it controls the governorship in all states except Guanabara. The President of the republic is head of the party and has the decisive voice in selecting its candidates. Other national directors of the party are chosen from ARENA members of the Senate and Chamber of Deputies.

ARENA came into existence late in 1965 as a result of efforts by the administration of Humberto CASTELLO BRANCO to reduce the number of political parties and to impose greater discipline on their members. Following the gubernatorial elections of October 3, 1965, in which two opposition candidates were victorious, the government issued the Second Institutional Act on October 27, dissolving all existing political parties in Brazil. Complementary Act No. 4 of November 30 provided for the formation of political organizations endorsed by at least 120 congressmen and 20 senators. Subsequently, more than twice the minimum number of legislators adhered to ARENA. The others entered the MOVIMENTO DEMOCRÁTICO BRASILEIRO. Throughout Brazil the members of ARENA were drawn primarily from officeholders elected on the tickets of the former UNIÃO DEMOCRÁTICA NACIONAL (National Democratic Union) and the former PARTIDO SOCIAL DEMOCRÁTICO (Social Democratic party). ARENA has only limited grass-roots support.

ROLLIE E. POPPINO

ALIANZA NACIONAL POPULAR (NATIONAL POPULAR ALLIANCE; ANAPO). Colombian political movement that arose from the ashes of the Presidency of Gen. Gustavo ROJAS PINILLA. Founded in 1960, it is led by the ailing Rojas and his daughter, María Eugenia Rojas de Moreno Díaz, seemingly to vindicate their reputations by regaining power through constitutional means. Its supporters have been united by their exclusion from NATIONAL FRONT patronage and by some personal loyalty to Rojas. Otherwise ANAPO has been a curious coalition of incompatibles: big landowners on the Colombian coast, militantly clerical priests in upland Boyacá, and self-proclaimed socialists in Bogotá. The leadership has been careful to avoid ideological definition in order to avoid offending any group, and it has not built more than a skeleton press for fear of inciting disunity. Its success has been in its organization. María Eugenia has been incomparably skillful and peculiarly accessible. ANAPO has been carefully financed at all levels through compulsory contributions imposed upon post holders, big business contributions, and the sale of membership cards in the municipalities. A Cardex system was imported from the United States to keep track of the movement of members.

From 1962 on ANAPO, or Anapista, candidates were elected to Congress, although they were compelled constitutionally to run under the umbrella terms "Conservative" or "Liberal," that is, as Anapista Conservatives or Anapista Liberals (*see* CONSERVATIVE PARTY:

COLOMBIA; LIBERAL PARTY: COLOMBIA). In 1966 ANAPO presented a last-minute and almost unknown presidential candidate, José Jaramillo Giraldo, who secured 28 percent of the vote. The gap between promise and performance in social legislation of the National Front played into the hands of ANAPO, so that slowly it gained a majority in Congress and control of the municipal councils of all the departmental capitals but one. The defeat of Rojas in the 1970 election compaign by Misael PASTRANA BORRERO by the slight margin of approximately 60,000 votes was greeted with accusations of electoral fraud and intimidation and with complaints of exclusion from television time. In 1971 in a short ceremony in Leiva, Boyacá, the Anapista movement was converted into a formal party that would disregard electoral legislation insisting on either Liberal or Conservative appellations for candidates. The defeat of ANAPO in the municipal and departmental elections of April 1972, when it received 538,394 votes to 2,204,812 for the Liberals and Conservatives, exposed its weaknesses: an unreliable middle-level leadership, a lack of ideological distinctiveness, and an inability to maintain grass-roots enthusiasm between presidential elections.

C. G. ABEL

ALIANZA POPULAR REVOLUCIONARIA AMERICANA (AMERICAN POPULAR REVOLUTIONARY ALLIANCE; APRA). Peruvian political party, also known as the Partido Aprista Peruano (PAP), founded in Mexico in 1924 by exiled Peruvian intellectuals. APRA has had a very stormy history. It has enjoyed irregular spurts of legality (1930–1932, 1933–1934, 1945–1948, 1956–   ), and although it has been the largest political party for most of the past forty years, it has never gained power. The party has simultaneously been accused of being communist and fascist, and it has been advertised as both the potential savior and the certain ruin of Peru. These contradictions stem in part from the party's doctrinal reliance on the thinking of Manuel GONZÁLEZ PRADA, Karl Marx, Lenin, the Chinese Kuomintang, and other assorted philosophies, all pragmatically adopted by APRA's leader, Víctor Raúl HAYA DE LA TORRE, to the needs of Peru and the party.

APRA's history can be divided roughly into three stages: the formative (1924–1930), the militant (1930–1945), and the conciliatory (1945–   ). The first was highlighted by a rejection of affiliation with the Third International, the development of a "maximum" program, and the attempt to create a network of intellectually related political parties throughout Latin America to fight United States imperialism and its allies, Latin America's governing classes. The "intellectual and manual workers of America" were to constitute the organization's vanguard and were to work for the implementation of a maximum program applicable to all Latin America. The program contained five essentially unoriginal principles: (1) control of Yankee imperialism, (2) internationalization of the Panama Canal, (3) political and economic unity of Latin America, (4) nationalization of land and industry, and (5) solidarity of all oppressed people and classes. The program's more controversial provisions have since been abandoned, along with attempts to form a sort of Latin

American Aprista International. In fact, APRA has succeeded in establishing itself only in Peru, where it emerged as a force following the overthrow of Augusto LEGUÍA in 1930.

The organization of APRA in Peru and its participation in the 1931 election mark the beginning of the second stage. With the early radicalism tempered by electoral realities, the party platform's nonrevolutionary but reformist proposals ("minimum" program) were meant to please APRA's middle-class membership and segments of organized labor without alarming the electorate. However, the credibility of the program's mildness had already been undermined by the fiery speeches of many Aprista leaders, which sounded uncompromisingly hostile to the oligarchy, the Army, the church, and foreign capital and attacked anyone opposed to the radical transformation of Peruvian society. It was the oratory that especially alarmed the Army and the oligarchy. Convinced of the party's radicalism, they helped elect the populist military hero and APRA opponent Luis M. SÁNCHEZ CERRO in the 1931 election. The next fourteen years were for APRA both trying and glorious. They were trying because the party suffered persecution, most seriously under Sánchez Cerro (1931–1933) and less so during the regimes of Oscar BENAVIDES (1933–1939) and Manuel PRADO (1939–1945). They were glorious because despite the suppression APRA continued to thrive, emerging in 1945 as the most powerful political force in Peru. Those years also left wounds that have not yet healed. The Army's opposition to APRA stiffened, and segments of the oligarchy became firmly convinced of the party's "diabolical" intentions.

To counter the opposition of the Army and to quell the fears of the conservatives, APRA attempted in the 1940s to change its radical image. It repeatedly guaranteed the institutional integrity of the Army and abandoned such demands as redistribution of wealth, separation of church and state, and control of foreign capital. In addition, to regain legality and the opportunity to participate in presidential politics, APRA entered into alliances with politicians willing to ensure it that opportunity, whatever their ideology. Begun in the 1930s, this strategy reached maturity in 1945 with an agreement that marked the beginning of the party's conciliatory stage and was generally supported by the party membership. However, the 1956 *convivencia* with Manuel Prado, a wealthy oligarch, disillusioned many of the party's younger members. Some of them joined radical organizations, while others entered the ranks of ACCIÓN POPULAR (AP).

In spite of its conciliatory approach APRA failed throughout the 1960s to win the coveted Presidency, mainly because of continued military opposition. Thus, in 1962 the Army canceled the election returns (favoring Haya de la Torre), and in the next year's balloting it supported AP's Fernando BELAÚNDE TERRY, who won. In 1968, when a split within AP seemed to ensure an Aprista victory in 1969, the Army took power.

APRA's future is uncertain. Its top leadership has not changed significantly in forty years, and its power base has not been enlarged. In fact, it is perhaps being eroded by aggressive leftist organizations and, more seriously, by the military government that took power in 1968. For example, the government's efforts to win the loyalty of the sugar workers in the north, traditionally APRA's greatest asset, may, if successful, do irreparable damage to the party. However, in the past APRA's resilience and remarkable discipline allowed it to overcome persecution, internal dissension, and defections, and any report of the party's imminent demise must now be considered premature.

Bibliography. Enrique Chirinos Soto, *El Perú frente a junio de 1962,* Lima, 1962; Felipe Cossío del Pomar, *Víctor Raúl,* Mexico City, 1961; Víctor Raúl Haya de la Torre, *Pensamiento político de Haya de la Torre,* 5 vols., Lima, 1961; Alfredo Hernández Urbina, *Los partidos y la crisis APRA,* Lima, 1956; Harry Kantor, *The Ideology and Program of the Peruvian Aprista Movement,* Berkeley, Calif., 1953; Robert McNicoll, "Intellectual Origins of Aprismo," *Hispanic American Historical Review,* vol. XXXIII, no. 3, August 1943, pp. 425–440; Fredrick B. Pike, "The New and Old Apra: Myth and Reality," *Inter-American Economic Affairs,* vol. XVIII, no. 2, Autumn, 1964, pp. 3–45; Víctor Villanueva, *La tragedia de un pueblo y de un partido,* Santiago, 1954.

ORAZIO A. CICCARELLI

ALLENDE, IGNACIO DE (1769–1811). Mexican independence leader. The creole son of a peninsular Spanish merchant, Ignacio de Allende was born in the prosperous BAJÍO town of San Miguel el Grande (now San Miguel de Allende). Ignacio was a virile youth whose horsemanship and bullfighting prepared him to become a militia officer (1795). Two of the factors that later convinced him to rebel stand out. First, the royal amortization of ecclesiastical funds in 1804 struck hard at Allende's family, as it did at other wealthy proprietors throughout the viceroyalty whose lands were mortgaged to the church. Second, in 1806 Viceroy José de Iturrigaray cultivated Allende and other officers during maneuvers at Jalapa. Allende therefore deeply resented the *gachupín* (Spanish) coup that overthrew Iturrigaray in September 1808. These circumstances, together with events in Spain, made Allende a principal actor in the Querétaro conspiracy. He emerged at the outbreak of rebellion in September 1810 as second in command to Miguel HIDALGO Y COSTILLA.

Allende brought his military training and influence over Bajío militia units to the independence movement. However, he chafed at Hidalgo's dependence upon an enormous horde, which alienated potential creole supporters, and resented the superior role that the priest played in the development of strategy. Allende was overruled on his desire to take Mexico City after the victory at Monte de las Cruces, to hold Guanajuato against the Spanish commander Félix María Calleja in November, and to divide the horde into multiple armies in January 1811. He finally wrested command from Hidalgo but only after the horde's catastrophic defeat at Calderón on January 17. Allende led the insurgent remnants north but was captured in March at Baján on his way to seek aid in the United States. Taken with other leaders to Chihuahua, he was tried and shot in June. His head was hung on the Alhóndiga in Guanajuato until after independence, when his remains were enshrined with those of other patriots.

HUGH M. HAMILL, JR.

ALLENDE, PEDRO HUMBERTO (1885–1959). Chilean composer. Born in Santiago de Chile, he studied both in his native country and in France, where he met Claude Debussy, who praised him for his concerto for cello and orchestra (1915). Allende was a prominent teacher under whose guidance most of the Chilean composers of the succeeding generation were trained. His works reflect French impressionism and Chile's folk music traditions. The most valuable are his *Tonadas* for piano and the symphonic poems *Escenas campesinas* (1913) and *La voz de las calles* (1920). He also wrote a number of vocal compositions and a concerto for violin and orchestra (1940).

JUAN A. ORREGO-SALAS

ALLENDE [GOSSENS], SALVADOR (1908–1973). President of Chile (1970–1973). Born in Santiago, Allende was educated at schools in Talca, Valdivia, and Valparaíso and at the University of Chile, from which he graduated as a medical doctor in 1932 with a thesis on mental hygiene and delinquency. He soon turned to politics and was an active member of the Socialist party from its foundation in 1933 on, first entering Congress in 1937 as a deputy for Valparaíso and Quillota (*see* SOCIALIST PARTY: CHILE). As founder and regional secretary of the Valparaíso branch of the party, Allende played an important part in the electoral victory of Pedro AGUIRRE CERDA in 1938 and resigned his seat in Congress in September 1939 in order to accept appointment as Minister of Health. He held

Salvador Allende. [United Press International]

this post until October 1941, and again from December 1941 to April 1942. Meanwhile, he did not neglect his other interests: he took a leading part in several medical congresses, served as a doctor in a number of Chilean institutions, edited medical journals, and published the book *La realidad médico-social chilena* (1940), which won a literary prize.

In 1943, as secretary-general of the Socialist party, Allende led the official wing against Marmaduke Grove. Two years later he returned to Congress, serving as senator for the southern provinces (1945–1953), Tarapacá and Antofagasta (1953–1961), and Aconcagua and Valparaíso (1961–1969). In 1969 Allende secured the highest vote of the fourteen candidates standing for the Senate in Aysén, Chiloé, and Magallanes. His twenty-five years in the Senate, during which he served on many committees and as both Vice President and President of the chamber, gave Allende an unrivaled knowledge of the Chilean political system, though he had a more checkered career in the Socialist party. In 1948 Allende and Raúl Ampuero left the party in protest at its support of President Gabriel GONZÁLEZ VIDELA and founded the Partido Socialista Popular, but four years later Allende disagreed with that group's decision to back Carlos IBÁÑEZ for the Presidency and rejoined the main Socialist party. It says much for his standing and his powers of persuasion that the party then adopted him as its own presidential candidate in 1952. Although he came in last in the contest, Allende was now the leading Socialist figure, and his position was enhanced by his role in the formation of the FRENTE DE ACCIÓN POPULAR (FRAP) and by the reunification of the Socialist factions in 1957. He reached the apex of his political career to that time as the FRAP candidate for the Presidency in 1958, losing only narrowly to Jorge ALESSANDRI.

After the CUBAN REVOLUTION of 1959, Allende became a great admirer of Fidel CASTRO and paid many visits to Cuba, but this attitude did not entirely please Ampuero, now secretary-general of the Socialist party and its emerging leader. Nevertheless, Allende was still the obvious FRAP candidate for the presidential election of 1964, but his campaign, based on "the Cuban example," proved disastrous. The Cuban missile crisis had undercut FRAP's appeal, and Christian Democracy presented a formidable challenge to Marxism as the force for change in Chile (*see* PARTIDO DEMÓCRATA CRISTIANO), while Allende himself was nervous and defensive in his reaction to anti-Communist propaganda. Eduardo FREI's dramatic victory marked a low point for Allende's political fortunes, and the aftermath of the election suggested that he was a spent force, as Ampuero left the party with a splinter group and mutual recrimination broke out between Socialists and Communists (*see* COMMUNIST PARTY: CHILE). Again, however, Allende's resilience, his position as the best-known figure on the Chilean left, and his acceptability to many political factions as the standard-bearer made him a presidential candidate for the fourth time, in 1970. He now led the Unidad Popular (Popular Unity) coalition of Socialists, Communists, Radicals, and others (*see* RADICAL PARTY: CHILE) and won a very narrow victory, to assume office in November 1970 as the first Marxist head of state in the world to win power democratically.

Allende promised to pursue socialism in Chile by constitutional means and embarked on a sweeping program of state control, nationalizing mineral resources, foreign banks, and monopolistic enterprises. He also redistributed income, raised wages and controlled prices, and accelerated land reform. By 1972 the effect had been to polarize political opinion around government and opposition and to create a serious economic situation. Faced with a Congress he did not control, harassed on the left by revolutionary groups urging more violent change than he perhaps contemplated, supported by a heterogeneous coalition of parties that was rent by division, and caught in an economic crisis of severe proportions, Allende had increasing difficulty in maintaining control of the country. Growing opposition culminated on September 11, 1973, in a violent military coup. Allende refused to resign and allegedly committed suicide.

Bibliography. Salvador Allende, *Primer mensaje del Presidente Allende ante el Congreso Pleno,* Santiago, 1971; Harold Blakemore, "Chile: Continuity and Change on the Road to Socialism," *Bank of London & South America Review,* vol. VI, no. 61, January 1972, pp. 2–10; Federico Gil, *The Political System of Chile,* Boston, 1966; Ernst Halperin, *Nationalism and Communism in Chile,* Cambridge, Mass., 1965; Sergio Guilisasti Tagle, *Partidos políticos chilenos,* 2d ed., Santiago, 1964.

HAROLD BLAKEMORE

ALLIANCE FOR PROGRESS. Program to vitalize the social and economic development of Latin America initiated in 1961 with the leadership and support of the United States. In the period after World War II the amount of United States economic assistance to Latin America was relatively small, and American officials maintained that the development of Latin America would best be achieved by private capital, both foreign and domestic (*see* FOREIGN INVESTMENT). By the end of the 1950s, however, largely as a result of the hostile reception given Vice President Richard M. Nixon on his tour of Latin America in 1958 and the rise of Fidel CASTRO in Cuba, policy makers in Washington had become convinced of the need for a reassessment of the American position regarding public economic assistance to Latin America. Meanwhile, in 1958, President Juscelino KUBITSCHEK of Brazil proposed the adoption of a large-scale hemispheric development program to be called Operation Pan America. A Committee of Twenty-One was subsequently created by the ORGANIZATION OF AMERICAN STATES (OAS) to plan further action on the basis of Operation Pan America. One of the first concrete results of these events was the establishment of the INTER-AMERICAN DEVELOPMENT BANK in 1959–1960. The Act of Bogotá, adopted at the third meeting of the Committee of Twenty-One in 1960 and signed by all the members of the OAS, committed both the United States and Latin America to work for economic development and social reform in the region. The Charter of the Alliance for Progress was signed by all the members of the OAS except Cuba at Punta del Este, Uruguay, on August 17, 1961. The Punta del Este meeting had been a response to President John F. Kennedy's call to "all people of the hemisphere to join in a new alliance for progress . . . a vast cooperative effort unparalleled in magnitude and nobility of purpose, to satisfy the basic needs of the American people for homes, work and land, health and schools."

The objectives of the Alliance, as set forth in the Declaration to the Peoples of America that accompanied the Charter, reflected the conviction of the drafters that economic development and social justice might be realized simultaneously and that both could be achieved within a democratic framework. Among the goals of the Alliance were the following: to strengthen democratic institutions; to accelerate economic and social development; to provide decent homes for the Latin American people; to encourage AGRARIAN REFORM programs; to ensure fair wages and satisfactory working conditions for all workers; to wipe out illiteracy; to reform tax laws; to stimulate private enterprise in order to encourage economic development; to solve the problems created by excessive price fluctuations for basic commodity exports; and to accelerate the ECONOMIC INTEGRATION of Latin America. The declaration further stated that these changes could come about only through self-help efforts by each country. However, the efforts of the Latin American nations had to be reinforced by external assistance, and the United States pledged itself to provide a major part of the minimum sum of $20 billion that Latin America would require over the next ten years. The Charter itself specified that the Latin American states would aim at an annual increase of at least 2.5 percent in per capita product. The Charter also provided for the preparation of national development plans by the signatory states.

From its inception the Alliance encountered many severe. if not crippling, problems. One of these was the inadequacy of the machinery for its implementation, which in turn reflected a halfhearted commitment to multilateralism on the part of the United States and some of the Latin American countries. The Punta del Este Meeting created a Panel of Nine Experts, the members of which took part in the evaluation of national plans and made recommendations to the various lending agencies. The desire for a more authoritative body led to the establishment of the COMITÉ INTER-AMERICANO DE LA ALIANZA PARA EL PROGRESO in 1964.

Meanwhile, Latin America made only sluggish progress toward reaching the goals of the Alliance, which increasingly were viewed as unrealistic. Between 1961 and 1967 only seven of the nineteen countries recorded an annual growth rate of 2.5 percent or more. Although significant gains were made during this period in increasing tax revenues and making tax systems more equitable, relatively little was accomplished in the areas of education, housing, and agrarian reform. The occurrence of several military coups in Latin America in the early 1960s also belied the avowed devotion of many of the signers of the Charter to democratic institutions. In addition, the willingness or ability of Latin American governments to embark upon and persist in politically hazardous reformist courses seemed debatable.

The volume of external assistance also proved disappointing to Latin Americans. It has been estimated that between 1961 and 1968 net official capital flow to Latin America from the United States and international financial institutions averaged approximately $920 million per year. Not only were the sums disbursed lower than had been anticipated, but they were not evenly distributed among the Latin American states. Between 1961 and 1966, for example, United States commitments to Panama and Chile totaled respectively $89.7 and $84 per capita, while only $20.4 per capita was committed to Brazil, although this country was the recipient of the largest amount of United States aid. Some critics of the Alliance in the United States charged that funds were wasted on unproductive projects or on excessive personnel in United States aid agencies; others complained that United States assistance had served mainly to bolster existing elites.

Although in 1967 President Lyndon B. Johnson affirmed the support of the United States for the Alliance beyond the ten-year period originally envisioned, by 1970 enthusiasm for the Alliance had waned in both the United States and Latin America. This was due in part to the disappointing results of the Alliance and to a growing belief that its various goals might be incompatible. Moreover, United States fears that violent revolution or Castroite upheaval might take place in Latin America had dimmed by the end of the decade, and the region in general seemed to evoke little interest in Washington. In his first major address on Latin America (October 31, 1969), President Nixon asserted that his administration was guided by the principles of the Alliance, but he also hinted at its impending demise by declaring that the 1970s should be "a decade of Action for Progress in the Americas."

Bibliography. John C. Drier (ed.), *The Alliance for Progress: Problems and Perspectives,* Baltimore, 1962; Lincoln Gordon, *A New Deal for Latin America: The Alliance for Progress,* Cambridge, Mass., 1963; Simon G. Hanson, *Five Years of the Alliance for Progress: An Appraisal,* Washington, 1967; Abraham F. Lowenthal, "Alliance Rhetoric vs. Latin American Reality," *Foreign Affairs,* vol. XLVIII, no. 3, April 1970, pp. 494–508; Warren Nystrom and Nathan A. Haverstock, *The Alliance for Progress: Key to Latin America's Development,* Princeton, N.J., 1966; Harvey Perloff, *Alliance for Progress: A Social Invention in the Making,* Baltimore, 1969; William D. Rogers, *The Twilight Struggle: The Alliance for Progress and the Politics of Development,* New York, 1967.

TAYLOR K. COUSINS

ALMAGRO, DIEGO DE (1475–1538). Castilian partner of Francisco PIZARRO in the conquest of Peru. Diego de Almagro arrived in Panama with Pedro Arias de ÁVILA's expedition in 1514. He became Pizarro's junior partner in the management of *encomiendas.* When the two men turned their efforts toward exploration (1524–1528), Pizarro assumed military leadership while Almagro recruited men and equipped the expeditions. After Pizarro's force left for Peru in 1531, Almagro followed with reinforcements but arrived too late to share in the division of ATAHUALPA's ransom. After the occupation of Cuzco (1533), Pizarro sent Almagro to assist Sebastián de BENALCÁZAR in opposing Pedro de ALVARADO's invasion of Quito.

Returning to Cuzco, Almagro learned that King CHARLES I had given him an extensive grant south of Pizarro's, and he set out on an unrewarding 2,400-mile expedition to Chile (1535–1537). Reentering

Peru, he raised MANCO INCA's siege of Cuzco, claimed the governorship of the city, and arrested Francisco Pizarro's brothers Hernando and Gonzalo for resisting his authority (*see* PIZARRO, Gonzalo). Attempts to reconcile Francisco Pizarro and Almagro failed except to free Hernando, who promptly raised an army and defeated Almagro's "men of Chile" on the plains of Las Salinas (April 6, 1538). Hernando's execution of Almagro the following July was disastrous for the Pizarros, resulting in a twenty-year imprisonment for Hernando in Spain and the assassination of Francisco (1541) by vengeful *almagristas,* who declared Almagro's mestizo son, known as El Mozo (the Lad), Governor of Peru. The *almagristas* were decisively defeated in the Battle of Chupas (1542), after which El Mozo was executed.

WILLIAM S. DUDLEY

ALMEIDA, JOSÉ AMÉRICO DE (1887–   ). Brazilian novelist and politician, member of the Brazilian Academy of Letters. He was born in Paraíba, graduated from the Recife law school, and for many years practiced law. Active in the REVOLUTION OF 1930, he later became the Governor of Paraíba, a government minister, and a senator. He was the first of the neoregionalist novelists of the NORTHEAST to deal with the vast geographic, economic, and social problems of that area. Before José Lins do REGO [Cavalcânti] wrote his novels of the sugarcane cycle, Almeida had written about a great plantation in his novel *A Bagaceira* (1928). In it two types of life are contrasted: that of the patriarchal, autocratic structure of the sugar plantation on the rich lands near the coast, in which the conditions of slavery still existed, and that of the hinterland with its relatively democratic society. The periodic droughts with their devastating effects on the land and people furnish a secondary theme. In 1935 Almeida published two other regional novels, *O Boqueirão* and *Coiteiros.* Although there had been other regionalist novels in Brazil, the sociological approach he employs (previously seen in his essay *A Paraíba e Seus Problemas*) gives his work its originality. The most important influences on him were probably the theories of Gilberto FREYRE and *Os Sertões* by Euclides da CUNHA.

RAYMOND S. SAYERS

ALONSO, AMADO (1896–1952). Spanish-born Argentine scholar and critic. A disciple of Ramón Menéndez Pidal in the Centro de Estudios Históricos of Madrid, he devoted his life to linguistic research and teaching and was a major influence in Hispanic letters. He served as director of the Institute of Philology at the University of Buenos Aires and in 1939 founded the *Revista de Filología Hispánica* (later *Nueva Revista de Filología Hispánica*), which became the most important review of its kind in Latin America.

Alonso is widely known for studies of phonetics and dialectology and for pioneer work in stylistics in the tradition of Karl Vossler, Charles Bally, and others. Among his best-known works are *El problema de la lengua en América* (1935), *Poesía y estilo de Pablo Neruda* (1940), and *Castellano, español, idioma nacional* (1942). His literary criticism is also deservedly famous. From 1946 on Alonso taught at Harvard University.

RACHEL PHILLIPS

ALTIPLANO. South American plateau enclosed by two parallel mountain chains, the Cordilleras Occidental and Real, lying about 13,000 feet above sea level. It is approximately 520 miles long and 80 to 100 miles wide and comprises an area of about 50,000 square miles. More than two-thirds of the altiplano is located in Bolivia; the rest, in Peru.

Although the altiplano is situated in the latitude of the tropics, it is cold because of its altitude. The terrain is dry most of the year, and even the heavy rains that fall between December and February have no lasting benefit since they are rapidly absorbed by the porous soil. Consequently, the altiplano is almost permanently parched. In spite of these difficult conditions, the altiplano has served as the center for a series of advanced civilizations, including the Inca (*see* INCAS). Even today this region has the highest rural population in Bolivia. Nevertheless, the altiplano is not very hospitable. Except for coarse grass and hardy shrubs, it is virtually bare of vegetation. The potato is the most important domesticated crop, and, along with a variety of other tubers and a few cereals, it constitutes the inhabitants' major source of nourishment.

The altiplano's animal life is equally sparse. Llamas, alpacas, and vicuñas are the most valuable indigenous fauna. While cattle are uncommon because the altiplano does not have suitable pasture, sheep have been replacing llamas and vicuñas as a source of both fiber and food, particularly in the northern altiplano.

ORAZIO A. CICCARELLI

ALVARADO, PEDRO DE (1485–1541). Spanish conquistador. A prototype of the ambitious and restless conqueror, Alvarado arrived in Hispaniola in 1510. After commanding a ship in the expedition of Juan de Grijalva to explore the coast of Yucatán and Mexico, he joined the army of Hernán CORTÉS in 1519. During the conquest of New Spain, Alvarado became Cortés's principal captain and was left in command in Mexico City–Tenochtitlán while Cortés traveled to the coast to deflect a rival Spanish expedition. Alvarado bore the responsibility for provoking a rebellion of Aztec nobility (*see* AZTECS), which led to the death of MOCTEZUMA and the expulsion of the Spaniards from the Valley of Mexico in June 1520.

Throughout the final conquest of Mexico, Alvarado displayed skill, boldness, and audacity as a soldier. He led an expedition to Tehuantepec in 1523 and then moved on to conquer Guatemala and El Salvador. In 1524 he became Governor and Captain-General of Guatemala, a position he held until his death. Because of opposition from the *audiencia,* he voyaged to Spain (1526–1528), where his titles and honors were confirmed. In 1534 he sailed to Ecuador with an army of 2,500 men, seeking a share of the former Inca empire (*see* INCAS). Both Diego de ALMAGRO and Sebastián de BENALCÁZAR anticipated his arrival, and rather than risk an armed conflict with them, Alvarado accepted payment in exchange for his army and supplies.

Alvarado returned to Spain between 1536 and 1539, again receiving ratification of his authority in Guatemala. He undertook an exploration of the South Sea Islands in 1541 but was persuaded by Viceroy Antonio de MENDOZA to travel overland to look for the legendary Cíbola. While on his way to the north, he participated in the Mixtón War, an Indian rebellion in New Galicia. He was killed accidentally at the end of a battle. His wife succeeded him as Governor of Guatemala.

EDITH B. COUTURIER

ÁLVARES CORREIA, DIOGO. *See* CARAMURÚ.

ALVEAR, MARCELO T[ORCUATO] DE (1868–1942). President of Argentina (1922–1928). Alvear came from a distinguished family. His grandfather, Carlos María de Alvear, was the Supreme Director in Buenos Aires in 1815. His father, Torcuato de Alvear (1822–1890), played a major role in the physical transformation of Buenos Aires while serving as Municipal Attendant (1883–1887). Marcelo entered politics at an early age; even before he graduated from law school in 1891 he helped form the Unión Cívica de la Juventud, became the secretary of Leandro ALEM, and participated in the revolution of 1890 against President Miguel JUÁREZ CELMAN. When the Unión Cívica split, he stayed with Alem to organize the Unión Cívica Radical (UCR; *see* RADICAL PARTY: ARGENTINA). The following year, 1892, he was imprisoned and exiled for his political activities, but undaunted he participated in the revolution of 1893. In 1906, after a courtship of eight years in Europe, during which he followed his future bride from one singing engagement to another, he married a famous Portuguese soprano of Italian parentage, Regina Pacini. His friendship with Hipólito YRIGOYEN dates from 1889; it became closer after 1897, when he served as Yrigoyen's second during a duel with Lisandro DE LA TORRE. Alvear was the Argentine representative in Paris from 1917 to 1922, and in opposition to the policy of President Yrigoyen he clearly indicated his sympathies for the Allied cause. His stand did not affect his relations with Yrigoyen, who was responsible for the Alvear–Elpidio González ticket of the UCR that won the elections of 1922.

As President, Alvear demonstrated that he was a liberal in the nineteenth-century sense of the word. He respected freedom of the press, favored a minimum of state interference in the economy, emphasized the importance of law and legal institutions, and stood for economic development, a balanced budget, and a strong currency. His budgets did show a surplus, and he used the money to build roads, schools, and hospitals, aid agriculture, establish the YACIMIENTOS PETROLÍFEROS FISCALES on a firm foundation, pay the interest due on the debt of the state railroads, and reduce the external debt of the country. He also consolidated the short-term debt of Argentina and abandoned Yrigoyen's protectionist trade policies.

It is difficult to assess Alvear's political influence. Some feel that he was not an effective leader. He was used, they claim, by his Cabinet ministers and especially by Drs. Tomás Le Breton and Vicente C. Gallo, two of his three Ministers of the Interior, and he remained aloof from the internecine party struggles that led to the division of the UCR in 1924 into two rival factions, the pro-Yrigoyen Personalistas and the anti-Yrigoyen Antipersonalistas, or Principistas. Others attribute the split in the UCR to Yrigoyen's conduct as President, his efforts to govern secretly during the first years of the Alvear administration, and his refusal, along with that of the Antipersonalistas, to cooperate with Álvear for the restoration of party unity in 1925.

Upon leaving office in 1928, Alvear sold all his properties and left for Europe. Three years later he returned to reorganize the UCR, but he never did bring the Radicals together in a revitalized party.

JOSEPH T. CRISCENTI

AMADO, JORGE (1912–   ). Brazilian novelist. Born in Bahia, the son of a cacao planter, he graduated from the Rio de Janeiro law school. For a time he was a member of the Communist party and was eventually elected to the national Chamber of Deputies as a Communist. Meanwhile, he was writing the remarkable series of novels that have made him the most popular contemporary Brazilian writer. They belong to two basic groups: those that represent the life of the poor in the old capital, Salvador, whose *joie de vivre* is not overcome by the conditions in which they exist; and those that deal with the cacao-planting region in which he spent his childhood. The earlier novels about Salvador, such as *Jubiabá* (1935) and *Mar Morto* (1936), emphasize social injustice and introduce colorful aspects of the life of a people who are still close to Africa. Such later books about Salvador as *Os Velhos Marinheiros*, 1961 (*The Two Deaths of Quincas Wateryell* and *Home Is the Sailor*), *Os Pastores da Noite*, 1964 (*Shepherds of the Night*), and *Dona Flor e Seus Dois Maridos*, 1966 (*Dona Flor and Her Two Husbands*) develop in greater depth the rich mine of customs and folklore that make the old city unique in Brazil. In his novels of the cacao cycle, especially *Terras do Sem Fim*, 1942 (*The Violent Land*) and *São Jorge dos Ilhéus* (1944), Amado achieved unusual power and epic scope. *Seara Vermelha* (1946) is more typically a novel of the NORTHEAST. Amado's later novels, beginning with *Gabriela, Cravo e Canela*, 1958 (*Gabriela, Clove and Cinnamon*), are in a newly humorous vein.

RAYMOND S. SAYERS

AMADOR GUERRERO, MANUEL (1833–1909). First President of independent Panama (1904–1908). Amador was born in Colombia. After establishing his residence in Aspinwall (Colón), he became a physician. Later he became chief of medical services for the PANAMA RAILROAD. A Conservative, he was the most active figure in the isthmian independence movement and was elected President by the Constituent Assembly of 1904.

As chief executive, Amador disbanded the armed forces and authorized a police corps of 700 men. By the end of his Presidency a secondary school and 222 primary schools were in operation, as were 2 normal schools, a vocational school, and a music conservatory. Colón and Panama City gained water and sewer systems, and streets were paved in both cities. The Canal Zone was created in 1904. Amador established a precedent by inviting United States supervision of the presidential election of 1908 in accordance with Article 136 of the 1904 constitution.

Important negotiations were undertaken with the United States and Costa Rica. Misunderstandings with Canal Zone officials led to the Taft Convention (1904) regulating international commerce, the postal service, and parity of the dollar with the Panamanian monetary unit. Amador attempted to demarcate the Costa Rican boundary. A treaty was negotiated and approved by the National Assembly but was rejected by Costa Rica.

LARRY L. PIPPIN

AMARAL, TARSILA DO (1890–1973). Brazilian painter. Born in Capivari, São Paulo, she began her art studies in São Paulo with Pedro Alexandrino and Georg Fischer Elpons, a German painter resident in Brazil who acquainted her with impressionism. Traveling to Europe in 1920, she studied first with Émile Renard at the Académie Julian in Paris and later with André Lhote, Albert Gleizes, and Fernand Léger, who introduced her to cubism. Her painting *The Negress* (1923) reveals the influence of Léger but also anticipates the concern with Brazilian themes that would be one of her dominant characteristics. She exhibited her work for the first time in 1922 and had her first one-woman show at the Galerie Percier in Paris in 1926.

Tarsila, as she is usually known, returned to Brazil in 1923. Two experiences the following year, the carnival in Rio de Janeiro and a tour of the historic cities of Minas Gerais during Holy Week, aroused in her a new appreciation for the forms and vivid colors of Brazilian popular arts that she would incorporate in her future work. She illustrated a book of poems, *Pau Brasil* (1925), by the writer Oswald de Andrade, whom she would later marry, and the title—meaning "Brazilwood," from which the country derives its name—came to be used to refer to her work of this period and to a literary movement associated with modernism (*see* MODERNISM: BRAZIL). Three years later her painting *O Abaporu* (*The Indian Cannibal*), showing a creature with a tiny head and an immense body and feet, gave rise to the literary movement known as anthropophagism. Founded by Andrade and Raúl Bopp, anthropophagism extolled the Indian as a primitive being for whom happiness is the only aim. In the 1930s Tarsila's work entered a new phase as she began painting canvases showing an interest in social problems, notably *Workers* and *Second Class*. However, she soon returned to her earlier style, landscapes being prominent in her later work.   HELEN DELPAR

AMAZON RIVER. Largest river system in the world, draining most of northern South America. Flowing some 3,900 miles from the ANDES MOUNTAINS to the Atlantic, the Amazon is fed by 1,100 tributaries, some silted and others clear. The river dominates southeastern Colombia, eastern Peru, and the Brazilian states of Pará, Amazonas, and Acre, as well as the territories of Amapá and Roraima, and parts of Maranhão, Goiás, and Mato Grosso. The *várzea* (floodplain) is a maze of channels forming a water network navigable by ocean steamer 2,300 miles upstream to Iquitos, Peru. Its generally fertile, annually replenished alluvial soils have made the *várzea* the center of permanent settlement. The interfluves are an upland area of fragile and infertile soils, tropical rain forest, and sparse population. The Amazonian climate is hot and humid but varies in precipitation and season. The population of Pará, Amazonas, Acre, and the Brazilian territories is only a little more than 3 million (1970), of whom 1.1 million live in Belém, Manaus, and Iquitos.

The effective discovery, exploration, and naming of the river date from Francisco de ORELLANA's expedition of 1541–1542. The presence of the legendary Amazons has never been substantiated. Brazilian claim to the entire basin, established in 1639, was confirmed by treaty in 1750, although specific boundaries have been ratified in the twentieth century.

Members of various religious orders, of whom the Jesuits were the most influential, arrived in the early seventeenth century. Amazonian colonial history is replete with clashes between Portuguese settlers and Jesuits over control of the Indians. The reforms of the Marquês de POMBAL, which brought administrative and economic change to the basin, also resolved this conflict by expelling the Jesuits in 1759 (*see* JESUITS, EXPULSION OF: BRAZIL).

Brazilian independence in 1822 brought little change to the basin, but the sporadic violence of the 1821–1840 period, known as the Cabanagem, had severe social and economic consequences. Beginning as a quarrel over spoils of office, the Cabanagem developed into a full-fledged race and class war that left about 30,000 dead. Belém was repeatedly sacked and burned, and pillage, murder, and chaos were commonplace all along the river.

Economic recovery began with an increased world demand for rubber (*see* RUBBER BOOM: BRAZIL). The boom, which lasted from about 1875 to 1911, brought new wealth to a few, ostentatious display in Belém and Manaus, and a perpetuation of feudallike social conditions. Many rubber gatherers were destitute refugees from the NORTHEAST, looking for work but finding isolation, exploitation, and death. The rubber boom collapsed in 1911–1912, with prices falling drastically. Even Henry Ford's attempt at rational planting between 1925 and 1946 could not revive the industry, and today the Amazon Basin cannot meet Brazil's needs for natural rubber. New crops have replaced rubber, the most important being jute and black pepper, introduced by Japanese colonists. The Amazonian export economy has traditionally centered on extractive forest products, and subsistence agriculture has been barely adequate to feed the local population.

Since World War II there have been sporadic but increasing attempts at industrialization and economic diversification, financed by both national and foreign capital, with emphasis on the former. This interest has been encouraged by federal attention to Amazonian development since 1964. The SUPERINTENDÊNCIA DO DESENVOLVIMENTO DA AMAZÔNIA (SUDAM) has been responsible for encouraging and guiding investments through technical assistance, feasibility studies, and recommendations for loans from the Banco da Amazônia, a government-operated credit facility.

AMAZON RIVER

There have been a number of government programs and projects to encourage development of the basin. A major reason for governmental interest is a desire to weave the area more closely into the Brazilian fabric in order to discourage foreign covetousness.

To encourage industrial development and strengthen ties with the rest of Brazil, transportation has been developed by means of airplane and highway. Perhaps the most striking change has been the opening of the Belém-Brasília highway, a major freight route from the south and an encouragement to squatter and rancher colonization along its sides. Other major links will be the Santarém-Cuiabá road and the well-publicized Transamazonian Highway, but it will be a long time before waterways cease to be the most popular mode of transportation.

The Amazon remains Brazil's "land of the future." How successful the many and varied schemes may be in developing the area and combating the internal colonialism that has made the north dependent on the southern metropolis remains to be seen. The Amazon has seen economic booms before, but none have had long-range beneficial effects. However, with agricultural diversification, industrialization, a transportation revolution, new integration with the rest of Brazil, government colonization schemes, increased technical aid and credit facilities, and radical transformation of the environment itself, change is inevitable. Its value remains to be judged.

See also PETRÓPOLIS, TREATY OF.

Bibliography. Brasil, Instituto Brasileiro de Geografia e Estatística, *A Grande Região Norte,* Rio de Janeiro, 1959; Ernesto Cruz, *História do Pará,* 2 vols., Belém, 1963; Mathias Kiemen, O.F.M., *The Indian Policy of Portugal in the Amazon Region, 1614–1693,* Washington, 1954; Artur Cezar Ferreira Reis, *A Amazônia e a Cobiça Internacional,* São Paulo, 1960; Henry Major Tomlinson, *The Sea and the Jungle,* New York, 1961; Charles Wagley, *Amazon Town: A Study of Man in the Tropics,* New York, 1964; Alfred Russell Wallace, *Travels on the Amazon,* London, 1889.

ROBIN L. ANDERSON

AMERICAN POPULAR REVOLUTIONARY ALLI-ANCE. *See* ALIANZA POPULAR REVOLUCIONARIA AMERICANA.

AMUNÁTEGUI, MIGUEL LUIS (1828–1888). Chilean historian and politician. Amunátegui served his country in numerous capacities. He sat for many years as a Liberal member of the Chamber of Deputies (*see* LIBERAL PARTY: CHILE) and several times held ministerial office. In 1875 he was offered, but declined, the opportunity of becoming the Liberal candidate for the Presidency.

Amunátegui's most important historical works were *La reconquista española* (1851), *Los tres primeros años de la revolución* (1851), *La dictadura de O'Higgins* (1853), *Los precursores de la independencia de Chile* (1870–1872), and *La crónica de 1810* (1876). In addition, he published numerous books and articles on topics ranging from philology to the frontier dispute with Argentina. Amunátegui must be regarded as second only to Diego BARROS ARANA among the great nineteenth-century historians of Chile.

SIMON COLLIER

ANAPO. *See* ALIANZA NACIONAL POPULAR.

ANCHIETA, JOSÉ DE (1534–1597). Jesuit missionary known as the Apostle of Brazil. Anchieta was born in the Canary Islands and studied at the University of Coimbra in Portugal. About 1553 he left for Brazil, where he taught at the Jesuit college of São Paulo. He served as a missionary in São Vicente, Rio de Janeiro, and Espírito Santo and was Provincial of the Society of Jesus in southern Brazil from 1577 to 1587. A leader in the attempt to teach the Amerindians to read and write, he devised a Tupí grammar (*see* TUPÍ-GUARANÍ), published in Coimbra in 1595.

KENNETH R. MAXWELL

ANDEAN GROUP (GRUPO ANDINO). Subregional grouping within the LATIN AMERICAN FREE TRADE ASSOCIATION (LAFTA), composed of Bolivia, Chile, Colombia, Ecuador, Peru, and Venezuela. The Andean Group grew out of the desire of the member states for an association that would enable them to confront the LAFTA Big Three—Brazil, Mexico, and Argentina—on a more equal footing. The subregional grouping was created in 1966 and was formally established with the signing of the Cartagena Agreement on May 26, 1969. The pact aroused some opposition from private business and industrial sectors, especially in Venezuela, which did not join the Andean Group until February 1973.

The Cartagena Agreement provides for the gradual elimination of all barriers to trade among the member nations by 1980 (1985 in the case of Bolivia and Ecuador) and for the establishment of a common external tariff by 1985. Bolivia and Ecuador, as the least-developed members of the group, are to be accorded special treatment. In addition, the Andean Group proposes to stimulate the industrial development of the member states through sectoral agreements giving each country exclusive access to a protected market for a designated group of products during a limited period of time. The member states also drew up (1970) a code regulating foreign investment in the region. To provide financing for industry and other development projects, the Andean Development Corporation (Corporación Andina de Fomento) was established in 1968, with capital derived from both private and public sources in the member states.

RODNEY D. ANDERSON

ANDES MOUNTAINS. The Andes stretch for about 4,000 miles from the northern to the southern end of South America on the west side of the continent. This region includes a broad diversity of landscapes, from turbulent rivers to coastal fiords, from humid to arid lands, and from desolate windswept plateaus to fertile basins.

Twelve Andean peaks rise above 20,000 feet in elevation. The Andes were elevated to their present height at about the same time as the Rocky Mountains in North America. Great masses of folded sedimentary rocks enclose a central granitic core. Numerous snow-covered volcanic cones and frequent tremors attest to the continuing crustal instability of the Andes and their fringes. Earthquakes destroyed several important cities in the colonial period and continue to pose a threat to human life and property.

These mountains do not form a single chain but are

broken into many different structural units that can be grouped into three main regional sections. The southern Andes extend from about 30° south latitude to Tierra del Fuego along the border between Chile and Argentina. Aside from some miners, these southern mountains are sparsely populated, serving as a great divide between the populous Central Valley of Chile and the piedmont oases of Argentina on the eastern side. The central Andes run from Ecuador into northwestern Argentina and are densely settled at high elevations. The ALTIPLANO, a lofty tableland in western Bolivia, is the most extensive flat area in the whole Andean system. The upper Marañon, Huallaga, Apurímac, Urubamba, and other rivers have etched out extraordinary canyons. In the northern Andes of Colombia and Venezuela discrete ranges are flanked on all sides by humid tropical lowlands. The snow line and upper limit of settlement descend to altitudes below 10,000 feet in this northern section, which thus differs from Peru and Bolivia, where farming occurs even above 14,000 feet above sea level. Unpredictable drought, frost, and hail are climatic adversities that occur in the mountains and not in the adjacent plains.

More people live in the Andes than in any other large highland region of the world. The inhabitants are largely Indian and mestizo peasant farmers, most of whom do not speak Spanish as their first language, if they speak it at all. In Peru and Bolivia the unusually large chests and torsos of the native inhabitants show evolutionary adaptation to the high elevation. Visitors to the region frequently suffer from *soroche* (mountain sickness), characterized by nausea, headache, and often nosebleed.

Agriculture is the main activity of the people who live in the Andes as far south as northwestern Argentina. Beginning at about Copiapó, Chile, the Andes contract to a single mountain range, and the climate becomes increasingly severe toward the south, so that agriculture is impossible at high elevations. Northward, however, the vertical zonation of climate and fertile tracts of land have favored dense sedentary populations since long before the Spanish conquest. Within 20° of the equator the base of the Andes has temperatures consistently high enough to permit many tropical crops, including bananas, manioc, and cacao. Above 3,000 feet a temperate climate that is especially suitable for coffee and maize prevails. In the cool lands above this zone, potatoes, wheat, barley, and quinoa (a domesticated chenopod) are among the dominant crops. The high grass-covered slopes beyond the limit of farming are dedicated to raising sheep, cattle, and, in Peru and Bolivia, the alpaca.

The more densely packed rural concentrations in the Andes are found where sizable areas of level land occur. Among the important districts are the Mérida Basin in Venezuela, the basin of Cundinamarca in Colombia, and the basins of Quito, Ambato, and Cuenca in Ecuador. In Peru parts of the Mantaro, Santa (Callejón de Huaylas), and Urubamba (Vilcanota) Valleys are heavily populated by peasants, as are the Lake Titicaca and Cochabamba Basins in Bolivia and the basins of Jujuy and Salta in Argentina.

Taken as a whole, the Andes have a serious shortage of good land for agriculture, arising from increasing population pressure, inefficient methods, and mounting soil erosion caused by centuries of ruthless forest exploitation. Large landholdings are still dominant despite some agrarian reforms that have been made and many others on paper (*see* AGRARIAN REFORM). The essential tasks of plowing, harvesting, and milling are largely carried on with methods and devices either passed down from preconquest times or introduced centuries ago from preindustrial Europe. Many peasants, especially in the central Andes, live in grinding poverty, with low dietary levels, a lack of consumer goods, and poor health conditions. Migration from marginal farms to cities is an accelerating trend.

The Andes have long been exploited by those seeking mineral riches. Silver was formerly mined in large quantities at Potosí, Bolivia; gold, especially in Colombia; and mercury at Huancavelica, Peru. Copper and iron ore deposits in Peru and Chile and tin in Bolivia are the most important mineral exports today. Other exports from these mountains are coffee, primarily from Colombia, and wool from Peru and Bolivia. Formerly cinchona bark was a product in world demand.

Rural settlements are typically clustered, either in manor estates or in independent hamlets. Agricultural villages are a legacy of the sixteenth-century reductions, and many are simply clusters of farm folk. Larger towns are centers of administration and periodic markets, still an important system of exchange in the Andes. Cities such as San Cristóbal in western Venezuela, Pasto in southern Colombia, Cuenca in Ecuador, Huancayo in central Peru, and Cochabamba in Bolivia dominate large regions economically, politically, and culturally. Some of these urban foci—Popayán and Tunja in Colombia, Ayacucho and Cuzco in Peru, and Sucre in Bolivia—have maintained their colonial physiognomy and charm. Two of the world's highest cities are Cerro de Pasco in Peru and Potosí in Bolivia, mining centers above 14,000 feet in elevation. Four cities above 5,000 feet have at least half a million people: Bogotá, Medellín, Quito, and La Paz.

The Andes have always constituted a formidable barrier to land movement both across and within it. A curious juxtaposition of primitive and modern modes is found; pack trains of mules and llamas may plod along narrow trails within a short distance of airports accommodating the most modern jet aircraft. Although vehicle roads are of limited mileage, poorly maintained, and often blocked by landslides in the rainy season, the truck is now the backbone of the Andean transport system. The age of railway building has passed, yet the lines that have been constructed continue to link the Andes to other regions: Bogotá with the Magdalena Valley; Quito with the port of Guayaquil; the Mantaro Valley of Peru with Lima; Cuzco and the Titicaca area with the southern Peruvian coast; and La Paz, Oruro, and the rest of the Bolivian altiplano with Arica and Antofagasta in Chile. Two railroads cross the cordillera between Chile and Argentina. Aviation has ended the extreme isolation of many larger mountain centers. Linkages between Bogotá and Medellín, Lima and Cuzco, Quito and Guayaquil, and La Paz and Cochabamba may be made in less than an hour's flying time, a trip that takes a day by truck or bus, and at least a week by mule.

In addition to being a well-defined physical region, this great mountain system also has some measure of cultural unity that transcends national boundaries. The tradition of indigenous civilizations, notably the Inca (*see* INCAS) and CHIBCHA, and the partial or total Indian racial composition of the majority of its inhabitants contribute to an Andean highland identity. Indigenous place names dot the land, and highlanders have a somewhat sibilant manner of speaking Spanish that sets them apart from people of other regions. Generally, these mountains are bastions of traditional form and substance in social and religious matters. In agriculture the Andean peasant emphasizes self-sufficiency, hand labor, and serious attention to cereals and tubers. Many traits or customs are localized, seen only in parts of the Andes; for example, the llama and the QUECHUA language do not occur in Venezuela, Colombia, southern Chile, or Argentina, and the *chaquitaclla,* or native foot plow, is a tool restricted to Peru and Bolivia. Yet cultural similarities in the Andes are sufficiently numerous to make this region a useful generalization for more than merely its highland physiography.

The seven countries that have portions of the Andes within their borders have differed in the degree of highland influence in national life. Bolivia and Colombia have probably been the most dominated by mountain-bred attitudes; Chile and Argentina, the least. Regional changes in economic development and population movement are apparent in Venezuela, where the Andean portion has lagged behind other areas of the country. Likewise in Ecuador, commercial agriculture in the coastal region, reinforced by newly exploited petroleum deposits in the Oriente, offsets the traditional dominance of the sierra region (*see* ORIENTE: ECUADOR; SIERRA: ECUADOR). In Peru the desert coast continues to receive streams of highland migrants looking for jobs in the rapidly expanding cities. In Bolivia the eastern plains have become the land of opportunity as mineral deposits in the altiplano become exhausted.

Bibliography. I. Bowman, *The Andes of Southern Peru,* New York, 1916; O. Dollfus, *Le Pérou,* Paris, 1968; P. James, *Latin America,* 4th ed., New York, 1969; H. Osborne, *Indians of the Andes,* Cambridge, Mass., 1952; E. Romero, *Biografía de los Andes,* Buenos Aires, 1965.

DANIEL W. GADE

ANDRADA E SILVA, JOSÉ BONIFACIO (1763–1838). Brazilian mineralogist, teacher, poet, author, and controversial political figure, known as the Patriarch of Brazilian Independence for his leadership in the Brazilian independence movement. Educated at the University of Coimbra, he was admitted to the Portuguese Academy of Sciences in 1789 and the following year was commissioned to undertake a scientific excursion through Europe to broaden his knowledge of mineralogy and natural history. After more than ten years of work and travel, including study in Paris and Freiburg, he returned to Portugal a renowned scholar and scientist. In Portugal he accepted high posts, including a professorship at Coimbra and the office of General Intendant of Mines.

José Bonifacio returned to Brazil in 1819 after a thirty-six-year absence, quickly becoming involved in the national independence movement. With the Portuguese Cortes (Parliament) threatening to reestablish the former colonial relationship, in late 1821 he called upon Prince Regent Pedro (later PEDRO I) to defy the Portuguese government and remain in Brazil as a means of achieving independence and avoiding national disintegration. On January 9, 1822, Pedro announced his decision to stay in Brazil ("*o Fico*"), and a week later he appointed José Bonifacio Minister of the Kingdom and of Foreign Affairs. As head of the Cabinet, José Bonifacio was involved in decisions leading to Pedro's declaration of independence on September 7, 1822 (*see* YPIRANGA, GRITO DE).

Elected to the General Constituent and Legislative Assembly, José Bonifacio and his brothers, Martim Francisco and Antônio Carlos Ribeiro de Andrada, were among the more progressive delegates, writing a liberal constitutional project in 1823 and advocating the abolition of the slave trade. On July 15, 1823, José Bonifacio was dismissed as head of the Cabinet, but for several months he and his brothers fought growing Portuguese influence in Pedro's government. In November 1823, the Emperor closed the Assembly and exiled the Andradas and their associates, but in 1831, upon his abdication, he appointed José Bonifacio tutor to his children, including the five-year-old PEDRO II. In December 1833, José Bonifacio was dismissed from the latter post by the ruling Liberals because of his alleged participation in a plot to restore the former Emperor to his throne. He was the author of scientific, historical, and political works, including pamphlets proposing the abolition of the slave trade and the incorporation of Indians into the national community.

ROBERT CONRAD

ANDRADE, CARLOS DRUMMOND DE (1902–   ). Brazilian poet and prose writer. Born in Itabira, Minas Gerais, he took a degree in pharmacy in Belo Horizonte in 1921 but then entered the field of journalism. While living in Belo Horizonte, he founded the modernist magazine *Revista de Antropofagia* (*Review of Cannibalism*) with other important Minas writers (*see* MODERNISM: BRAZIL). There, too, he met Mário de ANDRADE, with whom he began a long-lasting correspondence. Although he had not participated in the Modern Art Week (1922), he became thoroughly imbued with the modernist spirit, as is seen in his famous *pièce de scandale,* "Uma Pedra no Meio do Caminho" (1928), and in his first collection, *Alguma Poesia* (1930), dedicated to Mário de Andrade. His best early poetry is reminiscent of his childhood and the past, and the manner is flippant, often ironic. From the start his style and control of language were evident. Through the years his poetry became more serious, and in later years philosophical. One volume, *A Rosa do Povo* (1945), expresses a leftist ideology, but the sense of conviction diminishes in later volumes. However, the reminiscent tone, the irony, and the humor are always present. Among Andrade's other works are *Brejo das Almas* (1934), *Sentimento do Mundo* (1940), *Fazendeiro do Ar* (1955), and *Boitempo* (1968). He is also an essayist — *Confissões de Minas* (1944), *Passeios na Ilha* (1952), and *Fala, Amendoeira* (1957) — and the author of an excellent collection of short stories, *Contos de Aprendiz* (1951).

RAYMOND S. SAYERS

ANDRADE, MÁRIO [RAÚL] DE [MORAIS] (1893–1945). Brazilian poet, writer of fiction, critic, and musicologist. Born in São Paulo, Andrade studied at the São Paulo Conservatory, where he later taught. He was the first director of the São Paulo Department of Culture, the founder of the Brazilian Society of Ethnography and Culture, and professor of art history at the short-lived University of the Federal District.

Andrade took an active part in the Modern Art Week (1922), and he preached the doctrines of modernism (*see* MODERNISM: BRAZIL) in his volumes of criticism and literary history, *A Escrava Que Não É Isaura* (1925), *O Empalhador de Passarinho* (1944), and *Aspectos da Literatura Brasileira* (1943), as well as in his letters, especially the *Cartas a Manuel Bandeira* (1958). The poems in *Paulicéia Desvairada,* 1922 (*Hallucinated City*), express the whimsical irreverence of early modernism; they are written in the free verse and unconventional syntax the modernists cultivated. Andrade's love of São Paulo is a basic element in this and later volumes of poetry, including *Losango Cáqui* (1926), *Clã de Jabuti* (1927), and *Lira Paulistana* (1947). He was an innovator in fiction. In his collections of short stories, the last of which were *Os Contos de Belazarte* (1934) and *Novos Contos* (1947), he wrote about the native and immigrant groups of São Paulo. The novel *Macunaíma* (1928), which he also called a rhapsody, recounts the history of Brazil through the life of its mythical hero. The novel *Amar, Verbo Intransitivo* (1927), a satire on Brazilian family life, was translated into English as *Fräulein.*

Andrade was also one of the founders of Brazilian ethnomusicology, and he was very influential in the assertion of musical nationalism in the 1920s and 1930s. His lifelong investigations into Brazilian folk and popular music produced essays of great insight. His first monograph, *Ensaio sôbre a Música Brasileira* (1928), considers the relationship he feels ought to exist between art music and popular (folk) music and analyzes the rhythmic, melodic, harmonic, textural, instrumental, and formal characteristics of Brazilian music. Andrade was actively involved in the organization of the Congresso da Língua Nacional Cantada (1937). One of his lasting projects was the founding of the Discoteca Pública de São Paulo, which with the help of Oneyda Alvarenga has accumulated the best collection of recorded Brazilian music. Andrade's main musical publications include *Música, Doce Música* (1933), *O Samba Rural Paulista* (1937), *Danças Dramáticas do Brasil* (1958), and *Música de Feitiçaria no Brasil* (1958).

RAYMOND S. SAYERS AND GERARD H. BÉHAGUE

ANDRADE, ROBERTO (1852–1939). Ecuadorian politician, historian, and novelist. Andrade was born in Imbabura Province. Influenced by Juan MONTALVO's tracts, he conspired with other youths to assassinate President Gabriel GARCÍA MORENO. Another committed the act while Andrade stood on the sidelines, but Andrade basked in reflected glory all his life. An active Liberal (*see* LIBERAL PARTY: ECUADOR), he took part in the revolution against Ignacio VEINTEMILLA in 1882, fled to various Central American countries, was among the political prisoners freed in Quito by the Liberal Radicals in 1895, and served in the 1896 National Congress.

As a historian Andrade suffered from a fanatic bias. He hated Juan José FLORES, García Moreno, and such aspects of the church as the exploitation of the lower classes by the convents of Quito. His seven-volume *Historia del Ecuador* (1936) is largely a synthesis of earlier works combined with gossip, but it gave rise to a school of anti-García literature and psychohistory, as well as a second school enraged by Andrade's interpretation and bent upon canonizing García Moreno. Andrade's history of Ecuador for children became an official text and appeared in ten editions during the Liberal Radical era. A notable contribution was Andrade's realistic political tale, *Pacho Villamar* (1900), a bridge between the romantic and the modern Ecuadorian novel.

LOIS WEINMAN

ANDREONI, JOÃO ANTÔNIO (real name of ANDRÉ JOÃO ANTONIL, 1649–1716). Italian Jesuit. Author of the famous *Cultura e Opulência do Brasil por Suas Drogas e Minas,* published in Lisbon during 1711 under the pseudonym André João Antonil, Andreoni was born in Lucca, Tuscany, and studied law at the University of Perugia before joining the Society of Jesus during 1667. In Rome he became acquainted with Antônio VIEIRA, S.J., whom he accompanied to Brazil in 1681. He taught at the Jesuit college in Bahia (modern Salvador) and served as secretary to several Jesuit provincials. He probably began *Cultura e Opulência* about 1693, and the book was completed in stages over the next ten years.

The work was divided into four parts, the first and most substantial of which was concerned with sugar production (*see* SUGAR INDUSTRY: COLONIAL BRAZIL). It was based on Andreoni's observations in Bahia, most especially his visit to the famous Jesuit sugar mill of Sergipe do Conde. The second part dealt with tobacco cultivation, the third with the recently discovered gold mines, and the fourth with ranching, colonial trade, and revenues. The first edition was destroyed shortly after its printing, the Portuguese authorities fearing that the information it contained would be of value to Portugal's enemies. Their fear was not entirely unjustified, for the French were attacking Rio de Janeiro in 1711, and there was unrest in several parts of the colony. Only six copies of the original edition exist today, although there have been several reeditions. *Cultura e Opulência* is a prime source for the social and economic history of colonial Brazil.

KENNETH R. MAXWELL

ANDUEZA PALACIO, RAIMUNDO (1843–1900). President of Venezuela (1890–1892). Before succeeding to the Presidency in 1890, Andueza Palacio had had an active political career. A close associate of Juan C. FALCÓN during the latter's Presidency, he also served in various legislative and administrative posts in the era of Antonio GUZMÁN BLANCO's predominance. Despite this political experience, however, his Presidency ended in economic and political chaos, and he was forced from office by the Legalist Revolution led by Gen. Joaquín CRESPO.

JOHN V. LOMBARDI

ANGOSTURA, CONGRESS OF. Congress that convened in Angostura (now Ciudad Bolívar, Venezuela) in February 1819. It represented Simón BOLÍVAR's first serious effort to create a regular institutional base for the independence movement after his return to Venezuela in 1816. Patriot-held territory had steadily expanded in eastern Venezuela and the Orinoco plains, and the holding of a congress would demonstrate both the solidity of the new regime and its commitment to legal forms. The most heavily populated areas remained largely in royalist hands, but elsewhere elections for deputies were held.

The opening of the Congress on February 15 was marked by numerous festivities and by a notable address of Bolívar. He reviewed the problems facing Spanish America, emphasized the need to tailor institutions to the specific environment in which they would operate, and presented his own proposals for a Venezuelan constitution. These featured a strong executive, a hereditary Senate, and a fourth branch (the "moral power") with special responsibility for education and morals.

The Congress confirmed Bolívar as supreme civil and military head. Subsequently it adopted a constitution for Venezuela that followed Bolívar's recommendations in broad outline though not in all details (for example, it postponed adoption of the moral power). However, this constitution was short-lived, for Venezuela itself was absorbed into the larger union of Gran Colombia that the Congress proclaimed in December 1819 at Bolívar's behest (*see* COLOMBIA, GRAN). The Congress of Angostura continued meeting until July 1820, when it was dissolved to make way for the Congress of Cúcuta (*see* CÚCUTA, CONGRESS OF), which would be Gran Colombia's constituent convention.

DAVID BUSHNELL

ANTIOQUIA. Department in northwestern Colombia characterized by its diversity of geography, climate, industrial development, and agriculture. The first settlers, seeking gold, arrived in Antioquia in the sixteenth century. Although gold was found in the region, primitive mining techniques, labor shortages, inadequate transportation networks, and the absence of surplus capital to rectify these deficiencies inhibited spectacular exploitation of the mineral. The relative isolation of the region permitted the evolution of a distinctive cultural type, drawing from the traditions of Spanish, Indian, and Negro slave elements. The so-called *raza antioqueña* is usually described as ambitious, hardworking, and particularly able in trade and commerce.

Antioquia is but one of several *antioqueño* departments of Colombia. In the nineteenth and twentieth centuries a steady stream of *antioqueño* migrants has pushed southward along the slopes of the Cordillera Central and Cordillera Occidental and into the CAUCA VALLEY, carrying with it those cultural characteristics that have led *antioqueños* to be called the Yankees of South America. More recently these peoples have turned their attention to the settlement and exploitation of the tropical lowlands north to the Gulf of Urabá.

The department of Antioquia presents a series of contrasts. It is both urban and rural, includes both mountainous and tropical lowland terrain, is a major center for manufacturing, and offers an important and diversified contribution to Colombian agricultural production.

About 1.5 million persons, or 48 percent of Antioquia's population, reside in the 344-square-mile metropolitan area of Medellín, capital of the department. Some 25 percent of Colombia's industrial labor force are employed in Medellín, and of these 36 percent are employed by the textile industry. Although textiles are the leading industry in Antioquia, plastics, metal products, chemicals, machinery, and equipment show a greater rate of growth.

Agriculture is Antioquia's largest single source of employment, occupying about 44 percent of the work force in contrast to the 15 percent engaged in manufacturing. Antioquia is best known as an important coffee-producing region. Its 50,000 growers annually produce more than 100,000 tons of coffee beans, representing approximately 16 percent of the total Colombian output. *See also* COFFEE INDUSTRY (COLOMBIA).

In addition to coffee, livestock, bananas, and African palms have been developed as major export commodities. In 1962 the Corporación Financiera Colombiana and private investors joined to invest $40 million to develop banana production in the vicinity of the Gulf of Urabá. The investment enabled farmers to purchase plots at an average cost of $110 per acre. Currently more than 40,000 acres are producing bananas on farms ranging in size from 12 to 750 acres.

JAMES H. NEAL

ANTONIL, ANDRÉ JOÃO. *See* ANDREONI, JOÃO ANTÔNIO.

AP. *See* ACCIÓN POPULAR.

APATZINGÁN, CONSTITUTION OF. *See* CONSTITUTION OF APATZINGÁN.

APONTE LEDÉE, RAFAEL (1939–   ). Puerto Rican composer. Born in Guayama, he studied from 1957 to 1965 at the Royal Conservatory of Madrid and later with Alberto GINASTERA in Buenos Aires. Outstanding among his works are an elegy for strings, *Tema y seis diferencias* for piano, and *Impulsos* for orchestra (1967).

APRA. *See* ALIANZA POPULAR REVOLUCIONARIA AMERICANA.

ARAMBURU, PEDRO [EUGENIO] (1903–1970). Argentine army officer and provisional President (1955–1958) after the coup that overthrew Eduardo LONARDI. General Aramburu's government represented an attempt to normalize society by the suppression of Peronist elements (*see* PERONISM). The Peronist constitution of 1949 was decreed inoperative, more than 300 business firms were intervened, an extensive purge of the armed forces was carried out, and citizens who had held official positions in the government of Juan D. PERÓN were decreed ineligible for political posts. The most severely affected by such policies were labor groups (*see* CONFEDERACIÓN GENERAL DE TRABAJO). Convinced that the Argentine economy was in crisis, Aramburu implemented an austerity program that included wage controls. To encourage foreign investment he denationalized the Central Bank and joined the World Bank and the International Monetary Fund.

Aramburu withstood pressures from more extreme anti-Peronists and turned the government over to civilians elected with Peronist support in 1958. Establishing the Unión del Pueblo Argentino (UDELPA), he ran unsuccessfully as its "Gaullist" presidential candidate in 1963. Amid reports of his increasing tolerance toward Peronism and rumors that he would emerge after a coup as an interregnum figure prepared to turn power over to civilians once again, Aramburu was kidnapped and assassinated in June 1970, precipitating the fall of the government of Juan Carlos ONGANÍA.

NOREEN F. STACK

ARANA [OSORIO], CARLOS (1918–   ). President of Guatemala (1970–   ). A right-wing army officer, Arana took office in July 1970. His pledge of social reform was regarded by critics as window dressing. He nevertheless adopted Julio César MÉNDEZ MONTENEGRO's Five-Year Plan and added some touches of his own. The plan stresses rural development, particularly modernization and diversification, but does not include land reform. Relative prosperity continued from the latter years of the Méndez term.

Arana's "pacification" of Guatemala converted it into a police state. In November 1970, he declared a state of siege that continued for a year, and an obedient legislature adopted a "constitutional dictatorship." Aided by stringent curfew rules and rigorous news censorship, he began a campaign of extermination against guerrillas and "habitual criminals" (those with records of more than ten arrests). The police inaugurated a terror in the course of which they made unexplained roundups, searched private homes, and detained citizens indefinitely without trial.

Murder became commonplace, the toll of deaths from private vendettas, gang atrocities, and police actions reaching the hundreds. Attacks were not confined to Communists, guerrillas, and "habitual criminals" but included individuals of political orientation ranging from moderate to far left, from all levels of society, in all parts of the country. Murders of leaders of the democratic opposition, such as Adolfo Mijangos López, a crippled lawyer-deputy ruthlessly machine-gunned in his wheelchair, seemed particularly ominous. It appeared that Arana intended to liquidate all opposition before the scheduled 1974 election to make way for an unopposed right-wing government.

WILLIAM J. GRIFFITH

ARANGO, DOROTEO. *See* VILLA, FRANCISCO.

ARANHA, OSWALDO (1894–1960). Brazilian statesman and diplomat. Aranha's career was closely identified with that of Getúlio VARGAS, his lifelong friend and political leader. Born in Alegrete, Rio Grande do Sul, Aranha studied law in Brazil and France before entering politics in his home state. As state secretary of the interior (1928–1930), he actively supported Vargas's unsuccessful presidential campaign and played a major role as coordinator of the revolution that brought Vargas to national power in November 1930 (*see* REVOLUTION OF 1930). In the provisional government (1930–1934), Aranha served successively as Minister of Justice and Finance Minister, consolidating the authority of the regime and dealing with Brazil's critical Depression-era foreign debt problems. As Ambassador to Washington from 1934 to 1937, Aranha became a friend of President Roosevelt and a firm advocate of the GOOD NEIGHBOR POLICY. Surprised by the coup d'état that established the ESTADO NOVO in Brazil,

Aranha broke with Vargas, but in 1938 he accepted the post of Foreign Minister, which he held until 1944.

In the Ministry of Foreign Affairs Aranha worked persistently in support of Pan-Americanism, close relations with the United States, and Brazil's participation as one of the Allies in World War II. His reputation as an international statesman was reaffirmed by his Presidency of the General Assembly of the United Nations in 1947–1948. During Vargas's last administration Aranha returned to the Cabinet as Finance Minister in 1953. Although he remained active in the PARTIDO TRABALHISTA BRASILEIRO, he held no public office after the death of Vargas in 1954.

ROLLIE E. POPPINO

ARANTES DO NASCIMENTO, EDSON. *See* PELÉ.

ARAUCANIANS. Chilean Indians who once inhabited the whole of Chile from Coquimbo down to Chiloé. Found today only on reservations in the south, they are a peasantlike people who retain many of their traditional beliefs; they still practice, for instance, a Siberian type of shamanism. Although subjugated by the Inca empire, they were influenced by it only peripherally (*see* INCAS). They never abandoned their independent village-farming culture to create chiefdoms, as might have been expected. The southern groups, particularly the Mapuche, fought the Spaniards with great success, holding the line of the Bío-Bío River against all attack. They showed remarkable ingenuity in adapting the white man's tactics, quickly developing a cavalry of their own and a reliable war organization. It was not until 1866 that the Republic of Chile gave up the idea of conquest and adopted a reservation policy for the southern Mapuche. Neither the Spaniards nor the Chileans ever forced their surrender. *See* LAUTARO.

BURR C. BRUNDAGE

ARAÚJO LIMA, PEDRO DE (MARQUÊS DE OLINDA, 1793–1870). Brazilian statesman, senator, and Regent of the empire. The descendant of aristocrats of the NORTHEAST, Araújo Lima studied at Coimbra, where he received a doctorate in canonical law in 1819. In 1821 he was a member of the Portuguese Cortes (Parliament), representing his native Pernambuco, and in 1823 was elected to the Brazilian Constituent and Legislative Assembly. He served briefly as Minister of Empire just after the Emperor's dissolution of the Constituent Assembly in November 1823, retiring then from politics for a tour of Europe, only to be elected to the Chamber of Deputies in 1826. Having headed a second Cabinet in 1827–1828, he became a senator in 1837. Although he actively opposed the policies of Diogo Antônio FEIJÓ, the latter appointed him Minister of Empire on September 18, 1837, putting him constitutionally in line to succeed to the office of Regent upon Feijó's retirement the following day. As Regent, Araújo Lima attempted to end the FARROUPILHA REVOLT of Rio Grande do Sul and to suppress uprisings in other parts of the country, but Liberal antagonism deprived him of his high office by the early proclamation of the majority of PEDRO II on July 23, 1840.

In 1841 Araújo Lima was given the title of Visconde de Olinda (Marquês de Olinda in 1854), and he became a member of the Emperor's Council of State, where he exercised a conservative influence. In the years 1848–1849, 1857–1858, 1862–1864, and 1865–1866 Olinda again headed national ministries, on the last two occasions as a Liberal, although throughout his political life his tendencies were strongly conservative.

ROBERT CONRAD

ARAWAK. Distinct linguistic group inhabiting parts of northern South America and the Greater Antilles. Portions of the group left the mainland of South America, moving along the Antillean island chain, sometime before the Christian era. They followed the Ciboney into the Antilles and ended by pushing them into western Cuba. Interisland trade in large canoes (forty men apiece) was common, but Arawak villages were generally set back from the coasts for fear of marauding Caribs (see CARIB). They grew MAIZE and bitter manioc and used irrigation. They were organized in chiefdoms; Hispaniola, for instance, had six. Every person possessed one or more *zemis,* guardian spirits inhering in small wood, stone, or bone objects. The importance of a person's *zemis* was coincident with his rank, and the chief's *zemis* played the part of state deities. Connections of the island Arawak with Mesoamerica have been suspected, particularly because they knew and used the ball court and yokes that are found throughout Mexico.   BURR C. BRUNDAGE

ARBENZ GUZMÁN, JACOBO (1913–1971). Guatemalan army officer and President (1951–1954). Social snubs after María Cristina Vilanova, daughter of a wealthy El Salvador family, married the undistinguished young Guatemalan officer explain in part the vaulting ambition and hostility toward the established order that shaped the couple's joint career. Arbenz was a leader of the October 1944 revolution. As Minister of Defense under Juan José ARÉVALO, he aspired, with aid from Communists, to become President. The assassination of the favored candidate removed his chief obstacle. Arbenz won the election of 1950 and was inaugurated on March 15, 1951.

Agrarian reform and Communist influence immediately became major issues. Arbenz allowed a Communist party to operate openly and to publish a newspaper that followed the Moscow party line. He appointed Communists to administer major social and economic reforms, and would not tolerate protests against these policies from any source. The agrarian reform law of 1952 epitomized the issues. Some opponents attacked the law in order to defend the status quo; others questioned its viability as a fundamental reform. Some proponents of land reform found the law more a vindictive act punitively administered to enhance Communist power than a constructive measure to remedy a major national ill.

Brutal repressive measures adopted in 1953 following an attempted coup increased public alienation from Arbenz. When the Communists advised the arming of workers and peasants for defense of the regime against a small invading force under Carlos CASTILLO ARMAS in June 1954, the Army defected. Its ultimatum forced Arbenz to resign on June 27 and accept exile.

WILLIAM J. GRIFFITH

ARCE, MANUEL JOSÉ (1786–1847). President (1825–1829) of the Federation of Central America (see CENTRAL AMERICA, FEDERATION OF). Arce was born in San Salvador, in the province of El Salvador of the Kingdom of Guatemala. His early life was unremarkable, but his identification with provincial uprisings (1811, 1814) popularly associated with independence and his military and diplomatic exploits after independence made him the chief rival of José Cecilio del VALLE, the Central American savant, in the Federation's first presidential election. Although Valle lacked only one electoral vote for the absolute majority required for election, the Congress selected Arce in a deal-tainted decision.

Bickering between Arce and the Liberal state authorities of Guatemala produced accusations that the President had betrayed his Liberal supporters and embraced conservatism. Arce feared a plot against the Federation, and after some maneuvering and several confrontations he seized the Guatemalan chief of state (1826), whose Liberal government was soon replaced by a Conservative regime. Liberal partisans who had gathered in El Salvador violated the frontier, and Arce took the field against them. Invasion drew counterinvasion until a Liberal force under Francisco MORAZÁN captured Guatemala City in April 1829, exiled Arce and his principal collaborators, and installed Liberals in both state and federal governments.

Sheltered in neutral Soconusco and allegedly aided by rebellions at Trujillo and Omoa, Arce launched an unsuccessful military campaign to regain office. In 1843 he returned to El Salvador, but a suspicious Francisco Malespín forced him to flee to Guatemala, where he organized an abortive invasion of El Salvador. When Malespín fell in 1845, Arce returned to El Salvador and died there, virtually unnoticed, on December 14, 1847.

WILLIAM J. GRIFFITH

ARCHITECTURE (BRAZIL). Because Brazil did not immediately reveal the potential for wealth that characterized the Spanish viceroyalties, it was somewhat neglected by its Portuguese masters in the early decades of the sixteenth century. Only a few buildings of this epoch survive, but period prints show that little attempt was made to transfer to the colony Portugal's ornate Manueline Gothic style.

Although city planning and building were generally considered functions of defense and therefore were handled by military architects, the religious orders undertook extensive building programs by mid-century. Representative architects were A. Pires, D. Jácome, M. Fernandez, and Francisco Pereira dos Santos, a Capuchin monk active in Olinda. The Portuguese experience of violent earthquakes discouraged domed and vaulted construction, but colonial architecture showed a marked preference for windowed facades and belvederes. The simple facades of seventeenth- and eighteenth-century coastal baroque churches closely reflected contemporary Portuguese models, and on occasion arches and portals were even imported from Europe. By contrast the interiors of these churches were sumptuously and richly decorated with sculptures, columns, portals, and coffered ceilings.

An outstanding example of the coastal baroque is the Church of São Pedro dos Clérigos in Recife. Begun in 1728 and designed with an octagonal nave by Manoel Ferreira Jacomé, it resembles the oval church of the

The Presidential Palace in Brasília, designed by Oscar Niemeyer and completed in 1960. [United Press International]

same name in Oporto, Portugal, which is the principal achievement of the Italian Niccolò Nasoni (Nazzoni). An exception to the sober exteriors of the coast is that of the church of the Third Order of St. Francis in Bahia. Consecrated in 1703 and designed by the Brazilian-born Manoel Gabriel Ribeiro, it has a richly decorated facade suggesting Spanish colonial baroque.

The discovery of gold and diamonds in the inland province of Minas Gerais starting in the 1690s encouraged large-scale building in Ouro Prêto, Congonhas do Campo, Sabará, Mariana, and other towns. In this inland region eighteenth-century church architecture came to be characterized by a rococo exuberance that eventually influenced the coastal cities. The ultimate expression of the style can be seen in the work of the architect and sculptor Antônio Francisco LISBÔA, known as O Aleijadinho (the Little Cripple), whose masterpiece is the Church of São Francisco in São João del Rei.

After the Portuguese court of the future JOÃO VI fled Napoleon and settled in Rio de Janeiro in 1808, there was an upsurge of building in the new capital. Neoclassicism flourished and was confirmed by the artists and architects of the artistic mission imported from France in 1816, notably Auguste-Henri-Victor GRANDJEAN DE MONTIGNY. As the century wore on, the city plan and the buildings more and more bore the stamp of Paris and other European centers.

Eclecticism began to give way in 1928, when the Russian-born Gregori Warchavchik (1896–   ) built in São Paulo the first house exemplifying the principles of functional architecture. His partner and

colleague Lúcio COSTA headed a team of architects—including Oscar NIEMEYER, Jorge Moreira Machado (1904–   ), and Affonso Reidy (1909–1964)—who designed the landmark Ministry of Education and Health building in Rio de Janeiro, for which Le Corbusier was a consultant. Important features were the use of movable louvers (*brise-soleil*) for protection against the sun and of *azulejos* (ceramic tiles) designed by artist Cândido PORTINARI, as well as a tropical garden setting conceived by the landscape architect Roberto Burle Marx (1909–   ). Attention should also be drawn to the achievements of Rino Levi (1901–1965) and of the brothers who formed the influential MMM group: Marcelo Roberto (1908–1964), Milton Roberto (1914–1953), and Maurício Roberto (1921–   ).

Contemporary Brazilian architecture finds its ultimate expression in the artificially created capital Brasília (1960). The overall plan for the city was laid out by Costa along intersecting axes suggesting a bird or plane in flight. The design of most of the public buildings is the work of Niemeyer, imaginatively extending and adapting ideas reflecting the influence of Le Corbusier, modifying orthodox functionalism with curved echoes of Brazil's baroque age.

Bibliography. Germain Bazin, *L'architecture religeuse baroque au Brésil,* 2 vols., Paris and São Paulo, 1956–58; Leopoldo Castedo, *The Baroque Prevalence in Brazilian Art,* New York, 1964; Philip L. Goodwin, *Brazil Builds,* New York, 1943; Pál Kelemen, *Baroque and Rococo in Latin America,* New York, 1951; Henrique E. Mindlin, *Modern Architecture in Brazil,* New York, 1956.   STANLEY HOCHMAN

ARCHITECTURE (SPANISH AMERICA). Spanish American architecture developed in a field considered to be vacant; unhindered by native tradition, it expressed the rational ideals of an educated elite. Town planning and architecture were united as nowhere else in the world. In 1573 ordinances for the laying out of new towns dictated a uniform town plan of a rectangular grid oriented to the favorable winds as suggested by Vitruvius, with a *plaza de armas* square at the center. Blocks were divided into quarters and land granted with the obligation to build. The ancient Hellenistic house plan filled the blocks, turning inward toward courtyards and closing off the street with blank walls or a line of shops. Decorative details were in the Plateresque or baroque style. *See also* CITIES, STRUCTURE OF.

Major building began in the newly conquered lands in the first years of the sixteenth century, most importantly in Santo Domingo with the palace of Diego Columbus (begun in 1510), in up-to-date Renaissance style, and the late Gothic rib-vaulted Cathedral (begun about 1521). The thoroughly Spanish style of the early years is shown in the sculptured portal of the Montejo house in Mérida, Yucatán, of about 1550.

The principal structures of sixteenth-century Mexico were rural monastic establishments of the Dominicans (Yanhuitlán) in Oaxaca, the Franciscans (Huejotzingo, Tepeaca, Tlaxcala), and the Augustinians (Acolman) in central and western Mexico. The standard ensemble consisted of a single-aisle church with adjoining cloister and monastery, and an enclosed area before the church with an open chapel and corner chapels.

Colonial building in South America also began with monastic constructions, of which San Francisco in

Quito (ca. 1564) was the most influential. The facade of this church shows a Flemish version of Italian style. Spanish styles, which were dominant in Mexico and the Caribbean, had to compete with other styles, especially Italian and Flemish, in South America. The facade of San Francisco, with its symmetry, heavy rusticated banding, and curved pediment, was the model for church facades until about 1700, San Francisco in Lima (ca. 1657–1675) being a major example. Farther south Jesuits were responsible for most of the serious building in Argentina, Paraguay, and Chile, beginning with La Compañía in Córdoba (ca. 1645–1671). The Jesuit Andrés Blanqui made important contributions in the GUARANÍ missions and the Cathedral of Córdoba (ca. 1687–1758), using an Albertian Renaissance style.

After 1570 the major impulse throughout Spanish America was toward cathedral building: Guadalajara (1571–1618), Mexico City (begun 1563), and Puebla (begun 1555–1558). The latter two were redesigned about 1585 by Claudio Arciniega to produce a basilican design. At about the same time Francisco Becerra designed the Cathedrals of Cuzco (1582–1654) and Lima (1582–1622).

George Kubler, the foremost authority in this area, divides Andean baroque building into four phases: I. Cuzco, 1651–1669, during which the Cathedral was completed and the Compañía church and the Merced cloister were built. II. Lima, 1657–1675, when the new Church of San Francisco was built. III. Cuzco, 1673–1700, under Bishop Manuel de Mollinedo, when more than fifty churches were built, the most important being the Belén and San Pedro in Cuzco and the parish church of San Sebastián. Fine churches were built under Cuzco influence in Lampa, Ayaviri, and Asillo near Lake Titicaca. IV. Lima, 1700–1740, in which a late baroque sculptural style appears in the Torre Tagle Palace and Santa Rosa de las Monjas, and an ultra-baroque (sometimes called Churrigueresque) ornamental style in San Agustín and La Merced. The ultra-baroque scarcely penetrated South America except in interior furnishings and altars. Elaborate planiform ornament, a widespread style that is independent of the ultrabaroque, was more popular in the Andean region, as in the Cathedral of Cajamarca (begun in 1699) and San Lorenzo, Potosí (1728–1744). Similar textilelike effects are found in La Merced, Antigua Guatemala (about 1680), and the Cathedral of Zacatecas (dedicated 1752).

During the eighteenth century the ultrabaroque was popular in Mexico. The most famous examples are both ascribed to Spaniards: Santa Prisca in Taxco (1748), attributed to Diego Durán Berruecos, and the Sagrario (1749–1768) in Mexico City, by Lorenzo Rodríguez. The final phase of the ultrabaroque is represented by the Pocito Chapel (1779) in Guadalupe, by the creole Francisco Antonio Guerrero y Torres, in which massive forms and unconventional plans are dramatized by ornaments of linear and textural patterns.

Beginning in the 1790s Spanish America turned toward neoclassic forms. In Mexico City the Valencian Manuel TOLSÁ designed the School of Mines, and his pupil Francisco Eduardo Tresguerras designed numerous buildings in the BAJÍO region, the Church of El Carmen in Celaya (1803–1807) and the house of the

Counts of Rul in Guanajuato being good examples. Tresguerras never left Mexico, but most of the major neoclassic buildings in Spanish America were designed by Europeans. The Spanish Capuchin monk Domingo de Petrés designed the Cathedral of Bogotá (ca. 1805) with some baroque elements but with neoclassic restraint. Joaquín Toesca, a Spanish-trained Italian, designed the Cathedral (now remodeled) and La Moneda Palace (now the Presidential Palace) in Santiago, Chile, in Palladian neoclassic style. The strict antiquarian version of the neoclassic style in Latin America is represented by the twelve-columned facade added in 1822 to the eighteenth-century Cathedral of Buenos Aires by the French architect Próspero Catelin (d. 1870). The neoclassic style remained dominant until the advent of the early-twentieth-century revival styles exemplified by Adamo Boari's Palace of Fine Arts (1904–1934) in Mexico City and the colonial revival style of the Municipal Palace in Lima (1945).

Spanish American architecture since 1945 has been dominated by three main concerns: urbanization, the use of new forms and technology in an international style, and a search for a native or regional idiom. Urbanization, which has important pre-Columbian and colonial roots in Spanish America, has taken various forms since World War II. Great public housing schemes have been constructed to help cope with the explosive growth of cities. Two architects have been responsible for especially large projects: Carlos Raúl VILLANUEVA in Caracas and Mario Pani (1911–   ) in Mexico City. Both designers mix colossal blocks with smaller structures in a low-cost international modern style. The Cerro Piloto and 23 de Enero projects in Caracas (both 1955–1957) are typical of Villanueva's work. The grandest of Mario Pani's projects is Tlatelolco, housing 70,000 persons on 198 acres. More than half of the area is in lawns and parks, making the density of more than 450 persons per acre seem less crowded. All services are provided: thirteen schools at all levels, clinics, clubs, shopping areas. Pani, with Enrique del Moral and Mauricio Campos (who died early in the project), also designed the University City in Mexico City (1946–1954). New university facilities have been built in many other Latin American countries, including an important one by Villanueva in Caracas. In 1957 Pani designed Satellite City on the northern edge of Mexico City; it is distinguished by an entrance monument, designed by Mathias Goeritz, of five concrete towers in various colors reaching as high as 190 feet. The landscaping of Satellite City was designed by Luis Barragán, best known for his development of El Pedregal (from 1948) on the outskirts of Mexico City. The work of both Pani and Villanueva is noteworthy for its incorporation of natural features and archaeological and artistic elements.

The main impulse toward new forms and technology emanated from Le Corbusier's work in Rio de Janeiro in 1936. The style taught by Le Corbusier has had some close followers, such as Juan O'Gorman (1905–   ) in his earlier work in Mexico, but the style has often been used with great freedom. Concrete structures inspired by Le Corbusier's later work are the Provincial Government House, Santa Rosa, La Pampa, Argentina (1956–1963), by Clorindo Testa (1923–   ), and Emilio Duhart's United Nations Building in Santiago,

Chile (1966). Among the leaders of this movement in Argentina have been Antonio Bonet and Amancio WILLIAMS. New forms of striking freedom and originality are exemplified by the Marulandia development in Bogotá, designed by Rogelio Salmona and Hernán Vieco, and by Cuban architecture of the early 1960s, notably the Plastic Arts School by Ricardo Porro and the Ballet and Music Schools by Vittorio Garatti, all in Havana. Thin concrete shell vaults by the Spanish-born Félix Candela (1910–   ), done in collaboration with various architects, are the dominant new form in Mexican building. The Church of the Miraculous Virgin (1955) in Mexico City is a good example.

The search for a native idiom has led architects back to pre-Columbian and folk architecture; Spanish colonial architecture has been rejected as a foreign intrusion. Alberto Arai's fronton courts at the National University of Mexico (1954), derived from the AZTECS, and Salvador Ortega's Social Security Buildings in Villahermosa, Tabasco (1967), reflecting ancient temples of the MAYAS and Zapotecs, are among the most sophisticated examples. In 1943 the influential Uruguayan architect Julio Vilamajó (1894–1948) designed houses and hostels at Villa Serrana, Minas, Uruguay, using thatch, logs, and stone, formalizing the traditional folk materials and forms.

Bibliography. Francisco Bullrich, *New Directions in Latin American Architecture,* New York, 1969; H.-R. Hitchcock, *Latin American Architecture since 1945,* New York, 1955; George Kubler and Martin Soria, *Art and Architecture in Spain and Portugal and Their American Dominions, 1500–1800,* Baltimore, 1959; C. B. Smith, *Builders in the Sun: Five Mexican Architects,* New York, 1967; Harold E. Wethey, *Colonial Architecture and Sculpture in Peru,* Cambridge, Mass., 1949.

TERENCE GRIEDER

ARCINIEGAS, GERMÁN (1900–   ). Colombian writer. Arciniegas served as Minister of Education from 1941 to 1945. He has contributed to *El Tiempo* of Bogotá and to the journal *Cuadernos del Congreso por la Libertad de la Cultura* of Paris, of which he was a director. The preoccupations evident in all his writing stem from a liberal political outlook and a deep feeling of Americanism. His reflections on the situation of Latin America are best expressed in his essays "América, tierra firme" (1944), "Ese pueblo de América" (1945), "Entre la libertad y el miedo" (1952), and "América mágica" (1959). He has written a novel, *En medio del camino de la vida* (1949), and several biographies and works of historical reconstruction including *Los comuneros* (1939), *Los alemanes en la conquista de América,* 1941 (*Germans in the Conquest of America*), and *Biografía del Caribe,* 1945 (*Caribbean, Sea of the New World*).

RACHEL PHILLIPS

ARDÉVOL, JOSÉ (1911–   ). Spanish-born Cuban composer and conductor. Born in Barcelona, he moved to Havana in 1930 and shortly thereafter became a Cuban citizen. He has been a leader of Cuban musical life, a founder of the Grupo Renovación (1924), a teacher at the Municipal Conservatory of Havana, and a conductor. In addition, he has built up an extensive

catalog of compositions including works for a variety of chamber ensembles, three symphonies, pieces for solo piano, and two concerti grossi.

JUAN A. ORREGO-SALAS

ARENA. *See* ALIANÇA RENOVADORA NACIONAL.

ARÉVALO [BERMEJO], JUAN JOSÉ (1904–   ). President of Guatemala (1945–1951), elected after Jorge UBICO was overthrown in 1944. Arévalo was Guatemala-born, but he completed his education in Argentina and was a university professor there when he was recalled to Guatemala as the revolutionaries' presidential candidate. He won an overwhelming victory and on March 15, 1945, took office under a new constitution.

Arévalo tried to restructure Guatemalan society to afford larger economic benefits and greater social justice. To that end he created the Guatemalan Institute of Social Security and the Institute for the Development of Production, enacted a labor code, instituted educational reforms and health and sanitation projects, and began an ambitious program of major road building. Arévalo expressed the nationalism inherent in the revolution by renewing with Great Britain the dispute over Belize and by regulating foreign capital enterprises. He maintained an open society with freedom of speech and press.

Arévalo's policies aroused opposition of both a political and a military character. In crises of either nature the Communists were his most dependable supporters. For their assistance he tolerated them and rewarded a few individuals with high administrative posts, but he did not allow them formal organization or an opportunity to work openly. Arévalo and Jacobo ARBENZ GUZMÁN both survived suspicion of complicity in the assassination of Francisco Arana, Arévalo's probable successor, Arbenz to become President in 1951 and Arévalo to travel as Ambassador at Large. Arévalo's candidacy for the Presidency in 1963 induced Col. Enrique PERALTA AZURDIA to stage a coup to forestall the election.

WILLIAM J. GRIFFITH

ARGENTINA SINCE 1820. Argentina emerged from the long struggle against Spain with little to show for the effort except independence. Politically the nation, with an area of more than 1 million square miles, was in chaos. The city of Buenos Aires was inhabited by a literate, liberal, and relatively sophisticated population that looked to Europe for economic and social incentive as well as political ideology. The coastal oligarchy was totally estranged from the poor, ignorant, and isolated people of the interior provinces, who violently resisted its foreign-influenced culture, economics, and politics. In their resistance they adhered to local, informal, nativist political-military leaders called *caudillos.*

Economic activity was limited almost entirely to the importation of foreign manufactures for the upper-class population of the city of Buenos Aires and the exportation of hides and tallow. In the interior, which had attained a higher degree of self-sufficiency, the pastoral industry was supplemented by the manufacture of textiles and other products.

Between 1829 and 1852 a supreme *caudillo,* Juan

ARGENTINA
Area: 1,072,162 sq. mi.   Population: 23,362,204 (1970 est.).

Manuel de ROSAS, subdued the city of Buenos Aires and established his authority over the settled portion of the interior. He capitalized upon the xenophobic tendencies of the interior population by proclaiming his adherence to provincial self-government while in reality exercising a decidedly centralist authority.

Although the Generation of 1837, which succeeded Rosas in power after his ouster in 1852, inaugurated a system of aristocratic, liberal politics and laissez faire economics, rapid development did not begin until 1870. There were several reasons for the delay: the interior provinces remained inaccessible to the coast and were thinly settled; transportation was possible only by mule train or cumbersome two-wheeled carts, which were very slow and extremely expensive;

factional violence resumed in the provinces when Rosas' iron rule was removed; and the Indians vigorously contested the gradually expanding frontier. Even within the relatively densely populated province of Buenos Aires, the only significant industrial activity was that of slaughtering cattle and salting the meat.

Between 1880 and 1914 many of the impediments to economic growth were removed. Broken only by temporary recessions, development continued until 1930. Specifically, six achievements contributed to the breakthrough:

1. Political peace was attained in 1880 by the separation of Buenos Aires from the province of the same name and the organization of the city as a federal district, capital of the republic.

2. Vast new lands suitable for livestock grazing and agriculture were made available for exploitation by the subjugation of the Indians by Gen. Julio A. ROCA. *See* CONQUEST OF THE DESERT.

3. Dramatic technological advances were made in agriculture, livestock raising, and the methods of processing the raw materials of those two sectors.

4. Argentina became more fully incorporated into the international market structure that resulted from the long period of comparative peace between 1815 and 1914.

5. Large amounts of European, especially British, capital were invested in agricultural and pastoral enterprises and the establishment of social overhead services.

6. Emigration from Italy and Spain brought many workers to underpopulated Argentina. *See* IMMIGRATION (ARGENTINA).

As the liberal oligarchy entrenched itself politically, dissatisfaction increased among the growing urban middle class and others who objected to the fraudulent electoral practices of the era and to an economic system based on "boom and bust," which saw a period of frenzied speculation followed by collapse in 1889–1890. The dissidents formed a new party, the Unión Cívica, to oppose the oligarchy. An attempt at revolution in July 1890 resulted in the retirement of President Miguel JUÁREZ CELMAN, but he was replaced by another conservative, Carlos PELLEGRINI.

After the suppression of the revolution of 1890 internal dissension caused the Unión Cívica to split into two opposing sections. One allied itself with the oligarchy; the other, far larger segment formed the Unión Cívica Radical (UCR; *see* RADICAL PARTY: ARGENTINA). The tendency to internecine feuding has been a consistent characteristic of Radicalism from 1890 to the present day and is largely responsible for the failure of the movement to function effectively even when unopposed by other parties. Conservative politicians continued to employ fraud as a means of controlling elections and thereby the government.

Hipólito YRIGOYEN, a provincial politician, soon emerged as leader of the Radicals, exercising a near-total dominance over the party for forty years. Acting the role of *caudillo*, he demanded that the Radicals combat electoral corruption by abstaining from voting and work to attain power by revolution. In 1912 electoral reform began, not as a direct result of Radical policy but because of the action of the conservative president Roque SAENZ PEÑA, a member of the Unión Nacional. Saenz Peña apparently was motivated by disapproval of the sham that was representative government in Argentina and by a belief that the desires of the middle class and other excluded groups should be given an opportunity for peaceful expression. Unquestionably there was also a preference that change, inevitable in the long term, be initiated by conservatives rather than by means of eventual Radical violence. The Saenz Peña law of 1912 instituted compulsory, secret, universal suffrage for males over the age of eighteen. In 1912 Radicals won their first congressional seats, and in 1916, utilizing their formidable party machinery throughout the country, Yrigoyen was elected President for the term 1916–1922.

The performance of the Radical administrations from 1916 to 1930 failed to fulfill the expectations and hopes of the middle and lower classes. The nation prospered during World War I, in which Argentina was neutral and sold its beef, hides, and wheat to the Allies. The primarily foreign-born owners of industrial and commercial establishments also prospered as the wartime cessation of imports forced the development of domestic production. But neither these entrepreneurs nor the urban workers witnessed any genuine redistribution of wealth, lessening of the power of the great landowners, or modification of the long-standing and harsh antilabor legislation enacted by previous conservative regimes. Although business was given some freedom of action, labor was strictly controlled. When severe strikes occurred in early 1919, Yrigoyen did not hesitate to utilize the Army and turn the capital into a battleground (see SEMANA TRÁGICA). Nor did Yrigoyen hesitate to intervene frequently in the provinces, a practice he had criticized when used by conservatives. Yrigoyen did broaden the electoral base, but in the most literate, most highly industrialized, and most affluent nation of Latin America at that time much more ought to have been accomplished.

With the end of the war the importation of European goods was resumed, and some new and expanded domestic industries were forced to curtail operations. Many others, however, were able to retain their markets and continue growing. The war had, for the first time, succeeded in partially breaking the grip that the agricultural and pastoral sectors had maintained upon the entire economy since the mid-nineteenth century. Economic nationalists correctly declared that only with the attainment of complete self-sufficiency would true independence exist.

The onset of the world depression in early 1930 severely damaged Argentina's international trade, still the keystone of its economy. As nations began erecting tariff barriers to protect their own endangered producers, Argentina experienced a sharp decline in exports and was forced to meet terms dictated by the foreign consumers of its meat and grain (see ROCA-RUNCIMAN TREATY). The decline meant lower foreign exchange earnings, disappearance of credit, and devaluation of the peso. The Depression stimulated domestic industry as it became more difficult to obtain and pay for imported manufactures, but the lack of domestic raw materials such as coal, oil, and iron, inadequate tariff protection, and a shortage of credit prevented the realization of the full growth potential. A measure of stability was provided to the economy as a whole by the increased state regulation imposed by the authoritarian administrations of the Concordancia,

which ruled throughout the decade. See also CASTILLO, Ramón S.; JUSTO, Agustín P.; ORTIZ, Roberto M.; URIBURU, José Félix.

World War II restored prosperity to the economy and provided additional stimulation to industrialization as imports that had continued through the 1930s were reduced. The military governments that were in power beginning in mid-1943 continued state control and sought to encourage production. They were dismayed by the inferior economic and military position of Argentina in relation to Brazil, which as a close wartime ally of the United States received vast quantities of arms, supplies, and even entire hydroelectric and steel plants. President Juan D. PERÓN undertook an intensive economic development program especially intended to attain self-sufficiency through industrialization. Some gains were made, but Argentina continued to lag in fuel production and heavy industry. Credit was in short supply because of opposition to foreign investment, and the wartime accumulation of foreign exchange reserves that could have been applied to internal development was used to purchase the antiquated foreign-owned transportation systems.

By 1955, when Perón was deposed, agricultural production had fallen and wages were inflated, and an austerity program was recommended by the economic expert Raúl PREBISCH. New foreign investment was needed, but only hesitant steps were taken to obtain it because of the nationalistic outcry against "imperialism." Post-Perón regimes alternated between encouraging and discouraging such investment (see ARAMBURU, Pedro; FRONDIZI, Arturo; ILLIA, Arturo; LONARDI, Eduardo; ONGANÍA, Juan Carlos). By the early 1970s additional strides toward self-sufficiency had been made, but to a considerable degree the economy was still dependent upon imports.

Equal in complexity to the persistent economic problems have been the problems created by the changing social composition of Argentina. Before World War II society seemed stable. The old oligarchy retained much power and influence, although it yielded increasingly to the rising middle class. After 1930 both sectors lost much direct political influence to the military. The lower class had gradually benefited from the overall improvement in the standard of living, but it had made few of the real gains of the laboring classes in the United States and Western Europe.

Foreign immigration had declined after the enactment of restrictive legislation in the early 1930s. Beginning in the middle of that decade, large numbers of migrants had come from the interior provinces to work in the service industries, frigoríficos (meat-packing plants; see FRIGORÍFICO), and factories of the coastal cities. They lacked unions and were denied the free use of strikes as a means of protesting their subsistence wages and intolerable working conditions. Thoroughly dissatisfied and eager for change, they responded dramatically to Juan D. Perón when he first evidenced sympathy for their cause. The improvement of the circumstances of the lower class was perhaps the greatest achievement of Perón; subsequent administrations wavered between supporting or opposing those gains.

Argentina's complex social and economic problems persisted into the 1970s without prospect of facile resolution, and the nation's political future remained equally cloudy. Seven years of military rule, following the ouster of Arturo Illia in 1966, brought neither sustained economic growth nor social justice nor political peace, while the continuing mystique of PERONISM was dramatically illustrated by the outcome of the March 1973 election, in which the Peronist candidate, Héctor J. CÁMPORA, received nearly half of the popular vote. Cámpora took office on May 25, but there was growing conflict between rival Peronist groups. Perón himself was welcomed back to Argentina on June 20. The strife continued, and on July 13 Cámpora resigned so that Perón might run for the Presidency. Meanwhile, Raúl Lastiri, President of the Chamber of Deputies, served as interim President. New elections were scheduled for September 23, and on August 4 Perón and his wife Isabel were nominated as the presidential and vice-presidential candidates of the Peronist party.

See also AGRICULTURE (ARGENTINA); CATTLE INDUSTRY (ARGENTINA).

Bibliography. Samuel L. Baily, *Labor, Nationalism and Politics in Argentina,* New Brunswick, N.J., 1967; H. S. Ferns, *Argentina,* London, 1969; Aldo Ferrer, *The Argentine Economy,* Berkeley, Calif., 1967; José Luis Romero, *A History of Argentine Political Thought,* tr. by Thomas F. McGann, Stanford, Calif., 1963; James R. Scobie, *Argentina: A City and a Nation,* New York, 1964; Arthur P. Whitaker, *Argentina,* Englewood Cliffs, N.J., 1964.

EUGENE G. SHARKEY

ARGENTINE CONFEDERATION. Confederation formally constituted when all the Argentine provinces except Buenos Aires accepted the constitution proclaimed by Justo José de URQUIZA on May 25, 1853. Elections held in November resulted in the designation of Urquiza and Dr. Salvador María del Carril as President and Vice President, respectively, and in a Congress divided into several factions. Unable to use the capital-designate, the city of Buenos Aires, the central government established itself temporarily in Paraná, the capital of Entre Ríos, and embarked upon a program to bring the province of Buenos Aires into the Confederation, to foster immigration and economic development, to tie the interior provinces and even Bolivia more firmly to the economic and political orbit of the littoral provinces, to reorganize the national finances, and to eliminate, reduce, or check Brazilian influence in the RÍO DE LA PLATA. Explorations shattered dreams of using water routes to bring the interior provinces and Bolivia closer to the Paraná River, the railroad from Rosario to Córdoba was never begun, and immigration remained insignificant. No national currency was created, although Brazilian loans for this purpose had been obtained early in 1853. A system of differential tariffs did foster the growth of the port of Rosario as a rival of Buenos Aires, education at all levels was encouraged, foreign relations were put on a firm footing, and the government agreed to pay the Argentine external debt.

The fate of the Confederation was partially decided when both Brazil and Great Britain departed from their policy of keeping the Confederation and the province of Buenos Aires apart, and shifted their support to the *porteños.* Other factors included the political rivalries within the Confederation, the reluctance of Buenos Aires to join the Confederation and the greater financial resources of the former, and the presidential and

congressional elections of 1859. Acting on the instructions of Congress, Urquiza exhausted peaceful means before undertaking a military campaign that persuaded Buenos Aires, defeated at the Battle of Cepeda (1859), to join the Confederation. About the same time Urquiza decided on constitutional grounds to favor Dr. Santiago Derqui rather than Del Carril for the Presidency. Elected president, Derqui endeavored to create his own political party, the Constitutional, and to counter the military influence of Urquiza with that of Gen. Juan Sáa. This led to a series of political maneuvers that threatened the entry of Buenos Aires into the Confederation and ended in the defeat of the Confederation at Pavón (1861) after Urquiza's retirement from the field. The supremacy of Buenos Aires in the Argentine Republic was now assured, and the following year the Governor of the province, Bartolomé MITRE, became President of the nation.

JOSEPH T. CRISCENTI

ARGUEDAS, ALCIDES (1879–1946). Bolivian historian and novelist. Arguedas, one of the few Bolivians to achieve international renown, was born in La Paz and was educated first in Bolivia and then in France, where he spent many of his adult years. Until his death he led a very active political and literary life. After receiving a law degree in 1903, he served in the diplomatic corps (in France, England, Spain, and Colombia), was a newspaper correspondent for *La Nación* of Buenos Aires, served in the Bolivian Congress, headed the conservative Liberal party for several years, and served in the Ministries of Agriculture and Foreign Relations.

However, it was mainly through his many writings that Arguedas gained his fame abroad and became a controversial figure at home. The work that made his reputation was *Pueblo enfermo* (1909), a literary-sociological treatise intended to diagnose the defects of the Bolivian people. Arguedas was unrelenting in his criticism but concluded that the centuries of subservience forced on the people were solely responsible for their "sickness." He reached a similar conclusion in his historical works. Arguedas was not a trained historian but had come to history through the realization that only by studying Bolivia's past could its realities be properly analyzed. Finding no adequate texts, he wrote a multivolume history of the country along with a one-volume general survey, *Historia general de Bolivia: El proceso de la nacionalidad, 1809–1921* (1922), which remains the best-known text of its kind. In these works Arguedas emphasized the negative features of Bolivia's past because he believed that this approach would lead to a search for positive solutions. In fact, his works created awareness in a whole generation of Bolivians seeking practical and at times revolutionary answers to the nation's problems. He also wrote *Raza de bronce* (1919), an early novel of the Indianist school, in which he describes the suffering and exploitation of the Indians.

ORAZIO A. CICCARELLI

ARGUEDAS, JOSÉ MARÍA (1911–1969). Peruvian novelist. Arguedas devoted his life to the vindication of the QUECHUA language and literature and to the integration in his novels of the divided world of Peru. He was brought up by Quechua foster parents in an

Andean village and began his formal education in Spanish at the age of fourteen. His early anthology *Canto Kechwa* (1938) includes texts and translations of Quechua poetry. He continued this anthropological and academic work throughout his life, meanwhile exploring in his novels the dilemma of the Indians in Peru and the agony of their situation as he saw it. Among his novels are *Agua* (1935), *Yawar fiesta* (1941, revised 1958), *Los ríos profundos* (1958), *Todas las sangres* (1964), and *El zorro de arriba y el zorro de abajo* (1968–1969).

RACHEL PHILLIPS

ARIAS [MADRID], ARNULFO (1901–   ). Panamanian political leader. The charismatic Arias was elected to the Presidency on three occasions but was forced out of office each time. The younger brother of Harmodio ARIAS, he was born in Coclé Province. He was educated in the United States, receiving a bachelor's degree from the University of Chicago and a degree in medicine from Harvard University.

Arias rose to prominence as a result of the successful coup against President Florencio Arosemena on January 2, 1931. The coup was planned by Acción Comunal, a secret patriotic society founded by Arias and other Panamanians educated in the United States and opposed to American intervention in Panamanian affairs. Too young to be eligible for the Presidency himself, Arias played an important role in the election of his brother Harmodio Arias to the Presidency in 1932 and that of his successor Juan Demóstenes Arosemena in 1936. During the 1930s Arias served as Minister of Agriculture and Public Works and represented Panama in several European capitals and in the League of Nations. His exposure to European fascism is believed to have influenced him in its favor.

Elected to his first presidential term in 1940, he initiated a regime that was labeled racist and xenophobic. A new constitution, promulgated in January 1941, extended the presidential term from four to six years. Foreign businessmen, especially Chinese, were forced to sell or transfer ownership of their commercial establishments to Panamanians, and thousands of Negroes of West Indian origin lost their citizenship. A secret police force was created. At the same time social security was instituted, and paid vacations were authorized.

To many it also appeared that in international affairs Arias displayed an undisguised sympathy for the Axis. He equivocated regarding an American request for 134 defense sites outside the Canal Zone and refused to allow the arming of Panamanian-flag merchant vessels. Arias was ousted in October 1941, amid reports that the coup had been inspired by the United States.

Arias returned from exile in 1945 and ran for the Presidency in 1948. His opponent was declared the winner, but the decision was reversed in 1949, and he was belatedly inaugurated with the support of the National Police. Arias's second term was notably corrupt. When he engaged in such dictatorial tactics as replacing the 1946 constitution with his own 1941 document, dissolving the National Assembly, and suspending the Supreme Court, the police overthrew him with the support of most political parties.

Arias was stripped of his political rights in 1951, but they were restored in 1960. After an unsuccessful bid for the Presidency in 1964, he won the presidential contest of 1968. However, eleven days after taking office, he was overthrown in a military coup.

LARRY L. PIPPIN

ARIAS [MADRID], HARMODIO (1886–1962). Panamanian political leader and President (1932–1936). Born in Penonomé, Arias was the older brother of Arnulfo ARIAS. He was trained as an international lawyer, having been educated at Cambridge University and the University of London. In 1920 he became Panama's first delegate to the League of Nations and later served in the National Assembly.

Arias's rise to power was spurred by the coup of January 2, 1931, in which Arnulfo Arias played a leading role. The elder Arias was elected to the Presidency the following year in a remarkably honest election. During his administration a deteriorating economic situation necessitated an emergency program of public works. Arias's rural programs included the relocation of some landless farmers in agricultural colonies. In 1935 he founded the University of Panama. He intervened in the 1936 presidential election by jailing the members of the National Electoral Board in order to assure the victory of his handpicked candidate. In foreign affairs the Arias administration negotiated with the United States the HULL-ALFARO TREATY, which superseded important parts of the HAY–BUNAU-VARILLA TREATY of 1903.

Arias remained an influential political figure after leaving the Presidency, his power being based on his growing domination of the press (four newspapers), radio, and television. His three sons, Harmodio, Jr., Gilberto, and Roberto, were also prominent in politics and government. In 1959 Roberto Arias, husband of the ballerina Margot Fonteyn and then Ambassador in London, was implicated in an abortive Castroite invasion of Panama.

LARRY L. PIPPIN

ARIZAGA, RODOLFO (1926–   ). Argentine composer. Arizaga was born in Buenos Aires, where he first studied composition with Luis Gianneo. He then worked in Paris with Nadia Boulanger, Olivier Messiaen, and Maurice Martenot. In addition to achieving note as a composer, he has been an esteemed music critic of the daily newspaper *El Clarín*. His extensive catalog comprises works for almost every medium, including music for the stage, *Judas* (1952), an opera, *Prometeo* (1958), and a cantata, *El martirio de Santa Olalla,* on texts by Federico García Lorca, which received the Municipal Prize of Buenos Aires in 1952.

JUAN A. ORREGO-SALAS

ARLT, ROBERTO (1900–1942). Argentine writer. Arlt's novels reflect pessimism and bitterness at a society that he interprets in a nightmare vision of contemporary reality. The cynicism of his work expresses the frustrations of the middle class in Buenos Aires in the 1930s. However, a lyrical imagination also illumines his novels, which include *El juguete rabioso* (1927), *Los siete locos* (1929), *Los lanzallamas* (1931), and *El amor brujo* (1932). *Aguafuertes porteñas* (1933) and *El jorobadito* (1933) are collections of his short stories. Arlt also wrote interesting plays, among them, *África, 300 millones,* and *La isla desierta.*

RACHEL PHILLIPS

ARMED FORCES. Although there is a tendency to make sweeping generalizations about the Latin American armed forces, in fact few accurate generalizations can be made. Among those that can be made are the following: (1) The armed forces of all but two or three countries are actors in the political process and have been ever since the achievement of independence. (2) While the coup d'état and military rule are the most visible forms of political action on the part of the armed forces, they are not the only means by which the military participates in or exerts an influence on politics. There are other less spectacular, less visible, but nonetheless effective means: the vetoing or proscribing of particular policies or actions by civilian governments, the issuing of public and private warnings to politicians and political groups, and the giving or withholding of support. In the main, the coup d'état and military rule occur when the other means of influencing politics prove inadequate or insufficient to promote the interests that the armed forces are seeking to preserve or advance. (3) There is great variation from one Latin American country to another in the degree of military involvement in politics. In a very few countries the armed forces are apolitical. In others the armed forces' involvement is limited, almost never extending to the staging of a coup d'état. In still others the degree of involvement is substantial, with the military dominating politics. (4) The armed forces are not monolithic entities. Differences of opinion on political and nonpolitical issues exist among the members of the armed forces. There are both interservice and intraservice rivalries and conflicts. (5) It would be incorrect to think that all members of the armed forces in countries with politically active armed forces are politicians or are inclined toward political activity. Those who are inclined toward political involvement constitute a very small proportion of the total military personnel. In the main, it is only senior officers who are political activists, and only some of them. While there are notable exceptions, enlisted men, junior officers, and midcareer officers are not political activists, although they may have political views and may become activists as they advance through the ranks. (6) Today's military is very different from the one that existed in the first decades following the wars of independence. Throughout most of the nineteenth century the armed forces, with the landed aristocracy and the Roman Catholic Church, formed the conservative triarchy that dominated society and was dedicated to the defense of the status quo. Since the late nineteenth century the armed forces have become complex professionalized institutions, and their political stance and political involvement have been varied and multifaceted. Furthermore, the armed forces have become predominantly middle-class institutions. (7) There is considerable debate as to whether the armed forces are agents of societal modernization. The debate turns on the question of whether the armed forces are what Martin C. Needler has called "predatory reactionaries" or "modernizing patriots."

Reasons for political involvement. Theories and explanations concerning the Latin American armed forces' involvement in politics abound. Alexander T. Edelmann, in *Latin American Government and Politics* (rev. ed., Homewood, Ill., 1969, pp. 164–167), cites the traditional explanations: the wars of independence, which gave military leaders recognition and a sense of self-confidence and led them to assert a "right" to be taken into account in the organizing and governing of the new nations; the absence of a tradition of military subordination to civilian authority; a socioeconomic environment more conducive to authoritarianism, military or civilian, than to democracy; the influence of German and Italian military missions that trained many of the Latin American armed forces in the last years of the nineteenth and first years of the twentieth century; boredom on the part of military personnel who have rarely been called on to perform military tasks, such as engaging in combat with foreign enemies; the tradition of the military as "guardian of the nation," "ultimate arbiter," or "guardian of the constitution"; and crises and disorder created by social and economic change. These factors may partially explain the involvement, but they do not provide a total explanation.

Also helping to account for the prominent position that the armed forces have in the political process is the dearth of strong, well-organized political groups. Kalman Silvert makes this argument concerning the political influence of students in Latin America. He declares: "The ascription of great political influence to student organizations implies that these organizations are surrogates for other interested social groups. It also suggests that if young persons can gain sufficient influence to change, on occasion, the course of national political life, then, . . . other power centers must be in such disarray as to elevate the relative power of any organized group" ("The University Student," in John J. Johnson, ed., *Continuity and Change in Latin America,* Stanford, Calif., 1964, pp. 207–208). In other words, students—and the same goes for the armed forces—derive disproportionate political strength and influence, first, from the fact that they are well organized and, second, from the fact that most other groups in society are poorly organized or not organized at all for the purpose of making demands on or giving support to the political system. From this it follows that if other groups were as well organized as the students, the armed forces, and the church, these established groups would have less political strength than they do.

Going farther toward explaining the military's role is the legitimacy vacuum that marks the political systems of most Latin American countries—that is, the absence of any single authority or means of decision making that is unversally or even widely accepted as the most effective and appropriate for the society. As Needler puts it: "Militarism [in the form of involvement in politics and military rule] . . . is an unavoidable concomitant [of the legitimacy vacuum]. Where authority is not respected, force must be resorted to. Where force is used, the army necessarily has the last word. In this type of situation, the army is in politics whether it wants to be or not" (*Latin American Politics in Perspective,* rev. ed., Princeton, N.J., 1967, pp. 38–39). When the legitimacy vacuum is recognized, it becomes apparent that military involvement in politics is more the product of the nature of Latin American political systems than that of attitudes and desires on the part of the armed forces themselves.

The coup d'état. The coup d'état is an established feature of Latin American politics. It is an accepted means of changing governmental personnel. Typically, the coup is bloodless or nearly so, with the armed forces or a segment of them confronting the incumbent President with an ultimatum to quit. Often, the ultimatum is backed by a minor show of force or a threat to employ it. Usually, the incumbent has no alternative but to yield.

A coup is neither quickly conceived nor quickly executed. Furthermore, it is not an exclusively military phenomenon. Civilians are generally involved in the planning of the coup, and on occasion the events that prompt the military to execute a coup are contrived by civilians. (Thus, the coup and the military's general participation in politics should not be regarded as something which, in all instances, is imposed on a civilian population that to a man is wholly opposed to it.) The coup is a movement that develops over time, being launched by a small nucleus of disgruntled individuals who recruit others to their cause until they have sufficient strength to overthrow the incumbent government. The coup conspirators are rarely a homogeneous, cohesive lot. The conspirators tend to agree on only one point: the ousting of the incumbent President. Once the coup has been executed, disagreement frequently develops among those who executed it. Generally, the reins of government are relatively quickly returned to civilian hands.

What effect, intended or otherwise, does the coup have? Needler concludes, in a study of the fifty-six coups from 1935 through 1964, that the effect was to thwart change—social, economic, and political. That conclusion is supported by Edwin Lieuwen's study of the seven coups that took place between 1962 and the end of April 1964.

José Enrique Miguens asserts in "The New Latin American Military Coup" (*see* Bibliography) that the kind of coup just described, which he calls the "classical coup," has been replaced by a new variety, the "professional military coup," which emerged in the late 1960s. (The Argentine coup of 1966 and the Bolivian, Panamanian, and Peruvian coups of 1968 were, according to Miguens, professional military coups.) The two kinds of coups differ in fundamental respects. The professional coup is planned and executed by a small number of senior officers, and civilians are not involved. The government established in the wake of the professional coup is one that intends to retain power for an extended period. It restricts political party activity. It has definite objectives that include modernization or what the officers conceive of as modernization. Those staging the professional coup tend to regard themselves as the only segment of the population capable of governing. By contrast, those who executed classical coups believed that "the army was a provisional instrument for reestablishing order in the country but was not considered qualified to govern. The majority of officers inwardly felt that governing was a task for politicians (ibid., p. 10)."

The military and modernization. A detailed analysis of military governments and the behavior of the armed forces since 1945 provides no conclusive evidence as to whether the Latin American armed forces are predatory reactionaries or modernizing patriots. Evidence can be marshaled to support the view that the armed forces are agents of modernization, and evidence can be found to support the contrary view. What one is left with after reviewing the historical evidence is that the armed forces may promote modernization and sometimes have done so. However, historical evidence provides no basis for concluding that the Latin American armed forces are the institutions best equipped to promote modernization or the ones most likely to do so.

Certainly, the fact that the officers of the Latin American armed forces increasingly are being drawn from middle-class and lower-middle-class families does not guarantee that the armed forces will become agents of modernization. Those individuals may continue to identify with their origins. They may, however, drop that identification and come to identify with their profession and its interests, which are not in all cases compatible with modernization.

The future. It seems safe to assume that the Latin American armed forces will continue, as in the past, to be prominent actors in the political process in all but a handful of countries. The forms of involvement may remain the same or change somewhat, but the involvement will continue. Leaving aside the question of whether the armed forces are agents of modernization, as societal modernization proceeds (assuming that it does), the armed forces will not be neutral observers. Whether they seek to promote it, shape it, slow it, or block it, the armed forces will be caught up in that process, will be affected by it, and will play some part in the process. The reason is simple. The armed forces are and will remain a part of society, not apart from it.

Bibliography. Richard N. Adams, "The Development of the Guatemalan Military," *Studies in Comparative International Development,* vol. IV, no. 5, 1968–69, pp. 91–110; Luigi R. Einaudi and Alfred C. Stepan, *Latin American Institutional Development: Changing Military Perspectives in Peru and Brazil,* Santa Monica, Calif., 1971; John J. Johnson, *The Military and Society in Latin America,* Stanford, Calif., 1964; Edwin Lieuwen, *Arms and Politics in Latin America,* rev. ed., New York, 1961; id., *Generals vs. Presidents: Neo-Militarism in Latin America,* New York, 1964; José Enrique Miguens, "The New Latin American Military Coup," *Studies in Comparative International Development,* vol. VI, no. 1, 1970–71, pp. 3–14; Martin C. Needler, "Political Development and Military Intervention in Latin America," *American Political Science Review,* vol. LX, no. 3, September 1966, pp. 616–626; Eric A. Nordlinger, "Soldiers in Mufti: The Impact of Military Rule upon Economic and Social Change in the Non-Western States," *American Political Science Review,* vol. LXIV, no. 4, December 1970, pp. 1131–1148; José Nun, "The Middle-Class Military Coup," in Claudio Véliz (ed.), *The Politics of Conformity in Latin America,* New York, 1967, pp. 66–118; Alfred Stepan, *The Military in Politics: Changing Patterns in Brazil,* Princeton, N.J., 1971; David Wood, *Armed Forces in Central and South America,* Adelphi Papers, no. 34, London, 1967.

JAMES D. COCHRANE

AROSEMENA, JUSTO (1817–1896). Panamanian statesman. Born in Panama City, Arosemena was a member of a wealthy and influential creole family; his father, Mariano Arosemena, was a key figure in the declaration of Panamanian independence from Spain in 1821 and was later prominent in isthmian politics. A moderate Liberal, the younger Arosemena was also active in Panamanian political life, sat in the Colombian Congress on numerous occasions, and held several diplomatic posts. After the Conservative restoration of

1886, he retired from public life, becoming the chief legal adviser of the Panama Railroad Company in 1888 (*see* PANAMA RAILROAD).

Arosemena's most important work is *El estado federal de Panamá,* which he wrote in 1855 to urge passage of a bill pending before the Colombian Congress that provided for the creation of a self-governing state out of the four provinces into which Panama was then divided. In his treatise Arosemena extolled the superiority of the federal form of government and cited the special needs of Panama that made the adoption of such a system imperative. Otherwise, he warned, Colombia would lose the isthmus. Panama was made a federal state the same year, and Arosemena served briefly as provisional head of its government.

HELEN DELPAR

ARREOLA, JUAN JOSÉ (1918–   ). Mexican writer. His works combine fantasy, humor, intellectual games, and a skillful technique, always expressing an existential attitude toward man and the modern world. His short stories were collected in *Confabulario total, 1941–1961* (1962), and the novel *La feria* appeared in 1963. In 1954 he wrote a farce for the theater, *La hora de todos.*

RACHEL PHILLIPS

ARROYO DEL RÍO, CARLOS ALBERTO (1893–1969). President of Ecuador (1940–1944). A successful Guayaquil lawyer and writer, as the head of the Liberal Radical party (*see* LIBERAL PARTY: ECUADOR) in 1934–1935, he led the congressional opposition that forced President José María VELASCO IBARRA to dissolve Congress and declare a dictatorship. Arroyo del Río was still the leader of his party in 1941, when its accumulated errors fell on his head. He had demonstrated his loyalty to traditional values when he presided over an extraordinary congress in February 1939, scrapped a socially oriented constitution written the year before, and reinstated President Eloy ALFARO's constitution of 1906. Using party machinery assembled in 1901, he had won the 1940 presidential election by fraud. Then his managerial ability was eclipsed by an incident beyond his control: Ecuador's defeat in the border war with Peru in 1941. *See* ECUADOR-PERU CONFLICT.

The protocol signed at Rio de Janeiro the following year confirmed Ecuador's disastrous loss of 5,392 square miles of territory, and the people found a scapegoat in President Arroyo del Río. The Ecuadorian Democratic Alliance, a coalition ranging from Conservatives (*see* CONSERVATIVE PARTY: ECUADOR) to Communists, was formed to unseat him, and the Army forced his resignation in May 1944. Although vitriolic attacks plagued him for the rest of his life, Arroyo del Río displayed unusual restraint in answering his critics and quietly practiced law in Guayaquil until his death.

LOIS WEINMAN

ART (BRAZIL). The development of Brazilian culture and art was fixed to some extent in 1494, when the Treaty of Tordesillas (*see* TORDESILLAS, TREATY OF), by which Spain and Portugal divided the non-Christian world, shifted a large part of the South American continent from the Hispanic to the Portuguese zone. When colonists and Catholic missionaries began to arrive from the mother country in the early decades of the sixteenth century, they were accompanied by craftsmen and artists whose task was to transfer aspects of Portuguese civilization to the New World.

But what of the culture they found? There were three basic cultural areas. The tropical forest culture of the Indians of Brazil was not as highly developed as that of the civilizations of Mexico or the Andean region. Nevertheless, many of the ceramic pre-Columbian objects (the only ones to survive the climate and the periodic flooding) excavated in the Amazonian forest suggest by their form and decoration skilled artisans in the service of a structurally complex society. Burial urns, idols, and vases found near the mouth of the Amazon are often completely covered with geometric painted or champlevé designs; the area around Santarém has yielded unpainted pottery characterized by complex forms and naturalistic representations. Petroglyphs, crudely carved clubs, and aligned boulders are the only signs of ancient artistic development in the central plateau, the second cultural area. In the south, although the pottery is artistically uninteresting, there are important stone carvings of idols, conical mortars with pestles, and perforated disks evidently used as jewelry.

In many remote areas of contemporary Brazil government-protected Indian tribes living in basically neolithic societies continue to produce handicrafts in ceramic, stone, wood, and feathers according to primeval traditions. These art forms have had little influence on present-day Brazilian art. However, there is a flourishing popular art tradition stemming from the African influx and European mass immigration. In addition to providing widely differing regional pottery, basketwork, and objects made from tin cans and wood, it often produces the paintings, sculptures, and colorful ex-votos of countryside chapels.

The importance of art in colonial Brazil grew with the wealth of the seacoast settlements of Bahia (Salvador), Pernambuco, Cabo Frio, Rio de Janeiro, and São Vicente. Religious art was of course the major vehicle of expression. Although in the sixteenth century most religious art was still imported from Portugal, there are surviving examples of magnificent terra-cotta statues (1560) made in São Vicente and other coastal towns by João Gonçalvo Fernandes.

Most art works that have come down to us, however, date from the seventeenth century. They include the sculpture of Friar Agostinho da Piedade (d. 1661), notably his expressive terra-cotta *St. Peter Repentant* in the Church of Nossa Senhora de Montserrate in Bahia, and of his Brazilian-born disciple, Friar Agostinho de Jesus (ca. 1600–1661). Mention should also be made of Domingos da Conceição da Silva (1643–1718), whose *Virgin of Monserrat* in the Benedictine monastery of Rio de Janeiro foreshadows Brazilian baroque.

The best-known painter of the period was a German-born Benedictine monk, Ricardo do Pilar (d. 1700), examples of whose work can be seen in the São Bento monastery in Rio. The Dutch occupation of parts of Brazil from 1625 to 1654 (*see* DUTCH IN BRAZIL) brought the arrival of six artists in the entourage of the governor Count Johan Maurits van Nassau-Siegen. Among them were Albert Eckhout (fl.

1637–1664) and Frans Post (1612–1680) of Leiden, remembered for his many landscapes of Pernambuco. Dutch influence may have been responsible for a growing interest in portraits and battle scenes.

The discovery of gold in the Cataguases backlands at the end of the seventeenth century led to the establishment of cities in Minas Gerais, Mato Grosso, and Goiás. Scope was given to the talent of painters, wood-carvers, architects, and sculptors, who established new departures in Brazilian art. Chief among these was the almost-legendary architect and sculptor Antônio Francisco LISBÔA, who because of his deformities (possibly due to leprosy) was known as O Aleijadinho (the Little Cripple). His masterpiece is the group of twelve prophets (1800–1805) in front of the Church of Nosso Senhor Bom Jesus de Matozinhos in Congonhas do Campo, Minas Gerais. The greatest painter in colonial Minas Gerais was probably Manoel da Costa Ataíde (1762–1830), who created the magnificent rococo ceiling of the church of the Third Order of St. Francis built in Ouro Prêto by his friend O Aleijadinho. The Portuguese José Soares de Araújo (d. 1799) is known for his *Chariot of Elias,* which he painted in the Carmo in Diamantina, Minas Gerais.

In eighteenth-century Rio de Janeiro the better-known artists included José de Oliveira (ca. 1690–1770) and Manoel da Cunha (1737–1809). The latter is noted for his murals and altarpieces and as a portraitist; born a slave, he eventually won his freedom because of his success as an artist. In the same period the work of Leandro Joaquim (1738–1798) marked the transition to the neoclassicism that found expression in the art of Manoel Dias de Oliveira (1764–1783), José Leandro de Carvalho (d. 1834), Antônio Alves, and Antônio Joaquim Franco Velasco (1780–1833). In Bahia the Portuguese-educated painter José Joaquim da Rocha (1737?–1807), whose masterwork is the vault of Nossa Senhora da Conceiçao, founded a school of illusionist architectural perspective decorators.

The Napoleonic invasion of Portugal caused the royal court to flee to Brazil and establish itself in Rio de Janeiro in 1808. When, in 1815, the colony became a realm in the Kingdom of Portugal, the future JOÃO VI wished to furnish his capital with artistic adornments. In 1816 an artistic mission that included the architect Auguste-Henri-Victor GRANDJEAN DE MONTIGNY, the painters Jean-Baptiste DEBRET and Nicolas-Antoine Taunay (1755–1830), and the latter's brother, the sculptor Auguste-Marie Taunay (1768–1824), was imported from France. Received with limited enthusiasm in a country otherwise occupied, the mission broke off without achieving anything more noteworthy than the establishment of an Academy of Fine Arts that produced historical and genre painting. In sculpture the mission introduced the academic neoclassicism representative of the work of Marc Ferrez (1788–1850) and Honorato Manoel de Lima (d. 1863). An unfortunate result of its influence was a misguided attempt to transform national baroque monuments.

Contacts with Europe were to favor the romantic trend that can be seen in the work of the painters Manuel de Araújo Pôrto Alegre (1806–1879), Pedro Américo (1843–1905), Vítor Meireles de Lima (1832–1903), and José Ferraz de Almeida Júnior (1850–1899). The influence of both impressionism and Art Nouveau can be seen in the paintings of Eliseu

Lighted cross surmounting the Cathedral of Brasília. [*United Press International*]

d'Angelo Visconti (1866–1944), who also decorated the Municipal Theater of Rio de Janeiro and other public buildings.

In 1913 the Lithuanian-born painter Lasar SEGALL visited Brazil and liked it so much that he returned after World War I and exposure to German expressionism to establish himself in São Paulo. Emiliano DI CAVALCANTI acquired the techniques of Fauvism and cubism in Paris and applied them to paintings of Brazilian popular life. Folklorism dominated the later paintings of Anita MALFATTI, whose Berlin-acquired expressionism irritated critics in 1917. Tarsila do AMARAL adapted cubist techniques to anthropophagism, a mildly aggressive national movement that attempted to focus on the materials for a native culture.

The artistic stranglehold of academicism was broken with the Modern Art Week held in São Paulo in 1922 (*see* MODERNISM: BRAZIL). Its art shows, concerts, and prose and poetry readings had cultural repercussions that were soon felt in neighboring South American countries.

Brazil's outstanding twentieth-century artist, often linked in a triad with Segall and Di Cavalcanti, is Cândido PORTINARI, who combined native realism with abstract techniques, reporting on the exciting popular life around him. Other painters of note are Milton Rodrigues da Costa (1915–   ), the landscape architect Roberto Burle Marx (1909–   ), and Alfredo Volpi (1896–   ), whose reduction of folkloric symbols led him to concretism.

Among Brazil's outstanding twentieth-century sculptors are Vítor Brecheret (1894–1955), a leading defender of modern sculpture during the 1920s; Bruno Giorgi (1905–   ), whose well-known bronze *Warriors* stands in the Plaza of the Three Powers in Brasília; and Lígia Clark (1920–   ).

Significant changes in Brazilian cultural life were

made by the opening of influential museums in São Paulo and Rio de Janeiro and by the inauguration of the Bienal in São Paulo in 1951. In recent years the figurative art and abstractionism of Arcangelo Ianelli (1922–   ), the constructivism and fantasy of Ivan Ferreira Serpa (1923–   ), and the nonobjectivism of Iberê Camargo (1914–   ) have attracted favorable attention.

Bibliography. Pietro Maria Bardi, *The Arts in Brazil,* tr. by John Drummond, Milan, 1956; id., *New Brazilian Art,* New York, 1970; Gilbert Chase, *Contemporary Art in Latin America,* New York, 1970; Roberto Pontual, *Dicionário das Artes Plásticas no Brasil,* Rio de Janeiro, 1969.

STANLEY HOCHMAN

ART (SPANISH AMERICA). One of the first concerns of the Spanish conquerors of America was to destroy the indigenous art and substitute their own, art being considered the principal expression of ideology. Indian temples were pulled down and churches built on the ruins. As early as 1527 the Franciscan Pedro de Gante set up a school in Mexico City to train Indians to make religious furnishings and images. The enclosed yards of the early monastery churches in Mexico were ornamented with stone crosses, such as those found at Acolman and Atzacoalco near Mexico City, and the open chapels were decorated with carving, most impressively at Tlalmanalco in the 1560s. After 1570 Europeans increasingly received the major commissions.

Colonial painting, later almost entirely in Spanish hands, began about 1566 with the work of the Fleming Simon Pereyns, who did the altar paintings in the Franciscan church of Huejotzingo in Mexico. Colonial painting began in the Andes with the Italian Jesuit Bernardo Bitti (1548–ca. 1610), who designed altars and decorated them with sculptures and fine paintings in Lima, Cuzco, La Paz, Potosí, and other places. Mexico remained the main center of colonial painting with a style generally following Sevillan modes. The Sevillan Alonso Vázquez was in Mexico from 1603 until his death in 1608, bringing with him the early baroque style; *St. Michael Casting Out the Devil,* in the Academy of San Carlos in Mexico City, is typical. Baltasar de Echave Orio came to Mexico about 1580 with a late mannerist style and founded a dynasty of painters who were his sons and pupils. His son Baltasar de Echave Ibía and his pupil Luis Juárez (both ca. 1585–1645), both born in Mexico, carried on the Sevillan style. A third important painter of this period, also born in Mexico, was the Dominican Alonso López de Herrera (1579–ca. 1648), best known for his large and emotional *Assumption of the Virgin* (1622).

Sevillan baroque influence was renewed by Sebastián de Arteaga, who arrived in Mexico about 1640 and died there in 1653. Arteaga was a follower of Zurbarán, as is evident in his *Incredulity of St. Thomas.* Zurbarán himself sent paintings to America, as surviving examples in Mexico, Guatemala, and Lima testify.

Cristóbal de Villalpando (ca. 1652–1714) was "the most elegant and virtuoso artist Mexico produced," according to Martin Soria. A pupil of Echave Ibía's son, Villalpando continued the inherited style in a bright painterly version. His fresco *Heavenly Glory,* in the

dome of the Cathedral of Puebla, is an important link in the mural tradition in Mexico.

The dominant figure in eighteenth-century Mexico was Miguel Cabrera (1695–1768), the head of a large workshop producing religious paintings. He was best as a portraitist, *Sor Juana de la Cruz* being among his finest works. The portrait, despite the frequent representation of religious persons, was the main opening for the secular patronage of art. In Spain portraits had been confined mostly to the court, and they remained uncommon in Spanish America before the eighteenth century, religious subjects being predominant.

Painting in the Andes after Bitti was dominated by American-born artists. Three artists were outstanding during the seventeenth century: Gregorio Vázquez Ceballos (1638–1711) in Bogotá, Miguel de Santiago (ca. 1625–1706) in Quito, and Melchor Pérez Holguín (ca. 1660–after 1724) in Potosí. Holguín drew mainly from Bitti's mannerist style and from European prints, while the other two reflected Murillo's sentimental baroque style. Although Cuzco was a major center of art production, no painter there rivaled Holguín in quality. Diego Quispe Ttito, one of the best known, is noted for his allegories of the months in the Cathedral of Cuzco. Cuzco was also a major center of folk images carrying on the tradition of medieval European popular religious prints.

The last phase of colonial art adopted the neoclassic style, inspired by the newly discovered wonders of Athens and Pompeii. Neoclassicism affected every art to some degree, leading to severe linear styles based on antiquity or on Palladio. King CHARLES III's expulsion of the Jesuits in 1767 (*see* JESUITS, EXPULSION OF: SPANISH AMERICA), which was concerned only incidentally with the order's domination of art, removed the chief rival of the national government for control of the arts and for a time virtually eliminated the arts in Paraguay and Chile. The Academy of San Carlos was founded in Mexico in 1785 to centralize art under government patronage, and Spanish teachers, notably Manuel TOLSÁ and the painter Rafael Ximeno y Planes, were sent to teach the new style.

With independence the new American nations retained Charles III's policies of patronage of the arts. The Mexican Academy survived and continued to import Spanish teachers such as Pelegrín Clavé (1810–1880) throughout the nineteenth century. Academic ideals remained in the ascendancy. The academy stressed intellectual, as opposed to manual, knowledge: anatomy, the classical orders of architecture, erudite subject matter. Drawing, which was considered intellectual, was emphasized over color, which was considered emotional. Both Juan Cordero (1824–1884) and Clavé, bitter rivals for the directorship of the academy (which Cordero never attained), exemplify the style, especially in their numerous portraits.

The new republics encouraged the arts, usually by financing the essential European training. Even an artist as American in orientation as Juan Manuel Blanes (1830–1901) studied in Europe during the 1860s, meagerly supported by the Uruguayan government. The principal exception was José María VELASCO, who was trained by an Italian teacher, Eugenio Landesio, in the academy in Mexico City. The general rule was an Italian training before about 1870 and a Parisian training after that date. Cordero, Blanes, and the Peruvian Daniel Hernández (1856–1932) are among those who studied in Italy. Epifanio Garay (1849–1903) of Colombia, the Chilean Pedro Lira (1845–1912), and Arturo Michelena (1863–1898), Martín Tovar y Tovar (1828–1902), and Cristóbal Rojas (1858–1890), all of Venezuela, are among the many who received a conservative academic training in Paris. A later generation, at the turn of the twentieth century, returned from Europe with an impressionist training. Martín Malharro (1865–1911) and Fernando Fader (1882–1935) of Argentina, the Mexican Joaquín Clausell (1866–1935), and Pedro Blanes Viale (1879–1926) of Uruguay are among the major exponents of the style. Venezuela produced an important impressionist movement, including Antonio Edmundo Monsanto (1890–1947), Rafael Monasterios (1884–1961), Manuel Cabré (1890–   ), and Armando REVERÓN, who advanced the style in distinctive ways.

Several important art societies were established in the years around 1900. An early and significant group, the Society for the Stimulation of the Fine Arts, was founded in Buenos Aires in 1877. Its school and gallery were a center for progressive art. Fernando Fader, Collivadino, Quirós, and others formed the Nexus group in Buenos Aires in 1907 to advance the impressionist style. In 1910 the students at the Academy of San Carlos in Mexico City organized around Dr. ATL under the name Artistic Center to urge public mural commissions, a project forestalled by the MEXICAN REVOLUTION. In 1913 the students of the Venezuelan Academy of Fine Arts left to found studios and an annual exhibition under the name Fine Arts Circle. All these groups manifested a desire for new institutional foundations for progressive styles. The first stylistic results were impressionist and postimpressionist.

The institutional changes of the turn of the century laid foundations for creative progress in the 1920s. Paris was still the main training center, but cubist and expressionist styles had replaced the academic style there. Modern Art Week, held in São Paulo, Brazil, in 1922, had repercussions in other countries (*see* MODERNISM: BRAZIL). Emilio PETTORUTI introduced cubism to Buenos Aires in 1924. Joaquín TORRES-GARCÍA developed a humanistic constructivist style in Europe before returning to Uruguay in 1932. The geometric abstract wing of modern art bore fruit, especially in Argentina, in the work of Julio Le Parc (1928–   ), Ary Brizzi (1930–   ), and many others, and in Venezuela, where Alejandro Otero (1921–   ) and Jesús Soto (1923–   ) became outstanding. The teachings of Torres-García gained numerous followers, among them Julio Alpuy (1919–   ). Surrealism and psychological abstraction attracted few Latin American painters, although the Chilean Roberto MATTA made an important contribution. Wifredo LAM, whose Afro-Cuban subjects developed out of the work of Picasso, is another well-known artist with surrealist connections.

Mexico City produced the only art movement to rival the school of Paris. The mural movement sometimes called the Mexican Renaissance was organized under the Ministry of Education directed by José VASCONCELOS. Government sponsorship was essential to the grand scale and continuity of the movement. The basic theory of the movement was expressed as early as 1921, before any murals had been painted, by David Alfaro SIQUEIROS: art should be at the service of the people and should consist of exterior murals on social themes using modern industrial materials and techniques. Most of the earlier works were in the traditional technique of fresco. Great works were painted by José Clemente OROZCO and Diego RIVERA from 1922 into the 1940s in both Mexico and the United States. Siqueiros's major contribution began in 1930, and he continued to develop into the 1970s. The Mexican movement is the major expression of twentieth-century social ideals in art, but its influence on world art, especially on the art of the United States, although very great, has not as yet been properly assessed.

In the 1960s and 1970s Mexican painting has been dominated by two major trends, one deriving from Orozco and the other principally from Rufino TAMAYO. José Luis CUEVAS developed an elegant style of drawing grotesque subjects based on Orozco's early watercolors and later drawings. Rafael Coronel (1932–   ), Alberto Gironella (1929–   ), Leonel Góngora (1933–   ), a Colombian resident in Mexico from 1960 on, and Francisco Corzas (1936–   ) represent a wide range of related visions, Hispanophile and retrospective. The other major wing is coloristic in the manner of Tamayo and is indebted to international abstract movements. Pedro Coronel (1923–   ), Luis López Loza (1939–   ), Manuel Felguerez (1928–   ), and Antonio Peláez (1921–   ) are varied exponents of this approach.

During the 1960s New York replaced Paris as the major international art center, although Mexico City remained an independent center. The New York school includes many important Latin American artists, among them Armando Morales (Nicaragua, 1927–   ), MARISOL, the Venezuelan sculptor, and Fernando BOTERO, a Colombian painter of satirical images.

Since 1950 a completely new set of art institutions has come into existence. National museums and museums of modern art have been founded in many of the major cities. Large corporations and their foundations have begun to patronize the arts, rivaling or surpassing the state as a patron. International biennial exhibitions, among them those in São Paulo, Mexico City, Buenos Aires, and Córdoba, now set styles and standards, taking over the role once played by the Paris Salons.

Bibliography. S. L. Catlin and T. Grieder, *Art of Latin America since Independence,* New Haven, Conn., 1966; Leopoldo Castedo, *A History of Latin American Art and Architecture,* New York, 1969; G. Chase, *Contemporary Art in Latin America,* New York, 1970; George Kubler and Martin Soria, *Art and Architecture in Spain and Portugal and Their American Dominions,* Baltimore, 1959; Bernard S. Myers, *Mexican Painting in Our Time,* New York, 1956; E. W. Weismann, *Mexico in Sculpture,* Cambridge, Mass., 1950.

TERENCE GRIEDER

ARTIGAS, JOSÉ GERVASIO (1764–1850). National hero of Uruguay. Artigas was both the dominant personality of the independence movement in Uruguay and an early leader of the federalist cause in the civil wars of Argentina. Born in Montevideo into a prominent landowning and military family of the colonial Banda Oriental, he received an adequate formal education. From an early age, however, he showed a preference for life in the open on his family's cattle estates, perfecting him-

José Gervasio Artigas. [*United States Information Agency*]

self in all the skills of the GAUCHO population. In due course he went into business on his own, as a smuggler among other things. But he subsequently distinguished himself as a military officer for the Spaniards, working to establish order and promote new settlements in the countryside and serving ably against the British invasions of 1806–1807.

Although Montevideo failed to follow the revolution that broke out in May 1810 in Buenos Aires, scattered uprisings began occurring in the interior of the Banda Oriental, and early in 1811 Artigas threw in his lot with the patriot forces. Initially he accepted the authority of the Buenos Aires junta, and he served with the army that it sent to besiege Montevideo. But a serious complication appeared when the Portuguese, seeing an opportunity to gain their old ambition of a foothold on the RÍO DE LA PLATA, launched an invasion ostensibly to "pacify" the Banda Oriental. Hence there arose a three-way struggle involving Spaniards, Portuguese, and creole patriots. Nor did the patriots long remain united. The government at Buenos Aires, which had other problems to deal with, sought more than once to buy time by negotiating truces with its enemies in a manner that suggested to Artigas (who early established his leadership over the local contingents) a lack of firm commitment to the liberation of the province.

The distrust of Buenos Aires on the part of Artigas and his followers was intensified by an underlying conflict over forms of government. The dominant sentiment at the former viceregal capital favored strong centralist rule, whereas the outlying provinces leaned increasingly toward some type of federalism. In the Banda Oriental,

federalism derived added strength from the traditional commercial and political rivalry between Montevideo and its hinterland on one side and Buenos Aires on the other. Artigas himself emerged as one of the foremost exponents of federalism, and the rejection of the federalist delegation that he sent to the Argentine National Assembly of 1813 forcefully dramatized the growing division.

Meanwhile, the war dragged on. The Portuguese withdrew in 1812, under British pressure, and Montevideo fell to Buenos Aires forces two years later, by which time the Buenos Aires leadership had declared Artigas an outlaw with a price on his head. Yet Artigas largely controlled the countryside beyond Montevideo, and when Buenos Aires finally withdrew its forces early in 1815, he gained mastery of the entire Banda Oriental. His prime concern was to promote economic recovery after so much fighting, and his measures were both soundly conceived and socially progressive; his offer of land to the landless has been cited as an early precedent for AGRARIAN REFORM. At the same time, he continued to work for a broader union of the Río de la Plata provinces on the basis of federalism. Under the leadership of Artigas as Protector, a Federal League was created; at the height of its influence it extended as far as Córdoba in central Argentina.

Artigas's power was not destined to last. A new and massive Portuguese invasion that began in 1816 proved more than he could handle, especially since Buenos Aires refused to lend effective aid. Montevideo fell in January 1817. Artigas continued the struggle for three more years, but his position was also weakening in the adjoining Argentine provinces as the Federal League disintegrated under the combined impact of internal rivalries and Buenos Aires's hostility. Finally defeated on all fronts, Artigas went into exile in Paraguay, where he lived until his death in 1850. He thus had no direct part in the eventual establishment of an independent Uruguay, with the aid of British mediation, at the conclusion of the war of 1825–1828 between Brazil and Argentina. Indeed, he had not aimed at separate nationhood for the Banda Oriental but rather for its inclusion as an autonomous province within a larger Platine confederation. However, his own opposition to the pretensions of Buenos Aires had helped to make that outcome inevitable.

Bibliography. Eduardo Acevedo, *José Artigas: Su obra cívica, alegato histórico,* 3 vols., 3d ed., Montevideo, 1950; John Street, *Artigas and the Emancipation of Uruguay,* Cambridge, England, 1959; Nelson de la Torre et al., *Artigas: Tierra y revolución,* Montevideo, 1967.

DAVID BUSHNELL

ASBAJE Y RAMÍREZ DE SANTILLANA, JUANA DE. *See* JUANA INÉS DE LA CRUZ, SOR.

ASOCIACIÓN DE MAYO. Argentine society identified with the Generation of 1837. It was composed essentially of university students and writers who, inspired by French romanticism, wanted to advance the economic and cultural development of Argentina. It evolved from the informal meetings of Juan Bautista ALBERDI, Juan María Gutiérrez, and Esteban ECHEVERRÍA held at the home of Mme. Mendeville, wife of the French Consul, from 1835 to 1837. In June

1837, the group, having grown in size, moved to the Librería Argentina of Marcos Sastre. Here, under the leadership of Echeverría, they formed the Salón Literario for the purpose of reading and discussing European literary and philosophical works. Initially, they proposed to cooperate with the dictator Juan Manuel de ROSAS for the "peaceful progress of civilization" on the basis of law and reason. Rosas watched them curiously until they began to study the possible application of Saint-Simonian ideas to Argentina, then closed the bookstore. Undiscouraged, some of the group founded a small periodical, *La Moda,* which appeared from October 1837 to April 1838. In May 1838, at the suggestion of Echeverría that they imitate the Young Italy movement of Mazzini, they organized the Joven Argentina, or Asociación de Mayo. Outside Buenos Aires provincial chapters were started by such young students and writers as Domingo Faustino SARMIENTO in San Juan and Nicolás AVELLANEDA in Córdoba. On July 9, the members assembled in Buenos Aires adopted the political program which Alberdi and Echeverría had prepared and which was to appear, with a dedication to Gen. Juan Lavalle, as the *Dogma socialista* in 1846. In this and other works they showed that they had read and absorbed Saint-Simon, Leroux, Fourier, Lamennais, Hegel, and Savigny. What they sought was the reconciliation of all political parties in Argentina, political stability, the organization of Argentina on a democratic basis, and the economic advancement of the country. Disappointed at the failure of Rosas to seek their advice and support, they began to meet secretly and to plot with General Lavalle for the overthrow of Rosas. Lavalle was defeated in 1839, but by then many had sought safety abroad.

JOSEPH T. CRISCENTI

ASOCIACIÓN LATINOAMERICANA DE LIBRE COMERCIO. *See* LATIN AMERICAN FREE TRADE ASSOCIATION.

ASSIS FIGUEIREDO, AFONSO CELSO DE (VISCONDE OURO PRÊTO, 1836–1912). Brazilian statesman and last Prime Minister of the empire. Born in Ouro Prêto, then capital of Minas Gerais, Assis Figueiredo was educated at the Law Faculty in São Paulo. In 1864 he was elected to the Chamber of Deputies from Minas Gerais, beginning a long political career in which he advocated liberal causes. From August 1866 until July 1868 he was Naval Minister, playing an important role during a critical phase of the PARAGUAYAN WAR. With the fall of Zacarias de Goes and the rise of the Visconde Itaboraí in 1868, he joined José Thomaz Nabuco de Araújo's Liberal Center, which supported electoral reform, abolition of the National Guard, and a free birth law.

In 1876 he was reelected to the Chamber, and in 1879–1880, having been elevated to the Senate and granted the title Visconde Ouro Prêto, he served as Finance Minister, supporting electoral reform and economic changes intended to eliminate the perennial national deficit. During the unrest following the abolition of slavery (*see* ABOLITION OF SLAVERY: BRAZIL), he participated prominently in a Liberal party congress that formulated a program of progressive reforms. These included a broadening of the electorate, provincial autonomy under the imperial system, free-

dom of worship and of education, and a law to facilitate the acquisition of land. On June 7, 1889, Ouro Prêto organized a Liberal Cabinet, and in subsequent elections he gained a solid Liberal majority in the Chamber, virtually assuring action on the Liberal program in the special session scheduled to begin on November 20, 1889. This was prevented, however, by the republican coup of Nobember 15 of that year. After an exile of nearly two years, Ouro Prêto devoted his talents to the monarchist cause.

ROBERT CONRAD

ASTURIAS, MIGUEL ÁNGEL (1899–1974). Guatemalan writer. Asturias studied law at the University of San Carlos of Guatemala and from 1923 to 1926 attended the courses of Georges Raynaud at the Sorbonne on the ancient religions and cultures of Central America. His first book, *Leyendas de Guatemala* (Madrid, 1930, with a prologue letter by Paul Valéry), shows a continuing interest in the landscape, myths, and stories of his native land. He returned to Guatemala in 1933 and began an active public career as a federal deputy (1942), the founder of the Popular University of Guatemala, Cultural Attaché in Mexico (1946–1947) and Argentina (1948–1950), and Ambassador in San Salvador (1953–1954).

Asturias's first novel, *El señor presidente,* now widely translated, was published in Mexico in 1946; it uses surrealist techniques to describe the morally sick atmosphere of life in a Latin American dictatorship, undoubtedly based on the tyranny of Manuel ESTRADA CABRERA. *Hombres de maíz* (Buenos Aires, 1949) presents the problem of the persecuted Indian and mestizo minorities in a contrapuntal interweaving of the mythic world of the MAYAS and the reality of contemporary Guatemalan society. Later novels seem to sacrifice literary values to social and political content. A trilogy denouncing exploitation by the banana companies in the Caribbean, consisting of *Viento fuerte,* 1950 (*Strong Wind*), *El papa verde,* 1954 (*Green Pope*), and *Los ojos de los enterrados* (1955), is a cogent attack on colonialism. *Weekend en Guatemala* (1956) is a collection of eight stories, most with political intent. More recent novels are *El Alhajadito* (1961) and *Mulata de tal,* 1963 (*Hulata*).

Asturias published poetry of considerable merit, often based on popular and folkloric themes, including *Sien de alondra* (1949) and *Ejercicios poéticos en forma de soneto sobre temas de Horacio* (1951). He also wrote plays, including *Soluna* (1957), and he published an anthology entitled *Poesía precolombina* (1961). In 1966 he was named Ambassador in Paris; he won the Lenin Peace Prize in 1966 and the Nobel Prize for Literature in 1967.

RACHEL PHILLIPS

ASUNCIÓN. Capital of the Republic of Paraguay, situated on a bay in the Paraguay River some 180 miles north of the confluence of the Paraguay with the Paraná River. In 1968 it had a population approaching 400,000, or about 17 percent of that of the nation.

Founded in 1537, Asunción was an unimposing river town, the capital of a backward and isolated province, in 1811, when Spanish power was overthrown. From a town with a population of about 10,000 in 1811, Asunción grew to be a city of perhaps 25,000 by the 1850s, when, under the aegis of Carlos Antonio LÓPEZ (1844–1862), many large and handsome public buildings were constructed, giving the capital an urban aspect for the first time. The great surge in growth of the city is a twentieth-century phenomenon, occurring mostly after 1920.

Asunción is not only the nation's administrative center but the home of most of Paraguay's nascent industries. The city covers a very large area for its population and is devoid of the slums that fester in other large South American cities. From Palma and Estrella Streets, which form the geographical and commercial heart of the city, stretch out minor streets shaded by orange trees, which scent the air with their fragrance. Except for a season of intense heat from December to February, the climate is temperate and pleasant.

JOHN HOYT WILLIAMS

ATACAMA DESERT. Rainless, barren coastal desert in northern Chile stretching from the Peruvian border southward for about 600 miles to the vicinity of Copiapó. In appearance the desert is forbidding, but mineral deposits of copper and natural nitrate have made it economically important. From a nearly straight coastline, an escarpment rises abruptly directly from the sea or from narrow marine terraces to a plateau level 2,000 to 3,000 feet above the Pacific Ocean. Mountain peaks above the plateau surface reach as high as 9,000 feet. Between this coastal range and the ANDES MOUNTAINS lies a long depression that is divided into shallow bolsons (dry basins).

Tucked into irrigable mountain valleys of the Andes front are small, remote agricultural settlements that continue a largely self-sufficient way of life not greatly different from the one they followed long before the arrival of the Spaniards. By contrast, the other settlements of the Atacama have a precarious existence, depending upon the fortunes of mining and relying completely upon piped-in water. Copper and, to a lesser extent, gold and silver were extracted from the Atacama by the early nineteenth century, but it was nitrates that made the desert valuable, beginning in the 1870s. After 1910 technological innovations permitting the extraction of copper from low-grade ores made copper mining again the main economic activity of the Atacama, where enormous but low-grade reserves are now mined at Chuquicamata and El Salvador. Copper is Chile's main export. *See also* COPPER INDUSTRY (CHILE); NITRATE INDUSTRY (CHILE).

DANIEL W. GADE

ATAHUALPA (d. 1533). The last of the Inca rulers of Peru (*see* INCAS), executed by Francisco PIZARRO. Atahualpa was a grandson of Topa Inca Yupanqui, conqueror of Chile and Quito, and the favorite but illegitimate son of HUAYNA CAPAC, who ruled over the Incas during the late fifteenth century. Atahualpa had two brothers, the illegitimate MANCO INCA, who later led a rebellion against the Spaniards, and the legitimate heir to the throne, Huascar. At his death Huayna Capac divided his realm between Atahualpa, who received dominion over Quito, and Huascar, who was to rule Peru from Cuzco. After five uneasy years, hostilities broke out (1530) because of Atahualpa's aggressive policies. Atahualpa defeated one of Huascar's armies at Ambato and established his headquarters at Cajamarca while sending troops to Cuzco.

By the time Pizarro's expedition arrived at Cajamarca in 1532, Cuzco had fallen and Huascar was Atahualpa's prisoner. The Spaniards boldly ambushed Atahualpa, massacred his bodyguards, and held him prisoner. Pizarro then accepted Atahualpa's offer to fill a room with gold in exchange for his freedom. While his subjects were carrying out this task, Atahualpa ordered the murder of Huascar to prevent him from conspiring with the Spaniards. The arrival of Diego de ALMAGRO's party (1533) caused Pizarro to distribute the spoils before the collection was completed, but the danger of freeing a potential enemy outweighed the virtue of a kept promise. Atahualpa was tried and executed on the pretext that he had encouraged an Inca uprising.

WILLIAM S. DUDLEY

ATL, DR. (born GERARDO MURILLO, 1875–1964). Mexican painter and a major figure in Mexican cultural life throughout the first half of the twentieth century. Although he painted few murals, his admiration for Italian Renaissance murals, especially those of Michelangelo, inspired a generation of painters and their governmental patrons. As a landscape painter he is important in his own right.

He was born Gerardo Murillo in Guadalajara but adopted the name Atl, which means "water" in Nahuatl. His lifelong fascination with natural forces originated in walking trips in the hills of western Mexico. He was pensioned to Europe for art studies and returned to Mexico in 1904 with a passion for mural painting. Dr. Atl taught at the Academy of San Carlos and gained for himself and five collaborators a commission for murals in the Bolívar Auditorium of the National Preparatory School, where they began work in November 1910. The MEXICAN REVOLUTION delayed the project for twelve years, and Diego RIVERA ultimately painted the wall. Dr. Atl's most famous mural is the Tiffany glass curtain of the National Theater in the Palace of Fine Arts, on which he depicted the snow-capped volcanoes that guard Mexico City.

Dr. Atl was active in the revolution as a propagandist for Venustiano CARRANZA, publishing the newspaper *La Vanguardia,* on which José Clemente OROZCO worked, and as an organizer of pro-Carranza labor battalions. After the revolution he dedicated himself to studies of folk art, published as *Las artes populares de México* (1921), and wrote with Manuel Toussaint *Iglesias de México* (6 vols., 1924–1925).

He always preferred pastel and crayon to oil or fresco and made his own oil crayons, calling them Atl-color. Stupendous landscapes, devoid of human artifacts, with a curving horizon as if seen from outer space, were his specialty. He was obsessed by volcanoes and made a study of Paricutín as it grew in 1943. A long series of art works records this event.

TERENCE GRIEDER

AUDIENCIA. Initially an appellate court in colonial Spanish America. The first *audiencia* was established in Santo Domingo in 1511 to obviate the necessity of bringing lawsuits to Spain. Others were soon erected in centers of growing Spanish population until there were several *audiencias* within each viceroyalty, one being found in the principal city of each of the important provinces. Early *audiencias* included those of Mexico City (1528), Panama (1538), Lima (1542), Los Confines, or Guatemala (1548), and Bogotá (1549).

The *audiencia* quickly acquired much wider powers. To its judicial functions were added legislative and executive powers, and it became an advisory council to the viceroy or captain general (depending on its location) and shared many of his responsibilities. Although officially it was a court of appeal, it worked in practice as a general administrative board.

Theoretically all the *audiencias* held equal jurisdiction under the COUNCIL OF THE INDIES, but in practice they differed widely from one another. Those in the viceregal capitals, Mexico City and Lima, were more powerful and important, and the other *audiencias* tended to become subordinate to them. The power of a particular *audiencia* at a given time depended upon many variables, such as its location, the ability of its judges, called *oidores* (*see* OIDOR), and the strength and personality of the viceroy.

As a court of law the *audiencia* decided appeals from inferior tribunals in both criminal and civil cases. In most instances its decision was final, but important cases in which large sums of money were involved or severe punishments were recommended could be appealed to the Council of the Indies. The *audiencia* acted as a court of first instance in all cases within the city where it was situated as well as in cases that dealt with the usurpation of royal authority.

The *audiencia* took part in the legislation and administration of its area. One of its major responsibilities was the protection of the Indians. It assessed all legal and ecclesiastical fees and the Indian tribute. It authorized and regulated the REPARTIMIENTO, or distribution, of Indians for labor, and controlled the division of lands. The *audiencia* was given the responsibility for supervising the conduct of all royal officials by means of a VISITA, or tour of inspection through the province undertaken by an *oidor* to investigate all the economic, religious, and judicial conditions. It was also empowered to review the decisions of *visitas* and *residencias* (*see* RESIDENCIA) and to put them into effect. When the viceroyalty or captaincy general was vacant, the *audiencia* assumed all the powers of the office.

The viceroy or captain general presided ex officio over the *audiencia* of the area, while in the lesser *audiencias* one of the *oidores* served as president. The *audiencia* included a number of lesser officials, such as a *fiscal* appointed to protect the royal financial interests, who also acted as public prosecutor; a *relator*, who was a lawyer charged with preparing summaries of the cases; *receptores*, who traveled to collect evidence; and several notaries.

The *audiencia* and the viceroy shared the apex of colonial government. Sometimes they worked in harmony, while at other times great conflicts arose. Although the viceroy or captain general presided, he did not have a voice or a vote in the *audiencia* unless he was a lawyer. Theoretically, therefore, he could not interfere in the administration of justice. This division of jurisdiction was circumvented somewhat in practice, since the viceroy could decide whether a case was administrative or judicial in character and hence could intervene if he wished. In executive and administrative matters, the position of the *audiencia* depended largely on the relative strength of the *oidores* and of the viceroy at the particular time. The viceregal *audiencias* officially exercised only judicial authority, leaving the legislative and executive to the viceroy, but he was required to consult the *audiencia* in making important decisions and hence was forced to share his power. The viceroy's power was also constrained by the *audiencia*, since it could hear appeals against his actions and investigate his behavior, as it could for all royal officials. The *audiencia* also shared the viceroy's executive prerogatives, since it was empowered to try to effect its own decisions. It was allowed to enact local legislation subject to the approval of the King and the Council of the Indies, thus being converted into a legislative body as well.

The Spanish crown tried to divide the authority and responsibility for government because it had a deep distrust of initiative on the part of colonial officials, who it feared would try to usurp some of the royal power. It successfully divided the power to rule between the viceroy and the *audiencia*, which functioned as the principal check on the arbitrary exercise of power by the viceroy. The *audiencia* played a crucial role in colonial administration not only because it served as a foil to the viceroy but because it provided continuity from one viceregal regime to another. The *audiencias* constituted the most durable and stable branches of colonial government.

In the later colonial period the importance of the *audiencia* declined somewhat, along with that of the viceroy. In order to increase royal revenue in the seventeenth century the crown began to sell royal offices, thus removing from the jurisdiction of the *audiencia* and of the viceroy the authority to appoint lesser local officials. The powers of the *audiencia* declined even more in the eighteenth century with the introduction of the INTENDANCY SYSTEM because the intendants tried to evade viceregal and *audiencia* controls to deal directly with the ministries in Spain. Nevertheless, the *audiencias* survived until the end of the colonial period, and new ones were created in an effort to increase the efficiency of colonial administration.

Bibliography. Leon G. Campbell, "A Colonial Establishment: Creole Domination of the Audiencia of Lima during the Late Eighteenth Century," *Hispanic American Historical Review*, vol. LII, no. 1, February 1972, pp. 1–25; C. H. Cunningham, *The Audiencia in the Spanish Colonies as Illustrated by the Audiencia of Manila, 1583–1800*, Berkeley, Calif., 1919; Charles Gibson, *Spain in America*, New York, 1966; C. H. Haring, *The Spanish Empire in America*, New York, 1947; J. H. Parry, *The Audiencia of New Galicia in the Sixteenth Century*, Cambridge, England, 1948; id., *The Spanish Seaborne Empire*, New York, 1970; John Leddy Phelan, "Authority and Flexibility in the Spanish Imperial Bureaucracy," *Administrative Science Quarterly*, vol. V, no. 1, June 1960, pp. 47–65.

ELIZABETH WILKES DORE

AUTÉNTICO PARTY (CUBA). Popular name for the Partido de la Revolución Cubana, or Cuban Revolutionary party. The party was founded in 1934 by Dr. Ramón GRAU SAN MARTÍN and his followers in the Directorio Estudantil (Student Directorate), a university-based organization which had been dedicated to the overthrow of the dictatorship of Gerardo MACHADO. For several years the new party operated clandestinely, but it emerged as a strong political force in the late 1930s.

Called Auténtico in reference to the authentic revolution desired by the Cuban patriot José MARTÍ, the party followed the democratic left or populist position in Latin American politics. The Auténticos proposed structural reforms involving government intervention in the economy. As economic nationalists they advocated diversification of the economy and limitations on foreign-owned enterprises. The party was strongly represented in the Constituent Assembly that drafted Cuba's economically and socially progressive new constitution (*see* CONSTITUTION OF 1940: CUBA).

The Auténticos became the chief political rivals of both President Fulgencio BATISTA and the Cuban Communists. From 1944 to 1952 the party dominated national politics under the presidential administrations of Ramón Grau San Martín and Carlos PRÍO SOCORRÁS. This period was characterized by political democracy, the enactment of a few reform provisions of the constitution, and scandals involving corruption in government.

Auténtico political domination ended in 1952, when General Batista ousted President Prío by force and established a dictatorship that endured until 1959. After initial hesitation the party took the course of clandestine revolutionary opposition and reached a working agreement with Fidel CASTRO's July 26 movement in 1958. Since Castro's consolidation of political control in early 1959, the party has ceased to exist in Cuba.

DAVID A. CRAIN

AUTONOMOUS REGIONAL CORPORATION OF THE CAUCA VALLEY. *See* CORPORACIÓN AUTÓNOMA REGIONAL DEL VALLE DEL CAUCA.

AUZA-LEÓN, ATILIANO (1930–   ). Bolivian composer. Born in Sucre, he studied there and later with Alberto GINASTERA and others in Buenos Aires. In 1955 he was appointed professor of music in Bolivia and ever since has been a promoter of contemporary music in his native country. Outstanding among his works are *Nebulosas* for piano and string quartet (1952), *Anfiblástula* for piano (1965), a trio for winds (1965), and a concerto for violin and orchestra (1966).

JUAN A. ORREGO-SALAS

AVELLANEDA, NICOLÁS (1836–1885). President of Argentina (1874–1880). Avellaneda was born in Tucumán. After receiving his law degree from the University of Córdoba, he went to Buenos Aires and quickly became a regular contributor to *El Comercio del Plata* (1859–1860) and *El Nacional* (1859–1861). Within a few years he was teaching economics at the University of Buenos Aires. In 1866 he became minister of government for Governor Adolfo Alsina of Buenos Aires, and two years later he became Minister of Justice and Public Education for President Domingo Faustino SARMIENTO. In 1870 he was briefly the head of the Ministry of Finance.

His candidacy for the Presidency, announced in Córdoba in 1873, received the endorsement of Sarmiento. Alsina, another contender for the office, withdrew in favor of Avellaneda when he realized that he lacked a national following. Supported by a loose coalition of provincial parties called the Partido Nacional, Avellaneda won the elections in all the provinces except Buenos Aires, San Juan, and Santiago del Estero. The corruption evident during the elections served as a pretext for ex-President Bartolomé MITRE and his followers to revolt in 1874. Avellaneda took office in October, and the revolution collapsed shortly afterward with the defeat of Mitre and his supporters at Junín and Santa Rosa (December 7, 1874).

Although Avellaneda's first Cabinet consisted primarily of *provincianos,* the most important member was Minister of War Alsina, the *porteño* leader of the Partido Autonomista, whose support and advice the President needed and sought. As the Partido Autonomista was beginning to disintegrate into numerous factions, both Avellaneda and Alsina wanted to strengthen it and to persuade it and the Partido Nacional, which was boycotting elections, to challenge each other at the polls rather than on the battlefield and to share some public offices with the minority party. The federal government was to guarantee honest elections. To bring about the desired conciliation, Avellaneda annulled the decision of the Council of War to exile Mitre and the other military officers involved in the revolution of 1874 and urged Congress to pass a general amnesty law. In 1877 Mitre accepted the policy of conciliation that Avellaneda and Alsina advocated, and Congress reinstated all the officers who had been discharged from the Army because of their participation in the revolution and, on July 26, passed a general amnesty law for past political and military crimes. However, the death of Alsina in the last days of 1877 upset the existing political equilibrium. Avellaneda emerged from the ensuing reshuffling of political alliances as the head of a new party composed of Autonomistas and a faction of the Partido Nacional. Political crises also occurred over the presidential election of 1880, in which Julio A. ROCA opposed Carlos Tejedor, Governor of Buenos Aires Province, and over the decision to federalize the city of Buenos Aires, an event that took place in September 1880, a month before Roca's inauguration.

Politics so dominated the Avellaneda administration that it is easy to overlook the economic crisis that plagued it, particularly from 1874 to 1876. Avellaneda personally directed a program of economic austerity and was responsible for laws to encourage immigration and colonization (*see* IMMIGRATION: ARGENTINA), protect local manufacturers from imports, and suspend the conversion of paper money into gold. These policies, together with an improved balance of trade, contributed to the economic recovery that began in 1877.

JOSEPH T. CRISCENTI

ÁVILA, PEDRO ARIAS DE (PEDRARIAS; PEDRARIAS DÁVILA; ca. 1440–ca. 1530). Spanish conqueror and official. Born in Segovia of Jewish origin, he served as an officer against the Moors in Africa in 1510. He was married to Doña Isabel de Bobadilla y de Peñalosa, a strong-willed woman who bore him eight children and insisted on accompanying him to the New World, a singular act at that time. On July 27, 1513, he received a commission to assume the governorship of Darién as a result of complaints by Martín Fernández de Enciso against Vasco Núñez de BALBOA, news of whose discovery had not yet reached Spain. Sailing from Sanlúcar de Barrameda on April 12, 1514, he arrived on June 29 with 1,500 men.

Pedrarias has been universally condemned as a hard, cruel, and rapacious governor, the worst the Indies had ever known. In his youth he had been called El Galán (the Gallant One) and El Justador (the Jouster), tributes to his gallantry and prowess; in his later years he was deservedly referred to as Furor Domini (Wrath of God). Pedrarias instituted a RESIDENCIA against Balboa but was unsuccessful in convicting him of any misdeeds. Biding his time and waiting until Balboa relaxed his guard, Pedrarias accused him of treason and, after a trial, ordered him beheaded in January 1519. In that year he founded Panama City, the oldest existing European settlement on the American mainland. Four years later, in 1523, he seized control of Nicaragua, where he died. He had been made Governor in 1527 after having been superseded in Panama by Pedro de los Ríos.

MARTIN TORODASH

ÁVILA CAMACHO, MANUEL (1897–1955). President of Mexico (1940–1946). Ávila Camacho was born in Teziutlán, Puebla, the son of a farmer, Manuel Ávila Castilla. After graduating as an accountant, he joined the MEXICAN REVOLUTION in 1914 with the rank of sublieutenant. Six years later Lázaro CÁRDENAS named him chief of his general staff. In the campaign against the CRISTERO REBELLION in Jalisco, he distinguished himself for his use of peaceful methods; he used the same methods with equal success in 1932 in Tabasco while opposing the anticlericalism of Governor Tomás Garrido Canabal. In 1933 he rose from the position of First Undersecretary of War to Undersecretary; in January 1938 he became Secretary of War; and on March 1, 1938, he received the rank of general of division.

Because of his ties with Cárdenas and his conciliatory spirit, he became the official presidential candidate on November 3, 1939. He was elected on July 7, 1940, and took office the following December; meanwhile, a threatened revolt by the defeated candidate Juan Andreu Almazán failed to materialize. As President, Ávila Camacho put a halt to the radicalism of Cárdenas in order to assure the survival of the revolution and to prepare the nation for World War II, in which Mexico finally took part as a belligerent when some oil tankers were sunk by German submarines. He discouraged the collective EJIDO but created the Mexican Institute of Social Security.

The President's brother, Maximino Ávila Camacho, who was Secretary of Communications from 1941 until his death in February 1945, was a bitter foe of the leftist Vicente LOMBARDO TOLEDANO.

MOISÉS GONZÁLEZ NAVARRO

AYACUCHO, MARSHALS OF. See MARSHALS OF AYACUCHO.

AYACUCHO, BATTLE OF. Last great battle of the independence struggle in South America, fought in the highlands of south central Peru on December 9, 1824. It was the culmination of the campaign, launched by Simón BOLÍVAR with the able assistance of Gen. Antonio José de SUCRE, that in August had produced the

victory of Junín (see JUNÍN, BATTLE OF). In October Bolívar departed for Lima, leaving the army in the hands of Sucre though expecting to rejoin him later. The same month, Viceroy José de la Serna with a royalist army of more than 10,000 men set out from Cuzco in pursuit of the patriots; there followed a period of marching and countermarching as the rival forces maneuvered for position.

Instructed by Bolívar to use caution, Sucre kept basically on the defensive, but early in December he received full authorization to give battle. Although he had only about 6,000 men, he decided to do so and chose the small plain of Ayacucho as the site for a stand. Before the royalists could bring all their forces onto the field from adjoining heights, Sucre directed José María Córdoba with the Colombian infantry to attack those already on the plain and sent cavalry against others still descending from the heights. The royalist units that penetrated the plain behind Sucre's left flank were successfully repulsed. The battle was skillfully directed, brief, and decisive. La Serna, wounded, was taken prisoner. A capitulation signed the same day provided for the evacuation of Peru by the royalists but gave generous terms to the defeated army.

DAVID BUSHNELL

AYALA, ELIGIO (1880–1930). Paraguayan educator, politician, Liberal party leader, and President (1923–1924, 1925–1928). Born in the interior, Ayala was educated in Asunción at the Colegio Nacional and at the National University, from which he received a doctorate in law and social sciences in 1904. He taught at the Colegio Nacional and worked for the National Archives and the Ministry of Justice, after which he became a Senator. Between 1904 and 1911 he took part in a number of political insurrections as a militant Liberal; then, disillusioned, he traveled to Europe, where he spent the next eight years studying and writing. He returned to Paraguay at the urging of President Manuel GONDRA in 1920 to become Minister of the Treasury. In 1923 he was chosen provisional President and two years later was elected constitutional President, becoming one of the few men to complete his full term in that post. After stepping down in 1928, he returned to the Treasury and later filled several diplomatic posts.

Considered one of the most constructive leaders of the Liberal party, Ayala brought Paraguay its first four years of domestic peace in a generation. A contributor to many periodicals, upon his death he left a number of unpublished manuscripts dealing with Paraguay's social problems. See LIBERAL PARTY (PARAGUAY).

JOHN HOYT WILLIAMS

AYALA, EUSEBIO (1875–1942). Paraguayan educator, politician, and President (1921–1923, 1932–1936). Born outside Asunción, Ayala was educated at the Colegio Nacional and the National University, from which he was graduated as a doctor of law in 1900. He taught at the Colegio Nacional and traveled widely in Europe and the Americas. In 1908 he took part in the successful Liberal party revolt and a year later became Minister of Justice. Later he served as Minister of the Treasury and Minister of Foreign Affairs, in which post he ably represented Paraguay at many international conferences. See LIBERAL PARTY (PARAGUAY).

In 1921, while serving in the Senate, he was elected

President of Paraguay for a two-year term, during which he was kept busy crushing almost continual revolts. After his term was completed, he traveled to Europe. While in Paris, he received word that the CHACO WAR had erupted and that he had been drafted as the Liberal party presidential candidate. He won the election and upon his return to Paraguay capably directed the nation's massive war effort. In February 1936, he was forced to resign the Presidency as the result of a military revolt led by Col. Rafael FRANCO, who was angered by the terms of the Chaco truce of 1935. Ayala went into exile in Buenos Aires, where he died in 1942, the same year his beloved Liberal party was banned by the dictator Higinio MORÍNIGO.

JOHN HOYT WILLIAMS

AYALA, PLAN OF. Revolutionary program issued by Emiliano ZAPATA on November 28, 1911. In it Zapata disavowed Francisco I. MADERO as President of Mexico because the latter, in Zapata's opinion, had not fulfilled the promises of the MEXICAN REVOLUTION in imposing José María Pino Suárez as Vice President. The plan recognized Pascual Orozco as chief of the Liberating Revolution; if he did not accept, Zapata himself was to be chief. The plan also demanded the immediate restitution to towns and poor farmers of fields, waters, and timber of which they had been despoiled by landowners, CIENTÍFICOS, and bosses. To meet the needs of those who lacked lands because land was monopolized by a few, one-third of the holdings of the monopolists would be expropriated with prior indemnification; those who opposed the plan would lose all their property.

The origin of the Plan of Ayala is generally attributed to Professor Otilio Montaño, a schoolteacher executed by the *zapatistas* in 1917 on charges of treason. Orozco never repudiated the part of the Plan of Ayala that recognized him as head of the revolution of the south, but Zapata later disavowed Orozco and indeed had his father shot. Zapata's tenacity forced Venustiano CARRANZA to issue the law of January 6, 1915, the starting point of Mexico's agrarian legislation, which had a more precise juridical formulation than the embryonic one contained in the Plan of Ayala.

MOISÉS GONZÁLEZ NAVARRO

AYLLU. Basic social institution of the pre-Columbian Peruvian Indians. The typical *ayllu* was a grouping of people who believed themselves descended from a common ancestor. At the heart of the system were the ancestor's bones, or mummy, which were carefully protected and venerated. Thus, it can be viewed as a vague and widely extended family; descent was patrilinear. The *ayllu* generally appears to have been endogamous. It held all lands in common ownership and periodically reassigned land parcels in accordance with changes within its population. In times of crisis it could elect a war leader not necessarily from within the *ayllu*. The INCAS were organized in ten *ayllus*, which together were grouped in two moieties; this duplication was a common way of fitting *ayllus*, which otherwise acted like villages, into larger urban contexts.

BURR C. BRUNDAGE

AYMARÁ. Indian culture and language centered in the Bolivian highlands. Aymará groups (Colla, Lupaca, Pacasa, and others) first appear in history as subjects of the Inca empire. At that time they formed populous chiefdoms around the great lake areas that today support a radically smaller population. Conquered by the formidable Inca emperor PACHACUTI, they rose in revolt and were with difficulty again crushed by his son, Topa Inca. Although the Incas began the destruction of Aymará culture and manpower, the Spaniards practically completed it. Hundreds of thousands died in the colonial mines of Potosí and Carabaya. In 1780 the Aymará took part in the great rebellion against the Spaniards. They are today a dour people leading lives of unremitting toil. As in the past they raise potatoes and quinoa and still herd llamas and some alpacas. Because they live on the treeless puna at an elevation of about 12,000 feet, there is little or no surplus of time or goods; their culture perforce stresses the material. The Aymará religion has been basically the practice of magic. The anthropologist Harry Tschopik has called their culture "apprehensive." *See also* INCAS.

BURR C. BRUNDAGE

AYORA, ISIDRO (1879–). President and dictator of Ecuador (1926–1931). Born in Loja, Ayora received a medical degree from the Central University of Quito in 1905 and was serving as rector of the university when the revolution of July 1925 took place. A military junta appointed Dr. Ayora provisional President on April 1, 1926, and Ayora proceeded to launch a productive dictatorship.

Ecuador was suffering from a decline of the cacao trade, with a resultant shortage of foreign exchange and domestic inflation (*see* CACAO INDUSTRY: ECUADOR). The removal of the Moratorium Law (*see* PLAZA, Leonidas) had already forced banks of issue to close their doors. Now Ayora fined and liquidated the Banco Comercial y Agrícola, arbiter of Ecuadorian politics since 1912, closed unfriendly newspapers, and jailed many rich men who had prospered under bank rule. Rigid collections at the Guayaquil customhouse produced a treasury surplus by August 1926. Then Edwin W. Kemmerer of Princeton University and his team of economists arrived to set up a Central Bank, advise on public works, and draw up tax laws. Kemmerer left behind four American experts to supervise old and new agencies of fiscal and banking control, and government income soared.

Ayora also inaugurated pensions for city workers, a development bank, and Ecuador's first labor code. In 1929 a constituent assembly incorporated these and other progressive laws in a new constitution and elected Ayora to a four-year term. However, it also weakened the office of chief executive so that Congress easily overthrew Ayora's Minister of Government in 1931. This act, which was tantamount to a vote of no confidence, forced Ayora from the Presidency.

LOIS WEINMAN

AZEVEDO, ALUÍSIO [TANCREDO GONÇALVES DE] (1857–1913). Brazilian novelist and diplomat, one of the founders of the Brazilian Academy of Letters. Born in Maranhão, he eked out a meager living from his writing from 1880 to 1895, at which time he abandoned the struggle and entered the consular service. During these fifteen years he wrote fourteen books, including his three masterpieces, *O Mulato* (1881), *Casa de Pensão*

(1884), and *O Cortiço*, 1890 (*A Brazilian Tenement*), books that entitle him to be called Brazil's greatest naturalist writer. His fiction, written under the influence of Eça de Queiroz's *O Crime do Padre Amaro* and *O Primo Basílio*, exhibits the determinism, the acceptance of scientific theories, and the interest in deviant behavior characteristic of the school of naturalism. *O Mulato* is a thesis novel in which racial and social prejudice and clerical hypocrisy in provincial Maranhão are attacked. Because important *maranhenses* thought they were represented in it, he was forced to leave São Luís, the state capital, and go to Rio de Janeiro. *O Cortiço* contrasts the degeneracy of a bourgeois Rio family with the vitality of the residents of a teeming slum, or *cortiço,* depicted as a melting pot in which Negroes, mulattoes, and whites, Brazilians and foreigners, are fused into one race. The power of the characterizations and the rich descriptions of slum life give this novel a unique place in Brazilian literature.

RAYMOND S. SAYERS

AZTECS. The Aztecs claimed to have come from Chicomoztoc (Seven Caves), situated in a land called Aztlán in the far northwest. Modern scholarship suggests Michoacán or Jalisco as possible locations of Aztlán. The Aztecs were traditionally organized in seven tribal groups, generally listed as the Xochimilca, Chalca, Tepaneca, Acolhua, Tlalhuica, Tlascalteca, and Mexica. In 1168 they moved out of Chicomoztoc and headed for Tula, the capital of the empire of the TOLTECS, which had recently fallen, releasing floods of barbarian Chichimec bowmen, along with neo-Toltec refugees, into the areas south and southeast of Tula (*see* CHICHIMECS). From Tula the Aztecs moved to the great basin of Mexico, where in due time, after they had been instructed in the arts of civilized living by the predecessor peoples, they settled in cities. This basin and the areas adjoining it to the southeast thus became the heartland of the new Aztec culture.

History. The history of the Aztecs is an amazingly contentious one. Their cities, rapidly growing in population, fought each other consistently and with venom. Nevertheless, the period saw a homogeneous culture of remarkable vitality taking shape. The Mixteca-Puebla artistic style and the late Toltec institutions contributed to its formation.

The Aztec city Culhuacán claimed the first hegemony over the area but could not maintain the claim. Then, under the descendants of Xolotl, the old Chichimec chieftain, the city of Tezcoco (Texcoco) announced its imperial prerogatives. This was challenged by the redoubtable Tepaneca ruler Tezozomoc, whose city, Azcapotzalco, for a short time became the political center, only to fall in its turn to a coalition of three cities, Tezcoco, Mexico-Tenochtitlán, and Tlacopan. Some of the Aztec cities outside the basin, such as Tlascala (Tlaxcala), Huexotzinco (Huejotzingo), and Cholula, were able to escape absorption by this coalition. The three-city league remained the arbiter of Aztec destinies from 1428 until the destruction of Mexico by Hernán CORTÉS in 1521.

Mexico-Tenochtitlán is generally thought of as the predominant Aztec city, but this was true only during the reign of MOCTEZUMA II. Tezcoco, raised to heights of magnificence by the great ruler Nezahualcoyotl (1402–1472), was equally as important and far larger.

In addition, it possessed a ruling house with the most impressive royal pedigree of all the cities.

The Mexica were the poorest of the original seven tribes and the last to enter the valley. They were a predatory people and so antagonized their early neighbors as to be crushed and scattered by them in the year 1349. They moved after that through several stages of servitude and finally settled ingloriously on two mud flats in Lake Tezcoco that belonged to Azcapotzalco. Thus were founded, side by side in the lake, the twin Mexican cities Tlatilulco (Tlatelolco) and TENOCHTITLÁN.

The list of Mexican rulers of Tenochtitlán, which ultimately became the more important of the two cities, is as follows:

Acamapichtli (founder of the line but not an elected *tlatoani,* or ruler)	ca. 1375–1404
Huitzilihuitl	1391–1414
Chimalpopoca	1415–1427
Itzcoatl	1427–1440
Moctezuma I (Ilhuicamina)	1440–1468
Axayacatl	1469–1481
Tizoc	1481–1486
Ahuitzotl	1486–1502
Moctezuma II	1503–1520
Cuitlahuac	1520
Cuauhtémoc	1520–1521

From 1369 to 1427 Mexico paid tribute to Azcapotzalco and fought valiantly for that city in its wars of conquest. In 1428, with the aid of Nezahualcoyotl of Tezcoco, Mexico crushed Azcapotzalco and achieved its independence. The two allied cities were joined by Tlacopan to form a tripartite league that in letter, if not in spirit, lasted until the coming of Cortés. Fighting together, these confederate cities began a career of conquest that finally created a significant empire. Moctezuma I was the greatest of all the Mexican rulers, ranking with Nezahualcoyotl of Tezcoco, and under him the imperial Mexican state was fully formulated. He was aided in this by his brother and colleague Tlacaelel, an aggressive and commanding personality. In 1473 the Mexican island city Tlatilulco attacked Tenochtitlán and was defeated, to become thenceforth a mere ward in the amalgamated city.

Lake Tezcoco flooded in 1499, and Mexico was inundated and ruined. It had been reconstructed in *tezontli* stone by the opening of the reign of Moctezuma II. This ruler succeeded in reducing the two sister cities of the confederation to subservient status and thus transformed an Aztec empire into one that was strictly Mexican. In 1517 news of the Córdoba expedition to Yucatán filtered into the center of Mexico, and in 1518 Juan de Grijalva sailed up past the Aztec and Totonac cities of the Veracruz coast. Cortés himself landed in 1519, the year in which, according to Aztec prophecy, the god QUETZALCOATL would return to claim the throne of Mexico. This coincidence of myth and history had the effect of paralyzing Moctezuma's will to resist, and on November 9 Cortés entered the city of Mexico after a daring march upland through Tlascala and Cholula, both of which he subdued en route. Most of Mexico's former subjects and allies fell away from her and welcomed the Spaniards as saviors. Cortés arrested Moctezuma in his own palace and held him captive until his death before the *noche triste* (June 30, 1520), at which time the Spaniards were ejected from the city by a Mexican people who had recovered their confidence under a new ruler, Cuitlahuac. Cortés persisted in his efforts to take the city of Mexico and, aided by a huge army of Indian allies, finally succeeded. CUAUHTÉMOC, the last Mexican ruler, surrendered on August 14, 1521, after truly heroic resistance. The city was completely destroyed.

Economy. The city of Mexico lay approximately 1 mile offshore and probably had a population of close to 100,000. Tezcoco was considerably larger. Where the water was sufficiently sweet in Lake Tezcoco, cities were founded offshore and surrounded themselves with *chinampas,* large strips of lake mud and compost raised well above the surface and acting as permanently irrigated gardens. The great surplus of food produced by this specialized mode of agriculture goes far to explain the burgeoning of Aztec culture. MAIZE was the principal crop, but squash, beans, and chili peppers were also staples. Maguey was raised everywhere on the dry slopes, providing the Aztecs with a coarse thread, needles, fuel, thatching, and above all the intoxicating drink pulque (in NAHUATL, *octli*). There were no draft animals, and all distance carrying was done by a professional class of porters. The lake cities possessed large fleets of dugouts, which made transportation easy. Commerce was active and was carried on by merchants (*pochteca*) organized socially into guilds. In the latter years of the empire the *pochteca* became indispensable to the state as intelligence gatherers or spies. There was no network of imperial roads as in the Inca empire, and there were post-runner systems only on a few main-traveled routes (though performance here seems to have equaled the famed *chasqui* system of the INCAS). Commerce was mainly in private hands, though it never went counter to state policy.

Social organization. The typical Aztec state showed a pronounced tendency toward plural leadership, generally dual or quadruplicate. Mexico, for instance, had the custom of electing a council of four princes along with the ruler, the *tlatoani,* each with a distinctive title. Power resided in this council upon the death of a *tlatoani,* and it was the council that guided the discussions leading to the election of his successor. Priestly offices were as a rule distinct from these aforementioned executive offices, but there was one curious quasi-priestly position in Mexico permanently held in fief by one family—the office of *cihuacoatl.* In priestly terms this was an oracular office, and its incumbent wore the regalia and clothing of the goddess Cihuacoatl; in executive terms the office was viceregal. Thus, including the electoral college of the four princes, the *cihuacoatl,* and the *tlatoani,* the ruling body in Mexico was composed of six offices. Additionally, a Mexican *tlatoani,* to be elected properly, had to have the approval of his two co-emperors in Tezcoco and Tlacopan.

The typical Aztec society comprised at the top a warrior caste (the *teteuctin*) and an aristocracy (the *pipiltin*). A person could belong to both at once, of course, and the magnates generally did. The *teteuctin* were divided into war lodges, of which the two predominant ones were the eagle knights and the jaguar knights. Priests appear to have been a special social class. The typical city was organized around one central temple and then subdivided into wards, or CALPULLI.

Commoners (*macehualtin*) were held in contempt by the upper groups, but a *macehualli* who performed notably on the battlefield could be raised into the knightly rank, as could also merchants. Conversely, a *teuctli* could be deprived of his right to wear his knightly accouterments and be demoted into the vulgar class for cowardice or other egregious actions. The *macehualli* was a member of a certain *calpulli* and was assigned by that body an appropriate amount of land to cultivate and pay tribute on. Under him in the social scale was the landless day laborer, the *tlalmaitl,* who belonged to no *calpulli.* Slaves (*tlatlacotin*) existed in large numbers and formed an important article of commerce. A slave could purchase his freedom.

Religion and mythology. In terms of their pantheon of deities, the Aztec cities were eclectic, and pan-Mesoamerican gods such as Quetzalcoatl, Xipe Totec, Tlazolteotl, and Tlaloc were honored everywhere. The Aztecs also possessed gods who referred peculiarly to their Chichimec past, such as HUITZILOPOCHTLI, Camaxtli, and Mixcoatl. The god Tezcatlipoca presided over providence and assigned at whim good and evil destinies to men, from rulers down to commoners. Goddesses were as prominent as gods.

Aztec mythology was rich. The overriding concept was that of four past aeons, each created by a special god and later destroyed. The present age was the fifth one and was called into being when two gods sacrificed themselves in the fire at TEOTIHUACÁN and rose out of the ashes to become sun and moon. Added to this was the concept that the gods needed mankind's services and maintained their vitality only when given hearts as food and blood as drink; on this the Aztecs built their appalling cult of human sacrifice. While war could be mounted purely to gain land or prestige, it was also institutionalized as the means of acquiring ever-increasing numbers of prisoners who were to die that the gods might dine appropriately. A tournament war for the sole purpose of shedding blood on the battlefield and taking captives was known as a *xochiyaoyotl* (flower war). Warfare for the Aztecs was a most sacred activity and had been so designated by the gods. The state existed for the purpose of making war.

The arts. The Aztecs were a restrained people. They viewed life as a harsh lot imposed on the individual, and their pleasures and relaxations were correspondingly explosive. Choral dancing was essentially an act of worship and was exceptionally sophisticated and elegant. The game of *tlachtli,* played with a solid-rubber ball, was used for many ends, including pure sport, gambling, divination, and adjudication. The love of bright colors among the Aztecs was almost a hunger, and flowers were in constant use as adornment. Aztec poetry was generally limited to the themes of the transience of life and the warrior's greatness. The Nahuatl tongue has exceptional plasticity and can achieve oratorical effects of the highest order.

Aztec art is direct, unsophisticated, and monumental—a unique idiom. The visitor to the Aztec Hall of the Museo Nacional de Antropología in Mexico City will be aware of the heavy formalism of much of that art and, in such pieces as the Coatlicue, of an overpowering sense of death and terror.

Bibliography. A. J. O. Anderson and C. Dibble, *Florentine Codex,* 12 vols., Santa Fe, N.Mex., 1950–70; B. C. Brundage, *A Rain of Darts: The Mexica*

Aztecs, Austin, Tex., 1972; A. Caso, *Los calendarios prehispánicos,* Mexico City, 1967; C. Gibson, *The Aztecs under Spanish Rule,* Stanford, Calif., 1964; Francisco López de Gómara, *Cortés: The Life of the Conqueror by His Secretary,* tr. by L. B. Simpson, Berkeley, Calif., 1964; M. León-Portilla, *Aztec Thought and Culture,* Norman, Okla., 1963; H. B. Nicholson, "Religion in Pre-Hispanic Central Mexico," *Handbook of Middle American Indians,* vol. X, Austin, Tex., 1971, pp. 395–446; J. Soustelle, *The Daily Life of the Aztecs,* Harmondsworth, England, 1964.

BURR C. BRUNDAGE

AZUELA, MARIANO (1873–1952). Mexican novelist. Born in Jalisco, Azuela was trained as a doctor. His first novel, *María Luisa* (1907), was based on an article written during his student days. He was a liberal opposed to the regime of Porfirio DÍAZ, and his next novels, *Los fracasados* (1908) and *Mala yerba* (1909), show the development of the characteristics found in all his later work: social satire, a crude realism of expression, and a classic view of the novel form. *Andrés Pérez, maderista* (1911) begins a cycle of novels of the MEXICAN REVOLUTION that was to reflect Azuela's growing disappointment with the revolution's achievements.

Under Francisco I. MADERO, Azuela was political leader of Lagos de Moreno and director of education in Jalisco; when Madero was assassinated (1913), he joined the revolutionary forces of Julián Medina as a military doctor. He was exiled to Texas and there wrote his most famous novel, *Los de abajo,* 1916 (*Underdogs*), which was followed by *Los caciques,* 1917 (*The Bosses*), *Las moscas,* 1917 (*The Flies*), and the collection of stories *Domitilo quiere ser diputado* (1918).

In 1917 Azuela settled in Mexico City; his later novels evoke the atmosphere of city life. *La malhora* (1923), *El desquite* (1925), and *La luciérnaga* (1932) show experimentation with avant-garde literary techniques, but the chronicle form and the political and social satire of earlier works reappear in later novels. These include *Pedro Moreno, el insurgente* (1934), *Avanzada* (1940), *Nueva burguesía* (1941), *La mujer domada* (1946), *Sendas perdidas* (1949), and the posthumous *La maldición* (1955) and *Esa sangre* (1956). Azuela also wrote a volume of literary criticism, *Cien años de la novela mexicana* (1947), and made dramatic versions of some of his novels. His complete works were published in three volumes from 1958 to 1960.

RACHEL PHILLIPS

B

Babylonian Captivity

Bustos Domecq, Honorio

BABYLONIAN CAPTIVITY. Designation subsequently applied by Portuguese patriots to the sixty years (1580–1640) during which Portugal and its empire were incorporated in the Hapsburg dominions following the union of the Spanish and Portuguese crowns in the person of PHILIP II of Spain. For Brazil the period was marked by substantial opportunities, especially in the south, where a thriving contraband trade with Buenos Aires and Peru developed, and the *paulista* BANDEIRAS accelerated their exploration and slave raiding in the interior of the continent. Cattle ranching expanded in the region of the SÃO FRANCISCO VALLEY, and the sugar industry in Bahia and the NORTHEAST, which had been growing rapidly since 1570, reached major proportions (*see* SUGAR INDUSTRY: COLONIAL BRAZIL). Important judicial and administrative reorganization was undertaken; a RELAÇÃO (high court) was established in Bahia (modern Salvador, 1609), and the first inquisitorial visitation to Brazil took place (1591–1593; *see* INQUISITION, HOLY OFFICE OF THE). Spain's attempts to suppress the revolt of the Netherlands, however, caused severe repercussions for Portugal and its overseas possessions, where the Dutch were heavily involved commercially. Moreover, by the 1620s the disadvantages of the union with Spain were becoming more evident. With the ending of a Spanish truce with the Dutch in 1621 and the formation of the aggressive Dutch West India Company the same year, it was Brazil that bore the brunt of the renewed Dutch offensive. Bahia was lost temporarily in 1624, and in 1630 Pernambuco (modern Recife) fell. The Dutch based in Pernambuco took over most of the Northeast sugar-producing region. *See also* DUTCH IN BRAZIL.

The military pressure on the Spanish monarchy meanwhile led to added tax burdens on Portugal and caused increasing dissatisfaction with the Spanish connection. A successful uprising in Portugal during 1640 resulted in the reestablishment of Portugal's independence and the proclamation of the Duke of Braganza as King JOÃO IV. There was little immediate improvement in the Portuguese position in Brazil, but largely through the Brazilians' own efforts the Dutch were expelled from Pernambuco in 1654 after a decade of bitter warfare.

See also SEBASTIAN.

KENNETH R. MAXWELL

BÁEZ, BUENAVENTURA (1810–1882). President of the Dominican Republic (1849–1853, 1856–1857, 1865–1866, 1868–1873, 1876–†878). Báez alternated in the Presidency with Pedro SANTANA during the classic era of Dominican *caudillismo* and in the process helped retard the economic and institutional growth of the infant republic.

A mulatto landowner from the southern coastal area of the country, Báez himself felt he had no choice in the policies he pursued. Coming to power initially in the chaotic 1840s and 1850s, he was preoccupied with restoring a measure of order and economic solvency to the nation and with repelling the invading

Haitians, whose assaults had not ceased with the end of their occupation in 1844. He also had to deal with the imperialistic ambitions of the French, Spanish, British, and North Americans, all of whom were looking for fresh conquests and investment opportunities in the Caribbean.

Repeatedly exiled abroad or to his estate by his archenemy Santana, Báez returned to power following the Spanish occupation of 1861–1865. Now seeking an American protectorate, he approached the United States with a plan for annexation that barely failed of passage in the United States Senate. During his last term in office Báez also had the dubious distinction of helping snuff out some of the earliest sparks of Dominican liberalism.

HOWARD J. WIARDA

BÁEZ, CECILIO (1862–1941). Paraguayan diplomat, educator, philosopher, historian, and President (1905). Báez, who received a doctorate in law in 1893, had one of the most versatile political careers in Latin America. He began as an official in the Ministry of the Interior, became Minister to Washington and Mexico, next Minister of Foreign Affairs, then President of the Republic; he went on to be Paraguayan Minister successively to London, Paris, and Rome and, finally, Paraguayan Delegate to the League of Nations. In addition, he was at various times a professor of history, sociology, law, and philosophy at the National University, which he served as rector from 1929 until his death. One of the leading positivists of the Americas, Báez was an extremely prolific writer, leaving more than a score of major works dealing with philosophy, history, diplomatic affairs, and, most notably, the thorny problem of the CHACO boundaries, on which subject he is considered the leading Paraguayan authority.

JOHN HOYT WILLIAMS

BAHIA. See SALVADOR.

BAJÍO. Region in western Mexico, distinctive as an important grain-producing zone. The Bajío is a nearly flat area made up of the alluvial bottoms of ancient lakes into which flowed the rivers that descended along the southern slope of the sierra of Zacatecas. These lakes dried up when they were channeled by the Lerma River. The importance of the Bajío derives from its agricultural production and high demographic concentration as well as from its being the hub of heavily traveled routes that link the center of Mexico with the west and northwest of the plateau and with the regions leading to the Sierra Madre del Sur and the valley of the Río de las Balsas. The eastern Bajío (Celaya and Salamanca) is distinguished from the western Bajío (from Irapuato to León), but economic indicators such as rural emigration, salaries, and relative importance of various crops suggest that there is only one bloc, stretching from the plains emanating from the basin of Querétaro to those located to the north and south of Lake Chapala. Because of the low elevation near Chapala, wheat cultivation disappears and cane sugar appears. Some of the most important episodes in Mexican history took place in the Bajío: the beginning of the war for independence, the end of the empire of MAXIMILIAN, and the Battles of Celaya (see CELAYA, BATTLES OF),

decisive in the course of the MEXICAN REVOLUTION of 1910. The Cristeros (see CRISTERO REBELLION) were extremely powerful in this region, as was SINARQUISMO, the most important right-wing mass movement of the twentieth century.

MOISÉS GONZÁLEZ NAVARRO

BALAGUER, JOAQUÍN (1907–   ). President of the Dominican Republic (1960–1962, 1966–   ). Reelected for another four-year term in 1970, Balaguer remained in many ways an enigma. Scholar, intellectual, poet, and university professor, he had been elevated by the dictator Rafael Leonidas TRUJILLO MOLINA to the Vice Presidency and later to the Presidency of one of the most tyrannous and unintellectual regimes in Latin American history. Ruling during one of the bloodiest and most corrupt periods of Trujillo's long rule, Balaguer was apparently untainted by the degeneration that surrounded him. Ousted from the Presidency in the wake of the strong *antitrujillista* sentiment that exploded in 1961–1962, Balaguer was subsequently returned to office in two presidential elections that offered undoubted proof of his popular support. Though a mild, ascetic, and meek man hardly in keeping with the older Dominican tradition of rough-and-tumble *caudillos,* Balaguer remained a shrewd, skillful, cunning politician, able to dominate stronger and more charismatic personalities, not only surviving but thriving in the dangerous and shifting quicksands of Dominican politics.

Vice President at the time the dictator's brother Héctor Trujillo was serving as puppet President, Balaguer succeeded to the Presidency upon Héctor's resignation in 1960. When the elder Trujillo was assassinated the following year, Balaguer attempted to preside over the difficult postdictatorial transition, ruling first with the son and heir "Ramfis" Trujillo, then on his own, and finally sharing power with a six-man Council of State. Amid these fast-moving developments Balaguer's political skills were put to the test. After eight months, however, he was driven from office and into exile, paving the way for new elections in 1962.

Returning to the country following the revolution of 1965 (see DOMINICAN REVOLT), Balaguer again became a presidential candidate. Running a skillful, well-financed campaign and profiting from the shift of many Dominicans from bloodshed and revolution, as well as from the campaign of terror and intimidation launched against his opponents, Balaguer presented himself as the candidate of peace, moderation, and normalcy. In 1966 he handily beat Juan BOSCH and was again installed in the Presidential Palace.

In office on his own for the first time, Balaguer proved a remarkably durable President. Warding off attacks from left and right, cleverly manipulating appointments and programs, and playing one faction or individual off against another while steering a middle course, Balaguer both persisted and grew stronger. Ruling in a highly personalist and paternalistic manner, he sought to juggle political forces, meanwhile reinvigorating the economy and developing the country. His opponents continued to claim that Balaguer had sold out democracy, civil liberties, and the country and that powerful United States interests and "uncontrollable" military-civilian forces were in effect running the nation. There was truth in these charges, but there was also something to say for Balaguer's accomplishments. In 1970 Balaguer won another term as President in a plebiscite boycotted by the principal opposition.

HOWARD J. WIARDA

BALBOA, VASCO NÚÑEZ DE (1475–1519). Spanish explorer. Balboa was born in Jerez de los Caballeros in the province of Badajoz. During his early years he served as a page to Don Pedro Puertocarrero, lord of Moguer. In 1500 he sailed from Spain with Rodrigo de Bastidas, a wealthy notary, to trade for pearls along the north coast of South America behind the island of Margarita, where Columbus had learned these jewels were to be found. Settling in Santo Domingo as a planter, he fell into debt. To escape his creditors he stowed away on a ship owned by Martín Fernández de Enciso that was carrying relief provisions to a party which had sailed for Darién under the command of Alonso de OJEDA. Meeting the survivors of that expedition, Enciso forced them to return to San Sebastián, the town Ojeda had founded on the east side of the Gulf of Urabá. Upon their return they found the settlement destroyed by the natives. Balboa recalled from his voyage with Bastidas that a town existed on the west shore of the gulf, and the party sailed across the gulf to the vicinity of the Darién River, where they founded the town of Santa María de la Antigua del Darién.

Balboa then turned his attention to the neighboring region of Coiba. He made an alliance with the local chief, Careta, who sealed it by offering his daughter in marriage to Balboa and arranged an alliance with another powerful cacique, Comogre. This led to a fortuitous occurrence. The eldest of Comogre's sons, disgusted by the greed of the Spaniards, declared that he would lead them to a land on the other side of the mountains that was so rich in gold they would be sated with the metal. Balboa now determined to find this land of gold and, accompanied by 190 armed Spaniards as well as by natives, left Darién on September 1, 1513. The party plunged into the jungle and climbed mountains in what is still some of the most difficult terrain in the world. On the morning of September 27, accompanied only by his dog, Balboa climbed the "peak in Darién" and became the first European to look upon the Pacific from its eastern shore. He and his men spent some days marching to the sea so as to take formal possession. This act took place on September 29, St. Michael's Day, and Balboa called the place the Golfo de San Miguel.

Balboa spent a month amassing gold and pearls before he began the return journey to Darién, which he reached on January 19, 1514. Not only could he announce the triumph of the discovery of the South Sea, but the feat had been accomplished without the loss of a single Spanish life. The triumph was short-lived. Heeding the complaints of Enciso, who was still smarting because Balboa had deposed him, and of others who were filled with envy, King Ferdinand II appointed Pedro Arias de ÁVILA as Governor. Pedrarias, filled with hatred and envy, bided his time and then tricked Balboa into relaxing his guard. Arrested by Francisco

PIZARRO, Balboa was tried for treason and beheaded in Acla during the period between January 13 and 21, 1519.

MARTIN TORODASH

BALDOMIR, ALFREDO (1884–1948). President of Uruguay (1938–1943). Baldomir was born in Montevideo. During more than three decades as a military engineer and architect, he rose to the rank of general and also served as Minister of National Defense during the period 1935–1936. Among other positions he held in the early 1930s were those of chief of military construction and chief of police for the capital.

The brother-in-law of President Gabriel TERRA, Baldomir was the first popularly elected President to serve under the 1934 constitution. Whereas his predecessor had governed by decree after the 1933 coup, Baldomir encountered strong opposition from the Blancos (see BLANCO PARTY: URUGUAY), manifested both in the blocking of legislation and in criticism of the government's cooperation with the United States in World War II. After a particularly harsh Blanco attack on the government's break with the Axis Powers in January 1942, Baldomir dissolved the General Assembly, postponed the elections scheduled for the following March, and replaced the three Blancos in the Cabinet with members of his own Colorado party (see COLORADO PARTY: URUGUAY).

When elections were held in November 1942, voters once again favored the Colorados and by a margin of more than 3 to 1 approved a set of constitutional amendments designed to prevent minority opposition from obstructing government action. Among the changes was a Senate based upon proportional representation rather than the 50-50 party distribution established in the 1934 constitution.

LEE C. FENNELL

BALLAGAS, EMILIO (1908–1954). Cuban poet. Ballagas was born in Camagüey. His first poems appeared in the review *Antenas* (1928–1929). He developed as an important exponent of both the so-called pure poetry in the European symbolist tradition, with *Júbilo y fuga* (1931), and "black" poetry inspired by African rhythms and religion, with *Poesía negra* (1934), *Antología de la poesía negra hispanoamericana* (1935), *Lira negra* (1945), and *Mapa de la poesía negra americana* (1946). His volumes *Elegías sin nombre* (1936), *Nocturno y elegía* (1938), and *Sabor eterno* (1939) reflect disappointments in love and metaphysical anguish, but his last volumes show a renewed Catholic faith, as in *Nuestra señora del mar* (1943) and *Cielo en rehenes*. Ballagas's collected poetry appeared in 1955.

RACHEL PHILLIPS

BALLIVIÁN, JOSÉ (1804–1852). Bolivian military leader and President (1842–1847). Ballivián, born in La Paz of distinguished parents, was one of the ablest military men of his age and became one of Bolivia's most enlightened nineteenth-century presidents. Mostly self-educated, he entered the Army at an early age and through it sought glory and advancement. He took part in the early attempts by the Spanish crown to suppress rebellion in the Río de la Plata area, but later he joined the rebels and participated in many of the military campaigns that finally brought independence to Bolivia.

Ballivián was an early supporter of Andrés SANTA CRUZ, but after his mentor's defeat at Yungay in 1839 he rebelled against him. Later, during his own administration, he expended a great deal of energy to ensure that Santa Cruz did not return to Bolivia.

Ballivián's military fame rests on his important victory in the Battle of Ingavi (1841) against an invading Peruvian army. The victory enhanced his prestige and helped him gain the Presidency in 1842. He ruled autocratically until 1847, displaying little faith in his people's ability to rule themselves and confident that Bolivia's salvation could be ensured only by strong military rule. Nevertheless, he proved to be a relatively enlightened administrator. He devoted considerable attention to education, launched a road-building program, financed the exploration of uncharted regions of the country, and generally encouraged efforts to integrate the nation and make it more accessible to the outside world. However, throughout his regime he was plagued by military revolts, which eventually led to his resignation (1847) and to a self-imposed exile, first in Santiago and later in Rio de Janeiro, where he died.

ORAZIO A. CICCARELLI

BALMACEDA, JOSÉ MANUEL (1840–1891). President of Chile (1886–1891). Born into an aristocratic family in Santiago and educated at a Catholic seminary, Balmaceda entered Congress in 1864 as deputy for Carelmapu, retaining his seat until 1882. It was also in 1864 that he accompanied ex-President Manuel MONTT on a diplomatic mission to Lima, an influential event in his early life. Through eloquence and ability he soon established a reputation in the advanced wing of the Liberal party (*see* LIBERAL PARTY: CHILE) and in the Club de la Reforma, the meeting place of those seeking to reform the constitution of 1833 by reducing presidential power, ensuring free elections, and diminishing the power of the church (*see* CONSTITUTION OF 1833: CHILE). Appointed Envoy Extraordinary to Buenos Aires in 1878, he kept Argentina neutral during the WAR OF THE PACIFIC to Chile's benefit, and as Foreign Minister in 1881 he again showed his diplomatic talents by preventing the calling of an inter-American conference to intervene in the peace settlement, thus enabling Chile to dictate its own terms to Peru and Bolivia. Elected deputy for Santiago in 1882 and appointed Minister of the Interior, Balmaceda piloted through Congress controversial clerical reforms. He thus became the Liberal idol to succeed President Domingo Santa María, although a small group in the party, led by Miguel Luis AMUNÁTEGUI, objected to the way his candidacy was imposed.

Balmaceda assumed office in 1886, seeking to reunite the Liberals and bring the Radicals and the National party into the government, leaving only the Conservatives in opposition (*see* CONSERVATIVE PARTY: CHILE; RADICAL PARTY: CHILE). He began his term in an atmosphere of conciliation in order to secure maximum support for his real program, the investment of nitrate revenues in permanent public improvements (*see* NITRATE INDUSTRY: CHILE). In 1887 a new Ministry of Public Works was created, and by 1890 its budget had been increased four times. Educational expenditure tripled in the same period, and there was an unprecedented expansion of construction and communications,

José Manuel Balmaceda. [Organization of American States]

as schools were built, railway and telegraph networks were expanded, and public amenities grew.

Balmaceda's obsession with this vast program made him impatient of criticism, and he came to see often-justified attacks on it as affronts to himself. Moreover, the program depended on nitrate income, and most of the industry lay in foreign, mainly British, hands. The world nitrate market was unstable, and the creation of new companies in the 1880s by John Thomas North, the "Nitrate King," threatened to overstock it: the traditional reaction of producers in these circumstances was to reduce output until supply and demand again coincided. To counteract this threat to government income, Balmaceda made a number of speeches against foreign interests in Chile and tried to break North's growing monopoly in nitrates by encouraging Chilean investors and North's British competitors.

Nevertheless, the nitrate issue was overshadowed by internal political events. Balmaceda failed to unite the political factions, and by 1888 he had abandoned the dream of Liberal unity. Moreover, he lost the support of important groups and eventually his congressional majority through his vacillating and imperious behavior and their unwillingness to compromise. A long-maturing conflict between President and Congress now came to a head. During the nineteenth century constitutional precedents that were not embodied in law had developed and had come to be accepted; for example, ministers, though appointed by Presidents, had to be acceptable to Congress. Second, political opinion now demanded an end to executive interference in elections, a means whereby Presidents secured progovernment majorities in Congress. Formerly Balmaceda had supported these views; as President he stood firmly by the prerogatives conferred on him by the constitution and accepted the practices of his predecessors. Conflict became inevitable when Balmaceda refused to dismiss ministers censured by Congress, and Congress suspected that he intended to interfere in the elections of 1891 in order to impose his chosen successor. Late in 1890 Congress refused to pass essential laws for 1891, and on January 1, 1891, Balmaceda unconstitutionally extended existing laws.

A week later the Chilean Navy, with many Congressionalists on board, left Valparaíso to begin civil war. The Army remained loyal to Balmaceda. The revolutionaries seized the northern nitrate provinces, but neither side could attack the other, since Balmaceda lacked ships to move his army north, his opponents lacked arms to ship an army south, and the barren ATACAMA DESERT lay between them. Eight months of stalemate ended when the Congressionalists acquired arms from Europe, landed near Valparaíso late in August 1891, and routed Balmaceda's armies at Concón and Placilla. Balmaceda took refuge in the Argentine Embassy, where, on September 19, he committed suicide, leaving behind him a remarkably accurate prophecy of Chile's future political development. The dynamism of his life and the drama of his death gave Balmaceda a posthumous reputation as the most progressive statesman of nineteenth-century Chile and as a visionary whose defeat in 1891 was a catastrophe for the republic.

Bibliography. J. Bañados Espinosa, *Balmaceda, su gobierno y la revolución de 1891,* 2 vols., Paris, 1894; Harold Blakemore, "Chilean Revolutionary Agents in Europe, 1891," *Pacific Historical Review,* vol. XXXIII, no. 4, November 1964, pp. 425–446; id., "The Chilean Revolution of 1891 and Its Historiography," *Hispanic American Historical Review,* vol. XLV, no. 2, August 1965, pp. 393–421; F. A. Encina, *Balmaceda,* 2 vols., Santiago, 1952; Maurice Hervey, *Dark Days in Chile,* London, 1892; Hernán Ramírez Necochea, *Balmaceda y la contrarrevolución de 1891,* 2d ed., Santiago, 1969; J. M. Yrarrázaval, *El presidente Balmaceda,* 2 vols., Santiago, 1940.

HAROLD BLAKEMORE

BALTA, JOSÉ (1814–1872). President of Peru (1868–1872). A *limeño* of humble origins, the colorful and temperamental Balta rose to the Presidency of Peru after a long career of political and military intrigue. He was neither the head of a political party nor the representative of a special interest group or political ideology, although he leaned toward conservatism. Balta was an unknown entity when he came to office in 1868, except for the fact that he had been instrumental in the overthrow of the liberals in 1867.

Peruvian historians are divided in their assessment of Balta's four-year regime. There is less controversy over the argument that Balta, an untutored soldier, was the wrong leader for those times of serious economic difficulties. To be sure, he took great care in selecting his ministers. However, to the key Ministry of Finance he appointed Nicolás de PIÉROLA, with whom he shared the vision of quick material progress. This called for heavy expenditures at a time when retrenchment would have been advisable. He dreamed of crisscrossing Peru with railroads that would open it up to greater development and to the establishment of political order. To these ends he allocated 128 million soles, most of it borrowed in Europe. He increased the foreign debt from £4 million to £50 million, thus placing Peru more than ever at the mercy of foreign creditors. Railroads were favored to the neglect of everything else—education, agriculture, industry, health. Yet they failed to provide the economic and political benefits that had been envisioned. On the contrary, the expenditures brought Peru to the threshold of bankruptcy and of political chaos. The deepening political divisions were reflected in the bloody Gutiérrez brothers' revolt of 1872, during which Balta was assassinated by the rebels. *See also* DREYFUS CONTRACT; MEIGGS, HENRY.

ORAZIO A. CICCARELLI

BALTIMORE AFFAIR (1891–1892). Diplomatic incident between Chile and the United States. During the Chilean revolution of 1891, the American Minister in Chile, Patrick Egan, sympathized with President José Manuel BALMACEDA and, on his defeat, offered asylum to some Balmacedists, thus arousing hostility in Santiago. Shortly afterward, Capt. Winfield S. Schley of the U.S.S. *Baltimore,* then in Chilean waters, unwisely gave shore leave to part of his crew; a brawl took place, two sailors died, and several were wounded. The Chilean Foreign Minister, M. A. Matta, brusquely dismissed the State Department's protest, and on December 9, 1891, President Benjamin Harrison promised to consult Congress "for such action as may be necessary" if Chile did not send a satisfactory reply. Matta then sent a telegram to Chile's unaccredited Minister in Washington, imputing dishonesty to Egan and bluster to Harrison, and a serious crisis developed. The Chilean government dismissed Matta, but its request that Secretary of State James G. Blaine accept withdrawal of parts of the telegram was flatly refused, as was a request for Egan's recall.

On January 25, 1892, Harrison sent the full correspondence to Congress, threatening war unless Chile met all American demands, but the same day the Chilean government expressed regret for the incident, withdrew both the telegram and the request for Egan's recall, and offered compensation. Bitterly resented in Chile, the incident left a legacy of anti-Americanism for the rest of the decade.

HAROLD BLAKEMORE

BANANA INDUSTRY (CENTRAL AMERICA AND THE CARIBBEAN). Originally a Spanish transplant from the Canary Islands, bananas thrived in the American tropics as though they were indigenous. Wild and cultivated, they became a domestic food source and an article of trade, but extreme perishability restricted their range to local distribution.

Progressively during the latter half of the nineteenth century Caribbean growers found an export market for bananas. However, the natural ripening span of the fruit imposed a rigid limit on the interval between lading and marketing that effectively restricted distribution to the United States. By 1898 imports for shipside sale or limited dispersion around Gulf and Atlantic port cities reached an annual total of approximately 16 million stems.

Consolidation of two of the better-organized operations in 1899 to form the UNITED FRUIT COMPANY initiated the large-scale integrated phase of the banana industry. Increasingly sophisticated production techniques, progression from sail to steam propulsion and then to swift refrigerated cargo vessels, and the development of auxiliary services to facilitate the coordination of widely separated activities neutralized some hazards in the industry and widened the range of feasible fruit distribution to include Europe.

Commercial banana culture gave a fresh thrust to economic development in tropical America. In Jamaica it rallied the economy from a depression caused by the decline of the old sugar culture after the emancipation of the slaves. In Central America generally and to an important extent in Colombia and Ecuador, it opened and brought to high productivity previously unpopulated and worthless tropical lowland areas. Circumstances allowed American tropical countries virtually to monopolize production of the new export commodity. Costa Rica led world banana production by 1909, Honduras gained that position in the 1940s, and Ecuador attained first rank in 1951. In 1969 bananas ranked first among the exports of Honduras and Panama and held second rank in Costa Rica and fourth in Jamaica and Guatemala. That year banana production was estimated at 1,350,000 metric tons in Honduras, 967,000 metric tons in Costa Rica, and 900,000 metric tons in Panama.

Banana prosperity was checked by plant disease. Panama disease, a fusarium that attacks rhizomes and roots, appeared as early as 1915, and sigatoka, an airborne fungus that destroys leaves and dwarfs the fruit, appeared about 1930. Particularly during the 1930s and the early 1940s, these diseases devastated plantations in Jamaica, Colombia, Panama, Costa Rica, Honduras, and Guatemala, but the development of production in Ecuador largely offset the decline elsewhere. Cultivation in Jamaica, Colombia, and Honduras generally succumbed to Panama disease, but in Panama, Costa Rica, and Guatemala the companies shifted operations from the Caribbean to the Pacific side. Subsequently abandoned areas were reoccupied, as spraying controlled sigatoka, flood fallowing temporarily rehabilitated acreage polluted by Panama disease, and the disease-resistant Cavendish and Valerie varieties proved suitable for commercial production.

Banana cultivation developed under disparate systems of organization, labor, and land tenure. The most publicized system is the huge corporately owned and operated plantation. Units of this type were established to produce and ship fruit, but since they were situated in isolated and primitive environments, they were forced also to undertake a wide variety of sustaining functions. Among other auxiliary enterprises, they developed local food production, transport and communications systems, living quarters for workers and supervisory personnel, health services, recreational facilities, school systems, and certain devices for governance. They have often been regarded as separate entities related to the governments that hold jurisdiction over them in ways subsumed in the term "banana republic."

Elsewhere individual small cultivators dominate an important segment of banana production. In Jamaica former slaves acquired small holdings near the north coast and began to cultivate and sell bananas. Although large-scale operations appeared as the export business developed, small producers remained the principal suppliers. A similar pattern developed in Ecuador. In both cases independent buyers purchase fruit and assemble cargoes for client shippers.

The current trend is away from production by large plantations in favor of individual cultivators. Sustained criticism of the companies' internal involvements, labor disputes involving nationals, and progressively mounting pressure applied by increasingly nationalistic governments persuaded the companies that direct production had ceased to be desirable or feasible. At the same time, matured communities in the plantation areas composed of experienced cultivators made corporate production no longer necessary. The companies therefore have moved to dispose of land and appurtenances to individual cultivators and of internal auxiliary enterprises to governments or other appropriate agencies. The role they appear to reserve for themselves is to provide technical advice and service to local producers, buy their crops, assemble and prepare cargoes, and ship and market the fruit.

See also BANANA INDUSTRY (ECUADOR).

Bibliography. Preston E. James, *Latin America,* 4th ed., New York, 1969; Charles D. Kepner, *Social Aspects of the Banana Industry,* New York, 1936; Charles D. Kepner and Jay H. Soothill, *The Banana Empire: A Case Study of Economic Imperialism,* New York, 1935; Stacy May and Galo Plaza, *The United Fruit Company in Latin America,* New York, 1958; Robert C. West and John P. Augelli, *Middle America: Its Lands and Peoples,* Englewood Cliffs, N.J., 1966; Charles Morrow Wilson, *Ambassadors in White: The Story of American Tropical Medicine,* New York, 1942; id., *Empire in Green and Gold: The Story of the American Banana Trade,* New York, 1947.

WILLIAM J. GRIFFITH

BANANA INDUSTRY (ECUADOR). Ecuador is the world's largest exporter of bananas, although its relative importance declined from 28 percent of world trade in the early 1960s to approximately 20 percent in the early 1970s. Bananas have composed as much as 65 percent of the nation's exports, but their share has fallen to slightly below half. Banana production in Ecuador is almost unique in Latin America, since it developed and continued to flourish on relatively small-scale farms. Today the industry is facing increased competition because of a resurgence of banana exports from traditional suppliers as well as the emergence of new exporters. To continue to export at the present rate the nation will have to make significant changes in production techniques as well as greatly improve marketing facilities.

The banana was introduced into the country during the colonial period and since then has been an important constituent of the national diet, especially in the coastal plain (*see* COSTA: ECUADOR). Although the UNITED FRUIT COMPANY established a banana plantation in Ecuador in 1933, it was not until after World War II that there was a rapid expansion in production for export. Growth was due largely to difficulties experienced in the world's largest commercial banana-producing region, Central America. Panama disease and sigatoka had wrought great damage to export banana production in Central America, as had periodic hurricanes. Furthermore, the rise in nationalism was making it difficult for the plantations to operate without growing government intervention. *See* BANANA INDUSTRY (CENTRAL AMERICA AND THE CARIBBEAN).

Ecuador provided a good physical environment for commercial production. Rich alluvial soils derived from the volcanic highlands are found along the piedmont of the ANDES MOUNTAINS and cover the floodplains of rivers that flow to the Pacific. The climate is tropical, with ample rainfall in most parts of the coastal plain. Windstorms are rare, and at the time the industry was expanding, Panama disease and sigatoka presented no problems. To avoid the political complications that had arisen in Central America, the banana companies did not open plantations. The early United Fruit Company plantation was turned into an experimental farm, and small owner-operated farms were encouraged. The banana companies continue to offer technical advice and to operate marketing facilities at the ports.

Bananas are both highly perishable and low in value compared with their weight. Commercial production needs a well-integrated transportation network. To facilitate this the government invested in a series of roads that permitted bananas to be trucked to Guayaquil and the other major banana port, Esmeraldas. Production has also been encouraged by the sale of government land on liberal credit terms as well as the formation of a government banana board in which considerable power has been vested.

The major region of banana production is the Guayas Basin, where rivers as well as roads permit the easy transport of bananas to the port of Guayaquil. Roads have been extended northward, and two towns, Quevedo and Santo Domingo, have experienced huge population increases with the development of banana production in their hinterlands. An older area of banana production is found near the port of Esmeraldas, but it has lost relative importance to the Guayas Basin because sigatoka is more difficult to control there. A third small area of production is situated in the extreme south, near Puerto Bolívar, where the crop is raised under irrigation. Higher production costs due to irrigation are compensated for by the relative freedom from sigatoka and consequent relief from the expense of spraying.

Although sigatoka has been brought under control by spraying, little has been done to halt the spread of Panama disease. There has been a considerable increase in the use of Panama disease–resistant Cavendish-type bananas, which have overtaken the Gros Michel in importance. In 1966 the National Banana Board prohibited further plantings of the Gros Michel varieties and, in a step to control production, restricted banana farms to a maximum of 200 hectares. The growth in production of the more easily damaged Cavendish-type banana has radically altered banana marketing in Ecuador, since they must be exported in boxes. Ecuadorian producers suffer from poor quality control, which is ascribed to the small size of the production units and to the inability of growers to buy irrigation equipment to water plants during dry periods. The methods of marketing bananas from farm to port cause much damage to the fruit, especially to the delicate Cavendish banana. Presently bananas are loaded on trucks and hauled over rough roads to the docks. Of the total banana production, about 30 percent is exported, and approximately 25 percent is consumed fresh domestically. Most of the remainder either rots or is fed to cattle. Factories that produce banana wine, dehydrated bananas, and banana flour have been established, but they consume only small amounts of fruit. Clearly there is a need for greater control of production.

World production of bananas is growing at least as rapidly as demand, and the successful competitors in the search for markets will have to maintain low production costs, avoid excessive wastage, and market a high-quality exportable fruit. With the recent revitalization of banana production along the Caribbean coast of Central America, Ecuador is put in a difficult position. The quality of fruit shipped from Central America is better than that of Ecuador's fruit, and shipping charges to United States Atlantic and Gulf ports are lower. Ecuador grows a tasty fruit, but often the banana arrives at its destination bruised. Although the bruises do not affect taste, the high standards of appearance required by United States consumers have meant that Ecuadorian bananas have been declining in importance in United States markets. Fortunately, consumers in Europe still are not so demanding, and that market remains firm. Ecuador is attempting to open new markets, particularly throughout the Pacific, and it has begun to sell to Chile and Japan.

Bibliography. Charles R. Gibson, *Foreign Trade in the Economic Development of Small Nations: The Case of Ecuador,* New York, 1971; Luis Aníbal Mendoza, *Geografía económica del Ecuador,* Guayaquil, 1966; James J. Parsons, "Bananas in Ecuador: A New Chapter in the History of Tropical Agriculture," *Economic Geography,* vol. 33, 1957, pp. 201–216; D. A. Preston, "Changes in the Economic Geography of Banana Production in Ecuador," *Transactions of British Geographers,* no. 37, December 1965, pp. 77–90; United States Department of Agriculture, Economic Research Service, *World Demand Prospects for Bananas in 1980,* Foreign Agricultural Economic Report No. 69, February 1971.

MORTON D. WINSBERG

BANCO INTERAMERICANO DE DESARROLLO. *See* INTER-AMERICAN DEVELOPMENT BANK.

BANDEIRA [FILHO], MANUEL [CARNEIRO DE SOUSA] (1886–1968). Brazilian poet, essayist, journalist, professor, and member of the Brazilian Academy of Letters. Born into an old family of Recife, he was tubercular in his youth and spent a year in a Swiss sanatorium. He went to Rio de Janeiro, where he became a journalist and later taught in the College of Pedro II and the University of Brazil. In spite of the excellence and quantity of his prose, exemplified in his autobiography, *Itinerário de Pasárgada* (1954), and his classic *Guia de Ouro Prêto* (1938), he is best known as a poet. He began his career as a symbolist, as is evident in *A Cinza das Horas* (1917), *Carnaval* (1919), and *O Ritmo Dissoluto,* published in *Poesias Completas* in 1924. However, in the last two volumes a new feeling for Brazilian values and innovations in technique that show the influence of modernism can be detected (*see* MODERNISM: BRAZIL). His recollections of his childhood in Recife furnished the themes of some of his most notable poems, such as "Na Rua do Sabão," "Evocação do Recife," and "Profundamente." In succeeding volumes like *Lira dos Cinquent' Anos* and *Belo, Belo,* published in the *Poesias Completas* of 1940 and 1948 respectively, alongside the nostalgic verse about a dead past, a growing disillusionment, a recurring note of irony, and a lessening of sentimentality become evident. Bandeira wrote poems in prose, repunctuated newspaper articles into verse, produced "Compositions" which are concretist in effect, and transcribed lyrics that came to him in dreams.

RAYMOND S. SAYERS

BANDEIRAS. Quasi-military expeditions originating in São Paulo that penetrated deep into the interior of South America and succeeded in establishing Portugal's claims well beyond the theoretical line of the Treaty of Tordesillas (*see* TORDESILLAS, TREATY OF). São Paulo, though only 50 miles from the Atlantic, was situated on the interior escarpment with land and riverine access to the continental interior and the RÍO DE LA PLATA Basin via the Tieté and Paraná Rivers. Since the local economy yielded only a bare subsistence and the region was inhabited by a strongly mixed Euro-Amerindian population, the organization of slaving forays provided one of the few sources of profit for the inhabitants. Although the first expeditions took place in the late sixteenth century, they were most intense between 1628 and 1641. The *bandeiras* might contain as many as 3,000 men and remain in the interior years at a time. The *paulistas,* who were accompanied by large numbers of Indian auxiliaries, themselves adopted many Amerindian techniques of travel and warfare. Slaves obtained were sold on the Brazilian littoral to sugar planters; monetary gains were never excessive, however, as Indian slaves always fetched less than Africans. With the capture of Portugal's African slave depots by the Dutch in the seventeenth century, the *paulista* traffic increased considerably. Indian missions operated by the Jesuits were a favorite target of *bandeira* raids, but the Jesuits armed the Indians and were able to defeat the *paulistas* near the Mbororé River in 1641. With the recapture of Angola by Salvador Correia de Sá (1648) the *paulistas* turned to geopolitical explorations on behalf of the Portuguese authorities. The most famous was the 8,000-mile *bandeira* of Antônio Rapôso Tavares between 1648 and 1652, which traveled from São Paulo to Mato Grosso and the Bolivian Andes, returning to the Atlantic by way of the AMAZON RIVER. *Paulistas* also found employment as agents of internal repression, as in the campaign against the fugitive slave settlement of PALMARES (1692–1694). And increasingly the *paulistas* set out in search of precious metals. At the end of the seventeenth century they discovered the rich gold fields of Minas Gerais, and some years later those of Goiás and Mato Grosso. With the gold rush that followed, the old *paulista* dominance of the interior was broken. The great age of exploration found its fulfillment in 1750, when the boundaries of Portuguese America that the *bandeiras* had done much to establish were agreed on and recognized by the Treaty of Madrid (*see* MADRID, TREATY OF).

KENNETH R. MAXWELL

BANKING. Although the first banks in Brazil and Argentina were established during or shortly after the independence period, the development of banking in the Latin American republics dates generally from the third quarter of the nineteenth century, when economic expansion and increased foreign trade called for changes in monetary systems and the establishment of new institutions for the provision of credit (*see* TRADE: 1810–1940). Before the establishment of banks some banking functions were performed by mercantile houses, particularly those engaged in trade between Great Britain and Latin America, which made advances in connection with commercial operations and in some cases issued certificates of deposit.

Neither the first Banco do Brasil, established in 1808 soon after the arrival of the Portuguese court, nor the Banco de Buenos Aires, founded in 1822 and financed largely by Anglo-Argentine merchants, was destined to survive. In Brazil, however, new and more successful ventures in commercial banking were undertaken from the mid-1830s onward, and domestic banking was firmly established by 1862, when it first met foreign competition. In Argentina, the Banco de la Provincia de Buenos Aires, created in 1854, played an important part in the financial history of the republic during the next forty years, and it remains one of the largest commercial banks in the country.

From the 1880s onward domestically financed banks multiplied rapidly in all the more highly developed countries of the region. Many of them operated with too little capital and collapsed either as a result of their own ill-advised speculations or in one of the periodic financial crises, one of the worst of which, that in the RÍO DE LA PLATA countries in 1891, ruined even the semiofficial banks. The smaller banks often merged with larger and more stable institutions, and many of the most important domestic banks now operating date from the late nineteenth century. This period also saw the creation of the first mortgage and savings banks in the more highly developed countries.

Although the tendency toward regionalism was always present and many small local banks existed, local banking institutions remained relatively weak. As a result of this weakness and in the absence of any legislation to prevent countrywide banking, branch banking developed on European lines instead of toward the multiplicity of unit banks characteristic of the United States. In most countries there are two or three commercial banks far larger than any of the others, and often one official or semiofficial commercial bank has far more branches and a much greater volume of deposits than any of its rivals.

Foreign banks. While the earliest banks in the more advanced republics were financed domestically, the establishment of sound banking institutions generally owed much to foreign banks, which in many cases were actually the first in the field. The earliest of them was the London, Buenos Ayres and River Plate Bank, formed in London in 1862 by a group of merchants interested in Río de la Plata trade. Others followed rapidly with branches in Brazil and in Mexico, where the first real bank was a branch of the London Bank of Mexico and South America. British banks dominated the field in foreign trade for about twenty-five years and spread to all parts of the continent where there were British trading or investment interests. A Bank of Tarapacá and London, for example, was set up in 1888 to serve the nitrate industry in northern Chile (*see* NITRATE INDUSTRY: CHILE). The various British banking interests were ultimately absorbed into the Bank of London and South America.

German banks were among the first and most vigorous competitors of the British. As the stream of immigration strengthened still further the links between Europe and Latin America, banks were established to serve the common interests of the migrants and their relatives and to foster trade between the mother countries and Latin America. By the outbreak of World War I in 1914 banks capitalized from Britain, Germany, France, Spain, Italy, Belgium, the Netherlands, Portugal, and Scandinavia were all represented in Latin America. After the war new investment in banking, as in other fields, was to an increasing extent non-European. United States banks could not establish branches abroad until after the passage of the Federal Reserve Act in 1913. In the following year the National City Bank of New York set up a branch in Argentina and subsequently established a wide network of branches in Latin America, as have some other major United States banks. Canadian banks were also active in this period, especially in the Caribbean. A growing Japanese trading and immigrant interest in Latin America was reflected in the establishment of the first branches of Japanese banks in Brazil and Argentina in 1918.

Government control. In the nineteenth century, little control was exercised over the operation of banks once they had received a charter or license, and even this was not always necessary. Banking legislation was generally confined to a few paragraphs in the commercial code. Note-issuing franchises were granted on widely differing bases. The privilege of note issue was gradually removed from private banks, although in some countries it was taken away only at a comparatively late date. The sole right to issue notes in Venezuela was not given to a central bank until 1941, and in Honduras two private banks had the privilege of issue until 1950.

While in the more advanced countries of Latin America official or semiofficial banks enjoying a privileged position and carrying out some of the functions later associated with central banks existed before World War I, the creation of central banks as such dates from the 1920s. Before then the management of the currency was often in the hands of an exchange office whose function was to exchange domestic paper money, gold, and foreign exchange. If these operations had been strictly carried out, the money supply would simply have varied in accordance with the balance of payments, but the consequences of deflation proved to be unpalatable, and reserves of gold and foreign exchange were inadequate to allow the exchange offices

to maintain convertibility. In general the abuse of paper money by governments and the pressure of debtors' and exporters' interests created a strong bias toward currency depreciation.

In the early 1920s a series of missions led by Professor Edwin W. Kemmerer of Princeton University resulted in the establishment of central banks in the west coast republics of South America: Colombia (1923), Chile (1925), Ecuador (1927), Bolivia (1928), and Peru (1931). These institutions performed useful services for the commercial banks, but their only weapon of monetary management was the discount rate, which proved totally inadequate. During the Depression years of the early 1930s these banks at first attempted to enforce deflation and maintain the external value of their currencies, but in the end public opinion and exhausted reserves forced them to desist; expanded credit policies and exchange control followed. The Kemmerer banks were conceived to operate in a world of automatic economic adjustments in which governments played a relatively unimportant part. Government representation on the board of directors was shared with representatives of the associated banks, private shareholders, and other interests, and the banks' financial relations with the government were narrowly circumscribed. Successive modifications of the statutes of these banks have radically altered their character and given them more effective instruments for carrying out government exchange and credit policies.

The Banco de México, established in 1925, also operated on orthodox lines in its early years but subsequently was granted extremely wide powers that enabled it to play a key role in the financial system built up after 1940. In Argentina the Banco Central was established in 1935 on a plan drawn up by Sir Otto Niemeyer of the Bank of England. This institution, already one of the most efficient and powerful in Latin America, was nationalized in 1946 and given extensive new powers. In both Brazil and Uruguay central banking functions continued until recently to be carried out by a state-owned or state-controlled bank of a composite character. In Uruguay note issue and exchange control were managed by the state-owned Banco de la República, which was also the largest commercial bank in the country. Brazil evolved an institution *sui generis*, the Banco do Brasil, in which the state owned 51 percent of the shares. Like the official bank in Uruguay, it is the largest of the commercial banks, and it also carried out central banking functions through various specialized departments, although note issue remained with the Treasury. These somewhat anomalous situations were corrected when separate central banks were established in Brazil in 1965 and Uruguay in 1967. The only Latin American country now without a central bank is Panama, which is in an exceptional position in that the greater part of the currency in circulation consists of United States dollars.

The central banks now play a key role in the financial structure of most of the Latin American republics and, although enjoying little independence from governments, are among the most respected and efficient institutions in the public sector. Besides being instruments for the execution of the government's monetary policy, administering exchange control and in other ways acting as agents of the government, in conjunction with other official banking institutions they carry out other aspects of government economic policy, such as the implementation of agricultural price support policies. Supervision of private banks, if not carried out by the central bank itself, is delegated to a superintendency of banks or a similar organization. Comprehensive banking legislation, generally introduced at the same time as the establishment of central banks and since greatly modified, provides for the security and liquidity of the banking system by such means as prescribing minimum capital requirements, the ratio between capital and reserves and deposit-taking capacity, and cash reserve ratios.

Developments since 1945. Economic growth after World War II was naturally accompanied by a rapid expansion of commercial banking services, and in several countries the increase in the number of banks and banking offices was such that the chief commercial centers at least could be described as overbanked. In Uruguay, which supported more than eighty banks in 1962, the monetary crisis of the mid-1960s was followed by a deliberate attempt on the part of the authorities to eliminate redundant banking offices and to reduce by means of mergers the number of banks, which fell to twenty-eight by 1973. In Brazil the new central bank, with the aim both of strengthening the banking system and of increasing efficiency by lowering the banks' overheads, also encouraged amalgamations, and the number of commercial banks declined from 336 in 1964 to 123 in 1973.

Postwar developments have thus enhanced the dominant role within the private banking sector of the large banks based in the chief commercial centers. Another result has been to diminish the relative importance of foreign or foreign-controlled banks, which in a number of countries have also been affected by government restrictions. These restrictions have included limitations or absolute bans on the extension of foreign banks' branch systems, limits on the percentage of capital of local banks that may be owned by foreign banks, and the restriction to local banks of certain types of business, for example, the acceptance of savings deposits. In Mexico, where only one foreign (United States) bank survived the difficult conditions of the 1930s, the establishment of new banks or related financial enterprises by foreigners is effectively prohibited. In Cuba after 1959 and in Chile under the regime of Salvador ALLENDE (1970–1973), foreign banks were expropriated or purchased as part of a policy of bringing into public ownership the whole banking system. Where direct banking operations are not allowed, foreign banks are generally permitted to maintain representative offices.

Apart from Cuba and Chile, nationalization of the private deposit-taking banks has been carried out only in Costa Rica (1948). In Argentina under the first regime of Juan D. PERÓN and again with Perón's return to power in 1973, the deposits of private banks were "nationalized" under legislation that declared that deposits could be accepted only for the account of the Banco Central, which in turn granted rediscount quotas to the private banks, whose lending capacity thus depended on the extent of their own resources and these rediscount quotas.

Official control over, and participation in, the banking system has in any case continued to grow through the strengthening of the control mechanisms of the central banks and the growth of official banks. As mentioned above, banks owned by the central government (or by state or provincial governments) carry out an important role in commercial banking.

Specialized credit institutions. In addition to playing an important role in commercial banking, the state has been active in the establishment of specialized credit agencies. The creation of agricultural, industrial, and mining credit banks in the Latin American republics dates generally from the 1930s, when the disastrous effects of the Great Depression emphasized the need to diversify economies in order to encourage new industries and support small producers. In Peru a Banco Agrícola was set up in 1931; in addition to providing credit for all branches of agriculture it was authorized to import seeds, buy equipment, and perform other services of a similar nature. At least 20 percent of its capital was to be earmarked for unsecured loans to farmers who would otherwise have little or no opportunity of obtaining capital. A Banco Industrial was authorized in 1933 and began operations in 1937, and a Banco Minero, created to sustain and encourage the smaller domestic mining companies, began operations in 1941. Institutions with a similar purpose were established in many other Latin American republics at about the same time. In practice their usefulness was limited by scanty resources and a lack of an effective capital market. In countries where there was already a well-developed state-owned banking system, the creation of new institutions was less necessary. In Argentina, for example, the Banco de la Nación has a special responsibility for agriculture, to which it makes medium- and long-term loans of up to five and fifteen years, respectively, but a separate Banco Industrial was created for providing medium- and long-term credit to industry and mining. The latter was transformed in 1971 into the Banco Nacional de Desarrollo with wider powers for financing development projects.

Development banks or corporations have much wider functions than the specialized credit agencies. They are intended, within the framework of the government's plans for economic development, to mobilize capital from various sources for strengthening the country's economic infrastructure and developing key sectors where private enterprise is unable or unwilling to act. Notable among such institutions are Mexico's NACIONAL FINANCIERA, founded in 1934, and the Chilean CORPORACIÓN DE FOMENTO DE LA PRODUCCIÓN, established in 1939. In Brazil the leading development institution is the Banco Nacional do Desenvolvimento Economico (BNDE), which since its creation in 1950 has played a major role in financing developments in transport, electrical energy, and basic industry, especially iron and steel (*see* IRON AND STEEL INDUSTRY: BRAZIL), providing both local and foreign currency financing at long term and also equity capital. Its activities are supplemented by those of regional development banks, including the Banco de Crédito da Amazônia, established in Belém in 1942, and the Banco do Nordeste do Brasil, set up with its head office in Fortaleza in 1952. Elsewhere the activities of the Corporación Venezolana de Fomento (CVF), established in 1946, are particularly noteworthy; this institution played a major role in financing the expansion initially of electricity supplies and subsequently of a wide range of agricultural and industrial developments. Most countries now have one or more official development banks or corporations. The most effective of them have a regular income from budgetary sources or, as in the case of Nacional Financiera, an ability to raise long-term funds on the local capital market or abroad, and have built up over the years highly competent professional staffs. Much useful work in improving standards in Latin American development institutions has been done by the INTER-AMERICAN DEVELOPMENT BANK, which has given direct help in organizing banks in Ecuador, Honduras, Panama, Paraguay, and other countries and has mounted a major effort in training officials of Latin American development banks. It has also used local development banks as a channel for its own lending in the Latin American republics.

Other financial intermediaries. Before World War II commercial banks were virtually the only private financial institutions of importance, although private mortgage and savings banks had long been in existence in several countries. The postwar development of other private financial intermediaries has been the consequence, on the one hand, of economic growth and diversification and, on the other, of controls on commercial banking imposed by legislation and the dictates of monetary policy. In Peru, for example, commercial bank loans may not be granted for periods of more than one year. Some other countries have relaxed such restrictions with the aim of releasing funds for the development of agriculture and industry; in Colombia, for example, the orthodox tradition was breached in 1950 when commercial banks were authorized to make industrial development loans of up to five years, rediscountable in the Banco de la República. Colombia has since elaborated a system of "channeled" lending whereby banks devoting a specified proportion of their loans to development financing benefit from lower cash reserve requirements. In general, the frequent renewal of short-term borrowings also means that commercial banks are making a larger contribution to longer-term financing than may be apparent at first sight. Nevertheless, it remains a basic principle that the chief function of commercial banks is to provide short-term credit and carry out related ancillary business. The capacity of commercial banks to engage in long-term financing is in any case limited by their dependence on short-term deposits. The imposition of maximum interest rates on deposits has also tended to divert funds elsewhere, especially in times of high inflation, and commercial banks have also had to bear the brunt of credit controls imposed by the monetary authorities. This situation led in Latin America, as in other parts of the world, to the establishment of other financial institutions, less rigidly controlled, which were able to attract an increasing part of the deposits of the public. Commercial banks themselves set up subsidiary finance companies to obtain a share in remunerative types of business from which they would otherwise have been excluded.

There has thus grown up, especially in the more highly developed republics, a large number of institutions, which may generally be described as *financieras,* carrying out a wide range of functions from consumer credit to genuine investment banking. Although initially at least they tended to escape many of the controls imposed by central banks in furtherance of monetary policy, subsequent legislation brought them more and more under central bank control. In general, they are prohibited from accepting checking deposits.

The growth of private financial institutions other than commercial banks was essentially a feature of the late 1950s and early 1960s. In Brazil the *sociedades de crédito, financiamento e investimento* increased from 30 in 1951 to nearly 300 in 1966 but declined to about 180 at the end of 1971. These *sociedades* provided financing for a wide variety of purposes and financed themselves largely by the sale of acceptances; by the late 1960s the total of such acceptances equaled about 28 percent of total commercial bank loans to the private sector. In 1965 a new capital market law drew a distinction between finance companies and investment banks. The activities of the former increasingly became confined to the financing of durable consumer goods, while the investment banks, which by 1971 numbered about thirty-five, had as their proper sphere of action the provision of medium- and long-term credit, as well as equity financing for development purposes, and were also authorized to engage in other capital market operations.

In Mexico the development of privately owned *financieras* was encouraged by legislation going as far back as 1941. It was intended that these institutions should concentrate on long-term operations, financing themselves with long-term funds such as the issuance of debentures, leaving short-term business to commercial banks, but this distinction was by no means successfully maintained. For carrying out their specific purpose of promoting industrial and other developments in the private sector they were given broad powers to organize business enterprises, participating in their equity, to underwrite share issues and extend medium- and long-term credit, to accept time deposits from the public, and to market their own obligations. Many of the small *financieras* concentrate on the financing of sales of durable consumer goods. Of the existing 100-odd institutions of this type, about half a dozen transact most of the business and have some claim to be regarded as private development banks, although in fact they engage in almost the whole range of financial transactions other than checking deposit business. These large *financieras* are linked to the major commercial banks. By the mid-1960s the assets of the *financieras* equaled those of the commercial banks, and they subsequently exceeded them by a substantial margin.

Institutions for the provision of consumer credit exist in most of the other republics. One other country in which the *financieras* have made a noteworthy contribution toward economic development is Colombia, where the creation of private finance corporations as a means of mobilizing domestic savings for economic development was suggested in 1952 by a mission from the International Bank for Reconstruction and Development (World Bank). The first of these corporations, the Corporación Financiera Colombiana de Desarrollo Industrial (CFC), was founded in Bogotá in 1959; it was followed by the Corporación Financiera Nacional (CFN) in Medellín. Both corporations began operations in 1960. Subsequently such corporations were founded in Cali, Manizales, and other cities.

Bibliography. Banco Central de la República Argentina, *La creación del Banco Central y la experiencia monetaria argentina entre los años 1935–1943,* Buenos Aires, 1972; Antonín Basch and Milic Kybal, *Capital Markets in Latin America,* New York, 1970; *Brasil Financeiro 1971/72,* São Paulo, 1971; Wendell C.

Gordon, *The Political Economy of Latin America*, New York, 1965; Inter-American Development Bank, *The Mobilization of Internal Financial Resources in Latin America*, Washington, 1971; David Joslin, *A Century of Banking in Latin America*, London, 1963; David H. Shelton, "The Banking System: Money and the Goal of Growth," in Raymond Vernon (ed.), *Public Policy and Private Enterprise in Mexico*, Cambridge, Mass., 1967.

H. A. HOLLEY

BANZER [SUÁREZ], HUGO (1926–   ). Bolivian army officer and President (1971–   ). A graduate of the Colegio Militar, Banzer was just beginning his career in 1952, when the Army was dissolved by the MOVIMIENTO NACIONALISTA REVOLUCIONARIO (MNR) upon taking power. When the Army was reorganized in 1953, Banzer returned to its officer corps in spite of his steadfast refusal to join the government party. Although Banzer had a reputation for being an institutionalist-minded officer who eschewed politics, he supported the overthrow of the MNR regime in the November 1964 coup led by the Air Force commander René BARRIENTOS and the Army commander Alfredo OVANDO CANDIA. Banzer served for a time as Minister of Education under Barrientos and as director of the Colegio Militar during the government of General Ovando (1969–1970). He was relieved of this post at the beginning of January 1971 by Ovando's leftist successor, Gen. Juan José TORRES. After leading an unsuccessful revolt against Torres on January 10–11, 1971, Banzer went into exile in Argentina. From there he conspired against the Torres regime, joining forces with the MNR and its traditional opponent, the Falange Socialista Boliviana.

When Banzer entered the Bolivian department of Santa Cruz, he was arrested on August 18, 1971. The next day the revolt he had been planning went into operation, and he was freed and took command of rebel forces. By August 21 the rebels had seized La Paz, and on the following day he became President, although some student resistance continued on August 23.

Banzer formed a Cabinet of military men and members of the MNR and the Falange, the country's two largest parties, which announced the formation of the Nationalist Popular Front to seek political stability, economic development, and the orderly continuation of the social changes originally launched by the MNR regime. Banzer announced that he would maintain the expropriation of the Gulf Oil Corporation's holdings, carried out originally by Ovando. Protests against oppressive actions by the Minister of the Interior, Col. Andrés Selich, including one by the Auxiliary Archbishop of La Paz, led to a political crisis and the dismissal of Colonel Selich in November 1971. Meanwhile, the alliance of the military leaders with the two hitherto bitterly competing political parties remained uneasy, and by late 1973 the MNR had broken with Banzer.

ROBERT J. ALEXANDER

BARBOSA, RUY (1849–1923). Brazilian statesman, jurist, and publicist who gained international renown by his eloquent pleas for the rights of weak nations at the Second Hague Conference in 1907. A native of Salvador, Bahia, and a lawyer by profession, he entered na-

Ruy Barbosa. [Museu Imperial, Petrópolis, Rio de Janeiro]

tional politics through the movement to abolish slavery (*see* ABOLITION OF SLAVERY: BRAZIL). He was a member of the imperial Parliament before 1889 and represented the state of Bahia in the Brazilian Senate from 1891 to his death in 1923.

A liberal in the classic nineteenth-century mold and a monarchist in principle, he joined the republicans only a few days before the fall of the empire. As Vice Chief and Finance Minister in the provisional government of Marshal Manuel Deodoro da FONSECA he instituted far-ranging economic and financial reforms with limited success. He was the chief architect of the new constitution (*see* CONSTITUTION OF 1891: BRAZIL), modeling it after that of the United States, whose political institutions he greatly admired.

A courageous and outspoken defender of civil liberties, he vehemently opposed dictatorship and involvement of the military in politics and as a consequence was exiled in 1894–1895. His oratory and erudition at the Hague Peace Conference, where he was appointed a judge of the Permanent Court of Arbitration, made him a national hero. In 1910 he launched Brazil's first truly national party, the Civilistas, but was unsuccessful in his bid for the Presidency that year and again in 1919.

A founding member of the Brazilian Academy of Letters and its one-time president, he was a prolific writer whose works on jurisprudence, politics, and sociology total more than 150 volumes.

ARNOLD J. MEAGHER

BARRETO, AFONSO HENRIQUES DE LIMA (1881–1922). Brazilian novelist. Born in Rio de Janeiro, he was a Negro, the son of the administrator of the Rio insane asylum and the grandson of slaves on both sides of the family. He was educated in the College of Pedro II and completed two years at the Polytechnical School. He left it because of lack of success with certain subjects, became a clerk in the Ministry of War, and began to write for the newspapers. An alcoholic, he himself was interned more than once in the Rio asylum with a diagnosis of alcoholism. His father died insane. Lima

Barreto was an affectionate admirer of the humble people of Rio and loved Rio's suburbs. He was a bitter satirist of Brazilian institutions and the Brazilian political system, hating as well what he considered the sham of the intellectuals. He resented the color prejudice that he saw everywhere in Rio life, as is evident in *Recordações do Escrivão Isaías Caminha* (1909) and *Clara dos Anjos,* published posthumously in 1948. The hero and heroine of these novels, respectively, are subjected to deep humiliation because of their color. His best novel, *O Triste Fim de Policarpo Quaresma* (1915), is a bitter picture of a Brazilian patriot who gradually loses faith in the country and the myths by which it lives. His other great novel, *Vida e Morte de Gonzaga de Sá* (1919), though less satirical, is equally pessimistic. He was also an accomplished short-story writer.

RAYMOND S. SAYERS

BARRIENTOS [ORTUÑO], RENÉ (1919–1969). Bolivian army officer and President (1966–1969). A native of Cochabamba, Barrientos attended the Colegio Militar and was a junior officer at the time of the revolution of April 1952, which was led by the MOVIMIENTO NACIONALISTA REVOLUCIONARIO (MNR). He joined the MNR, and when the armed forces were reorganized a year after the revolution, he became a leading figure in its "military cell," rising by the early 1960s to be chief of that organization. In addition, he served simultaneously as commander of the Air Force.

As the 1964 presidential election approached, Barrientos made no secret of his political ambitions. Although another man was at first chosen to be the vice-presidential candidate on the MNR ticket headed by President Víctor PAZ ESTENSSORO, the National Committee of the party finally made Barrientos the vice-presidential nominee. He was elected, along with Paz Estenssoro, in June 1964.

By that time, however, Barrientos was plotting to overthrow the President. This plot reached fruition on November 5, 1964, when Barrientos and Gen. Alfredo OVANDO CANDIA led a successful military coup. Barrientos and Ovando served as Co-Presidents for a time, but Barrientos resigned this post to run for the Presidency in the elections of June 1966. Barrientos won over several opponents. His administration was marked by very strong measures against the Miners Federation, which led to virtual military occupation of the mining camps. It was also characterized by Barrientos's constant attempts to win support among the Indian peasants. Speaking QUECHUA himself, he took a great interest in the projects of his government in cooperation with the U.S. Agency for International Development to increase marketing facilities, carry out extension work, and encourage the Indians to shear the wool of their flocks of sheep and llamas and sell it.

In 1967 the Barrientos government was faced with the attempt led by Ernesto (Ché) GUEVARA to launch a guerrilla war in the department of Santa Cruz. There is little question that Barrientos's support of the agrarian reform which had been carried out by the MNR, coupled with his continuing interest in the welfare of the peasants, was a major factor in his success in crushing Guevara's movement, which culminated in the guerrilla leader's death after he had been captured. The following year the Barrientos regime was rocked by scandal when it was divulged that the Minister of the Interior, Alcides Arguedas, had sold Guevara's diary to the Cuban government. When dissident military officers threatened to use this incident to bring Barrientos down, he flew to Cochabamba, where he mobilized military units and his peasant followers and succeeded in calling the bluff of the would-be rebels.

Barrientos died under mysterious circumstances in April 1969. After addressing a meeting in a soccer stadium, he took off in his helicopter and crashed some miles away. It is still not clear whether his machine collided with electric wires, according to the official version, or whether he was shot.

ROBERT J. ALEXANDER

BARRIOS, EDUARDO (1884–1963). Chilean writer. Born in Valparaíso, he was General Director of Libraries, Minister of Education, editor of the newspaper *La Mañana,* and a member of the literary group known as Los Diez. He published several volumes of short stories including *Del natural* (1907); *El niño que enloqueció de amor* (1915), a masterful psychological study of awakening love; *Páginas de un pobre diablo* (1923); *Y la vida sigue* (1925); *La antipatía* (1933); and *Tamarugal* (1944). His novels are *Un perdido* (1918), the story of the disintegration of a personality; *El hermano asno* (1922), a penetrating study of an emotionally unbalanced friar; *Gran señor y rajadiablos* (1948), a prose epic of the Chilean landowner; and *Los hombres del hombre* (1950), a fantasy on the fragmentation of the main character. Among his plays are *Mercaderes en el templo* (1910), *Por el decoro* (1913), *Comedias originales* (1913), *Vivir* (1916), *Lo que niega la vida* (1917), and *Teatro escogido* (1947).

RACHEL PHILLIPS

BARRIOS, GERARDO (1813–1865). President of El Salvador (1860–1863). A Liberal, he began his career as a partisan of Francisco MORAZÁN, President of the Federation of Central America (*see* CENTRAL AMERICA, FEDERATION OF), held elective posts in both state and federal governments, participated in military campaigns, and when Morazán was driven into exile, accompanied him as far as Costa Rica. He rejoined Morazán in Costa Rica in 1842, and after the defeat and execution of the *caudillo* he was among the prisoners returned to El Salvador.

During the next fifteen years Barrios was active in the affairs of El Salvador and also of Honduras and Nicaragua. He held governmental administrative and military positions and was several times a designate, or alternate, for the Presidency of El Salvador. He aided Liberal revolutionary movements in neighboring states and on several occasions originated or joined conspiracies to seize the government of El Salvador. As a unionist disciple of Morazán, he participated in several mid-century efforts at unification in Central America.

After twice holding interim power, Barrios was elected President of El Salvador in 1860. He gave impetus to coffee planting and is credited with founding the modern industry (*see* COFFEE INDUSTRY: CENTRAL AMERICA). His feud with the clergy over prerogatives left deep domestic resentments, although these ostensibly were healed by the concordat signed in April 1862. He angered José Rafael CARRERA of Guatemala, who attacked El Salvador in 1863 and caused his overthrow. Barrios escaped but later fell into the hands of his enemy and successor as President of El Salvador, Francisco Dueñas, who executed him on August 29, 1865.

WILLIAM J. GRIFFITH

BARRIOS, JUSTO RUFINO (1835–1885). Dictator-President of Guatemala (1873–1885) whose extensive innovations earned him the sobriquet "Reformer." Barrios was born in San Lorenzo to well-to-do parents whose properties extended into Mexico. He studied law in Guatemala City and became a notary, but in 1862 he returned to the family holdings. From there he joined a Liberal revolution and became an associate of Miguel García Granados, with whom he overthrew President Vicente Cerna in June 1871. García Granados headed the new provisional government, but Barrios proved to have the stronger personality. Military and political successes increased his influence, and when elections were held in April 1873, he won the Presidency.

Barrios established a dictatorship no less rigorous than the one he had helped to overthrow. He virtually liquidated the Conservative opposition, dealt harshly with critics, and extended his controls to local affairs through appointed *jefes políticos* (departmental governors) vested with broad delegated powers. He replaced with unified law codes the unmanageable patchwork inheritance of unrepealed Spanish laws encrusted with fragmentary enactments added by temporizing legislatures since independence. A constituent assembly in 1879 drafted a constitution to accord with the Barrios style of strong central rule, and under it he was overwhelmingly elected in 1880. For the remainder of his tenure he maintained a charade of constitutionalism.

The Barrios reforms largely conformed to nineteenth-century Latin American Liberal-positivist thought. He regarded the Catholic Church as the fount of Conservative reaction and believed that Liberal success required the destruction of its political and economic power and the limitation of its social influence. To this end he suppressed the tithe, quashed the regular orders, nationalized church properties, and subjected clerics to the jurisdiction of civil courts. Companion legislation guaranteed the free exercise of all religions and established civil jurisdiction over such traditional church functions as marriage, education, and the recording of vital statistics.

Barrios considered popular education an essential reform. He instituted a system of free public elementary schools that he hoped to make universal, established secondary schools and a central normal school, and created a Ministry of Public Instruction. He brought the University of San Carlos under government control and reoriented it toward utilitarian ends.

Material progress was the goal Barrios pursued most assiduously. In the hope of facilitating economic development he founded a short-lived national bank and encouraged several private banking enterprises. He promoted coffee cultivation, made public lands easily accessible to prospective cultivators, enacted legislation intended to ensure them an ample supply of Indian labor, and took steps that led to the creation of a Ministry of Agriculture. He encouraged immigration both for the direct contribution foreign settlers were expected to make to production and for the beneficial example it was assumed they would set for nationals.

Barrios recognized that improved transportation and communications were essential to development. He established a labor levy for roadwork and by this means opened cart roads to connect departmental capitals and trunk routes leading through the western highlands, toward both oceans, and in the direction of El Salvador. He encouraged railroad construction and saw lines completed between Retalhuleu and the port of Champerico and between the capital, Escuintla, and the port of San José. He established and gave his name to Guatemala's first deepwater port on the Caribbean and with forced contributions from Guatemalans built a railroad to link it with the capital.

Like other Central American strong men, Barrios manipulated the external affairs of his country to his own advantage. He maintained congenial regimes in neighboring states and replaced executives who displeased him. He settled a long-standing boundary dispute with Mexico in 1882 in a fashion, his critics alleged, that favored his own property holdings more than the interests of the nation. He proclaimed the restoration of the Central American union in 1885, but the other states did not respond in unanimous accord. When he attempted to force his will by military action, he was killed at Chalchuapa near the Salvadoran frontier.

Barrios shaped the Liberal-positivist Guatemala that endured until 1944. He destroyed the traditional elite but created another of consciously favored entrepreneurs whom he heralded as architects of the new Guatemala. He despised Indians for their lack of enterprise, their "laziness," and their social "vices" and drove them to labor directed by the "enlightened" segment of society, as was their duty. He legislated universal education but was unable to produce the means, material or human, to fulfill the dream. His regime is perhaps epitomized in his reform of the university, which, in the judgment of one critic, sacrificed

Justo Rufino Barrios. [*Library of Congress*]

humanist tradition and converted it into "a factory of vulgar professionals."

Bibliography. Paul Burgess, *Justo Rufino Barrios: A Biography,* Philadelphia, 1926; Chester Lloyd Jones, *Guatemala Past and Present,* Minneapolis, 1940.

WILLIAM J. GRIFFITH

BARROS, ADHEMAR DE (1901–1969). Brazilian industrialist and politician. A populist leader, three times Governor of São Paulo, and a perennial aspirant to the Presidency of Brazil, Barros encouraged the rapid postwar industrial growth of his home state. His political style was expressed in the campaign slogan "He steals but gets things done." Barros was born in Piracicaba and studied medicine in Brazil and Germany. Entering politics in 1932, he served one term in the state legislature (1934–1937). He achieved national prominence in 1938, when President Getúlio VARGAS appointed him Interventor (Governor) of São Paulo, a post he held until 1941.

In 1945 Barros founded the Social Progressive party, which he dominated for the next twenty years. Elected to the governorship for a four-year term (1947–1951), he supported Vargas's successful presidential campaign in 1950. An early advocate of air transportation, Barros was instrumental in creating the state-owned airline Viação Aérea de São Paulo (VASP), which he used to further his political and business interests. He was narrowly defeated by Jânio QUADROS in the gubernatorial elections of 1954, but he was elected mayor of the city of São Paulo in 1958 and was returned to the governorship for the third time in 1962. Barros ran unsuccessfully for the Presidency in 1955 and 1960. Although he played an active role in planning the revolution of 1964, Barros later resisted the economic policies of the revolutionary government. Consequently, in 1966 he was deposed and deprived of political rights. He died in exile in Paris.

ROLLIE E. POPPINO

BARROS ARANA, DIEGO (1830–1907). Chilean historian, educator, and diplomat. After studying, like many other eminent Chileans, at the Instituto Nacional in Santiago, Barros Arana was prevented from pursuing his education further by ill health. This did not deter him from becoming one of the two or three most distinguished nineteenth-century Latin American historians. His first historical essays were published in 1850. Although he is remembered today chiefly as a scholar, Barros Arana's contributions to public life were considerable. A fervent Liberal (*see* LIBERAL PARTY: CHILE), he took an active part in opposing the administration of Manuel MONTT and was forced into exile at the end of 1858. He returned to Chile in 1861, having traveled in Argentina, England, France, and Spain. In 1863 he was appointed rector of the Instituto Nacional, a position he held for ten years before being dismissed at the behest of the Conservative Minister of Education, Abdón Cifuentes. Between 1876 and 1878 Barros Arana acted as Minister Plenipotentiary in Argentina, Uruguay, and Brazil, with instructions to negotiate a settlement of outstanding frontier questions with Argentina. He was later widely blamed for the Chilean abandonment of claims to the greater part of Patagonia, ratified in the treaty of 1881. The civil war of 1891 found Barros Arana in opposition to the regime of José Manuel BALMACEDA, and he was forced to go into hiding. Between 1893 and 1897 he served as rector of the University of Chile.

Barros Arana's output of historical works was substantial. His most notable books were the *Historia general de la independencia de Chile* (4 vols., 1854–1858), *Compendio de historia de América* (1865), *Historia de la guerra del Pacífico* (2 vols., 1880–1881), *Historia general de Chile* (16 vols., 1884–1902), and *Un decenio de la historia de Chile* (2 vols., 1905–1906). These works, together with his uninterrupted series of monographs and articles, make Barros Arana's claim to be regarded as the greatest Chilean historian impossible to dispute. The immense *Historia general de Chile,* his masterpiece, is an extraordinarily accurate and detailed narrative of Chile's history from pre-Columbian times to 1833. Its sixteen massive volumes have never been surpassed for quality (or for length) in Chilean historical writing.

SIMON COLLIER

BASADRE, JORGE (1903–   ). Peruvian historian. Born in Tacna in 1903 during the Chilean occupation of that region, Basadre is Peru's most renowned twentieth-century historian. He entered the University of San Marcos in 1919 and was later to be associated with the institution in a number of capacities. Basadre was part of the generation of the *centenario* (centenary of independence), which rose in the halls of San Marcos in the 1920s. Influenced by the Mexican and Russian revolutions, by the social unrest produced by World War I, and by the movement for university reform emanating from Argentina (*see* EDUCATION: UNIVERSITY), the members of this generation came to be known for their active nationalism and for their concern with social and political reforms. From this generation emerged some of Peru's best historians.

Basadre received his doctorate in literature in 1928 and immediately began teaching history at San Marcos. His concern with academic freedom led him to long years of absence from Peru. During those years he continued his teaching and other scholarly pursuits in European and American universities. In 1943 he took the job of reconstructing the National Library in Lima, which had been destroyed by fire. In 1945 he was appointed Minister of Education, a post he held for three months, and in 1956 he occupied the same ministerial position.

It is as a historian, however, that Basadre will be best remembered. Among his many works the monumental *Historia de la república del Perú* (17 vols., 6th ed., 1968) will remain the definitive general history of Peru for the foreseeable future. The work, which now covers the period from 1822 to 1933, will undoubtedly be expanded.

ORAZIO A. CICCARELLI

BATISTA, CÍCERO ROMÃO. *See* CÍCERO, PADRE.

BATISTA [ZALDÍVAR], FULGENCIO (1901–1973). President and dictator of Cuba. Born in Oriente Province to a lower-class family of mixed racial ancestry, Batista obtained little formal schooling as a child and early in life was forced to obtain numerous odd jobs to support himself. At the age of twenty he joined the Army, in which he learned typing and shorthand. Consequently he served as a stenographer and secretary, positions that gave him a firsthand acquaintance with the politics of the Cuban Army.

In 1933, following the fall of the dictator Gerardo MACHADO and the establishment of the government headed by Carlos Manuel de Céspedes, a group of sergeants formed a conspiracy to revolt against the commissioned officers of the Cuban Army. Batista was initially secretary to the group, but by the time the plot was carried out in September, he had emerged as the leader of the discontented sergeants. The Céspedes government disintegrated in the wake of the sergeants' coup, while civilian anti-Machado elements made common cause with the sergeants. A five-man commission was named to assume power, but five days later one of its members, Ramón GRAU SAN MARTÍN, became provisional President. However, the United States, following the advice of Ambassador Sumner WELLES, refused to recognize the provisional government because of its apparent radicalism and failure to impose order, and Batista, by now a colonel and the most powerful man in Cuba, forced Grau to resign in January 1934.

Batista continued to dominate Cuban political life for the remainder of the decade. Miguel Mariano Gómez, son of former President José Miguel GÓMEZ, was elected to the Presidency in January 1936 but soon clashed with Batista, who was chief of staff, over military interference in the educational system. In December 1936 Gómez was impeached by Congress, in which Batista supporters were in the majority, and was succeeded by Vice President Federico Laredo Bru, who was more willing to play the role of puppet President. Batista now began to evince concern for social and economic reforms and formed an alliance with the Communist party, which was legalized in 1938. He also sponsored the meeting in February 1940 of a Constituent Assembly that drafted a new constitution providing for social, economic, and political reforms that would have cured many of Cuba's ills had they been fully implemented. Shortly after the 1940 constitution (*see* CONSTITUTION OF 1940: CUBA) was promulgated, Batista ran for the Presidency as the candidate of a coalition of the Democratic, Liberal, and Communist parties. He easily defeated Grau San Martín, now the leader of the Auténtico party (*see* AUTÉNTICO PARTY: CUBA).

During Batista's term of office, which coincided with World War II, he took full advantage of all the opportunities to enhance his power and prestige as a democrat. He reaped the fruits of wartime economic expansion, enjoyed emergency legislation that gave him additional powers to impose political and economic controls, and became a valuable ally of the United States by cooperating in intelligence operations in the Caribbean. He also appointed two members of the Communist party to his Cabinet.

The 1940 constitution prevented Batista from running for reelection, but he attempted to continue to wield power by backing one of his closest associates, Carlos Saladrigas. In spite of Batista's attempt to control the election, however, Grau San Martín was elected by a substantial majority. Respecting the voters' decision, Batista withdrew from political power for the next eight years. During that time the Auténticos ousted most of Batista's supporters from the bureaucracy as well as those who had gained command positions in the armed forces.

In 1952 Batista entered the presidential race, along with two other candidates, but this time he had little chance of winning. Rather than wait for the election to decide his political future, Batista, with the help of key officers, staged a coup d'état on March 10, by gaining control of Camp Columbia, headquarters of the Cuban Army. Faced with a complete revolt of his armed forces, President Carlos PRÍO SOCARRÁS went into exile and left the country in the hands of Batista and his allies in the military. The unexpected turn of events triggered widespread opposition from student groups, legislators, and political parties, but Batista's promise to bring an end to corruption in Cuba and his smooth political touch soon defused all immediate threats to his regime.

Under pressure from the United States, Batista called for new elections in 1954. In this farcical electoral contest only factions of the political parties participated, and the controlling hand of the regime made Batista the sure winner. His second term in office was filled with violence and corruption. The most significant event of this period was the struggle between Fidel CASTRO and the Cuban government. Castro, an irreconcilable opponent of the March 10 coup d'état, made his first attack on the Batista regime on July 26, 1953, but was unsuccessful. After spending some time in exile in Mexico, he returned in 1956 to organize a guerrilla army in the Sierra Maestra with the purpose of overthrowing Batista. By 1958 Batista had alienated much of the Cuban middle class, allowing Castro to gain the support of many professionals and students in the cities. Assassination, bombings, and widespread burning of sugar plantations became common occurrences. Batista's administration was weakened to the point that on January 1, 1959, he decided to flee the country.

Bibliography. Fulgencio Batista, *Cuba Betrayed,* New York, 1962; Edmund Chester, *A Sergeant Named Batista,* New York, 1954; Hugh Thomas, *Cuba: The Pursuit of Freedom,* New York, 1971.

J. CORDELL ROBINSON

BATLLE [Y ORDÓÑEZ], JOSÉ (1856–1929). President of Uruguay (1903–1907, 1911–1915) and the father of modern Uruguay. He was twelve when his father, Lorenzo Batlle, became President of Uruguay (1868–1872), and he grew up in the Colorado party (*see* COLORADO PARTY: URUGUAY). He left the University of Montevideo before completing studies for a law degree, but in 1880 he studied at the Sorbonne and the Collège de France in Paris, preparing himself for a career in diplomacy and political journalism. In 1886 he founded the daily newspaper *El Día* to serve as the editorial voice of the Colorado party. Starting as political chief of the department of Minas, he rose in public posts to the office of senator. In 1903 he was elected to his first term as President of Uruguay. Soon after taking office, he was confronted by an unsuccessful Blanco revolution headed by Aparicio SARAVIA (*see* BLANCO PARTY: URUGUAY).

By the time Batlle became President, he was known throughout the republic as a champion of ORGANIZED LABOR, his column and editorials in *El Día* consistently calling for shorter workweeks and legalization of the right to strike, positions considered radical in the 1890s and early 1900s. During his first presidential term he fought for congressional enactment of an eight-hour–workday law, a fight that took eight years. The constitution then provided a four-year term of office, with a ban on consecutive reelection. Batlle prepared to step down in 1907 and then to offer himself as a candidate for the 1911–1915 presidential term. He asserted that if reelected in 1911, he would press for an eight-hour–workday law. In 1915 Batlle had such a law enacted at a time when other Latin American nations accepted the age-old dawn-to-dusk workday with little organized protest.

In 1905 Batlle had a Colorado senator introduce a bill to convert the 1885 marriage annulment law (the first such law in Latin America) into a full divorce law. In 1907 the measure was enacted, putting Uruguay in the vanguard of Latin American nations in giving women some legal and economic emancipation. Batlle was the first Latin American statesman to call publicly for women's rights.

Except for Montevideo, Uruguayan cities had only primary schools. In 1906, by presidential decree, Batlle established secondary schools in every provincial city, and the growth of agriculture gave the government a budgetary surplus with which to build schools and complete public works. Batlle also urged the Congress to create government corporations to compete with private corporations in supplying vital services and goods and to lower prices to fit the purchasing power of average citizens.

In his second term, in January 1912, Batlle signed into law a measure creating the Banco de Seguros del Estado (State Insurance Bank). By 1936 this government agency was writing three-fourths of the insurance issued in Uruguay, including fire and life insurance. In 1912 Batlle also successfully lobbied for publicly owned electric power. In 1915 the government took ownership of the telephone services, creating the Administración General de las Usinas Eléctricas y los Teléfonos del Estado, known as UTE. By 1954 Uruguay's per capita telephone ratio was second only to that of Argentina in Latin America, and in 1965 it surpassed the Argentine ratio.

During the four years between his presidential terms, Batlle studied European government and discovered that in Switzerland a plural Presidency had replaced the one-man chief executive. After returning to office, he proposed in 1913 that Uruguay adopt the Swiss system of a collegiate head for the executive branch of government, or COLEGIADO.

Some Colorados and most Blancos fought the proposed collegiate Presidency during years of congressional committee debate. When Batlle threatened to run for a third term in 1919 if a new constitution were not adopted, opponents gave in. The constitution of 1918 created a nine-member National Council of Administration, but it also added a President, giving Uruguay a two-headed executive branch. Batlle presided over the National Council of Administration in 1926 in his last governmental post.

Batlle died on October 20, 1929, the maker of modern Uruguay. Various welfare benefits, which were focused on social security payments for all retired workers, had become central to Uruguayan public life. Batlle's firm belief in secular control of political affairs had resulted in the peaceful separation of church and state in the 1918 constitution. His policies of economic nationalism through public corporations had greatly lessened foreign economic influence within Uruguay. Years after his passing, in 1951, Uruguayans were still *batllistas* enough to vote into existence another constitution with a plural Presidency, this time without any chief executive. This experiment in government lasted through 1966, when inflationary pressures forced a return to a single-Presidency constitution. Batlle's ideals became a political and social philosophy, *batllismo,* which even in the 1960s and 1970s had a continuing hold on segments of the population.

Bibliography. Marvin Alisky, *Uruguay: A Contemporary Survey,* New York, 1969; Russell H. Fitzgibbon, *Uruguay: Portrait of a Democracy,* New Brunswick, N.J., 1954; Roberto B. Giudici and Efraim González Conzi, *Batlle y el batllismo,* Montevideo, 1928; Milton I. Vanger, *José Batlle y Ordóñez of Uruguay: The Creator of His Times,* Cambridge, Mass., 1963.

MARVIN ALISKY

BATLLE BERRES, LUIS (1897–1964). President of Uruguay (1947–1951). The nephew of President José BATLLE, he was born in Montevideo and became a newspaperman. He was a member of the Chamber of Representatives during the years 1923–1933 and 1942–1947, serving as President of the Chamber from 1943 to 1945. Batlle Berres was elected Vice President in 1946 and succeeded to the Presidency upon the death of Tomás Berreta in August 1947.

The administration of Batlle Berres was a period of political peace and economic prosperity. This stability

José Batlle [y Ordóñez]. [Organization of American States]

attracted to Uruguay a considerable amount of foreign capital seeking safety in a world concerned with the cold war and, after mid-1950, the Korean war. Batlle Berres was an outspoken defender of democracy and civil liberties, and relations with Argentina were frequently strained by his administration's insistence upon granting political asylum to opponents of the government of Juan D. PERÓN.

A major division in the governing Colorado party (*see* COLORADO PARTY: URUGUAY) became evident in 1948, when Batlle Berres founded his own daily newspaper, *Acción,* to support the faction known as List 15. *El Día,* the traditional Colorado daily on which Batlle Berres had worked more than ten years, supported the rival List 14 headed by the sons of Batlle y Ordóñez. These two *sublemas* became permanent factions of the party (*see* LEMA SYSTEM).

After leaving the Presidency and following the 1951 constitutional change to a plural executive, Batlle Berres was elected in 1954 to the National Council of Government. He was President of that governing body during 1955–1956.

LEE C. FENNELL

BAY OF PIGS INVASION. After Fidel CASTRO seized power in Cuba in 1959, the United States became increasingly alarmed by the expropriation of American-owned property on the island, by Cuban ties with the Soviet Union, and by Cuban revolutionary activities in Latin America. An effort by the United States to persuade the ORGANIZATION OF AMERICAN STATES to take action against Cuba at the Seventh Meeting of Consultation of Ministers of Foreign Affairs in San José, Costa Rica, in August 1960, failed (*see* SAN JOSÉ MEETINGS). The Eisenhower administration then turned to unilateral plotting aimed at the overthrow of the Cuban government with the aid of Cuban refugees, and by the fall of 1960 approximately 1,500 Cubans were being trained in Guatemala by the Central Intelligence Agency, initially to conduct a guerrilla campaign; only later was it decided to mount a direct invasion of the island. When President Kennedy took office in 1961, he found preparations for the invasion under way and allowed it to proceed, though stipulating that American forces were not to be employed. After an air strike on Cuba on April 15 by Cuban pilots based in Nicaragua, an invasion force of about 1,300 men landed on April 17 at the Bay of Pigs (Bahía de Cochinos) on the south coast of Cuba west of Cienfuegos. The invaders were quickly defeated, and nearly 1,200 were taken prisoner. On May 1, his prestige enhanced by his recent victory, Castro announced that Cuba was a socialist state.

The United States was widely criticized for sponsoring the invasion in violation of repeated pledges never to intervene unilaterally in the affairs of another American state. Critics also charged that American planners erred by placing excessive reliance on conservative Cubans in preference to more radical leaders, by expecting that the invasion would trigger armed uprisings against the Cuban government while failing to take steps to ensure that such uprisings would occur, and by underestimating Castro's capacity to deal with the crisis. Others blamed the failure of the invasion on President Kennedy's decision to cancel a second air strike, scheduled to coincide with the start of the invasion.

Efforts to secure the release of the prisoners were soon initiated. A Tractors for Freedom Committee launched after Castro proposed their release in return for 500 bulldozers foundered on the shoals of domestic politics. The prisoners were released in December 1962, through the intercession of the New York lawyer James B. Donovan, in exchange for $53 million in food, drugs, and medical supplies.

RICHARD B. GRAY

BECERRA, GUSTAVO (1925–). Chilean composer. Born in Temuco, he studied at the National Conservatory of Music in Santiago with Pedro Humberto ALLENDE and Domingo SANTA CRUZ. In 1952 he became a member of the Music Faculty of the conservatory, and from 1959 to 1963 he was director of the Instituto de Extensión Musical. In 1971 he was appointed Chilean Cultural Attaché in Germany. One of the most prolific Chilean composers, Becerra has written four symphonies (1955, 1958, 1960, 1964); six concerti for solo instruments and orchestra, of which three are for guitar; and more than forty major chamber music compositions, as well as a long list of choral and solo vocal works, incidental music for the theater, and an opera, *La muerte de Don Rodrigo* (1958). Becerra's music spans a wide stylistic range, moving from a clearly neoclassicist approach to the use of a variety of avant-garde techniques.

JUAN A. ORREGO-SALAS

BELALCÁZAR, SEBASTIÁN DE. *See* BENALCÁZAR, SEBASTIÁN DE.

BELAÚNDE, VÍCTOR ANDRÉS (1883–1967). Peruvian professor of law, diplomat, and writer. Belaúnde was born in Arequipa of a once-wealthy aristocratic family. He studied international law at the University of San Marcos and became a leading spokesman for the *arielistas,* a talented group of intellectuals who sought to emphasize spiritual values over economic considerations. Belaúnde was one of the first *arielistas* to return to the Catholic faith; he became the church's most respected layman and its most active advocate of Christian humanism.

Although most of the *arielistas* were members of the establishment, they criticized it. Belaúnde, for one, in 1917 denounced the oligarchy-controlled universities for their irrelevance. In a 1914 lecture at San Marcos he attacked the ineffective ruling class for its lack of moral leadership and for allowing the dangerous growth of presidential power at the expense of Congress. As one of the first Peruvian intellectuals to concern himself with the middle class, he appealed to the oligarchy to help relieve the plight of the middle class and to seek cooperation with it.

Belaúnde's career as lawyer, professor, diplomat, and writer spanned more than sixty years. He taught both in Peru and in the United States; he wrote extensively and capably on history, law, philosophy, and politics; he served in the 1931 Constitutional Assembly, where his oratorical talents were fully displayed; he founded the periodical *Mercurio Peruano* and pursued other journalistic interests; and he occupied a number of diplomatic posts in Europe and the Americas. Finally, from 1949 to 1966 Belaúnde represented his country in the United Nations, serving also as President of the General Assembly in 1959.

ORAZIO A. CICCARELLI

BELAÚNDE TERRY, FERNANDO (1912–). President of Peru (1963–1968). Born in Lima of an aristocratic Arequipa family, Belaúnde Terry studied both in France and in the United States and in 1935 received a degree in architecture from the University of Texas. Soon thereafter he returned to Peru and quickly became a respected teacher and one of the country's most successful architects. Belaúnde began his political career in 1945 as a deputy to Congress and burst onto the national scene in 1956, when he ran for the Presidency. His candidacy was put forward by a young people's movement of students, intellectuals, and technicians. Belaúnde's reformist program won him a remarkably large following, but he placed second in the three-man race.

Encouraged by the election's results, Belaúnde undertook an extensive tour of the nation to preach his romantic vision of Peru, contained in his book *La conquista del Perú por los peruanos* (1959), and to broaden the popular base of his new party, ACCIÓN POPULAR. His charismatic qualities and his tireless campaigning through some of Peru's most remote regions won him enthusiastic national support. An attempt to discredit his movement by labeling it communist failed when his uncle, Víctor Andrés BELAÚNDE, Peru's most distinguished Catholic layman, ridiculed the charge.

In 1963 Belaúnde was elected President after winning the support of the armed forces and of the Christian Democratic party. His five-year administration began amid great expectations but quickly lost its luster. His reform program was emasculated by a hostile Congress, and Belaúnde himself began to appear indecisive and ineffective. Finally, in 1968, with his party divided and the economy in crisis, Belaúnde was replaced by a military junta.

ORAZIO A. CICCARELLI

BELGRANO, MANUEL (1770–1820). Argentine military and political leader of the independence period. Among the leaders of Argentine independence, only José de SAN MARTÍN enjoys more universal esteem than Manuel Belgrano. Yet Belgrano's total contribution is not easy to characterize. After studying in his native Buenos Aires and in Spain, he was admitted to practice law, but he was intensely interested in economic matters and became the secretary of the *consulado* (merchant guild) established in Buenos Aires in 1794. In that position he worked diligently to promote new industries and advances in education.

On the eve of independence Belgrano was one of the sponsors of the abortive project to establish a constitutional monarchy in America under Princess CARLOTA JOAQUINA DE BORBÓN Y PARMA, sister of Spain's captive FERDINAND VII. Following the May 1810 revolution in Buenos Aires, he served briefly on the governing junta, but he was soon thrust with little real preparation into a military role as head of an expedition to compel Paraguay to accept the junta's authority. His forces were defeated early in 1811, but his diplomacy helped prepare the way for Paraguay's subsequent revolt against Spanish rule.

After several lesser military and diplomatic assignments, Belgrano commanded patriot armies against the royalists, with mixed success, in northwestern Argentina and Upper Peru (Bolivia) from 1812 to 1814. He next formed part of a mission in Europe that labored futilely to effect a compromise with Spain. Again in Argentina in 1816, he exerted his influence at the Congress of Tucumán in favor of the formal declaration of Argentine independence and the proposal to create an independent monarchy under an Inca prince (*see* INCAS; TUCUMÁN, CONGRESS OF). Belgrano's closing years were devoted largely to further service on the northern front and to mediation in domestic political quarrels. He never did develop exceptional military talent, but his human and leadership qualities helped compensate for this lack. He died in Buenos Aires in June 1820.

DAVID BUSHNELL

BELIZE (BRITISH HONDURAS). As a separate entity Belize originated in the activities of seventeenth-century British buccaneers. Seeking protection behind coral reefs and profit from cutting logwood, sea rovers first settled at the mouth of the Belize River about 1640. Their numbers swelled when British suppressive measures required by the Treaties of Madrid of 1667 and 1670 drove other buccaneers to woodcutting. Great Britain considered that the recognition of its title to de facto possessions in America by the Madrid treaties legitimized the woodcutters' occupancy, but Spain continued to regard them as illegal interlopers subject to expulsion.

Late-eighteenth-century treaties legalized British woodcutting. Spanish concessions between 1763 and 1786 allowed British subjects to cut logwood and mahogany between the Hondo and Sibun Rivers but specifically reserved Spanish sovereignty and prohibited concessionaires from engaging in any activity that might suggest permanent tenure. The designation "settlement" rather than "colony" recognized the anomalous status of Belize. Joint Spanish-English inspections soon ended, and by custom the settlers elected magistrates representing the woodcutting interests to conduct local affairs. No local executive functioned until 1784, when Britain named a superintendent, subordinate to the Governor of Jamaica, to regulate the settlers' affairs. Spain failed to name a counterpart, and the office remained exclusively British.

By the early nineteenth century Belize had expanded territorially and functionally. Despite Spanish protests, British woodcutters extended their operations to the west and south far beyond the treaty limits. However, their dominance in settlement affairs ended when Belize developed an entrepôt trade with Central America, contraband before independence in 1821 and legal thereafter. Metropolitan interests established commission and branch houses that, with support from crown-appointed superintendents, gained ascendancy over the old woodcutting-mercantile aristocracy.

Subtle changes occurred also in the political status of the settlement. Spanish desistance from customary actions indicative of sovereignty and the repulse of an attacking Spanish force in 1798 allowed the settlers to assert possession by right of conquest and British authorities to perform acts of de facto sovereignty. Neither assumption, however, was validated by treaty.

Belize fell immediately into controversy with independent Mexico and Central America. The claim of the succession states that they had inherited Spain's titles in the area and the Superintendent's aggressive reassertion of British title to the Bay Islands and British protection over the Mosquito Kingdom opened a dispute over British tenure and boundaries. Central Americans also branded the Belize commercial monopoly as intolerable exploitation and actively sought means to circumvent it.

These issues were largely quiescent by 1860. Treaties with Mexico in 1826 and with Guatemala in 1859 ostensibly resolved the tenure and boundary questions favorably and allowed Britain in 1862 officially to proclaim Belize a colony. The British failure to assist in the construction of a means of transport between Guatemala and the Caribbean, however, gave Guatemala basis later to claim reversion of the rights it had surrendered. Belize's monopoly of Central American trade was broken during the 1850s, and its commerce sharply declined. Two quests largely epitomized the subsequent history of the colony. The first was for a means of livelihood; the second, for recovery of self-government, surrendered to the crown in 1871 after a dispute over defense appropriations.

Economically, with old industries largely moribund, hope focused on the development of agriculture. The colony proved unattractive to immigrants, however, and imported agricultural labor was unsuccessful. Varied forest products such as lumber, gums, resin, and chicle; sugar produced on small plots near Corozal by tenant Yucatecan émigrés; citrus fruits grown in the Stann Creek area; and an embryonic boom in bananas along the coast, first smothered by overproduction and then blighted by Panama disease—all raised some hope of economic revival. Nothing, however, afforded a stable economic base.

The colony, oriented to woodcutting and dependent on natural waterways for internal transport, found difficulty in reshaping its facilities to serve other pursuits. Grants from the Colonial Development and Welfare Fund in the twentieth century helped to provide some needed infrastructure, notably roads and bridges, but recurrent hurricanes inflicted losses that more than offset these gains. In 1961, for example, a hurricane virtually obliterated the capital.

Irreconcilable demands frustrated a return to representative government from 1890 to 1931. Then, acquiescence being forced by hurricane disaster, the Belize Council acceded to the home government's *quid pro quo* that the Governor be granted reserve powers. The constitution of 1954 established universal adult suffrage and a Legislative Assembly with an absolute majority of elected members; that of 1960 inaugurated responsible government. The movement for independence has been obstructed by partisan ambivalence on continuance of the British imperial connection and possible union with Guatemala or the ORGANIZACIÓN DE ESTADOS CENTROAMERICANOS. Further impediments are extreme poverty and a culturally heterogeneous population, estimated at 116,000 in 1968. Some also question the ability or the desire of the former colony to sustain its independence against a contiguous republic that considers it a purloined dependency.

Bibliography. J. A. Calderón Quijano, *Belice 1663(?)–1821: Historia de los establecimientos británicos del Río Valis hasta la independencia de hispano-américa,* Seville, 1944; Wayne M. Clegern, *British Honduras: Colonial Dead End, 1859–1900,* Baton Rouge, La., 1967; Isidro Fabela, *Belice: Defensa de los derechos de México,* Mexico City, 1944; A. R. Gibbs, *British Honduras: An Historical and Descrip-*

tive Account of the Colony from Its Settlement in 1670, London, 1883; D. L. Gordon, *The Economic Development Program of British Honduras,* Washington, 1954; R. A. Humphreys, *The Diplomatic History of British Honduras, 1638–1901,* London, 1961; J. L. Mendoza, *Britain and Her Treaties on Belize,* Guatemala City, 1947; D. A. G. Waddell, *British Honduras: A Historical and Contemporary Survey,* London, 1961.

WILLIAM J. GRIFFITH

BELLO, ANDRÉS (1781–1865). Venezuelan educator, legal expert, and man of letters. Bello was born in Caracas, where he received his education, studying law and medicine at the university. Educated in the tradition of his time, he was an enthusiastic reader of the classics and philosophy. When the German naturalist Alexander von HUMBOLDT visited Caracas in 1799, he was befriended by Bello, who was also interested in science.

In 1810, with the beginning of the revolutionary movement in Venezuela that led to independence from Spain, Bello was named by Simón BOLÍVAR, who had once been his student, to head a mission to London. He remained there for the next nineteen years, working as a teacher, journalist, and translator and continuing his studies of languages and literature. During this period he published "Alocución a la poesía," 1823 ("Allocution to Poetry"), and his famous *silva* "A la agricultura de la Zona Tórrida," 1826 ("Agriculture in the Torrid Zone"). In the second poem he glorifies country life over that of the city, stresses the wealth and fertility of the New World, and repeatedly emphasizes the theme of patriotism. While living in London, Bello published three important journals: *Censor Americano* (1820), *Biblioteca Americana* (1823), and *Repertorio Americano* (1825).

At the invitation of the Chilean government Bello left London in 1829 and went to Chile, where he undertook editorial duties and occupied a position in the Ministry of Foreign Affairs. He later became the founder of the University of Chile and served as its rector from 1843 to 1865. One of the most knowledgeable contemporary experts in law, he wrote *Principios del derecho de gentes* (1832) and a Chilean civil code (1855). Among his other publications are *Principios de la ortografía y métrica* (1835), *Análisis ideológico de los tiempos de la conjugación castellana* (1841), and *Gramática de la lengua castellana destinada al uso de los americanos* (1847), all works on the Spanish language. He wrote as well a work on philosophy, *Filosofía del entendimiento* (1843), and *Resumen de la historia de Venezuela,* published posthumously.

DANIEL R. REEDY

BELO HORIZONTE. Capital and principal city of the state of Minas Gerais, Brazil. It is located near the Serra do Curral at an elevation of 2,700 feet in the gold- and iron-mining region, and its elevation gives it a mild, subtropical climate. The city's construction, in accordance with Brazil's tradition of building new capitals to reorient the focus of the population, was started in 1893 on the site of the Arraial del Curral del Rei by Governor Afonso PENA. The city was inaugurated by Governor Bias Fortes on December 12, 1897. Its original name, Cidade de Minas, was later changed to Belo Horizonte.

The city was designed by the engineers Aarão Reis and Francisco Bicalho, who were inspired by the design of Washington. The streets were laid out in a grid pattern with broad avenues radiating diagonally across the grid from the center of the city. The sections that have grown up outside the perimeter of the original city are less orderly and contrast with the well-planned older area.

Since its completion Belo Horizonte has grown into the most important industrial and commercial center of the state. Its industrial sector includes food-processing, textile, metallurgical, and petroleum plants. Two railroads and a number of asphalt highways link the city with other parts of the state and nation. The city is also served by two airports, six daily newspapers, a number of hospitals and other medical facilities, radio and television stations, and three universities. Of the four largest Brazilian cities, Belo Horizonte has the fastest growth rate. The population increased from 693,328 in 1960 to 1,232,708 in 1970, or by 77.79 percent.

LAWRENCE J. NIELSEN

BELZÚ, MANUEL (1808–1865). Bolivian dictator. Belzú, one of Bolivia's most colorful *caudillos,* is best remembered as the man whose flagrant despotism gave rise to the expression *belcismo.* Born in La Paz, Belzú, a CHOLO, received practically no formal education in addition to what he acquired in the army barracks where he spent most of his life. In fact, he joined the Army at an early age, fought briefly in the War of Independence, and in 1841 distinguished himself at the Battle of Ingavi against an invading Peruvian army. In 1847 he led a revolt against President José BALLIVIÁN, and in 1848, following a brief civil war, he assumed the Presidency of Bolivia and ruled until 1855.

During his seven-year regime Belzú established a reign of terror in which spies were placed everywhere, the constitution was repeatedly violated, and hundreds of people were either killed or exiled. The reason for the longevity of his administration, however, is to be found in his expert manipulation of the cholos. Belzú made himself their spokesman and defender and pitted them against his wealthy opponents, whom he accused of enriching themselves illegitimately at the expense of the poor. By so doing, Belzú made the cholos more conscious than ever of their numerical strength and established such a close rapport with them that on more than one occasion his regime was saved by their timely intervention. However, opposition to Belzú's terrorism and despotism reached such proportions that in 1855 he resigned. Before leaving for Europe he reportedly remarked that "Bolivia is totally incapable of being governed." Nevertheless, in 1865 he attempted to regain power but was killed in La Paz during a meeting with President Mariano MELGAREJO.

ORAZIO A. CICCARELLI

BENALCÁZAR (BELALCÁZAR), SEBASTIÁN DE (ca. 1495–1551). Spanish conquistador who subjugated the Amerindians of Quito (Ecuador) and Popayán (Colombia). Benalcázar fought in the Nicaraguan and Honduran campaigns (1524–1527), became an encomendero, and joined the Peruvian expedition of Francisco PIZARRO and Diego de ALMAGRO. He participated in the Cajamarca massacre (1532) but received only a small share of ATAHUALPA's ransom. Pizarro effectively deprived Benalcázar of future shares of the INCAS' treasure by naming him base commander in the Pacific coast town of Piura (San Miguel). Benalcázar readily left his post for Quito to suppress Rumiñavi, an Inca general who had risen in revolt after the capture of Atahualpa. Almagro later assisted Benalcázar in thwarting the invasion of Pedro de ALVARADO (1534) and named him Deputy Governor of Quito, empowering him to carry the conquest northward.

Anxious to break free of Pizarro's hegemony, Benalcázar set out to conquer the tribes of Popayán and Cali for himself (1536–1537). He left Popayán in 1538 in search of an El Dorado (*see* DORADO, EL), marching as far as the recently founded Santa Fé de Bogotá, where he met rival expeditions led by Gonzalo JIMÉNEZ DE QUESADA and Nikolaus FEDERMANN (1539); all three claimed a share of the CHIBCHA conquest. Emperor Charles V (King CHARLES I) ignored Benalcázar's claim to Bogotá but named him Governor of Popayán (1540). Benalcázar later proved his loyalty by supporting the royalist leaders during the Peruvian civil wars. He died in Cartagena while en route to Spain to appeal a death sentence imposed by a *residencia* judge for conspiracy to murder a subordinate, Jorge Robledo.

WILLIAM S. DUDLEY

BENAVENTE, TORIBIO DE (also known as MOTO-LINÍA) (ca. 1499–?1569). Franciscan missionary. Born in Benavente, León, Spain, he was one of the first twelve Franciscans to arrive in New Spain in 1524. Adopting the name Motolinía, which in Nahuatl meant "poor," he devoted the rest of his life to the task of evangelization, traveling extensively in New Spain and Guatemala and living in complete poverty. Motolinía first worked in the area adjacent to Mexico City as guardian of the main Franciscan convent in the city and the one in Huexotzingo (1528). In these roles he opposed the reprehensible actions of the first *audiencia* of Mexico. About 1530 he organized a mission to Guatemala that was abandoned shortly thereafter. Around this time he suggested the foundation of Puebla as a city for Spanish settlers. In the following decade he traveled through several regions of New Spain carrying on his missionary activities, and in 1542 he became vice commissary of the Franciscan province of Guatemala and Yucatán. He was elected head of the custody of Guatemala in 1544. Although welcomed by the Spanish settlers there, he left Guatemala in 1545, probably because of clashes with the Dominicans. From 1548 through 1551 he was provincial of the Franciscan order in New Spain and later held several other positions.

Motolinía developed a strong animosity against Bartolomé de LAS CASAS, although both were devoted to the defense of the Indians. In 1555 Motolinía wrote a letter to King CHARLES I in which he criticized the *Confesionario,* or confessional rules issued by Las Casas governing the granting of absolution to penitents, and harshly censured him. Motolinía was the author of *Historia de los indios de la Nueva España,* which remained unpublished until the nineteenth century, and *Memoriales,* published in 1903. Both works recorded, although without much order, the customs of the AZTECS and other Indian cultures and the situation of the Indians after the Spanish conquest.

ASUNCIÓN LAVRIN

BENAVIDES, OSCAR (1876–1945). Peruvian army officer and President (1933–1939). Born in Lima, the socially prominent Benavides studied at military schools in both Peru and France. In 1911 he led Peru's troops in a brief and successful war against Colombia in the Amazon region, and in 1913 he became the Army's chief of staff. The following year, spurred on by colleagues of the CIVILISTA PARTY, he headed a military coup against the popular reformist government of Guillermo Billinghurst. In 1915 he relinquished power to a civilian President, the Civilista José PARDO, and spent most of the following two decades either in exile or as Peru's representative to various European countries. When a conflict erupted once again with Colombia over the Amazon area of Leticia, he returned to Peru and in 1933 became Minister of Defense. On April 30 of that year, following the assassination of Luis M. SÁNCHEZ CERRO, he was elected President by Congress. He was later charged with complicity in the assassination, but the accusation was unfounded.

Benavides's six-year regime was highlighted by the signing of a peace treaty with Colombia, by honesty and efficiency in government, and by considerable economic, educational, and social progress. He did rule dictatorially, however, and persecuted the popular ALIANZA POPULAR REVOLUCIONARIA AMERICANA during most of his regime. In 1939 he voluntarily turned power over to a handpicked successor, Manuel PRADO, and took ambassadorial positions in Spain and Argentina. He returned to Lima in 1944.

ORAZIO A. CICCARELLI

BENEDETTI, MARIO (1920–   ). Uruguayan writer. A poet and author of prose fiction generally based on the psychological observation of characters in urban environments, he is best known for his novels *Esta mañana* (1949), *El último viaje* (1951), *¿Quién de nosotros?* (1953), *Montevideanos* (1959), and *La tregua* (1960).

RACHEL PHILLIPS

BERNARDES, ARTUR DA SILVA (1875–1955). President of Brazil (1922–1926). Born in the state of Minas Gerais, Artur Bernardes was graduated from law school in 1900. Elected to Congress in 1909, he subsequently served as secretary of finance (1910–1914) and Governor (1918–1922) in Minas Gerais. Becoming the São Paulo–Minas Gerais presidential candidate in the 1922 election, Bernardes defeated former Vice President Nilo PEÇANHA, candidate of the opposition Republican Reaction.

As President, Bernardes faced formidable obstacles. He inherited an ailing economy: coffee sales, the major source of Brazilian income, were extremely low, and the country found itself heavily in debt. In addition, much of the military opposed him. Between Bernardes's election and inauguration, junior officers unsuccessfully revolted to protest what they felt was Brazil's political decadence (*see* COPACABANA REVOLT). During his administration other unsuccessful military revolts erupted, most notably in 1924 in São Paulo and Rio Grande do Sul.

Bernardes responded to the uneasy situation by governing for almost four years under a state of siege, generally restoring order. Following a generally deflationary policy, the Bernardes administration turned the economy around, with coffee sales reaching a new high

in 1926. The President also effected major educational and judicial reforms. Ending his administration in relative peace, he turned the Presidency over to Washington Luis PEREIRA DE SOUSA, a *paulista*, in 1926.

In 1929 Bernardes was elected to the federal Senate. After supporting the unsuccessful 1932 Constitutionalist revolution against President Getúlio VARGAS, he was exiled from Brazil, returning in 1935 to be elected a federal deputy. With the establishment of the ESTADO NOVO dictatorship in 1937, he withdrew from politics until 1945, when he founded the conservative Partido Republicano.

JOHN E. PICHEL

BETANCOURT, RÓMULO (1908–   ). President of Venezuela (1959–1964). Born in Guatire, Miranda, Betancourt received his education in Caracas. His political career began in 1928, during the regime of Juan Vicente GÓMEZ, when a group of university students planned a student week in which a harmless cultural festival became an anti-Gómez political rally. Betancourt, along with other participants, was arrested and then allowed to go into exile when public reaction to the arrests seemed strong. This group of students, the politicians of which have come to be known as the Generation of 1928, produced two Venezuelan Presidents and other important political leaders.

Betancourt passed the years of exile traveling around Latin America and the Antilles, learning and speaking about the Latin American political condition. Upon the death of Gómez in 1935, he returned to Venezuela to found a political group known as the Organización Venezolana (Orve). This party and the other political groups founded in the aftermath of the Gómez regime caused such difficulties for the government that they were suppressed in 1937 and their leaders sent into

Rómulo Betancourt. [*Organization of American States*]

exile. Betancourt remained in hiding in Caracas, writing articles for the press. Deported in 1939, he spent some time in Chile and Argentina before reentering Venezuela in 1941, when he supported the candidacy of Rómulo GALLEGOS and helped found ACCIÓN DEMOCRÁTICA (AD). With the failure of negotiations between AD and President Isaías MEDINA ANGARITA over the choice of Medina's successor, Betancourt took AD into the coalition of politicians and army officers that overthrew the Medina government in 1945.

As President of the junta which governed from 1945 to 1947, Betancourt helped adopt a series of radical social, political, and economic reforms. Although these two years alienated many of his political supporters and helped bring on the coup d'état of 1948, AD made such remarkable progress in organizing the peasants, especially because of its sponsorship of a radical AGRARIAN REFORM program, that the party's infrastructure remained reasonably intact after the military overthrew the government of Rómulo Gallegos in 1948. During the years of the military junta and the dictatorship of Marcos PÉREZ JIMÉNEZ, Betancourt remained in exile as titular head of AD. After the 1958 revolution that ousted Pérez Jiménez, Betancourt returned to Venezuela and led his party to an electoral victory that put him in the Presidency for the term 1959–1964.

The five years of his Presidency were plagued by guerrilla violence, several attempts on his life, strong opposition from business and oil interests, and several party divisions. Although Betancourt found it necessary to suspend constitutional guarantees and to jail or exile his intemperate opposition, he did keep the country from a violent revolution or a military coup d'état. His Presidency saw the development of the new type of petroleum arrangement with foreign companies known as the service contract. In 1965 he turned over the Presidency to the winner of a free election, Raúl LEONI, also of Acción Democrática. For most of the next few years Betancourt remained outside the country, traveling in Europe away from the public eye. By 1972, however, he was back in Caracas, active in the party politics preceding the elections of 1973. *See also* PETROLEUM INDUSTRY (VENEZUELA).

JOHN V. LOMBARDI

BIDLACK TREATY (NEW GRANADA TREATY). Agreement signed on December 12, 1846, between Benjamin A. Bidlack, the United States representative in Bogotá, and the Foreign Minister of New Granada (Colombia). In addition to regulating commercial relations between the two countries, the treaty provided that "the right of way or transit across the Isthmus of Panama upon any modes of communication that now exist, or that may be hereafter constructed, shall be open and free to the government and citizens of the United States." The United States promised New Granada to guarantee "the perfect neutrality of the before-mentioned isthmus, with the view that the free transit from the one to the other sea may not be interrupted or embarrassed in any future time while this treaty exists." In addition, the United States agreed to assure the sovereignty of New Granada over this area. Initiation for the treaty came not from the United States but from New Granada, which feared future British domination of Panama. The United States thus formally committed itself for the first time to come to the aid of a Latin American country if its independence were threatened. It is to be noted, however, that the United States did not insist upon or acquire exclusive transit or canal rights.

Starting in 1856, when two warships were dispatched to Panama in the wake of the WATERMELON RIOT, the United States intervened on the isthmus on numerous occasions in order to ensure uninterrupted transit during periods of internal disturbance in Panama. The United States paid less attention to its guarantee of Colombian sovereignty over the isthmus and in fact violated this provision of the treaty by encouraging Panama's secession from Colombia in 1903.

RICHARD B. GRAY

BILBAO, FRANCISCO (1823–1865). Chilean writer and political radical. Bilbao first won public attention in 1844, when his strongly worded article "Sociabilidad chilena" ("Chilean Society") was condemned as blasphemous, immoral, and seditious by the Chilean courts; Bilbao was fined, and the article was publicly burned. In 1845 Bilbao went to Paris, where he made contact with and came under the influence of Lamennais, Michelet, and, in particular, Edgar Quinet. The revolution of 1848 made a deep impression on him, as did many of the more radical and utopian ideas that came to the surface at that moment.

Returning to Chile early in 1850, Bilbao was given employment in the Statistics Office, but his main interests lay elsewhere. He now turned his attention to forming a radical political movement to press for an out-and-out liberalization of the conservative political system established by Diego PORTALES. With the help of a number of friends, notably Santiago Arcos, he was instrumental in creating, in April 1850, the Sociedad de la Igualdad (Society of Equality), which soon came to have a membership of around 6,000, including many artisans. The movement, which advocated radical and utopian ideals, quickly came to be associated with the more general opposition to the presidential candidacy of Manuel MONTT. Its demonstrations and picturesque French-style ceremonies did much to antagonize the government and, perhaps, to amuse the public. In November 1850 the society was suppressed, and Bilbao went into hiding. He took part in the abortive mutiny of April 20, 1851, in Santiago and afterward fled in disguise to Peru. He never returned to his native land.

After a somewhat stormy residence in Peru, Bilbao revisited Europe (1855–1857) before settling finally in Argentina, where he died. His later years were devoted mostly to writing. He was the author of numerous articles and several books. His earlier writings, couched in a highly florid and lyrical style, were concerned primarily with attacking the clerical and aristocratic aspects of Latin American life and with advocating the introduction of a vastly increased measure of political democracy. Later, in such works as *La América en peligro* (1862) and *El evangelio americano* (1864), he became obsessed by the contrast between the United States, prosperous and free, and the "Dis-United States" of Latin America. Bilbao has often been regarded as a precursor by modern radical and left-wing movements in Chile, with varying degrees of justification.

SIMON COLLIER

BIOY CASARES, ADOLFO (pseudonym, HONORIO BUSTOS DOMECQ) (1914–   ). Argentine writer. In his first and less well-known period he wrote such novels and stories as *Prólogo* (1929), *Caos* (1934), *La nueva tormenta* (1935), *La estatua casera* (1936), and *Luis Greve, muerto* (1937). A second, more interesting period begins with the novel *La invención de Morel* (1940) and its sequel, *Plan de evasión* (1945), both dealing with fantastic worlds created according to precise laws that lend verisimilitude to absurdity. The same vein runs through the stories of *La trama celeste* (1948), *Historia prodigiosa* (1956), *Guirnalda con amores* (1959), and *El lado de la sombra* (1962). His novel *El sueño de los héroes* (1954) describes a magic adventure in the suburbs of Buenos Aires. Under the pseudonym Honorio Bustos Domecq he collaborated with Jorge Luis BORGES in *Seis problemas para don Isidro Parodi* (1941), and this collaboration has continued to produce stories and novels whose curious analytical atmosphere recalls the technique of the detective story and science fiction. Bioy Casares also collaborated with his wife, Silvina Ocampo, in writing a detective story, *Los que aman, odian* (1946). A more recent work is *Diario de la guerra del cerdo* (1969).

RACHEL PHILLIPS

BLACK LEGEND. Thesis that the Spanish conquistadores treated the Indians with great cruelty and that later Spanish administration of the Americas was oppressive and corrupt. This view was spread especially by the European rivals of Spain. Jealous of the Spanish empire and the New World riches carried in Spanish galleons, the Low Countries, England, and France repeated and embellished the Black Legend (Leyenda Negra) for two centuries.

The chief source of the Black Legend is the *Very Brief Account of the Destruction of the Indies* by Bartolomé de LAS CASAS. Las Casas, the Protector of the Indians, composed this hard-hitting pamphlet between 1540 and 1542 and read it at the Spanish court to influence King CHARLES I to issue the NEW LAWS in defense of Indian rights. In 1552 Bishop Las Casas had the *Very Brief Account* printed in Seville, and by 1626 it had been translated into six European languages. In it Las Casas described the Spanish conquests in the New World, with many examples of Spanish cruelty; he stated that 15 or 20 million Indians had perished—an exaggeration, like most sixteenth-century statistics.

In 1598 a Latin edition of the *Very Brief Account* was printed in Frankfurt, with illustrations of the most sensational episodes by Théodore de Bry. De Bry's engravings, reprinted ten times before 1648, greatly increased the emotional impact of Las Casas' work; they even seem to have replaced the text as a source for some later anti-Spanish historians. The Black Legend was also reinforced by reports of the Spanish massacre of French settlers at Fort Caroline, Florida, in 1565, and by Girolamo Benzoni's popular *La historia del mondo nuovo* (1565). Early Dutch and French translations of the *Very Brief Account* (1578, 1579, etc.) are considered part of a propaganda war against Spain that accompanied the rebellion of the Low Countries.

At this time the Low Countries and England had religious as well as political motives for spreading the Black Legend. Spain was attacked as the champion of the Counter Reformation and the stronghold of the Inquisition (*see* INQUISITION, HOLY OFFICE OF THE). Collections of voyages, such as the *Grands voyages* and *Petits voyages* of Théodore de Bry and his successors (1590–1634), contained many accounts of Spanish excesses. The Dutchman Jan Laët (1630) disparaged Spain, and the English ex-Dominican Thomas GAGE (1648) especially emphasized Spanish cruelty. English editions of Las Casas' *Very Brief Account* were given titles like *The Tears of the Indians: Being an Historical and True Account of the Cruel Massacres and Slaughters of Above Twenty Millions of Innocent People* (1656). Seventeenth-century Italian writers denounced the conquest because they opposed Spanish policies in Italy.

In the eighteenth century champions of toleration cited the Spanish conquest as representing the opposite of their rationalist ideals. Voltaire's drama *Alzire* (1737) contrasts a bloodthirsty conquistador with a noble Indian rebel. Guillaume-Thomas Raynal's *Histoire philosophique et politique* (1770) portrays Spain as the enemy of civilization. In America nonconformist creoles repeated Las Casas' charges to justify their rebellion. For example, in 1798 Juan Pablo Viscardo y Guzmán accused Spain of "ingratitude, injustice, servitude, and desolation." Simon BOLÍVAR in his Jamaica Letter (1815) and the Argentine manifesto justifying independence from Spain (1816) expressed the same view. After winning independence, Latin American liberals called for the de-Hispanization of their new nations.

On the other hand, it was during the eighteenth century, according to Rómulo D. Carbia, that a reaction against the Black Legend achieved success. Even earlier some conquistadores, among them Bernal DÍAZ DEL CASTILLO (shortly after 1552), had defended their expeditions. The Franciscan missionary Toribio de BENAVENTE had sharply criticized Las Casas in his famous letter to Charles I (1555). At the end of the sixteenth century the historian Antonio de HERRERA Y TORDESILLAS, although he borrowed from Las Casas' unpublished *History of the Indies,* declared that the bad acts of a few should not tarnish the good deeds of many.

Herrera's reasoning was followed by a new school of historians, whose attitude was less factional than that of earlier writers. In his *Dictionnaire historique et critique* (1695–1697), Pierre Bayle found cruelty in Indian life as well as among Spaniards, while the *Nouveau dictionnaire historique* (1765) advocated a neutral stance toward the conquest. William Robertson, in his influential *History of America* (1777), praised Spain and criticized Las Casas for exaggeration. Juan Bautista Muñoz developed Robertson's arguments with richer documentation in his *Historia del nuevo mundo* (1793), concluding that little credit should be given the *Very Brief Account.* In the nineteenth century William H. PRESCOTT, and in the twentieth Edward Gaylord Bourne and Lesley B. Simpson, among others, defended Spanish colonial policy— defended it so vigorously that critics charge them with fostering a "White Legend" that exonerated the conquistadores from all accusations of wrongdoing.

Is the Black Legend true or false? Supporting it is the eyewitness testimony of Las Casas and others, testimony that, except for the inflated statistics, many scholars accept. These scholars also emphasize Spanish exploitative legislation, which authorized the conscription of Indian labor for mines and estates; and they point to the astounding decline in the Indian population. Skeptics rebut this evidence with well-documented proof of the concern of the Spanish crown about the treatment of the Indians, concern reflected in the New Laws of 1542 and in the Ordinances of Discovery and Settlement of 1573, supposedly ending conquest "by fire and by sword." They stress the struggle for justice carried on by Antonio de Montesinos, Bartolomé de Las Casas, Francisco de Vitoria, and other Spaniards. Each side cites case histories of good or bad treatment of the Indians; no clear verdict has been reached.

Thus the Black Legend remains a source of lively controversy. Disagreement over what to do when twentieth-century man stumbles upon primitive tribes suggests the difficulty of judging past Spanish conduct. In any event Spain can no longer be considered unique in its treatment of the inhabitants of the New World. The responsibility for mishandling relations with the less-developed countries of Asia and Africa and with the American Indians must be shared by all the former colonial powers, including the United States.

Bibliography. Edward G. Bourne, *Spain in America, 1450–1580,* New York, 1962; Rómulo D. Carbia, *Historia de la leyenda negra hispano-americana,* Buenos Aires, 1943; Charles Gibson (ed.), *The Black Legend,* New York, 1971; Lewis Hanke, "A Modest Proposal for a Moratorium on Grand Generalizations: Some Thoughts on the Black Legend," *Hispanic American Historical Review,* vol. LI, no. 1, February 1971, pp. 112–127; Benjamin Keen, "The Black Legend Revisited: Assumptions and Realities," *Hispanic American Historical Review,* vol. XLIX, no. 4, November 1969, pp. 703–719; id., "The White Legend Revisited: A Reply to Professor Hanke's 'Modest Proposal,'" *Hispanic American Historical Review,* vol. LI, no. 2, May 1971, pp. 336–355; William S. Maltby, *The Black Legend in England: The Development of Anti-Spanish Sentiment, 1558–1660,* Durham, N.C., 1971; Lesley B. Simpson, *The Encomienda in New Spain,* Berkeley, Calif., 1929.

GEORGE SANDERLIN

BLANCO PARTY (NATIONAL PARTY, URUGUAY). The National party, whose members are commonly known as Blancos, is the more conservative and rural-oriented of Uruguay's two major political parties. Although historically the party has almost always been in the role of opposition, it was the governing majority during the 1959–1967 period.

Like the rival Colorados (*see* COLORADO PARTY: URUGUAY), the Blancos trace their political heritage to the first half of the nineteenth century. The followers of Gen. Manuel ORIBE, whose centralizing aims led to a revolt after he became President in 1835, became known as Blancos as a result of the white hatbands they wore for identification on the battlefield. The Blancos began using the term "Partido Nacional" unofficially in 1857 and adopted it as the party's formal name in 1872.

Armed conflict between Blancos and Colorados was common throughout the nineteenth century. As early as mid-century, however, the parties began to reach periodic political agreements under which the Blancos would accept the dominant role of the Colorados in return for concessions such as cash indemnities and guaranteed Blanco control of specific departments. Although these periods of truce were usually short-lived, they may have helped establish the foundations of the principle of *coparticipación.* This belief that the minority should be guaranteed representation in government is strongly reflected in Uruguay's twentieth-century constitutions and electoral practices. The last major Blanco revolt against a Colorado government occurred in 1904. Aparicio SARAVIA, a wealthy landowner who was the major National party leader during the late nineteenth century, led the unsuccessful revolt and was mortally wounded in battle.

Among twentieth-century Blanco leaders, none has had as much influence upon the party as Luis Alberto de HERRERA. A participant in the Blanco revolts of 1897 and 1904, he became chairman of the National party Executive Committee in 1920 and remained the dominant figure in the party until his death in 1959. Opposition to Herrera's conservative policies, to his occasional collaboration with the Colorados, and to his personalistic leadership of the party produced recurring factionalism among Blancos. Some anti-Herrera factions, such as the Independent Nationalists, organized as separate parties while other groups opposed his leadership from within as *sublemas* (*see* LEMA SYSTEM).

In March 1959 the Blancos became the governing party for the first time in almost a century. The National party's electoral victory over the Colorados in November 1958 was the combined result of popular disillusionment with the Colorados and frustration over persistent economic problems, defection of the Federal League for Rural Action (LFAR) from its traditional support of the Colorados, and a new coalition under which the Independent Nationalists adhered to the Blanco *lema.* Herrera, head of the winning 1958 *sublema,* died five weeks after his party took control of the government. After his death intraparty divisions and realignments soon made the Blanco government as sharply factionalized as the previous Colorado administration.

The National party won the 1962 election by fewer than 11,000 votes, compared with its margin of more than 100,000 in 1958. During the 1963–1967 Blanco administration inflation and unemployment increased, and the government was confronted with a greater number of strikes and demonstrations than during the first administration. In 1966 Uruguayan voters chose both to return the Colorados to power and to replace the COLEGIADO with a conventional Presidency. Although in 1971 the Blancos again placed second in the presidential election, the party won in fourteen of the nation's nineteen departments.

Bibliography. Lorenzo Carnelli, *El radicalismo blanco,* Montevideo, 1925; Manuel Fonseca, *La política de coparticipación,* Montevideo, 1951; José Monegal, *Esquema de la historia del Partido Nacional,* Montevideo, 1959; Juan E. Pivel Devoto, *Historia de los partidos políticos en el Uruguay,* 2 vols., Montevideo, 1942.

LEE C. FENNELL

BLEST GANA, ALBERTO (1830–1920). Chilean novelist and diplomat. Blest Gana was born in Santiago and died in Paris. A graduate of the Escuela Militar (1846), he continued his studies in France until 1851. Upon his return to Chile, he served as an instructor in the Escuela Militar and as a member of the cartography team. The latter assignment made it possible for him to see much of the country and its people. Afterward he served in the Ministry of War, and he remained in the Army until 1855. In 1866 he entered the diplomatic corps.

An admirer of Honoré de Balzac, Blest Gana tried to emulate *La comédie humaine* by recording the life of the Chilean people in a long list of realistic novels. This he began to do while he was still in the Army. Of his novels, the best-known and most popular is *Martín Rivas* (1862), a *novela de costumbres* (local-color novel) about Santiago around the time of the revolution of 1851. Other works from his Army days are *Una escena social* (1853), *Engaños y desengaños* (1855), and *Los desposados* (1855). In 1858 he published *El primer amor, La fascinación, Juan de Aria,* and *El jefe de la familia,* and in 1860 he won the University Prize with *La aritmética en el amor.* There followed six more novels, of which four, including *El loco Estero,* 1909 (*The Madman Estero*), were written in Paris.

GERARDO SÁENZ

BOGOTÁ. Capital and largest city of Colombia and capital of the department of Cundinamarca. It is located almost at the geographical center of Colombia on a large *sabana* (savanna) 8,600 feet above sea level.

Bogotá was founded as Santa Fé de Bogotá, probably in 1539, by Gonzalo JIMÉNEZ DE QUESADA. CHARLES I gave the city a coat of arms and made it the seat of the *audiencia* of New Granada in 1548. Bogotá became the capital of the Viceroyalty of New Granada in 1717 and the capital of Gran Colombia (present-day Colombia, Venezuela, and Ecuador) in 1821 (*see* COLOMBIA, GRAN; NEW GRANADA, VICEROYALTY OF). With the dissolution of Gran Colombia in 1830, Bogotá continued as capital of New Granada, which later was renamed Colombia.

Bogotá has been the scene of many political crises, including the BOGOTAZO riots of April 9, 1948. The fear of similar destructive outbreaks may have contributed to the exodus of the more affluent citizens from their traditional central-city residences to suburban communities of the North American type that now constitute the northern part of the city. More than 40 percent of Colombia's economic output originates in Bogotá, and because of its early establishment as an educational and cultural center the city has become known as the Athens of Latin America.

In 1954 the Colombian Congress created the special district of Bogotá, comprising six boroughs and the city of Bogotá. The district is an independent and autonomous entity governed by a mayor appointed by the President. The population of the district in 1970 was slightly in excess of 2.5 million.

JAMES H. NEAL

BOGOTÁ CONFERENCE (1948). Ninth International Conference of American States. The conference was held in Bogotá, Colombia, from March 30 to May 2, 1948, and was attended by representatives of all the American republics. The major achievement of the conference was the drafting of the Charter of the OR-GANIZATION OF AMERICAN STATES (OAS), providing a legal framework for a permanent inter-American organization. Also agreed upon was the Pact of Bogotá, incorporating into one treaty all former inter-American agreements on the peaceful settlement of disputes between American nations. Despite Latin American hopes the American delegation, which was headed by Secretary of State George C. Marshall, made it plain that the United States would not establish the same kind of intensive program of government-to-government aid for Latin America that it was then undertaking in Europe through the Marshall Plan. It was stressed that Latin America would have to rely primarily on private foreign investment to stimulate its internal economic growth.

The conference was interrupted by the BOGOTAZO, a near week of rioting, burning, and looting that followed the assassination (April 9, 1948) in Bogotá of the popular Colombian reformist leader Jorge Eliécer GAITÁN.

RODNEY D. ANDERSON

BOGOTAZO. Outbreak of violent rioting in Bogotá, Colombia, following the assassination on April 9, 1948, of the charismatic Liberal leader Jorge Eliécer GAITÁN (*see* LIBERAL PARTY: COLOMBIA). The disturbances took place while the Colombian capital was playing host to the Ninth International Conference of American States (BOGOTÁ CONFERENCE).

Gaitán, a leftist who probably would have been elected President of Colombia in the next election, was mortally wounded near his office in downtown Bogotá by Juan Roa Sierra, a young man with a record of mental instability who was immediately beaten to death by an outraged mob. As the news of Gaitán's wounding and death became known, angry crowds looted stores, opened prisons, and attacked and burned the offices of the Conservative daily *El Siglo* and the home of the right-wing Conservative Laureano GÓMEZ (*see* CONSERVATIVE PARTY: COLOMBIA) as well as churches and public buildings in the center of the city. Some policemen joined the rioters, and the task of restoring order fell to the armed forces. Meanwhile, Liberal and Communist spokesmen, having taken over the radio stations, called for the overthrow of Conservative President Mariano OSPINA PÉREZ. The latter steadfastly refused to resign, although he did appoint a bipartisan Cabinet on April 10.

The period of most serious disorder lasted for approximately thirty hours, although occasional acts of violence occurred for several days afterward, and the inter-American conference formally resumed its deliberations on April 14. Estimates of the loss of life in Bogotá differ, ranging from 500 to 1,200; the death toll as a result of outbreaks in other cities was probably in the thousands. Moreover, the Bogotazo served to exacerbate partisan hatreds and to ignite two decades of violence in rural Colombia (*see* VIOLENCIA, LA).

The responsibility for the assassination of Gaitán and the subsequent disorders has never been fully elucidated, and the findings of a Scotland Yard investigation have not been released. At the time Colombian Conservatives, along with Secretary of State George C. Marshall, who attended the inter-American conference, blamed local Communists and the Soviet Embassy in Bogotá for both the assassination and the rioting.

Liberals accused Conservative extremists of arranging the murder. Others have asserted the involvement of Venezuela's ACCIÓN DEMOCRÁTICA (AD) party, whose leader, Rómulo BETANCOURT, was the head of his nation's delegation to the conference. Accusers of the AD claim that party leaders had been conspiring with Gaitán to overthrow the Colombian government and that, after his death, Venezuelan newspapers and radio stations incited the rioters to take such action. Fidel CASTRO, who was present in Bogotá at the time, has also been accused of complicity in both the murder and the rioting. Most objective analysts agree that although the Communists were quick to exploit Gaitán's death, the rioting was basically the result of existing political tensions and social and economic ills.

HELEN DELPAR

BOLAÑOS, CÉSAR (1931–). Peruvian composer. He was born in Lima, where he studied with Andrés SAS. Later he worked at the RCA Institute of Electronic Technology in New York and the institute of the Di Tella Foundation in Buenos Aires with Alberto GINASTERA. In addition to a number of works for chamber ensembles and orchestra, such as *Divertimento III* (*Density 1*), in which he employs aleatory resources, he has produced electronic music such as *Intensidad y altura,* based on a poem by César VALLEJO, and works based on the relationship of image and sound.

JUAN A. ORREGO-SALAS

BOLÍVAR, SIMÓN (1783–1830). South American independence leader. The future Liberator was by his birth a native of Caracas and a member of the creole landowning elite of colonial Venezuela. Orphaned before his tenth birthday, he nevertheless received a respectable education, which included an early exposure to the thought of the Enlightenment and to the teachings of Rousseau, who was a favorite of his tutor, Simón Rodríguez (*see* ENLIGHTENMENT: SPANISH AMERICA). In 1799 he made his first trip to Europe, where he remained until 1802; while in Madrid, he married the daughter of a prominent Caracas family, who died soon after the couple returned to Venezuela. He then made a second trip to Europe, during which he traveled widely, became acquainted with notable figures of the day, and made a vow in Rome to work for the freedom of Spanish America.

Bolívar was back in Venezuela in 1807. He devoted himself to agricultural and commercial interests and took part in the revolutionary ferment unleashed by the Napoleonic invasion of Spain in 1808 and the resulting imperial crisis. He welcomed the establishment of a junta in Caracas in April 1810 and, as an officer in the colonial militia, prepared to serve the new regime. But his first major assignment was a diplomatic mission to Europe, where he sought to attract the sympathy of the British government and established contact with MIRANDA.

Following his return to Venezuela in December 1810, Bolívar was one of the patriots who worked for a formal declaration of independence, which was issued on July 5, 1811. Almost immediately thereafter, he helped suppress a counterrevolutionary outbreak at Valencia. He was less fortunate in 1812 against the major royalist offensive launched by Juan Domingo Monteverde. On July 6, he was forced to abandon the key fortress of Puerto Cabello, whose command had been entrusted to him. Yet when Miranda a few weeks later signed a capitulation with Monteverde, Bolívar suspected betrayal and was one of the officers who joined together to block Miranda's departure, in effect delivering him to the royalists.

Bolívar himself soon left Venezuela, going by way of Curaçao to New Granada. After brief service with the New Granadan patriots, he obtained their support for an invasion of Venezuela that led him back in a lightning campaign to Caracas, which he entered on August 6, 1813. In the course of this campaign, at Trujillo, he issued his decree of war to the death, promising to execute all Spaniards not actively supporting the patriots. He established the second Venezuelan republic, which he ruled as virtual military dictator. However, the restored patriot regime was steadily undermined by such royalist leaders as José Tomás BOVES, who exploited racial and social tensions to rally much of the lower-class population against the generally aristocratic patriot leadership. In June 1814, Boves routed Bolívar at the Battle of La Puerta, opening the way to Caracas and forcing Bolívar and other patriots to retreat into the northeastern corner of Venezuela.

Bolívar eventually fled again to New Granada, where he served the federalist United Provinces in subduing centralist Cundinamarca (Bogotá), but he did not relish involvement in such internecine quarrels, which were irretrievably weakening New Granada at a time when Spanish forces threatened reconquest. In mid-1815 he therefore withdrew to Jamaica. There he composed his notable Jamaica Letter, in which he analyzed the state

Simón Bolívar. [*Radio Times Hulton Picture Library*]

of Spanish America, set forth his own political principles, and expressed firm confidence in final victory. Moving on to Haiti, he obtained assistance from President Alexandre Sabès PÉTION for a new attempt at freeing Venezuela. The first effort, begun in May 1816, failed to establish a patriot foothold, but with new help from Pétion he was back for good by the end of the year.

Bolívar established contact with other, scattered insurgent forces active in eastern Venezuela but, faced with dissension from rival leaders, transferred his operations to the lower ORINOCO RIVER. His efforts were crowned by success when Angostura (now Ciudad Bolívar) surrendered to the patriots in July 1817. Angostura became the provisional capital of independent Venezuela. Bolívar also won the collaboration of José Antonio PÁEZ, who had already carved out a patriot stronghold farther west, in Apure. Thanks to Páez, who enjoyed great popularity among the *llaneros* (plainsmen), and to such measures of Bolívar as the decree of October 1817 promising a bonus in land and cattle to patriot soldiers, the republican cause obtained a steadily wider popular following. However, Bolívar did not have much success against the Spanish regulars under Gen. Pablo Morillo who controlled most of the Venezuelan highlands.

By his installation of the Venezuelan Congress of Angostura in February 1819 (*see* ANGOSTURA, CONGRESS OF), Bolívar moved to give the patriot regime a regular legal basis. At the opening session he delivered his Angostura Address, which spelled out in concrete detail his belief in a system founded on representative and republican principles but with a strong central executive and pronounced aristocratic features, such as a hereditary Senate. Although Bolívar thus rejected political democracy, he included a vigorous plea for the abolition of slavery. This plea redeemed a pledge he had made to Pétion and heightened the "popular" character of his movement, but it also reflected his own sincere convictions.

In May 1819, abandoning his efforts to regain Caracas, Bolívar turned westward to invade the heart of New Granada. His victory at the Battle of Boyacá on August 7 (*see* BOYACÁ, BATTLE OF) was followed by the occupation of Bogotá and most of the surrounding provinces. Leaving the New Granadan officer Francisco de Paula SANTANDER in charge of organizing the newly liberated territory, Bolívar first hastened back to Angostura, where he induced the Congress to decree the union of Venezuela, New Granada, and Quito (Ecuador) as the Republic of Colombia, or Gran Colombia, as it was subsequently termed (*see* COLOMBIA, GRAN). He then turned once more to the military struggle, which was interrupted by an armistice (November 1820–April 1821) but culminated in victory at the Battle of Carabobo in June 1821 (*see* CARABOBO, BATTLE OF). The greater part of Venezuela and New Granada was then free. Bolívar paused to be inaugurated as the first constitutional President of Gran Colombia when elected to that position by the Congress of Cúcuta (*see* CÚCUTA, CONGRESS OF), but he left Santander as Vice President in charge of the home front while he set off to complete the struggle against Spain.

Bolívar conceived a pincers movement against Quito, which was still in Spanish hands: while Antonio José de SUCRE led an army up from Guayaquil, he would move overland through southern New Granada. As Bolívar was delayed by royalist resistance, Sucre reached Quito first, but Bolívar staged his triumphal entry soon afterward and also took steps to assure the incorporation into Gran Colombia of Guayaquil, which had functioned as an independent province since staging its own revolution in October 1820. This objective was accomplished on the eve of Bolívar's meeting at Guayaquil, in July 1822, with José de San MARTÍN. Although he did not wholly share San Martín's views on the future organization of Spanish America and apparently did not offer the Argentine liberator all the aid the latter considered necessary for the attainment of final victory in Peru, there was never any doubt as to Bolívar's ultimate commitment to a policy of continental cooperation. Indeed, the following year, after San Martín had withdrawn and the Congress in Bogotá had voted due authorization, Bolívar himself moved south to take command in the Peruvian theater.

Arriving in September 1823, Bolívar first had to deal with the struggle raging among Peruvian patriots between supporters and opponents of President José de la RIVA-AGÜERO. This was soon settled, at Riva-Agüero's expense, but in February 1824 the patriot cause suffered a major setback when an army mutiny at Callao delivered that strategic port and indirectly Lima as well to the enemy. Given dictatorial powers by the Peruvian Congress, Bolívar established his government at Trujillo in northern Peru. Then, once preparations were sufficiently advanced, he set forth on the campaign in the Peruvian highlands that produced the victory of Junín (*see* JUNÍN, BATTLE OF) and, in December 1824, the decisive defeat of the royalists at Ayacucho (*see* AYACUCHO, BATTLE OF). Bolívar was not present at the second battle; he had returned to Lima, which meanwhile the patriots had recovered. But the victorious commander was his most trusted lieutenant, Sucre.

While in Lima, Bolívar attended to problems of internal organization and, just two days before Ayacucho, issued an invitation to the Spanish American nations to attend a conference in Panama City for the purpose of cementing a permanent political and military alliance. Significantly, he did not invite the United States to participate. When Santander issued an invitation to Washington, Bolívar accepted the decision, but his own vision of inter-American cooperation was limited essentially to the Spanish American peoples. However, the PANAMA CONGRESS, which took place only in 1826, failed to live up to Bolívar's expectations.

It was Sucre once again who overcame the last important stronghold of royalist authority, Upper Peru, in the first part of 1825, but Bolívar followed him to take part in organizing the area, which became a separate nation named in his honor. He returned to Peru early in 1826, but at the Bolivians' request he drafted their first constitution, which was adopted with only minor alterations. Although it featured a life President who selected his own successor, it was in many respects decidedly liberal, thus reflecting the mixture of authoritarianism and sincere republicanism characteristic of Bolívar's thinking. Bolívar also obtained its adoption in Peru, and he hoped it would serve as a model for revamping the institutions of Gran Colombia as well; Bolivia, Peru, and Colombia he then hoped to join together in an ambitious Confederation of the Andes.

Neither the Bolivian constitution nor the Confederation of the Andes aroused much enthusiasm in Colombia, and Peru revoked Bolívar's constitution soon after he departed to deal with the rapid deterioration of stability in Colombia itself. The Colombian crisis was triggered by the autonomist revolt in Venezuela in April 1826 under José Antonio Páez; but it was soon aggravated by the distrust inspired in Santander and other Colombian liberals by the Bolivian constitution and by indications that Bolívar hoped to see it copied in Colombia if necessary by unconstitutional means. When Bolívar reached Caracas in January 1827 and made peace by pardoning Páez's rebellion, their fears increased and soon spilled over into open opposition. Bolívar felt compelled to return to Bogotá and assume personal command. He placed his hopes in a constitutional reform convention that met at Ocaña in April 1828, but when it dissolved with nothing accomplished, he established a frank military dictatorship that hardened after the attempt made on his life on September 25, 1828. Bolívar not only restricted political liberties but suspended many of the liberal reforms previously adopted in Gran Colombia, especially in religious and financial matters. He did not necessarily oppose these in principle but had concluded that they were premature and, as such, an undesirable source of internal dissension.

Dictatorship did not bring stability, which was undermined by scattered liberal revolts. A brief war with Peru in 1828–1829 added to Bolívar's problems, and at the end of 1829 Venezuela rebelled again, this time for definitive separation. The meeting of still another constitutional convention in Bogotá early in 1830 was incapable of halting the dissolution of Gran Colombia. Bolívar himself resigned the Presidency in despair, resolving to go into exile. Shortly afterward, Ecuador formally moved to secede, while in New Granada the party of Santander returned to political activity, hoping to settle old scores. Amid this panorama of growing strife and political disintegration, Bolívar died, at Santa Marta on the Colombian coast, in December 1830.

Bibliography. Víctor Andrés Belaúnde, *Bolívar and the Political Thought of the Spanish American Revolution,* reprint, New York, 1967; Simón Bolívar, *Selected Writings of Bolívar,* 2 vols., New York, 1951; id., *Escritos del Libertador,* Caracas, 1964–; Salvador de Madariaga, *Bolívar,* London and New York, 1952; Gerhard Masur, *Simon Bolivar,* 2d ed., Albuquerque, N.Mex., 1969; Daniel F. O'Leary, *Bolívar and the War of Independence,* Austin, Tex., 1970.

DAVID BUSHNELL

BOLIVIA SINCE 1828. What is today the Republic of Bolivia was the Upper Peru of the Spanish colonial period. Until 1776 it was governed from Lima, but with the creation of the new Viceroyalty of the Río de la Plata (*see* RÍO DE LA PLATA, VICEROYALTY OF) that year, its jurisdiction was transferred to Buenos Aires. However, when the people of Buenos Aires undertook the struggle in 1810 that led to the independence of the Río de la Plata area, there was little impact on Spanish power in Upper Peru. It was not until Simón BOLÍVAR sent his young general Antonio José de SUCRE to Upper Peru in 1825 that this region declared its independence.

Bolívar issued a new and complicated constitution, under which Sucre became the first President, agreeing

to serve for two years. In 1828, before his term was completed, he was forced to resign when he was defeated by a combination of local uprisings and an invasion from Peru.

Age of the caudillos. For most of the rest of the nineteenth century, Bolivia was ruled by a series of colorful *caudillos*. In most cases, however, their advent to or exit from power meant little to the Indians who made up the great majority of the population. Isolated by their languages (QUECHUA and AYMARÁ) from the Spanish-speaking whites and mixed-blood cholos (*see* CHOLO), they sought to have as little as possible to do with politics and the struggles for power among rival leaders. It may well be that the majority of them did not even know that they were living in a country called Bolivia.

The first of the long line of *caudillos* was Andrés SANTA CRUZ, a cholo claiming descent from the INCAS, who had for a short time served as President of Peru. He seized control of Bolivia in 1829 and held it for a decade. In 1836 he succeeded in organizing a PERU-BOLIVIA CONFEDERATION and assumed the post of lifetime Grand Protector of the new state.

The Confederation proved to be short-lived. Chilean troops invaded it and at the Battle of Yungay (1839) defeated Santa Cruz, who fled to Europe. Thereupon, Bolivia and Peru once again went their separate ways. Under the leadership of Gen. José BALLIVIÁN, the Bolivians were able to repulse a new invasion from Peru in 1841. Ballivián ruled for six years and was succeeded by Manuel BELZÚ, a cholo who incited his followers to attack many of the white and near-white large landlords. Belzú was succeeded by several other *caudillos* whose periods in power were short-lived. Mariano MELGAREJO, who stayed in office from 1864 until 1871, was the last of them.

Melgarejo's rule was marked not only by outrageous

BOLIVIA

Area: 424,164 sq. mi.   Population: 5,063,000 (1971 est.).

cruelty and debauchery but, more important, by his government's seizure and sale of Indian communal lands. The process of despoiling the Indians of the lands which their ancestors had held under the Incas, the titles to which had been recognized by the Spanish crown, was initiated in this period. During the decades after 1871 virtually all Indian communities disappeared, and their land was taken by white and cholo landlords. Only in the most isolated parts of the ALTIPLANO (high plateau) did the Indians continue to keep their ancestral holdings.

In 1879 Bolivia experienced a major national disaster. In the decades preceding that year, Chilean entrepreneurs, often in partnership with British capitalists, had been inaugurating the exploitation of the natural nitrate resources in the Bolivian coastal province of Atacama, centering on the port of Antofagasta, and in the Peruvian province of Tarapacá. They had worked under concessions granted by the Bolivian and Peruvian governments. In 1878, however, President Hilarión Daza of Bolivia decided to impose a new export tax on the Chilean nitrate entrepreneurs. *See* NITRATE INDUSTRY (CHILE).

Chile used this tax increase as a *casus belli,* and its troops descended on Antofagasta. Peru backed Bolivia, but its Army and Navy were no match for those of Chile, which not only seized Tarapacá but also sent its Army on to take the Peruvian capital, Lima, in 1881. As a result of this WAR OF THE PACIFIC, Bolivia lost its coastal province and outlet to the sea. It was not until 1904 that Bolivia formally forswore claims to the region and that Chile in return paid an indemnity of $1.5 million and agreed to make the former Peruvian port of Arica a free port for the transport of Bolivian products. In spite of this recognition of the facts of the case, the Bolivians have never given up their aspiration to acquire once again a port on the Pacific.

Twenty years after the War of the Pacific, a sizable portion of Bolivian national territory was lost to Brazil. The eastern department of Acre, in the Amazon Basin, was isolated from the seat of government in the altiplano, and when sizable numbers of Brazilian rubber seekers began settling in the area in the 1890s, Bolivia was unable to control their activities effectively. However, the Bolivian government's efforts to do so provoked a maneuver on the part of the Brazilians that was reminiscent of what had occurred in Texas more than half a century before. The Brazilian settlers declared Acre an independent country in 1899, shortly afterward asking for annexation by Brazil, a request to which the Brazilian government "graciously" acceded. Bolivian President José Manuel PANDO recognized the Brazilian annexation in the Treaty of Petrópolis (1903). *See* PETRÓPOLIS, TREATY OF. The present area of Bolivia is 424,164 square miles.

Conservatives and Liberals. Meanwhile, some semblance of political party activity had emerged in the wake of Bolivia's defeat in the War of the Pacific. Two parties, the Conservatives and the Liberals, were organized. The former remained in power until 1899, when their rivals, under Pando's leadership, succeeded in ousting them. The Liberals stayed in power until 1920. Pando and his successor, President Ismael MONTES, were the outstanding figures of the Liberal period.

The advent to power of the Liberals coincided with important changes in the Bolivian economy. Since the early days of Spanish colonial rule Bolivia had been one of the world's major producers of silver. Although silver mining had seriously declined, exports of tin began to mount in the late 1890s. This metal was in growing demand overseas, and foreign capital, particularly British and American, began to come into the country to help exploit Bolivia's tin resources. *See* TIN INDUSTRY (BOLIVIA).

The Liberal regime strongly encouraged the development of the tin-mining industry. It kept taxes on the industry very low, helped to bring about the construction of a railroad from the Bolivian altiplano to the port of Antofagasta in order to facilitate the export of the mineral, and otherwise favored the tin-mining interests. By the end of the Liberal period, the industry was largely in the hands of three firms, organized respectively by Simón I. PATIÑO, a Bolivian cholo, who became one of the world's richest men; Carlos Aramayo, also a Bolivian, although with financial interests in several other Latin American countries; and Mauricio Hochschild, a man of Austrian birth and Argentine nationality, who had interests in many other countries in both the Old and the New Worlds. Extensive British and American capital was also invested in all three of these enterprises.

The Liberal regime, with its belief in free enterprise, also intensified the despoiling of the Indian communities of their land. President Montes personally seized the lands belonging to one of the largest Indian communities on the shores of Lake Titicaca.

Republican period. In 1920 discontent with the Liberal regime boiled over, and the Liberals were ousted from power (forever, as it turned out). A new party, the Partido Republicano, had been formed under the leadership of Bautista Saavedra. It gathered together the remnants of the old Conservative party as well as many artisan groups that had arisen in La Paz and other cities. The ex-Conservatives, largely big landlords and businessmen, tended to constitute the right wing of the Partido Republicano; the artisans, its left wing.

Saavedra became the first Republican President. He was succeeded in 1926 by Hernando Siles, who ruled until he was overthrown in 1930. During this period the expansion of the mining industry reached its culmination. New firms, principally American, opened up mines exploiting tungsten, lead, and copper as well as tin. In 1922 the Standard Oil Company of New Jersey received large petroleum concessions in the southeastern part of the country. Bolivian politics came to hinge in large part on the rivalries among competing foreign economic interests. The Republican Presidents borrowed excessively large sums of money abroad during the 1920s, some of which went into public works but much of which went to build up what was publicized as the strongest army in South America.

This "strongest army" proved to be a complete failure when it was called upon to fight in the disastrous CHACO WAR with Paraguay, over the ill-defined border in the hot lowlands lying between the two countries. The war raged from 1932 to 1935 and was the largest conflict fought between any two Latin American countries in the twentieth century.

The Bolivian Army was completely defeated in the Chaco War. More important, the conflict shook the existing institutions of Bolivian society to their foundations. Young officers returning from the war brought home an attitude of rebellion toward the ruling economic and social elite (although most of them were in fact part of it), which they felt had betrayed their country and was responsible for the miserable state in which the great majority of the people lived. Fighting beside Indian troops in the Chaco War had made these officers very much aware of the plight of the Bolivian masses.

Post-Chaco War period. Soon after the war young military officers brought Col. David TORO to the Presidency. He announced the establishment of a "socialist republic," formed a Ministry of Labor for the first time, and nationalized the oil concessions of the Standard Oil Company. However, Toro's war record was something less than spectacular, and furthermore he began to move to the right. About a year after he took power, Toro was overthrown by Col. Germán BUSCH, one of the few real heroes of the Chaco War. Busch issued the country's first labor code and encouraged for the first time the establishment of unions among the tin miners. He also insisted that the tin companies sell all the foreign exchange they earned to the Banco Central and that any person or corporation in need of foreign currency buy it from the bank.

After the death of Busch in 1939, conservative military men took charge under Gen. Carlos Quintanilla. In 1940 elections were held, and another relatively conservative general, Enrique PEÑARANDA, was elected President. Meanwhile, several new parties had been established by young ex-officers and intellectuals. These included the Partido de Izquierda Revolucionaria (PIR), "independent Marxist" but Stalinite; the Partido Obrero Revolucionario, Trotskyite in orientation; the Falange Socialista Boliviana, a fascist-oriented party patterned after the Spanish Falange; and the MOVIMIENTO NACIONALISTA REVOLUCIONARIO (MNR), a nationalist party with a vaguely social orientation.

In December 1943, General Peñaranda was overthrown by a coup in which young military men cooperated with the MNR. During the following two and one-half years the government of Maj. Gualberto VILLARROEL encouraged union organization and summoned a congress of Indians, at which peasants from all over the country for the first time presented the government with the complaints and aspirations of the indigenous population.

Major Villarroel was overthrown in July 1946. For almost six years thereafter, conservative governments were again in control. However, the MNR gained the backing of most of the country's urban workers and large elements of the middle class during this period. Several insurrections led by the MNR failed. Then, on April 9, 1952, there began an MNR-led revolt that succeeded, and Víctor PAZ ESTENSSORO, the principal MNR leader, returned from exile to assume the Presidency.

The MNR remained in power for more than a dozen years. During that period it carried out a program of AGRARIAN REFORM that returned to the Indians most of the land in the altiplano which had been taken from them in the past; it nationalized the Big Three tin-mining companies; and it undertook a major economic development program in the Oriente (eastern Bolivia). It also maintained a relatively democratic political regime. These measures of the MNR government constituted a real revolution. They destroyed once and for all the power of the rural landholders and the mining interests that had dominated the republic during most of its existence. However, efforts to destroy the influence of the military in politics proved abortive. *See also* ORIENTE (BOLIVIA).

In November 1964, the MNR government of Paz Estenssoro was overthrown by the armed forces. During the next seven years a series of military regimes, under Generals René BARRIENTOS, Alfredo OVANDO CANDIA, and Juan José TORRES, controlled the country. Although they did not undo the basic changes enacted by the MNR regime, they did little to build upon them. The government of General Torres was dominated largely by left-wing dissidents from the MNR, together with pro-Moscow and pro-Peking Communists and various brands of Trotskyites.

In August 1971, the regime of General Torres was overthrown by a military coup led by Col. Hugo BANZER and supported by the MNR and its traditional rival, the Falange Socialista Boliviana. The new regime promised to carry out policies that would fulfill the promises which had been put forward by the MNR in 1952 and had not been fully met. Twenty years after the revolution the population of Bolivia, estimated at 4,804,000 in 1969, was still the most impoverished in South America, its per capita income being calculated at $170 in 1968.

Bibliography. Robert J. Alexander, *The Bolivian National Revolution*, New Brunswick, N.J., 1958; Charles W. Arnade, *The Emergence of the Republic of Bolivia*, Gainesville, Fla., 1957; J. Valerie Fifer, *Bolivia: Land, Location, and Politics since 1825*, Cambridge, England, 1972; Enrique Finot, *Nueva historia de Bolivia*, 2d ed., La Paz, 1954; Herbert S. Klein, *Parties and Political Change in Bolivia, 1880–1952*, Cambridge, England, 1969; James M. Malloy and Richard S. Thorn (eds.), *Beyond the Revolution: Bolivia since 1952*, Pittsburgh, 1971; Harold Osborne, *Bolivia: A Land Divided*, London, 1954; Cornelius Zondag, *The Bolivian Economy, 1952–1965: The Revolution and Its Aftermath*, New York, 1966.

ROBERT J. ALEXANDER

BONILLA, POLICARPO (1858–1926). President of Honduras (1894–1899). An ambitious young lawyer, Bonilla became head of the Honduran Liberal party when its founder, Céleo Arias, died in 1890. The next year the Nationalist party candidate, Ponciano Leiva, won the presidential election from Bonilla by fraudulent means. Upon taking office, Leiva dissolved the Liberal party and, in 1892, forced most of its leaders to seek sanctuary in Nicaragua. Nicaraguan President José Santos ZELAYA supported Bonilla in the two years of civil war that followed, and in February 1894 Bonilla captured the Honduran government. *See* LIBERAL PARTY (HONDURAS); NATIONAL OR NATIONALIST PARTY (HONDURAS).

Bonilla quickly proved himself a consummate legal and institutional architect. The government was completely restaffed with technocrats who enacted the creed of nineteenth-century Honduran Liberals into law in the 1894 constitution. To expedite economic reforms and control the countryside Bonilla greatly augmented executive power at the expense of other branches of government. Under his administration the Honduran north coast first rose to prominence as a banana-producing area. Bonilla was also an ardent proponent of Central American federation. In 1895 he sponsored a unionist congress at Amapala, and in 1898 he promoted an attempt to make a Central American constitution binding.

Bonilla devoted his later years to unionism and to Liberal party organization. After an unsuccessful bid for the Presidency in 1923, he retired to New Orleans, where he died in 1926.

GENE S. YEAGER

BORDABERRY, JUAN MARÍA (1928–). President of Uruguay (1972–), elected in November 1971 for a five-year term. Bordaberry ran as a vice-presidential candidate on the Colorado party slate headed by President Jorge PACHECO ARECO (*see* COLORADO PARTY: URUGUAY), with the understanding that he would become President if the *lema* and *sublema* won (*see* LEMA SYSTEM), but voters failed to approve the constitutional amendment allowing Pacheco Areco's reelection.

A rancher from the interior, Bordaberry is an expert in agricultural economics and served as Minister of Agriculture and Livestock under Pacheco Areco from 1969 until the 1971 election. He had been affiliated with the National party before assuming the Cabinet post, serving as a Blanco senator from 1963 to 1965 (*see* BLANCO PARTY: URUGUAY). Bordaberry became the leader of the Federal League for Rural Action (LFAR) after the death of Benito NARDONE in 1964.

During the 1971 campaign Bordaberry fully supported the record of the Pacheco Areco administration and pledged to continue essentially the same policies if he became President. The most significant and controversial of these policies were a program of economic austerity and a hard line vis-à-vis the activities of the Tupamaro guerrillas (*see* TUPAMAROS) and other civil disorders. By the end of 1972 the armed forces, given sweeping powers by Bordaberry, had apparently crushed the Tupamaros. However, the previously apolitical military now began to evince an interest in political matters, condemning financial corruption in government and private business and the general malaise of the country. In February 1973, when Bordaberry appointed the retired general Antonio Francese Minister of Defense with instructions to curb military intervention in politics, the armed forces staged a brief revolt, and Bordaberry was compelled to accept Francese's resignation. In the ensuing weeks the ascendancy of the armed forces was confirmed until Bordaberry was pressed into dissolving Congress on June 27, 1973, thereby ending a forty-year period of constitutional rule in Uruguay. The President's action was precipitated by the refusal of Congress to take action against the leftist senator Enrique Erro, who had been accused by the military of maintaining contact with the Tupamaros.

LEE C. FENNELL

BORGES, JORGE LUIS (1899–). Argentine writer. Born in Buenos Aires, he studied in Argentina, England, and Switzerland, where he came into contact with German expressionism. He returned to Argentina in 1921 and was one of the founders of the avant-garde review *Proa* (1924). Borges has served as professor of English literature at the University of Buenos Aires,

president of the Argentine Association of Writers (1950–1953), director of a film company, and director of the National Library (1955). His work expresses his intellectual brilliance as well as his agnosticism, and in it he displaces the traditional elements of space, time, and identity.

His earliest prose writings appeared in the reviews *Prismas, Nosotros,* and *Martín Fierro,* and his poems in *Fervor de Buenos Aires* (1923), *Luna de enfrente* (1925), and *Cuaderno San Martín* (1929). He first explored his metaphysical preoccupations in essays, which appeared in *Inquisiciones* (1925), *Tamaño de mi esperanza* (1926), *El idioma de los argentinos* (1928), *Evaristo Carriego* (1930), *Discusión* (1932), *Historia de la eternidad* (1936), *Nueva refutación del tiempo* (1947), *Otras inquisiciones* (1952), *Nuevas inquisiciones* (1960), and *Macedonio Fernández* (1962). In these as in the short story, for which he has received his greatest acclaim, his recurring themes are the infinite, the eternal return, the coincidence of the biography of one man with the history of all men, the modification of the real by the unreal, and the universe as a chaotic labyrinth that only the subjective intelligence can put in order.

Borges's best-known works are *Historia universal de la infamia* (1935), *El jardín de senderos que se bifurcan* (1941), *Ficciones* (1944), *El aleph* (1949), *El hacedor* (1960), and *Antología personal* (1961). In collaboration with Silvina Ocampo and Adolfo BIOY CASARES, he published *Antología de la literatura fantástica* (1941); in collaboration with Bioy Casares, *Cuentos breves y extraordinarios* (1956); and with D. Ingenieros, *Antiguas literaturas germánicas* (1952). In recent years he has lectured widely in the United States. In 1965, along with Samuel Beckett, he was awarded the Formentor Prize.

Much of Borges's work has been translated into English. Almost all his stories are included in three collections: *Labyrinths* (1961), *Ficciones* (1962), and *The Aleph and Other Stories* (1970).

RACHEL PHILLIPS

BORNO, [JOSEPH] LOUIS (1865–1942). President of Haiti (1922–1930). Born into the mulatto ÉLITE in Port-au-Prince, Borno studied law in Paris, wrote several works on law, and became a prominent diplomat, serving as envoy to the Dominican Republic and to the Permanent Court of International Justice and as Foreign Minister in the Haitian Cabinet. At first the American intervention of 1915 was distasteful to Borno, but he came to believe that more could be gained for Haiti through conciliation than by resistance. He was elected President and assumed office on May 15, 1922.

President Borno cooperated closely with the United States High Commissioner, Gen. John H. Russell, forming what critics termed a joint dictatorship. In place of a National Assembly, Borno appointed a legislative Council of State that served at his pleasure and reelected him in 1926. He refused to call the Assembly and was irked by the free press. He hoped to produce a responsible middle class in order to achieve national stability, but Haiti failed to provide the training necessary for the development of a democratically active bourgeoisie.

Violence against Borno's regime in 1929 led to the American appointment in 1930 of an investigating commission, headed by W. Cameron Forbes, which recommended that a neutral be selected temporary President until the Assembly could be elected and choose a permanent President. Reluctantly, Borno accepted Eugène Roy, who succeeded him on May 15, 1930. Borno died in Port-au-Prince on July 29, 1942.

JOHN E. BAUR

BOSCH, JUAN (1909–   ). Dominican writer and President (1963). A mercurial political figure whose significance reaches beyond his native country, Bosch personifies the frustration of Latin America's democratic left, the seemingly ingrained United States opposition to revolutionary social democratic solutions in the hemisphere and willingness to intervene militarily to prevent movements espousing them from coming to power, and the gravitation toward radical-nationalist solutions of those once considered in the middle of the road.

Bosch was a long-time exile from the dictatorship of Rafael Leonidas TRUJILLO MOLINA, living a social democratic exile's life in Cuba. Venezuela, and Costa Rica. A talented author and intellectual, he won fame as an essayist and short-story writer, wrote books on Cuba and Costa Rica, and penned numerous studies and exposés of the Trujillo regime. Returning to the Dominican Republic in 1961 following Trujillo's assassination, Bosch launched the campaign that in the December 1962 elections would bring him to the Presidency. Promising to carry out a democratic social revolution in the Dominican Republic, Bosch appealed chiefly to peasants and workers and won the elections overwhelmingly with their support.

Bosch proved to be less able as an administrator than as a campaigner, and his reforms failed to get under way. Lacking prior governmental experience and the aid of the country's traditional ruling elements, he was unable effectively to manipulate the levers of power. At the same time, conservative reaction to him and his programs was vehement. After seven tumultuous months in office, Bosch was overthrown.

From exile Bosch began preparing to restore constitutional government, not by elections but by a coup d'état of junior military officers. On April 24, 1965, the revolt began, with widespread popular support. Fearing that a Constitutionalist triumph would mean a "second Cuba," the United States intervened militarily on April 28 to contain the revolution. Bosch bitterly denounced the United States for its action.

Later that year Bosch returned to the country and launched a rather lackluster campaign for the Presidency. His opponent, Joaquín BALAGUER, ran a skillful campaign and also benefited from the popular wish for a respite from upheaval and revolution as well as from the intimidation of Bosch supporters in the interior. These factors combined to help defeat Bosch and his party in the 1966 elections.

Bosch then went into voluntary exile to travel, think, and write. He produced a long historical study of the Caribbean as an imperial frontier and another analyzing the development of Dominican society. He also penned *El Pentagonismo: Sustituto del imperialismo,* 1961 (*Pentagonism: A Substitute for Imperialism*), and in a series of writings he asserted that democratic solutions were bankrupt and a "dictatorship with popular support" was necessary. Returning to Santo Domingo,

Bosch, the great *caudillo* of the left and revolutionary forces in his country, began to plan for the implementation of this new revolutionary ideology.

See also DOMINICAN REVOLT; PARTIDO REVOLUCIONARIO DOMINICANO.

HOWARD J. WIARDA

BOTERO, FERNANDO (1932–   ). Colombian painter. Born in Medellín, Botero went to Bogotá in 1951 and had his first one-man show there; he then left for Spain, where he studied at the Academy of San Fernando and copied in the Prado Museum for a year. He visited Paris and spent eighteen months in Florence before returning in 1955 to Colombia, where a show of his work was unsuccessful. Discouraged, he moved to Mexico City and in 1957 had a one-man show in the Pan American Union in Washington that was well received. In 1960 he moved to New York, where he settled.

Despite Botero's international experience, his art is thoroughly Latin American. Baroque subjects and style stand behind his work; *Our Lady of Colombia, Prelates Bathing in a River, Adam,* and *Eve,* all of the 1960s, are examples. Favorite Renaissance and baroque paintings are given disturbing and humorous modern interpretations, as in *The Mona Lisa Age Twelve* and *Mrs. Rubens.* His still life with fruit is memorable, as is a sinister one with a pig's head. All the images are grossly inflated on large canvases and painted with sumptuous color that disguises a mordant humor. Botero's method is very direct, bordering on folk simplicity, but it is achieved by great sophistication. His work has been widely shown since 1960, with one-man shows in New York (Center for Inter-American Relations), Madrid, and other places.

TERENCE GRIEDER

BOURBON REFORMS. The Bourbon dynasty was established in Spain in 1700 with the advent of Philip V of Anjou (r.1700–1746), grandson of Louis XIV, to the throne. Because of the War of the Spanish Succession (1701–1714), no effective governmental policy was shaped until the second decade of the eighteenth century. The Bourbons introduced the French concept of a centralized government and gradually replaced outmoded Hapsburg institutions. Throughout the century they reorganized the governmental structure, the economic system, and the relations between church and state and modified the intellectual orientation of Spain and its empire. In the administrative field the council system was replaced by ministries and a Council of State. After 1717 the COUNCIL OF THE INDIES was largely replaced by the Ministry of Marine and the Indies. The INTENDANCY SYSTEM was introduced in the colonies to replace the corregidores (*see* CORREGIDOR); in general, it produced a more efficient and more highly centralized government. New viceroyalties were created in South America in order to gain greater control over neglected areas. The Casa de Contratación, which had regulated trade, was slowly phased out after having been transferred to Cádiz in 1717 and was abolished in 1790.

This step implied a reorganization of the trade system itself, a process that required several decades of experimentation. The fleet system, disrupted by continental wars, was abandoned in 1740 in northern South America and in 1789 in Veracruz. Trade was entrusted to companies which carried on business with certain areas of the empire and which put an end to the monopoly of Cádiz as the only outlet for commerce with the colonies. The CARACAS COMPANY was one of the most successful of the trading companies. CHARLES III (r. 1759–1788) proceeded with trade reforms aimed at regaining control over the American market and creating a market for Spanish industries. He gradually reopened inter-American trade and liberalized trade with Spain and friendly nations until, in 1778, he allowed "free" trade in a system that, if not perfect, was more flexible than before and provided a remarkable increase in imports, exports, and revenue for Spain. Smuggling was never uprooted, for it was a chronic disease in Spanish America. A reorganization of the fiscal system was carried on at the same time. Whereas some taxes were eliminated, others were collected more efficiently, much to the distress of the colonists. The crown undertook the monopoly of some products such as tobacco, playing cards, *aguardiente* (spirits), and salt, which became very reliable sources of income. As a result of state protection of Spanish industries, some of their Spanish American counterparts declined under the Bourbons. Mining received a great deal of attention from the crown, which sought to improve its conditions and obtain larger revenues (*see* MINING: COLONIAL SPANISH AMERICA). The Bourbon policies were rewarded with the largest yields in mining and minting recorded in the colonial period. On the other hand, agriculture remained largely neglected.

In their relations with the church the Bourbons, although preserving the orthodoxy of the faith, achieved a large degree of freedom from papal influence. The Concordat of 1753, obtained by Ferdinand VI (r. 1746–1759), gave the crown great control over the temporal affairs of the church, which Charles III increased. By the end of the first decade of the nineteenth century the Jesuits had been expelled from Spain and the Indies (1767; *see* JESUITS, EXPULSION OF: SPANISH AMERICA) and suppressed as an order with Bourbon help (1773), the immunities of the clergy had been greatly reduced, and part of the wealth of the church in Spain and the colonies had been expropriated (1797, 1804) by the crown in order to solve its own economic crisis. *See also* CATHOLIC CHURCH (COLONIAL PERIOD).

The Bourbon reforms sought not greater autonomy for the colonies but a more profitable system for the mother country. Nor did the Bourbons encourage greater participation of American-born colonists in the government. Although many governmental posts were filled by them, the intendants were Spaniards, and some of the reforming *visitadores* (inspectors), such as Areche in Peru and José de GÁLVEZ in New Spain, were anticreole. As a result, enmity between Spaniards and creoles grew stronger as the century neared its end. Important reforms in the military and defensive system were adopted during the reigns of Charles III and Charles IV. There was much concern about the defense of the empire's frontiers and strategic areas. Militias were reorganized, and a military class enjoying special prerogatives was created. Although there was great interest in furthering education, medicine, and the fine arts and in forming a few centers of social welfare, such as the *montepío* (widows' benefit fund), the Bourbon reforms never reached some of the basic

social inequalities of colonial life. Society continued to be hierarchically divided into many socioracial groups, and suggestions to soften or eliminate these cleavages went unheeded. The Indians and *castas* (mixed bloods), although forming the majority of the population, continued to bear the burden and the social stigma of personal taxes and continued to be excluded from governmental posts and other privileged occupations. The Bourbon reforms did not solve all the problems of Spain or the colonies, but they created a new climate of administrative concern and responsibility that had been missing under the later Hapsburgs. *See also* ENLIGHTENMENT (SPANISH AMERICA).

Bibliography. D. A. Brading, *Miners and Merchants in Bourbon Mexico,* London, 1971; Nancy Farriss, *Crown and Clergy in Colonial Mexico, 1759–1821,* London, 1968; J. R. Fisher, *Government and Society in Colonial Peru: The Intendant System, 1784–1814,* London, 1970; T. S. Floyd (ed.), *The Bourbon Reforms and Spanish Civilization,* Boston, 1966; R. D. Hussey, *The Caracas Company, 1728–1784,* Cambridge, Mass., 1934; John Lynch, *Spanish Colonial Administration, 1782–1810,* London, 1958; L. N. McAlister, *The Fuero Militar in New Spain,* Gainesville, Ga., 1957; A. P. Whitaker, *The Huancavelica Mine: A Contribution to the History of the Bourbon Renaissance in the Spanish Empire,* Cambridge, Mass., 1941.

ASUNCIÓN LAVRIN

BOVES, JOSÉ TOMÁS (1782–1814). Leader of royalist guerrillas in Venezuela. Boves, Spanish-born but of relatively humble origin and with both contraband experience and a jail sentence on his record, was engaged in commerce on the Venezuelan LLANOS (plains) at the outbreak of revolution. He was jailed, again, by the patriots under the first Venezuelan republic, but he obtained his release as it fell. He then joined the royalist forces, and when Simón BOLÍVAR returned to found the second Venezuelan republic in 1813, Boves appealed successfully to social and racial antagonisms, rousing the lower-class population against Bolívar and other patriot leaders, who were predominantly of the creole aristocracy. His greatest strength was among the rough *llanero* cowboys, whom he formed into irregular units that harried the patriots with devastating effect. To his followers he offered plunder without limit, while inflicting extreme, though erratic, bursts of cruelty upon creole republicans. His triumph in the Battle of La Puerta in June 1814 finally destroyed Bolívar's army and delivered Caracas into his hands. In December 1814, while suppressing last-ditch resistance in eastern Venezuela, Boves himself was killed in battle.

DAVID BUSHNELL

BOYACÁ, BATTLE OF. Battle fought on August 7, 1819, at the bridge of Boyacá, 10 miles southwest of Tunja on the road to Bogotá. It was the victorious culmination of a campaign begun by Simón BOLÍVAR late in May on the Venezuelan LLANOS (plains). Bolívar's army, which included Venezuelans and New Granadans and a select corps of British legionaries, first had to cross the eastern plains in the rainy season, when rivers overflowed their banks; it then scaled the ANDES MOUNTAINS over a path that went through rugged and largely uninhabited terrain, reaching an elevation of more than 13,000 feet. Despite major hardships and attrition, the army finally emerged in the mountain valleys east of Tunja, and although the first engagements were inconclusive, the patriots consolidated their foothold in eastern New Granada.

By skillful maneuvering Bolívar occupied Tunja on August 5, placing himself between the major royalist army under Col. José María Barreiro and the viceregal capital. Two days later, when Barreiro sought to outflank Bolívar and secure the road to Bogotá, the final battle was joined. The armies came together as they approached the bridge by which the main road crossed the small Boyacá River. Numerically they were about equal, roughly 2,850 patriots opposing 2,700 royalists, but the patriots were in better fighting condition. Moreover, when the royalist advance guard (following a brief initial clash) passed over the bridge, they benefited from the resulting division of enemy forces. Fighting lasted only two hours. Neither side suffered major casualties, but the greater part of the royalist army, including Barreiro, was taken prisoner.

On August 10, Bolívar entered Bogotá unopposed. The victory delivered central New Granada to the patriots, who were to use it as a strategic base and source of supplies and recruits for subsequent campaigns. Equally important, with the 1819 campaign the initiative passed permanently into Bolívar's hands. At Boyacá began the almost unbroken series of successes that eventually led to Ayacucho (see AYACUCHO, BATTLE OF).

DAVID BUSHNELL

BOYER, JEAN-PIERRE (1776–1850). President of Haiti (1818–1843). Boyer, a mulatto, was born in Port-au-Prince. At sixteen he joined the French Army, in which he rose rapidly. Returning to Saint-Domingue from his sojourn in France in 1791, he fought for the mulattoes and went into exile after their defeat by Toussaint LOUVERTURE. Boyer returned in Gen. Charles-Victor-Emmanuel Leclerc's invasion force as a captain, but after it became clear that Leclerc planned to reduce mulatto ascendancy, Boyer, who was an aide to Alexandre Sabès PÉTION, deserted and fought for independence.

When Haiti was divided into a black kingdom and a mulatto republic, Pétion, as President of the republic, named Boyer secretary, chief of staff, and, finally, general. Acknowledged as Pétion's heir, Boyer became President in April 1818. Boyer's army scattered the rebels of an opportunistic southern brigand known as Goman, reunited Haiti in 1820, and in 1822 annexed the Spanish part of Santo Domingo, frustrating Dominican attempts to achieve freedom.

In 1825 Boyer approved a French treaty recognizing Haitian independence. To restore agriculture, which had declined under Pétion, he tried in vain to impose a strict rural code regimenting laborers. Boyer did little for mass education during Haiti's formative years, while his policies let mulattoes perpetuate minority control of politics and national resources (see ÉLITE). Haiti's longest regime ended when Boyer was deposed in 1843. He died in Paris on July 9, 1850.

JOHN E. BAUR

BRADEN, SPRUILLE (1894–   ). American engineer, industrialist, and diplomat. In the midst of a very successful career in copper mining, finance, and industry in the United States and Latin America, Braden became a delegate to the Seventh International Conference of American States at Montevideo in 1933 (see MONTEVIDEO CONFERENCE) and the Pan American Commercial Conference in 1935. From that year until 1938 Ambassador Braden was chairman of the delegation to the Chaco Peace Conference (see CHACO WAR). He later served as Ambassador to Colombia and Cuba, and in 1945 he was appointed Ambassador to Argentina, where his open support of democratic governments was taken as an affront by the dictatorial regime of President Edelmiro J. Farrell and Vice President Juan D. PERÓN.

Returning to Washington in September 1945 to become Assistant Secretary of State for Latin America, Braden gave strong support to multilateral intervention on behalf of democratic principles. Although not originated by Braden, the idea became known as the Braden Corollary to the GOOD NEIGHBOR POLICY. A major application of the corollary was the publication of the United States Department of State *Blue Book* on Argentina twelve days before Argentine presidential elections in February 1946. The document's purpose was to influence the Argentine electorate against voting for Perón, who was charged, along with other Argentines, of having actively supported the Axis during World War II. Instead of helping to defeat Perón, the *Blue Book* was used by the candidate to arouse the national pride of the Argentine voters against outside interference, and Perón was elected. Braden resigned as Assistant Secretary of State for Latin America in 1947.

After his retirement from government service, Braden opposed communism and socialism in the hemisphere and was closely associated with the anti-Castro United States Citizens' Committee for a Free Cuba, established in 1963. A volume of memoirs, *Diplomats and Demagogues*, appeared in 1971.

RICHARD B. GRAY

BRÁS, VENCESLAU. *See* BRAZ, WENCESLAU.

BRASÍLIA. Capital of Brazil. Situated in the center west at an elevation of 3,300 feet, Brazil's new capital was designed and built under the direction of Lúcio COSTA and Oscar NIEMEYER. Brazilians from Tiradentes to Juscelino KUBITSCHEK had dreamed of relocating the national capital from the coast to the interior, and wrote that dream into the 1891, 1934, and 1946 constitutions. It remained for Kubitschek to translate that dream into reality. While campaigning for the Brazilian Presidency in Jataí, Goiás, in 1955, Kubitschek announced that he intended to relocate the capital in the interior as part of his constitutional obligations. After creating the Companhia Urbanizadora da Nova Capital (NOVACAP) in 1956, Kubitschek led the groundbreaking ceremonies on November 3, 1956.

Laborers flocked from all over Brazil, but primarily from the NORTHEAST, to build the city. The city was planned on two axes at right angles to one another. The residential districts are in the north-south axis, and the east-west axis contains the political, administrative, economic, cultural, and recreational centers. Other residential areas were built in satellite cities around the main city. Although many public buildings were still incomplete, the city was formally inaugurated on April 21, 1960.

After the inauguration of Brasília its population increased from 141,742 to 544,862 in 1970, or by a phenomenal 284.4 percent. The city is connected to the other major population centers by railroad and asphalt highways. It contains most, if not all, of the services one would expect to find in a modern city and is the home of thirteen hospitals and the University of Brasília as well as the center of national government.

LAWRENCE J. NIELSEN

BRAZ, WENCESLAU [PEREIRA GOMES] (VENCES-LAU BRÁS, 1868–1966). President of Brazil (1914–1918). Born in Itajubá, Minas Gerais, Braz graduated from the São Paulo law school in 1890 before entering politics as a member of the Partido Republicano Mineiro (Republican party of Minas Gerais). An able if lackluster politician, he rose rapidly in party councils. After serving in the state assembly, in the Governor's cabinet, and in Congress, Braz became Governor of Minas Gerais in 1908. Under the prevailing political system, whereby the Presidency of the republic usually alternated between ex-governors of São Paulo and Minas Gerais, Braz's two-year term as head of Brazil's most populous state made him eligible for the highest office in the land. However, in 1910 he was elected to the Vice Presidency on the ticket with Hermes da FONSECA. Braz spent his four years as Vice President quietly in Itajubá.

In 1914, at the age of forty-six, he was called back to the national arena to run for the Presidency. As the administration candidate, his election was a foregone conclusion. Braz's term of office coincided almost exactly with World War I. Reflecting the preponderantly Allied sympathies of the Brazilian people, President Braz encouraged the production of raw materials for the Allied cause and, in October 1917, took Brazil into the war against Germany. After leaving the Presidency on November 15, 1918, Braz lived inconspicuously in Itajubá, where he died on May 16, 1966, at the age of ninety-eight.

ROLLIE E. POPPINO

BRAZIL COMPANY (COMPANHIA DO COMÉRCIO DO BRASIL). Chartered company set up in 1649 during the critical years following the reestablishment of Portugal's independence from Spain (1640), with the objective of building a powerful fleet and protecting the Brazil trade. The idea for a company on the model of the Dutch West India Company, which had seized most of the NORTHEAST of Brazil after 1630 (see DUTCH IN BRAZIL), was backed by the famous Jesuit Antônio VIEIRA, who hoped that the capital of new Christians (Jews forced to convert to Christianity) and Portuguese Sephardic Jews would underwrite the project (the company's charter offered guarantees against the confiscation by the Inquisition of money invested). The company was granted a twenty-year monopoly of the trade in wine, olive oil, flour, and codfish to Brazil; was allowed to raise taxes on Brazilian sugar, tobacco, cotton, and hide exports; and was given the monopoly of the export of brazilwood from Rio de Janeiro, Bahia (modern Salvador), Ilhéus, and Pernambuco (modern Recife). In return the company was expected to construct and support thirty-six warships that were to

escort shipping to and from Brazil, a fleet, or convoy, system thus being inaugurated in the trade with Portuguese America. There was great opposition to the company in both Portugal and Brazil. In 1656 the exemption from inquisitorial investigation was removed, and two years later the company lost its monopoly of supplying Brazil. It was never able to meet its obligation with respect to warships. The fleet protection functions were incorporated during 1662–1663 into the royal administration under a newly established *junta do comércio,* the shareholders being compensated by holdings in the royal tobacco monopoly. In this guise the company continued until it was finally abolished in 1720. The convoy system continued until it was abolished by the Marquês de POMBAL in 1765.

KENNETH R. MAXWELL

BRAZILIAN COMMUNIST PARTY. *See* PARTIDO COMUNISTA BRASILEIRO.

BRAZILIAN DEMOCRATIC MOVEMENT. *See* MOVIMENTO DEMOCRÁTICO BRASILEIRO.

BRAZILIAN LABOR PARTY. *See* PARTIDO TRABALHISTA BRASILEIRO.

BRAZIL SINCE 1822. More than three centuries of Portuguese rule in Brazil came to an end on September 7, 1822, when Dom Pedro (later PEDRO I), scion and Regent of the house of Braganza, declared Brazil's political independence (*see* YPIRANGA, GRITO DE). This dramatic act, taken on the advice of his Austrian wife, Leopoldina von Hapsburg, and his Brazilian-born Prime Minister, José Bonifacio de ANDRADA E SILVA, occurred at Ypiranga, on the outskirts of the city of São Paulo (150 years later Pedro's remains were permanently enshrined at that site). By his decisive action

BRAZIL

Area: 3,286,488 sq. mi.   Population: 93,204,379 (1970).

the Prince Regent rejected the final effort of the Portuguese Cortes to reduce Brazil to colonial status, seized the leadership of the widespread Brazilian independence movement, and preserved the institution of monarchy in Brazil. Within three months he was acclaimed and crowned Pedro I, Emperor of the sovereign nation of Brazil, which included all Portuguese America and the Cisplatine province of Uruguay. Although the transition from colonial kingdom to independent empire was accomplished without civil war, it took nearly a full year to drive the Portuguese garrisons out of Bahia and the northern coastal provinces. An imperial navy, commanded and largely manned by Britons and North Americans, was assembled to harass the Portuguese Fleet from the AMAZON RIVER to the mouth of the Tagus, while in Bahia Brazilians marshaled the largest army ever committed to combat in the wars for independence in South America. In August 1825, the mother country acknowledged the independence of its former colony.

The new empire of Brazil had an area of approximately 3 million square miles and contained some 4 million inhabitants, of whom perhaps half were slaves and one-fourth were the black or brown descendants of slaves from Africa. Brazilian society was predominantly rural and was concentrated heavily along the coastal strip and in the province of Minas Gerais, although a few isolated clusters of population were scattered throughout the interior from the Amazon to the Río de la Plata. The large northern, northeastern, central, and southern regions of Brazil shared a common language and political heritage but otherwise were distinct entities, separated by great distances and the lack of easy communications except by sea. In the interior goods were transported in riverboats or on pack animals over trails impassable by wheeled vehicles. Although Brazil was politically independent, its economy remained colonial, with primary emphasis on the production of plantation crops for export to European markets. The overriding importance of export agriculture to the economy, society, and political order was shown in the choice of a sprig of coffee and a sheaf of tobacco leaves as emblems on the imperial shield of Brazil. The small minority of rich and wellborn who owned the land and monopolized education controlled the wealth of the empire and were the only politically active element in the population. The bulk of the freeborn Brazilian people, without access to land or schooling, were politically inert and perceived little need or opportunity to change their station in life. The Negro slaves, other than the tiny minority who might gain freedom by purchase or manumission, could look forward only to continued drudgery and bondage.

The relative ease with which Brazil achieved political independence stands in marked contrast to the quarter century of political unrest and turmoil that followed. During those years nearly every province of the empire rebelled against the central government at least once. Uruguay succeeded in breaking away from Brazil in 1828 after a costly three-year campaign, and in Rio Grande do Sul the FARROUPILHA REVOLT raged for a full decade (1835–1845) before the province was pacified. For much of the time between 1822 and about the mid-century the real authority of the court extended little beyond the city of Rio de Janeiro and its environs.

The difficulties of adjustment to self-rule in Brazil were exacerbated in large part by Pedro I (r. 1822–1831), whose autocratic manner, foreign birth, dynastic ties with Portugal, and disdain for legislative curbs on his authority ill-suited him for leadership of the now intensely nationalistic, self-confident Brazilian elites in a constitutional monarchy. Pedro's popularity waned steadily as he broke with the Constituent Assembly (1823), exiled its most outspoken leaders including his former friend and mentor, José Bonifacio, and dictated his own constitution (1824), which he proceeded to ignore at will (see CONSTITUTION OF 1824: BRAZIL). His abiding interest in the problems of the Braganza dynasty in Portugal, his callous treatment of the widely admired Empress, Leopoldina, who died in 1826, and his continued preference for Portuguese rather than Brazilian advisers further alienated the public, which blamed him totally for the loss of Uruguay. In these circumstances the landed gentry and the armed forces gradually withdrew their support. Unable to rule, on April 7, 1831, Pedro abdicated in favor of his young son, Pedro de Alcântara (see PEDRO II), and sailed for Europe, where he spent the remaining three years of his life securing the throne of Portugal for his daughter.

For nine years, during the minority of the Prince, Brazil experimented with republican rule in all but name. The country was governed by a series of Brazilian-born Regents and a Parliament of property owners, whose chief concern was to prevent the fragmentation of the empire, as advocates of federalism and republicanism kept the provinces in a state of agitation. The Additional Act (1834) to the constitution, providing for provincial legislatures and a measure of local autonomy, failed to stem the tide of unrest. Finally, an effective symbol of national unity was found in the boy Emperor. In July 1840, before his fifteenth birthday, he was declared of age and placed on the throne as Pedro II. Within a decade war-weary rebels accepted the peace of the empire, royal institutions were consolidated, and a vigorous young monarch assumed full responsibility as chief of state. The reign of Pedro II (1840–1889) was to be longer than the tenure of any other head of government in the Western Hemisphere.

Beneath the surface of politicomilitary crises that had marked the years of the Regency and continued into the 1840s, significant changes were occurring to pave the way for a long generation of political stability under Pedro II. Coffee became the leading export crop (see COFFEE INDUSTRY: BRAZIL), and the increasingly affluent coffee planters who extended their orchards the length of the Paraíba Valley and into the hill country of Minas Gerais and São Paulo joined the traditional sugar planters of the NORTHEAST as staunch supporters of the central government. At the same time antimonarchists and the regular armed forces were gradually excluded from the political scene following the creation of the civilian National Guard (1831), which in effect placed the police power in the hands of the strongest monarchist landholders in each province. Such rural bosses preserved the status quo in their respective localities. The imperial aristocracy, the life-term senators, and the officers of the National Guard were drawn from their ranks, while their sons and nephews, trained at the law schools of São Paulo or Recife, represented them as members of the Liberal or Conservative parties in the provincial assemblies and the Chamber of Deputies. The capstone of the rural-based political structure was the Emperor, who preserved the balance between conflicting regional and partisan interests through judicious exercise of his constitutional *poder moderador* (moderating power) to appoint and transfer provincial governors, to select the Prime Minister, and to rotate the parties in office.

Brazil enjoyed four decades of domestic peace and a generally expanding economy following the last provincial revolt in 1849. The alliance between the crown and the rural elites held firm through confrontation with Great Britain (1845–1850), foreign wars in Argentina (1851–1852) and Paraguay (1864–1870; *see* PARAGUAYAN WAR), the revival of republicanism, and friction between church and state in the 1870s. It eventually collapsed, and the empire fell in 1889, because the established political leadership failed to curb the growing assertiveness of the armed forces and was unable to resolve the slavery question without undermining the monarchy itself.

The African slave trade and the persistence of slavery as a legal institution posed the most perplexing dilemmas facing Brazil's leaders in the nineteenth century. Humanitarian considerations and concern over the Africanization of Brazil clashed with the perennial need for labor in the plantation economy. Thus, despite the pledges of the Portuguese crown before 1822 and of the Brazilian court thereafter to restrict the traffic, well over 1 million slaves were taken to Brazil between 1800 and 1850, bringing the number of bondsmen to 3 million in a total population of about 7 million. During that half century the crown was simply unable to enforce laws or treaties against the traffic over the objections of the planters. And as long as new levies of slaves arrived each year, slave owners had no need to question the assumption that they would be ruined without a continuing supply of servile labor. At the same time, however, Brazil was under mounting pressure from Great Britain, which led the crusade against the slave trade and vowed, in 1845, to exterminate it by force if necessary. The government of Brazil protested and procrastinated, but was finally obliged to concede. The QUEIROZ LAW, formally prohibiting all further importation of slaves from Africa, was enacted on September 4, 1850, and within three years the traffic was suppressed. For twenty years, however, nothing was done to free the blacks still in bondage, and as long as slavery persisted, no adequate alternative source of plantation labor was available to Brazil. The trickle of immigrants from Europe tended in large part to remain in the coastal cities or to settle in isolated colonies in the forests of southern Brazil. At the close of the Paraguayan War the question of emancipation became a major issue, which the Parliament dealt with primarily in economic terms. The FREE BIRTH LAW (1871) provided for gradual emancipation of slaves with compensation to their owners. Within a few years, however, this approach was under fire from the younger generation of politicians, led by Joaquim NABUCO and Ruy BARBOSA, who denounced slavery on moral grounds and demanded its immediate and total abolition. Their campaign attracted enthusiastic support in the cities and among small property owners throughout Brazil. As the large landholders continued to resist meaningful change in the laws affecting slavery, abolition became increasingly associated with the call for a change in the system of government, for it was

endorsed by the small republican movement and by positivist officers in the Army (*see* POSITIVISM: BRAZIL), who looked upon human bondage and monarchy as equally outmoded in the Western Hemisphere.

By the GOLDEN LAW of May 13, 1888, the remaining 700,000 slaves in Brazil were emancipated. The freedmen were turned out to fend for themselves, the abolitionists congratulated each other for their humanitarianism, and the disgruntled ex-slaveholders, who had received no compensation for their lost property, withdrew their support from the monarchy, which fell without defenders eighteen months later. *See also* ABOLITION OF SLAVERY (BRAZIL).

The overthrow of the empire and creation of the republic by Marshal Manuel Deodoro da FONSECA on November 15, 1889, did not immediately affect the basic social and economic order of Brazil, although they brought many surface changes and shattered the centralized rule of the imperial era. The Army would henceforth be a major force in national politics, but after five years of turmoil and violence under two inexperienced military Presidents, the armed forces withdrew from the limelight and civilian spokesmen for the now-fashionable Republican party assumed formal leadership of the nation.

The regime, since known as the FIRST REPUBLIC (Old Republic), endured until 1930 as a loose federation of quasi-sovereign states, usually dominated by the rural gentry of São Paulo and Minas Gerais. Despite their avowed dedication to the concepts of "order and progress," the traditional elites remained impervious to new ideas and to new forces seeking to enter the political arena. Nonetheless, in their pursuit of policies designed to promote and protect the coffee export industry, they unwittingly encouraged trends that would in due course make the rural-based political system unviable. By insisting upon balanced budgets and a strong currency, which had the effect of raising the cost of imports, the central government provided a barrier behind which a nascent domestic manufacturing industry developed. This contributed to the growth of an urban wage-earning working class, particularly in the cities of São Paulo and Rio de Janeiro, and to the emergence of a highly vocal, affluent group of native entrepreneurs who were soon objecting to the export mentality and political monopoly of the planter oligarchy. Equally far-reaching consequences stemmed from the government's encouragement of immigration from Europe as a source of cheap labor for the coffee plantations. During the years of the First Republic 3 million immigrants entered Brazil, bringing not only their brawn but a broad range of technological skills, European tastes, and great expectations for a better life. While some of them stayed in the coffee zone, the majority moved to the cities, where social mobility was easier but still was discouraged by the regime, which regarded "the social question" as a matter for the police. Their frustration added to the climate of unrest that characterized the cities of Brazil after World War I. The most dramatic protest against the status quo, however, was the series of revolts carried out after 1922 by younger army officers (*tenentes*) calling for political reforms and social justice (*see* TENENTISMO). These unsuccessful revolts were the prelude to the REVOLUTION OF 1930 that toppled the First Republic.

After 1930 Brazil experienced a profound, and largely nonviolent, social and economic revolution that is identified with Getúlio VARGAS, who dominated the political scene for a quarter of a century. He served continuously as chief of state until 1945, ruling most of that time without the restraints of elections, parties, or Congress, and was returned to office by popular vote in 1951. Under Vargas's direction the structure of the First Republic was dismantled, political primacy passed from the rural gentry to the urban middle class, and power was transferred from the states to the central government. Capitalizing upon the grievances of the urban population, Vargas encouraged the growth of the private industrial sector and greatly expanded the role of the government in the fields of labor, education, public health, and social welfare. A vast federal bureaucracy was formed to manage the new services, which attracted hundreds of thousands of migrants from rural areas to the burgeoning cities. Price supports and marketing assistance were provided to growers of coffee, cotton, and other agricultural exports, which continued to earn nearly all Brazil's foreign exchange, but none of the labor benefits or social legislation enjoyed by city workers were extended to the rural lower class. Nor was there any threat to the traditional land tenure pattern. Under Vargas the state also undertook a considerable expansion of the economic infrastructure, initiating the search for domestic sources of fuel, launching the integrated iron and steel plant at VOLTA REDONDA (see IRON AND STEEL INDUSTRY: BRAZIL), and improving land, air, and sea transportation facilities. During the later years of the authoritarian ESTADO NOVO (New State), Vargas catered increasingly to his labor following and appealed to the growing spirit of nationalism among all Brazilians, strengthening their conviction that Brazil was destined to become a world power.

After World War II, in which Brazil participated as one of the Allied nations, the Estado Novo was replaced by a system of open representative democracy that was to survive less than twenty years. The constitution of 1946 provided for the customary separation of executive, legislative, and judicial authority but retained the social, economic, and electoral reforms enacted during the Vargas years (see CONSTITUTION OF 1946: BRAZIL). A dozen new political parties competed for the allegiance of the voters, who now included all literate adults. Populist coalition politics, increasingly frantic appeals to xenophobic nationalism, and a pattern of frequent military intervention became the norm. The first populist President was Vargas, to whom the voters turned after five years of the lackluster administration of Eurico Gaspar DUTRA for easy solutions to the problems of inflation and lagging economic growth. In the eyes of his admirers, Vargas's last term was a success if only because it produced the national petroleum monopoly, PETRÓLEOS BRASILEIROS, S.A., in 1953. However, his inability to find a formula for simultaneous economic development and stability caused his downfall under military pressure. Vargas committed suicide in August 1954.

The most successful of the freely elected Presidents was Juscelino KUBITSCHEK (1956–1961), who combined developmentalism and nationalism with infectious confidence in Brazil's destiny to spark an unprecedented burst of economic growth. Kubitschek substantially fulfilled his promise to give Brazil "fifty years of progress in five," primarily in the areas of steel, transportation, and electric power. In terms of its psychological impact, his major accomplishment was doubtless the construction of Brasília, on the inland plateau between Minas Gerais and Goiás, which was inaugurated as the new capital of Brazil on April 21, 1960. Brasília was to serve as the hub of a network of interregional highways opening vast reaches of the interior and linking all the states of Brazil. The establishment of a national automotive industry with a monopoly of the Brazilian market assured that the vehicles traveling the new highways would be Brazilian-made. The price paid for Kubitschek's impressive building program was greatly increased foreign indebtedness and a new wave of inflation, which were to pose serious problems for his successors and the nation.

The now-customary politicomilitary crisis did not occur during the electoral campaign of 1960 but arose in August 1961, when President Jânio QUADROS resigned after only seven months in office, leaving it to Vice President João Goulart. The latter, a former protégé of Vargas and head of the PARTIDO TRABALHISTA BRASILEIRO, was considered too radical a leader by the military ministers, who called on Congress to block the succession. Congress refused. After a week of frantic maneuvering, a compromise was reached whereby Goulart took office with reduced powers at the head of a parliamentary regime. For the next sixteen months his principal objective was to regain full presidential authority, which was restored to him by a nationwide plebiscite in January 1963. By this time Brazilians of all political leanings were convinced that the country was in a prerevolutionary situation, and it was generally assumed that the revolution would come from the left. Goulart contributed to this assumption by word and deed. Harried by radical extremists within his own party who were seeking to win over his labor following, Goulart was unable to establish a working agreement with the badly splintered Congress to deal with the pressing problems of spiraling inflation and economic recession. Rather, he became increasingly demagogic in his appeals for support from urban workers and from the rural populace, which had been aroused by calls for agrarian reform. Badly frightened, conservatives and moderates turned to the military for rescue. Goulart's fate was sealed when he interfered with the execution of military discipline and turned directly to the enlisted ranks of the armed forces for political backing. On March 31, 1964, the Army rebelled, and within forty-eight hours it had taken control of the government.

The military administrations in power since 1964 — under Presidents Humberto CASTELLO BRANCO (1964–1967), Arthur da COSTA E SILVA (1967–1969), and Emílio Garrastazu MÉDICI (1969–1974) — have been concerned chiefly to purge Brazil of subversion and corruption and to provide a climate of political stability that would permit them to control inflation and foment a sustained high rate of rational, coordinated economic development. To achieve their political objectives they have concentrated power heavily in the hands of the President, canceled the mandates and political rights of hundreds of elected officials and critics in all areas of public life, imposed press censorship, suppressed armed opposition, imposed an artificial two-party system, and established indirect elections for most public executive offices. In the economic sphere they have maintained strict controls over wages and salaries, revised and tightened the tax system, engaged in economic planning to a greater extent than ever before in Brazil, vastly increased the rate of public investment in the economy, and provided optimum conditions for private investment, both domestic and foreign. The institutional changes have been incorporated into the constitution of 1967 and the extensive amendments of 1969 (*see* CONSTITUTION OF 1967: BRAZIL). The goals of the post-1964 regimes have for the most part been met or surpassed, with the result that Brazil has one of the highest rates of economic growth of any nation in the world. The military has vowed to remain in power until its reforms are irreversible.

See also AGRICULTURE (BRAZIL); IMMIGRATION (BRAZIL); INDUSTRY (BRAZIL); NEGRO IN BRAZIL.

Bibliography. José Maria Bello, *A History of Modern Brazil, 1889–1964,* Stanford, Calif., 1966; Sergio Buarque de Holanda (ed.), *História Geral da Civilização Brasileira,* 6 vols., São Paulo, 1960–; E. Bradford Burns, *A History of Brazil,* New York, 1970; Bailey W. Diffie, "Colonial Brazil," in *Latin American Civilization: Colonial Period,* Harrisburg, Pa., 1945; Gilberto Freyre, *New World in the Tropics,* New York, 1959; Celso Furtado, *The Economic Growth of Brazil,* Berkeley, Calif., 1963; C. H. Haring, *Empire in Brazil,* Cambridge, Mass., 1958; Rollie E. Poppino, *Brazil: The Land and People,* New York, 1968.

ROLLIE E. POPPINO

BRITISH HONDURAS. *See* BELIZE.

BROUWER, LEO (1939–   ). Cuban composer and guitarist. Brouwer was born in Havana. After beginning his music education at the conservatory there, he enrolled at the Juilliard School in New York, where he studied with Vincent Persichetti and others in 1959 and 1960. Some of his works have been presented in such important European festivals as those at Aldeburgh and Berlin. His most recent style is based on an exploration of new sounds and structures in which improvisation and strict adherence to the written text alternate. Good examples of this are his compositions *Cantigas del nuevo tiempo* (1970) and *Exaedros I* and *II* for guitar (1970). In addition, he has written numerous chamber music and orchestral compositions as well as incidental music for the theater.

JUAN A. ORREGO-SALAS

BRYAN-CHAMORRO TREATY. Financial and political difficulties in Nicaragua caused the regime of President Adolfo DÍAZ in December 1912 to propose to the United States the sale for $3 million of the sole right to contruct an interoceanic canal through the country. As signed by both parties on August 5, 1914, the treaty also provided for the lease by Nicaragua to the United States for ninety-nine years of the Great Corn and Little Corn Islands and for the right to establish a naval base on the Gulf of Fonseca, with the privilege of renewal of the grants for a similar period. The treaty was ratified by the United States Senate in 1916. Since Costa Rica, El Salvador, and Honduras had protested against the treaty because of infringement of their rights on the gulf, a proviso was added that

the convention was not intended to affect any existing rights of the protesting states. Nevertheless, Costa Rica and El Salvador carried their protest to the CENTRAL AMERICAN COURT OF JUSTICE in order to prevent Nicaragua from following through on the provisions of the treaty. Costa Rica argued that a treaty of 1858 between Nicaragua and Costa Rica had provided for consultation between the two countries before any contracts were signed in constructing a canal. Since in 1888 President Cleveland had acknowledged the validity of the treaty, Costa Rica seemed to have a good case. El Salvador petitioned the Court on the ground that it had equal rights with Honduras and Nicaragua in the Gulf of Fonseca. In 1916–1917 the Court upheld Costa Rican and Salvadoran claims, but neither the United States nor Nicaragua accepted the decision. The $3 million loan did help to restore solvency to Nicaragua, but the United States never exercised its options under the treaty, and both countries agreed to abrogate it in 1970.

RICHARD B. GRAY

BUCARELI [Y URSÚA], ANTONIO MARÍA (1717–1779). Spanish colonial administrator. The colonial career of Bucareli after the Peace of Paris (1763) was indicative of the interest of CHARLES III in men of military background and his concern for improving the defenses and finances of the overseas kingdoms. Of noble lineage, Bucareli had fought with distinction in Italy and Portugal and had served as inspector of coastal fortifications in Granada before being appointed Governor and Captain General of Cuba in 1766. There he became familiar with the chronic financial straits of his administrative superiors in New Spain, as he dealt with the new INTENDANCY SYSTEM and the economic changes that had been introduced in Cuba following the English occupation (1762) of Havana. After five years, though anxious to return to Spain and military duties, he reluctantly accepted the responsibility of the Viceroyalty of New Spain, then undergoing reorganization under the *visitador* José de GÁLVEZ. An efficient administrator rather than an innovative thinker, Bucareli improved the fortifications at Perote, Jalapa, at Acapulco, and at San Juan de Ulúa and brought greater efficiency to the collection and disbursement of revenue without making any basic changes in the structure. Charitable institutions and public works, including the thoroughfare that today bears his name, were stimulated. Enjoying wide popularity, Bucareli exercised his task with vigor until his death of pleurisy in April 1779.

ALAN KOVAC

BUCARELI CONFERENCES. Series of meetings (May 14–August 15, 1923) held in a building on Bucareli Avenue, Mexico City, between commissioners representing the United States and Mexico to discuss differences between the two nations stemming from Mexican agrarian and petroleum policies. Secretary of State Charles Evans Hughes wished to obtain a treaty commitment from Mexico that it would not violate the property rights of American citizens in implementing its policies, but President Álvaro OBREGÓN realized that it would be politically unwise to give such a commitment. As a result, the United States did not resume diplomatic relations with Mexico, which had been severed after the revolution that brought Obregón to power in 1920.

The Bucareli conferences were held in order to find a way out of the impasse. Considerable controversy has arisen over the discussions and the resulting agreements, which consisted of two treaties and an "extraofficial pact" with two sections. One of the treaties provided for a Special Claims Commission to consider claims against Mexico by American citizens for losses between 1910 and 1920. The other treaty provided for a General Claims Commission to deal with the claims of citizens of both nations for losses after 1868.

The first section of the extraofficial pact dealt with the exploitation of Mexico's petroleum resources by foreign firms. Ever since the constitution of 1917 (see CONSTITUTION OF 1917: MEXICO) had vested direct ownership of Mexico's subsoil wealth in the nation, which might grant concessions for its exploitation, the position of companies that had obtained oil lands or rights prior to 1917 had been seriously threatened. Difficulties were ostensibly eased by the extra-official pact, which ratified recent decisions of the Mexican Supreme Court to the effect that the constitutional provision was not to be applied retroactively in cases in which owners of oil lands or rights had performed "positive acts" in order to exploit them before 1917.

The second section of the pact dealt with compensation to Americans whose lands had been expropriated to form *ejidos* (communal holdings; see EJIDO). It was asserted that the United States in principle did not accept the compensation of its citizens by bonds; however, the commissioners agreed that American citizens would accept bonds for *ejidos* up to a maximum of 1,755 hectares (approximately 4,335 acres). According to one interpretation of this agreement, if American-owned holdings in excess of 1,755 hectares were expropriated, compensation was to be in cash.

After the Bucareli agreements had been approved by Presidents Obregón and Coolidge, the United States resumed diplomatic relations with Mexico on August 31, 1923. Later there would be debate over whether the extraofficial pact, which did not receive treaty status, was binding on Mexico.

HELEN DELPAR

BUENOS AIRES. Capital of Argentina. In 1580, forty-four years after the failure of Pedro de MENDOZA to establish a settlement on the RÍO DE LA PLATA, Juan de Garay arrived from Asunción with 300 settlers, cattle, and horses to lay the foundations of the Argentine capital and livestock industry. The Diocese of Buenos Aires was created on March 30, 1620, and until August 4, 1858, it included the provinces of Entre Ríos, Corrientes, and Sante Fe. The city was authorized to have its own *audiencia* in 1661. With intermittent legality Buenos Aires became a transit point for Negroes, often from Rio de Janeiro, bound for the slave marts in Chile, Peru, Bolivia, and the interior cities. Portuguese merchants and contrabandists trading with Portuguese and Spanish merchants in the interior began to establish their residence in Buenos Aires after 1618. Between 1713 and 1739 some of the British merchants participating in the Negro slave trade under

privileges granted by Spain to the British South Sea Company also settled in Buenos Aires. During the same period resident merchants began to ship hides and tallow to Europe and to import European goods for the local market or for Chile, Asunción, Charcas, and the interior cities.

From its designation as the capital of the newly created Viceroyalty of the Río de la Plata (see RÍO DE LA PLATA, VICEROYALTY OF) in 1776 until the outbreak of war between Spain and Great Britain in 1797, the city enjoyed considerable growth. Its population, which was composed of whites, Negroes, mestizos, and Indians, increased from 24,000 in 1776 to about 35,000 in 1794. Indicative of the new ferment were the creation of the *consulado* (merchants' guild) on January 30, 1794, and the opening of trade in jerked beef, wheat, and flour with Spain and Cuba. Aware of the city's strategic importance, the British captured it in 1806 but were soon expelled.

The independence movement began in Buenos Aires on May 25, 1810. During another period of advance in the 1820s, when foreigners, mostly French and English, dominated the commercial life of the city, the University of Buenos Aires, two agricultural schools, a theater, two banks, two newspapers, and a state library were started. In 1857 improvement of the city's port facilities was seriously undertaken. By 1870 the Colón Theater, a music hall, and the Cathedral had been completed, some streets had been lighted with gas, telegraph lines had reached Montevideo and Rosario, several newspapers had attained a daily circulation rate of 20,000, and the ships of seven steamship lines were calling regularly at the port. What remained unchanged were the high crime rate and the unsanitary conditions.

The city developed rapidly after it became the federal capital in 1880. Starting as the terminus of a 6-mile line in 1857, it became the hub of a railroad system with 17,357 miles in 1910 and 27,250 miles in 1955. By 1930 Buenos Aires had 30 percent of the industrial plants in Argentina and was attracting 20 to 25 percent of the foreign capital invested in the country. In 1869 the city had 187,346 inhabitants, or about 13 percent of the population of Argentina; in 1947, 3,000,371, or 28.7 percent. In 1970 greater Buenos Aires had a population of 8,352,900 out of a total Argentine population of 23,360,000.

See also PORTEÑO.

JOSEPH T. CRISCENTI

BULNES, MANUEL (1799–1866). President of Chile (1841–1851). Like Joaquín PRIETO, his uncle and immediate predecessor in the Chilean Presidency, Bulnes was a military man who came originally from Concepción. His career as a soldier was a notable one, culminating in his command of the second and final Chilean expeditionary force sent to destroy the PERU-BOLIVIA CONFEDERATION. Bulnes's victory in the Battle of Yungay (January 20, 1839) made him a national hero and an obvious candidate for the Presidency. His two administrations were marked by the foundation of the University of Chile (1842), the annexation of the Strait of Magellan territory (1843), the encouragement of German immigration in the south, and the building of the first Chilean railroad (1851). Bulnes fostered a somewhat more tolerant political atmosphere than had been apparent under his predecessor, although strict legislation on local government (1844) and the press (1846) showed that the main principles of the conservative political system were far from being discarded.

The final years of Bulnes's Presidency were overshadowed by the strident Liberal opposition to the presidential candidacy of Manuel MONTT (*see* LIBERAL PARTY: CHILE), which came to a head with the insurrection of April 20, 1851, in Santiago and the outbreak of full-scale civil war in September of that year. On completing his term of office, Bulnes assumed command of the government's forces and crushed the main rebellion in the Battle of Loncomilla (December 8, 1851); this ensured the survival of the Montt administration.

SIMON COLLIER

BURGOS, LAWS OF. *See* LAWS OF BURGOS.

BUSCH, GERMÁN (1904–1939). Bolivian army officer and President (1937–1939). The son of a German physician and his Bolivian wife, Busch was a graduate of the Colegio Militar and one of the few real Bolivian heroes in the CHACO WAR with Paraguay (1932–1935). Later he was one of a group of younger officers who carried out a coup d'état on June 20, 1936, that placed Col. David TORO in the Presidency.

Although Toro's regime at first proclaimed itself socialist and nationalist, it tended to move increasingly to the right, generating discontent among elements that had originally supported it. As a result, on July 13, 1937, there was another coup, which placed Busch in the Presidency. He gathered about him a group of left-wing intellectuals, of whom the two best-known were Gustavo Navarro (generally referred to by his pseudonym, Tristan Marof), a pioneer in trying to organize a socialist movement in Bolivia, and Víctor PAZ ESTENSSORO.

The Busch regime produced a number of innovations: it promulgated Bolivia's first detailed body of labor legislation; it brought about the enactment of a new constitution, patterned after that of Mexico, that contained extensive social and economic chapters; and it allowed union organization to begin among the tin miners. Finally, Busch took steps to limit the power of the Big Three tin-mining companies, which had dominated national politics for two generations. Busch established the government-owned Banco Minero, which undertook the sale abroad of the production of small- and medium-size tin firms, as well as helping to finance them. Even more important, on June 7, 1939, President Busch issued a decree

providing that the Big Three turn over to the Banco Central all the foreign exchange they earned and seek from the bank any foreign exchange they might need for making purchases abroad, paying debts and dividends, and so on. This decree aroused particularly strong hostility among the mining firms.

President Busch died on August 23, 1939, only a few weeks after issuing the foreign exchange control decree. Although the official cause of death was given as suicide, there were allegations at the time that the President had been murdered because of the danger he represented to the entrenched economic and social groups of the country.

ROBERT J. ALEXANDER

BUSTAMANTE [I RIVERO], JOSÉ LUIS (1894–   ). Peruvian scholar, diplomat, jurist, and President (1945–1948). Bustamante was born in Arequipa of modest middle-class parents. Educated in Cuzco and Arequipa, he spent most of his adult life in distinguished service to his country. He taught at the National University of San Augustín in Arequipa (1930–1934), served briefly as Minister of Education in 1931, and represented Peru in Bolivia, Paraguay, and Uruguay between 1934 and 1945.

In 1930 Bustamante participated in the revolt of Arequipa that ended Augusto LEGUÍA's eleven-year dictatorship (1919–1930). In fact, he apparently wrote the manifesto that stirred mass support for the rebels. In spite of this and other forays into politics, however, Bustamante developed a reputation for evenhandedness and neutrality. Precisely because of these characteristics he was elected President in 1945 by a coalition of forces seeking to restore democracy to Peru.

Bustamante's trying three years as President are described in his *Tres años de la lucha por la democracia en el Perú* (1949). He placed most of the blame for his overthrow by a military coup on the Apristas (*see* ALIANZA POPULAR REVOLUCIONARIA AMERICANA), but it appears that he contributed to the downfall of his administration by being markedly indecisive in confronting the then-traditional rivalry between the Apristas and the military-oligarchy coalition.

After 1948 Bustamante retired to private life and devoted most of his energies to the practice of law. He became a member of the International Court of Justice at The Hague in 1961 and its President in 1967.

ORAZIO A. CICCARELLI

BUSTOS DOMECQ, HONORIO. *See* BIOY CASARES, ADOLFO.

Caamaño, Roberto
CVC

C

CAAMAÑO, ROBERTO (1923–). Argentine composer. Caamaño was born in Buenos Aires, where he studied composition at the National Conservatory of Music. In 1960 he was appointed professor of composition at the conservatory, in 1961 artistic director of the Teatro Colón, and later dean of the Faculty of Music of the Catholic University in Buenos Aires. As of 1972 he was a member of the board of directors of the International Music Council of UNESCO. His catalog includes compositions for chamber ensembles, among which his quintet for piano and strings (1962) is the most outstanding; and orchestral works such as a suite (1949), a Magnificat for chorus and orchestra (1954), and a concerto for piano and orchestra (1957). JUAN A. ORREGO-SALAS

CABALLERO, BERNARDINO (1840–1912). Paraguayan war hero, politician, and President (1880–1881, 1881–1886). One of the few Paraguayan heroes to survive the disastrous PARAGUAYAN WAR (1864–1870), Caballero rose from the rank of sergeant to that of general during its course, taking part in most of the major battles. After the war, in 1870, he and Cándido Barreiro founded the Club del Pueblo, from which the Colorado party evolved. Waving the "bloody shirt," Caballero and Barreiro denounced the rival Gran Club del Pueblo as the lackey of the Brazilian occupation authorities. Several revolts led by the club occurred, but they were crushed with the aid of Brazilian troops. Then, in 1877, President Juan Bautista Gill was assassinated, and the next year Barreiro was made Presi-dent with Caballero as Minister of the Interior. When Barreiro died in 1880, Caballero filled out the rest of his term. Elected President on his own account in 1881, he served his full term. In 1887 he created the Asociación Nacional Repúblicana to institutionalize his political organization, and he remained head of the party until his death. From 1880 until the Liberals overthrew Colorado rule in 1904, Caballero dominated Paraguayan politics through his charismatic personality and control of his party. *See* COLORADO PARTY (PARAGUAY); LIBERAL PARTY (PARAGUAY). JOHN HOYT WILLIAMS

CABEZA DE VACA, ÁLVAR NÚÑEZ (1490?–1557). One of the first Spanish explorers of the North American Southwest and Governor of Paraguay. A native of Jerez de la Frontera, Cabeza de Vaca fought in the Italian wars and as a loyalist against the Comuneros in Spain. He was rewarded with an appointment as royal treasurer of the Pánfilo de NARVÁEZ expedition that left Spain in 1527 to conquer the Gulf of Mexico coast from Florida to Mexico. Narváez landed his expedition near Tampa Bay and marched northwest, but his men suffered greatly from hunger and Indian attacks. They put to sea on rafts, hoping to sail to Mexico, only to be shipwrecked near Galveston Island. Only Cabeza de Vaca and three others survived the entire ordeal. They became slaves of Indians, and in this capacity Cabeza de Vaca became adept as a trader and faith healer. He led the three others to New Spain (1536) after seven years of wandering with various Indian tribes. In 1537 he returned to Spain, and three years later he was appointed successor to Pedro de MENDOZA as Governor of the Río de la Plata region. Upon his arrival in Asunción, he met the survivors of the Mendoza-Ayolas expeditions under the command of Domingo Martínez de Irala, the deceased Juan de Ayolas's lieutenant. Cabeza de Vaca's strict enforcement of crown policy outraged Irala, who finally imprisoned the Governor and sent him to Spain for trial (1545). Cabeza de Vaca was condemned for numerous misdeeds as Governor, upon evidence supplied by his enemies, and died old and impoverished, having failed to clear his name, in spite of his loyalty to the crown during long years of service. WILLIAM S. DUDLEY

CABILDO. Municipal or town council, the lowest level of the administrative hierarchy in colonial Spanish America. The *cabildo,* or *ayuntamiento,* as it was sometimes called, was a local unit of government similar to that of medieval Castilian towns. Beginning in the first decades of colonial rule, municipalities were established in America and regulated by royal laws. Community government was thus fairly uniform throughout the colonies. Authority was vested in two basic types of officials, *regidores* (aldermen; *see* REGIDOR) and *alcaldes ordinarios* (magistrates), both of whom were voting members of the *cabildo.* The number of *regidores* and alcaldes who served on the council ranged between five and twelve, depending on the size and importance of the town. In cities and large towns the CORREGIDOR presided over the council, and in the sixteenth century there were frequent jurisdictional conflicts between the corregidor, a crown representative, and the *cabildo,* which spoke for the town's citizenry. A number of municipal officers of lesser importance, including local treasury officials, the city attorney, and the *cabildo* notary, also participated in council meetings.

The *cabildo* had various functions in the political, social, and economic spheres. Political authority was exercised by virtue of its right to select certain municipal officers and by its representation of community interests before outside authorities. In this capacity, *cabildos* often sent *procuradores* (representatives) to royal and viceregal courts. Within its local political jurisdiction, the *cabildo* also had the right to convene *cabildos abiertos* (open assemblies) of the town's *vecinos* (residents) to discuss matters of general concern. The *cabildo*'s social functions consisted of protecting the city's poor and small tradesmen, promoting education and public charity, and sponsoring fiestas to celebrate important events. The economic activities of municipal government were the most far-ranging. The *cabildo* issued land grants, established and enforced price controls on retail goods and services, regulated intracity commerce and manufacturing, collected certain taxes such as the ALCABALA, and financed public works. An important part of *cabildo* activity was the raising of municipal revenue to finance its operations. Income came from many sources: the *sisa* (excise tax on wine), the periodic auction of the meat supply contract, the dues levied on grain sold in the local granary, local fines, and rent on municipal property.

The *cabildo* underwent considerable change during three centuries of colonial rule. At the outset of Spanish colonization it served as the earliest institution with general authority over a newly conquered area. Following the arrival of royal officials, the jurisdiction of the *cabildo* was limited to an urban community, but it retained a large degree of authority and local autonomy. In the early and middle sixteenth century *cabildo* members were elected from the local elite. In the late sixteenth century, however, the *regimiento* (office of *regidor*) began to be filled by royal grantees. By the early seventeenth century *regimientos* had become proprietary and sometimes hereditary. In the crown's effort to raise revenue, these offices were increasingly sold for large sums of money. The effect of granting and later selling *cabildo* offices was twofold. First, the appeal to royal favor for grants of office weakened the autonomy of local administration, which had already been partly curtailed by royal legislation in the middle of the sixteenth century. Second, the sale and inheritance of *regimientos* tended to fix the composition of the *cabildo* and reduce the number of citizens who could hope to serve on the council. In the seventeenth century, as municipal administration was controlled increasingly by a small circle of the town's wealthy families who could afford the high price of office, the council tended to become less responsive to community interests. Furthermore, the increasingly static composition of the *cabildo* was reflected in the growing inefficiency and inaction of municipal government. Ceremonial questions and intercity rivalries took precedence over more useful administrative activity. *Libros de cabildos,* in which the minutes of the meetings were recorded, became filled with little more than copies of titles of officials and records of sales of offices.

By the eighteenth century most *cabildos* lacked the means to raise sufficient revenue to administer even a limited municipal government. Corrupt and inefficient, they were finally subordinated to intendants and their subdelegates, who under the centralizing tendency of BOURBON REFORMS took control of local administration in the 1780s (*see* INTENDANCY SYSTEM). As a result of administrative reform, the financial affairs of municipalities were improved and local government was partly revived. *Cabildos* gradually assumed greater responsibility, which frequently led to jurisdictional conflict between *cabildos* and intendants. By the late colonial period *cabildos* had come to represent creole interests over those of the crown, and when Spanish authority began to crumble in 1808, they played a key role in organizing local support for widespread political and economic reform. *Cabildos abiertos* became the focal points of colonial dissension and unrest. It was in a *cabildo abierto,* in fact, that independence was first declared in Buenos Aires in 1810.

Bibliography. Julio Alemparte, *El cabildo en Chile colonial,* Santiago, 1940; C. Bayle, *Los cabildos seculares en la América española,* Madrid, 1952; John Lynch, "Intendants and Cabildos in the Viceroyalty of Río de la Plata, 1782–1810," *Hispanic American Historical Review,* vol. XXXV, no. 3, August 1955, pp. 337–362; John P. Moore, *The Cabildo in Peru under the Bourbons,* Durham, N.C., 1966; id., *The Cabildo in Peru under the Hapsburgs,* Durham, N.C., 1954; Fredrick B. Pike, "Aspects of Cabildo Economic Regulations in Spanish America under the Hapsburgs," *Inter-American Economic Affairs,* vol. XIII, no. 4, Spring, 1960, pp. 67–86.

BROOKE LARSON SHUTE

CABOCLO. In colonial Brazil, a term (literally, "copper-colored") used to refer to an acculturated Indian. It later came to denote a mixed-blood of European and Indian ancestry and at present is widely used to refer to any lower-class rural male.

CABRAL, MANUEL DEL (1907–). Dominican writer whose poetry and poetic prose reflect an authentic Antillean culture. His major works include *Trópico negro* (1942), *Sangre mayor* (1945), *De este lado del mar* (1948), *Los huéspedes secretos* (1951), and *Pedrada planetaria* (1958). *Compadre Mon* (1943) is an epic-lyric poem that creates the myth of a popular hero. Cabral's two anthologies, *Antología tierra* (1959) and *Antología clave* (1957), cover a variety of themes, including the vein of so-called black, African-inspired poetry in which he excels. His poetic prose appeared in two volumes, *Chinchina busca el tiempo* (1945) and *30 parábolas* (1956).

RACHEL PHILLIPS

CABRAL, PEDRO ÁLVARES (ca. 1467–ca. 1520). Portuguese admiral and discoverer of Brazil. Cabral sighted the coast of South America in April 1500 while sailing to India and claimed the territory for the King of Portugal. This landfall six years after the signing of the Treaty of Tordesillas has provoked much debate among historians as to whether the Portuguese had prior knowledge of the location of the South American coast while they were negotiating the treaty (*see* TORDESILLAS, TREATY OF). In fact, the discovery had been almost inevitable since Vasco da GAMA's articulation of a sea passage to the Cape of Good Hope that avoided the difficult passage down the African coast in the face of contrary winds.

Cabral's was the first voyage after Da Gama's discovery of the westerlies, and his route took him close to the mainland. The discovery was called the Land of the True Cross but soon became known as Brazil, after the red dyewood that was its first valuable export to Europe. A report of the discovery by Pedro Vaz de Caminha forms the first chronicle of Portuguese America. Cabral himself remained only a few days before continuing the voyage to India, and he was never to return to Brazil. Cabral's landfall is situated in the present-day state of Espírito Santo.

KENNETH R. MAXWELL

CABRERA INFANTE, GUILLERMO (1929–). Cuban novelist. Born in Oriente Province, he moved to Havana with his family in 1941 and began writing in 1947 after giving up his hopes for a career in medicine. In 1950 he entered a school of journalism, and in 1954 he began to write cinema criticism for the review *Carteles* under the pseudonym G. Cain. He took over the editorship of *Carteles* in 1957, won literary prizes for his stories, and founded Cinemateca de Cuba, which he directed from 1951 to 1956. In 1959 he was an official director of culture and a director of the Cinema Institute and of the literary review *Lunes de Revolución.* In 1962 he went to Belgium as Cultural Attaché, but he gave up diplomacy in 1965; since then he has lived in England and Spain.

Cabrera Infante published a collection of translations of short stories from various languages, *Así en la paz como en la guerra* (1960); *Un oficio del siglo XX* (1963),

a volume of cinema criticism; and *Tres tristes tigres,* 1964 (*Three Trapped Tigers*), a novel whose brilliance won him prizes and fame. In this work the resources of language, wordplay, and pun are handled with a virtuosity that at once re-creates the atmosphere of pre-revolutionary Havana and explores the theme underlying the new novel in Latin America—language as the ultimate reality of literature and of man.

RACHEL PHILLIPS

CACAO INDUSTRY (ECUADOR). Estates on the costa (*see* COSTA: ECUADOR) produced cacao as early as the sixteenth century, and the native *cacao nacional* was of such excellent quality that it brought top prices even in the 1880s. However, it would grow only in deep silt along riverbanks. Demand for chocolate by 1890 had caused planters to introduce ordinary cacao seedlings from Trinidad; hence plantations expanded to the hills of Colonche and to the Andean foothills bordering the Guayas Lowland, and by 1894 Ecuador produced more cacao than any other country in the world.

Ecuadorians owned the estates, financed production, and controlled the trade. The Banco Comercial y Agrícola de Guayaquil, managed by Francisco Urbina Jado, serviced the exporters, and the Association of Agriculturists of Guayaquil had a government subsidy through which it could control exports by 1913. Incoming foreign exchange came under the joint influence of these two organizations, as did the Liberal Radical party (*see* LIBERAL PARTY: ECUADOR), the military, and the government itself. The leadership of Urbina Jado provided Ecuador with the longest period of political stability it had ever known. Cacao revenue was the key. After 1918 cacao profits receded because of post-World War I stockpiles, the destruction of the cacao trees by fungus diseases, and world competition. Foreign exchange shortages led to general discontent, and in 1925 the *quiteños* (people of Quito) reasserted themselves, overthrowing the last of the Presidents controlled by telegraph from the cacao exporters' bank.

Although exports and income fell drastically, cacao remained Ecuador's leading export until the 1930s. Then growers reluctantly abandoned the search for a cure for the diseases and began to plant banana shoots between the rows of cacao trees.

LOIS WEINMAN

CÁCERES, ANDRÉS (1833–1923). Peruvian military hero and President (1886–1890, 1894–1895). Born in Ayacucho, Cáceres, the son of an *hacendado* (landowner), entered the Army in 1854. He participated in the internal conflicts of the 1850s and distinguished himself in the wars against Ecuador (1859) and Spain (1866), rising to the rank of colonel by the time the WAR OF THE PACIFIC broke out in 1879. In that war, amid the humiliating military defeats and civilian bickering, he emerged as one of the heroes who helped salvage a degree of dignity for Peru. With his Indian guerrilla fighters, he inflicted considerable losses on the Chileans and aroused popular pride by refusing to accept peace with Chile long after the outcome of the conflict had been determined.

In 1886 Cáceres was elected President by an enthusiastic electorate. For the next four years he worked successfully to rehabilitate the economy. Unfortunately for Peru, he proved unable to work with civilian politicians, for whom he had undisguised contempt. He believed in military discipline as the best tool to correct Peru's ills and argued that since the soldiers had rescued the nation from complete humiliation in the War of the Pacific, they should rule in times of peace. His attitude was not fully shared by the populace that had once revered him. When, in 1894, he attempted to perpetuate a military dictatorship, dissidents formed a national coalition headed by Nicolás de PIÉROLA and, in one of Peru's bloodiest civil wars, overthrew Cáceres in 1895. The hero of the War of the Pacific died in 1923, his political failures gradually becoming obscured by the memories of his brilliant military career.

ORAZIO A. CICCARELLI

CÁCERES, RAMÓN (1866–1911). President of the Dominican Republic (1906–1911). Cáceres was a young and well-to-do Dominican idealist when he assassinated the dictator Ulises HEUREAUX in 1899. This act catapulted him to national prominence in the years of chaos following Heureaux's death; in 1904 he became Vice President and in 1906 succeeded to the Presidency.

During Cáceres's rule the Dominican Republic enjoyed one of the stablest, freest, and most prosperous periods in its history. Cáceres himself was an affable aristocrat, a man who knew enough to trust subordinates with the technical skills that he himself lacked. He reformed the constitution, extended the power of the central government, built public works, and brought some of the foreign concessionaires under the control of the state. Cáceres benefited from the prosperity resulting from the establishment of a United States customs receivership in 1905, but he also had to cope with the nationalistic resentment that the United States presence engendered. He put down numerous plots against his government but was fatally shot in 1911—ending, in a sense, as he had begun. His assassination led to a renewed period of chaos, paving the way for the full-scale United States military occupation of 1916–1924.

HOWARD J. WIARDA

CACIQUE. Local strong man in Spanish America. Of ARAWAK origin, this term was first heard by conquerors of the Windward Islands and referred to the head of an Indian village or tribe. From the Caribbean the word spread to New Spain and other Spanish colonies.

During the colonial period local native rulers served as intermediaries between Spanish society and the subordinate Indian population. In return, the caciques received special privileges, such as exemption from tribute payments and forced labor service.

The term cacique gradually lost its association with Indian leadership and came to denote any person of influence in the political and administrative affairs of a town or district. Cacique has pejorative connotations, implying the practice of nepotism and fraud under a cloak of legality. The cacique is sometimes contrasted with the CAUDILLO, whose power extends over a larger territory, such as a province or a nation.

The closest Portuguese word for a local boss is *coronel,* but it lacks the racial heritage of the Spanish term. *See* CORONELISMO.

ALAN KOVAC

CACM. *See* CENTRAL AMERICAN COMMON MARKET.

CACOS. Mercenary force of illiterate northern Haitian peasants. Cacos first appeared in Haitian politico-military history in 1868, when they were hired to effect a coup. A simple mountain people who gained a taste for loot, they became increasingly celebrated in the period from 1900 to 1915, when they fought without ideology for the ÉLITE. Cacos followed a traditional route to Port-au-Prince through Cap-Haïtien, Gonaïves, and Saint-Marc. Their willingness to fight, albeit with inferior arms, intensified violence and instability and placed the capital at the mercy of their employers. The activities of the Cacos were a factor in the decision of the United States to intervene in Haiti in 1915.

In order to remove the Caco menace, American Marines were moved inland beyond the initially held ports. The unpopularity of the *corvée* (forced road work), reimposed by the United States in 1918, led to a full-scale fanatical Caco uprising during which atrocities were reported on both sides. With improved communications the central government was able to suppress the Cacos, and the modern weapons of the American-trained Garde d'Haïti prevented their resurgence.

JOHN E. BAUR

CAEM. *See* CENTRO DE ALTOS ESTUDIOS MILITARES.

CAFÉ FILHO, JOÃO [FERNANDES CAMPOS] (1899–1970). President of Brazil (1954–1955). Born in Natal, Rio Grande do Norte, on February 3, 1899, Café Filho was raised as a Protestant and was educated in Natal and Recife. He began his public career as a trial lawyer and opposition journalist in the NORTHEAST. A supporter of the Liberal Alliance headed by Getúlio VARGAS, Café Filho served for a time as police chief in Natal following the REVOLUTION OF 1930 that brought Vargas to power. Returning to the opposition, he was elected to Congress in 1934 but was exiled for six months for denouncing the dictatorship established by Vargas in 1937. With the resumption of democratic rule, Café Filho served in the Constituent Assembly of 1946 and in Congress until 1950, when he was elected Vice President of Brazil on a coalition ticket with Vargas. He assumed the Presidency upon the suicide of Vargas on August 24, 1954.

As chief of state during a prolonged political crisis, Café Filho preserved constitutional government and presided over the bitterly contested presidential elections of October 1955. He took a leave of absence on November 8, 1955, after suffering a mild heart attack, and was later barred from resuming his post. He retired from politics in 1956 and became a minister of the Tribunal de Contas of the state of Guanabara in 1961. His memoirs, *Do Sindicato ao Catete,* were published in 1966. Café Filho died in Rio de Janeiro on February 20, 1970.

See also GOULART, João; KUBITSCHEK, Juscelino; LOTT, Henrique.

ROLLIE E. POPPINO

CAFUSO (CAFÚS). *See* ZAMBO.

CALCAÑO, JOSÉ ANTONIO (1900–   ). Venezuelan composer. Born in Caracas, Calcaño studied there, then worked for a while at the Music Academy of Bern, Switzerland. He had an outstanding career as a teacher, music historian, and choral director in addition to contributing compositions of a distinctly Venezuelan character. Best known among these are the ballet *Miranda en Rusia,* commissioned by the Ballet Russe of Monte Carlo, and the cantata *Desolación y gloria,* dedicated to the memory of Simón BOLÍVAR. Calcaño also wrote *La ciudad y su música* (1958), a book surveying musical life in Caracas from the late colonial period to the present.

JUAN A. ORREGO-SALAS

CALDERA [RODRÍGUEZ], RAFAEL (1916–   ). President of Venezuela (1969–1974). The principal leader of Venezuela's Social Christian party, the COMITÉ DE ORGANIZACIÓN POLÍTICA ELECTORAL INDEPENDIENTE (COPEI), Caldera received his university education in the last years of the regime of Juan Vicente GÓMEZ and the early years of the administration of Eleazar LÓPEZ CONTRERAS, graduating from the Central University of Venezuela in 1939. An expert on labor law, he spent his nonpolitical career teaching in the university. While still a student, in 1936, he founded the Unión Nacional Estudiantil to protest the position of the regular Federación de Estudiantes Venezolanos in favor of secularized education and the elimination of religious schools. In 1946 Caldera founded COPEI, which became an opposition party to the ACCIÓN DEMOCRÁTICA (AD)–dominated government between 1945 and 1948. Although Caldera had served as Attorney General of the revolutionary junta in 1945, he resigned the following year because of the increasingly socialist bias of the junta and the poor treatment his party received in the coalition government.

Caldera ran for President in 1947 as a compromise candidate supported by COPEI and the Unión Republicana Democrática (URD), but lost to the Acción Democrática nominee, Rómulo GALLEGOS. He ran again for the Presidency in 1958 and 1963, losing both times to AD candidates. In 1968 he won the Presidency and the next year was installed for a five-year term. Although unable to command a solid majority in Congress, Caldera nevertheless managed to keep the government moving through the use of shifting coalitions. His government raised the participation of the nation in oil company profits and managed to pacify most of the guerrilla forces in the countryside. In 1973 his government appeared reasonably stable and likely to complete its term peacefully.

JOHN V. LOMBARDI

CALDERÓN GUARDIA, RAFAEL ÁNGEL (1900–1971). President of Costa Rica (1940–1944). Educated in Belgium as a physician, Calderón dedicated himself to medicine and politics upon his return to Costa Rica. In the 1930s, as a member of the Legislative Assembly and later as its President, he worked to improve housing, sanitation, and medical facilities. After his election as President of Costa Rica in 1940, he continued this emphasis by furthering social security legislation and a workers' code. He received support both from conservative political groups and from the small Costa Rican Communist party. In 1944 he turned the Presidency over to Teodoro PICADO, a close associate in the Republican party, but he remained a powerful figure in national

politics. At the next elections, in 1948, Calderón aspired to return to the Presidency but was defeated by Otilio ULATE. The refusal of the government to admit Ulate's electoral victory led to the revolution of 1948. When José FIGUERES and his Army of National Liberation gained control of the country, Calderón and his most determined followers went into exile.

Calderón's reputation as a controversial figure in Costa Rica is due not only to his role in the revolution of 1948 but also to two unsuccessful invasions he led from Nicaragua in an effort to regain power (December 1948 and January 1955). He returned from exile for the first time in June 1958 and resumed his opposition to Figueres and his PARTIDO LIBERACIÓN NACIONAL (PLN). As Republican party candidate in the presidential campaign of 1962 he won 35 percent of the votes but lost to Francisco ORLICH of the PLN.

CHARLES L. STANSIFER

CALI. Capital of the department of Valle del Cauca and the third largest city in Colombia. Cali is a center of trade, industry, and transportation for western Colombia.

Although Cali was founded by Sebastian de BENALCÁZAR in 1536 as a center through which the wealth of northwestern South America could be transshipped to the Pacific Ocean, it was destined to languish in the shadow of Popayán, the political, ecclesiastical, and economic center of the region in the seventeenth and eighteenth centuries.

Citizens of Cali were early supporters of the patriot cause and formally declared independence from Spain on July 3, 1810. In the nineteenth century the highly politicized and racially variegated population of Cali provided leadership and manpower for the various parties and factions in the regional and national civil wars. In the twentieth century the completion of a railroad from Cali to the Pacific port of Buenaventura in 1914, the development of the *antioqueño* coffee economy to the north, and progressive community leadership served as catalysts to the development of Cali.

An economically sluggish community of 20,000 at the beginning of the twentieth century, Cali had by mid-century become one of the most nearly economically self-sufficient urban areas on the continent and counted a population of nearly 1 million in 1972. Cali was given a major face-lifting as part of the preparations for the Pan American Games held there in 1971.

JAMES H. NEAL

CALLES, PLUTARCO ELÍAS (1875–1945). Mexican revolutionary leader and President (1924–1928). Calles was born in Guaymas, Sonora. His father's name was Plutarco Elías, but he adopted the last name of Juan de Dios Calles, who took him in at an early age. A primary school teacher at eighteen, Calles became famous for his severity and austere manner and was known as "the old man" before he was fifty. José María Maytorena, future Governor of Sonora, introduced Calles to Francisco I. MADERO when the latter captured Ciudad Juárez in 1911. Upon joining the MEXICAN REVOLUTION, Calles failed in his efforts to capture Naco and in his desire to become a member of the state legislature of Sonora. He did acquire a certain military importance because of his long defense of Naco against Maytorena after the latter had broken with

Venustiano CARRANZA and allied himself with Francisco VILLA. A short time later Calles became Governor of Sonora. A highlight of his administration was his anti-alcoholic campaign (suppression of bars and a ban on the manufacture of all kinds of alcoholic beverages), which failed despite fines, jail sentences, and even executions. President Carranza named Calles Secretary of Industry and Commerce. At this time Calles did not hide his sympathy for the Soviet Union and showed himself to be openly anticlerical. When Carranza attempted to send troops to Sonora in mid-1919, allegedly to take part in a campaign against the Yaqui Indians, Calles opposed him and precipitated the break of the Sonora triumvirate—himself, Álvaro OBREGÓN, and Adolfo de la Huerta—with Carranza in the Plan of Agua Prieta (April 23, 1920).

After Calles was elected to the Presidency in 1924, his main source of support was the labor leader Luis MORONES, on whose group he conferred many favors. Thanks to the support of United States Ambassador Dwight W. MORROW, he was able to check the pretensions of the United States government, which through Secretary of State Frank B. Kellogg was demanding fulfillment of the Bucareli agreements (*see* BUCARELI CONFERENCES). Calles also severely suppressed the CRISTERO REBELLION and founded the Bank of Mexico, the Agricultural Credit Bank, and the National Irrigation Commission.

The assassination of Obregón in 1928 shortly before he was to return to the Presidency led Calles to explain in his last presidential message (September 1, 1928) that, the age of the *caudillos* having ended, Mexico would no longer be the "country of one man" but a "nation of institutions." He complemented this document, praised by some as a work worthy of the jurist Emilio Rabasa, with a statement on December 7 of the same year in which he promised that he would not attempt to be a political factor and that he would not take up arms again unless the nation's institutions were threatened. However, he did take charge of military operations in March 1929 in order to quell the rebellion of various military chiefs unhappy over the imposition of the official presidential candidate. In his capacity as "Maximum Chief of the Revolution," Calles dominated the administrations of Emilio PORTES GIL, Pascual ORTIZ RUBIO, and Abelardo RODRÍGUEZ, most visibly in the case of Ortiz Rubio. Everything indicated that this domination would continue during the Presidency of Lázaro CÁRDENAS, but Calles clashed with him because of the support given by Cárdenas to numerous strikes (one of which affected the telephone company, in which Calles was a stockholder). Cárdenas expelled Calles from Mexico in 1936. He was permitted to return by Cárdenas's successor, Manuel ÁVILA CAMACHO. He died in November 1945 on the fiftieth anniversary of the coronation of the Virgin of Guadalupe (*see* GUADALUPE, VIRGIN OF), an event celebrated with solemn ceremonies that contrasted strongly with Calles's well-known anticlericalism.

Bibliography. Vito Alessio Robles, *Desfile sangriento*, Mexico City, 1936; Djed Bórquez, *Calles*, Mexico City, 1923; Luis L. León, "El presidente Calles," *Historia Mexicana*, vol. X, no. 2, October–December 1960, pp. 320–331; Ramón Puente, *Hombres de la Revolución: Calles*, Los Angeles, 1933.

MOISÉS GONZÁLEZ NAVARRO

CALPULLI. Aztec social grouping (translated as "great house"), larger than the family and smaller than the state. Considering that the territorial aspect of the *calpulli* is so prominent, our nearest equivalent is perhaps a city ward. Nevertheless, a *calpulli*, like a clan, could break its ties with the land and move on, carrying its god with it, without losing its customary structure. In an Aztec city it was centered in the shrine of the tutelary god. Membership in the *calpulli* was based on birth, and it apparently included a prestigious family from which it elected its customary leader; this official carried out the wishes of the *tlatoani*, or city ruler, regarding work in his ward whether the matter concerned the allotment of labor, provision of services, or organization for war. The *calpulli* not only lived in a distinct section of the city but possessed, in collective ownership, its own agricultural lands outside the city, from which it made usufructuary assignment to its members. *See also* AZTECS.

BURR C. BRUNDAGE

CALVO DOCTRINE. International legal principle that maintains that no nation has the right to exert diplomatic pressure or employ armed force against another nation in order to pursue private claims or collect debts owed to its citizens. The doctrine is named after the Argentine jurist Carlos Calvo (1824–1906), who asserted that nineteenth-century European interventions in Latin America had been based not on law but on the power of the strong over the weak and had violated the principle of the equality of sovereign states. The Calvo

Plutarco Elías Calles. [*Organization of American States*]

Doctrine was the source of the Calvo clause, a clause inserted in a contract between a government and a foreign national or corporation, which stipulates that the latter renounces any claim to diplomatic assistance from his own government in the event that litigation arises from the contract. Several nations, including Mexico, have incorporated the Calvo clause into their constitutions.　　　RODNEY D. ANDERSON

CÂMARA, HÉLDER [PESSOA] (1909–　　). Roman Catholic Archbishop of Olinda and Recife, Brazil. Dom Hélder Câmara was born in Fortaleza, Ceará, in the NORTHEAST. Ordained a priest in 1931, he spent the first five years of his ministry in his native city, taking an active part in INTEGRALISMO, Brazil's version of fascism. After he was transferred to Rio de Janeiro in 1936, his militant anticommunism surrendered to a passionate concern for the poor. Spending much of his time in the *favelas,* the shantytown suburban slums (*see* FAVELA), he organized the São Sebastião Crusade, which built houses for *favela* families.

Shortly after becoming Auxiliary Bishop of Rio de Janeiro in 1952, he founded the National Conference of Brazilian Bishops and has been largely responsible for its moderately progressive stand on social issues. Immensely popular, he was offered the mayoralty of Rio de Janeiro by President Juscelino KUBITSCHEK, and Jânio QUADROS asked him to be his running mate in the 1960 presidential elections. He declined both offers. Early in 1964 Câmara was named Archbishop of Olinda and Recife and immediately became involved in local social and economic problems. He organized the poor into self-help groups and enlisted middle-class liberals in bringing moral pressure on the power elite. The program was harassed by right-wing terrorists who machine-gunned Câmara's residence and murdered one of his priests.

An outspoken critic of Brazil's military regime, Câmara is a moderate who rejects violence and seeks radical reforms within existing structures. In recent years he has gained a reputation as a religious spokesman for the Third World, and in 1970 he was nominated for the Nobel Peace Prize.　　　ARNOLD J. MEAGHER

CAMPESINO. In Spanish America, a countryman, a lower-class resident of a rural area. The term is also used to designate a peasant. In Bolivia, where the name "Indian" often has pejorative connotations, the revolutionary government that took power in 1952 officially adopted the term *campesino* to refer to an Indian peasant. The corresponding Portuguese word is *camponês.*

CÁMPORA, HÉCTOR J[OSÉ] (1909–　　). President of Argentina (1973). Elected in March 1973 for a four-year term, Cámpora was supported by a broad coalition of pro-Peronist forces in Argentina's first national election in eight years (*see* PERONISM). His inauguration on May 25, 1973, represented both the end of seven years of military rule and the return to power of the followers of former President Juan D. PERÓN.

Born in the town of Mercedes in the province of Buenos Aires, Cámpora attended the University of Córdoba and received a degree in dentistry in 1934. Joining the Peronist movement in the mid-1940s, he was elected to the national Chamber of Deputies in 1946. He served as President of the Chamber from 1948 to 1952, when he was elected to a second six-year term as deputy. Imprisoned by the military following the 1955 coup that overthrew the Perón government, Cámpora escaped with a group of other Peronists in 1957 and fled to Chile. He returned to Argentina under an amnesty in 1963 and resumed his active role in the Peronist movement. In 1971 Perón appointed Cámpora his delegate in Argentina and in late 1972 chose him as the Peronist candidate for the Presidency.

Cámpora campaigned for the Presidency on the basis of his loyalty to the movement's exiled leader. With no attempt to disguise his subservience, he used as his major campaign slogan "Cámpora in government, Perón in power." Although Peronists by and large represented no more than 25 to 30 percent of the electorate during other post-1955 elections, Cámpora drew nearly 50 percent of the vote in a field divided among a number of candidates. The Radical candidate Ricardo Balbín placed second with only about 25 percent of the vote (*see* RADICAL PARTY: ARGENTINA).

Dissension within the Peronist movement, apparent before Cámpora's inauguration, continued after May 25, 1973. Perón himself returned to Argentina on June 20, and on July 13 Cámpora resigned so that new elections might be held and Perón chosen for the Presidency.

LEE C. FENNELL

CAMPOS, ROBERTO [DE OLIVEIRA] (1917–　　). Brazilian economist and diplomat. Roberto Campos was born in Cuiabá, Mato Grosso, and entered the Brazilian foreign service in 1939. Beginning in the mid-1940s, when he completed undergraduate studies and graduate training in economics in the United States, his assignments usually involved him in questions of economic development policy. During the 1950s Campos served as a member of the Brazil–United States Commission for Economic Development, and he was a founder, economic director, and later president of the Brazilian National Bank for Economic Development. His first book, *Planning of the Economic Development of Underdeveloped Countries,* was published in 1952. An advocate of inter-American economic cooperation, he was one of the early promoters of the ALLIANCE FOR PROGRESS.

In 1961 Campos was appointed Ambassador to the United States. Following the revolution of March 31, 1964, he was recalled to Brazil to become Minister of Planning and Economic Coordination in the Cabinet of President Humberto CASTELLO BRANCO. In this post Campos bore primary responsibility for the fiscal and investment policies of the revolutionary government, designed to reduce monetary inflation gradually while encouraging industrial expansion by private enterprise through heavy public expenditures in the areas of power, steel, and transportation. He left office at the end of the Castello Branco administration in March 1967 to accept the presidency of a private investment bank.

ROLLIE E. POPPINO

CAMPOS-PARSI, HÉCTOR (1922–　　). Puerto Rican composer. Born in Ponce, he studied at the New England Conservatory in Boston and later with Nadia Boulanger in Paris and Aaron Copland in Tanglewood.

Campos-Parsi has been a leading force in Puerto Rico's musical life as a composer, music critic, teacher, and concert manager. Outstanding among his works are his sonata for piano (1953), *Divertimiento del Sur* (1953), *Duo trágico* for piano and orchestra (1965), and *Petroglifos* for violin, cello, and piano (1967).

JUAN A. ORREGO-SALAS

CAMPOS SALLES, MANOEL [FERRAZ DE] (1841–1913). President of Brazil (1898–1902). The son of a wealthy coffee planter, Campos Salles was born in Campinas, in the province of São Paulo. Upon graduation from the São Paulo law school in 1863, he entered politics as a member of the Liberal party. Ten years later he was a founding member of the Republican party of São Paulo, and thereafter his public life was identified with that political body. In 1885 he was one of the first three Republicans elected to the imperial Parliament. Following the establishment of the republic on November 15, 1889, Campos Salles served as Minister of Justice in the Cabinet of provisional President Manuel Deodoro da FONSECA until his election to the Constituent Assembly, where he helped draft the new constitution (*see* CONSTITUTION OF 1891: BRAZIL). After five years in the Senate, he became Governor of São Paulo in 1896.

As senator and Governor during years of civil war and political turmoil, Campos Salles consistently supported the republican regimes in Rio de Janeiro. Picked as the government's candidate for the Presidency, he won office easily in 1898. His administration was noted for its austere fiscal policies, carried out by Minister of Finance Joaquim MURTINHO, and for introducing the system of "governors' politics" whereby the selection of presidential candidates was based on a consensus among the governors of the larger states. Campos Salles retired to private life after leaving office but was reelected to the Senate in 1909 and was appointed Ambassador to Argentina in 1912.

ROLLIE E. POPPINO

CANDOMBLÉ. A highly ritualistic and formalized cult of African origin, *candomblé* was brought to Brazil by slaves from the West African kingdom of Yoruba (*see* NEGRO IN BRAZIL). Centered in Bahia, *candomblé* uses the Yoruban language, called *nagô* in Brazil; African deities are worshiped, and the chants and prayers of the cult are similar to those of Africa. Today frequent contact with Africa reinforces the cult's origins. Most of the faithful consider themselves Catholics, and Catholic saints are equated with the cult's divinities (*orixás*). Thus, Xangô, the god of lightning, is identified with St. Jerome; and Ogun, the god of hunting, with St. Anthony. Although the use of women as priestesses, the adoration of all gods in one ceremony rather than separately as in Africa, and the syncretistic blending of indigenous and Catholic practices reflect the modification of *candomblé* in Brazil from its African origins, religious expression and ritual remain remarkably similar in both areas.

The cult of *candomblé* is divided into sects, each of which occupies its own *terreiro* (land or place). Public ceremonies are presided over by the *pai* or *mãe de santo* (father or mother in sainthood). Although these priests and priestesses are not in themselves considered to be divine, it is only through their intercession, be-

cause of their peculiar sensitivity and knowledge, that the gods can mount their "human horses." Once "possessed," in a trancelike state the faithful are dressed in the colors and garments of their gods, acting out their defined roles. As such, they are viewed not as men or women but as gods, until concluding ceremonies expel the divinities from the temple. Through a hierarchy of officials, from the *filhas de santo* (daughters and keepers of the temple) to the *oguns* (drummers), the ceremony follows an elaborate and prescribed ritual.

Contrary to popular belief in Brazil, *candomblé* is not an orgiastic spectacle. Similar and rapidly spreading cults are known as *xangô* in Pernambuco, *macumba* in Rio de Janeiro, and voodoo in Maranhão, but the most traditional and purest African expression of the cult is that of *candomblé*.

JOSEPH A. ELLIS

CANTINFLAS (b. MARIO MORENO, 1911–). Mexican comedian. Cantinflas was born in Mexico City to a large and humble family. In 1929 he took part as a soldier in a battle in the state of Chihuahua. As a very young man he made his debut in Mexico City's traveling tent shows, where he created the character of Cantinflas, who speaks a great deal and says little. Compared by some to characters in the plays of Ionesco, Cantinflas originated as an exponent of the language and dress of the Mexico City type known as the *peladito*.

Cantinflas then moved on to the legitimate stage, comic bullfights, and motion pictures, first acquiring popularity in Mexico and later throughout Spanish America and in Spain. His first great successes—*Ahí está el detalle* and *El gendarme desconocido*—were followed by parodies of foreign works, such as *Los tres mosqueteros* and *Romeo y Julieta*. He also appeared in two international films, *Around the World in Eighty Days* and *Pepe*. In 1945 he clashed with the CONFEDERACIÓN DE TRABAJADORES DE MÉXICO over its reluctance to recognize a newly formed union of motion-picture workers, the Sindicato de Trabajadores de la Producción Cinematográfica. His latest films—*El padrecito, El profe, El señor doctor,* and *Su excelencia*—seek to convey a "message," adapted to current conditions in Mexico, which he views optimistically. One of the best-paid actors in the world and so popular in Mexico that he has won votes in presidential elections, Cantinflas is also well known for his works of charity, some of which are spectacular.

MOISÉS GONZÁLEZ NAVARRO

CAPISTRANO DE ABREU, JOÃO. *See* ABREU, JOÃO CAPISTRANO DE.

CAPITÃO MOR. In colonial Brazil, the royal governor of a subordinate captaincy. Following the establishment of the governor-generalship of Brazil at Bahia (modern Salvador) in 1549, the *capitães mores* gradually took over leadership in both the old private and the newly settled captaincies. With the gradual elaboration of royal administration, however, captains general were appointed to head provincial governments, and by the eighteenth century the title *capitão mor* was held either by the governor of an unincorporated settlement or by the commandant of a company of *ordenanças* (second-line militia).

KENNETH R. MAXWELL

CAPOEIRA. Presently a form of dance in Brazil but at one time a system of personal attack and defense similar to karate, *capoeira* has its roots in African traditions. Predominantly Bantu in origin and viewed as a pastime activity in Africa, *capoeira* became a means of defense against police persecution in colonial Brazil. For a long period the word had negative connotations, *capoeira* being considered a dangerous and disorderly activity. During carnival and holiday times in Rio de Janeiro gangs attacked revelers, using *capoeira* tactics; as a result, it was outlawed.

Legalized once again in 1961, *capoeira* has become highly ritualistic and formalized. Youths between ten and twelve years of age are rigorously initiated by a master, or teacher, of *capoeira*. Rapid movements, acrobatics, muscular force, and agility are essential to learning the many steps and turns. Accompanied by percussion instruments and the *berimbau* (a one-stringed bowlike instrument), the dancers "fight" each other, timing their movements and responses to the rhythm and never making bodily contact with one another. As a form of dance, *capoeira* is both graceful and impressive, complicated in its movements and fascinating in its intensity.

JOSEPH A. ELLIS

CAPTAINCY SYSTEM (DONATARY CAPTAINCY SYSTEM). First institutional framework for the settlement and colonization of Portuguese America. The donatary captaincy system was an elaboration of a medieval Portuguese technique for the repopulation and economic development of vacant lands and had been used previously in the colonization of the Atlantic islands. It had the advantage, from the crown's point of view, of requiring very little expenditure by the royal exchequer. In 1534–1535 King João III (r. 1521–1557) allocated fifteen captaincies to twelve donataries along the coast of Brazil from the AMAZON RIVER to São Vicente. The donatary was given wide powers, including the right to confer and sell deeds with full title (the Portuguese SESMARIA land-grant system). Only two of the attempts to colonize Brazil by this method were successful, however, that of Martim Afonso de SOUSA in São Vicente and that of Duarte COELHO in Pernambuco.

The general failure of the early captaincies and the continued threat to the Portuguese position in Brazil from other Europeans, especially the French, led the crown to establish direct royal control in 1549 under the auspices of the first Governor-General, Tomé de SOUSA. Those private captaincies that survived to the eighteenth century were eventually suppressed during the Pombaline epoch (1750–1777; *see* POMBAL, Marquês de). An exception was Itanhaém in São Paulo, which lasted until 1791.

KENNETH R. MAXWELL

CARABOBO, BATTLE OF. The battlefield of Carabobo, lying southwest of Valencia on the road to the Venezuelan LLANOS (plains), was the scene of two major engagements in the war for the independence of northern South America. The first, in May 1814, was a victory for Simón BOLÍVAR that merely delayed the defeat of the second Venezuelan republic. The second, which is the one usually referred to as Battle of Carabobo, finally assured Venezuelan independence.

Even before the expiration of the armistice negotiated with the royalists at Trujillo in November 1820, Bolívar was preparing for a final campaign against the Spanish forces still occupying Caracas and the core area of north central Venezuela. Once the armistice ended in late April 1821, Gen. José María Bermúdez on instructions from Bolívar attacked Caracas from the east and briefly took it. Though forced to withdraw, he gave Bolívar time to bring together separate armies from the west.

The Spanish commander, Miguel de la Torre, chose to make his stand on the plains of Carabobo, but he had inferior forces (roughly 5,000 men against 6,500) and little hope for success. On the morning of June 24, while Bolívar threatened the Spanish center, he sent Gen. José Antonio PÁEZ with more than half the patriot forces, including the British legion, around the Spanish right flank to attack from the rear. For this maneuver it was necessary to use a narrow path over difficult terrain, and the element of surprise was only partial. The fighting was bitter but was ultimately decided in the patriots' favor by Páez's *llanero* cavalry. The royalists' retreat ended only when La Torre reached the coastal fortress of Puerto Cabello. Bolívar reentered Caracas in triumph on June 28.

DAVID BUSHNELL

CARACAS. Capital of Venezuela. Located in a valley of the Cordillera de la Costa, Caracas enjoys a temperate climate thanks to its 3,000-foot elevation. Founded in 1567, it has grown from a struggling, backward colonial village into a cosmopolitan modern metropolis.

Throughout the colonial period Santiago de León de Caracas served as the administrative and religious center of the province of Caracas. Although always one of Venezuela's principal cities, it became preeminent from the energetic commercial monopoly of the CARACAS COMPANY in the mid-eighteenth century, from the imperial reorganization of the late eighteenth century that concentrated the bureaucracy in the city, and from the generation of 1800–1830, which made Caracas the locus of political control. The emergence of Caracas as the chief city of Venezuela was validated throughout the nineteenth century by rival *caudillos* who fought each other for the chance to command the national capital. No *caudillo* ever succeeded in capturing control of Venezuela without the acquiescence of the capital's political, economic, and administrative apparatus, even though some of them preferred to reside outside the city.

Throughout the nineteenth century and into the first decades of the twentieth, Caracas maintained much of the flavor and configuration of a colonial town, but the explosive economic growth spurred by the petroleum boom that began in the mid-1920s led to rapid expansion. Enclosed by the mountain ranges of the Cordillera de la Costa and the Serranía del Interior and centered on the western edge of the Caracas Valley, the city could expand only a short distance southward and then east along the valley floor. By the 1970s the metropolitan area had grown to absorb into its urban sprawl the towns from La Vega to Petare and encompassed almost 2 million people, including most of Venezuela's foreign-born population. To be sure, this growth carried with it the familiar problems of inadequate transportation, insufficient water and sanitary facilities, and unplanned squatter settlements. Yet with all its congestion and chaotic expansion, its high-rise apartments and office buildings, its large squatter settlements on the hillsides and in the gullies, Caracas remained the charming, exciting, and indispensable center of Venezuelan life.

JOHN V. LOMBARDI

CARACAS COMPANY (REAL COMPAÑÍA GUIPUZCOANA DE CARACAS). At the beginning of the eighteenth century, one of the less-developed areas in the Spanish empire was the province of Venezuela. Its trade with Spain was virtually nil while the Dutch in neighboring Curaçao conducted a successful contraband commerce in cacao. To remedy this situation King Philip V allowed the operation of a private trading company, the Caracas Company, granting it the right to trade with Venezuela in return for uprooting smuggling from its coasts. The company was formed with Basque capital raised in the province of Guipúzcoa and its port, San Sebastián. It began functioning in 1730 with a fleet of twelve ships.

The company built warehouses in several ports of Venezuela and northern Spain and engaged in the export of cacao and the import of supplies from Spain, bypassing trade with Cádiz. It proved to be a successful operation; in addition to buying and setting the price of cacao, it exported tobacco, indigo, and hides and created a remarkable economic expansion in Venezuela. In 1742 the crown granted the company a monopoly of trade. This concession provoked protests from several sectors of the population and an unsuccessful revolt in 1749. In 1751 the company's board of directors was transferred to Madrid, and in 1752 Venezuelan shareholders were allowed to participate in its operations. Small merchants were given cargo space and guaranteed fixed prices for their cacao in 1759. The growing orientation of King CHARLES III toward free trade resulted in the company's decline. Its monopoly grant was revoked in 1781, and it dissolved into smaller firms. The company's greatest contribution was the revival of Venezuelan trade with Spain and the consequent economic growth of the area, which enabled this province to finance its own administrative expenses and become a captaincy general and an intendancy. *See also* BOURBON REFORMS.

ASUNCIÓN LAVRIN

CARACAS CONFERENCE (1954). Tenth International Conference of American States, held in Caracas, Venezuela, on March 1–28, 1954. The conference centered in the United States delegation's efforts to obtain support for a resolution declaring that domination by the "international communist movement" of any American state would constitute a threat to the other American states and would call for appropriate action in accordance with existing treaties. Concerned about Communist influence in the regime of Jacobo ARBENZ GUZMÁN in Guatemala and the supposed threat that this posed to the strategic interests of the United States in the Caribbean, Secretary of State John Foster Dulles himself went to Caracas to sponsor the resolution, which did not mention Guatemala by name. Initially only six countries, all dictatorships, supported the Dulles proposal. Though most Latin American delegates saw the United States position as symptomatic of its overemphasis on the threat of communism and feared that the resolution might be interpreted to justify intervention in the internal affairs of an American state, Dulles's threats to withhold economic aid brought most delegations around. Afterward several delegates expressed bitterness over the pressure applied by Dulles. The resolution was eventually approved, with some modification, by a vote of seventeen to one; Argentina and Mexico abstained.

Because of the resentment engendered by Dulles and the fact that the resolution as approved called only for consultation to consider action if the need arose, the United States victory was reduced to some extent. In the end the United States found it expedient to use other means than collective action to deal with Guatemala; it helped finance and support the successful counterrevolutionary movement of Carlos CASTILLO ARMAS in June 1954.

RODNEY D. ANDERSON

CARAMURÚ (b. DIOGO ÁLVARES CORREIA, d. 1557). Portuguese adventurer and patriarch of Portuguese America. His origins, the date of his arrival in Brazil, and the etymology of his name are all uncertain. A Portuguese sailor, probably shipwrecked some time between 1509 and 1511, Caramurú became well established among the Amerindians and served as an important intermediary between them and later European arrivals. He may have acted as an agent for logwood traders and established himself with his Indian wife southeast of All Saints Bay. The donatary of the captaincy of Bahia, Francisco Pereira Coutinho, granted him land titles, although the donatary himself was much less successful in his activities than Caramurú. With the establishment of the Governor-General of Brazil in Bahia (modern Salvador) in 1549, Caramurú worked closely with the Jesuit missionaries, especially Manuel da NÓBREGA.

KENNETH R. MAXWELL

CARBALLIDO, EMILIO (1925–   ). Mexican dramatist. Born in Córdoba, Veracruz, Carballido studied the drama and English literature at the National University of Mexico. He then worked for a year in Jalapa as subdirector of the School of Drama at the University of Veracruz. He next taught at the School of Dramatic Arts of the National Institute of Fine Arts and later returned to the University of Veracruz as a professor and a member of the editorial board. He spent the year 1950 in New York on a scholarship from the Rockefeller Foundation, traveled in Europe and Asia, and received drama awards in Mexico and elsewhere.

Carballido has written short stories and short novels in which his dramatic interests are apparent in realistic plots with psychological overtones: *La veleta oxidada* (1956), *El norte* (1958), *La caja vacía* (1962), and *Las visitaciones del diablo* (1965). He is best known for his drama, marked sometimes by a scenic neorealism and sometimes by a search for poetic fantasy. His plays include *Rosalba y los Llaveros* (1950), *La zona intermedia* (1950), *La danza que sueña la tortuga* (1955), *Felicidad* (1957), *La hebra de oro* (1956), and *Las estatuas de marfil* (1960). Several of his works have appeared in English translation in the volume entitled *The Golden Thread and Other Plays* (1970).

RACHEL PHILLIPS

CÁRDENAS, LÁZARO (1895–1970). Mexican revolutionary leader and President (1934–1940). Cárdenas was born in Jiquilpan, Michoacán. His father was a weaver and the owner of a small store and billiard parlor; his mother, Felicitas del Río, supplemented the family income by working as a seamstress. Cárdenas worked in the tax collector's office, in the local jail, and in a printing plant. In July 1913 he joined the MEXICAN REVOLUTION in Apatzingán, being promoted to the rank of second captain in September. He fought against Emiliano ZAPATA in Xochimilco in September 1914 and against Francisco VILLA in March 1915. Cárdenas became Governor of his native state for the first time on June 17, 1920. He fought, with only slight success, the rebellion of Adolfo de la Huerta in 1923. Later he was chief of military operations in Michoacán, Huastecas, and Tehuantepec. He was promoted to the rank of division general on April 1, 1928. Plutarco Elías CALLES, trusting in his proven loyalty, gave him command of an army to combat the rebellion of 1929.

Having been elected Governor of Michoacán on September 15, 1928, he supported legislation on sharecropping and idle lands, hastened the distribution of *ejidos* (*see* EJIDO), limited the number of priests who could function legally within the state, increased the number of schools, and encouraged the creation of workers' and peasants' organizations. During his four-year governorship, he obtained leaves of absence to fight the Cristeros (*see* CRISTERO REBELLION) and to serve as president of the Partido Nacional Revolucionario (National Revolutionary party, PNR) and as Secretary of the Interior. He was Secretary of War from January 1 to May 15, 1933. On December 6 of that

year he was nominated as the presidential candidate of the PNR.

During his presidential campaign he pledged to combat alcoholism and religious fanaticism, both of which were strongly opposed by Calles, who was still his protector, but, in contrast to Calles, he also pledged to provide land, water, and credit to those who needed them. After Cárdenas took office on December 1, 1934, he supported numerous strikes, thereby making inevitable a rupture with Calles, whom he expelled in mid-1936, together with some of his closest partisans; governors, deputies, and municipal presidents friendly to Calles were also removed from their posts. Now the master of the situation, Cárdenas greatly accelerated the distribution of *ejidos* and established collective *ejidos* in territories devoted to the cultivation of cotton and henequen (*see* AGRARIAN REFORM). In 1936 he endorsed the birth of the CONFEDERACIÓN DE TRABAJADORES DE MÉXICO, which gave him useful support when he expropriated Mexico's foreign-owned oil properties on March 18, 1938. The same year he established the Confederación Nacional Campesina (National Confederation of Peasants) and transformed the PNR into the Partido de la Revolución Mexicana (Party of the Mexican Revolution). From this point on, although he was still able to protect the rights of the Civil Servants Union and to turn over operations of the railroads to the workers, he was obliged to contain his radicalism. Conflict with the church was muted during the Cárdenas administration, but controversy continued over a 1933 amendment to the constitution providing for "socialistic" education in public schools. In international affairs Cárdenas opposed fascist attacks in Ethiopia, Spain, Austria, China, and Czechoslovakia, but he also opposed the Soviet invasion of Finland and gave refuge to Leon Trotsky.

After stepping down from the Presidency on November 30, 1940, he was named chief of the Pacific military command late in 1941. From September 1942 to August 1945 he was Secretary of Defense. Later he served as director of the Tepalcatepec River project, created in 1947 to improve conditions in the drainage basin of the river and its tributaries. A recipient of the Stalin Peace Prize, Cárdenas was a supporter of the revolution of Fidel CASTRO in Cuba.

Bibliography. Victoriano Anguiano, "Cárdenas y el cardenismo," *Problemas Agrícolas e Industriales de México,* vol. VII, no. 3, July–September 1955, pp. 183–218; Joe C. Ashby, *Organized Labor and the Mexican Revolution under Cárdenas,* Chapel Hill, N.C., 1963; Lázaro Cárdenas, *Obras,* Mexico City, 1972; Eduardo J. Correa, *El balance del cardenismo,* Mexico City, 1941; William Cameron Townsend, *Lázaro Cárdenas, Mexican Democrat,* Ann Arbor, Mich., 1952; Nathaniel and Sylvia Weyl, *The Reconquest of Mexico,* London, 1939.

MOISÉS GONZÁLEZ NAVARRO

Lázaro Cárdenas. [*Organization of American States*]

CARDOZO, EFRAÍM (1906–1973). Paraguayan educator, man of letters, diplomat, and political leader. Cardozo was born in Villarrica, the son of a director of schools and famous historian. He received his advanced education in Asunción, graduating as a doctor of law and social sciences from the National University in 1932. A man of frenetic and acute intellectual activity, he had already edited and directed several professional and intellectual journals. The first several of his score of books were written in the 1930s on the CHACO boundary question, and in 1933 he was appointed to the Paraguayan Boundary Commission. In 1938 he was one of four Paraguayan delegates to sign the peace treaty ending the CHACO WAR (1932–1935) and then was elected to the Senate and the directorship of the Liberal party. *See* LIBERAL PARTY (PARAGUAY).

In the administration of President José Félix ESTIGARRIBIA (1939–1940), Cardozo was successively Minister of Justice, Education, and Foreign Affairs and special Minister to Argentina. Beginning in 1940, he spent ten years in exile in Buenos Aires, writing on Paraguayan history and against military dictatorship, then exemplified by Higinio MORÍNIGO (1940–1948). In 1954, back in Paraguay and once more titular head of the Liberal party, he became professor of colonial history at the National University. From that time on he was recognized as Paraguay's leading historian and continued to lead his party's legal opposition to the rule of Gen. Alfredo STROESSNER, who rose to power in 1954.

JOHN HOYT WILLIAMS

CARÍAS ANDINO, TIBURCIO (1876–1969). President of Honduras (1933–1948). Carías first entered National party politics in 1903 as a supporter of Manuel Bonilla. After two decades of factional disputes, during which he spent several periods of exile in El Salvador and Guatemala, Carías emerged as the leader of his party and in 1924 obtained a plurality of votes as the National party's presidential candidate. But Liberal obstructionism in the Honduran Congress, followed by United States mediation, resulted in the accession of Carías's running mate, Miguel Paz Baraona, to the Presidency. In 1928 Carías again sought office but lost to the Liberal candidate, Vicente Mejía Colindres. In both 1924 and 1928 Carías resigned himself peacefully to the election results. *See* LIBERAL PARTY (HONDURAS); NATIONAL OR NATIONALIST PARTY (HONDURAS).

In 1932 Carías was elected President of a country rent by political factionalism and stagnating in the Depression. The new regime, which took office in 1933, adopted policies of political repression and economic retrenchment in dealing with those problems. Labor organization and freedom of the press were sharply curtailed throughout the Carías years. Carías proved himself a master of CONTINUISMO, a policy that found favor among the many Hondurans exhausted by years of turmoil. In 1936 his supporters, arguing that the "prolongation of power is prolongation of peace," drafted a new constitution that extended the President's term of office to 1943. In 1939 this term was further extended to December 31, 1948.

An aged Carías still commanded a sizable Nationalist following when, in 1954, he sought to regain office. But younger, more progressive Nationalists, among them Juan Manuel GÁLVEZ and Abraham Williams, renounced Carías's repressive policies and left the regular party. An election marked by labor and student violence reflecting general discontent with conservative rule resulted in Carías's defeat.

GENE S. YEAGER

CARIB. Large linguistic grouping of South American Indian tribes centered mainly in the Guianas. The island Caribs, who left the mainland about a century before Columbus and pushed north into the Lesser Antilles, evicting the ARAWAK, are, however, the better known. They quickly became a skilled maritime people and made long voyages, even as far as the coast of Yucatán, raiding for captives in elaborately decorated sailing canoes. Valor was the highest virtue, and war the true center of their culture. Male captives were tortured and then cooked and eaten; women were kept as servile domestics. The men lived apart in lodges while the women labored, lived in separate houses, and tended the fruit plantations. The men spoke Carib, and their wives Arawak. The population dwindled rapidly after the intrusion of the white man, and there are no pure-blooded Caribs left in the islands.

BURR C. BRUNDAGE

CARIOCA. Word used to designate a native of the city of Rio de Janeiro or an aspect of the city's culture. Of Tupí origin, *carioca* has been in use since the colonial period and originally had pejorative connotations.

CARLOTA JOAQUINA DE BORBÓN Y PARMA (1775–1830). Queen of Portugal, Brazil, and Algarve. The daughter of Charles IV of Spain and María Luisa of Parma, she married the future Portuguese king JOÃO VI in 1785 and accompanied the Portuguese court to Brazil in 1807–1808. After Napoleon deposed and imprisoned the Spanish royal family in 1808, Carlota Joaquina saw herself as the logical legal Regent of the Spanish realm. Although she had partisans throughout Spanish America, Carlota Joaquina directed most of her efforts toward either Buenos Aires or Seville and Cádiz, where Spanish resistance to Bonaparte was centered. João at first favored her aspirations, perhaps as a disguise for Portuguese expansion into the long-coveted RÍO DE LA PLATA region, as she suspected. But while British Admiral Sir William Sidney Smith favored the idea, the British diplomatic representative, Viscount Strangford, always opposed her project. This official British disapproval, together with the bitter estrangement of the royal couple, eventually persuaded the Prince Regent to withdraw his support.

Carlota Joaquina received an initially enthusiastic response from Spanish Americans such as the Argentine Rodríguez Peña brothers and Manuel BELGRANO. However, agreement between absolutist and reformer proved impossible, given Carlota Joaquina's autocratic principles and Spanish loyalties, as she showed in denouncing an agent, James Parossien, to Spanish authorities in 1809 and in attempting to aid loyalists in Montevideo after the revolution of May 1810. Portuguese diplomatic efforts in Spain to secure her recognition there as Regent also failed. After 1814 Carlota Joaquina's participation in politics was less active, and her private life more notorious, until the return of the royal family to Portugal in 1821.

L. SHARON WYATT

CARO, MIGUEL ANTONIO (1843–1909). Colombian scholar, political thinker, and chief executive (1892–1898). Caro was born in Bogotá, the son of José Eusebio Caro (1817–1853), Colombia's best nineteenth-century romantic poet and a notable Conservative ideologue (*see* CONSERVATIVE PARTY: COLOMBIA). Young Miguel Antonio was reared by his maternal grandfather, Miguel Tovar, a jurist of note, and educated by the Jesuits.

Caro's political career dates from 1864, when he began publishing articles in various Conservative periodicals. From 1871 to 1876 he published *El Tradicionista,* a newspaper that advocated an end to Colombian federalism and the creation of a Catholic political party. In its pages can be found Caro's political philosophy, which was based on the concept of an intransigent Conservative polity that employed the church as an instrument of its power. In 1885 he wrote the draft of what would be the constitution of 1886, his greatest political contribution (*see* CONSTITUTION OF 1886: COLOMBIA). From 1892 to 1894 Caro held executive power as Vice President while the titular President, Rafael NÚÑEZ, remained in retirement in Cartagena; upon the latter's death in 1894, Caro succeeded to the Presidency, and there is little doubt that he sought to dominate his successor, Manuel Antonio Sanclemente.

Caro's partisan exclusivism and political intolerance have been blamed for the coming of the civil war of 1895 as well as the WAR OF THE THOUSAND DAYS. He is better remembered as a scholar. In 1870 he helped found the Colombian Academy, and he won election to the Royal Spanish Academy. His translation into Spanish of Virgil's *Aeneid* is considered one of the finest extant. Caro's poetry is less outstanding, but his works on Spanish grammar and philology are still classics.

J. LEÓN HELGUERA

CARPENTIER, ALEJO (1904–   ). Cuban novelist, musicologist, and postrevolutionary Ambassador in Paris. Carpentier was born in Havana. In 1921 he began the study of architecture, which he did not complete; the next year his first articles were published in *La Discusión.* He became active in politics and was imprisoned in 1927 for his activities as founder of a minority party. The composer Amadeo ROLDÁN wrote scores for several of his texts, among them *El milagro de Anaquilla* and *La Rembaramba,* and together they organized the first concerts of the so-called new music.

In Carpentier's first novel, *¡Ecué-Yamba-O!* (1933), a series of scenes of Afro-Cuban life, stylistic and documentary values take precedence over literary qualities. After a long silence, interrupted only by a study of Cuban music, *La música en Cuba* (1946), he published *El reino de este mundo,* 1949 (*The Kingdom of This World*), which presents the thesis of *lo real maravilloso* (marvelous reality) as a distinctive trait of America. This novel deals with the revolution of Santo Domingo, uniting the historical and the imaginary, the magic of folklore, and the desire for freedom and justice. In *Los pasos perdidos,* 1953 (*The Lost Steps*), the marvelous reality of America comes face to face with the rational and mechanical world of Western civilization. In *El siglo de las luces,* 1962 (*Explosion in a Cathedral*), an incident on Guadeloupe during the French Revolution is used to contrast the point of view of the European Enlightenment and the magical, vital American reality. Carpentier has also written shorter works, several of which were published together as *Guerra del tiempo* (1958).

RACHEL PHILLIPS

CARRANZA, VENUSTIANO (1859–1920). Mexican revolutionary leader and constitutional President (1917–1920). He was born in Cuatro Ciénagas, Coahuila, on November 29, 1859. His father, Jesús Carranza, fought on behalf of the Liberal cause in the War of the Reform (*see* REFORM, THE) and gave financial assistance to Benito JUÁREZ during the French intervention. After studying in Saltillo, the younger Carranza attended the National Preparatory School in 1874 but was unable to complete his studies because of an eye ailment. His first post in his long political career was the municipal presidency of Cuatro Ciénagas in 1887. In 1893 Carranza and his brothers, together with Francisco Z. Treviño, Francisco Urquizo, and Emilio Salinas (the latter two fathers of the Constitutionalist generals of the same names), rose in revolt against the Governor of Coahuila in a movement that, as Carranza explained personally to President Porfirio DÍAZ, was not predatory since they were all men of substance. The President yielded partially to their demands by not imposing his candidate for the governorship. Later Carranza again occupied the municipal presidency of Cuatro Ciénagas (1894) and served as interim Governor of Coahuila (1908) and as a senator in the waning days of the Díaz regime.

Carranza visited Francisco I. MADERO while the latter was in prison in Monterrey in June 1910, and in January 1911 he joined the Mexican revolutionary junta in San Antonio, Texas. In February of that year Madero named him provisional Governor of Coahuila and commander of the Third Military Zone (Coahuila,

Venustiano Carranza. [*Organization of American States*]

Nuevo León, and Tamaulipas). After he had taken part in the capture of Ciudad Juárez in May 1911, Madero named him Secretary of War in the provisional government, thereby arousing the resentment of Pascual Orozco, who thought that he should have received the post. On May 28, 1911, Carranza became interim Governor of his native state. In reaction to Madero's murder, he issued the Plan of Guadalupe (March 26, 1913), in which he disavowed Victoriano HUERTA as President of the republic as well as the legislative and judicial powers. The plan also named Carranza First Chief of the Constitutionalist Army. Upon the occupation of Mexico City by the Constitutionalist Army, Carranza was to become interim President and to hold elections as soon as peace had been consolidated. Only four of the twenty-seven governors repudiated Huerta. Carranza launched the struggle against Huerta with a small group of supporters and finally defeated him.

Carranza then clashed with Francisco VILLA, who maintained an independent attitude toward him (*see* AGUASCALIENTES CONVENTION; CELAYA, BATTLES OF). Others did not break openly with Carranza, but there were a variety of elements within Constitutionalist ranks, and some enacted agrarian, anticlerical, and, to a lesser extent, labor measures that undermined Carranza's authority. In foreign affairs, Carranza was able to deal successfully with several incidents involving Great Britain (the murder of William S. Benton by Villa) and the United States (the occupation of Veracruz, the self-kidnapping of consular agent William Jenkins; *see* VERACRUZ, OCCUPATION OF). He also succeeded in maintaining Mexican neutrality during World War I. Toward the end of 1915 he developed a policy that aimed at establishing his leadership not only over Mexico's revolutionaries but also over those of Latin America as a whole. In particular, he advocated the doctrine that foreigners in Latin American countries should not be allowed to enjoy greater rights than nationals.

At the end of 1916 he convoked a constituent congress, from which emerged the constitution promulgated on February 5, 1917 (*see* CONSTITUTION OF 1917: MEXICO). After his election to the Presidency, he gave slight impetus to the EJIDO, broke with the labor movement (mid-1916), and failed in his effort to impose a civilian successor. The triumvirate of Plutarco Elías CALLES, Álvaro OBREGÓN, and Adolfo de la Huerta easily defeated Carranza, who was murdered in San Antonio Tlaxcalantongo, a village in the mountains of Puebla, on May 21, 1920.

See also PERSHING PUNITIVE EXPEDITION.

Bibliography. Félix F. Palavicini, *El Primer Jefe,* Mexico City, 1916; Francisco L. Urquizo, *Venustiano Carranza: El hombre, el político, el caudillo,* Pachuca, 1935; Blas Urrea, *La herencia de Carranza,* Mexico City, 1920.
                                    MOISÉS GONZÁLEZ NAVARRO

CARRERA, JOSÉ MIGUEL (1786–1821). Chilean independence leader. Carrera, the principal rival of Bernardo O'HIGGINS in the struggle for the independence of Chile, was born in Santiago of a long-established aristocratic family. He received his higher education in Spain, where he also obtained military experience in fighting against the Napoleonic invaders. He returned to Chile in mid-1811 and threw himself into the revolu-

tionary movement that was then under way. With his good family connections (including two brothers who were also military officers), personal magnetism, and ample ambition, he had forced the dissolution of Congress by the end of the year and concentrated authority in his own hands.

Carrera claimed to offer a more vigorous revolutionary leadership and is generally classified as more "radical" than his principal rivals, but his ideas and objectives were not precisely formulated. Faced with a royalist invasion from Peru in 1813, he took the field against the enemy but was later deposed from power, O'Higgins being named general in chief in his place. In July 1814, Carrera seized power again. Incipient civil war between Carrera and O'Higgins was abruptly halted by news that the Viceroy of Peru had denounced a truce (Treaty of Lircay) previously signed by the royalists. O'Higgins then formally recognized Carrera's authority. Unfortunately, in October 1814, O'Higgins suffered a disastrous defeat at Rancagua that caused the final collapse of the patriot regime and also inspired new complaints against Carrera, whose failure to relieve Rancagua effectively contributed to the debacle.

Both leaders fled to Argentina, where they aligned themselves with opposite tendencies in Argentine politics. Carrera prospered briefly, then spent some time in the United States. Returning to Argentina in 1817, he was refused permission to proceed to Chile, where O'Higgins was now in control. Impelled by anger and frustration, Carrera became deeply enmeshed in the internecine struggles of the RÍO DE LA PLATA area and never returned to Chile. Instead, his involvement in the civil wars of the period, together with the animosity of his Chilean enemies, led to his execution in Argentina in 1821.
                                    DAVID BUSHNELL

CARRERA, JOSÉ RAFAEL (1814–1865). Conservative Guatemalan *caudillo.* Of mixed Spanish, Indian, and Negro stock, Carrera was the first of four long-term dictator-presidents who dominated the country between independence and 1944. He rose to prominence as the leader of a back-country revolt. The insurrection began when scandalized rural folk resisted attempts by the Liberal reformers Mariano GÁLVEZ in Guatemala and Francisco MORAZÁN in the Federation of Central America (*see* CENTRAL AMERICA, FEDERATION OF) to modernize their society, especially church-state relationships. A concurrent outbreak of cholera, which appeared to validate the canard that the leaders intended to destroy the population along with ancient customs, threw the countryside into a frenzy of fear and defiance. Carrera drove Gálvez from office in February 1838, and in March 1840 he repelled Morazán's last effort to take and hold the Guatemalan capital; thereafter he controlled the country.

Carrera came to power an illiterate, but he was astute and intelligent. At first he was content to manipulate figurehead officials, but in December 1844 he claimed the Presidency. The Liberals forced him into exile briefly in 1848, but their inability to consolidate their position allowed him to return in 1849. He regained the Presidency the next year and held office until his death.

Carrera's period of dominance, known as the thirty-year regime, was an unrelieved absolutism. He made Indians and mestizos a force in politics, and their

José Rafael Carrera. [*Radio Times Hulton Picture Library*]

readiness to support him nurtured an upper-class fear of a caste war that allowed him to become military master of the state and arbiter of its policy. He imposed internal order at the sacrifice of personal liberty, enforced conformity that stifled originality and initiative, and demanded adulation that precluded any hint of criticism.

Carrera's major goal was to restore the conventional attributes of Gautemalan life that Liberal reforms had threatened. He reinstalled an archbishop, gave the Catholic Church a place in government, reinstituted ecclesiastical *fueros* (corporate privileges), permitted monastic orders to reestablish communities, and in 1852 signed the first concordat between an independent Latin American nation and the Vatican. He revived the Sociedad Económica and the Consulado de Comercio, corporate special-interest groups organized during the later colonial years, and restored their quasi-public functions including economic development of the state. Education, however, he allowed to languish. Despite his Indian following, he accepted the colonial concept that Guatemala sheltered two disparate cultures, one of which had to patronize, chastise, and drive the other to do its duty.

Carrera's administration sought development by evolutionary process rather than by revolutionary change. He improved roads and ports, particularly on the Pacific side, and sponsored public works such as the theater in Guatemala City that bore his name. Faced with a decline of the market for cochineal, the principal export, he made efforts to diversify Guatemala's agriculture. Coffee had made Costa Rica prosper, and Carrera took steps compatible with his conservative philosophy to foster its cultivation in Guatemala. His measures chiefly benefited nationals, for he favored neither foreign capital nor foreign immigration.

Carrera was an exponent of Guatemalan nationalism. Under his influence Guatemala left the Federation of Central America on April 17, 1839, and on March 21, 1847, he declared it a sovereign republic. A Liberal separatist movement in western departments of the state was crushed mercilessly. He also successfully resisted attempts by the Belgian government to alienate the district of Santo Tomás, which had been granted for development in 1842 to the Belgian Colonization Company.

Although Carrera proclaimed Guatemalan nationhood in 1847, conforming constitutional revision was delayed. In 1851 an *acta constitutiva* established a government headed by an all-powerful President, with an Assembly of Notables representing the privileged corporations (including clergy, the university, the Sociedad Económica, and the Consulado de Comercio) and the traditional elite, whose principal function was to elect the President. Under that document Carrera was elected in 1851. In 1854 his tenure was extended for life with authority to choose his successor.

Carrera was the dominant figure in Central America during most of his tenure. He intervened repeatedly in neighboring countries to secure friendly governments, and he defended himself successfully against attack by hostile rivals. He cooperated with other Central American states to drive William WALKER from Nicaragua, but he took no leading role in the effort. In 1859 he signed a treaty acknowledging British tenure in, and the boundaries of, Belize (British Honduras), the interpretation of which became the subject of lasting dispute.

Carrera died on April 14, 1865. Vicente Cerna, one of his generals, succeeded him and continued his policies until the Liberal revolution of 1871 drove him from office.

Bibliography. José Rafael Carrera, *Memorias del General Carrera, 1837 á 1840,* ed. by Ignacio Solís, Guatemala City, 1906; Manuel Cobos Batres, *Carrera,* 3 parts, Guatemala City, n.d.; Lorenzo Montúfar y Rivera Maestre, *Reseña histórica de Centro-América,* 7 vols., Guatemala City, 1878–88; Pedro Tobar Cruz, *Los montañeses,* Guatemala City, 1958.

WILLIAM J. GRIFFITH

CARRERA ANDRADE, JORGE (1903–). Ecuadorian poet and diplomat. A native of Quito, he studied in Barcelona, Berlin, Paris, and London. He has lived for many years in Europe and has traveled widely as a diplomat. His best volumes of poetry are *Estanque inefable* (1922), *Boletines de mar y tierra* (1930), *Biografía para uso de los pájaros* (1937), *Microgramas* (1940), *Lugar de origen* (1945), *El visitante de niebla* (1947), and *Edades poéticas* (1958), the definitive edition of his poems. He also published *Guía de la joven poesía ecuatoriana* (1939), *Rostros y climas* (1948), *Poesía francesa contemporánea* (1951), and translations of the poems of Paul Valéry.

RACHEL PHILLIPS

CARRILLO, JULIÁN (1875–1965). Mexican composer. Carrillo was born in Ahualulco, San Luis Potosí, of

Indian extraction. He studied composition in Mexico City with Melesio Morales and graduated from the National Conservatory there in 1899. That year he received the President Díaz Prize for study in Europe. He then worked at the Leipzig Conservatory with Becker (violin) and Salomon Jadassohn (theory and composition); soon afterward he joined the Gewandhaus Orchestra as a violinist under Arthur Nikisch. In 1905 he returned to Mexico City, becoming professor of composition of the National Conservatory, whose directorship he assumed in 1913–1914. His prominence is due mainly to his contributions to the field of theory through the development of the so-called Sonido 13 method, involving the use of microtones. The application of such principles to his own compositions began in 1925, when he wrote *Preludio a Colón.*

Carrillo's compositions include two symphonies (1901, 1905), *Quinteto atonal a Debussy* (1917), and a triple concerto for flute, violin, cello, and orchestra (1918), which are good examples of his work prior to his use of microtonality. Outstanding compositions of the microtonal period are *Sonata casi fantasía* (1926), a concertino (1927), *Horizontes* (1947), two concerti for violin and orchestra, and *Mass in Memoriam of Pope John XXIII.*

JUAN A. ORREGO-SALAS

CARRIÓN, BENJAMÍN (1897–   ). Dean of twentieth-century Ecuadorian literature. Born in Loja, Carrión studied there and in Quito, worked in the diplomatic service, and published his first books in Europe, where he established an international reputation. He returned to Ecuador in 1928, helped found the Socialist party, and served as Minister of Education in 1932. Carrión rapidly emerged as Ecuador's cultural leader. It is said that all the great names in twentieth-century Ecuadorian poetry, theater, and plastic arts have been discovered, helped, and encouraged by him. He has written that small countries cannot compete with large nations on a material basis but that they can on spiritual and cultural grounds. The government-supported Casa de Cultura which Carrión founded (1943–1944) is a monument to that ideal. A center for Ecuadorian intellectuals, it organizes lectures, courses, and concerts, publishes books, and houses museum collections.

Carrión's writing embraces poetry, essays, political polemics, and novels. All of it reflects his fight for justice and a better life for the poor, and much of it is colored with his Communist orientation. Among his works are *Los creadores de la nueva América* (1928), *Mapa de América* (1930), and *El nuevo relato ecuatoriano* (1951–1952). Founder and director of the daily *El Sol,* which appeared in Quito in 1950, he lives in the capital and continues to be considered the best literary critic in Ecuador.   LOIS WEINMAN

CARVALHO E MELO, SEBASTIÃO JOSÉ DE. *See* POMBAL, MARQUÊS DE.

CASA DE CONTRATACIÓN. *See* COMMERCIAL POLICY (COLONIAL SPANISH AMERICA).

CASAS, BARTOLOMÉ DE LAS. *See* LAS CASAS, BARTOLOMÉ DE.

CASO, ALFONSO (1896–1970). Mexican archaeologist and anthropologist. A native of Mexico City, Caso was one of the celebrated Seven Sages, a group to which Manuel Gómez Morín and Vicente LOMBARDO TOLEDANO also belonged. He received a degree in law in 1919, having written a thesis called "What Is Law?" Caso was a professor of the philosophy of law at the National School of Jurisprudence and of epistemology at the Faculty of Philosophy and Letters of the National University of Mexico. During the administration of President Plutarco Elías CALLES (1924–1928) he served as director of the National Preparatory School. His interest in archaeology arose as a result of a visit to the ruins of Xochicalco; he then decided to study with Herman Beyer, who strongly influenced his archaeological formation, just as his brother Antonio CASO had influenced his philosophical orientation. In 1929 Caso joined the staff of the National Museum as an archaeologist, becoming head of the department the following year. From 1931 to 1940 he conducted explorations in the archaeological zone of MONTE ALBÁN in the state of Oaxaca, and his discoveries there made him famous. During the administration of Lázaro CÁRDENAS (1934–1940) he was named Director of Higher Education and Scientific Investigation. In 1939 he founded the National Institute of Anthropology and History and later the National School of Anthropology and History. Caso became rector of the National University of Mexico in 1944 under very difficult circumstances because of the anarchy in the university after the fall of the rector Rodulfo Brito Foucher. He remained in that post until March 1945, giving the university the organization it retains at present. During the administration of Miguel ALEMÁN (1946–1952) he founded the Secretariat of National Property and the National Indigenist Institute, having transformed his activities from those of an archaeologist to those of a social anthropologist. Among his best-known writings are *El teocalli de la Guerra Sagrada* (1927); *Las estelas zapotecas* (1928); *El pueblo del sol* (1953), illustrated by Miguel COVARRUBIAS; *Los calendarios prehispanicos* (1967); and *El tesoro de Monte Albán* (1969).

MOISÉS GONZÁLEZ NAVARRO

CASO, ANTONIO (1883–1946). Mexican philosopher and educator, older brother of the anthropologist Alfonso CASO. The first professor of philosophy at the National University of Mexico as reconstituted by Justo SIERRA in 1910, Caso evinced a lifelong commitment to teaching. He brought to the classroom the intellectual enthusiasm of the Ateneo de la Juventud, in which he participated with José VASCONCELOS and Sierra, criticizing positivism (*see* POSITIVISM: MEXICO) and the excessive rationalism of the CIENTÍFICOS of Porfirian Mexico (*see* DÍAZ, PORFIRIO). Instead they offered the intuitionism of Henri Bergson and other currents of thought emphasizing the senses and the unconscious in the formation of knowledge.

Caso's first book, *Problemas filosóficos* (1915), proposed the heart and experience as the keys to metaphysical knowledge and borrowed from William James a distrust of reason and an interest in religious experience. He combined this with the concepts of "disinterest" and "Christian charity" to form his own pragmatic theory of values in *La existencia como economía, como disinterés y como caridad* (1919) and *El concepto de la historia universal* (1923). For Caso the human will is tempered by charity, and pragmatic utility is determined by society rather than the individual, an idea taken from Émile Durkheim. In *Discursos a la nación mexicana* (1922), Caso used these concepts to promote Mexican nationalism by urging a heroic activism and a spirit of disinterest by public officials.

ALAN KOVAC

CASTAS (CASTES). *Castas,* along with Indians and Spaniards, constituted one of the three categories used by colonial officials as a way of defining tribute obligations and military service and of keeping records. Individuals who were included in the category *castas* were some combination of European, Indian, or African, as well as free blacks. The fact that all the *castas* except mestizos paid tribute, along with the Indians, placed them on a lower rung of the social hierarchy. Although the *castas* were not legally superior to the Indians, they enjoyed a higher status because they were Spanish-speaking and often were employed in more prestigious jobs.

Another use of the word *casta* describes a group known as *gente de casta limpia,* which included Europeans and *castizos,* individuals born of a mestizo mother and a Spanish father, who were of legitimate birth. The term *casta,* however, defies precise definition, as it could be used to describe legal, social, racial, or ethnic characteristics, or a combination of all of these.

EDITH B. COUTURIER

CASTELLANOS, GONZALO (1926–   ). Venezuelan composer and conductor. He was born in Canoabo, where he studied piano and organ with his father. Later he worked with Vicente Emilio Sojo in Caracas before traveling to Paris, where he joined the Schola Cantorum. He also received training in conducting from Sergiu Celibidache. Castellanos later became conductor of the Venezuela Symphony Orchestra and of the Collegium Musicum of Caracas. Outstanding examples of his works are his *Suite caraqueña* and his *Symphonic Fantasy* for piano and orchestra.

JUAN A. ORREGO-SALAS

CASTELLO BRANCO, HUMBERTO [DE ALENCAR] (1900–1967). President of Brazil (1964–1967). Humberto Castello Branco was born in Fortaleza, Ceará, into a traditional military family. He entered the Army in 1918 and was commissioned in 1921. Known primarily as a school officer, he taught at the Military School, served on the staff of the French military mission to Brazil, attended the French War College, the United States Army Command and General Staff College, and the Brazilian General Staff College, where he remained as an instructor. During World War II he was chief of operations of the Brazilian Expeditionary Force in Italy. After 1945 he alternated between field commands and the General Staff College, where he was commander in 1955. As director general of army education in 1960, he was closely associated with the Brazilian War College.

From his post as Army chief of staff during the latter months of the administration of João GOULART, Castello Branco coordinated military elements plotting the overthrow of the regime, and after the revolution of March 31, 1964, he was picked by its military and civilian leaders to become President. Retiring from the Army with the rank of marshal, Castello Branco was elected by Congress on April 11 and took office as President of Brazil on April 15, 1964. While attempting to preserve the essence of democratic government, he was nonetheless responsible for sweeping political purges and for the reorganization of political parties and the concentration of power in the hands of the executive that were incorporated into the constitution of 1967 (*see* CONSTITUTION OF 1967: BRAZIL). He left office on March 15, 1967, and died four months later in an air crash.

ROLLIE E. POPPINO

CASTES. *See* CASTAS.

CASTE WAR OF YUCATÁN (1847–1853). Civil war between the MAYAS from the central and eastern portions of the Yucatán Peninsula and whites, mestizos, and western Mayas. It had its origin in a variety of circumstances, the most important of which was probably the recent expansion of sugar production under creole direction in an area where white authority previously had been unknown. The war broke out in the summer of 1847, while Yucatán had temporarily withdrawn from the federal union and the Mexican Army was trying to stop Gen. Winfield Scott's advance into central Mexico (*see* MEXICAN WAR). The Mayan rebels were aided and supplied by British interests in British Honduras, which wished to extend their control into Yucatán.

The war was extremely brutal, with great fear existing among the white elements of the peninsular society. Within a year the Indian armies had occupied territory close to Mérida and Campeche. Soon thereafter, however, Yucatán negotiated its reentry into the Mexican republic, and federal aid was forthcoming to combat the rebellion. Arms were also received from Cuba by the government of the state, and some foreign soldiers joined the Army to defeat the Indians. The Mayas were on the defensive by 1849. In 1853 a treaty was negotiated with one faction of the Indians, and the action diminished considerably. Nevertheless, two factions continued the struggle in a sporadic fashion in central and eastern Yucatán for another half century.

CHARLES R. BERRY

CASTILE. Region in Spain, formerly a kingdom. The territory once known as Old Castile was originally divided into several counties that were united in the tenth century by Fernán González, who declared the title Count of Castile hereditary in his family. The title of King was assumed in the eleventh century by Ferdinand I, who ruled from 1035 to 1065. After the Kingdom of Toledo was reconquered from the Moors in 1085, it was annexed to Castile, constituting the region known as New Castile. The Kingdom of León was permanently united to Castile in 1230 during the reign of Ferdinand III, who also reconquered most of Andalusia, including the city of Seville. As a consequence of the marriage (1469) of Isabella, heiress to the throne of Castile (*see* ISABELLA I), and Ferdinand, heir to the throne of Aragon, these two kingdoms became joined by a dynastic tie.

By the end of the fifteenth century Castile occupied two-thirds of the Iberian Peninsula, and its population may have numbered 6 to 7 million. The experience of the reconquest not only had created a social order that prized aristocratic and military qualities but also had engendered a crusading spirit that became evident in the fifteenth-century conquest of the Canary Islands and the subsequent settlement of the New World. In contrast to the case of mercantile Aragon, the most important economic sector in fifteenth-century Castile was the sheep industry.

Castile's political and cultural hegemony over the rest of Spain was bolstered by its preponderant role in the conquest and colonization of America. Until the eighteenth century Spain's New World possessions were regarded as the patrimony of the sovereigns of Castile, and Queen Isabella's will specified that since the discovery of America had been undertaken and financed by Castilians, its exploitation should be reserved to them alone. Accordingly, most Spanish emigrants to America were Castilians, and the institutions and laws of the New World were patterned on those of Castile, which was also given a monopoly of colonial trade with the establishment of the Casa de Contratación in Seville.

HELEN DELPAR

CASTILLA, RAMÓN (1797–1867). Peruvian statesman and President (1845–1851, 1855–1862). Since his death more than a century ago, Ramón Castilla, perhaps Peru's most capable and revered nineteenth-century ruler, has become a national folk hero. He is fondly remembered for his homespun qualities and for his chauvinistic love of Peru. He thought Lima more beautiful than Paris and refused to be awed by monarchs and princes. Essentially a democrat, he liked to consider himself part of the masses, although his background was bourgeois. He was proud of being a mestizo and sought to make his life the vindication of a group vilified for

Ramón Castilla. [Radio Times Hulton Picture Library]

centuries. Throughout his public life, which spanned nearly fifty years, he worked tirelessly to preserve the independence of Peru and to create a more powerful nation.

Born in Tarapacá, now a Chilean province, Castilla became involved in the wars of independence at an early age, fighting for the royalists in Chile and Peru. In 1822 he joined José de SAN MARTÍN's liberation army, and for the next twenty-three years he participated in the political and military intrigues that made Peru's history chaotic. In the process he came to be associated with the great names of the age, such as San Martín, Simón BOLÍVAR, Agustín Gamarra, and Andrés SANTA CRUZ, and contributed to the creation of the Peruvian Army and to the early search for nitrate deposits in the south. Most of his actions during those years were dictated by a budding nationalism that was later to become the basis of his regimes. For example, he took part in the initial rebellion against Bolívar's domination of Peru. He helped defeat a separatist movement in the south, campaigned against foreign alliances he deemed harmful to Peru's independence, and contributed substantially to the collapse of the Bolivian-dominated PERU-BOLIVIA CONFEDERATION. In the process he was repeatedly wounded and suffered imprisonment, humiliation, and exile. From his experiences he learned the value of pragmatism and the art of political survival, qualities that contributed to his rise to power. In 1845, in fact, following another civil war, he was elected President. For the next two decades he worked to accomplish his goal of creating a better Peru.

The major criticism leveled against Castilla, whose regimes coincided with the GUANO-based economic boom, has to do with his laissez-faire economic philosophy and his shortsighted view of Peru's economic needs. Such shortcomings can easily be blamed on the general economic ignorance of the day. Nevertheless, Castilla's careless handling of the nation's guano resources and revenues did help to undermine Peru's economy seriously and to place it at the mercy of foreign capitalists.

These economic failures, however, cannot obscure Castilla's great political and social accomplishments. He reestablished, especially during his first administration, a degree of law and order unknown in more than twenty years. More important, as a pragmatist whose only ideology was a greater Peru, he successfully mediated the liberal-conservative conflicts responsible for much of the nation's chaos. The highlight of his policy was the moderate constitution of 1860, which remained in force until 1920. He also helped revive and modernize the coastal economy. He consolidated the internal debt and launched an extensive system of public works that included the building of the Lima-Callao railroad (1851), the first in South America; the construction of dock facilities at Callao; and increasing attention to steam navigation.

Castilla freed the Indians from the centuries-long custom of tribute payment and finally brought black slavery to an end (1854). He has been criticized, however, for contributing to the importation and enslavement of Chinese workers. He is, in fact, to be partially blamed for the origins of the practice, although most of the coolies were not brought to Peru until after he had left office. Internationally, through a policy of military preparedness, he changed Peru's status from a victim state to one of the great Pacific powers. Moreover, he placed Peru in the forefront of the struggle against imperialism and sought to revive the Bolivarian ideal of Hispanic-American unity. These are impressive credentials. Yet, to the historian Jorge BASADRE, Castilla's greatest contributions to Peru consisted of giving the nation the image of greatness and of inspiring a faith in its future which Peru had never had and which it was not to regain.

Bibliography. F. Mario Bazán, *Comentario en torno a Castilla,* Lima, 1958; Víctor Andrés Belaúnde, *El libertador Mariscal Castilla,* Lima, 1951; Instituto Libertador Ramón Castilla, *Archivo Castilla,* 4 vols., Lima, 1956–63; Miguel A. Martínez, *La vida heróica del gran mariscal don Ramón Castilla,* Lima, 1952; Carlos Wiesse, *Biografía en anécdotas del gran mariscal don Ramón Castilla,* Lima, 1924.

ORAZIO A. CICCARELLI

CASTILLO, RAMÓN S. (1873–1944). Argentine jurist and chief executive (1940–1943). A Conservative from the province of Catamarca, Castillo was elected Vice President in the fraudulent election of 1937. In July 1940 he received delegated presidential powers from President Roberto M. ORTIZ and acted as chief executive until the military overthrew his government on June 4, 1943.

The impact of World War II dominated Castillo's administration. Steadfastly maintaining Argentine neutrality, he had to contend with increasing pressure from the United States and from American-linked interests in Argentina to break relations with the Axis. Convinced that neutrality offered a means for national development and alarmed by the polarization occurring over the war issue, Castillo governed under a state of siege after the Pearl Harbor attack. The Argentine merchant marine was set up during his administration.

In domestic politics Castillo's government represented a turning away from Ortiz's policy of checking electoral fraud. The political impasse that ensued in the Radical-controlled Congress (*see* RADICAL PARTY: ARGENTINA) contributed to a deteriorating situation. The selection by Castillo of Robustiano Patrón Costas as the official presidential candidate in 1943 crystallized the currents of opposition and led to the military coup that displaced him.

NOREEN F. STACK

CASTILLO ARMAS, CARLOS (1914–1957). Guatemalan army officer and President who came to power by "liberating" Guatemala in 1954. After surviving an abortive coup in 1950 and subsequently escaping from the penitentiary, Castillo Armas had an almost legendary reputation for valor and persistence. His invasion in June 1954 posed only a token military threat, but the crisis it provoked forced Jacobo ARBENZ GUZMÁN to resign. The "liberation" made Castillo interim President. He claimed regularized status after a plebiscite in which only oral votes were counted, and a constituent assembly convoked to draft a new constitution fixed a term of office. With parties of the left banned and those of the right blocked, his National Democratic Movement party won the election he held in December 1955.

Castillo's major goal was to extirpate communism in Guatemala. He prohibited activity by political parties, labor unions, and other organizations suspected of infiltration until they could be purged. Since most Communist leaders had abandoned the country with Arbenz, the search for minor functionaries, collaborators, and suspected sympathizers suggested a witch-hunt. Some innovations of the revolutionary era were left untouched by Castillo Armas, but others suffered from Communist associations. The Institute of Social Security and the Institute for the Development of Production, for example, Castillo retained. However, labor unions were reorganized and shorn of some advantages, and the original owners regained much of the land Arbenz had distributed. Castillo inaugurated an agrarian reform of his own that was vaunted as superior to its predecessor in that it conferred title rather than lifetime usufruct. Other development projects Castillo devised were cut short when he was assassinated on July 26, 1957.

WILLIAM J. GRIFFITH

CASTRO, CIPRIANO (1858–1924). Dictator of Venezuela (1899–1908). The last of the *caudillo* revolutionaries and the first in a long series of Venezuelan leaders from the Andean region of Táchira, Castro led a successful revolt against the reigning general, Ignacio Andrade, in 1899. From then until 1908 Castro ruled Venezuela with such maleficent style and verve that he is universally recognized as one of the most corrupt, inefficient, and irresponsible Latin American dictators. Famous for his cavalier treatment of foreign diplomats and businessmen, Castro brought on the second Venezuelan incident (1902), which involved the intervention of British and German warships at Puerto Cabello to force payment of certain debts. In the end the intervention gained the support of Italy, and Venezuela's entire Caribbean coast was blockaded. Eventually the claims were settled in the Permanent Court of International Arbitration, which awarded the claimants about 20 percent of their demands. An international consequence of Castro's intransigence was the formulation of the DRAGO DOCTRINE (1902), which claimed that public debts could not be collected from American republics by armed force.

Perhaps Castro's most important domestic contribution resulted from his sponsorship of and reliance on a *tachirense* compatriot, Juan Vicente GÓMEZ, whose superior administrative and political abilities helped bring Castro to power and keep him there against the inevitable host of challengers. When Castro's extravagant life-style undermined his health, he left the government in the loyal hands of Gómez in 1908 and went to Europe in search of a cure. After a delay of about a month, however, Gómez took over the government for himself and ordered a permanent European exile for his benefactor.

JOHN V. LOMBARDI

CASTRO [RUZ], FIDEL (1926–   ). Cuban revolutionary leader and the Prime Minister of Cuba (1959–   ). The central figure of recent Cuban history, Castro was the third of seven children born to a moderately well-to-do Spanish immigrant landowner and his second wife. After attending primary school near his home in Oriente Province, Castro completed his elementary and secondary studies in Catholic institutions, including the prestigious Jesuit-run Colegio Belén in Havana. In 1945 he entered the University of Havana

Law School, where he plunged into revolutionary student politics. His political talents matured in a milieu of violent campus political activism. The previous two decades had witnessed a popular struggle against the dictatorship of Gerardo MACHADO and a rising current in favor of social reform and economic nationalism. Student politics reflected these events and became characterized by intense factional rivalry among self-styled revolutionary nationalist action groups.

While a law student, Castro became affiliated with an organization known as the Revolutionary Insurrectional Union, composed of students, former students, and politicians and linked with the government of Ramón GRAU SAN MARTÍN. His leadership talents and marathon oratorical performances propelled him into prominence among aspiring student politicians. Like many student leaders and faculty members, he deemed it necessary to carry a firearm in an atmosphere that sometimes produced political assassinations. At this time he also began to adopt his now-characteristic bohemian, unconventional style in manner and appearance.

Extracurricular political activism involved Castro in two international incidents. In 1947 he participated in the abortive Cayo Confites expedition against the dictatorship of Rafael Leonidas TRUJILLO MOLINA in the Dominican Republic. To elude capture by alerted Cuban Coast Guard patrols, Castro reportedly jumped ship and swam ashore carrying a heavy automatic weapon on his back. In April 1948 he toured Venezuela, Panama, and Colombia with three student companions. In Bogotá they participated in the newly formed Congress of Latin American Students organized by Cuban and Argentine students. This anti-imperialist gathering had been scheduled to coincide with the Ninth International Conference of American States (BOGOTÁ CONFERENCE). The assassination of Jorge Eliécer GAITÁN, the popular left-wing leader of the Colombian Liberals (*see* LIBERAL PARTY: COLOMBIA), occasioned destructive rioting and bloody clashes. Castro and other Cuban students were hunted by Colombian authorities for alleged participation in the ensuing disturbances but eventually escaped and returned to Cuba.

Castro resumed his university studies in 1948. Upon graduating in 1950 with a doctor of laws degree, he became a practicing attorney who specialized in cases for poor clients. During his university days he had become a supporter of Senator Eduardo CHIBÁS, a popular spokesman for political and social reform. Consequently he joined Chibas's Ortodoxo party (*see* ORTODOXO PARTY: CUBA) and became active in its Havana organization. Castro was slated to be an Ortodoxo candidate for Congress in the general elections scheduled for June 1952 that ex-President Fulgencio BATISTA's coup d'état of March 10 canceled.

Outraged, the young attorney wrote a strong letter of warning to Batista and filed a brief declaring the seizure of power illegal. When peaceful measures failed, Castro organized a revolutionary conspiracy with a number of radical young Ortodoxos and his younger brother Raúl CASTRO. The rebels intended to capture the Moncada military barracks in Santiago and set off a general uprising. On July 26, 1953, Castro led about 170 rebels in an unsuccessful assault on the fortress. Only 61 of the original force survived the attack and subsequent violent reprisals during the Army's roundup of participants.

Castro narrowly escaped assassination through the

Fidel Castro. [*United Press International*]

intervention of family friends and the humane impulses of his arresting officer. After spending several months in prison, he stood trial in October. Using smuggled notes prepared during his confinement, the rebel leader acted in his own defense and delivered a five-hour address now known by its closing statement, "History Will Absolve Me." The speech, a defense of the historical right to rebel against tyranny, also contained a statement of his revolutionary program. While proposing a return to democratic legality under the 1940 constitution (*see* CONSTITUTION OF 1940: CUBA), Castro advocated profound socioeconomic reforms and hinted that he would adopt policies radically different from those of past Cuban governments. He condemned the rich and comfortable elements for supporting dictators and expressed an interest in Cuba's long-neglected lower classes.

Sentenced to fifteen years, Castro spent the next nineteen months in confinement on the Isle of Pines. During this period he read avidly while making new plans to carry out his revolution. In May 1955 the Batista regime, in an effort to bolster its position, granted a general amnesty to political prisoners. During the first two months following his release Castro again concluded that his goals could be realized only through violent revolution. In July he left Cuba for Mexico to prepare his followers for a new assault against the regime.

In Mexico Castro's group underwent military preparation in guerrilla tactics under the leadership of Col. Alberto Bayo, a Loyalist veteran of the Spanish Civil War. The group consisted of Cuban political refugees, some veterans of the Moncada assault, and an Argentine-born physician, Ernesto GUEVARA. In March 1956 Castro severed his formal ties with the Ortodoxo party and established his own independent July 26 revolutionary movement. Then, in late November 1956, Castro and eighty-one armed men sailed from Yucatán on a small, leaky yacht, the *Granma*. The invaders reached Oriente Province on December 1, two days behind schedule. Their arrival was to have coincided with a local uprising, but the revolt had been crushed, and the invaders were met by alerted Cuban air and land forces. Only twelve men, including the

Castro brothers and Guevara, escaped from the ensuing clash and ultimately reached safety in the nearby Sierra Maestra.

While living precariously in this rugged terrain, Castro received supplies and recruits from his July 26 urban network and built a guerrilla force around his twelve-man nucleus. The guerrilla leader also gained cooperation and the bulk of his recruited guerrilla force from local peasants by promising and often effecting land reform in the rebel zone. Batista's massive effort to exterminate the guerrillas in 1957 failed. Publicity obtained from interviews by foreign journalists and news of rebel successes dispelled the government's official claims of victory and Castro's death. Castro thus became the central focus of growing popular resistance to the repressive Batista regime.

Castro's distaste for anti-Batista leaders from traditional Cuban political groups delayed initial attempts at forming a united opposition front. Finally, in April 1958 a unity pact was signed on Castro's terms. In the summer he also signed a secret agreement with the Cuban Communist party, then called the Popular Socialist party (PSP), which had initially denounced his activities as bourgeois putschism (*see* PARTIDO COMUNISTA DE CUBA). In August, Castro's guerrilla forces left their defense perimeter and took the offensive. By this time the regime had alienated itself from the populace through an excessive use of repressive terror. Batista's demoralized army put up ineffectual resistance to the rebels, who numbered fewer than 1,000 men, and the regime collapsed at the end of 1958. After capturing the city of Santiago, Castro made a triumphant tour across the island, entering Havana on January 8.

Castro's assumption and consolidation of power proceeded step by step throughout 1959. Initially the victorious guerrilla chief turned control of the new revolutionary government over to his more moderate middle-class allies from the traditional political groups. Meanwhile, he maintained control of the Army and enjoyed mass popular support as well as the loyalty of many intermediate-level government officials. He undermined the moderate leaders by arbitrarily announcing government policy on nationwide television and criticizing what he termed halfway measures. In February he assumed the office of Prime Minister.

Premier Castro's far-reaching AGRARIAN REFORM, his other measures involving considerable government regulation of the economy, and his apparent willingness to accept Communist participation in the revolutionary process alarmed moderate and conservative elements. In July Castro replaced provisional President Manuel Urrutia with Osvaldo DORTICÓS TORRADO, a Castro supporter and one-time Communist party member. Soon the regime took repressive measures against other prominent outspoken anti-Communists. Throughout 1959 Castro's followers consolidated their position by capturing control of the schools, civic and professional groups, and mass organizations such as the CONFEDERACIÓN DE TRABAJADORES CUBANOS. Moreover, Castro assumed the title Maximum Leader and reversed his earlier stand on holding elections.

The Cuban Prime Minister, a revolutionary nationalist, obviously had as his objective a social revolution—a radical transformation of Cuban society in behalf of the poor. Initially his movement lacked solid ideological underpinnings and was vaguely labeled "humanism." However, Castro gradually moved in the direction of Marxist socialism during the next two years. Since his university days his exposure to Marxism had been passing and unsystematic. At times he displayed a willingness to accept Communist support, but he also occasionally took anti-Communist positions. Nevertheless, the radical nationalist and social goals of his revolutionary program facilitated an accommodation between his regime and the Communists. While the PSP enthusiastically backed the revolutionary government, Castro unhesitatingly utilized its well-organized party machinery.

Throughout 1960 and 1961 the once-binding ties between Cuba and the United States deteriorated to the point of rupture as Castro moved ever closer to a Marxist position and an alliance with the international Communist bloc (*see* BAY OF PIGS INVASION). Finally, in an effort to commit the USSR to economic and military support of his revolution, Castro publicly declared himself a Marxist-Leninist in December 1961. He then proceeded to complete the nationalization of the Cuban economy and to establish a one-party regime with the political apparatus dominated initially by the PSP.

Cuban communism under Castro has reflected the peculiar background and style of the guerrilla leader and his young nationalist followers, who are newcomers to Marxism-Leninism. Castro has vigorously maintained his personal control of the revolution and asserted Cuba's political independence within the world Communist movement. In March 1962 he purged certain veteran Communist leaders who were overstepping their authority and restored control of the party to his "new Communist" followers. On ideological issues involving domestic and foreign policy, particularly revolutionary tactics in Latin America, Castro has frequently clashed with Moscow, Peking, and the traditional Latin American Communist parties. Castro's brand of communism emphasizes a pragmatic and experimental approach to building socialism. Therefore he has refused to be bound by textbook formulas of Marxist political and economic theory.

Castro's tactical preference for the Cuban model of guerrilla warfare over the more flexible political approach preferred by most pro-Soviet Communist parties led to sharp ideological disputes that reached their zenith in the period 1966–1968. During this time Castro criticized the USSR for its aid to anti-Communist regimes in Latin America and its lack of substantial support for revolutionary governments and movements in the Third World. Since 1968, however, Castro has taken a more flexible line on the question of revolutionary tactics while concentrating on domestic economic matters. Consequently, his relations with the Soviet Union and the Latin American Communist parties have improved substantially.

Castro's personality and style of leadership have exercised a profound effect on the course of the CUBAN REVOLUTION. His charismatic mass appeal and oratorical talents have enabled him to sustain over a long period the initial revolutionary enthusiasm of a still-considerable number of Cubans despite economic setbacks. These factors, combined with Castro's inclination to direct the revolution personally, have made him the central factor in the Cuban political process.

Castro's two-year guerrilla experience in the Sierra Maestra reinforced his basic nonconformist style and outlook. He still affects an unconventional appearance by continuing to wear army fatigues and a heavy beard. Furthermore, his rural guerrilla experience prejudiced him against the sedentary life and urban values in general. Castro is uncomfortable and impatient with bureaucracy; he feels free to cut through red tape and personally go to the heart of problems by intervening in all aspects of the revolutionary process. This highly personalized style has often led to abrupt changes of policy. The sudden abandonment of programs is followed by an enthusiastic promotion of new ones. It is Fidel Castro who clearly directs and personifies the Marxist social revolution that present-day Cuba is experiencing. His influence upon the course of events in contemporary Cuba provides strong evidence that politically gifted individuals can shape history.

Bibliography. Fidel Castro, *Selected Works, I: Cuba, Revolutionary Struggle,* ed. by Roland E. Bonachea and Nelson P. Valdés, Cambridge, Mass., 1972; Jules Dubois, *Fidel Castro: Liberator or Dictator?,* Indianapolis, 1959; Theodore Draper, *Castro's Revolution: Myths and Realities,* New York, 1963; K. S. Karol, *The Guerrillas in Power,* London, 1970; Lee Lockwood, *Castro's Cuba; Cuba's Fidel,* New York, 1967; Herbert Matthews, *Fidel Castro: A Political Biography,* London, 1969; Gerardo Rodríguez Morejón, *Fidel Castro: Biografía,* Havana, 1959; Andrés Suárez, *Cuba: Castro and Communism, 1959–1966,* Cambridge, Mass., 1967.

DAVID A. CRAIN

CASTRO, JUAN JOSÉ (1895–1968). Argentine composer and conductor. Born in Avellaneda, he first studied in Argentina with Constantino Gaito and later in Paris with Vincent d'Indy. Like his brothers José María and Washington, he was both a conductor and a composer of international repute. For many years after 1930 he conducted at the Teatro Colón in Buenos Aires. He was also permanent conductor of the National Symphony Orchestra of Argentina, the Havana Philharmonic Orchestra, the SODRE Orchestra of Montevideo, the Victorian Symphony Orchestra in Melbourne, Australia, and the Puerto Rico Symphony Orchestra. In 1959 he was appointed dean of the Conservatory of Puerto Rico and became a close associate of Pablo Casals.

His catalog of works includes several operas, among which *La zapatera prodigiosa* (1943) and *Bodas de sangre* (1952), both based on plays by Federico García Lorca, and *Proserpina y el extranjero* (1951) are the most outstanding. In addition, he wrote chamber music, piano compositions, works for voice, five symphonies, a concerto for piano and orchestra (1941), *Corales criollos* (1953), a concerto for violin and orchestra (1962), and numerous dramatic works.

JUAN A. ORREGO-SALAS

CASTRO, JULIÁN. President of Venezuela (1858–1859). Castro began his career as a military officer in the republican armies of Venezuela. A reasonably capable officer, he participated in the Revolución de las Reformas (Revolution of the Reforms) of 1835–1836 and joined the Liberal party at its inception in 1840. By virtue of his association with the Liberals he rose to prominence in the years of the Monagas dynasty (1848–1858). When Liberals and Conservatives began conspiring to overthrow José Tadeo MONAGAS, Castro joined them and became titular head of the revolution that ousted Monagas in March 1858.

As head of the revolutionary government (1858–1859), Castro allowed himself to be dominated by the Conservative element of the anti-Monagas fusion. He permitted a campaign of reprisals against the Liberal collaborators of the Monagas regime and through his ministers became involved in a serious altercation with the French and British diplomatic agents. This incident, caused by the government's demand that José Tadeo Monagas and other prominent Liberals who had sought refuge in the French Legation be turned over to the authorities, resulted in a short blockade of Venezuela's two major ports in 1858. In the end, José Tadeo was surrendered, but with guarantees of his safety and quick transportation out of the country. Castro governed Venezuela while the Constitutional Convention of Valencia created the constitution of 1858, which would provide the excuse for the Federal Wars.

By August 1859, Castro's flirtation with the now-rebellious Liberals had led to his ouster in a Conservative coup d'état. He reappeared as a general in the Liberal armies of Antonio GUZMÁN BLANCO a decade later but never again played a central role in politics.

JOHN V. LOMBARDI

CASTRO [RUZ], RAÚL (1931–   ). Cuban revolutionary leader and Defense Minister. Raúl Castro's career has been closely linked with that of his older and more famous brother, Fidel CASTRO. The youngest son in a large family, Raúl, like Fidel, attended the University of Havana and became involved in revolutionary student politics. Throughout the years the younger Castro has been regarded as more radical in his political views than his brother. While a student, he sometimes participated in the activities of Communist front groups and briefly belonged to the party's youth wing. Raúl was active in the revolutionary movement against Fulgencio BATISTA led by his brother. He survived both the unsuccessful attack on the Moncada army barracks on July 26, 1953, and the disastrous invasion landing of a small guerrilla force on the east coast of Cuba in November 1956.

The younger Castro lacks the popular appeal of his brother, but he proved his mettle as a superior military commander who won the respect of his men during the armed struggle against Batista. Since Fidel Castro's consolidation of power in 1959, Raúl has become the No. 2 man within the revolutionary regime in terms of position and influence. He has exercised control over the Rebel Armed Forces, a mainstay of the regime, and has long served as Minister of Defense in the Castro Cabinet. Raúl is also a member of the Secretariat and the Political Bureau of the new PARTIDO COMUNISTA DE CUBA. In 1959 he married Vilma Espín, a veteran member of the July 26 movement who now heads the Federation of Cuban Women.

DAVID A. CRAIN

CASTRO ALVES, ANTÔNIO (1847–1871). Brazilian poet. Born in the province of Bahia and educated in Salvador and in the law schools of Recife and São

Paulo, he devoted the better part of his short life to the abolition movement. He suffered a hunting accident that led to amputation of part of a leg and died several months later of tuberculosis. During his lifetime he was known as the poet of the slaves, although the one volume he published, *Espumas Flutuantes* (1870), contains none of his antislavery poems but is rather a collection of poems on love and nature. His poems on slavery, published posthumously in *A Cachoeira de Paulo Afonso* (1876), *Vozes de África* (1880), and *Os Escravos* (1883), became known through his recitations. "O Navio Negreiro," about a slave ship, became popular as a parlor elocutionary exercise. Castro Alves was the leader of the *condoreiros,* a group of romantic poets whose inflated, rhetorical verse carries a social message and recalls Victor Hugo. The personal poetry of *Espumas Flutuantes,* subtly impregnated with the sensual charm of the Brazilian landscape, is more delicately cadenced than his antislavery poems. All his poetry shows his great mastery of sensuous imagery. His historical drama, *Gonzaga ou a Revolução de Minas* (1875), though ostensibly dealing with the problems of slavery and Portuguese tyranny in colonial Brazil, may also be interpreted as a republican attack on the monarchy.

RAYMOND S. SAYERS

CATAVI MASSACRE. Title frequently given to a clash that took place on December 21, 1942, in the Catavi camp of Patiño Mines, between Bolivian soldiers and the tin miners and their families. Deaths among the mining folk were estimated in the hundreds, including a number of women and children.

The clash took place as a result of the miners' attempts to unionize in the face of opposition from the government of Gen. Enrique PEÑARANDA. The first major attempt to organize the miners had taken place during the administration of President Germán BUSCH (1937–1939). However, the Miners Federation established at that time met stiff opposition in the years that followed.

Labor and living conditions were particularly bad in the mining camps. The camps were located in isolated, bleak parts of the ALTIPLANO (high plateau), at exceptionally high altitudes. Housing was very bad, medical care inadequate, and schools few and of poor quality. Wages were very low, and working conditions were hazardous to the health and safety of the workers. The situation culminated late in 1942 in a strike among the miners. A demonstration of unarmed strikers and their families on December 21 was confronted by the local military detachment, and when the people refused to disperse, the military fired.

The Catavi massacre had a far-reaching impact both within Bolivia and abroad. It brought about the first substantial contact between the left-wing nationalist party, the MOVIMIENTO NACIONALISTA REVOLUCIONARIO (MNR), and the miners, when union leaders asked MNR deputies for support. MNR members of Congress interrogated government leaders and created an atmosphere that contributed greatly to the overthrow of Peñaranda and the first advent to power of the MNR itself.

The massacre aroused widespread protest abroad. The United States labor movement demanded that the United States government insist on the improvement of conditions in the mining areas before signing a contract with Bolivia to purchase tin. As a result, an official mission, with United States labor participation, was dispatched to Bolivia and made a widely publicized and highly derogatory report. Some improvement in conditions in the mining camps came about as a result.

ROBERT J. ALEXANDER

CATHOLIC CHURCH (COLONIAL PERIOD). The Catholic Church in Latin America was one of the main supports of the Spanish and Portuguese empires in the New World. The alliance of church and state under the PATRONATO REAL forged by Ferdinand II and ISABELLA I was transmitted to the Indies, where the church was even more closely allied to civil government than in Spain. As in the mother country, the only central authority whose officials were present in all parts of the realm was the church. Hence its influence was in many respects more pervasive than the crown's. In addition, clerics often served as royal officials or assisted civil authority in some other manner. This reflected the similarity of royal and ecclesiastical objectives and resulted in a high degree of cooperation, particularly in the early years of conquest and colonization. As the colonial period advanced, this identification of purposes diminished and tension and conflicts encouraged by overlapping jurisdiction increased.

Clerics first came to the New World as early as Christopher COLUMBUS's second voyage in 1493. The tremendous missionary opportunities presented by the American discoveries encouraged an increasing migration of religious, particularly Franciscans, Augustinians, Dominicans, and Mercedarians. The same phenomenon occurred in Brazil after 1500, although not on the same scale as in the Spanish possessions.

The influx of clerics to the New World and the demands of the American enterprise required administrative organization. As early as 1504 the Spanish crown obtained papal permission for the creation of an archbishopric and two bishoprics on the island of Hispaniola. These sees were not filled, for King Ferdinand refused to nominate any candidates until he obtained the broad patronage rights that the crown enjoyed in the Kingdom of Granada. By then population had shifted sufficiently in the Antilles so that new dioceses had to be designated. In 1511 an Archdiocese of Santo Domingo was created with two suffragan sees, one in Hispaniola and the other in Puerto Rico. Expansion to the mainland resulted in the creation of the Diocese of Darién in 1513. The most important dioceses were those established in the civilian administrative centers. In 1530 Mexico City was designated a see, while Lima became one in 1539. Until 1545 the American episcopacies were subordinate to Seville. By the end of the colonial period there were 10 archdioceses and 38 dioceses in Spanish America. The first Brazilian diocese was established at Bahia in 1551, followed by the episcopacy of Rio de Janeiro in 1577. The prelates who occupied these sees were selected by the Pope from three nominees proposed by the monarch. Lesser ecclesiastical officials were selected in a similar manner by the vice-patrons and church hierarchy. Church officials consequently were more likely to be loyal to Madrid than to Rome. In addition, the authority of the COUNCIL OF THE INDIES extended into the ecclesiastical sphere as a result of its having authority in such matters as the granting of licenses for religious to travel to the New World and for papal documents to be published there.

In the early years of the Spanish empire the energies of both civil and ecclesiastical officials were absorbed by the enormous task of Christianizing and Hispanicizing the Indians. This undertaking was complicated by debates in Spain and America over the justness of the Spanish conquest and enslavement of the Indians. Disputes arose over the capacity of the natives to become good Christians. The crown responded to the New World controversies by issuing such measures as the LAWS OF BURGOS in 1512 and the NEW LAWS in 1542, which were aimed at regularizing relationships between Indians and Spaniards, particularly with respect to the exploitation of native labor under the encomiendas (see ENCOMIENDA) and the obligation of the encomenderos to Christianize their charges. In 1537 Pope Paul III in the bull *Sublimis Deus* held that the Indians were capable of self-government, in addition to being capable of becoming true Catholics. The concern of the monarchy over such questions resulted in the debates in 1550 in Valladolid between Bartolomé de LAS CASAS, who defended the rationality of the Indians, and Juan Ginés de Sepúlveda, who adhered to the Aristotelian theory of natural servitude. Similar questions were to preoccupy the Portuguese, particularly as a result of Franciscan and Jesuit pleas for protection of the Indians. These appear to have had limited impact on the actual treatment of the Indians, and the Laws of Burgos, the New Laws, and the Portuguese regulations of 1624 aroused such opposition from the colonists that they were, for the most part, unenforceable. The Indian policy of the crown and church depended to a large extent on the will of the local encomendero, *doctrinero,* and corregidor. Central authorities were unable to eliminate abuse of the Indians.

Doubts concerning the capacity and rationality of the Indians led to attempts to exclude natives from the clergy. While there were exceptions, including three bishops of Mexico, in general Indians were discouraged or prohibited from entering the priesthood. The decisions of various religious orders and the secular clergy were confirmed by royal orders in 1578 that forbade the admission of mestizos, mulattoes, or Indians, although the prohibition against mestizos was relaxed in 1588, only to be reasserted by PHILIP II in 1590. Such regulations were occasionally ignored, especially if the individual belonged to a family of some status. While the predominance of Spanish clergy may have ensured that the church would serve the imperial system well, such prohibitions contributed to the identification of the church as a foreign institution and helped perpetuate a dependence on a nonnative clergy that still persists.

After the initial period of accomplishment, attention was turned to consolidation and institutional development. Religion became more formalized, missions more structured, and the church more urban-oriented. The increasing attention paid by Spanish American society to economic pursuits was reflected in the acquisition by ecclesiastical institutions of rural and urban real estate.

Beginning in the latter part of the sixteenth century, the crown attempted to expand its authority in the ecclesiastical sphere through such proposals as a patriarchate and vicarship of the Indies. In the seventeenth century the concept of the economic authority of the king, by which matters previously covered by ecclesiastical immunity fell within royal cognizance, was introduced. Royal control over the church in Brazil also increased, although metropolitan authority in that colony was not as effective as in Spanish America. The special problems of Brazil, especially the French and Dutch incursions and the migration of individuals of Jewish background, resulted in greater religious diversity and possibly more tolerance.

The authority and influence of the church in Spanish America came under serious attack in the eighteenth century. Not only were secular functions of the church restricted, but the crown intervened in areas previously regarded as falling within ecclesiastical jurisdiction, particularly clerical discipline. The crown was motivated by a general desire to increase the benefits to the mother country of the empire and to secure it against foreign depredations. Bourbon ecclesiastical reforms were aimed at reducing the independence of the church and churchmen. While there had been complaints throughout the colonial period about the clergy, it was not until the eighteenth century that royal regulations really began to be effective. Religious orders that were not under episcopal authority were ordered to give up their Indian parishes, and the Jesuits were expelled in 1767 (*see* JESUITS, EXPULSION OF: SPANISH AMERICA).

In Brazil regalism combined with the increasing secularization of life to weaken the church. Distance and the limited number of clergy had always restricted the influence of that institution and increased the dependence of clerics on civil authority. The first Trentian seminary for the training of ecclesiastics was not created until 1739. The expulsion of the Jesuits antedated that in the Spanish possessions by eight years and resulted in a decay in education and the destruction of a considerable number of missions (*see* JESUITS, EXPULSION OF: BRAZIL).

Such actions were, in part, the result of the crown's feeling that its exploitation of colonial resources was impeded by ecclesiastical influence and wealth. Initially church revenues flowed mainly from imposts collected and disbursed by royal officials. Donations and bequests, in addition to the tithes, all contributed to church wealth. The inalienability of ecclesiastical land, together with the astuteness of some churchmen, resulted in the emergence of their institutions as the richest in Latin America. Rural and urban real estate provided capital to invest, sometimes in moneylending. Individual clerics also engaged in financial dealings and sometimes amassed personal wealth. A goodly number of the ecclesiastical hierarchy had personal investments in the colonies and at times also served as commercial representatives for interests in Spain.

Royal efforts to diminish the economic importance of the church were not particularly successful. In 1617 regulations raised the crown's share of the tithe, while in the 1730s church endowments were declared to be no longer tax-exempt. By the end of the century such holdings were taxed at 15 percent of their value. In the early nineteenth century the monarchy attempted to divert ecclesiastical capital into the royal treasury more directly than before.

Perhaps the greatest riches the colonial churches possessed were the result of intellectual and artistic pursuits. The task of converting the Indians led the early missionaries not only into mastering the native languages but also into collecting information about the indigenes' history and culture. The knowledge gathered still serves as an important source, particularly for the pre-Columbian and conquest periods. Education was the exclusive responsibility of the church, and through its efforts Iberian culture and traditions were communicated to the American population. By the end of the colonial period there were twenty-five universities and more than fifty *colegios* (secondary schools) in Spanish America. In the eighteenth century such institutions functioned to disseminate Enlightenment thought. Rather than serving as a force of obscurantism, ecclesiastics in many instances promoted new ideas. *See* ENLIGHTENMENT (BRAZIL); ENLIGHTENMENT (SPANISH AMERICA).

Ecclesiastical architecture and art also communicated European cultural values. Although some indigenous elements were included, the dominant styles were non-American. The seventeenth century witnessed the construction of many churches and cathedrals that reflected baroque and rococo styles. Such buildings encouraged the development of colonial sculpture and painting.

As an institution the Catholic Church supported Spain in the struggles for independence. Such a position aroused the enmity of the governments of the new nations, which was reinforced by conflicts over the transference of the *patronato real*. In 1816 Pope Pius VII urged Spanish American prelates to encourage loyalty to FERDINAND VII. With the rising tide of liberalism in Spain, however, Rome began taking a more ambivalent stance, and by 1823 it recognized the changed nature of the American situation by dispatching an apostolic vicar, Archbishop Giovanni Muzi, to Argentina and Chile. The hostility of the governments of those areas was sufficient to prevent Muzi from accomplishing his purposes. A papal brief of Leo XII in 1824 supporting Ferdinand VII only increased animosity toward the church, and fears of schism caused a reevaluation of papal policy. In 1829 a papal nuncio, Pietro Ostini, was sent to Rio de Janeiro with authority for all Latin America. With the accession of Pope Gregory XVI in 1831 progress began to be made to restore some of the ground lost by the church. Throughout, Rome's objective was to eliminate the patronal rights originally granted to Ferdinand and Isabella. Disputes over this question continued well into the nineteenth century.

The attitude of individual clerics toward independence varied from strong opposition to active support. In general, the higher clergy tended to favor continued Spanish control, although one prelate, Bishop José Cuero y Caicedo, acted as President of the revolutionary junta of Quito. Among the lower clergy most were probably supporters of the status quo or neutral, although this group produced such revolutionary leaders as Miguel HIDALGO Y COSTILLA and José María MORELOS Y PAVÓN. Ecclesiastical involvement in the independence movement was greater in areas where the sentiment to break away was strongest, as in the Río de la Plata, where priests served in the *cabildo abierto* of May 25, 1810, the 1812 and 1813 Buenos Aires Assemblies, and the Congress of Tucumán, which declared the region's independence (*see* TUCUMÁN, CONGRESS OF). In Peru and Colombia the clergy reflected the stronger allegiance to the mother country of the populace, although there were clerics who

promoted and fought for independence. These differences of loyalty caused discord within the church at a time when anticlericalism was rife. In general, the identification of the church with the royalist cause prejudiced the new republics against the church, and it never regained its previous preeminent position.

See also INQUISITION, HOLY OFFICE OF THE; MISSIONS (SPANISH AMERICA); RELIGIOUS ORDERS (COLONIAL PERIOD).

Bibliography. Michael B. Costeloe, *Church Wealth in Mexico: 1800–1856,* Cambridge, Mass., 1968; Mariano Cuevas, *Historia de la iglesia en México,* 5 vols., Mexico City, 1946–47; N. M. Farriss, *Crown and Clergy in Colonial Mexico, 1759–1821: The Crisis of Ecclesiastical Privilege,* London, 1968; Richard E. Greenleaf (ed.), *The Roman Catholic Church in Latin America,* New York, 1971; León Lopétegui, Félix Zubillaga, and Antonio de Egaña, *Historia de la iglesia en la América española desde el descubrimiento hasta comienzos del siglo XIX,* 2 vols., Madrid, 1965–66; Robert Ricard, *The Spiritual Conquest of Mexico,* tr. by Lesley B. Simpson, Berkeley, Calif., 1966; Rubén Vargas Ugarte, *Historia de la iglesia en el Perú,* 5 vols., Burgos, 1953–62; Antonio Ybot León, *La iglesia y los eclesiásticos españoles en la empresa de Indias,* 2 vols., Barcelona, 1954.

MARGARET E. CRAHAN

CATHOLIC CHURCH (NATIONAL PERIOD). The formal religious commitment of most Latin Americans is to the Roman Catholic Church. Church sources claim 241 million Catholics out of the 268 million inhabitants of the twenty republics. The proportion of Catholics for the four largest countries is cited as 92 percent in Argentina, 90 percent in Brazil, 95 percent in Colombia, and 87 percent in Mexico. What might be interpreted as near unanimity, however, is hardly an accurate indicator of the dynamics of contemporary Catholicism. Catholics engaged in active practice of religion are fewer by far in number, with notable percentage differences according to country, age group, sex, and social condition. The chief social and political significance of the figures given above probably is that they show the lack in Latin America of the genuine and marked diversity of creeds found in Europe and North America. This relative absence of diversity must be taken into consideration as one of the most important background elements in any explanation of the development and present condition of the Catholic Church in Latin America.

An analysis of the church is undertaken here in two parts. The first deals with the evolution of the political and legal status of the church. The second offers some appraisal of the institutional force and influence of the Catholic Church in Latin America today.

Legal status. There are variations in status according to the public law of each nation, but three main categories establish essential distinctions: (1) an official church recognized either by constitutional stipulation, as in Argentina, or by concordat, as in Colombia; (2) a church separate from the state and enjoying a broad freedom of action, as in Chile; (3) a church separate and operating under substantial legal restrictions on its activity, as in Mexico. These are existing solutions to long-standing problems that date from the beginning of the republican period in Spanish-speaking America.

While some parallel problems arose occasionally in imperial Brazil, the more dramatic conflicts have taken place in the Spanish-speaking republics. The conflicts originated not over whether there should be church-state ties but rather over what the nature of those ties should be.

Regalism is the term generally used to describe the position taken by most of the early republican governments regarding the church. In the regalist view the church is a public institution. Accordingly, its officials must be accountable to public authority, and its real property and other resources must be employed in response to public policy. In the colonial era the crown had exercised full control over the church (*see* PATRONATO REAL). The early governments claimed the same power. Whereas many Latin American churchmen accepted the claim, the official attitude of the church, especially at Rome, opposed it. The Roman position was that the royal rights of control over church personnel and property had inhered in the person of the monarch by specific grants from Popes Alexander VI and Julius II at the beginning of the colonial period. As personal prerogatives of the King these rights could not be handed on to successor authorities. The republican answer was that the rights inhered in sovereignty itself. Resulting conflicts touched on several aspects of national and international church administration but endured longest in connection with episcopal appointments. Throughout the nineteenth century most governments insisted on some voice in the selection of bishops. For example, the Argentine constitution of 1853 (*see* CONSTITUTION OF 1853: ARGENTINA) spells out the roles of the President, the Senate, and the Supreme Court in the selection process as a part of the public law of the nation. Rome resisted this and similar assertions in other national constitutions as an unacceptable unilateral imposition of a solution. However, a large measure of harmony was often obtained in practice through a modus vivendi between the two parties. At the same time the church made evident its strong preference for the formal bilateral settlement of these questions through a concordat, as with Colombia in 1887. Much more recently, bilateral settlement has been possible through an instrument designated simply *acuerdo* (agreement), as in Venezuela in 1964 and Argentina in 1966, which grants the government a veto power over appointments but leaves initiative in the matter with the church.

In the nineteenth century the position of the church was also involved in questions of freedom of conscience and worship and eventually in the issue of separation of church and state. Most early constitutions honored freedom of conscience, but many recognized only a qualified freedom of worship. This could come as a limitation of public worship to Catholics (while others were obliged to worship in private) or some other device that restricted without denying other forms of worship. A growing liberalism, however, sought to eliminate this favored position of the Catholic faith. More important, challenges to traditional doctrine and practice made the church an issue in the prolonged civil strife of several countries, notably Mexico, Colombia, Ecuador, and Venezuela.

One result of the strife was to establish alliances between church forces and those of conservatism. Where the political competition developed between Liberal and Conservative parties, the Conservatives became, with few exceptions, the champions of the church and in turn received the church's endorsement or other form of approval. Today the Liberal-Conservative dichotomy has largely withered away, and with it the church-Conservative alliance, but at least in Chile and Colombia the Conservatives remained the church party well into the twentieth century (*see* CONSERVATIVE PARTY: CHILE; CONSERVATIVE PARTY: COLOMBIA).

Contemporary social critics reacted to the civil-ecclesiastical issues of the nineteenth century in a variety of ways, of which three main trends are found in the works of Francisco BILBAO (1823–1865), José Manuel Estrada (1842–1894), and Miguel Antonio CARO (1843–1909). The Chilean journalist Bilbao saw Catholicism as the fundamental underpinning of a social system that was evil and cruel. Justice demanded the destruction of the system and its replacement with one that was consistent with the promises of the wars of liberation. The necessary preliminary to this revolution was the removal of the influence of the church. Exactly the opposite view was taken by the liberal Estrada, law professor at the University of Buenos Aires. For him the liberal, progressive society that he believed to be developing in Argentina needed a strong moral force as its base. He saw this necessary force in the Catholic religion. The Colombian statesman Caro helped to weld together in the 1886 constitution (*see* CONSTITUTION OF 1886: COLOMBIA) the forces of conservatism and Catholicism. Caro saw the latter as a kind of moral and social cement to hold together a society to be reconstructed out of the divisiveness and fragmentation that a long period of civil strife had produced. Caro, moreover, linked the reconstruction to a return to Spanish values as the natural inheritance of Latin America, values which, according to him, an exotic liberalism had been seeking to supplant.

The concerns of these men were formulated vis-à-vis the nineteenth-century church with its emphasis on dogmatic unity and its seemingly monolithic structure. Neither friend nor foe views the church in the same light today. The rigidity of past positions on the part of both the church and its critics has given way, especially since the Second Vatican Council. This change has left the church a less polemical subject than before, but it has not necessarily reduced its institutional vitality.

Institutional significance. Drastically altered relations between episcopacy, clergy, and laity are generally supposed to mark present-day Catholicism with a diminished role for authority and greater individual freedom, less indoctrination and more "conscientization" (learning), fewer legalisms and greater social dedication. It is hoped that the training of the clergy will make them knowledgeable not only about theology but also about sociology and economics. Many concrete examples can be cited to support these suppositions. These examples must be understood, however, in the light of two important background considerations.

One is that Latin America has been going through several decades of still-inconclusive social change. It would be strange if the church were immune to the ferment. Hence it is logical to find priests and other church personnel engaged in helping to organize labor unions, student groups, peasant cooperatives, low-cost housing projects, and campaigns against illiteracy. The other consideration is that in Catholic church structure responsibility for actions and hence authority for decisions reside in the bishop of the diocese. This authoritarian factor need not militate against social change, but it can have other consequences.

In general bishops have given their collective support to programs of social change. National hierarchies, as in Chile and Brazil, have endorsed progressive positions and have sought to stimulate the civic conscience. In consonance with papal pronouncements the Latin American bishops' meeting of 1968 (Second Latin American Episcopal Conference; *see* CONSEJO EPISCOPAL LATINOAMERICANO) committed the church to work for social improvement as well as religious renewal. Where difficulties have arisen, they have generally come as clashes between the authority of a bishop and the actions or commitments of clergy. The most famous of these clashes involved the Colombian priest Camilo TORRES, who joined a guerrilla force in 1965 and was killed in 1966. His name has become a symbol for "revolutionary" clergy. Groups of such clergy organized on various bases exist today in Chile, Colombia, Peru, Argentina, and Brazil. It is impossible to generalize about them beyond the statement that they are impatient with the rate of change their ecclesiastical superiors have accepted.

In the main, however, more conventional relations between bishops, priests, and laity continue to characterize church organization. Social impact continues or is expanding in the maintenance of hospitals, clinics, orphanages, and so on, in which the religious orders have traditionally had a major role. A somewhat recent innovation has been social science research sponsored by national hierarchies or by certain dioceses. The religious orders, as exemplified by the Jesuits' Centro Bellarmino in Chile and the Center for Research and Social Action organization throughout the hemisphere, have also contributed substantially to this activity. Research has probably made churchmen more aware of the magnitude of social problems in areas where church doctrine is also involved, notably in matters of marriage and family. If the traditional doctrinal opposition to contraception has not changed, there is undoubtedly greater sophistication within the church regarding the population problem and the economic, social, and health factors affecting the family. Moreover, church concern for these factors seems to have supplanted the one-time concentration on canon law aspects of marriage.

The traditional Catholic role in education has also been reexamined in many countries with resultant expansion in certain fields and with controversy both within and outside the church on what the role should be. The principal activity was in the maintenance of primary and secondary schools to a large extent through the religious orders (Catholic but not necessarily parochial schools as in North America), with the most conspicuous element at the *colegio* (preuniversity) level. The public school systems of a number of countries have also been open to religious doctrine classes. At the university level the Catholic institution is somewhat of an innovation, since in most countries the Catholic university has made its appearance only in the last fifty years. Official sources list fourteen pontifical, or papal-connected, universities, and the number of institutions sponsored by religious orders is rising.

Numerous controversies over the whole range of educational endeavor can only be summarized here. On the one hand, extraecclesiastical critics maintain that in modern society the education function is so central in importance that the state cannot share this responsibility with others. At the university level, for example, they stress the fact that university degrees are an important part of certification for the public practice of a profession. Church spokesmen emphasize traditional Catholic contributions and the pluralism of modern society. On the other hand, intrachurch critics dwell on the obligation to diffuse evangelical effort throughout society and question whether church personnel and resources should be concentrated in the narrower confines of school and university. It is probable that the debate will continue. At the same time, as long as the church makes these resources available in societies where demands for education are increasing, it is likely that a major church role will continue. Even in some nations where legal constraints operate against religious orders the role seems to be prospering.

National differences in these matters and others continue to be noticeable. Nevertheless, the church in Latin America within the past two decades has acquired a new kind of organizational unity. This is in the Consejo Episcopal Latinoamericano (CELAM), which brings together the various national entities, offers a center in its Bogotá headquarters for consultation, and maintains expert staff to study, evaluate, and inform on questions of common concern. CELAM is not a governing body of the Latin American church, but it can often be regarded as the collective voice of those who hold traditional governing power in the church.

Bibliography. Francisco Bilbao, "Sociabilidad Chilena," in *Obras Completas,* vol. I, Santiago, 1897; Hélder Câmara, *Revolução dentro de la Paz,* Rio de Janeiro, 1968; Juan Casiello, *Iglesia y estado en la Argentina,* Buenos Aires, 1948; Consejo Episcopal Latinoamericano, *Documentos de Medellín,* Bogotá, 1969; José Manuel Estrada, *La iglesia y el estado,* Buenos Aires, 1929; Germán Guzmán Campos, *Camilo, el cura guerrillero,* 2d ed., Bogotá, 1967; Melchor Ocampo, *La religión, la iglesia y el clero,* 2d ed., Mexico City, 1958; Dalmacio Vélez Sarsfield, *Derecho público eclesiástico,* Buenos Aires, 1871.

JOHN J. KENNEDY

CATTLE INDUSTRY (ARGENTINA). To most people the clearest mental picture of Argentina is the flat and fertile PAMPA with its cattle. Such an impression is not without firm foundation, since Argentina has had an enormous cattle population for centuries. Tough Andalusian and Portuguese longhorn cattle were introduced in the latter part of the sixteenth century. With little competition from indigenous herbivores for their forage and with few natural enemies, feral cattle multiplied rapidly. There are estimates that there were more than 30 million of these wild cattle by the end of the eighteenth century. This lean stock with its bony frame and long legs, yielding only a small quantity of tough meat, bore little resemblance to modern breeds of cattle, which were introduced in the nineteenth century. However, the wild cattle served their purpose well, for in the seventeenth and eighteenth centuries Europe demanded thick cattle hides and Argentina could supply large quantities. During this period the GAUCHO, Argentina's nomadic mestizo horseman, reached the zenith of his importance. It was he who, risking danger from Indian attack, ventured onto the yet-unclaimed pampa to kill and skin the cattle, usually leaving the carcasses to wild dogs. Toward the end of the eighteenth century dried and salted meat began to grow in importance as an export, primarily to nations with large slave populations, such as Brazil. At this time cattle *estancias* (ranches) began to be carved from the pampa.

The industrial revolution had great direct and indirect effects upon the Argentine cattle industry. In the nineteenth century, often through the efforts of a growing number of Anglo-Argentine cattlemen, modern British beef breeds were introduced. In addition, barbed-wire fences were strung, new pasture grasses were sown, and in many other ways a more scientific approach to cattle production emerged. In 1876 the first successful shipment of refrigerated fresh beef crossed the Atlantic, and Argentina entered a new era of economic development. It soon became the chief purveyor of beef to Great Britain, and it was that nation which largely organized the Argentine meat-packing industry as well as the railroads that carried cattle to slaughter and the shipping lines that transported the beef overseas.

Modern cattle spread quickly over the pampa, and a specialized cattle industry evolved. The poorly drained and consequently low-quality grasslands of the southeastern pampa developed as the breeding zone, while the better-drained, drier areas of the northwestern pampa, where alfalfa could be grown, became the fattening zone. Although even today many cattle are born and raised to slaughter weights in the breeding zone, a large percentage of yearlings are sold and sent by train to be fattened on the alfalfa pastures of the fattening zone. After reaching maturity, usually in two years, cattle are transported to *frigoríficos* (meat-packing plants; *see* FRIGORÍFICO), situated at a port. The majority of *frigoríficos* are within the metropolitan area of Buenos Aires, but important plants also are found in Rosario and Bahía Blanca.

Originally beef was sent to Europe as frozen quarters, but as soon as it became technologically feasible to ship the quarters chilled, this type of beef, favored by the British consumer, dominated international trade. For most of the twentieth century beef has been Argentina's most important export, particularly during the two world wars. In most of this period Great Britain remained Argentina's major customer for beef, but after World War II the situation began to change. Britain began to negotiate preferential trade agreements with nations such as Australia and Ireland, both with rapidly expanding cattle industries. This forced Argentina to turn increasingly to the European continent for markets, and today that area takes well over half the nation's beef exports. Continental Europe's demands for beef differ from that of Great Britain. Leaner meat is desired, in the form of processed and frozen cuts, not chilled quarters.

The Argentine beef industry is beset by many problems. Its traditional trade partner, Great Britain, is buying beef elsewhere. Italy and West Germany, now important buyers, are within the European Economic Community and turn increasingly to France and the Netherlands for beef because of preferential trade agreements. Since World War II Argentine governmental policies have favored industry over agriculture, and

cattlemen claim that taxes and low profits make investment in their *estancias* unprofitable. Consequently, there has been little effort to fertilize pastures, feed cattle supplementally, engage in herd improvement, and intensify cattle production in other ways as well as to improve the quality of the beef. Packers recognize that foreign markets now demand cuts of beef that are processed, as well as cooked, canned, or frozen, where the cattle are slaughtered. Yet they will not make the investment to change unless they are promised greater profits, something the Argentine government has denied them. Meanwhile, since the Argentine population is growing at a more rapid rate than the cattle population, domestic consumption of beef is taking a greater percentage of total production. For the past two decades, to meet export commitments, the Argentine government periodically has been forced to decree meatless days. Until greater incentives are found to improve cattle production and meat packing, Argentina will encounter difficulty in maintaining its foreign market for beef.

Bibliography. Alfonso Arnolds, *Geográfica económica argentina,* Buenos Aires, 1963; Horacio C. E. Giberti, *Historia económica de la ganadería argentina,* Buenos Aires, 1961; Simon G. Hanson, *Argentine Meat and the British Market,* Palo Alto, Calif., 1938; Mauricio Lebedinsky, *Estructura de la ganadería: Histórica y actual,* Buenos Aires, 1967; Morton D. Winsberg, *Modern Cattle Breeds in Argentina,* Lawrence, Kans., 1968.

MORTON D. WINSBERG

CAUCA VALLEY. The Cauca Valley is a structural depression running in a north-south direction between the Cordillera Occidental and the Cordillera Central of the Colombian Andes. It has a length of approximately 250 miles and reaches a maximum width of 25 miles. Although the valley extends into ANTIOQUIA, as a separate cultural region it has a northern terminus in the city of Cartago and a southern terminus in Popayán. The Cauca River, which eventually joins the MAGDALENA RIVER, flows through the center of the valley. Rich volcanic ash fills the upper portion of the basin, providing excellent soil for agriculture. The climate is somewhat modified by the height of the valley, which is 5,500 feet at Popayán and drops to approximately 3,000 feet at Cali.

Europeans first entered the valley in 1536 under the command of Sebastián de BENALCÁZAR, who founded Cali, designating it the center for commercial activities in the region. In the seventeenth and eighteenth centuries, however, the valley was dominated by interests in Popayán, and most of the valley was pastoralized. After 1850 a stagnant economic situation was enlivened by the emergence of a modernizing elite, composed of immigrant and native families, which diversified and modernized agricultural production, improved communications, and lobbied for an improved transportation network.

The completion of a railroad between the valley and the Pacific port of Buenaventura in 1914 stimulated economic development in the upper portion. Today most of the land is still used for extensive cattle production. Nevertheless, there has been enormous investment in more intensive agriculture, particularly sugarcane. Most of Colombia's sugar is now produced in the region, and large quantities of cotton also are raised. Industrialization has gone on rapidly, and Cali, the region's most dynamic city, grew in population from 200,000 in 1950 to almost 1 million in 1972. The Cauca Valley contributes about 20 percent of Colombia's industrial production, the principal products being food, chemicals, metals and machinery, and paper. Since 1954 economic and social planning has been coordinated through the CORPORACIÓN REGIONAL AUTÓNOMA DEL VALLE DEL CAUCA, which also has undertaken flood control projects as well as land reclamation and hydroelectric development.

MORTON D. WINSBERG AND JAMES H. NEAL

CAUDILLO. Spanish term for "leader," often used in Spanish America to denote a strong man or dictator. The word is derived from the Late Latin *capitellum,* a diminutive of *caput* (head). The Spanish American *caudillo* is frequently identified as a military chieftain, and it is true that many outstanding *caudillos,* particularly in the first half of the nineteenth century, won national or regional power as a result of their exploits as leaders of armed men. Among these were *caudillos* who had distinguished themselves during the wars for independence, such as José Antonio PÁEZ of Venezuela and Andrés SANTA CRUZ of Bolivia, or who were leaders of provincial armed bands in the RÍO DE LA PLATA region, such as the redoubtable Juan Facundo Quiroga of La Rioja Province in Argentina. However, the term can also be applied to autocratic civilian leaders, such as Rafael NÚÑEZ of Colombia and Hipólito YRIGOYEN of Argentina.

HELEN DELPAR

CAVALCANTI, EMILIANO DI. *See* DI CAVALCANTI, EMILIANO.

CAVIEDES, JUAN DEL VALLE Y (1650?-?1697). Spanish-born Peruvian poet. Juan del Valle y Caviedes, usually referred to as Caviedes, was born in the Andalusian village of Porcuna, Jaén Province, but at an early age made his way to the Viceroyalty of Peru, where he spent the remainder of his life, dying before the end of the seventeenth century. Most of the information on his life comes from his poems, particularly an autobiographical piece that he wrote to Sor JUANA INÉS DE LA CRUZ. His testament, dated March 26, 1683, has also been discovered.

Because of the caustic nature of the satire in many of his poems, Caviedes's works were not published during his lifetime, but they did circulate surreptitiously in manuscript form. The satirical poems particularly, with their acerbic attacks on many aspects of Peruvian viceregal society, show his admiration for the famous Spanish poet Francisco de Quevedo. Caviedes's most famous collection, the *Diente del Parnaso,* contains some fifty poems that attack many aspects of seventeenth-century Peruvian society, especially medical doctors who are considered to be the messengers and agents of death. Among the doctors attacked by Caviedes in his poems were some of the most famous physicians of viceregal Lima: Dr. Francisco de Bermejo y Roldán, who was the Viceroy's physician, and Francisco Vargas Machuca, rector of the University of San Marcos and official doctor of the Inquisition (*see* INQUISITION, HOLY OFFICE OF THE). Caviedes's verses also attack professionals of all types, including lawyers,

priests, and tailors, people with physical deformities, and women, especially ugly women and prostitutes.

More than 300 poems were written by Caviedes on a variety of subjects. Particularly noteworthy are the poems on religious and amorous themes and some occasional poems written in honor of famous persons or for special events. His poetic production is typical of baroque conceptism, for many of his works are filled with satire, plays on words, conceits and puns, allusions, and popular subject matter. Caviedes was also the author of three short dramatic pieces: *Bayle del amor alcalde, Bayle del amor tahur,* and *Bayle cantado del amor médico.*

DANIEL R. REEDY

CAXIAS, DUQUE DE (LUIS ALVES DE LIMA E SILVA, 1803–1880). Brazilian soldier and Conservative politician. The son of Francisco de Lima e Silva, a prominent general and member of the Regency from 1831 to 1835, Luis Alves de Lima e Silva studied at the Military School in Rio de Janeiro and saw his first action in the struggle for independence in 1823. In 1840 he was appointed President and military commander of the rebellious province of Maranhão, re-establishing peace there in 1841 after seizure of the town of Caxias, for which he was granted the title Barão (later Conde, Marquês, and Duque) de Caxias. The following year he successfully ended Liberal rebellions in the provinces of Minas Gerais and São Paulo, and from 1842 to 1845 he commanded imperial forces in the victorious struggle against the Farroupilhas in the province of Rio Grande do Sul (*see* FARROUPILHA REVOLT). In 1867 he succeeded President Bartolomé MITRE of Argentina as commander of Allied forces in the PARAGUAYAN WAR, resigning from that position in January 1869 after the capture of Asunción and the dispersion of Paraguayan forces.

Caxias was a member of the Conservative party and held high positions in government, including a seat in the Senate from 1845 until his death. Appointed Minister of War in the Cabinet of the Marquês de Paraná in 1855, he became President of the Council of Ministers (Prime Minister) in 1856 following the latter's death, holding that office again in the years 1861–1862 and 1875–1878.

ROBERT CONRAD

CELAM. *See* CONSEJO EPISCOPAL LATINOAMERICANO.

CELAYA, BATTLES OF. Two battles fought in the Mexican city of Celaya, generally considered the turning point in the contest between Venustiano CARRANZA and Francisco VILLA. According to the *carrancista* general Álvaro OBREGÓN, the strategic importance of Celaya, which is located in the state of Guanajuato, lay in its being a railroad junction and an important agricultural center that could supply large armies. In the first battle (April 6–7, 1915), Obregón's forces, consisting of 6,000 cavalry and 5,000 infantry who had 86 machine guns and 13 cannons, faced approximately 20,000 *villistas,* mainly cavalry, with 22 cannons. At first the victory seemed to be Villa's, but he was ultimately unsuccessful, apparently because he lacked a general reserve and failed to engage in maneuvers in order to obtain the advantage in at least one sector. Villa lost 1,800 dead, approximately 3,000 wounded, and 500 taken prisoner; Obregón's casualties were 557 dead and 365 wounded. In the second battle (April 13–15, 1915), Obregón's army consisted of 8,000 cavalry and 7,000 infantry. Despite the rash charges of the *villista* cavalry, 4,000 of Villa's men were killed, 5,000 were wounded, and 8,000 were captured; Obregón estimated his casualties at 138 dead and 414 wounded. The Battles of Celaya are regarded as the most important in Mexican history because of the large number of combatants and the heavy casualties suffered by Villa.

The Battles of Trinidad and León, which took place in Guanajuato from April 29 to June 5, 1915, also resulted in a defeat for Villa. An apparently important factor in the outcome was the failure of Emiliano ZAPATA to cut Obregón's communications with Veracruz, where Carranza's headquarters was located. In addition, Villa did not follow the advice of Gen. Felipe Angeles that he force Obregón to move away from his base. It was during these battles, on June 3, that Obregón lost his right arm.

MOISÉS GONZÁLEZ NAVARRO

CENTER OF HIGH MILITARY STUDIES. *See* CENTRO DE ALTOS ESTUDIOS MILITARES.

CENTRAL AMERICA, FEDERATION OF. The Federation of Central America was the national successor to the Spanish colonial Kingdom, or Captaincy General, of Guatemala. After declaring their independence from Spain in 1821 and briefly joining the Mexican empire under Agustín de ITURBIDE, five provinces (Guatemala, El Salvador, Honduras, Nicaragua, and Costa Rica) opted for separate nationhood in 1823, adopted a republican form of government, and drafted a constitution creating the Federation of Central America.

The new government faced overwhelming problems. Fear of tyranny led the constitution framers to create a figurehead President, a largely advisory Senate, and an all-powerful Assembly. Guatemalan Conservatives expected that the large delegation assured to their state in the Assembly would perpetuate their colonial preponderance in government; Liberals hoped the strength of the provinces would neutralize the influence of Guatemala. The national government lacked resources adequate to overcome ideological divisions, regional jealousies, and individual ambitions. Want of revenue, dispersion of power to the states, and lack of a regular force for police actions undercut its effectiveness.

The Federation soon sacrificed any advantage gained from a bloodless origin. A tainted election made Manuel José ARCE President, and soon his actions led the Liberals to charge betrayal. Liberal partisans gathered in El Salvador and under Francisco MORAZÁN invaded Guatemala, overthrew Arce (April 1829), exiled him and his collaborators, and restored both Guatemalan and national governments to Liberal control. The following year Morazán was elected President; he was reelected in 1834, when death removed the President-elect, José Cecilio del VALLE.

Morazán's federal administration and ideologically related state governments inaugurated thoroughgoing programs of Liberal reform, a major aspect of which was shearing the Catholic Church of wealth and temporal power. This breach of tradition and the rapid pace and drastic character of other changes disturbed and scandalized conservative citizens of all levels.

Other circumstances contributed to unrest. Doubts arose that the nation was capable of maintaining its territorial integrity when, following the secession of Chiapas, Great Britain scorned Central American assertions of proprietorship over Belize (British Honduras), Mexico forced an arrangement on Soconusco that allowed its subsequent incorporation, Colombia seized the Bocas del Toro region, and the British re-established their influence on the Mosquito Coast. Arce's military threat to regain the Presidency, accompanied by rebellions by Vicente Domínguez and Ramón Guzmán at Trujillo and Omoa, fed fears that the republic might succumb to subversion. Dissatisfaction with the situation of the federal capital was not stilled by its removal from Guatemala City, nor did a revision of the constitution satisfy the widely held conviction that the federal system required an extensive overhaul.

Poverty prevented the government from improving its power base. A foreign loan contracted in 1824 to launch the new republic was floated only in part, and the Arce government squandered the proceeds. Appropriation by the states of the federal revenues deprived the national government of expected income and forced it, especially when burdened with extraordinary expenditures for military operations, to levy assessments on the states that only Guatemala paid regularly and to exact forced loans from wealthy nationals and resident foreigners. With its credit gone, the patience of many inhabitants exhausted, and foreign claimants threatening action, the government lacked the means to discharge its functions effectively.

The appearance of cholera in Guatemala in 1837 threw an already distressed people into panic. Popular uprisings, countered by force, soon engulfed the union in civil war. States seceded, elections were not held to fill federal offices, and by 1838 for practical purposes the Federation had ceased to exist. Morazán made a last desperate effort to subdue the enemies of the union by military action, but he was decisively defeated by José Rafael CARRERA at Guatemala City in March 1840, and shortly thereafter he went into exile. His return and attempt by force to restore the Federation ended with betrayal and execution in Costa Rica in 1842.

Although the Federation commanded little loyalty during its lifetime, the ideal of union did not die with its disappearance. Several subsequent attempts to reestablish a union reached the agreement stage, and a few even began a tentative operation, but none embraced all five Central American countries and none long survived. Union by military conquest was also attempted several times but never with success. The most promising of the collaborative movements appear to be the current limited association called the ORGANIZACIÓN DE ESTADOS CENTROAMERICANOS (ODECA) and the economic arrangement called the CENTRAL AMERICAN COMMON MARKET. Any optimism these ventures may inspire, however, must be tempered by the record of failure that attended all earlier unification attempts.

Bibliography. Pedro Joaquín Chamorro Zelaya, *Historia de la federación de la América Central, 1823–1840,* Madrid, 1951; Alberto Herrarte, *La unión de Centroamérica, tragedia y esperanza: Ensayo político-social sobre la realidad de Centroamérica,* Guatemala City, 1955; Mary P. Holleran, *Church and State in Guatemala,* New York, 1949; Thomas L. Karnes,

The Failure of Union: Central America, 1824–1960, Chapel Hill, N.C., 1961; Alejandro Marure, *Bosquejo histórico de las revoluciones de Centro-América,* 2 vols., Guatemala City, 1877–78; Salvador Mendieta, *La enfermedad de Centro-América,* 3 vols., Barcelona, 1934; Mario Rodríguez, *A Palmerstonian Diplomat in Central America: Frederick Chatfield, Esq.,* Tucson, 1964; Robert S. Smith, "Financing the Central American Federation, 1821–1838," *Hispanic American Historical Review,* vol. XLIII, no. 4, November 1963, pp. 483–510.

WILLIAM J. GRIFFITH

CENTRAL AMERICAN COMMON MARKET (MERCADO COMÚN CENTROAMERICANO; CACM). Intergovernmental system that developed under the patronage of the United Nations ECONOMIC COMMISSION FOR LATIN AMERICA (ECLA). The ministers of economy from the five countries of Central America, organized in 1952 as the Central American Committee on Economic Cooperation (CCE), spearheaded the movement. With technical assistance from ECLA, CCE made a series of background studies; established two regional service institutions, an Advanced School of Public Administration in Costa Rica and an Institute for Industrial Research and Technology in Guatemala; and drafted two agreements, a multilateral treaty for attaining free trade in ten years and a convention allowing designation of certain enterprises as "integration industries" so that they might enjoy protected access to the regional market, both of which became operative on July 9, 1959.

Guatemala, El Salvador, and Honduras threatened the cooperative fabric early in 1960 when they formed a separate economic association to achieve a common market within five years. CCE hastened to draft new agreements to reconcile the apparent dissatisfaction. It presented eight multilateral treaties, three of which became operative. The key instrument in this series was a General Treaty of Central American Economic Integration, signed in December 1960 by all the countries except Costa Rica. Ratification by Guatemala, El Salvador, and Nicaragua made it effective June 3, 1961; Honduras ratified in 1962, and Costa Rica in 1963.

This treaty replaced the previous similar instrument. It shortened to five years the period for reaching the common market, constituted the ministers of economy as a Central American Economic Council, created an Executive Council to administer the general treaty, and created a Permanent Secretariat to supervise all regional integrations and to service the Economic and Executive Councils. It also provided for a Central American Bank for Economic Integration (CABEI) that was set up by a simultaneously signed convention. An agreement establishing a Central American Clearing House within the CABEI was signed in June 1961.

Progress toward free trade was rapid, but it was not attained by the goal year 1966. By that time most items figuring in regional commerce were free-traded, and most countries had established uniform tariff duties on nearly all goods. The exceptions in both cases, however, represented so large a proportion of the total trade and so important a segment of total revenue that the appearance of near completeness was in part illusory. Overt results of the effort, nevertheless, were impressive. The value of all exports and imports increased sharply, but most significant, the share of regional trade within the total increased at more than twice the overall rate. Moreover, growth in the volume of trade was accompanied in three of the five countries by a decline in export concentration.

Despite its impressive showing the CACM encountered obstacles. A major difficulty was that the regional annual deficit in the balance of payments increased from an average of $52 million during the CACM's first three years to $175 million during its sixth and seventh. An important contributing cause was a drop in agricultural prices and a corresponding deterioration in the terms of trade, but adjustments to regional integration also played a role.

The crisis produced by the growing deficits in the balance of payments emphasized the fact that the CACM benefited participating members unevenly. It was charged, for example, that commodities fabricated in Central America of imported materials and only slightly enhanced in value were being sold within the region at prices artificially elevated by a common protective tariff, thereby depriving the purchasing countries of tariff revenues formerly collected on similar imported articles. The CACM area has not yet felt the full impact of import substitution, but as the trend develops, it will inevitably mean higher prices and a further disturbing effect on the balance of payments.

Attempts to correct balance-of-payments deficits and loss of customs revenues revealed a further weakness. A protocol signed at San José in June 1968 sharply increased regional tariffs on nonessential goods, but commercial interests delayed ratification because resultant higher prices on affected goods would reduce sales volume. Noting this inaction, Nicaragua unilaterally reimposed preexisting tariffs (1969) but rescinded the action under pressure.

One other incident revealed the fragile nature of economic unity. The so-called FOOTBALL WAR of 1969 between El Salvador and Honduras temporarily disrupted the CACM, and although the members formally resubscribed in December 1969, Honduras appears determined to use the incident to bargain for improved status. The questions remain whether conflicts can be successfully reconciled and whether interest groups and individual states will forgo immediate advantage for a long-term gain to allow the movement to proceed. *See also* REGIONAL INTEGRATION.

Bibliography. James D. Cochrane, *The Politics of Regional Integration: The Central American Case,* Tulane Studies in Political Science, vol. XII, New Orleans, 1969; Franklin D. Parker, *The Central American Republics,* New York, 1964; Joseph Pincus, *The Central American Common Market,* Washington, 1962; Mario Rodríguez, *Central America,* Englewood Cliffs, N.J., 1965.

WILLIAM J. GRIFFITH

CENTRAL AMERICAN COURT OF JUSTICE. Device for the peaceful resolution of controversies, created by the treaty structure adopted by the Central American countries at the Washington Conference of 1907. Its five justices, one elected by each national legislature for a five-year term, drew salaries from a common treasury to which each country contributed. It sat in Cartago, Costa Rica, until destruction of the city by earthquake in 1910 forced a move to San José. The Court was constituted as a supranational body. To it the members pledged "to submit all controversies or questions which may arise among them." It was to remain above political and personal influence and represent the "national conscience of Central America."

The Court's authority and integrity were soon tested. When revolution in Honduras in 1908 threatened a general war, it intervened successfully and averted hostilities. It debased itself, however, when the justices acted as partisan representatives of their countries and ultimately accepted the illegal replacement of a colleague after a change of government. It forfeited its last vestige of repute when it ruled in the BRYAN-CHA-MORRO TREATY case in 1917 that the canal agreement between Nicaragua and the United States injured both Costa Rica and El Salvador but declined to declare the treaty void. Nicaragua ignored the decision and withdrew from the Court. It expired the following year.

The ORGANIZACIÓN DE ESTADOS CENTROAMERICANOS (ODECA) has incorporated the regional court ideal. The revised charter of 1965 established a new Central American Court of Justice.   WILLIAM J. GRIFFITH

CENTRO DE ALTOS ESTUDIOS MILITARES (CENTER OF HIGH MILITARY STUDIES; CAEM). School created in 1958 through the efforts of Gen. José del Carmen Marín for the purpose of preparing the Peruvian high command for national defense. However, CAEM's orientation was altered almost immediately, and it became a school for the study of social, political, and economic questions. The syllabus pays a good deal of attention to history, international relations, the social sciences, geography, and economic planning. The faculty, including both full-time and guest lecturers, contains civilian intellectuals and university professors of a definite left-wing orientation. A significant number of them, for example, have had connections with the Movimiento Social Progresista (MSP), a loosely organized group of leftist intellectuals.

CAEM's deviation from the traditional concept of military training stems from the belief that the nation is threatened as much by internal socioeconomic conflicts as it is by external aggression. Therefore, the officer corps must be made aware of those conflicts and be asked to seek solutions to them before they endanger the nation's security. As a result, CAEM has created a socially conscious officer corps convinced that reforms are essential to prevent political violence and social conflict. Because of this concern the armed forces lent their support to the progressive Fernando BELAÚNDE TERRY in 1963. However, his failure to implement reforms, and a concern over growing political tensions proved to be two important reasons for the establishment of a military government in 1968. That government's continuing implementation of reformist legislation attests to the widespread influence CAEM has had on the armed forces.   ORAZIO A. CICCARELLI

CERRO CORPORATION. Enterprise formerly known as the Cerro de Pasco Mining Corporation, launched in 1902 by a group of United States financiers headed by J. P. Morgan. Its initial investment of $10 million was intended to exploit newly discovered copper deposits in the central highlands of Peru. The creation of the corporation inaugurated a new era of mining development in Peru. Its capital resources, together with a very liberal mining code, quickly made it the largest

single operation in Peru. The corporation's interests include mining, smelting, refining, milling, railroads, port facilities, hydroelectric plants, and, up to 1969, agriculture and stock-raising properties. It became the largest producer of copper, lead, and zinc, with sales of nearly $160 million and a labor force of 15,000. In 1960 it acquired a 22 percent interest in the Southern Peru Copper Corporation, which is exploiting one of the world's largest copper deposits.

The Cerro Corporation's employment practices were relatively good. Nevertheless, its extensive economic power and its traditionally poor community relations made it an easy target for nationalists. As a result, the corporation's history in Peru was marked by continual labor and community tension, often leading to bloodshed. The worst outbreak occurred in 1930, when clashes between strikers and Army troops were responsible for the death of two American citizens and a score of Peruvians. The corporation's difficulties repeatedly strained United States–Peruvian relations. Nonetheless, its economic status was never seriously threatened by any Peruvian government. Even the 1969 expropriation of its agricultural holdings in the central highlands, valued at $12 million, did not herald a drastic future diminution of the corporation's economic power in Peru. In 1972 the company offered to sell its mining and smelting operations in Peru to the government, but withdrew its offer in 1973 amid charges of bad faith on both sides.

ORAZIO A. CICCARELLI

CERVETTI, SERGIO (1940–   ). Uruguayan composer. Cervetti was born in Dolores. After starting his training in his native country, he went to the United States, where he studied with Ernst Křenek at the Peabody Conservatory in Baltimore. In 1969 he lived in Berlin as an artist in residence of the Deutscher Akademischer Austauschdienst, and later he joined the faculty of Brooklyn College. He has written a sonata for piano, a divertimento for string quartet, *Five Episodes* (1965) for violin, cello, and piano, and *Zinctum* (1967) for string quartet.

JUAN A. ORREGO-SALAS

CGT. *See* CONFEDERACIÓN GENERAL DE TRABAJO.

CHACABUCO, BATTLE OF. First major engagement fought by José de SAN MARTÍN on Chilean soil after crossing the Andes from Argentina. It took place on February 12, 1817, in the hills of Chacabuco, a natural obstacle along the route that led from Santiago to the Andean passes. San Martín's forces, numbering about 3,500, had met only scattered resistance on the way, but when news of their approach reached Santiago, royalist units marched out to make a stand at Chacabuco. It was a potentially favorable position, but San Martín hastened to give battle before the Spanish could properly concentrate their forces.

Early on February 12, one patriot division under the Chilean leader Bernardo O'HIGGINS moved directly against the enemy while a larger force under the Argentinian Miguel Soler took an alternate route to attack from the side and rear. Contrary to orders, after a preliminary exchange of fire O'Higgins impetuously launched a frontal assault without waiting for Soler and was repulsed. But San Martín threw himself into the fray; and when Soler's force finally did enter the battle, it was too strong for the outnumbered royalists, who withdrew with heavy losses. Two days later San Martín entered Santiago. Fighting in Chile was not over, for the royalists eventually reorganized their forces and a year later were threatening to retake Santiago. But the threat was dispelled by the decisive victory of San Martín at Maipú on April 5, 1818.

DAVID BUSHNELL

CHACO. Vast, sparsely populated lowland plain in the interior of South America lying mostly within eastern Bolivia, western Paraguay, and northern Argentina. Stretching from the foothills of the ANDES MOUNTAINS to the Paraguay River, the Chaco, or Gran Chaco ("great hunting ground"), is arid to semiarid in the west, becoming humid in the east. The rivers that cross its nearly level surface in braided, often-changing courses overflow annually during the hot, rainy summer and form large, shallow lakes and vast marshy areas. The extent and depth of the flooding decrease in the west. Winters are mild and dry; the land becomes dusty and many watercourses dry up completely.

The natural vegetation reflects these climatic transitions and seasonal changes. In the eastern Chaco there are large marshes and woodlands, including stands of quebracho trees, whose wood contains a very high percentage of the tannin used in tanning leather. In the western Chaco thorny, deciduous wood and brush lands are interrupted by irregular patches of dry, coarse savanna grasses.

The original inhabitants of the Chaco were nomadic tribes of GUARANÍ-speaking hunters. Between 1932 and 1935 Paraguay and Bolivia fought over the Chaco in a war that left both countries exhausted and impoverished (*see* CHACO WAR). Paraguay gained territory, but the known oil reserves, which have never proved as rich as had been expected, remained in Bolivia's possession. With economic development handicapped by climate,

transportation facilities, insects (especially locust plagues), and remoteness from major markets, the main areas of permanent settlement in the Chaco are now on its eastern and southern margins. Notable exceptions are the Mennonite colonies established in the twentieth century by German-speaking farmers (*see* MENNONITES IN PARAGUAY). The main agricultural products of the Chaco are cotton and some food crops. Much of the central and western Chaco is used only for very extensive grazing of low-quality cattle.

DANIEL W. GADE

CHACO WAR. Conflict between Bolivia and Paraguay (1932–1935) over possession of the CHACO north of the Pilcomayo River (Chaco Boreal). The origins of the Chaco War are to be sought in the conflicting boundaries and jurisdictions of the colonial era, when the Chaco was at various times under the authority of the *audiencia* of Charcas (modern Bolivia) and of the Governor of Paraguay. Lack of natural wealth, coupled with hostile Indians and climate, left the area a void buffer zone until the 1880s, when interest in it escalated as a result of Bolivia's loss of its coast to Chile in the WAR OF THE PACIFIC (1879–1883) and Paraguay's territorial losses in the PARAGUAYAN WAR (1864–1870). Bolivia sought a new outlet to the sea via the RÍO DE LA PLATA system and a new sense of national pride. It began erecting *fortines* (small forts) along the Pilcomayo in 1906, penetrating progressively to the southeast. Attempts at arbitration failed, and Paraguay, alarmed by the advance in what it had always considered its patrimony, offered Bolivia a free port on the upper Paraguay River, which Bolivia immediately rejected. Paraguay then began building its own *fortines* to block further Bolivian expansion and settled a large group of Canadian Mennonites in the Chaco to stake an effective claim. *See* MENNONITES IN PARAGUAY.

As armed clashes began in 1927, an arms race was launched in both countries. Bolivia, with a larger population and a larger army led by the German general Hans Kundt, seemed the inevitable victor when actual war began with a battle at Fortín Pitiantuta in June 1932, but the nationalism of the Paraguayans and their renowned fighting qualities prevailed as the conscript Indian soldiers from the Bolivian highlands found themselves unable to cope with the climate and Paraguayan ferocity. Disregarding the advice of many in his Cabinet and the Army command, the Paraguayan president Eusebio AYALA allowed Col. José Félix ESTIGARRIBIA to fight the offensive war he wished to wage against the superior enemy. Estigarribia was a military genius who understood better than Kundt that a war in the Chaco must be one of maneuver rather than siege. Expanding his force from 4,100 to more than 70,000, Estigarribia gradually drove the Bolivians back to the west, capturing almost all their *fortines* and destroying their best units.

In 1935, with Paraguay in control of virtually the entire Chaco to the Bolivian foothills, a truce was agreed upon, though it was unpopular among Paraguayans who sought "total victory." Essentially the same terms were incorporated in the 1938 peace treaty, which gave the lion's share of the disputed territory to the victor. In addition to the catastrophic financial cost of the war for two poor nations, some 50,000 Bolivians and 35,000 Paraguayans died in the conflict. The long-term result of the war for Paraguay was the saddling of

CHACO

the country with a politically minded, victorious army, and for Bolivia the beginning of demands for social change that burst forth in the revolution of 1952.

Bibliography. Carlos José Fernández, *La guerra del Chaco,* 4 vols., Buenos Aires, 1956–; Roberto Querejazo C., *Masamaclay,* La Paz, 1965; David Zook, *The Conduct of the Chaco War,* New Haven, Conn., 1960.

JOHN HOYT WILLIAMS

CHAMORRO, EMILIANO (1871–1966). Nicaraguan Conservative politician and President (1917–1921, 1926). Chamorro was the leading spokesman for Nicaraguan Conservatives during the entire first half of the twentieth century. He began his career as a rebel against the Liberal dictator José Santos ZELAYA and contributed to Zelaya's defeat in 1909. Afterward he accommodated himself to the occupation of his country by United States Marines, serving as Minister in Washington twice (1913–1916, 1921–1923) and as President of Nicaragua (1917–1921). As Minister he signed the controversial BRYAN-CHAMORRO TREATY, which granted the United States the exclusive privilege of constructing a canal across Nicaragua in return for a payment of $3 million.

Soon after the withdrawal of United States troops in 1925, Chamorro came to power by revolution but resigned after failing to gain diplomatic recognition by the United States. Until his death he tried unsuccessfully to restore the Conservatives to the dominant political position they had enjoyed during the period of United States occupation. Finally, despairing of an all-out contest with his Liberal party opponents, Chamorro signed the so-called Pact of the Generals in 1950 with President Anastasio SOMOZA GARCÍA. This agreement softened Conservative opposition in return for a certain percentage of governmental positions. Chamorro's career indicates that his role as Conservative leader was that of an opportunistic activist rather than that of a formulator of policy.

CHARLES L. STANSIFER

CHAMORRO CARDENAL, PEDRO JOAQUÍN (1924–   ). Nicaraguan journalist and writer. A member of the well-known, traditionally Conservative Chamorro family, Pedro Chamorro is a bitterly partisan opponent of the Somoza political dynasty in Nicaragua. His crusading opposition as editor of *La Prensa,* Nicaragua's most widely circulated newspaper, has led to his being jailed several times. *La Prensa* was founded in 1926, and Chamorro became editor after the death of his father, Pedro Joaquín Chamorro Zelaya, also a journalist and writer, in 1952. In 1959 he took part in an unsuccessful revolution against the regime of Luis SOMOZA DEBAYLE. The story of Chamorro's unsuccessful campaign against the Somozas is found in his *Estirpe sangrienta: Los Somoza* (1957) and *Diario de un preso* (1963). His anti-Marxist, pro-Christian, Conservative views are in *5 PM* (1967), a collection of his newspaper editorials. In the electoral campaign of 1966–1967 Chamorro coordinated the unsuccessful effort of the National Union of the Opposition (UNO) against the candidacy of Anastasio SOMOZA DEBAYLE.

CHARLES L. STANSIFER

CHAPETÓN. Term used in Spanish South America since the sixteenth century to describe the immigrant recently arrived from Europe, especially from Spain. It is a word of disparagement indicating lack of familiarity with the ways of the country. Hence it suggests a person who is inexperienced and unskilled, one who makes his way with difficulty: a greenhorn, a tenderfoot. Some authors suggest an origin from *chapín* (a clog with cork soles), a clumsy and noisy type of feminine footwear. The derivative *chapetonada* has as its most common meaning an illness, a fever, or an itchy skin irritation affecting newcomers to America and attributed to the change in climate. It can also mean being bowlegged or having crooked feet.

NORMAN MEIKLEJOHN

CHARLES I (1500–1558). King of Spain (1516–1556) and Holy Roman Emperor as Charles V (1519–1556). Born in Ghent, Charles was the son of Archduke Philip, who died in 1506, and of Joan the Mad, daughter of Ferdinand II of Aragon and ISABELLA I of Castile. He inherited the throne of Aragon, along with its Italian possessions, upon the death of Ferdinand in 1516 and was called upon to rule in Castile because of his mother's derangement. From his paternal grandparents, Mary of Burgundy and the emperor Maximilian, he inherited the Low Countries and the Hapsburg dominions in central Europe as well as a claim to the imperial title, to which he was elected in 1519.

Charles arrived in Spain in 1517, speaking no Spanish and surrounded by Flemings who proceeded to lay claim to the highest offices and honors in Castile. One of them was granted the first license to ship Negroes from Africa to the Indies and promptly sold it to some Genoese in Andalusia. Nationalist resentment burst forth in Castile in the revolt of the Comuneros (1520), which took on a more radical aspect in some areas. The nearly simultaneous uprising (1519) of the Germanía (Brotherhood) of Valencia was a popular rebellion against the local aristocracy. The defeat of both uprisings served to strengthen absolute monarchy, especially in Castile.

Although Charles developed a liking for Spain, he spent less than sixteen years there. Because of his far-flung concerns—his long rivalry with Francis I of France over hegemony in Italy, the expansionism of the Turkish empire, and his futile efforts to extirpate Lutheranism from Germany—Spanish interests were often ignored or neglected. The funds to finance Charles's ambitious imperial policy were obtained primarily from his European kingdoms and to a lesser extent from his New World colonies. In addition, he was forced to borrow heavily and on ever-worsening terms from German and Genoese bankers.

Probably as a result of the cosmopolitan nature of his empire, in the early years of his reign Charles followed a relatively liberal policy with respect to trade and settlement in the Indies, which he opened to his non-Castilian subjects. He also awarded concessions in America to the German banking firms of Fugger and Welser, the latter receiving the right to establish a colony in Venezuela.

Charles evinced concern for the welfare of the American Indians, whose plight was graphically depicted in the celebrated tract *Very Brief Account of the Destruction of the Indies,* which its author, Bartolomé de LAS CASAS, presented to him in 1542. The same year he issued the humanitarian NEW LAWS, but their hostile reception in America led to their modification several years later. In 1555–1556, weary and disillusioned, Charles renounced his possessions in Spain and the Low Countries in favor of his son, the future PHILIP II, and retired to the Hieronymite monastery of Yuste in Spain, where he remained until his death.

HELEN DELPAR

CHARLES III (1716–1788). King of Spain (1759–1788). The son of Philip V and Isabella of Parma (Elizabeth Farnese), he was King of Naples and Sicily from 1734 to 1759, when he succeeded his half brother Ferdinand VI in Spain. The most capable of the Spanish rulers of the eighteenth century, he was an example of the enlightened absolutist king. With the aid of able ministers, Charles set himself the task of reforming Spain and its colonies. His domestic and colonial policies were aimed at achieving more efficient government, greater welfare for the Spanish people, and the economic expansion of Spain. The results of his policies were mostly positive. Higher revenues were obtained after the fiscal system had been revamped. Industry was expanded under state protection in the peninsula, although sometimes at the expense of its development in the colonies. Trade with the American possessions was increased by ending all restrictions between 1765 and 1789. However, Spain's participation in the American War of Independence (1779–1783) led to the introduction of paper currency and foreign loans, which undermined the economy in the long run.

Charles's clerical policies were regalist, in that he used the church as an instrument of royal policy and approved legislation that curtailed clerical prerogatives. In 1767 the Jesuits were expelled from Spain and its possessions (*see* JESUITS, EXPULSION OF: SPANISH AMERICA). Charles promoted the modernization of the universities and educational methods and encouraged the *sociedades económicas*. He signed the Family Compact with France in 1761 to counterbalance British power, going to war with Britain in 1762 as a result and losing Florida. This province was recovered during the American War of Independence. *See also* BOURBON REFORMS.

ASUNCIÓN LAVRIN

CHATFIELD, FREDERICK (1801–1872). British consular official known in Central America as Great Britain's "eternal agent." He arrived in Guatemala in 1834 and, except for one leave of absence (1840–1842), remained as Consul and Consul General until he was recalled in 1852. Chatfield sought Central American adherence to the draft treaty of amity and commerce he carried. In this task he failed. His instructions enjoined him from discussing British tenure in Belize; the Central American negotiators made the resolution of that issue a precondition to further discussions. Failure in this assignment wounded Chatfield's pride, dashed his hope of elevation to diplomatic status, and embittered him against Central American nationalists.

Chatfield first believed that Liberal unionists could be reconciled to expanding British interests in Central America. However, anti-British sentiment developed as Chatfield supported the territorial and commercial pretensions of Belize, denied Central American title to the Bay Islands and the Mosquito Coast, and called for warships to support the claims of British bondholders. As a result, he became convinced that the Federation of Central America was inimical to British interests (*see* CENTRAL AMERICA, FEDERATION OF). He therefore formed a working alliance with Conservatives, which gave rise to the charge that he destroyed the union.

Chatfield maintained a self-complacent air of superiority in all his relationships. His personal arrogance, his ready tutorial lectures, and his meddling in internal affairs made him the "enemy" to many Central Americans when Ephraim George Squier, the United States Minister, in 1849–1850 engaged him in a brief but spectacular diplomatic duel that resulted in the recall of both men.

WILLIAM J. GRIFFITH

CHÁVEZ, CARLOS (1899–   ). Mexican composer, conductor, and teacher. Chávez was born in Mexico City into a mestizo family. Although he studied for a short time with Manuel PONCE, he can be considered self-taught. His early musical development coincided with the MEXICAN REVOLUTION, and his first compositions—the ballets *El fuego nuevo* (1921), *Los cuatro soles* (1926), and *Horse Power* (1927)—were inspired by its ideas. In addition to his creative activity, Chávez became a powerful leader of Mexico's musical life: he was director of the National Conservatory of Music, founder and first director of the National Institute of Fine Arts, and conductor of the Orquesta Sinfónica de México (later renamed the Orquesta Sinfónica Nacional). His influence as a composition teacher is reflected in the outstanding composers who were his pupils.

An extended catalog of works has contributed to Chávez's international reputation, as have his appearances as conductor with the leading European and American orchestras. He is the author of an opera, *Love Propitiated* (1953–1956); six symphonies, among which Symphony No. 2 (*India*; 1936) is the best known; a concerto for four horns and orchestra (1938), a concerto for piano and orchestra (1940), and a concerto for violin and orchestra (1950); and an extended list of chamber works and solo instrumental compositions including three string quartets and six piano sonatas. He has also written many books on music.

JUAN A. ORREGO-SALAS

CHAVÍN DE HUANTAR. Archaeological site in the highlands of Peru and an art style named for it. The Chavín complex and the associated art style date from 900–200 B.C. The ruins of Chavín de Huantar, just east of the Callejón de Huaylas, lie at an elevation of about 10,000 feet and include the remains of several platform mounds and a plaza area. These masonry structures are unique in being honeycombed by passageways, rooms, and ventilation flues. There are at least three floor levels in these cavernous galleries. At an interior intersection in the heart of one of the massive platforms stands the famous Lanzón, or "Smiling God" (J. H. Rowe's designation), one of the most important as well as impressive religious artifacts from the pre-Columbian New World. Chavín art is distinctive; jaguars, eagles, and serpents, as well as grotesque anthropomorphic beings composed of parts of the aforesaid animals, are depicted in intricate, closely packed, and flowing lines. Pottery forms are simple and monumental. It is a reasonable surmise that the great spread of Chavín influence in the arts implies also the spread of a cult. Archaeologists see this, however, as a missionary and not a militaristic movement.

BURR C. BRUNDAGE

CHIARI [REMÓN], ROBERTO F[RANCISCO] (1905–). President of Panama (1960–1964). Chiari was born in Panama City. His father, Rodolfo Chiari, was President of Panama from 1924 to 1928, and the Chiari family wealth (derived from sugar and dairying) had nourished Liberal party activities on the isthmus for decades. In 1949 Chiari, as Second Vice President, was placed in charge of the executive branch after the ouster of the acting President, Daniel Chanis, by the National Police. Five days later, the Supreme Court ruled that Chiari was ineligible for the Presidency, and he resigned.

In 1960 he was elected to the Presidency as the candidate of a four-party coalition of which his own Partido Liberal Nacional was a part. Meeting the first challenge of his Presidency, he brought Panama out of a recession through a $206.7 million development plan benefiting rural and urban areas. The program was financed through tax reforms and international borrowing. Chiari personally intervened in the settlement of a 1960–1961 strike of 10,000 banana workers in western Panama when the work stoppage threatened to disrupt the national economy.

Most of Chiari's efforts were concentrated on gaining more favorable interpretations of treaties with the United States. As a result, the United States position softened on the sovereignty (flag) question. Hoping for better relations and possibly a new treaty, President Chiari paid an official visit to the United States. In spite of his efforts, relations with the United States worsened after the 1964 FLAG RIOTS, in which twenty-seven persons were killed.

LARRY L. PIPPIN

CHIBÁS, EDUARDO (1907–1951). Cuban politician and founder of the Ortodoxo party (*see* ORTODOXO PARTY: CUBA). Eduardo (Eddie) Chibás's involvement in politics began in the late 1920s, when he was a student activist. An impassioned idealist, he participated in revolutionary student organizations such as the Directorio Estudiantil (Student Directorate), which employed terrorism against the dictatorship of Gerardo MACHADO. In 1933 Chibás took part in the coup against the Céspedes government, in which his wealthy father held a ministerial post.

Chibás eventually joined Ramón GRAU SAN MARTÍN's Auténtico (*see* AUTÉNTICO PARTY: CUBA) and won a Senate seat in the 1944 elections. Disillusioned with corruption in Grau's administration, he led a bolt from the Auténticos in 1947 and organized the Ortodoxo party. In 1948 he carried his opposition to the Auténticos into the presidential election as the Ortodoxo candidate. After an unsuccessful but respectable showing in the election, he pursued his campaign for moral reform through weekly radio broadcasts that specialized in sensational exposés of dishonest public officials in the government of Carlos PRÍO SOCORRÁS.

Chibás's idealism and charismatic manner attracted a considerable following. His Sunday night broadcasts reached receptive listeners disillusioned with the spectacle of graft and unfulfilled hopes that two

Auténtico administrations had generated. Subsequently Chibás became the idol of many reform-minded students and intellectuals. In 1951 Chibás, apparently frustrated by his inability to substantiate certain accusations, fatally shot himself after making a recording for his weekly broadcast. His dramatic suicide had a major impact upon his followers. In death he became a political martyr and a rallying symbol of the younger generation that became active in the revolutionary struggle against the dictatorship of Fulgencio BATISTA (1952–1959).

DAVID A. CRAIN

CHIBCHA. Formerly numerous pre-Columbian Indian group in the Cundinamarca and Boyacá areas of Colombia. Present-day Bogotá was the seat of one of the two major Chibcha chieftains, the Zipa; another chief, the Zaque, lived to the north. Sun worship was the predominant religion. The Chibcha seem to have been culturally more closely related to Mexico than to the central Andes, especially in such institutions as periodic markets and human sacrifices. Gold was important to the nobles for prestige purposes. Warfare was endemic among the lesser chiefs, but owing to the fragmentation of their political life they were easily conquered by the Spaniards. Perhaps the most noteworthy aspects of their culture were the elaborate organization of the priesthood and the complicated set of taboos and discipline connected with it.

BURR C. BRUNDAGE

CHICHÉN ITZÁ. Archaeological site in northeastern Yucatán, today visited by tourists driving out from Mérida. It was an important Mayan ceremonial center in the Late Classic period (A.D. 300–900). In the tenth century it was invaded by Toltec warriors and under their aegis became a notable pilgrimage center. While the NAHUATL-speaking Toltecs acted the part of conquering lords, the bulk of the population continued to be Mayan and eventually gave their language to the intruders. Sometime in the thirteenth century the city foundered and gave way to Mayapán, a city to the west. The interest in Chichén Itzá, for the tourist as well as the scholar, is in its two contrasting building styles, classic Puuc Mayan and the later Toltec. It is the buildings of the latter period that are the most attractive to the visitor because of the excellent restorative work done on them; the Castillo, the Temple of the Warriors, the *tzompantli* (skull-rocks), and the ball court are all splendid monuments. Nearby there were two deep pools, or *cenotes,* one of which gave the site its only dependable water supply. The larger of the two was joined to the ceremonial center by a causeway and is known as the Well of Sacrifice; into it were hurled living human sacrifices and rich objects. Dredging and scuba diving have accounted for the retrieval of many interesting and valuable artifacts. *See also* MAYAS; TOLTECS.

BURR C. BRUNDAGE

CHICHIMECS. Term used to designate any of the peripatetic Indian tribes north and west of the Toltec and Aztec empires. The name itself is NAHUATL and means "People of the Dog." These scattered and no doubt linguistically disparate peoples are described as nearly naked and without any formal shelters except caves and temporary brush huts. They were hunters and superior marksmen with the bow and arrow and possessed rudimentary chiefdoms. They worshiped astral deities, especially the sun. They were warlike and acted occasionally as subject mercenaries for the Toltec lords, and thus certain groups were in a position to acquire higher cultural skills; in the main, though, they appear to have resisted civilization strenuously. The Aztecs claimed with pride Chichimec ancestry. *See also* AZTECS; TOLTECS.   BURR C. BRUNDAGE

CHILEAN DEVELOPMENT CORPORATION. *See* CORPORACIÓN DE FOMENTO DE LA PRODUCCIÓN.

CHILE SINCE 1823. In 1823 the republic of Chile was approximately one-third its present size of nearly 300,000 square miles, hemmed in on the east by the ANDES MOUNTAINS and on the west by the Pacific Ocean, while to the north the ATACAMA DESERT provided the most natural, though ill-defined, of frontiers. To the south the Bío-Bío River marked the limit of settlement apart from isolated outposts such as Valdivia and Osorno, for beyond the river lay dense forests peopled only by Araucanian Indians (*see* ARAUCANIANS). But between Copiapó on the rim of the northern desert and Concepción on the Bío-Bío stretched the Central Valley of Chile, 700 miles long but rarely more than 100 miles wide, blessed with a Mediterranean climate, fertile valleys, wooded slopes, and fresh rivers rising from the snow-capped Cordillera de los Andes. This clearly defined central region was the real Chile, and it has remained the essential heart of the nation to the present.

The society of this region was basically rural. The *hacendado* (landowner) ruled the national life in all its branches, while an illiterate peasantry obeyed. From colonial times to the twentieth century, Chile's social structure was dominated by a distinctive and extreme form of land monopoly and a sharply marked social cleavage between master and man, and it was only in the late nineteenth century that the rise of new urban and industrial classes began to blur these sharp divisions. At the time of independence (1818), Chile's population was about 500,000, apart from some 100,000 unassimilated Indians beyond the Bío-Bío; this half million was divided into some 150,000 whites and 350,000 mestizos. Fewer than thirty towns existed, and most of these are better described as large villages with populations of about 3,000. Santiago, the capital, had perhaps 40,000 inhabitants; Valparaíso, the chief port, had about 7,000; and Concepción and Valdivia, frontier towns and military garrisons, each had between 5,000 and 6,000. At the apex of society stood the close-knit aristocracy of land, some 200 families of quite remarkable social solidarity. Below them, but linked to their social betters by interest and conviction, were creole mineowners, merchants, small-scale industrialists, and professional people (lawyers, clerics, and army officers), while the mestizo masses, illiterate and inert, were the rural workers, miners, laborers, and servants. This hierarchic social order was supported by a strong church.

The fall of Bernardo O'HIGGINS, Supreme Director of Chile from independence to 1823, ushered in a period of confusion. Within the ruling groups opinions were

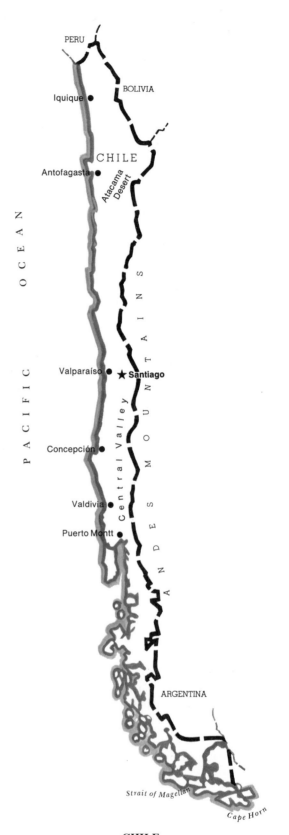

CHILE

Area: 292,258 sq. mi.   Population: 8,834,820 (1970 est.).

sharply divided on constitutional and religious issues. It was a time of heady oratory and utopian ideas about the capacity and the will of a newly independent people to build a new nation, but while Chile searched for a suitable constitutional form, political instability obtained and economic life languished. A conservative reaction set in, finding its embodiment in Diego PORTALES. Backed by the landed oligarchy and assisted by able lieutenants such as Mariano Egaña and Manuel Rengifo, Portales put an end to confusion and set Chile on a course that earned it a unique reputation in Spanish America for orderly government and internal peace. The constitution of 1833 was a major factor in this development: it recognized Chilean society for what it was rather than for what it might be and realistically established a system of government in accordance with the circumstances (*see* CONSTITUTION OF 1833: CHILE). Suffrage was limited to the propertied and literate classes; enormous powers were conferred on the President, in whose hands lay control of the armed forces, local administration, and the major part of central government; and an aristocratic bicameral legislature was established to work with the executive. As long as legislature and executive saw eye to eye on basic issues, the system worked well, but it contained a contradiction that later came to a head. Presidents increasingly saw themselves as the embodiment of the impersonal power of the state and as the guardians and promoters of its welfare; Congress, often representing more limited interests, did not always agree with a President's methods or aims. It thus became necessary for Presidents to secure majority support in Congress by interfering in elections, and this in turn created opposition both within the Congress itself and in public opinion. Yet for long periods the constitution worked well, and the country progressed under the double stimulus of political stability and economic development. Only four Presidents held office between 1831 and 1871, as each incumbent served two consecutive terms of five years each, and this continuity in government was a further favorable factor.

The chief event of the Presidency of Joaquín PRIETO (1831–1841) was a war between Chile on the one hand and Peru and Bolivia on the other, as the Bolivian dictator Andrés SANTA CRUZ sought to unite Chile's neighbors in the late 1830s (*see* PERU-BOLIVIA CONFEDERATION). Chile finally triumphed, thus taking the first step toward hegemony on the Pacific coast of South America, and even the assassination of Portales in 1837 did not disturb the republic, so firmly had he laid its foundations. Manuel BULNES, victor over Santa Cruz in war, became the next President (1841–1851), and his regime was marked by considerable economic progress and by the expansion of Chile's frontiers. By the 1840s Chile had become the world's leading copper producer, as mines in Atacama and Coquimbo were opened up, and it retained this position until the 1870s (*see* COPPER INDUSTRY: CHILE). In the 1840s and 1850s Chilean agriculture received a powerful stimulus from the gold discoveries in California and Australia. The country's geopolitical situation was turned to good advantage, since no other granary was better placed to feed the rapidly rising populations of the gold fields, and as agriculture expanded, so did the commerce of Valparaíso, a thriving township of 35,000 by 1850. Im-

provements in maritime communications played their part. In 1840 William WHEELWRIGHT, an American citizen, founded the Pacific Steam Navigation Company, based in Liverpool, establishing a regular steamship service between Europe and Chile. He also stimulated the mining of coal, as fuel for his ships, in the province of Arauco and built Chile's first railway, from Copiapó to Caldera, in 1851. In the same period the frontier of settlement was moved south of the Bío-Bío, as the Chilean government encouraged German immigration to Valdivia and Osorno. The settlements were small in number but significant in influence, their pattern of family farms contrasting strongly with the great estates of the Central Valley. The coming of steamships made the Strait of Magellan strategically vital to Chile, and in 1843 Bulnes affirmed Chilean rights by sending an expedition to establish forts in the region. Furthermore, as mineral riches became more apparent in the desert north of Chile, Bulnes claimed the 23d parallel south as the country's northern frontier.

Economic advances under Bulnes were paralleled by a revival of political activity, notably in the growth of liberal ideas imported from Europe, particularly after 1848. While Liberal politicians increasingly opposed the absorbing power of the presidential system (*see* LIBERAL PARTY: CHILE), Francisco BILBAO and Santiago Arcos founded the Society of Equality in 1850 to change society itself. But this step was premature. Although such new social forces as mining entrepreneurs, bankers, and businessmen were emerging, the old aristocracy showed remarkable resilience in absorbing them into its ranks, and the masses remained in the rural economy.

Under Manuel MONTT (1851–1861), an outstanding administrator and Chile's first civilian President, material progress continued after an abortive revolution in 1851 had been crushed. The telegraph appeared and spread rapidly, the great central railway was inaugurated from Santiago and reached Rancagua by 1859, and the line to Valparaíso was begun. Gas lighting appeared in the streets of the capital, public libraries were established, and the educational system was expanded. Commercial treaties were signed with a number of countries, and more liberal tariff policies were adopted. Banking institutions were developed, and a new civil code was decreed. This was the work of Andrés BELLO, the great Venezuelan jurist who lived in Chile from 1829 to his death in 1865, served as the first rector of the University of Chile (founded in 1842), and exercised a profound intellectual influence on his adopted country.

During Montt's term, however, significant political changes occurred. Montt was an authoritarian; together with his Minister of the Interior, Antonio VARAS, he governed autocratically despite the growing opposition of the Liberals, who in the late 1850s would find an unexpected ally in anti-Montt Conservatives. Beginning with a minor conflict in the church in 1857, a violent dispute developed between Montt and the ultramontane Archbishop of Santiago, Rafael Valentín Valdivieso, on the rights and prerogatives of church and state. The Conservative party, hitherto a supporter of the government, split into a pro-Montt section, now known as the National party, and an anti-Montt movement that kept the name Conservative party (*see* CONSERVATIVE PARTY: CHILE). Conservatives and Liberals thus joined forces against Montt, while more advanced Liberals subsequently broke away from their own party to form the Radical party (*see* RADICAL PARTY: CHILE). Government repression of opposition activities led to revolution, but the Army stood firm, and after months of fighting order was restored. However, political peace was secured only by the withdrawal of Varas from the presidential contest in 1861, and Conservatives and Liberals together supported a compromise candidate, José Joaquín PÉREZ, the last President to rule for ten years (1861–1871).

Liberal reforms were effected under Pérez, but since government depended on a fusion of Conservatives and Liberals, compromise policies obtained. Thus, in 1863 non-Catholics were given the right to practice their religion, but they still had to do so in private. A constitutional amendment prohibiting one man from serving two consecutive terms was passed in 1867, but more serious curtailment of presidential power had to wait, as did further restriction of church authority. Under Pérez, Chile was involved in its second war since independence, this time as Peru's ally against Spain (1864–1866). Valparaíso was bombarded by a Spanish squadron in 1866, but Spain's withdrawal from a ridiculous enterprise enhanced Chilean prestige in the Americas. Meanwhile, liberal opinion was growing in the political nation, and in 1873 the Conservative-Liberal fusion broke down. President Federico ERRÁZURIZ ZAÑARTU (1871–1876) governed with Liberals, Radicals, and Nationals, and a series of constitutional amendments markedly advanced legislative power over that of the executive during his Presidency.

At the same time, the country began to suffer from the impact of the world depression of the 1870s: Chilean copper production declined as the easiest ores were worked out and rich deposits in Spain and the United States came into their own, and there was a general economic recession. The recession reached its lowest point under President Aníbal Pinto (1876–1881), and in 1878 the government made the fateful decision to base its monetary system on inconvertible paper money, a factor that contributed to future instability and continuing inflation. The country quickly recovered from economic depression in 1879, however, when the WAR OF THE PACIFIC with Peru and Bolivia broke out. The origins of the war were many and complex, revolving around long-standing frontier disputes and Chilean economic penetration of Peruvian and Bolivian nitrate areas (*see* NITRATE INDUSTRY: CHILE). But the results were clear and definite: Chile, victorious on land and sea, compelled its adversaries to sue for peace, taking as spoils of war the Bolivian territory of Antofagasta and the Peruvian province of Tarapacá, regions rich in nitrates. Although the industry remained in foreign hands, Chilean revenues from export taxes on nitrate shipments increased enormously, amounting over the next forty years to roughly half of government income and supplying much of the capital for such public works as railways, docks, and public buildings and for the expansion of education.

Meanwhile, under President Domingo Santa María (1881–1886) the anticlerical aspect of the Liberal movement reached its apogee with the passage of laws reducing the power of the church. Civil marriage and registry and secular cemeteries were decreed, but with the attainment of these reforms one of the binding elements of Liberal opinion disappeared, leaving constitutional issues uppermost, notably the balance of power between legislature and executive. President José Manuel BALMACEDA (1886–1891) greatly improved communications and educational systems, using nitrate revenues for the purpose, but he alienated Congress by his strict insistence on presidential power and finally lost the confidence of its majority. An acute constitutional conflict developed in 1890, and neither President nor Congress would yield. Finally, in 1891, Balmaceda committed an unconstitutional act that precipitated civil war, and a bloody conflict ensued. The victory of Congress and the suicide of Balmaceda late in 1891 profoundly changed the spirit, though not the letter, of the constitutional system of Chile. Thereafter, to 1924, the balance of power lay decisively with the legislature, as Presidents accepted congressional vetoes of their appointed ministries, which changed with bewildering rapidity. In a multiparty system with a weak Presidency, government depended on changing alliances and coalitions, as the ruling classes played a game of pure politics while national issues were neglected. And those national issues increasingly revolved around social and economic conditions.

Between 1895 and 1920 Chile's population increased from 2.7 million to 3.7 million, and urbanization was accelerated. The population of Santiago rose from 258,000 in 1895 to 425,000 in 1920, while that of Valparaíso increased from 132,000 to 220,000. The growth of economic activities, particularly mining and construction, had already caused considerable rural migration in the latter half of the nineteenth century, and the proportion of the rural population declined from 73 percent of the total population in 1875 to 54 percent in 1920. With population rising at a high absolute rate and urbanization increasing rapidly, the country continued to depend on a rigid economic structure, its landholding system still being dominated by large and often unproductive estates and its export trade being confined largely to one commodity, nitrates. Working conditions in the mines and on the land were equally bad, and the laboring and lower-middle classes were the persistent victims of currency depreciation. Popular reaction expressed in strikes was bloodily suppressed, and workers turned to resistance organized in trade unions and later in political parties.

The impact of World War I, which disrupted the Chilean economy, catalyzed discontent, and Arturo ALESSANDRI, presidential aspirant in 1920, won a narrow victory on a program of radical reform. But he could not implement it; with Congress controlled by the opposition little was done, and the economic situation continued to deteriorate. Finally, after some political confusion, the Army intervened to begin a process of national regeneration. In 1925 Alessandri promulgated a new constitution in place of that of 1833. The constitution of 1925 restored a strong Presidency and separated church and state, but the continuation of a multiparty system still obliged Presidents to rely on congressional support from diverse groups and thus often made it necessary for them to bargain and compromise their programs (*see* CONSTITUTION OF 1925: CHILE). Moreover, in 1927 the constitutional system broke down when Carlos IBÁÑEZ, a leader of the military intervention three years earlier, maneuvered himself into the Presidency and established a quasi-dictatorial government. Although Ibáñez gagged the opposition and put politics into cold storage, he promoted economic growth, encouraging large-scale United States investment in manufacturing and mining. Chile enjoyed a temporary boom, and the role of the state in economic development was enhanced. Competition from synthetic nitrates had long since undercut Chile's natural production, but large-scale copper mining had now taken its place. Then the Great Depression hit Chile, as it did every other country, creating large-scale unemployment as capital inflows stopped and production ground to a halt.

Faced with popular revolt, Ibáñez resigned in 1931, and there followed a bewildering fifteen months of political chaos. Finally, in 1932, constitutional order was restored and Alessandri was reelected President. His second term pulled Chile out of the economic depression through brilliant financial management and the recovery of world trade, but Alessandri had now moved to the right, and repression of workers resulted in the formation of a Popular Front, composed of the Socialist party (founded in 1933), the revived Communist party (founded in 1922), and the old Radical party (see COMMUNIST PARTY: CHILE; POPULAR FRONT: CHILE; SOCIALIST PARTY: CHILE). The Popular Front won the presidential election in 1938 with Pedro AGUIRRE CERDA, and although the combination lasted only until 1941, it powerfully accelerated the process of state intervention in the economy through the CORPORACIÓN DE FOMENTO DE LA PRODUCCIÓN (Chilean Development Corporation), founded in 1939. Meanwhile, an economic boom during World War II saw widespread development of manufacturing. The processes of population explosion and urbanization now gathered further momentum. Between 1930 and 1960 Chile's population grew from 4,287,000 to 7,374,000, and that of Santiago from 600,000 to 1,700,000. Whereas in 1930 only 28 percent of Chileans lived in towns with populations of more than 20,000, by 1960, 66 percent did. By 1945 Chile was virtually self-sufficient in manufactured consumer goods, and more than 80 percent of the people were literate, but Chilean society remained sharply divided between a minority of 20 percent who led a reasonable existence and the 80 percent who did not. Inflation remained a recurrent problem, eroding apparent gains made by the working and middle classes, and such basic structural defects of the Chilean economy as the unproductive landholding system, a critical dependence on copper exports, and sharply skewed income distribution were largely ignored by successive governments from the 1940s to the 1960s. At the same time, a growing national consensus for fundamental change emerged, as the left-wing parties, Socialist and Communist, gathered strength and the PARTIDO DEMÓCRATA CRISTIANO (Christian Democratic party) emerged in the 1960s as a new center party, supplanting the Radicals. Under President Eduardo FREI (1964–1970), an ambitious program of social and economic reform was initiated by the first Christian Democratic government in Latin America. It failed in its objective of transforming Chile in six years, but it underlined a new national commitment to basic reform and paved the way for the election in 1970 of Salvador ALLENDE, the first Marxist head of the state in the world to come

to power in a democratic election, as the leader of a left-wing coalition that included Communists and Socialists.

The Allende government's first two years in office were marked by extensive nationalization of privately owned assets and a considerable redistribution of income, accompanied by a sharp polarization of political attitudes and increasing fears that Chilean liberties might not survive. Throughout its history Chile has preferred the path of evolution to that of revolution and has contained acute stresses in the social and economic fabric largely within a constitutional framework. Mounting opposition to Allende's program, however, culminated in September 1973 in a military coup and his suicide.

Bibliography. Harold Blakemore, "Chile," in Harold Blakemore and Clifford T. Smith (eds.), *Latin America: Geographical Perspectives,* London, 1971, pp. 475–565; Alberto Edwards Vives, *La fronda aristocrática en Chile,* Santiago, numerous editions; F. A. Encina and L. Castedo, *Resumen de la historia de Chile,* 3 vols., Santiago, numerous editions; Federico Gil, *The Political System of Chile,* Boston, 1966; Ernst Halperin, *Nationalism and Communism in Chile,* Cambridge, Mass., 1965; Julio César Jobet, *Ensayo crítico del desarrollo económico-social de Chile,* Santiago, 1951; G. M. McBride, *Chile: Land and Society,* New York, 1936; F. B. Pike, *Chile and the United States, 1880–1962: The Emergence of Chile's Social Crisis and the Challenge to United States Diplomacy,* Notre Dame, Ind., 1963.

HAROLD BLAKEMORE

CHILPANCINGO, CONGRESS OF. Congress convoked by José María MORELOS Y PAVÓN, the leader of the Mexican rebels in the struggle for independence, to serve as the government of the insurgent movement. The town of Chilpancingo, Guerrero, was chosen as the site of the Congress; the first session was held on September 14, 1813. Membership consisted of eight delegates and substitutes, including some of the leading insurgents, but it was not until late October that all the members assembled. One of their first acts was to appoint Morelos Generalissimo of the insurgent government, which position he accepted conditionally. This mandate was later revoked as opposition to him developed in the far from harmonious legislature.

Early in 1814 the Congress had to leave Chilpancingo; as the theater of military operations shifted, it was continually on the move. During one of these moves, in November 1815, Morelos was captured while trying to protect the fleeing delegates. The Congress then lost its incentive, and it was dissolved in Tehuacán, Puebla, the following month. Although its effectiveness was impeded by its lack of harmony and its forced peregrinations, the Congress issued a declaration of independence on November 6, 1813, later promulgated the CONSTITUTION OF APATZINGÁN, and otherwise helped formulate a political doctrine for the rebel cause, which the earlier movement initiated by Miguel HIDALGO Y COSTILLA had lacked.

CHARLES R. BERRY

CHIMU. Aggressive pre-Columbian coastal kingdom in Peru, of the Late Intermediate period (A.D. 1000–1476). It was finally incorporated by the INCAS under

PACHACUTI and his son, Topa Inca, into their empire. The ancient capital, the ruins of which are now referred to as Chan Chan, covered 6 square miles or more near Trujillo, north of Lima. Chimu claimed to have been created by invading peoples from the sea, who thus superimposed themselves on the established MOCHICA culture of the area. A dynasty of nine rulers of this refounded state could be counted down to and including Minchançaman, who was conquered by Topa Inca about 1470. Before its defeat by the Incas, the kingdom probably extended from Chira to Supe, roughly the northern half of the coast of northern Peru. Earlier road systems between the numerous coastal valleys were well maintained by Chimu. Canals increased the irrigation potentialities of the state, and fortifications provided security. The kingdom derived its art style in pottery from the predecessor Mochica culture, but in general preferred mass production of items to esthetic excellence.   BURR C. BRUNDAGE

CHOCANO, JOSÉ SANTOS (1875–1934). Peruvian poet. Chocano, Peru's foremost poet in the modernist literary movement (*see* MODERNISM: SPANISH AMERICA), was born in Lima. He entered the University of San Marcos but was a poor student and soon abandoned his studies. As a result of his involvement in political activities, he was imprisoned for six months in 1894. During his imprisonment he composed two volumes of poetry, *En la aldea* (1895) and *Iras santas* (1895). The second volume was printed in red ink and is filled with Chocano's feelings on political tyranny and oppression.

Following the publication of *El fin de Satán y otros poemas* (1901), Chocano began an erratic diplomatic career. He was sent to Madrid with the Peruvian diplomatic mission in 1905 and remained there for three years during the zenith of his literary career, publishing *Alma América* (1906) and *Fiat lux* (1908). His poetic production then declined in quality, if not in quantity. After spending two years in Mexico during the MEXICAN REVOLUTION, he moved to Guatemala and then to Costa Rica, where he remained until 1921. At the time of his return to Peru in 1922, he was publicly crowned National Poet by the government of President Augusto LEGUÍA.

In a heated argument over a political matter, Chocano shot and killed a young man in October 1925. After a year in prison, he was freed but was forced to leave Peru for Chile, where he spent the rest of his life. On December 13, 1934, he was attacked and killed by a disillusioned partner in one of the poet's fantastic projects to find buried treasure. Before his tragic death, Chocano published *Primicias de oro de Indias* (1934). Several volumes of his works were published posthumously: *Poemas del amor doliente* (1937), *Memorias* (1940), *El alma de Voltaire* (1940), and four volumes of *Oro de Indias* (1940–1941). He also wrote several dramatic pieces, but these were largely unsuccessful.
                                          DANIEL R. REEDY

CHOLO. Term applied in Peru and Bolivia to a person holding an intermediate position between the Indian and the MESTIZO. The cholo's origins place him in the indigenous class, but his desire to better himself and his acquisition of nonindigenous cultural attributes identify him with the mestizo culture. The term may be used with contempt, although there are those who consider the cholo the only true Peruvian, the person who has harmoniously combined within himself the various cultures and habits of Peru. The word may also be used as a synonym for mestizo.

The term is used in other Latin American countries, notably Ecuador, Chile, Argentina, and Costa Rica, to denote a lower-class person of mixed blood.
                                          ORAZIO A. CICCARELLI

CHÔRO. Term conveying various meanings in Brazilian popular music. Generically, *chôro* denotes ensemble music performance in an urban context, with a marked preference for a soloist against the performing group. Specifically, it refers to an ensemble of musician serenaders (*chorões*) that developed during the second half of the nineteenth century. One of the first known *chôros* in Rio de Janeiro was organized by the popular composer Joaquim Antonio da Silva Callado (1848–1880). At that time the instrumental ensemble generally included flute, clarinet, ophicleide, trombone, *cavaquinho* (a ukulele type of instrument), guitar, and a few percussion instruments (in particular, the tambourine). The repertoire of such ensembles consisted mostly of dances of European origin performed at popular festivities. For the serenades, the function of the band was to accompany the sentimental songs performed by a solo singer (*see* MODINHA). No special music was composed for the *chôros*, but such designations as *polka-chôro*, *valsa-chôro*, and the like indicate the process of nationalization undergone by European dances.

In the twentieth century the *chôro* or *chorinho* has been closely connected with other typical popular dances of urban Brazil, such as the maxixe, the *tango brasileiro*, and the SAMBA. They all present the same rhythmic patterns (syncopated binary figures), although tempo is a distinguishing feature. The originality of the *chôro* of the 1930s and 1940s (those of Pixinguinha and B. Lacerda, for example) resides in the typical virtuoso improvisation of instrumental variations and the imaginative resulting counterpoint.
                                          GERARD H. BÉHAGUE

CHRISTIAN DEMOCRATIC PARTY. *See* PARTIDO DEMÓCRATA CRISTIANO.

CHRISTOPHE, HENRY (1767–1820). Haitian revolutionary leader, President, and King. Christophe was born a free Negro on Grenada on October 6, 1767, four years after Great Britain acquired the island. He served at sea as a cabin boy and worked in a hotel. He then joined a French regiment of free Negroes and was wounded aiding Americans in the siege of Savannah in 1779.

In 1793 Christophe joined Saint-Domingue's revolutionary forces as an infantry captain. His aggressiveness led to his promotion to major by Toussaint LOUVERTURE. When the latter became Governor-General, Christophe rose to the rank of colonel. Louverture charged him with rebuilding the colony's agriculture, which had collapsed during the rebellion. Noted for methodical industry, Christophe succeeded in this first of his rural reforms. Abandoned plantations were taken over by the government and rented to army officers, who provided for the welfare of the regimented field hands with part of the revenue produced by their labors.

In 1802, when Gen. Charles-Victor-Emmanuel Leclerc tried to restore full French control, Christophe, under Louverture's orders, refused to turn Le Cap (modern Cap-Haïtien) over to him and fired the city. Leclerc outlawed him but rescinded the order when Christophe surrendered, though Christophe refused to betray his former commander, Louverture. When France restored slavery in other islands, reopened the African slave trade, and slaughtered black troops at Le Cap, Christophe joined his new superior, Jean-Jacques DESSALINES, to drive the French from Saint-Domingue, now renamed Haiti.

With victory, Christophe returned to his northern command. During the tyrannical reign of Dessalines, he feared the Emperor's growing distrust and opposed his negative policies. After Dessalines's murder the mulatto Alexandre Sabès PÉTION attempted to make Christophe a puppet President, retaining real power for himself as head of the Constituent Assembly. Christophe rejected this ruse, and civil war followed. Haiti was divided into a northern Negro realm, and a southern mulatto republic. The south deposed and outlawed Christophe, and Haiti sank into fourteen years of struggle between two nearly balanced states, neither strong enough to crush the other.

Christophe had himself proclaimed President in February 1807. Fearing a French invasion, he kept a large army. His trade and cultural relations with Britain were generally better than those with the United States. Neither of these countries nor France recognized him. Believing that the prestige of monarchy would advance Haiti, he proclaimed a kingdom in 1811, became Henry I, and created a working aristocracy. A monarch who

loved ostentation, he built several palaces, the finest of which was Sans Souci, perhaps the most magnificent building in the Caribbean. For defense, Henry constructed an engineering marvel, the Citadel, where he planned to retreat for a last stand if the French attempted reconquest. In order to restore Haitian prosperity, the King amplified the rural code, subjecting northerners to virtual serfdom while increasing agricultural output. Meanwhile, his police oversaw the details of daily life.

Although Christophe was a tyrant who could barely sign his name, he emphasized education and imported British teachers, missionaries, and advisers. He had the latest world news read to him, while his printing press showed that he realized the power of favorable publicity.

When military conquest of the south proved impossible, Christophe offered union under his aegis to Pétion and, later, to Jean-Pierre BOYER; both haughtily spurned his suggestion. In later years Henry grew more suspicious and ill-tempered and ruled through fear. When he suffered a paralytic stroke on August 15, 1820, fear dissolved and revolts broke out. Realizing that he was helpless, Christophe shot himself on October 8, 1820. Boyer soon moved north in triumph. Haiti's only king had ceased to reign; his interim of prosperity would not soon be repeated.

Bibliography. Hubert Cole, *Christophe: King of Haiti,* New York, 1967; Earl Leslie Griggs and C. H. Prator, *Henry Christophe and Thomas Clarkson: A Correspondence,* Berkeley, Calif., 1952; W. W. Harvey, *Sketches of Hayti,* London, 1827; Thomas Madiou, *Histoire d'Haïti,* Port-au-Prince, 1847–48; Vergniaud Leconte, *Henri Christophe dans l'histoire d'Haïti,* Paris, 1931.

JOHN E. BAUR

CHUMACERO, ALÍ (1918–   ). Mexican poet. The best known of the poets who identified themselves with the review *Tierra Nueva* (1940–1942), Chumacero cultivates pure poetry in the style of Xavier VILLAURRUTIA. His works include *Páramo de sueños* (1944), *Imágenes desterradas* (1948), and *Palabras en reposo* (1956). Along with Octavio PAZ and others he edited *Poesía en movimiento, México 1915–1966* (4th ed., 1970).

RACHEL PHILLIPS

CIAP. *See* COMITÉ INTERAMERICANO DE LA ALIANZA PARA EL PROGRESO.

CÍCERO, PADRE (b. CÍCERO ROMÃO BATISTA; 1844–1934). Popular mystical and political figure of northeastern Brazil, still idolized by the people of the SERTÃO. Padre Cícero was propelled into fame and legend after the 1889 "miracle of Joazeiro do Norte," in which, during communion, the host reputedly was transformed into blood. As news spread through the sertão, the tiny town in the Cariri Valley in Ceará was inundated with pilgrims, growing to 30,000 in 1914. Padre Cícero's miracle was never accepted by the church, despite considerable effort, and he was suspended and threatened with excommunication for insisting on its validity and for his political activities. His mystique and power grew nonetheless.

Padre Cícero became involved in politics both be-

Henry Christophe. [Photographie Bulloz]

cause of his relations with the church and because of his attempts to improve conditions for his followers. He became a powerful political force, strong enough to cause the downfall of the state government in 1914. He has been described as a messiah, but such a label is too simplistic to explain his movement. His actions were closely tied to the maneuvers of José Gomes PINHEIRO MACHADO in state and national politics, to the changing economy of Ceará, and to his shifting relationship with the church hierarchy. His followers did not seek to destroy the political or social order but demanded a greater share of the goods of society. Under Padre Cícero's leadership, Joazeiro (now Juàzeiro) developed into the agricultural, industrial, commercial, and artisan center of the sertão. ROBIN L. ANDERSON

CIENTÍFICOS. Term, meaning "scientifics" or "scientists," applied to a group of men who were influential in the latter half of the administration of Porfirio DÍAZ in Mexico, from approximately 1892 to 1911. They first became prominent as a group in 1892, when they were instrumental in organizing a political party to work for Díaz's reelection. With that accomplished, the party disappeared, but the *científicos'* influence and leadership remained as they helped shape the programs of the government. Prominent members of the group were Justo SIERRA, Francisco Bulnes, Rosendo Pineda, Manuel Zamacona, Pablo Macedo, and José Ives Limantour, Minister of the Treasury. Other members were of the same type—intellectuals, lawyers, and bureaucrats. They were imbued with the concepts of positivist philosophy and social Darwinism and advocated a stable, efficient government that would provide order and material progress. Many of the group were wealthy or became wealthy and were closely linked to foreign business interests. Their emphasis on efficiency and progress led them to denigrate the Indian and mestizo elements as retrograde and to work for the establishment of a creole oligarchy. Toward the end of the Díaz regime a few members began to defect or at least to criticize some aspects of the dictatorship.
See also POSITIVISM (MEXICO). CHARLES R. BERRY

CIEZA DE LEÓN, PEDRO DE (1518?–1560). Spanish soldier-historian of the Peruvian conquest. Cieza de León served under the founding Governor of Cartagena, Pedro de Heredia, and joined his successor, Juan de Vadillo, in an expedition up the CAUCA VALLEY (1537–1538). At Cali he shifted his allegiance to Lorenzo de Aldana and Jorge Robledo, representatives of Francisco PIZARRO opposed to Sebastián de BENALCÁZAR. Significantly, Cieza de León's habit of keeping a careful diary recommended him to Pedro de la Gasca, whom he served as official chronicler during the struggle against Gonzalo PIZARRO (1547–1548).

Uniquely combined military and literary talents gave Cieza de León the extraordinary opportunity of composing a firsthand history of the Peruvian conquest and civil wars, which he accomplished with uncommon veracity and impartiality. The product of his labors, *Crónica del Perú,* was written in four parts. The first was a geographical description of Peru from Colombia to Bolivia, published in 1553; the second, a description of Inca civilization (*see* INCAS), went unpublished until 1873. The third part, an account of the Peruvian con-

quest considered lost for centuries, was finally found and was published piecemeal (1946–1958) in the *Mercurio Peruano.* The fourth part was a narrative of the civil wars comprising five books, three of which have been found and published. Cieza de León's work is considered indispensable as a primary source for the study of Peruvian history.
WILLIAM S. DUDLEY

CIMARRÓN. In colonial Spanish America, a fugitive slave, a maroon. Considerable numbers of black slaves ran away into the bush throughout the colonial period and resumed life as they had known it in Africa. The nature of much of the terrain and the sparseness of the population facilitated this kind of total escape from the world of the master, but what made escape possible also made survival precarious. The *cimarrones* had to defend themselves against pursuit by establishing themselves in almost inaccessible places and erecting a *palenque* (palisade) around their settlement. For this reason, maroon settlements were commonly referred to in Spanish America as *palenques.*

The *cimarrones* were also exposed to a lack of food, a problem they resolved by raiding nearby plantations and stealing foodstuffs, clothing, tools, animals, and other slaves. Settlers feared the *cimarrones* and easily believed that they were conspiring with slaves and Indians and Englishmen to rise up and kill all the Spaniards and take over the land.

Royal legislation decreed the pursuit and capture of *cimarrones* and the destruction of their *palenques,* but such expeditions proved unpopular because they were costly, dangerous, and frequently ineffective. When a *palenque* proved impregnable, the crown could be persuaded to declare it a free town and its inhabitants freed men on condition, principally, that they become law-abiding and admit no new runaways. A number of such villages in Ecuador, Colombia, and Panama have survived into the twentieth century as incomparable laboratories for the study of Afro-American culture.
NORMAN MEIKLEJOHN

CITIES, STRUCTURE OF. Since the form of the city is shaped by both past and present forces, the modern Latin American city reflects both the original nucleus laid down in the colonial period and additions over time to that core.

Morphology. In the Spanish American city the colonial past is most clearly preserved in the heart, which was commonly laid out in a gridiron of square and rectangular blocks divided by narrow streets in response to regulations ultimately codified in the 1573 ordinances. These set out instructions not only for the siting of towns but also for their platting in a precise manner, including the location and proportions of the main plaza and the disposition of public buildings around it. Although the regulations were not applied uniformly and in some cases were ignored, the layout of the typical colonial town was more or less that intended by Spanish law. However, there was commonly little order to the street network on the town periphery, which was often the location of rude Indian dwellings along haphazard streets.

The towns of colonial Brazil, laid out without such royal orders, commonly lacked a rigid gridiron form, developing instead in response to local influences such as terrain, the routing of roads, the location of port facilities, and so forth. But here, as elsewhere in Latin America, the heart of the modern city is an artifact of the colonial period.

There was little population growth in most Latin American cities in the colonial period. Low levels of commercial and industrial activity, little migration into the city from either the interior or abroad, and low natural population increases kept the typical colonial city small and relatively insignificant. Mexico City was an exception, as were some mining towns that exhibited rapid growth in a short period of time. By 1650, for example, the silver town of Potosí in Upper Peru (modern Bolivia) had grown to 160,000, making it by far the largest city in Latin America at that time.

Movement within the colonial towns was either pedestrian or equine, directed toward a single focus of commercial activity, usually centered in or near the principal plaza. As a consequence of such limited mobility, the towns slowly grew outward in a roughly concentric fashion and, as shown in the accompanying figure, did not lose their essentially mononuclear form.

Although population increases and the growth of commerce and industry began significantly to change the *size* of cities in the latter nineteenth century (well after independence for most countries), their *shape* was influenced particularly by changes in the dominant transportation modes and by the growth of urban land speculation. The horse-drawn tram was introduced into

a number of the major cities after about 1870. Because of the inherent limitations of this mode of transport, however, it had only a minor effect upon the shape of the city. Its service was commonly too infrequent and too slow to enable workers dependent upon jobs in the central city to move into more distant suburbs; suburban railroad service was infrequent before the twentieth century. The cities therefore maintained their nuclear shape, albeit with minor linear expansion at the parts of the city edge where horse-tram service was available.

What changed the nuclear city to a linear star-shaped one was the electric trolley, introduced into the major Latin American cities in the first decades of the twentieth century. Faster and more dependable than the horse tram, the trolley permitted workers to live farther from the city center on relatively cheap land made available to them with the growth of urban real estate speculation. Rising incomes, population increases and crowding in the central city, and expanded suburban railroad service in a few instances all stimulated the development of the periphery, ultimately leading to the incorporation of older small outlying towns into the expanding city.

The introduction of public bus service in Latin American cities came in the 1920s and 1930s, and its widespread adoption, especially after about 1945, led to the residential development of large tracts that had been too far from trolley or railroad lines for such use. The private automobile, because of its absolute and relatively high cost in most countries, has yet to have a major impact upon the shape of most cities.

The smaller cities, without the influence of the trolley and the railroad, have been slow to exhibit the breakdown of the more traditional colonial form. Indeed, the mobility of the bus is reinforcing an essentially concentric growth pattern in them today.

The influence of terrain upon the shape of the city is obvious in some instances. The mountains of Rio de Janeiro, the valley of Caracas, the peninsular location of Montevideo, the narrow valley of Quito, and the ravine in which La Paz is sited all had considerable influence upon the morphology of the city. In contrast, terrain played a relatively insignificant role in Buenos Aires, Lima, Bogotá, São Paulo, and Mexico City compared with that of transportation, speculation, and the pattern of landownership.

Land uses. A segregation of land uses within the city was already well developed in the Indian towns and cities of pre-Columbian America. At Teotihuacán, for example, there was occupational specialization by barrio (neighborhood) as well as a definite religious center and market areas. In the Aztec capital of Tenochtitlán, merchandise was sold in streets and quarters exclusively assigned to those goods. It is highly likely that all the major Indian centers exhibited a roughly similar functional segregation of land uses.

In both the Spanish and the Portuguese colonial towns, the central focus was the principal plaza with its church, government buildings, shops, and homes of the wealthy, who sought a central location in order to have maximum access to all that the city offered. Normally, the center city was the location of those public services, such as paved streets, municipal water, garbage collection, and street lighting, that existed in the colonial town.

The poorer lived farther from the center, as did the

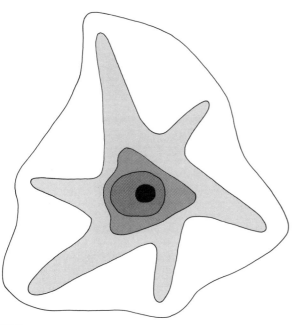

■ Colonial core (pedestrian).

▨ Colonial expansion (pedestrian).

▨ Late nineteenth century (horse tram).

▨ Early twentieth century (trolley and railroad).

☐ Post-1945 (bus and automobile).

Physical evolution of the Latin American city.

Indians. As the colonial town grew, new residential barrios that also supplied the low-order everyday goods and services needed on a neighborhood level were formed on the town's edge. Within the barrios there commonly developed a strong sense of community, and the city was socially segregated along these barrio lines; even today the barrio remains the major social subdivision of the Latin American city. Major commercial and many industrial activities remained in the central city, which was also the most densely settled residential area.

The central business district (CBD) of the Latin American city is still thriving and growing, for except in a few major cities, such as Caracas, there has not yet been the growth of significant outlying shopping centers to compete with the traditional commercial core. The continued focusing of transportation routes on the CBD and the low per capita ownership of automobiles helps maintain traditional central-city functions even in the largest and relatively more affluent metropolitan areas such as Buenos Aires, Rio de Janeiro, and Mexico City.

As industry developed in the city, certain districts came to have a strong industrial character. Noxious industries and those requiring much space, such as stockyards, typically were located on the edge of the city even in the colonial period and had to be relocated as the city expanded. In the late nineteenth century port districts evolved into important industrial zones, since imported raw materials, especially coal for fuel, were often essential to large-scale industrial production. Recently, planned industrial areas have been developed on the periphery of some cities, but except for large-scale, noxious, or port-oriented industries there has typically been little segregation of small-scale industry in the city.

Superficially, the major modern Latin American cities are striking because of the large numbers of modern high-rise office and apartment buildings. However, except for some public housing projects, such buildings serve primarily the more affluent commercial and high-income residential groups. Their predominance in the city center and in the more affluent districts attests to this condition. Elsewhere, major housing shortages are common, leading to the continued proliferation of the central-city slum with its high population densities and, especially since the 1950s, to the development of large numbers of squatter settlements.

The generic name of these settlements varies by country, but a common characteristic is their location on marginal lands, mostly on the periphery of the built-up zone but also in the older parts of the city along railroad tracks, on vacant parcels of public property, or on lands unsuitable for more conventional land uses, such as steep slopes. Public ownership of the land is most common, but in many cases the settlements are on privately owned land on some of which rent is paid. The occupancy of the land has typically been piecemeal, although there are instances of planned "invasions" of vacant land.

The dwellings themselves are constructed of whatever materials are available, such as scrap wood, cardboard, flattened tin cans, and cloth. Over time, the tendency is for the dwellings to become more substantial as the residents acquire better building materials and as additional public services are provided to the area. Typically, public services are limited, with few sources of water, only limited provision of electricity,

and no paving, sewers, or garbage collection. It is significant that the occupants of squatter settlements are generally underemployed rather than unemployed and that the existence of these marginal dwelling tracts is more often a consequence of the housing crisis than of unemployment.

Today the poor live throughout the city, while the wealthy are restricted to favored fringe areas and traditional central-city enclaves. As a generalization, the typical Latin American city exhibits traces of (1) a *concentric* pattern of residential segregation outward from the city center, (2) discrete socioeconomic *sectors* of residential occupancy, and (3) a segregation of land uses into discrete *nuclei* of residential, commercial, and manufacturing land uses.

Increasingly common to all the major cities of Latin America are the worldwide problems of traffic congestion and environmental deterioration. The narrow colonial streets of the center city, highly unsuited to modern modes of transportation, are heavily over-utilized because of the great vitality of the CBD. In response to the traffic problem, cities have increasingly turned to forms of rapid transit. Buenos Aires was the first to employ the subway (1913), and Mexico City inaugurated its first line in 1970. Caracas is installing a subway, and other cities have them under consideration. Most cities, however, rely increasingly upon the overburdened bus and, to a more limited extent, upon suburban train service.

The city is burdened increasingly by the unrestrained growth of the periphery and by the lack of financing to maintain existing buildings and services and to provide adequate public services to a rapidly growing population. Rapid growth has led to insufficient open space for parks and playgrounds, large areas of vacant, unimproved speculative landholdings, and the proliferation of cheaply built, unattractive residential barrios and squatter settlements. All indicators point to steadily worsening conditions and suggest that the Latin American city is in a crisis situation.

See also POPULATION.

Bibliography. J. M. Houston, "The Foundation of Colonial Towns in Hispanic America," in R. P. Beckinsale and J. M. Houston, *Urbanisation and Its Problems,* Oxford, England, 1968; Homer Hoyt, "The Residential and Retail Patterns of Leading Latin American Cities," *Land Economics,* vol. XXXIX, no. 4, November 1963, pp. 449–454; William Mangin, "Latin American Squatter Settlements: A Problem and a Solution," *Latin American Research Review,* vol. II, no. 3, Summer, 1967, pp. 65–98; Leo F. Schnore, "On the Spatial Structure of Cities in the Two Americas," in Philip M. Hauser and Leo F. Schnore (eds.), *The Study of Urbanization,* New York, 1965; T. Lynn Smith, "The Changing Functions of Latin American Cities," *The Americas,* vol. XXV, no. 1, July 1968, pp. 70–83; Dan Stanislawski, "Early Spanish Town Planning in the New World," *Geographical Review,* vol. XXXVII, no. 1, January 1947, pp. 94–105; Ruben D. Utria, "The Housing Problem in Latin America in Relation to Structural Development Factors," *Economic Bulletin for Latin America,* vol. XI, no. 2, October 1966, pp. 81–110.

CHARLES S. SARGENT

CIVILISTA PARTY. Most important political organization in Peru between 1899 and 1919. Founded in

1871, the Civilista party reflected the desire of the oligarchy of merchants, bankers, and landowners to bring order to the chaotic GUANO-oriented economy and to subordinate the unruly military *caudillos* to civilian control. The party's power base was principally in the cities and ports, and although it generally lacked widespread popular support, it compensated for this deficiency with social prestige, economic power, and political expertise.

In 1872 the party succeeded in electing its founder, Manuel PARDO, to the Presidency (1872–1876). However, when the Civilistas' antimilitarism was credited in part with Peru's humiliating defeat by Chile in the WAR OF THE PACIFIC (1879–1883), the party rapidly declined. Party members continued to hold important political posts, but it was not until after 1899 that the newly reorganized Civilistas gained control of the electoral machinery and returned to power. Until 1919 they dominated politics and made a number of important contributions, particularly in the early years of the twentieth century, to the nation's political stability and socioeconomic progress. Nonetheless, the party's internal divisions and its failure to respond adequately to the social and political forces created by the expansion of manufacturing, transportation, mining, and commercial agriculture brought about its downfall. In 1919 a spokesman of the new forces, Augusto LEGUÍA, came to power on an anti-Civilista platform, and in his eleven-year tenure he completed the dismantling of the Civilista party.

ORAZIO A. CICCARELLI

CLARK MEMORANDUM. Written by J. Reuben Clark, Jr., Undersecretary of State, at the request of the Secretary of State, the memorandum was intended to clarify the status of the MONROE DOCTRINE in the application of American foreign policy. The memorandum was presented to the Secretary on December 17, 1928, but was not made public until 1930. The Undersecretary declared that the doctrine had nothing to do with the relationship between the United States and Latin American nations, except in cases in which they became involved with European governments in arrangements that threatened the security of the United States. Even if this should happen, the doctrine was to be applied against the European country, not the Latin American one. In other words, "the Doctrine states a case of United States vs. Europe, not of United States vs. Latin America." Furthermore, it was clear that the Monroe Doctrine was not to be considered a pledge by the United States to other American states to protect them on demand from real or imaginary wrongs inflicted by European powers, and that it was not to be viewed as an obligation by the United States to any American state to intervene for its protection. Clark stated that the so-called ROOSEVELT COROLLARY to the Monroe Doctrine, which authorized the United States to intervene in the case of financial or other difficulties in weak Latin American states to prevent European interference, was contrary to the principles of the Monroe Doctrine.

RICHARD B. GRAY

CLAVER, ST. PEDRO (1580–1654). Spanish Jesuit who ministered to the poor, especially the blacks, of Cartagena, in what is now Colombia. Born in Catalonia, Pedro Claver entered the Society of Jesus in 1602 and was ordained a priest in 1616. His preferred and almost exclusive ministry was to black slaves, whose slave he declared himself to be. That Claver chose this ministry may be attributed in great part to the influence of a remarkably creative and apostolic Jesuit, Alonso de Sandoval, who laid the theoretical and methodological groundwork for a ministry to the African slaves in his work *De instauranda Aethiopum salute* (1627). However, neither Sandoval nor Claver ever questioned the institution of slavery.

Whenever a slave ship entered the harbor, Claver would hasten to climb aboard and bring solace to the aged and the infants, the sick and the dying. Once the slaves had been conducted to barracks, Claver went among them again, giving them an intensive initiation into the mysteries of the Christian faith. In between slave ship arrivals, Claver pursued the catechization of the blacks who remained in Cartagena and its environs, hearing their sins in confession, preaching to them, and giving them Holy Communion. He visited and tended the sick and the destitute in the slave quarters and in the city's hospital, its leprosarium, and its jails.

During his lifetime Claver was reputed to be a saint by all classes of Cartagena society. Not many years after he died in 1654, the case for his canonization was initiated, and in 1888 Pope Leo XIII declared him a saint of the Roman Catholic Church.

NORMAN MEIKLEJOHN

CLAVIJERO, FRANCISCO JAVIER (1731–1787). Mexican Jesuit historian. Born in Veracruz of Spanish parents, Clavijero was educated in the Jesuit College of Puebla and entered the order in 1748. His intellectual brilliance was recognized immediately, and he obtained the chairs of letters and philosophy in the College of San Ildefonso in Mexico City. He also taught in the Colleges of Valladolid and Guadalajara, introducing the concepts of modern philosophers such as Bacon, Descartes, and Leibniz and explaining the Copernican system. His teaching career was cut short by the decree of expulsion of the Jesuit order issued by King CHARLES III in 1767 (*see* JESUITS, EXPULSION OF: SPANISH AMERICA). With the rest of the members of the order he went to Italy. There he wrote his *Historia antigua de México* (*The History of Mexico*), a history of pre-Columbian civilizations in Mexico and of the conquest. He had had the opportunity of studying Indian codices in the College of San Gregorio and the manuscript collection of Indian antiquities and history owned by the savant Carlos de SIGÜENZA Y GÓNGORA. Clavijero also knew several Indian languages.

Completed in 1779, his *Historia* was translated into Italian and published in 1780–1781. He also wrote *Historia de la Baja California* and other minor works. However, the *Historia antigua de México,* 1789 (*The History of Lower California*) remains his best work. In it he described the physical environment of ancient Mexico, the main Indian groups and their interrelations, Aztec civilization (*see* AZTECS), and the Spanish conquest. His style was clear and modern. Viewing Indian cultures sympathetically, he recognized and praised their contributions to the Mexican nationality. Clavijero adopted a nationalistic attitude by analyzing and destroying the inaccurate concepts of the natural inferiority of the American continent spread in Europe by Cornelius de Pauw, Buffon, and other writers.

ASUNCIÓN LAVRIN

CLAYTON-BULWER TREATY. This important and controversial treaty between the United States and Great Britain was signed on April 19, 1850, in an effort to reach a compromise on the differences and rivalries of the two powers in Central America. Both governments agreed that neither would seek or keep exclusive control over any interoceanic canals to be built, and that neither would erect or maintain any fortifications along or near the canal; nor would either seek dominion over Nicaragua, Costa Rica, the Mosquito Coast, or any other part of Central America. In addition, both parties agreed that all advantages secured from any of these governments, if a canal should be built, would be offered on equal terms to the other. Each agreed to use its influence over said governments to facilitate the construction of the canal and the establishment of free ports at either end. They further agreed that the canal, when built, would be protected from interruption or seizure and that it would be kept open for general use. They also stated that they would extend their protection to any other form of communication, such as a railway across the isthmus, with particular reference to Tehuantepec and Panama. The United States expected that the British would withdraw from the Mosquito Coast and the Bay Islands, but this did not happen.

Secretary of State John M. Clayton was widely criticized in the United States for allowing the country in violation of the MONROE DOCTRINE to agree to an extension of British influence by means of a protective partnership over an interoceanic canal. A joint enterprise never developed, however, and the treaty was finally abrogated by the Hay-Pauncefote Treaty in 1901, clearing the way for the United States to build the canal on its own (*see* PANAMA CANAL).

RICHARD B. GRAY

CNT. *See* CONVENCIÓN NACIONAL DE TRABAJADORES.

COBO, BERNABÉ (1580–1657). Jesuit chronicler. Born in Lopera, Jaén Province, Cobo sailed from Spain in 1596 en route to northern South America. However, he evidently got no farther than Trinidad; from there he went to Hispaniola and eventually to Lima, where he enrolled in the Jesuit-run College of San Martín. From 1601, when he entered the Jesuit novitiate, until 1622, when he became a full member of the order, he not only continued his studies but also traveled extensively throughout the viceroyalty. By the late 1620s he had begun his history of the New World, for in 1629 he traveled to the Viceroyalty of New Spain to continue his research there. In 1642 he returned to Peru, where he remained until his death.

Cobo completed his *Historia del Nuevo Mundo* in the 1630s but continued revising it for many years; the prologue, dedicated to Juan SOLÓRZANO PEREIRA, is dated 1653. The original history consisted of forty-three books, divided into three parts, of which only seventeen are extant. The first part, published as *Historia del Nuevo Mundo* in four volumes in 1890–1893, contains descriptions of the geography, minerals, flora and fauna, and native inhabitants of the New World and concludes with an outstanding discussion of the culture of the INCAS. A portion of the second part was published as *Historia de la fundación de Lima* in 1882. Cobo's work is highly regarded not only be-

cause of the author's long and wide-ranging experience in America at a time relatively close to the conquest but also because of his extensive use of manuscript materials.

HELEN DELPAR

COCHRANE, THOMAS (LORD COCHRANE; 10TH EARL OF DUNDONALD; 1775–1860). British admiral and soldier of fortune who fought for the independence of both Spanish America and Brazil. The most eminent of the European adventurers who participated in the Latin American independence struggle, Cochrane was a member of a noble Scottish family who entered the British Navy and distinguished himself in the Napoleonic Wars. He also served in Parliament and became a noted critic of naval abuses.

In 1817 Lord Cochrane accepted an invitation to enter the service of Chile. Soon after his arrival in 1818, he was placed in command of Chile's fledgling Navy, composed of a heterogeneous assortment of warships, most of whose experienced seamen were also foreigners. Converting them into a disciplined force, he harassed the Spanish-held ports of Peru and Ecuador and played a key role in taking the royalist stronghold of Valdivia in southern Chile. In 1820 he headed the fleet that conveyed José de SAN MARTÍN northward to invade Peru. However, he quarreled bitterly with San Martín over the latter's cautious strategy and over pay and other support for his squadron. After cruising along the Pacific coast as far as Mexican waters, he returned to Chile in 1822.

Cochrane then transferred his services to Brazil, where he aided the emperor PEDRO I in the War of Independence against Portugal. By the end of 1825, however, he had quarreled with the Brazilians also and returned to Europe, where he fought for a time for Greek independence from Turkey and eventually reentered the British Navy.

DAVID BUSHNELL

COELHO, DUARTE (d. 1554). Portuguese founder and colonizer of Pernambuco, Brazil, and one of the most successful of the donatary captains (*see* CAPTAINCY SYSTEM). After extensive travels and service in Asia, Africa, and Europe, Duarte Coelho was rewarded with the grant of 60 leagues of coast in Pernambuco and Alagôas in 1534. He took his family and settlers and founded Olinda in 1537. One of the ablest colonizers, he probably used capital accumulated in India to establish sugar mills and import African slave labor. The establishment of the governor-generalship at Bahia (modern Salvador) in 1549 resulted in a struggle for the retention of the captaincy's autonomy from the new royal administration, a struggle in which Coelho was only partly successful.

KENNETH R. MAXWELL

COFFEE INDUSTRY (BRAZIL). The genesis of the Brazilian coffee industry is obscured in legend. It is believed by many that coffee was introduced into Brazil when Francisco de Melo Palheta brought about 1,000 beans and five plants to Pará from French Guiana in 1727. Whatever its origins, the coffee industry grew until in 1750 Pará exported 12 tons of coffee beans to Portugal. At the same time, coffee production spread to Ceará, Amazonas, Bahia, and Pernambuco. In 1761 the first seedlings were planted in Rio de Janeiro, and coffee culture slowly spread from Rio westward into Minas Gerais and southward down the Paraíba Valley into São Paulo, reaching the Campinas area by 1809. In spite of the growing production of coffee, Brazil did not become America's leading coffee producer until the industry of the hemisphere's primary producer, Haiti, was destroyed in the wake of independence in the late 1790s. By the 1840s Brazil had become the world's leading producer.

The coffee industry continued to expand until the turn of the twentieth century, and Brazil's share of total world production climbed to about three-quarters. In the last decades of the nineteenth century, however, production outstripped coffee consumption, and Brazil began to accumulate large surpluses. To meet the economic crisis caused by overproduction, the three leading coffee-producing states, Rio de Janeiro, Minas Gerais, and São Paulo, set up a valorization program in the 1906 TAUBATÉ CONVENTION. The states agreed to purchase most of the coffee harvests and hold them until the proper price level was reached. Also, planting new coffee orchards was prohibited. Valorization was overwhelmed in the late 1920s by a rash of bumper crops and the collapse of the world economy in 1929.

In spite of the economic situation created by the worldwide depression, Brazilian coffee production remained high, although a slight drop in the average yearly production from the 1928–1932 level of 21,883,-000 sacks of 132 pounds each to an average of 19,344,-000 sacks for the 1932–1936 period was recorded. To meet the problems of the coffee industry, the government of Getúlio VARGAS established the National Coffee Department (DNC) in 1933 to regulate the industry and reach an equilibrium between production and export capacity. Excess coffee was burned or dumped into the sea. Old orchards were uprooted, and a ban was placed on planting new orchards. In 1941 Brazil joined other American coffee producers to form the Inter-American Coffee Board and set production quotas. After the fall of the Vargas dictatorship, the government of Eurico Gaspar DUTRA abandoned (1946) the controls Vargas had placed on the industry. By 1952 the coffee industry was again in crisis, and Vargas, who had returned to power in the presidential election of 1950, created the Brazilian Coffee Institute (IBC) to improve Brazil's position in the world coffee market. At the same time, the various post-World War II governments attempted to end what Juscelino KUBITSCHEK called the "tyranny of coffee" by promoting industry and diversification of the export economy. In 1972 the Brazilian government announced that industrial goods might top coffee on the export list. This did not mean a serious decline in coffee production, which totaled 1,726,000 tons in 1970–1971, but an increase in the export of manufactures. The leading coffee-growing states are Paraná, São Paulo, Minas Gerais, and Espírito Santo, but new lands in Mato Grosso are being opened up to coffee culture.

The effects of the coffee industry are varied and widespread. Coffee cultivation changed the face of the countryside. In some areas poor planting techniques, erosion, and soil exhaustion resulted in ecological disaster. The coffee "rush" led to a shift in Brazil's economic center from the northeastern agricultural region to the southeast. A new aristocracy of coffee barons was born. In the nineteenth century the demand for labor led to a concentration of the slave population in the coffee region of the south. As it became apparent that slavery was doomed, the planters tried various schemes of acquiring free contract labor, including importing Chinese. After abolition in 1888 (*see* ABOLITION OF SLAVERY: BRAZIL), the coffee industry attracted growing numbers of immigrants, especially Italians (*see* IMMIGRATION: BRAZIL). The soaring population and wealth produced by coffee influenced the rapid growth of São Paulo and the founding of new towns. Accompanying the rise of the coffee industry were a transportation revolution and the growth of the port of Santos, as roads and railroads were opened up to allow coffee to reach the world market.

Bibliography. Luis Amaral, *História Geral da Agricultura Brasileira,* vol. III, Parte Especial, *O Café,* São Paulo, 1940; Roberto Cochrane Simonsen, *Aspectos da História Econômica do Café,* São Paulo, 1940; Affonso de Escragnolle Taunay, *História do Café no Brasil,* 15 vols., Rio de Janeiro, 1939.

LAWRENCE J. NIELSEN

COFFEE INDUSTRY (CENTRAL AMERICA). Coffee is the most generally cultivated commercial crop in Central America. It ranks first in value among the exports of Costa Rica, El Salvador, and Guatemala and usually second or third among those of Honduras and Nicaragua; total coffee production in the five republics was estimated at 388,200 metric tons in 1970. Extensive areas in the region afford ideal growing conditions, including elevations that produce premium grades.

Coffee was known in Guatemala and Costa Rica during the eighteenth century, but its cultivation as a Central American commercial crop began in Costa Rica soon after independence, when it promised to become that country's first suitable money crop. First shipped abroad in 1825, coffee had become Costa Rica's chief export by 1829. Early cargoes went to the west coast countries of South America, but shipments made to Great Britain in 1845 opened the European market, and large-scale exports began.

Other Central American countries followed Costa Rica's lead. El Salvador began commercial coffee production during the 1860s, and Guatemala about a decade later. In both countries coffee became the leading export during the latter half of the nineteenth century. Nicaragua first acquired the bean in 1850, but commercial production there and in Honduras was a twentieth-century development. The governments of Costa Rica and Guatemala actively fostered coffee development. Costa Rica offered free land to entrepreneurs who would set out coffee trees and began the construction of cart roads leading to Limón on the Caribbean and Puntarenas on the Pacific. Guatemala offered public lands for sale at reasonable prices and enacted labor laws that assured producers an adequate supply of Indian labor.

Coffee cultivation attracted both national and immigrant entrepreneurs. The steady movement of Costa Rican coffee planters outward from the older settled areas gave that country one of the few "solid frontiers" of occupation in Latin America. This development reversed the characteristic trend in the Meseta Central (Central Plateau) from small to larger landholdings. In El Salvador the local aristocracy first sensed the possibilities of coffee production and established large coffee *fincas* (plantations). Imitators on a smaller scale followed their lead until coffee growing was widely practiced. The wealth, however, became concentrated in the hands of the so-called "fourteen families" who own most of the plantations. In Guatemala nationals dominated production in the central and western highlands, and descendants of immigrants, principally Germans, in the slopes overlooking the Pacific and in much of the highland area between Huehuetenango and Alta Verapaz. Before World War II these immigrant proprietors owned nearly half of the large Guatemalan coffee properties and produced nearly two-thirds of the national crop. The government took over most German properties during World War II and operated them as national *fincas*, but in 1958 it sold some to private individuals.

Coffee production is a labor-intensive industry. Most operations including seeding, planting, cultivation, picking, and sorting are performed by hand. In some establishments depulping and drying likewise require much hand labor, but on the larger *fincas* these operations, as well as the polishing that prepares the bean for market, are mechanized. Labor systems have varied from the use of paid agricultural workers characteristic of Costa Rica to the Guatemalan pattern of maintaining *colonos* who live on the land for year-round tasks and employing *jornaleros*, day laborers acquired by varying proportions of attraction and coercion, for seasonal labor. The large pool of cheap labor has been an advantage in cost competition, but it has to be reckoned a factor retarding national development.

Coffee was the first bulk commodity Central America produced for export. The primitive transportation systems at first afforded conveyance only by Indian carriers or on muleback. At this stage easy access to the Pacific gave El Salvador a cost advantage over other Central American producers. In 1846 Costa Rica completed a cart road to Puntarenas that eased transport to the Pacific, and completion of the railroad to Puerto Limón in 1890 shifted the major outlet to the Atlantic. In Guatemala coffee production spurred the construction of outlet railroads on the Pacific side and in Alta Verapaz. Completion of the Guatemalan railroad to the Caribbean in 1908 and extension of the line to El Salvador in 1929 gave shippers of both countries rail access to both Pacific and Caribbean ports.

Central American countries produce less than 10 percent of Latin American coffee, but their premium grades enjoy a preferential market. They are parties to international coffee agreements and accept assigned market quotas (*see* INTERNATIONAL COFFEE AGREEMENT). Their coffee growers maintain associations that are affiliated with the Federación Cafetelera de América, a regional organization of Middle American associations with its seat in San Salvador.

Bibliography. Preston E. James, *Latin America,* 4th ed., New York, 1969; Franklin D. Parker, *The Central American Republics,* London, 1964; Robert C. West and John P. Augelli, *Middle America: Its Lands and Peoples,* Englewood Cliffs, N.J., 1966.

WILLIAM J. GRIFFITH

COFFEE INDUSTRY (COLOMBIA). Coffee represents approximately 30 percent of the agricultural output of Colombia and is its major export commodity, the value of exports exceeding $461 million in 1970. Colombian coffee is characteristically of the mild "washed" Arabica variety and is grown on small mountainside farms from 3,000 to 6,000 feet above sea level. Owing to exceptionally favorable natural conditions in the Colombian highlands, relatively efficient production is possible even on small-size plots using intensive labor techniques. Thus about 87 percent of the coffee farms are worked directly by their owners, and 42 percent of the total area in coffee cultivation is worked by the owners without outside labor. The number of coffee farms is slightly above 300,000, of which more than 110,000 are of less than 1 hectare and only 843 of more than 50 hectares. Some 93 percent of Colombia's coffee comes from farms producing less than eighty-five bags of coffee per year. Colombia's total annual production is in excess of 8 million bags. Because of the year-round moderation of the climate and rainfall distribution, planting can take place in almost any month.

Coffee first came to Colombia from the French Antilles in the second half of the eighteenth century. By 1808 there was some small-scale cultivation in the Cúcuta Valley in the region known as Santander, and in 1813 Ignacio Ordóñez de Lara could report that he had 7,000 plants on his hacienda, El Peñón, in the district of Cúcuta. From Santander the cultivation of coffee spread to Cundinamarca and, by 1932 Antioquia and the neighboring department of Caldas were producing 46.9 percent of Colombia's coffee. In contrast to the situation that prevailed in other departments, most coffee in Antioquia and Caldas was cultivated on small family farms.

The Colombian government early recognized the potential importance of coffee production. In 1821 national legislation erected barriers to the importation of foreign coffee, and in 1824 coffee producers were granted immunity from ecclesiastical taxes. The first recorded exportation of Colombian coffee was in 1834, but coffee did not become an important item of trade until late in the century. The dollar value of coffee exports first exceeded $100,000 in 1845; it did not exceed $1 million until 1872.

In 1927 the Federación Nacional de Cafeteros de Colombia (Federacafé) was established as a nonprofit, nonpolitical organization. Federacafé protects the interests of the small coffee growers, develops the coffee economy, and supervises Colombia's participation in the international coffee market. It is governed by an eleven-man board of directors, with six members representing the growers and five the government. Federacafé performs a variety of activities, including research through the federation's coffee experimental station in Chinchiná and banking through the Banco Cafetero. The most important function of the federation is guaranteeing a support price for coffee, thus avoiding drastic fluctuations in the purchasing power of the growers.

Extreme fluctuations in coffee prices have been minimized through Colombia's participation in the INTERNATIONAL COFFEE AGREEMENT of 1962. The agreement functions through a system of export quotas decided upon annually by producing and consuming countries. A selectivity mechanism diminishes or increases export supplies in relation to declining or rising coffee price levels. Although the agreement has generally succeeded in stabilizing prices, some fluctuation remains and is subsequently reflected in the rate of growth of the Colombian economy. Thus a decline in the value of coffee exports in 1971 by 13 percent in relation to 1970 was reflected in a major deceleration, while an increase by 25 percent in foreign currency earnings from coffee in 1972 caused considerable improvement in the domestic economy. A long-run stabilization of Colombian coffee prices at a high level is expected as a result of an increasing demand for coffee in Western Europe and Japan, a situation that is counteracting the stagnant demand registered in the United States coffee market in recent years. Total Western European coffee consumption now accounts for a larger volume than that of the United States.

To minimize further the domestic repercussions of fluctuations in international coffee quotations, Colombia has successfully implemented a drive toward export diversification that is beginning to exhibit significant results. In 1969, 1970, and 1971 the share of the value of coffee exports was respectively 57, 62, and 53 percent of the total, as contrasted with 75 percent in 1954 and an average of 66 percent for the decade of the 1960s.

Bibliography. Robert C. Beyer, "The Quality of Coffee: Its Colombian History," *Inter-American Economic Affairs,* vol. II, Autumn, 1948, pp. 72–80; id., "Transportation and the Coffee Industry in Colombia," *Inter-American Economic Affairs,* vol. II, Winter, 1948, pp. 17–30; William Paul McGreevey, *An Economic History of Colombia, 1845–1930,* Cambridge, England, 1971; Diego Monsalve, *Colombia cafetera,* Barcelona, 1927.

JAMES H. NEAL

COLEGIADO. The term *colegiado* refers to either of two forms of plural executive under which Uruguay was governed during the periods 1918–1933 and 1952–1967. During the earlier period executive power was divided between an elected President and a bipartisan National Council of Administration; under the more recent form, all executive authority was vested in a nine-member bipartisan National Council of Government.

After the concept of a plural executive had been advocated for years by the leader of the Colorado party (*see* COLORADO PARTY: URUGUAY), José BATLLE (President of Uruguay, 1903–1907 and 1911–1915), a diluted version eventually was incorporated in the 1918 constitution. The Presidency was retained, but the President was now to be popularly elected rather than chosen by the legislature as in the past, and he would have control over only the Ministries of Foreign Affairs and Interior and those dealing with national defense. Parallel to the President and sharing the executive power was a popularly elected nine-member National Council of Administration, whose membership was renewed by thirds every two years in elections that would give one of the three positions to the minority party. The Council had control of the Ministries of Public Instruction, Public Works, Finance, Labor, Industry, Public Welfare, and Health. The Council was abandoned after President Gabriel TERRA's coup d'état in 1933.

After eighteen years of a conventional Presidency, Uruguay readopted the plural executive in a more nearly complete form. The constitution of 1951 abolished the Presidency as it had traditionally existed, replacing it with the National Council of Government. All executive power rested in the Council, whose Presidency was rotated annually among members of the majority faction. In contrast to the earlier *colegiado,* this Council was renewed in its entirety every four years in elections that guaranteed six seats to the majority party and three to the second party. A constitutional amendment to return to a single executive was rejected in the 1962 election, but four years later voters approved a new constitution that replaced the National Council of Government with a strong President.

LEE C. FENNELL

COLOMBIA, GRAN (OR GREATER). Political union of present-day Colombia, Venezuela, Ecuador, and Panama that was established in 1819 and broke up in 1830. Since 1810 the patriots of Venezuela and New Granada had often lent each other military and other support, but formal unification was not attempted until December 1819. Then, at the urging of Simón BOLÍVAR, the Congress of Angostura (*see* ANGOSTURA, CONGRESS OF) proclaimed the union not just of Venezuela and New Granada but of all the former Viceroyalty of New Granada (that is, the Presidency of Quito, or Ecuador, as well). The nation received the name Republic of Colombia; "Gran" would be added later, to distinguish it from the Colombia of today.

The Congress of Angostura adopted a provisional organization that entailed separate Vice Presidents for Venezuela and Cundinamarca (New Granada). A permanent constitution, liberal but rigidly centralist, was enacted in 1821 by the Congress of Cúcuta (*see* CÚCUTA, CONGRESS OF), which elected Bolívar and Francisco de Paula SANTANDER as the first constitutional President and Vice President for all Colombia. However, Bolívar left the conduct of government to Santander so that he could continue to direct the struggle against Spain, including the final liberation of Ecuador, whose incorporation in Gran Colombia had been decreed without the vote of Ecuadorian representatives.

Santander worked ably to consolidate the institutions adopted at Cúcuta and extend the program of liberal reform also begun there; but internal dissensions accumulated, especially in Venezuela and Ecuador, which resented subordination to the central authorities in Bogotá. Thus the revolt of José Antonio PÁEZ in Venezuela in 1826 was followed by further defiance of the national administration in Ecuador. Order was restored temporarily when Bolívar returned from Peru, conciliated Páez, and assumed the Presidency in person. Neither a special convention held at Ocaña in 1828 to consider constitutional reform nor the establishment of a conservative dictatorship by Bolívar provided any lasting solution, and although a brief war with Peru in 1828–1829 resulted in Colombian victory, it placed additional strains on Bolívar's government. Páez revolted again, and Venezuela formally seceded in April 1830. In May 1830, Ecuador followed Venezuela's example. What remained of the original union made no attempt to stop them and instead reconstituted itself as the Republic of New Granada.

DAVID BUSHNELL

COLOMBIA SINCE 1830. The transfer of power from Spanish hands to those of the creole elite in Colombia was complete by 1824. Despite liberal social legislation enacted by the neophyte Congresses, the social structure inherited from colonial days was hardly affected. Indeed, slavery became more severe as a result of the Manumission Law of 1821, which provided for the emancipation of the children of slaves at the age of eighteen. Because of the imminent demise of the institution, those remaining in bondage tended to be exploited with less humanity than before. The condition of the country's Indian population deteriorated, too, with the passage of laws aimed at abolishing the Indians' reservation lands. In both cases the change was due to the removal of Spanish control over the creole elite. The elite's unwillingness to distribute the tax burden equitably, the continuation of a dependent export economy, and the huge deficits created by the wars of independence all served to destroy Gran Colombia by 1830 (*see* COLOMBIA, GRAN).

Following two years of civil strife three nations emerged from the ruins: New Granada, Ecuador, and Venezuela. New Granada, as present-day Colombia (which included Panama until 1903) was then called, chose Gen. Francisco de Paula SANTANDER as its chief executive. Ruling until early 1837, he stabilized the fiscal system and generally imposed strong central control over the country's variegated regions. With his successor, José Ignacio de Márquez (1837–1841), the Santanderian consensus came to an end. Regionalism, frustrated by a decade of official indifference to local aspirations, burst out in a wave of violent rebellions, known as the revolt of the Supremos (1839–1842). The rebellions were finally suppressed, though at considerable cost in lives and treasure, by Generals Pedro Alcántara Herrán and Tomás Cipriano de MOSQUERA.

The repressive policies of the early years of Herrán's Presidency (1841–1845) gradually gave way to a restoration of civil liberties, though within a framework of centralized authoritarian rule. Elected as guarantor of this conservative polity, General Mosquera departed from it by 1846, espoused economic and political liberalism, and sponsored an ambitious public works program. He also abandoned his predecessors' diplomatic isolationism and negotiated the Mallarino-Bidlack Treaty of 1846 with the United States (*see* BIDLACK TREATY).

The liberal Mosquera regime (1845–1849) was followed by that of Gen. José Hilario López, elected in 1849. López, supported by the former rebels of 1839–1842, the bulk of the university youth, and the artisans of the major cities, purged the bureaucracy of most of its experienced officials and appointed to public office only men acceptable to the recently created Liberal party (*see* LIBERAL PARTY: COLOMBIA). His exclusivism and partisanship encouraged the growth of the opposition Conservative party (*see* CONSERVATIVE PARTY: COLOMBIA), also newly founded. In the main the López administration (1849–1853) sought to extinguish the principal legacies of colonial rule: the political role of the church and the Army, slavery, and the communal land tenure system of the Indians. The church was hobbled (1853), the Army was much reduced in size (1853), slavery was abolished (1851), and much of the Indian land was divided and sold to local magnates.

Gen. José María OBANDO inherited the social and political tensions created by these policies when he became President in 1853. Socially and politically conservative, although nominally a Liberal, Obando was unable to ease the mounting pressures upon his regime. In April 1854, a barracks revolt led by Gen. José María Melo (perhaps tacitly approved by Obando) overthrew the government. Obando was placed under house arrest, the Congress was dissolved, and the capital and its hinterland fell to Melo, who declared himself dictator. Both Liberal and Conservative elites united in opposition to his rule and, after much campaigning, defeated him in December 1854. A bipartisan regime removed Obando from office, exiled Melo, and brought a truce between the two parties that lasted until 1856.

Victorious in the elections of that year, Conservative Mariano Ospina Rodríguez came to power. His Presidency (1857–1861) was marked by a revival of social and political tensions. He sought to employ the clergy as instruments of Conservative partisanship and refused to accept constitutional changes enacted in 1858 that gave greater autonomy to the states. By 1860 he had so antagonized the Liberals and the Governor of the state of Cauca, General Mosquera, that civil war ensued.

This conflict, called the Federal War because of the Liberal party's espousal of states' rights, lasted amid great bloodshed until the end of 1862. In its wake came Liberal victory, the revival of Mosquera's prestige, and a virulent assault upon the church. The most important aspect of this assault was the destruction of the church's economic base. Ecclesiastical properties, both rural and urban, were auctioned off between 1861 and 1880, often at a fraction of their value, by the Liberal governments.

COLOMBIA
Area: 439,737 sq. mi.   Population: 21,772,000 (1971 est.).

Once back in power, the Liberals were determined to retain their control at any cost. They enacted the constitution of 1863, in which the states were granted nearly sovereign powers, individual liberties were expanded, and the federal and state governments were authorized to exercise the right of "inspection" over religious cults. Mosquera's dominance, and that of the moderate Liberals, ended with his overthrow by a coup d'état in May 1867, clearing the way for the doctrinaire Radical Liberals to assume control of the party and the nation. In the succeeding decade five Radical Presidents sought to rule from a power base made increasingly untenable as federalism degenerated into intense localized factionalism. Vindictive anticlerical legislation continued to harass priests and bishops in most of the country and tore at the social fabric. The embattled clergy looked to a Conservative revival as their only means of preserving secular power.

The deepening elitist dissatisfaction with Radical dominance was also influenced by economic factors. When the republic was established in 1831–1832, it relied on gold exports for foreign exchange. In 1850 tobacco replaced gold, and its sale in Europe produced a measure of prosperity and supported steamboat transportation on the main river, the MAGDALENA RIVER. Tobacco remained the staple crop until the market collapsed in 1876. Massive land transfers (the Indians' lands after 1850 and those of the church after 1861) were of immense significance in the creation of latifundia and the expansion of cattle raising at the expense of foodstuff agriculture. Basic commodity prices rose sharply in the cities and towns, causing severe distress to the artisan and salaried classes. In the countryside many smallholders and ·Indian farmers were forced into peonage.

The political reflection of these stresses and of the need for a redirection of national priorities was the Independent party, a dissident faction of the Liberals. Its guiding light, Rafael NÚÑEZ, won the Presidency in 1880 with help from moderate Conservatives. At the end of his term in 1882 he concluded that Radical intransigence precluded any substantive compromise. By aligning his party even further with the Conservatives, he was able to regain power in 1884. The disgruntled Radicals revolted in 1885, but they were defeated and Núñez undertook his reconstruction of the body politic.

Under the centralist and authoritarian 1886 constitution (*see* CONSTITUTION OF 1886: COLOMBIA), the national executive became the real ruler of the nation, limited only by poor communications in maintaining its will over the hinterland. A concordat negotiated in 1887 restored the church to preeminence in education and thus to its position as principal arbiter of the country's social development. A return to more traditional policies, both in politics and in society, was inevitable.

The exclusion of the Liberals from power was more marked after they revolted against Núñez's successor, Miguel Antonio CARO, in 1895. It became nearly complete after the War of the Thousand Days (1899–1902; *see* THOUSAND DAYS, WAR OF THE), the final gasp of nineteenth-century Colombian liberalism. The next year saw the loss of the Isthmus of Panama, which seceded from Colombia with the aid of the United States.

To Gen. Rafael REYES, President from 1904 to 1909, fell the awesome task of reconstruction. The nation's economy was shattered by the war, its transportation system in shambles, and its morale strained. Reyes, whose regime became more and more dictatorial, was nonetheless able to restore a large measure of stability. His government foundered upon the rocks of an impoverished and imperfectly functioning fiscal structure rather than an effective political opposition.

By 1910 Colombia's political elites had regrouped. In almost undisputed dominance was the Conservative party. It ruled for two decades (1910–1930) through its provincial clients, by its manipulation of place and privilege, and because of the support of the urban and rural clergy. Basic to Colombia's economic development after 1905 was the rise of coffee as the nation's main cash export (*see* COFFEE INDUSTRY: COLOMBIA). Notwithstanding the severe economic crisis brought on by World War I (1914–1918), the Colombian government, by dint of stringent economies and careful management, kept its credit intact. The sharp economic dislocations caused by the war were reflected in labor violence from 1918 to 1920 in the capital and along the Magdalena and the Caribbean coast.

Cushioning Colombia's continuing poverty was the sum of $25 million received from the United States. Paid between 1922 and 1926, this "conscience money" for the United States role in the Panamanian secession of 1903 stimulated the sluggish Colombian economy. Most of the money was spent in modernizing the banking and transportation systems, which in turn improved Colombia's external credit somewhat. As a result, between 1922 and 1928 national, provincial, and even municipal governments were able to borrow considerable sums from United States banks.

In 1929, coinciding with the onset of world economic depression, came a deep split in the Conservative ruling elite. The church was badly compromised by the necessity of supporting first one and then another Conservative presidential hopeful, and its political influence was damaged. In addition, many Conservatives became convinced that only a Liberal President could stem burgeoning labor unrest and economic recession. As a result, Enrique OLAYA HERRERA won the Presidency in 1930.

The Olaya years (1930–1934) were a fragile buffer against the winds of economic and social change. Yet, in fact, the twentieth century, in the guise of Colombia's greater dependence upon foreign exchange and capital, had reached the country. Labor violence, which in the latter 1920s had contributed to the fall of the Conservatives, diminished after 1931, when labor unions were legalized. However, violence of a political origin increased, only to abate during the Leticia border dispute with Peru (1932–1934).

Alfonso LÓPEZ was elected to the Presidency in 1934. His administration, called the Revolution on the March, enacted the first mild AGRARIAN REFORM law, initiated social security legislation, and until 1937 placed itself on the side of change. A masterful politician, López found himself violently opposed by both left and right. He perceived greater strength in the right (within both the Liberal and the Conservative parties) and eventually gave way to it.

His successor, Eduardo SANTOS, during his Presidency (1938–1942) represented a definite shift away from the reformism of López, in part because of the effect of World War II on the coffee export economy. A second presidential term for López (1942–1945) revealed the incompatibility of the Liberal party's right and left wings and the inability of the President to maintain his momentum during a second time in power. Thanks to the Liberal division a Conservative resurgence, spurred by the vitriolic rhetoric of Laureano GÓMEZ, was rewarded in the election of Mariano OSPINA PÉREZ in 1946. A minority President, Ospina Pérez rode out the storm of the BOGOTAZO (April 9, 1948) and, after suppressing many civil rights, was succeeded in 1950 by Gómez.

Gómez, a brilliant opposition leader and polemicist, could not manage both internal Conservative and external Liberal contention while chief executive. His only definable policy was one of keeping power at the expense of public liberties. His repressive measures fanned the rural and urban violence that had risen sharply after mid-1948 and reached an apex during his rule (1950–1953; see VIOLENCIA, LA). A conflict-weary Colombia welcomed Gen. Gustavo ROJAS PINILLA's coup of June 1953, which sent Gómez into exile.

The Rojas Pinilla regime (1953–1957) represented a right-wing response, similar to that of Juan D. PERÓN in Argentina, to Colombia's mounting social and economic dilemmas. The reluctant military furnished nominal leadership, but the grass-roots administration was in the hands of Conservatives. As violence returned after mid-1954, the Rojas government sought to sponsor a "third force" answer to the country's pressing problems. Considerable amounts of capital were expended on road construction. The reaction of the business establishment became negative, and in May 1957 Rojas was ousted from power.

An interim military junta ruled from May 1957 to August 1958, when Alberto LLERAS CAMARGO took the presidential oath of office. He was to be the first of four NATIONAL FRONT Presidents. Created in 1956–1957 by the heads of the Conservative and Liberal parties, this system provided for alternate Liberal and Conservative Presidencies and for party parity in the Congress and in public administration. Ruling from 1958 to 1962, Lleras Camargo generated the creation of a greatly expanded professionalized bureaucratic structure independent of traditional political loyalties, began the nominal land reform still in process, and delivered a much calmer nation to his successor, Guillermo León VALENCIA.

It fell to Valencia, whose term lasted from 1962 to 1966, to end the worst remnants of the rural violence, mainly banditry by then, in which task, aided by a much-modernized military, he was successful. He was also able, through his shrewd political manipulations, to keep his opponents unbalanced while continuing the restructuring innovations of his predecessor. On the economic front Valencia was less successful, and the Colombian peso was sharply devalued.

Carlos LLERAS RESTREPO, who followed Valencia in office (1966–1970), had, together with Rafael Reyes and Alfonso López, the greatest impact on Colombia in the twentieth century. Lleras Restrepo devoted his considerable energy to implementing measures designed to lessen Colombian dependence upon coffee exports and vigorously espoused public and private investment in industrial development. The Lleras Restrepo regime secured much-needed foreign loans for this purpose. However, his rigid policy of holding industrial and other wages down in order to curb inflation and his frequent use of police power engendered deep discontent, which surfaced in the 1970 presidential elections.

Misael PASTRANA BORRERO barely won that contest against the populist forces of Rojas Pinilla's ALIANZA NACIONAL POPULAR. Pastrana loosened but maintained the economic direction set by Lleras Restrepo despite strong political pressure from both left and right. Inflation, the population explosion, especially in the overflowing cities, rural depression, and persistent unemployment did little to lighten his task.

Bibliography. Gustavo Arboleda, *Historia contemporánea de Colombia,* 6 vols., Bogotá, Popayán, and Cali, 1918–35; Robert H. Dix, *Colombia: The Political Dimensions of Change,* New Haven, Conn., 1967; Vernon L. Fluharty, *Dance of the Millions: Military Rule and Social Revolution in Colombia, 1930–1956,* Pittsburgh, 1957; José María Henao and Gerardo Arrubla, *History of Colombia,* tr. by J. Fred Rippy, Chapel Hill, N.C., 1938; Eduardo Lemaitre, *Reyes,* Bogotá, 1952; Luis Ospina Vásquez, *Industria y protección en Colombia 1810–1930,* Bogotá, 1955; Luis F. Sierra, *El tabaco en la economía colombiana del siglo XIX,* Bogotá, 1971.   J. LEÓN HELGUERA

COLOMBO, CRISTOFORO, OR COLÓN, CRISTÓBAL. *See* COLUMBUS, CHRISTOPHER.

COLÔNIA DO SACRAMENTO. Exposed Portuguese outpost on the north shore of the RÍO DE LA PLATA opposite, and only 15 miles from, Buenos Aires. Intended as a contraband entrepôt, the small fortified town was a constant challenge to the Spanish authorities throughout its existence (1680–1777). A key bargaining point in diplomatic negotiations (Utrecht, 1713–1715; Madrid, 1750; El Pardo, 1761; San Ildefonso, 1777), Colônia changed hands numerous times by treaty or by force of arms. The problem of the vulnerability of the outpost was never solved by the Portuguese, and they failed to close the gap between it and the frontier of their settlement in Rio Grande do Sul. Its isolation was increased with the fortification of Montevideo (1724) and Maldonado (1740) by the Spaniards. Besieged in 1681, 1705, 1735–1737, and 1762 and effectively blockaded by Spanish warships after 1763, the town capitulated to Spain for the fourth and last time in 1777. The loss was recognized by Portugal in the Treaty of San Ildefonso (*see* SAN ILDEFONSO, TREATY OF).

Portugal's desire to establish "natural" frontiers for Brazil at the Río de la Plata was revived in the 1790s by Dom Rodrigo de Sousa Coutinho, the Portuguese Colonial Secretary, and with the establishment of the Portuguese court in Rio de Janeiro in 1808 the Luso-Brazilians again took the offensive in the south, annexing the Banda Oriental in 1821. Revolt by the Spanish-speaking settlers of the region, clashes with the government of Buenos Aires, which also was interested in expansion, and British intervention led to the establishment of the independent buffer state of Uruguay in 1828.

See also MADRID, TREATY OF.

KENNETH R. MAXWELL

COLONIAL BRAZIL. *See* BANDEIRAS; CABRAL, PEDRO ÁLVARES; CATHOLIC CHURCH (COLONIAL PERIOD); DUTCH IN BRAZIL; MINING (COLONIAL BRAZIL); SUGAR INDUSTRY (COLONIAL BRAZIL).

COLONIAL SPANISH AMERICA. *See* AUDIENCIA; BLACK LEGEND; BOURBON REFORMS; CATHOLIC CHURCH (COLONIAL PERIOD); COMMERCIAL POLICY (COLONIAL SPANISH AMERICA); ENCOMIENDA; MINING (COLONIAL SPANISH AMERICA); NEW GRANADA, VICEROYALTY OF; NEW SPAIN, VICEROYALTY OF; PERU, VICEROYALTY OF; RÍO DE LA PLATA, VICEROYALTY OF.

COLONO. Term widely used in Latin America to refer to several different kinds of farmers or rural workers. In Peru and Bolivia it was applied to a peasant who was allotted a small parcel of land on a hacienda and, in Peru, received a low wage in exchange for contributing his labor to the owner's fields and performing other services. The term is also used in Guatemala and El Salvador to designate a peasant with similar obligations. In Colombia a *colono* is a squatter, and in the RÍO DE LA PLATA countries the word can apply to an inhabitant of a rural immigrant colony. In southern Brazil he is a small farmer, while in the state of São Paulo he is a plantation worker who assumes responsibility for a certain number of coffee trees or of other crops and is given a portion of the harvest in return.

HELEN DELPAR

COLORADO PARTY (PARAGUAY). The Colorado party evolved from the Club del Pueblo, formed by Cándido Barreiro and Gen. Bernardino CABALLERO after the PARAGUAYAN WAR in 1870. Opposing the Gran Club del Pueblo, which they accused of being the vehicle of lackeys of the victorious Allies and which was to evolve into the Liberal party, the Barreiro-Caballero group managed after several abortive revolutions to place Barreiro in the Presidency in 1878. From that date until 1904 the Colorado party (the Asociación Nacional Republicana as officially constituted in 1887, but named for its official color, red) overcame Liberal revolts and ruled the nation. With no ideology save the retention of power, Caballero became the power behind the throne, making and unmaking Presidents within his own party until a successful Liberal revolt and invasion by exiles in 1904. Despite attempts at revolution the Colorados were out of office for more than a generation. Only when the dictator Higinio MORÍNIGO (1940–1948) turned to the Colorado party for mass support did it regain power, and despite civil war and subversion it held that power until Gen. Alfredo STROESSNER seized the government in 1954. Stroessner, himself a Colorado and now chief of the party, has been in power ever since. *See also* LIBERAL PARTY (PARAGUAY).

Generally, the Colorados have been associated with conservative policies and look to the rural areas for much of their support, relying on the rural Colorado militia as well as the Army to keep "order." The party is still opportunistic rather than ideological, rhetorically stressing nationalism, patriotism, and the heritage of the dictator Francisco Solano LÓPEZ.

JOHN HOYT WILLIAMS

COLORADO PARTY (URUGUAY). Members of the Colorado party have governed Uruguay almost con-tinuously since independence. The Colorados established themselves early as the stronger of the nation's two major political groups and during almost a century and a half have lost control of the government for only a few brief intervals.

Although both the Colorado party and its traditional antagonist, the Blanco party (*see* BLANCO PARTY: URUGUAY), trace their origin to the personal rivalries of their early leaders, the Colorados have often been representative of urban interests and have at times adopted more liberal positions than the rural-based Blancos. The social and ideological base of the party became more clearly defined early in the twentieth century, when a series of Colorado administrations converted Uruguay into the hemisphere's first welfare state.

The Colorado party took shape during a successful revolt (1836–1838) against President Manuel ORIBE, whose efforts to assert government control over the countryside had aroused the wrath of his predecessor, Fructuoso RIVERA. Rivera's followers wore red hatbands to distinguish themselves on the battlefield from their opponents, who wore white bands. From that point forward the two political groupings have been known as the Colorados and the Blancos.

Although the Colorados succeeded in dominating the government during most of the nineteenth century, their control was challenged by recurring Blanco uprisings. When intervals of calm existed, they often were the result of monetary and political concessions to the opposition. The latter decades of the century saw a series of dictatorial Colorado administrations that presided over a measure of economic development but did little to promote social welfare or political democracy.

The man who brought about a significant transformation in both the party and the nation was President José BATLLE. An ardent spokesman for political and social reform, Batlle became President in 1903 and remained the dominant figure in the party until his death in 1929. Under his leadership the Colorados became more effectively organized, adopted democratic procedures of internal party operation, and developed a coherent social and economic program.

As President during the years 1903–1907 and 1911–1915 and as a strong influence upon other Colorado administrations, Batlle promoted a number of political, social, and economic changes that made Uruguay a model of political democracy and social reform in Latin America. Political reforms, many of them incorporated in the constitution of 1918, included an expanded suffrage, proportional representation, a popularly elected Presidency, and a decentralization of executive authority through the creation of the bipartisan National Council of Administration. Batlle worked to broaden the nation's economic base through selective nationalization in public utilities and other areas considered to be of prime social importance, a system of protective tariffs, and increased governmental involvement in various areas of the economy.

The strength of Batlle's leadership and the radicalism of his ideas produced a great deal of factionalism within the Colorado party. Not only was there opposition to some of Batlle's major proposals, such as the COLEGIADO, but after his death factionalism continued as a result of conflicting interpretations of his political philosophy. Since the 1940s the two major factions of the Colorados have been List 14 and List 15; the former was originally led by Batlle's sons and the latter by his nephew, Luis BATLLE BERRES. List 123, which won the Presidency in 1966 and 1971, was a coalition of List 14 and several minor Colorado factions.

Bibliography. Russell H. Fitzgibbon, "Adoption of a Collegiate Executive in Uruguay," *Journal of Politics,* vol. XIV, no. 4, November 1952, pp. 616–642; Göran G. Lindahl, *Uruguay's New Path: A Study in Politics during the First Colegiado, 1919–33,* Stockholm, 1962; Aldo E. Solari, *Estudios sobre la sociedad uruguaya,* Montevideo, 1965, vol. II, pp. 123–170; Philip B. Taylor, "The Uruguayan Coup d'État of 1933," *Hispanic American Historical Review,* vol. XXXII, no. 3, August 1952, pp. 301–320; Milton I. Vanger, *José Batlle y Ordóñez of Uruguay,* Cambridge, Mass., 1963.   LEE C. FENNELL

COLUMBUS, CHRISTOPHER (ITALIAN, CRISTOFORO COLOMBO; SPANISH, CRISTÓBAL COLÓN; 1451–1506). Discoverer of America. Although there has been much controversy about Columbus's place of birth, it is generally accepted that he was born in Genoa in 1451. He spent his early years in his father's weaving trade and as a sailor on Mediterranean ships. Shipwrecked in 1476, he came ashore in Portugal, which at that time was the center for the study of navigation and maritime exploration as a result of the efforts of Prince HENRY the Navigator. Columbus's brother Bartholomew, who was residing in Lisbon, obtained a position for him as a chart maker in the establishment in which he himself was employed. In 1479 Christopher married Doña Felipa Perestrello e Moniz, the daughter of a Portuguese nobleman, who bore him one son, Diego, in 1480. Doña Felipa died in 1485, the year in which John II of Portugal, on the counsel of his advisers, turned down Columbus's project to reach the Indies by sailing west. Columbus left Portugal for Spain that year and took as his mistress Beatriz Enríquez

Christopher Columbus. [Italian Cultural Institute]

Harana, who bore him a second son, Ferdinand.

Early in 1492 the Catholic Kings, Ferdinand II of Aragon and ISABELLA I of Castile, after years of importuning granted Columbus's pleas for backing. Contracts were signed in April 1492. The recruiting of men and the outfitting of three ships then began at the port of Palos, but it was not until August 2 that everything was ready and the fleet sailed. The first leg of the voyage took Columbus to the Canary Islands. After refitting and victualing, the ships left for a westward crossing that was completed on the morning of October 12, 1492, when a landfall was made on Guanahani, an island of the Bahama group, which Columbus named San Salvador. The fleet touched at other islands in the Bahamas and on October 28 made a landing in Cuba, which Columbus believed to be China. Not finding any gold or the Great Khan, he proceeded to Haiti, which he named La Isla Española (Hispaniola), arriving on December 6, 1492. On Christmas Day the flagship, the *Santa María,* ran aground on a coral reef and had to be abandoned. A fortified town was then built on the shore. Named Villa de la Navidad, it was the first attempt by the Spaniards at a permanent settlement in the New World. (Samuel Eliot Morison has located it near the present-day fishing village of Limonade Bord-de-Mer.) Thirty-nine men under the command of Diego de Harana were left behind to man the fort, constructed largely with timber from the *Santa María.*

With high hopes because of the first definite evidence of the existence of gold, Columbus was anxious to report his discovery to the Spanish sovereigns without delay and sailed for home on January 4, 1493. Again, he was fortunate in deciding to sail north as far as the latitude of Bermuda, where he found the prevailing westerlies and made a very fast crossing. A fierce storm was encountered just before the Azores were sighted on February 15. On March 4 he anchored in the Tagus River and was granted an audience by King João of Portugal. Four days later the *Niña* left Lisbon for Spain and anchored at Palos on March 15, 1493. Columbus was received at court by Ferdinand and Isabella, who granted him a coat of arms and the titles Admiral of the Ocean Sea, Viceroy, and Governor. A report of the voyage was sent to Rome, and Pope Alexander VI issued four bulls, the most important of which fixed as a demarcation line between Spanish and Portuguese discoveries a meridian that passed 100 leagues west of the westernmost island of the Azores, confirming to Portugal all lands east of it and to Spain all lands west of it. (The line of demarcation was pushed westward to the meridian 370 leagues west of the Cape Verde Islands by the Treaty of Tordesillas in 1494; *see* TORDESILLAS, TREATY OF).

Columbus sailed from the port of Cádiz on his second voyage in a flotilla of seventeen ships on September 25, 1493. The island of Dominica was the first landfall, made on November 3. On subsequent days other islands in the Lesser Antilles were discovered, and the first battle with the natives was joined on November 14 in the sea off St. Croix. Puerto Rico was discovered on November 19, and an overnight stop was made to take on fresh water. The fleet then proceeded to the previously discovered island of Hispaniola. On November 28, Columbus anchored at La Navidad and learned that the fortified settlement had been destroyed and all the Spaniards killed. He set sail toward the east and on January 2, 1494, established a trading post base that he named Isabela. Meanwhile, Alonso de OJEDA was sent in command of a party to search for gold in the interior of the island. On January 20, Ojeda returned with the first real evidence of the existence of the metal in quantity. Enough was gathered for a large token shipment to Spain in a fleet of twelve ships that left on February 2 under the command of Antonio de Torres and arrived at Cádiz on March 7.

Columbus, leaving his brother Diego in command at Isabela, left Hispaniola on April 24 with three caravels to explore Cuba (which he still believed to be the mainland of Asia) and find the Great Khan. The exploration began on the south coast at the location of the present-day United States naval base on Guantánamo Bay, named Puerto Grande by Columbus, and continued to Cabo Cruz, at which point Columbus decided to set sail for the island of Jamaica, where he hoped to find gold. The expedition arrived at Jamaica on May 5 and explored the island until May 13. Not finding any gold, Columbus resumed the exploration of the south coast of Cuba. Neither gold nor evidence of Chinese civilization was discovered, and after sailing as far as Bahía Cortés, Columbus set sail for Jamaica to complete his exploration of that island. Finally, on September 29, disabled by multiple ills, Columbus was carried ashore at Isabela, where he was greeted by his brother Bartholomew, who had arrived during his absence. Together with his brother, Columbus spent the year 1495 subjugating the island of Hispaniola, enslaving the natives, and forcing them to gather gold for the Spaniards. On March 10, 1496, he sailed back to Spain, arriving at Cádiz on June 11, 1496.

The third voyage did not get under way until May 30, 1498. With six ships Columbus sailed from Sanlúcar de Barrameda on a more southerly course than that followed on his previous trips. At Gomera, in the Canaries, three of the ships were sent on to Santo Domingo. Columbus, with the three remaining ships, made a landfall at Trinidad on July 31. He made his first landing on an American continent on August 5, 1498, on the south shore of the Peninsula of Paria, formal possession of which was taken on the following day. After exploring the Gulf of Paria, he sailed northward to Hispaniola, arriving in the harbor of Santo Domingo on August 31. There he learned of the mutiny led by Francisco Roldán, stemming from the dissatisfaction of men who were disappointed with the meager financial rewards of exploration and settlement. Although an accommodation was eventually reached with Roldán, complaints against Columbus and his brother were accumulating at court. These complaints prompted Ferdinand and Isabella to appoint a royal commissioner, Francisco de Bobadilla, to investigate conditions on the island. He arrived on August 23, 1500, and after gathering information decided to send the two Columbus brothers back to Spain for trial. Early in October Christopher and Diego were placed in chains and sent back on a caravel. The admiral and his brother were landed at Cádiz some three weeks later and were held captive until December 12. Five days later, though, they were graciously received by the royal family and restored to the good graces of the sovereigns. Bobadilla was recalled from the Indies in September 1501, and Nicolás de Ovando was named Governor. Columbus petitioned the sovereigns for permission to make a fourth voyage, and on March 14, 1502, authorization was given.

This fourth and last voyage began with four ships. They sailed from Seville on April 3, 1502, but did not leave Cádiz until May 9 and then were forced to take refuge for two days at La Caleta until favorable winds arrived. On June 15, after his fastest crossing, Columbus landed at Martinique. Two weeks later, having cruised through the Lesser Antilles and past Puerto Rico, Columbus arrived at Santo Domingo. He was not permitted to disembark or to take refuge from a hurricane that was in the offing. However, his ships rode out the storm in safety. The ships then sailed westward across the Caribbean and arrived at Bonacca (Guanaja), opposite Honduras, on July 30. Columbus then commenced in earnest upon a search for a westward passage to India. The ships beat to windward in terrible weather for four weeks until Cape Gracias a Dios was rounded. The search for a strait continued southward past Nicaragua and Costa Rica along the coast of Veraguas and Panama. After an unsuccessful attempt to establish a trading station, Columbus, remembering the disastrous experience at La Navidad, sailed northward on May 1, 1503. On June 25, with two ships and 115 men, Columbus landed at Jamaica. The ships, practically foundering and beyond repair, were run aground. Diego Méndez was sent in an Indian dugout canoe to Hispaniola to secure help. Ovando temporized for months and did not permit Méndez to return with a relief ship until late in June 1504, after Columbus had been marooned on the island for more than a year. Upon his arrival at Santo Domingo, Columbus, his son, and his brother chartered a ship for the voyage back to Spain and left on September 12. They reached Sanlúcar de Barrameda on November 7, 1504.

The last voyage of the admiral had ended. He spent the next year and a half following the court in its peregrinations across the country, in a vain attempt to obtain from the crown what he considered was rightfully his under the agreements reached with Ferdinand and Isabella covering pecuniary matters and hereditary privileges for his family. His health, weakened by the vicissitudes endured during the voyages, began to fail. On May 20, 1506, with his sons and his brother Diego at his bedside, he uttered the seven last words of Christ and died. His remains are entombed in the Cathedral of Santo Domingo in the Dominican Republic.

Bibliography. Antonio Ballesteros y Beretta, *Cristobal Colón y el descubrimiento de América,* Barcelona and Buenos Aires, 1945; Fernando Colón, *The Life of the Admiral Christopher Columbus by His Son Ferdinand,* tr. by Benjamin Keen, New Brunswick, N.J., 1959; Bartolomé de las Casas, *Historia de las Indias,* ed. by Agustín Millares Carlo, Mexico City, 1951; Samuel Eliot Morison, *Admiral of the Ocean Sea: A Life of Christopher Columbus,* 2 vols., Boston, 1942; Samuel Eliot Morison (ed.), *Journals and Other Documents on the Life and Voyages of Christopher Columbus,* New York, 1963; Charles E. Nowell, "The Columbus Question: A Survey of Recent Literature and Present Opinion," *American Historical Review,* vol. XLIV, no. 4, July 1939, pp. 802–822; *Raccolta di documenti e studi pubblicati dalla R. Commissione Colombiana,* Rome, 1892–1894; Martin Torodash, "Columbus Historiography since 1939," *Hispanic American Historical Review,* vol. XLVI, no. 4, November 1966, pp. 409–428.

MARTIN TORODASH

COLUMBUS, ARCHIPELAGO OF. *See* GALÁPAGOS ARCHIPELAGO.

COLUNA PRESTES. *See* PRESTES COLUMN.

COMIBOL. *See* CORPORACIÓN MINERA DE BOLIVIA.

COMISIÓN ECONÓMICA PARA AMÉRICA LATINA. *See* ECONOMIC COMMISSION FOR LATIN AMERICA.

COMITÉ DE ORGANIZACIÓN POLÍTICA ELECTORAL INDEPENDIENTE (COPEI). Venezuelan political party. Founded officially in 1946, the party later changed its name to Partido Social Cristiano. Until 1968 COPEI was the largest and most consistent rival of ACCIÓN DEMOCRÁTICA (AD). Led by Rafael CALDERA, COPEI played an active role in national politics throughout the 1950s and 1960s. Then, in 1968 the party elected Caldera President, thus capturing control of the government from AD. Essentially a Christian Democratic party, COPEI has managed to keep its defections to a minimum by good internal discipline and by taking an increasingly radical stance on social, political, and economic issues.

JOHN V. LOMBARDI

COMITÉ INTERAMERICANO DE LA ALIANZA PARA EL PROGRESO (INTER-AMERICAN COMMITTEE OF THE ALLIANCE FOR PROGRESS; CIAP). The permanent executive committee of the INTER-AMERICAN ECONOMIC AND SOCIAL COUNCIL of the ORGANIZATION OF AMERICAN STATES (OAS). Founded in 1964, the Committee grew out of dissatisfaction with existing machinery for implementing the ALLIANCE FOR PROGRESS. In 1963 former Presidents Juscelino KUBITSCHEK of Brazil and Alberto LLERAS CAMARGO of Colombia, who had been given the task of recommending steps to improve the Alliance, proposed the formation of a committee that would provide vigorous multilateral direction for the Alliance. CIAP was organized the following year, being composed of a Chairman and seven members, one of whom represented the United States. Its principal function came to be the annual review of the social and economic performance of each Latin American country. It did not receive the authority to determine the allocation of Alliance funds, as Kubitschek and Lleras Camargo had recommended, but in 1968 it was empowered by the United States Agency for International Development (AID) to evaluate requests for loans and technical assistance before action by AID.

CIAP was originally a special committee of the OAS Economic and Social Council, but both the Committee and the Council were upgraded as a result of the amendments to the OAS Charter that went into effect in 1970, and the Committee was given responsibility for overseeing all matters related to hemispheric development. In a speech on October 31, 1969, President Richard M. Nixon proposed further expansion of CIAP's responsibilities. However, its future was cast into question by the announcement in October 1972 of the impending resignation of its Chairman, Carlos Sanz de Santamaría, a former Finance Minister of Colombia. Sanz, who had been Chairman of CIAP since its inception, coupled his announcement with a call for a "new phase" in inter-American relations to reflect changing political and economic conditions in the Western Hemisphere and the world.

HELEN DELPAR

COMMERCIAL POLICY (COLONIAL SPANISH AMERICA). In the Venetian tradition, Spain claimed a monopoly over commerce with its American empire, and control of trade and navigation was still more narrowly confined to the ports of Seville and Cádiz in southern Andalusia. The monopoly was enforced, though with ever less effectiveness, to the end of the colonial period; in the eighteenth century trade with America was finally permitted from nearly all Spanish ports in keeping with ideas of modern nationalism.

When gold was discovered in Hispaniola about 1500, thereby stimulating trade, the need arose for a regulatory agency to control traffic and commerce and to collect royal taxes. On the advice of certain officials the crown established the Casa de Contratación at Seville in 1503, decreeing that henceforth all ships for the Indies must clear the Casa upon departure or return, paying whatever taxes were due the crown. Cádiz became the second official port for the Indies in 1508; these two ports controlled the Indies trade for the next two centuries.

At first the duties of the Casa multiplied faster than its staff; its three main officials — the *contador* (comptroller), treasurer, and factor — were responsible not only for registering cargoes and passengers and collecting taxes but also for adjudicating maritime civil suits and for training pilots. When corsairs made the Atlantic insecure, the crown ruled in 1522 that only fleets of at least ten ships could sail to the Indies; by 1543, with mounting insecurity and the great discoveries of precious metals, a half-dozen armed vessels accompanied annual fleets to America. The Casa assumed responsibility for providing ship's stores and armament, which together with its other duties soon proved too burdensome for a single agency.

The commercial policy reached its fullest development under PHILIP II (r. 1556–1598) and continued effectively until about 1625. The Casa was gradually transformed from a small general agency to a large specialized body under the direction of a president. It relinquished judicial cognizance over private mercantile suits in 1543, and it lost to other royal officials the financing and provisioning of fleets in the 1580s and the arming of fleets in 1607. At the same time the Casa staff was increased to handle the growing volume of commerce, and in 1580 it additionally assumed cognizance over maritime criminal cases. To ease the problem of logistics for a single large fleet, the King decreed in 1564–1565 that two fleets would sail annually, one to Veracruz, New Spain, and the other to Cartagena and Panama. Although the fleets left Spain at different times, they were to rendezvous at Havana and return to Spain together, thus providing the best possible defense for the returning bullion. Regularized commerce gave rise in America to annual fairs where goods from Spain were exchanged for precious metals and raw materials. The most famous of these fairs was held in Portobelo (Puerto Bello), Panama, the entrepôt after 1597 for most of Spanish South America; here goods and bullion valued at up to 20 million pesos changed hands within a few weeks, during which time a miserable shanty port became a bustling tent city swarming with thousands of sailors, soldiers, merchants, and officials. On the departure of the galleons to Havana, Portobelo relapsed into its customary somnolence.

During the seventeenth century the Casa, the fleets, and the colonial fairs declined owing to Spain's decreasing production and to increased smuggling in America. Though effective for defense (the return fleet was captured only three times in more than 200 years), the fleet system was inadequate to meet the needs of an expanding colonial market increasingly penetrated by cheaper and better foreign goods. In 1687 the Casa counted 110 employees, most of whom had bought offices without duties. Philip V (r. 1700–1746) tried to eliminate smuggling by means of a Caribbean patrol supported from the Havana dockyards and by private companies that contracted to defend and develop certain areas. But smuggling could not be thus uprooted, and in 1748 the fleet system was officially abandoned. The remainder of the century saw the increased sailing of single vessels, which, as a result of legislation enacted between 1765 and 1789, could sail from almost any Spanish port to many American ones. Castilian exclusivism was thus abolished, and the Casa, transferred to Cádiz in 1717, declined under the multiple-port policy. Meanwhile, the Spanish monopoly on trade was occasionally suspended, particularly in time of war during the last decades of the eighteenth century. In November 1797, while Spain was at war with Great Britain, the crown opened the ports of Spanish America to neutral shipping. The royal order was revoked in 1799, and an effort was made to restore the old monopoly upon the conclusion of hostilities in 1802. With the renewal of war in 1804, however, neutrals were again permitted to trade with the Indies. The French invasion of Spain in 1808 had the effect of permanently rupturing the monopoly.

See also BOURBON REFORMS.

Bibliography. Cayetano Alcázar Molina, *Los virreinatos en el siglo XVIII,* Barcelona and Buenos Aires, 1945; Clarence H. Haring, *Trade and Navigation between Spain and the Indies in the Time of the Hapsburgs,* Cambridge, Mass., 1918; Roland Hussey, "Spanish Colonial Trails in Panama," *Revista de Historia de América,* no. 6, August 1939, pp. 47–74; Allyn C. Loosley, "The Puerto Bello Fairs," *Hispanic American Historical Review,* vol. XIII, no. 3, August 1933, pp. 314–335; J. Múñoz Pérez, "La publicación del reglamento de comercio libre de Indias de 1778," *Anuario de estudios americanos,* vol. IV, 1947, pp. 615–664; Ernesto Schäfer, *El consejo real y supremo de las Indias,* 2 vols., Seville, 1935–47.   TROY S. FLOYD

COMMUNICATIONS. *See* PRESS; RADIO AND TELEVISION.

COMMUNISM. Communism in Latin America differs from country to country. Although it is an international phenomenon, the nature of its growth has been determined by political and social events in each nation. Consequently it is difficult to treat Latin American communism historically without finding exceptions to general patterns of development. Nonetheless, because the Communist party is an international one and because there is generally a party line emanating from Moscow, there are similarities in all Latin American Communist parties. In addition, the fact that the objectives of the various parties also are the same makes possible a general examination of the growth and development of communism in Latin America.

The Communist movement reached Latin America shortly after the successful conclusion of the Bolshevik revolution in Russia. There were, however, a number of groups and political parties that adhered to Marxist concepts even before the Third International was established in 1919. Many of these were affiliated with labor unions. Among the earliest Communist parties in Latin America were those of Argentina (1918), Mexico (1919), and Brazil (1922), the last of which had anarchist antecedents. Between 1920 and 1922 the Socialist parties of Uruguay and Chile moved into the international Communist movement by joining the Third International and renaming themselves Communist parties.

Throughout the 1920s Communist parties attempted without much success to establish themselves as political powers in their respective countries. Latin America was somewhat isolated from events in Europe, Asia, and North America, and Communist leaders found it difficult to determine the nature of the party line, much less to follow it. At the same time, some of the orders that came from the Soviet Union worked to the detriment of the Latin American Communist parties. For example, the directive that all parties must have the word "Communist" in their official titles drove some elements that were devoted to socialism away from the Communist movement. Another problem of the 1920s was frequent internal quarreling. The Latin American penchant for personalism dictated a situation in which individuals vied for control of each party. In addition, many members from parties that originally had been Marxist and were then converted to Communist parties soon became disenchanted with the orientation of communism and left the membership. Finally, the titanic Stalinist-Trotskyist clash that afflicted international communism inhibited the Latin American Communist movement.

To make matters more difficult Socialist elements that at first had tolerated communism began to turn against it, as both groups sought to gain adherents from the same social and economic classes. Antagonisms spread rapidly, and after the first flush of Communist success old-line Socialists regrouped and challenged communism for control of the left-wing reform movement.

In the early 1930s expansion was hindered also by the direction taken by most parties in accordance with the so-called third-period line laid down by the Communist International at its Sixth Congress (1928). The Communists decided to isolate themselves and attempted to gain political ascendancy without the encumbrance of other reform elements. Consequently, rather than infiltrate existing labor unions, as had been the practice in the early years of the movement, Communists now formed their own unions. They remained aloof from left-wing elements that would cooperate with them because they feared that coalition with non-Communist forces would weaken their cause. Other parties could claim credit for any changes that might be won by the coalition, and Communists did not want to elevate the prestige of parties they might ultimately have to confront once the moderates and conservatives were destroyed. It was this attitude that led the Communists to denounce Marmaduke Grove's short-lived Socialist

Republic of Chile in 1932. Communist leaders, alone among left-wing forces in Chile, assailed the effort as bourgeois and declined any support for it. At the same time, Víctor Raúl HAYA DE LA TORRE's efforts to establish socialism in Peru were scorned by the Communists, who made no effort to take advantage of a cooperative socialist approach.

The failure of this policy soon became obvious as communism showed no signs of progress. While the party was having difficulty in strengthening its position with the proletariat, conservative governments dealt it several paralyzing blows. In Chile, El Salvador, Paraguay, and Guatemala, Communist parties were suppressed. By 1935 it was apparent that a new tactic was needed not only in Latin America but throughout the world, and the Seventh Congress of the Communist International (1935) called for the formation of popular fronts wherein Communists would cooperate with other left-wing elements, in a direct reversal of the previous policy. Even before the congress took place, the PARTIDO COMUNISTA BRASILEIRO had encouraged the establishment of the National Liberating Alliance (March 1935), which named the Communist leader Luis Carlos PRESTES its honorary president. However, the increasing militancy of the alliance led to its suppression in July 1935, and abortive revolts in Natal, Recife, and Rio de Janeiro the following November in which the Communists were implicated were followed by severe anti-Communist repression.

The country in which the new policy bore the greatest fruit was Chile, where the Communists (*see* COMMUNIST PARTY: CHILE) participated in the Popular Front of 1938 (*see* POPULAR FRONT: CHILE), which elected its candidate President. Ironically, it was now the Socialist party's turn to remain aloof (*see* SOCIALIST PARTY: CHILE), and only after some tenacious bargaining by the Radical party (*see* RADICAL PARTY: CHILE) would the Socialists enter the coalition. Inside the front the Communists were overshadowed by the larger Radical and Socialist parties. Disappointed by their lack of influence, the Communists began to challenge frontist policies within months after the impressive electoral victory. Ultimately they pulled out completely, as did the Socialists. Their disaffection was only partly the result of their disillusionment with the front; of more immediate consequence was their continuing quarrel with the Socialists.

Nonetheless, Popular Front activity benefited the Communist movement not only in Chile but in all Latin America. It brought a measure of respectability to communism and reduced the antagonism of opponents in other parties who still recalled the isolationist days and Communist association with violence as a tool for political success. The Communists also used their frontist experience further to infiltrate labor unions and through them to enhance their political position.

The advent of World War II brought a halt to Communist advances. Because of the nonaggression treaty between Germany and the Soviet Union, the official party line called for opposition to the capitalist Allies and support for the Nazis. Almost all other left-wing parties in Latin America gave allegiance to the Allies, although they did not necessarily alter their opposition to capitalism. In this case they saw democratic capitalism as the lesser evil. In some countries such as Argentina, Uruguay, and Chile violent confrontations between Nazi groups and Socialists became common-

place, but the Communists did not take part. Once Germany marched into the Soviet Union, however, the party line changed immediately, and Latin American Communists gave wholehearted support to the Allied cause. The Communists were now willing to work not only with moderates and Socialists but even with Catholic organizations, conservative groups, and military dictators as long as these elements supported the Allied war effort. Their earlier condemnation of the Allied democracies, particularly the United States, now turned to lavish praise. To facilitate cooperation with erstwhile enemies the new policy even called for dropping the name "Communist" from official party listings and replacing it with "Socialist." For some old-line Communists such a swift reversal was too much to accept, and they left to become incorporated into Socialist parties. However, the discipline and organization of the party prevented these defections from becoming too great, and the vast majority of members took the policy change in their stride.

In this wartime atmosphere Communist parties met with less antagonism than ever before. Conservative and Liberal, Socialist and Communist, all were ostensibly united in the great struggle against fascist totalitarianism. Friendly feelings were generated even among directors of United States enterprises and United States diplomats. United States cooperation with the Soviet Union during the war also reduced the level of anticommunism in Latin America. By the end of the war the Communists had firmly established their presence in Latin America. Their parties were now legal in many Latin American countries, and even when they did not enjoy legal status, they did not meet the same kind of violent opposition they had encountered earlier.

Following 1946, however, Communist influence in general tended to decline. From the high point reached immediately after World War II communism met challenges from a variety of sources. As the Communists resumed their anticapitalist position, Latin Americans became less inclined to cooperate with them, while the United States, engrossed in the cold war, was fearful of Communist expansion in the hemisphere. The Communist party of Brazil was outlawed in 1947 and that of Chile in 1948, and both countries severed diplomatic relations with the Soviet Union. Although their participation probably was slight, Communists were blamed for the tragic outburst in Bogotá in 1948 that destroyed a portion of the city and killed and injured many citizens during the Ninth International Conference of American States (*see* BOGOTÁ CONFERENCE; BOGOTAZO).

Despite the fact that social and economic conditions in much of the area seemed to favor Communist success, the movement was able to make headway in only three countries after 1946, and in each of these it attached itself to another party or another movement. In Guatemala a social revolution, long overdue, burst forth in the mid-twentieth century. Because of their superior organization, Communists soon gained control of the labor movement in that nation and seemed well on the road to complete government control when a military uprising overthrew the sympathetic government of Jacobo ARBENZ GUZMÁN in 1954 and ushered in a period of rampant anticommunism.

In Cuba the revolution led by Fidel CASTRO aided the Communist party immeasurably, but the party (known as the Popular Socialist party from 1944 to 1961) was of little assistance to Castro during his struggle for power and in fact had not vigorously opposed the dictator Fulgencio BATISTA prior to his overthrow at the hands of the Castroites. Fortunately for Cuban communism no other political force in the country was as well organized following Castro's victory; the party joined Castro almost by default. Even in Cuba, however, the party was not strong enough to dominate the government, and the personalism of Castro continued to pervade the political scene. *See also* PARTIDO COMUNISTA DE CUBA.

Finally, communism's most remarkable success came in Chile, not by violence or revolution but rather through a peaceful, honest election. The Chilean Communist party joined a coalition of left-wing parties, particularly the Socialist party, which was successful in electing Salvador ALLENDE, a Socialist, President in 1970. The Communists were influential in the government, but Allende, being a Socialist, continued to oppose some Communist policies. Allende was not willing to follow the international Communist line as slavishly as the Chilean Communists, but in basic Marxist objectives he shared Communist aspirations.

Outside these three countries communism has not prospered dramatically. Although some Communist parties have participated in guerrilla warfare, which has been notably unsuccessful, others have avoided violence, thereby antagonizing more militant radicals. In countries in which right-wing and moderate governments have been dominant, such as Paraguay, Argentina, and Brazil, communism has found it difficult to advance.

One of the failings of the Communist movement has been its preoccupation with urban groups such as factory workers, students, and intellectuals. Most of Latin America remains agricultural and rural, so that communism's failure to direct its major thrust into rural regions denies it not only a majority of the population with which to work but also an area in which some of the greatest problems and most inhuman suffering exist.

Communism has had some scattered success in Latin America, but non-Communist parties have been more successful in winning and maintaining the support of the Latin American population. This is partly due to the fact that communism has an international character, whereas Socialist and Christian Democratic movements have been national in scope. NATIONALISM remains an exceptionally strong force in Latin America, and a national party still is far more attractive to the average citizen than a party controlled from outside the region.

Bibliography. Luis E. Aguilar (ed.), *Marxism in Latin America,* New York, 1968; Robert J. Alexander, *Communism in Latin America,* New Brunswick, N.J., 1957; Juan José Arevalo, *Anti-Kommunism in Latin America,* New York, 1963; Dorothy Dillon, *International Communism and Latin America,* Gainesville, Fla., 1962; Ernst Halperin, *Nationalism and Communism in Chile,* Cambridge, Mass., 1965; Rollie E. Poppino, *International Communism in Latin America,* Glencoe, Ill., 1964: Hernán Ramírez Necochea, *Origen y formación del partido comunista de Chile,* Santiago, 1965; Karl M. Schmitt, *Communism in Mexico: A Study in Political Frustration,* Austin, Tex., 1965.

JACK R. THOMAS

COMMUNIST PARTY (CHILE). The Chilean Communist party (Partido Comunista de Chile) was founded in January 1922, when Luis Emilio RECABARREN's Partido Obrero Socialista became affiliated with the Third International and changed its name. It secured one seat in the Senate and two seats in the Chamber of Deputies in the congressional elections of 1926, and in 1927 it adopted the revolutionary road to communism as its strategy. From 1927 to 1931 Carlos IBÁÑEZ persecuted the party and obliged it to work in secret. In these years, the party was split between Stalinists and Trotskyists, and Manuel Hidalgo led a group of Trotskyists out of the party. The party's "revolutionary" period (1927–1935) was undistinguished, its presidential candidate in 1932 finishing last with 1.2 percent of the vote. In the mid-1930s, however, the party played a leading role in the formation of the Popular Front with the Socialist and Radical parties, to secure Pedro AGUIRRE CERDA's election in 1938 (*see* POPULAR FRONT: CHILE; RADICAL PARTY: CHILE; SOCIALIST PARTY: CHILE). It refused seats in Aguirre Cerda's Cabinet while it built strength at lower levels. In 1946, having backed Gabriel GONZÁLEZ VIDELA for the Presidency, it accepted three seats in the Cabinet. Its ministers were dismissed after five months, however, as a result of growing right-wing alarm, especially after the municipal elections of 1947, in which the party doubled its vote.

As the cold war developed, the Chilean Communists launched a series of strikes. González Videla retaliated by arresting thousands of Communists and, in 1948, secured passage of the Law for the Defense of Democracy, which banned public activity by the party. Although the party worked clandestinely for the next ten years, it retained its organization and extended its membership; it also purged its ranks of those advocating revolutionary violence. In 1952 the party supported Salvador ALLENDE against Carlos Ibáñez, reaffirming its policy of seeking power with other left-wing forces through the ballot box. In 1958 it allied itself with the Socialists in the FRENTE DE ACCIÓN POPULAR (FRAP) to support Allende against Jorge ALESSANDRI and, with the repeal of the Law for the Defense of Democracy, returned openly to the political scene. Despite acute differences with the Socialists in the period 1958–1970, the alliance was re-formed for the presidential election of 1970 in the coalition Unidad Popular (Popular Unity). Allende's victory finally vindicated the party's strategy for winning power in Chile. Allende owed much to the strong local organization of the Communist party, the largest in Latin America, and gave it three seats in his Cabinet.

See also CORVALÁN, Luis.　　HAROLD BLAKEMORE

COMMUNIST PARTY OF BRAZIL. *See* PARTIDO COMUNISTA DO BRASIL.

COMMUNIST PARTY OF CUBA. *See* PARTIDO COMUNISTA DE CUBA.

COMONFORT, IGNACIO (1812–1863). President of Mexico (1855–1858). Born in the state of Puebla, Comonfort was a minor functionary for much of his life. He fought in the MEXICAN WAR and then served as collector of customs in Acapulco, where he came under the influence of Juan Álvarez. He helped write the Plan of Ayutla in 1854, gave his support to the rebel cause, and quickly rose to prominence as a moderate Liberal and one of the leading generals. With the triumph of the Liberals, he entered Álvarez's Cabinet as Minister of War and was designated provisional President when Álvarez retired in December 1855. The Reform began during his Presidency (*see* REFORM, THE): the Lerdo law was promulgated, the constitution of 1857 was issued (*see* CONSTITUTION OF 1857: MEXICO), and Comonfort moved decisively to suppress a Conservative-clerical rebellion in the city of Puebla in the spring of 1856.

As the movement demonstrated more radical tendencies, Comonfort's moderate position prompted him to enter into an agreement with the Conservatives, which resulted in a counterrevolution in December 1857. He remained briefly as chief executive of the Conservative government, but in January 1858 he resigned and went into exile in the United States. When the French intervened in Mexico, Comonfort returned to fight for the government of Benito JUÁREZ, was rehabilitated, and became a general in the Republican Army. He was killed in a minor engagement in November 1863.   CHARLES R. BERRY

COMPADRAZGO. Spanish term for the system of ritual kinship in Latin America (Portuguese *compadresco*). In Latin America, as in other Roman Catholic cultures, an individual acquires one or two godparents on several occasions of spiritual significance such as baptism, confirmation, and matrimony. By acting as a child's baptismal sponsors, the godfather (*padrino, padrinho*) and godmother (*madrina, madrinha*) become his coparents and assume the responsibility of watching over his spiritual and material well-being. At the same time the child's parents and godparents, who refer to each other as *compadre* (male) and *comadre* (female), form a close bond based on their willingness to render mutual aid and support. When *compadres* are blood relatives, as is often the case, the system serves to reinforce existing ties of consanguinity. It has also been common for lower-class parents to seek their child's godparents among individuals of a higher social and economic position for the benefits that such an association might bring them and their child. At present *compadrazgo* appears in its most traditional form in peasant communities.   HELEN DELPAR

COMPANHIA DO COMÉRCIO DO BRASIL. *See* BRAZIL COMPANY.

COMUNEROS, REVOLT OF THE (NEW GRANADA). Popular rebellion that began in March 1781 in the town of Socorro. *Comunes,* or juntas, were organized by Juan Francisco Berbeo and strengthened by the leadership of José Antonio Galán. The rebellion originated in the enforcement of a tax for the maintenance of naval defense in the Caribbean. Additional grievances were seen in the creation of a head, or poll, tax, the operation of a state monopoly of salt, tobacco, and liquor, and the doubling of the price of tobacco and liquor. The Comuneros claimed allegiance to the King, but several acts of violence were committed against royal officials and properties. Viceregal authorities in Santa Fé de Bogotá, trying to prevent the enlargement of the movement, acceded to the demands of the Comuneros. Among these were the abolition of the tax for defense,

the setting of a fixed poll tax on Indians and mulattoes to prevent abuses by the corregidores (*see* CORREGIDOR), the setting of the ALCABALA (sales tax) at 2 percent, the return of land improperly taken from the Indians, and priority for creoles over Spaniards in certain governmental offices. After the Comunero forces had been dispersed and the authorities had obtained the peaceful surrender of many leaders, the concessions made earlier were rescinded. Galán, who refused to accept governmental terms, was captured and executed with three other leaders in 1782. Those who participated in the rebellion, especially the Indians and mestizos, knew about the contemporary uprising of José Gabriel Condorcanqui TUPAC AMARU in Peru and were encouraged by it, but there was no direct connection between the two movements.

ASUNCIÓN LAVRIN

COMUNEROS, REVOLT OF THE (PARAGUAY). Confrontation (1717–1735) between the citizens of Asunción and the royal authorities of Peru and Buenos Aires. The origin of the revolt can be ascribed to the rivalry between the Jesuits and the citizens of Asunción for control over the Indian population. In 1717 the Jesuits obtained the support of Governor Diego de los Reyes y Balmaseda to allocate captured Indians to their missions and not to the laymen's labor force. Challenging the Governor's decision, the *cabildo* of Asunción demanded and obtained from the *audiencia* of Charcas the recall of Reyes; he was succeeded by the Panamanian José de Antequera y Castro, who had been Protector of the Indians for the *audiencia*. The *cabildo* refused to obey orders from Lima to reinstate the Governor and in 1724 expelled the Jesuits from Asunción and defeated troops sent from Buenos Aires by a partisan of Reyes. In 1725 Governor Bruno Mauricio de Zavala of Buenos Aires was able to take Asunción. Antequera, who had escaped to Charcas, was imprisoned and sent to Peru, where he was executed in 1731.

Zavala returned to Buenos Aires in 1725, but the rebellious citizens, led by Fernando de Mompox, a friend of Antequera, resisted the readmission of the Jesuits. A governing *común,* or junta, took power in Asunción, its members adopting the name of Comuneros and resisting royal authority on the basis of sixteenth-century ideas that the will of the *común* was superior to that of the King. The government of the junta was anarchical, and it became chaotic after the news of the death of Antequera was received in 1732. The Jesuits were reexpelled, and some of them were killed. There were rioting and looting in the city. Order and royal authority were restored when Governor Zavala, with an army of 8,000 men consisting mostly of Indians provided by the Jesuits, was able to crush the Comunero forces early in 1735.

ASUNCIÓN LAVRIN

CONFEDERACIÓN DE TRABAJADORES CUBANOS (CONFEDERATION OF CUBAN WORKERS; CTC). The structure of the ORGANIZED LABOR movement in Cuba is characterized by national federations based on local industrial unions. The incorporation of these federations into the present nationwide Confederation of Cuban Workers took place in January 1939. This course was decided upon by Cuban labor leaders attending the founding meeting of the Confederation of Latin American Workers (CTAL) in Mexico City. From its establishment until 1946 the CTC was under the control of Cuban Communists headed by Lázaro Peña. The Communists formed a working alliance with Fulgencio BATISTA, Cuba's political strong man of the mid-1930s and early 1940s, and in turn were permitted a free hand in the labor movement. During Batista's administration (1940–1944) the CTC was the recipient of paternalistic favors accorded by the Ministry of Labor.

In 1946 the reformist Auténtico party (*see* AUTÉNTICO PARTY: CUBA) took control of the CTC from the Communists. While under Auténtico domination the CTC was affiliated with the non-Communist Inter-American Regional Organization of Workers (ORIT) and dropped its ties to the Marxist CTAL. During the Batista dictatorship of 1952–1958 Auténtico labor leaders such as Eusebio Mujal reached a modus vivendi with the government, and organized labor was again rewarded with government favors, such as a dues checkoff. After the overthrow of Batista, David Salvador, acting for Fidel CASTRO's July 26 movement, took control of the CTC. However, Castro's leftward drift in 1959 brought the Communists back into control in November. Since that date the CTC has functioned as the political and economic arm of the Castro regime among Cuban workers.

DAVID A. CRAIN

CONFEDERACIÓN DE TRABAJADORES DEL PERÚ (WORKERS CONFEDERATION OF PERU; CTP). Since 1930 the history of the labor movement in Peru has been the story of the conflict between the ALIANZA POPULAR REVOLUCIONARIA AMERICANA (APRA) and the Communist party. The major prize in their struggle, especially since 1944, has been control of the Confederación de Trabajadores del Perú, a national labor confederation founded in 1944 during President Manuel PRADO's administration. The organization contains both white- and blue-collar workers grouped into individual unions and regional and industrial federations. CTP is governed by an officer board of 25 members and an assembly of delegates of about 200 members. The confederation's officers are elected and policy is discussed at a national congress that is supposed to be held every three years. Since its creation CTP has been the most powerful labor organization in Peru, representing from 200,000 to 400,000 members, or at least three-fourths of the union membership in the country.

The first secretary-general of CTP was the Communist Juan P. Luna. His party's domination of the organization was short-lived, for soon after APRA was legalized in 1945 it gained control of CTP. APRA retained control until 1948, when the dictator Manuel A. ODRÍA once again outlawed the party and attempted to rid CTP of Aprista influence. His failure to do so led to the suspension of the confederation until 1956, when it was again reorganized by the newly legalized APRA party. Since then the CTP has remained in Aprista hands, but the party has not often been able to use the organization to achieve political objectives. This inability was clearly demonstrated by APRA's dismal failure to rouse the CTP membership to a general strike to protest the 1962 military coup.

ORAZIO A. CICCARELLI

CONFEDERACIÓN DE TRABAJADORES DE MÉXICO (CONFEDERATION OF MEXICAN WORKERS; CTM). Mexico's leading labor confederation. The CTM was a direct outgrowth of the Confederación General de Obreros y Campesinos de México (General Confederation of Mexican Workers and Peasants), which was dissolved in February 1936 at a congress attended by 1,500 delegates representing 600,000 workers. Vicente LOMBARDO TOLEDANO became secretary-general of the new confederation. Its ultimate goal was the complete abolition of capitalism, but its immediate objectives were the struggle for political and economic liberation and the fight for the right to strike and against all churches and religions. Recognizing the international character of the labor and peasant movement, the CTM proclaimed a strategy based on direct action and constant opposition to any collaboration with the bourgeoisie. The president of Mexico, Lázaro CÁRDENAS, prevented its becoming involved in the organization of the peasants, whom Cárdenas decided to enroll in the Confederación Nacional Campesina (National Peasants Confederation).

In 1936 the CTM organized a strike in the Laguna District (Coahuila-Durango), from which came the expropriation of the lands of the region. Its effort to organize a popular front the following year failed when Cárdenas entrusted that task to the Partido Nacional Revolucionario (National Revolutionary party). When the latter transformed itself into the Partido de la Revolución Mexicana (Party of the Mexican Revolution), the CTM was the principal organization in the party's labor sector though not the only one. With the expulsion of Lombardo Toledano in 1948, the CTM's dependence on the government became more marked, and it substituted a nationalist rhetoric for Marxism. In return, it received generous rewards in the form of political posts, and its leaders grew old in their jobs. In 1973 CTM leaders placed its membership at 2 million.

MOISÉS GONZÁLEZ NAVARRO

CONFEDERACIÓN GENERAL DE TRABAJO (GENERAL CONFEDERATION OF LABOR; CGT). One of Argentina's most important interest groups, the CGT has passed through four well-defined stages (1930–1943, 1943–1955, 1955–1961, and 1961–   ) since its foundation in 1930 by the merger of Socialist and anarchosyndicalist labor groups in an effort to avoid disunity and doctrinal quarrels.

Because of the circumstances of its formation, the CGT originally was predicated on labor's independence from all political parties and ideological groups. Its initial five years, coinciding with the world economic crisis, were devoted to elaborating minimum economic demands. In the mid-1930s, however, with economic recovery under way and the antipathy of the government obvious, the question of political alliance as a tactic was reopened and led to a victory for the revisionists.

Although Socialists (*see* SOCIALIST PARTY: ARGENTINA) dominated labor organization for the rest of the decade, they were challenged increasingly by the Communist unions organized in "new" industries such as construction and textiles. By the end of the 1930s the Socialist unions themselves had divided, and the Communists joined one sector when two rival CGTs were established in March 1943. Oriented mainly toward

Europe in the 1930s, neither Socialists nor Communists made any effort to organize the Argentine internal migrants who streamed from the interior to the better-developed littoral.

The years between 1943 and 1955 marked a new era in the Argentine labor movement as it became identified increasingly with the Peronist government (*see* PERONISM). After Juan D. PERÓN's appointment as head of the National Labor Department (later Secretariat of Labor and Welfare) in 1943, his office initiated a program that sought to enforce existing labor legislation, guarantee rural labor the right to organize, integrate labor representatives into the government, and establish special labor tribunals. Although many old-time labor leaders were impressed by Perón's concrete achievements on behalf of labor, not all unions supported his efforts. Even after Perón's fall from power on October 9, 1945, the CGT Central Committee voted only narrowly for a general strike call for October 18. However, workers anticipated the committee and, on October 17, swarmed into the center of Buenos Aires, successfully demanding Perón's return and sealing his compact with the *descamisados*.

In the five years following Perón's 1946 electoral victory as the candidate of a coalition including a new Labor party, he consolidated his labor support chiefly in three ways. First, he sought to break the power of Labor party members who were unwilling to pledge primary loyalty to him. Second, a tremendous drive was undertaken to unionize labor, including the neglected internal migrants. Third, an attempt was made to control unions independent of the CGT, usually by the establishment of "parallel" unions that were accorded official bargaining powers.

A significant point in the Perón-labor relationship was reached during the extraordinary congress held by the CGT in 1950, when the group modified its statutes to include a specific endorsement of Perón's justicialist philosophy. Although labor unions in Argentina had always been ideologically oriented, so close a relationship with a government had never existed, and the question of primary loyalty became even more difficult. After 1948, when real wages began to fall, the government was increasingly hard-pressed in its attempts to satisfy its supporters. One means of dealing with the problem was to emphasize symbols of the government's concern. Hence the figure of Eva PERÓN was progressively idealized. It also helped to have "loyal" union leadership. This in turn led to a divergence between leaders and rank and file. Although the rank and file continued to support Perón, it also insisted on the need to strike if negotiations proved unsatisfactory. In these circumstances it looked to informal leaders more deeply committed to unions than to Peronism.

After Perón's fall the CGT was subjected to six years of governmental intervention (1955–1961). During the government of Eduardo LONARDI a period of grace evolved as he encouraged younger, more moderate Peronists at the expense of "hard liners." His careful policy proved successful when workers replaced the holdover secretary-general of the CGT with two younger Peronists.

Such an approach contributed to Lonardi's overthrow, and the succeeding government of Pedro ARAMBURU instituted a policy known to Peronists as the "revenge." Viewing Peronism as a superficial imposition without real roots in the working class, the government believed that with the elimination of "bad" leaders Peronist sympathies would disappear. Consequently the CGT was intervened, and Peronist leaders were jailed. These steps produced greater unity among Peronist workers and their leaders than had existed in years, and when attempts were made to normalize the labor unions, a sixty-two–union Peronist majority (the "sixty-two") emerged, in contrast to a nineteen-union Communist bloc (the "nineteen") and a thirty-two–union sector (the "thirty-two") that was both anti-Peronist and anti-Communist.

Under Arturo FRONDIZI an organizational shift occurred within the CGT as a weakened "nineteen" reorganized as the Movement of Syndical Unity and Coordination (MUCS), the "thirty-two" virtually disappeared, and non-Peronist labor groups organized themselves as "Independents." At the same time, Peronist labor, disillusioned with a government it had helped elect, escalated opposition from strikes to factory occupations. The most significant accomplishment of this period was the initiation of the process that ended government intervention and closed the CGT's third phase. Early in 1963 the first ordinary congress of the CGT to meet since 1955 was convened, and the twenty seats on the General Secretariat were divided equally between the "sixty-two" and the Independents. At the same time, José Alonso, the "sixty-two" candidate, was elected secretary-general.

If Frondizi's plan succeeded in uniting labor at least organizationally, subsequent events prevented its depoliticization. Deprived of legitimate electoral channels, Peronists were left with only labor unions as an institutionalized forum. Consequently, labor action plans reflected not only economic concerns but political goals as well, and the fundamental internal problem of the CGT was the tension developing from the contradictions between its economic and its political ends.

Arturo ILLIA sought to use such tensions to his party's benefit. What resulted instead was a 1964 fight plan that drove the Independents from the CGT, saw 3.2 million workers occupy 11,000 plants, and gained Illia the wrath of military and business sectors for his failure to suppress it.

The administration of Juan Carlos ONGANÍA, by contrast, sought the unity of labor in order to control it. Although Onganía was initially successful, the pressures of political concerns caused a further division in 1968, when Raimundo Ongaro established an "oppositionist" CGT (Paseo Colón) as a rival to a participationist sector (CGT Azopardo) led by Augusto VANDOR.

The assassinations of Vandor (June 1969) and Alonso (August 1970) were severe blows to government attempts to integrate labor. The violence of the demonstrations during the CORDOBAZO in May 1969 indicated a breakdown of communications between leaders and rank and file. Attempts by the government of Alejandro LANUSSE to make Peronist labor a part of the Great National Accord contributed instead to increasing division within the labor movement by suggesting a sellout. Thus old problems still prevailed as the 1970s opened.

Estimates of CGT membership are unreliable, particularly for the Perón period. The number of members was placed at about 300,000 in 1940 and at 1.5 million in 1947. Current membership is estimated at 2 million.

Bibliography. Samuel L. Baily, *Labor, Nationalism and Politics in Argentina,* New Brunswick, N.J., 1967; Alberto Belloni, *Del anarquismo al peronismo,* Buenos Aires, 1960; Roberto Carri, *Sindicatos y poder en la Argentina,* Buenos Aires, 1967; Sebastián Marrota, *El movimiento sindical argentino,* 3 vols., Buenos Aires, 1960–69; Miguel Murmis and Juan Carlos Portantiero, "El movimiento obrero y los orígenes del peronismo," *Documento de trabajo,* Centro de Investigaciones Sociales, Instituto Torcuato di Tella, no. 57, Buenos Aires, 1967.

NOREEN F. STACK

CONFEDERACIÓN REGIONAL OBRERA MEXI-CANA (REGIONAL CONFEDERATION OF MEXI-CAN LABOR; CROM). Mexican labor confederation founded in 1918. CROM reached the peak of its power during the Presidency (1924–1928) of Plutarco Elías CALLES as a result of the threefold role played by Luis MORONES, who was leader of CROM and of the Partido Laborista Mexicano (Mexican Labor party) and Minister of Industry, Labor, and Commerce. In 1926 it claimed a membership made up of 15 labor federations and 105 unions in the Federal District as well as 1,000 unions of industrial workers and 1,500 peasant organizations throughout the rest of the country. During this period posts for labor delegates in various diplomatic missions were created for the benefit of CROM leaders.

CROM clashed with the Partido Nacional Agrarista (National Agrarian party) because the party did not favor the affiliation of the *ejidatarios* (*see* EJIDO) with labor unions, given their peculiar juridical position. Although CROM declared itself socialist as well as syndicalist, it cooperated with the government in accordance with the policy of "multiple action," which was aimed at defending not only national sovereignty but also the sources of public wealth, which were the target of attacks by international capitalism. It refused to affiliate with the Red International of Labor Unions because the latter rejected its insistence on autonomy of action. It maintained good relations with the International Federation of Trade Unions but did not join it because it did not accept CROM's position on the rights of regional labor organizations. CROM did join the Pan American Federation of Labor, which it considered the only group capable of containing imperialism. The political defeat of Morones in the late 1920s signified the decline of CROM, which soon lost its hegemony in the Mexican labor movement.

MOISÉS GONZÁLEZ NAVARRO

CONFEDERATION OF CUBAN WORKERS. *See* CONFEDERACIÓN DE TRABAJADORES CUBANOS.

CONFEDERATION OF MEXICAN WORKERS. *See* CONFEDERACIÓN DE TRABAJADORES DE MÉXICO.

CONQUEST OF THE DESERT (1879–1880). The elimination of the Indian frontier in Argentina. This was the work of Gen. Julio A. ROCA, although others, notably Juan Manuel de ROSAS, Justo José de URQUIZA, and Bartolomé MITRE, had tried to solve the Indian problem in the postindependence era. The aims of Roca were to end the practice of paying the Indians for peace, to force the Indians to accept the authority of the national government, and to occupy the pampas (*see* PAMPA) as far as the Negro River. The campaign was preceded by extensive preparations, by a drought that weakened the Indian will to resist, and by a decline in the Indian population living in the area. As early as 1876 military patrols were sent into the pampas to collect data for topographical maps, and in 1878 small expeditionary forces left Bahia Blanca, Córdoba, and San Luis to study the features of the terrain to be traversed and occupied. To finance the expedition, Congress passed Law 947 (October 5, 1878), a modification of Law 215 (August 25, 1867). Both laws proposed moving the frontier to the Negro and Neuquén Rivers. The law of 1878 established the boundaries of all the provinces with claims to the Indian country (Buenos Aires, Mendoza, Córdoba, and San Luis), and to finance the cost of the campaign it authorized the sale of 4,000 bonds, each worth 400 pesos fuertes and each redeemable in the public land the Army was to bring under national control. The expeditionary force of 6,000 men invaded the Indian territory from four distinct points, and it reached its destination without experiencing any serious threats.

JOSEPH T. CRISCENTI

CONSEJO EPISCOPAL LATINOAMERICANO (LATIN AMERICAN BISHOPS COUNCIL; CELAM). Organization of Latin American bishops that seeks to coordinate Catholic activities and to encourage study and action with respect to problems of interest to the church in Latin America. CELAM was an outgrowth of the First Latin American Episcopal Conference, which met in Rio de Janeiro in 1955. It is composed of representatives of the episcopal conferences of the Latin American countries, with each national conference electing one delegate and one alternate, and is headed by a president and two vice presidents. At the Seventh Annual Meeting of CELAM in 1963 the first of several specialized departments were created; these cover such fields as pastoral planning, liturgy, vocations, education, and social action. The General Secretariat of CELAM is located in Bogotá, Colombia.

Almost since its formation CELAM has been dominated by bishops considered progressive, such as Bishop Manuel Larraín of Talca, Chile, who served as first vice president from 1956 to 1964 and as president from 1964 until his death in 1966. The influence of the progressives was also evident at the Second Latin American Episcopal Conference, which was convened in Bogotá by Pope Paul VI on August 24, 1968. The conclusions of the conference strongly affirmed the bishops' commitment to the struggle for social justice in Latin America.

See also CATHOLIC CHURCH (NATIONAL PERIOD).

HELEN DELPAR

CONSELHEIRO, ANTÔNIO (b. ANTÔNIO VICENTE MENDES MACIEL; 1835–1897). Perhaps the most colorful and controversial figure in the history of northeastern Brazil as well as the leader of the Canudos rebellion, with which his name is inextricably linked and which was immortalized in the Brazilian classic *Os Sertões,* by Euclides da CUNHA. The nickname "the Counselor" derived from his role as arbiter of disputes among his followers.

Born in Ceará, he left home during an interfamily feud to become an ascetic wanderer, traveling throughout the SERTÃO, preaching, building chapels, and acquiring a devoted, fanatical following. Regarded as a prophet and leader, he appealed to the mysticism of the *sertanejos* (backlanders) through his teachings, appearance, and the many miracles attributed to him. With his long blue canvas robe, flowing hair and beard, and piercing gaze, he was an arresting figure.

After some twenty years of wandering, he brought his thousands of followers to Canudos, Bahia, in 1890, and later clashed with the state government and ecclesiastical authorities. Mistakenly feared as a monarchist rebel by the republican government, the Counselor died shortly before his settlement was destroyed by the Brazilian Army after a series of bloody assaults in 1896–1897. He was more than a simple lunatic, fanatic, or messianic figure. He and his rebellion must be seen in the light of the change from monarchy to republic and the radical economic shift then moving the locus of power from the NORTHEAST to the southern coffee lands. These changes, together with the repeated droughts and epidemics of the sertão, provided the atmosphere for rebellion.

ROBIN L. ANDERSON

CONSELHO ULTRAMARINO. *See* OVERSEAS COUNCIL.

CONSERVATIVE PARTY (CHILE). A major force in Chilean politics for more than a century, the Conservative party arose in the 1850s, during the Presidency of Manuel MONTT. Before that time conservatives generally supported firm government, believed in the value of tradition, recognized the authority of the church, and, in fact, represented the upper classes. Under Montt some conservatives became estranged from the government, primarily because of a series of conflicts over the relationship between secular and religious authority. Conservatives with the government were henceforth known as the National party; those supporting the church kept the name Conservative party. Though the Conservative party was the fervent defender of the church against state encroachment, it differed little in social composition from its ideological opponent, the Liberal party, and government in the 1860s actually depended on a coalition of these major parties (*see* LIBERAL PARTY: CHILE). In the 1870s, however, Liberal pressure for clerical reform again brought theological issues to the fore. In 1873 the Conservatives left office, to become the solid core of opposition to Liberal governments until 1891. They bitterly opposed the secular reforms enacted by Domingo Santa María in the early 1880s and were prominent in the coalition against José Manuel BALMACEDA in the revolution of 1891.

The party opposed Arturo ALESSANDRI's first administration (1920–1925) but loyally supported his second (1932–1938), and it backed Gustavo ROSS for the Presidency, at the cost of losing its youth wing, the Falange Nacional. Generally in opposition in the 1940s and 1950s, the party kept considerable support at the polls, securing twenty-two seats in the Chamber of Deputies and six in the Senate in 1957. It backed Jorge ALESSANDRI for the Presidency in 1958 and Eduardo FREI of the PARTIDO DEMÓCRATA CRISTIANO in 1964.

Its increasing isolation from a rapidly changing Chile, however, was revealed in the congressional elections of 1965, when its representation in the Chamber of Deputies slumped to three. The other great traditional party of Chile, the Liberal party, having suffered a similar eclipse, the two united in the new National party in 1966, and the Conservative party ceased to exist.

HAROLD BLAKEMORE

CONSERVATIVE PARTY (COLOMBIA). One of Colombia's two traditional political parties, the Conservative party can trace its history at least as far back as the mid-nineteenth century. The existence of a political entity of that name was affirmed in the first issue (May 21, 1848) of a Bogotá newspaper called *El Nacional,* whose editors declared that its purpose was to defend the rights and principles of Colombia's Conservative party. The Conservatives of the mid-nineteenth century were the political heirs of Colombians who had supported the successful presidential candidacy of José Ignacio de Márquez in 1836 and rallied around his administration when it was seriously threatened by a revolution from 1839 to 1842. At that time Márquez and his supporters were known as *ministeriales* by their antagonists.

Doctrinal uniformity was no more a characteristic of Colombian conservatism in the nineteenth century than it would be in the twentieth. In general, however, Conservatives were staunch defenders of Roman Catholicism and sought a protected position for the Catholic Church in Colombia. Conservatives were also likely to favor a centralized form of government, although without the complete extinction of sectional autonomy. Finally, they generally evinced greater concern for order and for the sanctity of the right to property than did their Liberal contemporaries (*see* LIBERAL PARTY: COLOMBIA). Party organization was rudimentary during the nineteenth century, although conventions or gatherings of party notables were frequently held before presidential elections in order to determine party policy.

After the mid-nineteenth century Conservatives held power from 1857 to 1861 under President Mariano Ospina Rodríguez, whose term was marred by a successful Liberal revolution. Although a Conservative revolt in 1876–1877 was unsuccessful, the party was able to regain control of the government in 1885–1886 in alliance with Liberal President Rafael NÚÑEZ and his followers, who were known as Independents. A National party was launched to perpetuate the alliance of Conservatives and Independents, but it proved short-lived as the Conservatives quickly became dominant in both the party and the government. The Conservatives remained in power until 1930, when the emergence of two Conservative presidential candidates permitted the victory of Liberal Enrique OLAYA HERRERA.

Between 1930 and 1970 the Conservative party changed little. Organization was informal and fragile. A National Directorate, elected either by a vote of members of Congress or by a national convention composed partly or wholly of departmental delegates, sat uncomfortably upon a network of departmental directorates. These were in some cases appointed from Bogotá, but in the majority they were elected by departmental conventions with municipal representation. Municipal directorates correspondingly were elected by a vote of local Conservatives except in emergencies, when they were appointed by departmental directorates. This pattern was paralleled in cases of dissident Conservative movements, as with the *alzatista* group in the years 1951–1952.

Party financing was always haphazard, depending largely upon improvised collections at cocktail parties among the leadership and among sympathetic industrialists, financiers, and big landowners. Small contributions might be obtained at municipal bazaars and rallies, but there was no attempt to build a permanent paid-up membership.

The ideology of the Conservative party continued to be flexible. Its programs asserted that it was a decidedly Catholic party but not a clerical one and that its ideology was founded in the encyclicals of the popes, particularly Leo XIII. This left it considerable freedom of movement. The party could include large Medellín textile capitalists who looked to a conflict-free politics in which business could flourish, priests in the department of Norte de Santander who proclaimed a militant Carlism, and some army officers of semiclandestine but belligerent falangism. Secessionist movements to the right, especially the *derechista* groups of the mid-1930s, were quickly brought into line either by a quiet preemption of their ideological novelties on the part of the National Directorate or by the threat of sanctions by a formidable alliance of local bishops and Conservative chiefs. Between 1924 and 1970 the Conservatives borrowed doctrines from Action Française, Mexican counterrevolutionary movements, Portuguese corporatism, Spanish falangism, social Catholicism, and Christian democracy. Not even the last of these importations made a permanent impression. The appeal to the traditional *mística* (mystique) of the party and to ancestral memories of moments of profound political allegiance and identification has proved much more powerful than the new ideologies, whose reception for the most part has been restricted to big-city circles.

The lack of cohesiveness of the organization caused a certain unpredictability in electoral turnouts. When the national organization failed to satisfy the demands of its departmental counterpart, the response to exhortations to preelectoral activism was lukewarm, and abstention followed. The same pattern applied to the municipalities.

The leadership of the party has always been a matter of dispute. Even Laureano GÓMEZ, who revived conservatism as a plausible opposition party, was never the undisputed chief. A lack of patronage made loyalty in opposition contingent. In power the proportions of patronage exercised by the President and the National Directorate were ill defined. Party leadership has generally been contested by a small circle made up of the President, ex-Presidents, presidential aspirants, and regional party bosses, usually from the departments of Cundinamarca and ANTIOQUIA. Entry to the circle has been difficult for outsiders, but a shrewd regional organizer of considerable rhetorical skill such as Gilberto Alzate Avendaño might slowly penetrate it.

Over the years the Conservative party has been strongest in the departments of Antioquia, Nariño and Huila, and its following traditionally has been predominantly rural. Until the 1950s in most parts of Colombia the clergy was relied upon to keep the rural turnout high by sermonizing against liberalism and by

magnifying the threat of Communist penetration as a consequence of Liberal toleration. The depth of clerical identification with conservatism in some rural areas during the Violencia exacerbated local bitterness (*see* VIOLENCIA, LA). The church has been careful in the NATIONAL FRONT to avoid overassociation with one party to the exclusion of any other, partly for fear of exposing divisions within itself. Conservative efforts to win a larger part of the growing urban electorate have been modest in proportions and marginal in effect. The experience of the elections between 1962 and 1970 suggested that the superior organization of the ALIANZA NACIONAL POPULAR (ANAPO) at the grass roots was whittling away the traditional Conservative vote. The 1972 elections suggest some reversal of that trend and the possibility that a new organizational effort was beginning to pay off.

The Conservatives in 1972 seemed to have little new to offer the electorate. Programmatically they were not particularly distinguishable from the Liberals. However, their emphasis in agrarian legislation has been upon the improvement of credit facilities and other rural services rather than on redistribution. In early 1972 there was some debate as to whether the party wished to espouse a rather unclearly articulated "Brazilian" model of economic growth. Some doubts were expressed about the capacity of a leadership that had not changed substantially in twenty years to capture the imaginations of the traditional following or of "new" urban groups.

Bibliography. Rafael Azula Barrera, *De la revolución al orden nuevo: Proceso y drama de un pueblo,* Bogotá, 1956; Abel Carbonell, *La quincena política,* 5 vols., Bogotá, 1952; Laureano Gómez, *Discursos,* Bogotá, 1971; Jaime Jaramillo Uribe, *El pensamiento colombiano en el siglo XIX,* Bogotá, 1964; Carlos Martínez Silva, *Obras completas,* ed. by Luis Martínez Delgado, 9 vols., Bogotá, 1934–38; Mariano Ospina Pérez, *El gobierno de Unión Nacional,* 9 vols., Bogotá, 1946–50; id., *Una política conservadora para Colombia,* Bogotá, 1969; Gonzalo Restrepo Jaramillo, *El pensamiento conservador: Ensayos políticos,* Medellín, 1936.

C. G. ABEL AND HELEN DELPAR

CONSERVATIVE PARTY (ECUADOR). Ecuador's Conservative party, which is based on Catholic theology, appeared in 1830. The party has had its stronghold in the sierra, where the colonial elite enjoyed land and labor and shared in the status conferred upon that region by the *audiencia* of Quito, the archbishopric, and the great estates of the regular clergy (*see* SIERRA: ECUADOR). Their heirs in republican Ecuador remained at the top of a quasi-feudal society. Slow evolutionary shifts in the society were deemed healthy by nineteenth-century Conservatives, but such shifts were checked in the Conservative heartland by enforcement of the tithe, a continuation of the colonial Indian tribute, and *concertaje* (debt peonage). By abolishing these practices in 1897, 1898, and 1918, respectively, and by creating a lay state, the Liberal Radicals weakened the Conservative party economically and ideologically (*see* LIBERAL PARTY: ECUADOR).

After the assassination of their nineteenth-century standard-bearer, Gabriel GARCÍA MORENO, the Conservatives fought a losing battle with the Liberals. From 1875 to 1895 they had to depend upon center coalitions in order to dominate national politics; after 1895 they supplied no President until 1956, when Camilo PONCE was elected by a Conservative-dominated coalition called the Popular Alliance. Since maintenance of the existing social order is a luxury twentieth-century development-conscious countries can ill afford, Ecuador's electorate will no longer give broad support to the Conservatives.

LOIS WEINMAN

CONSTITUTION OF APATZINGÁN (1814). Provisional constitution issued on October 22, 1814, by the Mexican insurgent Congress of Chilpancingo while its headquarters was located in Apatzingán, Michoacán (*see* CHILPANCINGO, CONGRESS OF). The principal authors of the document were Carlos María de Bustamante, Ignacio López Rayón, Father Vicente de Santa María, Andrés Quintana Roo, José María Liceaga, José María Cos, and José Manuel Herrera. The United States Constitution had some slight influence on the writers, but they drew more heavily on the French revolutionary constitutions of 1791 and 1795, the Spanish constitution of Cádiz of 1812, and López Rayón's own tentative plan of government, which he had written in 1812.

The constitution of Apatzingán consisted of 242 articles and established a republican form of government of three separate branches (executive, legislative, and judicial). The Congress was to dominate the government and choose the three members of the plural executive and the five members of the judicial branch's review tribunal. Sovereignty was to reside in the people. Although there was no opportunity for the constitution of Apatzingán to become operative or to be adapted into a definitive charter, it was important in that it raised the morale of the insurgents by giving dignity and legality to their cause.

Soon the Congress once more became itinerant. It was dissolved a year later after the defeat and capture of José María MORELOS Y PAVÓN.

CHARLES R. BERRY

CONSTITUTION OF 1824 (BRAZIL). Based upon the project of the Constituent Assembly of 1823, this constitution was written by Emperor PEDRO I with the aid of ten appointed counselors and promulgated on March 25, 1824. A moderate document under the circumstances, it provided for a centralized monarchist state, weak provincial and local governments, and a restricted electorate, yet contained many guarantees. These included freedom of the press and of worship, sanctity of the home, protection from arbitrary arrest, the right of bail, and the right to primary instruction and to property. The enormous powers granted to the Emperor were of two kinds: the *poder moderador* (moderating power) and executive powers. The latter included the right to appoint judges, clergymen, and diplomatic, military, and government personnel; to direct foreign relations, make alliances, and declare war and peace; and to grant titles and honors. The *poder moderador,* based on a concept of the French philosopher Benjamin Constant and regarded as the key to the political system, gave the Emperor the right to appoint senators, to call special legislative sessions, to sanction laws, to dissolve the Chamber of Deputies, to name and dismiss ministers of state, to suspend judges, and to pardon criminals.

The legislative power was delegated to an appointed Senate and an elected Chamber. Elections were indirect (until the electoral reform of 1881), and only "active" citizens (with substantial monetary incomes) could vote or hold public office. Weak legislative councils were established in the provinces, but the Additional Act of 1834 replaced these with more powerful assemblies. A ten-member Council of State was established to advise the monarch, particularly on issues of war and peace and the use of the *poder moderador.* The constitution of 1824 said nothing about slavery, but references to freedmen implied its existence. Largely respected by PEDRO II, it remained the basic law of Brazil until the advent of the republic in 1889.

ROBERT CONRAD

CONSTITUTION OF 1830 (URUGUAY). The nation's first constitution after the definitive establishment of its independence in 1828 enjoys the distinction of being among Latin America's most durable charters, having survived all motions for its reform until 1918. The draft of the constitution was prepared by a seven-man committee appointed by the Uruguayan Assembly late in 1828 and presided over by Jaime Zudañez. As secretary, José Ellauri played a major role in the formulation of the working draft, which he presented to the Assembly on March 7, 1829. During the Assembly's discussion of the various articles of the draft Santiago Vásquez exercised considerable influence, on the strength of his having participated in the elaboration of the Argentine constitution of 1826. Although the Assembly completed its work on the constitution on September 10, 1829, it went into force only after being approved in Rio de Janeiro on May 26, 1830, by representatives of the governments of Brazil and Argentina, as had been provided for in the preliminary agreement that ended the Cisplatine War in 1828.

The constitution called for a unitary representative republican regime with a division of powers between the executive, the legislature, and the judiciary and stipulated that the Oriental State of Uruguay consisted of nine departments. Executive power was to be exercised by a President elected by the legislature for a four-year term and empowered to appoint and dismiss his Cabinet, which was limited to a maximum of three members. The legislature was composed of a Chamber of Deputies directly elected from each department in a number proportional to the population and a Senate indirectly elected on the basis of one senator per department. In an effort to curb the prevalent *caudillismo,* military personnel were excluded from service in the legislature. The legislature chose the members of the High Court of Justice, and the Court supervised the other organs of the judicial power. The departments were headed by political chiefs with police powers, who were appointed by the President. For the handling of the details of local administration the traditional *cabildos* (municipal councils) were replaced by locally elected economic administration boards of five to nine members chosen for a three-year term.

The constitution guaranteed most of the usual civil rights, but it provided for a restricted suffrage by excluding salaried servants, wage-earning peasants, the unemployed, the illiterate, and those seriously delinquent in paying their taxes; in addition, candidates to the legislature or the Presidency had to meet certain financial qualifications. The constitution established the Roman Catholic faith as the state religion but guaranteed freedom of religion. Amendment of the constitution required action by three successive legislatures.

JOHN H. HANN

CONSTITUTION OF 1833 (CHILE). One of the key political documents of the national period of Chilean history, the constitution of 1833 remained operative until 1925. It is difficult to exaggerate its importance in the nineteenth-century political development of Chile. In September 1831 the Chilean conservatives, who had come to power the previous year, set up a Grand Constituent Convention to amend the short-lived liberal constitution that had been enacted in 1828. In the event, and after several months of debate and close committee work, the convention produced a substantially different kind of document. The new constitution was formally promulgated by President Joaquín PRIETO on May 25, 1833.

The constitution contained a strong, though by no means exclusive, emphasis on presidential authority. The President of the republic, who was indirectly elected, was allotted a five-year period of office but was allowed to stand for immediate reelection at the end of his first term (Article 61). In practice this provision led to the four "decennial" Presidencies of Prieto (1831–1841), Manuel BULNES (1841–1851), Manuel MONTT (1851–1861), and José Joaquín PÉREZ (1861–1871). The President was given extensive emergency powers (Articles 82:xx and 161), and his authority was further entrenched by the fact that he directly appointed each provincial intendant, who was defined as his "natural and immediate agent" (Article 116). The constitution established a bicameral legislature consisting of an indirectly elected Senate and a Chamber of Deputies. The President, however, could veto any bill, delaying its enactment until the subsequent session of Congress; a vetoed bill had to be reintroduced within two years and had to obtain a two-thirds majority in both chambers before it could be overridden (Articles 40–51). Congress was left with the power to approve the budget, taxation, and the military establishment on an annual or eighteen-month basis. A powerful Council of State, consisting of the members of the Cabinet and eminent representatives of the national life, was set up to advise the President, who was obliged to consult it on legislative matters (Articles 102–107). The constitution gave the right to vote to all Chilean males over the age of twenty-five who had the appropriate property qualification, which was determined by a separate law (Article 8). The Roman Catholic Church was established as the official religion of the state, and the public exercise of any other religion was prohibited (Article 5).

The constitution of 1833 was regarded by Chilean conservatives as a notable achievement, and it won applause from many Latin American jurists. Most Chilean liberals, however, considered it at best an imperfect and at worst an entirely odious document. It soon became one of the main targets for the opposition. In the more tolerant political climate that developed in the 1860s under Pérez, however, a number of amendments were proposed, some of which were later enacted. In 1871 the President was deprived of the right to stand for immediate reelection. In 1874 the length of a senator's term was reduced from nine years to six, and elections to the Senate were made direct. Further reforms during the Presidencies of Domingo Santa María and José Manuel BALMACEDA eroded presidential authority, made the process of amending the constitution simpler, and extended the suffrage by lowering the voting age to twenty-one and by removing the property qualification. The document that was finally replaced in 1925 bore many formal resemblances to the original draft of 1833; its spirit, however, had changed drastically.

Bibliography. José María Cifuentes, "La constitución de 1833," *Boletín de la Academia Chilena de Historia,* año 1, no. 1 (1933); Luis Galdames, *Historia de Chile: La evolución constitucional desde 1810 hasta 1833,* Santiago, 1925; P. V. Shaw, *The Early Constitutions of Chile,* New York, 1930.

SIMON COLLIER

CONSTITUTION OF 1853 (ARGENTINA). One of the key documents of Argentine history. During the long dictatorship of Juan Manuel de ROSAS Argentina lacked a proper constitution. One of the principal themes of the exiled liberals who opposed Rosas was the need to "organize" Argentina by giving the country a fundamental law. Some three months after the overthrow of Rosas at the Battle of Caseros (February 3, 1852), delegates from the provinces of Argentina concluded the Agreement of San Nicolás, enabling a constituent convention to draft a constitution. This convention met at Santa Fe between November 1852 and May 1853. The most notable advice its members received was a hastily written treatise sent to the convention by the distinguished liberal exile Juan Bautista ALBERDI. This book, *Bases y puntos de partida para la organización política de la república argentina,* exercised a considerable influence on the discussions at the convention, although Alberdi himself was not present.

The constitution that emerged from the Santa Fe discussions struck a balance between federalist and centralist conceptions of political organization. Argentina's form of government was defined (Article 1) as "representative, federal, republican," and provincial constitutions were required to conform to this principle. The federal government, however, was given wide powers of intervention in provincial affairs "to reestablish public order when perturbed by sedition, or to attend to national security when menaced by an external attack or danger" (Article 6). These federal powers of intervention were often used in succeeding decades right up to 1930 and subsequently as well. The constitution created a fairly standard division of powers: it set up a bicameral legislature roughly on the United States model, with a Chamber of Deputies elected on the basis of population and a Senate composed of two representatives from each province. The head of state, to be known as the President of the ARGENTINE CONFEDERATION, was given a six-year term of office and was not eligible for immediate reelection.

Inevitably the constitution reflected the recent vicissitudes of Argentine history. It was felt necessary to prohibit provinces formally from making war on each other (Article 106), while the executive, whether federal or provincial, was expressly debarred from receiving "extraordinary faculties" or "the totality of public power," ominous expressions that had underpinned the Rosas regime. The liberal emphasis on increasing the national population also found a place in the document. Article 25 specifically enjoined on the federal government the task of encouraging "European immigration" (*see* IMMIGRATION: ARGENTINA). Resident foreigners were granted full civil rights and were permitted to naturalize themselves after two years in the country. Once naturalized, they were entitled to a ten-year optional exemption from military service (Articles 20, 21). Article 67 emphasized the liberal program for the economic development of the country.

The Santa Fe convention and the 1853 constitution were boycotted by the province of Buenos Aires. In 1860, after the Battle of Cepeda, modifications to the constitution were made to enable Buenos Aires to enter the Argentine Confederation. A number of powers given to the federal government in 1853 were returned to the provinces, and the word "Nation" replaced "Confederation" in the President's title. In addition, the controversial Article 3, declaring Buenos Aires to be the capital of the Confederation, was replaced by an article that effectively postponed the decision; only in 1880 did Buenos Aires finally become a federal district. There were several minor amendments to the constitution in 1866 and 1898.

The constitution of 1853 has operated in Argentina since its enactment except during periods of military rule and from 1949 to 1955, when it was temporarily replaced by the Peronist constitution (*see* PERONISM). Its most recent "restoration" occurred in 1973.

Bibliography. Julio B. Lafont, *Historia de la constitución argentina,* 2 vols., 3d ed., Buenos Aires, 1953; James R. Scobie, *La lucha por la consolidación de la nacionalidad argentina, 1852–1962,* Buenos Aires, 1964.   SIMON COLLIER

CONSTITUTION OF 1857 (MEXICO). Document adopted by the Constitutional Congress which was assembled in keeping with the Plan of Ayutla and which met for a year beginning February 18, 1856. The constitution was promulgated on March 11, 1857, and was made operative the following autumn. The majority of the delegates were moderates, but radical Liberals played an important role. Divided into eight titles or chapters, the constitution represents the triumph of liberalism and federalism in Mexico. Much emphasis was given to civil guarantees. The principle of the inviolability of property was tempered by the denial to civil and ecclesiastical entities of the right to own real estate. Religious toleration was rejected by the moderates in the debates and thus was not included in the constitution. Provision was made for an elected judiciary, a unicameral Congress (amended in 1874 to provide for a bicameral Congress), indirect election of the President, and the abolition of military and ecclesiastical privileges.

The church and other conservative elements considered that they were grossly mistreated by the new charter and engaged in a campaign to nullify it, which led to civil war between December 1857 and December 1860. During this struggle and the ensuing republican attempt to expel the French, the constitution of 1857 acquired an aura of sanctity, and to a large degree the strife centered on upholding the Liberal and republican principles embodied in the document. The constitution remained in effect until 1917, although it was frequently amended and was mostly a dead letter during much of the thirty-five-year rule of Porfirio DÍAZ. The spirit of the charter was not totally extinguished during this period, however, and the attempt to revitalize it accounts for much of the anti-Díaz agitation in the years 1900–1910 and for the movement led by Francisco I. MADERO.

See also REFORM, THE.   CHARLES R. BERRY

CONSTITUTION OF 1886 (COLOMBIA). The constitution of 1886 was drafted by an eighteen-member Council of Delegates in the aftermath of the 1885–1886 revolution, during which the Liberal party lost control of the government to a coalition of Conservatives and dissident Liberals known as Independents (*see* CONSERVATIVE PARTY: COLOMBIA; LIBERAL PARTY: COLOMBIA). The chief author of the constitution was the Conservative man of letters and future President Miguel Antonio CARO. The new constitution differed in several respects from its Liberal predecessor of 1863. It converted Colombia's nine "sovereign" states into nine departments headed by governors appointed by the President. Whereas the 1863 document provided for a two-year presidential term, the 1886 constitution provided that the President, who was to be elected indirectly, was to serve six years; in addition, presidential powers were greatly expanded. The right to vote for President and members of the Chamber of Representatives was restricted to those who could meet a property or literacy qualification. Finally, the new constitution declared that Roman Catholicism was the religion of the nation, that public authorities were empowered to enforce respect for it, and that public education was to be directed in accordance with its tenets; at the same time, religious freedom was guaranteed.

Colombia still is governed by the 1886 constitution, but important amendments have been made during the twentieth century. In 1910 the presidential term was reduced to four years; the terms of senators were reduced from six years to four, and those of members of the Chamber of Representatives from four years to two. In addition, both the President and senators, formerly chosen by departmental assemblies, were to be elected directly.

More fundamental changes were made in 1936 during the reformist administration of Alfonso LÓPEZ. Universal male suffrage was introduced. Property was declared to have a social character, which implies obligations, and the legislature was given the right to expropriate property for reasons of "public utility and social interest." The amended constitution also provided that labor was to enjoy the "special protection" of the state, and the right to strike was guaranteed except in public services. Moreover, the status of the church was reduced in several ways; for example, the statement that Catholicism was the religion of the nation was dropped, as was the requirement that public education be directed in accordance with the Catholic religion. However, when the constitution was amended to incorporate the provisions of the NATIONAL FRONT of 1957, Catholicism was again declared to be the religion of the nation. The 1957 amendments also conferred upon women, who had been granted the right to vote in 1954, political rights equal to those of men.

                    HELEN DELPAR

CONSTITUTION OF 1891 (BRAZIL). Following the overthrow of Emperor PEDRO II of Brazil in 1889, the provisional government of Manuel Deodoro da FONSECA appointed a five-man committee of jurists, which drafted a republican constitution. Minister of

Finance Ruy BARBOSA significantly revised the committee's proposals, giving the ultimate document a stronger presidential flavor than the committee had recommended. Promulgated on February 24, 1891, the new constitution—presidential, federal, and republican in nature—provided the framework for Brazilian government throughout the FIRST REPUBLIC until 1930.

The constitution conceded the twenty Brazilian states a great amount of political and economic autonomy. They could levy import and export taxes on goods shipped abroad, and they were given authority over the mineral deposits within their boundaries. Each state maintained its own militia, which provided additional leverage in its dealings with the national government. However, the powers delegated to the President somewhat tempered this federalism and guaranteed the strength of the federal government. The chief executive could proclaim a state of siege in any part of the country, intervene in the states' internal affairs, and supplant elected governors. In addition, the executive branch dominated the legislative and judicial branches of the federal government.

The constitution remained in effect until 1930, when a revolution overturned the government of Washington Luis PEREIRA DE SOUSA and ended the First Republic (see REVOLUTION OF 1930). The new President, Getúlio VARGAS, suspended the constitution by decree on November 11, 1930, and it was replaced by a new one in 1934.

JOHN E. PICHEL

CONSTITUTION OF 1917 (MEXICO). Until the drafting of the constitution of 1917, Mexico's revolutionary ideology even in its most radical aspects was the work of the rising urban middle class, which also claimed to protect the rural masses and the growing body of industrial workers while respecting and increasing Mexico's capitalist structure.

On September 14, 1916, a Constituent Congress was convened by the Ministry of the Interior (Gobernación). Only Constitutionalists attended the convention, which met at Querétaro on December 1, 1916. Defeated leaders—Victoriano HUERTA, Francisco VILLA, Emiliano ZAPATA—were excluded because they represented "low social depths." The Huichol Indian Victoriano Huerta was said to be descended from a tribe of cannibals, Villa had spent half his life "in vulgar and unspeakable crime," and Zapata was a rival of the terrible nineteenth-century cacique Lozada. Venustiano CARRANZA, on the other hand, was of a "good and honorable family."

The Constituent Congress divided itself into right and left wings. The former was headed by Félix Palavicini, José Natividad Macías, Luis Manuel Rojas, and others. These were professional men who had been deputies in the anti-Huerta Liberal Renovating bloc in the Congress of 1913 and had later supported Carranza. Palavicini made it clear that Carranza had never advanced a "socialist" program calling for large-scale land distribution or the aggrandizement of the labor unions. Macías pointed out that Carranza was not so foolish as to believe that he could overcome the natural laws by altering the social structure overnight, nor was Carranza a utopian who wished to level "all differences in aptitudes." Carranza aspired to the happiness of the greatest number, inspired by "science, morality, and justice." In the left wing, which included the majority of the delegates, among the outstanding figures were young military men such as Francisco J. Múgica, Esteban B. Calderón, and Heriberto Jara. They were supported by Álvaro OBREGÓN, who had declared, shortly before the Congress met, that the new charter should benefit the "laboring classes."

The draft constitution presented by Carranza modified the 1857 constitution (see CONSTITUTION OF 1857: MEXICO) only slightly, but the left wing gave it a radical character. In contrast to the freedom of instruction enshrined in Article 3 of the 1857 constitution, the 1917 document granted the state the power to offer instruction, permitting private education only when it adhered to constitutional provisions on the subject. Article 27 was revised by a large number of delegates and even some private citizens led by Pastor Rouaix, Carranza's Secretary of Agriculture, who was simultaneously a delegate. The article asserted that ownership of lands and waters was vested originally in the nation, which had the right to transmit ownership to private citizens; the state might impose on private property whatever restrictions public interest might dictate. The article permitted expropriation with indemnification, whereas the 1857 constitution required prior indemnification. In addition, Article 27 included the agrarian law of January 6, 1915, and provided for dividing latifundia in order to create small holdings, thereby linking the agrarian banners of the revolution of the south (the EJIDO) and the revolution of the north (small private property). Article 123 limited the maximum hours in the working day, recognized the right of workers to form unions and to strike, and established the principle of equal salaries for equal work for male and female workers. Article 130 denied juridical personality to churches and forbade the formation of political groups using words related to religious creeds in their names. In short, the anticlerical laws of the Reform (see REFORM, THE) were incorporated in the new constitution.

Bibliography. Djed Bórquez, *Crónica del constituyente,* Mexico City, 1937; H. N. Branch, *The Mexican Constitution of 1917 Compared with the Constitution of 1857,* Washington, 1926; Félix F. Palavicini, *Historia de la constitución de 1917,* Mexico City, 1938; Pastor Rouaix, *Génesis de los artículos 27 y 123 de la constitución política de 1917,* Puebla, 1945.

MOISÉS GONZÁLEZ NAVARRO

CONSTITUTION OF 1925 (CHILE). Chile's present constitution, promulgated in 1925, was adopted to replace the constitution of 1833 not only because that charter no longer reflected Chilean realities but because its operation had been perverted in the period 1891–1925 (see CONSTITUTION OF 1833: CHILE). The successful revolution of 1891 against José Manuel BALMACEDA had been fought in part for two objectives. One was to implant a parliamentary system in which ministers would be responsible to the legislature and not, as hitherto, to the executive; the other, to end executive interference in elections in order to secure a pliant Congress. After 1891 little change was made in the written constitution, but no ministry could survive without congressional approval and Presidents lacked their former power to guarantee congressional support. In a multiparty system, government depended on unstable political combinations and the legislature was supreme. Moreover, executives lacked the basic safe-guard of a genuine parliamentary system in case of a conflict of powers: the right to dissolve the legislature and call for fresh elections. The period 1891–1925, therefore, was characterized by governmental instability, and this precisely at a time when strong government was required. For Chile was changing, and changing fast. Population and urbanization were both increasing rapidly, and the rise of working classes, unrepresented in the political system, posed a new challenge to the old order, as social stability deteriorated and pressure for change increased.

Not until 1925, after a period of some turbulence, did Chile obtain from President Arturo ALESSANDRI an instrument of government more appropriate to the circumstances. Alessandri set up a 200-member consultative commission to draft the new constitution, although the effective work was done by a smaller committee dominated by Alessandri himself. Its proposals were approved by plebiscite in August 1925, and the new constitution went into effect immediately. Its object was to restore the balance between executive and legislature. The President was to be elected for a six-year term by direct vote, not indirectly as hitherto, but he could not stand for immediate reelection. Ministers, chosen by him, were not answerable to Congress, although Congress retained the right of impeachment of ministers and President alike, and ministers could not simultaneously hold congressional seats. The powers of Congress to delay legislation, especially money bills, were reduced, and a permanent qualifying tribunal to oversee elections took away from Congress and out of politics what had been a much-abused power. Church and state were separated, a provision resisted by Catholics but approved by the hierarchy in return for state subsidies to the church for a period of five years. Equally significant features of the constitution emphasized the state's preferential interest in social security and public health, including its prerogative to limit private property rights for the common good.

While going some way toward restoring the balance between the legislature and the executive, the constitution had weaknesses, as time was to reveal. The provision for presidential elections that stipulated that a candidate without a clear majority of the votes was not deemed elected unless his victory was ratified by Congress weakened the position of such candidates. Although Congress invariably accepted the candidate with the largest popular vote, bargaining between President-elect and parties in Congress was often necessary. Similarly, the separation of dates of various elections, while encouraging democratic practices and giving the electorate frequent opportunities to express its opinion, made electioneering a permanent feature of the political scene, and this was not conducive to firm government. Above all, the persistence of a multiparty system, which was almost inevitable with proportional representation, forced Presidents to bargain with different groups and try to balance diverse interests in compromise programs of public action. The positive emphasis on state intervention in the economy also had important results. As such intervention grew, increasing numbers of Chileans were linked directly with the government to support a system which might at times seem inefficient but at least was democratic in form and remarkably stable in operation.

Bibliography. Arturo Alessandri Palma, *Recuerdos de gobierno,* vol. II, Santiago, 1967; Ricardo Donoso, *Alessandri, agitador y demoledor,* vol. I, Mexico City, 1952; Federico Gil, *The Political System of Chile,* Boston, 1966; Julio Heise-González, "La constitución de 1925 y las nuevas tendencias político-sociales," *Anales de la Universidad de Chile,* Año CVIII, no. 80, 1950, pp. 95–234; Frederick M. Nunn, *Chilean Politics, 1920–1931: The Honorable Mission of the Armed Forces,* Albuquerque, N.Mex., 1970.

HAROLD BLAKEMORE

CONSTITUTION OF 1940 (CUBA). In 1940 the Republic of Cuba adopted a new constitution to replace its original fundamental law of 1901. Past abuses of presidential power and severe economic crises had led to revolutionary ferment in the 1930s in favor of basic structural changes in the existing system. These factors prompted Cuba's political strong man, Fulgencio BATISTA, to hold elections for a Constituent Assembly in 1939.

The new constitution bore the imprint of reform-oriented groups such as the Auténtico party (*see* AUTÉNTICO PARTY: CUBA). The recently legalized Communist party also participated in the assembly and gave its support to reform provisions. Of the 286 articles of the constitution, a significant number were devoted to social and economic improvements and political measures such as a semiparliamentary governmental structure designed to limit the executive power. An advanced labor code was incorporated into the constitution. A provision for restricting large landholdings also was included. However, most social or economic statements envisioned future legislative enactment. Many of these articles reflected a spirit of NATIONALISM directed against foreign economic domination of Cuba and called for government regulation of economic life in the public interest.

In the succeeding years (1940–1952) relatively few of the constitution's social and economic reforms were enacted. Furthermore, Presidents Ramón GRAU SAN MARTÍN, Carlos PRÍO SOCORRÁS, and Fulgencio Batista frequently circumvented checks on presidential authority. In 1952 the constitution was suspended following Fulgencio Batista's military coup and establishment of a dictatorship. Reinstatement and implementation of the 1940 constitution became a major announced goal of Fidel CASTRO's revolutionary movement against Batista.

DAVID A. CRAIN

CONSTITUTION OF 1946 (BRAZIL). The fourth constitution of the republican era was drafted by a panel selected by the Brazilian Institute of Lawyers and was approved by the newly elected Congress, which met as a constituent assembly. It weighted the union in favor of the federal government at the expense of the states, whose constitutions were to be written to comply with the federal document. The federal government was empowered to intervene in the affairs of the states in a variety of instances, for example, "to maintain the national integrity." The constitution declared Brazil to be a republic and provided for the separation of powers, but it did not greatly circumscribe the increased arena of executive authority that had developed during the administrations of Getúlio VARGAS. As a balance to this, the presidential term was limited to five years, and the

President could not succeed himself, although the Vice President could. The President and Vice President did not run on the same ticket and in practice came from different parties and even different coalitions of parties. Representatives to the Chamber of Deputies had a four-year term; senators, eight.

In conformity with the desire to create a national political focus, the constitution provided that candidates for federal office must be nominated by parties with a national rather than a regional base; despite this restriction a plethora of parties appeared, and a twenty-year period of coalition politics resulted. The electoral decree of 1945, which had freed political prisoners, had also defined the electorate, and this portion of the decree was incorporated into the new constitution. The franchise excluded illiterates and enlisted men in the armed forces. The constitution remained in effect until 1966.

FRANCESCA MILLER

CONSTITUTION OF 1967 (BRAZIL). Promulgated on January 24, 1967, by the administration of President Humberto CASTELLO BRANCO and approved by a margin of 2 to 1 by Congress, the fifth constitution of the republic incorporated the reform program of the new regime and provided for its legal continuity. It altered the balance of power between executive, legislature, and judiciary to enhance the authority of the President, and between national government and state government to reinforce federal supremacy. One of its most controversial provisions required the indirect election of the President (by an electoral college composed of Congress and delegates named by the state assemblies), governors (by state legislatures), and mayors of state capitals.

As in the 1946 constitution (*see* CONSTITUTION OF 1946: BRAZIL), the President could not succeed himself, but the powers that accrued to him in a "state of emergency," which he could and did declare, were pervasive. Illiterates continued to be excluded from the franchise.

In 1969 the fifth constitution was so drastically amended as to be virtually abrogated in a document that further circumscribed the powers of Congress, severely restricted the immunity of its members, and strengthened the government in its dealings with threats to the established order.

FRANCESCA MILLER

CONSULADO. Merchants' guild and court established by royal permission in several entrepôts in Spain during the late Middle Ages. The *consulado* responded to the need to protect seaborne trade, adjudicate disputes, and in general increase profits and promote mercantile interests. The first *consulado* for the Indies was established in Seville in 1543 after the discovery of precious metals had resulted in greater trade and attracted corsairs. The guild henceforth financed the annual fleets to America and controlled the profitable and limited cargoes they carried. For about a half century maritime commerce in America was handled by factors of the Seville merchants, but its increased volume, further enlarged by trade with the Philippines, led to the establishment of *consulados* in Mexico City (1594) and Lima (1613).

The control of commerce by three *consulados* depended on the system of annual fleets, which funneled trade into Portobelo and Veracruz, the two outlets for bullion from Peru and Mexico. The *consulados* were thus defenders of royal mercantile policy, helped enforce laws against smuggling, and assisted in meeting expenses of fortifications, road building, and coastal patrols. They also furnished royal subsidies. Since, owing to high risk and low velocity, only wealthy merchants could engage in the Indies trade, the *consulados* represented the mercantile elite.

The expansion of trade during the eighteenth century was accompanied by an increase in the number of *consulados* in Spain and America, although rebellions and administrative reforms delayed the establishment of the new American *consulados* until the 1790s. Between 1793 and 1795 *consulados* were established in Caracas, Guatemala City, Buenos Aires, Havana, Cartagena, Santiago de Chile, Guadalajara, and Veracruz. They did not long survive independence and the opening of Latin America to foreign merchants.

TROY S. FLOYD

CONTINUISMO. Practice whereby Latin American chief executives remain in office beyond the expiration of their initial terms through seemingly constitutional means. Since constitutions frequently forbid the election of an incumbent President to a second consecutive term, the method most frequently employed is amendment of the constitution to permit his reelection. An alternative is to draw up an entirely new constitution providing for a lengthened presidential term or permitting consecutive reelection.

Although *continuismo* has occurred throughout Latin America, it has appeared most frequently in Central America and the Caribbean. In the former region, for example, four dictators who came to power in the 1930s—Jorge UBICO of Guatemala, Maximiliano HERNÁNDEZ MARTÍNEZ of El Salvador, Tiburcio CARÍAS ANDINO of Honduras, and Anastasio SOMOZA GARCÍA of Nicaragua—made use of various constitutional devices to remain in office for years: Ubico and Hernández were overthrown in 1944, and Somoza was assassinated in 1956, while Carías Andino left the Presidency voluntarily in 1948. An example of *continuismo* in South America occurred when a 1949 reform of the Argentine constitution (*see* CONSTITUTION OF 1853: ARGENTINA) made President Juan D. PERÓN eligible for a second consecutive term, to which he was elected in November 1951.

HELEN DELPAR

CONVENCIÓN NACIONAL DE TRABAJADORES (NATIONAL CONVENTION OF WORKERS; CNT). Formed in 1966, the CNT is the latest in a series of Communist-oriented confederations that have dominated the Uruguayan labor movement since the 1940s. The first modern labor confederation in Uruguay was the Unión General de Trabajadores (UGT), formed in 1942 by some thirty unions representing 40,000 workers. One of the UGT's first demands was the reestablishment of Uruguay's diplomatic relations with the USSR, which had been suspended since the mid-1930s; the organization later announced that it was Moscow-oriented. Various groups withdrew from the UGT over the years, and by the early 1960s the confederation was defunct and had been replaced by the Central Única de Trabajadores, which attained a membership of 50,000 and was the direct predecessor of the CNT.

Estimates of the CNT's membership and support vary widely, but it clearly was the dominant voice of organized labor during its first few years of existence and in 1970 claimed to be the spokesman of more than half of the nation's 800,000-member work force.

The CNT called a number of brief nationwide strikes during the administration of President Jorge PACHECO ARECO, protesting both the government's wage freeze and its tough stance against strikes and protests. In 1969 the organization announced a set of generally radical demands including the nationalization of private banks, foreign trade, all transportation, and basic industries. The CNT is affiliated with the Moscow-oriented World Federation of Trade Unions.

LEE C. FENNELL

COPACABANA REVOLT. Brazilian military revolt of 1922. In Rio de Janeiro, on July 5, 1922, Realengo Military School cadets and Fort Igrejinha (Fort Copacabana) troops staged an antigovernment revolt—an outgrowth of growing dissatisfaction with what the rebels considered Brazil's political decay. The leaders had not formulated a specific program or ideology but felt that the armed forces could regenerate the nation through modernization and industrialization. They hoped that their example would provide the impetus for a general military uprising that would overthrow the government.

Instead, the government quickly suppressed the cadets and isolated the fort. No other military units joined in the insurrection, and by that evening only the fort remained in revolt. The following day, after 145 of the 162 rebels had surrendered, the remaining 17 (11 officers and 6 enlisted men) decided to dramatize their protest. They placed a piece of the Brazilian flag across their chests and marched out to fight the more than 1,000 government troops positioned on the beach. A civilian, Octávio Correa, joined the band as it proceeded. In the ensuing skirmish 16 of the rebels were killed, while 2 (Eduardo GOMES and Antônio Siqueira Campos) survived, although they were seriously wounded.

The heroics of the Eighteen of Copacabana provided the first expression of Brazil's TENENTISMO reform movement. The 1922 uprising initiated a series of revolts that culminated in the REVOLUTION OF 1930 and the demise of the FIRST REPUBLIC.

ALLAN K. JOHNSON

COPÁN. Mayan site in western Honduras, on the Guatemala border, dating from the Classic period (A.D. 300–900). The acropolis lies on the banks of the Copán River, which has eaten away the ruins, disclosing a massive vertical cut useful for stratigraphic purposes. Copán was a huge center, almost rivaling TIKAL. The acropolis alone covers 12 acres of ground and features the remarkable Hieroglyphic Stairway, which furnishes us with the longest Mayan text extant. Copán was evidently a center for priestly learning, for the year computations found here on the stelae are of rare accuracy. *See also* MAYAS.

BURR C. BRUNDAGE

COPEI. *See* COMITÉ DE ORGANIZACIÓN POLÍTICA ELECTORAL INDEPENDIENTE.

COPPER INDUSTRY (CHILE). Copper mining has a very long history in Chile, dating to the beginning of the colonial period. The main areas of exploitation were the provinces of Atacama and Coquimbo, where rich veins of easily extracted copper oxide were worked in numerous mines. The first great age of Chilean copper came after independence, as industrializing Europe demanded increasing supplies of the metal. From the 1820s to the 1870s average annual production rose from 3,000 to nearly 46,000 metric tons, and by the 1860s more than half of Chile's total export trade by value came from copper. Chile's share of world production reached its peak of 44 percent in the 1860s and stood at about 35 percent in the 1870s. By then, however, the easy ores were petering out and, with some few exceptions, Chilean mining methods were rather crude. At the same time, international competition grew, particularly from Spain and the United States, and Chile's share of the world market fell to 16 percent in the 1880s and to 6 percent in the 1890s. Fortunately for Chile, the decline of copper was paralleled by the rise of nitrates. *See* NITRATE INDUSTRY (CHILE).

The revival of copper in the twentieth century took place in circumstances very different from those of its earlier exploitation. In the first period mining was largely Chilean-owned and was characterized by accessible oxide ores, a large labor force, and simple technology. In the second great phase it was based on low-grade porphyry ores needing heavy capital investment, a much smaller labor force, and far more sophisticated mining and refining techniques. Hence foreign capital came to dominate the industry, since the required funds and expertise were lacking in Chile. There was also some shift in location, from the traditional copper-mining province of Coquimbo to the vast porphyry deposits of Potrerillos in Atacama, Chuquicamata in Antofagasta, and El Teniente in O'Higgins. American interests acquired all three. Chuquicamata, today the world's largest opencast mine, was bought by the Guggenheim interests in 1911 and began production in 1915, only to be sold in 1923 to the Anaconda Copper Mining Company. El Teniente, the largest underground copper mine in the world, was acquired by the Braden Copper Company in 1904 and sold to the Guggenheims in 1908; it began production in 1912 and was transferred to the Kennecott Copper Corporation in 1915. Work at Potrerillos was begun in 1916 by the Andes Copper Mining Company, a subsidiary of Anaconda, though production was delayed until 1926 by World War I and the ensuing slump in copper prices. These three mines formed the Gran Minería in Chilean copper, accounting for more than 80 percent of total production from the 1920s to the present, though in 1959 Potrerillos was closed as the nearby mine El Salvador was opened up.

Chilean production rose from 130,000 metric tons in 1922 to 600,000 in 1963, and the significance of copper in the Chilean economy rose likewise. By the late 1960s copper accounted for 60 percent of Chilean exports by value and 80 percent of government tax receipts, though for only 8 percent of the gross domestic product. Given this significance and the fact of foreign control, it was not surprising that demands for a greater national share in Chilean copper grew, as did demands for increased production to raise foreign exchange earnings. In 1966 President Eduardo FREI's government passed a law for the Chileanization of the Gran Minería, whereby the state acquired an approximate half interest in the mines, and the companies, in return for tax and other concessions, undertook to invest a further $500 million by 1971, to increase output to 1.1 million metric tons annually by that date, and to increase the amount of ore refined in Chile to 55 percent. For many Chileans the law did not go far enough, and in 1969 plans were announced for complete, but gradual, nationalization with compensation in the 1970s.

Again, however, arrangements were overtaken by events when Salvador ALLENDE assumed the Presidency of Chile in 1970. Immediate nationalization of the Gran Minería was part of his program, and this was effected in 1971 with the virtually unanimous support of the Chilean Congress. Although compensation was supposed to be fixed by an independent tribunal, great pressure built up in Chile for no compensation to be paid at all, in view of alleged excess profits made by the companies in the past. This is precisely what happened, apart from a derisory payment to one company, and as of 1972 the American companies were engaged in legal proceedings against the Chilean government. The industry was also disrupted by nationalization, but whatever the immediate future, Chile, with perhaps a third of the world's known reserves of copper, must remain heavily dependent on the mineral for a very long time to come.

Bibliography. Leland R. Pederson, *The Mining Industry of the Norte Chico, Chile,* Northwestern University Studies in Geography, No. 11, Evanston, Ill., 1966; C. E. Reynolds, "Development Problems of an Export Economy: The Case of Chile and Copper," in M. Mamalakis and C. E. Reynolds (eds.), *Essays on the Chilean Economy,* Homewood, Ill., 1965, pp. 207–398; Raúl Sáez, *Chile y el cobre,* Santiago, 1965; Mario Vera, *La política económica del cobre en Chile,* Santiago, 1962; Benjamín Vicuña Mackenna, *El libro del cobre i del carbon de piedra en Chile,* Santiago, 1883.

HAROLD BLAKEMORE

CORDERO, ROQUE (1917–   ). Panamanian composer. Cordero was born in Panama City, where he pursued his early musical studies. In 1943 he traveled to the United States and studied in Minneapolis with Ernst Křenek (composition) and Dimitri Mitropoulos (conducting). On his return to Panama he became director of the Instituto Nacional de Música and conductor of the Orquesta Nacional de Panamá. In 1966 he returned to the United States, where for three years he served as associate director of the Latin American Music Center of Indiana University and professor of composition at its School of Music. In 1969 he was appointed music adviser to the Peer International Corporation in New York.

One of the most prominent composers of his generation in Latin America, Cordero is the author of numerous works, including two symphonies (1945, 1956), a concerto for violin and orchestra (1962), two string quartets (1960, 1968), a quintet for piano, violin, cello, flute, and clarinet (1949), *Permutaciones 7* for chamber ensemble (1967), and many other compositions reflect-ing an extremely personal and free use of serial methods of composition.

JUAN A. ORREGO-SALAS

CÓRDOBA. City in Argentina, founded in 1573 by Spaniards arriving from Chile by way of Santiago del Estero. In 1623, ten years after being established, a seminary became the foundation for the University of Córdoba. Jesuits controlled the university until 1767, Franciscans from 1767 to 1808, and the state thereafter. In 1622 a customhouse was established in the city, and a heavy duty was levied on merchandise bound from Buenos Aires for Peru. The city was not too far from Esquina de Medrano, where travelers on the road from Buenos Aires to San Luis, Mendoza, and Chile could take the branch to Córdoba, Tucumán, Salta, and Peru. The city prospered from its location as a transit point and from the ample pasturage around it. By the end of the eighteenth century the province was used during the winter months to fatten mules sent from the littoral for Bolivian and Peruvian markets and was supplying the province of Santa Fe with cattle, sheep, and horses. Neither the urban nor the rural population were early supporters of the wars of independence.

By 1847 the city was considered one of the most prosperous in Argentina. Its population of 13,000 to 17,000 consisted primarily of mestizos. Foreigners began to arrive between 1864 and 1868. They were mainly Englishmen attracted by the rich agricultural land and by the prospect of a railroad reaching the province from Rosario. The inauguration of the railroad from Rosario to Córdoba in 1870, the national exposition of 1871, and the elimination of the Indian menace in 1879–1880 (*see* CONQUEST OF THE DESERT) marked the beginning of a new era in the history of the city. Immigrants, especially Spaniards and Italians, flocked to it. Its population grew from 28,523 in 1869 to 65,097 in 1890, 104,894 in 1914, 369,886 in 1947, and 889,000 in 1960. Industrialization took place essentially after World War II, when automotive, chemical, and agricultural machinery firms moved into the city.

See also CORDOBAZO.

JOSEPH T. CRISCENTI

CORDOBAZO. Massive rebellion in the Argentine city of Córdoba (May 29–30, 1969), which reflected deeply rooted discontent with the government of Juan Carlos ONGANÍA. Beginning as a diffuse protest, it culminated on May 29, when workers and students took control of a 150-block area in the city's center with the complicity of residents. Although there were clear antecedents to the event, including the emergence of a dissident sector within the CONFEDERACIÓN GENERAL DE TRABAJO, the death of a student protester, revised Saturday pay policies, and various police-union confrontations, none of them adequately accounted for the tremendous outburst of violence, which left fourteen dead and stunned the country, including labor leaders.

Government explanations stressing extremist agitation overlooked more fundamental factors. Córdoba's students had from the outset been the most vehement protesters against the government's university policy. Furthermore, since 1967 the Governor of Córdoba had been a symbol of what were regarded as corporativist tendencies within the government. Most important, however, was Córdoba's role as the new industrial center of Argentina. One of Argentina's traditional cities, Córdoba in little more than a decade had acquired modern overtones including an articulate, well-organized industrial working class, which on the rank-and-file level apparently believed that the country's economic development was being sought at labor's expense and without consultation on priorities.

NOREEN F. STACK

CORFO. *See* CORPORACIÓN DE FOMENTO DE LA PRODUCCIÓN.

CORONADO, FRANCISCO VÁSQUEZ DE (1510?–1554). Explorer of the American Southwest. Born into a noble family of Salamanca, Spain, Coronado emigrated to New Spain (Mexico) in 1535 and became Governor of New Galicia, in western New Spain, in 1538. In 1539 the Viceroy put him in charge of an expedition to conquer the Zuñi pueblos of western New Mexico, which the Spaniards erroneously believed to be large and wealthy cities comprising a kingdom called Cíbola. He reached the Zuñi pueblos in midsummer of 1540 and quickly brought them under control, but upon learning that they were much smaller and poorer than he had expected, he pushed on to the pueblos of central and north central New Mexico. In them he found no more treasure than he had found in the Zuñi pueblos, but he did find a Plains Indian who told him that to the east lay a country called Quivira whose inhabitants were so wealthy that their plates and bowls were made of gold. In the spring of 1541 Coronado set out for Quivira, taking the Plains Indian along as a guide. After traveling southeast into central Texas and then north, probably as far as Kansas, he reached Quivira. He found it to consist of several villages of thatched huts, inhabited by a tribe of Indians possessing no metal more precious than copper. Disappointed again, Coronado turned back to New Mexico and, after spending the winter there, led his men back to New Galicia in the spring of 1542. Two years after his return he lost the governorship of New Galicia, and he lived out his life in relative obscurity in Mexico City.

TIMOTHY C. HANLEY

CORONELISMO. Form of political bossism on the municipal and regional level characteristic especially of the hinterland regions of most of the Brazilian states. *Coronelismo*, in its mature form under the FIRST REPUBLIC (1889–1930), was fundamentally a system for the regimentation of political forces, based on a compromise between two centers of power, which involved a reciprocal exchange of benefits between the dominant oligarchs on the state level and the dominant potentates in each municipality or region. As a reward for the delivery of sufficiently large blocs of votes to assure the triumph of the incumbents' slates of candidates on both the state and the national level, the *coronel* (colonel), or de facto local chief, enjoyed a relatively free hand in the exercise of governmental functions and control over patronage appointments of immediate concern to his own bailiwick.

This compromise was made necessary by the superimposing of relatively advanced forms of representative government on a nation in which a considerable portion of the electors were dependents of a semi-feudal economic and social structure that was incompatible with the functioning of a political system dependent on a contest for power by widely based, organized parties appealing directly to the entire electorate. The fragility of the organs of central government on both the national and the state levels made it advisable for their dominant oligarchies to recognize the autonomous personal power wielded on the municipal and regional levels by prestigious local magnates in order to marshal the votes they needed.

Although associated primarily with the First Republic, *coronelismo* survived after 1930, especially in the more isolated regions of rural Brazil.

JOHN H. HANN

CORPORACIÓN AUTÓNOMA REGIONAL DEL VALLE DEL CAUCA (AUTONOMOUS REGIONAL CORPORATION OF THE CAUCA VALLEY; CVC). Administratively autonomous agency established in Colombia to promote unified development of the natural resources of the upper CAUCA VALLEY. The creation of the CVC by the legislative decrees of October 22, 1954, and July 5, 1955, represented a significant departure from traditional concepts of development, public administration, and public finance. In a nation of unitary-centralist traditions the CVC epitomizes the concept of territorial decentralization of services. In addition to its administrative autonomy and juridical status, the CVC has its own sources of revenue and provides services that hitherto were customarily the exclusive responsibility of the central government.

The initiative for the creation of the CVC was indigenous to the region served. Beginning in 1928, the departmental government of Valle del Cauca commissioned a series of studies on the potential for regional economic development. In 1954 a departmental planning committee created the year before published a plan for development. Although advice was sought from such foreign authorities as David E. Lilienthal, the first Chairman of the Tennessee Valley Authority, much of the engineering reconnaissance and analysis was provided by local experts, notably the engineering firm of Olarte, Ospina, Arias, & Payán (OLAP).

Among the functions assigned to the CVC are the generation, transmission, and distribution of electric power; flood control; irrigation; the distribution of water for industrial and public supply purposes; land reclamation; soil conservation and reforestation; the regulation of forest reserves; mineral resources development; port and transportation systems improvement; and cooperation in the development of education, public health, and community action programs.

JAMES H. NEAL

CORPORACIÓN DE FOMENTO DE LA PRODUC-CIÓN (CHILEAN DEVELOPMENT CORPORATION; CORFO). Governmental organ, established in April 1939 to promote national economic development, with extensive powers of planning and investment. It was set up shortly after a severe earthquake struck south central Chile, and congressional opposition to the creation by the Popular Front government (*see* POPULAR FRONT: CHILE) of such an instrument of state intervention in the economy was overcome only by adding the necessary legislation to a bill for the reconstruction of the devastated areas. From its foundation on, CORFO played a crucial role in the growth of the Chilean economy through its promotion of mining, agriculture, industry, and commerce. It was under its aegis that heavy industry, including the great steel plant at Huachipato, was established in the 1940s and 1950s in the Concepción industrial zone. This was CORFO's most spectacular achievement, but the range of its activities is very wide. Its directorate consists of representatives of the government, Congress, the leading Chilean industrial, commercial, and farming organizations, the state banks, and the Chilean trade unions. As an agency for national economic planning, CORFO has long been regarded as a model for other Latin American countries.

HAROLD BLAKEMORE

CORPORACIÓN MINERA DE BOLIVIA (MINING CORPORATION OF BOLIVIA; COMIBOL). Corporation organized in October 1952, when the government of President Víctor Paz ESTENSSORO nationalized Bolivia's Big Three tin-mining companies, Patiño, Hochschild, and Aramayo. The properties of the Big Three were turned over to COMIBOL.

The new government mining firm was faced with monumental problems. The private companies had removed not only all available cash but even geological maps needed for efficient operation. They had also ordered all foreign technical and managerial personnel to leave the country or lose their pension rights; as a result, COMIBOL's high-ranking personnel was relatively untrained. Moreover, COMIBOL was saddled with excess personnel as a result of the government's decision that all workers dismissed between 1946 and 1952 for political or trade union activity must be reemployed without dismissing any others. In addition, the government established the so-called Control Obrero system, whereby there was in each mine and in COMIBOL itself a workers' representative who had virtual veto power over any action of the management. Production costs were greatly increased by the maintenance of company stores, where workers could buy goods at far below market prices, and by a large-scale breakdown of labor discipline.

The result of these and other problems was a disastrous fall in the production of the COMIBOL mines. By 1960 the output of the mines had fallen to about half of what it had been in 1951. The firm also suffered continuous financial deficits, although a price stabilization program launched at the end of 1956 by President Hernán SILES brought some improvement in COMIBOL finances.

When Paz Estenssoro returned to the Presidency in 1960, he was determined to rationalize COMIBOL's activities. Under the so-called Operación Triangular (Triangular Plan), COMIBOL received new financing through the INTER-AMERICAN DEVELOPMENT BANK and technical help from West German mining firms. COMIBOL agreed to reduce its excess personnel and to abolish Control Obrero. The plan soon began to produce results in terms of increasing production. After 1962 the output of the tin-mining industry began to rise, albeit slowly.

However, Operación Triangular resulted in frequent conflicts with the unionized workers. One of these, late in October 1964, helped bring about the overthrow of the government of President Paz Estenssoro. As a result of further clashes with the government of his successor, René BARRIENTOS, the Miners Federation was largely destroyed and the mining camps were virtually occupied by the military. It was not until Gen. Alfredo OVANDO CANDIA became President in 1969 that the reestablishment of the Miners Federation was permitted.

COMIBOL was the center of violent controversy under President Ovando when the government decided to turn over the Matilda mine, one of the newest and richest owned by COMIBOL, to a private firm. This action was reversed under Ovando's successor, Gen. Juan José TORRES. Most of the Bolivian tin-mining industry remains in the hands of COMIBOL. *See also* TIN INDUSTRY (BOLIVIA).

ROBERT J. ALEXANDER

CORREGIDOR. District administrator in the Spanish colonies who until the mid-eighteenth century governed a territorial subdivision (*corregimiento*) within the jurisdiction of an AUDIENCIA. There were two types of corregidores, the corregidor associated with a municipality and the *corregidor de indios*. The office of town corregidor was the more prestigious post.

As superior administrator and judge of a municipal district, the corregidor was appointed by the crown or viceroy to serve a term of three to five years. Town corregidores were usually Spanish-born trained lawyers. They presided over *cabildos* (*see* CABILDO) and often wielded considerable power on a local level, particularly if they were able to balance the authority of the viceroy against that of the *audiencia*. The office of corregidor was increasingly sold in the seventeenth century.

Corregidores de indios administered local government in rural districts populated by Indians. They usually had no particular training for their duties and were appointed for shorter terms (two to three years) by the viceroy or the *audiencia*. Since their salary was small, usually derived from local Indian tribute, the *corregidores de indios* often engaged in illegal practices to augment their income. It was not uncommon, for example, for corregidores forcibly to distribute goods to Indians at exorbitant prices. They had a notorious reputation for tyrannical rule and massive exploitation of the local native population.

From an administrative point of view, the corregidor was the only royal official in the early period who, like the parish priest, counterbalanced the authority of encomenderos in administering the affairs of rural areas (*see* ENCOMIENDA). The *corregimiento* was one of the least supervised and efficient institutions of colonial government, however, and in the eighteenth century it was supplanted by new administrative districts called intendancies (*see* INTENDANCY SYSTEM).

BROOKE LARSON SHUTE

CORTÁZAR, JULIO (1914–   ). Argentine writer. Born in Brussels, Cortázar has won universal acclaim for his short stories and novels, which show his innovations in narrative technique, his brilliant synthesizing of a rich background of reading, and his preoccupation with metaphysics, language, and the structure of the modern novel. In 1938, using the pseudonym Julio Denis, he published *Presencia,* a book of verse, which was followed in 1949 by *Los reyes,* a dramatic poem in prose based on the myth of the Minotaur. In 1951 he moved to Paris, where he translated the complete works of Edgar Allan Poe, and that year he published his own *Bestiario,* which marked his emergence into the literature of the fantastic. Collections of stories in the same whimsical-realistic vein followed: *Final de juego* (1956), *Las armas secretas* (1959), and *Todos los fuegos el fuego* (1966).

Cortázar's gift for capturing the essence of his fellow countrymen while emphasizing the absurd and fantastic elements of existence is seen in the novels *Los premios,* 1960 (*The Winners*), *Historias de cronopios y de famas,* 1962 (*Cronopios and Famas*), and, above all, *Rayuela,* 1963 (*Hopscotch*), in which the circular structure, with its possibilities for a double reading, presents a kaleidoscopic vision of the empty dialectic of our civilization. Among his later works are *Vuelta al día en ochenta mundos* (1966), *62-Modelo para armar* (1968), and *Último round* (1969). Stories from several collections were published in English as *End of the Game and Other Stories* (1967).

RACHEL PHILLIPS

CORTÉS, HERNÁN OR HERNANDO (1485–1547).

Conqueror of New Spain. Born of minor nobility in Medellín, Estremadura, Cortés studied briefly at the University of Salamanca. He went to Hispaniola in 1504 and participated in the conquest of Cuba in 1511. By the time he embarked on the conquest of New Spain in 1519, he had accumulated nearly fifteen years of

Hernán Cortés. [*New York Historical Society*]

experience as an encomendero, official, and soldier.

Cortés undertook the conquest of the mainland under the patronage of the Governor of Cuba, Diego Velázquez. He set out from Cuba in February 1519 and cruised along the coast of the Gulf of Mexico, picking up a survivor from an earlier expedition in Yucatán as well as an Indian interpreter, MALINCHE. When the expedition landed on the Veracruz coast, Cortés formed a new government, declaring his independence from Velázquez, and then scuttled his ships, making it impossible for members of his army to return to Cuba.

On his route up to the Valley of Mexico to the seat of MOCTEZUMA's Aztec domains (*see* AZTECS), Cortés allied himself with various dissident tributary tribes, such as the Totonacs and the Tlaxcalans. The small Spanish army (probably about 550 men) entered Mexico City in November 1519 and took Moctezuma prisoner. The Spaniards ruled through him until May 1520, while discontent increased among the Aztec nobility and priesthood. Cortés was obliged to leave Mexico City because a rival expedition had been sent by Velázquez to supersede him (*see* ALVARADO, Pedro de; NARVÁEZ, Pánfilo de). In his absence a rebellion of the Aztec nobility held the Spanish garrison captive. Upon Cortés's return, Moctezuma was killed, and the Spaniards were expelled on June 30, 1520. From July to September 1520, the Spaniards took refuge in Tlaxcala, gathered reinforcements, constructed ships to navigate Lake Texcoco, and organized their allied Indian troops for a siege of Mexico City. For seventy-five days the defenders of the city fought so valiantly under the leadership of CUAUHTÉMOC, nephew of Moctezuma, that the city was destroyed before the Aztecs submitted. By 1524 Cortés and his lieutenants had completed the conquest of the whole central region from Guatemala to Acaponeta and along both coasts, including all the kingdoms that had been tributary to Moctezuma.

Between 1522 and 1524 Cortés governed the area personally as Captain General. He organized the religious conquest of New Spain (the name he gave the new domains), brought colonists, new plants, and domestic animals, and established the foundations of Spanish rule in the former Aztec domains. He also distributed the Indians among the various Spanish conquerors and settlers. Between 1524 and 1526 Cortés undertook the conquest of Honduras. While he was away from Mexico City, his enemies triumphed, and his power was eroded by various decrees of the crown.

During a visit to Spain between 1528 and 1530 Cortés retained the title Captain General, but real power was given to an *audiencia.* Nevertheless, he received the title Marqués del Valle de Oaxaca and seigneurial rights (the right to collect tribute and to exercise juridical powers) to about twenty-one villages in the regions of Oaxaca, Cuernavaca, and Toluca.

Cortés remained in Mexico between 1530 and 1540, sending out new expeditions of exploration and establishing industries in his own territories. He discovered Lower California in 1536, but other voyages of discovery were frustrated by Nuño de GUZMÁN, whose domain of exploration conflicted with the aspirations of Cortés. Cortés also quarreled with Antonio de MENDOZA. He participated in one of the campaigns of CHARLES I in 1541, but despite his services he was unable to obtain his demands for greater power in New Spain. His political supporters at the Spanish court were alleged to have been instrumental in bringing about the *visita* of 1546, which investigated the Mendoza regime. Cortés died in Spain in 1547, and his remains were taken to Mexico in 1566.

Cortés's reputation as the most able and just of the Spanish conquerors survives his many detractors. His estate, the Marquesado del Valle, was a unique example of the seigneurial regime in the New World and continued to function until the first third of the nineteenth century. His activities as a colonizer, explorer, and philanthropist, although less dramatic than his leadership of the conquest, were outstanding contributions to the future development of Mexico.

Bibliography. Hernán Cortés, *Cartas de relación de la conquista de la Nueva España escritas al Emperador Carlos V y otros documentos relativos a la conquista,* Graz, 1960; Bernal Díaz del Castillo, *Historia verdadera de la conquista de la Nueva España,* Madrid, 1940; Bernardo García Martínez, *El Marquesado del Valle,* Mexico City, 1969; Francisco López de Gómara, *Historia de la conquista de México,* Mexico City, 1943; William H. Prescott, *History of the Conquest of Mexico,* New York, 1843; Spain, Consejo Superior de Investigaciones Científicas, Instituto Gonzalo Fernández de Oviedo, *Estudios cortesianos,* Madrid, 1948; Henry R. Wagner, *The Rise of Fernando Cortés,* Berkeley, Calif., 1944. EDITH B. COUTURIER

CORVALÁN [LÓPEZ], LUIS (1916–   ). Chilean Communist leader. Born in Puerto Montt, Corvalán was educated at a school in Tomé and the teachers training college in Chillán. After qualifying as a teacher in 1934, he taught for a year in Iquique and Valdivia but was struck off the teachers' register for his political beliefs and activities. He then turned to journalism, and it was by this means that he rose in the Communist party, which he had joined in 1932 (*see* COMMUNIST PARTY: CHILE). He worked on newspapers in Santiago, Antofagasta, and Iquique and in 1945 became director of *El Siglo,* the leading Communist daily, a post he held for three years. When the government of Gabriel GONZÁLEZ VIDELA outlawed the Communist party with its Law for the Defense of Democracy in 1948, he was arrested and interned until 1952, when the law was applied less rigidly.

Corvalán was very active in the party in its period of clandestine operation in the 1950s, and in 1957 he became its secretary-general, the key post in the party hierarchy. In 1961 he was elected to the Senate for Ñuble, Concepción, and Arauco, and in 1969 for Aconcagua and Valparaíso. Meanwhile, he traveled widely in Europe, Asia, and Latin America as the Chilean Communist party delegate to conferences. Throughout his career he remained a consistent and outspoken mouthpiece within the party for ideological fidelity to Moscow and a firm advocate of union with other left-wing Chilean parties to attain power by the ballot box. HAROLD BLAKEMORE

COSÍO VILLEGAS, DANIEL (1900–   ). Mexican economist and historian. Beginning as a teacher of ethics at the National University at the age of seventeen, Cosío soon became influential in Mexican life and letters. He combined his early career as a banker

and economist with stimulation of social science study in Latin America through translations and original works published by the Fondo de Cultura Económica, a publishing house he founded in 1934, and in *El Trimestre Económico,* a journal he codirected for twelve years. During this time he also served as a professor at the National University and as director of its School of Economics.

Cosío played an important role in attracting Spanish intellectuals to Mexico, first as a visiting professor in Madrid (1933), then as Ambassador to Portugal (1936). With the Spanish philosopher José Gaos he helped found the Casa de España, of which Alfonso REYES was president. Mexican intellectuals soon were incorporated into the Casa, which was renamed El Colegio de México in 1940 and became an outstanding research and teaching institution in the fields of history, philology, and the social sciences. Cosío, who was president of El Colegio from 1958 to 1963, also directed the reviews *Historia Mexicana* and *Foro Internacional* for a decade. His seminar on modern Mexican history at El Colegio produced the nine-volume *Historia moderna de México* (1955–1972), and his seminar on contemporary Mexican history is continuing the study in the post-1910 period. Cosío's scholarly works include *Los Estados Unidos contra Porfirio Díaz,* 1956 (*The United States versus Porfirio Díaz*); and *La constitución de 1857 y sus críticos* (1957). His articles on national affairs (1968–1971) for the newspaper *Excelsior* were published as *Labor periodística, real e imaginaria* (1972). ALAN KOVAC

COSTA, LÚCIO (1902–   ). Brazilian architect and city planner. Born in Toulon, France, of Brazilian parents, Costa received his primary and secondary schooling in Europe. He studied architecture at the Escola Nacional de Belas Artes in Rio de Janeiro and served as the school's director in 1930–1931. By that time he had come under the influence of Gregori Warchavchik, a Russian architect who was an exponent of functionalism and who built the first modern house in Brazil (São Paulo, 1928). In the mid-1930s Costa headed the team of architects, including Oscar NIEMEYER, who planned the Ministry of Education and Health building (1936–1943) in Rio, notable as an embodiment of the ideas of Le Corbusier and considered a landmark in the development of modern architecture in Brazil. Costa also collaborated with Niemeyer in the design of the Brazilian Pavilion for the New York World's Fair of 1939.

Costa's best-known achievement is his design of the pilot plan for Brazil's new capital city, Brasília. His proposal, submitted on five medium-size cards, won the approval of five members of the six-man international jury that awarded him the prize in 1957. The pilot plan provided for a clearly articulated city whose shape would resemble that of an airplane; the fuselage of the airplane was to constitute a monumental axis containing government buildings, while the wings, or residential axis, were to be dominated by superblocks with polyclass housing units. The failure of Brasília to reflect fully the aspirations of its planners, particularly because of the proliferation of shantytowns on the outskirts of the city, subsequently brought criticism of Costa for ignoring the social realities of Brazil in his plan. HELEN DELPAR

COSTA (ECUADOR). Region along the Pacific Ocean composed of flatlands, a hilly belt, and the Guayas Lowland. The lowland runs 300 miles from south to north and extends to alluvial fans along the base of the ANDES MOUNTAINS. South of the Gulf of Guayaquil the cold HUMBOLDT CURRENT cools the air and prevents rainfall. Hence the southern littoral is arid. North of Manta warm currents prevail. Abundant sun and rain, diurnal temperatures of 80°F, and rich alluvial soil make the Guayas Lowland ideal for tropical agriculture. *See* BANANA INDUSTRY (ECUADOR); CACAO INDUSTRY (ECUADOR).

The population of the costa is racially mixed and of low density. The African presence dates from 1570, when slaves shipwrecked off the coast of Esmeralda Province landed and overcame the local inhabitants. They dominated the area politically and ethnically, sending two caciques (chiefs) to the *audiencia* of Quito in 1600. From Manabí southward Indians and Spanish landlords held their own, but both fused with the African to produce the coastal worker known as the *montuvio*. Always in short supply, the *montuvio* has earned wages five times as high as those of his Andean counterpart. He has known some mobility and independence, but debt peonage persisted on the costa into the twentieth century.

Export wealth and access to foreign influence have made the costa economically attractive and the focus of Liberal politics and labor organization (*see* LIBERAL PARTY: ECUADOR). Increasing numbers of people are leaving the sierra to settle there, especially in the port of Guayaquil, Ecuador's largest and economically most important city.   LOIS WEINMAN

COSTA (PERU). Narrow, 1,400-mile-long coastal region. The costa is desert, but more than fifty rivers flow from the mountains to the sea, and most of them provide water for irrigated agriculture. Temperatures of the region, which is dominated by the cool HUMBOLDT CURRENT offshore, are about 10°F lower than what would be expected for the latitude, and there are long periods of cloudy weather.

The costa, which occupies only about 12 percent of Peru and contains nearly 35 percent of its people, is politically and economically Peru's most important region. The southern section, from the Chilean border to Nazca, is especially narrow and dry, but the central (Nazca-Trujillo) and northern (Trujillo–Ecuadorian border) regions are heavily populated, agriculturally productive, and considerably industrialized. The irrigated valleys produce cotton, sugar, and other cash crops, which, with coastal petroleum production, make up a very important portion of Peru's exports; and the cities, particularly the Lima-Callao area, are the industrial centers of the nation. The costa's importance has been further enhanced by the recently developed fish-meal industry. This has led to the mushrooming of urban centers such as Chimbote, and it has made Peru the world's largest fish-meal exporter. Consequently, the now-traditional political and economic preeminence of the coast is not likely to diminish in the near future. *See also* FISHING INDUSTRY (PERU).

ORAZIO A. CICCARELLI

COSTA E SILVA, ARTHUR DA (1902–1969). President of Brazil (1967–1969). The son of a storekeeper in Taquari, Rio Grande do Sul, Costa e Silva was the first member of his family to follow a military career. He attended military school in Pôrto Alegre, enlisted in the Army as a cadet in 1918, and received his commission in 1921. Lieutenant da Costa e Silva took part in the revolutionary movements of 1922, 1924, and 1930 (*see* TENENTISMO; REVOLUTION OF 1930). Thereafter he advanced steadily as a line officer, becoming a specialist in mechanized warfare. As the senior army general supporting the revolution of 1964, Costa e Silva was head of the short-lived Supreme Revolutionary Command and became War Minister in the Cabinet of President Humberto CASTELLO BRANCO. He was instrumental in the decision to enact the Second Institutional Act and a series of complementary measures in the period 1965–1966 that enhanced the authority of the executive at the expense of the legislature and the civilian political sector.

Emerging as the only candidate to succeed Castello Branco, he was duly elected by the Congress in October 1966 and took office as President of Brazil on March 15, 1967. Although he promised to "humanize" the revolution, Costa e Silva proved politically inflexible and reacted to opposition by students and Congress with harsh measures, culminating in the Fifth Institutional Act of December 1968, which dismissed Congress and gave him authority to rule by decree. Costa e Silva was incapacitated by a stroke on August 29, 1969, and died in Rio de Janeiro on December 17, 1969.

ROLLIE E. POPPINO

COSTA RICA SINCE 1823. Isolated from the favored centers of the Spanish empire in the Americas, Costa Rica received little preparation for independence and little or no contest from Spain when separation was declared. In 1823 Costa Rica was a province—the smallest and the most distant from the capital, Guatemala City—of the Federation of Central America, which had come into existence after the separation from Spain two years before (*see* CENTRAL AMERICA, FEDERATION OF). But given the weakness of the Federation and the physical isolation of the towns of Costa Rica from Guatemala, Costa Rica actually began to govern itself. After the collapse of the Federation in 1838, independence became a necessity. Ten years later, after a confusing interlude of dictators and constitutional conventions, Costa Rica formally declared itself an independent republic.

Although during this period the other Central American countries were frequently involved in wars among themselves and engaged in numerous efforts to revive the Central American union, Costa Rica generally remained aloof. One notable exception occurred in 1842, when Francisco MORAZÁN, former President of the Federation and the hero of the unionist ideal, attempted to use Costa Rica as a base for reunifying the isthmus. He took over the Presidency, but opposing Costa Rican forces captured and executed him in September 1842. Costa Rica was also involved in the National War against William WALKER and the filibusters in 1856–1857. Walker's forces invaded Costa Rica from Nicaragua in 1856 but were repulsed. Costa Rica's President, Juan Rafael Mora, took command of an allied Central American army that forced Walker to surrender in 1857.

At the time of the establishment of the Federation

of Central America in 1823, the province of Costa Rica had a population of only about 60,000. No one of its four principal towns in the Meseta Central (Central Plateau) area had a population of more than 5,000. Despite its small size and a heritage of poverty and neglect from the colonial period, Costa Rica made rapid strides as an independent nation. The discovery and development of coffee as a cash crop had much to do with this progress. A colonial officer had brought coffee plants to Costa Rica from Cuba in the late eighteenth century. Exportation of the commodity began in 1825, and by 1829 it was the leading export of the country. Costa Rica, the first Central American country to grow coffee in abundance, now strongly endorsed its production. Owing to high quality, a result of ideal soil and climate conditions in the Central Plateau, Costa Rican coffee enjoyed a preferred status in the European market. The cultivation of coffee stimulated road building and port development, especially that of Puntarenas on the Pacific coast, and also furnished revenue. Moreover, it encouraged the growing population to move outward in search of new coffee lands, in contrast to the usual Latin American pattern of inward population growth. Coffee also widened the gap between rich and poor. Still, since landownership was never as highly concentrated in Costa Rica as it was in most other Latin American countries, the coffee oligarchy did not create a rigid social class structure. This was a factor favoring the establishment of democratic institutions. *See also* COFFEE INDUSTRY (CENTRAL AMERICA).

The homogeneity of Costa Rica's population also strengthened the nation's hopes for stable, democratic government. Without large numbers of Indians or former slaves, Costa Rica began independent life with a population overwhelmingly Spanish in origin. Moreover, since the population was concentrated almost wholly in the Central Plateau, there was little difficulty in communication. No region of the country could contest the supremacy of the plateau. Relatively equal land distribution, population homogeneity, absence of regional rivalries, and isolation from Central American wars were all factors contributing to Costa Rica's early peaceful evolution. In the country's political history the election of 1889 stands out as a landmark in the achievement of democracy. The election was seriously contested with a free press, and the government party, having lost, peacefully turned the government over to its opponents. On only two occasions thereafter (in 1917 and 1948) did irregularities occur in the electoral process.

In the late nineteenth century the stimulus of coffee revenues and dynamic leadership resulted in rapid economic change. Tomás GUARDIA, the last of the Costa Rican *caudillos,* who was in power for most of the time between 1870 and 1882, encouraged transportation development by contracting with Minor Cooper KEITH for the construction of the Northern Railway, which linked the Central Plateau with the Atlantic coast. Completion of the railway not only greatly stimulated the towns of Turrialba and Limón but also facilitated the exploitation of the humid Atlantic coastal lowlands, which had been largely ignored. This area proved to be ideal for the production of bananas, which soon rivaled coffee as Costa Rica's principal export. The railroad was finished in 1890, and by 1913 Costa Rica was the leading banana exporter of the world. Soil exhaustion and plant disease seriously reduced Atlantic banana production in succeeding years, but the UNITED FRUIT COMPANY, the leading banana producer in Costa Rica, began to move operations to the Pacific coast after the signing of the Cortés-Chittenden contract in 1936. This contract, which required the company to furnish hospitals, schools, and recreational facilities in the area of the new plantations, stimulated the economic development of the Puerto Quepos – Golfito area. In the 1960s some of the abandoned lands of the Atlantic region were returned to banana production. *See also* BANANA INDUSTRY (CENTRAL AMERICA AND THE CARIBBEAN).

Politically, the era between 1889 and 1940 was one of tranquillity, and consolidation of the democratic process. It could well be called the era of Don Cleto and Don Ricardo, because Cleto GONZÁLEZ VÍQUEZ and Ricardo JIMÉNEZ OREAMUNO, two of Costa Rica's most distinguished and respected political leaders, held presidential office five times in this period, although neither served for two successive terms. They neither promised nor effected significant changes, although both attempted to foster Costa Rica's development by paying attention to schools and roads. Their respect for individual liberties and their toleration of opposition helped to solidify Costa Rica's political institutions. Their relative timidity in fostering change permitted the national legislature to assume a stronger role in political life than is customary in most Latin American countries.

By 1940, when Rafael CALDERÓN GUARDIA was elected to the Presidency, demands for change rose to the surface. Calderón attempted to satisfy these demands through social security legislation and a new workers' code, but in 1948 he alienated many Costa Ricans by his attempt to return to the Presidency despite his electoral defeat. The resulting revolution drove Calderón and much of his party into exile and brought José FIGUERES and his PARTIDO LIBERACIÓN NACIONAL

COSTA RICA
Area: 19,576 sq. mi.   Population: 1,786,000 (1971 est.).

to national prominence, inaugurating a period of even more rapid change. Beginning in 1948 the Costa Rican government gave women the right to vote, abolished the Army, broadened social security, and nationalized banks and power companies. These developments were accompanied by the creation of autonomous government agencies for the management of electric power, railroads, insurance, banking, and other aspects of economic life. Autonomous agencies also were created to administer national planning, higher education, social security, tourist promotion, and the like. These agencies served to counterbalance the power traditionally shared by the executive and legislative branches of the government.

In population Costa Rica has always been the smallest of the five Central American republics. However, its population is growing at a more rapid rate; indeed, the country has often registered the highest annual increase in population in the world since World War II, at times exceeding 4 percent. The population rose from 800,875 in 1950 to 1,000,000 in 1956, 1,433,058 in 1965, and an estimated 1,798,000 in 1970. This extremely rapid growth resulted in a very young population (57 percent under nineteen years of age in 1963) and in consequent pressure on schools and other facilities. To take care of the increase in population the government, recognizing the weak international market for coffee and bananas, placed its hopes on industrialization. Only 11 percent of the labor force was employed in manufacturing in 1950, but this figure rose to approximately 15 percent by 1970. Although membership in the CENTRAL AMERICAN COMMON MARKET opened up a wider market for the country's furniture, wood, fertilizer, and food-processing industries, Costa Rica had trade deficits with its Common Market partners as well as chronic balance-of-payments problems. In June 1971, Costa Rica dealt the Common Market, already weakened by the effects of the FOOTBALL WAR, a blow by imposing customs guarantees that were in effect tariffs on Common Market goods. The measure was soon rescinded, but the issues that motivated it had not been resolved by 1972.

Bibliography. John P. Bell, *Crisis in Costa Rica: The Revolution of 1948,* Austin, Tex., 1971; John and Mavis Biesanz, *Costa Rican Life,* New York, 1945; Howard I. Blutstein et al., *Area Handbook for Costa Rica,* Washington, 1970; Charles F. Denton, *Patterns of Costa Rican Politics,* Boston, 1971; Clarence F. Jones and Paul C. Morrison, "Evolution of the Banana Industry of Costa Rica," *Economic Geography,* vol. XXVIII, no. 1, January 1952, pp. 1–19; Stacy May et al., *Costa Rica: A Study in Economic Development,* New York, 1952; Carlos Monge Alfaro, *Historia de Costa Rica,* San José, many editions; Robert E. Nunley, *The Distribution of Population in Costa Rica,* Washington, 1960.

CHARLES L. STANSIFER

COTAPOS, ACARIO (1889–1969). Chilean composer. Born in Valdivia, he was self-taught as a musician and was a pioneer of radicalism in Chilean music. He lived in France and Spain for many years and was active in New York at the time of the foundation of the League of Composers. In general his works are programmatic and descriptive. The best known of these are *Voces de gesta,* a tragedy in three parts based on texts by Ramón

del Valle-Inclán; *El pájaro burlón,* a stage poem on his own libretto; and *Sonata-Fantasía* for piano. In 1960 he received the National Prize for the Arts in Chile.

JUAN A. ORREGO-SALAS

COUNCIL OF THE INDIES. The Royal and Supreme Council of the Indies (*El Consejo Real y Supremo de las Indias*), the chief governing body for Spanish America, was established in 1524 after the conquest of New Spain. Virtually all aspects of government fell within its purview. It supervised the Casa de Contratación, recommended to the King candidates for civil and ecclesiastical offices, reviewed the performance of civil incumbents after and sometimes during tenure, and drafted the colonial ordinances, subsequently codified as the RECOPILACIÓN DE LEYES DE LAS INDIAS. It also sat as a supreme court hearing appeals from the American *audiencias* (*see* AUDIENCIA). Its decisions in all matters were subject to approval of the King.

Though the Council sometimes passed unrealistic legislation in its immature years, the gradual acquisition of detailed knowledge and the appointment of councilors with experience in America ultimately made the agency highly effective. In *El consejo real y supremo de las Indias* (2 vols., 1935–1947), Ernesto Schäfer concluded that in spite of the shortcomings of various members the Council maintained a high level of justice, helped prevent mistreatment of the Indians, and appointed capable men to fill the high-level positions in the Indies. During the seventeenth century the Council was affected by the malaise that imbued Spain in its descent from power. Its grasp of colonial affairs and its labors slackened, while its membership rose from 30 in 1598 to 100 about 1690, reflecting favoritism, nepotism, and the sale of offices, most of which were sinecural or honorific. Under the national ministerial system established in the eighteenth century, the Council became more bureaucratic than deliberative. It was belatedly abolished in the nineteenth century by Isabella II.

TROY S. FLOYD

COVARRUBIAS, MIGUEL (1904–1957). Mexican writer, artist, ethnologist, and archaeologist. A self-taught artist, at sixteen he was teaching art in the national education project initiated by Minister of Education José VASCONCELOS. In 1923 he went to New York with a portfolio of caricatures that gained him commissions from *Vanity Fair* and the *New Yorker.* These led to a book of caricatures, *The Prince of Wales and Other Famous Americans* (1925). His discovery of Harlem led to his second book, *Negro Drawings* (1927). Covarrubias alternated between the literary world and the traditional societies of the "underdeveloped" world, exemplified in New York by Harlem.

In 1930 he and his wife made a study of Bali on a Guggenheim fellowship. The resulting book presented material on "a living culture that is doomed to disappear under the merciless onslaught of modern commercialism and standardization." In 1939 Covarrubias painted six widely disseminated illustrated maps of the Pacific Basin for the Golden Gate Exposition in San Francisco. He also illustrated a variety of books, among them John Huston's *Frankie and Johnny* (1930), in his Harlem style, and Shui Hu-chuan's *All Men Are Brothers* (1948), in mock-Chinese style.

In 1940 he returned to Mexico. The rediscovery of his homeland led to *Mexico South* (1946), a classic account of the Tehuantepec region. He discovered the traditional societies of the pre-Columbian past; the famous site of Tlatilco was saved and named by Covarrubias. Tlatilco led to a perceptive study of Olmec art (*see* OLMECS). Covarrubias's volumes *The Eagle, the Jaguar, and the Serpent* (1954) and *Indian Art of Mexico and Central America* (1957), which he both wrote and illustrated, are standard studies. He left an important body of paintings, drawings, and illustrations in addition to his books.

TERENCE GRIEDER

CREOLE (CRIOLLO). In colonial Spanish America, a native-born white person, as distinguished from one born in Spain. Creoles dominated the economic life of colonial Spanish America, although they had to endure competition from whites born in Spain, who were particularly active in commerce, and from upwardly mobile nonwhites; most of the wealthy people in the colonies were creoles, although, by no means were all creoles wealthy and creoles were to be found at all economic levels. Socially, creoles occupied a status superior to that of nonwhites but inferior to that of whites born in Spain, who were known as *peninsulares*. In the political sphere, creoles occupied most posts in the lower levels of the colonial bureaucracy. Posts in the higher levels, however, usually went to *peninsulares;* creoles received a fair number of appointments as judges in the *audiencias* (*see* AUDIENCIA), mainly in the eighteenth century, but almost none as viceroys, captains general, or intendants. An analogous situation prevailed in the church; many priests were creoles, but a substantial majority of episcopal appointments went to *peninsulares*. In the militia, on the other hand, the creoles found the road to advancement more open.

Not surprisingly, the creoles came to harbor an intense resentment against the *peninsulares* and to regard them as pushy, arrogant, and avaricious. Their rivals paid back their resentment with contempt and regarded the creoles as superficial and lazy. Creole resentment agianst *peninsulares* and against the way *peninsulares* blocked their advancement in the bureaucracy was one cause of the Spanish American wars of independence, for which creoles provided most of the leadership.

In modern Spanish America, the term creole is used to describe something typical of or native to a country or region.

TIMOTHY C. HANLEY

CRÉOLE. Hybrid language of Haiti, consisting of French vocabulary and phonology with a West Africa–based grammar. There are five dialects of Haitian Créole, the Port-au-Prince variety being the most prestigious. Créole's origin is obscure. Some experts believe it evolved from French dialects or a lingua franca that French sailors brought to Saint-Domingue. It may have grown out of an Afro-Portuguese pidgin developed by slavers whose cargoes were sold to the French. Other students think that it may have evolved from a simplified French used by masters to communicate with their slaves. For Haiti's peasants, it is the only tongue; while acknowledging the prestige of French, they often consider it a language of deception. Educated Haitians employ Créole informally with peer groups and use standard French on formal occasions.

Créole is the repository of Haiti's rich folklore and expresses its national consciousness. Only recently was it completely reduced to writing. It may yet become the vehicle to educate the masses, once publication and standardization enhance its standing. By now half of Haiti's radio advertising is in Créole, a vibrant, constantly growing tongue that borrows much from French to meet the changing needs of its more than 4 million speakers.

JOHN E. BAUR

CRESPO, JOAQUÍN (1845–1898). President of Venezuela (1884–1886, 1892–1898). Crespo gained his Liberal credentials in the Federal Wars (1858–1863) fighting beside Juan C. FALCÓN and Antonio GUZMÁN BLANCO. Loyal to Guzmán Blanco, he received his reward by serving as puppet President from 1884 to 1886. His administration witnessed a major decline in coffee prices. After the withdrawal of Guzmán Blanco in 1888, Crespo tried unsuccessfully to obtain the Presidency. Unhappy with the post-Guzmán Blanco politics of more successful generals, Crespo in 1892 led a revolt called the Legalist Revolution, which deposed the government and allowed him to be named provisional President in 1892 and then to be elected President for the term ending in 1898. His second presidential term is best known for Venezuela's boundary dispute with Great Britain over the Guiana territory, where gold had been discovered. Although the dispute was settled peacefully by arbitration, Venezuela had to relinquish some of its territorial claims. After the end of his term Crespo became involved in the military defense of his successor, Ignacio Andrade, and was killed in battle in 1898.

JOHN V. LOMBARDI

CRIOLLO. *See* CREOLE.

CRISTERO REBELLION. During the MEXICAN REVOLUTION the long-standing struggle between church and state was exacerbated by the collaboration of some Catholics with the dictator Victoriano HUERTA. Various chiefs of the Constitutionalist Army expelled foreign priests as well as Jesuits regardless of nationality and performed other anticlerical acts, such as closing churches and forbidding confessions and the collection of parish fees. The 1917 constitution included several anticlerical provisions, including Article 130, which authorized the state legislatures to limit the number of priests (who had to be Mexicans by birth) and did not confer juridical personality upon churches (*see* CONSTITUTION OF 1917: MEXICO).

The Catholic hierarchy protested the constitution in 1917 and again in 1926, when the government of President Plutarco Elías CALLES attempted to force priests to register with civil authorities and enforce the anticlerical provisions of the constitution. As the controversy continued, the bishops closed the churches on July 25, 1926, thereby discontinuing public worship in Mexico. Those who actively supported the Catholic position during the conflict became known as Cristeros, the name being derived from the slogan "Long live Christ the King." Urban Cristeros were organized in the National League for the Defense of Religious Freedom, founded in 1925, which launched a boycott of goods and services as a means of defeating the government. In rural areas, especially in the BAJÍO and the states of Michoacán, Colima, and Jalisco, Cristeros resorted to arms. The conflict between the government and the church ended when, on June 22, 1929, the hierarchy accepted a statement by President Emilio PORTES GIL to the effect that the government did not seek to dominate the church by means of the civil inscription of priests. The Cristeros who were under arms accepted the surrender only reluctantly, and a number of them were subsequently murdered on the instructions of local officials.

See also MORROW, Dwight W.

MOISÉS GONZÁLEZ NAVARRO

CROM. *See* CONFEDERACIÓN REGIONAL OBRERA MEXICANA.

CROWDER, ENOCH H[ERBERT] (1859–1932). American army officer and diplomat. A graduate of the United States Military Academy in 1881, he earned a law degree in 1886. In 1891 he joined the office of the advocate general of the United States Army, and during the Spanish-American War he was sent to the Philippines as judge advocate general. After returning to the United States in 1903, he was appointed assistant to the judge advocate general of the Army. Later he served for two years as a military observer with the Japanese Army during the Russo-Japanese War.

During the second United States intervention in Cuba (1906–1909), Crowder was adviser to the Department of State and Justice in the provisional government and was named President of the Advisory Law Commission appointed by Governor Charles E. MAGOON in 1906 to reform Cuban law. In 1910 he attended the Fourth International Conference of American States in Argentina, and the same year he served briefly as United States Minister to Chile. After his return to the United States in 1911, he became judge advocate general of the United States Army. During World War I Crowder administered the Selective Service Act as provost marshal general. In 1919 he was sent to Cuba to help revise the nation's electoral laws, returning unexpectedly in 1921 to assist the island through the serious financial crisis that followed the so-called dance of the millions. He remained in Cuba as the personal representative of Presidents Wilson and Harding to the administration of Alfredo ZAYAS and worked, with only temporary success, for the reform of the Cuban government. In 1923 he was named Ambassador to Cuba, a post he held until his retirement in 1927.

RICHARD B. GRAY

CRUZ, OSWALDO [GONÇALVES] (1872–1917). Brazilian physician credited with eradicating yellow fever, smallpox, and malaria from the city of Rio de Janeiro and stopping epidemics of these diseases throughout Brazil. Born in São Luis do Paraitinga, São Paulo, Oswaldo Cruz obtained his medical degree from the Faculty of Medicine of Rio de Janeiro at the age of twenty. From 1896 to 1898 he studied bacteriology and experimental pathology at the Pasteur Institute of Paris. On his return to Brazil in 1899 he achieved prominence by controlling an epidemic of bubonic plague in Santos, the port of São Paulo.

In 1902 President Francisco de Paula RODRIGUES ALVES committed the federal government to eradicating tropical disease and appointed Dr. Cruz Director General of Public Health. Under Cruz's leadership an aggressive program, backed by public legislation, was launched in Rio de Janeiro and its vicinity to kill the *Stegomyia* mosquito, destroy its breeding grounds, vaccinate the people, and quarantine the sick. Deaths attributed to yellow fever in Rio de Janeiro dropped from 584 in 1903 to zero in 1906. By 1908 yellow fever, smallpox, and malaria were under control throughout Brazil.

The conquest of these dreaded diseases constituted a major turning point in the medical history of Brazil and contributed to increased European immigration and rapid settlement and industrialization of traditionally fever-infested areas. To this day Oswaldo Cruz is a household name among grateful *cariocas,* and his memory is fittingly preserved in the internationally renowned school of experimental tropical medicine of Rio de Janeiro, the Instituto Oswaldo Cruz.

ARNOLD J. MEAGHER

CRUZ, RAMÓN ERNESTO (1903–   ). President of Honduras (1971–1972). Cruz began his career teaching in a rural primary school and later became professor of law, economics, and sociology at the University of Honduras in Tegucigalpa. In 1943 he was appointed Appellate Court magistrate for Tegucigalpa, and three years later he joined the diplomatic corps, serving first as Minister and then as Ambassador to El Salvador. Subsequently he resumed his academic and legal careers as dean of the department of juridical and social sciences of the University of Honduras and Supreme Court magistrate.

In 1963 the National party chose Cruz as its presidential candidate, but a military coup canceled the election. At this juncture he abandoned his private life to devote all his time to party work. Nominated to the Presidency again in 1971, Cruz won a narrow victory over the Liberal candidate. His six-year term, which began on June 6, 1971, was threatened by an incipient land war, student unrest, and continuing border incidents with El Salvador. Perhaps the most serious task faced by Cruz, however, was that of reconciling a growing desire for national autonomy with a pressing need to participate in the CENTRAL AMERICAN COMMON MARKET. On December 4, 1972, however, Cruz was ousted in a military coup led by Gen. Oswaldo LÓPEZ ARELLANO, who was to serve as President for the rest of Cruz's term. *See* LIBERAL PARTY (HONDURAS); NATIONAL OR NATIONALIST PARTY (HONDURAS).

KENNETH V. FINNEY

CRUZ, SOR JUANA INÉS DE LA. *See* JUANA INÉS DE LA CRUZ, SOR.

CRUZ E SOUSA, JOÃO DA (1861–1898). Brazilian poet. Considered one of the greatest poets of his country, Cruz e Sousa was born in Santa Catarina, the child of emancipated slaves, and throughout his adult life had to struggle against color prejudice and poverty. He was well educated by the former owners of his parents, a cultured couple who treated him with great affection, and as a youth he moved in the intellectual circles of the provincial capital. When he went to Rio de Janeiro to live, however, the only position he could obtain was that of clerk in the railways, and his resultant financial problems were increased by his marriage to a Negro woman who suffered from attacks of insanity and from tuberculosis, the disease that was to kill them both. Though he always had a small group of admiring friends, he was not widely appreciated until after his death. He began to write when the formal rigidity and cold platitudes of Parnassianism were in vogue, and his symbolist poetry, composed between 1893 and 1898 (to be found chiefly in *Broquéis*, 1893, *Faróis*, 1900, and *Últimos Sonetos*, 1905), was too novel and too difficult to gain immediate recognition. The powerful rhetorical language, the vagueness of statement, and the startling images, coupled with an anguished pessimism of theme, retarded his acceptance as a great poet. In addition to a volume of prose pieces, *Tropos e Fantasias* (1895), Cruz e Sousa left two volumes of prose poems, *Missal* (1893) and *Evocações* (1898).

RAYMOND S. SAYERS

CTC. *See* CONFEDERACIÓN DE TRABAJADORES CUBANOS.

CTM. *See* CONFEDERACIÓN DE TRABAJADORES DE MÉXICO.

CTP. *See* CONFEDERACIÓN DE TRABAJADORES DEL PERÚ.

CUARTELAZO. Barracks revolt, the word being derived from the Spanish *cuartel* (barracks). The *cuartelazo* in Latin America ordinarily begins with the rebellion of the officers and men of a garrison who then march upon key government and communications centers. If the *cuartelazo* is the result of a well-coordinated conspiracy involving other officers and civilians, or if the leader's *pronunciamiento* (pronouncement) finds an echo in other garrisons, its prospects of success are greatly enhanced. A successful *cuartelazo* occurred in Peru after the army garrison in Arequipa revolted against President José Luis BUSTAMANTE on October 27, 1948, and proclaimed Gen. Manuel A. ODRÍA as supreme head of the revolution. When the general in command of the troops in Lima refused to take action against the rebels, Bustamante was forced to retire from the Presidency. In Cuba, Fulgencio BATISTA staged a successful *cuartelazo* on the night of March 10, 1952, by taking over, with his military supporters, the Camp Columbia army base in Havana; President Carlos PRÍO SOCORRÁS soon took refuge in the Mexican Embassy and on March 13 left for Mexico.

HELEN DELPAR

CUAUHTÉMOC (1495?–1525). Last Aztec emperor. A member of the Aztec royal family, Cuauhtémoc succeeded to the throne in late 1520 or early 1521, at the time when Hernán CORTÉS and his Spanish army of conquest were preparing to lay siege to the Aztec capital, TENOCHTITLÁN. He prepared for the coming siege by sending many of those who could not fight into the mountains and bringing warriors into the city, and by stockpiling food and weapons. When the Spaniards instituted their siege, he defended the city with great stubbornness, but his forces were worn down by hunger and disease and by the attacks of their enemies, who demolished Tenochtitlán building by building in order to break down the resistance of the defenders. Cuauhtémoc

consistently refused to surrender. Finally, after two and one-half months, the Spaniards overran the last section of the city that still held out, and Cuauhtémoc was captured. After taking him prisoner, the Spaniards burned the bottoms of his feet in an effort to make him reveal the location of treasure they believed he had hidden; his disclosure that the hiding place was the bottom of Lake Texcoco did them no good. Cuauhtémoc survived this torture; but four years later, while accompanying Cortés on an expedition to Honduras, he was accused of conspiring with other Indian leaders on the expedition to kill Cortés and his Spanish companions, and he was executed.

In 1951 bones alleged to be those of Cuauhtémoc were discovered in Ixcateopan, Guerrero, Mexico. Pro-Indian elements accepted the find as authentic, while pro-Spanish elements branded it as fraudulent. An investigating commission ruled that the authenticity of the discovery could not be confirmed.

TIMOTHY C. HANLEY

CUBAN REVOLUTION. On assuming power in Cuba early in 1959, Fidel CASTRO gave no indication that he was leading the first socialist revolution to have been made without the participation of the local Communist party. Foreign response, particularly the negative response of the United States, to such early "liberal" reforms as the Agrarian Reform Law of 1959 (*see* AGRARIAN REFORM) played a significant role in determining the increasingly radical course of the revolution. The Cuban leaders became convinced that to heed what they considered unreasonable American protests and demands would be to make further reform subject to the dictates of the United States. With the ensuing breach in Cuba's traditionally close commercial and political relations with the United States, the Cubans turned increasingly to the socialist nations.

These developments were still in the future in the first months of 1959, when the new regime purged the police, military, and judiciary of those who had cooperated with Fulgencio BATISTA; the worst offenders faced the firing squad. In March the management of the United States–owned telephone company was intervened, telephone rates were cut, and a general reduction in rents was decreed. The Agrarian Reform Law of May 17 founded the National Institute of Agrarian Reform (INRA) to administer laws limiting land ownership to 1,000 acres or, in cases of exceptionally high productivity, to 3,333 acres. Some 33,000 new farmers were created as lands were distributed to tenants in 67-acre lots. Numerous cooperatives were organized, while holdings that could not easily be broken up, such as cattle ranches, were taken over by INRA and converted into state farms. Although the law affected only about 10 percent of the farms in Cuba, these farms controlled 40 percent of the land. Properties of the UNITED FRUIT COMPANY, the Pingree Ranch, and the King Ranch of Texas were affected, and when the United States government responded with a demand for prompt compensation, Cuba rejected the demand.

Initially Castro's foreign policy was in a state of flux. On the one hand, much of his mid-April visit to the United States was spent defending his neutralist, nationalist revolution. On the other hand, Cuba invaded the Dominican Republic, desiring to portray itself as a liberator in the eyes of Latin America, where Rafael

Leonidas TRUJILLO MOLINA was despised as a tyrant. The invasion was badly defeated, and a Dominican protest was debated in the ORGANIZATION OF AMERICAN STATES (OAS).

Liberals in the Cuban government, fearing a collision with the United States and considered "subservient to imperialism," began to resign. Lacking national support, their gestures merely quickened the leftward pace of the revolution. Sabotage increased, and the death penalty was restored for crimes against the national economy and the revolution. The end of June 1959 saw defecting Air Force Maj. Pedro Díaz Lanz and President Manuel Urrutia both denouncing Communist activity. On July 17, Castro forced Urrutia out of office. The new President was Osvaldo DORTICÓS TORRADO, a former Communist who was then president of the National College of Lawyers. At the same time, the military's influence in INRA increased; land reform was accelerated, and the legal niceties of taking inventories and issuing receipts and bonds were often overlooked. At the Tenth Congress of the CONFEDERACIÓN DE TRABAJADORES DE CUBA in November, Castro was able to ensure the inclusion on the Executive Committee of several members who would not oppose Communist control of the unions. The elimination of anti-Communists from the unions followed.

Domestically, government by decree continued at the end of 1959 as the Minister of Labor was empowered to seize firms that were judged to be malfunctioning; the government was thus enabled to nationalize many hotels that had fallen on evil days because of the lack of tourists. Laws against foreign companies were tightened: oil companies were asked to drill immediately, and land belonging to the Bethlehem Steel Corporation and the International Harvester Company was seized. Florida-based light planes dropped incendiary bombs, and sabotage spread. Habeas corpus was suspended indefinitely, facilitating a wave of arrests on suspicion of conspiracy. Internationally, Cuba began looking to Western Europe to float a $100 million loan and buy arms. However, pressure from the United States dried up credit and supplies.

Finally, in February 1960, Anastas Mikoyan, Deputy Chairman of the Council of Ministers of the USSR, arrived in Havana and concluded a trade agreement. Russia agreed to buy 425,000 tons of sugar in 1960 and 1 million tons in 1961, to sell oil below United States prices, and to lend Cuba $100 million at an annual interest rate of 2.5 percent. To judge from the arms visible in the hands of the newly organized militia, Cuba apparently signed an arms agreement with Czechoslovakia during this period as well. This was the beginning of a new pattern of trade for Cuba: previously two-thirds of its trade had been with the United States; after 1960 two-thirds was with Communist nations.

By this time the United States image of Castro had changed from that of constitutional democrat to that of Communist subversive. The Central Intelligence Agency drew up contingency invasion plans and began to train exiles in Guatemala. Cuba discovered this and broke relations with Guatemala at the end of April.

When Texaco, Shell, and Standard Oil of New Jersey refused a Cuban demand that they refine Soviet oil, Castro responded on July 1 by taking over their refineries. On July 6 the United States cut Cuba's sugar quota by 700,000 tons. Six days later Castro announced that the Soviet Union would buy the sugar and defend Cuba. *See also* SUGAR INDUSTRY (CUBA).

International tension formed the backdrop for further encroachment on civil liberties in Cuba. The first newspaper to cease publication was the *Avance,* in January; *El País* and *Prensa Libre* were closed shortly thereafter. In March television stations came under government control, and by May no free media existed. A confrontation with the Catholic Church occurred at the end of May, when a mass for the victims of communism was broken up by militia men singing the "Internationale." Private schools began to be closed, and nongovernmental organizations to be banned. July witnessed the government take-over of the university; most first-rate staff went into exile. With the departure of eleven justices of the Supreme Court in November, "prorevolutionary" rather than "anti-Batista" sentiments came to dominate the judiciary. Finally, Committees for the Defense of the Revolution were created on a neighborhood basis by the government to report and enforce decrees.

Economically, the second half of 1960 was a period of large-scale changes. By the end of the year the government had taken over nearly all Cuba's major enterprises, including American properties valued at $1 billion and most of the large sugar estates, which were organized into cooperatives under INRA direction. These, along with other agricultural cooperatives, were eventually converted into state-owned people's farms. The dislocations were so great that the Cuban Communist party, known as the Popular Socialist party, (PSP), warned Castro that "private enterprise is still necessary. . . ." In an unprecedented move, however, the PSP placed itself under Fidel's leadership at the end of August 1960. In October the Urban Reform Law required tenants to purchase their dwelling units from the government on a monthly basis; the government would reimburse the owners. The same month the Chinese signed an agreement to buy 500,000 tons of sugar annually for five years and provide a credit of $60 million. The United States responded with an embargo on all trade with Cuba, except foodstuffs and medicines, and the permanent elimination of the sugar quota. The slack was picked up by the Soviet Union, which agreed to accept 2.7 million tons of sugar for 1961, and by China, with an additional 500,000 tons. United States diplomatic relations with Cuba were finally severed on January 3, 1961.

In mid-April 1961, the long-expected United States–sponsored invasion of Cuba was ineptly launched and quickly defeated, exploding the United States myth of Castro's unpopularity (*see* BAY OF PIGS INVASION). At a triumphant May Day celebration Castro officially announced that Cuba was socialist and that henceforth there would be no elections, as the revolution reflected the will of the people and had given each Cuban a rifle.

The invasion was followed eighteen months later by a second confrontation. An insecure Cuba accepted Soviet strategic missiles and watched helplessly as the United States forced their withdrawal. Just as the first experience fixed Cuba's attitude toward the United States, the second meant that Castro would never totally trust the Soviet Union or follow Moscow's ideological line or those in Cuba who did.

Difficulties with the Soviet Union as well as with Latin American Communist parties also arose as a result of Castro's material and moral support of leftist insurgents in the region. This support rested on the conviction that the Cuban experience could be duplicated elsewhere in Latin America. To achieve this goal, Ernesto (Che) GUEVARA, Régis DEBRAY, and others formulated a revolutionary strategy that envisioned operations on a continental scale to weaken the reaction of the United States; armed struggle was to be initiated by guerrillas in rural areas who would constitute the nucleus of a people's army. Although Castro apparently wavered in his support of the revolutionary movements of Latin America in the mid-1960s, he vigorously reasserted his position at the First Tricontinental Conference, held in Havana in January 1966, and on other occasions. By the end of 1969, however, Castro's militancy seemed to be diminishing, and in January 1970 he was publicly attacked by the Venezuelan guerrilla leader Douglas Bravo for cutting aid to insurgent groups.

Throughout the 1960s organizational problems plagued the new socialist state. Castro's July 26 movement lacked any formal organization, while the PSP was tightly organized but lacked national heroes. During the fall of 1961 Castro attempted to solve the problem by merging all political entities into one unit: the Integrated Revolutionary Organizations (ORI). Aníbal Escalante, an old Moscow-line Communist, was put in charge of organization, and 900 nuclei were formed throughout the country. Indoctrination courses were held in the old Jesuit headquarters. Within nine months Castro purged Escalante and accused him of placing the nation in a "sectarian straitjacket," distorting the history of the revolution, and losing touch with the masses. ORI was later replaced by the United Party of the Socialist Revolution (PURS), which in turn yielded to the PARTIDO COMUNISTA DE CUBA (Communist party of Cuba; PCC) in 1965. The PCC served as a counterweight to Cuba's 200,000-man Army, the largest in Latin America, but *fidelistas* as opposed to old-guard Communists were placed firmly in control. Hence, Cuba was to be not a satellite but an independent socialist state. The final reorganization appeared to give Cuba more liberal censors in art, literature, and film than those in other socialist countries.

Economic reorganization presented heartbreaking problems. Whereas the revolution and the end of the sugar quota were to have meant liberation from a one-crop economy, industrialization, and instant wealth, the initial result was a drop in production and food rationing. A second Agrarian Reform Law of October 1963 limited private holdings to 166 acres. The reform still left nearly 200,000 farmers, or 80 percent of the 1959 total, producing 90 percent of the coffee and tobacco, 70 percent of the fruit, and 25 percent of the sugarcane. When coupled with rationing, this permitted a large black market. In 1968, in an effort to liberate the new socialist man from the influence of the *petit bourgeoisie,* fruit stands, cockpits, pawn shops, music schools, laundries, and garages were confiscated, leaving only fishermen, farmers, and a few doctors in the private sector.

Industrialization proceeded slowly because of a lack of skilled personnel and Cuba's inability to pay the Soviet Union and the Eastern bloc for imports. As a result, after a massive effort to achieve rapid industrialization in the early 1960s, Castro was forced to reemphasize sugar, which continued to account for 80 percent of Cuban exports. The Soviet Union, Cuba's principal trading partner, now filled the political and economic role once held by the United States. One solution for Cuba would be to improve relations with the United States and maintain a more neutralist position. Such a shift was hinted at by the antihijacking agreement of February 1973. The impediment has been United States insistence that Cuba sever its military ties with the Soviet Union and stop aiding revolutionary elements in Latin America.

Cuba's new socialist man benefits from extensive free education; he has excelled in international sports competition; he enjoys free medical care, electricity, water, and, in many cases, living quarters. He also avoids the former chronic 25 percent nonharvest unemployment rate.

Bibliography. K. S. Karol, *Guerrillas in Power: The Course of the Cuban Revolution,* tr. by Arnold Pomerans, New York, 1970; Carmelo Mesa-Largo (ed.), *Revolutionary Change in Cuba,* Pittsburgh, 1971; Andrés Suárez, *Cuba: Castro and Communism, 1959–1966,* tr. by Joel Carmichael and Ernst Halperin, Cambridge, Mass., 1967; Jaime Suchlicki, "An Assessment of Castroism," *Orbis,* vol. XVI, no. 1, Spring, 1972, pp. 35–57; Hugh Thomas, *Cuba: The Pursuit of Freedom,* New York, 1971; Daniel Tretiak, "Cuba and the Communist System: The Politics of a Communist Independent, 1967–1969," *Orbis,* vol. XIV, no. 3, Fall, 1970, pp. 740–764; Nelson P. Valdés and Edwin Lieuwen, *The Cuban Revolution: A Research-Study Guide, 1959–1969,* Albuquerque, N. Mex., 1971; Desmond P. Wilson, Jr., "Alternative Futures in the Cuban Revolution," *Orbis,* vol. XV, no. 3, Fall, 1971, pp. 842–855.

JAMES L. DUDLEY

CUBAN REVOLUTIONARY PARTY. *See* AUTÉNTICO PARTY (CUBA).

CUBA SINCE 1902. On May 20, 1902, the United States military government of Cuba came to an end. The departing Governor, Gen. Leonard WOOD, had shown a great deal of ability in reorganizing the political and economic life of the country, and from all appearances Cuba seemed to be ready for a stable and independent future. Under the American administration roads and bridges were built, a communication system was

CUBA

Area: 44,218 sq. mi.   Population: 8,553,395 (1970 est.).

established, hospitals were founded, and attempts were made to eradicate such diseases as yellow fever. General Wood was also successful in establishing a public school system, a workable judicial system, a post office, and a customs agency. All these institutions were patterned after United States models.

The transition from United States rule to Cuban self-government was rather swift. The first step was taken in June 1900, when municipal officials were elected. In September elections were held to choose thirty-one delegates for the Constituent Assembly. The Assembly met in November 1900 and adopted a constitution similar to that of the United States, including a Cuban version of the Bill of Rights. In addition, as a price for independence, the Assembly agreed to attach to the constitution a number of stipulations governing future relations between Cuba and the United States. This addendum is generally known as the PLATT AMENDMENT. After the constitution was approved in June 1901, the Cubans began preparations for the selection of a Congress and a President. Both existing political parties, the Nationalist and the Republican, endorsed Tomás ESTRADA PALMA, who was elected the first President of the republic.

The birth of the Cuban nation occurred at a time of great optimism and confidence. The new President had been a prominent figure in the struggle against Spanish rule and enjoyed the respect and admiration of both his people and the Americans. Cuba possessed many of the elements on which to build a stable and prosperous nation; newly liberalized immigration laws attracted numerous immigrants, sugar production increased rapidly (*see* SUGAR INDUSTRY: CUBA), and large amounts of United States investment capital were introduced to the island in the first years of independence. The special relationship that the United States had designed between the two countries proved to be beneficial to Cuba in those initial years after 1902. As an example, the reciprocal treaty of 1903 provided for a 20 percent reduction in United States tariffs on all Cuban exports entering the United States.

By 1905, however, the bouyancy and enthusiasm of the first years of independent life had begun to fade as a realignment of the political groups created a Moderate party, which was conservative, and a Liberal party, which favored more radical changes. The Moderates selected Estrada Palma for a second term, and the Liberals supported the candidacy of José Miguel GÓMEZ. The 1905 presidential election was marred by illegal and extralegal practices engaged in by both parties. After the Moderates claimed victory, the Liberals went to court to seek a cancellation of the election results. When the courts validated the election of Estrada Palma, the Liberals began a rebellion against the government in August 1906. Estrada Palma then called upon the United States to intervene under the terms of Article 3 of the Platt Amendment.

Although President Theodore Roosevelt was reluctant to intervene, peace-making efforts by Secretary of War William Howard Taft and Acting Secretary of State Robert Bacon proved unsuccessful, and Taft issued a proclamation of intervention on September 29, 1906. This second intervention lasted until January 28, 1909, administered at first by Taft and later by Charles E. MAGOON. Magoon sought to solve the political conflict by appointing a substantial number of Liberals to public positions in an attempt to balance their political power vis-à-vis the Moderates, who had monopolized official posts under the administration of Estrada Palma.

In 1908 the United States administration in Cuba sponsored new elections for both local and national offices. For the Presidency there were two candidates, Gen. Mario García MENOCAL of the Conservative party (made up of former Moderates) and José Miguel Gómez of the Liberal party. In this election the Liberals captured the Presidency as well as many municipal offices. The United States withdrew several months later, and Cuba again had the opportunity of governing itself.

At the end of Gómez's four-year term Alfredo ZAYAS, his Vice President and political rival within the Liberal party, sought the nomination for President. He obtained the honor but with only lukewarm support from the outgoing chief executive. In the meantime the Conservatives chose Mario García Menocal as their candidate, and many Liberals who could not tolerate the candidacy of Zayas openly backed Menocal. As a result Menocal easily won over Zayas. It was ironical that after eight years in office Menocal supported Zayas for the Presidency in 1920 rather than the candidate of his own party.

During the latter part of Menocal's second term Cuba enjoyed a time of prosperity generally referred to as the "Dance of the Millions," stemming from the high war-induced price of sugar, but by the beginning of the Zayas administration there were ominous signs of deterioration. A small elite of former revolutionary leaders, whose election to public office depended almost solely on the support of those who were in a position to control the electoral machinery, continued to rule the country. Corruption was rampant from the lowest level of the government to the Presidential Palace. Economically Cuba also was faltering, and a sharp drop in sugar prices in 1920 was followed by many bankruptcies and foreclosures, a process that permitted United States banks and other business interests to increase their stake in Cuba's sugar industry. *See also* CROWDER, Enoch H.

The elections of 1924 brought to power Gerardo MACHADO, a Liberal who had campaigned for honesty in government and against the traditional political establishment. Soon, however, Machado was consolidating his power and silencing all forms of opposition to his regime. Toward the end of his term he forced a constitutional amendment extending the presidential period of office to six years. He was then reelected without a contest in November 1928. Machado's indiscriminate hunger for power, combined with growing economic problems because of the Depression, gave rise to political unrest that the government attempted to stop by violent repression. Between 1930 and 1933 opposition to Machado developed among students, the middle classes, and other influential groups to such an extent that his regime depended heavily on the support of the armed forces. Machado's position deteriorated further after the arrival in May 1933 of United States Ambassador Sumner WELLES with instructions to mediate between Machado and opposition leaders. In August 1933, when the Army commanders withdrew their support, Machado was forced to flee the country, leaving the Presidency in the hands of Carlos Manuel de Céspedes.

The vacillating Céspedes was unable to fill the power

vacuum that was produced with Machado's departure. In early September a group of noncommissioned Army officers took control of Camp Columbia, the main army headquarters of Cuba, and ousted the officer corps from all positions of command. The Céspedes government soon collapsed, and on September 10, 1933, Dr. Ramón GRAU SAN MARTÍN was named provisional President. In the confused and fluid circumstances of the last months of 1933, as the nationalist Grau regime attempted to restore order, the leading sergeant in the September revolt, Fulgencio BATISTA, began to emerge as the strong man of Cuba. When the United States refused to recognize the Grau government, Batista shifted his support to Col. Carlos Mendieta for President.

For the next ten years Cuba was ruled for all practical purposes by Batista. During the first six years he remained behind the scenes as chief of staff of the Army, refusing to accept a Cabinet position and preferring to rule through puppet Presidents. In 1940 Batista decided to run for the Presidency after a new constitution had been drafted and proclaimed (*see* CONSTITUTION OF 1940: CUBA). With all the sources of political power in his hands Batista had very little difficulty in winning the election against the candidate of the AUTÉNTICO PARTY (*see* AUTÉNTICO PARTY: CUBA), Ramón Grau San Martín. Batista's first constitutional rule was a complete success in terms of his personal prestige and influence. Nevertheless, when he tried to have a prospective puppet elected to replace him in 1944, he was surprised by the victory of Grau San Martín, who had waged an energetic campaign against the continued rule of Batista and his clique of former sergeants.

Between 1944 and 1952 Cuba was in the hands of the Auténticos, who began their eight-year rule amid promises of reforms and social and economic justice. In the administrations of both Grau San Martín (1944–1948) and Carlos PRÍO SOCARRÁS (1948–1952) the old revolutionaries of the early thirties succumbed to the Cuban political practice of milking the national treasury. Perhaps the prosperity of the post-World War II years was too much for the aging reformers, who did carry out a number of needed programs, although these were insignificant when compared with the widespread graft and political violence of the era.

It was this corruption and lawlessness that Batista used as an excuse for staging a coup d'état on March 10, 1952. Until then Batista had been running for the Presidency against two other candidates, Carlos Hevia and Roberto Agramonte, but he was expected to come in third. The coup, staged with the support of Army officers, brought down the government of Prío Socarrás and ended the Auténtico party's rule. Large sectors of society immediately expressed their opposition to Batista and his new government; in vain some groups threatened violence, while others appealed to the courts. Fidel CASTRO, a candidate for Congress in the canceled elections, organized an attack on two army barracks on July 26, 1953, but this act was a complete failure, resulting in the incarceration of Castro and the death of many of his followers.

Batista succeeded in cajoling sufficient influential elements to his side with promises of a better deal. The United States government was satisfied by the promise of elections, which were held in 1954. Batista was elected President with only token opposition, as most of the leading political figures either refused to participate or remained in exile. After 1954 Batista seemed well entrenched, although opposition to his regime never subsided completely.

The failure of the barracks attack in 1953 and Castro's imprisonment did not diminish his determination to bring down the Batista government, and when he was amnestied and released, he went to Mexico to prepare an invasion of Cuba that he hoped would result in a national uprising. In December 1956 Castro landed in Oriente, the easternmost province of the island, and succeeded in reaching the mountainous region of the Sierra Maestra, where he organized a guerrilla war against Batista troops. At first Batista pretended to ignore the existence of Castro and his guerrilla fighters, but by 1958 his bloody rule had alienated large segments of the politically active middle class, and these turned to Castro, providing him with financial support and aiding the struggle through terrorist activities in the urban areas. Throughout 1958 both sides engaged in torture, bombings, burnings, assassination, and kidnapping. In the meantime, Batista's army, handicapped by corruption and a lack of capable leadership, was unable to sustain an effective campaign against the guerrilla forces. Demoralized, the army fell back until it appeared that a collapse was imminent. Realizing the unfavorable situation facing him, Batista left the island unexpectedly after a New Year party on January 1, 1959.

With the departure of Batista, Castro took control of the country and initiated a revolutionary upheaval that drastically transformed the social, economic, and political sources of power in an effort to create a socialist society (*see* CUBAN REVOLUTION). By the early 1970s the rural proletariat of the prerevolutionary era was working under improved conditions on lands now owned by the state; schools were available to the poor in rural areas as well as in the cities; medical services were within reach of most of the population; Negroes, discriminated against in the past, were playing a larger role in the affairs of the country; and the corruption and moral decay prevalent in the 1950s, particularly in Havana, had all but disappeared. Nevertheless, the revolution had fallen short of several of its major goals. Cuba continued to be dependent on sugar as its main source of foreign exchange, while the familiar lines at the doors of countless shops bore witness to the constant shortages of consumer goods. Although the Castro government had destroyed most of the elements of class stratification in existence before 1959, it appeared that the new leadership and bureaucracy had formed, in effect, a new elite that enjoyed many of the prerogatives formerly the exclusive preserve of the privileged classes. After more than a decade of Castro's rule many Cubans still preferred to leave when possible in search of a freer and perhaps better life elsewhere.

Bibliography. Luis E. Aguilar, *Cuba 1933: Prologue to Revolution,* Ithaca, N.Y., 1972; Charles Edward Chapman, *A History of the Cuban Republic,* New York, 1927; Ramiro Guerra y Sanchez et al., *Historia de la nación cubana,* 10 vols., Havana, 1952; Lester D. Langley, *The Cuban Policy of the United States,* New York, 1968; Wyatt MacGaffey and Clifford R. Barnett, *Twentieth-century Cuba: The Background of the Castro Revolution,* Garden City, N.Y., 1965;

Ramón E. Ruiz, *Cuba: The Making of a Revolution,* New York, 1970; Robert F. Smith, "Twentieth-century Cuban Historiography," *Hispanic American Historical Review,* vol. XLIV, no. 1, February 1964, pp. 44–72; Hugh Thomas, *Cuba: The Pursuit of Freedom,* New York, 1971.
                                                J. CORDELL ROBINSON

CÚCUTA, CONGRESS OF. Constituent congress of Gran Colombia (*see* COLOMBIA, GRAN), held from May to October 1821. The primary mission of the Congress was to adopt a permanent frame of government for Gran Colombia in place of the provisional structure adopted by the Congress of Angostura in December 1819 (*see* ANGOSTURA, CONGRESS OF). Although Ecuador had not been represented at Angostura and was still unrepresented at Cúcuta, the Congress first reaffirmed the formal act of union among Venezuela, New Granada, and Ecuador by which Gran Colombia had been created. It then adopted a definitive constitution that was wholly centralist, concentrating all real authority in the national Congress and chief executive at Bogotá, but at the same time was conventionally liberal in most details of government procedure and in individual rights. One of the few obvious exceptions was the failure to include any guarantee of religious freedom.

The Congress also enacted a series of reforms of generally liberal inspiration that included a law freeing all children born in the future of slave parents; the abolition of the Inquisition (*see* INQUISITION, HOLY OFFICE OF THE) and Indian tribute; and the enforced closing of all small convents, their assets to be applied to the support of secondary education. Finally, so that the new constitution could take effect promptly, the deputies themselves elected Simón BOLÍVAR and Francisco de Paula SANTANDER to serve respectively as the first President and Vice President under its terms.
                                                DAVID BUSHNELL

CUESTAS, JUAN LINDOLFO (1837–1905). Chief executive of Uruguay (1897–1903). Born in Paysandú, Cuestas held several posts in private banks and in the government before being named Minister of Finance in 1880. Later, as Minister of Justice, Worship, and Public Instruction under President Máximo Santos, he came into conflict with devout Catholics over such measures as a law (1885) making civil marriage compulsory.

After serving briefly as Minister of Finance and Minister to Argentina in 1886–1887, Cuestas entered the national legislature and in February 1897 was chosen President of the Senate. By virtue of this position he became chief executive upon the assassination of President Juan Idiarte Borda on August 25, 1897. One of Cuestas' first acts was to reach a settlement in September with Nationalist revolutionaries (*see* BLANCO PARTY: URUGUAY) led by Aparicio SARAVIA, who had taken up arms the previous March. Supported by the Nationalists and by some of his fellow Colorados (*see* COLORADO PARTY: URUGUAY), Cuestas sought to secure his election to the Presidency upon the expiration of the Idiarte Borda term in February 1898. However, the resistance of the Colorado majority in the national legislature (the body that elected the President) led to its dissolution by Cuestas on February 10, 1898. He then worked out an *acuerdo* (accord) dividing the legislative seats between the Nationalists and his Colorado backers. A legislature elected under the terms of the

acuerdo named Cuestas President for a four-year term beginning March 1, 1899.

As President, Cuestas proved an able administrator, and he was proud of having balanced the budget by the end of his term. The principal achievement of his administration was construction of the port of Montevideo. Although Cuestas hoped that his Minister of Government, Eduardo MacEachen, would be his successor, he acquiesced in the victory of José BATLLE and immediately departed for Europe, where he died.
                                                HELEN DELPAR

CUEVAS, JOSÉ LUIS (1933–   ). Mexican painter. The best known of the younger Mexican artists, Cuevas was born in Mexico City and has remained there. At ten he had rheumatic fever, and he began drawing during his long convalescence. He studied briefly at La Esmeralda art school beginning in 1946, but he is essentially self-taught. The influences he admits are the early watercolors of José Clemente OROZCO, Picasso and Goya, and the writings of Kafka and Dostoyevsky.

Cuevas has always worked mainly in black and white, sometimes enriched with a wash. Ink, watercolor, and lithography have been his mediums. The human figure is his sole subject. The art critic José Gómez-Sicre has written of his "seeking out prostitutes, fortune-tellers, peddlers, beggars, dwarfs, abnormal children and the like" as his subjects. An older brother's medical and psychiatric studies provided entry into hospitals and asylums that gave him true images of the desperation and bitterness which have always dominated his work. Cuevas was the leading artist in the group called La Nueva Presencia, formed by artists interested in the human figure.

At twenty-one, in 1954, Cuevas had an exhibition in the Pan American Union in Washington that made him well known. He showed in Paris the next year. His reputation continued to grow, enhanced by the publication of sixty drawings in *The Worlds of Kafka and Cuevas* (1957).
                                                TERENCE GRIEDER

CUNHA, EUCLIDES DA (1866–1909). Brazilian essayist, historian, journalist, and engineer. Da Cunha was born in the province of Rio de Janeiro. During his years at secondary school and the Military School, he came under the influence of the leading Brazilian positivist, Benjamin Constant Botelho de MAGALHÃES, and became a republican and an abolitionist. After graduating from military school, he remained in the Army until 1896, when he went to São Paulo as an engineer in the Department of Public Works. Meanwhile he had been writing for the newspapers, and in 1897, when the federal government sent troops to the state of Bahia to reestablish control over the town of Canudos and the surrounding territory, he accompanied them as a correspondent for the newspaper *O Estado de São Paulo.* He recorded in his dispatches the last days of the struggle and kept a diary that was published posthumously as *Canudos: Diário de uma Espedição* (1939). Having returned to São Paulo, he was sent in 1899 to São José do Rio Pardo to rebuild a bridge, and during his three years there he wrote his masterpiece, *Os Sertões,* 1902 (*Rebellion in the Backlands*), dealing with the Canudos rebellion, which established his literary reputation and earned him election to the

Brazilian Academy of Letters and the Brazilian Historical and Geographical Institute. In 1904 he was appointed to a commission charged with establishing the frontier between Peru and Bolivia, and spent a year on the Amazon, where he wrote the official report, *Relatório da Comissão Mista Brasileiro-Peruana de Reconhecimento do Alto-Purus* (1906). This was followed by *Peru vs. Bolívia* (1907), a treatment of the frontier issues. His last two volumes, *Contrastes e Confrontos* (1907) and *À Margem da História* (1909), are collections of newspaper articles on various subjects. In 1909 he was appointed to the chair of logic in the College of Pedro II, which he occupied briefly until his assassination in Rio by an army officer over a personal dispute.

The fame of Euclides da Cunha rests on *Os Sertões,* generally considered Brazil's greatest book. Critics differ as to its genre, calling it variously a sociological study, a work of history, a novel, and even an epic poem, though all agree as to its power, originality, and beauty of style. There is no doubt that, in spite of the care he took with form and language, he considered it a scientific study of the ecology and sociology of a forgotten part of Brazil. He was as familiar as was possible in Brazil with the scientific knowledge of the day and knew the theories of Comte, Spencer, and Darwin as well as the contemporary anthropologists. He believed in natural selection, the influence on human development of heredity and environment, and European racial superiority, theories that serve as the ideological underpinning of the book; yet they do not vitiate it, for the reality he describes is more powerful than his theories. The subject is the military campaign against the rebels of a drought-stricken region in Bahia who were led by

Antônio CONSELHEIRO. The struggle cost the lives of countless peasants and required four military campaigns, in which thousands of soldiers were deployed, to quell. The account of the savage, bloody campaign is not the most important aspect of the book, the purpose of which rather is to inform the Brazil of the coast and the large cities about the other, unknown Brazil with its undeveloped economy and its impoverished rural masses. *Os Sertões* is divided into three parts: Land, Man, and The Struggle. The harsh geology and botany of the region are strikingly portrayed in the first section, and the inhabitants, underfed and undersized but strong, tenacious, and resistant, are shown in the second. Although Euclides da Cunha accepted the racial theories of the day, the pages on these mestizo *sertanejos* are full of praise for them. The book is now read as a great literary creation. Not only are scenes, characters, and types vividly portrayed, but the baroque style is brilliant and powerful, glittering with images and an unusual vocabulary including regionalisms, archaisms, neologisms, and scientific terms, all appropriate to the tragic subject.

Bibliography. Olímpio de Souza Andrade, *História e Interpretação de "Os Sertões,"* 3d ed., São Paulo, 1966; Euclides da Cunha, *Obra Completa,* ed. by Afrânio Coutinho, 2 vols., Rio de Janeiro, 1966; Wilson Martins, "O Significado de Euclides da Cunha na Literatura Brasileira," *Revista Interamericana de Bibliografia,* vol. XVI, no. 3, July–September 1966, pp. 249–261; Clovis Moura, *Introdução ao Pensamento de Euclides da Cunha,* Rio de Janeiro, 1964.

RAYMOND S. SAYERS

CUZCO. Capital of the Inca empire and still the largest city of the Peruvian sierra, its population being estimated at over 95,000 in 1971–1972. It lies at approximately 11,500 feet at the western end of the Huatanay Valley. Cuzco sprang into prominence during the reign of VIRACOCHA, the eighth Inca ruler, who acceded to the throne about A.D. 1400. Under his son, PACHACUTI, the city was reconstructed and became a notable center. It was considered to be peculiarly sacred and was conceived to be centered within the four quarters of the Inca empire.

Cuzco was not a city in the accepted sense, nor was it a ceremonial center, as were the famous Mayan sites. It was a park reserved for Incas of the blood and the members of their ruling house. The sacred area lay between two branches of the Huatanay River and was tabooed to peoples and classes uncongenial to the Incas. At the base of this sacred triangle were the steep heights of Sacsahuamán, on the summit of which perch today the fantastic ruins of Cuzco's great fortress.

The area around which the Inca emperors had their palaces is still the open center of the city, the Plaza de Armas. The most interesting of the ruins is Coricancha, the "Golden Yard," an ecclesiastical center wherein were enclosed the apartments of the various Inca gods, including those of Inti, the sun god. This site was taken over by the Dominicans, who superimposed their wood and adobe structures on top of the Inca stone walls. *See also* INCAS.

BURR C. BRUNDAGE

CVC. *See* CORPORACIÓN AUTÓNOMA REGIONAL DEL VALLE DEL CAUCA.

Euclides da Cunha. [*Bibliothèque Nationale, Paris*]

D

Darío, Rubén
Duvalier, Jean-Claude

DARÍO, RUBÉN (b. FÉLIX RUBÉN GARCÍA SAR-MIENTO, 1867–1916). Nicaraguan poet, journalist, critic, short-story writer, and diplomat, best known as the outstanding Spanish American modernist poet (*see* MODERNISM: SPANISH AMERICA). Darío was born in Metapa (now Ciudad Darío), Nicaragua, on January 18, 1867, and died in León, Nicaragua, on February 6, 1916. His parents separated after his birth, and he was reared in León by Bernarda Sarmiento de Ramírez, a maternal grandaunt, and her husband, Félix Ramírez. Rubén was a precocious child and was already known as a poet by 1879, when *El Termómetro,* a León newspaper, published his first contribution in verse. He was only fourteen when he joined the editorial staff of *La Verdad,* another León daily. A year later he was in Managua, working in the National Library. In 1883 he was in El Salvador, where the Salvadoran president, Rafael Zaldívar, had him enrolled in a San Salvador school. Back in Managua in 1884, he worked as a journalist, and his prose and verse appeared in such periodicals as *El Ferro-Carril* and *El Diario Nicaragüense.* At the same time, he became a voracious reader in the National Library. He was already familiar with the Spanish classics, and he now took a special interest in French writers. Meanwhile, his reputation as a poet kept growing.

In 1886 he went to Chile, carrying letters of recommendation that helped him establish contact with Chilean intellectuals. He spent a short time in Valparaíso and then moved to Santiago. Thanks to a letter of recommendation from Eduardo Poirer of Valparaíso, he soon began to write for *La Época,* one of the better-known Santiago newspapers.

The cosmopolitan life of Santiago was the kind of environment Darío needed in order to flourish. Despite his poverty, it did not take him long to establish himself as a writer. He was not successful as a journalist, but he won a poetry prize offered by *La Época,* and in 1887 he published *Abrojos,* a book of verse in the romantic tradition. In addition, he widened his horizons with a renewed interest in contemporary French writers. Moreover, he made friends among the intellectuals, including Pedro Balmaceda, son of the President, who allowed him to use his library. However, Darío was not the man to fill the post of journalist for *La Época.* For this reason, he returned to Valparaíso and a job as customs inspector that Balmaceda helped him obtain. Then he worked for the *Heraldo* in Valparaíso. In 1888 the publication of *Azul,* a collection of his short stories and poems, brought him into the international limelight when the great Spanish writer Juan Valera praised it in *El Imparcial* of Madrid. A harbinger of a new poetics with an esthetic tenor, it reflected the influence of the French writers whom Darío had read, including romantics, Parnassians, and symbolists.

Still in Valparaíso, Darío decided to leave Chile, but before his departure he met the publicist José Victorino Lastarria, who was a friend of the editor of the Buenos Aires *La Nación,* a newspaper for which Darío wanted to work. The publicist recommended Darío to *La Nación,* so that by the time the poet left Chile he already had the desired position. This post with the news-

Rubén Darío. [*Organization of American States*]

paper became a lifelong assignment for Darío. Leaving Valparaíso in February 1889, he went home but did not stay long in León. His next stop was El Salvador. Friends took him to meet Francisco Menéndez, then President, and by the time Darío left the President, he was head of the newspaper *La Unión.* During his stay in San Salvador, Darío renewed an old acquaintance with Rafaela Contreras, and after a courtship of a few weeks the poet married her on June 21, 1890, before the civil authorities. But a coup d'état the next night postponed the church ceremony. President Menéndez was dead. Although the general who led the revolt, Carlos Ezeta, was also the poet's friend, Darío left for Guatemala. Here he met the President, Manuel Lisandro Barillas, who asked him to write a report of the Salvadoran revolt. This the Nicaraguan did, and Barillas put him in charge of *El Correo de la Tarde,* a semiofficial newspaper that Darío soon made into a literary periodical. During the early days of 1891 he finally married Rafaela in a religious ceremony. His job with *El Correo* lasted only until June 1891, and by August he was in Costa Rica with his wife. He worked as a journalist in San José and spent some time on the staff of *El Heraldo.* At this time also, Darío and his wife became the parents of a son, Rubén Darío Contreras. The added responsibility made the poet's life more difficult, and in May

1892 he left his family in San José and returned to Guatemala. He had scarcely arrived when he received his first diplomatic appointment, being named one of the members of the Nicaraguan delegation to the Christopher COLUMBUS quadricentennial celebration in Spain.

Darío was already known as a poet in Spain because of Valera's favorable review of *Azul.* As a result, he was able to meet some of the outstanding intellectuals of the day, including Marcelino Menéndez y Pelayo, Emilio Castelar, and Valera. After the celebration he embarked for Nicaragua. However, the ship stopped at Cartagena, Colombia, where Darío visited Rafael NÚÑEZ, titular President of Colombia. Núñez, who was also a writer, took a great interest in the young man and arranged for him to be Consul General of Colombia in Buenos Aires. But fate had dealt Darío a cruel blow during his trip. When he arrived in León, he learned that his wife had died in El Salvador, where she had gone to be with relatives. Not long afterward he was back in Managua, where he married Rosario Murillo under nightmarish circumstances: the poet was drunk and threatened with death if he refused to marry her. As a consequence, the poet spent the rest of his life apart from his wife, who survived him. After he recovered from the wedding, he headed for Buenos Aires via New York and Paris, a long route popular among Spanish Americans of that time.

In Paris Darío met some of the outstanding intellectuals thanks to Enrique Gómez Carrillo, a noted Guatemalan journalist, and the Spanish writer Alejandro Sawa. He was introduced to Paul Verlaine, who was too drunk to talk with the Nicaraguan. Since he had money, Darío enjoyed himself. Arriving in Buenos Aires in 1893, he took over the consular post but continued to write for *La Nación* as well as for *La Tribuna* and *El Tiempo.* During this time he founded, with the Bolivian poet Ricardo Jaimes Freyre, the *Revista de América* (1894). In 1896 he published *Los raros* and *Prosas profanas.* The first is a collection of articles on American and European writers. The second is one of his most important volumes of poetry. In *Prosas profanas* Darío brought the pioneer poetics of *Azul* to maturity. By incorporating the metrical freedom of the French romantics, the plastic innovations of the Parnassians, and the musical and other sensory effects of the symbolists into his Spanish heritage, the poet helped liberate Spanish verse from its conservatism in meter and language. Unfriendly critics called the new poetry "decadent" and "modernist," both terms of censure in Spanish. Although Darío could scarcely be considered decadent with a work like *Prosas profanas,* he was modern. Consequently, the term "decadent" gradually lost ground as applied to the new poetics. At the same time, "modernist" was made a badge of honor by Darío and those who wrote as he did.

In 1898, after the Spanish-American War, *La Nación* sent Rubén Darío to Spain to report on the situation in the country after the disastrous defeat. He stayed in Madrid until April 1900. His writings of this period make up the volume titled *España contemporánea* (1901). In 1905 he published *Cantos de vida y esperanza,* generally considered his most outstanding book of poems. In this collection Darío continued writing according to the theory he had brought to fruition in *Prosas profanas.* At the same time, he added a new humanity to his poetry. The Spanish defeat in 1898 had brought a rude awakening to many Spanish American intellectuals, including Darío. They suddenly realized that the United States could no longer be regarded as a trustworthy older brother. Instead, it appeared to be a giant capable of devouring Spanish America. In addition, many Spanish Americans who had previously been more deeply interested in Europe and the United States began to develop a new awareness of Spanish America as their home and Spain as their mother country. All these trends were reflected by Darío in *Cantos de vida y esperanza.*

In 1907 Darío visited Nicaragua and was apotheosized by the government and the people. Before his departure he was appointed head of the Nicaraguan Legation in Madrid. Two years later he wrote "Canto a la Argentina," one of his most famous poems. In 1910 he was appointed special Ambassador to the centennial of Mexican independence. Then, when his ship stopped at Havana, he learned that Nicaragua had a new government. Although his appointment was no longer valid, he still went as far as Veracruz. On being informed that he would not be received by the Mexican President, he returned to Havana. Without the means to return to Europe, he was stranded in Cuba for two months until Gen. Bernardo Reyes of Mexico sent him the necessary funds.

After the Mexican debacle Darío returned to Paris, where, in 1911, he joined the publishers of *Mundial,* a literary magazine. In 1912 the publishers took him on an advertising tour to the New World. Unfortunately, Darío became ill in Buenos Aires. In the meantime he gave the text of his *Autobiografía* (1912) to *La Nación,* and it was published as a serial in the Buenos Aires magazine *Caras y Caretas.*

In 1913 Darío was back in Paris. Though he was ill, the following year he left for America on a lecture tour. In February 1915, he spoke at Columbia University, but he caught pneumonia and was hospitalized. The President of Guatemala then had him taken to Guatemala City. He stayed there until December, when he was taken to Nicaragua, where he died.

Bibliography. Rubén Darío, *Obras completas,* Madrid, 1950; Ricardo Gullón, *Direcciones del modernismo,* Madrid, 1963; Arturo Marasso, *Rubén Darío,* Buenos Aires, 1945; Antonio Oliver, *Este otro Rubén Darío,* Barcelona, 1960; Pedro Salinas, *La poesía de Rubén Darío,* Buenos Aires, 1948; Diego M. Sequeira, *Rubén Darío criollo,* Buenos Aires, 1945; Arturo Torres-Ríoseco, *Rubén Darío,* Cambridge, Mass., 1931.

GERARDO SÁENZ

DARTIGUENAVE, PHILIPPE SUDRÉ (b. 1863). President of Haiti during the American occupation. He was born in Sud Department, a member of the mulatto ÉLITE. At the beginning of the American occupation, in 1915, the National Assembly chose him President. Dartiguenave approved a treaty with the United States that virtually reduced Haiti to tutelage. Following a clever policy, he encouraged Haitian legislators to resist American pressure while suggesting to the occupiers the need for suppressing the Assembly and governing with a presidentially appointed Council of State. Under the 1918 constitution, the President was granted power to decide when legislative elections should take place and meanwhile to govern with an appointed Council. Subsequently, Dartiguenave postponed elections.

Once firmly in power, he argued with the Americans, while the nation experienced a respite from military action and the occupiers achieved progress in public works, sanitation, and education. Dartiguenave often appealed over the heads of his American advisers to the United States government, with varying success. He failed to gain reelection in 1922 and left office on May 15 of that year.

JOHN E. BAUR

DAVIDOVSKY, MARIO (1934–). Argentine composer. Davidovsky was born in Buenos Aires, where he undertook his early music studies. In 1958 he traveled to the United States to complete his training, and it was then that he started developing a deep interest in electronic music. Two consecutive Guggenheim fellowships (1960–1962) allowed him to increase his knowledge in this field. In 1964 he was appointed guest lecturer at the University of Michigan, and later he joined the Columbia-Princeton Electronic Music Center. In 1971 he was awarded the Pulitzer Prize. In addition to a few orchestral and chamber music compositions and pure electronic music, Davidovsky has written six compositions combining conventional instruments with electronic tapes, entitled *Synchronisms,* which are his best-known works.

JUAN A. ORREGO-SALAS

DÁVILA, PEDRARIAS. *See* ÁVILA, PEDRO ARIAS DE.

DEBRAY, [JULES] RÉGIS (1940–). French scholar and student of revolutions. A member of an intellectual family, Debray was a student at the University of Paris of Louis Althusser, a well-known Marxist philosopher. Reportedly he also belonged to the French Young Communists, but he soon became disillusioned by the conservative approach of the orthodox pro-Moscow Communists.

From 1961 to 1967 Debray spent long periods in Cuba, during which he familiarized himself with the details of the CUBAN REVOLUTION and became acquainted with Fidel CASTRO and Ernesto (Che) GUEVARA. The result of his studies was a slender volume, *Révolution dans la révolution?* (published in French, Spanish, and English in 1967). The degree to which the Cubans circulated this book indicated that it presented the accepted theories of the Cuban regime at the time. In it Debray advanced the *foco* (focus) theory of guerrilla warfare, which held that urban activists could, by establishing a *foco* in a remote rural area, begin to undermine the authority of the existing government. From that stage they would pass to guerrilla warfare and, finally, embark on all-out war. All of this, Debray argued, could be accomplished without the leadership of a revolutionary party: the party would evolve from the revolutionary army.

Meanwhile, Debray, carrying credentials as a journalist, had gone to Bolivia to join the guerrilla forces that Guevara had organized there. While attempting to leave on a mission for Guevara, he was arrested on April 20, 1967, in southeastern Bolivia and was jailed until his release in 1970 by the leftist government of Gen. Juan José TORRES. Debray then went to Chile, where he interviewed Socialist President Salvador ALLENDE. This interview was published as *Entretiens avec Allende sur la situation en Chili*, 1971 (*The Chilean Revolution: Conversations with Allende*).

ROBERT J. ALEXANDER

DEBRET, JEAN-BAPTISTE (1768–1848). French painter. A disciple and relative of David, Debret had attained considerable success as a painter when the death of his only son and the fall of Napoleon led him to join the team of French artists and craftsmen that traveled to Brazil in 1816 under the leadership of Joachim Lebreton (1760–1819). Remaining in Brazil until 1831, Debret played a key role in the organization of the Academia de Belas Artes, which was definitively installed in 1826 after much acrimony between the members of the French mission and their Brazilian and Portuguese critics. Active as a teacher as well, Debret trained a generation of Brazilian painters and in 1829 organized the first exhibit of fine arts to be held in Brazil. He is also known for his three-volume *Voyage pittoresque et historique au Brésil* (1834–1839), the illustrations of which vividly depict Brazilian types and scenes.

HELEN DELPAR

DEGOLLADO, SANTOS (1811–1861). Mexican soldier. A native of Guanajuato, Degollado was orphaned at an early age. For a while he attended the Military Academy in Mexico City, but he was largely self-educated. By 1828 he was in Morelia, where he became a notarial clerk, a profession he exercised for two decades. By the late 1840s he was holding minor political offices in Michoacán as a follower of Melchor OCAMPO, the leader of the Liberals in that state. He joined the Liberal Army in the revolution of Ayutla and was soon promoted to the rank of general. Degollado served as Governor of Jalisco for nine months in 1855–1856, and he was elected Governor of Michoacán in 1857. In March 1858, Benito JUÁREZ brought him into his Cabinet as Minister of War. Degollado was put in charge of the western military operations during the War of the Reform (*see* REFORM, THE), and although he won few victories, he played a crucial role in the final triumph of the Liberals. In June 1861, upon learning of the assassination of Ocampo, Degollado requested and received permission from the Mexican Congress to lead an expedition to destroy the guerrilla band that had executed his friend. In the operation his column was ambushed, and he was captured and executed by the guerrillas, led by the Conservative general Leonardo Márquez.

CHARLES R. BERRY

DE LA TORRE, LISANDRO (1868–1939). Founder of the Progressive Democratic party in Argentina. The son of a livestock breeder and a member of an aristocratic family, he was born in Rosario, in the province of Santa Fe, and received a law degree from the University of Buenos Aires in 1888. He supported the Unión Cívica of Leandro ALEM during the revolution of 1890, and when the Unión Cívica split, he stayed with Alem to form the Unión Cívica Radical (UCR; *see* RADICAL PARTY: ARGENTINA). In 1893 he led the UCR in Rosario in a revolution against the provincial government, and he might have succeeded but for the intervention of the national government. Three years later he went to Buenos Aires to oppose Gen. Julio A. ROCA's bid for the Presidency in the pages of *El Argentino*. That year the two men he admired, Alem and Aristóbulo del Valle, died. De la Torre now attempted to fill the vacuum they left in the party leadership, but he was unable to persuade Hipólito YRIGOYEN, *caudillo* of the Radicals in the province of Buenos Aires, to follow him. Disappointed, he returned to Rosario in 1897, determined never again to help the UCR.

In the following years De la Torre started *La República*, traveled to Europe and the United States, became president of the Rural Society of Rosario, and began to buy the Estancia de Pinas, located between Córdoba and La Rioja. He also directed a provincial movement for municipal reform, an overhaul of the tax system, greater self-government in the rural districts, and minority representation in the legislature.

In 1908 he formed the Liga del Sur (Southern League) to represent the middle-class farmers of Italian origin in the southern half of the province. By 1912, when he was elected to Congress, he was bitterly anti-UCR and anti-Socialist. With the approach of the presidential elections of 1916, he organized the Progressive Democratic party, fundamentally a Federalist party uniting Conservatives and other elements interested in economic progress and honest government. A heterogeneous collection of provincial groups endorsed his candidacy for the Presidency, but he carried only three provinces: Catamarca, San Luis, and Tucumán. After the elections the Conservatives left the party. Bitter, De la Torre decided never to support them again and retreated to Pinas. His self-imposed retirement from politics was interrupted when his party, reduced to his province, elected him in 1922 to a four-year term as provincial representative.

In 1930 he rejected an opportunity to help an old friend, Gen. José Félix URIBURU, who had just overthrown Yrigoyen, to form a new government and to succeed him in the Presidency. Instead, he brought the Socialist and the Progressive Democratic parties (*see* SOCIALIST PARTY: ARGENTINA) together in the Democratic Socialist Alliance and entered the presidential race of 1931 on a platform calling for the organization of cooperatives, lower freight rates, more roads, and the breaking up of large estates. The UCR refused to endorse him because of his hostility to Yrigoyen. De la Torre was defeated in the presidential contest by Agustín P. JUSTO, but he returned to Congress as a senator from Santa Fe, and for the first time in his career he was a popular national figure. Now, with the aid of intellectuals and youths of a leftist orientation, he persuaded the Progressive Democratic party to adopt a program that was anti-imperialist and anti-monopolist, advocated national economic independence, and defended the small cattle producers. His attacks on the government, especially during a sensational debate over the meat industry in 1935, increased his popularity among the democratic elements. However, the assassination of a friend and fellow senator, Enzo Bordabehere, on the floor of the Senate during the debate led him to withdraw from public life two years later. On January 5, 1939, he committed suicide.

JOSEPH T. CRISCENTI

DEMOCRATIC ACTION. *See* ACCIÓN DEMOCRÁTICA.

DEMOCRATIC PARTY (CHILE). The Chilean Democratic party was founded in 1887 by Radicals, led by Malaquías Concha, who were critical of their party's preoccupation with the middle classes and its neglect of workers' interests (*see* RADICAL PARTY: CHILE). Looking back to Francisco BILBAO, they hoped to create a political instrument for the working classes to effect social and economic reform. The first Democrat was elected to Congress in 1894, when Ángel Guarello entered the Chamber of Deputies for Valparaíso; subsequently, in 1912, he became the party's first senator.

The Democratic party faced a critical dilemma: as a minor party it could hope only to share power with others; yet many members opposed such an accommodation as a betrayal of principle. This split plagued the party throughout its existence, as it changed alliances according to circumstances and grew only modestly. Although Guarello and Malaquías Concha held Cabinet posts in the governments of Juan Luis Sanfuentes (1915–1920) and Arturo ALESSANDRI (1920–1925), the party vacillated wildly in the 1920s and 1930s, causing serious internal divisions. By the early 1930s the bulk of the party, with twelve seats in the Chamber of Deputies in 1932, had moved right, but three splinter groups, each holding one seat, had broken away. A degree of reunification took place in 1941, but latent internal divisions weakened the party's appeal. It split again, decisively, in 1952, into the Partido Democrático del Pueblo and the Partido Democrático de Chile, both of which joined the FRENTE DE ACCIÓN POPULAR (FRAP) in 1956, and in the presidential election of 1958 the two parties divided their support among three candidates. Finally, in September 1960, the Partido Democrático Nacional was formed; it secured less than 2 percent of the vote in the congressional elections of 1969.

HAROLD BLAKEMORE

DESCAMISADOS. *See* PERONISM.

DESERT, CONQUEST OF THE. *See* CONQUEST OF THE DESERT.

DESSALINES, JEAN-JACQUES (1758–1806). Liberator of Haiti. Dessalines was born a slave in Grande-Rivière-du-Nord and became the field hand of a free black. His early suffering may have accounted for his later desire for vengeance against whites, mulattoes, and free Negroes. Without intellectual or sympathetic ties to French culture or a chance to observe any but its most corrupt institutions, he developed into a cruel, vain, shrewd, and ruthless man with no vision for Haiti's future except that of an extremely antiforeign policy. He was a military genius, perhaps a better tactician than his superior, Toussaint LOUVERTURE, whose conciliatory policies he deprecated. After Gen. Charles-Victor-Emmanuel Leclerc exiled Louverture, Dessalines emerged as the architect of Haitian victory. On January 1, 1804, he proclaimed independence, adopting the prehistoric Indian name Haiti, meaning "mountainous."

Once in power, Dessalines made himself Emperor Jacques and ruled without a nobility. His massacre of whites, after promising mercy, and his antimulatto policy perhaps exceeded the atrocities of the Europeans. He soon reduced his fellow blacks to state serfdom. In 1805 he vainly attempted to reconquer the Spanish two-thirds of the island, fearful of a French attack from that area. His government, Haiti's first, set patterns of racial legislation, crystallized black-mulatto feuds, and emphasized isolation. After having alienated his army, Dessalines was ambushed, murdered, and mutilated near Port-au-Prince on October 17, 1806. Later he was proclaimed a national hero.

JOHN E. BAUR

DIANDA, HILDA (1925–   ). Argentine composer. Born in Córdoba, she studied in Buenos Aires with Honorio SICCARDI and in Europe with Francesco Malipiero and Hermann Scherchen. In the Electro-Acoustics Studio of the Italian Radio and Television Network and in Darmstadt, Germany, she developed her technique in electronic music. In 1964 she was appointed professor of composition at the University of Córdoba in Argentina. The best known among her works are *Díptico* (1962) for chamber ensemble, *Núcleos* (1963) for orchestra, *Resonancias I, II,* and *III* for various instrumental combinations (1964, 1965), and *A-7* (1966) for cello and electronic tape.

JUAN A. ORREGO-SALAS

DÍAZ, ADOLFO (1874–1964). Nicaraguan Conservative politician and President (1913–1917, 1926–1928). Díaz was the Conservative leader most trusted by United States Department of State officials and consequently acted as President twice during the United States occupation of Nicaragua. Indeed, as provisional President following the Liberal party collapse of 1909–1912, Díaz confessed his inability to control the country and asked for military intervention. United States troops helped pacify Nicaragua during Díaz's first regular Presidency (1913–1917), despite continuing domestic unrest and severe financial difficulties as a result of debts from previous civil wars and wartime disruption of Nicaragua's commerce.

In the mid-1920s, when Conservative-Liberal rivalry brought Nicaragua to the brink of anarchy and resulted in a second United States occupation, Díaz once again was called upon to serve as President. In this brief term (1926–1928) he temporarily pacified the country by supporting the Henry L. Stimson mission in its efforts to conciliate the rival factions, by asking for occupation by United States Marines once again, and by agreeing to cooperate with the United States in training a National Guard. He also agreed to United States supervision of the election of 1928, which was won by the Liberal party. Warfare between the guerrilla forces of Augusto César SANDINO, who refused to accept Stimson's mediation, and the National Guard grew more serious after Díaz's retirement from the Presidency.

CHARLES L. STANSIFER

DÍAZ, PORFIRIO (1830–1915). Mexican soldier and President. Díaz, a mestizo, was born into poverty in the city of Oaxaca. His father died when he was young, and he had to work to support his mother. His cousin Agustín Domínguez, the future Bishop of Oaxaca, served as his benefactor and saw that he received an education. The young Díaz transferred from the seminary to the state institute to study law and there came under the influence of Liberals, including Benito JUÁREZ and Marcos Pérez, the leader of the Oaxacan Liberal faction. The revolution of Ayutla interrupted his studies, and he joined the Liberal Army. During the War of the Reform (*see* REFORM, THE), he fought in many engagements and rose to the rank of general, to which he was appointed in 1861. In the war against the French, he fought in the sieges of Puebla (1862, 1863). Designated commander of the Army of the East in 1864, he established his headquarters in Oaxaca. When that city fell to the French early in 1865, he was taken prisoner. Making his escape late that year, he carried on guerrilla warfare against the French in Guerrero and Oaxaca and consolidated his forces to begin what he considered the reconquest of Mexico. His campaign in the south culminated in June 1867 with the capture of Mexico City.

Díaz was a national hero as a result of his loyalty to the Liberal cause and his successful military campaigns. After the war he retired from the Army and took up agriculture, keeping his eyes on the Presidency. He was an unsuccessful candidate for that office in 1871, and the so-called La Noria rebellion failed to remove Juárez and place Díaz in power. Again Díaz retired to private life to plan his political career. In the 1875 elections he ran for the Presidency in a campaign dedicated to "effective suffrage, no reelection." Defeated a second time, he and his supporters mounted the revolution of Tuxtepec, which was successful in removing Sebastián

LERDO DE TEJADA and placing Díaz in the Presidency. Díaz served as President from 1876 to 1880 and from 1884 to 1911.

During this long period Mexico was transformed into a stable, economically progressive nation but at the expense of freedom. Railroads were built, mining was revitalized, and an oil industry was begun. Much of this economic activity was generated by foreign capital. So strong was the influence of foreign investment that many became concerned that Mexico was being sold to alien investors. Political stability was maintained, and opposition suppressed. Security of property was enhanced by Díaz's Guardias Rurales (rural police force). The labor movement was retarded through measures that were often brutal. Land became concentrated in the hands of a few, while the peasants lived in miserable conditions. There developed a definite anti-Indian, pro-white racial cast to Díaz's government, largely as a result of the positivism practiced by his close advisers and supporters, the CIENTÍFICOS (*see* POSITIVISM: MEXICO). The anticlerical provisions of the constitution of 1857 were largely ignored as the church was allowed to regain much of its wealth and influence through Díaz's policy of conciliation (*see* CONSTITUTION OF 1857: MEXICO).

Díaz's last decade in office witnessed growing opposition from labor, liberals, and radical groups inside and outside Mexico. In 1908 he granted an interview to a United States journalist, James Creelman, who published it in *Pearson's Magazine*. In it Díaz, then approaching seventy-eight years of age, stated that he had achieved his goals, would not run for reelection in 1910, and welcomed the formation of political parties. A few months later, he retracted his statements. Opposition came out into the open, Francisco I. MADERO began his political campaign, and scattered fighting broke out late in 1910. When Ciudad Juárez fell to the rebels in May 1911, Díaz resigned and sailed for France, where he spent the remaining four years of his life.

See also MEXICAN REVOLUTION; RÍO BLANCO STRIKE.

Bibliography. Carleton Beals, *Porfirio Díaz, Dictator of Mexico*, Philadelphia, 1932; Alberto M. Carreño (comp.), *Archivo del general Porfirio Díaz: Memorias y documentos*, 30 vols., Mexico City, 1947–; Daniel Cosío Villegas, *The United States versus Porfirio Díaz*, Lincoln, Nebr., 1963; Daniel Cosío Villegas et al., *Historia moderna de México*, 9 vols., Mexico City, 1955–72; Jorge Fernando Iturribarría, *Porfirio Díaz ante la historia*, Mexico City, 1967; Salvador Quevedo y Zubieta, *Porfirio Díaz, Septiembre 1830–Septiembre 1865: Ensayo de psicología histórica*, Paris, 1906; José C. Valadés, *El porfirismo: Historia de un régimen*, 2 vols., Mexico City, 1941–48.

CHARLES R. BERRY

Porfirio Díaz. [*Organization of American States*]

DÍAZ DEL CASTILLO, BERNAL (1495?–?1584). Spanish conquistador and chronicler. Popular chronicler of the conquest of New Spain, Bernal Díaz claimed to have arrived in the New World with the expedition of Pedro Arias de ÁVILA in 1514 and to have participated in the explorations of the Gulf coast of Mexico in 1517 and 1518. Throughout the conquest of Mexico he served as a common soldier under the command of Pedro de ALVARADO and was rewarded with an encomienda in Tabasco in 1522. Díaz participated in the Honduras expedition with Hernán CORTÉS and made two trips to Spain, in 1539 and in 1550. After settling in Guatemala in 1541, he possessed encomiendas and served as an active member of the *cabildo* (municipal council).

Díaz began writing his account of the conquest of Mexico more than forty years after the events, partly in order to memorialize his own deeds. While writing his chronicle, the history of Francisco López de Gómara came to his view. He determined to continue his own history because he wished to correct errors and because he felt that Gómara had exaggerated the role of Cortés and minimized the part played by other Spanish soldiers. In fact, Díaz often refers to decisions reached collectively by consultations with the army rather than to decisions reached alone by Cortés. His manuscript was substantially completed by 1568 and was sent to Spain in 1575. Both Antonio de HERRERA Y TORDESILLAS and Juan de Torquemada used Díaz's manuscript in their own histories, and Fray Alonso de Remón published it in 1632.

Díaz's *Historia verdadera de la conquista de la Nueva España* (*The Discovery and Conquest of Mexico*) remains, along with the letters of Cortés and the history of Gómara, the chief source of the conquest of Mexico from the Spanish viewpoint. Díaz's eye for detail and ability to create a mood, his gifts as a storyteller, his respect for his Indian adversaries, and his exciting descriptions of the events of the conquest are the distinguishing qualities that are characteristic of his history.

EDITH B. COUTURIER

DÍAZ ORDAZ, GUSTAVO (1911–). President of Mexico (1964–1970). Díaz Ordaz was born in San Andrés Chalchicomula (now Serdán), Puebla; his father was employed first as a farmer, later as a civil servant. In 1937 Díaz Ordaz received his law degree in Puebla, where he worked as a public prosecutor; he also served as president of the Central Board of Conciliation and Arbitration in Puebla and on the state's Supreme Court. From 1943 to 1946 he was a federal deputy; from 1946 to 1952 he was a member of the Senate. He became First Undersecretary of the Ministry of the Interior (Gobernación) in 1953 and Secretary in 1958.

When Díaz Ordaz took office as President in 1964, Mexico's much-vaunted political stability was entering a period of crisis. In 1965 physicians seeking wage increases challenged the authorities. Later, student conflicts erupted in Michoacán, Sinaloa, and Mexico City and appeared aimed at sabotaging the Mexico City Olympics of 1968; the last of these student outbreaks was severely repressed in Tlatelolco. In 1970 the second federal labor code, superseding one enacted in 1931, took effect; its goal was to narrow the gap between most Mexicans and the favored minority. During his administration Mexico signed the Treaty of Tlatelolco, banning nuclear weapons from Latin America.

Díaz Ordaz ended his term on the defensive, maintaining that revolutionary changes should be gradual. He admitted that despite Mexico's labor and agrarian policies it had been impossible to impede the concentration of wealth because of the need to hasten the formation of capital.

MOISÉS GONZÁLEZ NAVARRO

DI CAVALCANTI [DE MELO], EMILIANO [AUGUSTO] (1897–). Brazilian painter and caricaturist. Di Cavalcanti was born in Rio de Janeiro. The first exhibition of his work took place in 1916, when his caricatures were displayed in the Salão das Humoristas of the Liceu de Artes e Ofícios in Rio. Abandoning thoughts of a legal career, he devoted himself to art but rebelled against what he considered the sterile academicism then dominant in Brazilian painting. In 1922 he played a leading role in the organization of Modern Art Week, a series of art shows, poetry readings, and the like in the São Paulo Municipal Theater that had an impact on Brazilian cultural life comparable with that of the 1913 Armory Show in the United States.

During the first of several trips to Europe, in 1923–1925, Di Cavalcanti had the opportunity to study the work of dead masters and to discover contemporaries like Picasso and Matisse. Although the influence of Picasso can be seen in Di Cavalcanti's work, he remained an eminently national painter in both theme and spirit. He is known especially for his portrayals of women, such as the oil *Five Young Ladies from Guaratinguetá* (1930), and of Brazilian blacks and mulattoes. Notable for their bright colors and sinuosity, his paintings are frankly sensual; yet they simultaneously convey the painter's underlying irony and sympathy for his subjects. He has written two volumes of memoirs, *Viagem de Minha Vida* (1955) and *Reminiscências Líricas de um Perfeito Carioca* (1964).

HELEN DELPAR

DOCTRINAS. *See* MISSIONS (SPANISH AMERICA).

DOLLAR DIPLOMACY. Policy associated especially with President William Howard Taft and his Secretary of State, Philander C. Knox, whereby the United States government encouraged American bankers to make loans to Central American and Caribbean governments, supplanting European capital in those countries. The objectives of dollar diplomacy were to improve the financial and political stability of this strategic area and to forestall intervention by European governments acting at the behest of disgruntled creditors. Meanwhile, American creditors would be guaranteed a satisfactory return on their investments through United States collection of customs in the countries involved. By its supporters dollar diplomacy was considered a means of achieving foreign policy objectives by the use of capital investment rather than by military or strictly diplomatic means, but the term has often been extended to be almost synonymous with economic imperialism.

During the Taft administration (1909–1913) dollar diplomacy was employed most strenuously in Nicaragua, which began to receive American loans in 1911; a customs collectorship was established the same year. Features of dollar diplomacy also be seen in United States policy toward the Dominican Republic under Theodore Roosevelt and toward Haiti under Woodrow Wilson. Taft's policy of promoting private American investment in China was also known as dollar diplomacy.

HELEN DELPAR

DOLORES, GRITO DE. Exhortation given by Miguel HIDALGO Y COSTILLA, curate of the Mexican town of Dolores (now Dolores Hidalgo), which began a rebellion against the Spanish government of New Spain on

September 16, 1810. The event has been celebrated throughout Mexico's national history as its principal patriotic holiday.

The sequence of events during the early hours of September 16, after news had reached Hidalgo that the Querétaro conspiracy had been exposed, is difficult to reconstruct. Moreover, contemporary accounts disagree about what the curate said in his extemporaneous appeal. There may well have been several *gritos:* one from the window or door of Hidalgo's house to explain his decision to revolt to early Sunday morning parishioners and another, hours later, in front of the church to animate a nuclear force of 600 men that had been assembled to begin the revolt.

That Hidalgo openly repudiated the Spanish King and called for Mexican independence, his actual goal, at any time that day is most unlikely. Hidalgo, Ignacio de ALLENDE, and other conspirators had agreed that "independence" was an abstraction of little consequence to the Indians and *castas* (mixed-bloods) of the BAJÍO region who were expected to serve as cannon fodder. Traditional protest rhetoric, an end to tribute, and a "red scare" charge that the *gachupines* (Spaniards) intended to deliver Mexico to Napoleon composed the basic message. Hidalgo's climax probably rang with "Long live FERDINAND VII! Long live America! Long live the Catholic religion! and Death to bad government!" Later in the day a standard with an image of the Virgin of Guadalupe was adopted as the banner of the insurrection (*see* GUADALUPE, VIRGIN OF). "Long live the Virgin!" was probably not incorporated into the revolutionary slogans until then.

HUGH M. HAMILL, JR.

DOMÍNGUEZ, MANUEL (1869–1935). Paraguayan educator, diplomat, and political figure. Born in the village of Itaguá, near Asunción, Domínguez studied in Pilar and Asunción, receiving his doctorate in law from the National University in 1899. For several years he taught various subjects at the Colegio Nacional, of which he became director. Later he was professor of constitutional law at the National University and eventually served as its rector.

A philosophical positivist, Domínguez entered political life quite early in his career. He was a Senator, Director of the National Archives, Foreign Minister, Vice President (1903–1904), and at various times Minister of Public Education and Culture, the Treasury, and Justice. Like his contemporary Cecilio BÁEZ, he was much concerned with the CHACO boundary question, a subject on which he labored for many years. He and Báez produced the best Paraguayan defenses of the country's Chaco claims, and their works are historically valuable today. Domínguez was personally active in the Chaco problem and served Paraguay competently as a delegate to conferences dealing with the dispute before the CHACO WAR erupted in 1932. He founded and edited the periodical *El Tiempo* in 1891 and wrote more than a dozen major books dealing mostly with history and Paraguayan diplomacy.

JOHN HOYT WILLIAMS

DOMINICAN REPUBLIC SINCE 1821. From a survey of Dominican history it is possible to place this small Caribbean nation within a distinctly Latin American descriptive framework of periodic violence, governmental instability, widespread social inequality, and economic stagnation. Yet the congruity of the development process of the Dominican Republic and that of many other Latin American countries cannot conceal certain unique national characteristics that hold the key to the sources of its tragic history.

The most advantageous beginning for a description of Dominican independent history is 1821, with the formal separation of the Spanish-speaking two-thirds of the island of Hispaniola from the mother country. The successful uprising against Spain left the former colony weak and vulnerable to invasion and control by those with greater resources. Neighboring Haiti, which occupies the remaining third of the island, showed great interest in extending its dominance and, under Gen. Jean-Pierre BOYER, proceeded to take complete control of the Dominican Republic.

The take-over of the entire island by the predominantly black Haitians created difficulties that were never resolved. At the root of the Haitian failure was the legacy of hatred left by the cruel generals Jean-Jacques DESSALINES and Henry CHRISTOPHE prior to 1821. The deep-seated enmity of the Dominicans for their black conquerors was increased by Boyer's decision to revive forced labor as well as by the continuation of senseless violence and pillage by Haitian administrators and military personnel. In such oppressive conditions it was not long before a call for a truly independent Dominican nation would be heard. It came from Juan Pablo DUARTE and his secret society of liberators (*see* TRINITARIA, LA). The Haitians, under a new leader, Gen. Charles Hérard, attempted to contain the rising revolutionary fervor of the Dominican people, but in February 1844, Duarte's forces ousted the Haitian invaders.

Despite the heroism and foresight that Duarte and his followers showed in launching the revolution, the great Dominican leader was unable to ward off the power-hungry advances of two *caudillos,* Pedro SANTANA and Buenaventura BÁEZ, who controlled Dominican politics from 1845 to 1878 and effectively stifled the democratic dream of Duarte. During the era of the "twin *caudillos*" the Dominican Republic fell increasingly into internal and international bankruptcy. The results of this inept management appeared not only in the impoverished state of the government's coffers but also in the expanded foreign interest and

DOMINICAN REPUBLIC

Area: 18,816 sq. mi.   Population: 4,006,405 (1970).

intrigue that surrounded Dominican politics. In an attempt to stabilize the faltering economy and to secure a protector against Haiti's continual assaults, President Santana permitted Spain to reannex the Dominican Republic in 1861.

Like the Haitian invasion, the reimposition of Spanish rule on the Dominican people created serious problems. As the occupation forces spread across the countryside causing ill-feeling and heightening tension, revolutionary efforts were made to rid the nation of these new foreign interlopers. In 1865 the Dominicans, led by the brilliant general Gregorio Luperón, were victorious for a second time in forcing the evacuation of the Spanish.

The Dominican people had now rid themselves of the Spanish twice, but their future was still neither secure nor bright as Buenaventura Báez continued to take the nation down the road to financial ruin and international dependence. Báez, who had already served two terms as President, captured the executive office three more times before his final ouster in 1878. During his last three terms he committed his country to damaging and unpayable foreign loans and almost succeeded in having the United States annex the Dominican Republic (the United States Senate rejected the treat signed by the Grant administration). By the time that Báez left Dominican politics, the country was sorely in need of an enlightened leadership that would bring some order to the shambles left by the politics of occupation, *caudillismo,* and interventionism. Moreover, the chaos in the political sphere was reflected in a disrupted social system and a backward economy.

The resourceful leadership that the Dominican people so desperately needed never materialized. Instead, the Dominicans had to endure the seventeen-year reign (1882–1899) of the black leader Ulises HEUREAUX. The paradoxical dictatorship of Heureaux was a unique period in Dominican history in that he combined a fierce, repressive rule with the introduction of many social and economic changes. Although assessments of his regime emphasize the violent excesses, the huge spy nets, the phenomenal economic losses, and the continued reliance on foreign financial assistance, the fact remains that under Heureaux education progressed steadily, transportation and communication links were expanded, preferential trade agreements were negotiated, and the bureaucracy and the Army were substantially overhauled. Yet despite these modernizing efforts, the Dominican Republic at the turn of the twentieth century languished in a state of political and financial collapse. With the assassination of Heureaux in 1899 the Dominican people and their leaders came to recognize the dire straits into which *caudillo* politics had led them. More important, many Dominicans again came to the conclusion that the most advantageous method of attaining economic stability and social development was through the guidance and assistance of a foreign power.

Foreign intervention in the name of financial solvency and economic prosperity came in 1905 with the establishment of a United States customs receivership. Embroiled in a political upheaval caused by two rival factions, the Dominicans turned over to the United States the collection of their customs and the servicing of their $29.5 million domestic and foreign debt. *See also* ROOSEVELT COROLLARY.

The receivership of 1905, for all the future implications it held for United States–Dominican relations, was on the whole successful in that it substantially reduced the country's debt burden. The social and political scene also seemed to benefit from the American presence. The administration of President Ramón CÁCERES was perhaps the most visionary and democratic in the nation's history. Unfortunately, Cáceres was assassinated, leaving the Dominican Republic again without effective leadership.

The death of Cáceres placed the Dominican Republic in a familiar position of having to fill a power void. The rival factions of Juan Isidro Jiménez and Horacio VÁSQUEZ attempted to fill this void but only brought the country another period of chaos. Domestic politics became so confused and unstable that the role of the United States shifted from customs collection to the control of national elections and, in 1916, to the occupation of the country.

With the initiation of the United States occupation, the Dominican Republic experienced its third foreign intervention since independence. As might have been expected from the popular reaction to past invasions, the Dominican people did not relish the new American presence on their soil. Although the American Governor, Capt. Harry S. Knapp, was a compassionate and understanding administrator, resistance movements sprang up throughout the nation. The United States Marines responded to these rebel groups with force but succeeded only in intensifying the ill-feeling of an already-hostile population.

Despite considerable anti-American bitterness, a number of social and economic improvements were made in agriculture, sanitation, road building, and education by American technicians. However, the modernizing and humanitarian assistance offered by the United States did not halt the tide of nationalism mounting among the Dominican people. By 1921 the United States had come to realize that its interests demanded an early departure from the Dominican Republic. In anticipation of the American withdrawal, which took place in 1924, Dominican political life revived as national leaders sought to use the expected exodus of the occupation forces to turn the country away from the despotism and stagnation of the past. The hopes of these leaders and of the United States were not realized. For six years under President Horacio Vásquez the Dominican Republic remained in a state of political impotence, as the stability that the United States presence had brought gave way to incompetent national administration.

With the advent of the 1930s the Dominican Republic witnessed the rise to dominance of a man who would alter the pattern of internal chaos and debility and fill the leadership void that had left Dominican politics fragmented. This man was Gen. Rafael Leonidas TRUJILLO MOLINA, who for thirty-one years controlled Latin America's most thoroughgoing dictatorship. The Trujillo era can best be examined by analyzing the extent of the dictator's control and its effect on the nation. It can be stated without exaggeration that Trujillo's control over the Dominican Republic was nearly complete. Trujillo and his family directly or indirectly owned, managed, regulated, or manipulated every major economic concern in the nation, from the sugar, cement, and tobacco industries to small shops and rural haciendas. Politics was not a means of determining policy alternatives but a way for Trujillo to further his own wealth and power. Education became a propaganda outlet for the Trujillo ideology. The roles of the police and the military were twisted from the administration of justice and the protection of the frontiers to internal surveillance and repression. The Dominican Republic became Trujillo's private estate, as the semi-educated dictator amassed about $100 million through his control of almost three-fourths of Dominican economic activity.

The dominance of Trujillo did not make his regime immune from errors of judgment, strategy, and tactics. By the late 1950s, after a number of years of economic growth and prosperity, the Trujillo government showed obvious signs of weakness. In the years before his death Trujillo became the object of intense criticism by journalists, church leaders, political exiles, neighboring governments, and his previously staunch ally, the United States. Faced with a declining economy, charges of suppression of political enemies, and widespread governmental ineptitude, Trujillo fought back, at times by conducting an expensive public relations campaign and at others by having critics murdered. Despite his attempts to preserve his dominance, however, world opinion became increasingly adverse and an internal resistance movement intent on overthrowing his dictatorship became active. It came as no surprise to some and caused great relief to many when Trujillo was assassinated on May 30, 1961.

The death of Rafael Trujillo and the eventual departure of his family once again left the Dominican Republic without substantial leadership. But even more than leadership the nation lacked understanding, training, and organization for self-government. Trujillo's control had been so pervasive that the Dominican people were unequipped for nation building and unaccustomed to the functioning of democratic government.

After a period of provisional rule the Dominican people in 1962 chose Juan BOSCH as their first freely elected President in more than thirty years. Bosch, the populist candidate of the PARTIDO REVOLUCIONARIO DOMINICANO (PRD), came into office after having won approximately 62 percent of the popular vote. This strong showing created hope in the Dominican Republic and throughout the world that a new era of reform democracy was about to begin.

President Bosch attempted to fulfill the hopes of his supporters by proposing radical land reforms, increasing educational expenditures, seeking the formation of peasant leagues and cooperatives, and intensifying efforts at tax equalization. From the start he encountered numerous obstacles. His abrasive and aloof style served to alienate possible allies and bewilder close admirers. The snubbing of the Catholic Church and the land and tax reforms struck fear in higher social circles. Finally, Bosch's left-wing position and rhetoric made the Dominican Republic's armed forces and its primary financial backer, the United States, extremely uneasy.

The revolutionary changes that Bosch sought to incorporate in the Dominican Republic widened the gap between the elite landholding, business, and military classes and the populist coalition of peasants, labor, and students. Every day of Bosch's Presidency brought new rumors of coups and counterrevolution. In September 1963, these rumors ended as the military forced Bosch from office and squelched any hope of democratic change.

Even though Bosch's dream of fulfilling the demands of the Dominican populace did not come true, the spirit of reform, participation, and social justice that he engendered did not die. The elite-oriented government of the businessman Donald Reid Cabral that replaced Bosch was successful neither in steering the Dominican consciousness away from political matters nor in crushing the desire for a fundamental restructuring of society. By April 1965, Reid Cabral could no longer contain the explosive elements in the situation. The result was civil war, followed by the landing of American troops (*see* DOMINICAN REVOLT). After months of stalemated fighting, an agreement was reached under United Nations and ORGANIZATION OF AMERICAN STATES auspices that ended hostilities and eventually the United States presence while also establishing a provisional government under the moderate leader Héctor GARCÍA-GODOY.

The Dominican Republic in the post-civil war period can best be described as a nation experiencing political fatigue, simmering frustrations, and uncertainty as to the future. Emphasis was again placed on internal stability and economic development; intense political involvement was reduced to a minimum. The most obvious sign of this changing mood was the election in 1966 and again in 1970 of Joaquín BALAGUER as President. Balaguer, a former puppet President under Trujillo, recognized this shift in national attitude away from violence and revolution and used it adroitly in defeating Juan Bosch and the PRD.

The Dominican Republic after the election of Balaguer in 1966 experienced a relatively placid political climate along with noticeable social and economic gains. The opposition to the Balaguer government was generally vocal but ineffectual as the PRD, the Christian Democrats, numerous Communist splinter groups, and the right vied for attention and influence. Outbreaks of violence also occurred, but they did not reach the intensity of 1965 or garner a wide range of support as in the past.

On the economic scene it was possible to judge more accurately the present state of the nation and the modernizing goals being sought. President Balaguer's administration made sizable advances in raising the gross national product by about 6.5 percent yearly, foreign investment began to return, the construction of two large hydroelectric dams was in progress, and agricultural output increased considerably. Although the economy still remained dependent in large measure on sugarcane, there were renewed efforts at diversification. New crops were introduced, and new mining and tourist incentive laws passed. The number of construction permits continued to increase, more jobs became available, and the economy entered a boom period. At the same time programs in housing, health, education, and other areas were accelerated. Despite these encouraging signs, the 4,011,589 inhabitants (1970) of the Dominican Republic were still beset by high unemployment and illiteracy rates, inadequate social programs, underdeveloped resources, and a continuing dependence on United States economic aid and political support.

Bibliography. Samuel Hazard, *Santo Domingo, Past*

and Present, New York, 1873; H. Hoetink, *El pueblo dominicano, 1850–1900,* Santiago, Dominican Republic, 1971; Rayford Logan, *Haiti and the Dominican Republic,* New York, 1968; John Bartlow Martin, *Overtaken by Events: The Dominican Republic from the Fall of Trujillo to the Civil War,* New York, 1966; Selden Rodman, *Quisqueya: A History of the Dominican Republic,* Seattle, 1964; Otto Schoenrich, *Santo Domingo: A Country with a Future,* New York, 1918; Sumner Welles, *Naboth's Vineyard: The Dominican Republic, 1844–1924,* 2 vols., New York, 1928; Howard J. Wiarda, *The Dominican Republic: Nation in Transition,* New York, 1969.

MICHAEL J. KRYZANEK

DOMINICAN REVOLT (1965–1966). The civil-military junta governing the Dominican Republic from September 1963 to April 1965 derived its original support from most of the country's business community, the traditional oligarchy, and the armed forces. Headed by the businessman Donald Reid Cabral, the regime also won the backing of the United States government and the friendship of Ambassador William Tapley Bennett.

The government faced severe economic and social problems still unsettled from the era of the dictator Rafael Leonidas TRUJILLO MOLINA, and its response to its financial difficulties was an austerity program that hit hardest at the urban poor, though it did result in loans and aid from the United States and the International Monetary Fund. Widespread corruption and the repressive behavior of many police and military units led to growing opposition, and Reid's attempts to curb military corruption by removing the worst offenders from command only earned him the loss of armed forces support as well. In January 1965, a drought and a simultaneous drop in world market prices for Dominican exports combined to halt a modest economic recovery. When Reid announced the postponement of a promised presidential election and his own candidacy, the opponents of the regime put their varied coup plans into operation.

The plotters ranged across the political spectrum. On the far and fragmented left there were the Castroite June 14 movement, the Moscow-line Popular Socialists, and the ultramilitant Dominican Popular movement. On the far right disgruntled military and police officers were joined by some former National Civic Union (UCN) politicians. The most significant groups were those supporting the return of either of two former Presidents, Juan BOSCH and Joaquín BALAGUER. The Bosch faction was spearheaded by his PARTIDO REVOLUCIONARIO DOMINICANO (PRD) and featured a coalition with Christian Socialists, foreign liberal groups, some middle- and upper-class elements, and several key military commanders and junior officers. It was by far the largest and best-organized and -prepared of the antijunta groups.

On April 24, 1965, an attempt by Reid to head off the Boschist military plotters backfired, and the revolt was set in motion. When the most important commanders (Air Force Gen. Juan de los Santos Céspedes and tank force Gen. Elías Wessin y Wessin) stood by while major units pledged their support for the coup, Reid turned to the United States Embassy. Bennett was absent, but top embassy and State Department officials agreed that the return of Bosch would not be in United States interests. However, Boschist forces seized the Presidential Palace, arrested Reid, and established a Constitutionalist regime aimed at restoring Bosch and the 1963 constitution.

When the goal of the coup became clear to all, the anti-Bosch military leaders, who had been idle up to this time, began to act. They telephoned the palace but could not get the Constitutionalists' quick agreement to the formation of a provisional junta. General de los Santos and his colleagues then ordered an Air Force strafing run and naval bombardment of the palace and the Twenty-seventh of February army camp. What role United States Embassy officials played in this action is not certain, but some evidence suggests that even if they did not suggest the attack, they made it clear to Wessin, De los Santos, and others that the United States would back an effort by the military to prevent the restoration of Bosch. The embassy also appears to have encouraged the anti-Bosch officers (the Loyalists) in their decision to form a junta under Col. Pedro Benoit and thus present a government that could request United States aid.

The Constitutionalists and other leftists distributed arms to the civilian population and rallied their support for what now became an incipient civil war. The Loyalists, keeping up their bombardments, prepared a tank and troop assault that General Wessin would send across the Duarte Bridge.

Repeated appeals by the Constitutionalists to the United States Embassy to arrange a cease-fire and talks were turned away. After Ambassador Bennett accused the "rebels" of responsibility for the bloodshed, an angry army colonel, Francisco Caamaño Deño, and his associates rallied the Constitutionalist forces and surprisingly halted and routed the junta attackers at the bridge. A series of Constitutionalist victories throughout Santo Domingo led the Benoit junta and Ambassador Bennett to appeal to Washington for intervention.

Late on April 28, President Lyndon B. Johnson ordered United States Marines ashore and began a massive buildup of United States forces in the island nation. He explained the landings as humanitarian moves to protect United States and other nationals and the embassies, but the United States troops were told that the rebels were the "enemy" and the two countries' militaries shared the facilities at the San Isidro air base.

Simultaneously with the landings, Johnson sent former Ambassador John Bartlow Martin to make contact with the Constitutionalists and informed the ORGANIZATION OF AMERICAN STATES (OAS) Council of United States actions. On April 30, a cease-fire was arranged between the Dominican factions by the Papal Nuncio with United States backing. But United States troops repeatedly engaged rebel units and snipers as the United States proceeded to set up an international zone of refuge in the west, secure the Duarte Bridge in the east, then link these positions with a line of communication that cut the Constitutionalist-held territory into two parts by May 2.

The OAS Council voted to send Secretary-General José A. MORA to the scene, and opponents of the intervention convened a Meeting of Consultation to deal with the crisis. It sent a special committee to report on events and seek the return of normal conditions. Both the OAS committee and Martin concluded that the Constitutionalist movement was suspect (Martin said it was "Communist-dominated"). The determination to prevent a "second Cuba" highlighted a speech by President Johnson on May 2 that infuriated Bosch and his followers.

Both factions now established more complete "governments" with the Loyalists agreeing to a Government of National Reconstruction (GNR) under the leadership of Gen. Antonio Imbert Barrera, whom Martin favored for this job. These developments and continued United States–rebel fighting led the Constitutionalists to turn to the UN Security Council for help, and that body voted to send an observer mission, the first direct United Nations presence in any inter-American crisis.

Mid-May brought critical events: (1) McGeorge Bundy headed another United States team, this one with a plan, later abandoned, to create a provisional government under the former Bosch Minister of Agriculture Silvestre Antonio Guzmán; (2) the GNR criticized this move by the United States government but launched a full-scale assault on the rebels' northern sector with the help, authorized or not, of United States troops; (3) the United Nations team arrived and joined efforts to obtain another cease-fire; and (4) the OAS committee left Santo Domingo angry at the new "interferences" by both the United States and the United Nations. By May 20, the northern sector was under junta control, and United States officials pledged not to let the Loyalists go through their lines; thus a military stalemate was created after the loss of hundreds of lives. Faced now with United States pressure, Imbert agreed to the new cease-fire and subsequently to its extension.

A voluntary Inter-American Peace Force was finally, though narrowly, approved by the OAS, but only Brazil made a significant contribution, and a Brazilian became the nominal commander. Politically, with the collapse of the "Guzmán formula" the United States turned to direct cooperation with, or use of, the OAS. On June 2, an ad hoc committee headed by Ambassador Ellsworth Bunker was dispatched to seek a political settlement. In addition, the Inter-American Human Rights Commission was called in to investigate increasing reports of terrorism.

On August 8, the ad hoc committee, after extensive talks with many Dominicans, proposed its own formula for a settlement, which included an Act of Dominican Reconciliation and an Institutional Act as a temporary constitution. This "arbitration"was resented by both factions and by several OAS members. But the Constitutionalists, bottled up and fearful of further attacks, agreed in principle by the end of August, and the GNR, denied all financial support and labeled the "chief obstacle" to settlement by the United States, resigned on August 31.

On September 3, Héctor GARCÍA-GODOY became provisional President and began the tortuous task of preparing the nation for June elections. Full backing by the United States and the OAS enabled the government to survive rightist coup attempts and leftist agitation, to accomplish the exiling or stripping from power of the most objectionable Constitutionalist and Loyalist officers, and to hold perhaps the freest elections in the history of the Dominican Republic. Not accomplished, however, were the reintegration of "rebel" units into the military, the complete purge of antidemocratic officers from the armed forces, and the collection of all arms held by civilians.

The elections themselves resulted in the surprising victory of Balaguer and his Partido Reformista over Bosch and the PRD. However, Balaguer had campaigned effectively while Bosch stayed home and used radio and television out of fear for his life, and many may have concluded that the United States would still not tolerate Bosch as President.

The withdrawal of all foreign troops and missions continued from June into September and Balaguer's term. The Dominican Republic was left with an aborted revolution, most of the same old social and economic problems, and even greater political polarization, complete with continued terror and counterterror.

Bibliography. Juan Bosch, *Pentagonism: A Substitute for Imperialism,* New York, 1968; Center for Strategic Studies, *Dominican Action—1965: Intervention or Cooperation?,* Washington, 1966; Theodore Draper, *The Dominican Revolt: A Case Study in American Policy,* New York, 1965; Dan Kurzman, *Revolt of the Damned,* New York, 1965; Abraham F. Lowenthal, *The Dominican Intervention,* Cambridge, Mass., 1971; José A. Moreno, *Barrios in Arms,* Pittsburgh, 1970; Jerome Slater, *Intervention and Negotiation: The United States and the Dominican Revolution,* New York, 1970; Tad Szulc, *Dominican Diary,* New York, 1965.

N. GARY HOLTEN

DOMINICAN REVOLUTIONARY PARTY. *See* PARTIDO REVOLUCIONARIO DOMINICANO.

DOMINICANS (COLONIAL PERIOD). *See* RELIGIOUS ORDERS (COLONIAL PERIOD).

DONATARY CAPTAINCY SYSTEM. *See* CAPTAINCY SYSTEM.

DONOSO, JOSÉ (1925–   ). Chilean novelist. Donoso was born in Santiago. After graduating from high school, he went to Magallanes, where he worked for a time as a shepherd. Later he worked in the port of Buenos Aires. He continued his studies in Chile and at Princeton, and has been a journalist, has lived in Spain, and has taught at the literary workshop of the State University of Iowa. His writings include two books of short stories, *Veraneo y otros cuentos* (1955) and *El Charlestón* (1960), and the novels *Coronación* (1957), for which he won the William Faulkner Prize, *Este domingo* (1966), and *El lugar sin límites* (1966).

RACHEL PHILLIPS

DORADO, EL (THE GILDED ONE). Sixteenth-century Spanish designation for the king of an Amerindian empire supposedly possessing enormous wealth. In the twentieth century El Dorado has come to signify any proverbially rich city or region. The legend has a basis in fact. Each year the *zipa* (chieftain) of the CHIBCHA nation that inhabited the Colombian highland plateau of Cundinamarca (Bogotá) during the fifteenth century was coated with gold dust and then transported to the center of Lake Guatavita, where he swam, washing off the valued substance. Word of this spendthrift monarch spread to the Spaniards who arrived about 1509 on the Caribbean coast. The tale soon was so greatly exaggerated that the conquistadores did not even recognize its source in the prosperous Chibcha empire when they discovered it.

The El Dorado legend lured thousands of gold-hungry sixteenth-century adventurers to their deaths in the vast plains, mountains, and jungles of northern South America. Unproductive as these odysseys were in terms of treasure, they yielded invaluable information about the geography of the South American interior, revealing trails, rivers, and mountain passes later used to exploit and settle the continent. Also cherished for what it revealed about the heights and depths of human potential as seen in the character of these conquistadores, the El Dorado legend became enmeshed in Western literature; references to it appear in John Milton's *Paradise Lost,* Voltaire's *Candide,* and many other works. The willingness of sixteenth-century conquistadores to credit the existence of this fabulous kingdom has been attributed partially to their medieval notions about exotic animals, beings, and kingdoms. Furthermore, for Spaniards, their conquests of the awesome Aztec and Inca empires (*see* AZTECS; INCAS) seemed a fulfillment of the belief, inspired by the reconquest of Spain, in their destiny to achieve apparently impossible deeds through Christian faith and military valor. Finally, the conquistadores were inspired by the ideal of the chivalric quest as popularized in the contemporary romance *Amadís de Gaula* and its sequel, *Las sergas de Esplandián.*

The first probe for El Dorado was led by German conquistadores of the Welser banking house in Venezuela. The expedition of Ambrosius Ehinger (1529) was followed by those of Nikolaus FEDERMANN and Georg Hohemut (Hohermuth; 1535–1539). The Spaniard Gonzalo JIMÉNEZ DE QUESADA was the first European to enter the Bogotá plateau (1537), and he lost no time in dominating the Chibchas, taking possession of what gold he could find. Their treasure, however, came nowhere near the vast quantity captured in the Peruvian conquest.

Quesada along with others then speculated that El Dorado's kingdom might be located in yet-undiscovered mountain ranges east of the ANDES MOUNTAINS or in the vast lowlands of southern Venezuela and northern Brazil. The expedition of Gonzalo PIZARRO (1539–1542) reflected this thinking, but its only positive accomplishment was the launching of Francisco de ORELLANA's voyage down the AMAZON RIVER. The last German expedition from Venezuela, led by Philipp von Hutten (1541–1545), discovered the Omagua Indian nation near the headwaters of the Río Negro and spread the rumor that the Omagua king might be El Dorado. Pedro de Ursúa's trek into the Amazon from Peru (1560) was a deliberate attempt to find Hutten's El Dorado, but it ended in catastrophe with the rebellion of Lope de Aguirre.

In 1568 Jiménez de Quesada won a hereditary grant covering some 400 leagues of the eastern Colombian watershed between the Amazon and Orinoco flood basins (*see* ORINOCO RIVER). After the failure of his expedition (1569–1572), he bequeathed his grant to his niece's husband, a Spanish military officer named Antonio de Berrío. Berrío carried on Quesada's quest but concentrated his efforts far to the east of Quesada's grant, near the Venezuela-Guiana border. His failure produced the notion that El Dorado must be located still farther east, in the Guiana Highlands.

In 1595 the Englishman Walter Raleigh led an exploratory expedition to the Orinoco region, during which he captured and interrogated Berrío. Raleigh's imaginative plans linked the finding of El Dorado with an English take-over of Spanish America. When he returned to the Orinoco with a large expedition (1617–1618), one mishap after another ruined his mission and angered the Spaniards as well as King James I, who had Raleigh executed after his return to England (1618).

Bibliography. Walker Chapman, *The Golden Dream: Seekers of El Dorado,* New York, 1967; Pedro de Cieza de León, *Civil Wars of Peru: The War of Chupas,* tr. by Clements R. Markham, London, 1918; John Hemming, *The Conquest of the Incas,* New York, 1970; Frederick A. Kirkpatrick, *The Spanish Conquistadores,* Cleveland and New York, 1962; James Lockhart, *The Men of Cajamarca: A Social and Biographical Study of the First Conquerors of Peru,* Austin, Tex., 1972; Irving Leonard, *Books of the Brave,* Cambridge, Mass., 1949; William H. Prescott, *History of the Conquest of Peru,* vol. II, Boston, 1856.

WILLIAM S. DUDLEY

DORTICÓS TORRADO, OSVALDO (1919–). President of Cuba (1959–). Dorticós was born in Cienfuegos. After graduating from the University of Havana, he practiced law in his native city and participated actively in left-wing politics. In the late 1930s and early 1940s he held membership in the Partido Popular Socialista (Communist party; PSP) and reportedly served as secretary to Juan Marinello, a PSP leader and Cabinet minister during Fulgencio BATISTA's first administration.

During the popular struggle against the Batista dictatorship in the late 1950s, Dorticós, no longer affiliated with the PSP, served the rebel cause as a civic resistance leader in Cienfuegos. His association with Fidel CASTRO commenced in January 1959, when he was assigned the task of studying and drafting all laws for the revolutionary government. From this important but relatively obscure position, Dorticós soon rose to public prominence in revolutionary Cuba. In July 1959 Prime Minister Castro appointed him to replace the anti-Communist Manuel Urrutia as President of Cuba.

Conspicuous as a civilian among government leaders with a background in the rebel guerrilla movement, Dorticós only occasionally appears dressed in military fatigues. In spite of his past association with the PSP, he is politically identified with the Castroite revolutionaries rather than with the old-guard Cuban Communists. He has become more than a passive figurehead in the Castro regime. In addition to the Presidency he has held the post of Economics Minister. In 1965 he was also named to the Political Bureau and the Secretariat of the Central Committee of the new PARTIDO COMUNISTA DE CUBA.

DAVID A. CRAIN

DRAGO DOCTRINE. International legal principle that no state has the right to use armed force against another state in order to collect public debts. The doctrine was contained in an official communication on December 29, 1902, from Luis María Drago (1859–1921), Foreign Minister of Argentina, to the Argentine Minister in Washington. It was written in response to the blockade of Venezuelan ports instituted in December 1902 by naval units of Germany and Great Britain (later joined by Italy) to force the government of

Cipriano CASTRO to pay debts owed to their citizens. It was Drago's contention that such interventions violated the principle of the juridical equality of states since "the summary and immediate collection [of a debt] at a given moment, by means of force, would occasion nothing less than the ruin of the weakest nations, and the absorption of their governments . . . by the mighty of the earth." He also maintained that the territorial occupation implicit in armed intervention was contrary to the MONROE DOCTRINE.

The Second Hague Conference of 1907 adopted a modified version of the Drago Doctrine, known as the Porter Doctrine, after Horace Porter, the head of the United States delegation, which sponsored it. The Porter Doctrine is broader than the Drago Doctrine, since it covers all contractual debts, but it sanctions the use of force if the debtor nation refuses international arbitration or neglects to enforce a decision arrived at through such arbitration. However, few Latin American nations approved of the Porter Doctrine.

RODNEY D. ANDERSON

DRAKE, FRANCIS (ca. 1543–1596). English seaman. Born in Devon, Drake was the son of a yeoman farmer who was also a staunch Protestant. He first went to sea as the apprentice of the master of a coastal bark. By 1569 he had made two voyages to the Indies in association with his kinsman John Hawkins and had tested the reaction of Spanish officials to English intrusion into their jealously guarded colonial preserve. Drake now determined to strike a blow at Spanish prestige and economic power by capturing the Isthmus of Panama, the transshipment point for the treasure of the Peruvian mines. A voyage to Panama in 1572–1573 had mixed results: Drake failed to capture Nombre de Dios, and an attempt on a treasure-laden mule train misfired, but a raid on another mule train did yield some gold.

In late 1577 Drake embarked upon his most celebrated voyage as he sailed from Plymouth with five ships, including his own, the *Pelican* (soon to be renamed the *Golden Hind*). It is not clear whether the purpose of the voyage was exploration of unknown lands and waters, opening up trade with the Spice Islands, reprisals against Spain for injuries to England, or a combination of these. Drake sailed along the east coast of South America and passed through the Strait of Magellan. Driven southward by a gale, he was able to see that Tierra del Fuego consisted of islands and was not, as was commonly supposed, part of a southern continent. During the storm one of Drake's three remaining vessels was lost with all on board, and the *Golden Hind* lost sight of the third, which eventually made its way back to England. Moving up the west coast of South America, Drake did extensive damage to Spanish shipping in Valparaíso, Arica, and Callao, and captured a rich treasure ship off Cape San Francisco. He proceeded northward, sailing to a point between 42° and 48°N, and then turned south and found shelter at a place he called New Albion. After sailing westward across the Pacific, he obtained six tons of cloves at the Moluccas and began the homeward journey around the coast of Africa, being forced to jettison half the cargo of cloves en route. He reached Plymouth on September 26, 1580, having completed the second circumnavigation of the world, and was knighted by Queen Elizabeth the following April. In 1585, as open war between England and Spain drew near, Drake made another voyage to the Indies during which Santo Domingo and Cartagena were captured and looted and the fort and settlement at St. Augustine, Florida, were destroyed.

The years 1587–1589 saw some of Drake's most famous exploits, such as his destructive raid on the harbor of Cádiz (April 1587), as well as an abortive effort to capture Lisbon. The ill fortune that attended this venture was repeated during Drake's last voyage to the Indies in 1595–1596. He was accompanied by Hawkins, who died off Puerto Rico. Drake made an unsuccessful attempt to take San Juan, then turned to the principal objective of the expedition: Panama. After capturing Nombre de Dios, which was no longer the Caribbean terminus for transisthmian shipping, the English moved inland toward Panama City but were halted by the Spanish defenses. Drake fell ill of dysentery and died off Puerto Bello on the night of January 27–28, 1596.

To contemporary Spaniards, Drake was a fearsome rogue. In England, however, he is remembered as a daring and imaginative seaman who proved that humble origins need not be an impediment to leadership, who was conspicuously courteous to his foes, and who laid the foundations for England's future maritime greatness.

HELEN DELPAR

DREYFUS CONTRACT. The GUANO boom of the mid-nineteenth century launched Peru on a course of reckless spending that repeatedly brought the nation to the verge of bankruptcy. In 1869 President José BALTA's Minister of Finance, Nicolás de PIÉROLA, sought to stabilize the financial situation by signing a contract with the French commercial house of Auguste Dreyfus. The agreement, signed in Paris on July 5, 1869, became one of the most controversial documents in the economic history of Peru. According to its terms, Dreyfus was to receive 2 million tons of guano and become Peru's exclusive guano consignee in Europe and other parts of the world. In return, the firm was to advance the Peruvian government 2 million soles, payable in two installments, and promised to pay the government 700,000 soles per month until March 1871. In addition, Dreyfus was to assume the obligation of servicing Peru's foreign debt, which amounted to 5 million soles per year. (At this time the sol was roughly equivalent to the United States dollar.)

To the defenders of the contract, the agreement represented freedom from a chaotic financial situation. The granting of the guano franchise to one consignee ensured a steady and predictable source of income, thus giving the government the opportunity to balance the budget. Moreover, the contract ensured a more economical exploitation of guano resources and reestablished Peru's international credit. Opponents, representing mainly Peru's new enterprising capitalists, complained to the Supreme Court that their exclusion from the guano trade injudiciously undermined their economic interests, and those of the nation. The Supreme Court agreed. Nevertheless, in 1870 Congress, amid charges of bribery on both sides, approved the contract. Today there is general agreement among historians and economists that although the contract tied government revenues to foreign capitalists, it was beneficial because it broke the stranglehold that the numerous guano consignees had over the treasury.

ORAZIO A. CICCARELLI

DROUGHT POLYGON. Geometrically shaped administrative area in northeastern Brazil, supposedly delimiting the drought area of the SERTÃO. The Paraíba and upper São Francisco Rivers form most of the southern and western boundaries; the northern and eastern boundaries connect specific towns and cities, excluding the coastal areas. The polygon includes parts of Piauí, Ceará, Rio Grande do Norte, Pernambuco, Paraíba, Alagôas, Sergipe, Bahia, and Minas Gerais. The Drought Polygon Commission, the National Department of Works against the Drought (DNOCS), and the SUPERINTENDÊNCIA DE DESENVOLVIMENTO DE NORDESTE (SUDENE) represent the numerous governmental bodies created at various times to study and find solutions for the problems pertinent to the drought area of the NORTHEAST. With numerous internal variations, the area circumscribed by the Drought Polygon is characterized by irregularity in the amount and distribution of rainfall and by recurrent droughts of one to three years' duration. The area involved is roughly equivalent to the extent of the sertão and its xerophytic vegetation, but the Drought Polygon exists primarily as an administrative unit for delineating the area eligible for national aid.

ROBIN L. ANDERSON

DRUMMOND DE ANDRADE, CARLOS. *See* ANDRADE, CARLOS DRUMMOND DE.

DUARTE, JUAN PABLO (1813–1876). Leader of Dominican independence, the "Apostle of Our Liberty," as one of the books about him proclaims. Duarte was sent out of the country to be educated during the Haitian occupation of 1822–1844. Caught up in the romantic literary currents then stirring France and influenced by the ideals of liberty and equality, he returned to Santo Domingo and helped organize a secret society that led the fight for independence (*see* TRINITARIA, LA). Forced into exile in 1842, Duarte returned triumphantly two years later as the victory over the Haitians was being consolidated.

His triumph was short-lived. An amateur soldier whose romanticism and idealism were both admired and distrusted, Duarte soon fell out with the other leaders of the new nation. He was jailed and exiled by the strong man, Gen. Pedro SANTANA; as a prophet he was without honor in his own country. After a brief period in a home for indigent mariners in Germany, he spent fifteen years in ascetic reclusion in the jungles of Venezuela. Returning to the Dominican Republic in 1864 and, in the aftermath of the Spanish occupation, hoping still to establish the principles of liberty in which he believed so passionately, Duarte was again repudiated. He was able to inspire but not to lead or govern, and the provisional government soon saw an opportunity to drive him out. Returning to Venezuela, Duarte lived in poverty and obscurity for the rest of his life. Only later would he be honored in schoolboy essays as the father of his country.

HOWARD J. WIARDA

DUNDONALD, 10TH EARL OF. *See* COCHRANE, THOMAS.

DURÃO, JOSÉ DE SANTA RITA (1722–1784). Brazilian poet and theologian. Born in Minas Gerais, he studied in Lisbon and took a doctorate in theology at the University of Coimbra. After a short voluntary exile in Rome, he was granted a chair at Coimbra when he returned to Portugal. His epic, *Caramurú* (1781), was received so coldly that he destroyed his other poems. *Caramurú* recalls *Os Lusíadas* not only in its form, ten cantos in ottava rima, but also in several episodes. The hero, CARAMURÚ, is Diogo Alvares Correia, who is said to have been shipwrecked off the coast of Bahia, saved from death at the hands of hostile Indians, and then to have married a chieftain's daughter, Paraguaçu, and with her to have visited the court of Henry II of France. The book is a compendium of information about Brazil, its flora and fauna, and its indigenous inhabitants; the theme is the importance to Brazil of the mother country. Though it lacks the poetic charm of *O Uruguai*, by José Basílio da GAMA, *Caramurú* has forceful episodes and interesting descriptions and is one of the better epics in the tradition of Camões.

RAYMOND S. SAYERS

DUTCH IN BRAZIL. The Dutch became important participants in the trade with Brazil during the sixteenth century, providing ships, loans to sugar mill owners (*see* SUGAR INDUSTRY: COLONIAL BRAZIL), and acting as refiners and distributors of Brazilian sugar via Amsterdam. With the union of the crowns of Spain and Portugal in 1580 (*see* BABYLONIAN CAPTIVITY), Portugal became embroiled in the long struggle between Spain and the Netherlands. The 1620s saw the launching of a full-scale offensive against Portuguese America led by the Dutch West India Company (founded 1621).

In 1624 the Dutch seized Bahia, and in 1625 they attempted to take control of the fort of São Jorge da Mina (now Elmina) on the West African coast. The two-pronged attack revealed how keenly aware the Dutch were of the nature of the Atlantic interconnection between South America and Africa. The Spanish reacted rapidly. A fleet and expeditionary force composed of fifty-two ships and 12,000 men successfully relieved Bahia in 1625. Meanwhile, the Dutch expeditionary force met with annihilation at the hands of the Portuguese African auxiliaries on the Gold Coast. The scale and rapidity of Spain's response were conditioned not so much by solicitude for Brazil as by fear of an assault on Peru, the undisguised Dutch objective. The respite, however, was only temporary. In 1628 Piet Heyn took the Mexican silver fleet in the Cuban harbor of Matanzas. With some of the proceeds the West India Company launched a second and this time successful assault on Brazil, seizing Pernambuco (modern Recife) in 1630. The Dutch took São Jorge da Mina in 1637 and Angola in 1641. With the capture of São Luís do Maranhão the same year, Dutch Brazil controlled seven of the fourteen captaincies that had previously formed Portuguese America.

Given Dutch sea power, financial strength, and technical and business expertise, the fall of Pernambuco to the Dutch West India Company in 1630 appeared to mark the inauguration of a promising new colonial empire. In Count Johan Maurits van Nassau-Siegen the company acquired an able Governor who brought with him to America an entourage of scholars and artists, among them Frans Post and Albert Eckhout. Nonetheless, the problems were considerable, and with time they accumulated. Much destruction had accompanied the conquest. It is estimated that of 160 *engenhos* (sugar mills) operating before the war only 10 continued to function without interruption. Moreover, the millowners had difficulty in finding *lavradores* (tenant farmers) to raise the cane. Their debt position was aggravated after 1637 by the rapid falloff in sugar prices, a deflationary situation allowing creditors to gain at the expense of debtors. Governor Johan Maurits's prohibition of interest rates higher than 18 percent on loans unsecured by realty and 12 percent on those so secured compared unfavorably with the $7\frac{1}{4}$ percent charged by such Luso-Brazilian charitable institutions as the Santa Casa da Misericórdia, with its notorious laxity in collection and failure to require adequate security. The rates were far from modest when it is considered that the Dutch and Jewish merchants who made the loans to the planters and millowners were themselves borrowing in Amsterdam at little more than 3 to 4 percent.

Paradoxically, Dutch toleration of religious differences probably increased tensions, for the lines of religious demarcation tended to parallel those between town and countryside. To some extent they created an urban and rural dichotomy. The dominance of Portuguese colonial municipal institutions by planters and millowners had prevented the development of any serious divergence of interest between urban and rural sectors, just as speculative investment in cane fields during the boom years had probably integrated many of the more modest urban inhabitants into the sugar sector. The rise of Recife at the expense of the old capital of Olinda, where most of the planters had their town houses, together with the influx of Protestant Dutch and Jewish immigrants, broke the linkages that had given Catholic millowners and planters their control over the municipal council, the Santa Casa da Misericórdia, and the prestigious white lay religious brotherhoods and hence over the pricing of the export crop, access to loans, and preeminence in urban affairs. The division between the Catholic hinterland and urban Dutch and Jewish settlers was also one between debtors and creditors and between producers and distributors. Nor did the Dutch lessen the rift by becoming planters and mill operators themselves.

It was ominous for the invading power that with time the rural groups coalesced while the urban group fractured. In the rural areas declining economic conditions were aggravated by cultural and religious irritants. Any advantage the Dutch might have gained from toleration of Catholicism was undermined by the prohibition on the replacement of priests, the failure to extend toleration to Maranhão, and the activities of the Calvinist predikants. The religious assault was especially important because Catholicism in Brazil was institutionalized in such a manner as to make its domain as much social as spiritual. To interfere with its functioning was not a question of confronting a church isolated and separate from the people. Through the lay religious brotherhoods (*confrarias, irmandades*) Catholicism had become a vital element of social acculturation and spiritual amelioration for the black and mulatto population, providing marginal, repressed, and exploited groups (slaves included) with respected organs located at the center of colonial society. The new urban zone, on the other hand, presented a series of segmented and antagonistic groupings. The Protestant Dutch merchants grew increasingly antagonistic toward their Jewish competitors, who possessed the considerable advantage of long contacts with the sugar trade. Many of the Jewish settlers had originated in Portugal or had been forced converts there (new Christians). In many cases they had mastered both the Dutch and the Portuguese languages and had family connections with Portuguese Jewish capitalists, who had invested heavily in the Amsterdam sugar-refining industry. Jewish merchants in Pernambuco came to dominate tax farming and were major participants in the slave trade. The community exceeded 1,000, who were served by two synagogues. Attempted persecution by local Protestants was overruled in Europe.

Although the reestablishment of Portuguese independence from Spain in 1640 was enthusiastically supported in what remained of Portuguese America, the new regime was precarious in the extreme, and the break with Spain only encouraged the Dutch to further overseas activity against the Portuguese territories. In Lisbon the government was prepared to compromise, even to abandon the NORTHEAST to permanent Dutch control. In 1644, however, the Portuguese planters in Pernambuco took matters into their own hands and plotted an uprising. The initial plan miscarried, but a long and bitter struggle began, with the Brazilians increasingly turning to swift guerrilla activity against the urban-based Dutch and their mercenary troops. The Dutch seriously underestimated the threat, and instead of reinforcing the garrison the company withdrew Johan Maurits and reduced troop strength. The miscalculation is more surprising in retrospect than in the context of the time, for Dutch power was at its zenith.

Although the Dutch held onto the urban strong points for nine years, they increasingly lost control of the hinterland. In 1644 an uprising in Maranhão led to their expulsion from that region. In Pernambuco the mobilization of Amerindian, black, and mulatto auxiliaries proved decisive. Facing war with England and Europe and besieged within the confines of Recife, the Dutch were forced to capitulate in 1654 after the cutting of their seaborne lines of communication by a Portuguese squadron. The Dutch recognized the reconquest of Brazil in 1661.

Bibliography. Charles R. Boxer, *Salvador de Sá and the Struggle for Brazil and Angola, 1602–1686,* London, 1952; id., *The Dutch in Brazil, 1624–1654,* Oxford, 1957; Mircea Buescu, *Historia Econômica do Brasil: Pesquisas e Analises,* Rio de Janeiro, 1970; Pierre Chaunu, "Brésil et Atlantique au XVIIe siècle," *Annales,* 16th année, Paris, 1962, pp. 1176–1207; Frédéric Mauro, *Le Portugal et l'Atlantique au XVIIe siècle, 1570–1670: Étude économique,* Paris, 1960; José Antônio Gonsalves de Mello, *Tempo dos Flamengos: Influência da Ocupação Holandêsa na Vida e na Cultura do Norte do Brasil,* Rio de Janeiro, 1947; José Honório Rodrigues, *Historiografía e Bibliografía do Domínio Holandes no Brasil,* Rio de Janeiro, 1949; Engel Sluiter, "Dutch Maritime Power and the Colonial Status Quo, 1585–1641," *Pacific Historical Review,* vol. XI, no. 2, March 1942, pp. 29–41.

KENNETH R. MAXWELL

DUTRA, EURICO GASPAR (1885–1974). Army general and President of Brazil (1946–1951). Born in

Cuiabá, Mato Grosso, Dutra attended the military school at Rio Pardo, Rio Grande do Sul, enlisted in the Army in 1902, and received his commission as a cavalry lieutenant in 1910. His career for the next thirty-five years was spent in the Army, in which he was a loyal supporter of the established government. Dutra helped suppress the revolts led by junior officers in the 1920s (*see* TENENTISMO) and opposed the REVOLUTION OF 1930 led by Getúlio VARGAS, but he defended the Vargas regime during the São Paulo rebellion of 1932, the Communist revolt of 1935, and the attempted putsch by right-wing extremists in 1938 (*see* INTEGRALISMO).

His tenure as War Minister was the longest in the history of Brazil. He was appointed in December 1936 and held the post until August 1945, when he resigned to campaign for the Presidency on the ticket of the PARTIDO SOCIAL DEMOCRÁTICO. Dutra had been one of the architects of the ESTADO NOVO in 1937, but he encouraged the restoration of democratic rule in postwar Brazil and took part in the coup d'état that removed Vargas from power in October 1945. He was elected on December 2, 1945, and took office on January 31, 1946. During his administration a new constitution was promulgated (*see* CONSTITUTION OF 1946: BRAZIL), an open political climate prevailed, and the state increased its direct participation in the economy with the completion of the Paulo Afonso hydroelectric project and the national steel mill at VOLTA REDONDA. Dutra retired from active political life at the expiration of his term.   ROLLIE E. POPPINO

DUVALIER, FRANÇOIS (1907–1971). Physician and President of Haiti (1957–1971). Duvalier, a Negro, was born on April 14, 1907, and educated in the Faculty of Medicine, Port-au-Prince, where his medical career began at St-François-Xavier Hospital. Later he joined an American medical mission as director of malaria control. Duvalier served in the Haitian Cabinet as Labor and Public Health Secretary and gained national repute as a humanitarian for his fight against yaws. He wrote extensively on tropical medicine and Negro culture. His works stressed racial pride and Haiti's African heritage while often denouncing the role of mulattoes. Duvalier argued that VODUN had made basic contributions to national independence and unity. Later,

he became the first ruler since Faustin SOULOUQUE to support it openly.

In 1957, after months of violence and four short provisional governments, Duvalier was chosen President. Initially he presented programs for long-needed rural reforms in literacy, local government, and community development, but progress was disappointing. Resistance to his rule grew among black intellectuals, Catholic clerics, and businessmen. To neutralize the political power of the Army, he supported the strong-arm Tontons Macoutes, a well-organized spy organization loyal to him. His ousting of several clergymen brought excommunication from the Catholic Church. Popular for his prideful foreign policy and the prestige he offered to Vodun and CRÉOLE, he restored the life Presidency. When the health of "Papa Doc" failed, he prevailed upon the National Assembly to name his son, Jean-Claude DUVALIER, his political heir. Duvalier died of the effects of a stroke on April 21, 1971.

                                            JOHN E. BAUR

DUVALIER, JEAN-CLAUDE (1951–   ). President of Haiti (1971–   ). The son of François DUVALIER, he gained a reputation as a jazz buff and sportsman. In February 1971, his ailing father achieved a landslide plebiscite that allowed his son to succeed to his life Presidency. Upon the elder Duvalier's death on April 21, 1971, Jean-Claude, not yet twenty, became the youngest Latin American President and the first Haitian to succeed his parent in power, this despite Haiti's three early adventures in monarchy. The succession was also one of the few in Haitian history to be both legal and peaceful. Observers concluded that Duvalier was the necessary symbol for a Duvalierist legend and that he was being advised, if not completely governed, by members of the Council of State, particularly Luckner Cambronne, a product of the first Duvalier regime.

The new administration announced a Five-Year Plan for realistically modest internal improvements and encouraged foreign aid and investment. After a decade of decline, tourism began to increase, and isolation waned. As of 1973, however, the future role of the earnest but as yet unforceful Jean-Claude Duvalier remained unclear.

                                            JOHN E. BAUR

Echandi, Mario

Exploration and Conquest

ECHANDI, MARIO (1915–). President of Costa Rica (1958–1962). Echandi served as Minister to the United States in 1950 and as Foreign Minister in 1951. During the first Presidency of José FIGUERES (1953–1958), he was the outstanding opposition leader in the Legislative Assembly. This position helped gain him influence and standing that led to his electoral victory in 1958 as the presidential candidate of the National Union party, a coalition of conservative groups.

As President, Echandi made no attempt to dismantle the work of Figueres in the nationalization of banks, insurance, and power but concentrated on encouraging trade and industry. However, control of the Legislative Assembly by the opposing PARTIDO LIBERACIÓN NACIONAL blocked much of the government's program, and declining coffee prices from 1958 to 1961 interfered with the President's economic plans. Under Echandi's leadership Costa Rica showed only mild interest in the treaties negotiated by the other Central American nations to establish the CENTRAL AMERICAN COMMON MARKET.

CHARLES L. STANSIFER

ECHEVERRÍA, ESTEBAN (1805–1851). Argentine poet and man of letters. Born in Buenos Aires, Echeverría was one of the foremost figures of the early romantic movement in Spanish America. After abandoning his studies in Argentina at the age of eighteen, he made his way in 1825 to Europe, where he studied for five years in Paris, pursuing his interests in philosophy, political science, and literature, particularly the works of contemporary writers, of whom Lord Byron was his favorite. On his return to Buenos Aires in 1830, the romantic movement exploded with full force, and Echeverría is credited with introducing the ideas of the French romantics whose works he had read while in Paris. Between 1831 and 1837 Echeverría's verses appeared in newspapers and journals, and he published one collection of poems, *Los consuelos* (1834), which received the acclaim of his contemporaries. *Rimas* (1837), another volume of poems, which contains his most famous poem, "La cautiva" ("The captive"), won the praise of many of his associates in the literary-political group ASOCIACIÓN DE MAYO.

Although Echeverría's importance as a poet is undeniable, he is best known today for "El matadero" ("The Slaughterhouse"), written in 1838, a brief narrative work with allegorical overtones in which he attacks the despotic regime of Juan Manuel de ROSAS, the tyrannical *caudillo* of Argentina for twenty-three years (1829–1852). Echeverría skillfully combines subjective emotional sentiment with crude realistic details in a somber picture of life and political persecution under Rosas. Among his other literary works are a poem, *Elvira o La novia del Plata* (1832), and a sociopolitical work, *Dogma socialista* (1846). After participating in an unsuccessful revolt against Rosas in 1839, Echeverría fled to Uruguay, where he died on February 19, 1851.

DANIEL R. REEDY

ECHEVERRÍA [ÁLVAREZ], LUIS (1922–).
President of Mexico (1970–). Echeverría was born
in the Federal District. After graduating from law
school, he launched his political career in 1947, working
with Gen. Rodolfo Sánchez Taboada in the PARTIDO
REVOLUCIONARIO INSTITUCIONAL (PRI) while the
latter was president of the party. He also served in the
Navy Department after Sánchez Taboada was named
Secretary of the Navy. After occupying the position of
First Undersecretary in the Ministry of Education,
Echeverría was named administrative chief of the PRI's
Central Executive Committee in October 1957. He was
Undersecretary in the Ministry of the Interior (Gober-
nación) from December 1958 to November 1963 and
Secretary from November 1963 to November 1969.
When he was nominated as the PRI presidential can-
didate in 1970, he affirmed that the MEXICAN REVOLU-
TION and the constitution of 1917 (*see* CONSTITUTION
OF 1917: MEXICO) did not incline to the right, left, or
center "but onward and upward."

Upon taking office as President on December 1,
1970, Echeverría stated that the revolution had not
been imported and could not be exported. As President
he advocated a nationalistic form of capitalism that
alarmed foreign investors in Mexico. He supported
enactment of a federal AGRARIAN REFORM law designed
to protect the EJIDO, communal property, and the
authentic small landholding. Although he initiated a
"political opening" by freeing numerous political intern-
ees in 1968, he had to contend with a wave of assaults
which he attributed to a conspiracy to disturb the social
peace. On June 10, 1971, a bloody clash occurred in
Mexico City when a leftist student demonstration was
attacked while police stood by; as a result of the disturbance, the mayor of Mexico City (Jefe del Departamento del Distrito Federal) and the police chief were
forced to resign.

Echeverría traveled widely abroad during his administration. In the first months of 1972 he visited Japan
and Chile; in June of that year he went to the United
States, where he requested, with unusual frankness, a
solution to the problem of the salinity of the waters of
the Colorado River. In 1971 he had supported the
admission of the People's Republic of China to the
United Nations in an address before the United Nations
General Assembly, and on February 14, 1972, Mexico
announced that it would establish diplomatic relations
with Peking. In 1973 the President embarked on a
lengthy tour that took him to Canada, England, Belgium,
France, the Soviet Union, and China.

MOISÉS GONZÁLEZ NAVARRO

**ECONOMIC COMMISSION FOR LATIN AMERICA
(COMISIÓN ECONÓMICA PARA AMÉRICA LA-
TINA; ECLA).** Regional commission of the United
Nations. ECLA was created in 1948 and has its permanent Secretariat in Santiago, Chile. Its functions
are to collect and publish data on the economies of
Latin America, to provide technical advice and support
for economic planning by the Latin American states,
and to promote the general economic development of
the region. Under Dr. Raúl PREBISCH, Executive
Secretary of ECLA from 1948 through 1962, the Commission became a dynamic and influential force in the
economic development of Latin America. Its annual

economic surveys of Latin America and its other publications are often provocative and penetrating analyses
of economic problems in Latin America. It has been
at times openly critical of the industrial nations for
their economic relations with the developing nations
and in particular has maintained that the terms of trade
are inherently in favor of the more advanced nations
and against the countries producing primary products.
It has strongly advocated import substitution as a
means to overcome this weakness and became an
important proponent of the ECONOMIC INTEGRATION
of the region. *See also* INDUSTRY (LATIN AMERICA).

RODNEY D. ANDERSON

ECONOMIC INTEGRATION. Although discussions
about unity, usually political unity, and in some instances moves toward it have surfaced in Latin America
ever since independence, it is only since the late 1950s
that substantial, sustained action toward unity—in this
case, economic unity—has become a reality. During
the 1950s and 1960s several efforts at regional economic
integration were initiated: the CENTRAL AMERICAN COM-
MON MARKET (CACM); the LATIN AMERICAN FREE
TRADE ASSOCIATION (LAFTA); the ANDEAN GROUP;
(Grupo Andino); and, granting for the moment that the
British Caribbean is part of Latin America, the Caribbean Free Trade Association. At the PUNTA DEL ESTE
MEETING of Western Hemisphere Presidents in 1967,
the Latin American countries, in the Declaration of
Presidents, committed themselves to create by 1985
a common market that would encompass all Latin
America. Little or nothing has been done to give effect
to that commitment, but the commitment remains.

Economic integration. For the most part, the rationale for economic integration in Latin America was
provided during the late 1940s and 1950s by the Secretariat of the United Nations ECONOMIC COMMISSION
FOR LATIN AMERICA (ECLA). ECLA's position was
and remains that industrialization is the most promising
means for the countries south of the Rio Grande to
employ in order to achieve the level of development
each of them seeks. Industrialization, it was argued,
would increase employment, reduce economic dependence on agriculture, increase governmental revenues,
lessen dependence on the export of primary products,
improve the region's foreign trade position, and set in
motion a general developmental force or momentum.
In turn, according to ECLA, the key to industrialization was economic integration. While the national or
domestic markets of some of the larger countries would
allow them to achieve a reasonably high level of industrialization, the small size of the markets of the bulk
of the Latin American countries would not allow much
industrial development. ECLA saw economic integration—the merger of national markets and the creation of
a single, larger market free or virtually free of all internal trade barriers—as the only device that would allow
Latin America as a whole to achieve a high level of
industrial development. The larger market, it was held,
would enhance the attractiveness of Latin America to
both foreign and domestic industrial investors. Furthermore, it would allow existing industries to expand
and take advantage of economies of scale, thus reducing prices. Price reductions, in turn, by increasing consumption would lead to increased production. The

larger market would make possible the location in Latin America of industries that for economic reasons could not be established at all, or at least not as efficient, reasonable-cost operations in even the larger Latin American countries.

Although the rationale for integration in Latin America is primarily economic, it is not exclusively so. To some extent there is also a political rationale. There is a hope, among some an expectation, that economic unity will enhance Latin America's bargaining position, especially on economic issues, vis-à-vis the more developed, more politically powerful countries. Robert Burr states in *Our Troubled Hemisphere* (Washington, 1967, p. 200): One ". . . objective of economic integration is to provide the basis for political unity that will enable the Latin Americans to deal more effectively with the United States and other great powers."

Despite the logic of integration, it was not immediately accepted by the Latin American governments. It had to be sold to them, and that not very easy task was performed by the personnel of the ECLA Secretariat. In their task the ECLA personnel recruited allies in national governments, and they accepted a subregional approach to integration rather than the regionwide one they preferred; that is, they accepted the idea of several economic groupings or movements toward integration rather than a single one including all the Latin American countries. ECLA's first concrete success came in the late 1950s with the launching of a movement toward economic integration in Central America.

Undoubtedly, some at the national level, especially some politicians, accepted or tolerated integration not because they liked the idea of integration or accepted the rationale for integration, but because they saw it as a possible means of dealing with national economic problems that they could not solve or as a way to transfer from themselves responsibility or blame for these problems and the failure to meet them.

Integration movement at work. Although the several efforts at regional economic integration in Latin America have compiled markedly different records, all have made some progress toward the achievement of the goals they set for themselves. No one factor is responsible for the successes that have been scored, but one appears to have been extremely important. It is the low cost, economic and political, of the various actions that have been taken to promote integration.

A number of economic costs are or may be associated with regional economic integration: the cost of operating integration institutions, revenues lost from eliminating tariffs on intraregional trade, forced adjustments by various sectors of the economy, and capital flow from low-profit to high-profit areas within the integrating region. In the case of the movements toward integration in Latin America, economic costs have been avoided or kept at acceptably low levels. The costs of the integration institutions have been very small. The lifting of intraregional tariffs did not seriously reduce government revenues, in part because intraregional trade before the initiation of the movement toward integration had been low and therefore contributed little to governmental revenues and in part because imports into the integrating areas from nonmembers have increased, more than making up the revenues lost as a result of intraregional free trade.

Relatively few adjustments and almost no hard or difficult adjustments have been required by any sector of the economy. Capital flows from low-profit to high-profit areas have not been experienced, at least not to any notable extent.

While economic costs are visible and important, they are neither the only or necessarily the most important ones. Political costs are at least of equal importance, and a number of major potential political costs may be associated with integration: infringement on sovereignty, loss of control over national economic policy, and adverse effects on key political groups. There is little or no evidence that any of the countries participating in the movements toward integration were prepared to accept much in the way of political costs, which have been kept to a minimum. There have been no infringement on sovereignty, no loss of control over nation economic policy, and no adverse effect on key political groups.

Although achievements have been scored, problems exist. The problems are most notable in LAFTA and CACM, which are the oldest of the movements and therefore the ones that have accumulated most in the way of a record. The problems are of several kinds: in some instances, slowness in meeting treaty obligations; slowness in freeing intraregional trade; tensions of one sort or another among members of the integrative arrangements; some dissatisfaction with the economic yields from integration; and complaints about the distribution of benefits, the less-developed members of the efforts charging that they are contributing more to the development of the other members than integration is contributing to their own development.

The problems can be accounted for in two ways. One explanation, albeit a partial explanation and one that covers only some of the problems, is that the countries engaged in the integration of their economies are engaged in a process unfamiliar to them and that in many instances they have not yet learned how to respond and react to problems, demands, and unanticipated developments. In short, the countries are still feeling their way, still learning. The other explanation, and the one that appears to go further toward accounting for the continued existence of serious problems, has to do with the isolation from politics of the movements toward integration, a factor that facilitated the movements at their outset. Vincent Cable, in assessing the present state of CACM, calls for a turning away from easy, low-cost actions and points to the need for facing difficult political issues squarely. He writes in the *Bank of London and South America Review* (June 1969, p. 346): "The present situation calls for politically difficult decisions: a more resilient and more exigent tax structure; land reform to stimulate local agriculture; greater willingness to sacrifice pet industrial projects so as to allow neighbours to catch up; more will to control the location of new foreign-owned plants; a readiness to tackle balance of payments problems in a deteriorating world market without attacking CACM partners."

Essentially the same assessment—the need for difficult political decisions and high-level political support for integration—applies to LAFTA. To date most Latin American politicians have not made a real commitment to integration. Instead, they have been content to leave integration to others. A very notable exception is Eduardo FREI. While he was President of Chile (1964–1970), he was an ardent champion and supporter of Latin American integration, urging the Latin American countries to move more rapidly and creatively in the integration of their economies.

There is some surface evidence that the Andean Group has learned from CACM and LAFTA experiences and may be avoiding at least some of the errors, shortcomings, and weaknesses of the two longer-established efforts.

However they are accounted for, the movements toward integration are plagued with problems. That does not mean that the movements are on the brink of collapse. Quite the contrary. Although the problems are inhibiting operation and to some extent retarding further development, the movements will in all probability continue to exist for the simple but crucial reason that virtually all the members have at least a minimal commitment to integration, see no alternative to it, and believe that it is impossible for them to go it alone in their quest for development. What was true at the outset of the movement toward integration (a movement that is far from complete) remains true: the individual markets of the Latin American countries are, with only two or three exceptions, too small to allow for any substantial or even moderately substantial level of industrial development.

Limits of economic integration. Although it has sometimes been cast as a total solution to the problem of economic development, economic integration alone does not provide such an answer. There are limits, very great limits, to what regional economic integration can contribute or accomplish. A number of barriers to development, including some of the most serious and difficult to attack, are beyond the scope of integration.

Bibliography. Sidney Dell, *A Latin American Common Market?*, New York, 1961; David Felix, "The Political Economy of Regional Integration in Latin America," *Studies in Comparative International Development,* vol. V, no. 5, 1969–70, pp. 87–102; Ernst B. Haas and Philippe C. Schmitter, "Economics and Differential Patterns of Political Integration: Projections about Unity in Latin America," *International Organization,* vol. XVIII, no. 4, Autumn 1964, pp. 705–737; Walter Krause and F. John Mathis, *Latin America and Economic Integration: Regional Planning for Development,* Iowa City, Iowa, 1970; Gustavo Lagos, "The Movement toward Integration," in Samuel Shapiro (ed.), *Integration of Man and Society in Latin America,* Notre Dame, Ind., 1967, pp. 242–269; Miguel S. Wionczek (ed.), *Latin American Economic Integration: Experience and Prospects,* New York, 1966; id., *Economic Cooperation in Latin America, Africa, and Asia: A Handbook of Documents,* Cambridge, Mass., 1969.   JAMES D. COCHRANE

ECUADOR-PERU CONFLICT. In 1941 Ecuador and Peru went to war over the control of a vast expanse of land in the AMAZON RIVER Basin whose boundaries had been ill defined since colonial days. Other territory on the Pacific coast and in the interior province of Jaén was at stake, but it was control of some 120,000 square miles in the Oriente that was viewed by Ecuador as both a psychological and an economic imperative (*see* ORIENTE: ECUADOR).

As the source of the expedition that had originally discovered the Amazon, Ecuador saw itself as a rightful claimant to a share of the river. In addition, it considered an outlet to the Amazon an economic necessity, for this would give the country access to the Atlantic Ocean. For Peru the issue was equally emotional, especially in view of a defeat by Colombia (1932–1934) over control of Leticia, a town on the Amazon. Peru was not prepared to suffer a second humiliation.

In 1940–1941 clashes erupted between Ecuadorian and Peruvian border patrols, leading in 1941 to open conflict. The war was a short one, lasting until early 1942. First, the Ecuadorian forces were no match for the better-trained and -equipped Peruvian Army and Air Force. Second, with World War II in progress, the United States and the major South American powers desired to end the fratricidal conflict and reestablish hemispheric solidarity. Thus, at the conference of Western Hemisphere foreign ministers held in Rio de Janeiro in January 1942 (*see* RIO DE JANEIRO MEETING), Ecuador was prevailed upon to sign the Rio Protocol. This peace treaty, guaranteed by Argentina, Brazil, Chile, and the United States, gave Peru control of the upper Amazon Basin and cost Ecuador a net total of 5,392 square miles of territory, according to the estimates of its own representative at Rio, Julio Tobar Donoso. Subsequently, an Ecuadorian-Peruvian boundary commission was created to fix the new frontier line between the two countries. This task was made very difficult by the adamant refusal of Ecuador to recognize the protocol. Ecuadorians universally came to feel that they had been shortchanged in 1942, and the regaining of the lost territory became one of the few emotional political issues about which most Ecuadorians could agree.

ORAZIO A. CICCARELLI

ECUADOR SINCE 1830. The Republic of Ecuador, though small in area, is a heterogeneous country, bordered by Colombia to the north and Peru to the south. Three centuries of political, economic, and racial integration within the limits of the district of the *audiencia* of Quito, one of the subdivisions of the Spanish Empire, constituted its formative period. In 1809 the city of Quito was among the first in Spanish America to seek unsuccessfully, through revolution, the loosening of the political bonds subordinating it to Spain. On October 9, 1820, the province of Guayaquil declared its independence, but the Spanish forces in Quito did not surrender until May 24, 1822, after their defeat in the Battle of Pichincha by an allied army under the command of the Venezuelan general Antonio José de SUCRE (*see* PICHINCHA, BATTLE OF).

The immediate result of the Battle of Pichincha was the absorption of the district of Quito and the rest of the territory of what is now Ecuador by the Republic of Colombia, a state created by the Venezuelan liberator Simón BOLÍVAR, which also included present-day Colombia, Panama, and Venezuela (*see* COLOMBIA, GRAN). This political entity disintegrated eight years later, and on May 13, 1830, the independence of Ecuador was proclaimed. The Venezuelan general Juan José FLORES became its first President, and he was to control the destinies of the country until 1845. Flores had the support of the Army, but his political acumen had even more to do with his ability to perpetuate himself in power. His masterstroke came in 1834: the leader of the revolutionaries of the coastal zone, Vicente ROCA-FUERTE, a wealthy and influential oligarch, fell into his hands. Instead of having him shot, Flores made him President and then turned against the revolutionaries of the highlands, whom he utterly defeated in the Battle of Miñarica.

While Flores kept the command of the Army, Rocafuerte undertook to rule the country. He was fifty-one years old at the time, having spent only about twenty of these years in his homeland and having returned only recently after a fifteen-year absence abroad. His lack of understanding of conditions in the country and his vitriolic temper explain the arbitrary nature of his regime.

In 1839 Rocafuerte returned the Presidency to Flores while retaining the important post of Governor of Guayas Province (capital, Guayaquil). Rocafuerte expected to be the general's successor for a second presidential term, but Flores changed both his mind and the constitution in 1843 and had himself reelected for a third period. A revolution instigated by Rocafuerte broke out in Guayaquil in March 1845. The bloody fighting resulted in a stalemate. Unbeaten but unable to reimpose his authority, Flores signed an agreement by which he resigned the Presidency and obliged himself to spend two years abroad, in exchange for a series of guarantees and compensation.

The new regime, known as *marcismo* (for the March rebels), was dominated by the coastal oligarchy, although, with the defeat of Rocafuerte's candidate, José Joaquín de OLMEDO, by Vicente Ramón Roca in the presidential election, it soon broke up into rival factions. Another threat to stability appeared when the government failed to honor the agreement with Flores,

who then sought to invade the country. In 1849 Congress failed to elect a new President after 105 ballots, and Vice President Manuel Ascázubi took over as provisional President. A few months later he was overthrown by Gen. José María URBINA (1850).

Even though Urbina did not claim the Presidency for himself immediately, he dominated Ecuadorian politics during the 1850s. First he accepted as President Diego Noboa (one of the candidates of 1849), only to oust him in 1851. Urbina took over the Presidency himself in 1852 for a term of four years. In 1856 he passed the office to his friend Gen. Francisco Robles. Urbina's positive accomplishments include the abolition of slavery, and he never applied the death sentence for political reasons. On the negative side, his regime was marked by militarism and the injection of the church-state conflict into politics.

General Robles and *urbinismo* were brought down in 1859 by a combination of internal and external problems. The Peruvian President, Gen. Ramón CASTILLA, invaded the country and blockaded the port of Guayaquil. Robles and Urbina moved the government and the Army to that city in order to face the enemy, thus enabling Conservative malcontents in Quito to revolt (*see* CONSERVATIVE PARTY: ECUADOR). Nevertheless, Urbina defeated them, and their leaders fled abroad. One of them, Gabriel GARCÍA MORENO, went to Peru, where he approached General Castilla in search of aid and was rebuffed. In the meantime, Gen. Guillermo Franco overthrew President Robles in Guayaquil and entered into an agreement with Castilla. García Moreno, back in Quito, organized a new revolutionary force, recalled General Flores from exile to head it, and marched on Guayaquil. Flores defeated Franco, Castilla was forced to withdraw, and García Moreno became Ecuador's master for the next decade and a half.

By birth and family the new President belonged to the Guayaquil oligarchy, but he was educated in Quito and married there into the influential Ascázubi family. He thus enjoyed a double base of power. García Moreno had been an admirer of Rocafuerte and an enemy of Flores, but the latter became his most effective ally during the first years of his regime. Insofar as temperament and methods of government were concerned, García Moreno was very much like Rocafuerte, even though there was a striking parallel between the Flores and the García eras. Like the general, García Moreno retired from the Presidency after his first term, while retaining the essence of power; he too returned for a second term and then changed the constitution in order to get reelected for a third period. Shortly before his third inauguration, in 1875, García Moreno was murdered.

The first forty-five years of Ecuador's independent existence can be divided into three periods of equal length. The first period, the Flores regime, was marked by the consolidation of the new republic. The second, the fifteen years of *marcismo* dominated by the figure of Urbina, brought about the "nationalization" of the Army and government. The third, the García Moreno era, was characterized by the subordination of the military to civilian rule and by the integration of the church into the state: both Army and church were used to impose the authority of government. This enabled García Moreno to realize important and lasting public works and to promote education with vigor. Nonethe-

ECUADOR

Area: 109,483 sq. mi.   Population: 6,297,000 (1971 est.).

less, García Moreno had a blundering foreign policy, his violent temper must be blamed for a number of excesses, and his conviction that his compatriots were in need of moral regeneration made the church an instrument of petty oppression. Together with his public works and educational achievements, García Moreno left behind a legacy of bitter and lasting political hatreds.

His successor, Antonio Borrero, was a Moderate Conservative from Cuenca who lacked sufficient political support. General Urbina, after having failed in his attempts to oust García Moreno, reappeared on the scene and helped to overthrow Borrero in 1876. It was Gen. Ignacio VEINTEMILLA who reaped the benefits of this subversion. His dictatorship lasted until 1883, when a coalition of all political and geographic sectors in Ecuador was finally able to expel him from the country.

The next twelve years were marked by relative internal stability and the succession of three Moderates in the Presidency: José María Plácido Caamaño, Antonio Flores (the general's son), and Luis Cordero, from Guayaquil, Quito, and Cuenca respectively. But the hopes for a peaceful evolution of Ecuador were lost after the elections of 1892, in which the Moderate candidate defeated the Conservative Camilo Ponce Ortiz. While the Liberals refused to support the new government (see LIBERAL PARTY: ECUADOR), the Conservatives took up arms against it. After Cordero resigned in 1895, there was a Liberal outbreak in Guayaquil. In need of a leader with military experience, the rebels of the port city called back from exile the Liberal Radical Eloy ALFARO. In a campaign of several months' duration, the Radical caudillo defeated both the government and the Conservative forces and made himself the master of the country.

The political hegemony of the Ecuadorian Liberal Radical party was to last half a century (1895–1944). Within this time span three periods can be distinguished, the first one ending in 1912 and the second in 1925. Their common characteristics were systematized electoral fraud, lack of respect for civil rights, constant military coups, and social, economic, and diplomatic irresponsibility.

The first seventeen years witnessed the introduction of several Liberal reforms, aimed mainly at separating church and state and lessening the power of the church. Catholicism was no longer recognized as the official religion, the vast properties of the regular orders were nationalized, civil marriage and divorce were instituted, and a system of secular education was organized. In addition, the tribute paid by Ecuador's Indians since the sixteenth century was ended by decrees in 1895 and 1898.

This period was dominated by General Alfaro, who was President from 1895 to 1901 and from 1906 to 1911. At the end of his first term his handpicked candidate, Gen. Leonidas PLAZA, was elected. However, before Plaza took possession of the office, the caudillo changed his mind and attempted to convince the President-elect to resign. Plaza refused. Even though his relations with Alfaro became extremely strained, he was able to complete his term and transmit the office to the man of his own choice, Lizardo García. But within a few months Alfaro ousted García to regain the Presidency. Five years later the story repeated itself. Alfaro chose as his successor Emilio Estrada, who was duly elected. He then changed his mind and wanted to impede Estrada's inauguration. But the caudillo lost his grip on his own party and was deposed shortly before the expiration of his term. Estrada was inaugurated as President, only to die a few months later, an event that induced Alfaro to head a new revolt in Guayaquil. The movement failed, and the Radical leader and his principal followers were taken as prisoners to Quito, where they were lynched by a mob.

The elimination of Alfaro paved the way for Leonidas Plaza's second term, which simultaneously inaugurated a thirteen-year period dominated by the bankers and cacao barons of Guayaquil, whose prosperity increased with the opening of the PANAMA CANAL (see CACAO INDUSTRY: ECUADOR). Plaza was followed by Alfredo Baquerizo Moreno (1916–1920), and the latter by José Luis Tamayo (1920–1924). In November 1922, a general strike in Guayaquil was repressed bloodily. As a sequel, Tamayo's successor, President Gonzalo S. Córdova, was overthrown by a movement of young officers with socialist sympathies (July 9, 1925).

During the next fifteen years a decline in cacao production caused by fungus disease was followed by worldwide depression. A worse affliction was the combination of military insubordination, congressional irresponsibility, electoral fraud, socialist agitation, and oligarchical exploitation. A few of the chief executives were honorable and capable men who tried to do their best, but they were not allowed to remain in office. Among these special mention should be made of José María VELASCO IBARRA, who first reached the Presidency on September 1, 1934. He was sensitive to the dignity of his office and of the nation, incorruptible, and dedicated to furthering the interests of Ecuador. On the other hand, the wide backing that the electorate never denied him was not accompanied by sufficient support from influential pressure groups, among them the Army. Unable to resign himself to congressional obstruction, Velasco Ibarra attempted to resort to dictatorship, as in August 1935, a step that led to his overthrow by the military.

After a series of dictatorships and interim regimes, Carlos Alberto ARROYO DEL RÍO reached the Presidency in 1940 by defeating Velasco Ibarra through electoral fraud. He was the last Liberal Radical President. His term marked the low point in Ecuador's international relations. When the country was invaded by Peru in 1941, the Arroyo regime showed itself completely incompetent to deal with the emergency and was finally persuaded by United States diplomacy to submit to the aggressor's territorial demands. See ECUADOR-PERU CONFLICT.

Popular indignation increased until the Arroyo regime was overthrown in May 1944. The next twenty-eight years marked a new period in Ecuador's history, dominated by the personality of Velasco Ibarra, who occupied the Presidency from 1944 to 1947, from 1952 to 1956, from 1960 to 1961, and from 1968 to 1972. The military allowed him to complete only one of his terms, but he exercised a decisive influence throughout the period. It can be said that for those twenty-eight years the political life of Ecuador was geared to Velasco's ideas, statements, acts, and personality. Other constitutional Presidents were Galo PLAZA (1948–1952) and Camilo PONCE (1956–1960).

The era of Velasco Ibarra came to an end on February 15, 1972, through a military coup. Although this event is proof of the persistence of militarism, it is still true that the nearly three decades that preceded it constitute a period of transition from a situation of political, economic, and social irresponsibility within an "invertebrate" nation toward a new Ecuador, characterized by geographic and social integration and economic development. If in the past abundant resources of cacao, coffee, rice, bananas, and other export products allowed the country to overcome political mismanagement, from now on petroleum, natural gas, the fishing industry, a rapidly growing system of highways, and many other assets would furnish the means to achieve a fundamental transformation within the next three decades.

See also BANANA INDUSTRY (ECUADOR).

Bibliography. Gabriel Cevallos García, *Història del Ecuador,* Cuenca, 1964; J. L. R. [José María Le Gouhir Raud], *Historia de la República del Ecuador,* 3 vols., Quito, 1920–1938; José Alfredo Llerena, *Frustración política en veintidós años,* Quito, 1959; Oscar Efrén Reyes, *Los últimos siete años,* Quito, 1933; id., *Breve historia del Ecuador,* 2 vols., Quito, 1950; Luis Robalino Dávila, *Orígenes del Ecuador de hoy,* Quito, 1948–69; id., *Testimonio de los tiempos,* Quito, 1971; Ádám Szászdi, "The Historiography of the Republic of Ecuador," *Hispanic American Historical Review,* vol. XLIV, no. 4, November 1964, pp. 503–550.

ÁDÁM SZÁSZDI

EDUCATION (PRIMARY AND SECONDARY). Two major facts dominate the educational scene in Latin America: the demographic explosion (*see* POPULATION) and the rising expectations of the great masses of people for a better life. These expectations include a demand for wider and more democratic access to education, which is viewed as a means of attaining greater social, economic, and political satisfactions. The Latin American members of the ORGANIZATION OF AMERICAN STATES differ greatly in levels of economic development, forms of government, and ethnic heritage, all factors that influence primary and secondary education. They are similar, however, in the extraordinary proportion of their increasing populations in the school age group and in a lack of financial resources adequate to meet the problem of supplying educational opportunity.

The rate of population growth in recent years has approximated 3 percent annually. From a total population in 1965 of about 236 million, it is estimated that the population will reach 364 million in 1980. Because the school age group grows very rapidly, the central problem for the national governments is the high percentage of the population that is of school age in comparison with the percentage in the work force. In Venezuela, for example, 56.3 percent of the total population is less than twenty years of age. The problem is compounded by the relatively low educational qualifications of the work force and the consequent low productivity. The United Nations ECONOMIC COMMISSION FOR LATIN AMERICA estimates that even by 1980 three-fourths of the work force will have no more than a primary education. Of this three-fourths, probably one-third will have fewer than three years of elementary schooling and will be virtually illiterate.

In the general drive for development that exists in most of the countries, there is almost always a recognition of the crucial role of education in economic and social progress. Most of the countries have been characterized by rigid and inflexible social class divisions, but since World War II education has been widely recognized as a necessary condition for upward mobility. However, the variations among the countries are great. The CUBAN REVOLUTION, for example, resulted in the loss of a great part of the educated upper classes but in a successful mass movement for literacy. In stable and conservative Costa Rica, at another extreme, education is the highest priority of government, and education at all levels has developed rapidly. Countries with large Indian populations, such as Peru and Guatemala, confront the most difficult problems of education, and it is doubtful that solutions are in sight.

Legal and constitutional provisions for education: goals and administration. All Latin American national constitutions include provisions for education, usually stating the goals as the integrated development of the moral, civic, intellectual, and vocational capacities of the individual. Primary education is declared to be obligatory. The responsibility for the development of elementary and secondary education is placed in the Ministry of Education. In most countries higher education is stated to be autonomous and hence largely independent of the Ministry. Many constitutions provide excessively detailed statements of the structure and operating procedures for elementary and secondary education, and most countries also have a codified set of detailed statutes for the operation of the educational system, although some still have an unorganized maze of statutes and decrees, occasionally even contradictory.

Two aspects of the administration of education are noteworthy. First, in some countries the constitutional and legal provisions for elementary and secondary education may be considered more as national goals for education than as a legal description of the reality. In Guatemala, for example, the constitution makes primary school attendance obligatory, but educational statistics indicate that less than half of the primary school age group is in fact in attendance.

A second aspect of educational administration is the extreme centralization of the responsibility for elementary and secondary education in the national government and in the Ministry of Education. The power of the Ministry in many countries is concentrated in the person of the Minister of Education. Even in countries such as Costa Rica where legal responsibility for education is placed in the hands of a Council over which the Minister presides and where the Minister himself tries to delegate and to decentralize, in fact the Minister remains the point of decision for the infinite details of the national system of education. The exception is Uruguay, where elementary and secondary education are controlled by councils whose policy is carried out by the Ministry.

Preprimary and primary education. Preprimary education is considered a part of the educational structure in most countries, but it is optional rather than required. Most kindergartens are located in urban rather than rural areas, and most are private rather than public. There are few formal requirements for curriculum or the qualifications of teachers.

The provision of primary education requires a major

effort in every country. Usually the Ministry of Education includes an office for primary education that has the financial, organizational, curricular, and staffing responsibilities for all public primary education. In most countries there are private primary schools, but the percentage of the age group served by private primary schools is much smaller than at the secondary level.

The primary school program is usually six years long. One of the great problems in many countries, especially in the rural areas, is that many schools do not offer the full six-year program but only the first two or three years. To complete primary school in these areas a student must move to another rural area or to a city. The consequence is that only a small proportion of children complete primary education in many rural areas and in many countries. Moreover, students who attend primary school for only two or three years may lapse into functional illiteracy soon thereafter.

The curriculum of the primary school regularly consists of a large number of subjects each year, often as many as eight or ten. Although lip service is usually given to the provision of differentiated programs for rural and urban areas, the fact is that in many countries the program is uniform for all and is oriented primarily toward the city. The problems are particularly great in countries such as Guatemala and Peru in which there are large indigenous populations for whom Spanish is often a second language. The efforts toward radical solutions of these problems of the Indian peoples that are being carried out in Peru under the comprehensive educational reforms of 1972 are especially noteworthy. The provision of some bilingual primary education is a key aspect of the new program.

Primary school teachers in most but not all countries are trained in normal schools at the secondary school level. In some countries primary school teachers may attend schools of education or humanities in the universities, but this pattern is not usual. Salaries for primary teachers are low, in most countries below the average income, for example, of taxicab drivers. Most primary teachers are women. A major problem of primary education, as in every other field in which educated persons are involved, is the unwillingness of teachers to go to the rural areas. Part of the Iberian and colonial heritage, the concentration of both power and amenities in the metropolis is a powerful magnet for schoolteachers. Even in countries like Costa Rica in which salary bonuses and special retirement privileges are offered for service in rural schools, the problem remains a major one.

In most countries inadequate finances require excessively large primary classes. In Mexico, for example, even in cities classes in the elementary schools often consist of sixty to seventy students. A major problem in almost all countries is the high rate of student attrition in the system and the low production of primary school graduates. The reasons for this inefficient performance are easy to identify: the irrelevance of some of the curriculum to the very diverse needs of the students, the economic problems of the students, the lack of effective teaching and counseling, and perhaps the traditional acceptance of a high failure rate even in the elementary years. The concept of automatic promotion is spreading in Latin America, but it is still very much a minority view.

Secondary education. The patterns of secondary education in Latin America are more diverse than those of primary education. In general and in most countries, the pattern is that of two cycles, a first cycle of general education of three years and a second cycle of specialized education of two or three years. After the three years of general education a student may go into an academic program leading to the *bachillerato,* a diploma usually required for entrance to the university; this program often requires a choice in emphasis between the humanities and the sciences and leads to a humanistic or scientific program in the university. Parallel programs to the academic ones usually exist for primary school teachers, bookkeepers and secretaries, and various types of technicians.

Major variations from these programs are found in some countries. In Mexico, for example, the three years of general education are followed by a two- or three-year academic program in a *preparatoria,* a school that usually has close academic and administrative ties to an institution of higher education rather than being directly under the Ministry of Education. The Peruvian reform of the early seventies refers to the second cycle of secondary education as the first level of higher education even though it is still under the direction of the Ministry of Education. This program combines general education and vocational studies and leads to a *bachillerato profesional.* It is required for admission to a Peruvian university, but the university program has no necessary relation to the vocational program followed earlier.

Like the primary curriculum, the program of secondary education includes a large number of subjects. The method of teaching is still likely to emphasize memorization rather than problem solving, although there is widespread recognition of the weakness of this method. In contrast to the primary school, in which the teacher is likely to be full-time, the secondary school teacher is probably part-time and may well teach in a number of schools and also practice a profession. Many secondary teachers are professional men and university graduates who teach part-time. In most Latin American countries perhaps the greatest single weakness of secondary education is the absence of adequate numbers of qualified teachers, that is, teachers with special preparation in the subject they teach as well as with some training in pedagogy. There is still uncertainty in many countries as to what the education of a secondary teacher should be and especially as to what role the university should play in the preparation of secondary teachers.

Like the population of the primary schools, that of secondary education constantly increases despite the very high attrition rate. The causes of this high rate of desertion are similar to those in other segments of Latin American education: economic problems of the student, irrelevant programs, poor teaching, and the long tradition of acceptance of a high rate of academic failure.

Technical education. The emphasis on economic development in Latin America has led to a widespread concern over the shortage of qualified workers, especially in the various categories of technicians. There has been a rapid growth in the numbers of technical schools and in their enrollments, although the growth is perhaps small in relation to the needs. Technical education has been held back by its high cost and by a shortage of well-prepared vocational teachers, as well as by the Latin American distaste for manual labor and the widespread preference of students for academic programs and entry into the traditional professions of law, medicine, and engineering.

Current problems. There is general agreement among leaders in Latin American education concerning the problems and needs of elementary and secondary education. The problems of immense population growth and of demands for access to education require massive and sophisticated educational planning, especially since there is a great shortage of financial resources. The unsettled conditions of government in many countries handicap this effort. Regional and international cooperation and heavy financial aid are required. Some countries spend as much as 30 percent of their national budgets on education even in the face of competing needs for essential institutions of health and economic development. The excessive centralization of educational administration, the lack of decentralization and of diversification of programs, the rigidity of traditional practices of teaching, grading, and personnel management, the weakness of student counseling, and the lack of adequately prepared secondary teachers are widely recognized.

There is some pessimism in the face of these enormous problems, but on the whole the educational system appears to gain rather than lose ground in most countries. Education cannot make a maximum development in the unstable political and economic circumstances endemic in much of Latin America, and progress is slow. In the decades since World War II elementary and secondary education in most countries has made important progress both quantitatively and qualitatively.

Bibliography. Comisión de Reforma de la Educación, *Reforma de la educación peruana: Informe general,* Lima, 1970; Inter-American Development Bank, *Socio-economic Progress in Latin America,* Annual Report, 1971, Washington, 1972; Rodolfo Low-Maus, *Compendium of the Colombian Educational System,* Bogotá, 1971; Pan American Union, *América en cifras 1967. Situación cultural: Educación y otros aspectos culturales,* Washington, 1969; United Nations Economic Commission for Latin America, *Educación, recursos humanos y desarrollo en América Latina,* New York, 1968; George R. Waggoner and Barbara A. Waggoner, *Education in Central America,* Lawrence, Kans., 1971.

GEORGE R. WAGGONER AND BARBARA A. WAGGONER

EDUCATION (UNIVERSITY). Seniority among Spanish American universities belongs to Santo Tomás de Aquino, founded by papal bull in Santo Domingo (Hispaniola) in 1538. In 1551 the two most eminent of the colonial universities, Mexico and Lima, were created in the viceregal capitals under royal and pontifical auspices. Like those founded subsequently, they patterned their studies and corporate organization after the Spanish Universities of Salamanca and Alcalá de Henares. The religious orders—the Dominicans preeminently in the sixteenth century and the Jesuits by the seventeenth—were instrumental in almost all foundations (*see* RELIGIOUS ORDERS: COLONIAL PERIOD), but in many cases ecclesiastical control had lapsed by the end of the colonial regime. By the outbreak of the wars of independence early in the nineteenth century, Spanish America possessed more than twenty institutions granting academic degrees beyond the bachelor's degree. They were located in eighteen cities and towns, including Bogotá (founded 1563), Quito (by 1603), Córdoba (1613), Chuquisaca (modern Sucre, 1624), Guatemala City (1676), Havana (1721), and Caracas (1721). Brazil at this time had no comparable institution of higher learning.

Studies were organized under the three professional faculties of theology, law, and medicine; a fourth, arts, was often incorporated within a *colegio,* either attached to the university or independent. Some scholarly controversy surrounds the content and quality of the instruction offered. In general, however, neither medicine nor the natural sciences flourished under the Hispanic aegis; except for the study of Amerindian languages, much of the remaining academic work was rote and uninspired. Racial criteria for admission to degrees, such as insistence upon *limpieza de sangre* (purity of the blood), though not always enforced, made the universities generally the preserve of the sons of the creole elite.

Through the nineteenth century, following independence, new universities were founded at a more rapid pace than before, and the old ones were modified. Almost without exception, the rationalistic and anticlerical ideologies of new national leaders caused the universities to be placed ever more firmly under civil control. The apparent need for technical expertise brought about an increase in the number of professional faculties, now on the Napoleonic model; among them, however, law and medicine remained the most prestigious. Several national universities, including Buenos Aires (1821), Montevideo (1833), Santiago de Chile (1842), and those of El Salvador, Costa Rica, and Honduras, date from the postrevolutionary period. Despite the dedicated work of peripatetic European and Latin American scholars, few Spanish American universities could flourish intellectually amid the political turbulence, meager public revenues, and subsistence or export-oriented economies (with their rudimentary occupational requirements) that characterized the emerging republics. As under the colony, little research was undertaken, memorization and verbalization were the essence of study, and family and political ties bulked large in the selection of professorial cadres. In this period isolated faculties of law, medicine, and engineering were created in several Brazilian cities, but they were not grouped into universities until the present century: for example, Rio de Janeiro (1920), Minas Gerais (1927), and São Paulo (1934).

In the first two decades of the twentieth century the dizzying economic growth of Argentina and Uruguay engendered the rapid expansion of new urban middle-class groups. They sought through political mobilization to break the hegemony of traditional landowning strata and through higher education to enhance upward social mobility. The conjunction of political and social forces generated in its turn the University Reform movement, which was to have long-lived reverberations throughout the area. Antecedents can be found at the Universities of Montevideo and Buenos Aires, but the reform as such is commonly associated with the student uprising, initially in reaction to an unpopular proclerical rector, at the University of Córdoba in 1918.

The full program of the Córdoba students could be divided into three components: (1) The university's internal structure was to be reformed so as to afford students participation in self-governance and to make merit the prime criterion for professorial and administrative appointments. These measures, it was assumed, would ensure higher quality and greater flexibility of instruction. (2) The "social" university, which would abandon the "ivory tower" mentality of its predecessors to assume responsibility for monitoring and guiding national development, was to be created. This aim was to be met in a variety of ways, including facilitating university entrance to hitherto-disadvantaged social classes, taking instruction to the common people (the "popular university" programs, later of some significance in Peru and Cuba), carrying out research into national social problems, and insisting that the university take stands on contemporary public issues. (3) A pan-Latin American student movement was begun. Its loose ideology acquired elements of both *arielismo* and Marxism; it became anti-imperialist, antimilitarist, and, commonly, anti-United States.

The Argentine students gained many of their pragmatic objectives in the University Statute of 1919. As hoped, moreover, the reform took on Latin American dimensions with startling rapidity. As early as 1921 an international student congress was held in Mexico City. During the 1920s reformist groups were active in Montevideo, Lima, Mexico City, Havana, and Asunción and in the Chilean, Bolivian, and Brazilian universities. In nations that did not enjoy Argentina's parliamentary democracy (itself ended by military coup in 1930), attempts to implement elements of the reform led inevitably to conflict and repression, as in the Venezuela of Juan Vicente GÓMEZ (1928) and the Cuba of Gerardo MACHADO (1930–1933). Similar repression in Peru led directly to the founding, by exiles under Víctor Raúl HAYA DE LA TORRE, of the ALIANZA POPULAR REVOLUCIONARIA AMERICANA (APRA) in 1924. Indirectly, numerous Latin American political leaders, including Presidents Rómulo BETANCOURT and Raúl LEONI of Venezuela and Premier Fidel CASTRO of Cuba, received their basic schooling in practical politics as activists in university parties or movements.

Widespread politicization has continued to characterize university life since World War II. Boycotts, strikes, public demonstrations, and confrontations with police have been endemic and have led to prolonged disruption or closure of entire faculties. The causes of the disturbances have ranged from increased fares on public transportation to attempts to impose entrance examinations and "weeding out" procedures, the creation of private Catholic universities, and "imbalanced" public expenditures (for example, on the military or, in Mexico City in 1968, on the Olympic Games). Universities formed centers of resistance to the dictatorships of Juan D. PERÓN and Fulgencio BATISTA, and student groups were prominent in the coalitions that overthrew them (in 1955 and 1958, respectively). However, since the mid-1960s a number of Latin American governments, including Mexico, Venezuela, and the military regimes of Argentina and Brazil, have withdrawn the tacit or legal immunities of the universities; much of their prized "autonomy" has been curtailed.

Official (and, it would appear, unofficial) disenchantment had been anticipated by serious analysts, who well before this had begun to draw largely negative conclusions from nearly half a century of the University Reform. The academic standing of the "reformed" universities showed, on balance, relatively little change (although, as John P. Harrison has suggested, the same could be said of the "unreformed" ones). The expectation that the reform would serve as the vehicle of political and moral regeneration has been frustrated by a number of factors. The upper- and middle-status backgrounds of most students and the transience of the university experience itself have diluted the carry-over into adult life of student political and social attitudes. Within the university the factional spectrum of national political life is reproduced; the maneuvering is equally intense, time-consuming, of dubious purpose, and ultimately disillusioning. Ties between student political groups and national parties range from resented subservience (as with APRA in Peru and ACCIÓN DEMOCRÁTICA in Venezuela) to great discontinuity; few examples of a working modus vivendi are to be found. Similarly, alliances between students and ORGANIZED LABOR have been few and fleeting, a condition that the students' assumed role of intellectual and moral mentors has undoubtedly done much to bring about. As an interest group in national politics, the university, with its transient membership, slender financial resources, and nonstrategic position in the economy, is at a great disadvantage vis-à-vis the military, the church, business groups, and organized labor.

Student politics today are therefore polarized: the extremism of the very few and the apathy, cynicism, and confusion of the very many. But it is also clear that politicization is and has been more a symptom than a cause of deep crisis. The most elementary dimension of the crisis is the pressure of numbers on facilities and available funds. By 1968, according to the ECONOMIC COMMISSION FOR LATIN AMERICA, there were about 200 institutions of higher education in the region. More than half had been founded since World War II; of these, a significant proportion were begun under church or other private auspices. In 1950, 28,000 persons held university appointments; in 1968, 147,000. In the same period, however, the student population grew from 279,000 to 1,253,000. Although in 1968 the percentage of university students of the total student population, 2.4 percent, was still less than half the world figure of 5 percent, in the latter half of the 1960s the average annual increase was 12 percent, against the world average of 8.7 percent. Projections for the quinquennium 1970–1975 for the growth of the age group from fifteen to twenty-four were above 3 percent; thus no slackening of demand was likely. To be sure, immense variations exist among the Latin American nations, ranging in 1968 from 34 university students per 100,000 inhabitants in Haiti and 143 per 100,000 in Honduras to 1,123 per 100,000 in Argentina (the United States figure is 3,735 per 100,000). Similarly, Argentina has the highest ratio of university graduates to population, 78 to 100,000 (the ratio is 515 to 100,000 in the United States).

The problem of "wastage," or the dropout rate, is even more worrisome. It manifests itself, of course, throughout the educational systems from primary through university levels. It was calculated in 1963 that of 1,000 Latin American children beginning primary school, 30 would finish secondary school and only

1 would complete six years at a university. Variations must again be noted: the ratio rose as high as 7 to 1,000 in Argentina and Uruguay. In the years 1953–1959 almost 100,000 students were enrolled at the University of Buenos Aires; in the same period, more than 47,000 students withdrew. A total of 18,366 degrees were awarded; that is, there was a ratio of 2.5 *abandonos* (dropouts) to 1 graduate. The magnitude of personal frustration as well as the profitless expenditure of public funds cannot fail to be of concern.

It is apparent that in recent decades the Latin American universities have ceased to be status-confirming elitist strongholds. Their new functions, however, remain in great dispute and confusion. The traditional attraction of the faculties of law and medicine has come under criticism, and although their enrollments have not declined, they have begun to lose ground relatively to the social and natural sciences, engineering specialties, and, to some extent, agriculture. Many recommendations for reform, tending toward modernization on the North American model, have been made by UNESCO and the Council on Higher Education in the American Republics (CHEAR): increased library and laboratory resources, increased basic research, the elimination of part-time faculty and students, the shortening of professional courses and the introduction of new technical programs, entrance examinations and compulsory introductory study prior to admission to professional faculties, full-time administrative staff, and a diminution of faculty and university autonomy. Many such reforms have been implemented in the private universities and at such public institutions as Concepción in Chile, San Marcos in Lima, and the University of Costa Rica. Elsewhere, however, "North Americanization" has encountered resistance on cultural grounds. Moreover, the emigration in recent years of university-trained professionals (the brain drain) suggests that the expansion of Latin American higher education has not been accompanied by an expansion of occupational opportunities and an increase of social mobility dependent upon merit. Although it will not be possible to assess fully the educational reforms of the CUBAN REVOLUTION for some time, it should be noted in passing that the university student population in Cuba remained constant through the 1960s but that the allocation of students to programs of study was drastically altered by authoritarian means. As Alistair Hennessey remarks (*see* Bibliography), ". . . the Cuban assertion that university reform is impossible without a total social and political revolution has yet to be proved wrong."

Bibliography. H. R. W. Benjamin, *Higher Education in the American Republics,* New York, 1965; J. P. Harrison, "The Confrontation with the Political University," *Annals,* American Academy of Political and Social Science, 1961; Alistair Hennessey, "University Students in National Politics," in C. Véliz (ed.), *The Politics of Conformity in Latin America,* London, 1967; J. T. Lanning, *Academic Culture in the Spanish Colonies,* New York, 1940; United Nations, Economic Commission for Latin America, *Human Resources and Development in Latin America,* New York, 1968.

RONALD C. NEWTON

EISENHOWER-REMÓN TREATY. A second major alteration of the HAY–BUNAU-VARILLA TREATY of 1903 (the first occurred in 1936 in the HULL-ALFARO TREA-TY), this accord with Panama, signed on January 25, 1955, committed the United States to increase its PANAMA CANAL payments from $430,000 to $1,930,000 annually. The treaty also permitted Panama to tax the income of persons working in the Canal Zone, with the exception of United States citizens and armed forces personnel; provided for the transfer to Panama of lands as they were no longer required by the United States; called for the United States to surrender the privilege of requiring compliance with sanitation regulations in Colón and Panama City; changed the boundary between the Canal Zone and Colón; ended commissary privileges of Canal Zone employees who were not United States citizens and did not live in the zone; caused the United States to surrender its exclusive right to railroad building in the zone, although the existing PANAMA RAILROAD was not to be affected; authorized Panama to tax certain products going into the zone; and increased Panama's share in supplying the zone market. In exchange for these concessions Panama agreed to a renewable lease of fifteen years of about 19,000 acres near Río Hato for United States military maneuvers and training. Attached to the treaty was a Memorandum of Understandings Reached, which promised that an effort would be made to seek legislation in the United States Congress to equalize wage scales for all employees without respect to citizenship and to provide for equality of employment opportunities. Delays by the United States Congress in carrying out provisions of the treaty and increasing resentment of the United States in the zone, along with student riots and a break in diplomatic relations, resulted in new treaty proposals, which were still pending early in 1974.

RICHARD B. GRAY

EJIDO. In Mexico, a landholding community or the land owned collectively by the members of such a community. In the strict meaning of the term, *ejido* refers to only one type of communal property, lands situated at the exit of a town that were devoted to livestock. The confusion between *ejido* in this sense and lands distributed among members of a community probably arose from a bill presented in the Mexican Congress by Luis Cabrera on December 3, 1912. Cabrera asked that the restitution and grant of *ejidos* to the towns be declared a measure of public utility. The civil war prevented the approval of this proposal. It was not put into effect until Venustiano CARRANZA, while he was bottled up in the port of Veracruz, promulgated the law of January 6, 1915, as an opportunist measure in order to seize the agrarian banner from his rivals, Francisco VILLA and Emiliano ZAPATA. The law, which was Cabrera's handiwork, reflects the ideas of Andrés MOLINA ENRÍQUEZ: since the Indians, because of their lack of evolutionary development, had not adapted themselves to the concept of private property, their right to communal property ought to be recognized. Having been despoiled of their communal holdings by the Amortization Law of 1856 and the public land policy of the regime of Porfirio DÍAZ, they had been forced to become wage laborers on the haciendas. Both for reasons of justice and for the maintenance of peace, their lands should be restored. When it was not possible to prove that the Indians had been despoiled of their holdings, they were to be granted lands in fee simple, but an effort would be made to keep the lands from falling into the hands of speculators, as had occurred after 1856.

The law of 1915, which was incorporated into the 1917 constitution (*see* CONSTITUTION OF 1917: MEXICO), provided for the restoration to the villages of lands of which they had been illegally deprived after 1856; other communities might receive land through the expropriation of private holdings by the government. This law formed the basis of Mexico's AGRARIAN REFORM, which got under way on a large scale after 1920 and reached its apogee during the administration of Lázaro CÁRDENAS (1934–1940). Communities that petitioned for and received land might cultivate it collectively or in individual plots, the latter being the alternative chosen most frequently. The *ejidatario,* or member of an *ejido,* might not ordinarily sell, mortgage, or alienate his land in any way; if he failed to cultivate his parcel satisfactorily or died without heirs, it was to revert to the community. The agrarian code of 1934 set the minimum size of individual parcels at 4 hectares (9.9 acres) of irrigated land or 8 hectares (19.8 acres) of seasonal land; the size of the minimum individual plot was increased to 10 hectares (24.7 acres) in 1947. However, allotments were often smaller than the minimum because of a scarcity of land, and individual holdings have been further reduced by subsequent fragmentation.

MOISÉS GONZÁLEZ NAVARRO

ÉLITE. Politically, economically, and culturally dominant upper class of Haiti. This group evolved from the French colonial freedmen of mulatto and Negro origin who were educated and prospering before the French Revolution. Experts cite the following as characteristic of the élite: freedom from manual labor; monopolization of professions and of all but rudimentary education; ability to speak and write French; adherence to Catholicism rather than VODUN; usually a light complexion; a heavier, taller build than that of peasants, because of better nutrition; traditional etiquette; good dress; urban residence; a proud genealogy; and high regard for French culture but contempt for most foreign ways. Élite women, unlike the economically indispensable peasant women, customarily have not entered business.

Numbering about 5 percent of the population, the élite has usually dominated government, especially in the south, ridiculed Haiti's African heritage, and justified its rule by its superior education and wealth. Despite tendencies toward "pigmentocracy," the élite has recruited outstanding blacks who share its philosophy. Although condemning trade as materialistic, the élite struggles to improve standards, unlike the socially static peasantry.

This extralegal caste crystallized during the mulatto ascendancy of Alexandre Sabès PÉTION and Jean-Pierre BOYER. François DUVALIER's appeal to the Negro majority against it wrought some change, creating a new élite of politics and economics rather than of culture and tradition.

JOHN E. BAUR

EL SALVADOR SINCE 1823. El Salvador is the smallest and most densely populated of the Spanish American countries and the only Central American state without a Caribbean littoral. Its population, estimated at 3,390,-000 in 1969, is largely mestizo, with perhaps 10 percent of persons of pure European descent and 5 percent of native Indians. Its limited area, poverty of natural resources, and situation as a geographical link between Nicaragua, Honduras, and Guatemala have had an important bearing on its national development.

At Central American independence El Salvador had long been politically, economically, and ecclesiastically dependent on Guatemala, and resentment of this tributary status was becoming overt. The question of an independent bishopric for El Salvador, for example, strongly influenced that province's participation in the events of the independence period, but the insistence with which José Matías Delgado, aided by his nephew Manuel José ARCE and others, sought the position for himself makes it difficult to discern whether patriotism, regionalism, or personal ambition was the principal motivation.

El Salvador was a Liberal stronghold and chief sustainer of the Federation of Central America among the states (*see* CENTRAL AMERICA, FEDERATION OF). Fear of the extension of Guatemalan hegemony and frustration over the bishopric question helped determine this political stance. El Salvador contributed a number of the prominent Liberal leaders of the independence epoch, including Arce and Delgado. Dissident Liberals gathered in El Salvador after the breach with Arce in 1826, and there Francisco MORAZÁN organized them for the conquest of Guatemala in 1829. San Salvador became the federal capital in 1834 in an attempt to ease friction within the Federation, and the state provided the loyal base from which Morazán made his final efforts in 1840 to hold together the disintegrating union. El Salvador's role made it a battleground between Liberal and Conservative partisans from within, as well as from neighboring states, during the life of the Federation and after.

After the demise of the Federation, El Salvador was exposed to the full play of isthmian politics. The middle states of Central America—El Salvador, Honduras, and Nicaragua—several times attempted to reconstitute a union, habitually meddled in each other's affairs, and not infrequently shared responsibility for coups attempted against each other or against Guatemala. José Rafael CARRERA, the Conservative dictator of Guatemala for a quarter of a century after 1840, reciprocated the attentions paid him by intervening to support ideologically compatible regimes in neighboring countries. El Salvador was the focal point of much of this rivalry.

EL SALVADOR

Area: 8,260 sq. mi.   Population: 3,549,260 (1971).

The frequent changes of executives and constitutions resulted from outside pressures as well as from internal trends.

From 1840 to 1845 El Salvador suffered the machinations of the *comandante de armas,* Francisco Malespín, a friend of Carrera. Liberals drove Malespín from power in 1845, and Liberal and moderate regimes filled the next five years. When Doroteo Vasconcelos joined Honduras in an abortive attack on Carrera's Guatemala in 1851, he was removed from office and Francisco Dueñas began a series of two-year Presidencies that continued until 1860. Then Gerardo BARRIOS, the last of the *morazanista* Liberals, seized power, had the presidential term extended to six years, and had himself elected President.

Barrios attempted a regime in the style of his late mentor. He decreed law codes, feuded with the clergy, promoted the cultivation of coffee, and projected a plan for union among the middle Central American states. He incurred the displeasure of Carrera, who brought about his overthrow, and Francisco Dueñas, whom he had recently exiled, succeeded him. When Dueñas got him in his power in 1865, he executed him.

Dueñas returned El Salvador to Conservative government. The new constitution adopted in 1864 was the first to claim status as an independent republic. During the early months of 1871 Dueñas was overthrown by a Liberal, Santiago González, who assisted successful Liberal revolutions against Carrera-installed regimes in Honduras and Guatemala. Andrés Valle succeeded González, but Justo Rufino BARRIOS of Guatemala deposed him and installed his friend Rafael Zaldívar. When Barrios prepared to unify Central America by conquest, however, Zaldívar challenged him at Chalchuapa, where Barrios lost his life. Zaldívar was forced out of office; Francisco Menéndez succeeded him and was elected President for the period 1887–1891, but his term was cut short by Carlos Ezeta in 1890.

The Ezeta brothers tyrannized over the country until 1894, when a revolution brought Rafael Antonio Gutiérrez to power. In 1898 Gutiérrez in turn was overthrown by Tomás REGALADO, who allowed the election of Pedro José Escalón in 1903. Fernando Figueroa served a term (1907–1911), but Manuel Enrique Araújo (1911–1913) was assassinated and was succeeded by Carlos Meléndez (1913–1919); then successive elections gave terms to the latter's brother, Jorge Meléndez (1919–1923), his brother-in-law, Alfonso Quiñones Molina (1923–1927), and, finally, Pío Romero Bosque (1927–1931). Romero Bosque departed from custom by holding a genuine election. As none of the numerous candidates received a majority, the legislature elected Arturo Araújo, who was ousted by an uprising in December 1931, and Maximiliano HERNÁNDEZ MARTÍNEZ succeeded to the office.

Presidential succession gradually became more orderly after 1871, but changes of administration did not imply altered policy. All executives tended to represent the same interests whether they seized power or were chosen by the process called election. In the early part of the twentieth century each incumbent chose his successor from among his friends or relatives and, like the authors of coups, submitted his choice for a perfunctory affirmative vote.

Conditions in El Salvador before 1871 afforded little opportunity for development. Longer periods of calm and expanding cultivation of coffee after 1871 reversed the trend. The country began to prosper. The modern character of El Salvador was formed during these years. The working alliance between the planter elite and the military was forged and remained a fixture. The wealthy landowning class early recognized the opportunity afforded by coffee culture and began converting their extensive holdings into coffee *fincas* (plantations). Smaller operators followed their example, but the major profits went to the wealthy. The gulf between poor and rich widened.

The planter elite was enlightened enough to recognize that to maintain growth the country had to modernize. Cart roads were opened during the latter half of the nineteenth century; all-weather roads, during the early twentieth century. The first railroad began operation in the early 1880s; a line connected the port of Acajutla with Santa Ana and San Salvador by 1900; and another was completed in 1929 from the port of La Unión to San Miguel, San Salvador, and Zacapa and Puerto Barrios in Guatemala.

From 1931 to 1944 Hernández Martínez ran a repressive military dictatorship, the rigors of which were intensified by the effects of the Depression and the dislocations attendant on World War II. A general strike drove him from office in 1944, but Salvador Castañeda Castro, who succeeded him in 1945, was scarcely better. He was ousted by a military junta in December 1948.

Maj. Oscar OSORIO emerged as the leading figure of the junta and was elected to the Presidency under the banner of the new PARTIDO REVOLUCIONARIO DE UNIFICACIÓN DEMOCRÁTICA (PRUD). PRUD controlled elections, monopolized the legislature, and elected Osorio's successor, Lieut. Col. José María LEMUS. An unresponsive political system and lagging socioeconomic reform produced an insurrection that brought Lemus down in October 1960. After interim government by two juntas, Col. Julio Adalberto RIVERA, the candidate of the National Conciliation party (PCN), was elected for a five-year term in 1962. He was followed in 1967 by Col. Fidel SÁNCHEZ HERNÁNDEZ and in 1972 by Col. Arturo Armando MOLINA, both of the same party.

The regimes from 1944 on were of essentially the same type. They were headed by military officers of reformist bent allied with the planter elite. They exacted consent to moderate reform measures from the economic elite by playing on its fear of the Communist alternative. In compensation, the reformers avoided such drastic measures as land redistribution and major improvements in working conditions for urban labor that would profoundly affect established interests.

These regimes accomplished significant economic development. They built important public works, constructed low-cost urban housing units, gave labor the right to organize and regulated the working conditions and pay scales of both urban and rural workers, instituted social security, stimulated the establishment of new industries, and promoted the CENTRAL AMERICAN COMMON MARKET to broaden economic opportunity.

These measures opened opportunities that the economic elite were quick to recognize, and they were not without benefit to the poor. But in relation to numbers, and especially to expectation, the benefits were too few, and they came too slowly. The rate of growth under this arrangement did not keep pace with the population increase. Urban dwellers fared better than rural residents, but on the average the quality of life deteriorated. In desperation, and beginning under the Rivera administration with the encouragement of the government, Salvadorans emigrated, some 300,000 of them by a 1969 estimate to Honduras alone. The tragic result of that chain of circumstances was the so-called FOOTBALL WAR of 1969, which embittered relations and jeopardized the economic improvement attained by the Common Market.

See also COFFEE INDUSTRY (CENTRAL AMERICA).

Bibliography. Thomas P. Anderson, *Matanza: El Salvador's Communist Revolt of 1932,* Lincoln, Nebr., 1971; Dana G. Munro, *The Five Republics of Central America,* New York, 1918; Franklin D. Parker, *The Central American Republics,* New York, 1964; Mario Rodríguez, *Central America,* Englewood Cliffs, N.J., 1965.

WILLIAM J. GRIFFITH

EMBOABAS, WAR OF (1708). Civil strife in Minas Gerais growing out of a conflict between the *paulista* pioneers and outsiders who had streamed into the region in the gold rush. The etymology of the word *emboaba* is obscure, but it was clearly a derogatory term used by the *paulistas* for the newcomers. Strong cultural antagonisms were involved in the dispute, for the *paulistas,* whose language and life-style were strongly influenced by Amerindian example, contrasted sharply with the immigrants from the littoral and Portugal. Skirmishing led to the virtual expulsion of the *paulistas* by the *emboaba* forces led by Manuel Nunes Viana, who was then proclaimed acting Governor. Intervention by successive Governors of Rio de Janeiro eventually succeeded in defusing the crisis by deflecting *paulista* reprisals and granting amnesty. In 1710 the crown established the captaincy of São Paulo and Minas de Ouro with its headquarters in São Paulo.

KENNETH R. MAXWELL

EMPHYTEUSIS. System of land tenure dating back to the late Roman Empire that was introduced in Argentina in the 1820s by Bernardino RIVADAVIA. Various explanations have been advanced for his action. Some think that he was trying to prevent the sale of large tracts of public land to a few individuals, others that he expected to make land rents a primary source of government revenue, others that he wanted to encourage immigration and farming, and still others that he wanted to use the public land set aside as collateral for loans to the state. According to the land laws establishing emphyteusis in the province of Buenos Aires in 1824 and in all the Argentine provinces in 1826, all public land belonged to the state, and to assure that the state received the increase in the value of the land, the occupiers were to pay a rental based on an appraisal made every ten years by a committee of local landowners. The rental charge for pastureland was 8 percent of its value; for agricultural land, 4 percent. Leases for the land usually were made for twenty-year periods, but the government could terminate them at the end of ten years. The laws did not limit the number of acres a person could lease, nor did they prohibit subleasing.

Irrespective of the intentions of Rivadavia, farming failed to develop significantly, land was granted in enormous tracts to individuals close to the centers of authority, and land rentals were low and were collected infrequently. By 1827, 112 individuals had leased 6.5 million acres, and three years later 538 leaseholders held 20 million acres. The system of emphyteusis evidently lapsed after 1838, and the land laws of Rivadavia were repealed in 1869. During the administration of Juan Manuel de ROSAS the occupiers were permitted to secure title to the public land they used.

JOSEPH T. CRISCENTI

ENCOMIENDA. The institution of the encomienda has Spanish antecedents in the Roman *commendatio,* or *patrocinium,* which is one of the sources of feudalism. During the barbarian invasions clients commended themselves to powerful nobles and received protection in return for fidelity and determined services. The relationship between patron and client came to be called *encomendación* or *patrocinio* and took various forms as it developed. By the twelfth century the term "encomienda" was in use as a name for a special class of lordship. Its basis was the idea of protection and defense by a noble in return for the temporal cession of a domain or other forms of property by the crown, a magnate, a monastery, or a military order. The lord of the encomienda, called an encomendero (*comendador* in the military orders), received economic benfits from the land or settlements under his protection and defense.

The distinctive American form of encomienda developed in the Antilles, where the settlers whom Christopher COLUMBUS brought with him on his second voyage were unwilling to work and the problem of labor supply was solved by the use of Indian forced labor. The first to use the term encomienda was Governor Nicolás de Ovando, Comendador Mayor of the military order of Alcántara. Because Queen ISABELLA I considered the Indians free crown vassals, instructions were given Ovando to inform the native rulers that they were obliged only to pay tribute equal to that of other crown subjects and that they might refuse to render labor services except in public works or in the royal placer mines. Thereupon the Indians refused to have anything to do with the Spaniards. The result was a series of royal decrees starting in 1503 that created the system of encomienda. The encomienda was originally a formal grant of Indian crown vassals (it did not include Indian lands) to a favored Spanish conqueror or colonist. The Indians were initially required to perform labor services and give tribute to their Spanish encomendero. In return for this royal favor, the Spaniard who held Indians in trust for the crown was obliged to render military service in defense of the colony and had the responsibility of Christianizing his Indian charges. In granting encomiendas, the crown intended both to reward deserving conquerors and settlers and to incorporate the Indians into Christian civilization by placing them under the protection of responsible individuals.

Encomienda, so excellent in intent, proved to be an unmitigated disaster. Encomenderos ignored their duties and exploited the Indians assigned them unmercifully, contributing to the swift destruction of the native population. When the encomienda spread to the mainland with the conquests of Panama, Mexico, and Peru, it also served as a factor in the demographic catastrophe witnessed there.

The cruelty and avarice of the encomenderos were protested by the Dominicans beginning in 1511. Their accusations brought about the LAWS OF BURGOS in 1512–1513. Encomiendas were to continue, but the mistreatment of Indians was to end. The ordinances were promulgated, but because no provisions were made for their enforcement, they remained a dead letter. Continuous agitation by pro-Indian reformers led by Bartolomé de LAS CASAS finally resulted in the NEW LAWS of 1542–1543. The New Laws decreed better treatment for the Indians and looked to the gradual extinction of encomiendas by forbidding new grants and the transmission of existing encomiendas by inheritance. Encomiendas were to revert to the crown upon the death of the holders, and there was finally to be only one encomendero, the King. The crown was forced to compromise its position regarding inheritance of encomiendas when the encomenderos of Peru revolted and the threat of rebellion in Mexico caused the New Laws to be suspended, but the number of encomiendas diminished steadily after 1550. Moreover, labor and tribute exactions given encomenderos were more rigidly controlled by *audiencias* (*see* AUDIENCIA), and the power of the encomenderos was curbed by 1560 as new forms of labor exploitation arose and the encomienda was modified. Examples of encomiendas authorized by the crown were to be found in Paraguay as late as 1769, but it is safe to say that the institution of encomienda was extinguished prior to the independence period.

Bibliography. John Francis Bannon (ed.), *Indian Labor in the Spanish Indies,* Boston, 1966; Charles Gibson, *Spain in America,* New York, 1967; Lewis Hanke, *The Spanish Struggle for Justice in the Conquest of America,* Boston, 1965; C. H. Haring, *The Spanish Empire in America,* New York, 1947; Julio Jiménez Rueda, *Historia de la cultura en México,* Mexico City, 1951; Lesley Byrd Simpson, *The Encomienda in New Spain,* Berkeley, Calif., 1950; Luis G. de Valdeavellano, *Curso de historia de las instituciones españolas de los orígenes al final de la edad media,* Madrid, 1968; Silvio A. Zavala, *La encomienda indiana,* Madrid, 1935.

RALPH H. VIGIL

ENLIGHTENMENT (BRAZIL). The views of the European *philosophes* had considerable impact during the last two decades of the eighteenth century on a generation of young Brazilians educated at the University of Coimbra, which was reformed by the Marquês de POMBAL in 1772, and elsewhere in Europe. Strongly scientific and utilitarian in their interests, they produced an impressive body of literature. The eighteenth century also saw several major scientific expeditions to Brazil and the establishment of a series of short-lived scientific and literary societies there. The most famous of the expeditions was that of Alexandre Rodrigues de Ferreira, a native of Bahia (modern Salvador) and a graduate of Coimbra, who explored Amazonia from 1783 to 1792. The first of the Brazilian societies was the Academia dos Esquecidos (Academy of the Forgotten), which met in Bahia during 1724–1725 under the patronage of the Viceroy, the Conde de Sabugosa. The academy's principal objective, the writing of a collaborative history of Brazil, was not realized, but one of its members, Sebastião de Rocha Pita, did write *História da América Portuguêsa* (1730), noted for its patriotic hyperbole. Several other academies were founded later; among them was a Sociedade Scientifica established in Rio de Janeiro in 1772 and dedicated to

the study of natural history, chemistry, medicine, and agriculture.

With the encouragement of the Portuguese government, attempts were also made during the last decades of the eighteenth century to stimulate agriculture and make more effective use of the raw materials of Portuguese America, and during the period of control of the overseas department by Rodrigo de Sousa Coutinho, many young Brazilian scholars became involved in the making of colonial policy. The *Memorias* of the Royal Academy of Sciences (established in Lisbon in 1780) and the publications of Frei Mariano da Conceição Veloso's press of the Arco do Cego in Lisbon became major outlets for the new output of scientific works on Portugal and Brazil. The most renowned of these was the *Fazendeiro do Brasil* (1798–1806), a ten-volume compilation of treatises on tropical agriculture. Most of the edition was sent to Brazil, where local officials were instructed to distribute copies to landowners, but this was rarely done.

KENNETH R. MAXWELL

ENLIGHTENMENT (SPANISH AMERICA). The Enlightenment was the eighteenth-century intellectual movement that emphasized the preeminence of reason in the study of nature and the government of society, and the ascendancy of science over religion. It was introduced to Spain by the writings of Benito Feyjóo y Montenegro, and it was brought to maturity during the reign of CHARLES III, whose chief ministers were influenced by the stream of European thought. The sources of the Enlightenment in Spanish America are to be found in English, French, and German thought, channeled through Spain or acquired by direct reading and reelaborated by Spanish American thinkers, who created what has been called a Christian eclectic modernist philosophy. The Spanish Enlightenment emphasized administrative and economic reforms that would benefit society at large and the promotion of useful knowledge. Although religion was not attacked, ecclesiastical institutions were subjected to greater control by the crown. The Enlightenment was patronized by the state, which started to open its possessions to scientific curiosity after 1735, when the expedition of Charles-Marie de La Condamine traveled to Quito to measure the equatorial arc. Many other expeditions followed, among them those of Nikolaus von Jacquin to Venezuela (1755–1759), Hipólito Ruiz, José Antonio Pavón, and Joseph Dombey to Chile (1777–1788), Martín Sessé and José Mariano Mociño to California and Guatemala (1791, 1795–1804), Alejandro Malaspina (1789–1794), and Alexander von HUMBOLDT (1799–1804).

The tempo of the Enlightenment quickened in the 1770s. The spirit of reform was carried throughout Spanish America by such diligent viceroys as Manuel de Guirior in New Granada, Juan José Vertiz in Buenos Aires, Manuel de Amat y Junient and José Fernando Abascal in Peru, and the 2d Count of REVILLAGIGEDO in New Spain. The institutions that carried the task of disseminating the useful knowledge were the *sociedades patrióticas* or *económicas,* which sought ways to keep the interested minority informed of the latest technical, economic, agricultural, and industrial ideas. Schooling, especially elementary education, became more widespread, and the ideal, if not the reality, of a basic education was for the first time acclaimed as a social benefit. In the universities and religious colleges older Thomist concepts were replaced by the study of Condillac, Descartes, Newton, Buffon, Montesquieu, Bacon, and Leibniz, even though the acceptance of some philosophers was not universal. The private libraries of many clerical and civil authorities contained the most recent and often prohibited books of European philosophers and North American scientists. Experimentation and the study of nature became the concern of most educators and public administrators. Advances in the experimental sciences were impeded by economic limitations rather than by intellectual backwardness. The crown itself was open-minded enough to provide sums for the creation of botanical gardens in Guatemala and Mexico, the latter led by Martín Sessé; an astronomical observatory in Bogotá, headed by Francisco José de Caldas; and the study of the American flora carried on by José Celestino Mutis, who won European recognition. The application of new industrial techniques to vital sources of the economy was encouraged. Mining in Mexico and South America received the benefits of German missions organized after the Elhuyar brothers were sent to Germany to study (*see* MINING: COLONIAL SPANISH AMERICA). Fausto de Elhuyar directed the School of Mining founded in Mexico City in 1792.

The spread of knowledge entailed the foundation of newspapers on literature and science. In Mexico the *Gazeta de Literatura de México* (1788–1795) of José Antonio Alzate was a notable publication, as was the *Diario de México* (1805–1817), Latin America's first daily newspaper. The *Mercurio Volante* (1772–1773) of José Ignacio Bartolache was a medical journal. In Peru the *Mercurio Peruano* (1791–1795) was the leading publication. Havana had its *Papel Periódico* (1790–1804), while in Quito Francisco Javier Eugenio de Santa Cruz y ESPEJO published *Las Primicias de la Cultura* (1792). In New Granada there were the *Papel Periódico* (1791–1797) and the *Semanario* (1808–1811), edited by Caldas; and Guatemala had a *Gazeta* (1794–1816).

The Enlightenment and its ideas did not lack opposition, especially from the church. The Inquisition kept its eye on printed material and condemned those who advocated radical political ideas and social change (*see* INQUISITION, HOLY OFFICE OF THE). Some zealous ministers, such as Archbishop Juan González de la Reguera in Lima, obstructed the Enlightenment in Peru, but many in the hierarchy of the church supported the practical side of the new ideas as long as religious orthodoxy was not challenged. When the Enlightenment touched political reform, it sometimes became liberal and nurtured the ideas of the precursors of independence and the first generation of revolutionaries. The benefits of the Enlightenment were not even. Society was not radically changed; some of the reforms undertaken did not produce the expected results or had a very short testing time. Nonetheless, the intellectual awareness and activities of the last decades of the colonial period belie assertions of colonial obscurantism and ignorance prior to the independence of the colonies.

Bibliography. Pablo González Casanova, *El misoneísmo y la modernidad cristiana en el siglo XVIII,* Mexico City, 1948; Richard Greenleaf, "The Mexican Inquisition and the Enlightenment, 1763–1805," *New Mexico Historical Review,* vol. XLI, no. 3, July 1966, pp. 181–191; Richard Herr, *The Eighteenth Century Revolution in Spain,* Princeton, N.J., 1958; J. T. Lanning, *The Eighteenth Century Enlightenment in the University of San Carlos de Guatemala,* Ithaca, N.Y., 1956; R. J. Shafer, *The Economic Societies in the Spanish World, 1763–1821,* Syracuse, N.Y., 1958; Arthur P. Whitaker, "The Elhuyar Mining Missions and the Enlightenment," *Hispanic American Historical Review,* vol. XXXI, no. 4, November 1951, pp. 557–585; Arthur P. Whitaker (ed.), *Latin America and the Enlightenment,* Ithaca, N.Y., 1958.

ASUNCIÓN LAVRIN

ENRÍQUEZ, MANUEL (1926–). Mexican composer and violinist. Enríquez was born in Jalisco. After studying composition with Bernal Jiménez, he enrolled in the Juilliard School in New York, where he studied violin with Ivan Galamian and composition with Peter Mennin. He is an outstanding member of the young generation of Mexican composers as well as a violinist of stature. For many years he has been assistant concertmaster of the Orquesta Nacional de México. Among his best works are a concerto for violin and orchestra (1955), two symphonies (1957, 1962), two string quartets (1959, 1967), and *Transición* for orchestra (1965).

JUAN A. ORREGO-SALAS

ERCILLA Y ZÚÑIGA, ALONSO DE (1533–1594). Spanish soldier and poet. Ercilla was born in Madrid. At the age of fifteen he entered the service of the future king PHILIP II as a page and traveled with him throughout Europe. After having accompanied the Prince to England in 1553, Ercilla decided to leave court life for reasons that are not known. He obtained permission to join the armada of the Peruvian Viceroy and left Spain on October 15, 1555. In February 1557, he embarked from Callao, the viceregal port city, for Chile on the same ship with García Hurtado de Mendoza. On his arrival in Chile he joined in the many expeditions and military actions against the Araucanian Indians (*see* ARAUCANIANS).

Because of a dispute with another soldier, Ercilla was condemned to death, but he was later exiled to Peru and soon returned to Spain, arriving there in 1563. He married, was made a member of the Order of Santiago, and undertook numerous diplomatic missions for the King.

Ercilla's fame as a poet rests on his epic poem *La Araucana* (*The Araucaniad*), which he composed in three parts, published in 1569, 1578, and 1589, respectively. *La Araucana* deals with the Spanish conquest of the fierce Araucanian Indians. In true Renaissance epic fashion, Ercilla creates heroes of epic proportions, particularly the Indian leader Caupolicán, but the reader sees as well Ercilla's strong humanistic sense. In his prologue to *La Araucana,* Ercilla tells of how he composed passages of the poem while participating in military campaigns, writing on bits of letters and scraps of leather when paper was lacking. He also expresses his intention to give a true history in the poem of the deeds of the Spaniards and the glories of the Araucanians for the edification of Philip II, to whom the poem is dedicated.

DANIEL R. REEDY

ERRÁZURIZ ZAÑARTU, FEDERICO (1825–1877).
President of Chile (1871–1876). An ardent Liberal,
Errázuriz first entered Congress in 1849 (*see* LIBERAL
PARTY: CHILE). He took an active part in the insurrection of April 20, 1851, in Santiago and afterward
was exiled to Peru. Errázuriz held ministerial office
during the administration of José Joaquín PÉREZ. The
premature death in 1867 of the Conservative front-run-
ner, Manuel Antonio Tocornal, paved the way for
Errázuriz to become the presidential candidate of the
governing Liberal-Conservative fusion. He won the
1871 election without difficulty, but his quinquennium
in power was marked by contentious political realignments. In 1873 the strongly Conservative Minister of
Education, Abdón Cifuentes, was obliged to resign,
whereupon the Conservatives withdrew their support
from the government and went into opposition (*see*
CONSERVATIVE PARTY: CHILE). This crisis ended the
Liberal-Conservative fusion, which had governed Chile
for more than ten years. Errázuriz ruled thereafter
exclusively with Liberal support, strengthened in 1875
by the formation of the Liberal Alliance, a coalition of
the Liberal and Radical parties (*see* RADICAL PARTY:
CHILE). Errázuriz's Presidency thus saw the exclusion
of the Conservatives from office for the first time since
1830; they were not to return until after the civil war
of 1891.

SIMON COLLIER

ESCOBAR, LUIS ANTONIO (1925–   ). Colombian
choral conductor and composer. Born in Villapinzón,
he studied in the National Conservatory of Bogotá
and later at the Peabody Conservatory in Baltimore
with Nikolai Nabokov and in Berlin with Boris Blacher.
Upon his return to Colombia in 1953 he was appointed
a professor at the National Conservatory; he received
a Guggenheim fellowship in 1957. In 1971 he joined
the diplomatic service as Colombian Cultural Attaché
to West Germany. In addition to having been an outstanding choral conductor, he has been recognized as
a composer of three symphonies (1955, 1960, 1965), a
concertino for flute and orchestra (1951), *Juramento a
Bolívar* (1964), and numerous works for solo instruments, chamber ensembles, and chorus.

JUAN A. ORREGO-SALAS

ESCOBAR, MARISOL. *See* MARISOL.

**ESCOLA SUPERIOR DE GUERRA (NATIONAL WAR
COLLEGE; ESG).** A military school of this name
existed briefly in Brazil in the 1890s and again in the
1930s, but it did not survive long enough to affect the
training and outlook of the Brazilian officer corps. The
present ESG was founded in 1949 and became the
most important center in Brazil for the formulation and
study of the doctrine of national security and economic
development. The Escola Superior de Guerra combines
features of the United States National War College and
Industrial College of the Armed Forces, but it draws its
students about equally from the three military services
and from such civilian sectors as the federal bureaucracy, education, industry, and banking. Its purpose is
to train students for executive or advisory positions
related to the internal and external security and development of the nation. Civilian students are required to
have had university training and to have demonstrated

the capacity for leadership. Officer students usually
hold the rank of colonel or its equivalent, and graduation
from the ESG is normally a prerequisite for further
career advancement. An active alumni association
serves to keep former students abreast of current developments and to disseminate ESG doctrines among the
armed forces and civilian society. Many of the views of
the Escola Superior de Guerra became government
policy after the 1964 revolution, for key civilian and
military members of the administration of Humberto
CASTELLO BRANCO were former students, instructors, or
commandants of the school.

ROLLIE E. POPPINO

**ESPEJO, FRANCISCO JAVIER EUGENIO DE SANTA
CRUZ Y (1747–1795).** Ecuadorian writer and physician.
Born in Quito, the son of an Indian father and a mulatto
mother, Espejo was mostly self-educated, receiving a
degree in medicine in 1767 and a permit to practice in
1772. He also had a degree in civil and canon law.
Espejo was a versatile writer and a biting satirist who
left an extensive collection of works on medicine,
journalism, economic and social reforms, and religious
subjects. In 1779 he published *El nuevo Luciano de
Quito,* a satire on the clergy. His best medical work
is *Reflexiones acerca de . . . las viruelas* (1785), in
which he suggested the microbial and contagious character of smallpox. Espejo was critical of the backwardness of medicine and public health in Quito and worked
assiduously to obtain better medical services for the
quiteños.

Having been accused of writing a satirical attack on
King CHARLES III, he traveled to Bogotá in 1787 to
prove his innocence. While in Bogotá, he befriended
Antonio NARIÑO and Francisco Antonio Zea, precursors of Colombian independence. He also met the
Marqués de Selva Alegre, who supported Espejo's
plan to found a *sociedad patriótica* in Quito. This project
materialized in 1791. Espejo was the society's secretary and the editor of *Las Primicias de la Cultura de
Quito,* the first newspaper in Quito. After 1792 Espejo
nurtured ideas of independence. He was betrayed and
sent to jail in 1795 but was not tried. Released from
prison after a few months, he died shortly thereafter.
He is well remembered for his perceptive analysis of
colonial Quito and the number and sharpness of his
satirical writings.

ASUNCIÓN LAVRIN

ESTADO NOVO (NEW STATE). Avowedly totalitarian
dictatorship in Brazil (1937–1945). By coup d'état on
November 10, 1937, President Getúlio VARGAS overthrew the constitutional government of Brazil and kept
himself in power at the head of the regime known variously as Estado Novo and Estado Nacional (National
State). The constitution issued on the same date provided for the separation of executive and legislative
authority, but in fact for eight years Vargas ruled by
decree without Congress, elections, or political parties.
He justified creation of the Estado Novo on the grounds
that it averted a Communist seizure of power and forestalled the outbreak of class warfare in Brazil. The
first allegation was patently false, and the second was a
gross misrepresentation of the democratic process, but
both were accepted at face value by the armed forces
and by civilian groups that regarded democracy as out-

moded and the corporate state as the wave of the future.

The Estado Novo gave Brazil a highly centralized government that promoted industrialization, sponsored urban labor organizations, raised educational and health standards in the cities, and vastly expanded the state bureaucracy. Although it was obviously inspired by European models, the Estado Novo lacked the external symbols and ideology of the totalitarian dictatorships of the 1930s. Brazil's wartime contribution to the defeat of fascism in Europe led to widespread disillusionment with dictatorship at home. In response to growing public pressure, on October 29, 1945, the armed forces removed Vargas from office and guaranteed the return to democratic rule in the elections of December 2, 1945.

ROLLIE E. POPPINO

ESTÉVEZ, ANTONIO (1916–   ). Venezuelan composer. Born in Calabozo, he studied composition with Vicente Emilio Sojo in Caracas and later with Aaron Copland in the United States. For many years he was an oboist with the Venezuela Symphony Orchestra. After a period of writing music deeply inspired by his native country's folk and popular traditions, of which outstanding examples are his concerto for orchestra (1950) and his *Cantata criolla* (1954), Estévez turned to electronic music. In 1967–1968 he studied its technique in Paris and produced his *Cosmovivrafonía I* and *II* for electronic tape.

JUAN A. ORREGO-SALAS

ESTIGARRIBIA, JOSÉ FÉLIX (1888–1940). Paraguayan marshal and President (1939–1940). Born into an established family with a long military tradition, Estigarribia joined the Army in 1910. He received specialized training in Chile and France and directed the Paraguayan Military Academy (1921–1923). In 1927, as Chief of the General Staff, he was vocal in urging Paraguayan mobilization in the face of Bolivian advances in the CHACO. When the CHACO WAR broke out in 1932, Estigarribia was deputy commander of the Army. As a reward for his brilliant and aggressive campaigns he was raised to the rank of marshal by President Eusebio AYALA in 1935. After the war, as a national hero without interest in politics, he traveled abroad. Returning to Paraguay in 1938, he was a signatory of the Chaco peace treaty and shortly thereafter became Ambassador to the United States. While in the United States, he was nominated to the Presidency by the Liberal party and elected in 1939. Upon his return, Estigarribia discovered that, despite his democratic leanings, only strong rule could hold the country together while political and military factions were engaging in plots and counterplots. He assumed temporary dictatorial powers in order to advocate the drafting of a new constitution and a new plan for "orderly democracy." The constitution, with some recognizably fascist trappings, provided for a very strong executive who could use the state of siege as an effective political tool. A few weeks after the promulgation of the constitution of 1940, Estigarribia and his wife were killed in an airplane crash while en route to their vacation retreat at Lake Ypacaraí. *See* LIBERAL PARTY (PARAGUAY).

JOHN HOYT WILLIAMS

ESTIMÉ, DUMARSAIS (1900–1953). President of Haiti (1946–1950). Dumarsais Estimé was born in Verrettes and briefly taught school and practiced law there; he then entered the National Assembly, eventually becoming Speaker. During the regime of Sténio VINCENT he was Secretary of Education. In the wake of the 1946 revolution, which ended a thirty-one-year mulatto rule, Estimé, a middle-class Negro intellectual, became President on August 16. His administration advanced Haitian education and stimulated tourism. A world's fair held in Port-au-Prince in 1949 celebrated the city's bicentennial. Estimé also signed an agreement with the Export-Import Bank to finance the Artibonite Valley irrigation project.

Opponents charged President Estimé with encouraging the politicization of unions, granting special favors to friends, and advancing the mulatto ÉLITE while sponsoring ill-fated agricultural reform programs. His attempt to gain reelection failed when the National Assembly refused to remove a no-reelection clause. Estimé was forced to resign on May 10, 1950. He went into exile in New York, where he died of uremia on July 20, 1953.

JOHN E. BAUR

ESTRADA, CARLOS (1909–1970). Uruguayan composer and conductor. A native of Montevideo, he obtained most of his training in Paris, where he studied composition with Roger Ducasse and conducting with Albert Wolff and Paul Paray. For many years he taught composition and served as director at the National Conservatory of Music and was permanent conductor of the Municipal Symphony Orchestra in Montevideo. In addition, he appeared many times as a guest conductor of major orchestras in Europe. His works, in a neoclassical vein, include an oratorio, *Daniel* (1942); two symphonies (1951, 1967); compositions for string orchestra; a concertino for piano and orchestra (1944); and a variety of chamber music, songs, and piano music.

JUAN A. ORREGO-SALAS

ESTRADA CABRERA, MANUEL (1857–1924). Guatemalan dictator-President. A foundling who was educated by clerics, he became a lawyer but attained little distinction until José María Reyna Barrios made him Minister of the Interior and first designate, or alternate, for the Presidency. The assassination of Reyna Barrios in February 1898 brought Estrada Cabrera to power. An election made him constitutional President, and travesties of democratic procedure reelected him in 1904, 1910, and 1916.

During his early years Estrada Cabrera continued the neo-Liberal program of development. He improved public health, extended highway construction, completed the railroad between the capital and the Caribbean, constructed schools, and inaugurated Festivals of Minerva, celebrated in simulated Greek temples, for the cultivation and display of Guatemalan culture. Subsequently his interest lagged, and he attempted nothing constructive. Economic deterioration thus engendered was intensified by corruption in government and by devouring inflation that attended repeated issues of paper money.

Estrada Cabrera was unassuming at first, but he developed a megalomania that demanded abject adulation. His only concern was to remain in office, and opposition, criticism, or even suspected alienation drew ruthless retaliation. His regime became an absolute military despotism employing secret police, informers, and swift and often secret vengeance. He survived several armed uprisings and numerous attempts on his life. In 1920 opposition to his regime coalesced. The Unionist party joined forces with dissident labor and other groups to campaign for his overthrow. In April the legislature found him mentally incompetent and deposed him.

WILLIAM J. GRIFFITH

ESTRADA DOCTRINE. International legal concept concerning the diplomatic recognition of a new government. In contrast to the Tobar Doctrine (1907), named after the Ecuadorian diplomat Carlos R. Tobar, which holds that no government coming to power through revolution should be recognized, the Estrada Doctrine asserts that recognition of a new regime should be automatic. Furthermore, no declaration of recognition should be made, since such a declaration implies a judgment of a new government. The author of the doctrine was Genaro Estrada (1877–1937), Foreign Minister of Mexico from 1927 to 1932. Enunciated in 1930, the doctrine has been supported by many nations at various times, but Mexico, with certain exceptions (for example, Spain), has consistently applied this principle in its recognition policy and has forcefully supported it in the ORGANIZATION OF AMERICAN STATES (OAS). For example, Mexico maintained relations with Cuba despite the OAS decision, made at the WASHINGTON MEETING in 1964, to break relations with that nation.

RODNEY D. ANDERSON

ESTRADA PALMA, TOMÁS (1835–1908). President of Cuba (1902–1906). During Cuba's TEN YEARS' WAR (1868–1878) against Spanish rule, Estrada Palma served briefly as provisional President of the rebel republic. A Protestant, he later spent several years as principal of a Quaker school for boys in Central Valley, New York. In the 1890s, as head of a Cuban revolutionary junta headquartered in New York City, he was instrumental in securing United States support for the Cuban independence movement, providing newspapers across the country with sensational stories of Spanish atrocities and cruelty.

In 1901 Estrada Palma was chosen the first Cuban President, being supported by all Cuban factions and being acceptable to the Americans as well. During his administration programs begun by the United States occupation administration in sanitation, public health, and education were continued. Spanish immigrants and American investors found Cuba increasingly attractive, and the island seemed to be on its way to a mature and independent political life. However, Estrada Palma's nomination for a second term in 1905 as the candidate of the Moderate party and his subsequent reelection led to a rebellion in 1906 by the defeated Liberals that resulted in his resignation and a second American intervention. Estrada is generally considered to have been Cuba's most honest President and a man who unselfishly devoted his life to the freedom of his country.

J. CORDELL ROBINSON

EXPLORATION AND CONQUEST. *See* BALBOA, VASCO NÚÑEZ DE; BLACK LEGEND; COLUMBUS, CHRISTOPHER; CORTÉS, HERNÁN; DORADO, EL; GAMA, VASCO DA; JIMÉNEZ DE QUESADA, GONZALO; MAGELLAN, FERDINAND; PIZARRO, FRANCISCO; VALDIVIA, PEDRO DE; VESPUCCI, AMERIGO.

F

Fabini, Eduardo
Furtado, Celso

FABINI, EDUARDO (1883–1950). Uruguayan composer and conductor. Fabini was born in Solís. After early training in his native country, he studied in Europe. As a violinist he toured some European countries and the United States in 1926; he then returned to Montevideo, where he dedicated himself to composition and music education. Fabini's style is deeply rooted in the folk music of Uruguay, with an esthetic influenced by French impressionism. Outstanding among his works are his symphonic poems *Campo* (1922) and *La isla de los Ceibos* (1926).

JUAN A. ORREGO-SALAS

FACIO, GONZALO (1918–   ). Costa Rican politician and ambassador. Facio was perhaps the chief spokesman for José FIGUERES and the PARTIDO LIBERACIÓN NACIONAL (PLN) outside the country. He was one of the founders of the PLN during the early 1940s, fought alongside Figueres in the revolution of 1948, and served as Minister of Justice in the period of the revolutionary junta (1948–1949). As head of the Costa Rican delegation to the United Nations in 1948 and 1952 and as Costa Rican Ambassador to the United States and the ORGANIZATION OF AMERICAN STATES (OAS) from 1956 to 1958 and from 1962 to 1966, he continually pressed for cooperative action against dictatorial Latin American governments. In 1962–1963 he served as president of the OAS Council. He was also President of the Legislative Assembly of Costa Rica from 1953 to 1955. In domestic politics he generally represented the conservative wing of the PLN. Upon Figueres's election to the Presidency in 1970, Facio became Minister of Foreign Relations.

CHARLES L. STANSIFER

FALCÓN, JUAN C[RISÓSTOMO] (1820–1870). President of Venezuela (1863–1868). From his home base in the province of Coro, now the state of Falcón, Juan C. Falcón gained his reputation as a capable military man and a leading Liberal by serving the nominally Liberal governments of the brothers José Tadeo MONAGAS and José Gregorio MONAGAS. During the revolutionary government of Gen. Julián CASTRO, Falcón emerged as the champion of the Liberal elements in the *castrista* coalition, and when Castro's government turned against the Liberal section of the coalition during 1858, Falcón fled with other prominent Liberals into exile in the Antilles. By July 1859, he had accumulated enough resources to attempt an invasion of Venezuela, and by the end of the year he had joined his major rival within the Liberal camp, Ezequiel Zamora. The two Liberal chieftains agreed to reconcile their differences by naming Falcón chief of the Liberal-Federalist cause and placing Zamora in active and direct command of the military forces. Unfortunately, Zamora, a brilliant tactician, died in battle about a month later (January 10, 1860), leaving Falcón in complete control of the Federalist forces. By April the Federalists had suffered serious military setbacks, which forced Falcón to leave Venezuela for Colombia. From

Colombia he traveled again to the Antilles, where he managed to obtain supplies and financing, and with this support he reinvaded Venezuela in mid-1861.

By October 1861, Federalist military successes and the weakness of the Conservative government in Caracas had led to a series of peace conferences, culminating in a meeting between Falcón and the main Conservative leader, Gen. José Antonio PÁEZ, in December 1861. In spite of the strong incentives for a peaceful settlement, Páez would not agree to any arrangement that relegated him to a secondary position. Likewise, Falcón refused any agreement that signified less than a clear Federalist victory. The result was an intensification of warfare during all of 1862 and half of 1863, with increasing successes by the Federalist armies. Finally, in April 1863, the Federal Wars came to an official close with the celebration of the Treaty of Coche, which formalized the triumph of the Federalists and Falcón over the Conservative government of Páez. In the wake of this success, Falcón was named provisional President of Venezuela on June 15, 1863, and proceeded to reorganize the government to consolidate the gains of the Federalist armies. After sending Gen. Antonio GUZMÁN BLANCO to Europe to arrange for the foreign loans required to finance the government and economic recovery, Falcón called a constitutional convention for December 1863. By mid-1864 the Federalist constitution had been completed and promulgated, and on March 18, 1865, Falcón was elected constitutional President of Venezuela for a term of four years. On several occasions during the next three years Falcón left the Presidency in other hands in order to put down uprisings.

The Falcón administration saw the beginnings of economic recovery from the destruction and disorganization caused by the Federal Wars. Roads, telegraphs, and a railroad were begun, credit was reestablished, and commerce and finance were placed on a secure footing. Although these advances began under Falcón's administration, credit for their implementation is due in larger part to Guzmán Blanco, since Falcón disliked the tasks of administration and finance, felt uncomfortable in Caracas, and was delighted to leave actual management of economic affairs to others while he traveled about the country pacifying dissidents. This failure to keep up with and control the day-to-day operation of his government led rather quickly to a series of crises. The primary issue that divided Falcón's party into factions resulted from the activities of Guzmán Blanco in negotiating European loans, particularly in 1864 and 1866. Because Guzmán Blanco became wealthy on commissions from these transactions and because in 1866 he seemed able to force the Venezuelan government, in the hands of a delegate while Falcón was putting down revolts, to do his bidding, one faction of the Federalist party wanted Guzmán Blanco removed from his diplomatic post.

Falcón's failure to keep a close watch on his own people contributed to the division in the Liberal party that led to the collapse of his regime in 1868. Indeed, by the beginning of 1867 the failure of Falcón's fiscal policies, the reactivation of the Conservative party, and the increasing discontent among the Liberals opposed to Guzmán Blanco had resulted in the formation of a nucleus of serious opposition that talked of a fusion of parties to force changes on the Falcón government or perhaps to replace it. The final revolt, which led to Falcón's decision to separate himself from the Presidency, began in late 1867 and was taken over by Gen. José Tádeo Monagas, whose insistence on total victory for his movement made any agreement between Falcón's and Monagas's parties impossible. In June Monagas, as head of the Revolución Azul (Blue Revolution), took Caracas, and Falcón went into exile.

Bibliography. Lisandro Alvarado, *Historia de la revolución federal en Venezuela,* Caracas, 1956; Jesús A. Cova, *Archivo del mariscal Juan Crisóstomo Falcón,* 5 vols., Caracas, 1957–60; Jacinto R. Pachano, *Biografía del mariscal Juan C. Falcón,* 2d ed., Caracas, 1960; José Santiago Rodríguez, *Contribución al estudio de la Guerra Federal en Venezuela,* 2 vols., Caracas, 1933; George S. Wise, *Caudillo: A Portrait of Antonio Guzmán Blanco,* New York, 1951.

JOHN V. LOMBARDI

FALKLAND ISLANDS (known in Argentina as ISLAS MALVINAS). Archipelago belonging to Great Britain, located in the South Atlantic Ocean some 300 miles from the Strait of Magellan. There are two large islands, East Falkland (Gran Malvina) and West Falkland (Isla Soledad), each with an area of more than 2,000 square miles, and some 200 smaller islands. The date the islands were discovered by Europeans is uncertain, but England, France, Spain, and Portugal have asserted at some time that their navigators were the first to sight or visit them in the sixteenth century. There was little incentive to settle the islands, as their soil is generally poor for agriculture. For many years they were frequented by fishing vessels attracted by the hair seals, fur seals, white whales, and black whales found in abundance in their vicinity and near Bahía sin Fondo (now Golfo San Matías). They lacked importance until the 1760s, when the English under Commo. John Byron established a colony at Port Egmont and the French under Louis-Antoine de Bougainville founded Port Louis. In 1767 the Spanish crown placed the islands under the jurisdiction of the captain general of Buenos Aires. Spain acknowledged the English claims to the islands in 1771, a year after it had expelled the English garrison, but this was a premature gesture as the English voluntarily left the islands in 1774.

The Argentine government asserted its sovereignty over the islands in 1820, did nothing for the next three years, and then appointed a governor. A small colony established at Port Louis was destroyed in 1831 by a United States naval force during a dispute with Buenos Aires involving American rights in the islands and Argentine sovereignty over them. What was left evidently was a small Argentine military garrison. Two years later Britain repossessed the islands so that it could build a naval base to guard an important segment of its sea-lanes to Australia and New Zealand. Argentina did little more than protest until 1838, and then, under the guidance of Juan Manuel de ROSAS, it followed a seemingly contradictory policy. Rosas, it appears, was willing to surrender Argentine rights to the islands in return for the cancellation of the national debt with Baring Brothers. Nothing happened, and to this date the two countries have not settled their dispute over the islands. Stanley, seat of the British government in the islands, has a population of about 2,000. The main wealth of the islands consists of sheep, cattle, and horses. About three-fourths of these animals belong to the Falkland Islands Company. Contact with the outside world is maintained through Montevideo, Uruguay, and Punta Arenas, Chile.

JOSEPH T. CRISCENTI

FARROUPILHA REVOLT. The most serious and prolonged of the Brazilian provincial uprisings after independence, the Farroupilha revolt began in September 1835 in the province of Rio Grande do Sul in protest against the appointed provincial President and the centralist policies of the imperial government. Gaining control of the capital, Pôrto Alegre, the revolutionaries, who were known as Farroupilhas (ragamuffins), soon faced strong imperial counterattacks ordered by the newly elected Regent, Father Diogo Antônio FEIJÓ. Based in the port town of Rio Grande, imperial forces captured Pôrto Alegre, but on September 11, 1836, the Farroupilhas, still controlling much of the interior, proclaimed the República Rio-Grandense with the alleged aim of achieving federalist goals rather than permanent separation. Establishing a government and electing a President (Bento Gonçalves da Silva, then imprisoned in Bahia), the Farroupilhas continued their separatist revolt. In 1839, under the leadership of the youthful Giuseppe Garibaldi, the movement spread briefly into the province of Santa Catarina, where the República Juliana was established in the port town of Laguna.

With the declaration of the majority of the emperor PEDRO II in 1840, general amnesty was declared, but the Farroupilhas reaffirmed their independence with the creation of a constituent assembly. In November 1842 the Barão (later Duque) de CAXIAS was appointed President of the rebellious province, and in 1843 he began a successful campaign of pacification that ended in 1845 with the reincorporation of Rio Grande do Sul into the empire.

ROBERT CONRAD

FAVELA. Shantytown in Brazil, specifically a hillside slum in the city of Rio de Janeiro. The name is said to have been given to Providence Hill in Rio de Janeiro by veterans of the Canudos campaign against Antônio CONSELHEIRO who established a settlement there in the late 1890s. The last assault in the campaign had been made from a hill dubbed Favela Hill because the caatinga shrub *favela* grew there in abundance.

Favelas are characterized by a profusion of shanties made of wooden planks, scrap metal, cardboard, and similar materials and by the absence or inadequacy of municipal services, such as running water, electricity, and sewerage. In 1957 it was estimated that 650,000 of Rio's 2 million inhabitants lived in *favelas*. They are likely to be recent rural migrants who retain many elements of their rural culture in their new urban milieu. Carolina Maria de Jesus, a resident of a São Paulo *favela,* gave a moving portrait of the degradation and vice that she found there in *Quarto de Despejo* (1960), translated into English as *Child of the Dark* (1962).

HELEN DELPAR

FEBRERISMO. Socially conscious political movement arising in Paraguay after the CHACO WAR. The movement had its roots in the National Independent League founded in 1928 by Dr. Juan Stefanich, a nonpartisan group aiming at the general economic and social regeneration of Paraguay. The Chaco War deepened opposition to the traditional ruling elite and brought together individuals and groups seeking social change. The discontent found a leader in Col. Rafael FRANCO, a war hero who in 1936 headed the important National Veterans Association. Discontent with the Chaco truce of 1935 was the immediate cause of a planned coup. Franco was arrested and exiled, but the coup was launched in February 1936 by Col. Federico W. Smith and the officer corps. The successful revolutionaries recalled Franco and made him President.

In power the Febreristas, whose ranks included fascists, liberals, and even Communists, could agree only that Paraguay needed significant change. The Franco government took a strongly nationalist stance and promulgated a radical AGRARIAN REFORM law; other progressive measures included the nation's first genuine labor code. Dr. Stefanich, the ideologue of the movement, created the National Revolutionary Union to institutionalize Febrerismo, but before the organization could become a mass party, the government was ousted in August 1937 by another military coup. Out of power, with its leadership in exile, the Febreristas attempted several abortive revolutions and were proscribed by both Liberal and Colorado governments, being allowed only occasional legal existence between 1937 and 1967, when they were declared part of the legitimate opposition by President Alfredo STROESSNER. *See* COLORADO PARTY (PARAGUAY); LIBERAL PARTY (PARAGUAY).

JOHN HOYT WILLIAMS

FEDERMANN, NIKOLAUS (NICOLÁS FÉDERMAN) (1501–1542). German explorer of Venezuela and seeker of El Dorado (*see* DORADO, EL). In 1528 the Augsburg banking house of Bartholomäus Welser was awarded the right to govern Venezuela by Emperor Charles V (King CHARLES I). The Welsers chose Federmann to reinforce their Governor, Ambrosius Ehinger (Ambrosio Alfinger), at Coro on the Gulf of Venezuela. Upon his arrival in 1530, Federmann found Ehinger absent and was soon promoted to second-in-command of the colony. Ehinger returned but stopped only long enough to put Federmann in charge and continued on to Santo Domingo. In 1531 Federmann set out with a party of his own and returned six months later, having penetrated the Cordillera de Mérida foothills east of Lake Maracaibo. He returned to Spain and was met with the news of Ehinger's death. The Welsers then (1534) appointed him lieutenant of the new Governor, Georg Hohemut von Speyer (Jorge de Espira).

In 1535–1536 Federmann left Coro to begin a three-year trek to the Colombian highlands. He marched to the southeast, crossing the Apure and Meta rivers, and reached the upper Guaviare River. He then crossed the Andes Mountains and came out on the plains of Bogotá (1539). Federmann arrived only to find that Gonzalo JIMÉNEZ DE QUESADA had already conquered the CHIBCHA Indians. Jiménez de Quesada paid him 4,000 gold pesos to waive any possible claims. Federmann returned to Spain, where the Welsers accused him of desertion and dismissed him. Refused compensation, he never returned to South America.

WILLIAM S. DUDLEY

FEIJÓ, DIOGO ANTÔNIO (1784–1843). Brazilian statesman and Regent of the Brazilian empire. An illegitimate child, Feijó was trained in the priesthood, becoming a teacher of Latin and philosophy before turning to politics. In 1821 he was elected to the Cortes of Portugal from his native São Paulo, there defending the rights of Brazil before the demands of the Portuguese government. From 1826 to 1829 he participated in the first legislature as a deputy from São Paulo, gaining attention through his opposition to clerical celibacy and other unorthodox views on church matters, and in 1833 he was granted a seat in the Senate.

Following the abdication of PEDRO I in 1831, Feijó was appointed Minister of Justice in the revolutionary government. As Minister he acted decisively to suppress numerous rebellions of the army and the *exaltados* (radical liberals), creating a National Guard and reducing the size of the Army, while also resisting alleged plots to restore the former Emperor to his throne. Following the passage of the Additional Act of 1834, Feijó was elected Regent, holding that office from October 1835 until September 1837. Unable to suppress a rebellion in Pará and the FARROUPILHA REVOLT in Rio Grande do Sul and involved in conflicts with the Holy See, Feijó faced a hostile Chamber of Deputies and the bitter opposition of Bernardo Pereira de VASCONCELOS, Honório Hermeto Carneiro Leão, and other former political allies. In poor health, he finally resigned in favor of Senator Pedro de ARAÚJO LIMA some two years before the end of his four-year term. In 1842 Feijó was involved, along with Senator Nicolau Vergueiro, in an unsuccessful Liberal uprising in São Paulo, serving the movement as a writer until his arrest and brief exile to the province of Espírito Santo. Feijó's most significant writings are those dealing with the question of clerical celibacy.

ROBERT CONRAD

FERDINAND II. *See* ISABELLA I.

FERDINAND VII (1784–1833). King of Spain (1808, 1814–1833). Ferdinand was the son of Charles IV and María Luisa of Parma, who completely dominated her husband. She in turn was under the influence of her alleged lover, Manuel de Godoy, who became the chief minister in 1792. By 1807 Ferdinand had become an open enemy of Godoy and his rival for the favor of Napoleon. On March 17, 1808, partisans of Ferdinand engineered the Tumult of Aranjuez, which led to the dismissal of Godoy and to the abdication of Charles. By this time large numbers of French troops were in Spain as a result of the Treaty of Fontainebleau (1807), providing for the dismemberment of Portugal, and Napoleon soon decided to discard the Spanish Bourbons, both father and son, and to bestow the crown of Spain upon his brother Joseph, King of Naples.

His suspicions lulled by Napoleon's assurances, Ferdinand traveled to Bayonne, France, for an interview with the French Emperor in April 1808. There Napoleon induced Ferdinand to abdicate while Charles, who arrived later, was prevailed upon to resign his rights in favor of Joseph. Ferdinand was thereupon confined in Talleyrand's castle at Valençay. Meanwhile, a popular nationalist revolution against French rule broke out throughout Spain. These events also sparked uprisings against Spanish authorities in the colonies that terminated in the independence of Spanish America.

When Ferdinand returned to Spain in 1814, the French had been expelled, but the country was divided between conservatives and liberals who supported a constitution drafted by a Cortes in Cádiz in 1812. Although the liberals had demanded that Ferdinand swear allegiance to the constitution, he soon disavowed the work of the Cortes. Heading a regime characterized by fiscal penury and ministerial instability, Ferdinand nonetheless attempted the recovery of his American empire. On January 1, 1820, however, Maj. Rafael del Riego, commanding troops concentrated in Andalusia for embarkation to America, proclaimed the constitution of 1812. The military revolt was followed by several provincial risings that forced the King to agree to govern in accordance with the constitution. Dissension between moderate liberals and the more radical *exaltados*, aggravated by the anticonstitutional maneuvers of the King, kept Spain in turmoil until a French army crossed the border in 1823 and restored absolutism.

Ferdinand's last decade saw the King move toward an enlightened despotism that antagonized extreme royalists as well as liberals. The former found a champion in the King's younger brother, Don Carlos, who was expected to succeed to the throne upon the death of the childless Ferdinand. The king's fourth wife, María Cristina of Naples, gave birth to a daughter, Isabella, in 1830, but the right of a female to succeed to the throne was disputed. Conflict over the succession, which saw liberal elements ally themselves with María Cristina, gave rise to the Carlist Wars after the death of Ferdinand in September 1833.

HELEN DELPAR

FERNÁNDEZ FÉLIX, MIGUEL. *See* VICTORIA, GUADALUPE.

FERNÂNDEZ, OSCAR LORENZO (1897–1948). Brazilian composer and music educator, identified with the trend of musical nationalism in the 1920s and 1930s. Born in Rio de Janeiro, he studied at the National Institute of Music in Rio, where he was appointed professor of harmony in 1925. Very active in the musical life of that city, he was one of the founders of the Sociedade de Cultura Musical (1920), the promoter of the monthly journal *Ilustração Musical* (1930), and the founder and director of the Brazilian Conservatory of Music (1936).

His best-known works of the 1920s include *Canção Sertaneja,* Op. 31, for voice and piano; *Trio Brasileiro,* Op. 32, for piano, violin, and cello; and the *Suite Sinfônica sôbre Três Temas Populares Brasileiros,* all of which give evidence of his nativistic orientation. Opus 31 enjoyed wide popularity for its excitingly national character, conveyed by imitation of the folk guitar in the accompaniment. Although Lorenzo Fernândez rarely quotes directly from folk sources, the thematic material of the *Trio Brasileiro* presents obvious folk song peculiarities. His most successful orchestral scores, *Imbapara* and *Reisado do Pastoreio,* were written in 1929 and 1930, respectively. *Imbapara,* intended as an Amerindian choreographic tone poem, employs Indian music material collected by the Brazilian ethnologist E. Roquete Pinto. *Reisado* is a tripartite suite inspired by CABOCLO and Afro-Brazilian folk traditions. Its last movement, "Batuque," relies on the lively rhythmic patterns of the SAMBA. Lorenzo Fernândez's opera *Malasarte,* first produced in 1941, with a libretto based on José Pereira da GRAÇA ARANHA's drama, is one of the very few successful twentieth-century operas by a Brazilian composer. *Malasarte* had its origins in the folk music traditions of the country.

GERARD H. BÉHAGUE

FERNÁNDEZ DE LIZARDI, JOSÉ JOAQUÍN (1776–1827). Mexican novelist and journalist. Lizardi was born in Mexico City. One of the most prolific writers in Mexico on the eve of independence and during the first years of the republic, he is best known as the author of *El periquillo sarniento,* 1816 (*The Itching Parrot*), the first Spanish American novel. He wrote poems, fables, plays, novels, and a miscellany of other things, including translations and many newspaper pieces of an ephemeral nature. Some of these compositions appeared with the signature El Pensador Mexicano, a pseudonym he used often. Lizardi also published several newspapers, of which *El Pensador Mexicano* (1812–1814) is best remembered. Considering freedom of the press a serious matter, he criticized some of the political ills of the day. Then, in the ninth issue of the *Pensador,* he satirized the Viceroy and was placed in prison. In 1813 a new Viceroy set him free. Despite severe censorship he continued publishing periodicals. Among them were *Alacena de Frioleras* and *Caxoncito de la Alacena,* which he published alternately (1815–1816), and *El Conductor Eléctrico* (1820).

Lizardi's novels include *La Quijotita y su prima* (1818), *Noches tristes* (1818), and *Don Catrín de la fachenda* (1832). But *El periquillo,* a picaresque novel that continues his crusade against the social wrongs of the day, is his masterpiece.

GERARDO SÁENZ

FERRÉ [AGUAYO], LUIS A[NTONIO] (1904–   ). Puerto Rican businessman and governor (1969–1973). A graduate of the Massachusetts Institute of Technology (B.S., 1924; M.A. in civil engineering, 1925), Ferré began working in his family enterprises soon after graduation. He first ran for public office in 1940, when he was defeated as the Republican party's candidate for mayor of Ponce. He was a member of the Constitutional Convention (1951–1952) and served as representative-at-large (Statehood Republican party; SRP) from 1952 to 1956. He was the unsuccessful SRP candidate for Governor in 1956, 1960, and 1964.

Ferré was a member of the joint United States–Puerto Rico commission that studied the status of Puerto Rico from 1964 to 1966. One of the commission's recommendations was that a plebiscite be held to determine the will of the people on the matter. The SRP, in a convention held in January 1967, voted for abstention. Ferré, who led the forces against abstention, formed his own organization, United Statehooders, to support the statehood formula in the plebiscite. United Statehooders' good showing in 1967 encouraged Ferré to form his own party, the New Progressive party (NPP). Partly because of a split within the ruling Popular Democratic party, Ferré won the governorship and control of the lower chamber of the Legisla-

ture, although the NPP received only 44.7 percent of the vote.

Ferré's tenure as Governor was difficult. He faced an adverse political situation in the island and an uncertain economic situation in the United States. A series of government scandals tarnished his image as an honest and efficient administrator. In the 1972 elections he was voted out of office, and Senate President Rafael HERNÁNDEZ COLÓN was elected to succeed him.

An art lover, Ferré has donated a considerable part of his wealth to the Luis Ferré Foundation, which runs the Ponce Art Museum.

LUIS E. AGRAIT

FERREIRA DA SILVA, VIRGOLINO. *See* LAMPEÃO.

FIGARI, PEDRO (1861–1938). Uruguayan painter. Figari is remembered mainly as a postimpressionist painter, but he also had a distinguished career in public life. He was born in Montevideo, where he studied law and made a reputation as a defense lawyer. He founded the newspaper *El Diario,* and he was elected to the Chamber of Deputies. In 1915 he was appointed director of the Escuela de Artes y Oficios, where he instituted reforms in vocational and industrial training. He was a prolific writer on a variety of subjects, from education and the law to art and poetry. *El arte, la estética y el ideal* (1917) is perhaps his most lasting and influential book.

Painting was Figari's greatest interest and is the basis of his continuing fame. As a young man he studied art privately, but it remained a diversion until 1921. That year, at sixty, he moved to Buenos Aires and devoted himself exclusively to art. In 1925 he went to Paris for a stay of eight years during which he reached full maturity as a painter. He concentrated on the depiction of traditional Uruguayan life, fiestas, and domestic scenes, such as *La pulla* (*Sharp Tongue;* Montevideo, National Historical Museum), depicting gossips in a parlor. Uruguayan Negro subjects are frequent, as in several scenes of dancing entitled *Candombé.* His style is a very personal postimpressionism in thick paint and rich color. In 1933 he returned to Montevideo, where he continued to paint in his last years. Although Figari's art is too personal to have many followers, his paintings are among the most prized in South America.

TERENCE GRIEDER

FIGUERES [FERRER], JOSÉ (1906–   ). President of Costa Rica (1953–1958, 1970–   ). Beginning in 1948, José (Pepe) Figueres was the central figure in Costa Rican politics. After graduating from secondary school in Costa Rica, he lived for four years in Boston and New York, and he maintained close ties with the United States thereafter. He traveled and lectured frequently in the United States, serving once as visiting professor of government at Harvard University, and he married a North American.

As a young man Figueres paid greater attention to farming than to politics. He made his estate, called La Lucha sin Fin, the center of considerable experimentation with cabuya, a fibrous plant that served as a substitute for henequen in ropemaking during World War II.

Figueres's opposition to the controversial Rafael CALDERÓN GUARDIA regime (1940–1944) led him into politics. In 1942 he made a radio speech attacking Calderón that resulted in his being exiled to Mexico for two years. Upon his return to Costa Rica he opposed the government of Teodoro PICADO (1944–1948), a follower of Calderón, and became a leading militant in Democratic Action, one of the parent organizations of the PARTIDO LIBERACIÓN NACIONAL (PLN). Events of 1948 catapulted Figueres into national prominence. Calderón lost the presidential election of that year to Otilio ULATE, but the Legislative Assembly annulled the election and planned to turn the government over to Calderón. This irregular procedure, which violated the national tradition of peaceful presidential succession, so enraged Costa Ricans that a revolution ensued. Figueres managed the successful revolutionary campaign from his estate near Cartago, where he had cached arms and ammunition in anticipation of a crisis, and drove Calderón and Picado into exile.

Although the principal aim of the revolutionaries was to put Ulate in his rightful position, they delayed for eighteen months while a junta headed by Figueres ran the country. A new constitution, which opened the way to various reforms, such as the abolition of the Army and the granting of the vote to women, was proclaimed in 1949. Other important steps taken immediately made credit more readily available to small farmers and created an independent, nonpartisan Supreme Tribunal of Elections.

Both as President of the junta and as constitutionally elected President of the country (1953–1958), Figueres

José Figueres. [*Organization of American States*]

worked for the socialization of the economy. Through a system of autonomous agencies the government entered the fields of banking, insurance, electric power, and housing. Figueres also entered into negotiation to achieve greater control over such large foreign firms as the UNITED FRUIT COMPANY. In particular, he persuaded United Fruit to increase its payments to Costa Rica from 10 percent to 30 percent of its profits. This agreement paved the way for other banana-producing nations of Latin America to renegotiate contracts with the company.

In his second Presidency, which began in 1970, Figueres had less popular and legislative support than in 1953. As a result, even though he promised a war against poverty in his electoral campaign, changes were less dramatic than during his first Presidency. To be sure, nationalization of the Northern Railway Company, which took place in 1971, was a significant step along the lines Figueres had followed earlier. But the prominent issues of the second administration did not involve the degree of state control of the national economy but concerned the President's stand on such international questions as his effort to persuade the ORGANIZATION OF AMERICAN STATES to adopt rigorous measures against airplane hijackers and kidnappers and his decision to accord diplomatic recognition to the Soviet Union. Clearly, Figueres did not permit the weakness of Costa Rica in the international political scene to impede his ambition to speak for a larger Latin American constituency.

Ever since sharing exile in Mexico City with other Latin Americans hostile to dictatorship, Figueres was in the forefront of a hemispheric antidictatorial movement. His antipathy to dictators like Rafael Leonidas TRUJILLO MOLINA of the Dominican Republic, Anastasio SOMOZA GARCÍA of Nicaragua and his sons, Fidel CASTRO of Cuba, and Marcos PÉREZ JIMÉNEZ of Venezuela and his association with the antidictatorial and somewhat mysterious Caribbean Legion helped make Figueres a figure of international prominence. Leading opponents of dictators like Juan BOSCH of the Dominican Republic and Rómulo BETANCOURT of Venezuela spent periods of exile in Costa Rica and contributed their efforts to Figueres's school for the training of young leftist democrats, the Inter-American School for Democratic Education (EIDED).

Friction between Figueres and the Somozas reached a critical stage on several occasions: in 1949, when *calderonistas* attempted to overthrow the governing junta of Costa Rica from Nicaraguan soil; in 1955, when another group of Costa Rican exiles invaded Costa Rica from Nicaragua; and in 1959, when Pedro Joaquín Chamorro led a group of Nicaraguans based in Costa Rica against the regime of Luis SOMOZA DEBAYLE. All these invasion attempts failed. By 1971, however, Costa Rican–Nicaraguan relations had improved to such an extent that President Figueres paid a friendly visit to President Anastasio SOMOZA DEBAYLE in Managua.

Bibliography. Oscar R. Aguilar Bulgarelli, *Costa Rica y sus hechos políticos de 1948,* San José, 1969; Carlos Araya Pochet, *Historia de los partidos políticos: Liberación Nacional,* San José, 1968; Alberto Baeza Flores, *La lucha sin fin,* Mexico City, 1969; John P. Bell, *Crisis in Costa Rica: The Revolution of*

1948, Austin, Tex., 1971; Arturo Castro Esquivel, *José Figueres Ferrer: El hombre y su obra,* San José, 1955; Burt H. English, *Liberación Nacional in Costa Rica,* Gainesville, Fla., 1971; José Figueres, *Cartas a un ciudadano,* San José, 1956; Harry Kantor, "The Struggle for Democracy in Costa Rica," *South Atlantic Quarterly,* vol. LV, January 1956, pp. 12–18.

CHARLES L. STANSIFER

FINLAY, CARLOS (1833–1915). Cuban physician and epidemiologist. Finlay was born in Puerto Príncipe (now Camagüey) on December 3, 1833. After receiving a medical degree from Jefferson College in Philadelphia, he returned to Cuba to practice. He developed an interest in epidemiology while investigating epidemics of cholera and yellow fever that periodically plagued the island, and in 1881 he theorized that yellow fever was transmitted by the *Stegomyia* mosquito.

Finlay's theory was largely ignored, and twenty years later the prevailing opinion was still that the disease was caused by filth. However, after the United States military government had cleaned up the city of Havana, only to see a new epidemic break out, Gen. Leonard WOOD (also a doctor) ordered the commission headed by Dr. Walter Reed to test Finlay's conclusions. Finlay made his research available to the commission, and two American doctors, Jesse Lazear and James Carroll, volunteered to expose themselves to the bite of the *Stegomyia* mosquito. Both contracted the disease (Lazear died; Carroll recovered), proving that the major means of yellow fever transmission was indeed the bite of the female *Stegomyia,* providing she had also bitten another person suffering from the disease during the first three days of an attack.

Thanks to Finlay, yellow fever was quickly conquered not only in Cuba but in much of the tropics. Unfortunately, it is Dr. Reed, who had originally doubted Finlay's theory, to whom much of the world has given credit for this major contribution to the field of medicine.

KENNETH F. KIPLE

FIRST (or OLD) REPUBLIC (1889–1930). The first forty-one years of republican government in Brazil as distinct from the new republican regime established in 1930. On November 15, 1889, the Army with civilian backing proclaimed Brazil a republic. A series of military decrees and a new constitution (*see* CONSTITUTION OF 1891: BRAZIL) abolished titles of nobility, severed the ties between church and state, and provided for a federal republic with a strong Presidency.

Patriarchal Brazil was unprepared for liberal democracy. Within nine months the republic's first President, Marshal Manuel Deodoro da FONSECA, assumed dictatorial power. Threatened with civil war, Deodoro stepped down. Vice President Gen. Floriano PEIXOTO became President and quickly showed his inability to govern constitutionally. General unrest erupted into a full-scale revolt in 1893. The election of a civilian President resolved the crisis, but a revolt in the NORTHEAST marred attempts at national recovery.

From 1898 to 1909 three able civilians, representing the southern coffee interests, served in the Presidency. This was one of the most constructive periods in the nation's history. There was a surge of industrial de-velopment, coffee and rubber exports more than doubled (*see* COFFEE INDUSTRY: BRAZIL; RUBBER BOOM: BRAZIL), tropical diseases were eradicated, increased immigration swelled the coastal cities, and 342,000 square miles were added to the national territory in peaceful boundary settlements.

The two decades from 1910 to 1930 were plagued by a faltering economy and revolutionary ferment. Military discontent led to numerous revolts. Growing urban middle sectors were clamoring for a voice in the political process. Politicomilitary conflicts and economic unrest culminated in the successful REVOLUTION OF 1930.

ARNOLD J. MEAGHER

FISHING INDUSTRY (PERU). The HUMBOLDT CURRENT has made the 1,400-mile stretch of Peruvian coast the richest-known fishing bank on earth. The exploitation of this important resource began on a large scale only in the 1950s, as a result of a combination of fortuitous circumstances and a growing recognition of the economic benefits to be derived from its development.

Not until 1941 was a study made to discover the fishing capacities of Peruvian waters. In 1946 the first modern canneries were established, but capital investments were low and the industry was still considered a speculative venture. The uncertainties stemmed partially from the opposition of the politically powerful Compañía Administradora de Guano, which sought to discourage fish-meal production. The company feared that fish-meal manufacture would have a direct impact on the supply of GUANO, since both the industry and the guano-producing birds fed upon the same fish, anchovies.

The failure of the California sardine industry in the early 1950s spurred the development of the Peruvian fishing industry. Whole factories from the failed plants in California were transplanted to Peru along with considerable capital. Coincidentally, the 1950s witnessed the growing employment of fish meal by developed nations as a dietary supplement for livestock and poultry. The combination of these and other factors, along with the diminishing power of the Compañía Administradora de Guano, contributed to the remarkable expansion of the fishing industry until it made Peru the world's largest fishing nation. Thus, Peru's fish catch grew from 113,800 metric tons in 1950 to 2,186,600 tons in 1959. In 1968 it reached 10,262,661 tons, and by 1970 there had been a further increase, to 12,600,000 tons. Nearly 98 percent of the catch was anchovies, the key ingredient in the production of fish meal. Early in 1972, however, the anchovy virtually disappeared from Peru's coastal waters, having been driven away by a warm current that displaced the Humboldt Current.

In 1968 the fishing industry provided 27.1 percent of Peru's total exports (85.8 percent of this was fish meal), with a value of $234.3 million. The largest single importer of Peruvian fish meal was the United States, taking 26.4 percent of the total in 1968, followed by West Germany (19.11 percent) and the Netherlands (9.7 percent). In addition to fish meal, fishery exports included fish oil, frozen fish, and an increasing quantity of canned fish. Aside from the revenues engendered by such exports, the industry has been instrumental in fomenting related economic activities. It has stimulated the growth of more than twenty Peruvian ports; it has provided employment for thousands of Peruvians; and it has spurred the development of related industries such as shipyards, net factories, and factories manufacturing equipment for fish-meal production.

Because of Peru's growing economic dependence on the fish industry, the government gradually took a more active interest in its operations. The government, concerned with the ecological question of overfishing, established a closed season (*veda*) from March to August. In addition, it attempted to control cutthroat competition within the industry and encouraged the signing of agreements with other major fish-meal producing countries in order to stabilize the world's market price. The government also pressed for recognition of a 200-mile territorial limit, which caused clashes especially with United States fishing interests (*see* TERRITORIAL WATERS).

Finally, on May 8, 1973, the government announced the expropriation of all firms, whether foreign or domestically owned, engaged in the fishing and processing of anchovy into fish meal and fish oil products. These activities would henceforth be conducted by a state monopoly to be called Pesca-Perú. The government attributed its action to the indebtedness of the firms as well as to the recent disappearance of the anchovy. Five United States companies, with holdings valued at $40 million, were affected by the decree, as were several European, Argentine, and Japanese firms.

Bibliography. Anuario de Pesca, Lima, 1961–62; *Peruvian Times,* "Fisheries Supplement," Lima, 1967; Bobbie B. and Robert M. Smetherman, "Fish Meal and the Peruvian Economy," *Quarterly Review of Economics and Business,* vol. X, no. 3, 1970, pp. 35–45; United Nations Food and Agriculture Organization, *Yearbook of Fishery Statistics,* Rome, 1948–.

ORAZIO A. CICCARELLI

FLAG RIOTS. Series of riots that occurred in and near the United States–administered Panama Canal Zone on January 9–11, 1964, and left twenty-three Panamanians and four United States soldiers dead. Property damage in the zone alone amounted to more than $2 million. Diplomatic relations with the United States were severed by Panama on January 10 and were not reestablished until April 3.

Numerous concessions on the always-volatile issue of sovereignty over the Canal Zone had been made by the United States since President Eisenhower, in 1960, first authorized the flying of the Panamanian flag alongside the American banner at one location in the zone. Canal Zone Governor Robert J. Fleming, Jr., announced on December 30, 1963, that both flags would be displayed together at sixteen places in the Zone. No Canal Zone schools were included. When American students raised the United States flag at Balboa High School, a contingent of 150 students from the nearest Panamanian secondary school marched on Balboa High. Unable to raise their flag, the Panamanian students withdrew, charging that the police guarding the flagpole had defiled and trampled on Panama's colors. Their story spread throughout the capital, and that evening 3,000 vengeful Panamanians invaded the zone,

where they began to burn and sack United States property. Now in command of the zone, American troops forced the mob back into the republic. Further action by United States soldiers was limited to border areas, but Panamanian mobs swept over both Panama City and Colón, throwing Molotov cocktails at buildings and automobiles owned or operated by Americans. In addition to the 27 deaths, nearly 700 persons were wounded.

After three months of negotiations, relations with the United States were reestablished. Special ambassadors sought the prompt elimination of the causes of conflict between the two countries.

LARRY L. PIPPIN

FLEET SYSTEM. *See* COMMERCIAL POLICY (COLONIAL SPANISH AMERICA).

FLORES, JUAN JOSÉ (1801–1864). First President of Ecuador. Juan José Flores was the illegitimate son of a Spanish merchant and of Rita Flores, a native of Puerto Cabello, Venezuela. He was born in the same city on June 19, 1801. As a child he experienced poverty. At the age of fourteen, after working in the Spanish military hospital, he enlisted in the royalist army during the war of Spanish American independence. Two years later, by then a sergeant, he was taken prisoner by the patriot forces of Gen. Simón BOLÍVAR, whose army he joined. He fought as a cavalry officer in the decisive Battle of Carabobo (June 24, 1821), which assured Venezuela its independence, earning on the field the rank of lieutenant colonel (*see* CARABOBO, BATTLE OF).

At twenty-three Flores was a colonel and Governor of the province of Pasto in southern Colombia. Shortly thereafter he was appointed Intendant of Quito. By 1830 his authority had been extended to include all present-day Ecuador. He was second in command to Gen. Antonio José de SUCRE in the Battle of Tarqui (February 27, 1829), where the Colombian Army halted a Peruvian invasion, and was promoted to the rank of general.

Not long afterward Bolívar's Republic of Colombia (*see* COLOMBIA, GRAN) broke up into its component parts: New Granada (present-day Colombia and Panama), Venezuela, and Ecuador. At that time Flores exercised civil authority in Ecuador, he commanded the armed forces there, he had married into the Quito aristocracy, and his tact and manners had gained him influential friends all over the country. Only General Sucre could have been his rival, but Sucre was at that time in New Granada and was murdered on his way back, probably by agents of Gen. José María OBANDO. With almost no opposition, an assembly convoked by Flores declared Ecuador's independence on May 13, 1830, and chose the general as its first chief executive. A few months later he was elected constitutional President.

Although Flores failed in his attempt to integrate the province of Pasto in the new republic, he deserves credit for the organization of the state of Ecuador. His task was made easier by the backing of the majority of the ruling class and of the Venezuelan troops that constituted the backbone of his army. Nevertheless, in 1834 he had to face a revolt by the Liberals, erstwhile enemies of Bolívar (*see* LIBERAL PARTY: ECUADOR).

Juan José Flores. [Organization of American States]

In a quick campaign Flores retook the port city of Guayaquil, captured the revolutionary chief Vicente ROCAFUERTE, offered him the Presidency, and with his support turned against the revolutionaries of the highlands, whom he annihilated at Miñarica (January 18, 1835).

While Rocafuerte governed as President, Flores retained command of the Army. In 1839 the general returned to the Presidency, and Rocafuerte was shifted to the post of Governor of Guayas Province (capital, Guayaquil), the second most important political office in Ecuador at that time. Rocafuerte fully expected to keep on alternating in the Presidency with Flores, but the general thought otherwise and had himself reelected in 1843. This was the biggest, perhaps the only, blunder of Flores's political career, for he lost the support of the Guayaquil oligarchy (in any case Rocafuerte had only four years to live). An armed revolt, instigated by Rocafuerte, broke out in Guayaquil in 1845. Undefeated but unable to impose his authority, Flores agreed to spend two years in exile in exchange for a series of guarantees and compensation (June 1845).

Flores traveled to Europe. When the new government of Ecuador failed to honor the agreement, the general obtained the financial backing of María Cristina de Borbón, the Queen Mother of Spain, for an armed expedition, offering to make her son by a morganatic marriage King of Ecuador. The plan failed when the British government embargoed his ships. Flores returned to his native Venezuela and then spent several years in various Spanish American countries. In 1852 he attempted to invade Ecuador from Peru, but he was defeated by an erstwhile protégé, Gen. José María URBINA.

In 1859 the Peruvians invaded Ecuador, the government of which was assailed by revolutionaries and finally overthrown. The provisional government of Quito, headed by Gabriel GARCÍA MORENO, emerged from the resulting anarchy as the one with widest support. García Moreno had been an admirer of Rocafuerte and a rather violent enemy of Flores; but, in need of a military commander, he recalled the general from exile. On September 24, 1860, Flores took the city of Guayaquil and thereby put an end to the civil war.

General Flores presided over the convention that legalized the García Moreno regime in 1861. He commanded the Ecuadorian Army during a brief conflict with Colombia that ended in an Ecuadorian defeat at Cuaspud (December 6, 1863). The next year he was confronted with an attempt by General Urbina to invade the country from Peru. Flores defeated the revolutionaries but died on board the steamer that was carrying him back to Guayaquil (October 1, 1864).

His son, Antonio Flores Jijón, was President of Ecuador from 1888 to 1892.

Bibliography. Jacinto Jijón y Caamaño, *La expedición floreana de 1846,* Quito, 1943; Elías Laso, "Biografía del General Juan José Flores" (1865), *Boletín de la Academia Nacional de Historia,* vol. VIII, Quito, 1924, pp. 95–145; Luis Robalino Dávila, *Nacimiento y primeros años de la república,* Quito, 1964; Carlos A. Rolando, *Biografía del General Juan José Flores,* Guayaquil, 1930.

ÁDÁM SZÁSZDI

FLORES, VENANCIO (1808–1868). Uruguayan President, dictator, and military leader. Born in Trinidad, department of San José (now Flores), the son of a rancher, he was directed by his family toward service in the church, but he embarked on a military career in 1825 on joining the campaign to free Uruguay from Brazil. Starting as a common soldier, he rose to the rank of captain by 1830. His return to civilian life in 1831 was interrupted by Juan Antonio LAVALLEJA's revolt in 1832, as he rallied to the support of President Fructuoso RIVERA. Having been imprisoned by the government of Manuel ORIBE in 1836 at the start of Rivera's revolt against Oribe, Flores soon escaped to join Rivera's forces and after their triumph was named political chief in the department of San José. From the beginning of Rivera's war with the Argentine dictator Juan Manuel de ROSAS in 1839 he served with the Colorado forces (*see* COLORADO PARTY: URUGUAY) in the countryside until 1844, at which time he slipped through the siege lines to enter Montevideo, where he briefly held the post of general commander of the forces in the capital before returning to the countryside to attempt to raise a new army.

Forced by a wound that he received early in 1845 to seek refuge in Brazil, he returned to Montevideo to convalesce in September of that year. In 1851 he served with the forces of Justo José de URQUIZA that brought an end to the GUERRA GRANDE, after which he was appointed political chief in Montevideo. After serving briefly as Minister of War and Navy in the latter half of 1852 in the government of President Juan Francisco

Giró, he played a leading role as one of the Colorado leaders in the crisis between July and September of 1853 that terminated with Giró's ouster on September 25. He then served as the dominant member of the triumvirate that provisionally assumed control of the government and after the death of his two colleagues secured his election as constitutional President to fill out the remaining two years of Giró's term. The growing reaction in both Uruguay's traditional parties to the *caudillo* tradition that Flores represented, his reliance on a 4,000-man Brazilian force to maintain order, and a serious financial situation created such dissatisfaction with his regime that he was forced to resign on September 10, 1855. Nettled by the Conservative Colorados' hostility toward him, he soon reached an agreement with the rival Blanco *caudillo,* Manuel Oribe (*see* BLANCO PARTY: URUGUAY), to support Gabriel Antonio Pereira as a bipartisan candidate for the presidential term beginning in 1856. When Pereira began maneuvering to free himself from the tutelage of the two *caudillos,* Flores withdrew to Argentina to engage in ranching in Entre Ríos and subsequently joined the forces of Bartolomé MITRE in Buenos Aires to play an important role in the Battles of Cepeda and Pavón. Capitalizing on the goodwill of the triumphant Mitre and on the dissatisfaction in Rio Grande do Sul over the Blanco government's treatment of Brazilians in Uruguay, he launched a revolt against that government on April 18, 1863, that finally triumphed early in 1865 with the assistance of Brazil's armed forces. Although he assumed dictatorial powers in January 1865, he sought to unite the nation through a policy of toleration toward the ousted Blancos that extended even to those responsible for the massacre of Colorados at Quinteros in 1858.

As the leader of the Uruguayan contingent in the PARAGUAYAN WAR, he was absent from the country until December 1866, at which time he returned to assume direct political control. Growing dissatisfaction with the prolongation of his personal rule induced him to resign on February 15, 1868, after he had convoked elections. It is not clear whether he intended to be a candidate, inasmuch as he was assassinated four days later during a Blanco revolt led by former President Bernardo Berro, who paid with his life when the revolt was crushed the same day.

Bibliography. Alfredo Lepro, *Años de forja: Venancio Flores,* Montevideo, 1962; Isidoro de María, *Rasgos biográficos de hombres notables de la República Oriental del Uruguay,* 4 vols., Montevideo, 1939; Juan E. Pivel Devoto and Alcira Ranieri de Pivel Devoto, *Historia de la República Oriental del Uruguay,* Montevideo, 1945.

JOHN H. HANN

FLÔRES DA CUNHA, JOSÉ ANTÔNIO (1880–1959). Brazilian politician. Born in the state of Rio Grande do Sul, the charismatic José Antônio Flôres da Cunha carved out a public career of more than half a century. After two decades of politics, including service as state and federal deputy, this rugged frontiersman burst into national prominence during the 1923 Libertador revolution against Rio Grande do Sul's Republican government. Between 1923 and 1927 Flôres' aggressive leadership of Republican military forces was primarily responsible for thwarting repeated Libertador efforts, thereby earning him a congressionally awarded honorary generalship.

An organizer of the REVOLUTION OF 1930, Flôres also commanded a major detachment in the drive north from Rio Grande do Sul, leading to the overthrow of the FIRST REPUBLIC and the installation of Getúlio VARGAS as President. Appointed Interventor of Rio Grande, Flôres threw the state's critical military support to Vargas against São Paulo during the 1932 Constitutionalist revolution and crushed pro-São Paulo revolts throughout the state. However, political disagreements soon transformed Flôres and Vargas into antagonists. Flôres opposed Vargas's plans to establish a dictatorship, while Vargas saw Flôres as a prime obstacle to his plans. Ultimately outflanked militarily and politically, Flôres fled in 1937 into exile in Uruguay, where he continued his opposition, including support of the abortive 1938 Integralista revolt against Vargas's ESTADO NOVO dictatorship (*see* INTEGRALISMO). Returning to Brazil in 1942, he was imprisoned.

When electoral politics returned to Brazil in 1945, Flôres became the Rio Grande leader of the anti-Vargas UNIÃO DEMOCRÁTICA NACIONAL, serving as federal deputy from 1945 to 1958. However, after splitting with his party during the November 1955 military coup, Flôres failed in his final electoral bid in 1958.

CARLOS E. CORTÉS

FLORES MAGÓN, RICARDO (1873–1922). Mexican journalist and political leader. Born in the state of Oaxaca, Flores Magón was educated in Mexico City, where he pursued a law degree. He dropped out of the

Venancio Flores. [*Organization of American States*]

Escuela de Jurisprudencia and took up journalism, writing in opposition to the programs of Porfirio DÍAZ, first for *El Demócrata* and then in his own newspaper, *Regeneración,* which he helped found in 1900 in cooperation with his brother Jesús. He became active in the movement that organized the First Liberal Congress in 1901. Ricardo was imprisoned on various occasions and finally, in 1904, sought refuge in San Antonio, Texas. There he resumed publication of *Regeneración,* this time assisted by another brother, Enrique. The following year, he moved his operation to St. Louis in order to escape harassment by Díaz's agents. The paper was smuggled into Mexico, where it helped stimulate opposition to Díaz and served as the organ of the radical Liberals.

In 1906 Flores Magón and some of his associates fled to Canada. His activities included organizing a rebellion in Baja California in 1911. He also wrote some plays with revolutionary themes. Attracted to anarchism, he refused to cooperate with Francisco I. MADERO, whose movement he considered too mild and middle-class. When he published an anarchist manifesto in the United States in 1918, he was arrested for violating the Espionage Act of 1917, convicted, and imprisoned. He died mysteriously in the federal penitentiary in Leavenworth, Kansas, in 1922.

CHARLES R. BERRY

FONSECA, HERMES [RODRIGUES] DA (1855–1923). Brazilian soldier and President (1910–1914). Born into a prominent military family in São Gabriel, Rio Grande do Sul, Fonseca enlisted in the Army in 1871 and was commissioned a lieutenant in the artillery in 1876. As a captain and aide to his uncle, Marshal Manuel Deodoro da FONSECA, he took part in the revolution that overthrew the empire of Brazil in 1889. Thereafter he advanced rapidly, reaching the rank of marshal in 1906, at the age of fifty-one. During the administration of President Afonso PENA (1906–1909), Fonseca was Minister of War. In this post he presided over sweeping changes designed to professionalize the Army. In 1909 he was nominated as the official candidate for the Presidency of Brazil and ran successfully against Ruy BARBOSA in the most bitterly contested presidential campaign of the era.

As President, Fonseca left many questions of domestic politics to his friend Senator José Gomes PINHEIRO MACHADO and maintained the established policy of close relations with the United States. Although he was elected to the Senate shortly after leaving office, he did not serve. Fonseca spent the years from 1915 to 1920 in Europe but plunged into politics upon his return to Brazil. As president of the Club Militar in 1922, he tried overtly to enlist Army support for the opposition presidential candidate and was placed under six-month house arrest by President Epitácio PESSOA. Released in poor health, Fonseca retired to Petrópolis, where he died.

ROLLIE E. POPPINO

FONSECA, MANUEL DEODORO DA (1827–1892). Brazilian army marshal. A lifelong military man, Deodoro da Fonseca first distinguished himself in combat during the suppression of the Liberal Pernambuco revolt of 1848. He achieved national prominence as commander of the 2d Battalion of Voluntários da Patria in the PARAGUAYAN WAR and emerged from that struggle a colonel. Elected the first president of Rio de Janeiro's Club Militar, Deodoro became the chief spokesman for the interests of the military. In 1886 he became concerned that military prestige and power were being undermined by the imperial government. Convinced by leaders of the Republican party that only a republican government could end what he perceived to be the persecution of the Army and restore the military to its proper place in the nation, he led the successful revolt of November 15, 1889, that ousted Emperor PEDRO II and established the FIRST REPUBLIC.

Proclaimed provisional President and formally elected President on February 25, 1891, under the new constitution (*see* CONSTITUTION OF 1891: BRAZIL), Deodoro soon saw his support collapse. The reforms of his Finance Minister, Ruy BARBOSA, came under attack from the press and the Congress. A major stock market boom, the Encilhamento, shook the country's finances. Deodoro clamped a tight censorship on the press. Congress even refused to pass laws for the expenditure of funds requested by the President. Accustomed to the discipline and respect of military life, Deodoro countered by dissolving the Congress, promising to reconvene it again when the situation had improved. His opponents now had the issue they had been seeking. Major revolts occurred in Rio Grande do Sul and in the harbor of Rio de Janeiro. Deodoro's Vice President, Floriano PEIXOTO, turned against him. Extremely ill and wishing to avoid a bloody civil war, Deodoro resigned from the Presidency on November 22, 1891. He died in relative obscurity on August 22, 1892.

JOHN E. PICHEL

FOOTBALL WAR (HUNDRED-HOUR WAR; SOCCER WAR). Conflict between El Salvador and Honduras in 1969. Ostensibly the ill-tempered outgrowth of hotly contested soccer matches between two countries contending for a place in the World Cup tourney of 1970, it was in reality a product of tensions produced by unresolved social problems. It has been called the first war caused by the population explosion.

The major circumstance underlying the war was a densely populated El Salvador lying adjacent to a sparsely populated Honduras. Estimates for 1967 showed El Salvador to be some seven times as densely populated as Honduras. Each had an annual population growth of 3.3 per 1,000, and each hoped for rapid national development.

El Salvador afforded insufficient opportunity to provide for its burgeoning population. Dramatically increased agricultural production over a decade chiefly augmented export crops, while per capita food production declined. Housing, health facilities, and other services also failed to keep pace. Urban industry could not absorb the labor surplus, and coffee growers afforded neither land nor employment. Beginning in 1950 the government tried without substantial success to resettle surplus residents from densely populated areas on state-owned land in the northern part of the republic, and after 1965 it made a fruitless effort at broad land reform.

Disparate population densities and insufficient opportunity at home tempted Salvadorans by the thousands to cross the line into Honduras, often without the documentation required to legalize their status. From about 1966 onward the government officially encouraged Salvadorans to emigrate. Investigators in 1969 estimated the number of Salvadorans in Honduras at more than 300,000. President Julio Adalberto RIVERA of El Salvador characterized this emigration as a mobility of labor that allowed other CENTRAL AMERICAN COMMON MARKET countries to draw on El Salvador's human reservoir.

Honduras also felt social pressures resulting from a rapidly expanding population entertaining rising hopes for national development. Much of the country was poorly adapted to agriculture, and most of the arable land was already engrossed in large holdings. Salvadoran immigrants squatted on private holdings, occupied open land, or competed with native-born Hondurans for the limited employment the country afforded, chiefly on the banana plantations of the north. By consuming resources that might better the situation of Hondurans, they seemed to prejudice the country's prospects for development.

Liberal President Ramón VILLEDA MORALES took measures to relieve social pressures in Honduras. His agrarian reform law of September 1962 envisioned the distribution of public lands and private holdings that did not meet minimum production requirements. It helped Honduras to qualify for ALLIANCE FOR PROGRESS aid, but it made no provision for landownership by foreigners. Threatened native landholders argued that the law should first be applied against individuals occupying land illegally. This law and two measures enacted during the subsequent administration that restricted employment and individual enterprise opportunities for foreigners provided the basis for action against the Salvadorans in 1968.

Feeling between the two countries ran high in 1967. There were military provocations along the frontier and growing resentment in Honduras at the disparate benefits the two countries reaped from the Central American Common Market. When Honduran President Oswaldo LÓPEZ ARELLANO initiated a colonization project in the Aguán Valley, the large landholders renewed their protests against foreign squatters. In response, the government repatriated several thousand Salvadorans during 1968. Tensions mounted as communications media in both countries circulated atrocity stories and the crucial soccer matches approached. On June 4, 1969, Honduras announced new evictions of Salvadoran families and squatters. A few days later, latent resentments flared into violence after the first soccer game played in Tegucigalpa, and again a week later after the second game in San Salvador. Protests and mutual accusations followed, and on June 26 the states broke diplomatic relations. The ORGANIZACIÓN DE ESTADOS CENTROAMERICANOS (ODECA) and the ORGANIZATION OF AMERICAN STATES (OAS) tried to avert the impending war, but on July 14 the Salvadoran Army moved on Honduras.

The OAS peace machinery immediately went into action. Hostilities continued, however, until the belligerents accepted an OAS peace plan on July 19. On July 30, El Salvador agreed to withdraw its troops. It was estimated at the time of the cease-fire that about 2,000 soldiers and civilians, mainly Hondurans, had been killed.

The consequences of the war are not easily assessed.

The wounds are deep and will be slow to heal. ODECA and the Central American Common Market are threatened, and if passion prevails over reason, they may succumb. There may yet be a beneficial outcome, however, if insights gained in contemplating the experience result in action on social problems too long ignored and in adjustment of the mechanisms of Central American cooperation to assist initially handicapped participants, such as Honduras, to grow abreast of their more fortunate partners.

Bibliography. Franklin D. Parker, "The *Futbol* Conflict and Central American Unity," *Annals of the Southeastern Conference on Latin American Studies,* vol. III, no. 1, March 1972, pp. 44–59.

WILLIAM J. GRIFFITH

FOREIGN INVESTMENT. No one knows with precision just how much foreign investment there is in Latin America, and what is known is grossly underestimated. The evidence indicates a dramatic expansion from about $3 billion outstanding at the turn of the twentieth century to about $37 billion at the end of 1970. In that year foreign capital was divided equally between direct investment under the control of foreign owners and loan capital in the form of guaranteed external debt. In addition, there were large but unknown amounts of corporate securities and unguaranteed private debts of varying maturities in the investment portfolios of foreigners.

A brief history. By the end of the nineteenth century Great Britain had invested $2 billion in Latin America, France $600 million, and the United States $300 million. By 1914 Germany had joined the ranks with $1 billion, and total foreign investment had grown to $9 billion. Britain was the leader, but it slowly relinquished that position to the United States over the following thirty years.

The decade of the 1920s was one of rapid expansion as the United States emulated its rivals by expanding into overseas sources of supply and replacing European loan capital for financing Latin American governments. On the eve of the Great Depression, United States investments in Latin America were valued at $5 billion or $6 billion, a level not reached again for more than twenty years. With the crash came massive defaults on bonds, and United States direct investment declined by one-fourth, partly because of petroleum expropriations in Mexico and because of political instability or unattractive markets elsewhere.

World War II brought renewed United States interest. Although portfolio investment declined, direct investment expanded rapidly after the war. Meanwhile, Britain liquidated one-fifth of its holdings, and Germany and France virtually disappeared from the scene, the former in part through expropriations. United States firms expanded their direct investments, from $4.5 billion at the end of 1950 to nearly $13 billion by the end of 1971.

The current picture. Despite the reappearance of other countries in recent years, the United States is still dominant, owning two-thirds of all direct foreign investments in the Latin American republics. There has been a marked change in the sectoral distribution, as internal markets have attracted capital to a dynamic manufacturing sector, where United States direct investment grew from $800 million in 1950 to nearly $5 billion by

DIRECT FOREIGN INVESTMENT AND EXTERNAL DEBT IN LATIN AMERICA, 1970 *
(In millions)

| | Investing Country | | | | | | | | | | | |
	United States	United King-dom	Can-ada	Ger-many	Nether-lands	France	Japan	Italy	Swit-zer-land	Other Europe †	Total	Ex-ternal debt
Argentina	$ 1,280	$ 210	$ 20	$120	$ 70	$130	$ 20	$250	$140	$ 20	$ 2,260	$ 2,400
Brazil	1,850	220	770	600	200	330	260	180	170	200	4,780	3,600
Chile	750	10	...	30	...	10	40	...	...	...	840	2,400
Colombia	700	30	10	30	30	...	...	...	...	10	810	1,700
Mexico	1,790	140	40	80	20	30	100	30	100	10	2,340	3,800
Panama	1,250	20	10	40	...	20	10	...	20	...	1,370	200
Peru	690	30	30	20	...	10	40	...	20	...	840	1,130
Venezuela	2,700	430	100	10	560	...	10	10	10	10	3,840	700
CACM ‡	620	30	50	10	10	...	20	...	...	...	740	830
Other §	630	60	50	10	10	10	10	...	...	...	780	1,540
Total ¶	$12,260	$1,180	$1,080	$950	$900	$540	$510	$470	$460	$250	$18,600	$18,300

* United States data are rounded figures from the Department of Commerce. All other data are estimates by the author, based on a variety of unofficial sources. Direct investment is book value at year-end. It includes investment only from member countries of the Organization for Economic Cooperation and Development. Excluded are investments by the Latin American countries themselves and by countries of the Middle East, Africa, and Asia other than Japan. External debt is guaranteed debt, including undisbursed amounts but excluding nonguaranteed private debt.
† Austria, Belgium, Denmark, Norway, Portugal, and Sweden.
‡ Central American Common Market (Costa Rica, El Salvador, Guatemala, Honduras, and Nicaragua).
§ Other Latin American republics (Bolivia, Dominican Republic, Ecuador, Haiti, Paraguay, and Uruguay).
¶ Excludes Cuba.

1971, heavily concentrated in Brazil, Mexico, and Argentina. Even so, one-fourth of United States investment is still in the petroleum industry, and the large amount in Venezuela remains the largest sectoral concentration of United States capital in Latin America.

Others investors have returned in force. German and Japanese capital, in particular, is in a phase of very fast growth. Canada, the Netherlands, France, Italy, and Switzerland each hold direct investments ranging from $500 million to $1 billion. Belgium owns $100 million, and very small amounts belong to Austria, Denmark, Norway, and Portugal. Although the holdings of the British have declined, they still own more than $1 billion worth of direct investments in the Latin American economies. (See accompanying table.)

Like the Americans, the Europeans and the Japanese, attracted by internal markets, have concentrated their capital in manufacturing. Latin American industrialization and import substitution policies have offered the attractions of tax holidays, other subsidies, and lucrative markets protected from import competition. Public policy in the capital-exporting countries has stimulated the flow of private investment through tax exemptions, investment insurance, advisory services, and even government equity participations; and government loans and grants have often provided the foreign exchange with which Latin American countries have paid the interest and profits on a growing volume of foreign investment.

Subsidiaries of foreign firms are well entrenched in Latin American markets. Ford and Fiat, Volkswagen and Renault, Datsun and Toyota have taken on the protective coloration of national manufacture, and virtually every well-known automobile is assembled in some Latin American country. British firms manufacture diesel engines, chemicals, cosmetics, and textiles. German firms produce steel, chemicals, fibers, and pharmaceuticals. Japanese subsidiaries make steel and ships, machinery and textiles. And United States firms are almost everywhere: petroleum refining, chemicals, transportation equipment, pharmaceuticals, rubber goods, paper, machinery, and a wide variety of food products. The lists given here are only partial.

United States enterprises alone have 5,000 affiliates in the Latin American republics. Half of them are in manufacturing, where their sales run to $7 billion or $8 billion per year, an amount roughly equivalent to 6 percent of the gross product of their host area. Nine-tenths of their sales are in local markets—sufficient proof of the attraction for foreign investment. Nevertheless, these subsidiaries are even more important in the export trade. Producing only 10 percent of manufacturing output, they account for 40 percent of manufactured exports, and the fraction is growing. One-fourth of these exports go to the United States.

Latin American policy in general has sought to replace some direct investment with loan capital, and it has succeeded. Guaranteed external debt grew from $2,250 million at the end of 1950 to $18 billion at the end of 1970. In the former year debt was not quite one-third as large as direct investment, while in the latter the two were equal. United States investors, public and private, held claims against the Latin American republics in 1970 amounting to $24 billion. Half of it was direct investment, $5 billion was in United States government loans, $1 billion in privately held bonds, $3 billion in short-term nonliquid claims, and the other $3 billion in a variety of assets held by United States banks, business enterprises, and individuals.

As the cold war has faded, even the Communist bloc

has invested a bit, with the USSR financing some projects and Romania and Yugoslavia making joint-venture agreements in manufacturing and mining.

Effects of foreign investment. To the foreign investor his venture is an instrument of development that transfers technology, pays taxes, and creates employment while it earns a profit. To the host country the effects are ambiguous, and the intrusion of foreign enterprise has created a series of defensive reactions. It is feared that foreign firms may preempt scarce resources and exercise superior bargaining power based on size, brand name, and access to international credits and talents. They may engage in market-sharing arrangements whereby the Latin American subsidiary agrees to limit or avoid the exportation of its products to markets where they will compete with those of the parent company or other subsidiaries in the system. They may withdraw excessive profits or avoid tax payments through internal transfer-pricing techniques; thus a parent firm may charge excessively high prices for supplying a subsidiary with inputs, or a subsidiary may sell its products to the parent at prices lower than the world market prices in order to avoid export taxes or other taxes based on price. Regular transfers of profits, interest, and payments for technology add pressures to the balance of payments. Foreign firms may interfere in local politics, dominate key sectors of the economy, and bring on diplomatic pressure or reprisal from their home governments. Their global experience and facilities may prove too much for local competitors, forestalling the development of local entrepreneurs or indigenous technology.

For Latin American governments, many of these potential results are real: restrictive clauses in Mexico, high transfer prices in Colombia, political intrigue in Chile, and balance-of-payments problems everywhere. Every republic except Venezuela has had large current-account deficits over the past decade, due largely to transfers of investment income. Annual payments of profits, interest, and amortizations run to $5 billion for the republics taken together, an amount equal to 35 percent of their total exports of goods and services. Payments for technology associated with direct investment may run as high as one-third of the amount transferred on account of interest and profits.

Latin American policies for the future. Because powerful firms present a challenge to economic policy and to national autonomy, Latin American governments have begun to regulate the inflow of foreign capital. They have expropriated outright in a few cases, most recently in Peru, Bolivia, and Chile. More often they have decided to screen new investments, to insist on local participation in capital and management, to require gradual or selective transfer of control to locals, and to supervise the purchase of foreign technology.

Today Latin America can purchase the plant, equipment, and know-how traditionally associated with direct investment, and it can play European, Japanese, and American sources against one another. There are signs that foreign investment will continue to grow in the future, but the conditions of its entry are certain to be regulated more frequently and more effectively.

Bibliography. Marvin D. Bernstein (ed.), *Foreign Investment in Latin America: Cases and Attitudes,* New York, 1966; Inter-American Development Bank, *Multinational Investment, Public and Private, in the Economic Development and Integration of Latin America,* Bogotá, April 1968; Herbert K. May, *The Effects of United States and Other Foreign Investment in Latin America,* New York, January 1970; Organization for Economic Cooperation and Development, Development Assistance Directorate, *Stock of Private Direct Investments by D.A.C. Countries in Developing Countries, End 1967,* Paris, 1972; Osvaldo Sunkel, "Big Business and 'Dependencia,'" *Foreign Affairs,* vol. 50, April 1972, pp. 517–531; United Nations Department of Economic and Social Affairs, *Foreign Capital in Latin America,* New York, 1955, Sales No.: 1954. II.G.4; University of Chicago, Research Center in Economic Development and Cultural Change, "United States Business and Labor in Latin America," *United States–Latin American Relations,* 86th Congress, 2d Session, Senate Document No. 125, Washington, August 31, 1960; Raymond Vernon, *Sovereignty at Bay: The Multinational Spread of U.S. Enterprises,* New York, 1971.

CALVIN P. BLAIR

FRANCIA, JOSÉ GASPAR RODRÍGUEZ DE (1766–1840). Supreme Dictator of Paraguay (1814–1840). Francia was born in Asunción, the son of a Brazilian militia officer settled in Paraguay and an upper-class Paraguayan woman. He was educated in Asunción and then attended the University of Córdoba, where he received a doctorate in theology in 1785. Returning to Asunción, he taught theology at the seminary for a short time and then decided to practice law. As a lawyer he gained a reputation for honesty and sagacity as well as for moderate social activism, since he often defended the poor against the powerful without charge. In the years 1807–1809 he was engaged in politics, holding virtually every available post in the Municipal Council of Asunción. By 1810 there were no other political goals he could seek without moving to another province, as creoles were rarely allowed to serve the crown in their own provinces. In 1811, although he was probably aware of the plot that overthrew Spanish power in May, he was not among the revolutionaries. Almost immediately, however, they turned to him for guidance, and he joined the revolutionary junta.

As one of the few well-educated Paraguayans, a man of prestige and good reputation, and an experienced politician, Francia was indispensable. From 1811 to 1813 he used this advantage to become the dominant figure of the junta and to further his initially unpopular plan for national independence rather than union with, and subjection to, Buenos Aires, the old viceregal capital. In 1813 he and Col. Fulgencio Yegros were named Co-Consuls of the republic of Paraguay, and by the end of that year Francia had discredited Yegros and was master of the nation. In 1814 a 1,000-member congress elected Francia Supreme Dictator of the republic, and two years later another congress added the word "Perpetual" to the title.

With popularly granted, almost absolute power, Francia began his own revolution. He broke the traditional white elite by mandating miscegenation, took over active direction of the understaffed church, created a powerful army, reasserted Paraguay's claim to the contested Misiones region, and adopted a policy of partial isolation of the nation to protect it from foreign subversion from Brazil and Argentina and contamination by the anarchy prevailing in neighboring Argentine provinces. Francia ruled Paraguay as if it were his own ranch; hundreds of Paraguayans and foreigners were jailed, and in 1822 a score or more of his enemies were executed. He gave Paraguay peace in a strife-torn age but at the cost of hallowing iron rule, increasing nationalism to the point of collective paranoia, and introducing the Army into political life. He died peacefully in 1840 after a twenty-six-year rule that had made him famous in the Americas and Europe and had given the term "dictator" the meaning we ascribe to it today.

Bibliography. Justo Pastor Benítez, *La vida solitaria del Dr. José Gaspar de Francia, dictador del Paraguay,* Buenos Aires, 1937; Julio César Chaves, *El supremo dictador,* 4th ed., Madrid, 1964; Francisco Wisner, *El dictador del Paraguay: José Gaspar Francia,* Buenos Aires, 1957.

JOHN HOYT WILLIAMS

FRANCISCANS (COLONIAL PERIOD). *See* RELIGIOUS ORDERS (COLONIAL PERIOD).

FRANCO, RAFAEL (1896–   ). Paraguayan military hero, leader of the Febrerista party, and President (1936–1937). A native of Asunción, Franco entered the Army at the age of twenty and rose through the ranks, retiring as a major at the age of thirty-four. When the CHACO WAR erupted in 1932, he was recalled to active service with the rank of lieutenant colonel and was given command of a crack regiment. He proved to be a brilliant field commander, eventually assuming command of the 2d Corps, the best in the Army. At the war's end in 1935, Franco, the idol of the Army, became the head of the Paraguayan Military Academy. In that post he was increasingly disturbed by what he considered a betrayal of the Paraguayan victory by the ruling Liberal party.

Franco gathered around him like-minded individuals, many of them young officers who hoped to implement a social revolution. In February 1936, despite the fact that he had just been exiled, his Febrerista revolution occurred, backed by the National Veterans Association and the major part of the Army. Franco was recalled and became president, but before his AGRARIAN REFORM and other programs could be carried out, he was overthrown in August 1937 by a military coup. From exile he tried to direct several countercoups, but they failed, and only in the 1947 civil war did the Febreristas come near to seizing power again.

Franco was in exile most of the years after 1937, usually in Buenos Aires. His movement, now a political party despite schisms, is part of the legal opposition to President Alfredo STROESSNER and takes part in elections. *See also* FEBRERISMO.

JOHN HOYT WILLIAMS

FRAP. *See* FRENTE DE ACCIÓN POPULAR.

FREE BIRTH LAW (LEI DO VENTRE LIVRE; RIO BRANCO LAW). Sponsored by Emperor PEDRO II as a compromise measure intended to eliminate slavery slowly and without disastrous effects upon the agricultural economy, the Free Birth Law was sanctioned on September 28, 1871, by Princess Isabel after years of acrimonious national debate. The most significant piece of legislation passed during the Conservative ministry of Visconde do RIO BRANCO, it included the following major provisions: It freed the children of slave women born after the date of the law, obligating the mothers' masters to care for them until the age of eight, when they could either exchange them for 6 percent thirty-year government bonds or use their labor until they reached the age of twenty-one. It created an emancipation fund for the annual liberation of slaves in all the provinces. It granted slaves the legal right to keep savings acquired through gifts or inheritance and, with the consent of their masters, through their own labor. It gave slaves the right to buy their freedom when they could offer a sum of money equal to their "value." It freed government-owned slaves and those included in unclaimed inheritances or abandoned by their masters. It placed free persons under governmental supervision for five years, with the obligation to contract their labor or, if living as vagabonds, to work in government establishments. Finally, it ordered a nationwide registration of all slaves and provided that slaves whose masters neglected to register them within one year were to be considered free.

A decade after passage, the failure of the Free Birth Law to produce impressive results was widely recognized. Registration had proceeded slowly, the emancipation fund had freed only a few thousand slaves at high prices, and even most children, though legally free, were living as de facto slaves. Nevertheless, by identifying emancipation with the best interests of the nation and reducing the national commitment to the slave system, the legislation undermined slavery and helped prepare the way for the dynamic abolitionist movement of the 1880s.

ROBERT CONRAD

FREI [MONTALVA], EDUARDO (1911–   ). President of Chile (1964–1970). The son of a Swiss father and a Chilean mother, Frei was born in Santiago and educated at the Seminario Pontificio, the Instituto de Humanidades, and the Catholic University, graduating as the top student in law in 1933. It was at the university, in the Association of Catholic Students, that he formed close friendships with other young men who shared his questioning attitude toward Chilean problems and acquired political experience, first as provincial secretary of the association, a post that put him in touch with many parts of Chile, and then as president. Nominated in 1934 with Manuel Garretón to represent Chile at the Congress of University Youth at Rome, he visited France and Belgium as well as Italy, meeting many eminent Catholics, including Pope Pius XI, Cardinal Pacelli (later Pius XII), and the French philosopher Jacques Maritain, whose lectures he attended in Paris.

Returning to Santiago, Frei became closely involved with the Movement of Conservative Students, which at first was warmly welcomed as its youth wing by the Conservative party (*see* CONSERVATIVE PARTY: CHILE) but then was increasingly rejected as overly progressive. By 1937 the Falange Nacional, as the movement was now called, had established its own identity, and Frei stood as one of its candidates in the congressional elections of that year. He was then working in the desert north of Chile as director of the paper *El Tarapacá,* and although he failed to win a seat for the province of Tarapacá, the experience was valuable. The same year he produced his first book, *Chile desconocido,* a study of the poverty he had seen in those barren regions. Returning to Santiago in 1937 to practice law, Frei was one of the leaders of the Falange Nacional who broke with the Conservative party over its support of Gustavo ROSS as the presidential candidate in 1938. From 1940 to 1945 he held the chair of labor law at the Catholic University. Meanwhile, in 1941, he became president of his party, a post to which he was reelected for three consecutive terms. He had also emerged as a leading publicist of the party with his books *Aún es tiempo* (1942) and *La política y el espíritu* (1946). Now something of a national figure, Frei was appointed Minister of Public Works and Communications by President Juan Antonio RÍOS in May 1946, only to resign in January 1947 in protest at the government's handling of a labor demonstration in which a worker was killed.

In 1949 Frei was elected senator for Atacama and Coquimbo, the first member of his party to enter the Senate, and when his term expired in 1957, he was elected senator for Santiago. These active years of congressional life also saw the appearance of other books, notably *La verdad tiene su hora* (1955), which won a literary prize in 1956, and *Pensamiento y acción* (1958). The title of the former book was adopted as the campaign slogan for the presidential election of 1958 by the new PARTIDO DEMÓCRATA CRISTIANO (Christian Democratic party). Its candidate was Eduardo Frei, now clearly established as the key personality in the party. Though Frei ran third in the election, he doubled the vote his party had received in elections for Congress in 1957, and his qualities of leadership were also in evi-

Eduardo Frei. [David F. Laurash]

dence while the party was in opposition to President Jorge ALESSANDRI (1958–1964). Despite pressure by prominent party members, Frei held the party consistently to the tactical line of avoiding entangling alliances with other parties while it created a distinctive image as a party of reform within a democratic framework. This policy paid off in increasing support at the polls, culminating in his own great victory in the presidential election of 1964, which he won with a clear majority, 56.09 percent of the vote, the biggest margin for any Chilean President since 1931. His subsequent call for "a parliament for Frei" in the congressional elections of 1965 was answered when the Christian Democrats gained overall control of the Chamber of Deputies and increased their representation in the Senate.

Frei presided over the most thoroughgoing reform regime that Chile had ever seen. Ambitious programs of economic development, based on AGRARIAN REFORM, control of inflation, equity participation in copper mining, and industrial development, were matched by social projects to transform education, reform the law, improve health and housing, and promote communal self-improvement. Frei also pursued an active foreign policy, notably in Chilean initiatives to promote Latin American ECONOMIC INTEGRATION and further good relations with other countries. Nevertheless, his "revolution in liberty" (the slogan with which he fought the election of 1964) was only a qualified success. Hampered by obstruction in the Senate, by serious natural disasters (earthquake and drought), by a split in his own party, and, above all, by the sheer impossibility of fulfilling the expectations of immediate improvement that his electoral victories had aroused, his government lost much of its early popularity, and the Christian Democrats were defeated in the presidential election of 1970. However, Frei himself lost little and left office a highly respected and much-admired figure. He was elected to the Senate from Santiago in the March 1973 congressional elections.

Bibliography. Eduardo Frei, *Pensamiento y acción,* Santiago, 1958; Sergio Guilisasti Tagle, *Partidos políticos chilenos,* 2d ed., Santiago, 1964; Gerardo Mello Mourao, *Frei y la revolución latino-americana,* Santiago, 1966.

HAROLD BLAKEMORE

FRENTE DE ACCIÓN POPULAR (POPULAR ACTION FRONT; FRAP). Marxist coalition, formed in March 1956, that united a number of left-wing Chilean parties opposed to the government of President Carlos IBÁÑEZ (1952–1958). It included the two Socialist parties, the Partido Socialista Popular, led by Raúl Ampuero, and the Partido Socialista de Chile of Salvador ALLENDE (*see* SOCIALIST PARTY: CHILE); the two factions of the Democratic party (*see* DEMOCRATIC PARTY: CHILE); and, though banned from public activity, the Communist party (*see* COMMUNIST PARTY: CHILE). Very different from the Popular Front of the 1930s in that it avoided the parties of the center, such as the Radicals and the Falange Nacional (*see* POPULAR FRONT: CHILE; RADICAL PARTY: CHILE), FRAP sought to create a united political force of the left primarily on working-class support. At its foundation it had thirty-eight seats in the Chamber of Deputies and eight seats in the Senate, but these figures fell to seventeen and seven, respectively, in the elections of 1957.

FRAP recovered ground with the reunification of the Socialist factions in 1957, and in the presidential election of 1958 Allende was a very close second to Jorge ALESSANDRI in a four-cornered contest. In 1961 the FRAP parties secured thirty-three seats in the lower house and twelve in the Senate, and it had high hopes for the presidential election of 1964, with Allende again as its candidate against Eduardo FREI for the PARTIDO DEMÓCRATA CRISTIANO (Christian Democratic party) and Julio Durán, the Radical nominee of a loose coalition of the Radical, Conservative, and Liberal parties (*see* CONSERVATIVE PARTY: CHILE; LIBERAL PARTY: CHILE). These hopes increased when, a few months before the election, FRAP won a by-election in the normally right-wing constituency of Curicó, but this was a Pyrrhic victory.

Now deeply alarmed at the prospect of a FRAP President, the right-wing parties left their Radical colleagues to fight alone and threw their unsolicited support to Frei. His shattering triumph over Allende, followed by his party's remarkable success in the congressional elections of 1965, virtually destroyed FRAP, which indulged in sharp internal recrimination for some time. In the event, however, the component parts of FRAP, together with Radicals and dissident Christian Democrats, reunited in December 1969, not as FRAP but as Unidad Popular (Popular Unity).

HAROLD BLAKEMORE

FREYRE, GILBERTO [DE MELLO] (1900–   ). Brazilian anthropologist, sociologist, historian, and journalist. Freyre was born in Recife, Pernambuco, and educated there and in the United States at Baylor and Columbia Universities. His *Casa Grande e Senzala* (1933), translated into English as *The Masters and the Slaves* (1946), is a study of the development and structure of the patriarchal society of the Brazilian NORTHEAST in the colonial period. It strongly influenced Brazilian ideas about the contribution of the Portuguese, Indians, and Negroes to the making of the country (*see* NEGRO IN BRAZIL) and produced changes in methods of research in the social sciences. Freyre stressed the importance of the African element in all aspects of social life. He emphasized the theory that social history has greater significance than political history. The book is a mine of information on the traditional Brazilian family, rural slavery, the status of women, and many other subjects. In *Sobrados e Mocambos* (1936), translated as *The Mansions and the Shanties* (1963), he showed the disintegration of the patriarchal plantation (fazenda) system and the development of the nineteenth-century city, as typified by Recife, with its rich merchants, penniless proletariat, and incipient middle class, which included many educated mulattoes who were to occupy an important position in the national political life and to become the backbone of the imperial civil service. Neither of these books is pure history, for Freyre uses anthropology and sociology in his analyses with an ease that few professional historians can exhibit.

One of Freyre's more recent and most controversial theories is that of *luso-tropicalismo,* according to which the Portuguese were particularly well adapted for the colonization of the tropics because of the liberalizing influence of their traditional Catholicism and the strong Moorish and Jewish elements in their background. This is expressed in *New World in the Tropics* (1961)

and other works. Freyre's reliance upon newspaper advertisements, diaries, and collections of letters that he found in family archives helped to arouse the interest of other researchers in these important sources of information. Freyre's large bibliography includes a history of nineteenth-century Brazil based on oral documents, *Ordem e Progresso* (1959), translated as *Order and Progress* (1970); other books on the Northeast, such as *Vida Social no Brasil nos Meados do Século XIX* (1964), which is a translation of his published master's thesis, *Social Life in Brazil in the Middle of the Nineteenth Century* (1922), originally written in English; and a novel, *Dona Sinhá e o Filho Padre,* 1964 (*Mother and Son*).

RAYMOND S. SAYERS

FRIGERIO, ROGELIO (1914–   ). Argentine industrialist and publisher with wide experience in textiles, mining, agriculture, and livestock raising. A close friend of ex-President Juan D. PERÓN, Frigerio was associated with Perón's policy of increasing the economic role of the small Argentine-owned industries and businesses of the interior represented after May 1946 by the Confederación General Económica. The policy was undertaken against opposition by the large foreign-oriented, and often foreign-owned, industries of the city and province of Buenos Aires, represented by the Unión Industrial Argentina, which was intervened by Perón in December 1951.

Frigerio supported Arturo FRONDIZI after 1956, most effectively through the pages of his review *Qué Sucedió en Siete Dias. Qué* provided the vehicle that enabled Frondizi to make his successful appeal for support to the mass of *peronistas.* Frigerio also was a leader in the *integracionista* movement, intended to incorporate the *peronistas,* now without a legal party, into the body of the Unión Cívica Radical Intransigente (*see* RADICAL PARTY: ARGENTINA). Early in 1958 Frigerio traveled to Caracas, Venezuela, to talk with Perón in a successful effort to negotiate the basis for *peronista* support. After Frondizi's inauguration in May 1958, the President appointed him Secretary of Socioeconomic Affairs.

Because of Frigerio's close ties with Perón and his service as a link between the ex-President and Frondizi, the military considered him totally unsuitable to hold government office. In early 1959 *peronista*-led strikes resulted in violence, and Frondizi requested military assistance in restoring order. The *quid pro quo* demanded by the officers was dismissal of Frigerio. Frondizi acquiesced, although Frigerio continued to serve in an unofficial capacity until Frondizi himself was deposed in March 1962.

EUGENE G. SHARKEY

FRIGORÍFICO. Meat-packing plant using the newly invented methods of refrigeration that appeared in Argentina in the 1880s. To satisfy European demands for meat Argentina began in 1874 to ship its livestock on the hoof. In 1876, eight years after the failure of the first attempt to ship frozen meat, *Le frigorifique* sailed from Rouen for Buenos Aires with beef and mutton being preserved by a technique recently developed by Charles Tellier. It returned to France with mutton supplied by Eugène Terrason, the French owner of the Saladero San Luis in San Nicolás. Not all the meat arrived in a satisfactory condition. A year later *Le Par-*

aguay, with equipment reducing the temperature to a lower level than that of the Tellier system, stopped in Buenos Aires for a shipment of mutton from the Saladero San Luis, and when it reached Marseille, its cargo was still good. This success encouraged Terrason to build a meat-packing plant with refrigeration equipment at San Nicolás, to begin exporting frozen mutton (his first consignment probably reached its destination in 1883), and to form the Compañía Argentina de Carnes Congeladas in 1884.

Three other *frigoríficos,* two English and one French, were opened by 1887, but industrial expansion then ceased because the anticipated profits had failed to materialize. Part of the problem was that until the introduction of the Lincoln breed of sheep about 1884, the comparatively lighter Argentine sheep were not highly valued in English markets; in addition, ranchers were not breeding high-quality cattle, and the *frigoríficos* were unable to compete with on-the-hoof shipments. Shipments of live cattle came to an abrupt end when England, frightened by an outbreak of foot-and-mouth disease, closed its markets to them in 1890.

By then ranchers had discovered the value of alfalfa and the shorthorn. Exports of frozen meat rose from 0.2 percent of all meat exports in 1887 to 51 percent in 1897, and the *frigoríficos* were financially in sound health by 1900. That year chilled beef was shipped for the first time, and it became so popular that by 1905 it had supplanted frozen meat. Between 1902 and 1905 Argentine, English, and South African capitalists, working alone or in combination, built five new *frigoríficos.* American firms began to enter the field in 1908, beginning with the purchase of the Berisso *frigorífico* at La Plata by Swift and Company. Armour, Wilson, and Morris arrived a little later. By 1913 these American firms controlled 60 percent of the meat exports of Argentina. The advent of the *frigorífico* meant the eventual disappearance of ranchers who lacked the capital, technical skill, or willingness to breed the sheep and cattle that produced meat satisfying to the English palate. Success meant higher prices, increased land values, and new markets.

See also CATTLE INDUSTRY (ARGENTINA).

JOSEPH T. CRISCENTI

FRONDIZI, ARTURO (1908–). President of Argentina (1958–1962). A member of the Unión Cívica Radical (*see* RADICAL PARTY: ARGENTINA) from 1928 on, Frondizi supported electoral abstention during the fraudulent administrations of the 1930s but reversed his position after 1943 and both advocated and participated in political activity. In 1946 and 1948 he was elected a national deputy from the federal capital. In 1951 he was an unsuccessful vice-presidential candidate with Ricardo Balbín. He consistently opposed the political methods of Juan D. PERÓN, although he approved of many of his social and economic ideas and therefore received Perón's support in his campaign for the Presidency in 1958.

Preoccupied with economic affairs and strongly influenced by Marxism, Frondizi vigorously criticized the penetration of Latin America by foreign capital. In contradiction of that sentiment but in recognition of the reality of his nation's economic situation, he signed oil exploitation contracts with foreign companies during his Presidency. He also abandoned much of his stated desire for AGRARIAN REFORM, autarkical industrial development, and nationalization of domestic- and foreign-owned utilities and monopolies. Economic difficulties including severe inflation, unfavorable trade balances, and labor unrest plagued Frondizi from the beginning of his term. He felt compelled to call upon the military to maintain order during severe strikes early in his term, and military interference increased from then until his dismissal in 1962.

In the elections of 1973 Frondizi supported the Peronist candidate for the Presidency (*see* PERONISM).

See also FRIGERIO, ROGELIO.

EUGENE G. SHARKEY

FUENTES, CARLOS (1928–). Mexican writer. Born in Mexico City, the son of a career diplomat, Fuentes learned English at the age of four and speaks fluent French as well. He held minor diplomatic posts, attended law school, which he finished in 1955, and founded the *Revista Mexicana de Literatura.* Fuentes is one of the most innovative of the generation of novelists responsible for the burgeoning of the so-called new Latin American novel. Much of his work deals with the consequences of the MEXICAN REVOLUTION and the analysis of the Mexican character through the exploration of the past. Fuentes is a master of the short story (*Los días enmascarados,* 1954; *Cantar de ciegos,* 1965) and of the novella (*Aura,* 1962; *Cumpleaños,* 1969). He has made important contributions to the essay with *La nueva novela latinoamericana* (1969) and *Casa con dos puertas* (1970) and has also written plays, including *Todos los gatos son pardos* (1970).

His talent is best expressed, however, in the novel, where his technical expertise and stylistic power disguise the bitterness of his criticism of modern Mexican society. *La región más transparente,* 1958 (*Where the Air Is Clear*), shows a society whose members have made their fortunes by dubious means in the post-revolutionary era. Here and in *Las buenas conciencias,* 1959 (*The Good Conscience*), he exposes a society in which individuals have sacrificed ideals to personal gain. *La muerte de Artemio Cruz,* 1962 (*The Death of Artemio Cruz*), explores this idea in depth. *Cambio de piel,* 1967 (*A Change of Skin*), represents a more abstract approach to novel writing and attempts by advanced techniques to integrate past, present, and future in a mythic synthesis of Mexican history and culture. A recent work is *Zona sagrada* (1967). Fuentes lives in Mexico City, where he is active in leftist political and intellectual circles.

RACHEL PHILLIPS

FUERO. In Spanish America a body of special rights, privileges, and exemptions. In the Spanish colonies as in Spain *fueros* were granted to municipalities and to groups such as the clergy, the military, and the merchants' guilds. Members of groups enjoying *fueros* might be exempt from certain taxes; in addition, such groups maintained their own courts, which might have complete jurisdiction over civil and criminal cases involving their members. Furthermore, *fueros* might be extended to include relatives and servants of members of the group in question.

The existence of such corporate privileges, which traced their origin to the Middle Ages, ran counter to the ideas of liberals who upheld the principle of equality before the law. The nineteenth century witnessed long struggles by liberals to abolish *fueros,* particularly those of the clergy and the military. Thus the Spanish constitution of 1812 limited the military and ecclesiastical *fueros,* and they were abolished by the Cortes of 1820. In Mexico the Juárez law (1855) abolished all special tribunals except those of the clergy and the military, the powers of which were drastically reduced.

ALAN KOVAC

FURTADO, CELSO [MONTEIRO] (1920–   ). Brazilian economist and sociologist. Furtado was born in Pombal, Paraíba. A self-described man of the left, Furtado is representative of the social scientist administrators who worked to plan and implement the developmental nationalism that characterized Brazil in the 1950s and early 1960s. He received his bachelor's degree from the University of Brazil and did graduate work in economics at the University of Paris and Cambridge University. In his writings he advocates a mixture of state economic planning and private initiative in a formula designed to bring economic improvement and political participation to the disadvantaged of Brazil.

In 1959 he was named by President Juscelino KUBITSCHEK to set up the SUPERINTENDÊNCIA DO DESENVOLVIMENTO DO NORDESTE (SUDENE) for the impoverished nine-state region in the NORTHEAST. He was confirmed as Director of SUDENE by President Jânio QUADROS in 1961 and served in that capacity until barred from public office in 1964. As Director he obtained special ALLIANCE FOR PROGRESS funds in support of the program and represented Brazil on the COMITÉ INTERAMERICANO DE LA ALIANZA PARA EL PROGRESO. In the Jânio Quadros–Joâo GOULART administration he was Minister without Portfolio in charge of economic planning. In the midst of the economic and political crisis of 1962 he was asked by President Goulart to draw up a plan that would provide for rapid economic growth and simultaneously reduce the spiraling rate of inflation. Furtado and Minister of Finance San Tiago Dantas worked together to produce the Three-Year Plan (1963–1965), which was to be a key element in Goulart's administrative program. However, as Goulart's support for the plan diminished, Furtado left the Planning Ministry in 1963. In 1964 he was stripped of his political rights for ten years by Brazil's new military government.

Furtado's books include *A Economia Brasileira* (1954); *Formação Econômica do Brasil,* 1959 (*The Economic Growth of Brazil,* 1963); and *A Pre-Revolução Brasileira,* 1962, and *Dialética do Desenvolvimento,* 1964 (published together as *Diagnosis of the Brazilian Crisis,* 1965).

FRANCESCA MILLER

GACHUPÍN. In colonial Mexico, a usually pejorative term for a peninsular Spaniard. The term probably derives from the Aztec "he who wears spurs," and is the Mexican equivalent of the Peruvian CHAPETÓN, meaning "tenderfoot." The term *gachupín* appeared at the end of the sixteenth century and described a recent arrival from Spain. *Gachupín* and CREOLE constituted the two principal divisions of the white upper class. The antagonism toward *gachupines* can be traced to the resentment of the early settlers toward those who arrived later, either as royal officials sent to replace the conquerors or as new migrants trying to make their fortunes. Many *gachupines* were considered by the creoles to be lowborn, socially inferior, grasping, and uncultured. Whether as a representative of the upper class, as a foreman on a hacienda, or as a merchant who carried out *repartimientos* (forced sales; *see* REPARTIMIENTO) of commodities to Indian villages, the *gachupín* was hated by the lower classes. Creoles and mestizos resented what they claimed was a monopoly of high government and ecclesiastical posts by *gachupines* and considered the newcomers unfit to understand local conditions.

Resentment against Spanish rule, and *gachupines* in particular, culminated in the rebellion of 1810, which demanded "death to the *gachupines*." Hatred of the *gachupines* continued to be an issue in Mexican politics for some years after independence.

EDITH B. COUTURIER

GAGE, THOMAS (1603?–1656). English traveler. A member of a prominent Roman Catholic family, Gage studied at a Jesuit college for English boys in French Flanders. Instead of becoming a Jesuit, however, he developed a strong dislike for the order and by 1625 had donned the habit of a Dominican friar. In the latter year he embarked for the Philippines, where he intended to serve as a missionary, but while en route he heard discouraging reports about conditions there and got no farther than Mexico. Gage lived in Central America, primarily in Guatemala, until 1637, when he departed without giving notice, traveling to Panama and thence to Spain and England. In 1642 he abjured Catholicism, delivering a sermon of recantation in London on August 28. The reasons for his action are not clear: he may have been moved, as he said, by religious doubts and shock at the clerical immorality he had observed in America, but he may have also felt rancor against his superiors. He soon reaffirmed his recantation by marrying and by testifying against a former schoolmate, now a Jesuit, charged with the treasonable offense of saying Mass in England. From 1643 until the mid-1650s Gage was a parish rector in Kent.

Gage is best known for his account of his life and travels in the New World, *The English American* (1648), one of the few depictions of the Spanish colonies by a non-Spaniard. In a memorandum prepared for Oliver Cromwell in 1654, as in *The English American*, Gage expressed confidence that the poorly defended and thinly populated Spanish colonies would succumb to an English attack and that the Indians and Negroes would make common cause with the English. Acting on Gage's advice, Cromwell mounted an expedition against Hispaniola, which Gage accompanied as chaplain. Unable to capture that island, the attackers were more successful in Jamaica, where Gage died the following year.

HELEN DELPAR

GAITÁN, JORGE ELIÉCER (1898–1948). Colombian political leader. Gaitán was born in Bogotá. His father was a bookseller, and his mother a schoolteacher. He studied law in Bogotá and Rome, first making his name in a well-publicized criminal case. Gaitán came to prominence in congressional debates when he led an onslaught against the handling of strikes in the banana zone (1928–1929) by the administration of Miguel Abadía Méndez. The fact that his skill as a speaker was not matched by skill as an organizer accounts in part for the episodic character of his career. He was briefly a member of the Liberal party Directorate (*see* LIBERAL PARTY: COLOMBIA), senator, representative, and elected leader of the short-lived Unión Nacional Izquierdista Revolucionaria (1934–1935). During the governments of Alfonso LÓPEZ and Eduardo SANTOS, Gaitán was briefly mayor of Bogotá, Minister of Education, and Minister of Labor. His performance in these posts was not spectacular, but he used them to build a personal following across Colombia.

In 1946 Gaitán emerged as one of two Liberal candidates for the Presidency, both of whom were defeated by the Conservative Mariano OSPINA PÉREZ. In a period of rapid inflation, mounting unemployment, and growing class resentment, Gaitán used his rhetorical talent to become leader of the "popular" elements of liberalism against the "oligarchy." However, his programs were not markedly distinctive from those of the "oligarchs" he attacked. In 1947 he was recognized as undisputed party chief. While the Ninth International Conference of American States was deliberating in Bogotá (*see* BOGOTÁ CONFERENCE), Gaitán was assassinated (April 9, 1948). His death precipitated the wave of urban violence in Bogotá known as the BOGOTAZO. Gaitán has subsequently filled the role of a Liberal martyr, his years of "oligarchic" association having been long forgotten.

C. G. ABEL

GALÁPAGOS ARCHIPELAGO (ARCHIPELAGO OF COLUMBUS). Thirteen large and seventeen small islands lying 700 miles off the Ecuadorian coast. Bishop Tomás de Berlanga discovered the islands accidentally in 1535 and sent King CHARLES I an illustrated letter depicting desolation and many rocks. Spain showed little interest in the islands, and pirates and buccaneers used them as a base for operations against Spanish shipping. Sailors' tales characterized them as "enchanted islands" where strange currents confused navigation and settlements disappeared. Gen. José Villamil is given credit for taking possession of the islands in the name of Ecuador in 1832, but the islands were not given effective administration. One entrepreneur, Manuel J. Cobas, set up a small private state on San Cristóbal, coined money, and built a sugar mill.

Charles Darwin visited the islands in 1835 and, impressed by the interisland variation of turtles (*galápagos*) and other fauna peculiar to the islands, was inspired to many of his views on natural selection. Clipper ships and whalers followed; Herman Melville arrived in 1841 and later recorded his impressions in *Las Encantadas,* ten sketches published in 1854. Scattered colonists were joined by political prisoners from the mainland in the nineteenth and twentieth centuries. California tuna fishermen arrived in the 1930s but clashed with the *guayaquileño* Lorenzo Tous, who held the national fishing monopoly there. Ecuador declared the islands a national sanctuary in 1935, and tourism and scientific investigation rose sharply in the 1960s.

LOIS WEINMAN

GALINDO, BLAS (1910–   ). Mexican composer. Born in Jalisco of an Indian family, he studied in Mexico City with José Chávez and later in the United States with Aaron Copland. His early works stress the use of native Mexican elements. Later he adhered to a more neoclassical line, which eventually led him into the use of serial devices. His achievements as a composer have been widely recognized with prizes, honorary degrees, commissions, and grants. He has written orchestral music, including four symphonies; several concerti for solo instruments, of which two are for piano (1942, 1961), one for flute (1960), and one for violin (1962); and a number of dramatic works, ballets, music for the theater, chamber music, choral compositions, and solo piano works.

JUAN A. ORREGO-SALAS

GALLEGOS, RÓMULO (1884–1969). Venezuelan novelist and President (1948). Born in Caracas, Gallegos entered the Central University of Venezuela to study law, which he abandoned to devote himself to education. After holding various teaching positions, he entered politics and in 1931, during the dictatorship of Juan Vicente GÓMEZ, was elected senator for the state of Apure, though he went into voluntary exile in New York instead of taking up his position. He lived in Spain until the death of the dictator in 1935. After serving briefly as Minister of Education in the government of Eleazar LÓPEZ CONTRERAS, he was an important member of the opposition in Congress. As a leader of ACCIÓN DEMOCRÁTICA (AD), he was elected President of the republic by a large majority in 1947. Because his party's government was unable to work out a successful coalition arrangement and because many Venezuelans considered AD overly radical, he was ousted in a military coup in November 1948. After a decade of exile in Mexico and Cuba, he returned to Venezuela in 1958 following the fall of the dictator Marcos PÉREZ JIMÉNEZ and was awarded the National Prize of Literature for his novel *La doncella y el último patriota* (1957).

Gallegos began his literary career in 1909, when he helped found the review *La Alborada.* From 1912 to 1918 he belonged to the Circle of Fine Arts, and in 1913 he published his first book, *Los aventureros,* a series of narrations of the type that he later published in the review *Actualidades,* which he edited from 1919 to 1921. His first novel, *El último Solar* (1920), later reissued as *Reinaldo Solar,* is a fictional biography of his friend and colleague Enrique Soublette.

It was followed by two short novels, *La rebelión* and *Los inmigrantes* (both 1922), and *La trepadora* (1925), his first novel on a rural theme. In 1929 his reputation was consolidated with *Doña Bárbara*, and his two other masterworks were written shortly thereafter in Spain: *Cantaclaro* (1934) and *Canaima* (1935). His attempt to leave a vast national epic by describing and transforming every aspect of Venezuelan life inspired the diversity of his later novels: *Pobre negro* (1937), *El forastero* (1942), *Sobre la misma tierra* (1943), *La brizna de paja en el viento* (1952), *Una posición en la vida* (1954), and *La doncella y el último patriota*.

RACHEL PHILLIPS AND JOHN V. LOMBARDI

GÁLVEZ, JOSÉ DE (MARQUÉS DE LA SONORA, 1729–1786). Spanish colonial administrator. Born in Málaga, Gálvez was appointed *visitador* of New Spain by King CHARLES III in 1765 with a mandate to revamp the colonial administration. His extensive authority over fiscal matters provoked a conflict with Viceroy Cruillas, who was recalled by the King and replaced by Marqués Carlos Francisco de Croix, who had orders to cooperate with Gálvez. The *visitador* stayed in New Spain from 1765 to 1771, traveling widely and studying its problems and suggesting reforms. His recommendations were submitted to the crown in 1771. Gálvez endorsed free trade and a reduction in import and export duties. He also reorganized the monopoly on tobacco and the ALCABALA (sales tax). A stern official, he punished harshly a local revolt against the enforcement of the monopoly. He suggested the adoption of a mining code and a mining guild, the establishment of basic salaries for free rural and mining laborers, and the regulation of laborers' debts to control peonage.

Gálvez revitalized the many provincial municipalities, instituting the annual election of *regidores* (aldermen), and he recommended the establishment of the INTENDANCY SYSTEM. Having visited the northwest of New Spain, he supported the creation of an independent military government there to subject the Indians and check the expansion of Great Britain and Russia in the northern Pacific area. Thus he laid the foundation for the settlement of California. In addition, he reorganized the militias and made them open to all social classes. During his visit the Jesuits were expelled from New Spain, and Gálvez quelled sporadic resistance to the expulsion (*see* JESUITS, EXPULSION OF: SPANISH AMERICA). After his mission in New Spain, in 1775, he was appointed Minister of the Indies.

ASUNCIÓN LAVRIN

GÁLVEZ, JUAN MANUEL (1887–   ). President of Honduras (1949–1954). Gálvez was elected President of Honduras in 1948. Since he had been groomed by the National party to succeed perennial dictator Tiburcio CARÍAS ANDINO, few Hondurans expected his regime to differ from that of his conservative predecessor. But although Gálvez retained much of Carías's personalistic style, he initiated a program of economic development, economic diversification, and road construction that was distinctively his own. *See* NATIONAL OR NATIONALIST PARTY (HONDURAS).

Like Carías, however, Gálvez discouraged labor organization among banana workers. Honduran employees of American fruit companies consequently did not receive the benefits that workers in neighbor-

ing countries had won in the 1940s. When UNITED FRUIT COMPANY stevedores on the Tela docks went on strike in 1954, sympathy strikes erupted among employees of other foreign concerns. Honduras was soon bound up in a violent general strike encouraged by radio transmissions from leftist Guatemala. There followed two and one-half months of indecision and erratic bargaining until an agreement was achieved.

Gálvez's inept handling of the banana strike and his acquiescence in allowing Honduran territory to be used as a base for the overthrow of the regime of Jacobo ARBENZ GUZMÁN in Guatemala thoroughly discredited his government. As a result, the Liberal presidential candidate, Ramón VILLEDA MORALES, won a plurality of votes in the 1954 elections. Gálvez, now seriously ill, could not follow the contested election to its resolution in the Congress. Vice President Julio Lozano staged a coup that captured the government. *See* LIBERAL PARTY (HONDURAS).

GENE S. YEAGER

GÁLVEZ, MANUEL (1882–1962). Argentine novelist. Gálvez was born in Paraná. In his youth he published a collection of poetry, *Sendero de humildad* (1909), much influenced by the modernist movement (*see* MODERNISM: SPANISH AMERICA) and by the French symbolists. He took part in the rise of new literary trends at the turn of the twentieth century and with Ricardo Olivera published the review *Ideas*. His best work as a novelist is that of his early realistic period, during which he wrote *La maestra normal* (1914), *El mal metafísico* (1916), *La sombra del convento* (1917), and *Nacha Regules* (1918). Here he describes contemporary society with critical acumen and acute powers of observation. He attempts to define the national character as seen in lower- and middle-class surroundings, and portrays the intellectual minority as an effete and paralyzed segment of society. His last works include *Las dos vidas del pobre Napoleón* (1954), a cycle of five historical novels of the era of Juan Manuel de ROSAS, and *Tránsito Guzmán* (1956), which deals with the end of the dictatorship of Juan D. PERÓN. He also wrote a biography of President Hipólito YRIGOYEN.

Politically Gálvez was identified with the revisionist outlook of conservative groups who tried to vindicate the nineteenth-century dictator Rosas as genuinely representative of the interests of the nation. The quality of his novels is often impaired by digressions, anecdotes, and unnecessary episodes.

RACHEL PHILLIPS

GÁLVEZ, MARIANO (1794–1862). Guatemalan statesman. Gálvez was a foundling reared in Guatemala City by highly placed foster parents. Influential patrons and royal dispensations from the disabilities attendant upon irregular birth enabled him to acquire the best legal education the colonial Kingdom of Guatemala afforded. Gálvez promoted independence from Spain in 1821 and union with Mexico as a stability measure. After Central America was separated from Mexico, he held high office in both state and Federation governments (*see* CENTRAL AMERICA, FEDERATION OF). He was elected chief of state of Guatemala in 1831 and reelected four years later.

Gálvez tried to create in Guatemala a state of liberty

and enlightenment that would enable the inhabitants, Indians included, to attain the perfection heralded by philosophers of the Enlightenment. To that end, he stripped the Catholic Church of wealth and temporal power, established religious toleration, adopted trial by jury, planned a system of free public lay education at all levels, and initiated a variety of development projects, the most spectacular employing massive foreign colonization. Gálvez's reorientation of Guatemalan life was too abrupt and too extreme for the old elite and the conservative countryside to accept. Alienation grew into rebellion, and the fanatical José Rafael CARRERA rose to lead it. Cholera appeared, producing a rapidly mounting death toll. Government control measures misinterpreted as deliberate poisonings gave the impetus of desperation to the revolt. Aided by dissident Liberals, the rebels overthrew Gálvez in February 1838 and forced him into exile about a year later. He lived in Mexico until his death in 1862. His remains were repatriated to Guatemala in 1925.

WILLIAM J. GRIFFITH

GAMA, JOSÉ BASÍLIO DA (1740–1795). Brazilian poet. Born in Minas Gerais, he was a novice in the Jesuit seminary in Rio de Janeiro at the time of the expulsion of the Jesuits (1759; *see* JESUITS, EXPULSION OF: BRAZIL). He continued his education in Portugal, at the University of Coimbra, until he was imprisoned on the assumption that he was still within the Jesuit fold. He gained his liberty and the favor of the Marquês de POMBAL by dedicating a poem to the dictator's daughter at the time of her marriage and by writing an anti-Jesuit epic, *O Uruguai,* both in 1769. The subject of the epic, the subjugation by the forces of the Portuguese government of the Indians living in the Jesuit villages in southern Brazil, is less attractive than the freshness of the descriptions of nature and the characterizations of the Indian hero and heroine, who exemplify Rousseau's Noble Savage. Interesting, too, is the originality of the treatment of the traditionally popular epic form. Instead of the usual ten cantos in ottava rima, *O Uruguai* is in five cantos and blank verse. These technical modifications contained lessons for the coming generation of Portuguese and Brazilian romantic writers. Basílio da Gama's other important but shorter poem, *Quitúbia* (1791), is about an Angolan black who was an officer in the Portuguese forces during a war in 1744 with an African queen.

RAYMOND S. SAYERS

GAMA, LUIS (1830–1882). Brazilian poet, journalist, and abolitionist lawyer. The illegitimate son of a Portuguese aristocrat from Bahia and a free black woman, Luis Gama was born free in Bahia in 1830, but in 1840 was sold into slavery by his father and shipped to the port of Santos in São Paulo. Employed as a servant in the provincial capital, where he learned to read with the help of a student, he soon fled from his master's home, conscious of the illegality of his enslavement as the son of a free woman. In 1854, after six years in the militia, Gama reappeared in São Paulo, where he worked as a secretary and soon gained prominence as a man of letters. In 1869 he was a coeditor, along with Ruy BARBOSA, Joaquim NABUCO, and others, of the liberal antislavery journal *Radical Paulistano,* which supported the reformist program of the Liberal

Luis Gama. [Biblioteca Nacional, Rio de Janeiro]

Center, led by the prominent Liberal statesman José Thomaz Nabuco de Araújo.

As a self-educated lawyer, Gama specialized in the liberation of persons held, as he had been, in illegal slavery, particularly Africans kept as slaves in violation of the antitraffic law of November 7, 1831, which declared the freedom of slaves entering Brazil from that day forward. By 1880 the former slave, by then the unchallenged leader of the antislavery movement in São Paulo, was said to have aided the liberation of more than 1,000 persons. Gama was the author of *Primeiras Trovas Burlescas* (1859) and *Trovas Burlescas e Escritos em Prosa.* His poetry, of high literary merit, is characterized by its defense of the black race and its satirical assaults upon the national aristocracy. Gama died in 1882, just as the antislavery campaign was about to enter a decisive phase.

ROBERT CONRAD

GAMA, VASCO DA (1469?–1524). Portuguese nobleman who established the oceanic route to India (1498). Da Gama's voyage followed the pioneering rounding of the Cape of Good Hope (1487–1488) by Bartolomeu Dias, who supervised the fitting out of the Da Gama expedition. Da Gama's objectives were to make contact with the kingdom of Prester John, which was believed to exist in East Africa, and also to break the Venetian monopoly of the spice trade in Europe by obtaining these Asiatic products by sea and establishing an alternative route to the Middle Eastern overland connection. Unlike Dias, who had beaten down the West and South coasts of Africa, Vasco da Gama swung out into the Atlantic after passing the Cape Verde Islands and picked up the steady westerly winds, which took him comfortably to the tip of Africa, thus articulating the pattern of navigation that was to dominate South Atlantic sailing for generations. He explored the East African coast to Mombasa and Melinda, where he obtained the services of an Arab pilot who guided the fleet safely to Calicut. Despite the opposition of local Arab merchants he succeeded in obtaining a cargo of pepper and spices. He reached Lisbon after his epic two-year voyage in the summer of 1499.

KENNETH R. MAXWELL

GAMARRA, AGUSTÍN. *See* MARSHALS OF AYACUCHO.

GAMONAL. Term used in Peru, especially in the early twentieth century, to refer to a large landowner of the sierra who was the dominant political figure in his locality and used force and semilegal methods to expand his landholdings (*see* SIERRA: PERU). Descriptions of *gamonales* can be found in the novels of José María ARGUEDAS and Ciro ALEGRÍA. In Colombia the word is applied to any local political boss.

HELEN DELPAR

GARCIA, JOSÉ MAURICIO NUNES (1767–1830). Brazilian composer mostly of sacred music. José Mauricio was chapelmaster at the Cathedral of Rio de Janeiro when the prince Dom João (later JOÃO VI) and the Portuguese court arrived in Brazil in 1808. He had studied with Salvador José, a well-known music teacher, but his training was mostly empirical. In 1792 he had been ordained, the priesthood being the salvation of many musicians without fortune or noble birth. Throughout his career he took advantage of the patronage system operative at the court. Dom João appointed him musical director and chapelmaster of the Royal Chapel in 1808. José Mauricio became fashionable and famous for his improvisational skills in noble salons.

According to Cleofe Person de Matos, who compiled the thematic catalog of his production, some 237 of his works are extant. The oldest manuscript, the antiphon *Tota pulchra est,* dates from 1783. In 1790 he wrote the *Sinfonia Fúnebre* for orchestra. Most of his sacred works are for four mixed voices, but a few, such as *Missa dos Defuntos* (1809), call for an *a cappella* performance. The most productive period of his life was from about 1798 to about 1810. He was strongly influenced by the classic style of Haydn and Mozart, but at the same time an obvious operatic style permeates many of his liturgical settings. His output includes some 20 Masses, among them his Requiem of 1816 and the *Missa a Grande Orquestra* of 1826, more than 100 psalms, and dozens of hymns, motets, antiphons, litanies, graduals, and responsories. The opera *Le due gemelle* was produced in 1809, but the original manuscript has been lost. José Mauricio also wrote some modinhas (*see* MODINHA), whose character influenced many of his Mass arias.

GERARD H. BÉHAGUE

GARCÍA CATURLA, ALEJANDRO (1906–1940). Cuban composer. Born in Remedios, he studied first in Havana and then with Nadia Boulanger in Paris. He and his compatriot Amadeo ROLDÁN were the first Cuban composers to be recognized in Europe and the United States. His style adheres to a free use of Afro-Cuban folk devices within a harmony radically dissonant for his time. These characteristics are reflected in such works as the *Tres danzas cubanas* for orchestra (1927), the First Cuban Suite for piano and wind instruments (1930), and a number of solo piano compositions and songs.

JUAN A. ORREGO-SALAS

GARCÍA-GODOY, HÉCTOR (1921–1970). Dominican diplomat and provisional President (1965–1966). A member of one of the most prestigious families in the Dominican Republic, García-Godoy earned a reputa-

tion as a tactful, skillful diplomat and a man of moderate views. Serving as Foreign Minister in the leftist government of Juan BOSCH, but acceptable to the center and right because of his name and family connections, he was called to lead the country in the difficult aftermath of the revolution and United States intervention of 1965 (*see* DOMINICAN REVOLT).

Forced to deal with the continued presence and authority of the Inter-American Peace Force and the special ambassador and presidential representative Ellsworth Bunker, as well as with challenges from both the revolutionary left and the unregenerate right, García-Godoy presided over a government in almost constant danger of being undermined or overthrown. Although unsuccessful in carrying through any significant reforms, García-Godoy did help pacify the country, muted some of the conflict, helped arrange for new elections, and turned the reins of power over to his elected successor, Joaquín BALAGUER.

He was later appointed Ambassador in Washington by Balaguer. Leaving that post, García-Godoy returned to Santo Domingo to enter the 1970 presidential campaign. In the midst of the campaign he died.

HOWARD J. WIARDA

GARCÍA MÁRQUEZ, GABRIEL (1928–   ). Colombian novelist. García Márquez was born in Aracataca, a small town near the Caribbean coast of Colombia. In 1940 he went to Bogotá to study law but left the National University without taking his degree. His first stories appeared in *El Espectador* of Bogotá, where he also worked as a journalist and editor. In 1954 the newspaper sent him to Rome, but the next year it was closed down by the dictatorship of Gustavo ROJAS PINILLA and García Márquez suffered grave poverty in France. He returned to South America in 1958, settling in Caracas, where he worked for *Momentos* and *Élite,* and in 1959 was appointed to direct the news agency Prensa Latina in Bogotá. He resigned from this post in opposition to military interference in his work. In 1961 he moved to Mexico and later to Spain.

García Márquez has written long stories, *El coronel no tiene quien le escriba* (1961) and *Los funerales de la Mamá Grande* (1962); the novels *La hojarasca* (1955), *La mala hora* (1963), and his masterwork, *Cien años de soledad,* 1967 (*One Hundred Years of Solitude*); and a collection of seven stories, *La increíble y triste historia de la cándida Eréndira y de su abuela desalmada* (1972). He is one of the most innovative of the contemporary experimental novelists in Latin America and has mythologized the national character and troubled history of Colombia in his creation of Macondo, an archetypal village in which fantasy and reality continuously intermingle. Several of his stories were translated into English in *No One Writes to the Colonel and Other Stories* (1968).   RACHEL PHILLIPS

GARCÍA MENOCAL, MARIO. *See* MENOCAL, MARIO GARCÍA.

GARCÍA MORENO, GABRIEL (1821–1875). Ecuadorian statesman. Gabriel García Moreno, the son of Gabriel García Gómez, a Spaniard, and of Mercedes Moreno, was born in Guayaquil on December 24, 1821. At the age of fifteen he went to study in Quito. Two years later he received minor orders. He soon changed his mind about entering the priesthood, however, and went on to earn a doctorate in law. At about the same time he became involved in politics as a follower of Vicente ROCAFUERTE and an enemy of Gen. Juan José FLORES. His marriage in 1846 to Rosa Ascázubi gave him, through family connections, a solid political base in Quito. The key to success in Ecuadorian politics consisted in being able to control both the capital and the influential port city of Guayaquil, and García Moreno belonged to one of Guayaquil's most eminent families.

In 1850 he traveled to Europe via New York. On his return the following year, he intervened in favor of the readmission to Ecuador of the Society of Jesus. But the next President, Gen. José María URBINA, expelled the Jesuits once more, and García Moreno soon followed them into exile for his role in defending them. Elected to the Senate, he was not allowed to take his seat. He then made a second trip to Paris. After a year's residence there, he returned to Ecuador in 1856. The following year he was elected mayor of Quito and rector of the University of Quito.

As a senator (1857–1858), García Moreno became the most outspoken adversary of the government, which was facing an armed invasion by Peru. He fled to Peru in January 1859, but he was soon back in Quito as a member of a revolutionary junta. García Moreno was given command of the rebel forces, but the regular Army under General Urbina defeated him, and once more he fled to Peru. He sought the alliance of the Peruvians, then besieging Guayaquil; on being rebuffed, he devised a plan of turning Ecuador into a French protectorate in exchange for military aid. In the end, the government was overthrown by an ambitious general. From the resulting confusion and with the help of his old enemy General Flores, García Moreno emerged in September 1860 as the undisputed master of Ecuador.

García Moreno's tenure as President was confirmed by a convention in 1861. His regime was harsh, but he was able to repel General Urbina's attempts to invade the country and imposed discipline on the rebellious army officers. However, he embarked on two foolish adventures against Colombia, both of which ended in fiascoes. The concordat he negotiated with the papacy in 1862 regulated the relations between church and state. He recalled the Jesuits and also invited French teaching orders to Ecuador: his efforts in the field of education were perhaps his main contribution.

Since the constitution of 1861 did not allow the President to succeed himself, he had Jerónimo Carrión elected in 1865. The following year García Moreno traveled to Lima and Santiago on a diplomatic mission. Back in Quito, he found the Carrión government unfriendly, and his election to the Senate was impugned (August 1867). García Moreno fought back, and in the face of mounting opposition Carrión resigned. Although the next President, Javier Espinosa, was his own choice, García Moreno ousted him in a successful coup on January 16, 1869. A new constitution consolidated García Moreno's power. Free of visible political opposition, he dedicated the next six years to furthering higher education, particularly in medicine and the sciences. Ecuador's first railway was inaugurated, although the building of a highway from Quito to the coast was much more important.

In 1875 García Moreno had himself reelected. Four days before his inauguration, on August 6, he was hacked to death by a machete-wielding Colombian, a disappointed office seeker, instigated by half a dozen Liberal fanatics who looked on from a safe distance.

See also MONTALVO, Juan.

Bibliography. Wilfrido Loor, *Cartas de García Moreno,* 4 vols., Quito, 1954–55; Richard Pattee, *Gabriel García Moreno y el Ecuador de su tiempo,* Quito, 1941, Mexico City, 1944; Luis Robalino Dávila, *García Moreno,* Quito, 1948.

ÁDÁM SZÁSZDI

GARCÍA MORILLO, ROBERTO (1911–　). Argentine composer and conductor. García Morillo was born in Buenos Aires, where he studied with Constantino Gaito and André. His prestige as a composer is matched by his reputation as a music critic of *La Nación* and his work as a composition teacher at the National Conservatory of Music in Buenos Aires. As a composer he has received a number of prizes in Argentina and other countries. Outstanding among his works are three symphonies (1948, 1955, 1961); *Variaciones olímpicas* (1948) for orchestra; the cantatas *Marín* (1950), *El Tamarit* (1953), and *Moriana* (1958); and a long list of piano compositions including five sonatas and three sets of variations. In addition, he has published several books on music, including one on Carlos CHÁVEZ in 1960.

JUAN A. ORREGO-SALAS

GARCÍA SARMIENTO, FÉLIX RUBÉN. *See* DARÍO, RUBÉN.

GARCILASO DE LA VEGA (EL INCA, 1539–1616). Peruvian chronicler. Garcilaso was born in Cuzco, the illegitimate son of an Inca princess, the niece of HUAYNA CAPAC, and Capt. Sebastián Garcilaso de la Vega, a Spanish conqueror of illustrious lineage. The infant mestizo was baptized Gómez Suárez de Figueroa; he did not use his father's name until 1563. Although he was never legitimized by his father, who married a fourteen-year-old Spanish girl in 1549, Garcilaso was raised in his household. As a boy in Cuzco he had an opportunity to absorb information on Inca civilization from his mother's relatives (*see* INCAS); he also received instruction from several clerical tutors.

In 1560, the year after his father's death, Garcilaso went to Spain, where he remained for the rest of his life. He settled first in the Andalusian village of Montilla, was named a captain while taking part (1570) in the campaign against Morisco rebels in the Alpujarras, took minor orders, and in 1605 was appointed chief steward of the Hospital of the Immaculate Conception in Córdoba, where he died. During his long residence in Spain he made several unsuccessful efforts to secure favor or recompense from the crown in recognition of his father's services in America.

Garcilaso's first published work (1590) was a Spanish translation of the *Dialoghi d'amore* by the humanist Judah Abarbanel, a Portuguese Jew known as León Hebreo. In 1590 Garcilaso was already at work on an account of Hernando de SOTO's expedition to Florida (1539–1542), based largely on the recollections of one of De Soto's soldiers, Gonzalo Silvestre, who was a good friend of Garcilaso. Because of the nature of its sources and because of Garcilaso's style, *La Florida del Inca* (1605) has been criticized as being overly romantic and redolent of the tales of chivalry that Garcilaso himself denounces in the book. For these very reasons the book has been praised as a literary work.

Garcilaso's most famous and controversial work is his *Comentarios reales,* 1609 (*Royal Commentaries*), which describes Inca history and culture. It remains an important source of information about pre-Columbian Inca society, though many modern critics regard his portrait of the Incas as inaccurate and excessively idealized. The second part of the *Comentarios reales* appeared after Garcilaso's death under the title *Historia general del Perú* (1617). This volume, which recounts the conquest of Peru and the civil wars between Pizarrists and Almagrists, has never been considered authoritative, except for those episodes of which Garcilaso had personal knowledge.

Garcilaso, who wrote that he was proud of being a mestizo, is often viewed as a symbol and spokesman of the new race created by the union of Spaniard and Indian.

HELEN DELPAR

GARDEL, CARLOS (1887?–1935). The most famous Argentine interpreter of the tango. Gardel's parents, place and date of birth, and education are unknown. He himself claimed a number of birthdays and nationalities, and others have confused him with the son of his guardian, Berthe Gardés. What is clear is that at an early age he was abandoned by his parents, that he acquired an intimate knowledge of street life and orphanages, and that he joined the family of Berthe Gardés. His relations with Berthe were ambiguous, for neither accepted the other, and yet they maintained their interest in each other all their lives. Gardel's street life was not uneventful, for in 1907 he was released from the jail at Ushuaia, where he had served a sentence for some crime. In the following years his associations with the underworld were reinforced by his friendship with Héctor Béhéty, the Uruguayan rival of the Argentine Mafia chief, and Juan Nicolás Ruggiero, the boss for twenty years of the criminal world in the Buenos Aires suburb of Avellaneda. By 1913 Gardel had become so popular a singer that he was making recordings and frequent personal appearances in the Argentine interior. The tango, his favorite medium, was then beginning to acquire respectability and popularity, both of which were firmly established by 1916.

Many of the tangos written during this period, especially in 1916, when Hipólito YRIGOYEN became President, were actually political pieces endorsing the Unión Cívica Radical and its candidates (*see* RADICAL PARTY: ARGENTINA). This undoubtedly was the type of tango Gardel sang when he campaigned for the reelection of the political boss of Avellaneda, Alberto Barceló. In 1917 he sang *Mi noche triste* by Pascual Contursi. According to some authorities, this event marks the birth of the tango song. It also was the year in which Gardel made his first motion picture, *Flor de durazno.* The tango song was at the height of its popularity during the 1920s, when Gardel recorded many of the songs of the prolific Anselmo Aieta. Near the end of the decade Gardel met Mme. Backfield, who financed his tour in Europe in 1930 and many of his films. When he returned to Europe in 1933, he was at the peak of his

popularity. But the tango was no longer the same. It now reflected the reaction to unemployment and the harsh realities of the economic depression. Gardel was not keeping abreast of the changes when he accidentally met his death in Medellín, Colombia. The end of the tango era was marked by the closing of the Café El Nacional, "La Catedral del Tango," in 1952.

JOSEPH T. CRISCENTI

GAUCHO. Term used to describe the rural male in the RÍO DE LA PLATA countries. In Argentina the ancestry of the gaucho generally is traced to the Spanish conquerors and colonizers who found the Indian squaws attractive and to the Indian braves who proudly possessed white women. The gaucho was a mestizo, usually the illegitimate offspring of a union between a Spaniard or creole and an Indian. Early in the seventeenth century he received an infusion of Negro blood. By 1640 the rural population included Negroes, Indians, mestizos, and Spaniards. As there was not enough rural work to go around, many gauchos were unemployed and poor. The rest of society regarded them as despicable, an image they were never able to shed completely.

The word "gaucho" appears to have come into common usage in the eighteenth century. Until the 1840s it denoted a horse thief or cattle rustler, an unemployed rural inhabitant, a man who lived and formed a farming family in Indian country, a rancher who had cut himself off from civilization, a man who worked for pay but was not committed to a single employer, the proud man with *fueros personales* (personal rights) who lived and worked for pay as a peon on some ranch, a settler without land who was a herdsman, and the *agregado,* who worked on a ranch without pay for the privilege of using and living on some unused portion of it. The gaucho clearly was a native rural inhabitant who had developed a way of life different from that of the urban dweller. After 1840 Germans, Englishmen, and Irishmen who lived in the rural areas were called gauchos, as were farmers who were part-time construction workers. At the same time there appeared an urban gaucho, a poor man without an education whose way of life aroused the ire of the educated urban classes. He probably was a transplanted rural gaucho or a European immigrant who had arrived in the country without a penny, without any knowledge of the language, and without a patron.

At least three hypotheses have been advanced to explain the appearance of the gaucho. One finds his origins in the inability of the Spanish family to keep its members together and to influence their conduct and in the increasing tempo with which the wild cattle of the PAMPA were exploited for their hides. For this school, the gaucho first appeared in the eighteenth century in the province of Santa Fe. Another interpretation sees the gaucho as a by-product of the disintegration of the Indian family, especially on the pampa of the province of Buenos Aires. He is the illegitimate offspring of an Indian woman who lives on an encomienda, is not allowed to join her husband, and is encouraged to be sexually promiscuous. A third view is that the ancestors of the gaucho were Indian, mestizo, and white creole peons, who had been attracted to Buenos Aires from the various regions of Argentina by the increasingly important trade in cowhides. These people, joined by the Negro, mixed together to produce the gaucho, or the nomad who skillfully performed all kinds of rural tasks.

The gaucho is associated with the growth of the live-stock industry (*see* CATTLE INDUSTRY: ARGENTINA) and with forced military service on the frontier or in Indian country. By the second half of the eighteenth century the gaucho was serving in the Army, far from his family and loved ones, with poor horses, weapons, clothing, and food and with long intervals, sometimes years, between paydays. The rate of desertion was consequently high. With few variations, these conditions remained unchanged until the third quarter of the nineteenth century, when the economic transformation of Argentina greatly altered the conditions of rural life.

The gaucho has been a prominent, if often idealized, figure in Argentine literature. Outstanding works of poetry dealing with the gaucho include Hilario Ascásubi's *Santos Vega* (1872), a tale of a gaucho bandit distinctive for its depiction of rural scenes and customs, and the two-part epic by José HERNÁNDEZ, *Martín Fierro* (1872, 1879), which relates the story of a gaucho at odds with civilization. Prose fiction about the gaucho made its appearance with the melodramatic novels of Eduardo Gutiérrez, who described the adventures of Juan Moreira, a good gaucho unjustly persecuted by the authorities. Other novelists who subsequently turned to the gaucho theme were the Uruguayans Eduardo ACEVEDO DÍAZ and Javier de Viana (1868–1926) and the Argentines Benito Lynch (1885–1951) and Ricardo GÜIRALDES, whose *Don Segundo Sombra* (1926) is considered the masterpiece of the genre. The successful dramatization in pantomime (1884) of Gutiérrez's novel *Juan Moreira* (1880) ushered in a series of dramas dealing with the gaucho, the best of which is *M'hijo el dotor* by Florencio SÁNCHEZ, which was produced in Buenos Aires in 1903.

The gaucho has also played an important symbolic role in Argentine examinations of the national character. Some have extolled him as a freedom-loving democrat and as the source of all that is truly autochthonous in Argentine culture. To others, notably the nineteenth-century statesman and man of letters Domingo Faustino SARMIENTO, he has symbolized the forces of ignorance and barbarism that had to be extirpated before Argentina could become a modern nation.

Bibliography. Fernando O. Assunção, *El gaucho,* Montevideo, 1963; Madaline W. Nichols, *The Gaucho: Cattle Hunter, Cavalryman, Ideal of Romance,* Durham, N.C., 1942; Ricardo Rodríguez Molas, *Historia social del gaucho,* Buenos Aires, 1968.

JOSEPH T. CRISCENTI

GEFFRARD, NICOLAS FABRE (1806–1879). President of Haiti (1859–1867). Geffrard, of Negro and mulatto ancestry, was born at Anse-à-Veau on September 19, 1806. His father, one of the authors of the constitution of 1806, died the same year. Young Nicolas was adopted and educated by Colonel Fabre, a friend of his father. Entering the Army at fifteen, he rose slowly. Later, as general, he was court-martialed for political reasons but was saved from conviction by Faustin SOULOUQUE. In 1856, when Soulouque was Emperor, Geffrard won him

a victory at La Tabarra against the Dominicans and was created Duke of La Tabarra. Eventually alienated by Faustin's tyranny, Geffrard proclaimed the restoration of the republic in December 1858 and soon was chosen President.

Geffrard reduced the Army's size, making it a small corps of well-trained troops. He sponsored a liberal tariff and signed a trade treaty with the United States in 1862, after the latter recognized Haiti. In 1860 Geffrard concluded a convention with the Vatican that granted the Catholic Church special advantages and gave him church patronage. When Spain attempted to recolonize the Dominican area, Geffrard helped arm its rebels until the Spaniards withdrew in 1865.

In Geffrard Haitian education found a rare friend. Schools and their enrollment increased. Nevertheless, his tenure was marred by rebellions. The final one, early in 1867, forced his flight to Jamaica, where he died on December 31, 1879.

JOHN E. BAUR

GEISEL, ERNESTO (1908–). Brazilian general elected President of Brazil on January 15, 1974, for a five-year term to begin on March 15, 1974. Of German ancestry and a Protestant, Geisel is a native of Rio Grande do Sul. In 1955–1956 he served as superintendent of the President Bernardes oil refinery, and in 1957 he became a member of the National Petroleum Council. Closely associated with the Sorbonne group of officers who came to prominence after the 1964 military coup against President João GOULART, he held several important posts before being named head of PETRÓLEOS BRASILEIROS, S.A., the national petroleum corporation of Brazil, in 1969. Geisel's presidential nomination, which originated in the military high command, was subsequently ratified by the ALIANÇA RENOVADORA NACIONAL, the progovernment party, and by 400 of the 503 members of the electoral college that actually elects the President. Geisel's brother Orlando, also a general, was Army Minister under President Emílio Garrastazu MÉDICI.

HELEN DELPAR

GENERAL CONFEDERATION OF LABOR. *See* CONFEDERACIÓN GENERAL DE TRABAJO.

GESTIDO, OSCAR D[ANIEL] (1901–1967). President of Uruguay (1967). Gestido, a retired military officer, was elected President in 1966 but died in December 1967 after only nine months in office. He was the nation's first President following the 1952–1967 experiment with the COLEGIADO.

Born in Montevideo, Gestido entered the Military Academy at the age of sixteen and achieved the rank of general in 1949. Most of his military career was devoted to the Air Force, where among other positions he served as director of the military aviation school and director general of military aviation. After a special governmental appointment (1949–1951) as head of the national airlines, PLUNA, Gestido spent his last four years on active duty as inspector general of the Army.

After retiring from the military in 1955, Gestido served as head of the national railroads from 1957 to 1959 and was a member of the National Council of Government in the years 1963–1966. He became the leader of the List 14 faction of the Colorado party (*see*

COLORADO PARTY: URUGUAY) after the death in 1964 of César Batlle Pacheco; this group united with other moderate factions to form List 123 (Unión Colorada y Batllista), which in 1966 carried Gestido to the Presidency. His brief period in office was spent in trying to solve the nation's pressing economic and social problems within a framework of respect for civil and political liberties. Shortly before his death, however, the Gestido administration adopted tougher measures to control the growing problem of strikes and demonstrations.

LEE C. FENNELL

GILDED ONE, THE. *See* DORADO, EL.

GINASTERA, ALBERTO (1916–   ). Argentine composer. Born in Buenos Aires, he studied with Atos Palma, graduating from the National Conservatory of Music in 1938. He has twice been a recipient of Guggenheim fellowships (1946, 1969). In 1953 he was appointed a professor at the National Conservatory in Buenos Aires; later he was director of the Conservatory of La Plata and dean of the music department at the Catholic University in Buenos Aires, and in 1960 he became the director of the Instituto de Altos Estudios Musicales of the Di Tella Foundation in Buenos Aires. Since 1970 he has lived in Switzerland.

Ginastera's early music adheres to a national vein that gradually disappears from works written after the late 1940s. Good examples of this first period are his ballets *Panambí* (1937) and *Estancia* (1941). His later evolution led him from a neoclassical approach to a very free and personal use of serial and aleatory techniques, characteristic of most of his compositions since 1960. His three operas, *Don Rodrigo* (1964), *Bomarzo* (1967), and *Beatrix Cenci* (1971), are outstanding examples of this approach, as are his *Cantata for Magic America* (1961), concerto for piano and orchestra (1961), concerto for violin and orchestra (1963), and concerto for cello and orchestra (1970). Many works belonging to his transitional middle period have had a deep influence on Latin American music, among them his *Variaciones concertantes* (1953), two string quartets (1948, 1958), and sonata for piano (1952). These and many other compositions justify Ginastera's position as a leading force in contemporary music.

JUAN A. ORREGO-SALAS

GODOI, JUAN SILVANO (1850–1929). Paraguayan politician, man of letters, and diplomat. Born in Paraguay, Godoi was continuing his education in Argentina when the PARAGUAYAN WAR broke out. He returned to his prostrate country in 1870. Identified with the Paraguayan Legion, which had fought with the Allies against the dictator Francisco Solano LÓPEZ, Godoi helped write the constitution of 1870 and served as a member of Congress from then until 1877. When the political opposition took over the government in 1878, he helped finance an abortive revolt and was forced to return to Buenos Aires as an exile. There he lived and maintained a successful business. Godoi's home was the center of a literary circle and the locus of exile activity. He toured Europe, wrote histories of the war, and financed several luckless revolutions. Before he returned to his homeland in 1895, he founded two

periodicals, *Las Provincias* and *La Discusión*, in the Argentine capital. Back in Paraguay, he served as Director of the National Library, Museum, and Archives, created the Godoi Art Museum (now the Museo Nacional de Bellas Artes y Antigüedades), continued writing about the war and its heroes, and served in several diplomatic posts including that of Minister to Brazil. He died in Asunción.

JOHN HOYT WILLIAMS

GODOY ALCAYAGA, LUCILA. *See* MISTRAL, GABRIELA.

GOETHALS, GEORGE WASHINGTON (1858–1928). American army officer and engineer, known primarily for his brilliant supervision of the construction of the PANAMA CANAL. Goethals's preparation for this assignment came from many years of work in river improvement on the Ohio, Cumberland and Tennessee Rivers, including the Muscle Shoals Canal. He served as chief engineer of the 1st Army Corps during the Spanish-American War, as an instructor at the United States Military Academy, and as a member of the General Staff. In 1907 President Theodore Roosevelt appointed him chief engineer with full authority in the building of the Panama Canal. Goethals proved equal to the monumental task, which lasted from 1907 to 1914. He displayed great engineering skill in the construction of the locks, dams, and passages subject to frequent landslides and diplomatic skill in handling the army of 30,000 workers. After the opening of the canal in 1914 President Woodrow Wilson appointed Goethals the first Governor of the Canal Zone. The following year Congress promoted him to the rank of major general by a special act and formally extended him its gratitude. In 1916 he retired from the Army, and the next year from the governorship of the canal. During World War I he was recalled to active duty, first as director of the United States Shipping Board Emergency Fleet Corporation and then as acting quartermaster general and assistant chief of staff of the Army.

RICHARD B. GRAY

GOLDEN LAW (LEI AUREA). The final act in the long struggle to end Brazilian slavery, the Golden Law was passed overwhelmingly by both houses of the General Assembly and sanctioned by Princess Isabel on May 13, 1888. Strikingly less complicated than earlier slavery legislation, such as the FREE BIRTH LAW of 1871 and the Saraiva-Cotegipe law of 1885, the Golden Law briefly stated: "Article 1. From the date of this law slavery in Brazil is declared extinct. Article 2. All enactments to the contrary are revoked." Thus some 600,000 slaves were suddenly freed without compensation to their owners, and masters were deprived of the labor of free children as provided for in the Free Birth Law.

The Golden Law, particularly its failure to reimburse owners for their lost slaves, aroused bitterness among ex-masters and was one of the main causes of the fall of the empire eighteen months later. Yet, from the point of view of the slaveholding class, its passage was urgently required as a way to end the turbulence brought on by the antislavery campaign. Moreover, the law was a practical recognition that the slave system had virtually collapsed throughout the nation. After seven years of abolitionist unrest, in 1887 the slaves of the key province of São Paulo had abandoned the plantations en masse, urged on by the Caifazes, a conspiratorial organization led by Antônio Bento. With their labor force vanishing and their economy threatened, the planters and political leaders of São Paulo, led by Senator Antônio da Silva Prado, had changed sides in the abolitionist struggle in late 1887, provisionally freeing their remaining slaves as a means of keeping them at work, and joining leaders from other sections of the country, notably João Alfredo Correia de Oliveira (Prime Minister in 1888), in urging a rapid end to the slave system. With the spread of the runaway movement into other provinces early in 1888, Liberal and Conservative politicians from most parts of the country joined forces to declare slavery's demise as the only reasonable solution to the national crisis. *See also* ABOLITION OF SLAVERY (BRAZIL).

ROBERT CONRAD

GOMES, ANTÔNIO CARLOS (1836–1896). Brazilian composer particularly eminent in the writing of grand operas. Born in Campinas, São Paulo, he acquired his musical training at the Conservatory of Music in Rio de Janeiro. Stimulated by José Amat, the first administrator of the Imperial Academy of Music and National Opera, Gomes had his first opera, *A Noite do Castelo,* produced at the Teatro Lírico Provisório and published in 1861. His second work, *Joana de Flandres,* appeared in 1863. Both operas followed the model of the early-nineteenth-century Italian operatic genre. The success of these works prompted Gomes's nomination to a government fellowship to study in Milan in 1863. Thereafter he spent most of his time in Italy, making occasional trips to Brazil. He died in Belém, Pará, where he had gone to found and direct a conservatory.

In Milan Gomes continued his studies with Lauro Rossi until 1867. With the opera *Il Guarany* (1870), based on the Indianist subject of José Martiniano de ALENCAR's novel, he reached an unprecedented popularity for a Latin American composer. First produced at La Scala in Milan on March 19, 1870, the opera is preceded by an overture, written in 1871, that has become a sort of national anthem in Brazil. The main theme of the overture functions as a leitmotiv throughout the work, expressing the typical romantic stylization of "primitive" Indian music. The opera includes ballet scenes presenting a stylization of the exotic Aimoré tribal dances. *Il Guarany* was very successful throughout Europe, and Verdi himself called it the work "of a true musical genius."

Despite the success of *Il Guarany,* Gomes's masterpiece was *Fosca* (1873), whose libretto was written by Antonio Ghislanzoni, the librettist of Verdi's *Aïda. Salvatore Rosa* (1874), which premiered in Genoa with clamorous success, was the result of another collaboration with Ghislanzoni. However, Gomes's next lyric drama, *Maria Tudor* (1879), was badly received at its premiere at La Scala. The original subject for his next opera, *Lo schiavo,* in favor of the abolitionist movement in Brazil, was suggested to Gomes by Visconde de Taunay, but the librettist Paravicini transformed it into another Indianist work. Gomes's last important productions include the opera *Condor* (1891) and the oratoriolike work *Colombo* (1891), written for the fourth centenary of the discovery of America.

GERARD H. BÉHAGUE

GOMES, EDUARDO (1896–). Brazilian air force officer and political leader. Gomes was born in Petrópolis, in the state of Rio de Janeiro, enlisted in the Army in 1916, and was commissioned a lieutenant in the artillery in 1919. In 1922 Gomes became a national celebrity as one of the survivors of the COPACABANA REVOLT, which launched the revolutionary movements by junior officers in the 1920s (*see* TENENTISMO). Imprisoned for his role as an air observer in the revolt of 1924, Gomes was returned to active duty and was assigned in 1927 to army aviation, where he remained until the Brazilian Air Force was created as a separate service in 1941. Gomes was one of the pioneers of the military airmail service in 1931 and served as Air Force commander in northeastern Brazil during World War II.

During the waning months of the dictatorship of Getúlio VARGAS in 1945, Gomes helped organize the anti-Vargas political party, the UNIÃO DEMOCRÁTICA NACIONAL, and ran unsuccessfully as its presidential candidate in 1945 and 1950. He continued to serve as an officer and later as elder statesman of the party until its dissolution in 1965. After Vargas's suicide in 1954, Gomes was appointed Air Minister by President João CAFÉ FILHO. He retired with the rank of air marshal in 1961 but was recalled to serve again as Air Minister in the Cabinet of President Humberto CASTELLO BRANCO after the revolution of 1964.

ROLLIE E. POPPINO

GÓMEZ, JOSÉ MIGUEL (1858–1921). President of Cuba (1909–1913). Gómez served as a general in the WAR FOR CUBAN INDEPENDENCE and was civil Governor of Santa Clara during the United States occupation. In 1902 he supported Tomás ESTRADA PALMA as the first President of Cuba, but in 1905 he sought the Presidency himself as the Liberal party candidate. Estrada Palma's reelection led to a Liberal revolt and United States intervention. In 1908 Gómez was elected President for a four-year term.

The Gómez administration was characterized by widespread corruption, which was encouraged by economic prosperity stemming from rising sugar prices. There were scandals of all sorts, involving high government officials including Gómez himself, whose personal style seemed to encourage dishonesty in public life. In 1912 panic engulfed the island as Negroes throughout Cuba demonstrated and went on strike at the height of the sugarcane harvest. The Negro revolt was quickly suppressed, but not before the United States landed Marines in Oriente Province with the stated purpose of protecting sugar estates.

The Gómez administration is also remembered for the legalization of two of the most popular activities in prerevolutionary Cuba, cockfighting and the national lottery. The lottery in particular was destined to have a pernicious influence on Cuban social development; by creating a means of quick enrichment, it encouraged excessive reliance on luck and superstition. It also became a major source of political corruption.

J. CORDELL ROBINSON

GÓMEZ, JUAN VICENTE (1857–1935). President of Venezuela (1908–1910, 1910–1914, 1915–1922, 1922–1929, 1931–1935). With José Antonio PÁEZ and Antonio GUZMÁN BLANCO, Juan Vicente Gómez was one of the three great authoritarian rulers of Venezuela. Like his two predecessors, Gómez led a regime whose duration, comprehensiveness, and expertise moved Venezuela to a new level of national achievement. Gómez, an illegitimate mestizo cattle driver from the Andean state of Táchira, had acquired a respectable fortune by 1890, which he lost in support of an unsuccessful revolt in 1892. From exile in Colombia he restored his wealth, this time on the basis of energetic cattle rustling. His superior administrative and managerial ability enabled him to rebuild his fortunes to such an extent that by 1899 he was ready to support another revolution, this one led by Gen. Cipriano CASTRO. The success of the Castro revolution began Juan Vicente's long political career. Under Castro he served as Governor of the Federal District, Governor of Táchira in 1900, and First Vice President in 1903. From 1902 until 1908 he also served as commander of the Army. Throughout this period Gómez played the role of a loyal subordinate so successfully that when Castro had to leave Venezuela for Europe to recover his health, he confidently left the government in Juan Vicente's hands. No sooner had Castro arrived in Europe than he discovered that Gómez had begun to fill the state governorships with his own men, who could then control the elections of national legislators who would make Gómez President. Castro was directed to remain in exile, and Gómez took control of Venezuela, relinquishing power only upon his death in 1935.

In the twenty-seven years of his rule Gómez changed the face of Venezuela. While he himself had scaled the political heights as a rebellious *caudillo*, he eliminated the possibility of a recurrence of this kind of revolt. One of his primary interests was the creation of a stable, well-organized, well-equipped, and professional Army. His soldiers received the best equipment and the most modern training from Italian, German, French, and Peruvian experts, and by the late 1920s the Army had a virtual monopoly on the instruments of war. By raising the Army's technical sophistication to so high a level, Gómez guaranteed that no regional *caudillo* could match its expertise and equipment. This policy, very successful from Gómez's point of view, had serious consequences for the nation after his death when the Army began to be responsible for the kind of governmental instability that had once been caused by regional *caudillos*.

The creation of a professional Army cost a great deal of money, and fortunately for Gómez the world petroleum market stood ready to provide it. After the MEXICAN REVOLUTION began, foreign oil companies were anxious to find a new producing nation where the security and stability of their investments could be guaranteed. Venezuela under Juan Vicente Gómez could do just that. A policy of liberal concessions brought in Royal Dutch Shell before World War I, and after the war United States companies rushed in to compete with the British and the Dutch. In the early 1920s, as a token of goodwill, Gómez allowed the oil companies to draw up their own legislation and then made it law. Such legislation, together with the development of the Maracaibo oil fields, made Venezuela the largest exporter and second largest producer of oil by 1928. Even this record was surpassed in 1935 with the opening of the LLANOS oil fields in Apure. Naturally, such an able administrator as Gómez made the most of this wealth. He not only succeeded in paying all Venezuela's foreign and domestic debts but had money left over to carry out a large-scale public works program as well as the professionalization of the armed forces. The petroleum boom also provided abundant opportunities for graft on a grand scale, opportunities ably exploited by the favorites of the Gómez regime. One unfortunate consequence of this infatuation with oil revenue was the neglect of agriculture and the rural sector. By the end of the Gómez regime Venezuela, an essentially agricultural country, could no longer feed itself.

Within this environment the Gómez political system functioned smoothly. Serious dissent met with swift punishment, exile, or imprisonment. The press, rigidly controlled, praised Gómez and his works. The Army, content with the professionalization program, was led by officers chosen for their origin in the Táchira Andes and their loyalty to the chief. Politicians, who also

Juan Vicente Gómez. [Library of Congress]

frequently were *tachirenses*, could count on rich financial rewards for loyalty and swift retribution for signs of critical independence. Gómez's secret police and spy system diligently searched out enemies of the state. The success of this political system in the short run can be seen in the twenty-seven years of peace and profit Gómez provided. The three movements directed against him all failed miserably: one led by students in 1928, an invasion of Cumaná in 1929, and an attempted coup by Gen. Rafael Simón Urbina in 1931. Yet the opposition groups and individuals who spent their youth in exile and learned their political lessons under Gómez, especially the Generation of 1928, would carry out the liquidation of the Gómez system.

Although Gómez himself had little love for the pomp and ceremony of the Presidency and set up his residence in a country house near Maracay, he always retained control of either the Presidency or the Army. From time to time he had loyal subordinates fill the presidential chair, but none of them ever acted independently. Gómez was provisional President from 1908 to 1910 and constitutional President from 1910 to 1914. Although elected President for the period 1915–1922, he had Dr. Victorino Márquez Bustillos act as provisional President during this term. He again served as constitutional President from 1922 to 1929 but allowed one of his loyalists, Juan Bautista Pérez, a judge, to serve as President from 1929 to 1931; he returned to the presidential chair for the last time in 1931, occupying it until his death at the age of seventy-nine.

See also PETROLEUM INDUSTRY (VENEZUELA).

Bibliography. Miguel Acosta Saignes, *Latifundio*, Mexico City, 1938; Mario Briceño Iragorry, *Los Riberas*, Caracas, 1957; Daniel J. Clinton, *Gómez, Tyrant of the Andes*, New York, 1936; Domingo A. Rangel, *Los andinos en el poder: Balance de una hegemonía, 1899–1945*, Caracas, 1964; Laureano Vallenilla Lanz, *Cesarismo democrático: Estudios sobre las bases sociológicas de la constitución efectiva de Venezuela*, 4th ed., Caracas, 1961.

JOHN V. LOMBARDI

GÓMEZ, LAUREANO (1889–1965). President of Colombia (1950–1953). Gómez was born in Bogotá of parents from Ocaña, Norte de Santander. Educated in Bogotá, he first received public attention as a mouthpiece of generational resentments while editor of *La Unidad* (1909–1916). He was a Conservative deputy in the Cundinamarca Assembly (*see* CONSERVATIVE PARTY: COLOMBIA), a representative and senator several times, and Minister to Argentina (1923–1925) and to Germany (1931). In the vacuum of Conservative party leadership after the 1930 election he became recognized, though not universally, as leader of the party, a position he occupied until his Presidency. Gómez was responsible for cementing Conservative opposition to the governments of Enrique OLAYA HERRERA, Alfonso LÓPEZ, and Eduardo SANTOS. As Conservative chances of recovering power seemed to diminish, his opposition became more shrill, until in 1939 he was espousing falangist ideology and tactics of direct action. Gómez was the first to choose Mariano OSPINA PÉREZ as a candidate (1946) and succeeded him in 1950 after uncontested elections.

The acute violence that Gómez inherited did not abate during his term. He was probably the object of greater hatred among Liberals than any other Conservative (*see* LIBERAL PARTY: COLOMBIA) and was suspected of promoting falangism in the capital and clericalism in the countryside. There was little of legislative interest except constitutional reform proposals that polarized the Conservative party into two wings, one led by Gilberto Alzate Avendaño and the other by Jorge Leyva. Illness forced Gómez to step down in November 1951, and Roberto Urdaneta Arbeláez acted as President until June 1953. Rural violence and divided parties made Colombia increasingly unmanageable. A minor scandal in the Army led Gómez to attempt to reassume office, but he was ousted by a military coup led by Gen. Gustavo ROJAS PINILLA. In exile in Spain, Gómez concentrated on removing Rojas from power. He was largely responsible for facilitating a Conservative alliance with Liberals to depose Rojas and make possible a NATIONAL FRONT in 1958.

C. G. ABEL

GÓMEZ, MÁXIMO (1836–1905). Hero of Cuban independence. Born in Baní, Santo Domingo, Gómez began his military career at the age of sixteen by fighting the Haitians. He rose to become a commander, but in the civil war (1866) following Spain's withdrawal from Santo Domingo he lost everything. He then went to Santiago de Cuba, where he became a farmer and an avid supporter of independence.

Following the Grito de Yara of October 1868, which launched the TEN YEARS' WAR, he joined the army of Carlos Manuel de Céspedes, in which his qualities of leadership, iron will, and mastery of guerrilla warfare facilitated his rise to the rank of general and then to Secretary of War. After the Pact of Zanjón (February 1878), Gómez entered the Army of Honduras, where many of Cuba's revolutionary leaders were reunited. In 1885 he went to the United States to help encourage another Cuban revolution, and in 1892 he accepted a command in the army being organized by José MARTÍ.

Following Martí's death in 1895, control of the revolution passed into the hands of the generals and, after Antonio MACEO was killed the following year, largely into the hands of Gómez (*see* WAR FOR CUBAN INDEPENDENCE). However, Gómez, now sixty-three, decided against making himself dictatorial head of the revolution, encouraged the intervention of the United States, and did his best to cooperate despite American insults to himself and his army. His decision to accept only $3 million for the unpaid Cuban Army because he did not want the new government burdened with a great debt antagonized many of his followers and cost him his position as supreme commander. He remained, nonetheless, one of the most popular men on the island and, despite his foreign birth, the logical choice as Cuba's first President. Instead, he supported Tomás ESTRADA PALMA, saying, "Men of war for war and those of peace for peace."

KENNETH F. KIPLE

GÓMEZ FARÍAS, VALENTÍN (1781–1858). Mexican statesman. A native of Guadalajara, Gómez Farías was trained in medicine but early gave up practice as a medical doctor to enter politics. He was elected deputy to the 1822 Spanish Cortes but did not attend it. From the very beginning he was a Liberal and a federalist. He was a delegate in the Congress that wrote the constitution of 1824 and briefly served in Manuel Gómez Pedraza's Cabinet. His real importance dates from 1833, when he was elected Vice President. Antonio López de SANTA ANNA, the President, was absent during much of 1833–1834, and Gómez Farías served as acting President. During these periods he sponsored a liberal legislative program that had as its goal the weakening of the economic, political, and social power and influence of the Catholic Church in Mexico. These measures were unpopular with many, and the nation seemed headed toward civil war. In April 1834, Santa Anna took the reins of government and nullified the laws, and Gómez Farías went into exile.

An avowed nationalist, Gómez Farías again served as acting President in 1846–1847, during the MEXICAN WAR, and while Santa Anna, the President, was commanding the Army in the field. When the revolution of Ayutla began, he supported that cause and became active as one of the political leaders. He was a delegate to the Constitutional Congress of 1856–1857. One of his last public acts was taking the oath to support the constitution of 1857, which embodied the ideals of the program he had labored to realize more than two decades previously (*see* CONSTITUTION OF 1857: MEXICO).

CHARLES R. BERRY

GONÇALVES DE MAGALHÃES, DOMINGOS JOSÉ (1811–1882). Brazilian poet, dramatist, essayist, and diplomat. Born in Rio de Janeiro, he took a medical degree in 1832 but did not practice. In 1833 he went to Paris, studied philosophy, worked briefly in the legation, and traveled in Western Europe. In 1836 he founded the magazine *Niteroi,* together with Sales Torres Homem and Araújo Pôrto Alegre, and published *Suspiros Poéticos e Saudades,* a collection of lyrics that marks the beginning of romanticism in Brazil. Patriotically eager to establish a great literature in his country, he began to attempt other genres: the drama, in *Antônio José ou o Poeta e a Inquisição,* presented in 1838 by João Caetano, the country's leading actor; and the epic, in *A Confederação dos Tamóios* (1856), the theme of which, as in *O Uruguai* and *Caramurú,* is the contribution of the Indian to the formation of the Brazilian nationality. Unlike the earlier poems, but like *Os Timbiras* (1857), by Antônio GONÇALVES DIAS, it is strongly colored with anti-Portuguese feeling. But José de ALENCAR attacked this epic in ten cantos and unrhymed decasyllables as not being Brazilian enough, even though it had the official sponsorship of the Emperor. The works of Gonçalves de Magalhães, published in nine volumes (1864–1876), include other poems, a second play, and essays on history, literature, and philosophy. His importance is that of an innovator and trailblazer.

RAYMOND S. SAYERS

GONÇALVES DIAS, ANTÔNIO (1823–1864). Brazilian poet and dramatist. Born in Maranhão, the illegitimate son of a Portuguese shopkeeper and an Indian-Negro woman, he was educated by his white stepmother, who sent him to study at the University of Coimbra, where the lack of funds caused him many privations. He taught at the College of Pedro II in Rio de Janeiro, was attached to the diplomatic service, and traveled widely on official missions through the north of Brazil and in Europe. He was a man of varied culture, capable of teaching Latin and teaching and writing about history. He also wrote about ethnography and composed a dictionary of the Tupí language. The first great Brazilian romantic, he made the Indian and nature his principal subjects. He depicted the Indian as a Noble Savage oppressed by decadent civilized man, and thus the symbol of all Americans who struggled for freedom from foreign oppression; nature he saw as the symbol of a brave new world that invaders from other continents had desecrated. His *Primeiros Cantos* (1846) brought him the praise of the Portuguese poet and historian Alexandre Herculano. This was followed by *Segundos Cantos e Sextilhas de Frei Antão* (1848), into which he introduced the medievalism so dear to the hearts of the romantics; *Últimos Cantos* (1851); and *Os Timbiras* (1857), an unfinished Indianist epic. He was a master of the dramatic monologue, such as "Ainda Uma Vez Adeus," and the pure lyric, such as "Olhos Verdes," both poems of love. He wrote in many meters and forms, and he had an unrivaled ear for the music of the language. He died in a shipwreck.

RAYMOND S. SAYERS

GONDRA, MANUEL (1871–1927). Paraguayan scholar, statesman, and President (1910–1911, 1920–1921). The son of an Argentine father and a Paraguayan mother, Gondra began his career as an educator, spending years renovating the Paraguayan school system. As a military man who in his part-time service reached the rank of general, he reorganized the Army, and in 1912 he served as Minister of War. While teaching geography, he had become interested in the CHACO boundary question, and over the years he was to be one of the chief architects of Paraguay's claims to that region. Gondra was a leader of the Liberal party and twice was the party's successful presidential candidate, but his short coup-ridden terms are remembered chiefly for the honesty with which he infused his administrations. *See* LIBERAL PARTY (PARAGUAY).

Although Gondra was only moderately successful as a politician, he was a distinguished writer and diplomat. He served as a delegate to a number of international conferences and is perhaps best remembered for the Gondra Convention, approved at the Fifth International Conference of American States, held in Santiago, Chile, in 1923. The convention was intended to provide guidelines for the avoidance of conflict between American states. A linguist and critic of renown, Gondra assembled one of the finest libraries in South America, which was sold to the University of Texas after his death.

JOHN HOYT WILLIAMS

GONZAGA, TOMÁS ANTÔNIO (1744–1810). Brazilian poet. Born in Oporto, Portugal, he received his early education in Bahia, where his father was a judge. He went to the University of Coimbra in 1762 to study law and remained in Portugal until 1782, when he returned to Brazil to be a judge in Villa Rica (now Ouro Prêto). There he became a friend of the important poets of the Minas school, met a girl of fifteen to whom he became engaged, and apparently became the enemy of the despotic and corrupt Governor. He was implicated with his friends in the conspiracy known as the INCONFI-

DÊNCIA MINEIRA and was imprisoned in 1789; in 1792 he was sent to Mozambique, where he died. Meanwhile he had written in 1786 the thirteen *Cartas Chilenas,* satires on the Governor and his court, which contain precious glimpses of life in the small but wealthy city. Both before and after his imprisonment he was writing *liras* (lyric poems) to his young fiancée, Maria Doroteia (Marília). They were published in 1792, and in enlarged editions in 1799 and 1812. In Mozambique, separated from his fiancée, he married a wealthy widow and began a second, more prosperous career. The lyrics of *Marília de Dirceu,* which have been frequently reprinted, are among the most popular in the language. In spite of their neoclassicism in form and their tendency to employ many conventional *topoi* (recurrent themes and images handed down from the past), there is novelty in the directness of their approach, the language is simple, and the allusions to Brazilian life and nature are charming.

RAYMOND S. SAYERS

GONZÁLEZ PRADA, MANUEL (1848–1918). Peruvian man of letters and reformer. González Prada, one of Peru's most distinguished literary figures, remains the object of controversy a half century after his death. To some he is the symbol of the destructiveness of the twentieth-century Peruvian radicalism he helped inspire. To others he is an early symbol of a new Peru and the source of a new national spirit. These admirers reject some of his apocalyptic visions, but still they have sought inspiration from his rebelliousness and his intellectual honesty.

González Prada was born to an aristocratic family in Lima on January 6, 1848. Early in his life he displayed the anticlericalism and the iconoclasm that were to become two of his principal trademarks. A mediocre student but a voracious reader and a budding poet, he expressed a desire to study engineering in Belgium. Forbidden to do so by his strong-willed mother, he devoted himself to literature. He wrote poetry, criticism, and essays while retaining an avid interest in languages, science, and farming.

His voluminous writings and his tormented adult life can be divided into two periods. The first was dominated by the disastrous WAR OF THE PACIFIC (1879–1883) and its aftermath. The second was highlighted by a long trip to Europe (1892–1898) and by a gradual espousal of anarchism.

The War of the Pacific, which cost Peru some territory and a great deal of pride, traumatized González Prada. He shut himself in his home for the duration of the Chilean occupation of Lima, and for the next decade he sought to explain the reasons for the defeat. In a series of speeches and essays, reprinted in *Páginas libres* (1894), he analyzed Peruvian history and discovered in it only venality, corruption, and intellectual obscurantism. He accused first Spain and then the post-independence aristocracy, church, and military of turning Peru into such a sick organism that "everywhere you press it, pus comes out." They were responsible for the defeat and would continue to bring harm to the nation until they, along with other institutions of the past, were destroyed. This radical transformation, according to González Prada, was to be carried out by the uncontaminated segments of Peruvian society, the youth and the Indians. His exhortation "Old men

to the tomb, young men to work" became a battle cry for future reformers. And his view that the Indian was potentially the most dynamic force in the nation helped arouse considerable interest in the Indian's plight.

Many of González Prada's ideas were not original. However, his program for their implementation was. In 1891 he and many of his followers in the Círculo Literario, a literary organization advocating a radical departure from the literary styles of the day, formed the Unión Nacional. This party, whose radical platform had been written by González Prada, was immediately given a mortal blow by González Prada himself when, in 1892, he left for Europe, to remain there until 1898. His sudden departure and eventual abandonment of the party were not surprising. González Prada was not a political activist but a literary man. He was an effective propagandist and pamphleteer but a shy and retiring individual who lacked the personality of the political organizer.

González Prada's return from Europe marks the beginning of his anarchist phase. His basic philosophy is contained in *Horas de lucha* (1908), a compilation of speeches and essays. In them he continued to espouse the Indian cause, but he also intensified his relentless assaults on religion, the state, and the rich. He preached a bloody revolution led by the working class and the intellectuals with the ultimate aim of bringing greater happiness to all humanity. Although his writings are

Manuel González Prada. [*Organization of American States*]

Marxist in tone, he rejected all forms of socialism, believing that only anarchism would give the individual the unlimited freedom he deserved.

In subsequent years González Prada's anarchism deepened to the point where he called for "revolution by everybody against everything." Such nihilism appeared to be a symptom of a growing bitterness and misanthropy clearly displayed in his poetry. In one poem, for example, he saw himself trapped in the wrong century; in another he boiled the meaning of life down to three words: sad, ridiculous, and foul. And in his last poem he bade farewell to the world by claiming never to have loved it and by expressing loathing for life and contempt for all men.

In 1918 González Prada died. Since 1912 he had been the director of the National Library. Both there and in his home he had held court for young intellectuals like José Carlos MARIÁTEGUI and Víctor Raúl HAYA DE LA TORRE. To them he was the spirit of a new era, although to many other Peruvians he was slightly mad and very dangerous. To be sure, his pronouncements against religion and for bloody revolution were often irrational. However, his unyielding social consciousness made him one of Peru's most inspiring reformers.

Bibliography. Eugenio Chang Rodríguez, *La literatura política de González Prada, Mariátegui, y Haya de la Torre,* Mexico City, 1957; Manuel González Prada, *Páginas libres,* Paris, 1894; id., *Horas de lucha,* Lima, 1908; Adriana de González Prada, *Mi Manuel,* Lima, 1947; Luis Alberto Sánchez, *Don Manuel,* Lima, 1930.

ORAZIO A. CICCARELLI

GONZÁLEZ SUÁREZ, FEDERICO (1844–1917). Ecuadorian archbishop and historian. Born in Quito, he joined the Jesuit order, turned secular priest in Cuenca at twenty-eight, and commenced his writing career. Ecuadorian historians still relied upon the eighteenth-century Jesuit scholar Father Juan de Velasco, but as González Suárez perfected his own methodology, he increasingly questioned Velasco's citations, eulogies, tales of animals transformed into plants, and the like. He sought out primary sources in the Spanish archives and labored ten years before he began publication of his eight-volume *Historia general de la república* (1890–1903). Incomplete in that it did not include the wars of independence, and unbalanced in that it left out regional economic aspects, it radically changed Ecuadorian historiography.

González Suárez's role as moderator between Liberals and Conservatives dates from his inclusion in Gen. Ignacio VEINTEMILLA's Assembly of 1878 (*see* CONSERVATIVE PARTY: ECUADOR; LIBERAL PARTY: ECUADOR). He was Bishop of Ibarra in 1895, when armed Conservatives spilled over the nearby Colombian border attempting to turn back Liberal party reforms. González Suárez instructed his priests to have nothing to do with politics in the classroom, in political parties, or in the civil wars. Eloy ALFARO sought the bishop's counsel for a new law of patronage and in 1906 appointed him Archbishop of Quito. Until his death in 1917 he maintained, in spite of harsh criticism by the Conservatives, "We ecclesiastics ought not to sacrifice the nation to save the religion."

LOIS WEINMAN

GONZÁLEZ VIDELA, GABRIEL (1898–   ). President of Chile (1946–1952). Born in La Serena, González Videla studied at a local school and then at the University of Chile, graduating in law in 1922. He practiced in his hometown until 1930 and then was elected to Congress as a Radical deputy for La Serena (*see* RADICAL PARTY: CHILE), holding his seat until 1939, when he entered the diplomatic service. He rose rapidly to national prominence, serving as President of the Chamber of Deputies in 1933 and as president of the Radical party in 1932 and 1937. When Pedro AGUIRRE CERDA became President of Chile in 1938, González Videla was appointed Ambassador to France (1939–1941), and when Juan Antonio RÍOS succeeded Aguirre Cerda in 1942, he served in Rio de Janeiro until 1944. Despite this absence from Chile, he retained his position in the Radical party and in 1945 returned to active politics as a senator for Tarapacá and Antofagasta.

With the death of Ríos in 1946, González Videla secured the Radical party nomination for the Presidency but failed to secure a clear majority over the other three candidates. The issue then went to Congress, as the constitution prescribed, and he was confirmed as President through an agreement between the Radicals and Liberals (*see* LIBERAL PARTY: CHILE). Since the Communists had also backed him, his first Cabinet consisted of three Radicals, three Liberals, and three Communists, who now entered the government for the first time (*see* COMMUNIST PARTY: CHILE). But Communist success in the municipal elections of 1947 caused the Liberals to resign from the Cabinet and González Videla to reconstitute it with Radicals alone. In 1948 he put through the Law for the Defense of Democracy, outlawing the Communist party from public life, and broke off relations with Communist countries. Under González Videla the State Technical University and the steel complex of Huachipato were inaugurated, and women were given the vote in national elections.

HAROLD BLAKEMORE

GONZÁLEZ VÍQUEZ, CLETO (1858–1937). President of Costa Rica (1906–1910, 1928–1932). As historian, jurist, teacher, legislator, and President; González Víquez earned a place as one of the most distinguished Costa Ricans in recent history. He was President twice and, like his distinguished contemporary Ricardo JIMÉNEZ OREAMUNO (President 1910–1914, 1924–1928, 1932–1936), governed with wit, moderation, rectitude, and charm. Seldom did he need to raise his voice or dictate strong measures. He governed at a time when Costa Ricans expected and applauded these qualities and apparently preferred his emphasis on education and public health to profound social or economic change. The most serious problem he faced as President was the economic depression of 1929, and he handled this crisis with such grace and sympathy for the financially unfortunate that he suffered little loss of popularity. As an author, González Víquez made a substantial contribution to the history of his country's economic and political institutions and to regional history, especially in his studies of Puntarenas and San José.

CHARLES L. STANSIFER

GOOD NEIGHBOR POLICY. In his inaugural speech on March 4, 1933, President Franklin D. Roosevelt articulated a basic precept of his foreign policy: "In the field of world policy, I would dedicate this nation to the policy of the good neighbor—the neighbor who resolutely respects himself, and because he does so, respects the rights of others—the neighbor who respects his obligations and respects the sanctity of his agreements in and with a world of neighbors." The President subsequently made it clear that this Good Neighbor policy was to apply specifically to the Western Hemisphere. As it unfolded, it proved to be a policy that was (1) essentially negative, with a few exceptions, (2) largely unilateral despite lavish references to multilateralism, and (3) the genesis of a significant United States military involvement in Latin America. Above all, good-neighborliness was aimed at furthering the immediate interests of the United States, namely, trade expansion and, after 1936, the security of the hemisphere against Axis aggression and subversion.

By the time Franklin Roosevelt entered the White House, armed intervention of the kind sanctioned by the ROOSEVELT COROLLARY of 1904 no longer constituted an efficient instrument for dealing with Latin America. It was expensive and generally ineffective in guaranteeing order or in spreading democracy. As early as 1928 Roosevelt had insisted: "Single-handed intervention by us in the internal affairs of other nations must end; with the cooperation of others we shall have more order in this Hemisphere and less dislike." Both at the MONTEVIDEO CONFERENCE (1933) and at the Inter-American Conference for the Maintenance of Peace (Buenos Aires, 1936) the United States signed agreements disavowing the right of intervention in the affairs of the Latin American nations.

United States repudiation of intervention faced several tests in the 1930s, most notably in Cuba, where lawlessness and instability resulted from the unpopular government of Gerardo MACHADO, and in Mexico, where in 1938 President Lázaro CÁRDENAS expropriated the holdings of foreign oil companies. In both cases there was pressure for United States armed intervention, but less forceful diplomatic initiatives proved successful. Other examples of Roosevelt's noninterventionism are readily found. The final detachment of Marines left Nicaragua in 1933, and the following year the United States completed its withdrawal from Haiti, which had been occupied since 1915. With the abrogation of the PLATT AMENDMENT in 1934, the United States gave up its right to intervene in Cuba, while the HULL-ALFARO TREATY of 1936 had a similar effect with respect to Panama. All these cases underscore the negative character of the Good Neighbor policy. The United States was saying, in effect, that it would *not* send troops to collect debts; it would *not* seize customhouses; it would *not* intervene militarily in political affairs; it would *not* rush to the rescue of private United States firms.

There were, in addition, positive aspects of the Good Neighbor policy, including efforts to increase trade through negotiated tariff cuts and through the establishment of the Export-Import Bank. During the period from 1932 to 1942, United States trade with Latin American nations increased by 302 percent. *See also* TRADE (1810–1940).

Alarmed by the aggressive posture of Mussolini and Hitler, Roosevelt also began to seek hemispheric unity against possible European threats to the New World. At the Buenos Aires Conference in 1936 and at the

LIMA CONFERENCE of 1938, the principle of hemispheric solidarity and consultation in the face of direct or indirect threats to security was adopted. With the outbreak of World War II in 1939, the foreign ministers of the American states meeting in Panama agreed to maintain hemispheric neutrality, but after the entry of the United States into the war the foreign ministers recommended that their governments sever diplomatic relations with the Axis (*see* HAVANA MEETING; PANAMA MEETING; RIO DE JANEIRO MEETING).

Despite frequent references to multilateralism, however, the responsibility for implementing policies adopted at these and other gatherings rested with the United States. Only the United States had power and resources sufficient to accomplish the goal of hemispheric defense, and the Latin American nations were relegated to a minor supporting role because of their low military capability. Their principal contribution consisted of making bases and strategic materials available to the United States. However, Cuba and Brazil played a part in antisubmarine warfare, and Brazil and Mexico sent military units to the battlefronts.

The seeds of the massive military involvement of the United States in Latin America in the 1950s and 1960s were sown in the Good Neighbor period. Through a series of military mission agreements with Latin American nations, the United States sent military advisers to nearly every country. In the process the United States also supplanted existing Italian and German missions.

The Good Neighbor policy had smaller long-range importance than was claimed for it in the 1930s and 1940s. The United States attained its principal objectives, the promotion of immediate United States economic and security needs, and it is unlikely that Latin American cooperation with the United States during World War II could have been secured without the "good-neighborliness" of the 1930s. On the other hand, despite the fact that it advanced United States interests to speak of the equality of all American states and multilateral policy making, the United States resorted to unilateral armed intervention in Latin America on several occasions after World War II. Moreover, the Good Neighbor policy failed to focus attention on the internal problems besetting each hemispheric state: gross income inequities, feudalistic social structures, uneven development, and predatory militarism. While promoting American exports and security, the Good Neighbor policy helped maintain the socioeconomic and political status quo. Despite its immediate success, it is difficult to perceive enduring contributions of the policy to inter-American relations or to conditions in the hemispheric republics.

Bibliography. Edward O. Guerrant, *Roosevelt's Good Neighbor Policy*, Albuquerque, N.Mex., 1950; Sumner Welles, *The Time for Decision*, New York, 1944; Bryce Wood, *The Making of the Good Neighbor Policy*, New York, 1961.   GEORGE W. GRAYSON

GOROSTIZA, JOSÉ (1901–   ). Mexican poet. A native of Villahermosa, Tabasco, he has filled diplomatic posts in various countries and at the United Nations. He forms part of the literary generation associated with the review *Contemporáneos* (1928–1931) and is a member of the Mexican Academy of the Language. In prose he has published criticism, reviews, a story, and translations. His first collection of poetry, *Canciones para cantar en las barcas* (1925), showed his interest in Spanish poets of the Golden Age and in Góngora's popular poetry. Fourteen years later he published his masterpiece, *Muerte sin fin* (1939), a long metaphysical poem that describes an increasingly intense search for the universal and the eternal.

RACHEL PHILLIPS

GOU. *See* GRUPO DE OFICIALES UNIDOS.

GOULART, JOÃO [BELCHIOR MARQUES] (1918–   ). President of Brazil (1961–1964). João Goulart, a labor politician popularly known as Jango, was born at São Borja, Rio Grande do Sul. After graduating from the Pôrto Alegre law school in 1945, he became the close friend and protégé of his neighbor, Getúlio VARGAS. When Vargas returned to the Presidency in 1951, Goulart accompanied him as a member of the official household and vice president of the PARTIDO TRABALHISTA BRASILEIRO (PTB). Appointed Labor Minister in 1953, Goulart sought to incorporate organized labor into the PTB but was forced from office by military pressure. He became president of the party following Vargas's suicide in 1954 and was its successful candidate for the Vice Presidency of Brazil in 1955 and 1960.

The resignation of President Jânio QUADROS in August 1961 placed Goulart at the center of a national crisis, for the military Cabinet ministers insisted that he was too radical to be permitted to succeed to the Presidency. Nonetheless, Goulart became President on September 7, 1961, after the crisis was resolved by a compromise that introduced the parliamentary form of government, greatly reducing presidential authority. He retrieved full executive powers as the result of a nationwide plebiscite in January 1963, but he proved unable to cope effectively with the deteriorating economy and polarization of political forces in Brazil. His administration was overthrown by the revolution of March 31, 1964. He went into exile in Uruguay on April 2, 1964.

ROLLIE E. POPPINO

GRAÇA ARANHA, JOSÉ PEREIRA DA (1869–1931). Brazilian man of letters and diplomat. Born in Maranhão, he was a graduate of the law school of Recife, where he came under the influence of the monistic philosophy of Tobias Barreto. He began his professional career as a judge in Espírito Santo and then went into the diplomatic service, a course that led to his appointment as minister in several capitals. He was a founding member of the Brazilian Academy of Letters, with which he quarreled in 1924 because of his support of modernism (*see* MODERNISM: BRAZIL). Throughout his life he was the friend and confidant of other writers and diplomats, the most important of whom were Joaquim NABUCO and Joaquim MACHADO DE ASSIS. He was not essentially a novelist, but he wrote two novels, *Canaã*, 1901 (*Canaan*), and *A Viagem Maravilhosa* (1929). *Canaã*, though lacking as a work of art, is one of the few Brazilian novels of ideas. In large part it is a debate between two German immigrants of good family who represent respectively liberalism and authoritarianism, the contradictory aspects of the German psyche. The question

is the contemporary situation and possible future of a country with Brazil's racial composition. The novel is classified as symbolist. His play *Malasarte* (1911) is very much within the symbolist tradition, too. In his most important philosophical work, *A Estética da Vida* (1920), Graça Aranha argues that man can achieve integration into the universe through the esthetic approach to life.

RAYMOND S. SAYERS

GRACE, W. R., & CO. *See* W. R. GRACE & CO. (PERU).

GRANADA. Nicaraguan city, situated on the western shore of Lake Nicaragua. Granada was founded in 1524 by Francisco Hernández de Córdoba and quickly developed into an important trading center and port. Indigo, cochineal, cacao, staples, and hides came overland from the Central American Pacific region to Granada to be transferred via Lake Nicaragua and the San Juan River to ships bound for the Caribbean and ultimately for European markets. This route also proved accessible to pirates, who sacked the city several times in the seventeenth century. Granada's commercial importance gradually declined because of piracy and natural hindrances to navigation on the San Juan River and because of a decrease in the market for Nicaragua's traditional exports.

Since independence Granada's old families have formed a Conservative political bastion that has exercised considerable influence on Nicaragua's political life. In 1856 it was a major object of attack by William WALKER's filibusters, who were allied with the opposing Liberal faction. The filibusters nearly destroyed the city by fire. It nevertheless retains its colonial appearance because the principal buildings were rebuilt in the original style. Nicaragua's twentieth-century industrial and commercial expansion has centered on Managua, about 30 miles away, leaving Granada essentially as it was fifty years ago. In 1906 it had a population of about 16,000; in 1950, about 30,000; and in 1968 just over 40,000.

CHARLES L. STANSIFER

GRAN COLOMBIA. *See* COLOMBIA, GRAN.

GRANDJEAN DE MONTIGNY, AUGUSTE-HENRI-VICTOR (1776–1850). French architect. Grandjean de Montigny attended the École des Beaux-Arts in Paris, where he was a student of Charles Percier and Pierre Fontaine; he continued his studies in Italy, winning the Prix de Rome for architecture in 1799. From 1810 to 1813 he was employed as an architect by Jérôme Bonaparte, King of Westphalia.

Along with Jean-Baptiste DEBRET, Grandjean de Montigny was a member of the Lebreton mission, which arrived in Brazil in 1816; and he was promptly named professor of architecture. Remaining in Brazil until his death, he left a strong mark on the architecture of Rio de Janeiro. Among his many projects for that city were the design of the Academia de Belas Artes, inaugurated in 1826; construction of a building to house Rio's first large market; and the remodeling of the Seminary of São Joaquim for use as the Colégio Pedro II.

HELEN DELPAR

GRAU SAN MARTÍN, RAMÓN (1887–1969). President of Cuba (1933–1934, 1944–1948). Grau, a prominent

Havana physician and opponent of ex-dictator Gerardo MACHADO, was named a member of the five-man commission organized after the sergeants' revolt of September 1933 led by Fulgencio BATISTA. On September 10, 1933, Grau took office as provisional President of Cuba. The government headed by Grau was reform-minded and nationalistic, but although it was opposed by the Communist party, it was considered excessively radical by United States Ambassador Sumner WELLES. The unwillingness of the United States to recognize Grau, which carried with it refusal to negotiate a favorable commercial agreement, led to his resignation the following January. Grau remained a leader of the non-Communist left opposition to Batista in the next decade.

In 1944 Grau was elected President for a four-year term as the candidate of the Auténtico party (*see* AUTÉNTICO PARTY: CUBA), defeating the plan of the incumbent, Batista, to install a puppet government that would have permitted him to continue exercising political control. Although Grau's administration was received with jubilation by all sectors of Cuban society, he proved a great disappointment to the country. His Presidency became an orgy of corruption sustained by the economic prosperity of the post-World War II years and fed by the avarice of the old revolutionaries of the early 1930s. There was some progress in health, education, and housing, but it was obscured by the dishonesty in government. By mid-term Grau had lost much of his original support. The failure of his administration was a major blow to the development of democratic institutions and social justice in Cuba.

J. CORDELL ROBINSON

GREATER COLOMBIA. *See* COLOMBIA, GRAN.

GRITO DE DOLORES. *See* DOLORES, GRITO DE.

GRITO DE YPIRANGA. *See* YPIRANGA, GRITO DE.

GRUPO ANDINO. *See* ANDEAN GROUP.

GRUPO DE OFICIALES UNIDOS (UNITED OFFICERS GROUP; GOU). A secret lodge within the Argentine Army composed chiefly of colonels, the GOU was formally constituted in March 1943 as a result of dissatisfaction with the official presidential candidate and concern about increasing United States pressure on the Army to assume a pro-Allied position. The GOU was instrumental in planning the June 1943 coup against the government of Ramón S. CASTILLO and became an important part of the power struggle that ensued. The aims of the lodge reflected the preoccupation of young officers with the Army's role in the preservation of the nation's integrity. In the circumstances imposed by World War II, this meant continuing the traditional policy of noninvolvement in wars not directly bearing on Argentina's security, guaranteeing the country's economic independence, and maintaining the corollary belief that such independence would be viable only when Argentina developed an economy based on industry.

With Pedro Pablo RAMÍREZ installed as President after the June 1943 coup, a power struggle developed within the government. Not until October did members of the GOU succeed in strengthening their control of the Cabinet. The break in diplomatic relations with the Axis in January 1944 heightened rivalries within the GOU itself and led both to its formal dissolution and to the dismissal of some of its members from the government. The rivalries continued until the definitive predominance of Juan D. PERÓN, originator of the GOU, in October 1945.

NOREEN F. STACK

GUADALAJARA. Mexican city. Founded on its present site in 1542, Guadalajara became the capital of the province of New Galicia during the colonial period. Like Mexico City, it boasted a university. It later became not only the capital of the state of Jalisco but also the most important city, demographically and economically, of western Mexico. In 1970 its population was 1,196,218.

Guadalajara has had rail communications with Mexico City and Manzanillo since the era of Porfirio DÍAZ (1876–1911) and more recently with the northeast. It exercises a hegemony in culture and finance as well as in health services over the states of Colima, Nayarit, Zacatecas, Michoacán, and Guanajuato as well as over Sinaloa, Sonora, and Baja California. It is a great consumer of corn, milk, livestock, vegetables, and fruits. It imports milk from Zacatecas and Aguascalientes and absorbs a large amount of the cattle of Jalisco, Colima, Nayarit, and Michoacán. Its oil factories consume raw materials from Colima, and its food-processing plants the products of coastal Jalisco, Michoacán, and Colima. It is also an important shoe-manufacturing center. The economic expansion of Guadalajara has taken place at the expense of the commercial autonomy of the microregions that surround it and has brought about the disappearance of the traditional commerce of the region. Its industrial development is being channeled along the so-called industrial corridor that will link it with Ocotlán and La Barca.

MOISÉS GONZÁLEZ NAVARRO

GUADALUPE, VIRGIN OF. According to tradition, the Virgin Mary appeared to an Indian, Juan Diego, on a hill near Mexico City on three distinct occasions in December 1531, identifying herself by this name. Tradition states that, to prove she was the Virgin, she caused a painting of herself to appear on the inside of Juan Diego's cloak, and, indeed, a cloak with such a painting does exist and is preserved in the basilica dedicated to the Virgin. Devotion to the Virgin of Guadalupe began soon after 1531.

The cult proved especially attractive to the Indians for several reasons: the Virgin had appeared to a member of their own race, the painting of the Virgin showed her to be of rather dark complexion herself, and the spot where she had appeared had previously been sacred to one of their pagan goddesses. Through their acceptance of the cult of the Virgin, the Indians became more strongly attached to Christianity itself.

Devotion to the Virgin took firm root among all other elements of the population, too, and as national consciousness developed in the eighteenth century, the Virgin came to be thought of as the symbol of the nation, with the result that when the War of Independence broke out, the insurgents carried the image of the Virgin as their banner. In the nineteenth and twentieth centuries, although the Guadalupan cult has been rejected by Mexicans who have rejected Catholicism itself and although a few prominent Catholics have questioned the authenticity of the apparition, devotion to the Virgin has generally continued to be strong in Mexico.

The feast of the Virgin of Guadalupe is celebrated on December 12, said to be the date of the last and most important of the three appearances that the Virgin made to Juan Diego.

TIMOTHY C. HANLEY

GUADALUPE HIDALGO, TREATY OF. Also known as the Treaty of Peace, Friendship, Limits, and Settlement between the United States and Mexico, the document ending the MEXICAN WAR (1846–1848) was signed in the village of Guadalupe Hidalgo on February 2, 1848. According to its terms the Texas boundary between the two nations was established at the Rio Grande, and Mexico was required to cede New Mexico and Upper California (now the states of California, Arizona, New Mexico, Nevada, and Utah, and parts of Colorado and Wyoming). In addition, all claims to Texas were relinquished. In return the United States was to pay $15 million, of which $3 million would be available upon Mexican ratification of the treaty. The United States also agreed to assume $3,250,000 of claims outstanding from citizens of the territory against the Mexican government.

The United States negotiator of the treaty, Nicholas P. Trist, was successful in gaining Mexican acceptance of President James K. Polk's terms for settlement. In so doing, however, Trist had ignored instructions from Polk to break off discussions at a crucial point in the negotiations. Angered by Trist's insubordination but pleased with his work, Polk submitted the treaty to the United States Senate for approval, which was received on March 10, 1848. Trist, however, was peremptorily dismissed, and it was not until 1871 that a grateful Congress approved his claims for salary and expenses.

RICHARD B. GRAY

GUANABARA. Smallest Brazilian state, dominated by the metropolitan area of its capital city, Rio de Janeiro. Guanabara's 543 square miles were detached from the province of Rio de Janeiro in 1834 to form a "neutral county" around the capital city. With the advent of the republic, the area was designated the Federal District; and in 1960, with the removal of the national capital from Rio de Janeiro to Brasília, it became a state.

Guanabara is the most densely populated state in Brazil, with 4,315,746 inhabitants (1970). Despite a government program to eradicate the hillside slums known as *favelas* (*see* FAVELA) and to relocate the residents, 515,647 persons still live in the *favelas*. Geographically, Guanabara is dominated by its surrounding waters, the Atlantic Ocean to the south and the Bay of Guanabara to the east, and by its spectacular *morros* (mountains), the most famous of which are Sugar Loaf and the Corcovado. The climate and vegetation are subtropical, with rainy, cool weather prevailing from July through August, and hot, summer weather bringing thousands to Rio's beaches from December through March. The industrial, cultural, and educational activities of Guanabara are synonymous with those of Rio de Janeiro, making the state second only to São Paulo in industrial development and preeminent in the areas of communications, education, and service-oriented activities.

FRANCESCA MILLER

GUANO. In the nineteenth century Peru's social, economic, and political institutions were radically affected by guano (Quechua *huanu,* "dung"), deposits of bird manure greatly in demand as a fertilizer in Europe. For thousands of years birds had found sanctuary on Peru's offshore islands, attracted to the region by the presence of large schools of fish, which in turn had been attracted by great quantities of food brought there by the cold HUMBOLDT CURRENT. The steady accumulation of guano on the islands at a rate of more than 6 feet per century was aided by the near absence of rain and strong winds in the region.

Guano had been used as a fertilizer by the pre-Inca and Inca civilizations. In smaller quantities it continued to be used during the colonial period, especially in the south of Peru. By 1840 a series of experiments had revealed what had been known by the natives for hundreds of years: guano was a potent fertilizer. A ton of it had enough mineral sustenance for the production of 25 tons of any cereal. By 1841 its exportation to Europe began on a large scale, to continue until the 1880s, when it was replaced by nitrates.

The largest guano deposits were found on the three Chincha Islands, where they were supposedly more than 160 feet high. Annually, hundreds of ships overcame the stench to dock there in order to bring hundreds of thousands of tons of guano to European markets. The financial returns for the Peruvian government and for everyone else connected with the trade were substantial, but in the long run the economic boom did more harm than good to the Peruvian economy. Guano is still widely utilized as a fertilizer in Peru.

ORAZIO A. CICCARELLI

GUANTÁNAMO BAY. An important harbor on the southeast coast of Cuba, 5 miles wide and 12 miles long, Guantánamo Bay is about 40 miles east of Santiago de Cuba and 70 miles from the eastern tip of the island. The ports of Caimanera and Boquerón also are on the bay, and the city of Guantánamo is located about 12 miles to the north. The United States Marines discovered the usefulness of the bay in the Spanish-American War of 1898. After the war the bay became the site of a United States naval base originally granted to the United States by the PLATT AMENDMENT appended to the Cuban constitution of 1901 and by a formal treaty in 1903. The annual rental of the base was set at $2,000, although this amount was later increased.

The bay's strategic importance along one of the chief routes to the PANAMA CANAL has been a major consideration in United States relations with Cuba in the twentieth century. When the Platt Amendment was abrogated in 1934, the United States declined to give up the fortified base, and a treaty signed on May 29, 1934, assured the United States' continued presence at Guantánamo Bay. Toward the end of the dictatorship of Fulgencio BATISTA rebel followers of Fidel CASTRO seized United States sailors and marines outside the base and caused additional trouble by cutting off the base's water supply at times from July to November 1958 as a form of protest against North American support of the Batista government.

Ever since Castro took power in 1959, the naval base has furnished him an excuse for charges of Yankee imperialism. When the base's water supply was cut off again in 1964, the United States responded by making the naval installation self-sufficient in water through costly desalinization plants.

RICHARD B. GRAY

GUARANÍ. One of the two officially recognized languages spoken in Paraguay (the other being Spanish). Representing the southern branch of the TUPÍ-GUARANÍ linguistic family, which was spoken by Indians from the Amazon Delta south through Paraguay and what is now northeastern Argentina, the Guaraní tongue has been much changed in recent centuries. The Jesuits were the first Europeans to create a grammar for written Guaraní and to print books in that language, preserving its usage in their missions. The impact of Spanish on the language has been great. Originally a rather simple language composed of fewer than 1,000 words, the Guaraní lexicon now contains more than 50,000 words, most of which are derived from Spanish root words. For example, *sapatú* (shoe) is derived from the Spanish *zapato* and ends with the accented vowel characteristic of Guaraní. Today most Paraguayans speak Jopará, an urban Guaraní containing more words of foreign origin than the "purer," more indigenous variety heard mainly in rural areas.

Paraguay is an almost fully bilingual country, with Guaraní being the familial or informal language of communication. There is a Guaraní literature. Especially well represented are the poem and the song, to which this melodic tongue seems particularly well suited; and the Municipal Theater of Asunción often presents plays in Guaraní. During the PARAGUAYAN WAR (1864–1870) an Army newspaper, *Cabichuí*, was published mostly in Guaraní.

JOHN HOYT WILLIAMS

GUARDIA [NAVARRO], ERNESTO DE LA (1904–). President of Panama (1956–1960). Born in Panama City, De la Guardia received a master's degree from the Amos Tuck School of Business Administration of Dartmouth College in 1925. After serving as Consul General in San Francisco and holding several posts in the Ministry of Foreign Relations, De la Guardia embarked on a business career; at the time of his election to the Presidency he was general manager of a major brewery, Cervecería Nacional.

In 1956 De la Guardia was elected to the Presidency as the candidate of the government-backed Coalición Patriótica Nacional, which had been founded by President José Antonio REMÓN in 1952 and was one of the two parties permitted by law. As President, he was unable to take full advantage of a landslide victory and the overwhelming majority of forty-seven to six in the unicameral National Assembly. Factionalism developed within the official party, and several social welfare programs foundered. Although a minimum wage law was approved, nagging unemployment alleviated, and additional schools funded, the public became dissatisfied with the dominant party and De la Guardia restored the multiparty system.

De la Guardia's foreign policies, abetted by Egypt after the nationalization of the Suez Canal, were jingoistic. Officials winked at two invasions of the United States–controlled Canal Zone. In May 1958, students planted Panamanian flags at various points in the zone. The invaders returned in force in November 1959 and clashed with armed police and troops. Upon being turned back by barbed wire and bayonets, the mob attacked United States property in the republic. Eventually the United States appeased the rioters by raising the Panamanian flag alongside that of the United States at a special site, as visual evidence of Panamanian titular sovereignty over the Canal Zone. Meanwhile, tensions in United States–Panamanian relations over conflicting interpretations of the 1955 treaty were reduced when Washington authorized higher pay scales and better job classifications for Panamanians working in the zone.

De la Guardia was the first Panamanian President elected since 1932 to finish his term of office.

LARRY L. PIPPIN

GUARDIA, TOMÁS (1832–1882). Costa Rican President. Guardia was one of the most important and powerful Costa Rican leaders of the nineteenth century. His reputation as a strong personality was enhanced by his participation in the war against the filibuster William WALKER in 1856. Later, in 1870, he led a coup d'état to take over the Costa Rican Presidency, and he maintained himself in power as a dictator, excepting for two brief periods, until his death in 1882.

Like his contemporaries in other Central American countries and Mexico, Guardia subordinated the liberal ideas of democracy and individual freedom to rapid material progress. It was Guardia who brought Minor Cooper KEITH to Costa Rica and gave him every possible aid to complete the railway linking the Central Plateau with the Atlantic coast. Not only did the railway facilitate the export of coffee but it opened up the lands of the Atlantic coast to the widespread development of banana production. Although the constitution of 1871, which authorized Guardia's dictatorial rule, was a backward step in Costa Rica's progress toward democratic institutions, his action in breaking the control of the country's economic and political life by the oligarchy (he exiled many of his political opponents) helped to foster conditions for political development.

CHARLES L. STANSIFER

GUARNIERI, MOZART CAMARGO (1907–). Brazilian composer and conductor of Italian parentage whose successful career has made him one of the most distinguished nationalist composers in Brazil. Born in Tietê, São Paulo, he received his musical training in the city of São Paulo, first in piano and then in composition. In 1928 he met Mário de ANDRADE, who influenced him greatly and became his mentor. His first important compositions were written for the piano in 1928: *Dansa Brasileira, Canção Sertaneja,* and *Sonatina,* which was highly praised by Andrade. Among his pieces for voice and piano of 1928, *Lembranças do Losango Cáqui* (with text by Andrade) and *As Flôres Amarelas dos Ipês* were published locally. Upon the award of a fellowship from the State Council of Artistic Orientation in 1938, he went to Paris for further studies with Charles Koechlin and Charles Munch. At that time he received much encouragement from Nadia Boulanger. In 1942 he visited the United States and had several of his symphonic works performed in Washington, New York, and Boston. Later he became the permanent conductor of the São Paulo Symphony Orchestra. Along with Heitor VILLA-LOBOS he founded the Brazilian Academy of Music in 1945, and he has since been involved in various capacities in the major events of Brazilian musical life.

Guarnieri's production is impressive both qualitatively and quantitatively. He has been very prolific in the field of chamber music, with a series of three *Chôros* (1930; *see* CHÔRO), two sonatas for cello and piano (1931, 1955), several sonatas for violin and piano written between 1930 and 1959, string quartets, trios, and other works. His symphonic output includes a violin concerto (1940); several symphonies; the suites *Brasiliana* (1950), *Suite IV Centenário* (1954), and *Suite Vila Rica* (1958); and a *chôro* for clarinet and orchestra (1956). The collection of some fifty *Ponteios* for piano (1931–1959) is a unique stylistic blend of Brazilian lyricism and keyboard virtuoso effects. Guarnieri relies in most of his works on São Paulo's folk musical traditions, which he has assimilated into his highly personal style.

GERARD H. BÉHAGUE

GUATEMALA CITY. Capital of Guatemala and the largest city in Central America (1970 population estimate, 730,991). It was established on royal order in 1776 to replace Antigua, the old capital of the colonial Kingdom of Guatemala, which had been ruined by an earthquake in 1773. After independence it served for a time as capital of both the Federation of Central America (*see* CENTRAL AMERICA, FEDERATION OF) and the state of Guatemala, then of the state, and finally of the Republic of Guatemala. Fear of domination from Guatemala City helped to undermine the original Federation and impeded subsequent attempts at restoring the union.

The city was extensively damaged by disastrous earthquakes in 1917 and 1918, but it was rebuilt essentially of one-story structures dominated by church towers to resemble its colonial predecessor. Recent construction of multistoried steel and concrete buildings, particularly in the central part of the city, has substantially altered its aspect.

Guatemala City is more than a political capital; it is the heart of the country's commercial, industrial, social, and cultural activity. It is the focus of road, rail, and domestic and international air routes; the principal seat of four public and private universities, and the site of the major schools for artistic, vocational, and military training and institutions of cultural diffusion such as museums and learned societies. It is a center for such tourist attractions as the colonial ruins of Antigua, Lake Atitlán, the Quiché Indian market and religious center of Chichicastenango, and the Mayan ruins of TIKAL. It is also the seat of several agencies of the ORGANIZACIÓN DE ESTADOS CENTROAMERICANOS (ODECA) and the CENTRAL AMERICAN COMMON MARKET.

WILLIAM J. GRIFFITH

GUATEMALA SINCE 1823. Guatemala, with a population estimated at 5.3 million in 1971, was the most prestigious of the five states that formed the independent Federation of Central America in 1823 (*see* CENTRAL AMERICA, FEDERATION OF), and it retained its influence when both national and state governments established themselves in Guatemala City. Resentment of hegemony from Guatemala was a major cause of friction within the Federation.

Conflict between federal and state authorities and civil war dominated the early independent years. When Mariano GÁLVEZ became chief of state in 1831, he inaugurated an idealistic program of Liberal political and socioeconomic reforms. Although the majority of Guatemala's inhabitants were Indians of distinctive culture who lived outside Western-oriented life, Gálvez tried to bring the Enlightenment to the country, to install a popular representative democracy, and to attain rapid economic development. The pervasiveness of the changes he introduced and the degree to which Conservatives conceived them to pervert the accustomed order led first to protest and then to rebellion. José Rafael CARRERA rose to the leadership of the rebels who overthrew Gálvez in February 1838.

Carrera was an illiterate but astute rustic who set the pattern of long-term dictatorship in Guatemala. His influence among the rural masses gave him a power base that allowed him first to manipulate the government and then, in 1844, to assume the Presidency. Triumphant Liberals deposed and exiled him briefly in 1848, but he was recalled and restored to power and in 1854 was made President for life.

Carrera, with Conservative support, attempted to return Guatemala to a traditional pattern of life. He restored the Catholic Church to a position approaching its colonial ascendancy, restructured the government to make it the instrument of the elite and the privileged, and revived colonial institutions for encouraging economic development. In 1847 he proclaimed Guatemala a sovereign republic. Carrera died in 1865, but Vicente Cerna continued his policies. The Carrera period ended in 1871, when Miguel García Granados and Justo Rufino BARRIOS staged a successful neo-Liberal revolution. García Granados held the Presidency briefly and then ceded it to Barrios (1873).

Barrios accomplished a major reorientation of Guate-

GUATEMALA

Area: 42,042 sq. mi.   Population: 5,348,000 (1971 est.).

malan life. He humbled the entrenched elite, broke the power of the church, reestablished public lay education, promulgated a constitution (1876) that with frequent amendment endured until 1945, fostered the construction of improved means of communication and transport, and opened the resources of the country to exploitation by private initiative under conditions favorable to foreign immigrants and capital. He thought to re-create the Central American union under his tutelage, and when persuasion failed to attain his object, he lost his life in an attempt to establish his hegemony by force (1885).

Manuel Lisandro Barillas succeeded Barrios until José María Reyna Barrios, a nephew of Justo Rufino, was elected in 1892. Reyna Barrios's assassination in 1898 made Manuel ESTRADA CABRERA President, and repeated "reelections" maintained Estrada Cabrera until 1920, when the Assembly removed him by declaring him mentally incompetent. The Presidency then passed in succession and for varying time intervals to Carlos Herrera, José María Orellana, Lázaro Chacón, Baudilio Palma, Manuel Orellana, and José María Andrade. In 1931 Jorge UBICO was elected President and began the fourth of the extended dictatorships notable in Guatemalan history.

These neo-Liberal rulers made an ostentatious display of constitutionalism, but in reality they ignored the constitution or modified it to accord with their wishes. They gave lip service to democracy, but in practice they developed ruthless personal or military dictatorships. They worshiped material development and in fact did much to extend and diversify agricultural production, improve travel, transport, and communications facilities, construct public works, and establish modern financial institutions. But to achieve progress they exploited nationals, especially Indians; ruthlessly trampled on human rights and dignity; and, although they professed concern for education and culture, neglected schools and other institutions that served these ends. The good things of life were for the rich, the entrepreneurs, the collaborators, the sycophants; the role of the poor was to serve.

The record of the regimes after 1871 made clear the degree to which liberalism lost its idealism after independence. García Granados may have been a throwback to the humanistic postindependence school, but his successors under positivist influence showed marked callousness. New socioeconomic groups called into being by such innovations as lay education, mechanized transport, electrical communications, and industrial development found no fulfillment and no hope in the dreary materialism that came to characterize Liberal programs. Dissatisfaction with the deteriorating quality of life mounted as World War II brought economic dislocation, and conditions in Guatemala contrasted unfavorably with the idealistic pronouncements of Allied war leaders.

In June 1944, a general strike forced Ubico to resign. Under the interim regime of Federico Ponce Vaides, labor organized, political parties were formed, and an electoral campaign began. When Ponce tried to retain power, a coalition of young military officers, students, and laborers overthrew him, in October, and installed a three-man junta. A constituent assembly drafted a new constitution, Juan José ARÉVALO won the December elections overwhelmingly, and he was in-

augurated and the new constitution proclaimed on March 15, 1945.

Arévalo tried to accomplish the revolutionary changes the movement of 1944 had initiated. He strove to maintain the political freedom and personal liberties guaranteed by the constitution, exact responsible behavior from the Army, assure Guatemalans greater economic opportunity and a larger share of the return from exploitation of their resources and their toil, afford legal protection and a position of dignity for labor, and provide a growing range of social services to an increasing number of citizens, including welfare, health and educational facilities, and access to the instruments of culture.

Arévalo's program drew opposition from nationals and resident foreigners. During his six years in office he faced more than twenty attempts to oust him, and he had several sharp confrontations with foreign corporate critics. In these crises the Communists were his most reliable supporters. He accepted their aid as long as their positions coincided with his own; further he would not go.

The major crisis of the Arévalo administration was the assassination of Francisco Arana, chief of the armed forces, in July 1949. Jacobo ARBENZ GUZMÁN, Minister of Defense, was patently the beneficiary of the crime, of which it was assumed neither he nor Arévalo could be entirely innocent. Both survived the crisis of Army outrage, but Arévalo lost control of his administration. Arbenz became the open favorite of the Communists, and with their support he won the presidential election handily in 1950.

Arbenz ostensibly continued the legislative revolution Arévalo had begun, but his administration developed other overtones because of open Communist activity. An agrarian law, his chief reform measure, raised a storm of opposition, in part in defense of the status quo and in part because honest critics believed it to be a weapon wielded by the Communists to attain partisan ends rather than an instrument to achieve needed reform. The situation was not acceptable to many Guatemalans, and it became a diplomatic concern of hemisphere neighbors. However, many antireform elements took convenient shelter under the anti-Communist cloak.

The terror instituted by Arbenz after an unsuccessful attempt against his regime in 1953 further eroded his support. When Carlos CASTILLO ARMAS invaded the country from Honduras in June 1954 and the Army refused to allow workers and peasants to be armed, Arbenz had no defenders and was forced to resign.

Castillo Armas came to power on July 8, 1954, and held it until his assassination three years later. Luis Arturo González López, as acting President, presided over an election which Miguel Ortiz Passarelli appeared to win but which later was annulled. Guillermo Flores Avendaño organized new elections from which Miguel YDÍGORAS FUENTES emerged as victor.

The administrations from Castillo Armas through Ydígoras Fuentes were attempts to save something from the old order while conceding enough to current demands to maintain a viable administration. The effort succeeded only momentarily. The revolutionists of 1944 considered their movement aborted and the reforms begun so promisingly under Arévalo scrapped. During the Ydígoras Fuentes term frustration of the hopes for reform, shame over the role the President accepted for the country in the BAY OF PIGS INVASION, and disgust with corruption and inefficiency in the Army led to an unsuccessful coup. The disappointed participants in the coup became guerrillas, hoping to bring the government down in a quick blow, but that plan also miscarried.

The major problem of Presidents Enrique PERALTA AZURDIA (1963–1966), Julio César MÉNDEZ MONTENEGRO (1966–1970), and Carlos ARANA (1970–   ) was control of guerrilla and terrorist activity. Leftist guerrillas decided that their ends could be accomplished only by prolonged revolutionary activity that would destroy the old order and create a society structured as they desired; the result was a war to the death. The fact that the right countered with its own war-to-the-death policy that it appeared determined to execute against the center as well as all gradations of the left offered little encouragement to moderates or the democratic left for either the immediate or the distant future.

See also BANANA INDUSTRY (CENTRAL AMERICA AND THE CARIBBEAN); COFFEE INDUSTRY (CENTRAL AMERICA); LADINO.

Bibliography. Richard N. Adams, *Crucifixion by Power: Essays on Guatemalan Social Structure, 1944–1966,* Austin, Tex., 1970; Richard Gott, *Guerrilla Movements in Latin America,* Garden City, N.Y., 1971; Mary P. Holleran, *Church and State in Guatemala,* New York, 1949; Chester Lloyd Jones, *Guatemala Past and Present,* Minneapolis, 1940; Dana G. Munro, *The Five Republics of Central America,* New York, 1918; Franklin D. Parker, *The Central American Republics,* New York, 1964; Ronald M. Schneider, *Communism in Guatemala, 1944–1954,* New York, 1958; Nathan L. Whetten, *Guatemala: The Land and the People,* New Haven, Conn., 1961.

WILLIAM J. GRIFFITH

GUAYAQUIL. Major port and largest city of Ecuador. Francisco de ORELLANA successfully founded Santiago de Guayaquil in 1537 after two other attempts to create a port for Quito on the Gulf of Guayaquil had failed. During the colonial period the city suffered from attacks by Indians but more frequently by Spain's European enemies and by pirates. History also records recurrent fires and epidemic yellow fever. Yet in the eighteenth century the Spanish travelers Jorge Juan and Antonio de Ulloa reported it to be one of the most populous cities in the Indies, "full of outsiders." Shipbuilding, cacao exports (*see* CACAO INDUSTRY: ECUADOR), and a frenzied commerce accounted for the wealth and opportunity. Vested interests guarded the foreign trade monopoly Guayaquil held in the *audiencia* of Quito and circumvented Spanish mercantilism by a well-developed system of contraband. These traditions persisted in the national period, as did the influx of outsiders: Europeans, North Americans, Lebanese, and Chinese. In the second decade of the twentieth century the government, with the assistance of the Rockefeller Foundation, eradicated yellow fever and greatly improved public health in Guayaquil.

Guayaquil's expanding exports of cacao in 1900, rice in the 1930s, and bananas in the 1950s (*see* BANANA INDUSTRY: ECUADOR) led local bankers and businessmen to complain that they supported the whole nation and, in particular, the expenses of the Quito bureaucracy. Urban workers also became restless and in 1922 staged a general strike in which 1,500 people were killed. Guayaquil's population outnumbered Quito's in 1930, and demand mounted to keep revenue and political power at the port. Since Guayaquil's interests have always clashed with the conservatism and religiosity of Quito, Ecuador's history can be aptly described as a tale of two cities. By 1970 the population of the city was estimated at almost 1 million.

LOIS WEINMAN

GÜEMES PACHECO DE PADILLA, JUAN VICENTE. *See* REVILLAGIGEDO, 2D COUNT OF.

GUERRERO, VICENTE (1783–1831). Mexican soldier and President. A native of the state that now bears his name, Guerrero was born to a poor rural family and received little education. He joined the ranks of the insurgents at the beginning of the struggle for independence, distinguished himself in several actions, and rose to a position of command. He kept fighting in the Sierra Madre del Sur after the defeat and execution of José María MORELOS Y PAVÓN in 1815. Accepting the Plan of Iguala in 1821, he united his forces with those of Agustín de ITURBIDE to form the Army of the Three Guarantees (independence, religion, and equality of treatment for Spaniards and creoles). For a while he supported Iturbide as Emperor but soon went into opposition.

A York rite Freemason, he was instrumental in putting down the Conservative-centralist rebellion centering in the Scottish rite lodges that aimed at ousting President Guadalupe VICTORIA in 1828. Guerrero ran for the Presidency that year but was defeated by a narrow margin. However, the victor, Manuel Gómez Pedraza, was not allowed to take office, for Guerrero's supporters rebelled and installed him as President on April 1, 1829. The following December, Guerrero's Conservative Vice President, Anastasio Bustamante, ousted him. Guerrero sought refuge in his native Sierra Madre del Sur, a fugitive from Bustamante's ill will. Eventually he was enticed aboard a ship at Acapulco and betrayed to an officer in Bustamante's army. Taken to the city of Oaxaca, he was tried by a court-martial and executed by a firing squad on February 14, 1831.

Guerrero was a federalist and a Liberal and was firm in the defense of his principles. However, the 1829 rebellion nullifying the election of his opponent established a precedent that boded ill for the political stability of the nation which he had helped found and to which he devoted his talents.

CHARLES R. BERRY

GUEVARA, ERNESTO (CHE, 1928–1967). Argentine revolutionary leader and theorist. Guevara was born in Rosario, Argentina, the oldest son of upper-middle-class parents with leftist political leanings. He became an intensely idealistic youth whose adventurous personality reflected his struggle to overcome physical frailty and a chronic asthmatic condition. At twenty-four he interrupted his medical studies at the University of Buenos Aires to undertake a motorcycle and hitchhiking tour of South America with a companion. After sojourns in Chile, Peru, Ecuador, Colombia, and

Ernesto (Che) Guevera. [Bibliothèque Nationale, Paris]

Venezuela, he returned to Argentina and completed requirements for his degree in medicine.

Again Guevara set out northward across the continent. The conditions of the lower classes that he observed in several countries reinforced his basically left-wing views. Eventually his odyssey took him to Guatemala, where he became an interested witness to the revolutionary program of the leftist government of Jacobo ARBENZ GUZMÁN. When rebels sponsored by the Central Intelligence Agency overthrew Arbenz in late 1954, Guevara, who had offered his services to the regime, sought political refuge in the Argentine Embassy and soon managed to cross the border into Mexico. In 1955 he joined a group of exiled Cuban revolutionaries in Mexico City under Fidel CASTRO. Clandestine military training in guerrilla tactics followed. Guevara participated in the Castro group's seaborne landing on the coast of Oriente Province, Cuba, in December 1956.

Guevara, best known by his nickname, Che, was one of the few survivors who escaped from this disastrous event into the nearby Sierra Maestra. During the revolutionary guerrilla struggle waged by Castro's July 26 movement against the regime of Fulgencio BATISTA, Guevara served as a doctor and military commander with the rank of major.

Guevara emerged from the revolutionary war as an influential leader in the July 26 movement and a trusted confidant of Fidel Castro. On January 9, 1959, the new government officially declared him a citizen of Cuba. When Castro and his followers assumed full control of the Cuban government, Guevara became one of its more colorful figures. Throughout his association with the revolutionary regime, he frequently traveled abroad on diplomatic and commercial missions. From the be-

ginning Premier Castro entrusted Guevara with responsibilities in the fields of economic planning and finance. Guevara served as chief of the Industrial Department of the National Institute of Agrarian Reform (1959) and head of the National Bank (1959–1961), as well as Minister of Industry (1961–1965). Through his writings and public statements he soon became regarded as the foremost Castroite theorist on socialist economic development and revolutionary warfare. Representing the most radical tendencies within the Castro regime, he appeared to be oriented toward the Chinese position in the Sino-Soviet dispute and implicitly criticized Moscow for insufficient support of the new underdeveloped nations and revolutionary movements of the Third World.

Contrary to the policy of emphasizing sugar production that the Soviet Union urged upon Cuba in 1963, Guevara continued to favor massive industrialization. Moreover, he urged the use of moral rather than material incentives to stimulate worker productivity. He also emphasized the creation of a new "socialist man" in revolutionary Cuba even prior to achieving a full-fledged Communist society.

In his famous study *La guerra de guerrillas,* 1960 (*Guerrilla Warfare*), Guevara projected the Cuban example of hit-and-run tactics by small and mobile rural partisan bands as the proper pathway to revolutionary transformations in Latin America. Armed struggle, he argued, would be a more effective means of stimulating a revolutionary attitude in the masses than the long-term political tactics advocated by most Latin American Communist parties, which he accused of defeatism and passivity.

In early 1965 Guevara mysteriously disappeared from public view. Speculation arose that he had clashed with Castro over economic policy and had perhaps been purged to placate Moscow. Castro's explanation that the Argentine revolutionary had freely departed from Cuba to serve the cause of socialist revolution abroad was substantiated when he later appeared in Bolivia. Guevara spent some time in Africa with Congolese rebels. In 1966 he returned to Havana, where he made plans to put his military theories into effect in South America. With Castro's support he assembled a force of Cuban and Peruvian revolutionaries who entered Bolivia in late 1966. Augmented by some Bolivians, the group was forced to begin its guerrilla campaign in southeastern Bolivia in March 1967 after its presence was detected. On October 8, 1967, a government ranger unit wounded and captured Guevara, and he was executed in La Higuera the following day by a Bolivian army officer. Since his death Guevara has become a symbol worthy of socialist emulation in Cuba and a legendary hero to leftists in Latin America and elsewhere.

See also BARRIENTOS, René.

Bibliography. Hugo Gambini, *El Che Guevara,* Buenos Aires, 1968; Luis J. González and G. A. Sánchez Salazar, *The Great Rebel: Che Guevara in Bolivia,* New York, 1969; Ernesto Guevara, *Obra revolucionaria,* Mexico City, 1967; id., *The Complete Bolivian Diaries of Che Guevara and Other Captured Documents,* ed. by Daniel James, New York, 1968; id., *Venceremos! The Speeches and Writings of Che Guevara,* ed. by John Gerassi, New York, 1968; id., *Che: Selected Works of Ernesto Guevara,* ed. by

Rolando E. Bonachea and Nelson P. Valdés, Cambridge, Mass., 1969; id., *Guerrilla Warfare,* New York, 1969; Richard Harris, *Death of a Revolutionary: Che Guevara's Last Mission,* New York, 1970.

DAVID A. CRAIN

GUILLÉN, NICOLÁS (1902–   ). Cuban poet. Born in Camagüey, Guillén left his native province in 1921 to study law in Havana but lacked the money to continue after a year. In 1919–1920 he published poetry in *Camagüey Gráfico, Castalia,* and *Orto,* and in 1923 he began work as a journalist for *El Camagüeyano.* He became a civil servant in Havana in 1925. In 1930 the *Diario de la Marina* published a collection of his poems, *Motivos del son.* He attended the Congress in Defense of Culture in Spain in 1937 and joined the Communist party. In 1937–1938 he edited the review *Mediodía* in Havana, and in 1944 he served on the board of *Gaceta del Caribe.* From 1945 to 1948 he traveled widely in Latin America giving readings and lectures. Exiled from 1953 to 1958, he received the Lenin Prize in 1956. He has held important positions in postrevolutionary Cuba, including the presidency of the Union of Writers and Artists since its establishment in 1961.

Guillén has written in the vein of "black" poetry (*Motivos del son*); poetry of political and social protest, beginning with *West Indies Ltd* (1934); and poetry on universal human themes, best seen in *El son entero* (1947). He originated the *son,* a poetic form based on popular Afro-Cuban music and has used it as a vehicle for lyricism and for social protest. He writes excellently in traditional verse forms and is also the best of the poets who use Afro-Caribbean folkloric themes. Among other volumes of poetry are *Sóngoro Cosongo* (1931), *Cantos para soldados y sones para turistas* (1937), *España, poema en cuatro angustias y una esperanza* (1937), *La paloma de vuelo popular* (1958), *¿Puedes?* (1959), *Poemas de amor* (1964), *Antología mayor* (1964), *Tengo* (1964), and *El gran zoo* (1967). His prose includes *Estampa de Lino Dou* (1944) and *Prosa de prisa* (1962).

RACHEL PHILLIPS

GÜIRALDES, RICARDO (1886–1927). Argentine writer. Güiraldes was born in Buenos Aires. After spending some years in Paris, he settled on his family's ranch in the province of Buenos Aires. His early poetry provides the principal link in Argentina between modernism (*see* MODERNISM: SPANISH AMERICA) and the avant-garde poetry of the 1920s. His first collection of poetry, *Cencerro de cristal* (1915), was unsuccessful, as was his first prose publication, *Cuentos de muerte y de sangre* (1915), in which he first attempted to incorporate the language of the GAUCHO in a literary style. His later novels include *Raucho* (1917), an account of his youth; *Rosaura* (1922); and *Xaimaca* (1923), based on a long journey along the Pacific coast. In 1924 he returned to Buenos Aires and collaborated with Jorge Luis BORGES and others in the reviews *Martín Fierro* and *Proa.* He also founded his own publishing house. His greatest success was a nostalgic novel of gaucho life, *Don Segundo Sombra* (1926), published shortly before his death. Posthumously published works include *Poemas místicos* (1928), *Poemas solitarios 1921–1927* (1928), *Seis*

relatos (1929), *El sendero* (1932), *El libro bravo* (1932), *El pájaro blanco* (1952), and *Pampa* (1954).

RACHEL PHILLIPS

GUTIÉRREZ NÁJERA, MANUEL (1859–1895). Mexican poet, journalist, and writer of short stories. Gutiérrez Nájera was born in Mexico City. One of his country's outstanding romantic poets and a precursor of modernism, he was also a journalist and a short-story writer. He was sometimes known by the pseudonym "El Duque Job." Gutiérrez Nájera had no formal education. Privately tutored in Latin, French, and mathematics, he became a highly cultivated man through vast reading and began his career as a journalist while still in his teens. *See* MODERNISM (SPANISH AMERICA).

Although much of Gutiérrez's work is of a journalistic nature, a large part consists of short stories and poems, and it is this creative writing that gives him a place in Spanish American letters. Both prose and poetry reflect his preference for French writers. French romantics, Parnassians, and symbolists played a great role in forming the work that places him among the precursors of modernism. During his lifetime only a few of his short stories were collected as *Cuentos frágiles* (1883), and most were scattered in a variety of periodicals. After his death his friends had all his poems published as *Poesías completas* (1896). Since then scholars have collected much of his prose.

GERARDO SÁENZ

GUZMÁN, MARTÍN LUIS (1887–   ). Mexican writer. A native of Chihuahua, Guzmán studied jurisprudence in Mexico City and in 1911 began a political career working for the cause of Francisco I. MADERO. After Victoriano HUERTA's coup in 1913 he joined the revolutionaries in the north and was in close touch with Francisco VILLA. As a result he was imprisoned in Mexico City but was freed by the AGUASCALIENTES CONVENTION. He was exiled from 1915 to 1920 and published *La querella de México* (1915) in Spain. In 1917 he edited the New York Spanish review *El Gráfico* and wrote articles for the *Revista Universal,* in which they were published in 1920 as *A orillas del Hudson.* He returned to an active career in Mexico as a journalist and politician and, as a result, was exiled to Spain from 1924 to 1936. There he wrote *El águila y la serpiente,* 1928 (*The Eagle and the Serpent*), his reconstruction of the events from 1913 to 1915. *La sombra del caudillo* (1929) is a political novel, and *Mina el mozo, héroe de Navarra* (1932) and *Filadelfia, paraíso de conspiradores* (1938) are biographies.

Guzmán's best work is *Memorias de Pancho Villa* (*Memoirs of Pancho Villa*), a first-person narration of the life of his political idol, which first appeared in 1936 serially in *El Universal,* then in four volumes (1938–1940), and finally in five volumes (1951). In 1940 he began editing the literary journal *Romance* in Mexico City and in 1942 founded the weekly *Tiempo.* He became a member of the Mexican Academy of the Language in 1940 and has received prizes for literature. Recent works include *Muertes históricas* (1958), *Pábulo para la historia* (1960), *Necesidad de cumplir las leyes de Reforma* (1963), *Febrero de 1913* (1963), and *Crónicas de mi destierro* (1964).

RACHEL PHILLIPS

GUZMÁN, NUÑO DE (1485/1490–?1558). Spanish official and conqueror. Nuño de Guzmán, born to a prominent family in Spain, was both resident and diplomat at the court of CHARLES I and was appointed Governor of the Pánuco region (northeastern Mexico) in 1525. His appointment, like that of many others, was the result of a royal policy that sought to replace Hernán CORTÉS's men with trusted bureaucrats. Guzmán served as Governor of the Pánuco region from May 1527 until November 1528, expelling supporters of Cortés, redistributing encomiendas (*see* ENCOMIENDA), and regularizing and increasing the Indian slave trade from Pánuco to the West Indian islands. He personally profited from this trade.

From December 1528 to December 1529, Guzmán held an appointment as president of the first *audiencia* in Mexico City. During his tenure, he incurred the enmity of Bishop Juan de ZUMÁRRAGA for his excessive tribute collections from the Indians, slave trading, corruption, and dictatorial practices. An open quarrel with the bishop and fear of replacement by the crown led Guzmán to undertake the conquest of the Indians in northwestern Mexico in the region known as New Galicia, over which he ruled as its first Governor. Between 1530 and 1536 Guzmán explored as far north as the state of Sinaloa, founding five towns and one city, including Culiacán, Tepic, and Guadalajara.

Replaced as Governor of New Galicia, he was imprisoned during the time of his *residencia* (the official investigation into his activities). No final decision on his policies and activities as governor and president was ever rendered. Guzmán returned to Spain in June 1538, and his name appears as a member of the court until 1558.

EDITH B. COUTURIER

GUZMÁN BLANCO, ANTONIO (1829–1899). President of Venezuela (1870–1877, 1879–1884, 1886–1888). In the process of national political formation the era of Antonio Guzmán Blanco was one of the most important periods in modern Venezuelan history. Born into a prominent Venezuelan family, Guzmán Blanco grew up in an atmosphere of intense partisan politics. His father, Antonio Leocadio Guzmán, founder of the Venezuelan Liberal party and often a presidential candidate, led a life of political intrigue, propaganda, and agitation. In this environment Antonio Guzmán Blanco readily became an able, careful, and experienced politician. More cautious, more calculating, and less given to demagoguery than his father, he ruled Venezuela personally or through agents for almost twenty years.

Guzmán Blanco came to power as a result of the Federal Wars (1858–1863), in which he emerged as the chief adviser to the Liberal chieftain, Juan C. FALCÓN. With the triumph of Falcón in the wars and his installation as President of Venezuela in 1863, Guzmán Blanco remained a first-echelon adviser, especially on economic and financial affairs. Many observers believed that practically all Falcón's political maneuvers were the work of Guzmán Blanco. In any event, Guzmán Blanco, serving as Vice President under Falcón (1863–1868), made his debut as a national statesman by negotiating a large loan in England under terms that some of his contemporaries considered onerous for Venezuela. Although this transaction received the approval of the Venezuelan Congress, Guzmán Blanco was accused of making a fortune at the expense of the nation. During most of Falcón's Presidency Guzmán Blanco remained in Europe on financial business for the Venezuelan government, but with the collapse of the Federal regime and the triumph of the Revolución Azul (Blue Revolution) led by the aging José Tadeo MONAGAS, he returned in 1868 to consolidate the Liberal forces and regain power.

The death of Monagas in November 1868 greatly weakened the Revolución Azul, as his supporters quickly fell to quarreling. Although Guzmán Blanco made serious efforts to reach an accommodation with the leaders of the governing faction, he was eventually forced to go into exile in Curaçao, where he prepared a military campaign. By the end of 1869 Liberal revolts had broken out all over the country, and the Azul government had proved unable to respond effectively. In February 1870, Guzmán Blanco launched his revolution by landing on the coast of Coro. His forces, called the Amarillos (Yellows), captured Caracas in April, but the Azules (Conservatives) refused to accept their defeat and Guzmán Blanco was forced to spend several months mopping up pockets of resistance.

From June 1870 until the end of his last presidential term in 1888, Guzmán Blanco controlled Venezuelan politics and guided its economic growth. The tone of his governments was set at the very beginning of his regime when he established a policy of castigating the Conservative party and proscribing Conservatives in general while bringing into his administration any able Conservatives who were prepared to cooperate with him. Guzmán Blanco's second preoccupation was the economic condition of the country, and as early as 1870 he began reorganizing the public credit by entrusting

Antonio Guzmán Blanco. [Radio Times Hulton Picture Library]

the management of Venezuela's revenues to a private group whose main function was to lend the government money for operating expenses in return for the privilege of collecting 85 percent of the customs receipts. By 1871 he had also established the Dirección General de Estadística and ordered preparations for a national census.

In spite of these impressive beginnings Guzmán Blanco spent most of 1871 and 1872 putting down Conservative challenges to his regime that were supported by the church, which opposed his tampering with the terms of ecclesiastical loans. Eventually, with the failure and subsequent execution of their most prominent general, Matías Salazar, the Conservatives lost most of their strength. Because of the role played by the church and churchmen in the anti-Guzmán Blanco revolts, the government suppressed the seminaries and transferred all religious instruction to the Central University, which had been notoriously pro-Liberal. The religious question remained a serious problem for Guzmán Blanco for a number of years, culminating in the establishment of civil matrimony, civil registry of births and deaths, the suppression of convents, and the exile of the Archbishop of Caracas. The struggle with the church ended in 1876, when Guzmán Blanco induced the recalcitrant Archbishop to resign and then negotiated with the Papal Nuncio church acceptance of his reforms as well as the official disestablishment of the church.

During the seven-year period known as the Septenio (1870–1877), Guzmán Blanco attempted to make Venezuela an attractive place for foreign investment. Roads, telegraph lines, aqueducts, and port facilities were constructed with a view toward generating foreign interest in Venezuela, foreign immigration was encouraged, and the security of private property was assured. In political matters Guzmán Blanco proved himself no less adept. While maintaining tight control over the operations of government, especially the Army, he managed to create what was evidently conceived as a civic religion. Although hero worship in Venezuela began long before Guzmán Blanco gained control of the country, he organized it and endowed it with rituals and symbols. Of prime importance was the creation of a national pantheon where the remains of Venezuela's great leaders could be assembled and revered in appropriate splendor. The Church of the Santísima Trinidad was commandeered for the purpose, and the campaign was launched by an elaborate apotheosis of El Libertador, Simón BOLÍVAR. As part of this campaign, Guzmán Blanco sponsored or allowed to be sponsored numerous statues of the great men of the past. Erected in plazas in all parts of the country, these monuments invariably bore the name of the "Illustrious American," Antonio Guzmán Blanco, in addition to that of the Venezuelan hero being commemorated. The effect of this civic religion on Venezuelan affairs is difficult to judge, but it has continued as an active part of official Venezuelan political life to the present day.

Although plagued with minor revolts and a major unsuccessful rebellion in 1874, the years of the Septenio were remarkably peaceful and prosperous. Guzmán Blanco considered matters so well in hand that he permitted the election of Gen. Francisco Linares Alcántara to succeed him for a two-year term in 1877–1879 and left for Europe with diplomatic credentials. While Alcántara remained loyal to Guzmán Blanco, however, he flirted with opposition conspirators and allowed the Guzmán Blanco political coalition to disintegrate. By 1878 a full-scale revolt had broken out, and early in 1879 the anti-Guzmán Blanco forces controlled the capital. Then, with the return of the Illustrious American from Europe, his revived forces recaptured Caracas in the so-called Campaña Reinvindicadora. Guzmán Blanco was installed as provisional President in February 1879 and elected officially in 1880 for the term 1880–1882, and then for the 1882–1884 term.

The five-year period from 1879 to 1884, which was known as the Quinquenio, saw a continuation of the patterns of economic development established during the Septenio. Politically, however, the forces opposed to Guzmán appeared to have gained strength, even though his control of the telegraph and railroads allowed him to retain the upper hand. By 1884 he apparently believed the country was pacified sufficiently to allow him to put his follower, Gen. Joaquín CRESPO, in the presidential chair for a two-year term. But with the *caudillo* in Europe, Crespo, like his predecessors, began to act on his own account, to the extreme displeasure of Guzmán Blanco's friends. The result, in 1885, was the election of the Illustrious American for the term 1886–1888, a period known as the Acclamation. At the end of this term, weary of the problems of office and longing to return to Paris, Guzmán Blanco chose one more Venezuelan President, Gen. Juan Pablo ROJAS PAÚL, and left Venezuela for the last time.

Bibliography. German Carrera Damas, *El culto a Bolívar,* Caracas, 1969; Ramón Díaz Sánchez, *Guzmán: Elipse de una ambición al poder,* Caracas, 1950; Edward B. Eastwick, *Venezuela: O apuntes sobre la vida en una república sudamericana con la historia del empréstito de 1864,* Caracas, 1959; Luis Level de Goda, *Historia contemporánea del Venezuela, política y militar (1858–1886),* Barcelona, 1893; Rafael A. Rondón Márquez, *Guzmán Blanco, "el autocrata civilizador": Parábola de los partidos políticos tradicionales en la historia de Venezuela,* 2 vols., Caracas, 1944; George S. Wise, *Caudillo: A Portrait of Antonio Guzmán Blanco,* New York, 1951.

JOHN V. LOMBARDI

Hacienda
Hundred-hour War

H

HACIENDA. Large landed estate in Spanish America. Ordinarily a labor-intensive enterprise cultivating only a portion of the land under its control and producing for a small-scale market, the traditional hacienda not only provides its owner with an economic return but also confers upon him social prestige and political influence. The hacienda's labor force is typically composed of resident workers who till the owner's fields and perform other services in return for a daily wage, a parcel of land, and perhaps a ration of food or spirits. In the past such workers were frequently given loans or advances on their wages that resulted in their being bound to labor on the hacienda until the debts were paid (*see* PEON). Haciendas are frequently distinguished from plantations or other agricultural enterprises that are capital-intensive and emphasize the production of cash crops for a large-scale and often-distant market. It has been argued, however, that such a distinction suggests a dichotomy which does not always exist.

There are also several national variants that designate haciendas. In Chile, for example, a large landed property has generally been known as a *fundo,* while the corresponding term in Argentina is *estancia,* especially when the reference is to a cattle ranch. In Brazil, any large estate, regardless of function, is called a *fazenda.*

See also LATIFUNDIUM.

HELEN DELPAR

HAITI SINCE 1804. Haiti, the second nation in the New World to achieve independence, was the result of the only successful slave revolt in modern times and became the sole French-speaking republic in the Western Hemisphere. In 1804 it faced a heritage of anti-white sentiment, a growing mulatto-Negro schism, and an economy devastated by years of strife. Cultural institutions had crumbled before a new tradition of militarism in what had been the world's richest tropical colony. About 90 percent of the population was composed of illiterate ex-slaves. Lacking diplomatic recognition, Haiti suffered from an isolation and ostracism that still scar it. Nevertheless, its strategic location and commercial potential have made it subject to continual foreign attention.

In 1804 the architect of independence, Jean-Jacques DESSALINES, despite inexperience in statecraft, made himself Emperor. After his murder two years later, Haiti was divided into a northern Negro kingdom under Henry CHRISTOPHE and a mulatto republic, led by Alexandre Sabès PÉTION, in the south. These rivals faced similar problems: the decline of agriculture, the absence of normal foreign relations, and the need of instruction for a deprived people. Through regimentation Christophe improved the economy and encouraged education, neither of which flourished in Pétion's static realm. Sharecropping and small peasant landholding eventually replaced Christophe's state agrarianism, and Haiti today has a higher ratio of peasants than any other Latin American nation. However, two-thirds of the land is untillable, plots are too small to support the population, and the rugged terrain is eroded and badly deforested. Sugar has long since been surpassed by coffee, which is more easily cultivated on small holdings than sugar, which required large plantations.

During the quarter-century rule of Jean-Pierre BOYER, successor to Pétion, Haiti was reunited, and for twenty-two years it incorporated the Spanish two-thirds of Hispaniola, which finally won independence in 1844. Under Boyer the mulatto ÉLITE achieved hegemony and developed techniques to maintain minority rule. After Boyer's fall in 1843, a long era of Negro Presidents followed. The rule of Faustin SOULOUQUE saw Haiti's third and last experiment in monarchy (1849–1859) and its final attempt to incorporate the Dominican area.

During the period 1867–1915, Haiti experienced growing economic and political instability and, though at last recognized by major powers, faced the conflicting interests of Great Britain, the United States, and Germany. Several executives were ousted or murdered, and the average presidential tenure was only three years. This period also saw the rise of northern peasant mercenaries, the CACOS, who helped unseat several Presidents, thus lowering national prestige. American politicians suggested the acquisition of Môle-Saint-Nicolas in northwestern Haiti for its natural advantages as a naval and coaling station. Meanwhile, Germany's growing commercial and naval interests in the Caribbean in the early twentieth century aroused American concern, as did the financial irresponsibility of Haiti. American investments in agriculture and transportation slowly grew.

In 1915, when deposed President Vilbrun Guillaume Sam, who had executed 167 opponents, was murdered while a refugee in the French Legation, United States naval forces were landed and restored order. An American-imposed customs receivership, similar to one developed earlier for the Dominican Republic, was negotiated with a new government approved by the United States. For the next nineteen years the United States guided Haiti with the assistance of a more or less amenable Haitian regime. Stability was restored, and progress was achieved in public works, sanitation, vocational education, and control of the Cacos. A new constitution, approved by plebiscite in 1918, provided

for civil rights and popular elections and legalized foreign ownership of land for the first time since 1804.

Always unpopular with Haitians, the American occupation became distasteful to the American public as well, and two investigating commissions appointed in 1930 recommended withdrawal. Americans had wounded Haitian pride and failed to reduce monoculture or solve the educational needs of the common people, but the Garde d'Haïti, a well-trained constabulary, brought order. The last Marines left Haiti in August 1934.

In the atmosphere of the GOOD NEIGHBOR POLICY, Haiti agreed to a reciprocity treaty with the United States in 1935 and entered its trade sphere. Meanwhile, a crisis caused by the massacre of perhaps 20,000 Haitians in the Dominican Republic in 1937 was solved by President Sténio VINCENT's use of American, Mexican, and Cuban mediators.

After Vincent's retirement in 1941, his mulatto protégé and successor, Élie LESCOT, cooperated with the Allies during World War II, as Haiti had done in the first great war. His postponement of elections and failure to improve the nation's endemic problems led in 1946 to the first violent ouster of a President since 1915 and underlined the mulatto-black schism. Blacks now returned to power under Dumarsais ESTIMÉ, but inflation canceled the advantages of higher coffee prices. After the interim rule of a military junta, Paul E. MAGLOIRE came to power in 1950 making promises of reform, but corruption, bad times, and an attempt to perpetuate himself in office led to his removal in 1956. The following months were Haiti's most chaotic since 1915.

A result of disillusionment with military rule was the choice of the Negro physician-intellectual, Dr. François DUVALIER. The story of his consolidation of power is the history of Haiti from 1957 to 1971. He probably possessed the best opportunity since the days of his hero, Dessalines, to achieve black pride, economic progress, and the regeneration of the nation, but he failed to advance the peasantry through education or agrarian or political reforms. Duvalier, who emphasized VODUN and restored the life Presidency, antagonized Americans, the church, and black intellectuals.

Despite the often-sudden comings and goings of Presidents, Haiti's annual per capita income, less than $80, has remained the lowest in the Western Hemisphere. The country's health is also the worst. Although advancement in the control of yaws and malaria has been impressive, Haitians still suffer from tetanus, diarrhea, starvation, parasites, gastroenteritis, tuberculosis, venereal diseases, and tropical ulcers. They have the hemisphere's poorest nutrition, perilously low in protein for a manual-labor economy. Since land is limited, crop yield must be increased through irrigation, fertilization, pest control, and improved crop varieties. All this, like educational reform and public works, depends on wise, stable government, which has not been achieved. Observers know that the total environment must be improved if victory over any particular deficiency is to be won. Haiti's population explosion, long an omen for the world, has led to migration for jobs into other West Indian areas, especially to Cuba after 1910 and to the Dominican Republic during the Depression, with rude rejection in both cases.

HAITI

Area: 10,714 sq. mi.   Population: 4,243,926 (1971 est.).

Haiti has made unique and rich cultural contributions. Its literature is distinctive in both French and CRÉOLE, the novel being a social document stressing action and protest. Haitian folklore is especially imaginative and earthy. Foreign interest in Haitian society, religion, language, and folklore has passed through several stages since 1804. Originally it was characterized by ignorance, derision, and a stress on the sensational. In the early twentieth century it was noted for sentimental awe, but in recent years it has been expanded through sociological studies dealing with the total culture. Meanwhile, Haiti's folk painting was "discovered" by foreigners in the 1940s, when air and steamship lines escalated tourism.

Haiti's literacy rate, though not accurately known, is the lowest in the hemisphere, probably about 12 percent and concentrated in urban areas. Rural folk who can read tend to move to towns. Urbanized teachers dislike rural teaching, especially in Créole. Perhaps more serious is Haiti's brain drain. With a longer history of Europeanized learning than most Africans have had, Haitians disgusted with politics have sought professional opportunities in French-speaking Africa since the 1950s, thus aggravating Haiti's shortage of skilled persons.

As the 1970s began, Haiti was undergoing rapid changes, and once-rigid barriers of class had become more fluid, especially since Duvalier's advent. Nevertheless, hurdles still remained. Strong-man rule continued, partly because the country still lacked a responsible middle class, adequate education, continuity in public service, and genuine political parties. The population, which approached the 5 million mark in 1972, was 85 percent rural, and plantation workers were laid off for three to six months annually. Despite the promises of politicians, most Haitians remained outside the national mainstream.

Bibliography. Harold Courlander, *The Drum and the Hoe: Life and Lore of the Haitian People,* Berkeley, Calif., 1960; H. P. Davis, *Black Democracy: The Story of Haiti,* New York, 1936; Melville J. Herskovits, *Life in a Haitian Valley,* London, 1937; James G. Leyburn, *The Haitian People,* New Haven, Conn., 1945; Rayford W. Logan, *The Diplomatic Relations of the United States with Haiti, 1776–1891,* Chapel Hill, N.C., 1941; id., *Haiti and the Dominican Republic,* New York and London, 1968; Selden Rodman, *Haiti: The Black Republic,* New York, 1954; Robert I. Rotberg, *Haiti: The Politics of Squalor,* Boston, 1971; Richard P. Schaedel (ed.), *Papers of the Conference on Research and Resources of Haiti,* New York, 1969.

JOHN E. BAUR

HAVANA. Capital of Cuba. The present site of the city was chosen by Spanish settlers in 1519 because of its excellent harbor, protected from storms and easily defended. In the next decade the conquest of Mexico and the discovery of the Old Bahama Channel made Havana the most important port in the West Indies. Later the city served as the rendezvous point where the annual Spanish fleets to Mexico and Panama assembled for the return voyage to Spain. Realizing Havana's strategic importance in preserving the lines of communication between Spain and the mainland colonies, the crown attempted to protect the city against French

and later English attackers by constructing fortifications such as El Morro, a castle built in the 1590s. Even so, Havana was sacked by French corsairs in 1538 and captured by the English in 1762 during the Seven Years' War. The English occupied Havana for less than a year but triggered a commercial boom by opening the port to English and North American merchant vessels. The large number of African slaves imported during this period contributed to the subsequent expansion of sugar cultivation on the island.

In the nineteenth century the city received a face-lifting during the administration of Captain General Miguel de Tacón (1834–1838), who improved sanitation and law enforcement and built new thoroughfares and public buildings. By the second decade of the twentieth century North American influence on the architecture and life-style of the city could be detected, and new suburbs, such as the Vedado and Miramar, were attracting the more affluent. Always a mecca for tourists from the United States, during the 1950s Havana was notorious for its beggars and prostitutes as well as for its lavish hotels, nightclubs, and gambling casinos. The city deteriorated physically in the post-revolutionary era, but it remained the administrative and cultural center of Cuba. With a metropolitan population estimated at nearly 1.7 million in 1966, it was by far the largest city in Cuba, accounting for more than 20 percent of the population of the island.

J. CORDELL ROBINSON

HAVANA CONFERENCE (1928). Sixth International Conference of American States. All twenty-one American republics were represented at this meeting, which was held in Havana, Cuba, from January 16 to February 20, 1928. The most important items for discussion included reorganization of the Pan American Union and matters of an inter-American juridical nature. Resentful of the Caribbean policies of the United States, the Latin American delegates arrived determined to secure acceptance of nonintervention as a principle of American international law. Fully aware of the situation, the United States, in turn, sent a powerful delegation headed by Charles Evans Hughes. President Calvin Coolidge himself, accompanied by Secretary of State Frank B. Kellogg, traveled to Havana to give the inaugural address.

Instructed to steer the discussion toward noncontroversial subjects and to oppose any resolutions that might limit diplomatic freedom of action, the United States representatives encountered less formidable opposition than they had expected, for the Latin American nations were unable to unite among themselves. Nevertheless, El Salvador did move for approval of a project adopted by the International Commission of Jurists (which had met in Rio de Janeiro from April 18 to May 20, 1927) condemning intervention. Following a classic defense of American policy by Hughes, the conference shelved the issue. Further conflict arose when an Argentine effort to obtain a declaration condemning inter-American trade barriers provoked an attack against United States tariff policies. The conference did approve a Mexican resolution prohibiting the Pan American Union from exercising political functions.

WILLIAM R. ADAMS

HAVANA MEETING (1940). Second Meeting of Consultation of Ministers of Foreign Affairs of the American republics. Faced with the German occupation of France and the Low Countries and the threatened invasion of Great Britain, the American foreign ministers met in Havana, Cuba, on July 21–30, 1940, to consider the possible transfer of colonies in the Western Hemisphere belonging to the defeated European nations. At stake was one of the oldest principles of United States foreign policy, the no-transfer rule of 1811, which the Congress had reaffirmed in a joint resolution on June 17–18, 1940. Although reluctant to endorse a diplomatic principle associated with the MONROE DOCTRINE, the Latin American nations bowed to the will of the United States and adopted the Act of Havana Concerning the Provisional Administration of European Colonies and Possessions in the Americas. The act provided that in the event of a threatened change of colonial sovereignty the American republics would establish a provisional regime in the colony affected, to be governed in turn by an Inter-American Commission for Territorial Administration. In an urgent case any one of the American republics could act before the Commission met. Of equal significance, the ministers agreed in Resolution 15 to regard an act of aggression against an American state by a non-American power as a threat to each of them and to consult accordingly on measures for collective defense. Because the resolution contained for the first time a specific reference to non-American states, it is the opinion of some scholars that the Havana Meeting thereby converted the Monroe Doctrine into a multilateral instrument of hemispheric defense. The ministers also created an Inter-American Peace Committee to monitor hemisphere disputes, passed resolutions designed to curb Axis subversive activities in the Americas, and expanded the economic functions of the Inter-American Financial and Economic Advisory Committee.

WILLIAM R. ADAMS

HAYA DE LA TORRE, VÍCTOR RAÚL (1895–). Peruvian political leader. For more than forty years Haya de la Torre, the son of an aristocrat from Trujillo, has been one of Peru's most popular *caudillos*. He emerged as a political figure when, as a student at the University of San Marcos, he became involved in the movement for social and university reforms. In 1924, while in exile in Mexico, he founded the reformist ALIANZA POPULAR REVOLUCIONARIA AMERICANA (APRA), a party that became a reflection of Haya de la Torre's social consciousness and political ambition. A remarkable propagandist and organizer, he made his party the largest in Peru in spite of frequent government persecution. In the process he became a romantic hero to thousands of Peruvians and foreigners alike.

After 1954 Haya de la Torre entrusted the daily operations of the party to his subordinates, while retaining veto power over them, and devoted himself principally to travel, writing, and lecturing. One function he refused to abandon was that of presidential contender, although it had become obvious that the armed forces would prevent his election at any cost. Thus, while a less controversial Aprista might have succeeded in winning the Presidency, Haya de la Torre chose to be the party's candidate in 1962 and 1963, and

he would have been again in 1969 if the military had not assumed power. Although Haya's quest for the Presidency failed, as the founder of the first truly mass political party in Peru, he has an assured place in Peruvian history.

ORAZIO A. CICCARELLI

HAY–BUNAU-VARILLA TREATY. The result of Panama's successful revolt against Colombia in November 1903, this treaty, signed in Washington on November 18, 1903, by Secretary of State John Hay and Philippe Bunau-Varilla, the representative of the new republic, gave the United States the exclusive right to build a canal across the isthmus (*see* PANAMA CANAL). According to the treaty, the United States agreed to guarantee the independence of Panama and to pay the republic $10 million in gold, followed by an annual subsidy of $250,000, to commence nine years after ratification of the treaty. In exchange Panama granted the United States in perpetuity, "as if it were sovereign," the use, control, and occupation of a zone of land 10 miles wide, crossing the isthmus from Panama City to Colón. Land and waters outside the zone required for the construction, operation, or protection of the area were also to be included. Panama was granted the privilege of transporting its troops, ships, and arms at all times free of charge. All rights to the New Panama Canal Company (the successor to the French company that had begun the canal) and the Panama Railroad Company (*see* PANAMA RAILROAD) were included. The United States agreed to maintain the neutrality of the zone according to the terms of the Hay-Pauncefote Treaty. The United States was permitted to fortify the zone and to use its troops to defend the canal, and Panama was denied the right to tax United States ships on canal business and to levy duties on employees or their property in the zone. Ratifications of the treaty were exchanged by the United States and Panama on February 26, 1904. Although amended several times, the controversial treaty remains the basic document regulating United States–Panamanian relations in the Canal Zone.

RICHARD B. GRAY

HENRIQUE. *See* HENRY.

HENRÍQUEZ, CAMILO (1769–1825). Chilean friar and revolutionary publicist. Born in Valdivia, Henríquez received his higher education in Lima, where he joined the friars of La Buena Muerte and had problems with the Inquisition (*see* INQUISITION, HOLY OFFICE OF THE). Following a brief trip to Quito, he returned to Chile in 1810. There he collaborated wholeheartedly with the revolutionary cause as a patriot preacher, congressman, and journalist. He edited the first Chilean newspaper, *La Aurora de Chile* (1812–1813). Ideologically, he belonged to the radical wing of the patriots, seeking to prepare public opinion for outright independence and republican government as well as campaigning for liberal reforms and useful improvements. In Chilean factional struggles he strongly supported José Miguel CARRERA.

Following the collapse of the Patria Vieja in 1814, Henríquez took refuge in Argentina, where he continued to work in journalism and tried his hand unsuccessfully at writing plays. After the liberation of Chile, Bernardo o'HIGGINS invited him to return and made good use of his services as editor of the *Gaceta* and national librarian and in other capacities. Henríquez served as secretary of the Chilean Convention of 1822. He died in Santiago. DAVID BUSHNELL

HENRÍQUEZ UREÑA, PEDRO (1884–1946). Dominican linguist and literary critic. A native of Santo Domingo, he studied in the United States and Mexico and taught in universities throughout the Americas. He died in La Plata, Argentina. His most famous linguistic work is *Sobre el problema del andalucismo dialectal de América* (1932). His essays include *Apuntes sobre la novela en América* (1927), *Seis ensayos en busca de nuestra expresión* (1928), *La versificación irregular en la poesía castellana* (1933), and *Las corrientes literarias en la América hispana, 1949 (Literary Currents in Hispanic America).*

His brother Max Henríquez Ureña (1885–   ) also became well known as a scholar and critic. RACHEL PHILLIPS

HENRY (HENRIQUE), known as the NAVIGATOR (1394–1460). Portuguese Prince and promoter of navigation. Born in Oporto, the fifth son of JOÃO I and Philippa of Lancaster, Henry participated in the conquest of Ceuta in 1415, was created Duke of Viseu, and was made Governor of Algarve. There he established himself at Sagres and recruited a group of scholars who made advances in map making and shipbuilding, especially in the development of the caravel. While pressing for crusading expansion in North Africa, the Prince also initiated a program of geographical exploration in the Atlantic and along the west coast of Africa. His objects were to find the African sources of gold that had reached Ceuta by caravan routes and to locate the Christian kingdom of Prester John, the legendary King of Ethiopia. Whether Henry also conceived the plan of reaching India by the circumnavigation of Africa is disputed, with eminent authorities aligned on each side of the question.

Madeira was rediscovered in 1419, and colonization began in 1425. By 1432 the Azores had been discovered. Communication with Africa was opened after 1434, when Cape Bojador was rounded by Gil Eanes, an achievement not merely over a geographical barrier but over a more formidable psychological fear of the unknown. Portuguese ambitions in the Canaries were thwarted in 1436, when the Pope reaffirmed Castile's rights. In 1437 Henry led a disastrous expedition to Tangier. Cape Blanco (Cap Blanc) was discovered in 1441. Two years later Rio do Ouro (Río de Oro) was reached, and the slave trade, subsequently headquartered at Arguim (Arguin), was begun. During 1444 and 1445 the Senegal River and Cape Verde (Cap Vert) were discovered, and the island of Gorée, beyond which the African coast trends eastward, was reached, as was the Cape of Masts on the rich Guinea coast beyond the desert. The Gambia River was explored in 1455, and the Cape Verde Islands were discovered in 1456. On the last of the Henrician voyages in 1460, Sierra Leone, about 1,500 miles down the West African coast, the farthest point, was reached (although Henry indicated that the point may have been as far as Cape Palmas). MARTIN TORODASH AND KENNETH R. MAXWELL

HEREDIA Y HEREDIA, JOSÉ MARÍA (1803–1839). Cuban poet. Heredia was born in Santiago de Cuba, but he was not destined to spend more than twenty years of his life in his native land, and he traveled to the United States, Venezuela, Mexico, and other countries before his death in Mexico City on May 7, 1839. A student of the classics and a translator of Horace, Heredia studied law at the University of Havana, obtaining his degree in 1821 after having spent two years with his family in Mexico. Of the several poems he wrote there, his most famous, and one of his masterpieces, is "En el Teocalli de Cholula" ("On the Temple Mound of Cholula"), which he composed in December 1820.

On his return to Cuba, Heredia became involved in politics and the independence movement. He was later implicated in Simón BOLÍVAR's Soles y Rayos conspiracy for independence and was forced to go into exile in New York, where he lived for a year and a half. His famous poem "Niágara" ("Ode to Niagara") was written in June 1824 as he contemplated the falls. His first volume of poetry was published in New York in 1825.

At the invitation of the Mexican government, Heredia left the United States for Mexico, where he continued to conspire in Cuba's battle against Spain. He held several positions in the Mexican judiciary, worked as a journalist, and founded two journals, *El Iris* (1826) and *La Miscelánea* (1829–1832). After a brief return to Cuba under an amnesty in 1836–1837, Heredia wrote his *Ultimos versos*. He died a short time later at the age of thirty-five.

Some of Heredia's works are considered neoclassical in form, but in many ways he was one of the first romantic poets of Spanish America, particularly when such poems as "En una tempestad" ("In a Tempest") are considered. He also wrote *Ensayo sobre la novela* (1832) and *Poetas ingleses contemporáneos* (1832), and his speeches and correspondence have been published. DANIEL R. REEDY

HERNÁNDEZ, JOSÉ (1834–1886). Argentine poet, journalist, and soldier. Hernández was born on a farm in the San Martín district of the province of Buenos Aires. He is best known as the author of *El gaucho Martín Fierro,* 1872 (*The Gaucho Martín Fierro*), a long poem with epic qualities relating the story of a GAUCHO's misfortunes. Hernández was a captain in Gen. Justo José de URQUIZA's army and took part in the Battles of Cepeda (1859) and Pavón (1861). In 1869 he founded the periodical *El Río de la Plata,* which ceased publication within a short time because of its attacks on the government. In 1870 he fought with Ricardo López Jordán in the Entre Ríos campaign. After a brief stay in Brazil, he returned to the Río de la Plata and worked as a newspaperman in Montevideo and Buenos Aires, where he spent the rest of his life.

Hernández's provincial birth and his father's business as a cattle dealer brought him into contact with the vast PAMPA during his childhood. He became well versed in the lore of the gauchos and the Indians during his travels through the countryside. Having lived with the gauchos in the provinces, he later became their champion, and with *El Río de la Plata* he sought to ameliorate their condition. He continued his crusade for the gauchos in *El gaucho Martín Fierro*. A second part, *La vuelta de Martín Fierro* (1879), rounded out this eloquent plea for justice, which immortalized its author.

GERARDO SÁENZ

HERNÁNDEZ COLÓN, RAFAEL (1936–   ). Governor of Puerto Rico (1973–   ). The youngest person to be elected Governor of Puerto Rico, Hernández Colón is the son of a prominent lawyer who served as Associate Justice of the Supreme Court. He graduated with honors from Johns Hopkins University in 1956 and received a law degree (magna cum laude) from the University of Puerto Rico in 1959. In 1960–1961 he served as Associate Commissioner of Public Service, and from then until 1965 he practiced law and taught at the Catholic University Law School. Hernández Colón is the author of a textbook on civil proceedings. He served as Secretary of Justice under Governor Roberto SÁNCHEZ VILELLA from 1965 to 1967.

Hernández Colón was a close collaborator of Luis MUÑOZ MARÍN during the 1967 plebiscite campaign. When Sánchez's split with the Popular Democratic party (PDP) was formalized, Hernández Colón remained in the PDP and was elected to the Senate in 1968; later he was elected president of the upper chamber. Elected to preside over the PDP, he reorganized the defeated and debt-ridden party and in 1972 received its nomination for Governor. Hernández Colón defeated the incumbent, Luis A. FERRÉ, receiving more than 50 percent of the popular vote. The first months of his administration were marked by significant efforts in the area of consumer affairs, new measures dealing with drug addiction, and vigorous steps to promote further growth of commonwealth status.

LUIS E. AGRAIT

HERNÁNDEZ MARTÍNEZ, MAXIMILIANO (1883–1966). Dictator of El Salvador (1931–1944). His maintenance of the status quo and the brutality of his repression made reform at the end of his regime almost inevitable. Hernández Martínez succeeded Arturo Araújo in the Presidency in December 1931. He was elected to a term of his own to run from 1935 to 1939 and thereafter perpetuated himself in office by having constitutional conventions extend his term successively to 1945 and 1949.

The dictator's program was a typical conservative performance. To counter the Depression, he reduced expenditures by half but maintained payments and by a marketing arrangement tried to protect coffee growers. He continued public works, such as road building, and paid for them from current revenues, and he established a central bank and other institutions to stimulate credit and savings. His regime was most notable for brutality. He crushed the slightest disturbance, often with "exemplary punishment" to discourage imitators. He wiped out the peasant uprising of 1932 (organized by the Communists but in essence a demand by impoverished peasants for land), slaughtering thousands of harmless *campesinos*. In April 1944, he strangled in blood a protest against the second extension of his period of office.

A general strike forced his resignation on May 8, 1944.

He went into exile in Honduras, returning during the 1956 presidential campaign "to die in El Salvador," but formulation of criminal charges against him persuaded him to seek medical treatment abroad.

WILLIAM J. GRIFFITH

HERRERA, FELIPE (1922–   ). Chilean economist and financial expert. Born in Valparaíso, Herrera received degrees in social sciences and law from the University of Chile, where he taught economics from 1947 to 1958. He served as Undersecretary of Economy and Commerce (1952–1953), Minister of Finance (1953), and general director of the Central Bank of Chile (1953–1958). In addition, from 1953 to 1958 he represented Chile on the governing boards of the World Bank and the International Monetary Fund, and in 1958 he was named an executive director of the latter.

Herrera is best known as the first President of the INTER-AMERICAN DEVELOPMENT BANK, which he headed from 1960 to 1971. In this capacity he was in large measure responsible for the early successes of the Bank and for its role in the financing of social development projects in housing, education, and the like. He resigned in 1970 (effective in 1971), stating that he wished to return to academic life in Chile so as not "to be separated from my country in the new stage of its historic evolution which is beginning." Early in 1972 Herrera, who had once been a member of the Socialist party (*see* SOCIALIST PARTY: CHILE), was named candidate of the governing Popular Unity coalition for the position of rector of the University of Chile. In the balloting on April 27, 1972, he was defeated by the former rector, who was supported by the PARTIDO DEMÓCRATA CRISTIANO. In 1973 he rejected Salvador ALLENDE's offer of a Cabinet post.

RODNEY D. ANDERSON

HERRERA, LUIS ALBERTO DE (1873–1959). Uruguayan political figure. Leader of the Blanco party (*see* BLANCO PARTY: URUGUAY) from 1920 until his death, Herrera was a frequent presidential candidate on the Blanco slate, and shortly before his death he led the party to its first major electoral victory in almost a century.

Born in Montevideo, Herrera served as a cavalryman in the Blanco uprisings of 1897 and 1904 and spent several terms as a national legislator beginning in 1905. He became chairman of the party's Executive Committee in 1920 and remained the dominant figure in the party for the next forty years. As his party's major presidential candidate throughout the 1920s, 1930s, and 1940s, Herrera sometimes polled more votes than any other candidate but lost the elections because the total vote for the Blanco *lema* was less than that accumulated by the Colorado *lema* (*see* COLORADO PARTY: URUGUAY; LEMA SYSTEM). He was President of the National Council of Administration from 1925 to 1927 during the first COLEGIADO and served as a national senator in the years 1934–1940.

After almost a century in the role of opposition, the Blanco party won control of the National Council of Government in the 1958 elections. Herrera, who had fought for his party's causes for sixty years and led the winning 1958 slate, died less than six weeks after the Blancos took office in March 1959. In addition to his lifelong political activities, Herrera was a prolific writer of history and served abroad in several diplomatic posts.

LEE C. FENNELL

HERRERA, TOMÁS (1804–1854). Panamanian army officer and statesman. A veteran of the wars for the independence of South America, Herrera, who held the rank of colonel in the armed forces of New Granada (modern Colombia), was named Governor of Panama in 1831. Before he could assume his post, he had to overcome the military dictator, Col. Juan Eligio Alzuru, a Venezuelan who had seized power and separated Panama from New Granada on July 9, 1831. Herrera defeated and executed his rival, ending the secession after only forty-one days.

After the start of a Liberal revolution in the interior of Colombia in 1839–1840, a popular assembly in Panama declared for separation on November 18, 1840, naming Herrera provisional head of the new isthmian state, which was recognized by Costa Rica. As a result of discussions with two commissioners from New Granada, however, Herrera agreed to the reintegration of Panama with that nation in December 1841. Although the agreement provided that amnesty be extended to those implicated in the secession, Herrera was degraded and exiled. By 1844 he had been rehabilitated and was named Governor of Panama for the period 1845–1849. In 1849 he became Minister of War in the Cabinet of fellow Liberal José Hilario López. In 1854 Herrera, who was first presidential alternate (*designado*) of New Granada, took a leading role in the campaign against the dictator José María Melo and was mortally wounded on December 4, 1854, during the battle to capture Bogotá.

LARRY L. PIPPIN

HERRERA Y TORDESILLAS, ANTONIO DE (ca. 1549–1625). Spanish historian. A native of Cuéllar, Segovia Province, Spain, Herrera obtained from King PHILIP II in 1596 the coveted post of *cronista mayor* (official historian). His best-known work, published between 1601 and 1615, is *Historia general de los hechos de los castellanos en las islas y tierra firme del mar océano,* also known as the *Décadas,* which relates events of discovery, pacification, and settlement by Spaniards in America between 1492 and 1555.

When Herrera composed this history, he had available to him all the documents then in the possession of the crown and of the COUNCIL OF THE INDIES. He used them so extensively that for almost two centuries his work constituted an easy means of access to numerous unpublished documents and manuscripts. Using an analytical-synchronic approach, he described year by year the glorious accomplishments of the Castilians (acknowledging the sometimes cruel components) and their tragic impact on the Indians.

Herrera's *Historia general* revealed his erudition, style, sweep, and organizational ability, but it also left him open to the charge of plagiarism. Indeed, it was asserted that the work was little more than an esthetically pleasing mosaic of other people's documents. Modern scholars reject this charge as unduly harsh and anachronistic and credit Herrera with acknowledging his sources in introductory passages, indicating the place whence they had been obtained, and sometimes evaluating the documents and their authors.

Herrera's multivolume history is referred to as the *Décadas* not because the work is divided into ten-year periods but because each of the eight original volumes was divided into ten chapters.

NORMAN MEIKLEJOHN

HEUREAUX, ULISES (1845–1899). Dominican dictator (1882–1899). Known as Lilís, Heureaux, a black, rose to power by means of physical prowess, military skill, and an undoubted capacity for leadership. His rule was often cruel and barbarous, and he was unequaled in the techniques of dictatorship. Nonetheless, he provided the longest period of order and stability the Dominican Republic had experienced, and under his hegemony the Dominican process of national development and modernization began.

During Heureaux's rule the Army and the bureaucracy were centralized and modernized, the population increased, new communications and transportation grids were introduced, foreign capital was welcomed, the sugar *latifundio* was established, and the economy expanded. New avenues of social mobility were opened, and new social classes appeared: a business-commercial oligarchy, a rising middle class, and a new lower-class proletariat. All these changes carried enormous implications for future Dominican development.

These accomplishments came at a severe cost. Heureaux ruled in an authoritarian, patrimonialist fashion that enriched him, frequently at the expense of the country, and that snuffed out all liberal and democratizing tendencies. He secured ruinous loans that bankrupted the treasury, sold important concessions to foreign exploiters, and left behind him a political and institutional vacuum. In 1899 Heureaux was assassinated, bequeathing a mixed and varied legacy to his country.

HOWARD J. WIARDA

HICKENLOOPER AMENDMENT. Sponsored by Senator Bourke B. Hickenlooper (Republican, Iowa) as an amendment to the Foreign Assistance Act of 1962, the measure provided that the President of the United States should suspend financial assistance to the government of any country which (1) had nationalized or expropriated or seized ownership or control of any property owned in excess of 50 percent by United States citizens or businesses or (2) had imposed or enforced discriminatory taxes or restrictions on operations of the property to the extent that it would in effect be nationalized or expropriated, if adequate and speedy compensation under international law were not provided. "Adequate and speedy" was interpreted to mean action within six months and payment in convertible foreign exchange as required by international law. A similar suspension of aid was to continue as long as relief from taxes or other oppressive conditions was not forthcoming. The President was expressly prohibited from waiving these provisions, which were made retroactive to January 1, 1962. A tentative application of the amendment occurred in 1968–1969, when Peru confiscated the holdings of the INTERNATIONAL PETROLEUM COMPANY, a subsidiary of Standard Oil of New Jersey (Exxon Corporation), without compensation. The Nixon administration threatened to suspend economic aid and intimated that it would cut back on sugar purchases, but widespread reaction in Peru persuaded the State Department not to retaliate. The *Rockefeller Report on the Americas* (1969) called upon the executive branch to seek the repeal of the amendment in the interests of economic development and harmony in the Western Hemisphere.

RICHARD B. GRAY

HIDALGO. Term denoting a Spanish nobleman, probably derived from *hijo d'algo,* or son of [someone who was] something. Sixteenth-century Spanish society was made up of three estates: nobility, clergy, and commonalty. The nobility consisted of a tiny group of wealthy grandees and titled nobles and the remaining mass of hidalgos. Membership in the nobility was normally acquired by birth from noble stock, although it could be granted as a royal favor. It conferred quality and social status, regardless of personal merit, and entailed exemption from personal taxes and privileged treatment by the courts.

The conquerors and early settlers of America brought these social categories with them, and although only a few of them were of noble lineage, they all deemed themselves nobles by virtue of their extraordinary feats and valuable services to the crown. Indeed, royal grants of encomiendas confirmed them as a new aristocracy. Joining them later came the upper levels of the ecclesiastical and governmental bureaucracies and the wealthy landowners, miners, and merchants who married into the nobility or were willing to purchase a certificate of nobility. Finally, even without benefit of lineage, marriage, or concession, all Americans who were white, Spanish, and without taint of African, Jewish, or Moorish blood came to consider themselves hidalgos.

Besides the social, economic, ethnic, and religious implications of *hidalguía,* there developed a psychological meaning to the effect that true *hidalguía* is a quality of mind and soul, enabling all Spaniards to perform noble deeds when the occasion arises. The Portuguese counterpart of the Spanish nobleman was called a *fidalgo.*

NORMAN MEIKLEJOHN

HIDALGO Y COSTILLA, MIGUEL (1753–1811). Mexican priest and revolutionary. Miguel Hidalgo y Costilla was born on May 8, 1753, and lived his boyhood years on the hacienda of San Diego Corralejo, where his father was administrator. A creole with access to education, Miguel was sent to Valladolid (now Morelia) to study in a Jesuit academy in 1765. When the Jesuits were expelled two years later (*see* JESUITS, EXPULSION OF: SPANISH AMERICA), Miguel matriculated in the diocesan College of San Nicolás. Intellectually inclined, Hidalgo spent the next quarter century in Valladolid as student, teacher, and administrator. Along the way he became a priest. From 1790 to 1792 he was rector of the college, but mismanagement of funds and his espousal of Enlightenment philosophy led to his dismissal (*see* ENLIGHTENMENT: SPANISH AMERICA).

For the next eighteen years Hidalgo served three curacies in the Michoacán diocese. Tropical Colima (1792) was followed by a ten-year stint in San Felipe (1793–1803). There Hidalgo turned his house into a salon, produced French theatrical works (which he translated), organized an orchestra, gave dances, and promoted literary discussions. Charges of heterodoxy and libertinism brought on an investigation by the Inquisition (1800–1801), but Hidalgo was not brought to trial (*see* INQUISITION, HOLY OFFICE OF THE). In 1803 he moved to Dolores (now Dolores Hidalgo), east of the Guanajuato mines. There Hidalgo turned his restless energies to the development of local industries and handicrafts (ceramics, sericulture, tanning) designed to enhance the economy of his parishioners.

Hidalgo was a peripatetic whose desire for stimulating company brought him into contact with creole and peninsular intellectuals throughout the BAJÍO and Michoacán. As the crisis of empire engulfed New Spain in 1808, the curate from Dolores increased his interest in politics. When creole plotters in Querétaro organized a military revolt to oust the *gachupín* (Spanish) government in Mexico City, Hidalgo joined them. As much for his intellect, rhetorical skill, and charisma as for the psychological advantages of his cloth, Hidalgo emerged the leader. Ignacio de ALLENDE, a militia captain from San Miguel, became second in command.

Before plans were fully matured, a betrayal impelled the conspirators to revolt. Hidalgo's famous Grito de Dolores (*see* DOLORES, GRITO DE), an exhortation to his parishioners early in the morning of September 16, 1810, marked the decisive step. The priest appears to have couched his appeal in traditional protest language: "Long live the King [the exiled FERDINAND VII]! Long live the Catholic religion! and Death to bad government." Such abstractions as "independence"

Miguel Hidalgo y Costilla. [*Organization of American States*]

were avoided as meaningless to an untutored audience of Indians and *castas* (mixed-bloods). A banner bearing an image of the Virgin of Guadalupe was shortly added as the symbol of the revolt (*see* GUADALUPE, VIRGIN OF).

The 25,000 Indians and *castas* who joined Hidalgo's holy war of redemption during the first two weeks quickly blurred the original white creole motives for the rebellion. As the *jacquerie* moved through the Bajío, the fury of the tributary masses was difficult to control. Tensions between the leaders surfaced early: Allende's militia discipline was overruled by Hidalgo's confidence in the horde. On September 28, Guanajuato was attacked and the peninsulars' granary fortress, the Alhóndiga de Granaditas, was stormed. The massacre of Spaniards and the subsequent sack of the city set the temper of the Hidalgo revolt. After some rudimentary organization Hidalgo marched south and took Valladolid without violence. As he turned east toward the vice-regal capital in late October, the horde swelled to some 80,000.

Meanwhile, the royalists and defenders of the status quo had prepared resistance, both military and psychological. Viceroy Francisco Xavier Venegas pressed an intensive propaganda campaign through pamphlets and broadsides that revealed the human and physical destruction of the social revolution, frightened the masses with the horrors of Guanajuato, and exposed the threat to creole vested interests. The victory that Hidalgo won at Monte de las Cruces, on the divide between Toluca and Mexico City, on October 30 was not conclusive because the inhabitants of the Valley of Mexico, Indians and *castas* as well as *gachupines* and creoles, refused to join the intruders. Threatened on his northern flank by a trained army under the Spanish commander Félix María Calleja and disheartened by his reception in the valley, Hidalgo decided to retreat to Guadalajara without an assault on the capital.

From Guadalajara Hidalgo made further efforts to establish a separatist government. He confirmed the end to tribute payments and slavery and made a modest effort to protect the lands of Indian villages. Progress, however, was marred by Hidalgo's strong ego and the continued disputes with Allende over strategy. When Calleja threatened the insurgents early in 1811, Hidalgo's decision to risk his entire horde, now reconstituted and numbering up to 100,000, in a single pitched battle prevailed. This proved his undoing, for the Battle of Calderón on January 17 ended in an insurgent rout.

During the flight north the Allende faction suspended Hidalgo from command, although he continued as the revolt's figurehead. Allende's futile attempt to reach the United States was betrayed by a disgruntled lieutenant, and the major leaders of the insurrection were captured at Baján, north of Saltillo.

Hidalgo, Allende, and their companions were taken to Chihuahua for trial. With execution his inexorable fate and aware that his cause had met disaster, Hidalgo repented and apparently signed a retraction. Once defrocked, the former curate was shot on July 30 and decapitated. The heads of Hidalgo, Allende, and two other commanders were taken to Guanajuato and hung as grisly reminders on the corners of the Alhóndiga. The independence movement languished after

Hidalgo's death in spite of the well-disciplined efforts of José María MORELOS Y PAVÓN (1811–1815), for the creole majority remained disaffected. In 1821 a conservatively inspired independence was achieved by Agustín de ITURBIDE, a creole who had opposed Hidalgo and Morelos. After Iturbide's overthrow and the establishment of the first Mexican republic, Hidalgo emerged as the prime mover of independence. Modern Mexico venerates him as the Padre de la Patria and celebrates September 16 as the principal national holiday.

Bibliography. Luis Castillo Ledón, *Hidalgo: La vida del héroe,* 2 vols., Mexico City, 1948–49; Hugh M. Hamill, Jr., *The Hidalgo Revolt: Prelude to Mexican Independence,* Gainesville, Fla., 1966; Antonio Pompa y Pompa (ed.), *Procesos inquisitorial y militar seguidos a D. Miguel Hidalgo y Costilla,* Mexico City, 1960.

HUGH M. HAMILL, JR.

HIGHWAYS. A highway system is said to be mature if current planning and budgets are directed largely toward the completion of secondary roads, farm-to-market subsystems, and the relief of urban traffic congestion. Few major projects remain to complete the basic connectivity of the system. Such a system has a high ratio of paved to unpaved kilometers and a high density network per 10,000 inhabitants, as well as a high road density in proportion to the area of the country. The size and the state of the motor vehicle fleet are also a measure of the extent to which the system is in a position to augment the gross domestic product and to lower transport costs. A highway network is said to have good connectivity if it has many nodes with multiple connections from those nodes not only to a central focus but to all parts of the network.

In the current state of highway development, each of the nations of Latin America can be placed in one of four categories:

Category I, mature systems having good connectivity between most urban centers down to an average population of 25,000, excellent maintenance, many traffic-generating nodes, few areas beyond the reach of the network of highways, good-to-excellent vehicle fleets, and adequate highway construction budgets.

Category II, mature systems which, although they are well maintained, tend to be adequate only for reaching the capital city and certain other key centers down to about 100,000 population. Such systems are also characterized by relatively large areas with poor access, although the vehicle fleets are good to excellent in size and adequacy. Highway budgets are generally adequate.

Category III, the major developing highway systems in which until recently there was little if any connectivity between disparate subsystems in various parts of the nation. These systems still have large areas beyond the reach of existing highways. Generally, they have heavy construction budgets and relatively good fleets.

Category IV, systems that are hardly more than subsystems of market roads focused on a few of the nation's major centers. Freight and passenger movements are seriously impeded. Highway budgets are inadequate, vehicle fleets small, and general road maintenance erratic.

Table 1 classifies the nations of Latin America by

categories of highway development. Colonial areas, the Caribbean islands, the Canal Zone, and some of the smaller nations such as Guyana, Jamaica, and Trinidad and Tobago, are not included.

The Latin American highway system is expected to reach a state of relative maturity during the 1970s. Rapid expansion in the networks of Brazil, Ecuador, and Colombia, together with the completion of vital links between existing national systems along the spinal PAN AMERICAN HIGHWAY (usually referred to as the Inter-American Highway in Central America), will provide a highway complex with adequate connectivity and good access to most developed regions. Perhaps the most symbolic portion of this current phase of road development is the Transamazonian Highway, of which the first section—1,290 kilometers between Estreito, Maranhão, and Itaituba, Pará—was completed by 1972. Also significant is the construction of the 401-kilometer link between Chepo, Panama, and the Turbo-Medellín highway in Colombia, which will remove the Darién gap by the late 1970s and permit an overland connection between the North and South American highway systems. Tables 2 and 3 show the highway and fleet systems in the various Latin American countries in 1971. Table 4 gives the density of the networks in 1967, and Table 5 the state of the Pan American Highway system that year.

The Latin American highway system as a whole, regarded as a sum of all the national systems, is only minimally connective. Except along the Inter-American Highway in Central America, connections at national borders are generally inadequate. Essentially, the national systems were developed to permit integration from the capital city, to serve a major port of export, or to penetrate vital agricultural regions. Only during the 1960s did highway planners begin to concentrate upon attaining higher degrees of internal connectivity. As yet there is no continental commitment to higher connectivity, and until there is, a continental system as such cannot be said to exist.

Brazil. The National Highway Plan introduced in February 1967 provides for the completion of a comprehensive network of federal roads: (1) nine radial highways fanning out from Brasília, linking the national capital with the various state capitals and with the frontiers of Bolivia, Colombia, Paraguay, and Peru (14,500 kilometers); (2) fourteen north-south highways, largely in the east (27,400 kilometers); (3) nineteen east-west highways (18,400 kilometers); and (4) twenty-four highways linking the northeast to the southwest and the northwest to the southeast (20,900 kilometers). The purpose is to remove the relative isolation not only of undeveloped regions but of many of the older states, especially in the NORTHEAST.

The highest priority has been given to the Transamazonian Highway. The Humaitá–Pôrto Velho–Rio Branco section was in use in 1971. The Estreito-Itaituba section opened early in 1972, and the complete highway was to be open to traffic by early 1973. A second major Amazonian road, to link Cuiabá, Mato Grosso, with Santarém, Pará, was also under construction by 1972. A further highway, the Perimetral Norte, to link Macapá, Amapá, with Içana, Amazonas, via the state of Pará and the territory of Roraima, was in the planning stages in 1972. In general, this heavy highway

TABLE 1. CLASSIFICATION OF LATIN AMERICAN HIGHWAY SYSTEMS

Category	Countries	General characteristics
I	Mexico Venezuela Uruguay Chile Dominican Republic Puerto Rico	Mature, well-maintained highway systems with many nodes, good connections to lesser centers, few areas beyond reach, a good-to-excellent fleet, and adequate highway construction budgets
II	Argentina Panama Costa Rica El Salvador Guatemala Cuba	Mature, well-maintained highway systems with fewer nodes, the capital city as the center of the system and poor connections to lesser points, large areas with poor access, a good fleet, and fair-to-adequate highway construction budgets
III	Brazil Peru Colombia Nicaragua Ecuador	Developing system with many gaps, poor connections, difficult terrain, much of the national area beyond highway reach, a good fleet, and heavy construction outlays needed or under way
IV	Bolivia Paraguay Haiti Honduras	No true highway system with often-poor maintenance of existing highways, freight and passenger traffic seriously impeded, inadequate highway budgets, and a small fleet

construction into undeveloped regions was encouraged by the extraordinary success of the Belém-Brasília highway.

During the 1960s the road network in Brazil grew from 475,000 kilometers, of which 31,500 kilometers were federal highways and 84,000 kilometers state highways, to 1,140,000 kilometers (1971). Of the early 1960s network, only 11,500 kilometers were paved. By 1971, 53,000 kilometers were paved, and 5,000 kilometers were being paved. The federal system had grown to 55,000 kilometers, and the state systems to 135,000 kilometers. In the same period the motor vehicle fleet grew from 1.2 million to 3.4 million vehicles, of which 23 percent were trucks. Freight movement by highway rose by 230 percent in the 1960s to become the dominant mode of transport. Yet the highway system was still essentially immature. Large and continuing expenditures would be necessary to attain the degree of national integration called for by the National Highway Plan.

TABLE 2. LATIN AMERICAN HIGHWAY SYSTEMS, 1971
(In kilometers)

Country	Paved roads	All-weather roads	Unim-proved roads	Total	Estimated 1971 highway expenditures
Argentina	33,398	167,121	...	200,519	$280,228,000
Bolivia	950	14,242	10,409	25,601	...
Brazil	52,900	101,906	983,638	1,138,444	...
Chile	7,900	65,000	...	72,900	49,056,000
Colombia	6,000	37,000	3,000	46,000	...
Costa Rica	1,333	5,187	12,280	18,800	...
Dominican Republic	5,153	3,673	1,200	10,026	...
Ecuador	3,079	14,260	5,562	22,901	12,287,000
El Salvador	1,207	3,083	4,405	8,695	...
Guatemala	2,112	8,176	1,930	12,218	...
Haiti	550	950	1,650	3,150	...
Honduras	949	2,477	5,140	8,566	16,530,000
Mexico	43,360	28,720	1,950	74,030	149,012,000
Nicaragua	1,260	5,260	7,550	14,070	10,644,000
Panama	1,802	1,490	3,570	6,862	27,276,000
Paraguay	602	5,033	10,321	15,956	...
Peru	4,858	22,359	22,830	50,047	37,181,000
Puerto Rico	6,342	518	913	7,773	...
Uruguay	6,000	22,745	23,000	51,745	...
Venezuela	18,006	21,584	16,135	55,725	...

SOURCE: International Road Federation, *Staff Report*, Washington, 1971.

TABLE 3. HIGHWAY VEHICLE FLEETS, LATIN AMERICA, 1971

Country	Automobiles	Trucks and buses	Total
Argentina	1,403,295	745,463	2,148,758
Bolivia	21,364	23,716	45,080
Brazil	1,827,897	1,569,409	3,397,306
Chile	226,000	78,500	304,500
Colombia	146,000	135,000	281,000
Costa Rica	36,065	20,621	56,686
Dominican Republic	44,283	19,783	64,066
Ecuador	28,850	52,700	81,550
El Salvador	34,965	15,527	50,492
Guatemala	42,770	30,352	73,122
Haiti	12,000	6,500	18,500
Honduras	17,148	14,230	31,378
Mexico	1,368,038	614,890	1,982,928
Nicaragua	26,600	13,900	40,500
Panama	45,526	14,534	60,060
Paraguay	8,100	11,030	19,130
Peru	239,336	63,874	303,210
Puerto Rico	493,000	108,000	601,000
Uruguay	124,200	78,100	202,300
Venezuela	534,449	207,900	742,349

SOURCE: International Road Federation, *Staff Report*, Washington, 1971.

Mexico. By 1971 there were about 43,300 kilometers of paved highways and 28,700 kilometers of all-weather highways in Mexico, or about four times the 1950 total. In every sense a mature system, the Mexican highway system has Mexico City as its primary node, with secondary nodes at Monterrey, Guadalajara, and Veracruz. From this integrated triangle of adequate and well-connected highways, trunk highways lead to

TABLE 4. DENSITY OF HIGHWAY NETWORKS, 1967

Country	Kilometers per 10,000 inhabitants		Kilometers per 1,000 square kilometers		Area (in square kilometers)
	Paved	Total	Paved	Total	
Argentina	9.4	86.3	7.9	72.3	2,777.7
Bolivia	1.6	63.9	0.6	22.1	1,098.6
Brazil	1.9	64.2	1.9	64.6	8,512.0
Chile	7.3	62.6	8.8	75.5	756.9
Colombia	3.5	23.5	5.9	37.7	1,138.9
Costa Rica	7.6	112.6	23.9	354.3	50.7
Dominican Republic	12.2	24.4	97.6	194.6	48.7
El Salvador	3.7	27.1	55.0	399.8	21.4
Guatemala	3.6	28.2	15.8	122.1	108.9
Haiti	1.1	7.0	17.8	115.6	27.8
Honduras	1.7	17.8	3.7	38.9	112.1
Mexico	8.3	14.3	19.3	33.0	1,972.5
Nicaragua	5.9	39.0	8.1	53.5	130.0
Panama	9.8	49.5	17.1	86.9	75.7
Paraguay	1.4	58.0	0.7	30.8	406.8
Peru	3.5	34.6	3.4	33.3	1,285.2
Uruguay	5.6	135.8	8.3	202.2	186.9
Venezuela	17.5	52.1	18.0	53.4	902.1

SOURCE: United Nations Economic Commission for Latin America, *Economic Survey of Latin America,* Santiago, Chile, annually.

the Pacific, north to the United States border at such points as Tijuana, Nuevo Laredo, Ciudad Juárez, and Matamoros, and south to Guatemala as well as to Yucatán and Belize. Traffic in the north and west is heavy, generated by many local industries and by agriculture. To the south and east there are less industry and less traffic. Mountains generally extending from north to south make east-west movement relatively difficult, but the major remaining highway problems concern the improvement of the farm-to-market network.

Annual federal spending on highways represents about 6 percent of the budget. Partly as a means of financing the necessary expansion of primary routes, Mexico has built a series of toll roads centering on Mexico City. These include the Mexico City–Iguala expressway with a branch to Cuautla, the Mexico City–Puebla-Orizaba expressway, and the Mexico City–Querétaro-Irapauta expressway running north and west from the capital toward Guadalajara. In addition, there is a toll section south from the California border through Tijuana to Ensenada.

By 1971 the Mexican vehicle fleet had grown to almost 2 million vehicles, of which 615,000 were trucks and buses. The fact that more than 500,000 of these were registered in the Federal District (Mexico City and its environs) is an indication of the traffic problems of the capital. It is not surprising that an increasing share of highway spending has been allocated to urban traffic bypasses and local street systems.

Argentina. Argentina has the second most extensive highway system in Latin America, totaling more than 200,000 kilometers. In 1971 more than 33,000 kilometers were paved, and another 28,000 kilometers were graded and macadamized. During the 1960s there was

little extensive improvement in this highway network, but the vehicle fleet increased dramatically, from about 500,000 vehicles in 1960 to 2.1 million in 1971. An estimated 1.2 million of these vehicles were registered in greater Buenos Aires, indicating the vastly increased traffic density in South America's largest metropolis. About 745,000 trucks and buses were included in the total fleet.

Perhaps the most dramatic achievement of the 1960s

TABLE 5. PAN AMERICAN
(INTER-AMERICAN) HIGHWAY SYSTEM, 1967
(In kilometers)

Country	Paved	All-weather	Dry-weather	Impas-sable	Total
Argentina	4,774	692	58	...	5,524
Bolivia	636	2,005	130	1,356	4,127
Brazil	5,199	1,794	...	8,282	15,275
Chile	3,237	53	16	...	3,306
Colombia	1,588	618	...	479	2,685
Ecuador	129	1,043	...	...	1,172
El Salvador	309	...	...	...	309
Guatemala	351	153	...	...	504
Honduras	243	...	...	...	243
Mexico	4,438	...	...	...	4,438
Nicaragua	384	...	...	...	384
Panama	552	...	...	286	838
Paraguay	335	...	761	19	1,115
Peru	2,545	1,768	288	129	4,730
Uruguay	344	290	...	...	634
Venezuela	1,585	101	18	...	1,704

SOURCE: Organization of American States, *América en cifras,* Washington, annually.

was the completion of the tunnel between Santa Fe and Paraná, providing the first direct highway connection between the province of Entre Rios and the west bank of the Paraná River. The Zárate–Brazo Largo bridge and road complex over the lower Paraná was undertaken between 1970 and 1972. Major construction plans for the 1970s involved essentially secondary roads in the three leading provinces of Buenos Aires, Sante Fe, and Córdoba, together with a 600-kilometer interurban expressway from Santa Fe through Rosario to Buenos Aires, La Plata, and Mar del Plata. The expressway is the first major project in more than a generation to affect the connectivity of the Argentine highway system.

The moderate degree of connectivity of the highway system is due to the tendency of highway planners to use Buenos Aires as the node. With no secondary nodes and with relatively weak interstitial connections, the system serves the capital city well but does not provide adequate access for Rosario, a metropolitan center with a population of almost 900,000, and even less for Córdoba, a city of 850,000 inhabitants. In effect, roads parallel railways across the PAMPA. Below Bahía Blanca into Patagonia and north from Sante Fe into the Chaco, both largely undeveloped areas, highways are little better than tracks.

Venezuela. Though not one of the larger highway systems, the Venezuelan network is probably the best developed in Latin America. Of the 55,700 kilometers in place in 1971, 18,000 kilometers were paved and another 21,500 kilometers were macadamized, graded, or drained. Included in the total are toll expressways from Caracas north to the port of La Guaira and south and west through Maracay and Valencia and north again to Puerto Cabello. The tollway system is being extended east of Petare. Within the Caracas Valley freeways provide ready access to all parts of the built-up area.

Good highways extend from this central coastal complex through the LLANOS to Guayana, crossing the ORINOCO RIVER via a toll bridge at Ciudad Bolívar. The highway extends eastward along the coast to Cumaná, and there is an excellent highway running westward from Valencia through Barquisimeto to Maracaibo and beyond. Southwest to San Cristóbal at the Colombian border, the Pan American Highway passes through the ANDES MOUNTAINS. Although east-west connections are poor south of the Cumaná-Maracaibo corridor, few parts of Venezuela lie beyond the reach of well-designed paved highways.

In metropolitan Caracas, two out of five persons own automobiles. The vehicle fleet in 1971 numbered almost 750,000 vehicles, of which 208,000 were buses and trucks. 'Jitneys provide inexpensive passenger service to all parts of the nation.

Central America. Highway systems in Central America vary from the well-integrated network in El Salvador to the inadequately developed road complex in Honduras. The Inter-American Highway serves as the spine of all these systems, running from the Mexican border at Talisman in Guatemala through El Salvador, Honduras, Nicaragua, and Costa Rica to a point beyond Chepo in Panama, where it ends at the Darién gap. In a very real sense, this highway makes the CENTRAL AMERICAN COMMON MARKET possible. Of the 59,200 kilometers of roads in Central America, 8,700 kilometers are paved and another 25,600 kilometers are all-weather highways.

The vehicle fleet in Central America comprises 312, 238 automobiles, trucks, and buses, of which 43 percent are registered in Panama and Guatemala. Vehicles of Mexican and United States registration provide regular bus and truck service over Central American highways.

The Darién gap, some 401 kilometers of swamp and jungle, has remained until recently the most challenging obstacle to the completion of a true continental network. Although the Darién terrain was once thought to be too difficult for highway construction, final surveys were completed by 1970, and contracts were let. It was determined that only 22 kilometers presented any serious problems and that adequate rock fill was available nearby. By the mid-1970s, a usable all-weather road should be in place.

Andean countries. Colombia, Ecuador, Peru, Bolivia, and Chile contain some of the most difficult terrain in the world. The Andes, which stretch from Colombia southward to Tierra del Fuego, have peaks more than 23,000 feet high. Only here and there is it possible to find east-west passes across this formidable barrier. Highways tend to follow the chain of valleys from the Caribbean south and to extend along the narrow band of land hugging the Pacific.

The Colombian national highway system consists of a linear network centering on Cali in the Cauca Valley and extending from Popayán to the north of Medellín; a weblike network centering on Bogotá on the Gran Sabana; and a north coast network running from Santa Marta through Barranquilla to Cartagena, Sincelejo, and Montería. Most of the country's paved kilometers are part of these subsystems. Connections between the Cali-Medellín and the Bogotá networks are made at Ibagué on the Armenia road and at Honda on the Manizales road, over the high ridge of the Cordillera Central.

From Bogotá a good all-weather road runs through Tunja via Bucaramanga to Cúcuta at the Venezuelan border. Between Medellín and Turbo there is a road in passable shape that will serve as the major connection with the Inter-American Highway below the Darién gap. In addition, a good road extends from Medellín to Caucasia and Sincelejo, from which it is possible to reach the north coastal system. Southward from Cali and Popayán a good road passes through Pasto and Ipiales to reach the Ecuadorian border at Rumichaca. From Cali, too, a good truck route descends to the nation's largest port at Buenaventura. Thus, the highway system not only integrates the diverse sectors of Colombia but also provides good overland connections with neighboring countries.

The Colombian vehicle fleet is surprisingly small, consisting of 135,000 trucks and buses and 146,000 automobiles. The number of vehicles has been growing slowly in recent years.

Ecuador has three major regions: a sierra made up of connected valleys ranging around 9,000 feet high and centering on Quito; a costa consisting of terrain ranging from rain forest in the north to almost desert below Guayaquil, the country's largest city and port; and the Amazon lowlands on the eastern slope of the cordillera of the Andes (see COSTA: ECUADOR; SIERRA: ECUADOR). The Pan American Highway runs south from Rumichaca to Loja, but the connection to Peru through Macarà is best described as difficult. With the completion of an excellent highway north from Guayaquil to

Santo Domingo de los Colorados and the use of the easiest pass up to Quito, a good connection along the coast is now available and in heavy use. The new bridge across the Guayas River at Guayaquil, together with a network of farm-to-market roads in Guayas Province, has sharply lowered the cost of transport in Ecuador. The rapid extension of the highways has now brought the national system to a level of nearly 23,000 kilometers, of which about 3,100 kilometers are paved. Another 14,200 kilometers are all-weather roads. As yet there is little if any highway access to the Amazon lowlands. Ecuador's highway vehicle fleet is barely adequate.

Like Ecuador, Peru is divided into sierra, costa, and montaña (the Amazon area; *see* COSTA: PERU; SIERRA: PERU). However, there are neither large population centers nor good through highways in the sierra, so that the Peruvian network consists of the spine of the Pan American Highway, running from Tumbes near the Ecuadorian border south to Tacna. At points like Piura, Pacasmayo, Trujillo, Barranca, Lima, and Arequipa there are penetration roads from this spine into the sierra and occasionally beyond it. A sierra road dating well beyond the reign of the INCAS runs from Pucallpa through Huánuco, Huancayo, and Ayacucho to Cuzco, reaching Puno near the Bolivian border, but it is not designed for heavy traffic. At Puno there are connections with a road from Arequipa via Juliaca and by ferry or road to Quaqui and La Paz.

About 4,700 kilometers of the Pan American Highway are in Peru; of these, 1,800 kilometers are paved. All but 120 kilometers of the highway in Peru are passable at all times. The total Peruvian system of 50,000 kilometers serves more than 300,000 vehicles.

Few nations are more dependent upon and less well supplied with highway transport than Bolivia. The nation's only paved highway runs from Cochabamba to Santa Cruz east of the Andean range. There is also a passable road from La Paz via Oruro and Potosí to La Quiaca at the Argentine border, but here as along other stretches of Bolivian highway the driver must be ready for landslides and other dangers. Despite relatively heavy spending, the Bolivian highway system is inadequate, and the vehicle fleet is quite small.

From Arica below Tacna at the Peruvian border south to Puerto Montt in the Chilean fiord country, the Pan American Highway runs through the ATACAMA DESERT, then the Central Valley, and finally a succession of temperate valleys to reach the sheltered sea. The Chilean network is much more sophisticated than that of Peru, although, like Peru's, it consists of a north-south spine with east-west connectors and penetration roads. There are good parallel routes, especially in the Central Valley near Santiago, and few inhabited parts of the country are beyond the reach of all-weather highways. North of Santiago, there is a connection at San Felipe via Los Andes to Mendoza, Argentina. Another highway crosses the Andes farther south via Junín de los Andes.

Chile's vehicle fleet consists of more than 304,000 cars, trucks, and buses and is growing quite fast. More than 10 percent of the 73,000-kilometer highway system is paved, and the rest is generally passable in all weather, although there is heavy snow east and south of Santiago at the higher elevations.

Uruguay and Paraguay. There are no roads from Asunción, capital of Paraguay, to Brazil, although a road running south to Posadas on the Argentine side of the upper Paraná River connects with a tourist road to Puerto Iguazu, where a Brazilian through road is being improved. Indeed, the Paraguayan system consists of little more than this road and its tributaries. An all-weather road runs from Asunción via Resistencia and Santa Fe to Buenos Aires.

Uruguay has an excellent system centered on Montevideo, from which there are ferries and hydrofoils to Buenos Aires. At least four good highways lead to the Brazilian border to the north, although only the road through Pelotas to Pôrto Alegre is suitable for heavy traffic connections with the Brazilian federal highway network.

Paraguay's vehicle fleet is quite small, consisting of less than 20,000 units, much more than half of which are trucks and buses. By contrast, Uruguay's fleet is large and is growing fast. More than half of Uruguay's 51,745 kilometers of highways are paved or all-weather roads.

The Caribbean. Cuba, the Dominican Republic, and Puerto Rico have large and well-developed highway systems. By contrast, the Haitian economy is severely limited by the inadequacy of its highways. Cuba's 1,144-kilometer central highway serves as the backbone of a system of 7,000 kilometers of secondary roads, only a small proportion of which are paved. Although maintenance has been at least adequate since 1960, little if any expansion took place in the 1960s and no major plans have been announced for the 1970s.

The Dominican Republic possesses one of the better road networks in Latin America, a well-integrated system of 10,000 kilometers, of which almost 5,200 kilometers are paved. Although most of these highways extend to the east, few major areas are without good road access. In Puerto Rico, the next island in the chain of the Greater Antilles, some 6,300 kilometers of the 7,800 kilometers in the highway system are paved. The Puerto Rican system contains expressways and urban bypasses, and the metropolitan systems are well integrated with the highway network. There are more than ten times as many automobiles in Puerto Rico (493,000) as in the Dominican Republic (44,000).

Haiti, with 550 kilometers of paved highways in a network of 3,100 kilometers, is served by a fleet of 18,500 vehicles.

Bibliography. Robert T. Brown, *Transport and the Economic Integration of South America,* Washington, 1966; E. T. Haefele (ed.), *Transport and National Goals,* Washington, 1969; Richard M. Soberman, *Transport Technology for Developing Regions: A Study of Road Transportation in Venezuela,* Cambridge, Mass., 1966; Charles J. Stokes, *Transportation and Economic Development in Latin America,* New York, 1968; United Nations Economic Commission for Latin America, *El transporte en América Latina,* Santiago, Chile, 1965; George W. Wilson, Barbara R. Bergmann, Leon B. Hirsch, and Martin S. Klein, *The Impact of Highway Investment on Development,* Washington, 1967.

CHARLES J. STOKES

HOJEDA, ALONSO DE. *See* OJEDA, ALONSO DE.

HOLY OFFICE OF THE INQUISITION. *See* INQUISITION, HOLY OFFICE OF THE.

HONDURAS SINCE 1823. When final independence came to Central America in 1823, Honduras embraced approximately 60,000 square miles but contained probably fewer than 150,000 inhabitants, of mixed Indian, Iberian, and African ancestry. Most of these mestizos lived in pocket-sized villages nestled in isolated valleys scattered throughout the deeply corrugated mountain spine that dominates the interior. No roads linked these villages; horse and mule trains provided the only transportation.

The overwhelming majority of the villagers wrung a meager sustenance from small patches of corn and beans. Frequent floods, droughts, infertile soil, and rude farming skills made subsistence agriculture a precarious undertaking. Folk miners called *guirises* eked out a livelihood grubbing in abandoned colonial mines. Together, the peasants and folk miners made up the lower strata of Honduran society.

An occasional prosperous hacienda owner grazed cattle on suitable highland savannas or on the coastal plains. Landed creoles of this type dominated the rural society around their estates. In the more important "urban" centers, especially Comayagua and Tegucigalpa, bureaucrats manned small governmental and ecclesiastical outposts and a few merchants handled the limited trade. Unable to produce the cochineal, indigo, or cacao that other Central American countries exported to European markets, Honduras had little contact with the outside world. In this circumstance, the politicians, clergy, and businessmen were social and political dependents of the landed elite.

Until internecine struggles finally destroyed the Federation of Central America in 1839–1840 (*see* CENTRAL AMERICA, FEDERATION OF), "Liberals" usually controlled the government at Comayagua but effected little reform beyond reducing the already-weak authority of the Catholic Church. With the defeat of Gen. Francisco MORAZÁN by the Guatemalan strong man José Rafael CARRERA, "Conservatives" gained the upper hand and led their country out of the Federation. For the next thirty years, the Conservatives maintained nominal control, but actual power devolved on the dominant regional cattle barons. Personal jealousies

flared into meaningless armed struggles between rival elite factions, which often enjoyed the support of sympathizers in neighboring states. Banditry spread like cancer across the countryside in the atmosphere of violence.

In the 1850s the stream of forty-niners rushing to the California gold workings prompted an American diplomat-archaeologist, Ephraim George Squier, to promote the construction of an interoceanic railway across Honduras. However, a change in local administration, conflicting estimates of the cost of the enterprise, and monetary crises in New York and Europe delayed the project until the PANAMA RAILROAD and completion of the transcontinental railroad across the United States made the Honduran route nonessential for international transportation. The Honduran government nevertheless continued to dream of opening up its undeveloped hinterland by means of an interoceanic rail system. In the late 1860s it secured several large loans from European bankers, with which it constructed a mere 60 miles of track, from Puerto Cortés through and beyond San Pedro Sula, before funds ran out. This railway did little to ease the lack of transportation into the interior, where most of the people lived. The completion of the Panama Railroad (1855) and the inauguration of regular shipping from Panama to San Francisco made the island port of Amapala on the Gulf of Fonseca the preferred point of entry for goods and passengers for this area. On the other hand, the huge foreign debt incurred to construct this spur of rails hung like a dark cloud over Honduras for three-quarters of a century, inhibiting the inflow of capital.

In 1876 Marco Aurelio SOTO, a reform Liberal, assumed power in Honduras. With the collaboration of like-minded executives in neighboring states who discouraged exiles from continuing the practice of launching attacks from sanctuaries within their borders, Soto was able to pacify Honduras. Factional warfare and banditry virtually ceased during his Presidency (1876–1883). Convinced that emulation of advanced societies in Europe and North America would develop his undeveloped domain, Soto initiated an ambitious program to provide Honduras with a modern infrastructure. By 1880 most important towns and villages had been tied into a telegraph network with international cable connections to the United States and Europe. Soto also commenced construction of a cart road, the Southern Highway, from Amapala to Tegucigalpa, to which the seat of government had been transferred in 1880. Successors completed this vital artery and extended it to several other important districts. *See also* LIBERAL PARTY (HONDURAS).

Beginning in 1880 American capitalists, and later English ones, formed more than 100 companies to rework old silver and gold mines with modern techniques and imported machinery. With the important exception of the New York and Honduras Rosario Mining Company, most of the concerns failed before they produced much bullion, being overcome by steadily declining silver prices, monetary panics, and a recrudescence of domestic turmoil in Honduras from 1891 to 1894. The mining boom failed to realize early expectations, but many new roads were opened and old ones repaired to facilitate the importation of mining equipment, commerce was stimulated, and small-scale ancillary industries were created.

HONDURAS

Area: 43,277 sq. mi.   Population: 2,495,000 (1969 est.).

By 1900 bananas emerged as the most important Honduran export. For several decades before the turn of the century, ships touching north coast Honduran ports had purchased bananas from natives for sale in New Orleans and other Gulf Coast cities of the United States, but commercial production was delayed until rapid refrigerated shipping became a reality. American capitalists, who possessed the essential entrepreneurial skills and initial investment capital required to establish and manage the large banana plantations, the fleet of cargo ships, and the market outlets abroad, quickly gained control of the industry. By 1930 the two giants, the UNITED FRUIT COMPANY and the Standard Fruit Company, had made Honduras the leading banana exporter in the world, shipping almost 30 million bunches in 1930. By 1940, however, sigatoka and Panama diseases had ravaged the banana plants, and Honduras dropped behind Ecuador in production. *See also* BANANA INDUSTRY (CENTRAL AMERICA AND THE CARIBBEAN).

The development of the banana "enclave" on the north coast wrought important changes in Honduras. A major transfer of population occurred as laborers and service personnel migrated to the north coast from the interior. The demands of the banana plantations encouraged the growth of commercial and light industrial activity in the San Pedro Sula–Puerto Cortés area, causing a shift in the locus of economic power away from Tegucigalpa. The increased wealth accruing to Honduras widened the gap between the upper and lower classes; the banana tax revenue and the influence of foreign elites reinforced the dominant political and social position of the ruling class. Finally, the plantation system provided a fertile environment for developing a labor movement despite efforts by the dictator Tiburcio CARÍAS ANDINO (1933–1948) and his successor, Juan Manuel GÁLVEZ (1949–1954), to discourage union activity. In 1954 banana workers began a wildcat strike for higher wages and a shorter workweek. The strike spread to other industries; ultimately 50,000 wage earners, a sizable portion of the Honduran work force, walked off their jobs. Negotiations for settlement of the strike were prolonged because of the struggle of rival labor leaders for control of ad hoc unionization and because of the fruit companies' lack of good faith.

Since 1950 the government has taken a more direct interest in the development of the country. An ambitious road-building program funded by international agencies has begun integrating the country with all-weather roads and paved arterial highways. Exports of timber, coffee, cotton, and citrus fruits have been encouraged. An AGRARIAN REFORM law enacted under President Ramón VILLEDA MORALES (1957–1963) attempted to eliminate unproductive landholdings. Much-needed programs of public health and municipal sanitation services have been put into operation, causing a rapid population growth. By 1969 the population had reached almost 2.5 million.

By 1950 Central Americans, including Hondurans, had realized the obstacles to further economic development inherent in the small size of their countries. In an effort to overcome this problem, the five countries banded together to form the CENTRAL AMERICAN COMMON MARKET in the late 1950s and early 1960s. Although Honduran exports to the other partners in the

Common Market expanded encouragingly, the country's inferior industrial capacity caused imports to rise at a more rapid pace and the balance of payments to turn permanently against Honduras: in 1968 this imbalance amounted to more than $15 million. Moreover, a provision of the Common Market that eliminated all restrictions on workers seeking employment across frontiers led to a flood of Salvadoran peasants wanting land in relatively unpopulated Honduras. For these and other reasons, relations between Honduras and El Salvador became increasingly strained. Finally a minor incident triggered the so-called FOOTBALL WAR in 1969. In the uneasy aftermath of that conflict Honduras withdrew from the Common Market and reinstated tariffs on Central American imports. At first, officials appeared eager to make Honduras autarkic, but recent negotiations reveal that they are now attempting to use the threat of sabotage of the Common Market system as a means of exacting more favorable conditions for Honduras in its economic intercourse with its Central American neighbors.

Bibliography. Hubert Howe Bancroft, *History of Central America,* vol. III, New York, n.d.; Vincent Checchi et al., *Honduras: A Problem in Economic Development,* New York, 1959; Rómulo E. Durón, *Bosquejo histórico de Honduras, 1502-a–1921,* San Pedro Sula, 1927; Luis Mariñas Otero, *Honduras,* Madrid, 1963; Franklin D. Parker, *The Central American Republics,* London, 1964; Ephraim G. Squier, *Honduras: Descriptive, Historical, and Statistical,* London, 1870; Charles L. Stansifer, "E. George Squier and the Honduras Interoceanic Railroad Project," *Hispanic American Historic Review,* vol. XLVI, no. 1, February 1966, pp. 1–27; William S. Stokes, *Honduras: An Area Study in Government,* Madison, Wis., 1950.

KENNETH V. FINNEY

HOPKINS, EDWARD A[UGUSTUS] (1823–1888). North American entrepreneur and the first United States diplomatic agent to the Republic of Paraguay (1851–1855). An officer in the United States Navy, Hopkins resigned from the service in 1845 to pursue a dream of exploiting the untapped riches of South America and becoming wealthy in the process. He had economic interests in several American republics, but Paraguay attracted him the most, and in 1845 he obtained an appointment from President James Polk as special agent to Paraguay, basically to ascertain whether the United States should recognize that nation. In Paraguay he exceeded his orders and assured President Carlos Antonio LÓPEZ that the United States would soon recognize Paraguay, writing Secretary of State James Buchanan that Paraguay must be recognized because it was a modern, powerful state.

After his initial short visit, Hopkins made several other trips to Paraguay in the late 1840s, explored the country, and expounded on its commercial possibilities. In 1851 he was appointed United States Consul to Paraguay just as López was making him a special Paraguayan envoy to the United States. Hopkins promised United States recognition of Paraguay in return for a monopoly of steam navigation on the Paraguay River. He returned to the United States, set up a navigation company, and then went back to Paraguay with machinery and trade goods and the sought-for recognition. However, López soon lost his appreciation of Hopkins and, in 1855, had him expelled, revoking the steam navigation charter. Litigation, diplomatic difficulties, and arbitration dragged on for decades. Hopkins died in 1888, burdened with the debts occasioned by the collapse of his company.

JOHN HOYT WILLIAMS

HOSTOS [Y BONILLA], EUGENIO MARÍA DE (1839–1903). Puerto Rican educator, philosopher, sociologist, and man of letters. Born near Mayagüez, Hostos was sent to Spain at an early age, studying at a secondary school in Bilbao and at the University of Madrid. Disillusioned by the unwillingness of Spanish republican leaders to grant autonomy to Puerto Rico and Cuba, he left Spain in 1869 for New York, where he associated himself with the Cuban revolutionary junta there. The following year he embarked upon a long tour of South America to promote the cause of Antillean independence. In 1875 he was in Puerto Plata, Dominican Republic, where he briefly published a periodical, *Las Tres Antillas,* advocating the creation of a confederation comprising Cuba, Puerto Rico, and the Dominican Republic. After a sojourn in Venezuela during which he married the daughter of a Cuban *émigré,* he returned to the Dominican Republic. During his nine-year stay in that country (1879–1888), he wrought great changes in its educational system. He founded its first normal school, helped reorganize public instruction by using modern pedagogical methods, and introduced scientific and experimental techniques into the curriculum. Moreover, he helped expose all of Dominican society to the intellectual currents of the outside world, from which it had long been isolated.

Difficulties with the government of the Dominican dictator Ulises HEUREAUX led Hostos to accept the invitation of the Chilean government to undertake a program of educational reform there. He remained in the southern republic from 1889 to 1898, serving as rector of the Liceo Miguel Luis Amunátegui in Santiago and as professor of constitutional law at the University of Chile.

Despite his long absence from the Caribbean area, Hostos' concern for the political future of Cuba and his native Puerto Rico had not waned. Moved by the outbreak of revolution in Cuba and by the likelihood of United States intervention, Hostos left Chile for New York in April 1898. By the time he reached New York not only had the United States gone to war against Spain, but United States occupation of Puerto Rico was a certainty. Hostos now sought, without success, the rapid establishment of a civilian government in Puerto Rico by the United States and the holding of a plebiscite to determine the fate of the island. After the assassination of Heureaux in 1899, Hostos was invited to resume his educational labors in the Dominican Republic and remained there until his death.

Hostos was a prolific writer, and his *Obras completas,* published by the Puerto Rican government in 1939, fill twenty volumes. Among his best-known works are a critical essay on *Hamlet* (1873); *Moral social* (1888), in which he set forth a moral code for the individual in society; and *Tratado de sociología* (1904), based partly on his lectures on sociology at the Normal School in Santo Domingo. HELEN DELPAR

HUAYNA CAPAC (d. 1526). Eleventh Inca emperor. Beginning his rule in 1493 as a young boy, he successfully and spectacularly weathered the conspiracies usual for such royal beginnings and survived until 1526. While he was in Bolivia overseeing the expansion of tribute in precious metals, he received news that the whole northern part of the empire had revolted. In 1511 he moved to counter this threat. It was not until 1522, after years of desperate campaigning in Ecuador, that he was able to restore order. In 1524, however, he embarked upon a quixotic raid into the coastal lowlands of Ecuador in which his losses were compounded by the epidemic that preceded Francisco PIZARRO's arrival. The disease swept the length and breadth of the empire, radically weakening it. Huayna Capac himself died of it in Quito and inadvertently left the empire split between two sons, Huascar and ATAHUALPA. This split opened the door to Pizarro's entry in 1532, six years after the death of Huayna Capac. *See also* INCAS.

BURR C. BRUNDAGE

HUDSON, W[ILLIAM] H[ENRY] (1841–1922). Argentine-born writer and field naturalist. Hudson was born in a farmhouse called "The Twenty-Five Ombús" near Buenos Aires, the son of American parents who had emigrated to Argentina in the 1830s. He spent his boyhood on the pampas (*see* PAMPA), receiving a haphazard education and assisting his father in his rather unsuccessful ventures as a rancher and storekeeper. Hudson early developed a lifelong love of birds and in 1866 began to send collections of bird skins to the Smithsonian Institution in Washington. In later life he would become a strong supporter of measures to protect birds against unnecessary slaughter. In 1874 Hudson left Argentina and settled permanently in England, becoming a British subject in 1900.

A literary rather than a scientific naturalist, Hudson was able to convey in fresh and limpid prose what John Galsworthy called his "unspoiled unity with Nature." Several of his best-known works are set in the Río de la Plata region. These include *The Purple Land That England Lost* (1885), an episodic novel dealing with the adventures of a young man in Uruguay; *The Naturalist in La Plata* (1892) and *Idle Days in Patagonia* (1893), essays; *El Ombú* (1902), stories; and *Far Away and Long Ago* (1918), an autobiography. Hudson's most famous work of fiction is *Green Mansions* (1904), a novel set in the Venezuelan forest, which he never visited, and dealing with the mysterious bird girl, Rima. Hudson's essays on English themes include *Nature in Downland* (1900), *A Shepherd's Life* (1910), and *A Hind in Richmond Park* (1922).

HELEN DELPAR

HUERTA, VICTORIANO (1854–1916). Mexican general and President (1913–1914). Huerta was born in Colotlán, Jalisco, of Huichol Indian parents. He was a brilliant student at the Colegio Militar and distinguished himself alongside Manuel González in the Division of the West in 1880 and in the pacification of a Maya uprising in YUCATÁN (*see* MAYAS) at the beginning of the twentieth century. When Bernardo Reyes became Secretary of War, he recommended Huerta as Undersecretary, but Huerta was unable to fill this post since President Porfirio DÍAZ forced Reyes to resign. To the consternation of Reyes, Huerta then proposed arresting Díaz and the leading CIENTÍFICOS. Later Huerta worked in Monterrey as an engineer under Reyes's protection.

In 1911 Huerta used extreme severity in attempting to quell the uprising of Emiliano ZAPATA; the following year he opposed the rebellion of Pascual Orozco. In February 1913, President Francisco I. MADERO entrusted Huerta with the task of defeating a revolt initiated in Mexico City by Félix Díaz, nephew of the exiled dictator. Huerta, however, made common cause with the rebels, arrested Madero, who was murdered, and made himself President. As President, Huerta had the support of some intellectuals, who in the midst of the general militarization of the country drafted two moderate AGRARIAN REFORM laws. Defeated by the Constitutionalists, Huerta resigned on July 15, 1914, and fled to the United States. He attempted to return to Mexico but was arrested on June 27, 1915, in the company of his old enemy Pascual Orozco and died a prisoner in Fort Bliss, San Antonio, Texas. According to some accounts, he was poisoned; according to others, he died of the effects of an unsuccessful operation to alleviate the cirrhosis caused by his alcoholism.

See also VERACRUZ, OCCUPATION OF; WILSON, Henry Lane. MOISÉS GONZÁLEZ NAVARRO

HUIDOBRO, VICENTE (in full, VICENTE GARCÍA HUIDOBRO FERNÁNDEZ; 1893–1948). Chilean poet. Born in Santiago, he was educated by the Jesuits. An independent income enabled him to go to Paris in 1916 and explore its cultural atmosphere and enter its literary and artistic circles. Huidobro contributed to the review *Nord Sud*, edited by the French poet Pierre Reverdy, and collaborated with Hans Arp in *Tres inmensas novelas* (1934). He also expounded a literary doctrine, called *creacionismo*, which reacted against tradition and regarded each poem as an absolutely new creation and which he defended in his *Manifiestos* (*Manifestes*, 1925). In Madrid he collaborated in the review *Ultra*, which gave its name to the movement known as *ultraismo*, and in 1924 he founded in Paris the review *Création*. Huidobro then returned to Chile and entered politics, running unsuccessfully for the Presidency in 1925, but continued writing. He fought in the Spanish Civil War and was a reporter in World War II.

Huidobro's poetry appeared both in Spanish and in French. It includes *Las pagodas ocultas* (1914); *Adán* (1916); *El espejo de agua* (1916); *Horizonte cuadrado* (*Horizon carré*, 1917); *Poemas árticos* (1918); *Torre Eiffel* (*Tour Eiffel*, 1918); *De repente* (*Tout à coup*, 1925); *El pasajero de su destino* (1930); *Altazor o El viaje en paracaídas* (1931), his masterpiece; *Ver y palpar* (1941); and *El ciudadano del olvido* (1941), in which his vision is deepened. Among his better novels are *Mío Cid Campeador* (1929), *Cagliostro, novela-film* (1934), and *Sátiro o El poder de las palabras* (1939). He also wrote plays, but these were not successful. RACHEL PHILLIPS

HUITZILOPOCHTLI. Tutelary deity of the Mexica AZTECS who was later identified with the sun. The name means "Hummingbird of the Left," and "left" is a synonym of "south," hence the "Southern Hummingbird." His oracles had led the Mexica on their wanderings from Chicomoztoc until they finally found their capital city of Mexico. In Mexico Huitzilopochtli shared the summit of the centrally located temple pyramid with the rain god Tlaloc. Like Tonatiuh, the sun god, Huitzilopochtli was a fighting god. He thus had close connections, through capture of prisoners in war, with the sacrificial cult. One major cosmic myth shows him in battle with his siblings, the titanic Centzon Huitznahua, who have been thought by some scholars to represent the stars. These titans were led by their sister, a goddess named Coyolxauhqui, who was almost certainly the moon. Huitzilopochtli, here an avatar of the sun, bursts from the womb of his mother, Coatlicue, the Earth, defeats the enemy host, and decapitates Coyolxauhqui. BURR C. BRUNDAGE

HULL-ALFARO TREATY. Officially known as the General Treaty of Friendship and Cooperation between the United States of America and Panama, the agreement amending the HAY–BUNAU-VARILLA TREATY was signed in Washington on March 2, 1936, by Secretary of State Cordell Hull and the Foreign Minister of Panama, Ricardo J. ALFARO. The result of the new era of the GOOD NEIGHBOR POLICY and of many years of Panamanian dissatisfaction with the terms of the original treaty, the document made substantial concessions to Panama. The United States renounced its guarantee of the independence of Panama, the right to expropriate additional land for PANAMA CANAL use without restrictions, the right of eminent domain in the cities of Panama and Colón, and the unlimited right to defend the canal. The treaty provided, however, that if some unforeseen emergency developed, the two governments would consult about the use of additional lands and waters in the maintenance, sanitation, and efficient operation of the canal, as well as on defense matters. The annual annuity of $250,000 to the Republic of Panama was increased to $430,000, to compensate Panama for the depreciation of the American dollar since 1934. Additional concessions to Panama included restrictions on the sale of commissary goods in the Canal Zone, the prohibition of private businesses in the zone, and extension of commercial privileges in the zone, such as free sites for customhouses. The United States Senate withheld approval of the treaty until July 25, 1939, after negotiations between the two governments assured United States freedom to act without consultation in defense emergencies. RICHARD B. GRAY

HUMAITÁ. Fortress situated 20 miles north of the confluence of the Paraná and Paraguay Rivers in Paraguay, designed to control access to the country. A battery and guard post had been present at Humaitá since the late colonial period, but it was only in the 1850s, when Brazil obtained the right of free transit on the Paraguay River north to Mato Grosso, that the site was transformed into a major bastion. This "Sevastopol of the Americas" mounted 380 cannon, many of large bore, at the outbreak of the PARAGUAYAN WAR in 1864 and soon became the key defensive focus of Paraguay's war effort. In June 1867, the Allies began a costly thirteen-month siege of the fortress. After several sanguinary battles with the large garrison, which for a time was directed by the dictator Francisco Solano LÓPEZ in person, they choked off the fort. In July 1868, the last starving remnants of the garrison evacuated the fort, and the battles of the siege, which had claimed about 100,000 lives, were at an end. The ruins of Humaitá, especially those of the church near its center, are today virtually national shrines for Paraguayans. JOHN HOYT WILLIAMS

HUMBOLDT, ALEXANDER VON (1769–1859). German scientist, born in Berlin. After a thorough scientific education in his native country and several European trips, he was granted permission to visit the Spanish empire. Accompanied by the French botanist Aimé Bonpland, Humboldt left Europe in 1799, traveling to Venezuela, Cuba, New Granada, Quito, and Peru. On the return trip he traveled through Mexico, Cuba, and the United States, returning to Europe in 1804. Probably no other foreign traveler had so thorough an acquaintance with the Spanish possessions. His scientific curiosity led him to visit the Orinoco, Negro, and Marañón Rivers in South America, Indian villages in the jungles, the volcanic peaks of the Andean range, Mexican mines, and Cuban sugar mills. Wherever he went, he took geographical measurements, collected mineral, botanical, and zoological samples, visited centers of education, and befriended the local learned men. As a result, he gathered a vast amount of information about Spanish America, which he published in Europe in numerous books and essays.

Humboldt's best-known works on American subjects are the thirty-volume *Voyage aux régions équinoxiales du Nouveau Continent*, 1807–1834 (*Personal Narrative of Travels to the Equinoctial Regions of the New Continent*); *Essai politique sur le royaume de la Nouvelle Espagne*, 1811 (*Political Essay on the Kingdom of New Spain*), which is part of the former; and *Essai politique sur l'île de Cuba*, 1826 (*Political Essay on the Island of Cuba*). In these works he concerned himself not only with the description of the physical world but also with social, economic, and political conditions in the countries he visited, not failing to point out the obstacles to their development. Although he was not free of bias, his enlightened liberal mind was able to provide a balanced view of the last years of the Spanish empire that has remained an unmatched source of information.

ASUNCIÓN LAVRIN

HUMBOLDT CURRENT (PERU CURRENT). Pacific Ocean current named after Baron Alexander von HUMBOLDT, the German scientist who first measured its temperature. The Humboldt Current flows north along the coast of Chile and Peru to the Ecuadorian border, where it turns west. It is divided into the Peru Oceanic Current and the Peru Coastal Current. The latter, which is from 50 to 100 miles wide, shapes Peru's coastal climate and economy. Since its waters are cold (average temperature, 58 to 64°F), it cools the air above the sea, increasing its stability. The result is that, with most of the moisture provided by a thick fog which hovers for months over the region, the coast has been turned into a desert dotted with oases created by streams flowing from the Andes to the Pacific. Periodically the climatic stability of the region is upset by a warm current from the equator. At intervals of five to ten years, usually around Christmas, it displaces the cold Humboldt Current, causing gigantic flood damage.

One beneficial result of the Humboldt Current is that it makes the year-long temperature along the coast mild—sunny in the summer and cloudy and damp in the winter. More important, by bringing with it large quantities of marine organisms, the current has given rise to a biological chain leading next to fish and finally to birds, whose fecal material has accumulated in large quantities on coastal headlands. Known as GUANO, this material is used as a fertilizer both in Peru and overseas. The large fish concentration has also engendered the development of a fish-meal industry.

ORAZIO A. CICCARELLI

HUNDRED-HOUR WAR. *See* FOOTBALL WAR.

IBÁÑEZ [DEL CAMPO], CARLOS (1877–1960). President of Chile (1927–1931, 1952–1958). Born in Linares of modest farming stock, Ibáñez was educated locally before entering the Military School in 1896. Graduating in 1898, he became a lieutenant in 1900. As a member of a military mission to El Salvador (1903–1908), he distinguished himself in a short engagement with Guatemalan troops that won him a medal and a hero's reputation. Back in Chile and now a captain, he spent two years at the War Academy with other junior officers who with Ibáñez were to play a significant part in Chilean affairs. Various posts of military responsibility and promotion to major followed. In 1919–1920 Ibáñez served as prefect of police in Iquique; this firsthand experience of a depressed area probably did much to mold his outlook.

As commander of the Cavalry School in Santiago from 1921 on, Ibáñez witnessed the impasse between President Arturo ALESSANDRI and the Congress at a time of increasing civic unrest. In 1924, when Congress voted salaries for its members in defiance of the constitution while government servants, including army officers, had not been paid for six months, Ibáñez and other junior officers intervened. They demonstrated in Congress, and when the high command refused to discipline them, Alessandri asked for their demands. At this point Ibáñez, who had become prominent in the group, took command and with another officer drew up a list of demands for social as well as military reform. Forced to act, Alessandri appointed Gen. Luis Altamirano Minister of the Interior, vetoed the congres-

sional salary bill, and sent the list to Congress, which in one day approved laws embodying all the demands. At the suggestion of Ibáñez a military junta was established; when it refused to disband at Alessandri's request, the President threatened to resign but was offered instead a six-month leave of absence. The high command took over, but its conservatism perturbed the junior officers, who, led by Ibáñez and Marmaduke Grove, seized power early in 1925 and recalled Alessandri from Europe. However, Ibáñez was now convinced that only the rule of a determined man could regenerate Chile, and as Minister of War he worked to attain that objective. Alessandri's increasing distrust of Ibáñez eventually led to the President's resignation. Under his successor, the ineffectual Emiliano Figueroa, Ibáñez built up support, first at the War Ministry and then as Minister of the Interior. Figueroa's own resignation in 1927 left Ibáñez supreme, and he won the ensuing presidential election with 98 percent of the vote.

Ibáñez gave Chile four years of firm, honest, and repressive government. He reorganized provincial administration, ended the TACNA-ARICA QUESTION with Peru, modernized the police force, restructured education, and carried out other reforms. He began a vast program of public works, financed largely by foreign loans, and presided over a period of economic boom. He also put politics into cold storage, suppressed opposition newspapers, and exiled opposition leaders. The Great Depression then hit Chile hard, and material progress, the major justification for the Ibáñez dictatorship, disappeared as foreign investment dried up, unemployment

Carlos Ibáñez. [*Organization of American States*]

increased, and austerity was the rule. The violent repression of discontent created so serious a situation that in July 1931 Ibáñez resigned and left the country.

Ibáñez remained a force in Chilean politics after his return to the country in 1937, and in 1942, as the only opponent of Juan Antonio RÍOS, he secured 44 percent of the vote in the presidential election. Ten years later, at the age of seventy-four, he won the Presidency with almost 47 percent of the vote. His election was, in effect, an endorsement of a father figure who had stood above party irresponsibility, but it was almost a disaster. The aged President could not grapple with rampant inflation or cope with constantly changing Cabinets, though he created the Ministry of Mines, the State Bank, the Housing Corporation, and other enduring administrative organs. When Ibáñez died in 1960, his funeral was attended by some of the largest crowds ever seen in Santiago, but he had remained to the end the most isolated and enigmatic figure in modern Chilean history.

Bibliography. Raúl Aldunate Phillips, *Ruido de sables,* Santiago, 1970; Luis Correa Prieto, *El presidente Ibáñez, la política y los políticos: Apuntes para la historia,* Santiago, 1962; C. H. Haring, "The Chilean Revolution of 1931," *Hispanic American Historical Review,* vol. XIII, no. 2, May 1933, pp. 197–203; René Montero, *La verdad sobre Ibáñez,* Santiago, 1952; Frederick M. Nunn, *Chilean Politics, 1920–1931: The Honorable Mission of the Armed Forces,* Albuquerque, N.Mex., 1970; Aquiles Vergara Vicuña, *Ibáñez, césar criollo,* 2 vols., Santiago, 1931; Carlos Vicuña, *La tiranía en Chile,* 2 vols., 2d ed., Santiago, 1945; Ernesto Würth Rojas, *Ibáñez, caudillo enigmático,* Santiago, 1958.

HAROLD BLAKEMORE

IBARBOUROU, JUANA DE (1895–   ). Uruguayan writer, honored in 1929 with the title Juana de América. In 1947 she was made a member of the National Academy of Letters, and in 1959 she won the first National Prize of Literature to be awarded in Uruguay. Her work deals mainly with the different phases and aspects of love and was regarded as daring when it first appeared. She has published *Las lenguas de diamante* (1919), which was immediately successful; *Cántaro fresco* (1920), poems in prose; *Raíz salvaje* (1922); *La rosa de los vientos* (1930); *Los loores de Nuestra Señora y estampas de la Biblia* (1934); *Chico Carlo* (1944), autobiographical stories of her childhood; *Perdida* (1950); *Azor* (1953); and *Oro y tormenta* (1956). She has also written for children: *Ejemplario* (1927), stories; and *Los sueños de Natacha* (1945), plays.
RACHEL PHILLIPS

ICAZA, JORGE (1906–   ). Ecuadorian novelist. A native of Quito, he achieved fame with *Huasipungo,* 1934 (*The Villagers*), one of the cornerstones of American *indigenista* literature. This novel uses an impersonal technique without individual characterization to show the destruction of an Indian village by a combination of greedy landowners and foreign investors. Icaza's second novel, *En las calles* (1935), similarly presents the problem of social revolt in a small town. *Cholos* (1938) analyzes the social humiliation of the city halfbreed, and *Media vida deslumbrados* (1942) explores the racial inferiority complex of Indians and mestizos. *Huairapamushcas* (1948) returns with slight modifications to the problem of *Huasipungo.* Later works include two books of stories, *Seis relatos* (1952) and *Viejos cuentos* (1960), and a novel, *El chulla Romero y Flores* (1958).
RACHEL PHILLIPS

IDB. *See* INTER-AMERICAN DEVELOPMENT BANK.

ILLIA, ARTURO (1900–   ). President of Argentina (1963–1966). Illia's most decisive actions occurred in the foreign relations field. He canceled the American oil concessions negotiated by Arturo FRONDIZI, rejected further agreements with the International Monetary Fund, and emphasized Argentina's identity with developing nations.

In domestic terms his attempts at moderation led to a "do-nothing" image. Elected with only 26 percent of the vote as the candidate of the Unión Cívica Radical del Pueblo (*see* RADICAL PARTY: ARGENTINA), he was forced to govern without a congressional majority. Committed to a political solution of Argentina's problems and hoping to capitalize on divisions in the Peronist movement (*see* PERONISM), Illia promised Peronists legality. Nevertheless, when the 1965 elections resulted in a strong Peronist showing, he moved to polarize political opinion into rigid Peronist–anti-Peronist sectors.

Most dangerous for Illia, however, was his attitude toward the military. Although the Azul (Blue) military faction was clearly the stronger, the President consistently favored the Colorados (Reds). The elimination of the Azul commander in chief, Juan Carlos ONGANÍA, in late 1965 heralded Illia's political fall. When provincial elections showed that in a polarized atmosphere the Peronists might gain the important elections in 1967, the military deposed Illia.
NOREEN F. STACK

IMMIGRATION (ARGENTINA). Few elements in Argentina's past have contributed more toward shaping the contemporary scene than the massive influx of European immigrants during the late nineteenth and early twentieth centuries. While the sheer numbers of new arrivals were impressive in themselves, the impact of immigration upon Argentine development was exaggerated because of the small native population. In 1856 scarcely 1.2 million Argentines awaited the 6.5 million foreigners who would arrive by 1930.

The period of sustained, massive immigration extended roughly from definitive national political organization in 1862 until the world economic crisis of 1930. From the beginning of the independence movement in 1810 until 1862 immigration did not play a crucial role in national development. In the two decades after 1810 support for immigration constituted part of the Liberal credo, but government-funded schemes yielded only a few short-lived agricultural colonies in the mid-1820s. During the era of Juan Manuel de ROSAS (1829–1852) support for immigration ceased, since immigrants were considered unnecessary in the ranch-dominated grazing economy of Rosas' cattle civilization. Government policies aside, Argentina's unstable politics and economic backwardness made it an unattractive haven for prospective European immigrants prior to 1862.

With political order established after 1862, Argentina's controlling liberal elite attacked the problem of economic development. Central to its plans was the attraction of massive European immigration. Imported manpower, along with primarily British capital and technology, was to be employed to release the vast agricultural potential of the PAMPA. Some justified immigration on racial grounds, denigrating the native creole and Indian stock and lauding the "civilizing" virtues of Europeans, but the basic rationale was economic. Immigrants were to supply the work force absent in Argentina's sparsely settled rural expanses.

Starting slowly in the 1860s and 1870s, immigration reached major proportions in the 1880s, decreased somewhat during the domestic economic setback of 1890s, and then posted record marks between 1904 and 1914. After a hiatus induced by World War I, the European flow resumed until the Depression struck in 1930. Italians (47 percent) and Spaniards (32 percent) dominated the immigrant stream, while significant numbers also arrived from Poland, Russia, France, and Germany. Most of the immigrants tended to be lower-class skilled and unskilled males of working age whose primary motivation was economic and whose ultimate goal was to return home with sufficient capital to purchase land in their native villages. That many did make the return trip is indicated by the fact that from 1871 to 1913 Argentina retained only 56 percent of the new arrivals. Seasonal agricultural laborers called *golondrinas* (swallows) contributed heavily to the emigrant ranks.

In part, the expectations of the ruling elite were fulfilled. Immigrant labor propelled Argentina into the ranks of the world's premier agricultural exporters. However, the modernizing thrust of immigration stimulated other profound changes less palatable to the elite, changes that resulted in challenges by new groups to the elite's monopolization of the political and economic power structure.

Demographically, immigrants fueled the process of urbanization, which swelled the urban sector of the population from 29 percent in 1869 to 53 percent in 1914. Denied ownership of rural properties by short-sighted land policies, immigrants flocked to the federal capital and other major cities. By 1914 three of four adults in Buenos Aires were foreign-born. Economically, immigrants not only provided large shares of the rural and urban working forces but controlled much of the nation's commercial and industrial activity before 1930. Socially, the mutually supportive forces of immigration and economic modernization broke down the two-class structure inherited from colonial days. In the more complicated and flexible replacement that evolved, immigrants predominated in both the new middle groups and the rising urban proletariat. Politically, these two groups constituted a reservoir upon which new parties drew for support in offering alternatives to the traditionally closed political system. Culturally, the impact of immigration still lacks clear definition. While specific contributions in terms of language, food, dress, and the like can be cataloged, particularly from the Italian and Spanish communities, the final amalgam has yet to work itself out.

In the Depression years of the 1930s and on through World War II, immigration was almost nonexistent. The decade after 1947 witnessed a renewal of European arrivals, with Argentina's net gain exceeding 550,000, some 60 percent of whom were Italian.

Particularly notable since the war has been the increasing immigration from Argentina's neighbors; between 1945 and 1964 a total of 242,500 came from Paraguay, 101,200 from Bolivia, and 80,400 from Chile. Consisting primarily of poverty-stricken rural folk, most of this flow is clandestine and closely resembles the internal migration characteristic of Argentina since the 1930s. Both the foreigners and the native migrants gravitate toward urban centers, especially Buenos Aires, where they live in slum conditions.

Bibliography. Oscar E. Cornblit, "European Immigrants in Argentine Industry and Politics," in Claudio Véliz (ed.), *The Politics of Conformity in Latin America*, London, 1967, pp. 221–248; Gino Germani, *Política y sociedad en una época de transición*, Buenos Aires, 1962; id., "Mass Immigration and Modernization in Argentina," in Irving L. Horowitz et al., *Latin American Radicalism*, New York, 1969, pp. 314–355; José Panettieri, *Inmigración en la Argentina*, Buenos Aires, 1970; Carl Solberg, *Immigration and Nationalism: Argentina and Chile, 1890–1914*, Austin, Tex., 1970.

JAMES E. BUCHANAN

IMMIGRATION (BRAZIL). Brazil ranks fourth among the immigration countries of the Western Hemisphere, after the United States, Argentina, and Canada. In 1500, when the Portuguese first set foot on the shores of Brazil, the native Indians did not exceed 1.5 million in number. Today, owing largely to immigration, Brazil has a population of nearly 100 million. In the intervening four and three-quarter centuries more than 10 million free and compulsory immigrants from Europe, Africa, and Asia entered Brazil. The intermingling of the indigenous Indians with Europeans, Africans, and a sprinkling of Asians has created a distinct people and culture that can only be described as Brazilian.

Throughout Brazil's colonial era Portugal discouraged other nationalities from entering the country. Hence immigration consisted almost entirely of Portuguese and Africans (*see* NEGRO IN BRAZIL). Portugal did not have the human resources to colonize its new possession quickly, and it was not until gold was discovered in the interior in the 1690s that mass immigration began. In the 1740s immigration restrictions were relaxed, and Europeans other than Portuguese were encouraged to migrate to Brazil, but the only significant response was the arrival of 4,000 couples from the Azores and Madeira.

Contemporaneous with the arrival of the Portuguese but more extensive was the influx of African slaves to Brazil during the colonial period. It is estimated that 2.5 million Africans were transported to Brazil in colonial times, as compared with 1.5 million Portuguese. An estimate of the total population for 1800 gives the figure 3,617,900, more than half being slaves. This comparatively small population and its high proportion of blacks to whites were the principal factors in determining immigration policy during the nineteenth and twentieth centuries.

From the early 1800s to the present approximately 5.5 million immigrants came voluntarily to Brazil. The vast majority of this number entered in the years from 1887 to 1934 and settled almost exclusively in the four southernmost states of São Paulo, Paraná, Santa Catarina, and Rio Grande do Sul. Prior to 1887 immigration was a mere trickle, and since 1934 the movement has been severely curtailed by a quota system.

After Prince Regent João (later JOÃO VI) arrived in Brazil in 1808, the Brazilian government, hoping to introduce diversified agriculture, settle the frontiers, and "whiten" the race, launched a program of colonization that actively sought immigrants outside Portugal. From 1820 to 1847 the efforts of government and private colonization companies succeeded in enticing only 16,666 immigrants to Brazilian shores. The colonial heritage of slave labor, large estates, and lack of religious freedom, together with an image of a disease-infested tropical land, was an effective barrier that nullified the good intentions of national and local governments and prevented any sizable influx of immigrants for the first three-quarters of the nineteenth century.

The year 1850 marked a turning point in the history of Brazilian immigration and colonization. That year the slave trade was abolished, and plantation owners began to look to Europe as a source of labor. In the following decades immigration steadily increased, experiencing a sudden expansion with the emancipation of the slaves in 1888. Local and national governments, in conjunction with coffee planters, subsidized the immigration of agricultural workers. This brought to São Paulo the lion's share of immigration from 1889 onward.

The concerted efforts of federal, provincial, and private sectors produced immediate results. From 1890 to 1900 inclusive, 1,251,376 immigrants arrived. More than 1 million arrived in the decade prior to World War I, and in the following sixty years nearly 2.5 million newcomers, including 250,000 Japanese, entered the country. Southern Europeans predominated, numbering 80 percent of all immigrants. Portuguese comprised more than 30 percent of the total, and Italians were a close second, with slightly less than 30 percent. Next came the Spaniards, with approximately 14 percent, followed by proportionally smaller numbers of Japanese, Germans, Turks, Poles, Russians, French, North Americans, English, Jews, and Chinese.

Immigration has had a profound impact on Brazilian society. Although the African was the backbone of the colonial economy and deeply affected Brazilian folklore and popular music, it was the Portuguese who gave Brazil its language, its religion, its institutions, and most of its traditions and customs. Wave after wave of Europeans, particularly in the last 100 years, not only served to reaffirm and fortify European civilization in Brazil but accelerated the "whitening of the race," contributed substantially to the rapid growth of urbanization, and played a major role in the technological awakening that stimulated Brazil's thrust toward modernization.

Bibliography. Fidélis Dolcin Barbosa (ed.), *Semblantes de Pioneiros: Vultos e Fatos da Colonização Italiana no Rio Grande do Sul,* Pôrto Alegre, 1961; José Fernando Carneiro, *Imigração e Colonização no Brasil,* Rio de Janeiro, 1950; Manuel Diégues, Jr., *Imigração, Urbanização, Industrialização,* Rio de Janeiro, 1964; Maurilio de Gouveia, *História da Escravidão,* Rio de Janeiro, 1955; Lawrence F. Hill, "Confederate Exiles to Brazil," *Hispanic American Historical Review,* vol. VII, 1927, pp. 192–210; Michael G. Mulhall, *Rio Grande do Sul and Its German Colonies,* London, 1873; Rollie E. Poppino, *Brazil: The Land and People,* New York, 1968; Hiroshi Saito, *O Japonês no Brasil: Estudo de Mobilidade e Fixação,* São Paulo, 1961.

ARNOLD J. MEAGHER

IMMIGRATION (PARAGUAY). Immigration to Paraguay, which took place primarily between 1880 and 1950, was notable in two ways. First, the majority of the settlers were Germanic in origin. Between 1881 and 1948, twenty-one settlements were made in Paraguay by German-speaking immigrants. After the disastrous PARAGUAYAN WAR (1864–1870) had decimated the population, the government did its best to stimulate foreign immigration, especially of sturdy farm folk. The Germans answered this need, and their communities were settled in disputed border areas such as the CHACO or in thinly settled parts of the interior. The German-speaking Mennonite settlements of the Chaco (Menno, Fernheim, and Neuland) were the largest initial settlements, totaling 6,143 original settlers. These settlements in the hostile environment of the Chaco helped make that region a contributing part of Paraguay. The second characteristic of the immigration was the group or community basis of settlement. Not only did most Germans enter Paraguay and settle in colonies, but Czechoslovak, Sudeten, Polish, Russian, and Japanese communities were established as well. Other, unsuccessful attempts at group settlement were made by immigrants from England, France, Australia, Sweden, and Italy. Although these colonies failed, many individuals remained. Finally, after World War II a rather large wave of German immigrants (including some fanatical ex-Nazis) entered Paraguay, many to stay. These, however, came as individuals. It is estimated that in 1958 Paraguay contained 75,000 immigrants in a total population of 1,800,000. *See also* MENNONITES IN PARAGUAY.

JOHN HOYT WILLIAMS

IMMIGRATION (URUGUAY). European immigration has had a major impact upon Uruguayan culture and society. From a sparsely populated area characterized by cattle, gauchos (*see* GAUCHO), and traditional *criollo* values, Uruguay within a few decades was transformed into a modern urbanized nation.

Compared with the influx to other immigrant countries such as Argentina, the total number of Europeans coming to Uruguay was relatively small; fewer than 1 million immigrants are estimated to have arrived between 1836 and 1926. The small native population and the fact that most immigrants remained in the cities, however, meant that these newcomers would have a significant effect upon the country. Although the heaviest immigration did not occur until early in the twentieth century, by 1840 there were more foreign-born than native residents of Montevideo; in 1900 one-third of the total population was foreign-born, while a substantial part of the remainder consisted of first-generation Uruguayans.

Italy and Spain accounted for the greatest portion of the immigrants. From 50 to 75 percent of those entering the country between 1880 and 1926 came from these two nations, with Italians in the majority until about 1905 and Spaniards becoming the dominant group thereafter. Among other nations from which immigrants came in smaller but significant numbers were England, France, and Brazil. Immigration has declined in recent decades, but even in 1970 it was estimated that 14 percent of Uruguay's population was foreign-born.

LEE C. FENNELL

IMMIGRATION (VENEZUELA). Since its separation from Gran Colombia in 1830, Venezuela has received a small but steady stream of foreign nationals who have come to make their fortune, and sometimes their homes, in the country. Although throughout the nineteenth century the Venezuelan government constantly talked about the need for immigrants, its policies seemed to provoke little enthusiasm among the dispossessed of Europe, primarily because Venezuela wanted laborers who would help develop the land owned by the great *latifundistas*. Moreover, during most of the nineteenth century Venezuela required that immigrants be Catholics. By the beginning of the Federal Wars (1858–1863) Venezuela had received fewer than 60,000 immigrants, most of these Canary Island Spaniards. In 1842 the government sponsored a small colonization project, Colonia Tovar, which in 1844 brought about 400 Catholic Germans to settle on an inaccessible and unproductive part of the Tovar family estates. The colony survived, but just barely, keeping its population at about 500; it is now a quaint tourist attraction. By the end of the nineteenth century Venezuela had living within its boundaries about 35,000 foreigners, a third of whom were Spaniards and Colombians.

During the first third of the twentieth century Venezuela received an average net gain of more than 1,000 persons per year, but as a result of the oil boom and the conditions in Europe caused by the Spanish Civil War and World War II this figure grew considerably. By the first years of the military junta of Marcos PÉREZ JI-MÉNEZ the country was receiving a net gain of more than 20,000 people a year. Indeed, of all the Venezuelan governments that talked about immigration, the Pérez Jiménez regime seemed best able to attract large numbers of people. Between 1949 and 1957 about 350,000 more people entered than left Venezuela. The peak years were 1952–1957, with an average annual net gain

of more than 45,000. This sizable contingent of newcomers originated in Spain, Italy, and Portugal in a ratio of 7 to 3 to 1. Most of these immigrants settled in the Caracas area, where they entered, and in places dominated, the construction trades (especially finishing work), the taxi and jitney services, and the small neighborhood grocery stores. After the fall of Pérez Jiménez in 1958 this flow of people into Venezuela ended. Between 1958 and 1969 the net gain from foreign immigration barely reached 45,000 in all, and between 1960 and 1962 and again between 1967 and 1969 there was a net loss of foreign population. Beginning in 1960, however, Venezuela received each year perhaps 10,000 illegal Colombian immigrants, principally in the Andean states and Maracaibo, who presented the government with serious social, economic, and diplomatic problems.

In quantitative terms Venezuela has not been greatly affected by foreign immigration, with the possible exception of the Caracas area. But from the ranks of these immigrants, especially those produced by the Spanish Civil War and World War II, have come some of Venezuela's most capable educators, intellectuals, and businessmen.

JOHN V. LOMBARDI

INCA, EL. *See* GARCILASO DE LA VEGA.

INCAP. *See* INSTITUTE OF NUTRITION OF CENTRAL AMERICA AND PANAMA.

INCAS. The backgrounds of the Inca people are unknown. Their traditions told that under a leader named MANCO CAPAC they had emerged from caves in the sacred rock of Pacaritambo. Inspired by an oracle, they had then set off to fulfill their destiny, which was to found the city of CUZCO and from there to reach out and conquer the world. The truth of the matter would seem to be that they were at first a homeless and ill-assembled band of Peruvian highlanders who, about A.D. 1250, entered the upper end of the Huatanay Valley, where they succeeded in taking over the site of Cuzco from the Hualla Indians. They thereupon proceeded to practice the arts of guile and sudden war upon their near neighbors until over the years they had built the nucleus of a state. As far as can be known there was no immediate predecessor empire upon which they modeled themselves. This was a period, however, when other aggressive and warlike states were emerging in Peru, such as CHIMU and Tumbez on the coast and that of the Chancas in the sierra.

History. The Incas presented to the world a canonical list of their rulers as follows: Manco Capac was followed by his son, Sinchi Roca, and then by his grandson, Lloque Yupanqui. Not until we come to the fourth ruler, Mayta Capac, are we informed about the initiation of a militant policy; this ruler was remembered as a ferocious fighter who was born with all his teeth and at the age of two was an acknowledged champion. Under Capac Yupanqui the Inca nation for the first time carried arms outside the Huatanay Valley. His son was Inca Roca, who subdued the adjoining and crucial basin today called the Pampa de Anta. Yahuar Huacac (Blood Weeper) ends this preliminary and suspiciously neat dynastic list.

With the succeeding, and eighth, ruler, Inca history becomes more accessible. Viracocha Inca began to rule about 1400. Under him the Inca empire emerged as one of the important powers of the sierra. At the same time a religious upheaval affected the state, for this ruler had imported from the outside a new high god, VIRACOCHA, undoubtedly intending thereby to acquire new sanctions for the growing state. Viracocha Inca's reign, however, ended in disaster. The Chanca nation across the Apurímac River felt itself menaced and now moved to the attack. Viracocha Inca, hard-pressed, abandoned Cuzco, his capital, and retreated to the Yucay Valley.

This outstanding failure of Inca leadership brought to the fore the savior of the Inca nation, PACHACUTI. The Chancas were repelled in 1438, and Tahuantin-suyo, as the Inca empire was now called, entered upon its remarkable expansion. Pachacuti reformulated the state by infusing it with a remarkable dynamic, and by the end of his career he had expanded it territorially a hundredfold. His son, Topa Inca, was coregent with his father in the latter part of the reign, and on Pacha-cuti's death in 1473 he ruled alone. He successfully put down a desperate rebellion in the Titicaca area and added Chile to the empire. His death in 1493 left Tahuantinsuyo an empire extending from Ecuador to Chile and including all the former kingdoms of the Pacific coast. His son and successor was HUAYNA CAPAC, who spent much of his time fruitlessly cam-paigning in northern Ecuador. Huayna Capac's death in 1526 led to a bitter war between Huascar, his legiti-mate heir, and another son, ATAHUALPA. Atahualpa's forces defeated Huascar and seized the city of Cuzco in 1532 at the moment when Francisco PIZARRO and his handful of Spaniards entered Peru.

All who have read William H. PRESCOTT's *History of the Conquest of Peru* (1847) have been enter-tained and instructed by the account of Pizarro's daring and ridiculously easy conquest of Tahuantinsuyo, which began with the simple expedient of scattering the court and seizing the person of Atahualpa. There never was a pitched battle between the major Inca forces and the 200 Spaniards and their Peruvian allies. Dur-ing the time he was being held for ransom by the Span-iards, Atahualpa ordered the execution of Huascar, who was held by his captains. He himself was executed by Pizarro in 1533.

That year the Spaniards, accompanied by a puppet emperor whom they had seated on the Inca throne, entered Cuzco. Their extortionate policies produced the inevitable revolt, and in 1536 a revived Inca army laid siege to the Spaniards in Cuzco for a whole year. With the collapse of this siege, the remnants of the Inca house along with a few supporters faded over the passes of the Andes into the Urubamba wilderness. For thirty-five years these neo-Inca emperors played a game of hide-and-seek with the Spaniards. In 1572 the last Emperor, TUPAC AMARU [I], was captured, brought back to Cuzco, and executed there in the square. After this it can be said that the Incas ceased to exist.

Imperial structure. Of all American Indian groups the Incas created the most imposing imperial structure. They had a genius for large political conceptions and possessed the administrative ability to build and main-tain an empire that stretched for more than 2,000 miles. The nature of this state has been seriously misunder-stood in the past. Some have claimed it as socialistic. On the contrary, Tahuantinsuyo was a ruthless autoc-racy; all policy emanated from the Emperor and the Inca magnates on high, with only their interests and their security in question. Their great success in giving continuity to the state was due not to their charity in distributing benefits to their more than 6 million sub-jects but to their foresight in providing against rebel-lions. The conquered peoples were broken apart where necessary and moved as *mitmacs* (*see* MITIMA) to other provinces where their threat to the Incas became neg-ligible. The Incas retained the sons of local rulers as hostages in Cuzco and insisted on their learning QUECHUA as a second tongue. The Emperor mo-nopolized trade in luxury items such as coca, gold, beau-tiful girls, thus retaining for himself the major articles of prestige. Tribute was at the center of imperial planning, and failure on the part of a subject prince to produce the required amount was tantamount to treason. All sur-pluses of tribute that were not immediately needed in Cuzco were stored in provincial centers all over the empire. These stored surpluses were, however, always available. Incomes and disbursements were all pre-cisely recorded on *quipus* (mnemonic devices com-posed of varicolored knotted strings; *see* QUIPU), and any designated stores could be moved out at a moment's notice or, in case of local famine or disaster, disbursed on the spot. This close and speedy control of imperial resources was the secret of Tahuantinsuyo's strength.

An adequate system of communication enabled the imperial administration to move rapidly in response to crises. The Incas created a network of roads that fol-lowed close behind their advancing armies. These roads have been praised from the days of the Spanish conquest to the present. They were generally paved and graded and possessed gutters and culverts wherever needed. Steps and tunnels through sheer rock faces were not uncommon, and where canyon country had to be traversed, suspension bridges kept in constant repair spanned the gorges. Along these roads raced the *chasquis* (post-runners), carrying messages at top speed from one end of the empire to another. A message could arrive in Quito six days after it was dispatched from Cuzco. The relay runners, spaced at intervals of a few miles, shouted their messages to their reliefs and passed on to them the *quipus* that confirmed the oral message.

Warfare was an Inca specialty closely tied in with the road system and the warehouses along the route. An Inca army was a unique military institution in the pre-Columbian Western world. It was strengthened by provincial militias, was officered by a professional Inca officer class, and had at its center pure-Inca shock troops organized in two regiments. What we know of the record of these troops places them high in the his-tory of soldiering. They could mount difficult offensives, whether sieges or open-order attacks, and could main-tain pressure on the enemy over a period of days and in spite of heavy losses. They were skilled in stratagems and marched in order.

Religion. Inca religion supported the state. Inti, the sun god, was the father of all Incas, and it was he who had guided them in all the vicissitudes of their history. He was the symbol of their greatness, and therefore in every conquered province a cult of Inti was maintained to validate the Inca presence. But it was the creator god, Viracocha, who was placed as a patron deity over the empire as such. His cult appears to have been more or less limited to the royal family and thus to have been their possession. Other gods of the Inca pantheon were Mama Quilla, the moon and therefore Inti's consort; Illapa, the god of storm, rain, and thunder; Huanacauri, the war god; Pachamama, the great earth mother; and Mama Sara, the deity of MAIZE. Most of these deities were congregated together in Cuzco in the great ecclesiastical yard, or enclosure, called Coricancha (today the house and church of the Dominican order), where they could be easily manipulated. The gods of the conquered people were looked upon as generally conspiratorial and always dangerous.

While the Incas did not have an elaborate calendar as did the peoples of Mesoamerica, they had a splendid series of festivals ceremonially commemorating themselves, their history, the royal house, and the agricultural year. The Inti Raymi, or Sun Festival, was perhaps the most magnificent of them all, while the Situa, or Festival of Renewal, was the most dramatic.

Social organization. The Incas can be most conveniently viewed as a caste — compact, very few in number, and deriving their privileges from a divine source. Like other Peruvian peoples they were grouped in *ayllus* (*see* AYLLU), which in turn were collected into two moieties called Upper and Lower Cuzco. Only one of the *ayllus* could be considered outside and superior to this system; this was the royal family, or the Capac *ayllu*. All legitimate Incas claimed Inti as their father and Mama Quilla as their mother; in theory they were thus an extended family of semidivine blood. The Emperor was the *sapa capac Inca*, or "the magnificent and only Inca," and he was hailed as the *Intip churin*, or "the son of the sun." He kept the blood of his issue undiluted by marrying his full sister, but even in aristocratic levels beneath him a pure lineage was a desideratum. Inca youths were inducted into the ranks of Inca manhood in the testing ceremony of the *huarachicoy*. All non-Incas were thought to be contemptible, and the Emperor would include in his huge harem only such beautiful girls as could additionally claim royal blood from the ruling houses of the conquered peoples.

The most unusual social institution conceived by the Incas was the *panaca*. It was based on the concept that no Inca Emperor ever died, even though full mourning rites were always carried out for him by his son and successor. In the person of his mummy, he was supposed to be merely translated into a less active sphere of life and to maintain his state. His palace, his goods, and his retainers were not inherited by his successor but continued to belong to him. This imperial estate headed by a mummy was called a *panaca*, as was the family comprised of his immediate descendants. A majordomo stood in for the dead ruler, spoke for him, issued invitations to other magnates, presided over drinking bouts, carried the mummy on his back, and simulated for him all natural functions. Every Inca ruler, beginning with Manco Capac, possessed this type of dead household. The influence of the *panacas* seems to have been pernicious; they claimed sovereignty and inviolability and could nurse conspiracies and rebellions behind the stone walls of their *canchas* (enclosures). Loyalty to these royal mummies, which were hidden away in hamlets outside Cuzco, lasted well into the colonial period.

The arts. The Incas were as unimaginative in the arts as they were superb in administration; in this they are the very opposite of the gifted MAYAS of Mesoamerica. Inca walls, however, represent perhaps man's most feeling use of stone as stone. The Cyclopean rusticated walls of the Incas, such as those at Sacsahuamán, achieve a ponderous esthetic quality by the very inversion of artistry.

Bibliography. B. C. Brundage, *Empire of the Inca,* Norman, Okla., 1963; id., *Lords of Cuzco,* Norman, Okla., 1967; Garcilaso de la Vega, *Royal Commentaries of the Incas,* tr. by H. V. Livermore, 2 vols., Austin, Tex., 1966; J. A. Mason, *Ancient Civilizations of Peru,* rev. ed., Harmondsworth, England, 1968; J. H. Rowe, "Inca Culture at the Time of the Spanish Conquest," *Handbook of South American Indians,* vol. II, Washington, 1945, pp. 183–330; G. R. Wiley, *An Introduction to American Archaeology,* vol. II, *South America,* Englewood Cliffs, N.J., 1971, pp. 172–184.

BURR C. BRUNDAGE

INCONFIDÊNCIA MINEIRA (1788–1789). Plot for an armed uprising against Portugal organized by important members of the elite of Minas Gerais. The conspiracy was initiated after the arrival in mid-1788 of a new Governor with draconian instructions to impose a per capita tax (*derrama*) to make up the massive arrears resulting from the repeated failure of the captaincy of Minas Gerais to meet its obligation to pay 100 arrobas (1 arroba = 32 pounds) of gold to the royal treasury each year; this failure was due mainly to the exhaustion of alluvial gold in the captaincy but was attributed by the Portuguese government to the malfeasance of the *mineiros*. In addition, there was a coincident threat to collect the huge unpaid sums owed by the tax farmers of the region, principally on the import taxes (*entradas*) and the tithes (*dízimos*). The tax demands took place within a situation already agitated by a long and bitter dispute between the former Governor and the magistrates and among competing factions within the regional military officer corps. Moreover, the demands ignored the consequences of the falloff in gold production on the local economy.

The particular coupling of demands — the per capita tax, which fell on the whole population, and the collection of tax-farm arrears, which fell on powerful and opulent individuals — provided the latter with an opportunity to seek relief from their personal obligations under the guise of popular opposition to Portuguese rule. Among the major supporters in Minas Gerais of the plot for an armed uprising against the Portuguese crown in late 1788 were the great merchant contractors, who were also the most circumspect and veiled in their participation. Most prominent among the activists was a second lieutenant of dragoons, Joaquim José Silva Xavier, better known by his nickname, Tiradentes. He was to lead the rising in Vila Rica de Ouro Prêto, timed to coincide with the imposition of the *derrama.* Several other officers of the dragoons, including the commandant, were also involved in the plot. The ideologues were drawn from among the captaincy's leading intellectuals, among them the famous poets Cláudio Manuel da Costa, Tomas Antônio GONZAGA, and José Alvarenga Peixoto. The plan called for the proclamation of a republic modeled on the North American example and for the establishment of a university and factories and, not surprisingly, pardoned all debts to the royal treasury.

The uprising failed to materialize. The Governor decided not to impose the *derrama,* for he saw that the economic circumstances of the region made so large a demand insupportable. He did not, however, at the same time remove demands on the former tax farmers. The result of his action was to split the coalition of disparate interests joined in the plot, remove the occasion for the uprising, and give strong inducement for defection. Joaquim Silverio dos Reis, one of the principal debtors, went to the Governor posthaste and revealed in detail the plans of the conspirators, hoping by this display of "loyalty" to gain the objective he had entered the plot to achieve in the first place, namely, to escape from his debts to the treasury. The Governor, aware of his own weakness due to the unreliability of the regular forces at his disposal, worked skillfully to bring into the "royalist" group men whose commitment to independence was more material than ideological. Meanwhile, he secretly got in touch with the Viceroy, requesting that European troops be sent surreptitiously to Vila Rica and that detachments of reliable guards be posted between Vila Rica and Rio de Janeiro.

The conspirators were arrested without much difficulty, and a long and involved series of investigations led eventually to their trial and sentencing in 1792. Only Tiradentes was hanged, then beheaded and quartered, parts of his body being displayed in different sections of Minas Gerais as a warning to would-be rebels. Others were sentenced to death but granted clemency and banished instead to various parts of the Portuguese empire (mainly Angola). The movement in Minas had been highly important even in failure, for unlike previous plots it was fundamentally anticolonial and protonationalist and, above all, republican.

Bibliography. Autos da Devassa de Inconfidência Mineira, 7 vols., Rio de Janeiro, 1936–38; Herculano Gomes Mathias, "O Tiradentes e a Cidade do Rio de Janeiro," *Anais do Museu Histórico Nacional*, Rio de Janeiro, 1960, vol. XVI, pp. 53–103; id., "Inconfidência e Inconfidentes," *Anais do Congresso Comemorativo do Bicentenário da Transferência da Sede do Governo do Brasil da Cidade do Salvador para o Rio de Janeiro*, 3 vols., Rio de Janeiro, 1967, vol. III, pp. 229–299; Kenneth R. Maxwell, *Conflicts and Conspiracies: Brazil and Portugal, 1750–1808*. Cambridge, England, 1973.   KENNETH R. MAXWELL

INDIANS. *See* ARAUCANIANS; ARAWAK; AYMARÁ; AZTECS; CARIB; CHIBCHA; CHICHIMEC; CHIMU; GUARANÍ; INCAS; MAYAS; OLMECS; QUECHUA; TOLTECS; TUPÍ-GUARANÍ; TUPINAMBÁ.

INDIGENISMO. *Indigenismo* can be defined as "a political and social movement on behalf of the American Indian which seeks to elevate his precarious standard of living and to incorporate him materially and spiritually into the ordinary civic life of the country in which he resides while preserving his own culture and without diminishing his specific psychological personality" (*Diccionario Enciclopédico Uteha*, vol. VI, p. 276). Today *indigenismo* is considered a policy of change, to be carried out by the state and other institutions, with the objective of resolving the problems faced by the Indian populations of America.

Indian population. Basic to *indigenismo* is knowledge of the size of the Indian population. Unfortunately, census data quantifying this population are not now available. It is possible to obtain these figures in some countries, for example, where the Indians live apart in compact geographic areas or where the censuses have a sound technical foundation and are conducted by specially trained personnel. However, the kind of indicators generally used in censuses to identify the Indian population—language and type of dwelling, for example—cannot provide an exact enumeration. These problems arise as a result of the processes of assimilation and integration being undergone by Indians who live in the same geographic areas as whites and mestizos and have interethnic relations with them.

Various criteria are used in the determination of what is to be considered Indian. The most important are historicocultural aspects (indicators related to spiritual and material life, such as language, dress, and traditional customs), the conservation of certain forms and patterns of social life in which the self-image of the individual is identified with his community, and the consciousness or sentiment of belonging to the Indian population. These factors are not mutually exclusive. What is Indian is best defined by the definite predominance of one or more of these or by a combination of all of them. As a result, in order to obtain an accurate and valid census, a concrete methodology must be adopted, and the census takers must be well prepared.

The foregoing considerations explain the diversity of calculations regarding the size of the Indian population of Latin America, estimated at between 15 and 30 million. The higher figure includes groups in the process of integration and acculturation; the smaller, only the population that is definitely and totally Indian. An acceptable and realistic estimate might be 20 million. At present the Indian population is concentrated in Guatemala, Bolivia, Peru, and Ecuador.

History of *indigenismo*. The contemporary Indianist movement can be traced as far back as the sixteenth century. During the Spanish conquest and colonial period, characterized as they were by the subjugation and exploitation of the Indian, a variety of orientations toward him can be perceived, ranging from the inhuman assertions of Juan Ginés de Sepúlveda, who argued that the conquest was justified because the Indians were barbaric and inferior beings, to the humanitarian and understanding attitude of Bartolomé de LAS CASAS. This famous defender of the Indians attempted to protect them from mistreatment at the hands of the Spaniards and worked for the enactment of legislation, such as the NEW LAWS, favorable to the Indians. During the nineteenth century Indianist sentiment was marked by a romantic, unscientific attitude steeped in paternalism. The early twentieth century saw the beginning of a Marxist approach to *indigenismo*, which was evident in the work of the Peruvian José Carlos MARIÁTEGUI and his followers. It was, however, the MEXICAN REVOLUTION of 1910 that transformed *indigenismo*, fixing the bases upon which the contemporary movement would be established. The Mexican revolution sought the roots of Mexican nationality in the Indian past and directed the action of the state, first, at the assimilation of the Indian and, later, at his incorporation into national life. At this time distinguished thinkers throughout the continent struggled for the redemption of the Indian. Among these outstanding spokesmen of *indigenismo* might be mentioned the Ecuadorian Pío Jaramillo Alvarado, the Mexicans Manuel Gamio and Moisés Sáenz, and the Brazilian Marshal Cândido RONDON. Novelists such as Jorge ICAZA of Ecuador also focused attention on the Indian by depicting his exploitation by whites and mestizos. Later Mexican anthropologists such as Alfonso CASO and Gonzalo Aguirre Beltrán set forth precise concepts of Indianist theory; based on a realistic knowledge of Indian culture and of the social situation of the Indian, it sought his integration into national life while fully respecting his personality and culture.

The continental Indianist movement culminated in 1940 with the meeting of the First Inter-American Indigenist Congress in Pátzcuaro, Mexico. One of the concrete results of the congress was the foundation of the Inter-American Indigenist Institute (Instituto Indigenista Interamericano), established in the belief that the Indian problem was of continental significance. To date seventeen nations have become members of the institute. Its basic objectives are to keep the indigenist cause alive and to work for the improvement of Indian groups and for their integration into the active life of the American peoples, to spread the ideas and principles of *indigenismo,* to carry out research, to sponsor technical meetings and specialized congresses, to offer technical assistance, and to aid in the training of specialized personnel. In the fulfillment of the institute's mission, the review *América Indígena* has played an outstanding role, as has the *Anuario Indigenista.*

Contemporary *indigenismo.* The contemporary Indianist movement has its own essential peculiarities. It is not a response to any racial theory, nor is it racist. It is a result of the realities of Indian life, which in turn stem from the historical processes that halted the development of the Indians' cultures and simultaneously led to their marginality and exploitation, typical forms of colonialism starting with the Spanish conquest and lasting in some countries to the present day. Contemporary *indigenismo* rejects the argument advanced by conservatives who maintained in the past (much less so today) that the Indian ought to remain in his unfortunate condition since he was incapable of assimilating other cultures or of participating in national life. On the other hand, the movement does not seek the total absorption of the Indian into white-mestizo life as if he were a blank page on which the new culture could be imprinted. Nor does the movement wish to keep the Indians isolated from other human groups and "uncontaminated" by Western culture. Although there is some support for this basically conservative position, it is not realistic since the vast majority of the Indian population has already been obliged to take part, under negative and difficult conditions, in many of the forms of life of the white-mestizo culture. The only exceptions are the forest Indians who are completely marginal as a result of geography and the lack of adequate means of communication.

Modern *indigenismo* respects the human dignity of the Indian and of his communities and respects his culture regardless of its level of development. Its most widely accepted goal is the integration of the Indian into national life while at the same time according to his peculiar cultural traits the consideration to which they are entitled. The movement does not favor an authoritarian approach to the Indians, ordering them to submit to the dictates of officials and agencies in a manner reminiscent of the feudal past. It also rejects paternalistic methods of dealing with the Indians that treat them like infants or charity cases. When this approach is used, the Indians merely take what is offered; their

spirit of enterprise is undermined, and they are encouraged to become dependent on the handouts conferred by public charity. Contemporary *indigenismo* favors what might be called an active methodology that encourages Indian groups to express their needs and desires and to participate in the planning and execution of programs affecting them. As a result, their spirit of enterprise is stimulated, and their leaders acquire experience and a sense of responsibility that permits continuous development.

The contemporary movement recognizes the importance of programs in the fields of health, agriculture, housing, and so on, but it maintains that they must be well coordinated and integrated so as to achieve balanced results. In such an integrated endeavor, economic and educational programs will play a key role, education being considered in the broadest sense of the word to embrace efforts to create new habits and change attitudes. In the economic sphere, AGRARIAN REFORM constitutes one of the most effective means of improving the life of the Indian population since most of them depend upon agriculture.

Recently there has appeared a current of opinion which not only demands respect for and complete preservation of Indian cultures but which also rejects any strategy aimed at incorporating the Indian into what its proponents consider an unjust and problem-ridden society. In some respects this point of view coincides with the old conservative position. In reality it can be applied only to totally isolated forest tribes, for the others have already been integrated to some extent into other cultures in the most disadvantageous ways. This opinion may ultimately be a negative factor, even in the quest for a new, less unjust society, for in such a transformation the Indian would initially be an inactive element. The position of Alejandro Marroquín (see Bibliography) is well taken:

> It is absurd to demand the neutrality of the state in the face of the poverty, exploitation, and injustice in which most Indian communities find themselves. No one can be neutral before the tragic reality of the Indian. The neutrality that is propounded with the pretext of protecting his right of self-determination leads in effect to complicity with poverty, exploitation and injustice. What is needed is rapid and efficacious action that will put an end to the ills afflicting the Indian while respecting his dignity as a human being.

Contemporary *indigenismo* faces many serious problems. Indians continue to be discriminated against in many ways, as is shown by their poverty, by the inadequate services they receive, by their nonparticipation in civic life, and at times by paternalistic legislation and programs that treat them as if they were children. In addition, efforts to overcome their prostration and backwardness have had disappointing results. Programs, especially in the educational and economic fields, have been badly focused and inadequately financed; nor have there been available the trained and dedicated technical personnel to carry on this work. Meanwhile, the sectors that exploit the Indian population and benefit from its present plight have offered resistance, both openly and subterraneously. In general the non-Indian population has not demonstrated a positive attitude toward the integration of the Indian, nor has it acknowledged his values and rights. Political and philosophical positions have arisen that frequently disorient action or serve as instruments helpful to forces interested in avoiding substantive changes. Finally, as a result of the inefficacy of past programs and the continuation of negative factors, the attitudes of the Indians themselves have not changed. For all these reasons it may be said that *indigenismo* is in a state of crisis.

Bibliography. Gonzalo Aguirre Beltrán, *El proceso de aculturación,* Mexico City, 1957; id., *Regiones de refugio,* Mexico City, 1967; Alfonso Caso, *¿Qué es el INI?,* Mexico City, 1955; id., *Indigenismo,* Mexico City, 1958; Juan Comas, *Ensayos sobre indigenismo,* Mexico City, 1953; Julio de la Fuente, *Relaciones interétnicas,* Mexico City, 1965; Alejandro D. Marroquín, *Balance del indigenismo,* Mexico City, 1972; Gonzalo Rubio Orbe, *Promociones indígenas en América,* Quito, 1957.

GONZALO RUBIO ORBE

INDUSTRY (BRAZIL). The rise of Brazilian industry has occurred largely since the 1930s and has been greatly influenced by economic nationalism and government direction. In turn, industrial growth has had significant effects upon almost all aspects of Brazilian life. During the colonial period the evolution of native industry was hindered by the mercantilist policies of Portugal. After independence little progress was made in establishing any significant industrial sector. Throughout the imperial era (1822–1889) men such as Visconde MAUÁ attempted to build industrial plants in Brazil, but with limited success, largely because the upper class believed that Brazil's future lay in exporting raw materials and agricultural goods while importing manufactured goods from industrialized nations, primarily Great Britain.

After 1889 little industrial growth was achieved until the Presidency of Afonso PENA (1906–1909). Pena set out to improve Brazil's economic stature by ending the dominance of agriculture and dependence upon British manufactures. Among other things, he proposed protective tariffs and improved communication routes. Domestic industry was further stimulated during World War I, which restricted Brazil's access to manufactured imports and markets for its goods. However, industrial growth was hindered by the lack of machinery and capital. After the war the industrial nations regained their old markets in Brazil, while Brazilian industrial growth was virtually stopped by increased foreign competition and the abandonment of protective tariffs by the government of Epitácio PESSOA (1919–1922). After 1930, spurred by economic nationalism and the world depression, which again cut Brazil off from foreign sources of manufactured goods, the government of Getúlio VARGAS attempted to promote the growth of industry.

In the years just prior to World War II, Brazil's industry expanded rapidly behind high protective tariffs and with the assistance of the Vargas administration. As the war approached, the government intensified its efforts on behalf of the industrial sector, with the result that, in spite of the limited availability of capital goods during the war years, Brazilian industry again grew tremendously. However, even with government sponsorship of such sectors as the steel industry (*see* IRON AND STEEL INDUSTRY: BRAZIL), with the building of VOLTA REDONDA, industries producing primary necessities such as foods, textiles, and beverages remained the most important. In the immediate postwar years the government of Eurico Gaspar DUTRA adopted a laissez faire economic policy in a reaction to the statist policies of the Vargas dictatorship. In 1947, in the face of worsening trade relations with the industrial nations and rising monetary inflation at home, Dutra found it necessary to return to protectionist policies in order to foster and shelter Brazilian industry.

Since World War II all Brazilian governments have encouraged measures to expand and broaden the range of industrial production. Hydroelectric output has been greatly increased, while roads and railroads have been improved to attract additional industry. As a result of government economic planning, Brazil has become Latin America's most industrialized nation and now exports manufactured items such as buses, automobile parts, processed foodstuffs, and textiles to other nations, including the United States.

In 1971 Brazil produced about 5,900,000 tons of steel ingots and about 4,880,000 tons of rolled steel, compared with 5,370,000 and 4,225,000 tons respectively in 1970. The automobile industry, which was inaugurated during the administration of Juscelino KUBITSCHEK (1956–1961), produced more than half a million cars, buses, and trucks and more than 20,000 tractors. In other areas production for domestic consumption and export also increased. In 1971 Brazilian manufactured exports were valued at about $233 million.

Not only has the growth of Brazilian industry significantly affected the economy, but it has drawn a large portion of the rural population into such cities as São Paulo, Rio de Janeiro, and Belo Horizonte. With the increased population, a large section of which is literate, the political power of the urban electorate and urban industrial pressure groups has also increased.

Bibliography. Manuel Diégues, Jr., *Industrialização, Urbanização, Imigração,* Rio de Janeiro, 1962; Nícia Vilela Luz, *A Luta pela Industrialização no Brasil, 1808–1930,* São Paulo, 1961; Rollie E. Poppino, *Brazil: The Land and People,* New York, 1968; Roberto C. Simonsen, *Brazil's Industrial Revolution,* São Paulo, 1939.

LAWRENCE J. NIELSEN

INDUSTRY (LATIN AMERICA). Manufacturing has existed in Latin America from at least the last decades of the nineteenth century. In Argentina, Brazil, and Mexico, the larger countries of the region, textiles and food products were produced in workshops and small factories. In addition, workshops producing machine tools and spare parts were established to service sugar-refining mills, railroads, and so on. It would not be correct, however, to characterize developments before World War I as industrialization, since industrial growth depended almost entirely on agricultural exports, which represented the economies' leading sector, while workshops and small industries merely supplemented economies based on agriculture and commerce.

World War I, the Depression, and World War II brought industrial growth to most of the larger countries. The industrialization that occurred because of these factors external to the region has been labeled import-substitutive in nature, since its principal purpose was to substitute domestically produced goods for imports to supply an already-existing market. For example, in World War I, as fewer nonmilitary goods were produced in Europe and the United States and fewer ships were available to transport such goods to Latin America, imported manufactured goods became scarce and relatively expensive and the local manufacture of such goods increasingly profitable. Factories producing textiles, food products, and various other light consumer goods expanded their output during the war by using existing capacity more intensively. Because of import restrictions, machinery to enlarge the productive capacity of industries could not be imported at the time. In the decade following the war, however, when competing industries in the United States and Europe revived to the detriment of their counterparts in Latin America, some investment took place in a number of countries both to replace depreciated equipment and to anticipate expansion.

As a result of the Depression exports declined and there was little foreign exchange available for imports. The shortage of imported goods led at first to greater use of manufacturing facilities that had not been fully utilized in the preceding decade and later to the construction of new plants. Most of the new import-substitutive industrialization involved light consumer goods, but in some cases, such as Brazil, there was a relatively small development in the steel and capital goods industries. *See* IRON AND STEEL INDUSTRY (BRAZIL).

Industry was further encouraged by World War II, when it became difficult to import manufactured goods. Existing plants were used to capacity, and new facilities were added after it became possible to import capital goods. After the war Latin American governments deliberately fostered industrialization of an import-substitutive nature. Policy makers in the major countries of the region concluded that it was futile to continue to conform to the customary world division of labor, wherein Latin America was assigned the production of food and primary products, for which world demand was unstable and rose relatively slowly. They believed that industrialization would accelerate growth rates and make their economies less dependent on world economic conditions.

To encourage industrial development governments made use of protective tariffs, exchange controls, or both. They also utilized such means as preferences for the importation of capital goods; preferential import exchange rates for industrial raw materials, fuels, and intermediate goods; government loans; government construction of infrastructure projects (improved transportation, increased power facilities, and so on); and participation in heavy industries that were unattractive to private capital.

Industries were encouraged indiscriminately without consideration of the possibility of comparative advantage. In Argentina, Chile, and Venezuela consumer goods industries were the first to be promoted, beginning with goods requiring little in the way of technology and gradually expanding to include more complex durables. Finally, the industrial sector began to comprise such products as steel and chemicals. In Brazil this sequence was less pronounced since the government wished to encourage consumer, intermediate, and capital goods industries simultaneously.

Foreign capital played a crucial role in Latin American industrialization in the 1950s and 1960s. Although it contributed less than 10 percent of total savings per year, it helped establish such key industries as automobiles, shipbuilding, steel, and capital goods. Moreover, infrastructure projects and government-owned heavy industries needed foreign loans and technical assistance.

TABLE 1. THE LATIN AMERICAN ECONOMIES: CHANGES IN STRUCTURE AND GROWTH RATES

Principal sectors	Percentage distribution of gross domestic product		Annual growth rates	
	1950	1967	1950–1960	1960–1967
Agriculture	25.2	20.5	3.5	3.5
Manufacturing	19.6	24.1	6.2	5.8
Mining and construction	7.6	7.7	…	…
Other	47.6	47.7	…	…
Total	100.0	100.0	4.9	4.6

SOURCE: United Nations Economic Commission for Latin America, *Estudio económico de América Latina, 1968,* New York, 1969.

The impact of industrialization in Latin America is illustrated in Table 1. It will be noted that in the early post-World War II period manufacturing industry was already large in the region's gross domestic product (GDP), but it was still smaller than agriculture. By the late sixties, however, manufacturing had surpassed agriculture, contributing more than 24 percent to the GDP. For larger countries such as Argentina, Mexico, and Brazil the industrial sector's contribution to the GDP was about 30 percent in the late sixties.

The import-substitutive nature of the industrialization process can clearly be seen in the data for Brazil and Mexico. In Table 2 imports as a proportion of total supplies are presented for the two countries. It will be noted that, as a result of the industrial growth antedating World War II, the countries were almost self-sufficient in respect to consumer goods. During the 1950s greater self-sufficiency was reached in intermediate and capital goods.

A more concrete picture of the result of Latin America's industrialization emerges from selected production

TABLE 2. IMPORTS AS A PERCENTAGE OF TOTAL SUPPLIES

	Consumer goods	Intermediate goods	Capital goods
Brazil:			
1949	9.0	25.9	63.7
1964	1.3	6.6	9.8
Mexico:			
1950	2.4	13.2	66.5
1965	1.1	9.9	59.8

SOURCE: Ian Little, Tibor Scitovsky, and Maurice Scott, *Industry and Trade in Some Developing Countries,* New York, 1970, p. 60.

data. Production of motor vehicles rose from 60,900 in 1955 to more than 1 million in 1971. Between 1953 and 1969 steel output rose from 174,000 to 1.7 million tons in Argentina, from 1 million to 5 million tons in Brazil, and from 462,000 to 3.5 million tons in Mexico (*see* IRON AND STEEL INDUSTRY: MEXICO). Television receiver production rose from 29,000 to 664,000 sets in the period 1953–1964 in Brazil, and from 65,000 to 403,000 in Mexico.

Although industrialization has wrought drastic changes in the larger Latin American economies and has been responsible for a high rate of growth for two decades, it has also given rise to a considerable number of problems. Each Latin American country industrialized in an indiscriminate way without regard to comparative advantage. Since even the larger countries of the region have a relatively small market, either because of small populations or because of a low per capita income that limits purchasing power for industrial goods, across-the-board industrialization has created many high-cost and inefficient industries. The condition of these industries is due in part to their limited capital and lack of skilled manpower and in part to their inability to enjoy the economies of large-scale technology: unless production is of a certain size, fixed costs per unit of output are excessively high. In addition, some countries allowed many firms to produce for a limited market, thus increasing still further fixed costs per unit. In the mid-sixties, for instance, ninety firms produced different automobile models for a market of 600,000. Thus car prices were extremely high and completely uncompetitive internationally. Similar problems have been found in such industries as newsprint, chemicals, heavy electrical equipment, and various types of consumer durables and capital goods.

The stress on import substitution industrialization caused many countries to neglect exports. In countries in which traditional agricultural exports continued to be in great demand in the international market, industrialization policies hampered the growth of agricultural export supplies because relative price policies, the allocation of investment credit, and taxation were such as to discourage agriculture. In Argentina, for example, industrialization occurred at the expense of agriculture.

TABLE 3. CHANGES IN IMPORT COEFFICIENTS *

Country	1928	1938	1948–1949	1960	1967
Argentina	17.8	12.1	11.2	8.0	6.6
Brazil	11.3	6.2	6.6	7.8	5.6
Chile	31.2	14.9	11.5	15.7	15.7
Mexico	14.2	7.0	8.5	7.8	7.8
Latin America	...	...	10.2	10.0	9.9

*Value of imports as a percentage of GDP.
SOURCES: Joseph Grunwald and Philip Musgrove, *Natural Resources in Latin American Development,* Baltimore, 1970, p. 20; data for 1960 and 1967, United Nations Economic Commission for Latin America, *Estudio económico de América Latina, 1968,* New York, 1969.

The neglect of exports also manifested itself in the unchanging nature of Latin America's export structure. Whereas the contribution of industry to the GDP became dominant after World War II, there was little alteration in the composition of exports. For example, in the late 1960s food and primary products still accounted for more than nine-tenths of the exports of Argentina and Brazil.

The neglect of export stimulation and diversification has placed many countries of the region in a vulnerable position. Latin American policy makers originally thought that import substitution industrialization would make their countries less dependent on a fluctuating international trade. It became evident, however, that import substitution has limits and that the ratio of imports to the GDP could be decreased only to a certain point. As Table 3 shows, the import/GDP ratio declined at first and then leveled off; at the same time there was a notable change in imports, for the new industries required foreign raw materials, semifinished products, and capital goods. If exports declined or grew too slowly, the industrialized Latin American economies would not be able to finance the necessary imports and so might suffer a prolonged recession. It thus became evident that greater stress would have to be placed on export promotion and diversification, although high costs, red tape, and poor credit facilities made this difficult.

On the domestic scene, industry's low capacity to absorb labor has been one of the major disappointments and problems confronting Latin Americans. While the annual population growth for the region rose from 1.9 to 2.8 percent in the post-World II period, and while migration from the countryside to the cities increased dramatically, the number of industrial jobs grew far more slowly (see Table 4). In some countries such as Brazil the urban population growth rate was much higher than the Latin American average, often reaching 6 percent a year, while the employment growth rate in manufacturing was only about 2.5 percent. Table 4 also shows that the proportion of the Latin American labor force in manufacturing decreased somewhat and that 44 percent were artisans rather than factory workers. There is no definitive explanation for the disappointing employment performance of industry. Some economists believe that the nature of the technology of modern industry is characterized by a high capital/labor ratio and that this ratio is fairly rigid. Others believe that technological choices exist for various industries but that artificially cheap prices for capital and high prices of labor (the former being due to policies adopted to induce industrial investment through cheap credit and the latter to enforced labor legislation in the major Latin American countries) lead to the adoption of capital-intensive production techniques.

There is general agreement, however, that the failure of labor absorption by industry has caused social problems in urban areas. In addition, because of the high capital/labor ratio of industry income is concentrated in fewer hands, and this in turn may result in an inadequate growth of demand for industrial goods. That is, the low increment in demand resulting from the concentration in the distribution of income may make it difficult to maintain the growth momentum of industry beyond the initial import substitution phase.

By the late 1960s and early 1970s many countries of

TABLE 4. EMPLOYMENT AND POPULATION GROWTH IN
LATIN AMERICA

Principal sectors	Percentage distribution of economically active population		Yearly employment growth rates		Population growth rates	
	1950	1969	1950–1960	1960–1969	1950–1960	1960–1969
Agriculture	53.4	42.2	1.3	1.5		
Manufacturing	14.4	13.8	2.6	2.3		
(Artisan)	(7.5)	(6.1)	(1.5)	(1.6)		
Mining	4.9	5.5	2.0	2.2		
Construction			3.2	4.0		
Basic services	4.2	5.5	4.6	3.4		
Other services	23.1	33.0	4.7	4.6		
(Commerce and finance)	(7.8)	(10.1)				
Total	100.0	100.0			2.8	2.9
				(Urban)	(4.8)	(4.4)
				(Rural)	(1.4)	(1.4)

SOURCE: United Nations Economic Commission for Latin America, *Estudio económico de América Latina, 1968,* New York, 1969.

the region had begun to eliminate some of the more painful distortions that had accompanied industrialization. Tariffs were reduced, and steps were taken to lower the number of firms in industries in which scale economies were important so as to reduce the high cost and price structure facing the consuming public.

For a number of years the ECONOMIC COMMISSION FOR LATIN AMERICA and the INTER-AMERICAN DEVELOPMENT BANK have urged the creation of a common market as a means of producing ECONOMIC INTEGRATION. Exports thus would be increased and diversified, and the various economies of the region would become more nearly complementary. Another device is the so-called complementation agreement, whereby production is divided vertically, with one country manufacturing parts for assembly in another. However, little progress had been made in this direction by the early 1970s. In addition, the general disappointment in the achievements of the LATIN AMERICAN FREE TRADE ASSOCIATION had led some smaller countries, which acutely felt the need for larger markets, to integrate under the banner of the ANDEAN GROUP.

Meanwhile, the various countries sought new ways to promote industrial growth beyond the stage of import substitution. The administration of President Emílio Garrastazu MÉDICI of Brazil proposed a program to raise the participation of the labor force in the national product, develop the region of the AMAZON RIVER, and improve communications by extensive road building. Peru embarked on AGRARIAN REFORM and profit sharing, while President Luis ECHEVERRÍA of Mexico stressed income redistribution. Most governments also tried to promote nontraditional exports, but the degree to which the United States, European, and other markets would be open to them was still speculative in 1973.

It is uncertain whether such measures as these will be as effective as import substitution was in promoting industrial growth. It seems unlikely that large numbers

of new workers can be employed in industry or the services. Nor is it clear that agrarian reform will enable rural areas to absorb or at least retain labor. If not, then perhaps the employment problem can be solved only by population control.

See also INDUSTRY (BRAZIL); INDUSTRY (MEXICO); TRADE (SINCE WORLD WAR II).

Bibliography. Parts of this article were adapted from a larger survey by the author: Werner Baer, "Import Substitution and Industrialization in Latin America," *Latin American Research Review,* vol. VII, no. 1, Spring, 1972, pp. 95–122. *See also* Werner Baer, *Industrialization and Economic Development in Brazil,* Homewood, Ill., 1965; Carlos Diaz-Alejandro, *Essays on the Economic History of the Argentine Republic,* New Haven, Conn., 1970; Joseph Grunwald, "Some Reflections on Latin American Industrialization Policies," *Journal of Political Economy,* vol. 78, no. 4, part II, July/August 1970, pp. 826–856; A. O. Hirschman, "The Political Economy of Import-Substituting Industrialization," *The Quarterly Journal of Economics,* vol. LXXXII, no. 1, February 1968, pp. 1–32; Richard R. Nelson, T. Paul Schultz, and Robert L. Slighton, *Structural Change in a Developing Economy: Colombia's Problems and Prospects,* Princeton, N.J., 1971; Clark W. Reynolds, *The Mexican Economy: Twentieth Century Structure and Growth,* New Haven, Conn., 1970; United Nations Economic Commission for Latin America, *The Process of Industrialization in Latin America,* New York, 1965; United Nations, "Industrial Development in Latin America," *Economic Bulletin for Latin America,* vol. XIV, no. 2, second half of 1969, pp. 3–77.

WERNER BAER

INDUSTRY (MEXICO). During the colonial period Mexico developed a primitive textile industry that was modernized by Lucas ALAMÁN in 1830 with the creation of the Banco de Avío, a national credit bank to promote industrial and agricultural development. The growth of a consumer goods industry (foodstuffs, footwear, textiles, etc.) during the era of Porfirio DÍAZ (1876–1911) stimulated the development of heavy industry (steel, chemicals, cement, etc.), as did the increasing demands of Mexico's mines, railways, and construction industry. In order to accelerate industrial growth the government maintained high tariff barriers against products that competed with domestic goods, and on June 3, 1893, it granted tax exemptions to those who launched new industries.

During the violent decade of the MEXICAN REVOLUTION (1910–1920) the sugar industry of Morelos was destroyed. In the next decade President Plutarco Elías CALLES embarked upon a program of public works (roads and irrigation projects). In the 1930s President Lázaro CÁRDENAS contributed to Mexican industrialization by nationalizing the petroleum industry (*see* PETRÓLEOS MEXICANOS), creating the National Polytechnic Institute, and expanding the internal market through his agrarian and labor policies. His successor, Manuel Ávila Camacho (1940–1946), transformed the NACIONAL FINANCIERA so that it would encourage industrialization, in keeping with the prevailing opinion that this was the best means of achieving economic development and raising the standard of living. This objective was furthered by the effects of World War II, which brought an increase in prices and FOREIGN INVESTMENT and reduced the outflow of profits. The political subjugation of the labor movement was achieved, among other means, by the argument that since capital was now in Mexican hands, workers should not expect the same support as when it was controlled by foreigners. Perhaps the peak of industrial growth was reached during the administration of Miguel ALEMÁN (1946–1952), largely because of the expansion of foreign investment, the government's public works program, and increased capitalization achieved through savings that benefited industrialists but hurt persons on fixed incomes.

The diversification of Mexico's industry reflects the country's recent economic development. For example, the food-processing industry represented 40 percent of the value of manufactured goods in 1930 but only 25 percent in 1955; the share of the textile industry diminished from 30 percent in 1930 to 18.5 percent in 1955. On the other hand, the share of the construction industry increased from 2.3 percent in 1930 to 19.7 percent in 1955, and that of automobile assembly and the manufacture of machines and electrical appliances from 2.3 to 15 percent. Accordingly, the increase in the number of persons employed in the textile industry (from 53,347 in 1930 to 248,568 in 1955) and food processing (from 45,598 in 1930 to 294,191 in 1955) was smaller than that in the construction industry (from 3,910 in 1930 to 591,522 in 1955), chemicals (from 2,026 in 1930 to 87,776 in 1955), and electrical appliances (from 120 in 1930 to 53,200 in 1955). By 1969 there were 2,973,540 persons employed in Mexican industry, representing 23 percent of the labor force.

Industrialization has also benefited from the diversification of Mexico's economy as a result of the decline in the proportion of the population engaged in agriculture and the improvement of agricultural techniques, accompanied by an increase in agricultural productivity. Some authorities have pointed out weaknesses in the industrial sector: because of a reliance on subsidies and exemptions, Mexican industry can barely compete in the international marketplace; the domestic market is incapable of absorbing Mexico's industrial production; and industry is dependent on foreign technology.

See also IRON AND STEEL INDUSTRY (MEXICO).

Bibliography. W. P. Glade and Charles Anderson, *The Political Economy of Mexico,* Madison, Wis., 1963; Roger D. Hansen, *The Politics of Mexican Development,* Baltimore, 1971; E. López Malo, *Ensayo sobre localización de la industria de México,* Mexico City, 1960; Sanford A. Mosk, *Industrial Revolution in Mexico,* Berkeley, Calif., 1950; Manuel Germán Parra, *La industrialización de México,* Mexico City, 1954; Leopoldo Solís, *La realidad económica mexicana: Retrovisión y perspectivas,* Mexico City, 1970; Raymond Vernon, *The Dilemma of Mexico's Development,* Cambridge, Mass., 1963.

MOISÉS GONZÁLEZ NAVARRO

INGENIEROS, JOSÉ (1877–1925). Argentine psychologist, philosopher, and man of letters. Ingenieros, whose real surname was Ingegneros, was born in Palermo, Italy. His family settled first in Montevideo, then moved to Buenos Aires. As a medical student he was drawn to the field of psychiatry, and he became so proficient in it that he was appointed professor of experimental psychology in the Faculty of Philosophy and Letters at the University of Buenos Aires.

Ingenieros and Leopoldo LUGONES joined the Socialist party soon after it was founded (*see* SOCIALIST PARTY: ARGENTINA), and together edited a socialist journal, *La Montaña* (1897), but neither it nor their interest in Marxism lasted long. Ingenieros's deeper concerns and his willingness to tolerate all philosophical viewpoints became evident during his long editorship of the *Revista de Filosofía,* the important journal he founded in 1915. He himself was strongly influenced by positivism, then at the peak of its popularity in Argentina, as well as by evolutionism and even doctrinaire materialism. His favorite theories of evolution, to judge from his works on psychology and sociology and especially his *Principios de psicología* (1911), were those of Darwin and Spencer. His well-known *La evolución de las ideas argentinas* (2 vols., 1918–1920) illustrates how he could apply the concepts of positivism and evolutionism in historical analysis. In this study he elaborated upon a notion first expressed in 1838 by Esteban ECHEVERRÍA that the development of Argentina from 1810 to the era of Juan Manuel de ROSAS was affected by the clash of two diametrically opposed philosophies, one liberal and the other conservative, with the first representing the forces of progress and the second the colonial tradition. Rosas, he maintained, was able to restore the colonial regime because he was the agent of the *porteño* cattle breeders and their allies and of the Holy Alliance. For a long time his conclusions were widely accepted, although they were not based on archival research. In recent years they have lost much of their appeal.

JOSEPH T. CRISCENTI

INQUILINO. "Tied peasant," or tenant-laborer, of the traditional Chilean hacienda. The institution of *inquilinaje,* which is essentially similar to agrarian labor arrangements prevailing elsewhere in Latin America, grew up in colonial times and was universal in Chile by the end of the eighteenth century. It embraced (and embraces) a great variety of different conditions and practices. Basically, however, the *inquilino* was a laborer who was granted a parcel of land within a hacienda in return for accepting labor obligations toward the landowner. In theory he was free to leave the hacienda, but in practice his obligations toward the *patrón* tended to become hereditary. In general terms, the *inquilino* occupied a stable position within the Chilean estate, particularly when compared with the less-privileged day laborers or itinerant workers. *Inquilinaje* survived as a universal Chilean practice almost until the present day, but the process of AGRARIAN REFORM set in motion in 1967 by the Christian Democratic government heralded its eventual disappearance from the agrarian scene in Chile (*see* PARTIDO DEMÓCRATA CRISTIANO).

SIMON COLLIER

INQUISITION, HOLY OFFICE OF THE. The Inquisition was introduced into America in 1517 to preserve religious and hence political orthodoxy, so close was the union of church and state under the PATRONATO REAL. At first inquisitorial authority was exercised by secular and regular prelates, but tribunals of the Inquisition were established in Lima in 1570, Mexico City in 1571, and Cartagena in 1610. Although no tribunal was established in Brazil, inquisitorial investigations did take place, beginning in 1591. Inquisitors concentrated on rooting out Christian heretics and those who secretly practiced Judaism. The tribunals were also concerned with clerical misbehavior, establishing the purity of lineage of candidates for the priesthood, and maintaining intellectual orthodoxy, principally through the censorship of books. Although the Inquisition was concerned primarily with Europeans, Indians were tried for idolatry, polygamy, sacrifice, and other practices. However, after 1570 jurisdiction over Indian orthodoxy did not fall to the tribunal of the Inquisition but to episcopal officials.

As a result of recurrent jurisdictional disputes, the Holy Office exacerbated tensions between civil and ecclesiastical officials and among the latter. Greedy inquisitors and their informants sometimes profited from the denunciation of business competitors and the sequestration of their wealth. Corrupt inquisitors contributed to the ill repute of the institution, as did the harshness of their methods. Overall, the Inquisition helped maintain Spanish control in America by combating ideas regarded as spiritual or political heresies, particularly those propounded by the Protestant Reformation and the Enlightenment (*see* ENLIGHTENMENT: SPANISH AMERICA). This function it served until it disappeared in the chaos of the wars for independence.

MARGARET E. CRAHAN

INSTITUTE OF NUTRITION OF CENTRAL AMERICA AND PANAMA (INSTITUTO DE NUTRICIÓN DE CENTRO AMÉRICA Y PANAMÁ; INCAP). Regional office for the Americas of the World Health Organization (WHO), with its seat in Guatemala. It was established in 1946 by intergovernmental agreement, modified in 1949, and given permanent form by an agreement signed on December 18, 1953. INCAP is controlled by a Directing Council composed of representatives from each of the six member countries and the Pan American Sanitary Bureau, acting since 1947 as the executive organ for the PAN AMERICAN HEALTH ORGANIZATION. Its Director is appointed by the Pan American Sanitary Bureau with the approval of the Directing Council. The first Director was Dr. Nevin S. Scrimshaw, who was succeeded by Dr. Moisés Béhar of Guatemala. INCAP is supported by contributions from the member states, the Pan American Sanitary Bureau, and other sources.

INCAP works to advance nutritional science and promote its application in member countries. It conducts research and clinical and biological studies and trains technical personnel from the region and from other Western Hemisphere countries. It cooperates with universities, agricultural institutions, and other scientific groups. Perhaps the best-known accomplishment of INCAP is the development of Incaparina, a low-cost, culturally acceptable food or food supplement especially rich in protein, compounded of locally produced elements. Incaparina's ability to forestall and counteract protein deficiency makes it a valuable corrective to the low-protein diets characteristic of the region. The product has aroused much interest in other world areas where diets lack protein.

WILLIAM J. GRIFFITH

INSTITUTIONAL REVOLUTIONARY PARTY. *See* PARTIDO REVOLUCIONARIO INSTITUCIONAL.

INSTITUTO SUPERIOR DE ESTUDOS BRASILEIROS (ADVANCED INSTITUTE OF BRAZILIAN STUDIES; ISEB). Brazilian government agency that existed in Rio de Janeiro from 1955 to 1964. The ISEB was conceived as a center of political and social studies to analyze Brazilian problems and apply the techniques and data of the social sciences to questions of national policy. In this regard it functioned as a predominantly civilian-led counterweight to the armed forces' ESCOLA SUPERIOR DE GUERRA. For administrative purposes the ISEB was located within the Ministry of Education, but it was given complete autonomy to carry out research, teaching, and publication in the fields of economics, history, philosophy, political science, and sociology. Initially it attracted such prominent scholars as Anísio Teixeira, Hélio Jaguaribe, and Roberto CAMPOS, and its research publications contributed measurably to the formulation of a doctrine of rapid economic development. Intensely nationalistic from the outset, the ISEB became increasingly xenophobic and Marxist-oriented, with the result that it lost many of its original contributors. Considered subversive by the forces that overthrew the administration of João GOULART, it was abolished by one of the first decrees of the revolutionary government in April 1964.

ROLLIE E. POPPINO

INTEGRALISMO. Reactionary Brazilian movement whose goal was the "integral" state under a single authoritarian head of government. Headed by Plínio Salgado, a writer from São Paulo, the Acão Integralista Brasileira emerged in 1932. Patterned after European fascist movements, Integralismo attracted Brazilians with its doctrinal blend of Catholicism, anti-Semitism, mysticism, and extreme nationalism. In imitation of Continental fascist movements, Integralismo adopted its own symbol (the Greek letter sigma), shirt color (green), the mass street rally, and street violence. Democrats, Jews, Communists, and Masons were deemed the primary "enemies of the nation"; the motto of the movement was "God, Country, and Family."

Integralismo attempted to win over the middle classes, which feared the growing influence of bolshevism in Brazil. Indicative of the movement's extent and vitality was Salgado's candidacy for the Presidency in 1937; in a close election the Integralistas conceivably could have held the balance of power. On November 10, however, President Getúlio VARGAS dissolved the Congress and instituted his ESTADO NOVO dictatorship. The Integralistas hoped they would benefit from this coup, but Vargas declared political organizations illegal on December 2, 1937. Thwarted in their political designs, a group of Integralistas and anti-Vargas military men attacked the Presidential Palace on the night of May 10, 1938. They were repulsed, their leaders were arrested, and Plínio Salgado was exiled to Portugal. Integralismo as an organized political movement ceased to exist.

LESLIE S. OFFUTT

INTENDANCY SYSTEM. Administrative system of French origin that was introduced by the Bourbons in Spain and its empire with the purpose of making the government more efficient through a process of centralization. First tried in Cuba in 1764, it was established in Buenos Aires in 1782, in Peru in 1784, and in Chile and New Spain in 1786. Intendancies aimed at improving the collection of revenue, suppressing the economic and social abuses of the CORREGIDOR system, bettering the administration of justice, and achieving greater prosperity by stimulating agriculture, mining, and trade. Each intendancy comprised an area that had previously contained numerous *corregimientos* and was under the jurisdiction of an *intendente,* a Spanish officer appointed by the crown, who had complete control in matters of justice, war, fiscal policies, and general public administration. Intendancies were subdivided into *partidos* governed by *subdelegados* appointed by the viceroys.

The intendancy system was most successful in the increase of royal revenue provided by larger collections of *alcabalas* (sales taxes; *see* ALCABALA), levies on mineral production, and Indian personal tribute. Its success depended on the ability of each intendant. Unfortunately, at local levels many *subdelegados* continued the extortions of the corregidores. Therefore, the administration of justice and the treatment of the Indians improved little. The effectiveness of the intendancies was reduced by jurisdictional conflicts with viceroys, *audiencias* (*see* AUDIENCIA), and religious authorities. These contested the wide powers of the intendants, which overlapped many of their own functions. With minor revisions intendancies remained in effect until the end of Spanish rule.

ASUNCIÓN LAVRIN

INTER-AMERICAN COMMITTEE OF THE ALLIANCE FOR PROGRESS. *See* COMITÉ INTERAMERICANO DE LA ALIANZA PARA EL PROGRESO.

INTER-AMERICAN COMMITTEE ON PEACEFUL SETTLEMENT. Subsidiary organ of the PERMANENT COUNCIL of the ORGANIZATION OF AMERICAN STATES (OAS). Under the amended OAS Charter, which went into effect in 1970, the Committee is to aid the Council in working for the peaceful settlement of disputes among member states. The present Committee is the successor to the Inter-American Peace Committee. The formation of the earlier body was authorized by the HAVANA MEETING in 1940, but it was not formally constituted until 1948, when it was organized to help settle a conflict between Cuba and the Dominican Republic. Its area of responsibility was broadened by the Fifth Meeting of Consultation of Ministers of Foreign Affairs (Santiago, 1959), which empowered it to examine methods of preventing intervention from abroad against established governments, the relationship between violation of human rights and political tensions affecting the peace of the hemisphere, and the relationship between economic underdevelopment and political instability. In 1960, acting under its new mandate, the Committee investigated and verified Venezuelan charges against the Trujillo government in the Dominican Republic, concluding that the regime's violations of human rights were responsible for increasing tensions in the Caribbean area.

RODNEY D. ANDERSON

INTER-AMERICAN COOPERATION. *See* ALLIANCE FOR PROGRESS; ANDEAN GROUP; CENTRAL AMERICA, FEDERATION OF; CENTRAL AMERICAN COMMON MARKET; CENTRAL AMERICAN COURT OF JUSTICE; ECONOMIC COMMISSION FOR LATIN AMERICA; INTER-AMERICAN COMMITTEE ON PEACEFUL SETTLEMENT; INTER-AMERICAN DEVELOPMENT BANK; INTER-AMERICAN ECONOMIC AND SOCIAL COUNCIL; LATIN AMERICAN FREE TRADE ASSOCIATION; ORGANIZACIÓN DE ESTADOS CENTROAMERICANOS; ORGANIZATION OF AMERICAN STATES; PERMANENT COUNCIL; RIO TREATY; SERVICIO TÉCNICO INTERAMERICANO DE COOPERACIÓN AGRÍCOLA.

INTER-AMERICAN COUNCIL FOR EDUCATION, SCIENCE, AND CULTURE. Council of the ORGANIZATION OF AMERICAN STATES (OAS), directly responsible to the General Assembly. According to the amended OAS Charter, which went into effect in 1970, the purpose of the Council is "to promote friendly relations and mutual understanding between the peoples of the Americas through educational, scientific, and cultural cooperation and exchange between Member States." The Council is composed of one principal representative from each member state and holds at least one meeting a year at the ministerial level. Under the unamended OAS Charter, this body was called the Inter-American Cultural Council and was subordinate to the Council of the OAS.

RODNEY D. ANDERSON

INTER-AMERICAN DEVELOPMENT BANK (BANCO INTERAMERICANO DE DESARROLLO; IDB). Regional lending agency, the purpose of which is to promote the economic development of the Western Hemisphere states that are members. The IDB, which formally came into existence in 1960, is financed largely by capital shares subscribed by the member states, by the sale of its bonds on the international market, and by special funds.

Proposals for the establishment of an inter-American bank can be traced as far back as 1889, but they were renewed with greater urgency by the Latin American nations after World War II. At this time the United States was opposed to the creation of such a bank, arguing that ample funds for development projects were available through the International Bank for Reconstruction and Development (World Bank; IBRD). For their part the Latin Americans maintained that the IBRD was overly conservative in its lending policies and would not finance badly needed projects in housing, education, and the like. In 1958, however, at the urging of Undersecretary of State Douglas Dillon, the Eisenhower administration reversed its position, and by December 1959 a charter for the IDB had been drawn up and ratified by nineteen nations (*see* ALLIANCE FOR PROGRESS).

The Charter of the IDB provided that it would begin operations with capital resources of $1 billion. The Bank's ordinary capital resources accounted for $850 million of this sum, of which the United States subscribed $350 million in 35,000 shares of $10,000 each; Argentina and Brazil each subscribed 5,157 shares, and Mexico 3,315. The remaining $150 million was to be used by the Bank's Fund for Special Operations (FSO), which provides financing for development projects under more liberal terms than those accorded projects financed from the Bank's ordinary capital resources. Until the mid-1960s the Bank also administered the Social Progress Trust Fund (SPTF), which was financed by $525 million made available by the United States and was designed to contribute to Latin American development through long-term loans and technical assistance in such fields as low-cost housing, environmental sanitation, advanced education, and rural development for small farmers. By 1965 the resources of the SPTF were virtually exhausted, and the financing of the fields it covered was transferred to the FSO, whose resources were increased for the purpose.

By 1970 the total resources of the IDB had grown to nearly $6 billion. From 1961 through 1970, 622 loans, totaling more than $4 billion, were authorized in the following areas: infrastructure (transportation, communications, and electric power), 31 percent; agriculture and industry, 41 percent; social projects (urban housing and development, sanitation, and education), 25 percent; and miscellaneous, 3 percent. These loans helped finance projects with a total investment of $11 billion, thus indicating the catalytic nature of the bank's operations.

The diminution of the political and financial support of the United States for the Bank in the early 1970s led to efforts to broaden its resource base through increased participation by Japan and other capital-exporting countries. In 1972 Canada became a member, subscribing $300 million to the capital resources of the Bank.

Overall control of the Bank is vested in the Board of Governors. Each member of the Bank appoints one governor and one alternate, who serve five-year terms. The operations of the Bank are in the hands of a seven-man Board of Directors. One director is appointed by the member with the largest number of shares in the Bank; the others are elected by the governors of the other members. The governors also choose the Bank's President, who serves a five-year term. The first President of the IDB, Felipe HERRERA of Chile, was elected in 1961 and reelected to a second term; after his resignation in 1970, he was succeeded by Antonio ORTIZ MENA of Mexico.

Bibliography. Felipe Herrera, "The Inter-American Development Bank," in Claudio Véliz (ed.), *Latin America and the Caribbean: A Handbook,* New York, 1968, pp. 558–564; Inter-American Development Bank, *Proceedings: Eleventh Meeting of the Board of Governors,* Washington, 1970; John White, *Regional Development Banks: A Study of Institutional Style,* London, 1970; Miguel S. Wionczek (ed.), *Economic Cooperation in Latin America, Africa, and Asia: A Handbook of Documents,* Cambridge, Mass., 1969.

RODNEY D. ANDERSON

INTER-AMERICAN ECONOMIC AND SOCIAL COUNCIL. Council of the ORGANIZATION OF AMERICAN STATES (OAS), directly responsible to the General Assembly. According to the amended OAS Charter, which went into effect in 1970, its purpose is "to promote cooperation among the American countries in order to attain accelerated economic and social development." In carrying out its purpose, the Council reviews and evaluates the efforts of member nations and acts as a coordinating agency for all the economic and social activities of the OAS. The Council is composed of one principal representative from each member state, and it holds at least one meeting a year at the ministerial level. The COMITÉ INTERAMERICANO DE LA ALIANZA PARA EL PROGRESO (CIAP) is to act as the permanent executive committee of the Council as long as the ALLIANCE FOR PROGRESS is in existence. Under the unamended OAS Charter, the Economic and Social Council was subordinate to the OAS Council; its elevation to a status equal to that of the latter indicates the increased concern of the OAS with economic and social issues.

RODNEY D. ANDERSON

INTER-AMERICAN HIGHWAY. *See* PAN AMERICAN HIGHWAY.

INTER-AMERICAN TECHNICAL SERVICE FOR AGRICULTURAL COOPERATION. *See* SERVICIO TÉCNICO INTERAMERICANO DE COOPERACIÓN AGRÍCOLA.

INTER-AMERICAN TREATY OF RECIPROCAL ASSISTANCE. *See* RIO TREATY.

INTERNATIONAL COFFEE AGREEMENT. Market-stabilizing agreement signed in 1962 by the world's coffee-producing and -consuming nations. The objectives of the agreement were to achieve a balance between coffee supply and demand, lessen the hardships caused by coffee surpluses and excessive fluctuations in price, and maintain prices at equitable levels. The chief mechanism of the agreement for achieving its objectives was the periodic allocation of export quotas, adjusted to world demand, among the producing nations. By 1968 membership in the International Coffee Organization created by the agreement had increased to sixty-two nations. The agreement expired on September 30, 1968, and was renewed for five years.

The origins of the agreement can be traced to the Inter-American Coffee Agreement (1940), which apportioned the United States market among fourteen producing nations in Latin America. This agreement expired in 1948, but faced with excessive production and falling prices in the mid-1950s, the Latin American producers decided in 1957–1958 to establish export quotas among themselves. The following year they were joined by the major African producers, whose output represented 14 percent of the world total at the time.

With the signing of the 1962 agreement, the participation of the consuming countries, considered a necessity for the success of the quota system, was ensured.

The agreement functioned with considerable success during the 1960s, but by the beginning of the 1970s the conditions that had made it possible had changed; coffee, for example, was in relatively short supply. As a result, after 1970 the agreement began to be eroded by conflicts between the producing and consuming nations, especially over prices, and its future after 1973 was uncertain.

HELEN DELPAR

INTERNATIONAL CONFERENCE OF AMERICAN STATES, SIXTH. *See* HAVANA CONFERENCE.

INTERNATIONAL CONFERENCE OF AMERICAN STATES, SEVENTH. *See* MONTEVIDEO CONFERENCE.

INTERNATIONAL CONFERENCE OF AMERICAN STATES, EIGHTH. *See* LIMA CONFERENCE.

INTERNATIONAL CONFERENCE OF AMERICAN STATES, NINTH. *See* BOGOTÁ CONFERENCE.

INTERNATIONAL CONFERENCE OF AMERICAN STATES, TENTH. *See* CARACAS CONFERENCE.

INTERNATIONAL PETROLEUM COMPANY (IPC). Subsidiary of Standard Oil of New Jersey that began operations in Peru in 1914. Its investments rose from $14 million in 1919 to more than $250 million in 1968, making it one of the largest foreign concerns in Peru. IPC's record as an employer has been relatively good. It has paid higher wages than the national average, and it has provided adequate housing and labor conditions for its employees. Nevertheless, for more than forty years the company was one of the major targets of nationalists. The reasons for the attacks can be traced to the monopolistic powers of the company (it refined 98 percent of the crude oil in Peru) and, more important, to the manner in which it came to control its major holding of La Brea y Pariñas in northern Peru.

The company acquired the oil lands in 1924 from a British concern and, contrary to Peruvian law, claimed rights over the property's subsoil. This claim was based both on a 1923 international arbitration board decision (tainted by outside diplomatic pressure upon the board) and on the 1826 Peruvian government grant to the original owner. Although the property had been sold repeatedly, IPC and all its predecessors argued that the original grant had included control over the subsoil. A succession of Peruvian administrations, on the other hand, denied the validity of the claim. However, they were either unwilling or unable to press the issue forcefully. Finally, in 1968 the military junta took the step advocated by nationalists since the 1920s and expropriated the property. This action raised the question of proper reimbursement to the IPC. The junta agrees with compensation in principle, but it argues that before it can act, the IPC must pay for more than forty years of illegal exploitation of La Brea y Pariñas. The cost to the company surpasses the assessed value of the property. Thus the issue remains unresolved, and it continues to cloud United States–Peruvian relations.

ORAZIO A. CICCARELLI

IRIGOYEN, HIPÓLITO. *See* YRIGOYEN, HIPÓLITO.

IRON AND STEEL INDUSTRY (BRAZIL). Brazil has the largest-known iron reserves in the world, and new finds are reported periodically. Most of the known deposits are located in the state of Minas Gerais.

The iron and steel industry in Brazil is largely a child of the twentieth century. Although the Portuguese and Brazilian crowns attempted to promote the industry in the nineteenth century, little was accomplished. By the end of the 1920s a number of small iron and steel mills existed, many of them financed with a mixture of Brazilian and foreign capital. The largest of the firms was the Belgo-Mineira Company in Sabará, Minas Gerais. Between 1920 and 1929 annual iron and steel production increased from less than 5,000 tons to 91,000 tons.

Stimulated by the effects of the Great Depression, the outbreak of World War II, and economic nationalism, the government of Getúlio VARGAS called for dramatic increases in iron and steel output. Various programs resulted in an increase to about 150,000 tons by 1939. Vargas founded the National Steel Company in 1941. This company, financed largely by Brazilian and foreign public funds, built the integrated iron and steel complex at VOLTA REDONDA in the Paraíba Valley near Rio de Janeiro. Completed at a cost of well over $100 million in 1946, the plant had an initial capacity of 300,000 tons. Since 1946 government interest in the industry has not decreased. The production facilities at Volta Redonda have been expanded, other plants built (mostly in Minas Gerais, São Paulo, and Rio de Janeiro), and foreign and national investment in this sector of the economy encouraged. United States, German, and (in recent years) Japanese investments have contributed to the rapid growth of the industry.

Pig iron production in 1970 reached 4,205,247 tons, and steel ingot tonnage was 5,390,360. Iron ore exports stood at 118,083 tons. Per capita consumption of steel rose to approximately 160 pounds.

LAWRENCE J. NIELSEN

IRON AND STEEL INDUSTRY (MEXICO). Within Latin America Mexico ranks second only to Brazil in the production of iron and steel. Its closest rival, Argentina, produced in 1970 less than half the total Mexican production of both iron and steel. The iron and steel industry has become an important part of the Mexican government's drive toward greater import substitution, since increased production of these commodities not only has provided much-needed employment for thousands of Mexican workers but also has released scarce foreign exchange for the purchase of imports for which Mexico does not enjoy a comparative advantage.

Fundidora de Fierro y Acero, S.A., established in Monterrey in 1900, was the first integrated iron and steel mill in Mexico and in Latin America. Mexico's second integrated iron and steel mill was Altos Hornos de México, S.A. (AHMSA), located in Monclova, Coahuila, which began operations in 1944; by the mid-1950s AHMSA's output of steel and pig iron exceeded Fundidora's. In 1962 AHMSA obtained control of another mill, La Consolidada.

In the two decades since 1950 the growth of Mexican iron and steel has outstripped the growth of all other sectors of the Mexican economy. In 1950 annual output amounted to 227,000 metric tons of pig iron and 390,000 metric tons of steel. In 1970 production of iron and steel had grown by more than 1,000 percent and 900 percent, respectively, over the 1950 level of production to a record output of 2,353,000 metric tons of iron and 3,834,000 metric tons of steel. As a result, the percentage of Mexico's iron and steel consumption originating from imports declined from 55 percent in the 1940s to less than 20 percent in the 1960s. Indeed, in 1969 Mexico exported 349 million pesos worth of iron and steel.

The Mexican government's impressive success in stimulating industrial growth has been to a large extent dependent upon an expanded iron and steel industry. It is therefore not surprising to find that in recent years the Mexican government has been the primary force behind continued growth in this basic industry. The government not only is one of the largest customers for the increased production but has aided the industry through protective tariffs, import licensing, and tax exemptions. In addition, the government is the principal stockholder in AHMSA. Fundidora and the third largest firm, Hojalata y Lámina, S.A., are private, domestically owned corporations.

TAYLOR K. COUSINS

IRON AND STEEL INDUSTRY (VENEZUELA). Venezuela's major iron ore deposits are located in the Guiana (Guayana) Highlands. Although known since colonial times, they have been commercially exploited successfully only since World War II. The few prewar efforts to establish a viable iron ore extracting operation in the Guiana Highlands foundered on transportation, communication, and health problems. But with the impetus of wartime scarcity and high iron ore prices, United States firms began active programs in the region. The first United States enterprise was the Iron Mines Company, a subsidiary of Bethlehem Steel, which began efforts as early as 1933 near the town of El Pao, located close to the confluence of the Caroní and Orinoco Rivers (*see* ORINOCO RIVER). By the use of a combination of railroads, barges, and oceangoing ships the transportation dilemma had been solved by 1950, and commercial extraction could begin. In 1946 the Orinoco Mining Company, a subsidiary of United States Steel, discovered the Cerro Bolívar, a solid iron ore mountain near the Caroní-Orinoco nexus. Upon this basis the Orinoco Mining Company controlled 85 percent of Venezuela's output by 1960. Extraction of ore rose from a modest beginning of less than 200 metric tons in 1950 to more than 20 million metric tons in the 1960s and early 1970s.

More than 90 percent of the ore produced in Venezuela is shipped to the United States, and Venezuelan ore accounts for about 20 percent of United States iron ore imports. The Venezuelan government has taken over the task of building a national steel industry at Puerto Ordaz near the mining centers and has constructed a steel mill capable of processing 750 thousand tons of steel per year. Beginning production in 1962, the mill became a profitable operation in 1971. Its major products are steel pipelines and structural steel.

JOHN V. LOMBARDI

ISAACS, JORGE (1837–1895). Colombian novelist and poet. Isaacs was born, according to some of his biographers, in Cali, on April 1, 1837, and died in Ibagué on April 17, 1895. His father, a convert from Judaism, was an Englishman who had immigrated to Colombia via Jamaica. Isaacs' youth was spent on El Paraíso, a hacienda near the Cauca River. This environment was utilized in his novel *María*, 1867 (*María, a South American Romance*).

Isaacs was educated in Cali, Popayán, Bogotá, and London, where he studied medicine although he did not complete his studies. In 1860 he took up arms in a civil war in defense of the Conservative government. As a result of the war, his father lost his properties and the family was left penniless when he died in 1864. That year Jorge Isaacs went to Bogotá in the hope of rebuilding the family's fortune. Most of his literary activities date from this period.

In the Colombian capital Isaacs joined the literary group El Mosaico; there he read his poems, collaborated in the group's journal, *El Mosaico,* and published a collection of poetry (*Poesías*, 1864). While serving as a road inspector in the coastal area of Colombia in 1864–1865, he wrote the drafts of *María*, which he published in Bogotá in 1867. In the years 1871–1873, having abandoned the Conservative party and become a Liberal, he served as Colombian Consul in Chile, and on several occasions he was elected to the Colombian Congress.

The idyllic romance that Isaacs presents in *María*, considered by many critics Spanish America's most exemplary romantic novel, is filled with sentimentality, melancholy, local color, fatalism, exoticism, and many of the other characteristics of romanticism. The work also contains autobiographical features.

DANIEL R. REEDY

ISABELLA (ISABEL) I (1451–1504). Queen of CASTILE (1474–1504) and wife of Ferdinand II of Aragon (1452–1516). Isabella's marriage in 1469 to Ferdinand, heir to the Aragonese throne, served to unite the crowns of the two kingdoms. Isabella claimed the throne of Castile upon the death (1474) of her half brother Henry IV, but her right to the succession was contested by partisans of Henry's young daughter Joan, whose paternity was questioned by Isabella's supporters. There ensued a civil war, which Isabella won by 1479. The same year Ferdinand, who had been acknowledged as joint ruler with Isabella in Castile, became King of Aragon. During their reign Ferdinand and Isabella, dubbed *los reyes católicos* (the Catholic Kings) by Pope Alexander VI in 1494, succeeded in asserting royal authority in Castile at the expense of the nobility and the towns and in strengthening religious uniformity throughout Spain by establishing the Inquisition (1478) and by expelling unconverted Jews (1492). Isabella encouraged a moral and intellectual reformation of the Catholic Church, which also came increasingly under royal control.

Early in 1492, just after the fall of Granada, the last Moorish kingdom in Spain, Ferdinand and Isabella rejected Christopher COLUMBUS's project of seeking a western route to the Indies. Later, however, Isabella was persuaded to accept Columbus's terms and even offered to pledge her jewels to finance the voyage, but this did not prove necessary. Once the colonization of America was under way, the pious Isabella took seriously the crown's obligation to Christianize the

Indians, imposed by the papal bull of 1493 giving dominion over the Indies to the Kings of Castile. In a deathbed codicil to her will, she appointed Ferdinand Regent of the Indies, charging him to convert the Indians and to prevent their mistreatment. Earlier, however, she had sanctioned forced labor and even enslavement of the Indians under certain conditions.

Upon Isabella's death in 1504, the succession in Castile passed to her daughter Joan (Juana), who was the wife of Archduke Philip, son of the emperor Maximilian. However, Philip's sudden death (1506) and the evident mental deterioration of Joan resulted in Ferdinand's being named to rule Castile. When he died in 1516, the thrones of Castile and Aragon passed to Joan and Philip's son, who became CHARLES I of Spain.

HELEN DELPAR

ISAMITT, CARLOS (1887–   ). Chilean composer and ethnomusicologist. Isamitt was born in Rengo. After his graduation from the National Conservatory of Santiago, his career developed in a twofold manner: as a composer and as an ethnomusicologist deeply involved in the study of the music of the ARAUCANIANS. His papers and publications on the latter are considered basic to the study of South American tribal music. In 1965 Isamitt was awarded the National Prize for the Arts in Chile. Some of his compositions use Araucanian Indian devices, as in the well-known *Friso araucano* for voice and orchestra (1931). Others are based on a very abstract approach to composition somewhat related to atonality; a good example is his *Tres pastorales* for violin and piano (1939).

JUAN A. ORREGO-SALAS

ISEB. *See* INSTITUTO SUPERIOR DE ESTUDOS BRASILEIROS.

ISLAS MALVINAS. *See* FALKLAND ISLANDS.

ITURBIDE, AGUSTÍN DE (1783–1824). Mexican soldier and Emperor under the title Agustín I. Born in Valladolid (modern Morelia), Michoacán, Iturbide studied briefly in the seminary of that city, then worked on his father's hacienda, and at fourteen entered the colonial militia as a second lieutenant. When the rebel-lion led by Miguel HIDALGO Y COSTILLA began, Iturbide went to Mexico City and joined the royalists. He fought throughout the campaigns against Hidalgo and José María MORELOS Y PAVÓN and by 1820 was a colonel. When constitutionalism was revived in Spain in 1820, Iturbide joined in the movement to keep liberalism out of Mexico by declaring independence. With some duplicity he negotiated with Vicente GUERRERO, the principal insurgent, and convinced him to accept the Plan of Iguala, calling for independence under a monarchy, which Iturbide authored. After reaching agreement with the new Spanish Viceroy, Juan O'Donojú, in the Treaty of Córdoba, Iturbide secured Mexican independence on September 27, 1821. Iturbide assumed control of the new government as President of the Regency Council. A popular demonstration in Mexico City in May 1822 proclaimed him Emperor, and this was ratified on May 20.

As Emperor, Iturbide quarreled frequently with Congress and finally dissolved it in favor of a smaller body composed only of his supporters. A military rebellion spearheaded by Antonio López de SANTA ANNA was successful in forcing Iturbide to abdicate in March 1823. He and his family were pensioned and sent to Italy in exile, but Iturbide returned to Mexico in July 1824, ignorant of a resolution passed in Congress the previous April that declared him a traitor and outside the law. He was apprehended soon after landing on the coast of Tamaulipas, sentenced to death by the legislature of that state, and executed on July 19, 1824.

CHARLES R. BERRY

ITURRIAGA, ENRIQUE (1918–   ). Peruvian composer and teacher. Born in Lima, he studied privately with Andrés SAS and then at the National Conservatory of Music with Rodolfo Holzmann. Having received a grant from the French government, he went to France, where he worked with Arthur Honegger. Since 1957 he has taught at the university of Lima and has actively promoted contemporary music among laymen through lectures, concerts, radio programs, and the like. His catalog of works is short, but each example is carefully finished. Outstanding is his *Vivencias* for orchestra (1965).

JUAN A. ORREGO-SALAS

Jesuits (Colonial Period)
Justo, Juan B.

J

JESUITS (COLONIAL PERIOD). *See* RELIGIOUS OR-DERS (COLONIAL PERIOD).

JESUITS, EXPULSION OF (BRAZIL). The first Jesuits arrived in Brazil in 1549, and the order rapidly acquired lands, properties, and slaves, ostensibly to support its educational establishments and missionary activity. By the mid-eighteenth century Portuguese officials, like their Spanish counterparts, had come to view the order with suspicion and to regard the great complex of Spanish and Portuguese Jesuit missions, which stretched from the mouth of the AMAZON RIVER almost to the RÍO DE LA PLATA, as a threat to the interests of both nations. There was some substance to their concern. Since the *paulistas* were repelled in the mid-seventeenth century, the mission villages had been prepared to defend themselves and to do so effectively, as was shown by the mission Indians of Uruguay, who had taken up arms to oppose the terms of the Treaty of Madrid (*see* MADRID, TREATY OF). Moreover, real philosophical differences lay behind the views of the contending parties. The all-powerful Portuguese Minister the Marquês de POMBAL believed in the need to incorporate and Europeanize the Indians through inter-marriage and the secularization of the missions, so that population might be increased in the frontier regions. The Jesuits, on the other hand, saw that the removal of their protection would have disastrous consequences by exposing the Indians to ruthless exploitation and decimation.

Moreover, the consistent refusal of the Jesuits to pay either *dízimos* (tithes) or customs dues infuriated Pombal's brother, the new Governor of Grão Pará and Maranhão, who wanted to construct and finance an extensive network of fortifications out of the meager resources of the local treasury. It was precisely the Jesuits' real and supposed wealth and exemptions that made any action against them highly popular, for the activity of the Society of Jesus was by no means confined to the missions. Among the Jesuits' vast holdings in urban and rural property were some of the greatest landed estates in the Americas; the fazenda of Santa Cruz in the captaincy of Rio de Janeiro, for example, extended over 100 square leagues and was worked by 1,000 slaves. The Jesuits possessed at least seventeen sugar mills and were substantial participants in the trade in cacao and Amazon products.

That is not to say that the society did not perform vital services. The educational establishment was almost entirely supported and staffed by Jesuits, who operated nineteen *colégios* throughout the colony. The accumulation of property, moreover, had come more as a result of institutional stability, careful management, and the long-term accumulation of endowments and benefactions than from corruption of spiritual objectives by worldly materialism. In fact, the Jesuits' problem was probably the opposite; they were too pure, too successful in blocking the materialism of others, especially with respect to the exploitation of Indian labor. In any event, they were a sitting target for expropriation, for they served small or powerless constituencies, either the Amerindians or the sons of the elite, and they were few in numbers (474 in the province of Brazil, 155 in the province of Maranhão). They were also the victims of intrachurch rivalries that enabled action against them to be disassociated from any feeling that the church itself was under attack. Indeed, some of their most outspoken enemies came from within the ecclesiastical establishment.

The crisis came to a head as a result of an unsuccessful attempt to assassinate King Joseph I in 1758, although relations between the state and the Jesuits had been deteriorating since 1755. Whatever the truth of the involvement of the Jesuits in the abortive aristocratic plot (and their "guilt" was more that of association than of participation), Pombal used the attack on the King as a means both to crush aristocratic opposition and to expel the Jesuits from Portuguese territory in 1759. The expropriation of Jesuit properties followed and provided important windfalls to the hard-pressed treasury. Little is known about the distribution of property in Brazil, but clearly a major transference of titles took place, often at greatly underrated prices, with social and economic consequences no less important than the impact of the expulsion on educational and missionary activity.

Bibliography. Dauril Alden, "Economic Aspects of the Expulsion of the Jesuits from Brazil: A Preliminary Report," in Henry Keith and S. F. Edwards (eds.), *Conflict and Continuity in Brazilian Society,* Columbia, S.C., 1969, pp. 25–65; Serafim Leite, S.J., *Suma Histórica da Companhia de Jesús no Brasil,* Lisbon, 1965; id., *História da Companhia de Jesús no Brasil,* 10 vols., Lisbon and Rio de Janeiro, 1938–50; Kenneth R. Maxwell, "Pombal and the Nationalization of the Luso-Brazilian Economy," *Hispanic American Historical Review,* vol. XLVIII, no. 4, November 1968, pp. 608–631; Marcos Carneiro de Mendonça, *A Amazônia na Era Pombalina: Correspondência Inédita do Governador e Capitão-General do Estado do Grão-Pará e Maranhão, Francisco Xavier de Mendonça Furtado, 1751–1759,* 3 vols., Rio de Janeiro, 1963.

KENNETH R. MAXWELL

JESUITS, EXPULSION OF (SPANISH AMERICA). The Jesuit order, founded in 1540, was introduced in the Spanish dominions in 1572. Until their expulsion in 1767 the Jesuits distinguished themselves as teachers of creole youth and as missionaries among the Indians, especially in Paraguay, Sonora, and Lower California. The reasons for their expulsion are complex. They had won the enmity of other orders and many laymen on theological and economic grounds. They held allegiance to the Pope above that due to the monarch and supported the philosophy of populism in direct opposition to the enlightened despotism and regalism prevalent in the eighteenth century. The order was wealthy and exempt from tithing, and its members exerted an unusual influence on Spanish and colonial society as confessors and educators.

The Jesuits also became objectionable to some of the ministers of CHARLES III, such as the Conde de Campomanes and the Conde de Aranda, who considered the order an obstacle to social and economic reforms. It was rumored that the Jesuits had promoted a Guaraní uprising in Paraguay (1754–1756). However, the direct cause of their expulsion was the belief that they had instigated popular riots in Madrid (1766) against the Minister of Finance, the Marqués de Esquilache (Squillacci). Campomanes and Aranda recommended the expulsion of the Jesuits on the ground of conspiracy against the government. The expulsion was decreed on February 27, 1767. The order was kept in great secrecy to prevent resistance by the population. In the colonies the expulsion was carried out during the latter part of the year; a few local efforts to block it were quelled. The expulsion deprived Spanish America of a group of devoted teachers and dedicated missionaries.

ASUNCIÓN LAVRIN

JEWS IN LATIN AMERICA. Jews constitute less than 1 percent of the Latin American population, but their contribution to the economic and cultural development of that region is far greater than their total numbers convey. No Latin American nation is without Jews, but Argentina, Brazil, Uruguay, Mexico, and Chile are the only countries with large numbers; in several Central American countries their total number is less than 200. There were Jews in Latin America during the colonial period, as well as many *conversos,* or Christians of Jewish origin, but it was not until the end of the nineteenth century that Jews arrived in appreciable numbers. Today the Jewish communities of Latin America face much the same problems as do Jewish communities elsewhere, outside of Israel. Anti-Semitism periodically becomes acute, but the gravest problem is cultural assimilation.

Numerous opinions have been advanced concerning the arrival of the first Jews to the Western Hemisphere. One, which enjoyed wide circulation in the seventeenth and eighteenth centuries, was that certain groups of Indians were descended from one or several of the Ten Lost Tribes of Israel. The purported discovery of pre-Columbian artifacts with Hebraic inscriptions or motifs was advanced as proof of early Jewish contact. Evidence has been offered to establish that Christopher COLUMBUS was a *converso.* This view has been popular among some intensely nationalistic Spanish historians who wish to claim that Columbus was of Spanish rather than Italian origin. Few scholars regard the evidence presented as convincing, although it is well documented that several members of the crew on his first voyage were *conversos,* some of whom certainly continued secretly to adhere to Judaism. Thus, both Christians and Jews reached the Western Hemisphere at the same time.

Throughout the colonial period the Spanish crown sought to prevent both Jews and *conversos* from emigrating to the New World. Practicing Jews were prohibited from entrance, as were *conversos* and their descendants through the third generation. The desperation of Jews upon being expelled first from Spain and then from Portugal was so great that many were ready to take the constant risk of exposure to start a new life in the New World. Jews and *conversos* soon were living in all the colonies. Their influence was sufficiently great for Spain to install the Inquisition in the Western Hemisphere (*see* INQUISITION, HOLY OFFICE OF THE). In Mexico alone, between 1528 and 1795, approximately 1,300 people were accused of Judaizing and brought before the courts. One of the most famous cases to appear before the Holy Office was that of the

Governor of the Kingdom of Nuevo León, Luis de Carvajal y de la Cueva. The son of new Christians, Carvajal died in the prison of the Inquisition in 1591 after being found guilty of aiding Jewish apostates. His nephew, Luis de Carvajal (El Mozo), a practicing Jew, was burned at the stake in 1596 with other members of the family. Though probably an exaggeration, it was estimated that 2,000 of the 20,000 Europeans living in Mexico in the seventeenth century were *conversos*. Buenos Aires, in the seventeenth century extremely isolated from the mainstream of Spanish colonial life, became the refuge of many Portuguese *conversos* escaping the threat of being returned to Lisbon from Brazil to face the Holy Office.

The Portuguese, who gave temporary refuge to Spanish Jews after their expulsion from Spain in 1492, had a more indulgent attitude toward *conversos* emigrating to Brazil than the Spaniards did with respect to their colonies. As early as 1502 a Portuguese *converso,* Fernando de Noronha, was granted the right to exploit a large area in Brazil. Several other *conversos* were awarded large grants of land during the sixteenth century. Once the Inquisition had been installed in Portugal, many more *conversos* emigrated, and it was this group that played a major role not only in the economic development of Brazil but in that of the Spanish colonies as well.

During the Dutch occupation of Brazil (1630–1654; *see* DUTCH IN BRAZIL), practicing Jews of Portuguese descent, then residents of Calvinist Holland, arrived as merchants. Because of the greater religious tolerance of the Dutch during their occupation, a number of Portuguese *conversos* joined them in the open profession of Judaism. During this period of Dutch occupation the Jewish population reached approximately 1,000, and there were several synagogues in the colony. After the Dutch withdrawal most Jews left. The majority returned to Holland, but some settled in the Guianas, while others scattered throughout the Dutch, British, and French possessions in the Caribbean. A small group reached the Dutch colony of New Amsterdam, at the mouth of the Hudson River, and formed the first Jewish community in what later became the United States.

During the eighteenth century the power of the Inquisition diminished, and by its close a handful of practicing Jews, mostly merchants, were living throughout Latin America, some openly professing their religion. The majority were Sephardim, the descendants of Spanish and Portuguese Jews who had fled to northern Europe or to countries in the Mediterranean Basin. During the nineteenth century a small number of Ashkenazim, Jews whose ancestors had resided in northern Europe for centuries, began to arrive. Those who came were primarily from France, Germany, and Great Britain. In the nineteenth century the first formally established Jewish communities emerged. One of the oldest is that of Buenos Aires. Yet the first publicly announced Yom Kippur, the Jewish New Year, was not held until 1862. If it had not been for a mass migration of Jews that began in the last decade of the century, the small Jewish communities established in Latin America earlier would have become extinct through assimilation with the Christian majority, since Jews who migrated earlier in the century rarely came with families.

The great political and economic turmoil that arose in Central and Eastern Europe at the close of the nineteenth century and continued until after World War II, with its associated anti-Semitism, forced almost 3.5 million Jews to emigrate to the Western Hemisphere. The vast majority entered either the United States or Canada, but a significant minority reached Latin America and had an enormous impact on Jewish life in the region.

The evolution of Jewish communities in Latin America is similar to that of Anglo-America. The small Western European Jewish communities that had grown up earlier in the nineteenth century were engulfed by the large wave of Eastern and Central European Jews who arrived at the turn of the century. As in Anglo-America, friction developed between the better-educated, less religious, more cosmopolitan, and more affluent Western European Jews and their less educated, more Orthodox, highly parochial, and poorer Eastern and Central European coreligionists. In some countries each group formed its own religious and social organizations. Although the differences between the two groups have diminished markedly, there still remain communities that have "German" synagogues as well as "Russian."

Friction within the Jewish communities of Latin America was aggravated by the arrival of large numbers of Sephardic Jews from the eastern Mediterranean. Latin America experienced a far greater immigration of Sephardim than Anglo-America did. Fundamental differences exist between the Ashkenazim and the Sephardim. Aside from differences in religious ritual, the former employ Yiddish, a mixture of German and Hebrew, as a lingua franca. The Sephardim speak Ladino, a combination of medieval Spanish and Hebrew. In all Latin American countries with significant Sephardic populations, they maintain separate religious and social institutions. Intermarriage between Ashkenazim and Sephardim continues to be a rarity.

In 1970 the American Jewish Congress estimated that there were 778,000 Jews living in Latin America. Argentina, with 500,000 Jews, had the largest community. In fact, that nation's Jewish population is the world's fourth largest outside of Israel. Approximately 150,000 are living in Brazil, 50,000 in Uruguay, and 35,000 in both Mexico and Chile. Other countries with significant Jewish populations are Venezuela and Colombia, with about 12,000 each.

Latin American Jews are heavily concentrated in the larger cities, where they are commonly employed in tertiary activities, especially commerce. This is especially true of smaller Jewish communities. In Buenos Aires, which has a Jewish population in excess of 350,000, the range of employment is much broader, with widespread Jewish participation in services, industry, and the civil service. Argentina was the site of a philanthropic effort by a wealthy European Jew, Baron Maurice de Hirsch, to resettle his Eastern European coreligionists on the land in an attempt to dispel the prevailing view that Jews were only urban commercial people. Despite the purchase of more than 1.5 million acres of land and the establishment of a number of colonies between 1891 and 1936, at one time containing more than 40,000 Jews, the venture failed. Today fewer than 10,000 Jews remain in the colonies.

Because of the great importance attached to education among the Jews, the economic success of many of the immigrants, and the availability of a variety of educational facilities in the larger cities where most Jews live, their children have turned increasingly toward the professions. This is especially true of medicine and dentistry, although there is widespread Jewish participation in many other highly technical professions. Jews have also made an important contribution to Latin American arts, particularly in Argentina, where they have risen to prominence in art, the theater, film making, literature, and music.

Although Latin American constitutions no longer prohibit non-Christians from holding public office, few Jews have participated in politics, and even fewer have held high office. In Argentina several provincial governors have been Jewish, as have a few members of presidential Cabinets. The Brazilian Congress has had Jewish senators, and Presidents have appointed several Jews to their Cabinets. There are at least four Jewish generals in the Brazilian Army, although Jewish participation in the military of Latin America is extremely rare. There are a number of cases of Christians, with recent Jewish backgrounds, holding high office. Nicaragua has had a President, a Vice President, a Minister of Finance, and a mayor of Managua, all of Ashkenazim descent.

Religious anti-Semitism no longer is a major problem in Latin America, and the Catholic Church has no official position against the religion, although individual officials have occasionally made anti-Semitic statements. The common man generally has no knowledge of the religion, and the term "Russian" or "Turk" is often more commonly used in reference to Jews than the name "Jew." Strong Jewish resistance to assimilation, with its associated Jewish schools, social organizations, and economic institutions, is not looked upon with the hostility that it sometimes engenders in Anglo-America. Many groups that have come to Latin America have developed their own institutions, in the belief that the culture they brought with them was superior to that which they found on arrival. The prevailing anti-Semitism is primarily economic and is confined generally to the middle and upper classes. Jews are resented for their more rapid upward economic mobility, which is ascribed to dishonest business practices. Whereas many Jewish businessmen are not blameless, unscrupulous business practices are not found only among Jews. Political anti-Semitism has arisen among conservatives because of the worldwide identification of Jews with leftist political views, as well as the frequent association of the younger, Latin American–born urban Jews with national leftist groups.

The future of Judaism in Latin America is not bright, especially for the smaller Jewish communities. Great efforts are made periodically to assemble young Jews from small communities in the hope that matches can be made, while the wealthier send their children to Israel or the United States for their education. Nevertheless, the rate of intermarriage in the small communities is extremely high, and it is doubtful if Jewish life will survive much longer in a number of Latin American countries. Assimilation is slower in the larger communities, which continue to maintain a variety of institutions to preserve unity. Curiously, religion is seldom the cohesive force it is elsewhere, outside of Israel. In Buenos Aires, in 1970, there were only twenty-two rabbis: fifteen Orthodox, four Conservative, and three Reform. Most Jews maintain an ill-defined ethnic solidarity based largely upon their own feelings of separation and not due to any Christian efforts to isolate them. There are no external barriers to assimilation. Yiddish still is a unifying element among some Jews, but more common is a concern for the future of Israel, along with a vague sense of cultural superiority associated with being Jewish. Without the support of a religious base it appears inevitable that the present unifying elements will gradually lose their importance and assimilation will intensify.

Bibliography. Jacob Beller, *Jews in Latin America,* New York, 1969; Boleslau Lewin, *Los judíos bajo la Inquisición en Hispanoamérica,* Buenos Aires, 1960; Seymour Liebman, *The Jews in New Spain,* Coral Gables, Fla., 1970; Jacob R. Marcus, *The Colonial American Jew, 1492–1776,* Detroit, 1970; Morton D. Winsberg, "Jewish Agricultural Colonization in Argentina," *Geographical Review,* vol. LIV, no. 4, October 1964, pp. 487–501; Arnold Wiznitzer, *Jews in Colonial Brazil,* New York, 1960.

MORTON D. WINSBERG

JIMÉNEZ DE QUESADA, GONZALO (1509?–1579). Spanish conqueror of the CHIBCHA Indians and founder of Santa Fe de Bogotá and the Kingdom of New Granada. A graduate of the University of Salamanca and a lawyer, Quesada joined the expedition of Pedro Fernández de Lugo bound in 1535 for the conquest of Santa Marta. Lugo later named Quesada, the expedition's magistrate, his second in command. Searching for a wealthy Indian empire, Quesada led 600 men through terrible hardships in a year-long trek up the Magdalena River Valley. He emerged on an upland plain inhabited by the Chibcha Indians (1537), entering the domain of the dominant Chibcha chief, the *zipa,* whose forebears, unbeknownst to Quesada, were the source of the El Dorado legend (*see* DORADO, EL). In contrast to the *zipa,* the Chibcha chief of Tunja, who was known as the *zaque,* did not resist the Spaniards, who obtained a large booty of gold and emeralds from him.

After founding the town of Santa Fé de Bogotá, probably in April 1539, Quesada soon found his claim challenged by the arrival of the expeditions of Sebastián de BENALCÁZAR and Nikolaus FEDERMANN. The crown bypassed Quesada and awarded the governorship to Alonso Luis de Lugo, son of the deceased commander. Granted the empty title of marshal of Bogotá (1549), Quesada finally received (1568) a royal license to explore the Venezuelan LLANOS in search of El Dorado. He was granted a hereditary governorship over 400 leagues of territory between the Amazon and Orinoco Rivers. Quesada's resulting expedition (1569–1572) failed completely, and the grant passed to his niece's husband, Antonio de Berrío, after Quesada's death.

WILLIAM S. DUDLEY

JIMÉNEZ OREAMUNO, RICARDO (1859–1945). President of Costa Rica (1910–1914, 1924–1928, 1932–1936). For more than fifty years Jiménez occupied the first rank as a molder of Costa Rican public opinion. His major rival for political preeminence in the first third of the twentieth century was Cleto GON-

ZÁLEZ VÍQUEZ, who shared his overall political outlook and many of his characteristics. Jiménez's wit, oratorical skills, moral rectitude, and imperturbability left an imprint on Costa Rican folklore unmatched by that of any other leader. He served as a legislator and judge, and he was President three times (1910–1914, 1924–1928, 1932–1936). If few material or diplomatic accomplishments were linked with his name, it mattered little to his constituents, who apparently did not then expect solutions to social and economic problems. His presidential terms were characterized by few national or international crises. Still, as evidence of Jiménez's awareness of demands for social reform during his last Presidency, one might list his establishment of the National Bank of Insurance, a far-reaching measure limiting private enterprise in the insurance field, and his efforts in 1935 to distribute land to the landless. Political reform, such as the replacement of the electoral system with a direct presidential vote, which occurred during his first Presidency, was characteristic of Jiménez and his era. He had so little taste for personal glorification that he insisted that no school or public building be named after him and that his portrait not be displayed in government offices.

CHARLES L. STANSIFER

JOÃO (JOHN) I (1357–1433). King of Portugal (1385–1433). João, the illegitimate son of Pedro I (r. 1357–1367), became grand master, or head, of the military and chivalric Order of Avis at an early age. Upon the death of his half brother, Ferdinand I, in 1383, the Portuguese crown passed to Ferdinand's young daughter, Beatriz, who was married to Juan (John) I of Castile. Opponents of the Castilian connection turned to João, who was recognized as King by a Cortes at Coimbra on April 6, 1385, and defeated Juan at the Battle of Aljubarrota the following August. João was supported by the artisans and middle classes against the majority of the old nobility, who had taken the side of the Castilian invaders. His subsequent marriage to Philippa of Lancaster, daughter of John of Gaunt, helped secure an English alliance. Under the Avis dynasty founded by João, which ruled until 1580, Portugal acquired an African, Asian, and American empire.

KENNETH R. MAXWELL

JOÃO (JOHN) IV (1604–1656). King of Portugal (1640–1656). João, the 8th Duke of Braganza, was the son of a niece of King João III (r. 1521–1557) and therefore had a strong collateral claim to the Portuguese throne, which had been occupied by the King of Spain since 1580 (*see* BABYLONIAN CAPTIVITY). He was crowned King following the restoration of Portuguese independence in 1640.

During João's reign Portugal was deprived of most of its remaining possessions in Asia, was expelled from Arabia and the Persian Gulf, and temporarily lost Angola and São Tomé as well. However, the rebellion against the Dutch in Pernambuco reestablished Portuguese control of all Brazil in 1654, and the American colony became, in the words of the King, his "milch cow" (*see* DUTCH IN BRAZIL). João signed treaties with England in 1642 and 1654, the latter of which granted special privileges to English merchants resident in Portugal and extended tariff concessions to English goods. The King's daughter, Catherine of Braganza,

married Charles II of England in 1662. Members of the house of Braganza founded by João ruled Brazil as emperors from 1822 until 1889 and Portugal as kings until 1910.

KENNETH R. MAXWELL

JOÃO (JOHN) VI (1767–1826). King of Portugal (1816–1826). The son of Maria I and Pedro III, he married CARLOTA JOAQUINA DE BORBÓN Y PARMA in 1785. He became acting Prince Regent in 1792, when Maria became hopelessly insane, formally assuming the title only in 1799. Upon the death of Maria on March 9, 1816, he became King of Portugal, Brazil, and Algarve.

After 1806 João came under increasing pressure from Napoleon to conform to the Continental system and end the Portuguese alliance with Great Britain. João hesitated, fearing the probable loss of Portugal's overseas empire to the British; yet he realized that Portugal was incapable of resisting the French Army. After attempting a policy of apparent neutrality and placation of Napoleon, João ultimately resorted to an ancient plan for the transfer of the Portuguese royal family to Brazil, aided by the British. The seemingly precipitous flight of the entire court occurred as French troops entered Lisbon on November 29, 1807. João reached Bahia on January 22, 1808, and Rio de Janeiro on March 7.

Considered ineffectual in Europe, João is honored in Brazil for introducing a new era through political, economic, cultural, and educational changes intended to make Brazil a place suitable for royal residence and the administrative center of the empire; these culminated in the elevation of Brazil to the category of kingdom in 1815. João created a bureaucratic structure in Brazil, enlarged the judiciary, and founded the Royal Mint and the Bank of Brazil. He also established a military academy, a school of engineering and artillery, schools of anatomy, surgery, and medicine, a law faculty, the National Library, a botanical garden, and the Imperial Academy of Fine Arts (now the National School of Fine Arts). European artists, scholars, and scientists were invited to visit Brazil, and the printing press was introduced to the colony.

On January 28, 1808, João issued a decree opening Brazilian ports to trade with friendly nations; this decree is considered the basis of Brazilian economic autonomy, although at the time it meant in practice trade with Great Britain. A decree of June 11, 1808, reduced the import duties paid on Portuguese goods to 16 percent while other goods were charged 24 percent until the commercial treaties of 1810 between João and Great Britain provided for a low 15 percent duty on British goods, the Portuguese achieving parity with the British only in 1818. João stimulated the industrialization of Brazil by removing all previous restrictions on manufacturing on April 1, 1808, introducing machinery and new processes, and removing duties on primary materials. Agriculture benefited from efforts to help the declining sugar industry, the protection of rice from foreign competition, the cultivation of coffee, and the introduction of new products. Immigration, whether Portuguese or foreign, was encouraged; some settlers were even introduced at government expense and with generous land grants. *See* IMMIGRATION (BRAZIL).

Various motives have been advanced to explain João's activities in the territories adjoining Brazil. Reasons of security and perhaps a desire for revenge led to the occupation of French Guiana in 1808. João was also concerned with the RÍO DE LA PLATA, initially because of the Spanish-French alliance and after mid-1808 because of the possibility of revolutionary activity in that region. João considered supporting the aspirations of his wife, Carlota Joaquina, to the Spanish Regency since she was the sole member of the Spanish royal family not held prisoner by Napoleon. However, British opposition to this plan and the long-standing and bitter estrangement of the royal couple led João to hesitate about sending her to Buenos Aires, although unsuccessful diplomatic efforts continued in Spain and Great Britain to achieve her recognition as Regent. After May 1810, João was confronted with a revolution in Buenos Aires and the establishment of a royalist stronghold in Montevideo. At the request of the Spaniards, João intervened militarily in the Banda Oriental (modern Uruguay) in 1812, but the British arranged an armistice and the withdrawal of the Portuguese in 1813. Continued anarchy and incursions by Argentines and Uruguayans on his own southern frontiers led João to order a new intervention in 1816. Fighting continued until 1820, when the Uruguayan leader José Gervasio ARTIGAS was finally defeated. A congress of Uruguayan representatives then voted to accept annexation of the Banda Oriental to Brazil as the Cisplatine Province. Whatever João's true intentions, imperialist or protectionist, he did attain temporarily for Brazil the natural boundary of the Río de la Plata long sought by Portugal. Nevertheless, he was not successful in preventing the spread of revolutionary and republican ideas to his empire (*see* PERNAMBUCAN REVOLUTION).

In 1820 Portugal, affected by the loss of its political and economical preeminence in the empire, revolted. A Parliament was convened in which liberal ideas were proclaimed and a constitution demanded. A constitutional monarchy appealed to liberals, both Portuguese and Brazilian, in Brazil as well. There were even sympathetic revolts, such as the rebellion in northern Pará, to emphasize adherence to the Parliament. João was ultimately forced to accept the bases of the future constitution. On April 26, 1821, he further acceded to Portuguese wishes and left Brazil to return to Portugal, leaving the Crown Prince, the future Emperor PEDRO I, as Regent.

Bibliography. John Armitage, *The History of Brazil,* London, 1836; Sergio Buarque de Holanda (ed.), *História Geral da Civilização Brasileira,* vol. XI, *O Brasil Monárquico,* part 1, *O Processo de Emancipação,* São Paulo, 1962; Pedro Calmon, *História do Brasil,* vol. IV, *Séculos XVIII e XIX,* Rio de Janeiro, 1961; Manuel de Oliveira Lima, *Dom João VI no Brasil, 1808–1821,* 3 vols., 2d ed., Rio de Janeiro, 1945; Angelo Pereira, *D. João VI, Príncipe e Rei,* 3 vols., Lisbon, 1953–54; J. F. da Rocha Pombo, *História do Brasil,* vol. II, *O Brasil, Séde da Monarchia Portugueza: A independencia,* Rio de Janeiro, 1906–10; Francisco Muniz Tavares, *História da revolução de Pernambuco em 1817,* 3d ed., Recife, 1917; F. A. de Varnhagen, *História Geral do Brasil,* vols. V, VI, São Paulo, 1962.

L. SHARON WYATT

JONES-COSTIGAN ACT. Adopted on May 9, 1934, the act authorized the United States Secretary of Agriculture to fix quotas for sugar importation from United States possessions and Cuba (*see* SUGAR INDUSTRY: CUBA). Quotas were also established for continental sugar beet growers. Quotas from each region overseas were to be based on amounts imported into the United States during three typical years in the 1925–1933 period and were to meet estimated consumption requirements in the United States. Cuba, for example, was assigned an initial quota of 1,902,000 short tons, 22 percent of which could be refined sugar.

The immediate effect of the law was to raise the disastrously low price of sugar. The act guided United States–Cuban sugar policy for the next twenty-five years, although the Sugar Act of 1948 altered the basis on which quotas were assigned to Cuba. Additional benefits accrued to Cuba when President Roosevelt followed the act by reducing the tariff on sugar and by sponsoring the establishment of the second Export-Import Bank in March 1934 in order to lend money to the island republic.

The agreement was subsequently criticized for restricting Cuban sugar production and during the early years of the regime of Fidel CASTRO led to Cuban accusations of economic enslavement by the United States. By 1960 Cuba's quota amounted to 3,129,000 tons, or about one-third of United States sugar requirements. That year, however, relations with Cuba worsened to such an extent that on July 6 President Eisenhower suspended Cuban sugar imports into the United States. Cuba's quota was reassigned to foreign and domestic producers.

RICHARD B. GRAY

JUANA DE AMÉRICA. *See* IBARBOUROU, JUANA DE.

JUANA INÉS DE LA CRUZ, SOR (b. JUANA DE ASBAJE Y RAMÍREZ DE SANTILLANA, 1648–1695). Mexican poet, essayist, and dramatist. Sor Juana Inés de la Cruz was born in San Miguel de Nepantla. She died in Mexico City on April 17, 1695, during an epidemic.

Often called Mexico's tenth muse, she was an intellectual prodigy and reputedly learned Latin in twenty lessons at an early age. At sixteen she went to the Viceroy's palace as a lady of the Marquesa de Mancera and became a favorite of the court. She first entered the convent of the Discalced Carmelites, but illness forced her to leave the order, and she later entered that of St. Jerome, where she spent the remainder of her life. In the convent her intellectual interests did not wane, and she amassed a library of 4,000 volumes. Because of her talent as a poet she was often called upon to write *villancicos* (carols) and other pieces for special days of celebration in the church.

In response to a sermon by the Luso-Brazilian Jesuit Antônio VIEIRA, Sor Juana wrote her *Carta atenagórica,* 1690 (*The Athenagoric Letter*), which came to the attention of the Bishop of Puebla, who replied to her using the name Sor Filotea de la Cruz. Her subsequent "Respuesta a Sor Filotea de la Cruz," 1691 ("A Letter to the Bishop"), is an autobiographical essay that considers, in part, the subject of women's rights.

Sor Juana's fame as a writer is unsurpassed by that

of her contemporaries. In 1692 she published *El primero sueño* (*First Dream*), a long baroque poem with mystical overtones. Her lyric poetry is contained in *Poemas* (1692) and *Fama y obras póstumas* (1700). Her secular dramatic works include several minor pieces and two plays, *Los empeños de una casa* (*The Trials of a Noble House*) and *Amor es más laberinto* (*Love, the Greater Labyrinth*). Her religious works include her masterpiece, a sacramental play entitled *El divino Narciso* (*The Divine Narcissus*), *El mártir del sacramento* (*The Martyr of the Sacrament*), and *El cetro de José* (*Joseph's Scepter*).

DANIEL R. REEDY

JUÁREZ, BENITO (1806–1872). Mexican statesman. Juárez, a Zapotec Indian, was born in the isolated mountain village of San Pablo Guelatao in the state of Oaxaca. Orphaned at an early age, he lived with an uncle but at thirteen ran away to the city of Oaxaca, the state capital, where a sister worked as a servant for the wealthy Maza family. He found a benefactor in Antonio Salanueva, a bookbinder and a devoutly religious man. With his sponsor's encouragement he entered the diocesan seminary, from which he received a bachelor's degree in 1827. Then he entered the newly opened secular institute and pursued a degree in law, which he received in 1834. While working on his degree, he entered local politics to serve on the town council and in the state legislature. Juárez was early concerned with the inferior status and political exploitation of the Indians and defended several Indian villages in civil suits. In 1843 he married Margarita Maza, daughter of

the family for which his sister had worked. His political career advanced dramatically throughout the 1840s: he served as head of the Governor's secretariat, as delegate to the Mexican Congress during the MEXICAN WAR, and as acting Governor of Oaxaca. He was elected constitutional Governor in 1848 for a four-year term and established his reputation as a reformer. His program emphasized public works, more numerous schools, economic advancement, reorganization of the National Guard, and honest, efficient government. After his term ended, he became rector of the state's educational institute, his alma mater.

When Antonio López de SANTA ANNA was recalled to the Presidency in 1853 and developed his program of extreme centralism and reactionary conservatism, Juárez was exiled to New Orleans, where he and other Liberal republicans lived in poverty. Juárez returned to Mexico after the revolution of Ayutla began and joined the insurgents in the state of Guerrero. When the Liberals triumphed, Juan Álvarez designated Juárez as his Minister of Justice in the fall of 1855. In this capacity Juárez wrote the law which bears his name and which limited the jurisdiction of ecclesiastical and military tribunals and reformed the judicial system. He was then sent back to Oaxaca as Governor but re-emerged on the national scene in 1857, when he was elected Chief Justice of the Mexican Supreme Court. By virtue of the provisions for succession in the constitution of 1857 (*see* CONSTITUTION OF 1857: MEXICO), Juárez claimed the Presidency in 1858, when Ignacio COMONFORT helped implement a Conservative coup d'état.

As the Conservatives extended their control over central Mexico, Juárez and his supporters fled to the west and then to Veracruz, where he established his government. His administration became increasingly radical as the civil war was prolonged. Victorious in late 1860, he returned to Mexico City. Elections had been postponed during the war, but he ran as a candidate for the Presidency in 1861 and won. By now there was strong Liberal opposition to his continued hold on the government. These political questions were put aside the following year, when the government was confronted with the French invasion. In mid-1863, as the Interventionist Army occupied central Mexico, Juárez again found himself a refugee, this time in the far north, where he remained and directed the war effort until 1867, when MAXIMILIAN was defeated. Again he ran for reelection and won, arousing much opposition, and in 1871 he was elected to another four-year term, which had just begun when he died of a heart attack on July 18, 1872. During the five years of his administration after the defeat of Maximilian, he revealed himself to be less concerned with honest government and allowed the creation of a political machine to keep himself in power. But he is revered as the man who forged a nation, defeated a crack invading army, and endowed Mexico with the virtues of liberalism.

See also REFORM, THE.

Bibliography. Francisco Bulnes, *El verdadero Juárez y la verdad sobre la intervención y el imperio*, Paris, 1904; Benito Juárez, *Apuntes para mis hijos*, autobiography, many editions; Ralph Roeder, *Juárez and His Mexico: A Biographical History*, 2 vols., New York, 1968; Justo Sierra, *Juárez: Su obra y su tiempo*,

Benito Juárez. [*Juárez Sanctuary, Mexico City*]

vol. XIII, *Obras completas,* Mexico City, 1948; Charles A. Smart, *Viva Juárez! A Biography,* Philadelphia, 1963; Jorge L. Tamayo (ed.), *Benito Juárez: Documentos, discursos y correspondencia,* 11 vols., Mexico City, 1964–67.

CHARLES R. BERRY

JUÁREZ CELMAN, MIGUEL (1844–1909). President of Argentina (1886–1890). His paternal and maternal ancestors were among the original settlers of the city of Córdoba. Juárez Celman graduated from the Colegio de Montserrat, and in 1858 he entered the University of Córdoba to study law. He received a law degree in 1869 and a doctorate in jurisprudence in 1874; he took this long a time to complete his legal training because he had entered provincial politics in 1866 and his family responsibilities had increased with the death of his grandfather and mother during the cholera epidemic of 1867 (his father had died in 1847) and with his marriage to Elisa Funes Díaz of Córdoba in April 1872, four months before Julio A. ROCA married her sister Clara. Juárez Celman and Roca, whom he had met in 1867, were already close political collaborators. From 1874 to 1877 he represented the departments of Río Cuarto and Tercero Arriba (now Oliva) in the provincial legislature as deputy or senator. A member of the Partido Autonomista of Adolfo Alsina, he quickly established his reputation as a liberal and as a loyal and trustworthy friend. In 1877 he entered the provincial government of Dr. Antonio del Viso as minister of government, and the following year Roca joined the Cabinet of President Nicolás AVELLANEDA as Minister of War.

The ways in which Juárez Celman and Roca could help each other became apparent in 1880. Juárez Celman, some say, organized the league of governors that made possible the election of Roca to the Presidency and helped him suppress the *porteños* who rebelled against the federalization of their city, and Roca assisted him in winning and keeping the governorship of Córdoba. For the next three years Juárez Celman, now a member of the Partido Autonomista Nacional, tried to implement the program of the Generation of Eighty. He build schools, welcomed immigrants, established a civil marriage register, and began the modernization of the provincial capital and provincial institutions. In 1883 he entered Congress as a senator for Córdoba, and there he was the spokesman of Roca. He succeeded Roca in the Presidency after an electoral campaign noted for its violence and corruption. Gradually he replaced the governors of the provinces of Buenos Aires, Tucumán, Córdoba, and Mendoza with people he could trust. He also secured the passage of a civil marriage law (1888) and a commercial code (1889), and he launched an ambitious program to foster the economic development of the nation. Provincial governments followed his leadership, but above all it was Congress that showed unrestrained enthusiasm for the prevailing concept of "progress unlimited." Foreign loans were negotiated to finance the numerous public works projects, and the national and provincial governments issued increasing amounts of paper money. Some of the results were widespread corruption and speculation, inflation, a rash of strikes, and, finally, the financial and economic crisis of 1889–1890. The decline in the value of paper money, bonds, stocks, and real estate coincided with lower prices for Argentine exports. In 1889, in an attempt to avert bankruptcy, a vain effort was made to acquire 20 million gold pesos through the sale of public land in Europe.

As the crisis developed, there was a reaction, especially among the middle classes, to the corruption, the economic policies of the government, and the *unicato* principle of Juárez Celman whereby political power was concentrated in the party of the oligarchy. With the support of an important military element, the newly organized Unión Cívica (*see* RADICAL PARTY: ARGENTINA) started a revolt against the government on July 26–27, 1890. Roca and Vice President Carlos PELLEGRINI defeated the revolutionaries, but as they themselves were already dissatisfied with Juárez Celman's conduct, they forced him to resign ten days later, on August 6.

JOSEPH T. CRISCENTI

JULIÃO [ARRUDA DE PAULA], FRANCISCO (1915–). Brazilian politician and peasant leader. Julião was born in Bom Jardim, in the coastal sugar plantation zone of Pernambuco. The scion of a prominent landowning family, he attended private schools in Recife before graduating from the Recife law school in 1939. After practicing law for several years, Julião entered politics as a member of the Brazilian Socialist party. He was elected to the Pernambuco legislature in 1954 and was returned to office in 1958. Meanwhile, he began to build a reputation as a spokesman for the rural workers of the sugar zone and a champion of AGRARIAN REFORM.

In 1955 Julião was made honorary chairman of a peasant society, the Sociedade Agrícola e Pecuária dos Plantadores de Pernambuco, for his role in the expropriation of a large plantation that was turned over to former sharecroppers. Thereafter he gained international fame as an organizer and sponsor of peasant leagues in northeastern Brazil. He visited the People's Republic of China in the late 1950s and revolutionary Cuba in the early 1960s.

Julião was elected to the Brazilian Congress in 1962 but was deprived of office, jailed, and exiled after the revolution of March 31, 1964. In 1966 he was sentenced *in absentia* to seven years' imprisonment for having incited the peasants and attempting to overthrow the government. Julião lives in Mexico.

ROLLIE E. POPPINO

JUNÍN, BATTLE OF. Battle fought in the Peruvian central highlands in August 1824. Though a minor engagement in itself, it had significant consequences for the independence struggle in South America. The royalists had regained possession of Lima in February 1824, following the mutiny of the Callao garrison, and Simón BOLÍVAR then reestablished his headquarters at Trujillo on the northern Peruvian coast. Ably assisted by Gen. Antonio José de SUCRE, he prepared his forces for a new campaign and in mid-June took the offensive. With an army of 9,000 men he marched southeast toward a Spanish army of almost equal size under Gen. José Canterac, based in the valley of Jauja directly inland from Lima. In the late afternoon of August 6, the armies met on the plains of Junín, northwest of Jauja. Canterac sought to draw back to protect Jauja, but Bolívar insisted on giving battle with the patriot cavalry despite the unfavorable terrain. At first the patriots gave way, but the royalists overreached themselves and were thrown back in bitter hand-to-hand fighting with lance and saber. The royalists eventually broke and retreated, leaving the field to Bolívar.

The battle lasted roughly an hour and was essentially a cavalry skirmish; firearms were not used. Nonetheless, the victory served to restore the patriots' confidence, which had been undermined by the Callao mutiny and the loss of Lima. By the same token, it was a critical blow to the morale of the royalists, who did not make a serious stand again until Ayacucho (*see* AYACUCHO, BATTLE OF) and meanwhile also evacuated Lima.

DAVID BUSHNELL

JUSTICIALISM. *See* PERONISM.

JUSTO, AGUSTÍN P[EDRO] (1876–1943). President of Argentina (1932–1938). A professional soldier, civil engineer, and Minister of War in the Cabinet of Marcelo T. de ALVEAR, Justo shared with Gen. José Félix URIBURU the leadership of the 1930 military overthrow of the Radical administration of President Hipólito YRIGOYEN (*see* RADICAL PARTY: ARGENTINA). Uriburu represented the ardently conservative, Catholic upper class, while Justo was supported by the more moderate but equally dissatisfied middle class.

Uriburu established himself as provisional President, but his intellectual and personal deficiencies soon alienated his supporters. When general elections were called for November 1936, Justo emerged as the only military figure capable of the sophisticated exercise of fraud and manipulation necessary to undermine the liberal tradition as practiced by the Yrigoyen Radicals and to exclude that party from power. Justo was supported by conservative National Democrats, anti-Yrigoyen Radicals, and Independent Socialists grouped in a coalition called the Concordancia. The coalition dominated Argentine politics from 1932 until 1943.

Although Justo attained power fraudulently and his regime was thoroughly authoritarian, he did demonstrate vigor and achieve considerable success in softening the impact upon Argentina of the escalating world depression (*see* ROCA-RUNCIMAN TREATY). Most notable was the increase in the role of the state in regulating the economy. Following his succession by Roberto M. ORTIZ in 1938, Justo remained influential within the Army and until his death in 1943 exercised a moderating influence upon those officers who sought to intervene in the daily decisions of the civilian administrators.

EUGENE G. SHARKEY

JUSTO, JUAN B[AUTISTA] (1865–1928). Argentine Socialist. Justo was born on the family *estancia* of La Vanguardia, in the province of Buenos Aires. At the age of seventeen he entered the Medical School of the University of Buenos Aires, where he studied both surgery and psychology, and upon his graduation in 1888 he went to Europe to continue his studies. There he was introduced to socialism. Upon his return he helped Leandro ALEM organize the Unión Cívica Radical (*see* RADICAL PARTY: ARGENTINA), but he soon left it to form the Socialist Workers Center. By this time he evidently had come under the influence of Germán Ave Lallemant (1835–1910), a German engineer who had corresponded with Engels during the First International and who was to edit the Marxist journal *El Obrero* in 1890. In 1894 he founded the International Socialist Workers party, and on April 7 he began to publish *La Vanguardia,* the official organ of the party. The following year he left for Europe again, but this time he included the United States in his itinerary. He remained abroad long enough to translate the first volume of Karl Marx's *Das Kapital* (the translation appeared in 1898, and a corrected version in 1918). Shortly after his return, his party, now called the Argentine Socialist Workers party, changed its name to the Argentine SOCIALIST PARTY at a congress held in June 1896 and announced its entry in the electoral contest for congressmen from the city of Buenos Aires. Justo was a candidate, but he was not elected. It was not until 1904 that a Socialist, Alfredo L. PALACIOS, was elected to Congress. Eventually, Justo himself served in Congress, twice as a deputy and once as a senator for the federal capital. Outside Buenos Aires neither Justo nor his party enjoyed much popularity.

The political philosophy of Justo was a mixture of positivism, Darwinism, and Marxism. He outlined his views in *El realismo ingenuo* (1914). With its emphasis on facts and experience, *realismo ingenuo,* some maintain, is another way of saying common sense. Justo early abandoned the dialectical method of Marx for the precepts of Bernardino RIVADAVIA and Bartolomé MITRE. He favored free trade, public education for the workers, cooperatives, and the influx of foreign capital. He disapproved of imperialism and clericalism. He wanted to help the working class gain control of the state without resort to violence. The party he organized began as a party of the working class and was based on the native laborers and immigrants, especially German, who were arriving in large numbers. It gradually shifted its interest from social problems to the need for change in Congress itself.

JOSEPH T. CRISCENTI

KEITH, MINOR COOPER (1848–1929). North American and Costa Rican businessman. Through his uncle Henry MEIGGS, Keith took over a contract to build a railway from the Central Plateau of Costa Rica to the Atlantic coast. When he arrived in Costa Rica in 1871, he worked merely as a storekeeper in support of his brother, but upon his brother's departure in 1873 he took complete charge of the construction operation. The long struggle to bring the road to completion (it was finally completed in 1890) bound Keith's fortunes intimately to Costa Rica, although he later expanded his interests to include several other Latin American countries. His marriage to the daughter of a former President of Costa Rica further linked his destiny to the country.

Even before completing the railway, Keith was involved in numerous commercial enterprises. His most spectacular success was with bananas, which were ideally suited for growth in the humid lowlands of the Atlantic coast. Exporting bananas to New Orleans and Mobile, he made sufficient profits to continue railroad construction. The success of these ventures led to the organization of Keith's Tropical Trading and Transport Company, a parent of the UNITED FRUIT COMPANY, which was organized in 1899, and indirectly to Costa Rica's becoming the leading banana-exporting country in the world by 1913. *See also* BANANA INDUSTRY (CENTRAL AMERICA AND THE CARIBBEAN).

CHARLES L. STANSIFER

KINO, EUSEBIO FRANCISCO (1645–1711). Jesuit missionary. Born in Segno, Italy, he joined the Society of Jesus in 1665 and studied in the colleges of Trent and Ingolstadt, specializing in mathematics and geography. In 1678 he was appointed a missionary to Mexico, arriving there in 1681. That year he published his *Exposición astrónomica del cometa,* about the comet of 1680, which he had observed in Spain. In 1683 Kino joined the expedition of Adm. Isidro de Atondo to Baja California as royal cosmographer, but lack of supplies resulted in its failure. In 1687 Kino was commissioned to undertake missionary work among the Indians of Pimería Alta, in northwestern Mexico and southern Arizona. He founded the mission of Nuestra Señora de los Dolores, which remained his headquarters for the rest of his life.

In the ensuing years Kino founded numerous missions while he explored the vast area assigned to him. He undertook forty expeditions, exploring the Altar River Valley (1690), southern Arizona (1691), the Santa Cruz River (1691), the Gila River (1694), and the Colorado River (1700–1701). As a result of his travels Kino became convinced that California was a peninsula. His tireless missionary activities were carried out among the Yumas, Quiquimas, Cocopas, and other tribes. His life was devoted to church building, the work of conversion and baptism, and the organization of Indian communities. He became the protector of the Pima Indians against attempts to turn the missions over to the secular clergy and the encroachments of Spanish settlers. Kino mapped the territory he covered in his trips and wrote extensive reports and diaries of his travels. The best known of his foundations is San Xavier del Bac, near Tucson, Arizona. His missionary work was essential in the expansion of the frontiers of the Spanish possessions in northern Mexico.

ASUNCIÓN LAVRIN

KORN, ALEJANDRO (1860–1936). Argentine philosopher. Korn was born in San Vicente, Buenos Aires Province. There are many similarities between his career and that of José INGENIEROS. Both studied medicine and specialized in psychiatry; both shared the enthusiasm of their classmates for positivism, but Korn was later to dispute its merits with Ingenieros; and both, though Korn later than Ingenieros, were Socialists for brief periods. For many years after he graduated from medical school, Korn practiced medicine in various communities of the Province of Buenos Aires, and he devoted his leisure moments to reading historical works and the modern philosophers. Gradually he found formal philosophy more exciting than medicine, and in 1906 he became a professor of philosophy in the Faculty of Philosophy and Letters at the University of Buenos Aires. He eventually transferred to the University of La Plata. No one school of philosophy seems to have had a major impact on his thinking. His philosophy was a blend of his own reflections and those of the philosophers he read. Among the philosophers who influenced him were Henri Bergson, Benedetto Croce, William James, and, above all, Wilhelm Dilthey. Korn criticized positivism, but he never rejected it completely or ceased to admire one of its exponents, Juan Bautista ALBERDI. Some of his criticisms appear in his *Las influencias filosóficas en la evolución nacional* (1936), a brilliant effort, like that of Ingenieros, to identify the fundamental characteristics of Argentina.

JOSEPH T. CRISCENTI

KUBITSCHEK [DE OLIVEIRA], JUSCELINO (1902–   ). President of Brazil (1956–1961). Kubitschek was born in Diamantina, Minas Gerais, and was raised in humble circumstances by his widowed mother, a schoolteacher of Czech descent, whose surname he took as his own. Self-supporting from an early age, Kubitschek attended medical school in Belo Horizonte, graduating in 1927, and spent three years in Europe, where he trained in surgery in Paris and completed hospital internship in Berlin. He returned to Brazil late in 1930 to begin medical practice in Belo Horizonte. He also took a commission as a medical officer in the Minas Gerais state military forces and served in combat on the São Paulo border during the revolt of 1932.

Kubitschek entered politics in 1933 as secretary and protégé of Benedito Valadares, who had just been appointed Interventor (Governor) of Minas Gerais by President Getúlio VARGAS. In 1934 Kubitschek was elected to the national Congress, where he served until the coup d'état of November 10, 1937, by which Vargas became dictator of Brazil. After three years of private medical practice, Kubitschek was appointed mayor of Belo Horizonte, a post he held until the end of the Vargas dictatorship in 1945. As mayor he engaged the architect Oscar NIEMEYER to design several municipal projects, including the futuristic Pampulha church, since hailed as a masterpiece of modern Brazilian architecture. In 1945, with Valadares, Kubitschek was a founding member of the PARTIDO SOCIAL DEMOCRÁTICO (Social Democratic party, PSD) in Minas Gerais and was elected on its ticket to the Constituent Assembly,

where he took part in drafting the new constitution (*see* CONSTITUTION OF 1946: BRAZIL). He served in Congress until 1950, when he was elected Governor of his home state. As Governor of Minas Gerais from January 1951 until January 1955, Kubitschek pursued an ambitious development program that tripled the output of electric power and expanded the state highway network by five times. These accomplishments marked him as a forceful administrator and helped him win his party's nomination for the Presidency in February 1955.

Kubitschek's candidacy caused alarm among civilian conservatives and in some military circles, especially after he was endorsed by the PARTIDO TRABALHISTA BRASILEIRO (Brazilian Labor party) and João GOULART became his running mate. Nonetheless, he campaigned vigorously, promising to give Brazil "fifty years of progress in five." Kubitschek presented the voters with a list of some thirty "impossible" production targets, largely in the areas of transportation, basic industries, agriculture, and power, that he vowed to meet or surpass during the presidential term. He and Goulart won a plurality in the bitterly contested elections of October 3, giving rise to a spate of rumors of a coup d'état to bar them from office. Kubitschek took no part in the "countercoup" of November 11, 1955, carried out by War Minister Henrique LOTT to assure his right to the Presidency. Kubitschek and Goulart were inaugurated without incident on January 31, 1956.

Kubitschek's five-year administration represented

Juscelino Kubitschek. [*Organization of American States*]

the high point reached by Brazil under the open political system established in 1945. In an atmosphere of political peace in which civil liberties flourished and the rights of person and property were secure, there were an unprecedented rate of economic growth and a comparable rise in the spirit of nationalism. Kubitschek personified and stimulated these changes. Imbued with infectious optimism and confidence in Brazil's future as a world power, he convinced the Brazilian people of their ability to reach and sustain the high level of economic development necessary for the nation to achieve its destiny.

Most of Kubitschek's campaign promises were fulfilled. Highway mileage, electric power generating capacity, and steel production nearly doubled, while petroleum output soared and facilities for storing and transporting agricultural products were increased many times over. Even more striking achievements were registered in the private industrial sector, in which, for example, an entire new automobile industry was erected behind tariff walls. Kubitschek's greatest and most controversial project was the construction of Brasília on the inland plateau, to serve as the capital and hub of an interregional highway system linking all Brazil. The new capital, designed by Lúcio COSTA and executed in large part by Oscar Niemeyer, was inaugurated on April 21, 1960. To achieve its impressive record the Kubitschek administration invited foreign capital into Brazil on favorable terms, borrowed heavily abroad, tolerated a high level of corruption in public office, and left a legacy of monetary inflation. Kubitschek left office on January 31, 1961. In 1962 he was elected to the Senate from the state of Goiás, and early in 1964 he was nominated by the PSD for reelection to the Presidency. Opposed to the revolution of March 31, 1964, he was removed from the Senate and deprived of political rights for ten years by the revolutionary government.

Bibliography. J. W. F. Dulles, *Unrest in Brazil,* Austin, Tex., 1970; "JK Awakes the Giant," *Manchete,* special ed., 1960; Juscelino Kubitschek, *A Marcha do Amanhecer,* São Paulo, 1962; Rollie E. Poppino, "Brazil since 1954," in José Maria Bello, *A History of Modern Brazil, 1889–1964,* Stanford, Calif., 1966; R. M. Schneider, *The Political System of Brazil,* New York, 1971; T. E. Skidmore, *Politics in Brazil, 1930–1964,* New York, 1967.

ROLLIE E. POPPINO

L

Lacerda, Carlos
Lynch, Elisa Alicia

LACERDA, CARLOS [FREDERICO WERNECK DE] (1914–). Brazilian politician and journalist. Lacerda, the son of the writer-politician Mauricio Lacerda, was born in Vassouras, Rio de Janeiro. A militant Communist in the 1930s, he was a founding member of the conservative UNIÃO DEMOCRÁTICA NACIONAL (UDN) in 1945. Always a popular vote getter, Lacerda represented the UDN in the municipal assembly of Rio de Janeiro (1947–1951), in Congress (1954–1960), as Governor of the state of Guanabara (1960–1965), and as its nominee for the Presidency of Brazil (1964–1965).

Lacerda's career as a journalist and politician was built largely upon his persistent and unrestrained opposition to the person, policies, and political heirs of Getúlio VARGAS. An unsuccessful attempt on Lacerda's life by the Presidential Guard on August 5, 1954, precipitated the crisis that resulted in President Vargas's suicide. Lacerda opposed the election of Juscelino KUBITSCHEK and João GOULART and went into voluntary exile when their supporters seized power in November 1955. In 1960 Lacerda endorsed the candidacy of Jânio QUADROS but broke with Quadros after the latter's inauguration as President.

When Quadros resigned in August 1961, Lacerda backed the abortive effort to block Vice President Goulart's accession to the Presidency. He participated in the revolution of 1964 and nominated Humberto CASTELLO BRANCO for the Presidency. Lacerda soon broke with the revolutionary regime, however, and in 1967 tried to organize an opposition movement including followers of ex-Presidents Kubitschek and Goulart. Lacerda's political rights were canceled in December 1968.

ROLLIE E. POPPINO

LADINO. Spanish word signifying a sagacious, cunning, crafty person or one adept at learning languages. It is thought originally to have described the qualities of a person, or the person himself, who was quickly latinized after the Roman conquest. By extension it was applied to any person who quickly learned and adopted the attributes of a conquering people.

In Guatemala and to some degree elsewhere in Central America, the term formerly was used to mean a person of mixed blood, a mestizo. It now carries a purely cultural connotation, meaning a person, irrespective of racial origin, who culturally is not Indian. This is an inclusive category ranging from individuals of pure European descent to the biological Indian who has adopted cultural attributes that identify him with the European rather than the Indian way of life. Some of the cultural traits that mark this distinction are wearing European-type clothing rather than traditional Indian dress, speaking Spanish or another European language rather than an Indian tongue, wearing shoes rather than sandals or going barefoot, and sleeping on a bed raised from the floor.

To an Indian, to become "ladinoized" means to forsake a culture that henceforth will regard him as alien and to adopt another in which he will not be fully accepted. For the interval of transition, perhaps for his lifetime, he may count as a statistical ladino, but as an individual he remains in cultural limbo. It was estimated in 1966 that slightly more than 58 percent of the Guatemalan population could be considered ladino.

WILLIAM J. GRIFFITH

LAFTA. *See* LATIN AMERICAN FREE TRADE ASSOCIATION.

LAM, WIFREDO (1902–   ). Cuban painter. He is the best known of Cuba's modern painters, a group that includes Fidelio Ponce de León (1895–1949), Amelia Peláez (1897–1968), and Mario Carreño (1913–   ). Lam is unique in his powerful evocation of Afro-Cuban VODUN spirits in a style based on Picasso's and on West African inventions. Funny and frightening, his paintings appeal to current tastes for the psychological and the primitive.

Lam was born in Sagua la Grande and studied at the National School of Fine Arts in Havana, from which he was sent to Madrid. He worked independently in Madrid and had his first show there in 1928. His early work is in a subtle postimpressionist style. In the 1930s he turned to surrealist symbolism. In 1937 he went to Paris with a letter of introduction to Picasso, who befriended him, and the two showed together in New York in 1939.

During World War II Lam was in Cuba, and it was in this period that he turned to Afro-Cuban subjects. *The Jungle* (1943), in the Museum of Modern Art, New York, is his best-known painting. He continued to work in this manner, his style growing simpler and more abstract. He also did illustrations for André Breton's *Fata Morgana* and Aimé Césaire's *Retour au pays natal*.

TERENCE GRIEDER

LA MAR, JOSÉ DE. *See* MARSHALS OF AYACUCHO.

LAMPEÃO (b. VIRGOLINO FERREIRA DA SILVA, 1900–1938). Brazilian bandit. Despite the shortness of his career, Lampeão captured the Brazilian imagination and became the stereotype of the *cangaceiro* (outlaw) in the northeastern SERTÃO, where banditry was endemic. The commonly accepted legend tells that Lampeão and his two brothers joined a *cangaceiro* band in 1917 to avenge their father's death. He rose in command, eventually leading some 200 men and spreading terror, death, and destruction throughout the NORTHEAST, raiding from Bahia to Ceará. His death in 1938 was not popularly believed until his head was displayed in Salvador. He has become a folk hero and a legend in the sertão; ballads are sung, novels written, and motion pictures made of his exploits. Unfounded rumors continue to circulate that he still lives.

Lampeão has been described as a Robin Hood, a social bandit type, or a primitive rebel, but this aspect of his character showed only intermittently, as he usually made no class distinction in his raiding. Earlier bandits were usually paid political strong-arm men, employed by local political bosses (*coronéis*), but Lampeão and bandits like him operated independently in their own self-interest and had no permanent alliances with the political structure. The rampant banditry was a symptom of poverty, social and economic deprivation, and

political unrest in the sertão. Lampeão was the strongest and most colorful example of the northeastern bandit.

ROBIN L. ANDERSON

LANDA, DIEGO DE (1524?–1579). Bishop of Yucatán. Born in Spain, Landa traveled to New Spain in 1549, shortly after being ordained. He became guardian, or head, of the convent of Izamal in 1552 and, after having been appointed *custodio* (custodian) of Yucatán (1556) and guardian of the convent of Mérida (1560), he was elected provincial of the Franciscans in Yucatán in 1561.

Landa was an excessively zealous missionary, and the lack of subtlety and patience in his methods of Christianization earned him the criticism of other missionaries and laymen. Having discovered that many apparently converted Indians were still adoring their gods, he carried out an inquisitorial search in order to discover the source of paganism. It is reported that 157 Indians died during this process. Most of the written codices of the MAYAS were also destroyed. A report of this incident prompted an official investigation. Landa traveled to Mexico City and Spain in order to defend his behavior before the COUNCIL OF THE INDIES. He was exonerated and returned to Yucatán, becoming its bishop in 1572.

During his stay in Spain he wrote the work for which he is best known, the *Relación de las cosas de Yucatán,* a compilation of the history of the Mayas, which was published in part for the first time in 1864. The *Relación* describes the territory and the main features of Mayan civilization, the Spanish conquest, and the arrival of the missionaries. He took his data from a few extant codices and from oral tradition. The *Relación* partially made up for Landa's prior destruction of Mayan sources, and it remains an indispensable source for students of Mayan culture. An English translation by A. H. Tozzer appeared in 1941.

ASUNCIÓN LAVRIN

LAND REFORM. *See* AGRARIAN REFORM.

LANUSSE, ALEJANDRO (1918–   ). Argentine army officer and President (1971–1973). After his elevation to the position of commander in chief of the Army in 1968, Lanusse was instrumental in the ouster of President Juan Carlos ONGANÍA in June 1970 and the substitution of Marcelo Levingston. Faced by a deteriorating economic situation and Levingston's apparent desire for indefinite military rule, Lanusse led the movement to depose Levingston in March 1971 and assumed the Presidency himself.

Lanusse's basic commitment was to a return to the electoral process. Thus, as part of his Great National Accord, he scheduled elections for March 1973, legalized political parties, and made concrete overtures toward the incorporation of the Peronists into the legitimate political system (*see* PERONISM). Among the primary impediments to such an accord were continued economic stagnation and a soaring cost of living. In addition, several groups had become so deeply alienated that they were committed to terrorism. If in domestic policy Lanusse viewed his government as transitional, in foreign affairs he was far more assertive. Firmly believing in Argentina's "manifest destiny" in South America, he initiated a series of state visits, culminating in his trip in March 1972 to Brazil, Argentina's rival for continental supremacy. He left office on May 25, 1973, when his successor, Dr. Héctor J. CÁMPORA, was inaugurated.

NOREEN F. STACK

LANZA, ALCIDES (1929–   ). Argentine composer, conductor, and pianist. Born in Rosario, he studied composition in Buenos Aires with Julián Bautista and Alberto GINASTERA and conducting with Kinsky. After belonging for six years to the staff of the Teatro Colón in Buenos Aires, he traveled to the United States on a Guggenheim fellowship in 1965. Shortly thereafter, he joined the Columbia-Princeton Electronic Music Center in New York as a composer and teacher. Lanza joined the faculty of McGill University in Montreal in 1971. For a number of years the director of the New Sound Composers Group of New York, he has widely promoted avant-garde music in the United States. His catalog comprises a variety of solo instrumental works, sometimes combined with electronic sounds, such as his *Plectros II* for piano and tape (1966); numerous ensemble works with or without electronic sounds; orchestral compositions, such as a concerto for piano and orchestra (1964); and *Interferences I* and *II* for winds and percussions, respectively, with tape (1967).

JUAN A. ORREGO-SALAS

LA PAZ. Capital of Bolivia. The highest capital in the world, La Paz is Bolivia's largest city and its commercial, political, and manufacturing center. The city's nearly 500,000 inhabitants are wedged into a narrow valley in the ALTIPLANO (high plateau) at an average altitude of about 12,400 feet. The higher locations of the city are occupied mostly by Indians, while the lower districts house the more elegant homes and the most exclusive sports and social clubs.

La Paz was founded in 1548 as a convenient way station between the mines of Potosí, Lake Titicaca, and the viceregal capital, Lima. Moreover, its location in a natural basin 1,200 feet below the altiplano afforded the traveler some protection from the hostile elements above. Once established, the city came to control the trade to and from Lima, along with the profitable traffic in coca leaves between the YUNGAS and the altiplano. In 1899 La Paz became the de facto capital of Bolivia, and the executive and legislative branches of government were permanently established there. The Supreme Court continued to sit in Sucre, the de jure capital.

According to some observers, La Paz is not suited to the role of chief city because of its location and climate. However, it appears that as long as the valley communities along the eastern Andes remain isolated and underdeveloped, La Paz will continue to maintain its now-traditional preeminence.

ORAZIO A. CICCARELLI

LARRETA, ENRIQUE RODRÍGUEZ (1875–1961). Argentine novelist. Born into a well-to-do family, Larreta traveled as a youth to Europe, studied law, and entered the diplomatic service. His first novel, *Artemis,* which appeared in the review *La Biblioteca* in 1896, shows the beginnings of the deliberately refined style that reaches its apogee in his most successful novel, *La gloria de don Ramiro* (1908), the best prose example of modernism (*see* MODERNISM: SPANISH AMER-

ICA). In 1926 Larreta published *Zogoibi,* written in a realistic and psychologically analytical vein and presenting a nostalgic view of the recent Argentine past. He also wrote *Las orillas del Ebro* (1949), essays on contemporary life in Spain; the novel *Gerardo o La torre de las damas* (1953); the plays *La que buscaba don Juan* (1923), *El linyera* (1932), *Santa María del Buen Aire* (1935), and *Pasión de Roma* (1937); personal memoirs, *Tiempos iluminados* (1929); and an essay, "Las dos fundaciones de Buenos Aires" (1933). His book of sonnets, *La calle de la vida y de la muerte* (1943), shows the same qualities as his prose: evocative symbolism and pictorial impressionism, together with a deep knowledge of Spanish Renaissance poetry.

RACHEL PHILLIPS

LAS CASAS, BARTOLOMÉ DE (1474–1566). Spanish Dominican and Bishop of Chiapas, Mexico, who became the best-known champion of the Indians in the New World. Las Casas challenged the racist and imperialist assumptions of the conquistadores, emphasizing Christian teachings about the dignity of man, as developed by St. Thomas Aquinas, and defending Indian culture as the equal of the European. He wished to abolish the ENCOMIENDA, return Indian lands to the Indians, and limit Spanish activity to the peaceful preaching of the Gospel.

Las Casas was born in Seville in August 1474, the son of an "old Christian" mother and a businessman father descended from *conversos* (Jewish converts to Christianity). After receiving a sound Latin education

Bartolomé de las Casas. [*Organization of American States*]

in the cathedral academy, he went to Hispaniola in 1502 as a *doctrinero* (teacher of Christian doctrine). But his daily life was that of an encomendero (holder of Indians) even after he became the first priest ordained in the New World (1512). Alert and capable, he treated his Taino Indians humanely but profited from their labor. When the Dominicans denounced Spanish treatment of the Indians (1511), Las Casas at first disagreed with them. In 1513 he went as a chaplain on the conquest of Cuba and was given an encomienda there.

He was, however, increasingly troubled by Spanish exploitation of the Indians. Nine-tenths of the Tainos on Hispaniola had perished by now. In 1514 the forty-year-old Las Casas read a text from Ecclesiasticus 34 ("Tainted his gifts who offers in sacrifice ill-gotten goods") and experienced a profound conversion. He gave up his encomienda and journeyed to Spain to fight for Indian rights at court. There he secured the support of the Co-Regents, Francisco Jiménez de Cisneros and Adrian of Utrecht; in 1516 he was appointed Protector of the Indians.

Between 1516 and 1522 Las Casas proposed several substitutes for the encomienda, including the importation of black slaves, a suggestion he later regretted making, deciding that all slavery was unjust. He even headed one idealistic but ill-fated colonizing expedition in Venezuela (1520–1522). Then he entered the Dominican order (1524) and spent several years in meditation and self-education through extensive reading. He returned to an activist role in the 1530s, preaching against a proposed conquest of Indians in Nicaragua (1536) and organizing a Dominican mission to Tuzulutlán, the "Land of War," in Guatemala (1537–1539). The mission eventually succeeded, and the Land of War was renamed Verapaz (True Peace).

In the early 1540s Las Casas lobbied at the Spanish court for the abolition of the encomienda. For this purpose he wrote, and later printed, his *Entre los remedios* (*Eighth Remedy*) and his sensational *Brevísima relación de la destrucción de las Indias* (*Very Brief Account of the Destruction of the Indies;* tr. into Eng.), said to be one source of the BLACK LEGEND of Spanish cruelty. He was gratified by King CHARLES I's issuing the NEW LAWS (1542), which provided for the phasing out of the encomienda. In 1545–1546, Las Casas was back in the New World as Bishop of Chiapas, adjoining Verapaz. But Charles was soon forced by rebellious colonists to modify the New Laws. Las Casas failed to persuade his hostile congregation to restore wealth taken from the Indians, and in 1550 he resigned his bishopric.

That year, in Valladolid, Las Casas debated the justice of the Spanish conquest with Juan Ginés de Sepúlveda. Sepúlveda argued that the Indians were, in Aristotle's phrase, "slaves by nature," who must first be subjected, then converted. But Las Casas denounced war against the Indians as unjust, defended the rationality of the Indians, and even found excuses for their practice of human sacrifice. "All the races of the world are men," he declared, and therefore were equal in their capacity for improvement. Las Casas' ideas are said to be reflected in the Ordinances of Discovery and Settlement (1573), which prohibited conquest of the Indians "by fire and by sword."

During the last sixteen years of his life Las Casas blocked an attempt by the conquistadores of Peru to have their encomiendas made perpetual, organized new missions to the New World, and completed his major writings. He died in Madrid on July 18, 1566.

Las Casas wrote many letters and treatises, but his chief works are *Del único modo de atraer a todos los pueblos a la verdadera religión* (*The Only Method of Attracting All People to the True Faith;* written 1537?), the *Apologética historia* (*Apologetic History;* written 1550–?1559), and the *Historia de las Indias* (*History of the Indies;* written 1527–1564; tr. into Eng. in abridged form). *The Only Method of Attracting All People to the True Faith* advocates the conversion of all pagans by peaceful means alone. The *Apologetic History* presents an "anthropology of hope," comparing Indian and European cultures and affirming the Indians' potentiality to rise in the scale of civilization. The *History of the Indies,* covering the period 1492–1520, remained unpublished until 1875; it has been called by Samuel Eliot Morison "the one book on the discovery of America that I should wish to preserve if all others were destroyed."

Bibliography. Marcel Bataillon, *Études sur Bartolomé de las Casas,* Paris, 1965; Bartolomé de las Casas, *Obras escogidas,* ed. by Juan Pérez de Tudela, Madrid, 1957–58; Juan Friede and Benjamin Keen (eds.), *Bartolomé de las Casas in History,* DeKalb, Ill., 1971; Lewis Hanke, *Bartolomé de las Casas, Bookman, Scholar, Propagandist,* Philadelphia, 1952; id., *The Spanish Struggle for Justice in the Conquest of America,* Boston, 1965; George Sanderlin (tr.), *Bartolomé de las Casas: A Selection of His Writings,* New York, 1971; Henry Raup Wagner and Helen Rand Parish, *The Life and Writings of Bartolomé de las Casas,* Albuquerque, N.Mex., 1967.

GEORGE SANDERLIN

LASTARRIA, JOSÉ VICTORINO (1817–1888). Chilean writer and Liberal politician (*see* LIBERAL PARTY: CHILE). Lastarria occupied a large number of public and university posts and was several times a member of the Chamber of Deputies. In 1862 he served for three months as Minister of Finance, and for a year in 1876–1877 he was Minister of the Interior, but his gifts as an active politician were not outstanding. He is remembered chiefly for his widespread intellectual and literary activity. His numerous works include literary criticism, disquisitions on politics and constitutional history, impressions of travel, treatises on geography, and reflections of a philosophical nature. His philosophy of history was deeply influenced by the works of Auguste Comte, the founder of positivism.

Lastarria's role in nineteenth-century Chilean letters was not confined to authorship. He was an active editor of journals and reviews, perhaps the most notable of which was the *Revista de Santiago,* founded by Lastarria in 1848. He was an indefatigable literary "organizer"; in 1842 he founded the influential Literary Society of Santiago and so became a prime mover in the literary revival of that year. In 1859 he formed the Circle of Friends of Literature, in 1873 the Academy of Belles-Lettres, and in 1884 the Chilean Academy. His *Recuerdos literarios* (1878) contains an interesting account of these experiences. The importance of Lastarria's role as intellectual mentor to two generations of Chilean Liberals cannot easily be exaggerated.

SIMON COLLIER

LATIFUNDIUM. Latin word for a large landed estate (Spanish and Portuguese *latifundio*). The term has traditionally been applied to relatively unproductive holdings characterized by a dependent labor force, reliance on primitive technology, and low capital investment. Thus the Bolivian AGRARIAN REFORM decree of 1953 outlawed the latifundium but not the capital-intensive agricultural enterprise producing for a large market and employing wage-earning workers who had the right to organize and to bargain collectively.

The *minifundio* is a holding so small that it cannot yield an adequate livelihood to the owner and his family. *Minifundios* exist in many areas of Latin America, notably in Venezuela, Colombia, and Ecuador.

See also HACIENDA.   HELEN DELPAR

LATIN AMERICAN BISHOPS COUNCIL. *See* CONSEJO EPISCOPAL LATINOAMERICANO.

LATIN AMERICAN FREE TRADE ASSOCIATION (ASOCIACIÓN LATINOAMERICANA DE LIBRE COMERCIO; LAFTA). Regional grouping of eleven Latin American nations for the purpose of gradually eliminating tariffs and other restrictions on imports originating in the member states and encouraging the ECONOMIC INTEGRATION of their economies. The Association was established by the Montevideo Treaty (February 18, 1960), which was signed by Argentina, Brazil, Chile, Mexico, Paraguay, Peru, and Uruguay. These countries were later joined by Bolivia, Colombia, Ecuador, and Venezuela. The treaty, which went into effect in mid-1961, provided for the establishment of virtually free trade within the area of the member states by 1973. This goal was to be achieved by periodic negotiations to draw up (1) national schedules specifying the annual reductions in duties, charges, and other restrictions which each of the member states was to grant to the others; and (2) a common schedule listing the products from which the members collectively agreed to remove tariffs and other restrictions. Special arrangements regarding agricultural commodities were included, as well as concessions to countries "at a relatively less advanced stage of economic development." The treaty also contained several articles designed "to ensure the continued expansion and diversification of reciprocal trade" and "to facilitate the increasing integration and complementarity" of the economies of the member states.

Although intraregional trade increased after 1961, the treaty's goals were not met, as difficulties were encountered in obtaining continuing agreement from member nations on the items to be liberalized. As a result, in 1969 LAFTA members signed the Caracas Protocol, extending the deadline for the establishment of the free trade zone until 1980. Meanwhile, the heads of state of the American republics, meeting at Punta del Este, Uruguay, in 1967, had called for the establishment of a Latin American common market by 1985.

Among the most serious problems encountered by LAFTA was the fear of nations at an intermediate stage of development, such as Chile and Colombia, of being reduced to a position of dependency vis-à-vis the more highly industrialized Big Three—Brazil, Mexico, and Argentina. This fear led to the formation of the ANDEAN GROUP as a subregional unit within LAFTA in the late 1960s.   RODNEY D. ANDERSON

LAUTARO (1530?–1557). Araucanian Indian whose military prowess defeated the conquistador Pedro de VALDIVIA (*see* ARAUCANIANS). Lautaro was captured by the Spaniards during their campaigns to conquer and settle the region south of the Bío-Bío River in Chile (1545–1553). Valdivia took custody of the youth and made him his groom. By the time he escaped from the Spanish camp, Lautaro had become acquainted with Spanish speech, customs, and military tactics. After returning to his people, Lautaro convinced them that they must adopt new methods of fighting. On Christmas Day, 1553, Valdivia and forty men were wiped out by an Araucanian force instructed and led by Lautaro. As described superbly in the epic poem *La Araucana* by Alonso de ERCILLA Y ZÚÑIGA, Lautaro had informed his warriors that Spanish horses would tire under repeated attacks by fresh waves of infantry. He sent small groups of Indians successively to engage and exhaust the Spaniards and their horses. Finally, as Valdivia sounded retreat, the Araucanians attacked en masse, capturing and killing Valdivia. Later Lautaro defeated forces under Francisco de Villagra, causing the population of Concepción to flee northward to Santiago. Although Lautaro died in battle with the Spaniards at Peteroa (1557), his example long inspired the bellicose Araucanians, who were not subjected completely until the mid-nineteenth century.

WILLIAM S. DUDLEY

LAUTARO LODGE. A widespread phenomenon in Latin America during the independence period was the appearance of Masonic and quasi-Masonic lodges that served as both social clubs and secret political societies. The best known and most important was the Lautaro Lodge founded in Buenos Aires in 1812 by José de SAN MARTÍN and others. It was conceived as an offshoot of the lodges already established in Cádiz and London by Spanish Americans sympathetic to the idea of independence.

In October 1812 the Lautaro Lodge was instrumental in overthrowing the government of the First Triumvirate, whose dominant figure was Bernardino RIVADAVIA. Thereafter it displayed some of the characteristics of a shadow government, although internal dissension caused it to be virtually refounded in 1815. While San Martín was in Mendoza preparing his expedition to Chile, it played a vital role in mobilizing resources in his behalf. Moreover, he created branches in Mendoza and later in Chile (where a principal member was Bernardo O'HIGGINS) and Peru. But as San Martín moved farther afield, the original lodge became deeply involved in Argentine political problems and less responsive to his continental design; eventually it was discredited along with the directory regime that fell in 1820.

Whether the Lautaro Lodge (or Lodges) can be considered Masonic in a strict sense remains subject to debate. Many formulas and trappings were of Masonic inspiration, but the very secrecy of the organization makes it difficult to give a categorical answer. The primary function, in any case, was political: to promote Spanish American independence.

DAVID BUSHNELL

LAVALLEJA, JUAN ANTONIO (1784–1853). Uruguayan independence leader and soldier. Born in Santa Lucía, department of Minas, of Spanish parents who were wealthy ranchers, he enlisted in the patriot forces early in 1811, when the revolt against Spanish rule broke out in Uruguay. Rising to the rank of captain by 1814 in recognition of his valorous service, he remained a loyal follower of José Gervasio ARTIGAS through the vicissitudes of Artigas's conflicts with the government of Buenos Aires and resistance to the Luso-Brazilian invasion of 1816. Captured by a Brazilian patrol in 1818, Lavalleja spent the next three years in detention in Rio de Janeiro. Although he joined Fructuoso RIVERA's Union Regiment of Dragoons in the service of Portugal on his return to Uruguay in 1821, he was among the first Uruguayans to conspire to renew the struggle for independence when a schism developed between the Portuguese and Brazilian occupation forces as Brazil moved toward independence. While in refuge in Argentina through 1824, he played the leading role in organizing the independence movement that was formally launched by his landing on Uruguayan soil with thirty-two companions on April 19, 1825. His service to his nation during the Cisplatine War (1825–1828) represents the high point of his career.

Until the decisive patriot triumph at Sarandí he served as commander in chief of the Uruguayan forces, accepting a subaltern position when Argentine forces entered the fray. Upon the departure of the Argentine commander, Carlos María de Alvear, in the wake of President Bernardino RIVADAVIA's resignation in 1827, he reassumed supreme command of the patriot forces. In October 1827, in a move to consolidate his position politically, he dissolved the existing government, exercising dictatorial powers until after the establishment of peace in 1828.

Although Lavalleja served briefly as provisional President in 1830, his maneuvers during the period of provisional government (1828–1830) failed to bring him the coveted election as Uruguay's first constitutional President. Impelled by disappointed ambitions and distress over the disorganization and dominance by pro-Brazilian elements that characterized President Fructuoso Rivera's first Cabinets, he launched in 1832 and 1834 the first of the revolts against the nation's legal authorities that were to mar Uruguay's history for the rest of the century. From 1834 on he also served in some degree as an instrument for the designs of the Argentine dictator Juan Manuel de ROSAS in Uruguay. In 1836 he lent his support to President Manuel ORIBE against the revolt led by Rivera. After Oribe's defeat and resignation, Lavalleja returned with the Argentine forces that invaded Uruguay in 1839, serving as a scapegoat for the defeat suffered by those forces. During the ensuing years of the Guerra Grande he vegetated in Oribe's camp at Cerrito. He last appeared in national affairs as a colleague of his erstwhile rival, Rivera, in the triumvirate dominated by Venancio FLORES and supported by Brazil that was the provisional successor to the ousted legal government of President Juan Francisco Giró, a leader of the Blanco party (see BLANCO PARTY: URUGUAY), in whose ranks Lavalleja had long served. He died in Montevideo on October 22, 1853, shortly after assuming that post.

Bibliography. Luis Arcos Ferrand, *La cruzada de los treinta y tres Orientales,* Montevideo, 1925; Alfredo Raúl Castellanos, *Juan Antonio Lavalleja, libertador del pueblo oriental: Ensayo biográfico,* Montevideo, 1955; Enrique de Gandia, *Los treinta y tres Orientales y la independencia del Uruguay,* Buenos Aires, 1939; Eduardo de Salterain Herrera, *Lavalleja: La redención patria,* Montevideo, 1957; Juan Antonio Vázquez, *Lavalleja y la campaña de 1825,* Montevideo, 1927.

JOHN H. HANN

LAVISTA, MARIO (1943–). Mexican composer. Lavista was born in Mexico City, where he received his early training as a composer with Rodolfo Halffter and Héctor Quintanar, completing it with Karlheinz Stockhausen and Henri Pousseur in Europe. He can be considered the most experimentalist among the composers of the young generation in Mexico. Notable works are *Homage to Beckett* (1968) for triple chorus, twelve microphones, and three loudspeakers; *Bleu* (1969) for tape; and *Kronos,* in which he uses fifteen alarm clocks, microphones, and various loudspeakers.

JUAN A. ORREGO-SALAS

LAWS OF BURGOS. Spanish legislation of 1512–1513 that sought to eliminate the cruelties of the ENCOMIENDA system in the West Indies but was never enforced. The laws ordered the royal authorities to burn the lodges of the Indians and to move the natives, described as inclined to idleness and vice, to the vicinity of the Spanish communities, where they would be Christianized by continual association with the Spaniards. Encomiendas were to continue, and a third of the Indians were to work in the mines, but no encomendero might hold more than 150 Indians, and the natives were to be given hammocks in which to sleep. Moreover, pregnant women after the fourth month were not to be sent to the mines, and Spaniards who beat Indians or called them dogs were to be fined. Although Indians were to work nine months of the year for Spaniards, sons of chiefs were to be taught to read and write and then returned to their encomenderos so that they might teach the other Indians. Indians were also to be allowed to perform their native dances and were to be fed cooked meat at least on Sundays and feast days, and those found competent to govern themselves were to be allowed to live as free men. No less an authority than the historian Lesley Byrd Simpson has stated that to a modern reader these laws seem merely, "in their practicable measures, a cold-blooded sanctioning of current methods of exploitation."

RALPH H. VIGIL

LECHÍN [OQUENDO], JUAN (1915–). Bolivian politician and tin miners' leader. A veteran of the CHACO WAR, Lechín later became a professional soccer player and was employed as a clerk by Patiño Mines to justify his presence on the company's team.

When Maj. Gualberto VILLARROEL, backed by the MOVIMIENTO NACIONALISTA REVOLUCIONARIO (MNR), came to power in December 1943, Lechín, an MNR member, was made subprefect of Catavi. He gained fame when he threw out a representative of Patiño Mines who proposed to pay a "bonus," as had been customary with other subprefects. In 1945 Lechín was elected executive secretary of the Miners Federation, the tin workers' organization. He maintained this position when the pro-MNR government of Major Villarroel was overthrown in July 1946. The following year, he was elected a senator on the ticket of the Miners bloc.

During the next five years Lechín was several times deported by the conservative regimes of the period. In April 1952, he joined Hernán SILES to lead the MNR uprising that brought that party to power. He became Minister of Mines in the administration of MNR President Víctor PAZ ESTENSSORO and head of the new labor confederation, the Central Obrera Boliviana.

In 1956 Lechín was elected Vice President of Bolivia, representing the left wing of the MNR. He spent much of the next four years as Minister to Italy and the Vatican, without giving up the Vice Presidency. In 1960 he agreed to postpone his presidential ambitions for four years, on the promise that he would be the MNR candidate in 1964. However, when in 1963 Paz Estenssoro decided to run for a third term, Lechín broke with the MNR, forming his own party, the Partido Revolucionario de la Izquierda Nacional. He supported the coup against Paz Estenssoro in November 1964, but his Miners Federation soon broke with President René BARRIENTOS, and in a showdown in May 1965 the federation was temporarily crushed. Lechín went into exile.

When Gen. Alfredo OVANDO CANDIA seized power in 1969, Lechín threw his backing behind the new regime. Ovando allowed the reorganization of the Miners Federation, but it soon fell out with Ovando and supported his overthrow late in 1970 and the advent to power of President Juan José TORRES. Under Torres, Lechín played a leading role and was chosen President of the left-wing People's Assembly. After the overthrow of Torres in August 1971, Lechín went into exile in Chile.

ROBERT J. ALEXANDER

LEGUÍA, AUGUSTO (1863–1932). President and dictator of Peru. The product of a comfortably placed Lambayeque family, Leguía used his considerable business acumen, personal charm, and political agility to enter the best circles of Lima society. His active political career began in 1903. He served as Finance Minister in the administrations of Manuel Candamo and José PARDO, and in 1908 led the CIVILISTA PARTY to an easy victory in that year's presidential election. During his first administration (1908–1912) he displayed the iron determination and authoritarian tendencies that were to become the hallmark of his second administration (1919–1930). But whereas in 1908 his strong-arm tactics failed because of a watchful Civilista-dominated Congress, in 1919 he returned to power with the Civilistas divided and with the nation's institutions weakened. Once in office, he subverted all political institutions and proceeded to establish a dictatorial regime that lasted for eleven years (the Oncenio).

Leguía's goal during his second administration was to transform Peru into a truly modern capitalist society. He did, in fact, spark considerable economic progress, but the cost was the mortgaging of the nation's economy to foreign lenders and investors who also constituted Leguía's principal source of power. When the Depression came and the flow of foreign capital ended, Leguía was overthrown (1930). He was unceremoniously imprisoned in one of the jails he had made notorious during his regime, and in spite of his failing health he was held there until his death in 1932. He left a legacy of intolerance and institutional weakness from which Peru was slow to recover.

ORAZIO A. CICCARELLI

LEI AUREA. *See* GOLDEN LAW.

LEI DO VENTRE LIVRE. *See* FREE BIRTH LAW.

LEMA SYSTEM. Elected officials in Uruguay are chosen through a complicated process known as the double simultaneous vote, or simply the *lema* system. The method, in use since the 1920s, in effect combines a party primary and a general election. It tends to favor the larger parties while giving official recognition to factions within those parties.

The basis of the system is the *lema,* or party label. The major *lemas* always have been the Colorado party and the National (Blanco) party (*see* BLANCO PARTY: URUGUAY; COLORADO PARTY: URUGUAY), which together usually have accounted for more than 80 percent of the vote. However, within each party, or *lema,* separate factions present their own slates in the form of *sublemas.* Voters choose one of these *sublemas,* which often represent well-organized and relatively permanent factions within the party, and the vote for all *sublemas* is totaled to determine the vote for the *lema.* The winning slate for the Presidency (formerly for the majority on the National Councils) is that of the most strongly supported *sublema* within the *lema* whose factions yield the highest total vote. Legislative seats are distributed among the *lemas* and *sublemas* on the basis of proportional representation. Within a *sublema* seats are sometimes divided among several different candidate lists called *distintivos.*

In order to gain official recognition of a *lema,* a party must present to the Electoral Court six months before an election a statement of the party's principles, a list of at least 500 party members, and the names of party officials. Once registered, a *lema* becomes the official property of that party; no other party may use the title of an existing or former party, and a group wishing to run as a *sublema* under a particular party's *lema* must have that party's permission. While a party has sometimes denied a faction the use of its *lema,* the advantages of the accumulation of votes have encouraged toleration of a considerable diversity within each of the two major parties. *Sublemas* may be registered with the Electoral Court as late as thirty days before an election by submitting a statement of principles, a list of 50 members, and names of the faction's leaders.

LEE C. FENNELL

LEMUS, JOSÉ MARÍA (1911–   ). Salvadoran army officer and President (1956–1960). Lemus was elected President of El Salvador in March 1956 and inaugurated on September 14. He was the second member of the PARTIDO REVOLUCIONARIO DE UNIFICACIÓN DEMOCRÁTICA (PRUD) dynasty that ruled El Salvador during the 1950s. After a bitter electoral campaign, Lemus attempted conciliation and tried to attract able men to his Cabinet regardless of political affiliation. Resentment against PRUD was too strong for collaboration, however, and the heavy-handed PRUD conduct of the legislative elections of 1958 only increased it.

The Lemus program emphasized public works. The outstanding examples were installations at Lake Güija on the Guatemalan border to supply hydroelectric power, new port facilities at Acajutla, and a new highway along the Pacific littoral. These developments and the prospect of a CENTRAL AMERICAN COMMON MARKET attracted domestic capital into local enterprise, but economic optimism was dulled somewhat by a decline in coffee production and a drop in coffee prices.

Angered by PRUD's continuing rigid control of politics, students, intellectuals, and workers in 1959 formed the leftist- and reform-oriented Revolutionary Party of April and May (PRAM). Lemus branded the party Communist, but its reform appeal attracted a following. Lemus's predecessor, Oscar OSORIO, broke with him in 1959 to found PRUD Auténtico, and several other parties were formed. When PRUD swept another manipulated legislative election in April 1960, protest grew into insurrection. After a bloody suppression that invaded the National University, Lemus was arrested on October 26, 1960, exiled to Costa Rica, and replaced by a junta, which promised free elections.

WILLIAM J. GRIFFITH

LEÓN. Nicaraguan city. Throughout the colonial period León was the capital and most important city in the province of Nicaragua, which was under the *audiencia* of Guatemala. Francisco Hernández de Córdoba founded León in 1524 near Momotombo Volcano on the northern shore of Lake Managua. At first an outpost guarding the area against rival Spanish conquerors from Mexico to the north, it became Nicaragua's administrative and intellectual capital in the colonial period. Its commercial base was improved after a volcanic eruption in 1609 caused its citizens to move to its present location 19 miles from the Pacific Ocean. The move brought León closer to the important colonial shipbuilding port of El Realejo and to the agricultural heartland of the León-Chinandega plain.

After independence León became the nucleus of Liberal political groups that vied with Conservative Granada for preeminence. This rivalry between León and Granada, the leading commercial city, finally resulted in a compromise decision to move the nation's capital to Managua in the 1850s. León held tenaciously thereafter to its intellectual traditions, and it still is the seat of the National University, but national political and commercial leadership has passed to Managua. Since World War II a cotton boom in the León-Chinandega area has served to bolster León's commercial importance. It had a population of about 57,000 in 1906 and 62,000 in 1968.

CHARLES L. STANSIFER

LEONI, RAÚL (1906–1972). President of Venezuela (1964–1969). With his fellow ACCIÓN DEMOCRÁTICA (AD) member Rómulo BETANCOURT, Leoni joined in the 1928 student week that turned into a political rally against the dictator Juan Vicente GÓMEZ, and he is therefore considered a member of the Generation of 1928. Leoni participated prominently in anti-Gómez activities, and because of his political visibility the government of Eleazar LÓPEZ CONTRERAS had his election to Congress annulled in 1936. Leoni found it wise to go into exile in 1937–1938. From 1942 on he served on the Executive Committee of AD and as such was a civilian member of the revolutionary junta established in 1945 in the wake of the coup d'état against Gen. Isaías MEDINA ANGARITA. Leoni also served as Minister of Labor from 1945 until the end of the government of Rómulo GALLEGOS in 1948.

A loyal supporter of Betancourt throughout the latter's difficult Presidency and through the party crises and schisms of the early 1960s, Leoni received his reward in the form of the AD nomination for the Presidency and election for the term 1964–1969. His years in office were a muted and less violent continuation of Betancourt's. Most of his problems were internal political ones, the result of AD's failure to achieve a majority in Congress. By means of shifting coalitions Leoni managed to keep the government moving and the country away from a constitutional crisis. He presided over the elections of 1968, which saw the transfer of power by means of a free popular election from the hands of Acción Democrática to the COMITÉ DE ORGANIZACIÓN POLÍTICA ELECTORAL INDEPENDIENTE (COPEI) and its leader, Rafael CALDERA. Leoni's health declined, and he went to the United States for treatment. His condition worsened until he died in mid-1972.

JOHN V. LOMBARDI

LERDO DE TEJADA, SEBASTIÁN (1827–1889). Mexican statesman and President (1872–1876). Born in Jalapa, Veracruz, Lerdo studied for the priesthood but had a change of mind and entered the Colegio de San Ildefonso in Mexico City to pursue a law degree. He later taught in that college and from 1852 to 1863 served as its rector. Lerdo served as Minister of Foreign Relations in the Cabinet of Ignacio COMONFORT in 1857 and as a congressman in the period 1861–1863. After the fall of Puebla to the French in 1863, he fled with Benito JUÁREZ and then entered the Cabinet as one of the President's closest collaborators and principal supporters during the northern sojourn. In the 1867 elections he was chosen President of the Supreme Court and for a time also held concurrently a Cabinet post and served as a congressman, which provoked many complaints. In the 1871 elections he ran for the Presidency, was defeated by Juárez, but remained as President of the Court. By virtue of this position, he succeeded Juárez as President upon the latter's death in July 1872. Lerdo served as President until his overthrow by Porfirio DÍAZ in November 1876. He spent the remaining thirteen years of his life in exile in New York.

As a Liberal, Lerdo was firmly committed to the reform program of his party. His administration was not peaceful, for there were perplexing political problems such as that in the west concerning the creation of the state of Nayarit. His opponents charged him with political corruption.

See also REFORM, THE. CHARLES R. BERRY

LESCOT, ÉLIE (b. 1883). President of Haiti (1941–1946). Lescot was born in Saint-Louis-du-Nord and educated in Cap-Haïtien. He received a doctorate at Laval University in Quebec and continued his studies in Ottawa. Lescot served in several posts: he was a customs interpreter, a national deputy, a secondary school director, a judge, and Secretary of Public Education, Justice, and the Interior in various Cabinets. As envoy to the Dominican Republic (1937–1938), he helped settle a Haitian boundary dispute with that country. He also served as a diplomat in the United States before being elected President in April 1941. The choice of Sténio VINCENT, Lescot continued the policies of his predecessor. His government declared war on the Axis Powers in December 1941, and because of the war "emergency" placed Haiti in a state of siege. Constitutional guarantees were suspended, and elections were postponed. With United States encouragement, Lescot unsuccessfully attempted to grow a substitute for rubber during the wartime shortage and ruined valuable Haitian farmland in the process. An ill-advised campaign to eradicate VODUN also failed.

Resistance to the long rule of the mulatto ÉLITE, combined with charges of nepotism and financial ineptitude, led to a coup when the National Assembly refused to support him. Lescot resigned on January 11, 1946.

JOHN E. BAUR

LETELIER, VALENTÍN (1852–1919). Chilean writer and politician. After receiving a legal education, Letelier held a number of political and public offices in Chile, culminating in his appointment as rector of the University of Chile in 1906. A prominent member of the Radical party (*see* RADICAL PARTY: CHILE), he was among those who signed the act deposing President José Manuel BALMACEDA (January 1891), and he was later imprisoned and sent into exile for his opposition to the regime. Letelier was responsible for steering the Radical party toward an increased interest in social reform. In a memorable series of debates at the third Radical party convention (1906), he defended what was known as a "socialist" tendency in the party against the "individualist" position represented by the brilliant orator Enrique MacIver. Letelier's emphasis on social concerns won the day and had an important influence on the subsequent development of Chilean radicalism.

Letelier was a distinguished thinker and writer who produced numerous works on history, jurisprudence, social science, and philosophy. He is often considered to have been the outstanding Chilean representative of the positivist school.

SIMON COLLIER

LEY, SALVADOR (1907–   ). Guatemalan composer and pianist. Ley was born in Guatemala City and studied in Berlin with Klatte and Hugo Leichtentritt. In 1937, after teaching for five years in Guatemala, he established his residence in the United States. Returning to Guatemala in 1944, he became the director of the Conservatory of Music, a position he held until 1953. He later taught at the Westchester Conservatory in New York. Ley has an extended catalog of works in which vocal and piano music prevail, but he has also written for orchestra, solo instruments and orchestra, and a variety of chamber music combinations, as well as composing an opera, *Lera* (1960).

JUAN A. ORREGO-SALAS

LEZAMA LIMA, JOSÉ (1912–   ). Cuban writer. Born in Havana and trained in law, he has been Cultural Director of the Ministry of Education and has held important posts in the Academy of Sciences of Cuba. He has also been vice president of the Union of Writers and Artists since 1962. Lezama Lima founded four reviews: *Verbum* (1937), *Espuela de Plata* (1939–1941), *Nadie Parecía* (1942–1944), and *Orígenes* (1944–1956). From the publication of his earliest poems, *Muerte de Narciso* (1937) and *Enemigo rumor* (1941), with their metaphoric and imagistic originality,

he has been a leading influence on younger Cuban writers. Later volumes of poetry include *Aventuras sigilosas* (1945), *La fijeza* (1949), and *Dador* (1960). In 1938 he first published his famous *Coloquio con Juan Ramón Jiménez,* which later appeared in a book of essays, *Analecta del reloj* (1953). Other essay collections are *Tratados en La Habana* (1958) and *Islas* (1961). He has written some stories and the immense novel *Paradiso* (1966), all showing an extreme complexity of texture and metaphor. He has also written a study of the painter Aristides Fernández (1950) and *Antología de la poesía cubana* (1965).

RACHEL PHILLIPS

LIBERAL PARTY (CHILE). One of the two great traditional parties of Chile, the Liberal party emerged in the 1840s. Liberals were less traditionally minded than their Conservative rivals, less proclerical, much less authoritarian, and more open to outside ideas (*see* CONSERVATIVE PARTY: CHILE). They sought to amend the autocratic constitution of 1833, emphasizing individual liberty and equality before the law (*see* CONSTITUTION OF 1833: CHILE).

Liberals opposed the authoritarianism of Presidents Manuel BULNES (1841–1851) and Manuel MONTT (1851–1861), though supporting Montt against the church, but under the conciliatory José Joaquín PÉREZ (1861–1871) both Liberals and Conservatives upheld the established order. Some reforms were then achieved, notably the prohibition of consecutive presidential terms. Religious issues forced the Conservatives out of the government in 1873; from then to 1891 the Liberal party was supreme. Under Federico ERRÁZURIZ ZAÑARTU (1871–1876) religious *fueros* (corporate privileges) were abolished, and constitutional reforms strengthened the legislature at the expense of the executive. The Liberals also secured other cherished objectives under Domingo Santa María (1881–1886), when civil marriage and registry, secular cemeteries, and a reduction of church influence in education were secured. These aims had knit the party together; their achievement loosened its cohesion. Santa María's successor, José Manuel BALMACEDA (1886–1891), intended to reunite the party but succeeded only in dividing it further, and in the revolution of 1891 many Liberals opposed him. Further complications followed as the Balmacedists formed a distinct party known as the Liberal Democratic party.

Not until 1933 were the chief Liberal factions reunited. By then, with the rise of the middle-class Radical party (*see* RADICAL PARTY: CHILE) and the Marxist parties of the left, the Liberals had come to be associated with upper-class interests, particularly business, and were allied with the Conservatives on basic issues. Their somewhat more flexible attitudes, however, helped them to hold about 15 percent of the vote in elections until 1965, but congressional elections that year reduced their strength from twenty-eight to six seats in the Chamber of Deputies and from nine to five seats in the Senate. No longer a viable force alone, the Liberals merged with their historical adversaries, the Conservatives, to form the National party in 1966.

HAROLD BLAKEMORE

LIBERAL PARTY (COLOMBIA). One of Colombia's two traditional political parties, the Liberal party can trace its history to the factions that supported Francisco de Paula SANTANDER during his conflict with Simón BOLÍVAR in the 1820s. However, it was not until the late 1840s that that party took permanent shape, numbering among its adherents the surviving *santanderistas,* artisans and workers in Bogotá and other towns, and youthful reformers imbued with the ideas of contemporary French writers like Lamartine, Proudhon, and Eugène Sue. During the presidential term of Liberal José Hilario López (1849–1853), some of the measures advocated by the reformers became a reality, among them expulsion of the Jesuits, abolition of slavery, and fiscal decentralization, by which certain sources of revenue were allocated to provincial governments. Disagreement over the wisdom of further reform led to party division and eventually to loss of power to the Conservatives (*see* CONSERVATIVE PARTY: COLOMBIA), but a successful revolution brought a Liberal restoration in 1861. Party division between 1875 and 1885 again cost the Liberals their control of the government, and they remained in opposition until 1930, when they were able to exploit Conservative dissension to elect Enrique OLAYA HERRERA to the Presidency.

During the nineteenth century the Liberal party was identified with anticlericalism, federalism, and Manchesterian economic principles. However, although Liberals generally wished to reduce the spiritual and temporal power of the Catholic Church, they differed on the means of achieving this goal, with some supporting separation of church and state and others advocating strong governmental controls over the clergy. By the end of the century national party leaders were minimizing the "religious question." There was also disagreement over the proper division of powers between the national government and state or sectional governments. In economic matters articulate Liberals of the mid-nineteenth century were likely to be supporters of laissez faire, but by 1900 most Liberals had come to the conclusion that some state action was necessary to promote economic development. By 1922 the party was prepared to adopt a platform calling for the nationalization of public services and measures to ensure a more equitable distribution of wealth.

Until the last decade of the nineteenth century party organization was haphazard, and party decisions were made by informal groups, caucuses of members of Congress, and ad hoc committees of party notables. Steps to create a permanent party structure were initiated in 1891, and conventions with delegates from all the departments were held in 1892 and 1897.

The Liberal party did not change substantially after 1930. It has been divided, though not always formally, into two wings, the one more reformist and the other more conservative. In its structure and its financing the Liberal party has been identical to the Conservative party, being characterized by a pattern of directorates, conventions, and improvisation. The only major innovation in financing came in 1966, when Carlos LLERAS RESTREPO appealed directly to industry for campaign contributions.

Liberal ideology has been flexible. National Liberal leaders have claimed to be loyally if not militantly Catholic, but departmental leaders have frequently evinced an acute anticlericalism that awakened fears of a revival of the persecution of the church of the nineteenth century. Since the first administration of Alfonso

LÓPEZ (1934–1938), liberalism has been increasingly associated with economic interventionism, some social reformism, and political centralization. Between 1920 and 1970 individual Liberals looked for inspiration to agrarian socialism, Mexican revolutionism, the Peruvian ALIANZA POPULAR REVOLUCIONARIA AMERICANA, the Popular Fronts of France and Spain, diluted forms of Marxism, the ALLIANCE FOR PROGRESS, and the Chilean government of President Salvador ALLENDE. None of these has made a deep impression, and most have been only convenient debating tools at a given moment.

Liberal national leadership is less easily defined in regional terms than that of the Conservatives. Between 1924 and 1929 the party lacked both leadership and enthusiasm, although the Bogotá newspaper *El Tiempo* of Eduardo SANTOS kept the Liberal flag flying. The crisis surrounding the Depression produced a new generation of Liberal leaders, notably Alfonso López, Jorge Eliécer GAITÁN, and Gabriel Turbay. Both López and Santos had several outstanding protégés, of whom Alberto LLERAS CAMARGO and Carlos Lleras Restrepo were subsequently to become Presidents. Curiously, in the decade between the death of Gaitán (1948) and the beginning of the NATIONAL FRONT (1958) no new national figure emerged, although new local leaders, some of them associated with guerrilla organizations, proliferated. During the National Front some new national leaders, including Julio César Turbay and Virgilio Barco, have appeared, but entry to the leadership has not been easy. Even the son of López, Alfonso López Michelsen, was admitted to the leadership only after organizing a short-lived but electorally effective dissident Liberal movement, the Movimiento Revolucionario Liberal.

The Liberal party has been more generally associated with urban areas than the Conservative, although the picture can easily be overdrawn. A strong rural support base is a precondition of power in Colombia. The Liberals have this. They mobilized further rural support when López introduced universal male suffrage. Despite sanctions imposed against Liberals by some bishops and priests until the late 1950s, the party leadership could count upon a readily exploitable party mystique at a local level. The persistence of Liberal rural action in the Violencia (*see* VIOLENCIA, LA) after the closure of the National Directorate (1952) testified to local-level enthusiasm and fanaticism. Recent election results confirm the strength of rural liberalism.

During the government of Misael PASTRANA BORRERO, the Liberals lacked direction, at least until 1972. Some Liberals were dissatisfied with the tempo and scope of Pastrana's reform policy but were slow to express their opposition forcibly, partly for fear of exacerbating internal party divisions. In the latter half of 1972, however, party unity was achieved, at least temporarily. The two principal Liberal leaders, ex-President Carlos Lleras Restrepo and Julio César Turbay, made peace along with their respective followers, and Lleras Restrepo was named sole party head.

Bibliography. Robert H. Dix, *Colombia: The Political Dimensions of Change,* New Haven, Conn., 1967; Robert L. Gilmore, "New Granada's Socialist Mirage," *Hispanic American Historical Review,* vol. XXXVI, no. 2, May 1956, pp. 190–210; Carlos Lleras

Restrepo, *De la república a la dictadura*, Bogotá, 1955; Plinio Mendoza Neira and Alberto Camacho Angarita, *El liberalismo en el gobierno*, 3 vols., Bogotá, 1946; Gerardo Molina, *Las ideas liberales en Colombia, 1849–1914*, Bogotá, 1970; Eduardo Rodríguez Piñeres, *Diez años de política liberal, 1892–1902*, Bogotá, 1945; id., *El olimpo radical*, Bogotá, 1950; Alfonso Romero Aguirre, *Ayer, hoy y mañana del liberalismo colombiano*, 4 vols., 3d enl. ed., Bogotá, 1949.

C. G. ABEL AND HELEN DELPAR

LIBERAL PARTY (HONDURAS). Céleo Arias, the intellectual progenitor of the Honduran Liberal party, first succeeded in uniting unorganized constellations of nineteenth-century *rojos* (reds) around a central set of goals. Many of his plans for economic development, foreign investment, and secularization of education were given flesh during the Liberal administration of Marco Aurelio SOTO (1876–1883). The party itself, however, was still bound together on a highly personalistic basis. Although Policarpo BONILLA established a party office and regular party machinery in 1890, Liberals broke into factions after he left the Presidency in 1899. Liberals played a diminished role in Honduras politics until the end of the rule of Nationalist dictator Tiburcio CARÍAS ANDINO in 1948. *See* NATIONAL OR NATIONALIST PARTY (HONDURAS).

The National party splintered when Carías's successor, Juan Manuel GÁLVEZ, failed to deal effectively with rising feelings of nationalism and labor discontent. Ramón VILLEDA MORALES, a popular Liberal who had remained in Tegucigalpa during the long Carías interlude while other Liberals were in exile, rose to challenge the Nationalists in the 1954 elections. Villeda won an easy plurality but was denied the Presidency when Vice President Julio Lozano declared martial law, suppressed the Liberal party, and exiled Villeda. Villeda returned to win the Presidency in 1957. With the aid of a Liberal-controlled Congress, he initiated a program of modernization, land reform, and educational expansion, much of which was conceived and executed under ALLIANCE FOR PROGRESS auspices.

Although Honduran Liberals represent themselves as friends of labor and progress, often invoking the memory of Villeda, party objectives do not differ significantly from those of the National party. Many Hondurans point out that the Liberal party is distinguished only by its chronic inability to gain power.

GENE S. YEAGER

LIBERAL PARTY (LIBERAL RADICAL PARTY, ECUADOR). The Ecuadorian Liberal party emerged as forward-looking intellectuals of the early nineteenth century championed freedom of speech and press and a mild anticlericalism and rallied around the able Vicente ROCAFUERTE in the 1830s. In 1845 Liberals returned to power as the revolutionaries of March, but their era was marked by disorder. Regionalism, the rule of local *caudillos* by force of arms, and border wars helped account for the eleven Presidents and provisional juntas that ruled from 1845 to 1860. Liberalism was discredited, and a Conservative reaction set in that lasted until 1895 (*see* CONSERVATIVE PARTY: ECUADOR). Liberal opposition gained steadily after the death of Gabriel GARCÍA MORENO, the word "Radical"

being added to the party's name in 1878 to denote a vigorous anticlericalism. The Guayaquil commercial class used this ideological weapon, export wealth, and the leadership of Gen. Eloy ALFARO to carry out a successful revolution in 1895.

The era of the Liberal Radical party (1895–1944) was marked by the separation of church and state and by Guayaquil's control of politics. However, the Liberals lacked twentieth-century ideological weaponry, failed to recognize social and urban change dramatized by the 1922 Guayaquil strike, and were discredited by the 1925 coup that overthrew their President, Dr. Gonzalo S. Córdova. The ideological vacuum was filled by the Socialist and Communist parties, which were formed in the 1930s, but the Liberals maintained fraudulent election machinery to win through the election of 1940. Their last President, Carlos Alberto ARROYO DEL RÍO, failed Ecuador on the international front. Above all, the Liberal party declined because it did nothing to satisfy the demands of the lower classes or to close the gap between Ecuador and other developing nations.

LOIS WEINMAN

LIBERAL PARTY (PARAGUAY). The Liberal party had its origins in the Gran Club del Pueblo, established in 1870 by ex-legionnaires who had fought against the regime of Francisco Solano LÓPEZ in the PARAGUAYAN WAR (1864–1870). Ignoring accusations of treason from the rival Club del Pueblo, from which the Colorado party evolved, the Gran Club cooperated with the Brazilian occupation authorities and ruled the defeated nation until it was ousted by the Colorados in 1877. From then until 1904 the Liberals, as they became known, grew to be a mass party as they absorbed many anti-Colorado elements and lost their identification with the label "traitor." *See* COLORADO PARTY (PARAGUAY).

In 1904 the Liberals in Paraguay revolted, and Liberal exiles invaded the country from Argentina, toppling the Colorados. They ruled from that year until 1936, when they were overthrown by the radical new Febrerista movement (*see* FEBRERISMO). They have not been in power again. Their last serious thrust for power came in the bloody 1947 civil war, an attempt to oust the dictator Higinio MORÍNIGO, a Colorado. Split several times, the party has been best represented by the able historian Efraím CARDOZO, and it functions in open and legitimate, if not loyal, opposition to the regime of Gen. Alfredo STROESSNER, in power since 1954. Only slightly more progressive than the Colorado opposition, the Liberals have generally been less strong in the rural areas than their rivals but more powerful in the towns and cities outside the capital.

JOHN HOYT WILLIAMS

LIBERAL RADICAL PARTY (ECUADOR). *See* LIBERAL PARTY (ECUADOR).

LIMA, JORGE MATEUS DE (1895–1953). Brazilian poet, novelist, physician, and politician. He was born in Alagoas, studied medicine in Bahia and Rio de Janeiro, then returned to Alagoas to practice, remaining there, teaching and taking part in politics, until he was forced to flee to Rio in 1930. There he continued his medical career, taught in the university, and was elected president of the city council. He published *Poemas* in 1927;

in it the influence of modernism is revealed by his use of elements of Brazilian history and folklore and his portrayal of aspects of Negro life, as well as by the free verse in which most of the poems are written (*see* MODERNISM: BRAZIL). The influence of Walt Whitman is also present, and American imperialism is occasionally attacked. His most famous Negro poem, *Essa Negra Fuló*, appeared in 1928, and *Poemas Negros* in 1947. Initially a freethinker, he experienced a religious awakening in 1935, and thereafter his poetry was profoundly Christian, as in *A Túnica Inconsútil* (1938) and *Mira Coeli*, published in *Obra Poética* (1950). His most important book is *Invenção de Orfeu* (1952), an epic in ten cantos and a variety of meters and verse forms, which has been called the epic of the Brazilian spirit and praised as an affirmation of eternal and universal values. *Calunga* (1935) is a novel that belongs to the regional fiction of the NORTHEAST. *O Anjo* (1934) and *Guerra Dentro do Beco* (1950) are surrealistic and allegorical.

RAYMOND S. SAYERS

LIMA. Capital of Peru, founded by Francisco PIZARRO in 1535. Its coastal location was chosen because of the fertility of the valley watered by the Rimac River and the protected anchorage at nearby Callao. Laid out in characteristic Spanish style around a central plaza (Plaza de Armas), Lima (known as the City of Kings) was the major political center of South America during the colonial period. After independence, Lima lost that exalted position, but it has retained a considerable amount of Spanish colonial flavor amid the changes brought by modernization.

By far Peru's largest city, Lima is an expanding cosmopolitan center that has seen its population swell from about 400,000 in 1940 to nearly 2.5 million in the early 1970s. This rapid growth has caused the mushrooming of *barriadas* (shantytowns), which ring the city and accommodate more than 500,000 people. The poverty of the *barriadas* is visible to any visitor traveling the 10 miles from the modernistic José Chávez International Airport to the center of the city.

Along with its port of Callao, Lima has always been the financial, commercial, and industrial center of Peru. In addition, it has always dominated the political, social, and cultural life of the nation. To a large extent, its people have been under the impression that Lima is Peru, and they have acted accordingly. Such behavior has aroused profound jealousies in the provinces. These have led to abortive secessionist movements and to persistent demands for decentralization. With nearly 40 percent of the registered voters situated in Lima, however, it is unlikely that the imbalance will be corrected in the foreseeable future.

ORAZIO A. CICCARELLI

LIMA BARRETO, AFONSO HENRIQUES DE. *See* BARRETO, AFONSO HENRIQUES DE LIMA.

LIMA CONFERENCE (1938). Eighth International Conference of American States. All twenty-one American republics were represented at this conference, which met in Lima, Peru, on December 9–27, 1938, amid a growing threat of war in Europe. At the instigation of the United States, discussions in Lima focused on means of developing effective inter-American co-operation to check the spread of Axis trade and propaganda in the Western Hemisphere. Although Latin American fears of the United States had eased as a result of the GOOD NEIGHBOR POLICY, the formal defense pact Washington desired could not be obtained, largely because of Argentine resistance. Instead the delegates produced the Declaration of Lima, a bland reaffirmation of continental solidarity that provided for consultative meetings of the American foreign ministers in the event of a threat to the "peace, security, or territorial integrity" of any hemisphere republic. In deference to Argentina's wishes, no explicit reference to non-American powers was made.

WILLIAM R. ADAMS

LIMA E SILVA, LUIS ALVES DE. *See* CAXIAS, DUQUE DE.

LINIERS, SANTIAGO (1753–1810). Franco-Spanish military officer and Viceroy of Río de la Plata. Although he was of French origin (he was born in Niort), Santiago (Jacques) Liniers figured prominently in the antecedents of Argentine independence and, as an opponent, in the first stage of the movement itself. He joined the French Army at an early age but in 1774 entered the service of Spain. From 1788 until his death, he remained in the Río de la Plata, serving chiefly as a naval officer.

The high point of Liniers's military career came during the British invasions of the Río de la Plata in 1806–1807, when he was the principal organizer and hero of the reconquest and defense of Buenos Aires. His performance so overshadowed that of the titular Viceroy that the latter was irregularly deposed and his powers thrust upon Liniers. The Spanish government subsequently confirmed Liniers as acting Viceroy. The Napoleonic invasion of Spain, however, inevitably brought the loyalty of a French-born Viceroy under suspicion, apparently with some justification, and led to an abortive effort to depose him. By the time of the May 1810 revolution in Buenos Aires, he had been replaced by a new Viceroy sent from Spain, but this time Liniers unequivocally demonstrated his Spanish loyalty by joining in a premature counterrevolutionary movement in the interior province of Córdoba. It was quickly repressed, and he was among the ringleaders executed on August 26, 1810.

DAVID BUSHNELL

LISBÔA, ANTÔNIO FRANCISCO (O ALEIJADINHO, 1730/1738–1814). Brazilian architect and sculptor. Lisbôa, who was often known as O Aleijadinho (a nickname meaning "the Little Cripple"), was born in Ouro Prêto, in the state of Minas Gerais. He was the illegitimate son of the architect Manuel Francisco Lisbôa and a Negro slave girl. A lost document dated 1790 was cited by his first biographer (Rodrigo Brêtas, in the newspaper of Ouro Prêto, 1858), who quoted from it extensively. The anonymous contemporary author praised O Aleijadinho fulsomely, calling him "the new Praxiteles, [who] honors architecture and sculpture equally."

O Aleijadinho became a cripple in his mid-thirties and was described as "so sickly that he has to be carried everywhere and has to have his chisels strapped to him to be able to work." Despite the contemporary recognition of his genius, social malice added to his physical agonies. He was not permitted to join the artists' religious fraternity but was obliged to join a fraternity for mulattoes. Many commissions that he both designed and executed were assigned contractually to others while he was listed as a laborer.

In architecture classicistic mannerism persisted in Brazil into the eighteenth century. About 1760, particularly in Minas Gerais, where gold and diamond rushes made the state prosperous, the rococo style began to be employed. Essentially it was a style of elliptical curves and sinuous rhythms enriched with irregular ornament. Ultimately it was derived from the architectural designs of Francesco Borromini through the Portuguese works of Italians: Guarino Guarini in Lisbon in the seventeenth century and Niccolò Nasoni (Nazzoni) in Oporto in the eighteenth century. O Aleijadinho's works are outstanding in the rococo both for inventiveness and for harmony.

The undoubted architectural masterpiece of O Aleijadinho is the Church of São Francisco de Assis, Third Order, in Ouro Prêto (1766–1794). The ground plan is an attenuated rectangle. The central bay of the facade is a flat plane, and the lateral bays, concavely curved, end in round towers. A side view of the exterior offers an interesting rhythm of projections and recessions: the concave lateral bay of the facade, the convex curves of the tower, the flat nave wall, the polygonal forward thrust of the wider sanctuary area, its flat wall, and, finally, a slight, orthogonal saliency of a box-shaped, terminal spatial unit.

O Aleijadinho's designs are characterized by an effective blending of the straight and the curved. The facade of São Francisco, seen in elevation, is an interesting example. The flat central bay is flanked by Ionic columns in the round; the apertures offer a variety of curves, as does the cresting; and straight pilasters mark the junctures of the curved lateral bays and round towers. O Aleijadinho executed the rococo medallion above the portal depicting St. Francis receiving the stigmata, the other sculptural ornament in the same location, and all the interior sculpture.

O Aleijadinho's sculpture includes pulpits, portals, balconies, altars, statues, processional images, and caryatids. His sculpture always enhanced as well as harmonized with his architecture. The most dramatic example is his soapstone group of twelve prophets (1800–1805) for the Church of Bom Jesus de Matozinhos in Congonhas do Campo. The atrium of the church is enclosed by a low wall that is open in the front to a monumental multiflight stairway. The figures of the prophets are so disposed on the atrium wall and staircase railing that the ensemble has been compared to a tremendous ballet. Ascending and descending the winding staircase, one is offered innumerable compositional arrangements. It is as though one could view Auguste Rodin's *Burghers of Calais* from diverse angles *within* the group. The prophets' figures are in no way rococo. They loom above one's vision portentously as though hewn by a Romanesque Michelangelo.

Bibliography. Germain Bazin, "*Aleijadinho*" *et la sculpture baroque au Brésil,* Paris, 1963; Pál Kelemen, *Baroque and Rococo in Latin America,* New York, 1951; Hans Mann et al., *The 12 Prophets of Antônio Francisco Lisbôa, "O Aleijadinho,"* Rio de Janeiro, 1958.

EILEEN LORD

LITERATURE (BRAZIL). Brazilian literature is similar to the literatures of other American nations in that it has always been affected by cultural movements that originated in Europe and spread to other lands in which European languages are spoken. Such movements as the baroque, neoclassicism, romanticism, realism, and naturalism flourished in Brazil, usually under the same names. At first, and until after independence, there was no attempt to recognize the existence of a Brazilian literature as such; what existed was a literature written by Brazilians or by others about Brazil or in Brazil. The actual quantity of such literature produced during the first three centuries of the colony's existence was small partly because all books were printed in Portugal and subject there to the usual censorship until the beginning of the nineteenth century. There were no universities, and everyone who wanted an education, usually to work in the legal service of the government or higher echelons of the clergy, studied in Portugal. These Brazilians frequently remained in Portugal or even went to other colonies as civil servants. Therefore, there was but a small reading public in Brazil, and Brazilian books were read mostly in the mother country. Thus Brazilian literature not only was considered as a part of Portuguese literature but was in fact almost buried in the greater volume of that literature. Yet if there was no recognition of the existence of a Brazilian literature as such, there was recognition of the qualities in this literature that are different from those of other writings in Portuguese, namely, that it is also an American literature and exhibits the fact that it belongs to a new, utopian world with a new race of men and a new geography. This literature has developed a series of constants that reappear through the centuries: the idea of the magnificence and variety of nature in Brazil; the figure of the Indian, at first as a real though idealized being and then more frequently as a literary symbol, usually the Noble Savage; and that of the Negro, who is depicted both realistically and as a symbol.

The first example of Brazilian literature is a letter written to the King of Portugal by Pero Vaz de Caminha, who accompanied the expedition of discovery in 1500 and who describes in it what he saw on the new continent. This *Carta do Achamento* was only one of many accounts of travel in Brazil. There were other books that served the purpose of informing the Portuguese about the new world of Brazil, the most important being the *Tratado Descritivo do Brasil em 1587,* apparently by Gabriel Soares de Sousa, published in the nineteenth century. Except for this literary genre, some letters written by Jesuit priests, and poetry by José de ANCHIETA, a Jesuit missionary, there was little writing in the sixteenth century. Only in 1593 was the first work by a native written—Bento Teixeira's *A Prosopopéia* (1601), an epic in the tradition of Camões. The baroque seventeenth century was barren except for biographies, sermons, and other spiritual writings. The one great poet who wrote in Portuguese was a Brazilian, Gregório de MATOS [Guerra], a native of Bahia who was educated in Portugal and lived there for years. Father Antônio VIEIRA, his contemporary, though born in Portugal and an important Portuguese political figure, may also be claimed for Brazil because of the letters and sermons he wrote there. The sermons especially are baroque masterpieces with their sonorousness, imaginative metaphors, and brilliant construction. In the eighteenth century the most significant Brazilian baroque monument was not poetry or oratory but a history of the colony, *História da América Portuguesa* (1730), by another native of Bahia, Sebastião da Rocha Pita. Its theme is the greatness of Portuguese America. During the eighteenth century the discovery of gold brought greater wealth to support more extensive cultural activities. The most significant literary production was in poetry and came from the province of Minas Gerais, where a group of poets lived. The most important were Cláudio Manuel da Costa (1729–1789), Tomás Antônio GONZAGA, and Inácio José de Alvarenga Peixoto (1744–1793), who were later implicated in the Minas conspiracy. Along with José Basílio da GAMA and José de Santa Rita DURÃO, they represent neoclassicism, or *arcadismo,* a reaction against the baroque esthetic in the direction of simplicity of language and style and a search for a more personal subject matter. The first three are mainly lyric poets, but the last two wrote epics about episodes in Brazilian history.

When in 1822 Brazil achieved its independence, it also began the process of cultural emancipation. The first monument of romanticism was associated with France: *Suspiros Poéticos e Saudades* (1836), by Domingos José GONÇALVES DE MAGALHÃES, who was living there when he wrote much of the book. He was an innovator who wrote lyrics, plays, and an Indianist epic, and he was an ardent advocate of the new poetry. Together with Antônio GONÇALVES DIAS, he is representative of the first generation of romantics, whose poetry is concerned with nature and Indianism and often expresses religious feeling. Later romantics were disciples of Byron and Musset, whose egoism and cynicism they introduced into their poems; the most important were Antônio Álvares de Azevedo (1831–1852) and Luis José Junqueira Freire (1832–1855). Finally, under the influence of Victor Hugo and in response to the vast social and political questions being asked in Brazil, a group of socially conscious poets came to the fore to attack slavery and the monarchy. This group found its head in Antônio CASTRO ALVES, the leader of the *condoreiros.* During the romantic period the first real fiction and drama were written in Brazil. Among the different genres were the novel of manners and city life, whose exponents were Manuel Antônio de Almeida (1830–1861), Joaquim Manuel de MACEDO, José de ALENCAR, and Joaquim Maria MACHADO DE ASSIS; the historical novel, represented principally by Alencar and Franklin Távora (1842–1888); the novel of local color, by Alencar and Bernardo Guimarães (1825–1884); and the antislavery novel, by Macedo's *As Vítimas Algozes* (1869) and Guimarães's *A Escrava Isaura* (1875). During this period Brazil's theater was flourishing. In 1838 Brazilians saw their first two romantic plays, *Antônio José,* by Gonçalves de Magalhães, and *O Juiz de Paz na Roça,* by Luis Carlos Martins PENA. The latter's comedies of urban and rural life still have a place in the theater.

Though Machado de Assis towered above contemporary novelists after the publication of *Memórias Póstumas de Bras Cubas,* 1880–1881 (*Epitaph for a Small Winner*), there was at least one other remarkable novelist, Raúl Pompéia (1863–1895). His *O Ateneu* (1888) is not so much an account of life in a boys'

school as a symbolist study of human beings as they reveal themselves in a small, closed society, written with all the resources of a great stylist. Contemporary with these two figures are a group of naturalists who left priceless documentation for the student of Brazilian regional life and the Brazilian psychology of the period, especially Herculano Inglês de Sousa (1853–1918), Aluísio AZEVEDO, and Adolfo Caminha (1867–1897). They were followed by José Pereira de GRAÇA ARANHA, more of a symbolist than a naturalist; Henrique Coelho Netto (1864–1934), now remembered as a baroque stylist; and Afonso Henriques de Lima BARRETO, whose humble birth and African heritage marked him throughout his life. It is necessary, too, to mention some of the important writers of nonfiction: Francisco Adolfo Varnhagen (1816–1878) and João Capistrano de ABREU, historians; Joaquim NABUCO, memorialist and biographer; Sílvio Romero (1851–1914), literary historian; and Euclides da CUNHA, author of a great sociological study, *Os Sertões* (*Rebellion in the Backlands*). More recent writers of nonfiction who have had a powerful influence on Brazilian thought are Paulo Prado (1869–1943), who analyzes the Brazilian psyche in *Retrato do Brasil* (1928), and Gilberto FREYRE, whose studies of plantation life influenced writers of the NORTHEAST.

After romanticism the first important movement was Parnassianism, which espoused an ideal of formal perfection as a reaction to the freedom that the romantics sought. Its three great figures were Olavo Bilac (1865–1918), Raimundo Correia (1859–1911), and Alberto de Oliveira (1859–1937). A slightly later, overlapping group was the symbolists, represented by João da CRUZ E SOUSA and Alphonsus de Guimarães (1870–1921). Neosymbolism continued to be an important force all through the modernist period. In 1922 Modern Art Week brought to the attention of literate Brazil the idea that something new had been happening in the arts; namely, that there was a new movement which was called *modernismo* (modernism) and which was repudiating established artistic values and setting up new canons. Emphasizing the importance of a new understanding of Brazil, the adoption of new literary forms, and the use of Brazilian Portuguese as the medium of literary expression, writers and critics like Mário de ANDRADE and Oswald de Andrade (1890–1954) led this new movement, which soon affected all Brazil. Modernism has been a dominant force ever since, and even a countermovement, that of the Generation of 1945, has not succeeded in shaking its principles. Under its banner have marched great poets, novelists, and critics. If there are today groups of concretist poets and postmodernist novelists like Clarice Lispector, João GUIMARÃES ROSA, Autran Dourado, or Fernando Sabino, they would not be the writers they are had it not been for modernism. *See* MODERNISM (BRAZIL).

Brazilian drama has developed since World War II. The first dramatist of note among the moderns was Nelson Rodrigues (1912–   ), who startled Rio with his *Vestido de Noiva* (1943), a play that marks a great technical advance in the Brazilian theater. Others are Jorge Andrade (1922–   ), who has chronicled aspects of life in rural São Paulo; Alfredo Dias Gomes (1922–   ), whose theater is one of social protest; and Antônio Suassuna (1927–   ), who draws heavily on the rich folklore of the Northeast. Women writers have come to the fore, too. Whereas in the past there was only a handful of names, such as Teresa Margarida da Silva e Orta (1711–1793), Francisca Júlia (1871–1920), Júlia Lopes de Almeida (1862–1934), and Auta de Sousa (1876–1901), since modernism there have been many women writers, among them Cecília Meireles (1901–1964), one of the greatest poets of the century; Adalgisa Nery (1905–   ) and Henriqueta Lisboa, also poets; Raquel de QUEIROS, a novelist of the Northeast; Lúcia Miguel-Pereira (1903–1959), novelist and critic; and Clarice Lispector, Nélida Piñón, and Maria Alice Barroso, novelists. It is also necessary to point out the importance of the Negro writer in Brazil. The two greatest Brazilian novelists, Machado de Assis and Lima Barreto, were blacks, or, to be more exact, mulattoes; the greatest romantic poet, Gonçalves Dias, had African and Indian blood; the greatest symbolist poet, João da Cruz e Sousa, was the child of slaves; and the great critic and leader of modernism, Mário de Andrade, was also a mulatto, as is the contemporary stage director, producer, and playwright Abdias do Nascimento. *See also* NEGRO IN BRAZIL.

Bibliography. Manuel Bandeira, *Brief History of Brazilian Literature,* tr. by Ralph Dimmick, Washington, 1958; Afrânio Coutinho, *An Introduction to Literature in Brazil,* tr. by Gregory Rabassa, New York, 1969; Afrânio Coutinho (ed.), *A Literatura no Brasil,* 6 vols., 2d ed., Rio de Janeiro, 1968; Sábato Magaldi, *Panorama do Teatro Brasileiro,* São Paulo, 1962; Jacinto do Prado Coelho, *Dicionário de Literatura,* 2 vols., 2d ed., Oporto, 1969; Sílvio Romero, *História da Literatura Brasileira,* 5 vols., 3d ed., Rio de Janeiro, 1943; Raymond S. Sayers, *The Negro in Brazilian Literature,* New York, 1956.

RAYMOND S. SAYERS

LITERATURE (SPANISH AMERICA, to 1910). The early periods of Spanish American literature have been treated in different fashions by literary critics and historians. Some have tended to think of literary figures in relation to the century in which they wrote, that is, the literature of the seventeenth or eighteenth century, or in terms of a generational plan. Other literary historians have chosen to group all the literature prior to political independence from Spain under the heading "Literature of the Colonial Period," which is perhaps more a political than a literary term. Still other critics refuse to consider any grouping except by country, arguing that a concept of Spanish American or Latin American literature has no meaning and that the early preindependence literature of Spanish America represents little more than a slavish imitation of Spain's major writers.

One approach to Spanish American literature that has won some acceptance is based on period or epoch style: pre-Columbian, or pre-Hispanic, literature; literature of the exploration and conquest (sixteenth century); the baroque period (seventeenth and early eighteenth centuries); neoclassicism, or the Enlightenment (eighteenth and early nineteenth centuries); romanticism (1830–1880s); realism-naturalism (1880–1910); and modernism (1888–1910). Whatever arbitrary dates are affixed to these periods, there must obviously be exceptions because of the number of countries involved. These dates are intended to encompass the major nucleus of each period.

Pre-Columbian period. Prior to the period of exploration and conquest, there existed an oral literary tradition among some of the aboriginal civilizations of the New World. The MAYAS used ideographs that in some cases have been deciphered. This literary tradition, both oral and written, was most prevalent among the QUECHUA speakers of the Inca empire (*see* INCAS), the Mayas, the Maya-Quichés, and the NAHUATL-speaking AZTECS. Among the most significant works are the Quechua drama *Apu Ollantay,* which is considered to be pre-Hispanic; the Nahuatl poetry of the Aztecs; and the Maya-Quiché *Popul Vuh,* or *Libro del Consejo,* as well as a kind of tragedy with the name *Rabinal Achí.*

Exploration and conquest. The literature of exploration and conquest in the sixteenth century is based primarily on the chroniclers and two major poets. The figures who come to the fore among the chroniclers are Christopher COLUMBUS, whose *Journal* describes his explorations and experiences, and Hernán CORTÉS, whose *Cartas de relación,* 1519–1536 (*Five Letters of Relation to the Emperor Charles V*), gives a vivid account of his adventures to King CHARLES I of Spain. One of the most readable accounts is that of Bernal DÍAZ DEL CASTILLO, author of *Verdadera historia de la conquista de Nueva España,* published posthumously in 1632. Fray Bartolomé de LAS CASAS is probably the most famous chronicler of the New World because of the popularity of his *Brevísima relación de la destrucción de las Indias* (1542, published 1552). The Inca GARCILASO DE LA VEGA was a native of the New World, having been born in Cuzco, the son of an Inca princess and a Spanish captain. This mestizo writer produced several important works, of which the most famous are *La Florida del Inca* (1605) and the *Comentarios reales,* 1609 (*Royal Commentaries*).

La Araucana, 1569, 1578, 1589 (*The Araucaniad*), by Alonso de ERCILLA Y ZÚÑIGA, is in a sense a rhymed chronicle of the conquest of Chile, but it represents as well the high point of the renaissance epic in Spanish. Pedro de Oña (Chile, 1570–?1643) wrote an epic poem, having been inspired by that of Ercilla, entitled *Arauco domado,* 1596 (*Arauco Tamed*). He also composed several other poems of significance.

Baroque period. By the beginning of the seventeenth century intellectual life in the viceregal capitals was becoming quite active, and the currents of the baroque found enthusiastic followers in the colonies. Bernardo de Balbuena (Mexico, 1562?–1627) wrote one of the best descriptive epics of his time, *La grandeza mexicana* (1604). He is also known for his epic *Bernardo, o Victoria de Roncesvalles* (1624). Diego de Hojeda (Peru, 1571–1615) wrote a religious epic, *La cristiada* (1611), on the life and Passion of Christ.

The two major writers of lyric poetry in the baroque period are Mexico's "tenth muse," Sor JUANA INÉS DE LA CRUZ, and Juan del Valle y CAVIEDES of Peru. Sor Juana's poetry, prose, and drama place her at the forefront of the writers of the century. *El primero sueño,* 1692 (*First Dream*), a long poem with religious-mystical overtones, is one of the masterpieces of baroque narrative poetry in Spanish. Caviedes was a satirical poet whose works are akin in concept and form to the poetry of the Spaniard Francisco de Quevedo. Another Peruvian, Pedro de PERALTA BARNUEVO, was a savant who wrote literary as well as scientific works. His literary works show him to have been a transitional figure between the baroque and the Enlightenment (*see* ENLIGHTENMENT: SPANISH AMERICA). In addition to several plays, he wrote an epic poem, *Lima fundada* (1738), on Francisco PIZARRO's conquest of Peru. In addition to Sor Juana and Peralta Barnuevo, the major figure in the theater is Juan Ruiz de Alarcón (Mexico, 1580–1639), who spent much of his life in Spain, where such dramatic works as *La verdad sospechosa* won the admiration of his Golden Age contemporaries.

A Mexican contemporary of Sor Juana, Carlos de SIGÜENZA Y GÓNGORA, was one of the foremost intellects of the seventeenth century. He wrote several works in verse, of which the gongoristic *Primavera indiana* (1668) is the best known. His *Infortunios de Alonso Ramírez* (1690) is a kind of first-person forerunner of the modern novel in Spanish America. The creole Chilean writer Francisco de Pineda y Bascuñán (1607–1682) wrote a prose work entitled *Cautiverio feliz* (1650?), which tells of a man's captivity among the Araucanian Indians (*see* ARAUCANIANS). Religious prose writers of this period are best represented by Madre Castillo (Sor Francisca Josefa de la Concepción de Castillo y Guevara; Colombia, 1671–1742) and her *Afectos espirituales* (written about 1694). Concolorcorvo, whose real name was Alonso Carrió de la Vandera (Spain, 1715?–?1778), wrote an account of a journey from Montevideo to Lima entitled *Lazarillo de ciegos caminantes* (1773) that is noteworthy for its satire of society.

Neoclassicism, or the Enlightenment. The literature of this period in Spanish America reflects the classical molds of French and Spanish models. This was a period of transition between the exaggerated rococo style and the beginnings of romanticism. Only a few major writers need be cited as representatives of neoclassicism. In poetry, José Joaquín de OLMEDO of Ecuador is well known for "La victoria de Junín: Canto a Bolívar," 1825 ("The Victory of Junin"), which is a good example of heroic verse in a classical style. Andrés BELLO of Venezuela was, like Olmedo, a leader in the battle for independence from Spain. He was trained in the classical tradition, and his poems, such as "A la agricultura de la Zona Tórrida," 1826 ("Agriculture in the Torrid Zone"), and "Alocución a la poesía," 1823 ("Allocution to Poetry"), are highly considered examples of the contemporary style.

The man considered to be the first novelist of Spanish America is José Joaquín FERNÁNDEZ DE LIZARDI, also known as El Pensador Mexicano. In addition to other prose writings, including two other novels, he composed a picaresque novel, *El periquillo sarniento*, 1816 (*The Itching Parrot*), that satirizes life in Mexico.

Manuel Eduardo de Gorostiza (1789–1851) of Mexico is the best dramatist of this period. Of his several plays, *Contigo pan y cebolla* (1833) is the most widely respected.

Romanticism. Several poets of the romantic period are worthy of note. Esteban ECHEVERRÍA of Argentina was one of the first writers of the movement. His poem "La cautiva," 1837 ("The Captive"), is his best-known work in verse, but he also wrote a narrative poem, *Elvira o La novia del Plata* (1832), and a famous short story, "El matadero," 1838 ("The Slaughterhouse"), in which he attacked political authoritarianism. Cuba produced two important romantic poets. Plácido

(Gabriel de la Concepción Valdés, 1809–1844), a mulatto, is best known for such poems as "Jicotencal" and "Plegaria a Dios" ("Prayer to God"). Gertrudis Gómez de Avellaneda (1814–1873) spent much of her life in Spain but was named Cuba's national poetess. In addition to her many volumes of poetry, she wrote several plays and novels. Her novel *Sab* (1841) deals with racial conflict.

Of a later generation of romantics is José HERNÁNDEZ of Argentina, whose long poem *El gaucho Martín Fierro* (1872) and its sequel, *La vuelta de Martín Fierro* (1879), are considered classics of GAUCHO poetry. His Uruguayan contemporary Juan ZORRILLA DE SAN MARTÍN also wrote an important epic poem, *Tabaré* (1888), on an indigenous theme.

The novel and short story were fertile genres during the romantic period. José MÁRMOL of Argentina produced one of the most important political novels of the time, *Amalia* (1851). His contemporary fellow countryman Domingo Faustino SARMIENTO spent his life in politics, but he wrote, among other works, a novelesque volume, *Facundo o Civilización y barbarie* (1845), that is considered a classic.

Juan León MERA of Ecuador produced an important Indian novel, *Cumandá* (1879), but the Colombian Jorge ISAACS wrote the masterpiece of the sentimental romantic novel in Spanish America, *María* (1867), which he patterned on French romantic models. Alberto BLEST GANA of Chile wrote several novels, some of which are romantic while others are realistic. Among his romantic novels are *La aritmética en el amor* (1860), *Una escena social* (1853), and *Juan de Aria* (1858). Mexico's leading romantic novelist was Ignacio Manuel Altamirano (1834–1893), who is best known for the novels *Clemencia* (1869) and *El Zarco*, which was published posthumously in 1901.

The Peruvian Ricardo PALMA represents another aspect of the inventive nature of the romantics who chose new molds for their works. His various series of *Tradiciones peruanas,* short prose pieces, were unique in their time and have won Palma a place of honor among the major writers of the nineteenth century.

In the drama, two compatriots of Palma, Felipe Pardo y Aliaga (1806–1868) and Manuel Segura (1805–1871), are the best representatives of the romantic interest in *costumbrismo,* a literary genre typified by an emphasis on aspects of local color and the customs of a specific region or locale. *Los frutos de la educación* (1829) by Pardo y Aliaga and Segura's *El sargento Canuto* (1839) and *Ña Catita* (1856) are their most representative works.

The two major essayists of the time are Juan MONTALVO of Ecuador, who published *Siete tratados* in 1882, and the Puerto Rican Eugenio María de HOSTOS, whose *Moral social* (1888) is his most important work.

Realism and naturalism. Among the principal novelists of realism in Spanish America are José López Portillo y Rojas (Mexico, 1850–1923), Tomás Carrasquilla (Colombia, 1858–1940), and the Peruvian Clorinda MATTO DE TURNER. Portillo y Rojas wrote *La parcela* (1898), but he is best known for some of his short prose works. Carrasquilla produced several novels, of which *Frutos de mi tierra* (1896) and *La marquesa de Yolombó* (1929) are the best known, as well as short stories. Clorinda Matto de Turner's most famous novel is *Aves sin nido,* 1889 (*Birds without Nests*), considered the first *indigenista* novel in Spanish America.

The influences of naturalism are seen in the novels of several Spanish American authors. Eduardo ACEVEDO DÍAZ of Uruguay wrote several novels of the gaucho type in which he introduced naturalism to his country. Another Uruguayan, Carlos REYLES, wrote several naturalistic novels: *Por la vida* (1888), *Beba* (1894), and *Raza de Caín* (1900). His compatriot Javier de Viana (1868–1926) published many volumes of short stories, including *Campo* (1896), *Gurí* (1901), *Macachines* (1910), *Leña seca* (1911), and *Yuyos* (1912). The short stories in *Sub terra* (1904) and *Sub sole* (1907), by the Chilean Baldomero Lillo (1867–1923), give ample evidence of the influence of Émile Zola and the Goncourt brothers. Lillo's most famous short story is "La compuerta número 12."

Florencio SÁNCHEZ of Uruguay is the most important dramatist of this period and the first important figure of the modern theater in Spanish America. Among his best works are *M'hijo el dotor,* 1903 (*My Son the Lawyer*); *La gringa,* 1904 (*The Immigrant Girl*); and *Barranca abajo,* 1905 (*Down the Gully*).

Modernism. Modernism (1888–1910) was the first literary movement to begin in Spanish America and then spread throughout the Hispanic world. The movement's undisputed leader was Rubén DARÍO, a Nicaraguan, whose volume of prose and verse *Azul,* published in Chile in 1888, marked the beginning of the movement. Darío traveled throughout Spanish America and Europe and was in touch with other modernist writers. He published several other important volumes —*Prosas profanas* (1896), *Cantos de vida y esperanza* (1905), *El canto errante* (1907)—as well as books of essays and short stories.

The precursors of modernism were the Cuban José MARTÍ, the author of *Ismaelillo* (1882), *Versos sencillos* (1891), and *Versos libres* (1913); another Cuban, Julián del Casal (1863–1893), who wrote *Hojas al viento* (1890), *Nieve* (1892), and *Bustos y rimas* (1893); the Colombian José Asunción SILVA, the best representative of the early stages of the movement; and Manuel GUTIÉRREZ NÁJERA of Mexico, who is as highly considered for his short stories (*Cuentos frágiles,* 1883) as he is for his poetry.

The second group of modernists in the field of poetry includes Leopoldo LUGONES, Ricardo Jaimes Freyre, Amado NERVO, José Santos CHOCANO, Guillermo Valencia, and Julio Herrera y Reissig, among many others. Lugones, the author of *Las montañas del oro* (1897), *Los crepúsculos del jardín* (1905), and *Lunario sentimental* (1909), among many other works in prose and verse, was the leader of the modernist writers in Argentina. Ricardo Jaimes Freyre (Bolivia, 1868–1933) lived for several years in Buenos Aires, where he knew Darío. His *Castalia bárbara* (1899) is one of the important volumes of modernist poetry. Julio Herrera y Reissig (Uruguay, 1875–1910) belongs to the modernist group whose works, such as *Los maitines de la noche* (1900–1903) and *Los éxtasis de la montaña* (1904), show the influence of the French symbolists.

The Peruvian José Santos Chocano, known as the Cantor de América, was the modernist poet who most often utilized autochthonous elements in his poetry. Of primary interest is the collection entitled *Alma América* (1906). Guillermo Valencia (Colombia, 1873–1943) cultivated exotic themes in many of the poems in his collections. His best book is *Ritos* (1899, 1914), but he also published *Poesías* (1912), *Poemas* (1918), and *Catay: Poemas orientales* (1929). The leader of the Mexican poets of this generation of modernists is Amado Nervo. His preoccupation with the mystical aspects of religion is evident in several of his works. Nervo also wrote short stories that belonged to the modernist movement.

Among other writers of the modernist movement are Manuel Díaz Rodríguez (Venezuela, 1868–1927), novelist and author of *Idolos rotos* (1901) and *Sangre patricia* (1902); Enrique LARRETA of Argentina, author of one of modernism's best novels, *La gloria de don Ramiro* (1908); and the Uruguayan José Enrique RODÓ, whose *Ariel* (1900) marks an important moment in the development of the essay in Spanish America.

See also MODERNISM (SPANISH AMERICA).

Bibliography. Fernando Alegría, *Historia de la novela hispanoamericana,* Mexico City, 1965; Enrique Anderson-Imbert, *Historia de la literatura hispanoamericana,* 2 vols., 2d ed., Mexico City, 1970; José Juan Arrom, *Historia del teatro hispanoamericano (época colonial),* 2d ed., Mexico City, 1967; John Englekirk et al., *An Outline History of Spanish American Literature,* 3d ed., New York, 1965; Jean Franco, *An Introduction to Spanish American Literature,* London, 1969; Pedro Henríquez Ureña, *Las corrientes literarias en la América Hispana,* 3d ed., Mexico City, 1969; Willis Knapp Jones, *Behind Spanish American Footlights,* Austin, Tex., 1966; Luis Leal, *Breve historia de la literatura hispanoamericana,* New York, 1971; id., *Historia del cuento hispanoamericano,* 2d ed., Mexico City, 1971.   DANIEL R. REEDY

LITERATURE (SPANISH AMERICA, since 1910). By 1910 the modernist movement no longer seemed forward-looking, and this led to a reaction against its estheticism (*see* MODERNISM: SPANISH AMERICA). Its elitist values were rejected by writers who looked to daily life for inspiration and by thinkers who turned to the reality of America as a continent unique in its development and characteristics. The modernists had taught men to take literature seriously, however, and thus authors started to explore the problems and values of Latin American nations. The way was prepared for the *criollista* strain that replaced modernism by focusing on the political, social, and geographic reality of the Hispano-American continent (*see* CREOLE). Three cataclysmic events also helped to break the European-inspired ways of thought of earlier generations: the MEXICAN REVOLUTION (1910), World War I (1914–1918), and the Russian Revolution (1917). Old values had failed, and a new spirit of independence and appraisal marked Latin American literature from 1910 onward.

Mexico. The Mexican novel after 1910, showing the impact of the revolution that changed the political and economic structure of the country, was concerned either with the dramatic events themselves or with their effect on everyday existence. Mariano AZUELA, the most prolific author, used at first realistic and later more experimental narrative techniques. José Rubén ROMERO considered the revolution's implications for life in provincial backwaters, Martín Luis GUZMÁN treated the perspective of the great leaders, and Gregorio LÓPEZ Y FUENTES dealt with events from a sociological point of view. The revolution also provides the background for *Al filo del agua*, 1947 (*The Edge of the Storm*), the most famous novel of Agustín YAÑEZ, although he used avant-garde techniques to interpret Mexican reality.

Realism continued to influence José Revueltas (1914–), producing as well *Juan Pérez Jolote* (1952), the anthropological but almost novelistic study by Ricardo Pozas (1910–). A variety of techniques emerged after 1950: the fantastic and humorous stories of Juan José ARREOLA, the mythical interpretation of Juan RULFO, and the novels of Sergio Fernández (1926–), Luis Spota (1925–), Rosario Castellanos (1925–), Sergio Galindo (1926–), and most notably, Carlos FUENTES, now widely translated and internationally famous. A younger group of experimental novelists is headed by Salvador Elizondo (1932–) and Gustavo Sainz (1940–).

Mexico's best-known essayist is Alfonso REYES, whose multiplicity of themes makes him a cultural leader of the continent. José VASCONCELOS is important as both politician and writer; Leopoldo Zea (1912–) has written on the theme of national identity, as has Octavio PAZ.

Among the writers attempting to create a Mexican theater, Rodolfo USIGLI and Celestino Gorostiza (1904–1966) are outstanding. Younger dramatists, such as Elena Garro (1920–), Luisa Josefina Hernández (1928–), Emilio CARBALLIDO, and Jorge Ibargüengoitia (1928–), are influenced by the notion of the absurd.

Among the Mexican poets who reacted against modernism were Juan José TABLADA, who turned to the Orient for new forms and themes, and the more important Ramón LÓPEZ VELARDE, whose poetry focuses on the melancholy charm of daily life. Some poets grouped themselves around the journal *Contemporáneos* (1928–1931), the most famous being Xavier VILLAURRUTIA, José GOROSTIZA, and Jaime Torres Bodet (1902–). Carlos PELLICER is another fine poet of this generation. Alí CHUMACERO is the leading poet of still another group whose voice is the magazine *Tierra Nueva* (1940–1942). Jaime Sabines (1926–), Tomás Segovia (1927–), and Marco Antonio Montes de Oca (1932–) are important younger poets.

Central America. Fiction writing in Guatemala has produced the interesting psychological stories of Rafael Arévalo Martínez (1884–) and the mythicosocial novels of Miguel Ángel ASTURIAS, one of the leading writers of the century. In El Salvador poverty is treated imaginatively in the stories of Salvador Salazar Arrué (1899–), who is known as Salarrué. The best-known novelist in Costa Rica is José Marín Cañas (1914–), and Panama has an excellent prose writer in Rogelio Sinán (1904–). The Central American countries also have many writers who explore social and political problems and who focus on the sufferings of the indigenous population; among them are Víctor Cáceres Lara (1915–) and Ramón Amaya Amador, both of Honduras.

Central American poetry is represented by Rafael Arévalo Martínez, Rafael Cardona (Costa Rica, 1892–), Ricardo Miró (Panama, 1883–1940), Luis Cardoza y Aragón (Guatemala, 1904–), Claudia Lars (El Salvador, 1899–), José Coronel Urtecho (Nicaragua, 1906–), and, more recently, Ernesto Mejía Sánchez (Nicaragua, 1923–), among others.

Cuba and the Caribbean. In the early part of the twentieth century Cuban novelists were preoccupied with political problems and the need for social reform; this concern produced novels about the lives of blacks and mulattoes. The most famous of these writers are Ramón Guirao (1908–1949); Lydia Cabrera (1900–), who collected stories of ethnographic interest; and Alejo CARPENTIER, whose first novel is based on Afro-Cuban themes. With his later works Carpentier became one of the greatest modern novelists. Lino NOVÁS CALVO is an assiduously realistic writer whose work, along with that of José LEZAMA LIMA, Guillermo CABRERA INFANTE, and Severo Sarduy (1937–), ensures Cuban prose fiction a leading place in the hemisphere. And the Cuban José Triana (1932–) is a fine playwright. In the Dominican Republic Juan BOSCH, though best known as a political figure, is an excellent short-story writer.

Poetry in the Caribbean countries has been vigorous since the decline of modernism. In Cuba the traditional verse of José Manuel Poveda (1888–1926) and his contemporaries gave way to the "new" (that is, experimental) poetry of Mariano Brull (1891–1956), Regino Pedroso (1896–), and Eugenio Florit (1903–), and in the 1920s to the "black" poetry of Emilio BALLAGAS and Nicolás GUILLÉN, which was inspired by African religion and rhythms. Manuel del CABRAL of the Dominican Republic and Luis PALÉS MATOS (1898–1959) of Puerto Rico are outstanding in both "black" poetry and "pure" poetry in the European symbolist tradition. Newer names are Cintio Vitier (1921–), Eliseo Diego (1920–), Fayad Jamis (1930–), Roberto Fernández Retamar (1930–), Pablo Armando Fernández (1930–), and Heberto Padilla (1932–), all of Cuba.

Venezuela. The novel is dominated by Rómulo GALLEGOS, whose work presents the epic of Venezuela's land and culture. Other novelists are Teresa de la Parra (1891–1936) and the more realistic José Rafael Pocaterra (1889–1955). Arturo USLAR PIETRI is influenced by avant-garde movements, while Miguel Otero Silva (1908–) and Ramón Díaz Sánchez (1903–) continue to write in the realistic tradition.

The most important poets are Andrés Eloy Blanco (1897–1955) and Jacinto Fombona Pachano (1901–1951). Miguel Otero Silva and Antonio Arraiz (1903–) employ more experimental techniques, and Ida Gramcko (1925–) is one of the most original of the many younger poets. Juan Calzadilla (1931–) and Pedro Duno (1933–) also stand out among their contemporaries.

Colombia. José Eustasio RIVERA was the first regionalist writer in Colombia, and José Restrepo Jaramillo (1896–1945) showed originality of theme and technique. Prose fiction manifested an interest in local color and a sociological point of view with the work of Eduardo Arias Suárez (1897–) and César Uribe Piedrahita (1897–1951) and in regionalism with that of Antonio Cardona Jaramillo (1914–) and Eduardo Zalamea Borda (1907–). A more universal writer is Eduardo Caballero Calderón (1910–). Manuel Zapata Olivella (1920–) is among the interesting younger writers, of whom the most outstanding is the internationally known Gabriel GARCÍA MÁRQUEZ, one of the best novelists of the day. Colombia also has a brilliant thinker and essayist in Germán ARCINIEGAS.

Colombian poetry is notable for the modernist Porfirio Barba Jacob (pseudonym of Miguel Ángel Osorio, 1883–1942), the lyrical re-creation of landscape by José Eustasio Rivera, the experimentalism of León de Greiff (1895–   ), and the poets grouped around the journals *Los Nuevos* and the later *Piedra y Cielo,* whose main promoter was Eduardo Carranza (1913–   ).

Ecuador. Ecuador produced a moderately good writer of the early twentieth century in Gonzalo Zaldumbide (1885–   ). Pablo Palacio (1906–1946) wrote stories and novels with a perceptively human approach. A more lasting impression was made by the *indigenista* novels of Jorge ICAZA, who defended the Indian against exploitation. Demetrio Aguilera Malta (1905–   ) also wrote about the sufferings of the underprivileged, and Enrique Gil Gilbert (1912–   ) among others has continued the use of prose fiction for sociopolitical ends. Adalberto Ortiz (1914–   ) explores the frustrations of the black minority, and Pedro Jorge Vera (1914–   ) the pyschological depths of his characters.

Ecuadorian poetry enjoyed a modernist phase, followed by the experimentation of some minor writers. Jorge CARRERA ANDRADE is the best known among many poets of quality, and Alejandro Carrión (1915–   ) is highly esteemed.

Peru. The first major fiction writer was Ventura García Calderón (1886–1959), who was at once regional in focus and universal in interest, while Augusto Aguirre Morales (1890–   ) used archaeology and imagination to reconstruct the world of the INCAS. The best known of the realistic writers is Ciro ALEGRÍA, whose sympathy for the Indians makes his novels valuable from a sociological as well as an artistic point of view. The same is true of José María ARGUEDAS. Among younger writers of note are Carlos Zavaleta (1928–   ), José Durand (1925–   ), Enrique Congrains Martín (1932–   ), and the justly celebrated Mario VARGAS LLOSA.

Peruvian poetry enjoyed a brief period of modernism, after which more experimental verse appeared in the magazine *Amauta* (1926–1930), edited by José Carlos MARIÁTEGUI. César VALLEJO is the leading Peruvian poet of the century and one of the greatest in Spanish. Carlos Oquendo de Amat (1909–1936) left interesting work, and Emilio Adolfo Westphalen (1911–   ) is another poet of merit. Magda Portal (1901–   ) is an interesting sociopolitical poet; among younger writers the guerrilla poet Javier Heraud (1942–1963) is outstanding.

Bolivia. Bolivian reality is admirably described in the novels of Armando Chirveches (1883–1926), who was followed by writers in the naturalist and *indigenista* traditions. The CHACO WAR (1932–1935) inspired Oscar Cerruto (1907–   ) and Augusto Céspedes (1904–   ), among others. Later authors often focus on social issues.

Bolivian poetry is noteworthy for the modernist Ricardo Jaimes Freyre (1868–1933) and Claudio Peñaranda (1884–1924), the experimental Rafael Ballivián (1898–   ), and the woman poet Yolanda Bedregal (1916–   ).

Chile. Twentieth-century Chile has produced several outstanding prose writers: Eduardo BARRIOS, noted for psychological realism; Pedro PRADO, whose poetic prose is dense with philosophical preoccupations; and Jenaro Prieto (1889–1946), who exhibits a fantastic vision of reality. Psychological regionalism is found in the novels of Rafael Maluenda (1885–   ), and a more limited regionalism in those of Mariano Latorre (1886–1955), but the best writers of these years are the psychological novelist Joaquín Edwards Bello (1888–   ) and Manuel ROJAS. María Luisa Bombal (1910–   ), who writes admirably on a smaller scale, is one of several fine contemporary women authors. After a period of socially directed creole literature, Chilean novelists returned to more general themes and psychological penetration with Fernando Alegría (1918–   ), the younger José DONOSO, and Jorge Edwards (1931–   ), among others.

Chilean poetry has been rich in this century, from the universal humanitarianism of Gabriela MISTRAL to the romantic excesses of Pablo de Rokha (1894–   ) and the cosmopolitan originality of Vicente HUIDOBRO. The giant of contemporary Latin American poetry is Pablo NERUDA, around whom grew minor poets of value, such as Humberto Díaz Casanueva (1908–   ). Some surrealist poets formed a group around the journal *Mandrágora* (1938–1941), and some later poets found inspiration in folklore. From this starting point Nicanor PARRA developed his antipoetry and, together with Enrique Lihn (1929–   ), Efraín Barquero (1931–   ), and others, continues to give vitality to Chilean poetry. Notable dramatists are Luis Alberto Heiremans (1928–   ), Egon Wolff (1926–   ), and Fernando Debesa (1921–   ).

Argentina and the Río de la Plata region. Regional nationalism inspired the gifted Argentine writer Ricardo GÜIRALDES, who was concerned with his country's identity. Later writers of the area turned their attention to one or another region or to national problems. Among them are Natalicio González (Paraguay, 1897–   ), Adolfo Montiel Ballesteros (Uruguay, 1888–   ), Alberto Gerchunoff (Argentina, 1883/1884–1950), and the popular Benito Lynch (Argentina, 1885–1952). The Uruguayan Juan Carlos ONETTI explores the urban reality of Montevideo and Buenos Aires; Leopoldo Marechal (Argentina, 1898–   ) wrote *Adán Buenosayres,* a novel with symbolic overtones; and Jorge Luis BORGES dominates Latin American prose with his short stories and essays. Among other first-rate novelists are Ernesto SÁBATO, who evinces tendencies toward surrealism and existentialism, and Eduardo MALLEA, who develops existentialist ideas in a series of powerful works. Silvina Ocampo (Argentina, 1906?–   ) and Adolfo BIOY CASARES are writers of quality closely associated with Borges. A more objective vision is found in Enrique Amorim (Uruguay, 1900–1960) and a large number of Argentine writers, among whom Roberto ARLT and Augusto ROA BASTOS are outstanding. A slightly younger generation has produced H. A. Murena (Argentina, 1924–   ); Julio CORTÁZAR, whose philosophicofantastic *oeuvre* is justly famous; and Mario BENEDETTI.

The Río de la Plata area has had a strong poetic tradition since modernism and a surprising trio of women, Delmira AGUSTINI, Juana de IBARBOUROU, and Alfonsina STORNI. Carlos Sabat Ercasty (Uruguay, 1887–   ) wrote with a spontaneity that influenced the young Neruda. Enrique Banchs (Argentina, 1888–   ) showed an early promise that was not fulfilled, writing in a classical style shared by Baldomero Fernández Moreno (Argentina, 1886–1950). Avant-garde experimentalism is associated with Julio J. Casal (Uruguay, 1889–1954) and flourished in the reviews *Proa* and *Martín Fierro,* both of Buenos Aires, with which Oliverio Girondo (Argentina, 1891–   ) and Borges were closely associated. Noteworthy poets include Ildefonso Pereda Valdés (Uruguay, 1899–   ), who writes with a strong social commitment, and Ricardo E. Molinari (Argentina, 1898–   ), who is associated with the avant-garde group.

The theater has flourished with the works of Chilean-born Armando L. Moock (1894–1943), Samuel Eichelbaum (Argentina, 1894–   ), Conrado Nalé Roxlo (Argentina, 1898–   ), and an increasing number of younger playwrights. Among essayists and critics of the first rank are Ezequiel MARTÍNEZ ESTRADA, Emir Rodríguez Monegal (Uruguay, 1921–   ), and Emma Susana Speratti Pinero (Argentina, 1919–   ).

Bibliography. Fernando Alegría, *Historia de la novela hispanoamericana,* Mexico City, 1966; id., *Novelistas contemporáneos hispanoamericanos,* Boston, 1964; Enrique Anderson Imbert, *Historia de la literatura hispanoamericana,* Mexico City, 1961; Germán Bleiberg and Julián Marías, *Diccionario de literatura española,* 3d ed., Madrid, 1964; Jean Franco, *An Introduction to Spanish-American Literature,* New York, 1969; Orlando Gómez-Gil, *Historia crítica de la literatura hispanoamericana,* New York, 1968; Emir Rodríguez Monegal, *Narradores de esta América,* Montevideo, n.d.; Leopoldo Zea, *The Latin American Mind,* Norman, Okla., 1963.

RACHEL PHILLIPS

LIVESTOCK INDUSTRY (URUGUAY). Throughout its history Uruguay has been heavily dependent upon its livestock industry. In this century livestock products have normally comprised two-thirds of the value of the nation's agricultural output and at least two-thirds of its exports. Until recently wool dominated exports, but in the 1960s the value of beef exports grew while that of wool exports remained relatively constant. Since 1950 the livestock industry of Uruguay has been characterized by economic stagnation—part of the general malaise of the national economy.

Prior to independence Uruguay was occupied by wild creole cattle, the descendants of cattle released in the early days of colonization. Gauchos (*see* GAUCHO) followed the herds and slaughtered the animals for their hides, which were brought to the coast for export. Toward the end of the eighteenth century *saladeros* were opened to produce salt beef for Brazil and Cuba, where it was in demand as a food for slaves. To assure a steady supply of cattle for the *saladeros,* located on the coast or along the URUGUAY RIVER, large ranches began to be laid out and the wild cattle were domesticated. The importance of large ranches was enhanced by a general growth in wool exports throughout the nineteenth century as well as by the sale of fresh beef to Western Europe, made possible by the development of the refrigerated ship. During this period the British played an enormous role in Uruguayan agriculture, acquiring much land, building meat-packing plants, and financing railroads.

Generally the physical environment of Uruguay is better suited to grazing than to crop production, but there are handicaps to raising livestock. Most soils are thin, and the climate does not permit the commercial growth of forage as nutritive as alfalfa. Rainfall is frequently irregular in summer. During severe droughts millions of livestock can be lost. The physical environment influenced stockmen to choose sheep over cattle as their principal source of income, sheep being better adapted to pasture conditions, but the high Uruguayan per capita beef consumption has necessitated the maintenance of large herds of cattle. Approximately 90 percent of the land in farms is in pasture. No section of the nation specializes in either sheep or beef cattle, although there is a slightly higher relative importance of beef cattle in the area south of the Negro River, which is relatively tick-free. Dairy, hog, and poultry production is concentrated near the large urban market of Montevideo.

Low productivity in the livestock industry cannot be ascribed to the physical environment. The problem is both cultural and economic. Landownership remains highly concentrated, the owners of the large ranches normally being economically conservative. Their large estates produce sufficient income for them and their families to enjoy the amenities they desire. These usually include a town house in Montevideo, where they reside most of the year. Unfortunately, there are insufficient profits to provide a decent life for the ranch employees. AGRARIAN REFORM programs have been enacted, but implementation is slow. Little effort has been made to improve stock other than the initial steps taken in the nineteenth century when creole cattle and sheep were replaced with British breeds. Few stockmen have attempted to develop modern improved pastures, supplemental feeding during the winter or periods of drought is rare, and lack of shelter has caused a high mortality rate among the animals. The slow maturation rate of beef cattle because of these and other factors, which could be alleviated through better management, has contributed to a very low yield of beef per acre.

Uruguay's economic policy has also greatly reduced the possibility for an increase in livestock productivity. Since 1950 the government has pursued a policy of encouraging high-cost import substitution industries, which provide employment to the nation's rapidly growing urban population. The attraction of urban jobs induced a large number of underpaid farm laborers to abandon the land. Unemployment rates rose in the cities, since the number of new jobs could not keep pace with the applicants, and the farm economy suffered because of the absence of labor. The industrialization program has been undertaken largely at the expense of the agricultural economy, which has been heavily taxed. Controls have been placed on the price of domestic beef. The low price stimulates a high per capita consumption and a consequent reduction in surpluses that might have been available for export. Several meat-packing plants that processed beef for export were closed in the late 1960s. An outbreak of foot-and-mouth disease among British cattle in 1969 caused that nation, a large purchaser of Uruguayan beef, to place a temporary embargo on trade. Although the embargo has been lifted, the future sale of Uruguayan beef to Europe is clouded by British participation in the European Common Market as well as by the emergence of a large and efficient beef cattle industry in, among other nations, Australia, Ireland, Yugoslavia, and France. World prices of wool have declined with the decrease in demand induced by the growth in importance of synthetic fibers. Throughout this difficult economic period Uruguay has endeavored to maintain Latin America's most elaborate social service program largely at the expense of agriculture.

The future of Uruguay's livestock industry depends upon the solution of the nation's overriding problem, the achievement of a logical balance between urban and rural economic development. If the urban sector continues to be favored without a radical change in rural institutions, the rural sector will have no incentive to develop. If the rural sector is favored over the urban, there will be an increase in hardship among the urban population, which today constitutes more than 80 percent of the nation's population.

Bibliography. Russell H. Brannon, *The Agricultural Development of Uruguay,* New York, 1968; Jorge Chebataroff, *Tierra uruguaya: Introducción a la geografía de la República Oriental del Uruguay,* Montevideo, 1960; United States Department of Agriculture, Economic Research Service, *A Survey of Agriculture in Uruguay,* ERS-Foreign 299, April 1970; United States Department of Agriculture, Office of Foreign Agricultural Relations, *The Agriculture of Uruguay,* by Constance H. Farnworth, Foreign Agriculture Bulletin 3, August 1952.

MORTON D. WINSBERG

LIZARDI, JOSÉ JOAQUÍN FERNÁNDEZ DE. *See* FERNÁNDEZ DE LIZARDI, JOSÉ JOAQUÍN.

LLANOS. Sparsely populated grass-covered plains extending across northern South America from the ANDES MOUNTAINS to the Atlantic Ocean. Stretching across eastern Colombia and through Venezuela, they are bounded on the north by coastal mountains and on the south by the Guiana Highlands. These gently rolling plains of tall, coarse grasses and some scrubby trees are marked by low mesas and flat alluvial lands over which meander the many tributaries of the ORINOCO RIVER, which drains this region. The tropical wet and dry climate of the region causes alternate floods and droughts in the low-lying llanos. With the rains of the high sun period (April to November), the broad lowlands along the streams are inundated. The waters slowly recede and evaporate, and by the peak of the dry season the ground is parched and hard, the grasses are brown and brittle, and the scrub trees have shed their leaves.

The traditional and dominant use of the llanos is extensive cattle raising despite the handicaps of floods and droughts, low-quality forage, insects and diseases, and poor transportation. Ranch headquarters and small river towns form the only population clusters. Since the 1950s large dam projects have permitted the development of irrigated agriculture on the northern edge of the Venezuelan llanos. Important petroleum reserves underlie the llanos, and a large field has been tapped in eastern Venezuela (*see* PETROLEUM INDUSTRY: VENEZUELA).

DANIEL W. GADE

LLERAS CAMARGO, ALBERTO (1906–　). President of Colombia (1945–1946, 1958–1962). Lleras Camargo was educated at a prominent elite school,

the Colegio del Rosario in Bogotá, and at the Externado de Derecho. His talent was soon recognized by the owner of *El Tiempo,* Eduardo SANTOS. He was briefly on the newspaper's editorial staff. Lleras was secretary-general of the Liberal party (1930–1933; *see* LIBERAL PARTY: COLOMBIA), a member of the Chamber of Representatives (1931–1933), and subsequently its President. He was appointed Secretary-General of the Presidency (1934–1936) and Minister of Government (1936–1938) by President Alfonso LÓPEZ. Lleras and Darío Echandía were the main architects of López's reformist program. Lleras was partly responsible for Liberal sponsorship of the first Colombian syndical confederation, the Confederación de Trabajadores Colombianos (CTC), which he vainly hoped would be a dependable *lopista* support base. When Santos assumed power in 1938, Lleras founded *El Liberal,* a *lopista* paper that survived in Bogotá until 1951.

Lleras was again a central figure in the second López administration. As Minister of Government he broadcast extensively to reassure Colombians of continuing tranquillity when López was kidnapped in 1944. On López's retirement in 1945 Lleras succeeded him as interim President, providing a breathing space and free elections in which the Conservative Mariano OSPINA PÉREZ gained power (*see* CONSERVATIVE PARTY: COLOMBIA). From 1948 until 1954 Lleras, who had been a delegate to the MONTEVIDEO CONFERENCE in 1933 and served briefly as Minister in Washington in 1943, was Secretary-General of the ORGANIZATION OF AMERICAN STATES.

Lleras returned to Colombia in 1954 and emerged as the Liberal leader of attempts to form a civilian coalition of Liberals and Conservatives against Gen. Gustavo ROJAS PINILLA. He flew twice to Spain for meetings with Laureano GÓMEZ. At the first meeting,

Alberto Lleras Camargo. [*Organization of American States*]

in Benidorm in 1956, party collaboration to oust Rojas was agreed upon; at the second, in Sitges in 1957, Lleras and Gómez agreed to a policy of joint presidential candidacies and parity of the parties in power. After the fall of Rojas, a military junta governed in an interim capacity and held elections. Lleras emerged as the only candidate acceptable to the majority groups of both parties. His reputation was enhanced when he was arrested two days before the election during an abortive coup by dissident military.

Defeating the dissident Conservative candidate, Jorge Leyva, Lleras entered office in 1958. He succeeded in his first objective: he demonstrated that a NATIONAL FRONT was workable, and he accomplished an adroit balancing act between, above, and within the parties. He had limited success in reducing the Violencia (*see* VIOLENCIA, LA), partly by introducing a rehabilitation policy designed to relieve the areas of most acute violence. He was careful to avoid reprisals against *rojistas*. His decision to allow Rojas to return to Colombia to stand trial aroused considerable criticism. Many feared that the National Front would be brought into disrepute if *rojistas* were allowed to air their grievances against its leaders in public and over the radio. Under United States influence Lleras engaged in Colombia's first tentative AGRARIAN REFORM and established Acción Comunal, a movement intended to develop rural areas by equipping villages with the technical means upon which a system of self-help could be based. Inflation and the shadow of the CUBAN REVOLUTION contributed to a series of urban disturbances. Relative peace made it possible in 1959 to lift the state of siege imposed by Ospina in 1949 except in departments of continuing violence.

Unlike López and Gómez, Lleras has never been a demagogue. He has perhaps typified the style of the Colombian politician who shuns appeals to sectarian passions. His periodic resurgences have come at moments when a dispassionate, conciliatory figure who could rise above apparently irreconcilable divisions was needed. His frugality and honesty are proverbial. In recent years he has directed the continental journal *Visión* from the United States. The frequency of his residence in the United States and the pervasiveness of North American influences in his political style and thinking have aroused fears, from orthodox Catholics as well as from leftists, of excessive United States influence on his policy. It is sometimes said that he is better known outside Colombia than inside.

Bibliography. Alberto Lleras Camargo, *Sus mejores páginas,* Bogotá, 1959(?); Ministerio de Trabajo, *El pensamiento social de Alberto Lleras,* Bogotá, 1960; República de Colombia, *Un año de gobierno, 1945–1946: Discursos y otros documentos,* Bogotá, 1946.

C. G. ABEL

LLERAS RESTREPO, CARLOS (1908–   ). President of Colombia (1966–1970). Born in Bogotá, where he had a conventional education, Lleras Restrepo emerged as a Liberal student leader in the late 1920s (*see* LIBERAL PARTY: COLOMBIA) and was soon in departmental politics in Cundinamarca, where as secretary of government he was briefly concerned with conflicts between sharecroppers and landowners in coffee areas. He served as representative, senator, Director of the National Census, director of *El Tiempo* (1941), Minis-

ter of Finance under Eduardo SANTOS and Alfonso LÓPEZ, and president of the Liberal National Directorate. After the assassination of Jorge Eliécer GAITÁN in 1948, Lleras Restrepo emerged as the most vociferous Liberal opponent of the governments of Mariano OSPINA PÉREZ and Laureano GÓMEZ. In 1952 Lleras went into voluntary exile after the burning of his house by a mob. His political participation has been discontinuous. He has been a member of the board of directors of the Federación Nacional de Cafeteros de Colombia, and he has been intimately connected with banking interests.

As a party leader acceptable also to Conservatives, Lleras emerged as the triumphant NATIONAL FRONT presidential candidate in 1966. The choice of Lleras suggested an activism in government and a sensitivity to economic problems not possessed by his predecessor, Guillermo León VALENCIA. A change in budget priorities from public order to social welfare was reflected in an ambitious social policy that featured an enthusiastic experiment in AGRARIAN REFORM, new tax legislation, the use of "autonomous institutions" acting as spearheads for reform, and the formation of a land users' organization. The Lleras government was perhaps more important for its attempts at reform than for its achievement.

During the administration of Misael PASTRANA BORRERO, Lleras spent some time studying agrarian reform programs in Rome with the Food and Agriculture Organization of the United Nations. In 1972 he was named sole head of the Liberal party. A proposal by Lleras that both parties support a single presidential candidate in 1974 was rejected, and on June 30, 1973, he lost a bid for the Liberal presidential nomination to Alfonso López Michelsen, the son of Alfonso López.

C. G. ABEL

LOBATO, JOSÉ BENTO MONTEIRO (1882–1948). Brazilian man of letters and book publisher. Born in the state of São Paulo, he studied law at the São Paulo law school, became a district attorney in a small town and then a farmer, but later returned to the capital, where he made his name known as a crusading journalist. His first collection of short stories, *Urupês* (1918), shocked the country by its realistic presentation of the depressed living conditions of rural Brazil. *Cidades Mortas* (1919), *Negrinha* (1920), and other books about provincial Brazil met with equal success. Although these books express indignation at the stagnation of the country and its waste of human lives, Lobato was also capable of writing in an original, rich comic vein. His style is direct, at times brilliant, and free from the artificiality affected by many of his contemporaries. A publishing company that he founded, A Editôra Revista do Brazil, published *A Vida e Morte de Gonzaga de Sá* by Afonso Lima BARRETO, a writer whom he much admired. He wrote a book about future racial conflict in the United States, *O Choque das Raças ou o Presidente Negro* (1926), but came to admire the country during his stay there as commercial attaché from 1927 to 1931. Though not a participant in Modern Art Week (1922), because of his ideas and style he should be considered a precursor of Brazilian modernism (*see* MODERNISM: BRAZIL).

RAYMOND S. SAYERS

LOMBARDO TOLEDANO, VICENTE (1894–1968). Mexican labor leader and intellectual. Lombardo Toledano was born in Teziutlán, Puebla, of a middle-class family of Italian origin. He began to earn his living in Mexico City by giving lessons and working on the newspaper *El Universal*. His initial orientation, because of the influence of his teacher Antonio CASO, was intuitionist and Christian. In those days he thought that the profit sharing established by Article 123 of the constitution (*see* CONSTITUTION OF 1917: MEXICO) was based on the false theory of Marxism, and he considered the introduction of foreign capital to Mexico a necessity. He received his law degree in 1919; in 1923 he was named secretary of education of the CONFEDER-ACIÓN REGIONAL OBRERA MEXICANA (Regional Confederation of Mexican Labor; CROM) and interim Governor of Puebla. He was a member of the Municipal Council of Mexico City in 1924 and sat in Congress the following year. He left the CROM on September 19, 1932, declaring himself a radical Marxist, though not a Communist; he would later clash with the Communist party on several occasions. With some dissident CROM unions he organized in 1933 the Confederación General de Obreros y Campesinos Mexicanos (General Confederation of Mexican Workers and Peasants), which was converted into the CONFEDERACIÓN DE TRABAJADORES DE MÉXICO (Confederation of Mexican Workers; CTM) in February 1936. Lombardo Toledano was secretary-general of the CTM for five years, during which he launched the Universidad Obrera (Workers University) as an auxiliary of the CTM and founded the Confederación de Trabajadores de América Latina (Latin American Labor Confederation). Having been expelled from the CTM early in 1948, he founded the Partido Popular (Popular party) shortly afterward, adding the word Socialist to its name in 1960. He was the Popular party's presidential candidate in 1952 but was later abandoned by a considerable number of his followers.

MOISÉS GONZÁLEZ NAVARRO

LONARDI, EDUARDO (1896–1956). President of Argentina (September–November 1955). A career army officer until complicity in an anti-Peronist plot (*see* PERONISM) forced his retirement in 1951, General Lonardi initiated fighting in the interior city of Córdoba on September 16, 1955, and was propelled into the Presidency when Juan D. PERÓN went into exile.

As President, Lonardi sought to establish a kind of national reconciliation through an approach he summarized as "neither victors nor vanquished." Thus, while attempting to discredit the *peronistas,* he sought in general to coopt rather than exterminate Peronism. Clear evidence of this tendency was his approach to Peronist-dominated labor (*see* CONFEDERACIÓN GENERAL DE TRABAJO). Another effort to establish a broad consensus for his government was the establishment of the National Consultative Council, an advisory board composed of representatives of all political parties except Peronists and Communists. The lines of Lonardi's economic policy remain unclear, for he fell from power soon after contracting an analysis of the economic situation by Raúl PREBISCH. Failure to yield to the pressures of more militant anti-Peronists within the government led to his removal from office by the military.

NOREEN F. STACK

LÓPEZ [PUMAREJO], ALFONSO (1886–1959). President of Colombia (1934–1938, 1942–1945). López was born in Honda, Tolima, and educated in Bogotá and the United States. His father, Pedro A. López, was a prominent magnate in the coffee and import-export businesses. From his teens Alfonso López worked in the family firm and briefly managed its New York and Bogotá branches. Although he had sat in the Tolima Assembly in 1915, he was better known as a businessman than as a politician until 1929. He came to prominence and established a permanent stake in a political career when at the 1929 Liberal Convention (*see* LIBERAL PARTY: COLOMBIA) he asserted unequivocally that liberalism, which had been out of power for two generations, should prepare to reassume it. In an uneasy alliance with *El Tiempo,* López restored the morale of liberalism, although he was slow to accept the candidacy of Enrique OLAYA HERRERA for the 1930 election. Olaya appointed López Minister to London in 1931. López returned to Colombia as the Liberal presidential candidate for 1934. The Conservatives (*see* CONSERVATIVE PARTY: COLOMBIA), led by Laureano GÓMEZ, abstained, and López assumed power on a program entitled "Revolution on the March."

Despite his business background, López was identified with the more radical branch of the Liberal party. His first government borrowed much of its vocabulary from Mexico. Its action was, by the criteria of Colombia in the mid-1930s, startlingly dramatic. López selected several little-known ministers, including Darío Echandía, Alberto LLERAS CAMARGO, and Jorge Soto del Corral, to implement a program of income tax reform, universal male suffrage, some military and educational innovations, a constitutional reform that modified church-state relations, and a small AGRARIAN REFORM. Further reformism was hampered by the size of the national budget. Despite the limited nature of the reforms, they were denounced by vocal Conservative opponents as prefiguring an anticlerical and anti-Conservative persecution comparable to that of the mid-nineteenth century. The less reformist Liberals who surrounded Olaya feared the effects of civil disorder on business and industry. The flirtations of López with the nascent Communist party and with militant trade unionism compounded these fears, and under congressional pressure López soft-pedaled his program from 1937 on. The pace was already slackening when Eduardo SANTOS succeeded López in 1938.

López returned to power in violent elections in 1942. His second administration lacked the dynamism of the first. A series of strikes and scandals demoralized the government and were exploited systematically by Gómez. Concern for his wife's health led López to leave Colombia in 1943 for several months, and Echandía acted as President. Tranquillity was not restored. Conditions deteriorated to such an extent that López was kidnapped while attending army maneuvers near Pasto in a small localized military coup (1944). Echandía assumed power in Bogotá. The uprising met with little military support in the rest of Colombia and flickered out. Released by loyal troops, López returned to Bogotá. This series of crises prompted a tired López to retire before the expiration of his term in 1945, leaving Lleras Camargo as interim President. After 1945 López took part in national politics only sporadically. Between 1946 and 1948 he represented

Colombia at the United Nations General Assembly.

López's experience of the 1940s led him to canvass the possibility of a NATIONAL FRONT in the 1950s. The National Front owes more to the inspiration of López than to that of any other single Colombian politician. López was, with the possible exception of Gen. Rafael REYES, the most original political figure in Colombia in the first half of the twentieth century, but as he himself came to recognize, he bore some of the responsibility for destabilizing Colombian politics in the 1940s. His mantle was assumed by his son, Alfonso López Michelsen, founder of the Movimiento Revolucionario Liberal, who was the successful Liberal presidential candidate in 1974.

Bibliography. Hugo Latorre Cabal, *Mi novela: Apuntes autobiográficos de Alfonso López,* Bogotá, 1961; Alfonso López Michelsen, *Los últimos días de Alfonso López y cartas íntimas de tres campañas políticas (1929–1940–1958),* Bogotá, 1961; *Mensajes del Presidente López al Congreso Nacional,* 4 vols., Bogotá, 1934–1938; Jaime Quintero, *Consacá,* Cali, 1944; Eduardo Zuleta Angel, *El presidente López,* Bogotá, 1966.

C. G. ABEL

LÓPEZ, CARLOS ANTONIO (1792–1862). First President of Paraguay (1844–1862). Carlos Antonio López was born in Asunción of a modest family of good lineage. He was educated at the convent school of Recoleta and the Seminary of San Carlos, where he completed studies in philosophy and theology in 1810 and took minor orders. In 1814 he won a competition for the chair of arts at the seminary, and in 1817 that of theology. By 1820, however, López had turned toward a career in law and gained renown as a skillful attorney. In late 1820 the dictatorship of José Gaspar Rodríguez de FRANCIA became more repressive when a plot against the despot's life was discovered and he took savage reprisals. As the upper class was being decimated by Dr. Francia, López retired to his family home in Recoleta, where he maintained a cautious silence. In 1826 he married the wealthy Juana Pabla Carillo, who brought him as dowry an *estancia* (ranch) in Rosario. The couple retired there, and López dedicated himself to running the *estancia,* at which he exhibited his customary talent. He fathered five children, including the eldest, the favored Francisco Solano LÓPEZ, who succeeded him in 1862.

In September 1840, Francia died, and López returned to the capital to witness the scramble for power. In February 1841, Col. Mariano Roque Alonso emerged as the dominant force. An uneducated soldier, he hired López as his secretary. In March a 500-member congress was called. It created a two-man consulate composed of Alonso and López, who were to rule jointly for three years. In 1844 another congress elected López President of Paraguay, and he set himself the task of changing the nation. El Ciudadano (the Citizen), as he became known, using the prosperity bequeathed by Francia, opened the country to foreign trade and won recognition of Paraguayan sovereignty by most nations. In 1845 he began publishing the first Paraguayan periodical, *El Paraguayo Independiente,* which under his direction became the mouthpiece for his policies

and for an intense nationalism. López jealously guarded the contested frontiers, expanded and modernized the Army, and brought foreign technicians, engineers, and military experts to Paraguay. With these men and native talent, he built one of South America's first railroads and telegraph networks, huge fortifications such as HUMAITÁ (in 1864 it mounted 380 cannon), a shipyard for the construction of steam-powered merchant and war vessels, a gun factory at Itá, and an arsenal and iron foundry at Ybycuí. New roads, canals, and impressive public buildings were constructed. Agriculture also flourished, and crop diversification, stimulated by growing foreign trade, led to a large output of yerba maté, tobacco (which won a gold medal for excellence in Paris in 1855), sugarcane, manioc, cotton, corn, and rice. By 1862 Paraguay was, by South American standards, a modern, powerful nation with a population of about 500,000 and a school system famous in Latin America. López ruled as an autocrat, though he created and used a genuine bureaucracy, something unknown under Dr. Francia.

Despite diplomatic problems with the United States and Brazil, López had an admirable record of international as well as domestic peace. In 1853 he sent his son to Europe to seek naval vessels, technicians, and arms. Francisco Solano visited industrial establishments in England and on the Continent and was absent almost two years. López also used his son as a mediator in the civil wars of the Argentine Confederation in 1859 and as commander in chief of the Army in the last years of his rule. He was a wise and benevolent despot, but he bequeathed the prosperous nation to Francisco Solano, whose actions would cause the disastrous PARAGUAYAN WAR (1864–1870).

See also HOPKINS, Edward A[ugustus]; WATER WITCH INCIDENT.

Bibliography. Julio César Chaves, *El presidente López,* 2d ed., Buenos Aires, 1968; Juan F. Pérez-Acosta, *Carlos Antonio López: Obrero-máximo,* Asunción, 1948.

JOHN HOYT WILLIAMS

LÓPEZ, FRANCISCO SOLANO (1826–1870). Dictator of Paraguay (1862–1870). The first son of Carlos Antonio LÓPEZ, he was born in Asunción and raised at the family *estancia* (ranch) in Rosario, north of the capital. He obtained his early education from his father, who in 1840 entered politics and in 1844 was elected President of the republic. From then until 1862 Francisco Solano remained in the shadow of his father, the President-dictator.

In 1845 the President declared war on the dictator Juan Manuel de ROSAS of Argentina, promoted his nineteen-year-old son to the rank of brigadier general, and sent him with an army into neighboring Corrientes Province. After a short, tranquil campaign the Paraguayan forces returned home. Francisco Solano henceforth became the regime's troubleshooter. As part of his program to modernize Paraguay, the President sent his son on a mission to Europe in 1853. Francisco Solano visited England, France, and Spain, negotiating contracts with immigrants and technicians and buying arms and a naval vessel on which his party returned to Paraguay early in 1856. He also brought with him his most interesting acquisition, his Irish-born mistress Elisa Alicia LYNCH, whom he had met in Paris.

In 1859 Carlos Antonio sent his son to Buenos Aires to mediate a settlement between the warring Argentine Confederation and the province of Buenos Aires, a task he handled with some skill. In 1862 the President died, leaving Francisco Solano as Vice President, commander of the Army, and member of a triumvirate that was to rule until a congress could choose a successor to the Presidency. With this power base, Francisco Solano had no difficulty in inducing the Congress to hail him as President. During his first years in power, the country was moderately prosperous, and he continued his father's program of modernization. At the same time, however, he greatly increased the size and weaponry of the Army and conceived a false vision of himself as arbiter of affairs in the RÍO DE LA PLATA region. In the early 1860s Brazil, with which Paraguay had had serious border problems and clashes since the colonial era, was interfering blatantly in the domestic affairs of Uruguay, and Francisco Solano believed that it was time these machinations were halted lest Paraguay, like Uruguay a buffer state between Brazil and Argentina, later receive the same treatment. When Brazilian troops invaded Uruguay in 1864 and the emperor PEDRO II ignored a Paraguayan ultimatum, Francisco Solano seized a Brazilian vessel and invaded Mato Grosso while preparing another, larger invasion of Rio Grande do Sul. In an almost heroic miscalculation, he ignored Argentine protests and marched this second force across the Argentine province of Misiones; the result was war with that nation as well.

Beginning in 1864, the PARAGUAYAN WAR, involving

Francisco Solano López. [*Radio Times Hulton Picture Library*]

Uruguay, Brazil, and Argentina in alliance against Paraguay, devastated the Guaraní republic. To López's credit as a leader, the people remained faithful to him with a rare fanaticism, seeing the war through his eyes as a struggle for national existence. Despite his paranoic killing within his own Army and territory, Paraguay stayed with him until March 1, 1870, when a last battle was fought at Cerro Corá, in the rugged north of Paraguay. There López, the only head of state in hemispheric history to die in battle, received a fatal Brazilian lance thrust. Regardless of the national suicide committed in his name, Francisco Solano is a national hero in modern Paraguay and the virtual patron saint of the now-ruling Colorado party. *See* COLORADO PARTY (PARAGUAY).

Bibliography. Cecilio Báez, *El mariscal Francisco Solano López,* Asunción, 1926; R. B. Cunninghame Graham, *Portrait of a Dictator: Francisco Solano López,* London, 1933; Juan O'Leary, *El mariscal Solano López,* 2d ed., Madrid, 1925.

JOHN HOYT WILLIAMS

LÓPEZ, NARCISO (1798–1851). Venezuelan soldier, filibuster, and precursor of Cuban independence. Born in Venezuela, López early developed a taste for adventure and military life. He distinguished himself in the fighting against Simón BOLÍVAR and then went to Spain, where he performed admirably against the Carlists. He was named Governor of Valencia in 1839 and became a general the following year.

In 1841 he returned to America with the new Captain General of Cuba, Gerónimo Valdés. In Cuba he married into a wealthy family and received from Valdés several honors and offices. In 1843, however, Valdés lost his position, and López consequently lost his offices. Soon thereafter López began planning a revolution to free Cuba from Spain. It proved abortive, and in 1848 he was forced to flee to the United States.

There he found powerful supporters, among them Governor John A. Quitman of Mississippi, and was able to organize three successive filibustering expeditions against his adopted homeland. The first (July 1849) was prevented from sailing by United States authorities; the second (May 1850) saw Cárdenas captured, but López withdrew after the citizenry proved unenthusiastic about their "liberation"; and the third (August 1850) failed largely because two internal uprisings scheduled to coincide with the landing of López's forces were discovered and crushed. López himself was captured, convicted of treason, and publicly garroted.

López is viewed today by some as a precursor and martyr of Cuban independence, but most see him as an agent of United States annexationism. It is interesting that the flag López designed for Cuba has flown over the island since its first day of independence in 1902.

KENNETH F. KIPLE

LÓPEZ ARELLANO, OSWALDO (1921–   ). Honduran air force officer and President (1964–1971, 1972–   ). López Arellano, the dominant military officer in Honduras since the late 1950s, joined the Army in 1939. Three years later, after attending flight school in Tucson, Arizona, he transferred to the Air Force. By 1956 he had become Minister of Defense.

In November 1957, fellow officers selected López

to fill a vacant seat on the junta that had earlier deposed the dictator Julio Lozano. He served for a month until the military allowed Ramón VILLEDA MORALES to assume the Presidency. On October 3, 1963, Colonel López, now chief of the armed forces, declared that a Communist take-over of Honduras was imminent, overthrew the Villeda administration, and canceled elections scheduled for the following month. After serving as head of a de facto military government for eight months while a new constitution was being written, López was elected President.

Burdened by a stagnant economy, the López regime was beset by widespread labor difficulties, agitation for agrarian reform, and rising tension with El Salvador. The government's attempt to relieve pressure for a radical redistribution of land by repatriating all Salvadoran immigrants who lacked proper papers provoked El Salvador into launching the undeclared FOOTBALL WAR in 1969. Under pressure from the United States and the ORGANIZATION OF AMERICAN STATES, this border conflict ended in an uneasy truce, but it led López to withdraw his country from the CENTRAL AMERICAN COMMON MARKET.

Under considerable pressure not to continue in office when his term expired in 1971, López returned the government to civilian control under a coalition of Liberals and Nationalists. On December 4, 1972, however, President Ramón Ernesto CRUZ was ousted by the armed forces in a bloodless coup, and López Arellano was installed as President to complete Cruz's term. *See* LIBERAL PARTY (HONDURAS); NATIONAL OR NATIONALIST PARTY (HONDURAS).

KENNETH V. FINNEY

LÓPEZ BUCHARDO, CARLOS (1881–1948). Argentine composer. After studying in his native Buenos Aires, he went to Paris to work with Albert Roussel. Upon his return he became a leading figure of Argentine music and an active promoter of the music of his day. He was appointed director of the National Conservatory of Music, which now bears his name in memory of his services to the institution. López Buchardo's style is markedly Argentine in character within the harmonic and orchestral framework of impressionism. The list of his works comprises operas, operettas, songs, works for orchestra and for solo piano, and music for schools. Especially well known are his *Escenas argentinas* for orchestra (1920).   JUAN A. ORREGO-SALAS

LÓPEZ CONTRERAS, ELEAZAR (1883–1973). Venezuelan army officer and President (1936–1941). A professional soldier whose military experience spanned the *caudillo*-led armies of Cipriano CASTRO and the technocratic military of Juan Vicente GÓMEZ, López Contreras gained a distinguished record as Director of War in locating and purchasing military supplies in Europe from 1914 to 1920. In recompense for his loyalty and recognition of his abilities, López Contreras served as Minister of War and Marine from 1931 until Gómez's death in 1935. As Minister of War he became the logical choice to succeed Gómez, and his authority, assumed at the time of Gómez's death, was confirmed by Congress, which elected him President in 1936.

Although López Contreras wanted to preside over a revival of political discourse, he could not tolerate the powerful popular opposition organized by the new

mass-appeal parties such as ACCIÓN DEMOCRÁTICA. Soon after his election as President, he began to curtail political activities that he regarded as unpatriotic and suppressed a twenty-seven-day strike in the oil fields. He then found it useful to exile some members of the opposition. Nevertheless, the López Contreras years saw greater political freedom and political activity than any of the years under Gómez. His administration enacted a comprehensive three-year program to help improve the social, material, and educational conditions of the country. He also allowed a stronger, more nationalistic oil law to be passed in 1938, although he failed to enforce it.

Like many of his presidential predecessors, López Contreras was a strong supporter of the cult of Simón BOLÍVAR. At the end of his term he refused reelection and imposed his own Minister of War, Isaías MEDINA ANGARITA, as his successor. He ran once again for President in 1945 but was exiled after the coup d'état of that year.

JOHN V. LOMBARDI

LÓPEZ MATEOS, ADOLFO (1910–1969). President of Mexico (1958–1964). Born in Atizapán de Zaragoza in the state of México, López Mateos was a scholarship student at the Colegio Francés and also studied at the Preparatory School in Toluca. He was a supporter of the presidential candidacy of José VASCONCELOS in 1929, but in 1934, having recently graduated from law school, he worked as private secretary to the president of the Partido Nacional Revolucionario. A protégé of Isidro Fabela, he was rector of the Toluca Institute in 1941 and represented the state of México in the Senate from 1946 to 1952. He managed the presidential campaign of Adolfo RUIZ CORTINES in 1952 and upon the latter's election was named Minister of Labor, becoming noted for his adroit and conciliatory policies in that post.

López Mateos's nomination as the presidential candidate of the PARTIDO REVOLUCIONARIO INSTITUCIONAL in 1958 broke the recent tradition of elevating Secretaries of the Interior (Gobernación) to the Presidency. The tenor of his administration was suggested by the fact that during his campaign he was surrounded by members of the bourgeoisie. As President he severely opposed the striking railroad workers in 1959; in 1962 their leader, Demetrio Vallejo, was convicted of "social dissolution" for his role in calling the strike, and the artist David Alfaro SIQUEIROS was sentenced to eight years in prison for organizing a student riot in 1960 (Siqueiros was freed in 1964).

At the instigation of the President, in 1962 Congress enacted a law providing for profit sharing by workers in accordance with Article 123 of the constitution (*see* CONSTITUTION OF 1917: MEXICO). López Mateos also nationalized the electric power industry, revitalized the distribution of ejidos (*see* EJIDO), and ended the program of internal colonization initiated by his predecessor. Another achievement of the administration was the enactment of a measure to increase minority representation in the Chamber of Deputies by giving minor parties seats in that body in addition to those won at the polls.

In an effort to diversify Mexican trade López Mateos traveled to South America, Asia, and Europe. In 1963 he reached agreement with the United States for the return to Mexico of the border area known as El Chamizal.   MOISÉS GONZÁLEZ NAVARRO

LÓPEZ VELARDE, RAMÓN (1888–1921). Mexican writer. Born in Jerez (now García), Zacatecas, he studied law in San Luis Potosí and practiced it in Aguascalientes and Mexico City. His poetry, which marks the break with modernism in Mexico (*see* MODERNISM: SPANISH AMERICA), is characterized by a vague preoccupation with the themes of time and death, a warm sensuality, and a deep attachment to his surroundings. He wrote with concern for richness of language and symbolist imagery. Two volumes of verse appeared in his lifetime, *La sangre devota* (1916) and *Zozobra* (1919), and other volumes posthumously: *El minutero* (1923), poetic prose; *El son del corazón* (1932); *El don de febrero* (1952), essays; *Poesías, cartas y documentos* (1952); and *Prosas políticas* (1953).

RACHEL PHILLIPS

LÓPEZ Y FUENTES, GREGORIO (1897–1966). Mexican novelist. Born in the state of Veracruz, he was a journalist by profession. His first publications were modernist poems in *La siringa de cristal* (1914) and *Claros de selva* (1922; *see* MODERNISM: SPANISH AMERICA). His first successful novel was *Campamento* (1931), which deals, as do almost all his novels, with the MEXICAN REVOLUTION. It was followed by *¡Mi general!* (1934), *El indio* (1935), *Huasteca* (1939), *Los peregrinos inmóviles* (1944), *Entresuelo* (1948), and *Acomodaticio: Un político de convicciones* (1943).

RACHEL PHILLIPS

LOTT, HENRIQUE [BATISTA DUFFLES TEIXEIRA] (1894–   ). Brazilian soldier and politician. Born in Sítio on the Minas Gerais border, Lott attended military school in Rio de Janeiro, enlisted in the Army in 1911, and was commissioned in 1916. A thorough professional, he devoted himself exclusively to military duties and consistently supported the established government through the revolts of the 1920s, the REVOLUTION OF 1930, and the São Paulo rebellion of 1932. Lott excelled as student and instructor at the General Staff College, and he also attended the French École Supérieure de Guerre and the United States Army Command and General Staff College. He became a general at fifty.

Lott's involvement in politics began with his appointment as War Minister in August 1954, following the suicide of Getúlio VARGAS. Although he had been selected by President João CAFÉ FILHO for his reputation as an apolitical officer, Lott became a controversial political figure in November 1955, when he led the coup d'état that deposed the acting President and guaranteed the inauguration of Juscelino KUBITSCHEK and João GOULART as President and Vice President of Brazil. Kubitschek retained him as War Minister. In 1959 Lott retired from active duty with the rank of marshal but continued as War Minister until February 1960, when he resigned to campaign unsuccessfully for the Presidency of Brazil. Lott opposed the military intervention against Vice President Goulart in 1961 and the revolution that overthrew the Goulart administration in 1964. His proposed candidacy for the governorship of Guanabara in 1965 was blocked by the revolutionary government.

ROLLIE E. POPPINO

LOUVERTURE (L'OUVERTURE), [DOMINIQUE] TOUSSAINT (1743–1803). Haitian revolutionary leader. Louverture was born near Le Cap (modern Cap-Haïtien). Originally known as Toussaint Bréda for his master's Bréda plantation, he later adopted the name Louverture, meaning "opening," perhaps because admiring Frenchmen praised his opening the enemy lines. The eldest of eight children, he was a small, sickly boy who developed his body through strenuous exercise. From his godfather he learned French, Latin, and geometry, and from his father herbal lore, which was useful in doctoring livestock. Although Louverture's language was CRÉOLE, he knew French well enough to read Abbé Guillaume Raynal's classic work on colonialism, which may have convinced him that he was the black Spartacus the abbé prophesied would free his race. As coachman, veterinarian, and steward, he was highly respected by his peers.

As a royalist during the Haitian revolution, he joined forces with the black leader Jean-François and received a high military post. When the French Republic fought Spain in 1793, Louverture joined the Spanish Army with his 600 well-trained Negroes. Never a bigot, he accepted any able man who served his military, political, and economic objectives, and he condemned unnecessary violence and vengeance.

By 1794 Louverture's was the best-disciplined Negro force in Spanish service and had won brilliant victories. Now he decided to rejoin France at its lowest fortunes in Saint-Domingue. This required courage, foresight, and subtlety. He feared the British, who had invaded the island to aid the whites, and knew that under Spain he would never rise to the station of Jean-François. Perhaps France's emancipation of the slaves also entered his calculations. He negotiated with Gen.

Toussaint Louverture. [*Organization of American States*]

Étienne Leveaux while technically loyal to Spain, then killed those who refused to join him in returning to the service of France. His sudden abandonment disorganized Spanish efforts, and he was able to force their evacuation of the north. Now he turned against the British invaders, dedicating two years to their defeat.

The smoldering rivalry between mulattoes and Negroes ignited when the former, led by André Rigaud, refused to recognize Louverture's authority after Leveaux gratefully made him lieutenant governor of Saint-Domingue and thus the most important black on the island. In 1800 Louverture defeated Rigaud, who left for France. In addition, he cleverly forced his French competitors for power to return to Europe.

In 1801 Louverture invaded the eastern two-thirds of the island (Santo Domingo), which had been ceded to France by Spain in the Treaty of Basel (1795). He feared that Napoleon would take advantage of the weak Spanish force there in order to use that territory as a base to invade Louverture's strongholds to the west. Having pacified and unified the island, Louverture turned to restoring the once-vaunted agricultural affluence of Saint-Domingue. He requested the return of French émigré planters, for he needed their skills and prestige. Blacks were regimented as plantation laborers and punished for inefficient work. Results were good, and prosperity began to return.

In 1800 Louverture's handpicked convention wrote a constitution for the island, giving lip service to French sovereignty while naming him Governor for life. Resenting this action and Louverture's general defiance, Napoleon sent his brother-in-law Gen. Charles-Victor-Emmanuel Leclerc to subdue Saint-Domingue. When Louverture resisted his landing, Leclerc declared him outlawed. Louverture eventually surrendered but soon was tricked into a meeting at which he was arrested and sent to Fort de Joux in the French Alps, where he sickened and died on April 7, 1803.

Louverture's dream of liberty, prosperity, and respect for his people inspired foreign intellectuals to applaud him as a symbol of black heroism in plays, poems, oratory, and biography while rebellious slaves elsewhere knew his name. His charisma, courage, intellect, and statecraft reveal a complicated giant.

Bibliography. C. L. R. James, *The Black Jacobins: Toussaint L'Ouverture and the San Domingo Revolution,* New York, 1938; Charles Moran, *Black Triumvirate: A Study of L'Ouverture, Dessalines, Christophe,* New York, 1957; Horace Pauléus Sannon, *Histoire de Toussaint Louverture,* 3 vols., Port-au-Prince, 1920–33; Katharine Scherman, *The Slave Who Freed Haiti,* New York, 1954; T. Lothrop Stoddard, *The French Revolution in San Domingo,* Boston, 1914.

                                                    JOHN E. BAUR

LUGONES, LEOPOLDO (1874–1938). Argentine poet, essayist, and writer of short stories. Lugones was born in Río Seco (now Villa de María) in the province of Córdoba. In 1896 he moved to Buenos Aires, where he worked as a journalist. During this time he met Rubén DARÍO, the leader of the modernist literary movement, when the two were employed as postal clerks (*see* MODERNISM: SPANISH AMERICA).

At one time Lugones was an active member of the Socialist party (*see* SOCIALIST PARTY: ARGENTINA), but he left its ranks and after 1910 was a staunch nationalist. Eventually he supported authoritarian governments and was actively engaged in political life prior to his death. Lugones held posts as visitor of secondary education (1900) and Inspector General of Education (1904). On four occasions he traveled to Europe; in Paris, from 1911 to 1914, he edited the *Revue Sud-américaine.* He was also the founder of the Argentine Society of Writers (1928). From 1915 until his death he served as director of the Biblioteca de Maestros in Buenos Aires. He died by his own hand near Buenos Aires on February 19, 1938.

Lugones's position among the modernist poets of Spanish America is second only to that of Darío. After meeting Darío in 1896, Lugones published a volume of poetry, *Las montañas de oro* (1897). This was followed by one of his most important works, *Los crepúsculos del jardín* (1905), which shows the influence of the French symbolists, as does his next work, *Lunario sentimental* (1909). *Los crepúsculos* contains his famous poem "El solterón" ("The Bachelor"), considered one of the masterpieces of Spanish American poetry. Lugones's *Odas seculares* (1910) marks his movement into nationalist themes, which he continued to develop in several later volumes.

In prose Lugones published *La reforma educacional* (1903), *El imperio jesuítico* (1904), and three collections of short stories: *La guerra gaucha* (1905), *Las fuerzas extrañas* (1906), and *Cuentos fatales* (1924). He also wrote more than twenty other volumes of essays, poetry, and miscellaneous writings.

                                                    DANIEL R. REEDY

LYNCH, ELISA ALICIA (1835–1886). Irish-born mistress of the dictator Francisco Solano LÓPEZ of Paraguay. Elisa Lynch married a French army doctor at the age of fifteen. Three years later her husband deserted her, and she lived with several lovers in Paris. There, in 1853, she met López, the son of the dictator Carlos Antonio LÓPEZ, who was in Europe on official business. The younger López fell in love with the beautiful red-haired woman, and she became his adoring mistress. She soon returned with him to Paraguay and, despite gossip, lived openly in Asunción as the mistress of the President's son.

Between her arrival and the outbreak of the PARAGUAYAN WAR in 1864, Elisa bore López five children and, upon his accession to the Presidency in 1862, became de facto first lady. During the war she was often with her lover, first at the fortress HUMAITÁ and then on the disastrous and sanguinary retreat into the northern jungle. There, in 1870, she witnessed López's death in battle and buried him and their first-born son herself on the banks of the Aquidabán River. She is said to have amassed huge landholdings and a great treasure in gold, silver, and jewels. At the end of the war she was deported, losing most of her wealth. She lived out the rest of her life in Paris and Jerusalem, where, in 1886, she died penniless and largely forgotten.

                                                    JOHN HOYT WILLIAMS

Macció, Rómulo

Music (Spanish America)

MACCIÓ, RÓMULO (1931–). Argentine painter and a leader of New Figurative art. Macció was apprenticed at fourteen to a publicity agency and worked as a graphic designer and set designer. He is self-taught as a painter. He began exhibiting in 1956 and has presented many exhibitions internationally. In 1961 he won the International Prize of the Instituto Torcuato di Tella in Buenos Aires and in 1967 the Grand Prize of the National Salon of Argentina.

In the early 1960s Macció was a member of the Nueva Figuración group with Ernesto Deira, Jorge de la Vega, and Luis Felipe Noé, and he has remained faithful to the principles of that movement: to seek a union of the human image with the psychological effects of abstract expressionism. His series *To Live* (1963), in circular, octagonal, or square canvases, reveals the anxiety of his images in their titles, for example, *To Live, at All Costs.* His work has been compared to the stories of Jorge Luis BORGES. This connection was made explicit in Macció's titling a 1966 New York exhibition with the Borges title *Fictions.*

TERENCE GRIEDER

MACEDO, JOAQUIM MANUEL DE (1820–1882). Brazilian novelist, dramatist, poet, biographer, historian, and politician. Born in the province of Rio de Janeiro, he took a degree in medicine but did not practice. He taught geography and Brazilian history at the College of Pedro II and several times was elected to the provincial and national legislatures. The author of the first popular Brazilian novel, *A Moreninha* (1844),

he wrote a naïve kind of fiction that photographed amusingly Brazilian types and scenes, but he was superficial, and as Brazilian readers became more sophisticated, he lost his public. Among his fiction there is one collection of three antislavery novellas, *As Vítimas Algozes* (1869), which deals with a more serious theme and has more power than the others. He wrote several plays, at least one of which, *A Torre em Concurso* (1863), is still amusing, and two books of nonfiction about Rio, *Passeio pela Cidade do Rio de Janeiro* (1862) and *Memórias da Rua do Ouvidor* (1878), which are still lively reading. *A Carteira do Meu Tio* (1855), *Memórias de um Sobrinho do Meu Tio* (1867–1868), and *A Luneta Mágica* (1869), which are political satire thinly disguised as fiction, are interesting statements about social and political life during the empire.

RAYMOND S. SAYERS

MACEO, ANTONIO (1848–1896). Cuban nationalist hero. Maceo was born a mulatto in Santiago de Cuba, of a family fated to lose its father and eleven sons in the struggle for Cuba's independence. During the TEN YEARS' WAR (1868–1878) Maceo rose quickly in the rebel ranks by virtue of his reputation as a brilliant strategist, coupled with a fearlessness and audacity that marked him as a natural leader of men. Known as the "Titan of Bronze," Maceo was feared not only by the Spaniards but also by other rebel leaders, who suspected him of wishing to turn Cuba into a black republic.

Maceo refused to accept the Pact of Zanjón (February 1878), asserting his conviction that independence and peace were inseparable. Although forced from the island soon after the armistice, he continued to plan new revolutions. While residing in Costa Rica he accepted José MARTÍ's offer to assume leadership of the revolutionary forces, and 1895 found him again fighting on the island (*see* WAR FOR CUBAN INDEPENDENCE). He waged a brilliant guerrilla war so fiercely that the Spanish command feared him above all other rebel leaders.

The arrival of the Spanish general Valeriano Weyler in Cuba began a duel between Maceo and Weyler. It was largely due to Maceo's success that Weyler implemented his "reconcentration" policy, hoping to force Maceo to capitulate or cross into Spanish-controlled territory. He succeeded. Maceo and his men were surprised in an attempt to link up with the forces of Máximo GÓMEZ, and the man often called the greatest military leader in Cuba's history was killed.

KENNETH F. KIPLE

MACHADO, GERARDO (1871–1938). President and dictator of Cuba (1925–1933). Born in Las Villas Province, Machado served as mayor of Santa Clara and in the Cabinet of President José Miguel GÓMEZ. Meanwhile, he was also active as a businessman and was closely connected with the Havana subsidiary of the Electric Bond and Share Company. Although Machado was considered an unsavory character by many, in 1924, against heavy odds, he sought the presidential nomination of the Liberal party, posing as the heir to Gómez. He won not only the nomination but also the Presidency, having promised to clean up Cuban politics. Nevertheless, corruption continued unabated, and before long Machado was maneuvering to consolidate his power. He persecuted and bribed his enemies with promises of lucrative jobs and the enjoyment of graft. The officer corps of the Army, which had opposed his election, became his main base of support through increased privileges and material rewards.

Machado's rule was not challenged until he succeeded in having his term of office extended by means of a constitutional amendment. It was then that the middle class, students, professional men, and labor leaders turned against him. The ABC, a secret society made up mainly of young professional men and organized to seek his downfall through acts of violence, created a virtual reign of terror from 1931 to 1933. Meanwhile, the United States government, influenced by American business interests, continued to support Machado until it became obvious that his position was becoming increasingly untenable. In August 1933 Machado resigned under pressure from the United States and fled from the country.

See also WELLES, Sumner.

J. CORDELL ROBINSON

MACHADO, JOSÉ GOMES PINHEIRO. *See* PINHEIRO MACHADO, JOSÉ GOMES.

MACHADO DE ASSIS, JOAQUIM MARIA (1839–1908). Brazilian writer of fiction, drama, poetry, criticism, and essays. He was born and died in Rio de Janeiro, the son of a Portuguese mother and a mulatto father; he was an epileptic and had a speech defect. Largely self-taught, by the time he was fifty he was ac-

knowledged to be Brazil's greatest writer; he was also in the civil service and before his death had attained the highest position open to him in it. His wife, Carolina, was a Portuguese woman of excellent family, and his friends were the leading intellectuals of the country. He was the founder and perpetual president of the Brazilian Academy of Letters. In 1856, with the publication of a poem in a periodical, he began his lifelong contributions to the journals of Rio, which included short stories, novels, criticism, and regular columns.

Machado was known at first as a poet and critic, and his first published volume was a collection of poems, *Crisálidas* (1864). Later he brought out *Falenas* (1869), *Americanas* (1875), and *Poesias Completas* (1901). His criticism includes a long attack (1878) on Eça de Queiroz's *O Primo Basílio* and two frequently cited studies of Brazilian literature, "O Instinto da Nacionalidade" (1873) and "A Nova Geração" (1879). His *crônicas,* or newspaper columns, represent a genre of which he is the master in Brazil. His first volume of short stories, *Contos Fluminenses,* appeared in 1872. Of his 200 short stories, the best collections are *Histórias sem Data* (1884) and *Várias Histórias* (1896). His original plays, chiefly brief comedies dealing with a single situation, are printed in *Teatro* (1910). His career as a novelist began in 1872 with *Ressurreição.* His first great novel, *Memórias Póstumas de Brás Cubas,* 1880–1881 (*Epitaph of a Small Winner*), marks the beginning of the second, more powerful phase of his career, during which, in addition to the short stories already mentioned, he wrote other novels, *Quincas*

Joaquim Maria Machado de Assis. [Organization of American States]

Borba, 1891 *(Philosopher or Dog), Dom Casmurro,* 1899 *(Dom Casmurro), Esaú e Jacó,* 1904 *(Esau and Jacob),* and *Memorial de Aires* (1908).

Machado was a man of culture with a passionate interest in music and philosophy. He was an admirer of Schopenhauer, Pascal, the English novelists of the eighteenth century, and Thackeray, and his work contains many allusions to the Bible, Shakespeare, and other writers. He is a moralist who skeptically observes the human comedy, satirizes what he sees, and regrets that its actors are content with mediocre roles when they might be heroic. His subject matter, especially in his novels, is Rio and its aristocratic society whose wealth was based on property and, until 1888, the possession of slaves, and which, because of social position, family connections, and money, had an opportunity for achievement that was denied other classes; yet the life of the aristocrat, as he sees it, is an exercise in futility. Except for Rubião, the schizophrenic protagonist of *Quincas Borba,* his characters have few visions of grandeur or even illusions and are fundamentally egotistic. Machado does not espouse social causes in his fiction, although he wrote two short stories, "Pai contra Mãe" and "O Caso da Vara," which are among the saddest presentations in literature of the cruelty of slavery. His plots are usually simple, even banal. The theme of love recurs constantly, with the stress on fickleness, infidelity, and deception, and the resultant disillusionment and unhappiness. Nevertheless his best works seem to be much more modern than those of such great contemporaries as Aluísio AZEVEDO in Brazil or Eça de Queiroz in Portugal. Frequently, as in the short stories "Missa do Galo" and "Uns Braços" or in the novel *Dom Casmurro,* the relationship between two characters remains ambiguous. His interest in cases of madness, which can be seen also in "O Alienista" (translated into English in *The Psychiatrist and Other Stories,* 1963), is shared by other writers of the time, but his studies in alienation and solitude bring him close to modern writers, as do the style and structure of his novels, which owe much to Laurence Sterne. In three major novels he uses a narrator who is also a character; elsewhere he likes to indulge in the irony of reminding his reader that books are not life but art and that the author may take the liberty of intervening in them at will. His chapters are brief, sometimes even without words; his sentences are short, frequently punctuated with semicolons; and his images and metaphors are often startling.

Bibliography. Helen Caldwell, *Machado de Assis: The Brazilian Master and His Novels,* Berkeley, Calif., 1970; José Aderaldo Castello, *Realidade e Illusão em Machado de Assis,* São Paulo, 1969; Joaquim Maria Machado de Assis, *Obra Completa,* ed. by Afrânio Coutinho, 3 vols., Rio de Janeiro, 1959; Lúcia Miguel-Pereira, *Machado de Assis,* 5th ed., Rio de Janeiro, 1955; J. Galante de Sousa, *Bibliografia de Machado de Assis,* Rio de Janeiro, 1955; Luiz Vianna Filho, *A Vida de Machado de Assis,* São Paulo, 1965.

RAYMOND S. SAYERS

MACHU PICCHU. Modern name of a spectacular Inca site overlooking the Vilcanota (Urubamba) River in south-central Peru. The ancient name is not known, nor are there any clear-cut references to it in the literature of the early Spanish conquerors. The site, perched on a sharp saddle pinched in by a great U curve of the river below, was discovered by Hiram Bingham in 1911. All its central parts have been cleared and reconstructed.

Most of the literature on Machu Picchu is unreliable. Most probably it was a sacred site inhabited and serviced by priestesses. It was reached by an Inca road run through an incredible wilderness of mountains; along this road (which had no economic function) there are other ruins, not so spectacular as Machu Picchu but still impressive in their isolation. This road no doubt carried the emperors out to Machu Picchu for purposes of worship and oracular reading. The great rock of Huayna Picchu, up which some of the more daring tourists today climb, was probably the embodiment of the *huaca* (supernatural power) that was the object of the Incas' veneration. There is today a quite adequate government hotel next to the ruins. Most visitors make the round trip in one long day, traveling by narrow-gauge railroad between Cuzco and Machu Picchu. *See also* INCAS.

BURR C. BRUNDAGE

MACIEL, ANTÔNIO VICENTE MENDES. *See* CONSELHEIRO, ANTÔNIO.

MADERO, FRANCISCO I[NDALECIO] (1873–1913). Mexican revolutionary leader and President (1911–1913). Madero was born in Parras, Coahuila. His grandfather, Evaristo Madero, was the head of one of the most powerful families in northern Mexico. From 1887 to 1892 Madero and a younger brother, Gustavo, studied economics and commerce in France, and later they spent a year studying agriculture at the University of California in Berkeley. Back in Mexico, Madero stimulated the development of the Laguna District (Durango-Coahuila), first as administrator of his father's property and later working his own lands. Through his own efforts he was able to acquire a fortune of more than 500,000 pesos. As a child, Madero gave evidence of a generous nature; as a young man, he was influenced by intuitionist philosophy in its least sophisticated manifestations (theosophy and spiritism) and by homeopathic medicine. For all these reasons he was frequently called a lunatic.

Madero entered political life in 1904 by taking part in municipal elections in San Pedro, Coahuila. Beginning in 1905, he gave financial assistance to the group headed by Ricardo FLORES MAGÓN. In 1908 Madero published the first edition of *La sucesión presidencial en 1910,* in which he accepted the reelection of President Porfirio DÍAZ but sought freedom in the selection of the Vice President, perhaps believing that the demise of the nearly octogenarian Díaz would soon occur. In the face of Díaz's indifference, he formed the Partido Nacional Antirreeleccionista (National Antireelectionist party) in 1909; perhaps judging from his own background, he hoped that the party would be composed of independent men who did not need to earn their livelihood from the public treasury and might even be capable of accumulating "honorable fortunes." Nominated to the Presidency by a party convention in April 1910, Madero was harassed by the authorities during his campaign but succeeded in arousing enthusiasm in the large cities with speeches in which he emphasized political freedom as the basis of the solution to all the country's problems.

Francisco I. Madero. [*Organization of American States*]

Madero was arrested in Monterrey in June 1910 but was able to flee to the United States in October, having finally decided to embark on an armed struggle against the regime and setting forth his goals in the Plan of San Luis Potosí (*see* SAN LUIS POTOSÍ, PLAN OF). He returned to Mexico with a few supporters in February 1911, as the revolution he had called for got under way (*see* MEXICAN REVOLUTION). The capture in May of Ciudad Juárez, Chihuahua, in which Pascual Orozco distinguished himself, gave a strong impetus to the revolution. As a result of treaties signed in that city on May 21, 1911, Porfirio Díaz resigned the Presidency on May 25 and was succeeded by an interim President, Francisco León de la Barra. During De la Barra's Presidency Madero put an end to the Partido Nacional Antirreeleccionista and formed the Partido Constitucional Progresista (Constitutional Progressive party), which nominated him for the Presidency and José María Pino Suárez of YUCATÁN for the Vice Presidency in August–September 1911. Flores Magón broke with Madero in May 1911; Emiliano ZAPATA, in November of that year.

Madero occupied the Presidency from November 6, 1911, until he resigned on February 19, 1913; on February 22 he was murdered. His agrarian policy consisted of reorganizing the Caja de Préstamos, parceling the *ejidos* (*see* EJIDO), and surveying and selling public lands. He also created a Department of Labor. In March 1912 his former subordinate Pascual Orozco rebelled against the government, charging Madero with nepotism; later, in the Pact of the Empacadora (March 25, 1912), he accused the President of having launched the revolution with American help. Madero succeeded in defeating Orozco in an energetic military campaign headed by his future executioner, Victoriano HUERTA. In February 1913, Félix Díaz, a nephew of the exiled dictator, began an uprising which Huerta exploited to his own advantage and which ended in the murder of the President and Vice President Pino Suárez. A crucial role in the tragedy was played by the American Ambassador, Henry Lane WILSON, who a few days after Madero's death denied that the latter had been the "apostle of liberty"; in Wilson's opinion, he had merely been a man of disordered intellect.

Bibliography. Charles C. Cumberland, *Mexican Revolution: Genesis under Madero*, Austin, Tex., 1952; Roque Estrada, *La Revolución y Francisco I. Madero*, Guadalajara, 1912; Francisco I. Madero, *La sucesión presidencial en 1910: El Partido Nacional Democrático*, San Pedro, Coahuila, 1908; id., "Mis memorias," *Anales del Museo Nacional de Arqueología, Historia y Etnografía*, vol. I, 4th epoch, 1922, pp. 7–30; Stanley R. Ross, *Francisco I. Madero: Apostle of Mexican Democracy*, New York, 1955; Alfonso Taracena, *Madero: Vida del hombre y del político*, Mexico City, 1937; José C. Valadés, *Imaginación y realidad de Francisco I. Madero*, Mexico City, 1960.

MOISÉS GONZÁLEZ NAVARRO

MADRID, TREATY OF (1750). Formal recognition by Spain of the expansion of Portuguese America beyond the theoretical line of the Treaty of Tordesillas of 1494 (*see* TORDESILLAS, TREATY OF). The treaty was the result of three years of arduous negotiation, conducted for the Portuguese by Alexandre de Gusmão, the Brazilian-born private secretary of King João V, and Don José de Carvajal y Lencastre, President of the COUNCIL OF THE INDIES, for Spain. Both Iberian powers were anxious to settle their differences in America, and the accession of Ferdinand VI of Spain (r. 1746–1759) with his Portuguese wife, Maria Barbara, provided a favorable setting. Spain gained recognition of its supremacy in the RÍO DE LA PLATA with Portuguese agreement to abandon Colônia do Sacramento, the fortified contraband entrepôt opposite Buenos Aires. The Portuguese established their claim to much of Amazónia, gained the territory of the seven missions of Uruguay (the Jesuit Amerindian villages along the banks of the URUGUAY RIVER), and achieved the recognition of boundaries essentially those of present-day Brazil, which guaranteed their possession of the gold and diamond regions of Minas Gerais, Goiás, and Mato Grosso.

Strong opposition to the treaty soon emerged, from the Jesuits, the Amerindians of the missions, and the newly appointed Portuguese Secretary of State, Sebastião José de Carvalho e Melo, the future Marquês de POMBAL. The treaty was abrogated by the accord of El Pardo (1761), but its territorial arrangements were upheld in most respects by the Treaty of San Ildefonso of 1777 (*see* SAN ILDEFONSO, TREATY OF).

KENNETH R. MAXWELL

MAGALHÃES, BENJAMIN CONSTANT BOTELHO DE (1836–1891). Brazilian positivist, educator, republican, and revolutionary general. Born into a poor family of Rio de Janeiro Province, Benjamin Constant turned to the Army for an education. After studying at the Military School, he began a long and influential pedagogic career, teaching science and mathematics at institutions in Rio de Janeiro and even tutoring the Emperor's grandchildren, despite his known adherence to republicanism and the positivist doctrines of Auguste Comte (see POSITIVISM: BRAZIL).

Rising in military rank and prestige after service in the PARAGUAYAN WAR (1864–1870), he gained an eager following among the students of the Military and Polytechnical Schools, converting some to positivism and the republican cause. In 1886 he intervened in the "military question," strongly defending the honor and dignity of the armed forces, then allegedly threatened, and in 1889 he openly associated himself with the vigorous new republican movement. In October of that year, at a banquet for visiting Chilean naval officers, Benjamin Constant denounced the monarchist regime, and on November 11, at a meeting of revolutionary conspirators, including Ruy BARBOSA, Quintino Bocaiúva, and Marshal Manuel Deodoro da FONSECA, he urged an end to the monarchy as well as to the ruling Liberal Ministry of Visconde de Ouro Prêto (Afonso Celso de ASSIS FIGUEIREDO). He participated in the republican revolt of November 15, 1889, at the head of an army brigade, becoming Minister of War in the first republican regime.   ROBERT CONRAD

MAGALHÃES E SOUSA, FERNÃO DE, or MAGAL-LANES, FERNANDO DE. See MAGELLAN, FERDI-NAND.

MAGDALENA RIVER. Colombia's principal river, the Magdalena was discovered and named for St. Mary Magdalene on April 1, 1501, by the Spanish conqueror Rodrigo de Bastidas. The river is approximately 950 miles long, flowing into the Caribbean in a south-north direction. It is divided into three main stretches. The first, extending from the source of the river in the extreme southwest of Huila Department, flows about 135 miles to the city of Neiva. The second, from Neiva to the city of Honda, a distance of 231 miles, is partially navigable in shallow-draft vessels. It is only on the third stretch, known as the lower Magdalena and extending approximately 588 miles from Honda to the mouth of the river (the Bocas de Ceniza), that large-scale river shipping is feasible.

The river and its valley served as the main arterial route into the interior of Colombia almost from the time of their discovery. The settlement patterns of much of Colombia's Andean highlands follow the Magdalena and its 500 tributaries. For the first three centuries river navigation was by dugout canoe. Steam navigation was firmly established by the late 1840s after several unsuccessful attempts in the 1820s and 1830s, and to this day stern-wheelers (now diesel-powered) ply the lower reaches of the Magdalena.

Colombia's main Caribbean port cities—Barranquilla, Cartagena, and Santa Marta—are all connected by water to the Magdalena, whether directly or indirectly. The great river produces an abundant variety of edible fish that support much of the Magdalena Valley's population. With the development of rail, air, and road transportation, however, the Magdalena has been superseded as Colombia's main highway.

J. LEÓN HELGUERA

MAGELLAN, FERDINAND (Portuguese, FERNÃO DE MAGALHÃES E SOUSA; Spanish, FERNANDO DE MAGALLANES; ca. 1480–1521). Portuguese navigator. Born near Oporto, Magellan entered royal service and was educated as a page. In 1504 he enlisted under Francisco de Almeida, the first Viceroy of Portuguese India. He was sent to Sofala, Mozambique, with Nuno Vaz Pereira to help build a fortress there and then returned to India, where he fought against the Moslems at Diu. In August 1509, Magellan, along with Francisco Serrão, was sent on a reconnaissance expedition under Diogo Lopes de Sequeira to Malacca. He accompanied the new Viceroy, Afonso de Albuquerque, in the successful assault against Goa. He also took part in the taking of Malacca in August 1511 and then may have sailed as a captain under Antônio d'Abreu, along with Serrão, in search of the Spice Islands. This expedition reached Amboina, but Serrão was shipwrecked on the return voyage. Serrão offered his services to the ruler of Ternate, remained there for the rest of his days, and corresponded with Magellan, who had returned to Portugal and remained there for about a year. Magellan left for action in Morocco and received a wound that left him slightly lame. Owing to a contretemps over a cattle sale, he then left Africa and returned to Lisbon. He applied for a minute increase in his *moradia* (pension) but was refused it by King Manoel—an evidence of displeasure that meant an end to any career under the Portuguese flag. In 1517 he denaturalized himself and with a Portuguese astronomer, Ruy Faleiro, offered his services to Spain. He managed to convince the King, on the basis of letters from Serrão, that the Spice Islands lay within the sphere assigned to Spain by the Treaty of Tordesillas (see TORDESILLAS, TREATY OF). In the same year, 1517, he married Beatriz Barbosa, by whom he had a son, Rodrigo, who died in infancy; in 1522 Beatriz died.

Magellan left Sanlúcar de Barrameda with five ships on September 20, 1519. After stopping at Madeira, the fleet crossed the Atlantic, reached Brazil, explored the RÍO DE LA PLATA, and at the end of March reached the Bay of San Julián, where Magellan decided to winter. A mutiny was put down there, and one ship was lost. On October 21, 1520, the entrance of what proved to be the Strait of Magellan was reached and negotiated, the Pacific being entered on November 28. Sailing on a course of north and then northwest and west, Magellan reached Guam on March 6, 1521, having sighted only two other islands, both uninhabited, on a voyage of almost 100 days. On March 16, 1521, the Philippines were discovered. Unfortunately, Magellan made an alliance with a local chieftain and lost his life in an attack on the island of Mactan on April 27, 1521. After voyaging through the Moluccas, the survivors, by now left with only one ship, the *Victoria,* under the command of Juan Sebastián del Cano, sailed back to Spain by way of the Cape of Good Hope. Eighteen men disembarked on September 6, 1522, having completed the first circumnavigation of the globe.

MARTIN TORODASH

MAGLOIRE, PAUL E[UGÈNE] (1907–   ). General and President of Haiti (1950–1956). A Negro, Magloire was born in Cap-Haïtien. Although he briefly taught in his native city (1929–1930), his career was almost entirely in the Army before he entered politics. Graduating from the National Military Academy, he entered the Army and was commissioned in 1931. By the early 1940s he had been commander of the National Penitentiary, police chief of the capital, and commander of military forces at the Presidential Palace. He joined dissident officers who forced President Élie LESCOT to resign in a bloodless coup in January 1946. Magloire became a member of the military triumvirate that ruled Haiti until the National Assembly chose Dumarsais ESTIMÉ as President on August 16.

When Estimé was deposed in 1950, the three-man junta reassumed power, with Colonel Magloire, a Negro respected by mulattoes, in prime position. On October 8, he won the first popular presidential election in Haiti's history despite his opponent's claim of fraud. Although Magloire promised educational and other reforms and guaranteed civil liberties, charges of gross corruption and the suppression of the opposition were made, and seem valid. Opposition to his reelection led to his resignation at the end of his term in December 1956. The Army's attempt to restore their strong man led to a general uprising that paralyzed the nation; as a result, Magloire resigned again on December 12 and went into exile.   JOHN E. BAUR

MAGOON, CHARLES E[DWARD] (1861–1920). American lawyer, administrator, governor, and diplomat. Magoon practiced law in Lincoln, Nebraska, from 1882 to 1899, when President McKinley appointed him to the Bureau of Insular Affairs, newly established in the War Department, to handle legal matters resulting from United States acquisition of the Philippines and Puerto Rico and intervention in Cuba. Serving in the role of law officer for the Bureau until 1904, Magoon gave detailed opinions on the relationship of United States laws to the laws of these areas. His next assignment was as General Counsel to the Isthmian Canal Commission (1904–1905); he was later a member of the Commission and simultaneously Governor of the Canal Zone and United States Minister to Panama (1905–1906).

In 1906 Magoon was sent to Cuba as military Governor, under the provisions of the PLATT AMENDMENT, after President Tomás ESTRADA PALMA had resigned early in his second term in the midst of an uprising by opponents of his reelection. Under Magoon's administration financial reforms were introduced, new laws enacted, sanitation advanced, public order restored, yellow fever eliminated, and the school system reorganized. Presidential and congressional elections were held in November 1908, and in January 1909 Governor Magoon turned the administration of the country over to the newly elected President, José Miguel GÓMEZ. Magoon's record in Cuba has often been criticized by Cuban historians, who have accused him of encouraging political corruption and of creating jobs for political purposes.   RICHARD B. GRAY

MAIGUASHCA, MESÍAS (1938–   ). Ecuadorian composer. Born in Quito, he began his studies at the conservatory there and continued them at the Eastman School of Music in Rochester, New York. For a summer he worked in Aspen, Colorado, with Darius Milhaud, and later with Alberto GINASTERA in Buenos Aires. His music bears some traces of the Ecuadorian vernacular within the use of advanced techniques. Although he has written mainly for small ensembles and for voice, he is well known for his *Huacayñan,* a suite for orchestra (1962).

                JUAN A. ORREGO-SALAS

MAIZE. Staple grain first domesticated in pre-Columbian Mexico. It quickly spread to all areas of the New World that could climatically and culturally adopt it. Along with the cultigens squash, beans, and chili peppers, it forms part of a significant food complex upon which all the great cultures of pre-Columbian America depended. Richard S. MacNeish, in his significant researches in the Valley of Tehuacan, in Mexico, has dated the first wild maize (a highland grass) to 5200 B.C. and its earliest appearance as a domesticated plant to 3400 B.C. It is a reasonable conjecture that highland Mexico was thus the home of the first Indian corn. About 2500 B.C. hybridization of local strains began, resulting in a great augmentation of food supplies; on this base the high cultures of Nuclear America were built. Maize first appeared in Peru about 2000 B.C.

                BURR C. BRUNDAGE

MALFATTI, ANITA (1896–1964). Brazilian painter. Born in São Paulo, the daughter of an Italian engineer resident in Brazil, she studied in Berlin and Dresden, where she came under the influence of the expressionist Lovis Corinth, and in the United States, where she became acquainted with cubism. In December 1917 she exhibited her work in São Paulo in what is considered the first significant, if not the earliest, modern art show in Brazil. Although Lasar SEGALL had shown his paintings in 1913, they evoked relatively little controversy. However, Anita Malfatti's exhibit became a *cause célèbre* when the man of letters José Bento Monteiro LOBATO, while praising her talent, denounced modern art in *O Estado de São Paulo,* equating it with paranoia. Her show thus had a polarizing effect on art-conscious Brazilians and stimulated the artistic rebelliousness that burst forth in the São Paulo Modern Art Week of 1922 (*see* MODERNISM: BRAZIL), to which she also contributed. She continued to paint in various styles until the 1960s, and a retrospective show at the Seventh Bienal (1963) in São Paulo contained thirty-nine paintings and seven drawings.   HELEN DELPAR

MALINCHE (MARINA, MALINTZIN; d. 1528 or 1529). Aztec woman who served as interpreter to Hernán CORTÉS during the conquest of Mexico. Malinche was born somewhere within the Aztec empire some years prior to the Spanish conquest. While still a child she was sold as a slave and taken to Tabasco, on the Gulf of Mexico. Cortés arrived in Tabasco in 1519, and after he had defeated the Indians in battle, they gave Malinche to him, along with some other women. Once Cortés had penetrated into Aztec territory, Malinche, who knew both NAHUATL (the Aztec language) and Maya (the language spoken in Tabasco), was able to function as interpreter, working in conjunction with one of Cortés's men who knew both Maya and Spanish. She was indirectly responsible for the famous massacre in the town of Cholula, where Cortés killed thousands of natives after being told by her that they were plotting against him, which may or may not have been true. During the conquest she was Cortés's mistress, but after the conquest Cortés married her off to Juan Jaramillo, one of his followers. By Cortés she had a son named Martín, and by Jaramillo a daughter named María. As a reward for the help she had given the Spaniards during the conquest, Malinche was given the income from two Indian towns. In modern Mexico, the term *malinchista* is used to designate a person who rejects the national heritage and prefers that which is foreign.

TIMOTHY C. HANLEY

MALLEA, EDUARDO (1903–   ). Argentine writer. Mallea was born in Bahía Blanca. Beginning in 1916 he studied in Buenos Aires, where he frequented the *Martín Fierro* group. In 1926 he published his first book, *Cuentos para una inglesa desesperada*. He traveled in Europe, returning to Argentina in 1934, and published two important works, *Historia de una pasión argentina* (1935) and *La ciudad junto al río inmóvil* (1936), which reflect the complex and changing reality of the country in those years of crisis. Mallea became the most vigorous of the writers associated with the review *Sur,* edited by Victoria Ocampo, and despite his evasive, sometimes abstract style, his work is a firm denunciation of the false system of values he saw around him.

Of his many novels the most noteworthy are *Fiesta en noviembre* (1938), *La bahía del silencio* (1940), *Todo verdor perecerá* (1941), *Las águilas* (1943), *Los enemigos del alma* (1950), *Chaves* (1953), and *Simbad* (1957). *La sala de espera* (1953) is a collection of short stories. In 1965 he published *Poderío de la novela,* a collection of essays. Several of Mallea's works were translated into English as *All Green Shall Perish and Other Novellas and Stories* (1966).

RACHEL PHILLIPS

MAMELUCO (MAMALUCO). In colonial Brazil a name applied to a person of mixed European and Amerindian ancestry. Since the same word can also mean "Mamluk," or "Mameluke," it may have acquired a new meaning after its importation in Brazil. A Tupí derivation has also been suggested.

MANAGUA. Capital of Nicaragua, located on the site of an Indian town on the southern shore of Lake Managua. Still only a village at the end of the colonial period, it served as a neutral meeting ground for the rival political factions from León and Granada, Nicaragua's leading cities in the early nineteenth century. In 1858 the Nicaraguan government agreed on Managua as the capital, replacing León. By 1896 it had a population of 25,000, or less than León but more than Granada. Growth was rapid thereafter, especially after the completion in 1898 of a railway to the coffee-growing area of the department of Carazo, making Managua a distribution center for Nicaragua's rapidly expanding coffee exports.

Completion of the Pacific Railway in 1903 stimulated the city's growth by linking Lake Nicaragua to the Pacific port of Corinto via Managua. In 1920 it had a population of approximately 59,000. An earthquake in 1931 and a fire five years later damaged or destroyed most of the city's principal buildings. Managua's population reached 80,000 in 1940 and 353,000 in 1970, far outdistancing its Nicaraguan rivals. Despite its late start, by the mid-twentieth century Managua had become a typical Latin American primate city, absorbing the country's people, capital, and talent. One out of every six Nicaraguans lived in Managua in 1970. The city, which had been completely rebuilt after the disasters of the 1930s, was largely destroyed by earthquakes in December 1972.   CHARLES L. STANSIFER

MANCO CAPAC. Reputed first ancestor of the INCAS. The myth tells that, following the world flood, eight semidivine beings, brothers and sister-wives, emerged from clefts in the sacred rock of Pacaritambo. The four brothers were Manco Capac, Ayar Cachi, Ayar Ucho, and Ayar Auca. The sun god Inti, who was their father, gave them the mission to make a journey and found a city called CUZCO, from which they would then reach out to conquer the world. They were to know where the designated founding should take place when Mama Huaco, one of the sister-wives, would sink her golden digging stick deep into the ground. Led by Manco Capac, the Incas, as prophesied, founded Cuzco. Manco Capac was kept and worshiped in the form of a stone by his *panaca,* the family comprised of his immediate descendants. He was accounted the first emperor. Insofar as there is any historicity at all to the figure of Manco Capac, he was probably of the Tambo tribe, one of the component groups of the Incas.

BURR C. BRUNDAGE

MANCO INCA (ca. 1516–1545). Inca Emperor, crowned at Cuzco in December 1533, who with Francisco PIZARRO's blessing sought to reestablish Inca administration of the empire (*see* INCAS). The native aristocracy was divided over recognizing his authority, some Indian tribes reasserted their pre-Inca independence, and, worst of all, Spanish support and consideration soon began to wane. Provoked by extreme ill treatment at the hands of the Spaniards, especially the Pizarros, Manco Inca turned against them and, in 1535, escaped from Cuzco. During the decade that followed, he organized a resistance movement that produced two important campaigns (1536, 1538). In both instances he was able to raise large armies of loyal Indians and to cause grave concern to Spanish leaders and citizens. Ultimately, his troops were no match for the Spanish and their Indian allies, including many Incas and even his own brother, Paullu.

Manco withdrew to Vitcos, in the Vilcabamba Valley, and established a tiny native state where the Inca religion and Inca culture were preserved. Successive Spanish leaders attempted by diplomatic means to bring about a reconciliation with Manco, but each time negotiations fell through. Attempts were also made to reduce him by force, but he consistently managed to elude his would-be captors. He was treacherously killed by fugitive partisans of his friend Diego de ALMAGRO after he had given them sanctuary and royal hospitality for two years. His Inca state survived another twenty-five years until Viceroy Francisco de TOLEDO suppressed it and executed his son and successor, TUPAC AMARU.

NORMAN MEIKLEJOHN

MANN, THOMAS C[LIFTON] (1912–   ). United States diplomat and lawyer. Born in Laredo, Texas, Mann received a law degree from Baylor University in 1934 and practiced law in Laredo for eight years. His first diplomatic assignment was to the American Embassy in Uruguay in 1942–1943. Joining the State Department in 1944, he became a foreign service officer in 1947. He served briefly as Deputy Assistant Secretary of State for Inter-American Affairs in 1950–1951, was assigned to the American Embassy in Guatemala in 1955, and became Ambassador to El Salvador that year, serving there until 1957. His next posts were as Assistant Secretary of State for Economic Affairs (1957–1960) and Assistant Secretary of State for Inter-American Affairs (1960–1961), a position he resumed in 1964 after serving from 1961 to 1963 as Ambassador to Mexico. In the period 1965–1966 he was Undersecretary of State for Economic Affairs.

Mann is best known for his role as one of President Johnson's principal advisers on Latin American policy. Although in his speeches the Assistant Secretary praised the principles of nonintervention and the cause of democracy, he took a hard line against the threat of communism in the Western Hemisphere. He justified the successful effort of the United States to aid in the overthrow of the leftist government of Jacobo ARBENZ GUZMÁN in Guatemala in 1954, and he was a major decision maker in the United States intervention in the Dominican Republic in 1965 to prevent a left-wing movement from taking over the country (*see* DOMINICAN REVOLT). He returned to private life in 1966.

RICHARD B. GRAY

MAR, SERRA DO. *See* SERRA DO MAR.

MARIÁTEGUI, JOSÉ CARLOS (1895–1930). Peruvian Marxist, political analyst, and organizer. Mariátegui occupies a leading position among twentieth-century Peruvian public figures. As a journalist he was one of the most thoughtful and incisive social and political analysts of his age. As a political organizer he inspired the creation of the Communist and Socialist parties of Peru. Most important, as a socialist intellectual he was the first to provide a Marxist interpretation of Peruvian history and to originate socialist studies in Peru.

Mariátegui's rise to prominence was marked by triumphs over poverty and personal tragedies. He was born in Lima in 1895 (a recent study, however, places his birth at Moquegua in 1894), and his already-poor middle-class homelife was adversely affected by his father's disappearance. Nevertheless, he finished primary school and in 1909 went to work for Lima's *La Prensa* as a proofreader. His years of activity between 1909 and 1919 were described by Mariátegui himself as his "stone age," a period of literary adolescence whose frivolity he decried. Nonetheless, they were important formative years. He wrote for a number of publications on a variety of subjects, published poetry, and contributed to the creation of short-lived but at times important newspapers. Throughout this period he displayed political acumen, but it was not until 1918 that he began to reveal a measure of real social awareness. As a budding socialist, he contributed articles to two of his cocreations, *Nuestra Época* and *La Razón,* in which he supported the demands of labor and preached university reforms. However, his socialism did not become rooted on solid foundations until he went to Europe in 1919 on a government fellowship. He had been critical of the new Augusto LEGUÍA government, and the fellowship was offered as an alternative to prison.

In the four years spent in Europe, Mariátegui traveled extensively and studied in France, Italy, and Germany. Along with a family, he acquired a considerably more solid Marxist education and returned with both to Peru in 1923. From that year until his death in 1930 he made the propagation of socialism his major goal. His vehicle for this undertaking was the press, and he used it as adeptly as anyone. His essays and articles consisted of rational, in-depth analyses of Peruvian and world events rather than fiery revolutionary propaganda. This lack of inflammatory jargon was perhaps instrumental in convincing the government that Mariátegui was not to be feared.

Mariátegui's literary and political activities became especially pronounced after 1924 when the amputation of a cancerous leg forced him to spend the rest of his life in a wheelchair. Rather than being overcome by self-pity, Mariátegui decided that only renewed journalistic activity would make his physical impediment less tragic. Thus, in 1925 he published a collection of essays titled *La escena contemporánea.* In 1926 he reached his journalistic apex with the creation of *Amauta,* a socialist publication containing contributions from the most influential intellectuals of the Americas. In 1928 he published his most acclaimed work, *Siete ensayos de interpretación de la realidad peruana* (*Seven Interpretive Essays on Peruvian Reality*). Coolly received at first, it has become Mariátegui's most enduring contribution to Marxist historical studies.

The work is a compilation of seven previously published essays. The first represents an economic analysis of Peruvian history from the days of the INCAS to the 1920s. The next six deal respectively with the Indian, landholding, education, religion, regionalism and centralism, and literature. Each topic is too vast to be explored adequately in one essay. In addition, the study suffers from marked historical subjectivity and at times from a lack of realism, as when Mariátegui suggests a return to the Incas' communist socioeconomic system. Mariátegui himself acknowledged the absence of historical objectivity, and he made it clear that his intent was not historical accuracy and thoroughness but the propagation of the socialist ideal. Nevertheless, the shortcomings cannot diminish the brilliant originality and the undisputed value of the undertaking. It was, after all, the first socialist interpretation of the Peruvian past.

In 1928 Mariátegui and seven associates founded the Socialist party in response to a directive from the Third International. The party was intended to be a counterweight to Víctor Raúl HAYA DE LA TORRE'S ALIANZA POPULAR REVOLUCIONARIA AMERICANA, to which Mariátegui had briefly belonged and which had definitely broken with the Comintern in 1927. The International, however, was displeased with Mariátegui's creation. It objected to the name "Socialist" adopted by the new party and also to its ideological orientation, which tried to appeal to the workers, the peasants, and the *petite bourgeoisie.* Mariátegui resisted pressures to conform to orthodox international Communist ideology on the ground that it did not reflect

Peruvian reality. In April 1930, while preparing for a trip to Buenos Aires, he died. With his death the party split into a Communist and a Socialist organization.

Mariátegui's unorthodox Marxism and his alleged romantic nationalism drew criticism from orthodox believers long after his death. He was dismissed as a "populist" rather than a scientific socialist. Time, however, and the emergence of new Marxist currents such as the Chinese have raised Mariátegui's ideological stock in international circles. He is now considered the undisputed Marxist guiding light not only of Peru but perhaps of all South America.

Bibliography. Armando Bazán, *Biografía de J. C. Mariátegui,* Santiago, 1939; Eugenio Chang Rodríguez, *La literatura política de González Prada, Mariátegui y Haya de la Torre,* Mexico City, 1957; José Carlos Mariátegui, *Siete ensayos de interpretación de la realidad peruana,* Lima, 1928; María Wiesse, *José Carlos Mariátegui: Etapas de su vida,* Lima, 1945.   ORAZIO A. CICCARELLI

MARINA. *See* MALINCHE.

MARISOL (b. MARISOL ESCOBAR, 1930–   ). Venezuelan sculptor. Marisol is an important sculptor in the New York school identified especially with Pop Art. She was born of Venezuelan parents in Paris but was raised in Venezuela. She then studied painting in New York with Kuniyoshi and Hans Hofmann. Inspired by an exhibition of pre-Columbian sculpture, she turned in 1954 to terra-cotta sculpture. *Printer's Box* and *Purgatorio,* compartmented boxes with pottery and brass figures, are typical of her work of the 1950s. About 1960 she began making life-size painted wood figures with all sorts of materials added: plaster, metal door locks and knobs, a real bicycle. The figures, usually retaining parts of the original block form, are in the cubist-constructivist tradition of Joaquín TORRES-GARCÍA. The amusing topicality of her subjects (*The Kennedys, John Wayne*) made her one of the best-known New York artists of the 1960s, but her genuine formal qualities may give her a more lasting importance. Psychological overtones and elements of fantasy and the grotesque enrich her basically humane art, as seen in *The Party,* a large sculptural group, and *Baby Boy.*   TERENCE GRIEDER

MÁRMOL, JOSÉ (1817–1871). Argentine novelist and poet. Mármol was born in Buenos Aires and died there. While still in his teens, he became an opponent of Juan Manuel de ROSAS. Attacking the dictator with his pen, he found himself in prison in 1839. He then spent thirteen years as an impoverished exile in Montevideo, producing an endless barrage of prose and verse that earned him the title of Rosas' poetic scourge. All his verse is written in the romantic vein, and *El peregrino* (1847), his longest poem, is an imitation of Byron's *Childe Harold.* "Rosas, el 25 de mayo de 1850," another poem, is a frontal attack on Rosas, whom he considered second only to Satan. Mármol also wrote two plays in verse, *El poeta* (1842) and *El cruzado* (1851), but his most famous work is *Amalia,* 1851 (*Amalia, a Romance of the Argentine*), a romantic historical novel.

Amalia, whose present-day value is more historical than artistic, takes place in Buenos Aires in 1840, while Rosas was in power, and shows the dictatorship as the bloody regime it was. At the same time, the author explains that he has used a retrospective point of view aimed at posterity. Unfortunately, the style and technique of the novel discouraged the readers of the day for which he wrote. As a consequence, *Amalia* is now usually remembered only for its chronological significance as the first novel in Argentine literature.   GERARDO SÁENZ

MARQUÉS, RENÉ (1919–   ). Puerto Rican writer. In 1954, after studying in Puerto Rico, Spain, and the United States, he became director of the Experimental Theater of the Puerto Rican Atheneum and was awarded a Guggenheim fellowship that allowed him to write his novel *Víspera del hombre* (1959). Marqués has also written stories and essays but is best known as a dramatist, showing in his plays his constant preoccupation with his country's political and social problems. Several of his plays appeared first on the New York stage. The best known include *El hombre y sus sueños* (1948), *Palm Sunday* (1949), *El sol y los MacDonald* (1950), *La carreta* (1952), *La muerte no entrará en palacio* (1957), *Los soles truncos* (1958), *Un niño azul para esa sombra* (1959), and *La casa sin reloj* (1961). He has also published collections of stories, including *Otro día nuestro* (1955) and *En una ciudad llamada San Juan* (1960), and the anthology *Cuentos puertorriqueños de hoy* (1959). Marqués is a supporter of Puerto Rican independence.   RACHEL PHILLIPS

MÁRQUEZ, GABRIEL GARCÍA. *See* GARCÍA MÁRQUEZ, GABRIEL.

MARSHALS OF AYACUCHO. The 1824 Battle of Ayacucho finally broke Spanish power in Peru. Three of its leading participants were Marshals José de La Mar (1776–1830), Augustín Gamarra (1785–1841), and Andrés SANTA CRUZ (1792–1865). Until 1841 these same men were to be leading figures during one of Peru's most chaotic periods. *See* AYACUCHO, BATTLE OF.

La Mar, a creole career army officer who had fought against Napoleon's armies in Spain, supported the royalist cause in Peru until 1821, when he surrendered Callao to José de SAN MARTÍN's liberation army and then joined it. Subsequently, he participated in the liberation of Ecuador and distinguished himself in the Battles of Junín and Ayacucho (*see* JUNÍN, BATTLE OF). In 1827 a liberal congress elected him President of the republic. His rule was short-lived owing to an unsuccessful war against Simón BOLÍVAR's Gran Colombia (*see* COLOMBIA, GRAN) and to a series of military conspiracies spearheaded by Gamarra and Santa Cruz, among others. In 1829 La Mar was exiled to Costa Rica, where he died the following year.

From 1829 to 1841 Peru's political history was shaped largely by the clashing personalities and ambitions of Gamarra and Santa Cruz, a Bolivian by birth who played a key role in Peruvian history. Both marshals were mestizos, and both had fought for the royalists until after the arrival of San Martín in 1821. Both had participated in the political intrigues of the young republic, and both wished to create a federation of Peru and Bolivia.

From 1829 to 1833 Gamarra ruled over a chaotic nation, and then the Liberals forced him into exile. Santa Cruz, unable to become President of Peru, settled for Bolivia. Beginning in 1828, he established a dictatorship there, and in 1836 he conquered politically torn Peru and created the PERU-BOLIVIA CONFEDERATION. Few persons besides Santa Cruz and none of the neighboring nations were happy with the arrangement. By 1839 discontented Peruvians led by Gamarra, together with Chilean troops, brought the experiment to an end. Santa Cruz was exiled, and Gamarra was elected President by a grateful Congress. Shortly thereafter, in 1841, Gamarra died during an attempted invasion of Bolivia. With Gamarra's death and Santa Cruz's exile the political power of the Marshals of Ayacucho came to an end, and the ideal of a Peru-Bolivia Confederation was laid to rest.

ORAZIO A. CICCARELLI

MARTÍ [Y PÉREZ], JOSÉ [JULIÁN] (1853–1895). Cuban revolutionary leader, essayist, and poet. José Martí, the national hero of Cuba, was born on January 28, 1853, in Havana, the son of Mariano Martí y Navarro, a noncommissioned officer in the Spanish Royal Artillery, and of Leonor Pérez y Cabrera. The parents of eight children in all, Martí's father came from Valencia, Spain, and his mother from Santa Cruz de Tenerife, Canary Islands.

Martí as a revolutionist. Martí's early schooling in Havana was obtained at San Anacleto and San Pablo, where he came under the influence of Rafael María de Mendive, a teacher, poet, and critic of the Spanish regime in Cuba. Mendive induced Martí's parents to permit him to continue his education by enrolling him in the Instituto de Segunda Enseñanza de la Habana

José Martí. [*Richard B. Gray*]

in 1866. In the period 1867–1868 Martí attended St. Paul's School, a branch of the institute under the direction of Mendive. Martí and his good friend Fermín Valdés Domínguez became the devoted followers of Mendive, who encouraged his young disciples in their anti-Spanish activities. The time was ripe for protest, for the rebellion of Carlos Manuel de Céspedes had started in 1868 what became known as the TEN YEARS' WAR. In 1869 Valdés and Martí published their first political tract, *El diablo cojuelo* (*The Limping Devil*), a short collection of anecdotes and puns on freedom of the press. Martí followed this publication with a one-issue newspaper, *Patria Libre,* which contained his first drama, *Abdala,* a thinly disguised political message.

On October 4, 1869, Martí was arrested on a charge of treason for having written a letter critical of the Spanish authorities, and on April 5, 1870, he was sentenced to six years in prison, first at hard labor in a stone quarry in Havana and then on a farm on the Isle of Pines. On January 15, 1871, he was deported to Spain, where he was given complete freedom.

On May 31, 1871, Martí enrolled at the University of Madrid as a first-year law student, at the same time continuing to attack Spanish rule in Cuba in letters to newspapers and in such works as *El presidio político en Cuba* (1871), in which he complained of the treatment of political prisoners on the island, and *¡27 de noviembre!* (1872), a condemnation of the shooting by firing squad of eight medical students in Havana. For reasons of health he transferred in 1873 from the University of Madrid to the University of Saragossa, where the climate was friendlier to Cuban exiles. When the first Spanish republic was proclaimed in February 1873, Martí took advantage of the change in government to urge in *La república española ante la revolución cubana* that the Spanish government recognize Cuban independence. The University of Saragossa granted Martí a law degree on June 30, 1874, and a degree in liberal arts later that year. He then left for Mexico, arriving on February 8, 1875, to join members of his family. Through a friend, Manuel Mercado, he obtained a job writing for *La Revista Universal,* a major newspaper in Mexico City; this was to be the first of many newspaper assignments.

Curiosity about the political situation in Cuba caused him to return to Havana under an assumed name in January 1877. He stayed only a month and then was on his way to Guatemala to teach in a high school in the capital city. Although he was engaged to be married, he took time from his teaching duties for a brief romance with María Granados, the daughter of a former President of Guatemala. His obligation to marry Carmen Zayas-Bazán led him back to Mexico at the end of 1877. After the wedding he returned to Guatemala with his Cuban wife to resume teaching.

In mid-1878 the couple departed for Havana as a result of a general amnesty given to political exiles upon the signing (February 10, 1878) of the Pact of Zanjón ending the Ten Years' War. Martí sought employment as a lawyer in order to support his wife and newly born son José (November 22, 1878), but obstacles in certification prevented him from doing so. His opposition to the Spanish regime was now manifested in public debates with Hispanophiles and conspiracies with well-known opponents of the regime, such as Juan Gualberto Gómez. Both men were detained for conspiracy on

September 17, 1879, and a week later Martí was deported once again to Spain. For most of the remaining fifteen years of his life Martí remained in exile, returning to Cuba only in 1895, the year he died.

By January 1880 Martí was in New York, which was to be his headquarters for the final war of liberation of Cuba from Spain. From 1880 to 1895 he marshaled forces for the revolution, writing letters, making speeches, collecting money, and traveling widely up and down the Atlantic coast, organizing groups of Cubans in exile in New York, Tampa, and Key West. During this period he also served as Vice-Consul and Consul for Uruguay in New York and as a delegate to the First International Conference of American States, held from October 2, 1889, to April 19, 1890, in Washington. It was at this conference that Martí met Gonzalo de Quesada y Aróstegui, a Cuban who was secretary to the Argentine delegation. Quesada became one of Martí's closest associates in the revolutionary movement, the heir to his personal papers, and Cuba's first Minister to the United States.

On April 10, 1892, the Cuban Revolutionary party was officially proclaimed, with Martí elected as chief delegate (president) and Quesada as secretary. Martí's revolutionary thought is expressed in the *Resoluciones* (November 28, 1891), *Bases y estatutos secretos del Partido Revolucionario Cubano* (January 5, 1892), and *Manifiesto de Montecristi* (March 25, 1895). These documents served to describe party objectives and to unite the Cubans in exile, to form the Cuban Revolutionary party, and to inform the Cuban people that the final struggle for independence was about to begin. A major theme of Martí's political thinking was the expectation that a free Cuba should seek governmental forms derived from native institutions rather than from borrowings from alien cultures. His ideal republic, as can be noted in much of his writing, called for compulsory voting, liberty within the framework of the law, and service and self-sacrifice by the individual. He favored a radical revolution in education in order to substitute physics, scientific agriculture, and practical arts for the traditional subjects of logic, theology, and rhetoric. However, his reputation for anticlericalism did not extend to teaching against religion in the schools. Martí feared United States domination of Cuban politics and economics, and he frequently warned of the dangers in one-crop economies (sugar in the case of Cuba), which made weak nations vulnerable to powerful neighbors.

After many years of effort on behalf of the Cuban revolution, Martí and his collaborators decided on 1895 as the year to start another armed rebellion (*see* WAR FOR CUBAN INDEPENDENCE). Although an attempt on January 12, 1895, to send an expedition to Cuba from Fernandina, Florida, failed, Martí pressed on with an order, signed January 29, 1895, for a general uprising in Cuba. Antonio MACEO and Flor Crombet were engaged to invade the island from Costa Rica, and Juan Gualberto Gómez was notified to start the revolt inside Cuba. On January 31, 1895, Martí left the United States to meet Gen. Máximo GÓMEZ in the Dominican Republic. Together they proclaimed the Cuban uprising on February 24 and worked out the wording for the *Manifiesto,* which was announced on March 25. Preparations were made for a small expeditionary force, consisting of Gómez as leader,

Martí, and a handful of others for an invasion of Cuba from the Dominican Republic. The task force of six men finally reached the shores of Cuba and landed at Playitas, near Punta Maisí, on April 11. They got in touch with Maceo's forces, and Martí was commissioned a general in the field. On May 19, 1895, Martí was shot and killed in a skirmish with Spanish forces near Dos Ríos.

Martí as the national hero. After his death in 1895 Martí was highly praised by his fellow revolutionists, who proceeded to carry the rebellion to a successful conclusion in 1898 with the aid of the United States. For the next thirty years Martí's reputation abroad was almost greater than in Cuba. In the 1930s, however, a rediscovery of Martí as *the* national hero occurred, and since that time there has been an outpouring of homage to his memory. The apotheosis of Martí can be dated from the reference of Martí's favorite disciple, Gonzalo de Quesada y Aróstegui, to him as the "Apostle." Although Martí was memorialized in statues, busts, monuments, coins, and stamps prior to the Martí renaissance, it was during the 1930s that his writings and works about him began to appear in large volume, reaching a high point in the 1953 centennial celebrations of his birth. In 1954 Fermín Peraza Sarausa reported in his bibliography the existence of more than 10,000 entries on Martí, including more than 200 full-length biographies. Martí was idealized as the universal man and compared favorably with national heroes around the world.

Martí's status survived the transition in 1959 from a republican form of government in Cuba to that of a Communist dictatorship. He was cited by Fidel CASTRO as the "intellectual author" of the present CUBAN REVOLUTION. Although Martí is buried in a massive mausoleum in Santiago de Cuba, the city of Havana has done the most to memorialize him in stone. A 465-foot obelisk of Isle of Pines marble, with a 55-foot statue of Martí by the sculptor Juan José Sicre at the entrance, is the nation's impressive tribute to its founding father. Although Martí is not generally known in the United States, the city of New York has placed a very large statue of him on horseback, executed by Anna H. Huntington, at the Avenue of the Americas entrance to Central Park.

Martí's literary work. Martí's reputation as a writer is derived mainly from his journalistic efforts and his poetry. His political writings were important at the time but now are mainly of historical interest. His plays *Abdala* (1869), *Adúltera* (1872), and *Amor con amor se paga* (1875) are light creations, as is his novel *Amistad funesta* (1885), which he wrote in seven days.

For fifteen years Martí wrote articles interpreting the United States to the Spanish-speaking world. With great skill and sensitivity he wrote at length of the political, social, and economic changes taking place in the United States in the 1880s and 1890s and assessed the nation's strengths and weaknesses with critical but not unsympathetic understanding. Martí greatly admired and wrote enthusiastically of Abraham Lincoln, Henry David Thoreau, Peter Cooper, and Walt Whitman, and he also wrote entertainingly of Buffalo Bill, Jesse James, Coney Island, the Oklahoma land rush, and the Brooklyn Bridge. For the benefit of his North American audience he wrote about Benito JUÁREZ, Cecilio Acosta, Simón BOLÍVAR, José de SAN MARTÍN, the Andes, and other Latin American topics. He was a regular correspondent for the New York *Sun, La Nación* of Buenos Aires, *La Opinión Nacional* of Caracas, and *Patria,* the official paper he founded in New York for the Cuban revolution. His prose was distinctive, sometimes telegraphic, sometimes turgid and convoluted, but often serene, beautiful, and deeply moving.

Martí was also a master poet, lionized by the great literary figures Rubén DARÍO, Gabriela MISTRAL, Miguel de Unamuno, Fernando de los Ríos, Rufino Blanco-Fombona, and Amado NERVO as an initiator of modernism in Spanish American poetry (*see* MODERNISM: SPANISH AMERICA). His first major poetic work consisted of fifteen poems on fatherly love, published in 1882 in a little book entitled *Ismaelillo* (a nickname for his son). They are distinctive for their simplicity and sincerity. In 1891 he published *Versos sencillos,* a widely read collection of poems on friendship and love. Many of his poems were gathered after his death and published in special collections, such as *Versos libres* (1933), on the theme of freedom, and *Flores del destierro* (1939), on exile. Martí also wrote short stories for children in the four issues of his short-lived magazine *La Edad de Oro* (1889). Although he is the national hero of Cuba, his vision was never narrowly nationalistic. His humanity, vividly expressed by his life and writings, is a gift for all men and all times.

Bibliography. The America of José Martí, tr. by Juan de Onís, New York, 1954; Richard B. Gray, *José Martí, Cuban Patriot,* Gainesville, Fla., 1962; Andrés Iduarte, *Martí, escritor,* Mexico City, 1945; Jorge Mañach, *Martí, Apostle of Freedom,* tr. by Coley Taylor, New York, 1950; Fermín Peraza Sarausa, *Bibliografía martiana,* 2d ed. rev., Havana, 1956; Gonzalo de Quesada y Miranda, *Martí, hombre,* Havana, 1940; Gonzalo de Quesada y Miranda (ed.), *Obras completas de Martí,* 74 vols., Havana, 1936–49; Ivan A. Schulman, *Símbolo y color en la obra de José Martí,* Madrid 1960.

RICHARD B. GRAY

MARTÍNEZ ESTRADA, EZEQUIEL (1895–1964). Argentine poet and essayist concerned with the search for a national identity. He spent some years working as a postal official before his literary talent was recognized. From 1924 to 1946 he served as a professor of literature at the National University of La Plata, and for a short time he taught at the National University of the South in Bahía Blanca. He edited the review *La Vida Literaria* and was twice president of the Argentine Society of Writers (1942–1943, 1944–1945). He traveled extensively in Latin America and Europe, visiting countries on both sides of the Iron Curtain.

Martínez Estrada's early volumes of poetry brought him acclaim and awards: *Oro y piedra* (1918), *Nefelibal* (1922), *Motivos del cielo* (1924), *Argentina* (1927), and *Humoresca* (1929). His poetry shows a realistic and ironic vein in reaction to the lingering traces of modernism (*see* MODERNISM: SPANISH AMERICA) and the experimental vanguardism of his contemporaries. But his pessimistic and intellectual turn of mind was better expressed in his later essays. He also wrote plays, including *Títeres de pies ligeros* (1929), *Lo que no vemos morir* (1941), *Sombras* (1941), and *Cazadores* (1957), but they were only moderately successful. His

most individual contribution is the controversial series of essays that began in 1933 with *Radiografía de la pampa* (*X-Ray of the Pampa*). This is a penetrating, pessimistic exploration of the Argentine identity crisis. His deep understanding of the national spirit is also shown in *La cabeza de Goliat* (1940), an examination of the phenomenon of Buenos Aires, and in his second great work, *Muerte y transfiguración de Martín Fierro* (1946), which explores the presence of the GAUCHO as a constant in the national soul.

RACHEL PHILLIPS

MARTINS PENA, LUIS CARLOS. *See* PENA, LUIS CARLOS MARTINS.

MARTYR, PETER (PIETRO MARTIRE D'ANGHERA or D'ANGHIERA, 1457–1526). Italian-born historian of the New World. Although his name is usually given as Pietro Martire d'Anghera, his birthplace was in Arona. Because of political upheavals, he left Lombardy in 1477 for Rome, where he became one of the leading preceptors among the academicians of the period. In 1487 he accompanied the Conde de Tendilla, the Ambassador from Ferdinand II and ISABELLA I, back to Spain. Upon his arrival he took holy orders and secured the favor of Isabella and the friendship of Christopher COLUMBUS. In 1520 he was appointed historiographer and also became secretary to the COUNCIL OF THE INDIES. From these vantage points he collected the vast amount of material embodied in *De orbe novo,* the work that made him the first historian of America.

His information was obtained firsthand from the leading participants in the voyages of discovery. Although his *modus operandi* was partly responsible for the errors he made because he relied too heavily on the self-serving versions of the discoverers themselves, his material was authentic, fresh, and readable; his judgment of its importance was perceptive and prescient. The first decade, or part, appeared in Seville in 1511; the completed series of eight decades, in 1530. An English-language edition of the Latin original was published in 1912 (reprinted 1970); a Spanish translation was published in 1944. Peter Martyr's work remains valuable as an example of the spirit of the intellectually curious men of Europe in the early sixteenth century.

MARTIN TORODASH

MASCATES, WAR OF (1709–1711). Bitter struggle between the Pernambucan sugar planters and the urban population of Recife in colonial Brazil. The etymology of *mascate* is uncertain, but the word was used to designate a peddler or itinerant merchant, who was generally an immigrant from Portugal. The dispute also focused on the rivalry between the old capital of the captaincy, Olinda, dominated by the plantation aristocracy, and Recife, the thriving seaport that had been the capital of Dutch Brazil; the dispute was doubtless made worse by the traditional hostility between debtors and creditors, a constant factor of stress in the relations between the urban merchants and the rural planters. The royal decision to raise Recife to the status of an independent municipality in 1709 provoked a rising of the planters, which was followed by a counterrising against them by the townspeople and garrison of Recife, producing a small-scale civil war. The planters were eventually suppressed by a new royal Governor aided by Amerindian and black auxiliaries in 1711. The "war" is sometimes seen as a protoindependence movement, but it is probably more important for its revelation of the tensions never far from the surface in Brazilian colonial society.

KENNETH R. MAXWELL

MATA, EDUARDO (1942–   ). Mexican composer and conductor. Born in Mexico City, he studied at the National Conservatory with Rodolfo Halffter among others, later with Julián ORBÓN, and in the United States with Gunther Schuller. In 1965 he was appointed chief of the Music Section of the National University of Mexico and permanent conductor of the Orquesta Sinfónica de Guadalajara. He was later named conductor of the Orquesta Sinfónica de la Universidad de México. Outstanding among his works are three symphonies (1962, 1965, 1967), his *Improvisación* for clarinet and piano (1961) and for violin and piano (1965), and his sonata for cello and piano (1966).

JUAN A. ORREGO-SALAS

MATOS [GUERRA], GREGÓRIO DE (1633–1696). Brazilian poet. Born in Bahia, he was the outstanding representative of the baroque spirit in Brazilian poetry and comparable to the Spanish poet Quevedo, some of whose poems in translation have been attributed to him. He studied law at the University of Coimbra and after thirty years as a civil servant in Portugal returned to Brazil, where he was given employment in the Archdiocese of Bahia. There, because of his caustic satires on the local inhabitants and the violence of his language, he was nicknamed "Boca do Inferno" (Hell's Mouth). He was soon deprived of his ecclesiastical position and was sent to Angola, where he remained until a year before his death. He is best known for his satires, in which he struck at all his fellow Bahians: the local aristocracy who claimed to descend from the first settlers and Indian chiefs; the ignorant Portuguese immigrants, often criminals in exile, who arrived penniless and soon were able to return to Portugal with their pockets full of money; the mulatto men, whom he considered insolent; and the higher clergy in general. He is also the author of beautiful love poems and devotional verse. Like other baroque poets, he was both pious and sensuous, religious, and sometimes pornographic. He used all the techniques and artifices of the *conceptistas,* the Iberian metaphysical poets: startling metaphors and images, puns, plays on words, anadiplosis (a variety of which may be observed in his echo sonnets), hyperbaton, and oxymoron.

RAYMOND S. SAYERS

MATTA [ECHAURREN], ROBERTO [SEBASTIÁN ANTONIO] (1912–   ). Chilean painter. Matta is the best-known Latin American painter in a surrealist style, seeking psychological rather than material truth or, as he says, the representation of "nonanthropomorphic man." He was born in Santiago, where he studied architecture. In 1934 he went to Paris to work with Le Corbusier, but he soon turned to painting. Federico García Lorca sponsored his first exhibit during a visit to Spain in 1935. In Paris Matta was associated with André Breton, Max Ernst, and Joan Miró,

and in New York during World War II with Marcel Duchamp and Yves Tanguy. After the war he lived in Rome until 1954, when he settled permanently in Paris and became a French citizen. In 1957 he had a retrospective one-man show at the Museum of Modern Art in New York.

Matta's paintings have been consistently "metaphysical," with biomorphic or mechanistic forms in brilliant, subtly modulated colors. *Listen to Living* (1941; New York, Museum of Modern Art) suggests volcanoes and natural forces. *To Cover the Earth with a New Dew* (1953) is a landscape of transparent forms with a science-fiction quality. In 1966 Matta showed six large paintings in New York that condemned American violence, as in *Vietnam* and *Alabama* (both 1965), using forms based on weapons and suggesting abstract violence, a subject that has preoccupied him in recent years.

TERENCE GRIEDER

MATTO DE TURNER, CLORINDA (b. GRIMANESA MARTINA MATTO, 1854–1909). Peruvian novelist, essayist, and journalist. Clorinda Matto de Turner was born in Cuzco and died in Buenos Aires. She is best known as the author of *Aves sin nido,* 1889 (*Birds without Nests*), the first *indigenista* novel. The daughter of a well-to-do family, she married Joseph Turner, an English doctor, in 1871.

In 1884, three years after the death of her husband, she published *Tradiciones cuzqueñas* in Cuzco with a prologue by Ricardo PALMA. A second volume appeared in Lima in 1886. That year she also published *Don Juan de Espinosa Medrano,* a biographical study of the seventeenth-century Peruvian writer El Lunarejo, and *Elementos de literatura,* a manual of literature for women. Then came *Aves sin nido,* a novel of social protest in which life in the provinces is shown to be plagued by cruel and immoral members of the government and the clergy who abuse the Indian and tread on the sanctity of the home with impunity. A blend of romanticism and realism, the novel lacks the polish of experienced writing but compensates for this defect with courage and humanity.

Other works followed, including *Índole* (1891), a novel; *Hima Sumac* (1892), a play; and *Herencia* (1895), another novel. But the author's activities had earned her excommunication from the Catholic Church (1892), and she was also ostracized by society. In 1895 she left Peru for Argentina, where she continued to write until her death.

GERARDO SÁENZ

MAUÁ, VISCONDE (IRINEU EVANGELISTA DE SOUSA, 1813–1889). Brazilian merchant, banker, industrialist, and railroad tycoon. Born into a poor and obscure family of Rio Grande do Sul, Irineu Evangelista de Sousa acquired fame and power and huge economic holdings through wide-ranging business activities. Apprenticed to a merchant of Rio de Janeiro in 1824, at sixteen he was employed by a British importing firm, in which he learned English and gained respect for British political and business methods, and was soon a partner and sole manager. In 1846, already prosperous, he established an iron foundry, gaining an assured market through a contract to supply pipes for a new water system in Rio de Janeiro. Acquiring concessions for a gas lamp system, a tramway line, and a monopoly on Amazon steamship navigation, he was soon investing in banks, railroads, gold mines, tanneries, agricultural estates, and other enterprises. His political and business activities extended into the RÍO DE LA PLATA region. Involved in arms dealings in Uruguay, he acquired a banking concession in Montevideo, and his Uruguayan holdings came to include railroads, gasworks, docks, livestock farms, and meat-processing plants.

In 1854, having constructed Brazil's first railroad line from the port of Mauá on the Bay of Guanabara to the nearby mountains, he was granted the title Barão Mauá, and in 1874 the title of Visconde Mauá for his part in laying the first submarine cable between Europe and Brazil. In 1856 he entered the Chamber of Deputies, where he represented Rio Grande do Sul until 1873. Mauá's economic liberalism and his far-flung activities caused resentment in both Brazil and Uruguay and aroused opposition in traditional economic sectors. These factors and the losses he incurred in the Río de la Plata region during the PARAGUAYAN WAR (1864–1870) were allegedly among the causes of the decline of his fortunes in the early 1870s, which ended in bankruptcy in 1878. During his last years, powerless and obscure, he gained a living for his family through a modest investment business.   ROBERT CONRAD

MAXIMILIAN (1832–1867). Austrian archduke and Emperor of Mexico. Ferdinand Maximilian Joseph, younger brother of Emperor Francis Joseph of Austria, was born in Vienna on July 6, 1832. Trained for a career in the Navy, he later became Governor of Lombardy-Venetia. In 1857 he married Charlotte (Carlota, 1840–1927), daughter of Leopold I of Belgium. As the French intervention in Mexico took form, Maximilian was considered a candidate for the Mexican throne. The invitation was formally offered by a Mexican Junta of Notables in July 1863, after the French had occupied Mexico City. A delegation was sent to Miramar, Maximilian's home near Trieste, to present the invitation, and in April of the following year the Archduke accepted. He and Charlotte arrived in Mexico City in June. Supported by the French Army, Maximilian set about establishing his control over Mexico but ran into difficulty from all sides: his liberalism alienated the Mexican Catholic hierarchy, overtures to Mexican republicans generally were of no avail, and the French soon grew weary of their Mexican venture and planned to withdraw.

Charlotte returned to Europe in mid-1866 to try to convince Napoleon III to maintain his support, but she met with failure and lost her mind. Many of Maximilian's military and civilian advisers, both Mexican and foreign, tried to induce him to abdicate. Instead he decided to fight, and with his Austro-Mexican Conservative Army he made an effort to hold the empire together. After his capture by the Republican Army at Querétaro in May 1867, he was tried by a court-martial and sentenced to death. Despite many appeals throughout the world for clemency, he was executed by a firing squad on June 19, 1867.

CHARLES R. BERRY

MAYAS. The ancient Mayas are known to us almost exclusively through the efforts of archaeologists. Because their hieroglyphic inscriptions have not yet been adequately translated, little is known of their history. This grave imbalance in our knowledge is only partially redressed by our possession of such works as Bishop Diego de LANDA's *Relación de las cosas de Yucatán* (written 1566), the *Popul Vuh,* the *Annals of the Cakchiquels,* the *Title of the Lords of Totonicapán,* and the *Books of Chilam Balam.* These works, all written after the Spanish conquest, in any case relate facts and surmises only from the late period when Mexican influences were strong; they say little or nothing about the more important Classic period.

In spite of this deficiency, the material remaining tells us a lot. There are indications that Mayan civilization originated under the impact of the La Venta culture of the Veracruz and Tabasco lowlands (*see* OLMECS). The concept of a ceremonial center, jaguar symbolism, the stela cult, hieroglyphic writing, stone incense burners, cotton clothing, and an involved calendric system are undoubted exports from that area.

History. The area inhabited by the Mayas, while extensive, was relatively compact. It can be usefully divided into three zones, which also in a very rough and casual way correspond to three chronological periods archaeologically defined.

(1) The south (called the Guatemalan Highlands) includes the cordillera, or volcanic uplands, in Guatemala and the country declining to the shores of the Pacific. In Middle and Late Preclassic times (600 B.C.– A.D. 200) proto-Mayas in the area were already defining their civilization, centering it around the great and as yet only partially excavated site of Kaminaljuyú.

(2) The center (called the Southern Lowlands) is roughly the southern half of the peninsula of Yucatán. It is an area of rolling hills, in part covered with tropical forests; in the popular mind this is the region *par excellence* of Mayan splendor. Here have been discovered and unearthed the great ceremonial centers TIKAL, Uaxactun, Piedras Negras, Palenque, and, just to the southeast, COPÁN, Quiriguá, and many more. These sites are from the Classic period (300–900), and taken together they reveal a civilization artistically sophisticated and confident of itself.

In the early part of the Classic period the Mayan sites in the Guatemalan Highlands came under powerful influences from the Mexican city TEOTIHUACÁN far to the northwest. They were thus bastardizing their culture at the very moment when the sites on the Southern Lowlands were embarking on an isolated and unique style of life, little influenced by the outside. At the end of the Classic period and after an amazing *floruit* of 600 years all these great ceremonial centers in the Southern Lowlands were almost simultaneously abandoned to the encroachments of the jungle.

The suddenness of this collapse has puzzled scholars. Epidemic has been advanced as a cause. Other factors suspected have been soil exhaustion, climatic change, conquest, civil war, and social senility. While none of these can be dismissed out of hand, there is much to commend in Sylvanus G. Morley's belief that the flight of population from the sites must be connected with the failure of the priesthood to retain the loyalties of the people whose surplus labor and religious interest they monopolized. S. F. de Borhegyi presents an interesting modification of this theory: he speculates that the social system broke down when the increasing size of the ceremonial center forced a swelling population in the surrounding villages to subdivide and establish daughter villages farther and farther removed from the ceremonial center. Inconvenience of commutation to the major ceremonial center then forced the substitution of even smaller and more locally oriented centers. This decentralization ended with the withering of the major centers. However, the new local cult centers were unable to carry the great inherited load of cult, astronomical calculation, and administration of labor, and they in turn disappeared. However, the suddenness of the collapse at the end of the Classic period is not easily explained by any theory. What can be stated is that the baroque complications of Classic Mayan culture must have been finally beyond the comprehension of the Mayan peasant upon whose surplus MAIZE and labor it rested.

(3) The north (called the Northern Lowlands) is a limestone plain in northern Yucatán devoid of surface runoff and bearing a scrubby growth quite unlike the rain forest to the south. Mayan sites appear here as early as they do in the center but do not bear comparison with them either in variety or in esthetic merit. What is striking, however, about these northern sites is the heavy Mexican influence that affected them at the beginning of the Postclassic era (900–1527). Actual invasion by NAHUATL-speaking TOLTECS is certain. These warlike people from the city of Tula brought with them their full paraphernalia of war, human sacrifice, *tzompantli* (skull-rocks), Chacmools (statues of reclining figures), and the overriding cult of QUETZAL-COATL (in Mayan, Kukulcán). The city of CHICHÉN ITZÁ particularly attests to Toltec domination. The extension of Toltec influences was at the same time also being felt among the Mayas of the Guatemalan Highlands.

It is at this point that a few sparse historical items become available. In the north a Toltec group known as the Itzás moved in under their leader Kukulcán, seizing the Mayan site of Chichén Itzá and splendidly reformulating it as another Tula. When Chichén Itzá declined, Toltec power moved west to Mayapán, which was a true city enclosed by a defensive wall. The Itzás had a checkered career after they lost Chichén Itzá, finally moving south into Petén, where they endured in a crude independence until conquered by the Spaniards in 1697. But Mayan civilization as a culture able to build magnificent sites and carry on calendric observations had disintegrated well before the coming of the first Spaniards. Even a much-reduced Mayapán had fallen a century before the Spanish conquest, and the Mayas whom Pedro de ALVARADO met in the Guatemalan Highlands were also radically weakened.

Conquest of the Mayas by the Spaniards was arduous and fitful. Lack of precious metals and of large concentrated populations rendered the area unattractive to the typical conquistador. Though the first white man was cast ashore in eastern Yucatán in 1511, conquest was not attempted until 1527, by Francisco de Montejo, one of the trusted captains of Cortés. The Mayas reacted vigorously and kept the small Spanish contingents constantly engaged until 1534. That year Montejo withdrew his forces, depleted by the defections of those who had heard of the recent fabulous successes of the PIZARRO brothers in Peru. In 1541 Francisco de Montejo's son, of the same name, renewed Spanish efforts to control Yucatán, founded the capital city of Mérida in 1542, and received the final surrender of the stubborn Mayan chiefs of Yucatán in 1546. (The splintered Mayan tribes of the Guatemalan Highlands had been subdued by Pedro de Alvarado by 1528.)

Social organization. The most significant social fact about the ancient Mayas was their settlement pattern. Mayan farming groups appear to have clustered in small village-type communities widely scattered about in the bush or the forest and practicing slash-and-burn agriculture. Their surplus labor, which appears to have been considerable, supported the imposing ceremonial centers whose ruins are now so well known. These aggregations of burial mounds, temples, and sacred precincts were not true cities for they were not permanent places of residence and work. Rather they were centers where powerful priesthoods officiated and to which the dispersed population was summoned to participate in periodic and varied rituals and building projects. Among the masses there must have been part-time specialists in masonry and the graphic and plastic arts whose anonymous donated labor built and decorated such wonderful sites as Tikal, Piedras Negras, Copán, and Chichén Itzá.

Religion. In spite of the plethora of remains in the cult centers, surprisingly little is known about the Mayan religion. The burning of the Mayan codices by Bishop de Landa in the sixteenth century effectively closed us off from an adequate knowledge of the Mayan pantheon; as a consequence much of what appears in popularizations concerning the Mayan religion is suppositious. A few statements can be made. A god of rarefied priestly formation was Hunab Ku, whom the priests cast in the role of creator. More impressive, because more concrete, was Itzamná, a Jovian figure (perhaps originally a personification of the sky) who lorded it over the other gods. He was benevolent and had varied characteristics. His name means "iguana house," and J. E. S. Thompson speculates that it refers to the universe conceived of as a dwelling constructed of the body of a cosmic dragon. Itzamná controlled the waters in the sky and had very close connections with Kinich Ahau, the sun god. When conceived of as Kinich Ahau, he had as his consort the ambivalent goddess Ixchel, who may have been the moon and patroness of women; she was also the mistress of floods and destroying waters. Chac, the rain god of the peasants, was important to the Mayas, especially to those of the Northern Lowlands, where rain was seasonally scarce. The maize god was represented as a handsome young man. Ah Puch, the god of death, had all the sinister qualities expected of a lord of the underworld. Kukulcán (the god of that name and not the earthly ruler) was probably the lord of the winds and was intimately associated with the rain god. Many other deities are known by name, but trustworthy information about them is generally lacking.

Conception of time. Few myths concerning the gods have been preserved, possibly because of the overshadowing sense of time possessed by the Mayas. Time to the Mayas had the quality of the divine; in fact they shared with other peoples of Mesoamerica the myth of the destruction of previous aeons and subsequent reactivations of the universe. The Mayas believed that each day, year, and *katun* (sacred period, consisting of 7,200 days, or approximately 20 years) possessed its own complexion of good or evil.

This preoccupation with time led to priestly speculations of major importance, which in turn created the well-known stela cult. At the end of each *katun* a dated commemorative stone stela, often copiously decorated in relief, was erected in the ceremonial center. Later some of the centers even erected stelae marking shorter time periods, such as halves and quarters of the *katun*. Over these periodic and sequential parts of the sacred realm of time successive gods presided. The notational system that placed events in a chronological schema was of admirable ingenuity. Positional notation and the zero sign were used by the Mayas at the beginning of the Classic period, though almost certainly these arithmetical tools had been passed on to them by the peoples of the La Venta culture.

There were four important cycles in Mayan calendrics: the solar year (365 days), the Sacred Round, or *tzolkin* (260 days), the Venus cycle (584 days), and a lunar series by which eclipses could be predicted. The combination of the first two revolving on each other gave a sacred century of approximately 52 years, generally referred to as the Calendar Round.

While it is possible for us to read the hieroglyphics that relate to dating, we are not so fortunate with regard to the remainder of the signs. Advances in decipherment of meaning are slowly being made, but there is still no certainty that the equivalents in the Mayan tongue will ever be known. The earliest Mayan glyphs come from the Preclassic period in the Guatemalan Highlands. Whatever its origins, Mayan writing is the most elaborate and sophisticated of all such systems in Mesoamerica.

Technology. Lacking the wheel and metallurgy, Mayan technology was primitive. This did not affect, however, the elaboration of Mayan architecture. The stone temples were undoubtedly modeled on the humble thatched hut, which was the common domicile then as now, but they were perched on pyramidal substructures, sometimes of great height, thereby acquiring dignity. Mayan architecture is characterized by interior corbeled vaulting, narrow transverse rooms, the lavish use of mortar and stucco, rubble fill within the walls, a strip of facade molding at median height, exotic roof combs and flying facades, stelae placed most often at the foot of stairs, rectangular plazas partially enclosed by shrines, and causeways connecting sacred areas. The arch was not known. Ball courts, astronomical observatories, and sweathouses, while offering variety, were integrated parts of whole religious complexes.

The arts. In the arts, the Mayas must be placed in the front ranks not only for excellence but for virtuosity. Their masterworks were produced in many genres—in the relief carving of Tikal and Piedras Negras, the full-round stone sculpture of Copán, the easy and lovely frescoes of Bonampak, the delicacy of Palenque stucco modeling, and the detail of the Jaina clay figurines.

Bibliography. S. G. Morley and G. W. Brainerd, *The Ancient Maya,* 3d ed., Stanford, Calif., 1956; F. C. Scholes and R. L. Roys, *The Maya Chontal Indians of Acalan-Tixchel,* 2d ed., Norman, Okla., 1968; H. J. Spinden, *A Study of Maya Art, Its Subject Matter and Historical Development,* Cambridge, Mass., 1913; J. E. S. Thompson, "Maya Hieroglyphic Writing," *Handbook of Middle American Indians,* vol. III, Austin, Tex., 1965, pp. 632–658; id., *Maya History and Religion,* Norman, Okla., 1970; A. M. Tozzer (ed.), *Landa's Relación de las Cosas de Yucatán: A Translation,* Cambridge, Mass., 1941.

BURR C. BRUNDAGE

MDB. *See* MOVIMENTO DEMOCRÁTICO BRASILEIRO.

MEDELLÍN. City of Colombia. Located in the valley of Aburrá among the highlands of the Cordillera Occidental, Medellín contains approximately 1 million inhabitants. It has a benign climate, with an average mean temperature of 55°F, as well as abundant water and extensive hydroelectric resources. These, together with the enterprise of its inhabitants, have made the city and its surrounding satellite towns Colombia's most important industrial complex. Medellín's main industry is textiles, but the city's 1,870 factories also produce metal furniture, foodstuffs, tobacco products, liquor, chinaware, cement, rubber goods, and electric products.

The city is the capital of the department of ANTIOQUIA and the seat of its archdiocese. Medellín's location is such as to dominate almost all its hinterland, and communications by road, rail, and boat are generally adequate. Medellín, founded in 1616 by Francisco Herrera Campuzano, since the late colonial period has been the heartland of the Antioquian region and the spiritual capital of Antioquia, Caldas, and Risaralda Departments. It is also the educational center for northwestern Colombia, containing 5 universities, 80 normal schools, and 266 secondary schools; in addition, more than 300,000 children attend primary school in Medellín.

Despite the industrial growth of Medellín, the strong civic spirit of its citizens has preserved much of the beauty of its location, and its thousands of well-kept gardens, many filled with exquisite orchids, have given Medellín the fitting title of City of Flowers.

J. LEÓN HELGUERA

MÉDICI, EMÍLIO GARRASTAZU (1905–   ). President of Brazil (1969–1974). Before reaching the Presidency at the age of sixty-three, Médici had spent his entire life as a professional soldier. Born in Bagé, Rio Grande do Sul, he entered military school in Pôrto Alegre at twelve, enlisted in the Army at eighteen, and was commissioned a lieutenant in the cavalry at twenty-one. Displaying no interest in politics, he received routine assignments and promotions until he attended the Army's General Staff College during World War II. Thereafter, he held a series of general staff appointments as an intelligence officer.

Médici became a general in 1961. He supported the revolution of March 31, 1964, from his post as commander of the Military School, and was assigned as Military Attaché in Washington by the first revolutionary government. Under President Arthur da COSTA E SILVA, Médici held Cabinet rank for two years as chief of the National Intelligence Service and then was given command of the powerful Third Army in Rio Grande do Sul. Selected by the military high command in October 1969 to succeed Costa e Silva in the Presidency, Médici was nominated by the majority party, the ALIANÇA RENOVADORA NACIONAL, elected by Congress on October 25, and inaugurated five days later for the term ending March 15, 1974. As President he reiterated the regime's dedication to economic progress and national integration and launched the Trans-amazonian Highway project in order to promote the occupation and development of the vast basin of the Amazon River.   ROLLIE E. POPPINO

MEDINA, JOSÉ TORIBIO (1852–1930). Chilean scholar. A man of outstanding achievement, Medina was the author of more than 400 works in the fields of bibliography, history, literary criticism, folklore, geography, numismatics, biography, anthropology, and natural history. On several visits to Europe, in particular to Spain, he collected or copied an immense number of manuscripts relating to Chilean and Latin American history. Perhaps his most notable works were the series of detailed histories of the branches of the Inquisition (*see* INQUISITION, HOLY OFFICE OF THE) in the Spanish colonies and his minutely accurate bibliographies of the output of the Spanish American and Philippine printing presses of the colonial period. Another of his important bibliographical works is the seven-volume *Biblioteca Hispanoamericana, 1493–1810* (1898–1907). Many of these works were printed by Medina on his own press.

Medina was showered with honors and distinctions by the international academic world. He also held a number of public offices: adviser to the Chilean Army during the WAR OF THE PACIFIC, Secretary of the Chilean Legation in Spain (1884–1886), and mayor of Santiago during the civil war of 1891. His support of President José Manuel BALMACEDA obliged him to live abroad until 1895. Medina donated his enormous collection of books and manuscripts to the National Library of Chile, where it is housed today in an ornately decorated room bearing his name.

SIMON COLLIER

MEDINA ANGARITA, ISAÍAS (1897–1953). Venezuelan army officer and President (1941–1945) who advocated increased political freedom and greater popular participation in politics. A native of the state of Táchira with a good military record, Medina served as Minister of War under Eleazar LÓPEZ CONTRERAS. Unfortunately his good intentions did not make him able to cope with the complexities and pressures of Venezuelan politics in the post-Gómez era. Nevertheless, under his administration a petroleum law that gave even better terms to the nation was adopted in 1943. He also oversaw a constitutional reform making elections to the Chamber of Deputies direct, and he allowed women to vote in municipal elections. In 1945 his administration adopted an AGRARIAN REFORM law. That year Venezuela also declared war on the Axis.

Despite his goodwill and his desire for democratic government, Medina failed to satisfy an important sector of the Army and the leaders of ACCIÓN DEMOCRÁTICA, who combined to overthrow his government on the eve of the elections of 1945. Medina was then sent into exile.

See also PETROLEUM INDUSTRY (VENEZUELA).

JOHN V. LOMBARDI

MEETING OF CONSULTATION OF MINISTERS OF FOREIGN AFFAIRS, FIRST. *See* PANAMA MEETING.

MEETING OF CONSULTATION OF MINISTERS OF FOREIGN AFFAIRS, SECOND. *See* HAVANA MEETING.

MEETING OF CONSULTATION OF MINISTERS OF FOREIGN AFFAIRS, THIRD. *See* RIO DE JANEIRO MEETING.

MEETING OF CONSULTATION OF MINISTERS OF FOREIGN AFFAIRS, SIXTH AND SEVENTH. *See* SAN JOSÉ MEETINGS.

MEETING OF CONSULTATION OF MINISTERS OF FOREIGN AFFAIRS, EIGHTH. *See* PUNTA DEL ESTE MEETING.

MEETING OF CONSULTATION OF MINISTERS OF FOREIGN AFFAIRS, NINTH. *See* WASHINGTON MEETING.

MEIGGS, HENRY (1811–1877). North American railroad builder. A remarkable man, Meiggs was, like Commodore Vanderbilt and John D. Rockefeller, the personification of nineteenth-century Yankee ingenuity. He shared their confidence in the power of material progress to right most wrongs and tried to spread this gospel to Peru, where he became a potent economic and social influence.

Meiggs, a native New Yorker, moved to California in the 1840s. When his ingeniously built economic empire collapsed, he hurriedly left the state and went to Chile, where he acquired a reputation as a daring railroad builder. Called to Peru in the 1860s, he found his grandiose railroad projects wholeheartedly supported by governments which believed that the GUANO-induced economic boom would finance an indefinite amount of public works. Between 1869 and 1872, during the Presidency of José BALTA, Meiggs was asked to initiate an expensive system of railroad building through some of the most difficult terrain on earth. The undertakings themselves were a test of man's vision and ingenuity, but the economic feasibility of such construction was suspect from the beginning, for the railroads could not be operated profitably in the then-foreseeable future. More than 140 million soles were spent on ten projects, the most imposing and expensive ones being the Arequipa-Puno and Callao–La Oroya lines, which cost nearly 60 million soles. The money was obtained by increasing Peru's foreign debt from £4 million in 1870 to £50 million in 1872. Paradoxically, the railroads proved not to be the harbinger of great progress and political peace. On the contrary, this construction brought bankruptcy, civil war, and international humiliation.

ORAZIO A. CICCARELLI

MELGAREJO, MARIANO (ca. 1820–1871). Bolivian dictator. Called by a French biographer "the romantic tyrant" and by his enemies "the scourge of God," Melgarejo was the most notorious of a long series of *caudillos* who dominated Bolivia during most of the nineteenth century. He joined the Army when he was seventeen, and during the civil wars among *caudillos* he rose steadily from private to sergeant to officer to become the country's youngest general. He became an important supporter of Manuel BELZÚ, who controlled Bolivia during the 1850s and early 1860s. Finally turning against his patron, Melgarejo seized power for himself in 1864.

During most of his seven years in power, Melgarejo

was faced with rebellions in various parts of the country. He was forced to move from city to city, dealing with recalcitrants. Those who failed in their revolts against him were submitted to ferocious cruelty. His companion during most of this time was his mistress, Juana Sánchez, who reportedly matched him in cruelty. Melgarejo did not allow any concepts of loyalty to Juana to interfere with his seduction of other women, who not infrequently were ladies of the best families.

A number of Melgarejo's acts had important consequences after his period in power. He sold disputed lands to Brazil. He granted, for a price, rights along the coast to Chilean entrepreneurs who wanted to exploit the rich nitrate deposits in the province of Atacama. Disputes over these grants about a decade later led to the WAR OF THE PACIFIC, as a result of which Chile deprived Bolivia of Atacama and its port, Antofagasta.

Also of major significance for Bolivia's future was Melgarejo's onslaught on Indian communal lands. In spite of extensive land grants made by the Spanish crown to the conquistadores and their descendants and of land seizures carried out by early *caudillos* during the first decades of independence, a large part of the ALTIPLANO (high plateau) remained in Indian hands when Melgarejo came to power. He proceeded to seize these lands ruthlessly on a large scale and to sell them to the highest bidders. This began a process that within a few decades was to deprive virtually all Indians of the Bolivian altiplano of their land.

Melgarejo was overthrown by a military uprising in 1871.

ROBERT J. ALEXANDER

MELLA, JULIO ANTONIO (1905–1929). Cuban Communist leader. A gifted speaker and organizer with a magnetic personality, Mella first rose to prominence in the movement for university reform. In 1923 he organized the first National Congress of Students. While Mella was editing the periodical *Juventud,* his leftist political leanings were strengthened by his association with Carlos Baliño, a veteran promoter of Marxian socialism who had recently embraced bolshevism. With Baliño, Mella became a cofounder of the Cuban Communist party in 1925, and he was elected its first secretary-general.

Mella took charge of the education of party members and gave weekly classes in political instruction in Havana labor unions. He also promoted student agitation against the dictatorship of President Gerardo MACHADO. Within a few months he was arrested on a bomb-plot charge after leading a student strike that shut down the University of Havana. While in prison Mella organized a nineteen-day hunger strike that attracted national and international publicity. Shortly thereafter he was deported to Mexico, where he engaged in anti-Machado propaganda and became active in the Mexican Communist party, briefly serving as its secretary-general.

On January 10, 1929, Mella was assassinated on the streets of Mexico City. The question of whether he met death at the hands of Machado's police agents or at those of a rival Communist faction is unresolved. Since his death Mella has become a hero of the Cuban Communist party and holds similar status under the revolutionary government of Fidel CASTRO.

DAVID A. CRAIN

MELO FRANCO, AFRÂNIO DE (1870–1943). Brazilian diplomat and politician. A native of Paracatú, Minas Gerais, and a member of the São Paulo law school class of 1890, Melo Franco began his career as a public prosecutor in his home state. He was Secretary to the Brazilian Legation in Montevideo in 1896. Returning to Minas Gerais, he took an active role in politics, being elected in 1902 to the state legislature and in 1906 to the first of several successive terms in the national Congress. In the years 1918–1919 he was Minister of Transportation in the Cabinet of acting President Delfim Moreira. President Artur da Silva BERNARDES appointed Melo Franco head of the Brazilian delegation to the Fifth International Conference of American States, held in Santiago in 1923, and shortly thereafter sent him to Geneva as Ambassador to the League of Nations, a post he retained until Brazil's withdrawal from the world body in 1926.

One of the leaders of the Liberal Alliance, which backed Getúlio VARGAS's unsuccessful campaign for the Presidency of Brazil in 1930, Melo Franco endorsed the revolution by which Vargas came to power later that year (*see* REVOLUTION OF 1930). He served as Minister of Foreign Affairs under Vargas until 1933, but his greatest diplomatic triumph came with the settlement of the Leticia dispute between Colombia and Peru shortly after he left the Foreign Ministry. Melo Franco represented Brazil at the LIMA CONFERENCE in 1938 and was presiding officer of the Inter-American Juridical Committee at the time of his death.

ROLLIE E. POPPINO

MÉNDEZ MONTENEGRO, JULIO CÉSAR (1915–). President of Guatemala (1966–1970). A civilian, Méndez was elected in 1966 as the presidential candidate of the leftist Revolutionary party (PR) in substitution for his assassinated brother. He took office on July 1, 1966. Méndez offered amnesty to the guerrillas and inaugurated a Five-Year Plan for socioeconomic reform, particularly in rural areas, in order to correct conditions that were exploited by the guerrillas to attract support. The guerrillas spurned the offer, convinced that their goals could be reached only by revolutionary activity.

Méndez also prepared the "iron fist" he had promised as the alternative to amnesty. He appointed tough Col. Carlos ARANA to command the counterinsurgency operation. Advised by United States Green Berets, Arana launched a punishing offensive against the guerrillas, coupled with an Army civic action program to undermine their support. Later he abandoned civic action as too slow and organized paramilitary units of peasants thought to be linked with Mano Blanca (White Hand), the rightist terrorist group. Action in the hills accompanied violence in the city, where right and left matched outrage with outrage. When Arana was linked with a Mano Blanca abduction of the Archbishop of Guatemala to discredit the government, Méndez removed him from command and sent him abroad. Among the murder victims in the capital were the Ambassadors of the United States and West Germany.

Arana returned in 1970 for the presidential campaign. He was lightly regarded, but the violence and terror enhanced the appeal of his law-and-order stance. In the March election he won a surprising plurality, and the PR-dominated legislature dutifully elected him President for the second consecutive constitutional succession.

See also PERALTA AZURDIA, Enrique.

WILLIAM J. GRIFFITH

MENDOZA, ANTONIO DE (1490–1552). First Viceroy of New Spain. Antonio de Mendoza is credited with establishing the foundations of viceregal rule in Mexico between 1535 and 1550. His superb political skills, his understanding of the possible limits to his power, his enjoyment of the confidence of the King, and his large personal entourage made it possible for him to survive many threats to his position.

Born to an aristocratic family in Granada, Antonio de Mendoza began his career as a diplomat at the court of CHARLES I. He undertook missions to Flanders and to Hungary before his appointment as Viceroy of New Spain. As an administrator, Mendoza displayed remarkable talents, changing existing legislative and judicial procedures in order to facilitate the execution of royal policies. He fostered both Spanish and Indian local governmental institutions and reformed the operation of the treasury by improving record keeping, organizing the collection of tribute, and establishing the first mint. He encouraged silver mining by sponsoring mining laws (which were codified in 1550) and establishing a foundry in Mexico City in 1539. Mendoza attempted to enforce better treatment of the Indians by regulating the conditions of their labor and by hearing their grievances regularly. He established a school at Tlaltelolco for the education of the sons of the Indian nobility. However, he opposed the abolition of the ENCOMIENDA, for he believed that Spain could not colonize the New World without the use of forced Indian labor.

In order to increase economic activity in New Spain as well as on his own lands, Mendoza imported merino sheep and established the first center for the weaving of woolen cloth. The exploration of the northern area of New Spain and the conclusion of the conquest of Yucatán were carried out under his leadership. In 1551 Mendoza left Mexico to become the Viceroy of Peru, but served there only a year before his death.

EDITH B. COUTURIER

MENDOZA, PEDRO DE (1487–1537). Founder of the first settlement of Buenos Aires. Pedro de Mendoza was born in Almería, Spain, of a wealthy family with influence at the court of Emperor Charles V (King CHARLES I). A gentleman of the royal household and a veteran of the Italian wars, Mendoza was one of the few wellborn conquistadores. In exchange for financing an expedition, Mendoza was commissioned to settle the RÍO DE LA PLATA region, to found three forts, and to take possession of 200 leagues of Chilean coastline below Diego de ALMAGRO's grant. Gentlemen and nobles hastened to sign on as Mendoza assembled one of the best-equipped expeditions ever sent to the Indies, with 11 ships, 100 horses, and 1,200 settlers. The expedition set sail in August 1535 and paused for refitting at Rio de Janeiro, where Mendoza's suspicious and jealous nature prompted him to order the murder of his second in command, Juan Osorio.

Mendoza's fleet arrived at the south bank of the Río de la Plata in 1536 and founded Santa María del Buen Aire a short distance from the present site. As the Spaniards built their mud-hut fort and village, they deplored the lack of sedentary Indians suitable for enslavement. The local Querandí tribe was nomadic, and its members fiercely resisted Spanish attempts to force them to supply food and labor. The Querandí besieged the starving community, and the syphilis-racked Mendoza lost heart after stout resistance. He abandoned the settlement and died en route to Spain. Meanwhile, members of Mendoza's expedition had founded Asunción (1537).

WILLIAM S. DUDLEY

MENNONITES IN PARAGUAY. Beginning in 1926 Paraguay accepted a large number of German-origin Mennonites from Canada and Russia as immigrants. Settling on a community basis, they were attracted to Paraguay by offers of cheap or free land, freedom from military service, and general autonomy in most matters. In return, the Mennonites were to settle the empty and often hostile or contested frontier regions. The three large CHACO settlements of Menno (1926), Fernheim (1930), and Neuland (1947) had a combined initial complement of 6,143 settlers. Despite the brutal environment they have made the Chaco productive and an integral part of Paraguay's economic life for the first time. By 1958 Paraguay contained more than 12,000 Mennonites, of whom 8,672 lived in the Chaco. Other Mennonite colonies in eastern Paraguay are Friesland (1958 population, 955), Volendam (1,067), Bergthal (700), and Sommerfeld (700).

The Mennonites comprise the largest single coherent foreign community in Paraguay, and despite their charitable missions and their fruitful agricultural labor, which has gained them respect, they willingly stand apart from their Paraguayan neighbors and Paraguayan society. With their different creed, language, and customs, they will no doubt be considered foreigners for a long while to come.

JOHN HOYT WILLIAMS

MENOCAL, MARIO GARCÍA (1866–1941). President of Cuba (1913–1921). Menocal was forced at an early age to emigrate with his parents during the TEN YEARS' WAR (1868–1878) for Cuban independence. While in exile, he was educated in the United States, obtaining an engineering degree from Cornell University. In 1895 he returned to Cuba and actively participated in the renewed revolution against Spanish control (*see* WAR FOR CUBAN INDEPENDENCE). Following the Spanish-American War General Menocal held minor public posts under the United States military government and later served as the successful manager of a large sugar plantation for a North American firm.

Menocal rose to national prominence in the Conservative party and made an unsuccessful bid for the Presidency in 1908. In 1912 the Conservatives under Menocal returned to power. Assuming office in 1913 following a corruption-tainted Liberal administration, Menocal's "reform-minded" administration ultimately proved to be susceptible to the shortcomings of its predecessor. In 1916 he won a second term amid outcries of electoral fraud that culminated in an unsuccessful Liberal revolt and threats of intervention by United States military forces.

Strong-arm rule, vote fraud, and graft characterized Menocal's second administration. In foreign affairs he cooperated closely with the United States during World War I. At this time Cuba enjoyed unparalleled economic prosperity caused by inflated wartime sugar prices, but a ruinous financial crash occurred in Menocal's last year in office. After the end of his second presidential term in 1921 Menocal continued to exercise a substantial influence in Conservative and national politics.   DAVID A. CRAIN

MERA, JUAN LEÓN (1832–1894). Ecuadorian poet, novelist, and conservative politician. Mera was born in Ambato and died in nearby Atocha. He is best remembered as the author of *Cumandá* (1879), a romantic novel. A self-taught man, he spent most of his early life in rural communities with his mother, who had been abandoned by the boy's father before his birth. At twenty he spent a short time in Quito studying painting. Then he went to Atocha, where he began to publish in local newspapers. In 1858 he published his first book of poems, called *Poesías*. The following year he became a lieutenant in the militia.

In 1860 Mera entered political life with a series of posts that included those of treasurer for the province of Tungurahua and secretary of the Council of Government headed by Gabriel GARCÍA MORENO. He represented Ambato in the Constituent Assembly of 1861, and his good relations with García Moreno continued during the latter's administration. The last office he held was that of Minister of Finance, in 1891.

However, it is as a writer that Mera is usually remembered. He wrote several short novels, including *Entre dos tías y un tío* (1889), a *novela de costumbres* (local-color novel), but it was *Cumandá* that won him international status. Though praised by such Spanish writers as Juan Valera and José María de Pereda, it remains a romantic novel with the weaknesses of the genre as well as a few defects of its own.

GERARDO SÁENZ

MERCADO COMÚN CENTROAMERICANO. *See* CENTRAL AMERICAN COMMON MARKET.

MESA DA CONSCIÊNCIA E ORDENS. Portuguese tribunal responsible for religious affairs and the administration of military orders in the colonies and the mother country. Established in 1532 and composed of both lay and ecclesiastical officials, it was intended to advise the monarch on all matters relating to his conscience. In 1576 the University of Coimbra came under its jurisdiction.   KENNETH R. MAXWELL

MESTIZO. In Spanish America a person of mixed racial origin, particularly one of white and Indian ancestry. The name is derived from the Low Latin *misticius* (mixed). During the colonial period mestizos, though included among the CASTAS, did not suffer as many legal disabilities as did Indians, blacks, and mulattoes. However, they were ordinarily viewed as shiftless and troublesome, in part because they were usually of illegitimate birth. Even so, a Euromestizo (a person predominantly European in racial and ethnic qualities) might be regarded legally and socially as a white, particularly if his parents were married; on the other hand, an Indomestizo (one whose culture and physical appearance were predominantly Indian) would probably be classified as an Indian.

Although legal discrimination against mestizos ended after independence, some Spanish Americans continued to denigrate both Indian and mestizo. However, by

the 1920s this position was being undermined by the development of NATIONALISM and by the conviction that Europe was decadent and that the center of Western civilization was shifting to the Americas. In Mexico, for example, José VASCONCELOS stressed the newness and uniqueness of the American peoples and the positive features of the Indian contribution as he prophesied the emergence of a "cosmic race" in Latin America. Whereas some Spanish American writers espoused INDIGENISMO by exalting the Indian and his culture, most saw the future of their country in *mestizaje* (race mixture), although the concept eluded precise definition, especially in its cultural sense.

In the Andean countries of South America the word CHOLO is sometimes used as a synonym for mestizo. In Brazil the Portuguese word *mestiço* is a generic term for mixed-bloods of all types; during the colonial period a person of Indian-white origin was referred to as a CABOCLO or a MAMELUCO.   ALAN KOVAC

MEXICAN REVOLUTION. The Mexican revolution began in 1910 after Francisco I. MADERO disavowed the regime of Porfirio DÍAZ in his Plan of San Luis Potosí and called for revolution (*see* SAN LUIS POTOSÍ, PLAN OF). Díaz was forced to resign the following May, but his departure merely marked the end of the first phase of the revolution (*see* CARRANZA, Venustiano; HUERTA, Victoriano; VILLA, Francisco). The most violent period of the revolution came to an end in 1920 and was followed by a decade of consolidation under the so-called Northern dynasty headed by Álvaro OBREGÓN and Plutarco Elías CALLES. During the administration of Lázaro CÁRDENAS (1934–1940), Mexico experienced a period of radical social change, highlighted by the distribution of millions of hectares of land to the peasantry, government support for the aspirations of industrial workers, and the nationalization of the oil industry on March 18, 1938.

The revolution assumed a different character in southern Mexico than it did in the north. In the south the revolution was related to the nineteenth-century caste wars; from this point of view, Vicente GUERRERO and Juan Álvarez can be considered precursors of Emiliano ZAPATA. To be precise, however, the revolution of the south should really be considered the revolution of the southwest since southeastern Mexico remained almost aloof from it; in fact, the state of Oaxaca, which had preserved a large part of its communal property, went so far as to declare itself neutral. In the north, a region that had experienced great economic development during the era of Porfirio Díaz, a wide range of social groups took part in the revolution: landowners with a bourgeois mentality, such as the Madero family; small rural proprietors, such as Álvaro Obregón; a dependent middle class; migratory workers from the Laguna District; and cowboys and peons, among whom Villa recruited many of his followers. Also worthy of note was the presence of numerous lawyers and professors. Later, workers and artisans participated in large, well-organized groups: the pro-Carranza "red battalions" of the syndicalist Casa del Obrero Mundial (House of the World Worker).

Among the most important causes of the revolution were the inequitable distribution of land and the domination of key sectors of the Mexican economy by foreigners. On the eve of the revolution in 1910, Mexico's 200 million hectares (500 million acres) of territory were distributed approximately as follows: public lands, 10 percent; latifundia, 54 percent; small private holdings, 20 percent; communal holdings, 6 percent; and uncultivated lands, 10 percent. One-fourth of the national domain was in the hands of foreigners, mainly Americans in the north and Spaniards or descendants of Spaniards in the central part of the country.

In general, foreigners dominated the most important activities of the Porfirian economy. In 1911 they owned 98 percent of the railroad shares, 97.5 percent of the petroleum shares, and 97.4 percent of the mining shares. The proportion of stock held by citizens of the United States was as follows: mining, 78 percent; railroads, 72.4 percent; foundries, 72.2 percent; and rubber, 68.2 percent. Xenophobia was directed against the Chinese, especially in the north, because they had acquired a comfortable economic position through their industry and frugality. There was also hostility toward Spaniards, not only because it was easy to exploit traditional grudges but also because they were present daily in various roles: as administrators of haciendas, barkeepers, owners of urban pawnshops, and so on. In the international background of the Mexican revolution a struggle over petroleum can be perceived, with the United States pitted against Great Britain, which had been favored by Díaz as a counterweight to the growing economic power of the northern republic.

In these circumstances the political banner unfurled by Madero in 1910—"Effective Suffrage. No Reelection"—served only to unleash broader and more profound aspirations. Meanwhile, supporters of the old regime sarcastically remarked that a more accurate motto for Madero would have been "Effective Looting. No Restitution"; what the masses really needed was "No Poverty and Effective Food."

In writing the constitution of 1917 (see CONSTITUTION OF 1917: MEXICO) the classes that participated in the struggle reconciled their differences; the institutions created in it reflect their relative strength and social role while leaving the door open for future readjustments in an unstable equilibrium. Accordingly, the current predominance of bourgeois interests does not imply the demise of the revolution since it was always bourgeois, except in the south, where emphasis was placed on the defense of communal property. Under Cárdenas the Mexican revolution politically liquidated the hacienda, an act that brought, among other consequences, the destruction of the corporate society inherited from the colonial regime and the establishment of the formal liberty of a society of classes.

See also AGRARIAN REFORM; EJIDO.

Bibliography. Marjorie Ruth Clark, Organized Labor in Mexico, Chapel Hill, N.C., 1934; Howard F. Cline, Mexico: Revolution to Evolution, 1940–1960, London, 1962; Moisés González Navarro, México: El capitalismo nacionalista, Mexico City, 1970; José E. Iturriaga, La estructura social y cultural de México, Mexico City, 1951; Alfonso López Aparicio, El movimiento obrero en México, Mexico City, 1958; Lucio Mendieta y Núñez, El problema agrario en México, 8th ed., Mexico City, 1964; Stanley R. Ross (ed.), Is the Mexican Revolution Dead?, New York, 1966; Nathan L. Whetten, Rural Mexico, Chicago, 1948.

MOISÉS GONZÁLEZ NAVARRO

MEXICAN WAR (1846–1848). War fought between Mexico and the United States that resulted primarily from the annexation of the former Mexican province of Texas to the United States in December 1845. A mission to Mexico undertaken by John Slidell failed because the war party led by Mariano Paredes came to power, and President James K. Polk sent United States troops into disputed territory between the Nueces and Rio Grande Rivers. Hostilities began early in April 1846 along the Rio Grande. There were several campaigns, including Maj. Gen. Zachary Taylor's invasion of northern Mexico, Brig. Gen. Stephen W. Kearny's seizure of New Mexico, and the activities of Capt. John C. Frémont and Commo. John D. Sloat in California. In March 1847, troops under Gen. Winfield Scott took Veracruz and began to march into the interior. As the United States Army approached the Valley of Mexico, several hotly contested battles were fought: Churubusco, Molino del Rey, and Chapultepec. Mexico City fell on September 14, 1847.

Antonio López de SANTA ANNA, in exile when the war began, returned to Mexico in September 1846 and was designated President and commander in chief of the Mexican forces. He opposed Taylor's advance in the north, but after the Battle of Buena Vista he retreated into central Mexico and confronted Scott's invasion. The war was terminated by the Treaty of Guadalupe Hidalgo of February 2, 1848, by which Mexico gave up all claims to Texas and ceded the remainder of its territory between Texas and the Pacific Ocean in exchange for $15 million and the assumption by the United States government of unpaid claims of American citizens (see GUADALUPE HIDALGO, TREATY OF). The last American troops were withdrawn in August 1848.

CHARLES R. BERRY

MEXICO CITY. Capital of Mexico. The pre-Hispanic city TENOCHTITLÁN was founded about 1325 on the principal island of the largest of the lakes in what is commonly called the Valley of Mexico. The Hispanic city was founded on the same site by Hernán CORTÉS in 1521. In both cases the prehistoric name of the spot—Anahuac, which means surrounded by water—corresponded with geographic reality. In the eighteenth century the city's appearance underwent considerable change as numerous public buildings were constructed or renovated. With the nationalization of ecclesiastical properties in 1859, many convents and even some churches were torn down. In their place streets were laid out and houses constructed. During the era of Porfirio DÍAZ (1876–1911) various streets and public buildings were improved, and drainage works begun during the colonial period were completed (1900).

The valley has an area of about 5,000 square miles; it is roughly elliptical, stretching in a north-south direction. The city occupies 87 square miles, but the metropolitan area (the delegaciones Atzacapozalco, Gustavo A. Madero, Ixtacalco, Ixtapalapa, Coyoacán, and Obregón, together with the municipalities Tlalnepantla, Naucalpan, Texcoco, and others) totals approximately 215 square miles. Mexico City is not only the political capital of Mexico and of the Federal District but also the country's geographic, commercial, and intellectual center. As a result, in 1970 this small area held more than 8 million people, or 15 percent of the population of Mexico. This was the largest concentration of human beings at such a high altitude (7,347 feet above sea level) in the world.

MOISÉS GONZÁLEZ NAVARRO

MEXICO SINCE 1821. The birth of an independent Mexico in 1821 was accompanied by overwhelming enthusiasm, but the anarchy that dominated the first thirty-three years of the national period resulted in the diminution of this optimism. During this period four constitutional systems, two centralist and two federalist, were established, in addition to the last dictatorship of Antonio López de SANTA ANNA (1853–1855). Two of the numerous holders of executive power were shot: the emperor Agustín de ITURBIDE and President Vicente GUERRERO, precisely the two men who had been the authors of independence. Only two Presidents served out their full terms: Guadalupe VICTORIA (1825–1829), who headed the first federalist republic; and José Joaquín de Herrera (1848–1851), who ruled during the second federalist republic and surrendered power peacefully to his successor. Throughout these years, from the promulgation of the Plan of Veracruz (December 6, 1822) until the Plan of Ayutla (March 1, 1854), Santa Anna dominated the national scene, and the Conservative statesman Lucas ALAMÁN was correct in writing that the history of the period could properly be called "the history of the revolutions of Santa Anna."

The history of this third of a century is usually summarized by a series of dichotomies: republic against monarchy; federalism against centralism; democracy against oligarchy; the middle class against the clergy, army, and landowners; partisans of the United States against European sympathizers. A simplistic scheme would indicate that the same forces were consistently allied, so that on the one hand there emerged a constellation comprising federalism, a democratic republic, liberalism, and a pro-American bourgeoisie, and on the other a constellation comprising monarchism, a centralized republic, and a conservative, Europeanizing oligarchy.

Mexico obtained its independence in 1821 with Iturbide's Plan of Iguala, but not its liberty; that is, Mexico was separated from Spain, but the status quo was preserved. The efforts of some to preserve the legacy of

Iguala and of others to destroy it engaged the country for a third of a century. This struggle between progress and backwardness, to use the language of Dr. José María Luis MORA, is personified by Mora himself and by Alamán. The principal obstacles to the triumph of progress were the military and the clergy.

The situation created by the continuous civil wars of the period was complicated by Mexico's international struggle. First, it was necessary to save the country from reconquest by Spain, which was supported by the Holy Alliance. Great Britain collaborated with Spanish America by denying its support to Spain, while the United States aided with the MONRÓE DOCTRINE. Mexico's defeat of the Spanish expedition of 1829 constituted the country's only completely successful defense of national territory in the face of foreign invasion. In contrast, the United States, in its westward march to fulfill its "manifest destiny," took advantage of Santa Anna's defeat at San Jacinto in 1836 to support the annexation of Texas in 1845. With Mexico's defeat in the war against the United States in 1847 (*see* MEXICAN WAR), many despaired of the possibility of Mexico's saving itself by its own efforts.

These thirty-three years of apparent anarchy in reality foreshadowed the elements that would come to a head in the struggle initiated in the revolution of Ayutla against Santa Anna. For the first time a profound change in the political life of the country could be perceived, not only because of the language of the Plan of Ayutla but also because of the appearance of a younger generation of Liberals who united with the veteran exponents of liberalism in opposition to an older generation that fought in the Conservative camp.

The fundamental political problem solved during the era of the Reform (*see* REFORM, THE) was that of Mexico's form of government. From this time on the republican-monarchical antinomy was resolved definitively in favor of a republican solution. This aspect of Mexico's struggle coincided with the conflict between Europe (represented primarily by France) and the United States. The collapse of the empire of MAXIMILIAN in 1867 meant that Mexico would remain within the sphere of influence of the northern republic.

As important as the question of Mexico's form of government (and in part mingled with it) was the struggle between the civil and ecclesiastical powers. The timid victory achieved by the moderate Liberals in the constitution of 1857 (*see* CONSTITUTION OF 1857: MEXICO) was strengthened by the reform laws of 1859, the work of the more radical "pure" Liberals. Thus, the reform initiated by Valentín GÓMEZ FARÍAS and Mora in 1833 reached its culmination a quarter of a century later with the establishment of a secular civil power superior to the church.

Mexico emerged from the struggles of the Reform and the empire with the facade of a republican, federal, liberal, and democratic nation. In economic matters, the consecration of complete freedom with respect to property, labor, interest, and enterprise, the conception of self-interest as the motor of the economy, and the desire for unlimited production prefigured some of the elements of modern capitalism converted into partial reality by the era of Porfirio DÍAZ (1876–1911).

With the defeat of Maximilian, the Liberal party, republican by a large majority, undertook direction of the country. The capture of Ciudad Juárez in May 1911

MEXICO

Area: 761,604 sq. mi.   Population: 48,225,238 (1970).

marked the end of the Liberal era, which can be divided into two stages: the restored republic (1867–1876) and the Porfiriato (1876–1911). The victory over the empire gave new hope to a country exhausted by civil war and foreign intervention, even though the hour of triumph also saw disunity within the victorious party and Benito JUÁREZ had to repress several rebellions, among them that of La Noria, led by Díaz.

Upon the death of Juárez on July 18, 1872, Sebastián LERDO DE TEJADA, one of the members of the group called Paso del Norte and President of the Supreme Court, succeeded to the Presidency. On September 25, 1873, Lerdo incorporated the anticlerical reform laws into the constitution of 1857. The same year he defeated a great Indian uprising led by Manuel Lozada and inaugurated the Mexico City–Veracruz railroad. However, Lerdo was unable to prevent the conquest of power by Porfirio Díaz in a second rebellion. Díaz would remain in power for a third of a century.

The Porfiriato can be divided into three stages: pacification (1876–1884), apogee (1885–1905), and crisis (1905–1911). Díaz pacified the country and maintained his power by the use of armed force, but he also won his enemies over through a policy of conciliation. Equally effective in pacification was the economic expansion of Mexico spurred by foreign capital. To encourage foreign investment Díaz secured legislation (June 21, 1885) providing for conversion of the foreign debt. After that he obtained new loans abroad (a total of £31 million through mid-1911) and guaranteed a climate of confidence for foreign investors, to whom the doors of the country were opened ever wider.

The celebration in 1910 of the centenary of the beginning of the independence movement represented the Porfiriato's last opportunity to present a magnificent facade, for the edifice was definitively cracked. Despite the air of self-congratulation that characterized the celebration, the social evils eating away at the country were already known abroad.

The revolution initiated by Francisco I. MADERO in November 1910 triumphed because of the alliance of peasants, workers, and the middle classes (*see* MEXICAN REVOLUTION). The new constitution (*see* CONSTITUTION OF 1917: MEXICO) established the institutions that would give shape to that alliance: a system characterized by a mixed economy that, upon the liquidation of the hacienda, would open the doors to industrialization (*see* INDUSTRY: MEXICO).

An optimistic official balance sheet drawn up on the fiftieth anniversary of the revolution set forth the country's advances since 1910. In the occupational structure, the agrarian population no longer predominated to the extent it had before the revolution, a majority having turned to industry and the service sectors. The gross national product had multiplied five times. A large part of this increase could be attributed to the greater participation of the industrial sector in the total value of national production. By 1960, 2.5 million hectares (6.2 million acres) of land had been irrigated; as a result, Mexico not only could feed itself but could supply raw materials to industry. Mining had ceased to be the principal source of the country's wealth; because of its dependence on international markets, the mining industry, with the exception of iron (*see* IRON AND STEEL INDUSTRY: MEXICO), was rela-

tively stagnant. Although the railroads had made comparatively few gains, in contrast with the Porfirian era, the road network increased from 431 miles in 1925 to about 30,000 miles in 1960, or more than twice the length of the railroads.

Nevertheless, these economic gains were greatly debated, especially after the crisis of 1968. Indeed, it was maintained that Mexico's economic development had been based on the sacrifice of low-income workers. Moreover, this development was achieved thanks to a dangerously high foreign debt, which, together with the domination of technology by foreign firms, had annulled the significance of the fact that the infrastructure (petroleum, railways, electricity, and so on) was in the hands of the state. It also was pointed out that the demographic explosion had counteracted the effectiveness of policies affecting labor (such as the establishment of a minimum wage and, more recently, profit sharing), the agrarian sector (encouragement of the EJIDO), and education (rural schools and literacy programs). In addition, the political stability enthusiastically hailed as one of the great achievements of contemporary Mexico, starting with the creation of the official party in 1929 (*see* PARTIDO REVOLUCIONARIO INSTITUCIONAL), was seen by some as one of the causes of the country's rigidity, impeding the independent life of agrarian and labor groups.

President Luis ECHEVERRÍA (1970–   ) reverted to the nationalism of 1910, which had contained traces of xenophobia and had been strengthened during the administration of Lázaro CÁRDENAS. However, in the alliance of classes that characterized the regime derived from the Mexican revolution, it was a segment of the native bourgeoisie that initiated the new nationalism.

Bibliography. Cincuenta años de Revolución, Mexico City, 1960–62; Daniel Cosío Villegas (ed.), *Historia moderna de México*, Mexico City, 1955–72; Moisés González Navarro, *Raza y tierra*, Mexico City, 1970; Moisés González Navarro and Stanley Ross, *Historia documental de México*, Mexico City, 1964; Jesús Reyes Heroles, *El liberalismo mexicano*, Mexico City, 1957–61; Justo Sierra, *México: Su evolución social*, Mexico City, 1900–02; id., *Juárez: Su obra y su tiempo*, Mexico City, 1905–06.

MOISÉS GONZÁLEZ NAVARRO

MIER [NORIEGA Y GUERRA], [JOSÉ] SERVANDO TERESA DE (1763–1827). Mexican priest and man of letters. Born in Monterrey, Mier entered the Dominican order at an early age and later received a doctorate in theology. On December 12, 1794, he delivered a sermon in Mexico City in which he expressed doubts about certain aspects of the apparition of the Virgin of Guadalupe (*see* GUADALUPE, VIRGIN OF) and asserted that Christianity had been introduced to America by the apostle Thomas long before the Spanish conquest. As a result of this sermon Mier was deprived of his title of doctor and sentenced to banishment and imprisonment in Spain. From 1795 to 1810 he led an adventurous life in Europe, frequently being jailed and just as regularly escaping from captivity.

Upon learning of the uprising of Miguel HIDALGO Y COSTILLA in 1810, Mier went to London, where he devoted himself to the cause of Mexican independence. Having taken part in Francisco Xavier Mina's ill-fated expedition to Mexico in 1817, he was tried by the Inquisition (*see* INQUISITION, HOLY OFFICE OF THE), and after the dissolution of that tribunal in 1820 he was put on board a ship for Spain. However, he escaped in Havana, traveled to the United States, and made his way back to Mexico after independence had been achieved. Suspected of conspiring against the emperor Agustín de ITURBIDE, he was jailed for the last time in 1822. As a member of Mexico's Second Constituent Congress in 1823, he declared himself a partisan of a moderate form of federalism that would deny the attributes of sovereignty to the federated states.

Mier's writings include a two-volume *Historia de la revolución de Nueva España* (1813), the first history of Mexico's independence movement, and two picaresque autobiographical works, generally printed under the title *Memorias*.   HELEN DELPAR

MIGNONE, FRANCISCO (1897–   ). Brazilian pianist and composer of Italian parentage. Most of his works reflect a conscious striving for easy understanding and appreciation. Consequently he draws heavily upon folk and popular musical sources, either by direct quotation or by re-creating the essence of the folk-popular material in a technically refined style. His first successful attempts at composition were in the urban popular musical idiom of his time. He graduated in flute, piano, and composition from the São Paulo Conservatory in 1917. In 1920 he left for Milan for further studies under Vincenzo Ferroni. He then wrote his first opera, *O Contratador de Diamantes* (1921), with a libretto by Gerolamo Bottoni, which premiered in Rio de Janeiro in 1924. Of this work a well-known symphonic piece, *Congada,* was performed in Rio de Janeiro by the Vienna Philharmonic Orchestra under Richard Strauss.

Before Mignone returned to Brazil in 1929, he spent some time in Spain, where he completed his opera *L'innocente,* premiered in Rio in 1928 with great success. His friendship with Mário de ANDRADE influenced his conversion to musical nationalism, which dominated his artistic production from about 1930 to about 1959. During this long period Mignone wrote in many different genres. The chief works of national expression include four *Fantasias Brasileiras* for piano and orchestra (1929–1936); the ballets *Maracatu do Chico-Rei* (1933), *Leilão* (1941), and *O Espantalho* (inspired by two paintings of Cândido PORTINARI); the tone poems of Afro-Brazilian inspiration *Babaloxá* and *Batucajé* (both 1936); the oratorio *Alegrias de Nossa Senhora* for solo, chorus, and orchestra; and numerous piano pieces, among them nine *Lendas Sertanejas* (1923–1940), twelve *Valsas de Esquina* (1938–1943), and twelve *Valsas-Chôros* (1946–1955).

The works of the 1960s reveal Mignone's gradual abandonment of national musical expression. Among these we find six masses for mixed voices *a cappella,* a double concerto for violin, piano, and orchestra (1966), and several sonatas for various media. Compositional processes, such as atonality and serialism, or twelve-tone technique, are used in some of these works in an unorthodox manner.   GERARD H. BÉHAGUE

MINAS GERAIS. With an area of 226,805 square miles (6.9 percent of Brazil's surface area), or roughly the same as the total area of the Iberian Peninsula, Minas Gerais is Brazil's fifth largest state. Climatic conditions range from semiarid in the northern portion to semitropical in the west. The diversified geography, which includes both plains and mountains, supplies not only mineral wealth and fertile farm and pasturelands but also numerous rivers that provide water for agriculture, some transportation routes, and hydroelectric power. However, much of the hydroelectric potential of the state remains to be tapped. In 1970 Minas Gerais was the second most populous state in Brazil, had the largest cattle herd, and was first in steel, cement, and milk production. The state also produces significant portions of Brazil's rice, bean, corn, and coffee output.

The history of Minas Gerais began with the discovery of gold in the late seventeenth century, which was followed by a rapid influx of population and the establishment of numerous villages and towns. Within a few years diamonds also were discovered in large quantity. Although mining continued as the main economic activity until the late eighteenth century, a vigorous agricultural and pastoral economy evolved to supply the demands for food, leather, and animal power in the mining centers. *See* MINING (COLONIAL BRAZIL).

With the collapse of mining, agriculture became the economic mainstay of the province in the nineteenth century. In the twentieth century, industry, especially iron and steel (*see* IRON AND STEEL INDUSTRY: BRAZIL), and banking have joined agriculture to produce the material wealth of the state.

Between 1872 and 1970 the population of the state grew from 2,039,735 to 11,645,092. In the same period the average population density increased from 8.99 per square mile to 51.34 per square mile. In 1970, 47.04 percent of the population resided in rural areas, and 1,106,722 (9.5 percent) made their homes in Belo Horizonte, the capital city. The state's population increase is reflected in the proliferation of municipal governments, which increased in number from 72 in 1872 to 722 in 1970.

LAWRENCE J. NIELSEN

MINING (COLONIAL BRAZIL). The most dramatic and decisive consequence of the exploration of the interior of colonial Brazil was the discovery of gold during the 1690s by *paulista* prospectors. Gold was found initially in the streams along the flanks of the Serra do Espinhaço, which runs north and south between present-day Ouro Prêto and Diamantina across the great interior plateau and forms the watershed between the São Francisco and Paraguay–Río de la Plata river valley systems. Most of the gold was obtained by washing and panning; it was sifted in *bateias* (large, shallow bowls) in which the water and gravel were rotated so that the gold was separated out to sink to the bottom. As the *cascalho* (gravelly subsoil) containing the gold was often under sand, earth, or clay, diggings were necessary, and the owners of slave gangs stood at a considerable advantage. Streams might be diverted to allow access to the placers, and hydraulic machines and troughs constructed to facilitate the sifting of the gold-bearing *cascalho.*

Situated in hostile mountain country, heavily wooded at the beginning of the eighteenth century, the goldfields were several hundred miles inland and difficult of access. By 1700 the overland route from São Paulo was connected to the small coastal town of Parati, south of

Rio de Janeiro, to which it was linked by coastal shipping. From Bahia the mines were reached via Cachoeira, and then inland to the São Francisco River at Arraial de Matias Cardoso, and upriver to the junction with the Rio das Velhas. Within a few years a new, more direct route to Rio de Janeiro was opened from the landward side, crossing the coastal mountain ranges and the valley of the Paraíba to the Bay of Guanabara, where barges linked the end of the mule route at Pôrto Estrella to the city. The news of the discovery spread rapidly once the gold began to arrive regularly in Lisbon. Portuguese immigrants, adventurers, renegade friars, slave owners, and prospectors from the Brazilian littoral flooded into the interior and the turbulent mining camps of Ribeirão do Carmo, Vila Rica de Ouro Prêto, and Sabará in a major gold rush.

In 1718 alluvial gold was accidentally discovered in Cuiabá, and subsequent strikes were made by *paulistas* in Goiás in 1725 and in Guaporé (now Rondônia) in 1734. As had occurred earlier in Minas Gerais, the strikes were followed by gold rushes.

After 1700 gold mining in Minas Gerais was regulated by a mining code promulgated that year which remained in force until the end of the colonial period. The code provided that the first individual to discover gold in an area could select the site of the first two *datas* (mining allotments). The third went to the crown and was immediately auctioned off; the fourth went to the *guarda mor* (King's representative). After the initial distribution of *datas,* miners were free to augment or otherwise modify their holdings.

The crown had the right to a *quinto* (fifth part) of gold production, but collection proved difficult. An attempt by the crown to modify the system of collection in order to increase revenue led to a serious uprising in Vila Rica de Ouro Prêto, the main gold-mining town, in 1720. After the uprising was savagely suppressed, Minas Gerais was placed under a newly formed captaincy with its own Governor, who was provided in the 1730s with a regular military force, the much-feared and respected Minas Dragoons.

During the late 1720s diamonds were discovered in the Tejuco region of Minas Gerais, the Governor of the captaincy, Dom Lourenço de Almeida, at first feigning ignorance as to their identification while busily acquiring as many as possible. The diamond district was demarcated in 1734 and placed under an intendant virtually independent of the Governor of Minas Gerais and the Viceroy in Bahia.

From 1740 to 1772 diamond mining was a government monopoly that could be carried on legally only by contractors. Despite draconian measures to enforce the monopoly, however, illicit mining flourished, its practitioners being known as *garimpeiros*. Starting in 1772, the mines were operated directly on behalf of the crown.

Brazilian gold production was high from the beginning of the eighteenth century until the 1760s, when the falloff was rapid owing to the exhaustion of alluvial deposits. The volume is not easily assessed, as methods of fiscalization varied and there was much fraud and contraband. During the 1750s, when production was probably at its height, the royal *quinto*, which represented a minimum 20 percent of total output, was running at over 100 arrobas of gold per annum (1 arroba = 32 pounds). Diamond production is measured not so much by volume as by the price of cut diamonds on the

Amsterdam market, and the problem for the Portuguese authorities was to restrict output in order to keep prices up.

Bibliography. Charles R. Boxer, *The Golden Age of Brazil, 1695–1750,* Berkeley, Calif., 1962; João Pandiá Calógeras, *As Minas do Brasil e Sua Legislação,* 3 vols., Rio de Janeiro, 1904–05; Manoel Cardozo, "The Brazilian Gold Rush," *Americas,* vol. III, no. 2, October 1946, pp. 137–160; Caio Prado Junior, *The Colonial Background of Modern Brazil,* tr. by Suzette Macedo, Berkeley, Calif., 1969; Carlos Prieto, *Mining in the New World,* New York, 1973; Roberto C. Simonsen, *História Econômica do Brasil, 1500–1820,* 5th ed., São Paulo, 1967; João Camillo de Oliveira Torres, *História da Minas Gerais,* 5 vols., Belo Horizonte, 1962.

KENNETH R. MAXWELL

MINING (COLONIAL SPANISH AMERICA). Gold and silver mining was the most important industry in colonial Spanish America. Great deposits of precious metals, discovered in the Sierra Madre Occidental in New Spain (Mexico) and in the ANDES MOUNTAINS in New Granada (Colombia) and Upper Peru (Bolivia), obviated the need for Spain to exploit extensively other forms of wealth, although tin and copper were mined in Peru, especially during the eighteenth century, and dyestuffs and agricultural products surpassed minerals in value toward the end of the colonial period.

No great bonanzas were discovered before the 1540s. Gold was discovered in Hispaniola by 1500, and Spaniards worked the Aztec mines of Taxco and Pachuca in southern New Spain after 1521, but these mines could not compare with the discoveries made about twenty years later. In 1540 Jorge Robledo, a lieutenant of Sebastián de BENALCÁZAR, found gold at Anserma in the upper Cauca Valley in western New Granada. Within a decade mining camps dotted the Cauca and Magdalena Valleys, which comprised the richest goldfield in Spanish America. In 1545 an Indian llama driver showed his Spanish master silver deposits in the great cone-shaped mountain of POTOSÍ in Upper Peru. Potosí contained fabulous wealth in a half-dozen great veins that ran into the mountain for many miles. A third great strike in 1546 at Zacatecas, New Spain, set off a rush that extended, within a few years, to Guanajuato, where equally valuable silver deposits were found.

At first, Spanish mineowners employed Indians in the mines who had been assigned them as a reward for royal service, but about 1550 the Indians were placed directly under the crown, and a system of labor called the MITA in South America and the REPARTIMIENTO in New Spain was established. About the same time Indian slave labor was abolished. Under the new system, a certain number of Indian males were assigned to the mines from designated villages to work several months on salary. After the sixteenth century the labor system was further modified: in New Spain the tendency was toward free labor and profit sharing; in New Granada Negroes replaced Indians, who were virtually eliminated by disease; and in Upper Peru free labor made strong inroads, although the *mita* persisted until virtually the end of the colonial era.

Few changes were made in the methods of tunneling, the pick and bar work, the carrying of ore on men's backs, and the grinding by mills turned by the power of animals or water. Only in the late eighteenth century were windlasses and drainage pumps developed that made the industry less dependent on simpler forms of power. Refining, however, was improved in 1556 by the introduction of the patio process by Bartolomé de Medina, who used mercury as an amalgamating agent in the Pachuca mines of New Spain. The patio process, also introduced at Potosí after mercury was discovered at Huancavelica in the 1560s, permitted working lower-grade ore and greatly increased the production of silver. Huancavelica and Almadén, Spain, furnished mercury for the mines.

The mining fields stimulated the economy for hundreds of miles around. Potosí drew upon Chile for wine, Córdoba for mules, and Paraguay for yerba maté; livestock were driven into the Cauca-Magdalena Valleys from Ecuador, cacao was brought from the Maracaibo Basin, and cloth was supplied from the textile factories of Bogotá and Tunja. In New Spain grains and tropical fruits were shipped to the mines from Tabasco, Puebla, and the Bajío, and livestock and wine came from the north.

Potosí was the leading silver producer during the colonial period, and annual production there sometimes totaled 7 million pesos before 1635. New Spain produced 2 million pesos yearly, chiefly in silver, until about 1700, while New Granada's production, mainly in gold, varied between 900,000 and 1.7 million pesos. Production rose during the eighteenth century in New Spain and New Granada, as old mines were worked more efficiently and new fields were opened in Nuevo León and Chihuahua in New Spain and in Chocó in western New Granada. New Spain produced between 13 million and 20 million pesos annually from 1750 to 1810, and production in New Granada attained 2 million pesos in certain years. Meanwhile, production in Potosí tended to decline owing to excessively long tunnels, the great Indian revolt of the 1780s led by José Gabriel Condorcanqui TUPAC AMARU, and the official redirection of bullion through Buenos Aires with the establishment of the Viceroyalty of the Río de la Plata in 1776, which ruptured credit relations between Lima merchants and Potosí miners. On the average, the crown exacted a royalty of one-fifth from mining production, and the Spanish Hapsburgs' primacy in Europe depended on the great income from these three mining fields.

Bibliography. P. J. Bakewell, *Silver Mining and Society in Colonial Mexico: Zacatecas, 1546–1700,* New York, 1971; D. A. Brading, *Miners and Merchants in Bourbon Mexico, 1763–1810,* London, 1971; Gwendolin B. Cobb, "Supply and Transportation for the Potosí Mines, 1545–1640," *Hispanic American Historical Review,* vol. XXIX, no. 1, February 1949, pp. 25–45; Nicolás Martínez Arzanz y Vela, *Historia de la villa imperial del Potosí,* Buenos Aires, 1944; Clement G. Motten, *Mexican Silver and the Enlightenment,* Philadelphia, 1950; Carlos Prieto, *Mining in the New World,* New York, 1973; Vicente Restrepo, *Estudio sobre las minas de oro y plata de Colombia,* Bogotá, 1888; Robert C. West, *Colonial Placer Mining in Colombia,* Baton Rouge, La., 1952.

TROY S. FLOYD

MINING (LATIN AMERICA). The search for mineral wealth in Latin America has been a recurring theme since pre-Columbian times. Soft metallics such as gold, silver, lead, tin, and copper were sought by many indigenous groups prior to contact with Europeans. Some gathered gold nuggets and wore them unworked for adornment. Others, such as the AZTECS, Tarascans, MAYAS, Coclés, Chibchas (*see* CHIBCHA), and INCAS smelted, alloyed, and shaped metals to produce a variety of decorative objects. All high-culture groups regularly traded these metals and semiprecious gems such as amber, jade, and turquoise. The Aztecs and Tarascans, in particular, actively sought to extend their political control over areas of soft metallic deposits. Hard metallics such as iron were apparently unknown, although in Ecuador platinum nuggets were shaped and worked with gold. Information on nonmetallics is more scanty. Pottery clays were worked rather ubiquitously, and along the west coast of South America GUANO deposits were mined for fertilizer. Obsidian and other stones used for implements and weapons were quarried and traded among some groups. In areas of maize consumption limestone was used to remove the outer kernel covering prior to its preparation as a food. Petroleum from surface seeps was occasionally used as a medicine, but there is no indication that oil or coal was used for light or as a fuel.

One of the principal aims of the European conquest of Latin America was the search for precious metals, primarily gold and silver. Although placer gold was found over a wide area, most deposits were quickly depleted. Vein mining for silver was much more permanent but was confined largely to central and northern Mexico and the highlands of Peru and Bolivia. In Mexico major silver deposits were discovered at Taxco (1534), Zacatecas (1546), Guanajuato (1550), Pachuca (1552), San Luis Potosí (1592), and Santa Eulalia (now Aquiles Serdán), near Chihuahua (1703). In Peru and Bolivia the sites of principal silver ore deposits included POTOSÍ (1545), Castrovirreyna (1555), Oruro (about 1595), and Cerro de Pasco (1630).

In Brazil only minor placer gold deposits were discovered early in the colonial period, but with the gold finds later in Minas Gerais (1690s), Cuiabá (1718), and Goiás (1725) the metal became important economically. During the eighteenth century Brazil's production of gold, derived largely from placer deposits, equaled nearly one-half of the world's output. Diamonds, also discovered in Minas Gerais (1729), along with gold spurred further exploration of the Brazilian interior and led to the establishment of numerous mining communities.

Throughout the colonial and independence periods until the latter part of the nineteenth century mining activities in Latin America were confined largely to the more valuable metals. Iron ore was discovered in northern Mexico (1552) and in Minas Gerais, Brazil (1590), but neither deposit was utilized in any degree. Lead, tin, copper, and zinc were of local importance only. Mining and refining techniques were dependent largely on Indian labor and knowledge, although later German technology became increasingly important. One important technique was the use of mercury as an amalgam in smelting ores, particularly silver. Mercury discovered at Huancavelica, Peru (1563), was shipped to other parts of Spanish Latin America for this purpose.

Mining activities began to expand in the latter part of the nineteenth century to include new minerals and new areas of production. The impetus for acceleration was derived mainly from increased foreign investment, which provided capital, technology, and management, and from the demand for mineral products in the United States and Western Europe. For example, in 1897 the investments of United States citizens in Latin American mining totaled about $80 million; in 1929 they approximated $800 million. Improved transport facilities also stimulated mining activity. Petroleum, whose existence had long been known, began to be exploited along the Gulf coast of Mexico, the Caribbean coast of Colombia, the eastern LLANOS and Maracaibo Basin of Venezuela, and the northwest coast of Peru. Still later petroleum was discovered in northeastern Brazil, in the CHACO of Bolivia, and in Argentina. In Mexico, the value of lead, zinc, and copper production surpassed that of silver and gold by about 1900, and by 1881 the iron ore deposits of Durango were more extensively worked. In Peru the CERRO CORPORATION, founded in 1902, consolidated numerous mining claims and installed modern equipment to recover not only silver but also other minerals, including copper, lead, zinc, bismuth, and gold. In Bolivia tin ores along the eastern border of the ALTIPLANO were rediscovered and became the principal export of the nation. In Chile, *caliche* deposits of sodium nitrate, of which the country had a virtual world monopoly, had been mined since the early nineteenth century, but the greatest levels of production were reached in the latter part of that century and the early twentieth century (*see* NITRATE INDUSTRY: CHILE). Copper, like sodium nitrate, had been mined earlier, but major increases in production did not occur until the twentieth century, when foreign mining companies

opened new deposits and expanded others. The Chilean iron ore industry also began about this time. In Brazil the iron ore deposits around the southern end of the Serra do Espinhaço were apparently first worked about 1817, but large-scale usage did not begin until after World War I. Deposits of other minerals were also found in Brazil, but their exploitation was minimal.

By 1940 Latin America had firmly established itself as one of the mineral-rich regions of the world. Mining production had increased continually and contributed significantly to the gross national product of several nations. Much of the gain in mining activity resulted from foreign company investment, and a number of governments were increasingly concerned about the heavy investments in that sector of their national resources; in 1943 United States companies' investments in mining approximated $1 billion. Bolivia and Mexico nationalized their petroleum industries in 1937 and 1938, respectively, and other countries began placing greater restrictions on foreign investments and requiring a larger share of the profits from these ventures. Table 1 shows the production of selected minerals.

Mineral production increased continually in the post-World War II period. The traditional metallogenic regions of Mexico, Peru-Bolivia, and Brazil remained principal source areas of silver, gold, lead, and zinc, although many of the mines became more costly to operate because of lower-grade ores and greater mining depths. In Mexico and Peru-Bolivia many mines were closed, and relatively few new ore bodies were exploited. In Brazil, however, there was a significant expansion of production and ore body development.

TABLE 1. PRINCIPAL MINERALS MINED IN LATIN AMERICA
(1939 or nearest available year)

Mineral	Latin America's percentage of world production	Percentage of total Latin American output by major producing nations						All others
		First		Second		Third		
Antimony	55	Bolivia	53	Mexico	41	Peru	4	2
Bauxite	26	Surinam	50	British Guiana	48	Brazil	2	...
Bismuth	37	Peru	97	Bolivia	3	...	...	...
Cadmium	20	Mexico	100	...	...	...	...	...
Chromite	6	Cuba	96	Guatemala	3	Brazil	1	...
Copper	20	Chile	78	Mexico	10	Peru	8	4
Diamonds	3	Brazil	90	British Guiana	8	Venezuela	2	...
Gold	7	Mexico	32	Colombia	19	Chile	10	39
Iron	2	Chile	67	Brazil	16	Cuba	12	5
Lead	13	Mexico	86	Peru	10	Argentina	4	...
Manganese	6	Brazil	62	Cuba	33	Chile	4	1
Mercury	4	Mexico	99	Bolivia	1	...	...	...
Molybdenum	4	Mexico	64	Peru	32	Chile	4	...
Petroleum	16	Venezuela	63	Mexico	13	Colombia	7	17
Platinum	6	Colombia	99	Panama	1	...	...	...
Silver	42	Mexico	68	Peru	17	Bolivia	7	8
Tin	16	Bolivia	95	Argentina	4	Mexico	1	...
Tungsten	7	Bolivia	67	Argentina	32	Peru	1	...
Vanadium	7	Peru	82	Mexico	18	...	...	...
Zinc	12	Mexico	66	Chile	20	Peru	14	...

Since data for most metals are based on smelted production by the country where smelted, production data for Latin America are underestimated. In addition to the minerals listed, the following were mined: gypsum, phosphate rock, feldspar, fluorspar, asbestos, coal, salt, emeralds, and other precious and semiprecious gems.

SOURCE: United States Department of the Interior, Bureau of Mines, *Minerals Yearbook, 1940,* Washington, 1940.

TABLE 2. PRINCIPAL MINERALS MINED IN LATIN AMERICA
(1969 or nearest available year)

Mineral	Latin America's percentage of world production	Percentage of total Latin American output by major producing nations						All others
		First		Second		Third		
Antimony	32	Bolivia	76	Mexico	19	Peru	5	...
Asbestos	9	Bolivia	100	...	...	...	...	...
Bauxite	43	Jamaica	45	Surinam	27	Guyana	19	9
Bismuth	51	Peru	35	Bolivia	34	Mexico	31	...
Copper	17	Chile	70	Peru	20	Mexico	7	3
Gold	2	Colombia	23	Mexico	19	Brazil	18	40
Iron	11	Brazil	38	Venezuela	28	Chile	16	18
Lead	13	Mexico	42	Peru	40	Argentina	7	11
Manganese	15	Brazil	87	Mexico	6	Guyana	4	3
Mercury	10	Mexico	85	Peru	13	Colombia	1	1
Molybdenum	7	Bolivia	94	Peru	3	Mexico	2	1
Petroleum	13	Venezuela	72	Mexico	8	Argentina	7	13
Salt	6	Mexico	40	Brazil	20	Chile	16	24
Silver	33	Mexico	46	Peru	37	Bolivia	6	11
Tin	18	Bolivia	91	Brazil	8	Mexico	1	...
Tungsten	10	Bolivia	56	Peru	19	Brazil	14	11
Zinc	12	Peru	50	Mexico	40	Argentina	4	6

Since data for most metals are based on smelted production by the country where smelted, production data for Latin America are underestimated. In addition to the minerals listed, the following were mined: gypsum, phosphate rock, fluorspar, platinum, coal, chromite, vanadium, diamonds, and other precious and semiprecious gems.

sources: Statistical Office of the United Nations, Department of Economic and Social Affairs, *United Nations Statistical Yearbook, 1970,* New York, 1971; United States Department of the Interior, Bureau of Mines, *Minerals Yearbook, 1969,* Washington, 1971.

Elsewhere mineral production was either maintained or expanded (*see* Table 2).

Mining became important in several new areas. Bauxite mining, formerly confined to the Guianas, was developed in Jamaica, which has become the world's leading producer. In Mexico sulfur production began in the Isthmus of Tehuantepec. In Venezuela the iron deposits of the northern Guiana Highlands were developed. Brazil began the exploitation of a number of metallic minerals along the northern and western fringe of the Brazilian highlands and along the southern edge of the Guiana Highlands. Coal deposits whose existence had been long known but little worked because of low quality, particularly those of southern Argentina, southern Brazil, northern Colombia, and central Peru, were more fully exploited. The search for petroleum continued into new areas. Exploration in southern Colombia, eastern Ecuador, and adjacent Peru gave further confirmation of the belief that extensive petroleum deposits of commercial quality underlie the Amazon Basin. Exploration along the Caribbean coast of Central America indicates the presence of oil-bearing strata, but no commercial production has resulted.

Geologic and mineralogic data are incomplete or totally lacking for many parts of Latin America. No general inventory of the area's known mineral resources has been made; knowledge of nonmetallics is particularly scanty. From 1959 to 1969, however, the United Nations Development Program (Special Fund) contributed nearly $42 million for mineral surveys in Latin America, or 32 percent of all sums granted for such programs. Most authorities believe that reserves of many minerals will increase substantially through new discoveries and through the application of improved mining technology whereby low-grade deposits are reclassified as commercially exploitable. The relation of Latin America's known reserves of selected minerals to those of the world is shown in Table 3, and reserves of unknown amount are listed in Table 4.

Although mining employs only a small percentage of the labor force in any country, it contributes greatly to the area economy in terms of value of exports. For Latin America as a whole, more than 20 percent of all exports by value consists of minerals. Some countries depend upon mineral exports for the bulk of their foreign exchange. Percentages of total exports for selected countries in 1969 (or the nearest available year) were as follows: Venezuela, 97; Chile, 88; Bolivia, 80; Surinam, 80; Trinidad, 77; Jamaica, 55; Peru, 43; and Guyana, 42.

Technology used in mining varies generally with the scale of operation. Large-scale enterprises are usually of foreign investment origin, although now they may be partially or totally controlled by the host government. Exploitation is based on extensive mineralogic surveys and employs advanced extractive and processing techniques. The result is high productivity at low cost and a competitive position in the world markets. Formerly management and technical personnel were foreign, but nationals in the mining country are assuming many of their functions. At the other end of the scale is folk mining, which is confined to high-grade ores, uses limited technology, and is labor-intensive.

TABLE 3. KNOWN RESERVES OF MINERALS IN LATIN AMERICA

Mineral	Percentage of world reserves	Principal Latin American nations with known reserves
Copper	30	Chile, Peru
Bauxite	20	Jamaica, Surinam, Guyana
Manganese	18	Brazil, Bolivia, Mexico
Tin	15	Bolivia
Iron	15	Brazil, Bolivia, Venezuela
Molybdenum	15	Chile, Peru
Lead	14	Mexico, Peru, Argentina
Zinc	13	Mexico, Peru, Bolivia

Production costs are high, and yields are low. Ventures of this type are generally feasible only when they are subsidized or when high world prices prevail.

Many Latin American nations have revised their mining policies and begun to assume a more active role in the industry. Policies have varied from country to country, but all show a trend toward (1) greater participation of the government in mining activities, by serving either as part or complete owner of the operations or by employing such restrictive regulations as those limiting the percentage of net income that may be removed from the country; (2) obtaining of a greater share of profits; and (3) greater integration of the industry into the national economy. Of particular concern are the large mining ventures that have shipped minerals to other nations in a raw or semiraw state. Examples of revised mining policy include (1) the nationalization of the larger tin-mining companies in Bolivia (1952) and a new mining code (1971); (2) restrictions on sulfur exports from Mexico to conform with increases in proved reserves (1956–1966) and numerous other policies to encourage Mexican participation in mining and processing nationally; (3) the nationalization of the Cuban mineral industry (1960–1961); (4) the adoption of a "no more concessions" policy for Venezuelan iron and nickel deposits (1960), an announced policy of reversion of petroleum concessions at their termination date (1971), and the requirement that crude oil must be refined within national borders as soon as practicable; (5) the Chilean copper agreement in which the government became part owner of the copper companies (1966) and the nationalization of the copper companies (1971); (6) the mining code of Brazil (1967) designed to spur mineral exploration and production, the formation of a government-controlled mineral resource company (1969), and the general governmental policy of state-operated mining and processing concerns; (7) the nationalization of the principal bauxite deposits in Guyana (1971); and (8) the partial nationalization of Peruvian petroleum operations (1968) and preparation of a new mining code (1972).

Prospects for the mining industry are uncertain. Factors indicating that production will continue to rise include (1) the expansion of proved reserves and discoveries of new deposits; (2) the limited but progressive vertical integration of minerals in the growing Latin American manufacturing complex; (3) the increasing demand for minerals in the United States, Western Europe, and Japan; and (4) the development of improved mining and processing techniques. Factors that may hinder production include (1) the shortage of capital and organizational ability, particularly as the rate of new United States investments declines; (2) the limited increase in value of most raw minerals since 1950; and (3) the instability of world market prices for minerals. Probably overshadowing all other factors are government policy and action. Policies that encourage capital investments, mineralogic surveys, and equitable taxation can stimulate production greatly. Policies that reflect extreme economic nationalism or improper institutional and legal structures may result in diminished output.

See also COPPER INDUSTRY (CHILE); IRON AND STEEL INDUSTRY (BRAZIL); IRON AND STEEL INDUSTRY (MEXICO); IRON AND STEEL INDUSTRY (VENEZUELA); PETROLEUM INDUSTRY (LATIN AMERICA); PETROLEUM INDUSTRY (VENEZUELA); TIN INDUSTRY (BOLIVIA).

Bibliography. Modesto Bargalló, *La minería y la metalurgía en la América Española durante la época colonial*, Mexico City and Buenos Aires, 1955; Dudley T. Easby, Jr., "Pre-Hispanic Metallurgy and Metalworking in the New World," *Proceedings of the American Philosophical Society*, vol. CIX, no. 2, April 1965, pp. 89–98; "Mining in Latin America," *Economic Bulletin for Latin America*, vol. XIV, no. 2, second half 1969, pp. 78–109; J. Fred Rippy, *Globe and Hemisphere: Latin America's Place in the Postwar Foreign Relations of the United States*, Chicago, 1958; United Nations, Department of Economic and Social Affairs, *Mineral Resources Development with Particular Reference to the Developing Countries*, New York, 1970; United States Department of the Interior, Bureau of Mines, *Minerals Yearbook*, Washington, varying dates; id., *Mineral Facts and Problems*, Washington, 1970.

DON R. HOY

TABLE 4. MINERAL RESERVES OF UNKNOWN AMOUNT IN LATIN AMERICA

Mineral	Principal Latin American nations with known reserves
Silver, gold	Mexico, Peru, Bolivia
Tungsten	Bolivia, Brazil
Nickel	Cuba, Brazil, Venezuela, Guatemala
Antimony	Bolivia, Mexico
Mercury	Mexico
Bismuth	Mexico, Peru, Bolivia
Sulfur	Mexico, Peru, Bolivia
Nitrates	Chile
Phosphate rock	Peru, Brazil

MINING CORPORATION OF BOLIVIA. *See* CORPORACIÓN MINERA DE BOLIVIA.

MIRAMÓN, MIGUEL (1831–1867). Mexican soldier. Born in Mexico City, Miramón began his military career at the age of fifteen, when he entered the Military Academy. The following year saw him fighting against United States forces in the MEXICAN WAR. After the war he taught in the academy. He fought against the Ayutla rebels and also saw action in the Puebla revolt on the side of the Conservatives in 1856. During the War of the Reform (*see* REFORM, THE), he played an important role, serving as President of the Conservative government during most of 1860 and the remainder of the time as one of the leading generals. In the latter capacity, he led his army against the Liberal seat in Veracruz on two occasions but was forced to withdraw. Though ultimately defeated in the crucial Battle of Calpulálpam, he nevertheless won many victories.

After the Liberals' triumph, Miramón went into exile in Europe, where he worked to establish a monarchy in Mexico. In 1863 he returned to Mexico to offer his services to the empire. MAXIMILIAN sent him to Berlin to study tactics. When the French began to withdraw, Miramón returned to Mexico and was given command of one of Maximilian's divisions. He was wounded and captured in the siege of Querétaro. Like Maximilian, he was tried by a court-martial for treason and was executed with the Emperor on June 19, 1867. Miramón was one of the most energetic and sincere members of the Conservative party and was widely respected for his bravery and loyalty.

CHARLES R. BERRY

MIRANDA, FRANCISCO DE (1750–1816). Venezuelan precursor of independence and leader of the first Venezuelan republic. The archconspirator and early protagonist of Latin American independence, Francisco de Miranda was born in Caracas, the son of a Canary Islander who had settled in Venezuela and become a successful merchant. He obtained his higher education in Caracas, then moved to Spain, where he purchased a commission in the Spanish Army. He fought in North Africa and also, during the American Revolutionary War, in the Caribbean. He rose to the rank of colonel but made numerous enemies in Spanish service and in

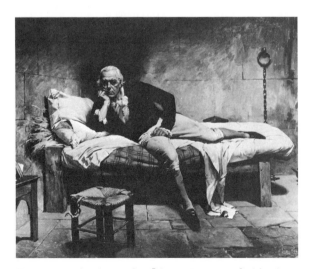

Francisco de Miranda. [*Organization of American States*]

1783, with charges of assorted irregularities hanging over him, fled to the United States.

Miranda traveled widely in the United States, met influential men, and discussed the possibility that Spanish America might emulate the independence of the English colonies. But whether he was already firmly committed to that objective is unclear. Indeed, when he moved to England early in 1785, he approached the Spanish Ambassador with a view to having his name cleared and receiving an honorable discharge from the Spanish Army. Without waiting for a final answer (which would be unfavorable), Miranda left England for a grand tour of the Continent, during which he perfected his knowledge of the world by a careful observation of people and places, made the acquaintance of influential persons, even becoming a favorite of Catherine the Great, and more than once again broached the subject of Spanish American independence.

Miranda was back in England in 1789. Over the following years he completed his transformation into a hardened revolutionary, seeking support from European rulers and conspiring with any other disaffected creoles who came his way. Although he took time out to fight in the French Revolution, rising to a general's rank in the French Army, London eventually became his principal base of operations. The British government, appreciating his potential nuisance value, gave him intermittent support and encouragement but refused to commit itself unequivocally to his schemes. In 1798 he attempted unsuccessfully to enlist the support of American Federalists for an Anglo-American campaign to revolutionize the Spanish colonies.

In 1805 Miranda recrossed the Atlantic, aiming to try his luck with the United States. He obtained no official cooperation, but he succeeded in raising a volunteer force, and in February 1806 he set out on the ship *Leander* from New York to the West Indies for an attack upon Venezuela. On his second attempt he made a successful landing and briefly captured Coro, but the inhabitants failed to rally to his support, British naval units in the Caribbean did not give the help he had hoped for, and he ultimately returned to London, to take up where he had left off.

Just when it appeared that Britain was finally ready to adopt his schemes for revolutionizing Spanish America, the Napoleonic invasion of Spain abruptly transformed Spain into a British ally. However, the outbreak of revolution in Venezuela in 1810 finally gave him his chance. By the end of the year he was again in his native land, where his accumulated revolutionary experience and prestige gave him a position of leadership within the patriot camp, and he used it to press for an outright declaration of independence. On July 5, 1811, that objective was achieved. Soon afterward Miranda was given the task of suppressing a counterrevolution in Valencia, and he succeeded in doing so. Yet his long absence from Venezuela, combined with personal differences, prevented him from obtaining the full confidence of other patriot leaders. Over his objections (and those of Simón BOLÍVAR), the Venezuelan Congress adopted a weak federal form of organization for the nation, and it refused to give him supreme political power until the disastrous earthquake of March 1812, following a royalist offensive launched from western coastal Venezuela by Juan

Domingo Monteverde, had created a crisis situation.

Although Miranda was granted dictatorial authority, he could not turn back the royalist challenge. Probably no one could have done so, but when Miranda capitulated to Monteverde on July 25 and prepared to leave Venezuela (presumably hoping to continue the struggle elsewhere), there were those who suspected treason. A group including Bolívar forcibly prevented his departure. Miranda was then arrested by the royalists in violation of the capitulation and was shipped to a Spanish prison, where he died in 1816. His service as a leader of independent Venezuela was thus crowned with failure, but no other Spanish American had done so much to lay the groundwork for revolution prior to the final outbreak of the movement in 1810.

Bibliography. Láutico García, *Francisco de Miranda y el antiguo régimen español,* Caracas, 1961; Francisco de Miranda, *The New Democracy in America: Travels of Francisco de Miranda in the United States,* Norman, Okla., 1963; William S. Robertson, *The Life of Miranda,* 2 vols., Chapel Hill, N.C., 1929; Joseph F. Thorning, *Miranda: World Citizen,* Gainesville, Fla., 1952.

DAVID BUSHNELL

MISSIONS (SPANISH AMERICA). Since a prime justification of Spain's dominion in the New World was the Christianization of the Indians, considerable attention was paid by ecclesiastical and royal officials to the discharge of the missionary obligation. The chief means of conversion were the *doctrinas,* missions, and reductions, which together with the encomiendas (*see* ENCOMIENDA) aimed at making the Indian a good Christian and a loyal subject of Spain.

Doctrinas were territorial and jurisdictional units designated as the missionary area of a priest or priests. They emerged in the 1520s in New Spain to fulfill the encomendero's responsibility for the spiritual welfare of his charges. Under this system Indians were organized into villages according to Spanish traditions of town life. Churches, schools, rectories, hospitals, and *obrajes* (textile factories; *see* OBRAJE) were built by native labor. The parish priest (*doctrinero*) was paid by the encomendero from Indian tribute, although the cleric sometimes exacted additional fees. In the sixteenth century the *doctrinero* was usually an Augustinian, Dominican, Franciscan, or Mercedarian. In the 1570s King PHILIP II moved to bring Indian parishes firmly under episcopal and hence royal control by directing that *doctrinas* be turned over to secular priests. The crown also began favoring the missions, in which civil involvement was greater, as better fulfilling royal needs, particularly in frontier areas.

While various orders established missions throughout Spanish America, the Franciscans and the Jesuits were the most active. As in the case of the *doctrina,* the purpose of the mission was to Christianize and Hispanicize the Indian. Among the notable examples of this type was the architecturally pleasing chain of Franciscan missions that studded the California coast. In the missions the Indians worked, studied, and were socialized in a highly structured, paternalistic environment.

Jesuit missionary efforts were concentrated in South America and reached their culmination in Paraguay, where the Society of Jesus created more than fifty missions, known as reductions, some of which contained as many as 8,000 inhabitants. Geographically isolated and economically self-sufficient, the Jesuit reductions were relatively independent of episcopal and royal control. With the expulsion of the Jesuits in 1767 (*see* JESUITS, EXPULSION OF: SPANISH AMERICA), these settlements were turned over to secular clerics and civilian authorities and declined rapidly.

MARGARET E. CRAHAN

MISTRAL, GABRIELA (pseudonym of LUCILA GODOY ALCAYAGA, 1889–1957). Chilean poet. Born in Coquimbo Province, Gabriela Mistral devoted herself to literature and education, first teaching in elementary schools in rural Chile and then becoming a grade school director and the principal of the Liceo de Señoritas in Santiago. In 1922 she went to Mexico at the invitation of José VASCONCELOS, then Minister of Education, to advise him on his program of educational reform. In 1925 she entered the Chilean diplomatic service and served as a consul throughout Europe and the Americas until her death. In 1945 she was awarded the Nobel Prize for Literature.

Gabriela Mistral's poetry is marked by an intense lyricism; it explores love in all its forms, sexual, maternal, and humanitarian. Her first literary triumph came in 1914, when she won the first prize in the Floral Games of Santiago for *Los sonetos de la muerte,* written after the suicide of the man she loved. This tragic love and her idealism create the melancholy atmosphere of much of her work, especially *Desolación* (1922), *Ternura* (1924), and *Tala* (1938), although the last of these transcends human wretchedness in a metaphysical response to the universe. This feeling becomes more apparent in *Lagar* (1954). Gabriela Mistral's love for children caused her to write children's stories, published with other short prose pieces in *Páginas en prosa* (1965). Her *Poesías completas* appeared in 1958.

RACHEL PHILLIPS

MITA. Peruvian equivalent of the Mexican REPARTIMIENTO. A system of forced wage labor resting upon previous native customs of public service, the *mita* was regularized under Viceroy Francisco de TOLEDO in the 1570s. In general, all formally free, unskilled, adult males over eighteen were required to perform labor services for the Spaniards in the mines, textile mills, farms and ranches, and public works. In contrast to conditions under the *repartimiento,* which used about 4 percent of the available Indians for a work period of about one week at any one time, the *mitayos* in Peru labored for months and about 14 percent of the Indians were used in the labor allotments. The Indians of Peru were also forced to travel great distances to assigned places of work, while in Mexico the labor *repartimiento* was usually filled by Indians in districts near the location of the work. Because the pay received by the Indians did not exceed the tribute dues they were obliged to pay, debt servitude was usual and the Indians were no better off under the *mita* than under the ENCOMIENDA. Although the *mita* was reformed by royal decrees in 1601 and 1609, it was still in existence in modified form until the 1820s, when it was finally abolished by leaders in the struggle for independence.

RALPH H. VIGIL

MITIMA. Spanish form of the QUECHUA word *mitmac*, meaning "one newly arrived in a region." It was the policy of the Inca emperors to detach segments of the population (usually the most intransigent) from a newly conquered province and to settle them in other provinces. Their places were then taken by more dependable and acculturated Quechua-speaking groups, who acted as informers for the government and instructors to the new subjects. In any move, however, a *mitmac* group retained its own tribal identity, dress, and local fetishes; this prevented it from making common cause with the tribes surrounding it. In short, the *mitmac* system was an aspect of the Inca security system. *See also* INCAS.

BURR C. BRUNDAGE

MITRE, BARTOLOMÉ (1821–1906). Argentine historian and President (1862–1868). Mitre's youth was entirely overshadowed by the long dictatorship of Juan Manuel de ROSAS, on whose brother's *estancia*, ironically enough, he spent some four years of his childhood. In 1831 Mitre's father moved to Uruguay, and it was in Montevideo that the young Bartolomé grew up. As an adolescent and young man in the Uruguayan capital, he studied at the Military School, served in the armies of Gen. Fructuoso RIVERA, and apprenticed himself to literature by writing poetry. In 1842 he married Delfina de Vedia, who died in 1883. In 1843 Rosas and his Uruguayan allies laid siege to Montevideo; Mitre became a lieutenant colonel in the artillery and served with distinction in the defense of the city, as did the Italian patriot Giuseppe Garibaldi, with whom he became friendly. In 1846 he left Montevideo, hoping to take up arms against Rosas in the Argentine province of Corrientes, but the army he intended to join had vanished before he arrived. He spent the next few years

Bartolomé Mitre. [Organization of American States]

living in Bolivia, Peru, and Chile, following a variety of occupations.

Together with Domingo Faustino SARMIENTO and many other Argentine expatriates, Mitre sailed from Chile in 1851 to join Gen. Justo José de URQUIZA, the *caudillo* who was to lead the final great revolt against Rosas. Mitre served in Urquiza's Grand Army and fought at the Battle of Caseros (February 3, 1852). With Rosas out of the way, Mitre returned to Buenos Aires and entered politics, adopting a very hostile line toward Urquiza, as did many liberal intellectuals. When the province of Buenos Aires declared its independence of Urquiza's projected ARGENTINE CONFEDERATION, Mitre was made minister of the interior (government) in the provincial administration. He took a prominent part in defending the city against Urquiza's blockade in 1853 and the following year was appointed minister of war. The year 1857 saw him as minister of foreign relations and the interior. By now Mitre was one of the most prominent political figures in the state of Buenos Aires. Opinion in the state was divided between the "autonomists," who were prepared to contemplate a permanent separation from the rest of Argentina, and the "nationalists," who wanted reunification on terms favorable to Buenos Aires. Mitre was a nationalist. It fell to him to lead the province's forces when Urquiza reopened hostilities in 1859. The defeat of Buenos Aires at the Battle of Cepeda in October 1859 was followed by the incorporation of the province into the Confederation on terms acceptable to the nationalists. Mitre was elected Governor of Buenos Aires in May 1860.

The settlement between Buenos Aires and the other thirteen provinces of Argentina augured well for the future, but it broke down in 1861 in a further spasm of civil war. Once again Mitre commanded the army of Buenos Aires, but this time he won, for at the Battle of Pavón in September 1861 Urquiza withdrew from the field and from political life, leaving Mitre as the dominant figure in Argentina. His statesmanlike and conciliatory attitude prevented any general recrudescence of civil war, and in 1862 a new federal congress elected him President of what from now onward was to be known as the Argentine Republic. The country was now finally reunited and the disastrous legacy of Rosas overcome.

In the Presidency Mitre turned his attention to implementing the political and economic program that he and other liberal exiles had dreamed of during the Rosas period. He encouraged foreign trade, planned new railroads, watched thousands of immigrants arrive (*see* IMMIGRATION: ARGENTINA), and took steps to eliminate what remained of *caudillo* rule in the interior. With the outbreak of the PARAGUAYAN WAR in 1865 and the formation of the Triple Alliance, Mitre became commander in chief of the Allied armies. He spent most of the remainder of his term of office on active service, as the Allies made their slow advance along the line of the Paraguay River. The death of his Vice President obliged him to return to Buenos Aires in January 1868. His successor in the Argentine Presidency, later that year, was Sarmiento.

Mitre was still a comparatively young man when he left office, and many years of active political life remained to him. At the end of Sarmiento's term of office in 1874, Mitre stood once again for the Presidency but was defeated by Nicolás AVELLANEDA. His followers refused to accept this defeat, and Mitre placed himself at the head of an armed rebellion that was crushed by the government. Mitre was condemned to death, but the sentence was subsequently commuted to an eight-year exile, which itself was effectively quashed by President Avellaneda. In 1880, when Buenos Aires rose against the government on the issue of federalization, Mitre played a principal part in negotiating an end to the rebellion despite his deep sympathies for the stand taken by his native city.

During the prosperous 1880s Mitre found himself increasingly dissatisfied by the governments of the day, and in 1889–1890 he took part in the formation of the Unión Cívica (Civic Union), a strong opposition group whose nominal leader he became. Mitre was on a visit to Europe in 1890 when the opposition rose in revolt, but soon after his return to Argentina the following year he split the Unión Cívica by concluding an agreement with the governing parties. His own "National" Civic Union thereafter supported the government, while Leandro ALEM's "Radical" Civic Union remained in opposition to the regime (*see* RADICAL PARTY: ARGENTINA). By now Mitre was the grand old man of Argentine politics; his eightieth birthday in 1901 brought innumerable tributes from far and wide.

Mitre's political career was notable enough, but he was also a talented and indefatigable journalist, writer, and historian as well as a persuasive orator. In 1870 he founded *La Nación,* one of Latin America's greatest newspapers. He produced poetry, essays, a novel, and numerous translations. His *Historia de Belgrano y de la independencia argentina* (1876–1877) and his *Historia de San Martín y de la emancipación sud-americana* (1888–1889) place him in the very highest rank of Latin American historians of his era. In all, his achievement was a formidable one, almost unrivaled in nineteenth-century Argentina.

Bibliography. Archivo del General Mitre, 28 vols., Buenos Aires, 1911–14; W. H. Jeffrey, *Mitre and Argentina,* New York, 1952.   SIMON COLLIER

MNR. *See* MOVIMIENTO NACIONALISTA REVOLUCIONARIO.

MOCHICA. Archaeological complex centered in the valley of Moche, on the north coast of Peru, but also extending to adjacent valleys. It is dated to A.D. 200–700. Moche appears to have been a powerful emergent state, both militaristic and confident. One of the ruins from that culture is the famous Huaca del Sol, a vast truncated pyramid of adobe bricks. Nearby is the Huaca de la Luna with its interesting remnants of murals depicting anthropomorphized weapons attacking humans. The people of Moche were outstanding as potters. Their stirrup-spouted pots are represented in every important collection of pre-Columbian art and depict with wonderful vigor and naturalism portraits of commoners and rulers, animals, grotesques, sexual acts, genre scenes, and architectural items. Few cultures in the history of world art have survived so magnificently on the basis of a limited art form.

BURR C. BRUNDAGE

MOCTEZUMA (MONTEZUMA, MOTECUHZOMA; d. 1520). Aztec emperor. Moctezuma became Emperor in 1502 or 1503, having previously held the office of high priest. He favored the hereditary nobility over other elements of the population, and he carried out the traditional Aztec practice of making war against enemy peoples in order to obtain captives for religious sacrifice. It was his misfortune to be on the throne when a Spanish army of conquest under Hernán CORTÉS landed in Mexico in 1519. Moctezuma decided the strangers might be representatives of the god QUETZALCOATL, who, according to tradition, would one day come from his home in the east to rule the country. He therefore allowed Cortés and his men to enter his capital, TENOCHTITLÁN, and received them as honored guests. Nonetheless, the Spaniards felt insecure, and after they had been in Tenochtitlán a week, they seized Moctezuma and held him as a hostage. They required him to swear allegiance to the King of Spain and for several months controlled the Aztec empire through him. This state of affairs ended when the people of Tenochtitlán revolted against the Spaniards. Moctezuma, at the insistence of Cortés, appealed to his people to leave the Spaniards in peace, but they refused to obey him and showered him with missiles. Felled by a stone, he died a few days later. Some accounts claim he lost his will to live and died from his wound; others assert that he was killed by the Spaniards, his usefulness to them having come to an end. *See also* AZTECS.

TIMOTHY C. HANLEY

MODERNISM (BRAZIL). *Modernismo* carries different meanings in Portuguese and Spanish. In Spanish it refers to a movement that began in the 1890s and continued to the middle of the second decade of the twentieth century. Reflecting the influence of French Parnassianism and symbolism and *fin de siècle* decadence, it subscribed to the doctrine of art for art's sake. Brazilian *modernismo,* though it had antecedents in the symbolism of the beginning of the century and in the attitudes and ideas of important writers of the period from 1900 to 1910, should be associated with the great change that took place in Brazil during World War I, shaking the economic system, bringing about social realignments, and challenging the cultural and intellectual hegemony of Rio de Janeiro. It was a movement that affected all the arts and caused the Brazilians to reexamine their relations with Europe and their national past. The consequences were far-reaching in that they revolutionized both the form and the substance of artistic production and caused the appearance of the most interesting generation of writers, painters, composers, and eventually dramatists that Brazil had ever known.

The movement is usually considered to have commenced in 1922 with Modern Art Week (*Semana de Arte Moderna*), which consisted of festivals of all the arts and was celebrated in the São Paulo Municipal Theater. Among the important participants were the writers Mário de ANDRADE, Oswald de Andrade, and Guilherme de Almeida; the painter Emiliano DI CAVALCANTI; and the composer Heitor VILLA-LOBOS. Other figures connected with *modernismo* are the painter Tarsila do AMARAL, the poets Manuel BANDEIRA and Carlos Drummond de ANDRADE, and the critic Alceu Amoroso Lima. It has been said of the modernists that their only resemblance to one another lies in their common espousal of the cause of artistic freedom. Originally influenced by the German expressionists and by the Italian futurists through the work of Anita MALFATTI and Oswald de Andrade, respectively, they also were affected by the early-twentieth-century European interest in primitivism, which they associated with Brazil's almost extinct Indians and its vigorous Negro population. They were nationalists who believed it the artist's duty to discover the esthetic and human values peculiar to his own country, an attitude that stimulated them to great enthusiasm about the new Brazil with its rapidly growing cities, its changing population, and its manifestations of incipient industrialization. In their attack on the past, the modernists challenged everything that the symbolists and Parnassians had stood for, including their choice of language; they insisted that the Portuguese of a Brazilian writer should be that spoken in Brazil. They aimed at a colloquial and even slangy style, which was uniquely appropriate for their humor and irony. Metrical and verse forms were to be free and determined by the needs of the subject. These theories are exemplified in the work of Mário de Andrade, whose best stories and poems deal with life in São Paulo. His novel *Macunaíma* is an allegorical history of Brazil written in a language fabricated out of regional dialects, and his treatise *A Escrava Que Não É Isaura* is a defense of the modernist esthetic.

The modernists broke into several groups—namely, Pau Brasil (Brazil Wood), the Verdeamarelistas (the Green and Yellows), and that associated with the *Revista de Antropofagia* (*Review of Cannibalism*)—all of which preached a reexamination of the values of the Brazilian past, with the Verdeamarelistas developing into Integralistas, or fascists. From the *Antropofagia* group came one of the country's great literary monuments, a neo-Indianist poem by Raúl Bopp entitled *A Cobra Norato.* The group connected with the magazine *Festa* continued the symbolist tradition. In the NORTHEAST an independent group grew up around the figure of Gilberto FREYRE, in whose *Manifesto Regionalista* (1926) we find the codification of the ideas of the novelists of the Northeast together with an affirmation of the doctrine of the necessity of an appreciation of old Brazilian values.

Modernismo flourished almost unchallenged from 1930, eight years after the Modern Art Week, to 1945, at which time a reaction set in with the appearance of the gifted Generation of 1945. Nevertheless, the leading modernists continued to dominate the literary scene for many years and to influence their younger contemporaries. The achievement of *modernismo* was as great as that of romanticism in the previous century: it brought about an artistic revival that, in the words of one critic, reflected faithfully the soul of the country, and it made clear once and for all the cultural independence of Brazil.

See also LITERATURE (BRAZIL).

Bibliography. Elizabeth Bishop and Emanuel Brasil (eds.), *An Anthology of Twentieth Century Brazilian Poetry,* Middletown, Conn., 1972; Mário da Silva Brito, *História do Modernismo Brasileiro,* vol. I, *Antecedentes da Semana de Arte Moderna,* São Paulo, 1958; Antônio Cândido and José Aderaldo Castello, *Presença da Literatura Brasileira,* vol. III, *Modernismo,* São Paulo, 1964; Afrânio Coutinho (ed.), *A Literatura no Brasil,* 2d ed., vol. V, *Modernismo,* Rio de Janeiro, 1970; Giovanni Pontiero (ed.), *An Anthology of Brazilian Modernist Poetry,* Oxford, 1969; Wilson Martins, *The Modernist Idea: A Critical Survey of Brazilian Writing in the Twentieth Century,* tr. by Jack E. Tomlins, New York, 1970. RAYMOND S. SAYERS

MODERNISM (SPANISH AMERICA). The modernist movement was the first literary movement to have its inception in Spanish America, from which its influence subsequently spread to Spain. The undisputed founder and leader of the movement was Rubén DARÍO, whose publication in 1888 of *Azul,* a volume of verse and prose, marked the beginning of modernism in Spanish American letters. Modernism was not exclusively a movement in poetry, its principal genre, but included the short story and some novels, although it did not find fertile expression in the essay or the drama.

The influence of French Parnassian and symbolist writers was strong on the modernists in their formative period. Like their French models, they utilized new themes and subject matter in their works, and they began as well to experiment with new poetical forms. In this early stage there were a marked predilection for elegance of style and a concern for form that were associated with a kind of artificial refinement in taste, including aristocratic symbols of elegance such as the Wagnerian swan and the French fleur-de-lis. In a later stage there was a more clearly defined reorientation toward Spanish America.

The desire to achieve perfection of poetic form was clearly due to the influence of the French Parnassians, whose motto "Art for Art's Sake" was adopted by the Spanish American modernists. This attempt to achieve perfection of form stimulated a desire to renovate and change poetic form from its original concepts. In poetry the modernists experimented with new forms while they revitalized old ones. In both prose and verse new rhythms began to appear. The influence of the Parnassians also accounts in part for the modernist interest in the past. The Middle Ages, ancient Greece, the biblical past, and the elegance of eighteenth-century France appear in these works.

The modernists largely turned away from America, away from local color and folk heroes and toward a created world of fantasy and illusion. This desire to escape from the mundane world around them prompted the creation of an ivory-tower concept of existence, with the result that many writers chose to write about fairies, gnomes, princesses, or exotic myths.

One of the most obvious stylistic features of modernism is the superabundance of sensory images. This refinement is seen in the use of words that transmit visual effects of brilliance or color—jewels, precious stones, gold and other fine metals. These chromatic effects are combined with other sensory images to form synesthesias, which abound in modernist works. The emphasis on sensory images immerses the reader in a complete sensory perception of the world created by the author.

The exotic also attracted many modernist writers, whose works are filled with references to places in the Orient and to Oriental art. Some poets attempted to imitate the form of Japanese poetry. Other writers chose to depict the Middle East or the Scandinavian countries. There is also a marked sensualism and eroticism, not typical of romanticism, in some modernist works that describe the beauties of the body and the glories of the flesh. In general, the modernist writers broke with the literary molds of the past and allowed their imagination full rein in their desire to create a new literature in Spanish.

The four writers most often considered precursors of modernism have in common their deaths before 1896, when the movement was in its most fertile period. José MARTÍ, the Cuban patriot, contributed three volumes: *Ismaelillo* (1882), *Versos sencillos* (1891), and *Versos libres,* published posthumously in 1913. His compatriot Julián del Casal (1863–1893) was an enthusiastic reader of the French Parnassians, as his volumes *Hojas al viento* (1890), *Nieve* (1892), and *Bustos y rimas* (1893) demonstrate. He adapted some Japanese poetic forms into Spanish. José Asunción SILVA published only a small volume of poems (*Poesías,* 1886), but he was an innovator with his metrical experimentation, and he composed some of the most lyrical poems in the language. The Mexican Manuel GUTIÉRREZ NÁJERA was also a precursor of the movement. He founded the modernist journal *Revista Azul* (1894–1896) and is highly regarded for his short stories, *Cuentos frágiles* (1883), as well as for his poetry.

Rubén Darío's initial success with *Azul* in 1888 was enhanced by his publication of *Prosas profanas* (1896), and he won even more widespread acclaim with *Cantos de vida y esperanza* (1905). He traveled extensively in Spanish America and Europe, where he was in touch with many writers of the movement.

Amado NERVO best represents modernism in its full development in Mexico. Of his several collections of poetry, *Perlas negras* (1898) and *La amada inmóvil* (1920) are among the best known. Nervo also published several volumes of prose. His religious inclinations, which give a note of mysticism to many of his poems, are one of his most distinguishing features as a modernist writer.

Ricardo Jaimes Freyre (Bolivia, 1868–1933) lived in Argentina, where he met and collaborated with Darío. His poems in *Castalia bárbara* (1899) contain many exotic references to Nordic mythology. His *Leyes de la versificación castellana* (1912) shows his interest in the theory of metrics and poetic forms.

Leopoldo LUGONES of Argentina occupies a place of importance close to that of Darío in the modernist movement. Although he wrote numerous volumes of prose and poetry, his most important books of verse are *Las montañas de oro* (1897), *Los crepúsculos del jardín* (1905), and *Lunario sentimental* (1909). Erotic themes predominate in *Los crepúsculos del jardín,* which also contains his famous poem "El solterón" ("The Bachelor").

More akin to symbolism is the poetry of Julio Herrera y Reissig (Uruguay, 1875–1910), as may be seen in his collections *Las pascuas del tiempo* (1900), *Los maitines de la noche* (1900–1903), and his most important work, *La éxtasis de la montaña* (1904). The Colombian Guillermo Valencia (1873–1943), another important modernist poet, wrote several volumes of poems that show his interest in exotic places: *Ritos* (1899, 1914), which contains some works translated from other sources; *Poesías* (1912); *Poemas* (1918); and *Catay* (1929). José Santos CHOCANO, the Peruvian Cantor de América, was more interested in autochthonous America than were other modernists, as demonstrated by poems in his most important volume, *Alma América* (1906): "Los pantanos," "La magnolia," and "El sueño del caimán."

Other writers associated with modernism are José Enrique RODÓ, essayist and author of *Ariel* (1900); Enrique LARRETA, whose novel *La gloria de don Ramiro* (1908) is an excellent example of the modernist esthetic, although such is not the case in his other

major works; and Rafael Arévalo Martínez (Guatemala, 1884–   ), whose short story "El hombre que parecía un caballo" (1915) is considered the best example of its type at the close of the movement. Manuel Díaz Rodríguez (Venezuela, 1868–1927) wrote two novels that are modernist in style: *Ídolos rotos* (1901) and *Sangre patricia* (1902).

The announcement of the beginning of the end of the modernist movement came in a now-famous sonnet by Enrique González Martínez (Mexico, 1871–1952), "Tuércele el cuello al cisne" ("Wring the Neck of the Swan"), which appeared in his volume *Los senderos ocultos* (1911). For many critics this short poem symbolizes the end of modernism in Spanish America.

Bibliography. Ned J. Davison, *The Concept of Modernism in Hispanic Criticism,* Boulder, Colo., 1966; Ricardo Gullón, *Direcciones del modernismo,* Madrid, 1963; Max Henríquez Ureña, *Breve historia del modernismo,* 2d ed., Mexico City, 1962; Evan A. Schulman, *El modernismo hispanoamericano,* Buenos Aires, 1969.

DANIEL R. REEDY

MODINHA. Brazilian sentimental art song cultivated in the eighteenth and nineteenth centuries by Portuguese and Brazilian composers. During the second empire in Brazil, it acquired the character of the Italian opera aria, some aspects of which came to be identified later as "national" traits, and eventually became a folk song type of a strongly lyrical character. As a love song the *modinha* is closely related to another popular species, the *lundu,* a form of song and dance of African origin whose transformation made it a prestigious salon genre in Portugal and Brazil. The first collections were printed in Lisbon in the late eighteenth century. Typically, the *modinhas* in these collections are pieces for two voices in parallel motion with a keyboard or guitar accompaniment. The texts came from such well-known poets as Domingos Caldas Barbosa.

GERARD H. BÉHAGUE

MOLINA, ARTURO ARMANDO (1928–   ). President of El Salvador (1972–   ). An army colonel and former secretary of the incumbent President, Fidel SÁNCHEZ HERNÁNDEZ, Molina ran for the Presidency as the candidate of the government-backed National Coalition party. In the balloting held on February 20, 1972, he won a plurality over three other candidates, including José Napoleón Duarte, former mayor of San Salvador, who was supported by a left-wing coalition of which his own Christian Democratic party was a part. Congress declared Molina the winner several days later. Upon taking office for a five-year term on July 1, 1972, Molina pledged that his administration would pay special attention to the problems of public health, housing, unemployment, and AGRARIAN REFORM.

HELEN DELPAR

MOLINA ENRÍQUEZ, ANDRÉS (1866–1940). Mexican writer. A native of the state of Mexico, Molina received his training in law in Toluca. He wrote for several important newspapers and became prominent with the appearance in 1906 of *La Reforma y Juárez,* the fourth of his published books. The seminal *Los grandes problemas nacionales* (1909), his most important study, is a penetrating analysis of the social and economic problems of Mexico; it is particularly concerned with the role of the mestizo and the Indian, from whom Molina considered progress must emanate. This book became influential in shaping the ideology and programs of the MEXICAN REVOLUTION of 1910–1920. At first Molina Enríquez supported Francisco I. MADERO, but when he discovered Madero's hesitancy in providing a solution to the agrarian problem, he withdrew his support and in 1911 published the Plan of Texcoco, which among other things advocated the expropriation of large estates, their division, and distribution to landless peasants. For his opposition he was imprisoned for two years. Molina directly influenced the writing of Article 27 of the constitution of 1917, which dealt with the land question (*see* CONSTITUTION OF 1917: MEXICO). Although he wrote on other themes, such as ethnology and archaeology, he is noted primarily for his studies on agrarian and social problems. His last major work was the five-volume *Esbozo de la historia de los primeros diez años de la revolución agraria de México* (1932–1936). Molina taught for three decades in the Museo Nacional.

CHARLES R. BERRY

MONAGAS, JOSÉ GREGORIO (1795–1858). President of Venezuela (1851–1855). Like his brother, José Tadeo MONAGAS, José Gregorio fought in the wars of independence and became a strong supporter of the interests of the eastern provinces. In contrast to his more famous brother, however, he had no consuming ambitions and turned out to be practical, loyal, and reasonable. A man of principle, he joined enthusiastically in the formation of the Liberal party in 1840 and became a major political figure in the late 1840s and early 1850s by virtue of José Tadeo's reflected glory. Brought to the Presidency in 1851 to keep the country firmly in the hands of the Monagas family, José Gregorio proved himself a capable and reasonably honest President. Because of the anarchic conditions of Venezuelan politics and the continually declining economy, however, José Gregorio spent most of his term helping his brother keep the country at peace. The high point of his administration occurred in 1854 with the decision to abolish slavery in Venezuela in order to prevent dissident factions from exploiting the revolutionary potential of the remaining black captives. From the end of his presidential term until his death in 1858 José Gregorio played an important if minor role in the civil strife that led to the Federal Wars.

JOHN V. LOMBARDI

MONAGAS, JOSÉ TADEO (1784–1868). President of Venezuela (1847–1851, 1855–1858). One of the heroes of independence from the eastern region of Venezuela, José Tadeo Monagas and his family occupied a prominent position in politics for half a century. In 1831 he led an abortive uprising against the civilian-dominated government of Gen. José Antonio PÁEZ. Claiming that the Venezuelan government had sold out the heroes of independence by abolishing military *fueros* (corporate privileges) and had wounded the moral sensibilities of the people by ending ecclesiastical *fueros,* he called for the reintegration of Gran Colombia (*see* COLOMBIA, GRAN) and the restoration of the military and the church as the twin pillars of society. But with the news of the death of Simón BOLÍVAR the Gran Colombian dream died too, and Monagas then shifted ground, calling for a separatist government of the eastern provinces of Venezuela, to be named the state of Oriente, with himself as chief. Although able to involve such well-known eastern leaders as Santiago Mariño, the rebellion failed to gain enough momentum to succeed against Páez's superior force. In the end Monagas called off his revolt, and in return the government pardoned the rebels. The 1835–1836 Revolución de las Reformas (Revolution of the Reforms) brought out Monagas again in opposition to the civilian government of Dr. José María VARGAS. While Monagas still cherished his hope of establishing a state of Oriente, the Reformas revolt collapsed when Páez moved in support of the government. Again Monagas gave up the fight and received a pardon, although some of his more persistent corevolutionaries were caught in the vindictive reprisals of the victorious civilian Congress and government.

During the next decade Monagas remained quiet in his eastern stronghold, although his brother José Gregorio MONAGAS managed to establish a reputation as a Liberal. By 1846, when the country appeared to be on the verge of civil disturbances and economic depression seemed to be generating considerable resistance to the Páez hegemony, Monagas emerged as a compromise candidate for the Presidency. Although associated with the antigovernment uprisings of 1831 and 1835–1836, he had remained aloof from the Liberal party's violent polemics of the early 1840s. Moreover, Páez evidently thought that Monagas, while pacifying the rambunctious Liberals, would remain loyal to him. He erred in this calculation, for as soon as Monagas took office in 1847, he threw his lot in with the Liberals, and by 1848 he had so alienated the Conservatives that Páez rebelled unsuccessfully against the President he had placed in power.

Although José Tadeo Monagas held the presidential office only between 1847 and 1851 and then again from 1855 to 1858, the decade 1848–1858 was dominated by the operations of the Monagas clan. For a time he enjoyed the support of the Liberals, but as his inability to cope with the economic crisis became evident and his personalist family rule became more blatant, the Liberals became increasingly disillusioned with their erstwhile champion. Throughout the period of the Monagas family rule the government had to contend with a series of revolts and subversive plots engineered by the now-exiled *paecistas.* By 1858 the opposition had grown so strong with a fusion of Liberals and Conservatives that Monagas was forced to resign from the Presidency in March. Although a marginal participant in the subsequent Federal Wars and active in politics until his death, Monagas never again came to play a central political role.

See also CASTRO, Julián.

JOHN V. LOMBARDI

MONÇÃO. *See* MONSOON.

MONROE DOCTRINE. Statement enunciated in a message to Congress on December 2, 1823, by President James Monroe. In it Monroe declared that "the American continents . . . are henceforth not to be considered as subjects for future colonization by any European powers." This portion of the message was directed against a decree (1821) of Czar Alexander I conferring upon Russian subjects exclusive trading rights along the northwest coast of North America to

51° north latitude. The second portion of Monroe's statement reflected the concern of the President that the European powers united in the Quadruple Alliance, which had already authorized a French invasion of Spain to restore the absolute powers of King FERDINAND VII, might attempt to reimpose Spanish rule over the newly independent Spanish American states or bring them under French dominion. Asserting the differences between the political systems of the allied powers and those of the American nations, Monroe stated that the United States would consider any attempt by European powers "to extend their system to any portion of this hemisphere as dangerous" to the "peace and safety" of the United States.

Although the doctrine bears Monroe's name, it was fashioned as much by Secretary of State John Quincy Adams as by the President. Adams prevailed upon Monroe to issue a unilateral policy statement instead of a joint declaration with Great Britain, as had been proposed earlier by British Foreign Secretary George Canning. Adams also persuaded Monroe to refrain from pledging United States support for Greek revolutionaries seeking independence from Turkey and instead to promise that the United States would remain aloof from purely European affairs. He also prevented the inclusion of a pledge that the United States would not acquire additional territory.

Initial European respect for the policies embodied in Monroe's statement sprang not from fear of the President's initiative—after all the United States was a young country, inexperienced in international affairs and boasting only a modest military force—but from knowledge that Canning could use the British Navy to protect Latin America, with which Great Britain enjoyed extensive commercial ties. In fact, two months before Monroe made his historic speech, Canning induced the French to affirm in the Polignac Memorandum that France disclaimed any intention to invade Spain's erstwhile colonies. This stroke of the pen removed the threat of intervention by the most effective European army. Further, Monroe's declaration was not a doctrine in the sense that it became part of international law, for it was never formally agreed to by other powers. Nor was it incorporated into the statutes of the United States, although Congress on several occasions attempted to do so.

For Latin Americans the doctrine initially served to arouse unrequited hopes. At various times after its enunciation, the United States refused to grant assistance against European threats or actual interventions and resisted joining any alliance for that purpose. And although the Europeans did concentrate on Africa and Asia during the remainder of the nineteenth century, they did not hesitate to enter Latin America from time to time. The 1850 CLAYTON-BULWER TREATY between the United States and Great Britain recognized the latter's presence in Central America; in 1861 Spain reannexed Santo Domingo; and two years later French troops of Napoleon III placed the archduke MAXIMILIAN, an Austrian Hapsburg, on a Mexican throne in an effort to resurrect France's influence in America. Opposed by Mexican Liberals and by the United States, the French beat a hasty retreat with the termination of the American Civil War, aware that the United States had become strong enough to back the Monroe Doctrine with force.

A number of corollaries have been attached to the Monroe Doctrine. On December 2, 1845, President James K. Polk asserted what is known as the Polk Corollary when he declared that if any North American people desired to join the United States, the matter would be one for them and the United States to determine "without any foreign interposition." In his statement Polk was alluding not only to British and French efforts to prevent the recent annexation of Texas but also to the dispute with Great Britain over Oregon and to suspicions that the British might be bent on thwarting American ambitions in California. Probably thinking of California, he also announced the opposition of the United States to the cession of any territory in North America to a European power.

The ROOSEVELT COROLLARY of 1904 stated that if Latin American nations failed to keep their political and financial houses in order, the United States would reluctantly exercise "an international police power." This corollary gave rise to subsequent United States intervention in the Dominican Republic and other Latin American states. The CLARK MEMORANDUM of 1928, however, explicitly dissociated the Monroe Doctrine from the right of intervention.

Whereas the Monroe Doctrine had in the past been directed toward European powers, in 1912 a corollary advanced by Senator Henry Cabot Lodge of Massachusetts turned the policy toward Asia. Responding to a Japanese company's negotiations to purchase a large tract of land in Baja California, Lodge introduced in the Senate a resolution disapproving of the transfer of vital American areas to non-American private firms that could be serving as agents of foreign nations—a clear reference to Japan.

Post-World War II rhetoric has held that inter-American agreements, such as the RIO TREATY of 1947 and the Charter of the ORGANIZATION OF AMERICAN STATES (1948), have made the Monroe Doctrine multilateral. However, in spite of cooperative agreements, on a number of occasions, including the 1965 DOMINICAN REVOLT, the United States acted unilaterally to attempt to curb the perceived threat of a nonhemispheric power or foreign ideology from gaining a foothold south of the Rio Grande.

Strengthened by 150 years of tradition, the Monroe Doctrine now symbolizes the insistence of a superpower on keeping alien influence out of its region. The impossibility of such a paternalistic endeavor is transcended only by the intensity of the nationalistic reaction that it provokes.

Bibliography. Alejandro Álvarez, *The Monroe Doctrine: Its Importance in the International Life of the States of the World,* New York, 1924; Donald M. Dozer (ed.), *The Monroe Doctrine: Its Modern Significance,* New York, 1965; Frederick Merk, *The Monroe Doctrine and American Expansionism, 1843–1849,* New York, 1966; Dexter Perkins, *A History of the Monroe Doctrine,* rev. ed., Boston, 1955; William F. Reddaway, *The Monroe Doctrine,* 2d ed., New York, 1905.

GEORGE W. GRAYSON

MONSOON (MONÇÃO). In colonial Brazil, the annual river journey from São Paulo to the goldfields of Cuiabá, a freshwater voyage that outward-bound might take as long as the passage from Lisbon to India via the Cape of Good Hope, or five to six months. The original route passed by way of the Tietê, Paraná,

Pardo, Anhandui, Aquidauana, Paraguay, and Cuiabá Rivers, but after 1725 a 10-mile portage between the Pardo and the Coxim-Taquari was used to reach the Paraguay.

The canoe convoys left between March and mid-June in order to take advantage of the rivers in flood. The return from Bom Jesus do Cuiabá required only two months, and canoes left in June. The convoys, which might contain as many as 300 canoes carrying some 3,000 people, took merchandise, supplies, salt, and animals to Cuiabá and brought back gold. The route was fraught with danger. The voyagers faced many rapids and portages, and in the late 1720s they often had to battle with the ferocious aquatic Paiaguá (Payagua) Indians.

KENNETH R. MAXWELL

MONTALVO, JUAN (1832–1889). Ecuadorian man of letters. Born in Ambato, Montalvo was a distinguished stylist and political writer. Before finishing his studies at the Central University of Quito, he joined the Ecuadorian Legations in Rome and Paris, where he met Victor Hugo and the aging Alphonse de Lamartine. Montalvo returned to Ecuador an enemy of tyranny in all its forms. With his pen as his weapon, he attacked Gabriel GARCÍA MORENO and his clerical supporters. Espousing the theory that tyranny is the wickedness of a few but the cowardice of many, Montalvo castigated the conscience of the Ecuadorian people in his periodical *El Cosmopolita*. Soon he was in exile, supported financially by Generals Ignacio VEINTEMILLA and Eloy ALFARO. From Ipiales, Colombia, he published such propaganda as *La dictadura perpetua* (1874), which predicted García Moreno's death. When a fanatic assassinated García Moreno, Montalvo proudly said, "My pen killed him." He returned to Ecuador the following year to find a new dictator, General Veintemilla, in office. Montalvo refused to sit in Veintemilla's Congress and instead raised his pen in attack. In the *Catilinarias* (1880–1906), he called Veintemilla the "excrement of García Moreno" and was expelled again to Ipiales, traveling from there to Europe.

Montalvo's later years in Paris, where he died, produced the richly embroidered prose considered his best: *Siete tratados* (1882), essays on nobility and beauty; *Capítulos que se le olvidaron a Cervantes* (1895); and *El espectador* (1886–1888), about leisurely fashion and the faults of society.

LOIS WEINMAN

MONTEAGUDO, JOSÉ BERNARDO DE (1789–1825). Argentine patriot and revolutionary publicist. Monteagudo, who in his public career evolved from radical zealot to spokesman for constitutional monarchy and close associate of José de SAN MARTÍN and Simón BOLÍVAR, was born in Tucumán. He received university training at Chuquisaca (modern Sucre, Bolivia) and took part there in the abortive uprising of May 1809. Subsequently imprisoned, he escaped to join the patriot forces from Buenos Aires that invaded the region in 1810. Monteagudo ardently collaborated in the endeavor as a revolutionary propagandist. The expedition ended in defeat, but he soon made his mark again as a journalist and political activist in Buenos Aires. Monteagudo was an early and open exponent of an outright declaration of independence, and in 1812 he became associated with San Martín's LAUTARO LODGE.

An unfavorable turn of Argentine politics in 1815 forced Monteagudo into exile. He traveled to Europe, then returned to America, where he served the Chilean government of Bernardo O'HIGGINS and eventually accompanied San Martín to Peru. San Martín named him Minister of War, in which capacity he aroused considerable hostility by his harsh treatment of Spanish subjects. He likewise worked to promote the cause of constitutional monarchy, for despite his earlier republican leanings he had come to favor a monarchist solution, as did San Martín. But this, too, aroused resistance, and while San Martín was absent for the Guayaquil interview, Monteagudo was compelled to resign and leave Peru. He later returned to Lima as a collaborator of Bolívar, but in 1825 he was assassinated in circumstances that have never been fully clarified.

DAVID BUSHNELL

MONTE ALBÁN. The most spectacular archaeological site in all of Mesoamerica, located 3 miles southwest of Oaxaca, in southern Mexico. It was begun under the influence of Olmec culture, about 500 B.C., at which time it already showed evidences of a hieroglyphic system of writing and a calendar. It is assumed that, throughout most of its long history, the site of Monte Albán was a ceremonial center of the Zapotec Indians. The splendid ruins occupy the elongated top of a high hill overlooking Oaxaca and the valley bottoms on either side. The hilltop was artificially leveled, and the great platforms supporting the cult structures lined a truly vast axial plaza, about 1,000 by 650 feet. The site was to all intents and purposes abandoned, except for burial purposes, by A.D. 900. *See also* OLMECS.

BURR C. BRUNDAGE

MONTERREY. City in northeastern Mexico and capital of the state of Nuevo León. First founded in 1581 and resettled in 1596, it was Mexico's most highly industrialized city during the era of Porfirio DÍAZ (1876–1911) but is now only the economic center of northeastern Mexico.

With the loss of Mexico's northern territory to the United States in 1848, Monterrey became almost a frontier city, and during the American Civil War it had important commercial relations with the Confederacy. Its great development in the last quarter of the nineteenth century stemmed from the fact that it was the junction of several railroad lines and from its proximity to several important customhouses, the cotton of the Laguna District, the livestock and coal mines of Coahuila, the iron deposits of Durango, and the petroleum of northern Veracruz and southern Tamaulipas. By decreeing tax exemption for new industries in 1888, Governor Bernardo Reyes abetted the enterprising spirit of German, Italian, Spanish, and North American residents, who were later emulated by natives, Arabs, Syrians, and Lebanese.

The bases of Monterrey's industrial growth have been the brewery Cervecería Cuauhtémoc, the iron and steel mill Fundidora de Fierro y Acero, and the glassworks Vidriera Monterrey. The principal figures in these enterprises, among them Luis G. Sada of Cervecería Cuauhtémoc and Adolfo Prieto of the Fundidora, developed a paternalistic social policy that resulted in a confrontation with the leftist president Lázaro CÁRDENAS in 1936.

The city is dominated by a very active and well-organized bourgeoisie. Its celebrated Institute of Technology and Advanced Studies was founded in 1943. The population of Monterrey was 830,336 in 1970.

MOISÉS GONZÁLEZ NAVARRO

MONTES, ISMAEL (1861–1933). President of Bolivia (1904–1909, 1913–1917). Montes had training both in the law and in the military. He fought in the Bolivian Army during the WAR OF THE PACIFIC against Chile in 1879 and in the campaign against the Brazilians in Acre in 1903.

When the Liberals seized power in 1899, overthrowing the Conservative regime that had been in control for two decades, Montes became Minister of War. He was the principal lieutenant of the first Liberal President, José Manuel PANDO, and succeeded him as President of Bolivia in 1904, serving until 1909. After being out of office for one term, he returned to the Presidency, serving between 1913 and 1917.

The period in which the Liberals were in power was characterized by doctrinaire application of the party's principles. This was reflected in an anticlerical policy that brought the government into conflict with the Catholic Church on several occasions. It was also shown in the degree to which the Liberal administrations encouraged free private enterprise, both domestic and foreign. The Liberal regimes extensively aided the foreign tin-mining companies, levying very little taxation on them and extending them other favors.

Laissez faire economic principles also found expression in the Liberal governments' seizure of the remaining lands belonging to Indian communities and assignment of them to large private landholders. Montes himself seized some of the choicest remaining Indian communal properties, particularly along the borders of Lake Titicaca.

Upon leaving the Presidency for the second time, Montes was appointed Minister to Great Britain and France. When the Liberal regime was overthrown by a coup of the rival Partido Republicano in 1920, Montes stayed in Paris. He returned to Bolivia only in 1928.

ROBERT J. ALEXANDER

MONTEVIDEO. Capital of Uruguay. As the only major city in Uruguay, Montevideo dominates the nation's economic, social, and cultural as well as political life. In 1970 greater Montevideo had a population of about 1.5 million, or half the population of the nation.

Founded in 1726 as a Spanish outpost in the rivalry with Portugal over control of the Banda Oriental, Montevideo for more than a century was periodically under siege or occupation first by the Iberian powers and later by Great Britain, Argentina, Brazil, and rival Uruguayan factions. At the time of independence the city's population was only 9,000, or about 12 percent of the nation's total, but Montevideo's advantage as Uruguay's major seaport, combined with the impact of heavy European immigration in the late nineteenth and early twentieth century, transformed the city into a major metropolis. *See* IMMIGRATION: URUGUAY.

In addition to being a commercial and industrial center, Montevideo has beaches that attract thousands of tourists to the city each year, particularly from Argentina. The Uruguayan capital also has been the site of many important hemispheric conferences.

LEE C. FENNELL

MONTEVIDEO CONFERENCE (1933). Seventh International Conference of American States, which met in Montevideo, Uruguay, from December 3 to December 26, 1933. The most important result of the conference was the adoption of the Convention on the Rights and Duties of States, the eighth article of which stated: "No state has the right to intervene in the internal or external affairs of another." The decision of Secretary of State Cordell Hull, who headed the United States delegation, to accept the convention fulfilled a long-standing political objective of the Latin American nations. However, Hull added a reservation that lessened the significance of American adherence to the convention; in it the United States reserved its rights "by the law of nations as generally recognized." Further provisions of the convention substantially incorporated the Calvo clause (*see* CALVO DOCTRINE) and the ESTRADA DOCTRINE.

The conference also adopted resolutions recommending a reduction of trade barriers and the codification of international law, drafted a protocol designed to improve the inter-American conciliation system, and proposed the creation of an inter-American bank. Finally, it recommended adherence to a treaty of nonaggression and conciliation that had been signed the previous October by Argentina, Brazil, Chile, Mexico, Paraguay, and Uruguay. The conference failed, however, to obtain more than a brief respite in the CHACO WAR, then raging between Bolivia and Paraguay.

WILLIAM R. ADAMS

MONTEZUMA. *See* MOCTEZUMA.

MONTT, MANUEL (1809–1880). President of Chile (1851–1861). Montt was the key figure in mid-nineteenth-century Chilean history, not only because of his many constructive achievements but also because of the passionate opposition he aroused in many quarters. His political career provoked two civil wars and was also responsible for the emergence of clearly defined political parties in Chile.

Montt came from a well-connected but somewhat impoverished family and was to a certain extent a self-made man. Educated at the Instituto Nacional, he became its deputy rector in 1832 and its rector three years later. He served as senior official in the Ministry of the Interior during the final months of Diego PORTALES's second administration. Presidents Joaquín PRIETO and Manuel BULNES both gave him ministerial rank: he held the combined portfolios of the Interior and External Relations in 1840–1841 and again in 1845–1846. While Minister of Education (1841–1845), Montt gave decisive help to the career of the distinguished Argentine Domingo Faustino SARMIENTO, then in exile in Chile. Sarmiento repaid him with firm support during the difficult events of 1850–1851.

Toward the end of the Bulnes administration Montt emerged as the probable government candidate for the presidential succession. This prospect aroused considerable hostility from the Liberal opposition in Congress (*see* LIBERAL PARTY: CHILE) and provoked the formation, in April 1850, of the more radically inclined Sociedad de la Igualdad (Society of Equality) headed by Francisco BILBAO and others. Faced with this opposition, Bulnes gave official backing to Montt's candidacy, and the Sociedad de la Igualdad was suppressed. The opposition next turned to armed revolt. On April

Manuel Montt. [Radio Times Hulton Picture Library]

20, 1851, a mutiny led by Col. Pedro Urriola broke out in Santiago; 100 lives were lost before it was defeated. Thanks to the government's habitual practice of intervention, ably directed on this occasion by Montt's close associate Antonio VARAS as Minister of the Interior, the presidential election itself was a foregone conclusion. The Liberal opposition now rallied behind the figure of Gen. José María de la Cruz, intendant of Concepción, who placed himself at the head of a rebel army of 3,500 men. A secondary revolt broke out in La Serena. Chile was thus in the grip of civil war when Montt assumed office on September 18, 1851. Government troops under the outgoing President, Bulnes, were able to defeat Cruz in the Battle of Loncomilla (December 8, 1851), and the La Serena insurrection was crushed a few days later. The threat to the regime was averted; and in the aftermath of the civil war Montt took sweeping emergency powers.

In the Presidency, Montt combined an inflexible conservatism with an equally inflexible determination to stimulate the material progress of Chile. His government was one of the most active and enterprising in Chilean history. (The average age of Cabinet ministers during Montt's first quinquennium was thirty-six.) Montt placed considerable emphasis on national development through private enterprise but recognized that "the spirit of association" was weak in Chile and needed reinforcement by government action. During Montt's decade in power the important Santiago-Valparaíso railroad was nearly completed, while the first stage of the publicly financed railroad from Santiago to the south was also put in hand. Chile's first electric telegraph lines were installed, gas lighting appeared in the city streets, and the postal service was reorganized along British lines. In order to stimulate a more productive agriculture, the government established in 1856 the Caja de Crédito Hipotecario (Land Mortgage Bank). Private banking developed apace, and suitable legislation was enacted in 1860. Bulnes's policy of encouraging German immigration to the southern provinces was continued. The government also made serious efforts to expand and improve Chilean education, a particularly strong interest of Montt's.

The closing years of Montt's Presidency were clouded by an economic recession, which coincided with a marked revival of political tension. Political difficulties began in 1856 with a serious conflict between church and state. Montt's intransigent attitude toward the Archbishop of Santiago during this conflict had the effect of alienating a significant section of the ruling party. The disaffected group arrogated to itself the title Conservative party (*see* CONSERVATIVE PARTY: CHILE) and joined forces with the Liberals in an opposition alliance known as the Liberal-Conservative fusion. Montt's remaining supporters formed the National (or *montt-varista*) party. Throughout 1858 the chorus of opposition to Montt grew in volume. The politicians of the fusion, together with more radical elements, vociferously demanded fundamental changes in the constitution (*see* CONSTITUTION OF 1833: CHILE). Their case was most forcefully put in the short-lived journal *La Asamblea Constituyente*, edited by Benjamín VICUÑA MACKENNA. In December 1858, Montt ordered a state of siege and imprisoned Vicuña Mackenna and other leading members of his group. At the start of 1859 revolts against the government broke out in several Chilean cities. These were crushed without difficulty, except in the north, where a rich mining magnate, Pedro León Gallo, organized an army and occupied La Serena after defeating government troops in the Battle of Los Loros (March 14, 1859). Gallo's triumph was brief. On April 29, 1859, his army was destroyed in the Battle of Cerro Grande, and he himself fled to Argentina. Peace was gradually restored throughout the country, although in September the commander of the government forces at Cerro Grande, Gen. Juan Vidaurre Leal, lost his life in a mutiny in Valparaíso. A further round of civil strife seemed imminent over the question of the presidential succession, since Antonio Varas, who shared Montt's approach to government, appeared to be the most likely official candidate. In the event, however, Varas withdrew and the less contentious figure of José Joaquín PÉREZ was chosen by the National party as Montt's successor.

Following his retirement from the Presidency, Montt served as President of the Supreme Court, deputy, senator, and Councillor of State. In 1864–1865 he represented Chile at the American Congress in Lima convened by the Peruvian government and made a notable contribution to its work. His final years were tranquil: the intense political rivalries generated by his Presidency were quickly superseded, and many of his fiercest opponents came to recognize him as a man of great energy and vision. To Chilean historians, however, he remains a figure of controversy.

Bibliography. Alberto Edwards, *El gobierno de don Manuel Montt,* Santiago, 1933; Francisco Antonio Encina, *Historia de Chile,* vol. XIII, Santiago, 1949, vol. XIV, Santiago, 1950, pp. 5–186; Januario Espinosa, *Don Manuel Montt,* Santiago, 1944.

SIMON COLLIER

MORA [OTERO], JOSÉ A[NTONIO] (1897–). Uruguayan statesman and diplomat. Born in Montevideo, Mora graduated as a doctor of laws and social sciences from the University of Montevideo in 1925. He entered the Uruguayan diplomatic service a year later and subsequently served at posts in Spain, Portugal, Brazil, and Bolivia before becoming Ambassador to the United States in 1951. Mora also represented his country at the United Nations and in a number of inter-American conferences, gaining a reputation as a skillful mediator of international disputes. He acted as chairman of the Inter-American Peace Committee that successfully ended a dispute involving the Dominican Republic, Cuba, and Guatemala in 1950. As chairman of the PERMANENT COUNCIL of the ORGANIZATION OF AMERICAN STATES (OAS) in 1955, he helped resolve difficulties between Costa Rica and Nicaragua.

In 1956 Mora was elected to fill the unexpired term of Carlos Dávila as OAS Secretary-General, and on May 18, 1958, he began his own ten-year term in that position. Mora's hope of avoiding involvement of the OAS Secretariat in hemisphere political affairs could not be realized. As Secretary-General, he became personally and officially involved in several disputes, notably in the Dominican crisis of 1965, in which he played a direct role (*see* DOMINICAN REVOLT).

WILLIAM R. ADAMS

MORA, JOSÉ MARÍA LUIS (1794–1850). Mexican political theorist. Mora was the major Liberal thinker of nineteenth-century Mexico. Born into a wealthy creole family in the state of Guanajuato, he was educated in Mexico City at the Colegio de San Ildefonso, where he received a degree in theology in 1819. He was ordained a priest and taught at that college. Although he had not been involved in the earlier phases of the independence movement, he became active in the early 1820s, editing a newspaper advocating separation from Spain and serving in the provincial deputation of the state of México and then as a delegate in the first legislature of the state. The state's constitution, which he authored, was an expression of his liberalism. When the Zacatecas legislature sponsored an essay contest on the subject of the relation between church and state and the question of ecclesiastical wealth, Mora submitted a manuscript that was to become influential in later Liberal thought and programs. In it he upheld the anticlerical theory that the state could intervene in ecclesiastical affairs and that the wealth of the church should be appropriated by the state.

Mora was closely associated with the reform administration of Valentín GÓMEZ FARÍAS in 1833–1834. When it fell, he went to Paris, where he published three volumes of his *Méjico y sus revoluciones* (1836) and his *Obras sueltas* (1837), in which he analyzed Mexican history. Except for a brief period in the late 1840s when he served as the Mexican Minister to Great Britain, he remained in France until his death.

CHARLES R. BERRY

MORA FERNÁNDEZ, JUAN (1784–1854). Costa Rican political leader. After the declaration of independence by which Central America freed itself of Spain, there was much confusion among the towns as to their proper allegiance. Some preferred to be part of the Central American government being formed in Guatemala, some preferred a Mexican connection, and still others saw opportunities of local independence or even allegiance to New Granada (later Colombia) to the south. Their differing views led to hostilities. It was this uneasy situation that Mora Fernández found upon assuming the position of chief of state of Costa Rica in 1824. He was so successful in pacifying the rival factions and in laying the basis for a government independent of Mexico and Guatemala that his term was extended until 1833 without significant opposition. In the 1824–1833 period, while Costa Rica was technically a province within the Federation of Central America (*see* CENTRAL AMERICA, FEDERATION OF), Mora brought the first printing press to Costa Rica, arranged for mining machinery to be imported, and laid plans for the development of the port of Puntarenas. The port was necessary to facilitate the export of coffee, which had become Costa Rica's principal cash crop during the Mora period. When the Federation of Central America broke up in 1838, Costa Rica, partly because of Mora's tutelage, was ready to assume fully independent status.

CHARLES L. STANSIFER

MORAIS [BARROS], PRUDENTE [JOSÉ] DE (1841–1902). President of Brazil (1894–1898). Member of a landowning family in Itu, in the province of São Paulo, Prudente de Morais graduated from the São Paulo law school in 1863 and entered the Liberal party, on whose ticket he was elected to the provincial assembly in 1868. Seven years later he transferred to the Republican party of São Paulo and moved quickly into a position of leadership. In 1885 he was one of the first three Republicans elected to the imperial Parliament. When the empire was overthrown in November 1889, Morais became Governor of São Paulo. The following year he was elected as a senator to the Constituent Assembly and served as its President during the drafting of the constitution of 1891 (*see* CONSTITUTION OF 1891: BRAZIL). Morais was the only candidate to run against Marshal Manuel Deodoro da FONSECA in the indirect elections for the Presidency of Brazil. Defeated, he remained in the Senate until 1894 but then emerged as the official candidate and was elected without opposition as the first civilian President of the republic. During his administration the civil war in Rio Grande do Sul (1893–1895) was brought to a close, but political violence persisted within the Army and among the followers of Antônio CONSELHEIRO in Bahia until 1897. The assassination of the Minister of War gave Morais the opportunity to suppress military insubordination in his last year in office. After completing his term in ill health, Morais avoided public office but remained politically active, opposing the system of "governors' politics" introduced by his successor, Manoel CAMPOS SALLES.

ROLLIE E. POPPINO

MORAZÁN, FRANCISCO (1792–1842). President of the Federation of Central America (1830–1839). Considered the father of Central America for his major role in defending the original union of the five isthmian states, Morazán was born in Tegucigalpa, Honduras, on October 3, 1792. He received little formal schooling but educated himself sufficiently to practice law and secure a position in the municipal government of Tegucigalpa. His career as a minor bureaucrat was cut short when he enlisted in the local militia, then preparing to attack Comayagua, at that time the capital of Hon-

Francisco Morazán. [*Organization of American States*]

duras, in a conflict over whether or not Central America should be annexed to Agustín de ITURBIDE's Mexican empire. This prologue to Morazán's military career ended inauspiciously with his capture by the defenders of Comayagua, who favored annexation.

After the downfall of Iturbide's empire in 1823, the Central American states seceded from Mexico to form a separate republic. This turn of the political wheel netted Morazán the position of Secretary-General in the state government of Honduras in 1824. A year later he relinquished this post to become President of the state legislature. In the meantime, a struggle erupted between the "Conservative" federal government and the state of Guatemala, on the one hand, and the "Liberal" authorities in the outlying provinces. A military expedition from Guatemala City entered Honduras to oust the Liberal government at Comayagua. Officials there commissioned Morazán to recruit troops at Tegucigalpa to bring relief to the besieged capital, but as he returned with a small band of men, he encountered a unit of the Federal Army and exhausted his ammunition in a brief battle at La Maradiaga. He was forced to abandon the attempt to lift the siege, and the Liberal government eventually succumbed. Later he was arrested by the new government at Comayagua but was promptly released. At first he

contemplated emigrating to Mexico but instead recruited an army of 500 men, which he threw against the Conservative Army at La Trinidad. He won a decisive victory there, took Tegucigalpa without resistance, and made himself Chief of State of Honduras in late 1827.

The following year Morazán left Honduras in the hands of his Vice Chief and led an army into El Salvador, where he defeated a superior force at Gualacho on July 6, 1828. With these victories behind him, Morazán was able to subdue the rest of El Salvador and raise the so-called Protector of the Laws Army. Early in 1829 he took Guatemala City with this army after bitter fighting.

In 1830 Morazán won election as President of the Federation of Central America, defeating José Cecilio del VALLE. His fellow Liberals in the provincial capitals disestablished the Catholic Church, enacted radical programs for education and the judiciary, and attempted to promote economic development and immigration. Soon, however, the centrifugal strain of local power struggles, intermunicipal rivalries, resentment of the dominance of Guatemala, and Conservative hostility forced Morazán to take military measures to prevent the Federation from flying apart. In 1832 two filibuster expeditions were beaten back, and trouble was put down in El Salvador and Honduras, but the campaigns and the forced tax levies to finance them swelled Conservative support and divided the Liberals. The Indians, confused and enraged by certain reforms, were further agitated by antigovernment propaganda and a cholera epidemic. Soon Morazán found himself fighting a protracted guerrilla war against José Rafael CARRERA. Emboldened by the Carreran revolt in Guatemala, separatist movements erupted in Honduras, Nicaragua, and Costa Rica. At last encircled, Morazán lost a final battle to Carrera at Guatemala City in 1840 and went into exile, first in Panama and then in Peru.

In 1842 Morazán returned to Central America and helped dissident Costa Ricans overthrow their government. Without pausing to consolidate his control of Costa Rica, he renewed his struggle to forge a Central American nation by armed conquest, but elements within his own army rebelled and executed him by firing squad.

See also CENTRAL AMERICA, FEDERATION OF.

Bibliography. Robert Stoner Chamberlain, *Francisco Morazán: Champion of Central American Federation,* Coral Gables, Fla., 1950; Eduardo Martínez López, *Biografía del General Francisco Morazán,* Tegucigalpa, 1931; Arturo Humberto Montes, *Morazán y la Federación Centroamericana,* Mexico City, 1958; Mary W. Williams, "The Ecclesiastical Policy of Francisco Morazán and Other Central American Liberals," *Hispanic American Historical Review,* vol. III, no. 2, May 1920, pp. 119–143.

KENNETH V. FINNEY

MORELOS Y PAVÓN, JOSÉ MARÍA (1765–1815). Mexican independence leader. Morelos was born in Valladolid (now Morelia), Michoacán, the son of a mestizo father and a creole mother. Upon his father's death in 1779, the boy went to live with an uncle who operated a mule train and owned a hacienda near Apatzingán, where for the next eleven years Morelos worked as a farmer and as a muleteer on the route between Mexico City and Acapulco. In 1790 he left these occupations to enter the Colegio de San Nicolás in Valladolid, where he studied for two years. He then spent three years in the seminary in the same city. In December 1797, he was ordained a priest and assigned to a parish south of Valladolid, near the border of the state of Guerrero, an isolated, poor region in the unhealthy *tierra caliente* (hot country). Morelos remained there as a parish priest for almost thirteen years, until he enlisted in the movement for independence led by Manuel HIDALGO Y COSTILLA. He fathered two, perhaps three, illegitimate children during this period, one of whom, Juan Nepomuceno Almonte, later became important as a political and military figure and especially as an advocate of monarchy in Mexico.

When Morelos learned of the Hidalgo rebellion early in October 1810, he prepared to leave his parish to serve the rebels as a chaplain. Instead Hidalgo gave him a military commission and sent him into Guerrero to raise an army, gather supplies, and capture Acapulco. He was unable to take Acapulco, but by late 1811 he commanded a sizable army that controlled a wide arc of territory, including parts of the present states of Puebla, Oaxaca, Morelos, México, Guerrero, and Michoacán, which continued to be his principal area of operations throughout his campaigns. His second military campaign, beginning late in 1811, brought him control of the city of Oaxaca, where he established his headquarters for a time. By then, largely as a result of his victories, he was generally accepted as the leader of the insurgent cause. His third major campaign began early in 1813, with the goal of capturing Acapulco, which he finally accomplished in August after a four-month siege.

In September 1813, the Congress of Chilpancingo

José María Morelos y Pavón. [*National Museum of History, Mexico City*]

met under his sponsorship and protection (*see* CHILPANCINGO, CONGRESS OF). Briefly Morelos's political interests displaced his military concerns since the title Generalissimo conferred upon him by the legislature gave him authority over civil as well as military affairs. In November 1813, he began his fourth campaign, this time to capture Valladolid. But his army was defeated in late December, and from then until his capture twenty-three months later he was on the defensive, trying to protect the Congress as it moved from place to place to escape the royalist thrusts. He fell prisoner on November 5, 1815, while escorting the Congress on a long march to Tehuacán, Puebla. Taken to Mexico City, he was tried by the Inquisition, which convicted him of heresy and treason and ordered him degraded as a priest (*see* INQUISITION, HOLY OFFICE OF THE). Then he was turned over to the state, which also convicted him and ordered his execution by firing squad at San Cristóbal Ecatepec, outside Mexico City, on December 22, 1815.

Morelos had a genius for military command. More important, he injected into the insurgent movement a purpose and a political program that had been lacking under Hidalgo's leadership. The Congress was chiefly his idea, and it issued a declaration of independence and a provisional constitution. Furthermore, Morelos proclaimed the abolition of slavery and social equality. Although he was condemned by the church, he recognized it as a state church with its colonial privileges intact. After his capture the Congress was dissolved, and the insurgent army broke up into small scattered guerrilla bands. For the next five years the independence movement in Mexico was virtually dormant.

See also CONSTITUTION OF APATZINGÁN.

Bibliography. Rafael Aguirre Colorado et al., *Campañas de Morelos sobre Acapulco,* Mexico City, 1933; Luis Castillo Ledón (comp.), *Morelos: Documentos inéditos y poco conocidos,* 3 vols., Mexico City, 1927; Martín Luis Guzmán (ed.), *Morelos y la iglesia católica,* Mexico City, 1948; Ernesto Lemoine Villicaña (comp.), *Morelos: Su vida revolucionaria a través de sus escritos y de otros testimonios de la época,* Mexico City, 1965; Alfonso Teja Zabre, *Vida de Morelos,* 3d ed., Mexico City, 1959; Wilbert H. Timmons, *Morelos: Priest, Soldier, Statesman of Mexico,* El Paso, Tex., 1963; Ernesto de la Torre Villar, *La Constitución de Apatzingán y los creadores del Estado Mexicano,* Mexico City, 1964.   CHARLES R. BERRY

MORENO, MARIANO (1778–1811). Dominant figure in the first phase of the Argentine independence movement. Still the most controversial of the leaders of Argentine independence, he also had the briefest public career. He was a native of Buenos Aires, born in 1778 to a family of moderate means. Moreno received his higher education in the colonial university center of Chuquisaca, Upper Peru (now Sucre, Bolivia), where he earned degrees in theology and law and received a general exposure to the thought of the Enlightenment in the private library of a learned priest who befriended him (*see* ENLIGHTENMENT: SPANISH AMERICA). He also observed and took to heart the miserable condition of the Andean Indian masses. Indeed, he composed a dissertation on the abuses of Indian forced labor. Although he had begun to practice law in Upper Peru,

Mariano Moreno. [*Organization of American States*]

he returned in 1805 to Buenos Aires, where he continued private practice and also filled a number of official positions. In January 1809, he supported the abortive move to set up a governing junta in place of Viceroy Santiago LINIERS. Later that year he drafted the famous *Representación de los hacendados,* which was a denunciation of Spanish commercial restrictions and a skillful defense of the de facto opening of the port to British trade that the following Viceroy, Baltasar Hidalgo de Cisneros, had decided upon. Moreno still was not a widely known figure at the time of the May 1810 revolution, in which Cisneros himself was deposed and a creole-staffed junta was successfully established. However, he was named one of the junta's two secretaries, with special responsibility for political and military affairs.

The specific influence of Moreno on the course of the revolution is not easy to distinguish from that of the new government as a whole, but it was clearly great. In particular, he either initiated or gave effective support to a wide range of forward-looking measures, such as the junta's decree of press freedom, its elimination of distinctions between Indians and whites in militia organization, and the establishment of what became Argentina's National Library. To him is also attributed the authorship of a revolutionary "plan of operations" that, among other things, called for the use of terror against the enemies of the revolution and the promotion of insurrection in neighboring Brazil with a view to the eventual annexation of Rio Grande do Sul. The authen-

ticity of the plan has been denied by some; but terror was in fact displayed, in the execution of former Viceroy Liniers and other leaders of a counterrevolutionary movement in August 1810.

Then, too, Moreno made use of the official *Gazeta de Buenos Ayres,* which he edited, to prepare opinion for the frank acceptance of independence from Spain and the establishment of democratic and republican institutions. He even sponsored the first Latin American edition of Rousseau's *Contrat Social,* though omitting the section on religion lest it unduly alarm the more conservative creoles.

However, conservative elements *were* alarmed, not just by Rousseau but by the use of "Jacobin" terror and in general by what seemed the dangerous radicalism of men like Moreno. Their strength was greatest in the interior provinces, but Moreno's position was also weakening in the capital thanks to a combination of policy differences and personal or factional rivalries. Most serious was the disagreement between Moreno and the junta's President, Cornelio de Saavedra, which became an open break when Moreno moved to strip Saavedra of "viceregal" honors. He won the point, but his victory was short-lived. In response to an earlier summons from the junta, deputies chosen by the interior provinces were arriving in Buenos Aires and demanding to be incorporated into the junta itself. As they represented the very forces that distrusted Moreno's brand of activism, he employed delaying tactics, but on December 18, with strong support from Saavedra, the interior deputies were admitted to the junta. Moreno then felt compelled to resign from his position. He was offered an official mission to Europe, most likely as a discreet diplomatic exile, but his health was already failing, and he died at sea in March 1811.

Despite the brevity of his career and its ambiguous termination, Moreno left a strong imprint on the independence movement. Others continued the work he had started. Conservative writers have often minimized or denigrated his contribution, but Argentine liberals and leftists, each claiming him as a forerunner of their own positions, have ranked him second only to José de SAN MARTÍN among the heroes of the revolution.

Bibliography. Ricardo Levene, *Ensayo histórico sobre la revolución de Mayo y Mariano Moreno,* 3 vols., 4th ed., Buenos Aires, 1960; Manuel Moreno, *Vida y memorias del doctor Mariano Moreno,* London, 1812, and many later editions; William S. Robertson, "Mariano Moreno," chap. 5, *Rise of the Spanish-American Republics as Told in the Lives of Their Liberators,* New York, 1918; Eugene M. Wait, "Mariano Moreno: Promoter of Enlightenment," *Hispanic American Historical Review,* vol. XLV, no. 3, August 1965, pp. 359–383.

DAVID BUSHNELL

MORENO, MARIO. *See* CANTINFLAS.

MORÍNIGO, HIGINIO (1897–   ). Paraguayan military leader and President-dictator (1940–1948). An officer who had risen to high rank during the CHACO WAR, Morínigo was named Minister of War by President José Félix ESTIGARRIBIA in 1939 and remained in that office until the President died in an airplane crash in 1940. The Cabinet chose Morínigo to fill the rest of Estigarribia's term, and he did so with an iron hand.

President by accident and having little personal support, Morínigo announced that he was to lead the "Paraguayan revolution." Ideologically he leaned toward the right, a posture that pleased his brother officers, but he could not afford to lean too far to the right lest he sacrifice United States aid during World War II. With this aid he embarked upon massive public works programs. In 1943, as the only candidate, he was elected to a full term as President, and his major source of support, the military, was rewarded with more than half the annual budget. In 1945 Morínigo grudgingly declared war on the Axis Powers so that Paraguay could be a member of the United Nations.

Despite his seeming solidarity with the democratic world, Morínigo ran a thoroughgoing police state, complete with censorship, repression of labor, the peasants, and the political opposition, and an effective secret police, all of which induced many Paraguayans to go into exile. After the war he bowed to pressure to moderate his dictatorship, and unrest, always endemic, exploded. In 1947 there was a civil war in which various factions united in an endeavor to drive Morínigo from power. In desperation he turned to the conservative Colorado party for support. The Army and the Colorados finally prevailed over the rebels, and Morínigo, to keep his bargain, stepped down to allow a Colorado, J. Natalicio González, to assume the Presidency. Shortly thereafter Morínigo was invited to leave Paraguay by his erstwhile supporters, and he went into exile in Buenos Aires. He had given Paraguay substantial economic and some social progress but at the price of brutal political repression. The Colorados have been in power since 1948. *See* COLORADO PARTY (PARAGUAY).

JOHN HOYT WILLIAMS

MORONES, LUIS (1890–1964). Mexican labor leader. Morones was born in Tlalpan in the Federal District. His parents, Ignacio Morones and Rafaela Negrete, as well as his aunts and uncles, were textile workers from Guadalajara. Although his father, who had settled in Mexico City, wanted him to continue the family tradition, the younger Morones preferred to work as an electrician; he also studied stenography. Thanks to the help of his numerous aunts, he did not suffer great economic hardships. He joined the Casa del Obrero Mundial (House of the World Worker) in 1913. In December 1914 he took part in the establishment of the Sindicato Mexicano de Electricistas (Mexican Electrical Workers Union) despite the fact that he no longer worked for the electric light company because he had been dismissed as a dangerous agitator. In February 1915 he became manager of the Mexican Telegraph and Telephone Company. The following year he was expelled from the Casa del Obrero Mundial for having abandoned its apolitical character by adopting the so-called tactics of multiple action in order to take part in electoral politics.

In 1917 Morones founded the ephemeral Partido Socialista Obrero (Socialist Workers party); in May 1918 he founded the CONFEDERACIÓN REGIONAL OBRERA MEXICANA (Regional Confederation of Mexican Labor), and in December 1919 the Partido Laborista Mexicano (Mexican Labor party). During the Presidency of Plutarco Elías CALLES (1924–1928), he was Minister of Industry, Commerce, and Labor, and

his influence became so great that he was considered a possible successor to Calles. His political career declined after the assassination of Álvaro OBREGÓN in 1928, and attacks on his ostentatious and ill-gotten fortune became more severe. In 1936 he was expelled from Mexico together with Calles. Upon his return during the Presidency of Manuel ÁVILA CAMACHO (1940–1946), his conservatism became more marked.

MOISÉS GONZÁLEZ NAVARRO

MORROW, DWIGHT W[HITNEY] (1873–1931). American businessman and Ambassador to Mexico. Morrow became Ambassador in 1927. His predecessor, James Rockwell Sheffield, and Secretary of State Frank B. Kellogg had been planning an armed intervention of Mexico in order to secure Mexican compliance with the Bucareli agreements (*see* BUCARELI CONFERENCES). When the President of Mexico, Plutarco Elías CALLES, brought the matter to the attention of President Calvin Coolidge, Sheffield was removed.

A classmate of Coolidge at Amherst College and a graduate of Columbia University Law School, Morrow was a member of the banking firm of J. P. Morgan & Company (1914–1927) and a director of the General Electric Company and the Bankers Trust Company. He soon made himself popular in Mexico with his "ham and eggs" diplomacy, so called because of his preference for discussing business informally at simple meals. His article "Who Buys Foreign Bonds?" (published in *Foreign Affairs* in 1926) anticipated his rejection of the use of force to compel the payment of debts because, among other reasons, there was no "international sheriff." In accordance with this thesis, he made efforts to reconcile the interests of American investors in Mexico with Mexican sovereignty. In upholding the complaints of the oil companies, he took advantage of the fact that the Mexican Supreme Court had ruled that the petroleum laws should not be applied retroactively. Although he acknowledged the validity of Mexico's agrarian laws, he suggested to Calles that they be applied with moderation, an idea the latter attempted to put into practice through his influence on succeeding Presidents. Morrow also contributed to the modus vivendi that put an end to the CRISTERO REBELLION. Elected to the United States Senate as a Republican from New Jersey in 1930, Morrow died shortly after taking his seat.

MOISÉS GONZÁLEZ NAVARRO

MOSQUERA, TOMÁS CIPRIANO DE (1798–1878). Colombian general and political leader. Mosquera was born in Popayán to rank and wealth. His older brother, Joaquín (1787–1878), served as Vice President of the republic (1833–1835), while a younger brother, Manuel José (1800–1853), became Archbishop of Bogotá in 1835. Mosquera's formal education was interrupted by the wars for independence. While he saw duty briefly in the patriot army in 1815–1816, his real service began only in 1820. His family's social and economic importance ensured Mosquera's rapid rise in rank. A captain in 1820, he had become a lieutenant colonel by 1822 and a colonel by 1824. In the latter year his defense of Barbacoas cost him much of his left jaw and several teeth, causing him to have a speech defect for the rest of his life.

In 1826 Simón BOLÍVAR named the ambitious and

Tomás Cipriano de Mosquera. [J. León Helguera Collection]

energetic Mosquera intendant of Guayaquil, where he formally espoused Bolívar's dictatorship in August of the same year. He was later appointed intendant of Cauca, but on November 11, 1828, he suffered a defeat near Popayán at the hands of the anti-Bolivarian chief Col. José María OBANDO. After a diplomatic mission to Peru (1829–1830), Mosquera spent the next three years in Europe and the United States, traveling and studying military science. Upon returning to Colombia, he was elected to Congress, where from 1834 to 1837 he was a spokesman for economic and social reform and material development. An opponent of Francisco de Paula SANTANDER, Mosquera took an active part in securing the election of President José Ignacio de Márquez (1837–1841) and became an important member of his administration.

Mosquera was Minister of War when the revolt of the Supremos broke out in 1839. He took to the field in early 1840, and by the war's end in 1842 he had established a reputation for military prowess and arbitrary conduct. In 1845 Mosquera succeeded his son-in-law, Pedro Alcántara Herrán, in the Presidency. After 1846 he promoted policies of fiscal, political, and educational reform, which, while they enshrined the period as the century's most progressive, also split the ruling class, permitting a Liberal electoral victory in 1849 (*see* LIBERAL PARTY: COLOMBIA).

Unsuccessful in creating a party of progressive moderates like himself, Mosquera went to the United States, where he established a commission house in 1850. Its failure was imminent in 1854, when he returned to Colombia to lead an army against the dictatorship of José María Melo. As a senator (1855–1857), Mosquera espoused federalism and was instrumental in creating the state of Cauca, becoming its

Governor in 1858. While still Governor, he led a nationwide revolution, supported by the Liberal party, against the federal administration in Bogotá, which was headed by the Conservative Mariano Ospina Rodríguez (*see* CONSERVATIVE PARTY: COLOMBIA).

Occupying Bogotá in mid-1861, Mosquera, as acting President, inaugurated a harsh program of anti-clericalism that ended mortmain and destroyed the Catholic Church as an economic factor in Colombian society. Although he was able to defeat an Ecuadorian army at Cuaspud in December 1863 and to win the title of field marshal, Mosquera's authoritarianism clashed with the dogmatism of the Liberal leadership, and he was removed from the Presidency on May 23, 1867, during his fourth tenure of that office.

Mosquera was tried before the Senate and exiled to Peru, where he remained until 1870, writing his memoirs and justifying his conduct. Upon returning to Colombia, he was elected Governor of Cauca State (1871–1873), which he also represented in the Senate (1876–1877). He continued to be an active promoter of the economic development of the region until his death near Popayán in 1878.

Bibliography. Joaquín Estrada Monsalve, *Mosquera: Su grandeza y su comedia*, Bogotá, 1945; J. León Helguera and Robert H. Davis (eds.), *Archivo epistolar del General Mosquera*, 3 vols., Bogotá, 1966– ; Ignacio Liévano Aguirre, *El proceso de Mosquera ante el Senado*, Bogotá, 1966; Joaquín Tamayo, *Don Tomás Cipriano de Mosquera*, Bogotá, 1936.

J. LEÓN HELGUERA

MOSQUITO COAST. Territory of indefinite depth that extended along the Central American Caribbean littoral from Trujillo, Honduras, to the San Juan River. The inhabitants were Mosquito (Miskito) Indians, a people of mixed Indian and Negro ancestry. Especially after the conquest of Jamaica in 1655, British buccaneers, woodcutters, and traders frequented this coast. In time they built settlements, erected fortifications, and occupied the Bay Islands. The British dramatized their claim that, never having submitted to Spaniards, the Mosquitos maintained an independent native kingdom, by crowning each "King" as he succeeded to the chieftainship. Central Americans regarded these performances as travesties. In compliance with the Convention of London of 1786, Britain abandoned the Bay Islands and the Mosquito Coast and transferred its subjects to Belize.

After Central American independence, the expansion of Belize mahogany cutting and an aggressive revival of British claims by the Superintendent of Belize reestablished British control of the Mosquito Coast and the Bay Islands. The United States sought to halt this advance by the CLAYTON-BULWER TREATY in 1850, and Britain renounced its claims to the Bay Islands and the Mosquito Coast by individual treaties signed with Honduras (1859) and Nicaragua (1860). However, Britain maintained Nicaraguan Mosquitia as an autonomous Indian reservation until 1894, when Nicaragua incorporated it.

Honduras and Nicaragua long disputed the division of the former Mosquito Coast. An arbitral award made by King Alfonso XIII of Spain in 1906, confirmed by the International Court of Justice in 1960, established the boundary at the Coco River.

WILLIAM J. GRIFFITH

MOTECUHZOMA. *See* MOCTEZUMA.

MOTOLINÍA. *See* BENAVENTE, TORIBIO DE.

MOVIMENTO DEMOCRÁTICO BRASILEIRO (BRAZILIAN DEMOCRATIC MOVEMENT; MDB).

The only opposition party in Brazil, it has primarily an urban electoral following. The MDB was formed during the first half of 1966, in the wake of actions by the administration of Humberto CASTELLO BRANCO abolishing all existing political parties and requiring that new ones be sponsored by at least 120 congressmen and 20 senators. For the most part, the men attracted to the MDB had formerly represented the PARTIDO TRABALHISTA BRASILEIRO (Brazilian Labor party) in national, state, or municipal offices. In view of the fact that the President of the nation is elected by Congress, in which the administration's ALIANÇA RENOVADORA NACIONAL commanded a majority of 2 to 1, the MDB did not present a candidate to run against Arthur da COSTA E SILVA in 1966 or against Emílio Garrastazu MÉDICI in 1969.

Although initially the MDB enjoyed a majority in three state legislatures, its position was steadily undermined by purges of its officeholders carried out by the national government under the terms of the Second and Fifth Institutional Acts of 1965 and 1968. In 1970 the MDB still dominated the Guanabara Assembly, thereby assuring the victory of its candidate in the indirect gubernatorial elections, but elsewhere the party failed to elect a single governor. In the 1970 congressional contests the Movimento Democrático Brasileiro returned only about 90 of 310 congressmen and 6 of the 46 new senators.

ROLLIE E. POPPINO

MOVIMIENTO NACIONALISTA REVOLUCIONA-RIO (NATIONALIST REVOLUTIONARY MOVEMENT; MNR).

Most important political party of Bolivia since World War II. The MNR was established in 1941 by veterans of the CHACO WAR, which Bolivia fought with Paraguay between 1932 and 1935. It was one of several parties founded after the Chaco War as a result of the disintegration of the social and political fabric of Bolivia precipitated by that conflict. Not inspired by any philosophy from outside Bolivia, the MNR proclaimed itself to be nationalist and strongly opposed to the influence of the Big Three mining companies that dominated the tin industry (the country's major source of exports) and were to a considerable degree foreign-owned. *See* TIN INDUSTRY (BOLIVIA).

During World War II the Movimientistas were accused of being pro-Axis. This charge was reinforced by the party's opposition to the entry of additional Jews to Bolivia, on the ground that previous immigrants who had come ostensibly as agriculturalists had in fact settled as traders in La Paz and Cochabamba. However, the MNR leaders insisted that they were not pro-Axis but were opposed to the excessive influence of British and American capital in the nation's economy. Their subsequent behavior in the government indicated that they held no prejudice against Jews but, on the contrary, particularly favored the Jewish population.

Some of the young men who were to establish the MNR had held posts in the administration of President Germán BUSCH (1937–1939) and supported his nationalistic economic policies. With his death in August 1939 and elections in the following year, several future MNR leaders were elected to Congress, including Víctor PAZ ESTENSSORO, Hernán SILES, and Walter Guevara Arce.

The MNR was a minority party until the CATAVI MASSACRE in December 1942. The leaders of the tin miners, many of whose followers had been killed when troops fired on striking tin workers, sought out the MNR members of Congress. These deputies undertook the defense of the miners and vociferously denounced the government of Gen. Enrique PEÑARANDA. In December 1943 the MNR cooperated with a group of young officers, the Razón de Patria (RADEPA) lodge, to overthrow Peñaranda. In the new regime (1943–1946) of Maj. Gualberto VILLARROEL, MNR leaders for the first time entered the government. For the party's future, its most important activity during this period was in organizing tin miners. The Villarroel government encouraged the unionization of these workers, and in 1945 an MNR member, Juan LECHÍN, was elected executive secretary of the Miners Federation.

In July 1946 the Villarroel regime was overthrown. For almost six years thereafter, the MNR was in a political wilderness. Its leaders were in exile or underground, although the party organized general strikes on several occasions and a major insurrection, which was almost successful, in 1949.

The MNR presented Víctor Paz Estenssoro for President and Hernán Siles for Vice President in the 1950 election, although both were in exile. They got more votes than any other nominees, but President Mamerto Urriolagoitia, rather than admit the MNR victory, turned power over to a military junta. The military regime was overthrown in April 1952 in an insurrection led by the MNR, together with the national police. Siles and Juan Lechín led the MNR forces. With its victory they called Paz Estenssoro back from exile.

During the next twelve years the MNR brought about a fundamental revolution in Bolivia. This included an AGRARIAN REFORM, which gave the land of the ALTIPLANO (high plateau) to the Indians, from whom it had been taken during and after the Spanish conquest. The Indians were organized into unions (which, pending land distribution, negotiated rental terms with the landlords), militia groups (with arms taken from the defeated Army), and local units of the MNR. The MNR government's program also included nationalization of the Big Three tin-mining companies, Patiño, Hochschild, and Aramayo. It launched a large-scale economic development program in the Oriente (eastern Bolivia). It established a relatively democratic system of government; in the 1956 and 1960 presidential elections the MNR was faced with several rival candidates. However, in 1964 Lechín, who meanwhile had broken with the party, withdrew his candidacy, saying that President Paz Estenssoro had arranged for his own reelection. *See also* ORIENTE (BOLIVIA).

Although Paz Estenssoro was reelected in June 1964, he was overthrown on November 4 by the military, with the support of various opposition groups, including MNR dissidents. The overthrow of the MNR was due in large part to the split in its ranks. In 1960 Walter Guevara Arce, a party founder, had broken with it when he was denied the MNR nomination in favor of ex-President Paz Estenssoro. Four years later,

Juan Lechín had broken away to establish his own party, the Partido Revolucionario de la Izquierda Nacionalista (PRIN), when he too was refused the MNR nomination, in favor of the reelection of Paz Estenssoro.

Between November 1964 and August 1971 the MNR was again in the political wilderness. The party split into two factions, one led by Víctor Andrade, former Ambassador to the United States, and the other composed of younger MNR leaders who called themselves the Movimiento Revolucionario Pazestenssorista and set up separate groups. Meanwhile, the exiled MNR leaders sought to reestablish the party's unity. In August 1971 Gen. Juan José TORRES, who had the backing of the PRIN of Lechín and of pro-Moscow and pro-Chinese Communists and various Trotskyite factions, was overthrown. The groups supporting the rebel leader, Col. Hugo BANZER, included a major part of the Army, the MNR forces of Paz Estenssoro, and the MNR's traditional opponent, the Falange Socialista Boliviana. The MNR received three posts in President Banzer's new government. Late in 1973, however, Paz Estenssoro's withdrawal of support for the Banzer government provoked a split in the party.

Paz Estenssoro returned to Bolivia and undertook the job of reorganizing the party. In March 1972 it held its Twelfth Congress, which laid down the lines for resuming the transformation of the economy and society begun during the twelve years the party had been in power.

Bibliography. Robert J. Alexander, *The Bolivian National Revolution,* New Brunswick, N.J., 1958; James M. Malloy and Richard S. Thorn (eds.), *Beyond the Revolution: Bolivia since 1952,* Pittsburgh, 1971.

ROBERT J. ALEXANDER

MUÑOZ MARÍN, LUIS (1898–   ). Puerto Rican poet, newspaperman, and statesman. Luis Muñoz Marín, founder and leader of the Partido Popular Democrático (Popular Democratic party; PDP) and Puerto Rico's first elected Governor, led the country's rise from a poor and underdeveloped economy to a modern and highly industrialized society. The son of Luis MUÑOZ RIVERA, Puerto Rico's foremost autonomist leader in the nineteenth century and the first decade of the twentieth, Muñoz Marín spent much of his youth in the United States, where his father served as resident commissioner in Congress from 1910 until 1916. After his father's death he remained in the United States, leading a bohemian life and writing poetry and political commentary for the *Nation,* the *American Mercury,* and the *New Republic,* among others.

In 1931 Muñoz Marín returned permanently to Puerto Rico and joined the newly founded Liberal party. The next year he was elected Senator-at-Large. His early success in politics was due only partly to his family name and brilliant mind. Equally important were the friendships which he had made during his years in the United States and which now gained him access to the upper echelons of the Roosevelt administration, a circumstance much admired in the island. By 1936 his future could not have appeared brighter. Then things changed. His contacts with federal authorities began to wane when he refused to condemn the assassination of the chief of police unless the death of the two Nationalists who killed him was also condemned. He urged the Liberal party to boycott the 1936 elections, losing a close vote in the party's convention over the issue.

The Liberal party lost the elections, and Muñoz's career appeared to have reached its end. But Muñoz and a group of devoted followers, including Inés María Mendoza, who would become his second wife, began to crisscross the island talking to the *jíbaros* (countryfolk) about their problems and urging them not to sell their votes. In 1938 he founded the Popular Democratic party. He pledged himself to deal with Puerto Rico's awesome socioeconomic problems and to postpone the issue of political status. The PDP won a narrow victory in 1940, gaining control of the Senate and having the same number as the opposition in the House of Representatives, where a three-member splinter party delegation held the balance. Yet the impressive victory and Muñoz's skill made it possible for the PDP, with the aid of Governor Rexford Guy Tugwell, to effectuate a peaceful revolution, enacting into law numerous far-ranging economic, social, and political reforms. In 1948 Puerto Ricans elected their own Governor for the first time. Muñoz Marín received overwhelming support, losing in only one municipality.

After eight years as leader of the party in power Muñoz knew that he had to face the postponed status problem. An ardent independence backer in his early years, he began to realize the economic hardship that total separation from the United States would imply. At the same time he rejected the total assimilation that statehood would mean and feared the impact of federal taxation on the economy. However, continuance of colonial status was intolerable. The new Governor then proposed a process whereby Puerto Rico could achieve full autonomy; this process was implemented between 1950 and 1952. On July 25, 1952, Governor Muñoz Marín proclaimed the Estado Libre Asociado, and for the first time the Puerto Rican flag was hoisted officially.

Muñoz was reelected by a wide margin in 1956. In the 1960 election a new element was added. The Roman Catholic hierarchy not only objected to the PDP's opposition to religious instruction in public schools but also declared it a sin to vote for the PDP because of the party's stand on birth control. Despite this opposition the PDP won with more than 58 percent of the vote. In 1964 Muñoz, against the will of the party's assembly, refused renomination for a fifth term, and nominated his Secretary of State and right-hand man, Roberto SÁNCHEZ VILELLA, to succeed him. Muñoz accepted an at-large nomination for the Senate. After the elections Muñoz was named a member of a joint United States–Puerto Rico commission studying the status of Puerto Rico. The commission recommended that a plebiscite be held to determine the wishes of the people regarding this matter. Muñoz campaigned vigorously in favor of commonwealth status, and in the vote in July 1967 commonwealth status was endorsed by 60.4 percent of the voters.

In the meantime Sánchez Vilella had antagonized important and powerful sectors of the party. The rift became complete when the PDP denied him renomination. Sánchez then left the party and accepted the nomination of the People's party. Muñoz reassumed the leadership of the PDP and participated actively in the 1968 campaign. This time the PDP was voted out of office. Muñoz retained his at-large seat in the Senate but did not play an active role. After two years he resigned his seat and went to live in Europe, returning several weeks before the 1972 elections to help in the final phase of the campaign. The PDP regained control of the executive and both chambers of the legislative branch.

Although Muñoz has in a pragmatic fashion adapted many of his ideas to the changing realities of his country, there is a profound consistency in his thought and action in behalf of his people. In his last message to the Legislature as Governor he defined it thus: "Puerto Rico shall not only hunger for consumption, but also thirst for justice, art, science, comprehension and good human fellowship; it shall not be satisfied with material abundance without moral and spiritual excellence."

Bibliography. Thomas Aitken, Jr., *Poet in the Fortress: The Story of Luis Muñoz Marín,* New York, 1964; Robert J. Alexander, *Prophets of Revolution: Profiles of Latin American Leaders,* New York, 1962; Thomas Mathews, *Puerto Rican Politics and the New Deal,* Gainesville, Fla., 1960; id., *Luis Muñoz Marín: A Concise Bibliography,* New York, 1967; Luis Muñoz Marín, *The Commonwealth of Puerto Rico: A House of Good Will,* San Juan, 1956; id., "Development through Democracy," *Annals of the American Academy of Political and Social Science,* vol. CCLXXV, January 1953, pp. 1–8; Bolívar Pagán, *Historia de los partidos políticos puertorriqueños (1898–1956),* 2 vols., San Juan, 1959; Henry Wells, *The Modernization of Puerto Rico: A Political Study of Changing Values and Institutions,* Cambridge, Mass., 1969.   LUIS E. AGRAIT

MUÑOZ RIVERA, LUIS (1859–1916). Puerto Rican poet, newspaperman, and statesman. Muñoz Rivera first ventured into politics as a candidate for the Provincial Assembly in 1885. In 1887 he participated in the convention in Ponce that founded the Autonomist party under the leadership of Román Baldorioty de Castro. After Baldorioty's death in 1889 Muñoz Rivera moved from his small hometown of Barranquitas to the city of Ponce, where he founded and edited *La Democracia.*

He became convinced that the main problem facing the Autonomist forces was not lack of support in Puerto Rico, for they enjoyed a clear majority in the island, but rather their political weakness in Spain. He proposed that the Autonomist party make an alliance with the Liberal Fusion party of Práxedes Mateo Sagasta. In 1896 he journeyed to Spain and made the alliance with Sagasta. The pact caused a split within the Autonomist party, leading to the withdrawal of a group led by José Celso that opposed any agreement with a monarchical party. Sagasta came to power in Spain in August 1897. In December of that year the Autonomic Charter (Carta Autonómica) was decreed. This decree marked the culmination of the aspirations of the liberal creole group in the nineteenth century. In the new government Muñoz Rivera was named Secretary of Grace, Justice, and Government. The Autonomic Cabinet did not last long. In 1898 the island was ceded to the United States in the Treaty of Paris ending the Spanish-American War.

When the American military government was established, Muñoz, who differed in almost all respects with United States policy, reopened *La Democracia.* In 1901 he moved to New York, where he edited the *Puerto Rican Herald.* Three years later he returned to Puerto Rico to dissolve the Federal party, which he had created after the change of sovereignty, and join in the Unión de Puerto Rico with Rosendo Matienzo Cintrón and his followers in the hope of creating a broad-based political force that could channel effectively the generalized desire for change. The Unión became the dominant party in the island. In 1910 Muñoz Rivera was elected Puerto Rico's resident commissioner in Washington. From his seat in the House of Representatives he continued to battle for a fuller degree of autonomy. His efforts were partly successful with the approval in 1917 of the Jones Act, which contained a Bill of Rights, authorized popular election of both chambers of the Legislature, and granted American citizenship to Puerto Ricans. Muñoz Rivera did not live to see this triumph, for he had died five months before.

Muñoz Rivera published two books of poems, *Retamas* (1891) and *Tropicales* (1902). Some of his political writings were published by his son, Luis MUÑOZ MARÍN, in *Campañas políticas* (1925). His complete works (1889–1898) were published by the Institute of Puerto Rican Culture (1960–1964).

LUIS E. AGRAIT

MURILLO, GERARDO. *See* ATL, DR.

MURILLO TORO, MANUEL (1816–1880). President of Colombia (1864–1866, 1872–1874). Murillo was born of humble parentage in Chaparral, Tolima. Thanks to the patronage of the physician and botanical scholar Manuel María Quijano, he was able to attend the university in Bogotá; he received a doctorate in law in 1836. A follower of Francisco de Paula SANTANDER, Murillo was associated in his youth with various newspapers hostile to the administration of José Ignacio de Márquez (1837–1841). In 1839–1840 he took an active role in the revolt of the Supremos and barely escaped prison or exile. In 1844 he managed to secure a post as secretary to the Governor of Panama, and in 1847–1848 he edited the Liberal *Gaceta Mercantil* in Santa Marta.

During the Presidency of Liberal José Hilario López (1849–1853), Murillo served as Secretary of Finance and was the chief ideologue of the administration. He led the doctrinaire Liberals (*see* LIBERAL PARTY: COLOMBIA), known as Gólgotas, against the presidential candidacy of José María OBANDO in 1852 and opposed the Melo dictatorship in 1854. He ran unsuccessfully for the Presidency in 1856, was Governor of the state of Santander from 1857 to 1859, and, as a convinced federalist, joined Gen. Tomás Cipriano de MOSQUERA's revolution in 1860. During this period he also edited *El Tiempo,* the leading Liberal party organ in Bogotá.

Murillo was elected to the Presidency in 1863 while he was serving as Colombian Minister to the United States. During his first administration (1864–1866) he restored some peace to the war-torn nation by mitigating the stringent anticlerical measures imposed by his predecessor, General Mosquera. In 1867 he was instrumental in the overthrow of Mosquera's last government. As President for a second term (1872–1874), he improved public finances and promoted secular education. He remained the Liberal kingmaker until his death in 1880. A masterful political manipulator, Murillo nonetheless made the Liberal party so hermetic and exclusivist that Rafael NÚÑEZ was forced to go out of it and create his own.

J. LEÓN HELGUERA

MURTINHO, JOAQUIM [DUARTE] (1848–1911).
Brazilian politician and Finance Minister. Born in
Cuiabá, Mato Grosso, and trained in medicine, Murtinho established himself as a political figure at the provincial level before his election to the Senate of the Constituent Assembly. In that capacity he helped to draft
the republican constitution of 1891 (*see* CONSTITUTION
OF 1891: BRAZIL). At the same time he opened a medical clinic in Rio de Janeiro, which he continued to
operate until his death. In 1897 he became Minister of
Industry in the Cabinet of Prudente de MORAIS.

Murtinho is best remembered as the Finance Minister
and strongest member of the Cabinet of President
Manoel CAMPOS SALLES, a post he held from 1898 to
1902. As a proponent of free trade during a period of
monetary inflation and economic depression, Murtinho
imposed a policy of stringent fiscal austerity, cutting
public expenditures to the minimum and raising taxes
on imports, the principal source of revenue for the national government. He attracted much criticism for
his refusal to authorize new currency emissions and
for the public destruction of outworn paper money in
his successful campaign to restore the value of Brazil's
currency. The Brazilian tariff of 1900, which bears his
name, greatly increased the proportion of import taxes
to be paid in gold. It was regarded at the time as a free
trade measure but proved to offer protection to Brazil's
infant manufacturing industries. After leaving the
cabinet Murtinho returned to the Senate, where he
continued to expound classical economic theories.

ROLLIE E. POPPINO

MUSIC (BRAZIL). Relatively little is known about the
art music of the first two centuries of Brazilian history.
Throughout the colonial period (which lasted until
1822) most music making was related directly to church
services. With a few isolated exceptions, the extant
colonial repertoire therefore falls mainly in the category
of sacred music. The substantial documentation attest-
ing to important musical activities in Olinda and Recife,
Pernambuco, and Salvador, Bahia, has only recently
been compiled and studied.

The regular clergy were the first to organize Christian
religious life in Brazil. The Franciscans started using
music in the conversion of the Indians, but the Jesuits
had the strongest impact in bringing European musical
practices to the colony. By 1550 the Jesuit Manuel da
NÓBREGA had initiated musical instruction in Salvador.
Instrument making did not flourish until the eighteenth
century, when organs and other instruments were built
in Olinda and Minas Gerais.

The actual colonial music repertoire of which manuscripts exist in Brazil dates to 1759–1760. A recita-
tive and aria in the vernacular for soprano, first and second violins, and continuo, was written in Salvador in
1759. Although this piece was first considered anonymous, recently gathered evidence has shown that it was
composed by Caetano de Mello Jesus, the contemporary chapelmaster of the Cathedral of Salvador. The
second of the two oldest pieces is the Te Deum (ca.
1760) for mixed chorus and continuo by Luis Álvares
Pinto (1719–1789), a mulatto composer who was the
chapelmaster at the Church of São Pedro dos Clérigos
in Recife and the founder in that city of the all-impor-
tant Irmandade de Santa Cecília dos Músicos.

An exceptional musical life developed during the
latter part of the eighteenth century in Minas Gerais
as the consequence of the socioeconomic boom in the
province. According to the musicologist Francisco
Curt Lange (*see* Bibliography), who first uncovered the
primary sources of that repertoire, about 1,000 musicians were active in Minas between approximately
1760 and 1800, especially in the cities of Vila Rica
de Ouro Prêto, Sabará, Mariana, Arraial do Tejuco
(now Diamantina), and São João del Rei. Most of these
musicians were mulattoes who were associated with
local *irmandades* (brotherhoods), musical guilds relatively independent of the clergy. Among the composers whose works have come to light are José Joaquim Emerico Lobo de Mesquita (ca. 1740s–1805),
Marcos Coelho Netto (d. 1806), Francisco Gomes da
Rocha (d. 1808), and Ignacio Parreiras Neves (ca.
1730–ca. 1793). All of them cultivated a prevailingly
homophonic style in sacred works for mixed chorus
with orchestral accompaniment including violins, viola,
French horns, occasional oboes and flutes, and continuo. Practically all the pieces thus far discovered are
compositions for liturgical use (masses, motets, antiphons, novenas, and so on). The only work with text in
the vernacular is Parreiras Neves's *Oratoria ao Menino
Deos para a Noite de Natal* (1789), discovered in
Mariana in 1967. Only its soprano and instrumental
bass parts remain.

Among the chapelmasters at the Cathedral of São
Paulo, André da Silva Gomes (1752–1844) deserves a
special place not only as a prolific composer of sacred
music but also as an influential teacher. His *Missa a
8 Vozes e Instrumentos* displays a solid contrapuntal
style and a general harmonic richness.

Musical life in Rio de Janeiro began to flourish with
the transfer to that city of the Portuguese royal court in
1808. That year the prince Dom João (later JOÃO VI)
created the Royal Chapel, to which he appointed as
musical director and chapelmaster the mulatto composer José Mauricio Nunes GARCIA. José Mauricio is
rightly considered one of the glories of Brazil's musical
past. Some 237 works of his are extant, among them a
large number of masses, motets, and pieces for Holy
Week and other liturgical occasions. Such early sacred
pieces as *Crux fidelis* (1806) exhibit a profound devotional character, while the later compositions (for
example, *Missa Pastoril,* 1811) display in both choral
numbers and arias the operatic influence then common
in Europe in sacred works. José Mauricio's Requiem
(1816), written on the occasion of the death of Queen
Maria I, is generally considered his masterpiece. He
also wrote some secular pieces. Of interest are the
MODINHA *Beijo a Mão Que Me Condemna* and several
overtures, among which *Zemira* is still occasionally
performed in Brazil.

Professional European composers began to migrate
to Brazil during Dom João's residence in Rio. In 1811
the Portuguese opera composer Marcos Portugal
(Marcantonio Portogallo, 1762–1830) settled there,
adding great prestige to the musical life of the city. The
Austrian Sigismund von Neukomm (1778–1858) was
hired by the court from 1816 to 1821 to teach the young
prince Dom Pedro (later PEDRO I). Neukomm wrote
the oldest known piano piece (1819), using a tune from
a Brazilian popular *lundu.*

The nineteenth century was dominated by opera and

salon music. After independence the former Royal Theater became the Imperial Theater. The period of PEDRO II's reign (1831–1889) was characterized by the cultivation and official protection of Italian opera. Bellini's *Norma* received numerous performances. In the government-subsidized theaters (São Pedro de Alcântara, later Teatro Lírico Provisório) in Rio were produced the main operas from Rossini to Verdi. Particularly active at that time was Francisco Manuel da Silva (1795–1865), remembered today as the composer of the Brazilian national anthem. Da Silva attempted to stimulate the use of the vernacular in the operatic repertoire. In 1857, under the auspices of the Emperor, the Imperial Academy of Music and National Opera was founded with the same goal. After that date the first operas by Brazilian composers were presented. Such composers included Elías Álvares Lobo, Henrique Alves de Mesquita, and, above all, Antônio Carlos GOMES. Gomes had the most brilliant career of any composer of the hemisphere in the nineteenth century. One of his first successes came in 1861 with the presentation at the Teatro Lírico Provisório of his grand opera *A Noite do Castelo,* which was strongly influenced by contemporary Italian models and displayed the qualities of lyricism and dramatization essential for an opera composer. After studying at the Milan Conservatory, Gomes achieved his greatest success with the premiere of *Il Guarany* at the La Scala in Milan in 1870.

Regular concert life began to emerge in Rio only during the last three decades of the nineteenth century. Concert societies and clubs were founded, stimulating the appearance in Brazil of some of the most celebrated performing artists of the time (Sigismund Thalberg, Arthur Napoleão, Louis Moreau Gottschalk). At the same time several composers, including Leopoldo Miguéz and Henrique Oswald, cultivated prevailing European styles, using especially Wagnerian and early impressionist models. As a teacher of composition Francisco Braga (1868–1945) exerted a strong influence in the local extension of Wagnerian romanticism.

This is also the period of incipient nationalistic concern in Brazilian music. The first "nationalist" composition was published in 1869 by Brasílio Itiberê da Cunha (1846–1913), an amateur musician and a remarkable pianist. His piano piece *A Sertaneja* attempts to recreate in various ways the atmosphere of urban popular music, even quoting a characteristic popular tune, "Balaio, Meu Bem, Balaio." Alexandre Levy (1864–1892) wrote his most typically national compositions in 1890, among them the *Tango Brasileiro,* for piano, and the *Suite brésilienne,* for orchestra. The latter is the forerunner of many such pieces produced by later nationalist composers. Its last movement, "Samba," can be considered the first decisive step toward musical nationalism in Brazil. Rather than being based on the characteristics of the folk SAMBA, the movement draws on urban popular dance rhythms, such as those of the maxixe and the Brazilian tango.

By the start of the twentieth century art music in Brazil had begun to display a typical individuality. The composer Alberto NEPOMUCENO played a role of primary importance in the creation of genuine national music. Among his numerous compositions, the *Série Brasileira* (1892) and the prelude *O Garatuja* (1904), both for orchestra, the String Quartet No. 3 (1891), the

piano pieces *Galhofeira* (1894) and *Brasileira* (1919), and several art songs present folk or popular material or simply draw directly upon popular music. The last movement, "Batuque," of his *Série Brasileira* is symptomatic of the discovery of the rhythmic primacy of popular music, prefiguring similar accomplishments in subsequent twentieth-century compositions.

After 1920 the major exponent of Brazilian art music was Heitor VILLA-LOBOS. Extremely prolific and imaginative, he wrote about 1,000 works (if various arrangements of many pieces are considered) in all possible genres and media. The Modern Art Week that took place in São Paulo in 1922 under the leadership of Mário de ANDRADE, among others, was influential in Villa-Lobos's career. This event stimulated him in his already well-established quest for musical nationalism. The various facets of Villa-Lobos's creative power are revealed in his most important works of the 1920s: the *Nonetto* (*Impressão Rápida de Todo o Brasil*) of 1923; the series of *Chôros* (see CHÔRO), single-movement works for varying media, from solo guitar to full orchestra with choir, inspired by the urban popular musical atmosphere of the beginning of the century; and piano works, such as *Rudepoema* (1921–1926), *A Prole do Bebê* (No. 2, 1921; No. 3, 1926), and *Cirandas* (1926). The last period of his production (1930–1957) includes the nine pieces entitled *Bachianas Brasileiras,* thirteen of his seventeen string quartets, seven of his twelve symphonies, and numerous solo songs. The *Bachianas* were intended as a tribute to Johann Sebastian Bach and were written as dance suites preceded generally by a prelude and ending with a fuguelike or toccatalike movement (the well-known "Little Train of the Caipira" is the toccata movement of *Bachianas* No. 2). Actual baroque compositional processes are rather slender. The use of the fugue as a formal principle could be construed as a neobaroque device, demanding a clarity of horizontal movement and the use of systematic imitation. Ostinato figures and long pedal tones are also indicative of neoclassic devices.

Among Villa-Lobos's contemporaries, Oscar Lorenzo FERNÂNDEZ, Luciano Gallet (1893–1931), and Francisco MIGNONE represent the nativistic orientation of their time. Mignone, a pianist, flutist, and conductor, has cultivated a national style relying heavily on urban popular and folk musical expressions, as in his four Brazilian fantasias for piano and orchestra and the series of piano pieces *Lendas Sertanejas, Valsas de Esquina,* and *Valsas-Chôros.*

Among the most important composers of the next generation are Mozart Camargo GUARNIERI, Luis Cosme (1908–1965), Radamés Gnatalli (1906–   ), and José Siqueira (1907–   ). Very prolific, Guarnieri has achieved an international reputation. Cosme's best works include the ballet *Salamanca do Jaráu* (1933) and *Novena à Senhora da Graça* (1950), which is written in a freely adapted twelve-tone technique. Gnatalli has cultivated both popular and art music idioms, tending in his later works toward neoclassic conceptions.

The style of the younger composers first active in the 1940s alternated between musical nationalism and prevalent European techniques. Foremost among the influential European techniques were Schoenberg's dodecaphonic theories, first introduced in Brazil by the German composer Hans-Joachim Koellreutter. Cláudio SANTORO and César Guerra-Peixe (1914–   ) experienced such drastic stylistic changes. Edino Krieger (1928–   ), after some incursions into strict atonality, found interesting compromises within a modernistic neoclassic style, as in his First String Quartet (1956). Serial and experimental techniques of composition have been used by younger composers who became prominent in the 1960s. At that time São Paulo was the center of the Brazilian avant-garde. The group Música Nova there included Gilberto Mendes (1922–   ), Damião Cozzella (1930–   ), and Rogério Duprat (1932–   ). The credo of these men was a total commitment to the contemporary artistic world. Despite the limited means of the Brazilian musical scene, they advocated and used electronic musical resources, aleatory techniques, and indeterminacy, thus breaking categorically with the predominant trend of musical nationalism. Mendes's *Nascemorre* (1963), for microtonal voices, percussion, and tape, is the setting of a text by the concrete poet Haroldo de Campos. Marlos Nobre (1939–   ) appeared in the late 1960s as one of the most successful experimental composers in Brazil. He was a fellow of the Instituto de Altos Estudios Musicales of the Di Tella Foundation in Buenos Aires, under the directorship of Alberto GINASTERA. Nobre's most significant works include *Variações Rítmicas* (1963), for piano and percussion; a short cantata, *Ukrinmakrinkrin*, on a text in Xucurú dialect (1963); the ballets *Rhythmetron* (1968) for thirty-eight percussion instruments and *Convergências* (1968); *Concerto Breve* (1969); and *Ludus instrumentalis* (1969).

The folk music of Brazil is derived from Luso-Hispanic counterparts and from African music, especially that of West Africa, the Congo, and Angola. Amerindian elements are preserved mostly in instruments such as rattles. Folk song genres derived from the Iberian Peninsula include *romances* and *xácaras* of a narrative character and children's songs of Portuguese origin, which are remarkably consistent with the original versions. With its cultivated origin the *modinha* illustrates the transplanting of European musical culture into the folk and popular music of Brazil. In addition, folk rituals associated with Roman Catholic feasts are common throughout the country. There are many *bailados* (dramatic dances), the central subject of which is always religious (conversion or resurrection). The distinctive secular folk and popular dances are well known. Among them the *batuque* and the samba epitomize the important black contribution to Brazilian folk and popular musical traditions. Among urban dances that developed since the latter part of the nineteenth century are the maxixe, *maracatu* (Recife), *baião, marchas,* and *chôro.*

Bibliography. Renato Almeida, *História da Música Brasileira,* Rio de Janeiro, 1942; Oneyda Alvarenga, *Música Popular Brasileira,* Rio de Janeiro, 1950; Alceu Maynard Araújo, *Folclore Nacional,* vols. 1 and 2, São Paulo, 1964; Luiz Heitor Corrêa de Azevedo, *150 Anos de Música no Brasil, 1800–1950,* Rio de Janeiro, 1956; Gerard H. Béhague, *The Beginnings of Musical Nationalism in Brazil,* Detroit, 1971; Jaime C. Diniz, *Músicos Pernambucanos do Passado,* vols. 1 and 2, Recife, 1969, 1971; Francisco Curt Lange,

A Organização Musical durante o Período Colonial Brasileiro, Coimbra, 1966; Vasco Mariz, *Figuras da Música Brasileira Contemporânea,* Brasília, 1970.

GERARD H. BÉHAGUE

MUSIC (SPANISH AMERICA). According to archaeological remains and the testimony of early European observers, musical life was of the utmost significance and social importance in the Americas prior to the Spanish conquest. Since not a single example of pre-Columbian music has been preserved in notational form, only instruments found in excavations and performances by Indian groups that up to recent decades remained somewhat untouched by European influences have provided a basis for the study of music in primitive America. From these sources we know that this art played an integral part in the social and religious lives of many Indian cultures, such as those of the MAYAS, AZTECS, and INCAS.

Music practices in these communities were of an improvisatory character, but the improvisations followed certain patterns and were organized around the scales, to which wind instruments were fashioned with great precision. String instruments were unknown in pre-Columbian America, and the guitar and its derivatives, which nowadays occupy such an important position in Latin American folk music, were introduced by Europeans.

A considerable variety of percussions and winds was found in the Americas. Winds appear to have been more highly developed among the Andean cultures of South America, while percussions showed their splendor mainly in Mexico, in Central America, and among the peoples of the Caribbean islands and of the Orinoco and Amazon Valleys. Thus it was the dark sound of the *huehuetl,* the skinned cylindrical drum made of a hollowed-out tree trunk, and the lighter beats of the *teponaztli* that characterized Mexican Indian ritual music. On the other hand, the flute of the QUECHUA and AYMARÁ cultures of Peru and Bolivia, known as the *kena (quena),* is derived from examples of bone flutes found in graves of the fourth century A.D. Likewise, present-day panpipes used by the peoples of these regions are survivals of *antaras* from the archaeological past.

Music among the primitive inhabitants of the Americas was presumably monodic. Only at a later stage were rudimentary rhythmic supports provided for the voice by percussion instruments, while winds alternated with vocal sections in freely improvised episodes. Oral tradition suggests that music attached to ceremonial and folk festivities followed very simple patterns, usually of an alternating character with changing sections assigned to a solo singer interspersed with repeated episodes performed by the community. Pre-Columbian music was seldom separated from the dance or from the spectacular choreographic displays that so often accompanied the worship of gods and emperors.

In addition, many other forms of songs and dances were cultivated, some being linked to religious and social occasions and others to particular activities. Among these were love songs, epics celebrating martial exploits, songs to cure disease, harvest songs, and funeral chants.

Music resulting from a learned approach to composition had an early start in Spanish America. After the first school where music was taught had been established in Texcoco, near Mexico City, in the year 1523 by the Franciscan missionary Pedro de Gante, a continuing stream of evolution, mainly in the field of church music, can clearly be followed. Pedro de Gante succeeded in establishing a permanent choir of natives in the Cathedral of Mexico City a little more than ten years after Hernán CORTES's conquest of Mexico. This example was followed in other colonies. By 1591 a Spaniard called Luis Cárdenas was teaching music to the natives in Caracas, and as early as the middle of the sixteenth century Miguel Velásquez had been appointed to the Cathedral of Santiago de Cuba with similar duties. In 1556 a book containing chants used in the Ordinary of the Mass in Gregorian notation was printed in Mexico, and by the end of the century eleven more books with printed music were published in Spanish America.

In addition to plain chant, polyphonic music was performed increasingly in the churches. Composers in Mexico, Peru, Guatemala, and elsewhere mastered the craft of their age and contributed to the wealth of music in Spanish America with works in the best traditions of Europe. The compositions of Juan de Lienas (fl. ca. 1550), Hernando Franco (1532–1585), Fructus del Castillo (fl. ca. 1600), and Gutierre Hernández Hidalgo (1555–ca. 1620) are outstanding examples of the music of this period.

It was not until the second half of the seventeenth century that music resulting from the mingling of European and native traditions appeared, owing perhaps to a more liberal attitude of the church toward indigenous expression and also to the growing number of native composers who participated in colonial musical life. A number of songs and hymns set to Indian dialects are evidence of the rapprochement between native and Spanish cultures at the sophisticated level of art composition. Sometimes European melodies were adapted to words in Indian languages, and sometimes native melodies were used as the basis for three- or four-part choral settings.

Instrumental music was cultivated in Latin America during the colonial period, and the works of the most outstanding masters of the keyboard in Europe were often performed in the New World. In the early years of the eighteenth century opera also emerged in Latin American music. The earliest extant example was produced in 1701 in Lima. This was *La púrpura de la rosa,* a setting of the play of the Spanish poet Pedro Calderón de la Barca by the composer Tomás de Torrejón y Velasco (1644–1728), chapelmaster in the Cathedral of Lima in the late seventeenth century.

In addition, other forms of secular music were cultivated, particularly the *villancico,* a typical folk and art form that had been brought from Spain but soon developed in combination with Indian and Negro influences. Most of the *villancicos* preserved from the colonial period were intended for use at Christmas. Outstanding examples of these compositions are found among the preserved manuscripts of the Peruvian composers Juan de Araujo (ca. 1646–1714) and Tomás de Torrejón; the Mexicans Antonio de Salazar (fl. 1680), who set many texts of the famous poet Sor JUANA INÉS DE LA CRUZ, and José María Aldana (d.

1810); and the Cuban Esteban Salas (1725–1803).

As the church began to lose its power and as the secular character of European classicism gradually influenced music in Latin America, forms of music other than those meant for church usage increased in number. Along with the *villancico,* the cantata, as cultivated by José Orejón y Aparicio (ca. 1705–1765) in Peru, and various forms of instrumental dances gained popularity.

Romantic influences became evident during the independence era. By the decade 1810–1820, during which most of the revolts against Spain took place, Latin America was ready to receive the influences of Italian opera, which affected its nineteenth-century music so markedly. In general, music during this period imitated either Italian opera or romantic forms patterned after the reigning Parisian tastes of salon music and instrumental virtuosity. Along with Italian *bel canto,* reflected in most of the vocal compositions of this period, local replicas of the mazurka, minuet, polka, tarantella, and waltz, among others, and short instrumental pieces of a descriptive nature comprised the repertory of music cultivated in the salons of the time. The works of such composers as Laureano Fuentes (1825–1898) in Cuba, Santos Cifuentes (1870–1932) in Colombia, Gustavo E. Campa (1863–1934) and Ricardo Castro (1864–1907) in Mexico, and Amancio Alcorta (1805–1862) in Argentina are good examples of the imitation of European forms of music.

Simultaneously, during the second half of the nineteenth century, some composers attempted to use vernacular elements drawn from the folk music of their countries, thus showing real concern for the development of a mother tongue in art composition. Among these pioneers of musical nationalism were Ignacio Cervantes (1847–1905) in Cuba, Aniceto Ortega (1823–1875) in Mexico, José M. Ponce de León (1846–1932) in Colombia, and Enrique SORO in Chile.

What these composers initiated led to a confrontation of European traditions of art music with folk and popular music that had developed from the assimilation of Spanish music transplanted to the New World, from Indian and African sources, or from mixtures of all these elements. From the turn of the twentieth century until the early 1940s composers concerned with a nationalistic approach dominated music in each of the Latin American countries. In this respect the outstanding example of Heitor VILLA-LOBOS in Brazil was followed by such composers as Manuel PONCE, Silvestre REVUELTAS, and Carlos CHÁVEZ in Mexico; Guillermo URIBE HOLGUÍN and Antonio M. VALENCIA in Colombia; Eduardo FABINI in Uruguay; Alberto WILLIAMS, Carlos LÓPEZ BUCHARDO, and Juan José CASTRO in Argentina; Andrés SAS in Peru; Pedro Humberto ALLENDE and Carlos ISAMITT in Chile; and Amadeo ROLDÁN and Alejandro GARCÍA CATURLA in Cuba.

The work of each of these composers reveals a wide range of characteristics. This is easily explained in terms of the great variety of influences participating in the development of folk music in Spanish America. In some areas the Spanish traditions were mingled with Indian or African traditions, or both, while in others Indian and African traditions were weak or nonexistent and the accents of European folk music assimilated by the peoples of the New World predominated.

Sometimes the influences of Italian opera, French salon music, or jazz modified the styles of the composers' music.

Nevertheless, not all composers of this generation joined the nationalistic movement, and some even waged deliberate battles against musical nationalism. Prior to 1930 the names of Julián CARRILLO in Mexico, Juan Carlos PAZ in Argentina, and Domingo SANTA CRUZ in Chile were identified with an approach to composition that was substantially removed from any involvement with folk music. This group of composers pioneered a movement that was to dominate Spanish America after World War II.

Alberto GINASTERA, the leading figure of Argentine music, after a few early works of a marked nationalistic character, had by the late forties undergone a complete change that led him to the stage of abstraction and cosmopolitanism characteristic of all his subsequent compositions. Most of the composers of his generation elsewhere in Spanish America underwent a similar evolution, among them Antonio ESTÉVEZ from Venezuela, Roque CORDERO from Panama, Blas GALINDO from Mexico, Héctor TOSAR from Uruguay, Enrique ITURRIAGA from Peru, Juan A. ORREGO-SALAS from Chile, Roberto CAAMAÑO and Roberto GARCÍA MORILLO from Argentina, and José ARDÉVOL from Cuba.

The members of the next generation achieved recognition in the world of music as supporters of styles following the many methods of contemporary European music. Although they rejected all deliberate borrowings from folk and popular music, some of them were concerned with developing an idiom deeply attached to the essence of their national traditions and not to the external body of the vernacular expressions. Among the younger figures of this generation are Julián ORBÓN, Aurelio de la VEGA, and Leo BROUWER from Cuba; Luis Antonio ESCOBAR from Colombia; Mario DAVIDOWSKY, Antonio TAURIELLO, and Alcides LANZA from Argentina; Gustavo BECERRA and León SCHIDLOWSKY from Chile; José SEREBRIER and Sergio CERVETTI from Uruguay; and Manuel ENRÍQUEZ and Eduardo MATA from Mexico.

Bibliography. Gilbert Chase, *A Guide to the Music of Latin America,* 2d ed., Washington, 1962; George List and Juan Orrego-Salas (eds.), *Music in the Americas,* Bloomington, Ind., 1967; Otto Mayer-Serra, *Música y músicos de América,* 2 vols., Mexico City, 1947; Robert Stevenson, *Music in Aztec and Inca Territory,* Berkeley, Calif., 1968.

JUAN A. ORREGO-SALAS

NABUCO, JOAQUIM (1849–1910). Brazilian abolitionist, statesman, author, and diplomat. A descendant of prominent families of the NORTHEAST and the son of the Liberal senator José Thomaz Nabuco de Araújo, Joaquim Nabuco was one of the most effective and talented of the major abolitionist leaders. Under his father's influence he joined the struggle against slavery in the late 1860s while still a student, writing "A Escravidão," a brilliant antislavery tract, and contributing to the Liberal journal *A Reforma*. In 1879, newly elected to the Chamber of Deputies after a diplomatic assignment in Washington, he and other northern legislators renewed the antislavery struggle in the national legislature, and the following year, frustrated in his attempt to end slavery through legislation, he founded the Brazilian Antislavery Society and the monthly *O Abolicionista,* major steps in the establishment of a powerful antislavery movement.

Losing his legislative seat in 1881, he traveled to Europe, where he wrote his classic antislavery study, *O Abolicionismo* (1883), not only calling for an end to bondage but recognizing the need for democratization of the nation's political and economic systems. Through articles and speeches he supported the Liberal Dantas bill of 1884, which was intended to free slaves attaining the age of sixty, and in 1885 he regained his seat in the Chamber through a hard-fought campaign in Recife. Elected a third time to the Chamber in 1887, he participated prominently in the passage of the GOLDEN LAW, which ended slavery. *See also* ABOLITION OF SLAVERY (BRAZIL).

Joaquim Nabuco. [Museu Imperial, Petrópolis, Rio de Janeiro]

After abolition Nabuco opposed the powerful new republican movement, advocating federalization of the empire under the monarchy. With the fall of PEDRO II in 1889, he turned from politics to literature, writing his autobiographical *Minha Formação* (1900) and a multivolume political biography of his father, *Um Estadista do Império* (1897–1899). In 1899, after ten years of estrangement from the new regime, he agreed to serve the republic in its dispute with Britain over the Guiana border, and the following year, fully reconciled to the republic, he was appointed Minister to London. From 1905 until his death he was Ambassador to Washington, where he gained the reputation of a brilliant elder statesman and an ardent Pan-Americanist.

ROBERT CONRAD

NACIONAL FINANCIERA (NAFIN). National development corporation of Mexico. Nacional Financiera began to function in mid-1934 to reincorporate certain real estate into the private sector and to stimulate the stock market. This experimental stage ended with the law of December 30, 1940, which provided that its principal functions would henceforth be to regulate the stock market, to promote the investment of capital in the creation and expansion of industrial enterprises, and to act as the agent of the government in the emission of public securities. The first certificates of participation were issued the following year, and for the first time foreign and domestic capital began to be channeled systematically toward the development of industry. With the enactment of new legislation in December 1947 a third stage was initiated in order that the activities of NAFIN might be coordinated more rigorously with those of other credit institutions. NAFIN also increased its initial capital of 20 million pesos provided by the federal government (of which only 3 million were in cash) to 100 million pesos.

NAFIN has spurred the development of Mexico's most dynamic industries, those with the most advanced technology and the highest productivity; these include basic industries like petroleum and petrochemicals (*see* PETRÓLEOS MEXICANOS), iron and steel (*see* IRON AND STEEL INDUSTRY: MEXICO), and cement, and key industries, such as paper and cellulose, fertilizer, and electrical appliances. Four of the seven members of NAFIN's Board of Administration are elected by the private stockholders, the other three by the federal government, which always accounts for 51 percent of its capital in Series A shares.

MOISÉS GONZÁLEZ NAVARRO

NAHUATL. Uto-Aztecan language. It was the language of the TOLTECS and of the AZTECS, who appeared after the collapse of the Toltec empire. Nahuatl was also spoken on both coasts of Tehuantepec and in Veracruz. In the immediate postconquest period it was carried by the Aztecs, who were escorting and serving their new Spanish masters, even farther than the confines of their own empire. This is why, even in areas where it was never spoken, the map of Mexico and Guatemala is studded with toponyms in Nahuatl. Considering its remarkable plasticity, Nahuatl is still an easy language to learn. More than a million people in Mexico today speak it.

BURR C. BRUNDAGE

NARDONE, BENITO (1906–1964). President of Uruguay and leader of the Blanco party (*see* BLANCO PARTY: URUGUAY). Although a symbol of rural leadership and the political spokesman for ranchers and provincial interests, Nardone was born in Montevideo, the son of an Italian immigrant longshoreman. After graduating from the Montevideo school system, he became a newspaper reporter in that city; later, as an editor of provincial publications, he became active in rural politics.

In 1950 Nardone founded the Liga Federal de Acción Rural (Federal League for Rural Action; LFAR). In 1954 Nardone's *ruralistas* supported the Colorado party faction (*see* COLORADO PARTY: URUGUAY) led by Luis BATLLE BERRES, but soon thereafter Nardone became a Blanco and took the LFAR into the National party as followers of the long-time Blanco leader Luis Alberto de HERRERA.

Beginning in 1944, Nardone became a radio commentator, widely known as Chicotazo (the Whip-Cracker). His daily broadcasts over Radio Rural were repeated on affiliates throughout the republic. He offered market advice, grain and wool quotations, news summaries, and political commentary favoring agricultural interests, private enterprise, the reduction of welfare programs, and anticommunism.

In 1958 Nardone helped the Blancos end ninety-three years of government by the Colorados, and when the Blancos became the six-member majority in the National Council of Government in 1959, Nardone was elected Council chairman, or titular President of the republic. In April 1959, Herrera died, and Nardone became head of the National party's dominant faction.

In 1962 the Colorados again became the six-member majority and the Blancos the three-member minority in the National Council of Government (replaced by a chief executive in 1967). Nardone remained a Blanco leader and helped in the movement for a return to the single Presidency, though he died two and one-half years before the change was voted.

MARVIN ALISKY

NARIÑO, ANTONIO (1765–1823). Colombian precursor of independence and early patriot leader. The outstanding figure in the preliminary stages of Colombian independence, Nariño was born of an aristocratic family in Bogotá in 1765. Well educated, he became a prosperous merchant and held important official positions. He also read widely, in works of the Enlightenment among others (*see* ENLIGHTENMENT: SPANISH AMERICA), and formed a large personal library that served as the headquarters of a circle of public-spirited creoles dissatisfied with the colonial regime.

In December 1793, Nariño translated and printed the French Declaration of the Rights of Man. Although he quickly regretted his rashness and burned most copies, he was discovered, tried for sedition, and sentenced to exile in Spanish Africa. Nariño escaped when his ship reached Cádiz and traveled through Western Europe, seeking while in London to sound out the British on the possibility of aid for an eventual revolution in Spanish America. He subsequently returned to America and, after further traveling in disguise, openly presented himself to the viceroy of New Granada. He was not sent back to exile, but from 1797 to 1810 he remained in jail or under a form of house arrest.

The outbreak of the independence movement finally gave him his freedom. He became active as a revolutionary publicist, then obtained the Presidency of the state of Cundinamarca, comprising Bogotá and the immediately surrounding area. In this position he led the struggle for a strong centralized government in New Granada against the federalists who controlled most outlying provinces. The struggle degenerated in 1812 into civil war, which smoldered sporadically for several years. Nariño himself, however, was removed from the scene when he was captured leading an army against the royalists in southern New Granada.

Nariño spent another six years as a prisoner before he was released from jail in Spain in 1820. He returned to America in time to preside as acting Vice President of Gran Colombia over the opening of the Congress of Cúcuta (see CÚCUTA, CONGRESS OF), but he was defeated by Francisco de Paula SANTANDER in the election for constitutional Vice President. Becoming a focus of opposition to the new government, he found himself exposed to a campaign of personal vilification that, combined with failing health, greatly embittered his final days. He died in Leiva in December 1823.

DAVID BUSHNELL

NARVÁEZ, PÁNFILO DE (1480?–1528). Spanish conquistador and explorer. Born in Spain in either the province of Valladolid or the province of Segovia, Narváez went to the New World around 1498. He participated in the conquest of Cuba in 1511 and was the man chiefly responsible for bringing the island under Spanish control. In 1520 the Governor of Cuba sent him to Mexico with a large expedition to reassert the Governor's authority over Hernán CORTÉS, who had gone to Mexico to conquer the country in the Governor's name but once there had thrown off his allegiance to the Governor. In Mexico Narváez was defeated by Cortés and was held captive by him for two years; upon his release he returned to Spain. In 1528 he led a Spanish expedition to Florida. Landing near Tampa Bay, he heard from local Indians of a place called Apalache where gold was to be found in abundance. Striking inland, he reached Apalache (probably located near present-day Tallahassee) but found it to be a village of about forty small huts whose inhabitants possessed no gold. Narváez then made his way south to the Gulf coast, and, having long since lost contact with his ships, he had his men construct five small boats in which they set sail for Mexico. The boat in which Narváez was journeying was swept out to sea one night and was never seen again. The occupants of the other boats were forced to abandon their vessels for various reasons and went ashore, where almost all of them perished. Only Álvar Núñez CABEZA DE VACA and three others ever reached Mexico to reveal the fate of the expedition and its commander.

TIMOTHY C. HANLEY

NATIONAL ACTION PARTY. *See* PARTIDO DE ACCIÓN NACIONAL.

NATIONAL CONVENTION OF WORKERS. *See* CONVENCIÓN NACIONAL DE TRABAJADORES.

NATIONAL DEMOCRATIC UNION. *See* UNIÃO DEMOCRÁTICA NACIONAL.

NATIONAL FRONT. After the resignation of Gustavo ROJAS PINILLA in 1957, Liberal Alberto LLERAS CAMARGO and Conservative Laureano GÓMEZ (*see* CONSERVATIVE PARTY: COLOMBIA; LIBERAL PARTY: COLOMBIA) agreed on behalf of their parties to the Declaration of Sitges (July 20, 1957), which provided for coalition government in an attempt to end rural partisan conflict (*see* VIOLENCIA, LA) and bring political stability to Colombia. This National Front plan was submitted to Colombian voters in a constitutional plebiscite in December 1957 and was accepted overwhelmingly. Among its main provisions was a guarantee of parity whereby Conservatives and Liberals were to be represented equally in all elected and almost all appointed political positions in Colombia. It was also stipulated that the two political parties would alternate in the office of the Presidency every four years until 1974.

The coalition's first President was Lleras Camargo, who took office in August 1958 after a landslide victory. Despite a decrease in the Violencia, the front's popularity declined subsequently with the elections of Guillermo León VALENCIA and Carlos LLERAS RESTREPO. Voter abstention was widespread, and opposition groups developed. The next presidential candidate, Misael PASTRANA BORRERO, barely won over Rojas Pinilla in the 1970 elections. Threatening to resign, Lleras Restrepo pushed reforms through Congress in 1968 designed to make the transition from coalition rule less abrupt. A two-thirds approval of both houses was no longer required on most legislation. Moreover, in the 1972 congressional and municipal elections parity would not apply. However, in July 1972 President Pastrana announced that both parties had agreed to continue aspects of parity within the administration through 1978.

GERALD THEISEN

NATIONALISM. Nationalism is the most important single force affecting Latin America today. Almost all groups, regardless of their ideologies, appeal to nationalism and attempt to use it for their own purposes. Thus, both the Marxist Fidel CASTRO and the right-wing military rulers of Brazil invoke nationalism in an effort to unite their respective countries and to legitimize their political power. Yet although we know nationalism exists and is important, we do not know precisely what it is; scholars have not been able to give a precise, workable, universally accepted definition of the idea. Our purpose here is not to produce the long-sought-after definition of nationalism. Rather, our aim is to make a number of observations that will help us understand this elusive, complex, and widely used phenomenon as it developed in Latin America.

Let us begin by noting that nationalism is the major legitimizing concept that has come forth in independent Latin America to replace the formerly unquestioned authority of the Iberian monarchs. Between 1810 and 1825 all the Latin American countries except Cuba and Puerto Rico won their independence from Spain and Portugal. In so doing they broke the bonds of an all-embracing system of political, economic, and social authority that for more than 300 years had tied them to Iberia and held each of them together. The independence movements destroyed the unquestioned authority of the King, but they created no new form of legitimate authority. The critical issues facing the newly formed Latin American states were: Who should inherit the King's all-encompassing authority? Who should be the arbiter of disputes among groups and individuals within the newly born societies? How does a society create legitimate authority?

Since 1825 uncounted individuals and groups have struggled with each other in their efforts to establish a new basis for legitimate authority. The most significant result of this 150-year effort to replace the authority of the King has been nationalism. Therefore, the underlying function of nationalism in Latin America, though by no means its only function, has been to bind together the diverse elements of each society, to create a community toward which ultimate loyalty is given, to establish a nation. The nation is the community of ultimate loyalty because it represents a broad consensus of the members of a society on basic values and procedures. If the national consensual community we call the nation exists, it provides its members with a sense of identity and it becomes the source of legitimacy for the acts of men and governments.

In most Latin American countries no such broad consensus has emerged, and the nation, strictly defined, does not exist. With the possible exceptions of Mexico and Cuba, there is no widespread agreement on what values and procedures each national community should stand for; there are few common interests or genuinely representative institutions to incorporate the diverse elements of the fragmented societies. Competing nationalist groups claim that they speak for an emerging national consensus, and to support their claim they generally seek control of the state. If the nation does not exist, those in control of the state cannot in fact represent it, but those in control of the state have distinct advantages over their competitors in pressing their claim; by controlling the mass media, the police and the military, the financial system, and the various agencies of government they have the best chance to provide services and benefits to the public and in this way to gain widespread support. Thus, much of the study of nationalism focuses on those who control or seek to control the state.

In the abstract, nationalism in Latin America is the force engendered by those attempting to fill the legitimacy vacuum created 150 years ago. In each country nationalism has developed at a different pace, it has been used by different groups and individuals for different purposes, and it has produced widely divergent results. Because nationalism differs from time to time and from place to place, it must be studied within a specific historical and time context.

Colonial period (1492–1810). Modern nationalism did not emerge in Europe until the second half of the eighteenth century and in Latin America until the nineteenth century. During the colonial period, however, a number of issues and attitudes did develop that later helped define the nature and content of nationalism. First of all, this period constituted a specific past of 300 years of colonial rule associated with the Catholic Church, the Spanish and Portuguese monarchies, mercantilism, and a rigid social hierarchy with whites on top and Indians and Negroes on the bottom. This specific past helps explain, for example, the intense anticlericalism and antiracism of many Latin American nationalists.

When the ideas of the Enlightenment penetrated the area during the eighteenth century, positive feelings closely associated with the emergence of nationalism became manifest. The local elites developed a sense of separate identity, a feeling of distinctness from the mother country, an attitude of self-reliance associated with the local area or with a vague concept of Americanism. Many of these people also developed distinct anti-Spanish and anti-Portuguese attitudes. *See* ENLIGHTENMENT (BRAZIL); ENLIGHTENMENT (SPANISH AMERICA).

Independence period (1810–1825). The fifteen-year struggle for independence sharpened and intensified the vague sense of separateness and distinctness and the nascent anti-Spanish and anti-Portuguese attitudes of the preceding century. The independence struggle created sovereign states that became the geographical base for the national consensual community. In addition, it created a vacuum of legitimate authority that nationalism has attempted to fill.

Nineteenth century. As a result of independence, a native white elite replaced the Iberian colonialists at the top of the Latin American political and social hierarchy, and Great Britain replaced Spain and Portugal as the direct "colonial" economic power. Native white elites in collaboration with foreign partners dominated all aspects of society and maintained much of the colonial structure intact with themselves rather than the Spanish and Portuguese in control. They divided into such groups as conservatives and liberals, federalists and centralists, but they united in the face of any challenge from below. This system of neocolonialism pervaded Latin America throughout the nineteenth century and, in most areas, into the twentieth century.

A number of nationalists among these elites believed that the best way to create the nation was to develop their societies by utilizing foreign money, foreign expertise, foreign culture, and foreign political institutions and ideas. Nationalism was for them a modernizing and Europeanizing device. But these nationalists failed to create the nation-state for a variety of reasons. The rugged geography of the region, encompassing the high mountains of the Andes and the Sierra Madre and the jungles of the Amazon Basin, made communication difficult and encouraged localism. The strength of personalism discouraged the development of loyalty to a national community. Rigid class distinctions further divided the population, and the church's cosmopolitanism seemed to dictate ultimate loyalty to something beyond the nation-state. Finally, many Latin Americans rejected the colonial past as a cultural and spiritual basis for unity; until they found a substitute sense of unity, the development of nationalism was unlikely.

Although the nineteenth-century nationalists failed to create nations, there were a number of developments, particularly during the second half of the century, that contributed to the growing strength of nationalism. A half-dozen local wars stimulated the sense of solidarity and identification within the respective participant states. The drive to modernize produced many of the physical prerequisites (railroads, roads, harbors, etc.) for the development of an integrated national community. And finally, 400 years of racial mixture produced the mestizo (part Indian and part European) who had no roots in the past and who looked to the emerging nation-state for a sense of communal identity.

Twentieth century. The embryonic feelings of nationalism manifested by the nineteenth century elites became more pronounced, varied, and widespread during the twentieth century. The emergence of new forms of nationalism, such as economic and popular nationalism, was closely related to the process of modernization that had begun during the later part of the nineteenth century. European countries, particularly Britain, needed the raw materials and markets that Latin America could supply. The new demands stimulated the commercialization of agriculture, the development of mining, and the growth of cities. Many people were uprooted from their traditional society and thrust into a new and unfamiliar urban environment. These rootless middle and lower socioeconomic groups articulated new forms of nationalism as they sought to establish a national community that represented their ideas and interests.

1900–1930. New and old issues influenced the development of nationalism during this period. One of the most important new issues was the dramatic expansion of United States political and economic influence into the Caribbean and Central America. Between 1898 and 1930 the United States directly encouraged the separation of Panama from Colombia, and it occupied Cuba, Haiti, the Dominican Republic, and Nicaragua. These activities added a strong anti-American dimension to nationalism that focused not only on the political and economic influence of the United States but also on its materialistic cultural impact.

The second issue of importance during this period was control of the economy. As middle-sector groups gained political power in Argentina, Mexico, Chile, and Uruguay, they set forth the ideas that the nation owned the subsoil and natural resources of a country and that the good of the nation must prevail over the individual's right of private property. This idea was first clearly expounded in Article 27 of the Mexican constitution of 1917 in terms of the "social function" of property (*see* CONSTITUTION OF 1917: MEXICO). The idea is important to nationalism because it provides the basis for the nationalization of vital resources, land reform, and the preeminence of the nation-state over foreign interests.

Race also became an important issue for nationalists during this period. With the influx of large numbers of European immigrants into Argentina, Uruguay, and southern Brazil and with the increased blending of races in the rest of Latin America, the question arose as to who constituted the nationality. Many, though not all, answered that the genuine nationality must draw on the strengths of all racial and national elements to create the "cosmic race."

1930–1945. Economic nationalism during this period intensified as the Depression cut off world trade and nearly destroyed the one-product export economies of Latin America. In addition, the governments of Bolivia and Mexico, believing their sovereignty to be threatened, nationalized large American- and British-owned oil companies.

The issue of race and nationality took on a new dimension. Formerly the issue was one of the blending of Indians and Europeans to make a mestizo cosmic race. In this period, Brazilians such as Gilberto FREYRE began to talk about the virtues of the mixture of black and white and the resulting "racial democracy."

Fascism in Europe stimulated a number of Latin American right-wing elements to set forth a nationalism that associated Christianity, Hispanic values, the corporate state, and rule by an elite. In countries such as Mexico and Argentina the left attempted to enunciate an antifascist popular nationalism in opposition to the new right-wing nationalism.

The GOOD NEIGHBOR POLICY and World War II muted the anti-United States feelings that had been growing since the turn of the century, but the war also created conditions for the future intensification of an anti-United States economic nationalism. The war created demand abroad for Latin American resources and stimulated economic development. Also, it created a shortage of imported manufactured goods normally supplied by the belligerent countries and thus stimulated Latin American industry.

Since 1945. The postwar conflict of interest between the United States and Latin America stemmed from a fundamental difference of opinion concerning the development of Latin America. Since 1945 most Latin American countries have wanted to continue the development of their industrial sectors because they have seen this as the only way to become modern countries independent of foreign economic control. The United States, however, has argued that the Latin American countries can best develop by continuing to export their raw materials. The power of the United States to impose its will on Latin America has caused great frustration and a strong anti-United States nationalism. Furthermore, the cold war and the effort to divide the world into Communist and non-Communist blocs has also had an impact on nationalism. Many Latin American countries have considered this effort to be opposed to their best national interests. Thus Juan D. PERÓN in Argentina, Jânio QUADROS in Brazil, and others have set forth a neutralist foreign policy as that best able to serve the interests of their countries.

Finally, popular nationalism, which emerged during the MEXICAN REVOLUTION of 1910, became more widespread and influential. Urban workers and to some extent rural peons gained political significance in Argentina, Bolivia, Cuba, and Chile and claimed to be the genuine representatives of the emerging nation. They have demanded incorporation within the national political structure and a voice in the formulation of the country's destiny.

Conclusion. Nationalism in Latin America has developed as a multifaceted phenomenon. Some types have emerged in response to external threats such as the economic and political penetration of the United States. Others have developed in response to internal situations related to development and to the growth of new socioeconomic groups. Nationalism has been used by a wide variety of people for many purposes, and it has influenced the behavior of different elements within the respective Latin American societies. Yet in all cases nationalism has become increasingly influential and widespread in Latin America, and it will continue to grow in importance in the coming decades.

Bibliography. Victor Alba, *Nationalists without Nations,* New York, 1968; Samuel L. Baily (ed.), *Nationalism in Latin America,* New York, 1971; E. Bradford Burns, *Nationalism in Brazil,* New York, 1968; Frederick C. Turner, *The Dynamic of Mexican Nationalism,* Chapel Hill, N.C., 1968; Arthur P. Whitaker and David C. Jordan, *Nationalism in Contemporary Latin America,* New York, 1966.

SAMUEL L. BAILY

NATIONALIST REVOLUTIONARY MOVEMENT. *See* MOVIMIENTO NACIONALISTA REVOLUCIONARIO.

NATIONAL LIBERATION PARTY. *See* PARTIDO LIBERACIÓN NACIONAL.

NATIONAL or NATIONALIST PARTY (HONDURAS). In 1902, after a long period of Liberal party domination in Honduras, President Manuel Bonilla (1903–1907) was able to weld shifting coalitions of *caudillos* into the first recognizable opposition party. It was not until February 1916, however, that the Honduran National party was formally constituted under the guidance of Francisco Bertrand. There followed a period of fragmentation in which several National parties worked at cross-purposes. *See* LIBERAL PARTY (HONDURAS).

Out of the political chaos of the early 1920s emerged an intellectual, Dr. Paulino Valladares, and a *caudillo,* Tiburcio CARÍAS ANDINO, who restored order to Nationalist ranks. After running unsuccessfully for the office in 1923 and 1928, Carías was finally elected President in 1932. Carías's long dictatorship (1933–1948) began a period of National party ascendancy that, with one Liberal interlude, has continued to the present. National party objectives are largely indistinguishable from those of the opposing Liberals; both parties advocate a program of economic development within a context of nationalism. Recent attacks on agricultural squatters by the administration of Nationalist Ramón Ernesto CRUZ, however, suggest that the National party is not as firm an advocate of AGRARIAN REFORM as its Liberal opposition.

GENE S. YEAGER

NATIONAL PARTY (URUGUAY). *See* BLANCO PARTY (URUGUAY).

NATIONAL POPULAR ALLIANCE. *See* ALIANZA NACIONAL POPULAR.

NATIONAL RENOVATING ALLIANCE. *See* ALIANÇA RENOVADORA NACIONAL.

NATIONAL WAR COLLEGE. *See* ESCOLA SUPERIOR DE GUERRA.

NAZCA. Culture complex, and in particular a polychrome pottery style, on the south coast of Peru dating from about 200 B.C. to A.D. 600. The style is easily recognized by its rich varieties of red, white, black, gray, and orange, its depiction of a peculiar cat god, and its near-modern painted stylizations of birds and fish. The Nazca pottery differs from the MOCHICA in being only seldom subject to modeling. In the Nazca culture area occur the peculiar rayed designs that cover large areas of the desert surface as seen from the air.

BURR C. BRUNDAGE

NEGRO IN BRAZIL. An important element of the Brazilian population since the sixteenth century, black Africans and their descendants have contributed greatly to the economic, artistic, and cultural development of the nation. During the first fifty years of Portuguese contact with Brazil (1500–1550) the native Indian population supplied the labor needed to collect brazilwood and to initiate the sugar industry (*see* SUGAR INDUSTRY: COLONIAL BRAZIL), and therefore the importation of African slaves was small. During the second half of the sixteenth century, however, tens of thousands of Africans were transported to Brazil, followed during the next 250 years by an even larger forced migration. No exact statistics are available, but it has been estimated that in the seventeenth century probably more than 500,000 slaves entered Brazil, in the eighteenth century almost 2 million, and during the first half of the nineteenth century probably more than 1 million, making a total of perhaps 3.5 million people. The Africans were embarked at the Cape Verde Islands and nearby Portuguese Guinea, on the coast of what is now Ghana, in the Bight of Benin and the Bight of Biafra and the nearby Portuguese-controlled islands of Príncipe and São Tomé, at Cabinda near the mouth of the Congo, and at the ports of Portuguese-dominated Angola and Mozambique. Most slaves who reached Brazil belonged to the main language groups of central and southern Africa, the Sudanic and Bantu.

For almost as long as slavery lasted, bondsmen performed most of the productive labor in Brazil in both urban and rural areas. In the sixteenth and seventeenth centuries the sugar industry absorbed most slaves, but in the eighteenth century there was a shift of economic interest and therefore of black workers into the new mining regions of Minas Gerais, Goiás, and Mato Grosso (*see* MINING: COLONIAL BRAZIL). With the decline of mining and the growth of a dynamic coffee industry early in the nineteenth century (*see* COFFEE INDUSTRY: BRAZIL), the province of Rio de Janeiro and adjacent regions of Minas Gerais, São Paulo, and Espírito Santo began to receive a majority of the slaves from Africa, and this tendency toward concentration of the slave population in the coffee region accelerated during the illegal phase of the African slave trade (1831–1850) and during the succeeding large-scale north-south domestic slave trade (1851–1881). An important result of this concentration was a waning of proslavery sentiment in noncoffee regions that significantly strengthened the antislavery movement in the years between 1865 and 1888 (*see* ABOLITION OF SLAVERY: BRAZIL). Although most slaves labored on plantations, tens of thousands lived in cities, where they were employed as porters, artisans, servants, peddlers, day laborers, seamstresses, and textile workers.

Several modern students of Brazil, notably Gilberto FREYRE and Frank Tannenbaum, have claimed that the Brazilian slave was mildly treated in comparison with his counterpart in the United States. Impressed by comparatively harmonious race relations in Brazil, Tannenbaum alleged in his influential study *Slave and Citizen* (1947) that unlike the slave in the United States, the Brazilian bondsman was protected by legal, religious, and patriarchal traditions and institutions. In Brazil, claimed Tannenbaum, the human character of the slave was respected despite his slave status. Manumission was thus significantly easier and more common than in the United States, slave marriages were more generally encouraged, the slave family was more respected, and, once free, the black or mulatto encountered comparatively few obstacles to social elevation and material success.

Recent research has shown, however, that in some ways the Brazilian slave system was even more brutal than its North American counterpart. Because of unfavorable physical conditions on Brazilian plantations and a persistent imbalance of the sexes, slaves in Brazil were not born as fast as they died, and Brazilian slavery therefore depended upon the African slave trade long after the American South was being supplied almost solely by natural increase. Over the centuries, therefore, Brazil received perhaps ten times as many Africans as the North American colonies, but, owing to a high death rate and a low rate of reproduction, the Brazilian slave population of 1860 was only about half as large as the North American slave population of that date. Although manumission was more common in Brazil than in the United States, as Tannenbaum claimed, most Brazilian slaves had little hope of freedom, and hundreds of thousands imported illegally after November 7, 1831, were actually kept in illegal bondage. Moreover, the free black population developed only very slowly during the first three centuries of Brazilian history, a fact which suggests that freedom was granted far less often than historians have assumed. As late as 1798 probably only about a fifth of the blacks and mulattoes of Brazil were free, despite the ease with which the free could increase their numbers through natural reproduction. Contrary to the claim of Tannenbaum, moreover, family relationships among slaves in Brazil were unstable, and most slaves were never granted the sacrament of marriage. In 1887, for example, only about 13 percent of Brazil's slaves (all sixteen or older, since babies born after September 1871 had been liberated by the FREE BIRTH LAW) were married or widowed, and abundant information pertaining to earlier periods shows that this paucity of marriages among black captives was not a situation peculiar to the last phase of slavery. Furthermore, until 1869 no Brazilian law prohibited the separation of slave families, and many families were in fact broken up by the internal slave trade. Even the punishments normally inflicted upon slaves in Brazil appear to have been more severe than those suffered by slaves in the United States, although atrocities were of course committed in both countries.

Brazilian slaves reacted far more radically to their plight than slaves in the United States, perhaps because their conditions were less tolerable. Suicides were more common in Brazil than in the United States, flight and rebellion were more frequent, and runaway slave settlements such as the famous *quilombo* of PALMARES (a rare phenomenon in the United States) were a common feature of the Brazilian countryside as long as slavery lasted. In Brazil, finally, there was a significant gap between protective laws and customary practices, between the theoretical guardianship of the Catholic Church and the church's normal failure to interfere with slavery or even to assure the sacraments and the integrity of the Christian slave family.

Despite the slave system and other social and historical handicaps, Brazilian blacks and mulattoes have made great contributions to the national culture. African foods, religious rites, dress, music, and dance have survived, particularly in the NORTHEAST, and African words have enriched the national language. The greatest Brazilian sculptor of the colonial period, O Aleijadinho (Antônio Francisco LISBÔA), was a mulatto, as was the internationally known novelist Joaquim Maria MACHADO DE ASSIS. The mulattoes Luis GAMA, André REBOUÇAS, José do PATROCINIO, and Francisco José do Nascimento, to cite only the most famous, played important roles in the struggle to end slavery, and such

descendants of Africans as Evaristo de Moraes and Edison Carneiro have made significant contributions to the historiography of slavery and to an understanding of the black cultural contribution to Brazilian society.

Brazil is justifiably famous for its harmonious race relations. Intermarriage, if not the rule, is common; outright segregation is rare; Jim Crow laws are nonexistent; and the national consensus against public discrimination on the basis of color was formalized in 1951 by the Afonso Arinos law. Since 1930, in fact, Brazilians of all classes and races have adhered to a cult of racial equality that has probably advanced racial democracy and instilled some pride and identity in the nonwhite portion of the population. Nevertheless, harmony between the races has been emphasized to the point of exaggeration. The recent sociological studies of Octavio Ianni, Florestan Fernandes, Fernando Henrique Cardoso, and other scholars have shown that serious forms of discrimination do exist in Brazil and that color prejudice creates serious barriers to the advancement of nonwhites, particularly in São Paulo and the three southernmost states, where whites predominate. However, discrimination is the result not only of prejudice but, as much or even more, of severe class disparities in part inherited from the slave system. Freed from slavery but not from the consequences of their servile past, black Brazilians have remained poor and socially deprived, thus tending to confirm the well-established biases of the white community and to compound the problems that blacks encounter in their efforts to improve their economic and social status. Many nonwhites, particularly mulattoes, have of course taken respectable places in Brazilian society, but most Brazilians descended from black Africans (well over a third of the population) are members of the lower class, and although many whites are scarcely more prosperous, the upper class is predominantly of European descent. The history of blacks in Brazil is principally the history of slavery, of the struggle for freedom, and (since 1888) of the ordeal of the descendants of slaves in a class society in which archaic social patterns have given way only slowly to modernizing influences.

Bibliography. Leslie Bethell, *The Abolition of the Brazilian Slave Trade,* Cambridge, England, 1970; Fernando Henrique Cardoso, *Capitalismo e Escravidão,* São Paulo, 1962; Robert Conrad, *The Destruction of Brazilian Slavery: 1850–1888,* Berkeley, Calif., and London, 1972; Carl N. Degler, *Neither Black nor White: Slavery and Race Relations in Brazil and the United States,* New York, 1971; Florestan Fernandes, *The Negro in Brazilian Society,* New York, 1969; Octavio Ianni, *As Metamorfoses do Escravo,* São Paulo, 1962; Joaquim Nabuco, *O Abolicionismo,* London, 1883; Agostinho Marques Perdigão Malheiro, *A Escravidão no Brasil: Ensaio Histórico-jurídico-social,* 2 vols., 2d ed., São Paulo, 1944; Raymond S. Sayers, *The Negro in Brazilian Literature,* New York, 1956; Stanley J. Stein, *Vassouras: A Brazilian Coffee County, 1850–1900,* Cambridge, Mass., 1957; Emilia Viotti da Costa, *Da Senzala à Colônia,* São Paulo, 1966.

ROBERT CONRAD

NEGRO IN SPANISH AMERICA. The history of Spanish America is to a great extent the story of the three basic racial types—Negroid, Mongoloid, and Caucasoid—meeting and mingling on a large scale. Like the other two groupings, the Negroid was present from the very beginning. Two of the men accompanying Christopher COLUMBUS were probably black, and it has been argued that Pedro Alonso Niño, one of the admiral's pilots, was of African descent. Certainly there were Negroes with Vasco Núñez de BALBOA in Panama, with Hernán CORTÉS in Mexico, Hernando de SOTO in Florida, and Francisco and Gonzalo PIZARRO in Peru, while Esteban, a black, was instrumental in Spain's early exploration of present-day Arizona and New Mexico.

Slave trade. Even these first blacks in the Americas were mostly slaves. Negro slavery was an old institution in Spain and one the Spaniards naturally turned to in the New World after the indigenous American population proved to be poor slave material. They had a whole new world to exploit and colonize but few persons to perform the labor. The African, familiar with an agricultural way of life in his homeland, provided an effective, if unhappy, solution. Thus began the slave trade, a massive intercontinental movement that witnessed the transfer of millions of Africans to the Americas over a period of almost four centuries.

An extensive traffic in Negro slaves to Europe was begun by the Portuguese during their fifteenth-century explorations of the African coast. Spain rapidly became Portugal's best customer and following the discovery of the New World wasted little time in introducing black slavery there. As early as 1501 Governor Nicolás de Ovando received permission from the Spanish crown to ship peninsular-born Christianized slaves to the Indies, and in 1518 King CHARLES I granted the first license to transport slaves directly from Africa to the Americas. Thus Spain was the first of the European countries to initiate an Atlantic slave trade. It would also be the last to end this traffic some three and one-half centuries later.

During much of this period, however, control of the trade rested not in the hands of Spain but in those of foreigners. First the Portuguese and later the Dutch, French, and English would vie with one another for the *asiento*, a system whereby the Spanish crown granted to individuals and to companies the privilege of transporting African slaves to its American colonies. The *asiento* was coveted not only as a profitable undertaking in its own right but also as a screen for the introduction of contraband goods into Spain's empire. Hence the breakdown of Spain's commercial monopoly in the New World is closely connected with the slave trade. Slaves, of course, were also smuggled into the Americas by Spaniard and foreigner alike, and many of the slaves received by Spanish America were illegally imported.

In 1789 King Charles IV decreed an end to the *asiento* system and made the slave trade a free one. The action was taken largely to aid Cuban planters who wished to expand their island's labor force and make Cuba a major sugar producer. Hence Spain's Atlantic slave traffic began increasing in volume at a time when most nations were in the process of abolishing the slave trade. Denmark in 1802 became the first to do so, followed by Great Britain in 1807, the United States in 1808, Sweden in 1813, the Dutch in 1814, and the French in 1818. By the mid-1830s Portugal and most of the newly independent Latin American countries agreed to prohibit their citizens from engaging in the trade. However, Spain, despite promises to abolish its

slave traffic in the Anglo-Spanish treaties of 1817 and 1835, remained unwilling and unable to make them good, with the result that Cuba, plagued by a scarcity of slave labor, continued to import contraband slaves on an extensive scale until the middle 1860s.

This shortage of slaves on the island of Cuba underlies another paradox of the Atlantic slave trade: despite its lengthy duration Spain's colonies received a surprisingly low percentage of the total number of Africans introduced to the New World. Although this total has been placed as high as 20 million, a recent study has indicated that 10 million is probably closer to the truth, with only 1.5 million, or 15 percent, reaching the Spanish Americas. Of these, more than half were received by Cuba and the other Spanish islands of the Caribbean, a third went to the South American continent, with the Viceroyalty of New Granada taking the great majority, while the remainder, perhaps 15 percent, went to Mexico and Central America.

Slavery. In the New World Africans became the sowers of America, cultivating crops of sugar, maize, tobacco, cotton, and cacao throughout the vastness of the hemisphere. Yet, because of the African's skills and adaptability, he could also be found hammering at a blacksmith forge in Lima, herding cattle in the Argentine pampas, panning gold in New Granada, fishing off the Mexican coasts, building fortresses in Havana, driving carriages in Quito, doing military duty, and pushing back the frontier. The Negro's early experience in America, then, was a diverse one and not confined to agricultural slavery.

Nor is it true that the African accepted his enslavement passively. The slave trade is a story studded with incidents of slave mutiny and suicide, while the story of slavery is one of more mutinies, slave revolutions, and constant fear on the part of whites in regions that had large slave populations. As early as 1550, for example, slaves revolted and destroyed Santa Marta in present-day Colombia. Many others "revolted" by running away and became *cimarrones* (*see* CIMARRÓN), wild Negroes forming their own communities in remote corners of the Antilles and the mainland.

It is difficult to generalize about the well-being of the African under slavery in Spanish America. As a rule, where black populations were large and where large plantations developed for the intensive cultivation of a cash crop, as in nineteenth-century Cuba, brutal methods of control were practiced. But even then, for slaves not subject to the pressures of capitalistic agriculture conditions were significantly better than they were for the plantation workers. Again, for slaves employed in mining, life was normally brutal and short, yet those engaged in subsistence agriculture or employed as domestics in the cities probably enjoyed a span of life similar to that of their white masters. Thus local conditions, which varied from region to region and within a region from task to task, had more to do with the slave's well-being than all the laws, priests, and government officials combined, no matter how well intentioned.

Very early in his New World experience the African found himself being severely punished, mutilated, or even killed for seemingly trivial offenses. He was prohibited from consuming intoxicants, bearing arms, riding horses, or walking the streets at night, while the male was discouraged from seeking sexual contacts with Indians and whites alike. Later, when the large plantations (particularly sugar) came into being, conditions grew even worse, and the blacks employed on them died at a rate so terrible as to make a mockery of the legend of the humaneness of Spanish slavery.

On the other hand, there seems little doubt that the Spanish were relatively liberal on the question of manumission and self-purchase, a practice called *coartación*. Masters often provided for their slaves' freedom in their wills, and some fortunate, enterprising slaves were able to buy their freedom, with the result that large populations of freed blacks could be found throughout colonial Spanish America. However, this apparent liberalism has often tended to conceal the fact that frequently those manumitted were the sick, the old, and the disabled whose freedom relieved their masters of the responsibility of caring for them.

For those who were freed during colonial times, prospects were far from bright. Their Negro parentage meant that they remained in the lowest state of the realm, living under a separate legal code, subject to stricter royal authority, and often legally barred from entering the "better" professions.

Wars for independence and emancipation. Freedom was also achieved by fighting for it. During the Spanish American wars for independence, thousands of slaves became free men by virtue of their service in the armies of liberation. Later, the TEN YEARS' WAR in Cuba (1868–1878) would result in the beginning of the end of slavery for that country, where many slaves and free blacks formed a large portion of the fighting force (*see* ABOLITION OF SLAVERY: CUBA). In the final drive for freedom (1895–1898) it has been estimated that 80 to 85 percent of the soldiers in the revolutionary army were blacks or mulattoes.

The great numbers of freedmen created by the wars of liberation and the liberalism of the times, coupled with the effectiveness of Great Britain in pressing the newly independent nations of the Americas to abolish their respective slave trades, gradually led to complete abolition: Santo Domingo, 1822; Federation of Central America, 1824; Chile, 1823; Mexico, 1829; Bolivia, 1831; Uruguay, 1842; Colombia, 1851; Ecuador, 1852; Argentina, 1853; Venezuela, 1854; Peru, 1854; Paraguay, 1869; Puerto Rico, 1873; and Cuba, 1886.

For most of the free coloreds, however, this change in status did little to improve their lot. The Negro remained, as before, on the bottom rung of the social ladder performing the least prestigious and most menial economic tasks, and although the mulatto was a step above, he too felt the sting of a prejudice, which if not so overt and pronounced as, for example, in the United States, was nonetheless very real.

Nevertheless, a few were able to make real social and economic gains. As heroes of the wars of independence, José Padilla rose to become a Colombian admiral, Manuel Piar became a general in the early Venezuelan campaigns, and the name of Col. Leonardo Infante grew to legendary proportions by virtue of his heroic exploits. Two mulattoes, Pedro SANTANA and Buenaventura BÁEZ, and two blacks, Gregorio Luperón and Ulises HEUREAUX, dominated the politics of the Dominican Republic during the second half of the nineteenth century, while in Cuba one of Latin America's finest generals, Antonio MACEO, a mulatto, was a leader in the war for independence. For others, social barriers proved flexible as they managed to amass some wealth; hence the truism "money whitens," illustrated by the adage, "A rich Negro is a mulatto, and a rich mulatto is a white man."

It can be seen, then, that whiteness is the ideal and thus the key to social mobility in Spanish American society. Because of this, it is fortunate that as a result of miscegenation the definition of a Negro has become an exceptionally fluid one. Racial mixing means that the phenotypical characteristics of the Negro (texture of hair, shape of nose and lips, color of skin) have become less pronounced in the population, permitting many some social mobility. Then, too, the desire to marry whiter than oneself—black to mulatto, mulatto to white—is strong, which further blends the Negroid features with those of the white.

Thus neither phenotypical characteristics nor ancestry (since mulattoes often take great pains to conceal their family origins) can be very rigid determinants of whiteness or blackness, and many are able to pass for white. This passing, of course, is made easier by the extent of a man's prestige, his wealth, and the social company he keeps.

Demographic experience of the black in the Americas. The enormous racial mixing that has occurred in the Spanish Americas has been denounced by some as creating "a mongrel race" or "demographic disaster." Others, such as the famous Mexican philosopher José VASCONCELOS, have viewed it as putting in motion a process that will ultimately blur all racial distinctions and produce one great race, a "cosmic race." Regardless of which view one has, in retrospect the massive amount of interbreeding that has taken place between African, Indian, and European seems to have been inevitable.

The peculiar circumstances of the slave trade (which dictated that far more males than females were brought to the New World), along with the peculiar circumstance of slavery (which often found the black female the sexual property of her white master), meant that the Negro male, unable to construct a familiar family structure in the New World, was forced to turn to the Indian to correct the imbalance of the sexes. The interbreeding of white master and black female, black male and Indian female, and, of course, white male and Indian female, along with the further mixing of the offspring of these unions, gradually brought about a vast degree of heterogeneity in racial composition for Spanish America. However, the degree of assimilation varies so from region to region that each requires separate consideration in quantitative terms. Yet even quantitative data can only suggest an approximation of reality. In the early New World censuses (sixteenth to eighteenth century) it often happened that Africans were classified as Negroes only if they were slaves, while most censuses taken since independence have no straightforward classification of race, leaving the decision to the whim of the census taker.

Philip Curtin's recent study, *The Atlantic Slave Trade: A Census* (Madison, Wis., 1969), has suggested that perhaps 10 million Negroes were brought from Africa to the New World throughout the slave trade period; of these Spanish America received some 1.5 million, or about 15 percent. By the early nineteenth century there seem to have been only 775,000 persons classified as Negroes in Spanish America, or approximately half of the number originally imported. However, another 5 million persons were categorized as "mixed," containing a variety of white, Negro, and Indian strains. Throughout the nineteenth and twentieth centuries the number of persons of African descent continued to grow, so that by the mid-twentieth century the figure stood at some 10 million persons in those countries that had once made up Spain's New World empire. The experience in the various regions follows.

The Caribbean: Cuba, Puerto Rico, and Santo Domingo. These Spanish islands together imported more than 800,000 slaves, the bulk of them, or about 700,000, going to Cuba and, of these, roughly 600,000 reaching the country late in the slave trade period (1790–1865). Puerto Rico's case was similar, with about 70,000 of the 80,000 slaves the island imported reaching its shores between the years 1765 and 1835. Only the Dominican Republic received most of its slaves (about 30,000) much earlier in the slave trade period.

Besides the importation from Africa, both the Dominican Republic and Cuba have more recently been the recipients of great numbers of Haitian workers and, in the case of Cuba, workers from Jamaica as well. Thus by the mid-twentieth century the Dominican Republic found that about 72 percent of its population, or more than 2 million persons, was of Negro descent, while about 11 percent of the total population, or 220,000, was classified as Negro. At the same time, Cuba classified about 25 percent of its population, or roughly 1.5 million persons, as Negro or colored, while Puerto Rico found 20 percent of its population, or 400,000 individuals, to be nonwhite.

Undoubtedly, however, the enumeration of blacks and mulattoes in the population of Cuba and Puerto Rico was incomplete. There exist other estimates that, in Cuba's case, for example, place the percentage of the population with distinctly Negroid characteristics at closer to 50 percent, with another 20 percent or so estimated as mulatto, a situation more closely resembling that of the Dominican Republic and, one suspects, the truth as well.

Mexico and Central America. Together this region imported about 230,000 slaves, more than 200,000 of them going to Mexico and most of these arriving before the end of the seventeenth century. The existence there of a large Indian population to absorb them over the centuries has resulted in very few Mexicans' possessing predominantly Negroid characteristics, perhaps only 10,000 to 14,000, as of a 1940 estimate. These, combined with a few hundred thousand persons who could be classified as Afro-crosses, make up perhaps 5 percent of Mexico's population. They can be found today living along the Pacific and Gulf coastal lowlands, with the states of Veracruz and Guerrero containing the largest number of Negroid types.

Central America, on the other hand, although it imported few slaves, has a much larger Negro population than one would suspect. In 1940 Nicaragua, Honduras, and Costa Rica had an estimated combined Negro and mulatto population of almost 250,000, constituting, respectively, 9 percent, 6 percent, and 4 percent of their populations.

Again, as in the case of the Haitian and Jamaican migration to Cuba, internal movement has been responsible for greatly modifying the ethnic map. Some blacks reached Honduras as runaway slaves from neighboring Belize. Later the British deported many black Caribs (runaway slaves who had interbred with the remnants of the CARIB Indians) from St. Vincent and others of the Windward Islands to Roatán Island, from which some found their way to mainland Honduras. Then, as the banana plantations began springing up throughout Central America, more labor was required to work them than the sparsely populated region could supply. Again it was the Caribbean Negro, mostly from the British islands, who supplied the labor and became part of the Central American population.

Viceroyalty of New Granada: Colombia, Venezuela, Panama, and Ecuador. Together these four countries may have imported as few as 320,000 slaves. Nevertheless, the region today has a population of more than 5 million Negroes and Afro-crosses. Although this growth has been largely internal, again there have been additions to the population from the outside world. This occurred notably in the Panama region, where Caribbean blacks were first brought in to build the PANAMA RAILROAD in the 1850s. Later more were imported to help the French attempt a canal, while some 20,000 flowed in from British and French islands to help the Americans finish it (*see* PANAMA CANAL). After the work was completed, many of these blacks drifted away to work on banana plantations, so that when the canal's defenses required supplementing in 1939, even more blacks were imported.

Viceroyalty of Peru: Peru and Chile. Together these countries probably imported no more than 100,000 slaves, with Peru taking the overwhelming majority (perhaps 95 percent). Most of these were brought in very early in the colonial period, with the great majority having been imported by the end of the seventeenth century. In 1940 Peru had about 29,000 members of its population classified as pure Negro, while in 1950 it was estimated that about 110,000 persons in the country were either Negro or of African descent. Chile, by contrast, imported only about 6,000 slaves; yet it saw its African population grow by natural means to perhaps 22,000 by 1620 and then decrease as it was absorbed, so that by the mid-twentieth century there were only about 4,000 persons in Chile of recognizable African descent.

Viceroyalty of Río de la Plata: Argentina, Uruguay, Paraguay, and Bolivia. The number of slaves who were imported to the Río de la Plata will never be known. Much of its slave trade was contraband, with Negroes entering the region from Brazil instead of Africa, while others were transshipped after Montevideo was made the sole port of entry for slaves sent to the area (1791) and became the focus of an inland slave trade not only to the provinces of the Río de la Plata but to Chile and Peru as well. It has been estimated that perhaps the entire region received 100,000 slaves who were retained in the area. As of 1940 there were approximately this number of Negroes and Afro-crosses in the region, with Uruguay having about 60 percent of the total, Bolivia about 14 percent, Argentina 16 percent, and Paraguay 10 percent.

Blacks in Spanish America since emancipation. Emancipation solved few problems either socially or economically for the Negroes in Spanish America. In the cities most continued to form a class of artisans, day laborers, and domestics. Some became small merchants; few became large ones. It was in the rural areas, however, that the great majority of Negroes remained, for an agricultural way of life was all they knew. A few became small landowners, most worked as laborers, and many found themselves caught up in a system of debt peonage, which prompted more than one late-nineteenth- and early-twentieth-century observer to suggest that the Africans of Latin America were still enslaved.

The general instability that characterized Spanish American political life during these years militated against efforts to improve the lot of the black or mulatto. His children were debarred from many schools, his level of living was the lowest, and his opportunities were few. Those of African descent who achieved political power, such as Rafael Leonidas TRUJILLO MOLINA, a mulatto, seemed for the most part to reflect not the aspirations of the colored masses but rather the values of the white elite. Thus Trujillo prohibited black immigration to the Dominican Republic but encouraged white immigrants to come in a determined campaign to "whiten" the country's population.

Yet, gradually, with or without a campaign, the population of Spanish America has become whiter, and as this has occurred, political, social, and economic opportunities for persons of African descent have increased accordingly. Today it is commonly asserted that if a black or mulatto experiences limitations, they are no longer racial ones but rather of a social and economic nature. Certainly, as the African has been increasingly absorbed, strictly Negro institutions have disappeared. Gone are the Negro churches, the Negro newspapers, and the Negro schools from Spanish America. Negroes and mulattoes are increasingly found in all walks of life: the military, politics, education, business. Spanish America is still no racial paradise, but generally speaking, those of African descent have been assimilated into national societies and cultures.

Bibliography. Philip D. Curtin, *The Atlantic Slave Trade: A Census,* Madison, Wis., 1969; David Brion Davis, *The Problem of Slavery in Western Culture,* Ithaca, N.Y., 1966; Magnus Mörner, "The History of Race Relations in Latin America: Some Comments on the State of Research," *Latin American Research Review,* vol. I, no. 3, Summer 1966, pp. 17–44; id., *Race Mixture in the History of Latin America,* Boston, 1967; José Antonio Saco, *La historia de la esclavitud de la raza africana en el Nuevo Mundo y en especial en los paises Americo-Hispanos,* 4 vols., Havana, 1938–40; Frank Tannenbaum, *Slave and Citizen: The Negro in the Americas,* New York, 1947; Wilbur Zelinsky, "The Historical Geography of the Negro Population of Latin America," *Journal of Negro History,* vol. XXXIV, no. 2, 1949, pp. 153–221.

KENNETH F. KIPLE

NEPOMUCENO, ALBERTO (1864–1920). Brazilian composer and conductor who played a major role in the development of musical nationalism at the beginning of the twentieth century. Born in Fortaleza, Ceará, he studied in Europe at the most celebrated music schools of the time (Santa Cecilia, Rome; Stern Conservatory, Berlin; Paris Conservatory). When he returned to Brazil in 1895, he had already written some compositions of a national character: the String Quartet No. 3 (*Brasileiro*), the piano piece *Galhofeira,* and a large number of songs in Portuguese. In Rio de Janeiro he directed the Association of Popular Concerts, promoting the performance of the works of local art music and popular composers and thus appearing as the main champion of the Brazilian composer.

Nepomuceno's extensive production reveals his eclecticism. He wrote in all the traditional musical forms or genres. Of all his works only the *Série Brasileira* and the prelude *O Garatuja,* both for orchestra, and the piano piece *Brasileira,* in addition to the compositions previously mentioned, present folk or popular material or simply draw directly upon popular music. The *Série Brasileira* (1892) brought him greater national recognition than any of his subsequent compositions. This suite was the first attempt to depict typical aspects of Brazilian life. Although Nepomuceno did not escape the domination of European music of his time, he was attentive to his own environment.

GERARD H. BÉHAGUE

NERUDA, PABLO (pseudonym of NEFTALÍ RICARDO REYES BASOALTO, 1904–1973). Chilean poet. He was born in Parral, Linares Province. From 1920 to 1927 he lived in Santiago, where he published his first books: *La canción de la fiesta* (1921); *Crepusculario* (1923); *El hondero entusiasta* (1923–1924); *Veinte poemas de amor y una canción desesperada* (1924), one of his best-known works; and *Tentativa del hombre infinito* (1925). These works show his gradual development from modernist imitation (*see* MODERNISM: SPANISH AMERICA) to a personal and free poetic expression. These years also produced a short novel, *El habitante y su esperanza* (1925), and the lyric prose pieces of *Anillos* (1926), written in collaboration with Tomás Lago. In 1927 Neruda began serving as a consul in the Far East, in China, Ceylon, and Burma. In *Residencia en la tierra I* (1933) his intense originality was expressed in surrealism. From 1934 to 1938 Neruda was consul in Spain, where he came into contact with Spanish writers of the generation of 1927 and edited the review *Caballo Verde para la Poesía.* He also published *Residencia en la tierra II* (1935), *Las furias y las penas* (1936), and the volume *España en el corazón* (1937), which gave vent to his despair at the impending defeat of the republic in the civil war. *Tercera residencia* (1942) contains the 1936 and 1937 volumes and other poems.

Neruda settled in Mexico in 1941, published *Tercera residencia* and *Dura elegía* (1942), and later returned to Chile, by now a member of the Communist party. He was elected to the Senate in 1945 but because of his political affiliations was forced into exile in 1948, and he did not return to Chile until 1953. *Himno y regreso* (1947) and *Que despierte el leñador* (1948) heralded the great work of 1950, *Canto general.* The same year Neruda was awarded the Stalin Peace Prize. In 1971 he received the Nobel Prize for Literature.

Among Neruda's later works are *Todo el amor* (1953); *Las uvas y el viento* (1954); *Odas elementales* (1954, 1955, 1957), celebrating the humblest created objects; *Estravagario* (1958); *Navegaciones y regresos* (1959); *Memorial de la isla Negra* (1964); and a play, *Fulgor y muerte de Joaquín Murieta,* first presented in 1967.

RACHEL PHILLIPS

NERVO, AMADO (1870–1919). Mexican poet. Nervo was born in Tepic. After studying in Jacona and Zamora, he wrote his first articles for a newspaper in Mazatlán. In 1894 he settled in Mexico City, where he worked for *El Imparcial,* also acting as its European correspondent in the period 1900–1901. His first success was the novel *El bachiller* (1895), which was followed by two volumes of poetry, *Perlas negras* (1898) and *Místicas* (1898). Nervo was one of the founders of the *Revista Moderna* (1898–1911), a celebrated outlet for modernist writers (*see* MODERNISM: SPANISH AMERICA). In 1905 he entered the diplomatic service and was sent to Spain, where he was able to continue his association with European writers, as well as expatriate Latin Americans such as Rubén DARÍO. These years produced volumes of poetry in which a tendency toward a somewhat sentimental mysticism is apparent: *Poemas* (1901), *El éxodo y las flores del camino* (1902), *Lira heróica* (1902), *Las voces* (1904), and *Los jardines interiores* (1905). Nervo also wrote *Crónicas de Europa* (1905–1907) and some didactic works.

Succeeding years saw the publication of the more traditional, introspective poetry of *En voz baja* (1909), *Serenidad* (1914), *Elevación* (1917), and *Plenitud* (1918) as well as *Juana de Asbaje* (1910), his most important critical work. In addition, Nervo wrote a number of short novels: *El diablo desinteresado* (1916), *El diamante de la inquietud* (1917), *Una mentira* (1917), *Un sueño* (1917), and *El sexto sentido* and *Amnesia* (both 1918). In 1918 he was named Minister in Argentina and Uruguay, and *El estanque de los lotos* (1919) and the posthumous *El arquero divino* (1922) both appeared in Buenos Aires. The twenty-nine volumes of his complete works, edited by Alfonso REYES, were published between 1926 and 1928.

RACHEL PHILLIPS

NEW CASTILE, VICEROYALTY OF. *See* PERU, VICEROYALTY OF.

NEW GRANADA, VICEROYALTY OF. Jurisdiction comprising the northern region of South America, created in 1717. Its capital was Santa Fé de Bogotá. The reason for its creation lies in the condition of the area. In 1700 the region was sparsely populated in the interior and poorly developed. Commercial activities centered in the coastal towns of Portobelo and Cartagena, the rendezvous for the Spanish fleets and the outlet for Peruvian mining wealth. The area was subjected to constant piracy and was too far from Lima for effective administration. In 1723 the viceroyalty was suppressed, and captaincies general were reestablished. With the beginning of war with Great Britain in 1739, however, the strategic position of New Granada led to the reinstallation of the viceroyalty with minor readjustments. Thus, the Presidency of Panama was ended in 1751, while prosperous Venezuela was allowed increasing autonomy. Quito remained a presidency within the viceroyalty.

New Granada successfully withstood the attacks of the English admiral Edward Vernon, and its several viceroys improved its administration and promoted economic development. Among the most notable viceroys were Pedro Messía de la Cerda and Manuel de Guirior. The creation of state monopolies and the enforcement of certain taxes caused the revolt in 1781 of the comuneros, which expressed a growing feeling of discontent (*see* COMUNEROS, REVOLT OF THE: NEW GRANADA). Toward the end of the eighteenth century the viceroyalty was one of the main cultural centers of the Spanish empire.

ASUNCIÓN LAVRIN

NEW GRANADA TREATY. *See* BIDLACK TREATY.

NEW LAWS. Body of legislation issued by the Spanish crown in 1542–1543. After discussing the responsibilities and duties of the COUNCIL OF THE INDIES and the American *audiencias* (*see* AUDIENCIA) and their relationship, the New Laws created the Viceroyalty of Peru and the *audiencias* of Lima and Guatemala. They then concerned themselves with fundamental reforms in the regulation of the work, tribute, and encomiendas of Indians (*see* ENCOMIENDA) and forbade any future enslavement of Indians. The release of slaves and free Indians to whom title could not be proved was ordered, compulsory personal services were ended, and tribute and services were to be regulated by the *audiencias* and were to be less than that formerly paid to caciques. In addition, new grants of encomiendas were forbidden, existing encomiendas were to be of moderate size and were to revert to the crown upon the death of their holders, and all encomiendas held by civil servants and ecclesiastics were to be transferred to the crown.

When the New Laws caused a revolt in Peru and a flood of protests in the other Spanish colonies, the crown retreated and compromised. Encomiendas continued when the crown allowed the right of succession by heirs, but the laws against Indian slavery and enforced personal services remained and were reaffirmed. Moreover, the New Laws did curb the power of the encomenderos, and encomiendas gradually escheated to the crown between 1550 and 1800.

RALPH H. VIGIL

NEW SPAIN, VICEROYALTY OF. In colonial Spanish America, a political unit that included modern-day Mexico, Central America, the southern half of the United States, the Antilles, and the Philippine Islands. The governors and royal *audiencias* of these territories were technically subordinate to the Viceroy and the royal *audiencia* of New Spain, but they governed with considerable independence from them. In practical terms the viceroyalty, which was established in 1535, corresponded to central and southern Mexico, that is, the area extending from San Luis Potosí, Zacatecas, and Culiacán in the north to the Isthmus of Tehuantepec in the south.

The viceroyalty's principal sources of wealth were its rapidly Christianized population, its silver mines, and its stock ranches. In addition to these, New Spain could boast of the Castilian sophistication of its aristocracy, the beauty of its cities, public buildings, churches, and monasteries, the quality of its educational institutions, the works of numerous scholars and artists, the particular luster of the nun-poet Sor JUANA INÉS DE LA CRUZ, the zeal of its early missionaries, and the statesmanship of a number of its bishops, judges, and viceroys.

After a period of decline in the late seventeenth and

early eighteenth centuries, the reforms effected by the royal visitor José de GÁLVEZ between 1765 and 1771 assured an impressive future for the viceroyalty. But New Spain's steady growth in the ensuing forty years was brought to a halt by the independence movement that began in 1810 and triumphed in 1821.

NORMAN MEIKLEJOHN

NEW STATE. *See* ESTADO NOVO.

NICARAGUA SINCE 1823. At the time of Central America's separation from Mexico, in 1823, Nicaragua was one of the five provinces in the United Provinces of Central America (*see* CENTRAL AMERICA, FEDERATION OF). A weak financial base and partisan regional rivalries prevented this confederation from stabilizing itself, and when it broke up, Nicaragua was forced to go its separate way. Nicaraguans proclaimed their independence in 1838 and adopted a republican constitution to govern the state, which had roughly its present boundaries and contained approximately 100,000 inhabitants. By far the majority of Nicaragua's citizens, mostly mestizos, lived in the fertile lowlands between Lakes Managua and Nicaragua and the Pacific Ocean. The Atlantic coastal region had been unattractive to settlement because of a very humid climate, hostile Indian tribes, and the proximity of Caribbean-based pirates. Liberals from the old colonial capital, León, an intellectual and religious center, dominated the new government, but not without serious opposition. The commercial center, Granada, served as the Conservative power base.

The rivalry between León and Granada was exacerbated by the tendency of politics to cross national boundaries and involve sympathizers from sister states in the old Central American confederation. Both Liberal and Conservative groups received support occasionally from El Salvador and Honduras, intensifying partisan feeling. In brief moments of peace, delegates from these three states frequently met in an effort to re-create the lost union. This was to be a recurring theme in Central American history, with Nicaragua, having suffered much from Central American wars, often in the vanguard of unionist movements.

Once the pattern of international Liberal-Conservative rivalry was established, it was not an unusual step for the Liberals to ask for help from a group of North American filibusters in 1854. However, the filibusters, who were led by William WALKER, took advantage of Nicaragua's weakness and took over the country. Walker became President of Nicaragua in 1856, at which time Nicaragua's factions temporarily set aside their differences and began a campaign to rid themselves of the intruder. With the help of forces from other Central American states whose leaders had reason to fear the loss of their own independence, they defeated Walker in 1857. Two subsequent Walker invasions were repulsed.

Following the Walker episode, Nicaragua settled into a period of relative tranquillity known as the Thirty Years (1863–1893). In this period the Conservative party predominated, but no one individual insisted on remaining in power and the government remained open to moderate social and economic change. The problem of León-Granada rivalry was mitigated by making neutral Managua the capital. The long period of peace

enabled Nicaraguans to encourage foreign investment, especially in coffee plantations in the Pacific region and in railroads. On the Atlantic coast, concessions enabled timber cutting, gold mining, and banana production to begin in earnest. This was the period when coffee cultivation, introduced for the first time in the 1850s near Managua, began to expand rapidly and give Nicaragua a reliable source of foreign exchange. Early-nineteenth-century products like indigo, cacao, and hides declined as exports. By 1904, when reliable statistics on exports first became available, coffee made up 25 percent of Nicaragua's exports. *See* COFFEE INDUSTRY (CENTRAL AMERICA).

Both the exploitation of Nicaragua's resources and the modernization of its transportation system were vastly accelerated when the Liberal dictator José Santos ZELAYA took over in 1893. In addition, the Zelaya regime was responsible for a secularizing trend, which resulted in the separation of church and state, the acceptance of civil marriage and divorce, and an emphasis on state-controlled education. Educational and transportation facilities were given particular attention. In the international sphere, Zelaya led a movement that resulted in a brief union (1896–1898) of Nicaragua, El Salvador, and Honduras and was instrumental in establishing Liberal governments in the Central American states. Nicaragua was probably at the peak of its international prestige under Zelaya's leadership at the beginning of the twentieth century. Zelaya's dictatorial methods, however, provoked opposition, and he fell from power in 1909, in a revolution that received the direct support of the United States.

Throughout the nineteenth century a recurring theme in Nicaraguan history was the canal question. The possibility of a canal across the Central American isthmus via the San Juan River and Lake Nicaragua was recognized early by the major powers, and as a consequence weak Nicaragua found itself a pawn in

NICARAGUA

Area: 50,193 sq. mi.   Population: 1,911,543 (1971 est.).

their rivalry for control over this route. In 1848 Great Britain temporarily seized the town of San Juan del Norte at the mouth of the San Juan River, and the same year the United States began seriously to contest British supremacy on the Central American isthmus. The United States and Great Britain settled their differences by signing the CLAYTON-BULWER TREATY in 1850. According to its terms, the two powers promised not to acquire territory in Central America and not to build a fortified canal. This agreement helped to preserve Nicaraguan sovereignty, but in effect it postponed the opportunity for cashing in on its most valuable resource, the canal route. It soon became obvious that the canal was beyond the financial reach of private enterprise and that the United States would not build a canal which it could not fortify and control. Hopes for a Nicaraguan canal were renewed as various technical studies emphasized the superiority of the Nicaraguan route, as commerce steadily increased in the late nineteenth century, and especially as new Anglo-American negotiations resulted in freedom for the United States to build a fortified canal. However, these hopes were crushed when Panamanian independence in 1903 and Washington politics resulted in the construction of the canal in Panama instead of Nicaragua.

The canal question has remained an issue in the twentieth century with the same result—no canal. With United States Marines in occupation of Nicaragua, discussions began in 1913 for the construction of a second isthmian canal. The resulting BRYAN-CHAMORRO TREATY granted exclusive privileges to the United States for canal construction and also allowed it military privileges on Nicaragua's Corn Islands in the Caribbean and in the Gulf of Fonseca on the Pacific coast. The hostility of Nicaragua's immediate neighbors to these privileges granted to the United States was a hindrance to Nicaragua's relations with the Central American countries and a formidable obstacle to union plans. No serious effort to build a canal was ever undertaken under this treaty, and the two countries finally agreed to abrogate it in 1970.

Nicaragua's chief problem in the first half of the twentieth century was the overwhelming presence of the United States in its political and economic life. The removal of Zelaya in 1909 opened the way for the new situation to develop. With Zelaya gone, the Conservative party regained its ascendancy, and when the Liberals threatened to return by revolution, the Conservatives, under President Adolfo DÍAZ, asked for military protection by the United States. Thus began, in 1912, the long period of occupation of Nicaragua by United States Marines. The Marines were not finally withdrawn until 1933. In the meantime, Nicaragua surrendered control over the collection of customs and much of its financial system to United States officials. In addition, United States investment in various segments of the Nicaraguan economy increased to such an extent as to expand the total United States influence to an unprecedented degree. Militarily, the peak of United States presence occurred in 1930–1931, when approximately 5,000 Marines were in Nicaragua in the unsuccessful effort to defeat the Nicaraguan guerrilla leader Augusto César SANDINO. The 1928 and 1932 presidential elections were held under the supervision of the Marines, resulting in victories by the Liberal party. Military intervention ended in January 1933,

when Juan Bautista SACASA was inaugurated as President and the National Guard, trained by United States military officers as a peace-keeping force, took over the responsibility of maintaining order.

The National Guard proved to be the instrument for Anastasio SOMOZA GARCÍA's rise to power in 1936 and the basis for the maintenance of control over Nicaragua by the Somoza family ever since. Somoza García was dictator from 1936 until his assassination in 1956, whereupon his son Luis SOMOZA DEBAYLE assumed command. Another son, Anastasio SOMOZA DEBAYLE, took over as President in 1967.

There have been the usual problems of dictatorial rule. Opponents who overstep the unwritten limits of criticism of the regime have been subjected to harassment, jail, and even torture. The success of any project, intellectual, charitable, social, or entrepreneurial, depends on the goodwill of the highest level of government, which makes for efficiency once approval is given but discourages independent thinking and initiative. The Somoza dictatorship was a factor in heightened tension between Nicaragua and Costa Rica in the 1950s and 1960s, although a 1971 summit conference between President Somoza and President José FIGUERES of Costa Rica served to improve relations.

The Somozas have justified their dictatorship on the ground that Nicaragua's principal requirement is rapid economic growth. For the most part, statistical indices of Nicaragua's economy since the mid-1930s do indicate steady and dramatic growth. Nicaragua's total foreign trade amounted to only $10,227,806 in 1936 (approximately the same as it was in the decade between 1910 and 1920), but it rose to $47 million in 1948 and to a startling $320 million in 1966, when it leveled off. Since Nicaragua's population only doubled in this period, from approximately 900,000 in 1936 to 1.7 million in 1966, and since inflation was moderate, a rapid increase in per capita exports and imports took place. The most rapid increase in the country's goods and services in its history, according to available statistics, occurred between 1960 and 1965, when the average annual increase was 8.3 percent, the largest increase of all the Latin American nations in this period.

Much of Nicaragua's economic growth in the early 1960s can be traced to the agricultural sector, especially to cotton, which enjoyed a boom starting after World War II. In 1954 cotton made up 31 percent of Nicaragua's exports, but by 1958 its share had risen to 39 percent and by 1965 to 46 percent. From 1954 to 1965 the share of the old reliable export of coffee had fallen from 46 percent to 18 percent. Banana production on the Atlantic coast was curtailed in the 1930s because of plant diseases, and by 1940 bananas had ceased to be of importance in Nicaragua's export picture.

Since 1965 the industrial sector has expanded more rapidly than the agricultural sector. In 1965 industrial production was valued at $59 million, or approximately one-third that of agricultural production; by 1970 its value had reached $104 million, or approximately one-half that of agricultural production, which had increased by only $2.5 million (from $186 million to $188.5 million) in the five-year interval. From 1965 to 1970, however, the average annual increase in total goods and services dropped to half that of the previous five years, or about 4 percent per year. These figures, of course, tell us little about distribution of income or the degree of dominance of the Nicaraguan economy by the Somoza family and coterie. Neither do they settle the controversy over whether or not the Somoza dictatorship is an economic necessity in Nicaragua's stage of development. They do indicate that a remarkable economic growth has taken place in the country since the mid-1930s.

Bibliography. Emilio Álvarez Lejarza, *Las constituciones de Nicaragua,* Madrid, 1958; Alejandro Cole Chamorro, *145 años de historia política de Nicaragua,* Managua, 1967; Isaac J. Cox, *Nicaragua and the United States,* Boston, 1927; Carlos Cuadra Pasos, *Historia de medio siglo,* Managua, 1964; José Dolores Gámez, *Historia de Nicaragua desde los tiempos prehistóricos hasta 1860,* Managua, 1889; International Bank for Reconstruction and Development, *The Economic Development of Nicaragua,* Baltimore, 1953; Ephraim George Squier, *Nicaragua: Its People, Scenery, Monuments, and the Proposed Nicaraguan Canal,* 2 vols., New York, 1852; William Walker, *The War in Nicaragua,* Mobile, 1860.

CHARLES L. STANSIFER

NIEMEYER [SOARES FILHO], OSCAR (1907–).

Brazilian architect. Niemeyer was born in Rio de Janeiro of well-to-do parents. In 1930, already married, he began his architectural studies at the Escola Nacional de Belas Artes, graduating in 1934. Upon his own insistence he joined the staff of the school's former director, Lúcio COSTA, in 1932.

The single greatest influence upon Niemeyer's art is the work and theories of Le Corbusier, who visited Brazil for one month in 1936 for consultation on the projected Ministry of Education and Health building in Rio de Janeiro. Three years later, Niemeyer was appointed head of the design group for this building. In addition to Costa and Niemeyer, several other architects of note in Brazil's subsequent architectural boom worked on the building (1936–1943). Niemeyer's commissions, both public and private, have since been numerous and have often overlapped. His early works are elegant and inventive derivatives of Le Corbusier's buildings with stilts, solids alternating with voids, honeycomb frames with movable louvers (*brise-soleil*) in front of recessed windows, decorative murals in tile, and his own special concern for integrating the arts: architecture, painting, sculpture, and, when possible, landscape gardening. Examples of such designs are the Maternity Clinic (1937), the Ministry of Education and Health building, and the Sul America Hospital (1952), all in Rio de Janeiro.

Niemeyer's rapid rise to fame is attested by his appointment to collaborate with Lúcio Costa on the Brazilian Pavilion for the New York World's Fair of 1939. The final form (1947) for the United Nations headquarters in New York is a felicitous combination of designs by Niemeyer and Le Corbusier. The new capital, Brasília, was planned from 1957 to 1959, Costa being the chief planner and Joaquim Cardozo the chief engineer. Niemeyer was responsible for designing all the important federal buildings and several others; he worked with the assistance of about sixty architects.

During World War II he spent time researching esthetic problems in experimental projects that led him away from the austere functionalism of the International Style. The change is not a total abandonment of the International Style's esthetic but rather the additional use, by way of the engineer's esthetic, of the poetic and the symbolic. Although the expression of this trend appears frequently in secular buildings such as in the exotic colonnade screening the facade of the presidential Palace of the Dawn (1959) in Brasília, the most memorable effects are in ecclesiastical monuments.

Niemeyer was comissioned to design several buildings along the shores of an artificial lake at Pampulha, a newly developed suburb of Belo Horizonte. One of these is the little Church of St. Francis of Assisi (1943). It is a most ingenious combination of traditional elements, modern structure, and subtle symbolism. In ground plan it is the Constantinian Latin-cross type (T shape) such as Old St. Peter's in Rome, omitting the apse. In elevation its nave is like Eugène Freyssinet's airship hangars at Orly, and the transept restates segments of the parabolic curve in escalloped echoes. The transept's roof overlaps that of the nave with a narrow clerestory band created between them. Light from this clerestory falls on the interior, like a luminous veil between the end of the nave and the sanctuary, which is the center of the transept. The salient ends of the transept serve as sacristy and vestry and recall the sanctuary-flanking disposition of pastophoria in fifth-century Syrian churches. Outside there is a modern version of an Italian Romanesque freestanding bell tower. This small gem of a church was almost razed during a puzzling storm of clerical disapproval. No small part of the loss would have been the tile mural by Cândido PORTINARI, who depicted the life of St. Francis on the transept's external rear wall.

The tiny Presidential Chapel (1958) in Brasília is helicoid like a snail's shell and suggests a snug retreat for private spiritual regeneration. Its inhospitably lightless portal signals a dark night of the soul preceding a mystical experience or warns that the entry of the uninvited would be a violation. Around the bend from that shadowed entrance the interior of the chapel is brightly illuminated by an unseen window in the wall of a curved cul-de-sac to one's left.

The Chapel of Our Lady of Fatima (1959), also in Brasília, has a triangular roof raised like a canopied cloth of honor on three triangular piers over a U-shaped cella at its center. Inside a fresco by Alfredo Volpi continues the illusion of a temporary tent. Thus the tent of Abraham is symbolically made one with Christianity's triune God.

The Cathedral of Brasília (1959) is approached through a subterranean passage that leads to a circular nave about 10 feet underground. At ground level twenty-one buttresses rise from the top of the nave wall, sweep upward and inward, and then curve slightly outward to hold and surround like a thorny corona a round concrete slab of roof. Since the interstices between the buttresses are glazed, gazing upward from the subterranean floor of the nave is like looking through a nimbus of ribbed light at a circular opening to an invisible beyond. At night a view of the starry firmament would also appear to be pierced by a darksome porthole. The most obvious prototype of the above-ground structure is the tepee with its central smoke hole plugged. Reference has been made to the religious concept of the sacred mountain, which is true enough on the exterior, but the interior of the cathedral is more expressive of an incorporeal, gloriously ascensional leap through the light of structured reason to blind faith.

Bibliography. Oscar Niemeyer, *Minha Experiência em Brasília,* Rio de Janeiro, 1961; Stamo Papadaki, *Oscar Niemeyer,* New York, 1960; id., *Oscar Niemeyer,* Ravensburg, 1962.

EILEEN LORD

NITRATE INDUSTRY (CHILE). The ATACAMA DESERT of northern Chile contains the world's largest deposits of sodium nitrate, a rich natural fertilizer and a basic ingredient of gunpowder. Before the WAR OF THE PACIFIC, in which Chile took the area from its northern neighbors, Peru held the richest fields, in Tarapacá, and Bolivia had deposits in Antofagasta, though Chilean and British capital and Chilean labor were important in their exploitation. Until the mid-1870s the Peruvian government limited its interest to exacting duties on nitrate exports, but financial difficulties persuaded it, in 1875, to bring nitrates under state control. Certificates were issued to the owners of the nitrate works (*oficinas*) in return for their properties, to be redeemed with cash once the government secured a European loan. This, however, it failed to do, and great uncertainty resulted. A severe earthquake, restricting production, occurred in 1877, and the outbreak of the War of the Pacific in 1879 was the last straw for many producers. The certificates they held, the title deeds to the *oficinas,* were transferable to third parties, and many owners sold out for what they could get, particularly since none knew Chile's postwar intentions. In this way, speculators, notably John Thomas North, bought certificates very cheaply, acquiring the best of the *oficinas* for subsequent sale to limited liability companies North founded in the 1880s. The gamble paid off when, in 1881, the Chilean government resolved to return the industry to private hands on the basis of the Peruvian certificates, a decision much criticized by later historians but one taken in the age of laissez faire by a government which believed in that philosophy and which was not encouraged by Peru's abortive attempt at state control. As a result, Chile's nitrate industry remained largely in foreign hands; the government exacted export duties and did little else, though President José Manuel BALMACEDA made a halfhearted attempt to reduce the foreign monopoly.

Yet the industry was crucial to Chile: between 1880 and 1920 export duties on nitrates provided more than half of government revenue, furnishing capital for public works and obviating the necessity for heavy internal taxation. Chile dominated the world market in nitrates, accounting for 73 percent of world supplies in 1894 and 56 percent in 1914, but boom followed slump with alarming regularity. The major markets for nitrates were the agricultural industries of Europe and America, and their periodic depressions immediately affected nitrates. From time to time, when world markets were overstocked, producers formed combinations to limit output and thus raise prices, but these were palliatives for a basic problem, the comparative inelasticity of world demand.

Chile's great dependence on nitrates was cruelly revealed during World War I, when the German market was abruptly cut off, closing half the *oficinas* in Tarapacá and putting 40,000 men out of work within a few months. Worse was to follow. Spurred by necessity

during the war, German scientists perfected techniques for making synthetic nitrates in commercial quantities, and these techniques spread. Although the quantity of nitrates shipped from Chile in the postwar period did not fall significantly, its share of world production, both natural and synthetic, declined from 90 percent in 1919 to 24 percent in 1929. By this time also, United States capital had largely replaced British in the industry, the Guggenheim interests being predominant. In 1931, when the Great Depression had already disrupted world trade, President Carlos IBÁÑEZ tried to reorganize the industry by the formation of a state monopoly, the Compañía de Salitre de Chile (COSACH), absorbing the thirty-four private companies but allowing them to hold shares in COSACH. The experiment failed, and COSACH was liquidated in 1933, when Gustavo ROSS formed the Corporación de Ventas de Salitre (COVENSA), a looser sales organization empowered to make agreements on finance and production with the *oficinas,* which were returned to private hands.

Improved cost-effective techniques enabled Chile to retain a small proportion of the world market, but production became concentrated in two or three modernized *oficinas,* and many others closed down. Today Chilean nitrates hold about 4 percent of the world market. In 1971 the last chapter in the industry's history was written when President Salvador ALLENDE nationalized remaining foreign interests.

Nitrates dominated the economic life of Chile for almost half a century, as copper does today, and the history of the industry provides a classic example of the short-run advantages and long-term dangers of national dependence on the export of one commodity.

Bibliography. Guillermo E. Billinghurst, *Los capitales salitreros de Tarapacá,* Santiago, 1889; Harold Blakemore, "John Thomas North, the Nitrate King," *History Today,* vol. XII, no. 7, July 1962, pp. 467–475; M. B. Donald, "History of the Chile Nitrate Industry," *Annals of Science,* vol. I, no. 1, January 1936, pp. 29–47, no. 2, April 1936, pp. 193–216; R. Hernández, *El salitre,* Valparaíso, 1930; J. Fred Rippy, "Economic Enterprises of the Nitrate King and His Associates in Chile," *Pacific Historical Review,* vol. XVII, 1948, pp. 457–465; L. S. Rowe, *Early Effects of the European War upon the Finance, Commerce and Industry of Chile,* New York, 1918; E. Semper and E. Michels, *La industria del salitre en Chile,* tr. and augmented by J. Ganderillas and Orlando G. Salas, Santiago, 1908.　HAROLD BLAKEMORE

NÓBREGA, MANUEL DA (1517–1570). Portuguese missionary and first Jesuit Provincial of Brazil. Nóbrega was born of the lower nobility in the northern Portuguese province of Minho. Educated at the Universities of Salamanca and Coimbra, he joined the Society of Jesus in 1544. In 1549 he was chosen to head the first Jesuit mission to Brazil, which sailed to Bahia (modern Salvador) in the fleet carrying the first Governor-General, Tomé de SOUSA. Soon after their arrival it became evident that the Jesuits considered their primary task the conversion and protection of Brazil's Indian populations. Emphasis was placed upon learning the native languages and on isolating the Indians from the colonists by gathering them into Jesuit-operated villages (*aldeias*).

In 1553 Nóbrega was appointed Provincial of Brazil, and the same year he left Bahia to open a missionary front in the south, in the captaincy of São Vicente (modern São Paulo). In 1554, under Nóbrega's direction, the mission and *colégio* (secondary school) of São Paulo were established near the incipient village of Piratininga. Nóbrega returned to Bahia in 1556, but in 1560 he was back in São Paulo, relieved of the office of Provincial. From 1561 until his death Nóbrega was involved in the effort to recapture the Bay of Guanabara from the French and to establish the Portuguese and Jesuit presence firmly there through the newly founded (1565) city of Rio de Janeiro and the Jesuit *colégio* he established in Rio in 1567. Nóbrega served as rector of the *colégio* until his death on October 18, 1570.

The most important writings of Manuel da Nóbrega are his collected letters and two works on Brazil, *Informação das Terras do Brasil* (1549) and *Diálogo sôbre a Conversão do Gentio* (1556–1557).

FREDERICK V. GIFUN

NORTHEAST. Region of Brazil comprising the states of Maranhão, Piauí, Ceará, Rio Grande do Norte, Paraíba, Pernambuco, and Alagoas and the island of Fernando de Noronha. There are many variations and subregions in the 373,465 square miles composing the Northeast, which contains nearly 20 million people (1970), or 21 percent of the Brazilian population. It is an area of widespread and severe poverty, with a high infant mortality rate, inequitable land distribution, overpopulation, hunger, and disease. Despite increasing official attention in this century, it remains a national problem area.

The Northeast consists basically of two very different physical, social, and economic units: the coastal strip and the interior SERTÃO. The coast is a humid area of intense agricultural exploitation. The sertão is a hot, dry land subject to periodic droughts, with generally poor soils, xerophytic vegetation, and relatively low population density.

The coast has been the center of sugarcane plantations since the sixteenth century; it was here that African slavery was instituted, leaving an indelible mark on society and the economy (*see* NEGRO IN BRAZIL; SUGAR INDUSTRY: COLONIAL BRAZIL). Agriculture has been large-scale and permanent. In the sertão economic activity centers on extensive livestock grazing, extractive products, and subsistence agriculture.

The northeastern coast was one of the first areas of Brazil to be explored by the Portuguese discoverers after 1500. This area became the first site of economic exploitation of the colony with the brazilwood trade. Within a few decades attention turned to sugar, and Brazil soon became the world's leading sugar producer. The society that grew up around sugar had a plantation orientation strongly reminiscent of the antebellum South in the United States. The colonial capital was in Bahia, an indication of the importance of the Northeast.

The sertão became a major cattle region, supplying food and draft animals to the coast, but aside from cattle raising, the interior remained underdeveloped. Brazil lost its sugar monopoly in the mid-seventeenth century as Caribbean islands came into production, but sugar remained the leading crop of the Northeast and the source of most of Brazil's revenue until the late nine-

teenth century, when the economic and political locus of power shifted to the southern coffee lands.

The African influence on the coast is strongly felt in racial composition, food, music, language, and religion. In the sugar zone large holdings still remain, and sharecropping is the most common form of tenure. Large holdings also dominate the sertão, but the population tends to be seminomadic.

Much of northeastern history has been punctuated by violence. There were numerous slave uprisings of varying intensity, and the first third of the nineteenth century saw a series of regional revolts. Perhaps the most famous revolt was the Canudos rebellion of 1896–1897, led by Antônio CONSELHEIRO, during which three federal campaigns were repulsed. In addition to such organized violence, the sertão has had a long history of banditry and general lawlessness. Social unrest has been a tradition in the sertão and has been attributed to messianism and fanaticism. *See also* CÍCERO, Padre; LAMPEÃO.

There is a strong regional attachment among the Northeasterners. Climatic and economic conditions have forced large numbers to leave the Northeast in search of work and food, but many return as soon as possible, and the others still remember their origins fondly. One of the most famous such migrations was the exodus to the AMAZON RIVER to tap rubber in the 1880s and 1890s, but the move to the industrializing central south in more recent times has been far greater.

There have been numerous attempts to alleviate the problems of the Northeast, mostly unsuccessful. The greatest progress toward this goal has been made since 1955 by the SUPERINTENDÊNCIA DO DESENVOLVIMENTO DO NORDESTE (SUDENE). Through programs such as school construction, agricultural improvement, development of mineral and other natural resources, fiscal incentives for industrialization, and increase of hydroelectric power, SUDENE hopes to develop the Northeast so that it will no longer be a net drain on the nation. Solutions to some of the problems have been found, but the Northeast remains a source of frustration, despair, and unrest in Brazil.

Bibliography. João Capistrano de Abreu, *Caminhos Antigos e Povoamento do Brasil,* Rio de Janeiro, 1960; Manuel Correia de Andrade, *A Terra e o Homem no Nordeste,* São Paulo, 1963; Josué de Castro, *Death in the Northeast: Poverty and Revolution in the Northeast of Brazil,* New York, 1969; Euclides da Cunha, *Os Sertões,* tr. by Samuel Putnam as *Rebellion in the Backlands,* Chicago, 1944; Gilberto Freyre, *The Masters and the Slaves,* New York, 1964; Harry W. Hutchinson, *Village and Plantation Life in Northeastern Brazil,* Seattle, 1957; Alexander Marchant, *From Barter to Slavery: The Economic Relations of Portuguese and Indians in the Settlement of Brazil, 1500–1580,* Baltimore, 1942.

ROBIN L. ANDERSON

NORTHEAST DEVELOPMENT AGENCY. *See* SUPERINTENDÊNCIA DO DESENVOLVIMENTO DO NORDESTE.

NOVÁS CALVO, LINO (1905–   ). Cuban writer. Born in Galicia, Spain, Novás Calvo emigrated to Cuba at the age of seven and made it his home until 1960, when he settled permanently in the United States. His first publication was a poem, written in the avant-garde style, that appeared in the *Revista de Avance* in

1928. From 1931 to 1933 he was foreign correspondent for the review *Orbe* and lived in Madrid, where he published a novel, *El negrero, vida novelada de Pedro Banco Fernández de Trava* (1933). He translated various novels of Huxley, D. H. Lawrence, and Faulkner into Spanish, wrote for the *Revista de Occidente* under the protection of Ortega y Gasset, and stayed in Spain during the civil war as a foreign correspondent in the Republican zone. In 1939 he returned to Cuba, where he continued writing and teaching until 1960. He has written a considerable number of short stories and is one of the best contemporary writers in this genre.

RACHEL PHILLIPS

NUCLEAR AMERICA. Term used by archaeologists to refer to the area of the high civilizations of pre-Columbian America (Mayan, Mexican, Chibcha, and Inca). Under this rubric is implied a loose set of cultural relationships within the area, as well as a powerful focus of influences emanating outward and affecting other areas of the New World.

BURR C. BRUNDAGE

NÚÑEZ [MOLEDO], RAFAEL (1825–1894). President of Colombia (1880–1882, 1884–1894). Still a controversial figure eight decades after his death, Núñez has been variously described as an ambitious renegade who betrayed his party and as an enlightened statesman who saved Colombia from political strife and economic stagnation. Born in the coastal city of Cartagena, Núñez was trained as a lawyer. In the 1850s he was appointed to a minor post in Panama, where he married for the first time. His wife was the sister-in-law of a prominent Panamanian politican through whose influence Núñez won a seat in the Chamber of Representatives in Bogotá. In 1853 he served briefly as Secretary of Government under President José María OBANDO. A Liberal (*see* LIBERAL PARTY: COLOMBIA), he again held Cabinet posts in the bipartisan regime (1855–1857) of Conservative Manuel María Mallarino (*see* CONSERVATIVE PARTY: COLOMBIA) and in the provisional government established by Tomás Cipriano de MOSQUERA after the successful Liberal revolution of 1860. As Secretary of the Treasury and Public Credit, he wrote a well-known defense (1862) of the recent decree nationalizing church property.

From 1863 until 1874, Núñez lived abroad, first in the United States and later in Le Havre and Liverpool, serving as Colombian Consul in both cities and contributing articles to Colombian periodicals on current events in Europe. Upon his return to Colombia, he was nominated to the Presidency by dissident Liberals unhappy with the development policies and political practices of recent Liberal administrations and desirous of seeing a native of the coastal region as chief executive. Núñez lost his first presidential bid after an acrimonious campaign, but he was successful in 1879. By this time he had the support not only of the dissident Liberals, who were now known as Independents, but of many Conservative leaders as well. Upon taking office on April 8, 1880, Núñez stressed the need to stimulate Colombia's economic development, and to achieve this goal he requested the enactment of a protective tariff and the creation of a National Bank. Both requests were granted by Congress in 1880. Núñez and his followers also showed themselves sympathetic to the church and obtained the repeal of recent anticlerical measures.

Núñez retired from the Presidency at the expiration of his two-year term but was reelected in 1883, having received the official endorsement of the Conservative party. Although he called himself an "irrevocable member of Colombian liberalism" in his inaugural address, most Liberal leaders, including some repentant Independents, feared that Núñez would eventually turn over control of the government to the Conservatives. These fears were realized in 1885–1886, when an uprising in the state of Santander led to a Liberal revolution against the Núñez government, in the course of which the President turned to the Conservatives for assistance in crushing the insurrectionists.

Núñez proceeded to announce the demise of the Liberal constitution of 1863 and sponsored the drafting of a new charter that was both authoritarian and centralist (*see* CONSTITUTION OF 1886: COLOMBIA). The regime instituted by its adoption, backed by both the Conservatives and the remaining Independents, was known as the Regeneration. Núñez was elected President for a six-year term by the eighteen-member body that drafted the constitution, but he served for only about a year, departing for Cartagena in 1888 and leaving the government in the hands of the presidential alternate, Carlos Holguín. While in retirement he made his views known in Bogotá by means of telegrams and newspaper articles. In 1891 he was elected to another six-year term but remained in Cartagena while Vice President Miguel Antonio CARO acted as chief executive. He was preparing to return to Bogotá to heal dissension among supporters of the Regeneration when he died on September 18, 1894.

Always enigmatic and dubious of man's ability to discern truth or even of its existence, Núñez never formally embraced conservatism and denied that he had betrayed the Liberal principles of his youth. It was his contention that he had rejected only what he had come to regard as the pernicious federalism and anticlericalism upheld by Liberal extremists, to which he attributed Colombia's political instability and continuing underdevelopment. By the late 1880s he had become convinced that political tranquillity was Colombia's greatest need and that religious belief was the wellspring of social order. Núñez was also a competent poet.

Bibliography. Nicolás del Castillo, *El primer Núñez,* Bogotá, 1971; Indalecio Liévano Aguirre, *Rafael Núñez,* 3d ed., Bogotá, 1946; Rafael Núñez, *Ensayo de crítica social,* Rouen, 1874; id., *La reforma política en Colombia,* 7 vols., Bogotá, 1944–1950; Gustavo Otero Muñoz, *Un hombre y una época: La vida azarosa de Rafael Núñez,* Bogotá, 1951; Joaquín Tamayo, *Núñez,* Bogotá, 1939; José Ramón Vergara, *Escrutinio histórico: Rafael Núñez,* Bogotá, 1939.

HELEN DELPAR

OAS. *See* ORGANIZATION OF AMERICAN STATES.

OBANDO, JOSÉ MARÍA (1795–1861). Colombian general and political leader. Obando was born near Popayán. Although he was raised in comfortable circumstances, his illegitimate birth excluded him from full membership in the local elite. The wars of independence, which had a markedly social character in southern Colombia, put Obando on the royalist side and, from 1819 to 1822, saw him emerge as the charismatic leader of the Indian and Negro masses of the region.

Simón BOLÍVAR coopted Obando into the army of Gran Colombia in 1822 (*see* COLOMBIA, GRAN), and he did much to bring his native region under republican rule. A colonel by 1828, Obando sided with Francisco de Paula SANTANDER in the latter's struggle against the Bolivarian dictatorship and defeated Bolívar's southern agent, Tomás Cipriano de MOSQUERA, in November 1828. Bolívar recognized Obando as the leading power broker of the south, but he was soon accused of the murder (June 4, 1830) of Marshal Antonio José de SUCRE; the charges were never proved.

Obando successfully combatted the government of Rafael Urdaneta in Bogotá (1831) and, as acting President, headed the caretaker regime established prior to the return of Santander. In 1832 Obando was sent to detach his native region from Ecuador, to which it had been attached during the conflict with Urdaneta, and to reincorporate it into Colombia. He remained the leading figure of the south until 1836, when his defeat in a presidential election badly eroded his prestige.

José María Obando. [J. León Helguera Collection]

An uprising in Pasto Province in 1839 brought about a revival of the charges against Obando in the Sucre murder. By July 1840 he had sparked the entire south into rebellion against the government of José Ignacio de Márquez. He lost his army in October 1840, but he escaped captivity and rekindled his revolt in early 1841, only to be decisively defeated in July.

Obando fled to Peru, where he remained in exile until 1849, engaging in journalistic polemics with Mosquera. Returning to Colombia as a martyrlike figure in the eyes of the Liberal party (*see* LIBERAL PARTY: COLOMBIA), he was given military and diplomatic posts by the administration of José Hilario López and easily swept to victory in the presidential election of 1852. Obando took office on April 1, 1853, at a time when the Liberal party was gripped by intense factionalism which pitted doctrinaire Liberals known as Gólgotas against the more moderate Draconianos, who numbered in their ranks the military, the urban artisans, and Obando himself. On April 17, 1854, Obando was offered dictatorial powers by Gen. José María Melo; when the President refused, Melo assumed them himself.

Melo was removed from power by a combined Liberal-Conservative military effort in late 1854 (*see* CONSERVATIVE PARTY: COLOMBIA), but Obando was charged with complicity in the coup and was tried for high treason by the Senate. Although he was absolved, he was forced to retire from the Presidency. Obando returned to political life in 1860, when he joined the successful federalist revolt led by his old adversary, Mosquera. He died in a skirmish on the outskirts of Bogotá on April 29, 1861.

J. LEÓN HELGUERA

OBRAJE. Cloth production was the most widely developed manufacturing industry in the Spanish colonies, and woolen cloth was of chief importance, although cotton and silk also were woven. Production of cloth, which chiefly involved washing, carding, spinning, and weaving, took place in *obrajes*, or sweatshops, owned in some instances by Indians and mestizos. Workers might be free indebted laborers, people of color, convicts sold by the AUDIENCIA into service, Chinese slaves brought from the Philippines to Mexico, or, in Peru, REPARTIMIENTO Indians sent to labor in the textile mills. It was also permissible in Peru to draft children ten years old to work in *obrajes*, and it was not uncommon to find children of six working in the mills in defiance of regulations.

Once inside the mill, which colonial writers compared to a prison workshop, the Indians often never left until they died. Half-naked workers labored from before sunrise until twilight, and the double doors of the *obraje* remained shut and guarded by Negroes or mulattoes to prevent escape. Severe whippings and fines were common for failure to meet the daily production quota, and the low wages paid in supplies allowed the manufacturer to keep his laborers forever in debt. Decrees to eliminate the extortion and abuses in the *obrajes* were circumvented by manufacturers who bribed mill inspectors, and the exploitation of cloth workers continued throughout the colonial period.

RALPH H. VIGIL

OBREGÓN, ÁLVARO (1880–1928). Mexican revolutionary leader and President (1920–1924). Obregón was born on a farm in Álamos, Sonora, that was the property of his parents, Francisco Obregón and Cenobia Salido. As a child he came into contact with the Mayo Indians, whose language he seems to have learned. His earliest schooling was given to him by his

sisters. At the age of ten he moved with his family to Huatabampo, where he completed his elementary education. He soon began to work in a carriage shop and in a cigar factory, both of which he owned himself. Later he took charge of a flour mill in Álamos and worked in a sugar mill in Navolato. In 1903 he married Refugio Urrea, who died in 1908. Four years earlier he had gone into farming; first he rented a small property, and later he acquired national lands that formed the basis of his farm, La Quinta Chilla.

Obregón did not take up arms when Francisco I. MADERO launched the MEXICAN REVOLUTION in 1910, but the Partido Nacional Antirreeleccionista later brought him to the municipal presidency of Huatabampo. When Pascual Orozco rose in revolt against Madero in mid-April 1912, Obregón formed an army of 300 men, most of whom were Mayo Indians, to oppose Orozco; all were farmers, and the majority were property owners, but only 6 had firearms. The government of Sonora called the group the 4th Irregular Battalion of Sonora and put Obregón in command. The murder of Madero in 1913 forced Obregón to pursue a military career. In this manner the group of military men and politicians who ruled Mexico from 1920 to 1935 was formed. Obregón was promoted to division general on June 29, 1913, at the head of the Army Corps of the Northwest. With Venustiano CARRANZA, he occupied Mexico City on August 20, 1914. During his stay in the capital he adopted a policy of anticlericalism

Álvaro Obregón. [Organization of American States]

and exacted forced loans from foreigners as well as natives (though he did not include citizens of other Latin American nations among the former).

From April 6, 1915, to July 10, 1915, he inflicted a series of defeats on Francisco VILLA at Celaya, Trinidad, and Aguascalientes (*see* CELAYA, BATTLES OF). In December 1915 he rejected a Yaqui demand that "all, elements foreign to their race" be expelled from their territory; this was one of several differences he had with that tribe. In March 1916 he married for the second time. The same month Carranza named him Secretary of War, and shortly afterward he organized the Partido Liberal Constitucionalista. His relations with Carranza having cooled, he resigned his Cabinet post on April 30, 1917. He then began to develop his agricultural and industrial properties in Sonora, but in 1919 he initiated a campaign for the Presidency. After the assassination of Carranza in May 1920, Adolfo de la Huerta occupied the Presidency from June 1, 1920, to November 30, 1920, and was succeeded by Obregón for the subsequent four-year term. After defeating an uprising headed by De la Huerta in late 1923, Obregón eliminated numerous military chiefs. During his administration the Partido Nacional Agrarista, formed by former supporters of the late Emiliano ZAPATA, gained strength, Villa was murdered, and the way was left open for the succession of Plutárco Elías CALLES, to whom Obregón bequeathed the Bucareli agreements (*see* BUCARELI CONFERENCES), which paralyzed the application of Article 27 of the constitution to the advantage of North American investors. Having decided to return to the Presidency, Obregón eliminated his former subordinates, Francisco R. Serrano and Arnulfo Gómez, in 1927. While he was President-elect, he was assassinated on July 17, 1928, by León Toral, who apparently wanted to avenge the persecution of the church.

See also CONSTITUTION OF 1917 (MEXICO).

Bibliography. Narciso Bassols Batalla, *El pensamiento político de Álvaro Obregón,* Mexico City, 1967; *Discursos del General Obregón,* Mexico City, 1932; Feliciano Gil, *Biografía y vida militar del general Álvaro Obregón,* Hermosillo, 1914; Álvaro Obregón, *Ocho mil kilómetros en campaña: Relación de las acciones de armas, efectuadas en más de veinte estados de la república durante el período de cuatro años,* Mexico City, 1959; Aarón Sáenz, "Álvaro Obregón," *Historia Mexicana,* vol. X, October–December 1960, pp. 309–319.

MOISÉS GONZALÉZ NAVARRO

OCAMPO, MELCHOR (1814–1861). Mexican statesman. Ocampo's origins are obscure. He was raised by a wealthy woman, who perhaps was his mother, on her hacienda in Michoacán. Ocampo graduated from the seminary in Morelia and studied for a law degree. After a trip to Europe in 1840–1841, he managed the estates his benefactress left him when she died and also entered politics, serving as a deputy and senator in the Mexican Congress, as a reform-minded Governor of Michoacán, and briefly in 1850 as Minister of the Treasury. With other prominent Liberals he was exiled by Antonio López de SANTA ANNA in 1853. Ocampo went to New Orleans, where he and Benito JUÁREZ became friends, and later to Brownsville, Texas. When the Liberals came to power in 1855 as a result of the

revolution of Ayutla, Ocampo, by then back in Mexico, entered the Cabinet of President Juan Álvarez, but he quarreled frequently with his more moderate colleagues and soon resigned. He was a delegate to the Constitutional Congress of 1856–1857 and helped write the constitution of 1857 (*see* CONSTITUTION OF 1857: MEXICO). When Ignacio COMONFORT conspired with the Conservatives, Ocampo joined Juárez and served in the Cabinet of the Liberal government throughout the Three Years' War (*see* REFORM, THE). His liberalism, of the radical *puro* variety, led him to play a major role in shaping the reform program. Upon the triumph of the Liberals late in 1860, Ocampo resigned and returned to his hacienda in Michoacán. There he was captured by a Conservative guerrilla force and executed on June 3, 1861.

CHARLES R. BERRY

ODECA. *See* ORGANIZACIÓN DE ESTADOS CENTRO-AMERICANOS.

ODRÍA, MANUEL A[POLINARIO] (1897–1974). Peruvian dictator. Born in the Andean town Tarma, Odría spent most of his adult life in the Army. He attended various military schools in Peru and later taught at and directed both the Escuela Militar de Chorrillos and the Escuela Superior de Guerra. He participated in the 1941 war against Ecuador and reached the rank of general and chief of staff of the Army by 1946. In 1948, encouraged by the anti-Aprista oligarchy, he led a military coup against the democratically elected government of José Luis BUSTAMANTE and for the next two years ruled by decree. In 1950 he arranged his election to the Presidency for a six-year constitutional term.

The Ochenio, Odría's eight-year dictatorship, was marked by the violent persecution of the ALIANZA POPULAR REVOLUCIONARIA AMERICANA (APRA). Its leaders were jailed, exiled, or killed, and Víctor Raúl HAYA DE LA TORRE was forced to spend six years as a prisoner in the Colombian Embassy in Lima.

At first Odría enjoyed popular support. The Korean war, along with heavy foreign capital investments, encouraged an expansion of the economy. The resulting prosperity allowed Odría to launch important socio-economic programs that benefited especially the population of Lima, including the shantytown dwellers. After 1953, however, the end of the Korean war brought an economic recession. Public works projects diminished, and so did Odría's hold on power. In 1956, abandoned by important segments of the armed forces and the oligarchy, Odría's corrupt regime ended with the election of Manuel PRADO. Nevertheless, Odría managed to retain strong support among Lima's slum dwellers, as indicated by the 1962 and 1963 presidential returns and by the decisive role Odría's party, the Unión Nacional Odriísta, played in Congress until the military coup of 1968.

ORAZIO A. CICCARELLI

O'HIGGINS, BERNARDO (1778–1842). Principal hero of Chilean independence. The future liberator of Chile was born in 1778, at Chillán, the illegitimate son of Ambrosio O'Higgins, an Irishman who entered Spanish service and eventually rose to be Captain General of Chile and Viceroy of Peru. Although he had little direct contact with his father, the latter saw to it that young

Bernardo O'Higgins. [Radio Times Hulton Picture Library]

O'Higgins received a good education. Indeed, he completed his studies in England, where he came under the influence of the Venezuelan precursor Francisco de MIRANDA and also began his transformation into a partisan of revolution.

Back in Chile in 1802, O'Higgins proceeded to claim an estate bequeathed to him by his father. He became an *hacendado* (landowner) and, in due course, a minor official in southern Chile. When the independence movement began, with the creation of a Chilean governing junta in September 1810, O'Higgins welcomed the move and promptly organized a military force in support of the new regime. He was subsequently elected to the Chilean Congress, where he showed himself to be a convinced patriot and an advocate of liberal reforms. But he distrusted the more radical and highly ambitious José Miguel CARRERA, who in 1811 obtained control of the revolutionary movement, and he played an important part in the maneuverings of hostile factions that continued until and even after the landing in March 1813 of an expedition sent by the Viceroy of Peru to return Chile to obedience.

A force commanded by O'Higgins fought and won the first skirmish with the invaders, but the Chileans continued to be distracted by internecine wrangling, as first Carrera was deposed and O'Higgins was named general-in-chief and then Carrera regained supreme power. Though rivals, the two men still professed their resolve to fight together against the enemy. At length, however, in the Battle of Rancagua (October 1814) the Chileans suffered a crushing defeat. The loss was due in considerable part to Carrera's failure, for reasons still debated, to bring timely aid to the forces of O'Higgins,

who at Rancagua made a heroic two-day stand even in defeat. O'Higgins's pleas to continue fighting to defend Santiago were then rejected by Carrera, who saw no chance of success. Shortly afterward, both men fled to Argentina along with countless others, leaving Spanish rule securely reestablished in Chile.

When the opportunity presented itself, O'Higgins joined eagerly with José de SAN MARTÍN in preparing the campaign of 1817 that led back across the Andes and produced the victory of Chacabuco on February 12 (*see* CHACABUCO, BATTLE OF). O'Higgins played a leading part in that engagement and a few days later was made Supreme Director of Chile with San Martín's blessing. As such, he devoted himself energetically to creating an independent government, although the formal declaration of Chilean independence was actually made only on the first anniversary of Chacabuco. O'Higgins likewise continued to press the war against the royalists and, after the Battle of Maipú (April 1818) had eliminated any major threat from the enemy on Chilean soil, to assist San Martín's preparations for the invasion of Peru.

In October 1818, O'Higgins promulgated a provisional constitution for Chile. Under it he remained as Supreme Director and appointed the Senate; in practice, he retained semiautocratic authority. O'Higgins actively encouraged commerce and foreign investment, and he sponsored a number of progressive reforms ranging from the abolition of bullfighting to the authorization of Protestant cemeteries and the abolition of entailed estates. However, the last-named measure was suspended by the Senate, which did not prove wholly subservient. It finally dissolved itself in 1822, when a new Congress elected by limited popular suffrage convened to draft a supposedly permanent constitution. The Congress produced a more liberal, though highly centralist, frame of government; and O'Higgins continued to serve as chief executive under its terms.

But O'Higgins's political position had been weakened: he was too liberal for some Chileans and too autocratic for others, and for many he was associated vaguely with Argentine influence. In November 1822, a revolt began at Concepción in the south, where complaints against the government in Santiago were aggravated by regional jealousies. Led by the liberal general Ramón Freire, the movement gathered strength until O'Higgins felt compelled to resign in January 1823. He ultimately went into exile in Peru, where he briefly returned to military service under Bolívar's command in the final stages of the independence struggle, and then lived quietly until his death in 1842.

Bibliography. Simon Collier, *Ideas and Politics of Chilean Independence, 1808–1835,* London, 1967; Jaime Eyzaguirre, *O'Higgins,* 6th ed., Santiago, 1965; Jay Kinsbruner, *Bernardo O'Higgins,* New York, 1968.

DAVID BUSHNELL

OIDOR. Judge of an AUDIENCIA in colonial Spanish America. *Oidores* almost always were professional lawyers, and practically all the *oidores* in the early colonial period were Spaniards, partly because of the crown's desire to control the *audiencia* closely and partly because few creoles were graduates of law schools. In the later colonial period creoles came to play a greater role in the *audiencias,* and by the end of the eighteenth century they dominated most of them.

The *oidores* were appointed and removed by the King and the COUNCIL OF THE INDIES and might correspond directly with the central authorities in Spain, going over the head of the viceroy. In order to increase royal revenue in the seventeenth century, the crown began to appoint men to the position of *oidor* in return for a large donation to the royal treasury. Thus in effect the position came to be sold. Under the Bourbons, in the late eighteenth century, efforts were made to curtail this practice, but they seem to have had little effect, and hence less distinguished and responsible men came to fill the office.

The government tried to prevent the *oidores* from establishing ties to the community in which they served or from falling under influences that might prejudice them. Neither they nor their children could enter into business or trade, borrow or lend money, own property, hold an ENCOMIENDA, marry within the province, or engage in enterprises of discovery or settlement without the permission of the King. Nor could they maintain close friendships in the New World, serve as godfathers, attend weddings or funerals, receive gifts or fees, or serve in the province of their birth. They were not permitted to attend any kind of social gathering, and the only relaxation allowed was attendance at religious festivals. All the *oidores* lived together in a house attached to the court, and even their dress was prescribed. To try to ensure their honesty the salaries of the *oidores* were considerably higher than those of any other colonial official except the viceroy. Nevertheless the crown could not enforce all the strict prohibitions, which one by one came to be disregarded until they were completely forgotten.

ELIZABETH WILKES DORE

OJEDA (HOJEDA), ALONSO DE (1466–?1516). Early explorer of the Spanish Main. A client of the Duke of Medina Celi, Ojeda became a ship captain in the fleet that sailed with Christopher COLUMBUS's second voyage to the West Indies (1493). Columbus chose Ojeda to lead an exploration of the Cibao region of Hispaniola. In doing so, Ojeda earned Bartolomé de LAS CASAS' enmity for his infamous mutilation of native prisoners. Columbus, however, commended Ojeda and sent him back to Spain for reinforcements. Instead, Ojeda took the opportunity to obtain royal permission for a West Indies voyage of his own (1499), despite the explicit challenge to Columbus's authority. Accompanied by Amerigo VESPUCCI and Juan de la Cosa, he sailed along the Guiana and Venezuelan coasts, discovering pearl fisheries at Margarita and originating the name Venezuela (Little Venice) to describe stilted-hut Indian colonies spotted in Lake Maracaibo. Given jurisdiction by the crown over the Caribbean coast of Colombia from Cabo de la Vela to the Gulf of Urabá, he founded a colony (1510) on the east coast of the gulf. The settlement was called San Sebastián, perhaps because the Spaniards hoped that the arrow-martyred saint would protect them from the poisoned arrows of the Indians of the area. Ojeda himself was wounded and was saved only by drastic cauterization. Later the same year he left his men under the command of his lieutenant Francisco PIZARRO and departed for Santo Domingo to seek additional men and supplies. He reached Hispaniola but never returned to San Sebastián, which was soon abandoned.

WILLIAM S. DUDLEY

OLAYA HERRERA, ENRIQUE (1881–1937). President of Colombia (1930–1934). Born in humble circumstances in Guateque, Boyacá, Olaya Herrera joined the Liberal operation in the War of the Thousand Days in Cundinamarca (*see* LIBERAL PARTY: COLOMBIA; THOUSAND DAYS, WAR OF THE) and came to prominence by editorializing against graft in the administration of Gen. Rafael REYES (1904–1909). In 1909 Olaya led a demonstration that precipitated the downfall of Reyes and was rewarded with a short spell as Minister of Foreign Relations in the government of Carlos E. Restrepo (1910–1914). Like Restrepo, Olaya consistently advocated a policy of rapprochement between the parties, even defying the official Liberal line during the government of Pedro Nel Ospina (1922–1926) by accepting the post of Minister in Washington, where he remained until 1929.

Olaya emerged as the candidate of a Liberal-led coalition on a National Concentration ticket and defeated a divided Conservative party in 1930 (*see* CONSERVATIVE PARTY: COLOMBIA). He contrived a careful balancing act throughout his Presidency (1930–1934), neither offending nor satisfying established interests in either party. His administration was characterized not by innovation but by an attempt to cushion Colombia against the effects of the Depression. Olaya used his banking contacts in the United States and cultivated close relations with the United States Ambassador in Bogotá to procure favorable terms for Colombian interests. He laid himself open to charges of being a tool of United States imperialism, especially in his handling of oil contracts. Olaya's government was not free of violence. Liberal efforts to gain hegemonic control of local government in Boyacá and the Santanderes gave rise to Conservative revanchists' violence, incited in part by self-styled Carlist priests. Only a border confrontation with Peru over the long-disputed Leticia territory halted the violence. The Leticia conflict was settled to Colombia's satisfaction with the assistance of the League of Nations.

In the first government of Alfonso LÓPEZ, Olaya came to represent the less reformist groups of the Liberal party. He was briefly Minister of Foreign Relations and then Ambassador at the Vatican. Proclaimed as the Liberal candidate for the 1938 election, he died in Rome in 1937 before leaving Italy to campaign.

C. G. ABEL

OLD REPUBLIC. *See* FIRST REPUBLIC.

OLINDA, MARQUÊS DE. *See* ARAÚJO LIMA, PEDRO DE.

OLMECS. The first civilization in Mesoamerica, considered by most archaeologists to have been the mother culture from which the Mayan was derived. The culture was indigenous to the swampy lowlands of the Veracruz-Tabasco coast and is thought to have begun at the site of La Venta about 1000 B.C. or a trifle earlier and to have ended in 300 B.C. The Olmec art style is distinctive and by now well documented. Basically a sculptural art both in the round and in relief, it is amazingly naturalistic, using rich, loose curvilinear forms and lines. Its subject matter is often the so-called were-jaguar, a sexless being with an embryonic face and everted lips but with the fangs of a jaguar. The bodies of these figures are often fleshy-appearing and rather limp. Even more spectacular than this common motif are the great stone heads, sometimes weighing up to 20 tons, which apparently were portraits, all of them wearing the ball-game helmet. The facial features resemble those of no other known American Indian group. The heads found in La Venta were rafted in from quarries, about 80 miles away, where the nearest available stone was to be found. Hieroglyphs have been found from the Olmec culture, and almost certainly the Long Count calendar known from the much later Mayan period was invented by them (from the Olmec site of Tres Zapotes comes the date 31 B.C.). Olmec influences spread into Puebla, Guerrero, Oaxaca, and down the Pacific coast as far as El Salvador.

BURR C. BRUNDAGE

OLMEDO, JOSÉ JOAQUÍN DE (1780–1847). Ecuadorian poet and public official. Olmedo was born in Guayaquil and died there. He received his education in Guayaquil, Quito, and Lima, where he studied in the Colegio de San Carlos. His advanced studies were undertaken in the University of San Marcos, where he specialized in mathematics and philosophy. He received a law degree from the university in 1805.

Olmedo's career as a public figure began with his election in 1810 as a representative to the Spanish Cortes, where he was named Secretary of the Assembly. After Guayaquil's declaration of independence in 1820, Olmedo became its political chief and cooperated with Simón BOLÍVAR, who was continuing his wars of independence in South America. Following Bolívar's victory at Junín in August 1824 (*see* JUNÍN, BATTLE OF), Olmedo began his famous poem "La victoria de Junín: Canto a Bolívar" ("The Victory of Junín"), which he later published in two editions (London and Paris, 1826). Bolívar himself read and made suggestions on the manuscript before publication. The Liberator seemed particularly interested in knowing how his role in the battle would be presented, and he reputedly made several suggestions that enhanced his importance in the poem.

In 1825 Bolívar named Olmedo Minister Plenipotentiary from Peru in the courts of London and Paris. In London he met and became a friend of another important figure of the time, Andrés BELLO. After Olmedo's return to Ecuador in 1828, he was twice elected Governor of Guayas. His last years were devoted to politics and writing.

In addition to "La victoria de Junín," Olmedo composed other poems typical of the neoclassical style then in vogue. One of his best works is "Al General Flores, vencedor en Miñarica," 1835 ("To General Flores"). With Bello, Olmedo is considered one of the leading literary figures of the time and a worthy American representative of the Enlightenment (*see* ENLIGHTENMENT: SPANISH AMERICA).

DANIEL R. REEDY

ONETTI, JUAN CARLOS (1909–   ). Uruguayan writer. Born in Montevideo, Onetti moved to Buenos Aires in 1929 and has since alternated between the two capitals. He worked for the Reuters agency and served as editorial secretary of the leftist Uruguayan review *Marcha* and of *Vea y Lea* of Argentina. His novels show the influence of Céline and of North American writers, especially Faulkner, and have been characterized as existentialist by some critics. His fictional world is an original one, and *La vida breve* (1950) is generally considered his best work. Other novels are *El pozo* (1939), *Tierra de nadie* (1941), *Para esta noche* (1943), *Los adioses* (1954), *Una tumba sin nombre* (1959), *El astillero* (1961), *El infierno tan temido* (1962), *Tan triste como ella* (1963), and *Juntacadáveres* (1964).

RACHEL PHILLIPS

ONGANÍA, JUAN CARLOS (1914–   ). Argentine army officer and President (1966–1970). The emergence of Onganía as President after the June 1966 coup against the government of Arturo ILLIA formalized the strong influence he had had on public affairs since assuming the leadership of the Azul (Blue) faction of the Army in 1962. The first six months of the "Argentine revolution" under Onganía were devoted to a consolidation of authority that involved the uprooting of the entire political structure and the elaboration of a policy emphasizing concentration on economic development. Minister of Economy and Labor Adalberto Krieger Vasena instituted a belt-tightening program that by 1968 had succeeded in lowering the cost of living, increasing the gross national product, and making Argentina's monetary position comparatively strong.

In sociopolitical terms the government suffered from a long process of attrition. Students were alienated when university interventions reversed a long-standing tradition of student participation in university government. Liberal political sectors were distrustful of what they saw as corporative tendencies in the regime. Not overtly hostile to labor, Onganía could not control the divisions that developed in that sector (*see* CONFEDERACIÓN GENERAL DE TRABAJO). Furthermore, his economic policies tended to sacrifice labor's interest to general economic growth. The government never recovered from the violent form that the inevitable opposition took, and pressure mounted until Onganía was ousted by a military coup in June 1970.

See also ARAMBURU, Pedro; CORDOBAZO.

NOREEN F. STACK

ORBÓN, JULIÁN (1925–   ). Spanish-born Cuban composer. Orbón was born in Avilés. When he was very young, his family settled in Havana, where he studied composition with José ARDÉVOL and later with Aaron Copland in Tanglewood. From 1944 to 1955 he was the director of the Conservatorio Orbón in Havana; he spent part of his time in Mexico working with Carlos CHÁVEZ. In 1958 he was the recipient of a Guggenheim fellowship. Many of his works have been commissioned by performers and foundations from Spain, the United States, and Cuba. In 1954 he received the Landaeta Prize for composition in Venezuela for *Tres versiones sinfónicas* (1953). Among his many other works are a symphony (1944), a concerto grosso (1955), *Monte Gelboé* (1962) for tenor and orchestra, a string quartet (1951), *Cantigas del rey* (1960), and Partita No. 2 for chamber ensemble (1966). In the 1960s he became a resident of the United States.

JUAN A. ORREGO-SALAS

ORELLANA, FRANCISCO DE (1511?–1546). Spanish conquistador and the first European to navigate the

AMAZON RIVER. Placed in charge of the third founding of Guayaquil (1537), he resigned his post in 1540 to join Gonzalo PIZARRO's expedition from Quito in search of El Dorado (*see* DORADO, EL) and a fabled Land of Cinnamon, reputedly located east of the ANDES MOUNTAINS. Orellana reinforced Pizarro with a band of seamen and shipbuilders from Guayaquil and was named second in command. After seven arduous months, the expedition arrived at the Coca River. Pizarro sent Orellana downstream on a hastily constructed brigantine to obtain food rumored to be near the confluence of the Coca and Napo Rivers.

Orellana departed in December 1541, after promising to return as soon as possible, but he never did. He yielded to the arguments of his companions, who asserted the impossibility of navigating upstream, and continued with the current until he reached the mouth of the Amazon (August 1542). From there he sailed northwestward to Cubagua and Santo Domingo, and finally to Spain, where he defended himself against charges of deserting Pizarro, told fables about female warriors, and requested permission to colonize the Amazon. CHARLES I granted him the governorship of "New Andalusia" and commissioned him to found towns and settle colonists along the Amazon's right bank.

After many delays Orellana's expedition arrived at the Amazon Delta but failed to find the main channel. The party disintegrated, and Orellana died of illness and grief, but his reputation as the discoverer and navigator of the Amazon River was fully established.

WILLIAM S. DUDLEY

ORELLANA, JOAQUÍN (1933–   ). Guatemalan composer and violinist. Orellana was born in Guatemala City, where he studied with Castañeda. He is a member of the violin section of the National Symphony Orchestra of Guatemala. Orellana has assembled a small but distinguished catalog of compositions including orchestral, chamber, and choral music. Well known among these is his string trio, written for the Third Inter-American Music Festival, held in Washington in 1965.

JUAN A. ORREGO-SALAS

ORGANIZACIÓN DE ESTADOS AMERICANOS. *See* ORGANIZATION OF AMERICAN STATES.

ORGANIZACIÓN DE ESTADOS CENTROAMERICANOS (ORGANIZATION OF CENTRAL AMERICAN STATES; ODECA). International organization, the most recent venture in the long search for Central American unity. The member states are Costa Rica, El Salvador, Guatemala, Honduras, and Nicaragua; Panama participates in some functions, but has not accepted full membership. ODECA was created in October 1951, when the five Central American foreign ministers signed the Charter of San Salvador on behalf of their governments. It was modified by a new charter signed in Panama City on December 14, 1962, which came into force on May 30, 1965.

Unlike previous plans, ODECA does not envision immediate political unification. Rather, it affords a mechanism to enable the Central American states "to resolve their problems and defend their interests through collective and systematized action." The Organization seeks to strengthen ties between the states, but its objective is regional economic, social, and cultural development attained through joint action rather than political consolidation. Nevertheless, unionists hope that cooperative action in other fields may prepare the way for the ultimate restoration of a single Central American nation.

ODECA is structured for consultation and cooperation. The supreme organ, assumed to be used only rarely, is the Meeting of Heads of Government. The principal organ for the conduct of affairs is the annual Meeting of Ministers of Foreign Affairs. The permanent active body is the Executive Council, also composed of the foreign ministers or their appointed representatives, which meets at least once each week to direct and coordinate ODECA policy.

The major areas of ODECA interest are assigned to councils. The Economic Council is identical in membership with the Economic Council of the CENTRAL AMERICAN COMMON MARKET, and it also meets at least once each year to plan, coordinate, and execute the economic integration program. The Cultural and Educational Council is composed of the ministers of education of the five republics or their representatives, who attempt through agreement on common purposes and organizational patterns to attain educational and cultural unity. The Defense Council, composed of the ministers of defense, is concerned with joint security problems and regional defense. The Legislative Council is composed of three members of each legislative assembly; it meets once each year to advise on legislative matters and to explore the possibilities of uniform legislation in Central America. The amended charter provides for a Central American Court of Justice, consisting of the presidents of the supreme courts, who meet as necessary.

The Central American Bureau, the general secretariat of ODECA, has its seat in San Salvador. It coordinates and assists the work of the various organs and collects and disseminates information. It is presided over by a Secretary-General, elected by the Executive Council for a four-year term. The incumbents since 1955 have been José Guillermo Trabanino (El Salvador), Marco Tulio Zeledón (Costa Rica), Rafael Huezo Selvas (Guatemala), Albino Román y Vega (Nicaragua), and Manuel Villacorta Vielmann (El Salvador).

ODECA became operative on December 14, 1951. Before the first regular Meeting of Ministers of Foreign Affairs took place, however, the appearance of unity was broken. Learning that El Salvador intended to introduce an anti-Communist resolution at the meeting, the government of Jacobo ARBENZ GUZMÁN withdrew Guatemala from ODECA. The other foreign ministers decided to continue ODECA according to plan and invited Guatemala to reconsider its decision. Under Carlos CASTILLO ARMAS, who overthrew Arbenz in 1954, Guatemala rejoined ODECA. The threat of war between Nicaragua and Costa Rica early in 1955 caused another postponement of the projected Meeting of Foreign Ministers, but ODECA finally became a functioning body when this meeting took place in Antigua, Guatemala, in August of that year.

ODECA has successfully promoted cooperation in many areas. On several occasions it has cooled tensions that threatened violence within the region, and it has sponsored discussion among many Central American groups with kindred interests. The concerns submitted for regional treatment range from the operations of governmental ministries, through enterprises of such far-reaching import as educational integration at all levels, to the problems common to major industries of the region.

A recrudescence of the characteristics that impeded previous unity movements has plagued ODECA also. The unwillingness of the Arbenz government in Guatemala to have its actions publicly scrutinized by its neighbors is one such instance. The impasse produced by Guatemalan and Costa Rican support of rival candidates in the election of a second Secretary-General in 1959–1960 is another. Finally, the mechanisms and officials of ODECA were unable to avert hostilities between El Salvador and Honduras in 1969, to reconcile the hard feelings that survived the war, or to mitigate the underlying conditions that caused it (*see* FOOTBALL WAR).

Bibliography. Franklin D. Parker, *The Central American Republics,* New York, 1964; Mario Rodríguez, *Central America,* Englewood Cliffs, N.J., 1965; Marco Tulío Zeledón, *La Odeca: Sus antecedentes históricos y su aporte al derecho internacional americano,* San José, 1966.

WILLIAM J. GRIFFITH

ORGANIZATION OF AMERICAN STATES (ORGANIZACIÓN DE ESTADOS AMERICANOS; OAS). The Organization of American States was established at the Ninth International Conference of American States, held in Bogotá, Colombia, in 1948 (*see* BOGOTÁ CONFERENCE). Membership at that time consisted of the twenty Latin American republics and the United States. Since then the OAS has admitted Trinidad and Tobago, Barbados, and Jamaica. The government of Cuba was excluded from the OAS at the PUNTA DEL ESTE MEETING in 1962.

The origin of the OAS can be traced to the First International Conference of American States, which met in Washington in 1889. The conference was held at the instigation of the United States, which wished both to increase its trade with Latin America and to work for the preservation of peace in the region. The principal accomplishment of the conference was the establishment of the International Union of American Republics, the purpose of which was the prompt collection and distribution of commercial information. The Commercial Bureau of the American Republics was set up in Washington to serve as the organ of the Union; the name of the Bureau was changed to the Pan American Union at the Fourth International Conference of American States (Buenos Aires, 1910).

Between 1890 and 1945 the inter-American system was given shape by a series of conferences, agreements, and agencies. In 1945, however, a long-felt desire to strengthen the system was given greater urgency by concern that the new world organization projected at Dumbarton Oaks might constitute a threat to the existence of the regional system. Accordingly, the Inter-American Conference on Problems of War and Peace, held in Mexico City in February–March 1945, agreed to take steps to draft a collective security treaty, a treaty coordinating existing procedures for the peaceful settlement of disputes, and a charter to give legal form to the inter-American system. The first of these instruments, the RIO TREATY, was achieved at the Inter-American Conference for the Maintenance of Peace

and Security in Rio de Janeiro in 1947; the second and third resulted from the Bogotá Conference.

Under the Charter drafted at Bogotá, the supreme organ of the OAS was to be the Inter-American Conference. Although it was to convene every five years, only one such conference, the CARACAS CONFERENCE (1954), was held. Meetings of Consultation of Ministers of Foreign Affairs were to be held to consider problems of an urgent nature and of common interest to the American states and to serve as the Organ of Consultation in accordance with the Rio Treaty. The permanent executive organ of the OAS was to be the Council, which was the successor of the Governing Board of the Pan American Union. The latter became the central and permanent organ of the OAS, as well as its Secretariat, and was to be directed by a Secretary-General elected by the Council for a ten-year term.

Alberto LLERAS CAMARGO of Colombia was the first Secretary-General of the OAS, serving from 1948 until his resignation in 1954. When his successor, Carlos Dávila Espinoza of Chile, died in office in 1955, José A. MORA of Uruguay was elected to fill the unexpired term and was then reelected in 1958. He was succeeded in 1968 by Galo PLAZA of Ecuador, who was elected over two rivals after a bitter struggle.

A major revision of the OAS Charter was approved at the Third Special Inter-American Conference in Buenos Aires in 1967 and went into effect in 1970. Under the amended Charter, the Inter-American Conference has been replaced as the supreme organ of the OAS by the General Assembly, composed of all the member states, which is to meet annually. In addition, the powers of the Council, renamed the PERMANENT COUNCIL, have been reduced, and the Secretariat is no longer to be known as the Pan American Union. The Secretary-General is to be elected for a five-year term by the General Assembly and may be reelected once. Finally, the extended chapters on economic and social standards in the amended Charter reflect the greater interest of the American states in economic development, social justice, and regional integration.

The record of the OAS in preserving hemispheric peace has been mixed. It has been most effective in solving conflicts between the smaller Caribbean and Central American nations in which the United States has not deemed its vital interests to be deeply involved. On the other hand, the United States has frequently attempted, with only partial success, to manipulate the OAS for its own purposes and on occasion has ignored it. Thus the American-sponsored BAY OF PIGS INVASION of Cuba in 1961 and the United States intervention in the Dominican Republic in 1965 were clear violations of the OAS Charter, which strictly forbids intervention in the internal affairs of a sister republic without collective agreement. For their part the Latin American republics have repeatedly asserted the principle of nonintervention and have sought to use the machinery of the OAS to restrain the United States.

The effect of the recently adopted amendments remains to be seen, but they appear to be designed to lessen the direct influence of the United States in the OAS and to diminish what had become the increasingly important political role of the Council. In any case, despite ratification of the amendments Latin American discontent with the OAS has not been eliminated, and further reform seems likely.

Bibliography. M. Margaret Ball, *The OAS in Transition,* Durham, N.C., 1969; Gordon Connell-Smith, *The Inter-American System,* London, 1966; John C. Dreier, *The Organization of American States and the Hemisphere Crisis,* New York, 1962; id., "The Council of the OAS: Performance and Potential," *Journal of Inter-American Studies,* vol. X, no. 1, January 1968, pp. 1–14; Jerome Slater, *The OAS and United States Foreign Policy,* Columbus, 1967; Ann Van Wynen Thomas and A. J. Thomas, Jr., *The Organization of American States,* Dallas, 1963.

RODNEY D. ANDERSON

ORGANIZATION OF CENTRAL AMERICAN STATES. *See* ORGANIZACIÓN DE ESTADOS CENTRO-AMERICANOS.

ORGANIZED LABOR. Labor movements of some description exist in every Latin American country except Haiti. Most industrial and transportation workers, substantial numbers of white-collar employees, and some agricultural laborers are in unions. By the early 1970s the strongest and best-organized labor movements were to be found in Mexico, Argentina, Venezuela, Chile, Bolivia, Colombia, and Peru. The Brazilian labor movement, although strong numerically, was relatively weak because of the stringent government controls to which it was subjected. In Cuba, where organized labor was also numerically very strong, it had little autonomy and was unable effectively to present workers' demands and aspirations because of its complete subjection to the governing PARTIDO COMUNISTA DE CUBA. In the rest of the countries organized labor was relatively small and weak, reflecting a lack of economic development or particular political circumstances that limited the effectiveness of the trade unions.

Organized labor in Latin America had its origins in the second half of the nineteenth century. During the period before World War I the trade union movements of the region were generally under anarchosyndicalist influence. This was explainable in part by the bitter resistance to unionization by both employers and governments. It was also explainable in terms of the typical industrial establishment of the time: a workshop rather than a large factory. The workers tended to be in close personal contact with the owners, and there was no need for the rule of law in labor relations that became evident when enterprises grew larger.

The anarchosyndicalists believed in direct action. Although this sometimes involved sabotage and violence, its most characteristic feature was the presentation of demands to employers on a "take it or leave it" basis, as well as a refusal by union leaders to enter into written agreements with employers because such agreements represented "class collaboration," to which the anarchosyndicalists were bitterly opposed. Thus, in the pre–World War I period there was relatively little real collective bargaining.

During and after World War I anarchosyndicalist influence tended to decline rapidly, and other political tendencies became dominant. The war had impelled the first wave of industrialization in Latin America. The factory was beginning to take the place of the workshop. In the factory, where workers had little or no direct contact with the employer, there was a need for a set of rules to govern labor relations that both the employer and the workers could understand and for an institution for applying these rules. These were provided by the collective contract and grievance machinery.

Another factor altering the political complexion of organized labor was a change in the attitude of governments toward trade unionism. Starting in Mexico during the first decade of the MEXICAN REVOLUTION and in 1924 in Chile, governments slowly began to take a more tolerant attitude toward the labor movement. They began both to encourage it and to try to control it. By the end of the 1930s almost all Latin American countries had labor codes that authorized unionization under stated circumstances, provided machinery for collective bargaining, and even permitted strikes under certain conditions.

As a result, by the period of World War II labor relations in Latin America were characterized by collective bargaining whereby unions and employers reached agreements. In some countries, such as Mexico and Argentina, these agreements tended to be voluminous and to cover most of the important aspects of labor-management relations. In other countries they were more rudimentary. Some kind of machinery for presenting and processing individual workers' grievances was also developed, either in the collective agreements themselves or on a more informal basis.

Governments have generally played a larger role in collective bargaining in Latin America than in the United States. Most labor codes provide for some degree of mandatory government mediation of disputes over the terms of a contract and frequently also for government participation in the grievance procedure. Beyond this it is not unusual for high government officials, including the Minister of Labor and even the President, to intervene informally in economically damaging strikes.

Various political tendencies appeared in organized labor after World War I. In Argentina, the Socialist party was dominant during most of the period between the two world conflicts (*see* SOCIALIST PARTY: ARGENTINA). In a number of other countries the Communists were of particular importance. In Peru, Venezuela, Bolivia, and Costa Rica, national revolutionary parties (such as ACCIÓN DEMOCRÁTICA in Venezuela and the ALIANZA POPULAR REVOLUCIONARIA AMERICANA in Peru) either were dominant or struggled with the Communists for control of organized labor. In Mexico, after the establishment in 1929 of the party that became the PARTIDO REVOLUCIONARIO INSTITUCIONAL, the labor movement was closely associated with it. More recently, the Christian Democrats and other Catholic-oriented groups, the followers of President Juan D. PERÓN in Argentina, and the followers of the late President Getúlio VARGAS in Brazil have been important.

A number of factors have contributed to the high degree of politicization of Latin American organized labor. One important factor was certainly the early hostility of governments toward unionization, which drove the unions to seek support from other politicians who might be more sympathetic to their cause. Another factor has been the financial weakness of the unions. Until recent years unions in Latin America generally did not have the checkoff (deduction of dues by the employers), and workers, given their low wages and general lack of acquaintance with financial contributions to institutions, were a precarious source of voluntary dues.

Hence, the labor movements often had to look outside their own membership for support and found it in governments or in political parties friendly to organized labor.

Until recent decades politicization also reflected the relative lack of industrialization in the Latin American economies. Manufacturing tended to be confined to a few cities, and within each city there were heterogeneous industries. Thus, the most logical grouping of unions was on a citywide basis. Nationwide industries did not exist, and there were no national industrial unions.

Citywide groups lent themselves more to political activities than to serving their members' collective bargaining needs. An official of a citywide body who came from one particular industry could not be expected to be familiar with the situation in a variety of industries. He could, however, express the aspirations and demands of the working class, as a group, in political terms.

This situation has been changing since World War II. With the geographical spread of industry in various countries and the increase in the number of plants in particular industries (textiles, metalworking, etc.), it became possible to establish national unions. Being more or less homogeneous, these unions were more likely to concentrate on collective bargaining, negotiating agreements with employers (or assisting their constituent locals to do so) or helping with the grievance procedure. Hence, they tended to pay greater attention to economic matters than to political ones.

Finally, politicization has been maintained because many Latin American political parties have carried on intensive activities within the unions. They have recruited members, offered lists of candidates in union elections, and otherwise attempted to influence unions' policies. This has been true not only of the Communists but also of the national revolutionaries and Christian Democrats and, in some cases, of the Socialists, Radicals, and other parties.

The status of organized labor in Brazil and Cuba is worthy of special comment. In the former, labor works under the handicap of the abortive corporative state system originally established by President Vargas in the late 1930s. Although this system provided that all workers contribute financially to the unions, making them relatively strong financially, it almost completely deprived the unions of collective bargaining rights, consigning their role to that of social service agencies for their members. Rigid government controls were established over union finances and elections. Although the unions strove for a greater degree of autonomy between 1945 and 1964 and collective bargaining became common in the larger cities, since the military coup of April 1964 the system established by Vargas has been enforced with new rigor, and the unions have very little freedom of action.

In Cuba under Fidel CASTRO, the CONFEDERACIÓN DE TRABAJADORES CUBANOS and its affiliates have been assigned the role common for labor movements in Communist countries. They do not engage in collective bargaining (abolished in 1961), their major functions being to stimulate the workers to produce more goods and to serve as a propaganda instrument for spreading government and party directives to the workers. The unions are maintained quite frankly under the absolute control of the Communist party.

Various Latin American and inter-American labor confederations have existed during the last half century. The first successful attempt to establish a hemispheric trade union confederation was made in 1918, with the Pan American Federation of Labor (PAFL), established principally on the initiative of the American Federation of Labor (AFL) and the CONFEDERACIÓN REGIONAL OBRERA MEXICANA. It functioned for only a decade, although officially it did not disappear until after World War II. The PAFL consisted principally of union groups in the United States, Mexico, Central America, and the Caribbean. Its principal activities were helping its weaker members financially and otherwise and protesting to the United States government against the "big stick" in various parts of the Caribbean and against the threat of further United States intervention in Mexico.

In 1929 two new Latin American labor confederations were established. One was organized by the remaining anarchosyndicalist union groups in the area, under the name Asociación Continental Americana de Trabajadores (ACAT). It never had great weight in hemispheric labor affairs, although on paper at least it continues to exist today. The second group was the Confederación Sindical Latino Americana (CSLA), organized by the Communists. Its establishment reflected the so-called third period in Communist history, during which the Communist International instructed all national affiliates to establish separate trade union movements under strict party control. Such groups had been set up in virtually every country in Latin America in which a Communist party existed at that time, and these were brought together in the CSLA. This confederation was a victim of the switch in the Comintern line in 1934–1935 to a Popular Front policy, at which time the national labor groups controlled by the Communists generally merged with those of other political colorations.

The nearest thing to overall unity among the Latin American unions took place in 1938, with the establishment of the Confederación de Trabajadores de América Latina (CTAL). At its founding congress in Mexico, trade union groups from most Latin American countries and of varied political orientation (Communist, Socialist, national revolutionary, Liberal) were brought together. This was the culmination of Popular Frontism in the trade union field. In the years that followed, the CTAL was converted into a completely Communist-controlled group, and within a few years after the end of World War II, when Communist influence in Latin American organized labor shrank drastically, it was converted into little more than a general staff for Communist groups operating in the trade unions of the area.

After World War II the AFL renewed its interest in contacts with Latin American unionism. It appointed Serafino Romualdi, of the International Ladies Garment Workers Union, as its Latin American representative. He established contact with anti-Communist elements within CTAL and trade union groups that did not belong to it. Within less than two years his efforts had borne fruit in the form of a new Confederación Interamericana de Trabajadores (CIT), which included not only trade union confederations from a dozen Latin American countries but also the AFL and its Canadian counterpart. The CIT continued in existence until 1951, when its place was taken by the Organización

Regional Interamericana de Trabajadores (ORIT). The ORIT was the Western Hemisphere regional affiliate of the new International Confederation of Free Trade Unions, which the British and American union movements had been largely instrumental in establishing when they withdrew from the Communist-controlled World Federation of Trade Unions.

During the early 1950s the ORIT was faced with a potentially serious rival. This was the Agrupación de Trabajadores Latino Americanos Sindicalizados (ATLAS), organized by supporters of Argentine President Perón, under the direction of the CONFEDERACIÓN GENERAL DEL TRABAJO. However, the ATLAS collapsed with the fall of the Perón regime.

In 1955 still another Latin American confederation, the Confederación Latino Americana de Sindicalistas Cristianos (CLASC), was established. The CLASC was organized as the Latin American regional grouping of the International Federation of Christian Trade Unions. It grew slowly, but by the late 1960s it had affiliates in most of the Latin American countries. It assumed a distinctly left-wing position, being particularly critical of what it alleged was the dominance of its rival, the ORIT, by the United States unions.

By the early 1970s the ORIT and CLASC were the only functioning regional labor confederations. The ORIT was still the larger of the two, having the largest elements in organized labor in Mexico, Venezuela, Peru, Colombia, and most of the English-speaking countries and territories in and around the Caribbean. It had at least some affiliates in most of the rest of the Latin American countries. The CLASC had the largest labor confederation in Ecuador and at least some representation in most of the other countries. The Argentine, Chilean, and Bolivian labor movements were largely outside both regional groupings.

See also CONFEDERACIÓN DE TRABAJADORES DEL PERÚ; CONFEDERACIÓN DE TRABAJADORES DE MÉXICO; CONVENCIÓN NACIONAL DE TRABAJADORES; POLITICAL PARTIES.

Bibliography. Victor Alba, *Politics and the Labor Movement in Latin America,* Stanford, Calif., 1968; Robert J. Alexander, *Organized Labor in Latin America,* New York, 1965; Moisés Poblete Troncoso and Ben G. Burnett, *The Rise of the Latin American Labor Movement,* New York, 1960; Serafino Romualdi, *Presidents and Peons: Recollections of a Labor Ambassador,* New York, 1967.

ROBERT J. ALEXANDER

ORIBE, MANUEL [CEFERINO] (1792–1857). Uruguyan independence leader, second President, and founder of the Blanco party (*see* BLANCO PARTY: URUGUAY). Born in Montevideo into a long-established family that had strong links to the military service, he joined the forces fighting for Uruguay's independence soon after the launching of that struggle in 1811. Having begun his service in the army of José Rondeau, commander of the patriot forces in Uruguay, he was among the Uruguayans who did not follow José Gervasio ARTIGAS in the latter's conflict with the forces from Buenos Aires, although he rejoined the Uruguayans when the *porteños* abandoned Montevideo to them. Soon after the fall of Montevideo to the Portuguese at the start of 1817, he defected from Artigas's army to serve in the forces of Buenos Aires with the rank of captain, which he had held in Uruguay's army. Return-

ing to Montevideo in 1821 at the start of the schism between the Portuguese and the Brazilian forces of occupation, he enlisted in the Portuguese Army and joined the Uruguayans there conspiring for independence.

Upon the departure of the Portuguese, he withdrew to Buenos Aires early in 1824, becoming an enthusiastic supporter of Juan Antonio LAVALLEJA's plans to liberate his native land. Landing in Uruguay in April 1825 as one of the more prominent members of the famous Thirty-three, he took part in the major engagements of the Cisplatine War (1825–1828) at the head of one of the Uruguayan units.

Despite his ties with Lavalleja, Oribe, as a devotee of order and authority, defended the cause of legality during Lavalleja's revolts against Fructuoso RIVERA, who rewarded his loyalty by naming him Minister of War and Navy in October 1833 and by approving his election to succeed him in the Presidency for the term beginning on March 1, 1835. Oribe's efforts to establish an effective central government, exercising real authority in the countryside as well as in the capital and thereby thwarting Rivera's design to maintain his hegemony in the rural districts, together with his publication of financial mismanagement during Rivera's Presidency, drove Rivera to launch a revolt in 1836, which eventually forced the resignation of Oribe in October 1838. In the heat of this conflict Oribe and his supporters gave shape to the Blanco party, emphasizing the maintenance of legality and order in a somewhat authoritarian sense, stressing nationalism, and making the wearing of the party color, white, mandatory for all civil and military personnel, after the fashion decreed by the Argentine dictator Juan Manuel de ROSAS.

Manuel Oribe. [*Organization of American States*]

After resigning, Oribe and a large number of his followers emigrated to Buenos Aires, where, at the suggestion of Rosas, he reassumed the title of legal President, even though he had accepted an appointment from Rosas to head the army from Buenos Aires that defeated the Coalition of the North in 1840 and 1841. During this campaign his reputation was stained by a series of executions carried out by the army under his command. He also led the Argentine forces that defeated Rivera's army in Entre Ríos in 1842, thereby making possible his return to Uruguay and rapid conquest of most of the countryside. In 1843 he began a nine-year siege of Montevideo and organized a Blanco-dominated government headquartered in Restauración that claimed to be the legal government. Even though it became increasingly obvious that the prolongation of the struggle was not in the best interest of his native land, he remained faithful to his alliance with Rosas until almost the end of the Guerra Grande, negotiating a treaty of peace with Justo José de URQUIZA only when the alliance between Urquiza, Brazil, and Montevideo made further resistance pointless.

Although he returned to private life in 1851, he was forced into exile in Europe during the political crisis of mid-1853 under pressure from the Colorados (see COLORADO PARTY: URUGUAY), who feared his reemergence as the military leader of the Blancos. He returned to Uruguay in August 1855, just prior to the ouster of President Venancio FLORES, with whom he entered the Union Pact a few months later. Under this agreement the two rival *caudillos* pledged their support for the election of Gabriel Antonio Pereira as President in opposition to the Conservative Colorados, who had been largely responsible for Flores's resignation and Oribe's exile. Oribe died on November 12, 1857, after a short illness.

Bibliography. Lorenzo Carnelli, *Oribe y su época,* Montevideo, n.d.; Aquiles B. Oribe, *Brigadier general D. Manuel Oribe: Estudio científico acerca de su personalidad,* 2 vols., 2d ed., rev., Montevideo, 1912; Setembrino Pereda, *Los partidos históricos uruguayos,* Montevideo, 1918; José P. Pintos, *El brigadier general don Manuel Oribe,* Montevideo, 1859; Mario Andrés Raineri, *Oribe y el estado nacional,* Montevideo, 1960; Guillermo Stewart Vargas, *Oribe y su significación frente á Rozas y Rivera: Ensayo,* Buenos Aires, 1958.

JOHN H. HANN

ORIENTE (BOLIVIA). Term applied to the eastern two-thirds of Bolivia, stretching from the Amazon Basin in the north to the CHACO in the south. In the north the Oriente consists of dense tropical forests. Several decades ago this region was important economically as a producer of rubber, quinine, and Brazil nuts, but these industries have long since declined. The central portion, whose vast open plains produce most of Bolivia's meat, also contains the department of Santa Cruz, the largest department in Bolivia and the most productive in the Oriente. The southern part of the Oriente is dominated by the savannas and woodlands of the dry Chaco, where herds of wild cattle and goats are to be found.

Although the entire Oriente is generally underdeveloped and underpopulated, the department of Santa Cruz experienced considerable growth after the MOVIMIENTO NACIONALISTA REVOLUCIONARIO (MNR)

revolution of 1952, with the help of United States loans, grants, and technical assistance. Great increases were recorded in the production of rice and sugar, the two principal commercial crops of the Oriente, and the exploitation of petroleum deposits near Santa Cruz was initiated by the Bolivian Gulf Oil Corporation. The Santa Cruz region, along with other parts of the Oriente, also saw colonization—spontaneous, semidirected, and directed—by highland Bolivians and Okinawans, the latter being extremely successful in the cultivation of rice. Although Santa Cruz, now the third largest city in Bolivia (estimated 1969 population, 108,720), is linked to Cochabamba by a highway completed in 1953, the Oriente suffers from a scarcity of internal communication arteries. In fact, except for some major roads, transport within the Oriente is still conducted largely by means of rivers. Two recently completed railroads, financed by Brazil and Argentina in anticipation of increased resource exploitation, connect Santa Cruz with those two countries, but traffic is still light.

ORAZIO A. CICCARELLI

ORIENTE (ECUADOR). Densely forested region east of the ANDES MOUNTAINS comprising almost half the national territory (56,000 square miles). Rain forests cover the eastern slopes of the cordillera but give way to flat jungle lands crossed by numerous rivers. These in turn form the drainage basin of the upper AMAZON RIVER, where a sweltering climate and hostile natives have prevented effective settlement by outsiders.

Administration from Quito was marked by initial expansion followed by contraction. Governor Gonzalo PIZARRO led a Spanish expedition east in 1540–1541, and his lieutenant, Francisco de ORELLANA, sailed on to the mouth of the Amazon. The *audiencia* at Quito in the sixteenth century actively administered only Quijos Province immediately to the east. In 1591 King PHILIP II created a sprawling province called Maynas along the broad basins of the Amazon, Marañon, and Ucayali Rivers, thus extending Quito's Oriente halfway across the continent. All Quijos and Maynas might have fallen to present-day Ecuador had its neighbors not intervened (see ECUADOR-PERU CONFLICT). By 1950 only an abbreviated Oriente remained. Lying along the Andean piedmont, it was populated by some 80,000 aborigines and was not incorporated into the national life.

The Oriente's prospects for the future changed on March 29, 1967, when Texaco and Gulf technicians brought in a 500-foot gusher of oil near the Colombian border. The Oriente is now claimed to hold one of the world's largest oil reserves, and output reached approximately 200,000 barrels per day in 1973.

LOIS WEINMAN

ORINOCO RIVER. Approximately 1,500 miles in length, the Orinoco rises in the heavily forested Serra Parima in the border region between Brazil and Venezuela. It flows northwest, then north, forming for a time the border between Venezuela and Colombia, and then northeast along the southern edge of the Venezuelan LLANOS. It finally empties into the Atlantic across an extensive and swampy delta region. In its early course a branch known as the Casiquiare separates from the main stream and ultimately connects with the AMAZON RIVER system. The principal tributaries of the Orinoco are the Guaviare, Vichada, Meta, and Arauca, all originating in Colombia, and the Apure, which is fed by streams originating both in the western highlands of Venezuela and in northeastern Colombia. The most important river ports are San Fernando de Apure, located on the Apure in the heart of the Venezuelan llanos; Ciudad Bolívar, which can be reached by oceangoing vessels and serves as both the political and commercial center of eastern Venezuela and the traditional gateway to Venezuela's Guiana Highlands; and Puerto Ordaz, especially constructed to handle Guiana iron ore for export overseas.

The Orinoco system is the third largest in South America, after the Amazon and Paraná-Paraguay systems, and it played an important part in early Spanish explorations of the continent. For most of its course the Orinoco flows through very thinly inhabited territory, but together with its tributaries it is today a significant artery of communication both for interior Venezuela and for much of eastern Colombia.

DAVID BUSHNELL

ORLICH, FRANCISCO (1907-1969). President of Costa Rica (1962-1966). After studying business administration in the United States as a young man, Orlich put his training to good use in administering his family's extensive commercial and agricultural enterprises in Costa Rica. Meanwhile, from 1928 to 1940 he served as a municipal official in his native San Ramón. As a deputy in the Legislative Assembly in the 1940s, he helped organize the Democratic Action party, a forerunner of the PARTIDO LIBERACIÓN NACIONAL (PLN), but it was the revolution of 1948 that brought him to national political prominence. In that struggle he fought alongside José FIGUERES as a commander of the Army of National Liberation. In 1955, when an invasion force from Nicaragua threatened the Figueres government, Orlich took supreme command. In 1958 he was the PLN presidential candidate, but because of a party split he lost to Mario ECHANDI. Four years later, however, he soundly beat Rafael CALDERÓN GUARDIA for the Presidency.

Orlich's principal accomplishment as President was to bring Costa Rica, despite its traditional isolationism, into full-fledged membership in the CENTRAL AMERICAN COMMON MARKET in 1963. In refusing to establish diplomatic relations with Fidel CASTRO of Cuba, Enrique PERALTA AZURDIA of Guatemala, and the 1962 military junta of Peru, Orlich maintained the PLN tradition of opposition to dictatorial regimes. Domestically, it was Orlich's misfortune that his four years in office (1962-1966) coincided with low coffee prices, declining banana crops, and the eruption in 1963 of the volcano Irazú, which severely disrupted agriculture.

CHARLES L. STANSIFER

OROZCO, JOSÉ CLEMENTE (1883-1949). Mexican painter. Orozco is widely considered the most important of the mural painters of the Mexican Renaissance. This reputation rests on the vast series of murals begun in 1923, the year he turned forty without having yet painted a mural.

Orozco was born in Zapotlán, Jalisco, but grew up in Mexico City, where he took a degree in agronomy. In his twenties he began turning toward art and attended classes at the Academy of San Carlos (1908-1914).

He became a close friend of Dr. ATL, and in the period 1914-1915 he was in Orizaba producing cartoons and drawings for *La Vanguardia,* a paper issued by Dr. Atl in support of Venustiano CARRANZA. During this period Orozco produced mainly political cartoons (this despite his lack of personal politics) and watercolors of prostitutes. His first one-man show, held in 1916 in Mexico City, included these two kinds of work as well as drawings for the oil of *San Juan de Ulúa.* The reception of this show discouraged Orozco to the degree that he gave up art and worked in California as a photofinisher during the years 1917-1919. Some favorable critical notice and the beginning of government-sponsored mural projects brought him back to art. His first murals were done in 1923 in the National Preparatory School, where he painted Michelangelesque figures inspired by Dr. Atl's ideas. Only *Maternity* survives intact from this phase. The others were partly or totally repainted by Orozco in 1926. During 1924, irritated by attacks on his work and with termination of his contract certain, Orozco painted the second floor of the same building with savage cartoon murals satirizing the church, the bourgeoisie, justice, and all corrupt social systems. Themes such as *Social and Political Junk Heap* that first appeared here became basic in Orozco's imagery. A fresco entitled *Omniscience* (1925), in the House of Tiles, summed up his debt to Dr. Atl, and one in Orizaba at the Industrial School (1926) introduced tragic peasant and worker figures caught up in the MEXICAN REVOLUTION. A long series on the revolution ensued: the third floor of the National Preparatory School and a repainting of all but one of the compositions on the first floor of that building, as well as a series of drawings and oil paintings up to 1933, of which the most famous is *Zapatistas* (New York, Museum of Modern Art). The somber, idealistic new murals on the ground floor of the National Preparatory School are among Orozco's finest works.

From 1928 to 1934 Orozco was in the United States, first in New York, where his work was shown in 1928. During these years he painted three important mural series: at Pomona College in California (*Prometheus,* 1930), at the New School for Social Research in New York, and in the Baker Library, Dartmouth College (1932-1934). The first may be the most effective, but the Dartmouth murals allowed him to work out many themes that he later developed. Orozco visited Europe in 1932 and 1934. When he returned to Mexico in 1934, it was to embark on a fifteen-year period of tremendous creative power. *Katharsis,* in the Palace of Fine Arts, opened the period with a colossal "junk heap" of prostitutes, weapons, flames, and men in murderous struggle. Between 1936 and 1939 Orozco painted in Guadalajara at the university, the Government Palace, and the Hospicio Cabañas orphanage, where walls, vaults, pendentives, and dome exceed 1,200 square meters. The Hospicio Cabañas frescoes are Orozco's finest, a spiritual and moral history culminating in the *Man of Fire* in the dome.

In 1940 he painted the library at Jiquilpan, Michoacán, in large black drawings of revolutionary themes and an allegorical scene, and a six-panel portable mural, *Dive Bomber,* for the Museum of Modern Art in New York. His late work was done in Mexico City: the Supreme Court; unfinished murals in the chapel of the Hospital of Jesús Nazareno; a rejected mural on panels celebrating the end of World War II, unique in being entirely joyous; and an exterior mural in an architectonic style for the Normal School. His final murals were on historical themes: *Juárez and the Reform* in the National Museum of History and *Hidalgo and the Liberation* in the Senate Chamber of the Government Palace in Guadalajara.

Besides his mural paintings, Orozco did important easel paintings, watercolors, and drawings. Scarcely any work by Orozco is beautiful, but in their idealism and profound conviction his paintings and drawings are unique and overpowering.

Bibliography. J. Fernández, *José Clemente Orozco: Forma e idea,* Mexico City, 1942; Bernard S. Myers, *Mexican Painting in Our Time,* New York, 1956; Alma Reed, *José Clemente Orozco,* New York, 1956.

TERENCE GRIEDER

ORREGO-SALAS, JUAN A[NTONIO] (1919–   ). Chilean composer and teacher. Orrego-Salas was born in Santiago. While studying music with Pedro Humberto ALLENDE and Domingo SANTA CRUZ, he enrolled in the School of Architecture and obtained a diploma as an architect in 1943. Holding first a Rockefeller fellowship and then a Guggenheim, he studied composition in the United States from 1944 to 1947 with Randall Thompson and Aaron Copland and musicology with P. H. Lang. Returning to Chile, he joined the Faculty of Music at the University of Chile and continued to serve as conductor of the Catholic University Choir, which he had founded in 1938. Later he served as music critic of *El Mercurio* in Santiago, editor of the *Revista Musical Chilena,* director of the Instituto de Extensión Musical, and chairman of the music department of the Catholic University of Chile. In 1954 he received a second Guggenheim fellowship, and in 1961 he joined the faculty of the School of Music at Indiana University in the United States and was appointed director of its Latin American Music Center.

The list of Orrego-Salas's works comprises four symphonies (1949, 1954, 1961, 1966), a concerto for piano and orchestra (1950), *Canciones castellanas* (1947), *Missa* for chorus and orchestra (1969), *Words of Don Quixote* (1971) for baritone and chamber orchestra, *Variaciones serenas* for string orchestra (1971), solo piano works, choral compositions, two ballets, music for the screen, and incidental music for the theater. In 1971 the Catholic University of Chile conferred an honorary doctorate on him.

JUAN A. ORREGO-SALAS

ORTIZ, FERNANDO (1881–   ). Cuban scholar and man of letters. Ortiz is one of the most talented and many-sided intellectual figures of twentieth-century Cuba. Having studied law in Spanish universities, he briefly represented newly independent Cuba as a consular official in Italy and was appointed public prosecutor for Havana in 1906. Ortiz also taught law at the University of Havana and in 1910 became president of the Economic Society, editing its publication *Revista Bimestre Cubana.* During the next two decades he intermixed scholarly pursuits with public service. Ortiz served several terms in Congress, during which he championed the cause of political reform. In 1923, when corruption in public life had reached alarming

proportions, he headed the Committee of National-Civic Restoration.

Ortiz's writings, which span more than five decades, include works on such varied subjects as Cuban history, criminology, ethnology, archaeology, linguistics, and contemporary social and political problems. At an early date he focused on social aspects of the colonial period, particularly the Negro in Cuba. Ortiz founded the Cuban Folklore Society in 1923 and the Society for Afro-Cuban Studies in 1926. In his later years he devoted most of his scholarly attention to the numerous artistic manifestations of Afro-Cuban culture.

Ortiz is well known outside Cuba for his study *Contrapunto cubano del tabaco y del azúcar,* 1940 (*Cuban Counterpoint: Tobacco and Sugar*), in which he examined the economic, political, and social consequences of the sugar monoculture. An intense nationalist, Ortiz was frequently critical of Cuba's economic and political dependence on the United States.

DAVID A. CRAIN

ORTIZ, ROBERTO M[ARCELINO] (1886–1942). President of Argentina (1938–1940). An Antipersonalista Radical (*see* RADICAL PARTY: ARGENTINA), Ortiz headed an official slate in the blatantly fraudulent presidential election of 1937. Although as President he was content to continue the economic and social policies of his predecessor, Agustín P. JUSTO, after consolidating his support among the military he concentrated on shifting the political balance in the country to the Radicals. To this end he employed federal intervention following Conservative victories in fraudulent provincial elections.

When Ortiz vowed to continue such policies, Conservative elements mounted a counterattack designed to discredit his administration as corrupt. Seriously ill, Ortiz delegated presidential authority to his Conservative Vice President, Ramon S. CASTILLO, and thus ironically enabled the Conservatives to regain ascendancy. Although he later made dramatic initial steps to return to the Presidency, he succumbed to diabetes in July 1942, leaving behind an increasingly fractionalized and visibly corrupt political system.

NOREEN F. STACK

ORTIZ MENA, ANTONIO (1908–   ). Mexican lawyer and public official. Born in Parral, Chihuahua, Ortiz Mena received a degree in law from the National University of Mexico in 1932. Shortly afterward he was named legal counsel to the Federal District, a position he held until 1938. Later he was deputy director and director of the Bank of Public Works (1942–1952) and Director of the Social Security Institute (1952–1958). As Secretary of Finance and Public Credit (1958–1970), he was credited with guiding Mexico through a period of remarkable economic development. In 1970 he was elected President of the INTER-AMERICAN DEVELOPMENT BANK to succeed Felipe HERRERA and took office in March 1971.

RODNEY D. ANDERSON

ORTIZ RUBIO, PASCUAL (1877–1963). President of Mexico (1930–1932). Born in Morelia, Michoacán, Ortiz Rubio received an engineering degree in Mexico City on November 24, 1902, and was a contributor to the opposition newspapers *El Antirreeleccionista* and

México Nuevo. He joined the MEXICAN REVOLUTION with the rank of first captain of engineers on April 10, 1911. Having been elected to Congress, he was jailed by the government of Victoriano HUERTA in 1913. After being freed on January 1, 1914, he joined the Constitutionalist ranks, undertaking duties that were more civilian than military in nature, such as the emission of paper money that supposedly could not be counterfeited. Having served as a deputy to the Constituent Congress, he took office on August 6, 1917, as Governor of his native state. Although he failed in his effort to create an autonomous university of Michoacán because of controversy over his choice of a rector, he established the Popular University of Michoacán in 1919. He also encouraged a temperance campaign and initiated the distribution of *ejidos* (*see* EJIDO).

Upon the triumph of the anti-Carranza Agua Prieta movement of 1920 (*see* CARRANZA, Venustiano), Ortiz Rubio was named Minister of Communications and Public Works, but he resigned in March 1921 because of difficulties with Adolfo de la Huerta. He then carried on his engineering profession in Europe. In 1923 he was named Minister to Germany, and he held the same position in Brazil from 1926 to 1929. After taking office as President on February 5, 1930, he promulgated the first federal labor code and adopted the ESTRADA DOCTRINE, but he slowed down AGRARIAN REFORM. He resigned on September 2, 1932, under pressure from Plutarco Elías CALLES.

MOISÉS GONZÁLEZ NAVARRO

ORTODOXO PARTY (CUBA). Popular name for the Partido del Pueblo Cubano. In 1947 Senator Eduardo CHIBÁS led a schism from the Auténtico party (*see* AUTÉNTICO PARTY: CUBA) of President Ramón GRAU SAN MARTÍN over the issue of corruption in government. Chibás and his followers officially adopted the name Cuban People's party and designated themselves Ortodoxos (orthodox followers of José MARTÍ). The Ortodoxo platform paralleled the original moderate leftist and nationalist Auténtico program. The party encompassed varying political tendencies from moderates to leftists who were disillusioned with the Auténticos' failure to implement profound social reforms.

Stressing moral regeneration, the Ortodoxos entered the 1948 elections using a broom as their symbol. Chibás, the party's presidential candidate, polled 16 percent of the vote in a field of several candidates. In 1951 Chibás committed suicide, but the party continued to gain electoral support. Roberto Agramonte, the Ortodoxo candidate in 1952, was considered by some observers likely to defeat both the Auténtico nominee and Gen. Fulgencio BATISTA. After Batista's coup d'état, which indefinitely postponed the elections, some young Ortodoxos were involved in the abortive revolutionary attempt of July 26, 1953. Their leader, Fidel CASTRO, had been slated to run as an Ortodoxo congressional candidate in 1952.

In March 1956 Castro officially broke with the Ortodoxos to form his own revolutionary organization. The Ortodoxos, with other anti-Batista political factions, ultimately signed a pact with Castro's July 26 movement in 1958. Before Castro's establishment of a single-party dictatorship, the Ortodoxos were represented in the first post-Batista Cabinet by Agramonte.

DAVID A. CRAIN

OSORIO, OSCAR (1910–1969). President of El Salvador (1950–1956). A career military officer, Osorio headed the military junta that exercised interim power after the overthrow of Salvador Castañeda Castro in 1948. He was the presidential candidate of the PARTIDO REVOLUCIONARIO DE UNIFICACIÓN DEMOCRÁTICA (PRUD), won the election of March 1950, and was inaugurated on September 14.

Osorio tried to establish a revolutionary image for his regime, and there was in fact some innovation. The junta instituted social security, and his own regime inaugurated a low-cost housing program, legalized labor unions, and for the first time allowed labor to organize. Much of his program, however, was more conventional. He attempted to diversify the economy by establishing the Salvadoran Institute for Development of Production (INSAFOP), which promoted tourism and fishing, and encouraged the establishment of light processing industries. His major completed projects were low-cost urban housing and the harnessing of the Lempa River for hydroelectric development and irrigation.

The threat of Communist subversion from Guatemala greatly concerned Osorio. Direct negotiation produced no abatement, and his plan to bring the issue before the ORGANIZACIÓN DE ESTADOS CENTROAMERICANOS (ODECA) temporarily disrupted Central American cooperation. His roundup of suspects in El Salvador, however, forestalled any infiltration attempt there.

During the Osorio regime, PRUD maintained absolute control of all political machinery. The opposition charged that congressional elections were rigged and refused to participate. The presidential campaign in 1956 also ended in an opposition boycott, and the PRUD candidate, Minister of the Interior José María LEMUS, swept the election. Osorio later broke with Lemus and formed a rival party.

WILLIAM J. GRIFFITH

OSPINA PÉREZ, MARIANO (1891–   ). President of Colombia (1946–1950). Born in Medellín in 1891, Ospina Pérez came of a prominent *antioqueño* politico-commercial family. His grandfather, Mariano Ospina Rodríguez, was President from 1857 to 1861, and his uncle, Pedro Nel Ospina, from 1922 to 1926. Educated in mining and engineering in Medellín, Louisiana, Wisconsin, and Liège, he managed various family interests, especially in coffee and urban construction, and participated actively in Medellín and *antioqueño* politics. In 1923 he was elected senator, and in 1926 he was appointed Minister of Public Works. For four years he was manager of the Federación Nacional de Cafeteros de Colombia.

Considered as a possible presidential candidate for the elections of 1930 and 1938, Ospina was chosen in 1946 by the Conservative Convention as the candidate to oppose a divided Liberal party (*see* CONSERVATIVE PARTY: COLOMBIA; LIBERAL PARTY: COLOMBIA). The selection of Ospina suggested a moderation and willingness to compromise that would not alienate Liberals. Ospina's government was characterized by a very limited reformism: abolition of the intoxicant *chicha*, measures providing for free overalls and shoes for factory and mine workers, some minimal social insurance, and a qualified welcome to the first international mission led by Lauchlin Currie. Governmental action was increasingly nullified by a Liberal majority in Congress and in Bogotá. Growing rural violence became a semigeneralized phenomenon after the assassination of Jorge Eliécer GAITÁN in 1948. Ospina survived the wreckage of the BOGOTAZO, admitting Liberals to the Cabinet and leaving the oft-quoted adage "Better a dead President than a fugitive one" for subsequent repetition. Ospina survived his term in office only by closing Congress and imposing a state of siege. His subsequent political activity has been intermittent, but his wife, Berta Hernández de Ospina Pérez, since 1950 has established herself as a political leader in her own right.

C. G. ABEL

OURO PRÊTO, VISCONDE. *See* ASSIS FIGUEIREDO, AFONSO CELSO DE.

OVANDO CANDIA, ALFREDO (1917–   ). Bolivian army officer and President (September 1969–October 1970). Ovando became a career military officer in his youth and rose more or less normally through the grades until the revolution of 1952, in which the Army was defeated by forces led by the MOVIMIENTO NACIONALISTA REVOLUCIONARIO (MNR). The new government temporarily dispersed the officer corps. When the Army was reconstituted in 1953, most of the reinstated officers were people loyal to the MNR. However, Ovando was an exception, being reinstated because of his reputation as an apolitical officer who would support the regime in power.

By 1964 Ovando was commander in chief of the Army. That year he became a principal architect of the coup that ousted President Víctor PAZ ESTENSSORO in November. For some time thereafter he served with its other major figure, Air Force Gen. René BARRIENTOS, as Co-President of the republic. When elections were called in 1965, Ovando stepped aside to let Barrientos run, Ovando remaining as Army commander. In that post he directed the virtual military occupation of the tin mines and the destruction of the miners' unions.

In April 1969 President Barrientos died in a helicopter crash, under mysterious conditions. General Ovando allowed Vice President Luis Adolfo Siles to assume the Presidency. In September 1969, however, Ovando overthrew Siles. His first act was to annul the petroleum code that had been in effect for thirteen years. Soon thereafter he announced the expropriation of the holdings of the Gulf Oil Corporation, a step that mobilized substantial support among nationalists. However, before the end of his regime he had made arrangements for a Spanish firm in which Gulf had a substantial interest to take over the concession.

In an effort to gain the support of organized workers, Ovando withdrew troops from mining areas, allowing the reconstitution and federation of the miners' unions. Nevertheless, he came into increasingly sharp conflict with leftist workers and students. In September 1970, he aroused special opposition by deporting four radical priests. Finally, on October 4, 1970, a coup of right-wing army officers, who argued that Ovando had lost control, overthrew the regime. After confusion and conflict among military and civilian units, Gen. Juan José TORRES seized control with the support of left-wing labor and student groups. President Torres named Ovando Ambassador to Spain. He stayed in Spain after Torres was overthrown in August 1971.

ROBERT J. ALEXANDER

OVERSEAS COUNCIL (CONSELHO ULTRAMARINO). The major administrative arm of the Portuguese monarchy for the overseas territories. Modeled on the short-lived India Council (1604–1614), which was itself modeled on the Spanish COUNCIL OF THE INDIES, the Overseas Council first met in December 1643. With the exception of ecclesiastical affairs the Council deliberated on all colonial matters, meeting on Monday, Tuesday, and Wednesday to discuss Asia and East Africa, on Thursday and Friday to deal with Brazil, and on Saturday to dispose of matters concerning West Africa and the Cape Verde Islands. Three councillors were reckoned a quorum. After 1736, with the appointment of a Secretary of State for the overseas dominions, the administrative authority of the Council was gradually undermined, and during the period of the control of the Portuguese government by the Marquês de POMBAL (1750–1777) the Council's business was reduced to little more than routine concerns.

KENNETH R. MAXWELL

OVIEDO [Y VALDÉS], GONZALO FERNÁNDEZ (1478–1557). Spanish historian and official. Born in Madrid, Oviedo was the son of Miguel de Sobrepeña and Juana de Oviedo. He became a page to the Duque de Villahermosa and later served the infante Don Juan. His career in America began with his appointment as inspector of the mines of Darién in the expedition of Pedro Arias de ÁVILA (Pedrarias). The party left for the Isthmus of Panama in April 1514 and arrived in late June, to be welcomed by Vasco Núñez de BALBOA, who was deposed as Governor by Pedrarias. Deciding to report the latter's misconduct to the King, Oviedo left for Spain in October 1515 and temporarily retired from governmental service after Ferdinand II's death. During this sojourn he published what was probably the first novel written in America in Spanish, *Claribalte,* and had a confrontation with Bartolomé de LAS CASAS in which he opposed conversion of the natives. In 1520 he returned to Darién, but his wife's death and a quarrel with Pedrarias prompted him to leave for Spain.

In 1526 Oviedo's most popular work, the *Sumario de la natural historia de las Indias,* was published. Four years later he was appointed Chronicler of the Indies. The *Historia general y natural de las Indias,* his magnum opus, was first published in Seville in 1535; the completed work covers the period 1492–1548. It is an invaluable contemporary source that has placed him in the first rank of early Spanish historians. Oviedo died in Santo Domingo.

MARTIN TORODASH

PACHACUTI (ca. 1391–ca. 1473). True founder of the Inca empire and its ninth ruler. Pachacuti (Earthquake) was the throne-name taken by Inca Yupanqui, one of the sons of the Inca ruler VIRACOCHA. He rose to prominence at the time when his father abandoned the Inca capital, CUZCO, in the face of an attack by the Chanca state. He saved the city, deposed his father, and reconstituted the state on a fully imperialist pattern, then spent most of the rest of his reign in conquest. By the time of his death the Inca empire had been extended to include all the Peruvian coastal states of importance as well as the highlands from Ecuador to Bolivia. In addition, he had made advances into the upper montaña, or eastern foothills of the Andes.

Pachacuti remade Cuzco not only physically but spiritually by interpreting it as the central *huaca,* or sacred site, of the Peruvian world. He reorganized Inca religion from top to bottom, giving it a structure that supported and furthered his imperial aspirations; in the process he also reworked the official mythology. He organized the communications systems (roads and posts) and the warehousing of tribute. He provided for the security of the empire by moving dissident populations about and by requiring the use of QUECHUA, the Inca tongue. From his death until the entry of Francisco PIZARRO in 1532, the Inca empire merely continued along the lines which he had traced for it. Pachacuti was the single most influential American Indian in the history of the New World.

See also INCAS.   BURR C. BRUNDAGE

PACHECO ARECO, JORGE (1920–   ). President of Uruguay (1967–1972). Born in Montevideo, Pacheco Areco joined the staff of the Montevideo daily *El Día* in the 1940s and rose from reporter to executive publisher. Prior to the 1966 election he served four years in the national Chamber of Representatives.

Elected Vice President in 1966, Pacheco Areco succeeded to the Presidency upon the death of Oscar D. GESTIDO in December 1967. The new President faced a nation plagued by economic problems and social disorder. In addition to a ruinous rate of inflation and recurring labor strikes and student demonstrations, there was an increasing amount of urban guerrilla activity. By mid-1968 Pacheco Areco had set the tone of his administration through crackdowns on unauthorized strikes and demonstrations, a tough policy toward the TUPAMAROS, and a variety of measures aimed at economic stabilization. Throughout his administration this hard line produced a considerable amount of opposition within the President's own Colorado party while gaining him a measure of support among the more conservative Blancos (*see* BLANCO PARTY: URUGUAY; COLORADO PARTY: URUGUAY).

Arguing the need for continuity of leadership in a time of national crisis, Pacheco Areco sought a second term in 1971 through a proposed constitutional amendment allowing reelection of the President. Voters rejected the amendment, but the solid victory of the slate headed by the President was regarded as a popular vote of confidence in his policies. With the outcome of the election, the Presidency for 1972–1977 went to Pacheco Areco's chosen successor, Juan María BOR-DABERRY.   LEE C. FENNELL

PACIFIC, WAR OF THE. *See* WAR OF THE PACIFIC.

PADROADO REAL. *See* PATRONATO REAL.

PÁEZ, JOSÉ ANTONIO (1790–1873). Venezuelan general of the independence movement and President. Páez, whose contribution to Venezuelan independence was second only to that of Simón BOLÍVAR, was born near Aricagua on the edge of the Venezuelan LLANOS (plains). Of humble origins and having only the most rudimentary education, he worked for a time as a ranch hand. When the independence movement began in 1810, he threw in his lot with the patriots, and after the collapse of the second Venezuelan republic in 1814 he was one of those who succeeded in establishing and gradually expanding a patriot foothold on the llanos. Once Bolívar returned to Venezuela from the Antilles and established a solid base of operations in the interior of the country, Páez agreed to recognize his leadership. However, Páez still enjoyed a degree of independent authority by virtue of the ascendancy he had acquired among the rough *llanero* cowboys through his intimate knowledge of the region and its inhabitants and his acknowledged prowess in horsemanship and fighting.

Páez took part with Bolívar in the decisive Battle of Carabobo (1821), which assured the independence of Venezuela even though pockets of royalist resistance remained (*see* CARABOBO, BATTLE OF). When Bolívar

José Antonio Páez. [*Organization of American States*]

then carried the war to other fronts, Páez stayed behind in Venezuela, where his influence transcended the series of subordinate positions entrusted to him. He had further taken advantage of the military land bonus and related speculations to become wealthy. Moreover, he shared the widespread resentment of Venezuelans over their subjection to the central government of Gran Colombia at Bogotá (*see* COLOMBIA, GRAN). Called to Bogotá himself in 1826 to answer charges of misconduct, he launched a revolt for greater autonomy that ended in January 1827 in return for an amnesty from Bolívar. But when a new movement developed late in 1829 to make Venezuela entirely separate, Páez placed himself at its head and quickly led it to a successful conclusion.

In 1831 Páez became the first President of Venezuela, and until 1848 he controlled the country either as President himself or through handpicked presidential candidates. The Páez era, known as that of the Conservative oligarchy, was made possible by a coalition of conservative *caraqueños,* many of whom had not participated actively in the independence movement, the Venezuelan commercial and financial elite, and the agents of British or German investors. Supported by a postwar prosperity based on strong coffee prices, the Conservative oligarchy brought peace and prosperity to much of Venezuela.

To be sure, Páez found it necessary to meet the challenge of several military revolts and the formation of a major opposition party. Perhaps the most significant revolt occurred in 1835–1836, when a group headed by Santiago Mariño and José Tadeo MONAGAS rebelled against Páez's handpicked successor, Dr. José María VARGAS, on the grounds that the Páez government had failed to reward the military heroes of independence, discriminated against the followers and relatives of Bolívar, and had sought refuge among the remnants of the *godo,* or pro-Spanish, party. This rebellion, known as the Revolución de las Reformas (Revolution of the Reforms), had strong regionalist overtones, based as it was in the eastern section of Venezuela, which traditionally has had an identity and a cohesiveness all its own. Páez, through careful negotiation and able military tactics, put the revolt down with remarkable leniency, but his civilian supporters refused to show magnanimity toward the rebels and carried out a policy of expulsions and reprisals whose victims would continue to disturb the political and social peace of the Conservatives for decades.

Although Vargas was forced out of office in 1836, the Conservatives continued to rule through the person of Gen. Carlos SOUBLETTE, Páez's most trusted associate and Vice President under Vargas. In the subsequent presidential period (1839–1843), General Páez once again sat in the presidential chair; during these years the ascendancy of the commercial-mercantile elite reached its high point. Indeed, the "old Patriots," the family and friends of Bolívar's clan, and a sizable portion of the *caraqueño* landed elite became so deeply alienated from the Páez government that they organized the Liberal party, headed by the talented demagogue Antonio Leocadio Guzmán, to contest the electoral power of the old general. Although the Liberal party was too weak seriously to challenge Páez's chosen successor, Soublette, at the polls, the events of Soublette's Presidency (1843–1847) helped mobilize and consolidate the opposition. Most of this opposition resulted from a worsening economic crisis that began about 1840 and continued throughout the 1840s and into the 1850s. The Liberals, who claimed to represent debtors and agriculturists, clamored for debt relief and an agricultural land bank to save them from bankruptcy caused by declining coffee prices and high interest rates. The Conservatives, as representatives of the commercial class, staunchly opposed any relaxation of the legal means of collecting debts or foreclosing on defaulting farmers. Thus the increasingly depressed economic conditions helped fuel long-standing party, personal, and regional resentments. When the midterm legislative elections turned out to be corrupt and failed to deliver the Liberal party the triumph they had expected, some socially prominent Liberals cooperated in an abortive uprising that, before it died out, showed some potential for a social revolution.

By 1847, when Páez had to choose a new presidential candidate, the stability and coherence of his Venezuela appeared to be seriously threatened. In an apparent effort to mollify the Liberals without losing control of his government he chose Gen. José Tadeo Monagas, one of the leaders of the Reformista revolt of the mid-1830s and a man widely believed to be associated to some degree with the Liberal cause. Páez evidently thought he could control the eastern chieftain and make him into another tool of the *paecista* regime.

No sooner had Monagas been elected President for the period 1847–1851 than he proceeded to chart an independent course, replacing Conservatives with proscribed Liberals in his government and in general reorganizing the state in his own image. By early 1848 this process had gone so far that Páez revolted against the government he had picked. Unfortunately Páez soon discovered that the charisma he had acquired during his career as a guerrilla fighter and patriot captain had been dissipated during his years in power. Defeated in 1848 by Monagas's troops, Páez fled to Colombia, then to St. Thomas in the Virgin Islands, where he reorganized his forces. He returned to Venezuela in 1849 to try to regain past glory, but his time was past and his defeat resulted in capture. After considerable discussion among the leaders of Monagas's government, Páez was expelled from the country in May 1850. From 1850 until his recall to Venezuela by the revolution of 1858, Páez spent most of his time in New York, keeping in close touch with his Conservative supporters in Venezuela. His return to the country in 1858 in the wake of the successful revolution led by Gen. Julián CASTRO was a triumphal but short-lived occasion. Complicated and unstable political and military alliances forced him to retire from Venezuela once again in July 1859. Because of the continued inability of any one faction to control the country, however, the Conservatives called on Páez for the last time in 1861 and gave him supreme command of the armed forces. Throughout the period of the Federal Wars (1858–1863) the Conservative-Centralist group used Páez as much as possible against the Liberal-Federalist group, but many Conservatives had no desire to see Páez back in full command. Nevertheless, the failure of the anti-Páez Conservatives to control events led to his proclamation as dictator of Venezuela in 1861. Throughout 1861, 1862, and much of 1863 the Páez dictatorship had to contend with dissension within its own ranks and the increasing success

of the Federalists under Gen. Juan C. FALCÓN. In mid-1863, after several negotiations failed, Páez and Falcón came to an agreement that ended the Federal Wars, provided for the definitive exile of Páez in the United States, and brought an end to the Conservative oligarchy. Páez spent the last ten years of his life in New York and died there on May 7, 1873. By 1888 his reputation had been rehabilitated by Antonio GUZMÁN BLANCO, and his position as one of Venezuela's great heroes firmly established.

Bibliography. Robert B. Cunninghame Graham, *José Antonio Páez,* London, 1929; John V. Lombardi, *The Decline and Abolition of Negro Slavery in Venezuela, 1820–1854,* Westport, Conn., 1971; José Antonio Páez, *Autobiografía del General José Antonio Páez,* 2 vols., New York, 1869; Caracciolo Parra-Pérez, *Mariño y las guerras civiles,* 3 vols., Madrid, 1958–60; Robert Ker Porter, *Caracas Diary (1825–1842),* ed. by Walter Dupouy, Caracas, 1966.

DAVID BUSHNELL AND JOHN V. LOMBARDI

PAHO. *See* PAN AMERICAN HEALTH ORGANIZATION.

PALACIOS, ALFREDO L[ORENZO] (1880–1965). Argentine Socialist legislator, lawyer, and educator. From his first election to the Chamber of Deputies in 1904 until his death, Palacios pursued one of the longest and most colorful careers in Argentine political history. He was often at odds with the leadership of the party, but for almost two-thirds of a century he was an eloquent advocate of Socialist causes both in and out of Congress (*see* SOCIALIST PARTY: ARGENTINA).

When Palacios won a congressional seat in 1904, he became the first Socialist to be elected to national office in South America. In addition to many terms in the Chamber of Deputies (his last election to that body was in 1963), he served in the Senate during the 1932–1943 and 1961–1962 periods. He was a candidate for the Presidency in several elections and served as Ambassador to Uruguay from 1955 to 1957. During his years in Congress he introduced a number of bills to improve living conditions of the Argentine working class, some of which became models for similar legislation in neighboring countries.

The early difficulties of Palacios with the party leadership were due primarily to his insistence upon fighting duels, an Argentine tradition strongly denounced by the Socialist party. Later in his career he moved more and more to the left of the party leadership, helping to precipitate several formal divisions within the movement. His strong endorsement of the CUBAN REVOLUTION in the early 1960s gained him a considerable following among Argentine university students.

In addition to his active career in politics, Palacios taught law and served as dean of the Faculty of Law of the University of Buenos Aires and as rector of the National University of La Plata. A prolific writer on political and constitutional themes, he was the author of more than fifty books.

LEE C. FENNELL

PALÉS MATOS, LUIS (1898–1959). Puerto Rican poet. Palés Matos was born in Guayama. His first book of poetry, written in modernist style (*see* MODERNISM: SPANISH AMERICA), was *Azaleas* (1915). About 1921 he and J. J. de Diego Padro tried to launch *diepalismo,* a literary movement that used sounds to reflect reality.

When this experiment failed, he initiated the style that came to be known as black poetry, using motifs and rhythms based on Negro folklore in the Caribbean area. His first such poem was "Pueblo negro," published in 1926 in *La democracia*. Among other volumes are *Tuntún de pasa y grifería* (1937) and *Poesía 1915–1956* (1957).

RACHEL PHILLIPS

PALMA, RICARDO (1833–1919). Peruvian man of letters. Born in Lima, Palma was an active participant in Peru's political, cultural, and literary life until his death in 1919. In his youth he took part in an unsuccessful revolt against Ramón CASTILLA that earned him exile to Chile in 1860. Subsequently he served on several diplomatic missions, and in 1867 he participated in the antiliberal revolt that brought José BALTA to the Presidency. In 1868 he became Balta's secretary and also served as senator from Loreto. In the 1870s he joined with Nicolás de PIÉROLA in the struggles against the CIVILISTA PARTY, and in 1881, during the WAR OF THE PACIFIC, he took up arms in defense of Lima against the invading Chilean Army. After the war he was assigned the task of rebuilding Lima's National Library, which had been thoroughly vandalized by the Chilean occupation forces. By the time Palma retired as its director in 1912, the library's holdings surpassed by far the prewar levels.

It is as a literary figure, however, that Palma enjoys the greatest renown. He was a prolific poet, playwright, essayist, and journalist. His most acclaimed work is *Tradiciones peruanas,* a series of short, often satirical, and eminently readable prose sketches mixing fact with fancy. Published between 1872 and 1918, the *Tradiciones* covers Peruvian history from the INCAS to the national period. Some critics have seen the work as a confirmation of the persistence of a colonial mentality in Peru. Nevertheless, as a literary work the *Tradiciones* represents one of the richest Latin American contributions to the Spanish language.

ORAZIO A. CICCARELLI

PALMARES. Group of fugitive slave settlements in Pernambuco whose existence (ca. 1605–1695) spanned almost the entire seventeenth century and came to be regarded as a threat to Portuguese America no less important than the Dutch conquest (*see* DUTCH IN BRAZIL). Palmares was much more than an isolated and small-scale QUILOMBO, many of which existed throughout Brazil while slavery lasted. With a population ranging from 6,000 to 30,000, it was organized as a centralized kingdom with an elected ruler, Ganga Zumba, who appointed officeholders in the numerous confederated settlements that composed the Palmares complex. Palmares formed a type of African-inspired black counterculture to the slavocratic Portuguese coastal zone. When Palmares proved resistant to Dutch and Portuguese military expeditions, the Governor of Pernambuco contracted *paulista* forces under the command of Domingos Jorge Velho, who after a two-year campaign dispersed the *palmaristas* and captured the ruler Zambi (1694–1695).

KENNETH R. MAXWELL

PAMPA. Broad natural region situated entirely within Argentina, not to be confused with the Argentine province La Pampa. Approximately 250,000 square miles in area, it is shaped like a crescent, its outer margin being approximately 400 miles from Buenos Aires. The northern edge of the arc is at the Paraná River (*see* PARANÁ-PARAGUAY RIVER BASIN). Curving gradually west and then southward, it terminates approximately at the port of Bahía Blanca.

Physically the region is flat to gently undulating, although in a few places low mountains rise above the plain. The plain itself is formed from deep layers of alluvium swept down from the ANDES MOUNTAINS to the west. In much of the pampa the alluvium is covered by a layer of loess, fine windblown material that settles over the region from the west. The climate is humid subtropical, although total annual precipitation decreases gradually toward the interior, with an accompanying decrease in reliability. The arriving Europeans encountered a vast grassland, although botanists debate whether this represented the climax vegetation or was a plant association formed by the continual burning of the vegetation by the pre-Columbian Indians. The soils of the pampa are highly organic and often are rich loams.

A combination of topography, climate, and soils has made the pampa one of the regions of the world most suitable for agriculture, comparable with the Corn Belt of the United States and the plains of the Danube or the Ukraine. However, until the end of the nineteenth century it was little utilized except for extensive grazing of cattle and sheep. The underutilization of so rich a natural region can be attributed to its isolation from the large concentrations of world population as well as to the small population in Argentina and the low volume of international trade in agricultural commodities. By the end of the nineteenth century, however, a demand arose in the industrializing European countries, particularly Great Britain, for meat and wheat. The pampa was able to meet this demand as a result of a massive influx of European immigrants and capital (*see* IMMIGRATION: ARGENTINA). Since most of the land had been incorporated into the private domain early in the nineteenth century, much of the conversion to modern agriculture was done by tenant farmers under onerous agreements. The large landowners leased blocks of land to tenants who plowed under the coarse native grasses and planted wheat or other grains. At the termination of the lease they were obliged to plant improved grasses or alfalfa, permitting the owners to turn their stock onto much-improved pasture.

Over the years tenancy on the pampa has declined, and many former tenants have moved to the cities. There has, however, been no significant decrease in the importance of the large estate. Although most estates are engaged in highly commercial agriculture and the pampa may be subdivided into subregions, each with its own type of agriculture, the region is not an efficient producer of agricultural products. There has been some subdivision of rural properties in parts of the pampa, but vast changes in its cultural and economic institutions are necessary before this rich agricultural region reaches its full potential as a food producer.

See also AGRICULTURE (ARGENTINA).

MORTON D. WINSBERG

PAN. *See* PARTIDO DE ACCIÓN NACIONAL.

PANAMA CANAL. Constructed between 1904 and 1914, the Panama Canal decreased by 7,873 miles (12,676 kilometers) the sea distance between New York and San Francisco. Construction cost nearly $400 million and took the work of 40,000 men. The canal is 50 miles long (80 kilometers) and contains six pairs of locks that raise and lower the ships making the transit. At the Gatun Locks at the Caribbean entrance of the canal, for example, ships are raised or lowered 85 feet (26 meters) to or from the level of the sea. The locks are 110 feet (33.5 meters) wide, or more than sufficient for the earlier vessels but too narrow for the largest ships being built today. Between thirty and forty oceangoing vessels make the transit each day, taking seven to eight hours. More than half the total volume of trade passing through the canal is going to or coming from the United States.

The canal is located in the Canal Zone, comprising 647 square miles of land and water running from 3 marine miles off each entrance of the canal at the mean low-water mark. The zone is approximately 10 miles wide and includes Gatun Lake, a man-made lake 166 square miles in size. The zone does not include Panama City and Colón, although both cities are located close to the entrances of the canal, on the Pacific and Caribbean sides respectively. In 1970 the total population of the zone, including military dependents, was 44,198, of whom 32,552 resided in the Balboa District in the Pacific sector of the zone. The rest lived in the Cristobal District in the Caribbean sector of the zone. Approximately one-third of the area of the zone is taken up by United States Army, Navy, and Air Force bases. Canal administration is located in the town of Balboa at the Pacific entrance to the canal. The only other town sites of any significance are Gamboa, located near the terminus of Lake Gatun, and Cristobal, located near the Caribbean entrance to the canal. The entire area is an official United States government preserve; private enterprise exists only on lands rented from the Canal Zone government and is usually related directly to the servicing of the operations of the canal.

The Panama Canal is operated by the Panama Canal Company, an independent corporation of the federal government of the United States. The company comes under the legal jurisdiction of the Canal Zone government, which is headed by a Governor appointed by the President of the United States. The Canal Zone government and the Panama Canal Company are both directly responsible to the Secretary of the Army. Generally the Governor has been a military man and is the ex officio president of the canal company. The Secretary of the Army appoints the thirteen-member board of directors of the canal company. The Canal Zone government and the Panama Canal Company are therefore independent of each other's operations but are in fact part of the same chain of command.

History. Centuries ago Spain recognized the possibility of a canal through the Isthmus of Panama connecting the two oceans, but such a plan was not technologically feasible at that time. In the late nineteenth century a private French concern headed by Ferdinand de Lesseps attempted to build a sea-level canal across Panama, then a province of Colombia, but failed. By this time the United States government had also become interested in building a canal. After considerable study and political maneuvering, Panama was chosen over Nicaragua as the best site for such a canal. When the Colombian Senate rejected a treaty giving the United States the right to build the canal, the Theodore Roosevelt administration gave its support to a successful separatist revolt in Panama in November 1903. The United States quickly recognized Panamanian independence and signed the HAY–BUNAU-VARILLA TREATY granting the United States the right to build the canal.

The canal is in large measure responsible for Panama's relative prosperity (it has one of the highest per capita incomes in Latin America), but the Panamanians are not always disposed to view the canal in material terms, and United States–Panamanian relations have become increasingly difficult. Perhaps the major issue between the two nations has been the Hay–Bunau-Varilla Treaty itself, which Panamanians generally insist was negotiated under duress. The other major sources of conflict between the two countries have been the overt discrimination practiced against Panamanians in jobs and wages and against Panamanian blacks in general, commercial competition by Canal Zone commissaries with Panamanian shops, and the question of sovereignty over the land in the Canal Zone. Racial discrimination was officially abolished in the 1950s,

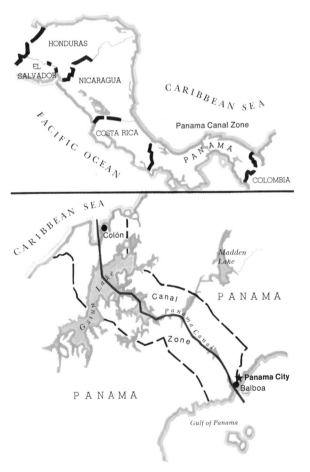

PANAMA CANAL

Panama Canal. [*Public Information Office, Panama Canal*]

and the EISENHOWER-REMÓN TREATY of 1955 ended commercial and job discrimination. The most controversial issue, however, has been that of sovereignty. The 1903 treaty gave the United States the right to act "as if it were sovereign" in the Canal Zone. Panama has always insisted that it has residual sovereignty, that is, that the Canal Zone lies on Panamanian soil. The issue is an emotional one in Panama, stemming as it does from its growing sense of national pride, and it led to major riots against United States policy in November 1959 and January 1964 (*see* FLAG RIOTS). Out of the violence came renewed efforts to negotiate a new treaty agreeable to both nations. In June 1967 three new treaties dealing with the existing canal, the military bases, and a new sea-level canal were announced. Under the new treaty arrangements Panama would have been recognized by the United States as the titular sovereign of the Canal Zone, would have been given a voice in the operations of the canal and the Canal Zone, and would have received an increased share in the revenues. As an obvious warning to the Panamanians, however, the treaty dealing with a sea-level canal specifically spelled out four possible routes for the new canal, only two of which are in Panama (the others are located on the Colombian border with Panama and on the Costa Rican–Nicaraguan borders). Opposition within both nations prevented the ratification of the treaties. In February 1974, however, the two countries signed an agreement on eight principles to serve as guidelines for the negotiation of a new treaty.

Bibliography. Charles D. Ameringer, "Philippe Bunau-Varilla: New Light on the Panama Canal Treaty," *Hispanic American Historical Review,* vol. XLVI, no. 1, February 1966, pp. 28–52; Ira E. Bennett, *History of the Panama Canal: Its Construction and Builders,* Washington, 1915; Miles P. DuVal, *Cadiz to Cathay: The Story of the Long Diplomatic Struggle for the Panama Canal,* Stanford, Calif., 1940; Lester D. Langley, "U.S.–Panamanian Relations since 1941," *Journal of Inter-American Studies and World Affairs,* vol. XII, no. 3, July 1970, pp. 339–366; Sheldon B. Liss, *The Canal: Aspects of United States–Panamanian Relations,* Notre Dame, Ind., 1969.

RODNEY D. ANDERSON

PANAMA CITY. Capital of Panama and the cultural, commercial, and industrial center of the republic. Panama is served by major air and maritime routes. It is linked by highway with Colón as well as with Central and North America, and with Colón by rail.

Founded by Pedro Arias de ÁVILA in 1519 on the Pacific coast, Panama City was sacked and burned in 1671 after its capture by Henry Morgan and rebuilt at a more easily defensible site 5 miles away. The city's prosperity has been due to its position on a narrow isthmus between the Atlantic and Pacific Oceans.

Panama grew wealthy as the transshipment point for Peruvian silver en route to Spain, but the city declined after 1740 when ships were permitted to sail directly to Peru around Cape Horn. Panama revived a century later when gold was discovered in California. To expedite the movement of passengers and cargo, the PANAMA RAILROAD was built from Colón to Panama City between 1850 and 1855. Once the United States transcontinental railroad was completed (1869), however, hard times returned to Panama. The construction (1883–1914) of an interoceanic canal brought years of intermittent prosperity to Panama City (see PANAMA CANAL). This has been continued until the present by the wars of the twentieth century.

Historical landmarks in the city include the church of San José (1674) and the Cathedral (1760). Portions of the old wall surrounding the inner city are still visible, as are the breastworks of the Spanish seawall. The population of Panama City, estimated at 389,000 in 1969, is cosmopolitan, with Negro and Indian strains predominating.

LARRY L. PIPPIN

PANAMA CONGRESS. First in a series of inter-American conferences that initiated the beginning phase of Pan-Americanism (1826–1888). In 1824 Simón BOLÍVAR, liberator of Spanish South America and then President of Gran Colombia and Peru, invited the Spanish American nations to meet in a conference to seek the establishment of a confederation that would provide mutual security in defense of their newly won independence and conciliate differences between states in the hemisphere. Representatives of Central America, Gran Colombia, Mexico, and Peru attended the Congress, held in Panama from June 22 to July 15, 1826, along with unofficial representatives of Great Britain and Holland. After considerable debate in Congress, the United States, which had been invited later, appointed two delegates, but one, Richard C. Anderson, died en route, and the other, John Sergeant, missed the session in Panama but went to Tacubaya, Mexico, to await a scheduled resumption of the Congress, which never took place.

The Congress drew up a Treaty of Perpetual Union, League, and Confederation providing that the signatory states would aid one another with military and naval forces if attacked by a foreign power, attempt to settle disputes without recourse to war, grant reciprocal citizenship rights, and renounce the slave trade. Although this and other treaties of the Congress were ratified only by Gran Colombia, the Congress did establish the goal of hemispheric unity and set a precedent for subsequent meetings of Spanish American nations to solve their common problems.

RODNEY D. ANDERSON

PANAMA MEETING (1939). First Meeting of Consultation of Ministers of Foreign Affairs of the American republics. The Panama Meeting, the first held in accordance with the Declaration of Lima approved at the LIMA CONFERENCE (1938), met in Panama from September 23 to October 3, 1939, with the objective of preserving American neutrality in the face of the outbreak of World War II in Europe. In addition to adopting a General Declaration of Neutrality, the foreign ministers approved the Declaration of Panama, which established a neutral zone extending approxi-

mately 300 miles off the shores of the entire hemisphere, excluding Canada, within which the belligerent nations were to commit no hostile actions. In order to clarify the problems of neutrality confronting the Americas, an Inter-American Neutrality Committee of seven noted jurists was commissioned to draw up recommendations. An Inter-American Financial and Economic Advisory Committee to study the economic problems stemming from the war was also created at the meeting.

The belligerents refused to recognize the Declaration of Panama, and its ineffectiveness was shown the following December, when the German pocket battleship *Graf Spee* engaged in battle with three British cruisers within sight of the harbor of Montevideo.

RODNEY D. ANDERSON

PANAMA RAILROAD. Transcontinental railroad 47 miles long, crossing the Isthmus of Panama between Colón and Panama City. Including spurs and sidings, the line owns 142 miles of track. Construction was begun in 1850 and completed in 1855 at a cost of $7.4 million. Promoters of the railroad were William H. Aspinwall, founder of the Pacific Mail Steamship Company, the New York capitalist Henry Chauncey, and the archaeologist-traveler John Lloyd STEPHENS, who obtained the concession from New Granada (Colombia). Laborers for the construction of the railroad were imported from several areas, including Colombia, Jamaica, Ireland, and China. Reports of heavy mortality among the railroad workers were probably exaggerated, though many Chinese coolies fell ill or committed suicide from melancholy.

The fact that construction of the railroad coincided with the California gold rush helped to make it an extremely profitable operation from the start, as did the high rates charged for passengers and freight. The best year was 1868, when the stockholders received a 44 percent return on their investment. Profits declined sharply after 1869, when a transcontinental railroad was completed in the United States. Most of the railroad's revenue came from hauling California-bound passengers, agricultural commodities, forest products, gold, and silver. Panamanians who had previously profited from the traffic of passengers and freight along the old Chagres River route were hard hit by the railroad, and resentment over the economic distress caused by the railroad probably contributed to the tensions between Americans and Panamanians that led to the WATERMELON RIOT of 1856.

The French canal company headed by Ferdinand de Lesseps acquired control of the railway stock in 1881 at a cost of $18 million in order to construct a projected sea-level waterway generally along the railroad route. In 1904 the United States government acquired the railway and other French interests in Panama for $40 million. A considerable portion of the roadbed was relocated because of American plans for a lakes-and-locks canal. By 1942 a transisthmian highway was competing with the railroad for both passengers and freight. In 1954 the Panama Canal Company announced plans for replacing the railroad, by now operating at a loss, with a new transisthmian highway on the roadbed of the rail route. The United States Congress has not complied with its request. *See also* PANAMA CANAL.

LARRY L. PIPPIN

PANAMA SINCE 1903. From 1821, when it declared its independence from Spain, until 1903, Panama was part of Colombia. Separatist sentiments were voiced on occasion during the nineteenth century, but it was not until 1903 that Panama became an independent republic. *See* AROSEMENA, Justo; HERRERA, Tomás.

The independence of Panama in 1903 represented a convergence of frustrations. Panamanians dissatisfied with Colombian rule favored the secession of the isthmus. The United States was unhappy over the recent rejection by the Colombian Senate of the Hay-Herrán Treaty, which provided for American construction of a transisthmian canal. Stockholders in the New Panama Canal Company, which had acquired the property and rights of the unsuccessful French canal-building venture, wished to sell them to the United States lest they revert to Colombia. The result was a successful conspiracy to detach Panama from Colombia. The extent to which American officials in Washington were implicated in the plot has long been a subject of controversy. However, when the plot unfolded on November 3, 1903, American employees of the Panama Railroad Company (*see* PANAMA RAILROAD) assisted the conspirators, and American naval vessels on the scene later prevented the landing of Colombian troops. A new treaty granting the United States the right to construct an interoceanic waterway under conditions more favorable to it than those included in the Hay-Herrán Treaty was quickly negotiated by Philippe-Jean Bunau-Varilla, a former engineer for the French canal company who had played a key role in the conspiracy of November 3 and was named Minister to Washington by the fledgling republic.

According to United States interpretations, the HAY–BUNAU-VARILLA TREATY granted the United States control "in perpetuity" over a 10-mile-wide corridor across the isthmus. Panama also became a protectorate of the United States, which pledged itself to guarantee Panamanian independence. President Manuel AMADOR GUERRERO enjoyed United States protection but protested when the United States attempted to apply its Dingley tariff to products entering the Canal Zone. President Theodore Roosevelt sent Secretary of War William Howard Taft to the zone in 1904 to work out a tariff agreement, and the resulting instrument remained in force for twenty years.

The cost of the PANAMA CANAL, which was completed in 1914, approached $400 million. This input of dollars, together with the expenditures of the construc-

tion force, created a persistent "canal economy," that is, an overwhelming economic dependence on the waterway for income, revenue, and employment. Another consequence of the construction of the canal was the importation of thousands of workers from all parts of the world. Nonwhites, mainly English-speaking blacks from the Antilles, found themselves victims of racial discrimination and prejudice by American foremen, engineers, and administrators. Panamanians experienced similar treatment at the hands of Americans.

In 1908 Amador was succeeded by José de Obaldía, a Conservative, but the opposition Liberal party won the presidential election in 1912, and personalist factions of that party retained the Presidency until 1931. The chief figure in the long dominance of the Liberal splinter parties was Belisario PORRAS, who was chief executive on three occasions, serving for a total of more than nine years (1912–1916, 1918–1920, 1920–1924).

In 1931 the hapless elitist regime of Florencio Arosemena was ousted in a coup carried out by Acción Comunal, a secret patriotic society formed by Arnulfo ARIAS and other United States–educated Panamanians, whose goal was to gain control of the government following the expiration of the Taft Convention and the refusal of President Calvin Coolidge to renew it. As Arnulfo Arias was only twenty-nine years old and was therefore ineligible for the Presidency under the 1904 constitution, his brother Harmodio ARIAS took over until Presidential Alternate Ricardo J. ALFARO arrived from the United States. Alfaro finished Arosemena's term with a Cabinet chosen by the revolutionary group. Because of the prominence of Arnulfo Arias and the worldwide economic crisis, President Alfaro found it a difficult time to be in office. As the youthful Arnulfo was still ineligible for the Presidency in 1932, Harmodio Arias became the candidate of the revolutionaries.

To mitigate the impact of the economic depression and consequent high unemployment, President Arias traveled to the United States for direct discussions with President Franklin D. Roosevelt. An outgrowth of these talks was an eventual renegotiation of portions of the 1903 canal treaty. Under the resulting HULL-ALFARO TREATY, the United States relinquished its guarantee of Panamanian independence, and commercial interests in Panama gained a larger share of the Canal Zone market. Anticipating increased revenues, both direct and indirect, from the canal operation, Arias resorted to public works projects as a means of creating employment.

Since Harmodio Arias's term ended before his brother became eligible for the Presidency, Juan Demóstenes Arosemena served as a stand-in for Arnulfo in 1936. During Arosemena's administration important advances were made in education. He ordered the construction of a normal school in Santiago and founded a school for girls in Panama City. Departments were added to the recently established University of Panama (the university was opened in 1935, incorporating a school of law and political science, founded in 1918, and schools of land surveying and pharmacy established in 1920). By this time some progress had been made toward implementing the constitutional goal of free and compulsory primary education for all. Public schools were attended by the socially mobile middle and lower classes, while the wealthy were enrolled in private institutions.

PANAMA
Area: 29,208 sq. mi.   Population: 1,428,082 (1970).

The 1940 political campaign was one of the most acrimonious ever waged in Panama. Liberals hoped to end their "dark decade" out of power by choosing the formidable ex-President Alfaro. As the government candidate, the fascist-leaning Arnulfo Arias had insurmountable advantages, including endorsements from the two major newspapers. Once in office, Arias considered his election a mandate for change and within three months promulgated a new and highly nationalistic constitution. In addition, he displayed undisguised sympathy for the Axis cause in World War II.

On October 9, 1941, Arias was removed from office. Under his successor, former Minister of Government Ricardo Adolfo de la Guardia, relations between Panama and the United States improved greatly. When Japan attacked Pearl Harbor, De la Guardia declared war on the Axis Powers and detained their nationals. During his administration a wartime economy caused population shifts and increased demands for social welfare measures. Students and teachers were restless. De la Guardia placated the students by extending autonomy to the University of Panama, and the professors gained a tenure plan. The sizable wartime monetary surplus was invested in such public works and social services as roads, schools, and hospitals.

When it became apparent in 1945 that Arias supporters in the National Assembly were going to force his removal from the Presidency, De la Guardia, backed by seven elitist political parties, revoked the 1941 constitution. He called for the election of a Constituent Assembly to name a provisional President, prepare a new constitution, and schedule a presidential election. On June 15, 1945, De la Guardia was succeeded by the Assembly's choice, Enrique A. Jiménez. By March 1, 1946, the Constituent Assembly had completed its work and the constitution was proclaimed. New elections were not called, however, and Jiménez remained in the Presidency until 1948. The President attempted to alleviate the housing shortage and to impede the formation of slums resulting from wartime-induced migration into urban areas, mainly the terminal cities, Panama City and Colón. Funds for public housing and slum clearance were allocated, and some new residential areas were opened for the lower and middle classes. A treaty providing for the retention of 13 of 134 defense sites outside the Canal Zone granted in 1942 and for a 19,000-acre bomber base at Río Hato was negotiated with the United States in 1947. Diplomatic blundering cost the Jiménez administration the public support it had enjoyed, and the treaty was unanimously rejected by the National Assembly, seriously worsening relations between the two countries.

The first presidential elections in eight years were held in May 1948. The aged politician Domingo Díaz Arosemena was the government candidate, and the popular, demagogic Arnulfo Arias was his inevitable opponent. The results of the vote count were not revealed until July, when it was announced that Díaz had won a thin victory. Arias did not accept the decision of the National Electoral Board, but Díaz took office, calling for better relations with the United States and greater emphasis on agriculture. The abandonment of agricultural activities in the hope of a daily wage in the zone or in the terminal cities had reduced the country's capacity to feed itself. Much of the food consumed had to be imported, draining foreign exchange.

In August 1949, a few agitated months after taking office, President Díaz died. Vice President Daniel Chanis was unable to rise to the challenge presented by the Presidency. He attempted to consolidate political power in his own hands by calling for the resignation of the head of the National Police, José Antonio REMÓN. The maneuver failed, and Chanis resigned four months after assuming the Presidency. Second Vice President Roberto F. CHIARI took over the presidential chair, but his tenure was jeopardized by a Supreme Court decision restoring the Presidency to Chanis, who, after claiming that he had been coerced by Remón into resigning, withdrew his resignation. At this point in the growing political crisis, Remón staged his second coup within a week by turning over the Presidential Palace to ex-President Arnulfo Arias. To legitimize the police action, ballots from the 1948 presidential election were hastily recounted, revealing that Arias had been the victor.

In his second regime (1949–1951) Arias was handicapped by his dependence on the National Police. His tenure lacked the dynamism of his first regime. When he mounted an attack on the press, dissolved the National Assembly, neutralized the Supreme Court, and attempted to restore his authoritarian constitution of 1941, he was impeached. Vice President Alcibíades Arosemena succeeded him, giving Remón additional time to form a winning coalition for the 1952 presidential contest. The police chief, capitalizing on his close connections within the elite, won handily over the Liberal Roberto F. Chiari.

The Remón administration set the pattern for the 1950s. The development of natural resources was promoted. Efforts were made to attain self-sufficiency in agriculture, especially in rice and sugar production, and coffee was exported for the first time. Administration recovery programs reduced the internal debt by bringing budgetary deficits under control. Taxes were increased and collected, and public funds were handled honestly. Revenues were disbursed for public works projects in both rural and urban areas. An effort was undertaken to make effective citizens of the rural poor through agricultural and land distribution programs and of the urban poor through an endeavor to end racial discrimination. The surprisingly adept President was able to engage Washington in a renegotiation of portions of the 1903 treaty, an effort accompanied by a noisy reaffirmation of isthmian nationalism. As the final details of the monumental EISENHOWER-REMÓN TREATY were being arranged, the dynamic President was assassinated by assailants whose identity was never clearly revealed. The Remón term was finished by Second Vice President Ricardo Arias Espinosa, in collaboration with Cecilia Remón, the politically active widow of the slain President.

An electoral reform law, approved during the Remón Presidency, allowed only two parties, the Partido Liberal Nacional (National Liberal party; PLN) and the official Coalición Patriótica Nacional (National Patriotic Coalition; CPN). In the 1956 presidential election the government candidate, a conservative businessman named Ernesto de la GUARDIA, was easily swept into office. In spite of his overwhelming majority in the National Assembly, however, De la Guardia had difficulty in retaining his office because of dissension both inside and outside his coalition. He did little to maintain an image of the CPN as a party of the people. In 1959 he used force and tear gas to break up a "hunger march" of 1,500 protesters, some underpaid and the remainder jobless. Student pressure on the regime was relentless. Ten deaths were recorded in May 1958 before De la Guardia arranged a pact between students and the leaders of the National Guard (formerly the National Police). The three leading guard commanders would resign at the end of each presidential term, allowing the incoming chief executive to select new leaders, thus reducing the influence of the guard in political life. Relations with the United States were allowed to drift to their lowest level since 1947. Panamanians were disappointed with the 1955 treaty as implemented. Violent confrontations between Panamanian mobs and United States armed forces occurred along the Canal Zone boundary in 1959. American property in Panama was attacked, and the United States flag was defiled.

The sugar baron Roberto F. Chiari of the PLN was the beneficiary of the eclipse of the CPN. He won the Presidency in 1960 and conducted a moderate reform administration, financed through new and higher taxes as well as foreign loans. His housing plans benefited the urban masses, while heavy expenditures were made in rural education, electrification, public health, and road construction. Chiari was unable to improve diplomatic relations with the United States; in fact, he severed relations during his last months in office (*see* FLAG RIOTS).

President Chiari backed Interior Minister Marco A. ROBLES for the Presidency in 1964. Opposition came from ex-President Arnulfo Arias, who had recently regained the political rights of which he had been deprived following his impeachment in 1951. In a close race Robles was declared the winner. A man of modest means, President Robles tried to improve the living standards of the wretched urban dwellers. Three new treaties were negotiated with the United States during his term, but they were not submitted to the National Assembly for ratification. Robles feared the impact that the treaty debates would have on the upcoming national elections. Finally, he lost control of the Assembly. That body went on to impeach and replace him, but the action was honored by neither the National Guard nor the Supreme Court.

In his fourth campaign for the Presidency, Arnulfo Arias was able to count on the support of several elitist parties. Oligarchic dissatisfaction with the candidate that Robles had chosen overcame decades of distrust and suspicion of the authoritarian Arias. Arias, now sixty-seven years old, was the winner in 1968. The alacrity with which he attempted to consolidate his power over the National Assembly, Supreme Court, and National Guard dismayed his oligarchic supporters. Dissatisfied with their reassignments, some guard officers organized a barracks revolt, wresting the Presidency from Arias on the eleventh day of his third term.

Power struggles within the National Guard left political authority in the hands of Lieut. Col. Omar TORRIJOS by the end of 1970. On October 11, 1972, he began serving a six-year term as Panama's "maximum leader" with the powers of chief executive in accordance with a new constitution drafted by an Assembly of Community Representatives. Demetrio B. Lakas and Antonio Sucre were sworn in as President and Vice President, respectively, also to serve six-year terms.

Claiming that its revolutionary ideology was neither communistic nor capitalistic, the Torrijos regime demonstrated a reliance on private enterprise for the development of the economy. Dependence on an anachronistic canal economy, featuring the "export" of services to the Canal Zone, had led the country into troublesome and recurrent deficits in its balance of payments, aggravated by heavy foreign-debt servicing. To alleviate this situation, the Torrijos government attempted to improve Panama's foreign trade position by expanding exports of traditional agricultural commodities, especially bananas and sugar. In an attempt at diversifying the economy, a 1970 law on industrial incentives, which focused on industrialization and mining, eased conditions under which foreign companies could locate in Panama. A 1970 banking law made Panama a financial center for Latin America, causing a sharp increase in the number of local banks and a doubling of money on deposit. Plans were made for the creation of a stock exchange. To relieve a chronic unemployment problem, Torrijos also furthered public works projects, including a $150 million highway through Darién Province, a $60 million international airport, a $40 million hydroelectric dam, and a $28.5 million water supply system for the capital.

Bibliography. John and Mavis Biesanz, *The People of Panama*, New York, 1955; Jules Dubois, *Danger over Panama*, Indianapolis, 1964; Lawrence O. Ealy, *Yanqui Politics and the Isthmian Canal*, University Park, Pa., 1971; Junta Nacional del Cincuentenario, *Panamá: 50 años de república*, Panama City, 1953; Jean Gilbreath Niemeier, *The Panama Story*, Portland, Oreg., 1968; Larry L. Pippin, *The Remón Era*, Stanford, Calif., 1964; Joaquín A. Ortega C., *Gobernantes de la república de Panamá, 1903–1968*, Panama City, 1965; Special Operations Research Office, *Area Handbook for Panama*, Washington, 1962.

LARRY L. PIPPIN

PAN AMERICAN HEALTH ORGANIZATION (PAHO). Specialized organization of the ORGANIZATION OF AMERICAN STATES (OAS) concerned with problems of public health in the Western Hemisphere. Incorporated as a special organization when the OAS was established in 1948, PAHO has complete autonomy within that organization. Its functions are to provide the OAS with technical advice on matters of public health, to coordinate the health policies of all the American republics, and to carry on campaigns to control and eliminate such diseases as yellow fever, smallpox, typhus fever, and malaria. It has also been instrumental in the control of foot-and-mouth disease and has trained veterinarians to serve in this field.

The historical antecedents of PAHO began with the International Sanitary Convention, adopted by a group of American states meeting in Rio de Janeiro in 1887. The Pan American Sanitary Code was signed in 1924 and was ratified eventually by all the American republics. It is still in effect, modified by the Protocol of 1952. At the Tenth Inter-American Sanitary Conference in 1947 the Pan American Sanitary Organization (now PAHO) was created, and in 1949 it assumed the Western Hemisphere functions of the World Health Organization. It therefore serves all the nations of the hemisphere, whether or not they are members of the OAS. Its Secretariat is the Pan American Sanitary Bureau, founded in 1902, which carried out official inter-American health programs prior to the founding of PAHO.

RODNEY D. ANDERSON

PAN AMERICAN HIGHWAY. System of roads linking the mainland republics of Latin America and the United States. The highway project was a result of the Fifth International Conference of American States (Santiago, 1923), which recommended the holding of a conference to "study measures best adapted to developing an efficient program for the construction of automobile highways within the different countries of America, and between such countries." The project was furthered by a series of highway congresses and by the signing of the Pan American Highway Convention at the Inter-American Conference for the Maintenance of Peace (Buenos Aires, 1936).

Although the Pan American Highway was conceived originally as a road connecting the capitals of the American republics, it evolved into a highway system that includes alternate roads of international significance. The overall plan of the highway and international junction points have been determined by international agreement, but each nation designates highway routes within its territory and is responsible for its part of the system. The portion of the highway from Nuevo Laredo, Mexico, to Panama is known as the Inter-American Highway. By 1963 the United States Congress had appropriated more than $170 million for construction of the Inter-American Highway south of Mexico. In South America the highway system stretches from Colombia along the west coast of the continent to Chile, where it crosses the ANDES MOUNTAINS to Argentina and then moves along the east coast to Brasília; there are connections to Caracas, La Paz, and Asunción.

The only portion of the highway still incomplete in 1973 was the so-called Darién gap, extending for 250 miles through nearly impenetrable swamp and tropical rain forest in Panama and northwestern Colombia. In 1971 the United States, Panama, and Colombia signed agreements to close this last link; construction was expected to take from five to ten years.

See also HIGHWAYS.

HELEN DELPAR

PAN AMERICAN INSTITUTE OF GEOGRAPHY AND HISTORY. Specialized organization of the ORGANIZATION OF AMERICAN STATES (OAS). Established as an inter-American institute in 1928 during the Sixth International Conference of American States (HAVANA CONFERENCE), the Pan American Institute of Geography and History (PAIGH) became a specialized organization of the OAS in 1949. The purpose of the Institute is the promotion, coordination, distribution, and publication of geographical and historical studies in the American states. Its own research studies are carried out at the request of the member states: the OAS countries and Canada. Several organs make up the organization: the General Assembly (composed of a representative from each member country), the Executive Committee, the National Departments, the General Secretariat, and commissions on cartography,

geography, and history. PAIGH also directs the Training Center for Evaluation of Natural Resources, the purpose of which is to study the natural resources of Latin America as the basis of a program of economic development. The National Departments are the nucleus of PAIGH, encouraging geographic and historical research within the various countries. The Institute has published many important works, an example being the studies of the wars of independence by the Special Committee of the Historical Commission. PAIGH is one of several OAS agencies working to promote mutual understanding through cultural cooperation among the diverse peoples of the Americas.

RODNEY D. ANDERSON

PANDO, JOSÉ MANUEL (1848–1917). Bolivian army officer and President (1899–1904). Pando served Bolivia in a number of capacities. As an expert artillery officer he distinguished himself in the WAR OF THE PACIFIC, emerging from the conflict as one of Bolivia's few heroes. As an explorer of the eastern Beni region, he recognized the economic and political necessity of opening up the uncharted regions of the Oriente. As a politician he participated actively in the political intrigues of his day, leading a series of Liberal revolts against the entrenched Conservative power structure. In 1899 he led a successful revolt, as a result of which he became President and served in that capacity until 1904. *See also* ORIENTE (BOLIVIA).

During his administration Pando worked to develop the ALTIPLANO (high plateau) through the expansion of mining, railroads, and steam navigation on Lake Titicaca. In addition, confident that real economic progress would only follow the establishment of normal diplomatic relations, he sought to resolve outstanding differences with Chile and Brazil. In the case of Chile the difficulties stemmed from the War of the Pacific. He laid the groundwork for the agreement which was signed in 1905 by his successor and which reestablished a degree of diplomatic normalcy. As for Brazil, the tensions had arisen over control of the rubber-rich Acre region. Brazilian rubber prospectors had declared Acre independent in 1899. When two Bolivian military expeditions failed to reestablish Bolivian control of the region, Pando in 1903 signed the Treaty of Petrópolis, whereby most of Acre went to Brazil in return for $10 million and a railroad that was to serve as Bolivia's commercial outlet to the Amazon. *See* PETRÓPOLIS, TREATY OF.

After 1904 Pando continued to be involved in politics, but he never returned to power. In 1917 he was assassinated.

ORAZIO A. CICCARELLI

PARAGUAYAN WAR (WAR OF THE TRIPLE ALLIANCE). When Francisco Solano LÓPEZ succeeded his father, Carlos Antonio LÓPEZ, as President-dictator of Paraguay in 1862, he inherited a self-sufficient, nationalistic state with a strong army. At that time, Uruguay, created as a buffer state between Argentina and Brazil in 1828, was torn by political strife in which Brazil was deeply involved. Fearful that the domination of Uruguay by Brazil would be prejudicial to Paraguayan interests and overestimating the influence he should and could apply, López decided to halt Brazilian "subversion" in Uruguay and in this way become the arbiter of the region. Diplomacy failed, but the Paraguayan Army was greatly increased, and when, in 1864, Brazil actually invaded Uruguay to implement its hegemony, López without hesitation initiated hostilities, detaining a Brazilian vessel and invading Mato Grosso, where his army scored an immediate success. Overconfident of the neutrality of Argentina, López sent an army across that nation to attack the Brazilians in Rio Grande do Sul. Argentina declared war, and a puppet government in Uruguay followed suit. In May 1865, the three Allies signed the "secret" Triple Alliance, providing for final boundary adjustments that seemed to Paraguayans to mean dismemberment when the terms soon became common knowledge.

Paraguay had two advantages when the war began: an army of some 60,000 relatively well-armed and trained soldiers (South America's largest) and the huge fortress complex HUMAITÁ, blocking ascent of the Paraguay River with its 380 cannon. In April 1866, the Allied Army, consisting mostly of Brazilians, invaded Paraguay under the command of Argentine President Bartolomé MITRE. The fighting was savage, and the Paraguayans contested every foot of their beloved soil, suffering and causing horrible casualties. From June 1867 to July 1868, the Allies besieged Humaitá from land and river, and by the time the fortress fell, the Paraguayan Army had been reduced to a remnant. At the head of the Army, López led a long, sad, and sanguinary retreat to the north, hounded by the Allied Army, now commanded by Brazilian generals. Moving the capital from Asunción, which fell to the Allies in January 1869, to Luque and then to Pirebebuy, López kept gathering recruits, many of them mere boys, in order to continue the struggle. While the Allies claimed that the war was against López and not the Paraguayan people, Paraguayans were convinced that their nation's existence was at stake, and they continued to fight. Finally, with a small nucleus of troops, López was surprised at Cerro Corá, deep in the interior, by Brazilian cavalry, and there, on March 1, 1870, he died in battle, along with his Vice President and his eldest son.

López's death ended the war, but the occupation of Paraguay continued for six years, and boundary adjustments stripped the country of considerable territory. Paraguay was devastated: of a population of about 525,000 in 1865, only 220,000 survived the war, and few of them were men. In addition, more than 100,000 Allied soldiers died in combat or from disease in this, Latin America's bloodiest war. At the least it should be said that the war greatly retarded Paraguay's progress. Also, by glorifying the military and its leaders, including López himself, the war helped condition Paraguay to accept the "man on horseback" who would so often dominate its history.

Bibliography. Juan Beverina, *La guerra del Paraguay,* 5 vols., Buenos Aires, 1921; Pelham Horton Box, *The Origins of the Paraguayan War,* 2 vols., Urbana, Ill., 1927; Augusto Tasso Fragoso, *História da Guerra entre a Tríplice Aliança e o Paraguai,* 5 vols., Rio de Janeiro, 1934; Charles Kolinski, *Independence or Death: The Story of the Paraguayan War,* Gainesville, Fla., 1965; George F. Masterman, *Seven Eventful Years in Paraguay,* 2d ed., London, 1870.

JOHN HOYT WILLIAMS

PARAGUAY RIVER. *See* PARANÁ-PARAGUAY RIVER BASIN.

PARAGUAY SINCE 1811. National history began for Paraguay on the night of May 14–15, 1811, when in a bloodless coup the creole military leaders of the province took effective power from the last Spanish Governor, Bernardo de Velasco. The coup was undertaken in order to prevent the Governor from inviting Portuguese forces in neighboring Brazil to enter Paraguay and help protect the province from the revolutionaries of Buenos Aires, who a few months before had invaded Paraguay unsuccessfully. Having repulsed an invasion from the south, the Paraguayan revolutionaries forestalled an occupation from the northeast. In rejecting potential domination by its larger neighbors, Paraguay set a pattern that it would follow for a century.

Inexperienced in administration, the revolutionaries turned to Dr. José Gaspar Rodríguez de FRANCIA for aid in governing the province. By 1813 Francia, a staunch nationalist and a power seeker, dominated the government and had induced the people to declare their independence of all outside powers as the Republic of Paraguay. The following year he was chosen Supreme Dictator of the republic by a 1,000-member congress, and in 1816 the word "Perpetual" was added to his title by another congress. The dictatorship of Dr. Francia lasted for twenty-six years, until his death in 1840. In this period national sovereignty was made a fact rather than an assertion, and Paraguay prospered, enjoying both internal and external peace. However, the price was high: political oppression, little contact with the outside world, and capricious personal rule.

Initial uncertainty after Francia's death gave way to a consulate composed of Col. Mariano Roque Alonso and Carlos Antonio LÓPEZ, which lasted from 1841 until the latter's election as the first President of the republic in 1844. While the rule of Francia, El Supremo, was characterized by isolation, that of López, El Ciudadano (the Citizen), was marked by openness to outside influences, ideas, and technology. The period of his rule (1844–1862) was one of growth, progress, and modernization, presided over and directed by the corpulent, patriarchal dictator. In those years Paraguay received some European immigrants, was recognized as an independent nation by most of the world's powers, and was transformed by a large number of European and North American technicians, engineers, and advisers under contract to the government. Still troubled by disputed borders, López built up and modernized the Army and defied the encroachments of hostile Brazil and Argentina.

When López died in 1862, a prosperous, populous, and nationalistic Paraguay passed to his eldest son, Francisco Solano LÓPEZ, a man of little talent and much ambition, who sought to use the leverage he thought his nation possessed to become the arbiter of affairs in the RÍO DE LA PLATA region. This gross overestimation of his nation's importance, coupled with a lack of tact and a colossal ego, led him and his nation to war in 1864. This, the horrendous PARAGUAYAN WAR, temporarily ended the rivalry between Argentina and Brazil, which Carlos Antonio had effectively exploited, and united them, together with Uruguay, against Paraguay. The war dragged on for almost six years, from 1864 to 1870, devastating Paraguay and ending only when Francisco Solano met his death in battle on the banks of the Aquidabán River.

In 1870 Paraguay was prostrate, with more than half of its population dead, its livestock decimated, much of its territory taken by the peace treaty of that year, and a large Brazilian occupation army on its soil. From this nadir in its national fortunes Paraguay slowly and painfully moved toward recovery, hampered by corrupt, coup-ridden politics and chronic bankruptcy.

Shortly after the war two political clubs evolved into the two major political parties of modern Paraguay, the Liberals and the Colorados. From 1877 until 1904 the Colorado party was in power, waving the "bloody shirt" as the patriotic heir of Francisco Solano López and conducting rigged elections. The salient figure of the Colorado ascendancy was Gen. Bernardino CABALLERO, war hero and cofounder of the party, who after serving as President himself (1880–1881, 1881–1886) made and unmade Presidents within his own party until the Liberal revolt of 1904 terminated Colorado rule. *See* COLORADO PARTY (PARAGUAY); LIBERAL PARTY (PARAGUAY).

The Liberal party, which dominated Paraguayan politics from 1904 until 1936, was only slightly less corrupt, personalistic, and opportunistic than the Colorados. The major problems faced by the Liberal Presidents, of whom there were nineteen in thirty-two years, were repression of Colorado revolts and subversion and an inexorable Bolivian advance in the CHACO. The first problem was handled as a matter of course, but the Chaco question led to war. The CHACO WAR (1932–1935) began because of confused and conflicting boundary and jurisdictional claims that dated from the colonial era. The virtually unpopulated Chaco, the major portion of which was assumed by most people to be an integral part of Paraguay, became important to the Bolivians after they lost their Pacific coast to Chile in the WAR OF THE PACIFIC (1879–1883). Armed clashes beginning in 1927 caused an arms and propaganda race, and incidents between garrisons in the Chaco soon evolved into open conflict and war. Although initially the weaker of the contenders, Paraguay, ably led by Col. (later Marshal) José Félix ESTIGARRIBIA, halted the Bolivian advance and in two years of brutal fighting drove the enemy back to the foothills of the Andes. A truce ending hostilities was signed in 1935, and the final peace treaty came three years later. Paraguay was conceded virtually the entire contested territory.

The cost of the war in money, resources, and lives was staggering for the Guaraní republic, and it caused social unrest that culminated in the Febrerista revolt of 1936, led by the social activist Col. Rafael FRANCO and other veteran officers. The Febreristas, who were in power only a year, were a strange coalition united only in their conviction that the traditional ruling parties of Paraguay were bankrupt. They aimed to regenerate the nation, but their rule was too short to achieve much of the social revolution they envisioned, and their overthrow led Paraguayan politics back into a familiar path. *See* FEBRERISMO.

After a short period of rule by the popular Marshal Estigarribia, terminated by his death in an airplane crash, Gen. Higinio MORÍNIGO, another war hero, be-

PARAGUAY

Area: 157,047 sq. mi.   Population: 2,303,000 (1969 est.).

came President. Morínigo, a thorough despot, governed until 1948. Attempting to prolong his rule in the face of rising opposition and the civil war of 1947, he turned to the Colorado party for mass support, but the party and the military soon forced him to leave the country.

Since Morínigo's regime the Colorado party has held power in Paraguay, and the most notable of the party's modern chiefs, Gen. Alfredo STROESSNER, who seized power in 1954, retains it today. The period of Stroessner's rule, after the early years of severe repression of his enemies, has been one of domestic peace and notable material progress. There have been no coups or serious threats to order. New roads and schools, a moderate AGRARIAN REFORM program, and a recent relaxation of political suppression have marked the Stroessner period. Opposition political parties, including the once-feared Febreristas, function openly, and the Liberal party captured one-third of the National Assembly seats in the 1968 election. In that year the Paraguayan population numbered 2,231,000, of whom about 400,000 lived in the capital, Asunción. The population is growing by an estimated 3.1 percent annually and is expected to reach 3,361,000 by 1980.

Paraguay is the best and most complete example of the mestizo nation. The vast majority, perhaps 95 percent, of the people have both Spanish and Guaraní ancestors, and most are truly bilingual. The predominant racial strain in the mestizo is the Indian, as relatively few Spaniards settled in Guaraní lands during the colonial period; yet there is a fierce pride in Paraguayan *mestizaje,* and the people are equally proud of both components of their racial history. In addition to the overwhelmingly mestizo element, there are perhaps as many as 40,000 "pure" Indians, most of whom live primitive lives in the Chaco and the extreme north. There is also a "foreign" element, numbering as many as 50,000, composed of German, French, Welsh, North American, and other immigrants and their offspring.

Although many of these are second- and third-generation Paraguayans, they are frequently considered outsiders, or gringos. *See also* GUARANÍ; IMMIGRATION (PARAGUAY); MENNONITES IN PARAGUAY.

Paraguay is an overwhelmingly agricultural land. The chief economic activities beyond subsistence farming are the gathering and exportation of agricultural and forest products. Paraguay exports large amounts of yerba maté, citrus and citric extract, oils for perfume, lumber, tannic acid derived from the quebracho tree, jaguar and other exotic skins, and meat extract. There is little industry aside from a few light enterprises such as Coca-Cola bottling plants and handicraft workshops in the Asunción area. Future economic development will probably be directed at more rational and efficient exploitation of nature's bounty. More efficient sugar plantations, such as that at Tebicuari, aim at producing low-cost sugar for the United States and other foreign markets, and cattle ranching has been the object of considerable investment and technological improvement. Basically, for the foreseeable future Paraguay will remain an economic satellite of Argentina, which produces much of the manufactured articles consumed in Paraguay and in return absorbs much of its smaller neighbor's exports. The standard of living, still low, has risen considerably, as has the annual per capita income ($229 in 1968).

Bibliography. Justo Pastor Benítez, *Formación social del pueblo paraguayo,* Asunción, 1955; Efraím Cardozo, *Breve historia del Paraguay,* Buenos Aires, 1967; Carlos Centurión, *Historia de la cultura paraguaya,* 2 vols., Asunción, 1961; Andrés Riquelme, *Apuntes para la historia política y diplomática del Paraguay,* 2 vols., Asunción, 1960; Harris G. Warren, *Paraguay: An Informal History,* Norman, Okla., 1949.

JOHN HOYT WILLIAMS

PARANÁ-PARAGUAY RIVER BASIN. The Paraná-Paraguay River Basin is the second largest in South America, the Amazon Basin being the largest. Situated in the southern portion of the continent, it is composed of two major rivers, the Paraná and the Paraguay, which join near the Argentine city of Corrientes. From that point the Paraná continues to Buenos Aires, where it enters the RÍO DE LA PLATA, a saltwater estuary that connects with the Atlantic Ocean.

The drainage basin may be divided into several important subregions. The largest and most important of these is the Gran CHACO, a low interior plain formed from debris swept down from the ANDES MOUNTAINS. In the north, at the juncture of Paraguay, Bolivia, and Brazil, is the low and swampy Pantanal do Rio Negro. Farther to the east is the Mato Grosso, a tropical grassland. Southward, situated primarily in eastern Paraguay and the southern states of Brazil, is the Paraná Plateau, a region of rich soils weathered from volcanic material. Tropical climates dominate the basin, the winter dry period becoming more severe as one progresses westward.

Except for minor economic development in eastern Paraguay and the province of Misiones in Argentina, the drainage basin was little exploited by Europeans during the colonial period. The Brazilian mestizos known as *bandeirantes* (*see* BANDEIRAS) made raids into the area to capture and enslave the TUPÍ-GUARANÍ, who were the inhabitants of the basin before the arrival of the Europeans. At the opening of the national period

there were probably fewer inhabitants in the basin than when the Europeans first arrived. During the early nineteenth century some commercial livestock production commenced in the Argentine province of Entre Ríos, but what little agriculture was found in most of the basin was of a subsistence nature.

In the twentieth century the basin began to be settled more intensively. Extensive grazing of low-grade cattle is now the dominant use of the land, although there are some intensive irrigation agriculture within the Gran Chaco and much coffee cultivation on the Paraná Plateau. Lumbering has become a major industry on

PARANÁ-PARAGUAY RIVER BASIN

this plateau, which has one of the largest stands of commercial pine in South America. Minerals play a minor role in the basin's economy, although the search for petroleum has been intensive. Transportation has always presented a grave problem to economic development. A heavy load is placed on the river system, but the Paraguay is navigable only as far as Asunción by shallow-draft ocean vessels. Beyond that point small riverboats can reach into Brazil. The upper Paraná has a series of falls shortly above its confluence with the Paraguay and is navigable only with the greatest difficulty. The newest focus of economic interest is the development of hydroelectricity along the upper Paraná and its tributaries, and in 1973 Brazil and Paraguay agreed to construct a giant hydroelectric plant at Itaipu on the upper Paraná.　　　MORTON D. WINSBERG

PARANHOS, JOSÉ MARIA DA SILVA. *See* RIO BRANCO, VISCONDE DO.

PARANHOS JÚNIOR, JOSÉ MARIA DA SILVA. *See* RIO BRANCO, BARÃO DO.

PARDO [Y BARREDA], JOSÉ (1864–1947). President of Peru (1904–1908, 1915–1919). Born in Lima, the aristocratic José Pardo (son of Manuel PARDO, founder of the CIVILISTA PARTY) had the physical and mental vigor, family prestige, social connections, and wealth to make himself one of the most influential politicians of his age. He studied at the University of San Marcos and subsequently engaged in a variety of business enterprises through which he rebuilt the family fortune, depleted during the ruinous WAR OF THE PACIFIC (1879–1883). He also taught at the University of San Marcos and served in a number of diplomatic posts. His rapid rise to the Presidency began in 1903, when he was appointed Minister of Foreign Relations and head of the Cabinet. Pardo was elected to the Presidency in 1904 after the death of President Manuel Candamo. He was not the popular choice (his organization controlled the electoral machinery), nor did he have the unanimous support of his party. In fact, he and his young Civilista followers had been strenuously opposed by the party's old establishment. Nevertheless, Pardo's four-year regime was very progressive, spurring economic growth and educational and social reforms.

In 1915 a convention of Civilistas and members of two smaller parties again brought Pardo to the Presidency. The convention, which lacked true popular representation, had been called to bring order after three years of political turmoil. The choice of Pardo was meant to achieve this goal, but in his four-year regime he was faced with serious problems emanating from World War I, labor unrest, and university revolts. Nonetheless, Pardo ruled capably though not always wisely. In 1919 he was overthrown and exiled. He returned to Peru after the fall of Augusto LEGUÍA in 1930 and died in Lima in 1947.

ORAZIO A. CICCARELLI

PARDO, MANUEL (1834–1878). President of Peru (1872–1876). A Lima aristocrat and a self-made millionaire, Pardo was the first civilian President of Peru and certainly one of its most capable leaders. Educated in South America and Europe, he chose a career in business rather than the more traditional path of government, church, or the military. The great energy he

brought to his profession and the great success he enjoyed in it (he had amassed a fortune by the age of twenty-five) made him, more than any of his contemporaries, the symbol of a modern and capitalist Peru. He brought the same energy, along with a vision of a better Peru, to politics. As mayor of Lima he modernized the city, opened schools, and provided basic social services, thus gaining the great affection of the masses. In 1871 he founded the CIVILISTA PARTY, to which he imparted his reformist economic and political philosophy, and in 1872 led it to victory in the presidential election. In the ensuing four years he introduced economic and educational reforms, streamlined the government bureaucracy, and diminished the power of the military. In 1878, while he was serving as President of the Senate, he was assassinated by a disgruntled army sergeant who blamed Pardo's military policies for his failure to be promoted to officer rank.

ORAZIO A. CICCARELLI

PARDO. Term widely used in Latin America to refer to a person of mixed racial origin, particularly a mulatto. Like other nonwhites in the Spanish colonies, *pardos* experienced both legal and social discrimination and were ordinarily excluded from the universities, the clergy, and certain occupations (*see* CASTAS). There is evidence that *pardos* had greater opportunities for upward mobility during the latter part of the eighteenth century, and a royal decree of February 10, 1795, allowed them to purchase exemption from their condition of inferiority. Such concessions to *pardos* were vehemently opposed by American-born whites (creoles; *see* CREOLE), notably in Venezuela.

HELEN DELPAR

PARRA, NICANOR (1914–   ). Chilean poet. Born in Chillán, Parra has enriched Chilean poetry with his interest in folklore and with his antipoems, which combine colloquial language with a sense of the absurd. His work is not a denial of poetry but a new and ingenious expression of pessimism and irony in the dehumanized world of technology. He has lectured and taught widely in the United States. Among his publications are *Cancionero sin nombre* (1937), *Poemas y antipoemas* (1954), *La cueca larga* (1958), *Versos de salón* (1962), *Canciones rusas* (1967), and *Los profesores* (1971).

RACHEL PHILLIPS

PARTIDO APRISTA PERUANO. *See* ALIANZA POPULAR REVOLUCIONARIA AMERICANA.

PARTIDO COMUNISTA BRASILEIRO (BRAZILIAN COMMUNIST PARTY; PCB). The Brazilian Communist party, founded in 1922, has been an illegal political party for most of its existence. Prior to the REVOLUTION OF 1930, led by Getúlio VARGAS, sectarian differences between Trotskyites and Stalinists kept party membership limited. Under the leadership of Luis Carlos PRESTES, whose guerrilla role in the 1920s gained him wide popular support, the party was strengthened. By 1935, with an "anti-imperialist" program based upon nationalization of foreign companies and an end to the landed oligarchy, the PCB organized the short-lived Aliança Nacional Libertadora (National Liberation Alliance), a popular front. Premature revolts in November 1935 by militant members in Rio de Janeiro, Natal, and Recife, which some believe were instigated by Vargas, led to swift reprisals and suppression of the PCB by the Vargas regime.

Prestes was imprisoned in 1936, and after Brazil joined the Allies during World War II, leadership of the PCB passed to Diógenes de Arruda Câmara. Its program became one of antifascism. In 1945, after the military coup against Vargas and the granting of amnesty to Prestes, the now-legal PCB scored impressively in national elections. Outlawed by the government of President Eurico Gaspar DUTRA in 1947, the PCB was again forced underground. During the 1950s the party sought worker and peasant support; internal struggles for control were not resolved until 1957, when Prestes and his "Bahia" group regained control from the "Stalinist" Arruda Câmara.

By 1962 Prestes' program, which called for peaceful revolution through a united front ("nationalist and democratic" in nature), had been rejected by a small party faction advocating armed revolt. Taking the former party name, the PARTIDO COMUNISTA DO BRASIL (PCdoB), this group disavowed cooperative efforts by the PCB with the government of President João GOULART. Since the military coup of 1964, the PCB, its leadership suppressed and its orthodox ideology challenged by newer Marxist currents, has lost much of its appeal and popular support, particularly among younger groups.   JOSEPH A. ELLIS

PARTIDO COMUNISTA DE CUBA (COMMUNIST PARTY OF CUBA; PCC).

Cuba's original Communist party was founded in 1925. Initially crippled by repression, the party went underground but emerged after the mid-1930s as one of the strongest Communist parties in the Western Hemisphere. As a result of a fruitful working relationship with Fulgencio BATISTA, who was elected to the Presidency in 1940 with Communist help, the party gained legalization, representation in Congress and the Cabinet, and domination of the CONFEDERACIÓN DE TRABAJADORES CUBANOS. After 1944 the party was known as the Popular Socialist party (PSP). The party's gains under Batista were eradicated after 1946 because of the anti-Communist initiatives of the administrations of Ramón GRAU SAN MARTÍN and Carlos PRÍO SOCORRÁS. After Batista's return to power in 1952, the PSP was outlawed.

The PSP initially denounced Fidel CASTRO's anti-Batista revolutionary activities as putschist, but in mid-1958 it formed a secret eleventh-hour alliance with his July 26 movement. The party reached the height of its influence in 1961 after the BAY OF PIGS INVASION, when Castro declared his a socialist revolution and created the Integrated Revolutionary Organizations (ORI) as a forerunner to a United Party of the Socialist Revolution (PURS). The PSP initially dominated the ORI, but in early 1962 Castro denounced the sectarianism of some former PSP officials and restored control to non-PSP groups within his revolutionary movement.

In October 1965 PURS officially assumed the name Communist party of Cuba. The new PCC is an elitist party with a highly selective membership, although efforts to increase party membership were reported in the early 1970s. Affiliated to the party are a number of mass organizations that contain a large portion of Cuba's population. In Cuba, as in most Communist countries, the top party and government leaderships overlap.

See also MELLA, Julio Antonio; RODRÍGUEZ, Carlos Rafael.   DAVID A. CRAIN

PARTIDO COMUNISTA DO BRASIL (COMMUNIST PARTY OF BRAZIL; PCDOB).

The Partido Comunista do Brasil was formed in 1962 by a dissident faction of the PARTIDO COMUNISTA BRASILEIRO (PCB). This faction, led by Maurício Grabois, Pedro Pomar, and João Amazonas, rejected the cooperative united-front party program then being espoused by Luis Carlos PRESTES and his controlling group within the PCB. Adopting a pro-Chinese stance, the PCdoB advocated armed struggle as the only means through which Brazil could be freed from its "imperialistic" and "capitalistic dependency" status. Initially, the PCdoB called for revolutionary organization among the rural peasantry. Internal differences over tactics, the failure during the 1960s of rural guerrilla movements to radicalize the peasantry, and successful governmental counterefforts have resulted in suppression and fragmentation of the party since 1964.

In 1966 a small group of militants differed over tactics and broke away from the PCdoB, forming the Partido Comunista Revolucionário (PCR), which has focused upon the sugarcane workers of the NORTHEAST. Similarly, another faction under the leadership of Jacob Gorender and Mario Alves split from the PCdoB, again over the issue of tactics, and formed the Partido Comunista Brasileiro Revolucionário (PCBR). This group merged with the Movimento Revolucionário–26 (MR–26 or MAR) and later committed sporadic acts of urban violence. When Carlos Marighela left the PCB, after calling for armed struggle during the Havana meeting of the Latin American Solidarity Organization in 1967, he led the urban-based *paulista* Açao Libertadora Nacional (ALN). Killed by the police in 1969, Marighela through his speeches and writings provided theoretical justification and inspiration for the Brazilian groups advocating armed violence. More recently, the Vanguardia Armada Revolucionária–Palmares (VAR–Palmares), named after the seventeenth-century black slave republic, gained headlines and some prominence through urban terror and sensational kidnappings.

Nevertheless, differences over tactics and ideology have prevented these groups and the PCdoB from posing a serious challenge to the present government. Drawn largely from student and intellectual circles and reflecting the urban middle class, these elitist cell-like organizations have had little impact on the Brazilian masses.   JOSEPH A. ELLIS

PARTIDO DE ACCIÓN NACIONAL (NATIONAL ACTION PARTY; PAN).

Mexican political party organized by Manuel Gómez Morín between 1938 and September 14–17, 1939. Its name was inspired by the sympathy of PAN leader Efraín González Luna for the Action Française. It supported the opposition candidate Juan Andreu Almazán in the presidential election of 1940, but it survived his defeat and succeeded in its goal of becoming a permanent party. Gómez Morín, who had distinguished himself as the author of the laws creating the Bank of Mexico in 1925 and the Agrarian Credit Law of 1926 and as rector of the National University in 1933, counted upon the support of his former students in the organization of the party, which also included some prominent intellectuals of the eras of

Porfirio DÍAZ, Francisco I. MADERO, and Victoriano HUERTA. Among the rank and file were descendants of landowners, bankers, industrialists, and merchants, as well as individuals of more modest economic circumstances affiliated with Catholic groups. In practice its ideology of political humanism, which emphasizes respect for the common good and the human being, took the form of tenacious opposition to the socialist education prescribed by a constitutional amendment in 1933; the party also defended the private landholding in opposition to the EJIDO.

Since 1943, when the PAN took part in elections for deputies to Congress, it has nominated candidates for the Presidency and Congress and to a lesser extent for governorships and seats in the municipal councils and state legislatures. By 1972 the number of PAN deputies in Congress had risen to twenty, thanks to the system of "deputies of party," introduced in 1962, whereby minority parties are awarded seats in the lower house of Congress in addition to those won at the polls. The PAN won control of the municipal presidencies of Tijuana and Mexicali in 1968 and of Mérida in 1969, partly because of support from dissidents of the PARTIDO REVOLUCIONARIO INSTITUCIONAL.

MOISÉS GONZÁLEZ NAVARRO

PARTIDO DE LA REVOLUCIÓN CUBANA. *See* AUTÉNTICO PARTY (CUBA).

PARTIDO DEL PUEBLO CUBANO. *See* ORTODOXO PARTY (CUBA).

PARTIDO DEMÓCRATA CRISTIANO (CHRISTIAN DEMOCRATIC PARTY; PDC). Chilean political party that resulted from the merger in July 1957 of the Falange Nacional and the Partido Conservador Social Cristiano. Of the two components the Falange was the more important. Its intellectual origins lay in papal encyclicals on social reform and in the work of contemporary Catholic thinkers, notably Jacques Maritain. In the early 1930s a group of Catholic students, among them Eduardo FREI and Radomiro Tomic, set up a youth movement within the Conservative party to influence it on social issues (*see* CONSERVATIVE PARTY: CHILE), but by 1938 the movement had broken with the parent body and become a separate party, taking the name Falange Nacional as a reflection of events in Spain.

Until the 1950s it was a minor party, though Frei held Cabinet office in 1945–1946, but after the PDC was founded, the new party made a progressive impact at the polls from 1957 to 1969. Its strongly reformist program, democratic principles, excellent organization, and skillful leadership offered Chileans a viable alternative to the Marxist left and the discredited right, and in 1964 Frei won the presidential election with 56.1 percent of the vote, to become Latin America's first Christian Democratic President. A year later the PDC won eighty-two seats in the lower house of Congress, obtaining a clear majority, and twelve seats in the Senate. Its government, in power from 1964 to 1970, began a large-scale program of change and development in education, housing, AGRARIAN REFORM, and many other fields. But opposition in the Senate, natural disaster in the form of a serious drought (1967–1968), and a split in the party, which lost its left wing to the opposition, combined to make the government's performance fall far short of its promise. In 1970 Tomic, the PDC candidate for the Presidency, came in third in the presidential election, although the party remained the largest and best organized in Chile.

HAROLD BLAKEMORE

PARTIDO LIBERACIÓN NACIONAL (NATIONAL LIBERATION PARTY; PLN). Costa Rican political party. Since it was founded in 1951 by José FIGUERES and others, it has been the principal party of the nation. The party's origins date to the early 1940s. At that time groups of young intellectuals, dissatisfied with the administration of Rafael CALDERÓN GUARDIA, formed the Center for the Study of National Problems. The unification in 1943 of this group with a young activist political organization called Democratic Action created a powerful force for the reform of the traditional Costa Rican political system. The exhilarating victory of Figueres in the revolution of 1948 both produced a charismatic hero and mobilized the reform spirit. After the party's organization by formal charter in October 1951, Francisco ORLICH became president of the party and Figueres became its first presidential candidate in the election of 1953.

Since 1953, when Figueres led the PLN to a 65 percent victory at the presidential polls, the party has captured the Presidency three additional times. In 1962 Orlich won with 50 percent of the vote, and in 1970 Figueres won with 53 percent. In 1974 the PLN candidate Daniel Oduber Quirós defeated several other candidates to win the Presidency with 43 percent of the vote. A split within the party caused defeat in 1958, and poor campaign strategy reportedly caused defeat in 1966. From 1953 until 1974, when it failed to win a majority, the PLN had control of the Legislative Assembly. Also, it has been the only Costa Rican party to garner support in all regions and municipalities. From the beginning the party has had a strong ideological, reformist orientation. These factors—continuous organization, strength throughout the country, and ideological orientation—lead to the conclusion that the PLN is the first modern political party in Central America. Since much of the party's original program, such as nationalized banking institutions and the extension of social security, has been enacted into law, the chief problem facing its leaders in the 1970s is the maintenance of enthusiasm for public administration of this program. Moreover, as the party's leaders grow old, they face increased pressure from younger members for positions of influence and responsibility.

CHARLES L. STANSIFER

PARTIDO REVOLUCIONARIO DE UNIFICACIÓN DEMOCRÁTICA (REVOLUTIONARY PARTY OF DEMOCRATIC UNIFICATION; PRUD). Dominant political party in El Salvador during the administrations of Oscar OSORIO (1950–1956) and José María LEMUS (1956–1960). The methods it employed and the success it attained gave El Salvador, in effect, a one-party system. Ostensibly PRUD represented the aspirations of popular groups frustrated since 1931 by the conservative regimes of Maximiliano HERNÁNDEZ MARTÍNEZ and Salvador Castañeda Castro. It sought to attain a leftist image and to be regarded as a revolutionary party. Some of its early reform measures contributed to building that image. In reality, however, it was a coalition of the military and aristocracy such as traditionally had controlled the country.

PRUD's dilemma was to sustain a revolutionary appearance while maintaining the traditional socioeconomic order. The argument to the elite was that either the Army and the upper classes would modernize the country or the Communists would direct the process and destroy the existing order. The Communist-inspired uprising of 1932 and the threat of Communist infiltration from Guatemala during the 1950s instilled sufficient fear to win elite acquiescence in moderate reforms in return for military cooperation in restraining violent outbreaks. Such radical measures as land redistribution and a major improvement in the condition of the urban working class, although regarded by many as essential to any significant improvement in the situation of the masses, were not on the PRUD agenda.

PRUD gave strong emphasis to public works and an unusually important place to private capital. The latter characteristic was evident in the encouragement of new industries such as tourism, fishing, and light fabrication enterprises and of diversified agricultural production. PRUD also urged the formation of the CENTRAL AMERICAN COMMON MARKET as a means of enhancing economic opportunity.

Perhaps more than to ideological commitment, PRUD directed its energies to maintaining itself in power. It was dominated by a reformist military group dedicated only to the forms of democracy. In the management of elections it proved to be as efficient, ruthless, and relentless as its predecessors. It controlled the central election board that supervised elections, and it threw all the weight of the government and the Army behind party candidates.

PRUD's insensitivity to popular sentiment, its disregard of criticism, the heavy-handedness of the party leaders, and their arbitrary conduct of national affairs finally brought the political situation to a crisis. Popular demonstrations against the regime grew in size and menace until the party lost power when Lemus was ousted in October 1960. The National Conciliation party, which replaced it, was more a change in the leadership of the "revolution" than an ideological shift.

WILLIAM J. GRIFFITH

PARTIDO REVOLUCIONARIO DOMINICANO (DOMINICAN REVOLUTIONARY PARTY; PRD). The PRD is the most important party in a country where political parties have never counted for very much. It is a left-of-center, radically nationalist, and reform-oriented party with probably the strongest organization and mass following in the Dominican Republic, but whether party politics and electioneering represent a major and viable path to power in that country remains uncertain.

Founded as an exile organization in 1939 by Juan BOSCH, the party suffered the vagaries of an exile existence for a long time, eventually establishing branch organizations in several Caribbean capitals and in New York. In 1961, following the assassination of the dictator Rafael Leonidas TRUJILLO MOLINA, the PRD was established in the Dominican Republic. It grew rapidly on the basis of its social democratic platform, mass appeal, and strong leadership and organization; and in 1962 it, along with Bosch, swept to an overwhelming 2-1 electoral victory. With Bosch in the Presidency, the party organization was neglected and allowed to run down. Once Bosch was ousted, however,

the party revived and regained the widespread support of many intellectuals, the masses, and much of the middle class. It was the PRD which launched the uprising of 1965 designed to restore constitutional government but which instead provoked civil war and United States intervention (*see* DOMINICAN REVOLT).

Persecuted by Dominican police and military elements, torn by dissension, and apparently declining in popularity, the party and Bosch lost the 1966 elections and abstained from participation in 1970. Along with Bosch, the party abandoned its advocacy of a parliamentary or electoral path to democracy in favor of other means and of a "dictatorship with popular support." Later, however, not only did Bosch retreat from this position, but in November 1973 he resigned from the PRD, announcing that he would form a new political party.

HOWARD J. WIARDA

PARTIDO REVOLUCIONARIO INSTITUCIONAL (INSTITUTIONAL REVOLUTIONARY PARTY; PRI). Dominant political party of Mexico. After the triumph of the Constitutionalist revolution against Victoriano HUERTA in 1914, the self-destruction of Mexico's military chiefs began. From this struggle Álvaro OBREGÓN emerged as the outstanding figure, a position he retained until his assassination in 1928. With the demise of Mexico's last military *caudillo*, President Plutarco Elías CALLES proceeded to organize the Partido Nacional Revolucionario (National Revolutionary party; PNR), in essence a coalition of national parties, such as the Labor and Agrarian parties, and of the very numerous regional parties in Mexico. The PNR was created in Querétaro in March 1929 with the motto "institutions and social reform." Recognizing the absolute autonomy of the confederated parties in local matters, the PNR urged the fulfillment of Articles 27 and 123 of the constitution of 1917 (*see* CONSTITUTION OF 1917: MEXICO) along with the protection of industry. The PNR was thus a polyclass party affiliated with the state.

In 1937, at the instigation of President Lázaro CÁRDENAS, the PNR held internal elections for the purpose of dividing its membership into agrarian, labor, and military sectors. Cárdenas reluctantly agreed to the creation of a fourth sector, the popular sector. On March 30, 1938, twelve days after the expropriation of the oil industry, an assembly was convened in which the PNR converted itself into the Partido de la Revolución Mexicana (Party of the Mexican Revolution; PRM), composed of agrarian, labor, military, and popular sectors. The military sector disappeared at the beginning of the administration of Manuel ÁVILA CAMACHO (1940–1946). On September 16, 1941, there began the reorganization of the popular sector, a task that concluded with the creation of the Confederación Nacional de Organizaciones Populares (National Confederation of Popular Organizations; CNOP) on February 28, 1943. It was said at the time that the CNOP filled a gap in the revolutionary family by allowing the middle class to occupy a place alongside the proletariat.

On January 18, 1946, the PRM was transformed into the PRI, made up of three sectors, agrarian, labor, and popular. Although theoretically the only organization in the agrarian sector should be the Confederación Nacional Campesina (National Peasants Confederation), the leader of the Central Campesina Independente was recently elected to Congress on the PRI ticket. The CONFEDERACIÓN DE TRABAJADORES DE MÉXICO (Confederation of Mexican Workers) is the dominant group in the labor sector. The popular sector is divided into ten branches: civil servants, cooperativists, small farm owners, small merchants, small industrialists, intellectuals and professionals, youths, women, artisans, and nonsalaried workers.

In its declaration of principles the PRI indicated that the ideals of the MEXICAN REVOLUTION had crystallized into institutions which it was necessary to preserve and protect: the EJIDO (though, in contrast with the PRM, the PRI did not emphasize the collective ejido); the labor union, along with the right to bargain collectively and to strike; and the right of the nation to control Mexico's subsoil wealth and to direct education. The PRI has controlled the political rivalries of the revolutionary family, but it has not destroyed them, and social conflicts have also reappeared within its ranks, especially in the popular sector, where owners coexist with wage earners. At the beginning of Miguel ALE-MÁN's Presidency (1946–1952), Mexico's bourgeoisie rejected a political confrontation with the PRI; it abandoned the PARTIDO DE ACCIÓN NACIONAL (National Action party), preferring to accomplish its goals by means of pressure groups, such as the bankers' association and chambers of commerce and industry. For this reason it has not been necessary to create, as some have suggested, a new fourth sector, that of "private enterprise."

Bibliography. Frank R. Brandenburg, *Mexico: An Experiment in One Party Democracy,* Ann Arbor, Mich., 1955; Vicente Fuentes Díaz, *Los partidos políticos en México,* Mexico City, 1956; Pablo González Casanova, *La democracia en México,* Mexico City, 1965; Moisés González Navarro, *La Confederación Nacional Campesina: Un grupo de presión en la reforma agraria mexicana,* Mexico City, 1968; L. Vincent Padgett, *The Mexican Political System,* Boston, 1966; Robert E. Scott, *Mexican Government in Transition,* Urbana, Ill., 1964.

MOISÉS GONZÁLEZ NAVARRO

PARTIDO SOCIAL DEMOCRÁTICO (SOCIAL DEMOCRATIC PARTY; PSD). The largest political party in post-World War II Brazil. When the formation of political parties was authorized in May 1945 after more than seven years of dictatorship, the PSD was the stronger of the two parties organized and led by Getúlio VARGAS. As the "official" party, it attracted men who served the regime in public office at the national, state, and municipal levels throughout Brazil. It also gained considerable support from the armed forces, the business community, and rural political bosses who wished to be associated with the established government. In common with the other parties created at that time, the PSD espoused the principles of representative democracy but had no other ideological basis. It nominated Vargas's personal choice for the Presidency, War Minister Eurico Gaspar DUTRA, and continued to back his successful campaign after Vargas was deposed in October 1945.

In the elections of December 2, 1945, the party gained a majority in the Constituent Assembly, and in January 1947 it won twelve governorships and elected legislators in all twenty states. Thereafter its numerical superiority gradually declined, but in coalition with the Vargas-created PARTIDO TRABALHISTA BRASILEIRO,

the PSD shared power in the administrations of Vargas (1951–1954), Juscelino KUBITSCHEK (1956–1961), and João GOULART (1961–1964). When the PSD was dissolved following the Second Institutional Act of October 27, 1965, most of its members joined the new ALIANÇA RENOVADORA NACIONAL.

ROLLIE E. POPPINO

PARTIDO TRABALHISTA BRASILEIRO (BRAZILIAN LABOR PARTY; PTB). The Brazilian Labor party was founded by Getúlio VARGAS on March 26, 1945, and was composed initially of men who had endorsed and participated in the organized labor apparatus and social welfare agencies of his regimes since 1930. The PTB also attracted the mass of the urban working class and others who were personally loyal to Vargas. Its program called for the preservation and extension of the social legislation of the ESTADO NOVO under a democratic government. The PTB ran third among the eleven parties competing in the Constituent Assembly elections in 1945, increased its share of the vote in the state and municipal contests of 1947 and 1948, and backed Vargas in his successful bid for the Presidency in 1950. After Vargas's suicide in 1954, João GOULART became president of the party and its winning candidate for the Vice Presidency of the nation in 1955 and 1960. As the result of elections and the influx of officeholders from other parties, the PTB continued to increase its representation in Congress, replacing the UNIÃO DEMOCRÁTICA NACIONAL as the second party in 1962 and outstripping the PARTIDO SOCIAL DEMOCRÁTICO in the final months of the Goulart administration (1961–1964). The PTB was heavily purged following the revolution of March 31, 1964. When political parties were dissolved by the Second Institutional Act of October 27, 1965, the surviving PTB members in Congress entered the opposition MOVIMENTO DEMOCRÁTICO BRASILEIRO.

ROLLIE E. POPPINO

PASTRANA BORRERO, MISAEL (1923–   ). President of Colombia (1970–   ). Born in Neiva, Pastrana studied law and economics at the Jesuits' Universidad Javeriana, receiving his doctorate in 1945. Subsequently, he served on the staff of the Colombian Embassy at the Vatican. In the late 1940s he was Secretary-General to the President under Mariano OSPINA PÉREZ and then briefly under Laureano GÓMEZ. From 1950 through 1956 he was employed in a variety of governmental positions, serving as alternate delegate to both the United Nations and the ORGANIZATION OF AMERICAN STATES, as well as on the staff of the Minister of Foreign Affairs in Bogotá. Under Liberal President Alberto LLERAS CAMARGO (*see* LIBERAL PARTY: COLOMBIA), he was Minister of Development, Minister of Public Works, and Minister of Finance and Public Credit. Beginning in 1966, Pastrana served for several years as Minister of Government (Interior) in the Cabinet of Liberal President Carlos LLERAS RESTREPO. During the period 1968–1969 he was in Washington as the Colombian Ambassador.

Pastrana then returned to Colombia to be the NATIONAL FRONT coalition's Conservative party candidate for President (*see* CONSERVATIVE PARTY: COLOMBIA). Two Conservatives who had fought his nomination, Evaristo Sourdis and Belisario Betancur, opposed him in the general election, being joined by the flamboyant ex-dictator Gustavo ROJAS PINILLA. The results were close and disputed. In the end Pastrana won over Rojas by only about 60,000 of 4 million votes cast. Pastrana experienced difficulty as a minority President, although prospects generally brightened in the second half of his administration. More important, the strength of Rojas's ALIANZA NACIONAL POPULAR declined markedly in the 1972 elections.

GERALD THEISEN

PASTRY WAR (1838–1839). Brief encounter between Mexico and France that originated in claims, many of them exaggerated, of French citizens against the Mexican government for property lost or damaged in civil and military disturbances. The action takes its name from the claim of a French baker in Tacubaya who demanded 60,000 pesos as compensation for pastries he had lost. In February 1838, a French squadron appeared at Veracruz to present an ultimatum to the Mexican government demanding settlement of the claims by mid-April. Mexico refused to negotiate unless the squadron was withdrawn, which the French would not do. When the deadline expired, the French blockaded Veracruz. Five months after the blockade had been placed, France sent emissaries to Mexico City to open negotiations. These failing, the French bombarded San Juan de Ulúa on October 27. The commander of the fortress surrendered, and the Governor of Veracruz capitulated. The national government named Antonio López de SANTA ANNA the new commandant of the port, and he issued a declaration of war on October 30. Once again negotiations failed, and the French landed troops in the city of Veracruz on December 5. Santa Anna lost a leg in the fighting. With the British Ambassador as mediator, treaties were signed on March 9, 1839, and ratified by the Mexican Congress ten days later. Mexico agreed to pay claims in the amount of 600,000 pesos within six months and to submit other claims and questions to arbitration. France agreed to return ships and cargoes seized during the blockade and to withdraw its forces.

CHARLES R. BERRY

PATAGONIA. Arid plateaus south of the Colorado River, Argentina, bordered on the east by the Atlantic Ocean and on the west by the ANDES MOUNTAINS. The coastline, especially south of the 44th parallel, is indented by numerous bays and coves and presents a forbidding appearance because most of it is lined with rocks. The area was first visited by Ferdinand MAGELLAN in 1520, and the earliest attempt to explore, conquer, and settle it from the sea, the first of many failures, was made by Simón de Alcazaba in 1534. In the seventeenth century Spaniards, seeking the mythical city of the Caesars, penetrated Patagonia from the sea, from the north, and from Chile. Chilean Jesuits, beginning with Nicolás Mascardi, who founded a mission in 1670 on the shores of Lake Nahuel Huapí, continued the fruitless search for the city until the end of the following century. The most important Jesuit was the Englishman Thomas Falkner. Sent by the Spanish government, he established the mission Nuestra Señora del Pilar de Vulcán in 1740, and from there he was able to collect the data he needed for the first map of the region and for his scientific book, *A Description of Patagonia, and the Adjoining Parts of South America* (1774). Among the other Englishmen who were at-

tracted to Patagonia the most noteworthy were Robert Fitzroy and Charles Darwin, who discovered and explored the Chubut River in 1833, and George C. Musters, who crossed and recrossed the ground between Punta Arenas and Carmen de Patagones in 1869 and 1870, taking notes for his classic study, *At Home with the Patagonians* (1871). Another result of English activities in the region was the founding of Port Madryn by Welsh settlers in 1865.

In the nineteenth century Argentina, Chile, and France competed for control of Patagonia. The Argentine dictator Juan Manuel de ROSAS, claiming the entire territory to the Strait of Magellan, tried to occupy it, but he only reached the Negro River in 1833. A decade later Chilean explorers were moving up the coast from Punta Arenas, and in 1873 Chile started to build a fort at the mouth of the Santa Cruz River. It was demolished by the Argentines, but in 1874 Chile claimed the region south of the Santa Cruz. A war between the two countries was narrowly averted in 1878. The Chilean threat spurred the Argentine government to renew its efforts to take actual possession of Patagonia. Argentine occupation of the area was not completed until the end of the century, but in 1884 the national territories of La Pampa, Neuquén, Río Negro, Chubut, Santa Cruz, and Tierra del Fuego were created and given the boundaries the provinces of the same names generally have today. The new western boundary of Argentina was disputed by Chile, and this issue was not settled until 1902.

Until recently most of the wealth in Patagonia has consisted of sheep, although there are large herds of cattle and horses and a significant agricultural sector. Oil was discovered at Comodoro Rivadavia on December 13, 1907, six years after the founding of the city, and oil production has increased steadily over the years. In 1947 an iron-ore deposit was found at Sierra Grande in Río Negro Province. As part of its industrial promotion plan for Patagonia, the Argentine government concluded contracts in 1972 for the construction of the facilities and for the machinery needed to exploit the iron-ore field; for a hydroelectric complex at El Chocón–Cerros Colorados, an aluminum plant at Puerto Madryn, and an oil refinery at Plaza Huincul; and for the development of the petroleum and natural gas deposits at San Sebastián.

JOSEPH T. CRISCENTI

PATIÑO, SIMÓN I[TURRI] (1860–1947). Bolivian tin magnate. Patiño, who was to be the pioneer in developing the exploitation of Bolivia's tin resources and who died a multimillionaire, was a CHOLO, or Bolivian of mixed European and Indian ancestry. Born near Cochabamba, he received very little schooling and worked for some time as a store clerk. It was in this capacity that he is said to have accepted a miner's claim in payment of a debt and then acquired the claim for himself.

Patiño discovered that the area to which he had acquired title was rich in tin. It is recounted that for some years he and his wife exploited their first mine with very primitive equipment. However, Patiño had some notion of the potentialities of what he possessed, and he soon sought both technical assistance and financial backing in Great Britain and the United States.

By the first decade of the twentieth century, the growth of the Bolivian tin-mining industry was fully under way, and by the end of that decade, Patiño was reported to be a millionaire. Soon afterward he went to Europe, where he served as a diplomatic agent for Bolivia, a useful cover for managing his rapidly expanding financial interests. By the 1920s, controlling well over half the tin production of his native country, he had also invested in tin mining in Malaya and in smelting installations in Germany and Great Britain, as well as in a large variety of other enterprises in various parts of the world.

Patiño lived in Europe in the grand style. He had palatial homes in Paris, Biarritz, and Nice. His wealth won him entry into European society, and several of his five surviving children married scions of the nobility. However, his social success in Europe was not matched in his native country. When he returned to Bolivia for a short while in 1924, he found that all his wealth was not sufficient to win acceptance for a cholo of humble origins in the provincial white and near-white aristocracy of Cochabamba. As a result, Patiño returned to Europe and never again set foot in his native country. He lived in France until the fall of that country to the Nazis in 1940 drove him to set up residence in New York, where he died.

On his death Patiño was probably one of the world's richest men. His compatriots had little love for him, rightly accusing him of having drained vast riches from his native country and of having done little with those riches to develop Bolivia or to improve the levels of living of its people. During most of his life, his Bolivian enterprises went virtually untaxed, and Patiño invested nothing in the country except for a huge mansion that he constructed in Cochabamba. *See also* TIN INDUSTRY (BOLIVIA).   ROBERT J. ALEXANDER

PATROCINIO, JOSÉ DO (1853–1904). Brazilian antislavery leader, journalist, orator, and poet. The son of a slave-owning priest and planter and a black fruit vendor, José do Patrocinio was born in his father's vicarage in Campos, Rio de Janeiro Province. Brought up in Campos and on a nearby plantation, he was introduced as a child to the realities of slavery in both rural and urban settings. At thirteen he began an apprenticeship in the Misericordia Hospital in Rio de Janeiro, and in 1872 he entered the Faculty of Medicine as a pharmacy student, earning his diploma but lacking funds to establish himself in his profession. Having tutored briefly, in 1877 he joined the staff of the *Gazeta de Noticias* on the strength of his poetic talent. In 1881, already famous, he acquired the abolitionist *Gazeta da Tarde,* maintaining it as the leading antislavery journal in Rio until he replaced it with the equally effective *Cidade do Rio* in 1887. He was an active head of the Sociedade Central Emancipadora in 1880, cofounder of the Confederação Abolicionista in 1883, and coauthor with André REBOUÇAS of the *Manifesto da Confederação Abolicionista* of the same year. He served as an abolitionist emissary to Europe and with his presence helped to spur antislavery movements in Ceará in 1882, in his native Campos in 1885, and in the port of Santos in 1886.

With the end of slavery in 1888 (*see* ABOLITION OF SLAVERY: BRAZIL), Patrocinio became a supporter of Princess Isabel, then under attack by a growing republican movement, but after the fall of the empire on November 15, 1889, he declared his loyalty to the new republican regime. A critic of the dictatorial Floriano PEIXOTO, he was exiled in 1892 with other "conspirators" to the state of Amazonas. Amnestied, he returned to Rio, only to be forced into hiding with the beginning of the naval revolt in September 1893. From October of that year until March 1895 publication of the *Cidade do Rio* was suspended by order of the government, but after the reestablishment of constitutional government Patrocinio was able to continue his journalistic career until his death in 1904.

                                      ROBERT CONRAD

PATRONATO REAL. System of patronage under which the Spanish crown was granted privileges with respect to ecclesiastical appointments, benefices, and finances in compensation for assuming certain obligations dealing with the maintenance of the Catholic Church and its ministers. The Spanish Kings also assisted in preserving the integrity of the Catholic faith and encouraging its spread. As a result of the relationship thus established, civil and ecclesiastical authority became intermingled, giving rise to conflicts over jurisdiction.

As the *patronato real* evolved, secular authority over clerics was gradually increased. This was especially true in the Spanish possessions in America, which had closer contact with Madrid than with Rome. There the rights of patronage were delegated by the King to royal representatives, primarily the viceroys, presidents, and governors. The crown expected these vice-patrons to preserve and maintain royal prerogatives under the *patronato real,* and their efforts in this area were examined at the time of their *residencias* (*see* RESIDENCIA).

The discovery of America gave rise to conflicting claims by Spain and Portugal to the New World. These were resolved in 1493 by Pope Alexander VI, who confirmed Spain's sovereignty in the New World. In return, the Spanish monarchy assumed responsibility for Christianizing the new lands. Thus Spain's claim to America was inextricably tied to the missionary task of the church (*see* MISSIONS: SPANISH AMERICA). To regularize this relationship and to respond to special conditions in the Indies, papal concessions were sought by the Spanish monarchy. The Alexandrine bulls of 1493 granted Ferdinand II and ISABELLA I the patronal rights enjoyed by the Portuguese monarchs in their overseas possessions. These were extended by the bull *Eximiae devotionis* (November 16, 1501), by which royal officials collected ecclesiastical tithes and controlled their disbursement. This was an innovation that did not exist in Spain. In 1508 the papal brief *Universalis ecclesiae* conferred on the Spanish Kings the right of presentation to all benefices in their possessions in America. This ensured that the church would develop as an integral part of the Spanish colonial system.

Considerable growth of patronal authority occurred during the reigns of PHILIP II (1556–1598) and CHARLES III (1759–1788). Under the former a patriarchate of the Indies was proposed but because of the opposition of Rome was never instituted. The concept of the King as vicar of the church in the Indies and of a royal "economic authority" emerged in the seventeenth century to justify civil intervention in the ecclesiastical sphere. This concept was used by Charles III as the legal basis for the expulsion of the Jesuits in 1767 (*see* JESUITS, EXPULSION OF: SPANISH AMERICA).

In Brazil the *padroado real* operated in much the

same manner as the *patronato real* in the Spanish colonies, but the Portuguese monarchs exercised their prerogatives as administrators of the Order of Christ. Because of the loose grip of Portugal on Brazil, patronal authority was not as effective in regulating the church as it was in Hispanic America.

The question of the transmission of the *patronato real* to the Spanish American republics arose at the time of independence. The new governments argued that such rights were inherent in sovereignty; the church argued that patronal rights were personal grants to the Spanish Kings and consequently lapsed with the end of monarchical control. Disputes over this question marked the histories of each of the new republics.

MARGARET E. CRAHAN

PAZ, JUAN CARLOS (1897–1972). Argentine composer. Born in Buenos Aires, he studied there with Constantino Gaito and sprang to the fore of Argentine musical life with the founding in 1937 of the Grupo Renovación. His early works adhere to a neoclassical style with strong polyphonic characteristics; he later moved on to atonality and then to an almost exclusive reliance on twelve-tone techniques, which he always used with a highly progressive and personal spirit. Outstanding among his compositions are his *Ten Pieces on a Twelve-tone Row* for piano (1936), *Dedalus* (1950), *Continuidades* for orchestra (1966), and *Music for Piano and Orchestra* (1965). He also wrote several books on music.

JUAN A. ORREGO-SALAS

PAZ, OCTAVIO (1914–   ). Mexican poet and prose writer. Paz's first poems appeared in *Barandal* (1931–1932) and *Cuadernos del Valle de México* (1933–1934). His first volume of poetry, *Luna silvestre,* was published in 1933, but its poems are omitted from *Libertad bajo palabra* (1960; revised 1968), which contains his collected poems from 1935 to 1957. Two later volumes contain the rest of his poetry to 1969: *Salamandra* (1962) and *Ladera Este* (1969). His prose works range from essays on contemporary political and social events, such as *El laberinto de la soledad,* 1950 (*The Labyrinth of Solitude*), *Corriente alterna* (1967), and *Posdata* (1970), through esthetics and literary criticism (*El arco y la lira,* 1956, 1967; *Las peras del olmo,* 1957; *Cuadrivio,* 1965; *Puertas al campo,* 1966), to art criticism (*Marcel Duchamp o El castillo de la pureza,* 1968) and structuralism (*Claude Lévi-Strauss o El nuevo festín de Esopo,* 1967; *Conjunciones y disyunciones,* 1969). Paz has translated poetry, including the work of Matsuo Basho, and has been responsible for the propagation of Mexican poetry in general and the work of younger poets in particular.

In 1937 Paz went to Spain, where he sympathized with the Republicans in the civil war. He was a Guggenheim fellow in the United States in 1944–1945 and came into contact with the surrealist group in Paris in 1945. The next year he entered the Mexican foreign service and thereafter traveled widely, visiting India and Japan in 1952 and becoming Ambassador to India in 1962. His studies of Oriental philosophy, art, and literature have had a deep effect on his work since this time. Paz resigned his diplomatic post in 1968 in protest against the Mexican government's repression of student demonstrations. He has held important university posts in Great Britain and the United States, including the Simón Bolívar chair at Cambridge University (1969–1970) and the Charles Eliot Norton professorship of poetry at Harvard (1971–1972). He is the editor of the review *Plural* (1971).

RACHEL PHILLIPS

PAZ ESTENSSORO, VÍCTOR (1907–   ). Bolivian political leader and President (1952–1956, 1960–1964). Paz Estenssoro, who presided over the beginning of one of the most profound revolutionary changes to take place in Latin America in the twentieth century, was born in the department of Tarija. After completing his university education in economics, he served as an officer in the Bolivian Army during the CHACO WAR with Paraguay (1932–1935). Two years later he became an economic adviser to President Germán BUSCH. He is generally credited with having drafted the decree of July 1939 that required the tin-mining companies to sell all their foreign exchange to the Banco Central.

In 1940 Paz Estenssoro was elected as an independent member of the Chamber of Deputies. In the following year, he and several other deputies took the lead in forming a new party, the MOVIMIENTO NACIONALISTA REVOLUCIONARIO (MNR). This party, as its name implied, favored economic nationalism and was particularly opposed to the influence of the Big Three tin-mining companies, Patiño, Aramayo, and Hochschild. *See* TIN INDUSTRY (BOLIVIA).

In December 1943 the MNR cooperated with young

Víctor Paz Estenssoro. [*Radio Times Hulton Picture Library*]

military men organized in the Razón de Patria (RADEPA) lodge to overthrow President Enrique PEÑARANDA and install Maj. Gualberto VILLARROEL in his place. Paz Estenssoro became Minister of Finance in the new government. However, as the result of opposition from the United States government, the MNR members of the government were forced to resign early in 1944. They returned some months later, after the United States had recognized the Villarroel government. Paz Estenssoro resigned from the Cabinet just a few days before Villarroel was overthrown in July 1946.

For the next six years Paz Estenssoro remained the most outstanding leader of the MNR. In 1951, while in exile in Buenos Aires, he ran for President of Bolivia, with Hernán SILES as his vice-presidential running mate. They won at least a plurality, although the government of President Mamerto Urriolagoitia insisted that the MNR candidates had not received the 50 percent plus one required by the constitution. In the face of this situation, Urriolagoitia turned power over to a military junta.

On April 9, 1952, the MNR began an uprising against the junta. After it succeeded, Juan LECHÍN and Hernán Siles, who led the revolt in La Paz, summoned Paz Estenssoro back from exile to assume the Presidency to which the MNR maintained he had been elected the year before. During Paz Estenssoro's first presidential term (1952–1956) the achievements of his government included extension of the right to vote to the illiterate Indians, nationalization of the Big Three mining companies, an AGRARIAN REFORM that began the process of returning the land to the Indians, and a substantial program of economic development, particularly in the Oriente (the eastern part of the country). *See* ORIENTE (BOLIVIA).

When his term expired in 1956, Paz Estenssoro handed over the office to his elected successor, Siles. Soon after Siles took office, Paz Estenssoro was named Bolivian Ambassador in London, and he remained in that post during most of the Siles administration.

There was a struggle for the MNR nomination for President in 1960. Walter Guevara Arce, a founder of the MNR and Minister of Foreign Affairs under Paz Estenssoro, sought the nomination, as did Paz Estenssoro himself. When Guevara Arce was defeated, he withdrew to form the Partido Revolucionario Auténtico. During his second administration (1960–1964), Paz concentrated on economic development problems. The so-called Operación Triangular (Triangular Plan) for rehabilitating the tin mines was worked out with the INTER-AMERICAN DEVELOPMENT BANK, the United States government, and West German mining engineering firms. Although implementation of the plan reversed the decline in production that had been occurring since 1952, it also caused conflicts with the miners, who turned against the regime. Paz also pushed an agricultural development and colonization program in the Oriente.

Paz Estenssoro was elected to a third presidential term in June 1964, but he was overthrown in a military coup the following November and went into exile in Lima. During the next seven years he taught economic development in several Lima universities and undertook some short-term jobs for the United Nations. At the same time, he kept in close touch with the MNR underground in Bolivia, trying to bring together the various factions into which the party had split. He was finally able to return to Bolivia in August 1971, after a conspiracy among the MNR, the Falange Socialista Boliviana, and a faction of the Army led by Col. Hugo BANZER had been successful. Paz Estenssoro was reelected national chief of the MNR at its Ninth Extraordinary Congress, held in La Paz in March 1972. He withdrew his support from the Banzer government in November 1973, thereby splitting the MNR, and was expelled from Bolivia the following January.

Bibliography. Robert J. Alexander, *Prophets of the Revolution,* New York, 1962; José Fellman Velarde, *Víctor Paz Estenssoro: El hombre y la revolución,* 2d ed., La Paz, 1955.

ROBERT J. ALEXANDER

PCB. *See* PARTIDO COMUNISTA BRASILEIRO.

PCC. *See* PARTIDO COMUNISTA DE CUBA.

PCDOB. *See* PARTIDO COMUNISTA DO BRASIL.

PDC. *See* PARTIDO DEMÓCRATA CRISTIANO.

PEÇANHA, NILO (1867–1924). Vice President of Brazil, elected in 1906, who assumed the Presidency upon the death of Afonso PENA in 1909. Of humble origin, he was born in Campos, Rio de Janeiro. He studied law in São Paulo but received his degree in Recife in 1887. In the closing years of the empire he was an outspoken proponent of abolition and republicanism and was the founder of the Republican Club of Campos. With the advent of the new regime he represented his native state in the Constituent Assembly (1890–1891). In 1903 he was elected a senator, a position he relinquished the same year to become Governor of the state of Rio de Janeiro. As Governor, he initiated a policy of fiscal reform and was in 1905 a signatory of the coffee valorization plan (*see* TAUBATÉ CONVENTION). Elected Vice President in 1906, he was instrumental in establishing the Ministry of Agriculture.

Peçanha's brief term as President (June 14, 1909–November 15, 1910) was marked by virulent preelection strife over the issue of militarism in government. A skilled politician and conciliator, he created a balanced Cabinet and successfully presided over the elections of 1910, which drew a record number of voters to the polls. He was again elected Governor in 1914 but did not complete his term, being called upon by President Wenceslau BRAZ in 1917 to fill the post of Foreign Minister. Leaving office with the Braz administration in 1918, he was once more elected to the Senate. In 1921 he emerged as the leader of the Republican Reaction coalition that opposed the candidacy of Artur da Silva BERNARDES. He died in the city of Rio de Janeiro on March 31, 1924.

FRANCESCA MILLER

PEDRARIAS. *See* ÁVILA, PEDRO ARIAS DE.

PEDRO I (1798–1834). First Emperor of Brazil and, as Pedro IV, King of Portugal. The son of King JOÃO VI of Portugal and CARLOTA JOAQUINA DE BORBÓN Y PARMA, Pedro married Archduchess Maria Leopoldina of Austria in 1819; after her death in 1826, he wedded Amelia

Pedro I. [Organization of American States]

of Leuchtenberg. João invested Pedro with full governing powers as Regent of Brazil on April 22, 1821. An astute politician, João advised Pedro to lead the independence movement if Brazil should rebel against Portugal.

As Regent, Pedro had to contend with various difficulties: financial problems, the suspicions of Brazilian and Portuguese liberals that he was attempting to usurp the power of the new Portuguese Parliament, the countermanding of his orders by the Parliament, dissension between Portuguese and Brazilians, and military disturbances. Gradually Brazilians became alienated by the Parliament's efforts to restore a colonial regime to their country and began to envision a separation from Portugal under the leadership of Pedro. On January 9, 1822, Pedro issued his famous *"Fico"* ("I am staying") statement in response to Brazilian requests that he refuse to comply with parliamentary orders to return to Portugal. Thereafter, he began to consolidate his control over Brazil, allowed only the Portuguese decrees he authorized to be promulgated, reorganized the Cabinet, placing José Bonifacio de ANDRADA E SILVA at its head, and reduced the number of Portuguese troops in Brazil. On May 13, 1822, he accepted the title Perpetual Defender of Brazil from the Masons, and on June 3 he agreed to convoke a General Constituent and Legislative Assembly for Brazil. Pedro also had to resolve disputes in provincial governments, which occasioned his journey in September to São Paulo, during which independence was declared. *See* YPIRANGA, GRITO DE.

On October 12, 1822, Pedro was crowned Constitutional Emperor and Perpetual Defender of Brazil. His reign was troubled. His Portuguese ties, his supposedly autocratic tendencies, war with Argentina, and scandals concerning his private life with his wives and mistresses gradually reduced his popularity and alienated the people. Politics provided an immediate and enduring source of controversy. Although true political parties did not yet exist, numerous ambitious men, including José Bonifacio de Andrada and his brothers Antônio and Martim, and contentious factions agitated for their particular ideas and did not hesitate violently to criticize the Emperor himself, especially for suspected absolutist intentions. After much acrimonious debate, quarreling, and delay in the Assembly over the production of a constitution, Pedro forcibly dissolved the body on November 12, 1823, and exiled certain leaders, including the Andradas. He then presented a constitution to Brazil on March 25, 1824, which governed the country until the overthrow of the empire (*see* CONSTITUTION OF 1824: BRAZIL). It was most noteworthy for creating the fourth, or moderating, power, which was invested in the Emperor. However, Pedro's critics felt that he did not even observe his own constitution, for he did not hesitate to dismiss the Congress, as in 1829. Disturbances included apparently republican-inspired uprisings, such as the revolution of 1824 in the NORTHEAST.

Political turmoil was increased by nationalistic sentiment. Brazilians were sensitive on this issue and disliked Pedro's Portuguese connections. Pedro had extended citizenship to any Portuguese who wished it, even if they had initially fought against independence. Pedro had been born in Portugal, of course, and his closest friends included many Portuguese. And finally, after Portugal recognized Brazilian independence on August 29, 1825, João insisted that Pedro remain heir to the Portuguese throne. Moreover, Pedro obligated Brazil to assume payment of Portugal's war debts to Great Britain, totaling £1.4 million, and promised £600,000 to João for former crown property in Brazil. Nevertheless, when João died in 1826, Pedro deferred to Brazilian feeling and abdicated the Portuguese throne in favor of his daughter, Maria II. Unfortunately, the child's rights were usurped by her uncle Miguel in 1828. Pedro's continuing interest in the ensuing civil war in Portugal was resented by Brazilians, who thought that their Emperor should devote his full attention to Brazilian problems. One of these was the revolt of the Cisplatine Province in 1825 with the aid of Argentina, which wished to annex it. The unpopular war was eventually resolved by negotiations under the mediation of Great Britain, which resulted in the creation of a new buffer state, the Republic of Uruguay, with the signing of a preliminary convention of peace on August 27, 1828. This loss of territory did not enhance the Emperor's position.

Political agitation increased in 1830 and 1831 with a further breakdown in respect for public authority as Brazilian admiration for the French revolution of 1830 led to more violence, clashes between Brazilians and naturalized Portuguese increased, and Cabinets rose and fell from power. When the military joined the people in demanding that a Brazilian ministry be restored, Pedro refused to accede to their demands, feeling that his personal honor and integrity were at stake and that he would no longer be able truly to rule if he were to do so. Lacking military support, Pedro had no choice but to abdicate in favor of his Brazilian-born son, PEDRO II, on April 7, 1831. Pedro's last years were spent in consolidating Maria's throne in Portugal.

Bibliography. John Armitage, *The History of Brazil, from the Period of the Arrival of the Braganza Family in 1808, to the Abdication of don Pedro the First in 1831 . . .* , 2 vols., London, 1836; Pedro Calmon, *Vida de D. Pedro I, o Rei Cavaleiro*, 3d ed., Oporto, 1952; Tobias do Rego Monteiro, *História do Império: A Elaboração da Independência*, Rio de Janeiro, 1927; id., *História do Império: O Primeiro Reinado*, Rio de Janeiro, 1939; Octavio Tarquinio de Sousa, *História dos Fundadores do Império do Brasil*, vols. II–IV, *A Vida de D. Pedro I*, 3d ed., rev., Rio de Janeiro, 1957.

L. SHARON WYATT

PEDRO II (1825–1891). Second and last Emperor of Brazil (1831–1889). The son of PEDRO I and Archduchess Leopoldina of Austria, Pedro II was born in Rio de Janeiro and was thus the first native Brazilian monarch. Upon his father's abdication in 1831, he succeeded to the throne at the age of five. The first nine years of his reign coincided with the turbulent era of the regencies, which ended in 1840 with the declaration of his majority at the age of fourteen. Pedro was educated by private tutors, including José Bonifacio de ANDRADA E SILVA, early revealing the devotion to study characteristic of him for the rest of his life. From 1840 to 1847 he underwent a political apprenticeship allegedly under the influence of a palace coterie, but by the latter year he was independently exercising the great powers granted to him by the constitution of 1824 (*see* CONSTITUTION OF 1824: BRAZIL). In 1843 he married Princess Thereza Christina of Naples; their two sons died in infancy, placing Pedro's elder daughter, Princess Isabel, in immediate line to the throne. In pursuit of scholarly interests or medical care, Pedro made three trips abroad before his exile in 1889, visiting Europe, Palestine, Egypt, and the United States and making the acquaintance of noted scientists, poets, scholars, and national leaders, including Walter Scott, Henry Wadsworth Longfellow, Alexander Graham Bell, and Queen Victoria.

Unlike his father, Pedro normally ruled with wisdom and caution, gaining the reputation of a fair and moderate leader dedicated to science and the cultural development and progress of the nation. In politics he was inclined toward neutrality, favoring neither major party, Liberal or Conservative, maintaining a free press and other constitutional guarantees, and allowing the unrestricted development of a Republican party after 1870. Yet Pedro was also capable of arbitrary decisions and of a stubborn pursuit of unpopular policies. Possessing the constitutional right to appoint Cabinet ministers at will, regardless of the partisan composition of the Chamber of Deputies, on several occasions he replaced Prime Ministers (Presidents of the Council of State) with members of the minority party, either to advance personal policies or to end a political impasse, but also allegedly because the Brazilian political system provided no other way to prevent the perpetuation of a single party in power. Pedro followed this policy in 1862, when he replaced the Conservative Duque de

Pedro II. [Library of Congress]

CAXIAS with the Liberal Zacarias de Goes; in 1868, when a Ministry headed by Zacarias de Goes was replaced by one led by the Conservative Visconde Itboraí; in 1878, when Caxias was succeeded by Visconde Sinimbú; in 1885, when the Conservative Barão Cotegipe replaced José Antônio Saraiva; and finally in 1889, when the Liberal Visconde Ouro Prêto (Afonso Celso de ASSIS FIGUEIREDO) formed the last Cabinet of the empire, replacing João Alfredo Correia de Oliveira. These sudden political shifts caused discontent among the offended parties, particularly in 1868 and 1889, and are regarded as one cause of Pedro's fall from power in the latter year.

Pedro's long reign was characterized by national development and social change but was also studded with critical and violent events. These included the FARROUPILHA REVOLT (1835–1845) in Rio Grande do Sul and frequent rebellions in other parts of the country, ending with the Liberal Praieira revolt of 1848–1850 in Pernambuco. They also included wars carried on in the RÍO DE LA PLATA region, notably the struggle that ended the rule of Juan Manuel de ROSAS of Argentina in 1852 and the more costly PARAGUAYAN WAR (1864–1870). Also unsettling to the regime was Pedro's bitter dispute with the Bishop of Olinda, Dom Vital Maria Gonçalves de Oliveira, over the question of Freemasonry, which began in 1872 as a minor local controversy and developed into a conflict involving Pope Pius IX. Destructive too was the "military question," a series of disputes between 1883 and 1889 regarding the honor and rights of army officers, which embittered the officer corps and undermined its support of the government. Particularly significant was the struggle over slavery, which slowly declined during the second half of the nineteenth century, hastened by the QUEIROZ LAW of 1850 and the FREE BIRTH LAW of 1871, initiated and supported by the Emperor. The abolitionist movement of the 1880s and the GOLDEN LAW of 1888, sanctioned by Princess Regent Isabel during Pedro's absence in Europe, undoubtedly weakened Pedro's support among the planter class, and this loss of confidence was accentuated in the final months of his reign as the Liberal regime of Visconde Ouro Prêto moved toward the enactment of important social and economic reforms. Pedro fell from power on November 15, 1889, in an almost bloodless coup backed by the Republican party and sailed into permanent exile two days later. Although some abolitionists and monarchists supported his return, Pedro was unwilling to engage in conspiracies or to reassume power without a clear mandate from Brazil. He died in Paris on December 5, 1891.

Bibliography. Robert Conrad, *The Destruction of Brazilian Slavery, 1850–1888,* Berkeley, Calif., and London, 1972; Richard Graham, *Britain and the Onset of Modernization in Brazil, 1850–1914,* London, 1968; C. H. Haring, *Empire in Brazil,* Cambridge, Mass., 1958; Heitor Lyra, *História de Dom Pedro II, 1825–1891,* 3 vols., São Paulo, 1938–40; Anyda Marchant, *Viscount Mauá and the Empire of Brazil,* Berkeley, Calif., 1965; Joaquim Nabuco, *Um Estadista do Império,* 4 vols., São Paulo, 1949; Mary Wilhelmine Williams, *Dom Pedro the Magnanimous, Second Emperor of Brazil,* Chapel Hill, N.C., 1937.

ROBERT CONRAD

PEIXOTO, FLORIANO (1839–1895). President of Brazil (1891–1894). Born in the province of Alagoas, Floriano Peixoto first achieved recognition for bravery in battle during the PARAGUAYAN WAR, emerging in 1869 as a lieutenant colonel. He attained the rank of brigadier general in 1883. A last-minute supporter of the forces that overthrew Emperor PEDRO II in 1889, he became Vice President under President Manuel Deodoro da FONSECA following the establishment of the FIRST REPUBLIC in February 1891. When Deodoro resigned in November 1891, Floriano became President.

After reinstating the Congress dissolved by Deodoro, Floriano deposed all but one of the state governors and replaced them with his men, creating much opposition. The press bitterly attacked the President; civilians voiced fears of a military dictatorship. Responding to nationwide chaos, Floriano ruled with an iron hand, censoring the press and imprisoning or deporting many of his detractors. When a long-standing local dispute in Rio Grande do Sul erupted into full-scale civil war in February 1893, promonarchist naval forces under Adm. Custodio de Melo seized the opportunity and revolted against the Floriano government in September 1893, triggering rebellion throughout the country. Republican forces, heretofore distrustful of the President, united behind Floriano, who crushed both the dissidents in the rebellious states and the naval revolt, which collapsed in May 1894. For his prompt action in restoring peace, Floriano became known as the "Consolidator of the Republic." His power and prestige at their peak, he turned the Presidency over to Brazil's first civilian chief executive, Prudente de MORAIS, on November 15, 1894.

JOHN E. PICHEL

PELADO. Term (literally, "bare" in Spanish) widely used in Spanish America to refer to someone without financial resources, especially one whose pretensions do not correspond to his actual situation. In Mexican literature *pelado* designates a member of the lower classes, particularly one characterized by picturesque language and rustic humor and genius. This usage can be found in the writings of Guillermo PRIETO, Manuel Payno, Luis Inclán, Victoriano Salado Álvarez, and Mariano AZUELA.

The term was given further refinement by the Mexican psychologist Samuel Ramos in *El perfil del hombre y la cultura en México,* 1934 (*Profile of Man and Culture in Mexico*). Treating the *pelado* as a psychological type, Ramos saw his pretensions about his resources and status as symptoms of a deeper malaise. According to Ramos, the *pelado,* suspicious and lacking faith in himself, views the world as conspiring against him; he constructs a fictitious reality in order to live and struggles to maintain it under the threat of exposure. As a result of the ensuing tension he is subject to violent verbal and physical outbursts. "Virility" is an important part of the fiction, and the language of the *pelado* is full of explicitly sexual terms and innuendoes.

ALAN KOVAC

PELÉ (b. EDSON ARANTES DO NASCIMENTO, 1940–). Brazilian soccer star. Pelé was born in Três Corações, Minas Gerais, the son of a minor-league soccer player. He left school after the fourth grade and by the age of ten had become the protégé of Waldemar de Brito, coach of the Bauru, São Paulo, soccer club; at fifteen he was one of the best players on the Bauru club. After being rejected by a São Paulo club, Pelé was hired by the Santos team (for which he has played ever since) and became a star within a year.

Pelé attracted world attention in 1958, when he sparked the Brazilian national team to victory during the World Cup series held in Sweden; two subsequent victories by Brazilian teams (1962, 1970) of which Pelé was a member gave Brazil permanent possession of the Rimet Trophy Cup. Recognizing the passing of his prime, Pelé subsequently announced his withdrawal from the Brazilian team being organized for World Cup competition in 1974. With an annual income of more than $500,000, drawn from salaries, bonuses, advertising fees, and business interests, Pelé remains modest and soft-spoken, permitting neither fame nor wealth to interfere with his family life.

JOSEPH A. ELLIS

PELLEGRINI, CARLOS (1846–1906). President of Argentina (August 6, 1890–October 12, 1892). His father, an engineer, the son of Italians, was born in Savoy four years after it had been ceded to France and arrived in Argentina in 1828. His mother, María Bevans, was a descendant of John Bright. The younger Pellegrini was born and educated in the city of Buenos Aires. His legal studies at the University of Buenos Aires, begun in 1863, were interrupted for about a year by the PARAGUAYAN WAR and by his numerous duties as an employee in the national administration. He went to work in the Ministry of Finance in 1867, and undoubtedly with the support of Vice President Adolfo Alsina, whose partisan he had been since 1860, he held the position of Undersecretary of Finance from 1868 to 1872. In 1869 he received his law degree and joined the editorial staff of the newly founded newspaper *La Prensa*. Three years later, on his third attempt, he was elected to the provincial legislature as a deputy, but he held office only for about a year. In January 1873, he became a congressional deputy for Buenos Aires, a post he held until 1881. He endorsed the candidacy of Alsina for the Presidency in 1874, but another close friend, Nicolás AVELLANEDA, won the election.

Shortly after a trip to Europe in 1876, Pellegrini was forced by the death of Alsina to assume a more prominent role in politics and to strengthen his ties with a childhood friend, Gen. Julio A. ROCA. Together they prevented the breakup of the Partido Autonomista Nacional, and they helped Avellaneda bring about conciliation with the Partido Nacionalista in 1877. In the last months of the Avellaneda administration, Pellegrini succeeded Roca as Minister of War and helped defeat the *porteño* revolution against the federalization of the city of Buenos Aires. In 1881–1882, as a national senator for Buenos Aires, he firmly established his reputation as an expert in economic matters. In 1885 Roca sent him to London and Paris, where he obtained a loan of £8.4 million for the government. Upon his return Roca made him Minister of War.

In 1886 Miguel JUÁREZ CELMAN and Pellegrini, candidates of the Partido Autonomista Nacional, were elected President and Vice President respectively. Within a few years a commercial crisis, the drying up of Argentine credit in Europe, and the secret government emissions of paper money led Pellegrini to withdraw his support of Juárez Celman. He and Roca forced the President to resign in 1890; at the same time they defeated a revolt, led by Leandro ALEM, against the government. As President, Pellegrini successfully endeavored to stabilize the currency and to maintain the credit rating of Argentina in foreign money markets. He founded the Caja de Conversión (Conversion Fund) and the Banco de la Nación Argentina. His policies, together with the growing importance of agricultural exports, helped lay the basis for nearly three decades of economic growth. He failed to achieve some of his other goals, such as greater tolerance for political adversaries and the peaceful solution of political differences.   JOSEPH T. CRISCENTI

PELLICER, CARLOS (1899–   ). Mexican poet. Born in Villahermosa, Tabasco, he served as secretary to José VASCONCELOS and became famous as a museum curator. At first he was connected with the poets of the *Contemporáneos* group but later broke away from them. He is a Catholic and a liberal, and his most important contribution has been his vision of external reality and the Mexican landscape. *Material poético, 1918–1961* (1962) contains most of his work: *Colores en el mar y otros poemas* (1921), *Piedra de sacrificios* (1924), *Seis, siete poemas* (1924), *Hora y 20* (1927), *Camino* (1929), *5 poemas* (1931), and *Práctica de vuelo* (1956). Later volumes are *Con palabras y fuego* (1963) and *Teotihuacán y 13 de agosto: Ruina de Tenochtitlán* (1965).   RACHEL PHILLIPS

PELUCÓN. Nickname, meaning "big wig," first applied to Chilean conservatives (especially the more traditional members of the landed aristocracy) in the 1820s. The term derived from their supposed fondness for the large powdered wigs common in colonial times. The *pelucones* were among the prime movers in the rebellion of 1829–1830 that overthrew the liberal government of the day and introduced the conservative political system associated chiefly with Diego PORTALES.   SIMON COLLIER

PEMEX. *See* PETRÓLEOS MEXICANOS.

PENA (PENNA), AFONSO (AFFONSO) [AUGUSTO MOREIRA] (1847–1909). President of Brazil (1906–1909). A native of Santa Barbara, Minas Gerais, Pena graduated from the São Paulo law school in 1870 and entered politics as a member of the Liberal party. In 1879 he was elected to the imperial Parliament, where he served continuously until the fall of the empire in November 1889. During that decade he held three Cabinet positions and was a member of the parliamentary commission to codify the civil law of Brazil. Returning to Minas Gerais, Pena was elected a state senator and presiding officer of the state constituent assembly (1890–1891). In 1892 he was elected to serve out the unexpired portion of the term of the Governor of Minas Gerais. In that post he was responsible for the law authorizing construction of Belo Horizonte as the new state capital.

Always a staunch supporter of constitutional legitimacy, Pena gave full support to the administration of President Floriano PEIXOTO during the civil war (1893–1894). After leaving the governorship, Pena was president of the Bank of the Republic until 1899 and again state senator until 1903. In the latter year he was elected to complete the term of the deceased Vice President, and in 1906 he became the first man from his state to occupy the Presidency of Brazil. Pena's administration was noted for its protection of coffee prices and for the extension of railroads and the telegraph into the interior of Brazil. He died in office before the expiration of his term.   ROLLIE E. POPPINO

PENA, LUIS CARLOS MARTINS (1815–1848). Brazilian dramatist and diplomat. Born in Rio de Janeiro, he was the creator of the Brazilian theater. He wrote comedies of manners depicting rural and urban customs, some perennially popular, and melodramas that have seldom been produced. The comedies, farcical and satirical in nature, utilize familiar situations and devices such as mistaken identity, disguises, and eavesdropping, but they retain interest because of the freshness of their satire and because of their authentic portrayal of Brazilian characters. They are a valuable record of Brazilian life in the first part of the nineteenth century. *O Juiz de Paz na Roça* was produced in 1838; that year *Antônio José* by Domingos José GONÇALVES DE MAGALHÃES also appeared. Other plays by Martins Pena that are still staged with success are *A Família e a Festa da Roça* (1840), *O Judas em Sábado de Alelúia* (1844), and *Os Irmãos da Almas* (1844). His influence is obvious in all later comic writers of the century, and especially in Joaquim Manuel de MACEDO and Joaquim França Júnior.   RAYMOND S. SAYERS

PEÑARANDA, ENRIQUE (1892–1970). Bolivian army officer and President (1940–1943). Peñaranda was a professional military man. In the latter part of the CHACO WAR he became the commander in chief of the Bolivian forces and in this capacity led them to some of their few last-minute victories. He seems to have played little or no part in the military coups in the closing months of the war and the years immediately afterward. When general elections were called in 1940, a few months after the suicide of President Germán BUSCH, Peñaranda ran as the candidate of the more conservative elements. He won by a large margin over his only opponent, the left-wing sociology professor José Antonio Arze.

Peñaranda had to face the problems resulting from World War II. He also tried to take advantage of the war to further the economic development of the country, albeit on a modest scale. After the Japanese conquest of Malaya, Bolivia was the only Allied source of tin. Hence, the United States sought agreement with Peñaranda for the sale of the country's tin output at relatively low prices that would not inflate the costs of the war. Peñaranda later maintained that he had agreed to such arrangements in part to contribute to the Allied war effort and in part because of promises by President Roosevelt that Bolivia would be compensated after the war for sacrifices it had made during the conflict. Peñaranda also felt the need to settle the question of the former properties of the Standard Oil Company, which had been expropriated by one of his predecessors. An agreement was finally reached on terms of compensation, which Peñaranda later argued provided Standard Oil with less than the value of its installations. This arrangement was facilitated by loans from the Export-Import Bank of Washington to the government of Bolivia.

The downfall of Peñaranda was provoked in part by the CATAVI MASSACRE, a bloody clash between striking tin miners and the armed forces in December 1942, which aroused a storm of indignation and considerably strengthened the opposition, particularly the MOVIMIENTO NACIONALISTA REVOLUCIONARIO (MNR). The MNR entered into a conspiracy with discontented younger military men that led, in December 1943, to the ouster of Peñaranda.

ROBERT J. ALEXANDER

PENINSULAR. In colonial Spanish America a native of the Iberian Peninsula, that is, a Spaniard. The term was used to distinguish European-born Spaniards from American-born whites of Spanish origin. *See also* CHAPETÓN; CREOLE; GACHUPÍN.

In Brazil a native of the Kingdom of Portugal was called a *reinól* (plural, *reinões*).

PENNA, AFFONSO. *See* PENA, AFONSO.

PEON. Word (Spanish *peón*) applied widely in Spanish America to any unskilled laborer, particularly in rural areas. The term is used more specifically to refer to an individual living in the condition of debt peonage. Where peonage exists, debts incurred by landless hacienda workers are used by the landowner as a means of retaining their services. A worker might incur a debt by obtaining a loan or an advance on his wages from the landowner in order to cover an extraordinary expense, such as the baptism of a child or participation in a religious fiesta. The landowner, supported by the law or by his influence in the locality, may then oblige the worker to remain in his service until the debt is paid. Since it is unlikely that the worker will ever be able to pay off his debt, the landowner is assured of inexpensive labor for an indefinite period of time, a consideration of great importance where manpower is scarce. Although there are many gaps in the study of peonage, the institution has been traced to the seventeenth and eighteenth centuries in Mexico and Andean South America. Peonage survived in many countries until the twentieth century.

HELEN DELPAR

PERALTA AZURDIA, ENRIQUE (1908–   ). Guatemalan army officer and President. Peralta seized power from Miguel YDÍGORAS FUENTES on March 30, 1963. His rightist military dictatorship continued until the end of June 1966. Moving to thwart the subversion he believed imminent, Peralta declared martial law, suspended the constitution, and banned political activity. When he considered the situation safe, he restored constitutional guarantees and permitted a constituent assembly to draft a new constitution that took effect in September 1965.

The activity of guerrilla bands was the principal threat to Peralta. Bombings, kidnappings, assaults, and assassinations in the capital and forays in the mountains of Izabal and Zacapa constantly challenged the government. Peralta maintained an anti-United States posture throughout his administration. He was careful, however, not to endanger ALLIANCE FOR PROGRESS funds, which were restored after newly inaugurated President Lyndon B. Johnson recognized his government on the basis of his promise to hold elections. Peralta did, however, refuse United States military aid in dealing with the rebels.

Peralta announced elections for March 1966. He backed one military officer, the old party of Carlos CASTILLO ARMAS supported another, and the leftist Revolutionary party (PR) backed its civilian leader Mario Méndez Montenegro. When Méndez was assassinated in October 1965, the PR immediately nominated his brother, Julio César MÉNDEZ MONTENEGRO. The guerrilla factions were divided over the expediency of participating in the elections, and Guatemalan Labor (Communist) party expatriates from Mexico came to reconcile the rift; in early March 1966, twenty-six of them were captured and shot. In a free election, with guerrilla support, Méndez won a surprising plurality of the votes, and on May 5 Congress elected him.

WILLIAM J. GRIFFITH

PERALTA BARNUEVO [Y ROCHA], PEDRO DE (1663–1743). Peruvian savant. Peralta, one of the leading intellectual figures of viceregal Peru, was born in Lima, where he spent his entire life. He received degrees in Roman and canonical law and the arts at the University of San Marcos and demonstrated a remarkable mastery of classical and modern languages; his first published poem was written in Greek. He was also knowledgeable in mathematics, medicine, the natural sciences, and engineering. In 1709 he occupied the chair of mathematics at San Marcos and was given the title Chief Cosmographer and Chief Engineer of Peru. Later, in 1715, he became rector of the university, where he helped end corrupt practices.

Because of the menace of pirates and foreign invaders along the coast of Peru, Peralta wrote *Lima inexpugnable* (1740), in which he dealt with the need for better defenses for the city. His interest and research in metallurgy resulted in *Arte o cartilla del nuevo beneficio de la plata en todo género de metales fríos o calientes* (1738). In addition, he submitted articles on astronomy to the French Academy of Sciences and published a small volume entitled *Observationes astronomicae* (1717).

Of his projected monumental history of Spain, only the first volume, *Historia de España vindicada* (1730), was published. Peralta's fame as a poet rests mainly on his long epic *Lima fundada o La conquista del Perú* (1732), in which he recounts the deeds of Francisco PIZARRO. He also wrote poems in Italian and French, as well as several dramatic pieces, including *Triunfos de amor y poder* (1710) and *Afectos vencen finezas* (1720). His best-known play is *La Rodoguna* (1708?), an adaptation of Corneille's *Rodogune*. In 1738 he published *La pasión y triunfo de Cristo,* a collection of prayers or meditations for which he was summoned before the Inquisition, where the matter was later dropped (*see* INQUISITION, HOLY OFFICE OF THE). For the most part, Peralta's works mark the apex of the baroque-rococo style.

DANIEL R. REEDY

PEREIRA DE SOUSA, WASHINGTON LUIS (1870–1957). President of Brazil (1926–1930). Born in the state of Rio de Janeiro, Washington Luis was graduated from law school in São Paulo in 1891. After serving as president of a municipal council, deputy in the São Paulo legislature, and Governor of that powerful coffee state, he was elected President of Brazil in 1926.

The new President inherited a relatively stable political and economic situation. He suspended the state of siege established during the previous administration and restored press freedom. Aided by all-time high coffee sales, he embarked upon an ambitious program of road building, notably the construction of the Rio de Janeiro–São Paulo highway. His policy of monetary stabilization helped strengthen public finances; budgets were kept in balance. However, the worldwide depression of 1929 wrecked his economic program and left Brazil with a massive coffee surplus in the face of falling prices. São Paulo planters clamored for a federal guarantee of coffee prices, and when Washington Luis refused to take such action, he alienated many of his staunchest supporters.

In this unstable atmosphere the 1930 presidential succession question arose. Politicians in the large states of Rio Grande do Sul and Minas Gerais opposed Washington Luis's choice of a successor, Governor Júlio Prestes of São Paulo, and nominated Governor Getúlio VARGAS of Rio Grande as the candidate of the new Liberal Alliance. On March 1, 1930, in an election filled with corruption on both sides, Prestes was elected President, with the opposition claiming fraud. On October 3, 1930, an opposition revolution broke out in Minas Gerais, Rio Grande do Sul, and Paraíba. Wishing to avoid a potentially bloody civil war, high-ranking officers deposed the President, im-

prisoned him, and, after a brief delay, turned the Presidency over to Getúlio Vargas. With Washington Luis's overthrow, the FIRST REPUBLIC came to an end. Sent into exile, the ex-President lived in the United States and Europe before returning to Brazil in 1946.

JOHN E. PICHEL

PÉREZ, CARLOS ANDRÉS (1922–   ). President of Venezuela (1974–   ). A native of the Andean state of Táchira and the son of a coffee grower, Pérez is a long-time member of ACCIÓN DEMOCRÁTICA and a close associate of ex-President Rómulo BETANCOURT. Exiled from Venezuela during the dictatorship of Marcos PÉREZ JIMÉNEZ, Pérez served as Minister of the Interior during Betancourt's administration (1959–1964), becoming known for his strong stand against leftist terrorists and guerrillas. In the presidential election held on December 9, 1973, Pérez won an impressive 48.6 percent of the vote in a field of twelve candidates, while his closest rival, Lorenzo Fernández of the ruling COMITÉ DE ORGANIZACIÓN POLÍTICA ELECTORAL INDEPENDIENTE (COPEI), trailed by nearly 500,000 votes. Pérez took office in March 1974 for a five-year term.

HELEN DELPAR

PÉREZ, JOSÉ JOAQUÍN (1801–1889). President of Chile (1861–1871). After a short period in the infant Chilean diplomatic service, Pérez entered politics as a member of the Chamber of Deputies. He first attained ministerial rank in 1844, during the administration of Manuel BULNES. In the Presidency of Manuel MONTT he served as senator and Councillor of State. As a member of Montt's National party but known for his moderate views, Pérez proved to be the ideal politician to replace the controversial Antonio VARAS as the government candidate in the 1861 presidential election. His inauguration marked a decisive shift in Chilean politics, a shift symbolized by the notable amnesty law of October 1861. The political atmosphere now became a great deal more relaxed. Pérez himself was neither as inflexible nor as energetic as his predecessor. In 1862 he dispensed with the support of the National party and called the opposition Liberal-Conservative fusion into the government. The fusion naturally won a handsome majority at the congressional elections of 1864 and backed Pérez to the end of his administration. At the end of Pérez's first term Chile briefly went to war with Spain. A Spanish naval squadron bombarded Valparaíso for three hours on March 31, 1866.

SIMON COLLIER

PÉREZ JIMÉNEZ, MARCOS (1914–   ). Venezuelan army officer and President (1952–1953, 1953–1958). A product of the professional military schools and the new military attitudes cultivated by the regime of Juan Vicente GÓMEZ, Pérez Jiménez graduated from the Escuela Militar de Venezuela in 1934 and went to Peru for more specialized military training. By 1945, when Pérez Jiménez first participated in national party politics in the movement to depose Gen. Isaías MEDINA ANGARITA, he had taught a number of courses on military subjects in the military academies of Peru and Venezuela. Raised to the rank of major, he began in 1946 a series of visits to the United States, Mexico, Argentina, Peru, Bolivia, and Chile, where he collected a number of military honors and decorations. This active and successful military career prepared him to assume the central role in the military junta that replaced the first ACCIÓN DEMOCRÁTICA (AD) government of Rómulo GALLEGOS in 1948. In 1950, after the assassination of the President of the junta, Lieut. Col. Carlos Delgado Chalbaud, Pérez Jiménez moved gradually to dominate the junta until in 1952 he was made provisional President of the republic. In 1953 the Congress made him constitutional President.

Pérez Jiménez's regime earned the reputation of being one of the most repressive in Venezuela's history. His elaborate police and spy organization hunted out dissident intellectuals, students, and politicians. The shaky peace thus established allowed him to carry out his development program, which consisted of the construction of huge public works in the city of Caracas, the encouragement of a massive immigration of Spaniards, Portuguese, and Italians to Caracas (*see* IMMIGRATION: VENEZUELA), the development of a fledgling iron and steel industry (*see* IRON AND STEEL INDUSTRY: VENEZUELA), and the studied neglect of the rural sections of agricultural Venezuela. With none of the finesse of his more able predecessor Gómez, Pérez Jiménez soon exasperated even his natural allies by his arbitrary actions and corrupt administration. In December 1957 he held a plebiscite to decide whether he should continue in office and announced the results before the votes could have been counted. In January 1958 a coalition of political parties, business groups, the Catholic Church, and elements of the armed forces forced him to flee the country for a comfortable exile in the United States. Extradited to answer charges of peculation and corruption, he spent a long time awaiting trial and arguing his case. Finally he was sentenced to a short term and then sent into exile again in 1969. He nevertheless managed to win a seat in the 1969 congressional elections, although the courts refused him permission to take it. His political popularity, especially in Caracas, had grown to such an extent in 1972 that he was seriously considered a possible candidate for the presidential elections of 1973, but he was barred from seeking the Presidency by a constitutional amendment.

JOHN V. LOMBARDI

PERMANENT COUNCIL. Organ of the ORGANIZATION OF AMERICAN STATES, directly responsible to the General Assembly. In the amended OAS Charter, ratified in 1970, some of the Council's major functions were transferred to other bodies. Others are still in the process of being clearly defined.

The Permanent Council is composed of representatives, with the rank of ambassador, from each of the member states. A chairman presides over the Council for a six-month term; the office rotates among the representatives, following the alphabetical order in Spanish of the names of their respective countries. The Permanent Council has the authority to act as the provisional Organ of Consultation in case of an armed attack within the territory of an American state (*see* RIO TREATY). It is also authorized to assist the member states in the peaceful settlement of disputes; in the performance of this function, it is aided by the INTER-AMERICAN COMMITTEE ON PEACEFUL SETTLEMENT, which is a subsidiary organ of the Council. The Council also takes cognizance of any matters referred to it by

the two higher OAS organs, the General Assembly and the Meeting of Consultation of Ministers of Foreign Affairs. Among the functions it no longer performs are determining the financial contributions of the member states and preparing the budget of the OAS. In addition, two of the three organs previously subordinate to the Council, the INTER-AMERICAN ECONOMIC AND SOCIAL COUNCIL and the Inter-American Cultural Council (now the INTER-AMERICAN COUNCIL FOR EDUCATION, SCIENCE, AND CULTURE), have become autonomous bodies coequal with the Council. The third organ, the Inter-American Council of Jurists, has been abolished, and its functions transferred to the Inter-American Juridical Committee.

RODNEY D. ANDERSON

PERNAMBUCAN REVOLUTION. Unsuccessful republican revolt in the captaincy of Pernambuco, Brazil, in 1817. Although the city of Recife in Pernambuco was prospering as a result of the opening of Brazilian ports to ships of all nations in 1808 by JOÃO VI, Brazilians there felt that the Portuguese benefited most from the increase in trade. Resentment against the government further contributed to anti-Portuguese sentiment, for Brazilians believed that provincial officials were inept and corrupt and that Pernambuco did not receive adequate attention from the capital. The influence of the Masons and clergy in promoting republican ideas was also apparent.

After receiving warnings of an impending revolt, the Governor ordered the arrest of the suspected leaders on March 6, 1817. The resistance of army officers who were members of the conspiracy led to the premature outbreak of a full-scale revolt and the expulsion of the Governor. The rebels instituted a provisional government for their new republic, consisting of five representatives, one from each of the important elements of the captaincy: clergy, merchants, planters, military, and judiciary. To gain support, the leaders raised military pay while abolishing revenue taxes. They invited neighboring captaincies to join them, and Paraíba, Rio Grande do Norte, and Alagoas did so. After news of the revolution spread to Bahia, its governor, the Conde dos Arcos, took the first stringent measures against it by sending troops overland and ships to blockade the port. When Rio de Janeiro learned of the revolution on March 25, the populace as a whole, whether Brazilian or Portuguese, backed João fervently, offering equipment and money to support an expedition or volunteering to serve in it. The revolution was thoroughly crushed in May, and severe reprisals, including executions and confiscation of property, were taken against those involved or suspected of complicity.

L. SHARON WYATT

PERÓN, [MARÍA] EVA [DUARTE DE] (1919–1952). First lady of Argentina (1946–1952). The second wife of Juan D. PERÓN, Evita Perón became one of the most formidable political figures in modern Argentina because of her ability to identify herself with and capitalize on the aspirations of the Argentine working class. A one-time radio and motion-picture actress, she was the mistress of the widowed Perón for eighteen months before marrying him on October 22, 1945. Rejected by and rejecting Argentina's social elite, she worked indefatigably to convert herself into a symbol of the *descamisados* (shirtless ones) and to ensure their allegiance to Perón (*see* PERONISM). Greatly expanding the role traditionally accorded to Presidents' wives, she spearheaded the movement for woman suffrage, organized a women's division of the Peronist party, centralized the country's social welfare services under her control through the Eva Perón Foundation, and acted as a mediator between labor unions and the government. A veto by Perón's military supporters prevented her candidacy for the Vice Presidency in 1951.

An imposing mythology has been forged around her figure. She has been elevated by Peronists to popular sainthood, immune from criticism. On the other hand, an antimyth stresses her early career as an entertainer, her "resentment," her financial irresponsibility, and her "fanaticism." Her symbolic role even after death is shown by the removal of her remains from Argentina after Perón's ouster and their secret burial in Italy. In 1971 they were returned to the exiled dictator. Overshadowing the uses to which she has been put is the fact that her picture is prominently displayed in innumerable Argentine homes.

NOREEN F. STACK

PERÓN, JUAN D[OMINGO] (1895–   ). President of Argentina (1946–1955, 1973–   ); dominant political figure of its contemporary era. Born in the province of Buenos Aires into a rural middle-class family that combined Italian and Spanish-creole antecedents, Perón spent part of his youth in isolated PATAGONIA before entering the Military Academy in 1911. His thirty-two-year military career before his emergence as a political figure was highlighted by athletic championships, the authorship of military histories and armed forces manuals, command of mountain troops in the Andes, and a tour of duty in Italy. The fact that these activities occurred during a time when the Argentine Army was acquiring an increasing sense of responsibility for the country's future in addition to its purely military concerns provided a consistent framework for Perón's political career. Thus the series of events that culminated in his election as President began in 1943, when he organized the GRUPO DE OFICIALES UNIDOS, a military lodge designed to spread a particular sense of mission within the Army.

If Perón shared his fellow officers' commitment to Argentina's need for self-development, in the wake of the 1943 coup that overthrew Ramón S. CASTILLO he displayed an outstanding perception of the sociopolitical circumstances of the country. Convinced of the need for a mass base for the new government, committed to a national unity based on a balancing of various interest groups, and concerned with securing his own position in the power struggle within the government, Perón focused his attempts to realize his goals in the National Labor Department, which he took over in October 1943. *See also* CONFEDERACIÓN GENERAL DE TRABAJO.

Perón's position was consolidated by subsequent appointments as Minister of War, Vice President, and President of the Postwar Council, established in August 1945 to plan the protection of Argentina's economy in the post-World War II era. However, increasing opposition within the armed forces to his growing dominance led to his removal from all offices on October 9, 1945. Threatened with a loss of the gains

they had achieved through Perón, workers staged a massive demonstration on October 17 that convinced the military of the necessity of his return and led directly to his presidential candidacy in the elections of February 1946. Opposed by a coalition formed by all of Argentina's major political parties actively supported by Spruille BRADEN, former American Ambassador to Argentina and now Assistant Secretary of State for Inter-American Affairs, Perón relied on a loosely knit grouping of the newly formed Labor party, dissident Radicals (*see* RADICAL PARTY: ARGENTINA), and political independents. After a campaign in which he pledged economic nationalism, social justice, and the protection of national sovereignty, he was elected in the cleanest elections since 1916.

Perón's attempts at consolidating his control during the next three years were eased by Argentina's strong financial position resulting from the war and its aftermath. Using accumulated reserves, he purchased the country's railroads from their British owners. Relying on the devastation of Eastern European grain fields, he established the Argentine Institute for Trade Promotion (IAPI), which, acting as a middleman between Argentine producers and European buyers, sought as a single seller to maximize Argentine profits and redirect them into the industrial sector. At the same time general prosperity allowed Perón to continue policies of wage increases and expanded fringe benefits for workers.

Perón's ability to fulfill his campaign promises in

Juan D. Perón. [*Organization of American States*]

turn facilitated his extension of political control. Great advances were made in the organization of labor, not only by expanding existing unions but also by organizing previously neglected internal migrants. Parallel to Perón's attempts to eliminate opposition within the labor movement was the tighter organization of his political supporters by the establishment of the Peronist party. As in the case of labor, Perón's wife Eva PERÓN made an important contribution as head of the Women's Peronist party set up after the enfranchisement of women in 1947. Neither Perón nor his political opponents valued the concept of a loyal opposition, and his political astuteness, the general sense of accomplishment in Argentina during these years, and the ineptness of the anti-Peronist forces combined to make these forces increasingly ineffective.

As these political successes were being formalized in the 1949 constitution and Perón's doctrine of justicialism (*see* PERONISM), the country's economic outlook weakened. The redirection of resources toward industrialization had been only partially successful. Although the consumer goods industry boomed (by 1955 it would supply 99 percent of Argentina's needs), little had been done to lay the basis for heavy industry. Furthermore, with war-accumulated credits spent, Argentina was dependent on agricultural production to garner foreign exchange. However, agriculture had declined. Farmers, resentful of IAPI's pincer squeeze, had curtailed production; both money and men had fled the countryside. Two years of severe drought aggravated the crisis.

Perón responded on various levels. He dismissed his original economic team and stressed agricultural production in a Second Five-Year Plan. Foreign investment was encouraged, and an Export-Import Bank credit was arranged. At the same time Perón curtailed public expenditures and urged workers to increase productivity.

Accompanying these attempts at economic retrenchment were steps toward the bureaucratization of both labor and the Peronist party. Loyalty to Perón became a primary value. In the increasing use of symbolism and ritual Eva Perón was a key figure. Identifying Perón with the nation and herself with the workers, she sought to strengthen the bonds between the two.

Perón's emphasis on organization, derived from his military background, was heightened by these economic and political developments as well as by the successful foiling of an anti-Peronist coup in 1951, Eva Perón's death in 1952, and the initiation of his second term as President the same year. Secure politically and considering labor's position to be consolidated, Perón turned to a more generalized and more broadly extrapolitical organization of society. Thus the Confederación General Económica (CGE), representing small business interests, was set up, and attempts at national conciliation were made through efforts to attract former political opponents. Most important, however, was a growing concentration on the mobilization of youth. Both confident and bored after nearly a decade of political success, Perón had become increasingly preoccupied with ensuring his place in the country's history. In youth he saw an opportunity to project the continuation of the "new" Argentina into the future.

At this point, however, a serious communications breakdown occurred between Perón and the people. His inability to overcome the animosities formed during his earlier consolidation of power had the effect of increasing the importance of loyalty as the first criterion in the selection of Peronist elites. The fact that loyalty to the regime seemed the only conspicuous virtue displayed by many Peronist leaders served further to isolate Perón and to increase his vulnerability to charges of corruption and immorality in the regime. In these circumstances the disadvantages of Perón's tactical emphasis on maneuverability became obvious. Unable to impress Argentines with the overall consistency of his policies, he appeared instead to have abandoned the workers, to have categorically embraced economic liberalism, and in general to have proved long-standing anti-Peronist charges of opportunism. Increasingly frustrated, Perón proved unable to control either a conflict in 1954–1955 with the Catholic Church over clerical intromission into politics or a controversy in 1955 over oil contracts with North American companies. The final result of this process was the neutralization, if not alienation, of large segments of the population. In September 1955 the military, threatened by Perón's seeming acquiescence in the establishment of workers' militias, was able to topple his government.

In exile Perón continued to influence Argentine politics. The unwillingness of post-1955 governments to accept Peronists on an equal footing with other sectors of society converted Perón into a living myth and assured him great flexibility in conducting from afar an increasingly diverse movement. Hence, the willingness of the government of Alejandro LANUSSE to end Perón's forced exile presented a dilemma, for however much Perón might look forward to the "great return," once inside the country his options would be circumscribed.

The Lanusse government allowed Perón to return to Argentina in November 1972 for a short stay, but his authentic homecoming did not take place until June 20, 1973, several weeks after the inauguration of Peronist President Héctor J. CÁMPORA. An estimated 2 million persons gathered near the Ezeiza Airport to welcome Perón, but the reception was marred by gun battles between rival Peronist groups that left at least twenty persons dead; Perón's plane, meanwhile, was diverted to another airport. The following day he urged his followers to end their feuding.

As strife continued, Cámpora resigned on July 13 to enable new presidential elections to be held in September, with Perón as the candidate of his party. On August 4, the Peronist party duly nominated Perón and his wife Isabel as its presidential and vice-presidential candidates. In the election held on September 23, Perón won more than 60 percent of the vote, running well ahead of his closest rival, the Radical Ricardo Balbín. Perón took office on October 12.

Bibliography. Robert J. Alexander, *The Perón Era,* New York, 1951; Joseph Barager (ed.), *Why Perón Came to Power,* New York, 1968; Fritz L. Hoffman, "Perón and After," part I, *Hispanic American Historical Review,* vol. XXXVI, 1956, pp. 510–528; part II, ibid., vol. XXXIX, 1959, pp. 213–333; Félix Luna, *El 45,* Buenos Aires, 1969; Jorge Abelardo Ramos, *Revolución y contrarevolución en la Argentina,* Buenos Aires, 1961; Arthur P. Whitaker, *Argentine Upheaval: Perón's Fall and the New Regime,* New York, 1956.

NOREEN F. STACK

PERONISM. Argentine sociopolitical movement centering on the figure of Juan D. PERÓN. Simply stated, the significance of Peronism rests in the fact that it provided the vehicle by which the Argentine working class became an undeniable power factor in society. In this respect it is most clearly reflected in the transformation of the term used to describe Perón's working-class followers, *descamisados* (shirtless ones), from one of denigration to one of pride. However, although this may signify what happened, how it happened is fundamental to an understanding of the movement's complexity and diversity.

As World War II was terminated in Europe, Argentina entered the second decade of a process that had worked fundamental, if not readily perceptible, changes in society. Politically, electoral fraud had been so extensive that disillusionment with liberal democracy was increasing. Socially, in response to the Depression and later to the industrial development encouraged by the war, there was occurring a vast population shift that would uproot masses of Argentines from the interior and relocate them in the more highly developed littoral. Economically, while the maintenance of Argentina's position in the world market had seemed to require extensive concessions to foreign demands, such as the ROCA-RUNCIMAN TREATY, these in turn, supplemented by the impact of the war, led to a nationalistic reaction, particularly in the Army. Juan Perón emerged from the Army as a charismatic leader, manipulating and satisfying this new configuration of forces.

From the outset Peronism was a coalition of various groups: sectors of the Army concerned with the unity and security of the nation in the broadest terms; nationalists of the left and right who were determined to withstand North American and British imperialist pressures; "new" industrialists seeking the development of their nascent industries; both organized and unorganized labor attempting to correct their differing degrees of marginality from power structures; and, finally, any number of "unclassifiable" citizens disillusioned with the corruption, venality, hollow verbosity, and drifting that dominated the country. In consolidating his support from these groups, Perón successfully isolated oppositionist forces and gained ascendancy both within and among various sectors by appearing to be at worst the less objectionable of two alternatives. Within this coalition, however, during the first six years of Perón's political activity (1943–1949), the position occupied by labor seemed outstanding. Because of both the number of people involved and their previous lack of direct access to the government, the economic and psychological gains this sector achieved were impressive.

Two events of 1949, the constitutional revision and Perón's formal elucidation of the Peronist philosophy of justicialism, clarify the kind of relationship that existed between Perón and labor and the way he envisioned the Peronist movement as a whole. The Peronist constitution institutionalized labor's gains. Thus, these advances were not simply gifts bestowed by Perón; instead, they had become constitutionally sanctioned rights of the worker. The 1949 document formalized other socioeconomic preoccupations of Peronism, such as the social function of property and capital, the rights of the elderly and the family, the right to education, and the state's right to intervene in the economy and to control natural resources. However, it did not attempt to overturn completely the

country's past traditions; rather, it preserved intact most of the juridical structures of the 1853 constitution (*see* CONSTITUTION OF 1853: ARGENTINA).

If the constitution provided Peronism with a link to the past, Perón's address outlining justicialism represented a bridge to the future. According to Perón, two pairs of opposing forces were constantly struggling for supremacy in society: idealism and materialism, individualism and collectivism. Each of the four elements had a legitimate role to play, but the ascendancy of any one or combination of two resulted in tyranny. Justicialism, or the third position, sought a balance that was not static and centrist but dynamic and fluid.

The substance of what Perón said was not new. Balanced unity as a goal and tactical maneuverability as a means had been the underpinnings of Peronism since its inception. What was seen here was a shift of emphasis. On one level, an immediate one, it paralleled the constitution in its attempt to legitimize the Peronist program. At the same time it inaugurated a new phase of Peronism. Labor, as the most disadvantaged element at the onset of Peronism, had merited special consideration. Now stronger and better organized with its position consolidated, it could enter into the balance of the "new" Argentina on an equal footing with other sectors.

The final years of Peronism in power were marked by Perón's attention to the organization of society on a broader scale. With this came the conversion of the Peronist philosophy into the "national doctrine." When Perón could not make this leap into belief plausible to Argentines, his government was overthrown in 1955 and Peronism became an oppositionist force.

Peronism in opposition exhibited both parallels with its past and variations on it imposed by changing times and circumstances. By far the most consistent element was Perón's tactical approach. Thus, he sought to control the movement by maintaining himself as the ultimate arbiter. Moreover, no person, faction, or sector was allowed to gain such prominence that he or it could either dominate or secede from the movement as a whole.

The variations stemmed from factors both internal and external to Peronism. Of those arising from within Peronism, the most fundamental had roots dating to the period 1943–1955. Perón created the Peronist party. He did not create the Argentine labor movement. And it was Peronized labor that proved both the most resistant to efforts by post-1955 governments to neutralize the Argentine working class as a power factor and the most difficult for Perón to maintain under his complete control. Labor, then, produced the mainstream of the neo-Peronist movement.

Primary among the external factors that contributed to the modifications of Peronism was the refusal of post-1955 governments to regard Peronism as a legitimate force in society. It was this "illegitimacy," added to the aura of martyrdom surrounding Perón, that fostered the identification of revolutionary youth groups with Peronism.

When elections were held in March 1973 after seven years of military rule, the Peronist candidate, Dr. Héctor J. CÁMPORA, won and, on May 25, was inaugurated as President. However, strife within the Peronist movement made his tenure difficult, and he resigned on July 13 to enable Perón himself to run for the Presidency in new elections. He won the election by a land-slide, but as he took office on October 12, it was by no means clear that he would be able or indeed willing to satisfy all the aspirations of his variegated following.

Bibliography. George Blanksten, *Perón's Argentina,* Chicago, 1953; Antonio Cafiero, *Cinco años después,* Buenos Aires, 1961; Gonzalo H. Cárdenas et al., *El peronismo,* Buenos Aires, 1969; Alberto Ciria, *Perón y justicialismo,* Buenos Aires, 1971; Carlos S. Fayt, *La naturaleza del peronismo,* Buenos Aires, 1967; Gino Germani, *Política y sociedad en una época de transición,* Buenos Aires, 1962; Peter Ranis, "*Peronismo* without Perón," *Journal of Inter-American Studies,* vol. VIII, no. 1, January 1966, pp. 112–128.

NOREEN F. STACK

PERSHING PUNITIVE EXPEDITION. A military ex-pedition initially composed of 4,800 American troops under the command of Gen. John J. Pershing, it was sent into Mexico on March 15, 1916, in pursuit of the Mexican revolutionary leader Francisco (Pancho) VILLA. Villa and his followers had been responsible for the murder of seventeen American mining engineers in Santa Ysabel, Sonora, on January 10, 1916, and for a raid on the border town of Columbus, New Mexico, on March 9, 1916. Seventeen Americans were killed, and parts of the town were burned during the raid. The *villista* depredations were the result of Villa's resent-ment at the decision of President Wilson to extend American recognition to the government of Villa's rival, Venustiano CARRANZA, in 1915.

Pershing was ordered to disperse the *villistas,* but his movements were restricted by Carranza, who re-sented the American presence on Mexican soil. On April 12, 1916, Pershing's men skirmished with Mex-ican civilians and soldiers at Hidalgo del Parral, Chi-huahua, killing about forty Mexicans. On June 21, twelve American soldiers were killed and twenty-four captured by Mexican troops at Carrizal, Chihuahua. Despite American outrage over the Carrizal incident, Wilson followed a policy of restraint because of the threat of American involvement in World War I.

A commission of Mexican and American members met in New London, Connecticut, on September 6, 1916, to negotiate a settlement. Although Carranza rejected a formula reached by the commissioners for the withdrawal of the troops, Wilson decided to remove them, and the soldiers began to leave Mexico on Feb-ruary 5, 1917.

RICHARD B. GRAY

PERU (NEW CASTILE), VICEROYALTY OF. In colonial Spanish America, a political unit that included all present-day Spanish South America except the coast of Venezuela. The Viceroyalty of Peru was established in 1542. The territories of modern Colombia, Ecuador, and Panama were detached from its jurisdiction in 1739, as were the territories of modern Argentina, Uru-guay, Paraguay, and eastern Bolivia in 1776.

Considered Spain's most precious New World pos-session because of its mineral wealth, Peru was also the most difficult to govern. Enormous distances and extraordinarily rough terrain greatly limited its effec-tive control. There remained traces of divisiveness and insubordination, a possible legacy of the colony's tur-bulent beginnings. The lust for wealth and profit, fed by the mines, contributed to the harsh exploitation of the native population, which had been only belatedly, and even then poorly, Christianized and Hispanicized. The very location of Lima on the Pacific coast, while sug-gesting a commercial entrepôt between highland Peru and Spain, made communication with the home govern-ment extremely time-consuming. Nevertheless, colo-nial Peru enjoyed fairly high cultural attainments: beau-tiful public buildings, churches and monasteries, ed-ucational institutions that produced their quota of learned men, chroniclers and scholars, poets and artists, mystics and even saints.

Late-eighteenth-century efforts by the crown to in-stitute needed reforms in the viceroyalty met with con-siderable resistance and limited success. In 1780 the long suffering of the Indians was interrupted momen-tarily by a violent and tragic rebellion led by José Ga-briel Condorcanqui TUPAC AMARU, a probable descen-dant of the last Inca (*see* INCAS). Because of these many circumstances Peru was slow to experience a sense of national identity and remained the last bastion of loy-alty to Spain in continental America.

NORMAN MEIKLEJOHN

PERU-BOLIVIA CONFEDERATION. In 1836 Bo-livian President Andrés SANTA CRUZ exploited politi-cal divisions in Peru to gain control of the country and to bring into reality his dream of a Peru-Bolivia Con-federation. This Confederation, which represented in part Santa Cruz's desire to revive the Inca imperial ideal (*see* INCAS), met with the immediate opposition of Argentina and Chile. The latter was especially worried by the Confederation's threat to its strategic and eco-nomic interests. Strategically the Confederation could reduce Chile to a second-rate Pacific power; economi-cally it endangered Chile's trade relations, especially in view of Santa Cruz's plan of making Arica, Cobija, Callao, and Paita free ports in the direct trade with Europe. Santa Cruz had imposed heavy tariffs on all goods from Europe that touched other Pacific ports before reaching any Confederation port. This obviously represented a direct threat to the merchant class of Chile and to the bustling port of Valparaíso. Diego PORTALES, the dictator of Chile and himself a mer-chant, brought Chile into war against the Confedera-tion in 1836 and was followed a year later by Argentina, although the latter played only a minor role in the con-flict.

In spite of Santa Cruz's strenuous attempts to avoid war, Chile invaded Peru, first unsuccessfully in 1837 and then again in 1838. The latter invasion, assisted by Peruvian exiles, occurred at a time of growing discon-tent, especially in the northern region of Peru, which had never been an enthusiastic supporter of Santa Cruz. At the Battle of Yungay in 1839 the Confederation's army was defeated by the combined Chilean-Peruvian forces. The defeat was accompanied by rebellions in the north of Peru, in Lima, and eventually in Bolivia itself. Santa Cruz was forced to flee, and the Confed-eration came to an end, with Chile the major bene-ficiary of its dissolution.

ORAZIO A. CICCARELLI

PERU CURRENT. *See* HUMBOLDT CURRENT.

PERU SINCE 1826. Peru's national history has fre-quently been viewed as a continuing effort by a power-ful oligarchy, aided by the armed forces, to suppress the large and inert masses. While this dualistic view may be applied accurately to nineteenth-century Peruvian society, it fails to appreciate the important economic and social developments of the last seventy years. The rise of a middle class and of a labor movement and the growing consciousness evidenced by the peasants and the urban masses have noticeably altered the nature of Peruvian life.

Nineteenth century. Peru emerged from the wars of independence economically bankrupt and politically divided. The mines were ruined, and the end of Spanish mercantilism had brought few benefits to a country removed from convenient trade routes. Politically, the usual liberal-conservative struggles plagued the nation. At the same time, military *caudillos,* laying moral claim to political authority, took advantage of divisions among the civilian elite to gain power. As a result, between 1826 and 1895 eighteen military *caudillos* ruled the nation. They presided over a long series of civil wars, several international conflicts (with Colombia, Bolivia, and Chile), and an attempted confederation with Bolivia (1836–1839). To be sure, they were on the whole honorable and patriotic men, but most of them were ill equipped to rule. The most notable exception was Ramón CASTILLA, a mestizo who for nearly two decades (1845–1862) provided the nation with forceful and progressive government. *See* MARSHALS OF AYACUCHO; PERU-BOLIVIA CONFEDERATION.

Military domination did not, of course, imply a threat to the status quo. The *caudillos* sought the support of the landed aristocracy (some even entered its ranks) and in return protected its basic economic interests. Certainly, aspirations for social reform pervaded some liberal circles. However, a social revolution was not advocated, and none took place. In fact, in spite of liberal legislation to combat it, the colonial structure of *latifundismo,* based on the servile labor of the masses, became more deeply entrenched, although the membership of the oligarchy changed during the nineteenth and twentieth centuries. One example of misguided liberal legislation was Simón BOLÍVAR's decree (1824) breaking up Indian communities in order to create in Peru a nation of small farmers. However admirable, the decree, supported by the liberals, led to the despoilment of entire Indian communities and to both the creation of new haciendas and the enlargement of existing ones.

Even the economic windfall that came to Peru through the sale of GUANO beginning in the 1840s ultimately strengthened the oligarchy, although it also engendered new economic interests. As a potent fertilizer in great demand in Europe, guano generated large quantities of revenue, which was employed by various administrations in an attempt to bring peace and progress to Peru. For example, Castilla, whose regimes coincided with the first twenty years of the guano craze, spent approximately $23 million on projects beneficial to every social class, but particularly the landed oligarchy. Castilla's extravagant expenditures were continued by subsequent administrations, culminating in that of President José BALTA (1868–1872). Balta mortgaged the nation's production and sale of guano to the French Dreyfus Company for the building of spectacular but then-unproductive railroads connecting the costa (coast) and the sierra. *See* COSTA (PERU); DREYFUS CONTRACT; MEIGGS, Henry; SIERRA (PERU).

The sudden inflow of revenue from guano and, to a lesser extent, from nitrates created almost overnight a

PERU

Area: 496,224 sq. mi.   Population: 13,567,939 (1972 est.).

new capitalist class of commercial and banking interests with headquarters in Lima. Allied with the landed oligarchy, it created the first Peruvian political party, the CIVILISTA PARTY, which advocated national development and antimilitarism. In 1872 the party gave Peru its first civilian President, Manuel PARDO, but it was not until after 1899 that the Civilistas came to dominate Peruvian politics.

The exploitation of guano and nitrates had other long-lasting repercussions. It created a psychological atmosphere that encouraged successive administrations to act as if the guano boom would never end and thus to reject the necessity for a systematic policy of development. It also established the coast as the undisputed economic center of the nation, while the sierra was relegated to a permanent secondary position. Finally, guano opened Peru up to the heavy incursion of foreign capital (British, French, and later United States), thus reinforcing Peru's colonial economic status as a supplier of raw materials to industrial powers.

The artificial prosperity created by guano finally came to a crashing end with the WAR OF THE PACIFIC (1879–1883) and the displacement of guano by Chilean nitrates in the world market. The humiliating defeat in the war by Chile and the subsequent economic depression triggered a far-reaching reevaluation of Peruvian realities. The postwar period was one of the most intellectually fertile eras in Peru's history. The ideas of neopositivists like Manuel Vicente Villarán and Javier Prado, who favored improving the condition of the masses as well as economic growth, gave rise to the relatively advanced social legislation Peru boasted by 1915, while the fiery prose of Manuel GONZÁLEZ PRADA helped inspire radical ideologues such as the brilliant Marxist José Carlos MARIÁTEGUI and the eclectic Víctor Raúl HAYA DE LA TORRE. Although the degree of their reformist zeal varied, both the neopositivists and the radicals criticized the militarism of the nineteenth century, the continuing colonial social structure, the venality of the oligarchy, and the exclusion of the Indians from national participation. These themes, together with those advanced more recently, such as opposition to social inequality and imperialism, have constituted the basis of political divisions in Peru to the present day.

Twentieth century. The intellectual ferment of the postwar years stimulated the passage of progressive social, economic, and political legislation, especially between 1895 and 1908. The benefits from that legislation, however, were somewhat diminished by the fact that most of the period between 1899 and 1919 was dominated by the Civilista party. As representatives of banking, merchant, and plantation interests, the various Civilista administrations protected those interests. They encouraged export agriculture from the coast (cotton and sugar) and later fostered mineral production through the granting of concessions to foreign investors. In the process, the Peruvian economy was revived, but the revival benefited mostly narrow interest groups.

Nevertheless, the economic revival of the early 1900s, together with World War I and internal migration to the coast, encouraged the rise of a middle class and of a labor movement. The middle class, composed mainly of bureaucrats, professional people, white-collar workers, small landowners, businessmen, and miners, was not large, nor did it have much class consciousness. Most of its members were dependent on the oligarchy and foreign interests and thus did not seek the destruction of either one. However, the middle class did demand a greater share of the benefits and of the political power then monopolized by the oligarchy. The labor movement, which had begun to develop only after the War of the Pacific thanks to foreign capital investments in manufacturing (Lima-Callao), sugar refining (central and northern Peru), mining (central Peru), and transportation (central and southern Peru), was small and badly organized and thus was not a threat to the oligarchy. However, it was an important new political factor because of its ability to organize even small strikes and because of its potential for violence.

At first the Civilistas, prodded by the neopositivists, met some of the demands of these new groups by passing significant social legislation. But as the party grew more conservative and less responsive, it lost its vitality and eventually its considerable unity. Thus, in the 1919 presidential election its candidate lost to an opportunistic ex-Civilista, Augusto LEGUÍA, who exploited the political and economic aspirations of the new social forces to create a new political alliance. Campaigning on an antioligarchy platform, he advanced a slogan, "Patria Nueva," that appealed to members of the middle class, including students and lower-ranking military officers, to segments of organized labor, and to disaffected members of the oligarchy.

In his eleven-year dictatorship (1919–1930), Leguía attempted to create a modern capitalist nation in order to strengthen his newly developed political base and to diminish permanently the traditional oligarchy's political power. To achieve his aims Leguía granted carte blanche to foreign investors, mostly from the United States, at the cost of Peru's financial independence. The resulting inflow of foreign capital spurred the rise to prominence of capitalist interests closely tied to foreign investments and strongly antagonistic to the Civilista oligarchy. In addition, it permitted Leguía to expand and pamper the bureaucracy and the Army and to inaugurate an extensive public works system that enhanced his middle- and working-class support. Moreover, Leguía's encouragement of foreign capital investment in plantation agriculture, mining, and manufacturing also contributed to the well-being of the social classes represented by these interests.

Leguía's policies toward the Civilista oligarchy had no lasting effects. While he was able to make anti-Civilismo quite fashionable and succeeded in liquidating the Civilista party, he proved unable to weaken permanently the oligarchy because he allowed it to share in the economic prosperity of the 1920s. Thus, with the end of Leguía's rule in 1930, the oligarchy regained power, although it exercised it less conspicuously than in the past.

The success of Leguía's political coalition throughout the 1920s was ensured by the persecution of both traditional and new political parties, including the ALIANZA POPULAR REVOLUCIONARIA AMERICANA (APRA). APRA was an eclectic leftist organization founded in Mexico in 1924 by Víctor Raúl Haya de la Torre. His intention of creating a middle- and working-class coalition brought the party into conflict first with Leguía, over control of the middle class, and later with the Communists and the Socialists, over control of the working class.

While the prosperity of the 1920s persisted, Leguía's position was unchallenged, but when the Depression struck, his regime was brought to an end. The middle and working classes, disenchanted with capitalism and with the existing social system, lent their support to organizations advocating reform. Important segments of the middle class joined the ranks of APRA, while the working class divided its loyalties among the APRA, Communist, and Socialist parties. But the threat to the status quo presented by the political and social unrest of the Depression and highlighted by the remarkable growth of APRA was met by an alliance between the traditional oligarchy and the armed forces. The success of this coalition was first evidenced in 1931, when the populist military hero Luis M. SÁNCHEZ CERRO, leader of the 1930 revolt against Leguía, defeated Haya de la Torre in a presidential election which, despite Aprista claims, was one of Peru's fairest.

A strong nationalist, suspicious of APRA's internationalism and antimilitarism, Sánchez Cerro throughout his regime (1931–1933) tried to destroy APRA. His dual approach, also employed by subsequent military administrations, included both repression of the party and the passage of progressive social legislation. This strategy failed, for even though APRA was forced underground until 1945, it continued to prosper.

With the end of World War II in 1945, a popular front seeking to reestablish political democracy emerged in Peru. The front's candidate, José Luis

BUSTAMANTE, supported by the newly legalized APRA party, gained the Presidency, while APRA won control of Congress and later of the Cabinet. For three years APRA wielded considerable political power. To the surprise of most observers, the party's vaunted radicalism proved to be a myth. APRA merely worked to strengthen its influence over its middle- and working-class supporters. In spite of this moderation, however, the party's old rivalries with the Army (dating back to 1932) and with the oligarchy (represented by the newspapers *El Comercio* and *La Prensa*) resurfaced, and they led to a military coup in 1948 and to the outlawing of the party.

Except for its tireless suppression of APRA, Manuel A. ODRÍA's military dictatorship (1948–1956) proved to be relatively mild. Moreover, since its first five years coincided with the economic prosperity engendered by foreign investments and the Korean war, the dictatorship was credited with the launching of extensive public works projects and with the passage of important social legislation beneficial to the urban masses and the blue-collar workers.

In the 1956 presidential election the political divisions that had persisted since 1930 became blurred with the signing of the *convivencia*. This alliance between important segments of the oligarchy and APRA ensured the election of ex-President Manuel PRADO (1956–1962) and the legalization of APRA. However, it also finally dispelled the myth of APRA's radicalism. The party's leadership denied that the *convivencia* constituted a departure from its basic ideology. Actually, APRA had always been more moderate than its propaganda had indicated. In fact, its radical image had served to isolate the true left and to make Peruvian politics relatively moderate and devoid of ideological extremes. A similar role came to be played by the equally moderate ACCIÓN POPULAR of Fernando BELAÚNDE TERRY, which emerged after 1956 as a major political force and won the Presidency in 1963.

The period after 1930, then, saw Peru undergo considerable political transformation. During these years important social and economic changes also occurred. Although Peru was still an incipient industrial nation, its reliance on several exports (cotton, sugar, minerals, and later fish meal) gave it a strong economic base not critically affected by the price fluctuations of a single product. The nation's wealth, however, remained unequally distributed, especially between the coast and the sierra. The result was a demographic dislocation, with hundreds of thousands of *serranos* migrating to the coastal region. Affected also by the nationwide high birthrate (31 per 1,000), the population of Lima zoomed from about 400,000 in 1940 to nearly 2.5 million by 1970, with more than 600,000 people living in the *barriadas* (shantytowns) that ring the city. Such dislocation put an added strain on the national budget and constituted a source of concern, even though the *barriada* dwellers proved to be rather conservative and unorganized, judging from their repeated support of Odría in the presidential elections of 1962 and 1963. Nevertheless, their increasing consciousness made them a powerful new political force.

Migration to the coastal region was caused principally by deteriorating conditions in the sierra. The situation there became critical as a result of the peasants' growing militancy, exemplified by the invasion of haciendas, the creation of peasant leagues, and the outbreak of guerrilla warfare in the south (1964–1965). Although quickly suppressed by the Army, the outbreak raised the specter of protracted armed conflict. The outcome was the recognition that one of Peru's most immediate needs was land reform. Even the oligarchy has accepted its inevitability and demonstrated a readiness to sacrifice the *gamonales* (bosses) of the sierra in order to protect its coastal property.

The armed forces also recognized the necessity for reform. Its members, however, became divided on the course such reforms should take. The more radical "Nasserist" elements, usually the product of the CENTRO DE ALTOS ESTUDIOS MILITARES (CAEM), advocated sweeping changes, while the moderates proposed a more evolutionary approach. At first the moderates prevailed. In the 1963 presidential election the armed forces supported the candidacy of the progressive Belaúnde Terry, who was elected. However, Belaúnde's administration (1963–1968) proved too timid to overcome an obstructionist Congress and allowed its progressive program to be sabotaged. This, plus a serious political and economic crisis (which led to a 40 percent devaluation of the sol in 1967), prompted the armed forces to overthrow Belaúnde in 1968.

The armed forces' action was motivated by two other important factors: a desire to forestall an almost certain Aprista victory in the presidential election of 1969; and a desire to prevent anarchy and bloodshed, which, according to the military, the failure of Belaúnde's reform program made inevitable.

For the time being, the more radical wing of the armed forces seems to have won control of the military junta set up in 1968 under the leadership of Juan VELASCO ALVARADO. Since its inception the military government has adopted a series of radical measures. It has enacted land, financial, credit, and industrial reforms, has nationalized sizable foreign holdings, has extended some controls over foreign and national capital, and is attempting a more egalitarian distribution of wealth. On the basis of this legislation the Velasco government can be called revolutionary. It has attacked some of the major sources of discontent such as social inequality, oligarchic domination, and economic colonialism. Whether it will continue to do so remains to be seen.

See also AGRARIAN REFORM; FISHING INDUSTRY (PERU); SELVA (PERU).

Bibliography. Jorge Basadre, *Historia de la república del Perú,* 17 vols., 6th ed., Lima, 1968; François Bourricaud, *Power and Society in Contemporary Peru,* New York, 1962; Carlos Dellepiane, *Historia militar del Perú,* 2 vols., Lima, 1943; Robert Marett, *Peru,* New York, 1969; José Pareja Paz Soldán (ed.), *Visión del Perú en el siglo XX,* 2 vols., Lima, 1962; Fredrick B. Pike, *The Modern History of Peru,* New York, 1962; Emilio Romero, *Historia económica del Perú,* Lima, 1949; César Antonio Ugarte, *Bosquejo de la historia económica del Perú,* Lima, 1926.

ORAZIO A. CICCARELLI

PESSOA, EPITÁCIO [DA SILVA] (1865–1942). Brazilian jurist and President (1919–1922). Born into a prominent family at Umbuzeiro, Paraíba, Pessoa was educated in Pernambuco, graduating from the Recife law school in 1886. Three years later the new republican Governor appointed him secretary-general of Paraíba, from which post he ran successfully for the Constituent

Assembly in 1890. Although he was inconspicuous among the drafters of the constitution of 1891 (*see* CONSTITUTION OF 1891: BRAZIL), Pessoa came to national attention the following year as an outspoken critic of the Floriano PEIXOTO government. He resigned in 1901 to accept appointment as Chief Justice of the Supreme Court and later as Attorney General of the republic. After the Third International Conference of American States in 1906, Pessoa chaired the committee of jurists selected to study the codification of international law.

Returning to politics in 1912, he was elected to the Senate from Paraíba. Pessoa headed Brazil's delegation to the Paris Peace Conference following World War I and was in France when he was elected to serve out the unexpired term of President Francisco de Paula RODRIGUES ALVES. Pessoa's administration attended to the problems of the drought-ridden NORTHEAST. On leaving the Presidency, he was appointed to the Permanent Court of International Justice at The Hague, on which he served until 1930. During his last years Pessoa suffered from Parkinson's disease.

ROLLIE E. POPPINO

PESSOA [CAVALCANTI DE ALBUQUERQUE], JOÃO (1878–1930).
Brazilian politician. Born in Umbuzeiro, Paraíba, he was the nephew of Epitácio PESSOA. In 1903 he received his degree from the law school at Recife. Pessoa practiced law in Recife until 1911, when he moved south to Rio de Janeiro to assume the post of naval auditor. In 1918 he was promoted to auditor general and in 1920 was appointed to the office of the Minister of the Supreme Military Tribunal. Pessoa was noted for his inflexibility in discharging the obligations of the latter office. He was elected Governor of Paraíba for the 1928–1930 term. While serving in that post, he joined Getúlio VARGAS on the Liberal Alliance ticket in the 1930 presidential compaign, after the Governor of Pernambuco, Estácio Coimbra, refused to accept the vice-presidential spot.

When the administration-backed slate, headed by Júlio Prestes, defeated the Liberal Alliance ticket, Vargas and Pessoa seemed disposed to accept the verdict of the polls, although many of their supporters urged revolution. All attempts to calm the revolutionary fervor were brought to naught by the assassination of João Pessoa in Recife on July 26, 1930. While his death at the hands of the bitter son of a local political enemy was not atypical in the clan-dominated political climate of the NORTHEAST, the assassin was linked to a group supported by Prestes and President Washington Luis PEREIRA DE SOUSA. Pessoa's assassination helped coalesce the wavering advocates of revolution. Vargas could not stem the tide and therefore decided to ride with it.

LAWRENCE J. NIELSEN

PÉTION, ALEXANDRE SABÈS (1770–1818).
President of Haiti (1807–1818). Born in Saint-Domingue and educated in Paris, Pétion supported the mulatto leader André Rigaud during the Haitian revolution. A skilled artilleryman, he returned to Saint-Domingue with Gen. Charles-Victor-Emmanuel Leclerc's French invasion force of 1801, but when it became clear that France intended to deny mulatto aspirations along with those of blacks, he joined with Negro leaders to achieve independence.

Under Jean-Jacques DESSALINES as Emperor, Pétion commanded the south, and upon Dessalines's death he contrived to make Henry CHRISTOPHE a figurehead President through mulatto control of the Constituent Assembly. Christophe rejected the scheme, and civil war split Haiti until 1820. Pétion headed a republic in the south, where his constitution made him President with greater powers than he had planned for Christophe; yet he failed to defeat his foe and unite Haiti.

As President for life and champion of the mulatto ÉLITE, Pétion allowed agriculture, commerce, and learning to decline. Generally irresolute, perhaps because of ill health, temperament, and fear that action would bring a revolt of the unwilling Negro majority, he failed to reconcile freedom with authority. During a period of adversity for Simón BOLÍVAR (1815), Pétion granted him a haven, money, arms, and a press. After a long illness, Pétion died in Port-au-Prince on March 29, 1818.

JOHN E. BAUR

PETRÓLEOS BRASILEIROS, S.A. (PETROBRÁS).
National petroleum corporation of Brazil. Before World War II all the petroleum products used in Brazil were imported, refined, and distributed by private companies. The search for domestic oil reserves by the National Petroleum Council resulted in the discovery of the Lobato oil field in Bahia in 1939, but production could not keep pace with Brazil's growing needs for fuel. The question of national self-sufficiency and control of the oil industry became the most emotion-charged political issue of the immediate post-World War II years. In October 1953, after an intensive six-year campaign, the Congress created Petrobrás as a mixed-capital corporation in which the national government holds the controlling interest and minority shares may be sold only to native-born Brazilian citizens. Existing private oil refiners and retailers were not affected, but Petrobrás was given a monopoly over the discovery, processing, and transportation of Brazilian oil.

Under the overall supervision of the National Petroleum Council and the immediate direction of a retired military officer, Petrobrás has entered every phase of the oil industry. Although it searches for oil in all parts of Brazil, its field operations are concentrated along the northeastern coast, where the Bahian field has been expanded and new wells opened in the coastal strip and offshore waters of Alagoas, Sergipe, and Espírito Santo. Petrobrás also operates its own tanker fleet, a chain of gasoline stations, and major petrochemical complexes near Salvador, Bahia, and in Cubatão, São Paulo.

ROLLIE E. POPPINO

PETRÓLEOS MEXICANOS (PEMEX).
National petroleum corporation of Mexico. On December 28, 1933, President Abelardo RODRÍGUEZ decreed the formation of a corporation to regulate the internal market for petroleum and its derivatives in order to ensure an adequate supply and to train Mexican technicians. In October 1934 this corporation was given the name Petróleos de México, S.A. (Petro-Mex). After the expropriation of Mexico's foreign-owned oil holdings by President Lázaro CÁRDENAS on March 18, 1938, the government organized Petróleos Mexicanos, which had the same functions as Petro-Mex, and Distribuidora de Petróleos Mexicanos, which was given responsibility for the distribution of Mexico's oil and its derivatives.

The two were unified on August 8, 1940, as Petróleos Mexicanos.

The beginnings of Pemex were difficult because of the boycott of Mexican oil by the expropriated firms and because of the necessity of changing from production for export to production for domestic consumption; problems were also caused by the need to fuse many firms into a single enterprise and to readjust working conditions. In 1958 Pemex was entrusted with the production of basic petrochemicals, which became Mexico's most dynamic industrial sector. By the early 1970s Pemex was Mexico's outstanding enterprise because of the size of its revenues and the value of its assets and because it was the principal contributor to the public treasury and the major source of direct and indirect employment. Nevertheless, its financial position had suffered strong pressures because of its lack of liquidity, and from time to time labor corruption reared its head. By 1973 Mexico imported oil only for regions distant from the producing areas and special lubricants not produced in Mexico.

MOISÉS GONZÁLEZ NAVARRO

PETROLEUM INDUSTRY (LATIN AMERICA). The petroleum industry has different characteristics in different regions of Latin America. Petroleum is above all an international industry, with crude oil the first-ranking commodity in world trade. All Latin American countries consume petroleum products in rapidly increasing volumes, but only nine produce crude oil, and of these nine only four produce more than they consume. Venezuela is the only Latin American country prominent in the world petroleum export trade, producing more than 70 percent of all Latin American oil while consuming only about 8 percent. Venezuelan production and exports have increased much less rapidly than those of the world oil industry as a whole. In recent years Venezuela has dropped from first to third among exporters and from third to fifth or sixth among world producers.

Table 1 presents 1971 statistics on the petroleum industry in each of the Latin American countries. Total oil production was just over 5 million barrels per day, while consumption was almost 3 million, providing an export surplus of 2 million barrels per day. Estimated crude oil reserves as of the end of 1971 were 36.3 billion barrels, indicating a ratio of 20 to 1 between total reserves and annual production.

Oil production varies greatly among the countries. About 70 percent of the oil is produced in Venezuela, 8 percent in Argentina, 8 percent in Mexico, 4 percent in Colombia, and 3 percent in Brazil, the remaining 7 percent being divided among Trinidad, Peru, Chile, Bolivia, and Ecuador. The major consuming countries are Brazil, Mexico, and Argentina, which account for just over half of total consumption. Other relatively large consumers are Venezuela, Puerto Rico, Colombia, and the Netherlands Antilles, but in these areas consumption includes not only domestic use but also some intra-industry use of crude oil for the refining of petroleum for the export of fuels. Chile and Peru complete the list of countries consuming more than 100,000 barrels of oil per day. Chile's relatively small consumption reflects its lesser degree of dependence upon petroleum fuels, since, unlike most of the other countries, it has relatively abundant supplies of low-cost coal and harnessed waterpower.

Of the three major consuming countries, Argentina and Mexico have managed to achieve almost 90 percent self-sufficiency in oil supply, whereas Brazil, which with its very sparse endowment of known oil resources must import 70 percent of its oil needs, is by far the largest net importer. Since no oil is produced in Central America, all the countries between Mexico and Colombia rely entirely upon imports. If we exclude Puerto Rico and the Netherlands Antilles (where the oil demand is almost entirely for refinery input for re-export), the total import needs of the Central America–Caribbean area countries are only 356,000 barrels per day. The further elimination of Cuba, which at present does not participate in the commercial world petroleum market but barters sugar for Soviet petroleum, would reduce net imports from free-market sources to 266,000 barrels per day.

Of the South American nations, only Uruguay, Paraguay, and the Guianas are completely dependent upon imports. Colombia is the second largest oil exporter in Latin America, although with its 107,000 barrels per day of export capacity it ranks a poor second to Venezuela. Bolivia's production is only 35,000 barrels per day, but since its domestic consumption is lower than that of any other South American country except Paraguay, it still provides an export surplus of 22,000 barrels per day. In 1971 Peru and Ecuador were supplying less oil than they consumed, but large new discoveries in both countries since 1970 would soon permit these countries to provide growing exports of oil.

Oil reserves are crucial to the long-run position of a national petroleum industry. Venezuela, with 70 percent of Latin American production, has only 54 percent of Latin American oil reserves. Another 13 percent of the reserves is in Mexico, and Ecuador now has 11 percent, the other 22 percent being divided among the remaining six producing lands.

A nation cannot become an important oil exporter without very large reserves. Table 1 shows that the known reserves endowment of Latin America is very uneven, five-sixths of the reserves being in South America. Apart from Venezuela and eastern Mexico, the petroleum resource endowment of Latin America is unusually poor. By way of contrast, 1971 crude oil reserves were 324 billion barrels in the Middle East, 85 billion in the U.S.S.R. and Asia, 60 billion in the United States and Canada, and 47 billion in Africa.

Table 1 also shows data on refineries and petrochemical plants. In 1971 there were twenty-eight refineries in the Mexico–Central America–Caribbean area and sixty-one in South America. However, throughput capacity, or the capacity of a refinery for processing a given volume of crude oil, was much more evenly divided: 2.5 million barrels per day in the north and 2.8 million in the south. The two refineries in the Netherlands Antilles are among the world's largest, while those in Trinidad, Puerto Rico, Mexico, and the Bahamas are also relatively large. In South America only the Venezuelan refineries are of comparable size, the Amuay (Las Piedras) refinery of Exxon Corporation being the largest refinery in the world.

In the oil-exporting countries, refinery capacity is uniformly greater than domestic consumption. The major exporters, Venezuela and Colombia, ship most of their petroleum in the form of crude oil, but much of Venezuela's crude oil is sent to Caribbean-area refineries, where it is refined into petroleum fuel that is then

TABLE 1. PETROLEUM INDUSTRY IN LATIN AMERICA, 1971

Country	Oil production	Oil consumption	Net oil imports	Net oil exports	Estimated oil reserves, (billion barrels, Dec. 31, 1971)	Refineries Number	Refineries Throughput capacity (1,000 barrels per day)	Petrochemical plants Operating, 1971	New projects, 1972 New plants	New projects, 1972 Expansions	Total
	(1,000 barrels per day)										
Northern region:											
Mexico	427	480	53	...	4.5	6	533	29	4	5	9
Bahamas	...	47	47	...	...	2	266	...	...	...	...
Barbados	...	91	91	...	...	1	3	...	...	...	...
Bermuda	...	10	10	...	...	...	...	...	...	...	...
Costa Rica	...	8	8	...	...	1	8	...	...	...	...
Cuba	...	90	90	...	...	4	82	...	1	...	1
Dominican Republic	...	17	17	...	...	...	...	...	...	...	...
Guatemala	...	19	19	...	...	2	25	...	...	...	...
Haiti	...	4	4	...	...	...	...	...	...	...	...
Honduras	...	10	10	...	...	1	10	...	...	...	...
British Honduras	...	1	1	...	...	...	...	...	...	...	...
Jamaica	...	30	30	...	...	1	36	...	...	...	...
Nicaragua	...	9	9	...	...	1	22	1	...	...	...
Panama	...	84	84	...	...	1	75	...	...	...	...
Puerto Rico	...	161	161	...	...	2	155	13	1	3	4
El Salvador	...	9	9	...	...	1	13	1	1	...	1
Trinidad and Tobago	135	62	...	73	1.5	3	425	2	...	1	1
Netherlands Antilles	...	112	112	...	...	2	800	2	...	...	...
Total, northern region	562	1,244	682 *	...	6.0	28	2,453	48	7	9	16
Southern region:											
Bolivia	35	13	...	22	.3	5	16	...	2	...	2
Brazil	168	560	392	...	1.0	11	496	31	14	7	21
Chile	35	108	73	...	.2	3	115	2	3	1	4
Colombia	227	120	...	107	2.3	5	135	11	...	4	4
Ecuador	4	24	20	...	4.0	2	35	1	...	...	...
Guianas	...	22	22	...	...	...	...	...	...	...	...
Argentina	424	473	49	...	2.5	16	514	21	9	10	19
Paraguay	...	6	6	...	...	1	5	...	...	...	...
Peru	62	110	48	...	.5	5	90	1	5	...	5
Uruguay	...	45	45	...	...	1	40	1	...	...	...
Venezuela	3,548	249	...	3,299	19.5	12	1,343	4	6	1	7
Total, southern region	4,503	1,730	...	2,773 †	30.3	61	2,789	72	39	23	62
Total, Latin America	5,065	2,974	...	2,091 ‡	36.3	89	5,242	120	46	32	78

* 755 − 73 = 682.
† 3,428 − 655 = 2,773.
‡ 2,773 − 682 = 2,091.
SOURCE: *World Petroleum Report,* 1972, pp. 11, 13, 14.

exported to other markets, primarily in North America. Hence, for the Caribbean countries (excluding Cuba) oil consumption is 534,000 barrels per day, while refinery capacity is 1,685,000 barrels per day. Only the Guianas, Hispaniola, and British Honduras are entirely lacking in refineries. Other countries have refining capacities that vary from about 85 to 125 percent of their consumption. There appears to be no significant shortage of refining capacity anywhere, the largest discrepancy being the 64,000-barrel-per-day gap for Brazil.

There were 120 petrochemical plants in Latin America in 1971; of these, 72 were in South America. Expansion of capacity is proceeding at a rapid rate. During 1972, 46 new plants were under construction, and 32 existing plants were being expanded.

As of 1971 commercial production of natural gas in Latin America was not very far advanced, although large resources existed in Venezuela and their development was under discussion. It was expected that the natural gas deposits of Latin America would become increasingly important in the future. In addition to crude oil, Latin America contains deposits of oil shales and tar sands that might be converted into liquid fuels identical to those produced from petroleum. As of 1971 the world price of crude oil was so low that it was not economical to develop these resources; nevertheless, the oil shales of Brazil are the second most extensive in the world and contain reserves equivalent to perhaps 200 billion barrels of oil. Even more extensive are the tar sands of Venezuela, which contain some 700 billion

TABLE 2. LATIN AMERICAN PETROLEUM EXPORTS AND IMPORTS, 1970

Areas receiving exports	Exports from Caribbean area		Exports from rest of Latin America		Source of imports	Imports into Latin America excluding Caribbean area	
	(1,000 barrels per day)	Percent of total exports	(1,000 barrels per day)	Percent of total exports		(1,000 barrels per day)	Percent of total imports
United States	1,680	52	80	88	United States	50	6
Canada	480	15	...	...	Caribbean area	335	43
Other Western Hemisphere	335	10	5	6	Other Latin America	5	1
Western Europe	640	20	5	6	Western Europe	25	3
Africa	50	2	...	...	Middle East	150	19
Japan	45	1	...	...	North Africa	25	3
					West Africa	90	11
					U.S.S.R. and Eastern Europe	105	14
Total	3,230	100	90	100		785	100

SOURCE: *British Petroleum Statistical Review of the World Oil Industry, 1970.*

barrels of oil in place, but it may never be economical to recover more than a small fraction of the total deposit.

In terms of international oil trade patterns, Latin America may be divided into two regions. The northern, or "Caribbean," region has a large export surplus, while the southern region is a large net importer. In the north exports from Venezuela, Colombia, and Trinidad go mainly to North American, European, and African markets, either directly or after having been processed by Caribbean-area refineries. The southern region obtains its imports not only from the northern region but also from the Middle East, Africa, and Eastern Europe. Table 2 shows that in the north 52 percent of exports in 1970 went to the United States, 20 percent to Western Europe, 15 percent to Canada, 10 percent to southern Latin America, 2 percent to Africa, and 1 percent to Japan. The southern region obtained 43 percent of its imports from the north, 19 percent from the Middle East, 14 percent from Africa, 14 percent from the U.S.S.R. and Eastern Europe, and 9 percent from the United States and Western Europe combined. The southern region did not buy all its oil needs from the north, since it could then purchase oil more cheaply from Africa and the Middle East because of the combination of lower Eastern Hemisphere wellhead prices and relatively low tanker shipment rates that prevailed through 1971 despite increases in Eastern Hemisphere prices. Venezuela and Colombia, on the other hand, were more anxious to sell their oil in northern than in southern markets, since the protected price in the United States market was higher than prices in Latin America.

The future of the Latin American petroleum industry depends largely upon the ability of producers to develop new reserves. Consumption is increasing very rapidly in all countries. The growth of reserves and production is less certain. In the past Venezuela has dominated the industry, but a combination of economic, political,

and geological factors suggests that Venezuela's role in world oil will slowly decline. While new discoveries will no doubt continue to be made in Venezuela, maintenance of its output at present rates will make it difficult to increase or even replace its reserves in the long run. The major prospects for new discoveries are in offshore areas, particularly offshore Ecuador, Peru, Brazil, and Chile. Much of the new oil to be found in the Caribbean area will probably be offshore from Colombia and Venezuela. Oil prospecting in the interior of Brazil has been quite disappointing, but recent discoveries in Bolivia and in the interior of Peru suggest that new onshore areas in South America may yet prove productive.

In projecting the future of Latin American petroleum, much depends upon the political climate and the extent to which it encourages exploration and permits discovery and production. The pattern of regulation varies considerably. Since in almost all Latin American countries the state is considered to possess title to all mineral rights, the national government has a monopoly on the granting of access to oil lands. In most areas this means that private investors, domestic or foreign, must submit to detailed regulation of their exploratory, development, and production activities. In a few areas such as Brazil, Mexico, and Chile, all exploration and production is done directly by a state monopoly oil company. Even where the national company is not given a monopoly, it may still be given preference in taxation, land use, domestic marketing, and the like. Every Latin American oil-producing country now has such a national oil company.

State control may also be imposed over petroleum imports and over the prices at which crude oil and refined products transactions take place. Government monopoly is less common in the phases of refining and marketing. Refining is mostly in private hands, although it is subject to much regulation. Marketing is even more frequently entrusted to private investors; such

TABLE 3. PROJECTIONS OF PETROLEUM PRODUCTION, CONSUMPTION, IMPORTS, AND EXPORTS FOR LATIN AMERICA, 1971–1990
(Million barrels per day)

| | Production | | | | | |
	Venezuela	Other Latin America	Total	Consumption	Imports	Exports
1971	3.5	1.6	5.1	2.9	.8	3.0
1972	3.5	1.7	5.2	3.1	.9	3.0
1973	3.5	1.8	5.3	3.3	.9	2.9
1974	3.6	2.0	5.6	3.5	.9	3.0
1975	3.6	2.2	5.8	3.7	1.0	3.1
1976	3.6	2.4	6.0	3.9	1.1	3.2
1977	3.7	2.6	6.3	4.2	1.2	3.3
1978	3.7	2.8	6.5	4.4	1.3	3.4
1979	3.8	3.0	6.8	4.7	1.4	3.5
1980	3.8	3.2	7.0	5.0	1.6	3.6
1981	3.9	3.4	7.3	5.3	1.7	3.7
1982	3.9	3.6	7.5	5.6	1.9	3.8
1983	3.9	3.8	7.7	5.9	2.0	3.8
1984	4.0	3.9	7.9	6.3	2.2	3.8
1985	4.0	4.1	8.1	6.6	2.3	3.8
1986	3.9	4.3	8.2	7.0	2.4	3.6
1987	3.9	4.5	8.4	7.5	2.6	3.5
1988	3.8	4.8	8.6	7.9	2.7	3.4
1989	3.7	5.2	8.9	8.4	2.8	3.3
1990	3.6	5.6	9.2	8.9	3.0	3.3

SOURCE: Author's projections.

major international companies as Exxon and Shell are important factors in marketing in many countries, along with many privately owned local distribution outlets.

It is in connection with exploration and finding efforts, however, that most problems arise. In this context the major reasons for predicting a rather stagnant future for Venezuelan oil may be cited. First, the resource base has been rather thoroughly explored, and there is no great likelihood that many new giant fields will be found. Second, the policy of the present government is to reduce the degree of national dependence upon oil for public policy and conservation reasons. While other oil-exporting countries have been increasing output very rapidly, Venezuela has been content with a static rate. Third, in the early 1970s Venezuelan oil was overpriced in world markets, in view of (a) its high sulfur content and the high refining costs of treatment to meet air pollution standards in its main market and (b) declining tanker freight rates that reduced Venezuela's transportation cost advantage over Middle Eastern oil. Fourth, in order to implement its policy of assuming eventual control of all Venezuelan oil, the government has granted no new concessions since 1956, and existing concessions are to terminate in 1983–1984. Recent tax and regulatory decrees have discouraged additional development of petroleum resources.

Table 3 presents projections of the future of petro-leum in Latin America through 1990. Total output rises from 5.1 million barrels per day in 1971 to 9.2 million by 1990, but virtually all the increase is due to production in areas other than Venezuela. Venezuelan output is essentially static, while output in other areas is projected to increase by 4 million barrels per day.

Consumption should increase more rapidly than production, from 2.9 million barrels per day to 8.9 million. About one-third of the increase in consumption is supplied by an increase in imports, almost exclusively from the Eastern Hemisphere, which grow from 800,000 barrels per day to 3 million. Exports manage to increase slightly despite the rapid growth in consumption and are foreseen to rise from 3 million barrels per day in 1971 to 3.3 million by 1990.

See also PETRÓLEOS BRASILEIROS, S.A.; PETRÓLEOS MEXICANOS; PETROLEUM INDUSTRY (VENEZUELA); YACIMIENTOS PETROLÍFEROS FISCALES; YACIMIENTOS PETROLÍFEROS FISCALES BOLIVIANOS.

Bibliography. G. H. Barrows, *International Petroleum Industry,* New York, 1967; Z. M. Mikdashi, *The Community of Oil Exporting Countries: A Study in Government Cooperation,* Ithaca, N.Y., 1972; Edith T. Penrose, *The Large International Firm in Developing Countries: The International Petroleum Industry,* London, 1968; M. Tanzer, *The Political Economy of International Oil and the Underdeveloped Countries,* Boston, 1969.

HENRY B. STEELE

PETROLEUM INDUSTRY (VENEZUELA).

Petroleum is Venezuela's most important natural resource, its largest earner of foreign exchange, its greatest source of government revenue, and its most controversial political topic. Although Venezuelans have always known about their petroleum resources and have used asphalt seepages to caulk their boats since precolonial times, the petroleum boom became a reality only in the 1920s. Before that decade the major foreign exploitation of this product had been undertaken in the Andes by an American-affiliated company that had obtained a concession to develop the oil deposits. From the very beginning of foreign commercial exploitation, petroleum was a difficult international question. President Cipriano CASTRO, for example, found it difficult to compel the oil company working in the Andes to obey the regulations his government established.

Such an unhappy beginning was quickly forgotten during the years of the regime of Juan Vicente GÓMEZ (1908–1935), when petroleum policy was one of free and open access to Venezuelan resources. This era of oil exploitation may be divided into two periods. The first involved large-scale concessions to Venezuelans who quickly transferred their claims to foreign companies, especially British and Dutch affiliates. This system lasted through World War I until about 1923. Then Gómez began to channel all his concessions through the Compañía Venezolana de Petróleo, which in turn awarded the concessions to foreign companies. This device allowed Gómez to receive all the financial benefit accruing from the transfer of petroleum concessions. During this second phase, American oil companies managed to enter and, in the end, to dominate the Venezuelan oil market.

During the Gómez years a series of laws was adopted to govern the exploitation of oil resources. One, passed in 1920, placed some limitations on the companies' activities, but it was replaced in 1922 by a more agreeable instrument. The 1928 law, promulgated in 1930, contained a number of restrictions on company activities, but these came to naught when the oil interests protested, and they remained without effect to the end of the Gómez regime. After the death of Gómez in 1935, popular pressure forced the government of Eleazar LÓPEZ CONTRERAS to improve the government's participation in and supervision of the oil industry. Although López Contreras still granted concessions to companies, he insisted on bidding to obtain the best possible terms. A new, short-lived law required that the concessions be awarded in a checkerboard fashion, reserving alternate squares for future exploitation by Venezuela. This provision did not survive the next hydrocarbon law, adopted in 1943 under the government of Isaías MEDINA ANGARITA, which consolidated all previous legislation. All concessions then in existence, whatever their origin, were reissued for a forty-year period starting in 1943. In return for this extension royalty payments were increased, and the land tax on concessions was raised. Moreover, part of the petroleum thus produced had to be refined in Venezuela. Despite his nationalistic position on oil, however, Medina issued a large number of new concessions.

Although the revolutionary junta government of ACCIÓN DEMOCRÁTICA (AD) leaders and military officers that replaced Medina in 1945 initially alarmed the oil companies, its actions proved to be rather mild. In 1945, with the so-called 50-50 formula, it raised the income tax on oil revenues to a level that would return to Venezuela half of the oil companies' earnings. The next year it approved a collective labor agreement that greatly improved the salaries of petroleum workers, and in 1947 it took part of the royalty payments in kind and sold the oil on the world market to verify the prices the companies were reporting. It soon discovered that the companies had been understating their prices. This government also ended the policy of awarding concessions.

After the fall of the government of President Rómulo GALLEGOS in 1948, the dictatorship of Marcos PÉREZ JIMÉNEZ proceeded to suppress the labor movement in the oil fields and, in 1956–1957, awarded two large blocks of new concessions. With the ouster of Pérez Jiménez in 1958, however, the concession policy appeared to be ended for good. The AD governments of Rómulo BETANCOURT and Raúl LEONI continued the policy begun in 1945. In 1958 they raised the taxes to bring Venezuela's participation in petroleum profits to 60 percent. From 1959 on Venezuela encouraged the development of a government petroleum company, the Corporación Venezolana de Petróleos (CVP), to provide the government with a yardstick to evaluate the foreign companies and to serve as a school to create a technically trained national petroleum managerial force. The long-term goal of both the AD governments and the government of the COMITÉ DE ORGANIZACIÓN POLÍTICA ELECTORAL INDEPENDIENTE (COPEI) installed in 1969 appeared to be the gradual reduction of foreign control until the entire oil industry became Venezuelan. This process involved gradually increasing the taxes and requirements imposed on the oil companies while continuously improving the pool of Venezuelan technicians. Naturally, this process, carried out in full public view, caused serious internal political debate and equally complex international discussions. Venezuela became an active member of the Organización de Paises Exportadores del Petróleo (OPEP) and an active exponent of the producing countries' maintaining high stable oil prices.

Oil is produced in the sedimentary basins of Maracaibo, Falcón, Apure, and Oriente. In 1970 more than 80 percent of the petroleum came from Maracaibo, more than 17 percent from Oriente, and the rest from Apure and Falcón. Annual oil production rose from some 1 million barrels in 1920 to 137 million in 1930, 186 million in 1940, 542 million in 1950, 1,042 million in 1960, and 1,353 million in 1970. The income received by Venezuela from royalty payments and a variety of taxes exceeded $1.3 billion by 1971. With an annual government income of almost $2.2 billion in 1971, it was clear that the half of the national revenue derived from the petroleum industry had a substantial impact on Venezuela. Finally, Venezuela's desire to have the petroleum industry under its own control was still thwarted by the problem of refining. By 1970 only about one-third of the petroleum produced in Venezuela was refined in the country, and this with Venezuela-based refineries working at almost 90 percent of capacity.

Bibliography. Rómulo Betancourt, *Venezuela: Política y petróleo,* Mexico City, 1956; Edwin Lieuwen, *Petroleum in Venezuela: A History,* Berkeley, Calif., 1954; Héctor Malavé Mata, *Petróleo y desarrollo económico de Venezuela,* Caracas, 1962; Domingo F. Maza Zavala, *Venezuela, una economía dependiente,* Caracas, 1964.

JOHN V. LOMBARDI

PETRÓPOLIS, TREATY OF. Treaty of 1903 between Bolivia and Brazil. The late-nineteenth-century rubber boom made the AMAZON RIVER region very valuable economically (*see* RUBBER BOOM: BRAZIL). Suddenly international boundaries that had never been clearly defined became a source of dispute between Brazil and its neighbors (Bolivia, Peru, Ecuador, Colombia, Venezuela, and British Guiana). One of the more important disputes was with Bolivia over the Acre Territory, a poorly surveyed, rubber-rich area on the Brazil-Bolivia-Peru borders.

As *sertanejos* (Brazilian backlanders) occupied and developed Acre, the Bolivian government became fearful of Brazilian expansion into its claim. To counter this expansion, the Bolivian government made a contract in 1901 with American capitalists to develop Acre for Bolivia. In 1902, before the contract could be implemented, disgruntled Brazilians, led by Plácido de Castro, took over the Bolivian customhouse. In response, both Bolivia and Brazil sent troops to Acre, but diplomats of the two nations successfully forestalled the potential war.

In 1903, in the Brazilian city of Petrópolis, representatives of the two nations negotiated a settlement known as the Treaty of Petrópolis. The treaty stipulated that (1) Bolivia was to cede Acre (73,000 square miles) to Brazil, (2) Brazil was to cede lands bordering the Madeira River to Bolivia, (3) Brazil was to construct the Madeira-Mamoré railroad, and (4) Brazil would pay Bolivia a $10 million indemnity. Brazil fulfilled its treaty obligations, obtained favorable decisions concerning other disputed areas, and was enriched by rubber revenues. Bolivia lost a province but gained financial reimbursement and, through the railroad, an outlet to world markets.   ALLAN K. JOHNSON

PETTORUTI, EMILIO (1892–   ). Argentine painter. The principal exponent of cubist abstract painting in South America, Pettoruti was born in La Plata, where the provincial legislature recognized his ability with a grant for European study (1913–1923). He settled in Florence, where he participated in the futurist movement, but his work was never so greatly concerned with the depiction of motion as that of painters typical of the movement. He remained faithful to a synthetic cubist style that he developed independently, having become acquainted with the work of Picasso, Gris, and Braque only in 1923 while on a trip to Paris and Berlin.

Pettoruti returned to Buenos Aires in 1924 and held his first show at the Witcomb Gallery. Modernist theory had only recently been expounded by the new review *Martín Fierro*, and his exhibit became a rallying point for the modernists. Pettoruti remained a controversial figure in conservative circles. He was appointed director of the Museum of Fine Arts in La Plata in 1930 and again in the 1940s, both times to be removed by government intervention. Foreign recognition gained him some recognition at home. He was invited to the United States in 1941 for an eight-month visit and exhibitions organized by the San Francisco Museum of Art. He also had important one-man shows in Paris (1958), London (1960), and, finally, the National Museum of Fine Arts in Buenos Aires (1962). His earlier work, such as *Romantic Serenade* (1938), is lyrical in color and subject. More recent work, such as *Bird of Light* (1961), is more abstract and metaphysical.

TERENCE GRIEDER

PHILIP II (1527–1598). King of Spain (1556–1598). The son of Emperor Charles V (King CHARLES I) and Isabella, daughter of King Manoel I of Portugal, Philip was born and reared in Spain; he was preeminently a Spanish monarch and, in contrast to his peripatetic father, remained in the Iberian Peninsula from September 1559 until his death. Of his father's possessions, he received Spain and the Low Countries as well as Spain's territories in Italy and its overseas empire. When the King of Portugal died without issue in 1580, Philip, who was the nearest heir, quickly occupied the country and was recognized as its monarch in 1581.

Depicted as a despotic bigot by his foreign foes and subsequent detractors, Philip was devout, industrious, and conscientious, although his indecisiveness and compulsive attention to detail hampered his effectiveness as a monarch. As the champion of Roman Catholicism in Europe, he fought against the Turks, winning a decisive naval battle in the Gulf of Lepanto (1571); attempted unsuccessfully to check Calvinism and nationalist aspirations in the Netherlands; intervened on behalf of the French Catholic party and waged war (1589–1598) against Henry IV of France; and dispatched the ill-fated Armada against England (1588). Meanwhile, he vigorously defended Catholic orthodoxy in Spain, which became the citadel of the Catholic Reformation, and crushed a Morisco revolt in the Alpujarras region of Granada (1568–1570).

Interested in obtaining knowledge of his American possessions, Philip sponsored scientific expeditions in the New World, such as Francisco Hernández's investigation of the medicinal properties of the plants of New Spain in the 1570s, and ordered royal officials to prepare reports on the geography and history of the colonies. His reign coincided with the beginning of large-scale silver production in the New World, but the crown's share of the American treasure, coupled with its revenue from ordinary sources, proved inadequate to support the costs of Philip's far-flung military ventures, and the precarious financial structure inherited by Philip from his father was further undermined by borrowing and increased taxation. To augment royal revenue, early in his reign Philip introduced the sale of public offices in America. Despite the use of such expedients, the crown was forced to suspend payments to its creditors in 1557, 1575, and 1596. By the end of his reign Spain's political and economic decline had already been adumbrated.

Philip died at the Escorial, the palace-mausoleum-monastery that he built near Madrid. He was succeeded by his only surviving son, who became Philip III.

HELEN DELPAR

PICADO, TEODORO (1900–1960). President of Costa Rica (1944–1948). Before turning to politics, Picado was a teacher in several secondary schools and the director of the Instituto de Alajuela. In the third administration of Ricardo JIMÉNEZ OREAMUNO (1932–1936), he served as Minister of Education. Afterward he was a deputy and then President of the Legislative Assembly. A close associate of President Rafael CALDERÓN GUARDIA (1940–1944), Picado assumed the Presidency in 1944 and carried on where his predecessor had left off. However, declining coffee prices following World War II and financial maladministration contributed to popular dissatisfaction in the last years of his government. In 1948 Picado and the Legislative

Assembly attempted to deny the electoral victory of Otilio ULATE over Calderón, precipitating a revolution led by José FIGUERES. Both Picado and Calderón were driven from the country.

While in exile in Nicaragua, Picado made his living by writing articles, many of them valuable contributions to Costa Rican and Nicaraguan history, for the government newspaper, *Las Novedades*. He never returned to Costa Rica; his self-imposed exile continued until his death in Managua in 1960.

CHARLES L. STANSIFER

PICHINCHA, BATTLE OF. Battle fought just west of Quito in May 1822. It was the last major engagement of the independence struggle in Ecuador. The patriot forces were led by Gen. Antonio José de SUCRE, whom Simón Bolívar had dispatched to the aid of the port city of Guayaquil after its bloodless revolution of October 1820. With additional forces raised locally and the assistance of Peruvian and Argentine contingents as well, Sucre early in 1822 launched an invasion of the Ecuadorian highlands that was timed to coincide with Bolívar's own progress south from Popayán in New Granada. The resistance of royalist Pasto delayed Bolívar, but Sucre, after an early setback, advanced steadily toward Quito.

In the early morning of May 24, Sucre occupied a position on the slopes of Mount Pichincha, dominating the Ecuadorian capital from the west. There he was attacked by the main royalist army in a hard-fought battle that lasted about three hours, with the advantage shifting first to one side and then to the other. At one stage several patriot units broke and fled, but the issue was finally decided by a vigorous charge of Colombian infantry under José María Córdoba.

Although the royalist forces had only been defeated, not destroyed, their cause was hopeless. Recognizing this, Melchor de Aymerich, the President of Quito and the highest Spanish authority of the region, signed a full surrender the next day, thus finally assuring the independence of what is now Ecuador.

DAVID BUSHNELL

PIÉROLA, NICOLÁS DE (1839–1913). Peruvian statesman and President (1895–1899). As one of the most popular civilian *caudillos* in Peruvian history, Piérola was active in politics for more than half a century. Born in Camaná, the conservative, ambitious, and temperamental Piérola rose quickly in both the political and the business worlds. In 1869 he served as President José BALTA's Finance Minister, pursuing the then unfortunately common policy of easy loans and over-reliance on GUANO sales for governmental expenditures. During the WAR OF THE PACIFIC (1879–1883), he briefly made himself dictator but failed to reverse Peru's long slide to defeat. At the end of the war he devoted himself to the reorganization of his Democratic party, and in 1894 he entered the presidential campaign. When it became apparent that the army commanders had rigged the election, he led a national uprising that cost thousands of lives but ended more than a decade of military rule.

In 1895, as the duly elected President, Piérola was at the height of his popularity. By then the impetuosity of the 1870s had given way to statesmanship. He proved conciliatory toward his old nemesis, the CIVILISTA PARTY. Together they set the scene both for the be-

ginning of the economic revival of the nation, in a shambles since the end of the war, and for the development of stable institutions that ensured Peru's orderly development for more than twenty years. Piérola's administration was, in fact, one of the most productive in Peruvian history. In 1899 he peacefully transferred the presidential office to his successor. Although his popularity remained unabated, the Civilistas, having gained control of the electoral machinery, were able to deny him a chance to return to power.

See also DREYFUS CONTRACT.

ORAZIO A. CICCARELLI

PINHEIRO MACHADO, JOSÉ GOMES (1851–1915). Brazilian political figure. Born in Cruz Alta, Rio Grande do Sul, Pinheiro Machado attended the Military School in Rio de Janeiro in preparation for an army career but resigned because of parental objections and later switched to law. He graduated from the São Paulo law school in 1878 and entered private practice in Rio Grande do Sul, where he joined the Republican party. Elected as a senator to the Constituent Assembly, he helped draft the republican constitution of 1891 (*see* CONSTITUTION OF 1891: BRAZIL). Pinheiro Machado took an active part in the military phase of the revolution and civil war in Rio Grande do Sul (1893–1895), first to restore Júlio de Castilhos to the governorship and subsequently to defend the federal administration of Floriano PEIXOTO. Before peace was fully restored, he returned to the Senate, where for the next two decades he was the representative of Governor de Castilhos, and later of Governor Borges de Medeiros, to the national government.

After 1900 Pinheiro Machado was clearly the most powerful individual in the Brazilian Congress. He largely controlled its membership from his position as perennial chairman and absolute boss of the Credentials Committee, which seated only candidates who had been elected by his political allies. Although he was not able to secure the Presidency for himself, Pinheiro Machado gained the reputation of President maker because of his adept manipulation of the oligarchies that controlled state politics in Brazil during the years of the FIRST REPUBLIC. He was assassinated on September 8, 1915.

ROLLIE E. POPPINO

PINZÓN, VICENTE YÁÑEZ (ca. 1460–1509). Spanish navigator. Pinzón was one of three brothers in a Palos family of seamen that included Martín Alonso and Francisco Martín, all three of whom accompanied Christopher COLUMBUS in 1492. He achieved fame as the captain of the *Niña* and has the additional distinction of having always remained loyal to Columbus, unlike his brother Martín, who commanded the *Pinta*. An expedition of his own left Palos on November 18, 1499, with four ships on a voyage of discovery to the Indies. The party sailed southward and then southwest. Pinzón was blown off his course and reached the easternmost point of Brazil on January 20, 1500. (Pedro Álvares CABRAL did not arrive in Brazil until April, but word of his discovery reached Europe before Pinzón returned.) Unable to develop a trading relationship with the natives, the Spaniards sailed northward along the coast for 2,000 miles. They discovered the mouth of the Amazon, which Pinzón called Santa María de la Mar Dulce (St. Mary of the Sea of Fresh Waters) and believed to be part of the Ganges. He sailed through the Gulf of Paria to the Caribbean Sea and northwest to Santo Domingo, which he reached on June 23, 1500, and returned to Spain on September 30, 1500.

In 1508 Pinzón was authorized to make a voyage to the New World in search of the Spice Islands. He sailed from Sanlúcar de Barrameda on June 29 with Juan Díaz de SOLÍS and Pedro de Ledesma. After sailing around Cuba and following the Central and South American coastlines as far south as the Río Negro, the party returned to Spain on November 14, 1509.

MARTIN TORODASH

PIPIOLO. Nickname, meaning "novice," first applied to Chilean liberals in the 1820s. It is generally thought to derive from the relatively modest social background of some of the liberal politicians of the period. A newspaper with the title *El Pipiolo* published eight issues in 1827. Although the *pipiolos* lost power in the brief civil war of 1829–1830, the term itself survived and was later used for many decades to describe members of the Chilean Liberal party (*see* LIBERAL PARTY: CHILE).

SIMON COLLIER

PIZARRO, FRANCISCO (ca. 1470–1541). Spanish conqueror of the empire of the INCAS and founder of Lima, capital of Peru. An illegitimate son of Capt. Gonzalo Pizarro of the Royal Infantry, he was born in Trujillo, Estremadura. Pizarro went to the West Indies with the fleet of Governor Nicolás de Ovando of Hispaniola (1502). In 1509 he joined the expedition led by Alonso de OJEDA to the Gulf of Urabá; when Ojeda returned to Hispaniola for reinforcements, he left Pizarro as

Francisco Pizarro. [Organization of American States]

second in command, a clear mark of his respect for Pizarro's military qualities. Later Pizarro joined the expedition of Vasco Núñez de BALBOA that discovered the Pacific Ocean (1513). With the arrival of Governor Pedro Arias de ÁVILA (Pedrarias) in Darién in 1514, Pizarro shifted allegiance, and less than two years later he arrested Balboa at the behest of Pedrarias, who believed Balboa guilty of treason.

By 1522 Pizarro's seniority and military experience over twenty years had earned him considerable respect and prosperity. He had become an encomendero and *vecino* (resident) of Panama City, serving on the municipal council and as magistrate. He had adopted Diego de ALMAGRO as a junior partner in various enterprises, some of which were joined in by a third man, the schoolmaster-priest Fernando de Luque. Meanwhile, lands southwest of Panama had been discovered by Pascual de Andagoya (1522), but follow-up expeditions had failed. Pedrarias granted Pizarro and Almagro permission to undertake new discoveries, claiming a share of the anticipated profits. With Pizarro as military leader and Almagro in charge of logistics and recruitment, the partners began in 1524 two years of unrewarding exploration along the Pacific coast of Colombia. Finally, during the period 1526–1528 definite signs of a high Indian civilization were located in the village of Tumbes, an Inca outpost on the Gulf of Guayaquil. Needing reinforcements, Pizarro returned to Panama, found his funds exhausted, and sailed to Spain, where he spent a year obtaining royal favor, support, and recruits from his native province. Supplied with the titles of Governor, *adelantado,* and *alguacil mayor* of Peru, Pizarro returned to Panama. In January 1531, he led forth an expedition of 180 men and 27 horses while Almagro remained behind to follow with reinforcements. After arriving in Peru, Pizarro's force was joined by two groups from Nicaragua led by the veterans Sebastián de BENALCÁZAR and Hernando de SOTO. Pizarro then founded San Miguel (Piura) as a base and marched to Cajamarca in the northern highlands, where he found the court of ATAHUALPA, the recently victorious Inca who ruled over an empire weakened by years of civil war. Vastly outnumbered, Pizarro and his men audaciously lured Atahualpa's bodyguards into an ambush, massacred many, and captured Atahualpa, whom they held for ransom. While a huge sum was being collected, Almagro's force arrived, too late to merit a share of the ransom. Pizarro, rather than release Atahualpa as agreed, tried and executed him on charges that he had instigated rebellion. This deed has been judged a blunder because it destroyed what influence the Spaniards had gained over the Incas through their King and led ultimately to native rebellion.

There followed the Spanish capture of Cuzco (1533), the subjugation of the northern Inca kingdom of Quito by Benalcázar (1534), and the founding of Lima (1535). Pizarro's brother Hernando visited the imperial court and returned to Peru bearing a marquisate for Francisco and a commision of *adelantado* for Almagro, who was allotted 200 leagues to the south of Cuzco. Almagro immediately departed for Chile on a two-year expedition of discovery and in 1537 returned empty-handed after a 2,400-mile march of incredible difficulty. Upon arrival at Cuzco, Almagro raised the siege of MANCO INCA, imprisoned Hernando and Gonzalo PIZARRO, and claimed that city as part of his territory. The ensuing quarrel between the Pizarro family and the "men of Chile" embittered relations between the former partners. An attempted arbitration that released Hernando Pizarro failed to satisfy the *almagristas*. Finally, a civil war broke out among the Spaniards that delayed the pacification of Peru for twelve years. The first important leader to fall was Almagro, who was defeated, captured, and executed by Hernando Pizarro (1537–1538). The rancor spawned by these events culminated in the assassination of Francisco Pizarro by Almagro's mestizo son and some survivors of the Chilean expedition in the Governor's palace in Lima in 1541.

Bibliography. Pedro de Cieza de León, *Civil Wars of Peru: The War of Quito,* tr. by Clements R. Markham, London, 1913; id., *The War of Chupas,* London, 1918; id., *The War of Las Salinas,* London, 1923; John Hemming, *The Conquest of the Incas,* New York, 1970; Frederick A. Kirkpatrick, *The Spanish Conquistadores,* Cleveland and New York, 1962; James Lockhart, *The Men of Cajamarca: A Social and Biographical Study of the First Conquerors of Peru,* Austin, Tex., 1972; William H. Prescott, *History of the Conquest of Peru,* 2 vols., Boston, 1847.

WILLIAM S. DUDLEY

PIZARRO, GONZALO (1506?–1548). Younger brother of Francisco PIZARRO, he was best known for his search for El Dorado (*see* DORADO, EL) and his rebellion against royal authority. After Francisco's audience with Emperor Charles V (King CHARLES I) in 1529, Gonzalo returned with him to Panama and departed with the Pizarro–Diego de ALMAGRO expedition to Peru. He participated in the massacre at Cajamarca, the capture of ATAHUALPA, and the occupation of Cuzco (1532–1535). He aided his brothers Juan and Hernando in defending Cuzco against the siege of MANCO INCA and was arrested and imprisoned by Almagro upon the latter's return from Chile (1537). Gonzalo escaped in time to help defeat Almagro's men in the Battle of Las Salinas and was rewarded with land grants in the region of Charcas (Bolivia), which he conquered with his brother Hernando.

Appointed Governor of Quito (1539), Gonzalo immediately set out with a large expedition to explore the eastern slopes of the ANDES MOUNTAINS in search of El Dorado. Enduring many hardships, he discovered rich stands of cinnamon, reached the confluence of the Coca and Napo Rivers, and unintentionally sponsored Francisco de ORELLANA's epic navigation of the AMAZON RIVER. In 1542 Gonzalo returned to Quito with his depleted party and retired to his estates in Charcas. He later rebelled against the authority of Viceroy Blasco Núñez Vela, who was killed in battle with Pizarro's forces (1546). Gonzalo remained master of Peru until the army of Pedro de la Gasca, the King's representative, defeated his in battle (1548). Gonzalo Pizarro was then tried, condemned, and executed as a traitor.

WILLIAM S. DUDLEY

PLATT AMENDMENT. The Platt Amendment, designed to regulate the relations between the United States and Cuba, originated in an amendment to the Army Appropriations bill of 1901. Although it was named for Senator Orville H. Platt of Connecticut, chairman of the Committee on Relations with Cuba, its chief author was Secretary of War Elihu Root. Of the amendment's eight articles, the most important was the third, which authorized United States intervention "for the preservation of Cuban independence [and] the maintenance of a government adequate for the protection of life, property, and individual liberty." This clause was seen as a means whereby the United States might protect its interests in Cuba and forestall the danger of European intervention without invoking the MONROE DOCTRINE, which was not recognized by European nations. Under the terms of other articles, Cuba agreed to sign no treaty that might impair its independence and to limit its freedom to contract debts. In addition, the Isle of Pines was omitted from the boundaries of Cuba, its disposition to be determined later, and Cuba pledged the sale or lease of land for coaling stations or naval bases to the United States. The members of Cuba's Constituent Assembly reluctantly adopted the amendment as an appendix to the constitution of 1901, and it was incorporated into the permanent treaty between the United States and Cuba (1903). It was abrogated in 1934.

HELEN DELPAR

PLAZA [LASSO], GALO (1906–   ). Ecuadorian statesman. Plaza was born in New York while his father, former President Leonidas PLAZA, was Ecuadorian Minister to the United States. The younger Plaza had his primary and secondary schooling in Ecuador but returned to the United States for higher education. He attended the Universities of California and Maryland and Georgetown University, where he was a better football player than student. One lasting effect of Plaza's youthful residence in the United States was that he learned to speak English like a North American.

In 1930 Plaza entered the Ecuadorian diplomatic corps, becoming an attaché in the embassy in Washington. After a few years he withdrew from the foreign service to follow in his father's footsteps in politics. In 1936 he was elected mayor of Quito. Subsequently he became Minister of Defense, served as Ambassador to Washington, and was elected to the Senate. When presidential elections were held in 1948 after the overthrow of the dictatorship of President José María VELASCO IBARRA, Plaza, although an independent, ran as the candidate of the Liberal party (*see* LIBERAL PARTY: ECUADOR). Victorious over several other nominees, he governed with the support principally of the Liberals and the Socialists.

Galo Plaza's administration (1948–1952) was unspectacular, but it was an unusually democratic government for Ecuador. The opposition functioned freely, the press was unmuzzled, and there were no political prisoners. Emphasis was placed on expanding the national economy. As a result, the traditional exports of coffee and cacao increased substantially, a beginning was made in developing the banana industry, which subsequently became the major source of foreign exchange (*see* BANANA INDUSTRY: ECUADOR), and some progress was made in industrialization. However, the Plaza government made no serious effort to initiate basic reforms such as land redistribution. Apart from the fact that the President, as a large highland landholder himself, may not have particularly favored such a program, he undoubtedly felt that reformist measures would have aroused the kind of opposition that would

Galo Plaza. [*IPS*]

have made it impossible for him to complete successfully his term in office.

Several attempts were made by dissident military men to overthrow the government, but they were thwarted with relative ease. Plaza presided over free elections at the end of his term, and these brought back to the Presidency the hardy perennial candidate Velasco Ibarra, to whom he turned over his post in 1952.

After leaving the Presidency, Galo Plaza returned to live on his highland estate. He had already achieved a considerable reputation as a progressive landowner, having ended most of the semifeudal obligations that his tenants had traditionally owed to their *patrón*, and encouraging them to develop handicraft industries that would permit them to add to their income and raise their levels of living. He also had established schools on his hacienda and was known to be a scientific farmer. On a limited scale, he now carried out experiments in allowing his tenants to become owners of their own land.

Plaza's interests and activities were by no means confined to his private concerns. He remained a major element in national politics, although, unlike many other former Presidents, he did not try to get reelected to the Presidency. In the years following his presidential administration he served the United Nations in several capacities. Thus, he served with United Nations peacekeeping groups in Lebanon, the Congo, and Cyprus. During 1957 and 1958 he was head of a special working party of the United Nations ECONOMIC COMMISSION FOR LATIN AMERICA that drew up some of the suggestions which led a few years later to the launching of the LATIN AMERICAN FREE TRADE ASSOCIATION (LAFTA). Plaza strongly supported the idea of Latin American economic unity (*see* ECONOMIC INTEGRATION).

In February 1968, while serving in Cyprus, Plaza was elected by the Council of the ORGANIZATION OF AMERICAN STATES (OAS) to serve a ten-year term

as OAS Secretary-General, the successor to Dr. José A. MORA. In this post Plaza sought to exert a leadership role. He attempted to induce the United States to intensify its interest in and aid for Latin American economic development, while at the same time stressing the need for the Latin American countries to do the utmost to help themselves. He also used his influence to try to bring about a rapprochement between the OAS and Fidel CASTRO's Cuba, although this effort was resisted not only by the United States but also by many of the Latin American members of the OAS.

Bibliography. George I. Blanksten, *Ecuador: Constitutions and Caudillos,* Berkeley, Calif., 1951; Galo Plaza, *Problems of Democracy in Latin America,* Chapel Hill, N.C., 1955; id., *Latin America Today and Tomorrow,* Washington, 1971.

ROBERT J. ALEXANDER

PLAZA [GUTIÉRREZ], LEONIDAS (1865–1932). President of Ecuador (1901–1905, 1912–1916). Born in Manabí, Plaza appeared with Eloy ALFARO in an 1884 Liberal uprising, gained experience and the rank of general in El Salvador and Costa Rica, and fought with Alfaro in the Battle of Gatazo. He served in Alfaro's government, succeeded him as President (1901–1905), and presided over the completion of many Liberal Radical goals (*see* LIBERAL PARTY: ECUADOR). A breach between Plaza and Alfaro terminated with Alfaro's assassination and Plaza's reelection to the Presidency in 1912.

Plaza's second term coincided with the commencement of both World War I and rule by the Banco Comercial y Agrícola (*see* CACAO INDUSTRY: ECUADOR). As President, Plaza was relied upon to uphold the Moratorium Law, which suspended payment of gold by the banks indefinitely. This allowed favored banks to make loans to the government in unsupported paper currency. The government in turn supported a huge program of public works and railroads allocated on a regional basis to satisfy local political chiefs. Railroad politics, a swollen bureaucracy, and a prolonged *alfarista* uprising in Esmeraldas forced Plaza to contract new domestic and foreign debts. He managed skillfully, his key to success being his alliance with the cacao export bank. During the rule of succeeding bank-dominated Presidents to 1925, Plaza remained in control of the military. In the July revolution of that year he was arrested along with the bank manager, Francisco Urbina Jado, and the President of Ecuador and exiled.

LOIS WEINMAN

PLN. *See* PARTIDO LIBERACIÓN NACIONAL.

POINSETT, JOEL R[OBERTS] (1779–1851). American diplomat and politician, known also for introducing the brilliant poinsettia flower to the United States from Mexico. A South Carolinian by birth, Poinsett was sent in 1810 as a special commercial agent of the United States to Buenos Aires. Appointment as Consul General for the provinces of Buenos Aires, Chile, and Peru followed in 1811. The same year he was transferred to Chile, where his open sympathy and help for independence leaders, especially José Miguel CARRERA and his brothers, forced his return to Buenos Aires in 1814. Upon his return to the United States he won election in 1816 to the South Carolina General Assembly and reelection in 1818. From 1821 to 1825 he was a member of the United States Congress.

In 1822 President Monroe sent Poinsett on a short mission to Mexico, a visit that resulted in his *Notes on Mexico* (1824). His next assignment to that country was as the first American Minister, a post he held from 1825 to 1829. Assuming his usual active role, Poinsett supported President Guadalupe VICTORIA, the opponent of Conservative political forces in Mexico, and vied for influence with the British Chargé d'Affaires, H. G. Ward. Accused of interfering in Mexican politics, Poinsett was forced by a Conservative victory in 1829 to return to the United States.

Back in South Carolina, he became a leader of the Unionist party in opposition to the nullification movement. From 1837 to 1841, during the Van Buren administration, Poinsett was Secretary of War. After his retirement in 1841 he continued to make known his opposition to such matters as the MEXICAN WAR and secession.

RICHARD B. GRAY

POLITICAL PARTIES. In a number of Latin American countries political parties can be traced into the nineteenth century, but they have become far more important in recent years. Today parties can no longer be regarded merely as pressure groups or narrow personalistic factions. Rather, they have become central to existing political systems. Truly national, mass-based, popular parties are creatures of the modern era. Among their major characteristics are widespread popular appeal, effective organizational machinery, and an identifiable common ideology or set of policy goals. Moreover, they have endured over a period of years to win lasting electoral acceptance and register a meaningful impact on politics.

The historical genesis of Latin America's early parties came shortly after the winning of independence. By the 1850s political leaders in Colombia, Mexico, and several other countries had grouped themselves into Conservative and Liberal factions, establishing the traditional pattern that persisted into the twentieth century. Three basic issues generally divided these early parties. Conservatives were adamantly pro-clerical in upholding the interests of the Roman Catholic Church, championed a strong unitary form of centralized government, and supported the exercise of national control over economic policy. In marked contrast, the Liberals advocated church-state separation and the establishment of free secular education. They also sought a federal, decentralized governmental structure, while encouraging free trade, open immigration, and laissez faire economic policies.

Factional strife between Conservatives and Liberals was endemic, leading to prolonged and sometimes violent civil strife in Colombia, Uruguay, Venezuela, Ecuador, and elsewhere. By the early 1900s the major points of dispute began to recede, however, while increasing public participation in politics contributed to a fragmentation of the old elitist-controlled parties. The extension of suffrage, the rise of early industrialization, the beginnings of urbanization, and an influx of different political doctrines all contributed to a crumbling of traditional party patterns. Today only a few countries still retain the old Conservative-Liberal

division, most notably Colombia, Nicaragua, Paraguay, and, to some extent, Ecuador. *See* CONSERVATIVE PARTY (COLOMBIA); CONSERVATIVE PARTY (ECUADOR); LIBERAL PARTY (COLOMBIA); LIBERAL PARTY (ECUADOR).

By the close of World War II a number of modern mass-based parties had begun to emerge. Since then the overall role of parties has grown swiftly. At the same time, great variety has been evident throughout the hemisphere. Organizational bases differ extensively, and ideological or programmatic stances range from one extreme of the political spectrum to the other. Furthermore, individual party systems have taken a variety of forms. While the most common pattern is multiparty, there are examples of other types. One-party systems are not uncommon, being found most typically in noncompetitive, dictatorial regimes. Thus the Dominican Republic under Gen. Rafael Leonidas TRUJILLO MOLINA (1930–1961) and Colombia under Gen. Gustavo ROJAS PINILLA (1953–1957) saw official government parties dominating politics, with meaningful opposition prohibited or seriously curtailed. In Mexico, however, the long hegemonic control of the PARTIDO REVOLUCIONARIO INSTITUCIONAL (PRI) has been maintained despite the presence of several small opposition parties. For all practical purposes the Mexican system is one-party, yet it is quite different from a system in which the government prohibits any form of competition.

Two-party systems are increasingly rare, given a customary proliferation of parties and the progressive disappearance of the Conservative-Liberal division. Only Colombia and Uruguay have maintained two-party systems in recent years, with both nearing the vanishing point (*see* BLANCO PARTY: URUGUAY; COLORADO PARTY: URUGUAY). In the former the prolonged effort by national elites to maintain control through a two-party alliance has broken down. Uruguay has also experienced fragmentation, with the two traditional parties now divided into smaller cliques and factions, so that in practice there is a multiparty system. In short, the prevailing contemporary pattern is that of more than two parties. These include both fully modern, well-organized national parties and the so-called mini-parties, which appear and disappear with dismaying rapidity.

Two major aspects stand out in analyzing parties: structure and organization, and doctrine and ideology. The former, although frequently ignored, has proved crucial in winning elections and in governing. Types of party organization include personalist, or ad hoc, elitist-directed, and representational. Party organizations of the first type have been common for years and still persist in many countries. The personalist party, headed by a single *caudillo,* or chief, exists almost solely for the purpose of achieving the *caudillo*'s political ambitions. The leader's interests are decisive in party deliberations, there is little meaningful organization, and the directorship is composed of friends and colleagues selected by the *caudillo.* He enjoys a *patrón*-client relationship with his followers. Typical illustrations of the personalist party are the Unión Nacional Odriísta (UNO) of Manuel A. ODRÍA in Peru and the Federación Nacional Velasquista (FNV) of the five-time Ecuadorian president José María VELASCO IBARRA.

The elitist-directed party frequently has a detailed hierarchy of party structures, but these are not decisive in party affairs. In practice major decisions are taken by a small handful of politicians at the apex of the organizational pyramid. Upper echelons are oligarchical in outlook, with party assemblies and convocations providing a convenient rubber stamp for decisions already taken. The leadership is nondemocratic and self-perpetuating, composed of notables immune to rank-and-file opinion. Influence is often wielded by noted public figures not formally within the organizational hierarchy. Ex-presidents and former presidential nominees are powerful, while prominent businessmen and others in the socioeconomic elite may be instrumental in manipulating party policy. Like personalist parties, the directed ones often have brief political lives, although they are obviously less dependent upon the fortunes of a single individual.

In contrast, the representational party is oriented toward broad participation and attempts to articulate the interests of its membership. The party machinery reaches throughout the country, with local and regional organs regularly active. The selection of leaders is popular and representative, with party notables reaching positions of authority only after years of faithful service. Conventions and assemblies provide a forum in which a multitude of interests are represented. Strong labor, peasant, and youth wings frequently affect party decisions. Whereas the directed party resembles a head with no body, in the representational party all levels of activity become meaningful. A suggestive illustration is the 1963 national convention of Venezuela's ACCIÓN DEMOCRÁTICA (AD), where the wishes of the party founder, President Rómulo BETANCOURT, were rejected in the selection of a presidential nominee. Moreover, the party youth and labor branches played a large role in selecting the candidate.

The experience of recent years testifies to the significance of organization. At the same time, ideological or doctrinal considerations count. Especially since World War II, heightened attention has been given to the formulation of a coherent body of doctrine. At the extreme right are falangist-type parties that advocate an essentially corporative and quasi-fascist view. Admirers of ancient Spanish tradition and committed to an elitist hierarchical system, they revere the church and the heritage of *hispanidad* and seek a disciplined, orderly society. Prime examples are the Acción Revolucionaria Nacionalista Ecuatoriana (ARNE) of Ecuador and the Brazilian Integralistas (*see* INTEGRALISMO).

Traditional conservative parties, supportive of the status quo and concerned with preserving the existing system, are fundamentally resistant to popular demands for change and reform. In the contemporary setting they recognize that the maintenance of their traditional authority requires the articulation of some policy changes. Socioeconomic reforms may be yielded to reduce the pressure from below, but there is little inclination to encourage extensive improvement in the life of the masses. Among the many examples are the Conservative parties of Ecuador, Colombia, Honduras, and Nicaragua.

Reformist parties have become prominent, reflecting a growing social consciousness, the rise of the middle sectors, and the spread of public discontent. A number of Social Democratic parties have come to the fore in the last quarter century, including Venezuela's Acción Democrática, Costa Rica's PARTIDO LIBERACIÓN

NACIONAL (PLN), and, during its early years, the MOVIMIENTO NACIONALISTA REVOLUCIONARIO (MNR) of Bolivia. Stemming from Marxist origins, they supported fairly radical if democratic efforts to transform socioeconomic structures, later becoming more moderate and centrist in outlook. Reformist parties' criticisms of existing conditions are customarily sharp, but after their initial years the approach becomes increasingly gradualistic. Such parties encourage mass participation, stress the importance of democratic and representative institutions, and seek power by nonviolent, electoral means. (These parties are frequently but incorrectly referred to as Aprista parties. The term derives from the ALIANZA POPULAR REVOLUCIONARIA AMERICANA, or APRA, of Peru, once radical in outlook but subsequently conservative, wedded to the Peruvian establishment, and preeminently opportunistic.)

Another category of reformist parties, which arose in the 1960s, consists of the Christian Democrats. Inspired by progressive papal encyclicals and by the French New Catholic school of thought, they retain a commitment to Catholicism while seeking reforms quite similar to those of Social Democratic parties. AGRARIAN REFORM, industrial development, economic diversification, tax revision, and improved health and housing are among their major goals. They also share a commitment to the centrality of the state in the direction and implementation of national policy. Ideological statements pay tribute to moral and humanitarian values, further emphasizing the family and the sanctity of the home. The first Christian Democratic party to win power was the Chilean party under Eduardo FREI, who ruled from 1964 to 1970 (*see* PARTIDO DEMÓCRATA CRISTIANO). In 1969 Venezuela also inaugurated a Christian Democratic President, although the party, the COMITÉ DE ORGANIZACIÓN POLÍTICA ELECTORAL INDEPENDIENTE (COPEI), and its leader, Rafael CALDERA, were more centrist than their Chilean counterparts. Hemispherically the movement has also enjoyed some success in El Salvador and Peru. Contrary to the hopes of its theoreticians, however, the movement has failed to gain ascendancy in the majority of countries.

On the left of the spectrum stand a host of Marxist parties. The Marxist left is badly splintered, ranging from bourgeois, orthodox pro-Moscow Communist parties, as in Venezuela, Brazil, Argentina, and Bolivia, to radical and violence-prone movements in Chile, Guatemala, and Colombia. All stripes of factions may be found, even a Trotskyite group in Bolivia. The effect of the CUBAN REVOLUTION has been writ large on Latin American Marxism. In the early years after Fidel CASTRO's accession to power in 1959, the *fidelista* model was widely admired. Guerrilla warfare and peasant activism were advocated, and revolutionary bands took up arms in Venezuela, Guatemala, Colombia, Peru, and Bolivia. For such movements Revolution with a capital "R" was the order of the day, the ultimate objective being a drastic recasting of a nation's politics, economy, and social structure. After the failure of such movements to win power outside Cuba, attention turned in the 1970s to the case of Chile, where Socialist President Salvador ALLENDE, after winning democratic elections, undertook the task of building a socialist system by peaceful means.

Contemporary Latin American parties are by no

means fully responsive to national needs or to popular pressure for reform. Yet the most prominent ones (not coincidentally the most successful politically) have provided substantial impetus for change and progress. However, slow changes have often reflected the strength and durability of traditional social and economic forces as much as the shortcomings of political parties. As long as a political system operates within a constitutional framework and maintains a democratic process, the parties will continue to carry a major responsibility for national development and the improvement of living conditions.

Bibliography. Torcuato S. Di Tella, "Populism and Reform in Latin America," in Claudio Véliz (ed.), *Obstacles to Change in Latin America,* London, 1965, pp. 47–75; Burt H. English, *Liberación Nacional in Costa Rica,* Gainesville, Fla., 1971; Miguel Jorrín and John D. Martz, *Latin-American Political Thought and Ideology,* Chapel Hill, N.C., 1970; Ronald McDonald, "Electoral Systems, Party Representation and Political Change in Latin America," *Western Political Quarterly,* vol. XX, no. 3, September 1967, pp. 694–708; John D. Martz, *Acción Democrática: Evolution of a Modern Political Party in Venezuela,* Princeton, N.J., 1966; Robert E. Scott, "Political Parties and Policy-Making in Latin America," in Joseph LaPalombara and Myron Weiner (eds.), *Political Parties and Political Development,* Princeton, N.J., 1966, pp. 331–369; Edward J. Williams, *Latin-American Christian Democratic Parties,* Knoxville, Tenn., 1967.

JOHN D. MARTZ

POMBAL, MARQUÊS DE (SEBASTIÃO JOSÉ DE CARVALHO E MELO, 1699–1782). Dominant Minister in Portugal (1750–1777), generally known by the title Marquês de Pombal, which he received in 1770. Having previously served as Portuguese envoy in London and Vienna, he moved into a position of almost absolute power during the reign of Joseph I, especially after the Lisbon earthquake of 1755. A contemporary of the enlightened despots, Pombal had much in common with them. Anxious to reestablish Portugal's independence from what he regarded as excessive dependence on Great Britain, he instigated reforms in almost all aspects of metropolitan and colonial affairs.

For Brazil the Pombaline period saw a series of administrative, fiscal, and military innovations. The method of collecting the royal fifth in Minas Gerais was reformed, a basic annual contribution of 100 arrobas of gold (1 arroba = 32 pounds) replacing the previous capitation tax on slaves. Inspection houses were established in the major port cities to oversee the pricing of sugar and tobacco. A serious attempt was made to increase population by encouraging miscegenation between Indians and whites. In 1755–1756 a monopolistic company was established for Grão Pará and Maranhão, and the expulsion from Brazil of all *commissários volantes,* itinerant traders who had flooded the colony as commission agents of foreign, mainly British, merchant houses established in Lisbon, was ordered. The choice of Pará and Maranhão, the stronghold of Jesuit missionary activities and the scene of bitter Jesuit-colonist disputes, for the first monopoly company, one of the major objectives of which in the metropolitan setting was to encourage national merchant interests, thrust the "nationalizing" actions of

the Pombal administration into the midst of the geopolitical problems that had arisen out of the Madrid settlement and into conflict with the Jesuits, who had opposed the settlement all along (*see* MADRID, TREATY OF). Indeed, Pombal came increasingly to see the Jesuits, along with the English and the dispossessed traders, as a threat to his policy as a whole. And, given his power, the reality of the threat was of less importance than his perception of it. *See also* JESUITS, EXPULSION OF (BRAZIL).

The Spanish invasion of Portugal in 1762 was a rude awakening for the Portuguese government. Much greater circumspection became necessary in relations with Great Britain, whose military aid had become essential. The plan to establish privileged companies to cover all Brazil, a measure strenuously opposed by the British merchants in Lisbon, was abandoned, leaving only the far north and (since 1759) Pernambuco and Paraíba as monopoly zones. Nonetheless, the objective of reestablishing national control of basic resources and commerce continued under other guises. The capital of the Viceroyalty of Brazil was moved from Bahia (modern Salvador) to Rio de Janeiro in 1763. The fleet system was abolished in 1765. The Lisbon *junta do comércio* (board of trade) established by Pombal in 1755 took an active part in stimulating colonial economic development. Coffee, wheat, rice, flax, indigo, and cochineal were all encouraged by means of subsidy, technical assistance, and tariff manipulation. Most spectacular, however, was the success of the Company of Grão Pará and Maranhão in developing raw cotton production, which within two decades was to become a major item of Portuguese reexport to Britain and France. Loans bearing interest of only 3 percent and tariff manipulation aided the production of tobacco and hides in the Pernambuco region. Manufacturing and processing enterprises were encouraged, among them an iron foundry in the captaincy of São Paulo and a rice-processing plant in Rio de Janeiro. The fiscal system was thoroughly overhauled, modern bookkeeping techniques were introduced, and *juntas da fazenda* (treasury boards) were established for each captaincy. Many new auxiliary regiments were raised, and the military establishment was brought within the reforming purview of experts sent from Portugal. In 1771 the diamond district of Minas Gerais was taken from the administration of the contractors and placed under direct royal supervision. Like most of the measures, the new diamond regulations also provided for and welcomed participation by the most powerful regional magnates.

Pombal, who fell from power upon the death of the King in 1777, remains one of the most controversial figures in Portuguese history, and with good reason, for there was hardly an area of Portuguese life that he did not interfere with or seek to alter. In some ways his impact on Brazil was no less critical, and many elite elements gained much from his policies. He was very much aware of the need for circumspection in dealings with Brazil and on the whole treated Brazilians well.

Bibliography. Dauril Alden, *Royal Government in Colonial Brazil, with Special Reference to the Administration of the Marquis of Lavradio, Viceroy, 1769–1779,* Berkeley, Calif., 1968; João Lúcio d'Azevedo, *O Marquês de Pombal e a Sua Época,* 2d ed., Lisbon, 1922; Jorge Borges de Macedo, *A Situação Económica no Tempo de Pombal: Alguns Aspectos,* Oporto, 1951; id., "Portugal e a Economia 'Pombalina': Temas e Hipoteses," *Revista de História,* no. 19, São Paulo, 1954, pp. 81–100; Kenneth R. Maxwell, *Conflicts and Conspiracies: Brazil and Portugal, 1750–1808,* Cambridge, England, 1973; Marcos Carneiro de Mendonça, *O Marquês de Pombal e o Brasil,* São Paulo, 1960.

KENNETH R. MAXWELL

PONCE [ENRÍQUEZ], CAMILO (1912–   ). Lawyer, writer, and President of Ecuador (1956–1960). Ponce was born into the sierra elite (*see* SIERRA: ECUADOR). After study abroad he received a law degree from the Central University of Quito in 1938 and devoted himself to a successful practice and Conservative politics (*see* CONSERVATIVE PARTY: ECUADOR). In 1951 he founded the Social Christian Movement, a political party somewhat to the right of Chilean and European Christian Socialists. He was an admirer of José María VELASCO IBARRA during the latter's 1952–1956 administration, served as his Minister of Government, and received Velasco's support in the 1956 presidential campaign. Ponce was elected by a small margin and became the first Conservative President in Ecuador since 1895. He kept many of Velasco Ibarra's men in office, but he allied himself with *quiteños* on the extreme right and gradually favored them in government posts, thus irritating followers of Velasco Ibarra.

Ponce is remembered for giving Ecuador an orderly administration with a tight fiscal policy. Although banana exports increased, many *guayaquileños* objected to what they termed an austerity budget. Ponce also broke with his former friend and supporter, Velasco Ibarra. The break was so decisive that he resigned from office one day early rather than hand over the reins of government to Velasco Ibarra when he was reelected in 1960.

Although still an active politician, Ponce received a series of setbacks after 1960. He was badly defeated in the 1968 presidential election and could not muster sufficient support to confront the electoral forces of Asaad Bucaram in 1972. He nevertheless remained one of the most significant politicians on the Ecuadorian scene.

LOIS WEINMAN

PONCE, MANUEL (1882–1948). Mexican composer. Born in Fresnillo, Zacatecas, he studied composition with Enrico Bossi in Bologna and piano with Martin Krause in Berlin. After a period in Mexico, New York, and Havana, he returned to Europe, this time to study with Paul Dukas in Paris. His contact with French music brought a major change in his approach to music; after his early period, which dealt almost exclusively with popular music, he became concerned with the major forms of composition along stylistic lines deeply influenced by impressionistic esthetics. However, his popularity had been well established before the change, with songs such as "Estrellita" and "A la orilla de un palmar." Following this he built up a large catalog of works including more than 100 art songs, numerous works for the guitar, chamber music, and almost 100 solo piano works. Outstanding among these are his symphonic poem *Chapultepec* (1929), his twelve preludes and five sonatas for solo guitar, his *Suite en estilo antiguo* for orchestra (1935), his *Concierto del sur* for guitar and orchestra (1941), and his concerto for violin and orchestra (1943). He also wrote an opera, *El patio florido* (1913).

JUAN A. ORREGO-SALAS

PONCE DE LEÓN, JUAN (ca. 1460–1521). Spanish explorer. Born to a noble family in Santervás de Campos, Valladolid Province, he served as a page at court and in the campaign against the Moors in Granada. In 1493 he sailed from Cádiz with Christopher COLUMBUS on the second voyage, during which Puerto Rico was discovered on November 19. He returned to that island in 1508 after having helped to subdue the natives in the province of Higüey in eastern Hispaniola. He established a settlement, Caparra, near present-day San Juan, and served as Governor of Puerto Rico from 1509 to 1511. In 1512, hearing tales of a rich island called Bimini that supposedly contained a "fountain of youth," he obtained a commission to explore and colonize it. He sailed northward through the Bahamas and, during Easter (Pascua Florida), encountered the Florida coast, which was explored as far north as the outlet of St. Johns River east of present-day Jacksonville. The expedition, failing to find the legendary fountain and discovering the Indians to be hostile, gave up the search and turned back. Still believing the land to be an island, Ponce de León sailed around the tip of the peninsula and may have explored the west coast as far north as Tampa Bay or Apalachee Bay before heading for Cuba and Puerto Rico. During the next few years he served in various military pacifying expeditions in the West Indies. In 1521 he renewed his quest in Florida but once again encountered hostile natives. He was wounded in the thigh by an arrow and sailed for Cuba, where he died shortly afterward.

MARTIN TORODASH

POPULAR ACTION. *See* ACCIÓN POPULAR.

POPULAR ACTION FRONT. *See* FRENTE DE ACCIÓN POPULAR.

POPULAR FRONT (CHILE). The Chilean Popular Front (Frente Popular) was established in 1936 as a coalition of the Radical, Socialist, and Communist parties, other political groups, and organized labor to create a united opposition to the policies of President Arturo ALESSANDRI and his Finance Minister, Gustavo ROSS (*see* COMMUNIST PARTY: CHILE; RADICAL PARTY: CHILE; SOCIALIST PARTY: CHILE). Government economic policies and repression of discontent persuaded the Socialists, in February 1936, to call for the unity of left-wing forces and the Radical party, a call taken up the same month by the left-wing Radical deputy Justiniano Sotomayor at the party's Santiago assembly. The Communists were motivated not only by events in Chile but also by Moscow's new world strategy for Communist parties to ally themselves with other parties in "antifascist" fronts, as in Spain and France. The "fascist threat" in Chile was insignificant, but the policy suited the Communists' plans to make their party respectable, notably through association with the Radicals. The Radical party, however, was divided over cooperating with the left-wing parties.

Congressional elections in 1937 were the turning

point. Despite massive bribery by Ross, the front parties did well because of the popular enthusiasm the front had aroused. Radical skeptics now saw in the front the road to power, and with Ross himself proclaimed the right-wing candidate, the front parties met in April to select their nominee. Two days of debate ended dramatically when the Socialist contender, Marmaduke Grove, withdrew in favor of the Radical, Pedro AGUIRRE CERDA. Assisted by national reaction to the government's bloody repression of an abortive revolt by the Chilean Nazi party, the front won the election by a narrow margin. But the Popular Front did not long survive. Bitter rivalry between Radicals and Socialists and the Communists' refusal to enter the government created such problems for Aguirre Cerda that by January 1941 the front had virtually ceased to exist.

HAROLD BLAKEMORE

POPULATION. The population of Latin America in mid-1971 was 291 million, with a rate of growth that during the 1960s was 2.9 percent annually. By the end of the century the population should at least approach, and will probably exceed, 600 million. The region was the first of the underdeveloped areas of the world to undergo the first phase of the transition from the demographic conditions prevailing in preindustrial societies to those characteristic of industrially advanced societies, by the lowering of mortality rates, so that since the 1920s it has been the fastest-growing region in population. Two major population trends characterize Latin America: (1) a very rapid rate of growth (the population doubling within a quarter of a century), resulting from a relatively sharp decline in death rates, most pronounced in the immediate post-World War II period, while birthrates remained high; and (2) large-scale internal migration and population redistribution, with the rapid process of urbanization (notably rural-to-urban migration) clearly the major internal movement. The urban sector is increasing by 4 to 5 percent annually, so that the urban population doubles in fourteen to eighteen years.

Historical growth. Estimates of the pre-Columbian aboriginal population of Latin America vary from 8 million to 100 million. At least one-half, and probably two-thirds, of the inhabitants lived in the Aztec-Mayan and Inca regions (*see* AZTECS; INCAS; MAYAS). There was a significant, perhaps catastrophic, die-off of the Amerindian population as the result of European colonization, as diseases, the consequences of enslavement, starvation, and warfare took their toll. The decline of the native inhabitants probably continued until the middle or latter half of the seventeenth century. In many districts Amerindians disappeared entirely. Partly for this reason, African Negro slaves were introduced early in the colonial period, and 7 million to 20 million were imported before the slave trade was effectively abolished well into the nineteenth century. Because of very high mortality there was little if any natural increase among Negroes until the end of the colonial period. Virtually all the slaves went to the Antilles and the NORTHEAST of Brazil, whence they gradually spread to neighboring regions. (*See* NEGRO IN BRAZIL; NEGRO IN SPANISH AMERICA.) During the colonial period many Europeans, primarily Spaniards

TABLE 1. POPULATION GROWTH
(In millions)

Year	World	Latin America	Percentage of world population
1650	508	9.5	1.87
1750	711	10.5	1.48
1800	913	21	2.30
1850	1,131	33	2.92
1900	1,590	63	3.96
1920	1,811	91	5.02
1930	2,070	108	5.22
1940	2,295	130	5.66
1950	2,517	163	6.48
1960	3,003	213	7.09
1970	3,632	283	7.79

and Portuguese, also settled in Latin America.

The population of Latin America began to grow, at first very slowly, some time after the mid-seventeenth century. Table 1 compares the growth of the population of Latin America and the world since 1650. The major factor in population growth in Latin America has been natural increase, primarily the result of a decline in mortality, although immigration has been an important contributor in certain countries.

Beginning about the middle of the nineteenth century, immigration, primarily from Europe (especially Spain, Italy, and Portugal) and to a much smaller degree from Asia, became a significant growth factor in certain regions of Latin America. A total of at least 12 million, and perhaps 15 million, immigrants arrived. More than four-fifths went to Argentina and Brazil, and considerably smaller numbers to Cuba and Uruguay. Perhaps one-quarter to one-third of the immigrants eventually reemigrated. The wave of immigration ended with the economic depression of the 1930s, but a smaller movement, amounting to perhaps 1.5 million, occurred in the post-World War II period and continued through the 1950s. This movement was directed essentially to Argentina, Brazil, and Venezuela. *See* IMMIGRATION (ARGENTINA); IMMIGRATION (BRAZIL); IMMIGRATION (URUGUAY); IMMIGRATION (VENEZUELA).

During recent decades there has been significant emigration from Latin America, notably of Mexicans to the southwestern United States, Puerto Ricans to New York, West Indians primarily to Great Britain, and Cubans to Miami. At present, prospects for significant international migrations appear rather poor. Intraregional movements involving migrations between Latin American countries, although significant in the past, are coming under increasing restriction and supervision, but clandestine movements apparently still occur.

Distribution. The spatial distribution pattern of population in Latin America has several outstanding features:

1. *Sparse population density.* The overall population density is only half the world average. High den-

TABLE 2. POPULATION CHARACTERISTICS

	Population (in millions)		Density (in square miles), 1970 [c]	Current annual population percentage increase [d]	Birth-rate [abd]	Death rate [abd]	Infant mortality rate [abd]	Urban percentage, 1970 [e]	Percentage of annual increase, 1960–1970 [e]	
	1970 [a]	1980 [b]							Urban population	Rural population
Mexico	49.1	71.4	67	3.4	43	10	69	60	5.3	1.8
Guatemala	5.2	6.9	122	2.9	43	17	92	34	4.2	2.8
El Salvador	3.5	4.9	427	3.4	47	13	67	38	5.5	2.5
Honduras	2.6	3.7	60	3.4	49	17	44	32	6.5	2.6
Nicaragua	2.0	2.8	39	3.0	46	17	55	44	5.7	3.0
Costa Rica	1.7	2.7	88	3.8	45	7	67	35	5.0	4.0
Panama	1.5	2.0	49	3.3	41	9	41	48	4.9	1.6
Cuba	8.4	10.1	189	1.9	27	7	40	53	2.3	1.8
Dominican Republic	4.3	6.2	231	3.4	48	15	64	40	6.2	2.4
Haiti	4.9	6.8	453	2.5	44	20	190	17	5.9	1.8
Puerto Rico	2.7	3.1 [f]	826	1.4	25	6	24	44 [g]	1.5 [g]	−0.04 [g]
Venezuela	10.8	15.0	28	3.4	46	9	46	76	5.4	1.2
Colombia	21.1	31.4	49	3.4	44	11	78	58	6.1	1.6
Ecuador	6.1	8.4	54	3.4	45	11	91	38	6.2	2.4
Peru	13.6	18.5	28	3.1	42	11	73	52	6.0	1.6
Bolivia	4.9	6.0	10	2.4	44	19	77	35	4.1	1.5
Paraguay	2.4	3.5	16	3.4	45	11	84	36	5.6	2.6
Chile	9.8	12.2	34	2.3	33	9	92	74	3.9	0.8
Argentina	23.2	28.2	23	1.5	22	10	58	79	2.7	−0.2
Uruguay	2.9	3.3	41	1.2	21	9	49	81	2.2	−0.6
Brazil	95.3	124.0	28	2.8	38	10	93	48	4.6	1.5
Latin America [h]	283	378.4 [f]	36	2.9	38	10	81	54	4.3	1.5

[a] *Population and Vital Statistics Report,* United Nations Statistical Papers, Series A, vol. XXIV, no. 1, January 1972.

[b] *Datos básicos de población en América Latina, 1970,* Pan American Union, Department of Social Affairs, Washington.

[c] *Demographic Yearbook, 1970,* United Nations Department of Economic and Social Affairs, 1971. Based on data from Tables 1, 2, 13, 16, and 17.

[d] *World Population Data Sheet, 1971,* Population Reference Bureau, Inc., Washington, June 1971.

[e] Computed from data in *Datos básicos de población en América Latina, 1970* and *Demographic Yearbook, 1970,* Table 5. Data for certain countries do not cover the entire 1960–1970 period. Data for Puerto Rico are from *Statistical Abstract of the United States, 1971,* United States Department of Commerce, Washington, 1971.

[f] *World Population Prospects as Assessed in 1963,* United Nations Department of Economic and Social Affairs, Population Studies No. 41, 1966, Tables A3.8 and A3.2.

[g] Urban percentage is for 1960, and percentage of annual increase is for 1950–1960.

[h] Totals usually include other territories in addition to the countries listed.

sities occur only in the Antilles, El Salvador, and Guatemala, while Costa Rica is the only other country where the density exceeds the world average (*see* Table 2). In contrast, Bolivia, the most sparsely settled country, is included in the lowest group of countries in the world in population density. The Antilles is the most densely settled subregion, followed by mainland Middle America; South America is the most sparsely settled.

2. *Coastal and peripheral concentrations.* This feature is especially noticeable in South America, which has vast sparsely settled interior regions. The interior half of South America contains only slightly more than one-twelfth of the continent's population.

3. *Highland concentration within the tropics.* The ameliorating effects of altitude have made much of the highland Latin American tropics more attractive for habitation. Within the tropical environs at least half, and generally considerably more, of the national population resides in the highlands, except in the Antilles, Nicaragua, and Panama.

4. *Semi-isolated population clusters.* Population is concentrated in a small portion of the national area, with relatively empty spaces between population clusters. As a result, much of Latin America is still not effectively settled. International boundaries very rarely intersect even minor population clusters, and to a lesser degree this is true of national political subdivisions as well.

Some internal movements of the present and recent past are redistributing the population. The major movement is clearly the rapid process of urbanization. A countervailing trend is the movement toward a more even spread of the population throughout the individual countries as more sparsely populated districts are settled. There are significant migrations into newly developing areas, notably from the traditional highland areas of settlement into the lower altitudes and coastal plains of the humid tropics. However, the very extensive areas nearly devoid of settlement are absorbing only a negligible portion of the increases in the national populations. The least sparsely settled half of the area of Latin America still does not account for more than 5 percent of the total population.

Demographic characteristics. Since World War II the outstanding demographic characteristic of Latin America has been its prodigious rate of growth. The rate of population increase itself has been rising for several decades, and since 1920 the rate of population growth has increased by more than one-half, to approximately 3 percent annually. The current rate is highly likely to continue during the 1970s and then should begin a gradual decline. In contrast to the past, the level of fertility will be the major determinant of natural increase in Latin America because mortality has been reduced to a low level in most countries.

The individual countries of Latin America exhibit demographic characteristics that typify conditions prevailing in the underdeveloped world. However, Argentina and Uruguay in most demographic features resemble the developed countries, while Puerto Rico, Cuba, and Chile occupy an intermediate position between Argentina and Uruguay and the rest of the Latin American countries.

In most of Latin America fertility remains at a consistently high level, with birthrates of about 40 per 1,000 inhabitants or higher. Birthrates in Argentina and Uruguay approximate those of developed countries, while Cuba and, to a lesser degree, Chile have significantly reduced natality. Puerto Rico has undergone the most dramatic decline in fertility, the birthrate having been reduced by two-fifths since the late 1940s. Recent declines in natality in both Puerto Rico and Cuba have brought them almost to the level of the Río de la Plata countries.

Mortality has declined much more uniformly over Latin America; the decline has been especially pronounced since World War II. The overall death rate is now 10 per 1,000 inhabitants, although some countries, notably Haiti, the Dominican Republic, Bolivia, and parts of Central America, have a significantly higher mortality that is more typical of the Afro-Asian regions. All these countries are already growing at rates exceeding the world average, and an even more prodigious growth is likely to occur as mortality continues to decline. Infant mortality, one of the best indices of health conditions, has also been declining dramatically over much of Latin America. Nevertheless, the infant mortality rate is still at least three times greater than that prevailing in the advanced countries. The most marked declines in mortality in Latin America, in fact, have occurred among infants and young children. Despite this decline, two-fifths or more of all deaths in most Latin American countries still occur among children younger than five years of age. The reduction in mortality rates has significantly extended life expectancy in Latin America from about forty-five years or slightly greater in 1950 to slightly more than sixty years in 1970, but further improvements will be increasingly difficult and expensive. Toward the end of the century life expectancy in Latin America should approximate present-day levels in the developed world.

The youthful age structure of the population of Latin America generally reflects the high fertility that has prevailed in the region. From 40 to 45 percent of the population in most countries is younger than fifteen years of age. Argentina and Uruguay are the marked exceptions, with less than 30 percent in these young ages (this is comparable to the percentage in the developed countries). Cuba, Puerto Rico, and Chile are slightly below the Latin American average. On the other hand, because of relatively high mortality and because mortality rates for the older age groups have probably been lowered only slightly in the recent past, only about 3 percent of the population is older than sixty-five. The consequence of the youthful age structure is that only about 55 percent of the population is in the economically productive ages (fifteen to sixty-four years), in contrast to 60 to 65 percent in developed countries. Even more significant is the fact that, with declining mortality, ever-increasing numbers will be seeking employment and will also be entering the reproductive ages. Large increases in employment opportunities must be provided, and without basic social changes population increases in the future will be even greater.

See also PUBLIC HEALTH.

Urbanization. The second most important demographic trend in Latin America is the rural exodus, with the consequent rapid growth of urban centers, particularly the larger cities. This massive internal migration, amounting to perhaps 2 million or 3 million people annually, is the result of numerous and complex factors stemming from depressed rural conditions (especially in view of the rapid natural increase of the rural population) and the diverse and often disappointing appeal of urban opportunities. Urban growth is also due to natural increase, since in Latin America overall urban natality probably is still only somewhat less than in rural areas.

In 1970, 54 percent of the population of Latin America was classified as urban (the 50 percent mark was attained about 1965). Since World War II the urban population has been increasing by about 3 or 4 percentage points in each five-year period, and this rate of increase has been projected to continue at least until the end of the century.

The process of urbanization started earliest (about the World War I period) in Argentina and Uruguay, where approximately four-fifths of the population is urban, and developed later in Chile, Cuba, and Venezuela. The degree of urbanization is lowest in Hispaniola and in much of Central America, Bolivia, Paraguay, and Ecuador. In many of these countries with limited urbanization the growth of the urban sector was most pronounced during the 1960s.

An outstanding characteristic of the urban pattern in Latin America is the high degree of primacy, or the predominance of the largest city in the urban hierarchy. For the 1960s, in fifteen countries the largest city (the capital, except in Ecuador and Brazil) was at least 3.5 times larger than the second city in population. Furthermore, in about half of the countries the largest city was continuing to grow at a faster rate than the overall urban expansion. A number of larger cities in Latin America have sustained an annual population increment of 7 percent, which means that the city population doubles in about a decade. The rapid urban growth generally has resulted in the problem of overurbanization, with an excessive development of the service sector of the economy and an inadequate development of industry, housing, social services, and employment opportunities. The outskirts of many Latin American cities are now fringed by marginal slums in which sometimes as much as 10 to 30 percent of a city's population resides.

Bibliography. Glenn H. Beyer (ed.), *Urban Explosion in Latin America,* Ithaca, N.Y., 1967; Kingsley Davis, "The Place of Latin America in World Demographic History," *Milbank Memorial Fund Quarterly,* vol. XLII, 1964; Alfonso González, "Population Prospects for Latin America," *Revista Geográfica,* vol. LXXI, December 1969, pp. 75–92; Carmen A. Miró, "The Population of Latin America," *Demography,* vol. I, no. 1, 1964, pp. 15–41; T. Lynn Smith, *Latin America: Population Studies,* Gainesville, Fla., 1961; J. Mayone Stycos and Jorge Arias (eds.), *Population Dilemma in Latin America,* Washington, 1966; United Nations Economic Commission for Latin America, "The Demographic Situation in Latin America," *Economic Bulletin for Latin America,* vol. VI, no. 2, October 1961, pp. 13–51; id., "Geographic Redistribution of the Population of Latin America and Regional Development Priorities," *Economic Bulletin for Latin America,* vol. VIII, 1963, pp. 51–64.

ALFONSO GONZÁLEZ

PORRAS, BELISARIO (1856–1942). President of Panama (1912–1916, 1918–1920, 1920–1924). Born in Las Tablas, Porras was educated in Colombia and Belgium. As a leader of the Liberal party on the isthmus, he took part in the War of the Thousand Days (1899–1902; *see* THOUSAND DAYS, WAR OF THE) and later wrote a volume of memoirs (1922) describing his campaigns. Porras opposed the separation of Panama from Colombia, but in 1907 he was granted Panamanian citizenship by the National Assembly and remained prominent in Liberal politics.

During his long tenure as President, Porras was responsible for many public works and institutions. A 100-mile railroad was constructed in western Panama, and new facilities were provided for Santo Tomás Hospital in the capital. The public registry of property and of changes in civil status was instituted, and Panamanian law codes were drafted. A law faculty was created (it became the nucleus of the University of Panama, founded in 1935). A border controversy with Costa Rica drew the two nations into a short war (1921) after arbitration had failed to solve the dispute. Intervention by United States troops in the border province of Chiriquí lasted two years (1918–1920).

LARRY L. PIPPIN

PORRES, ST. MARTÍN DE (1579–1639). Patron saint of social service and interracial harmony. Born in Lima, he was the illegitimate son of Juan de Porres, a Spanish gentleman, and Ana Velásquez, a black freedwoman. Though his father acknowledged that the boy and his sister were his children, he left them in Lima in the care of their mother. At twelve Martín was apprenticed to a barber-surgeon, and at fifteen he entered the Third Order of St. Dominic, eventually pronouncing religious vows in the Dominican order's Rosario Convent in Lima. There he worked tirelessly as barber-surgeon and infirmarian for the numerous members of his religious community, for the countless sick poor of all races and racial mixtures who came to him or whom he found in the streets and in the vicinity of the order's hacienda in Limatambo, and for a few well-to-do friends and benefactors. He was instrumental in establishing a foundling home and orphanage for abandoned children.

Brother Martín became widely known throughout the city for collecting and distributing alms, feeding and clothing the poor, and healing the sick. He was even reputed to be a miracle worker and to have a miraculous way with animals. He led an extremely austere life in terms of food, clothing, and rest, mortified his flesh, spent many hours in prayer, and was the recipient of mystical experiences such as ecstasies and levitation. He was conscious of his color, but racial slurs he accepted as a reminder of his unworthiness before God. He was declared blessed in 1837 and a saint in 1962.

NORMAN MEIKLEJOHN

PORTALES, DIEGO (1793–1837). Chilean statesman. Often referred to by Chileans as the organizer of the republic, Portales may be said to have occupied the key position in the early part of the national period of Chile's history. There can be little doubt that he was principally responsible for laying the foundations of the conservative political system that enabled Chile to avoid the maelstrom of revolts and palace revolutions so common elsewhere in the Latin America of that period.

Portales was born into the Chilean creole aristocracy. His father was superintendent of the Royal Mint in Santiago, where Portales himself worked for a time as a young man. He took no part in the wars of independence

Diego Portales. [Bibliothèque Nationale, Paris]

and seems to have been indifferent to the patriot cause. In 1821 he was left a widower after less than two years of marriage; later he became somewhat hedonistic in his private life, a characteristic that contrasted sharply with the notorious austerity of his approach to public office. In 1822, having entered a trading partnership with José Manuel Cea, Portales moved to Lima, but he returned to Chile two years later; his commercial ventures were rarely successful. In August 1824 the firm of Portales, Cea and Company was entrusted by the government with the management of the *estanco* (state tobacco monopoly) in return for paying interest on the £1 million loan Chile had contracted in London in 1822. This contract aroused considerable public hostility, and in September 1826 it was revoked, much to Portales's disgust.

Over the next three years Portales and a group of associates, commonly known as *estanqueros,* formed an increasingly active and vocal opposition to the liberal governments of the day. The *estanquero* group, reacting against the climate of mild disorder that Chile was then experiencing, advocated the creation of a government based on a strong executive. Portales's chance came in September 1829, when the *estanqueros* joined forces with the conservative PELUCÓN faction and supporters of the exiled dictator Bernardo O'HIGGINS to overthrow the liberal regime. Portales swiftly assumed effective control of the rebellion launched from Concepción by Gen. Joaquín PRIETO and, with the retreat of the liberals from Santiago, became Minister of the Interior, External Relations, War, and Navy (April 6, 1830).

The final defeat of the liberal army at Lircay on April 17, 1830, guaranteed the survival of the new conservative regime. Portales remained at the head of the Ministry until August 1831, when he resigned all his portfolios except War, which he retained for an additional eleven months. At no time did he show the slightest interest in becoming head of state, though he briefly (and very unwillingly) held the office of Vice President until its abolition in 1833. After his retirement as Minister, he took almost no official part in the running of the country except as Governor of Valparaíso (1832–1833) until his return to power in September 1835.

Whether Portales was in the government or not, his influence was supreme. He was no philosopher, and his political ideas were never set out in systematic form, but a clear impression of their nature can be derived from his voluminous correspondence and from his activities as a statesman. Two fundamental notions lay close to the center of his thinking on politics. First, he wished to set up a strong, efficient, and scrupulously conscientious government that would guarantee uninterrupted political stability within a framework of settled law. Second, he believed very firmly in the maintenance of Chilean national sovereignty and, if possible, Chilean leadership on the west coast of South America. In 1822, in a famous letter to Cea, Portales defined his political ideal as follows: "a strong, centralizing government, whose members are genuine examples of virtue and patriotism." This, he believed, would "set the citizens on the straight path of order and the virtues. When they have attained a degree of morality, then we can have the completely liberal sort of Government, free and full of ideals, in which all the citizens can take part."

After 1830 the conservative regime, under Portales's

guidance, acted swiftly to repress liberal conspiracies and revolts and to dampen the ardor of the opposition press. The endemic banditry of the southern provinces was eliminated. New standards of efficiency and austerity were imposed in public administration. A well-trained national militia, the Civic Guard, was set up as a counterweight to the influence of the regular armed forces. Portales's vigorous Finance Minister, Manuel Rengifo, balanced the budget and began reducing the public debt. The constitution of 1833, while owing relatively little to Portales himself, provided the new regime with an appropriate and remarkably durable legal basis (*see* CONSTITUTION OF 1833: CHILE).

Portales's deep patriotism led him to work for the maintenance of real and effective independence for Chile. Foreign powers that made extravagant demands on the Chilean state were treated courteously but firmly. Steps were taken to build up Valparaíso as the leading entrepôt port on the west coast of South America, a tactic that was extremely successful. Furthermore, Portales kept a close watch on foreign developments that might threaten Chilean independence. His chief preoccupation on this score was Peru. Chile's relations with Peru were seriously strained in the early 1830s, in large part for commercial reasons. The situation was exacerbated by the ambitions of the Bolivian mestizo general Andrés SANTA CRUZ, who in 1836 united Peru and Bolivia in a Confederation under his own leadership (*see* PERU-BOLIVIA CONFEDERATION).

In September 1835 a brief flurry of opposition to the conservative government obliged Portales to resume his position as Minister of War and Navy; he took on the combined portfolio of the Interior and External Relations three weeks later. International affairs quickly came to engross his attention, since he held the view that the very existence of the Peru-Bolivia Confederation represented a permanent and unacceptable threat to Chilean independence. Chile, Portales wrote in September 1836, now needed to win her "second independence." On December 28 of that year, President Prieto declared war on the Confederation and took sweeping emergency powers. Chilean public opinion does not seem to have welcomed the outbreak of war. Several conspiracies, in which Santa Cruz may well have had a hand, were detected and repressed. Portales himself became a tragic victim of the most serious of these threats to the regime. In June 1837 the Maipú Regiment, under the command of Col. José Antonio Vidaurre, attempted to capture Valparaíso and seize control of the Chilean Fleet in a move to overthrow the government. On June 2, Portales arrived at Quillota, where the regiment was in camp, to inspect the troops. Unaware of the regiment's plans, he was arrested by Vidaurre's men and obliged to accompany the mutineers as they advanced toward Valparaíso. On June 6, while the opening shots were being exchanged between the rebels and the defenders of the port, Portales was taken from his carriage and cruelly murdered. He thus lived to see neither the defeat of the insurrection nor the subsequent Chilean victory over the Peru-Bolivia Confederation in 1839.

Bibliography. Francisco Antonio Encina, *Portales,* 2 vols., Santiago, 1934; Ramón Sotomayor Valdés, *El ministro Portales,* Santiago, 1954; Benjamín Vicuña Mackenna, *Diego Portales,* 2 vols., Valparaíso, 1863.

SIMON COLLIER

PORT-AU-PRINCE. Capital and largest city of Haiti, situated on the west coast at the head of the Bay of Léogane. It was founded by the French in 1749, and by 1770 it had become the capital of Saint-Domingue, chiefly because of the southward shift of the agricultural economy. The most fertile region of the colony was the 40-mile plain Cul-de-Sac, which lies east of the city; its sugar, cotton, indigo, and coffee production made Saint-Domingue the richest tropical possession of the eighteenth-century world. Its marshy, tropical climate made it unhealthy.

Captured by the British in 1794, the city was evacuated four years later. During the French Revolution it was briefly renamed Port Républicain. A center of the mulatto ÉLITE, Port-au-Prince became capital of Alexandre Sabès PÉTION's southern republic in 1807 and of all Haiti after 1820. Traditional northern jealousy of Port-au-Prince's prestige and power partly accounts for several rebellions that originated in the north. The city has often suffered from severe earthquakes and fires.

Considerably larger than other Haitian communities, Port-au-Prince doubled in population during the half century from 1920 to 1970. Its population in 1970 was estimated at 240,000.

JOHN E. BAUR

PORTEÑO. Spanish word meaning "of or pertaining to the port," specifically the port of Buenos Aires, which until the rise of Rosario in the late nineteenth century was the only significant maritime port of Argentina as well as the country's political and administrative center. Hence the term is used in Argentina, as both noun and adjective, to designate an inhabitant of the capital city or anything relating to the city of Buenos Aires.

Apart from its literal meaning, the term *porteño* has connotations evocative of the long-standing tension between Buenos Aires and the Argentine interior. By virtue of its location and commercial functions, Buenos Aires came to look outward and to follow closely the models and fashions of Europe. This cultural orientation, together with the possession of a disproportionate share of Argentina's material wealth and political power, nurtured a strong and all-too-evident feeling of superiority on the part of the *porteños* vis-à-vis the more isolated and less favored interior provinces. The latter, in turn, came to resent the *porteños* both for their pretentiousness and for their tendency to monopolize national resources, which continues to be perceived as a factor holding back the development of the interior.

DAVID BUSHNELL

PORTES GIL, EMILIO (1891–   ). President of Mexico (1928–1930). Portes Gil was born in Ciudad Victoria, Tamaulipas. His father, Domingo Portes, was of Dominican descent. After completing his preliminary studies in his native city, Portes Gil graduated as a lawyer from the Escuela Libre de Derecho in 1915. The same year he became subchief of the Department of Military Justice. He was later a judge, magistrate of the Superior Court of Sonora, consulting attorney to the Department of War, member of Congress, and Governor of Tamaulipas.

When the assassination of President-elect Álvaro OBREGÓN in 1928 created the need for the selection of a provisional President, Portes Gil emerged as a suitable candidate for several reasons: as a civilian he would check the ambitions of the military men; he had distinguished himself for his hostility to the CONFEDERACIÓN REGIONAL OBRERA MEXICANA (CROM); and the fact that he had placed special emphasis on the distribution of *ejidos* (*see* EJIDO) was pleasing to the Partido Nacional Agrarista. He took part in the organization of the Partido Nacional Revolucionario (PNR) and, with the help of Plutarco Elías CALLES, defeated the rebellion of 1929, which was launched by several army officers who opposed what they considered Calles's attempt to impose a successor to Portes Gil, first Aaron Sáenz and later Pascual ORTIZ RUBIO. He concluded his term on February 5, 1930. During the following six years he held several high offices, serving as Secretary of Foreign Relations and twice as president of the PNR. This purely political career came to an end in 1936, when he was accused of selecting overly moderate PNR candidates.

MOISÉS GONZÁLEZ NAVARRO

PORTINARI, CÂNDIDO [TORQUATO] (1903–1962). Brazilian painter. Portinari was born in Brodósqui (Brodowski), São Paulo, the son of agricultural workers who had emigrated from Italy. His formal education was rudimentary, but his passion for art became evident while he was still a boy when he helped restore the decorations of the local church. In 1918 he went to Rio de Janeiro, where he studied at the Liceu de Artes e Ofícios and at the Escola Nacional de Belas Artes. At this time he was most strongly impressed by the work of the Spaniard Ignacio Zuloaga and the Swede Anders Zorn, although he later described his disappointment at seeing Zuloaga's work in the original. In 1928 he was awarded a prize that allowed him to go to Europe, where he visited France, England, Spain, and Italy. He painted very little while abroad, but after his return to Brazil in 1930 he produced a massive outpouring of art, which revealed the influence of the Mexican muralists as well as the use of themes related to his childhood in the coffee-growing region of São Paulo. In 1935 his large oil canvas *Coffee* won an honorable mention at the International Exposition of the Carnegie Institute in Pittsburgh and brought him international recognition for the first time.

Portinari was later commissioned to do the murals for the Ministry of Education building designed by Oscar NIEMEYER; based on the theme "The Epic of Brazil," the murals show Brazilians at work in gold prospecting, sugar cultivation, and other activities. In 1939 he prepared three murals in tempera for the Brazilian Pavilion of the New York World's Fair, and in 1941 he completed four murals in the same medium for the Hispanic Foundation of the Library of Congress in Washington. He also did the decorations for Niemeyer's Church of St. Francis of Assisi in the Belo Horizonte suburb of Pampulha, including a superb exterior mural in blue and white tiles showing scenes from the life of the saint. During this period he also did a series of expressionistic paintings inspired by a drought in the northeastern state of Ceará, among them *Dead Child* and *Burial in a Net*. In 1948–1949 he executed murals on the saying of the first mass in Brazil for the Banco Boavista in Guanabara and on the popular hero Tiradentes for the Colégio de Cataguases in Minas Gerais. The mid-1950s saw him at work on the panels *War* and *Peace* for the United Nations headquarters in New York. In his last years he painted a large number of easel pictures, frequently returning to earlier subjects, his work now being marked by the use of more brilliant color.

Often considered Brazil's greatest modern painter, Portinari borrowed from cubism, expressionism, and other international styles, but in thematic material he remained rooted in the Brazilian soil, with which he experimented in order to obtain colors for his murals and canvases. He constantly attempted to improve his technique as a craftsman, and his death on February 6, 1962, was the result of a disease caused by metallic poisoning from the paints he mixed.

HELEN DELPAR

PÔRTO ALEGRE. Capital of the state of Rio Grande do Sul, Brazil. With a population of 885,567 (1970), Pôrto Alegre is the largest city in the south of Brazil. It is located on the Guaíba Estuary at the upper end of the Lagoa dos Patos in eastern Rio Grande do Sul. First settled by peasant colonists from the Azores in the 1750s, when it was known as Pôrto dos Casais, the city has since absorbed successive contingents of immigrants from Germany and Italy as well as colonists and migrants from all the southern states of Brazil. Pôrto Alegre has been a political capital since 1773 and has become the commercial and financial center of the state. The heaviest concentration of industries in southern Brazil, particularly food processing, leather goods and clothing, and metallurgy, is located at Pôrto Alegre. Although it is situated some 200 miles from the Atlantic, the city is a major port, serving as market and transfer point for cargoes brought by ocean vessels and by the large fleet of river boats that ply the extensive inland waterways of Rio Grande do Sul. As an educational and publication center, Pôrto Alegre exerts its influence well beyond the boundaries of Rio Grande do Sul. One of Brazil's largest publishing houses has its headquarters in Pôrto Alegre, and the city's two universities are regional centers of professional training in law, medicine, and the arts.

ROLLIE E. POPPINO

PORTOBELO. *See* COMMERCIAL POLICY (COLONIAL SPANISH AMERICA).

POSADA, JOSÉ GUADALUPE (1852–1913). Mexican engraver. Posada was the most famous designer of popular prints in Mexico, and in more than 15,000 prints he summed up the imagery of his country. Jean Charlot commented that Posada "functions in the history of Mexican art like the narrow neck of an hourglass, where the past is metamorphosed grain by grain into the future." Diego RIVERA and José Clemente OROZCO were proud to trace their art from Posada's, thereby signifying that they were making art for the people.

Posada was born in Aguascalientes, where he collaborated with his teacher, Trinidad Pedroza, on a satirical paper that was suppressed in the 1870s. He moved to León, where he remained until 1887, and then for twenty-six years did illustrations in Mexico City for the popular publications of Antonio Vanegas Arroyo. Covers of song sheets, single prints, cartoons, all printed on the cheapest paper, poured from his studio. The *calavera* (animated skeleton) had been invented earlier by Santiago Hernández, but it was Posada who made it a famous device. His grimly amusing visions of an antiworld of skeletons satirized every aspect of contemporary life, from bicycle riding to the dictator Victoriano HUERTA, attacked in the skull-spider *Calavera huertista*.

TERENCE GRIEDER

POSITIVISM (BRAZIL). In Brazil, as in Mexico and Chile, the positivist philosophy of Auguste Comte was a strong influence during the last decades of the nineteenth century. Never attracting a mass following, its doctrines were nonetheless fervently adopted by a small group of middle-class intellectuals and army officers, notably those who came under the influence of Benjamin Constant Botelho de MAGALHÃES at the Military School in Rio de Janeiro.

The first manifestations of Comte's philosophy appeared in theses and books in the 1850s and 1860s, and by 1876 the Positivist Association of Brazil had been formed by seven members, including Benjamin Constant, Miguel Lemos, and Raimundo Teixeira Mendes. In 1878 the Positivist Society of Rio de Janeiro replaced the original organization, the youthful Miguel Lemos assuming the presidency after his return from France in 1881.

Under the direction of Lemos and Teixeira Mendes, the society stressed religious, educational, and reformist activities during the 1880s. It supported republicanism and the abolitionist movement, effectively opposed the importation of Chinese workers as substitutes for slaves, and advocated the separation of church and state and related reforms. The orthodoxy of Lemos's positivism kept the movement small, but the participation of Benjamin Constant and Demetrio Ribeiro, two followers of Comte, in the republican revolt of 1889 gave the society significant influence in the first republican government, particularly during its early vital months. A lasting effect is to be found in the Brazilian flag, conceived by Teixeira Mendes and designed by the positivist painter Décio Vilares, which bears the positivist motto "Order and Progress." Although positivism continued to influence Brazilian politics well into the FIRST REPUBLIC, particularly in the southern state of Rio Grande do Sul, the religious and philosophical aspects of the surviving movement have outweighed the political in the twentieth century.

ROBERT CONRAD

POSITIVISM (MEXICO). The system of philosophy developed by the Frenchman Auguste Comte was introduced in Mexico by Gabino Barreda (1818–1881), who studied medicine in Paris from 1847 to 1851 and there came into contact with Comte. This philosophy divides the history of mankind into three periods, moving from superstition through abstract principles to reality and progress, stages that Comte described as theological, metaphysical, and positivist. Barreda adapted these to Mexican history to correspond to the colonial era, dominated by the church; the period following independence; and the contemporary implantation and strengthening of liberalism in the era of the Reform (*see* REFORM, THE). In 1868 Barreda founded in Mexico City the National Preparatory School, which became the center for the diffusion of positivist thought. Science, statistics, sociology, and political economy became important as tools useful for the study of society and for social and material progress. Order and progress were the keynotes and later provided the themes of and justification for the type of government imposed by Porfirio DÍAZ. The earlier Mexican positivists also had emphasized liberty, but during the Díaz regime the second generation of positivists, influenced by social Darwinism and the writings of Herbert Spencer, blamed concern with freedom for much of the turbulence and civil disorder that continued to impede Mexico's material development. They advocated instead government by the elite, which they equated with creole society. A clique of the later positivists, referred to as the CIENTÍFICOS, exercised great influence. In Mexico the religious overtones of positivism, important in Comte's scheme, were not present.

CHARLES R. BERRY

POTATO. Root crop (*Solanum tuberosum*) native to the dry altiplano of Peru and Bolivia. It was here, at 8,000 feet or more, that this staple was domesticated. The latest dating for its domestication is sometime shortly before 1800 B.C. The *taclla* (a QUECHUA word), or foot plow, was used in its cultivation. A common method of making potato meal (*chuño*) was to allow potatoes on a bed of grass alternately to freeze and thaw; the moisture was then pressed out, and the peels removed. The natives of the highlands developed an amazing number of varieties of this important cultigen. From here, with the advent of the Spaniards, potatoes spread all over the world.

BURR C. BRUNDAGE

POTOSÍ. City and department in Bolivia. The city was the largest silver-mining town in South America during the colonial period. Situated 13,400 feet above sea level, Potosí was founded in 1545, when silver was discovered near the peak of the *cerro rico*. Silver production increased rapidly, and by the end of the sixteenth century Potosí was the largest exporter of silver in the New World. During this period the town's population may have reached a peak of some 160,000 people, and Potosí became the largest commercial center in the Viceroyalty of Peru.

The highest level of silver production was reached in the period between 1572 and about 1630, when Potosí's annual output often exceeded 7 million pesos and accounted for approximately 70 percent of the yearly mineral exports of Peru. The sharp increase in silver production after 1572 was due to a number of factors. The introduction of mercury in the refining process allowed lower-quality ore, which was not suitable for smelting, to be profitably extracted. Of equal importance was the abundant supply of cheap mine labor that the MITA provided. This massive input of Indian labor, together with the relatively small capital investment necessary to mine silver ore at Potosí (there were few drainage problems requiring expensive capital equipment), minimized production costs and allowed a sustained growth of silver production until the middle of the seventeenth century. After the middle decades of the century, there was a sharp decline in output as silver ore was increasingly exhausted. Although production picked up again after 1740, Potosí never regained its former economic

position. During the wars for independence, Potosí's mining industry further declined, and by 1825 its population had fallen to 8,000. In 1964 the population of the city was estimated at 64,000, and that of the department at 624,439.

See also MINING (COLONIAL SPANISH AMERICA).

BROOKE LARSON SHUTE

PRADO [Y UGARTECHE], MANUEL (1889–1967). President of Peru (1939–1945, 1956–1962). Born in Lima, the aristocratic Manuel Prado was the son of President Mariano Ignacio Prado. He studied in Peru and France, earning a degree in engineering. Subsequently he taught higher mathematics and science at the University of San Marcos and later was exiled by Augusto LEGUÍA because of his CIVILISTA PARTY background. He was appointed president of the Central Reserve Bank of Peru in 1934 and became Premier and Finance Minister during the regime of Oscar BENAVIDES (1933–1939). In 1939 he was elected President for the first time. His administration was highlighted by a successful war against Ecuador and by an improvement in relations between the Peruvian establishment and the often-persecuted ALIANZA POPULAR REVOLUCIONARIA AMERICANA (APRA). The relationship between Prado and APRA blossomed in 1956 with the signing of the *convivencia* by which Prado, a member of the traditional oligarchy, guaranteed the formerly anti-oligarchy APRA legality in return for support in that year's presidential election. The consummation of the pact brought Prado victory and APRA legality after eight years of persecution.

Prado's second administration (1956–1962) began during an economic recession that was to persist for a few years. However, in the last three years of his term Peru witnessed a considerable economic recovery, spurred by austerity at home and higher world commodity prices, although this recovery did not diminish widespread rural unrest and frequent strikes. In 1962, shortly before the completion of his term, Prado was overthrown by the armed forces.

ORAZIO A. CICCARELLI

PRADO, PEDRO (1886–1952). Chilean writer. A native of Santiago, he founded the *Revista Moderna* and the group Los Diez and its review of the same name (1915). He first became known as a poet in 1908 with *Flores de cardo*, which was followed by *La casa abandonada* (1912); *El llamado del mundo* (1913); *Los pájaros errantes* (1915), a collection of poems in prose; *Androvar* (1925), a dramatic poem; *Camino de las horas* (1934); *Otoño en las dunas* (1940); *Esta bella ciudad envenenada* (1945), a collection of sonnets; and *No más que una rosa* (1946). Lyric emotion dominates his novels: *La reina de Rapa Nui* (1914), *Un juez rural* (1924), and *Alsino* (1920). In collaboration with the Mexican Antonio Castro Leal, he wrote *Karez-I-Roshan* (1921).

RACHEL PHILLIPS

PRD. *See* PARTIDO REVOLUCIONARIO DOMINICANO.

PREBISCH, RAÚL (1901–   ). Argentine economist. Prebisch graduated from the University of Buenos Aires with a doctorate in economics and was a professor of political economy there from 1925 to 1948. He also served as Undersecretary of Finance (1930–1932) under provisional President José Félix URIBURU and as general manager of the Central Bank of Argentina from its foundation in 1935 until 1943.

Prebisch is best known for his work as the Executive Secretary of the United Nations ECONOMIC COMMISSION FOR LATIN AMERICA (ECLA) from 1948 to 1962. Under his leadership ECLA encouraged the industrialization and ECONOMIC INTEGRATION of Latin America and supported social reform as a prerequisite for the economic development of the area. In *The Economic Development of Latin America and Its Principal Problems* (1950), he maintained that the theory of the international division of trade had worked to the disadvantage of Latin America, which was on the periphery of the world system, because it did not receive the benefits of increased productivity in a measure comparable to that of the industrial nations. He also asserted that industrial development was the best means whereby Latin America might share in the technical progress of the age and raise the standard of living of its people.

In 1955, after the overthrow of Juan D. PERÓN, the provisional government of Gen. Eduardo LONARDI asked Prebisch to assess the condition of the Argentine economy. In his report Prebisch excoriated the Perón administration, declaring that national production had declined to such an extent that recovery would require extraordinary measures. His recommendations included a reduction in the level of consumption, imposition of lower and, in his view, more realistic wage scales for labor, and encouragement of private investment. In 1962 Prebisch became Director General of the newly founded Latin American Institute for Economic and Social Planning, established under ECLA auspices to provide training and other services in the field of planning. From 1964 to 1969 he served as Secretary-General of the United Nations Conference on Trade and Development (UNCTAD).

RODNEY D. ANDERSON AND EUGENE G. SHARKEY

PRE-COLUMBIAN CIVILIZATION. *See* AYLLU; AZTECS; CALPULLI; CHICHÉN ITZÁ; CHIBCHA; CHIMU; COPÁN; CUZCO; INCAS; MACHU PICCHU; MAIZE; MAYAS; MOCHICA; MONTE ALBÁN; OLMECS; QUECHUA; QUIPU; TENOCHTITLÁN; TEOTIHUACÁN; TIKAL; TOLTECS.

PRESCOTT, WILLIAM H[ICKLING] (1796–1859). American historian. Prescott was born in Salem, Massachusetts, the son of a prominent New England judge. He studied to be a lawyer but had to abandon plans to enter the legal profession when he became permanently blind in one eye and intermittently blind in the other. He decided to devote his life to writing the history of Spain and Spanish America, and he produced the following major works: *History of the Reign of Ferdinand and Isabella the Catholic* (1838), *History of the Conquest of Mexico* (1843), *History of the Conquest of Peru* (1847), and *History of the Reign of Philip the Second, King of Spain* (1855–1858). Death prevented him from completing the fourth and final volume of the last of these works.

Prescott, following the fashion of his time and his own inclinations, concentrated on political and military history rather than social, economic, or administrative history and on narration rather than analysis. But his books, though limited in scope and depth, merit great respect for three reasons. First, Prescott told a story very well, aided by a fine pictorial imagination and a clear style. Second, he constructed his histories on a solid documentary base, using much primary source material never before employed. Third, he strove not only to be accurate in setting forth his facts but also to be fair-minded in judging the people and the civilizations he was describing. Because of these factors his books were landmarks when they appeared and are still useful today, although the sections of *History of the Conquest of Mexico* and *History of the Conquest of Peru* dealing with the civilizations of the AZTECS and INCAS are now outdated.

TIMOTHY C. HANLEY

PRESS. Generalizations about the press of Latin America must be drawn with the understanding that the area contains nineteen separate republics. Whereas Spanish is the language of a majority of the region's 283 million people, more than 90 million Brazilians speak Portuguese, while French is the preferred language of Haiti's literate minority. Another 15 million Amerinds—the indigenous population—have cultures and languages so different from those of the rest of Latin America that reaching them involves new concepts in communications.

Although several internationally recognized newspapers and magazines are published in Latin America, the area does not enjoy the wide periodical readerships found in Western Europe, Japan, and the United States. This situation is due in part both to the high level of functional illiteracy in most of Latin America and to the fact that a large proportion of the population lives in rural and semiurban areas where the press is not the principal link with the outside. According to a 1969 report, a village less than one hour by bus from Medellín, Colombia's second-largest city, reported 85 percent literacy, yet 51 percent of the peasants there said that they had never read a newspaper in their lives. According to another source, 80 percent of Latin America's inhabitants never see a daily newspaper. And as Latin America's urban population continues to grow, the challenge faced by print journalism will be to provide media to inform, educate, and entertain this semiliterate, often country-bred population.

Early history. The printing press came to Spanish America soon after the conquest, but the exact date of the arrival of the first press is uncertain. Bishop Juan de ZUMÁRRAGA is usually credited with being responsible for the introduction of the printing press to Mexico in the mid-1530s; however, the earliest extant printed work dates from 1539. The second American printing press was established in Lima, Peru, in 1584, and the third in Puebla de los Angeles, Mexico, in 1640. A printing press was installed in Guatemala in the second half of the seventeenth century, while another was at work in the Jesuit missions of Paraguay about 1700. Several other Spanish American cities, including Bogotá and Havana, acquired printing presses in the eighteenth century, but Brazil did not have a press until the arrival of the future JOÃO VI in 1808.

Latin America's first periodical was the *Gaceta de México y Noticias de Nueva España,* which appeared monthly under semiofficial auspices in Mexico City from January to June 1722. Before 1810 newspapers had been established in several other cities, including Guatemala City, Lima, Havana, Bogotá, Montevideo, and Quito. Mexico City was also the site of the first daily newspaper, the *Diario de México,* which was published from 1805 to 1817. Although colonial newspapers were subject to prior censorship by civil and ecclesiastical authorities, they not only reported news of recent events but also disseminated useful information regarding colonial commerce, mining, and agriculture and served to stimulate feelings of national identity among creoles. *See also* ENLIGHTENMENT (SPANISH AMERICA).

The periodical press in Latin America received a strong impetus from the events of the independence era. Many newspapers were founded in areas controlled by insurgent forces, often under the editorship of outstanding intellectuals such as the Chilean friar Camilo HENRÍQUEZ, who founded Chile's first newspaper, *La Aurora de Chile.*

In the era of the revolutions for independence and during much of the nineteenth century, the journalist and the entrepreneur were one and the same person, and newspapers concentrated on politics and polemics rather than on the reporting of news. Journalism and literature were closely allied as well, and such creative writers as José MARTÍ and Rubén DARÍO were frequently employed as journalists. As the decades passed, however, the publication of a newspaper became a complex and costly undertaking requiring the division of labor and a large capital investment for the installation of expensive machinery and physical plant.

The modern press. Modern metropolitan newspapers in Latin America fall into one of two categories: (1) large, prosperous institutions owned and operated by landowning, industrial, or military interests with the money and the influence to withstand most changes of political atmosphere; and (2) newspapers owned or influenced strongly by political groups or persons with political organizations. The latter depend for their income on party contributions or money from political organizations; when the winds of change make it politically unwise or financially impossible for them to find support, they are likely to disappear or change their political outlook.

Latin American newspapers cited among the world's elite in terms of influence and prestige are in the first category. Outstanding newspapers of this type include *La Prensa* and *La Nación* of Buenos Aires, *O Estado de São Paulo* of São Paulo, and *Excelsior* of Mexico City. Founded in 1869 by Dr. José C. Paz (1842–1912), *La Prensa* has frequently experienced the wrath of Argentine Presidents, ranging from Domingo Faustino SARMIENTO, a former journalist himself, to Juan D. PERÓN. In 1951, while Perón was President, the newspaper was confiscated and turned over to the CONFEDERACIÓN GENERAL DE TRABAJO to run. After the overthrow of Perón in 1955, the newspaper was returned to the Paz family. Argentina's second major daily, *La Nación,* was founded by ex-President Bartolomé MITRE in 1870. *Excelsior,* founded in 1917 by Rafael Alducín (1889–1924), is the Mexican daily with the largest circulation. *O Estado de São Paulo,* which was established in 1875 with the name *A Provincia de São Paulo,* is noted for its outstanding coverage of foreign and domestic news, sometimes being known as the *New York Times* of Latin America.

Other highly respected newspapers are *El Universal* and *Novedades* of Mexico City, the *Jornal do Brasil* and *O Globo* of Rio de Janeiro, *El Tiempo* of Bogotá, *El Comercio* of Lima, and *El Mercurio* of Santiago, Chile. The principal Cuban paper is the Havana daily *Granma,* the official organ of the PARTIDO COMUNISTA DE CUBA. It was founded in 1965 upon the merger of the Communist newspaper *Hoy* with *Revolución,* the organ of Fidel CASTRO's 26th of July movement. Leading magazines in Latin America include the news weeklies *Veja* (Brazil), *Primera Plana* (Argentina), and *Ercilla* (Chile); *O Cruzeiro* and *Manchete* (both Brazil), popular illustrated weeklies; *Marcha* (Uruguay), a leftist weekly influential among intellectuals; and *Sur* (Argentina), a literary monthly. *Visión,* which appears fortnightly in both Spanish and Portuguese editions and emphasizes economic and political developments, is truly continental in coverage, but it is largely owned by United States interests.

For news of the United States, Europe, and other parts of the world as well as of Latin America itself, Latin American newspapers rely almost exclusively on foreign news agencies. Thus a survey of the foreign news content of fourteen Latin American newspapers on June 30, 1965, showed that 40.8 percent was supplied by United Press International, 31.3 percent by the Associated Press, 18.6 percent by Agence France Presse, 1.6 percent by Reuters, 1.2 percent by the Italian agency ANSA, and more than 6 percent by others. This dependence on foreign news agencies often evokes concern or indignation, and efforts have been made from time to time to break the foreign monopoly. In 1959 the Cuban government set up its own international news agency and wire service, Prensa Latina. More recently, on August 21, 1973, the Peronist President of Argentina, Raúl Lastiri, forbade foreign news agencies to transmit Argentine news within Argentina.

Latin America's authoritarian tradition, frequent changes of government, and political instability have often compromised freedom of the press in the region, and dictators such as Perón of Argentina, Getúlio VARGAS of Brazil, and Gustavo ROJAS PINILLA of Colombia brought an eclipse of press freedom in the countries they dominated. No newspapers, no matter how substantial, can be immune from pressure by an unfriendly government. Methods of suppression need not always be so heavy-handed as outright closure. Offending newspapers may, for example, be subjected to government-induced labor troubles, customs delays in acquiring needed equipment, or reduction of ink and newsprint supplies. Moreover, the possibility that such penalties may be invoked encourages self-censorship on the part of periodicals. Prior censorship also exists, as in Brazil, where after 1968 newspapers frequently appeared with insignificant or incongruous stories in lead spaces because of a censor's decision to excise a story. The prospects for press freedom seemed especially dim in the mid-1970s, as newspapers in such traditionally free countries as Chile and Uruguay came under severe controls.

To resist political and economic pressure on the press and to fight for press freedom in the hemisphere are the major purposes of the Inter American Press Association (Sociedad Interamericana de Prensa, IAPA), which grew out of a series of inter-American press conferences held between 1926 and 1950. The present organization was established in 1950, largely at the instigation of journalists from the United States, at the Sixth Inter-American Press Congress in New York City. Although more than 1,000 Latin American and North American publications were members by the early 1970s, critics asserted that the domination of IAPA by owners and publishers had made it overly conservative.

The IAPA Committee on Freedom of the Press and Information reports annually on the status of press freedom in the Americas, conducts investigations into alleged infringements of press freedom, and attempts to keep public attention focused on the issue. Also associated with IAPA are the IAPA Technical Center, Inc., established in 1957 to provide technical information to IAPA members, and the Office of Certified Circulation, Inc., initiated in 1954 to make a circulation auditing service available to interested members.

A 1968 survey of ninety-four journalists on metropolitan newspapers in Buenos Aires, Mexico City, and La Paz indicated that the contemporary Latin American newspaperman is a relatively well-educated urban individual who derives social and economic benefits from his employment. He considers himself to be middle- or upper-class socially, is generally happy in his work, and exhibits a marked professional orientation. Somewhat similar conclusions were reached in a 1967 survey of Chilean journalists. However, both surveys showed that journalists were likely to hold several jobs, sometimes outside the media or on competing media. Another problem is the venality of some journalists.

Until relatively recently journalism schools in Latin America were few in number and consisted mainly of private institutions founded by persons whose qualifications and motives did not always coincide with the best interests of professional journalism. Courses and curriculum were haphazard, and the aims of training were often unrealistic and distorted. Although the number of Latin American schools of journalism grew from six in 1946 to eighty-one in mid-1969, graduates of journalism programs often prefer better-paying jobs in advertising or public relations to newspaper work. Newspapers and labor unions also offer instruction in journalism.

Journalism education and the increased professionalization of newspapermen are the goals of the Center for Higher Studies in Journalism for Latin America (Centro Internacional de Estudios Superiores de Periodismo para América Latina, CIESPAL). CIESPAL was created by the United Nations Educational, Scientific and Cultural Organization in 1959 following several international meetings at which it was concluded that action was needed to promote the development of the mass media through the education of better-qualified journalism instructors, the encouragement of greater professionalism among journalists, and systematic research into the problems of mass communications. CIESPAL has developed annual courses for professional journalists and journalism school instructors. Instructors from North America and Europe teach journalism at the appropriate intellectual and technical level for teachers and newspapermen selected to attend.

Bibliography. Ronald H. Chilcote, *The Press in Latin America, Spain and Portugal: A Survey of Recent Developments,* Stanford, Calif., 1963; J. Laurence Day, "The Latin American Journalist: A Tentative Profile," *Journalism Quarterly,* vol. XLV, no. 3, autumn, 1968, pp. 509–515; Eleazar Díaz Rangel, *Pueblos subinformados: Las agencias de noticias y América Latina,* Caracas, 1967; Mary A. Gardner, *The Inter American Press Association: Its Fight for Freedom of the Press, 1926–1960,* Austin, Tex., 1967; John Merrill, *The Elite Press,* New York, 1968; John Merrill, Carter R. Bryan, and Marvin Alisky, *The Foreign Press,* Baton Rouge, La., 1970; Raymond B. Nixon, *Education for Journalism in Latin America,* New York, 1970; Sergio de Santis, "The Latin American Press," in Claudio Véliz (ed.), *Latin America and the Caribbean: A Handbook,* New York, 1968, pp. 826–831.

J. LAURENCE DAY AND HELEN DELPAR

PRESTES, LUIS CARLOS (1898–   ). Brazilian political leader. Born in Rio Grande do Sul, Prestes was graduated from the Military School in 1918. In October 1924, he participated in a military revolt in Rio Grande do Sul. Pressed by loyalist troops, the rebels trekked north to the Iguaçu Falls to join another revolutionary force that had retreated from São Paulo following an unsuccessful revolt earlier that year. With Prestes as the recognized leader, this combined revolutionary army, known as the PRESTES COLUMN, marched through the interior of Brazil from 1925 to 1927, spreading a message of social reform and seeking peasant support. Because of his brilliant military leadership and championing of reform, Prestes became a nearly mystical figure known as the Cavalheiro da Esperança (Knight of Hope).

In 1927, under severe military pressure, he disbanded the column into Bolivia. Becoming a Buenos Aires resident, Prestes embraced communism and visited the Soviet Union, where he worked in factories and became a member of the eleven-man Executive Committee of the Comintern.

Returning to Brazil in 1935, Prestes became honorary president of the Aliança Nacional Libertadora (ANL), a leftist reform organization. Accusing the ANL of supporting the unsuccessful 1935 military uprising in Recife, Natal, and Rio de Janeiro, President Getúlio VARGAS outlawed the organization. Prestes was captured the following year and incarcerated until 1945, when he was granted political amnesty. With the legalization of political parties in 1945, Prestes reorganized the PARTIDO COMUNISTA BRASILEIRO (PCB) and was elected senator. In 1947 the Brazilian government, uneasy over the PCB's growth in power and popularity, outlawed the party, forcing Prestes into hiding. Although Prestes never again held public office, he remained the leading PCB spokesman. Over the years, however, he became a voice of caution and moderation among Brazil's divided Communists.

ALLAN K. JOHNSON

PRESTES COLUMN (COLUNA PRESTES). Expeditionary force of Brazilian rebels headed by Luis Carlos PRESTES. The Prestes Column was the final and most extraordinary chapter in the series of *tenente* (lieutenant) revolts that erupted in Brazil between 1922 and 1924 (*see* TENENTISMO). In 1924 rebellious troops, augmented by a few survivors of the COPACABANA REVOLT of 1922, rose in São Paulo and were able to hold the city against rescuing federal forces for several weeks. In October of that year, Luis Carlos Prestes, an army captain, instigated the rebellion of the battalion stationed at Santo Ângelo, Rio Grande do Sul. The Prestes forces fought their way north to the Iguaçu Falls to meet the rebels who had fled from São Paulo. The two groups of army rebels united under the leadership of Prestes to form the Prestes Column, now about 1,000 strong.

For more than two years this "invincible column" marched through the Brazilian backlands. During this trek of 14,000 to 18,000 miles, north to Piauí and back to the south central region, the column fought at least a dozen major military engagements and almost daily skirmishes. In seeking to spread its message of social reform and to recruit support among the peasants, the column had to contend with the backland power structure of local and regional leaders known as *coronéis,* mainly large landowners. The *coronéis's* effective maintenance of control over the peasants and the column's inability to establish contact with urban bases of support mitigated its impact. Plagued by military pressure, disease, and lack of supplies, the column disbanded into Bolivia in 1927.

Although the column failed to overthrow the government or mobilize the peasants, it created a revolutionary mystique for future Brazilian insurgents and elevated Prestes to the stature of Brazil's Cavalheiro da Esperança (Knight of Hope). In addition, many of the column veterans became leading figures in the *tenente* movement of the 1920s and 1930s.

ALLAN K. JOHNSON AND FRANCESCA MILLER

PRI. *See* PARTIDO REVOLUCIONARIO INSTITUCIONAL.

PRIETO, GUILLERMO (1818–1897). Mexican writer and politician. Prieto was born in Mexico City and spent most of his life there. When he was thirteen, his father died and he was on his own for a number of years, holding various jobs, reading widely, and obtaining what education he could. It was in this period that he began to write the popular poetry that brought him fame. At nineteen he became secretary to President Anastasio Bustamante and also began his career in journalism. Throughout his long life he wrote for many of the leading newspapers, served as editor of some, and helped found other important journals. In 1848 he became a deputy to the Mexican Congress, where he served almost continuously until his death, usually as a deputy but once as a senator, representing various areas including Jalisco, Puebla, Querétaro, San Luis Potosí, Guanajuato, and the Federal District. In addition, he served as Minister of the Treasury on four occasions (1852, 1855, 1858, 1861). As director of the national postal system in 1856–1857, he brought about significant reforms.

Prieto is an important figure in nineteenth-century Mexican letters, not so much because of the quality of his writings but because of his themes, his leadership in literary movements, and his literary journalism. Representative works are the *Memorias de mis tiempos* (2 vols., 1906) and the poetry in *Musa callejera* (2d ed., augmented, 1883).

CHARLES R. BERRY

PRIETO, JOAQUÍN (1786–1854). President of Chile (1831–1841). Born in Concepción, Prieto came from a distinguished family and followed a military career. He fought in the Battles of Chacabuco (1817; *see* CHACA-

BUCO, BATTLE OF) and Maipú (1818). By the end of the 1820s Prieto had become the most powerful general in Chile and, as commander of the Army of the South, occupied a key position in the country's life. A staunch supporter of the exiled dictator Bernardo O'HIGGINS, he placed himself at the head of the conservative rebellion of 1829 in the hope of bringing about an early restoration of his hero. This hope he soon abandoned. Although the subsequent reshaping of Chilean politics owed far more to Diego PORTALES than to Prieto, the latter proved to be the ideal figure to occupy the Presidency. He played a leading part in implanting the new institutions, not least after the death of Portales in 1837.

Prieto's was the first of the four "decennial" Presidencies of Chile. During his second term (1836–1841), Chile went to war with the PERU-BOLIVIA CONFEDERATION set up by Andrés SANTA CRUZ. The first Chilean expeditionary force, under Adm. Blanco Encalada, was obliged by Santa Cruz to accept a peace treaty (1837) that was immediately repudiated by the Chilean government. A second expeditionary force, led by Prieto's nephew, Gen. Manuel BULNES, occupied Lima and went on to defeat Santa Cruz in the Battle of Yungay (January 20, 1839), thus sealing the fate of the Confederation.

SIMON COLLIER

PRÍO SOCORRÁS, CARLOS (1903–   ). President of Cuba (1948–1952). Prío's participation in Cuban politics began when as a student he rebelled against the dictatorship of President Gerardo MACHADO. In 1933 he was a supporter of the barracks coup led by Sgt. Fulgencio BATISTA that temporarily brought Ramón GRAU SAN MARTÍN to power. A fiery young nationalist, Prío first entered public life as a Cuban delegate to the Seventh International Conference of American States in Montevideo in 1933 (*see* MONTEVIDEO CONFERENCE). He became active in the Auténtico political movement (*see* AUTÉNTICO PARTY: CUBA) and later served as Minister of Labor in the administration of Grau San Martín (1944–1948). As Labor Minister he proceeded after 1946 to purge the CONFEDERACIÓN DE TRABAJADORES CUBANOS (CTC) of Communist control.

In 1948 Prío succeeded Grau as President of Cuba. His administration, like that of his predecessor, enacted some social and economic provisions of the progressive 1940 constitution (*see* CONSTITUTION OF 1940: CUBA). However, both Auténtico administrations generally disappointed the hopes of reform-minded Cubans and were tainted with charges of corruption.

On March 10, 1952, Gen. Fulgencio Batista led a military coup that ousted Prío from office just prior to scheduled presidential elections that Batista, one of three candidates, had little chance of winning. Forced into exile in the United States during most of the 1952–1958 period, Prío actively plotted against Batista, giving financial aid to revolutionary groups including Fidel CASTRO's July 26 movement. Developments in Cuba following the CUBAN REVOLUTION and the rise to power of Castro in 1959 again compelled the former President to seek refuge in the United States.

DAVID A. CRAIN

PROTESTANTISM. As Latin America entered the 1970s, there were an estimated 5 million Protestants in communicant membership in seventeen countries, excluding British Honduras, the Guianas, and the islands of the Caribbean. The Protestant community was estimated to be three times this number, or some 15 million. To put these figures in perspective we should note that the estimated population of these countries was approximately 240 million. This means that Protestant communicants comprised 2 percent of the population, and the Protestant community some 6 percent. The average annual rate of growth of the entire population is 3 percent, but the rate of growth of Protestantism is 10 percent. A cautionary word about statistics: with current data-gathering policies it is impossible to determine the actual birth and death rates of any Latin American country. Only a few republics have religious censuses, and these are unreliable in the absence of field sampling. Attitudes of resistance to keeping statistics characterize even the largest Protestant groupings, while others reveal their figures only to trusted Protestant investigators. Lutherans count every live birth a member, while other Protestant bodies admit members only on confession of faith and water baptism. Protestant statistics generally include those fourteen years of age; with half of Latin America under the age of fifteen, the community is always larger than the body of communicants.

Political economy and Protestantism. Protestantism in Latin America can be divided for convenience into three historical ages. The imperial age runs approximately from the fifteenth through the eighteenth century. The doctrinal and territorial lines of present-day Christendom were drawn under policies of economic and political expansion of the European powers. Religion was sponsored by kings as a tool of empire. For example, Adm. Gaspar de Coligny, leader of France's Huguenots, obtained patents from King Henry III for the founding of a colony in South America. John Calvin of Geneva sent him 300 settlers, 2 ministers, and 14 ministerial students, who arrived in what is now the harbor of Rio de Janeiro on March 7, 1557. Suffering from attack by Indians, the ecological effects of the tropics, and internal dissension, they were driven out by the Portuguese by 1568 (*see* VILLEGAGNON, Nicolas Durand de). Similarly the settlements of Bahia (modern Salvador), Olinda, and Recife were attacked and occupied by Dutch Protestants between 1624 and 1630. The Dutch presence in Curaçao, Aruba, Bonaire, and some of the Leeward Islands of the Caribbean today attests to resettlement after their expulsion by the Portuguese in 1654. *See also* DUTCH IN BRAZIL.

The nineteenth century roughly coincides with the age of independence for the Latin American republics, and the social forces causing the breakup of the Portuguese and Spanish empires also aided the peaceful penetration of Protestantism. In a sense the struggle for independence can be described as an attempt to eliminate the middleman in commerce and to obtain the right to trade directly with the Protestant manufacturing powers of Europe. As a result, colonists from Protestant lands followed both flag and trade. Under the commercial treaty of 1810, for example, English property in Brazil was exempted from control by the Catholic Inquisition, and freedom of religion on Brazilian soil was guaranteed for Englishmen, including the right of assembly in Anglican churches and a resi-

EVANGELICALS * IN LATIN AMERICA

Country	Evangelicals			Population	
	Communicants (thousands), 1967	Annual growth rate (percent), 1960–1967	Index † of relative size	Total (millions), mid-1969	Current annual growth rate (percent)
Argentina	249.5	5.0	107	23.4	1.5
Bolivia	45.4	11.5	116	3.9	2.4
Brazil	3,313.2	11.0	375	88.3	3.2
Chile	441.7	8.5	485	9.1	2.2
Colombia	73.9	12.0	38	19.7	3.2
Costa Rica	14.2	7.0	89	1.6	3.5
Ecuador	12.6	15.0	22	5.7	3.4
El Salvador	35.8	5.5	109	3.3	3.7
Guatemala	77.2	9.0	158	4.9	3.1
Honduras	18.8	8.5	75	2.5	3.5
Mexico	429.9	11.0	91	47.3	3.5
Nicaragua	19.8	3.0	110	1.8	3.5
Panama	37.5	5.5	268	1.4	3.2
Paraguay	15.2	11.0	47	2.2	3.2
Peru	61.9	6.5	48	12.8	3.1
Uruguay	21.8	7.0	78	2.8	1.2
Venezuela	46.9	14.0	48	9.7	3.6
Total	4,915.3	10.0	204	240.4	3.0

* Protestants are called Evangelicals in Latin America.
† An index number of 100 = 1 percent of population.
SOURCE: William R. Read, Victor M. Monterroso, and Harmon A. Johnson, *Latin American Church Growth*, Grand Rapids, Mich., 1969, p. 49. Used by permission.

dent chaplain. The first such minister arrived in Rio de Janeiro in 1816, and the first Anglican church in all Latin America was erected in that city in 1819.

Commerce and colonization cannot be overemphasized as a source of Protestantism in Latin America. It was believed that colonists were a major resource in economic development, and members of any group associated with hard work and technical skill were especially prized. Brazil, Argentina, and Chile received thousands of immigrants of German Lutheran heritage by the end of the nineteenth century. The Emperor of Brazil paid the salaries of ministers for them out of his own pocket. The traveling expenses of Northern Presbyterian missionaries were met by the President of Guatemala in 1882. Today Argentina, Brazil, Chile, and Uruguay have the largest proportion of persons of European origin in their population as a result of an active encouragement of colonization. These countries also possess the highest percentages of Protestants, for although only a small number of the colonists were Protestants, all proved fertile soil for conversion, as attested by the Italians of São Paulo, Brazil. Arriving as Roman Catholics in the nineteenth and early twentieth century, they were converted in such numbers that they constitute the second largest Protestant body in Latin America in the Congregação Cristã do Brasil. The end of slavery in the United States by the Civil War brought many disaffected Southerners of Baptist, Methodist, and Presbyterian persuasion to Brazil. The eclipse of the European powers by the United States in commerce in this era also saw an increasing dominance of North American Protestantism, reflected in the influx of Lutherans of the Missouri Synod.

The twentieth century may be termed the age of development even though Latin American attempts to acquire self-sufficiency in manufacturing antedate this era. The significant Protestant fact of the twentieth century is the rise of Pentecostalism. A general movement of revitalization appearing in the United States, England, and the Scandinavian countries around the turn of the century, Pentecostalism represents a further elaboration of the principle of private interpretation. The fragmenting or sectarian effects of this "principle" have long been recognized in the history of Protestant denominationalism, especially in the dissenting churches of the Anabaptist tradition. Pentecostals emphasize private initiative under the personal guidance of the Holy Ghost, and "speaking in tongues" is the charismatic symbol of membership in the "priesthood of all believers." The significance of Pentecostalism is seen in the fact that more than 60 percent of Latin American Protestants are Pentecostal. Their fierce independence can be measured by observing that less than 10 percent of the foreign missionaries are associated with Pentecostals while nearly 45 percent are associated with traditional churches, which have less than one-fourth of the total number of Protestants. Pentecostalism is strongest in commercial and manufacturing centers, but it flourishes also in the developing frontier areas of Brazil, Ecuador, Mexico, and Peru as well as in the mining regions of Chile.

Politics and Protestantism. In many parts of Latin America Protestants have undergone bloody persecutions, and in Bolivia, Colombia, Ecuador, and Venezuela the violence of 1946–1961 may recur in the future. However, it is relatively safe to say that in most Latin American countries Protestants are accepted in much the same manner that Catholics are now accepted in the United States. Dating from just before the reign of Pope John XXIII, there has been an increasing rapprochement between the Catholic and Protestant clergy (with notable exceptions) as well as cooperation aimed at ameliorating the conditions of hunger, disease, and natural disaster. Persecutions historically brought the unanticipated consequence of rapid Protestant growth. For example, in 1932 the Governor of the state of Tabasco, Mexico, expelled both Catholic and Protestant clergy for seven years. By the end of that time the numbers of Protestant Otomí Indians had grown from a few hundred to more than 10,000 adult baptized members by their own missionary efforts. At present a representation of Baptists, Methodists, Lutherans, Seventh-day Adventists, and Presbyterians, among others, can be found in the highest political and professional positions in most of Latin America. There are not only Protestant councilmen, mayors, state and federal deputies, and senators but also bankers, lawyers, doctors, engineers, and military men from privates to admirals and generals.

Protestantism in Latin America has also adapted itself to the transformation of *caudillismo* into populist electoral politics. Native pastors often become clients of political patrons and provide votes in return for government favors to their churches. It would also appear that Protestantism helps develop political consciousness, inasmuch as many Latin American Protestants become almost xenophobically nationalistic. For instance, the Presbyterian Church of Brazil met in Vitória, Espírito Santo, in 1965 and passed resolutions demanding the halt of photomapping operations by the United States Air Force, denouncing United States intervention in the Dominican Republic and Vietnam, and protesting the Brazilian policy of *interdependência* with the United States for the promotion of hemispheric growth. The General Assembly also demanded that American missionaries be sent home and that the money supporting them be donated in one lump sum for the endowment of their own organizations. American Presbyterians were forbidden even to observe the proceedings on the ground that they were "spies" of the Central Intelligence Agency.

The political positions of Latin American Protestants are by no means uniform, however. In Brazil, for example, the so-called revolution of April 1964 found the Assemblies of God of Rio Grande do Sul supporting ousted President João GOULART, whose brother-in-law was Governor of their state, whereas to the north in Minas Gerais the Assemblies of God just as ardently supported the revolutionaries.

Economic process and Protestantism. Probably the greatest tangible accomplishment of Protestantism lies in the area of economic development, especially the infrastructural development of human resources. This begins with literacy and includes recruitment and training in dozens of technical skills as well as the provision of equipment and supplies. Most of the fewer than 6,000 missionaries labor in hospitals, orphanages, elementary schools, and technical institutes of all kinds and in Protestant-founded and -run secondary schools and universities, such as the Colegio Americano in Caracas, Venezuela. There are 360 Bible institutes, and a significant portion of the educational systems of Latin

America, like those of the United States and Europe, began in institutions to train ministers and Christian workers. The schools of the Seventh-day Adventists are the backbone of large networks of churches among the AYMARÁ and QUECHUA Indians in Bolivia, helping to bring these peoples into the modern economy. Many schools have become so important to the development of their countries that they have been nationalized, among them Mackenzie University in São Paulo, Brazil, to mention only one. A Presbyterian hospital in Guatemala was first nationalized and then sold into private practice when the vast extent of the foreign subsidy thus forgone was realized.

Increasingly national law demands that ownership and control of such strategic operations be vested in citizens of the respective countries. One of the most powerful radio stations in the world is HCJB of the World Radio Missionary Fellowship in Quito, Ecuador. Called the Voice of the Andes, it is staffed by more than 100 missionaries. When this organization tried to bring a similarly powerful and expensive transmitter into Brazil, the nationals on the governing board used their legal majority effectively to confiscate the entire operation. Traditionally conflicts have developed within Protestant ranks, between missionaries and their converts, over the control of lands, buildings, equipment, and funds as well as membership and executive personnel. It is the pattern that success at the institutional level eventually leads to autonomy for a national church. Foreign businessmen have had to learn to amortize their investments rapidly in the face of expropriation by host governments. Missionary enterprises have also had to face this desire for economic control or independence. It has been a bittersweet experience for missionaries all over the world, not only in Latin America, to realize that their converts are citizens in addition to being Christians.

At least 250 missionaries serve fewer than 136,000 Indians in the AMAZON RIVER Basin of Brazil. This is an uneconomical allocation of personnel in a country of some 100 million people who occupy 47 percent of the entire South American landmass. Similarly, 600 Wycliffe Bible Translators (Summer Institute of Linguistics) are allocated among the hundreds of tiny Indian linguistic communities of Mexico and Central and South America. However, the Indians of Latin America have a more profound and enduring need for the infrastructural spin-off correlated with missions than do European immigrants or their descendants. Speaking realistically, the Indian missions may be the best hope of preventing the eventual extinction of the Indians. At the same time the enduring need for their services prolongs the usefulness and careers of foreign missionaries.

Prospect. The realities of the economic and political process in the long run mean that Protestants are going to have to use modern data-gathering and communications techniques to match their trained personnel quickly and efficiently with areas of high developmental potential. In fact, this is coming about, for missions are an important step in the direction of state growth. Because of this fundamental truth there is an increasing convergence between Catholic and Protestant missions not only in Latin America but around the world. As one result of studies carried out by Catholic research centers in such places as Bogotá, Colombia, Cuerna-

vaca, Mexico, and Rio de Janeiro, Brazil, the Catholic Church now considers all Latin America to be mission territory. Less than 10 percent of the professing population have proved to be truly Catholic by church standards. In addition, it has proved to be almost impossible to recruit enough Latin Americans for the priesthood to minister to their own people. Today there are more Catholic than Protestant missionaries of European and United States origin in Latin America.

The entrance of hundreds of Latin American Roman Catholics into the International Full Gospel Businessmen's Association, a worldwide group of Pentecostal commercial entrepreneurs, is part of a larger interest in Pentecostalism on the part of Catholic clergy and laity alike, much of it within the framework of the Catholic Church itself. This is matched by the Pentecostal revitalization movements that are sweeping the ranks of established Baptist, Congregational, and Presbyterian churches in such widely separated countries as Argentina and Mexico. The great Pentecostal denominations of Chile, for example, began among the Methodists.

Matching Catholic interest in research and development are a number of Protestant study groups, among them the Center for Advanced Studies in Evangelism (CASE) in São Paulo, Brazil. Missions Advanced Research and Communications Center (MARC), a division of World Vision International of Monrovia, California, is part of a consortium engaged in revising the *World Christian Handbook,* at the same time conducting studies to assist churches and missions in planning, management, the obtaining of strategic information on the world, and the identification of areas of high church growth potential. In a pilot project on Brazil MARC has programmed computers with Brazilian census records, correlated the results with Brazilian economic and geographic microregions, and is training a corps of Brazilian field observers to update the information and utilize the results. To cite two other representative examples of modernization among missions, the School of World Mission, Fuller Theological Seminary, Pasadena, California, and the Jaffrey School of Mission, Nyack Missionary College, Nyack, New York, now employ anthropologists with doctoral degrees to train seasoned missionaries on home furlough in social science research methods.

In the light of this sample of Catholic and Protestant activity concerning Latin America, the "conservative" versus "liberal" debate within the World Council of Churches takes on new significance as it reaches a new intensity. "Liberals" in general identify the Christian message with economic and social as well as political development, most of them having reconciled the historic gospel with socialistic philosophies in the Third World of developing nations. "Conservatives," on the other hand, generally believe the essence of their task to lie in the work of conversion, although neither group is totally unconcerned with the priorities of the other. As Christendom entered the 1970s, the important post of director of the Division of Mission and World Evangelism of the World Council of Churches passed out of liberal hands into those of the conservatives. This move reflects the concern of veteran field missionaries around the world over the impact of nationalism upon Christian churches as well as missions. Growth frequently results in struggles between political factions in developing areas, resulting in repressive governmental policies that at times lead to expulsion or even bloody persecution. The desirability of a low profile in missions was outlined briefly but pungently by Ralph D. Winter in *The 25 Unbelievable Years* (*see* Bibliography). In many areas of the world, not excluding Latin America, missionaries have fulfilled their function so well that they have worked themselves out of a job.

Bibliography. H. Wakelin Coxill and Kenneth Grubb (eds.), *World Christian Handbook,* London, 1968; Prudencio Damboriena, S.J., *El Protestantismo en América Latina,* 2 vols., Bogotá, 1962; Christian Lalive d'Epinay, *Haven of the Masses: A Study of the Pentecostal Movement in Chile,* London, 1969; Walter J. Hollenweger, *The Pentecostals,* Augsburg, 1972; Kenneth Scott Latourette, *A History of the Expansion of Christianity,* New York, 1937–45; Emile G. Léonard, *O Protestantismo Brasileiro: Estudo de Eclesiologia e História Social,* São Paulo, 1963; William R. Read, Victor M. Monterroso, and Harmon A. Johnson, *Latin American Church Growth,* Grand Rapids, Mich., 1969; John Sinclair, *Protestantism in Latin America: A Bibliographical Guide,* Austin, Tex., 1967; Emílio Willems, *Followers of the New Faith: Culture Change and the Rise of Protestantism in Brazil and Chile,* Nashville, Tenn., 1967; Ralph D. Winter, *The 25 Unbelievable Years: 1945–1969,* Pasadena, Calif., 1970.

DONALD EDWARD CURRY

PRUD. *See* PARTIDO REVOLUCIONARIO DE UNIFICACIÓN DEMOCRÁTICA.

PSD. *See* PARTIDO SOCIAL DEMOCRÁTICO.

PTB. *See* PARTIDO TRABALHISTA BRASILEIRO.

PUBLIC HEALTH. The term "public health" may be defined as public services provided to prevent and to treat illness. The concept embraces more than precautionary measures to avoid illness, such as inoculations, attacks on specific causes of disease, and health examinations and health education. It includes also programs of environmental sanitation (housing, water supply, sewage disposal, and so on) and efforts to improve nutrition. In many parts of the world the success of the modern public health movement has been responsible for relieving vast human misery, offering the promise of a longer and better life, and, at the same time, contributing to the mixed blessing of an extraordinary rise in population.

Rise in population. In perhaps no other region of the world have advances in public health had a greater impact on population growth than in Latin America. Indeed, the rate of growth there exceeds that of any other major world region. In Europe the population doubles every 100 years and in North America every 63 years, but in Latin America it doubles every 24 years. Juan Bautista ALBERDI, the nineteenth-century Argentine political thinker, wrote "To govern is to populate." In the twentieth century some Latin American nationalists have equated an increasing population with ascending national power. Historically Latin American culture has always placed a high priority on virility and fecundity, and until recently there was little support for voluntary population control at either the grass-roots or the official level. Thus the birthrate has always been high in Latin America, and the "revolution" effected there by the use of modern public health procedures has been one of substantially reducing the death rate. In large part this has come about by reducing or eliminating the threat of deadly communicable diseases. *See also* POPULATION.

Communicable diseases in past centuries. Numerous early chroniclers commented on the excellent state of health of the aboriginal Indian population. Such deadly diseases as measles, plague, smallpox, Asian cholera, and possibly yellow fever and tuberculosis seem to have been unknown in the New World prior to the conquest. From the sixteenth through the nineteenth century, however, great epidemics repeatedly swept through Latin America, claiming hundreds of thousands of lives. Smallpox, yellow fever, and Asian cholera (not introduced until the nineteenth century) were the most destructive. Smallpox penetrated most parts of the New World during the sixteenth century; it was particularly lethal to Indians, since their systems lacked protective antibodies for this disease. Yellow fever was endemic in the Caribbean, Mexico, and Central America by the seventeenth century, and in Brazil great epidemics of this disease commenced by 1850. Cholera swept through Mexico and Central America in the 1830s and through Brazil in the 1850s. Official sources in Brazil estimated that there were more than 150,000 deaths from cholera in 1855–1856 alone. Most of the victims were Negroes, many of whom were slaves. Of all the major communicable diseases cholera was the first to disappear from Latin America; there has not been a single case reported there since the nineteenth century.

Communicable diseases in the twentieth century. In more recent years the most remarkable success in the field of public health in Latin America has been the substantial reduction in mortality caused by communicable diseases. The great epidemics of earlier centuries have been eliminated, and hundreds of thousands of lives have been spared. Control of yellow fever was the first great success in public health of the twentieth century. The *Aëdes aegypti* mosquito, the principal vector of the disease, has been eradicated from nearly 80 percent of the areas ecologically favorable to it in Latin America. An effective vaccine against yellow fever is now available. There has not been a single case of urban yellow fever reported in Latin America since 1954, but jungle yellow fever persists in the Amazon, Orinoco, and Magdalena Valleys. Since certain animals, particularly marmosets and howler monkeys, are readily susceptible to yellow fever and hence serve as a living reservoir of the virus, and since the *Aëdes aegypti* mosquito has returned to some areas from which it had been eradicated, one cannot be certain that Latin America has seen the last of its great epidemics of yellow fever.

There is reason to hope that smallpox will be eradicated from Latin America by the end of the 1970s. Brazil is now the only country of the region with endemic smallpox; 21,552 cases were reported there between 1966 and 1970. Man constitutes the only reservoir of the disease, and an effective vaccine offers the hope of complete protection. Since for most countries the threat of smallpox cases is now remote, some have followed the lead of the United States in no longer requiring compulsory vaccination for international travelers.

Tuberculosis remains one of the more serious public health problems in Latin America, and one that offers no prospect of a rapid solution. Reduction in mortality, which was rapid in the years 1948–1954, has recently proceeded more slowly. The disease remains a major problem in every country of the area despite the use of BCG vaccination, modern chemotherapy, and improved knowledge of the cure and prevention of the disease. In 1968 the mortality rate per 100,000 population was 21.3 in South America, 16.9 in Middle America, and 3.1 in the United States and Canada. In 1969 it was estimated by the Director of the PAN AMERICAN HEALTH ORGANIZATION (PAHO) that 1,250,000 cases were active in Latin America.

The current status of several other major communicable diseases varies. Leprosy is found in every nation of the Western Hemisphere with the exception of mainland Chile. In 1970 the total number of cases in Latin America was close to 200,000, of which more than 50 percent were reported from Brazil. Poliomyelitis appeared to be decreasing steadily until 1970, and there was even hope of complete eradication by the end of the decade. That year, however, the number of cases nearly doubled over the previous year. Cuba is the only Latin American nation with an adequate vaccination program for poliomyelitis. Yaws has declined spectacularly since 1950, when authorities estimated that there were 1 million cases in Haiti alone; in 1970 only 32 cases were reported there. Plague has been reported in fifteen countries of the Americas since 1900, but since 1959 the only cases have come from Bolivia, Brazil, Peru, Ecuador, and Venezuela. Measles is still a cause of high mortality and morbidity rates in Latin America, especially among poor children for whom malnutrition is a common problem. In keeping with a worldwide trend, there has been a sharp increase in the incidence of venereal disease. Louse-borne typhus still exists in Mexico, Peru, and Bolivia.

Parasitic diseases. Without question the major parasitic disease in Latin America is malaria. Throughout the Americas more than one-third of the population lives in areas that were malarious at one time. Recently important progress has been made. Malaria has been eradicated in the United States and Cuba. For the single year 1969, PAHO estimated that had it not been for the malaria eradication campaign, an additional 22 million cases and 220,000 deaths would have occurred. As it was, PAHO estimated that there were 1,200,000 cases of malaria and 3,000 deaths from the disease in 1969. Eradication has been complicated because of increased vector resistance to insecticides.

Next to malaria, schistosomiasis is the most serious parasitic disease of Latin America. In Brazil alone it affects between 6 million and 7 million persons, of whom nearly 120,000 are totally disabled and more than 1.5 million are partially disabled. The annual economic loss to Brazil is placed at $60 million. The disease is serious also in Venezuela and the Caribbean. Another parasitic disease, Chagas' disease, is found in almost every country of Latin America. At least 10 million Latin Americans suffer from this ailment; in some communities the incidence is almost 100 percent. In Venezuela some 20 percent of the rural population has Chagas' disease, and one-half of this group has suffered serious heart damage as a consequence. In general the eradication or control of parasitic diseases (with the exception of malaria) has had a low priority and has been neglected in some countries in spite of the diseases' enormous economic and public health importance.

Zoonoses. Diseases of animals that can be transmitted to man, or zoonoses, significantly affect both the public health and the economy of Latin America. In a part of the world where the majority of people suffer from undernutrition, the annual loss of meat and milk because of animal diseases substantially decreases the availability of proteins. It was estimated that in 1970 meat and milk losses due to brucellosis were nearly $10 million in Venezuela, while the Dominican Republic lost nearly $8 million from this disease. Furthermore, nearly 8,000 cases of brucellosis were reported among humans in Latin America that year. Bovine tuberculosis is endemic in most of South America; 20 to 40 percent of the animals in the dairy herds around Lima, Peru, suffered from this disease in 1970. Foot-and-mouth disease (*aftosa*), although not a disease of humans, causes an annual economic loss to South America of $400 million. It is the single greatest cause of inadequate production of animal protein in the continent.

Undernutrition. It could well be said that the main public health problem of Latin America is undernutrition, especially in children. More than two-thirds of the children suffer from varying degrees of undernutrition; this is the principal cause of death during the first year of life. Furthermore, 50 percent of the children of Latin America die before the age of fifteen as compared with 6 percent in the United States. The great majority of these Latin American children never enjoyed an adequate or proper diet. An important advance has been the development of low-cost vegetable proteins with a high nutritive value, the most noteworthy example being Incaparina. This product, which was developed by the INSTITUTE OF NUTRITION OF CENTRAL AMERICA AND PANAMA (INCAP), now enjoys wide acceptance beyond Central America.

Public health personnel. Although the number of medical schools in Latin America has more than doubled since World War II, there continues to be a severe shortage of physicians and dentists. Furthermore, more than 50 percent of the physicians are concentrated in capitals and large cities where less than 20 percent of the people live. Even scarcer than physicians are auxiliary medical personnel such as nurses, therapists, and technicians.

Future prospects. The spectacular success achieved in the twentieth century in controlling the ravages of communicable diseases is not likely to be matched as quickly or even at all in several other crucial aspects of public health. It seems all too clear that such factors as deficient sanitary engineering, dilapidated and unsanitary housing, low per capita income, low median educational levels, high malnutrition rates, and inadequate funding for public health programs—all of which seriously affect adversely future prospects for improved health care—will not yield rapidly to any easy solutions. For the time being Latin American populations will continue to be characterized as generally young, as growing at an accelerated rate, and as producing less than they need and certainly less than they demand. Despite some undeniable advances in public health, for the typical Latin American life expectancy at birth will continue to be less, and prospects for achieving good health lower, than for residents of the world's more highly developed regions.

Bibliography. Donald B. Cooper, *Epidemic Disease in Mexico City, 1761–1813: An Administrative, Social and Medical Study,* Austin, Tex., 1965; [A. A. Moll], *The Pan American Sanitary Bureau: Its Origin, Development and Achievements* (*1902–1944*), Washington. 1948; Pan American Health Organization, *Annual Report(s) of the Director, 1968, 1969, 1970,* Washington, 1970; id., *Quadrennial Report of the Director, 1966–1969,* Washington, 1970; id., *Special Meeting of Ministers of Health of the Americas,* Washington, 1969; Fred L. Soper, *Building the Health Bridge: Selections from the Works of Fred L. Soper, M.D.,* Bloomington, Ind., 1970; A. Curtis Wilgus (ed.), *The Caribbean: Its Health Problems,* Gainesville, Fla., 1965.

DONALD B. COOPER

PUERTO BELLO. *See* COMMERCIAL POLICY (COLONIAL SPANISH AMERICA).

PUERTO RICO. The easternmost and smallest of the Greater Antilles, the island of Puerto Rico has an area of 3,435 square miles; it is 100 miles long and 35 miles wide. Its population in 1970 was 2,712,033.

Discovered by Christopher COLUMBUS on November 19, 1493, the island was inhabited at the time by Taino Indians, a subculture of the Arawaks (*see* ARAWAK). Two earlier Indian groups had lived there: the Archaic and the Igneri. The Tainos were peaceful tillers of the soil, and their weapons were no match for those of the Spaniards. The native inhabitants, calculated to have numbered around 30,000, called the island Boriquén, or Land of the Noble Lord, and the words *borincano* and *boricua* are still used to identify a Puerto Rican.

Early colonial development. The colonization of Puerto Rico began in 1508, when Juan PONCE DE LEÓN founded Caparra. The colony served three basic purposes: it was a military outpost against the incursions of the man-eating CARIB Indians who inhabited the Lesser Antilles, an auxiliary base for the penetration of the Spanish Main, and a laboratory for experiments in the transfer of Spanish institutions and culture to the New World. The early colonial economy was based on the exploitation of gold placer deposits in the rivers, but by 1536 the deposits were largely exhausted. Attention was then turned to the cultivation of sugarcane as the new economic base of the colony. African slaves were introduced to provide labor, and the crown granted

credits to aid the budding enterprise. Yet lack of sufficient capital and an inflexible commercial policy that precluded direct entrance into the growing European market stunted the growth of a slave-based monoculture plantation system.

As other European nations began to develop an interest in the Caribbean, Puerto Rico gained an added role. Given its location, the island served a strategic function as a bastion against the incursions of foreign powers. To bolster its defenses the *situado,* a yearly subsidy from Mexico, was paid to Puerto Rico every year. The island's strategic importance was recognized by other European powers. Between 1595 and 1625 it was attacked three times. Sir Francis DRAKE tried to take it in 1595 and was repulsed. Three years later George de Clifford, 3d Earl of Cumberland, took San Juan and held it for some months before being forced to abandon the city because tropical diseases were decimating his troops. In 1625 the Dutchman Boudewijn Hendrikszoon took San Juan but was unable to defeat the defenders of El Morro Castle and finally left after burning the city to the ground.

As the economic importance of Puerto Rico declined, Spanish merchant vessels soon began to bypass the island. In 1662 the Governor complained that not a single merchant ship had arrived in eleven years. Since commerce with Spain was limited, the residents turned to a highly profitable contraband trade. English, French, and Dutch were quite content to trade their goods for the island's cattle and foodstuffs. Another profitable enterprise was based on letters of marque. In the seventeenth and eighteenth centuries Puerto Rico was a major privateering center, and Puerto Rican corsairs became a menace, especially to British trade.

During this period a social dichotomy developed between San Juan, the outpost of the empire, and the rural hinterland. San Juan, the walled city, its life dominated by the imperial bureaucracy, was part of a political structure that covered vast territories. In the hinterland a more rustic and carefree society emerged. Living in rather primitive conditions, the rural folk, unconcerned about the clashes of distant empires, developed their own norms.

Enlightened reforms. Although the view that Puerto Rico slept a peaceful colonial siesta during the seventeenth and eighteenth centuries is clearly inadequate, it is nonetheless true that it was not until the mid-eighteenth century that the tempo of social and economic change began to accelerate. By 1750 Puerto Rico had fourteen towns, compared with five at the beginning of the century. Attempts were made to divide the large haciendas into smaller farms, and coffee was introduced from the nearby French islands. In 1765 Field Marshal Alejandro O'Reilly arrived to inspect military conditions. O'Reilly was appalled by the general condition of the island, the poverty of its people, the decay of its defenses, and the extent and openness of illegal commerce. In his report to the Spanish monarch he made several recommendations: break up the large haciendas, promote the development of a sugar industry, liberalize trade restrictions, and encourage selective foreign migration. O'Reilly's enlightened proposals were only partially implemented by the royal decree of 1778. This decree opened the island to foreign migration, although it retained stiff restrictions, and formulated a new general agrarian policy.

PUERTO RICO

Area: 3,435 sq. mi.   Population: 2,712,033 (1970).

O'Reilly's military recommendations were implemented in time to help defeat a British attack under Gen. Sir Ralph Abercromby in 1797.

The creative century. At the beginning of the nineteenth century several developments converged to make possible new departures in the island's development. The creole elite became conscious of the difference between the PENINSULAR and the islander. Foreign immigration, spurred by the decree of 1778, exposed Puerto Ricans to new ideological currents, while the confused state of affairs caused by the Napoleonic invasion of Spain and the wars of independence in South America also stimulated change. Since commerce with the metropolis was disrupted, the colonial authorities were forced to legalize trade with the United States. This trade grew throughout the century as Puerto Rico exchanged sugar, molasses, and coffee for North American flour and manufactured goods. A writer of the time, José Julián Acosta, affirmed that "were it not for the consumer and productive market of the United States, there would have been no development of Puerto Rican agriculture." It should also be noted that Puerto Rico received at this time an influx of royalist *émigrés,* who became an important conservative force in the island.

Despite this conservative element the first decades of the century witnessed the consolidation and emergence of a strong creole liberal conscience. Don Ramón Power y Giral, named in 1809 to be a member of the Junta Suprema in Spain and elected a year later as a deputy to the Cortes, where he eventually rose to the position of Vice President, is typical of the new creole attitude. He sought concrete and tangible reforms rather than allowing himself to be seduced by abstract ideals or revolutionary rhetoric. He fully expressed the feeling of differentiation and uniqueness that had developed in the island, while at the same time he did not wish to sever ties with Spain. Some of the liberal reforms he advocated were decreed in the *Cédula de gracias* of 1815. Among other changes, foreign immigration was further encouraged, and free trade with friendly nations was permitted. The restoration of absolutism in Spain in 1823 slowed political development but did not affect adversely Puerto Rico's economic growth.

Pursuit of reform. By the 1850s a split had developed within the liberal creole forces. Some of them had become more radical and impatient in the face of the continuous frustration of liberal aspirations. Eventually members of this group became convinced that it was illusory to expect reforms from Spain and came to demand full independence. Ramón Emeterio Betances, a physician, emerged as the outstanding leader of this faction. From exile he inspired and planned an armed insurrection against the Spanish authorities. On the night of September 23, 1868, a group of rebels temporarily took the mountain town of Lares. The colonial authorities reacted vigorously and suppressed the uprising with relative ease. Despite its failure the Grito of Lares, as the uprising is known, has become a symbol to groups that favor independence for Puerto Rico.

The majority of the liberal forces, however, continued to follow a moderate policy and seek reforms in an evolutionist, pragmatic manner despite the increased persecution suffered because of the Lares uprising. This group achieved two important triumphs during the last three decades of the century. The first was the abolition of slavery in 1873; the second, the granting of the Autonomic Charter in 1898. In 1887 the Autonomist party had been founded under the leadership of Román Baldorioty de Castro to fight for the establishment of an autonomous regime. After Baldorioty's death in 1889 a young journalist named Luis MUÑOZ RIVERA emerged as the leader of the autonomist forces. Muñoz signed a pact with the Liberal party in Spain. After the party's leader, Práxedes Mateo Sagasta, became Prime Minister, his government granted autonomy to Puerto Rico, in 1898. Under the Autonomic Charter Puerto Rico had a bicameral legislature that could enact all laws except those reserved for the national Cortes and had the right to send deputies to the Cortes as well as the power to sign commercial treaties and impose import duties. Furthermore, only the provincial assembly had the power to initiate amendments to the charter.

Puerto Rico under United States sovereignty. The new government never had a chance to work, for the same year Puerto Rico was ceded to the United States by the Treaty of Paris ending the Spanish-American War. After two years of military government the Foraker Act was enacted in 1900 to provide for a civil government. This act established a presidential-type government. The Governor, his Cabinet, and the judges of the Supreme Court were all appointed by the President of the United States. The Cabinet and five additional presidential appointees constituted the upper chamber of the Legislature. The will of the people of Puerto Rico was represented only in the thirty-five-member House of Delegates. Economically, the island was incorporated within the United States tariff system, and the free movement of goods between Puerto Rico and the mainland was established.

The Foraker Act pleased almost no one in Puerto Rico. Among its many shortcomings was the fact that the island enjoyed less autonomy than it had under monarchical Spain. Once again Muñoz Rivera shouldered much of the burden of wresting concessions from the metropolitan power. In 1904 he dissolved his Federal party and joined other leaders in forming the Unión de Puerto Rico, which became the dominant party. In 1910 he was elected resident commissioner to Congress, and from his seat in the House of Representatives he led the fight for greater autonomy. In 1917 Congress approved the Jones Act. This law provided for popular election of both houses of the Legislature and appointment by the Governor, with the advice and consent of the Senate, of all members of his Cabinet except the Commissioner of Instruction and the Attorney General. It contained a bill of rights and granted American citizenship to Puerto Ricans.

The critical decade. While some political progress was thus achieved, the economic situation of the island began to deteriorate. From the relatively diversified agricultural economy of the nineteenth century, the island had been transformed into a monoculture economy producing sugar for the United States market. The critical stage was reached in the 1930s. The world depression hit Puerto Rico extremely hard. As the price and volume of its exports shrank, per capita income declined from $122 in 1930 to $86 in 1932. The economic disaster gave fresh urgency to the search for new political, social, and economic departures.

Once again there emerged the division between the

radical-activist tendency that had given rise to the Grito of Lares and the evolutionary-pragmatic tradition that had generally received greater popular support. The former was represented by Pedro Albizu Campos; the latter, by Luis MUÑOZ MARÍN. Albizu was the leader of the Nationalist party (NP). After its rejection at the polls in 1932, the NP opted for more direct forms of political action. Various instances of political violence were tied directly to members of the party, and the American authorities were rash and ruthless in their actions against its followers. The climate of violence reached a climax in 1937, when the police opened fire on an NP parade in Ponce, leaving seven dead and many more wounded. In the meantime, Albizu had been tried and found guilty in a federal court of conspiring against the United States. With its leader in prison the NP began a steady decline.

Muñoz era. The son of Muñoz Rivera, Muñoz Marín spent most of his youth in the United States, returning permanently to Puerto Rico in 1931. In 1938 he founded the Popular Democratic party (PDP) and led it to an astonishing if narrow victory. With the PDP in power Muñoz implemented a series of social and economic reforms that peacefully revolutionized the island. Puerto Rico changed from a poor agricultural economy with a per capita income of $121 in 1940 to a highly industrialized economy with a per capita income of $900 in 1965, at the end of the Muñoz era. Illiteracy was reduced from 41.5 to 15.1 percent, while college enrollment grew from 5,371 in 1940 to 40,000 in 1964. More important than statistics was the fact that Muñoz taught his people the value of the vote, the force of its mandate, and the strength of its will. In 1948 he became the first Governor to be elected by the people, and he won reelection in 1952, 1956, and 1960.

In 1940 and 1944 the PDP had declared that the political status of Puerto Rico would not be an issue in the elections, but after eight years in power the party had to deal with the need to end the existing colonial regime. By this time Muñoz had abandoned his preference for independence, but he feared the economic and cultural impact of statehood. He proposed a process whereby Puerto Rico would achieve a new type of political status. The process was implemented between 1950 and 1952. In 1950 Congress approved P.L. 600 "in the nature of a compact" to allow the people of Puerto Rico to form a government of their own choosing. The law would not go into effect unless the people of Puerto Rico approved it in a referendum. This they did, and they also elected a constitutional convention to draft a constitution. Once drafted, the constitution was submitted to the voters, and after the voters approved it, it was submitted to Congress. Congress approved the constitution with some changes, which were accepted by the convention. On July 25, 1952, Governor Muñoz Marín proclaimed the creation of the Estado Libre Asociado (Associated Free State). The relations between the United States and Puerto Rico are regulated by the United States–Puerto Rico Federal Relations Act, which consists of those sections of the Jones Act of 1917 not repealed by P.L. 600. Under it Puerto Rico has full autonomy in internal matters and shares with the United States a common currency, common defense, common market, and common citizenship. In 1953 the General Assembly of the United Nations

recognized that Puerto Rico had "achieved a new constitutional status" and "effectively exercised its right to self-determination." Furthermore, "the people of the Commonwealth of Puerto Rico have been invested with attributes of political sovereignty" and were no longer deemed a dependent territory. On July 23, 1967, a plebiscite was held to determine the people's choice of political status. The results were: commonwealth, 60.1 percent; statehood, 38.98 percent; independence, 0.6 percent.

Post-Muñoz era. In 1964 Muñoz would not accept renomination. He selected his Secretary of State, Roberto SÁNCHEZ VILELLA, to succeed him. Sánchez, an experienced and admired administrator, soon ran into trouble with various sectors of the PDP. The split grew when he divorced his wife and married a young assistant, Jeannette Ramos. Reversing his announced decision not to seek the nomination of his party in 1968, Sánchez campaigned strongly for it. When it was denied to him, he switched parties and ran for reelection as the candidate of the People's party. The split within the PDP was largely responsible for its losing the elections. Luis A. FERRÉ, a successful prostatehood businessman who had run unsuccessfully for the governorship three times, won in his fourth attempt under the banner of the New Progressive party.

Ferré's term in office was marked by adverse economic and political conditions. The PDP had retained control of the Senate, and public scandals in the government tarnished Ferré's reputation. In 1972 the PDP, under the youthful leadership of Senate President Rafael HERNÁNDEZ COLÓN, became the first party in Puerto Rican history to have recovered power once it had been voted out of office. At thirty-six Hernández Colón became the youngest Governor to be elected.

Bibliography. Tomás Blanco, *Prontuario histórico de Puerto Rico,* 2d ed., San Juan, 1943; Salvador Brau, *Historia de Puerto Rico,* New York, 1904; Antonio J. Colorado and Lidio Cruz Monclova, *Noticia y pulso del movimiento político puertorriqueño (1808–1898–1952),* Mexico City, 1955; Lidio Cruz Monclova, *Historia de Puerto Rico (siglo XIX),* 3 vols., 6th ed., Rio Piedras, P.R., 1970; Manuel Maldonado Denis, *Puerto Rico: Una interpretación histórico-social,* Mexico City, 1969; Arturo Morales Carrión, *Historia del pueblo de Puerto Rico (desde sus orígenes hasta el siglo XVIII),* San Juan, 1968; id., *Ojeada al proceso histórico y otros ensayos,* San Juan, 1971; United States–Puerto Rico Commission on the Status of Puerto Rico, *Selected Background Studies,* Washington, 1966.   LUIS E. AGRAIT

PUEYRREDÓN, PRILIDIANO (1823–1870). Argentine painter. Unlike his Uruguayan contemporary Juan Manuel Blanes, who expressed a middle-class view, Pueyrredón had the restrained formality of the wealthy class to which he belonged. He was a serious amateur in engineering, architecture, and painting. His training is unknown, and he may have been painting before his first European trip in 1846. The Spanish portraits of Vicente López and Federico de Madrazo were surely known to him, and his portraits suggest an acquaintance with the work of Velázquez. He improved noticeably in his later work.

Among Pueyrredón's portraits are *Manuelita Rosas*

(1850) and *Adela Eastman de Barros* (1865), both in the National Museum of Fine Arts in Buenos Aires. Manuelita, daughter of the dictator Juan Manuel de ROSAS, is a standing figure in a red gown, painted with a freedom and atmosphere rare in that period. The painting of the melancholy Señora de Barros has the restrained elegance of Spanish portraits. Pueyrredón also painted landscapes of ranch life with GAUCHO figures, such as *A Rest in the Country*. In addition, he occasionally made genre and local-color paintings.

TERENCE GRIEDER

PULGAR-VIDAL, FRANCISCO (1929–   ). Peruvian composer. Born in Huanuco, he studied composition in Lima with Andrés SAS and Rodolfo Holzmann and in Bogotá with Roberto Pineda-Duque. Throughout his career he has been concerned with developing a national idiom in music beyond the pure imitation of folklore. He has written works for piano, voice and piano, and orchestra, as well as two string quartets (1953, 1955). Outstanding among his orchestral works is *Apu Inqa* (1970), a cantata for soloists, chorus, and orchestra.

JUAN A. ORREGO-SALAS

PUNTA DEL ESTE MEETING (1962). Eighth Meeting of Consultation of Ministers of Foreign Affairs of the republics of the ORGANIZATION OF AMERICAN STATES (OAS). The meeting was convened by the OAS PERMANENT COUNCIL, in accordance with the Inter-American Treaty of Reciprocal Assistance (RIO TREATY), to deal with charges that the regime of Fidel CASTRO in Cuba represented a threat to the security of the American republics. However, Cuba and Mexico voted against the resolution to hold the meeting, and Argentina, Bolivia, Brazil, Chile, and Ecuador abstained.

The meeting was held in Punta del Este, Uruguay, on January 22–31, 1962. In the divided United States delegation, headed by Secretary of State Dean Rusk, some favored the imposition of diplomatic and economic sanctions on Cuba, while others preferred less drastic action. In the end, all the republics but Cuba approved a declaration stating that the principles of communism were incompatible with the principles of the inter-American political system. A proposal to exclude Cuba from the OAS was passed by a bare two-thirds majority, while Argentina, Bolivia, Brazil, Chile, Ecuador, and Mexico abstained. The arguments against the action ranged from the position that the OAS did not have the legal mandate, under the OAS Charter, to expel a member state to Mexico's stand that the Cuban people should be permitted to determine their own destiny. The meeting also voted, with four abstentions, to suspend trade with Cuba in arms and war equipment.

RODNEY D. ANDERSON

Quadros, Jânio

Quito

QUADROS, JÂNIO [DA SILVA] (1917–   ). President of Brazil (1961). Born in Campo Grande, Mato Grosso, Quadros was taken as a child to São Paulo, where he graduated from law school in 1939. He entered politics in 1947, when he was elected to the São Paulo city council. Thereafter he had a meteoric political career. Quadros gained fame as an unorthodox, invincible campaigner against the powerful political machine of ex-Governor Adhemar de BARROS. Backed by a succession of minor party coalitions, he was elected a state assemblyman in 1951, mayor of the city of São Paulo in 1953, and Governor of the state of São Paulo in 1954. Four years later he became a congressman from the state of Paraná on the ticket of the PARTIDO TRABALHISTA BRASILEIRO. His abilities as an honest, efficient administrator, demonstrated while he was Governor, earned Quadros the presidential nomination of the UNIÃO DEMOCRÁTICA NACIONAL in 1960.

Campaigning on a platform of nationalism, social justice, and honesty in government, Quadros received the largest vote ever cast for a Brazilian presidential candidate. He was inaugurated on January 31, 1961. As President, Quadros initiated an "independent" foreign policy and sent Vice President João GOULART on a state visit to the Soviet Union and the People's Republic of China. On August 25, while Goulart was still abroad, Quadros abruptly resigned without explanation and sailed for Europe. He returned in 1962 to run again for the governorship of São Paulo but was soundly defeated. After the revolution of March 31, 1964, his political rights were suspended for ten years.

ROLLIE E. POPPINO

QUECHUA. Language originally spoken in parts of the Peruvian sierra. It is not known whether in dialectical form it was also the mother tongue of the INCAS or whether it was subsequently adopted by them. The Quechua name for itself was *runa simi,* "the speech of men." At any rate it became the official language of the Inca empire, and its use was required of all the subject *curacas* (chiefs). Thus, when the Spaniards arrived, it was widely enough spread so that they also encouraged its use as a second language. Close to 2 million Indians of Peru, Ecuador, and Bolivia today speak Quechua, and there are some mestizos who prefer it to Spanish in their homes.

BURR C. BRUNDAGE

QUEIROS, RAQUEL DE (1910–   ). Brazilian novelist and journalist. Born in Ceará, she was one of the group of novelists of the NORTHEAST, publishing her first novel, *O Quinze,* in 1930. Its subject was the great drought of 1915 and its disastrous consequences for her state. Her next two novels, *João Miguel* (1932) and *Caminhos de Pedra* (1937), also take the Northeast as their subject, but a fourth, *As Três Marias,* 1939 (*The Three Marias*), only incidentally treats socioeconomic problems and rather is concerned with the situation of women and their attempt to lead their own lives, a topic that was expressed in *O Quinze* but with less maturity. In *As Três Marias* the heroine achieves liberation only when she leaves the provincial atmosphere of Fortaleza and goes to Rio de Janeiro to live. Rachel de Queiros published two plays about the Northeast, *Lampeão* (1953) and *A Beata Maria de Egito* (1958), and collections of her newspaper columns and memoirs.

RAYMOND S. SAYERS

QUEIROZ LAW. Sanctioned by Emperor PEDRO II on September 4, 1850, the Queiroz law (named for Minister of Justice Eusébio de Queiroz) was intended to supplement and strengthen the anti-slave-trade law of November 7, 1831, which had ordered the liberation of all slaves entering Brazil from that time forward. Declaring that slave trade was piracy in response to repeated British requests, the Queiroz law provided that Brazilian ships and all foreign vessels encountered in Brazilian waters that were known to be involved in slave trading, whether slaves were aboard or not, were to be seized by Brazilian authorities. Like the law of 1831, the Queiroz law authorized severe punishment for the owners and officers of such ships and their accomplices onshore, including heavy fines, long prison terms, and the obligation to finance the return to Africa of slaves seized.

The Queiroz law was the result of decades of British pressure against the Brazilian slave trade, culminating in mid-1850 in British seizures of Brazilian ships in territorial waters of the empire and in several violent exchanges between British warships and Brazilian shore batteries, notably at the ports of Paranaguá and Cabo Frio. The decision to end two decades of official tolerance of massive illegal slave traffic was reached in response to a British promise of July 13, 1850, to suspend naval incursions into fortified Brazilian harbors and to limit the boarding and seizure of slave ships to the open seas or ungarrisoned ports. Strongly enforced by Brazilian authorities, as the 1831 legislation had never been, the Queiroz law was the last important legislation directed against the slave trade, which was almost entirely suppressed by 1853.

ROBERT CONRAD

QUETZALCOATL. Ancient god of Mesoamerica whose name means "Feathered Serpent." It is believed that he may have been a sky dragon originally and was therefore to be connected with atmospheric effects. In one of his avatars he is Ehecatl, the Wind; in another he is Tlahuizcalpanteuctli, or Venus the Evening Star. Before the AZTECS took him over, he was worshiped by the TOLTECS and seems to have led them in war and in the arts of human sacrifice. Much confusion has arisen because one of his Toltec high priests, whose name was Topiltzin, was also called Quetzalcoatl. This priest tried to reform the sacrificial cult, failed, and was exiled. He sailed away into the Gulf of Mexico after announcing that he would return in a year named *ce acatl,* which was the year of his birth. According to the Aztec calendar, *ce acatl* turned out to be 1519, the year when Hernán CORTÉS landed near the site of Veracruz, thus leading MOCTEZUMA to believe that the Spaniards were followers of Quetzalcoatl, returning to claim their patrimony.

BURR C. BRUNDAGE

QUILOMBO. Fugitive slave settlement in colonial Brazil (in the seventeenth century more generally called a *mocambo,* a word of African origin, probably deriving from the Ambunda term for a hideout, *mu-kambo*). The establishment of *quilombos* was one of the commonest forms of slave resistance in colonial Brazil. Most were small predatory settlements situated close to urban centers. At times agglomerations of *quilombos* or *mocambos* might unite. Such was the case of the "Republic of PALMARES," situated in the interior of Pernambuco and emerging in the seventeenth century as a centrally ruled confederation with strong African characteristics. Palmares, however, was an exception. The slave hideouts were rarely allowed to remain in existence long, although suppression was difficult and the task was left to Indian auxiliary forces, bush captains, and often the half-Indian *paulista bandeirantes* (*see* BANDEIRAS).

KENNETH R. MAXWELL

QUIPU. Mnemonic aid used in pre-Columbian Peru. The *quipu* was a master cord from which other cords depended, either of slightly varying length or of a contrasting color. By tying knots in these cords, one could keep accurate counts in various categories. A reasonable assumption is that the *quipu* was originally a tally made by llama herders to keep track of categories among their flocks. The *quipus* were the basis of the Incas' administrative efficiency, for on them were recorded entries and disbursements of all items in the many warehouses of the empire, the numbers of subjects according to their ages, sex, occupation, and so on. All the provincial tallies were then summed up and sent as one tally to the central archives in CUZCO, thus keeping officials up to date on the resources available to the state. The *quipu* could also be used to jog the memories of historians recounting the deeds and enactments of the past. *See also* INCAS.

BURR C. BRUNDAGE

QUIROGA, HORACIO (1879–1937). Uruguayan writer. A native of Salto, he began writing in the modernist style (*see* MODERNISM: SPANISH AMERICA), publishing first in *La Revista* of Salto, but his work shows the development of an original style more akin to *indigenista* literature. His first volume was a collection of verse and prose, *Los arrecifes de coral* (1901). In 1902 he joined Leopoldo LUGONES's expedition to the jungle of Misiones, in which he spent four years and which provided the background for many of his stories. He spent the rest of his life either in Buenos Aires or in the jungles of Paraná.

Apart from two novels, *Historia de un amor turbio* (1908) and *Pasado amor* (1929), all Quiroga's work is in the short-story genre, and the atmosphere of mystery and terror of many of his stories shows his fascination with the work of Edgar Allan Poe. In the essay "Decálogo del cuentista" he expressed his ideas on the genre as an emotional unity and noted his favorite models: Poe, Maupassant, Kipling, and Chekhov. His collections include *Cuentos de amor, de locura y de muerte* (1917), *El salvaje* (1920), *Anaconda* (1923), *El desierto* (1924), *Los desterrados* (1929), and *Más allá* (1935). Quiroga's suicide in Buenos Aires ended a life dominated by pessimism and a tragic sense of existence.

RACHEL PHILLIPS

QUIROGA, VASCO DE (1470?–1565). Member of the second *audiencia* of New Spain and first Bishop of Michoacán. Born in Castile, Quiroga was a lawyer sixty years of age in 1530, when the crown requested his services as a judge in the second *audiencia* of New Spain. He served in the trial of the members of the first *audiencia* and of Bishop Juan de ZUMÁRRAGA, finding the former guilty and the latter innocent of the charges raised.

Vasco de Quiroga was the founder of the hospital-city of Santa Fe, a model Indian town in Coyoacán based on the social ideas of Plato and St. Thomas More, whose inhabitants were Christianized, educated, and taught various trades. In 1533 he was sent as a *visitador* (inspector) to Michoacán, where he introduced a similar system of hospital-cities among the Tarascan Indians, each town specializing in a different trade or agricultural crop. In 1535 Zumárraga proposed him for the bishopric of Michoacán, and after taking holy orders he was consecrated in 1539. He established the seat of the bishopric at Pátzcuaro, where he founded the school of St. Nicholas for Indian and Spanish boys, a school for girls, and a hospital. He worked assiduously for the exemption of the Indians from taxation and for their physical and spiritual welfare.

At seventy-seven he traveled to Spain, where he obtained exemption from personal services for the Indians of his hospitals and tried to recruit secular priests for his diocese because of the problems of jurisdiction that he encountered with the regular orders. Back in New Spain he participated in the First Provincial Council of 1555 and continued to found churches and hospitals until his death.

ASUNCIÓN LAVRIN

QUITO. Capital of Ecuador. Located 9,350 feet above sea level on the slopes of Mount Pichincha, it was the site, according to prehistoric accounts, of the kingdom of the Quitus, who were defeated after the arrival of the migrant Cara Indians about A.D. 800. The latter spread a loose confederation across the sierra, where it flourished until 1487 (*see* SIERRA: ECUADOR). The Inca HUAYNA CAPAC added the confederation to his empire (*see* INCAS), but in 1533–1534 the Incas fled before Sebastián de BENALCÁZAR, leaving Quito in ruins to the Spaniards. Spain made Quito the seat of a bishopric in 1545 and of an *audiencia* in 1563.

Quito's central Andean location and crystalline beauty attracted settlers. The Jesuits established a seminary in 1594, and the Dominicans a university in 1688. Church wealth was turned to music, a fine school of painting, and world-renowned baroque architecture. Explorers used Quito as a base to explore the Oriente, as they have ever since (*see* ORIENTE: ECUADOR). After independence the Central University produced scholars of varying ideologies, but Quito's extreme religiosity and the fact that its citizens included Ecuador's richest absentee landlords made it the center of conservatism. *Quiteños* mistrusted the coastal plutocrats and Guayaquil's urban masses and claimed cultural superiority. They found employment in the bureaucracy and in the military, where they could support Conservatives like Gabriel GARCÍA MORENO (*see* CONSERVATIVE PARTY: ECUADOR) and the later military juntas that took power to "save the nation" after 1925. Recently urban sprawl has taken Quito's population, estimated at more than 600,000 in 1970, to the limits of the intermontane basin in which it is situated.

LOIS WEINMAN

Radical Party (Argentina)
Rulfo, Juan

R

RADICAL PARTY (ARGENTINA). The Radical party, the first middle-class political movement in Argentina, has played a major role in the country's politics during the twentieth century. Although persistent fragmentation frequently has prevented Radicals from attaining or retaining control of the government, they have consistently represented a broader sector of Argentine opinion than any other political group.

The Radical party was formed in 1891, when a new political group, the Unión Cívica, divided over the question of whether to seek an accord with the governing oligarchy. Members opposed to the idea formed the Unión Cívica Radical (UCR) under the leadership of Leandro ALEM and called for "relentless struggle" against the conservative landed groups that controlled the government. This conflict between intransigence and compromise, between abstention and participation, long remained a divisive element among Radicals.

Rivalry between Alem and his nephew Hipólito YRIGOYEN weakened the UCR in the 1890s, as did the decision of Juan B. JUSTO to take his leftist following out of the party in 1894 and Lisandro DE LA TORRE's departure toward the center with his following in 1897. The defection of these groups and Alem's death in 1896 left Yrigoyen in clear control of the party. Convinced that the only way to achieve the UCR's goals of free elections and constitutional government was by overthrowing the incumbent regime, Yrigoyen repeatedly stressed the need for party "intransigence" and spent much of the next two decades plotting uprisings. After an unsuccessful Radical revolt in 1905,

however, pressure for a change of tactics began to grow within the party. A 1912 law that extended the suffrage and seemed to assure honest popular elections for the first time in Argentine history intensified the struggle within the UCR, and against Yrigoyen's advice Radicals entered and won several congressional and gubernatorial elections in 1912 and 1914. As the 1916 presidential election approached, Yrigoyen accepted the UCR's nomination and won narrowly.

Radical administrations governed Argentina for the next fourteen years, with Yrigoyen as President during 1916–1922 and 1928–1930 and Marcelo T. de ALVEAR in the Presidency during 1922–1928. Continuing disagreement among Radicals over Yrigoyen's leadership and the UCR's relations with other parties produced a major split in 1924, when the party divided into the UCR under Yrigoyen's continuing direction and the UCR Antipersonalista under the guidance of Alvear. Yrigoyen won easily over the Antipersonalista candidate in the 1928 election but was overthrown two years later by Argentina's first military coup since the mid-nineteenth century.

In the face of widespread electoral fraud employed by the conservative-military coalition that came to power after 1930, the UCR returned to its pre-1916 pattern of electoral abstention combined with revolutionary plotting. Despite the antagonisms of the 1920s, Alvear returned from Europe in 1931 to lead the reorganization of the UCR and after the death of Yrigoyen in 1933 became the party's dominant figure. The UCR began to participate in elections in 1935 and was the major opposition party until the military coup of 1943. The problem of internal divisions continued for the UCR during the 1930s, when the most important split was the formation in 1935 of the Fuerza de Orientación Radical de la Joven Argentina (FORJA) by a group that argued that both the government and the UCR were insufficiently nationalistic. After five years as a dissident faction within the UCR, FORJA became an independent political movement in 1940. When it formally disbanded five years later, many of its members joined the Peronist movement (*see* PERONISM).

The UCR was the center of the coalition formed against Juan D. PERÓN in the 1946 presidential election, although there were various dissident Radical groups that supported Perón. From Perón's election in 1946 until his overthrow by the military in 1955 the UCR formed the core of the opposition in Congress, in the press, and on the street. As a result, many Radical leaders were jailed or forced into exile.

Upon the fall of Perón the Radicals were the only major political group organized on a national scale, and they now had the added appeal of having led the besieged opposition to Perón. The two major leaders of this opposition began an intense rivalry for the party's presidential nomination, however, and in 1956 the UCR split once again into two parties. The Unión Cívica Radical Intransigente (UCRI) supported the nomination of Arturo FRONDIZI, while the Unión Cívica Radical del Pueblo (UCRP) supported that of Ricardo Balbín. Although the schism divided the UCR rather evenly, Frondizi won the 1958 election with an unprecedented margin by also obtaining the support of an estimated 1.5 million Peronists, who were prohibited from running their own candidate. In return, the Peronists two days after the election demanded full legality for their movement and participation in the government. When this was not granted, they withdrew their support, and for the next four years Frondizi's was a minority administration opposed by both the UCRP and the Peronists.

Frondizi was deposed by a coup in March 1962 and remained in military custody for more than a year. Oscar Alende, a former Governor of Buenos Aires Province, became the leader of the UCRI during Frondizi's absence and was the UCRI candidate in the 1963 presidential election. The election was won by the UCRP candidate Arturo ILLIA, however, and the UCRI now moved into the role of opposition. Frondizi, unable to regain control of his party, formed a new group in 1964 after the UCRI bloc in the Chamber of Deputies divided about evenly into Alende and Frondizi factions. Frondizi's new party, initially named Movimiento de Intransigencia Radical (MIR) but soon changed to Movimiento de Integración y Desarrollo (MID), sought to reestablish the type of Radical-Peronist coalition that had been achieved briefly in 1958. It was largely unsuccessful in this aim but quickly became the most vocal critic of the UCRP administration.

The military intervened once again in 1966 and ended the Illia administration halfway through its six-year term. When elections were next held in March 1973, the Balbín sector was again the strongest of several contending Radical groups, but its vote was far behind that of the winning coalition of Peronist parties. In the presidential election of September 23, 1973, Balbín won approximately 24 percent of the vote, running a poor second to Perón.

Bibliography. Mariano G. Bosch, *Historia del Partido Radical,* Buenos Aires, 1931; Alberto Ciria, *Partidos y poder en la Argentina moderna, 1930–46,* Buenos Aires, 1964; Roberto Etcheparreborda, *La revolución argentina del 90,* Buenos Aires, 1966; Alfredo Galletti, *La política y los partidos,* Buenos Aires, 1961; Félix Luna, *Diálogos con Frondizi,* Buenos Aires, 1963; Gabriel del Mazo, *El radicalismo,* 3 vols., Buenos Aires, 1957–59; Luis Alberto Romero et al., *El radicalismo,* Buenos Aires, 1968; Peter G. Snow, *Argentine Radicalism,* Iowa City, 1965.

LEE C. FENNELL

RADICAL PARTY (CHILE). Founded officially in 1863, the Radical party reflected the dissatisfaction of some Chilean politicians, such as Pedro León Gallo and Manuel Antonio Matta, with the lack of radicalism in the Liberal party (*see* LIBERAL PARTY: CHILE). They wanted drastic constitutional reform, stressing provincial rights, the strengthening of the legislature against the executive, a wider suffrage, and the destruction of church influence, especially in education. The party drew its strength from the provinces rather than from Santiago and appealed to the rising middle classes, not to the traditional aristocracy. Opposed to the government of Liberal-Conservative fusion in the 1860s (*see* CONSERVATIVE PARTY: CHILE), the Radical party played a major role in the clerical reforms of Domingo Santa María (1881–1886) but opposed José Manuel BALMACEDA in 1891. In the confused period from 1891 to 1920 the party was always in the opposite camp to the Conservatives: as the latter were linked by religious conviction, so the Radicals were bound by anticlericalism.

The party convention of 1906 revealed the first signs of serious disunity when Valentín LETELIER, arguing that social issues to win working-class support should figure in party programs, defeated Enrique MacIver, who emphasized traditional doctrinal issues. Now preeminently the party of Chile's middle class, the Radicals henceforth could not quite decide whether their future lay with the forces of conservatism or with those of change. The party reached a high-water mark in the 1920s, but it was divided in its attitude toward Carlos IBÁÑEZ; having first supported Arturo ALESSANDRI in his second administration, it then joined the Popular Front in 1936 (*see* POPULAR FRONT: CHILE). The election of Pedro AGUIRRE CERDA in 1938 inaugurated a period of Radical domination of politics that lasted until 1952 and gave the party enormous strength in government and administration. In the 1960s, however, the PARTIDO DEMÓCRATA CRISTIANO supplanted the Radicals in the center of the political stage, and, having begun the decade with a disastrous attempt to combine with the right-wing parties, the Radicals ended it firmly aligned with the left, coming full circle in 1971 with official acceptance of Marxism. The ensuing split of the party into Marxist and non-Marxist wings is probably a definitive rupture.

HAROLD BLAKEMORE

RADIO AND TELEVISION. Latin America's chief mass medium is radio. The wide distribution of inexpensive transistor radios in the late 1960s and early 1970s contrasted sharply with the slower growth of television receiver sales, which was due to the vast difference in price between the two appliances.

Radio. Newspaper readership has not been able to match the growth of radio listening because annual increments in literacy have not kept pace with annual net increases in population. More than half of the adults in Latin America are unable to read. Many ministries of education count as literate any citizen able to recognize a few words in print, such as his or her own name or hometown, but such marginal "literates" could not comprehend newspaper stories even if they had the spare money to buy a daily or weekly newspaper. Radio, by contrast, is limited only in regions where Indian languages predominate over Spanish or Portuguese.

Radio leaps across Latin American jungles and mountains that otherwise isolate clusters of peasants, capturing the attention of illiterates and semiliterates. Radio programming, however, tends to concentrate on music and continuing daily dramas, or soap operas, interspersed with commercials. Fewer than 10 percent of all radio stations maintain professional staffs of reporters and editors capable of providing reliable news roundups. Moreover, a majority of the radio stations of Latin America, unlike those in the United States, Canada, and Western Europe, do not purchase news agency services, stories supplied continuously via teletype printers. Only the largest stations in each republic invest in one or more of the news services: the Associated Press, United Press International, Reuters of Great Britain, Agence France Presse, ANSA of Italy, Prensa Latina of Cuba.

A second negative factor limiting news on radio in Latin America, government censorship or restrictions or management of news, can be found in a majority of the nations. With the exception of Cuba and, to a lesser extent, Peru, Brazil, and Haiti, most radio stations in Latin American nations are owned privately, only a handful of transmitters in each republic being owned outright by the government. Nevertheless, in most nations the government either supplies some of the news announcements to the commercial stations or insists on receiving air time for governmental broadcasts.

In August 1920, Latin America's first commercial radio stations offering daily service went on the air in Rio de Janeiro and Buenos Aires. Although most of the other Latin American nations soon got at least one experimental or amateur broadcasting station on the air, they did not follow Brazil and Argentina in providing daily commercial radio service until 1922, when Chile, Cuba, Puerto Rico, Uruguay, and Venezuela each got commercial radio stations with services seven days a week.

By the time Mexico City's first commercial radio station, CYL, began daily operation in 1923, only seven Latin American nations lacked daily broadcasting to mass audiences. Lima was among the last major Latin American cities to get a commercial radio station, OAX (later Radio Nacional), in 1925.

Brazil, Latin America's largest nation in land area (3,286,488 square miles) and in population (94 million), also has the greatest number of radio stations and radios in use of any Latin American country. In 1971 Brazil's National Telecommunications Council (CONTEL) reported 1,205 standard-band, or medium-wave, radio stations and 155 shortwave radio stations in operation. Some 15 million radios in homes were supplemented by an equal number of portable transistor radios.

Latin America's second most populous nation, Mexico, has 389 medium-wave radio stations serving almost 14 million radios in homes and offices, plus shortwave and FM broadcasting. Argentina has 11 million radios in homes and offices in daily use; Colombia, 4.5 million, Venezuela and Peru, 3 million each; Chile, 1.7 million; Cuba, 1.6 million; and Uruguay and Bolivia, 700,000 each.

The most popular stations with the largest audiences are in the largest cities, feeding affiliated stations in provincial cities through networks. In Brazil Radio Tupi and Radio Mundial head commercial networks, and Radio Nacional links governmental stations in Rio, São Paulo, Brasília, and provincial stations in twenty of the twenty-two states.

In Mexico the Radio Cadena Nacional and the Radio Programas de México are the largest radio networks. Mexico City's radio station XEW, with the most powerful medium-wave transmitter in the Western Hemisphere at 200,000 watts, reaches every state in Mexico and a bonus audience throughout Central America and the Southwest of the United States. It has repeater satellite transmitters in Guadalajara, Monterrey, Veracruz, and San Luis Potosí.

Argentina's Splendid, Mitre, and Belgrano radio networks are headed by stations of the same names in Buenos Aires. Colombia's five radio networks originate in Bogotá: Caracol, Cadena Nacional, Circuito Todelar, Sonar, and Tricolor.

On November 10, 1971, a presidential decree expropriated to the Peruvian government 25 percent of the stock in all privately owned radio stations and 51 percent of the stock in all privately owned television stations. In Cuba no privately owned radio or television stations survived the take-over by the government of Fidel CASTRO in 1959. In Brazil and Haiti the number of government-owned or -controlled radio stations has increased in recent years.

Television. Latin America's first television station, XHTV Channel 4, went on the air in Mexico City on August 31, 1950. Argentina received the second television station in Latin America in Buenos Aires, and Brazil the third one in Rio de Janeiro, both in 1951. By 1972, throughout Latin America 325 television stations were telecasting to almost 19 million video receivers, principally in urban areas. Although the high cost of television sets still keeps TV out of many homes, group viewing at schools, parks, lobbies, clubs, auditoriums, and other places and family and neighborhood viewing raise the total video audience to more than 50 million. Of the 19 million TV sets, three large nations account for 15.3 million: Brazil, 6.8 million; Argentina, 6 million; and Mexico, 2.5 million.

In Brazil there are no networks airing simultaneous nationwide hookups as in the United States. Rather, privately owned stations belong to associations, the largest being Diários Associados of the Assis Chateaubriand Corporation, with thirteen affiliated stations. As in most other Latin American nations, these Brazilian networks repeat programs from the major cities on provincial affiliated stations by means of videotape or film. Brazil's forty-nine television stations (plus 201 satellite repeater transmitters) include seven in São Paulo and five in Rio de Janeiro. In 1971 there were some 25 million viewers watching the 6.8 million sets in twenty states. There are two full-time educational stations, in São Paulo and Recife.

Mexico City televiewers have a choice of commercial Channels 2, 4, 5, 8, and 13, plus educational Channel 11. Through Emilio Azcárraga's Telesistema organization, videotapes of Channels 2, 4, and 5 are bicycled around the republic on thirty-eight provincial television stations. In the Federal District Channels 8 and 13 air greater numbers of Hollywood movies and United States–produced shows than do the other channels of Mexico City. The Telesistema video network has the largest news operation in Latin American television. Behind Jacobo Zabludovsky, commentator and editor of the 11 P.M. to midnight nightly news program "24 Hours," are dozens of reporters and technicians, including correspondents plugged in by telephone and satellite from Santiago, Lima, Buenos Aires, Los Angeles, Washington, and New York.

In Buenos Aires Channels 2, 7, 9, 11, and 13 each videotape popular programs for rebroadcast on stations in thirty-two provincial cities, including Ushuaia in Tierra del Fuego, where Channel 11 is the world's southernmost video station.

Until recently Chile was unique among Latin American nations in having its television stations licensed to universities but operated as combined commercial-educational channels. Advertising has vied with telecourses. Channel 9, owned by the University of Chile, was inaugurated in Santiago in 1959. Channel 13, the property of Catholic University of Chile in Santiago, began broadcasting in 1962. After the other Santiago station, Channel 7, began running an increasing number of governmental reports of the administration of Salvador ALLENDE in 1971, Marxists in the Cabinet endeavored to have the government control Channel 13 as well, but Catholic University successfully blocked the move. Chilean provincial television stations also are linked to educational institutions. Catholic University of Valparaíso has Channel 8, and the University of the North in Antofagasta has Channel 3, emphasizing Jesuit liberal views of the Catholic Church.

The pioneer full-time educational channel in Latin America is XEIPN Channel 11 in Mexico City, owned and operated by the National Polytechnic Institute, which first went on the air on March 2, 1959. The major educational channels in Latin America are Lima's Channel 13, owned and operated by the University of Lima, a private institution, and the Brazilian stations in São Paulo and Recife. These channels feature symphony orchestras, telecourses in literacy and languages, and adult education.

A majority of the commercial Latin American stations feature domestically produced programs during less than a third of their scheduled air time and foreign videotapes and films during more than two thirds. In late 1971 in Mexico City, Lima, Montevideo, Buenos Aires, São Paulo, and Rio de Janeiro, TV schedules showed such United States programs as "Bonanza," "The Lucy Show," "Dragnet," "Dean Martin," "I Dream of Jeannie," and "Ironside," dubbed into Spanish or Portuguese. "Civilization" by Kenneth Clark, the British series of thirteen programs, was aired on leading commercial stations with a Spanish narration in 1971 and 1972.

Censorship. During the era of Fulgencio BATISTA (1952–1958), Cuba's video and radio news was corrupted by bribes and governmental subsidies. Since 1959, under Castro, all radio and television stations have been operated by the government without the slightest hint of criticism of the Communist regime ever being aired.

Since October 1971, the Peruvian government has effectively eliminated meaningful criticism of the government from news and talk shows on television and radio. Since 1969 military censors in Brazil have forced governmental propaganda onto the air and kept criticism off it. The same can be said of Bolivian, Paraguayan, Haitian, Dominican, and Guatemalan broadcasting. In Nicaragua and Honduras entertainment and governmental coercion crowd most reporting and informational programming off the air.

Uruguay, Costa Rica, and Venezuela constitute the handful of Latin American nations not burdened with governmental interference in radio and television broadcasting to the detriment of artistic and journalistic freedom and innovation. In Mexico, Colombia, Chile, Ecuador, and El Salvador governmental public relations officials take air time on both radio and television to place the administration in the best possible light.

In sum, broadcasting in much of Latin America combines Hollywood reruns with governmental propaganda and old movies. There are few unfettered informational programs and domestic-culture creative shows.

Bibliography. Marvin Alisky, "Early Mexican Broadcasting," *Hispanic American Historical Review,* vol. XXXIV, no. 4, November 1954, pp. 513–526; id., "Mass Media in Central America," *Journalism Quarterly,* vol. XXXII, no. 4, Fall, 1955, pp. 479–486; id., "Broadcasting in Peru," *Journal of Broadcasting,* vol. III, no. 2, Spring, 1959, pp. 118–127; id., "The End of Nicaragua's Radio Freedom," *Journal of Broadcasting,* vol. V, no. 4, Fall, 1961, pp. 311–314; id., "Uruguay's Utopian Broadcasting," *Journal of Broadcasting,* vol. XIII, no. 3, Summer, 1969, pp. 277–283; John C. Merrill, Carter R. Bryan, and Marvin Alisky, *The Foreign Press,* Baton Rouge, La., 1970; John F. Newman, "Radio Newscasting in Latin America," *Journal of Broadcasting,* vol. X, no. 1, Winter, 1965–66, pp. 25–32; Standard Rate & Data Service, *Medios publicitarios: Centro América—Radio y televisión,* Evanston, Ill., 1971.
                                                    MARVIN ALISKY

RAILROADS. In Latin America railroads were built largely to meet short-range economic and political goals. What remains of the network begun in the mid-nineteenth century suffers from a basic inflexibility of routes, gauges, equipment, and service procedures. Designed to be an integral part of an ocean-rail interchange, the Latin American rail system has in recent years faced heavy competition from highway transport (*see* HIGHWAYS). Yet there have been both a basic reorientation of rail service and planning and an expansion of the rail network to serve new areas. Ahead lies the problem of providing rail service as part of a well-integrated national transport system. Even farther down the road is the possibility of a continental rail system, a less viable goal now than in the past.

Only Argentina, Brazil, Chile, and Mexico have rail networks of national coverage, with good connectivity and adequate roadbed, rail, and maintenance standards, as well as reasonable importance to the national economy. Elsewhere, as Robert T. Brown has observed (*see* Bibliography), there are four kinds of rail systems. The first is the resource-penetration rail line which, like the Southern Railway of Peru, operates from a seaport (Mollendo) to the minehead in the

TABLE 1. ARGENTINE RAIL SYSTEM, 1969–1970

Division	Route length		Freight volume (in millions of tons)	Passenger volume (in millions)
	Miles	Kilometers		
Belgrano	8,528	13,724	5.5	73.7
Mitre	3,878	6,242	4.2	109.1
Roca	5,669	9,124	5.1	115.9
San Martín	2,895	4,660	5.5	51.0
Sarmiento	2,389	3,845	1.5	113.5
Urquiza	2,208	3,553	1.4	28.1
Total	25,567	41,148	23.2	491.3
Gauge				
5′6″	14,582	23,468		
4′8″	2,078	3,344		
3′3⅜″	8,480	13,647		

SOURCE: *Jane's World Railways,* New York, 1971.

ANDES MOUNTAINS to the east. Second, there is the rail line which, like that from Guayaquil to Quito, Ecuador, is intended to reduce the isolation of the national capital by connecting it with the principal port city. The third type is the integrative system which, like much of the northern Chilean trackage, is intended to link a distant area to the center of the national population. Finally, there is the international railway, best typified by the International Railways of Central America, which serves as the principal freight link between Guatemala, El Salvador, and, to a limited extent, Honduras and the Atlantic coast at Puerto Barrios.

Argentina. The Argentine rail system, financed largely by British capital and generally complete by World War I, not only is mature, in the sense that little of the nation remains outside the existing network, but is relatively highly connective. There are three foci for the Argentine rail system. One of these is Buenos Aires, to which all but one of the rail lines lead and which is served by each of the nationalized rail transport companies. From Buenos Aires these lines stretch out like a vast semicircular web. The Mitre, Belgrano, Roca, Urquiza, Sarmiento, and San Martín companies, which are parts of the Empresa de los Ferrocarriles del Estado Argentino (EFEA), all operate from vast rail terminals located on the fringes of the central city.

The second and much smaller focus is Rosario, the second city, some 300 kilometers up the Paraná River northwest of Buenos Aires. Rosario is served by the Belgrano and Mitre companies, which have lines stretching out north, west, south, and southwest of Rosario. All the lines serving the Argentine Andean west pass through Rosario on their way to Buenos Aires. Rosario also has a line, the old Rosario–Puerto Belgrano line, that runs south to Bahía Blanca, the last large port before Patagonia, providing a cross-country link through Buenos Aires Province that avoids the federal capital. However, this line has seldom been of much economic value either to Rosario or to the nation as a whole.

Bahía Blanca, in southeastern Buenos Aires Province, is the third focus. Not only is it connected to Buenos Aires, Mar del Plata, and Rosario, but it has

rail links with the Chilean border beyond San Carlos de Bariloche and with Patagonia to the south.

Other major cities, such as Córdoba, Mendoza, Tucumán, and Paraná, either are at the end of single lines or developed rather later than the rail network and are eccentric with respect to the rail lines. Moreover, there is no rail bridge across the Paraná, and the Urquiza Railway, which serves Entre Ríos Province, uses car ferries. Statistics on the various lines are shown in Table 1.

Because of their essentially British origin, the Argentine railways were built to high standards, although service was worsening noticeably by the 1940s. Thus, although the Argentine railways are substantially better built and maintained than most other Latin American railways, there has been strong and continuous criticism of railway operations, especially since nationalization in the 1940s. A fairer assessment of the Argentine railway situation would require a careful consideration of the benefits the nation derives from dependable freight and passenger service as against the costs of alternatives and suggested improvements. By the late 1960s,

TABLE 2. OPERATING TRENDS OF THE
ARGENTINE RAIL SYSTEM

Year	Passenger-kilometers (in thousands)	Freight-ton-kilometers (in thousands)	Operating ratio
1952	13,451	15,255	1.17
1958	15,403	13,835	1.43
1960	15,685	15,158	1.57
1963	12,074	10,631	2.02
1968	14,747	13,397	1.44
1970	…	…	1.00 *

* Estimated.
SOURCES: United Nations Economic Commission for Latin America; Empresa de los Ferrocarriles del Estado Argentino.

TABLE 3. BRAZILIAN RAIL SYSTEM, 1969–1970

Division or ownership	Route length		Freight volume (in millions of tons)	Passenger volume (in millions)
	Miles	Kilometers		
Federal				
Northeast region (four lines)	4,622	7,438		
Central region (three lines)	5,550	8,933		
Central-South region (two lines)	1,100	1,771		
South region (four lines)	4,178	6,722		
Total, federal system	15,450	24,864	30.0	318.6
São Paulo State (five lines)	3,970	6,391	11.9	50.3
Other state and private	2,793	4,464		
Total	22,213	35,719		

SOURCE: *Jane's World Railways,* New York, 1971.

EFEA had dismissed excess personnel, upgraded mainline trackage, added significantly to rolling stock and motive power, and improved schedules, while at the same time reducing the operating ratio, or the proportion of operating revenues consumed by operating costs (*see* Table 2). Indeed, by 1971 EFEA was able to announce that it was covering the costs of operations from its revenues.

The giant railroad terminals in Buenos Aires—Retiro, Constitución, Once, Lacroze—still are great attractions for the railway buff. In addition to the suburban trains, which leave every few minutes filled with passengers, there are long-distance specials with sleeping cars, parlor cars, air-conditioned service, and all the polish of railroading at its best. Almost nowhere else in the Americas, with the exception perhaps of Toronto and Montreal, does old-fashioned railroading persist to the same degree.

Brazil. With the creation in 1958 of the Rede Ferroviária Federal (Federal Railway System; RFF), Brazil began a process of integration and improvement of the many pieces of short and long lines that had long characterized its rail system. Throughout the 1960s progress was made, especially in the north, in linking the diverse subsystems and in removing such operational barriers as varying gauges, equipment, and operating procedures. Late in the decade four operating regions were set up: Northeast, based on Recife; Central, based on Rio de Janeiro; Central-South, based on São Paulo, but excluding the five lines owned by the state of São Paulo; and South, based on Pôrto Alegre. These regions included almost 15,500 route miles. Another 3,970 route miles were under the management of the state of São Paulo. Late in 1971 São Paulo combined its five lines under one company, Ferrovias Paulistas, S.A. (Fepasa), and retained European rail-transport planners to develop a five-year plan for integrated service and a reduction of duplication. Almost 2,800 route miles remain under either private or smaller state management. In all, there are 22,213 route miles of rail lines in Brazil, making this the second largest rail system in Latin America (*see* Table 3).

During the 1960s rail traffic increased by 210 percent, almost matching the growth of highway traffic (*see* Table 4). Indeed, since 1968, partly because of extraordinarily large harvests in the south, traffic by rail has grown significantly faster than that by road.

Government policy has been to eliminate unprofitable lines, reduce staff, and thus decrease subsidies for operational purposes. Yet, given the enormity of the transport program undertaken, resources have hardly been sufficient to do more than finish such major projects as the São Paulo–Pôrto Alegre direct line, the Central do Brasil to the port of Sepetiba, and improvements in the Rio de Janeiro–São Paulo main line. By the late 1960s federal subsidies to the RFF had been reduced from 87 percent of expenditures to less than 40 percent.

Since 1967 the main government concern has been to induce cooperation among all transport modes, suppressing unnecessary competition. Investment planning for rail expansion has been made part of a larger planning scheme involving all transport modes. About 20 percent of the transport budget for the first five years of the 1970s was to be devoted to extending routes, acquiring new rolling stock, and building terminals and marshaling yards. The government has stated that the major goal is greater overall transport efficacy in the national development program.

TABLE 4. OPERATING TRENDS OF THE BRAZILIAN FEDERAL SYSTEM

Year	Passenger-kilometers (in thousands)	Freight-ton-kilometers (in thousands)	Operating ratio
1958	13,432	10,471	…
1960	15,395	12,079	2.39
1962	17,926	14,921	3.66
1964	…	15,287	3.51
1965	…	16,781	2.40
1968	21,560 *	18,120	1.92
1969	22,640 *	25,370	…
1970	23,750 *	26,910 *	1.40

* Estimated.

SOURCE: Fundacão Getúlio Vargas, *Realidade,* July 1970.

TABLE 5. MEXICAN RAIL SYSTEM, 1967

Division	Route length Miles	Route length Kilometers	Passenger volume (in thousands)	Freight volume (in thousands of tons)
Nacionales de México	10,614	17,082	34,839	34,695
Pacífico	1,612	2,594	983	4,156
Chihuahua al Pacífico	1,086	1,747	576	2,096
Sureste	507	816	841	622
Sonora–Baja California	388	624	362	438
Unidos de Yucatán	420	676	1,158	421
Coahuila y Zacatecas	115	186	131	175
Occidental de México	24	38	...	135
Tijuana y Tecate	49	79	...	403
Nacozari	83	134	36	18
Total	14,898	23,976	38,926	43,159

SOURCE: *Estadística Ferroviaria Nacional*, Mexico City, 1968.

Mexico. The Mexican rail system, which is composed of ten operating units, is a highly integrated transport network focused on Mexico City (*see* Table 5). Nearly 15,000 miles (24,000 kilometers) of rail connect almost all parts of the nation with the capital. Every major border crossing with the United States and all major ports are connected by this network. In general, the gauge is United States standard, but a little more than 5 percent of the route length consists of narrow-gauge lines.

Plans exist for bringing all the operating units under one management, but wage differentials, especially for the Pacific lines, are a major stumbling block. All rail service in Mexico has been nationalized since 1937, when the Ferrocarriles Nacionales de México were taken over by the government.

Although the operating ratio of Mexican railways has been low as compared with other Latin American systems (except for Argentina), substantial deficits are incurred in passenger rail service. The latest year for which data are available, 1969, shows a government support payment of 2,289 million pesos ($183 million).

As shown in Table 6, passenger traffic since 1960 has fluctuated in the neighborhood of 4 million passenger-kilometers. It is estimated that average revenue per passenger-kilometer covers only 75 percent of the marginal cost of the service. Rail fares remain low partly because the trains serve the poorest segment of the population, who cannot afford even the faster bus services that compete with rail. A government committed to social equalization can do little more than bear these costs.

Freight movements increased relatively fast in the 1960s and reached 21 million ton-kilometers by 1970. Agricultural products, metallic and nonmetallic minerals, and petroleum constitute 70 percent of the freight traffic. A review of the profitability of freight traffic by line and by category is under way. From the available evidence, movements of sugarcane, iron ore, and minerals apparently do not cover variable costs; whereas petroleum, industrial products, and finished goods not only cover out-of-pocket costs but contribute significantly to fixed costs. It is possible, then, that freight operations will break even.

There are no major plans for the expansion of rail lines or service. The Mexican rail system was built to meet political and economic needs that have changed considerably in recent years as rapid economic growth has taken place. To some extent, the system suffers from a complex of attitudes, legal restrictions, and public lack of concern that will make the effective modernization of the entire network difficult. Moreover, the highway network and services provide formidable competition. Yet it would be wrong to conclude that rail service in Mexico is dying. Between 1950 and 1970 passenger traffic increased by 50 percent, and freight movements doubled.

Chile. The Chilean rail network is basically a spinal north-south line with many vertebrae. The largest east-west line runs from Valparaíso through Santiago to connect at Los Andes with the Transandean Railroad to Mendoza, Argentina. Other connections run from Arica at the Peruvian border to La Paz, Bolivia, and from Antofagasta to a connection with the Bolivian state railway system.

TABLE 6. OPERATING TRENDS OF THE MEXICAN RAIL SYSTEM

Year	Passenger-kilometers (in thousands)	Freight-ton-kilometers (in thousands)	Operating ratio
1958	3,491	12,810	1.27
1960	4,128	14,004	1.16
1962	3,770	13,522	1.34
1964	4,097	16,330	1.35
1965	3,872	18,325	1.25
1968	4,252	20,733	1.43
1969	...	20,750	...
1970	...	21,006 *	...

* Estimated.

SOURCE: *Estadística Ferroviaria Nacional*, Mexico City, 1968.

TABLE 7. CHILEAN RAIL SYSTEM, 1967–1968

Division or ownership	Route length		Passenger volume (in thousands)	Freight volume (in thousands of tons)
	Miles	Kilometers		
Private lines	952	1,531	...	...
Government				
Arica–La Paz (Chile route only)	129	207	28	130
Northern network	920	1,481	470	7,511
Southern network	3,448	5,549	20,258	5,414
Iquique	70	113	20	324
Transandean	44	71	111	99
Total	5,563	8,952	20,887	13,478

SOURCE: *Jane's World Railways*, New York, 1971.

The Northern network (Red Norte) is a narrow-gauge line, but it carries the largest freight traffic load, or approximately 56 percent of the state railway total (*see* Table 7). This traffic consists mostly of raw minerals and mining supplies. The Southern network (Red Sur), a wide-gauge line, is one of the best-run rail services on the continent, operating almost at the standard of European railways. It carries an annual average of more than 20 million passengers, and there has been no noticeable trend for this number to decline. A significant portion of the service in and around Santiago is electrified. The remaining portions of the Chilean rail system are either short international connections, such as the 71-kilometer Transandean and the 207-kilometer Arica–La Paz lines, or privately held mining lines. It was anticipated that all private lines would be acquired by the government during the 1970s.

As shown in Table 8, in terms of passenger-kilometers and freight-ton-kilometers there has been a slow though noticeable upward trend in rail utilization since the late 1950s. Perhaps the lesson of the Chilean system is that if high standards of track construction and rolling stock maintenance are observed, it is possible to provide the kind of service that will attract users from competing modes or that at least will permit rail managers to retain a reasonably profitable share of the total freight and passenger movement. It should be added, however, that Chilean operating ratios have been relatively unfavorable in recent years.

Other rail systems. Among other Latin American nations with rail systems of more than 1,000 route miles are Cuba, Peru, Bolivia, Colombia, and Uruguay. Cuba's system has been modernized with the addition of new trackage to the east and with substantial purchases of Russian, Hungarian, East German, and British rolling stock. There is evidence that the Cuban economy's dependence on the rail system increased during the 1960s.

Peru's rail system is an example of almost complete disarticulation. A series of relatively short links from port to minehead combine to make up the more than 2,500 route miles. Included in this mileage are some of the highest rail passes in the world. The Central Railroad of Peru on its way from Lima to Huancayo crests at an altitude of 15,700 feet near La Oroya. The Southern Railroad between Arequipa and Juliaca reaches 14,700 feet along a tortuous route.

By the mid-1960s it had become clear that all but a few of the Peruvian rail lines had such poor operating ratios that widespread abandonment could not be avoided without a government take-over. Yet such is the geography of the sierra (*see* SIERRA: PERU) that in many cases abandonment would leave key centers without an alternative transport link to the world beyond. By 1972, besides attempting to encourage or coerce current managements to continue rail service, the military government of Peru had not determined how to retain rail service under a national transport plan.

Like Peru, Bolivia needs rail service, if only because of the extremely mountainous terrain. La Paz, the capital, is situated at an altitude between 13,000 and 14,000 feet. Yet a declining mining industry, an uncertain economy, and political instability have combined to make the position of private rail companies tenuous. Bolivia depends on important international rail connections to the sea — via Corumbá to São Paulo and Santos on the Atlantic, via La Quiaca to Buenos Aires, and through Chile to Arica and Antofagasta on the Pacific coast. In addition, the Southern Railroad of Peru connects with boat service on Lake Titicaca to provide a link through Arequipa and Mollendo to the Pacific.

TABLE 8. OPERATING TRENDS OF THE CHILEAN RAIL SYSTEM

Year	Passenger-kilometers (in thousands)	Freight-ton-kilometers (in thousands)	Operating ratio
1958	1,527	2,146	...
1960	1,906	1,953	1.53
1962	1,885	1,608	2.12
1965	2,221	2,156	1.93
1968	2,071	2,187	1.43

SOURCE: *Jane's World Railways*, New York, 1971.

TABLE 9. COLOMBIAN RAIL SYSTEM

Division	Route length Miles	Route length Kilometers	Passenger volume	Freight volume (in tons)
Pacífico	561	903		
Central	850	1,368		
Magdalena	264	425		
Antioquia	211	340		
Santander	249	400		
Total	2,135	3,436	3,690,000	3,240,000

SOURCE: DANE, *Informe,* 1969.

In both Peru and Bolivia transport planning has stressed road building, and it seems likely that rail service will continue to decline in relative importance, quality of service, and economic viability.

Alone among the Andean nations, Colombia has been engaged in major rail expansion. By the early 1970s it had developed an integrated national rail system. The most spectacular link was the Atlantic railway connecting the central division based on Bogotá with the Atlantic coast at Santa Marta. Finished in the early 1960s, this railway makes it possible for traffic to move not only from Bogotá but from Buenaventura on the Pacific coast, the nation's most important port, through Cali and Medellín, key industrial centers, to the north coast.

Although Colombia has more than 2,100 miles of track route in service (*see* Table 9), its mountainous characteristics, together with severe competition from road and air freight service, have not permitted economic operation of the railways. Passenger traffic reached a peak early in the 1960s and declined steadily thereafter (*see* Table 10). Freight movement, however, has begun to show some improvement. The availability of modern freight cars, continuing improvement in efficiency of operation, and better scheduling will probably lead to even faster growth. The most urgent needs are further track rehabilitation and rolling stock capable of handling the frequent 3 percent grades. However, a comparison of the experience of Colombia, Ecuador, Bolivia, and Peru suggests that a mountain rail system is so costly to build and operate that only under highly specialized conditions will benefits, however measured, equal (let alone exceed) costs. Colombia intends to succeed, but this will require considerable effort.

The Uruguayan rail system, focused on Montevideo, is in some sense modeled on the Argentine network, with which there are no interrail connections. Indeed, the connections with the Brazilian system are very inadequate. Designed to move grain to the docks at Montevideo and to provide for some passenger movement, the Uruguayan system is basically efficient. However, partly because of inflation and generally poor management, the Uruguayan operating ratios are extremely bad.

Elsewhere in Latin America, significant regular freight or passenger rail service is found only in Central America, Panama, and Venezuela. Except for the International Railways of Central America, the economic importance of these rail links is not great.

Economic perspectives. The obviously difficult situation in which Latin American railways generally operate is traceable to three factors: the failure to maintain many lines in effective operating condition, heavy competition with alternative transport modes, especially highways, and changes in economic geography that have rendered many nineteenth-century routes obsolete. Yet for Argentina, Brazil, Chile, and Mexico the rail systems are a vital part of the national economic structure, though not necessarily with present routes and rolling stock. It is estimated that a carefully planned 50 percent reduction in the Argentine network would provide a rail system that would meet that nation's transport needs. Although trackage should be reduced in certain parts of Brazil, the general problem is that of providing good connections between key production centers. Mexico and Chile have networks of about the correct extension, and the key problem is how to pay for operating costs.

Little expansion in rail networks can be expected during the 1970s. Certainly the dreams of international rail connections must now be abandoned. The integration of rail service into coordinated transport systems with the objective of minimizing transport costs is the likely path ahead. Sterile arguments about which mode is cheapest or yields the best development results must be replaced by a consideration of the transport tasks each nation faces and the alternative and integrated transport modes available to accomplish them.

TABLE 10. OPERATING TRENDS OF THE COLOMBIAN RAIL SYSTEM, 1958–1968

Year	Passenger-kilometers (in thousands)	Freight-ton-kilometers (in thousands)	Operating ratio
1958	...	654	...
1960	85	768	1.13
1962	623	918	1.21
1965	513	890	1.39
1968	352	1,125	0.92

SOURCE: DANE, *Informe,* 1968.

Bibliography. Robert T. Brown, *Transport and the Economic Integration of South America,* Washington, 1966; *Jane's World Railways,* New York, 1971; Charles J. Stokes, *Transportation and Economic Development in Latin America,* New York, 1968; United Nations Economic Commission for Latin America, *El transporte en América Latina,* vols. I and II, Santiago, Chile, 1965; id., "Public Enterprises: Their Present Significance and Their Potential in Development," *Economic Bulletin for Latin America,* vol. XVI, no. 1, first half, 1971, pp. 1–70.

CHARLES J. STOKES

RAMÍREZ, PEDRO PABLO (1884–1962). President of Argentina (June 1943–March 1944). A career army officer, Ramírez was appointed Minister of War in 1942. He then became the focal point of political and military maneuvering from which he emerged as President after the June 1943 coup against Ramón S. CASTILLO.

Ramírez's administration was characterized by divisions within the ruling group and a search for a commonly agreeable policy. Near unanimity was achieved in the elaboration of a response to the economic impact of World War II. With industry burgeoning, the government decided to seek means to protect its growth. Nationalist concerns were further indicated by the nationalization of foreign-owned utilities and transport.

There was greater division over the extent to which political reforms should be carried out. While some sectors maintained that a simple change of personnel and a guarantee of free elections would restore public confidence in the electoral system, others argued that the system itself had proved inadequate and that fundamental structural changes were required. The apparent ascendancy of the latter group after October 1943 heightened fears that the military government had no intention of returning to the electoral process.

Even greater dissension developed over foreign policy, as Argentina's commitment to neutrality in World War II became more difficult to maintain in the face of increasing United States pressure. The Ramírez government was placed in a compromising position after the arrest (November 1943) in Trinidad of Osmar Alberto Helmuth, an Argentine naval reserve officer and German agent, who was en route to Berlin to secure arms for Argentina. The danger that Helmuth's mission might be exposed, together with the threatened publication by the United States of documents incriminating Argentina in a recent coup in Bolivia, led the Ramírez government to sever diplomatic relations with the Axis on January 26, 1944. This act in turn produced a government crisis that ended in Ramírez's resignation in March. He was succeeded by the Vice President, Brig. Gen. Edelmiro J. Farrell, a good friend of Juan D. PERÓN, who soon became Minister of War and Vice President.

NOREEN F. STACK

RAMOS, GRACILIANO (1892–1953). Brazilian novelist. Born in Alagoas, he taught and worked as a civil servant in small towns in the NORTHEAST until 1936, when he was arrested for his political views and taken to Rio de Janeiro, where he remained until his death. In one small city, Palmeira das Índias, where he spent most of his time from 1910 to 1933, he came into contact with some of the other leading intellectuals of the Northeast, who lived there for some years. He joined the Communist party in 1945. The reception of his first novel, *Caetés* (1933), encouraged him to continue to write and publish. With other novelists of the group of the Northeast he shared a deep interest in the economic and social problems of the region, but he was also much concerned with problems of esthetics—plot construction, character development, and style—and he read widely and assimilated ideas and methods of foreign writers such as Dostoevski. His work has been divided into three parts: the novels of profound psychological analysis, *Caetés, São Bernardo* (1934), and *Angústia,* 1936 (*Anguish*); works concerned with the individual in his social relations, *Vidas Secas,* 1938 (*Barren Lives*), and *Insônia* (1947), a volume of short stories; and works that are autobiographical, *Infância* (1945) and *Memórias do Cárcere* (1953). Other collections of stories and articles have been published posthumously. Because of his style, vision, and psychological penetration, Ramos is one of the most admired contemporary novelists.

RAYMOND S. SAYERS

RAMOS ARIZPE, JOSÉ MIGUEL (1775–1843). Mexican political theorist and politician. A native of Coahuila, Ramos Arizpe was ordained a priest in 1803 after study in the seminaries of Monterrey and Guadalajara. He taught in the Seminary of Monterrey and was a member of the chapter of the Monterrey Cathedral. Elected a deputy to the Spanish Cortes in 1810, he was an active spokesman for American interests and reform in that body from 1811 to 1814 and again in the Cortes of 1820. He was one of the Mexican delegates imprisoned on the order of FERDINAND VII when that monarch was restored to his throne in 1814 and dissolved the Cortes.

Returning to Mexico in 1822, Ramos Arizpe was chosen a delegate to the Constitutional Congress and was the principal author of the constitution of 1824. The leader of the federalists in the Congress, he is often described as the father of Mexican federalism. Although his clerical career was frequently subordinated to his political activities, he held offices in the Puebla diocesan chapter, of which he was designated dean in 1831. He served as Minister of Justice for short periods in the administrations of Guadalupe VICTORIA, Antonio López de SANTA ANNA, and Valentín GÓMEZ FARÍAS and as a delegate from Puebla to the Congress of 1842.

CHARLES R. BERRY

REAL COMPAÑÍA GUIPUZCOANA DE CARACAS. *See* CARACAS COMPANY.

REBOUÇAS, ANDRÉ (1838–1898). Brazilian abolitionist, engineer, economist, teacher, and early advocate of land reform. A mulatto, Rebouças was the son of a magistrate and national deputy from Bahia, Antônio Pereira Rebouças. He was educated at the Military School in Rio de Janeiro as a mathematician and engineer, gaining a lifelong interest in literature, economics, politics, and music. Intimate with the talented and powerful, including the imperial family, he overcame racial prejudice to influence the key people of his time. Traveling to Europe in 1861 to study contemporary engineering projects, he returned to Brazil as the

PARAGUAYAN WAR (1864–1870) was beginning, playing a role as a planner of campaigns and adviser to Allied leaders remarkable for his age and rank (lieutenant). Having undertaken major engineering assignments during and after the war, he eventually withdrew into teaching, exercising a strong influence upon students at the Polytechnical School in Rio de Janeiro.

During the antislavery campaign (1880–1888), Rebouças donated his wealth and abundant talents to the cause with unwavering enthusiasm, writing articles, pamphlets, and manifestos, helping to organize abolitionist and immigration societies, advising and encouraging reformers, and traveling to Europe as an emissary of the Brazilian Antislavery Society. With the abolition of slavery on May 13, 1888 (*see* ABOLITION OF SLAVERY: BRAZIL), Rebouças and other members of the Confederação Abolicionista continued their call for reforms, including popular education and "rural democracy," the creation of small agricultural holdings to benefit ex-slaves, immigrants, and the rural poor.

Accompanying the emperor PEDRO II into exile after the republican revolt of November 15, 1889, Rebouças spent his last years in isolation in Europe, Africa, and Funchal, Madeira, where he died mysteriously just ten years after the Brazilian Chamber of Deputies voted to abolish slavery. Rebouças was the author of many articles, a diary, and a major book on agriculture and social problems: *Agricultura Nacional: Estudos Economicos, Propaganda Abolicionista e Democratica* (1883).   ROBERT CONRAD

RECABARREN [SERRANO], LUIS EMILIO (d. 1924).

Labor leader and founder of the Chilean Communist party (*see* COMMUNIST PARTY: CHILE). Born in Valparaíso, Recabarren became a printer. An admirer of Francisco BILBAO, he joined the Democratic party in 1894 (*see* DEMOCRATIC PARTY: CHILE) and tried for years to make it more militant than its middle-class leadership desired. A convinced socialist, he founded many newspapers to propagate his ideas and published numerous works on social questions.

In 1903 Recabarren left Santiago for the northern nitrate regions, to organize workers in unions and publicize socialist doctrines, and in 1906 he was elected deputy for Antofagasta, only to be debarred by Congress because of his militant activities. He played a major role in Chile's first important trade union, the Unión General de Trabajadores, and in 1912 led a like-minded group of members out of the Democratic party to found the Partido Obrero Socialista. The close links between the party and trade unionism were seen in the congress of the Federación Obrera de Chile (then Chile's most important union) held in Concepción in 1919, over which Recabarren presided, and in the federation's decision at its next congress, held in Rancagua in 1921, to affiliate with the Moscow-based Red Trade Union International.

A year later the convention of the Partido Obrero Socialista, also meeting at Rancagua, joined the Third International and changed its name to Chilean Communist party. Recabarren entered Congress as a deputy for Antofagasta (1921–1924) and paid a visit to the U.S.S.R. in 1924. Toward the end of that year he committed suicide, possibly disillusioned by the Soviet Union or by military intervention in politics in Chile.

HAROLD BLAKEMORE

RECIFE. Capital of the state of Pernambuco, Brazil. With a population of 1,078,816 (1970), Recife is the largest city and leading seaport of the NORTHEAST. It is located at the mouth of the Capiberibe River and is named for the reef that lies just offshore to provide a sheltered harbor for ocean vessels. Founded in 1535 as the port for the first permanent Portuguese colony in Pernambuco, Recife remained a small village until Pernambuco was conquered by the Dutch in 1630 (*see* DUTCH IN BRAZIL). The Dutch made Recife their capital and transformed it into one of the most modern cities in the Western Hemisphere. It continued to serve as the capital of Pernambuco after the Portuguese resumed control in 1654.

As the administrative center and entrepôt of the coastal sugar plantation zone, Recife has long exerted strong political, economic, and cultural influence throughout the Brazilian Northeast. The uprisings of 1817 and 1824, seeking to separate the Northeast from the rest of Brazil, took place in Recife. Since 1827 most of the political leaders of northeastern Brazil have been trained at its law school. The present University of Pernambuco, located in Recife, continues to attract students from all the northeastern states. Recife is the focal point of the railroad and highway systems that fan out across the states of Alagôas, Pernambuco, Paraíba, Rio Grande do Norte, and Ceará. The city is a minor industrial center and also serves as the regional headquarters for the church, the military, and the economic development agencies concerned with the Northeast.   ROLLIE E. POPPINO

RECOPILACIÓN DE LEYES DE LAS INDIAS. Compilation of laws enacted for Spain's American possessions and published in 1681. In Spain's New World possessions the laws of the mother country continued in force, but in response to local conditions and needs a complementary body of laws developed, emanating from the monarch himself, the COUNCIL OF THE INDIES, and the royal *audiencias* (*see* AUDIENCIA). However, given the tendency of Spanish rulers to govern by legislating and the tendency of those governed to disregard legislation and given also the often repetitious, detailed, and even trivial nature of this legislation, it is not surprising that the laws became so numerous that administrators, judges, and lawyers found it increasingly difficult to use them.

As early as the sixteenth century a need was felt for compilations that would make the laws easier to use. A number of compilations were attempted, but none were so successful or comprehensive as the *Recopilación de Leyes de las Indias*. It contained 6,377 laws distributed in nine books, 218 chapters, and many more subgroupings. Each law was numbered and preceded by a brief description, the name of the monarch by whose authority it had been promulgated, and the date of promulgation. These laws dealt with every aspect of colonial life: the church, the government, the judiciary, royal officials, education, public works, commerce, mines, factories, the treatment of Indians, royal revenue, and many others.

Royal legislation continued to be produced after 1681. Indeed, radically new legislation was enacted by the kings of the Bourbon dynasty (*see* BOURBON REFORMS). But no revision of the *Recopilación* or new comprehensive compilation was ever published. The *Recopilación* remained the greatest legal monument of the colonial era and made its influence widely felt in the legislation of the newly independent Spanish American nations.

NORMAN MEIKLEJOHN

REDUCTIONS. *See* MISSIONS.

REFORM, THE (LA REFORMA). Term applied to the period in Mexican history from the Liberal victory in the revolution of Ayutla in late 1855 to the end of the War of the Reform in late 1860, in its narrower limits, or to mid-1867 and the defeat of MAXIMILIAN in its broader application. Precedents may be found in the attempted reform of Valentín GÓMEZ FARÍAS in 1833–1834. The principal goals of the Liberals were the separation of church and state, the alienation of church property, the elimination of the social and political influence of the church, and the strengthening of middle-class and laissez faire capitalism in Mexico.

In its juridical aspect, the Reform is associated primarily with a group of laws that embodied these goals. The first two were issued in November 1855 and June 1856, respectively, by the governments of Juan Álvarez and Ignacio COMONFORT and bear the names of their authors, Benito JUÁREZ and Miguel Lerdo de Tejada, members of those Cabinets. The Juárez law limited ecclesiastical and military privileges in regard to special tribunals of justice and further reformed the judicial system. Its promulgation inspired a rebellion by Conservatives and supporters of the church in the city of Puebla in the spring of 1856, which was contained and then put down by Comonfort. Deciding that the church must bear the costs of defeating this rebellion, the national government decreed that church-owned property in Puebla should be sold; the money derived from the sale would be used to finance the military operation. This served as a prelude to the Lerdo law, which in effect extended the alienation of church property throughout Mexico and also included provisions prohibiting government ownership of real estate, such as the communal lands owned by Indian villages. The constitution of 1857 might also be considered a part of the Reform legislation (*see* CONSTITUTION OF 1857: MEXICO).

As these laws were issued and implemented, the clerical-Conservative faction became disturbed by the increasing radicalism and decided upon rebellion to halt the growth of liberalism. War broke out in December 1857 and lasted through December 1860. During this struggle, known as the War of the Reform or the Three Years' War, the Conservatives controlled Mexico City and the center of the nation, while the Liberals, led by President Juárez, established their headquarters in Veracruz and controlled the south, parts of the west, and most of the north.

In July–August 1859, the beleaguered Liberals advanced their reform program with another group of laws, issued from their eastern capital. These included decrees that nationalized church property, closed monasteries, and separated church and state; established civil registry and civil matrimony; secularized cemeteries; and regulated public holidays. One other decree, issued in 1863, which closed the convents, completed the reform program. Of these statutes, the most important and far-reaching were those that nationalized

ecclesiastical wealth. Whereas the Lerdo law of 1856 had been an economic measure, the later decree was political and was designed to so weaken the church that it could never again threaten the civil power. By its provisions church property not yet sold under the terms of the Lerdo law was confiscated by the government, which then put it up for sale and received the income; and the mortgages held by the church as a result of sales under the 1856 statute were taken by the civil government. Church libraries were confiscated, monasteries were sold, and chantries and pious funds were expropriated. Much of the property was bought by private citizens of average means, and much was used to endow education and agencies of general welfare.

The implementation of these laws was uneven because the Liberals did not control all the territory and because once again they found themselves on the defensive when the French intervened in 1862. When peace was finally established in 1867, attempts were made at full implementation. In 1873 the laws were incorporated in the constitution of 1857 as amendments.

Although Porfirio DÍAZ largely ignored the spirit of the Reform during the latter part of his long tenure and although much of the work of the reformers had to be redone in the revolution of 1910 (*see* MEXICAN REVOLUTION) and the constitution of 1917 (*see* CONSTITUTION OF 1917: MEXICO), the Reform was a watershed in the evolution of modern Mexico, giving impetus to the standard Liberal interpretation of Mexican history.

See also DEGOLLADO, Santos; LERDO DE TEJADA, Sebastián; MIRAMÓN, Miguel; OCAMPO, Melchor.

Bibliography. Jan Bazant, *Alienation of Church Wealth in Mexico: Social and Economic Aspects of the Liberal Revolution, 1856–1875*, Cambridge, England, 1971; Francisco Bulnes, *Juárez y las revoluciones de Ayutla y de Reforma*, Mexico City, 1905; Wilfrid Hardy Callcott, *Liberalism in Mexico, 1857–1929*, Hamden, Conn., 1965; Agustín Cue Cánovas, *La reforma liberal en México*, Mexico City, 1960; Luis G. Labastida, *Colección de leyes . . . relativos a la desamortización de los bienes de corporaciones civiles y religiosas y a la nacionalización de los que administraron las últimas*, Mexico City, 1893; Andrés Molina Enríquez, *Juárez y la Reforma*, 4th ed., Mexico City, 1961; Walter V. Scholes, *Mexican Politics during the Juárez Regime, 1855–1872*, Columbia, Mo., 1957.

CHARLES R. BERRY

REGALADO, TOMÁS (1861–1906). President of El Salvador (1898–1903). Regalado unseated Rafael Antonio Gutiérrez and seized the Presidency of El Salvador by a coup in 1898. Other Presidents have since been removed by force in El Salvador, but until 1944 no other individual succeeded in seizing the office for himself. Regalado's coup capitalized on divided opinion on El Salvador's entry into a new Central American union. By the Pact of Amapala, ratified by the Gutiérrez government on September 12, 1895, El Salvador joined Honduras and Nicaragua to form the so-called República Mayor. A federal constitution was drafted and became effective November 1, 1898. Regalado overthrew Gutiérrez a few days later, and the first major act of his government was to withdraw El Salvador from the union. This defection ended the República Mayor.

Regalado regularized his status and on March 1,

1899, began a constitutional four-year term. He chose not to have himself reelected, and in 1903 he allowed a peaceable selection of a President for the first time in half a century. Pedro José Escalón was chosen, and Regalado turned over the office to him, but he retained control of the armed forces and remained the real power behind the government.

Regalado maintained close relations with *émigrés* from Guatemala who were conspiring to overthrow the regime of Manuel ESTRADA CABRERA. He encouraged their plans for an invasion and promised them aid. In 1906 they attempted an invasion in which Regalado commanded the cooperating El Salvador troops. He was killed in the Battle of El Jícaro in July 1906.

WILLIAM J. GRIFFITH

REGIDOR. Voting member of the CABILDO. *Regidores* exercised both political and legislative authority in colonial Spanish America.

REGIONAL CONFEDERATION OF MEXICAN LABOR. *See* CONFEDERACIÓN REGIONAL OBRERA MEXICANA.

REGO [CAVALCÂNTI], JOSÉ LINS DO (1901–1957). Brazilian novelist, journalist, and critic. Born in Paraíba, he lived as a child on his grandfather's sugar plantation and watched with regret its decline as the old system of sugar production changed. His experiences are recounted nostalgically in the sequence of novels of his sugarcane cycle, *Menino de Engenho* (1932), *Doidinho* (1933), *Bangüê* (1934), *Usina* (1936), and *Fogo Morto* (1943), the first three of which were published in English as *Plantation Boy,* and later in his book of memoirs, *Meus Verdes Anos* (1956). In these books one sees the influence of his friendship with Gilberto FREYRE, whose *Casa Grande e Senzala* (1933) defended the human and especially the Brazilian values of the NORTHEAST, a region with its own character, vitality, and traditions. Rego Cavalcânti's *O Moleque Ricardo* (1935), which is about the life of the proletariat in Recife, was one of the first Brazilian proletarian novels. He also wrote books of psychological analysis, like *Eurídice* (1947), and books about the outlaws who once infested the region, such as *Pedra Bonita* (1938) and *Cangaceiros* (1953), but they are inferior to those dealing with plantation life.

RAYMOND S. SAYERS

REINÓL. *See* PENINSULAR.

RELAÇÃO. High court of appeals. The first *relação* established in Brazil was set up in Bahia (modern Salvador) in 1609. It was suspended in 1624, and its revenues were allocated instead to military expenditure during the period of struggle with the Dutch (*see* DUTCH IN BRAZIL). The court was composed initially of ten *desembargadores* (judges), who were university-trained lawyers with previous experience as magistrates, most usually by the eighteenth century as *ouvidores* (circuit judges). The Bahian *relação* was reestablished in 1652, and a second *relação* was instituted in Rio de Janeiro in 1751. The limit of the court's authority in civil cases was placed at 2,000 cruzados in real estate and 3,000 cruzados in chattels. Appeal in civil cases was to the Casa de Suplicação (High Court of Appeals) in Lisbon; there was no appeal in criminal cases. (Per-

sons with military or ecclesiastical privileges were, of course, eligible for trial by special courts.) The typical *desembargador* later went on to serve on high courts in Portugal. It was rare for a magistrate who had served in India to be appointed to Brazil, or vice versa, but magistrates with both Asian and American experience served in the metropolitan courts.

KENNETH R. MAXWELL

RELIGIOUS ORDERS (COLONIAL PERIOD). The conquest and colonization of America, as well as its political, economic, and religious integration into the Spanish and Portuguese empires, were to a large extent accomplished through the efforts of men and women who belonged to religious orders. The first friars came to the New World in 1493, and they and their successors participated actively in the explorations, discoveries, and subjection of the indigenous population. Until 1568 the Franciscans, Dominicans, Augustinians, and Mercedarians enjoyed considerable latitude as they pursued their missionary activities in the Spanish colonies. Such freedom was encouraged by the papal bull *Exponi nobis* (*Omnímoda*) of 1522, which gave regular clerics and prelates powers normally exercised by their secular counterparts. In some areas, as the only Spaniards they exercised total control over the native population.

As part of his imperial reforms King PHILIP II (r. 1556–1598) attempted to decrease the power of the religious orders in the Indies, primarily by turning over church benefices to the secular clergy. He also directed that no new religious foundations be established without prior royal and episcopal permission. These restrictions were, in part, inspired by the Council of Trent (1545–1563), which urged the expansion of episcopal authority to assist in the reformation of the Catholic Church. Although these and other directives could not be implemented throughout the Indies, they did cause some religious to regard themselves as under attack by both the monarchy and the secular clergy. As a result, the orders began to emphasize institutional consolidation and development, while their missionary zeal declined. The arrival of the Jesuits in the late 1560s in Peru and New Spain renewed missionary activity in Spanish America. By the mid-seventeenth century, however, the orders increasingly were concentrating their activities in urban areas. The establishment of missionary colleges by the Franciscans beginning in 1683 countered this trend to a limited extent. The secularization of Indian parishes was advanced by royal decrees of 1752 and 1754 ordering regulars to be replaced by diocesan clergy and by the expulsion of the Jesuits in 1767 (*see* JESUITS, EXPULSION OF: SPANISH AMERICA).

Religious orders transmitted to America their peninsular administrative structure. Each community had a superior, subordinate to a provincial who oversaw the foundations in a designated area. A major superior had authority over several provinces, while a vicar-general or commissary general had jurisdiction over the entire order in the Indies. The latter generally resided at court in Spain, where he came under the direct influence of the crown. Only the Jesuits, whose general resided in Rome and who took an additional vow of obedience to the Pope, escaped this influence.

The most active religious were the Franciscans, Dominicans, Augustinians, Mercedarians, and Jesuits, although Capuchins, Carmelites, Hieronymites, Hospitalers of St. John, Bethlehemites, Oratorians, Camillians, Conceptionists, Trinitarians, Brigittines, and members of the Company of Mary were also present. The Franciscans were among the earliest arrivals and hence were heavily involved in Christianizing the Indians. Their missions were scattered throughout the Spanish and Portuguese possessions and strongly influenced methods of conversion. They also contributed many bishops and archbishops to the American church, particularly in the sixteenth century. The Dominicans focused their attention on the Spanish and creole population, although the foremost defender of the Indians, Bartolomé de LAS CASAS (1474–1566), sprang from their ranks. Established in Santo Domingo in 1510, they expanded to the mainland in the company of the conquistadores. They founded convents in the main urban centers and were active in founding *colegios* (secondary schools) and universities and staffing them. The Augustinians combined missionary activity with scholarship and had foundations in New Spain, New Granada, Peru, Chile, Argentina, and the Philippines. They founded educational institutions, such as the Colegio de San Ildefonso (1598) in Lima, in addition to producing such scholars as the philosopher and canonist Alonso de la Vera Cruz and the historians Juan de Grijalva and Antonio de la Calancha. The Mercedarians established their first convent in the New World in Hispaniola in 1514 and from there spread to Central America, Mexico, Peru, Chile, Argentina, Bolivia, and Ecuador. In 1568 the crown attempted to limit their influence by directing that they no longer accept novices in America and by restricting the migration of members from Spain. The order, nevertheless, continued its missionary and educational work and in 1612 had more than 500 members in more than 120 convents and *doctrinas*. They also supplied university professors and were active in publishing.

The first Jesuits to come to America arrived in Brazil in 1549 to serve as missionaries. By the seventeenth century they had missions, urban parishes, and *colegios* throughout Latin America. Their most notable work was accomplished among the Indians of the Paraguayan region, whom they gathered into reductions with populations sometimes numbering several thousands. These missions were highly organized and relatively self-sufficient economically. The expulsion of the Jesuits from Brazil in 1759 and from the Spanish colonies in 1767 resulted in the decline of these and other establishments of the order (*see* JESUITS, EXPULSION OF: BRAZIL).

Of the less numerous orders in the New World, the Hieronymites and Bethlehemites are notable. The former, as the wealthiest and most powerful order in Spain, was called upon to contribute its resources and experience to the colonial enterprise. Hieronymites constructed a number of convents in the early period and also supplied some bishops. Their influence was never as great as it was in the mother country, in part because their energies were already profitably absorbed in the metropolis. The Bethlehemites were the only order of men founded in Spanish America in the colonial period, originating in the latter part of the seventeenth century in Guatemala. Their founder, Rodrigo de Arias Maldonado (1637–1716), directed them to care for the sick, particularly the indigent. In 1687 they received papal confirmation, and in 1696 royal approval.

Each of their hospitals was to have a school; some of these schools became noted for their courses in the natural sciences.

The Carmelites concentrated their efforts in Brazil, although they spread to Mexico, Panama, and New Granada. They preached devotion to Mary and proselytized for themselves and the Catholic faith. Royal pressure in the late sixteenth century restricted their activities. Although the Capuchins did not found any monasteries, they were active in Christianizing the Indians in New Granada. Members of the order from France were missionaries in the Antilles until the French Revolution. A few representatives of the Benedictines and the Camillians came to America; the latter, like the Bethlehemites and Hospitalers of St. John, were concerned principally with the care of the sick

Religious orders for women appeared in America in the first half of the sixteenth century to meet both spiritual and societal needs. Like the *beaterios* (houses for lay sisters) that preceded them, convents served not only those who desired to pursue a religious life but also women for whom there was no fixed role in society. Hence convents came to be populated by unmarried women, widows, divorcees, reformed prostitutes, orphans, and abandoned children. Such institutions also served as schools for girls, centers of artistic and cultural life, and sometimes as clinics. They were concentrated in the cities, particularly in the viceregal capitals, Lima and Mexico City. Their administrative organization generally followed that of the male orders. Most nunneries had a hierarchical structure; black-veiled nuns, mostly creoles and Spaniards, with some mestizas, had greater status and authority than white-veiled nuns, who were normally mestizas, Indians, and mulatas. Most convents had their complement of servants and slaves. Students were also sometimes resident in convents.

The quality of life in these institutions varied with the austerity of the rule followed and the backgrounds and resources of the nuns. This was also true of the religious orders of men, but given the restricted nature of the role of female religious, their lives revolved around the nunnery itself to a much greater degree. Hence, convents reflected secular life, with some nuns pursuing their interests independent of the community, living in their own apartments with their servants and passing their time in genteel pursuits. This practice gave rise to complaints and demands for reform of conventual life, which generally were not effective.

Conceptionists, Franciscans, Clarists, Capuchins, Dominicans, Carmelites, Hieronymites, Brigittines, and the Company of Mary all established nunneries in New Spain. Except for the Clarists of the First Order, who accepted only Indian women, most orders served the Spanish and creole populations. The founding of the Convent of La Encarnación in Lima in 1561 served as the impetus for the spread of nunneries throughout the viceroyalty. Like most later convents, it admitted mestizas but restricted Indians to the role of sisters or servants. Royal regulations prohibited the founding of nunneries in Brazil until the eighteenth century, when the Ursulines, Carmelites of St. Joseph, Conceptionists, and Poor Clares began to establish convents and schools.

Religious orders for men and women came to have

great importance in the economic life of the colonies. Convents amassed considerable wealth through contributions, inheritance, and purchase, in addition to their ordinary sources of income. They became the largest holders of liquid capital, which led them into money-lending. Not all convents possessed substantial incomes or were well run financially. Not only was moral reform sometimes needed, but fiscal reform as well. Attempts by the crown and some prelates to regulate the financial affairs of the convents, sometimes for the benefit of the latter and sometimes for the benefit of the former, were not always successful. Royal efforts sometimes alienated ecclesiastics and weakened church support of the metropolis. During the struggles for independence, however, most religious supported the Spanish cause, thus contributing to the orders' loss of influence in the national period.

See also MISSIONS (SPANISH AMERICA).

Bibliography. Fernando de Armas Medina, *Cristianización del Perú, 1532–1600,* Seville, 1953; Gerard Decorme, *La obra de los jesuitas mexicanos durante la época colonial, 1572–1767,* 2 vols., Mexico City, 1941; Serafim Leite, *Suma histórica da Companhia de Jesus no Brasil: Assistencia de Portugal, 1549–1760,* Lisbon, 1965; Magnus Mörner (ed.), *The Expulsion of the Jesuits from Latin America,* New York, 1965; John Leddy Phelan, *The Millennial Kingdom of the Franciscans in the New World: A Study of the Writings of Gerónimo de Mendieta,* Berkeley, Calif., 1956; Antonine Tibesar, "The *Alternativa:* A Study of Spanish-Creole Relations in Seventeenth-Century Peru," *The Americas,* vol. XI, no. 3, January 1955, pp. 229–283; id., *Franciscan Beginnings in Colonial Peru,* Washington, 1953; Rubén Vargas Ugarte, *Historia de la Compañía de Jesús en el Perú,* 4 vols., Burgos, 1963–69.

MARGARET E. CRAHAN

REMÓN [CANTERA], JOSÉ ANTONIO (1908–1955). President of Panama (1952–1955). Remón won a scholarship to the Mexican Military Academy and entered the Panamanian National Police in 1931 with the rank of captain. In 1947 he became first commandant, or head, of the police, a position that enabled him to play the role of kingmaker in Panamanian politics. In 1952 he was elected to the Presidency after waging an energetic campaign with the help of his wife.

Remón was probably the most effective chief executive Panama has had since World War II. He was able to put the internal and external finances of the nation in order through private borrowing, higher income tax schedules, and more efficient tax collection procedures. Public funds were honestly handled. Perennial unemployment problems were alleviated through an ambitious program of public works, including roads, an international air terminal, and new ministries, clinics, and schools. Remón also inaugurated the Colón Free Zone and the Institute for Economic Development. He gave added prestige to the police corps by increasing its armament and elevating it to the status of a national guard. Finally, he oversaw negotiations with the United States that resulted in the EISENHOWER-REMÓN TREATY (1955).

Remón was shot and mortally wounded on January 2, 1955, while at the racetrack in Panama City. The circumstances of the assassination have never been fully elucidated.

LARRY L. PIPPIN

REPARTIMIENTO. In the Spanish colonies, a general term for a division or distribution; also the forced sale of goods to Indians by corregidores (*see* CORREGIDOR). A more specific use of the term meant an allotment of Indians, and the terms ENCOMIENDA and *repartimiento* were used interchangeably in the West Indies. After the NEW LAWS of 1542–1543 abolished Indian slavery and forced labor, the *repartimiento* became an institution for the use of Indians in labor gangs to work in mines, factories, farms and ranches, and public works for a prescribed period of time. Thus compulsory paid labor regulated by statutes replaced forced personal services. The *repartimiento* in Peru came to be called the MITA, and in New Spain the *cuatequil.* By law *repartimientos* were authorized by royal authorities, and only a small number of the available Indians were to be used and paid the standard wage when needed.

The *repartimiento* system because of its abuses caused heavy loss of life among the Indians. Moreover, it was normal to harass Indians in every way possible and work them without rest. In 1601 the *repartimiento* was modified and replaced by a system that required a fourth of the able-bodied Indians of an area to hire themselves out at any one time to prospective employers. Compulsory labor thus remained but was free in that a choice of employer was permitted. However, in 1609 the *repartimiento* was restored for certain kinds of labor.

RALPH H. VIGIL

REQUERIMIENTO. Statement by which the Indians were required, first, to acknowledge the lordship of the Pope and the King of Spain over their lands and, second, to receive preachers of the Christian faith. If the Indians refused, the Spaniards might justly conquer and enslave them.

The jurist Juan López de Palacios Rubios composed the *requerimiento* (requirement) in 1513 at the command of King Ferdinand II, after Martín Fernández de Enciso had justified Spanish conquests in the New World before a conference of theologians. Enciso argued that just as Joshua had had the right to require the inhabitants of Jericho to surrender their city to the Jews because God had promised it to them, so the Spaniards were justified in requiring the Indians to surrender lands assigned to Spain by Pope Alexander VI in 1493. The *requerimiento* briefly defined the primacy of St. Peter over all peoples and explained that the Pope, his successor, had granted the New World to Spain. It concluded by calling upon a notary to witness that it had been read to the Indians.

Bartolomé de LAS CASAS did not know whether "to laugh or to weep" when he contemplated the *requerimiento* being read to Indians who did not understand a word of Spanish. Sometimes it was read to trees at midnight, preceding a surprise attack on a nearby village. One cacique thought that the Pope must have been "out of his mind" to give away lands belonging to someone else. Although denounced by Las Casas, the *requerimiento* continued to be used until it was superseded by the general law on exploration and conquest of 1573.

GEORGE SANDERLIN

RESIDENCIA. Formal investigation held in the Spanish colonies at the conclusion of an incumbent's term of office to assess his conduct. It was an inquiry to which every servant of the crown had to submit, and it was intended to aid the crown in keeping a strict control of its officials in the New World by providing a means for checking their honesty and efficiency.

To conduct a *residencia,* a specially designated commissioner, the *juez de residencia,* was required to travel to the district in question and there to issue a proclamation announcing the *residencia.* Anyone was free to present accusations or to give evidence. After the hearing the judge prepared his report and pronounced the sentence. In cases of misconduct the officeholder would be required to make restitution to persons whom he had mistreated, and he also could be penalized by heavy fines, confiscation of property, or imprisonment.

Although theoretically the *residencia* was supposed to prevent corrupt administration, in reality it was subject to many abuses. Too often the judge was the successor to the outgoing official and intended to employ the same practices as his predecessor. Moreover, the *residencia* frequently enabled dishonest officials to persecute honest ones. If the incumbent offended powerful interests in the district, the *residencia* often became a tool for revenge. A powerful official with influential friends might have the results of the *residencia* dispensed with, or he might reach an agreement with the judge, who realized that someday he too would have to submit to a similar hearing.

Unfortunately, because of its many abuses, one of the effects of the *residencia* was to discourage initiative on the part of officials who feared that any deviation from royal instructions might provide fertile ground for charges by their enemies. This prevented needed change from taking place in the administration of the colonies, with the result that stagnation often pervaded the political structures of the Spanish colonial empire.

ELIZABETH WILKES DORE

REVERÓN, ARMANDO (1889–1954). Venezuelan painter. One of the greatest impressionist painters, Reverón was born in Caracas, where he began studying at the Academy of Fine Arts at fifteen. In 1911 he went to Barcelona for art studies and then to the Academy of San Fernando in Madrid. In 1915 he returned to Caracas and six years later settled in Macuto, on the coast, where he increasingly withdrew into his work. He remained in touch with several members of the Caracas art world whom he described as having influenced him, especially Rafael Monasterios, Samys Mützner, and Emilio Boggio. From 1943 on he suffered from growing mental derangement and was frequently hospitalized, but he produced some of his best work during these years.

Reverón's career developed through four phases: an early Hispanophile phase; a blue period, of which *La cueva* (*The Cave,* 1919) is a famous example; a white period represented by many landscapes, such as *El arbol* (1931); and a later sepia period, of which *La maja criolla* (1940s) is an example. Reverón, in his hermitage, brought impressionism to a logical conclusion in painting pure light, especially in the white paintings in which the scene is almost washed out by brilliant tropical light. Landscapes and nudes were his subjects, with several self-portraits. Reverón was neglected during his lifetime but was the subject of a major retrospective exhibit in the Museum of Fine Arts in Caracas after his death in 1954 and in Boston in 1956. He is also the subject of an important monograph by Alfredo Boulton (Caracas, 1966).

TERENCE GRIEDER

REVILLAGIGEDO, 2D COUNT OF (JUAN VICENTE GÜEMES PACHECO DE PADILLA, 1740–1799). Fifty-second Viceroy of New Spain. Born in Havana, he took office in 1789 and with a zeal characteristic of an enlightened official undertook a complete revision of the social, financial, and administrative condition of New Spain. Revillagigedo ordered the first census of New Spain, using it to reorganize the militia. In order to strengthen the frontier, he gave special attention to the border garrisons and promoted the exploration of the Pacific coast by Galiana y Valdés in 1792. The collection of revenue and the administration of public funds were streamlined, resulting in larger yields than before. During Revillagigedo's administration the INTENDANCY SYSTEM was established in New Spain, and he suggested improvements in its organization. He also gave his attention to the condition of the Indians and established rules to prevent undue abuse of their labor. The provision of grain and meat for the capital was one of his main concerns, and he regulated the prices of basic foods. In addition, he suggested the construction of roads to benefit agriculture and mining and favored the enlargement of the textile industry. Mexico City benefited from paving and lighting projects, better policing, and the Viceroy's concern for problems of public health. There was hardly any branch of public administration that did not receive his attention, as is evident from the perceptive report he wrote in 1794 to his successor, the Marqués de Branciforte. He is regarded as one of the most efficient and honest viceroys ever appointed by the Spanish crown.

ASUNCIÓN LAVRIN

REVOLUTIONARY PARTY OF DEMOCRATIC UNIFICATION. *See* PARTIDO REVOLUCIONARIO DE UNIFICACIÓN DEMOCRÁTICA.

REVOLUTION OF 1930. Dramatic turning point in Brazilian history that terminated the FIRST REPUBLIC and ushered in the rule of Getúlio VARGAS. In 1930 Brazil was ripe for a change of leadership. There was increasing disaffection with oligarchical rule, manipulated elections, and the inability of government to bolster a faltering economy.

In the semipatriarchal system inherited from the empire the big states of São Paulo and Minas Gerais dominated national politics. This irritated leaders in other states, particularly third-ranked Rio Grande do Sul. In 1929 economic crisis stalked the nation, confidence in the government declined, and coffee barons withdrew their support. The urban population, traditionally ignored, was growing restless, and reform-minded army officers were impatient for change.

In this unstable situation President Washington Luis PEREIRA DE SOUSA made the unfortunate decision to nominate Júlio Prestes, a fellow *paulista,* as his successor, thereby defying the gentleman's agreement that rotated the Presidency between São Paulo and Minas Gerais. Indignant, the states of Minas Gerais and Paraíba supported the opposition candidate, Getúlio

Vargas of Rio Grande do Sul. The coalition, known as the Liberal Alliance, attracted reformers and malcontents throughout Brazil.

When Prestes won the election in March 1930, Vargas's supporters prepared to overthrow the government. The assassination of João PESSOA, a leader of the Liberal Alliance, triggered the revolt. As rebel units marched on the capital, the Army deserted the government, President Washington Luis was arrested, and on November 3, Vargas was placed in the Presidential Palace. Thus the First Republic came to an end, and a new era of centralized administration was inaugurated.

ARNOLD J. MEAGHER

REVUELTAS, SILVESTRE (1899–1940). Mexican composer. Born in Santiago Papasquiaro, Durango, he studied in his native country and later in Chicago and New York with Felix Borowski (composition) and Sametini (violin). In 1929 he became assistant conductor to Carlos CHÁVEZ in the Orquesta Sinfónica de México. His first compositions date from that time. Revueltas's works are distinctive for their originality, strength, and deep attachment to the spirit of Mexico. Among them are *Cuauhnahuac* (1933), *Sensemayá* (1938), *Homenaje a García Lorca* (1935), and *Eight for a Broadcasting* (1933).

JUAN A. ORREGO-SALAS

REYES, ALFONSO (1889–1959). Mexican writer. Born in Monterrey, he was the son of Bernardo Reyes (1850–1913), a prominent general and political leader of the era of Porfirio DÍAZ. The younger Reyes's life was devoted to diplomacy, literature, and education. He founded chairs in Mexican universities for the study of Spanish language and literature and formed part of a commission to study in European archives. From 1914 to 1924 he lived in Spain, where he wrote and worked for the Centro de Estudios Históricos. Reyes produced many valuable books of nonfiction, including *Visión de Anahuac* (1917), *La experiencia literaria* (1942), and *La X en la frente* (1952). He translated the works of writers as diverse as Mallarmé and Sterne; prepared critical editions of Spanish classical authors; wrote stories (*El plano oblicuo,* 1920), a play (*Ifigenia cruel,* 1924), and poetry inspired as much by classical models as by traditional and popular forms: *Huellas* (1922), *Yerbas de Tarahumara* (1934), *Cantata en la tumba de Federico García Lorca* (1937), *Algunos poemas* (1941), and others. In 1945 he was awarded a national prize for his book *La crítica en la edad ateniense* (1941). He is regarded as one of the outstanding scholars and thinkers of the twentieth century. Several of his essays have been translated into English and published in *The Position of America and Other Essays* (1950) and *Mexico in a Nutshell* (1964).

RACHEL PHILLIPS

REYES, RAFAEL (1850–1921). Colombian general and President (1904–1909). Reyes was born in Santa Rosa, Boyacá, into a family of some local prominence. He spent his early manhood in various commercial ventures in Amazonian Colombia and with his brothers established a trade route to Brazil. His years in the south, together with his marriage to a Popayán lady, influenced Reyes's style. Ebullient, vain, energetic, and brave, an authoritarian to the core, Reyes was in many

ways a latter-day version of Gen. Tomás Cipriano de MOSQUERA.

Reyes came late to political life, taking a leading role as a Conservative (*see* CONSERVATIVE PARTY: COLOMBIA) in the civil wars of 1885 and 1895. By the latter year his talents on the battlefield had made him a presidential contender, but the partisanship of President Miguel Antonio CARO frustrated such aspirations. It was only after the bloody WAR OF THE THOUSAND DAYS that Reyes could win the chief executive's sash.

The Reyes administration (1904–1909), known as the Quinquennium in Colombian history, was one of limited tolerance for the defeated Liberals (*see* LIBERAL PARTY: COLOMBIA), some of whom were appointed to political office, and considerable repression for the more intransigent Conservatives, some of whom were exiled to jungle incarceration. Imposing his own form of Carthaginian peace on the distracted and ruined country, Reyes sought to turn Colombian elites away from politics and toward the massive tasks of economic reconstruction. He sponsored technical education, a professionalized military, and ambitious transportation projects. Essentially Reyes was brought down by the ruinous fiscal situation of Colombia, but it was his effort to come to some accommodation with the United States over Panama that ostensibly triggered his ouster. University students in Bogotá led by Enrique OLAYA HERRERA demonstrated their disapproval of Reyes's regime so effectively on March 13, 1909, that he left the capital and resigned in July.

Reyes spent the next decade in exile in Europe, the United States, and South America, promoting Colombian products and seeking international support to rectify the "rape of Panama." Infirm and a political cipher, he returned to Bogotá in 1918 and died there in 1921.

J. LEÓN HELGUERA

REYES BASOALTO, NEFTALÍ RICARDO. *See* NERUDA, PABLO.

REYLES, CARLOS (1868–1938). Uruguayan novelist. Born into a wealthy family and mainly self-taught, Reyles made several trips to Europe and produced a considerable number of novels, mostly realistic in tone and using the Argentine countryside as a background, as in *Beba* (1894) and *El gaucho florido* (1932). He also wrote one of the most notable Latin American novels, *El embrujo de Sevilla,* 1922 (*Castanets*), which is purely Hispanic in theme but is written in a lyrical and vivid style much influenced by the modernist movement (*see* MODERNISM: SPANISH AMERICA).

RACHEL PHILLIPS

RÍO BLANCO STRIKE. Mexican textile workers in the region around Orizaba, Veracruz, influenced by men who had been associated with Ricardo FLORES MAGÓN and his brothers, went on strike late in 1906. Their demands included shorter hours, higher wages, accident compensation, payment in legal tender, and a pension program. The Veracruz workers were later joined by workers from some areas of the neighboring state of Puebla. An appeal was made to President Porfirio DÍAZ to serve as arbitrator; the decision he handed down upheld the millowners' position, which centered on an offer to reduce the working day to twelve and one-half hours. On the morning of January 7, 1907, violence broke out at a large factory in Río Blanco when a group of workers attacked the hated company store and an employee of the store killed one of the strikers. Then the workers attacked the municipal building. The violence quickly spread to other textile factories in the immediate vicinity of Río Blanco and also Nogales, involving more than 6,000 workers. Federal troops and Guardias Rurales (rural police) attacked the strikers, who were armed only with stones and clubs. The strikers included large numbers of women and children. There were many casualties, both killed and wounded, and the three principal strike leaders were executed. As a result of the brutal suppression of the strike the labor movement received a major setback in Mexico, and the remaining years of the Díaz administration witnessed no further major labor disturbances.

CHARLES R. BERRY

RIO BRANCO, BARÃO DO (JOSÉ MARIA DA SILVA PARANHOS JÚNIOR, 1845–1912). Brazilian diplomat. Born in Bahia, he became perhaps Brazil's most renowned diplomat. Trained in law, he taught history for a short time after 1868 before becoming a member of the Chamber of Deputies from Mato Grosso. In 1876 he was appointed Brazilian Consul in Liverpool, a position he held until 1891. He was named Barão do Rio Branco by Emperor PEDRO II in 1888. During the FIRST REPUBLIC he became director of the Immigration Service of Brazil in Paris. In 1893, owing to his reputation as a scholar of history and geography, he became involved in negotiating Brazil's boundary disagreements. Largely because of his negotiations, Brazil was awarded the Misiones territory from Argentina in 1895 and the Amapá area from French Guiana in 1900.

After only a year's service as Minister to Germany, Rio Branco returned to Brazil in 1902 as Minister of Foreign Affairs, a position he held until his death in 1912. He strove for three goals during his ministry: the establishment of Brazilian leadership in South America, foreign recognition of this leadership, and the settlement of all Brazil's frontiers. In the matter of the frontiers his major achievement was his negotiation on November 17, 1903, of the Treaty of Petrópolis (*see* PETRÓPOLIS, TREATY OF), in which Acre, claimed by both Bolivia and Brazil, was awarded to Brazil. Largely through his efforts similarly favorable settlements were reached between 1904 and 1909 with the Guianas, Ecuador, Venezuela, Colombia, Peru, and Uruguay. Rio Branco also strengthened ties between the United States and Brazil, supported Pan-Americanism, and by the successful and peaceful settlement of Brazil's boundaries, reinforced the nation's image abroad and at home.

LESLIE S. OFFUTT

RIO BRANCO, VISCONDE DO (JOSÉ MARIA DA SILVA PARANHOS, 1819–1880). Brazilian diplomat and statesman. Born in Bahia, Paranhos was educated at the naval and military academies in Rio de Janeiro. Making a name as a teacher, journalist, and provincial politician, he was elected in 1847 to the Chamber of Deputies from Rio de Janeiro Province. In 1851 he traveled to Uruguay as secretary to the Marquês de Paraná, beginning an outstanding diplomatic career

that involved him deeply in the affairs of the republics of the RÍO DE LA PLATA. From 1855 to 1857 and again in 1858 and 1861 he served as Minister of Foreign Affairs, negotiating important commercial and border treaties in Río de la Plata capitals. In 1864 he was again in Uruguay, where he helped to settle serious internal disputes and prepared Uruguay for membership in the Triple Alliance against Paraguay. Serving again as Foreign Minister in the Conservative Cabinet of Visconde Itaboraí, he was sent in 1869 as Minister Plenipotentiary to Asunción to negotiate an end to the PARAGUAYAN WAR, signing a peace treaty with that country during a final mission in 1871.

With this successful diplomatic background, on March 7, 1871, he was appointed President of the Council of Ministers (Prime Minister). The Rio Branco Cabinet, which lasted until June 1875, was one of the most successful regimes of the empire. Notable among its accomplishments was the passage of the FREE BIRTH LAW, intended to free the newborn children of slave women.

ROBERT CONRAD

RIO BRANCO LAW. *See* FREE BIRTH LAW.

RIO DE JANEIRO. Capital of the state of Guanabara, Brazil. With 4,296,782 inhabitants (1970), Rio de Janeiro is the second largest city in Brazil. Its metropolitan area, which spreads into the neighboring state of Rio de Janeiro, has more than 7 million residents and comprises one of the leading commercial and industrial complexes in Latin America. Rio de Janeiro, located on the Bay of Guanabara, is a major seaport as well as the focal point of all domestic and international airlines serving Brazil. Long the capital of Brazil, the city remains the semiofficial political and administrative nerve center of the nation. It has the highest concentration of cultural and educational institutions in Brazil. Its famous *favelas* (*see* FAVELA), sandwiched between middle-class residential districts, are glaring examples of urban poverty.

The site of Rio de Janeiro was discovered and named by Portuguese explorers early in the sixteenth century but was subsequently claimed by French colonists. The city grew out of a military camp, São Sebastião do Rio de Janeiro, founded by the Portuguese in 1565 during the campaign to expel the French. Rio de Janeiro became the capital of Brazil in 1763. The capital and its immediate hinterland, which were separated from the state of Rio de Janeiro in 1834, were known as the Federal District after the creation of the Republic of Brazil in 1889. With the transfer of the national capital to Brasília in 1960, the former Federal District became the state of Guanabara. Residents of Rio de Janeiro are known as *cariocas*.

ROLLIE E. POPPINO

RIO DE JANEIRO MEETING (1942). Third Meeting of Consultation of Ministers of Foreign Affairs of the American republics. At the instance of the United States the American foreign ministers convened in Rio de Janeiro, Brazil, on January 15–28, 1942, to consider in conformity with Resolution 15 adopted at the HAVANA MEETING (1940) the response of their countries to the Japanese attack on Pearl Harbor and the United States entry into World War II. While the agenda included proposed measures for preserving the territorial integrity of the American republics and strengthening economic solidarity, the principal issue became the severance of diplomatic relations with the Axis Powers. Nine Central American and Caribbean nations had already declared war on the Axis, and three more (Mexico, Venezuela, and Colombia) had broken relations, but Chile and Argentina refused to subscribe to a resolution explicitly demanding a diplomatic rupture. Chile, with a long and vulnerable coastline, feared Axis reprisal, but it was suspected that pro-Nazi sympathies dictated Argentina's intransigence. For the sake of unity, the conference on January 23 approved a mild resolution that merely recommended a break, permitting the two recalcitrant nations to maintain their ties with Germany. The meeting also recommended the severance of commercial and financial relations with the Axis Powers.

A number of resolutions dealing with greater economic cooperation were adopted, including one looking toward a solution of postwar economic problems. In order to strengthen hemisphere security the ministers established the Inter-American Defense Board to study and suggest defense measures and the Emergency Advisory Committee for Political Defense to study and coordinate antisubversive activities. Further accomplishments included settlement of the ECUADOR-PERU CONFLICT, creation of a committee to study juridical matters relating to the war, adherence to the Atlantic Charter, and endorsement of the GOOD NEIGHBOR POLICY as a "norm of international law of the American Continent."

WILLIAM R. ADAMS

RÍO DE LA PLATA. Estuary about 170 miles long, formed by the union of the Paraná and Uruguay rivers (*see* PARANÁ-PARAGUAY RIVER BASIN; URUGUAY RIVER). The Argentine side of the river is discolored by the silt that the fast current of the Paraná River carries down from Paraguay. Not too far from where the river flows into the Atlantic Ocean there is a group of small, rocky, and desolate islands that in bygone days alerted the experienced skipper of a sailing vessel to begin his sharp watch to the southwest for the black clouds announcing the approach of the dangerous and destructive wind known as the pampero. Other threats to safety were and are the numerous and shifting sandbanks and shoals. Near the other end of the estuary is the island of Martín García, which dominates the entrance to the Uruguay River and the deepwater channel called Guazú leading into the Paraná River. Running along the Uruguayan coastline for a significant distance before it turns toward Argentina is the access channel to the port of Buenos Aires known as Punta Indio. In spite of the navigational difficulties it presents, the river is not lacking in strategic importance. It provides countries on its borders with access to the sea, and it could be used to influence the economic and political destinies of the areas serviced by its tributaries.

The river was discovered by Juan Díaz de SOLÍS in 1516. He called it Mar Dulce, but it was known as Río de Solis until 1532, when the name Río de la Plata began to appear. Francis DRAKE visited the estuary in 1578. Two years later the second founding of the city of Buenos Aires took place. Montevideo appeared on the opposite shore in 1726. With its more secure and easily accessible harbor, Montevideo was preferred to Buenos Aires by ships from Europe, and a "war of the ports" soon developed.

Argentine-Uruguayan relations have been troubled for more than 100 years by a dispute over sovereignty over the river. Argentina maintains, in the Zeballos Doctrine, that the Uruguayan boundary is the coastline at low tide, thus placing the access channels to Buenos Aires and Montevideo under its control, but Uruguay insists that the demarcation line is midway between them. In the 1960s the problem was complicated by the realization that large oil fields may exist under the riverbed. The two countries, however, have already agreed on where the Río de la Plata meets the Atlantic Ocean and on calling it an "interior river." The major international powers do not accept this decision.

JOSEPH T. CRISCENTI

RÍO DE LA PLATA, VICEROYALTY OF. Last viceroyalty created in the Spanish empire, established in 1776. It covered the areas of Buenos Aires, Paraguay, Tucumán, the province of Cuyo, and the Presidency of Charcas (modern Bolivia). The viceroyalty was founded to defend the largely neglected and vulnerable southern coastline of the empire from possible British attack, to stop the encroachment of the Portuguese on the northern shore of the Río de la Plata, and to curtail the contraband trade enjoyed mostly by Portuguese Brazil. This vast region was brought under firm Spanish control after the arrival (1776) of the first viceroy, Pedro de Cevallos, with a large military and naval force. Among the immediate reforms adopted by Cevallos were the authorization to export silver bullion and the rechanneling of the export of silver from the Potosí mines, previously sent to Peru, through Buenos Aires. In 1778 the port of Buenos Aires was temporarily opened to registered vessels of friendly nations.

By the end of the eighteenth century the expansion of trade had created an unprecedented prosperity. The exploitation of cattle products was intensified. Hides and salted meat became major export products. The INTENDANCY SYSTEM was introduced in 1778, and in less than two decades the viceroyalty had become a flourishing outpost of the Spanish empire. In 1806 and 1807 the population of Buenos Aires successfully repelled two attacks by British forces seeking to establish a protectorate. These victories enhanced the growing feeling of creole self-assurance. In 1810, with Spain under Napoleonic rule, the creoles adopted an autonomous government. This act ended the viceroyalty and began the process of independence. *See also* SAN ILDEFONSO, TREATY OF.

ASUNCIÓN LAVRIN

RÍOS [MORALES], JUAN ANTONIO (1888–1946). President of Chile (1942–1946). Born in Cañete in the coal-mining province of Arauco, Ríos was educated locally and at the University of Chile, from which he graduated in law in 1914. A member of the Radical party (*see* RADICAL PARTY: CHILE), he was elected to Congress as a deputy for Arauco, Lebu, and Cañete in 1924, retained his seat (1926–1930), and was reelected for the period 1933–1937. He rose rapidly in the Radical party in the 1920s, becoming its president in 1927, but allegations that he supported the dictatorship of Carlos IBÁÑEZ (1927–1931) led to his expulsion from the party in 1931. During the Socialist republic of Carlos Dávila (1932), Ríos served as Minister of the Interior, and later as Minister of Justice in the provisional government set up between Dávila's fall and Chile's return to orderly rule at the end of the year. Readmitted to his party in 1933, Ríos soon reestablished his position as a leading Radical and was again party president in 1937. Though fervently anti-Communist, he supported the Popular Front in opposition to Arturo ALESSANDRI (*see* POPULAR FRONT: CHILE) and contested the Radical party nomination for the Presidency with Pedro AGUIRRE CERDA in 1938. He held no Cabinet office in the Popular Front government (1938–1941), but on the death of Aguirre Cerda he secured the Radical nomination for the presidential election of 1942. With the right-wing parties backing the ex-dictator Ibáñez, the Communists and Socialists threw their support to Ríos, who won by 260,034 votes to 204,653 (*see* COMMUNIST PARTY: CHILE; SOCIALIST PARTY: CHILE). Ríos continued the domestic policies of the Popular Front, emphasizing industrial growth through the CORPORACIÓN DE FOMENTO DE LA PRODUCCIÓN. In foreign affairs he broke off relations with the Axis Powers in January 1943, and he paid an official visit to Washington in October 1945. Like Aguirre Cerda, Ríos fell ill and died in office.

HAROLD BLAKEMORE

RIO TREATY. The Inter-American Treaty of Reciprocal Assistance, a collective security pact drafted at the Inter-American Conference for the Maintenance of Peace and Security, held near Rio de Janeiro from August 15 to September 2, 1947. The treaty went into effect in 1948 after its ratification by two-thirds of the signatory states.

Article 3 of the treaty provides that "an armed attack by any State against an American State shall be considered as an attack against all the American States," and that the Organ of Consultation shall meet immediately to decide upon measures to be taken. A meeting of the Organ of Consultation is also to be held "if the inviolability or the integrity of the territory or the sovereignty or political independence of any American State should be affected by an aggression which is not an armed attack or by an extra-continental or intra-continental conflict, or by any other fact or situation that might endanger the peace of America." According to Article 11, "the consultations to which this Treaty refers shall be carried out by means of the Meetings of Ministers of Foreign Affairs of the American Republics which have ratified the Treaty." This provision is reasserted in the Charter of the ORGANIZATION OF AMERICAN STATES, which stipulates that the meeting of consultation of foreign ministers shall serve as the Organ of Consultation. Under certain circumstances, the PERMANENT COUNCIL may serve as a provisional Organ of Consultation. Sanctions which may be imposed by the Organ of Consultation range from recall of chiefs of diplomatic missions to the use of armed force.

The Rio Treaty has been invoked in a number of instances since 1948, notably during the Cuban missile crisis of 1962, when the OAS Council, meeting as the provisional Organ of Consultation, authorized the use of force for the first time under the treaty to prevent Cuba from receiving military equipment from the Sino-Soviet powers and "to prevent the missiles in Cuba . . . from ever becoming an active threat to the peace and security of the Continent."

RODNEY D. ANDERSON

RIVA-AGÜERO, JOSÉ DE LA (1783–1858). Peruvian patriot and first President. The controversial Riva-Agüero was born in Lima, the son of a Spanish official. Educated in Spain, he fought briefly with the Spaniards against Napoleon but also became committed to the cause of greater Spanish American autonomy. In 1809 he returned to Lima and took part in the process of agitation and conspiracy that was gradually undermining the Spanish regime even while Peru remained the primary bastion of royalist power in South America.

After José de SAN MARTÍN's occupation of the Peruvian coast, Riva-Agüero collaborated actively with him as prefect of Lima. He was also developing a personal political following among his fellow Peruvians. Following San Martín's departure and a brief junta experiment, Riva-Agüero was made the first constitutional President of Peru, but his prestige declined as Peruvians increasingly looked to Simón BOLÍVAR to finish their independence struggle. Indeed, that struggle suffered important setbacks, and by the time Bolívar reached Peruvian soil in September 1823, Riva-Agüero's opponents had ordered him deposed and created a rival government. Bolívar sought to mediate the dispute but in effect supported the anti-Riva-Agüero faction. The Peruvian leader then entered negotiations with the Spanish Viceroy, proposing the establishment of a native monarchy under a Spanish prince, but was captured and exiled. He remained in Europe until 1833. He collaborated in the abortive PERU-BOLIVIA CONFEDERATION of Andrés SANTA CRUZ and was reexpelled at its collapse, but he spent his last years (1845–1858) in Peru, looking back on the events of his lifetime with a bitterness forcefully expressed in his memoirs.

DAVID BUSHNELL

RIVA-AGÜERO [Y OSMA], JOSÉ DE LA (1885–1944). Peruvian scholar and spokesman of conservatism. Riva-Agüero was born in Lima of an aristocratic family. His unusual intelligence was first displayed in 1905 upon the completion of his bachelor thesis at the University of San Marcos. The thesis was an impressively original and panoramic analysis of Peruvian literature that marked the beginning of a new era of criticism. Five years later he completed his dissertation, *La historia del Perú*. A history of Peruvian historiography, it was a seminal contribution to the intellectual, social, and political history of Peru. Riva-Agüero quickly became the leader of the *arielista* generation of 1900, which sought to emphasize spiritual values over economic considerations and to reject blind adherence to foreign currents. He and his contemporaries wished to discover Peru's authentic values by studying its past. The result was an acceptance and admiration of some of the Inca traditions (*see* INCAS) and a renewed vigorous appreciation of Hispanic contributions.

Riva-Agüero's political activities were less successful than his intellectual pursuits. He founded the Nationalist Democratic party (Futuristas), composed of gifted but politically ineffective intellectuals. In the

1930s he served capably as mayor of Lima and headed one of the Cabinets of President Oscar BENAVIDES. At the same time his traditional conservative ideology, which had led him to preach against democracy and advocate government by a virtuous and capable elite, emerged in the 1930s as a commendation of fascism, which he defended until his death in 1944.

ORAZIO A. CICCARELLI

RIVADAVIA, BERNARDINO (1780–1845). Argentine statesman, often regarded as one of the founders of the Argentine Republic. He was the son of a merchant from Spanish Galicia who had established himself in Buenos Aires, married a local girl, and become immersed in the public, legal, and commercial life of the city. The younger Rivadavia attended the Colegio de San Carlos from 1798 to 1803 without graduating, and six years later he married into the family of former Viceroy Joaquín del Pino. By 1809 he was well known as a merchant and merchants' lawyer, a patriot who had defended Buenos Aires during the British invasion of 1806, and an enemy of Manuel MORENO. After 1810 he dedicated himself primarily to the organization of the Argentine nation and to its economic and cultural development. Initially, his political career was influenced by a relative, Cornelio de Saavedra.

As Secretary of the First Triumvirate (1811–1812), he encouraged education, ranching, agriculture, mining, immigration, and foreign investments in Argentina, tried to reconcile competing political groups, and endeavored to restore peace and order. He continued these policies as a minister in the administration of Gen. Martín Rodríguez (1820–1824) and as President (1826–1827). Pro-British partly because of his long association with British merchants, he welcomed English commercial, mining, and immigration companies, negotiated a treaty of friendship, commerce, and navigation with Great Britain (1825), obtained a multipurpose loan from Baring Brothers, and exchanged ideas with Sir Woodbine Parish, the British chargé d'affaires, during the writing of the constitution of 1826. Among the measures he sponsored were the establishment of the University of Buenos Aires, the National Archives, and a postal service to the interior provinces; the creation of a national bank and a charitable society; the introduction of universal manhood suffrage and EMPHYTEUSIS in the province of Buenos Aires; the reorganization of the Army and the civil bureaucracy; and the abolition of the ecclesiastical tithes and FUERO. The Cisplatine War with Brazil over control of Uruguay (1825–1828) forced him to call the Congress that wrote the centralist constitution of 1826 and elected him President. He also nationalized the city of Buenos Aires.

Unable to persuade the provinces to accept the constitution and to obtain a favorable peace treaty with Brazil, he resigned and left for Europe in 1827, leaving his followers to form the Unitarian party (see UNITARIO). Today, some Argentines contend that he wanted to see democracy take root in Argentina, to prevent the concentration of wealth in a few hands, and to discourage immigrants from settling in and about the city of Buenos Aires. Others imply that he vacillated between republicanism and monarchism until 1820 and then endorsed centralism. Still others see him as a traitor.

JOSEPH T. CRISCENTI

RIVERA, DIEGO (1886–1957). Mexican muralist and painter. Rivera was born in Guanajuato and trained in the Academy of San Carlos in Mexico City. He received a scholarship to study in Europe and remained there from 1907 to 1921, mainly in Paris, where he was an early member of the cubist group. A self-portrait of 1913 is one of about eighty cubist paintings, an important contribution to the movement. He returned to Mexico in 1921 to participate in the revival often called the Mexican Renaissance. He was immediately a central figure, taking the Ministry of Education Building as his preserve. That building, where he worked off and on for many years, shows his gradual perfection of the fresco technique and an appealing narrative style, based on curvilinear simplification, that owes something to both cubism and Italian Renaissance frescoes. Inspired by travels during which he rediscovered Mexico, as well as by the folk imagery of José Guadalupe POSADA, Rivera invented a great range of images of Mexican history and people.

In 1926–1927 he painted the chapel of the Agricultural School in Chapingo with revolutionary scenes paralleled by allegories of natural generation and fruition represented by nude figures. Chapingo is widely regarded as his masterpiece, summing up his social message and his fascination with the human figure. In 1929 Rivera painted scenes from Mexican history in the loggia of the Palace of Cortés in Cuernavaca and began the staircase mural in the National Palace in Mexico City, where he was to work intermittently for the rest of his life. These designs reveal his ability to organize complex narratives full of historical detail on vast walls. In 1930 Rivera went to the United States and did murals in San Francisco, Detroit, and Rockefeller Center in New York, where his *Man at the Crossroads* was destroyed because it glorified communism. The mural was repainted for the Palace of Fine Arts in Mexico City. Rivera produced relatively few murals in his later years: a rejected set for the Hotel Reforma, two panels for the Institute of Cardiology (1943), a large mural for the Hotel del Prado (1947–1948), and now-damaged murals in a water distribution chamber of the Lerma waterworks. He returned to Aztec subjects in his last mural, a history of medicine in the Hospital de la Raza (1953–1955). At the waterworks he designed an influential stone mosaic. He continued to use mosaic on the Insurgentes Theater, but in a painterly way, returning to the rugged natural stone in a mural at the stadium of University City (1952).

Rivera's reputation rests as much on his oil paintings, watercolors, prints, and drawings as on his murals. These more modest works express a lyrical mood rare in his murals, and they are equally polished. The famous *Flower Vendor* (San Francisco Museum of Art) is a good example, ranking with his Chapingo murals.

Bibliography. Bernard S. Myers, *Mexican Painting in Our Time,* New York, 1956; Diego Rivera, *Diego Rivera: 50 años de su labor artística,* Mexico City, 1949; Bertram D. Wolfe, *Diego Rivera: His Life and Times,* New York, 1939.

TERENCE GRIEDER

RIVERA, [JOSÉ] FRUCTUOSO (ca. 1784–1854). Uruguayan independence leader and first President. Born in Uruguay, probably between 1784 and 1789, he enlisted in the patriot forces soon after the revolt

Fructuoso Rivera. [*Organization of American States*]

against Spanish rule began in 1811. He served so effectively at Las Piedras a few days later that he was raised at once to the rank of captain. After fighting against the first Portuguese intrusion of 1811–1812, he supported José Gervasio ARTIGAS in his resistance to the hegemony pretended by Buenos Aires and led the forces that triumphed at Guayabos. He played a prominent role in the Uruguayan resistance to the subsequent Portuguese invasion from 1816 to 1820, coming to terms with the intruders only when his forces constituted the last organized patriot opposition.

After signing the act incorporating Uruguay with Brazil, he was given command of the Union Regiment of Dragoons, a militia unit of Uruguayan-born soldiers. Having taken no part in the first conspiracies in 1823 for the renewal of the struggle for independence, he was decorated and promoted to the rank of brigadier general for his loyal service to Brazil during this crisis and, ultimately, in 1824, was named general commander of the forces in the Uruguayan countryside. However, when Juan Antonio LAVALLEJA launched his movement in 1825, Rivera, apparently by prior agreement, allowed himself to be captured by the patriots, becoming forthwith the second in command in the patriot forces and bringing to their cause his substantial following in the rural districts. His friction with Lavalleja and aversion to the prominent role assigned to the forces from Buenos Aires led him to withdraw from the campaign in 1826. Proceeding to Santa Fe, he obtained some assistance from Estanislao López in preparing for the conquest of the Brazilian missions region early in 1828, a feat that restored his prestige, gave him a loyal army as a base of power, and had a decisive influence on Brazil's resolution to end the war by recognizing Uruguay's independence.

In August 1829, Rivera became Minister of War in the provisional government, and on October 29, 1830,

he won election as the first constitutional President. He proved to be less able as a statesman than as a soldier. In choosing to operate during most of his term as a *caudillo* with his base of power in the countryside, he let pass the opportunity offered by the constitutionalization of the country to heal the schism, which had persisted since 1811, between the cultured elements of the capital and the frontiersmen of the countryside. His initial predilection for the pro-Brazilian clique among the nation's political leaders, his almost complete exclusion from power of the Lavalleja faction, and his careless handling of the nation's finances stimulated dissatisfaction and revolt. By his employment of Argentine UNITARIO *émigrés* in his forces and by his intrigues with the rivals of the Argentine dictator Juan Manuel de ROSAS in the River Provinces, as well as by his later alliance with adherents of the FARROUPILHA REVOLT of Rio Grande do Sul, he contributed to Uruguay's embroilment in the civil conflicts of both Argentina and Brazil. When Manuel ORIBE, his successor in the Presidency, sought to extend the government's control over the countryside, which Rivera continued to regard as his bailiwick, Rivera led a revolt in 1836 that eventually forced Oribe's resignation in 1838. In the course of this struggle the Colorado party began to take shape around Rivera, who is regarded as its founder (*see* COLORADO PARTY: URUGUAY). Its organizers assumed a liberal pose in reaction to President Oribe's Rosas-like authoritarianism and traditionalism and under Rivera's direction initially showed interest in federating Uruguay with some of the Argentine River Provinces and with Brazil's Rio Grande do Sul as well as Paraguay to form a third large state on the Atlantic coast of South America between Brazil and Argentina.

As a consequence of his triumph over President Oribe, Rivera was elected to a second presidential term, running from March 1, 1839, to March 1, 1843. Having declared war on Rosas ten days after his inauguration, Rivera launched the so-called Guerra Grande that was to end only in 1852. Although he routed an invading Argentine army in December 1839, he suffered a disastrous series of defeats between 1842 and 1845 that forced him to abandon the countryside to Oribe and his Argentine forces and to seek refuge in Brazil. He returned to the fray in 1846 at the head of a new Colorado army in the countryside, but he was removed from command in 1847, when after new reverses he attempted an unauthorized discussion of peace terms with Oribe. Condemned to exile for the next four years, he lived in Rio de Janeiro in failing health until the ban was lifted late in 1851. Even then, fearful of his potential for disturbing the peace, the Brazilian government blocked his return to Uruguay for some months. He was still on Brazilian soil in 1853 when he learned of his appointment to the triumvirate, dominated by Venancio FLORES, that was the provisional successor to the ousted legal government of President Juan Francisco Giró. He died near Melo on January 13, 1854, while still on his way to Montevideo to assume that post.

Bibliography. José Gervasio Antuña, *Un caudillo, el general Fructuoso Rivera, prócer del Uruguay,* Madrid, 1948; Alfredo Lepro, *Fructuoso Rivera, hombre del pueblo: Sentido revolucionario de su vida y de su acción,* Montevideo, 1945; Telmo Manacorda,

Fructuoso Rivera, el perpetuo defensor de la República Oriental, Madrid, 1933; José Luciano Martínez, *Brigadier general Fructuoso Rivera y la campaña de las Misiones: El hombre, el soldado, el gobernante*, Montevideo, 1961; Alberto Palomeque, *Guerra de la Argentina y el Brasil: El general Rivera y la campaña de Misiones (1828)*, Buenos Aires, 1914.

JOHN H. HANN

RIVERA, JOSÉ EUSTASIO (1889–1928). Colombian writer. Rivera was trained in law and held various political and diplomatic posts. He first published a volume of sonnets, *Tierra de promisión* (1921), based on the reality of the tropics, but is best known for his novel *La vorágine*, 1924 (*The Vortex*), set in forests between Colombia and Venezuela, which he had visited twice. There is much of autobiography in this book, which was also intended to expose the exploitation of the rubber companies, and it expresses Rivera's horrified fascination for the jungle. There is an unpublished play of the same title.

RACHEL PHILLIPS

RIVERA, JULIO ADALBERTO (1922–1973). Salvadoran army officer and President (1962–1967). His National Conciliation party (PCN) replaced the PARTIDO REVOLUCIONARIO DE UNIFICACIÓN DEMOCRÁTICA (PRUD) but continued the military reformist leadership of Salvadoran politics that had begun in 1950.

Rivera was a member of the five-man Civil-Military Directory which, in January 1961, recovered the "revolution" of 1950 from the more radical junta that had supplanted José María LEMUS. Like PRUD, the directory initiated reforms; then Rivera resigned and formed the PCN to defend the reform program. In manipulated elections held in December 1961, PCN candidates won all fifty-four seats in the Legislative Assembly. Rivera was the PCN candidate for a five-year term in the Presidency on a platform of full cooperation with the ALLIANCE FOR PROGRESS, and when opposition parties declined participation, he swept the April election and took office on July 1, 1962.

Rivera continued and expanded as Alliance for Progress projects the development program begun under PRUD administrations. He also sponsored such socioeconomic measures as regulating working hours and setting minimum wages for rural agricultural workers. When planters threatened to decrease food production in retaliation, he cautioned them that their continued existence depended on their acceptance of reform. He attempted to ease population pressure by colonizing state lands in the north, but when he attained only small success, he encouraged Salvadorans to emigrate.

For the 1967 election PCN nominated Col. Fidel SÁNCHEZ HERNÁNDEZ, another career military officer, for the Presidency. He won over the candidates of three other parties in the March elections.

WILLIAM J. GRIFFITH

ROA BASTOS, AUGUSTO (1918–   ). Paraguayan writer. He is the author of one of the most important novels of his country, *Hijo de hombre*, 1960 (*Son of Man*), a panoramic vision of Paraguay from the CHACO WAR through the social conflicts that followed it. He also published collections of short stories, including

El trueno entre las hojas (1953) and *El baldío* (1966). For many years he lived in exile in Buenos Aires, returning to Paraguay in 1966.

RACHEL PHILLIPS

ROBLES, MARCO A[NTONIO] (1905–   ). President of Panama (1964–1968). Born in Aguadulce, Robles was a Liberal party activist for more than thirty years before becoming President. Named Minister of the Interior and Justice in 1960, he was elected to the Presidency in 1964 as the candidate of a seven-party coalition.

Robles's middle-class–oriented regime was characterized by new initiatives to redistribute income through increased tax levies. His urban development plan called for a heavy investment of domestic and foreign funds in schools, streets, housing, health centers, and job training. Efforts were made to establish Panama as a major banking center for Latin America.

Robles identified Panama more closely with Central American integration, but his major efforts in foreign affairs were directed toward the United States. Treaties concerning the PANAMA CANAL, the status of United States military forces in the Canal Zone, and construction of a sea-level waterway were negotiated with the United States. As these treaties appeared unacceptable to opposition parties in an election year, however, Robles did not submit them to the National Assembly for ratification.

Accusing Robles of favoritism in the 1968 elections, the Assembly, where he no longer enjoyed a majority, impeached and replaced him. Even though the Assembly action was nullified by the Supreme Court, Robles's coalition was defeated in the 1968 presidential contest. After 1968 Robles lived in "voluntary exile" in the United States.

LARRY L. PIPPIN

ROCA, JULIO A[RGENTINO] (1843–1914). President of Argentina (1880–1886, 1898–1904). A native of Tucumán, he was a member of a distinguished provincial family of soldiers. One of six sons who chose a military career, his father served with José de SAN MARTÍN and later was aide-de-camp to several Unitarian generals (*see* UNITARIO). Roca initiated his own military career when he left the Colegio del Uruguay at the end of his second year to fight with his father for the ARGENTINE CONFEDERATION at Cepeda (1859) and Pavón (1861). Afterward, they joined the staff of Gen. Wenceslao Paunero and participated in the campaign against Ángel Vicente Peñaloza, the rural *caudillo* known as El Chacho. From 1864 onward Roca distinguished himself fighting in the PARAGUAYAN WAR, held assignments on the Indian frontier, organized topographical surveys of Indian territory, and carried out political missions for his superiors. That he himself was destined for the Presidency became clear when he defeated his *compadre* Gen. José Miguel Arredondo at Santa Rosa (December 6, 1874). His knowledge of the Indian country assured the success of the campaign he launched in 1879 to fix the national boundaries at the Negro River. This CONQUEST OF THE DESERT was financed by selling in advance the lands to be conquered. President Nicolás AVELLANEDA, also from Tucumán, made certain that Roca became President in 1880.

Roca's second administration began in 1898. He

never enunciated any abstract political principles; he stood essentially for peace, order, and prosperity. Prosperity was the trademark of both administrations. The first was characterized by inflation, the establishment of one legal currency for the country, a monetary crisis, and the issuance of paper money by both the national and provincial banks. The second saw the settlement of boundary disputes with Chile and Brazil and the enunciation of the DRAGO DOCTRINE. Roca chose his brother-in-law, Miguel JUÁREZ CELMAN, to succeed him in 1886, and Manuel Quintana in 1904.

JOSEPH T. CRISCENTI

ROCAFUERTE, VICENTE (1783–1847). President of Ecuador (1835–1839). Born in the colonial *audiencia* of Quito to wealth and prestige, Rocafuerte was educated in Madrid and Paris. He represented Guayaquil in the Spanish Cortes of 1814 and belonged to the generation of Spanish liberals who worked for a united republican Spain. He was forced to abandon Spain and this goal when the absolutist FERDINAND VII regained the throne. From 1814 to 1833 he devoted his energy and personal fortune to the tasks of the emerging New World nations. Mexico became his base of operations, and he served as Secretary to the Mexican Legation in London from 1824 to 1830.

Returning to Guayaquil in 1833, he joined the anti-Flores faction and headed the Liberals in the legislature and in a Guayaquil uprising (*see* LIBERAL PARTY: ECUADOR). The revolt led to his capture by Juan José FLORES and to an agreement between them whereby Rocafuerte assumed the Presidency. He established his reputation as founder of the republic by providing good fiscal organization and a stable currency, ordering urban convents to provide schools, founding naval and military colleges, and writing a penal code. Flores, once reinstalled in 1839, appointed Rocafuerte Governor of Guayas Province, but when Flores sought to continue himself in office for eight years, Rocafuerte left for Lima. From there his barrage of bitter publications helped launch a successful revolution against the dictator, and Rocafuerte was back to serve as President of the Senate in 1846. He died while on a diplomatic mission in Lima the following year.

LOIS WEINMAN

ROCA-RUNCIMAN TREATY. Trade agreement between Great Britain and Argentina signed in 1933. The effects of the world economic depression that began in the United States and Europe in late 1929 reached Argentina early in 1930. Exports began to fall, with resultant declines in agricultural prices, increased urban and rural unemployment, reduced government revenues, and the devaluation of the peso. The determinant of whether the Depression would accelerate to the point of complete national economic collapse or stabilize at an acceptable intermediate point was the capacity of the meat and cereal exporters to sustain a reasonable level of foreign deliveries.

The United Kingdom was the principal purchaser of these products, but also as a result of the world economic crisis the certainty of the British market was in doubt. British investors in Argentine railways, tramways, and power companies complained that they no longer received adequate returns on their money and were forced to pay high taxes to the Argentine govern-ment. British farmers and cattle raisers complained that at a time of collapsing prices their government continued to permit the importation of as much as 90 percent of all Argentine meat exports. In 1932 London yielded to the rising pressure of all discontented groups and held a conference of Commonwealth nations in Ottawa. The results of the conference can be summed by the precept "Buy from those who buy from us." The United Kingdom agreed to give Commonwealth meat and grain exports preference in the British market and to maintain existing tariffs on non-Commonwealth imports.

The Argentine response to the Ottawa agreement was one of extreme alarm. The government sent Vice President Julio A. Roca (who was the son of the President of the same name) to London to confer with Walter Runciman, President of the British Board of Trade. The negotiating position of Britain was clearly superior. Runciman declared that Britain bought more from Argentina than it sold to the latter. Argentina bought most of its manufactured goods from the United States, but the United States purchased no Argentine exports. Roca could have challenged Runciman on British statistics on the price paid for Argentine beef, which differed markedly from what Argentine exporters actually received. Moreover, Britain benefited from many invisible exports, such as the fees received for the use of British shipping by Argentine exporters. But Roca, aware of his inferior position, chose not to dispute with Runciman.

In May 1933, a treaty was signed. Britain made only one concession: to maintain quarterly imports of Argentine chilled beef at the amount imported for the corresponding quarter of the fiscal year ending June 30, 1932, and not to levy any new duties on Argentine meat or grain. Argentina agreed, first, to abstain from withdrawing earned exchange from Britain so that it could be applied to Argentine debts there. Second, 85 percent of the meat processed in Argentina was to be awarded to foreign *frigoríficos* (meat-packing plants; *see* FRIGORÍFICO), and the balance could be processed only by noncompetitive Argentine establishments. Argentina further agreed to reduce tariffs on British manufactured goods to 1930 levels; coal was to be admitted without duty. In a protocol to the treaty Argentina acquiesced to the clamor of British investors by agreeing to "accord . . . benevolent treatment" to British investments, that is, the railroads, tramways, and power companies.

EUGENE G. SHARKEY

ROCKEFELLER, NELSON A[LDRICH] (1908–   ). American public official. Born in Bar Harbor, Maine, Rockefeller graduated from Dartmouth College in 1930 and embarked upon a career in banking, international business, philanthropy, government service, and politics. He assumed an early interest in Latin America with his appointment to the board of directors of the Creole Petroleum Corporation, a subsidiary in Venezuela of the Standard Oil Corporation (founded by his grandfather, John D. Rockefeller, Sr.). In 1940 he created the Compañía de Fomento Venezolano as a development enterprise in Venezuela, and the same year he was appointed by President Roosevelt as coordinator of commercial and cultural relations between the American republics. Rockefeller later served briefly as Assistant Secretary of State for Latin American

Affairs (1944–1945).

In 1969, while serving his third term as Republican Governor of New York, he was sent as head of a fact-finding mission to Latin America for the purpose of making recommendations for United States foreign policy toward the area. The resulting *Rockefeller Report on the Americas* (1969) predicted that the decade of the 1970s would see the growth of NATIONALISM in Latin America, increasing frustration over lagging development, and continued control of governments by reform-minded military leaders. The *Report*'s recommendations included the appointment of a Secretary of Western Hemisphere Affairs and the creation of a civilian-directed Western Hemisphere Security Council, with headquarters outside the United States, "to cope with the forces of subversion."

RICHARD B. GRAY

RODÓ, JOSÉ ENRIQUE (1871–1917). Uruguayan essayist. Rodó was born in Montevideo and died in Palermo, Sicily. Best known for his writings of a philosophical nature, he was also one of the literary critics of the modernist period (*see* MODERNISM: SPANISH AMERICA), and he served as professor of literature in the National University (1898), director of the National Library (1900), and a member of Congress (1902). He spent most of his life in Montevideo and was one of the founders of the *Revista Nacional de Literatura y Ciencias Sociales* (1895–1897). His major works are mostly collections of shorter writings and include *Ariel* (1900), *Liberalismo y jacobinismo* (1906), *Motivos de Proteo,* 1909 (*The Motives of Proteus*), and *El mirador de Próspero* (1913).

It was *Ariel* that placed him in the international limelight and made him a hero to the youth of Spanish America. The best integrated of his major works and the one with which most people identify him, it takes its title from the name of the airy spirit in Shakespeare's *The Tempest*. Written in the form of a last lecture to his students by a revered teacher they call Próspero, it is a lesson for the youth of Latin America. In it Rodó extols the value of spirituality and idealism, which he contrasts with the vulgar materialism characteristic of the age. Because of certain passages in the book, many readers came to the conclusion that Rodó identified Hispanic culture with the values he upheld while viewing the United States as the embodiment of the materialism he disdained. In the words of W. Rex Crawford, *Ariel* became "the pillow-book of a generation of Latin American youth," but it has been criticized for its unawareness of the realities of Latin American life.

GERARDO SÁENZ

RODRIGUES, JOSÉ HONÓRIO (1913–   ). Brazilian historian. Elected to the Brazilian Academy of Letters in September 1969, Rodrigues is one of Brazil's most respected historians. Strongly influenced by the nineteenth-century historian of colonial Brazil, João Capistrano de ABREU, and by two contemporary social historians, Francisco José de Oliveira Vianna and Gilberto FREYRE, Rodrigues's writings are interpretive and analytical rather than descriptive and reveal his familiarity with European and North American historians and historiography.

A native of Rio de Janeiro and a graduate of the University of Brazil (1937), Rodrigues is self-taught as a historian of Brazil since he completed his formal education at a time when studies in Brazilian history were only beginning in Brazilian universities. He has held administrative positions at the Rio Branco Institute (1946–1956), the National Archive (1958–1964), and the Brazilian Institute of International Relations (1964–1968) and since 1953 has been a faculty member at both the University of the State of Guanabara and the Pontifical Catholic University of Rio de Janeiro. Among his more important works are *Teoría da História do Brasil* (1949; 2d ed., 1957), *A Pesquisa Histórica no Brasil* (1952), *Brasil e África,* 1961 (*Brazil and Africa*), *Aspirações Nacionais,* 1963 (*The Brazilians: Their Character and Aspirations*), *História e Historiadores do Brasil* (1965), *Interesse Nacional e Política Externa* (1966), and *Historiografia e Bibliografia do Domínio Holandés no Brasil* (various editions).

JOSEPH A. ELLIS

RODRIGUES ALVES, FRANCISCO DE PAULA (1848–1919). President of Brazil (1902–1906). Born in Guaretinguetá, São Paulo, Rodrigues Alves graduated from the São Paulo law school in 1870. Entering politics as a Conservative, he served in the provincial legislature from 1872 to 1879, as Governor of São Paulo in 1887, and in the imperial Parliament from 1885 to 1889. Following the overthrow of the empire, he joined the Republican party of São Paulo and thereafter usually held high state or national office. As a senator in the Constituent Assembly, Rodrigues Alves helped write the constitution of 1891 (*see* CONSTITUTION OF 1891: BRAZIL). Subsequently he alternated between the Senate and service as Minister of Finance under Presidents Floriano PEIXOTO and Prudente de MORAIS. As Governor of São Paulo after 1900, he worked closely with President Manoel CAMPOS SALLES, who chose him as the official candidate for the Presidency in 1902.

The chief accomplishment of Rodrigues Alves's administration was the transformation of Rio de Janeiro into a healthful and beautiful city as the result of projects carried out by Oswaldo CRUZ and Paulo de Frontin. After leaving the Presidency, Rodrigues Alves suffered from declining health, but he served a full term as Governor of São Paulo (1912–1916) and was active in the Senate. In 1918 he was selected as a compromise administration candidate to succeed President Wenceslau BRAZ. Although he won election easily, he was too ill to take the oath of office. Rodrigues Alves died in January 1919 without having assumed power for the second time.

See also TAUBATÉ CONVENTION.

ROLLIE E. POPPINO

RODRÍGUEZ, ABELARDO (1889–1967). President of Mexico (1932–1934). Born in San José de Guaymas, Rodríguez was the son of a mule team owner. He worked in the Cananea copper mines and, in January 1911, took part in the defense of Baja California against North American and Mexican filibusters. On March 1, 1913, he joined the 2d Sonora Battalion with the rank of lieutenant; on June 11, 1928, he reached the rank of division general. From 1916 to 1920 he fought a Yaqui Indian uprising in Sonora. In the latter year he defeated the pro-Carranza Governor of Baja California (*see* CARRANZA, Venustiano), the Northern District of which he governed from October 31, 1923, until May 1929. As Governor he encouraged industrialization and the establishment of agricultural colonies and stimulated the urban development of Mexicali and Tijuana, but he was criticized for protecting gambling and prostitution. Later he served as Undersecretary of War, Minister of Industry, Commerce, and Labor, and Minister of War.

While serving as President of Mexico from September 3, 1932, until November 30, 1934, he divided the Ministry of Industry, Commerce, and Labor into a Ministry of National Economy and a Department of Labor. In January 1934 an autonomous Agrarian Department replaced the National Agrarian Commission, and in March of that year the first agrarian code was promulgated. He attacked labor leaders severely and constantly and criticized the "socialist" education decreed by a constitutional amendment in 1933. Later he was Governor of Sonora. He successfully combined politics with business enterprises in fishing, cinematography, viticulture, maritime transport, and other fields.

MOISÉS GONZÁLEZ NAVARRO

RODRÍGUEZ, CARLOS RAFAEL (1913–   ). Cuban Communist leader. Rodríguez is one of the few veteran Communist party leaders who has attained an influential position in the political hierarchy of Fidel CASTRO's Cuba. He has the distinction of having held a Cabinet position under the governments of both Fulgencio BATISTA and Castro.

In 1936, while a university student, Rodríguez joined the Communist party. He graduated with a law degree and has intermittently served on the Law Faculty of Havana University. In 1939 he was elected to the Central Committee of the Communist party (after 1944, Popular Socialist party, or PSP). During Batista's first administration Rodríguez temporarily served as Minister without Portfolio.

In early 1958 when the PSP decided to support Castro's armed struggle against the Batista dictatorship, Rodríguez received the assignment of traveling to the Sierra Maestra to effect an alliance with the July 26 movement. Of all the PSP leaders Rodríguez developed the closest relationship with the Castroites. His ties with orthodox communism made him a useful liaison between the revolutionary regime and the international Communist movement. During 1959 Rodríguez edited the PSP daily organ *Hoy* and participated in drawing up government decrees such as the Agrarian Reform Law and economic and educational measures. From 1962 to 1964 he headed the Institute of Agrarian Reform (INRA), and later he served as Minister of Agriculture and Minister without Portfolio. Rodríguez also holds top-level positions within the new PARTIDO COMUNISTA DE CUBA, serving on the Secretariat and Political Bureau of the Central Committee. He was also named to one of the seven Vice Premier posts created in the government in 1972.

DAVID A. CRAIN

ROJAS, MANUEL (1896–   ). Chilean novelist. Rojas, who was born in Argentina, was awarded the Chilean National Prize for Literature in 1957 for *Hijo de ladrón* (1951), his most outstanding novel, which describes the life of a child reaching adolescence in a hostile urban environment. This theme was continued in *Mejor que el vino* (1958) and *Sombras contra el muro* (1964). Among other works are *Hombres del sur* (1926) and *El bonete maulino* (1943), both collections of short stories; the novels *Lanchas en la bahía* (1932) and *Punta de rieles* (1962); and the critical volume *Antología autobiográfica* (1962).

RACHEL PHILLIPS

ROJAS, RICARDO (1882–1957). Historian and critic of Argentine literature. Born in the city of Tucumán, he was educated in Santiago del Estero. Both his parents belonged to families which had their roots in colonial Tucumán and which had contributed to the wars of independence. In 1899, a year after he graduated from the Colegio Nacional de Santiago del Estero, Rojas started his legal studies at the University of Buenos Aires, but he soon abandoned law for literature. By the time his first book of verses, *La victoria del hombre,* appeared in 1903, he was a member of the well-known group of aspiring writers who met at the café La Brasileña, the café Los Inmortales, or the offices of *El Sol* to discuss literature, philosophy, Marxism, socialism, and anarchism. One product of these meetings was Rojas's decision to study Argentine literature.

Obtaining a leave of absence from his position in the Ministry of Public Education, he went to Europe in 1908 to search for the colonial antecedents of Argentine literature in the archives and libraries of Madrid, Seville, and Paris and to examine the European educational systems. Upon his return in 1909, he joined the faculty of the University of La Plata as a professor of literature and thus laid the foundations of the future Facultad de Ciencias de la Educación y Humanidades. At the same time he published *La restauración nacionalista: Informe de educación* (1909). It was less a description of education in Europe than an attack on education in Argentina. What Rojas wanted was for Argentine youth, mostly the sons of immigrants, to learn less about Europe and more about Argentina so that they would come to know and love the country of their birth. To advance his plan for the development of Argentine nationalism, he tried for five years to obtain financial support for the publication of a cheap student edition of the Argentine classics. He realized his dream when the first issue of the *Biblioteca argentina* (18 vols., 1914–1928) was sold in 1914. In all he published twenty-nine titles in the series.

In 1912 Rojas was appointed to a newly created professorship in Argentine literature, the first of its kind, at the University of Buenos Aires. In the ensuing years he trained innumerable scholars in all aspects of the new discipline and collected data for his pioneer work, *Historia de la literatura argentina* (4 vols. in 8, 1917–1922). In 1922 Rojas founded the Instituto de Literatura Argentina in the University of Buenos Aires, of which he was then dean and later rector (1926–1930). The purposes of the institute were to prepare bibliographies, collect documents on folklore, popular music, the theater, and literature, and publish monographic studies. According to some critics, Rojas's best work in prose is *El santo de la espada,* 1933 (*San Martín, Knight of the Andes*), dealing with José de SAN MARTÍN, but others prefer *El profeta de la pampa* (1945), on Domingo Faustino SARMIENTO.

The contributions of Rojas to scholarship are so important that it is easy to overlook his political career. In 1916 he was a member of the Comité Nacional de la Juventud, which sympathized with the cause of the Allies. His insistent urgings that a new political party was needed helped prepare the way for the Guardia Cívica that appeared during the SEMANA TRÁGICA (Tragic Week) of 1919 and became the Liga Patriótica Argentina. After the overthrow of Hipólito YRIGOYEN in 1930, he clearly identified himself with the Unión Cívica Radical (*see* RADICAL PARTY: ARGENTINA), became the secretary of its National Committee, and rose to the position of a party leader. Gen. José Félix URIBURU twice imprisoned him on the island of Martín García, and mostly because of his opposition to the ROCA-RUNCIMAN TREATY and because of rumors that he was involved in a revolutionary plot, President Agustín P. JUSTO sent him to Ushuaia, Tierra del Fuego, in 1934. While he was in Ushuaia, he wrote *Archipiélago* (1942).

JOSEPH T. CRISCENTI

ROJAS PAÚL, JUAN PABLO (1829–1905). President of Venezuela (1888–1890). Rojas Paúl was a loyal follower of Antonio GUZMÁN BLANCO, but his Presidency was somewhat more open than that of his predecessor. Allowing freedom of the press and some freedom to demonstrate, he found it necessary to defend the monuments of the Guzmán Blanco era against hostile mobs. In spite of the initial opposition of his major rival, Joaquín CRESPO, Rojas Paúl managed to pacify the factions of the Liberal-Federalist party and pass the Presidency on to his chosen successor, Raimundo ANDUEZA PALACIO. After his presidential term Rojas Paúl enjoyed an active political career in the Venezuelan Congress.

JOHN V. LOMBARDI

ROJAS PINILLA, GUSTAVO (1900–   ). Colombian army officer and dictator. Born in Tunja, Rojas Pinilla was educated at the Colombian Military Academy, receiving his commission in 1920. After an extended period of inactive duty, he served in a variety of positions, culminating in 1950 with his appointment to command the nation's military forces. In June 1953, supported by the Liberals and moderate Conservatives (*see* CONSERVATIVE PARTY: COLOMBIA; LIBERAL PARTY: COLOMBIA), the military deposed the authoritarian Conservative president Laureano GÓMEZ and installed Rojas in power. Confirmed to a four-year term as President, he began to rule dictatorially and to repress the established political parties. He was unsuccessful, however, in his attempt to secure solid populist support. In a situation of economic decline, his arbitrariness and seeming ineptness led to a national strike and rioting. In May 1957, under pressure from the armed forces and political leaders, Rojas resigned, turning power over to a military junta, and subsequently the NATIONAL FRONT coalition was established.

When Rojas returned from voluntary exile in 1959, he was tried before the Senate and stripped of his civil rights. Nevertheless, he ran for the Presidency and received more than 50,000 votes (2.5 percent) in 1962, and five years later the Supreme Court reinstated his civil rights. In 1970 Rojas lost to Misael PASTRANA BORRERO by only about 60,000 of 4 million votes cast in the contested presidential election. Prospects of his running for the Presidency in 1974 were uncertain as his health was poor, but his political party, the ALIANZA NACIONAL POPULAR (ANAPO), had become a major force through the efforts of his daughter, Senator María Eugenia Rojas de Moreno Díaz.

GERALD THEISEN

ROLDÁN, AMADEO (1900–1939). Cuban composer and conductor. Born in Paris of Cuban parents, he studied in Spain, learning composition with Conrado del Campo and violin with Bordas. In 1916 he received the Sarasate Violin Prize. Settling in Havana in 1921, he became the concertmaster of the Philharmonic Orchestra in 1924, assistant conductor in 1925, and permanent conductor in 1932. In 1934 he was appointed director of the Havana Conservatory and professor of composition. His compositions involve a successful use of Afro-Cuban folk devices and also reveal the influence of postimpressionistic esthetics. Outstanding among his works are his six *Rítmicas* (1930) for different instrumental groups, his *Overture on Cuban Themes* (1925), and his *Motivos de son* (1934) for voice, piano, and orchestra.

JUAN A. ORREGO-SALAS

ROMERO, JOSÉ RUBÉN (1890–1952). Mexican writer. Born in Michoacán, Romero was one of the most original poets and novelists of contemporary Mexico. His novels deal mainly with the environment of provincial Mexico during and after the MEXICAN REVOLUTION, and the most noteworthy, *La vida inútil de Pito Pérez*, 1938 (*The Futile Life of Pito Pérez*), is a picaresque novel of our days. Romero played an active part in the revolution and later devoted himself to diplomacy and letters. His works include several volumes of poetry, including *Poesía: Fantasías* (1908), and the novels *Apuntes de un lugareño* (1932), *Mi caballo, mi perro y mi rifle* (1936), *Anticipación de la muerte* (1939), *Algunas cosillas de Pito Pérez que se me quedaron en el tintero* (1945), and *Rosenda* (1946).

RACHEL PHILLIPS

RONDON, CÂNDIDO [MARIANO DA SILVA] (1865–1958). Brazilian soldier largely responsible for exploring the interior of Mato Grosso, extending telegraph communications, and peacefully subduing the forest Indians. Born of mestizo and Indian parents in Cuiabá, Rondon entered the Army at the age of sixteen and graduated from the Military School in Rio de Janeiro in 1890. A disciple of Benjamin Constant Botelho de MAGALHÃES, he was deeply committed to the secular and religious aspects of Comtian positivism (*see* POSITIVISM: BRAZIL).

In 1890 he was commissioned to extend telegraph lines and explore the interior, and he assumed leadership of the project in 1892. The Rondon mission furthered the exploration and pacification of the interior and collected data on the geography, geology, linguistics, ethnography, botany, and zoology of western Brazil. In his contacts with the Indians Rondon respected their rights, dealt fairly with them, and earned their confidence. His rule, "Die if you must, but never kill," became the motto of the Indian Protective Service created under his direction in 1910. In 1913–1914 he guided Theodore Roosevelt on the search for the River of Doubt.

Rondon's inspection of Brazilian frontiers between 1927 and 1930 was interrupted by the REVOLUTION OF 1930. He represented Brazil on the International Leticia Commission from 1934 to 1938. He is perhaps best known in Brazil as a peaceful bearer of civilization to the interior. Among the many honors and awards he received the greatest was the renaming of the Guaporé Territory as Rondônia in 1956.

ROBIN L. ANDERSON

ROOSEVELT COROLLARY. Formulated by President Theodore Roosevelt in 1904, this "activist" interpretation of the MONROE DOCTRINE held that the United States might, under certain circumstances, exercise an "international police power" in the Western Hemisphere. Specifically, Roosevelt maintained that under the Monroe Doctrine the United States was duty-bound to intervene unilaterally in the affairs of Latin American nations when their domestic politics or finances were in such disorder as to invite intervention by nonhemisphere powers. This new interpretation of the Monroe Doctrine became the policy mandate for numerous interventions in the Caribbean area. Among the most noted of these were the forced fiscal supervision of the Dominican Republic (1905–1941), the military occupation of that country (1916–1924), the military occupation of Haiti (1915–1934), and the armed intervention in Nicaragua (1912–1925, 1927–1933).

The benefits to the United States from the Roosevelt Corollary were never very obvious, and the distrust and ill will generated in Latin America as a result of its implementation made it a positive burden. The corollary was publicly repudiated by the Hoover administration with the publication of the CLARK MEMORANDUM in 1930 and was finally renounced by the Franklin Delano Roosevelt administration at the MONTEVIDEO CONFERENCE in 1933, when it abandoned the right of unilateral intervention in the internal affairs of other American states.

RODNEY D. ANDERSON

ROSA, JOÃO GUIMARÃES (1908–1967). Brazilian writer of fiction, physician, and diplomat. Born in Minas Gerais, he took his medical degree in Belo Horizonte and practiced until 1934, when he entered the diplomatic service. During World War II he was interned in Germany, where he had been stationed. He achieved great success with his first volume, *Sagarana* (1946), a collection of nine regional tales, the novelty of which was in the language. The author showed his acquaintance with the most local elements of the dialect of the Campos Gerais, the plains in northeastern Minas, and the most minute details of its geography and life. Ten years later he brought out his collection of seven novellas, *Corpo de Baile,* and his masterpiece, the enormous novel *Grande Sertão: Veredas* (*The Devil to Pay in the Backlands*). This book, like *Sagarana,* deals with the Campos Gerais, and the literary adaptation of the dialect of that region, in which it is written, has attracted the attention of all critics. It belongs to the *ciclo do cangaço,* or novels about outlaws, but it is more than a mere book of adventures, concerning itself rather with universal questions about life and about man's relation to his fellows.

RAYMOND S. SAYERS

ROSARIO. Major Argentine port in the province of Santa Fe. Rosario began as a small settlement around a chapel toward the end of the seventeenth century or during the first two decades of the eighteenth. In the first half of the nineteenth century it was known as the small village, built on a cliff overlooking the Paraná River (*see* PARANÁ-PARAGUAY RIVER BASIN), where boats from Montevideo could exchange their cargoes for products from the interior provinces. Fire destroyed it in 1819, but its strategic location always attracted settlers.

The city began to stir after Justo José de URQUIZA opened its port in 1852 to ships arriving directly from overseas. Its population grew from 600 in 1850 to 1,500 or 2,000 in 1852, and its port was quickly filled with small boats, owned and manned by Italians, carrying freight to and from Buenos Aires, Montevideo, and other points along the river. The port had its own customhouse in 1854. The city then showed signs of becoming the financial and commercial capital of the ARGENTINE CONFEDERATION. In 1856 Congress enacted the differential tariff, which penalized ships for stopping at intermediate points before reaching a port of the Confederation, and foreign commercial houses ended their indecision and established agencies in Rosario. In 1858, when Barão (later Visconde) MAUÁ opened his bank there, the city had a population of 22,751, or more than half that of the province. On the eve of the PARAGUAYAN WAR it had a cathedral, two flour mills, three *saladeros,* and a large foreign community consisting mainly of Germans, French, and Italians. When the war ended, it was connected with Buenos Aires by telegraph and with Córdoba by rail, and it had several new banks but no wharves or docks for steamers and sailing vessels. Its citizens challenged the traditional leadership of the city of Santa Fe in 1867, and their initial success introduced a new element in provincial politics still evident today. Two efforts were made to have Rosario named the federal capital, and the newspaper *La Capital* was founded with the aid of Urquiza to generate widespread support for the cause, but the requisite federal laws were vetoed by the incumbent Presidents in 1868 and 1869.

By 1908 Rosario had developed a manufacturing industry to serve its agricultural hinterland and port facilities to handle the exports of eight provinces. Its population grew from 91,669 in 1895 to 223,000 in 1914, 400,000 in 1930, and 750,000 in 1960. As early as 1930 it was exporting 42 percent of the corn and 35 percent of the wheat and linseed produced in Argentina. Subsequently (especially in 1972) the federal government adopted laws designed to give the port a greater percentage of the national export-import trade.

JOSEPH T. CRISCENTI

ROSAS, JUAN MANUEL DE (1793–1877). Argentine dictator and Governor of Buenos Aires (1829–1832, 1835–1852). Rosas has never ceased to arouse controversy in Argentina. By some he is regarded as an early hero of Argentine nationalism. Others look upon him as an execrable tyrant, best forgotten. He is unforgettable. His unmistakable mark was stamped on three turbulent decades of Argentine history.

Rosas was born into a distinguished family of the creole aristocracy of Buenos Aires, and at a very early stage he acquired a deep affection for and a consummate mastery of *estancia* activities. In 1813 he married Encarnación de Ezcurra, a formidable woman who was to be of great help to him in his later career. Around this time he left his father's *estancia* to branch out on his own, forming a business association with Juan Nepomuceno Terrero and Luis Dorrego in 1815. (In the early 1820s they were joined by Rosas' cousins Juan José and Nicolás Anchorena.) Rosas and his partners quickly built up an extraordinarily flourishing set of enterprises and were especially prominent in the export of salted meat. By the 1820s they constituted one of the most powerful economic interests in the province of Buenos Aires.

In 1806–1807 Rosas had fought in the defense of Buenos Aires against the British, but he took no part in the wars of independence. During the chaos of the "terrible year" 1820, when the government of Buenos Aires changed hands twelve times between February and October, he organized a GAUCHO militia in defense of the city and province. Effective power in Argentina had now passed to the *caudillos* of the provinces, conservative and "federalist" in outlook. These resisted the influence of Buenos Aires and proved too strong for the Unitarios ("centralists"; *see* UNITARIO), the liberals who, under Bernardino RIVADAVIA's leadership, tried to unify and reform Argentina in the 1820s. Rivadavia's downfall in June 1827 brought Rosas into prominence as commander of the Buenos Aires provincial militias. Argentina was once again plunged into civil war, the centralist cause having been taken up by the armies returning from the recent war between Argentina and Brazil: one army, under Gen. Juan Lavalle, seized power in Buenos Aires, while a second, commanded by the brilliant general José María Paz, won control of the provinces of the interior. Rosas now emerged into full view as the champion of federalism in Buenos Aires. Joining forces with the most powerful federalist *caudillo* in the provinces, Estanislao López of Santa Fe, he obliged Lavalle to negotiate his way out of politics (August 1829). The next step was for the provincial legislature of Buenos Aires to elect Rosas

Juan Manuel de Rosas. [*Organization of American States*]

as Governor with extraordinary powers (December 1, 1829).

Rosas now controlled Buenos Aires, while his ally López dominated the river provinces. General Paz, however, consolidated his hold on the interior, inflicting a severe defeat on its strongest *caudillo,* Facundo Quiroga of La Rioja, at Oncativo in February 1830. Buenos Aires, Entre Ríos, and Santa Fe concluded the Federal Pact (Pact of the Littoral) in January 1831 in order to combat Paz's League of the Interior. Following Paz's accidental capture (May 1831), a remarkable stroke of luck for the federalists, the league collapsed; Quiroga destroyed centralist resistance in the north; and the federalist *caudillos* were now supreme. But Rosas' position was by no means wholly secure; his tight grip on power and his persecution of Unitarios aroused opposition in political circles in Buenos Aires, and in December 1832 he resigned the governorship. In order to reestablish his political authority he took command of a successful campaign against the marauding PAMPA Indians (April 1833), while in Buenos Aires his supporters, ably coordinated by Doña Encarnación de Rosas, prepared the ground for his return to power. The murder of Quiroga in February 1835 produced the necessary crisis. In April Rosas took over as Governor again, entrusted with "the totality of public power" by a grateful legislature.

Rosas' dictatorship now assumed its full shape. The liberal opposition was relentlessly persecuted; the Mazorca, a ruthless band of official thugs, brutally intimidated any dissidents; and at times of crisis a veritable reign of terror was introduced. Rosas also fostered a somewhat grotesque cult of his own personality, and the red sash or ribbon of federalism, with suitably embroidered slogans, became an obligatory sartorial appurtenance. The church was obliged to play a part in this: Rosas' picture was displayed on its altars, and its priestly vestments incorporated the federalist emblem. Rosas and his wife (who died in 1838) carefully courted the urban lower classes of Buenos Aires, although many of his measures were in fact designed to benefit the aristocracy of *estancieros* from which he came. Massive tracts of public land were sold off at ludicrous prices; Rosas' relatives, the Anchorenas, did particularly well. Despite his fervent professions of federalist faith, Rosas did much to bolster the privileged economic position of Buenos Aires, which barred the river provinces and the interior from direct trade with the outside world. His one experiment in economic nationalism, the protective tariff of 1835, was abandoned in 1841. Politically, Argentina remained unorganized. The provinces were loosely associated under the Federal Pact or concluded bilateral treaties with Buenos Aires; Rosas was entrusted with the conduct of foreign affairs but did not become President of Argentina, preferring his title as Governor of Buenos Aires. He torpedoed such efforts as were made to provide the country with a proper constitution.

For much of the time Rosas was under attack from his centralist enemies. Their revolts were all crushed. His policies also brought him into conflict with foreign powers. In 1838 France mounted a blockade of Buenos Aires that lasted 949 days. In 1843 Rosas lent support to the Uruguayan Blancos led by Manuel ORIBE (*see* BLANCO PARTY: URUGUAY), then in opposition, and besieged Montevideo. The siege was to last more than nine years. This action caused Great Britain and France to impose a blockade of Buenos Aires; they captured the island of Martín García and broke into the Paraná River to trade with the river provinces. But Rosas held firm. In 1847–1848 the blockade was lifted. This Argentine triumph over the great powers pleased Gen. José de SAN MARTÍN, who died in France in August 1850 and bequeathed his sword to Rosas.

In 1850 Rosas seemed to be at the zenith of his power, but his insistence on maintaining the economic privileges of Buenos Aires was provoking dissatisfaction, not least in the river provinces. In May 1851 the *caudillo* of Entre Ríos, Justo José de URQUIZA, Rosas' most faithful henchman, withdrew his allegiance, concluded an agreement with Uruguay and Brazil (which had long resented Rosas' interference in Uruguay), and marched to relieve the besieged city of Montevideo. Once installed there, he organized a Grand Army of 24,000 men, including powerful Brazilian and Uruguayan contingents. This invading force met Rosas' troops at Caseros on February 3, 1852, and defeated them. Rosas wrote out his resignation and went calmly into exile aboard a British warship. He arrived at Devonport, England, on April 23, 1852, and soon afterward settled on a farm outside Southampton. There, in the company of his daughter Manuelita, he spent the last twenty-four years of his life. Rosas was buried in Southampton. His admirers have made efforts to have his remains repatriated, so far without success. The supreme exponent of the gaucho virtues (and vices) does not lack apologists in the nationalist-minded twentieth century.

Bibliography. L. W. Bealer, "Juan Manuel de Rosas," in A. C. Wilgus (ed.), *South American Dictators during the First Century of Independence,* Washington, 1937; Carlos Ibarguren, *Juan Manuel de Rosas: Su vida, su drama,* Buenos Aires, 1930; Ernesto Quesada, *La época de Rosas,* Buenos Aires, 1898; Emilio Ravignani, *Rosas: Interpretación real y moderna,* Buenos Aires, 1970.   SIMON COLLIER

ROSE OF LIMA, ST. (1586–1617). Patron saint of Peru. The daughter of Gaspardo de Flores and María de Oliva, she was born into a large family of straitened circumstances. The child was baptized Isabella, but her beauty quickly earned her the sobriquet Rose, which eventually replaced her given name. At a very early age she determined never to marry but to dedicate herself to God. She does not seem to have given serious thought to the cloistered life, preferring to stay at home, where she could contribute to the support of the family by the sale of her embroidery and of the flowers she raised. Striving in many ways to imitate St. Catherine of Siena, she joined the Third Order of St. Dominic, donned the Dominican habit, and lived as a recluse. She seldom left the family home, but spent most of her time at work in her garden or at prayer in her hermitage. She also ministered in a small way to the material and health needs of impoverished ladies and fallen women.

The young recluse was much given to austerity, eating little, sleeping even less, and torturing her body cruelly, to the point of being reported to the Inquisition (*see* INQUISITION, HOLY OFFICE OF THE). A group of theologians interrogated her and concluded that her behavior was prompted by the Holy Spirit. Her fellow *limeños* were so fired with enthusiasm for her legendary beauty and saintliness that when she died her funeral occasioned a near riot, and her body had to be buried

secretly. She was officially declared blessed in 1668 and a saint in 1671.   NORMAN MEIKLEJOHN

ROSS [SANTA MARÍA], GUSTAVO (1879-   ). Chilean Minister of Finance (1932–1937). Born in Valparaíso and educated at the local high school, Ross went into business, for which he had a remarkable talent. He developed large financial interests in Chile and Europe, but in 1927 he was exiled by Carlos IBÁÑEZ and spent the next few years abroad, mostly in Paris. There he came to the attention of Arturo ALESSANDRI, and when, in 1932, Alessandri became President of Chile for the second time, he appointed Ross to the key post of Minister of Finance. Ross's only previous experience of public office had been as a local councillor in Valparaíso, and his Cabinet appointment was very unpopular because of his extremely conservative views. Nevertheless, his financial expertise played a major role in Chile's recovery from the disastrous impact of the Great Depression. Helped by the general recovery in world trade, Ross brought order to Chilean finances, encouraged industrial expansion by skillful monetary and trade policies, and completely reorganized the nitrate industry (*see* NITRATE INDUSTRY: CHILE).

Ross's performance in office, his extreme opposition to the left-wing parties, and Alessandri's own support made him the candidate of the right in the presidential election of 1938 against the Popular Front's nominee, Pedro AGUIRRE CERDA (*see* POPULAR FRONT: CHILE). Although Ross was supported by the Conservative and Liberal parties, which also controlled Congress (*see* CONSERVATIVE PARTY: CHILE; LIBERAL PARTY: CHILE), and was assisted by vote buying on a large scale, he was defeated, securing 218,609 votes to Aguirre Cerda's 222,700.   HAROLD BLAKEMORE

ROTO. Chilean term for a member of the urban lower class, especially in Santiago. The expression has been used since colonial times and in some respects is comparable to the term "cockney" applied to a Londoner. Its connotations are by no means invariably pejorative. The Chilean *roto* is renowned for his sense of humor, his instinctive ability when confronted by technical problems, and his superb qualities as a fighting man.   SIMON COLLIER

RUBBER BOOM (BRAZIL). The major rubber-producing area of Brazil lies in the states of Amazonas, Pará, and Mato Grosso and Acre Territory. Brazilian rubber production rose dramatically, particularly after 1890, sparked by a series of technological inventions, such as the development (1823) of a process of impregnating textiles with rubber to make them impermeable, the discovery (1843) of the vulcanization process, the invention (1890) of the pneumatic tire, and the rapid development of the automobile industry, which increased world demand for rubber. Production climbed steadily from an annual average of 460 tons in the 1840s to more than 34,500 tons annually during the 1901–1912 peak years, accounting for 88 percent of the world's rubber supply. As world demand increased, rubber prices experienced a similar upsurge, rising from £45 per ton to £640 per ton between 1840 and 1909. During the boom Brazil exported more than $70 million worth of the "white gold." Rubber exports played an insignificant role in the Brazilian economy prior to 1890, but in 1912 rubber accounted for 40 percent of the nation's exports, being second only to coffee.

The tremendous expansion of rubber production also attracted a steadily increasing stream of immigrants to the AMAZON RIVER region. The population of the Amazon territory, which was 337,000 in 1872, increased threefold by 1906. Recognizing the profitability of rubber, the Brazilian government endeavored to settle its long-standing Amazonian border disputes, particularly in the rubber-rich Acre region, claimed by both Bolivia and Brazil. By 1890 nearly 60,000 Brazilians had swarmed into the disputed territory. Bolivian efforts to regain control of Acre triggered Brazilian-backed local rebellions in 1899 and 1902. The hostilities were finally terminated on November 17, 1903, when the two countries signed the Treaty of Petrópolis, which gave Brazil dominion over 73,000 square miles of Acre (*see* PETRÓPOLIS, TREATY OF).

The boom collapsed suddenly in 1913 as the result of increasing competition from the Far East. A shortage of manpower, the nomadic nature of the rubber gatherers, and a lack of technological innovations and rational organization severely restricted Brazil's ability to compete with Far Eastern rubber producers, who had successfully developed a highly productive plantation system based on transplanted Brazilian rubber plants. Large-scale Far Eastern rubber shipments commenced in 1910, and within three years Oriental rubber exports had surpassed those of Brazil. By 1919 the Far East accounted for 90 percent of the world's rubber supply, while Brazil's share of the world market had dropped to less than 10 percent. PAUL A. VIAFORA

RUGENDAS, JOHANN MORITZ (1802–1858). Bavarian painter. Rugendas was the most prolific and wide-ranging of the early-nineteenth-century *costumbrista* (local-color) artists. The son of the director of the Augsburg Academy of Art in Bavaria, he was trained in that school and in Munich. At eighteen he joined the expedition of Baron Georg Heinrich Lansdorff to Brazil, but he shortly left the group to work independently. In 1823 he returned to Europe with a collection of depictions of the newly opened lands, 100 of which eventually appeared as lithographs in his *Voyage pittoresque au Brésil* (Paris, 1834). Rugendas became a friend of Alexander von HUMBOLDT, who encouraged his project of a great volume on the Latin American countries, which occupied the rest of his life but never came to fruition.

In the years 1831–1834 he was in Mexico, which still has a large collection of his sketches and small oils (National Museum of History). Expelled for his involvement in revolutionary activities, he sailed to Chile, where he remained for twelve years except for excursions to Argentina (1837–1838) and Peru and Bolivia (1842–1844). In 1845 he sailed around the Horn to Buenos Aires and Montevideo, then went on to Brazil, where he painted a portrait of PEDRO II. He returned to Europe in 1847. Although he failed to find support for the great publication he envisioned, he received the patronage of the Bavarian state. His dashing reportorial style found little favor, and his last years were filled with discouragement.

Rugendas gives us an excellent picture of life in the new Latin American nations in such works as *Plaza de Armas, Lima* (Lima, Taurino Museum). As a teacher he helped to reestablish art institutions after independence. TERENCE GRIEDER

RUIZ CORTINES, ADOLFO (1891–1973). President of Mexico (1952–1958). Born in the city of Veracruz, Ruiz Cortines had a long career in public administration, during which he was closely associated with Miguel ALEMÁN, President from 1946 to 1952. He was Manuel ÁVILA CAMACHO's campaign treasurer in 1940, served as First Undersecretary of the Ministry of the Interior (Gobernación) from 1940 to 1944 while Alemán was Minister, and was Governor of his native state from 1944 to 1948. In the last of these posts he adumbrated some of his best-known positions, such as the mystique of labor, "the harmonious relationship between private and public action," and, above all, administrative honesty. During Alemán's Presidency, Ruiz Cortines was Minister of the Interior.

Nominated for the Presidency by the PARTIDO REVO-LUCIONARIO INSTITUCIONAL, Ruiz Cortines won approximately three-quarters of the votes cast on election day, July 6, 1952, defeating three other candidates. During his administration, the Falcón Dam on the United States–Mexican border was inaugurated, women were granted the right to vote, the Seguro Agrícola Integral was created to provide crop insurance for farmers, and nonpolitical civic betterment juntas were established to supplement the activities of municipal councils. He defended the right of nations to self-determination while the subject of Communist penetration in Guatemala was being discussed at the CARACAS CONFERENCE of 1954. In contrast to the optimistic Alemán, Ruiz Cortines was a pessimist who pointed out the disproportion between the growth of Mexico's population and the country's means of subsistence. To remedy rural poverty he advocated internal colonization and a "march to the sea" along the tropical lowlands of Mexico's Gulf coast. Between February and September 1958 he severely repressed a strike of railroad workers, telegraphers, and teachers, claiming that he wished to preserve Mexico's political liberty, which was being jeopardized by the struggle between reaction and promises of "sudden and profound social changes, artificially copied." MOISÉS GONZÁLEZ NAVARRO

RULFO, JUAN (1918–   ). Mexican novelist. Rulfo was born in Jalisco. His family was ruined by the MEXICAN REVOLUTION, and the child was brought up in an orphanage. In 1933 he moved to Mexico City. Rulfo held various administrative posts in the Immigration Department (1935–1945), with the B. F. Goodrich Company (1947–1953), with the Papaloapan Commission, and, most recently, in the Indigenist Institute. Rulfo's literary reputation depends basically on two books: *El llano en llamas* (1953), a collection of short stories; and the novel *Pedro Páramo* (1955). Rulfo's works are rooted in his native province but transcend the particular with their universality and awareness of human suffering. His style is simple, although his novelistic technique in *Pedro Páramo* is complex and firmly within the modern experimental tradition. Here Rulfo uses a dreamlike framework to explore the inauthenticity of the past through the eponymous protagonist, who symbolizes the now-dead Mexico of the landowning cacique. Several of his shorter works were published in English as *The Burning Plain and Other Stories* (1967). RACHEL PHILLIPS

S

Saavedra Lamas, Carlos

Superintendência do Desenvolvimento do Nordeste

SAAVEDRA LAMAS, CARLOS (1878–1959). Argentine lawyer and statesman. Saavedra Lamas served as the Foreign Minister in the conservative regime of Agustín P. JUSTO from 1932 to 1938. During this period he was active in the cause of world peace; in 1933 he drew up an antiwar pact that was subsequently signed by thirteen Latin American nations, the United States, and Italy. As the presiding officer of the Chaco Peace Conference in 1935 he helped bring to an end the CHACO WAR between Bolivia and Paraguay. He also presided over the Assembly of the League of Nations in 1936. That year he was awarded the Nobel Peace Prize for his efforts over the years for world peace. In addition, he played a major role in the Inter-American Conference for the Maintenance of Peace, which met in Buenos Aires on December 1–23, 1936, to discuss collective security in the case of non-American aggression in the hemisphere. A vigorous spokesman for Argentine leadership in inter-American affairs, Saavedra Lamas often came into conflict with the United States and had an intense dislike for what he called "Monroeism," that is, what he considered the traditional United States policy of keeping Latin America in tutelage.

RODNEY D. ANDERSON

SÁBATO, ERNESTO (1911–). Argentine writer. Born in the province of Buenos Aires, Sábato first studied physics and visited Europe in 1935. After gaining his doctorate at the National University of La Plata, he continued his studies at the Curie Laboratory in Paris. An intellectual crisis brought him into contact with surrealism and made him decide to devote himself to literature. His first novel, *El túnel* (1948), is the amplification of a short story, and like *Sobre héroes y tumbas* (1961), it was immediately successful. These are dense existentialist novels in which the Argentine setting assumes universal and symbolic proportions. Sábato also has written an important book of criticism on the novel, *El escritor y sus fantasmas* (1963), and a more general essay, *Tango: Discusión y clave* (1963).

RACHEL PHILLIPS

SABOGAL, JOSÉ (1888–1956). Peruvian painter. The major figure in the Peruvian *indigenista* art movement of the 1930s, Sabogal was born in Cajabamba in northern Peru. In 1908 he traveled to Europe and North Africa, and beginning in 1912 he studied for three years in the National School of Fine Arts in Buenos Aires. He taught for a period in Jujuy, Argentina, and traveled extensively in Peru and Bolivia. In 1919 he exhibited in Lima paintings done in Cuzco, a region that especially interested him. From 1922 until 1943 he was a teacher and later director (1933–1943) of the National School of Fine Arts in Lima, a position that made him the most influential artist in the country. In 1922 he visited Mexico, where the mural movement was just getting under way. The nationalist, nativist, social-realist aims of that movement were accepted by Sabogal as his own. Indian figures and Andean landscapes were the subjects he stressed. An important group of followers, among them Julia Codesido (1892–), Camilo Blas (1903–), and Enrique Camino Brent (1909–1960), made the *indigenista* movement the most important painting style in Peru since independence.

As a painter Sabogal is overshadowed by his followers and by Jorge Vinatea Reinoso (1900–1931) of Arequipa, who was probably the best painter in the style. Sabogal's best paintings are his earlier works, such as *Elections in the Sierra,* and his woodcuts. He inspired a revaluation of native themes and of the folk arts that had lasting effects on Peruvian art and life.

TERENCE GRIEDER

SACASA, JUAN BAUTISTA (1874–1946). Nicaraguan Liberal party politician and President (1933–1936). Sacasa first rose to prominence in Nicaraguan politics as Vice President under Carlos Solórzano in 1926. When this government fell to a coup d'état led by the Conservative *caudillo* Emiliano CHAMORRO, Sacasa quickly became the rallying point of the Liberal party opposition. However, because of his Liberal party antecedents and his willingness to accept Mexican aid, the United States opposed him and maneuvered Adolfo DÍAZ into the Presidency in place of Chamorro. Again, in 1928, the United States opposed his presidential candidacy, but when a Liberal won, Sacasa became the Nicaraguan Minister in Washington. Finally, through elections closely supervised by the United States in 1932, Sacasa won a substantial victory over the opposing ticket of Díaz-Chamorro.

Sacasa took office early in 1933, when warfare between the guerrilla forces of Augusto César SANDINO and United States Marines was diminishing. Nevertheless, forces were at work in Nicaragua that prevented him from ever consolidating his power. These were the *sandinistas* and the National Guard, the latter a powerful police force trained by the United States and led by Anastasio SOMOZA GARCÍA. Sandino was in the process of negotiating the terms of peace with Sacasa when he was assassinated by members of the National Guard in February 1934. Sacasa's ineffective efforts to punish the assassins revealed that the National Guard rather than the Presidency was the true power nucleus in Nicaragua. Finally, in 1936, Somoza ousted Sacasa by coup d'état, and Sacasa went into exile in the United States.

CHARLES L. STANSIFER

SAENZ (SÁENZ) PEÑA, ROQUE (1851–1914). Argentine President (1910–1914) who secured the passage of the law bearing his name providing for the compulsory vote and the secret ballot. His parents, Luis Saenz Peña and Cipriana Lahitte, belonged to old aristocratic families in the city of Buenos Aires. The younger Saenz Peña began his legal studies at the University of Buenos Aires in 1871, and although he put his books aside to defend the national government during the revolution of 1874, he received his law degree in 1875. A year later he was elected deputy to the provincial legislature on the ticket of the Partido Autonomista Nacional. In 1879 he fought in the armed forces of Peru and Bolivia in their war with Chile (*see* WAR OF THE PACIFIC). He was named Undersecretary of the Ministry of Foreign Relations in 1881 and served briefly as Minister in 1890. As a member of the Argentine delegation, he attended the South American Congress of International Private Law (1888), the First International Conference of American States (1889–1890), and the Second Hague Conference (1907).

In 1891 he was the candidate of the Modernistas for President. As they had anticipated, he withdrew from the presidential race when ex-Presidents Julio A. ROCA and Bartolomé MITRE advanced the candidacy of his father, but he retained his seat in the national Senate, where he represented his native province, until political differences with his father, then the President, led him to resign in December 1892. He retired to the Estancia Ibicuy in Entre Ríos. After his return to the federal capital in 1895, he received a number of diplomatic assignments, but there was time for politics and public lectures. By 1903 his attacks on authoritarianism and personalism, his advocacy of free suffrage and majority rule, convinced many that he could spearhead the assault on the existing corrupt system of political control. Two groups of reformers, the Partido Republicano of Emilio Mitre and Carlos PELLEGRINI's faction in the Partido Autonomista Nacional, successfully combined their forces in 1906 and 1908 to elect Saenz Peña to Congress as a deputy for the federal capital. In 1909 he agreed to become a candidate for President. His party, the Unión Nacional, was a coalition of all the provincial parties, some forced to join by the federal government, and of independent groups. Official coercion and personal popularity explain the election results and the absence of any dissenting electoral vote.

Saenz Peña returned from Italy, where he was the Argentine Ambassador, to take office on October 12, 1910. His electoral reform measure, written with the apathetic voter in mind, became law on February 13, 1912. It contained three parts: (1) the Minister of War was to prepare voting registers on the basis of the military enlistment records; (2) officials selected by the judicial branch of the government were to organize and conduct the elections; and (3) voting was to be secret and compulsory for all males over the age of eighteen, and one-third of the deputies elected were to represent minority groups. In foreign affairs Saenz Peña successfully conciliated Argentina's neighbors and averted a possible naval armaments race with Brazil. At home he was unable to solve the problems of permanent unemployment and low wages or to reduce significantly the number of strikes. He died in office.

JOSEPH T. CRISCENTI

SAHAGÚN, BERNARDINO DE [RIBEIRA] (1500?– 1590). Spanish missionary and ethnographer. Born in Sahagún, León, he professed as a Franciscan in 1524 and arrived in New Spain in 1529. In 1536 he was a teacher at the College of Santiago Tlaltelolco, where Spanish missionaries instructed their Indian disciples in all the branches of classical knowledge. It was probably at the request of Toribio de BENAVENTE that Sahagún started the methodical gathering of data for the writing of a book on Aztec culture (*see* AZTECS). This work was started in the late 1540s, and Sahagún devoted to it the following three decades of his life. He gathered his information from the elders of Indian towns orally or through paintings. A team of Indian Latinists collected the data and put it into NAHUATL and Latin. Sahagún then revised the information and organized it. It was not until the late 1560s that Sahagún decided to translate into Spanish the material gathered in Nahuatl.

The most complete version of Sahagún's work is known as the Florentine Codex, or *Historia general de las cosas de Nueva España* (*General History of the Things of New Spain*), written in Spanish and Nahuatl and profusely illustrated. There is also a preliminary version known as the *Primeros memoriales*. Although the work of translation into Spanish found some opposition among Sahagún's Franciscan superiors in the early 1570s, it was almost finished by 1577. That year a royal decree ordered the confiscation of the work, which remained largely unknown until the eighteenth century and was first printed in 1829–1830. The Florentine Codex is divided into twelve books, which cover the ecological setting of Aztec civilization, its religious and philosophical ideas, and its social organization until the conquest of Mexico. Sahagún wished to vindicate Aztec culture, and his work not only achieved that purpose but remains the most notable source of information about the Aztecs.

ASUNCIÓN LAVRIN

SALGADO, PLÍNIO. *See* INTEGRALISMO.

SALLES, MANOEL CAMPOS. *See* CAMPOS SALLES, Manoel.

SALVADOR. Capital of the state of Bahia, Brazil. Salvador is Brazil's fifth largest city, with a population of 1,007,744 according to the census of 1970. The city is known variously as São Salvador; Bahia, the popular name; and Salvador, the current official designation. Salvador was founded in 1549 and served as the capital of the colony until 1763. One of Brazil's oldest cities and a former center of sugar cultivation and the African slave trade, it is the most "African" of major Brazilian cities. A leading tourist attraction, it preserves in its architecture and urban structure much of the flavor of its colonial past.

Salvador is located on a peninsula and faces west into All Saints Bay. The natural features of the peninsula—narrow coastal strip, abrupt escarpment, and plateau—have led to the distinctive division of the city into upper (*cidade alta*) and lower (*cidade baixa*) levels. These are connected by inclined planes and elevators, including the Elevador Lacerda, which provides the major link between the separate public transportation systems of the upper and lower cities. In the lower city the activities of the port, which is one of the busiest in Brazil, determine the predominance of export firms, commercial houses, and the wholesale trade. The major exports are agricultural, with industry geared primarily to food- and crop-processing operations. The upper city contains most of the retail trade and administrative and business offices, as well as the principal residential areas (*bairros*), which as in most Brazilian cities proceed from the richest, in the south, to the poorest, in the north.

FREDERICK V. GIFUN

SAMBA. Originally a generic term designating, along with *batuque,* the choreography of certain round dances imported from Angola and the Congo. A characteristic element of the folk samba and of all Afro-Brazilian dances is the *umbigada,* a sort of "invitation to the dance" manifested by the touching of the couple's navels. It appears, therefore, as a diagnostic trait defining the origin of a dance. Singing always accompanies the dancing. Mostly in binary rhythm, the samba presents a highly syncopated accompaniment. The dance had been urbanized by the late nineteenth century. The twentieth-century rural samba is defined by its choreography rather than by its musical structure and is substantially different from the urbanized version. Mário

de ANDRADE showed that the texts are simpler than those of the urban forms, being rather short and using systematically the traditional seven-syllable verse of the Portuguese language. The melodic line in the rural samba presents a descending character, a probable West African retention. In time the melody acquired the syncopated rhythm that at first pertained to the accompaniment alone.

A particularly important feature of the samba is the responsorial singing that has influenced the structure of the urban samba, that is, alternating stanzas and refrain. Even today this practice is very common in carnival sambas, the stanza being sung by a soloist and the refrain by a chorus. A special kind of urban samba called *samba de morro* and sometimes *batucada* has been cultivated among the people inhabiting the hillside slums of Rio de Janeiro (*see* FAVELA). Its accompaniment is performed exclusively by percussion instruments.

In the 1930s and 1940s the classic urban samba acquired the character of a ballroom type of sung dance, with the backing of a fairly colorful orchestra whose percussion section was considerably reduced in comparison with the concurrent carnival samba. Typically, ballroom samba lyrics dealt with love and unhappiness, often melodramatically. Among the most important composers of urban sambas are José Barbosa da Silva, known as Sinhô; Noel Rosa; Ari Barroso, the author of *Aquarela do Brasil;* and Dorival Caymmi.

The urban samba remained basically unchanged until the advent of *bossa nova.* The first major album of *bossa nova* was João Gilberto's *Chega de Saudade,* released in March 1959. At that time the composer Antônio Carlos Jobim appeared as one of the major innovators. The innovations involved above all the attempt to integrate melody, harmony, and rhythm. The singing style was marked by a subdued tone with a characteristic nasal production. *Bossa nova* sambas such as "Garôta de Ipanema," "Desafinado," and "Samba de uma Nota Só" became internationally famous in the 1960s.

GERARD H. BÉHAGUE

SÁNCHEZ, FLORENCIO (1875–1910). Uruguayan dramatist. Sánchez was born in Montevideo and died in Milan. Renowned as a playwright, he was also a journalist and worked for newspapers in Uruguay and Argentina. He began writing in Minas at the age of fifteen. Later he moved to Buenos Aires, where he worked for the government. He also contributed to *El Siglo* and *La Razón* of Montevideo, *El País* and *El Sol* of Buenos Aires, and *La República* of Rosario, Argentina.

Although Sánchez began his dramatic work with a piece for the Centro Internacional de Estudios Sociales in Montevideo before 1900, his best work was done after 1902. This period began with the presentation of *M'hijo el dotor,* 1903 (*My Son the Lawyer*), a three-act play, and ended with the two-act *Un buen negocio* (1909). In the interim he produced sixteen other plays. Among the outstanding works in this group are *La gringa,* 1904 (*The Immigrant Girl*), in four acts; *Barranca abajo,* 1905 (*Down the Gully*), in three acts; and *La tigra,* 1907 (*The Tigress*), three tableaux. In all his works he portrays man struggling against poverty, vice, disease, and injustice.

GERARDO SÁENZ

SÁNCHEZ, LUIS ALBERTO (1900–   ). Peruvian man of letters. Sánchez, a middle-class *limeño,* was a major political and literary force in Peru for forty years. He belonged to the generation of the *centenario* (centenary of independence), which rose in the halls of the University of San Marcos in the early 1920s. Its members, influenced by the Mexican and Russian revolutions and by the social unrest caused by World War I, demonstrated a preoccupation with social and political inequality. This concern led many of them to participate directly and at times militantly in Peruvian politics. The ALIANZA POPULAR REVOLUCIONARIA AMERICANA (APRA), founded in 1924, was one of the results of this participation, and Sánchez, a lawyer, professor, and writer, became one of its major spokesmen. He was a member of the party's National Committee for a combined total of more than twenty years and was one of its representatives in Congress a number of times (1931–1936, 1945–1948, 1963–1968). He served as Ambassador to Colombia and Mexico and twice (1946–1948, 1961–1964) as rector of San Marcos. However, during APRA's long years of illegality and persecution he repeatedly suffered exile.

Along with his political activities, Sánchez served on the faculty of a number of universities in North and South America and proved to be a prolific author. Many of his writings could be described as high-level Aprista propaganda, but many others demonstrate his abilities as a literary critic and historian. Among his major works are *La literatura peruana* (6 vols., 1950) and *Historia general de América* (2 vols., 6th ed., 1956), which outlines the Aprista conception of the history of the New World.

ORAZIO A. CICCARELLI

SÁNCHEZ CERRO, LUIS M[ANUEL] (1889–1933). President of Peru (1930–1931, 1931–1933). The dark-skinned, delicately built Sánchez Cerro was born in Piura. He graduated from the Escuela Militar de Chorrillos in 1910 and spent most of the rest of his life as a conspirator, specializing in clandestine meetings and the planning of coups, an experience that proved invaluable during his own presidential administrations.

A temperamental man of quickly changing moods, Sánchez Cerro was highly ambitious and self-confident, qualities that fed his rather simplistic economic and political views. His education was limited, and his speech full of popular expressions. He was highly superstitious, and his tastes and behavior reflected his lower-middle-class mestizo background. Nevertheless, these qualities, together with his leadership of the military-civilian junta that in August 1930 ended the eleven-year dictatorship of Augusto LEGUÍA, contributed to his rise as a popular *caudillo.* Even the failure of his first regime (August 1930–March 1931) did not diminish his considerable mass appeal. Thus, in the 1931 presidential election he won a resounding victory against another popular *caudillo,* Víctor Raúl HAYA DE LA TORRE, head of the ALIANZA POPULAR REVOLUCIONARIA AMERICANA (APRA).

In the following seventeen months (December 1931–April 1933), Sánchez Cerro sacrificed his populist program and the better interests of Peru in an attempt to destroy APRA, which he considered the greatest single threat to Peruvian nationality. The result was one of the most violent periods in Peruvian history, culminating in Sánchez Cerro's own assassination by an Aprista in April 1933.

ORAZIO A. CICCARELLI

SÁNCHEZ HERNÁNDEZ, FIDEL (1918–   ). Salvadoran army officer and President (1967–1972). His administration continued government by the coalition of the reformist military and economic elite that had been in power since 1950.

The slow pace of reform under Sánchez Hernández caused widespread dissatisfaction. Within its first year the administration faced a general strike and a teachers' strike. Its major reform measure was a minimum wage law for urban and rural labor that set standards considered high for Central America. The President's National Conciliation party (PCN) appeared to be losing its monopoly control. The Christian Democratic party gained four congressional seats in the elections of March 1968 and won 151 of 261 municipal governments, including half of the largest cities, among them the capital. Christian Democratic deputies also gained some PCN deputies' support to oust the administration's congressional Executive Committee, which they charged with manipulation to restrict debate.

The major event of the administration was the FOOTBALL WAR with Honduras. Tensions increased until diplomatic relations were broken on June 26, 1969; then military operations began. Inflamed nationalism brought the regime instant popularity, but the country could ill afford the staggering cost of the war and of care for the repatriated population as well as the economic contraction resulting from the disruption of the CENTRAL AMERICAN COMMON MARKET.

The PCN maintained strength to win the February 1972 presidential elections. Col. Arturo Armando MOLINA won a plurality of votes over two other candidates, and Congress then elected him President. A revolt against Sánchez Hernández by the unsuccessful candidates failed to attract popular support, and Molina took office in July 1972.

WILLIAM J. GRIFFITH

SÁNCHEZ VILELLA, ROBERTO (1913–   ). Governor of Puerto Rico (1965–1969). Born in Ponce, Sánchez Vilella studied engineering at Ohio State University, from which he graduated in 1934. He had accepted a job with the Tennessee Valley Authority, but in Washington he met Luis MUÑOZ MARÍN, who convinced him to return to Puerto Rico. When Muñoz Marín founded the Popular Democratic party (PDP) in 1938, Sánchez became a close collaborator. With the PDP in power after 1940 he occupied a succession of political and administrative jobs. He was Vice Commissioner of the Interior (1941–1942), administrator of the city of San Juan (1946–1947), Executive Secretary of Puerto Rico (1949–1951), and Secretary of Public Works (1951–1959). From 1952 to 1964 he also served as Secretary of State.

Sánchez was nominated as the PDP gubernatorial candidate in 1964. The party won an impressive victory at the polls, and Sánchez interpreted the election as a mandate for change, for "new faces, new ideas." This "new style" antagonized members of the party's old guard, and soon he began to experience difficulties with some PDP leaders. His troubles deepened when he divorced his wife and married a young assistant, Jeannette Ramos. After his remarriage Sánchez, who had announced that he would retire at the end of his term in office, gave signs of increased political activity. Later he decided to seek renomination. After he lost his bid for renomination, he left the PDP and ran on the ticket of the People's party (PP), originally a pro-statehood party whose founders had transferred control and leadership to the Governor in a notarized document. The PP gained 10 percent of the vote, and there is little doubt that Sánchez's attacks on the PDP were a significant factor in the latter's defeat.

In the 1972 elections Sánchez ran for a seat as representative-at-large. While the PP received only 2,910 votes, Sánchez polled more than 57,000 votes as a result of ticket splitting; this is a remarkable number in Puerto Rico, where voting a straight ticket is the rule. Nonetheless, since the PP failed to maintain its registration as a party, Sánchez was unable to gain a seat in the Legislature. The matter was appealed to the courts.

LUIS E. AGRAIT

SANDINO, AUGUSTO CÉSAR (1893-1934). Nicaraguan guerrilla leader. Sandino's reputation in Latin America as a patriot and defender of Latin American independence against foreign intervention rests on his stubborn resistance to the occupation of Nicaragua by United States Marines. When the United States special emissary Henry L. Stimson negotiated an end to the Nicaraguan civil war of 1926–1927, Sandino alone among the Liberal leaders refused to lay down his arms. He vowed never to do so until foreign troops left Nicaraguan soil. His recalcitrance was based on a sense of nationalism rather than on any clear-cut political outlook, although as a worker in the Mexican oil fields in the years 1923–1926 he had become well acquainted with radical, anticapitalist views. To Washington officials who had dispatched a small peace-keeping force to Nicaragua in 1926, Sandino's resistance branded him as an irresponsible bandit and necessitated stern measures to force him to yield. More Marines arrived. In company with the Nicaraguan National Guard, which was being prepared at that time for just this purpose of pacification, they sought to crush Sandino and his small band. After suffering heavy losses in several pitched battles, Sandino retreated into the mountains of Nueva Segovia in the remote border area near Honduras and adopted guerrilla tactics.

Fighting grew more bitter as Sandino's successful resistance to superior forces and more sophisticated weaponry became a source of embarrassment to the Marines· and as the continuing pressure on Sandino forced him into acts of violence against ranchers and miners in order to maintain his band. By 1931 Nicaragua was engulfed in another civil war, and 5,000 Marines were in the country trying through air power and heavy patrols to clear the countryside of *sandinistas*. Sandino still refused to buckle. Moral support came to him from all over Latin America, and he acquired arms and ammunition by raiding enemy columns in traditional guerrilla fashion. In Nueva Segovia the rugged terrain and the loyalty of the local people protected him from Marine incursions. The expense of maintaining so many troops abroad and acute embarrassment over the failure to eliminate Sandino caused general disillusionment in Washington. Finally, in January 1933, the Marines were

withdrawn under orders of President Herbert Hoover, and the pacification of Sandino was left to the Nicaraguan National Guard. With Anastasio SOMOZA GARCÍA in command of the Guard, the Nicaraguan government prepared to put an end to the Sandino campaign.

Sandino now became a key figure in the struggle between rival political factions in Nicaragua. A national hero to many Nicaraguans, he was just an obstacle to the consolidation of power by the Juan Bautista SACASA administration, which had come to office following the elections of 1932. To Somoza of the National Guard, Sandino was a constant menace to the stability of the country. Sacasa preferred to negotiate with Sandino, but Somoza wanted to crush the guerrilla leader by force. Now that the Marines were gone, Sandino was prepared to negotiate, but he did not propose to put himself and his men at the mercy of the National Guard. Sandino insisted on a kind of special autonomy for an agricultural colony he wished to establish in his Nueva Segovia bastion and a private guard of approximately 100 men to protect it. Sacasa accepted these terms, but Somoza and the National Guard were known to be vehemently opposed to them, especially after Sandino also insisted on additional arms. Negotiations were still proceeding on these matters when, in February 1934, members of the National Guard captured and executed Sandino and several of his aides shortly after they had concluded a negotiating session at the Presidential Palace.

Although Sandino's elimination by assassination proved to be an immediate stepping-stone for Somoza's rise to the Presidency of Nicaragua, in the long run Sandino's martyrdom in Latin America was assured by his cruel death. Latin Americans who disapproved of Sandino's methods while he was alive could forget them and elevate him to hero status after his death. Also, Sandino's failure to offer any clear-cut political program during his long years in the mountains did not hinder Latin Americans of all political persuasions from admiring his tenacity in resisting external intervention.

Bibliography. Gustavo Alemán Bolaños, *Sandino, el libertador: La epopeya, la paz, el invasor, la muerte,* Mexico City, 1952; Joseph O. Baylen, "Sandino: Patriot or Bandit?" *Hispanic American Historical Review,* vol. XXXI, no. 3, August 1951, pp. 394–419; Carleton Beals, *Banana Gold,* Philadelphia, 1932; Ramón de Belausteguigoitia, *Con Sandino en Nicaragua: La hora de la paz,* Madrid, 1934; Lejeune Cummins, *Quijote on a Burro: Sandino and the Marines, a Study in the Formulation of Foreign Policy,* Mexico City, 1958; Neill Macaulay, *The Sandino Affair,* Chicago, 1967; Gregorio Selser, *Sandino, general de hombres libres,* Buenos Aires, 1959; Anastasio Somoza, *El verdadero Sandino, o El calvario de las Segovias,* Managua, 1936.

CHARLES L. STANSIFER

SAN ILDEFONSO, TREATY OF (1777). Accord between Spain and Portugal settling hostilities in South America and drawing boundaries in the so-called debatable lands. Armed clashes had resumed between the two Iberian powers in South America during the 1770s, the Portuguese retaking the parts of Rio Grande do Sul lost to Spain in 1762. In retaliation CHARLES III sent the largest expeditionary force ever assembled in Spain for American service. Under the command of

Don Pedro de Cevallos the Spaniards met with rapid success, taking Santa Catarina without a casualty in 1776. Colônia do Sacramento capitulated in 1777, and Cevallos razed the Portuguese outpost to the ground, ending the existence of a long-time irritant to Spanish territorial claims in the New World. Cevallos was about to move on Rio Grande when word arrived from Europe of a new settlement, made possible by changes in both the Portuguese and the Spanish administrations. The retirement of the Marqués de Grimaldi, the Spanish Foreign Minister, and the fall from power of the Marquês de POMBAL had opened the road to compromise. By the Treaty of San Ildefonso, Spain returned Santa Catarina and recognized essentially the same boundaries as had been envisioned by the Treaty of Madrid (1750; *see* MADRID, TREATY OF), with the exception of the loss by Portugal of the territory of the seven missions of Uruguay. Portugal ceded Colônia and its claim to a frontier on the RÍO DE LA PLATA.

KENNETH R. MAXWELL

SAN JOSÉ. Capital of Costa Rica. San José is the largest and most important city in the country. Located on the Central Plateau at an altitude of 3,870 feet, it enjoys a year-round temperate climate. Midway between the oceans, it is far enough west to avoid the torrential rains of the Atlantic zone and far enough east to avoid the periodic droughts characteristic of the Pacific zone. Since the other three cities of the Central Plateau (Cartago, Alajuela, and Heredia) share these conditions, the explanation for San José's preeminence must be sought in its history.

In 1738 a small church was constructed on the site of San José, and church authorities began a campaign to urge the farmers of the surrounding area to move nearby. Because San José's central location was well suited to the churchmen's purpose and because Cartago, the colonial capital, was stagnant, the policy gradually worked. Still, in 1751 San José was reported to have only eleven houses. Liberalization of Spanish trade policies in the second half of the eighteenth century stimulated commercial activity, especially in sugar and tobacco, and increased San José's importance. San José's economic future was assured with the development of coffee as a cash crop in the early nineteenth century because the city was in the heart of the region's best coffee lands. When the opportunity of independence came in 1821, *josefinos* assured their city's political future by being first to declare themselves free of Spanish control and first to oppose union with Mexico. The reward for this early display of Costa Rican patriotism was the conferring of the title capital on San José by Costa Rica's first congress. At that time the city had approximately 3,000 inhabitants. After a brief interlude, when Costa Ricans experimented with the idea of rotating the capital among the four principal cities of the Central Plateau, San José became the permanent capital in 1834.

Throughout the nineteenth century growth occurred slowly because of Costa Rica's isolation, lack of strategic significance, and poor transportation facilities. By 1910, with railroads linking the capital to ports on both coasts, San José's population had reached only approximately 30,000. By 1950 the population was 180,000, or 21.2 percent of the total population of the country, and the city was taking on the characteristics of a typical Latin American metropolis. The most rapid growth occurred in the two decades following 1950: by 1970 San José had a population of 440,000, or 24.5 percent of the country's population.

CHARLES L. STANSIFER

SAN JOSÉ MEETINGS (1960). Sixth and Seventh Meetings of Consultation of Ministers of Foreign Affairs of the republics of the ORGANIZATION OF AMERICAN STATES, held in August 1960 in San José, Costa Rica. At the Sixth Meeting sanctions were imposed on the Dominican Republic upon the presentation of evidence that Rafael Leonidas TRUJILLO MOLINA, long-time dictator of that nation, was behind an attempted assassination of Rómulo BETANCOURT, reformist President of Venezuela. Called under the auspices of the Inter-American Treaty of Reciprocal Assistance (RIO TREATY), the meeting condemned the Dominican Republic for its violation of the nonintervention clause of the treaty and agreed that member nations should immediately sever diplomatic relations with that country as well as partially suspend economic relations, including all trade in arms.

Immediately upon the conclusion of the Sixth Meeting, the Seventh Meeting was convened in San José to consider the problem of Communist encroachment in Cuba. U.S. Secretary of State Christian Herter had supported the sanctions against the Dominican Republic in the hope of winning support for some form of collective action against Cuba. Instead, the Latin American delegates opposed such action. Herter finally agreed to a resolution condemning the intervention by any extracontinental power in the affairs of Latin American nations, specifically mentioning the Sino-Soviet bloc but not mentioning Cuba by name. The resolution reaffirmed the principle of nonintervention by any American state in the affairs of another American state.

RODNEY D. ANDERSON

SAN JUAN DE PUERTO RICO. Capital of Puerto Rico. The second oldest capital in the Western Hemisphere, San Juan was founded in 1521. That year Caparra, the island's first permanent settlement, founded by Juan PONCE DE LEÓN, was moved from several leagues inland to an islet in the nearby bay. At first the new town was called Puerto Rico, and the island was called San Juan, but the names were subsequently inverted.

The new town did not grow rapidly. It had 320 inhabitants at its foundation and added only 180 in its first fourteen years. By the beginning of the seventeenth century the population had grown to 1,600. Demographic sources show a fluctuating population pattern during the rest of that century, but by the end of the eighteenth century the population was on an evident upswing. In 1783 the population was 6,462, and by 1860 it had grown to 18,259. An 1899 census taken immediately after the change of sovereignty showed that the population of San Juan stood at 32,048. Population growth in the twentieth century has been explosive. During the second decade San Juan surpassed the 50,000 mark. The 1970 census put the population of the city proper (excluding other municipalities of the metropolitan area) at 463,000.

San Juan has historically exerted an attraction for unwanted visitors. The town was first invaded by CARIB

Indians in 1529. Sir Francis DRAKE attacked it in 1595 but was repelled. In 1598 an Englishman, George de Clifford, 3d Earl of Cumberland, landed his troops six leagues east of the city and took it in a land attack. He held San Juan for three months before being forced to leave because tropical diseases were decimating his troops. A Dutch commander, Boudewijn Hendrikszoon, was able to capture the city in 1625 but could not force the troops garrisoned at the fortress of El Morro to surrender. Before leaving, he took time to burn the city. In 1797 Sir Ralph Abercromby made another unsuccessful attempt to take San Juan.

Such foreign interest in San Juan persuaded the Spaniards to fortify the city. The defense works were begun in 1533 with the construction of La Fortaleza, now the Governor's office and residence, and were finished in the nineteenth century. In 1539 the construction of El Morro, at the very entrance of the bay, was begun. With the construction of walls in the seventeenth century and of the fort of San Cristóbal, designed to afford protection from an attack by land, the old city became a completely walled enclave. At the beginning of the twentieth century the walls facing land were demolished to make room for further urban growth, but the remaining walls and forts offer some of the best examples of Spanish military architecture to be found anywhere in the Americas.

LUIS E. AGRAIT

SAN LUIS POTOSÍ, PLAN OF. Revolutionary program issued in November 1910 by Francisco I. MADERO in which he called for the overthrow of President Porfirio DÍAZ of Mexico. Madero drew up the plan after he had lost all hope that Díaz would permit a free choice for the Vice Presidency for the forthcoming six-year term and thereby build a bridge between the present dictatorship and a future democracy. He discussed the draft of the plan in October with Federico González Garza, Roque Estrada, Juan Sánchez Azcona, and Enrique Bordes. The plan was published in San Antonio, Texas, whither Madero had fled after escaping from prison in San Luis Potosí, but to prevent international complications it was dated October 5, 1910, the last day he had been in the Mexican city.

In the plan Madero declared that the recent presidential, judicial, and congressional elections were null and void and designated November 20, 1910, as the starting date of the revolution. Although he disavowed the Díaz regime, he offered to recognize obligations contracted by the government before November 20. Denouncing the fact that many small landowners, mainly Indians, had been despoiled of their lands by abuse of the surveying laws, he offered to restore such lands to the original owners and to pay them an indemnity. Finally, Madero declared that, in addition to the constitution and other existing legislation, the principle of no reelection of the President, Vice President, state governors, and municipal presidents would be the supreme law of the land.

MOISÉS GONZÁLEZ NAVARRO

SAN MARTÍN, JOSÉ DE (1778–1850). Argentine general and leader of the independence movement. The principal figure of the independence struggle in southern South America, José de San Martín, was born on February 25, 1778, at Yapeyú in what is now north-eastern Argentina. The son of a Spanish military officer, he left America at the age of eight when his father returned to Spain. There he trained for a military career, and from 1808 to 1811 he served with distinction as a Spanish army officer against the forces of Napoleon.

Though he loyally supported the mother country against France, San Martín did not favor either the traditional absolute monarchy or the existing colonial system. He was already an adherent of constitutional liberalism, and at some point he had further become associated with a lodge founded in Cádiz by other American creoles to work for the cause of Spanish American autonomy. In 1811 he resigned from Spanish service ostensibly to go to Peru, the main bulwark of loyalism in South America. However, after a brief stay in London, where he was again in touch with disaffected Spanish Americans, he sailed for Buenos Aires, arriving in March 1812. He was almost immediately taken into the service of the revolutionary regime established there two years before, and as an experienced professional soldier he was a valuable acquisition.

On a personal level, the long-absent San Martín strengthened his ties with the land of his birth by his marriage in September 1812 to María de los Remedios Escalada, of an upper-class Buenos Aires family. (Four years later she bore him a daughter, Mercedes.) Moreover, he promptly became involved in the internal politics of the area by helping to found the LAUTARO LODGE, a secret organization that aimed to give more forceful leadership to the patriot cause and aligned itself with the opposition to the government then in power: the

José de San Martín. [Radio Times Hulton Picture Library]

so-called First Triumvirate, dominated by Bernardino RIVADAVIA. From the standpoint of San Martín and the *lautarianos,* Rivadavia was more deeply concerned with local Buenos Aires interests than with the broader design of Spanish American liberation, and in a bloodless coup of October 1812 they succeeded in deposing the Rivadavian faction.

San Martín's first important military contribution had been to organize a crack corps of mounted grenadiers within the patriot armed forces. On February 3, 1813, he fought and won his first actual engagement on American soil by defeating a royalist force that came up the Paraná River and attempted a landing at San Lorenzo, just above Rosario. The main theater of war, however, was at this stage in Upper Peru (modern Bolivia) and northwestern Argentina, where the struggle in the latter part of 1813 was not going well. Accordingly, the government at Buenos Aires dispatched San Martín to stabilize and strengthen the patriots' military position in the northern provinces. He ably fulfilled the assignment until ill health interrupted his efforts in mid-1814. He retired briefly to the province of Córdoba for rest and recuperation, but meanwhile he was evolving in his mind the strategic plan that would crown his contribution to the independence movement. Like others before him, he saw that the ultimate objective must be to overcome the royalists' stronghold in Peru, but he realized that the path heretofore chosen, through the mountains of Upper Peru, though the most direct was also the most difficult. More promising was the route that led westward from Argentina to Chile and from there by sea to the Peruvian coast.

Having asked for and obtained reassignment to the governorship of Cuyo, at the foot of the Andes in western Argentina, San Martín began preparing the execution of his design with meticulous care. The collapse of the existing Chilean patriot regime in October 1814 was an obvious setback, partially offset by the arrival in Cuyo of Chilean *émigrés,* including Bernardo O'HIGGINS, who were eager for a chance to reconquer their homeland. But San Martín did not neglect the political dimensions of the struggle in his concentration on military preparations. When representatives of the Argentine provinces met in 1816 at the Congress of Tucumán (*see* TUCUMÁN, CONGRESS OF), he placed his influence strongly on the side of an outright declaration of independence from Spain, which the Congress issued on July 9. He also supported the move to establish a limited monarchy under a prince of the Inca royal family (*see* INCAS). Although the latter scheme did not prosper, San Martín continued to regard a liberal constitutional monarchy of one sort or another as the best hope for stability in the new nations of Spanish America.

In January 1817, San Martín at last set out on his expedition to Chile, taking the main part of his army over a pass nearly 15,000 feet above sea level on the north side of Mount Aconcagua. On February 12, he defeated the royalists in the Battle of Chacabuco (*see* CHACABUCO, BATTLE OF), which opened the way to Santiago. This did not end enemy resistance, but Chilean independence was assured by a second major victory at Maipú in April 1818. San Martín was content to see O'Higgins assume the government of Chile as Supreme Director, and both men took part in sponsoring an Argentine-Chilean mission to Europe that sought support of the major powers for a solution to the struggle against

Spain on the basis of creating independent American kingdoms. An even more immediate concern was San Martín's next military objective, the liberation of Peru. When his original sponsor, the government in Buenos Aires, became too deeply embroiled in domestic quarrels to continue effective support and instead called on San Martín to help it repress local enemies, he simply struck out on his own. With the cooperation of the Chilean government of O'Higgins and a fleet commanded by the Scottish admiral Thomas COCHRANE, he sailed northward from Chile and in September 1820 landed with an army on the Peruvian coast.

Although San Martín did not neglect military measures, he hoped that the royalists might now be ready for a peaceful settlement. He entered negotiations with them, proposing that Peru be converted into an independent monarchy under a prince of the Spanish royal family. These negotiations came to nothing, but opinion in Peru was steadily turning in the patriots' favor. The Spaniards saw fit to evacuate Lima, allowing San Martín to enter it unopposed. He then formally declared Peruvian independence on July 28, 1821, and he accepted the supreme political as well as military command under the title Protector of Peru.

In the newly liberated areas San Martín proceeded to establish a government, raise forces, and enact a series of liberal reforms such as the abolition of Indian tribute and forced labor and the gradual emancipation of Negro slaves under the free-birth principle. Nevertheless, he inevitably aroused some degree of resentment simply because he was a non-Peruvian, while his monarchist ideas provoked the distrust of doctrinaire republicans. His slowness in pressing the military struggle against the royalists, who still dominated the Peruvian Andes, led to further criticism. Yet San Martín's cautious policy did not lack justification, since the enemy forces were both numerous and well entrenched.

San Martín thus faced serious problems in Peru by the time he departed for a private meeting with Simón BOLÍVAR, whose forces had just completed the liberation of Ecuador. Their interview took place at Guayaquil in late July 1822. Historians are still debating the substance of their discussion, but presumably it covered both the future organization of Spanish America and the military situation in Peru. Suffice it to say here that while each man was committed in principle both to a successful conclusion of the war and to a policy of continuing close association among the Spanish American peoples, there was disagreement on many details. Nor is it clear whether San Martín had decided even before the meeting to withdraw and leave to Bolívar the task of finishing the liberation of Peru or whether this decision resulted (as some have argued) from a conviction he formed at Guayaquil that Bolívar in practice was not prepared to cooperate wholeheartedly with him against the royalists in Peru. But withdraw he did, resigning as Protector of Peru on September 20, after his return to Lima, and then leaving the country for good. Whatever the precise motivation, San Martín's voluntary departure stands out as a remarkable instance of personal and political self-denial.

San Martín stopped for a time in Chile, then returned to Cuyo, where he sought to isolate himself from the internecine quarrels of the Argentine patriots. Yet his mere presence in his homeland was an unsettling factor, giving false hopes to some and being viewed by others as a threat to their position. In due course, in February 1824, San Martín sailed for Europe, giving as his ostensible reason the need to arrange for the education of his daughter, whom he took with him. (His wife had died the year before.) Obviously, that was not his only reason, for the move emphasized his disengagement from Argentine petty politics yet permitted him to bring to bear what influence he could, in Europe, on behalf of the larger interests of Spanish America.

Toward the end of 1828 San Martín made a final trip to America, to examine the course of affairs at first-hand and perhaps to offer his services again if it seemed that he could usefully contribute to the internal peace and institutional consolidation of the new nations. He got as far as Montevideo, soon decided there was nothing he could accomplish, and returned to Europe in mid-1829 without even setting foot on Argentine soil. Thereafter he lived mainly in France and in retirement, though not in isolation. At the time of the French and English interventions in the RÍO DE LA PLATA area in opposition to the government of Juan Manuel de ROSAS, San Martín gave effective moral support to Rosas as the defender of American sovereignty; and he willed his sword to the Argentine dictator as a special tribute. He died in Boulogne on August 17, 1850.

Bibliography. Bartolomé Mitre, *Historia de San Martín y de la emancipación sudamericana,* still the classic work, available in many editions including a condensed English translation by William Pilling, London, 1893; José Pacífico Otero, *Historia del libertador don José de San Martín,* 4 vols., Buenos Aires, 1932; A. J. Pérez Amuchástegui, *Ideología y acción de San Martín,* Buenos Aires, 1966; Ricardo Piccirilli, *San Martín y la política de los pueblos,* Buenos Aires, 1957; Richard Rojas, *San Martín, Knight of the Andes,* New York, 1945.

DAVID BUSHNELL

SAN SALVADOR. Capital of El Salvador and the second largest city in Central America. Its population in 1969 was estimated at 349,333.

San Salvador was founded in 1525 and after some vicissitudes was officially recognized in its present situation in 1545. Within the colonial Kingdom of Guatemala the city served as the capital of the province of El Salvador and, after 1786, of the Intendancy of San Salvador. After independence it served as the capital of the state of El Salvador, as capital of the Federation of Central America from 1835 to 1839 (*see* CENTRAL AMERICA, FEDERATION OF), and thereafter as capital of the state and the Republic of El Salvador. The city suffered an extraordinary number of natural disasters, particularly earthquakes. The most severe earthquakes following independence occurred in 1839, 1854, 1873, and 1917. The devastation in 1854 was so massive that Cojutepeque functioned as the capital until 1858.

San Salvador is the focus of virtually everything in El Salvador. It is the seat of both departmental and national governments and the center of political activity for the country. It is also the social and artistic capital, the seat of the principal educational and cultural institutions, the hub of road, rail, and air transportation, and the banking, industrial, and commercial center of the republic. Its industrial growth has encouraged migration from the countryside in excess of its employment capacity. Despite extensive construction of low-cost housing, the squalor and misery of the very poor contrast sharply with the elegant abodes of the wealthy.

WILLIAM J. GRIFFITH

SANTA ANNA, ANTONIO LÓPEZ DE (1794–1876). Mexican soldier and President. Santa Anna dominated Mexican politics from the late 1820s to the mid-1850s. Because of his role and influence, this period is frequently called the age of Santa Anna. He was born in Jalapa, Veracruz, and maintained a close association with that area during most of his active career. Santa Anna became an infantry cadet when he was sixteen; from then until his final overthrow in 1855 much of his fame and political career centered on his connection with the Army. He fought against the insurgents during the struggle for independence but joined Agustín de ITURBIDE's army and accepted the Plan of Iguala in 1821. Two years later, he played a major role in overthrowing Iturbide and establishing the republic. During the following decade he shifted his allegiance frequently and was instrumental in causing much of the political turbulence in the new nation. His actions must be explained largely by his ambition for power.

In the elections of 1833 he was chosen President, but he remained at his hacienda, Manga de Clavo, and allowed his Vice President, Valentín GÓMEZ FARÍAS, to act for him, a practice that would become habitual in his various terms in office. When Gómez Farías undertook an unpopular reform program, Santa Anna left retirement in 1834, took over the government, and nullified the reform measures that had been enacted. He took command of the Army to put down the Texas

Antonio López de Santa Anna. [New York Historical Society]

rebellion in late 1835, besieged the Alamo early in 1836, and a month and a half later was captured by Sam Houston at the Battle of San Jacinto. Eventually he was sent to Washington, where he conferred with President Andrew Jackson and was then allowed to return to Mexico. He was in disgrace upon his arrival because of his loss of Texas, but before long he had become a hero once more as a result of his action in the PASTRY WAR.

Santa Anna served as President briefly in 1839 and again for varying lengths of time in the period 1841–1844. It was in this period that he attempted to construct a centralist state and establish a rigid conservatism. This failing, he was driven from office and was sent into exile in Havana. When the MEXICAN WAR began, he intrigued with President James K. Polk to be allowed to return to Mexico to help work for the defeat of his country. He was passed through the American naval blockade, but when he arrived, he instead accepted the Presidency and took command of the Army to defeat the forces of the United States. He resigned when the Treaty of Guadalupe Hidalgo (*see* GUADALUPE HIDALGO, TREATY OF) was negotiated and went into exile in Jamaica. In 1853 he was recalled by the Conservatives to become dictator; this time there were many trappings of monarchy. But the financial situation, the disaffection of many elements, and the resolve of the Liberals determined that his dictatorship would be of short duration and that he would no longer be a dominant figure in Mexican politics. Santa Anna was overthrown as a result of the revolution of Ayutla and left Mexico in 1855 for exile in St. Thomas. He returned to Mexico in 1864, ostensibly to support the empire, but was allowed to stay only briefly. He attempted to return once more in mid-1867, this time as a mediator between the *juaristas* and the moderate Liberals. Imprisoned in San Juan de Ulúa for six months, he was then sent into exile to Nassau. He was finally allowed to return to Mexico in 1872 and died four years later.

A brief sketch cannot do justice to the colorful personality or the military-political career of Santa Anna. That he was a popular figure is indicated by the frequency with which he was called upon to take control of the government and stabilize the political situation. He was an opportunist who could gauge public opinion astutely. A talented military commander, he could weld an army with his personal magnetism.

See also ALAMÁN, Lucas.

Bibliography. Wilfrid Hardy Callcott, *Santa Anna: The Story of an Enigma Who Once Was Mexico,* Hamden, Conn., 1964; José Fuentes Mares, *Santa Anna: Aurora y ocaso de un comediante,* Mexico City, 1959; Oakah L. Jones, Jr., *Santa Anna,* New York, 1968; Antonio López de Santa Anna, *The Eagle: The Autobiography of Santa Anna,* ed. by Ann Fears Crawford, Austin, Tex., 1967; José C. Valadés, *Santa Anna y la guerra de Texas,* Mexico City, 1936.

CHARLES R. BERRY

SANTA CRUZ, ANDRÉS (1792–1865). Bolivian statesman. Santa Cruz, perhaps Bolivia's most capable President, was born in La Paz. The son of a minor Spanish official and of a mother who claimed direct descent from the INCAS, he cut his education short in order to pursue a military career. He joined the Army

Andrés Santa Cruz. [*Photographie Bulloz*]

in 1809, and during the War of Independence he remained loyal to the crown, fighting and distinguishing himself in the conflict. In 1817 he was captured by the Argentinians but managed, after a tortuous and difficult escape, to rejoin the royalist forces in Peru in 1820. Soon after, following his capture by José de SAN MARTÍN's liberating forces, he, like many other royalist officers, embraced the rebel cause, bringing to it the same enthusiasm he had given the royalist cause. San Martín appointed him commander of the division sent to assist Ecuador's struggle for independence. Later, he participated in the Battle of Junín and contributed indirectly to the rebel victory at Ayacucho that sealed Peru's independence. For all these accomplishments he was promoted to the rank of grand marshal. *See* AYACUCHO, BATTLE OF; JUNÍN, BATTLE OF.

To be sure, Santa Cruz did not limit his activities to military matters. He vigorously involved himself in political intrigue. In 1823 he led a movement against the Liberals in Peru that brought José de la RIVA-AGÜERO to the Presidency. In 1826 Simón BOLÍVAR named him President of Peru's Council of Ministers, a post Santa Cruz hoped to use as a stepping-stone to the Peruvian Presidency. The opportunity was denied him by a Liberal Congress fearful of Santa Cruz's strong will and conservatism. In spite of this rejection Santa Cruz continued to cherish the dream of becoming the ruler of Peru. Even after he assumed the Presidency of Bolivia in 1829, he intrigued and plotted until he achieved his goal in 1836.

Santa Cruz had been offered the Presidency of Bolivia because no other man seemed able to end the political, economic, and military chaos that gripped the young republic soon after independence. Within a short time he accomplished the task by dictatorially reducing the constitution to a few articles and by using his notorious cruelty to cow his real or suspected enemies into submission. Thus, at a time when confusion reigned in most of Latin America, Bolivia enjoyed a period of peace and order perhaps unequaled in its history.

But Santa Cruz's regime brought progress as well as peace and order. He established schools, including universities at La Paz and Cochabamba, a medical school, a military college, and a national college of science. He introduced new penal, civil, mining, and commercial codes, reorganized finances, encouraged trade and manufacturing, ordered Bolivia's first census, had the first general map of Bolivia drawn up, and launched a necessary road- and bridge-building program.

Santa Cruz also paid a great deal of attention to the Army, even cutting the salaries of other bureaucrats in order to buy equipment for it. The reasons were threefold: to maintain the loyalty of the Army; to stop, if necessary, certain ambitious Peruvian generals who wished to annex Bolivia; and to carry out Santa Cruz's own ultimate ambition of uniting Bolivia and Peru. This last goal was finally achieved with the creation in 1836 of the PERU-BOLIVIA CONFEDERATION.

The Confederation, which partly reflected Santa Cruz's desire to re-create the old Inca empire, was to last only three years, mainly because of the opposition of Chile and Argentina. Chile in particular saw its economic and strategic position as a Pacific power threatened by the new alliance. Thus, from the beginning Chile lent assistance to Peruvian opponents of Santa Cruz, and it was the first, in 1836, to declare war on the Confederation, followed a year later by Argentina. Santa Cruz did not wish war. He tried to reach a compromise at almost any cost, but to no avail. Finally, in 1839 the Confederation was brought to an end following the defeat of its forces at Yungay by a combined Chilean-Peruvian army. Immediately thereafter, a revolt broke out in Bolivia that forced Santa Cruz to flee to Ecuador. In 1843 he was captured in Peru while attempting to invade Bolivia, where he had continued to enjoy strong support. His captors turned him over to the Chilean government, whose continuing strong antipathy for Santa Cruz had been especially instrumental in thwarting his return to power. After nearly three years of imprisonment he was finally exiled to Europe.

In Europe Santa Cruz lived very modestly until the Bolivian government appointed him its representative to various European courts. In 1855, relieved of his diplomatic functions, he sailed to Argentina to launch his last unsuccessful assault on the Bolivian Presidency. His political comeback thwarted, he devoted his energies to a real estate enterprise in Argentina that made him wealthy enough to retire to France. There he died in 1865 and was buried in Versailles.

Bibliography. Federico Bascón C., *Siete capítulos en la vida del Gran Mariscal Andrés Santa Cruz,* La Paz, 1965; Jorge Cornejo B., *La Confederación Peru-Boliviana,* Cuzco, 1935; Alfonso Crespo, *Santa Cruz, el condor indio,* Mexico City, 1944; Julio Díaz A., *El Mariscal Santa Cruz y sus generales,* La Paz, 1965; Agustín Iturricha, *Historia de Bolivia bajo la administración del Mariscal Andrés Santa Cruz,* 2 vols., Sucre, 1920; Lane C. Kendall, "Andrés Santa Cruz and the Peru-Bolivia Confederation," *Hispanic American Historical Review,* vol. XVI, no. 1, February 1936, pp. 29–48; Oscar de Santa Cruz (ed.), *El Mariscal Andrés Santa Cruz y el Gran Perú,* La Paz, 1924.

ORAZIO A. CICCARELLI

SANTA CRUZ, DOMINGO (1899–   ). Chilean composer and educator. Born in La Cruz, he studied first in his native country with Enrique SORO and then in Spain with Conrado del Campo. He has been the most powerful leader of Chile's musical life since 1917, when he founded the chorus of the Bach Society in Santiago. For a time he was a member of the diplomatic service, from which he retired in 1927. In 1928 he directed the reorganization of the National Conservatory in Santiago. In 1930 he established the Faculty of Fine Arts and Music of the University of Chile; two years later he was elected its dean, a position he held through successive reelections until 1953. He again served as dean from 1962 until his retirement in 1969. In 1940 he created the Instituto de Extensión Musical, and in 1946 the Institute for Musical Research, and from 1955 to 1958 he served as president both of the International Music Council of UNESCO and of the International Association of Music Education. In 1951 he was awarded the National Prize for the Arts in Chile.

As a composer Santa Cruz has always supported a cosmopolitan position marked by moderate radicalism and austere linear characteristics. Works illustrating these traits are his *Cantata de los ríos* (1941), *Égloga* (1949), *Lamentations of Jeremiah* (1969) for chorus and orchestra, his four symphonies (1946, 1948, 1967, 1968), his three string quartets (1923, 1947, 1959), and his variations for piano and orchestra (1943), in addition to numerous vocal, choral, and chamber music compositions.

JUAN A. ORREGO-SALAS

SANTANA, PEDRO (1801–1864). Dominican political leader. Santana was the great *caudillo* of the Dominican Republic's first twenty years. Unlike the wily but uncharismatic Buenaventura BÁEZ, with whom by force of arms he alternated in office, but like the contemporary Mexican *caudillo* Antonio López de SANTA ANNA, whose name was so similar to his own, Santana was tough, courageous, and magnetic, a man able to attract support in moments of crisis and equally adept at using public office for private gain.

His first term in office lasted from 1844 to 1848, coming on the heels of his seizure of power from liberal idealists like Juan Pablo DUARTE who had led the struggle for independence from the Haitians and had proclaimed the new republic. Santana felt that, because of the repeated invasions of its more powerful neighbor, Haiti, the Dominican Republic could not afford the luxury of democracy, and he thus sent the Congress home and rewrote the constitution, making the Presidency virtually all-powerful. On numerous occasions Santana rallied his people against the Haitians, riding these crests of popularity in and out of office.

His second term lasted from 1853 to 1856, and his third from 1859 to 1861. Convinced like Báez of the need for a foreign protector to help guard the country against Haitian assaults, Santana turned first to the United States and then to Spain, paving the way for the Spanish occupation of 1861–1865, during which Santana was named Captain General. Called upon by Spain to put down his own insurgent countrymen, Santana went into battle halfheartedly and eventually retired to his estate infirm and disillusioned.

HOWARD J. WIARDA

SANTANDER, FRANCISCO DE PAULA (1792–1840). Colombian general and political leader of the independence and early national periods. Francisco de Paula Santander was born on the eastern border of New Granada to a family of upper-class provincial landowners. His formal education was interrupted by the outbreak of the independence movement, and he subsequently saw active service both in the civil conflicts of New Granada patriots and against Spain.

After the royalists reconquered most of the colony in 1815–1816, Santander helped organize resistance on the thinly settled eastern plains (llanos). Eventually joining forces with Simón BOLÍVAR, he took part in the campaign of 1819 that culminated in the decisive victory of Boyacá (*see* BOYACÁ, BATTLE OF). Bolívar then assigned him to administer the liberated portions of New Granada, and in recognition of his capable performance in this task he was elected in 1821 Vice President of Gran Colombia (*see* COLOMBIA, GRAN). Since Bolívar, the titular President, remained with the armies fighting against Spain, Santander was left in full charge of government affairs on the home front.

Santander again proved a capable administrator. He

Francisco de Paula Santander. [*J. León Helguera Collection*]

also showed an interest in liberal reforms (to promote education and economic development and limit clerical influence) and a regard for constitutional formalities that won him fame as the "Man of Laws." However, he was sometimes criticized for pushing reforms too rapidly, and he was also troubled by separatism in Venezuela. In 1827 Santander was replaced at the head of the government by Bolívar himself, who had returned home at last and now proceeded to establish a conservative dictatorship. Santander became a rallying point for Bolívar's opponents, and when some sought to assassinate Bolívar in September 1828, Santander (though apparently innocent) was formally exiled.

Although Santander was still absent when Gran Colombia disintegrated in 1830, his sympathizers ultimately emerged in control of the separate Republic of New Granada and elected him to serve as its first constitutional President, beginning in 1832. As a firm and experienced administrator, Santander got the new government off to a good start, but his programs were somewhat more moderate than in Gran Colombia, with the principal exception of education, which again received his special attention.

Politically, President Santander showed little real disposition to conciliate the former followers of Bolívar, and he answered conspiratorial threats with public executions. Nevertheless, when his own one-time collaborator José Ignacio de Márquez, whom he now opposed, won the presidential election of 1836, Santander dutifully turned over the office to him the following year.

Santander returned briefly to private life, then entered the Chamber of Representatives, where he took a leading role in opposition to the Márquez administration. He was still serving in Congress when he died, in Bogotá, on May 5, 1840. His political followers later formed the nucleus of the Liberal party (*see* LIBERAL PARTY: COLOMBIA), which has conventionally claimed Santander as its founder.

Bibliography. David Bushnell, *The Santander Regime in Gran Colombia,* Newark, Del., 1954; Laureano Gómez, *El mito de Santander,* 2 vols., Bogotá, 1966; Julio Hoenigsberg, *Santander ante la historia,* 3 vols., Barranquilla, 1969–70.

DAVID BUSHNELL

SANTIAGO. Capital of Chile, situated at elevations of 1,600 to 2,600 feet at the northern end of the great Central Valley of Chile. To the east it is flanked by the Cordillera de los Andes, some of whose peaks at this point rise to 20,000 feet and form an impressive and majestic back cloth to the city. To the west, at a slightly greater distance from the urban area, lies the lesser Cordillera Marítima. Santiago is traversed by the Mapocho River, which at certain times of the year scarcely merits the title of river at all; at other periods, however, it is swollen with the waters of the melting Andean snows. Two hills rise close to the central area of the city: the 3,000-foot Cerro San Cristóbal and, on the fringe of the business district, the smaller Cerro Santa Lucía.

It was below this latter hill that Santiago was founded on February 12, 1541, by the Spanish conquistador Pedro de VALDIVIA. Almost from the first it became the effective capital of the new colony. From 1561 on it was the seat of a bishopric, and from 1609 a royal *audiencia*.

In May 1647 an earthquake devastated the settlement. Santiago's very modest appearance was slightly altered toward the end of colonial times with the construction of proper embankments for the Mapocho and several new public buildings, the most notable of which was the Casa de la Moneda (Royal Mint); in the 1840s this became the Presidential Palace. The population on the eve of independence was around 30,000.

Only in the second half of the nineteenth century did Santiago begin to lose its colonial character. Street lighting, the paving of roads, and the building of sumptuous mansions by members of the aristocracy all contributed to the reshaping of the city. The municipal improvements carried out under the reforming intendancy of Benjamín VICUÑA MACKENNA were especially remarkable: the Cerro Santa Lucía, a notorious eyesore, was transformed into a delightful urban park, complete with statues, awesome ramparts, and baroque arches. The dignified Municipal Theater and the Congress were also completed in the 1870s. At the turn of the century the population of the capital stood at around 300,000.

The expansion of Santiago in the first seven decades of the present century was phenomenal. Upper- and middle-class residential development spread rapidly beyond the line of Vicuña Mackenna's *camino de cintura* (ring road) to the east and advanced remorselessly toward the foothills of the Cordillera, bringing into existence the *barrio alto* (upper district). Expansion was also considerable to the north of the Mapocho and in the south of the city, particularly in the populous commune of San Miguel. In the 1950s and 1960s migrations from the countryside produced a large number of shantytowns (*callampas*), although a serious attack on this problem was mounted by the Christian Democratic government of President Eduardo FREI (*see* PARTIDO DEMÓCRATA CRISTIANO). In recent years, pollution has become a major problem; the Santiago smog is as̆ disagreeable as any in the Western Hemisphere. At the end of the 1960s the population of Santiago was approaching 3 million.

SIMON COLLIER

SANTO DOMINGO [DE GUZMÁN]. Capital and largest city of the Dominican Republic and the oldest permanent European settlement in the New World. Though historically the name "Santo Domingo" has often been used to refer to the entire island of Hispaniola or to the whole country of the Dominican Republic, nowadays it more commonly refers only to the capital city.

Founded in 1496 at the mouth of the Ozama River on the country's south coast, Santo Domingo served as the base for later Spanish expeditions to other islands and the mainland and, initially at least, as Spain's administrative base in the Americas. The first hospital and monastery were built in Santo Domingo, the first university chartered, and the first *audiencia* created. It was the scene of Spain's first social, economic, and political experiments in the Americas and also of the New World's first revolution.

After the first flourishing decades Santo Domingo declined as an administrative and political center. Depopulated, ignored by Spain, and occasionally attacked by foreign corsairs, it sank into decay and abandonment for the rest of the colonial period. Early in the nineteenth century it was captured by the Haitians.

Once independence was achieved, Santo Domingo gradually regained some of its former importance. Its population increased, and it eventually replaced Santiago, the largest city of the northern Cíbao, as the economic, political, and cultural center of the country.

In 1936 its name was changed to Ciudad Trujillo to honor the ruling dictator, Rafael Leonidas TRUJILLO MOLINA; it reverted to its former name after Trujillo was assassinated in 1961. By 1970 Santo Domingo was a sprawling metropolis of approximately 400,000 inhabitants and unquestionably the chief city of the Dominican Republic.

HOWARD J. WIARDA

SANTORO, CLÁUDIO (1919–   ). Brazilian composer and conductor of international repute. Four stylistic trends can be seen in Santoro's musical production (1938–1968). From an atonal dodecaphonic musical language in the early 1940s, he entered a neo-romantic phase, then adhered to a subjective nationalism in the 1950s, and finally developed into serialism and aleatory techniques in the 1960s. Born in Manaus, Amazonas, Santoro acquired his musical training first at the Federal District Conservatory in Rio de Janeiro and then with the German composer Hans-Joachim Koellreutter, an expert in Schoenberg's method of composition. In 1947 he studied in Paris with Nadia Boulanger and at the Paris Conservatory with the conductor Eugène Bigot. He took a very active part in the group Música Viva, organized in the late 1930s by young musicians around Koellreutter.

Santoro's first works—a sonata for violin solo, two sonatas for violin and piano, *4 Peças para Piano Solo*, and the First String Quartet, all written between 1940 and 1943—attest to his experimentation with atonality and twelve-tone writing. His participation in the Congress of Progressive Composers, held in Prague in 1948, which condemned dodecaphonic music, influenced his future orientation. His Sinfonia No. 4 (*Sinfonia la Paz*) was recorded in 1954 by the State Orchestra of the U.S.S.R. The many national and international prizes received by Santoro include a prize from the Chamber Music Guild of Washington (1944), an award from the Guggenheim Foundation (1946), an international prize for peace (Vienna, 1952), and the First Prize from the Brazilian Ministry of Education (Brasília, 1960). After founding and directing the music department of the University of Brasília (1962–1965), Santoro became musical director at the Berlin Opera. His enormous musical production includes eight symphonies, three piano concertos, two oratorios (*Odes a Stalingrado*, 1947; *Berlim, 13 de agôsto*, 1961), ballets, and many chamber music pieces for various media. His most recent works using aleatory techniques include *Intermitências II* (1967), *Agrupamento em 10* (1966), *Interações Assintóticas* (1970), and the *Cantata Elegíaca* (1970), based on a text by Luiz de Camões.

GERARD H. BÉHAGUE

SANTOS, EDUARDO (1888–1974). Colombian newspaper publisher and President (1938–1942). Born in Bogotá of patriarchal *santandereano* parentage, Santos was educated at the Colegio del Rosario and in Paris, retaining pronounced French sympathies. Enrique OLAYA HERRERA appointed him head of the archives in the Ministry of Foreign Relations in 1911. He built his political reputation as a sustained opponent of the

Conservative "hegemony" (*see* CONSERVATIVE PARTY: COLOMBIA) in the editorial columns of *El Tiempo*, which he owned from 1913 until his death. A member of the Republican Union until 1921, he then became a virulent Liberal (*see* LIBERAL PARTY: COLOMBIA) and made *El Tiempo* the spearhead of militant liberalism. Santos entered the Olaya administration briefly as Minister of Foreign Relations (1930) and then as Governor of Santander (1931). Subsequently he headed the Colombian delegation at the League of Nations (1931–1933) and led the Colombian team during negotiations (1933–1934) in Rio de Janeiro to settle the dispute with Peru over Leticia. His career reached a peak when, after the death of Olaya, he emerged as the Liberal presidential candidate and was elected unopposed in 1938.

The government of Santos was handicapped by wartime conditions and marked a further deceleration of the already-faltering "Revolution on the March" of Alfonso LÓPEZ. There was little opportunity for innovative legislation, since tax revenue was almost at a standstill owing to dwindling coffee returns during World War II. Yet, under the guidance of Minister of Finance Carlos LLERAS RESTREPO, several semiautonomous interventionist institutes were founded to stimulate municipal development, credit, and public housing. Although underfinancing rendered these almost ineffective, they provided an important precedent for later governments. Santos collaborated wholeheartedly with the Allies, breaking diplomatic relations with the Axis after Pearl Harbor. After the end of his term of office, Santos sat on the Liberal National Directorate for short periods, but his influence was felt mainly through *El Tiempo*. His attempt to rally a demoralized liberalism to a crusade of "Faith and Dignity" during the government of Laureano GÓMEZ met with little success. Santos was subsequently identified with all governments of the NATIONAL FRONT, embracing that of his protégé, Carlos Lleras, with the greatest enthusiasm.

C. G. ABEL

SANTOS-DUMONT, ALBERTO (1873–1932). Brazilian inventor, engineer, and aviator. Santos-Dumont was born on his parents' coffee plantation in Palmira (now Santos Dumont), Minas Gerais. His father, an engineer, encouraged Santos-Dumont's early aptitude for mechanics and in 1891 sent him to Paris to study. In France he joined the international coterie of pioneer aviators, making his initial balloon ascent in 1897. Santos-Dumont was the first to turn the internal combustion engine to practical use in aviation and, after a series of near catastrophes in 1899 and 1900, successfully navigated his gasoline-powered balloon over an oval course stretching from Saint-Cloud around the Eiffel Tower and back to win the Deutsch Prize in 1901. With the prize came international recognition, and in the next few years he garnered many awards in Europe and the United States. He turned from balloons to airplanes in 1906 with the construction of the 14 Bis, which won him the Archdeacon Prize in October of that year. His Demoiselle, built in 1908, is considered the prototype of all subsequent monoplanes. The French government awarded him the Legion of Honor in 1909. During World War I he was accused of espionage by that government, but he was exonerated and later was decorated for his work in aeronautical design on behalf of the Allies.

In his last years Santos-Dumont suffered great mental anguish at the destructive use to which his beloved air machines had been put, a dismay that was heightened on a visit to Rio de Janeiro in 1928 when he witnessed the fatal crash of an airplane loaded with welcoming friends. A member of the Brazilian Academy of Letters, he is known to his countrymen as the Father of Aviation. He wrote two books, *Dans l'air* (1904) and *O Que Eu Vi e o Que Nós Veremos* (1918).

FRANCESCA MILLER

SÃO FRANCISCO VALLEY. Major river basin in Brazil. The valley occupies much of the semiarid DROUGHT POLYGON of the NORTHEAST. It takes its name from the São Francisco River, which rises in the Brazilian highlands in the state of Minas Gerais and flows nearly 2,000 miles generally northward through Bahia, where it turns sharply to the east to enter the Atlantic between the states of Alagoas and Sergipe. Settlement of the valley was begun in the seventeenth century by gold seekers from São Paulo and cattlemen from the coast of Bahia and Pernambuco, who converted it into a vast pastoral region. The valley remains primarily a grazing area for livestock, although agriculture flourishes wherever irrigation is possible. The leading agricultural products are the carnauba palm, cotton, and food crops such as beans and manioc.

The river, too shallow for navigation in its lower reaches, is navigable for more than 1,200 miles upstream and has long served as the principal inland artery linking northeastern and southern Brazil. The economic development of the valley has been accelerated by the opening of all-weather highways and by the construction of two large dams on the São Francisco River, at Paulo Afonso about 200 miles from the sea, in 1950, and at Três Marias, 1,500 miles upstream, in 1960. The dams control the flow of water for navigation and irrigation and supply electricity to the residents of the valley. Juàzeiro, Bahia, is the largest city and commercial center in the São Francisco Valley.

ROLLIE E. POPPINO

SÃO PAULO. Name of a state and its capital city in southeastern Brazil. São Paulo is the most heavily populated and economically developed state in Brazil. The living standards and levels of income and education of the population compare favorably with those of Western Europe. Although São Paulo was the site of the first permanent Portuguese settlement in the New World (1532), it was a backwater in colonial days. It developed rapidly as a coffee-producing region in the nineteenth century, and has become the most highly industrialized state of Brazil in the twentieth. São Paulo leads Brazil in the production of food crops and cotton and accounts for more than half of the country's industrial output. Its 17,716,816 inhabitants (1970) represent nearly one-fifth of the population of Brazil.

The city of São Paulo, founded in 1554, remained little more than a frontier community until about a century ago. Since that time, as the result of the heavy influx of foreign immigrants before World War I and of Brazilians migrating from rural areas in recent decades, the city has experienced uninterrupted demographic growth. As the administrative, financial, commercial, and transportation hub of the state, it attracted the bulk of the new industrial enterprises, to become the principal manufacturing center in the nation by 1920. With

5,901,533 residents in the city proper and a total of 8,031,486 in the metropolitan area in 1970, São Paulo ranks as the largest city in Brazil and one of the major urban areas of Latin America.

ROLLIE E. POPPINO

SARAVIA, APARICIO (1855–1904). Uruguayan political leader and military chief of the National party (*see* BLANCO PARTY: URUGUAY). Saravia was born of a Brazilian father in the department of Cerro Largo. From 1893 to 1895 he was in Brazil, where he fought on behalf of federalist revolutionaries in Rio Grande do Sul. Back in Uruguay, he launched a brief revolt against the government of the Colorado Juan Idiarte Borda in November 1896 (*see* COLORADO PARTY: URUGUAY). The following March he led a more carefully planned and widely supported revolution, the outcome of which was still unresolved when Idiarte Borda was assassinated on August 25, 1897. Idiarte Borda's successor, Juan Lindolfo CUESTAS, quickly made peace with the revolutionaries. The settlement reached on September 18, 1897, provided for the appointment of Nationalist political chiefs (*jefes políticos*) to six of Uruguay's nineteen departments and for the enactment of electoral legislation guaranteeing minority representation in the Assembly.

Now at the peak of his influence, Saravia retired to his ranch, where he regularly received Nationalist emissaries from Montevideo. Like most Nationalists, he supported the Cuestas administration and the policy of *acuerdos* (accords) that divided legislative seats between Nationalists and Colorados. During the political maneuvering that preceded the presidential election of 1903, he disapproved of the candidacy of José BATLLE, but his failure to indicate his own preference contributed to Batlle's victory.

Saravia's suspicions of Batlle were confirmed when one of his first acts as President was to appoint Nationalists not in Saravia's confidence as political chiefs of two of the Nationalist departments. A threatened revolt in March 1903 was narrowly averted by a compromise, but disagreement over the terms of the compromise resulted in a full-scale Nationalist revolution in 1904. When Saravia was wounded at Masoller on September 1, 1904, and died soon afterward, the revolutionary forces disintegrated, and Uruguay's last civil war came to an end.

HELEN DELPAR

SARMIENTO, DOMINGO FAUSTINO (1811–1888). Argentine educationist, writer, and President (1868–1874). Together with Bartolomé MITRE, Sarmiento must be regarded as one of the two most brilliant and active Argentines of the nineteenth century. He was born in the provincial city of San Juan, and received a local education; indeed, he was largely self-taught. From 1829 on he fought on the liberal, centralist side in the civil war that was raging throughout Argentina. Two years later, following the defeat of El Rodeo de Chacón in Cuyo, he fled to Chile, where he eked out a living as a schoolmaster: he had already conceived a passion for education that was to remain with him for life. A serious illness gained him permission, in 1836, to return to San Juan. Once there, he started a newspaper, only to see it closed down after six weeks. In 1840 the worsening political climate sent him back to Chile.

Journalism now became a major outlet for his abundant energies; he edited and contributed to several newspapers, including *El Mercurio* and *El Progreso*. In 1845 the latter serialized his most famous single work, *Facundo*, an essay on the bloody career of the federalist *caudillo* Facundo Quiroga that was also, more significantly, a ferocious attack on the dictatorship of Juan Manuel de ROSAS. (Rosas is believed to have regarded the work as the best attack on him he had seen!) In 1842 Sarmiento was appointed director of a newly established teacher-training institution in Santiago. The Chilean government sent him in 1845 on a mission to study educational practices in Europe and North America. The visit lasted three years and produced an important effect on Sarmiento's outlook: his adoration of Europe was now tempered by a much stronger enthusiasm for the United States, which he felt was more progressive than the nations of the Old World. On his return to Chile Sarmiento lent his support to the political aspirations of his good friend Manuel MONTT, elected President in 1851, and resumed his journalistic war against Rosas.

In 1851 Gen. Justo José de URQUIZA mounted what was to be the final revolt against the dictator. In company with Mitre and other exiles, Sarmiento sailed to Montevideo in September that year in order to join forces with the rebel *caudillo*. Urquiza gave Sarmiento the job of editing and printing the official bulletin of his Grand Army; after the victory at Caseros (February 3,

Domingo Faustino Sarmiento. [*Organization of American States*]

1852), he went to Rosas' house at Palermo, sat at his desk, and wrote several letters to his friends. Relations between Sarmiento and the victorious Urquiza were far from cordial, and he returned almost immediately to Chile. Only in 1856, when he became director of schools in the province of Buenos Aires, did he finally settle in his native land.

The long struggle between Buenos Aires and the remaining thirteen provinces of Argentina ended in 1861–1862 with the effective triumph of Buenos Aires. When Mitre was elected Governor of the province in 1860, Sarmiento briefly acted as his minister of the interior (government). Following the Battle of Pavón in September 1861, he played a notable part in imposing order in the provinces of the interior. From February 1862 to April 1864 he served as Governor of San Juan, where he was as active as ever in education and journalism. When Gen. Ángel Vicente Peñaloza (El Chacho) of La Rioja formed his Reactionary Army to oppose the federal government, Sarmiento played a leading role in repressing the rebellion. El Chacho was finally hunted down by federal forces in November 1863 and was put to death with considerable cruelty. Whether this was done on Sarmiento's direct orders is disputed; it is certain that he fully approved of the action. El Chacho's head was subsequently displayed on a pike.

In 1864 Sarmiento was appointed Minister Plenipotentiary to the United States, traveling to his new post via Chile and Peru. Three years later he revisited Paris, where he strongly defended Benito JUÁREZ's execution of the Emperor MAXIMILIAN in a conversation with Thiers. In 1868, at the close of Mitre's term of office. Sarmiento was elected President of Argentina; the news of his election reached him as he was on his way home from the United States.

Sarmiento's Presidency was commendably vigorous. He continued Mitre's work in promoting the development of Argentina in accordance with the liberal priorities he had sketched out in Part 3 of *Facundo* and elsewhere. Trade expanded, railroad building increased, immigration was fostered (*see* IMMIGRATION: ARGENTINA), and steps were taken to beautify and modernize Buenos Aires. The year 1869 saw the first Argentine census. As might be expected, Sarmiento laid particular stress on education: the number of schools as well as the number of pupils nearly doubled. The most notable episode in Sarmiento's later political career was a brief and stormy spell as Minister of the Interior between August and October 1879, when he accused President Nicolás AVELLANEDA of open intervention in favor of the presidential candidacy of Gen. Julio A. ROCA; this was precisely what he himself had done on behalf of Avellaneda in 1874. In his final years Sarmiento held various offices, including those of director of schools for the province of Buenos Aires and grand master of Argentine Freemasonry. In 1884 he revisited Chile. He died while on a visit to Paraguay for reasons of health.

Sarmiento was an aggressive, egotistical man, sometimes nicknamed Don Yo on account of his frequent references to himself. His writings, later collected into fifty-three volumes, were copious; they included books and essays on a wide variety of subjects, not least education. Sarmiento's main claim to literary immortality rests on *Facundo*. With its interwoven contrasts between civilization and barbarism, frontier and metropolis, Europe and America, town and country, GAUCHO and intellectual, it is a classic of Argentine and Latin American literature.

Bibliography. A. W. Bunkley (ed.), *A Sarmiento Anthology,* Princeton, N.J., 1952; Frances W. Crowley, *Domingo Faustino Sarmiento,* New York, 1972; D. F. Sarmiento, *Life in the Argentine Republic in the Days of the Tyrants,* Mrs. Horace Mann's translation of Parts 1 and 2 of *Facundo,* New York, 1868; id., *Obras completas,* 53 vols., Buenos Aires, 1884–1903.

SIMON COLLIER

SARMIENTO DE GAMBOA, PEDRO (ca. 1530–after 1591). Spanish navigator, cosmographer, and historian. Born in Alcalá de Henares, Sarmiento led a varied and adventurous life after traveling to the Indies in the 1550s. In 1567–1568 he took part in an expedition that discovered the Solomon Islands. In 1579, after Francis DRAKE's raid on Callao, he was put in command of an expedition to explore the lands and waters around the Strait of Magellan, then considered the only means of access to the Pacific. Sarmiento spent the rest of his life in an unsuccessful effort to fortify and colonize the strait. While returning to Spain from South America in 1586, he was captured by ships belonging to Sir Walter Raleigh and taken to England, where he had an opportunity to converse with Raleigh and Queen Elizabeth. He was released in October 1586 with a message for King PHILIP II, only to be seized in France by a company of Huguenots and held for ransom for more than three years. He was twice (1565, 1578) condemned for sorcery by the Inquisition in Lima (*see* INQUISITION, HOLY OFFICE OF THE).

Sarmiento was a trusted adviser of Viceroy Francisco de TOLEDO of Peru, who arrived in Lima in 1569, and accompanied him as cosmographer on his five-year tour of inspection of the viceroyalty. Commissioned by Toledo to write a history that would prove conclusively Spain's right to rule Peru, Sarmiento produced in 1572 a work, *Historia Índica* (*History of the Incas*), that is the antithesis of the *Royal Commentaries* which GARCILASO DE LA VEGA would publish three decades later. Based on Toledo's inquiries into the Inca past, known as the *Informaciones,* as well as on Sarmiento's own investigation, the *History* traces Peruvian history to the Spanish conquest and depicts the INCAS as cruel tyrants and usurpers who could not be considered the legitimate lords of Peru. The *History* was sent to Spain, but it was neglected until 1893, when it was discovered in the library of the University of Göttingen. It was first published in Berlin in 1906.

HELEN DELPAR

SARMIENTOS, JORGE (1933–). Guatemalan composer. Born in San Antonio, he studied first at the National Conservatory in Guatemala City and then with Darius Milhaud and Nadia Boulanger in Paris. He has had a distinguished career as a conductor and percussionist in addition to composing such works as a concertino for marimba and orchestra (1958) and a concerto for timpani and orchestra (1965).

JUAN A. ORREGO-SALAS

SAS, ANDRÉS (1900–1967). French composer and musicologist, long resident in Peru. Born in Paris, he traveled to Lima in 1924, invited by the Peruvian government to join the faculty of the National Conservatory. With his wife he established his own music academy in 1929. In 1951 he became director of the National Conservatory. Always interested in Peruvian Indian and popular music, Sas wrote extensively on this subject, and his compositions generally reflect many stylistic features of the music of the Peruvian highlands. Outstanding among these are his *Tres estampas del Perú* (1936) for orchestra, his *Sonata-Fantasía* for flute and piano (1934), and his sonata for piano (1936). He was also responsible for the transcription into current notation of the first Peruvian opera, *La púrpura de la rosa* (1701), by Tomás de Torrejón y Velasco.

JUAN A. ORREGO-SALAS

SCHICK GUTIÉRREZ, RENÉ (1909–1966). Nicaraguan civil servant and President (1963–1966). Minister of Education and Foreign Relations during the regime of Luis SOMOZA DEBAYLE (1956–1963) and President from 1963 until his death in August 1966, Schick was closely identified with the Somoza dynasty. Before serving as a public official, he worked as an administrator of the Somoza family enterprises. During his Presidency, the National Guard, the political and military power base of the country, continued under the command of Anastasio SOMOZA DEBAYLE. Although Schick did nothing to break the power of the Somoza family over the political and economic life of the country, his modesty and fairness, plus the respect which he insisted upon for the government's opponents, won him a respected place among Nicaragua's Presidents. Since his regime coincided with a period of increasing exports and prosperity and of relative calm on the international isthmian scene, Schick never faced serious internal or external opposition.

CHARLES L. STANSIFER

SCHIDLOWSKY, LEÓN (1931–   ). Chilean composer. Born in Santiago, he studied there with Juan A. Allende-Blin and Free Focke and later in Detmold, Germany. In 1963 he was appointed director of the Instituto de Extensión Musical and shortly thereafter joined the Faculty of Music of the University of Chile. In 1968 he received a Guggenheim fellowship. From his very early works Schidlowsky's style was shaped along personal and progressive lines; although he was not fully committed to any particular method of avant-garde composition, he was closer to the Webern-Berg idiom than to any other. Among his outstanding works are *Cantata negra* (1957), *Amatorias* (1963) for voice and chamber ensemble, a concerto for six instruments (1957), *Kadish* for cello and orchestra (1968), *Llaqui* (1965), *La noche de cristal* (1961), and *Hexá-foros* (1968).

JUAN A. ORREGO-SALAS

SEBASTIAN (SEBASTIÃO, 1554–1578). Childless King of Portugal (1557–1578) whose defeat and death at Al-Qsar al-Kbir, Morocco (August 4, 1578), left the aged Cardinal King Henry (Henrique) as the last monarch of the house of Aviz. Severely weakened by Sebastian's rash and badly planned crusade against Islam, which had cost half the state's annual revenues and 7,000 lives in addition to his own, Portugal was in no condition to resist the military power and bribery of PHILIP II when Henry died in 1580. During the sixty years of so-called BABYLONIAN CAPTIVITY under the Hapsburg kings of Spain and Portugal, the belief that

Sebastian had not died and would return to reclaim his throne became associated with popular nationalistic desires and acquired strong messianic overtones. Several impostors attempted to exploit the myth, and it was used to aid the restoration movement in the 1640s, to the benefit of the Duke of Braganza (*see* JOÃO IV).

KENNETH R. MAXWELL

SEGALL, LASAR (1891–1957). Brazilian painter. Born in Vilna, Lithuania, Segall attended the Berlin Academy of Art from 1907 to 1909 but rebelled against the prevailing academicism and moved to Dresden, where he met George Grosz and Otto Dix. After a short stay in the Netherlands he traveled to Brazil in 1912. The following year his paintings were shown in São Paulo and Campinas; these were the first modern art shows in Brazil, but they had less impact than the controversial exhibit by Anita MALFATTI in 1917. Back in Germany during World War I, he was interned as a Russian subject but was allowed to return to Dresden in 1916. Until 1923 he was associated with the German expressionist movement, but his work was always imbued with a compassion for humanity, as shown in his somber studies on universal themes, such as *Sick Family* (1920). Moving to Brazil in 1923, he married Jenny Klabin, a Brazilian noted as a translator, and became a Brazilian citizen. He participated actively in the artistic life of his adopted country and in 1932 was a founder of the Sociedade Pro-Arte Moderna, helping to decorate the society's quarters. In the early 1930s he also began his well-known landscapes of Campos de Jordão and a series of portraits of the artist Lucy Citti Ferrara. The album *Mangue* (1944) contained illustrations depicting the prostitutes of a red-light district in Rio de Janeiro.

Throughout his career Segall's work had revealed his consciousness of Jewish suffering, and starting in 1936 he returned to this theme in a powerful series of oils inspired by events in Europe, among them *Pogrom* (1936–1937), *Emigrants' Ship* (1939–1941), and *Concentration Camp* (1945). The years after 1949 were devoted to the series *Wandering Women* and *Forests*.

HELEN DELPAR

SELVA (PERU). Forested area of eastern Peru. Occupying 60 percent of Peru and containing only about 10 percent of its population, the selva has been touted by some observers, perhaps unrealistically, as the country's greatest future source of wealth. Its chief commercial center is Iquitos (population, 55,000), a port on the AMAZON RIVER that played an important economic role during the rubber boom early in the twentieth century. The major part of the region's 285,000 square miles of thickly forested, often poorly drained terrain is unfit for large-scale agricultural production. Much of it is still largely unexplored and is inhabited by primitive tribes. The other part of the selva, the montaña, is the section whose economic potential has inspired great optimism. Situated on the eastern slopes of the ANDES MOUNTAINS up to an altitude of several thousand feet, it is endowed with fertile soil, a favorable climate, valuable commercial forests, and considerable oil resources. For years isolated groups have cultivated commercially small quantities of such products as sugar, tea, cacao, and tobacco. However, the surface of the montaña, consisting of swift rivers and deep canyons, makes penetration nearly impossible. For more than 100 years governments have been attempting to encourage colonization. In the last three decades a few roads have been built, and settlements have been established, the most important one being at Tingo María. Nevertheless, the optimistic future envisioned for the montaña will not be realized until better communications with other regions are established.

ORAZIO A. CICCARELLI

SEMANA TRÁGICA (TRAGIC WEEK). Name given by the press to the violent and disorderly week of January 7–14, 1919, in the city of Buenos Aires. The sequence of events is still imperfectly known, and their significance is not clear. What occurred evidently resulted from a confluence of diverse forces. The upheaval began outside the metallurgical plant of Pedro Vasena e Hijos, located near the Riachuelo, where a strike had been in progress since December 2, 1918. The plant was protected by an armed security force authorized by the government. Outbursts of shooting occurred on January 3 and on January 5. On Tuesday, January 7, a shot was heard as a wagon under armed escort made its way to the Vasena plant; in the ensuing melee three innocent bystanders, including an eighteen-year-old boy, and one worker, were killed, and twenty to thirty-six persons, mostly policemen and firemen, were wounded. On Thursday, the day of a general strike by the Sociedad de Resistencia Metalúrgicos and the Federación Obrera Regional Argentina del IX Congreso, a large crowd gathered before 10 A.M. at a Socialist center for the funeral of the boy. By the time they were told that the procession would begin at 2 P.M., they were restless. It was hot, and at the request of some workers and to avoid trouble, the firemen and the police were confined to their stations. The dispersing crowd broke into three segments.

One segment, containing the Socialists and anarchists, paralyzed the municipal transportation system. Another tried to storm the Vasena factory, firing upon the security forces there; in the disturbance that followed the arrival of police reinforcements, twenty-three to twenty-eight persons were killed and thirty-six wounded. Those forming the funeral cortege set fire to a church, shot at the firemen sent to put it out, and fought with the police in the cemetery. By 7 P.M. five policemen were dead, and many more were wounded. Various figures are given for the fatalities among the demonstrators.

About that time Gen. Luis J. Dellepiane, commander of the 2d Division at the Campo de Mayo, sent his troops into the city to reestablish order and asked the Minister of War to approve his initiative. On Friday there were no newspapers, and telephone and railroad service was suspended; the soldiers and policemen patrolling the city, along with some civilians, attacked union leaders and union centers. The following day Vasena capitulated to union demands. On Sunday, acting on reports from the Montevideo police of a Communist plot to seize the two capitals, the police arrested allegedly pro-Soviet Russian Jews, and on Tuesday they attacked the local anarchist newspaper without authorization. Three days later the city had returned to normal, and the soldiers were back in their barracks.

Dellepiane is credited with saving the hesitant government of President Hipólito YRIGOYEN, which he could have overthrown. Poorly paid and their morale low, the police showed little discipline when attacked by the workers. In addition, there was no permanent police chief for the first part of the week. The struggle between the Socialists, anarchists, and syndicalists for control of the labor movement also contributed to the crisis.

JOSEPH T. CRISCENTI

SENADO DA CÂMARA. Municipal council, a vital administrative organ in Portuguese metropolitan and colonial society providing for urban government by locally elected officials. In the colonial setting the *câmara* often became a powerful mouthpiece for dominant local interests, especially in the second half of the seventeenth century, when the colonial *câmaras* played a prominent role in financing defensive measures against the Dutch (*see* DUTCH IN BRAZIL). The *câmara* was responsible for the leasing and distribution of municipal lands, levied municipal taxes, and regulated the prices of necessities. Colonial *câmaras* were often represented in Lisbon by a *procurador* (attorney), and in 1653 the *câmara* of Bahia was granted the right to send representatives to the Portuguese Cortes. The *câmara* was composed of several *vereadores* (aldermen), who held office for one year and were elected by a complicated process from among the local *homens bons* (worthy men), as well as a procurator, a secretary, and several municipal officials without voting rights. During the eighteenth century some check was placed on the pretensions of the municipal councils with the modification of election procedures, the introduction of the *juiz de fora* (royal magistrate) as presiding officer (a change that took place in 1696 in the case of Bahia), and the loss by the port city *câmaras* of their role in fixing the prices of sugar and tobacco because of the establishment of *mesas de inspeção* (inspection boards) in 1751.

KENNETH R. MAXWELL

SEREBRIER, JOSÉ (1938–   ). Uruguayan composer and conductor. He was born in Montevideo, where he studied composition and conducting with Guido Santórsola. Later he received conducting lessons from Antal Dorati and Pierre Monteux and composition lessons from Aaron Copland and Vittorio Giannini in the United States. Serebrier has conducted some of the major orchestras in the United States, Latin America, and Europe. He has been the recipient of two Guggenheim fellowships, an assistant to Leopold Stokowski in the American Symphony Orchestra, and composer in residence of the Cleveland Orchestra under George Szell. His work as a composer includes some early examples of a neoclassical character, strongly rhythmical and dissonant, and from there evolves into the use of aleatory devices. Outstanding in his catalog are a symphony (1957), *Poema elegíaco* (1962), and more recent contributions, such as *Erótica* (1968) and *Colores mágicos* (1971) for harp, orchestra, and sinchroma (a machine designed to react to sound and project colors and images on a screen).

JUAN A. ORREGO-SALAS

SERRA DO MAR. So-called coastal mountain range of southeastern Brazil. The Serra do Mar is the principal topographical feature of the Brazilian coast from northern Rio Grande do Sul into the state of Espírito Santo.

It was given its name by early Portuguese navigators who viewed it from the Atlantic and assumed it was a mountain chain. The Serra do Mar is in fact the jagged upper rim of the inland plateau, which slopes downward to the south and west. In a few places the rim has been worn away by the sea to form spectacular bays, such as those at Rio de Janeiro and Vitória, but elsewhere it is an escarpment rising sharply from the sea or from a narrow coastal strip to elevations ranging from 1,000 to 3,000 feet, with occasional higher peaks. It reaches its maximum proportions along the Atlantic shoreline of Paraná and São Paulo, where from the coast it presents an irregular wall of eroded rock cliffs and steep jungle-covered slopes.

From time immemorial the Serra do Mar has served as a barrier to penetration and travel inland from the Atlantic, and in modern times it is a major obstacle to engineers pushing rail and highway routes over it. Because of the Serra do Mar, rivers rising only a few miles from the coast of Brazil must flow inland more than 1,000 miles into the Paraná–La Plata Basin to reach the sea.

ROLLIE E. POPPINO

SERTÃO. The term "sertão" (plural, sertões) has two distinct but interrelated meanings. Historically, the sertão has meant the interior, or backlands, of Brazil. The term can apply equally to Amazonian rain forest (*see* AMAZON RIVER), arid desert, grasslands, and mountains. The spices from the colonial Amazon were *drogas do sertão*; the *sertanejo,* the inhabitant of the vast interior. The sertão of northeastern Brazil (*see* NORTHEAST) is a far more specific term, referring to the extremely arid interior and including parts of Piauí, Ceará, Rio Grande do Norte, Paraíba, Pernambuco, and Bahia. Typical landforms are planated surfaces, crystalline massifs, and *chapadas* (sedimentary plateaus). The climate is hot and dry; the periodic droughts, lasting up to three years, disrupt agriculture, thin the herds, kill the crops, and cause intense human suffering. The vegetation is *caatinga*, a scrubby xerophytic plant community.

Economic activity depends heavily on the availability of water from rain, contact springs, or semipermanent streams. The best areas are planted in sugar and coffee; the less desirable land is used for arboreal cotton, manioc, beans, and other food crops. Carnauba palms scattered in relatively humid areas provide valuable wax. Most of the sertão is used only for ranching: cattle where water is commonly available, sheep and goats in the poorest pastures.

The inhabitant of the sertão is a man facing extreme adversity. Despite the difficulty in coping with the environment, people are deeply attached to the sertão and will often return from their flights to escape the droughts. The sertão remains a problem area that continues to defy attempts to rationalize its use.

ROBIN L. ANDERSON

SERVICIO TÉCNICO INTERAMERICANO DE COOPERACIÓN AGRÍCOLA (INTER-AMERICAN TECHNICAL SERVICE FOR AGRICULTURAL COOPERATION; STICA). STICA was founded in December 1942 by the Paraguayan government and the Institute of Inter-American Affairs in Washington. Originally designed as a measure of World War II cooperation to stimulate the production of food and other materials needed in the fight against the Axis, STICA still functions today, in part with North American agronomists and technical experts, to better the lot of Paraguay's farmers. With bilateral funds, STICA created an Institute of Agronomy and established model and experimental farms and ranches to improve the breed of Paraguayan cattle and to develop new hybrid seeds. It also helps further the agrarian reforms of President Alfredo STROESSNER, providing credit and technical advice to farmers and helping settle squatters and new colonists on their own land. STICA is the main instrument for the renovation of Paraguayan agriculture and ranching, contributing greatly to their development. In addition to its aid to farm families, it focuses its attention on such major areas as weed control, the development of nontoxic insecticides, the demonstration of the use of fertilizers, and the introduction of more modern farm machinery.

JOHN HOYT WILLIAMS

SESMARIA. Land concession that served as the basic title to landed property in colonial Brazil. The grant of *sesmarias* in the settlement and development of territory had a long tradition in Portugal and the Atlantic islands before it was used in Brazil. The donataries were given the right to grant *sesmarias* in 1532, but after the establishment of royal administration in 1549 it was the Governors-General who enjoyed this prerogative (*see* CAPTAINCY SYSTEM). The law of 1375 on *sesmarias* had been intended as a means to improve agricultural output and encourage effective land use by the redistribution of lands that were unoccupied or were inadequately cultivated on condition that they be put to use within a stated period. In Brazil these stipulations as to effective occupation and use often remained dead letters, as huge tracts of land were accumulated by powerful colonial families. The crown's attempts in 1695, 1697, and 1699 to limit the size of holdings, and in 1699 to expropriate uncultivated land, met with no success.

KENNETH R. MAXWELL

SICCARDI, HONORIO (1897–   ). Argentine composer. Born in Buenos Aires, where he studied with Felipe Boero and Gilardo Gilardi, he later received some training in Italy from Francesco Malipiero. Siccardi was an active member of the Grupo Renovación after its establishment in Buenos Aires in 1937. His extended catalog of works comprises two *Suites Argentina* for orchestra (1945–1946); a symphony (1950); a chamber opera, *Mador* (1956); a concerto for violin and orchestra (1942); a concerto for piano and orchestra (1950); numerous chamber music works including seven string quartets; music for solo piano; and songs. He also wrote several textbooks and translated into Spanish many books on music.

JUAN A. ORREGO-SALAS

SIERRA, JUSTO (1848–1912). Mexican writer and educator. The son of the important Yucatecan writer and politician of the same name, Justo Sierra was born in Campeche. After the death of his father in 1861, he was taken to Mexico City; he received a degree in law from the Colegio de San Ildefonso a decade later. Sierra began writing for important newspapers while still a student, achieving some fame through these journalistic efforts, his poetry, and his fiction. He later entered politics, frequently serving as a deputy in Congress and also occupying a seat on the Supreme Court. He was best known, however, as an educator and historian. Sierra was Minister of Public Instruction from 1905 to 1911. His chief accomplishment in this field was the reorganization of the National University, but he also worked to bring about curricular reform and the dissemination of education. His zeal and achievements in these endeavors place him alongside Gabino Barreda and José VASCONCELOS in Mexico's triumvirate of great educational reformers.

Also far-reaching in influence on succeeding generations of intellectuals was his historical writing, principally *México: Su evolución social* (1900–1902), a cooperative multivolume work which he directed and for which he wrote a substantial and important part, later brought together and published separately as *Evolución política del pueblo mexicano,* 1910 (*The Political Evolution of the Mexican People*). In this study Sierra ushered in a new phase of Mexican historical writing with a synthesis emphasizing the importance of the mestizo. His other great history, *Juárez: Su obra y su tiempo* (1905), was written in collaboration with Carlos Pereyra. Sierra was appointed Ambassador to Spain in 1912 and died that year in Madrid.

See also CIENTÍFICOS.

CHARLES R. BERRY

SIERRA (ECUADOR). The highland of Ecuador is composed of two parallel ranges of mountains and a series of ten intermontane basins. These basins, often made intensely fertile by ash and lava deposited from surrounding volcanoes, support dense populations of Indian farmers. Only the basins of Quito and Cuenca have attracted significant numbers of people of Spanish ancestry, and they live primarily in the cities. A strong provincialism, preservation of Indian and Spanish traditions, and the influence of the Catholic Church distinguish the area.

Gold lured the Spaniards to the highland in 1534, but the climate and availability of a large submissive Indian work force led to lasting settlement. Huge grants of labor and land went to relatively few men. These emerged as the elite *terratenientes* (landowners) of Ecuador, who traded subsistence commodities grown on their great estates, filled public offices, and dedicated themselves to the preservation of the past. Even today the highland produces little for export.

During the colonial period the Indian, conditioned by Inca rule (*see* INCAS), labored under the ENCOMIENDA and MITA systems. Debt peonage followed, and the Indian paid tribute to the Ecuadorian government until 1895. Wages on some haciendas were as low as 50 centavos (5 cents) a day in 1955. Intensely concerned with mere existence, the Indian turned for vitality to ancient communal practices, spoke QUECHUA, and practiced a combination of Catholic and indigenous religions. Today illiterate, apolitical, and effectively immobilized, he shuns even the Ecuadorian Communist party and instead buttresses the conservatism of the sierra elite.   LOIS WEINMAN

SIERRA (PERU). Region with an average altitude of 13,000 feet. The sierra is characterized by pronounced ecological diversity. Stretching from approximately 6,500 to 22,180 feet, it is crisscrossed by numerous mountain chains, by basins of differing fertility, and by a varied flora and fauna. The sierra can be divided roughly into two parts: the páramo, the humid and fertile highland extending from the Ecuadorian border to Cajamarca; and the puna, a beautifully windswept and dry highland crossed by many fertile valleys that sink thousands of feet below the plateau. The puna, which extends from central Peru to the southern border, begins close to the upper limits of most crop production (about 14,000 feet) and is devoted almost exclusively to grazing.

The sierra contains most of Peru's population (about 55 percent), although an increasing number is continuing to migrate to the coast. Its economy is essentially based on mining, agriculture, and grazing, and most of its products are produced for local consumption. Mine products represent the region's major export. Wool and cattle also constitute important commercial commodities sold to the coast. The sierra also produces a variety of crops, including potatoes, barley, alfalfa, corn, wheat, rice, and sugarcane. However, its true agricultural potential has been inhibited by antiquated production methods, by a lack of adequate transportation, and by archaic landholding systems.

The sierra's predominantly Indian population is concentrated in villages at altitudes between 9,000 and 10,000 feet, and except for the major population centers, such as Cajamarca, Huancayo, Cuzco, and Arequipa, it has been relatively isolated from the rest of the nation. This factor partially explains the sierra's continuing cultural and political traditionalism.

ORAZIO A. CICCARELLI

SIGÜENZA Y GÓNGORA, CARLOS DE (1645–1700). Mexican scientist and intellectual. Born in Mexico City, he belonged to a distinguished family and was educated by the Jesuits, but was dismissed from the order. In 1672, after ordination as a secular priest, he was appointed to the chair of mathematics and astrology of the University of Mexico, which he held for more than twenty years. He was also appointed Royal Cosmographer, probably in 1689. In 1690 he published *Libra astronómica y filosófica,* in which he argued against Father Eusebio Francisco KINO's explanation of the character of a comet visible in 1680–1681, giving to this phenomenon a scientific explanation.

Sigüenza had a vast knowledge of history and geography. Among his many works are biographies of St. Francis Xavier and Hernán CORTÉS, a book of poetry, and a description of the French defeat in Santo Domingo in 1691. Sigüenza also had a keen interest in Mexican archaeology and the cult of the Virgin of Guadalupe (*see* GUADALUPE, VIRGIN OF). One of his greatest contributions to history was the rescue of the records of the Municipal Council of Mexico City, endangered by fire during the popular riots of 1692. As Royal Cosmographer he accompanied the 1693 expedition led by Andrés de Pez, which carried out the mapping and reconnaissance of Pensacola Bay in Florida. Sigüenza acted as chaplain of the Hospital del Amor de Dios, where he resided after 1682. He donated his vast library to the Jesuits and may have been allowed to join the order at the end of his life. Few men in colonial Mexico equaled Sigüenza y Góngora in versatility and intellectual talent.   ASUNCIÓN LAVRIN

SILES [ZUAZO], HERNÁN (1914–   ). President of Bolivia (1956–1960). The illegitimate son of Hernando Siles, President of Bolivia from 1928 to 1930, Siles served in the CHACO WAR. He was elected to Congress as an independent in 1940 and the following year was one of the founders of the MOVIMIENTO NACIONALISTA REVOLUCIONARIO (MNR).

During the 1940s he emerged as the chief lieutenant of Víctor PAZ ESTENSSORO, head of the MNR. In 1951 he was the party's candidate for Vice President, and although he was victorious, his victory was not recognized by the government of President Mamerto Urriolagoitia. In April 1952 he joined the tin miners' leader Juan LECHÍN to lead the successful revolution of the MNR against the military junta that had seized power after the 1951 election. In the succeeding government of Paz Estenssoro, Siles served as Vice President.

In 1956 Siles was elected as the MNR candidate for President. He launched a program for price stabilization to counteract the runaway inflation then gripping the country. When Lechín challenged this program, Siles went to the tin mines and broke an attempted general strike called by Lechín. During the rest of his administration Siles consolidated the revolutionary reforms begun by Paz Estenssoro.

Siles supported the reelection of Paz Estenssoro in 1960, but when the latter sought election to a third term in 1964, Siles opposed him and began to conspire with Gen. René BARRIENTOS against the President. Although Siles supported the coup against the MNR regime in November 1964, he soon fell out with the new government and went into exile, remaining away from Bolivia for most of the next five years. He returned for a few months to support the government of Gen. Juan José TORRES, who came to power in November 1970.

During the period after the overthrow of the MNR regime, Siles sought to help reestablish the unity of the MNR. In January 1971 he and ex-President Paz Estenssoro signed a tentative agreement to this end. However, when the faction of the MNR led by Paz Estenssoro cooperated with a military movement to overthrow the Torres government, Siles remained in exile in Chile.

ROBERT J. ALEXANDER

SILVA, JOSÉ ASUNCIÓN (1865–1896). Colombian poet. Silva is considered one of the most important precursors of the modernist movement in Spanish American literature (*see* MODERNISM: SPANISH AMERICA). He was born in Bogotá, the son of a wealthy family. His father was at the center of El Mosaico, a literary group in which Jorge ISAACS participated. His earliest poetic composition, "Primera comunión," was written in 1875 when he was ten years old. Because of his delicate features and physical attractiveness, he was unpopular with his fellow students and was often called El Niño Bonito and José Presunción. He soon abandoned formal studies but continued to read classical writers in Spanish, French, and English.

From 1883 to 1886 Silva traveled in Europe, where he became acquainted with Oscar Wilde and Stéphane Mallarmé. When his family's fortune was lost in the Colombian civil war of 1885, he was forced to return home. His attempts at a business career failed, and after the death of his sister Elvira he was forced to take a position as Secretary of the Colombian Legation in Venezuela (1894–1895). His greatest period of literary productivity came after Elvira's death and during his year in Venezuela, but he unfortunately lost three manuscripts, including some short stories, in a shipwreck while returning to Colombia in 1895. Silva's attempt to rebuild his economic fortunes failed, and he committed suicide on May 23, 1896, for unknown reasons.

Aside from one novel, *De sobremesa,* which was published posthumously in 1925, Silva is best known for his poetry (*Poesías,* 1886). "Día de difuntos" ("Day of the Dead") shows the influence of Edgar Allan Poe's "The Bells," and some of his poems are considered to be among the most musical and rhythmic in the Spanish language. Especially well known is "Nocturno III," which Silva supposedly wrote on the death of Elvira. "Vejeces," "Los maderos de San Juan" ("The Firewood of St. John"), and "Ronda" ("Round") are also among his best poems.

DANIEL R. REEDY

SILVA HENRÍQUEZ, RAÚL (1907–   ). Cardinal Archbishop of Santiago. Born in Talca, Silva Henríquez studied at the Liceo Alemán and the Catholic University, graduating in 1930. The same year he entered the Salesian Congregation, and in 1938 he was ordained. He spent many years in teaching, serving as director of a number of educational institutions, and he also played a leading role in national and international Catholic philanthropic organizations. His appointment as Bishop of Valparaíso in 1959 gave him a prominent position in the Chilean hierarchy, and he attained its highest position in 1961 on his elevation to the Archbishopric of Santiago. The following year he was designated Cardinal by Pope John XXIII.

Within the Catholic hierarchy of Latin America, Silva Henríquez is a liberal, strongly believing that the modern church must involve itself in social and economic reform, and he has expressed this belief in deeds as well as in words. In the early 1960s, following the lead of the Bishop of Talca, Manuel Larraín, who turned over church land to a peasant cooperative, he set up a significant land reform project with two large estates in the Santiago diocese, and with Larraín he established the Instituto de Promoción Agraria, a pioneer agency for land reform.

HAROLD BLAKEMORE

SILVA PARANHOS, JOSÉ MARIA DA. *See* RIO BRANCO, VISCONDE DO.

SILVA XAVIER, JOAQUIM JOSÉ. *See* INCONFIDÊNCIA MINEIRA.

SINARQUISMO. Vigorous counterrevolutionary mass movement that arose in central Mexico in May 1937, with the formation of the Unión Nacional Sinarquista, just as President Lázaro CÁRDENAS was exerting his greatest efforts to carry out his AGRARIAN REFORM program. Although the young leaders of the movement included descendants of large landholders and small farmers, most of its members were peasants who had not received land or who had received land but had not attained economic success. A fifth of Mexico's *ejidatarios* (*see* EJIDO) lived in the states of Guanajuato, Querétaro, Jalisco, and Michoacán, but in 1941 they had received only one-tenth of the funds lent by the National Bank of Ejidal Credit.

The nucleus of the *sinarquista* movement was in León, Guanajuato, the great artisan city in central Mexico. It took hold in regions where the CRISTERO REBELLION still smoldered and where there was a large percentage of illiterates. *Sinarquismo* advanced its own agrarian program in opposition to that of Cárdenas: to distribute land as private property, not to "lend" it to *ejidatarios* after it had been "stolen" from its owners. To combat the Communist cry "Proletarians All," the *sinarquistas* raised the slogan "Proprietors All."

In July 1938 the movement launched, without success, an ambitious program of colonization in the dry coastal regions of Baja California and Sonora and in the arid coast of Tamaulipas. In 1940, certain of imminent success, in part because of their belief in a Nazi victory in Europe, the *sinarquistas* prophesied that by 1960 they would have solved Mexico's agrarian problems through the exploitation of large tracts of public lands, which would be well watered and served by good transportation systems. Every family would have a piece of land, agricultural production would have increased, illiteracy would have virtually disappeared, and political corruption would have come to an end. The Unión Nacional Sinarquista declined as a result of the Nazi defeat and its own internal divisions, caused by the decision of some to participate directly in politics. The movement was also noted for its hatred of Miguel HIDALGO Y COSTILLA and Benito JUÁREZ.

MOISÉS GONZÁLEZ NAVARRO

SIQUEIROS, DAVID ALFARO (1896–1974). Mexican muralist and painter. Born in Chihuahua, Siqueiros was raised mainly in Mexico City, where he attended the Academy of San Carlos. He followed Dr. ATL to Orizaba with the forces of Venustiano CARRANZA in 1913 and reached the rank of captain. In 1919, with the end of the fighting, he was assigned a sinecure in the Mexican Embassy in Paris to continue his art studies. In Barcelona in 1921 he published one issue of *Vida Americana* containing a manifesto calling for artists to abandon oil painting in favor of exterior public murals in the service of society, their style to be dictated by their message. His life reflected a consistent effort to fulfill these ideals.

In 1922 he returned to Mexico and began painting murals in the National Preparatory School, the unfinished *Burial of a Worker* being the best. From 1925 to 1930 he was active mainly as a labor organizer, becoming secretary-general of the Confederación Sindical Unitaria, until he was arrested and confined to Taxco in 1930, where he began to paint again. He exiled himself to California in 1932. As a teacher of mural painting at the Chouinard Institute in Los Angeles, he used photographic techniques for designing, group work modeled on industrial crews, and new industrial materials and techniques, such as spray guns. In 1936 he founded the Experimental Workshop in New York to develop weather-resistant materials for exterior murals. Plastic-based industrial paints were first used for art by Siqueiros and his collaborators.

Late in 1936 he joined the Republican Army in Spain as a lieutenant colonel. He did not return to art until 1939, when he painted *Portrait of the Bourgeoisie* in pyroxylin on cement in the Electrical Workers Union Building in Mexico City. He was implicated in the assassination of Trotsky and remained in exile from 1941 to 1943, painting murals in Argentina and Cuba and an important one in pyroxylin on masonite in a school in Chillán, Chile. In Mexico City in 1944 he began a series of murals in the Palace of Fine Arts, *The New Democracy* being the first and a series glorifying CUAUHTÉMOC being done between 1951 and 1960. During the 1950s he also executed important murals in the National Polytechnic Institute, the National University of Mexico, and social security hospitals. That at the university is an exterior relief mosaic.

In 1960 Siqueiros was imprisoned for political agitation for four years, during which he painted prolifically. He had always been a major painter of easel works, although murals were his principal interest. Upon his release he completed the historical mural in the National Museum of History and began *The March of Humanity in Latin America,* completed in 1971 in an urban project on the Avenida de los Insurgentes Sur in Mexico City. This colossal work, covering more than 50,000 square feet in plastic paints on asbestos and cement with many three-dimensional elements of metal, is the product of a team of technicians using modern industrial tools and materials. Dramatic light and sound and a tilted rotating platform for observers make the murals a theatrical experience related to cinema, in line with Siqueiros's lifelong search for an art of total emotional engagement for a mass audience. Although the style is often abstract, Siqueiros defined his art as realistic, in opposition to the esthetic formalism of the art of the schools of Paris and New York. Siqueiros's many technical innovations, his independence of international trends, and his position as the major artist dedicated to the expression of twentieth-century social ideals give him an important place in the history of modern art.

Bibliography. Mario de Micheli, *David Alfaro Siqueiros,* New York, 1971; Bernard S. Myers, *Mexican Painting in Our Time,* New York, 1956.

TERENCE GRIEDER

SLAVERY. *See* ABOLITION OF SLAVERY (BRAZIL); ABOLITION OF SLAVERY (CUBA); NEGRO IN BRAZIL; NEGRO IN SPANISH AMERICA.

SOCCER WAR. *See* FOOTBALL WAR.

SOCIAL DEMOCRATIC PARTY. *See* PARTIDO SOCIAL DEMOCRÁTICO.

SOCIALISM. Socialism first appeared in Latin America in the mid-nineteenth century in the form of European utopian socialism. Disenchanted young intellectuals of the Argentine generation of 1837 and the Chilean generation of 1842, as well as young Colombian Liberals (*see* LIBERAL PARTY: COLOMBIA), concluded that this new social philosophy was the answer to their national problems of poverty, illiteracy, and inequality. Typical of such men were the Chileans Santiago Arcos and Francisco BILBAO, who at first contented themselves with publishing tracts and articles condemning the conditions they found. Soon, however, they concluded that literary protest was not enough and moved to create a viable political force that would bring socialism to Chile.

As Chile's commerce and industry expanded, Arcos and Bilbao decided to make use of the increasing numbers of workers by forming in 1850 an organization that would contain artisans and laborers as well as intellectuals and literary figures. They named the organization the Sociedad de la Igualdad (Society of Equality). Arcos did not think that large numbers of workers alone would carry his programs into reality. He was convinced that politically aware workers such as European immigrants were a necessity for his movement. Europeans, he reasoned, would already have been exposed to one form of socialism or another and would not require the indoctrination necessary for indigenous laborers, who were less knowledgeable concerning political and social problems. The society was suppressed in less than a year, but its influence on Chilean socialists was considerable.

In the late nineteenth and early twentieth century a variety of socialistic philosophies, notably Marxism and anarchosyndicalism, appeared, particularly in countries that experienced heavy immigration from Europe. The new arrivals were frequently socialists themselves and, more militant than their mid-nineteenth-century counterparts, gained popularity with indigenous workers because of their dramatic demonstrations, riots, and strikes. Some political parties now came into existence to represent the various socialistic attitudes, but these generally had little impact on governments or on society. Before World War I socialists did not have much political success, although they were able openly to expound their philosophies. One of their greatest problems stemmed from a failure to unite in the common cause. They could not form a cohesive socialist movement because the various socialistic groups were antagonistic toward each other; Marxists and anarchists found it impossible to coexist. Consequently, even when a labor dispute that should have welded all socialists together developed, it seldom was possible to achieve concerted action.

Following World War I socialism was unable to make much headway because of the arrival of international COMMUNISM on the scene. The novelty of communism and its radical program appealed to many who had been Socialist party members. As individuals and as parties, Socialists moved into the Communist fold. In addition, Socialists had to face the competition of new left-wing non-Communist parties, such as the ALIANZA POPULAR REVOLUCIONARIA AMERICANA (APRA), which rapidly gained strength in Peru after its establishment in 1924. Although not a Marxist party, APRA came to be associated with socialism, since its ideals and objectives were similar. Finally, the Socialist parties were still generally rooted in utopian socialism and frequently lost sight of practical politics in flights of intellectual fancy.

Among the Socialist parties established before World War I, those of Argentina, Chile, and Uruguay were the most important. The Argentine party (originally called the Partido Socialista Obrero Argentino; *see* SOCIALIST PARTY: ARGENTINA) was founded in 1896 under the leadership of Juan B. JUSTO, a physician by profession. Rivalry between the Socialist party and the anarchists inhibited the socialist movement in Argentina, as did the relative isolation of the movement, which was confined almost entirely to Buenos Aires while the rest of the nation had no contact with it. The party professed a Marxist sympathy but was extremely moderate. Moreover, it was undercut on many issues by the powerful Radical party (*see* RADICAL PARTY: ARGENTINA). Con-sequently, although the Argentine Socialist party is the oldest in Latin America, it has seldom played a significant role in the political life of the nation.

The Socialist party of Uruguay, founded in 1910, grew out of the Karl Marx Center, a study group of which Emilio Frugoni was the secretary. The party succeeded in electing Frugoni to the national legislature in 1911. In 1921 the party was fragmented when a majority of the delegates to a party congress voted to join the Third International and adopt the name Communist party of Uruguay. The minority, which included Frugoni, constituted a new Socialist party.

The first important Socialist party in Chile was organized in 1912 when a group of Socialists in the Democratic party (*see* DEMOCRATIC PARTY: CHILE) decided that it was becoming too moderate and, led by Luis Emilio RECABARREN, broke away to form the Socialist Workers party (Partido Obrero Socialista). The new party quickly gained control of the labor movement, increasing its strength until it became a significant factor in left-wing Chilean politics. Unfortunately for the Socialists, the party leadership chose to adhere to the Communist International in 1922, forcing those who did not espouse communism to drop out and form a number of small, ineffective Socialist parties.

These small splinter parties of the 1920s served as a foundation for the creation in 1933 of the present Socialist party (*see* SOCIALIST PARTY: CHILE). From a modest beginning that year the party expanded rapidly until by 1938 it could boast of three senators and a dozen deputies in the national Congress. In 1936 the Communists dropped their isolationist stance and sought to cooperate with other left-of-center parties. Socialists, Communists, Radicals, and Democrats banded together to form the Popular Front, which won the 1938 presidential election (*see* POPULAR FRONT: CHILE).

The Popular Front experience proved to be no great asset to Chilean socialism, for quarrels developed over participation in the government and cooperation with the Communists. By World War II Chilean socialism had splintered once again, and for the next two decades Socialists expended their energies in creating new parties and battling inside the established party.

Meanwhile, Socialist parties had been established in Brazil, Panama, and other Latin American countries, while David TORO launched a government of "military socialism" in Bolivia in 1936. In Peru the Marxist intellectual José Carlos MARIÁTEGUI organized a Socialist party in 1928, but it adopted the Communist name after his death two years later. A number of Socialist parties appeared in Brazil in the 1920s and joined the National Liberating Alliance of 1934–1935, only to be crushed by Getúlio VARGAS after the abortive uprising of 1935. After Ecuador's first Socialist party entered the Third International, a new party of the same name was formed in 1930. In 1938 a coalition of Socialists and Communists won control of Congress but proved unable to agree on a presidential candidate. Six years later the Socialists joined Communists and other left-wing groups in a Democratic Alliance that restored the perennial *caudillo* José María VELASCO IBARRA to the Presidency. The alliance also dominated the Constituent Congress of 1944–1945, but Velasco Ibarra soon broke with both the Socialists and the Communists.

In the years since World War II Socialist forces have

fractionalized, fought among themselves, and altered their philosophies. Many have become far more radical than their ancestors, supporting Marxism and Castroism and lending support to communism. Whereas some of the traditional so-called Democratic Socialist parties continue to function, the trend has been toward parties that call themselves Popular Socialist. These Popular Socialist parties are more internationally oriented and are not averse to using violence as a means of gaining political power. The most spectacular success to be registered by any Socialist party was the election in 1970 of Salvador ALLENDE to the Presidency of Chile. Allende, a Marxist and a Socialist, was the candidate of a coalition composed of Socialists, Communists (*see* COMMUNIST PARTY: CHILE), and other left-wing groups.

Although Socialist parties, whether democratic or popular, have not grown dramatically in recent years, their programs and ideals have become firmly rooted in Latin American political thought through other parties and ruling cliques. ACCIÓN DEMOCRÁTICA (Democratic Action; AD) in Venezuela and APRA in Peru have fostered socialist programs and pursued socialist objectives. Even Peruvian military officers, traditionally conservative, espoused some socialist programs and attempted to put them into practice after taking power in 1968. Consequently, socialism continues to be an important political philosophy even in countries in which Socialist parties have little or no electoral importance.

Bibliography. Victor Alba, *Politics and the Labor Movement in Latin America,* Stanford, Calif., 1968; Luis E. Aguilar (ed.), *Marxism in Latin America,* New York, 1968; Régis Debray, *Conversations with Allende,* New York, 1971; Julio César Jobet, *Precursores del pensamiento social de Chile,* Santiago, 1955–56; Oscar Waiss, *Nacionalismo y socialismo en América Latina,* Buenos Aires, 1961.

JACK R. THOMAS

SOCIALIST PARTY (ARGENTINA). An outgrowth of, and a response to, massive European immigration (*see* IMMIGRATION: ARGENTINA), the Socialist party founded in Argentina in 1896 sought the transformation of society and control of the government by the proletariat. Insisting on the need to substitute ideas for men as the country's dominant political force, it focused its concern on socioeconomic issues and sought to use the national Congress as a forum, to further civic morality through popular libraries and its organ, *La Vanguardia,* and to organize the proletariat into labor unions.

The decade of the 1930s represented the peak of the party's strength. As a result of the Radical party's electoral abstention until 1935 (*see* RADICAL PARTY: ARGENTINA), Socialist representation in Congress increased, thereby providing the party with an arena for its interest in social welfare and in the exposure of governmental graft. However, because of its European orientation, its rejection of "creole" Argentina, its moderation on economic issues, and its debilitation by five major splits, the party's influence was confined primarily to Buenos Aires, where it increasingly represented the interests of middle-class groups. Progressively weaker since the 1930s, the party has participated in a long series of "popular front" attempts that have led to further incisions.

See JUSTO, Juan B.; PALACIOS, Alfredo L.

NOREEN F. STACK

SOCIALIST PARTY (CHILE). Founded in April 1933, the Chilean Socialist party (Partido Socialista de Chile) was the result of a fusion of a number of Marxist groups. It proclaimed itself the party of workers and intellectuals. The party supported the Popular Front of the 1930s and secured three seats in Pedro AGUIRRE CERDA's Cabinet (*see* POPULAR FRONT: CHILE). The collapse of the front in 1941 was followed by a split in the party in 1943, when one of its founders, Marmaduke Grove, opposed its support of Juan Antonio RÍOS and created the Partido Socialista Auténtico. The official party ran its own candidate against Gabriel GONZÁLEZ VIDELA in the presidential election of 1946 but won only 2.5 percent of the vote. A deeper internal division occurred in 1948 over the Law for the Defense of Democracy, which Salvador ALLENDE and Raúl Ampuero, two leading members, opposed to the point of leaving the party to found the Partido Socialista Popular. When that faction backed Carlos IBÁÑEZ for the Presidency in 1952, Allende returned to the parent body and persuaded it to nominate him as its own presidential candidate. He ran last, with 5.5 percent of the vote.

With Chilean politics in chaos, a movement toward reconciliation began, first in the FRENTE DE ACCIÓN POPULAR (FRAP) and then, in 1957, in the reunification of the Socialist parties. Though Allende failed to win the Presidency in 1958 and 1964, his party received 11 percent of the vote in congressional elections in 1961 and 1965 and raised its share to 14 percent in 1967. After the victories of the PARTIDO DEMÓCRATA CRISTIANO in 1964 and 1965, the Socialist party split again as Raúl Ampuero formed the Unión Socialista Popular, but this faction was annihilated in the congressional elections of 1969 while Allende's official party secured 11.5 percent of the vote. In 1969 the party joined Communists, Radicals, and other groups in Unidad Popular (Popular Unity), a coalition to fight the presidential election of 1970, and it secured Allende's fourth nomination as the left-wing candidate, but only after hard bargaining (*see* COMMUNIST PARTY: CHILE; RADICAL PARTY: CHILE). His victory was the Socialist party's greatest electoral triumph, though the historical division between moderates and extremists in the party had far from disappeared.

HAROLD BLAKEMORE

SOLÍS, JUAN DÍAZ DE (1470–1516). Spanish navigator. Born in Lebrija, Solís sailed with Vicente Yáñez PINZÓN on June 29, 1508, in search of the Spice Islands by a western route. The expedition commenced its explorations by circumnavigating Cuba, thus proving conclusively that it was an island. They then continued to the Gulf of Honduras and proceeded to follow carefully the Central and South American coastlines until approximately 41° south latitude, where they discovered the Río Negro. Strangely, they sailed past and did not discover the RÍO DE LA PLATA on this voyage.

In 1512, upon the death of Amerigo VESPUCCI, Solís succeeded to the post of Pilot Major of Spain. On November 12, 1514, King Ferdinand II commissioned him to take three ships for a period of two years to attempt to find a southwest passage to the Spice Islands. After entering the Pacific, he was to sail northward to the Isthmus of Panama and follow that latitude to his destination. Solís sailed from Sanlúcar de Barrameda on October 8, 1515, and arrived at the Río de la Plata, which he named El Mar Dulce (Freshwater

Sea), in February 1516. The expedition explored what seemed to offer a transoceanic passage as far as the territory of the Charruas. Disaster befell them when Solís rowed ashore on the Uruguayan coast and was killed and eaten by the natives in August 1516. Thoroughly demoralized, the Spaniards, under the command of his brother-in-law, Francisco de Torres, returned to Spain, arriving on September 4, 1516.

MARTIN TORODASH

SOLÓRZANO PEREIRA, JUAN (1575–1655). Spanish jurist and author of *Política indiana*. Solórzano was born in Madrid and earned a doctorate in law at the University of Salamanca. In 1609 he was selected for an appointment as *oidor* (judge), of the *audiencia* of Lima.

Solórzano spent eighteen intensely busy years in this post. In addition to his regular work he managed to write an erudite treatise in elegant Latin entitled *De Indiarum jure*. A Spanish edition of this work appeared in 1648 under the title *Política indiana*. An indispensable tool for understanding colonial Spanish America, the treatise was divided into six books in which the author examined consecutively Spain's title to the Indies, the native population, the ENCOMIENDA system, the church, the state, and the economy. *Política indiana* remains a priceless commentary on the laws of the Indies, a study that influenced the subsequent development of jurisprudence in America and in Spain.

During his stay in America, Solórzano also worked on a compilation of laws. In 1618 he sent to the COUNCIL OF THE INDIES the completed first volume of a projected six-volume collection, and in 1648 he submitted the completed six-volume work. The Council did not see fit to adopt Solórzano's compilation, but there is little doubt that it facilitated the work that finally did appear in 1681 (*see* RECOPILACIÓN DE LEYES DE LAS INDIAS).

Solórzano returned to Spain in 1627, served as a member of the Council of the Indies from 1629 until his retirement in 1644, and died in Madrid in 1655.

NORMAN MEIKLEJOHN

SOMOZA DEBAYLE, ANASTASIO (1925–   ). Nicaraguan military officer and President (1967–1972). As the son of Anastasio SOMOZA GARCÍA, the founder of the Somoza political dynasty in Nicaragua, Anastasio Somoza Debayle was born to special privilege and responsibility. Graduating from West Point in 1948, he returned to Nicaragua to assume high positions in the National Guard, which combines the nation's military and police power. At the age of thirty, while his father was still President, he became commander of the guard. When his father was assassinated in 1956, Somoza remained in command of the guard while his older brother Luis, a civilian, became President. He resigned from the guard in 1966 in order to be eligible constitutionally to run for the Presidency. Having easily won the election, he began a five-year term as President on May 1, 1967. Compared with the presidential terms of Luis SOMOZA DEBAYLE (1956–1963) and René SCHICK GUTIÉRREZ (1963–1966), the regime of Anastasio Somoza Debayle (1967–1972) brought a tightening of press censorship and political control. The death of Luis Somoza in April 1967 removed a restraining influence on the military-minded

Anastasio Somoza. Minor outbreaks early in his administration involving students, clerics, and laborers met with a quick, forceful response by the National Guard. A series of poor crop years lowered prices of Nicaragua's exports, and other economic problems heightened discontent toward the end of his administration. When Somoza's term expired in 1972, he turned over power to a bipartisan triumvirate and was immediately proclaimed a presidential candidate in elections scheduled for September 1974.

CHARLES L. STANSIFER

SOMOZA DEBAYLE, LUIS (1923–1967). Nicaraguan President (1956–1963). Of the two sons of Anastasio SOMOZA GARCÍA, founder of the durable Somoza political dynasty in Nicaragua, Luis was the older and the more liberal. A civilian, he attended several universities in the United States before returning to Nicaragua to serve as a Nationalist Liberal in the Congress. When his father was assassinated in 1956, Luis Somoza, as President of Congress and first designate (alternate) to the Presidency, automatically became President. He finished his father's term of office and was reelected with only token opposition. As he had promised from the beginning, he stepped down at the end of his elected term in 1963. His successor, René SCHICK GUTIÉRREZ, was a close associate of the Somoza family.

The Presidency of Luis Somoza was a period of gradual relaxation of the political repression characteristic of the previous twenty years. The Somoza family remained firmly in command, but Luis Somoza preferred to silence opposition by social action rather than by force. Steps were taken on behalf of housing improvement, social security, land reform, and university autonomy. The economy, as measured by an average annual increase in goods and services of approximately 8 percent, was healthy. Somoza contributed to improved Central American relations by accepting the International Court of Justice decision regarding Nicaragua's border dispute with Honduras and by working to avoid conflict with Costa Rica. This relaxation of international tensions contributed to the success of the negotiations for the CENTRAL AMERICAN COMMON MARKET, which Somoza supported. With respect to the problem of hemispheric relations with Fidel CASTRO, Somoza proved to be one of the most willing collaborators in the plans for the 1961 invasion of Cuba. Somoza died of a heart attack in April 1967.

CHARLES L. STANSIFER

SOMOZA GARCÍA, ANASTASIO (1896–1956). Nicaraguan dictator. Somoza dominated the Nicaraguan political scene from the early 1930s until his death in 1956. During this time he established one of the most enduring political dynasties that Latin America has experienced in the period since independence.

Educated in a business school in Philadelphia, Somoza dedicated himself to a military career upon his return to Nicaragua. He rose to prominence first as an officer and then as chief of the National Guard. The guard was created in the late 1920s, during the occupation of Nicaragua by United States Marines, as a force to put an end to Nicaragua's bitterly partisan political rivalries, always a disturbing element in Central American international relations. Since it combined both military and police functions, the guard under Somoza's direction soon became a more powerful political instrument than the Presidency itself. With the guard's backing Somoza ousted President Juan Bautista SACASA in 1936 and took over the Presidency himself. Although on two occasions Somoza allowed others to assume the Presidency, he reclaimed the office when the first showed a degree of independence and when the second died in office. Even while President, he did not relinquish control over the guard. Following Somoza's assassination in 1956, just after he had announced that he would seek still another presidential term, his sons Luis SOMOZA DEBAYLE and Anastasio SOMOZA DEBAYLE kept the Somoza system intact.

Somoza did not need strong-arm methods to maintain control. A comparatively well-paid bureaucracy, dependent on the dictator, provided jobs for the loyal and administered Somoza's will. The National Guard's monopoly of force discouraged violence against the regime. The Nationalist Liberal party became a disciplined instrument for the influencing of voters. Lastly, the numerous businesses and ranches owned or controlled by the Somoza family provided reliable support for the dictator. Also, by tempting Conservative opponents and independents with jobs and influence on a minor scale, Somoza weakened the opposition. Twice the Conservative party negotiated formal agreements with the Somoza government that provided it with a stated percentage of governmental posts in return for relaxation of opposition. These deals naturally divided Somoza's opponents, for of course some argued that to negotiate with Somoza for anything short of surrender sacrificed their principles as opponents of dictatorship.

Furthermore, Somoza was not indifferent to the

Anastasio Somoza García. [*Organization of American States*]

demands of Nicaraguans for social progress. A new labor code in 1944, an income tax law in 1952, the creation of a development institute in 1953, and similar measures improved economic and social conditions in the country and satisfied some demands for change. Needless to say, they did not immediately undermine the basis of Somoza's paternalistic system. Somoza's control over Nicaragua's economic production allowed attention to be paid to centralization and planning. One of the results was to expand cotton production starting in the late 1940s, with a resultant cotton boom in the next decade. By 1958 cotton outdistanced coffee, the traditional leader, in Nicaragua's export list. The figure for per capita exports increased from $12 in 1940, the fourth year of the Somoza government, to $53 in 1959, a remarkably rapid increase at least partially attributable to the new politicoeconomic climate of the Somoza regime.

In relations with foreign governments Somoza had a mixed record. He was wise enough to cultivate good relations with the United States, which reached one climax in 1939 when he paid a state visit to the United States and was elaborately received by Washington officials. Predictably he cooperated with the United States during World War II and the early years of the cold war. Dividends for this policy were collected in the form of loans and grants for highway and other development. However, the smaller powers of the Central American area were somewhat uneasy with such a powerful figure in their midst. In 1954 Somoza was involved in an incident that nearly precipitated war between his country and Costa Rica. Under his protection Costa Rican exiles hostile to President JOSÉ FIGUERES prepared and launched an invasion of Costa Rica from Nicaraguan soil. Quick action by the ORGANIZATION OF AMERICAN STATES prevented the incident from deteriorating into outright warfare between the two countries.

Of all the dictators of the Caribbean area during the 1930s and 1940s, Somoza was perhaps the most interested in social and economic measures. Dividends such as he provided help to explain a degree of popular satisfaction with the Somoza government and an acceptance of the loss of political and press freedom.

See also SANDINO, Augusto César.

Bibliography. Gustavo Alemán Bolaños, *Un lombrosiano: Somoza, 1939–1944,* Guatemala City, 1945; id., *Los pobres diablos, 1937–1944.* Guatemala City, 1947; Evans F. Carlson, "The Guardia Nacional de Nicaragua," *Marine Corps Gazette,* vol. XXXI, August 1937, pp. 7–20; Pedro Joaquín Chamorro Cardenal, *Estirpe sangrienta: Los Somoza,* Mexico City, 1957; Gratus Halftermeyer, *El General Somoza, su vida y su obra,* Managua, 1957; Patrick McMahon, "Somoza of Nicaragua," *American Mercury,* vol. LXXVIII, April 1954, pp. 132–136; Ramón Romero, *Somoza, asesino de Sandino,* Mexico City, 1959; Peter H. Smith, "Dictatorship and Development in Nicaragua: 1950–1960," *American Economist,* vol. VII, no. 1, June 1963, pp. 24–32.

CHARLES L. STANSIFER

SONORA, MARQUÉS DE LA. *See* GÁLVEZ, JOSÉ DE.

SORO, ENRIQUE (1884–1954). Chilean composer. Born in Concepción, he studied music with his father, an Italian composer who had settled in Chile, and completed his instruction at the Milan Conservatory in 1906. He was appointed professor of piano and composition at the National Conservatory in Santiago, of which he was the director for almost a decade (1919–1928). Soro received the National Prize for the Arts in 1948. His style is something of a holdover from late romanticism, at times with subtle touches of Chilean folk music. He wrote *Romantic Symphony* (1920), *Andante appassionato* (1915), *Danza fantástica* (1916), *Tres aires chilenos* (1943), a concerto for piano and orchestra (1919), two sonatas for cello and piano and two for violin and piano, and a large amount of piano music and songs.

JUAN A. ORREGO-SALAS

SOTO, BERNARDO (1854–1931). Costa Rican President. Upon the death of President Próspero Fernández in 1885, Bernardo Soto assumed the Presidency in his capacity as first designate, or presidential alternate. He was reelected the following year and served a four-year term. Soto continued the progressive work of his two predecessors, Fernández and Tomás GUARDIA, emphasizing the construction of new schools and hospital facilities. The well-known mental hospital Asilo Chapui was founded during his regime, as was the National Library. Soto's Minister of Education, Mauro Fernández, was a particularly active Cabinet officer who was responsible, with Soto, for the Fundamental Law of Public Instruction, which made education free and obligatory in Costa Rica. Furthermore, the educational budget was tripled between 1885 and 1888.

The presidential election of 1889, over which Soto presided, is generally considered a landmark in Costa Rica's political evolution. This is true in the sense that there was freedom of expression, political party organization along ideological as well as personalist lines, and a correct count of the votes. The political grouping that opposed the government's candidate won the election and took office peacefully. Any deviation from this procedure since 1889 has been condemned by Costa Rican public opinion.

CHARLES L. STANSIFER

SOTO, HERNANDO DE (1498?–1542). Spanish conquistador of Peru and explorer of North America. An Estremaduran hidalgo, Soto became a protégé of Pedro Arias de ÁVILA (Pedrarias) and sailed with his expedition to Panama in 1514. Soto's martial boldness during the Nicaraguan campaign (1524) won him the post of alcalde in León and a share of the best encomiendas of Nicaragua. With his partner Hernán Ponce de León, he contributed two ships, men, and horses to Francisco PIZARRO's Peruvian expedition, arriving at Puná Island in time for the march to Cajamarca (1532). Pizarro showed his respect for Soto's leadership ability by sending him with his brother Hernando to confront the Inca ATAHUALPA. Soto led Pizarro's cavalry in the massacre of Atahualpa's bodyguards, stoutly protested the latter's execution, and fought in the vanguard to clear the road to Cuzco (1533). Pizarro rewarded him with 17,740 gold pesos but denied further favors when Soto sought to join Diego de ALMAGRO's group. Rebuffed by Almagro, Soto returned to Spain, married a daughter of Pedrarias, and obtained the right to conquer and settle Florida (1537). Granted titles of *adelantado,* Marqués, and Governor of Cuba and Florida, Soto left his wife in charge at Havana while he embarked on a three-

year trek (1539–1542) from Tampa Bay to Arkansas. After rash decisions and numerous misfortunes had ruined the expedition, Soto died; his body was sunk in the Mississippi River. Ironically, he is famed more for his failure in North America than for his successes in Central America and Peru.

WILLIAM S. DUDLEY

SOTO, MARCO AURELIO (1846–1908). President of Honduras (1876–1883). The golden age of Honduran Liberalism, which flowered in the late nineteenth century, derived much of its substance and direction from neighboring Guatemala. Its main exponent, Marco Aurelio Soto, and his lieutenant, Ramón Rosa, received their formal education in Guatemalan schools and their practical grooming as members of Justo Rufino BARRIOS's Liberal Guatemalan bureaucracy. With Barrios's support Soto assumed the Honduran Presidency in 1876. *See* LIBERAL PARTY (HONDURAS).

Once installed in office, Soto launched an ambitious, if sometimes haphazard and corrupt, program of reform. Construction of a cart road connecting Tegucigalpa with the Pacific was begun, the postal system was regularized, and a telegraph network was created. Soto's most positive contribution lay in drafting the legislation with which his successors Luis Bográn (1884–1891) and Policarpo BONILLA (1894–1899) could pursue the integration and modernization of Honduras.

The improved communication system, coupled with the presence of a powerful and congenial Guatemalan neighbor, inaugurated a period of strong central government hitherto unknown in Honduras. But Barrios's influence could also have an unsettling effect on Honduran affairs. In March 1883, having incurred Barrios's disfavor, Soto resigned his office and left Honduras. Nevertheless, his involvement in Honduran politics continued. Eager to recapture the Presidency, Soto and his followers launched several abortive filibuster attempts and an unsuccessful election campaign in 1902.

GENE S. YEAGER

SOUBLETTE, CARLOS (1789–1870). President of Venezuela (1837–1839, 1843–1847). During the independence period Soublette emerged as a capable administrator. Simón BOLÍVAR quickly recognized his talents and used them consistently until Soublette threw his lot in with José Antonio PÁEZ and the Venezuelan separatists. From 1829 until his death in 1870 Soublette played a prominent role among the *paecistas*. A prime Conservative oligarch, Soublette could always be counted on to do what he was told and to do it well. His two presidential terms, the first from 1837 to 1839 as successor to Dr. José María VARGAS and the second in his own right in the period 1843–1847, were characterized by careful, cautious, conservative, but able administration. Always sensitive to the needs of his superiors, Soublette evidently never aspired to replace them, thus enhancing his value as a trustworthy subordinate. With the turmoil of the Federal Wars (1858–1863) and their aftermath, Soublette's fortunes followed those of his Conservative associates. He served in various important but secondary capacities in the armies of the Conservatives and in the fleeting *paecista* government of 1861–1863. He reappeared for the last time in the final Conservative government in 1869.

JOHN V. LOMBARDI

SOULOUQUE, FAUSTIN (ca. 1789–1867). President and Emperor of Haiti. Born a slave, Soulouque rose through the ranks of the Haitian Army to head the National Guard in 1847, when he was chosen as a compromise candidate for President. Proud, determined, and uneducated, Soulouque consolidated his power by iron rule. Like Jean-Jacques DESSALINES and Henry CHRISTOPHE, he considered monarchy a symbol of political success and in 1849 prevailed on the Senate to approve him as Emperor Faustin I. He created six princes and fifty-nine dukes, marquises, and barons.

Faustin, like earlier Haitians, feared that a foreign presence on Dominican soil would be a prelude to the conquest of Haiti. To forestall such an eventuality he invaded the east in 1849, but his badly equipped army failed, as it did again in 1855. Soulouque's domestic policies proved short-sighted, particularly his neglect of agriculture and mining. He and his wife were devout followers of VODUN and as a result were ridiculed by the ÉLITE and foreigners.

As Faustin's despotism increased without parallel gains for the nation, opposition mounted. In 1858 Nicolas Fabre GEFFRARD rebelled, declared the republic restored, and won when the imperial forces deserted Faustin. Faustin left for Jamaica on January 22, 1859, but returned to Haiti shortly before his death at his birthplace, Petit-Goâve, on August 6, 1867.

JOHN E. BAUR

SOUSA, IRINEU EVANGELISTA DE. See MAUÁ, VISCONDE.

SOUSA, JOÃO DA CRUZ E. See CRUZ E SOUSA, JOÃO DA.

SOUSA, MARTIM AFONSO DE (1500–1564). Experienced Portuguese sea commander who in 1531 led an expedition to Brazil charged with the discovery of new lands and the expulsion of the French from the territory claimed by Portugal. Martim Afonso explored the coast south to the RÍO DE LA PLATA, returning to send expeditions into the interior from the Bay of Guanabara and Cananéia, the major objectives of which were to seek possible sources of precious metals. Before returning to Portugal in 1533, Martim Afonso founded a small settlement on the island of São Vicente, the first Portuguese establishment in southern Brazil, situated near the present city of Santos in São Paulo State. The following year he was granted São Vicente as a hereditary captaincy by King João III. He never returned to Brazil, however, serving later in India and on the Council of State in Lisbon. São Vicente was competently administered by overseers. Sugarcane was introduced, and the construction of a sugar mill was financed by the Flemish capitalist Erasmus Schetz (see SUGAR INDUSTRY: COLONIAL BRAZIL).

KENNETH R. MAXWELL

SOUSA, TOMÉ DE (d. 1579). First Governor-General of Brazil (1549–1553). In 1549 Tomé de Sousa led a well-organized expedition that established the authority of the crown in the administration of Brazil and founded Salvador da Bahia as the administrative capital of Portuguese America. He arrived with some 1,000 men, among whom were 320 soldier-colonizers, military, fiscal, and judicial officials, artisans including stonemasons and tilemakers, and 400 *degregados* (convicts).

The Governor-General's instructions provided comprehensively for the defense, colonization, and Christianization of the Portuguese territory. To aid missionary activity he was accompanied by six Jesuits led by Manuel da NÓBREGA. Tomé de Sousa chose the site for the city of Salvador and began its construction. He also possessed the authority to make *sesmarias* (land grants; see SESMARIA) and sought to encourage the construction of sugar mills. Although donatary captaincies were not abolished, they were made subject to the Governor-General's authority (see CAPTAINCY SYSTEM).

KENNETH R. MAXWELL

STEPHENS, JOHN LLOYD (1805–1852). American explorer-archaeologist who first made Central America generally known in the United States and who inaugurated modern studies of the MAYAS. He was born in New Jersey, graduated from Columbia College, and after studying law settled in New York in 1825. There he began his practice and also engaged actively in Democratic politics.

Stephens's strenuous support of William L. Marcy in the gubernatorial campaign of 1834 earned him a claim to a later political favor, along with an infected throat that sent him abroad to recuperate. A trip to Europe, extended to the Near East and Egypt, awakened in him a passion for "antiquities" that led him to abandon the promising career in politics he had begun in New York. He found his tastes and enthusiasms matched in those of Frederick Catherwood, an artist he met in London, and their partnership, which subsequent collaboration made famous, was born. Mutual excitement generated by a report Catherwood had just seen on extraordinary ruins said to exist at Palenque, in the Mexican state of Chiapas, provided a direction for their joint venture.

Stephens's published accounts of his travels attained immediate popularity, and proceeds from sales soon gave him financial independence, enabling him and Catherwood to begin preparations for a Central American expedition. The death of the recently appointed Minister to Central America allowed Stephens to apply for and receive from President Martin Van Buren (August 1839) an appointment to find and negotiate with the Central American government that would give the two men the advantages of diplomatic status.

Stephens and Catherwood found Central America in ferment. José Rafael CARRERA, a Guatemalan guerrilla, terrorized the countryside and threatened the governments both of his own state and of the Federation of Central America (see CENTRAL AMERICA, FEDERATION OF). The distracted condition of the country and uncertainty as to the existence of a general government allowed time, while Stephens awaited a favorable opportunity to execute his diplomatic commission, for the travelers to investigate the ruins they had come to see. A detour from the usual route to Guatemala City took them to the ruins of COPÁN in Honduras, where Catherwood remained to make drawings—and later to discover and record the monuments at Quiriguá in Guatemala—while Stephens proceeded to Guatemala City. The impracticability of negotiation at that juncture gave Stephens the opportunity to visit the other Central American states and to record his view of the life and customs of the day as well as data from the first scientific examination of the proposed Nicaraguan canal route. On his return to El Salvador he encountered Francisco MORAZÁN, the defender of the Federation, reeling back to San Salvador after his decisive defeat by Carrera at Guatemala City and on his way to exile. Since no general government with which to negotiate remained, Stephens decided to return to the United States.

The two men made the homeward journey an extended exploration. They visited archaeological sites, the principal ones being Utatlán, Palenque, and Uxmal, before Catherwood's illness forced them to proceed to the United States. In 1841 they returned to Yucatán for a more extensive inspection of ruins. For ten months, between attacks of malaria, they explored and recorded known ruins of the peninsula, principally those of Uxmal and CHICHÉN ITZÁ, and some previously unknown sites. Stephens's separate two-volume accounts of these two expeditions, *Incidents of Travel in Central America, Chiapas, and Yucatán* (1841) and *Incidents of Travel in Yucatán* (1843), with illustrations by Catherwood, were both enthusiastically received; the first went through twelve editions and sold 20,000 copies within three months.

Stephens's association with Central America made it natural that he should be drawn into isthmian transportation projects. In 1849 he joined William H. Aspinwall and Henry Chauncey to incorporate the Panama Railroad Company (*see* PANAMA RAILROAD). As vice president and later as president of the company, he negotiated with the Colombian government a contract to clear the way for building a railway, and shortly thereafter he began construction of the line. The project bordered on failure in 1851, but fares collected from California-bound gold seekers for use of the completed segment of the line enabled him to revive the credit of the company and assure the success of the undertaking. He was not able to complete construction, however. Racked by malaria contracted in Central America, he weakened and finally collapsed. He was returned to New York, and there he died on October 13, 1852. His tomb was unmarked until October 7, 1947, when a memorial plaque was affixed to the vault identified as holding his remains.

Bibliography. John Lloyd Stephens, *Incidents of Travel in Central America, Chiapas, and Yucatán,* ed. by R. L. Predmore, New Brunswick, N.J., 1949; id., *Incidents of Travel in Yucatán,* 2 vols., New York, 1843; Victor Wolfgang von Hagen, *Maya Explorer: John Lloyd Stephens and the Lost Cities of Central America and Yucatán,* Norman, Okla., 1947.

WILLIAM J. GRIFFITH

STICA. *See* SERVICIO TÉCNICO INTERAMERICANO DE COOPERACIÓN AGRÍCOLA.

STORNI, ALFONSINA (1892–1938). Argentine poet. Born in Switzerland, she grew up in Argentina and became a teacher. Her deep poetic sensibility is shown in her first publication, *La inquietud del rosal* (1916), and she injected a new note of disillusionment into feminine erotic poetry in her later volumes: *El dulce daño* (1918), *Ocre* (1925), and *Mundo de siete pozos* (1934). Her last volume, *Mascarilla y trebol* (1938), published the year in which an incurable illness caused her to commit suicide, presents the tortured, intellectual poetry that is her best work.

RACHEL PHILLIPS

STROESSNER, ALFREDO (1912–   ). President of Paraguay (1954–   ). The son of an immigrant German brewer and a Paraguayan woman, Stroessner was born in Encarnación, in southeastern Paraguay. At the age of sixteen he entered the Paraguayan Military Academy, and when the CHACO WAR broke out in 1932, he was a lieutenant. A cited hero at the war's end in 1935, he was given a garrison artillery command and soon rose in rank. In 1948 he was made commander of the artillery, and in 1951 general of the army. In May 1954, he helped oust President Federico Chaves and became the only candidate for the Presidency. From 1954 on his power, based on the Colorado party and the Army, grew substantially. *See* COLORADO PARTY (PARAGUAY).

In the 1950s Stroessner gained an unsavory reputation for authoritarian rule, brutally suppressing revolts, plots, and invasions led by exiles, censoring the press, outlawing political opposition, and sending political prisoners to work camps in the CHACO. Reelected without opposition in 1958 and 1964, he allowed token opposition in the 1968 election and after it considerably moderated his regime; low-level dissent was tolerated. On February 11, 1973, he was elected to another five-year presidential term.

Stroessner has presided over a healthy economic growth in Paraguay and has pursued a policy of friendship with the United States, coupled with virulent anticommunism at home and abroad. A modern *caudillo,* fluent in German, Spanish, and GUARANÍ, he is relatively well liked by his people for the economic progress, new schools, and work ethic he has brought them. Though totally lacking in ideology, Stroessner will probably remain in office until his death.

JOHN HOYT WILLIAMS

SUCRE, ANTONIO JOSÉ DE (1795–1830). Venezuelan general of independence and first constitutional President of Bolivia. Sucre, the foremost of Simón BOLÍVAR's military lieutenants, was by birth a member of the local aristocracy of Cumaná in eastern Venezuela. He was only fifteen when the revolt against Spain began in 1810, but he joined the patriot forces and saw active service under the first and second Venezuelan republics. At the fall of the second republic in 1814, he fled to the Antilles, then proceeded to New Granada to continue the struggle, but was forced to take refuge again, in Haiti, at the end of 1815.

The next year Sucre was back in Venezuela. For a time he fought under the leadership of Gen. Santiago Mariño, but he abandoned Mariño when the latter challenged the leadership of Bolívar. Sucre transferred his own allegiance permanently to Bolívar, who was steadily expanding a foothold in Venezuela, and he ably fulfilled a succession of military assignments as well as a commission to Trinidad to obtain arms.

As Bolívar's chief of staff Sucre helped negotiate the armistice signed with the royalists in November 1820. Soon afterward, he was given an even more important mission as head of an expedition designed to aid the Ecuadorian port of Guayaquil, where a local uprising against Spanish rule had occurred the previous October, and then to march against the royalist forces in the adjoining highlands. His first invasion of the highlands was unsuccessful, but in 1822, reinforced by an auxiliary army sent from Peru by José de SAN

MARTÍN, he marched inland again and by his victory at Pichincha on May 24, 1822 (*see* PICHINCHA, BATTLE OF) secured the final liberation of Quito.

When Gran Colombia in turn sent troops to aid the liberation of Peru, Sucre went as their commander and as Colombian commissioner to the Peruvian patriots pending the arrival of Bolívar. He then served as Bolívar's closest collaborator in preparing and executing the campaign of 1824 that produced the total defeat of Spain. Sucre's crowning achievement was the Battle of Ayacucho, on December 9, 1824, in which he was in sole command on the American side since Bolívar had meanwhile returned to Lima (*see* AYACUCHO, BATTLE OF). The victory he won there led to the surrender of the principal Spanish forces still fighting in South America. After Ayacucho little more was left than to suppress last-ditch royalist resistance in Upper Peru (modern Bolivia), a task Sucre undertook early in 1825.

Sucre pledged that Upper Peru would have the right to decide whether to become a separate nation or to join with one of its neighbors. Although Bolívar questioned Sucre's authority for such a declaration, it was clearly the most realistic course to follow; and when the region opted for independence, Bolívar himself became its first ruler. On leaving again for Peru in December 1825, Bolívar transferred his authority to Sucre, who the following year was chosen first constitutional President of Bolivia under the terms of the constitution Bolívar had drafted for the new nation. Both before and after this election, Sucre worked earnestly to establish Bolivian institutions on a firm footing and to introduce progressive reforms in taxation, education, and other fields. Yet he was resented by many Bolivians as a foreigner, and he also found Bolívar's constitution unduly complicated. Peruvian hostility further undermined his position, and in August 1828 he resigned the Presidency.

Sucre hoped to settle in Quito, where his Ecuadorian wife awaited him. But with the outbreak of war between Gran Colombia and Peru his services were needed again. In the chief battle of the war, that of Tarqui (February 27, 1829), he defeated a Peruvian force invading Ecuador. In 1830 he served his country once more as President of the Congreso Admirable, which sought, unsuccessfully, to find a constitutional formula that might preserve the Colombian union. Its dissolution was already an accomplished fact when Sucre himself, on his way home to Quito from Bogotá, was assassinated at Berruecos, near Pasto, on June 4, 1830. Suspicion fell on Colombian liberals, who feared that Sucre might restore the fortunes of the Bolivarian party even after Bolívar's final resignation, and secondarily on Juan José FLORES, the first head of independent Ecuador. But the inspiration of the crime remains a subject of heated historical debate. *See also* OBANDO, José María.

Bibliography. Charles Arnade, *The Emergence of the Republic of Bolivia,* Gainesville, Fla., 1957; William Lofstrom, "Attempted Economic Reform and Innovation in Bolivia under Antonio José de Sucre, 1825–1828," *Hispanic American Historical Review,* vol. L, no. 2, May 1970, pp. 279–299; Alfonso Rumazo González, *Sucre, gran mariscal de Ayacucho,* Madrid, 1963; Guillermo A. Sherwell, *Antonio José de Sucre (Gran Mariscal de Ayacucho), Hero and Martyr of American Independence: A Sketch of His Life,* Washington, 1924.

DAVID BUSHNELL

SUCRE. Official capital of Bolivia. Situated northeast of Potosí at an altitude of 10,300 feet above sea level, Sucre has a population of about 60,000. The city was founded in 1538 and during its rather momentous history changed its name four times. It was first called Charcas, then Chuquisaca, later La Plata, and finally Sucre in honor of Antonio José de SUCRE, the Venezuelan soldier who liberated Bolivia from Spanish domination.

In colonial times Sucre served as the headquarters for the *audiencia* of Charcas. It was also the home of Sucre University, founded in 1624. On May 25, 1809, the people of Sucre rioted against royal authority. Although the disorder was quickly suppressed, Bolivians like to place the beginning of the War of Independence on that date. It was also in Sucre that Bolivia's declaration of independence was signed in 1825. Until 1899 Sucre served as the nation's only capital, but it was outstripped in importance by La Paz. Thus, following a brief civil war, La Paz was recognized as the de facto capital, and the executive and legislative branches of government were permanently established there. Sucre remained the de jure capital and the seat of the Supreme Court.

The declining political and economic importance of Sucre in the nineteenth and twentieth centuries was due largely to its isolation from Bolivia's economic centers.

Antonio José de Sucre. [*Organization of American States*]

This isolation has diminished in the past few decades, but it remains an obstacle to the city's growth. One beneficial outcome of isolation has been the city's ability to retain a degree of colonial charm.

ORAZIO A. CICCARELLI

SUDAM. *See* SUPERINTENDÊNCIA DO DESENVOLVI- MENTO DO AMAZÔNIA.

SUDENE. *See* SUPERINTENDÊNCIA DO DESENVOLVI- MENTO DO NORDESTE.

SUGAR INDUSTRY (COLONIAL BRAZIL). The first sugar mill in Brazil was reputedly established in São Vicente during the 1530s. Certainly the Flemish capitalist Erasmus Schetz is known to have had a mill in operation there by 1540. It was in the NORTHEAST that the expansion was most spectacular. Between 1570 and 1610 the number of sugar mills north of the mouth of the São Francisco River rose from 24 to 140. In the central zone, especially in Bahia, the number rose from 31 to 50 mills in this period. And to the south of Pôrto Seguro, whereas 5 mills had been functioning in 1570, 40 were in operation in 1610.

Portuguese interest in sugar cultivation dated from the successful introduction of cane into the Atlantic islands during the fifteenth century. Not only could Brazilian producers take advantage of the distributive networks and consumer acceptance that Portuguese Atlantic island sugar had achieved, but they also possessed formidable advantages over the islands that soon allowed them to undersell the sugar of Madeira in Lisbon by as much as 50 percent. Brazil also possessed relatively rapid access to Europe. In sailing time, for example, Pernambuco and Bahia were not at a serious disadvantage compared with the Caribbean. The Brazilian ports were well protected and at the hub of the major sugar-producing regions. Irrigation was unnecessary in Brazil, the planters thus avoiding one of the major expenses facing the sugar producers of the Atlantic Islands. Finally, the soils were exceptionally rich, and the black *massapé* of the Varzea of Recife and the Reconcavo of Bahia proved capable of sustaining continuous cultivation for as much as thirty years without serious deterioration. Some forty to fifty crops could be expected from one planting of cane.

The large mills were substantial establishments, with workshops, chapel, processing plant, *casa grande* (great house), and *senzala* (slave quarters). The complex might employ 15 to 20 Portuguese and more than 100 African and Indian slaves. The *engenho* (mill) was water- or oxen-powered, using the Sicilian vertical three-roller mechanism after about 1608. The Sicilian grinder was an important innovation that allowed continuous double crushing and increased juice output. The juice was transferred to the purging and boiling house, where it was placed in a series of large copper cauldrons, agents (generally lime) being added to bring the impurities to the surface, where they could be skimmed off. The juice was then ladled into a set of smaller cauldrons to cool. The Brazilian producers next separated the molasses in order to process the semicrystallized juice into white sugar. By 1618 the larger mills might be producing between 6,000 and 10,000 arrobas of sugar per annum (1 arroba = 32 pounds), and Portuguese America as a whole exporting some 1.2 million arrobas to Europe.

A permanent disciplined labor force was essential for the varied demands of cane growing and particularly for manning the mill during the harvest. For eight to nine months the mills ground day and night, the slaves working shifts from six to twelve o'clock and from twelve to six. Initially the workers were Amerindian. Vigorous opposition from the Jesuits notwithstanding, of the 253 slaves listed in the inventory of the great sugar mill of Sergipe do Conde in Bahia during 1572, 233 were Indian and only 20 were African. However, the increasing difficulty in obtaining Indian slaves and their susceptibility to disease (30,000 lost their lives in the Bahian epidemic of 1562) combined to stimulate the Atlantic slave trade in captive Africans. After 1570 the opening of extensive slave trading in Angola by Paulo Dias de Novais, together with the relative ease of the transatlantic connection (a mere thirty-five days between Angola and Pernambuco and forty days from Luanda to Bahia), encouraged the gradual substitution of Amerindians by Africans. Adopting the Indians' staple diet (especially manioc roots processed into coarse white flour or cassava), the black slaves came to provide the backbone of the rapidly expanding Brazilian sugar economy. Perhaps 10,000 Africans were imported between 1551 and 1575, and 40,000 between 1576 and 1600, the latter number making Brazil the largest recipient of slaves in the New World during this period. *See also* NEGRO IN BRAZIL.

In addition to the purchase of slaves, a large amount of capital was needed for hydraulic works, milling machinery, copper utensils, iron, barges, and oxen. Operating expenses for salaries of the sugar masters, bookkeepers, and overseers, food for the work force, and replacement of slaves might also be substantial. Increasingly in the seventeenth century the cost of firewood became a major item of expenditure. Initial investment funds came from a variety of sources. The proprietors (donataries) of the captaincies (*see* CAP- TAINCY SYSTEM), in association with foreign capitalists, were active during the early years. With the establishment of royal administration, officeholders invested heavily, the most notable being Governor-General Mem de Sá, who established the great Sergipe mill during the 1560s. Tax exemptions were granted to new owners, most often exemption from the *dízimos* (tithes), which in Brazil were administered by the King in his capacity as grand master of the Order of Christ, and in the case of sugar involved a tenth part of the crop. Loans were obtained from local and metropolitan merchants or from colonial institutions that acquired de facto banking functions, such as the charitable sodalities of the Santa Casa da Misericórdia (Holy House of Mercy) and the lay religious brotherhoods (*irman- dades* and *confrarias*). Land initially was cheap, often obtained in an outright grant (*see* SESMARIA) from the donatary or captain general, a gift with full title ostensibly on condition only that the land be placed into cultivation within a stated period and the *dízimos* paid. In subsequent sales land values were determined by the richness of the soil and the ease of access to water- power and communication.

The Italian Jesuit André João Antonil (João Antônio ANDREONI) considered the position of *senhor de engenho* as being comparable in status with that of fidalgo (gentleman or noble) in Portugal. "Lord of the mill," however, is not precisely analogous to "planta- tion owner" with its concomitant assumptions about a society composed of masters and slaves locked within large, vertically integrated latifundian estates. Social structure, land tenure, and production patterns were more complex. Some of the great mills did not produce their own cane at all, preferring to lease their lands to *lavradores* (tenant farmers) in exchange for an agreed portion of the crop. The *lavradores* were a very diverse group, and regrettably little is known about them. Some could be very substantial men, commanders of the military orders, municipal officeholders, and clergy. Others might be little more than poor sharecroppers with limited means, eking out a precarious existence. The terms of tenure also varied greatly. The millowner might retain seigneurial rights over land held by *lavradores,* which obliged the planters to have their cane ground at the mill (so-called captive cane), or he might lease land under terms of EMPHYTEUSIS (lease in perpetuity but with restrictions). More often the land was owned by the *senhor de engenho* and leased for various terms (from one to nineteen years) to slaveholding farmers, who in return paid half the crop to the *senhor de engenho* in addition to an agreed proportion of the other half, a proportion that might vary from one-third to one-fifteenth or even one-twentieth, depending on the profitability of sugar and the relative negotiating strength of the millowner and farmer. The costs of leases were based on the amount of cane that could be ground within twenty-four hours (*tarefa*), reckoned to be twenty-five to thirty-five cartloads of cane for a mill powered by oxen and forty to fifty for a water-powered mill. The *tarefa* varied from area to area and was more a measure of the productivity of the soil than of acreage. The prosperous *lavrador* might produce about forty *tarefas* per annum, which would require twenty slaves and four to eight oxcarts.

Nonetheless, sugar production was a precarious business even for the great millowners and much more so for the *lavradores* and sharecroppers. Margins of profit were probably small for the producer. Interest payments probably cut into a large portion of potential profits. Uncertainties of weather, crop disease, and miscalculation of the time of cutting and processing could all seriously affect the quality of the sugar. The Sergipe mill during the harvest of 1651–1652 lost thirteen days of milling through lack of wood, ten days because of mechanical difficulties, and four days because of a lack of cane, in addition to twenty-eight Sundays and twenty-one saints' days. The ostentation of the millowners has probably been exaggerated, certainly in comparison with contemporaneous consumption patterns of people of similar social position in Europe. The Dutch (*see* DUTCH IN BRAZIL) were surprised by the lack of furnishings and paintings in the homes of the colonial elite and the frugality of their diet.

Until the mid-seventeenth century Brazilian sugar dominated world markets, retaining high prices on the Amsterdam exchange. Prices collapsed after the 1650s as a result of rising competition from the Caribbean and tariff barriers in previously important markets in northwestern Europe. Sugar production continued to be important in Brazil, however, and there was a temporary recovery in prices at the end of the century as a result of wartime conditions in the North Atlantic. Prices declined throughout much of the eighteenth century, but a massive recovery began again during the 1780s, largely as a result of wartime conditions, and continued in the 1790s because of the great slave revolt in Haiti,

a major competitor. Production in the 1670s was probably about 2 million arrobas per annum; 100 years later, 2.5 million arrobas.

Bibliography. André João Antonil, *Cultura e Opulência do Brasil por Suas Drogas e Minas,* text of 1711 ed., tr. with commentary by Andrée Mansuy, Paris, 1968; Mircea Buescu, *História Econômica do Brasil: Pesquisas e Analises,* Rio de Janeiro, 1970; Alice P. Canabrava, "A Grande Propriedade Rural," *História Geral da Civilização Brasileira,* ed. by Sérgio Buarque de Holanda, São Paulo, 1960, vol. I, no. 2, pp. 192–217; Miguel Costa Filho, *A Cana de Açúcar em Minas Gerais,* Rio de Janeiro, 1963; Frédéric Mauro, *Le Portugal et l'Atlantique au XVIIe siècle, 1570–1670: Étude économique,* Paris, 1960; Maria Theresa Schorer Petrone, *A Lavoura Canaveira em São Paulo: Expansão e Diclínio 1761–1851,* São Paulo, 1968; Stuart B. Schwartz, "Free Farmers in a Slave Economy," *Colonial Roots of Modern Brazil,* ed. by Dauril Alden, Berkeley, Calif., 1972; Roberto C. Simonsen, *História Econômica do Brasil 1500–1820,* 5th ed., São Paulo, 1967.

KENNETH R. MAXWELL

SUGAR INDUSTRY (CUBA). Although the production of sugar was introduced in Cuba very early in the colonial period, it did not reach a significant level until the late eighteenth century, when sugar plantations numbered more than 100 and contained approximately 10,000 acres of cultivated cane. During this century the creole families who owned much of the land turned their estates over to cane when they realized that sugar was more profitable than cattle. Since the production of sugar required a substantial labor supply, large numbers of African slaves were imported and sold to the plantation owners.

By the early 1800s sugar was Cuba's main source of wealth. In the late 1820s there were about 1,000 sugar plantations concentrated in the western region of the island and covering an area of about 500,000 acres. Investments in sugar production soon reached $185 million, a sum many times larger than that invested in coffee or tobacco, and output per mill rose from 72 tons in 1830 to 120 tons in 1841 and to 316 tons by 1860. Much of the increase in production was the result of the construction of a railroad system and the mechanization of the industry.

Prior to the TEN YEARS' WAR (1868–1878), Cuban sugar was produced by 2,000 mills whose owners also grew their own cane, but after the war this pattern was altered by unforeseen developments. The war itself was a disrupting factor, but the most significant development was the emancipation of the slaves, upon whom the entire sugar industry had depended (*see* ABOLITION OF SLAVERY: CUBA). Furthermore, the successful production of beet sugar in Europe forced sugar prices down on the world market. As a result of these adverse conditions, the number of mills declined so that there may have been as few as 500 by 1894. In addition, the cultivation of sugar increasingly came to be in the hands of *colonos,* farmer owners or tenants of the mills, who turned their crop over to the mills for grinding. The process of concentration among the mills continued into the twentieth century, stimulated by technological innovations that led to further mechanization. Only companies that could acquire the necessary capital for the purchase of the new machinery survived, and by the

1920s only 180 mills were operating in Cuba.

Following the independence of Cuba in 1902 American corporations increased their investment in the Cuban sugar industry. It is calculated that by 1913 United States investment in Cuban sugar amounted to $200 million and that by 1919 United States investors controlled between 40 and 50 percent of the mills. The World War I years were very good for Cuba's sugar industry. The disruption of European beet production forced the Allied countries to rely on Cuba for most of their sugar supply, and the price of Cuban sugar rose substantially. Encouraged by the demand, the industry experienced a rapid expansion, mostly in the eastern areas of the island. In 1915 alone twelve new mills were founded; of these eight were financed by American capital.

The end of the war released Cuban sugar from all price restraints, allowing it to reach peak prices as it enjoyed a strong demand on the world market. During this time, called the "dance of the millions," almost every investor in sugar grew wealthy. However, the prosperous times did not last long, for Europe recovered rapidly, and by 1920 sugar was again plentiful. The average price of a pound of sugar fell from an all-time high of 22.5 cents in May 1920 to 3.75 cents by mid-December 1920. This drop caused widespread chaos and bankruptcies in the industry and opened the door to further United States control. In 1921 and 1922 the National City Bank took over the direction of nearly sixty sugar mills, while the Chase National Bank received titles to many mills in return for the settlement of debts.

In 1926, in an attempt to prevent another collapse of prices, the government initiated a system of production control. The 1927 crop was limited to 4.5 million tons, and each mill was given a quota. Similar measures were adopted in subsequent years, but they failed to achieve the desired goals. During the Depression Cuba also agreed to reduce tariffs on American goods in return for a preferential quota in the United States market. See also JONES-COSTIGAN ACT.

Historically the sugar industry of Cuba has played an important and even a dominant role in the development of the country. In 1958 it was estimated that the sugar industry produced from 20 to 25 percent of the national income; fully one-seventh of the island was covered by sugarcane, while the mills controlled 20.9 percent of the land area. The same year Cuba produced 5,964,000 metric tons of raw sugar, which brought in 594 million pesos of the 734 million pesos earned by all Cuban exports. United States companies produced approximately 37 percent of Cuba's raw sugar, and United States investment in the industry amounted to $300 million. In addition, the sugar industry affected to a considerable extent the employment pattern of the country. Unemployment decreased during the *zafra* (harvest season) to a low of 10 percent of the work force but rose after the harvest to about 20 percent. The "dead season" from May through October affected not only those who were directly involved in the production of sugar but also other areas of the economy. Transportation, for example, was greatly influenced by the harvest, and the rate of domestic consumption rose and fell with the sugar production schedule.

It was this dependency on the sugar industry that Fidel CASTRO and his revolutionary government sought to change in the 1960s. The Castro government imposed drastic reforms on the industry in an effort to escape the consequences of monoculture. The industry was placed under the control of the National Institute of Agrarian Reform (INRA), which proceeded to expropriate the cane-producing lands and all United States–owned mills. By November 11, 1960, the government was in possession of the entire sugar industry, but the wholesale expropriation of the *latifundios* of sugarcane and the nationalization of the mills temporarily disrupted the economy. This disruption was aggravated by an attempt by Castro to diversify agriculture quickly and to industrialize Cuba to lessen dependency on other countries. The economic realities of world trade, however, brought Cuba back to the realization that sugar was its best bet on the market. Under pressure from the Soviet Union, Cuba's financial sponsor, the Cuban government returned to sugar. The most dramatic evidence of this trend was the vain effort in 1970 to reach the goal of 10 million metric tons of sugar even at the expense of all other sectors of the economy.

Bibliography. Edward Boorstein, *The Economic Transformation of Cuba,* New York, 1968; Leland Jenks, *Our Cuban Colony: A Study of Sugar,* New York, 1928; Wyatt MacGaffey and Clifford R. Barnett, *Twentieth-century Cuba: The Background of the Castro Revolution,* Garden City, N.Y., 1965; Lowry Nelson, *Rural Cuba,* Minneapolis, 1950; Dudley Seers et al., *Cuba: The Economic and Social Revolution,* Chapel Hill, N.C., 1964.

J. CORDELL ROBINSON

SUPERINTENDÊNCIA DO DESENVOLVIMENTO DA AMAZÔNIA (SUPERINTENDENCY FOR THE DEVELOPMENT OF AMAZONIA; SUDAM). Brazilian agency responsible for the administration of developmental projects in Amazonia, an area of more than 5 million square kilometers (2 million square miles) with a population of some 8 million (*see* AMAZON RIVER). This area includes all the northern states and territories of Brazil and parts of the states of Maranhão, Goiás, and Mato Grosso. The SUDAM area is bordered by two other such administrative units, where the SUPERINTENDÊNCIA DO DESENVOLVIMENTO DO NORDESTE (SUDENE), for the NORTHEAST, and the Superintendência do Desenvolvimento da Região Centro-Oeste (SUDECO), for the rest of Mato Grosso and Goiás, function.

SUDAM was created in October 1966, replacing a similar agency dissolved after the revolution of 1964. Its headquarters is in Belém, Pará. Its primary responsibility is the administration of the Fiscal Incentive Law of October 1966 and a 1969 revision, dealing with general tax exemptions and tax deductions for investments. Depending on the date of creation, enterprises in SUDAM's area are either partially or entirely exempt from income taxes until 1982, provided that such enterprises are in the interest of regional development. SUDAM is responsible for determining the applicability and usefulness of the proposals and otherwise regulating the use of the tax exemption clause.

All corporate bodies in Brazil may invest 75 percent of their income tax in bonds of the Bank of Amazonia for a general developmental fund or 50 percent in farming, stockbreeding and industrial projects, and basic services that SUDAM declares to be of interest to the development of the Amazon Basin. The investment may be used for several projects, but in all projects at least one-third of the financing must be private. Much of the private capital comes from São Paulo and Rio de Janeiro, although foreign capital has also been encouraged. SUDAM gives priority to projects involving territorial occupation and using regional raw materials and labor.

SUDAM functions in both public and private sectors. To create the necessary infrastructure, it has emphasized transportation, hydroelectric power, communication, education, and health and sanitation. It has cooperated with surveys and planning for the Transamazonian and other highways that will open huge new areas to settlement and has approved projects for airports, ports, and improved river navigation facilities. With SUDAM cooperation the Brazilian television network has been extended across Amazonia. SUDAM has encouraged the training of laborers and technicians for the new jobs being created and has heavily financed research into the development of natural resources. With SUDAM's aid public health campaigns are more frequent and effective, and sanitation is improving markedly in the cities and towns.

SUDAM's role in the private sector is pronounced; perhaps half of the industries in the Amazon Basin have SUDAM backing. SUDAM has financed food-processing and beverage industries, light manufactures such as matches, jewelry and diamond cutting, textiles, garments, synthetic fibers, plastics, and foundries.

The agricultural and ranching sector has received most of SUDAM's attention. There has been considerable emphasis on developing ranching areas in previously deserted areas of the basin, using modern techniques to increase beef and milk production. At the same time there are restrictions to prevent the wholesale destruction of the environment. SUDAM has also been involved in encouraging the production of jute, pepper, and African oil palm.

There are projects to utilize the Amazonian forests for hardwoods and wood products, rubber and other gums and resins, brazil nuts, and other extractive products. Mineral prospecting and production have been encouraged, and SUDAM has assisted in aerial surveys designed to locate further natural resources. Fishing has also received SUDAM attention and support.

There is no doubt that SUDAM and the fiscal incentives it administers have brought a new degree of industrial and agricultural development to the Amazon. SUDAM has had to combat the problems of low population density, vastness of territory, and a developmental psychology of extractive enterprise, and it

has been able to encourage capital migration from the more affluent parts of Brazil to the north. SUDAM's methods of administering fiscal incentives are undergoing revision to cope with a burgeoning number of requests for assistance, and the next few years may see substantial policy changes. However, SUDAM's primary purpose will remain the development and national integration of the Amazon Basin.

Bibliography. Ernesto Bandeira Coelho, "SUDAM Mostra Sua Obra de Cinco Anos na Região," *SUDAM em Revista,* vol. 2 (10/11), 1971, pp. 15–19; Law No. 5174, October 27, 1966, of the Legislative Authority, *Diário Oficial,* October 31, 1966; SUDAM, *Regimento Interno,* Belém, 1970; id., *Relatório das Actividades da SUDAM no Exercício de 1969: Setor Público, Setor Privado,* Belém, 1970; id., *Plano de Desenvolvimento da Amazônia 1972–1974* and *Subsídios ao Plano Regional de Desenvolvimento 1972–1974,* 2 vols., Belém, 1971.   ROBIN L. ANDERSON

SUPERINTENDÊNCIA DO DESENVOLVIMENTO DO NORDESTE (NORTHEAST DEVELOPMENT AGENCY; SUDENE). Agency of the Brazilian government established in 1959 to plan and coordinate development programs and investments in the nine-state NORTHEAST. Designed by the economist Celso FURTADO, who served as the agency's director from 1959 to 1964, and inaugurated under the administration of President Juscelino KUBITSCHEK, SUDENE has received strong support from successive Brazilian administrations and has been considerably broadened in scope since 1964. As envisioned by its planners, SUDENE's purpose is to improve the quality of life for the peoples of the drought- and poverty-stricken Northeast through social service programs in education, sanitation, public health, and housing. In the effort to realize its human goals, SUDENE has set a priority on developing the basic components of the economic infrastructure such as hydroelectric projects, transportation, and the encouragement of new industry and buttressing of existing industry through tax incentives and direct aid. It has also worked to revitalize the traditional areas of agriculture, mining, fishing, cattle raising, and tourism.

As of 1972 more than 1,300 projects, three-quarters of them industrial, had been approved. SUDENE's most spectacular achievements are the expansion of the hydroelectric plant at Paulo Afonso Falls to a capacity of 1.2 million kilowatts and the construction of the Transamazonian Highway. The agency is financed by a mixture of international, federal, and state funds and works in conjunction with the federal Bank of the Northeast.   FRANCESCA MILLER

Tablada, José Juan

Tupinambá

TABLADA, JOSÉ JUAN (1871–1945). Mexican journalist and poet in touch with the currents of European literature and with Oriental verse forms. His first volume, *El florilegio* (1899), shows the influence of modernist writers (*see* MODERNISM: SPANISH AMERICA), but his most important collections are *Un día...* (1919), poems in the manner of the Japanese *haiku*, and *Li-Po y otros poemas* (1920). These volumes greatly affected contemporary Mexican poetry.

RACHEL PHILLIPS

TACNA-ARICA QUESTION. Territorial dispute between Chile and Peru (1883–1929), involving the coastal provinces of Tacna and Arica. During Spanish rule this territory belonged to Peru, but the boundaries remained undefined. After independence Peru held the provinces of Tacna, Arica, and Tarapacá, while Bolivia occupied the province of Antofagasta. In 1865 rich nitrate deposits were discovered in Antofagasta. Conflicts between Chile and Bolivia over possession of this valuable mining region led to the WAR OF THE PACIFIC (1879–1883), in which Chile defeated Bolivia and its ally, Peru. Under the terms of the Treaty of Ancón, which ended the war, Tarapacá was ceded to Chile, while Tacna and Arica were placed under Chilean control for ten years. At the end of this period a plebiscite was to be held to determine possession of the provinces.

The plebiscite was scheduled for 1893, but specific procedures could not be agreed upon between Peru and Chile. As the dispute continued, relations between the two countries worsened. From 1922 to 1926 the United States attempted to mediate the dispute. Although generally unsuccessful, United States mediation did revive direct negotiations between the two nations. In 1929 a settlement was reached whereby Tacna was returned to Peru with an indemnity of $6 million, while Chile retained possession of Arica. Resentments caused by this dispute damaged relations between Peru and Chile during the twentieth century.

RODNEY D. ANDERSON

TAMAYO, FRANZ (1879–1956). Founder of the Indianist movement in Bolivia. Tamayo was born in La Paz and was educated in Bolivia and Europe. Although he was a member of a distinguished upper-class family, he was considered a revolutionary, disdainful of the established order. Nevertheless, he operated within it. He repeatedly served in Congress and was chosen President of the Chamber of Deputies. He represented his country at the League of Nations and in 1932–1933 served as Foreign Minister in President Daniel Salamanca's Cabinet. In 1934 he was elected President, although because of a coup d'état he never took office.

Amid such "establishment" activities, he wrote for a prolabor newspaper and for other antiestablishment organs; he was one of the founders, guiding lights, and major celebrities of the Radical party, an organization of intellectuals with little support outside La Paz; and he emerged as one of the most outspoken Indianists in Bolivia, a factor clearly evident in his numerous literary works. He loathed everything Spanish and blamed Spain for Bolivia's innumerable problems. He believed that Bolivia's history since the conquest deserved no attention because it was dominated by Spain's corrupting influence. In his writing he repeatedly preached social revolution, and because of it he became a spokesman for a whole generation wishing to reform Bolivia's institutions.

ORAZIO A. CICCARELLI

TAMAYO, RUFINO (1899–   ). Mexican painter. The major Mexican painter to accept an international formalist style, Tamayo was born in Oaxaca but lived in Mexico City from the age of eight. He attended classes at the Academy of San Carlos and as a young man was put in charge of ethnographic drawing in the National Museum of Anthropology. This acquaintance with pre-Columbian ceramic sculpture, coupled with the influence of Picasso, is basic to his art. Tamayo showed for the first time in 1926 in Mexico City and New York, where he remained for two years and where he later spent much time. He taught art in New York beginning in 1938, and his reputation was made there.

Tamayo has painted several murals; important ones are a fresco of an Indian personification of *Music* (1933), *Birth of Our Nationality* (1952), and *Mexico Today* (1952). But easel painting is his forte, and he always remained apart from the mural movement. In 1960 he stated: "There is no place in art for political or ideological manifestations. Painting is painting. . . ." His work, most of it in oil, emphasizes color and poetic mood. *Woman with a Birdcage* (1941) recalls ancient Mexican ceramic figures in form and color. *Woman Reaching for the Moon* (1946) is a typical night subject, with softly modulated colors. Watermelons became almost a Tamayo trademark, obviously appealing to him for their rich color and their precise curves and angular cuts. Tamayo's colors grew richer in the 1960s, and his paint thicker. His influence has been great on such younger painters as Pedro Coronel (1923–   ), for whom he represents an alternative to the mural movement, a cosmopolitan style.

TERENCE GRIEDER

TARSILA DO AMARAL. *See* AMARAL, TARSILA DO.

TAUBATÉ CONVENTION. A meeting was held in Taubaté, São Paulo, in March 1906 to discuss the drastic decline of world coffee prices coupled with the rapid increase in Brazil's coffee production. At this meeting the governors of São Paulo, Rio de Janeiro, and Minas Gerais, in an effort to control the marketing of coffee and stave off panic by stabilizing coffee prices, developed a valorization plan. This plan provided that the state and federal governments would purchase the coffee beans when prices fell below a minimum and hold them off the market until prices rose again. Under this plan the federal government would collect a surtax on every bag exported, which it would use to amortize the cost of establishing the Emission and Control Bank, organized to handle the financial aspects of the valorization plan.

The price support provisions in this valorization scheme would have altered the government's monetary policy by setting a special exchange rate for coffee of 12 pence per milreis (the normal exchange parity was 27 pence). Therefore President Francisco de Paula RODRIGUES ALVES refused to endorse the Taubaté Convention. However, his successor in office, Afonso PENA, implemented the monetary reform proposed at

Taubaté, including establishing a conversion fund to handle finances. By loans from the federal government, both São Paulo and Minas Gerais were able to purchase excess coffee and keep it off the market. This, coupled with small harvests, made valorization an effective means of controlling prices. World War I, by cutting off the European market and thus reducing the volume of coffee exports, brought the collapse of the conversion fund and the Taubaté Convention plan.

LESLIE S. OFFUTT

TAURIELLO, ANTONIO (1931–   ). Argentine composer and conductor. Tauriello was born in Buenos Aires, where he studied piano with Walter Gieseking and Spivak and composition with Alberto GINASTERA. Since 1958 he has conducted in the Teatro Colón, served as assistant director in the Lyric Opera in Chicago, and conducted in New York and Washington. His work as a composer belongs to the so-called avant-garde in Latin America, yet he shows no dependence on any particular trend of twentieth-century music. The alternation of highly controlled episodes and free improvisation is perhaps one of the most characteristic features of his style. His works include *Transparencies* (1965), *Serenata II* (1967), a concerto for piano and orchestra (1968), *Ilinx* for clarinet and orchestra (1968), *Mansión de Tlaloc* (1970), and the opera *Las guerras picrocholinas* (1970), based on Rabelais's *Pantagruel*.

JUAN A. ORREGO-SALAS

TÁVORA, JUAREZ [DO NASCIMENTO FERNANDES] (1899–   ). Brazilian soldier and political figure. One of the outstanding reformist officers of the Brazilian Army, Távora played a prominent role on or near the political stage for more than forty years. Born in Jaguaribe Mirim, Ceará, he enlisted in the Army in 1916 and was commissioned in the engineers in 1920. Four years later he jeopardized a promising career to take part in the revolt in São Paulo and accompany Luis Carlos PRESTES on the long march through the interior of Brazil (*see* PRESTES COLUMN). In 1930 he was selected by Getúlio VARGAS to command the revolutionary forces in northern Brazil, a position that brought him the unofficial title of Viceroy of the North. Távora served briefly as Minister of Transportation in President Vargas's first Cabinet and was Minister of Agriculture from late 1932 to mid-1934, but for the next ten years he resumed his military career. He became a general in 1946.

As commander of the ESCOLA SUPERIOR DE GUERRA, Távora signed the Army manifesto calling for the resignation of President Vargas in 1954, and following Vargas's suicide he served as chief military aide to President João CAFÉ FILHO. Távora ran unsuccessfully for the Presidency as the candidate of the UNIÃO DEMOCRÁTICA NACIONAL in 1955 but was elected to Congress on the Christian Democratic party ticket in 1962. He endorsed the revolution of March 31, 1964, and was appointed Minister of Transportation and Public Works in the Cabinet of President Humberto CASTELLO BRANCO, a post he held until March 1967.

ROLLIE E. POPPINO

TEGUCIGALPA. Capital of Honduras. One of the salient features of Honduran history has been the shifting of the country's economic and political center of gravity. By the late nineteenth century Tegucigalpa, originally a mining center, had begun to eclipse the traditional capital, Comayagua. Centuries of human habitation had deeply eroded the valley in which Comayagua was situated, making water and food supplies precarious. Comayagua's liabilities were compounded when, in 1873, the fires of civil war gutted many of its buildings.

As Comayagua's fortunes declined, Tegucigalpa was emerging as an important trade center. The completion of the PANAMA RAILROAD in 1855 swelled the volume of Pacific trade, trade that Tegucigalpa, as the highland terminus of Honduras's road to the south, was able to dominate. Liberal President Marco Aurelio SOTO (1876–1883), recognizing the deficiencies of Comayagua and finding its conservative political ambience uncongenial, shifted the capital to Tegucigalpa in 1880. Following a period of indecision during which the Nationalist Ponciano Leiva returned the capital to Comayagua, the federal government came to permanent rest in Tegucigalpa. *See* LIBERAL PARTY (HONDURAS); NATIONAL OR NATIONALIST PARTY (HONDURAS).

Burgeoning commerce and a swelling bureaucracy proved so attractive to Hondurans that the population of the Federal District rose to almost 250,000 by 1968. Meanwhile, however, with the rise of bananas as an export crop, the center of gravity had again shifted. Modern Tegucigalpa remains a political, cultural, and banking center while lowland San Pedro Sula controls most of Honduras's industry and international commerce.

GENE S. YEAGER

TENENTISMO. Political movement stemming from the great social and economic tensions in Brazil in the 1920s. Literally defined, a *tenente* is a military lieutenant. In the context of twentieth-century Brazilian history, however, *tenentes* were a group of reform-minded, generally young military men and their close civilian allies. *Tenentismo* was a general philosophical-political movement that sought such reforms as governmental recognition of trade unions, the passage of minimum wage and child labor laws, the expansion of the electorate, the strengthening of central government, the encouragement of governmental ownership of natural resources, the eradication of political corruption, the strengthening of the military, and, through modernization and industrialization, the creation of a Brazilian economy less dependent on foreign capital.

The unsuccessful COPACABANA REVOLT of July 5, 1922, provided the first expression of *tenentismo*. On July 5, 1924, a second uprising occurred, this time in the city of São Paulo. Beleaguered, these rebels, under Maj. Miguel Costa, sought safety in the jungles of Paraná. In October 1924, a sympathetic military revolt erupted in Rio Grande do Sul, but, pressed by loyalist troops, these insurgents retreated north to the Iguaçu Falls, where they united with the São Paulo troops to form a revolutionary army in March 1925. Under the command of Luis Carlos PRESTES, this column marched through the interior of Brazil, attempting to spread the ideas of *tenentismo* and recruit peasant support. Military pressure and disease finally forced the column to disband into Bolivia in 1927. *See also* PRESTES COLUMN.

Most of the *tenentes* (Prestes, now a Communist, was a notable exception) participated in the REVOLUTION OF 1930, which overthrew the FIRST REPUBLIC, and obtained key posts in the revolutionary government. The heyday of *tenentismo* ended in 1933, by which time it had lost its cohesion, luster, and strength as a movement. However, many individual *tenentes* carved out long, successful political careers.

ALLAN K. JOHNSON

TENOCHTITLÁN. Capital of the Mexica AZTECS. founded on a mud flat in Lake Texcoco in 1369, and predecessor of modern Mexico City. There was an adjoining island called Tlatilulco. Both islands were inhabited by Mexica people, but in 1473 the inhabitants of Tlatilulco were defeated by Tenochtitlán. The city was divided into four large quarters, with the temples of HUITZILOPOCHTLI and Tlaloc in the center, and each quarter was further divided into CALPULLI. The population probably ran as high as 150,000. Access to the mainland was over causeways that also carried aqueducts. The city was besieged and destroyed by Hernán CORTÉS in 1521; very soon thereafter he began its reconstruction as a Spanish colonial city.

BURR C. BRUNDAGE

TEN YEARS' WAR (1868–1878). Conflict in Cuba sparked by Spain's "Glorious Revolution" (1868), which created a crisis of power in the mother country. Seizing the opportunity, Carlos Manuel de Céspedes, with other small planters of the island's Eastern Department, set in motion a revolution with a declaration of independence on October 10, 1868. This Grito de Yara brought still more planters, students, and blacks into the ranks of the revolution, and soon the rebels found themselves in control of the eastern portion of Cuba. A provisional government was organized, and it appeared briefly as if the revolution might succeed.

However, its leaders were not revolutionary enough. They hesitated to invade the Western Department and remained ambiguous on the question of abolition (*see* ABOLITION OF SLAVERY: CUBA). By so doing they retained the support of some of Cuba's wealthy planters and rich exiles in New York, but they sacrificed the support of many Cuban blacks (both slave and free) and any possibility of United States recognition. Moreover, the leaders were not united; many of them distrusted their two finest generals, Antonio MACEO and Máximo GÓMEZ, the former because he was a mulatto and the latter because he was foreign-born.

The other side experienced no such disunity. Peninsular-born Spaniards, working together within a militia institution called the Spanish Volunteers, freed soldiers from garrison duty, intimidated creoles, and helped hold the island until 1876, when Spain, with its own house in order again, was able to release Gen. Arsenio Martínez de Campos and 25,000 additional troops to put down the rebellion. It soon became apparent to the insurgents that victory was impossible, and they agreed to an armistice proposed by General Martínez de Campos (the Pact of Zanjón) in February 1878. The pact ended hostilities with promises of amnesty and widespread political reform.

KENNETH F. KIPLE

TEOTIHUACÁN. Famous archaeological site about 20 miles north of Mexico City. It is generally believed by scholars to have been the first true city (as opposed to ceremonial center) in the Western Hemisphere. It is thought to have been situated on an arm of the beautiful Lake Texcoco that has since disappeared. The area of the ancient city, which was built on a grid pattern, was more than 9 square miles. The community originated and grew to great size in the late Preclassic period (300 B.C.–B.C./A.D.) and to even greater size in the Classic (B.C./A.D.–A.D. 600), when it was the cultural pacesetter for all of Mesoamerica.

The layout of the city is most impressive. An axial thoroughfare, the Street of the Dead, is laid out in an orientation conforming almost exactly to magnetic north. On its east side lie the huge Pyramid of the Sun and the Ciudadela with its enclosed temple of QUETZAL-COATL. The Street of the Dead abuts on its north end the Pyramid of the Moon. The hills surrounding the great site today are arid and were probably stripped of their forest cover to provide for the needs of this city of possibly 60,000 to 80,000 inhabitants. The deforestation caused heavy erosion that silted up and pushed back the lake, and this may have initiated events leading to the decline of the city.

At its height Teotihuacán possessed a magnificent mural art, a distinctive architecture, a system of writing, a sacred calendar of 260 days, and a cult centered around the great agricultural deities. Its influences reached as far as the Guatemalan Highlands, where the site called Kaminaljuyú closely imitated it. About A.D. 600 the city was overwhelmed by Chichimec-like peoples from the north who had earlier moved into its ambit. Prestige then passed to cities like Cholula, which formerly had been within its hegemony.

The name Teotihuacán means, in NAHUATL, "where the gods were made." This is a reference to the cosmic myth containing descriptions of how the world came to an end and how two gods, more brave and pious than the rest, hurled themselves into a sacred fire in Teotihuacán, only to rise from its ashes as the sun and the moon, thus returning light to a re-created world.

BURR C. BRUNDAGE

TERRA, GABRIEL (1873–1942). President of Uruguay (1931–1938). Born in Montevideo, Terra was a lawyer and teacher who held a variety of political, administrative, and diplomatic posts. He served as Minister of Industries, Labor, and Education in the administration of President Claudio Williman (1907–1911), as Minister of the Interior under President Baltasar Brum (1919–1923), and as Minister to Italy. For five years prior to his election as President in 1930, he was a member of the National Council of Administration.

Terra, a member of the Colorado party (see COLORADO PARTY: URUGUAY), was elected at a time when both major parties were deeply fragmented and the nation faced severe economic troubles. Convinced that the COLEGIADO was a major obstacle to effective governmental action, the President in 1933 dissolved both the National Council of Administration and the legislature and called for a constitutional convention. The coup d'état was supported by Luis Alberto de HERRERA'S wing of the National party (see BLANCO PARTY: URUGUAY).

The new constitution abandoned the *colegiado* and concentrated executive power in the President. At the same time, it granted extensive powers to the legislature, guaranteed minority representation in the Cabinet, and stipulated that the Senate be equally divided between the two major parties. The constitutional convention named Terra President for the 1934–1938 term, during which he maintained a close censor-ship of the press, exiled a number of political opponents, and governed largely by executive decree.

LEE C. FENNELL

TERRITORIAL WATERS. Nine Latin American countries (Argentina, Brazil, Chile, Ecuador, El Salvador, Nicaragua, Panama, Peru, and Uruguay) claim 200 miles of territorial waters. In addition, in 1972 fifteen Caribbean nations, while claiming only 12 miles of territorial waters, declared sovereignty over 200 miles of "patrimonial" waters, wherein they assert exclusive rights to all natural resources. Meanwhile, most of the great maritime nations of the world, including the United States, claim no more than 12 miles. This discrepancy has given rise to a continuing controversy over fishing rights in the eastern Pacific between the United States and the CEP countries (Chile, Ecuador, and Peru).

Paradoxically, the idea of widening substantially the zone of jurisdictional waters was originated by the government of the United States. On September 28, 1945, President Harry S. Truman proclaimed that, in view of the mineral resources close to its coastline but beyond the 3-mile limit, the United States would regard "the natural resources and the seabed of the continental shelf beneath the high seas but contiguous to the coasts of the United States as appertaining to the United States, subject to its jurisdiction and control." Although in the proclamation the United States did not claim exclusive authority over fishery exploitation beyond established international boundaries, some Latin American nations interpreted it as doing so and thus moved to protect their own fishery resources.

On August 18, 1952, the CEP countries signed the Declaration of Santiago, by which they obliged themselves to maintain their jurisdiction over 200 miles of territorial waters in order to protect their natural resources. The 200-mile claim was based on the knowledge that the biological boundaries of the Peru Current (HUMBOLDT CURRENT) extend 80 to 100 miles from shore in summer and 200 to 250 miles in winter. Since the waters off the Peruvian and Ecuadorian coasts contain some of the richest tuna-fishing grounds in the world (see FISHING INDUSTRY: PERU), the two governments wanted to protect the area from unchecked exploitation by United States fishing vessels, which with the disappearance of the sardine industry in California in the early 1950s had increasingly turned to tropical tuna fishing. By 1967 these vessels were responsible for 75 to 85 percent of the tuna catch each year, worth $50 million.

The enforcement of the Santiago Declaration and the refusal of United States fishing vessels to purchase the required fishing license has led to the wholesale seizing and fining of United States boats. Most of them have been seized by Ecuador (seventy-four between 1961 and mid-1971) and Peru (thirty-eight in the same ten years), and the fines by mid-1971 amounted to $2,197,780; more than half of this sum was collected by Ecuador in the first four months of 1971. Although the total fines far surpassed the expected cumulative cost of licenses, the United States government and the American Tunaboat Association continue to discourage vessels from purchasing licenses lest such action be interpreted as recognition of the 200-mile limit. The United States government's opposition stems from its concern over the chaos such recognition would bring to traditional fishing grounds, and over the possible conflicts it would ignite in the development of undersea mineral resources.

Thus, since the early 1950s the United States has employed threats, persuasion, and diplomacy to force a reduction in the 200-mile limit. In 1954 it passed the Fishermen's Protective Act, which threatened legal action against countries seizing United States vessels and promised the reimbursement of fines to boat owners. This legislation made it economically feasible for unlicensed fishing vessels to continue violating the CEP countries' 200-mile limit, but as the seizures mounted in the 1950s and 1960s, the United States Congress repeatedly enacted legislation to reduce or curtail military and economic aid to the offending countries. For diplomatic reasons such legislation has been enforced only sparingly, but a 1973 law made mandatory the cutoff of foreign aid to countries that refused to refund fines collected from seized fishing boats.

The United States government has also tried to seek a satisfactory solution through the International Court of Justice, the United Nations, and the ORGANIZATION OF AMERICAN STATES (OAS), but to no avail. The CEP countries have refused to submit the issue to the International Court for arbitration, the United Nations has repeatedly failed to work out a satisfactory agreement, and the OAS has given moral support to the CEP claim. A major reason for the impasse is that retention of the 200-mile limit has become a symbol of anti-imperialism and a mark of the underdeveloped nations' determination to end the plunder, whether real or imagined, of their natural resources by foreign capitalists. The CEP countries have also justifiably insisted that conservation, ecology, and their very national development require the establishment of control over the ocean's resources. The remarkable economic success of the fish-meal industry in Peru, the recognition of the ocean's potential as a future source of protein for the under-nourished masses, the recent discovery of the technology required for the exploitation of mineral resources in the ocean's floor and subfloor, and the discovery of the ocean's far-from-limitless mineral and food resources have intensified their determination to maintain the 200-mile limit.

But compromise is not impossible. The 200-mile claim may be negotiable if a much broader area of jurisdiction than presently acknowledged is recognized and if effective international regulations on the uses of the ocean's resources can be established. Equally important may be United States willingness to remove its tariff on imported canned fish, which has helped retard the tuna fish industry in Peru and Ecuador by denying it the essential United States market. At this time, however, it is doubtful that United States fishing interests would willingly forgo protection from competition in exchange for protection from seizure. Consequently, the issue of territorial waters will probably continue to strain United States–Latin American relations.

However, in 1972 the United States was able to reach its first fishing accord with a nation claiming sovereignty over 200 miles of territorial waters. The treaty, which was negotiated with Brazil and entered into force on February 14, 1973, ignores the question of territorial waters, but it allows Brazil to regulate Amer-ican shrimp boats operating within 200 miles of the Brazilian coast by licensing them, limiting their number, and so on.

Bibliography. Teodoro Alvarado Garaicoa, *El dominio del mar,* Guayaquil, 1968; David C. Edmonds, "The 200 Miles Fishing Rights Controversy," *Inter-American Economic Affairs,* vol. XXVI, no. 4, Spring, 1973, pp. 3–18; Douglas M. Johnston, *The International Law of Fisheries,* New Haven, Conn., 1965; Bobbie B. Smetherman and Robert M. Smetherman, "The CEP Claims, U.S. Tuna Fishing and Inter-American Relations," *Orbis,* vol. XIV, no. 4, Winter, 1971, pp. 951–972.

ORAZIO A. CICCARELLI

THOUSAND DAYS, WAR OF THE (1899–1902). Civil war between Liberals and Conservatives in Colombia (*see* CONSERVATIVE PARTY: COLOMBIA; LIBERAL PARTY: COLOMBIA).   The war stemmed primarily from the dissatisfaction of Liberals over their party's virtual exclusion from public office since it lost power to the Conservatives in 1885–1886. Contributory causes were a depressed economy and the resulting instability of Colombia's unsupported paper currency; the belief of many Liberals that Conservative opponents of the government would remain neutral in the event of a revolution; and the recent installation in Venezuela of the regime of Cipriano CASTRO, who was sympathetic to the cause of Colombian Liberals. Even so, when the fighting began on October 17, 1899, most party leaders either disapproved of the appeal to violence or considered the moment inopportune because of the party's military unpreparedness. Despite some early victories, the Liberals were unable to topple the Conservative government, which was initially headed by the aged and ailing Manuel María Sanclemente. Sanclemente was deposed on July 31, 1900, by dissident Conservatives who hoped that his successor, José Manuel Marroquín, would be conciliatory to the revolutionaries; Marroquín, however, soon indicated that he would prosecute the war with even greater vigor than his predecessor. The fighting ended in 1902 after the two principal revolutionary generals, Rafael Uribe Uribe and Benjamín Herrera, signed peace treaties in which the Marroquín administration promised to institute political reforms. One contemporary estimated that as many as 80,000 men may have died in combat or of disease during the war; the damage to property was extensive, while the value of the Colombian peso plummeted as a result of uncontrolled emissions by the government. The secession of Panama in 1903 dramatically underscored the debilitation into which Colombia had fallen after three years of war.

HELEN DELPAR

TIAHUANACO. Archaeological site situated at an altitude of 13,000 feet on the south shore of Lake Titicaca in Bolivia. It was undoubtedly the capital of a notable empire, which is dated to A.D. 600–1000. The ruins visited today are those of a ceremonial, and probably a pilgrimage, center, but there is also evidence for positing large-scale residence in the immediate environs. Great stone monolithic figures have been unearthed here, and among the extensive building remains there are evidences of subterranean storerooms, stairways, and canals. The most famous megalith on the site is the Gateway of the Sun, on which is depicted one of the great deities of the place, surrounded by running and winged messenger demons. The influence of Tiahuanaco was carried probably by conquest and colonization outward to the southern coast of Peru and throughout Bolivia. In attenuated form this influence reached even into southwestern Argentina and the Atacama Desert.

BURR C. BRUNDAGE

TIKAL. Mayan archaeological site in the Petén of Guatemala. As it lies deep in the jungle rain forest, the tourist can reach it only by airplane. It is one of the most distinctive and architecturally interesting of all the great Mayan ceremonial centers of the Classic period (A.D. 300–900). One of the temple-platform complexes is estimated to have been 229 feet high. Eighty-six stone stelae, of which twenty-one bear reliefs and hieroglyphics, have been located in the ruins of Tikal. Tikal was one of the most extensive of the Mayan ceremonial centers, and archaeologically the area has as yet been barely scratched. All structures, both large and small, are oriented to within 10 degrees of the cardinal directions—but surprisingly these directions are taken from the magnetic and not the true north. *See also* MAYAS.

BURR C. BRUNDAGE

TIN INDUSTRY (BOLIVIA). Bolivia has always been a mining country. In the colonial period silver mines near Potosí provided a large part of the world's supply of that precious metal. During the first seventy-five years of independence silver continued to be the principal source of the country's foreign exchange, but in the late nineteenth century tin began to supplement silver as an important export, and within a couple of decades it had become the principal one. The world demand for this metal was growing, and Bolivia became one of its major producers.

The Bolivian tin-mining industry is located in the bleak ALTIPLANO (high plateau). The mines are at altitudes of 12,000 to 18,000 feet, making both working and living conditions peculiarly difficult. The situation in the mines is made even more trying by the extreme depth of many of the shafts. The mining camps have always been company towns, although some of them are located near cities, such as Oruro and Potosí. The labor force for the tin mines has traditionally been drawn from the Indian peasantry. Although the industry is old enough to have second- and third-generation mining families, many of them still maintain contact with their rural relatives and continue to speak Indian languages. Miners played a major role in organizing peasant unions after the national revolution of 1952.

One of the first tin "barons" was Simón I. PATIÑO, who together with his wife began exploiting a claim in the Catavi area in the 1890s. After some years he sought technical and financial help from British and United States investors. The final result was Patiño Enterprises, a firm with worldwide investments, which became by far the largest exploiter of Bolivian tin. Other entrepreneurs developed extensive interests in Bolivian tin during the early decades of the twentieth century. These included Carlos Aramayo, like Simon Patiño a Bolivian, and Mauricio Hochschild, an Austrian. Together, the Patiño, Aramayo, and Hochschild firms

came to constitute the Big Three of the Bolivian mining industry.

Tin mining reached its apogee in the 1920s, after which it began to decline. The early mines began to be worked out, with the percentage of tin in the ore dropping from as high as 20 to an average of 3.5 percent by the 1960s. The industry suffered particularly during the Great Depression, and revivals during World War II and the Korean war proved to be only temporary halts in a long-term decline in Bolivian tin mining.

The Bolivians have participated for four decades in the International Tin Council, which seeks to keep up the price of the metal and sets quotas for all major producers in the non-Communist world. Since World War II, Bolivia has generally not been able to meet its quota. Nevertheless, in the late 1960s Bolivia was providing about 15 percent of the production of the non-Communist world and was second only to Malaysia among the member states of the International Tin Council.

In 1952 the revolutionary government of President Víctor PAZ ESTENSSORO nationalized the Big Three tin-mining companies. However, it did not touch the smaller producers, the largest of which was W. R. Grace & Co. By 1968 the nationalized part of the industry turned out 63 percent of the country's production.

The part of the tin industry formerly belonging to the Big Three was turned over to a new government-owned company, the CORPORACIÓN MINERA DE BOLIVIA (COMIBOL). It was faced with immense difficulties, particularly during the first years of its existence, stemming from the departure of foreign technical and managerial personnel, serious labor problems, and the failure to make a profit or to make new investments to expand its activities. Foreign exchange earned through its tin exports was used for other sectors of the economy rather than to recapitalize the mining industry.

When Paz Estenssoro returned to the Presidency in 1960, he was determined to rehabilitate the industry. To this end his government entered in 1961 into an agreement with the United States, West Germany, and the INTER-AMERICAN DEVELOPMENT BANK in the so-called Operación Triangular (Triangular Plan). The United States government and the Bank agreed to finance the operation, while the Germans provided technical and managerial personnel. Operación Triangular was continued even after Paz Estenssoro was ousted by a coup d'état in November 1964. As a result, output recovered substantially. Whereas production of the Big Three in 1951 had been about 28,000 tons and COMIBOL by the early 1960s was producing only about half of that, the output of COMIBOL by 1969 had risen to just over 19,000 tons, of the country's total output of 30,220 tons.

Most Bolivian tin is refined in the United Kingdom, at a plant owned in part by Patiño Enterprises. During and immediately after World War II the United States government operated a refinery in Texas to which some of Bolivia's output was sent. In recent years the Bolivians have been working on plans for establishing a refinery in Bolivia to handle at least part of the country's output. Under the government of President Juan José TORRES (1970–1971), an agreement was signed with the Soviet Union to assist this enterprise.

Bibliography. Guillermo Bedregal, *Monopolios contra paises pobres: La crisis mundial de estaño,* Mexico

City, 1967; Fernando Baptista Gumucio, *Estrategia del estaño,* La Paz, 1966; Klaus Eugen Knorr, *Tin under Control,* Stanford, Calif., 1945.

ROBERT J. ALEXANDER

TINOCO, FEDERICO (1870–1931). President of Costa Rica (1917–1919). Tinoco's brief tenure as President came about as a result of a temporary breakdown in Costa Rica's usually orderly democratic processes. Alfredo González Flores became President in 1914 as a compromise choice when a three-way electoral race produced an impasse. As a consequence he never had a popular following. The outbreak of World War I, by cutting Costa Rica's opportunities to sell bananas and coffee to Europe, worsened the situation to such an extent that when Tinoco took over by coup d'état in January 1917, practically no Costa Ricans objected. However, Tinoco was no more successful than González in solving the country's desperate financial problems, and he therefore also lacked a popular following. His strong-arm tactics, which he resorted to in suppressing minor outbreaks, produced even greater antagonism. A yet more powerful opponent to Tinoco's consolidation of power was Woodrow Wilson, who steadfastly refused to recognize diplomatically his regime on the ground that he had come to power by violence. Tinoco did everything possible to conciliate the United States, from declaring war on Germany to hiring William Jennings Bryan and others to plead his case before Congress, but Wilson remained firm. Nonrecognition so encouraged Tinoco's opponents that they were able to force his resignation in August 1919. Thereafter he lived in exile in Paris until his death in 1931.

CHARLES L. STANSIFER

TIRADENTES. *See* INCONFIDÊNCIA MINEIRA.

TITICACA, LAKE. South American lake, the highest navigable freshwater lake in the world (12,500 feet). Its beautifully transparent waters, along with its thirty-six islands, cover an area of about 3,500 square miles. The lake is 138 miles long and at most 70 miles wide. Its shores, in marked contrast to most of the ALTIPLANO (high plateau), are moist, temperate, and very fertile and support a large and prosperous agricultural community. The lake is also the source of much of the fish consumed on the altiplano.

The lake is fed by twenty-five rivers and streams from the surrounding snow-capped mountains. Its only outlet is the Desaguadero River in the south, yet the lake has been steadily shrinking. This may be caused by seepage into the parched and spongy terrain of the altiplano.

Late Titicaca is shared by Peru and Bolivia. Their major lake ports of Puno and Guaqui, respectively, are connected by an efficient steamship navigation system established in 1873. This system serves an important economic function because it links the railroads from the coast of Peru to the southern altiplano.

Historically, Lake Titicaca has been sacred to both Quechua and Aymará Indians since, according to legend, the sun god emerged from it. Moreover, the lake was the center of the Inca civilization, whose traces are still very much in evidence.

ORAZIO A. CICCARELLI

TOLEDO, FRANCISCO DE (1515–1582). Viceroy of Peru (1569–1581). Toledo was among the most noteworthy officials of colonial South America. He brought to Peru the organization and stability that earlier governors and viceroys had failed to achieve because of civil war, rebellion, and the sheer magnitude of the problems. Soon after his arrival, Toledo embarked on an inspection tour that took him to Cuzco, Potosí, Chuquisaca, and then, some five years later, back to Lima via Arequipa. Thus well informed and assisted by very competent aides, he was able to establish regulations for the efficient administration of the viceroyalty from the *audiencia* level down to the local *cabildos* of both Spanish and Indian communities.

Toledo sponsored an investigation of Inca history (*see* INCAS) that convinced him that the Inca rulers had been mere usurpers and tyrants and that the Spaniards did indeed hold legitimate title to Peru. He declared war on the outlaw Inca TUPAC AMARU and had him captured, condemned for treason, and executed.

Toledo effected the relocation of 1.5 million Indians away from isolated mountain hamlets into new, more accessible villages; set up a system of native administration whereby the Indians were immediately controlled by Christianized native chiefs (*curacas*); and resolved the problem of free Indians who were reluctant to work, even for wages, by reinstating the preconquest system of draft labor, the MITA. Deserving of mention also are Toledo's mining code, which remained in force throughout the colonial era, and his intervention at the University of San Marcos, which freed that institution from the control of the Dominican order and launched it as an important center of colonial learning. He retired from the viceroyalty in 1581 and died in Spain shortly thereafter.

See also SARMIENTO DE GAMBOA, Pedro.

NORMAN MEIKLEJOHN

TOLSÁ, MANUEL (1757–1816). Spanish architect and sculptor. The principal neoclassic architect and sculptor in Mexico at the end of the colonial period, Tolsá was born near Valencia and trained in the academy there. In 1791 he was chosen as a teacher in the newly founded Academy of San Carlos in Mexico City. With his friend the painter Rafael Ximeno y Planes, he brought a neoclassic style to Mexico. He completed the Cathedral of Mexico City, but his major architectural work is the School of Mines (1797–1813), a more modest but refined design in the tradition of the Royal Palace in Madrid. Some of his private houses still stand, for example, at the corner of Argentina and Donceles in Mexico City.

In sculpture his major work is the bronze equestrian statue of King Charles IV of Spain, done between 1796 and 1803. It represents the King as a Roman emperor, a traditional idea. The statue originally stood in the Zócalo but is now at Avenida Juárez and Paseo de la Reforma. It was a great technical feat for its period.

Tolsá was the most ambitious and technically advanced artist at work in Spanish America in his time, and he set a standard that the Mexican Academy could attain only rarely in later periods. He left a few students, the best known being Pedro Patiño Ixtolinque (ca. 1774–1835), a conservative neoclassic sculptor. The important architect of the BAJÍO region Francisco Eduardo Tresguerras (1759–1833), best known for the

Church of El Carmen in Celaya, owes something of his pure neoclassic style to the teachings and example of Tolsá.

TERENCE GRIEDER

TOLTECS. A people of the early Postclassic period (A.D. 900–1527) who founded an empire that was the model upon which many of the Aztec states later were to pattern themselves. They spoke NAHUATL and were connected in some way with the Chichimec tribes of the northern steppe (*see* CHICHIMECS). The Toltecs settled in their capital, Tula, in the latter part of the ninth century. Tula is presently an archaeological site about 37 miles north of Mexico City and is well known to tourists. One of their great legendary rulers was Ce Acatl Topiltzin (*see* QUETZALCOATL), whose priestly office brought him into conflict with a party formed around the opposing cult of the violent god Tezcatlipoca. According to tradition, Topiltzin was expelled from the city in the year 987; from that time on Tula fulfilled its destiny as a center of warfare and of aggressive commerce until its fall in 1168.

The Toltecs were remembered as skilled craftsmen and possessors of great wealth. They were reputed wise in such esoteric areas as interpreting dreams, naming the stars, and manipulating the calendar. They ranged far and were seen in the most distant places. The site of CHICHÉN ITZÁ in Yucatán, a Toltec foundation, bears this out, as does the presence of the trading state of Acalan in southwestern Campeche. Their warriors were divided into knightly lodges totemically conceived; this was also true of the Aztecs, who copied them at a later date. As far as we can reconstruct the outlines of the Toltec state, there seem to have been two rulers, the *quetzalcoatl*, which title was the name of the divine plumed serpent, and the *huemac*, who may have been the war leader or executive ruler. This division of power may lie behind the legend of Topiltzin mentioned above. Rulers were alleged to have been replaced at the end of every 52-year cycle.

The end of the city of Tula was reported as a hideous enchantment cast upon its people by the god Tezcatlipoca; in a mad dance the Toltecs rushed about in demented fashion and finally spilled over into the surrounding deep gullies, settling to the bottom as rocks. The historical reality of Tula's end seems to point to years of drought, the revolt of important provincial rulers, and multiple incursions of Chichimecs, some of whom were the forerunners of the Aztecs. The ruins of Tula today are only moderately impressive. Architectural motifs there refer to the warriors of the various lodges and, in friezes of skulls and crossbones, to human sacrifice and death. Most impressive are the rigid stone figures of Toltec warriors that, as pillars, once supported the roof of the shrine of Quetzalcoatl.

See also AZTECS.

BURR C. BRUNDAGE

TORDESILLAS, TREATY OF. The discoveries of Christopher COLUMBUS prompted Ferdinand II and ISABELLA I to secure a monopoly for Spanish navigation and conquest from Pope Alexander VI, the Spaniard Rodrigo Borgia. He responded by issuing four bulls in 1493. The first two, *Inter caetera* and *Eximiae devotionis*, confirmed Castile's right to lands discovered or to be discovered in the west not infring-

ing upon the rights of another Christian ruler. The third, *Inter caetera*, fixed a north-south line of demarcation along a meridian passing 100 leagues west of the Azores and Cape Verde Islands, awarding to Spain all lands west and south of the line, Portugal being given all lands east and south. The fourth bull, *Dudum siquidem*, extended the Spanish grant to include any islands or mainland as far as and including India and the Indies.

Portugal, alarmed and failing to secure redress from the Pope, resorted to direct diplomacy, which resulted in the signing of the Treaty of Tordesillas on June 7, 1494. The line of demarcation was moved to 370 leagues west of the Cape Verde Islands, theoretically halfway across the Atlantic, thus placing all of Africa, India, and, as a result of Pedro Álvares CABRAL's discovery of 1500, Brazil within Portugal's sphere. The treaty was confirmed by a papal bull, *Ea quae,* in 1506. In 1529 the position was clarified in the Orient in the Treaty of Saragossa, whereby Spain, for 350,000 cruzados, renounced its claim to the Moluccas and recognized a new line running from north to south 297.5 leagues east of the Moluccas. The boundaries of Brazil were redefined in the Treaty of Madrid of 1750 (*see* MADRID, TREATY OF).

MARTIN TORODASH

TORO, DAVID (1898–   ). Bolivian army officer and President (1936–1937). Toro was a member of the high command of the Bolivian Army during the CHACO WAR with Paraguay (1932–1935) and was widely regarded as sharing responsibility for the poor showing of the Army. However, because of his rank and his capacity as a military politician, he was able to assume for a time the leadership of a group of younger officers who sought basic changes in Bolivian society.

On May 17, 1936, a military coup overthrew the existing government and made Colonel Toro President of the governing junta. He immediately proclaimed his intention of building a "socialist state." Toro established a Ministry of Labor for the first time, and named Waldo Álvarez, of the printing trades union, as its first Minister. The government nationalized the holdings of the Standard Oil Company of New Jersey, and although compensation was promised, an agreement on terms was not reached for half a dozen years. In April 1937 a government-backed Partido Socialista de Estado (State Socialist party) was created.

Soon after coming to power, Toro also announced plans for a corporative state. All interest groups—workers, employers, and members of the liberal professions—would be required to join unions (*sindicatos*). These would present labor and related problems to the state, which would be the final arbiter. The state itself was to be reorganized, with Congress being elected by the *sindicatos* rather than by the general citizenry. These plans never came to fruition. Colonel Toro became increasingly conservative and established relations with the Hochschild and Aramayo mining interests, which publicly proclaimed their support of his regime. As a result of Toro's move to the right and the corruption of the regime, discontent mounted among young officers and left-wing civilians who had first supported him. His regime was finally overthrown by a new military coup, led by Col. Germán BUSCH on July 13, 1937.

ROBERT J. ALEXANDER

TORRE, LISANDRO DE LA. *See* DE LA TORRE, LISANDRO.

TORRES [RESTREPO], CAMILO (1929–1966). Colombian revolutionary priest. Torres was born in Bogotá of upper-class anticlerical parents and studied at the National University. Having entered the church and studied sociology at Louvain, Father Torres became chaplain of the National University and cofounder of its Faculty of Sociology. He worked with the AGRARIAN REFORM agency, the Instituto Colombiano de Reforma Agraria (INCORA), and obtained official assistance to create a Unidad de Acción Rural in the eastern llanos. His experience of rural conditions reinforced his belief that only radical alterations of Colombian power structures could secure Catholic social justice. He concluded that sociology and Marxism provided the tools of a Christian social and political critique. In 1965 he called for the formation of a Frente Unido (United Front) composed of the nonaligned and of the "popular classes" disenchanted with the NATIONAL FRONT. He also founded a newspaper of the same name. He aimed at overthrowing the "oligarchy" by peaceful means, but if it were to resist violently, he saw no alternative to counterviolence.

His willingness to work with Communists and his espousal of violence against "legitimate" civil authorities brought Father Torres into conflict with the hierarchy, especially Luis Cardinal Concha Córdoba. Torres felt compelled to give up the priesthood. His campaign struck a sympathetic chord among the rapidly expanding university population and some younger clergy, but while he could arouse considerable enthusiasm at his rallies, he could muster only a handful of friends when he concluded finally that an intransigent National Front could be overthrown only by violence. He then joined the rural guerrillas. As a member of the Ejército de Liberación Nacional, he was killed in mysterious circumstances in a confrontation with a military unit in Santander in 1966.

Torres left no enduring organization. His influence was felt in a loosely knit group of priests called the Golconda, led until his death in 1972 by Bishop Valencia Cano of Buenaventura. Torres was rapidly acknowledged by the Latin American left as the protomartyr of the "rebel church," but perhaps he was more important for sowing self-doubts among the younger generation of Colombian priests.

C. G. ABEL

TORRES [GONZALES], JUAN JOSÉ (1921–   ). Bolivian army officer and President (1970–1971). A regular army officer, Torres was commander in chief of the armed forces after Gen. Alfredo OVANDO CANDIA seized power in September 1969. However, because of pressure from right-wing military elements he was removed from this post in July 1970.

Torres came to power after the ouster of General Ovando by right-wing military leaders on October 4, 1970. Dissidence among them, resistance from other military groups, and the mobilization of students and some workers made it impossible for Gen. Rogelio Miranda, who had overthrown Ovando, to take power. Torres finally mobilized the anti-Miranda elements and installed himself in the Presidency on October 8.

Students largely took control of La Paz after Torres's victory. They seized the Bolivian–United States Cultural Center and the newspaper *El Diario*, which was converted into a cooperative by its workers. Although Torres, as a specialist in counterinsurgency, had had a role in the campaign against Ernesto (Che) GUEVARA's guerrillas, in December he pardoned Régis DEBRAY, who had been sentenced to a long jail term after being picked up while on business for Guevara. Torres also granted a major demand of left-wing groups when he nationalized the Matilda mine, one of the largest in the country, which had previously been given to a private firm. The United States Steel Corporation had a large investment in the expropriated firm.

In February 1971 it was announced that a People's Assembly, consisting mainly of union representatives and students, would be organized. It finally met on June 23, and although it was heralded by the extreme left as a "dual power," it adjourned without taking any decisive step to play a role comparable to that of the soviets in the Russian Revolution of 1917. Of the 220 members of the Assembly, 60 percent were from urban unions and only 10 percent from peasant groups. Virtually all left and far-left parties had members, although the latter predominated.

Almost from its inception the new regime faced serious opposition, and Torres tried to purge the Army to remove possible sources of danger. However, on January 10, 1971, there was an attempted coup in La Paz, headed by Col. Hugo BANZER, who had just been dismissed as head of the Colegio Militar. On March 3 another attempted coup took place in Santa Cruz, after a march by 2,500 peasants through the city in protest against "the infantile left." Banzer was exiled after the failure of his coup, but he returned to Bolivia in August and succeeded in launching the military uprising that brought Torres's downfall. Torres went into exile in Chile.

ROBERT J. ALEXANDER

TORRES-GARCÍA, JOAQUÍN (1874–1949). Uruguayan painter. A principal figure in constructivist art and an influential theoretician and teacher, Torres-García was born in Montevideo of a Catalan father. At seventeen he was taken to Barcelona, where he spent much of his life. He was trained in the art schools of Barcelona and developed a conservative classical style. Torres-García had a lifelong devotion to the classical principles of order, measure, and ideas as essences. At forty he was a dominant figure in Catalan painting, but the abstract art that is his main contribution did not appear until later. He painted semiabstract cityscapes as early as 1917, with numbers and writing playing important parts. These soon gave way to a series of figure studies in what he called a "primitive" style of black line and neutral color, which in 1929 were transformed into the diagrammatic abstractions on which his fame rests.

Unlike his friend Mondrian, from whom he learned, Torres-García strove to humanize abstract art with symbols taken from daily experience: the clock as time, the compass as space, the hammer as human labor. Letters and numbers were given cosmic significance. In his later work imaginative portraits (*Raphael, Napoleon*) and geometrical landscapes are mixed with the abstractions, giving evidence of his love of the natural world and human history.

In 1932 Torres-García returned to Montevideo, where he founded the Association of Constructive Art. In 1944 he founded the Torres-García Workshop. Both schools have been widely influential. Torres-García was a prolific writer on art and also produced autobiographies (1917, 1939).

TERENCE GRIEDER

TORRIJOS [HERRERA], OMAR (1929–). Panamanian army officer and leader. Lieut. Col. Omar Torrijos and other officers of the National Guard overthrew President Arnulfo ARIAS in a military coup on October 11, 1968. Torrijos took full control of the government in February 1969, even though he did not move into the Presidency. That Torrijos, as commander in chief of the National Guard, had become a "strong man" was demonstrated by his handling of opposition to his regime. Suspending constitutional rights and ruling by decree, he imprisoned scores of opponents and held them without trial. The University of Panama was closed for six months while its student body was being purged of 3,000 students. Legislators were sent home, political parties were outlawed, and promises of early elections were broken. The press was brought under government control, either by forced sale or by the designation of editors. Priests unable to accept the harsh dictatorship were exiled; one was taken by uniformed men and, apparently, martyred.

By September 1970, Torrijos was ready for a confrontation with the United States on the PANAMA CANAL issue. He rejected three treaties that had been negotiated previously. In 1971 President Richard M. Nixon authorized a resumption of negotiations. The Torrijos regime placed much emphasis on the canal, as this issue united all Panamanians. Basically, the Panamanians wanted to regain control over the Canal Zone, conceded "in perpetuity" in 1903. They asked that a date be fixed for turning over the canal operation to Panama. Torrijos expected a larger share of canal revenues.

On domestic issues, Torrijos's government championed the interests of the poor over those of the former ruling elites. Rural squatters were given additional protection against removal, and a campaign to reduce illiteracy was initiated. On October 11, 1972, Torrijos's de facto powers were legitimized when he was sworn in for a six-year term as Panama's "maximum leader" in accordance with a new constitution drafted by an Assembly of Community Representatives.

LARRY L. PIPPIN

TOSAR, HÉCTOR (1923–). Uruguayan composer and pianist. Born in Montevideo, he first studied there with Humberto Baldi, then in the United States with Aaron Copland and Darius Milhaud, and in France with Arthur Honegger. In 1939 he was appointed professor of harmony and piano at the Kolischer Conservatory in Montevideo, and from 1961 to 1967 he taught composition at the Conservatory of Music in San Juan, Puerto Rico. He has twice been the recipient of Guggenheim fellowships and has traveled extensively in the Americas, Europe, and Asia as the guest of various organizations and as a concert pianist. Outstanding among his works are his Symphony No. 2 for strings (1950), *Sinfonía Concertante* (1957) for piano and orchestra, a Te Deum for bass, chorus, and orchestra (1960), *Stray Birds* (1965), and *Four Pieces*

for Orchestra (1967). Tosar's style is highly personal, uncommitted to any particular esthetic, and always deeply serious.

JUAN A. ORREGO-SALAS

TOURISM. An area as large as Latin America can be expected to contain a variety of tourism patterns, and a regional breakdown offers a convenient framework for understanding the Latin American tourism industry.

Tourist regions. As shown in the accompanying table, four major types of tourist regions are readily distinguishable.

Region I: The Caribbean. Most visitors to the islands are seeking refuge from cold winters farther north; they come primarily from the United States and to a lesser extent from Canada and Europe. Attractions such as historic sites, shopping, gambling, cultural events, and water-related activities provide additional diversion. While many visitors arrive on cruise ships and small private vessels, most fly. These relatively expensive modes of transportation, coupled with a paucity of medium- and low-cost accommodations, effectively restrict Caribbean travel to upper-middle and higher income groups. Island hopping is practiced by some seafaring passengers and by a few air passengers. More commonly, however, Caribbean tourists fly directly to one of the major resort islands such as Jamaica, Puerto Rico, and the United States Virgin Islands, stay at a single resort site between seven and ten days, and then fly directly home. In most cases their home is the United States. Some smaller islands and individual resorts cater to travelers who visit for extended periods (two to four months), while others focus upon the short-term visitor of a day or two.

In sum, although variations exist, most Caribbean tourists are wealthy, travel by airplane from the United States to one of the major resort islands, and come for the mild winter climate.

Region II: Mexico. Mexico, whose earnings from tourism are greater than those from all its exports, qualifies as a separate tourist region primarily because of its easy access to the enormous United States travel market. In addition to a sizable contingent of wealthy Americans who fly to Mexico for relief from northern winters, larger numbers arrive by automobile from middle- and even lower-income sectors. The majority of the latter group arrive during the summer months and are attracted by historic sites, the varied cultural and physical landscape, and shopping advantages. Although costs have been rising in recent years, Mexico still has much to offer the budget traveler, especially in comparison to the Caribbean region. While the Caribbean is located close to the United States, it is not accessible by land, thus necessitating more expensive air or water transportation costs. In addition, there is a dearth of moderately priced hotel and restaurant facilities on the islands, whereas Mexico has earned a well-deserved reputation for inexpensive accommodations.

Generally, tourists to Mexico are either wealthy United States citizens flying down for winter relief or middle-income families visiting a variety of places and events in their automobiles during the summer months.

Region III: South America. Whereas some intra-regional tourism exists and appears to be increasing in the countries of South America (this is true also of the

VISITORS TO TOURIST REGIONS OF LATIN AMERICA

Method of arrival	Region I: The Caribbean (1970)		Region II: Mexico (1971)		Region III: South America (1970 estimate)		Region IV: Central America (1970 estimate)	
Airplane	3,038,923	(69.4%)	1,018,017	(40.2%)	441,000	(97.8%) *	129,000	(62%)
Water	1,293,375	(29.5%)	8,672	(0.3%)	10,080	(2.2%)	16,800	(8%)
Land	None		1,490,251	(59.0%)	None		64,200	(30%)
Unclassified	39,921	(1.1%)	13,716	(0.5%)	None		None	
Total	4,375,219†		2,530,656		451,080		210,000	
Percentage of international visitors from the United States	70		88.2		41.1		54	

* The only reliable compiled figures available for South America were for air flights originating in the United States.

† Regional totals are merely a compilation of data from separate countries; hence a single traveler would be tallied each time he entered a country.

SOURCES: Data provided by the South American Travel Organization, Caribbean Travel Association, Secretaría de Integración Turística Centroamericana, and Departamento de Turismo, Mexico City.

Caribbean and Central America, but to a lesser extent), the tourist industry still is supported mostly by visitors from the United States and Europe. In most South American countries quality facilities are limited largely to the major urban centers. Consequently, most travelers take a grand tour type of vacation, spending two or three days in several airport cities such as Buenos Aires, Santiago, Lima, Bogotá, and Rio de Janeiro. However, not all visitors are discouraged by the limited facilities outside major centers, although relatively few tourists venture out on an uncharted course. And for tourists in South America, very little is charted in comparison with the wide range of choices in places to visit, means of transportation, and accommodations in other tourist centers such as Mexico, much of the Caribbean, and Europe.

Except for a very few well-known places, such as Viña del Mar in Chile, Punta del Este in Uruguay, Cuzco in Peru, and Copacabana near Rio de Janeiro, most of South America's potential tourist industry remains to be developed. For the present most visitors will be North Americans or Europeans, few in number, necessarily wealthy, and touring a relatively few major urban centers by airplane.

Region IV: Central America. The five countries of Central America have begun to organize their tourist industry relatively recently. Much effort has been expended to help the automobile-driving tourist family from the United States. From present indications Central America can expect this type of land travel to grow considerably in importance in the 1970s. The limited tourism that now exists usually involves wealthy Americans who spend time in a capital city or a seaside resort and less wealthy, highway-traveling Americans who concentrate on historic sites.

Current developments and anticipated trends. Many forces are acting to modify the existing patterns of tourism. The decade of the 1960s was a period of unprecedented growth for tourism throughout Latin America, but 1970 and 1971 were years of economic slowdown in the United States, and the growth of tourism was curtailed in most Latin American countries and actually decreased in some places. However, tourist travel fluctuated less than the overall regional economy.

An examination of visitor origins reveals that in many countries, as growth continues, United States citizens are beginning to comprise a relatively smaller percentage of the total number of visitors. In recent years a larger proportion of all visitors have been citizens of other Latin American countries, Europe, and Asia (especially Japan). The tourist industry is broadening its market.

The greater use of package tours and charter flights is another change that is beginning to affect the major tourist countries. The European experience has provided ample evidence that such arrangements have the potential for greatly enlarging tourist markets.

The development of entirely new tourist destinations is under way in more than half of the countries of Latin America. Ambitious attempts to open up heretofore unused or only lightly used areas testify to recent industry successes and to the growing determination of national governments to develop more fully the potential benefits of tourism. Among the new growth centers are the lakes district around San Carlos de Bariloche, Argentina; Yucatán and Baja California, Mexico; southern Brazil; western El Salvador; western Puerto Rico; interior Surinam; the Stann Creek region of British Honduras; and the ancient Mayan capital of Tikal in Guatemala.

There has been a dynamic new relationship between the tourist industry and national governments since the 1960s. With mounting pressures for economic improvements (jobs, housing, public services, and so on) and a growing realization that tourism can help provide them, virtually all Latin American governments have begun to organize and promote their tourist industries. Naturally, some countries have been slow to start and have provided only nominal assistance, while others have accorded tourism Cabinet-level priority and massive governmental support. Public involvement may take several forms: (1) comprehensive planning for an integrated industry; (2) aid in the development of the related infrastructure (public utilities, transportation, educational programs, and so on); (3) enactment of legislation offering incentives for growth; (4) direct planning and financing of advertising and promotion; and (5) financial support for new construction by direct government investment and by making easy credit available. Where governments have provided active and extensive support for the tourist industry, as in Mexico, Jamaica, and Puerto Rico, vastly expanded and improved benefits have resulted.

A 1972 survey of the national directors of tourist development in Latin America revealed four common needs for further expansion of tourism in their countries. Virtually all countries stressed the need for increased promotional advertising. The international travel industry is keenly competitive. Convincing information about travel opportunities in Latin America must reach potential tourists, especially since rivals in Europe, North America, and elsewhere already are promoting their attractions very effectively. Undoubtedly, tourist travel to Latin America will increase as propaganda efforts are intensified.

In addition to insufficient promotion, much of Latin America has serious shortages of adequate facilities for the accommodation and servicing of visitors. Until an area has enough first-class hotels and restaurants, tourists cannot be accommodated. Continued growth in an area can depend upon the construction of additional facilities.

Transportation inadequacies constitute another limitation. If a traveler cannot easily gain access to an area, he may be discouraged from entering it altogether, particularly if a competing area can be reached more easily. It is axiomatic that the most popular tourist destinations also have the best transportation connections. Much remains to be done to strengthen the passenger transportation system. Construction of new facilities to open up isolated areas and regional integration of existing travel networks are being emphasized.

A frequent plea was made by the national directors for increased and more clearly defined governmental support. Naturally, this sentiment was strongest in countries where the tourist industry was receiving only limited support. The establishment of quasi-governmental corporations was often mentioned as a worthwhile undertaking. Charging such public corporations with broad responsibility for developing a tourist industry has apparently been successful in several places.

Finally, the need for greatly expanded cooperation within the tourist industry is becoming widely recognized. The many private regional travel associations, aided by the ORGANIZATION OF AMERICAN STATES through the Inter-American Travel Congresses held every three to four years, can provide a framework for greatly expanding regional cooperation. Solutions could be found for many problems by approaching them regionally. This is especially true of promotional advertising and transportation. Other problems, such as antitourism feelings, outdated customs procedures, travel research, the training of workers, industry standards, rate structures, and complementary industries, all have regional expressions.

Bibliography. Georges Anderla, *Trends and Prospects of Latin American Tourism,* International Union of Official Travel Organizations, Geneva, 1968; Doreen Compton de Calvo, "Tourism in Latin America," *Bank of London and South American Review,* vol. III, no. 28, April 1969, pp. 200–212; Douglas Aircraft Company, *Focus on South American Tourism and International Air Travel,* Long Beach, Calif., 1969; International Civil Aviation Organization, *Development of International Air Passenger Travel—Latin America,* Montreal, 1968; Robert C. Mings, *A Bibliography of the Tourist Industry in Latin America,* Washington, 1970; Lyell H. Ritchie, *A Regional Study of Tourist Development in Central America,* Washington, 1965; Secretaría de Integración Turística Centroamericana, Secretariat, *Turismo: Solución inmediata,* Managua, 1971; United Nations Conference on Trade and Development, Secretariat, *The Development of Tourism in Mexico since the Early 1950's,* Geneva, 1971.

ROBERT C. MINGS

TOUSSAINT LOUVERTURE. *See* LOUVERTURE, TOUSSAINT.

TRADE (1810–1940). Between 1810 and 1940 the Latin American economies had a substantially "colonial" character. During this period most of them became strongly oriented to foreign trade and heavily dependent upon imported consumer durables, food, and machinery and upon exports of raw materials to pay for these imports. In their economic relations with the industrial powers the Latin American nations, as producers of raw materials, were vulnerable to sharp fluctuations in demand. Their agricultural products, with their relative inelasticity of supply, were particularly affected. In addition, in many cases the Latin American countries depended upon sales of only one or two commodities in only a few dominant markets in which they had to compete with many producers of the same raw materials. The industrial powers, on the other hand, were fewer in number, faced less competition, and had greater control over the supply of their products. There also was an important difference in scale. No Latin American market had half as much importance to any industrial power as any of the large markets in the more developed world had for Latin American countries. The industrial powers therefore held the whip hand over the many small Latin American economies. As a result, foreign trade became the primary preoccupation of Latin American elites, both because of their countries' acknowledged dependence upon it and because of the vulnerability of their trade position.

Comprehensive statistical statements on Latin American trade are as yet difficult to make, most particularly for the nineteenth century. The data are listed in currencies of fluctuating and uncertain value, and are not sufficiently uniform to permit easy aggregation. The Latin American figures are also usually deficient, masking a substantial amount of smuggling or understatement at customs offices. Comparisons of data among trade partners show discrepancies of as much as 300 percent. As yet there are no statistical summaries for the nineteenth century that include reliable data from all of Latin America's significant trading partners.

For the period 1810–1940 the foreign trade of Latin American nations was conducted primarily with nations outside the Latin American area. As of the 1920s less than 10 percent of Latin America's international trade was conducted within the area, and the percentage probably was not greater at any time before that. Intra-Latin American trade has been limited mainly because many of the nations produce many of the same products. Thus, the tropical countries of the Caribbean area throughout the period found complementarity with the United States and Europe rather than with each other. The most significant trade among Latin American nations before 1930 occurred between the temperate and tropical zones on the east and west coasts of South America.

Latin America's trade with world powers may be divided into the following phases: (1) 1810–1850, a period of relatively slow average growth, in which the most notable expansion occurred in countries with exportable resources in coastal areas (Argentina, Chile, Venezuela, Brazil, and Cuba) and in which Great Britain overwhelmingly dominated the import trade; (2) 1850–1880, a period of more rapid growth, extending first of all to Peru and then to Colombia, with Great Britain retaining dominance of the import trade while exports tended increasingly to flow to alternative markets in continental Europe and the United States; (3) 1880–1914, a period of dynamic growth of trade which affected almost all countries, but was most dramatically evident in the immigration-fed economies of Argentina and southern Brazil (*see* IMMIGRATION: ARGENTINA; IMMIGRATION: BRAZIL), and which was marked by competition among Great Britain, Germany, and the United States in the import trade; (4) 1914–1929, a period of United States dominance, aided by the disruption of traditional trade patterns during World War I; and (5) 1930–1940, the Depression decade, in which the value of Latin American exports dropped precipitously and Latin America was forced to abandon its former orientation toward the export of raw materials and move toward defensive autarky.

The first phase of trade (1810–1850) began with a burst of activity as British manufacturing and commerce sought alternative outlets to continental European markets during the Napoleonic era. However, Latin America proved a less lucrative market than British merchants first imagined, as its populations were small and generally poor. In addition, Latin American countries whose populations and marketable raw materials were concentrated in mountainous interiors (most Andean countries) found it difficult, because of high transportation costs, to generate exports. Mexico's foreign trade, which had grown notably between 1780 and 1810, stagnated after 1810 as its silver mines, flooded during the independence struggle, failed to regain their late-colonial production. The most notable growth of exports occurred in countries whose population and usable resources were located close to the coast. Trade grew particularly in Argentina (with cowhides comprising 65 percent of the total from about 1810 to 1853), Brazil (coffee and sugar), and Chile (silver, copper, and wheat). Venezuela's coastal coffee and cacao provided it with rapid trade growth in the 1830s, but the 1840s were marked by crisis and slower growth. After 1840 European demand for Peru's coastal GUANO provided that country with a British-managed commercial boom lasting to the latter 1870s. In the 1860s Argentina, Uruguay, Chile, Peru, and Venezuela all had per capita exports in excess of $10; with 30 percent of Spanish America's population, they provided nearly 40 percent of its exports. In all other

Spanish American countries exports were less than $5 per capita. Among these less successful exporters the trade balance was generally unfavorable, and continued importation was sustained only through heavy exports of specie, which, in countries lacking banking systems, meant economic constriction.

The 1850–1880 period was one of greatly increased orientation toward and effectiveness in exporting in Latin America. Until about 1845 some of the larger Latin American countries (principally Mexico, Colombia, Argentina, and Chile) attempted to provide infant industries with some tariff protection. But the falling prices of European textiles, the uninspiring performance of domestic industrial enterprise in competition with European manufacturers, perceptions of growing opportunities in the export market given the expansion of European population and industry, and the influence of the British example (particularly after the repeal of the Corn Laws) induced Latin American leaders during the 1840s to abandon the goal of domestic industry in favor of complete specialization in the export of raw materials. Under the banner of the international division of labor, Latin American leaders enthusiastically lowered tariffs in order to draw their countries into the welling tide of international commerce.

The foreign trade mania after 1850 had some negative effects. Increasing agricultural specialization in export products encouraged land concentration, a decline in production of domestically consumed foods, and a drop in the real income of rural labor. The external orientation and profits in the export-import sector also fostered conspicuous consumption among the upper classes. Between 1848 and 1860 imports from France, mostly luxury items, quadrupled. The mid-nineteenth-century export economies stimulated the founding of Latin America's first banks and the construction of its first railways. But transportation development was not always aided by the export economy. Some products, such as cinchona bark and indigo, were so low in volume and so unstable in markets that they did not serve as the basis for road building. In other cases where there were higher-volume exports, as in Chile's minerals or Brazil's coffee, railroads were built, but the external orientation of the lines made them of little use for integrating domestic markets.

Between 1810 and 1850 Great Britain completely dominated Latin American trade on the basis of the early entry of British merchants into the market in the Napoleonic era, strength in shipping, increasingly low costs in the manufacture of cotton textiles, and large supplies of capital that made the extension of credit easier than for competing nations. Throughout the 1810–1850 period Great Britain supplied much more to Latin America than it consumed of Latin America's exports, a large part of which was transshipped from British ports to continental European markets. Between 1850 and 1880, as a growing, increasingly urban-industrial continental European population provided increasing demand for Latin American primary products, the British lost some of their control of the Latin American export market. Much Brazilian coffee and Colombian tobacco now went directly to the Hanseatic cities, and wool from the RÍO DE LA PLATA to French ports. As trade diversified and grew, upper-class Latin Americans also took over some economic roles from British merchants. Some of them entered the export trade, and

FOREIGN TRADE OF MAJOR LATIN AMERICAN COUNTRIES, 1889–1938
(In millions)

Country	1889		1913		1929		1938	
	Imports	Exports	Imports	Exports	Imports	Exports	Imports	Exports
Argentina	$164.6	$122.8	$487.7	$510.3	$820.0	$907.3	$428.2	$409.2
Bolivia	6.0	9.0	21.3	36.5	25.9	50.8	25.0	34.8
Brazil	124.1	173.0	324.0	315.7	416.6	455.9	295.4	295.6
Chile	52.1	52.8	120.3	142.8	196.9	279.1	103.0	141.0
Colombia	9.8	13.5	27.6	33.2	122.0	122.5	89.1	80.8
Cuba	12.6	29.3	140.1	164.6	216.2	272.4	106.0	142.7
Mexico *	47.0	62.5	90.7	148.0	184.2	284.6	109.3	185.4
Peru	28.0	27.3	29.0	43.6	75.9	134.0	58.3	76.7
Uruguay	36.8	25.9	52.8	71.8	92.0	91.7	61.9	61.7
Venezuela *	16.7	20.2	77.8	28.3	87.4	150.2	97.5	280.4

* Economic year 1889–1890.

SOURCES: *The Stateman's Yearbook, 1892;* Pan American Union, Division of Economic Research, *The Foreign Trade of Latin America since 1913,* Washington, 1952; Republic of Peru, Ministerio de Fomento, *Extraco estadístico del Perú, 1920,* Lima, 1922.

even greater numbers became wholesale importers, dealing directly with commission houses in England and France.

The 1880–1914 period was one of dynamic trade expansion (the dollar value of the trade of the major countries for 1889, 1913, 1929, and 1938 is shown in the accompanying table). It also was marked by a notable change in the composition of imports. Before 1880 consumer goods, particularly textiles, overwhelmingly dominated Latin American imports. After 1880, as the Latin American countries built railways and undertook the first steps toward agricultural modernization and import-substituting manufacture, imports of machinery and industrial fuels became more notable. In 1850, 63 percent of Great Britain's exports to Latin America consisted of textiles and only 18 percent of metals and machinery; by 1913 textiles represented only one-third of British exports to Latin America, and metals and machinery were up to 27 percent. These figures actually may mask the change somewhat, as textiles were one of Britain's fortes. In 1867 less than 4 percent of Chilean imports consisted of agricultural and industrial machinery and tools; by 1908 their share had risen to nearly 20 percent. In Argentina the change came dramatically. Before 1900 two-thirds of its imports were for unproductive consumption; after 1905 more than half the imports were classified as investments in production. *See also* INDUSTRY (LATIN AMERICA).

In this period of expansion and change Great Britain faced serious challenges first from Germany, which sold aggressively, then from the United States, which was aided by its large consumption of Latin American exports. Despite its continuing failure to provide an attractive market for Latin American exports, Great Britain retained overall dominance of Latin America's import trade, with particular strength in southern South America. Its position was aided by long-established credit and marketing relations; the predominance

of British banking (established in many cases since the 1860s); heavy investments in mining and railways, which brought the purchase of British equipment in these fields; substantial purchases of Argentine cereals and beef, Bolivian tin, and Chilean nitrates, wool, and cereals; and sales of coal brought in backhaul. However, Britain was unable to keep up with Germany and the United States in sales related to technologies developed after the era of steam. The Germans dominated the chemicals trade and shared that in electrical equipment with the United States. The North Americans came to the fore in agricultural machinery and, with the development of automotive culture after 1900, in the sale of automobiles and petroleum products. During this period also the United States added to its dominance of Cuban trade by taking over the lion's share of Mexican commerce. Although European investors still controlled more than three-fifths of FOREIGN INVESTMENT in 1911, North American capital concentrated on mines and railroads, both of which stimulated imports of United States equipment. Direct railroad connection of Mexico to the North American economy and expanding mining and cotton production also favored Mexican–United States trade. In the years before World War I the United States also gained a slight edge in the imports of Venezuela and Colombia, but the British retained a leading sales position everywhere else in South America, even in Brazil, which sent three times as much of its exports to the United States as to the United Kingdom.

Although sales of the United States to Latin America grew significantly in the 1900–1914 period, its dominance over most Latin American trade was clearly established only with World War I, which temporarily eliminated its European competitors in both trade and investment. After the war the British and Germans returned to the scene, but they did not recover the strength of the prewar period. The United States remained the dominant consumer as well as the leading investor and supplier of Mexico, the Caribbean area, and northern South America. Aided by the PANAMA CANAL, the United States was now also the leading supplier of the Pacific coast of South America. Until World War II, however, the British continued to compete effectively in South America's richest markets (Argentina, Brazil, Chile, and Uruguay).

As producers of raw materials the Latin American countries have had to contend with the often-sudden entry into the market of new competitors in other parts of the world. Asian plantations, run with scientific efficiency under the British and other colonial rulers, periodically drove successful but improvidently managed Latin American exports from European markets. This happened to Colombian tobacco in the 1860s, Andean cinchona bark in the 1880s, and Amazonian rubber between 1905 and 1910 (*see* RUBBER BOOM: BRAZIL). Sales of Chilean wheat in Europe (1865–1925) fluctuated wildly, depending on the crops of larger producers. Special relations between Great Britain and the Commonwealth countries (most notably Canada and Australia) reduced the role of Argentine wheat in the British market, particularly during the Depression of the 1930s.

By contrast, in a few cases Latin American producers have sufficiently approached a monopoly to be able to protect themselves. After 1906 Brazil as a majority producer succeeded in its effort to hold up coffee prices by withholding coffee from the world market (*see* TAUBATÉ CONVENTION), but valorization had the long-range effect of encouraging the expansion of coffee production among lesser competitors in Latin America and Africa. A Cuban effort to restrict sales of sugar in the 1920s also had the effect of encouraging expansion among competitors.

Latin American exports have also been affected by the development in the industrial world of synthetics or other substitutes for basic export commodities. During the nineteenth century sugarcane had to make a place for the sugar beet, developed during the Napoleonic period; in the latter half of the nineteenth century coal-tar dyes displaced indigo and cochineal; and the Germans, cut off from Chilean nitrates in World War I, developed a substitute supply that ultimately undermined the Chilean industry (*see* NITRATE INDUSTRY: CHILE).

At least until World War II Latin America's trade position vis-à-vis the leading industrial nations seems to have been in a long-term decline. In 1950 Raúl PREBISCH of the ECONOMIC COMMISSION FOR LATIN AMERICA (ECLA) claimed that between 1876 and 1938 raw materials suffered a 36 percent decline in their terms of trade with manufactured goods; that is, a given unit of primary products in 1938 could buy on the average less than two-thirds as much in manufactures as it could in 1876. Over this period the prices of manufactures rose faster in prosperity and declined less in depression than those of raw materials. The ECLA calculations exaggerate the decline in Latin America's terms of trade, among other reasons because they do not take into account improvements in intrinsic value that have accompanied rising prices of manufactures. Nevertheless, it is clear that Latin America's trade position did decline after the heyday of 1880–1914, in part because of an overexpansion of capacity stimulated

by World War I. Wild fluctuations in demand and crisis in the early 1920s were followed by a period of expanding production and softening prices that culminated in the shock of the Depression of the 1930s. Between 1929 and 1932 the prices of the most important raw materials exported by Latin America dropped between 47 and 66 percent, and Latin America's capacity to import (taking into consideration volume of exports and lower prices of manufactures) dropped by nearly one-fourth. By curtailing Latin America's capacity to import, the crisis of the 1930s forced the area's leaders to begin to turn away from their former focus on raw materials exports and to give the highest priority to defensive industrialization. The larger countries, with import-substituting manufactures already well under way, expanded these activities. By 1940 Latin America had entered fully into an era in which traditional exports of primary products were used principally to subsidize imports of industrial raw materials and capital goods. This change foreshadowed Latin America's current emergence as an exporter of some kinds of manufactured goods.

Bibliography. P. T. Ellsworth, "The Terms of Trade between Primary Producing and Industrial Countries," *Inter-American Economic Affairs,* vol. X, no. 1, Summer, 1956, pp. 47–65; R. A. Humphreys (ed.), *British Consular Reports on the Trade and Politics of Latin America, 1824–1826,* London, 1940; Clarence F. Jones, *Commerce of South America,* Boston, 1928; Alan K. Manchester, *British Preëminence in Brazil: Its Rise and Decline,* Chapel Hill, N.C., 1933; Margaret Alexander Marsh, "Monoculture and the Level of Living: An Hypothesis," *Inter-American Economic Affairs,* vol. I, no. 1, June 1947, pp. 77–111; D. C. M. Platt, *Latin America and British Trade,* New York, 1973; Sergio Sepúlveda G., *El trigo chileno en el mercado mundial: Ensayo de geografía histórica,* Santiago, Chile, 1959; United States Tariff Commission, *The Foreign Trade of Latin America,* 3 parts, rev. ed., Report 146, 2d ser., Washington, 1942.

FRANK SAFFORD

TRADE (since World War II). Latin American trade has undergone rapid changes in volume and direction since World War II. The causes of these changes are many and varied, but they center in changes in world prices for Latin American exports, the relatively unchanging composition of Latin American imports and exports, and significant import substitution, especially in some important countries, as well as inflation, trade controls, and burgeoning population growth. These and other forces have led to a declining position in world trade, with subsequent relative losses of foreign currency earnings "needed" to import scarce capital goods and raw materials. Some countries have done much better than others, however, and no average accurately reflects the situation for each country.

Changes in per capita trade and gross national product. The value of Latin American traded goods (exports and imports) approximately doubled between 1948 and 1969 in dollar terms. As can be seen in Table 1, however, the distribution of total trade and of these changes between countries is uneven. Just four countries accounted for more than half of the total trade. The economic giants—Mexico, Brazil, and Argentina—and oil-rich Venezuela accounted for more than 56

TABLE 1. TRADE OF LATIN AMERICAN COUNTRIES, 1948 AND 1969
(In millions)

Country	1948			1969		
	Imports	Exports	Total	Imports	Exports	Total
Mexico	$ 560	$ 465	$1,025	$2,078	$ 1,430	$ 3,508
Costa Rica	42	46	88	245	194	439
El Salvador	41	45	86	214	202	416
Guatemala *	68	67	135	247	222	469
Honduras†	33	55	88	184	181	365
Nicaragua	28	19	47	177	155	332
Panama	64	25	89	294	117	411
Total, Central America*	276	257	533	1,361	1,071	2,432
Barbados†	26	12	38	91	37	128
Cuba‡	547	724	1,271	1,001	717	1,718
Dominican Republic	65	83	148	243	184	427
Haiti	31	30	61	38	38	76
Jamaica	79	46	125	442	257	699
Trinidad and Tobago	110	110	220	483	475	958
Total, Caribbean area‡	858	1,005	1,863	2,298	1,708	4,006
Argentina	1,562	1,629	3,191	1,576	1,612	3,188
Bolivia	79	98	177	167	181	348
Brazil	1,134	1,173	2,307	2,242	2,311	4,553
Chile	269	329	598	907	1,071	1,978
Colombia	324	277	601	686	608	1,294
Ecuador	53	50	103	262	183	445
Guyana	41	31	72	118	121	239
Paraguay	24	28	52	82	51	133
Peru	168	157	325	604	864	1,468
Uruguay	201	179	380	197	200	397
Venezuela	726	1,040	1,766	1,572	2,892	4,464
Total, South America	$4,581	$4,991	$9,572	$8,413	$10,094	$18,507

* 1968 trade figures used (1969 data unavailable).

† 1968 export trade figures used (1969 data unavailable).

‡ 1967 trade figures used (1969 data unavailable).

SOURCE: Kenneth Ruddle and Mukhtar Hamour (eds.), *Statistical Abstract of Latin America, 1969,* Los Angeles, 1970.

percent of total trade by value in 1969, but the most spectacular increase had been made by Peru, with a 400 percent increment, and the Central American countries generally.

A slightly different perspective is provided in Table 2, in which annual per capita growth rates of trade are compared with those of the gross national product (GNP) by country and region. Surprisingly, trade growth was greater than GNP growth for Latin America as a whole. However, the country deviations from the average were large. Several of the major countries were able to grow very respectably in per capita GNP while trade hardly increased at all. Brazil, Colombia, and Venezuela all fit this category. That these countries were able to do so well in terms of GNP growth is attributable to their effective import substitution programs, which resulted in the replacement of imports, mainly of manufactured goods, by domestic products. In Brazil exports were undynamic, whereas in Colombia and Venezuela exports grew much more rapidly

than imports. Mexico constitutes an intermediate case, in which GNP outperformed trade but trade growth was still fairly sizable. In a few countries, among them Cuba, Argentina, and Uruguay, per capita trade diminished during this period. In the case of Cuba there is a ready explanation: the CUBAN REVOLUTION and the subsequent boycott of trade by the United States and many Latin American countries. Argentina and Uruguay have both been beset by many ills which have made their economies and their trade stagnant and which are too complex to be treated here. Thus, while there was a correlation between growth in GNP and growth in trade per capita in some countries, there were enough variations from this pattern to call for further inquiry into whether or not Latin American trade performance was satisfactory. One indicator is Latin American performance vis-à-vis the rest of the world.

Latin America in comparison with the rest of the world. Latin America's relative share of total world trade has declined significantly since World War II. As shown in

TABLE 2. ANNUAL COMPOUND GROWTH RATES IN PER CAPITA TRADE AND GROSS NATIONAL PRODUCT IN LATIN AMERICA

Country	Compound annual growth rates (percent)			Imports as a percentage of GNP	
	Imports[a]	Exports[a]	GNP[b]	1948–1949	1969
Mexico	2.8	1.9	3.5	8.5	7.1
Costa Rica	5.1	3.5	1.5	27.9[c]	29.8
El Salvador	5.8	5.0	...	...	22.7
Guatemala[d,e]	5.0	4.5	1.3	11.0[c]	15.0
Honduras[e,f]	5.1	2.6	9.0	19.0[c]	28.5
Nicaragua	6.6	7.8	...	19.9[c]	24.3
Panama	4.2	4.3	−0.7	24.1[c]	32.1
Total, Central America[d]	5.4	4.6	...	...	23.0
Barbados[f]	5.0	4.3	...	...	67.9
Cuba[g]	0.4	−1.5	...	25.3[c]	...
Dominican Republic	3.1	0.8	0.5	16.8[c]	19.1
Haiti	−0.2	−0.1	...	...	9.4
Jamaica	6.6	6.6	...	31.1[c]	41.5
Trinidad and Tobago	4.5	4.4	3.3	...	62.2
Total, Caribbean area[g]	2.4	0.4	...	...	...
Argentina	−1.4	−1.4	0.6	11.2	7.9
Bolivia	2.6	2.0	...	...	18.5
Brazil	0.2	0.2	1.8	6.6	7.2
Chile	3.3	3.1	0.3	11.5	14.7
Colombia	0.5	0.7	1.9	10.6	11.1
Ecuador	5.3	3.2	2.1	12.1[c]	15.9
Guyana	2.1	3.6	1.7	...	50.2
Paraguay	3.1	0.02	2.7	17.9[c]	15.1
Peru	3.9	6.0	4.0	9.6	11.8
Uruguay	−0.9	−0.4	...	...	10.1
Venezuela	−0.2	1.1	2.7	20.5[c]	16.3
Total, South America	−0.1	1.1	...	...	10.3
Total average	3.5	3.1	2.6	16.7	23.4

[a] Based on 1948–1969 percentage changes unless otherwise noted.
[b] Based on 1953–1969 percentage changes unless otherwise noted.
[c] 1953 data used (1948–1949 data unavailable).
[d] Based on 1948–1968 trade figures.
[e] 1952 population figure used for GNP calculations.
[f] 1948–1968 trade figures used for export category.
[g] Based on 1948–1967 trade figures.

SOURCE: Werner Baer, "Import Substitution Industrialization in Latin America," *Latin American Research Review*, vol. VII, no. 1, Spring, 1972, pp. 95–122; United Nations, *Statistical Yearbook 1949–50*, New York, 1951; id., *Economic Survey of Latin America 1969*, New York, 1970; id., *Handbook of International Trade and Development Statistics, 1969*, New York, 1969; id., *The Latin American Economy in 1969*, New York, 1970; id., *Yearbook of International Trade Statistics 1969*, New York, 1971.

Table 3, not only has growth in export volume fallen short of the growth in exports of developed nations since 1955–1960, but it has lagged substantially behind that of other developing nations. Why has Latin America done so poorly? One explanation is that the Latin American countries have stressed import substitution growth and neglected their foreign sectors. Policies of "Supply the foreign market only after domestic needs are met," tariffs and quotas, overvalued exchange rates, and provision of ample cheap loans and credit for manu-facturing all gave import substitution incentives at the expense of more traditional primary export sectors.

This basic explanation does not conflict with the observation that all developing nations have been losing ground in their share of world trade because they are producers of primary products, which have low income elasticities of demand. Income elasticity of demand is important because it denotes the change in quantity demanded of a product in response to a change in income. In fact, whereas primary products often

TABLE 3. VARIATION IN VOLUME OF WORLD EXPORTS
(Annual growth rates)

Year	World total*	Developed countries	Developing countries	Latin America
1955–1960	5.9	6.6	4.3	4.3
1960–1965	7.0	7.4	6.1	3.3
1965	7.3	8.1	5.6	3.9
1966	7.6	8.3	4.4	3.8
1967	4.7	4.6	4.2	2.7
1968	12.0	13.2	8.1	1.8
1969	9.9	11.6	6.6	7.2†

* Excluding countries with centrally planned economies.

† January–September, 1969.

SOURCE: United Nations, *Economic Survey of Latin America 1969*, New York, 1970.

have lower income elasticities of demand than manufactured goods, they frequently constitute the best source of income and foreign exchange for Latin American countries. Moreover, not all primary products have low income elasticities. Handicraft culture goods, truck crops, strawberries, tomatoes, apples, peaches, and specialty goods such as lobster and seafood delicacies are only a few examples of high-elasticity products. Latin American countries have not turned to these partly because of the difficulty of introduction of new products and partly because of lack of foresight and discrimination against the export sector in an era stressing autarky and import substitution. Beef is another large-scale potential export. Although Argentina and Uruguay have tended to dominate this market in Latin America, the possibilities in Brazil, Colombia, and other countries are excellent once problems of disease control, processing, and marketing have been solved. Recent moves have been made in both these directions, for example, by Mexico in diversified spe-

cialty products and by Brazil in beef cattle. It remains to be seen how quickly results on a larger scale will materialize and what the United States reaction will be. Nonprice obstacles to such exports as beef are still very great in the United States and Europe. The 1972 United Nations Conference on Trade and Development was unsuccessful in gaining much cooperation from the advanced countries toward reducing these obstacles.

Composition of Latin American trade. The composition of Latin American trade changed only slightly between 1950 and 1968. Table 4 shows the structure of exports in 1955 and 1967. Some shift toward manufactured goods and away from primary products is apparent, but in comparison with all other developing countries Latin America still has a very large concentration of primary exports (85 percent versus 79 percent for all the others). Nonetheless, Latin American exports are growing slowly not so much because they are made up mainly of primary products as because Latin America has greatly discouraged exports in general without promoting primary goods with high income elasticities.

The composition of imports from 1951–1955 to 1961–1968 was also very stable. As shown in Table 5, crude materials and fuels constituted about half of all Latin American imports, capital goods a third, and durable and nondurable consumer goods the remainder. These figures reflect the great dependence of the Latin American manufacturing industry upon foreign inputs but tend to hide the tremendous import substitution in consumer goods that occurred in the larger countries over these years. In the less developed countries consumer goods imports still loom large. Thus, for example, Brazil and Paraguay were farther apart in this respect than Brazil and the United States.

Country shares. Latin American exports have been aimed predominantly at the United States and Western Europe, although their share of the total fell from 78 percent in 1959 to 68 percent in 1969. The percentage going to Japan, other Latin American countries, Eastern Europe, and mainland China rose significantly during the same period. The American share declined, while that of Western Europe increased. Between 1950 and 1969 the United States share fell from 48 to 34 percent. The Western European share rose from 30 to 34 percent in this period, while Canada's share increased from 2 to 3 percent. The reduced Latin Amer-

TABLE 4. COMPOSITION OF EXPORTS

Category	Percent 1955	Percent 1967
Primary products	90	85
Food	47	43
Crude materials	19	18
Fuels	24	24
Manufactures	9	15
Chemical products	1	2
Machinery	...	1
Other manufactures	8	12

SOURCE: United Nations, *Economic Survey of Latin America 1969*, New York, 1970.

TABLE 5. COMPOSITION OF IMPORTS
(Average annual percentages)

Periods	Crude materials and fuels	Nondurable consumer goods	Capital goods	Durable consumer goods
1951–1955	51	12	30	6
1960–1968	49	10	33	6

SOURCE: United Nations, *Economic Survey of Latin America 1969*, New York, 1970.

TABLE 6. TERMS OF TRADE OF SEVENTEEN LATIN AMERICAN COUNTRIES *

(Index: 1963 = 100)

Countries	Average annual indices		
	1951–1955	1956–1960	1961–1968
Metal-exporting countries			
Bolivia, Chile, and Peru	110	102	118
Coffee-exporting countries			
Brazil, Colombia, Costa Rica,			
El Salvador, and Guatemala	150	130	109
Banana-exporting countries			
Honduras, Panama, and Ecuador	131	119	104
Sugar-exporting country			
Dominican Republic	145	108	101
Cotton-exporting country			
Nicaragua	120	97	102
Countries exporting livestock products			
Argentina and Uruguay	103	86	96
Petroleum-exporting country			
Venezuela	141	131	90
Country with diversified exports			
Mexico	125	104	97
Fourteen countries (excluding Bolivia,			
Chile, and Peru)	129	115	97
Total, Latin America	127	113	100

* Argentina, Bolivia, Brazil, Chile, Colombia, Costa Rica, Dominican Republic, Ecuador, El Salvador, Guatemala, Honduras, Mexico, Nicaragua, Panama, Peru, Uruguay, and Venezuela.
SOURCE: United Nations Economic Commission for Latin America, *The Latin American Economy in 1969: An excerpt from ECLA Survey,* New York, 1970.

ican dependence upon the United States since 1950 reflected in part a return to the more normal pre-World War II trade patterns.

Latin American intraregional exports increased from 9.5 percent of total Latin American exports for 1946–1951 to 12.3 percent in 1969. Between 1960 and 1968 the intraregional export growth rate was 9.3 percent. Argentina, Venezuela, Brazil, and Mexico dominate intraregional exports, accounting for 63.1 percent of all such exports for 1967–1968.

Import trends have been very similar in configuration to export trends.

Export and import prices: terms of trade. The prices that Latin American countries obtain for their exports as compared with the prices they pay for their imports are of the utmost importance, especially for countries in which exports and imports represent a major share of national income. The relationship between what is paid for exports and what is paid for imports is called the terms of trade. Beginning with an arbitrary base year in which both prices equal an index of 100, the change in one is compared with the change in the other. Since the export price index is placed above the import price index (P_x/P_m), if export prices increase more than import prices following the base year, the index is greater than 100 and the terms of trade are said to improve. If import prices increase more than export prices, there is a deterioration.

Since World War II Latin American export prices have fluctuated widely but have fallen overall. Import prices, conversely, have been fairly stable but have risen slightly overall. The net outcome is therefore one of a falling terms-of-trade index, or a deterioration of about 27 percent, as shown at the bottom of Table 6 for all Latin America. The statistical picture for individual countries according to the type of major export is shown in the upper portion of the table. All the countries except those exporting metal products (Bolivia, Chile, and Peru) experienced declining and unfavorable terms of trade. Even Mexico, which is classified as having diversified exports, suffered a substantial worsening. The solution is clearly not only the diversification of exports but a switch to exports with a higher income elasticity and international demand. To achieve the necessary change in production structure and a lowering of import barriers for manufactures in North America and Europe will require time, and no rapid change can be expected.

Trade with socialist countries. Latin American exports to socialist countries, mainly the U.S.S.R. and Eastern Europe, increased by 411 percent and imports by 672 percent from 1955 to 1968 (exports and imports increased in value from $320 million to $1,690 million). Most of the increase was due to the shift in trade patterns after the Cuban revolution in 1959. In 1968, for example, 56 percent of all Latin American exports to socialist countries originated in Cuba, and 84 percent of all Latin American imports from socialist countries went to Cuba.

Conclusions. Most Latin American countries have had severe problems with their trade, as have other developing countries. Falling prices of primary products because of income-inelastic demands may continue to plague exports while Latin American demands for capital goods and strategic fuels will grow faster than income. The impetus to change the structure of exports toward manufactured goods should continue slowly. Competitive production and marketing problems are severe. Market barriers to imports of many manufactures are high in the United States and Europe and will probably remain so. Finally, given the tight import constraints faced by Latin America, we can expect to find continuing efforts to substitute domestic production for imports even where this will be of questionable value because the small size of markets will prevent the capturing of important economies of scale and lead to inefficiencies due to inexperience. Hitherto only Brazil and Mexico have succeeded in diversifying their domestic economies, and only Mexico in diversifying exports. Most of the countries are too small to achieve an integrated production structure, and that is why efforts to share production and markets in free trade areas and by other community arrangements (*see* ECONOMIC INTEGRATION) will be an important feature of endeavors as yet barely under way.

See also INDUSTRY (LATIN AMERICA).

Bibliography. Werner Baer, "Import Substitution Industrialization in Latin America," *Latin American Research Review,* vol. VII, no. 1, Spring, 1972, pp. 95–122; Joseph Grunwald, Miguel Wionczek, and Martin Carnoy, *Latin American Integration and U.S. Policy,* Washington, 1972; Kenneth Ruddle and Mukhtar Hamour (eds.), *Statistical Abstract of Latin America, 1969,* Los Angeles, 1970; United Nations Economic Commission for Latin America, *Economic Survey of Latin America 1969,* New York, 1970, id., *The Latin American Economy in 1969: An Excerpt from ECLA Survey,* New York, 1970.

DONALD L. HUDDLE

TRAGIC WEEK. *See* SEMANA TRÁGICA.

TRANSPORTATION. *See* AIR TRANSPORT; HIGHWAYS; RAILROADS.

TREJOS, JOSÉ JOAQUÍN (1916–   ). President of Costa Rica (1966–1970). A professional economist, Trejos served as dean of the Faculty of Economics of the University of Costa Rica and as a director of the Central Bank of Costa Rica before actively entering politics. His political naïveté proved to be an advantage in the campaign of 1966, since his opponent, Daniel Oduber of the PARTIDO LIBERACIÓN NACIONAL (PLN), presented a whirlwind professional campaign. Observers concluded that Costa Rican voters preferred Trejos's quiet, steady competence to Oduber's flamboyance. Perhaps, too, voters preferred his conservative economic outlook to Oduber's socialism.

As a coalition President representing several conservative groups, Trejos found it difficult to carry out any legislative program. During the Trejos administration the PLN held a one-member margin in the Legislative Assembly. As a result, Trejos's program for the reestablishment of private banking was defeated, as were most of his finance and tax proposals. However, a 5 percent sales tax law was passed in December 1966. Revenues were nonetheless insufficient to enable Trejos to balance the budget or to establish the fiscal soundness he worked for.

CHARLES L. STANSIFER

TRINITARIA, LA. Secret society organized by Dominican patriots in 1838 to drive out the Haitian occupation forces and secure independence for their country. Organized in three-man cells, La Trinitaria fashioned an elaborate system of codes and passwords and soon established branches in the country's major towns. The Trinitarios signed their loyalty to the movement in blood, and their rituals contained a mixture of political and religious symbols. The principal leaders (and the original Trinitarios) were Juan Pablo DUARTE, Francisco del Rosario Sánchez, and Ramón Mella.

Though the movement was persecuted by the Haitians, its ideals spread; eventually the Haitians were defeated, and independence was achieved. Almost immediately, however, the leaders of the movement and many of their visions were repudiated by the succession of men on horseback who came to power in the Dominican Republic. Nevertheless, the Trinitario ideals of democracy, representative government, and unfettered independence survived. Frequently in subsequent Dominican history these ideals inspired young patriots to try to throw off the yoke of domestic or foreign tyrannies and to reestablish the fundamental principles that had inspired the independence heroes. Many times these groups adopted the Trinitarios' name, mode of organization, and secret rituals. Though frequently thwarted, the inspiration of the Trinitarios is still strongly present in the Dominican Republic.

HOWARD J. WIARDA

TRIPLE ALLIANCE, WAR OF THE. *See* PARAGUAYAN WAR.

TRUJILLO MOLINA, RAFAEL LEONIDAS (1891–1961). Dominican dictator (1930–1961) and President (1930–1938, 1943–1952). Rafael Trujillo was born in San Cristóbal, Dominican Republic. His parents were middle-class, by the standards of the town, and did not belong to the white, aristocratic elite. Young Trujillo had only a modest formal education, but he was shrewd and astute and came to know intimately the strengths, weaknesses, and aspirations of his people and his country. Early in life he found employment as a telegraph operator and on one of the sugar estates, but it was not until the United States military occupation of 1916–1924 that the big opportunity in his life came. Trujillo enrolled as an officer in the peacekeeping constabulary created by the United States Marines, rose rapidly through the grades, and, after the occupation forces had left, became commander in chief of this newly powerful national army. In 1930, with the economy collapsing as a result of the Depression and with the elitist oligarchic system in disarray, he seized power, ruling until similar economic difficulties, coupled with political-diplomatic pressure exerted by the ORGANIZATION OF AMERICAN STATES, helped precipitate his assassination in 1961. *See also* SAN JOSÉ MEETINGS.

Trujillo's dictatorship was one of the tightest and most absolute the world had ever seen. He directed virtually all aspects of national life. The military remained the final basis of his power, and he dominated it absolutely, meanwhile modernizing and greatly expanding it. The governmental machinery—courts, Congress, elections, Cabinets, bureaucracy—was also dominated completely by Trujillo. Through his control of the Army and the government, he converted the national economy into his personal fief, again modernizing and developing the institutional and financial infrastructure, though chiefly for his own advantage. He also terrorized the population, created his own official party, the Partido Dominicano, to operate as a mechanism for extending his power and financial control, dominated education and intimidated intellectuals and the universities, manipulated the lives of both oppositionists and allies, used the United States and its cold war psychology to cement himself in power, and dabbled in the techniques of totalitarian thought control.

The Trujillo regime thus not only was one of the longest in Latin American history but may also have been among the strongest, most personal, and most pervasive anywhere in the world. Some have seen Trujillo as merely another in the long line of Dominican strong men on horseback, but it is clear that his rule went considerably beyond classic Latin American *caudillismo*. Others have seen in his dictatorship strong elements of modern totalitarianism, although it is equally clear that Trujillo was not a Dominican Hitler or Stalin.

The Trujillo regime was in essence a reflection of

Rafael Leonidas Trujillo Molina. [*Organization of American States*]

a classic Latin American authoritarian tradition, albeit "modernized" in a variety of ways. Trujillo's regime was bloody, to be sure, but he was as much a demanding "father" as an unmitigated oppressor, as much paternal as tyrannical. The way Trujillo governed, seeing his Army, his people, and his country as part of his private domain, is in accord with the classic mold of traditional patrimonialism. His system of economic monopoly, of centralism and absolutism, of privilege and favoritism, has its antecedents in the Spanish colonial system of royal, state-building central authority. In this sense Trujillo may be seen as trying to reestablish in his country the ancient Spanish system of power and grandeur after centuries of disorder and chaos. But Trujillo was also in a sense a modern, caught up in the newer currents of nationalism, populism, and developmentalism. He and his advisers were influenced by the newer currents of Catholicism and corporatism and sought to adapt the ancient Spanish ideals to twentieth-century trends. Trujillo's rule also reflected and symbolized the rise of the middle sectors to power and prominence in Dominican life and the eclipse of the older ruling elites.

It is not fatuous to remind ourselves that Trujillo was both a product and a reflection of his time and circumstances. Coming to power in a poor, weak, and chronically unstable country, he sought to restore order, reorient his countrymen, and develop the nation. He sought also to deal with the newer phenomena of rapid urbanization, industrialization, a rising working class, new and conflicting ideologies and movements, and diverse external pressures. Yet he did all these things within the classic Latin framework of corporatism, authoritarianism, hierarchy, and patrimonialism. Through his skill, drive, and undoubted capacities as a leader and organizer, Trujillo for a long time was able to hold these diverse threads together and blend and reconcile traditional and modern elements in a heterogeneous, overlapping pattern. Eventually, however, some holes began to appear and then grow larger in the Trujillo system, the dictator was assassinated, and the fabric of Dominican sociopolitical life again unraveled. The old accommodation network collapsed; a new one had to be created.

Bibliography. G. Pope Atkins and Larman C. Wilson, *The United States and the Trujillo Regime,* New Brunswick, N.J., 1972; Juan Bosch, *Trujillo,* Caracas, 1959; Robert Crassweller, *Trujillo,* New York, 1966; Arturo Espaillat, *Trujillo,* Chicago, 1963; Jesús de Galíndez, *La era de Trujillo,* Santiago, Chile, 1956; Abelardo Nanita, *La era de Trujillo,* Ciudad Trujillo, 1955; Germán Ornes, *Trujillo,* New York, 1958; Howard J. Wiarda, *Dictatorship and Development: The Methods of Control in Trujillo's Dominican Republic,* Gainesville, Fla., 1970.

HOWARD J. WIARDA

TUCUMÁN, CONGRESS OF. Argentine national Congress of 1816 that declared formal independence. Following the May 1810 revolution Argentina was ruled by a succession of revolutionary governments that successfully warded off counterrevolutionary moves but proved unable to place the new regime on a firm institutional footing. The Assembly of 1813, the first effective national Congress, failed to adopt a constitution or even to discard the fiction of loyalty to King

FERDINAND VII. These and other items of unfinished business were left to form the agenda of a new Congress, which convened in Tucumán in March 1816.

When the Congress met, the outlook for independence in Spanish America was scarcely favorable: in all major theaters except Argentina royalists had regained the upper hand. Nevertheless, the uncompromising attitude of the government in Madrid left little room for accommodation, and on July 9, 1816, the deputies at Tucumán formally declared the independence of the United Provinces of South America. The same deputies, however, predominantly favored the establishment of an independent monarchy as the system best able to assure internal stability and gain the sympathy of Britain and other European powers. The proposal that enjoyed the most widespread support was to crown an heir of the Inca royal family as constitutional monarch (*see* INCAS). However, there was strong opposition to the idea in some quarters, and it was not clear who the logical Inca candidate might be. Eventually, therefore, the plan was dropped.

Early in 1817 the Congress suspended its sessions in Tucumán. In April it reconvened in Buenos Aires. There the deputies continued to dabble in monarchist schemes, now oriented toward finding a European prince, and adopted a centralist constitution in April 1819. But this document was short-lived, for the following year saw the collapse of all central authority in Argentina and with it the final dissolution of the Congress itself.

DAVID BUSHNELL

TUPAC AMARU (ca. 1544–1572). Last Inca of Peru. The legitimate son of MANCO INCA, Tupac Amaru succeeded as ruler of the Inca state of Vilcabamba, north of Cuzco, in 1571, upon the death of his half brother Titu Cusi. Unlike Titu Cusi, who had been willing to negotiate with Spanish officialdom and to receive Christian missionaries at Vilcabamba, Tupac Amaru and his followers were hostile to European culture. The murder of an emissary from Viceroy Francisco de TOLEDO in March 1572 soon led to a successful Spanish campaign against the Inca enclave. Tupac Amaru was captured and brought to Cuzco, where he was accused of personal responsibility for recent outrages against Spaniards. After a brief trial he was sentenced to be beheaded, to the dismay of many Spanish clergymen, who asked that his life be spared on the grounds that he was innocent of the crimes attributed to him. Toledo, however, who wished to terminate the Inca dynasty once and for all, was unyielding, and the sentence was carried out in September 1572. Before his death Tupac Amaru, who had been baptized after his capture, reportedly made a speech denouncing the Indian religion. José Gabriel Condorcanqui TUPAC AMARU, who led a rebellion against Spanish officials in 1780, was the great-great-grandson of a daughter of Tupac Amaru.

HELEN DELPAR

TUPAC AMARU, JOSÉ GABRIEL CONDORCANQUI (ca. 1742–1781). Leader of the most important Indian revolt in eighteenth-century Spanish America. Born in Tinta, Peru, he inherited the paternal *cacicazgo* and claimed to be a direct descendant of the Inca TUPAC AMARU on his maternal side. Although his social position was high, he became concerned about the abuses suffered by the mass of Indians, especially the onerous working conditions in the *obrajes* (textile factories; *see* OBRAJE) and the forced service in the mines of Potosí. In 1776 the *audiencia* of Lima denied his petition that the Indians of Tinta be exempted from work in the mines. Since this legal attempt to obtain redress against the extortions of the local corregidor was ineffective, he resorted to more radical action. On November 4, 1780, he started an uprising, with formal demands for the abolition of the forced purchase of merchandise from the corregidores, the appointment of Indian alcaldes (magistrates), the lifting of certain tributes, and the creation of an *audiencia* at Cuzco. The rebellion originally proclaimed allegiance to the King, but in its last stages it developed separatist overtones. It spread rapidly in the provinces around Cuzco and resulted in the execution of one corregidor and the destruction of *obrajes* and other Spanish properties. Appeals for the support of some noble Indian sectors and the white creoles failed. Despite some early victories, the rebels were unable to capture Cuzco early in 1781, lacking the military ability to defeat the Spaniards. Tupac Amaru was captured, and after a summary trial he was executed on May 18, 1781.

ASUNCIÓN LAVRIN

TUPAMAROS. Urban guerrillas of Uruguay. The Tupamaros were founded in Montevideo in 1963 as Latin America's first Marxist rebels organized for guerrilla warfare in the cities rather than in the countryside. Following the Tupamaro example in Uruguay, other urban guerrillas appeared in Guatemala, Argentina, and Brazil in the late 1960s.

Taking their name from José Gabriel Condorcanqui TUPAC AMARU, the eighteenth-century Peruvian Inca who fought Spanish colonial practices, the Tupamaros sought a Robin Hood image and in their early operations robbed from the wealthy to aid the poor. In the mid-1960s, as inflation eroded the purchasing power of most Uruguayans, the Tupamaros moved from bank robberies to bombings and kidnappings, seeking a violent overthrow of Uruguay's mixed economy and the establishment of a completely socialist state.

In August 1968, the Tupamaros gained extensive national publicity by kidnapping presidential adviser Ulyses Pereira Reverbel and releasing him after five days. In July 1970, the Tupamaros kidnapped Dan Mitrione, a United States police administrator serving as an adviser on training in Montevideo, and killed him. Also that July, they kidnapped Brazilian Consul Aloysio Dias Gomide but released him in February 1971 after a ransom was paid. Claude Fly, United States agricultural technical adviser, was kidnapped in August 1970 and released the following March after he had a severe heart attack. British Ambassador Geoffrey Jackson, kidnapped in January 1971 and freed in September 1971 after 244 days of captivity, was the seventh prominent person abducted within two years as part of a Tupamaro campaign for public recognition.

In 1970, by presidential decree, the government abridged decades of complete press freedom by prohibiting news stories describing the Tupamaros as political crusaders; they now had to be identified as criminals sought for robbery and murder. In April

1972, the Tupamaros killed former Assistant Minister of the Interior Armando Acosta y Lara and a navy captain, engendering a new wave of criticism.

For months prior to the national elections of November 1971, the Tupamaros remained relatively quiet, but with the inauguration of President Juan María BORDABERRY in March 1972, they resumed terror tactics. On April 15, 1972, Bordaberry, supported by the Congress, declared an internal war against the Tupamaros with extensive police and military searches for the guerrillas taking place. By the fall of 1972 the government crackdown was widely believed to have seriously weakened the guerrilla organization. In September 1972 the Tupamaro leader Raúl Sendic, who had escaped from captivity in 1971, was recaptured.

MARVIN ALISKY

TUPÍ-GUARANÍ. Widely spread South American group of natives, all speaking dialects of the Tupían language. They lived along the lower Amazon, in eastern Brazil, and in Paraguay (where they were known as the Guaraní) and even included some peripatetic groups near the Bolivian montaña. The Chiriguanos, belonging to the latter category, were the only tribe ever successfully to invade the Inca empire. Peculiar to the Tupían peoples was a powerfully affective belief in the Land of the Grandfather, a mythical place ruled by the sky god. This utopian concept caused several of the groups to undertake long migrations in search of the promised blessings. The first unsettling contacts with white men motivated several of these semireligious peregrinations. GUARANÍ is still an important language in modern Paraguay, where it is the mother tongue of the mestizo population.

BURR C. BRUNDAGE

TUPINAMBÁ. Amerindian tribal grouping of the TUPÍ-GUARANÍ language family that inhabited the Brazilian littoral in the region of Guanabara, Cape Frio, and Bahia at the time of the arrival of the first Europeans. The Tupinambá of the Guanabara region were major enemies of the Tupiniquim to the south, and the conflict between the two groups became involved in the struggle between the French and the Portuguese for control of the region and the brazilwood trade, the former supporting the French and the latter the Portuguese. The defeat and expulsion of the French allowed the settlers of Rio de Janeiro to conduct several large-scale military campaigns against the Amerindians of the region between 1560 and 1575, and similar military pacification expeditions from Bahia forced the Tupinambá into the interior. The survivors eventually moved north into the Pará and Maranhão regions, where in the seventeenth century they were again harassed and displaced. A fierce, warlike people, they survived on subsistence hunting and fishing and the cultivation (by the women) of manioc, sweet potatoes, and beans. Contact with Europeans eventually was fatal to them, though the struggle was not always one-sided and they proved to be dangerous adversaries.

KENNETH R. MAXWELL

UBICO, JORGE (1878–1946). Dictator-President of Guatemala. Ubico was born in Guatemala City, received his early education in the United States, then entered the Escuela Politécnica in Guatemala City to prepare for a military career. He fulfilled numerous military and administrative assignments, the most important of which were tours as *jefe político* (political chief) of the departments of Alta Verapaz and Retalhuleu. As the candidate of the Liberal Progressive party (his own Progressive party joined with the Liberal party) in the election that followed the resignation of President Lázaro Chacón, he was overwhelmingly elected. He took office on February 14, 1931.

The administration of Ubico resembled that of his predecessors in the neo-Liberal line. He promoted physical improvements, particularly road and bridge building, encouraged the diversification of agricultural production, favored entrepreneurs and sacrificed labor, and deprecated intellectual endeavor. By probity, economy, and good management he restored the shattered finances of the country. He extended his term of office by extralegal "plebiscites" and maintained an oppressive military dictatorship that disregarded human rights and met dissent with increasingly brutal repression. Reputedly he admired the European fascist regimes, but in World War II he gave formal allegiance to the Allies.

Ubico's administration epitomized the stark barrenness of the successive neo-Liberal regimes. In June 1944, following a similar action in El Salvador, a general strike forced Ubico to resign. Leaving the government to his friend Gen. Federico Ponce Vaides, he went into exile in New Orleans, where he died in 1946.

WILLIAM J. GRIFFITH

UDN. *See* UNIÃO DEMOCRÁTICA NACIONAL.

UGARTE, FLORO (1884–   ). Argentine composer. Born in Buenos Aires, he studied there and in Paris. Ugarte actively participated in the creation of the National Conservatory of Music of Buenos Aires in 1924 and for a number of years was technical or artistic director of the Teatro Colón. He has written an opera, *Saika* (1959), a ballet, *El junco* (1944), many orchestral works inspired by Argentine folklore, a few chamber music compositions, songs, and solo piano music. In addition, he is the author of a treatise on harmony and acoustics and has translated Arthur Honegger's *Je suis compositeur* into Spanish.

JUAN A. ORREGO-SALAS

ULATE, OTILIO (1892–   ). President of Costa Rica (1949–1953). Ulate played a key role in the Costa Rican revolution of 1948. He was the victor in the presidential elections of 1948 over Rafael CALDERÓN GUARDIA, but the Legislative Assembly, partial to Calderón, annulled the elections. The result was a revolution led by José FIGUERES, who established a governmental junta after gaining control of the country. After eighteen months the junta turned the Presidency over to Ulate, who served as President until 1953.

Ulate owed his position to Figueres, but he was no follower of the socialist ideas of Figueres's PARTIDO LIBERACIÓN NACIONAL. A former deputy in the Legislative Assembly (1930–1938) and the publisher of the *Diario de Costa Rica,* he had a political outlook that was personalist and opportunistic rather than ideological. He was a conservative President who made little attempt to foster further social change. Consequently, the years of his administration, between the junta and the first Figueres Presidency, can be considered an era of consolidation with an emphasis on efficient public administration. An exponent of Central American union, Ulate participated fully in the discussions over a common market while President and afterward worked successfully for the establishment of a Central American Development Bank (*see* CENTRAL AMERICAN COMMON MARKET). President Figueres, as a conciliatory gesture, named Ulate Minister to Spain in 1971.

CHARLES L. STANSIFER

UNÁNUE, HIPÓLITO (1755–1833). Peruvian physician who exerted a great influence on the development of scientific interest and medical studies in Peru at the end of the eighteenth century. He received a degree in medicine in 1786 and a chair in anatomy in the University of San Marcos, Lima, in 1789. The opening of an anatomical amphitheater in the university in 1792 was due mostly to his persistent requests. His interest in introducing reforms in the teaching of medicine led him to organize, in 1794, a series of lectures on medicine and surgery given by the leading physicians of Lima. However, his suggestions for the creation of a new school of medicine were not carried through by the government because of a lack of funds, and the project had to wait more than a decade. In 1807 Unánue obtained the position of *protomédico* (royal physician) at the university, and with the support of Viceroy José Fernando Abascal he organized the new school of medicine, the College of San Fernando, which was opened in 1811 and which flourished during the ensuing decade.

Unánue is also well known for the many articles on scientific subjects that he published in the *Mercurio Peruano,* the journal of the Sociedad Económica de Lima. He wrote the essay "Observaciones sobre el clima de Lima" (1806), in which he developed the theory of the influence of climate on health. Unánue was not a true experimental scientist. His studies were not rigorous enough, and he accepted and perpetuated many erroneous concepts and practices. His main asset was his awareness of the growing importance of science in his time and his unrelenting interest in the creation of scientific consciousness in Peru.

ASUNCIÓN LAVRIN

UNIÃO DEMOCRÁTICA NACIONAL (NATIONAL DEMOCRATIC UNION; UDN). Major conservative party in post-World War II Brazil. Its program stressed the rule of law, freedom of the individual, and respect for private property common to nineteenth-century liberalism. Founded early in 1945 by men who opposed the dictatorship of Getúlio VARGAS, the UDN led the campaign for the return to democracy in Brazil. Its leaders included politicians who had been displaced by the REVOLUTION OF 1930; Eduardo GOMES and other revolutionaries of 1930 who had since broken with Vargas; and young reformers, such as the fire-brand journalist Carlos LACERDA. Its members were drawn heavily from the urban business community, the professions, and the middle-class bureaucracy, but its electoral strength rested largely on bloc votes delivered by rural political bosses.

Although the party's presidential candidates were defeated in 1945, 1950, and 1955, the UDN consistently polled the second largest vote in legislative elections at the national, state, and local levels. In 1960 the UDN nominated the political independent Jânio QUADROS for the Presidency and swept into power with his landslide victory, but it returned to its customary role in the opposition when Quadros resigned in August 1961. Two UDN governors, Carlos Lacerda of Guanabara and José de Magalhães Pinto of Minas Gerais, were active conspirators in the revolution of March 31, 1964, although Lacerda later led his wing of the party out of the revolutionary camp. Most of the UDN members in Congress entered the ALIANÇA RENOVADORA NACIONAL when the existing political parties were abolished in 1965.

ROLLIE E. POPPINO

UNIÓN CÍVICA RADICAL. *See* RADICAL PARTY (ARGENTINA).

UNIÓN CÍVICA RADICAL DEL PUEBLO. *See* RADICAL PARTY (ARGENTINA).

UNIÓN CÍVICA RADICAL INTRANSIGENTE. *See* RADICAL PARTY (ARGENTINA).

UNIÓN DE TRABAJADORES DE COLOMBIA (UNION OF COLOMBIAN WORKERS; UTC). Colombia's major labor collective bargaining association. The UTC was founded in June 1946 in response to national legislation (Law 6 of 1945) that permitted collective bargaining. Also significant in its creation was the wish of the Roman Catholic Church to construct a labor organization that might counter rising Communist influence among the Colombian working classes.

The sponsoring role of the church in the creation of the UTC, especially in the traditionally religious bastion of ANTIOQUIA, gave the UTC immediate social respectability in sharp contrast to Communist-dominated unions in Cundinamarca. It is important to note, however, that from its inception the UTC has sought to defend workers' interests, not those of a political party. Its consistently apolitical line has encouraged unity and added much to its prestige.

Initially financed by the church, the UTC eventually became self-supporting by levying modest dues on its membership. Although its financial resources are not such as to support affiliated workers in a long strike, the UTC can and has underwritten some work stoppages on a partial basis. As of 1963, 902 labor unions belonged to the UTC, including the bulk of Colombian ORGANIZED LABOR in the industrial and transport sectors. The UTC has generally negotiated successfully with industry and only in the more extreme cases has resorted to its final weapon, the strike.

J. LEÓN HELGUERA

UNITARIO. Member of one of the two unstable political factions (the other was the Federalist) that struggled for control of the political and economic destinies of Argentina after 1810. The ideological differences between the Unitarios (Unitarians) and the Federalists were rather insignificant until 1822 or 1823, and individuals moved freely from one to the other group. The existence of the two camps has been used in a variety of ways to explain Argentine history for most of the nineteenth century. The struggle between the Unitarians and Federalists may be viewed as one between civilization and barbarism, between the landed and cattle interests and the proletariat, and between a rich, urban minority seeking its inspiration in Europe and the Argentine masses led by their popular *caudillos*. Keenly aware of the historic antipathy between *porteños* (*see* PORTEÑO), natives of the city of Buenos Aires, and *provincianos,* those living elsewhere in Argentina, some equate Unitarians with *porteños* and Federalists with *provincianos*. The former, it is said, wished to monopolize the customs revenues of the port city, while the latter wanted the income distributed among them. The difficulty with this explanation is that it is possible to identify three distinct Federalist factions, one in the city of Buenos Aires, another in the upriver provinces, and still another in the interior provinces, and that a Unitarian element existed in all the provinces. A more recent interpretation attributes to the Unitarians an interest in national unity and the economic modernization of Argentina and condemns the Federalists for their alleged localism and backwardness. In this context the first Unitarians were Bernardino RIVADAVIA and the small group around him who strongly favored foreign capitalists and enterprises and who were willing to employ force, local or foreign, to achieve their goals. Their insistence on free trade probably was the only position that clearly set them apart from the Federalists, but even here, as on other Rivadavian proposals, they could anticipate support from many Federalists.   JOSEPH T. CRISCENTI

UNITED FRUIT COMPANY. Company created in 1899, when the Boston Fruit Company, incorporated by Capt. Alonzo D. Baker, Andrew W. Preston, and others, merged with Minor Cooper KEITH's varied Central American enterprises. The Boston company imported bananas from Jamaica for regional distribution by its subsidiary, the Fruit Dispatch Company. Keith grew bananas in Costa Rica and adjacent countries and shipped them to Southern ports. The merger combined such extensive growing, shipping, and distribution resources that United could anticipate supplying a national market in the United States from plantations sufficiently dispersed to assure continuous production despite local calamities.

The United Fruit Company was the strongest competitor in a high-risk industry. It increased its holdings in Jamaica, Costa Rica, Nicaragua, and Colombia and bought land in the Dominican Republic, Cuba, Panama, Honduras, and Guatemala. Size, efficiency, and a certain ruthlessness enabled it to squeeze out, buy, or merge with a number of rival concerns. In 1929 it effected an important merger with Samuel Zemurray's Cuyamel Fruit Company.

The locale of its operations forced United Fruit to become a land developer and colonizer. The Caribbean lowlands in Central America were a wilderness until United cleared forests, drained swamps, and often built soil by trapping silt from floodwater. The inability of local governments to extend services into those mortiferous zones required the company to undertake extensive sanitation projects and to provide all facilities to maintain health, comfort, and morale for whole communities of imported residents.

United initiated several auxiliary enterprises that were intended primarily for its own use but also had a quasi-public character. It built private rail lines to service all its plantations, and at various times it also built, controlled, or operated railroads serving the public in Colombia, Panama, Costa Rica, Honduras, Guatemala, and El Salvador. It also operated a fleet of vessels that carried freight and cruise passengers who made tourism a significant tropical industry. A charter ship rigged for refrigeration in 1903 inaugurated the age of refrigerated cargo and presaged the sleek, swift craft later built for the Great White Fleet. To coordinate its widely separated operations, United in 1910 inaugurated radio communication between the United States and Central America that in 1913 became its subsidiary Tropical Radio and Telegraph Company.

United managed to neutralize many hazards that bedeviled the early banana business, but it fell victim to plant diseases. The Gros Michel, the major commercial variety, proved fatally susceptible to Panama disease and sigatoka, which devastated plantations around the Caribbean. In some areas production declined almost to extinction. In Panama, Costa Rica, and Guatemala, however, United developed new centers of production in Pacific lowlands during the 1930s. The discovery that sigatoka could be controlled, that land could be reclaimed from Panama disease, and that disease-resistant varieties were commercially acceptable allowed the reoccupation of abandoned Caribbean plantations. A production shift to strategic materials such as sisal during World War II and a subsequent program of diversification aided this process.

The United Fruit Company has attracted a barrage of adverse criticism. Small among United States corporations operating abroad, it appears huge in its production areas, where it has often been called "the Octopus." It is criticized for having acquired without cost or at ridiculously low initial prices vast acreages of now-valuable plantations, for holding immense reserves of undeveloped land, for labor policies alleged to discriminate against nationals, for repeated interference in the internal affairs of host countries, and for removing wealth wrung from local resources without adequate return to the host country. It is also charged with having imported an alien population of English-speaking Caribbean blacks and of later abandoning them without means of livelihood when banana production shifted from Caribbean to Pacific lowlands. Finally, it has been accused of monopolistic control internally of banana production and such auxiliary services as railroads, port facilities, and international communications, and externally of ocean transport and the importation and distribution of bananas in the United States, if not the world.

Some, perhaps all, of these charges have had validity at some point in the history of the banana industry. Some recall situations that no longer pertain, some legitimately admit of divergent points of view, and others are perhaps not unfair current criticisms. The company's most insistent critics ignore such accomplishments as the restoration of the ruins of Zaculeu in Guatemala and the maintenance of the Pan American School of Agriculture in Zamorano, Honduras. Whether because of more equitable national contracts, a stockholders' suit and resultant court order, the pressure of public opinion, or its own free choice, the United Fruit Company abandoned many of the activities against which criticisms were directed.

In 1969, after a long and dramatic campaign, the AMK Corporation, a meat-packing and machinery-making conglomerate, acquired control of the United Fruit Company. In July 1970 the two companies merged as the United Brands Company.

See also BANANA INDUSTRY (CENTRAL AMERICA AND THE CARIBBEAN).

Bibliography. Charles D. Kepner, *Social Aspects of the Banana Industry,* New York, 1936; Charles D. Kepner and Jay H. Soothill, *The Banana Empire: A Case Study of Economic Imperialism,* New York, 1935; Stacy May and Galo Plaza, *The United Fruit Company in Latin America,* New York, 1958; Watt Stewart, *Keith and Costa Rica: A Biographical Study of Minor Cooper Keith,* Albuquerque, N.Mex., 1964; Charles Morrow Wilson, *Ambassadors in White: The Story of American Tropical Medicine,* New York, 1942; id., *Middle America,* New York, 1944; id., *Empire in Green and Gold: The Story of the American Banana Trade,* New York, 1947.

WILLIAM J. GRIFFITH

UNITED OFFICERS GROUP. *See* GRUPO DE OFICIALES UNIDOS.

UNITED STATES RELATIONS WITH LATIN AMERICA. *See* ALLIANCE FOR PROGRESS; CLARK MEMORANDUM; DOLLAR DIPLOMACY; GOOD NEIGHBOR POLICY; HICKENLOOPER AMENDMENT; MONROE DOCTRINE; PANAMA CANAL; ROOSEVELT COROLLARY.

URBINA, JOSÉ MARÍA (1808–1891). President of Ecuador (1852–1856). Born in Ambato, Urbina entered the Guayaquil Naval Academy at the age of fourteen but later joined the Army. When, in March 1845, the *guayaquileños* formed their own government and raised troops to defeat the dictator Juan José FLORES, Colonel Urbina ordered his garrison in Manabí to join the revolution. The March rebels won, but their liberal constitution was not entirely to the liking of Urbina, and when the new government launched a campaign against military privileges, Urbina convinced *guayaquileños* that they had a sacred obligation to form a second government. In February 1851, a popular assembly at Guayaquil named him chief of the armed forces and their native son, Diego Noboa, President. By July Urbina had Noboa on a ship bound for Chile and assumed a dictatorship. He thwarted an invasion by Flores, won over influential Ecuadorians, and convoked Ecuador's sixth constitutional convention, which elected him President.

Powerful enough to enforce liberal ideas, Urbina freed the slaves and raised taxes to reimburse their owners. He espoused relief for the sierra Indians (*see* SIERRA: ECUADOR), the real Ecuadorian work force, but Congress refused to discuss the matter. His expulsion of the Jesuits aroused the opposition and contributed to the downfall of his chosen successor, Gen. Francisco Robles. Urbina failed in several revolutionary attempts against Gabriel GARCÍA MORENO, and lived in exile until 1875. He helped install Gen. Ignacio VEINTEMILLA in 1876 and then resided in Guayaquil until he died at the age of eighty-three.

His son, Francisco Urbina Jado, became manager of the Banco Comercial y Agrícola and the key figure in Ecuador's political and economic life in the early twentieth century.

LOIS WEINMAN

URIBE HOLGUÍN, GUILLERMO (1880–1972). Colombian composer and conductor. Uribe Holguín was born in Bogotá. After initial studies there he enrolled in the Schola Cantorum in Paris, where he worked with Vincent d'Indy and others. In addition to composing, he conducted and taught, and he toured the United States, France, Spain, Germany, Austria, and Switzerland. He was also the author of a treatise on harmony (1936). His list of compositions is extensive, comprising eleven symphonies, seven concerti for solo instruments and orchestra, a large amount of chamber music, including ten string quartets, more than thirty solo piano works, and numerous songs. His style reflects the concern with music nationalism characteristic of his generation.

JUAN A. ORREGO-SALAS

URIBURU, JOSÉ FÉLIX (1868–1932). Argentine army officer and provisional President (September 1930–February 1932). On September 6, 1930, General Uriburu led a column of cadets from the Colegio Militar to the Casa Rosada and deposed the aged Radical President, Hipólito YRIGOYEN (*see* RADICAL PARTY: ARGENTINA). With a proclamation of martial law he ended almost seventy years of liberal government.

Although Uriburu had participated in the unsuccessful revolt of 1890 and had briefly toyed with radicalism, his instincts were with the aristocratic, conservative sector in which he had been raised. However, he possessed few intellectual capabilities beyond those of the professional soldier and was ignorant of the social, economic, and cultural aspects of the Argentines he presumed to govern. Equally ignorant of political theory, he developed a fascination with fascism, in the belief that it was an aristocratic movement that would solve all problems by eliminating politics. His ideas proved inapplicable, and his efforts merely alienated his fellow conservatives.

When Uriburu, confident that the deposed Radicals were impotent, called provincial elections in Buenos Aires in April 1931, the Radicals were victorious. Their success indicated an unmistakable rejection of his administration, which by then had become a harshly militaristic variation of the old pre-Radical conservative regimes. The ailing Uriburu was forced to abandon his plans for constitutional reform before holding a presidential election. In February 1932 he was succeeded by the victor in the November 1931 elections, Gen. Agustín P. JUSTO.

EUGENE G. SHARKEY

URQUIZA, JUSTO JOSÉ DE (1801–1870). Argentine statesman often regarded as the organizer of the Argentine nation. Urquiza was born in Concepción del Uruguay, Entre Ríos, the son of a country merchant and officer in the local militia. He attended the Colegio de San Carlos of Buenos Aires for two years and returned home to open a small business. By midcentury he had become the wealthiest landowner and rancher in Entre Ríos. After 1852 he invested his surplus capital in banks, agricultural colonies, salt meat–packing plants, ships, and a wide variety of other enterprises.

Between 1810 and 1850 Entre Ríos was a no-man's-land over which the enemies and allies of Buenos Aires as well as the other riverine provinces fought for control. When Urquiza became Governor in 1841, his aim was to restore the peace, order, and security of the province, and within a few years he succeeded. He directed provincial affairs until 1870, for his progressive administration was widely endorsed. What eventually undermined his popularity was his conduct in national affairs. Carrying out the promises he made on May 1, 1851, he defeated the dictator Juan Manuel de ROSAS at Caseros (1852) with the aid of Brazil and the Montevideo government and then organized the ARGENTINE CONFEDERATION. He also concluded an international treaty guaranteeing freedom of navigation on the Paraná River (see PARANÁ-PARAGUAY RIVER BASIN). As President (1854–1860), he tried unsuccessfully to bring the province of Buenos Aires into the Confederation, to solve the financial problems of the central government, and to foster the economic development of the interior provinces.

His influence was already declining when he failed to defeat Buenos Aires decisively at Cepeda (1859), fled from the battlefield of Pavón (1861), and abandoned the Federalist party. During the PARAGUAYAN WAR he was unable to contribute troops to the national forces because of political and economic discontent in Entre Ríos, but he did mobilize sufficient support to assure the election of Domingo Faustino SARMIENTO to the Presidency in 1868. On April 11, 1870, he and two of his sons were assassinated by the partisans of Ricardo López Jordán, who succeeded Urquiza as Governor of Entre Ríos.   JOSEPH T. CRISCENTI

URUGUAY RIVER. The Uruguay River forms the western border of Uruguay and is the source of the nation's name. During colonial times the area was known as the Banda Oriental (Eastern Shore); after independence it adopted the name República Oriental del Uruguay (Republic East of the Uruguay).

The river, which flows 1,000 miles from southern Brazil to the RÍO DE LA PLATA, was an important transportation route during the colonial and early national periods. Population centers and economic activity developed early along both sides of the river; Uruguay's largest cities after Montevideo—Paysandú and Salto—are river ports. Although rail and truck transportation have replaced much of the traffic on the Uruguay, the river is still an economic artery. It is navigable by oceangoing vessels as far north as Paysandú, and except for an area of rapids at Salto it can be managed by smaller commercial craft for several hundred miles beyond.

The lower 50 miles or more of the Uruguay, from the delta of the Paraná River (see PARANÁ-PARAGUAY RIVER BASIN) north to Fray Bentos, resembles a fluvial lake with a width of up to 8 miles. The stretch of some 70 miles between Fray Bentos and Paysandú is dotted with scores of islands of varying size; north of Paysandú, the river becomes considerably narrower. Uruguay's major internal river, the Negro, empties into the Uruguay River south of Fray Bentos.

LEE C. FENNELL

URUGUAY SINCE 1825. With the news headlines made by Tupamaro guerrillas in the late 1960s and early 1970s (see TUPAMAROS), Uruguay's image abroad incorrectly emphasized political confrontation. In fact, for most of this century Uruguayan political life has emphasized the peaceful resolution of major problems, the coexistence of two large political parties, and an open society in which civil liberties and welfare benefits have been the norm.

In 1825 thirty-three Uruguayan patriots, led by Juan Antonio LAVALLEJA, crossed the RÍO DE LA PLATA from Argentina at night to rally their countrymen against a Brazilian army of occupation. In 1828, after several years of fighting between the Uruguayans, their Argentine allies, and Brazil, British mediation brought about the recognition of Uruguayan independence. Thus Uruguay had firm support into nationhood, the guarantee of its territorial integrity by its larger neighbors. Under its first constitution (see CONSTITUTION OF 1830: URUGUAY), which remained in force until 1918, twenty-five governments administered the republic, rival leaders being able to redivide the spoils of public office and to reform public institutions without resorting to the writing of new constitutions, a practice in many other Latin American nations.

Uruguay's two major political parties (see BLANCO PARTY: URUGUAY; COLORADO PARTY: URUGUAY) were formed during a revolt (1836–1838) led by Fructuoso RIVERA, the nation's first President (1830–1835), against his successor, Manuel ORIBE, who became the founder of the Blancos. Oribe was forced to resign in 1838 and moved to Buenos Aires. Angered by Argentine support of the Blancos, Rivera declared war on the Argentine dictator Juan Manuel de ROSAS in 1839. Thus began the long conflict known as the Guerra Grande (Great War), during which Montevideo was besieged for nine years. The war became more than a struggle between Uruguayan Colorados and Blancos and their

URUGUAY

Area: 72,172 sq. mi.   Population: 2,921,000 (1971 est.).

respective Argentine allies, for the political and military contest developed into an economic contest between the capital city and the countryside. In 1851 a revolt in Argentina forced the withdrawal of Argentine troops, and the Blanco chief Oribe signed a treaty of peace on October 8, 1851.

From 1865 to 1870 the Colorado government of Uruguay, which had recently been installed with Brazilian aid, was allied with Brazil and Argentina in the PARAGUAYAN WAR against Paraguay. While the war was in progress, the Blancos tried unsuccessfully to oust the Colorados, but in 1872 both parties came to terms, and an era of measured progress began. A wave of immigration, especially of Italians, brought a new variety to society (see IMMIGRATION: URUGUAY).

In September 1904, at the Battle of Masoller, Colorado troops defeated the Blancos led by Aparicio SARAVIA, and the two major political forces have since coexisted peacefully in the government and in other areas of public life. Between 1830 and 1903, out of twenty-five governments, nine were overthrown and two were ended by assassination. By contrast, for forty years after 1903 only one coup, a bloodless and brief episode in 1933, occurred to disturb an otherwise-uninterrupted constitutional system. In 1973, however, President Juan María BORDABERRY, acting under military pressure, dissolved Congress and imposed a virtual military dictatorship.

The maker of modern Uruguay, José BATLLE Y ORDÓÑEZ, served as President from 1903 to 1907 and again from 1911 to 1915, helping to create public corporations to ensure Uruguay's economic independence from foreign investors and instituting programs that made the republic Latin America's first welfare state. Batlle died in 1929, but his influence remained strong, his dream of a plural Presidency (see COLEGIADO) forming the basis for a majority faction of the Colorado party. At Batlle's insistence the constitution of 1918 created a National Council of Administration, a nine-member head of the executive branch of government modeled after that of Switzerland but with the difference that a President was added, giving the government a two-headed structure. In 1933, driven by the economic depression, President Gabriel TERRA, who had been frustrated by the inaction of the National Council of Administration, removed it from power. The constitution of 1934 restored the single Presidency.

During Batlle's second term laws were enacted to create the State Insurance Bank, the State Mortgage Bank, and the State Electric Facilities Corporation. Uruguay thereby undertook governmental responsibility for low-cost fire insurance, social security retirement benefits, housing loans, and low-cost utility service. In 1915 the government established the Administración General de las Usinas Eléctricas y los Teléfonos del Estado (UTE) to provide low telephone rates.

The pattern of state intervention in the economy set by Batlle continued after his death. The government took over the national airline, PLUNA, in 1944 and the railroads in 1949. In 1947 the Congress created the Administración Nacional de Transportes (AMDET) as a major transportation corporation for greater Montevideo, where half the nation's population resides. The largest importer in Uruguay is the government corporation Administración Nacional de Combustibles, Alcohol y Portland (ANCAP). ANCAP has a monopoly on importing and refining crude oil but competes at the retail level with Shell, Exxon, and Texaco service stations. In addition, numerous boards and commissions regulate rents, control prices, and oversee tourist facilities.

With the public corporations added to the executive, legislative, and judicial branches of government, nearly one-third of the Uruguayan work force is employed by the state. Government employees belong to civil servant unions grouped into the Confederación de Organizaciones de Funcionarios del Estado and the Mesa Sindical Coordinadora, a trade union round table that speaks for employees of autonomous entities and decentralized services, such as the railroads and the telephone company. The largest labor federation is the Communist-oriented CONVENCIÓN NACIONAL DE TRABAJADORES.

The livestock industry is the most important sector of the Uruguayan economy, with wool accounting for 53 percent of total exports and beef for as much as 30 percent (see LIVESTOCK INDUSTRY: URUGUAY). In 1928 the government established the Frigorífico Nacional (Frigonal), which became the republic's largest meat-packing corporation. In 1958 a cooperative of employees bought out the Swift and Armour facilities, which became the Cerro Corporation. Ten years later the Anglo meat-packing plant at Fray Bentos became a cooperative. Dairy herds are often raised alongside beef cattle and sheep. In 1935 the government helped the National Council of Dairy Farmers to form a cooperative to buy out private commercial dairies. Called the Cooperativa Nacional de Productores de Leche (CONAPROLE), it still processes milk products and distributes them to retailers.

In 1951 voters approved a new constitution that replaced the office of President with a plural Presidency, the National Council of Government. It remained in force until the election of November 1966, when Uruguayans voted to adopt another constitution restoring the office of chief executive in place of the Council.

From 1952 to 1958 strikes for higher wages stimulated inflation, while the government continued to spend funds on welfare benefits that were beyond the means of the gross national product. In the elections of 1958 the political reversal of the century occurred. After ninety-three years of Colorado rule, the Blancos took control not only of both chambers of Congress but also of the six-member majority in the National Council of Government. With decisions delayed by debates, the Council fostered inefficiency in the operation of the telephone and electric services, railroads, airline, the petroleum and cement industries, the postal service, and other governmental entities. The Blancos again emerged as the majority party in the 1962 elections and continued to lead the National Council of Government and the Congress until 1967.

In November 1966 voters participated in a plebiscite to adopt or reject a new constitution whose principal change was the substitution of a President and a Vice President for the National Council of Government and a municipal *intendente* in each departmental capital for the departmental plural executive. The new constitution was adopted and the office of chief executive restored, 52 percent of the voters approving the change. The constitution set all elected terms of office at five years, instead of the traditional four.

In the 1966 election the Colorados and Blancos received 91 percent of the popular vote, but in November 1971 they received 82 percent. Between 1967 and 1971 the Frente Izquierdista de Libertad (Leftist Front of Liberty; FIDEL) had grown by absorbing the defunct Socialist party and the Communist party. In the 1971 campaign it drew the Christian Democratic party into an alliance called the Frente Amplio (Broad Front).

Of the ninety-nine members of the Chamber of Deputies, fifty were Colorados for the 1967–1972 term, forty-one were Blancos, five were members of FIDEL or Communists, and there were three Christian Democrats. For the 1972–1977 term the voters chose forty-one Colorados, forty Blancos, and eighteen Frente Amplio (FIDEL and Christian Democratic) deputies. There are thirty-one votes in the Senate, including that of the Vice President of the republic. For the 1967–1972 term the upper chamber had sixteen Colorados, thirteen Blancos, and one FIDEL member; for the 1972–1977 term, thirteen Colorados, twelve Blancos, and five Frente Amplio members (FIDEL and Christian Democrats).

When Oscar D. GESTIDO, a retired air force general who had been a civilian administrator for twelve years, was inaugurated as President on March 1, 1967, he faced the economic pressure of inflation and the task of unifying factions of his own majority Colorado party. He took action against smuggling from Brazil and induced the Congress to pass a law allowing citizens owing taxes to pay up promptly and be forgiven penalties as delinquents. The response in payments was strong. However, strikes and wage-price rises increased the cost of living for 1967 by 136 percent. Upon Gestido's death in December 1967, Vice President Jorge PACHECO ARECO became President and finished the five-year term with an outstanding record in reducing inflation from the high 1967 level to 14 percent for 1969. Nevertheless, since such a large proportion of the work force was employed either by the national or local governments or by government utilities and other public corporations and since about 250,000 Uruguayans were drawing social security pensions in a nation of only 2.7 million, Pacheco could not significantly reduce government payrolls or the budgetary deficit. He did attack inflation in June 1968 by establishing price and wage ceilings. As attacks of the Marxist urban guerrillas, the Tupamaros, increased after 1968, President Pacheco abridged Uruguay's long-standing press freedom by a decree (1970) preventing the Tupamaros from being described as social crusaders and requiring their identification as criminals wanted for murders, bank robberies, and kidnappings.

As strikes, inflationary pressures, and Tupamaro violence disturbed the tranquillity of traditionally democratic Uruguay, the campaign for the November 1971 elections found factions within the Colorado and Blanco parties in disagreement over public policies and the Frente Amplio making political inroads through a coalition of Communists, Socialists, and Christian Democrats. The Colorados failed to win a majority in either chamber of Congress, setting the stage for five years of parliamentary infighting. Under the electoral law each faction or *sublema* of the major parties can nominate its own presidential candidate, although the parties must combine their votes for purposes of computing proportional representation in Congress, the faction candidate with the highest popular vote being elected President (*see* LEMA SYSTEM). The Colorados received 681,624 votes, the Blancos 668,822, and the Frente Amplio 304,275. On March 1, 1972, Bordaberry, a leader of the moderate faction of the Colorado party, was inaugurated as President for the 1972–1977 term. Although he was evidently successful in subduing the Tupamaros, within a year of his inauguration his administration had fallen under the domination of the armed forces.

Bibliography. Marvin Alisky, *Uruguay: A Contemporary Survey,* New York, 1969; Russell H. Brannon, *The Agricultural Development of Uruguay,* New York, 1968; Russell H. Fitzgibbon, *Uruguay: Portrait of a Democracy,* New Brunswick, N.J., 1954; Simon G. Hanson, *Utopia in Uruguay: Chapters in the Economic History of Uruguay,* New York, 1938; Julio Martínez Lamas, *Riqueza y pobreza del Uruguay: Estudio de las causas que retardan el progreso nacional,* 2d ed., Montevideo, 1946; Juan E. Pivel Devoto and Alcira Ranieri de Pivel Devoto, *Historia de la República Oriental del Uruguay 1830–1930,* Montevideo, 1945; Philip B. Taylor, Jr., *Government and Politics in Uruguay,* New Orleans, 1960; Milton I. Vanger, *José Batlle y Ordóñez of Uruguay: The Creator of His Times,* Cambridge, Mass., 1963.

MARVIN ALISKY

USIGLI, RODOLFO (1905–   ). Mexican dramatist. Usigli is one of the most professional and widely translated of Mexico's dramatists. His many plays, which range from comedies and social and political satires to psychological and historical dramas, all show his technical expertise and intellectual curiosity. Among the best known are *El niño y la niebla* (written 1936), which involves some episodes of Mexico's recent history; *El gesticulador* (written 1937), an existential play with overtones of national criticism; and *Corona de sombra,* written 1943 (*Crown of Shadows*), an interesting reconstruction of the reign of MAXIMILIAN and Carlota. Usigli has been for some years Mexican Ambassador to Norway.

RACHEL PHILLIPS

USLAR PIETRI, ARTURO (1905–   ). Venezuelan novelist. A doctor of political science and doctor *honoris causa* in law, he has lived in Europe, traveled in the East, and held important political posts. His first publication, *Barrabás y otros relatos* (1928), was followed by one of the most famous Latin American novels, *Las lanzas coloradas,* 1931 (*The Red Lances*), which evokes the fight for independence. Uslar Pietri published some volumes of essays, including *De una a otra Venezuela* (1950), *Las nubes* (1952), and *Breve historia de la novela hispanoamericana* (1954); and a historical novel, *El camino de El Dorado* (1947). Later novels, such as *Un retrato en la geografía* (1962) and *Estación de máscaras* (1964), are often set in contemporary Venezuela. Volumes of short stories include *Treinta hombres y sus sombras* (1949) and *Pasos y pasajeros* (1967).   RACHEL PHILLIPS

UTC. *See* UNIÓN DE TRABAJADORES DE COLOMBIA.

Valdivia, Pedro de

Voodoo

VALDIVIA, PEDRO DE (1500?–1553). Conquistador from Estremadura, Spain, who led the conquest of Chile. After serving in the Spanish Army in Flanders and Italy, Valdivia went to America about 1535 and spent a year in Venezuela before moving on to Peru. He supported Francisco and Gonzalo PIZARRO against the followers of Diego de ALMAGRO (1537–1538) and thus obtained a commission to continue Almagro's abandoned Chilean conquest. Valdivia marched to the Central Valley of Chile and in 1541 founded Santiago. The next year he suppressed an *almagrista* rebellion among the Spanish residents of Santiago. The city endured starvation while successfully defending itself from an Indian siege in Valdivia's absence. After reinforcements arrived in 1543, Valdivia expedited the conquest and in 1545 began to recount the fortunes of his colony in the first of five letters sent to Emperor Charles V (King CHARLES I). When Gonzalo Pizarro rebelled in Peru, Valdivia sailed north to join Pedro de la Gasca's army and made signal contributions to Pizarro's defeat in 1548.

After obtaining confirmation of his governorship, Valdivia returned to Chile, where he put down a widespread Indian rebellion, sent explorers east of the ANDES MOUNTAINS, and pushed farther south, founding Concepción (1550) and Valdivia (1552). He met final defeat at the hands of the Araucanian Indians (*see* ARAUCANIANS), who captured and killed him, setting a bold precedent for their centuries of resistance to Spanish rule.

See also LAUTARO.

WILLIAM S. DUDLEY

VALENCIA, ANTONIO M[ARÍA] (1902–1952). Colombian composer and pianist. Born in Cali, he studied in Bogotá and at the Schola Cantorum in Paris. He founded the Conservatory of Cali in 1933 and served as director of the National Conservatory of Bogotá. Valencia's music shows a deep attachment to Colombian vernacular expressions. Outstanding in this respect are his *Emociones caucanas* (1938) for piano, violin, and cello, his orchestral work *Chirimía y Bambuco* (1942), and most of his piano music. He also produced sacred music, including a Requiem Mass (1943).

JUAN A. ORREGO-SALAS

VALENCIA, GUILLERMO LEÓN (1909–1971). President of Colombia (1962–1966). Born in Popayán, Valencia was the son of Guillermo Valencia (1873–1943), one of Colombia's famous poets as well as a Conservative political leader (*see* CONSERVATIVE PARTY: COLOMBIA). The younger Valencia was a lawyer, receiving his professional education at the University of the Cauca. His early government service was as a state legislator in Cauca and Cundinamarca and as a municipal councillor in Popayán. From 1939 to 1949 he was a member of the national Senate. When Congress was closed, he was sent abroad as Ambassador to Spain during 1952–1953.

Valencia was vocal in his opposition to the dictator Gustavo ROJAS PINILLA and gave his support to the organization of the NATIONAL FRONT coalition in 1957. As a Conservative more moderate than in his youth, he became the coalition's second President in 1962, receiving a majority of the vote. However, there was significant opposition to the National Front at the polls, in the candidacies of Jorge Leyva, Alfonso López Michelsen, and Rojas Pinilla. Moreover, about one-half of the eligible voters did not cast ballots.

Valencia's term in office was characterized both by various crises and by his unsatisfactory leadership. There was guerrilla activity in the countryside, and student riots erupted in the cities. Existing economic problems were compounded by a decline in the price of coffee. Valencia finished his four years as President without congressional support, ruling by decree. He was succeeded by the better-prepared Carlos LLERAS RESTREPO, who appointed Valencia Ambassador to Spain.

GERALD THEISEN

VALLE, JOSÉ CECILIO DEL (1776–1834). Central American savant and statesman. Valle was born into an aristocratic creole family in Choluteca, Honduras, on November 22, 1776. When he was thirteen, he and his family left the provincial ranching town for Guatemala City, and in 1790 he enrolled in the University of San Carlos. Under the tutelage of instructors influenced by the Enlightenment (*see* ENLIGHTENMENT: SPANISH AMERICA), the young scholar commenced a lifelong quest for practical knowledge sustained by rigorous self-discipline and burning ambition.

His education completed, Valle chose politics to exercise his ample talents. Until 1820 he diligently served the Spanish captains general in Guatemala City, with an eye toward securing a high administrative post in the mother country. His aptitude and industriousness ensured his rapid advancement in local politics.

As the Spanish colonial system deteriorated, Valle, acknowledged the most prominent savant in Central America and an authority in political economy, emerged as a leader of the moderate conservatives. In 1820 he was elected mayor of Guatemala City, where he served with distinction. When independence could no longer be averted, Valle placed himself at the head of the movement to blunt the chance that emancipation would become social revolution. From his position on the provisional junta that assumed control of Central American government on September 15, 1821, he guided the annexation movement that made Central America part of Agustín de ITURBIDE'S Mexican empire. Sent to Mexico City to represent the province of Tegucigalpa in 1822, Valle soon became Vice President of the Congress. Mistakenly imprisoned by Iturbide on charges of conspiracy against the empire, he was later released and made Secretary of Foreign and Domestic Affairs.

Upon the fall of the Mexican empire, Valle returned to Guatemala City and was made a member of the provisional triumvirate that governed Central America until elections could be held. When elections were held to choose the first President of the Federation of Central America in 1824–1825 (*see* CENTRAL AMERICA, FEDERATION OF), Valle won a plurality of the electoral votes, but his opponents in Congress denied him the Presidency on a technicality. Almost a decade later Valle won the election again but died before the ballots could be counted. KENNETH V. FINNEY

VALLEJO, CÉSAR (1892–1938). Peruvian poet. Born in Santiago de Chuco, he studied in the Universities of Trujillo and San Marcos and spent some years teaching in elementary schools. His first volume, *Los heraldos negros* (1918), shows the influence of the modernist movement (*see* MODERNISM: SPANISH AMERICA), together with the existential anguish that marks all his work. In 1920 he was unjustly arrested and imprisoned for being the "intellectual instigator" of a minor riot. In 1922 he won a national short-story prize with "Más alla de la vida y de la muerte," which reappeared in 1923 in *Escalas melografiadas*. His second book of poetry, *Trilce* (1922), reflects a new departure, with dislocated syntax, interior monologue, and hermetic symbolism that heighten the feeling of solitude and isolation of the human condition. In his last collection, *Poemas humanos* (1939), he returned, with a greater desire for communication, to the same themes of compassion and distress.

Vallejo spent many years in Madrid and Paris, earning his living as a journalist. During this period his loyalty to communism produced a journey to the U.S.S.R. and a socialist novel, *El tungsteno* (1931). He was devoted to the Spanish Republican cause and was broken by its impending defeat. He died in Paris. His *Poesías completas* appeared in 1949, but his French widow, Georgette, continues to obstruct critical consideration of his other works and loose notes.

RACHEL PHILLIPS

VALPARAÍSO. Principal port and second city of Chile. Built on the shoreline and hills surrounding its spacious bay, Valparaíso has long enjoyed a deserved reputation for character and picturesqueness. It is also a thriving industrial center and, with its adjacent seaside resort of Viña del Mar, a notable tourist attraction. The site of the modern city was first reconnoitered in 1536 by the Spaniard Juan de Saavedra, during Diego de ALMAGRO's unsuccessful expedition to Chile. The port's early development was slow in the extreme. For most of the colonial period it remained a very modest settlement, although this did not secure it immunity from the attentions of foreign marauders. Francis DRAKE sacked the township in 1578. Sir Richard Hawkins appeared in the bay in 1593, as did a Dutch expedition seven years later. On the eve of the wars of independence Valparaíso was still a very small community, with a population of about 5,000.

The opening of Chile to international trade following the attainment of independence brought a sudden burst of prosperity to Valparaíso. The bay now became crowded with shipping, and the population expanded dramatically, taking on a markedly cosmopolitan character. The oldest daily newspaper in the Spanish-speaking world, *El Mercurio*, was founded in Valparaíso in 1827, largely to cater to the growing commercial community. The port's leading position on the west coast of South America was systematically fostered and enhanced by Diego PORTALES. Its commercial district, with its numerous foreign business houses, took on a faintly English atmosphere. During the remainder of the nineteenth century the city prospered.

Practically defenseless in military terms, Valparaíso was bombarded for three hours by a Spanish naval squadron on March 31, 1866, during the brief war between Chile and Spain. Only two citizens lost their lives (the population simply retired to the surrounding hillsides), but the damage to property was considerable. Further destruction was caused by looting at the end of the civil war of 1891. These man-induced catastrophes were followed, on August 16, 1906, by the devastation of a large part of the city by a severe earthquake.

During the twentieth century Valparaíso has developed as one of the leading centers of industry in Chile and has long since eclipsed Concepción as the second city of the country. Its population at the end of the 1960s exceeded 250,000.   SIMON COLLIER

VANDOR, AUGUSTO (1920–1969). Neo-Peronist Metalworkers Union leader in Argentina. Representative of a group of leaders who achieved prominence after the fall of Juan D. PERÓN, Vandor, although a Peronist (*see* PERONISM), was loyal primarily to labor.

After the normalization of the CONFEDERACIÓN GENERAL DE TRABAJO in 1961, a split developed within the Peronist "sixty-two" unions over the degree of labor politicization. Vandor, seeking to avoid another CGT intervention, held that emphasis must be placed on concrete economic issues. In 1964 his forces defeated the more "political" sector in the election of the CGT secretary-general.

By 1966 Vandor was under increasing attack for his relative lack of ideology, his "empiricism," and his lack of theoretical planning. Thus, part of his 1964 force was led out of the CGT by José Alonso to form the "sixty-two *de pie*" ("On your feet for Perón"). More than a labor question was involved, for many Peronist politicians backed the Alonso "orthodox" movement in a desire to acquire a mass base for themselves and weaken a leader who showed strength in semi-independence of Perón. Other attempts to use Alonso came from groups as diverse as the Peronist revolutionary left and the Radical party (*see* RADICAL PARTY: ARGENTINA).

The Vandor-led "sixty-two" suffered another incision in 1968, when Raimundo Ongaro established the oppositionist "CGT Paseo Colón." Vandor's assassination in June 1969 was a severe blow to forces seeking labor's integration.   NOREEN F. STACK

VARAS, ANTONIO (1817–1886). Chilean politician. Closely associated throughout his career with Manuel MONTT, Varas served as Minister of the Interior from 1850 to 1856, in 1860–1861, and, briefly, in 1879 at the start of the WAR OF THE PACIFIC. Toward the end of the Montt administration, the ruling National (or *monttvarista*) party looked on Varas as the automatic candidate for the succession, although the close identity of his views with those of Montt made him entirely unacceptable to the opposition. In January 1861, Varas withdrew his candidacy as a way of preventing further civil strife, thus allowing the less controversial figure of José Joaquín PÉREZ to emerge as the government candidate.   SIMON COLLIER

VARELA [Y MORALES], FÉLIX FRANCISCO JOSÉ MARÍA DE LA CONCEPCIÓN (1788–1853). Cuban philosopher, man of letters, and abolitionist. Varela has been called "the man who taught Cubans how to think." A priest at the age of twenty-three, he became that year (1811) the first professor of philosophy in Havana. He shocked the city by eschewing the use of Latin in his lectures (the first of many educational reforms he would introduce), embarrassed the church by advocat-

ing sorely needed reforms within it, and stressed to his students concepts, derived from the Scriptures, of justice, equality, and freedom, urging them to seek these principles for Cuba by thinking in political terms and applying themselves to social problems.

As a Cuban representative in the liberal Cortes in Madrid (1820–1823), Varela not only favored an immediate end to the island's slave trade but proposed the abolition of slavery as well. He also came out strongly for semiautonomous status for Cuba under Spanish sovereignty. This was remembered by the autocratic king FERDINAND VII. In August 1823, when the conspiracy of the Soles y Rayos de Bolívar, which sought Cuban independence, was discovered and a movement begun to crush liberalism, Varela was forced to flee to the United States. He took up residence in New York, where he wrote prodigiously, published *El Habanero,* edited several reviews, and became vicar-general of the city. Later, exhausted by overwork and in failing health, he retired to St. Augustine, Florida, where he died and was buried.

                    KENNETH F. KIPLE

VARELA, JOSÉ PEDRO (1845–1879). Uruguayan educator. Although Varela lived only thirty-four years, he was second only to José BATLLE Y ORDÓÑEZ as a maker of modern Uruguay. Varela created the tradition that a public education is the political birthright of every citizen, a legacy culminating in the fact that present-day Uruguay leads other Latin American nations in literacy, with 92 percent of its citizens literate.

After graduating from the Montevideo school system, Varela in 1867 visited Europe and the United States, where he got to know the Argentine educator Domingo Faustino SARMIENTO, then serving as Argentine Minister in Washington. The young teacher adopted the elder statesman's plan for modernizing teacher training in South America.

Varela returned to Montevideo in 1868 to begin his career as an educator, forming the Society of the Friends of Popular Education with himself as secretary. In 1869, as the society's president, he established an experimental school to popularize new teaching methods. In 1874 his first book, *La educación del pueblo,* made the Uruguayan general public aware of modern pedagogy. His second book, *Legislación escolar* (1876), proposed a new school law, which President Lorenzo Latorre promulgated by executive decree the next year. Through his periodical *Enciclopedia de Educación,* Varela interested scores of young Uruguayans in a teaching career. School construction and teachers' salaries began to account for larger portions of the national budget. Varela helped commit Uruguay to an emphasis on education.

                    MARVIN ALISKY

VARGAS, GETÚLIO [DORNELLES] (1883–1954). President of Brazil (1930–1945, 1951–1954). Revolutionary leader, dictator, statesman, and President of his country longer than any other person in the history of Brazil, Getúlio Vargas dominated the national political scene for the last quarter century of his life. His name is given to the post-1930 "revolution" that shook the foundations of the established political, economic, and social order and moved Brazil into the forefront of the modernizing, industrializing nations of Latin America.

Vargas's personality was shaped by his family background and by his long apprenticeship in the autocratic Republican party regime in his home state. The third son of Gen. Manoel do Nascimento Vargas and Candida Dornelles Vargas, he was born on April 19, 1883, at São Borja, on the western border of Rio Grande do Sul. His parents were from politically antagonistic families in a region where partisan loyalties ran deep and political contests were often extensions of feuds between rival clans. In this environment Vargas early learned the arts of tact, compromise, and patience, which he was to use to excellent advantage throughout his political career. After an unsuccessful start toward a military career, he attended the Pôrto Alegre law school. During his senior year Vargas entered state politics, campaigning on behalf of the Republican party candidate for the governorship. In this capacity he came to the attention of the party boss Borges de Medeiros, and upon graduation in 1907 he was appointed a public prosecutor in Pôrto Alegre. He held the post until 1909, when he returned to São Borja to open a private law practice. From 1909 to 1912 Vargas also served in the state legislature, which met briefly each year to approve the Governor's budget. Then for several years he was barred from public office because he had mildly criticized Governor Medeiros's iron rule over the state and the party. In 1917, after making his peace with the Governor, he returned to the state legislature.

Vargas achieved national stature in 1922, with his election to Congress and appointment as chief of the Rio Grande do Sul delegation. In 1926 he became Minister of Finance in the Cabinet of President

Getúlio Vargas. [*Brazilian Consulate General, New York*]

Washington Luis PEREIRA DE SOUSA, and two years later he succeeded Medeiros as Governor of Rio Grande do Sul. In that office Vargas adopted a conciliatory attitude toward the opposition party and thus was able to unite the political forces of the state solidly behind his candidacy for the Presidency in 1930. As head of the reform ticket of the Liberal Alliance, Vargas was also supported by the Republican party machines of Minas Gerais and Paraíba, by opposition parties in the other states, and by the young military officers who had fought for political and social reforms in the abortive revolts of 1922 and 1924 (*see* TENENTISMO). Convinced that he would not be allowed to win, Vargas waged a quiet campaign and did not protest his defeat at the polls but permitted his backers to plan the revolution that broke out in October and carried him to supreme power in Brazil on November 3, 1930 (*see* REVOLUTION OF 1930). Vargas remained chief of state for the next fifteen years. He ruled by decree as provisional President until July 17, 1934, when constitutional rule was restored and the new Congress elected him to a four-year term. On November 10, 1937, Vargas presided over the coup d'état that made him dictator of the ESTADO NOVO (New State), which survived until October 29, 1945. In the post-World War II wave of democratic spirit he was deposed by the armed forces without recriminations. Vargas spent nearly five years in retirement at São Borja, but in 1950 he returned to the political fray as the candidate of the PARTIDO TRABALHISTA BRASILEIRO and was elected to the Presidency by a large plurality, taking office in January 1951. However, in an open political milieu he proved unable to cope with the problems of inflation, underemployment, and strident nationalistic demands for economic development, to which his own policies contributed. Within four years he had lost much public support and aroused the opposition of the military. Rather than resign under pressure, he took his own life on August 24, 1954.

It is difficult to assess the extent of Vargas's responsibility for the changes that occurred in Brazil during his tenure in office. He was first and foremost a political pragmatist with an all-consuming love of power, who came to the Presidency without firm ideological convictions or preconceived programs for reshaping Brazil. Yet he usually found it to his advantage to be identified with the forces of change, with the result that his fifteen-year rule after 1930 transformed Brazil into a modern state. Under his direction the central government and the urban working and middle classes gained power at the expense of the states and the rural oligarchy. Vargas put the government into business in the areas of transportation and steel production and greatly increased its regulatory powers over the economy, but he did not tamper with private property or seriously challenge the private enterprise system. He permitted urban labor to organize and brought it under government control. His administrations witnessed a vast expansion of the federal bureaucracy in response to the expanded role of the government in such fields as labor, education, and public health and encouraged the growth of the middle class with policies promoting manufacturing industries in private hands. Vargas resorted to nationalistic appeals, justifying his policies on the ground that they contributed to a stronger Brazil, one less dependent on foreign markets and sources of supply. In the last years of the dictatorship and increasingly after 1950, Vargas turned to populism, seeking a mass labor base for his administration. His final suicide message interpreted his career as a long crusade on behalf of the poor and humble of Brazil.

Bibliography. José Maria Bello, *A History of Modern Brazil, 1889–1964,* Stanford, Calif., 1966, chaps. 23–24; John W. F. Dulles, *Vargas of Brazil: A Political Biography,* Austin, Tex., 1967; Affonso Henriques, *Ascensão e Queda de Getúlio Vargas, o Maquiavélico,* 3 vols., Rio de Janeiro, 1966; Robert M. Levine, *The Vargas Regime: The Critical Years, 1934–1938,* New York, 1970; Karl Loewenstein, *Brazil under Vargas,* New York, 1942; Alzira Vargas do Amaral Peixoto, *Getúlio Vargas, Meu Pai,* Rio de Janeiro, 1960; Thomas E. Skidmore, *Politics in Brazil, 1930–1964: An Experiment in Democracy,* New York, 1967; John D. Wirth, *The Politics of Brazilian Development, 1930–1954,* Stanford, Calif., 1970.

ROLLIE E. POPPINO

VARGAS, JOSÉ MARÍA (1786–1854). President of Venezuela (1835–1836). A native of La Guaira, Vargas attended the Central University in Caracas and received a degree in medicine in 1808. He then went to Cumaná, where his incipient medical practice was cut short by the independence movement. Because of his involvement with the patriots in Cumaná he suffered imprisonment and then exile. Between 1814 and 1817 he studied surgery in Edinburgh; he then moved to Puerto Rico, where he practiced medicine until 1825. Returning to Caracas, Vargas quickly became one of the most able and respected leaders of *caraqueño* society. Simón BOLÍVAR appointed him rector of the Central University, where he initiated reforms in the curriculum.

By 1830 Vargas had entered politics and public affairs through his election to the Constitutional Convention of Valencia (1830) and then to the Council of Government, where he served as presidential adviser. His lack of military connections, his reputation for knowledge and moderation, and his political visibility induced his supporters to have him elected President of Venezuela to succeed Gen. José Antonio PÁEZ in 1835. Because of his lack of revolutionary credentials and his obvious alliance with the civilian arbiters of Caracas society, however, the military faction, consisting of prominent captains of Bolívar's army who were led by Gen. Santiago Mariño, launched a revolt against Vargas that succeeded on July 8, 1835. The Reformistas, as the victorious rebels called themselves, expelled Vargas from the Presidency and the country. But Páez, who had waited out the revolt, moved against the rebels in defense of the constitution. By routing Mariño's forces and restoring Vargas to the Presidency, Páez impressed upon the civilian elite of Caracas their dependence on his armies for their ascendancy. Once returned to power late in 1835, Vargas found himself unable to govern effectively, in part because he could not operate independently of Páez and in part because he could not agree with the reprisals taken by Congress against the Reformistas. By April 1836 he felt compelled to resign from the Presidency.

Although Vargas remained a controversial topic of political debate, his active political life had virtually ended with the exception of short terms as senator in 1839 and as a member of the Council of Government in 1847. His poor health forced him to travel to the United States, where he died in 1854.

Vargas's greatest contribution to the nation was his thorough revision of the Central University's organization and curriculum, which gave that venerable institution new courses in modern foreign languages and experimental medicine, a better arrangement for fixing the duties and responsibilities of faculty and students, and an admission policy that allowed blacks, *pardos* (mulattoes), Protestants, Jews, and foreigners to matriculate and receive degrees.

JOHN V. LOMBARDI

VARGAS LLOSA, MARIO (1936–   ). Peruvian novelist. Born in Arequipa, he began his studies in Bolivia and in Piura, Peru. In Lima he attended a military college that provided the background for his first novel, *La ciudad y los perros,* 1962 (*The Time of the Hero*). In 1958 he moved to Madrid and from there to Paris to gain his doctorate. He won the Leopoldo Alas Prize in Madrid with a book of short stories, *Los jefes* (1958), and his fame was enhanced by his second novel, *La casa verde,* 1966 (*The Green House*), which was awarded several prizes. In 1968 appeared the story "Los cachorros," and in 1969 the two-volume *Conversación en la Catedral.* Vargas Llosa transcends realism with a sure use of experimental techniques and a penetrating vision of Peruvian society.

RACHEL PHILLIPS

VARONA [Y PERA], ENRIQUE JOSÉ (1849–1933). Cuban intellectual, philosopher, and political figure. Born in Puerto Príncipe (now Camagüey) on April 13, 1849, he was destined to become one of Cuba's greatest intellectuals, with a career so prolific that at the time of his death his bibliography contained 1,880 items. Varona, who received his doctorate from the University of Havana, was greatly influenced by such men as Spencer, Comte, Ward, and Durkheim and is credited both with introducing positivism into Cuba and with being among its leading exemplars in Latin America. He is also remembered as the founder and editor of *La Revista Cubana.*

Varona served for a period as a deputy to the Spanish Cortes from the province of Camagüey and was an early advocate of autonomy for Cuba. Later he changed his mind, embraced the separatist cause, and joined José MARTÍ in New York, where he worked for independence by editing *Patria,* an organ of the revolutionary party.

Following the struggle for independence (*see* WAR OF CUBAN INDEPENDENCE), he accepted the post of Secretary of Education in the Cabinet of Gen. Leonard WOOD and reorganized the University of Havana. He also became the leader of the conservatives and a severe critic of almost every administration, denouncing corruption and deploring the dependence of the island on sugar, while urging economic diversity.

Varona served Cuba as Vice President during the years 1913–1917 under Gen. Mario García MENOCAL but was unable to make his views prevail. In part, this was because he had become identified with conservatism, but the failure was due mainly to his inability to arouse the many. Throughout his life his genius lay in inspiring the few—Cuba's intellectual elite.

KENNETH F. KIPLE

VASCONCELOS, BERNARDO PEREIRA DE (1795–1850). Brazilian political leader, cofounder of the Conservative party. Trained in law at the University of Coimbra, Vasconcelos was a major political figure from 1826 until his death in 1850. At first a liberal, by the early 1830s he was already displaying conservative tendencies, urging stern suppression of the *exaltados* (radical liberals) but also opposing the restoration of PEDRO I. As a member of a committee assigned to prepare constitutional reforms, he wrote in 1834 a preliminary version of the Additional Act, which amended the constitution of 1824 to allow greater provincial and local autonomy, abolition of the Council of State, a single elected Regent, and other significant changes (*see* CONSTITUTION OF 1824: BRAZIL).

Vasconcelos was a political ally of the prominent Liberals Evaristo da VEIGA and Diogo Antônio FEIJÓ until the latter's rise to the Regency in 1835, but from then until the triumph of the Conservatives in 1837 he was a bitter enemy of the ruling Liberals. One of the most active members of the movement known as *o regresso* (the regression), which evolved into the Conservative party, he opposed Feijó's unorthodox religious policies, his alleged leniency toward the FARROUPILHA REVOLT and other revolutionary movements, and the liberal application of the Additional Act by provincial assemblies. With the triumph of *o regresso* and Pedro de ARAÚJO LIMA's succession to the Regency in September 1837, Vasconcelos became Minister of Empire and of Justice. During his Ministry he created such public institutions as the College of Pedro II and the National Archive and advocated policies favoring the conservative planter class, including relegalization of the slave trade and contract labor legislation. On April 16, 1839, he resigned from the Ministry, but during the political crisis that led to the declaration of the majority of PEDRO II in 1840, he was again Minister of Empire, holding that office for only nine hours. Vasconcelos was a prime force in the movement that reestablished the Council of State in 1841, holding a seat on that imperial advisory body from 1842 until 1850.

ROBERT CONRAD

VASCONCELOS, JOSÉ (1882–1959). Mexican statesman and writer. Born in Oaxaca, he was trained as a lawyer by 1907 and took an active part in the MEXICAN REVOLUTION under Francisco I. MADERO and Francisco VILLA. He was named rector of the National University of Mexico by Álvaro OBREGÓN and from 1921 to 1924 had extraordinary success as Minister of Education, introducing important educational reforms with the help of such figures as Pedro HENRÍQUEZ UREÑA and Gabriela MISTRAL. He had to leave the country several times for political reasons and lived in Europe and the United States. In 1929 he made an unsuccessful bid for the Presidency, after which he was forced to go into exile once more. From Paris and Madrid he edited the review *La Antorcha*. He returned to Mexico in 1940 and served as director of the *Biblioteca México* until his death.

Vasconcelos was a member of the National College and of the Mexican Academy of the Language. His written work ranges from philosophy to sociology, history, and autobiography. In *La raza cósmica* (1925) and *Indología* (1926) he expounds his preoccupation with Latin American culture. His four autobiographical volumes, *Ulises criollo* (1935), *La tormenta* (1936),

El desastre (1938), and *El proconsulado* (1939), reflect his vigorous personality and the troubled times in which he lived. Vasconcelos's autobiography was published in abridged form in English as *A Mexican Ulysses* (1963).

RACHEL PHILLIPS

VÁSQUEZ, HORACIO (1860–1936). President of the Dominican Republic (1899, 1902–1903, 1924–1930). As a young idealist, Vásquez participated in several plots to overthrow the dictator Ulises HEUREAUX and first came to power in the aftermath of Heureaux's assassination. During the next sixteen years Vásquez was one of the country's principal leaders, and his followers, known as the *horacistas,* constituted one of its major "parties."

The Vásquez era was one of severe political instability but also of accelerated prosperity. It was, as well, a period of rising United States influence and of the emergence of a wealthy merchant and planter class. Vásquez was one of the principals during the United States occupation of 1916–1924, and he served on the negotiating committee that helped facilitate the United States withdrawal.

After Vásquez was elected to the Presidency in the United States–supervised elections of 1924, the United States Marines withdrew. His administration was honest and generally free, but to many Dominicans he remained a puppet of the Americans, who had unconstitutionally extended his term of office from four to six years. When the Depression struck, the perpetual feuding of the parties reasserted itself, and in 1930 a revolution was launched against his government. It was as a result of this revolt that Rafael Leonidas TRUJILLO MOLINA took power. Vásquez presided over the eclipse of an older, sleepier oligarchic era in Dominican social history and paved the way for the rise of a newer, more dynamic, and uncertain one.

HOWARD J. WIARDA

VÁSQUEZ DE CORONADO, FRANCISCO. *See* CORONADO, FRANCISCO VÁSQUEZ DE.

VAUDUN. *See* VODUN.

VEGA, AURELIO DE LA (1925–   ). Cuban composer, essayist, and teacher. He was born in Havana, where he began his musical training with Kramer while he was studying diplomacy. After receiving his doctorate in diplomatic studies, he continued his musical training in California with Ernst Toch. The list of his articles on music is as extensive as that of his compositions. His early works are of a marked neoromantic character, which gradually evolved into the use of serialism and aleatory techniques, including the electronic medium. Outstanding examples are an elegy for strings (1954), a string quartet (1957), a cantata (1958), a symphony (1960), *Analigus* (1965) for orchestra, *Labdanum* (1970), and *Intrata* (1972).

JUAN A. ORREGO-SALAS

VEGA, GARCILASO DE LA. *See* GARCILASO DE LA VEGA.

VEIGA, EVARISTO DA (1799–1837). Brazilian journalist and politician. Da Veiga acquired much of his liberal education in his father's bookshop in Rio de Janeiro. Prospering in his father's profession between

1823 and 1827, he gained control of the *Aurora Fluminense,* a newspaper of the capital, in 1828. He quickly made it an example of journalistic moderation and good taste, gaining a national reputation as a spokesman for liberalism, constitutional monarchy, and a free press. Already a major political personality, he was elected in 1830 to the national Chamber of Deputies from Minas Gerais, a position he held until his death.

In 1831 he became involved in the political turbulence that brought on the Liberal revolution of April 7, 1831, and the abdication of PEDRO I, rising to the height of national leadership along with Senator Nicolau Vergueiro, Father Diogo Antônio FEIJÓ, Bernardo Pereira de VASCONCELOS, and other Liberals. Averse to a republican solution to the political crisis, fearing national dissolution and militarism, he helped to moderate the revolutionary movement and to retain the monarchist system in the name of the five-year-old PEDRO II.

After the Liberal revolt, allegedly more frightened of anarchy than of despotism, he supported the moderately liberal Sociedade Defensora da Liberdade e Independência Nacional with its branch organizations throughout the provinces and was deeply involved in the subsequent political struggles between *exaltados* (radicals) and *caramurús* (conservatives), who until the death of Pedro I in 1834 urged the restoration of the former Emperor. Always wary of change, Evaristo da Veiga nevertheless played a role in the passage of the Additional Act of 1834, which liberalized the Constitution of 1824 (*see* CONSTITUTION OF 1824: BRAZIL) without eliminating the centralist and monarchist political system. A moderate throughout his brief career, he made bitter enemies, but his leadership helped cement political compromises and strengthen political institutions at a time when divisiveness threatened the unity of the Brazilian nation.

ROBERT CONRAD

VEINTEMILLA, IGNACIO (1828–1908). Ecuadorian military dictator who displaced President Antonio Borrero in 1876. Since Borrero, a compromise Moderate Conservative (*see* CONSERVATIVE PARTY: ECUADOR), had pleased no one, General Veintemilla had little difficulty in gathering support when he spoke in the Guayaquil barracks, convinced the city council to proclaim a new government, and set out for the Andes. There he won a bloody victory at Galte. For more than a year Veintemilla ruled as dictator, but his personal ambition disenchanted his Liberal followers, and they soon conspired against him (*see* LIBERAL PARTY: ECUADOR). Civilian and military dissenters were beaten in the army barracks, and many fled from Ecuador. Veintemilla proved his Liberal principles by striking out ruthlessly at the church. He jailed and exiled distinguished clergy and temporarily broke Ecuador's concordat with the Pope. A constitutional convention in which army delegates received five votes each met in 1878, and Veintemilla was duly elected President of Ecuador.

Veintemilla's able administration was marred by university uprisings and by invasions from Panama by Eloy ALFARO. Partly because the WAR OF THE PACIFIC dislocated the coastal trade of Peru, Bolivia, and Chile, but also because of a brisk export trade in cacao, coffee, ivory nuts, and hides, the economy flourished.

Nonetheless, the beating of the writer Miguel Valverde and the loss of army support ended Veintemilla's hopes for a second dictatorship. Beset in Quito by a frenzied crowd, Veintemilla left for Guayaquil and then, in 1883, for Lima. He later returned to Quito, where he resided until his death.

LOIS WEINMAN

VELASCO, JOSÉ MARÍA (1840–1912). Mexican painter. He specialized in landscapes and preferred those of his native Valley of Mexico. Velasco was born at Temascalcingo, near Mexico City, and was trained by the Italian landscapist Eugenio Landesio at the Academy of San Carlos in Mexico City. In 1868 he was named professor of perspective in the academy, a post he held for the rest of his life. In 1902 he was invalided by a heart attack that ended his career as a painter and teacher. Velasco disliked traveling, but he visited the United States twice (Philadelphia in 1876, Chicago in 1893) and Europe (1889) to exhibit and receive prizes.

Velasco's painting developed slowly and logically from early works that emphasize relationships of mass, as in *Former Convent of San Agustín* (1861), and details of landscape forms, as in his album of lithographs *Flora of the Environs of Mexico* (early 1870s), to an emphasis on sky and space in his last paintings, as in *The Hacienda of Chimalpa* (1893). Velasco is recorded as reading the Psalms before beginning important paintings, a practice that reflected his belief in a divine order in nature, the revelation of which was the mission of painting. The seriousness and objectivity of his work make his paintings modern, while Landesio's similar views are romantic. His most romantic paintings are those of trains (*The Bridge at Metlac,* 1881; *The Peak of Orizaba,* 1897). Velasco was respected during his lifetime, and his reputation has not declined.

TERENCE GRIEDER

VELASCO ALVARADO, JUAN (1910–   ). Peruvian army officer and President (1968–   ). Born in Piura of working-class parents, Velasco Alvarado joined the Army as a private in April 1929 and entered the cadet school in 1930. Four years later he graduated first in his class. From second lieutenant he rose steadily through the ranks until by 1963 he had been promoted to general of division. During those thirty years his assignments included teaching at the Escuela Superior de Guerra and the Escuela Militar de Chorrillos. He was also Military Attaché to France, Army delegate to the Inter-American Defense Board, and inspector general of the Army. By 1968, when he led a military coup against President Fernando BELAÚNDE TERRY, he was commander in chief of the Army and the senior general on active duty. The coup was motivated, among other things, by more than two years of political and economic crisis, but it was sparked by a supposedly unfavorable agreement signed by the government with the INTERNATIONAL PETROLEUM COMPANY.

The Velasco government, fiercely nationalistic and at first loudly anti-American, progressively won a greater degree of popular support. While attempting to maintain a balance between its moderate and its leftist supporters, it adopted a more independent foreign policy by establishing relations with the Soviet Union and other Communist countries. At home the Velasco government introduced a series of important measures, including agrarian, financial, and industrial reforms. These measures, plus the government's efforts to exercise stricter control over foreign capital, made it an object of great interest to other Latin American governments.

ORAZIO A. CICCARELLI

VELASCO IBARRA, JOSÉ MARÍA (1893–). Ecuadorian political leader. Velasco Ibarra received a law school education, and on his frequent "vacations" from politics he served as professor of law in Ecuador, Argentina, and other countries. He became provisional President of Ecuador for the first time in 1934, remaining in office for only a year. Upon being overthrown, he went into exile in neighboring Colombia. In 1944 he returned to Ecuador to lead the opposition to Carlos Alberto ARROYO DEL RÍO, a Liberal whose handling of the recent conflict with Peru had aroused strong nationalistic resentment (*see* LIBERAL PARTY: ECUADOR). He helped organize the Ecuadorian Democratic Alliance, including Conservatives (*see* CONSERVATIVE PARTY: ECUADOR), Socialists, Communists, and some Liberals. The alliance succeeded in bringing about Arroyo del Río's downfall in May 1944, and Velasco Ibarra became provisional President.

A coalition government, including all political groups supporting the coup, held elections for a Constituent Congress, which wrote a new constitution and elected Velasco Ibarra President under the new document. President Velasco Ibarra soon came to depend principally on the Conservative party, and he became increasingly dictatorial. In August 1947, he was overthrown by a military coup and went into exile in Argentina.

In 1948, after several provisional governments, Galo PLAZA was elected constitutional President. Four years later Velasco Ibarra returned home to run successfully for the Presidency against seriously split opposition. This time he stayed in office throughout his constitutional four-year term in spite of the fact that his administration was characterized by confusion, demagoguery, and considerable corruption.

In 1956 Velasco Ibarra turned the post over to his legally elected successor, Camilo PONCE, nominee of the Social Christian Movement, who was also backed by the traditional Conservatives. At the end of Ponce's term, Velasco Ibarra returned from Argentina to run for the Presidency once more and was victorious in the election of June 1960.

Velasco Ibarra again governed with demagoguery but without any well-defined program. He tried to reconcile conservative and radical elements among his followers in the face of growing concern among the military. With the connivance of Velasco Ibarra's Vice President, Carlos Julio Arosemena, the soldiers finally overthrew Velasco Ibarra in November 1961, and Arosemena assumed the Presidency.

Arosemena's tenure was short. Partly as a result of his frequent inebriation, he was ousted in 1963, and power was seized by a military junta. The soldiers remained in control until March 1966, when they were overthrown by a popular uprising. Shortly afterward, Velasco Ibarra returned from Argentina, landing in the port of Guayaquil, where he was greeted by wildly cheering crowds. His subsequent tour of the country was a triumph.

Virtually all other political leaders sought to prevent Velasco Ibarra from becoming President again. There was a proposal to call elections for a constituent assembly, which it was presumed Velasco Ibarra's followers could not win, and then have this body elect the new President. Popular pressure prevented such a stratagem, and in the presidential election held in 1968 Velasco Ibarra won.

The fifth Velasco Ibarra administration was no more successful than most of the previous ones. In mid-1970, the President proclaimed a dictatorship, with the support of the armed forces, in an attempt to forestall growing opposition. The following year the dictatorial regime was modified, and preparations began for election of Velasco Ibarra's successor.

It soon became clear that the likely winner in these elections was Asaad Bucaram, former mayor of Guayaquil and the candidate of the moderately left-wing Concentración de Fuerzas Populares. Bucaram's opponents alleged that he was not eligible for the Presidency, since he had been born in Lebanon. The dispute over Bucaram's qualifications presented the military with an excuse for ousting Velasco Ibarra in February 1972. The deposed President, as was his wont, sought refuge in Argentina. It seemed unlikely that he would get a sixth chance to be President.

José María Velasco Ibarra. [*Organization of American States*]

Velasco Ibarra was a peculiar phenomenon in Latin American politics. His appeal, principally to the lower classes, was never based on a well-defined program. None of his administrations had clear policies, and his ability to return so often to the Presidency was due to his oratorical power and his skill in arousing the hopes of the urban masses, despite his equally notable inability to satisfy these hopes once he had been elected.

Bibliography. George I. Blanksten, *Ecuador: Constitutions and Caudillos,* Berkeley, Calif., 1951; Lilo Linke, "Ecuador's Politics: President Velasco's Fourth Exile," *World Today,* vol. XVIII, no. 2, February 1962, pp. 57–69; George Maier, *The Ecuadorian Presidential Election of June 2, 1968: An Analysis,* Washington, 1969; José María Velasco Ibarra, *Conciencia o barbarie,* 2d ed., Quito, 1937; id., *Obra doctrinaria y práctica del gobierno ecuatoriano,* Quito, 1956; id., *Cuarta jornada,* Quito, 1961.

ROBERT J. ALEXANDER

VENEZUELA SINCE 1830. Venezuela, a country of approximately 352,000 square miles and more than 10 million people, has a history of such variety and complexity that it almost defies description. Since independence in 1810, Venezuela has grown from an essentially agricultural-pastoral domain ruled by a narrow elite into a bustling, industrializing, oil-rich country enmeshed in international political concerns and governed through competing popular parties with mass electoral appeal. This transformation of Venezuelan life in a little more than a century and a half came about through a kaleidoscopic combination of economic, social, and political forces. Behind the procession of presidents, generals, wars, revolts, economic booms and depressions, and international involvements lie a structure and a series of processes that help explain the apparently chaotic development of the country's past.

In 1830, with the disintegration of Simón BOLÍVAR's

VENEZUELA
Area: 352,144 sq. mi.   Population: 10,721,522 (1971 est.).

Gran Colombia (*see* COLOMBIA, GRAN), Venezuela took on its republican political personality and began its first cycle of historical development under the aegis of the patriot captain of the LLANOS, Gen. José Antonio PÁEZ. Lasting for about a generation between 1830 and 1858, this period, known as the conservative oligarchy, saw a postindependence coffee boom that brought rapid economic recovery accompanied by political tranquillity. Within this first generation Venezuela acquired many of the political, social, and economic characteristics that would last for a century or more. In the political sphere General Páez established the strong-man pattern in which the supreme *caudillo* ruled for long periods but allowed his more loyal subordinates to occupy the presidential chair from time to time, thereby preserving the forms of liberal constitutional government without being required to subscribe to the content. Thus, in an unhappy experiment in civilian executive rule, Páez first sponsored Dr. José María VARGAS as a substitute President in 1835; then he turned to the more reliable Gen. Carlos SOUBLETTE to be titular head of the government in 1837–1839 and again in 1843–1847.

Perhaps even more important than this presidential pattern was the consolidation of the position of Caracas as the economic-administrative capital of Venezuela. Although the preeminence of Caracas among Venezuelan cities dates from the seventeenth century, the coffee generation made Caracas's position unchallengeable; this primacy became even more marked during the next century. This development came about through an alliance of convenience between the commercial-mercantile elite, located in Caracas and living off the lucrative coffee export trade, and General Páez, the possessor of the requisite military force to keep the peace. While Páez mobilized the armies necessary to preserve peace, the elite administered the financial resources of the country as it saw fit. In return for power and the right to reward himself and his followers, the *caudillo* guaranteed peace and tranquillity and ensured that the commercial-mercantile elite would have the appropriate legal machinery to conduct its business. This marriage of convenience lasted, with some challenges, for about a generation and so helped fix the position of Caracas as the arbiter of Venezuela's destiny. Throughout the nineteenth century and well into the twentieth, the principal goal of all politically ambitious men was control of the administrative and financial resources of the capital city.

The Páez hegemony began to weaken in the 1840s and collapsed altogether in the 1850s. Although Páez had made some efforts to create a strong political structure of his own, he lacked the will, expertise, and technology to control his political environment. A decline in international coffee prices created a strong opposition group clustered around the demagogic but brilliant journalist Antonio Leocadio Guzmán, whose newspaper, *El Venezolano,* founded in 1840, became the standard bearer of the newly formed Liberal party. These Liberals, whose principal leaders came from landed agricultural families, mobilized only when the Páez arrangement with the commercial-mercantile elite failed to keep their own situation prosperous. A decline in coffee prices brought many planters close to bankruptcy, and their appeals to Páez for assistance went unheeded. The inevitable result was a strong opposition party whose agitation and propaganda caused serious social and political unrest.

Following traditional political practices, Páez chose Gen. José Tadeo MONAGAS to succeed to the presidential chair for the 1847–1851 term. Monagas, while willing to be designated President, had ambitions of his own and quickly shook off Páez's authority and began his own conquest of power by embracing the Liberals. For the next ten years the resistance of the commercial-mercantile elite, worsening economic conditions, the violent opposition of General Páez to the Monagas rule, and the claims of competing *caudillos* kept Venezuela in an almost perpetual state of warfare. Nevertheless, Monagas, like Páez before him, made every effort to maintain the forms of liberal constitutionalism. He installed his brother José Gregorio MONAGAS in the presidential chair for the 1851–1855 term and then reassumed the Presidency in 1855 in the hope of maintaining his hegemony. The dream ended in 1858 with the uprising of Gen. Julián CASTRO, which is generally regarded as marking the beginning of the Federal Wars.

The Federal Wars (1858–1863), ostensibly a contest between the exponents of a federal form of government (the Liberals) and the advocates of centralized government (the Conservatives), in reality represented the disintegration of the marriage between Páez and the Caracas-based commercial-mercantile elite and a contest to decide which group would now fill Páez's role. The wars themselves were extremely complex; they lasted at least five years and cost thousands of lives. They brought to the surface the social tensions inherent in any poor, hierarchically organized society, and they provided the opportunity for a new generation of military leaders to earn their laurels and validate their claims to Venezuela's political spoils.

The victors, under the military leadership of Gen. Juan C. FALCÓN, from the western province of Coro, officially came to power in 1863 and promptly selected Falcón as President. In traditional fashion the Liberal-Federalists proceeded to write a new constitution, symbolizing the new arrangement between the *caudillos'* force and *caraqueño* commercial expertise. Unfortunately, Falcón lacked the skill, interest, and resources to maintain and develop this arrangement. His passage through the Presidency lasted about five years, and then the Conservatives staged a final campaign to regain their position. Although they achieved a fleeting moment of success, their movement collapsed under the pressure of the Liberal-Federalist armies of Gen. Antonio GUZMÁN BLANCO, Falcón's ablest assistant and one of the finest administrative and financial minds ever to govern in Venezuela.

Like the coffee generation that preceded it, the Guzmán Blanco regime restored to Venezuela the peace and stability that had been destroyed during the Federal Wars. And like Páez, Guzmán Blanco made arrangements with the commercial-mercantile elite for their mutual benefit. Throughout the years of his command (1870–1888) the forms of liberal constitutional government were conspicuously and carefully observed while the realities of political activity conformed to the whims of the strong man. With the assistance of substantial economic recovery, Guzmán Blanco made a solid contribution to Venezuela's growth. To be sure, for the vast majority of Venezuelans conditions improved only minimally, but the administrative and financial accomplishments of the regime were undeniable.

During the Federal Wars the participants had formed so many factions and changed sides so often that differences between Liberals and Conservatives had begun to lose their meaning. Because Guzmán Blanco excoriated Conservatives in public but employed them in his administration, the distinction between political persuasions became more and more difficult to make during his years in power. Yet his elaborate political structure lacked the organization and technology to maintain itself once he removed himself from the scene to take up a comfortable self-imposed exile in Paris. His successors in the presidential chair gradually allowed his political apparatus to disintegrate until Cipriano CASTRO, an energetic general from the Andean region of Táchira, mobilized an effective and well-organized army to reimpose order on Venezuela's quarreling *guzmancista* elite. For more than eight years (1899–1908) Castro gloried in the role of supreme commander of Venezuela.

In many ways Cipriano Castro, a caricature of the traditional Venezuelan strong man with all his vices magnified and virtues diminished, symbolized the passing of an age, the end of the second cycle of Venezuelan history. Castro closed out an era when he left Venezuela for Europe in 1908 in search of a cure for his various ailments and left his Vice President and heretofore-loyal subordinate, Gen. Juan Vicente GÓMEZ, in charge. Although Gómez quickly formed a government in his own right and ordered Castro into permanent exile, he inaugurated a substantially different system of political management, much of which is still evident today.

It fell to Gómez to end for all time the traditional system of political competition. By carefully thought-out programs of road building and communications expansion he made certain that no enterprising political rival could marshal a dangerously large military force to challenge him. Any such attempt could be noted, reported, and suppressed in very short order by Gómez's military establishment. Moreover, Juan Vicente introduced the techniques of an efficient, ruthless secret police to ferret out those suspected of disloyal or dangerous plans. During his regime (1908–1935) Gómez perfected this system to such a degree that no serious opposition to his rule developed before his death. Although his success marks the end of the era of the *caudillo*, his technique had been foreshadowed by Guzmán Blanco, who also clearly saw the crucial importance of efficient communications in the suppression of revolts. But whereas Guzmán Blanco lacked the technology and the resources to carry out his conception fully, Gómez was able to acquire all the technology necessary through the greatly increased government revenues from the oil boom (*see* PETROLEUM INDUSTRY: VENEZUELA). Moreover, whereas Guzmán Blanco became a Europeanized Latin American who governed Venezuela to support his European residence and life-style, Gómez was completely dedicated to Venezuela, which he came to regard as his private preserve, to be cared for and managed as a personal estate. Thus, while Guzmán Blanco maintained the peace to use the country and magnify his stature abroad, Gómez established the peace so that he could live in the country as he chose.

The increased efficiency of Gómez's authoritarian government, the futility of *caudillo* revolts, and the ruthless ability of the secret police changed the rules of political activity. The increasing urbanization of the country brought about by a petroleum-fueled economic renaissance also helped to restructure political conflict. A new breed of political activists, university-trained and sophisticated in political theory and practice, emerged to challenge Gómez from within his tightly controlled autocracy. The principal leaders of this group gained their first notoriety in 1928 when they demonstrated as university students against Gómez's hegemony. Although suppressed, persecuted, imprisoned, and exiled, these men managed to begin the organization of broadly based, ideologically consistent political organizations, organizations strong enough to function without the direct presence of the main leadership and flexible enough to adjust to changing economic and political conditions. Although Gómez can hardly be regarded as a champion of the politics of the masses, his regime saw the creation of popular political action groups that after his death would help revise the organization of Venezuelan political life.

Even though the Gómez years present an unrelieved wasteland of political repression and personal aggrandizement, the first generation of the twentieth century saw Venezuela transformed from a minor agricultural country to a major world supplier of oil and a major target of foreign investors. By 1935 Venezuela had acquired a technologically sophisticated labor force in the petroleum industry, a colossal government income from oil royalties even under the generous terms of the Gómez oil concessions, and all the tensions of an industrializing society. Uninterested in resolving these problems, Gómez simply repressed them, leaving their solution to the inheritors of his patrimony after 1935.

Among the accomplishments of Juan Vicente's long reign should be counted his creation of a professional, well-trained, and politically active military establishment. Before Gómez armies were rarely professional, and generals spent most of their time in nonmilitary pursuits. By the careful cultivation of the armed forces and a conscientious professionalization campaign, Gómez created a new generation of military technocrats who often acted as if the interests of the military were synonymous with those of the country. Although Juan Vicente, one of the last of the nonprofessional generals, kept the new Army under control, his successors in the presidential office were less successful.

Thus the Venezuela that Juan Vicente Gómez willed to his followers in 1935 was a much-changed country from the one he took away from Cipriano Castro some thirty years before. His Minister of War, Gen. Eleazar LÓPEZ CONTRERAS, lacking the ability of the old *caudillo* and representing a break in the continuity of *gomecista* stability, tried to bend with the pressures of the new political groups organized by the members of the rebellious Generation of 1928. Allowed to operate freely, these leaders organized associations that rapidly took on all the trappings of modern political parties. They agitated, organized, propagandized, accused, and, worst of all, appeared to have real mass support. López, finding that he could bend no further, quickly curbed this democratic excess and carefully managed the trans-

fer of power to his comrade-in-arms and Minister of War, Gen. Isaías MEDINA ANGARITA, in 1941.

Although Medina's apparent moderation gave the Generation of 1928 some hope of reopening the political contest, they soon became disillusioned and supported a military coup d'état as the best means to political power in 1945. The movement, which led eventually to the Presidency of the folk hero of ACCIÓN DEMOCRÁTICA (AD), Rómulo GALLEGOS, established the new technocrats of the military profession as prime movers in political competition. By accepting the military coup as a means to political power, the civilian political parties legitimized the king-making role of the Army—a costly accomplishment. The brief interlude of AD government under Gallegos (1948) was notable for its intemperate haste for reform, its intolerance of sympathetic but critical political competitors, such as the COMITÉ DE ORGANIZACIÓN POLÍTICA ELECTORAL INDEPENDIENTE (COPEI), the Social Christian party of Rafael CALDERA, and its inability to control its military collaborators. In the end some of the Army's bright young men brought the Gallegos administration to an abrupt close with a coup d'état in 1948.

The regime that followed, led in the end by Gen. Marcos PÉREZ JIMÉNEZ, showed some striking parallels to that of Cipriano Castro. Like Castro, Pérez Jiménez represented a transition from one style of political competition to another. He was the last of the military strong men able to rule without mass popular support. Whereas Castro was an exaggeration of the nineteenth-century *caudillo*, Pérez Jiménez seemed a caricature of Juan Vicente Gómez. Although a representative of the new technocratic Army, Pérez Jiménez operated in the personalist style of the past. Indeed, it was this contradiction between old and new styles that allowed a combination of political parties, dissatisfied military professionals, disgusted businessmen, and disillusioned masses to topple him from power in 1958.

Although historical interpretation at such short range is extremely hazardous, it appears that the ouster of Pérez Jiménez marked the end of the third cycle of Venezuelan political development. After 1958 the rules of political conflict were redefined to exclude the authoritarian personalist ruler. Elections and the competition of mass-based political coalitions replaced the traditional methods of political combat. To be sure, the government of Rómulo BETANCOURT (1959–1964), the *caudillo* of AD, barely survived concentrated and effective assaults on its position, which were controlled only through harsh repressive measures. Yet the subsequent AD government of Raúl LEONI (1964–1969) had less trouble of this kind, and the transfer of power peacefully to the Social Christians of COPEI in the person of Rafael Caldera for the presidential term 1969–1974 seemed to validate the new political rules, as did AD's return to power in 1974 in the person of Carlos Andrés PÉREZ.

Underneath this varied and exciting political panorama the stubborn realities of class and economic underdevelopment changed more slowly. Although the petroleum revolution begun under Gómez made Venezuela first among Latin American countries in terms of per capita income and permitted the development of ambitious programs of social assistance, AGRARIAN REFORM, and industrial development, the disparities between rich and poor remained large in the 1970s. The agricultural and stock-raising sectors of this once predominantly agricultural country were in serious decline. Caracas, always the commercial and political center of the nation, continued to grow uncontrollably. To be sure, the standard of living had risen in recent decades, but the rural poor and the urban masses had received less than their rightful share. The tensions engendered by the spectacular economic growth since 1928 were kept under control thanks to expensive programs made possible by the oil boom. The fate of the country if the oil revenue were to cease was difficult to predict. Given the continuance of oil-generated resources, however, Venezuela should continue in this fourth historical cycle for some time.

See also IMMIGRATION (VENEZUELA); IRON AND STEEL INDUSTRY (VENEZUELA).

Bibliography. Carlos Acedo Mendoza, *Venezuela: Ruta y destino,* 2 vols., Barcelona, 1966; Robert L. Gilmore, *Caudillism and Militarism in Venezuela, 1810–1910,* Athens, Ohio, 1964; Francisco González Guiñán, *Historia contemporánea de Venezuela,* 15 vols., Caracas, 1909–25; Pedro Grases, *Investigaciones bibliográficas,* 2 vols., Caracas, 1968; John V. Lombardi, "Venezuela since Independence," in Charles C. Griffin (ed.), *Latin America: A Guide to the Historical Literature,* Austin, Tex., 1971; Donna Keyse Rudolph and G. A. Rudolph, *Historical Dictionary of Venezuela,* Metuchen, N.J., 1971; Venezuela, Presidencia, *Pensamiento político venezolano del siglo XIX: Textos para su estudio,* ed. by Pedro Grases and Manuel Pérez Vila, 15 vols., Caracas, 1960–62.

JOHN V. LOMBARDI

VERACRUZ, OCCUPATION OF. After the overthrow and murder of President Francisco I. MADERO of Mexico in February 1913, President Woodrow Wilson refused to recognize the successor regime of Victoriano HUERTA and recalled Ambassador Henry Lane WILSON, who had been deeply implicated in Madero's deposition. Convinced that Huerta was a sanguinary despot, President Wilson looked for an opportunity to intervene in Mexico on behalf of Huerta's Constitutionalist foes.

John Lind, former Governor of Minnesota whom Wilson had sent to Mexico as his special agent, advised the United States government on April 1, 1914, that, in view of an imminent attack by the Constitutionalists on the Gulf coast oil center of Tampico, the United States had the right to declare the neutrality of the port and the surrounding area. The same might be done in Veracruz, thereby preventing Huerta from receiving arms shipments from Europe. According to Lind, such action might constitute intervention, but intervention of a humanitarian nature.

The occasion for intervention was provided by the arrest in Tampico on April 9, 1914, of several American sailors and an officer who had been loading gasoline into a whaleboat flying the American flag. Rear Adm. Henry T. Mayo, commander of United States naval forces at the scene, accused Huerta's army of violating American territory, demanded an apology and severe punishment for the officials responsible, and insisted that the American flag be raised on a prominent part of the beach. Huerta rejected this ultimatum on the grounds that the Americans had landed without giving notice and without permission and proposed the submission of the matter to the Permanent Court of Arbitration at The Hague; he later suggested simultaneous salutes to the flags of both nations and finally reciprocal salutes.

As it became clear that no satisfactory settlement would be reached, President Wilson began to lay plans for intervention. The seizure of Veracruz was decided upon in order to prevent a shipment of German arms due to arrive soon in that port from reaching Huerta. American vessels attacked Veracruz on April 21, 1914, and the occupation was completed the following day with casualties of approximately 200 dead and 300 wounded on the Mexican side; the Americans lost 19 dead, and 47 were wounded. When the Constitutionalist chief Venustiano CARRANZA protested the occupation, Francisco VILLA asserted that Carranza's protest had only a personal character and blamed Huerta for having provoked the incident. Huerta vainly tried to win over his domestic enemies so that they might unite in the struggle against the United States, declaring that a "racial war" was imminent. According to the United States government, the intervention was directed not against the Mexican people but against Huerta and Veracruz would be evacuated when constitutional order was reestablished. The city was evacuated on November 23, 1914, after Huerta's flight from Mexico.

MOISÉS GONZÁLEZ NAVARRO

VERÍSSIMO, ÉRICO [LOPES] (1905–   ). Brazilian novelist. Born in Rio Grande do Sul, he spent most of his life there, writing and serving as editorial consultant to the publishing house O Globo and as editor of its magazine. He taught at the Universities of Wisconsin and California. Veríssimo may be considered the novelist of Rio Grande do Sul. In his early books, such as *Clarissa* (1933), *Caminhos Cruzados,* 1935 (*Crossroads*), *Música ao Longe* (1935), *Olhai os Lírios do Campo,* 1938 (*Consider the Lilies of the Field*), and *O Resto É Silêncio,* 1943 (*The Rest Is Silence*), he wrote of contemporary life in a small town and in the more cosmopolitan city of Pôrto Alegre, showing the contrast between the traditional culture of the interior of the state and the new customs and ideas of the capital. In 1949 he began a second phase of his career with the publication of *O Continente* (*Time and the Wind*), the first volume of a trilogy, *O Tempo e o Vento,* in which he presents the history of his native state from 1745 to 1945 through the biography of one of its leading families. The second and third parts of the trilogy are *O Retrato* (1951) and *O Arquipélago* (1961). They are constructed on a large scale with a great number of characters and countless scenes. The first volume especially has epic scope and sweep. He wrote many other books, including two of impressions of the United States, *Gato Preto em Campo de Neve* (1941) and *A Volta do Gato Preto* (1946).

RAYMOND S. SAYERS

VESPUCCI, AMERIGO (1454–1512). Italian-born navigator. Born in Florence, the third son of Stagio Vespucci, a notary, and his wife, Lisabetta Mini, Vespucci remained in Italy almost forty years, mainly in the employ of the Medici. He left in 1492 for Seville, where he was a shipping contractor, probably as an agent of the Florentine bankers. Vespucci made a voyage to the Pearl Coast of northern South America under Alonso de OJEDA, sailing from Cádiz on May 16, 1499, and returning on September 8, 1500. It is accepted that he explored the Brazilian coast on this voyage. However, an account was published in 1504 in which someone antedated this voyage to 1497, thus giving Vespucci credit for having reached the mainland before Christopher COLUMBUS.

Controversy has raged for years over whether Vespucci did in fact reach the mainland before Columbus and whether he made four voyages in all or two. It is generally acknowledged that he made another voyage in the service of King Manoel of Portugal, leaving Lisbon in May 1501 and returning there on September 7, 1505, after having discovered All Saints Bay and possibly sailing to the RÍO DE LA PLATA. Voyages in 1497 and 1503 are discounted.

Vespucci became a naturalized Castilian on April 24, 1505, and was named the first Pilot Major on March 22, 1508. His fame is due chiefly to Martin Waldseemüller, who misnamed the two newly discovered continents America in his *Cosmographiae introductio* (1507). Vespucci, however, was the first to refer to America as a "New World" (Mundus Novus), although he continued to call it, as Columbus had, Las Indias.

MARTIN TORODASH

VICEROY. The highest official in Spain's colonial hierarchy, the viceroy presided over the largest unit of government, the viceroyalty. Within the limits of his territory he had supreme authority in matters regarding political administration, the royal treasury, the defense of the realm, the secular dimension of the church, and the protection of the Indians. In his capacity as president of the royal AUDIENCIA of the kingdom in which he had his capital, he supervised the administration of justice.

The viceroy's authority was limited, however, by a number of inhibiting circumstances. The enormous expanse of the viceroyalty tended to restrict the full exercise of his authority to the area served by his royal *audiencia*. The manner of handling routine administration was determined by existing royal decrees and provisions. Although he could make laws and other executive decisions in emergency situations, he had to submit them to the King for approval. In governing, he had to consult the royal *audiencia,* which doubled as a council of advisers. His dealings with churchmen were often difficult because their respective areas of competence were not clearly defined. Indeed, jurisdictional overlapping was seemingly contrived by the crown precisely as a check. The viceroy's principal subordinates were appointed by the King and were free to communicate directly with him. At the end of his term the viceroy was subjected to a thorough review of his administration.

Given these and other constraints, only a few outstanding viceroys managed to govern effectively and creatively. The others limited themselves to holding actions. Outstanding sixteenth-century viceroys included Antonio de MENDOZA, first Viceroy of New Spain (1535–1550), and Francisco de TOLEDO of Peru (1569–1581). The late eighteenth century saw the appointment of a number of energetic and capable viceroys, notably Antonio María BUCARELI (1771–1779) and the 2d Count of REVILLAGIGEDO (1789–1794), both of New Spain.

NORMAN MEIKLEJOHN

VICTORIA, GUADALUPE (b. MIGUEL FERNÁNDEZ FÉLIX, 1785/1786–1843). Mexican soldier and statesman. A native of Durango, Fernández arrived in Mexico City in 1808 and studied law in the Colegio de San Ildefonso, but he left school to join the rebels fighting for independence. It was while serving in the army of José María MORELOS Y PAVÓN that he changed his name to Guadalupe Victoria, by which he was known thereafter. He was engaged in the campaigns in Oaxaca and Veracruz, especially in the strategic area around the Puente del Rey on the road from the coast to Jalapa. When the rebels were defeated, Victoria refused to surrender or accept amnesty and instead went into hiding in the mountains of the state of Veracruz, emerging in 1821 to accept the Plan of Iguala and to cooperate with Agustín de ITURBIDE in securing independence. He soon became disenchanted with Iturbide, however, and once more sought refuge in the mountains. He cooperated in the overthrow of the empire.

Because of his role in the independence movement and in the cause of republicanism, Victoria was elected by the states as the first President of Mexico under the constitution of 1824. His term ran from October 10, 1824, to March 21, 1829. As President he attempted to consolidate republicanism but was involved in putting down many disturbances, principally centering in the struggle between Conservatives and Liberals in the Scottish and York Masonic lodges. He promoted the candidacy of his Minister of War, Manuel Gómez Pedraza, as his successor in 1828–1829, but when Gómez Pedraza won the election, a rebellion placed Vicente GUERRERO in office instead. Victoria retired to his hacienda and, largely because of ill health, did not engage in politics actively thereafter.

CHARLES R. BERRY

VICUÑA MACKENNA, BENJAMÍN (1831–1886). Chilean writer and politician. In some respects the most remarkable Chilean of the nineteenth century, Vicuña Mackenna was a distinguished and highly prolific writer, an unceasingly active politician, a great reforming intendant of Santiago, and an outstanding patriot. Most of his numerous books were historical, his great biographies of Bernardo O'HIGGINS and Diego PORTALES and his histories of Santiago and Valparaíso being the most noteworthy. In politics Vicuña Mackenna was an ardent Liberal who twice knew exile during the administration of Manuel MONTT (*see* LIBERAL PARTY: CHILE). In 1875 he mounted a vigorous independent candidacy for the Presidency, withdrawing at the last moment. Between 1872 and 1875, as intendant of Santiago, he did much to transform the city, endowing it with parks, avenues, and the splendid urban folly of the Cerro Santa Lucía. During the WAR OF THE PACIFIC (1879–1883), Vicuña Mackenna expertly mobilized public opinion in favor of a vigorously aggressive war policy. For many Chileans he came to embody the widespread patriotic feelings of the time.

SIMON COLLIER

VIEIRA, ANTÔNIO (1608–1697). Portuguese missionary and orator, member of the Society of Jesus. Vieira was born in Lisbon of humble parents. At six years of age he was taken to Bahia (modern Salvador), where he remained for the next twenty-seven years. He received his education at the Jesuit College of Bahia and was in the city during the Dutch attack of 1624. Later he became a missionary to the Amerindians and African slaves, learning both TUPÍ-GUARANÍ and Kimbundu. He was an outstanding preacher whose sermons are among the finest literary productions in the Portuguese language.

While in Lisbon after the restoration of Portugal's independence from Spain in 1640, Vieira became an influential adviser to King JOÃO IV, who consulted him on matters of state and employed him on secret diplomatic missions to Paris and The Hague. Vieira saw that if Portugal were to survive as an independent state, it was necessary to protect the sailing route to Brazil and stop the harassment and losses of Brazil shipping. In consequence he strongly supported the establishment of the BRAZIL COMPANY and the inauguration of a protective fleet system. He also advised toleration of the new Christians, former Portuguese Jews who had been forcibly converted, in the hope that they would invest in the company.

Vieira returned to Brazil as a missionary in 1654, but his activity in defense of the Amerindians in Maranhão produced an uprising of the colonists and his deportation to Europe in 1661. Back in Lisbon he was arrested and tried by the Inquisition for Sebastianist beliefs, the Holy Office having long been opposed to his influence and support of the new Christians. A change of power in the royal court led to his release, whereupon he went to Rome to plead the case of the Portuguese Jews, who he hoped might be spared the rigors of the Inquisition. He returned to Brazil in 1681 and spent the remaining sixteen years of his life in Bahia.

KENNETH R. MAXWELL

VIGIL, FRANCISCO DE PAULA GONZÁLEZ (1792–1875). Peruvian priest, publicist, and political leader. A creole born in Tacna, Father Vigil in 1826 set aside the quiet life of a parish priest for that of a political activist. He was elected to Congress eight times, and there he joined the liberals in the protracted struggles against the conservatives. In 1845 he accepted the directorship of the National Library in Lima and retained it until his death in 1875. Those years of semipolitical retirement were also Vigil's most productive intellectually. Although his works are rarely read today, in the mid-nineteenth century they attracted much attention. Vigil drew heavily from both French and Spanish eighteenth-century intellectual currents to defend almost fanatically the virtues of reason, to advance the concepts of equality and liberty, and to attack vehemently the Catholic Church's usurpation of "civil" authority. He called upon the state to strip the church of all its temporal powers and to deny the clergy special privileges. He also advocated local control of the church, challenged papal authority, and launched repeated attacks on the wealth of the church and on its loss of authentic Christian principles. The result was the condemnation of most of his works and excommunication.

Although anticlericalism constituted Vigil's major crusade, he wrote on a variety of other subjects. He decried the extremes of wealth and poverty in Peru; demanded educational opportunities for all, including women; denounced the Army as an obstacle to progress because of its narrow class interests; and preached inter-American unity and solidarity. Clearly, Vigil was, at least by Peruvian standards, a very "modern" author.

He has justifiably been called Peru's greatest nineteenth-century liberal and a precursor of twentieth-century reformers.

ORAZIO A. CICCARELLI

VILLA, FRANCISCO (PANCHO VILLA; b. DOROTEO ARANGO; 1877–1923). Mexican revolutionary leader. Villa's parents were Agustín Arango and Micaela Arámbula, residents of the Río Grande Ranch near San Juan del Río, Durango. About 1894, while he was working as a peon, he wounded the landowner Agustín López Negrete in the defense of his sister; as a result, he fled and adopted the name Pancho Villa. Accounts of his life for the next fifteen years are a mixture of legend and history; he is pictured as a fugitive from justice, a cattle rustler, a worker in the United States, and a soldier in the United States Army during the Spanish-American War. When Francisco I. MADERO visited Chihuahua during his electoral campaign in mid-1910, Villa was already living in that city and was engaged in the livestock business, but shortly afterward he fled after killing a man in a quarrel. In mid-November 1910 he joined the MEXICAN REVOLUTION at the head of 15 men; soon he led 400 well-armed horsemen.

Villa took part in the capture of Ciudad Juárez in May 1911, supporting Pascual Orozco in his disagreements with Madero. The firmness of Madero inspired in Villa a profound admiration for him as well as a strong hatred for Orozco. Villa retired in June 1911, with the rank of colonel, to occupy himself in the cattle and meat business. When Orozco broke with Madero, Villa left the city of Chihuahua with 11 followers; in a short time his force numbered 500. He joined the army of Victoriano HUERTA, which was opposing Orozco, as a scout. As a result of a misunderstanding, Huerta almost had Villa shot, but instead he sent him as a prisoner to Mexico City, from which he escaped after

Francisco Villa (left). [Library of Congress]

Madero's murder. Villa accepted Venustiano CAR-RANZA's Plan of Guadalupe, but on condition that no generals not born in Chihuahua be sent to that state. Carranza named him commander of all the revolutionary forces in Chihuahua. On December 8, 1913, he was appointed provisional Governor of the state. He surrounded himself with former supporters of Madero, among them Gen. Felipe Ángeles, all of whom were viewed with suspicion by Carranza. Although the victory of Tierra Blanca is considered the most nearly perfect in Villa's military career, the capture of Zacatecas from the *huertistas* on June 23, 1914, was politically more significant, for despite the maneuvers of Carranza it put Villa in a position to take Mexico City two weeks before Álvaro OBREGÓN, who did not conquer Guadalajara until July 8, 1914.

Carranza promoted Villa to the rank of division general, but Villa's self-esteem had been wounded because Obregón and Pablo González had been promoted ahead of him. The AGUASCALIENTES CONVENTION proved unable to avoid the rupture between Villa and Carranza. Obregón's subsequent victories at Celaya, Trinidad, and León destroyed Villa as a decisive element in the Revolution (*see* CELAYA, BATTLES OF). The extension of de facto recognition to Carranza's government by the United States on October 19, 1915, and the aid provided by the United States to Plutarco Elías CALLES in the defense of Agua Prieta, which frustrated Villa's attempt to take the city, made him determined to seek vengeance against the United States. On January 10, 1916, a *villista* colonel murdered seventeen Americans near Santa Ysabel, Sonora, and two months later Villa raided the town of Columbus, New Mexico. Gen. John J. Pershing unsuccessfully pursued Villa for approximately a year (*see* PERSHING PUNITIVE EXPEDITION). After the murder of Carranza, Villa surrendered to Adolfo de la Huerta on July 8, 1920, and was given the hacienda of Canutillo in Durango. For the next three years he lived peacefully and prosperously. In 1923 he was murdered in the city of Parral, where he had gone on private business accompanied only by a small escort. His assassination caused a sensation, since the public assumed the complicity of persons such as Obregón or Calles who looked with disfavor upon Villa's sympathy for the presidential candidacy of Adolfo de la Huerta.

Bibliography. Nellie Campobello, *Apuntes sobre la vida militar de Francisco Villa,* Mexico City, 1940; Federico Cervantes, *Francisco Villa y la Revolución,* Mexico City, 1960; Clarence C. Clendenen, *The United States and Pancho Villa: A Study in Unconventional Diplomacy,* Ithaca, N.Y., 1961; Marte R. Gómez, *La reforma agraria en las filas villistas,* Mexico City, 1956; Martín Luis Guzmán, *Memorias de Pancho Villa,* Mexico City, 1938.

MOISÉS GONZÁLEZ NAVARRO

VILLA-LOBOS, HEITOR (1887–1959). Brazilian composer and conductor who achieved in a long career the highest international fame of all Latin American musicians. He wrote in practically all musical genres known in Western art music. He was extremely prolific, and his entire production includes more than 1,000 items, the great majority of them belonging to the mainstream of musical nationalism.

A native of Rio de Janeiro, he early joined the pop-

ular musicians known in Rio as *chorões* (*see* CHÔRO). This participation afforded him a practical knowledge of urban popular music, characterized by the improvisation and variations of simple, sentimental melodies associated with Afro-Brazilian rhythms. His first compositions, written in 1900–1901, were dedicated to and influenced by the *chôros* (for example, *Panqueca* and *Mazurka in D,* for solo guitar). Outside of some training in music theory, cello, and clarinet given by his father, his musical education remained unorthodox. Throughout his life he avoided contacts with the routine of academic teaching. Around 1905 he undertook a series of trips all over Brazil that lasted eight years and resulted in firsthand acquaintance with the rich musical heritage of the rural areas, so strongly present in his mature works. By the time he settled down in Rio in 1913, he had written some fifty-five compositions, among which the *Suite dos Cântigos Sertanejos* (1910), for small orchestra, seems to be the first instance of his elaboration of thematic material derived from folk music sources. From this early period date such varied pieces as the march *Pro pax* for band, the *Suite populaire brésilienne* for guitar, the operas *Aglaia-Izath* and *Elisa,* and a double quintet (manuscript lost), showing the composer's prevailing eclecticism. Although Villa-Lobos was still unaware around 1915 of Stravinsky's experiments, his works up to that time reveal a great tonal instability, thus indicating his desire for harmonic innovation, as Oscar Lorenzo FERNÂNDEZ has shown in "A Contribuição Harmônica de Villa-Lobos para a Música Brasileira," published in the *Boletín Latino-Americano de Música* (April

Heitor Villa-Lobos. [*H. Roger Viollet*]

1946). His friendship with the pianist Artur Rubinstein proved profitable to him, for Rubinstein included many of the composer's works in his concert tours and contributed greatly to the worldwide attention given to the Brazilian composer. Villa-Lobos began using typical Brazilian subjects in his tone poems and ballets of the late 1910s, such as *Saci-Pererê, Uirapurú,* and *Amazonas* (all 1917), and introduced systematically characteristic harmonic and rhythmic elements of popular music as well as tunes of children's songs in his piano pieces, such as *A Prole do Bebê* No. 1 (1918) and *Lenda do Caboclo* (1920), and in his String Quartets No. 3 and No. 4 (1916–1917).

In 1923 Villa-Lobos went to Paris with the intention of making his works known to the Parisian public, but it was only on the occasion of his second trip to the French capital in 1927 that he succeeded in asserting himself. A Villa-Lobos Festival at the Salle Gaveau in October 1927 was remarkably successful. The 1920s were particularly important for him, since he completed the series of the *Chôros,* considered, together with the *Bachianas Brasileiras,* his best contribution to modern music. Inspired by the native background of the *chôros,* he wrote sixteen compositions bearing this title. They are not in chronological order and are intended for the most varied media, from solo guitar (No.1) to full orchestra with mixed chorus (No. 10). The only common stylistic traits involve musical manifestations of various popular and primitive cultural traditions. *Rasga o Coração* (No. 10) reveals the assimilation of the most advanced compositional techniques of the time: predominance of rhythm and percussion instruments, polytonality, and atonality with tone clusters. The 1920s were also the years of Villa-Lobos's piano masterpieces, the *Cirandas* (1926), sixteen pieces of high virtuosity based on children's songs, and *Rudepoema* (1921–1926), dedicated to Rubinstein.

Villa-Lobos's gigantic production was dominated during the last twenty-seven years of his life by the series of *Bachianas Brasileiras,* his last seven symphonies, and his last thirteen string quartets. According to the composer, the *Bachianas* were inspired by the work of Johann Sebastian Bach, which he considered a universal source of music. From that mystic and utopian conception in which Bach appears as the essence of music was born this series of nine pieces. These works were intended not as a stylization of Bach's music but rather as an adaptation with unquestionable liberty of certain baroque contrapuntal procedures applied to Brazilian folk music.

The nationalistic phase of folkloric aspect represents the most original cycle of Villa-Lobos's output, but it also reveals artistic universality through the creation of formal elements suggested by the various popular music traditions. His influence in Brazil has been very strong, but only when a critical thematic catalog of his entire production is available will it be possible to define objectively his place in twentieth-century music.

Bibliography. Luiz Heitor Corrêa de Azevedo, *150 anos de Música no Brasil, 1800–1950,* Rio de Janeiro, 1956; Francisco Curt Lange, "Villa-Lobos, un Pedagogo Creador," *Boletín Latino-Americano de Música,* vol. I, April 1935, pp. 189–196; Vasco Mariz, *Heitor Villa-Lobos, Brazilian Composer,* Washington, 1970; Andrade Muricy, *Villa-Lobos; Uma Interpretação,* Rio de Janeiro, 1961; Museu Villa-Lobos, *Villa-Lobos: Sua Obra,* Rio de Janeiro, 1965; Lisa M. Peppercorn, *Heitor Villa-Lobos: Leben und Werk des brasilianischen Komponisten,* Zurich, 1972; David E. Vassberg, "Villa-Lobos: Music as a Tool of Nationalism," *Luso-Brazilian Review,* vol. VI, no. 2, December 1969, pp. 55–65.

GERARD H. BÉHAGUE

VILLANUEVA, CARLOS RAÚL (1900–   ). Venezuelan architect and urban planner. The son of a diplomat, Villanueva was born in London and studied architecture at the École Nationale des Beaux-Arts in Paris. In 1928 he opened an office in Caracas and became a leader in historical conservation as well as in the design of new buildings. His work has always been in large public commissions; two houses for his own family stand apart from the vast schemes of his other work. The bullring at Maracay (1931), in traditional style, utilizes modern concrete construction. The Escuela Gran Colombia in Caracas (1939) is in geometric modern style, great attention having been paid to functional planning. The first of Villanueva's several low-cost housing projects was El Silencio (1941), and most of his major work in recent years has been great public housing projects such as El Paraíso and 23 de Enero, all in Caracas.

The new University City, begun in 1944, is Villanueva's monument. The campus centers on the large auditorium, the Aula Magna (1952). Its facade is a powerful sculpture of concrete piers above a sheltering concrete marquee. The interior scale and acoustics of the 2,600-seat hall are enhanced by free-form panels by Alexander Calder hung from the walls and ceiling. The integration of painting and sculpture with architecture has been important in Villanueva's work. Those arts are part of the training in the new School of Architecture at the Central University of Venezuela, whose building Villanueva designed and where he is an influential teacher.

TERENCE GRIEDER

VILLARROEL, GUALBERTO (1908–1946). Bolivian army officer and President (December 1943–July 1946). A veteran of the CHACO WAR with Paraguay (1932–1935), Villarroel was a leading figure in a nationalistic military lodge known as Razón de Patria (RADEPA). The coup d'état that brought him to the Presidency was a joint enterprise of RADEPA and the civilian party MOVIMIENTO NACIONALISTA REVOLUCIONARIO (MNR).

Both RADEPA and the MNR were represented in Villarroel's first Cabinet. However, the United States refused to recognize the regime while the MNR remained in the administration, charging that the party was pro-Axis and had contacts with the military regime that had taken power in Argentina in June 1943. Hence the MNR ministers withdrew from the Cabinet for a time, returning only some months after the United States had recognized Villarroel.

The single most important accomplishment of the Villarroel government was its encouragement of unionization of the tin miners. Although the beginnings of a miners' federation had appeared in the late 1930s under President Germán BUSCH, the succeeding conservative governments hampered its further growth. In Villarroel's regime, the Federación Sindical de Trabajadores Mineros became firmly established under the leadership of a charismatic MNR chieftain, Juan LECHÍN. The Villarroel government also took the first step toward encouraging the organization of the Indians, who represented two-thirds to three-fourths of the population. In 1945 it summoned a congress of Indians, at which President Villarroel, the MNR chief Víctor PAZ ESTENSSORO, and others in the government listened for several days to Indian complaints and suggestions.

The Villarroel regime encountered fierce resistance not only from the tin-mining interests, the landlords, and the parties representing them but also from the pro-Communist Partido de la Izquierda Revolucionaria. The opposition was finally able in July 1946 to organize a rebellion, led largely by the market women of La Paz. When the military leaders refused to come to the President's support, mobs attacked the Presidential Palace, threw President Villarroel from the balcony into Plaza Murillo below, and hanged him to a lamppost in front of the palace. Six years later, when the MNR returned to power, that lamppost became a national shrine; a plaque in front of it recounts the martyrdom of Villarroel, and a soldier is on honor guard there twenty-four hours a day.

ROBERT J. ALEXANDER

VILLAURRUTIA, XAVIER (1903–1950). Mexican poet. Born in Mexico City, he began the study of law but abandoned it for literature. His first poems date from 1919. In 1927–1928 he helped edit the review *Ulises*, which was closely in touch with avant-garde trends in Europe and America. He was one of the leaders of the so-called *Contemporáneos* group (1928–1931) and worked for the renovation of the Mexican theater. In 1935 and 1936 he studied at the Yale University Drama School with a Rockefeller scholarship and in 1946 was named professor of acting at the National Drama School. He wrote for the reviews *Letras de México* (1937–1947) and *El Hijo Pródigo* (1943–1946) and in 1948 was awarded a prize for his poem "Canto a la primavera."

Villaurrutia was active as a dramatist, poet, and critic. His first book of poems, *Reflejos* (1926), shows the influence of Ramón LÓPEZ VELARDE, but an individual style had developed by the time of the publication of *Nostalgia de la muerte* (1938), in which his favorite themes of love, night, and death are developed with skill and rigor. Among his most successful plays are *Invitación a la muerte* (written 1940), *La hiedra* (staged 1941), and *La mujer legítima* (staged 1942). His best essays appeared in the collection *Textos y pretextos* (1940). His writings show his close contact with all literary developments.

RACHEL PHILLIPS

VILLEDA MORALES, RAMÓN (1908–1971). President of Honduras (1957–1963). Villeda Morales combined an active political life with a career in medicine. After studying in Honduras and Europe, he practiced pediatrics in Santa Rosa de Copán and later in Tegucigalpa during a long period of continuous National party government in Honduras. He thus managed to avoid exile for his Liberal convictions. *See* LIBERAL PARTY (HONDURAS); NATIONAL OR NATIONALIST PARTY (HONDURAS).

A persuasive orator, "Little Bird," as Villeda was affectionately known, emerged as a leading spokesman of the Honduran Liberals and party chairman in 1949. He founded the party's newspaper, *El Pueblo,* managed a vigorous campaign in the 1953 municipal elections for the Liberal slate, and was named presidential candidate the following year. Villeda won the 1954 race, but his failure to get a majority threw the election into the Congress. Nationalist senators absented themselves from the chamber to prevent a quorum, and in the stalemate that followed Vice President Julio Lozano usurped the government.

Three years later, Villeda came to power under the aegis of the military junta that overthrew Lozano. As President, he mounted a wide-ranging, ambitious developmental program to modernize the country's highway, port, and air terminal facilities. Education and public health received unprecedented attention. Progressive labor regulations and AGRARIAN REFORM legislation were enacted. Treaties were signed incorporating Honduras into the CENTRAL AMERICAN COMMON MARKET.

On October 3, 1963, only two months before scheduled presidential elections would have determined a successor, the chief of the armed forces, Oswaldo LÓPEZ ARELLANO, deposed Villeda to foil an alleged Communist take-over.

Dr. Villeda died of a heart attack in a New York hotel on October 8, 1971, shortly after arriving in the United States to represent his country before the United Nations.

KENNETH V. FINNEY

VILLEGAGNON, NICOLAS DURAND DE (1510–1571). Leader of attempted French colonization in the Bay of Guanabara and founder of the ambitiously named but short-lived Antarctic France. With both Catholic and Protestant support Villegagnon, who had behind him a brilliant military career in Algeria, Italy, and Scotland, left Le Havre in 1555 with settlers and convicts to settle in Brazil, where French brazilwood traders had been active for the past three or four decades. The colony was soon split by religious differences, which grew worse after the arrival in 1557 of Calvinist missionaries from Geneva, in the first missionary activity of Protestants overseas. Villegagnon's attempts to resolve doctrinal disputes only alienated the factions. The French presence meanwhile had galvanized the Portuguese into action, and in 1559 an expeditionary force led by Mem de Sá, the third Governor-General of Brazil, captured and destroyed Fort Coligny. Further military expeditions in 1564–1568 supported from Bahia and Espírito Santo as well as from São Paulo de Piratininga and São Vicente defeated the TUPINAMBÁ, the Amerindian allies of the French, and expelled Portugal's major European competitors from the region. The foundation of São Sebastião de Rio de Janeiro confirmed Portuguese domination.

KENNETH R. MAXWELL

VINCENT, STÉNIO [JOSEPH] (1874–1959). President of Haiti (1930–1941). A member of the mulatto ÉLITE, Vincent was born in Port-au-Prince. He was an able lawyer, a diplomat who represented Haiti in Paris, Berlin, and The Hague, and the founder of two political journals. During the American occupation Vincent served as a senator and as Secretary of State and Minister Plenipotentiary. As a member of the Patriotic Union, he supported the presentation to the United States of a memorial demanding its withdrawal. Although he was a leader of the anti-interventionist Nationalist party, he was never extremely anti-American. His long career revealed a shrewd, pragmatic politician and elitist.

After the resignation of Louis BORNO, Vincent was elected President for a six-year term in November 1930. His tenure was extended for five years by a plebiscite in 1935. When a second extension was suggested in 1941, Vincent decided to retire, claiming ill health as his motive.

During his long tenure, Vincent dealt successfully with the United States. His visit in 1934 to Franklin D. Roosevelt resulted in advancing the date of the withdrawal of the United States Marines. Under him Haiti benefited from more advantageous commercial relations. Vincent's eyesight failed shortly after he left office. He died in Port-au-Prince on September 3, 1959.

JOHN E. BAUR

VIOLENCIA, LA. Civil disorder experienced by Colombia for two decades beginning in the 1940s. The Violencia ("Violence") was characterized by attacks on Liberals in rural areas by Conservative authorities, particularly the police, and by retaliatory actions against Conservatives by Liberal guerrilla bands (*see* CONSERVATIVE PARTY: COLOMBIA; LIBERAL PARTY: COLOMBIA).

Although the causes of the Violencia are exceedingly complex, it was principally political in its origins, stemming from the "inherited hatreds" that traditionally had embittered relations between adherents of Colombia's two major parties. It was also nourished by social and economic tensions which had been accumulating in rural areas for years, especially as a result of increasing population pressure on land resources, and which had received insufficient governmental attention. Participants in the Violencia seemed overwhelmed by the conflict and often committed acts of hideous brutality that defied traditional controls. Such efforts as were made to control and direct the violence in order to achieve significant political or economic changes had little effect.

The Violencia is usually said to have begun during the administration of moderate Conservative Mariano OSPINA PÉREZ, who was elected to the Presidency in 1946. The Liberals had ruled Colombia since 1930, but in 1946 the party was divided because of the unwillingness of many party members to accept the candidacy of left-wing Jorge Eliécer GAITÁN.

On April 9, 1948, while the Ninth International Conference of American States was meeting in Bogotá (*see* BOGOTÁ CONFERENCE), Gaitán was assassinated in the streets of the capital. The immediate result was several days of rioting, known as the BOGOTAZO, which soon spread to the countryside and intensified existing violence. By late 1949 partisan passions had become so inflamed that the Liberals refused to take part in the presidential election held on November 27, 1949, and the ultra-Conservative Laureano GÓMEZ was elected without opposition. As Gómez took steps to impose an authoritarian regime on the country, rural violence continued unabated, approaching a state of civil war.

In June 1953 Gómez was overthrown by the armed forces with the support of the Liberals and many Conservatives, and Lieut. Gen. Gustavo ROJAS PINILLA took power. Some guerrillas surrendered under a guarantee of amnesty, and an attempt was made to bring social services to rural areas. Rojas also placed the police under military jurisdiction. Although the Violencia diminished temporarily, in 1954 more localized but serious fighting broke out and began to spread, as the Army was deployed into regions not under government control.

When Rojas resigned in 1957, the interim military junta again offered amnesty. After 1958 partisan political violence gradually gave way to institutionalized banditry, but by the mid-1960s it had been significantly reduced with the initiation of social and economic programs in rural areas by the army and civilian agencies. Even so, antigovernment guerrillas inspired by the Cuban experience were active at the end of the decade and continued to exist in the 1970s.

Violence occurred throughout most of rural Colombia, except for the Atlantic coast departments and the extreme southwest. It began in the eastern llanos (plains) and later became concentrated in the interior highlands, especially in the departments of Tolima, Caldas, and Valle del Cauca. The number of deaths was about 160,000, though some estimates are as high as 300,000. In addition, thousands of peasants were displaced, frequently selling or abandoning their farms and fleeing to the cities for safety.

GERALD THEISEN

VIRACOCHA. Incorporeal creator god who presided over the Inca empire. All other gods were his surrogates. He created all things in TIAHUANACO, the sacred site on the south shore of Lake Titicaca. Viracocha is sometimes credited with more than one creation. He appears also as a culture hero in a myth in which, in a triune form, he moved north from Tiahuanaco, giving peoples their languages, customs, and means of subsistence. His civilizing mission was completed when he came to Ecuador and there went down to the Pacific and disappeared into its vastness. The Incas believed that he would return and, with his archangelic retinue, would bring the present age to an end. The first Spaniards for a short while were thought to be Viracochas. The name Viracocha Inca was adopted by the ruler Hatun Topa Inca, during whose reign (ca. 1400–1438) the Inca empire was born. *See also* INCAS.

BURR C. BRUNDAGE

VISITA. In colonial Spanish America, an investigation to correct abuses or effect improvements in government. Any official, institution, or territory could be the object of a *visita,* but the decision to institute one and to appoint a royal *visitador* depended in most cases on the COUNCIL OF THE INDIES. To facilitate his getting to the cause of things the *visitador* was granted almost unlimited powers. Once his investigation was finished, he submitted a complete report of his findings to the Council for final action. General *visitas* involving branches of government or territories were rare and were especially difficult to carry out, because the problems were more diffuse and the solutions called for more elusive. In the eighteenth century general *visitas* of three viceroyalties were instituted with a view to making reforms in political organization and administration, defense, the collection of royal revenues, mining, education, and many other aspects of viceregal government. Local *visitas* authorized by the viceroy were limited to investigating reports of blatant illegality and scandal within the viceroyalty.

Potentially, the *visita* was a good instrument for improving the quality of government. As often as not, however, it failed to do so. This may be attributed to defects in the system itself, inadequacies on the part of *visitadores,* and the magnitude and complexity of the problems resulting from absolute and centralized rule carried out at long distance. At least equally responsible for the limited success of many *visitas* was the all-too-human weakness of men more strongly motivated by self-interest than by a spirit of service to King and kingdom. NORMAN MEIKLEJOHN

VODUN (VOODOO; VAUDUN). Syncretic folk religion of most Haitians. Vodun combines Catholic, African, and probably Islamic elements. Its devotees believe that God is paramount but not omnipotent. Since he is too busy for immediate concern with man's affairs, *loa,* or spirits, are vital. Hundreds of these evolved in Dahomey or later in Haiti and are thought to perform good and evil deeds. Their attributes equate them with Christian saints. Possession by *loa* occurs in regular, predictable fashion. Believers say *loa* once were living persons and now may possess a devotee, changing his characteristics. Through serving *loa,* the possessed may gain favors.

The Vodun *houngan* (priest) is central to Haitian rural life. He claims knowledge through visions and dreams and masters herbal lore, divination, and psychotherapy. Haitians resort to *houngans* before any major action, believing that no event lacks spiritual content. Vodun provides supernatural sanction for conduct and contact with ancestors, explains natural events, brings release from anxiety, and provides peasants with music, dance, and drama.

Once revolutionary in opposing slavery, this family-oriented faith does not threaten urban government or seek to improve the peasants' basic status. Since 1804 attempts to stamp out Vodun have failed, for it satisfies peasant needs, which an urbanized Catholicism has not. François DUVALIER tried to politicize Vodun, but it lacks hierarchy and centralization to serve as a political force. However, clear standards for *houngan* competence exist. JOHN E. BAUR

VOLTA REDONDA. Town on the Paraíba River in the state of Rio de Janeiro, Brazil. The name is often employed as a synonym for the government-owned National Steel Mill (Companhia Siderúrgica Nacional; CSN), which is located in Volta Redonda. The CSN was founded in 1941 and immediately began construction of the mill that was expected to make Brazil nearly self-sufficient in iron and steel products. The Volta Redonda site was selected with a view toward military defense as well as for access both to raw materials and to the major markets of São Paulo and Rio de Janeiro. Fifty miles inland behind the SERRA DO MAR, Volta Redonda was immune to attack by sea and yet was connected by rail with its source of coal, the port of Barra Mansa to the south, and the iron mines of Minas Gerais to the north.

When the Volta Redonda works went into operation in 1946, their annual output of some 300,000 tons was larger than the combined production of all private steel mills in Brazil. The facilities at Volta Redonda have been continually expanded. During the administration of President Juscelino KUBITSCHEK (1956–1961), installed capacity nearly doubled, increasing from some 700,000 tons to well over 1.3 million tons per year, and after the revolution of March 31, 1964, capacity and production more than doubled again, to mark Volta Redonda as a symbol of state enterprise in Brazil and the largest integrated iron and steel manufacturing complex in South America. *See also* IRON AND STEEL INDUSTRY (BRAZIL). ROLLIE E. POPPINO

VOODOO. *See* VODUN.

Wagner, Werner

W. R. Grace & Co. (Peru)

WAGNER, WERNER (1927–   ). German-born Argentine composer. Wagner was born in Cologne. When very young he went to Buenos Aires, where he studied composition with Jacobo Ficher. In addition to his career as a composer, he has been active as a manager and as a member of the Argentine Association of Young Composers. His works include two suites for orchestra (1952, 1956), *Poem for Violin and Orchestra* (1953), two string quartets (1959, 1962), and *Música a 12* for chamber ensemble (1968).

JUAN A. ORREGO-SALAS

WALKER, WILLIAM (1824–1860). United States filibuster. Educated as a lawyer in his native state of Tennessee and as a physician in France, Walker scorned both professions for a career as a filibuster. As a California resident shortly after the gold rush, he gathered a band of adventurers and invaded the Mexican territory of Baja California. Despite humiliating failure on that occasion he was ready to try again when a civil war in Nicaragua offered him the opportunity. In June 1855, he arrived in Nicaragua with fifty-eight followers and allied himself to the cause of the *democráticos* (Liberals), who were locked in a struggle with the *legitimistas* (Conservatives). Walker's band, supplemented by other adventurers recruited from the many travelers using the Nicaragua route to and from California, quickly made itself the fulcrum of power. After the death of the *democrático* leader Francisco Castellón, Walker took over as commander of the armed forces, Minister of War, and, in 1856, President. Now, however, the presence of Walker in the highest office of the country awakened a sense of nationalistic unity among Nicaraguans of all political groups and a fear of intervention in the neighboring countries of Central America. In the so-called National War these forces combined to defeat Walker. Help came also from the financier Cornelius Vanderbilt, whose transit route across Nicaragua suffered from Walker's interference. Walker surrendered to a United States naval officer on Nicaraguan soil in May 1857, but made two unsuccessful additional attempts to install himself in power in Nicaragua. He was captured and executed in 1860.

CHARLES L. STANSIFER

WAR FOR CUBAN INDEPENDENCE (1895–1898). The final struggle for Cuban independence began in early 1895 in Oriente Province. It was the result of a combination of factors, among them a spirit of nationalism created by the TEN YEARS' WAR, the failure of Spain to provide much-needed political and constitutional reforms, and the dependence of Cuba's economy on the United States rather than on Spain. Also, José MARTÍ's work in the United States had made the alternatives to independence—autonomy under Spain or annexation to the United States—unpopular in the minds of many Cubans.

Martí was killed in action soon after arriving in Cuba. Control of the revolution then passed to the generals Antonio MACEO, Máximo GÓMEZ, and Calixto García. In contrast to the situation in the Ten Years' War there was little hesitation about carrying the war to the west, where guerrilla tactics were employed. Property was destroyed, and the rural regions lapsed into anarchy, while the insurgents lived off the land, avoided open battle, and remained elusive.

To combat this type of warfare, Spain sent Gen. Valeriano Weyler to take command. He began fighting fire with fire by recruiting Cuban counterguerrillas and by implementing a policy of reconcentration, whereby entire populations were relocated to military areas. The idea was to isolate the rebels and deny them sustenance. Perhaps militarily sound, the policy nevertheless caused the death of thousands of those relocated, hardened the attitude of Cubans against Spain, supplied the material for atrocity stories in the United States press, and provided the excuse for intervention by the United States (April 1898). Spanish defeats in the Philippines and Cuba were followed by the signing of a peace treaty in Paris by Spain and the United States (December 10, 1898). The treaty provided for the independence of Cuba and for the cession of the Philippines, Guam, and Puerto Rico to the United States, which was to pay $20 million for the Philippines. After four years of American military rule under John R. Brooke and Leonard WOOD, Cuba became independent in May 1902, but the United States retained considerable control over the island by means of the PLATT AMENDMENT.

KENNETH F. KIPLE

WAR OF THE PACIFIC (1879–1883). War fought by Bolivia and Peru against Chile; one of the two most serious international conflicts in nineteenth-century Latin American history. The fundamental cause of tension between Chile and its northern neighbors was the situation in the ATACAMA DESERT just north of the 24th parallel, the boundary between Chile and Bolivia fixed by treaty in 1866. Chilean interests had come to predominate in the exploitation of the rich nitrate deposits of the region, the majority of whose population in 1879 was in fact Chilean (*see* NITRATE INDUSTRY: CHILE). In 1878 the Bolivian government of Col. Hilarión Daza imposed a new export tax of 10 centavos per quintal of nitrate. This tax contravened a treaty of 1874 under which Bolivia had agreed to exempt Chilean concerns from additional taxation for twenty-five years. When the main Chilean nitrate enterprise refused to pay the new tax, Daza made arrangements for its confiscation. In order to forestall this, a small Chilean force under Col. Emilio Sotomayor occupied the port of Antofagasta, north of the 24th parallel, in February 1879. Bolivia declared war on Chile on March 1. After a heroic but vain defense of the desert town of Calama, the Bolivians were compelled to withdraw from the Atacama region. Peru was drawn into the conflict, since in 1873 it had signed a secret treaty of alliance with Bolivia. In April, following frenzied but fruitless diplomatic activity, the Chilean government of President Aníbal Pinto formally declared war on both countries.

The first major actions of the war were fought at sea. On May 21, 1879, the Chilean warships *Esmeralda* and *Covadonga,* both of wooden construction, were attacked off Iquique by the Peruvian ironclads *Huascar* and *Independencia.* Although the Chileans were plainly outclassed, the *Esmeralda*'s commander, Capt. Arturo Prat, decided to fight to the end. Prat lost his life during a hopeless boarding operation when the *Esmeralda* was rammed by the *Huascar.* He has been regarded ever since as one of the supreme Chilean heroes. The *Esmeralda* sank, and most of her crew were lost, but by way of compensation the *Covadonga* lured

the *Independencia* onto a nearby reef, where she stuck fast.

The Chilean defeat at Iquique was followed by a Peruvian naval offensive, during which several Chilean ports were bombarded, but the loss of Captain Prat was soon avenged. At the Battle of Cape Angamos (October 8, 1879) the *Huascar* was cornered by the Chilean Fleet and forced to surrender after her gallant commander, Adm. Miguel Grau, had been killed in action. As a result of this victory, Chile gained command of the sea. This was to prove a decisive factor in the remainder of the war, for Chile was now in a position to go on to the offensive against the Allies.

The first major campaign on land took place in the Peruvian desert province of Tarapacá. Soon after the Battle of Cape Angamos, a Chilean force of more than 9,000 men set sail from Antofagasta, landed at Pisagua, and quickly consolidated its hold on the province. The Allies were obliged to fall back on Tacna-Arica. The reverses suffered in Tarapacá brought significant political changes in both countries. Daza was overthrown in Bolivia, while in Peru a popular and energetic war leader, Nicolás de PIÉROLA, rose to power as dictator.

The second major land campaign of the war began early in 1880, when a Chilean army of more than 12,000 men, under Gen. Manuel Baquedano, landed at Ilo, defeated the Peruvians at Los Angeles, near Moquegua, and marched southward through the desert to Tacna. The Allied forces were decisively beaten in the Battle of Campo de la Alianza (May 26, 1880), and at this point Bolivia abandoned the conduct of the war to Peru. Having taken Tacna, the Chileans moved down the railway line to the port of Arica. The town's strongly fortified 350-foot cliff top, the Morro, was widely believed to be impregnable, but the Chileans took fifty-five minutes to capture it, in a series of ferocious assaults on June 7. Col. Francisco Bolognesi, the Peruvian defender of the Morro, was shot by the victorious Chileans. Among those who fought on the Peruvian side in the battle was a future President of Argentina, Roque SAENZ PEÑA.

With Chile now in control of both the Bolivian and the Peruvian nitrate provinces, the United States government attempted to end the war by bringing representatives of the belligerent states together on board the cruiser *Lackawanna* off Arica (October 1880). The failure of this conference and repeated cries of "On to Lima!" from Chilean public opinion compelled the Pinto government to act against its own inclinations and organize a third campaign. At the end of 1880 a Chilean army of more than 26,000 men disembarked on the Peruvian coast to the south of Lima. General Baquedano, the victor of Tacna-Arica, was once again in command. Piérola had prepared two main lines of defense for the Peruvian capital. The first of these, at Chorrillos, was overrun by the Chileans on January 13, 1881. The second, Miraflores, fell two days later. Both battles were extremely bloody. Chilean losses totaled around 5,000 men; Peru lost perhaps twice that number. Lima surrendered and was immediately occupied by Chilean troops. A certain amount of looting occurred. Piérola withdrew to the interior, where his authority soon evaporated.

The war continued in a lower key for more than two years after the occupation of Lima. In the interior of

Peru the Chileans fought intermittently against guerrilla forces organized by such Peruvian leaders as Col. Andrés CÁCERES, the "wizard of the Andes." On July 9–10, 1882, a Chilean garrison of 79 men at Concepción, near Jauja, was surrounded by some 2,000 Peruvians and wiped out. But following the Chilean victory over Cáceres's forces at Huamachuco (July 10, 1883), it became glaringly apparent that no Peruvian leader, however intrepid, could reverse the result of the war. The Peruvian government bowed to the inevitable and accepted the stiff Chilean terms for peace. A treaty was duly signed at Ancón on October 20, 1883, after which the remaining Chilean occupation forces left for home. Peru ceded the province of Tarapacá to Chile, "unconditionally and in perpetuity," and handed over Tacna and Arica for a period of ten years, following which there was to be a plebiscite to determine the future status of those territories. No plebiscite was in fact organized. Chile kept Tacna and Arica beyond the stipulated time, and relations between the two republics were seriously embittered for nearly half a century. Not until 1929 was a compromise solution reached: Chile retained Arica, while Tacna reverted to Peru. *See also* TACNA-ARICA QUESTION.

The negotiation of a final settlement between Chile and Bolivia proved more thorny. A truce signed at Valparaíso on April 4, 1884, allowed Chile to remain in de facto control of the Bolivian Atacama. (The government of President José Manuel BALMACEDA in fact placed the territory under normal Chilean administration as the province of Antofagasta in 1888.) A full peace treaty was not concluded until October 20, 1904, when Chile agreed, among other things, to build a railroad from Arica to La Paz in return for Bolivia's final cession of the Atacama Desert and littoral. Bolivia thus forfeited its access to the sea and became a landlocked nation.

Bibliography. Diego Barros Arana, *La guerra del Pacífico,* 2 vols., Santiago, 1880–81; Gonzalo Bulnes, *Guerra del Pacífico,* 3 vols., Santiago, 1911–19; W. J. Dennis, *Tacna and Arica,* New Haven, Conn., 1931; V. G. Kiernan, "Foreign Interests in the War of the Pacific," *Hispanic American Historical Review,* vol. XXXV, no. 1, February 1955, pp. 14–36; Sir Clements Markham, *The War between Peru and Chile, 1879–1882,* London, 1882; Donald E. Worcester, "Naval Strategy in the War of the Pacific," *Journal of Inter-American Studies,* vol. V, no. 1, January 1963, pp. 31–37.   SIMON COLLIER

WASHINGTON MEETING (1964). Ninth Meeting of Consultation of Ministers of Foreign Affairs of the republics of the ORGANIZATION OF AMERICAN STATES (OAS). Convening in Washington, D.C., on July 21–26, 1964, as the organ of consultation in the application of the Inter-American Treaty of Reciprocal Assistance (RIO TREATY), the meeting considered the charge that the Cuban regime of Fidel CASTRO had conspired to overthrow the freely elected Venezuelan government of Rómulo BETANCOURT. An OAS investigating committee had confirmed that in 1963 Cuba had shipped a large quantity of arms to be used by Venezuelan guerrillas, presumably to disrupt the presidential election of that year. By a vote of fifteen to four, with one abstention, the meeting agreed that the OAS members should suspend diplomatic relations with Cuba and curtail all trade with that country except in foodstuffs, medicines, and medical equipment sent for humanitarian reasons. By the OAS Charter the vote was binding on all members. (The OAS had previously, at the PUNTA DEL ESTE MEETING in 1962, suspended Cuba from the Organization.) Mexico took the lead in arguing against the suspension of diplomatic relations, maintaining its traditional position that diplomatic recognition should imply neither approval nor disapproval of a government and that to withhold it for political reasons amounted to unwarranted intervention in the internal affairs of a country. Bolivia, Chile, and Uruguay voted with Mexico against the measure, and Argentina abstained. By the end of 1964, however, all but Mexico had withdrawn diplomatic recognition from Cuba.

RODNEY D. ANDERSON

WATERMELON RIOT. Racial disorder in Panama City (April 15, 1856) in which sixteen Americans and two Panamanians were killed. Establishments belonging to Americans were looted, and property of the United States–owned PANAMA RAILROAD was pillaged.

The disturbance began after a rowdy American transient, Jack Oliver, took a slice of watermelon from a Negro vendor but refused to pay. Oliver eventually drew a pistol, which was seized and fired by an onlooker. Soon afterward armed blacks ran wild through the area where nearly 4,000 American travelers had barricaded themselves in commercial firms and railway buildings. The state Governor, Francisco de Fábrega, failed to quell the melee, and, according to the American version, his police sided with local people firing on the besieged Americans.

An official report on the riot was made by United States Consul Amos B. Corwine, who urged American military intervention in the isthmus until adequate protection existed and reparations had been made. Accordingly, a detachment of 160 Marines landed on September 19 in Panama City, occupying the railroad station for three days, in the first armed intervention under a provision of the BIDLACK TREATY (1846) with New Granada (Colombia). That instrument gave the United States the right to intervene in order to guarantee "the perfect neutrality" of the isthmus, but the United States government now interpreted the provision as a right to intervene against internal disorders as well. The United States sued in the courts of New Granada, which after nine years of litigation awarded damages of more than $412,000 to the railway and other claimants.

LARRY L. PIPPIN

WATER WITCH INCIDENT. In 1852 the U.S.S. *Water Witch,* commanded by Thomas Jefferson Page, was chosen by the United States government to explore the RÍO DE LA PLATA system. She left port early in 1853 and after preliminary work reached Asunción in October. There the Americans were cordially received. They pressed north, steaming as far as Corumbá in Brazilian Mato Grosso. Based at Asunción, Page spent the year 1854 charting the waters of the Paraguay River and its tributaries. As a result of diplomatic difficulties with the Paraguayan dictator Carlos Antonio LÓPEZ, he later changed his base to Corrientes. Unaware that López had just closed Paraguayan waters to foreign warships, Page sent Lieut. William Jeffers north again on the *Water Witch,* and on February 1, 1855, the ship was fired upon by the Paraguayan battery at Itapirú. The helmsman was killed, and Jeffers returned fire but withdrew. In 1858 President James Buchanan was given funds by the United States Congress to outfit an expedition of retaliation. When part of the large punitive force reached Asunción late that year, López was conciliatory, and a few months later a treaty guaranteeing free navigation of the Paraguay River was signed.

JOHN HOYT WILLIAMS

WELLES, SUMNER (1892–1961). American diplomat and statesman. One of the architects of the GOOD NEIGHBOR POLICY under President Franklin D. Roosevelt, Welles was born in New York into an old and prominent family and graduated from Harvard University in 1914. After he had served extensively in Latin America as a career foreign service officer, Roosevelt appointed him Assistant Secretary of State in 1933. In the next decade he not only acted as a major Latin American policy adviser to Roosevelt but also was an important administration spokesman on international policy in the critical years preceding and during World War II. He is best known, however, for his role in developing the Good Neighbor policy of the Roosevelt administration.

Welles held that the inter-American system should be based on a "recognition of actual and not theoretical equality between the American Republics" and advocated "complete forbearance from interference by any republic in the domestic concerns of any other." He frequently served as a special envoy to Latin America. One of the best-known instances was his appointment as Ambassador to Cuba in 1933. He was instrumental in establishing the interim government headed by Dr. Carlos Manuel de Céspedes after the brutal regime of Gerardo MACHADO was overthrown in August. When Céspedes was replaced by Dr. Ramón GRAU SAN MARTÍN in September, Welles persuaded Roosevelt and Secretary of State Cordell Hull to withhold recognition of the new government. Whether Welles took this stand because the Grau regime was too radical to maintain order, as his cables to Washington indicated, or because he felt personally affronted by the coup against the government he had so strongly supported, is difficult to say. In any event, the Grau regime was replaced by one more agreeable to the United States shortly after Welles resumed his position in the State Department in December 1933. He resigned from the Department of State in 1943, reportedly over policy disagreements with Hull. Welles was the author of several books, including a two-volume history of the Dominican Republic, *Naboth's Vineyard: The Dominican Republic, 1844–1924* (1928).

RODNEY D. ANDERSON

WHEELWRIGHT, WILLIAM (1798–1873). North American entrepreneur. Born in Newburyport, Massachusetts, and educated at Andover Academy, Wheelwright went to sea at an early age. In 1823 his ship was wrecked on the coast of the province of Buenos Aires, and henceforth he was to become intimately connected with the economic development and modernization of Argentina, Chile, Peru, and Ecuador. Wherever he went, he established friendly relations with politicians, the military, and intellectuals. For a few years in the 1820s he served as United States Consul in Guayaquil

and participated in the coastal trade between Panama and Valparaíso. After he moved to Valparaíso in 1829, he revealed great entrepreneurial talents and energy. He founded immigrant colonies, improved the ports of Buenos Aires, Caldera, and Guayaquil, built gas or water works for Valparaíso, Copiapó, and Callao, and installed lighthouses and buoys along the Pacific coast of South America. In 1835, with the aid of British capital and foreign merchants in Chile, Peru, and Ecuador, he organized the Pacific Steam Navigation Company. The line was to serve the Pacific coast of South America and to connect with a railroad at the Isthmus of Panama. The first of four steamers, all built in Bristol, arrived in 1840, and they were allowed to sail beyond Callao to Panama in 1845. In 1855 the ARGENTINE CONFEDERATION contracted with Wheelwright and José de Buschenthal for the construction of a trans-Andean railroad connecting the Atlantic with the Pacific Ocean at Caldera. Actual work on the Rosario-Córdoba segment, authorized by the administration of Bartolomé MITRE, began in 1863, and the task was completed in 1870 at a cost of £6,400 per mile. Three years later the stretch from Buenos Aires to Ensenada was completed.

JOSEPH T. CRISCENTI

WILLIAMS, ALBERTO (1862–1952). Argentine composer. Born in Buenos Aires of British and Basque descent, he died there at the age of eighty-nine after an active life dedicated to composing, conducting, teaching, and writing poetry. He studied in the Paris Conservatory with Georges Mathias (piano) and César Franck (composition), among others. His early works are markedly French in character, but he later moved to a deliberate use of Argentine folk melodies and rhythms and then to the establishment of an idiom identified with his native country's vernacular by means of a subtle assimilation of its folk and popular music. He wrote a fair amount of orchestral music, including nine symphonies, a few sonatas for solo strings and piano, and an extended list of solo piano music and songs, in addition to textbooks dealing with theoretical aspects of composition and piano teaching.

JUAN A. ORREGO-SALAS

WILLIAMS, AMANCIO (1913–   ). Argentine architect. Williams has been one of the creative influences in South American architecture despite a paucity of constructed works. He studied at the University of Buenos Aires and was associated there with the Austral movement in the late 1930s. Williams's architecture has developed on the principles of Le Corbusier. The house built for his father, Alberto WILLIAMS, in Mar del Plata in 1945 is his best-known work. It is a long rectangle riding on a shallow arch over a ravine. The interior is flowing open space with continuous strip windows. Williams's unconstructed project of 1948 for an office building in which the blocks are suspended on cables within a colossal steel frame remains an impressive scheme. He has also done important designs for an airport and an auditorium, neither of which has been constructed.

TERENCE GRIEDER

WILSON, HENRY LANE (1857–1932). American politician and diplomat. Born into a well-to-do Indiana family, he became prominent in Republican politics in the state of Washington and was appointed Minister to

Chile (1897–1905) and Belgium (1905–1909) and Ambassador to Mexico (1909–1913). Although his tenure in Chile was not without accolades, his term as Ambassador to Mexico was surrounded by controversy. His main concern in Mexico was the expansion and protection of American business interests, which had grown in value to more than $1 billion by 1910. As he had developed a cordial working relationship with the President of Mexico, Porfirio DÍAZ, he was apprehensive about the anti-Díaz movement led by Francisco I. MADERO. His dispatches to the Department of State from June 1910 until the triumph of the *maderista* revolt in May 1911 show an increasing dislike and distrust of Madero. This attitude became even more pronounced during the Madero Presidency (1911–1913), especially when it became clear that the revolution of 1910 (*see* MEXICAN REVOLUTION) had unleashed anti-American sentiments that Madero would not or could not control.

Wilson welcomed the conservative Victoriano HUERTA–Díaz revolt against Madero in February 1913 and admitted publicly that he had been in contact with the rebels prior to their victory, a flagrant violation of good faith with the government to which he was accredited. Madero was captured and executed shortly thereafter by Huerta's troops, an act of brutality with which Wilson has become associated because of his refusal to intercede with Huerta to guarantee Madero's life. Despite the urging of Ambassador Wilson, the newly inaugurated United States administration of President Woodrow Wilson refused to recognize the Huerta regime and, obviously dissatisfied with him, accepted his resignation in October 1913. In his *Diplomatic Episodes in Mexico, Belgium and Chile* (1927), Wilson defended his actions as being in the best interests of the United States.

RODNEY D. ANDERSON

WOMEN. The history of women in Latin America is as diverse as the area's twenty varied societies. The historical roles, functions, and values of Latin America's women are subject to variables determined by place, time, ruralism, urbanization, society, the economy, secularism, religion, race, class, individual character, and family. To make generalizations about Latin American women from these variables, their position in education, the economy, the law, society, and politics must be examined.

Position to 1850. Women of each of Latin America's three races responded to contact with males and social groups of alien cultures in ways peculiar to their own cultures. Pre-Columbian Amerindian women of many indigenous societies had been accustomed to dominating their economies or to wielding extensive influence within their households and larger kin groups. On the other hand, Amerindian women had minimal political power and were either peripheral to or barred from most religious-ceremonial functions.

The ascribed social roles and actual behavior of women were separate from their basic sexual roles in marriage and motherhood. In terms of sexual behavior women also served other purposes. Among some Amerindian groups premarital virginity was highly prized for the economic and social alliances that marriage with an untouched maiden could effect. Among others premarital virginity had little import; indeed, the extensive GUARANÍ language–group tribes of present-day Paraguay and Brazil seemed to prefer not to wait for marriage but rather sealed alliances by giving virgin girls to their new allies. This friendly arrangement was one way by which Iberians solved the problem of the scarcity of their own women, but it also was the source of European condemnation of the "promiscuity" of Amerindians.

Sex and economics were often commingled in pre- and post-Columbian America. Slavery was an institution whereby several Indian groups had paid tribute to local overlords, and the practice continued after their contact with Iberians. Female slaves were sold to Iberians to perform numerous functions; many became the concubines of their masters, while others served at domestic and field tasks. Regardless of the means of acquisition—gift, purchase, tribute, persuasion, force—Amerindian women performed for their male overlords basic functions in a "womanless" Iberian society. Throughout the several centuries of colonial rule and the first century of independence Indian women and their offspring, in either casual or formal alliances, contributed from their cultures to the formation of mestizo societies, particularly in Mexico, Middle America, the Andean countries, and parts of the Río de la Plata region.

The scarcity of Iberian women in areas in which Indians did not predominate, particularly in plantation societies, was met by the importation of African females in the shipments of slaves to the New World. The treatment and position of females of African ancestry in the New World had much to do with the proportion of female to male imports. Planters preferred males to females, noting that females were less economical as labor units during pregnancy, postparturition, and child raising, and slavers normally imported two men for each woman. Since female slaves were knowledgeable about abortive and contraceptive techniques, they had fewer children. Nor did planters encourage either a high birth rate or a low rate of infant mortality.

African females in Latin America functioned both as slaves and as freedwomen, most often in domestic service. In such areas as Brazil, Colombia, Venezuela, and the Spanish Caribbean the small percentage of black females relative to African males, the fact that black females generally performed domestic functions, and the relative scarcity of white females worked to the black females' advantage. The black woman was accorded a higher status than her male counterpart and easier entrée into "white" society, and she experienced less discrimination than that shown black or mulatto males. Numerous scholars have recorded that black women, especially mulatto women, seemed to hold a special sexual fascination for Iberian and Ibero-American males.

Most African females, like their Amerindian sisters, usually had exerted considerable influence and even control over economic activities and household functions in their local groups, but ordinarily they were less involved in political and religious matters. To the degree that they were able to function in the New World as they had in their own African environment, they continued to perform in their ascribed roles. Usually their functions were determined by their status; slave women were responsible for domestic work, child rearing, and the like, while freedwomen and free black or mulatto women usually worked as street vendors, laundresses, bakers, and prostitutes. In Haiti, Cuba, Venezuela, Colombia, Ecuador, Peru, and especially Brazil, African women often controlled the production, distribution, and sale of market produce. Furthermore, in many of these societies and particularly in Brazil, black and mulatto women dominated socioreligious life (as they still do) by their roles as *maes de santos* in religious cults of African origin. Like their lower-class Amerindian counterparts, black women and their offspring through either casual or formal alliances contributed immeasurably to the formation of several Latin American societies. *See also* NEGRO IN BRAZIL; NEGRO IN SPANISH AMERICA.

The highest legal and social rankings in Latin American society accrued to males of Iberian ancestry and, by extension, to their women. Although there is little doubt that, especially in early generations, Iberian females were at a premium, the actual ratio (10:1) of male/female emigrants obscures the fact that actual sexual proportions in New World societies must have been closer because of the high mortality rate of males. Nonetheless, as with Amerindian and African women, Iberian females present paradoxes to the observer. Lower-class women seemed to enjoy fewer restraints on their social behavior and greater influence in economic activities than did their upper-class counterparts. Although both lower- and upper-class Iberian women tended to exert a significant amount of control over their households, upper-class women seemed to be more cloistered from mundane activities than their lower-class cousins. Evidence which would explain such paradoxes in status and rights, in theory and practice, and which would help us to understand why women's sexual role is only one factor among the many that define her situation in society is still wanting. The greater freedom accorded to women in the working classes may have stemmed from the fact that their tasks and their husbands' occupations often took them out of their homes. A different mode of sexual behavior for such women may have evolved because their work in fields, shops, and, later, factories put them into more frequent and closer contact with men than was normally the case for upper-class women.

By the end of the eighteenth century the American empires of Spain and Portugal had come under the influence of the Enlightenment, which served as a purveyor of concepts of liberty and equality (*see* ENLIGHTENMENT: BRAZIL; ENLIGHTENMENT: SPANISH AMERICA). The former ideal was expressed in the nineteenth-century independence movements, which resulted in the breaking of political ties between Latin American nations and their mother countries. The ideal of equality later found expression in matters of education, quickening social consciousness, religious and political freedoms, and discussions on the position of women. This last aspect was particularly evident in nineteenth-century Argentina, Chile, Peru, Mexico, and Cuba.

In general terms, prior to the middle of the nineteenth century Latin America's women, regardless of class, seem to have exerted considerable influence within their households; some enjoyed a modicum of economic input either through domination of economic ventures or as transmitters of properties, and a few occasionally dominated their larger kin groups either by force of personality or by virtue of their family's position. On the other hand, women were bereft of political power, rarely were part of the administrative machinery, and often were victims rather than beneficiaries of legal measures purportedly enacted on their behalf.

Position since 1850. Starting in the mid-nineteenth century, Latin American societies were affected by the triple processes of modernization, industrialization, and urbanization. Demands for an expanded labor force engendered new ideas and attitudes and contributed toward alterations in the societal perceptions of women. A greater number of schools opened their doors to girls as educators conceded that girls were educable and had the right to be educated. Laws were enacted that accorded women basic human rights and guarantees of civic liberties and laid the groundwork for increased female participation in political processes. In all these areas Argentina and Chile set examples for their neighbors.

By the first decade of the twentieth century Latin American women had begun to emerge from traditional patterns of life into new social, economic, political, civic, and cultural identities. They faced pressures on the customary pattern of male-female relationships in terms both of ascribed roles and of actual behavior. Changes that accompanied urbanization, modernization, and industrialization altered the living and working situations of many Latin American families and, consequently, of their women.

Education. Latin American nations have placed relatively few formal restrictions on women's access to education in this century, but conditions differ in various areas and in the educational opportunities available to men and women. Functional literacy and general intellectual achievement are much higher in urban than in rural sectors. Accordingly, the functional literacy and general intellectual achievement of women are much higher in urban areas, particularly those of Argentina, Chile, Uruguay, Mexico, and Cuba, than they are in the countryside. Education of the male has always taken precedence over education of the female in Latin America, and the ratios of male/female literacy therefore are in proportion to the actual educational opportunities available to each sex.

Argentina and Chile have been more the exception than the rule in Latin America regarding literacy and higher education for professional training. For example, in 1968 only 80.6 percent of Chile's male population was literate, whereas 88.1 percent of the women were literate; women comprised 46.1 percent of the university population, one of the highest percentages in the world. Furthermore, Chilean and Argentine women have done extremely well at the professional level; in both countries they comprise 20 to 55 percent in such fields as law, medicine, and dentistry. In other countries, such as Peru and Colombia, the figures are lower, although in recent years most Latin American countries have adopted a relatively vigorous policy to obliterate illiteracy. In general women, especially those of the lower-class laboring force, possess a much lower educational attainment than do their male counterparts. Much of the education adopted for these women is in the area of practical education. *See also* EDUCATION (PRIMARY AND SECONDARY); EDUCATION (UNIVERSITY).

Civic rights. Until the twentieth century Latin America's laws restricted women's basic rights, and men were granted the right to administer property and to supervise family welfare. After 1900 Chile, Argentina, and Uruguay led the way in granting women suffrage, in legalizing civil marriage, in upholding the right of women to apply for divorce, and in providing for the fair and equitable distribution of property. Even in conservative Ecuador, where wives are still considered legally incapable of entering into any property or commercial transaction, women are now allowed to file for divorce, although divorce is generally frowned upon there.

All these formal civic rights and restrictions primarily affect women of the upper and middle classes and, in racially mixed societies, the white population. The lower classes, regardless of color, seem to have a code of their own, since they usually cannot afford the cost of legal trappings for marriage, divorce, or other ventures that comprise civic rights. The lower classes formalize relationships to a much lesser extent than the upper classes and are seldom able to afford counsel for any legal matters. Among the lower classes the tenuousness of personal relationships tends to thrust the female into a position of exaggerated responsibility vis-à-vis her family, and she often assumes the role of both father and mother for her family in matters of civic rights.

Economics. In contemporary Latin America the employment and advancement of women workers have depended generally on the rate of social and economic advance of their countries as well as on the conditions under which all workers must function. Little has been done to train women for industrial tasks except in nations such as Argentina and Brazil where industrial development is important. Attitudes regarding the choice of workers remain very strong: certain tasks are considered suitable only for women, and others only for men. Furthermore, the lack of facilities to train women in industrial jobs has caused employers to consider them incapable of performing particular tasks. All these factors have resulted in and reinforced the practice of unequal pay for equal work.

According to reports of the United Nations and other international agencies, women in Latin America are less active economically in comparison with men than are women in any major area of the world. Latin American females as a whole comprise only 13 percent of the area's labor force; of those actively employed 40 percent work in domestic activities, while the rest are in retail work, office employment, primary school education, and other service sectors. In addition, a much larger group (percentage unknown) of women are engaged in agricultural work. Indeed, this is the largest source of employment, paid or unpaid, for females, although conditions vary from country to country. For example, some 32 percent of Peru's female workers are in agricultural activities, while in Chile the figure is only 4.7 percent. Apparently very few married Latin American women are employed (perhaps only 10 percent), so that the great majority of the paid female labor force are unmarried and contribute either to the support of parents and siblings or to that of their own families from informal alliances.

Paradoxically, Latin America boasts a high proportion of women in professions in comparison with the United States. Argentina, Chile, and Uruguay have substantial numbers of female doctors, lawyers, and professors. Females comprise about one-fifth of Argentina's doctors and lawyers, about two-fifths of its pharmacists, about one-third of its architects, and about one-half of its biochemists and dentists. Even in poor and highly rural Paraguay women comprise about two-thirds of the dentists, one-fourth of the doctors, and two-thirds of the pharmacists. This situation is due to the traditional belief that professional work indicates membership in the upper classes and also to "cosmopolitan" families' encouragement of their daughters' entrance into professional life (in addition, of course, to marriage and motherhood).

Despite the low percentages of women in the economically active labor force, more are now being employed, especially as the exodus from farms to towns continues. Yet there are some negative aspects to the growth in female employment. Women are employed often because they will accept lower wages than men and demand fewer employee benefits. Furthermore, the less white a woman is, racially or culturally, the lower her wages are likely to be. Lack of vocational training also makes women workers more vulnerable than men in matters of wages, job security, benefits, and the like. Also, women are still restricted by cultural customs and male prejudice to "traditional" occupations.

Politics. Despite a history of some female economic involvement Latin America has been notoriously conservative in welcoming women to political life. Although it is true that historically most Latin American nations circumscribed the political activities of their general populations, politics is the male stronghold that women have been slowest to breach. Now Latin American women are becoming increasingly active, particularly through associations, in the political life of their nations.

Some countries have moved further along this road than others. Argentina, which has long enjoyed female political participation and boasts a lengthy list of legislative acts favoring such participation, had made much progress, which Juan D. PERÓN and Eva PERÓN brought to culmination by giving women the franchise and by involving lower-class females in active political life. In Chile there is substantial female involvement in politics but to a lesser extent than in Argentina. Participation in politics, especially in elections, tends to increase among *chilenas* as socioeconomic status increases. In Mexico political privileges became most significant for women during the administration of Lázaro CÁRDENAS (1934–1940), who permitted the woman's wing of the revolutionary party to fight for suffrage, which was eventually granted in 1953. In Colombia, however, political education for women has remained negligible, and in neighboring Ecuador, where all voters must be literate, voting is compulsory for eligible men but optional and not particularly encouraged for women.

What does this variation portend for Latin American women? If we consider that political power is the ultimate measure of equality between the sexes, then Latin American females have far to go. Involvement in political parties is low, although increasing numbers of women have joined parties in most of Latin America. However, the tendency in most of the nations to separate women into their own cadres within parties has the effect of lessening their potential influence on party policy. Women have the right to hold political office, but they are usually found in small and insignificant numbers in the legislative, judicial, and especially executive branches of the government.

Social status. Prior to the twentieth century few women of the upper classes were seen at public affairs, and when they were, they were seldom alone. The seemingly free and open life of lower-class women was frowned upon. In marital relations the paterfamilias controlled the legal and social life of his wife and other females in his family, acquiring title to any properties that had been brought to the marriage and deciding every aspect of woman's social, economic, and political life. Juxtaposed to this condition was the ideal notion that woman was the core of home and society; to her all homage and respect were due, and to her accrued a substantial amount of authority over her family.

Industrialization, urbanization, modernization, and the accompanying changes these events implied for economic, political, and social mobility have significantly increased life's options for Latin American women. Cities have provided greater opportunities than the countryside for change by offering a freer, more relaxed atmosphere for unchaperoned contact between the sexes. As a result, traditional sexual attitudes and relationships have been weakened.

The growth of a middle class and the increasing number of females of all classes in the work force mean that women are earning wages and thereby achieving some freedom from familial economic constraints. Middle- and upper-class girls who work thus have leverage to extricate them from family pressures. Their wages also allow them to purchase birth control devices and to afford abortions and so escape unwanted marriages.

Changes in social status and mobility are slower among lower-class women because Latin American society makes it difficult for the masses to acquire elite status. In sociosexual terms, however, lower-class women have less distance to travel than other females in their societies, perhaps because the pattern of their social behavior has been legitimized as it has become more acceptable, and more often practiced, among middle- and upper-class women. On the other hand, since poorer women have less opportunity for economic advancement and political participation than middle- and upper-class women, their social situation is less likely to change.

In the Spanish Caribbean and in Brazil sexual-social relationships are complicated by color as well as by class. A wealthy mulatto woman of good family has a better opportunity to overcome her inferior position than has a black of similar standing.

Despite advances in attitudes and in daily practice, Latin American females of all classes still are defined and define themselves in terms of men and their relationships to men rather than in terms of their own identity. Even in Cuba it appears that advances toward equality are tempered whenever they are inconsistent with the goals of the CUBAN REVOLUTION. Whenever that occurs, it is certain that the woman remains secondary to any man.

Bibliography. Charles R. Boxer, *Race Relations in the Portuguese Colonial Empire, 1415–1810,* Oxford, 1963; Philip D. Curtin, "The Slave Trade and the Atlantic Basin: Intercontinental Perspectives," in Nathan I. Huggins, Martin Kilson, and Daniel Fox (eds.), *Key Issues in the Afro-American Experience,* New York, 1971, vol. I, pp. 74–95; Richard Konetzke, "La emigración de la mujeres españolas a América durante le época colonial," *Revista Internacional de la Sociología,* vol. III, 1945; Ann M. Pescatello, "The Female in Ibero-America: An Essay on Research Bibliography and Research Directions," *Latin American Research Review,* vol. VII, no. 2, Summer, 1972, pp. 125–141; Ann M. Pescatello (ed.), *Female and Male in Latin America: Essays,* Pittsburgh, 1973.

ANN M. PESCATELLO

WOOD, LEONARD (1860–1927). American army officer and administrator. Wood graduated from Harvard Medical School in 1884 and began his military service as a surgeon with the United States Army in the Southwest. He was transferred to Washington in 1895, became President McKinley's physician, and established a close friendship with Theodore Roosevelt. In 1898 Wood and Roosevelt formed the 1st United States Volunteer Cavalry (Rough Riders), with Wood in command. Such was Wood's success as a military officer that he was awarded a battlefield promotion to brigadier general, followed by appointment as Governor of the eastern sector of Cuba, promotion to major general, and, finally, appointment as military Governor of all Cuba, a post he held until authority was transferred to the newly formed government of Cuba on May 20, 1902. As military Governor, Wood carried on a massive public works campaign of improving sanitation, building railroads and highways, establishing public schools, reforming the judiciary, and eliminating mosquitoes, which had recently been discovered to be the carriers of yellow fever. *See also* FINLAY, Carlos.

Wood's next assignment, in 1903, was to the Philippines, where he was appointed Governor of Moro Province to pacify opposition to the American occupation. He headed the Philippine Division of the Army from 1906 to 1908. Upon his return to the United States he was placed in charge of the Department of the East (1908–1910, 1914–1917). During his tenure as Chief of Staff of the Army (1910–1914) his outspoken criticism of administration slowness in preparation for World War I caused President Woodrow Wilson to bypass him for Gen. John J. Pershing as leader of the American Expeditionary Force. After the death of Theodore Roosevelt in 1919, Wood became a leading candidate for the Republican nomination for President in 1920. Although he won in the primaries, he lost the nomination to Warren G. Harding. In 1921 Wood was appointed Governor General of the Philippines, a position he filled until shortly before his death.

RICHARD B. GRAY

WORKERS CONFEDERATION OF PERU. *See* CONFEDERACIÓN DE TRABAJADORES DEL PERÚ.

W. R. GRACE & CO. (PERU). W. R. Grace & Co. is the foreign concern with the longest history in Peru. It was formed by William Russell Grace (1832–1904), an Irish immigrant who entered the GUANO trade in the 1850s. By 1862 he had developed an import-export business between Callao and New York, and he then rapidly expanded the company's sphere of activities. In 1871 it acquired its first industrial plant in Peru, the Vitarte textile mill near Lima, and within ten years it came also to control vast sugar estates and the first large-scale sugar-refining plant in Peru. Although Grace left Peru in the 1860s and went on to become the first Roman Catholic mayor of New York in 1880, the business he founded continued to expand until it had spread over much of the west coast of South America. By 1935 in Peru alone it controlled forty-three companies, most of which it owned outright. Its activities came to encompass a near monopoly over passenger and freight traffic between the United States and Peru, half ownership of Pan American Airways, sugar and cotton estates, sugar refineries, paper and textile manufacturing plants, light and power properties, and petroleum resources.

As one of Peru's largest employers the company had a relatively good record. Moreover, as one of the largest foreign concerns it attempted to identify itself with Peruvian national interests, a policy reflected in the company's hiring of Peruvians for managerial positions. Nevertheless, its ability to influence so drastically both Peru's domestic industry and its foreign trade aroused nationalist demands for controls. Such demands were finally heeded in part when the military junta that assumed power in 1968 expropriated Grace's rich sugar plantations; other properties were nationalized in 1974. Although the Grace company was still engaged in manufacturing and mining in other Latin American countries in the early 1970s, it had sharply reduced its operations in the region.

ORAZIO A. CICCARELLI

Y

Yacimientos Petrolíferos Fiscales

Yungas

YACIMIENTOS PETROLÍFEROS FISCALES (YPF).
State petroleum corporation of Argentina. In 1922
President Hipólito YRIGOYEN, a Radical (*see* RADICAL
PARTY: ARGENTINA), created YPF under Army administration to control oil extraction, refining, and marketing. Col. Enrique Mosconi, an extraordinarily able
administrator, was appointed to head the organization.
The fiercely nationalistic Mosconi greatly enlarged
production and proportionately reduced the role of the
foreign corporations.

Yet maximum state production never exceeded one-
half of the domestic requirement. Although President Juan D. PERÓN continued and expanded the program to achieve petroleum self-sufficiency, by the
early 1950s labor unrest and mismanagement had
resulted in declining productivity and profitability.
In mid-1953 Perón reversed his nationalistic position
and negotiated with the Standard Oil Company of
California to exploit YPF reserves.

By 1958 YPF was producing only 40 percent of the
nation's daily consumption. President Arturo FRONDIZI
(1958–1962) campaigned on behalf of economic nationalism, but he also was forced to face the reality of
insufficient oil production and permitted numerous
foreign companies to exploit YPF fields on condition
that all the oil produced be sold by YPF.

President Arturo ILLIA (1963–1966), a staunch
economic nationalist, annulled the foreign contracts
and thereby caused a severe fall in production. Gen.
Juan Carlos ONGANÍA, who deposed and replaced Illia
in 1966, readmitted the foreign companies, albeit with

substantial restrictions. Since then there has been an
increase in production coupled with greater control
of foreign operations by YPF.

EUGENE G. SHARKEY

**YACIMIENTOS PETROLÍFEROS FISCALES BOLIV-
IANOS (YPFB).** Bolivian government corporation
established in 1937, when the government of Col.
David TORO expropriated the concessions of the Standard Oil Company of New Jersey in Bolivia. The YPFB
was given control over the former Standard Oil holdings.
For the next decade and a half the YPFB proved to be a
somewhat inefficient custodian of the country's oil
industry, and Bolivia became an importer of petroleum
and its derivatives. However, after the advent to power
of the MOVIMIENTO NACIONALISTA REVOLUCIONARIO
(MNR) government of President Víctor PAZ ESTENS-
SORO in 1952, Yacimientos was given substantial
additional financial resources, with the result that oil
output grew dramatically during the first years of the
MNR regime. Bolivia was converted for several years
into a net exporter of oil, and the YPFB built a sizable
new oil refinery near Sucre.

Nevertheless, the Paz Estenssoro government, which
sought to convert the oil industry into a major source of
exports, did not have faith in the ability of the YPFB to
achieve this objective. As a result, it wrote a new oil
code, which permitted the entry of foreign firms into
oil exploration and exploitation in competition with the
YPFB. Under the terms of this code, many firms sought
new sources of petroleum in the country, the Gulf Oil

Corporation being the only one to succeed on a large scale. For more than a decade Gulf developed its concessions and also undertook the construction of an oil pipeline to Chile, by means of which Bolivian oil could be exported.

One of the first moves of the government of Gen. Alfredo OVANDO CANDIA, who came to power late in 1969, was to annul the oil code; this step was followed by a decree nationalizing the Gulf holdings. When faced with the threat of an international boycott of Bolivian oil, Ovando offered a new concession to a Spanish firm in which Gulf had extensive interests. This agreement, however, was not ratified by the succeeding regime of Gen. Juan José TORRES, who came to power late in 1970. The regime of Col. Hugo BANZER, who took office in August 1971, announced soon after coming to power that it would not end the nationalization of the Gulf holdings. The former Gulf concession was added to the patrimony of the YPFB. The government firm also undertook, with Argentine help, the construction of a new pipeline from the Bolivian oil fields to Argentina.

ROBERT J. ALEXANDER

YANACONA (YANAKUNA). In pre-Columbian Peru one of a hereditary class of servants in the Inca empire (*see* INCAS) who had been removed from their ayllus (*see* AYLLU) and did not owe the MITA (labor service) to the state. The precise nature of the *yanacona's* status and functions is somewhat obscure. Yanaconas served the Emperor and the nobility, apparently working as agricultural laborers for the latter; whether craftsmen were also recruited from their ranks is unclear.

After the Spanish conquest of Peru, the same name was applied to Indians who had left their communities and attached themselves to Spaniards, whom they served as agricultural workers, miners, and so on. As *yanaconas* they were exempt from tribute and from labor service. After 1570 the government made an effort to limit their numbers and control their movements. By the end of the colonial period the term was being applied to laborers attached to agricultural estates by serflike bonds.

In republican Peru *yanaconas* were tenant farmers who received the use of a plot of land in return for surrendering part of their crop to the landowner and performing other services.

HELEN DELPAR

YÁÑEZ, AGUSTÍN (1904–). Mexican novelist. Born in Jalisco, he studied law in Guadalajara, taught there, and also edited the review *Bandera de Provincias*. He then continued his studies at the National University of Mexico and devoted himself to cultural and literary pursuits except for the years 1953–1959, when he was Governor of his native state. Yáñez has held a variety of educational posts, was named Minister of Education in 1964, and edited the complete works of Justo SIERRA. His novels and shorter works, which show his love for Jalisco, include *Genio y figuras de Guadalajara* (1941), *Flor de juegos antiguos* (1942), *Al filo del agua*, 1947 (*The Edge of the Storm*), *La tierra pródiga* (1960), and *Las tierras flacas*, 1962 (*The Lean Lands*). His best-known novel is *Al filo del agua*, which is technically ambitious and gives a brilliant picture of

life in a small provincial town at the outbreak of the MEXICAN REVOLUTION. Subjective and lyrical, Yáñez is one of the most perceptive novelists of the century.

RACHEL PHILLIPS

YDÍGORAS FUENTES, MIGUEL (1895–). President of Guatemala (1958–1963). His previous career included service as Director General of Roads under Jorge UBICO and as Minister to London under Juan José ARÉVALO and unsuccessful campaigns for the Presidency in 1950 and 1957. He won election in January 1958 and was inaugurated on March 2.

Ydígoras was a political anachronism striving for contemporaneity. His attempted reforms were thwarted by conservative opposition and falling coffee prices, and his frequent resorts to martial law to control public disorder recalled repudiated dictatorships. His attempts to rally support by challenging British possession of Belize proved more ridiculous than inspiring.

Ydígoras fashioned his own downfall. His involving Guatemala in the 1961 BAY OF PIGS INVASION of Cuba angered nationalists who resented the satellite role assigned to their country as well as leftists who identified the Cuban movement with their own thwarted revolution. Protesters who staged an unsuccessful coup in November 1960 were formed by Marco Antonio Yon Sosa and Luis Augusto Turcios Lima into a guerrilla group. The Bay of Pigs fiasco enhanced their appeal and also that of leftist political parties. In February 1962, the guerrillas launched a coup in the department of Izabal, aided by student demonstrations and a railway strike. Ydígoras responded by nationalizing the railroads and using the Army to crush the dissidents.

The approach of elections in 1963 brought a crisis. Activity by resurgent leftist parties and the declared candidacy of Arévalo raised conservative fears. On March 30, Enrique PERALTA AZURDIA, Minister of Defense, seized power; Ydígoras went into exile.

WILLIAM J. GRIFFITH

YPF. *See* YACIMIENTOS PETROLÍFEROS FISCALES.

YPFB. *See* YACIMIENTOS PETROLÍFEROS FISCALES BOLIVIANOS.

YPIRANGA, GRITO DE. Brazilian declaration of independence from Portugal on September 7, 1822. Throughout 1822 Brazilians grew increasingly unhappy with the treatment accorded them by the Portuguese. The Portuguese Parliament, while espousing liberal and constitutional ideas, pursued a repressive policy toward Brazil, refusing in effect to recognize Brazilian equality with Portugal within the empire, granted in 1815 by JOÃO VI, and wishing to reduce Brazil to colonial dependence once more. The treatment accorded Brazilian delegates to the Parliament, legislation damaging to Brazilian interests, and orders for Prince Regent Pedro (the future PEDRO I) to return to Europe revealed this intention. Brazilians led by Pedro and José Bonifacio de ANDRADA E SILVA were eventually convinced that the only course open was independence.

In September, Pedro traveled to São Paulo to resolve a dispute in the provincial government. His wife Leopoldina remained in Rio de Janeiro in charge of the government, along with José Bonifacio. They received the latest, humiliating orders of the Parliament, which allowed Pedro to continue as Regent only until the promulgation of the new Portuguese Constitution, subject to the King and Parliament and with a new Cabinet selected by Portugal. The Parliament also prohibited the future convening of a general council of provincial representatives in Brazil and ordered an investigation of the provincial government of São Paulo for requesting the Prince to stay in Brazil. These orders were sent to Pedro by special couriers, together with the opinions of Leopoldina and José Bonifacio that it was time to take the final step of breaking with Portugal. They reached Pedro, who was returning from Santos, on the banks of the Ypiranga, a small river not far from the city of São Paulo. After reading the dispatches, Pedro severed the ties between Brazil and Portugal with the dramatic *grito* (cry) "Independence or death!"

L. SHARON WYATT

YRIGOYEN (IRIGOYEN), HIPÓLITO (1852–1933). President of Argentina (1916–1922, 1928–1930). A controversial figure who has been called the "most loved and most hated man in Argentine history," Yrigoyen led the Radical party (*see* RADICAL PARTY: ARGENTINA) from political obscurity in the 1890s to national victory in 1916. Fourteen years later his second administration was brought to a premature end by the country's first military coup since the mid-nineteenth century.

Prior to the formation of the Unión Cívica Radical (UCR) in 1891, Yrigoyen was a schoolteacher and served single terms in the Buenos Aires provincial legislature (1878–1880) and the national Chamber of Deputies (1880–1882). Throughout his long political career he maintained ranching interests in Buenos Aires Province. Often described with such adjectives as "enigmatic" and "unfathomable," he was not an outstanding orator, nor did he possess other qualities usually associated with mass leaders; yet he attained extraordinary popularity. On the day of his first inauguration in 1916, members of the crowd unhitched the horses from his carriage and pulled it through the streets with their hands.

A nephew of Leandro ALEM, Yrigoyen challenged his uncle's leadership of the UCR from the time of its founding and became the dominant figure in the party after Alem's death in 1896. Over the next four decades the evolution of the Radical movement was strongly influenced by both Yrigoyen's values and his style. He was fond of saying that radicalism was not merely a political party but "the nation itself," but in the eyes of many other Radicals the party became much too closely linked with the personality of Yrigoyen.

A continuing source of conflict among Radicals was the relationship between the party and the broader Argentine political system. Yrigoyen always advocated a policy of "intransigence"; before 1916 this meant a refusal to participate in elections or in coalition governments while actively planning armed revolts. Other Radical leaders saw an inconsistency between Yrigoyen's tactics and the party's goals of free elections and constitutional government and argued increasingly for the pursuit of constitutional ends by constitutional means. This faction became dominant after a 1912 electoral reform brightened the prospects of winning office at

the polls, and in 1916 Yrigoyen became the party's candidate for President.

Attaining the Presidency did not alter Yrigoyen's position of intransigence toward other political groups. Arguing that all previous administrations had lacked legitimacy, he launched a series of federal interventions in the provinces designed to bring "national reparation" by eliminating the remaining centers of conservative strength. At the national level, his rhetoric and his personalistic governing style as well as his policies produced increasing opposition from other parties and within his own UCR. In Congress this hardening opposition thwarted a number of administrative proposals in the 1916–1922 period.

There were, of course, many positive sides to Yrigoyen's first administration. Perhaps the greatest contribution of the first Radical administration was psychological; it allowed large sectors of the population, particularly the urban middle class, to feel for the first time that they were an important part of the political system. There also were contributions of a more tangible nature. Yrigoyen showed a genuine, if rather paternalistic, concern for the condition of the working class that had not been common in previous administrations, although his record in this respect was marred by the violence of the SEMANA TRÁGICA. His also was a strongly nationalistic government, as indicated by its policy of neutrality in World War I and its proposals for the nationalization of petroleum. *See also* YACIMIENTOS PETROLÍFEROS FISCALES.

Yrigoyen chose as his successor Marcelo T. de ALVEAR, a moderate Radical who he hoped would heal the divisions within the party while remaining personally loyal. Shortly after the election of Alvear in 1922, however, it became evident that the new Radical President was not going to serve merely as a front for Yrigoyen's continued control of the party and the country. As Alvear's administration moved toward the political center, the Yrigoyenist faction of the UCR moved into a position of opposition, particularly after a formal party split in 1924.

Yrigoyen was elected once again to the Presidency in 1928, this time by a sweeping margin over the combined forces of the Antipersonalista Radicals and the Conservatives. Despite this popular mandate, Yrigoyen's second administration accomplished little. Seventy-six years old upon resuming the Presidency, Yrigoyen seemed oblivious to the variety of social, political, and economic problems that called for solutions, particularly the economic crisis that began in 1929. Even the sharp drop in UCR support evident in the 1930 congressional elections failed to shock the administration into meaningful action; instead, the government bloc in Congress spent months attempting to prevent opposition winners from being seated. The crisis continued to deepen, and on September 6, 1930, Yrigoyen was forced from office by the country's first military coup in almost seventy-five years. Despite Yrigoyen's overwhelming support two years earlier, his overthrow brought little public protest; events during the intervening two years had disillusioned all but the most loyal supporters of the aging UCR leader.

Bibliography. Jorge G. Fovie (ed.), *Discursos, escritos y polémicas del Dr. Hipólito Yrigoyen, 1878–1922*, Buenos Aires, 1923; Manuel Gálvez, *Vida de Hipólito Yrigoyen*, Buenos Aires, 1939; *Hipólito Yri-*

goyen: *Pueblo y gobierno*, 12 vols., Buenos Aires, 1951–53; Félix Luna, *Yrigoyen*, Buenos Aires, 1964; Rodolfo Puiggrós, *El yrigoyenismo*, Buenos Aires, 1965; Carlos J. Rodríguez, *Irigoyen*, Buenos Aires, 1943; Carlos Sánchez Viamonte, *El último caudillo*, Córdoba, 1930; Luis V. Sommi, *Hipólito Irigoyen*, Buenos Aires, 1947.

LEE C. FENNELL

YUCATÁN. Peninsula with an area of 55,400 square miles dividing the Gulf of Mexico from the Caribbean Sea. Located on it are the Mexican states of Yucatán and Campeche and the territory of Quintana Roo, as well as British Honduras and part of northern Guatemala. During the pre-Hispanic era, the Yucatán Peninsula was the center of Maya civilization (*see* MAYAS). Although this civilization was based exclusively on maize cultivation, it reached such a high level of development that the Mayas have been called the most brilliant indigenous people on earth. During the colonial period Yucatán was under the jurisdiction of the captaincy of Guatemala, but on August 25, 1823, it voluntarily confederated itself with "the other states of the Mexican nation." This act was the source of Yucatán's vigorous federalist sympathies, which led the state to secede from Mexico in 1847 (*see* CASTE WAR OF YUCATÁN). In reality, there was a marked conflict of interest between the Yucatecan cities of Mérida and Campeche. As a result, they vied with each other until Campeche was separated from Yucatán by means of the convention of May 3, 1858. The state of Yucatán was again dismembered in 1904 when the territory of Quintana Roo was formed out of the vast eastern region of the peninsula, which had remained in the hands of a rebellious Maya group after the Caste War.

The Caste War greatly affected the economy of the entire peninsula, and the dyewood, cotton, and sugar industries never quite recovered from its effects. However, henequen production became a major industry in the mid-nineteenth century as a result of the invention of a scraping machine and great demand for the fiber. Because of the henequen boom Yucatán was able to remain aloof from the MEXICAN REVOLUTION of 1910. In 1937 President Lázaro CÁRDENAS expropriated Yucatán's henequen plantations, which were converted into collective *ejidos* (*see* EJIDO). The expropriation of the plantations, coupled with Yuca-

tán's loss of its monopoly over henequen cultivation, severely depressed the area, which was unable to avoid the evils of monoculture.

As of 1969 there were about 625 miles of roads in the state, the most important of the federal highways being the road linking the state capital of Mérida with the port of Progreso. Yucatán was also served by airlines and a 465-mile rail network.

MOISÉS GONZÁLEZ NAVARRO

YUNGAS. Aymará term applied in Bolivia to the semitropical rugged valleys of the Cordillera Occidental, ranging in altitude from 3,000 to 6,500 feet. They exist in very limited areas (central La Paz and Cochabamba departments) and because of their lower altitude are ecologically quite different from the nearby ALTIPLANO (high plateau). For example, in contrast to the altiplano, the humidity in the yungas is high, the climate subtropical, and the vegetation dense. In fact, among the indigenous flora encountered in the yungas are several types of commercial trees, a variety of medicinal and aromatic trees and shrubs, numerous fruits and vegetables, and several kinds of spices. The two most important products of the region, however, are coffee and coca leaves. The coffee has been described as excellent, but it is not yet produced in large quantities. On the other hand, the coca leaves, from which cocaine is derived, are intensively cultivated and constitute an important item in Bolivia's internal economy. For hundreds of years the Indians have practiced the custom of chewing the leaves from morning until night. In fact, the coca traffic was economically important under the Incas, and the rise of La Paz to preeminence during colonial days was partially due to the large coca trade.

Aside from their commercial value, the yungas offer a refreshing contrast to the cold, dry, and thin-aired altiplano. Chulumani, the largest town in the yungas, is also Bolivia's most popular health resort. However, the fact that the 72-mile trip from La Paz to Chulumani is negotiated on a narrow gravel road through a series of deep valleys with precipitous drops in altitude from 15,000 to 4,000 feet explains the continuing isolation and economic underdevelopment of the yungas. This situation will probably remain unchanged in the foreseeable future.

ORAZIO A. CICCARELLI

Z

Zambo

Zumárraga, Juan de

ZAMBO. In colonial Spanish America a person of African and Indian origin. Like other CASTAS zambos were discriminated against socially and legally, and like the Indians they were obliged to pay tribute to the crown. Colonial authorities strongly opposed Afro-Indian unions, but they occurred nonetheless. In the late sixteenth century a "zambo republic" took shape on the Esmeraldas coast of Ecuador after a vessel carrying African slaves was wrecked and the survivors married local Indian women.

In Brazil the Afro-Indian mixed-blood is called a *cafuso* or *cafús*.

HELEN DELPAR

ZAPATA, EMILIANO (1879–1919). Mexican revolutionary leader. Born in Anenecuilco, Morelos, Zapata was able to overcome his humble beginnings by serving in the army and by working as a stableboy for local landowners. His work as a sharecropper allowed him to acquire sufficient savings so that he could proudly declare in mid-1911 that he had not joined the MEXICAN REVOLUTION because of poverty since he had lands and a stable, the result not of political activity but of "long years of honest labor."

When the sugar boom in Morelos impelled landowners to seize lands belonging to the towns, Zapata tenaciously defended the lands of Anenecuilco. The revolution initiated by Francisco I. MADERO in 1910 triumphed in Morelos thanks to the forces of Ambrosio Figueroa, originating in Guerrero, and to those recruited by Zapata in Morelos. In August 1911, Madero was still defending Zapata as an idol who was as popular among the traditionally exploited peons as he was hated by the landowners. The landowners regarded Zapata and his followers as mere criminals; in Morelos, they said, there was no agrarian problem because there was abundant and well-paid work on the sugar plantations.

Impatient at Madero's failure to solve the agrarian problem, Zapata ended by disavowing him as President in the Plan of Ayala (November 28, 1911; *see* AYALA, PLAN OF). Madero replied by suspending constitutional guarantees in the states of Guerrero, Morelos, and Tlaxcala and in some districts of Puebla (Acatlán, Chiautla, Matamoros, Atlixco, Cholula, Huejotzingo, and Tepexi) and of México (Chalco, Tenancingo, Sultepec, Temascaltepec, Tenango, and Lerma). Although this region was the heartland of the *zapatista* rebellion, the revolt also had repercussions in San Luis Potosí, Michoacán, Jalisco, Oaxaca, and Veracruz as well as in the outskirts of Mexico City. The revolution in the south, in contrast to the revolution of the north, had a peasant character and generally respected religion and the clergy, but it attacked the *gachupines* (*see* GACHUPÍN), a term that embraced all those who wore jackets and trousers.

Zapata recruited a goodly number of the chiefs of his revolutionary army among the migrant workers of the sugar mills; he made up his civilian ranks with professors, such as Otilio Montaño; lawyers, such as Antonio Díaz Soto y Gama; and engineers, such as Felipe Santibañez. The first formal act of land distribution took place in Ixcamilpa, Puebla, on April 30,

Emiliano Zapata. [*Organization of American States*]

1912. A manifesto issued in Milpa Alta in August 1914 explained that the revolution of the south did not struggle for illusory political rights, which did not give food, but for land and liberty. To this end, the properties of the enemies of the revolution would be confiscated, and those of lazy landowners would be expropriated.

Zapata succeeded in having the AGUASCALIENTES CONVENTION accept the agrarian principles of the Plan of Ayala, and Francisco VILLA and Zapata agreed, in the Pact of Xochimilco (December 4, 1914), to put the plan into effect. During his and Villa's military confrontation with Venustiano CARRANZA, Zapata contributed to Villa's defeat by failing to cut communications between Celaya and Carranza's headquarters in Veracruz. With the defeat of Villa, Zapata fell back to his mountains. In January 1915 the President of the Aguascalientes Convention, Eulalio Gutiérrez, accused Zapata of not having distributed any lands and of blowing up telegraph lines and railroads for his own gain. In the opinion of other chiefs of the convention, he was merely "a tyrant without God or law," while partisans of Carranza charged that his only talent was to dynamite undefended trains. Zapata was treacher-

ously assassinated in the hacienda of Chinameca on April 10, 1919.

Bibliography. Moisés González Navarro, "Zapata y la Revolución Agraria Mexicana," *Cahiers du monde hispanique et luso-brésilien,* vol. IX, 1967, pp. 5–31; Gildardo Magãna, *Emiliano Zapata y el agrarismo en México,* Mexico City, 1934–52; Antonio D. Melgarejo, *¿Los crímenes del zapatismo? (Apuntes de un guerrillero),* Mexico City, 1913; Jesús Sotelo Inclán, *Raíz y razón de Zapata,* Mexico City, 1970; John Womack, *Zapata and the Mexican Revolution,* New York, 1969.

MOISÉS GONZÁLEZ NAVARRO

ZAYAS, ALFREDO (1861–1934). President of Cuba (1921–1925). In 1905 the Liberal party selected Zayas as its vice-presidential candidate on the unsuccessful ticket headed by José Miguel GÓMEZ. The following year he joined the Liberal rebellion against Tomás ESTRADA PALMA's claim to a second term. Although he had broken politically with Gómez, he later agreed to serve a second time as his running mate in the United States–supervised election of 1908. For the next four years (1909–1913) he served quietly, hoping to replace Gómez at the end of the term. In 1912 he was successful in obtaining the Liberal party's nomination for the Presidency but lost in the general election when Gómez vacillated in supporting him. When Zayas was finally elected President in 1920, he was supported by the Conservatives and the outgoing administration, which placed the state's machinery at his disposal.

Zayas began his administration in the midst of a financial crisis caused by a sudden drop in the price of sugar on the world market. He was also faced with the threat of revolt by the Liberals, who claimed fraud in the election, and with increasing student unrest. Concerned about the situation, the United States dispatched Gen. Enoch H. CROWDER to Cuba in 1921, and Crowder remained as an adviser to Zayas in an attempt to prevent further fiscal and political deterioration. Pressed by Crowder, Zayas maintained a semblance of honesty in government until mid-1923, but a loan from American bankers and improving sugar prices proved too great a temptation for him. Toward the end of his term in office he embarked on a shameless program of personal enrichment that surpassed the record of previous Cuban Presidents.

J. CORDELL ROBINSON

ZELAYA, JOSÉ SANTOS (1853–1919). Nicaraguan dictator. Zelaya's long tenure as Nicaraguan chief of state (1893–1909) was a major turning point in the history of the country. His was the only Liberal regime from 1863, when the Conservatives began their so-called Thirty Years of political dominance, until the beginning of the Moncada administration in 1929. With a positivist outlook acquired through many years of study in France, Zelaya worked to separate church and state and to secularize and expand education. He also invigorated governmental agencies, libraries, and museums and attempted to modernize the Army, agriculture, and industry. Largely as a result of his initiative, railroad construction flourished and steamer navigation on Nicaragua's two great lakes was greatly expanded. Rigid adherence to international fiscal obligations and rising coffee exports kept Nicaragua's credit good.

Because of Zelaya's prestige in Central America, Managua became the rallying point for Liberal exiles from the whole isthmian region. He was so successful in installing governments friendly to himself in the other Central American countries that Nicaragua probably enjoyed greater international influence in the Zelaya years than at any other time in its history. However, his rivalry with Manuel ESTRADA CABRERA of Guatemala and his hostility toward the extension of United States influence in Central America in the later years of his regime proved to be his undoing. He fell from power in 1909, the victim of a revolution that received the outright support of the United States. Although the economic growth that Zelaya had fostered was stifled in subsequent years by United States intervention and the reopening of internal rivalries, the social changes that he had stimulated remained.

CHARLES L. STANSIFER

ZORRILLA DE SAN MARTÍN, JUAN (1855–1931). Uruguayan poet, lawyer, politician, and diplomat. Zorrilla de San Martín was born in Montevideo. Educated at the Jesuit school in Santa Fe, Argentina, he received a degree in law from the University of Chile in 1877. He then returned to Montevideo and in 1878 founded *El Bien Público,* a conservative periodical with a Catholic point of view. Exiled to Buenos Aires (1885–1887) during the regime of Máximo Santos, he later returned to serve in the national Congress. In 1891 he went to Spain to represent Uruguay at the quadricentennial celebration of the discovery of America. He remained in Spain until 1894, when he went to Paris as Uruguayan Ambassador. Later he taught at the National University in Montevideo.

Notwithstanding the numerous posts he held in the service of his country, Zorrilla de San Martín won fame primarily as a romantic poet. Among his works are *Poesías líricas* (1877), *La leyenda patria* (1879), *Tabaré* (1888), and *La epopeya de Artigas* (1900). Of these, it is *Tabaré* that has earned him the most lasting recognition. A long poem with epic qualities, it was intended as a resuscitation of the vanished world of the Charrúa Indians, who once lived in the land now occupied by Uruguay. As it turned out, perhaps because of the poet's romantic temperament, the poem is more elegiac than epic. Nevertheless, *Tabaré* is an admirable artistic accomplishment.

GERARDO SÁENZ

ZUMÁRRAGA, JUAN DE (1468–1548). First Bishop and Archbishop of Mexico. Born in Durango, Basque Provinces, he professed as a Franciscan near Valladolid, Spain. In 1527 he was appointed Bishop of New Spain and Protector of the Indians by King CHARLES I, arriving in Mexico with the members of the first *audiencia* in 1528. Zumárraga soon became involved in a bitter contest with the *audiencia* over treatment of the Indians. The confrontation reached a climax when the judges of the *audiencia* were excommunicated and the Franciscans retired to Texcoco. A letter (August 1529) by Zumárraga reporting the misdeeds of royal officials in New Spain was smuggled out of the colony and reached the crown, which ordered the formation of a second *audiencia.*

In 1532 Zumárraga traveled to Spain to defend himself against charges raised by the first *audiencia,* and there he was consecrated as a bishop (1533). After his return to New Spain he devoted himself to the organization of the church and to works of social relevance, such as the foundation of the Colleges of Santiago Tlaltelolco and San Juan de Letrán for Indian boys, schools for girls, and several hospitals. He also supported the foundation of a university and brought the first printing press to New Spain. He has been charged with the destruction of many Indian codices and temples in his missionary zeal, but his apologists state that such destruction began before Zumárraga's arrival in New Spain. He has also been charged with the burning of the Indian cacique Don Carlos and the establishment of inquisitorial practices in New Spain. In 1547 he was appointed Archbishop of New Spain.

ASUNCIÓN LAVRIN

Statistical Appendix

Table 1. Demographic Features

Country	Latest census	Census population	Midyear estimate of population, 1972 (in thousands)	Annual rate of increase, 1963–1972 (percent)	Area (in square kilometers)	Density, 1972 (population per square kilometer)
Argentina	9/30/70	23,362,204 [a]	23,923	1.5	2,776,889	9
Bolivia	9/5/50	2,704,165	5,194	2.6	1,098,581	5
Brazil [b]	9/1/70	93,204,379	98,854	2.9	8,511,965	12
Chile	4/22/70	8,834,820 [a]	...	...	756,945	...
Colombia	7/15/64	17,484,508	22,491	3.2	1,138,914	20
Costa Rica	4/1/63	1,336,274	1,842	3.2	50,700	36
Cuba	9/6/70	8,553,395 [a]	8,749 [a]	2.0	114,524	76
Dominican Republic	1/9/70	4,006,405	4,304	2.9	48,734	88
Ecuador [c]	11/25/62	4,649,648	6,508	3.4	283,561	23
El Salvador	6/28/71	3,549,260	3,760	...	21,393	176
Guatemala	4/18/64	4,287,997	5,409	2.9	108,889	50
Haiti	10/9/71	4,243,926 [a]	5,073	2.1	27,750	183
Honduras	4/17/61	1,884,765	2,687	3.1	112,088	24
Mexico	1/28/70	48,225,238	52,641	3.5	1,972,547	27
Nicaragua	4/20/71	1,911,543 [a]	1,988	...	130,000	15
Panama [d]	5/10/70	1,428,082	1,524	3.0	75,650	20
Paraguay	10/14/62	1,819,103	2,581	3.4	406,752	6
Peru [e]	6/4/72	13,567,939 [a]	14,456 [f]	3.1	1,285,216	11
Puerto Rico	4/1/70	2,712,033	2,809	1.3	8,897	316
Uruguay	10/16/63	2,595,510	2,956	1.2	177,508	17
Venezuela	11/2/71	10,721,522 [a]	10,969 [f]	3.4	912,050	12

[a] Provisional.

[b] Excludes Indian jungle population, estimated at 150,000 in 1956.

[c] Excludes nomadic Indian tribes.

[d] Excludes Canal Zone.

[e] Excludes Indian jungle population.

[f] Estimate not revised in accordance with latest census.

SOURCE: United Nations, Department of Economic and Social Affairs, Statistical Office, *Demographic Yearbook, 1972,* New York, 1973.

Table 2. Life Expectancy and Literacy

Country	Life expectancy at birth, 1968 (approximate number of years)	Literate persons aged fifteen and over, 1968 (percent)
Argentina	67.0	91.4 [a]
Bolivia	46.0	39.8
Brazil	56.0	69.6
Chile	62.0	89.6
Colombia	60.0	72.9 [b]
Costa Rica	63.3	85.8
Cuba	66.8 [c]	96.1 [d]
Dominican Republic	52.0	53.1
Ecuador	57.7	72.0
El Salvador	56.9	50.8
Guatemala	47.0	37.9 [e]
Haiti	47.5	18.8
Honduras	42.6	47.0 [a]
Mexico	60.0	77.5
Nicaragua	51.0	49.8 [e]
Panama	64.3	78.3
Paraguay	59.1	69.0
Peru	58.0	67.0
Puerto Rico	68.96 (male) [f]	
	75.18 (female) [f]	89.2 [g]
Uruguay	68.5	89.4 [e]
Venezuela	65.8	85.0

[a] 1960.

[b] 1964.

[c] 1965–1970.

[d] Persons aged ten and over, 1962.

[e] 1963.

[f] 1969–1971.

[g] Persons aged ten and over, 1970.

SOURCES: United Nations, Economic Commission for Latin America, *Economic Survey of Latin America, 1970,* New York, 1972; United Nations, Department of Economic and Social Affairs, Statistical Office, *Demographic Yearbook, 1972,* New York, 1973; Rolando E. Bonachea and Nelson P. Valdés (eds.), *Cuba in Revolution,* New York, 1972; United States Department of Commerce, Social and Economic Administration, Bureau of the Census, *1970 Census of Population: Detailed Characteristics, Puerto Rico,* Washington, 1973.

Table 3. Per Capita Gross Domestic Product

Country	Per capita gross domestic product (in purchasers' values expressed in current United States dollars)	
	1970 estimate	1971 estimate
Argentina	1,053	...
Bolivia	206	219
Brazil	402	...
Chile	755	632
Colombia	409	...
Costa Rica	544	584
Cuba	...	...
Dominican Republic	364	389
Ecuador	269	276
El Salvador	291	294
Guatemala	367	374
Haiti	92 *	...
Honduras	271	278
Mexico	682	717
Nicaragua	431	451
Panama	731	790
Paraguay	249	270
Peru	400	431
Puerto Rico	1,924	...
Uruguay	816	...
Venezuela	999	1,083

* 1969.

SOURCE: United Nations, Department of Economic and Social Affairs, Statistical Office, *Statistical Yearbook, 1972,* New York, 1973.

Table 4. Gross Domestic Product by Kind of Economic Activity in Current Prices

Country and unit of currency	Gross domestic product and year		Percentage distribution [a]						
			Agricul-ture [b]	Industrial activity [c]		Con-struc-tion	Whole-sale and retail trade	Transpor-tation and communi-cations	Other [d]
				Total	Manufac-turing indus-tries				
Argentina (1,000 million pesos)	80.4	(1969)	11	31	28	4	14	8	20
Bolivia (million pesos)	13,145.0	(1971)	16	30	14	4	13	8	29
Brazil (1,000 million new cruzeiros)	133.1	(1969)	13	22	20	1	10	4	27
Chile (million escudos)	120,445.9	(1971)	8	35	26	5	21	4	27
Colombia (million pesos)	130,590.9	(1970)	27	22	19	5	17	7	23
Costa Rica (million colones)	6,943.7	(1971)	22	21	...	5	17	4	31
Dominican Republic (million pesos)	1,633.0	(1971)	22	21	19	6	17	8	26
Ecuador (million sucres)	43,951.0	(1971)	24	18	15	5	11	6	28
El Salvador (million colones)	2,681.0	(1971)	27	21	19	3	23	5	21
Guatemala (million quetzales)	1,331.0	(1965)	29	16	15	2	28	4	22
Haiti (million gourdes)	1,652.9 [e]	(1970)	51	13	10	2	11	2	21
Honduras (million lempiras)	1,508.9	(1971)	32	15	12	5	12	6	21
Mexico (1,000 million pesos)	423.1	(1970)	11	29	23	5	33	3	20
Nicaragua (million córdobas)	6,471.0	(1971)	24	21	18	3	20	5	27
Panama (million balboas)	861.4	(1968)	23	17	15	6	9	4	34
Paraguay (million guaraníes)	83,735.9	(1971)	33	18	16	3	24	4	18
Peru (100 million soles)	250.1 [f]	(1971)	18	30	21	6	{	46	}
Puerto Rico (million U.S. dollars)	6,218.0	(1971)	3	27	23	8	20	6	36
Uruguay (100 million pesos)	499.7	(1969)	11	24	22	3	16	8	27
Venezuela (million bolívares)	52,350.0	(1971)	8	40	21	5	11	8	26

[a] Percentages do not add up to 100 because in many cases import duties are not included in the reported industrial groups.

[b] Agriculture, hunting, forestry, and fishing.

[c] Mining and quarrying, manufacturing, electricity, gas, and water.

[d] Finance, insurance, real estate, and business services; community, social, and personal services; and public administration and defense.

[e] Gross domestic product at constant prices of 1955.

[f] Gross domestic product at constant prices of 1970.

SOURCE: United Nations, Department of Economic and Social Affairs, Statistical Office, *Yearbook of National Account Statistics, 1972,* vol. III, New York, 1974.

Table 5. Structure of the Employed Population, 1969
(In percentages)

Country	Agri-culture	Industry * and basic services †	Services
Argentina	15.6	36.9	47.5
Bolivia	55.0	21.1	23.9
Brazil	46.6	23.3	30.1
Chile	22.5	31.6	45.9
Colombia	42.3	23.0	34.7
Costa Rica	49.3	19.6	31.1
Dominican Republic	59.8	14.2	26.0
Ecuador	52.5	20.4	27.1
El Salvador	56.1	19.1	24.8
Guatemala	64.7	15.5	19.8
Haiti ‡	81.2	6.7	12.1
Honduras	66.9	12.3	20.8
Mexico	47.2	23.3	29.5
Nicaragua	56.0	17.4	26.6
Panama	43.9	17.0	39.1
Paraguay	51.1	20.1	28.8
Peru	46.2	25.8	28.0
Uruguay	16.6	31.7	51.7
Venezuela	26.6	27.2	46.2

* Mining, manufacturing, and construction.

† Electricity, gas, water, sanitation, and transportation and communications.

‡ 1960.

SOURCE: United Nations, Economic Commission for Latin America, *Economic Survey of Latin America, 1970,* New York, 1972.

Select Bibliography of Bibliographies

GENERAL WORKS

Bayitch, S. A.: *Latin America and the Caribbean: A Bibliographical Guide to Works in English,* Coral Gables, Fla., 1967.

Griffin, Charles C. (ed.): *Latin America: A Guide to the Historical Literature,* Austin, Tex., 1971.

Gropp, Arthur E.: *A Bibliography of Latin American Bibliographies,* Metuchen, N.J., 1968.

————: *A Bibliography of Latin American Bibliographies: Supplement,* Metuchen, N.J., 1971.

Humphreys, R. A.: *Latin American History: A Guide to the Literature in English,* London, 1958.

Jones, Cecil Knight: *A Bibliography of Latin American Bibliographies,* 2d ed., rev. and enl., Washington, 1942.

Sable, Martin H.: *A Guide to Latin American Studies,* 2 vols., Los Angeles, 1967.

Sánchez Alonso, Benito: *Fuentes de la historia española e hispanoamericana,* 3d ed., rev., 3 vols., Madrid, 1952.

PERIODICAL PUBLICATIONS

Handbook of Latin American Studies, Cambridge, Mass., 1936–51; Gainesville, Fla., 1951–, annually.

Hispanic American Historical Review, Baltimore, 1918–22; Durham, N.C., 1926–, quarterly.

Índice Histórico Español, Barcelona, 1953–, quarterly.

Inter-American Review of Bibliography, Washington, 1951–, quarterly.

Latin American Research Review, Austin, Tex., 1965–, three times a year.

SPECIAL TOPICS

LITERATURE AND THE ARTS

Chase, Gilbert: *A Guide to Music of Latin America,* 2d ed., rev. and enl., Washington, 1962.

Foster, David William, and Virginia Ramos Foster: *Manual of Hispanic Bibliography,* Seattle, 1970.

Rela, Walter: *Guía bibliográfica de la literatura hispanoamericana, desde el siglo XIX hasta 1970,* Buenos Aires, 1971.

Simón Díaz, José: *Bibliografía de literatura hispánica,* 2d ed., rev. and enl., Madrid, 1960.

Smith, Robert C., and Elizabeth Wilder: *A Guide to the Art of Latin America,* Washington, 1948.

SOCIAL SCIENCES

Alfaro, Carlos: *Guía apostólica latinoamericana,* Barcelona, 1965.

Bayitch, S. A.: *Guide to Inter-American Legal Studies: A Selective Bibliography of Works in English,* Coral Gables, Fla., 1957.

Bernal, Ignacio: *Bibliografía de arqueología y etnografía: Mesoamérica y Norte de México, 1514–1960,* Mexico City, 1962.

Boggs, Ralph S.: *Bibliography of Latin American Folklore,* New York, 1940.

Chilcote, Ronald H.: *Revolution and Structural Change in Latin America: A Bibliography on Ideology, Development and the Radical Left (1930–1965),* Stanford, Calif., 1970.

Comas, Juan: *Bibliografía selectiva de las culturas indígenas de América,* Mexico City, 1953.

Harvard University, Bureau for Economic Research in Latin America: *The Economic Literature of Latin America: A Tentative Bibliography,* 2 vols., Cambridge, Mass., 1935–36.

Jones, Tom B., Elizabeth A. Warburton, and Anne Kingsley: *A Bibliography on South American Economic Affairs: Articles in Nineteenth-century Periodicals,* Minneapolis, 1955.

Kantor, Harry: *Latin American Political Parties: A Bibliography,* Gainesville, Fla., 1968.

Lauerhass, Jr., Ludwig: *Communism in Latin America—A Bibliography: The Postwar Years (1945–1960),* Los Angeles, 1962.

Lindenberg, Klaus: *Fuerzas armadas y política en América Latina: Bibliografía selecta,* Santiago, Chile, 1972.

Martínez, Hector, Miguel Cameo C., and Jesús Ramírez S.: *Bibliografía indígena andina peruana: 1900–1968,* Lima, 1969.

O'Leary, Timothy J.: *Ethnographic Bibliography of South America,* New Haven, Conn., 1970.

Sable, Martin H.: *Periodicals for Latin American Economic Development, Trade and Finance: An Annotated Bibliography,* Los Angeles, 1965.

—— and M. Wayne Dennis, *Communism in Latin America—An International Bibliography: 1900–1944, 1960–1967,* Los Angeles, 1968.

Trask, David F., Michael C. Meyer, and Roger R. Trask: *A Bibliography of United States–Latin American Relations since 1810,* Lincoln, Nebr., 1968.

Wish, John R.: *Economic Development in Latin America: An Annotated Bibliography,* New York, 1965.

INDIVIDUAL COUNTRIES

ARGENTINA

Geoghegan, Abel Rodolfo: *Bibliografía de bibliografías argentinas, 1807–1970,* Buenos Aires, 1970.

BOLIVIA

Siles Guevara, Juan: *Bibliografía de bibliografías bolivianas,* La Paz, 1969.

BRAZIL

Carpeaux, Otto M.: *Pequena bibliografia crítica da literatura brasileira,* 3d ed., rev. and enl., Rio de Janeiro, 1964.

Moraes, Rubens Borba de, and William Berrien: *Manual bibliográfico de estudos brasileiros,* Rio de Janeiro, 1949.

Sodré, Nelson Werneck: *O que se deve ler para conhecer o Brasil,* 2d ed., Rio de Janeiro, 1960.

CENTRAL AMERICA

Rodríguez, Mario, and Vincent C. Peloso: *A Guide for the Study of Culture in Central America: Humanities and Social Sciences,* Washington, 1968.

CHILE

Cruz, Guillermo Feliú: *Historia de las fuentes de la bibliografía chilena: Ensayo crítico,* 3 vols., Santiago, Chile, 1966–67.

Laval, Ramón A.: *Bibliografía de bibliografías chilenas,* Santiago, Chile, 1915.

Ruiz Urbina, Antonio, Alejandro Zorbas D., and Luis Donoso Varela: *Estratificación y movilidad sociales en Chile: Fuentes bibliográficas (desde los orígenes históricos hasta 1960),* Rio de Janeiro, 1961.

COLOMBIA

Giraldo Jaramillo, Gabriel: *Bibliografía de bibliografías colombianas,* 2d ed., rev., Bogotá, 1960.

Watson, Gayle Hudgens: *Colombia, Ecuador and Venezuela: An Annotated Guide to Reference Materials in the Humanities and Social Sciences,* Metuchen, N.J., 1971.

COSTA RICA

Dobles Segreda, Luis: *Índice bibliográfico de Costa Rica,* 9 vols., San José, 1927–36.

CUBA

Peraza Sarausa, Fermín: *Bibliografías cubanas,* Washington, 1945.

Valdés, Nelson P., and Edwin Lieuwen, *The Cuban Revolution: A Research-Study Guide (1959–1969),* Albuquerque, 1971.

DOMINICAN REPUBLIC

Florén Lozano, Luis: *Bibliografía de la bibliografía dominicana,* Ciudad Trujillo, 1948.

Hitt, Deborah S., and Larman C. Wilson: *A Selected Bibliography of the Dominican Republic,* Washington, 1968.

ECUADOR

Larrea, Carlos M.: *Bibliografía científica del Ecuador,* 5 vols., 1948–53.

Watson, Gayle Hudgens: *Colombia, Ecuador and Venezuela: An Annotated Guide to Reference Materials in the Humanities and Social Sciences,* Metuchen, N.J., 1971.

GUATEMALA

Valenzuela Reyna, Gilberto: *Bibliografía guatemalteca, y catálogo general de libros, folletos, periódicos, revistas, etc. (1861–1960),* 5 vols., Guatemala City, 1962–64.

HAITI

Bissainthe, Max: *Dictionnaire de bibliographie haïtienne,* Washington, 1951.

Duvivier, Ulrick: *Bibliographie générale et méthodique d'Haïti,* 2 vols., Port-au-Prince, 1941.

HONDURAS

Durón, Jorge Fidel: *Índice de la bibliografía hondureña,* Tegucigalpa, 1946.

García, Miguel Ángel: *Bibliografía hondureña*, 2 vols., Tegucigalpa, 1971–72.

MEXICO

González y González, Luis, Guadalupe Monroy, Luis Munro, and Susana Uribe: *Fuentes de la historia contemporánea de México: Libros y folletos*, 3 vols., Mexico City, 1961–62.

Millares Carlo, Agustín, and José Ignacio Mantecón: *Ensayo de una bibliografía de bibliografías mexicanas*, Mexico City, 1943.

Ross, Stanley R.: *Fuentes de la historia contemporánea de México: Periodicos y revistas*, 2 vols., Mexico City, 1965–67.

PANAMA

Susto Lara, Juan Antonio: *Panorama de la bibliografía en Panamá (1619–1967)*, Panama City, 1971.

PARAGUAY

Fernández-Caballero, Carlos F. S.: *The Paraguayan Bibliography: A Retrospective and Enumerative Bibliography of Printed Works of Paraguayan Authors*, Washington, 1970.

PERU

Herbold, Carl, and Steve Stein: *Guía bibliográfica para la historia social y política del Perú en el siglo XX: 1895–1960*, Lima, 1971.

Vargas Ugarte, Rubén: *Manual de estudios peruanistas*, 4th ed., Lima, 1959.

PUERTO RICO

Bird, Augusto. *Bibliografía puertorriqueña de fuentes para investigaciones sociales, 1930–1945*, 2 vols., Río Piedras, Puerto Rico, 1946–47.

Pedreira, Antonio S.: *Bibliografía puertorriqueña (1493–1930)*, Madrid, 1932.

Vivó, Paquita: *The Puerto Ricans: An Annotated Bibliography*, New York, 1973.

URUGUAY

Musso Ambrosi, Luis A.: *Bibliografía de bibliografías uruguayas*, Montevideo, 1964.

VENEZUELA

Sánchez, Manuel Segundo: *Bibliografía venezolanista*, Caracas, 1914.

Villasana, Ángel Raúl: *Ensayo de un repertorio bibliográfico venezolano: Años 1808–1950*, 4 vols., Caracas, 1969–70.

Watson, Gayle Hudgens: *Colombia, Ecuador and Venezuela: An Annotated Guide to Reference Materials in the Humanities and Social Sciences*, Metuchen, N.J., 1971.